ENCYCLOPÆDIA
Britannica

2003
BOOK OF THE YEAR®

Encyclopædia Britannica, Inc.
Chicago·London·New Delhi·Paris·Seoul·Sydney·Taipei·Tokyo

ENCYCLOPÆDIA
Britannica

BOOK OF THE YEAR®
2003

Foreword

The year 2002 was one of uncertainty. A rash of business scandals and bankruptcies, plummeting stock markets, the constant threat of terrorist attacks—punctuated by actual incidents—the continuing war in Afghanistan, and the sabre rattling in the direction of Iraq all contributed to a general sense of unease. As a result, immigration policies and national security measures were scrutinized, revised, and tightened. The pros and cons of the death penalty were again put under the microscope following the apprehension in the U.S. of a pair of homegrown snipers who had shot and killed unsuspecting passersby at random.

To highlight the major stories of the year, then, the editors of the 2003 *Britannica Book of the Year* have included Special Reports dealing with the immigration backlash, civil rights versus security, the death penalty, the wireless revolution, and modern warfare. The details of the Enron accounting debacle, which touched off an avalanche of other disclosures regarding irregularities in business practices and contributed to the downward spiral of the U.S. stock market, are recounted in a sidebar entitled, "Enron, What Happened?" A new graph appearing in "Economic Affairs: Stock Markets" details the activity of three major U.S. stock market indexes and illustrates the bumpy ride in financial markets during the year. Bad behaviour was rampant in 2003—just turn to our Sidebar about the Roman Catholic Church's long inaction against priests accused of sexually abusing minors, and our Special Report about the rising incidence of cheating in schools, academia, and elsewhere.

The cheating scandals also extended to the sporting world. The scandal surrounding the judging at the pairs ice-skating championship at the Olympics resulted in the awarding of gold medals to two pairs of athletes. A BBC television broadcast detailed the rampant corruption in British horse racing, and in the U.S. a breach in pari-mutuel wagering security shook the American turf scene. A football coach lost his dream job at Notre Dame after admitting that he had embellished his academic and athletic background. Scientific circles were aghast after it became known that a star research physicist at Bell Labs had falsified data in papers he published in top journals.

On a brighter note, some of the newer, thought-provoking trends in art are featured in a four-page photo essay. A Special Report on the XIX Winter Olympic Games in Salt Lake City, Utah, and a Sidebar on the association football (soccer) World Cup held in South Korea and Japan highlight the thrills and inspiration that one can derive from sporting events.

A calendar of events, biographies, obituaries, and coverage of every country in the world join these special features. I invite you to pull up a chair, relax, and enjoy your snapshot of 2002.

Karen Sparks, Editor

Contents

2003

Dates of 2002

A candlelight vigil in Canberra, Australia, commemorates the first anniversary of the September 11, 2001, attacks in the U.S.

January

> *I will not wait on events while dangers gather. I will not stand by as peril draws closer and closer. The United States of America will not permit the world's most dangerous regimes to threaten us with the world's most destructive weapons.*
>
> U.S. Pres. George W. Bush in his state of the union message before Congress, January 29

1 As the clock ticks over to 2002, the euro replaces the Deutsche Mark, the French franc, the Italian lira, the Spanish peseta, the Greek drachma, the Austrian schilling, the Belgian franc, the Finnish markka, the Irish pound, the Luxembourg franc, the Dutch guilder, and the Portuguese escudo as the official currency of these countries.

•

A law granting autonomy to the Indonesian province of Irian Jaya (West Papua) goes into effect, and the name of the province officially becomes Papua.

•

Military conscription officially ends in Spain.

Eduardo Duhalde, who lost the presidential election to Fernando de la Rúa in 1999, is chosen interim president of Argentina; he is sworn in the following day as Argentina's fifth president in the past two weeks, and he is expected to stay in office until elections are held at the end of 2003.

2 U.S. Senate Democrats announce that they plan to conduct hearings into the collapse of Enron Corp.

•

In spite of violent demonstrations to protest presidential elections that many felt were rigged, Levy Mwanawasa is inaugurated as president of Zambia.

3 The Netherlands renationalizes its rail network after years of private ownership during which service had deteriorated.

•

In the annual postseason Rose Bowl, the University of Miami (Fla.) defeats the University of Nebraska 37–14 to win the national college football Division I-A championship.

4 Nathan Ross Chapman becomes the first U.S. serviceman to die in combat in Afghanistan when a team of Americans and Afghans returning from a meeting are attacked.

•

Israel seizes a ship loaded with 50 tons of munitions that Israel says, and the captain of the ship later agrees, are destined for the Palestinian National Authority.

5 A 15-year-old student pilot steals a Cessna 172 and crashes it into a 40-story bank building in Tampa, Fla.

•

Historian Stephen Ambrose admits that some of the lines in his best-selling work *The Wild Blue* were inadvertently lifted from one of his sources, Thomas Childers's *The Wings of Morning* (1995). (*See* January 22.)

6 Argentina decouples the peso from the U.S. dollar, ending a policy that had been followed since 1991.

•

A UN official says that a disarmament program in Sierra Leone has successfully concluded, with most combatants in the civil war having turned their weapons over to UN peacekeepers.

•

Griffith Observatory in Los Angeles closes for renovation; the 67-year-old observatory, which has never been upgraded, is expected to reopen in 2005.

7 *The worst snowstorm in over three decades drops about 30 cm (12 in) of snow on Jordan and Lebanon. (Photo right.)*

•

At a conference of the American Astronomical Society in Washington, D.C., scientists present their findings that many gamma-ray bursts originated in nearby galaxy clusters and that evidence suggests that such bursts may result from supernova explosions.

•

Lucent Technologies names Patricia F. Russo, a former top executive at the company, its new CEO.

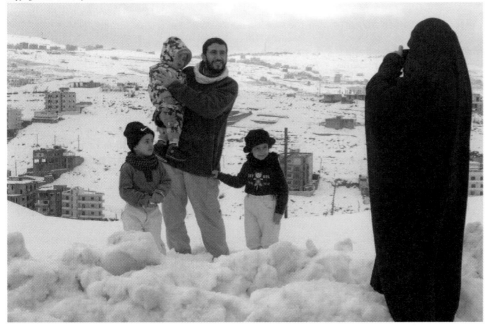

ing the banning of five organizations.

13 U.S. Pres. George W. Bush briefly loses consciousness while choking on a pretzel and falls, bruising his face; the only witnesses are the family dogs.

• After almost 42 years and exactly 17,162 performances, the curtain falls on *The Fantasticks* in the Sullivan Street Playhouse in Greenwich Village, New York City, for the last time.

• The 24th annual Dakar Rally finishes; the winners are Japanese driver Hiroshi Masuoka, in a Mitsubishi Pajero, Italian driver Fabrizio Meoni, on a KTM LC8 950 motorcycle, and Russian driver Vladimir Chagin, in a Kamaz 49255 truck.

14 The British government announces that the country is officially free of foot-and-mouth disease.

• Prime Minister Hamada Madi Bolero of Comoros announces his resignation as the first step toward the creation of a transitional government; on January 17 Pres. Azali Assoumani resigns for the same reason, and on January 20 the transitional government is formed, with Hamada Madi Bolero as both prime minister and president.

15 U.S. and Philippine military officials begin preparing joint operations against Abu Sayyaf, a militant Muslim organization that is believed to have ties to al-Qaeda.

• The world's largest drug company, Pfizer, announces plans to make its drugs available to low-income

• Apple Computer introduces its new iMac, featuring a flat-panel monitor on an adjustable "neck" attached to a hemispheric base.

• The foreign ministers of Myanmar (Burma) and Thailand begin talks to try to reach an accord on the repatriation to Myanmar of migrant workers, more than 400,000 of whom are registered in Thailand.

8 The U.S. Supreme Court issues a ruling that narrows the scope of the Americans with Disabilities Act, holding that a qualifying disability must not only impinge on one's ability to do one's job but also limit one's ability to function in everyday life.

• Rules quietly issued by the Vatican are made public; these new rules require that priests accused of pedophilia be tried by ecclesiastical courts overseen by the Holy See.

• Shortstop Ozzie Smith is elected to the National Baseball Hall of Fame.

9 Pres. Andrés Pastrana Arango of Colombia says that negotiations with the Revolutionary Armed Forces of Colombia (FARC) have failed, and he gives the rebel group 48 hours to vacate the area that Colombia had ceded to it during the peace talks.

• Archaeologists working on a site in Narsingdi, Bangladesh, find artifacts that date to 2,450 years ago, older than any found previously in the country; it is believed that they may presage discovery of part of the Brahmaputra civilization.

10 The U.S. begins taking al-Qaeda and Taliban prisoners to its naval base at Guantánamo Bay on the island of Cuba; the first 20 prisoners land the following day. (*See* January 23.)

• Officials of the accounting firm Arthur Andersen, which was the auditor of the collapsed energy company Enron, disclose that Andersen employees destroyed documents relating to

Enron, even after such documents had been subpoenaed by the Securities and Exchange Commission.

11 The Ford Motor Co. announces its biggest cutbacks in 20 years, including the closing of five plants and the discontinuation of four models—the Lincoln Continental, the Ford Escort, the Mercury Cougar, and the Mercury Villager.

• Astronomers say that if it were possible to view the universe from the outside, it would appear to be a pale green. (*See* March 7.)

12 After several days of violence in Belfast, N.Ire., a Roman Catholic mailman is killed; a Protestant group called the Red Hand Defenders claims responsibility and threatens to kill Catholic schoolteachers throughout the country.

• Pakistani Pres. Pervez Musharraf announces broad new restrictions on Muslim extremism, includelderly Americans for $15 a month per prescription.

•

Pat Cox of Ireland is elected president of the European Parliament in the third round of voting; Cox is viewed as more liberal than the outgoing president, Nicole Fontaine of France.

16 Riots break out in Lagos, Nigeria, as the Nigeria Labour Congress begins a general strike to protest an 18% increase in the price of gasoline and diesel fuel and a 40% increase in the price of kerosene.

•

Pres. Olusegun Obasanjo of Nigeria and Pres. Fradique de Menezes of São Tomé and Príncipe launch the Joint High Authority to manage oil exploration in the disputed Gulf of Guinea.

17 Argentina reopens its stock exchange and replaces the president of the central bank in an effort to gain some control over the continuing economic crisis.

•

In the Democratic Republic of the Congo, Mt. Nyiragongo, just outside the city of Goma, begins erupting; the following day almost the entire population of Goma flees as lava destroys much of the city.

•

The 100th anniversary of the first publication of *The Times Literary Supplement* is celebrated at Porchester Hall in London; literary luminaries in attendance include Martin Amis, Germaine Greer, Doris Lessing, V.S. Naipaul, and Salman Rushdie.

18 Pres. Ahmad Tejan Kabbah ceremonially declares that the civil war in Sierra Leone, which began in 1991, has ended.

•

AngloGold of South Africa allows its offer to buy Normandy Mining of Australia to expire, so Newmont Mining, based in Denver, Colo., becomes the buyer; when the deal is completed, it will make Newmont the largest gold-mining concern in the world.

•

Israeli tanks surround the headquarters of Palestinian National Authority head Yasir Arafat in the West Bank town of Ram Allah, effectively putting him under house arrest.

•

The second largest retailer in Japan, Daiei, asks banks to forgive its $3.2 billion in debt so that it will not go bankrupt.

19 At the World Cup swimming meet in Paris, Luo Xuejuan of China breaks the world record in the 50-m breaststroke with a time of 30.47 sec, and Yana Klochkova of Ukraine breaks the record, set in 1993, for the women's 400-m individual medley with a time of 4 min 27.83 sec.

•

Winning films at the Sundance Film Festival awards ceremony in Park City, Utah, include *Daughter from Danang, Personal Velocity, Amandla! A Revolution in Four Part Harmony,* and *Real Women Have Curves*.

•

A series of 2,000-year-old erotic frescoes, discovered in 1985 on the walls of a bathhouse in Pompeii, Italy, go on view to the public for the first time since AD 79.

20 A new constitution providing for a president to be elected for a seven-year term and a bicameral legislature is approved in a referendum in the Republic of the Congo.

•

At the Golden Globe Awards in Beverly Hills, Calif., best picture honours go to *A Beautiful Mind* and *Moulin Rouge;* best director goes to Robert Altman for *Gosford Park;* and the screenplay award goes to Akiva Goldsman for *A Beautiful Mind*.

21 U.S. Secretary of State Colin Powell announces that the U.S. will contribute nearly $300 million to the reconstruction of Afghanistan, close to one-fifth of what the UN estimates will be needed in the first year; the following day other countries agree to provide a total of $4.5 billion.

•

In the field of children's literature, the Newbery Medal is awarded to Linda Sue Park for *A Single Shard,* and David Wiesner wins the Caldecott Medal for his reworking of *The Three Pigs*.

22 The Kmart Corp. files for bankruptcy protection in the largest such action ever made by a retail company; it plans to remain in business and continue operating its stores, however.

•

The Hart Senate Office Building is finally declared free of anthrax contamination and reopens; it had been closed since mid-October 2001.

•

Philip Pullman wins the 2001 Whitbread Book of the Year Award, for books published in the U.K., for his young-adult novel *The Amber Spyglass;* it is the first time that a children's writer has won the prize.

•

Historian Doris Kearns Goodwin admits that she inadvertently copied some sentences from three other works in her 1987 book *The*

Fitzgeralds and the Kennedys. (*See* January 5.)

23 Daniel Pearl, a reporter working in Karachi, Pak., for *The Wall Street Journal,* is reported missing after he fails to return from what was thought to be a meeting with sources the previous day; on January 27 news organizations receive e-mail saying that Pearl has been kidnapped. (*See* February 12.)

•

The U.S. government, which has come under criticism for its treatment of al-Qaeda and Taliban prisoners being held at the military base at Guantánamo Bay, says it is suspending transport of prisoners there, as it has run out of space to put them. (*See* January 10.)

•

A panel of experts that works for the National Cancer Institute says that studies that have been relied upon as proof that mammograms prevent breast cancer deaths are so seriously flawed that they do not show whether such screening is beneficial.

•

The legislature of the Yugoslav republic of Serbia agrees to restore autonomy to the province of Vojvodina, which has a large Hungarian population.

24 Congressional hearings into the Enron collapse begin; corporate chairman and CEO Kenneth L. Lay had resigned the previous day.

•

U.S. special-operations forces conduct a successful commando raid on what they believe to be a Taliban stronghold in the Afghan town of Uruzgan, killing 21 and taking 27 prisoners; it later turns out that the raid had mistakenly been against anti-Taliban fighters.

The first of a planned seven German warships arrives off Djibouti, where they are to patrol the Horn of Africa, keeping an eye on developments in Somalia and Yemen and protecting shipping.

Leaders of 12 world religions gather in Assisi, Italy, to pray for peace; the event is organized by Pope John Paul II.

25 India test-fires an intermediate-range nuclear-capable missile; as India and Pakistan seem to be on the brink of war, the test is viewed with some alarm by the world community.

26 For the second consecutive year, Jennifer Capriati defeats Martina Hingis to win the Australian Open tennis tournament; on January 27 Thomas Johansson defeats Marat Safin to win his first Grand Slam title.

27 In Bodh Gaya, India, the Kalchakra festival, one of the largest Buddhist gatherings in the world, is canceled when the Dalai Lama falls ill.

PanCanadian Energy agrees to buy Alberta Energy; the new company, to be called EnCana, will be the biggest oil and gas company in Canada.

An accident at a munitions depot in Lagos, Nigeria, sets off dozens of large explosions, causing great damage and inciting panic; hundreds of people, many children, drown while fleeing across canals obscured by water hyacinths, and hundreds more are trampled to death.

The first Palestinian woman to act as a suicide bomber strikes in a shopping district in Jerusalem, killing one other person and injuring scores, including a man who had survived the World Trade Center attack on Sept. 11, 2001.

28 The Doha Round of World Trade Organization talks begins in Geneva, but the meeting gets off to a contentious start.

Verizon Wireless announces the first commercial third-generation (3G) wireless service in the U.S., available on the East Coast, in northern California, and in Salt Lake City, Utah; it will provide high-speed Internet access on cellular telephones.

Global Crossing, Ltd., a fibre-optics company with many high-profile investors, files for bankruptcy protection.

Siim Kallas takes office as prime minister of Estonia, replacing Mart Laar, who resigned on January 8 over the pace of reform.

29 U.S. Pres. George W. Bush delivers his first state of the union address to Congress; highlights of his speech include the creation of a new volunteer agency, the Freedom Corps, and the identification of Iran, Iraq, and North Korea as members of an "axis of evil."

Prime Minister Ilir Meta of Albania unexpectedly resigns his post in an acrimonious dispute with the head of his Socialist Party.

Japanese Prime Minister Junichiro Koizumi fires his popular and outspoken foreign minister, Makiko Tanaka.

30 Chile announces its plans to buy 10 F-16 fighter jets from the U.S.; it is the first time in over 20 years that the U.S. has approved the sale of sophisticated military equipment to a Latin American country.

The Taiheiyo coal mine—the last in Japan—closes, idling 1,000 miners; the 82-year-old mine is located near Kushiro on Hokkaido island.

31 *The World Economic Forum opens in New York City (rather than its usual venue, Davos, Switz.); among the opening-session speakers is the Irish rock star Bono. (Photo below.)*

Crossair, the designated successor airline to the bankrupt Swissair, announces plans that will make it Europe's fourth largest international airline, under the new name swiss.

An interview is published in which Israeli Prime Minister Ariel Sharon says that he regrets that Israel failed to take the opportunity to kill Palestinian leader Yasir Arafat in Lebanon 20 years ago.

Ecuador designates a 557-sq-km (215-sq-mi) area in the Amazon rainforest the Cofán Ecological Reserve after Field Museum scientists from Chicago assist Cofán Indians and Ecuadoran scientists by cataloging the species in the area and declaring it to be the most biologically diverse mountain range in the world.

AP/Wide World Photos

February

1 John Hume, the architect of the agreement that led to the power-sharing government in Northern Ireland, is presented with the Gandhi Peace Prize in New Delhi; the prize has been awarded annually since 1995.

Japanese Prime Minister Junichiro Koizumi names a second woman, Yoriko Kawaguchi, to be foreign minister in an effort to stem the political damage from his sacking of Makiko Tanaka; his approval ratings had fallen 36% since he removed the popular Tanaka from office.

•

The NCAA punishes the University of Alabama's football program for recruiting violations by banning it from bowl games for two years, putting it on probation for five years, and cutting the number of football scholarships it may offer.

2 In Amsterdam, Crown Prince Willem-Alexander of The Netherlands marries Máxima Zorreguieta, an investment banker from Argentina and the daughter of a government official for the military junta that ruled Argentina in 1976–83.

•

Former National Football League players Dave Casper, Dan Hampton, Jim Kelly, and John Stallworth and coach George Allen are elected to the Pro Football Hall of Fame.

3 In a dramatic upset, the New England Patriots defeat the St. Louis Rams 20–17 in the final seconds of the National Football League Super Bowl XXXVI.

•

In response to a recent Supreme Court ruling, the Argentine government offers a new economic plan that will allow the peso to float freely against the U.S. dollar; trading begins on February 11.

4 The eight-year investigation into corruption at the French oil company Elf Aquitaine comes to a close; trials of the more than 40 people implicated in the investigation are not expected to begin for many months.

•

Some 14,000 teachers go on strike in the Canadian province of Alberta; by February 21, when the govern-

ment orders them back to work, their numbers have swollen to 21,000.

5 The World Social Forum, an antiglobalization gathering of some 35,000 attendees, closes in Porto Alegre, Braz.; the summit is more successful in denouncing free trade and U.S. military action than in proposing solutions.

•

The government of Belgium apologizes for its role in the assassination in 1961 of Patrice Lumumba, the first prime minister of the Democratic Republic of the Congo.

•

Major League Baseball Commissioner Bud Selig abandons his plan to eliminate two baseball teams, the Minnesota Twins and the Montreal Expos, for the 2002 season; a court injunction had required the Twins to fulfill their lease by playing in the Metrodome throughout the season.

6 On the 50th anniversary of her accession to the throne of Great Britain, Queen Elizabeth II opens a cancer hospital; her accession came

when her father, King George VI, died of cancer. (*See* June 4.)

•

The *Journal of the American Medical Association* publishes a study indicating that close to 90% of medical experts who write treatment guidelines have undisclosed ties to pharmaceutical companies.

•

Democrat Nancy Pelosi of California becomes the first woman to join the leadership of the U.S. House of Representatives when she is sworn in as minority whip.

7 Engulfed in a scandal that broke with the trial for child sexual abuse of a former priest, John J. Geoghan, the Roman Catholic archdiocese of Boston announces that six priests have been suspended because of similar accusations; this is in addition to two priests who were suspended on February 2. (*See* February 21.)

•

The U.S. government says that Taliban prisoners being held at the U.S. military base at Guantánamo Bay in Cuba will be treated in accordance with the guidelines of the Geneva Convention but maintains that al-Qaeda prisoners are still exempt.

•

Pandeli Majko is appointed prime minister of Albania, replacing Ilir Meta, who resigned in January.

8 The XIX Olympic Winter Games open amid tight security in Salt Lake City, Utah.

Mullah Wakil Ahmed Muttawakil, the Taliban's foreign minister, surrenders to authorities of the new Afghan government in Kandahar.

•

The Alqueva dam in the Alentejo region of Portugal begins filling what will be the largest artificial lake in Europe, in spite of the objections of environmentalists, who protest that the lake will submerge the habitats of rare plants and animals as well as archaeological sites. (Photo below.)

9 Algerian forces say that they have killed Antar Zouabri, the leader of the Armed Islamic Group; under Zouabri, who became the rebel group's leader in 1996, the civil war in Algeria grew greatly in intensity.

•

Princess Margaret, the younger sister of the U.K.'s Queen Elizabeth II, dies.

10 Seven people are ax-murdered in a village near Moscow; the following day Pres. Vladimir Putin takes law-enforcement officials to task over increasing rates of violent crime.

•

At the Olympic Games, German skater Claudia Pechstein breaks her own world record in the 3,000-m speed-skating race with a time of 3:57.70; in the 5,000-m speed-skating race the previous day, American Derek Parra broke the world record, but about 20 minutes later Dutchman Jochem Uytdehaage rebroke the record with a time of 6:14.66.

11 In pairs figure skating at the Olympics, the gold medal goes to Russian skaters Yelena Berezhnaya and Anton Sikharulidze for a performance that most observers believe was inferior to that of Canadians Jamie Salé and David Pelletier, who are awarded the silver medal; a storm of protest ensues. (*See* February 15.)

•

The Roman Catholic Church creates four new dioceses within Russia; the Russian Orthodox Church views this as an attempt to convert Orthodox believers. (*See* March 2.)

•

NBC agrees to pay $7 million per episode to air a new season of the situation comedy *Friends*, with each of the six cast members to receive $1 million; this is a record price for a half hour of television.

•

The World Wildlife Fund Mexico releases information that 74% of the monarch butterflies in one colony and 80% of those in another were killed by a storm in mid-January in the largest die-off of migrating butterflies ever seen.

12 The first day of the Year of the Horse, 4700, is celebrated by Chinese people throughout the world.

•

In testimony before the Senate Budget Committee, Secretary of State Colin Powell says that the U.S. government is looking at options for engineering the overthrow of Saddam Hussein as ruler of Iraq.

•

Pakistani authorities arrest Muslim militant Ahmed Omar Sheikh, a leader in Jaish-e-Muhammad, whom they identified on February 6 as their chief suspect in the kidnapping of American journalist Daniel Pearl. (*See* January 23 and February 20.)

•

The Westminster Kennel Club Dog Show Best in Show prize is won by Surrey Spice Girl, a miniature poodle; the victory is something of a surprise, as Torums Scarf Michael, a Kerry Blue terrier, had been favoured to win.

13 The Lenten season begins in Spain with the traditional "burial of the sardine."

•

The Scottish Parliament passes the Protection of Wild Mammals Bill, which makes it illegal to hunt wild mammals with dogs and thereby effectively outlaws fox hunting in Scotland.

•

The day after Pres. Hugo Chávez announced his decision to let the bolívar float, the Venezuelan national currency falls in value by 19% against the dollar.

14 Emir Hamad ibn Isa al-Khalifah, ruler of Bahrain, proclaims himself king at the head of a constitutional monarchy; elections to the lower house of the new bicameral legislature are to be held in October.

•

The International Court of Justice (the World Court) invalidates a Belgian law that gave Belgium the right to try citizens of any nation for having committed war crimes against citizens of any nation.

•

NATO proposes to Russia the creation of a NATO-Russia Council to serve as a parallel organization to NATO's North Atlantic Council.

•

New York City's Metropolitan Opera debuts its version of Prokofiev's *War and Peace*, with its biggest cast ever: 52 soloists, 227 extras, 120 choristers, 41 dancers, and a horse.

15 After the International Olympic Committee asks the International Skating Union to look into the dispute over the pairs figure-skating awards, the ISU determines that the French judge was improperly influenced and announces that Jamie Salé and David Pelletier are to be awarded gold medals of their own. (*See* February 11 and July 31.)

•

Cassam Uteem resigns as president of Mauritius rather than sign into law an antiterrorism bill that he believes contains undemocratic clauses; the National Assembly elects Karl Offmann president on February 25.

•

Afghanistan's interim head of government, Hamid Karzai, announces that the killing the previous day of Abdul Rahman, the aviation and tourism minister, was a political assassination carried out by other government members.

•

After the chance discovery of a skull, authorities are horrified to discover that the Tri-State Crematory in Noble, Ga., has been piling bodies in the yard rather than cremating them; by early June, 339 bodies have been found on the crematory grounds.

16 Zimbabwe expels Pierre Schori, the head of a European mission to observe the presidential election; the European Union responds on February 18 by imposing

sanctions on the government of Pres. Robert Mugabe and withdrawing its team of observers. (*See* March 13.)

•

Ole Einar Björndalen of Norway becomes the first biathlete to win three Olympic gold medals in the same Games when he wins the 12.5-km competition, having previously won the 20-km and the 10-km events.

17 In their deadliest attack to date, Maoist rebels in Nepal kill 129, mostly police officers and soldiers, in Mangalsen, in the northwest.

•

Responsibility for airport security in the United States is transferred to the federal government.

•

In the Daytona 500 NASCAR race, there are nine crashes, one involving 18 cars, and the leader, Sterling Marlin, is sent to the end of the pack for making an unauthorized pit stop; the eventual winner is Ward Burton.

18 George Speight, who led a coup in Fiji in May 2000, pleads guilty to treason and is sentenced to death, but Pres. Ratu Josefa Iloilo almost immediately commutes the sentence to life in prison.

•

Point Given, winner of the Preakness and Belmont stakes, is named Horse of the Year for 2001; the horse was retired in the summer of 2001.

19 Rain and hail lead to floods and mud slides that kill 69 people in La Paz, Bol.; the storms are the worst La Paz has ever experienced.

•

Brazilian Pres. Fernando Henrique Cardoso says that

the water level in the reservoirs has recovered enough for him to end electricity rationing, imposed in May 2001, on March 1.

•

Health Minister C.P. Thakur confirms that there has been an outbreak of pneumonic plague in a remote region of India's Himachal Pradesh state.

20 A videotape that is delivered to Pakistani officials shows that kidnapped reporter Daniel Pearl has been killed. (*See* February 12.)

•

Jim Shea, Jr., wins the gold medal in men's skeleton and becomes the first third-generation Winter Olympian; his grandfather Jack Shea won two gold medals in speed skating in 1932, and his father, Jim Shea, Sr., competed in Nordic skiing in 1964.

•

A rare calendrical triple palindrome occurs at 8:02 PM, when the time and date are, in the European system, 20:02, 20/02/2002; such an occasion last occurred at 11:11 11/11/1111, and will next occur at 21:12 12/21/2112.

21 John Geoghan, a defrocked priest, is sentenced to 9–10 years in prison for the sexual molestation of a 10-year-old boy; revelations of Geoghan's long history of child molesting while serving as a priest have led to calls for Boston's Bernard Cardinal Law to step down and to the names of nearly 90 current or former priests being turned over to prosecutors. (*See* February 7 and March 8.)

•

Sarah Hughes, a 16-year-old skater from Great Neck, N.Y., exceeds everyone's expectations, including her

own, and skates a nearly flawless long program that includes two triple-triple combinations to win the Olympic women's figure-skating gold medal.

22 Jonas Savimbi, head of the rebel group UNITA, is killed by government soldiers in Moxico province, Angola; Savimbi had been waging war against the government of Angola since 1975. (*See* March 30.)

•

With the results of the December 2001 election still unclear, contender Marc Ravalomanana declares himself president of Madagascar; incumbent Pres. Didier Ratsiraka responds by declaring a state of emergency. (*See* March 4.)

•

Prime Minister Ranil Wickremesinghe of Sri Lanka and Velupillai Prabhakaran, leader of the Liberation Tigers of Tamil Eelam, sign a cease-fire agreement; the truce, brokered by Norway, will be monitored by Norway, Denmark, Finland, and Sweden.

•

In its first suit ever against the executive branch, the General Accounting Office sues U.S. Vice Pres. Dick Cheney over his refusal to release to Congress records of his energy task force meetings in 2001.

•

Japan notifies the International Whaling Commission that it plans to kill 50 more minke whales in 2002 than in the previous year and that, in addition, it intends to kill 50 sei whales; the sei whales are listed as endangered.

23 FARC guerrillas in Colombia kidnap Ingrid Betancourt, a high-profile presidential candidate; two days earlier government forces had renewed operations against the FARC after Pres. Andrés Pastrana Arango accused the rebel group of having hijacked a domestic airliner and kidnapped a senator. (*See* March 16.)

24 *Nature* releases a paper describing the successful cloning of a cat on Dec. 22, 2001; because coat colour in cats is only partly genetically determined, the kitten, named cc, does not physically resemble her genetic "parent."

•

On the final day of Olympic competition, Canada wins the gold medal in men's ice hockey for the first time in 50 years; three days previously the women's team from Canada, the birthplace of ice hockey, had also won gold.

•

Officials in Rio de Janeiro say that 40,000 people in the city have come down with dengue fever, but it is estimated that the number of cases throughout the state may already be as high as 100,000; 17 people have died of the disease.

•

The four surviving Mercury astronauts—John Glenn, Scott Carpenter, Wally Schirra, and Gordon Cooper—gather in Cape Canaveral, Fla., for a ceremony marking the 40th anniversary of the first U.S. manned flight to orbit the Earth.

25 A plan for peace in the Middle East proposed by Saudi Arabian Crown Prince Abdullah 'Abd al-'Aziz al-Sa'ud is seized upon eagerly throughout the Western world and by Israelis and Palestinians.

•

Representatives from the government, three armed rebel groups, and civic organizations open talks in Sun City, S.Af., that are meant to lead to peace and democracy in the Democratic Republic of the Congo; the inter-Congolese dialogue is facilitated by a former president of Botswana, Kutemile Masire. (*See* March 14.)

The Philippines celebrates a new national holiday in commemoration of the revolution that toppled Ferdi-

nand Marcos in 1986; the holiday was announced by Pres. Gloria Macapagal Arroyo on February 12.

26 U.S. Secretary of Defense Donald Rumsfeld disbands the Office of Strategic Influence after Pres. George W. Bush expresses his opposition to some of its proposed functions.

•

France begins a planned one-year celebration of the seminal Romantic writer Victor Hugo, who was born 200 years ago this day.

27 *A train carrying Hindu activists from Ayodhya, where militant Hindus have said they will illegally build a temple on the site of a 16th-century mosque that was pulled down by a mob in 1992, is set on fire by a Muslim mob in Godhra, Gujarat state, India, killing 58; the following day Hindu mobs rampage through nearby Ahmadabad in retaliation, and more than 60 Muslims are killed. (See March 1.) (Photo below.)*

At the Grammy Awards in Los Angeles, top winners are Alicia Keys, who wins five Grammys, including Song of the Year ("Fallin'") and best new artist, and the sound track for the movie *O Brother, Where Art Thou?*, which also takes home five awards, including Album of the Year; Record of the Year is U2's "Walk On."

•

Germany's Federal Statistics Office shows that Germany is officially in a recession.

•

On the centenary of the birth of the writer John Steinbeck, his hometown of Salinas, Calif., holds a tribute, one of more than 175 planned to take place throughout the United States this year.

28 The last day that national currencies may be used in the countries of the euro zone passes uneventfully; most people had fully switched to euros weeks before.

•

The Convention on the Future of Europe, meant to meet for one full year, is opened in Brussels by Valéry Giscard d'Estaing, who challenges the convention to produce a draft constitution for the European Union.

•

Envisat, a European satellite designed to monitor the environmental health of the planet, is launched by an Ariane rocket from French Guiana; it is the largest satellite the European Space Agency has put into orbit.

•

The journal *Nature* reports that scientists have found that the dinosaur *Tyrannosaurus rex* would have been incapable of running quickly or possibly at all, as an insufficient percentage of its body mass was in its leg muscles.

AP/Wide World Photos

March

1 The government of India sends armed forces to the city of Ahmadabad in an attempt to contain the violence of Hindu mobs seeking revenge for the Muslim attack on a train; in the past three days, more than 200 people have been killed in Gujarat state. (*See* February 27.)

• NASA scientists make public the first images and data from the *Mars Odyssey* spacecraft orbiting the planet; hydrogen measurements strongly suggest the presence of water ice.

• In Gary, Ind., Shauntay Hinton, representing the District of Columbia, is crowned Miss USA; she will compete in the Miss Universe contest in May.

2 By means of a satellite television linkup, Pope John Paul II leads prayers in several European cities: Athens, Budapest, Strasbourg, Valencia, Vienna, and Moscow; Russian Orthodox Patriarch Aleksey II characterizes the event as an unwelcome invasion. (*See* February 11.)

• NASA scientists receive a response from a radio signal sent to Pioneer 10, which was launched in 1972 and is on course for Aldebaran, in the constellation Taurus, a trip that will take two million years.

3 A referendum in Switzerland results in a narrow go-ahead for the government to apply for membership in the United Nations.

• Legislative elections in São Tomé and Príncipe are narrowly won by the Movement for the Liberation of São Tomé and Príncipe; the party leader, Gabriel Costa, is named prime minister on March 26.

• Austrian skier Stephan Eberharter clinches the men's overall World Cup title, and three days later Michaela Dorfmeister, also of Austria, clinches the women's overall title.

4 Ethnic Albanian leader Ibrahim Rugova is elected president of the province of Kosovo; the election, by the legislature, is expected to move Kosovo closer to secession from Yugoslavia.

• Murder charges are brought against Foday Sankoh, leader of the Revolutionary United Front rebel group in Sierra Leone, both by a war crimes tribunal formed by the UN and by the government of Sierra Leone.

• Two days after the declaration of a state of emergency in Madagascar by Pres. Didier Ratsiraka, the members of the alternative government appointed by Marc Ravalomanana take over government buildings as the armed forces stand aside. (*See* February 22.)

5 U.S. Pres. George W. Bush imposes tariffs of as much as 30% on steel imported from Europe, Asia, and South America, to begin on March 20 and last for three years; the European Union promises to lodge a complaint with the World Trade Organization.

• In primary elections in California, U.S. Rep. Gary Condit, at the centre of a scandal involving missing federal intern Chandra Levy, loses his bid to be the Democratic Party candidate for his seat in Congress to Dennis Cardoza. (*See* May 22.)

• The final flight of Ansett Airlines, founded in 1936 and at one time Australia's largest domestic carrier, transports passengers from Perth to Sydney.

6 The head of the U.S. Army Corps of Engineers, Michael Parker, is made to resign after he voiced reservations about the $450 million cut in the organization's funds envisioned by the budget proposed by Pres. George W. Bush.

7 Alan Greenspan, head of the U.S. Federal Reserve Board, indicates that he believes that the economic recession has ended.

• In the face of unceasing violence between the Israeli armed forces and Palestinians, U.S. Pres. George W. Bush sends his special envoy, Anthony C. Zinni, back into the fray.

• The scientists who announced in January that the universe is a pale green (*see* January 11) disclose that their conclusion resulted from faulty computation; the colour of the universe is in fact a very pale beige.

8 Kmart, which filed for bankruptcy protection in January, announces that it will close 284 stores in 40 states across the U.S.

•

Bishop Anthony J. O'Connell, who had been assigned to head the Roman Catholic diocese of Palm Beach, Fla., in 1999 after the previous bishop, Joseph Keith Symons, resigned after admitting having sexually molested boys, admits that he committed sexual abuse in the 1970s and resigns. (*See* February 21.)

9 Newspapers in the U.S. report that a Pentagon document discusses the use of nuclear weapons as a key element in military planning and indicates that possible targets would include Iran, Iraq, Libya, North Korea, and Syria.

•

The Mont Blanc tunnel between France and Italy, which had been closed since a truck fire took place in it in 1999, reopens; commercial traffic will be carefully regulated to prevent a recurrence of the disastrous fire.

•

Mexican authorities arrest Benjamín Arellano Félix, head of Mexico's most powerful drug cartel.

•

Following a highly contentious election, Melissa Gilbert defeats Valerie Harper for the position of president of the Screen Actors Guild.

10 Denis Sassou-Nguesso is overwhelmingly elected to continue in the presidency of the Republic of the Congo for a term of seven years.

•

In Barcelona, Spain, more than 100,000 people protest a plan to build dozens of dams on the Ebro River in order to provide water to parched regions of Spain farther south; protesters believe the plan would be an ecological disaster.

11 *As a culmination of observances of the six-month anniversary of the terrorist attacks of Sept. 11, 2001, a temporary memorial made of beams of light to illuminate the sky where the World Trade Center stood is lit. (Photo below.)*

•

A fire breaks out in a girls' school in Mecca, Saudi Arabia; in their panicked attempt to escape the school, the doors of which were kept locked, 14 girls are killed and some 50 injured, and accusations are later made that firefighters were prevented from rescuing the girls because the girls were not wearing *abaya* covering.

•

After weeks of high-profile speculation and hand-wringing about the fate of the acclaimed ABC late-night news show *Nightline,* David Letterman announces that he is declining ABC's offer to move his talk show to its network to replace *Nightline* and that he will remain with CBS.

12 Statistics Canada releases Canada's most recent census data: Canada in 2001 had a population of 30,007,094 and had a growth rate that matched the lowest rate in the country's history.

•

The nine members of the Organization of Eastern Caribbean States enact legislation permitting free movement of people between the member states without requiring the use of a visa or even a passport.

•

The Swiss-born Martin Buser wins the Iditarod Trail Sled Dog Race in 8 days 22 hours 46 minutes, breaking the record set by Doug Swingley in 2000 and becoming the first to finish in under 9 days.

•

Homeland Security chief Tom Ridge unveils a colour-coded system for terrorism alerts with specific meaning for local law-enforcement agencies; the code has five levels, ranging from a low of green to a high of red, and the present level is declared to be yellow, meaning an elevated risk of a terrorist attack.

13 Robert Mugabe is declared the winner of the presidential election in Zimbabwe; his opponent, Morgan Tsvangirai, says the election was flawed, and the U.S. agrees, but African nations hasten to send in congratulations and praise the election. (*See* February 16.)

•

Jamil Abdullah Al-Amin, a Muslim cleric who, as a prominent black activist in the 1960s, was known as H. Rap Brown, is sentenced to life in prison without parole for having murdered a sheriff's deputy in Fulton county, Ga.

14 Leaders of the two remaining republics in Yugoslavia agree to remake the country into a loose federation called Serbia and Montenegro.

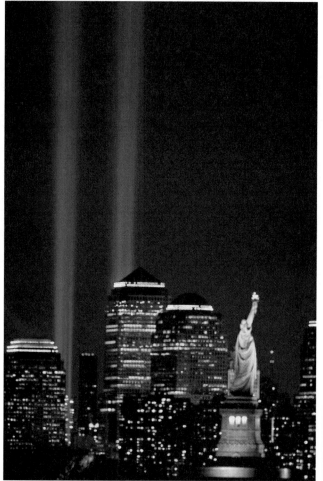

AP/Wide World Photos

●

The government of the Democratic Republic of the Congo pulls out of the peace talks in Sun City, S.Af., citing attacks by a Rwanda-backed rebel group in Katanga province. (*See* February 25.)

●

John C. Polkinghorne, an Anglican priest and former particle physicist, is named the winner of the Templeton Prize for Progress Toward Research or Discoveries About Spiritual Realities.

15 Israel pulls its armed forces out of every West Bank town except Bethlehem.

●

A number of its high-profile clients, including Sara Lee and Abbott Laboratories, sever ties with beleaguered accounting firm Arthur Andersen, as do several of the company's foreign subsidiaries.

●

A two-metre (seven-foot) bronze statue of John Lennon is unveiled at the airport in Liverpool, Eng., which is renamed the Liverpool John Lennon Airport; Liverpool was the hometown of the Beatles.

16 The outspoken Roman Catholic archbishop Isaias Duarte Cancino of Colombia is gunned down outside his church in Cali. (*See* February 23.)

●

An important Aymara religious icon, a monolith known as Bennett (after its American discoverer), is returned to its home in Tiwanaku, Bol., from which it had been taken to La Paz in 1932; the monolith, first erected in AD 373, is greeted with music and jubilation.

17 The Gravity Recovery and Climate Experi-

ment (Grace), sponsored by NASA and the German Aerospace Centre, is launched from the Plesetsk Cosmodrome in Russia; consisting of a pair of satellites, it will produce a gravity map of the Earth that is 100 times more detailed and accurate than any previous one.

●

The 17th biannual Arctic Winter Games, held simultaneously in Nuuk, Greenland, and Iqaluit, Nunavut, open; the games, continuing until March 23, include Dene and Inuit games and dog mushing as well as basketball, skating, and skiing.

18 Almost the entire population of Gibraltar turns out to protest the beginning of talks between Great Britain and Spain over the future status of the territory; it is believed that the talks are likely to lead to joint sovereignty, and the people of Gibraltar are adamantly opposed to Spain's playing any future role in its governance. (*See* February 16.)

●

The Rock and Roll Hall of Fame in Cleveland, Ohio, inducts Brenda Lee, Isaac Hayes, Gene Pitney, Chet Atkins, and Jim Stewart as well as the bands the Ramones, the Talking Heads, and Tom Petty and the Heartbreakers.

●

Maud Farris-Luse, recognized by the *Guinness Book of Records* as the oldest living person, dies in Michigan at the age of 115; the crown is now assumed by Japan's Kamato Hongo, age 114.

●

In the Chinese province of Yunnan, in the mountains near the border with Tibet, the county of Zhongdian officially changes its name to Shangri-La in hopes of drawing increased tourism.

19 The Commonwealth suspends Zimbabwe from membership for a period of one year after concluding that a high level of violence had made the presidential elections unfair.

●

The CEO of the computer company Hewlett-Packard, Carly S. Fiorina, says she has won a shareholder vote to allow a friendly merger with Compaq Computer.

●

The transport ministers of France and Italy break ground for a rail tunnel that will link Lyon, France, to Turin, Italy, and run 52.3 km (32.5 mi), 1.6 km (1 mi) longer than the Channel Tunnel.

●

Scientists say that the Larsen B ice shelf on the east coast of Antarctica, about 3,240 sq km (1,250 sq mi) in extent, has disintegrated with astonishing and unprecedented speed.

20 On the day of the vernal equinox, Farsi speakers throughout the world celebrate Noruz (Navruz), the traditional solar New Year's Day.

●

The government of Italy declares a state of emergency in regard to a flood of illegal immigrants; more than 20,000 illegal immigrants moved to Italy in 2001, and close to 5,000 have arrived since the beginning of 2002.

●

The Bipartisan Campaign Reform Act of 2001 is passed by the U.S. Congress; it is the first major change in campaign finance rules since 1974.

21 Heads of state or government of 50 countries begin two days of addresses before the UN International Con-

ference on Financing for Development, which opened in Monterrey, Mex., on March 18; the meeting is addressing the funneling of foreign aid to reduce worldwide poverty.

●

The oldest-known photographic image, made in 1825 by Nicéphore Niepce and showing a man leading a horse, is bought at auction by the National Library of France.

22 The World Meteorological Organization celebrates World Water Day by noting that, with agricultural output expected to rise 80% and water availability expected to increase only 12%, agriculture must learn to grow "more crop per drop."

●

The U.S. imposes tariffs that average 29% on softwood lumber imported from Canada, maintaining that Canada illegally subsidizes its lumber industry; American homebuilders are as incensed as Canadian officials, who promise to appeal to a NAFTA panel.

●

In Switzerland the Bergier Commission, which began work in 1996, releases its report, stating that the Swiss government worked secretly with Nazi Germany and that Switzerland refused refuge to thousands of Jews during World War II though it was aware of the concentration camps.

●

The Bundesrat, the upper house of Germany's legislature, passes a hotly disputed comprehensive immigration law that is intended to regulate the flow of foreign workers into the country.

23 Street Cry, owned by Sheikh Muhammad al-Maktoum and ridden by Jerry Bailey, wins the

Dubai World Cup, the world's richest horse race.

•

More than one million people in Rome demonstrate against government plans to rewrite labour regulations; government officials respond by accusing labour unions of complicity in the murder of Marco Biagi, and trade unions react by canceling talks planned with the government to try to resolve the dispute over the proposed new law.

24 In the longest Academy Awards ceremony in history, staged for the first time in the new Kodak Theatre in Hollywood, Calif., and hosted by Whoopi Goldberg, Oscars are won by, among others, *A Beautiful Mind,* director Ron Howard, and actors Denzel Washington, Halle Berry, Jim Broadbent, and Jennifer Connelly.

•

Shi'ite Muslims in Lebanon, Bahrain, and Iran observe the holiday of Ashura, when they commemorate the death of the Imam Husayn, son of 'Ali and grandson of Muhammad, in 670.

25 *A magnitude-6.1 earthquake destroys the densely populated village of Nahrin in the Hindu Kush mountain range in northern Afghanistan; about 1,000 people are believed dead. (Photo right.)*

•

Armed officials begin patrolling the shores of Lake Victoria in Uganda to look for crocodiles; 43 people have been killed by crocodiles in the past six months.

•

China launches its third unmanned spacecraft, Shenzhou III, from the Jiuquan Launch Centre in Gansu province.

26 Palestinian leader Yasir Arafat chooses not to attend an Arab summit meeting in Beirut, Lebanon, because Israeli Prime Minister Ariel Sharon has indicated that he might not permit Arafat to return to the West Bank once he has left.

•

The Finnish telecommunications company Sonera and the Swedish company Telia announce that they will merge; the union of the two formerly state-run monopolies will create the largest such company in the Nordic region.

Copyright AFP 2002, by Alexander Nemenov

•

A lawsuit is filed in a U.S. federal court on behalf of all living descendants of slaves and is seeking unspecified damages from FleetBoston Financial Corp., Aetna Inc., and CSX Corp., claiming that the predecessors of these companies profited from slave labour.

27 A Palestinian suicide bomber detonates his explosives in a hotel dining room in Netanya, Israel, as 200 people are sitting down to celebrate Passover, and at least 19 people are killed; Hamas claims responsibility and says it was done to derail the peace efforts.

•

A mentally ill man opens fire at a city council meeting in Nanterre, France, killing 8 council members and wounding 19 people; France, which has an extremely low crime rate, is horrified.

•

General Motors announces a plan to revive the Pontiac GTO model; the GTO, made from 1964 until 1974, was the original "muscle car."

28 Leaders at the Arab League summit meeting in Beirut, Lebanon, agree to a Saudi Arabian proposal to form normal relations with Israel if it will agree to conditions meant to lead to the creation of a Palestinian state, and they also unite in opposing any U.S. military action against Iraq.

•

Juliusz Paetz, archbishop of Poznan, Pol., resigns; he had been accused of sexually molesting teenage seminarians.

29 The Israeli army moves into the West Bank town of Ram Allah and storms the compound of Palestinian leader Yasir Arafat, imprisoning him in his office.

•

In the fourth suicide bombing in two weeks, Ayat al-Akhras, a Palestinian high-school student, detonates her explosives in the entrance to a grocery store in Jerusalem, killing 2 Israelis in addition to herself and wounding at least 30.

•

Direct commercial flights between Delhi and Beijing resume after a hiatus of 40 years.

30 Great Britain's beloved Queen Elizabeth, the Queen Mother, dies in her sleep at Windsor Palace at the age of 101.

•

After over two weeks of secret negotiations, military leaders of the government of Angola and of the UNITA rebel group sign a preliminary cease-fire agreement in the small town of Luena. (*See* February 22.)

•

Oxford defeats Cambridge by just two-thirds of a length in the 148th University Boat Race; Cambridge leads the series 77–70.

31 After a suicide bomber blows himself up in a restaurant in Haifa, killing 14 people, many of them Israeli Arabs, Israeli Prime Minister Ariel Sharon declares that Israel is at war.

•

Parliamentary elections held in Ukraine are won by the party of former prime minister Viktor Yushchenko.

April

1 After a weekend in which three French synagogues were set on fire and two other acts of violent anti-Semitism took place, Prime Minister Lionel Jospin calls out 1,100 extra police officers to guard synagogues and Jewish schools, declaring that any acts of anti-Semitism will be firmly pursued by the justice system.

•

Bishop Brendan Comiskey of the southeastern Irish diocese of Ferns announces his resignation, admitting that he had dealt inadequately with Sean Fortune, a priest who sexually assaulted dozens of boys for a period of about 10 years, before his suicide in 1999.

•

The National Collegiate Athletic Association championship in men's basketball is won by the University of Maryland, which defeats Indiana University 64–52; the previous day the University of Connecticut had defeated the University of Oklahoma 82–70 in the women's championship.

•

A team of Indian and British divers discover what they believe to be the lost city of Seven Pagodas off the coast of Mahabalipuram, India; the underwater site appears to be extensive.

•

Bel Canto, a novel by Ann Patchett, wins the 2002 PEN/Faulkner Award for fiction.

2 Israeli forces pursue Palestinian gunmen into Manger Square in Bethlehem, where the Palestinians seek refuge inside the Church of the Nativity, built over the spot that Christians believe to be the birthplace of Christ; the following day the Israeli army occupies Nablus, the second largest city in the West Bank, and thereby has gained control of every major centre in the West Bank except Hebron. (*See* April 4.)

3 A synagogue in Antwerp, Belg., is firebombed; earlier in the week a synagogue in Brussels had also been firebombed. (*See* April 4.)

•

Bayer A.G. and Exelixis Inc. announce that they have sequenced most of the genome of the tobacco budworm, an agricultural pest; it is hoped that the new information will allow them to create more effective pesticides.

4 The Israeli army completes its takeover of the West Bank when its tanks roll into Hebron; U.S. Pres. George W. Bush demands that Israel withdraw from the West Bank. (*See* April 2.)

•

Military leaders of the forces of the government and of UNITA sign a cease-fire agreement in Angola, the terms of which aim at the absorption of UNITA rebels into Angolan national life.

•

Arthur Andersen announces that it has reached an agreement to sell most of its tax business to another Big Five accounting firm, Deloitte & Touche.

•

A synagogue in the Paris suburb of Le Kremlin-Bicêtre is firebombed despite the presence of a police guard at the site. (*See* April 3.)

5 Representatives of the countries of the European Union and 10 Asian countries meet in the Canary Islands to make a plan to try to stem the flow of illegal immigrants to Europe; the Canary Islands are a frequent intermediate stop for such migrants en route to mainland Europe.

•

A team of Chinese researchers and a Swiss genomics company publish the genomes of two different strains of rice; it is believed that the information will be useful in developing more nutritious and efficient forms of rice and other cereals.

•

Oprah Winfrey announces that she is discontinuing her Oprah's Book Club, which has tremendously boosted the sales of each of its featured books.

6 José Manuel Durão Barroso is sworn in as prime minister of Portugal.

7 Two bombs go off in rapid succession in a nightclub in

Villavicencio, Colom., killing 12 people and injuring dozens more; it is believed that the FARC rebel group is behind the carnage.

8 An international commission announces that the Irish Republican Army has for the second time decommissioned a large quantity of arms; this is regarded as extremely propitious for the peace process in Northern Ireland.

•

Algeria's legislature approves a constitutional amendment that makes the Berber language, Tamazight, a national language.

•

In New York City the winners of the 2002 Pulitzer Prizes are announced: a record seven awards go to the *New York Times,* and other journalism awards go to the *Washington Post,* the *Los Angeles Times,* and *The Wall Street Journal,* and winners in arts and letters include Richard Russo for fiction and David McCullough for biography.

9 Mexico's Senate votes not to allow Pres. Vicente Fox to make a planned trip to the U.S. and Canada; it is the first time the Mexican Senate, which has had the power to do so since the 1850s, has exercised its right to curtail the foreign travel of the country's president.

•

Spain's top investigative magistrate opens an investigation into the country's second largest bank, Banco Bilbao Vizcaya Argentaria, which is suspected of money laundering and falsifying accounts.

•

David Duncan, a former partner at Arthur Andersen who was in charge of conducting the audits for the Enron Corp., pleads guilty to obstruction of justice, admitting that he made an

effort to destroy documents related to Enron's collapse.

•

The 72nd James E. Sullivan Award, to honour the most outstanding amateur athlete in the U.S., is awarded to Michelle Kwan; she is only the second figure skater ever to win the award.

10 At a NASA news conference, scientists describe research on two unusual stars based on data gathered by the Chandra X-ray Observatory that led them to think

AP/Wide World Photos

that the stars might be made of quarks in a form called strange quark matter; if true, the findings would change views on the nature of matter.

•

General Motors and the creditors of Daewoo Motor reach a detailed agreement on the takeover of Daewoo by General Motors.

11 A treaty that creates a permanent International Criminal Court, to be based in The Hague, is signed at

the United Nations headquarters in New York City; the U.S. government boycotts the ceremony.

•

A truck bomb explodes at a historic synagogue, which is said to have been originally built shortly after the destruction of the First Temple in Jerusalem in 586 BC, in Djerba, Tun.; 18 people, mostly German tourists, are killed, and the building is damaged.

•

The Walton Family Charitable Support Foundation, owned by the family that

owns the Wal-Mart store chain, donates $300 million to the University of Arkansas; it is the biggest gift ever given to a public university in the U.S.

12 After pro-Chávez forces fire on anti-Chávez demonstrators in Caracas, Venez., some military generals break ranks, and Pres. Hugo Chávez is forced from office; two days later Chávez resumes his post after popular demonstrations and the condemnation of regional

governments. (*See* October 5.)

•

Princeton University announces that it has hired the prominent African American scholar Cornel West away from Harvard University; West, star of Harvard's Afro-American studies department, had been publicly feuding with the university's president, Lawrence H. Summers, for several months.

13 The Permanent Court of Arbitration in The Hague delimits a 1,000-km (620-mi) stretch of border between Ethiopia and Eritrea, ending a dispute that led to war in 1998–2000.

•

Scotland defeats Sweden for the women's world curling championship; the next day Canada trounces Norway 10–5 for the men's title.

14 *In soon-to-be-independent East Timor's first presidential election, José Alexandre ("Xanana") Gusmão wins by a landslide; the turnout is better than 86%. (Photo left.)*

•

In winning the London Marathon, American Khalid Khannouchi breaks his own world record with a time of 2 hr 5 min 38 sec; Paula Radcliffe of the U.K. wins the women's race, with a time of 2 hr 18 min 56 sec, in the first marathon she has ever entered.

•

For the third time, Tiger Woods wins the Masters golf tournament in Augusta, Ga., becoming only the third person ever to win it in two consecutive years.

15 Pope John Paul II unexpectedly summons all 13

U.S. cardinals to Vatican City to discuss the burgeoning pedophile scandal; previous statements from Rome had seemed to downplay the significance of the issue. (*See* March 8 and April 24.)

•

The U.S. Food and Drug Administration approves the use of Botox for cosmetic purposes; Botox injections temporarily paralyze muscles and thereby smooth wrinkles.

•

Australian architect Glenn Murcutt is announced as the winner of the 2002 Pritzker Architecture Prize; the prize will be awarded in a ceremony on May 29.

•

The Ruth Lilly Poetry Prize is awarded to German-born American poet Lisel Mueller.

•

The 106th Boston Marathon is won by Rodgers Rop of Kenya with a time of 2 hr 9 min 2 sec; Margaret Okayo of Kenya breaks the course record for women with a time of 2 hr 20 min 43 sec.

16 A one-day general strike idles 13 million workers in Italy and virtually shuts down the country.

•

Dutch Prime Minister Wim Kok and his cabinet resign in order to take responsibility for mistakes made by the Dutch government when Dutch peacekeepers were unable to protect the Bosnian town of Srebrenica from being destroyed by Serbs in 1995.

17 A court in Madagascar orders a recount of the votes in the disputed presidential election; the following day Pres. Didier Ratsiraka and the self-declared president, Marc Ravalomanana, agree to form an interim government if the recount shows that neither candidate

got more than 50% of the vote. (*See* April 29.)

•

South African Pres. Thabo Mbeki announces that, in a change of policy, the government will make universally available the anti-AIDS drug nevirapine, which greatly reduces the chances that an infected mother will transmit the disease to her newborn baby.

•

In a settlement, the family of the Nigerian dictator Sani Abacha, who died in 1998, agrees to return to Nigeria $1 billion believed to have been plundered from the country by Abacha during his five years in power.

18 A U.S. fighter pilot in Afghanistan drops a 227-kg (500-lb) bomb on Canadian forces conducting training exercises, killing four Canadian soldiers; the pilot had mistakenly believed he was being fired upon.

•

After 29 years in exile, the former king of Afghanistan, Zahir Shah, returns to Kabul.

•

The U.S. Senate votes not to allow drilling for oil and gas in the Arctic National Wildlife Refuge; the plan had been the centrepiece of Pres. George W. Bush's energy policy.

•

The Organisation for Economic Co-operation and Development publishes its most recent blacklist of tax havens, containing 7 countries, down from 35 in its first list, in 2000: Andorra, Liberia, Liechtenstein, Monaco, the Marshall Islands, Nauru, and Vanuatu.

19 New constitutions are announced for each of the two entities making up Bosnia and

Herzegovina (the Federation of Bosnia and Herzegovina and Republika Srpska); the documents give Serbs, Croats, and Bosnian Muslims equal rights throughout the country.

•

The inter-Congolese dialogue in Sun City, S.Afr., ends without an agreement on an interim government to end the war in the Democratic Republic of the Congo.

•

Science magazine publishes an article describing the discovery of a new order of insects, *Mantophasmatodea*; the wingless mantislike insect order, found in the mountains of Namibia, is the first insect order discovered since 1914.

20 A meeting of finance ministers and central bankers of the Group of Seven advanced industrial nations in Washington, D.C., yields an agreement that will allow indebted countries to more easily renegotiate their payment schedules in order to lighten their burden.

21 In a shocking upset, the first round of presidential voting in France winnows the field of 16 candidates to the incumbent, Jacques Chirac, and extreme right-wing candidate Jean-Marie Le Pen.

•

Socialist Party candidate Peter Medgyessy is elected to succeed centre-right politician Viktor Orban as prime minister of Hungary.

•

Israel begins a partial withdrawal of its troops from the West Bank cities of Nablus and Ram Allah, bringing to a halt its ground invasion.

22 Martti Ahtisaari, a former president of

Finland, is appointed to head a UN fact-finding team that is to look into Palestinian allegations of a massacre in the West Bank refugee camp of Jenin.

•

The U.S. succeeds in orchestrating the ouster of José M. Bustani as director general of the 145-member Organisation for the Prohibition of Chemical Weapons; no successor is selected.

•

A. Alfred Taubman, the former head of Sotheby's auction house, is sentenced to a year and a day in prison and fined $7.5 million for leading a price-fixing scheme.

•

A federal ban on the use of motorized water scooters in U.S. national parks goes into effect.

23 Karen Hughes, counselor to the president of the U.S. and perhaps his most influential adviser, announces her resignation, effective probably in the summer; she feels that her family needs to return to its hometown in Texas.

24 *U.S. cardinals summoned by Pope John Paul II to Rome submit proposals for handling the issue of priests accused of sexual abuse, suggesting dismissal for serial offenders but discretion in cases that are not, in their words, notorious. (See April 15.) (Photo right.)*

As a wildfire near Denver, Colo., doubles in size, the town of Bailey is evacuated; the area is suffering from a prolonged drought that presages a bad fire season.

25 At a NASA news conference, scientists say they have measured the tempera-

AP/Wide World Photos

ture of the coldest white dwarf stars observed by the Hubble Space Telescope in the constellation Scorpius in the Milky Way and have concluded that the universe is about 13 billion years old, which agrees well with other recent estimates based on other ways of measuring.

A Russian rocket blasts off from the Baikonur Cosmodrome in Kazakhstan, carrying among its crew South African Internet millionaire Mark Shuttleworth, the second space tourist and the first person from Africa ever to go into space.

26 Argentine Pres. Eduardo Duhalde, after several attempts, finds a minister of the economy—Roberto Lavagna—who meets with the approval of everyone concerned; he also partially reopens the banks.

A recently expelled student, Robert Steinhäuser, goes on a shooting spree at a second-ary school in Erfurt, Ger., killing 17 people, 13 of them teachers, before turning a gun on himself; the country, which has a low violent crime rate and extremely tight gun laws, is shocked.

27 Pakistan's Supreme Court rules that the constitution allows Pres. Pervez Musharraf to hold his planned referendum on whether his presidency, which was set to end in October, should be extended for five years; the referendum, held on April 30, passes resoundingly.

In an auction of Texas longhorn cattle held by Red McCombs outside Johnson City, Texas, a record price of $59,000 is paid by Vicki Mosser for Day's Feisty Fannie, a heifer that sports horns close to 192 cm (76 in) from tip to tip, which makes her, in the words of her new owner, "the longest-horned longhorn that's ever been sold."

28 Israel agrees to end the blockade of Palestinian leader Yasir Arafat's compound in the West Bank town of Ram Allah, but the following day, Israeli forces seize control of Hebron.

A pipe bomb explodes in an outdoor market in Vladikavkaz, the capital of Russia's North Ossetian Republic, killing seven.

A storm system roars through the valleys of the Tennessee and Ohio rivers, spawning an exceptionally strong tornado in Maryland and killing four people throughout the area.

29 The U.S. regains its seat on the United Nations Human Rights Commission; it had unexpectedly lost its seat on the organization, which it helped found, on May 3, 2001.

The High Constitutional Court of Madagascar says that the recount of the vote shows that Marc Ravalomanana won an outright majority and was elected president; the incumbent, Didier Ratsiraka, who had agreed to the recount, does not accept the result. (*See* April 17.)

Australia's largest medical insurance company, United Medical Protection, files for bankruptcy.

30 In talks sponsored by the Red Cross, North Korea agrees to allow a search for Japanese citizens who Japan believes were kidnapped decades ago, and Japan agrees to search for Koreans taken to Japan before 1945.

Bernard J. Ebbers abruptly resigns as president and CEO of WorldCom, the telecommunications and Internet giant that he created and is replaced by John W. Sidgmore, a WorldCom vice chairman.

May

> *We do not want war. But if war is thrust upon us, we would respond with full might, and give a befitting reply.*
>
> Pakistani Pres. Pervez Musharraf, in his May 27 address to the nation

1 Throughout France more than a million people turn out in May Day demonstrations against right-wing presidential candidate Jean-Marie Le Pen. (*See* May 5.)

• A car bomb created by the Basque separatist organization ETA explodes outside a stadium in Madrid where soccer fans are lined up in anticipation of a game.

• At the National Magazine Awards ceremony, the big winners are *The Atlantic Monthly* and *The New Yorker*, while awards for general excellence go to *Newsweek, Entertainment Weekly, Vibe, National Geographic Adventure*, and *Print*.

2 Israeli forces withdraw from Yasir Arafat's compound in Ram Allah, and a firefight erupts at the Church of the Nativity in Bethlehem, resulting in some fire damage to the structure.

• Erik R. Lindbergh lands his Lancair Columbia 300 airplane at Le Bourget airport after a 17-hour flight that was a re-creation of the historic New York–Paris flight made by his grandfather, Charles Lindbergh, in 1927.

3 Eight rural mailboxes in a circular cluster of small towns in northwestern Illinois and northeastern Iowa are found to be booby-trapped with pipe bombs; each bomb is accompanied by a long, obscure antigovernment note. (*See* May 7.)

• Russia signs an agreement returning Cam Ranh Bay, after 1979 the largest Soviet naval base outside the Soviet Union, to Vietnam.

• Perry Christie becomes prime minister of The Bahamas after the opposition Progressive Liberal Party unexpectedly and overwhelmingly wins the general election.

• A funeral is held in Cape Town for Saartje Baartman, a Khoisan woman who left South Africa in 1810 and was exhibited in France as the "Hottentot Venus" for the rest of her life and after her death; Baartman's remains were returned by Paris's Musée de l'Homme to South Africa where her native Griqua people would decide on her burial.

4 In the 128th running of the Kentucky Derby, a longshot horse, War Emblem, wins; War Emblem had recently been purchased by Saudi Arabian Prince Ahmed ibn Salman and trained by Bob Baffert. (*See* May 18.)

5 Pres. Jacques Chirac wins reelection as president of France with 82% of the vote in the second round of balloting, as against 18% for Jean-Marie Le Pen; it is the

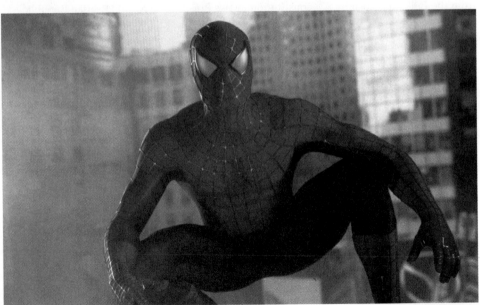

The Kobal Collection/Columbia/Marvel

largest margin of victory in France's history. (*See* May 1.)

•

The government of Nepal says that several recent battles with Maoist rebels have left 400 rebels dead, which, if true, would be a remarkable turnaround in battle fortunes; in recent months Prime Minister Sher Bahadur Deuba has cast the government's war with the Maoist rebels as part of the war on terror.

6 A leading candidate to become prime minister of The Netherlands, Pim Fortuyn, is assassinated; Fortuyn, an anti-immigration advocate with flamboyant views and lifestyle, had quickly risen to prominence in the previous weeks. (*See* May 8.)

•

Pres. Jacques Chirac names Jean-Pierre Raffarin interim prime minister of France, replacing Lionel Jospin.

Myanmar (Burma) announces that it is releasing rights activist Daw Aung San Suu Kyi from house arrest and allowing her to engage in political activity.

•

In its opening weekend in the U.S., the movie Spider-Man *smashes box-office records with a take of $115 million; it is the first movie to make more than $100 million in its first weekend. (Photo left.)*

7 A suicide bomber explodes his weapon in a gambling and billiards club outside Tel Aviv, Israel, killing 15 and wounding 58; Israeli Prime Minister Ariel Sharon cuts short his visit with U.S. Pres. George W. Bush and returns home the following day.

•

Lucas Helder, a student at the University of Wisconsin—Stout, is arrested in Nevada; he is believed to be

responsible for the pipe bombs found in various rural mailboxes in the Midwest. (*See* May 3.)

8 Abel Pacheco is inaugurated as the new president of Costa Rica.

•

A car bomb explodes outside the Sheraton Hotel in Karachi, Pak., killing 14 people, mostly French citizens working in Pakistan.

•

Volkert van der Graaf, a radical animal rights activist, is arraigned in Amsterdam in the assassination of politician Pim Fortuyn. (*See* May 6.)

•

Feyenoord Rotterdam beats Borussia Dortmund of Germany 3–2 in the association football (soccer) UEFA Cup final in Rotterdam, Neth.

9 A bomb explodes at a military parade in Kaspiysk, in the Russian republic of Dagestan, held to commemorate the end of World War II; 42 people, including 12 children and a number of members of a brass band, are killed.

•

Two men push into a bank in Mor, Hung., and open fire with automatic weapons, killing at least six people and deeply shocking a nation unaccustomed to violent crime.

•

Maryland Gov. Parris N. Glendening orders a moratorium on executions pending the completion of a study on whether racial bias is a factor in death penalty cases; Maryland is the second U.S. state to order such a moratorium, after Illinois in 2000.

10 Robert Hanssen, former FBI employee and double agent for the Soviet

Union, is sentenced to life in prison without possibility of parole.

•

After several false starts, the Israeli siege of the Church of the Nativity in Jerusalem is lifted with an agreement that many of the Palestinians within are to be exiled; the siege began on April 2.

11 Italian tenor Luciano Pavarotti cancels what would have been his final appearance at the Metropolitan Opera in New York City, pleading illness; he has announced that he will retire this year.

•

David Beckham, the star captain of the English national soccer team, signs a new contract with Manchester United.

•

Slovakia defeats Russia 4–3 to win its first world ice hockey championship.

12 Former U.S. president Jimmy Carter begins a five-day visit with Pres. Fidel Castro of Cuba. (*See* May 16.)

•

A runoff presidential election is held in Mali between Amadou Toumani Touré and Souomaïla Cissé; on May 24 it is declared that Touré is the winner.

13 A U.S. official arrives in India on a mission to defuse tension between India and Pakistan, which are believed to be on the brink of war, though Indian Defense Minister George Fernandes says in an interview that India will not attack Pakistan.

•

Sears, Roebuck & Co. announces that it has made a deal to buy mail-order retailer Land's End.

14 Ahmed Tejan Kabbah is commandingly reelected president of Sierra Leone; he is credited with having brought peace to the country.

•

Three Pakistani gunmen open fire on a bus and then on the family quarters of a military encampment in Kaluchak, in the Indian-administered area of Kashmir, killing 32 people, mostly women and children.

•

For the first time in Jordan's history, a court grants a woman a divorce from her husband; until a new law took effect in January, men could divorce their wives, but not vice versa.

15 Presidential press secretary Ari Fleischer says that U.S. Pres. George W. Bush was given information in August 2001 that Osama bin Laden was interested in hijacking aircraft in order to attack American interests.

•

Parliamentary elections held in The Netherlands result in 43 seats for the Christian Democrats in the 150-seat legislature and 26 for the List Pim Fortuyn, a better-than-expected showing; Prime Minister Wim Kok's Labour Party wins only 23 seats.

•

The Gold Medal for Architecture, awarded every six years by the American Academy of Arts and Letters, is presented to Frank O. Gehry in a ceremony in New York City.

16 *Granma*, the newspaper of the Cuban Communist Party, unexpectedly publishes the full text of a speech by former U.S. president Jimmy Carter in which he is critical of the Cuban government and supports a proposed referendum on civil rights that the newspaper has heretofore ignored. (*See* May 12.)

•

Scientists at the University of Hawaii announce that they have discovered 11 new moons orbiting Jupiter, giving it a total of 39.

17 Bertie Ahern is handily reelected prime minister of Ireland.

•

A U.S. proposal to exempt peacekeeping troops from prosecution before the new International Criminal Court is not accepted by the UN Security Council.

•

The German media giant Bertelsmann agrees to acquire the assets of Napster, a company that developed a World Wide Web file-exchange system, two days after takeover discussions had collapsed.

•

Legislators in Germany rewrite a clause of the Basic Law to require the government to respect the dignity of animals as well as people.

18 As Indian and Pakistani troops fire at each other across the line of control in Kashmir, India expels the Pakistani ambassador over the attack of May 14.

The World Health Organization agrees to delay the destruction of the last remaining stocks of smallpox virus, due to be destroyed at the end of the year to prevent the disease from ever occurring again, in order to allow time to develop vaccines and treatments in the event that some of the virus falls into the wrong hands.

•

Kentucky Derby winner War Emblem wins the Preakness Stakes. (*See* May 4.)

19 After two weeks of relative calm in Israel, a Palestinian suicide bomber disguised as an Israeli soldier blows himself up in a market in Netanya, killing two people and wounding dozens.

•

As questions as to whether the U.S. intelligence community should have been able to prevent the terrorist attacks of Sept. 11, 2001, are raised in Congress, Vice Pres. Dick Cheney says that there will almost certainly be more al-Qaeda attacks against the U.S.; the following day FBI Director Robert Mueller says that it is inevitable that there will be suicide attacks in the U.S. similar to those occurring in Israel.

•

Pope John Paul II canonizes Amabile Lucia Visintainer, known as Mother Paulina; she becomes the first Brazilian saint.

20 Thousands of people attend the celebration in Dili of the birth of a new nation, East Timor.

•

Officials in Tajikistan say that the country has agreed to cede 1,035 sq km (400 sq mi) of largely unoccupied territory to China, shortly after Kyrgyzstan agreed to cede 1,320 sq km (510 sq mi) of its territory to China; since Soviet times China has maintained that 30,000 sq km (11,500 sq mi) of territory in Central Asia belongs to it.

21 A moderate Kashmiri separatist leader, Abdul Ghani Lone, is gunned down in Srinagar in the Indian state of Jammu and Kashmir; it is unclear who the assassin is.

•

The brokerage firm Merrill Lynch & Co. agrees to pay a $100 million fine to settle a

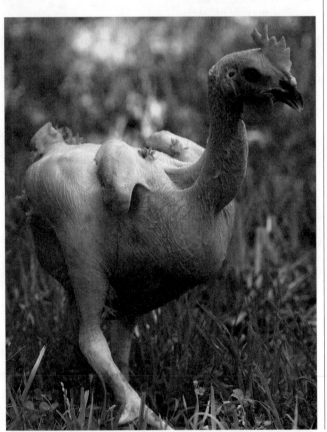

© Havakuk Levison/Reuters 2002

case in which it is accused of having publicly promoted stocks of companies whose business it wanted while privately denigrating those same stocks.

•

It is reported that scientists at Hebrew University in Israel have developed a featherless broiler chicken, claiming that broiler chickens tend to produce excessive body heat, so this benefits the chickens and of course eliminates the need for plucking. (Photo below.)

22 The skeletal remains of congressional intern Chandra Levy, missing since April 30, 2001, are discovered not far from her home in Washington, D.C.'s Rock Creek Park by a man walking his dog; it is later confirmed that she was murdered. (*See* March 6.)

•

In Birmingham, Ala., Bobby Frank Cherry is convicted of four counts of murder in the 1963 bombing of the 16th Street Baptist Church, in which four girls were killed; the former Klansman had hoped to shut down the civil rights movement with the violent act.

•

Pope John Paul II arrives in Baku, Azerbaijan, an almost wholly Muslim country, for a five-day trip that will also take him to Bulgaria.

•

Samuel D. Waksal resigns as CEO of ImClone, which is under investigation for having misled investors as to the regulatory status of its anticancer drug Erbitux; meanwhile, at the Gap, where stock prices have fallen precipitously of late, Millard S. Drexler unexpectedly resigns as CEO.

23 FBI Director Robert Mueller says that he is ordering an inquiry into complaints by senior Minneapolis agent Coleen Rowley that higher-ups had stymied her office's attempts to investigate suspected terrorist Zacarias Moussaoui before Sept. 11, 2001.

24 U.S. Pres. George W. Bush and Russian Pres. Vladimir Putin sign a treaty pledging the U.S. and Russia to deactivate nuclear warheads until, by 2012, there are no more than 2,200 active warheads each, at which point the treaty is to expire.

•

At an International Whaling Commission meeting in Shimonoseki, Japan, Japanese delegates, frustrated at their inability to get a proposal to end the moratorium on commercial whaling brought up for a vote, successfully lead the commission to deny whaling rights to native Arctic communities that depend on the whale for food. (*See* February 22.)

•

Sandra Baldwin resigns as president of the U.S. Olympic Committee after admitting that her résumé contained false information.

•

A baby that weighed only 283 g (9.97 oz) at birth in early February is sent home from the hospital in Florence weighing 1.9 kg (4.4 lb); she is believed to be the tiniest baby to have survived.

25 Lesotho holds parliamentary elections under a proportional representation system new to Africa, in which each balloter votes separately for the party of his choice and the district representative; the system is meant to discourage unrest by making it easier for smaller parties to gain seats.

•

New Zealand's Canterbury Crusaders defeat Australian rival the ACT Brumbies 31–13 in the Rugby Union Super 12 final in Christchurch, N.Z.

•

The first major Andy Warhol retrospective since 1989 opens to great fanfare in the Museum of Contemporary Art in Los Angeles.

26 In the race for the presidency of Colombia, Álvaro Uribe Vélez, who campaigned on a strong anticrime platform, is convincingly elected.

•

Near Webbers Falls, Okla., a river barge bumps into a support of a bridge over the Arkansas River, causing a section of the four-lane Interstate 40 to collapse into the river and a number of vehicles to plunge over the edge.

•

In the Indianapolis 500 auto race, Paul Tracy is penalized for having passed after a yellow caution flag was flown in the final laps of the race, and Brazilian Hélio Castroneves thereby becomes the first person since 1971 to win two consecutive Indy 500 races.

•

At the 55th Cannes International Film Festival, Roman Polanski's film *The Pianist* wins the Palme d'Or and the Grand Prix goes to Finnish director Aki Kaurismaki for *The Man Without a Past*.

•

Azali Assoumani is sworn in as president of the new Union of the Comoros after having been declared winner of a disputed second round of voting that took place in April; each of the three islands composing the union also will have its own president.

27 In a televised speech to the nation, Pakistani Pres. Pervez Mushar-raf urges dialogue with India over the Kashmir issue but asserts solidarity with Kashmiris resisting Indian rule, denies that Pakistan supports terrorist attacks across the line of control, and maintains that Pakistan is ready to fight if need be.

28 Both sides officially agree to the establishment of a NATO-Russia Council, permitting Russia to participate in many NATO discussions.

•

It is reported that Libya has offered to pay $2.7 billion to the survivors of the passengers on Pan Am Flight 103, which exploded over Lockerbie, Scot., in 1988, in return for the lifting of UN and U.S. sanctions against the country.

•

Palestinian leader Yasir Arafat signs a Basic Law, delineating rights of the people and responsibilities of the government, that was passed by the Palestinian Legislative Council in 1997.

29 The World Food Programme and the Food and Agriculture Organization issue a joint statement saying that some 10 million people in Malawi, Zimbabwe, Lesotho, and Swaziland face starvation because of the worst food shortages in 10 years.

•

In a cabinet reshuffle in Great Britain, Alistair Darling is named to replace Stephen Byers as transport secretary after Byers had resigned over, among other things, rail failures, and Paul Boateng becomes the first black member of the British Cabinet when he is named deputy treasury secretary.

•

Mohammad al-Fayed, owner of the genteelly satiric British magazine *Punch*, announces that he has had to close the magazine owing to lack of revenue and declining subscriptions; *Punch* was published from July 1841 to April 1992, then relaunched by Fayed in September 1996.

•

Black Sabbath vocalist Ozzy Osbourne and his family agree to a contract for a second season of MTV's surprise hit television show *The Osbournes*, chronicling everyday life in the rock star's household.

30 A ceremony is held to mark the conclusion of the cleanup operation at the site of the World Trade Center in New York City.

•

The Philip Morris Companies agree to sell the Miller Brewing Co. to South African Breweries.

•

The New England Journal of Medicine publishes the results of a small study of an experimental drug that appears to stop the progress of Type I diabetes.

31 Zimbabwe declares an AIDS-related national emergency in order to take advantage of trade rules that permit it to bypass patents and import cheaper generic versions of needed drugs; it is the first country to do so.

•

In first-round World Cup association football (soccer) play in Seoul, S.Kor., the sports world is stunned when Senegal defeats France, the reigning champion.

•

The Dr. Seuss National Memorial Sculpture Garden—featuring sculptures of the Cat in the Hat, Horton the Elephant, and the Lorax, among others—opens in Springfield, Mass.

June

" We are satisfied with this commitment.... There is
nothing that is human that can be regarded as perfect. "

Nigerian Pres. Olusegun Obasanjo, in Calgary, Alta.,
on the G-8 agreement to provide aid for Africa
in return for reforms

1 In a graduation speech at the U.S. Military Academy at West Point, U.S. Pres. George W. Bush declares that the Cold War policies of containment and deterrence are outdated and must be replaced by a policy of preemptive strikes.

•

Cuba begins use of the euro, a move that officials hope will encourage foreign tourism.

2 In rural southwestern Mexico, 16 people are jailed in connection with a massacre of 26 sawmill workers from the village of Santiago Xochiltepec two days previously; the event is believed to have stemmed from a feud, mostly over land, between neighbouring villages.

•

The 56th annual Tony Awards are presented at Radio City Music Hall in New York City; winners include the plays *The Goat, or Who Is Sylvia?, Thoroughly Modern Millie, Private Lives,* and *Into the Woods* and the actors Alan Bates, Lindsay Duncan, John Lithgow, and Sutton Foster.

3 *A rock concert and fireworks show at Buckingham Palace are a high point of the four-day official celebration of Queen Elizabeth II's golden jubilee, commemorating her 50 years on the throne. (Photo right.)*

•

Under threat of indictment for tax evasion, Dennis Kozlowski resigns as chairman and CEO of the industrial services manufacturing giant Tyco International Ltd.

•

Astronomers with the Sloan Digital Sky Survey report to the American Astronomical Society that they have for the first time seen a star cluster being pulled apart by the gravitational forces of the galactic disk of the Milky Way Galaxy.

•

Winners of the Council of Fashion Designers of America Awards include Narciso Rodriguez for women's wear and Marc Jacobs for men's wear; Rick Owens wins the Perry Ellis Award for newcomers.

4 Japan ratifies the Kyoto Protocol on global warming, improving the document's chances of becoming international law; Japan is the world's fourth-largest emitter of the greenhouse gas carbon dioxide, behind the U.S., the European Union (all of whose members have ratified the agreement), and Russia.

•

In a television interview, Pres. Jorge Batlle of Uruguay tearfully apologizes for having called Argentines "a bunch of thieves from start to finish"; his remarks had been made the previous day in a portion of an interview that he believed would not be broadcast.

5 Kim Hong Gul, the youngest son of South Korean Pres. Kim Dae Jung, is indicted on charges of influence peddling, accepting bribes, and tax evasion; another son is also under investigation.

•

R&B star R. Kelly is indicted in Chicago on charges of child pornography.

•

The space shuttle *Endeavour* takes off with a new crew for the International Space Station after a week of delays occasioned by bad weather and faulty equipment.

•

After seven months of protests, doctors in France reach an agreement with the state health insurer that allows them to raise their prices 8% for office visits and 43% for house calls, in return for which the doctors promise to help the government reduce health care costs.

6 In a nationally televised address, U.S. Pres. George W. Bush proposes the creation of a new cabinet post, the Department of Homeland Security, under which would fall the Customs Service, the Secret Service, the Immigration and Naturalization Service, and the Coast Guard but not the FBI or the CIA.

•

A judge in California fines the R.J. Reynolds Tobacco Co. $20 million for failing to honour the 1998 tobacco settlement; the company has continued to place advertisements in magazines that are read by a large proportion of teenagers.

•

It is reported that home arts maven Martha Stewart, a close friend of former ImClone CEO Samuel Waksal, sold all her ImClone

AP/Wide World Photos

stock shortly before an unfavourable ruling by the U.S. Food and Drug Administration was made public; on June 12 Waksal is arrested on charges of insider trading.

•

The 460-year-old Wye Oak, Maryland's state tree, is felled in a thunderstorm; the tree was 970 cm (382 in) in circumference and 29 m (96 ft) tall.

7 The leaders of Russia, China, Kazakhstan, Uzbekistan, Kyrgyzstan, and Tajikistan sign a charter that creates a new international organization, the Shanghai Cooperation Organization.

8 A government official in India says that Pakistani incursions into the Indian-administered portion of Kashmir have been halted and that this is a promising development; two days later India begins pulling back naval vessels from Pakistan's coast.

•

Two thousand people in Glenwood Springs, Colo., are evacuated from the path of the fast-moving Coal Seam Fire; another fire ignited on this day in the Pike National Forest near Denver, the Hayman Fire, grows within two days to become the largest wildfire in Colorado's history.

•

Serena Williams defeats her older sister, Venus, to win the women's French Open tennis title; the following day Albert Costa of Spain defeats his countryman Juan Carlos Ferrero to win the men's title.

•

Kentucky Derby and Preakness winner War Emblem stumbles coming out of the gate at the Belmont Stakes; the winner of the last of the Triple Crown horse races, Sarava, at 70–1, is the longest-shot horse ever to win the Belmont.

•

In Memphis, Tenn., Lennox Lewis defeats Mike Tyson by a knockout in the eighth round to retain his World Boxing Council and International Boxing Federation heavyweight titles.

•

Documenta 11, an exposition featuring the work of more than 100 international artists, opens in Kassel, Ger.; Documenta is a thorough survey of contemporary art that is mounted every five years.

9 The Sudan People's Liberation Army, fighting for autonomy for the non-Muslim south of The Sudan, says that it has seized control of the garrison town of Kapoeta, its biggest victory in two years.

•

Nature magazine publishes the discovery, by the Wellcom Trust Cancer Genome Project at the Sanger Institute near Cambridge, Eng., of a gene involved in malignant melanoma, the deadliest form of skin cancer; it is an early benefit of the completion of the human genome sequence.

•

Pak Se Ri of South Korea wins the Ladies Professional Golf Association championship by three strokes over veteran Beth Daniel; it is Pak's fourth major title and second LPGA championship in five years.

10 U.S. Attorney General John Ashcroft announces that with the arrest of former Chicago gang member Jose Padilla, who is using the name Abdullah al-Muhajir, the Department of Justice has broken up an al-Qaeda plot to detonate a so-called dirty bomb, a radioactive device, in the U.S.

•

For the second time in a week, Israeli forces surround the compound of Palestinian leader Yasir Arafat in Ram Allah.

•

The U.S. Supreme Court rules that the Americans with Disabilities Act does not require employers to give jobs to people whose health or safety would be compromised by doing the job.

11 Afghanistan's *loya jirga* is officially opened; the council will choose a government to rule Afghanistan for the next two years, until elections are held.

•

The U.S. House of Representatives passes a resolution recognizing the Italian-born Antonio Meucci as the inventor of the telephone.

•

In a castle near Glaslough, Ire., the former Beatle Sir Paul McCartney marries the former model Heather Mills.

12 The Los Angeles Lakers defeat the New Jersey Nets 113–107 to win the National Basketball Association championship for the third year in a row; also for the third time, Shaquille O'Neal is named Most Valuable Player of the finals.

•

The World Council of Religious Leaders begins a peace conference in Bangkok to seek ways to reduce sectarian conflict; the conference, attended by more than 100 leaders of different religions, is an outgrowth of the Millennium World Peace Summit in 2000.

•

Two crew members on the International Space Station, Daniel W. Bursch and Carl E. Walz, break the American space endurance record of 188 days 4 hours set by Shannon Lucid in 1996; by the time they return to Earth on June 19, their time aloft is 196 days; the world record is 438 days, held by Russian cosmonaut Valery V. Polyakov.

13 The U.S. formally withdraws from the Antiballistic Missile Treaty, signed in 1972 by U.S. Pres. Richard M. Nixon and Soviet leader Leonid Brezhnev; the following day Russia announces that it is abandoning the 1993 Start II accord.

•

Afghanistan's *loya jirga* elects Hamid Karzai to lead the transitional government for the next two years; the vote, monitored by the UN, gives Karzai 1,295 votes out of a total of 1,575.

•

The Detroit Red Wings defeat the Carolina Hurricanes to

win the Stanley Cup, the National Hockey League championship, for the third time in six years; the score of the final game is 3–1.

•

Astronomers announce that 55 Cancri, a star in the constellation Cancer, has been found to have a planet that has an orbit with similarities to that of Jupiter; it is the first extrasolar planetary finding of a system with a close resemblance to our solar system. (*See* June 18.)

14 A car bomb explodes outside the U.S. consulate in Karachi, Pak., killing 12 people and wounding more than 50.

•

The U.S. Conference of Catholic Bishops, meeting in Dallas, Texas, sets a new policy declaring that any priest who has ever sexually abused a minor may no longer engage in any ministerial duties, although it stops short of requiring that such a priest be defrocked.

15 The 89-year-old Big Five accounting firm Arthur Andersen is found guilty of obstruction of justice by a federal jury in Houston, Texas, and tells the government it will cease auditing public companies by the end of the summer and thus, in effect, go out of business.

•

Rolling Stones vocalist Mick Jagger is awarded a knighthood by Queen Elizabeth II "for services to popular music."

16 U.S. Pres. George W. Bush directs his top security personnel to develop a doctrine of preemptive action against nations and groups believed to be developing weapons of mass destruction or sponsoring terrorism.

•

The popular Italian stigmatic Padre Pio da Pietrelcina, who died in 1968, is canonized by Pope John Paul II in a ceremony in St. Peter's Square.

•

The CEO of Qwest Communications International, Joseph P. Nacchio, is forced to resign; Qwest's accounting practices are being investigated by the Securities and Exchange Commission.

•

For the first time, the U.S. Open golf tournament is played at a public facility, the Black Course at Bethpage State Park in New York; Tiger Woods becomes the first player since Jack Nicklaus in 1972 to win the Masters and the U.S. Open in the same year.

17 Thousands of construction workers walk off the job in Germany in a strike for higher wages; it is the first major strike in the construction sector in more than 50 years.

•

The government of Egypt announces the ousting of Muhammad Fahim Rayan, who has been chairman of EgyptAir, the national airline, since 1981, as part of a major revamping of the carrier.

18 A suicide bomber detonates an explosion on a morning rush-hour bus in Jerusalem, killing at least 19 people; the next day Israel announces that in retaliation it will begin seizing land held by the Palestinian Authority.

•

A team of European astronomers working at the Geneva Observatory say that they have found evidence that the star HD 190360a may have a planetary system even more like our solar system than that of star 55 Cancri. (*See* June 13.)

19 With the French in the lead, air-traffic controllers throughout Western Europe go on a brief strike to protest European Union plans to bring air-traffic control under a single framework by 2005; nearly 8,000 flights have to be canceled.

20 The day before an EU summit meeting in Seville, the whole of Spain is brought to a near standstill by a 24-hour general strike called by Spain's two largest unions in protest against changes imposed by the conservative government.

•

The U.S. Supreme Court rules that an evolving national consensus now considers that executing the mentally retarded violates the constitutional prohibition of cruel and unusual punishment; it does not, however, define mental retardation.

21 A.Q.M. Badruddoza Chowdhury resigns from the presidency of Bangladesh after the Bangladesh National Party accuses him of disrespecting the party's founder by failing to visit his grave.

•

In Arizona the Rodeo Fire, which started three days earlier, threatens the resort town of Show Low, while 14 km (9 mi) away the Chediski Fire is rapidly expanding.

•

The World Health Organization certifies that Europe is free of poliomyelitis; previously the Western Hemisphere and the Western Pacific had been certified.

22 A magnitude-6.3 earthquake hits northwestern Iran in the Qazvin region, destroying six villages and killing at least 235 people.

A pitcher for the St. Louis Cardinals professional baseball team, Darryl Kile, is found dead in his hotel room in Chicago the day before he was scheduled to pitch in a game against the Chicago Cubs; it is later determined that he suffered from clogged arteries and an enlarged heart.

•

Alvaro, conde de Marichalar, becomes the first person to cross the Atlantic Ocean on a Jet Ski when he arrives at a marina in Miami, Fla., four months after setting out down the Tiber River from Rome.

23 *In Arizona the Rodeo and Chediski fires merge, creating the largest wildfire in Arizona's history and passing in size Colorado's giant Hayman Fire; about 121,000 ha (330,000 ac) have been burned in Arizona. (Photo below.)*

24 U.S. Pres. George W. Bush makes a speech laying out a new Middle East policy in which he says that if the Palestinian people end terrorism, reform their economy, establish democracy, and change their leadership, the U.S. will support the creation of a provisional Palestinian state; meanwhile, Israeli forces occupy Ram Allah and surround Yasir Arafat's compound.

•

A law requiring some 3,000 white farmers in Zimbabwe to stop farming goes into effect in spite of the fact that Zimbabwe is facing a food crisis; these farmers are to vacate their land by August 10.

•

Albania's legislature elects Alfred Moisiu to succeed Rexhep Meidani as president.

•

Galileo Galilei, a new one-act opera by composer Philip Glass and director-librettist Mary Zimmerman, has its world premiere at the Goodman Theatre in Chicago.

Susan Jaffe gives her farewell performance with American Ballet Theatre in the title role in *Giselle;* she has danced with the troupe for 22 years.

25 WorldCom, the second largest U.S. long-distance-communication carri-er, says that it has overstated its cash flow by more than $3.8 billion during the past five quarters; the following day the Securities and Exchange Commission files fraud charges against the company.

•

A representative of the FARC rebel group in Colombia orders all the country's mayors and municipal judges to resign or face being killed or kidnapped; the group had previously issued this order to 120 mayors, and 8 have been killed so far this year.

26 A three-member panel for the U.S. Court of Appeals for the Ninth Circuit rules that the Pledge of Allegiance must not be recited in public schools because the phrase "under God," added to the pledge in 1954, violates the constitutional prohibition against government support of a particular religion.

•

China announces that it is undertaking a large-scale restoration of sacred buildings in Tibet, including the Potala Palace, the Norbuglinkha, and the Sagya Lamassery.

27 At the Group of Eight meeting in Calgary, Alta., a program is announced that will give billions of dollars in aid to African countries that adopt a wide range of reforms in their governments and economies.

The U.S. Supreme Court rules that a program in place in Cleveland, Ohio, whereby public-school money is given to students in the form of vouchers to be used at the private school of their choice does not violate the separation of church and state, even though some 95% of the vouchers are used to pay tuition at religious schools.

28 The Xerox Corp. announces that between 1997 and 2001 it overstated its equipment revenue by $6.4 billion and its pretax income by $1.4 billion, a much larger restatement than had been anticipated.

29 A North Korean patrol boat exchanges fire with a South Korean vessel, sinking it; each country blames the other for the incident.

30 The price of a first-class postage stamp in the U.S. rises 3 cents to 37 cents.

•

A part-time firefighter is charged with having started Arizona's Rodeo Fire in order to secure employment; earlier a U.S. Forest Service employee had been charged with setting Colorado's Hayman Fire.

•

In Yokohama, Japan, Brazil defeats Germany 2–0 to win the World Cup association football (soccer) championship.

David McNew/Getty Images

July

1 U.S. fighter airplanes strike a wedding party in Oruzgan province in Afghanistan, killing some 48 civilians; the following day, for the first time in the war, the government of Afghanistan demands an explanation.

•

A chartered Russian passenger airliner, Bashkirian Airlines Flight 2937, and a cargo plane operated by DHL International EC collide over Lake Constance, on the border between Germany and Switzerland; all 71 persons aboard the two airliners are killed. (Photo right.)

•

A new legal code, enshrining rights guaranteed in Western countries, goes into effect in Russia; it replaces a code written in 1960.

•

New rules designed to make immigration considerably more difficult go into effect in Denmark.

2 Adventurer Steve Fossett succeeds in becoming the first person to fly a balloon solo around the world when he crosses longitude 117° E off the south coast of Western Australia, where he had

started 13 days previously; it is his sixth attempt at the goal, and he traveled some 31,220 km (19,400 mi; [the circumference of the Earth at the Equator is about 40,070 km, or 24,900 mi]).

•

The United Nations releases a report ahead of the 14th International AIDS Conference that says that earlier analyses underestimated the spread of the disease and that it is now projected that the number of deaths from AIDS between 2000 and 2020 will reach 68 million.

•

Former Mexican president Luis Echeverría is called before a special prosecutor

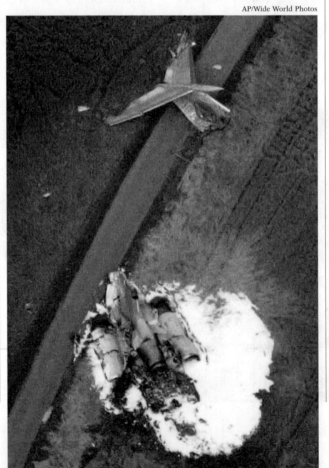

AP/Wide World Photos

to face questions about the government violence in the 1960s and '70s; it is the first time that a former head of state has been called to account in Mexico.

3 NASA launches a probe that constitutes the Comet Nucleus Tour (CONTOUR) mission; it is intended to intercept and probe, with cameras and chemical-measuring instruments, two nearby comets over the next four years. (*See* August 15.)

•

Texas Gov. Rick Perry declares 29 counties in central Texas a disaster area; 41 cm (16 in) of rain had fallen during the previous weekend in San Antonio, which normally sees 5 cm (2 in) of rain in the entire month of July.

4 A man armed with two handguns opens fire at the El Al Airlines ticket counter at the Los Angeles International Airport and kills two people before being killed himself by a security guard.

•

Greek police announce that they have in custody a member of the terrorist organization November 17 for the first time in the 27 years the group has been active. (*See* July 26.)

5 Dozens of people are killed when bombs explode in several areas where Algerians are celebrating the 40th anniversary of the country's independence; it is believed that Islamist rebels are behind the carnage.

The Constitutional Court in South Africa orders the government to provide nevirapine to HIV-infected pregnant women in state hospitals.

A new branch of the Imperial War Museum, the Imperial War Museum North, opens in Manchester, Eng., in a building designed by Daniel Libeskind and meant to echo the museum's theme—war and conflict in the 20th and 21st centuries.

6 Haji Abdul Qadir, a vice president of Afghanistan and one of the few Pashtun members of the interim government, is assassinated.

American tennis star Serena Williams defeats her sister, Venus, to win her first Wimbledon title; the following day Australian Lleyton Hewitt defeats David Nalbandian of Argentina to win the men's title in the most lopsided final at Wimbledon since 1984.

The Museum of Glass opens in Tacoma, Wash., featuring contemporary glass art and a glassblowing studio; it is linked to downtown Tacoma by the Chihuly Bridge of Glass, showcasing the work of Tacoma native Dale Chihuly.

7 A coal mine fire in Ukraine kills 35 miners, though 79 are saved; Ukraine has an unusually high rate of coal mine disasters.

American Juli Inkster wins her seventh major golf tournament when she defeats Annika Sörenstam of Sweden by two strokes to win the U.S. Women's Open; on the same day, Jerry Kelly defeats fellow American Davis Love III by two strokes to win the Western Open golf tournament.

8 The large German engineering company Babcock Borsig's attempt to avoid insolvency is unsuccessful, and the company becomes the fourth major enterprise in Germany to fail this year.

The on-line auction house eBay Inc. announces plans to buy PayPal, Inc., the most successful on-line payment service.

9 Bands, dancers, and military displays attend the inauguration of the African Union, the new international organization that replaces the Organization of African Unity, in Durban, S.Af.

Celebrations of Argentina's Independence Day turn into one of the largest protests to date against the continuing economic crisis.

U.S. baseball commissioner Bud Selig disappoints fans when he stops the All-Star Game after 11 innings, though the score is tied at 7–7; the teams' managers were concerned that they did not have enough substitute players, especially pitchers, to continue.

Standard & Poor's surprises the financial community by replacing seven non-American companies on its benchmark 500 index: Royal Dutch Petroleum, Unilever NV, Nortel Networks, Alcan Inc., Barrick Gold Corp., Placer Dome Inc., and Inco Ltd. are replaced by U.S.-based companies Goldman Sachs, United Parcel Service, Principal Financial Group, Prudential Financial, eBay Inc., Electronic Arts, and SunGard Data Systems.

10 The Nasdaq composite stock index ends the session at 1,346.01, its lowest close since May 19, 1997.

U.S. Navy officials confirm that marine archaeologist Robert D. Ballard has likely found *PT 109*, the patrol torpedo boat commanded by John F. Kennedy, in the Solomon Islands; the vessel was sunk by a Japanese destroyer in 1943.

11 *Nature* magazine publishes a paper that describes the finding in Chad of a hominid skull with a mix of hominid and apelike characteristics that is believed to be an astonishing six million to seven million years old; the find is described as revolutionary.

Moroccan soldiers seize the uninhabited islet of Perejil, claimed by Spain since 1668.

The Italian Parliament lifts the constitutional ban that since 1948 had prevented male members of the house of Savoy from entering Italy; the former ruling family of Italy lives in exile in Switzerland.

12 After weeks of confrontation and negotiations, the UN Security Council effectively permits UN peacekeeping troops from the U.S. to be immune from prosecution by the International Criminal Court for a period of one year, and the mandates for the peacekeeping missions in Bosnia and Herzegovina and the Prevlaka peninsula in Croatia are then renewed.

Vladimir Spidla is appointed by Pres. Vaclav Havel as prime minister of the Czech Republic.

13 In the city of Jammu in the Indian-administered part of Kashmir, a number of men invade a Hindu shantytown and, with automatic weapons and grenades, kill at least 27 people.

A wildfire begins in the Coast Ranges of southwestern Oregon and over the next few weeks grows to become one of the largest wildfires in the state's history, the Biscuit Fire.

14 Just before the annual Bastille Day military parade in Paris, a gunman attempts to assassinate French Pres. Jacques Chirac; no one is hurt.

15 The giant drug company Pfizer Inc. announces that it will buy Pharmacia Corp.; the combined company will be the largest pharmaceutical company in the world.

In Hyderabad, Pak., under extremely tight security, Ahmed Omar Saeed Sheikh is sentenced to death for the kidnapping and murder of American reporter Daniel Pearl.

In a plea agreement that surprises observers, John Walker Lindh, the American who was captured with Taliban forces in late 2001, pleads guilty to two charges and agrees to a 20-year prison term.

In the face of nationwide protests over the economy, in which two people were killed, Paraguayan Pres. Luis González Macchi declares a state of emergency.

16 The Irish Republican Army publishes a full apology to the families of those killed by IRA activities, in particular noncombatants; the apology comes just before the 30th anniversary of Bloody Friday, when a series of 22 IRA bombs killed 9 people and injured 130.

The Irish Hunger Memorial, a 0.2-ha (0.5-ac) artistic reproduction of an Irish hillside with a potato field and a fieldstone cottage, opens in New York City.

After nearly a month of relative quiet, a bus approaching a Jewish settlement in the West Bank is ambushed, and nine people are killed.

17 Spanish special forces, with backing from air and sea, retake the islet of Perejil from the occupying force of six Moroccan soldiers.

Two suicide bombers strike in a low-income immigrant neighbourhood in Tel Aviv, killing five people in addition to themselves.

Temperatures reach 30 °C (86 °F) in Buffalo, N.Y., where 100 years earlier Willis Haviland Carrier invented the first air conditioner; Carrier developed his device to stabilize lithographs at a printing company.

18 National and state legislators in India elect a new president, A.P.J. Abdul Kalam, a nuclear scientist and a Muslim.

Robert W. Pittman, one of the architects of America Online and a leading voice in favour of the merger of AOL with Time Warner, resigns as chief operating officer of AOL Time Warner in a major reorganization that sees almost all the top positions filled by Time Warner old-media veterans.

19 The findings of a yearlong inquiry into the activities of convicted mass murderer Harold Shipman are published by the leader of the investigation, Dame Janet Smith; she believes that Shipman, a doctor in Hyde, Eng., murdered at least 215 of his patients.

A panel of scientists studying the problem of how to prevent the northern snakehead, a voracious Chinese fish that has become established in a pond near Annapolis, Md., from spreading into rivers and streams recommends poisoning all the fish in the pond and then reestablishing the native populations.

The U.S. Department of Agriculture announces a recall of 8.6 million kg (19 million lb) of ground beef produced in a ConAgra Beef Co. plant in Greeley, Colo.; 19 people in six states had become ill from eating the meat, which was contaminated with *Escherichia coli* bacteria.

The International Spy Museum, featuring interactive exhibits and high-tech gadgets, opens in Washington, D.C. (Photo below.)

20 A preliminary peace agreement between the government of The Sudan and the Sudanese People's Liberation Army is signed after five weeks of negotiations; a week later Pres. Omar Hassan al-Bashir meets with rebel leader John Garang in Kampala, Uganda.

Under a deal brokered by the U.S., Spanish soldiers withdraw from the islet of Perejil and the status quo ante is restored.

21 The communications company WorldCom files for bankruptcy; at $107 billion, it by far surpasses Enron's ($63 billion) as the biggest bankruptcy filing in American history.

German race-car driver Michael Schumacher wins the French Grand Prix and secures the title for the season; he is the second person ever to win five Formula One world drivers titles.

Ernie Els of South Africa emerges the winner in the first four-man play-off in the history of the British Open golf tournament, defeating Australians Steve Elkington and Stuart Appleby and Thomas Levet of France.

22 Officials in Africa announce that a tentative agreement between Rwanda and the Democratic Republic of the Congo has been reached whereby Congo will demobilize guerrillas who threaten Rwanda, and Rwanda will withdraw its troops from the eastern portion of Congo; Pres. Paul Kagame of Rwanda and Pres. Joseph Kabila of Congo sign the agreement on July 30.

•

The U.S. government chooses to withhold previously approved funding for the UN Population Fund on the basis that it believes that the international organization condones the practice of mandatory abortions in China, in spite of the fact that its own investigative team found no evidence to support the contention.

23 U.S. Pres. George W. Bush signs a resolution approving the creation of a repository for radioactive by-products of the country's nuclear energy reactors under Yucca Mountain in Nevada, ending 20 years of discussion and debate over the best place to store such materials; they are currently housed in 131 temporary sites in 39 states.

•

An Israeli warplane fires a missile into the home of Hamas leader Sheikh Salah Shehada in Gaza City, killing at least 14 people, several of them children, in addition to Shehada.

•

Britain announces that Rowan Williams, a Welsh churchman of a notably liberal bent, will succeed George Carey as archbishop of Canterbury when Carey retires in October.

•

Pope John Paul II arrives in Toronto for the weeklong World Youth Day festival, which he addresses on July 25.

24 After falling for several weeks, the Dow Jones Industrial Average posts its second largest one-day point gain (488.95 points) since

the recovery from the market crash of 1987.

•

John Rigas, the founder and former CEO of Adelphia Communications Corp., and his sons Timothy and Michael are arrested on charges of embezzlement of hundreds of millions of dollars from the company, which filed for bankruptcy in June.

•

The UN Development Programme releases its annual Human Development Report, in which it ranks Norway as the most developed and Sierra Leone as the least developed countries in the world.

25 A group of American investors, led by the Texas Pacific Group, agrees to buy Burger King from the British liquor concern Diageo PLC.

•

In San Juan, P.R., thousands gather to commemorate the 50th anniversary of the island's becoming a U.S. commonwealth, while a similarly large group of independence advocates protest the same event.

26 In Indonesia Tommy Suharto (Hutomo Mandala Putra), the son of former president Suharto, is convicted of murder and sentenced to 15 years in prison for having hired assassins to kill a judge who had sentenced him to prison for corruption.

•

Police in Greece arrest Nikos Papanastasiou, who is believed to be one of the founders of the November 17 terrorist group. (*See* July 4.)

27 At an air show near Lviv, Ukraine, a Ukrainian air force Sukhoi Su-27 fighter jet performing

an acrobatic stunt crashes and skids into the crowd, killing 85 spectators in the world's most deadly air show accident to date.

28 After days of frantic efforts all nine miners trapped in a coal mine in Quecreek, Pa., after a wall leading into a flooded abandoned mine was breached on July 25 are rescued.

•

Thomas Middelhoff, the chairman and CEO of the German media conglomerate Bertelsmann AG, is forced out; Gunter Thielen is named as his replacement.

•

Qwest Communications International Inc., the dominant local phone service provider in 14 western U.S. states, announces that it incorrectly accounted for $1.16 billion in transactions between 1999 and 2001.

•

American Lance Armstrong coasts to his fourth consecutive victory in the Tour de France bicycle race.

29 A pod of 56 pilot whales strands itself on a Cape Cod Bay, Mass., beach; rescuers drive 46 of them back to sea, but the following day they wash up 40 km (25 mi) north, and volunteers are unable to save them.

•

Workers at the Edenhurst Gallery in Los Angeles discover that during the previous night two valuable Maxfield Parrish murals were stolen.

30 U.S. Pres. George W. Bush signs into law a broad new act intended to crack down on corporate fraud; it is believed to be the most far-reaching change in business regulation since the 1930s.

•

Vanguard Airlines Inc., which operates 70 flights a day in 18 cities and is based in Kansas City, Mo., announces that it is filing for bankruptcy and ceasing operations.

•

Uruguay closes its banks to prevent a run, and the following day it is announced that the banks will remain closed for the rest of the week. (*See* August 4.)

•

In Guatemala City, Guat., Pope John Paul II canonizes Pedro de San José Betancur, a 17th-century Spanish missionary and the first person from Central America to be canonized; the following day in Mexico City, the pontiff canonizes Juan Diego, an Aztec who is said to have received a vision of the Virgin of Guadalupe in 1531 but who is not universally believed to have actually lived.

31 A bomb explodes in the cafeteria at the Frank Sinatra International Student Center of the Hebrew University of Jerusalem, killing nine people, five of them Americans, and wounding dozens, among them a number of Israeli Arabs.

•

A clerk in the Ministry of Education in Beirut, Lebanon, guns down eight co-workers before running out of ammunition; it is thought that financial difficulties drove him over the edge.

•

Albania's legislature approves Socialist Party leader Fatos Nano as prime minister.

•

An Uzbek man believed to be a member of Russian organized crime is arrested in Italy on suspicion of having conspired to rig the outcomes of the pairs figure-skating and ice-dancing competitions at the Olympic Winter Games in Salt Lake City, Utah. (*See* February 15.)

August

> *The devastation caused by the flood offers much opportunity to build better, more sensibly, in a more intelligent manner. To build more beautiful buildings than some of those that have been destroyed.*
>
> Czech Republic Pres. Vaclav Havel, speaking to reporters on the aftermath of catastrophic flooding, August 27

1 WorldCom's former chief financial officer, Scott D. Sullivan, and its former controller, David F. Myers, are publicly escorted in handcuffs to a federal courthouse in New York City to face fraud charges. (*See* July 21.)

•

As it increasingly appears that the U.S. is making plans to invade Iraq, the Iraqi government for the first time since 1998 requests that the head of the UN team that is charged with inspecting Iraq for weapons violations go to Baghdad for negotiations.

•

The Education Ministry in Iran decrees that, for the first time since 1979, teachers and students in girls' schools in Tehran are permitted to remove their veils in the classroom.

2 Representatives of the Angolan government and of the UNITA rebels declare that the war between them, which began in 1975, is officially over. (*See* April 4.)

•

In response to the attack at the Hebrew University of Jerusalem on July 31, Israeli forces conduct a house-to-house search for explosives laboratories and suspected terrorists in the old city of Nabulus in the West Bank.

•

Health officials in the U.S. state of Louisiana report that a recent outbreak of West Nile virus has left 4 people dead and 58 people sick; with additional cases reported in Texas and Mississippi, it is the largest outbreak of the disease since it was first detected in the U.S. in 1999.

3 The Turkish Grand National Assembly passes a package of reforms that among other things abolishes the death penalty in peacetime and permits radio and television broadcasting in the Kurdish language; the hotly debated reforms are made with an eye toward Turkey's joining the European Union.

•

Chip Chip Hooray wins the Hambletonian final at the Meadowlands Racetrack in New Jersey; the same day Victory Tilly wins the Nat Ray final on the same track in 1 min 50.4 sec, a world trotting record.

4 The National Congress in Bolivia elects the political centrist Gonzalo Sánchez de Lozada president by a vote of 84–43 over the radical Indian coca champion Evo Morales; a close popular vote in June had thrown the election to the National Congress.

•

A bomb that kills 9 people on an Israeli commuter bus in Galilee inaugurates a series of Palestinian attacks over the next several hours that include a shootout and three ambushes, with a total death toll of 14.

•

The U.S. government announces that it will make a short-term loan of as much as $1.5 billion to Uruguay to enable Uruguay to reopen its banks, in spite of the assertion of the administration of Pres.

George W. Bush that lending money to countries with weak economies is counterproductive.

5 The newly elected legislature in Papua New Guinea unanimously chooses Sir Michael Somare to be the new prime minister; he is a founding father of independent Papua New Guinea.

•

Armed Pakistani militants attack a boarding school for children of Christian missionaries in the Himalayan foothills northeast of Islamabad; six Pakistani adults are killed on school grounds, but the attackers are unable to penetrate the school itself, and no children are hurt.

6 U.S. Pres. George W. Bush signs into law a measure that gives to the president sole authority to negotiate international trade agreements; presidents from 1975 to 1994 enjoyed this power, once known as "fast track."

Doctors at Mattel Children's Hospital at the University of California, Los Angeles, successfully complete the surgical separation of conjoined twins María Teresa and María de Jesús Quiej Álvarez, who were born joined at the top of the head on July 25, 2001, in Guatemala. (Photo right.)

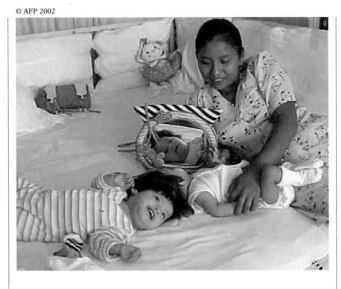

© AFP 2002

7 As Álvaro Uribe Vélez is sworn in as president of Colombia, scattered mortar shells fall in various places in Bogotá, killing 21 people and wounding at least 60; it is assumed that FARC guerrillas are behind the carnage.

•

Construction begins on the foundation of a light-water nuclear reactor in North Korea; the reactor is being built by an international consortium led by the U.S. under the terms of a 1994 agreement that also calls for North Korea to dismantle its graphite reactors and place its plutonium under international supervision.

•

The IMF agrees to loan $30 billion to Brazil in hopes of rescuing the country's flailing economy; the loan is nearly twice what analysts in Brazil had expected.

•

Jordan shuts down the local office of the Qatar-based satellite television network al-Jazeera the day after the network broadcast a program that criticized the late kings Hussein and Abdullah I as being too sympathetic to Israel.

8 In Zimbabwe 2,900 white farmers are ordered to vacate their farms by midnight, but nearly two-thirds defy the deadline. (*See* June 24.)

•

Following the successful July blockading of ChevronTexaco plants by unarmed women in southern Nigeria in order to force community development concessions from the oil company, hundreds more unarmed women blockade ChevronTexaco and Shell offices in southern Nigeria; order is restored by the following day.

•

Turkmen Pres. Saparmurad Niyazov announces plans to rename the months of the year for Turkmen heroes and symbols, beginning the year with a month named for himself.

9 A powerful explosion takes place outside a road-construction warehouse a few hundred metres from a major hydroelectric dam in Jalalabad, Afg.; at least 11 people are killed.

•

Pres. Denis Sassou-Nguesso of the Republic of the Congo announces that the transitional government has succeeded and democratic rule has been restored; the country's new constitution is to take effect at midnight.

10 On the second day of meetings in Washington, D.C., between Iraqi opposition leaders and U.S. government officials, Vice Pres. Dick Cheney is reported to have said via videoconference that the U.S. government intends to replace Iraqi ruler Saddam Hussein with a democratic government.

11 In Indonesia the People's Consultative Assembly approves constitutional amendments that provide for direct election of the president and eliminate reserved places in government for the military; in addition, the assembly rejects the proposed imposition of Islamic law (Shari'ah).

•

US Airways, the sixth largest carrier in the U.S., files for Chapter 11 bankruptcy protection but says it intends to continue operations.

•

Australian golfer Karrie Webb wins the Women's British Open tournament in Ayrshire, Scot.

12 Heavy rains continue to fall in the Czech Republic, and 50,000 residents of Prague are ordered evacuated to avoid flooding—the worst in over a century—which has killed more than 70 people as rivers in southeastern Russia and Eastern and Central Europe overflow.

13 Members of the militant Palestinian organizations Hamas and Islamic Jihad refuse to sign on to an agreement supported by Palestinian leader Yasir Arafat to stop attacks on civilians.

•

U.S. officials react with annoyance to reports that the European Union is urging aspiring members not to sign bilateral agreements with the U.S. to refrain from bringing any Americans before the new International Criminal Court. (*See* July 12.)

14 Pres. Alyaksandr Lukashenka of Belarus rejects the plan put forward by Russian Pres. Vladimir Putin for a union of Belarus and Russia in which Belarus would essentially be absorbed by Russia.

•

Javier Suárez Medina, a Mexican national who had been found guilty of having murdered an undercover narcotics officer in 1988, is executed in Texas over Mexico's strenuous objections.

•

The last major regional chain of discount department stores in the U.S., Ames Department Stores, Inc., based in the northeastern U.S., announces that it is going out of business and closing its 327 stores.

15 NASA announces that it has lost contact with its new Comet Nucleus Tour (CONTOUR) spacecraft; it is later found that the spacecraft may have broken apart.

•

The stage musical version of the 1988 John Waters movie *Hairspray,* starring Marissa Jaret Winokur and Harvey

Fierstein, opens to rave reviews in the Neil Simon Theater in New York City.

16 Pope John Paul II begins a three-day visit to his home country of Poland and celebrates an enormous open-air mass in Krakow on August 18.

After finding cracks in locomotives, Amtrak cancels all its high-speed Acela Express trains as well as a number of other trains, amounting to close to 20% of its service in the northeastern U.S.

The government of Zambia announces that it will not accept donations of genetically modified corn (maize) from the U.S. in spite of the danger of famine.

17 The Charles M. Schulz Museum and Research Center, which features exhibits devoted to the cartoonist and his *Peanuts* comic strip, opens in Santa Rosa, Calif.

The bodies of two 10-year-old girls, missing from near their homes in the town of Soham, Cambridgeshire, Eng., since August 4, are found buried in a wooded area a few kilometres outside town; the search for the girls had riveted Britain.

18 The relatively unknown American golfer Rich Beem defeats Tiger Woods by one stroke, winning the Professional Golfers' Association of America championship.

Israeli and Palestinian negotiators agree on a plan for Israeli forces to begin a withdrawal from the Gaza Strip and Bethlehem, provided Palestinian forces can maintain order.

CNN begins broadcasting portions of videotapes from a library of tapes made and maintained by al-Qaeda and acquired by a CNN reporter in Afghanistan; the broadcast tapes show, among other things, the apparent testing of chemical weapons.

The 43rd Edward MacDowell Medal, for outstanding contribution to the arts, is awarded to the photographer Robert Frank at the MacDowell Colony in Peterborough, N.H.

The *New York Times* announces that beginning in September it will include coverage of commitment ceremonies of gay and lesbian couples in the renamed "Weddings/Celebrations" portion of its Sunday Styles section.

19 A Palestinian newspaper reports that Abu Nidal, who was believed to have been behind many of the more notorious terrorist attacks from the early 1970s to the early 1990s, has been found dead in his home in Baghdad, Iraq.

A large Russian military helicopter, carrying 147 people, crashes in a minefield near the main military base in Chechnya; the death toll is well over 100.

The global mining conglomerate Anglo American PLC says that it has pulled out of the Zambian copper industry, finding it unlikely that it would profit from Zambia's copper mines.

20 Members of the Abu Sayyaf guerrilla group in the Philippines kidnap six Jehovah's Witnesses and two Muslims from the town of Patikul on the island of Jolo; two days later it is found

that the guerrillas have beheaded two of their captives. (*See* January 15.)

George Pell, the Roman Catholic archbishop of Sydney, Australia, takes a temporary leave of office while investigators look into allegations of child sex abuse made against him; he is cleared of the charges in October.

21 Pakistani Pres. Pervez Musharraf unilaterally imposes 29 amendments to the country's constitution; they have the effect of increasing the power of the presidency and the military at the expense of the legislature. (*See* April 27.)

Former Enron financial executive Michael J. Kopper enters a guilty plea in federal court and agrees to cooperate with investigators; he subsequently tells a federal judge that he paid large kickbacks to Andrew Fastow when Fastow was chief financial officer. (*See* April 9 and October 2.)

Canadian Prime Minister Jean Chrétien announces his plans to step down from office in 2004.

22 The U.S. government's September 11th Victim Compensation Fund announces its first awards to 25 families of people killed in the terrorist attacks in 2001.

The U.S. government exempts nearly 200 imported steel products from the steel tariffs it imposed in the spring.

Brazilian Pres. Fernando Henrique Cardoso decrees the creation of the Tumuc-Humac Mountains National Park, 3.9 million ha (9.6 million ac) of mostly virgin

rainforest on Brazil's border with French Guiana and Suriname; the new park, containing at least 8 primate species and 350 bird species, is the biggest tropical national park in the world.

A statue honouring Irish independence hero Michael Collins is unveiled in his home village of Clonakilty in West Cork; more than 5,000 people attend the ceremony, which takes place on the 80th anniversary of his assassination.

Controversial German filmmaker Leni Riefenstahl celebrates her 100th birthday; one week earlier her first movie in half a century, the documentary *Underwater Impressions*, had been broadcast on German television.

23 Georgian security forces move against Chechen guerrillas in Georgia's Pankisi Gorge as Georgian Pres. Eduard Shevardnadze accuses Russia of making raids in Georgian territory.

U.S. District Court Judge Miriam Goldman Cedarbaum rules that the rights to the majority of Martha Graham's dances belong to the Martha Graham Center of Contemporary Dance and not to her heir, Ronald Protas.

Science magazine publishes a report describing evidence that an asteroid hit the Earth some 3.5 billion years ago with 10 to 100 times the impact of the one believed to have ended the age of dinosaurs 65 million years ago.

24 The Carolina Courage wins the Women's United Soccer Association championship when it defeats the Washington Freedom 3–2 and takes home the Founders Cup;

Birgit Prinz is named Most Valuable Player.

•

Saud A.S. al-Rasheed, age 21, surrenders to authorities in Saudi Arabia after the U.S. Federal Bureau of Investigation had put out a worldwide alert for him, believing him to have connections with the hijackers of Sept. 11, 2001; Rasheed says he is wholly innocent and is later released.

25 The two leading candidates for chancellor of Germany, incumbent Gerhard Schröder and Edmund Stoiber, engage in a televised debate that is watched by eight million viewers; it is the first televised debate between political candidates ever held in Germany.

•

The Valley Sports American Little League team from Louisville, Ky., representing the U.S. Great Lakes, becomes the 56th Little League world champion when it defeats the team from Sendai, Japan, representing Asia, 1–0. (Photo below.)

26 The 10-day UN World Summit on Sustainable Development opens in Johannesburg, S.Af.

•

A judge in Spain bans the Basque political party Batasuna, accusing it of involvement in the terrorist activities of the separatist organization ETA.

•

The U.S. Court of Appeals for the 6th Circuit rules that the secret deportation hearings that took place in the wake of the terrorist attacks of Sept. 11, 2001, were unconstitutional, stating, "Democracies die behind closed doors."

27 A district court in Tokyo acknowledges for the first time that Japan engaged in germ warfare against China before and during World War II.

•

Two boys who were found guilty of having set the Internet café fire in Beijing that killed 25 people on June 16 are sentenced to life in prison.

•

Archaeologists working in the ancient town of Butrint in Albania announce their discovery of a large marble statue, possibly depicting the Roman goddess Minerva, believed to date to the time of the Roman emperor Caesar Augustus; it is the first major find at the site, which is a UNESCO World Heritage site and a national park.

28 A federal grand jury indicts a group of five men arrested near Detroit who the U.S. government believes are a terrorist "sleeper cell" associated with Salafiyya, an Islamic extremist movement.

•

Transparency International, based in Berlin, releases its Corruption Perceptions Index 2002, on which Bangladesh rates as the world's most corrupt country and Finland as the least.

29 Authorities in Germany say that investiga-

tors have found that the al-Qaeda cell based in Hamburg began planning the terrorist attacks of Sept. 11, 2001, as long ago as 1999.

30 The World Trade Organization rules that a tax break in the U.S. that is intended to promote exports is in violation of international trade treaties and that the European Union is entitled to penalize the U.S. as much as $4 billion.

•

German Defense Minister Peter Struck says that if the U.S. unilaterally attacks Iraq, Germany will withdraw from Kuwait its specialized unit dedicated to detecting biological, chemical, and nuclear weapons; the unit had been sent out in support of the campaign against al-Qaeda and the Taliban in Afghanistan.

•

Major League Baseball players and owners reach an agreement just a few hours short of a strike deadline; it is the first time in more than 30 years that a new labour contract has been signed in baseball without a strike.

31 Chechen fighters shoot down a Russian helicopter gunship, killing both pilots; it had recently been revealed that the large transport helicopter that crashed on August 19 was brought down by a shoulder-launched missile.

•

The Los Angeles Sparks defeat the New York Liberty 69–66 to win the Women's National Basketball Association championship for the second consecutive year.

•

The U.S.-based search engine Google becomes unavailable to Internet users in China; it is believed that the Chinese government is blocking access to the search engine.

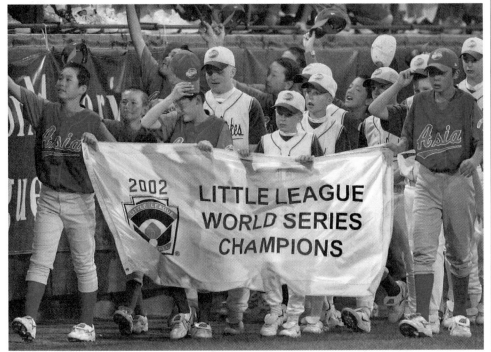

AP/Wide World Photos

September

1 At the UN World Summit on Sustainable Development in Johannesburg, S.Af., Israel and Jordan announce a plan to build a joint pipeline to pump water from the Red Sea into the rapidly shrinking Dead Sea in an effort to prevent the Dead Sea from drying up.

•

A fire starts in the Angeles National Forest in California and rapidly consumes about 4,450 ha (11,000 ac), forcing the immediate evacuation of at least 7,000 recreationists; it is one of three large fires in the Los Angeles area.

2 In the face of a governmental investigation into possible falsification of repair reports at nuclear plants in the late 1980s and '90s, the president and other top executives of the Tokyo Electric Power Co., Japan's biggest electric utility, admit that the company has falsified such reports and immediately announce their resignations.

•

In Los Angeles the new $195 million Cathedral of Our Lady of the Angels, conceived by Spanish architect José Rafael Moneo, is dedicated with a three-hour mass and a procession of 565 cardinals, bishops, archbishops, and priests.

3 Japan's main stock index falls to its lowest point in nearly 19 years, which raises fears of a banking crisis; banks in Japan typically hold a great deal of stock in their clients.

•

The first of four High Energy Stereoscopic System (HESS) telescopes, the most sensitive gamma-ray telescopes to be built so far, is inaugurated in Namibia; the telescope array is a joint European-African project.

4 Delegates at the World Summit on Sustainable Development agree on a plan that sets broadly drawn goals intended to reduce global poverty and preserve natural resources; the previous day Russia had announced that it will ratify the Kyoto Protocol.

•

On the Fox television show *American Idol*, a summer-long singing competition that was the most-watched television show of the summer, the winner is Kelly Clarkson; the voters, viewers of the show, voted via telephone.

5 In Kandahar, Afg., an assassination attempt on Pres. Hamid Karzai narrowly fails, and a car bomb explodes in Kabul, killing at least 26 people.

•

An enormous bomb is intercepted as it is being transported from the West Bank into Israel, and another bomb destroys an Israeli tank in Gaza; the Jewish High Holy Days begin at sundown the following day.

6 In Luanda, Angola, Pres. Yoweri Museveni of Uganda and Pres. Joseph Kabila of the Democratic Republic of the Congo sign a peace agreement that calls for Uganda to remove its troops from Congo and for Congo to take action against rebels who are hostile to the government in Uganda.

•

A grenade attack wounds a senior government official outside his home in Bishkek, Kyrgyzstan; opposition to the rule of Pres. Askar Akayev has been growing since March, and the country seems threatened by the outbreak of civil war.

7 Winning her third straight major championship, Serena Williams defeats her older sister, Venus, to win the U.S. Open tennis tournament; the following day Pete Sampras defeats Andre Agassi to win the men's championship.

•

Sir Simon Rattle conducts his first concert as chief conductor and artistic director of the Berlin Philharmonic.

8 Metropolitan Herman is installed as the third primate of the Orthodox Church in America in a ceremony in Washington, D.C.

•

In Indianapolis, Ind., Yugoslavia defeats Argentina to win the men's world basketball championship; on September 25 the U.S. beats Russia in the women's final in Nanjing, China.

9 *Martin Strel of Slovenia beats his own record for the longest swim when he becomes the first person to have swum the entire length of the Mississippi River; he began the 3,780-km (2,350-mi) swim on July 4. (Photo right.)*

10 Switzerland, the European centre of United Nations activities, joins the UN as its 190th member.

•

After days of severe storms that sparked flash floods that killed at least 21 people, rains in southeastern France ease; a day earlier a dam had given way, inundating the village of Aramon and leaving thousands without electricity or telephone service.

•

TRW Inc. announces that it has won the contract to build the James Webb Space Telescope for NASA; the new telescope will have a light-gathering area six times larger than that of the Hubble Space Telescope, which it is scheduled to replace in 2010.

•

U.S. government officials move the terrorism alert level up one step, from yellow (elevated) to orange (high); U.S. embassies around the world are closed, and Vice Pres. Dick Cheney is whisked to an undisclosed location.

AP/Wide World Photos

•

The government of Argentina orders banks to allow customers, starting in October, to make withdrawals from savings accounts, which have been frozen since the end of 2001.

11 Meeting in Ram Allah in the West Bank, the Palestinian Legislative Council, in an unprecedented show of strength, forces Palestinian leader Yasir Arafat to accept the resignation of his entire cabinet and schedule elections (later dropped) for 2003.

•

A great variety of solemn observances of the one-year anniversary of the September 11 terrorist attacks in the U.S. are held throughout the world.

12 U.S. Pres. George W. Bush addresses the General Assembly of the United Nations, enjoining the member nations to act quickly to force Iraq to disarm under threat of force and implying that the U.S. will act on its own if the UN does not do so.

•

L. Dennis Kozlowski, the former CEO of Tyco International Ltd., and Tyco's former chief financial officer, Mark H. Swartz, are indicted for fraud and racketeering, accused of having acquired $600 million in ill-gotten gains.

•

Archaeologists report their discovery in Vilnius, Lithuania, of some 100 skeletons believed to be remnants of Napoleon's Grand Army, almost the entirety of which likely died of cold and starvation in December 1812; nearly 2,000 skeletons had been discovered in the area in 2001.

•

In North Korea the Supreme People's Assembly issues a decree establishing an autonomous capitalist investment zone in the city of Sinuiju, on the Chinese border; the region is to be run by Chinese agricultural and industrial magnate Yang Bin.

13 American officials report that Ramzi ibn al-Shibh, believed to be a high-ranking al-Qaeda official and to have been closely involved with the Sept. 11, 2001, hijackers, has been captured and is in custody in Karachi, Pak.

•

Federal agents arrest five men in Lackawanna, N.Y., believing that they have ties to a terrorist group operating in the U.S.

14 In Las Vegas, Nev., Oscar de la Hoya defeats Fernando Vargas by technical knockout to add the World Boxing Association super welterweight (junior middleweight) title to the World

Boxing Council title that he already holds.

•

At the 18th International Association of Athletics Federations Grand Prix final in Paris, American sprinter Tim Montgomery runs the 100-m race in 9.78 sec, beating Maurice Green's three-year-old world record by one one-hundredth of a second.

•

In Uganda members of the Lord's Resistance Army, a rebel group that wants to replace the government with a theocracy based on the Ten Commandments, raids a Roman Catholic mission, kidnapping 2 priests and 45 civilians, and attacks a World Food Programme truck, killing the driver.

15 Elections in Sweden keep the centre-left Social Democrats, led by Prime Minister Göran Persson, in power.

•

In parliamentary elections in Macedonia, the ruling party is decisively defeated by a coalition led by the opposition Social Democratic Union, headed by Branko Crvenkovski.

•

Brazil closes down São Paulo's Casa de Detenção, the largest prison in Latin America, which was the centre of 2001's enormous prison uprising and, in 1992, the site of Brazil's biggest prison massacre.

16 Iraq notifies the United Nations that it is willing to allow UN weapons inspectors to return to the country "without conditions."

•

Peace talks between the government of Sri Lanka and the rebel Liberation Tigers of Tamil Eelam open at a naval base in Sattahip, Thai.; the cease-fire signed in February still holds.

The Pinakothek der Moderne, the largest museum of modern art in Germany, opens in Munich.

17 A Burundi government official says that gunmen massacred at least 183 people, 112 of them civilians, in Itaba commune in Gitega province on September 9; the number of dead is later reduced to some 173, and all are reported to have been unarmed civilians.

In Pyongyang, N.Kor., Japanese Prime Minister Junichiro Koizumi and North Korean leader Kim Jong Il agree to begin normalizing relations, and North Korea admits that its agents kidnapped 11 people from Japan during the late 1970s and early '80s.

NASA astronomers announce that the Hubble Space Telescope has detected clear evidence of medium-mass black holes, the existence of which was hinted at by data from the Chandra X-Ray and Roentgen Satellite (ROSAT) observatories.

18 *Nature* magazine publishes a paper on-line in which physicists working at CERN in Switzerland announce that they have created atoms of antimatter—specifically, atoms of antihydrogen; the researchers hope to test theories that antimatter should look and behave exactly like ordinary matter.

Ground-breaking ceremonies kick off the construction of a pipeline designed to carry oil from the Sangachal terminal in Azerbaijan to the port of Ceyhan in Turkey, traveling through Georgia and avoiding Russia and Iran; the pipeline is expected to start carrying oil in 2005.

Abu Salem, suspected of having been behind a series of high-profile murders and other terror attacks in India, including the worst bombings in the country's history, in 1993, is arrested in Portugal.

19 A coup is attempted in Côte d'Ivoire while Pres. Laurent Gbagbo is out of the country; Robert Gueï, who had become the military ruler of the country in a coup in 1999 but been forced out in 2000, is killed in the fighting.

In the second bombing in 24 hours, a suicide bomber detonates his weapons on a bus in Tel Aviv, Israel, outside the main synagogue, killing six passengers; the bombings mark the end of a period of 45 days with no attacks within Israel.

On the Transmigration of Souls, an orchestral and choral work commissioned from John Adams to commemorate the terrorist attacks of Sept. 11, 2001, premieres in New York City, conducted by Lorin Maazel.

20 The Israeli army demolishes all but a single building in the compound of Palestinian leader Yasir Arafat and imprisons him within the remaining building.

After months of resisting, the administration of U.S. Pres. George W. Bush accedes to Congress's demands for an independent investigation into possible intelligence failures in the period leading up to the terrorist attacks of Sept. 11, 2001.

A glacier in the Caucasus Mountains calves an enormous chunk of ice, which triggers mud slides that bury a village and tourist centres in Russia's republic of North Ossetia.

Nearly four weeks after his arrest, which caused an international outcry, AIDS activist Wan Yanhai is released from custody by Chinese authorities, apparently without restrictions.

21 The party of Prime Minister Mikulas Dzurinda, the Slovak Democratic and Christian Union, comes in only second best in parliamentary elections in Slovakia; Dzurinda is nonetheless reappointed prime minister on October 15.

The winners of the 2002 Albert Lasker Medical Research Awards are announced; they are James E. Rothman and Randy W. Schekman for basic medical research, Willem J. Kolff and Belding H. Scribner for clinical research, and James E. Darnell for special achievement.

Among the 16 people being inducted into the National Inventors Hall of Fame is Nils Bohlin, inventor of the three-point seat belt; he dies the same day in his native Sweden.

Miss Illinois, Erika Harold, is crowned Miss America in Atlantic City, N.J.

22 Elections in Germany keep Chancellor Gerhard Schröder in power.

The Emmy Awards are presented in Los Angeles, hosted by Conan O'Brien; winners include the television series **Friends** *(photo below) and* **The West Wing** *and the actors Ray Romano, Michael Chiklis, Jennifer Aniston, Allison Janney, Brad Garrett, John Spencer, Doris Roberts, and Stockard Channing.*

Germany defeats Chivas Regal (an international team) 8–6 to win Thailand's second annual King's Cup Elephant Polo Tournament; the game, first played in Mughal India but reinvented in Nepal in 1982, involves three players, each on an elephant with a

AP/Wide World Photos

mahout (handler), on each team and lasts 20 minutes.

23 U.S. officials issue a detailed plan to states on quick mass inoculation in the event of a biological attack involving smallpox; the states are instructed to prepare to vaccinate the entire population.

•

Russian Pres. Vladimir Putin and Azerbaijani Pres. Heydar Aliyev sign an agreement establishing the two countries' borders in the Caspian Sea and thus divide energy resources in the sea.

24 Argentina's economy minister, Roberto Lavagna, announces that Argentina will not use its foreign reserves to repay loans from the IMF and other multilateral lenders; Argentina has been complaining that the demands of the IMF are too burdensome.

•

Men with grenades and automatic weapons open fire in a Hindu temple complex in Gandhinagar, in Gujarat state in India, killing at least 30 people and wounding 74 before being killed themselves.

•

Oksana Fyodorova of Russia, who was crowned Miss Universe in May, is forced by the pageant to step down because it is believed that she is married and pregnant; Miss Panama, Justine Pasek, takes her place as Miss Universe.

25 As a rebellion in the interior of Côte d'Ivoire continues unabated, French troops rescue trapped students from the International Christian Academy in Bouaké, a school for the children of foreign missionaries in West Africa.

•

Armed men enter the offices of the Institute for Peace and Justice, a Christian charity, in Karachi, Pak., and tie up and murder seven employees; an eighth employee survives a gunshot to the head.

•

Jan Hendrik Schön, a star research physicist, is fired by Bell Labs, Murray Hill, N.J., for scientific misconduct; Schön, whose revolutionary work had been the object of keen excitement in scientific circles, is accused of having falsified data in 16 of the 24 suspect scientific papers he published in top journals from 1998 to 2001 and has shaken faith in the peer-review system for publishing.

26 Chechen fighters and Russian military forces engage in the biggest battle of 2002 in the Caucasus in the Russian republic of Ingushetia, leaving dozens dead.

•

U.S. Federal Reserve Board Chairman Alan Greenspan is given an honorary knighthood by the U.K.'s Queen Elizabeth II.

•

Federal prosecutors admit in a court document that they mistakenly turned 48 classified FBI reports over to accused terrorist Zacarias Moussaoui, who is conducting his own defense.

•

The son-in-law and three grandsons of former strongman U Ne Win are sentenced to death in Myanmar (Burma) for having plotted a coup against the government; the sentences are regarded as shockingly harsh.

•

SBC Communications Inc., the second biggest local telephone company in the U.S., says it has to lay off 11,000 employees, claiming that regulations that require it to sell access to its lines to

competitors at low prices are contributing to its financial difficulties.

27 East Timor becomes the 191st member of the United Nations just four months after becoming independent.

•

The Naismith Memorial Basketball Hall of Fame inducts players Earvin ("Magic") Johnson and Drazen Petrovic, coaches Larry Brown, Lute Olsen, and Kay Yow, and the Harlem Globetrotters; the following day the Hall of Fame's state-of-the-art basketball-shaped new home opens to the delighted public in Springfield, Mass.

•

The acquisition of the Pennzoil-Quaker State Co. by the Shell Oil Co. is approved by the Federal Trade Commission in the U.S.

•

A federal judge in Australia ceremonially delivers a 136,000-sq-km (52,500-sq-mi) tract of land in Western Australia to the Martu Aboriginal tribe, which had traditionally occupied the land before they were removed during the 1950s by the British government, which used the land as a missile test range.

28 Two bombs explode in a crowded movie theatre in Satkhira, Bangladesh, and shortly thereafter two more bombs explode at a circus in the same town; three people are killed and many more seriously wounded, and it is not clear who set the bombs.

•

The inaugural Maazel/Vilar Conductors' Competition—with a prize that includes $45,000, a conducting fellowship directed by Lorin Maazel, and a series of symphonic engagements—con-

cludes after 20 months and 362 contestants, with two winners: Xian Zhang, from China, and Bundit Ungrangsee, from Thailand.

29 The National Gallery of Art in Washington, D.C., opens to the public its new sculpture galleries, showcasing 900 works from the Middle Ages to the early 20th century.

•

West African leaders hold an emergency meeting in Ghana to discuss how to end the civil war in Côte d'Ivoire as American and French forces continue to evacuate foreigners from harm's way.

•

Israeli forces pull out of the largely destroyed compound of Palestinian leader Yasir Arafat, who emerges to the cheers of supporters.

•

The 34th Ryder Cup golf tournament, delayed for one year by the terrorist attacks of Sept. 11, 2001, concludes in Sutton Coldfield, Eng., with the European team defeating the heavily favoured Americans.

•

Port operators shut down 29 U.S. ports from Seattle, Wash., to San Diego, Calif., maintaining that longshoremen have been staging a work slowdown.

30 The European Union agrees to exempt U.S. soldiers from prosecution before the International Criminal Court, provided that accused Americans are tried in a U.S. court.

•

In an attempt to turn Japan's troubled economy around, Prime Minister Junichiro Koizumi replaces the country's conservative financial services minister with the reform-minded economic and fiscal policy minister, Heizo Takenaka.

October

1 Croatian Pres. Stipe Mesic appears before the international war crimes tribunal in The Hague to testify against former Serbian leader Slobodan Milosevic; it is the first time that a sitting head of state has testified before the war crimes tribunal, and it is regarded as an important precedent in international law.

•

The U.S. Northern Command, charged with the military protection of the entire U.S. and its territories as well as Canada and Mexico, opens near Colorado Springs, Colo.; it is the first time since the Revolutionary War that a single command centre has controlled the whole country's defense.

•

Reports say census takers in Russia's Taymyr autonomous *okrug* (district) have found a new ethnic group in northern Siberia, the Chalymtsy, who number about 130 and engage in hunting and subsistence agriculture.

2 *The former chief financial officer of the defunct energy* *giant Enron, Andrew S. Fastow, is arrested and charged in federal court with fraud, money laundering, and conspiracy. (See August 21.) (Photo below.)*

•

American and British scientists jointly announce that in separate projects, published in *Nature* and *Science,* they have sequenced the genome of the parasite that causes malaria as well as that of the *Anopheles gambiae* mosquito, which carries and transmits the disease.

3 Five people are randomly killed by a sniper in the suburbs of Washington, D.C., after another person had been killed the previous evening; the next day a seventh person is wounded.

•

Hurricane Lili weakens as it moves ashore in Louisiana; the previous day Russia's Mission Control Centre (MCC), near Moscow, had taken temporary control of the International Space Station while Lili threatened the MCC in Houston, Texas.

AP/Wide World Photos

4 King Gyanendra of Nepal dismisses Prime Minister Sher Bahadur Deuba and assumes direct power after Deuba recommends delaying parliamentary elections for a year; Deuba argues that the constitution does not give the king the power to fire an elected prime minister. (*See* October 11.)

•

As rhetoric between Pakistan and India again heats up, Pakistan test-fires a nuclear-capable medium-range missile.

5 Countrywide elections are held in Bosnia and Herzegovina.

•

South Korea's National Assembly overwhelmingly approves Kim Suk Soo as prime minister after having rejected Pres. Kim Dae Jung's first two choices earlier in the year.

•

Venezuelan Pres. Hugo Chávez announces that his government has foiled another attempted coup. (*See* April 12.)

•

A much-anticipated new museum, the Museum of

Sex, opens in New York City in what organizers suspect is a former brothel.

6 An explosion causes a fire and massive oil leak on the French oil tanker *Limburg* off the southeastern coast of Yemen; it is later determined that a terrorist attack caused the disaster.

•

Pope John Paul II canonizes Josemaría Escrivá de Bala-guer y Albás, the founder of the conservative Roman Catholic lay organization Opus Dei.

7 The Nobel Prize for Physiology or Medi-cine is awarded to Sydney Brenner, H. Robert Horvitz, and John E. Sul-ston for their discoveries regarding genetic regulation of organ development and the process of apoptosis, or programmed cell death.

•

Wolfgang Clement, the pre-mier of North Rhine-West-phalia, is named head of Germany's new "supermin-istry" for the economy and employment.

•

The American Astronomical Society announces that on June 4 researchers Michael Brown and Chadwick Trujil-lo discovered a Sun-orbiting object, which they named Quaoar, that is the largest body found in the Earth's solar system since Pluto was discovered in 1930.

8 U.S. Pres. George W. Bush invokes the Taft-Hartley Act, last employed in 1971, to per-suade a federal judge to issue an injunction tem-porarily halting the lockout of longshoremen that has shut down 29 West Coast ports for 10 days.

•

The Nobel Prize for Physics is awarded to Raymond

Davis, Jr., and Masatoshi Koshiba for their detection of cosmic neutrinos and to Riccardo Giacconi for his discovery of sources of cos-mic X-rays.

•

Two men open fire on U.S. marines engaging in training exercises in Kuwait, killing one soldier and wounding another before being killed themselves.

9 The U.S. Department of Justice indicts Enaam M. Arnaout on conspiracy, fraud, money-laundering, and racketeering charges, maintaining that the Chicago-based Benevolence International Foundation, a charity organization headed by Arnaout, contributed funds to support al-Qaeda.

•

The Nobel Prize for Econom-ics is awarded to Daniel Kah-neman and Vernon L. Smith, while the Nobel Prize for Chemistry goes to John B. Fenn, Koichi Tanaka, and Kurt Wüthrich for their work in developing techniques for identifying and mapping large biological molecules.

10 The Nobel Prize for Literature is awarded to the Hungarian writer Imre Kertész.

•

The International Court of Justice rules that the Bakas-si Peninsula in the Gulf of Guinea between Nigeria and Cameroon belongs to Cameroon; the peninsula is believed to contain rich oil deposits.

11 The Nobel Peace Prize is awarded to former U.S. president Jimmy Carter.

•

The U.S. Congress passes a bill by a wide margin grant-ing U.S. Pres. George W. Bush broad authority to use force against Iraq.

•

King Gyanendra of Nepal names Lokendra Bahadur Chand prime minister and appoints a nine-member cabinet as thousands of peo-ple demonstrate against the firing of the elected prime minister, Sher Bahadur Deuba. (*See* October 4.)

•

In Sholapur, India, five peo-ple are killed in riots that break out after a local newspaper reports that reli-gious commentator Jerry Falwell on the television show *60 Minutes* character-ized the Prophet Muham-mad as a terrorist and a vio-lent man.

•

The executive committee of New York City's Metropoli-tan Opera announces its appointment of opera star Beverly Sills as the Met's next chairman.

12 A car bomb explodes outside two nightclubs popular with foreigners on Bali, Indon.; at least 183 people, most of them Aus-tralian tourists, are killed. (*See* November 21.)

•

A large and distinctive new national performing arts cen-tre, the Esplanade–Theatres on the Bay, puts on a gala opening in Singapore.

13 Wampler Foods recalls a record 12.4 million kg (27.4 million lb) of poultry, all the cooked deli products produced in a plant in Fran-conia, Pa., since May; the poultry may be contaminat-ed with *Listeria monocyto-genes* bacteria.

•

Michael Schumacher wins the Japan Grand Prix auto race, his 11th victory for the year. (*See* July 21.)

•

During the Frankfurt (Ger.) Book Fair, Nigerian writer Chinua Achebe is awarded

the Peace Prize of the Ger-man Book Trade.

14 John Reid, the British secretary for Northern Ire-land, announces that the British government is sus-pending home rule and tak-ing over the government of Northern Ireland for the fourth time in less than three years.

•

Kenya's ruling party, Kenya African National Union, chooses Uhuru Kenyatta, son of the country's found-ing president, Jomo Kenyat-ta, as its candidate in elec-tions to replace retiring Pres. Daniel arap Moi. (*See* December 27.)

•

Workers in Denison, Iowa, are horrified when they open a Union Pacific railcar to find that it contains the remains of 11 would-be emi-grants from Mexico.

•

A new university, the Bulgari-an-Romanian Interuniversity Europe Centre opens its twin campuses in the Danube port cities of Ruse, Bulg., and Giurgiu, Rom.

•

The European Commission rules that only cheese made in Greece may be called feta; cheeses made in imitation of that cheese in other coun-tries must within five years be marketed under a differ-ent name.

15 A presidential election is held in Iraq in which the only candidate is Pres. Sad-dam Hussein; the following day it is announced that 100% of the electorate voted to retain him for another seven-year term.

16 Dutch Prime Minister Jan Peter Balkenende resigns three months after taking office as squabbling among the politically inexperienced members of coalition partner List Pim Fortuyn causes the collapse of the government.

•

The U.S. State Department announces that North Korea has admitted that it has been secretly developing a nuclear weapons program for several years, in violation of a 1994 agreement with the U.S. (*See* October 20.)

India announces that it will pull back its troops from the Pakistani border, where they have been deployed since shortly after the attack on the Indian Parliament building on Dec. 13, 2001; the following day Pakistan announces that it will follow suit.

•

The ruling People's National Party wins general elections in Jamaica, giving Prime Minister Percival J. Patterson an unprecedented third consecutive term of office.

•

The Bibliotheca Alexandrina, the successor to the fabled library of Alexandria, is officially dedicated by Egyptian Pres. Hosni Mubarak.

17 Officials representing the rebels in Côte d'Ivoire sign a truce agreement with West African mediators in Bouaké.

•

More than 20 years after he fled the country following his arrest for the murder of his former girlfriend Holly Maddux, onetime counterculture star Ira Einhorn is convicted of the 1977 murder in Philadelphia.

•

Le Monde publishes an interview with Romano Prodi, president of the European Commission, in which he characterizes the 1997 Stability and Growth Pact, which is the framework for the European single currency and which the European

Commission is empowered to enforce, as "stupid"; shock waves reverberate throughout Europe.

18 The Vatican rejects the policy drawn up by American bishops to address the problem of sexual abuse of minors by priests, indicating that the policy fails to safeguard the rights of accused priests.

The last major shirt-making factory in the U.S., a C.F. Hathaway Co. unit in Waterville, Maine, closes for good after 165 years of production.

•

The poet Quincy Troupe, who had become California's first official poet laureate on June 11, resigns after admitting that he had claimed on his résumé to have graduated from college, whereas he only attended.

19 The Treaty of Nice, which permits the European Union to add 10 new members, passes in a referendum in Ireland; the terms of the treaty required unanimous agreement by the member states, and Ireland had been the last holdout.

•

The first segment of the new Copenhagen Metro, featuring both subway and elevated train service, opens; Queen Margrethe II of Denmark is among the first passengers.

20 The U.S. announces that it considers a 1994 agreement under which it provided help to North Korea in building an energy infrastructure in return for North Korea's refraining from attempting to develop nuclear weapons to be effectively "nullified." (*See* October 16 and December 22.)

•

Iraqi Pres. Saddam Hussein announces an unprecedented amnesty of nearly all prisoners in the country.

•

Blue Stream, the deepest underwater pipeline in the world and a joint venture between Russia and Turkey, opens.

21 The UN Food and Agriculture Organization appeals for immediate food and agricultural aid, saying that more than 14 million people in sub-Saharan Africa are in danger of starvation and that famine also threatens in Afghanistan.

•

A three-tiered system of labels for organic foods denoting standards set by the U.S. Department of Agriculture goes into effect in American grocery stores.

•

The *Biblical Archaeological Review* announces the discovery of a stone ossuary with an ancient Aramaic inscription reading "James, son of Joseph, brother of Jesus"; some believe this is the first mention of Jesus Christ outside the Bible.

22 The New York Times Co. announces that it is buying out the Washington Post Co.'s share of the *International Herald Tribune;* the rival companies had co-owned the respected international newspaper for 35 years.

•

The Man Booker Prize for Fiction, Great Britain's top literary award, goes to Canadian writer Yann Martel for his novel *Life of Pi.*

•

The Royal Canadian Mounted Police file fraud charges against Garth Drabinsky and Myron Gottlieb, the founders of Livent Inc., one of North America's largest

theatre companies from the late 1980s until its demise in 1998.

•

Lithuania's legislature votes to adopt new rules that permit the use of the euro as legal tender in the country.

23 During a production of the popular musical *Nord-Ost* in a theatre in Moscow, more than 50 Chechen guerrillas storm the stage and take the actors and audience hostage. (*See* October 26.)

•

In a ceremony in Tokyo, the winners of the 2002 Praemium Imperiale Awards are presented with their medals for global achievement in the arts: Jean-Luc Godard in theatre/film, Norman Foster in architecture, Dietrich Fischer-Dieskau in music, Sigmar Polke in painting, and Giuliano Vangi in sculpture.

24 A man and a teenage boy, John Allen Muhammad and John Lee Malvo, are arrested near Myersville, Md., for the sniper killings that have left 10 people dead and 3 wounded and have terrified the area around Washington, D.C., since October 2 (*q.v.*).

•

In a ceremony in Ames, Iowa, soil scientist Pedro Sanchez is presented with the World Food Prize for having developed a low-tech, sustainable way for impoverished Africans to as much as quadruple their crop yields without exhausting the soil.

•

Elections are held in Bahrain to choose its first parliament since 1973, and for the first time anywhere in the Persian Gulf, women are allowed to vote and run for office in a national election.

•

Science magazine publishes a paper on-line that

describes an experiment in which scientists manipulated molecules to make a working logic circuit that is some 260,000 times smaller than the most advanced silicon circuitry.

25 Minnesota Sen. Paul Wellstone is killed when his campaign airplane crashes in northern Minnesota; the tragedy takes place less than two weeks before the election in which the prominent and outspoken liberal was expected to be returned to office.

•

Koki Ishii, a member of the Diet (parliament) who is head of an anticorruption task force in the Democratic Party of Japan, is stabbed to death as he is leaving his house to go to work; the following day a right-wing extremist admits to the assassination and turns himself in to police.

26 *Russian troops pump a gas intended to render people unconscious into the Moscow theatre in which Chechen guerrillas are holding the audience and performers hostage and then storm the theatre, freeing most of the 750 people, but at least 127 are killed by the disabling gas. (See October 23.) (Photo right.)*

•

Tens of thousands of people march in Washington, D.C., and in other cities across the U.S. to express their opposition to a possible war with Iraq.

•

The Breeders' Cup Classic Thoroughbred race is run at Arlington Park racetrack in Illinois, the winner is 43.5–1 long shot Volponi.

27 In Brazil's runoff presidential election, Work-ers' Party politician Lula (Luiz Inácio da Silva) wins by the largest margin of victory in the country's history.

•

In their first appearance in the World Series in their 42-year history, the Anaheim Angels defeat the San Francisco Giants in the seventh game to win the major league baseball championship in Anaheim, Calif.

28 The committee headed by Valéry Giscard d'Estaing unveils a draft constitution for the European Union; the document proposes a larger role in international affairs for the union.

•

Laurence Foley, a senior U.S. diplomat, is assassinated outside his home in Amman, Jordan; the attack is regarded as part of the worldwide terror campaign against Western targets.

The Prix Goncourt, France's top literary prize, is awarded to Pascal Quignard for *Les Ombres errantes.*

29 The Palestinian Legislative Council approves a new cabinet appointed by Yasir Arafat with two fewer ministers than the old.

•

The fifth annual Mark Twain Prize for American Humor is presented to Bob Newhart in a ceremony in the Kennedy Center in Washington, D.C.

•

A fire destroys the International Trade Center building in downtown Ho Chi Minh City, Vietnam, killing dozens of people.

30 Labour Party ministers in the coalition government of Israel resign, leaving Prime Minister Ariel Sharon without a majority; the ministers object to a budget that they see as favouring Israeli settlers in Palestinian regions over the poor of Israel.

•

Nine bombs go off in various places in Soweto, South Africa's largest black town-ship; the bombings are blamed on white extremists.

•

The government of the Central African Republic announces that it has retaken the capital, Bangui, from rebels who had seized the city nearly a week earlier.

•

Jam Master Jay, a deejay for the seminal rap group Run-D.M.C., is shot to death in his recording studio in Queens, N.Y.; friends and authorities are baffled.

31 George Carey retires as the archbishop of Canterbury, a position that he held for more than 11 years.

•

An earthquake in Italy causes the collapse of a nursery and elementary school in the small town of San Giuliano di Puglia, killing a teacher and 26 students who were gathered for a Halloween party; in the surrounding area scores of people are injured, two killed, and thousands left homeless.

AP/Wide World Photos

November

1 U.S. District Court Judge Colleen Kollar-Kotelly approves the antitrust settlement reached between the Department of Justice and Microsoft Corp., dismissing almost all the additional sanctions sought by the nine states that had not signed on to the proposed settlement.

In London, charges of robbery against Paul Burrell, who had been the butler of Diana, princess of Wales, are dropped after Queen Elizabeth II unexpectedly lets it be known that Burrell had told her that he was taking the princess's belongings for safekeeping after her death. (Photo right.)

Uniformed officers in Tokyo begin to fine violators of a ban on smoking in designated public areas; the ordinance, which went into effect on October 1, was introduced in response to complaints that people had been holding lit cigarettes at the same level as children's faces in crowded areas.

2 In Norwegian-brokered peace negotiations that were held in Thailand, the government of Sri Lanka and the Liberation Tigers of Tamil Eelam agree to set up a panel to discuss ways to share power.

A new moderate coalition government takes office in

© Michael Crabtree/Reuters 2002

the Indian state of Jammu and Kashmir, in spite of several attacks by Islamic militants.

In elections that began the previous day, the ruling coalition in the Czech Republic loses its majority in the Senate.

Police in London arrest five people they believe were planning to kidnap Victoria Beckham, wife of association football star David Beckham and former member of the Spice Girls; four additional suspects are arrested overnight but are later cleared of connection with the conspiracy.

3 Legislative elections in Turkey result in a resounding victory for the opposition Justice and Development Party; the party's leader, former Islamist Recep Tayyip Erdogan, has been barred from holding office, however.

A major earthquake, measuring an astonishing 7.9 in magnitude, occurs in Alaska; because its epicentre is in the state's sparsely populated interior, however, there are no casualties.

The Reventador volcano in Ecuador erupts, leaving the city of Quito covered with a thick layer of ash; residents are warned to remain indoors.

In the New York City Marathon, Rodgers Rop of Kenya wins with a time of 2 hr 8 min 7 sec; the fastest woman is Joyce Chepchumba, also from Kenya, who comes in at 2 hr 25 min 56 sec.

A missile fired by an unmanned U.S. Predator aircraft in Yemen kills six people, including a man known as Abu Ali, a top al-Qaeda figure.

4 Construction workers in Switzerland go on strike to protest the employers group's refusal to sign a negotiated contract; the last strike in Switzerland, also by construction workers, took place in 1947.

In Phnom Penh, Cambodia, Premier Zhu Rongji of China signs a framework agreement with the members of the Association of Southeast Asian Nations to set up a common free-trade area within the next decade.

5 In midterm congressional elections in the U.S., the Republican Party increases its majority in the House of Representatives and gains a majority in the Senate.

Harvey L. Pitt resigns as chairman of the U.S. Securities and Exchange Commission.

The European Court of Justice finds that bilateral aviation treaties between the U.S. and eight European countries violate European Union law.

Brazil's National Institute for Space Research releases the results of a satellite-data study of lightning incidence; it found that Brazil has more lightning strikes than any other country in the world.

6 In France's worst rail accident in five years, a train just outside a station in Nancy is engulfed in flames that are later determined to have been sparked by a kitchenette hot plate; 12 people die.

At the 36th annual Country Music Association Awards, musician Alan Jackson becomes only the third person to win five awards, including Entertainer of the Year and Single of the Year for his song "Where Were You (When the World Stopped Turning)."

7 The legislature of Latvia approves a new centre-right coalition government headed by Einars Repse.

The U.S. Food and Drug Administration approves a highly accurate test that can reveal in as little as 20 minutes whether a subject is infected with HIV; standard HIV testing usually requires a minimum two-day wait for results.

The University of Michigan announces that, having found that more than $600,000 in loans had been made to four university basketball players in violation of NCAA rules, it is imposing severe penalties on itself, including forfeiting all games in which those players were improperly involved and excluding itself from championship play for the coming season.

8 The UN Security Council unanimously approves a resolution sponsored by the U.S. and the U.K. requiring Iraq to submit to stringent weapons inspections, with deadlines for various related activities, or face "serious consequences."

Officials in Ecuador say that more than 1,000 people in the city of Ibarra have been made sick by contaminated municipal water after broken water pipes allowed purification systems to be overwhelmed by farm runoff after a storm.

9 In Dresden, Ger., the Zwinger Palace Museum's Old Masters Picture Gallery and the Semper Opera reopen for the first time since the summer floods.

10 The Arab League, meeting in Cairo, passes a resolu-

tion expressing support for weapons inspections in Iraq.

Police in Jordan begin a five-day siege of the city of Maan, looking for Islamic militants who have been terrorizing the country; firefights during the siege kill at least four people.

A severe storm front that had formed the previous day spawns some 88 tornadoes that over a 36-hour period cut a swath through Louisiana, Alabama, Mississippi, Georgia, Tennessee, Kentucky, Indiana, Ohio, and Pennsylvania, leaving at least 36 dead.

The constitutional ban on the return to Italy of members of the house of Savoy, Italy's former royal family, expires.

11 The UN presents a plan to both Greek and Turkish Cyprus, as well as Greece, Turkey, and the U.K., for reunification of Cyprus with a structure similar to that of Switzerland; acceptance of the plan is seen as vital to the island country's being invited to join the European Union.

Microsoft chairman Bill Gates pledges to donate $100 million from the Bill & Melinda Gates Foundation to combat the spread of HIV/AIDS in India.

12 The Qatar-based satellite television station al-Jazeera broadcasts a new audio tape that it says was made by Osama bin Laden and in which he praises recent terrorist attacks and threatens additional assaults; on November 18, U.S. intelligence officials say that they are convinced that the voice on the tape is indeed that of Bin Laden.

In a meaningless show of defiance, Iraq's National

Assembly rejects the UN resolution on weapons inspections but authorizes Pres. Saddam Hussein to make the final decision; the following day a letter is sent from Iraq accepting the resolution.

The United Nations Convention on International Trade in Endangered Species of Wild Fauna and Flora agrees to allow Botswana, Namibia, and South Africa to each hold a one-time sale of legal ivory mostly collected from elephants that died of natural causes; the sales are to take place after May 2004 if enough information on elephant populations and poaching levels has been gathered and if it has been determined that ivory-buying countries can control the domestic ivory trade.

The *Kenyon Review* literary magazine bestows its first Kenyon Review Award for Literary Achievement to American novelist E.L. Doctorow.

The British governmental organization English Nature designates Sherwood Forest, the legendary home of Robin Hood, a national nature reserve.

13 An aging single-hulled Bahamian-flagged tanker, the *Prestige,* which is carrying 77,000 metric tons of oil, begins to sink off the coast of Galicia, Spain; rescue workers frantically attempt to tow the leaking ship as far from the coast as possible. (*See* November 19.)

Great Britain's 50,000 full-time firefighters begin a 48-hour strike for higher pay; it is the first nationwide firefighter strike in 25 years.

14 Nancy Pelosi of California is elected to

succeed Richard Gephardt, who chose to step down, as leader of the Democratic Party in the U.S. House of Representatives; she is the first woman to be named leader of either party in either house of Congress.

•

Pres. Eduardo Duhalde of Argentina says that the country will be unable to meet the $805 million loan installment due today to the World Bank until the IMF restores a line of credit that it cut off almost a year ago.

•

Kai-Uwe Ricke, a top communications executive, is named to head Deutsche Telekom, Germany's telecommunications company.

15 At the end of the 16th Communist Party Congress in China, Hu Jintao is named the new leader of the Communist Party of China, replacing Pres. Jiang Zemin, who nevertheless will retain power behind the scenes.

•

Palestinian snipers kill nine Israeli soldiers and three civilians from an emergency response team in an ambush in the West Bank city of Hebron.

•

Joseph Parisi, editor of *Poetry*, announces that philanthropist Ruth Lilly has given the distinguished small journal a bequest that is likely to be worth at least $100 million and that makes it suddenly one of the world's richest publications.

16 Abdullah Gul, of the Justice and Development Party, is named prime minister of Turkey.

•

Unable to secure enough support in the parliament to carry out his policies, Pres. Leonid Kuchma of Ukraine dismisses the government of Prime Minister Anatoly

Kinakh and names Viktor Yanukovich prime minister in his place.

•

Police in Bishkek, the capital of Kyrgyzstan, detain more than 100 people and crush a protest calling for the resignation of Pres. Askar Akayev; regardless of concessions made by Akayev, protesters have been implacable since the killing of five protesters in March.

17 Voters in Peru, electing 25 new regional governments, choose the opposition party or independent parties over the party of Pres. Alejandro Toledo in almost every case.

•

An appeals court in Italy overturns the acquittal of former prime minister Giulio Andreotti on charges of complicity with the Mafia in the 1979 murder of a journalist and sentences him to 24 years in prison; politicians of all political bents condemn the development.

18 The European Union sets a tentative date of May 1, 2004, for 10 countries to become new members.

•

An advance team of UN weapons inspectors arrives in Baghdad, Iraq.

19 The U.S. Senate overwhelmingly approves the creation of a new cabinet department, the Department of Homeland Security, which will have a workforce of about 170,000; the House of Representatives had approved it the previous week.

•

The leaking oil tanker *Prestige*, being towed out to sea by order of the Spanish government, splits in two and sinks; the oil spill is believed

to be among the worst in history. (*See* November 13.)

•

Holland America Line announces that it is taking the cruise ship *Amsterdam* out of service for 10 days for disinfection as soon as it docks at Fort Lauderdale, Fla.; on the past four cruises, more than 500 people on the ship have come down with the Norwalk virus.

•

Astronomers at NASA say they have detected in the galaxy NGC 6240 two supermassive black holes that in several hundred million years will merge in a collision, the effects of which will be felt throughout the universe.

20 The National Book Awards are presented to Julia Glass for her first novel, *Three Junes*, Robert A. Caro for his nonfiction book *The Years of Lyndon Johnson: Master of the Senate*, Ruth Stone for her poetry collection *In the Next Galaxy*, and Nancy Farmer for her young-adult book *The House of the Scorpion*; novelist Philip Roth is given the Medal for Distinguished Contribution to American Letters.

•

The broadcasting authority in Turkey authorizes state radio and television stations to present a limited number of programs in Kurdish.

•

Major League Baseball commissioner Bud Selig announces that the Montreal Expos will play some of next season's "home" games in San Juan, P.R.

21 At a summit meeting in Prague, NATO extends an official invitation to Bulgaria, Estonia, Latvia, Lithuania, Romania, Slovakia, and Slovenia to become new alliance mem-

bers; they are expected to join in May 2004.

•

Zafarullah Khan Jamali is chosen by a narrow margin in Pakistan's Parliament to be prime minister; Jamali's name had been put forward by Pres. Pervez Musharraf, and he was chosen over Islamist candidate Fazlur Rahman.

•

Authorities in Indonesia arrest Imam Samudra, who they believed played a leading role in the Bali nightclub bombing (*See* October 12).

•

American missionary Bonnie Witherall is shot to death in Sidon, Lebanon; it is the first time in over 10 years that an American has been murdered in Lebanon.

22 Following a summit meeting between U.S. Pres. George W. Bush and Russian Pres. Vladimir Putin in St. Petersburg, both leaders promise to cooperate in matters of international terrorism and energy.

•

After the U.S. responds to news of North Korea's secret nuclear-weapons-development project by cutting off delivery of fuel supplies to North Korea, the Pyongyang regime says that it will not permit foreign inspectors to enter the country to verify that fuel supplies are being used for peaceful purposes.

•

Organizers of the Miss World beauty contest scheduled to be held on December 7 announce that the pageant will be moved from Abuja, Nigeria, to London; the decision came after more than 200 people were killed in violence touched off by a newspaper article expressing the opinion that the Prophet Muhammad would have approved of the contest.

•

Science magazine publishes three studies on dogs; one of them uses variations in mitochondrial DNA sequences to suggest that all dogs are descended from a population of wolves that lived in East Asia between 15,000 and 40,000 years ago.

23 Negotiators for dockworkers and terminal operators at the 29 ports on the U.S. West Coast that had closed in a contract dispute in October reach an agreement on a six-year contract.

•

After two weeks of delays caused by technical difficulties and bad weather, the space shuttle **Endeavour** *finally blasts off, carrying a replacement crew for the International Space Station and the first Native American astronaut, John B. Herrington, a registered member of the Chickasaw Nation. (Photo below.)*

24 Lucio Gutiérrez Borbúa, a leftist military man with virtually no previous political experience, is elected president of Ecuador in a runoff election.

•

Elections in Austria keep Chancellor Wolfgang Schüssel in office; only 10% of the popular vote goes to the far-right Freedom Party.

•

The Montreal Alouettes defeat the Edmonton Eskimos 25–16 in the Canadian Football League Grey Cup; it is Montreal's first CFL championship since 1977.

25 U.S. Pres. George W. Bush names Tom Ridge to be secretary of the new Department of Homeland Security.

•

Turkmenistan's Pres. Saparmurad Niyazov announces an amnesty for almost half the prisoners in the country; later he survives an assassination attempt when a man opens fire on his motorcade.

•

New York City authorities say they have broken up a credit-theft ring that has stolen the identities of more than 30,000 people.

26 The UN announces that for the first time half of all people with HIV infections are women and that some 42 million people worldwide have been infected.

•

Canadian Prime Minister Jean Chrétien accepts the resignation of Françoise

Ducros, his communications director, as a result of controversy that erupted over her off-the-record characterization of U.S. Pres. George W. Bush as "a moron."

•

The U.S.-based group Nature Conservancy announces that it believes that it has found evidence of a previously unknown population of orangutans in Kalimantan Timur on the island of Borneo in Indonesia; if confirmed, the discovery will increase the known number of orangutans in the world by approximately 10%.

27 UN weapons inspectors begin their work in Iraq under the new UN mandate; weapons inspectors under the previous mandate had left Iraq in 1998 because of the lack of cooperation of the Iraqi regime.

•

U.S. Pres. George W. Bush surprises observers by naming Henry Kissinger head of the independent investigation into the terrorist attacks of Sept. 11, 2001. (*See* December 16.)

28 Suicide bombers attack an Israeli resort

hotel in Mombasa, Kenya, killing 16 people, including themselves and members of a Kenyan dance troupe; at nearly the same time, shoulder-launched missiles are fired at an Israeli passenger jet leaving Mombasa, but this attack fails.

•

Javier Solana, secretary-general of the Council of the European Union, announces that the leaders of Serbia and Montenegro have agreed on the constitutional charter of the future union of Serbia and Montenegro.

29 The government of Italy releases the first of the money for the creation of the Moses Project, a plan to build barriers in the Adriatic seabed to protect Venice from tidal waters.

30 Turkey lifts a state of emergency that has been in place for 15 years in the largely Kurdish southeastern part of the country.

•

French romantic novelist Alexandre Dumas, who died in 1870, is reburied in the crypt of the Panthéon, France's official tomb of honour.

December

> *I want to say this about my state: When Strom Thurmond*
> *ran for president, we voted for him. We're proud of it.*
> *And if the rest of the country had followed our lead, we wouldn't*
> *have had all these problems over all these years, either.*
>
> —U.S. Senate Republican leader Trent Lott, at the centennial
> birthday celebration for Sen. Strom Thurmond, December 5

1 Prime Minister Janez Drnovsek of Slovenia wins a runoff election for president; he will take office on December 23, and Anton Rop replaces him as prime minister on December 11.

•

In the final set of the final match of the Davis Cup team tennis tournament, Mikhail Yuzhny of Russia defeats Paul-Henri Mathieu of France to bring Russia its first-ever Davis Cup victory. (Photo right.)

2 An open-ended general strike, intended to force Pres. Hugo Chávez into calling early elections, begins in Venezuela.

•

The health ministers of the members of the European Union approve a new rule that will ban tobacco advertising in magazines and newspapers as well as on the radio and the Internet and also prohibit tobacco-company sponsorship of major public events.

3 Rowan Williams is formally installed as the 104th archbishop of Canterbury in an ancient ceremony at St. Paul's Cathedral in London. (*See* October 31.)

•

United Nations weapons inspectors in Iraq engage in the previously unthinkable act of entering and searching one of Saddam Hussein's presidential palaces.

•

De Organizer, a one-act blues opera by James P. Johnston and Langston Hughes, is performed in Orchestra Hall in Detroit for the first time since its single performance at a convention of the Inter-

AP/Wide World Photos

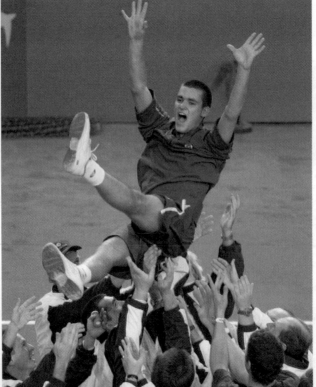

national Ladies' Garment Workers' Union in 1940.

4 The U.S. Air Transportation Stabilization Board rejects a plea by United Airlines for $1.8 billion in loan guarantees, saying the business plan submitted by the company is unsound.

•

Balkan Air Tour, the new national airline of Bulgaria, begins operations; it replaces the state-owned Balkan Airlines, which went bankrupt earlier in the year.

5 Negotiators for the government of Sri Lanka and the Liberation Tigers of Tamil Eelam announce an agreement to explore the creation of a united Sri Lanka with a federal structure.

•

U.S. Sen. Strom Thurmond celebrates his 100th birthday; he is the oldest person ever to have served in Congress and has been a member of the Senate longer than anyone else in history.

6 U.S. Pres. George W. Bush demands the resignations of Paul O'Neill as secretary of the treasury and Lawrence Lindsey as director of the National Economic Council.

•

The governments of Yugoslavia's constituent republics of Serbia and Montenegro accept a constitutional charter for a new state to be called Serbia and Montenegro; if accepted by the legislature of each republic, the new entity will become a reality.

•

Science magazine publishes an article saying that archaeologists at Florida State University believe they have found evidence of writing in pre-Columbian Mexico in Olmec artifacts dating to 650 BC; it had been believed that the earliest writing in Mexico was by the Zapotec culture in about 300 BC.

•

Researchers at the Information Technology Center of the University of Tokyo announce that in September they calculated the value of pi to a record 1.24 trillion places, using a Hitachi supercomputer for over 400 hours.

7 One day ahead of the Security Council deadline, Iraq delivers to the UN a 12,000-page declaration of its weapons-development programs.

•

Bombs go off almost simultaneously in four movie theatres in and around Mymensingh, Bangladesh, killing at least 15 people and wounding about 200; the movie houses were crowded with people celebrating the three-day Eid al-Fitr.

•

Two early paintings by Vincent van Gogh, *Congregation*

Leaving the Reformed Church in Nuenen and *View of the Sea at Scheveningen*, are stolen from the Van Gogh Museum in Amsterdam.

•

The Miss World contest, beset by controversy after religious violence led it to relocate to London from its planned venue in Nigeria, is won by Miss Turkey, Azra Akin. (*See* November 22.)

8 Serbia's third attempt to elect a new president again fails, with a turnout of 45%; the speaker of the parliament becomes acting president on December 30, while changes to the constitution are considered.

•

The annual Kennedy Center Honors are presented at the John F. Kennedy Center for the Performing Arts in Washington, D.C., in celebration of the artistic achievements of actor James Earl Jones, conductor James Levine, musical theatre star Chita Rivera, singer-songwriter Paul Simon, and movie star Elizabeth Taylor.

•

Conceptual artist Keith Tyson is awarded the Turner Prize, administered by Tate Britain in London; the work for which he won is entitled *The Thinker* and consists of a large block filled with computer parts.

•

The Times of London publishes a letter signed by directors of 18 major museums around the world asserting the right of museums to continue to hold antiquities that they have held for many years, even when they came from other countries.

9 United Airlines, the world's second largest airline, files for bankruptcy protection but continues operating.

•

U.S. Senate Majority Leader Trent Lott issues an apology

for remarks he made at Sen. Strom Thurmond's 100th birthday party in which he indicated continuing support for Thurmond's presidential candidacy in 1948, when Thurmond ran on a segregationist platform.

•

Representatives of the Indonesian government and of the Free Aceh Movement sign a peace treaty in Geneva providing autonomy and regional legislative elections for the district of Aceh on Sumatra and for negotiations on demilitarization.

•

The Right Livelihood Awards are presented in Stockholm to the Centre Jeunes Kamenge, a young people's centre in Burundi; Kvinna till Kvinna (Woman to Woman), a Swedish organization that works against ethnic hatred; Martin Almada, a Paraguayan human rights champion; and Martin Green, an Australian professor who specializes in the harnessing of solar energy.

•

Pres. Thabo Mbeki of South Africa, Pres. Robert Mugabe of Zimbabwe, and Pres. Joaquim Chissano of Mozambique officially launch the Great Limpopo Transfrontier Park, the largest game reserve in the world.

10 U.S. government officials report that Spanish warships the previous day had stopped a North Korean vessel flying no flag some 1,000 km (600 mi) off the coast of Yemen and found it to be carrying Scud missiles hidden under sacks of cement; the following day the shipment is released to Yemen, which maintains that it had legally bought the weapons.

•

Former U.S. president Jimmy Carter accepts his Nobel Peace Prize in a ceremony in Oslo.

•

U.S. Pres. George W. Bush selects a former head of the New York Stock Exchange, William Donaldson, to replace Harvey Pitt as head of the Securities and Exchange Commission and, in a policy change, promises to increase funding for the agency.

11 A joint congressional panel in the U.S. releases its final report on the Sept. 11, 2001, terrorist attacks; it recommends the creation of a new cabinet-level "director of national intelligence" to remedy the lack of coordination between the various intelligence agencies.

•

The U.S. reaches a free-trade agreement with Chile that, if approved, will immediately remove tariffs on the vast majority of items traded between the two countries.

12 A week after Congress decided to begin impeachment hearings against him, Paraguayan Pres. Luis González Macchi offers to leave office immediately after elections scheduled for April 2003 rather than wait for a further three months, as is customary.

•

The on-line search engine Google launches a new shopping site, different from other shopping sites in that it does not charge merchants to be listed; the new site is called Froogle.

13 U.S. Pres. George W. Bush announces a precautionary plan to give 500,000 military personnel smallpox vaccinations, to be followed by inoculations for as many as 10 million health care and emergency service workers; the general public is urged not to have vaccinations.

Pope John Paul II accepts the resignation of Bernard Cardinal Law, archbishop of the Boston archdiocese and the senior Roman Catholic prelate in the U.S. (*See* February 21.)

14 The Norwegian-registered *Tricolor*, carrying nearly 3,000 luxury cars, collides with a container ship and sinks in the North Sea, at the entrance to the Dover Strait between Great Britain and France.

Association football (soccer) star Ronaldo is named the male FIFA World Player of the Year for the third time in his career; two days later he is named European Player of the Year by *France Football* magazine.

15 Former U.S. vice president Al Gore says that he will not be a candidate for president in the elections of 2004.

In elections in the religiously polarized state of Gujarat in India, the Hindu nationalist Bharatiya Janata Party wins in a landslide over the secularist Congress Party.

16 Election officials in Equatorial Guinea announce that the winner of the previous day's presidential election was Pres. Teodoro Obiang Nguema Mbasogo, with more than 97% of the votes; the four opposition candidates, who had withdrawn on election day, citing voting irregularities and fraud, release a statement characterizing the election as invalid.

U.S. Pres. George W. Bush names Thomas Kean, a former governor of New Jersey, to head the commission to inquire into possible intelligence failures in the U.S.

prior to the Sept. 11, 2001, terrorist attacks; former secretary of state Henry Kissinger had surprised Bush by resigning as head of the commission on December 9.

17 In Pretoria, S.Af., an agreement is reached between Pres. Joseph Kabila of the Democratic Republic of the Congo and representatives of the two main rebel groups and the unarmed opposition whereby Kabila will be head of an 18-month transitional government, with each group contributing one vice president, at the end of which democratic elections will be held.

U.S. Pres. George W. Bush orders the Pentagon to have an antimissile shield system in place by the end of 2004.

Six members of the board of directors of WorldCom resign, leaving only three members, all recently appointed.

Australian surfer Layne Beachley wins her fifth consecutive world surfing championship in Maui, Hawaii.

18 The insurance holding company Conseco files for bankruptcy protection; it is the third largest bankruptcy filing in U.S. history, behind WorldCom and Enron.

Robert L. Johnson, founder of Black Entertainment Television, is awarded a new basketball franchise to be established in Charlotte, N.C., and thereby becomes the first African American majority owner in the National Basketball Association.

19 In presidential elections in South Korea the winner is Roh Moo Hyun, of the governing Millennium Democratic Party.

The Supreme Court of Venezuela orders the state-owned oil company, Petróleos de Venezuela, to cease striking and return to work; the order has no effect on the continuation of the general strike, now in its 18th day.

20 U.S. Sen. Trent Lott announces that he will step down as leader of the Republican Party in the Senate, though he will retain his seat; on December 23 Sen. Bill Frist is chosen to replace him as majority leader.

The U.S., the European Union, the United Nations, and Russia call for a Palestinian state to be created in three years; alone among the partners, however, the U.S. does not want a timetable for statehood to be set out at this time.

Pope John Paul II grants official recognition to a posthumous miracle attributed to Mother Teresa, the curing of cancer for a woman in India, and thus makes her eligible for beatification.

A court in France, after a 14-year investigation, finds American financier George Soros guilty of insider trading and fines him €2.2 million (about $2.3 million).

21 A helicopter carrying German peacekeepers crashes in Kabul, Afg., killing all seven aboard as well as two Afghani children on the ground.

After fighting extradition from Brazil for three years, Mexican pop star Gloria Trevi returns to Mexico to face charges of sex crimes against a girl; she and her manager, Sergio Andrade, have been publicly accused of having held young women for purposes of sexual exploitation.

22 North Korea announces that it has removed monitoring equipment installed by international inspectors to ensure that its supply of plutonium was not used in weapons production; the previous day it had begun removing monitoring equipment from a nuclear reactor.

In presidential elections in Lithuania, none of the candidates receives an absolute majority; a runoff between the top two finishers, Pres. Valdas Adamkus and Rolandas Paksas, will be held on Jan. 5, 2003.

23 A Ukrainian airplane carrying Ukrainian and Russian aeronautic specialists to Isfahan, Iran, for a test flight of an aircraft that is being jointly built by Ukraine and Iran crashes in central Iran; all 46 aboard are killed.

24 One week after the U.S. made pleas on his behalf, China releases from prison Xu Wenli, its best-known pro-democracy prisoner; he immediately moves to the U.S.

A new Metro railway system is ceremonially opened in Delhi, India; the following day, its first day of operation, the system is swamped by more than a million people who want to be first to ride the new trains.

Many of the 12,000 U.S. troops stationed in Kuwait awaiting a possible war against Iraq celebrate Christmas Eve with carols, donated gifts, and a visit from Santa Claus. (Photo right.)

25 Russia and Iran agree to speed up completion

of a nuclear power plant; the U.S. opposes this cooperation, fearing that Iran will use the plant to develop nuclear weapons.

26 In response to a request from Venezuelan Pres. Hugo Chávez, Brazil sends an emergency shipment of 520,000 bbl of gasoline to Venezuela, which is suffering shortages because of the nationwide general strike.

•

Millionaire Andrew J. Whittaker, Jr., is announced as the winner of the $314.9 million Christmas Day Powerball prize in West Virginia, the biggest undivided lottery jackpot ever; he plans to tithe the windfall to three churches.

27 In elections that are far from flawless but are far closer to free and fair than those in 1992 and 1997, Kenyans elect as their new president Mwai Kibaki of the National Rainbow Coalition, a collection of opposition parties. (*See* October 14.)

•

North Korea announces that it will expel all international nuclear inspectors; unless North Korea "cooperates, and cooperates fully," with International Atomic Energy Agency demands, the IAEA plans to declare before the UN Security Council that the country is in violation of international agreements.

•

Suicide bombers drive two explosives-laden vehicles into the headquarters of the pro-Russian government in Grozny, the capital of the Russian republic of Chechnya, destroying the building and killing 72 people.

•

Brigitte Boisselier, the CEO of Clonaid, a company founded by the Raelians, a religious group that believes that all humans were cloned from space travelers 25,000 years ago, announces that a cloned human baby has been born; the skepticism and condemnation that greet the announcement are later compounded by the group's failure to provide proof of the cloning by year's end.

28 Hundreds of French troops arrive in Côte d'Ivoire to reinforce the government forces in their civil war against three rebel groups.

•

As expected, the 27-m (90-ft) Australian yacht *Alfa Romeo* wins the annual Sydney–Hobart Race down the east coast of Australia.

•

Cyclone Zoe slams into the relatively inaccessible islands of Tikopia, Fataka, and Anuta in the Solomon Islands; Zoe is one of the most powerful cyclones ever recorded in the Pacific, and it will take days for relief ships to reach the remote islands.

29 The FBI issues an alert to the public and to law-enforcement agencies throughout the U.S. and the world to help find five men from the Middle East who are believed to have entered the U.S. illegally in the past few days; it is later learned that the alert was based on false information.

30 Gary Winnick announces that the following day he will resign as chairman of Global Crossing Ltd.; the bankrupt company's assets have been sold to Hutchison Telecommunications Ltd. and Singapore Technologies Telemedia.

•

Tyco International Ltd. announces that an internal investigation has found no systemic fraud but has revealed that for years, contrary to previous claims, the company engaged in accounting trickery to inflate its stated earnings.

31 A trial run of a new maglev (magnetic levitation) train, linking downtown Shanghai with Pudong International Airport, is enjoyed by Chinese Premier Zhu Rongji and German Chancellor Gerhard Schröder; afterward Schröder announces that China has awarded Germany a contract to expand the maglev rail system in the Shanghai area.

•

The stock market ends a year in which stock prices in the U.S. fell precipitously, the third consecutive year of decline on Wall Street.

© Chris Helgren/Reuters 2002

Disasters

The following list records the **MAJOR DISASTERS** that occurred in 2002. Events included in this feature involved the loss of **15 OR MORE LIVES** and/or **SIGNIFICANT DAMAGE** to property.

Aviation

January 27, Northeastern Chechnya. A military transport helicopter goes down near the village of Shelkovskaya, killing 21 persons; despite an initial report that the helicopter was shot down, Russian authorities later assert that the wreckage shows no signs that the aircraft was fired on.

January 28, Southern Colombia. An Ecuadoran airliner reportedly flying in heavy mist crashes on the slopes of the Nevado de Cumbal volcano; all 92 persons aboard the plane are killed.

February 12, Western Iran. An Iranian airliner flying in bad weather conditions with at least 117 persons aboard crashes in mountains near the city of Khorramabad; there are no survivors.

February 21, Near Arkhangelsk, Russia. A military cargo plane crashes while attempting to make an emergency landing; 17 persons die, most of them Russian naval officers.

March 14, Baez, Cuba. A single-engine charter plane crashes into a pond, reportedly after one of the plane's wings has broken off; at least 16 persons are killed.

April 15, Near Busan, S.Kor. An Air China Boeing 767 en route from Beijing to Busan slams into a hill while making its approach to land in rainy and foggy conditions; 39 of the reported 166 passengers and crew members aboard the plane survive the crash.

May 4, Near Kano, Nigeria. An airliner en route from Kano to Lagos crashes in a heavily populated suburb shortly after takeoff; at least 148 persons die.

May 7, Near Tunis, Tun. An Egypt Air Boeing 737-500 flying through fog, rain, and sandy wind blowing from the Sahara Desert crashes on a hillside while attempting to land; 18 persons are killed, and 25 are injured.

May 7, Near Dalian, China. A China Northern Airlines MD-82 jet goes down in the Bo Hai Sea, apparently after a fire in the plane's cabin; all 112 persons aboard the aircraft perish.

May 25, Off the coast of Taiwan. A China Airlines Boeing 747 bound for Hong Kong from Taipei with 225 persons aboard splits into four pieces over the Taiwan Strait; there are no survivors.

June 2, Near Ndalatando, Angola. A military helicopter crashes in bad weather; 20 persons die, including Lieut. Gen. José Domingues Ngueto, commander of the Kwanza-Bengo region.

July 1, Baden-Württemberg state, Ger. A midair collision between a Boeing 757 cargo plane and a Russian airliner near Lake Constance on the German-Swiss border claims the lives of all 71 persons aboard the two aircraft.

July 4, Bangui, Central African Republic. A cargo plane goes down in a residential area while attempting to land because of mechanical problems; 23 of the 25 persons aboard are killed, but no one on the ground appears to have been injured.

July 27, Lviv, Ukraine. A fighter jet crashes into spectators during an air show; 76 persons die, and more than 100 are injured; the jet was performing a low-altitude stunt when its wing hit the runway, causing the jet to cartwheel into the crowd.

July 28, Moscow. Shortly after takeoff from the Sheremetyevo airport, a cargo plane crashes in a forest, killing 15 persons.

August 22, Near Pokhara, Nepal. A small plane flying in bad weather slams into a mountain about 200 km (125 mi) west of Kathmandu; the 15 foreign tourists and 3 Nepalese crew members aboard are killed.

October 1, Near Panaji, Goa state, India. A midair collision between navy transport planes during an air show kills all 12 persons aboard both planes and 5 persons on the ground.

November 6, Luxembourg. A twin-engine passenger plane crashes in thick fog near Luxembourg's international airport, killing 18 of the 22 persons aboard the craft.

November 11, Manila. A twin-engine commuter plane goes down in Manila Bay shortly after takeoff, killing 19 of the 34 persons aboard; engine failure is the suspected cause of the crash.

December 23, Central Iran. A Ukrainian passenger plane en route from Kharkiv to the Iranian city of Isfahan crashes while preparing to land; all 46 persons aboard the plane—mostly Ukrainian and Russian aerospace scientists who were traveling to Iran to test a new airplane—are killed.

Fires and Explosions

January 21, Goma, Democratic Republic of the Congo. A river of lava from the Mt. Nyiragongo volcano sets off an explosion at a gas station in the centre of the city; some 50 persons looting fuel at the station are killed.

January 27, Lagos, Nigeria. A fire at a military arms depot sets off a series of huge explosions; bombs, shells, and rockets career into heavily populated neighbourhoods, causing thousands of residents to flee their homes; more than 1,000 persons die, many of whom are trampled to death or drowned while trying to cross two canals to safety; government officials maintain that the fire at the arms depot was accidental and not the result of sabotage.

February 18, Tangshan, China. A fire, probably caused by an electrical short circuit, destroys an illegal video-game parlour; at least 17 persons die.

March 6, Andhra Pradesh, India. An explosion in a village in the Karimnagar district of

A fighter jet crashes into spectators at an air show in Lviv, Ukraine, on July 27.

Andhra Pradesh kills at least 15 persons. The blast reportedly occurred as explosives were being unloaded from a van.

March 11, Near Chongqing, China. An explosion on a bus claims the lives of 21 persons; the bus is believed to have been illegally transporting fireworks.

March 11, Mecca, Saudi Arabia. A fire breaks out in a four-story building that houses a girls' school; 15 students die, most of them as they stampede to escape the blaze. Reports that Saudi religious police, or *mutaween*, prevented some girls from leaving the school because they were not wearing proper Islamic dress provoke harsh public criticism of the *mutaween*.

May 24, Northern India. An electrical short circuit ignites a fire that sweeps through a shoe factory in Agra, leaving at least 40 persons dead.

June 16, Beijing, China. An early-morning fire engulfs an unlicensed Internet cafe in the city's university district; 24 persons are killed, and 13 are injured.

July 7, Palembang, Indon. A fire reportedly caused by an electrical short circuit destroys a five-story karaoke bar, killing at least 46 persons; the bar lacked emergency exits and other safety features.

July 20, Lima, Peru. A blaze starts in an illegally operated disco after a bartender's fire-eating stunt goes awry; at least 30 persons die.

October 29, Ho Chi Minh City, Vietnam. Fire engulfs a six-story office building, killing more than 100 persons; the fire is reported to have started in the kitchen of a nightclub on the building's second floor.

November 1, El Jadida, Mor. An electrical short circuit apparently is the cause of a blaze at an overcrowded prison; at least 49 inmates are killed, most by smoke inhalation or in the stampede of prisoners attempting to escape the blaze.

November 30, Caracas, Venez. Flames engulf a crowded nightclub in the basement of a downtown hotel; at least 50 persons perish, according to official figures.

December 29, Northern Iran. A fire at a prison in the town of Gorgan claims the lives of at least 27 inmates and injures some 50 others; an electrical fault reportedly caused the fire.

December 31, Veracruz, Mex. An explosion of illegal fireworks engulfs an outdoor market and nearby buildings and cars; at least 28 persons die.

Marine

January 27, Southern Philippines. After experiencing engine trouble and encountering rough seas in the area, a ferry with some 70 persons aboard loses contact with coast guard officials; the boat is presumed to have sunk, and there are no signs of survivors.

March 7, Off the coast of the island of Lampedusa, Italy. An overcrowded wooden boat capsizes about 105 km (65 mi) south of Lampedusa, between Tunisia and Sicily; the boat is packed with passengers reportedly from North Africa and intent on entering Italy illegally; at least 50 persons perish.

Early April, Gulf of Aden. A boat carrying Somalis attempting to flee the ongoing civil war in their home country sinks in rough seas; more than 90 persons die.

April 6–7, Off the coast of southern Nigeria. A boat loaded with passengers and goods sinks between Port Harcourt and Nember, apparently after a leak developed and the boat's water pump failed; some 40 persons are feared dead.

April 11, Central Philippines. A fire breaks out on a ferry traveling between the island of Masbate and the port city of Lucena, forcing passengers to jump overboard; 23 persons are confirmed dead, and 32 are missing.

April 11, Central Tanzania. A ferry, possibly overloaded, capsizes on the Kilombero River near the town of Mahenge; at least 38 persons die.

May 3, Southeastern Bangladesh. A ferry sinks during a rainstorm on the Meghna River, killing at least 271 persons.

May 12, Off the coast of Birilan island, Phil. A ferry overturns and sinks after passengers, seeking shade, have gathered on one side of the vessel; 19 persons perish.

May 20, Lake Victoria. A boat returning to the mainland of Uganda from Kalangala Island experiences engine failure, capsizes, and sinks; 27 persons are feared dead.

June 11, Riau province, Indon. A passenger boat sinks in bad weather on the Kampar River on the island of Sumatra; 2 persons die, and 20 are missing and feared dead.

September 15, Off the coast of Sicily. A Tunisian-registered fishing boat carrying some 130 illegal immigrants from Liberia to Italy capsizes in a storm and sinks; at least 36 persons die.

September 26, Off the coast of The Gambia. In what is described as Africa's deadliest disaster at sea, a Senegalese ferry carrying more than twice its 550-passenger capacity capsizes in stormy weather; an estimated 1,200 persons die, according to the head of an official inquiry into the incident.

October 22, Caspian Sea. An Azerbaijani-owned ferry en route from Aqtau, Kazakhstan, to Azerbaijan's capital, Baku, capsizes and sinks in stormy seas hours after sending a distress signal; of the 51 persons aboard, only 9 are rescued, and one of the survivors later dies in a hospital.

November 13, Off the coast of West Bengal state, India. A cyclone strikes the Bay of Bengal, and scores of fishing boats sink during the storm; 10 deaths are confirmed, and at least 150 other fishermen are missing.

December 1, Off the coast of Libya. A fishing trawler with more than 100 illegal immigrants bound for Italy on board sinks in bad weather; 11 deaths are confirmed, and at least 50 are missing and feared dead.

December 14, Northwestern Liberia. An overcrowded ferry capsizes on the Mofa River near Robertsport; more than 100 persons are feared drowned.

December 18, Pará state, Braz. A ferry carrying more than twice its 150-passenger capacity capsizes on the Pará river near the town of Barcarena; at least 80 persons are missing and feared drowned.

December 31, Off the coast of Tanzania. An overloaded ferry capsizes, reportedly during a storm; up to 40 persons are missing and feared dead.

Mining and Construction

Early January, Democratic Republic of the Congo. Heavy rains trigger the collapse of a coltan mine; at least 30 miners are killed.

January 14, Yunnan and Hunan provinces, China. At least 43 miners die in two separate disasters. A gas explosion in an unlicensed coal pit in Yunnan claims the lives of 25 miners, and in Hunan at least 18 miners are believed to have suffocated following a gas explosion.

January 28 and 31, Central and Southwestern China. A total of 14 miners die in a gas explosion at a coal mine in Hengyang on January 28. Three days later a natural gas leak at a coal mine near the southwestern city of Chongqing causes 13 miners to suffocate, and another 8 are missing.

February 25, Damietta, Egypt. An aging residential building collapses, claiming the lives of 22 persons.

Early April, Jiangxi province, China. An explosion occurs while maintenance is performed at a coal mine; 16 miners die.

April 9, Heilongjiang province, China. Two explosions occur at different mines in the same city, Jixi, on the same day. In the largest blast, 24 miners are killed and 40 injured at a coal mine. In the second incident, also at a coal mine, 7 miners die and 4 are missing.

April 22 and 24, Sichuan province, China. A total of 11 miners are confirmed dead and 4 are missing in a gas explosion at a mine in Chongqing on April 22. Two days later a gas explosion at a coal mine in Panzhihua kills 23 miners.

June 20, Mererani, Tanz. An oxygen pump fails at a tanzanite mine, causing the deaths of 42 miners working some 125 m (410 ft) underground.

June 20, Heilongjiang province, China. In what is described as the fourth deadliest mining disaster in China's history, a gas explosion at the Chengzihe coal mine in Jixi leaves 111 miners dead and 4 missing.

June 22, Shanxi province, China. An explosion at a gold mine claims the lives of at least 36 miners; authorities later search for four persons, including the owner of the mine and his foreman, who are suspected of having hidden dozens of bodies in an attempt to cover up the accident.

July, Ukraine. Three separate mining disasters occur during a roughly three-week period. On July 7 in Donetsk, 35 miners die from smoke inhalation after a fire breaks out in their mine. On July 21 in the Dnepropetrovsk region, a methane gas explosion claims the lives of 6 miners, and another 28 are missing. At another mine in Donetsk on July 31, a gas explosion claims the lives of 20 miners.

July 23, Mhondoro, Zimb. A shaft caves in at an abandoned gold mine, killing at least 15 persons who are mining illegally at the site.

October 29, Nanning, Guangxi province, China. A fire at a coal mine claims the lives of 30 miners.

December 6, Near Taonan, Jilin province, China. A fire at the Wanbao coal mine, evidently started when machinery in the mine catches fire, kills at least 25 miners.

Natural

January, Mauritania. Heavy rains and extremely cold weather claim the lives of at least 25 persons and kill an estimated 80,000 head of livestock.

January 17–19, Goma, Democratic Republic of the Congo. The Mt. Nyiragongo volcano, 19 km (12 mi) north of Goma, erupts, and a river of lava some 50 m (165 ft) wide rolls through the city; hundreds of thousands of persons in the area are displaced, and at least 45 die.

Late January, Europe. Winds approaching 200 km/hr (120 mph) wreak havoc across the continent. At least 18 persons die, including 8 in Britain, 4 in Poland, and 3 in Germany. Hundreds of thousands are left without electricity, and travel is brought to a standstill in many areas.

February, Java, Indon. Weeks of heavy rains trigger floods and landslides on the island; at least 150 persons perish.

February 3, Central Turkey. An earthquake of magnitude 6 jolts the region; at least 43 persons die, more than 300 are injured, and some 600 buildings are destroyed.

February 6, Northern Afghanistan. During a blizzard an avalanche of snow blocks an entrance to the Salang Tunnel about 80 km (50 mi) north of Kabul; 4 persons are killed.

February 19, La Paz, Bol. A devastating storm—the most destructive in the history of the Bolivian capital—sets off flash floods and mud slides; 69 persons die, at least 100 are injured, and hundreds are left homeless.

March 3, Northern Afghanistan. A magnitude-7.4 earthquake shears off a cliff in the Hindu Kush mountains north of Kabul; the ensuing avalanche buries a village and claims the lives of at least 100 persons.

March 25–26, Northern Afghanistan. An earthquake of magnitude 6.1 and as many as six aftershocks jolt the region; the city of Nahrin and numerous mountain villages are destroyed; 1,000 persons die, and some 4,000 are injured.

April 2, Morobe province, Papua New Guinea. A landslide hits two villages in the province, killing 36 persons; another 28 are missing and feared dead.

April 12, Northern Afghanistan. A magnitude-5.8 earthquake strikes the mountainous Hindu Kush region; two villages, Doabi and Khoja Khesir, are devastated; at least 30 persons die, and some 100 are injured.

May 9–15, Andhra Pradesh, India. An unusually intense heat wave kills at least 1,030 persons in the southern Indian state.

Early June, Northeastern Nigeria. A heat wave claims the lives of more than 60 persons in the city of Maiduguri in Borno state.

Early to mid-June, Northwestern China. Torrential rains produce widespread flooding in the region; more than 200 persons die, including at least 152 in the worst-hit province, Shaanxi.

June, Southern Russia. Floods wreak havoc in the regions of Stavropol and Krasnodar and in the republics of Karachay-Cherkessia, North Ossetia, Ingushetia, and Chechnya. By June 24 some 70 villages are under water. At least 53 persons are confirmed dead, and 75,000 are homeless.

June–mid-August, South Asia. Monsoon floods submerge parts of Nepal, India, and Bangladesh. The death toll is highest in Nepal, where at least 422 persons perish and thousands are left homeless. In India nearly 400 persons are killed and some 15 million are displaced in Bihar and Assam states. At least 157 persons die in Bangladesh, where a third of the country is under water; about 6 million Bangladeshis are displaced.

June 4–5, Northwestern Syria. The Zeyzoun Dam, near the town of Hama, collapses after weeks of heavy rains in the area; several villages are flooded, and at least 28 persons are killed.

June 22, Northwestern Iran. An earthquake of magnitude 6.5 strikes an area between the cities of Qazvin and Hamadan and is followed by more than 20 aftershocks. At least 220 persons are killed, and 1,300 are injured. As many as 100 villages may have been flattened.

July, Algeria. A heat wave brings temperatures as high as 56 °C (133 °F)—the highest the country has seen in 50 years. At least 50 persons die.

July 2, Chuuk state, Federated States of Micronesia. Tropical Storm Chata'an wreaks havoc in the state; strong winds, rain, and landslides claim the lives of 47 persons.

Mid-July, Southeastern Peru. A severe cold snap kills at least 59 persons; more than 80,000 head of livestock, mostly llamas and alpacas, also perish.

July 19, Henan province, China. A storm produces high winds and egg-sized hailstones that batter the province; a number of buildings collapse, and power is temporarily cut off; 16 persons die, and some 200 are injured.

July 21–22, Eastern Cape and KwaZulu/Natal provinces, S.Af. Snowstorms dump up to 1 m (3.3 ft) of snow on parts of the provinces; thousands of homes and other buildings are damaged; 22 persons die.

August, Southern China. Torrential rains trigger landslides and floods across much of the region. At least 133 persons lose their lives, including 108 in Hunan province; more than 100 million persons are affected.

August 7, Eastern Tajikistan. A mud slide destroys some 56 homes in the village of Dasht in the Gorno-Badakhshan region; at least 20 persons die.

August 11, Uttaranchal state, India. Floods and mud slides wreak havoc in several villages after heavy monsoonal rains; at least 43 persons perish.

Mid-August, Central Europe and southern Russia. Extensive flooding inundates parts of Central Europe and Russia's Black Sea region after days of torrential rain. At least 18 persons are confirmed dead, and 25 are missing in Germany, where the worst flooding is occurring along the Elbe River and its Mulde tributary. Another 16 persons die in the Czech Republic, and at least 58 perish in Russia.

August 31–September 1, South Korea. The strongest storm to hit the Korean peninsula in 40 years claims the lives of at least 113 persons. Typhoon Rusa, moving across the southern part of the peninsula, brings extensive flooding and winds exceeding 200 km/hr (125 mph).

September 12, El Porvenir, Guat. A landslide that occurs following heavy rains buries a mountain village some 120 km (75 mi) south of Guatemala City; 26 persons are killed, and 7 are missing.

Mid-September, Sommières region, France. Torrential rains batter the region for days, triggering floods in which 23 persons lose their lives.

September 20, Southern Russia. An immense glacierborne landslide occurs in the Caucasus Mountains of North Ossetia; 16 deaths are confirmed, but according to officials, 132 are missing, including Russian action-film star Sergey Bodrov, Jr., who was making a movie in the area.

October 2, Northern Syria. A landslide causes several buildings to collapse; at least 20 persons are killed, and 30 are injured.

October 26–27, Northern Europe. A powerful storm rages across the region, killing 7 in Britain, 6 in France, at least 10 in Germany,

In Mossy Grove, Tenn., survivors of the November tornadoes that roared through the southeastern and midwestern U.S. clear up debris.

AP/Wide World Photos

5 in Belgium, 4 in The Netherlands, and 1 in Denmark.

October 29, Northern Colombia. A mud slide brought on by heavy rains sweeps through the village of Montecristo in the San Lucas Mountains; 6 deaths are confirmed, and at least 60 persons are missing and feared dead.

October 31, Central Italy. A severe earthquake shakes the mountainous Molise region northeast of Naples; in the town of San Giuliano di Puglia, 26 children and a teacher are killed when their school collapses. Some 11,000 in surrounding areas are left homeless.

November 3, Near Gilgit, Pakistan-administered Northern Areas of Jammu and Kashmir. A magnitude-4.5 earthquake rocks several mountain villages, killing at least 17 persons, and leaves some 1,600 families homeless.

November 9–11, Southeastern and midwestern U.S. A storm front that produces nearly 90 tornadoes cuts a broad swath of destruction from the Gulf of Mexico to the Great Lakes. The highest death toll is in Tennessee, where 17 persons are killed; 12 persons die in Alabama, 5 in Ohio, and 1 each in Mississippi and Pennsylvania. More than 200 persons are injured, and tens of thousands are without power.

November 17–25, Central Morocco. Heavy rain triggers flash floods in the region that claim the lives of at least 25 persons.

December 4–5, North and South Carolina. In one of the worst ice storms to strike the Carolinas in years, widespread power outages leave some 1.8 million customers without electricity; the storm, which brings heavy snow as well as ice to some areas, is blamed for at least 22 deaths.

December 8–9, Angra dos Reis, Braz. Mud slides brought on by torrential rains bury numerous houses; at least 34 persons are dead, and 40 are missing.

Late December, Northern Bangladesh. Unseasonably cold weather claims the lives of at least 100 persons by year's end.

Railroad

February 5, KwaZulu/Natal province, S.Af. A collision between a crowded passenger train and a stationary freight train claims the lives of 22 persons, as many as 16 of whom are schoolchildren; cables used in the railroad's signaling system reportedly were vandalized and stolen shortly before the disaster.

February 20, Near Cairo. In what is described as the worst rail disaster in Egypt's history, a fire sweeps through an overcrowded train en route from Cairo to Luxor; the blaze engulfs seven cars before conductors are able to detach them from the rest of the train; flames from a small stove started the fire; 363 persons perish.

May 25, Southern Mozambique. Two passenger cars of a train are entirely destroyed when they slam into freight cars parked at a rail station near the town of Moamba; 196 persons are killed, and hundreds are injured. It is Mozambique's worst rail disaster ever.

June 4, Uttar Pradesh state, India. An express train en route from Kanpur to Kasganj strikes a bus at a railroad crossing, throwing the bus into a canal; 34 persons die; a gatekeeper at the crossing reportedly failed to lower a gate as the train approached.

June 24, Central Tanzania. A passenger train experiences mechanical failure and careens backward down a hill until it slams into an oncoming cargo train; at least 280 persons die, and as many as 800 are injured.

September 9, Near Rafiganj, Bihar state, India. The Rajdhani Express train, while en route from Kolkata (Calcutta) to New Delhi, derails on a bridge and plunges into the rain-swollen Dhavi River; at least 106 persons die. There is some speculation that sabotage was involved, but local officials cite problems with the maintenance of the bridge.

Traffic

January 7, Northern Nigeria. A head-on collision between a bus and a minibus on a road near the village of Durbunde claims the lives of some 50 persons, many of them members of a wedding party.

January 7, Near Dhaka, Bangladesh. A speeding bus overturns and lands in a water-filled ditch; nearly 30 persons are believed killed.

February 13, Eastern Saudi Arabia. A collision between a bus and a truck on a road near the Saudi–United Arab Emirates border claims the lives of some 40 persons and injures 10. The bus was carrying Muslims to Mecca on the annual pilgrimage known as the hajj.

Mid-February, Peru. At least 38 persons die in separate traffic disasters. A bus traveling to Desaguadero in the south overturns, killing at least 23 persons. In the northeastern province of Ancash, a truck overturns, killing 15.

February 19, Chitwan, Nepal. A passenger bus en route from Kathmandu to Dhankuta falls from a highway into a stream; at least 40 persons perish.

March 13, Chincha, Peru. A bus runs off a rain-slicked highway, crashes into a gas station, and explodes; at least 35 persons die.

April 12, West Bengal state, India. A high-speed collision between a truck and a bus claims the lives of 21 persons and injures 15.

April 23, Central Russia. A steamroller falls from a truck onto a bus that the truck is passing; at least 15 persons on the bus are killed.

April 26, KwaZulu/Natal province, S.Af. After one of its tires bursts, a bus overturns and rolls down a cliff; at least 22 persons die, and more than 45 are injured.

May 26, Near Tacna, Peru. A truck loaded with passengers and farm produce experiences brake failure before crashing into a house and overturning; at least 21 persons perish.

June 10, Near Masvingo, Zimb. A collision between a bus and a truck claims the lives of at least 36 persons, most of them students.

June 11, Rutana province, Burundi. A United Nations-chartered truck transporting Burundian refugees home from Tanzania crashes after running off a road; 41 persons die, and 40 are injured.

Mid-June, Northern Egypt. Two trucks collide on a highway between Cairo and Alexandria; 19 persons—all of them farmworkers on their way to pick apricots—lose their lives, and 49 are injured.

June 30, Western Hungary. A bus carrying tourists from Poland to a Roman Catholic shrine in Bosnia and Herzegovina overturns, killing 19 persons and injuring 32.

Early July, Near Jember, East Java, Indon. A driver loses control of a bus after one of its tires blows out, and the bus falls into a ravine; at least 26 persons are killed.

July 18, Western Uganda. A collision between a runaway fuel truck and a passenger bus near Lutoto claims the lives of at least 60 persons.

August 6, Near Zinapecuaro, Mex. A bus crashes into a bridge after its brakes fail; 33 persons die.

August 18, Central Russia. Brake failure causes the driver of a bus to lose control of the vehicle; 24 persons die as the bus plummets into a ravine near the village of Yantikovo.

August 22, Western Nepal. While attempting to pass another vehicle, a bus leaves the road and falls into the Trishuli River; 45 persons are believed dead.

September 15, Catamarca, Arg. A bus loses its brakes on a mountain road and plunges into a gorge; at least 50 persons are killed and 25 injured.

November 20, Near Jabalpur, India. A bus overturns, and two gasoline-filled containers on board ignite a fire; 30 persons are killed, and 26 are injured.

November 24, Quezon province, Phil. While rounding a sharp downhill curve, a bus crashes through a railing and plunges into a ravine; at least 33 persons perish.

December 2, Chiapas state, Mex. A bus crashes on a mountain road near San Cristóbal de las Casas; 21 persons die.

Miscellaneous

March 14, Lucknow, India. Thousands of people are standing in line at a job-recruitment centre when a sewer drain collapses and the ground gives way beneath them; at least 23 persons die.

March 27, Dubai, U.A.E. Gates collapse at a dry dock, allowing seawater to flood the dock and submerge a number of ships under repair; 22 persons are killed, and 7 others are missing and feared dead.

May 26, Near Webbers Falls, Okla. An interstate highway bridge over the Arkansas River collapses after a barge being pushed by a towboat slams into one of the bridge's supports; at least 10 vehicles crossing the bridge plummet into the river. There are 14 confirmed deaths. The pilot of the towboat apparently blacked out just prior to the accident.

Early June, Saudi Arabia. At least 19 persons die from methanol poisoning after they drank cologne as a substitute for alcohol; 11 of the deaths occur in Mecca, the others in Jizan province.

September 24, Fangzhen, China. A guardrail in an unlighted stairwell at a middle school collapses as students are leaving for the day; 21 students die.

September 28, Lucknow, India. A stampede occurs at a railway station where thousands of people are in the process of returning home after having attended a political rally; at least 16 persons are killed, and 44 are injured.

December 1, Gaibandha, Bangladesh. A crowd of more than 10,000 people stampedes as guards open the gates of a mill where clothes donated by a charitable businessman are to be distributed; at least 30 persons die.

Young women return to school in Kabul, Afg.
AP/Wide World Photos

People of 2002

Nobel Prizes

Laureates in 2002 included a **PRESIDENTIAL PEACEMAKER**, a Hungarian **HOLOCAUST SURVIVOR**, pioneers in the study of **ECONOMIC DECISION MAKING**, and scientists who made pathbreaking discoveries concerning **PARTICLES** and **RADIATION** from **SPACE**, the **ANALYSIS OF PROTEINS**, and **PROGRAMMED CELL DEATH**.

PRIZE FOR PEACE

The 2002 Nobel Prize for Peace was awarded to Jimmy Carter, 39th president of the United States. The Norwegian Nobel Committee honoured his "decades of untiring effort to find peaceful solutions to international conflicts, to advance democracy and human rights, and to promote economic and social development." Among other things, the committee specifically cited Carter's role in the Camp David Accords between Egypt and Israel, as well as the projects of the Carter Center after he left office, including its work in monitoring elections and eradicating diseases. He was the third U.S. president, after Theodore Roosevelt (1906) and Woodrow Wilson (1919), to win the prize.

James Earl Carter, Jr., was born on Oct. 1, 1924, in Plains, Ga. He graduated from the U.S. Naval Academy in Annapolis, Md., in 1946 and served for seven years in the navy. Upon the death of his father in 1953, he returned to Georgia to manage the family's peanut farm. A Democrat, he was elected to the Georgia state Senate in 1962 and reelected in 1964, and he was elected governor in 1970. In 1976 he won the U.S. presidency. His most dramatic foreign-policy achievement was the 1978 Camp David Accords, in which Egyptian Pres. Anwar el-Sadat and Israeli Prime Minister Menachem Begin reached agreements that formed the basis of a peace treaty. Problems dogged the Carter presidency, however, among them the Iranian hostage crisis of 1979. Further, the administration was beset by domestic economic worries, and Carter lost his bid for reelection in 1980.

In 1982, in conjunction with Emory University in Atlanta, Ga., he founded the Carter Center, which served as the base for much of his subsequent work. Carter monitored various international elections, among them those in Nicaragua and East Timor. He also intervened in disputes involving North Korea, Haiti, Bosnia and Herzegovina, and other countries. In 2002 he became the first sitting or former U.S. president to travel to Cuba since Fidel Castro came to power. Beginning in 1984, Carter and his wife, Rosalynn, who was his partner in many of his undertakings, devoted one week of each year to Habitat for Humanity, a nonprofit Christian organization that builds affordable housing for the poor. A lifelong Baptist, he spoke freely of the role of religion in his life and work. Among his many books were *The Spiritual Journey of Jimmy Carter* (1978) and *Keeping Faith: Memoirs of a President* (1982).

In implied criticism of the policies of U.S. Pres. George W. Bush, the Nobel statement commented, "In a situation currently marked by threats of the use of power, Carter has stood by the principles that conflicts must as far as possible be resolved through mediation and international cooperation based on international law, respect for human rights, and economic development." At the same time, committee members emphasized that Carter had been awarded the prize on merit. Although Sadat and Begin had won the Nobel Prize for Peace in 1978, a technicality prevented Carter from also being considered at the time. He had been nominated virtually every year since, and many observers saw the prize as an honour long overdue.

(ROBERT RAUCH)

PRIZE FOR ECONOMICS

The Nobel Memorial Prize in Economic Sciences was awarded in 2002 to Israeli-born Daniel Kahneman and American Vernon L. Smith, who pioneered the use in decision making of psychological and experimental economics, respectively. The results of their work undermined two fundamental aspects of traditional economic theory—that in complex market situations people make rational decisions based on material incentives and that economics was a nonexperimental science that relied exclusively on field data.

Kahneman received the Nobel "for having integrated insights from psychological research into economic science, especially concerning human judgment and decision-making under uncertainty." He drew on cognitive psychology in relation to the mental processes used in forming judgments and making choices in order to increase understanding of how people make economic decisions. Kahneman's research with the late Amos Tversky on decision making under uncertainty resulted in the formulation of a new branch of economics, prospect theory, which was the subject of their seminal article "Prospect Theory: An Analysis of Decisions Under Risk" (1979). Previously, economists had believed that people's decisions are determined by the expected gains from each possible future scenario multiplied by its probability of occurring, but if people make an irrational judgment by giving more weight to some scenarios than to others, their decision will be different from that predicted by traditional economic theory. Kahneman's research (based on surveys and experiments) showed that his subjects were incapable of analyzing complex decision situations when the future consequences were uncertain. Instead, they relied on heuristic shortcuts, or rule-of-thumb, with few people evaluating the underlying probability.

Smith was awarded the Nobel "for having established laboratory experiments as a tool in empirical economic analysis, especially in the study of alternative market mechanisms." His early work was inspired by the classroom experiments of his teacher at Harvard University, E.H. Chamberlin, who tested the neoclassical theory of perfect competition. Smith improved on the process of testing the fundamental economic theory that under perfect competition the market price of any product or service establishes an equilibrium between supply and demand at the level where the value assigned by a marginal buyer is equal to that of a marginal seller. The results of Smith's experiments, published in 1962, involved the random designation of the roles of buyers and sellers with different and uninformed valuations of a commodity, expressed as a lowest acceptable selling price and highest acceptable buying price. He was able to determine the theoretical equilibrium, or acceptable market price. Unexpectedly, the prices obtained in the laboratory were close to the theoretical values. Many of his experiments focused on the outcome of public auctions; he showed that the way in which the bidding was organized affected the selling price. Smith also devised "wind-tunnel tests," where trials of new alternative market designs, such as those for a deregulated industry, could be tested.

Kahneman was born on March 5, 1934, in Tel Aviv, Israel, and was educated at Hebrew University, Jerusalem (B.A., 1954), and the University of California, Berkeley (Ph.D., 1961). He was a lecturer (1961–70) and professor (1970–78) of psychology at Hebrew University, and from 2000 he held a fellowship at that university's Center for Rationality. From 1993 Kahneman was Eugene Higgins Professor of Psychology at Princeton University and professor of public affairs at Princeton's Woodrow Wilson School of Public and International Affairs. He was on the editorial boards of several academic journals, notably the *Journal of Behavioral Decision Making* and the *Journal of Risk and Uncertainty*.

Smith was born on Jan. 1, 1927, in Wichita, Kan. He studied electrical engineering at the California Institute of Technology (Caltech; B.S., 1949), then switched to economics at the University of Kansas (M.A., 1951) and Harvard (Ph.D., 1955). Smith taught and did research at Purdue University, West Lafayette, Ind. (1955–67), Brown University, Providence, R.I. (1967–68), the University of Massachusetts (1968–75), Caltech (1973–75), and the University of Arizona (1975–01), where he was Regents' Professor of Economics from 1988. In 2001 he was named professor of economics and law at George Mason

University, Fairfax, Va. Much of Smith's commercial work was related to the deregulation of energy in the U.S., Australia, and New Zealand. He served on the editorial boards of several journals and wrote extensively on subjects ranging from capital theory and finance to natural resource economics and experimental economics.

(JANET H. CLARK)

PRIZE FOR LITERATURE

The 2002 Nobel Prize for Literature was awarded to Hungarian author and Holocaust survivor Imre Kertész. He was cited by the Swedish Academy for writing that "upholds the fragile experience of the individual against the barbaric arbitrariness of history." One of the many Eastern European writers who endured under the veil of communism, Kertész identified in part with the postwar literary generation that emerged in the wake of the 1956 uprising, including novelists Miklós Mészöly and György Konrád, poet Sándor Csoóri, and dramatist István

Csurka. After the violent Soviet suppression of the uprising, writers who remained in Hungary were subjected to the mandate of official censorship or risked arrest and imprisonment; others fell silent or were forced into exile. Preferring instead a form of self-imposed anonymity as protest against the communist dictatorship, Kertész was largely ignored for much of his career. With the fall of communism in Hungary following what was deemed the "quiet revolution" in 1989, Kertész resumed an active literary role—gaining national as well as international recognition as a writer—and at the age of 72 he became the first Hungarian to be named a Nobel laureate in literature.

Kertész was born on Nov. 9, 1929, in Budapest. He was 14 when he was deported with other Hungarian Jews during World War II to the Auschwitz concentration camp in Nazi-occupied Poland. He was later sent to the Buchenwald camp in Germany, where he was liberated in May 1945. Returning to Hungary, he worked as a journalist for the newspaper *Világosság* but

Imre Kertész

was dismissed in 1951 following the communist takeover. Refusing to submit to the cultural policies imposed by the new regime, Kertész turned to translation as a means of supporting himself without having to compromise his artistic integrity. Highly praised as a translator, he specialized in the works of German-language authors, notably Friedrich Nietzsche, Hugo von Hofmannsthal, Sigmund Freud, Arthur Schnitzler, and Ludwig Wittgenstein.

Kertész was best known for his first and most acclaimed novel, *Sorstalanság* (*Fateless*, 1992), which he completed in the mid-1960s but was unable to publish for nearly a decade. When the novel finally appeared in 1975, it received little critical attention but established Kertész as a unique and provocative voice in the dissident subculture within contemporary Hungarian literature. For Kertész the Holocaust was the definitive event of his life; in *Sorstalanság* he fused the experience of his youth with his determination to provide a truthful account of the persecution and near annihilation of Hungarian Jews during World War II. The adolescent narrator of *Sorstalanság* is arrested and deported to a concentration camp and confronts the inexplicable horror of human degradation not with outrage or resistance but with seemingly incomprehensible complacency and detachment. For the narrator the brutal reality of atrocity and evil is reconciled by his inherent and inexorable will to survive—without remorse or a need for retribution. With the publication in 1990 of the first German-language edition of the novel, Kertész began to expand his literary reputation in Europe, and the novel was later published in more than 10 languages, including English, French, Spanish, Italian, Dutch, Swedish, and Norwegian.

Sorstalanság was the first installment in his semiautobiographical trilogy reflecting on the Holocaust, and the two other novels—*A kudarc* (1988; "Fiasco") and *Kaddis a meg nem született gyermekért* (1990; *Kaddish for a Child Not Born*, 1997)—reintroduced the protagonist of *Sorstalanság*. In 1991 Kertész published *Az angol lobogó* ("The English Flag"), a collection of short stories and other short prose pieces, and he followed that in 1992 with *Gályanapló* ("Galley Diary"), a diary in fictional form covering the period from 1961 to 1991. Another installment of the diary, from 1991 to 1995, appeared in 1997 as *Valaki más: a változás krónikája* ("I—

Another: Chronicle of a Metamorphosis"). His essays and lectures were collected in *A holocaust mint kultúra* (1993; "The Holocaust as Culture"), *A gondolatnyi csend, amíg kivégzőoztag újratölt* (1998; "Moments of Silence While the Execution Squad Reloads"), and *A száműzött nyelv* (2001; "The Exiled Language"). In 1995 Kertész received the Brandenburg Literary Prize; the Leipzig Book Prize for European Understanding followed in 1997, and in 2000 he was awarded the WELT-Literature Prize.   (STEVEN R. SERAFIN)

PRIZE FOR CHEMISTRY

Three scientists—an American, a Japanese, and a Swiss—won the 2002 Nobel Prize for Chemistry for having developed techniques to identify and analyze proteins and other large biological molecules. John B. Fenn of Virginia Commonwealth University and Koichi Tanaka of Shimadzu Corp., Kyoto, shared half of the $1 million prize. The remainder went to Kurt Wüthrich of the Swiss Federal Institute of Technology (ETH), Zürich, and the Scripps Research Institute, La Jolla, Calif. The Royal Swedish Academy of Sciences, which awarded the prize, called their achievement a breakthrough that turned "chemical biology into the 'big science' of our time," allowing scientists to "both 'see' the proteins and understand how they function in the cells."

Fenn was born June 15, 1917, in New York City. After receiving a Ph.D. in chemistry in 1940 from Yale University, he spent more than a decade in industry before joining Princeton University in 1952. In 1967 he moved to Yale, where he became professor emeritus in 1987. In 1994 Fenn took a post as research professor at Virginia Commonwealth University. Tanaka, born Aug. 3, 1959, in Toyama City, Japan, earned an engineering degree from Tohoku University in 1983. He then joined Shimadzu, a maker of scientific and industrial instruments, and he remained there in various research capacities. Wüthrich was born Oct. 4, 1938, in Aarberg, Switz. He received a Ph.D. in inorganic chemistry in 1964 from the University of Basel and took his postdoctoral training in Switzerland and the U.S. In 1969 he joined ETH, and he became professor of biophysics in 1980. In 2001 he accepted a position at Scripps as a visiting professor.

Fenn's and Tanaka's prizewinning research expanded the applications of

mass spectrometry (MS), an analytic technique used in many fields of science since the early 20th century. MS can identify unknown compounds in minute samples of material, determine the amounts of known compounds, and help deduce molecular formulas of compounds. For decades scientists had employed MS on small and medium-size molecules, but they also dreamed of using it to identify large molecules such as proteins. After the genetic code was deciphered and gene sequences were explored, the study of proteins and how they interact inside cells took on great importance.

A requirement of MS is that samples be in the form of a gas of ions, or electrically charged molecules. Molecules such as proteins posed a problem because existing ionization techniques broke down their three-dimensional structure. Fenn and Tanaka each developed a way to convert samples of large molecules into gaseous form without such degradation. In the late 1980s Fenn originated electrospray ionization, a technique that involves injecting a solution of the sample into a strong electric field, which disperses it into a fine spray of charged droplets. As each droplet shrinks by evaporation, the electric field on its surface becomes intense enough to toss individual molecules from the droplet, forming free ions ready for analysis with MS. About the same time, Tanaka reported a different method, called soft laser desorption, in which the sample, in solid or viscous form, is bombarded with a laser pulse. As molecules in the sample absorb the laser energy, they let go of each other (desorb) and form a cloud of ions suitable for MS.

Wüthrich devised a way to apply another analytic technique, nuclear magnetic resonance (NMR), to the study of large biological molecules. Whereas MS excels at revealing kinds and amounts of molecules, NMR provides detailed information about their structure. Developed in the late 1940s, it requires placing the sample in a very strong magnetic field and bombarding it with radio waves. The nuclei of certain atoms, such as hydrogen, in the molecules respond by emitting their own radio waves, which can be analyzed to work out their structural details.

In the early 1980s, when Wüthrich began his prizewinning work, NMR worked best for small molecules. For large molecules such as proteins, the numerous atomic nuclei present produced an indecipherable tangle of radio signals. Wüthrich's solution, called sequential assignment, sorts out the tangle by methodically matching up each NMR signal with the corresponding hydrogen nucleus in the protein being analyzed. Wüthrich also showed how to use that information to determine distances between numerous pairs of hydrogen nuclei and thereby build up a three-dimensional picture of the molecule. The first complete determination of a protein structure with Wüthrich's method was achieved in 1985, and about 20% of protein structures known to date had been determined with NMR.

(MICHAEL WOODS)

PRIZE FOR PHYSICS

Three astrophysical pioneers won the 2002 Nobel Prize for Physics for discoveries about strange, elusive particles from the Sun and high-energy radiation from a variety of objects and processes in the universe. Raymond Davis, Jr., of the University of Pennsylvania shared half of the $1 million prize with Masatoshi Koshiba of the University of Tokyo. Each man led the construction of giant underground devices to detect neutrinos, ghostly subatomic particles that pass through Earth by the trillions each second. Riccardo Giacconi of Associated Universities, Inc., Washington, D.C., received the other half for seminal discoveries of cosmic sources of X-rays.

Davis, born Oct. 14, 1914, in Washington, D.C., received a Ph.D. in 1942 from Yale University. After wartime military service, he joined Brookhaven National Laboratory, Upton, N.Y., in 1948, where he remained until retirement in 1984. In 1985 he took a post as research professor with the University of Pennsylvania. Koshiba was born Sept. 19, 1926, in Toyohashi, Japan. After earning a Ph.D. in 1955 from the University of Rochester, N.Y., he joined the University of Tokyo, becoming professor in 1970 and emeritus professor in 1987. Giacconi, born Oct. 6, 1931, in Genoa, Italy, took a Ph.D. in 1954 from the University of Milan. In 1959 he joined the research firm American Science and Engineering, and in 1973 he moved to the Harvard-Smithsonian Center for Astrophysics. He directed the Space Telescope Science Institute from 1981 to 1993 and the European Southern Observatory for the six years following. In 1999 he became president of Associated Universities, Inc., which operates the National Radio Astronomy Observatory.

Scientists had suspected since the 1920s that the Sun shines because of nuclear fusion reactions that transform hydrogen into helium and release energy. Later, theoretical calculations indicated that countless neutrinos must be released in those reactions and, consequently, that Earth must be exposed to a constant flood of solar neutrinos. Because neutrinos interact weakly with matter, however, only one in every trillion is stopped on its way through the planet. Neutrinos thus developed a reputation as being undetectable.

Some of Davis's contemporaries had speculated that one type of nuclear reaction might produce neutrinos with enough energy to make them detectable. If such a neutrino collided with a chlorine atom, it should form a radioactive argon nucleus. In the 1960s, in a gold mine in South Dakota, Davis built a neutrino detector, a huge tank filled with over 600 tons of the cleaning fluid tetrachloroethylene. He calculated that high-energy neutrinos passing through the tank should form 20 argon atoms a month on average, and he developed a way to count those exceedingly rare atoms. Over a quarter century of monitoring the tank, he consistently found fewer neutrinos than expected. The deficit, dubbed the solar neutrino problem, implied either that scientists' understanding of energy production in the Sun was wrong or that something happened to the neutrinos en route to Earth in a way that made some of them seem to vanish.

In the 1980s Koshiba set up a different kind of detector in a zinc mine in Japan. Called Kamiokande II, it was an enormous water tank surrounded by electronic detectors to sense flashes of light produced when neutrinos interacted with atomic nuclei in water molecules. Kamiokande confirmed Davis's results, and, because it was directional, it eliminated any last doubt that neutrinos come from the Sun. In 1987 Kamiokande also detected neutrinos from a supernova explosion outside the Milky Way. After building a larger, more sensitive detector named Super-Kamiokande, which became operational in 1996, Koshiba found strong evidence for what scientists had already suspected—that neutrinos, of which three types are known, change from one type into another in flight. Because Davis's detector was sensitive to only one type, those that had switched identity eluded detection.

Giacconi began his award-winning work in X-ray astronomy in 1959, about a decade after astronomers had first detected X-rays from the Sun. Because X-rays emitted by cosmic objects are absorbed by Earth's atmosphere, this radiation could be studied only after sounding rockets were developed that could carry X-ray detectors above most of the atmosphere for brief flights. Giacconi conducted a number of these rocket observations, which led to the detection of intense X-rays from sources outside the solar system, including the star Scorpius X-1 and the Crab Nebula supernova remnant.

Giacconi's achievements piqued the interest of other scientists in the nascent field of X-ray astronomy, but their research was hampered by the short observation times afforded by rockets. For long-term studies Giacconi encouraged construction of an Earth-orbiting X-ray satellite to survey the sky. Named Uhuru (launched 1970), it raised the number of known X-ray sources into the hundreds. Earlier, Giacconi had worked out the operating principles for a telescope that could focus X-rays into images, and in the 1970s he built the first high-definition X-ray telescope. Called the Einstein Observatory (launched 1978), it examined stellar atmospheres and supernova remnants, identified many X-ray double stars (some containing suspected black holes), and detected X-ray sources in other galaxies. In 1976 Giacconi proposed a still more powerful instrument, which was finally launched in 1999 as the Chandra X-Ray Observatory.

(MICHAEL WOODS)

PRIZE FOR PHYSIOLOGY OR MEDICINE

Two Britons—Sydney Brenner and Sir John E. Sulston—and an American—H. Robert Horvitz—shared the 2002 Nobel Prize for Physiology or Medicine for discoveries about how genes regulate tissue and organ development via a key mechanism called programmed cell death, or apoptosis. Their research elucidated the exquisitely tuned process in which certain cells, at the right time and place, get a signal to commit suicide. As was observed by the Nobel Assembly at the Karolinska Institute in Stockholm, which awarded the $1 million prize, "The discoveries are important for medical research and have shed new light on the pathogenesis of many diseases."

Brenner was born Jan. 13, 1927, in Germiston, S.Af., and received a Ph.D. in 1954 from the University of Oxford.

Sydney Brenner

Sir John E. Sulston

H. Robert Horvitz

In 1957 he began work with the Medical Research Council (MRC) in the U.K., where he later directed its Laboratory of Molecular Biology (1979–86) and Molecular Genetics Unit (1986–91). In 1996 Brenner founded the California-based Molecular Sciences Institute, and in 2000 he accepted the position of distinguished research professor at the Salk Institute for Biological Studies, La Jolla, Calif. Sulston, who was born March 27, 1942, earned a Ph.D. in 1966 from the University of Cambridge. Following three years of postdoctoral work in the U.S., he joined Brenner's group at the MRC. From 1992 to 2000 he was director of the Sanger Institute, Cambridge. Horvitz, born May 8, 1947, in Chicago, took his Ph.D. in 1974 from Harvard University. In 1978, after a stint with Brenner at the MRC that had begun in 1974, he moved to the Massachusetts Institute of Technology, where he became a full professor in 1986.

Programmed cell death is essential for normal development in all animals. During the fetal development of humans, huge numbers of cells must be eliminated as body structures form. Programmed cell death sculpts the fingers and toes, for instance, by removing tissue that was originally present between the digits. Likewise, it removes surplus nerve cells produced during early development of the brain. In a typical adult human, about a trillion new cells develop each day; a similar number must be eliminated to maintain health and to keep the body from becoming overgrown with surplus cells.

To study programmed cell death in humans, Brenner, Sulston, and Horvitz relied on an animal model, the nematode *Caenorhabditis elegans*, a near-microscopic soil worm. In the early 1960s Brenner had realized the difficulties of studying organ development and related processes in higher animals, which have enormous numbers of cells. His search for a simple organism with many of the basic biological characteristics of humans led to *C. elegans*, which begins life with just 1,090 cells. Moreover, the animal is transparent, which allows scientists to follow cell divisions under a microscope; it reproduces quickly; and it is inexpensive to maintain. As researchers later learned, programmed cell death eliminates 131 cells in *C. elegans*, so that adults wind up with 959 body cells. Brenner's investigations showed that a chemical compound could induce genetic mutations in the worm and that the mutations had specific effects on organ development. His work "laid the foundation for this year's Prize," the Nobel Assembly stated, and established *C. elegans* as one of the most important experimental tools in genetics research.

Sulston in the 1970s mapped a complete cell lineage for *C. elegans*, tracing the descent of every cell, through division and differentiation, from the fertilized egg. From this he showed that, in worm after worm, exactly the same 131 cells are eliminated by programmed cell death as the animals develop into adults. Sulston also identified the first known mutations in genes involved in the process.

Beginning in the 1970s Horvitz used *C. elegans* to try to determine if a specific genetic program controlled cell death. In 1986 he reported the first two "death genes," *ced-3* and *ced-4*, which participate in the cell-killing process. Later he showed that another gene, *ced-9*, protects against cell death by interacting with *ced-3* and *ced-4*. Horvitz also established that humans have a counterpart to the *ced-3* gene. Scientists later found that most of the genes involved in controlling programmed cell death in *C. elegans* have counterparts in humans.

Knowledge about programmed cell death led to important advances not only in developmental biology but also in medicine. It helped, for example, to explain how some viruses and bacteria invade human cells and cause infections. In cancer and some other diseases, programmed cell death was seen to slow down, which allows survival of cells that normally are destined to die. In cancer the result is an excessive growth of cells that invade and destroy normal tissue. Some cancer treatments are based on the strategy of shifting the cell suicide program into higher gear.

(MICHAEL WOODS)

Biographies

The **SUBJECTS** of these biographies are the people who in the editors' opinions captured the **IMAGINATION** of the world in 2002—the most **INTERESTING** and/or **IMPORTANT PERSONALITIES** of the year.

Abdul Kalam, A.P.J.

In 2002 India made an unorthodox choice for president by electing a front-rank rocket scientist. A.P.J. Abdul Kalam, who was nicknamed Missile Man, had just retired from the country's space and defense research programs when the ruling National Democratic Alliance (NDA) government put forward his name for the presidency in the July election. Kalam won in a landslide and was sworn in as India's 11th president on July 25.

Avul Pakir Jainulabdeen Abdul Kalam was born on Oct. 15, 1931, in Rameswaram, Tamil Nadu state, India, to a Muslim family of modest means. He earned a degree in aeronautical engineering from the Madras Institute of Technology and joined the Defence Research and Development Organisation (DRDO) in 1958. He soon moved to the Indian Space Research Organisation, where his brilliance and leadership attracted notice. He was project director of SLV-III, India's first indigenously designed and produced satellite launch vehicle. Rejoining DRDO in 1982 he planned the Integrated Guided Missile Development Programme, which produced the missiles Agni, Prithvi, Akash, Trishul, and Nag that became household names in India. From 1992 to 1997 Kalam was scientific adviser to the defense minister, and in November 1999 he was named principal scientific adviser to the government with the rank of cabinet minister. He was awarded two of the highest national honours, Padma Vibhushan in 1990 and Bharat Ratna in 1997.

Kalam's interest was not confined to defense and space research. In 1998 he put forward a major plan for the application of science to problems of everyday life. He called it Technology Vision 2020 and described it as a road map for transforming India from a less-developed society into a developed one in 20 years. The plan called for, among other measures, increasing agricultural productivity, emphasizing technology as a vehicle for economic growth, and widening access to health care and education.

When the time came to nominate a successor to outgoing Pres. K.R. Narayanan, the NDA found that the arithmetic in the electoral college did not guarantee a safe passage for its candidate unless a section of the opposition also supported him. The government's failure to halt sectarian rioting in the western state of Gujarat—during which a large number of persons, mostly Muslims, had been killed—had prompted accusations that the NDA was anti-Muslim. The NDA hit upon Kalam's name. His stature and popular appeal were such that even the main opposition party, the Indian National Congress, also proposed his candidacy. He bested Lakshmi Sehgal, a token candidate put up by the Left parties, by a vote of 4,152–459 when polling took place in Congress on July 15. In his pronouncements following his victory, Kalam reiterated his resolve to work for Technology Vision 2020. In his autobiography, *Wheels of Fire* (1999), he had made a strong plea against "the culture of working only for material possessions and rewards."

(H.Y. SHARADA PRASAD)

Abdullah, Crown Prince

Crown Prince Abdullah, the de facto ruler of Saudi Arabia, emerged as a key political decision maker concerning Arab regional and international affairs in 2002. Following the 1995 stroke that afflicted his half brother, King Fahd, Prince Abdullah began running the daily affairs of the country. Though Abdullah was perceived as committed to preserving Arab interests, his goal was also to maintain good relations with the West, especially the U.S. Even before the Sept. 11, 2001, attacks by militant Islamists in the U.S., strains had appeared in Saudi-U.S. relations—the Saudis accused the new U.S. administration of Pres. George W. Bush of not being evenhanded in the Palestinian-Israeli conflict. During 2001 Abdullah twice declined U.S. presidential invitations to visit Washington, D.C.

The events of September 11 increased these strains, primarily because most of the suspects in the attack were Saudi nationals. Though Abdullah condemned these acts, Saudi-U.S. relations reached a low ebb in the first half of 2002. In a move to improve relations, Abdullah launched his proposal for a Saudi peace initiative. It was adopted during the Arab summit meeting held in Beirut, Leb., on March 27–28, 2002, as an Arab peace initiative. The plan called upon Israel to withdraw from the Palestinian and Syrian lands that it had occupied since 1967 and in return promised a full Arab normalization of relations with the Jewish state. He accepted a Saudi-Iraqi rapprochement, however, and publicly refused to support any attack on Iraq or the use of Saudi military facilities for such an act. The rift in Saudi-U.S. relations had mended by year's end after intensive diplomatic efforts.

'Abdullah ibn 'Abd al-'Aziz was born in 1923. He was one of King Abd al-'Aziz's 37 sons. As a result of his support of Crown Prince Faysal during Faysal's power struggle with King Saud, Abdullah was rewarded in 1962 with command of the National Guard, a force nearly as powerful as the Saudi army. He was appointed second deputy minister in 1975 by King Khalid after Faysal's assassination and was named crown prince and first deputy prime minister in 1982 by King Fahd. Abdullah, who continued to command the National Guard, served as regent in 1996 for a short period.

Abdullah was perceived by many as a man of integrity and as part of the "reformers" camp that supported gradual change in Saudi Arabia. In early 2002 he placed the institution responsible for the education of females—which had been overseen by the Saudi religious establishment—under the control of the central government as part of the Ministry of Education, which was responsible for the education of both male and female students. In August he backed the Justice Ministry's decision to license lawyers in a bid to regulate the Islamic justice system. In addition, he seemed to favour reducing state subsidies to private enterprises and moving toward an economic privatization program. In September he called on the religious establishment to be less rigid and open up in order to better serve the populace.

(MAHMOUD HADDAD)

Ashcroft, John

As U.S. attorney general, John Ashcroft was at the centre of policy changes adopted by the Department of Justice (DOJ) during 2002. Following the terrorist attacks in the U.S. on Sept. 11, 2001, he pressed for passage of the so-called USA PATRIOT Act, which expanded the government's power to detain noncitizens, conduct surveillance and search, and investigate persons suspected of involvement in criminal activity. Perhaps no actions were more controversial, however, than the administration's handling of some 1,200 people jailed after the attacks. These included immigration violators whose cases were heard in secret, a number of people held as material witnesses, and two U.S. nationals classified as "enemy combatants" and thus denied the legal rights of citizens. The DOJ vigorously resisted challenges to its actions from the courts and from members of the U.S. Congress and the press.

Ashcroft was born in Chicago on May 9, 1942, and grew up in Springfield, Mo. He was a graduate of Yale University (B.A., 1964) and the University of Chicago (J.D., 1967). Before entering politics in 1973, when he was appointed state auditor, he taught business law at Southwest Missouri State University. He was elected state attorney general in 1976 and reelected in 1980, and in 1984 he won the first of two terms as governor. As attorney general and governor of Missouri, he was known for fiscally and socially conservative policies, including restrictions on abortions. He was elected to the U.S. Senate in 1994 but was defeated in 2000, when he lost to a deceased candidate whose name remained on the ballot. Nominated by President-elect George W. Bush as attorney general, Ashcroft faced intense questioning in the Senate, particularly on his attitudes toward blacks and homosexuals and on his ability as a fundamentalist Christian to uphold U.S. law, but he was confirmed by a vote of 58 to 42.

Ashcroft took a number of positions favoured by the political right. In May 2002 the DOJ informed the U.S. Supreme Court that henceforth the government would consider the Second Amendment to the Constitution to give individual citizens the right to own guns, a reversal of a long-held more restrictive interpretation. Ashcroft approved giving agents of the FBI permission to monitor people in public areas—for example, in libraries and on the Internet—without evidence that a crime had been committed. Not all of Ashcroft's policies were well received, however. A number of local officials rebuffed his request that they call in Arab Americans for questioning, and courts ruled that he had overreached his authority in striking down an Oregon law permitting assisted suicide. When he announced a plan whereby workers with access to citizens' homes would be enlisted to report suspicious activity—the so-called Terrorism Information and Prevention System, or TIPS—it was denounced by both the left and the right and had to be substantially modified.   (ROBERT RAUCH)

Berry, Halle

American actress Halle Berry made Hollywood history in 2002, becoming the first black woman to win an Academy Award for best actress. Upon accepting the award for her performance in the 2001 film *Monster's Ball*, Berry delivered an emotional speech during which she proclaimed that the door had finally opened for women of colour hoping to be recognized for their talents as performers. "This moment is so much bigger than me," she said tearfully. With her Oscar win, Berry had succeeded in establishing herself as one of the biggest stars in the film business.

Berry was born on Aug. 14, 1966, in Cleveland, Ohio, to a white mother and an African American father. Although her ambition was to become a journalist, Berry began modeling at the age of 16. After finishing as first runner-up in the 1986 Miss USA pageant, Berry set her sights on a career in acting. She studied improvisation at the Second City comedy theatre in Chicago before moving to New York City to try to get work in televi-

sion. A regular role on the TV series *Living Dolls* ensued.

Her first major film role was as a drug-addicted prostitute in director Spike Lee's 1991 film *Jungle Fever*. This led to steady film work throughout the 1990s, including appearances in *The Flintstones* (1994), *Losing Isaiah* (1995), *Executive Decision* (1996), *Bulworth* (1998), and *X-Men* (2000). She also won an Emmy and a Golden Globe Award for her portrayal of the title character in the 1999 made-for-TV film *Introducing Dorothy Dandridge*. The parts did not always come easily, as Berry found that black actresses were often confined to a narrow niche in feature film roles. On one occasion she was turned down for a role as a park ranger because a studio executive was convinced that black park rangers did not exist. Despite her gritty debut screen role in *Jungle Fever*, Berry also had to fight against

AP/Wide World Photos

Hollywood headliner Halle Berry

the assumption that she was too pretty to play serious parts. Challenging roles eventually came her way, however. In *Monster's Ball* she played a death-row inmate's former wife who forges an unlikely relationship with a white prison guard who had participated in her ex-husband's execution.

Berry's personal life was also not without turmoil. Her much-publicized marriage to professional baseball player David Justice ended in 1997 after three trying years; a former boyfriend once hit her hard enough to cause permanent hearing loss; and in 2000 she was convicted on hit-and-run charges after leaving the scene of a traffic accident. She married jazz musician Eric Benet in 2001. By the end of 2002, she was making headlines again in Hollywood as the new "Bond girl." The 20th James Bond film, *Die Another Day*, in which Berry starred opposite Pierce Brosnan, was released in November.   (ANTHONY G. CRAINE)

Bjørndalen, Ole Einar

At the 2002 Winter Olympic Games in Salt Lake City, Utah, Norwegian biathlete Ole Einar Bjørndalen became only the third Olympian to win four gold medals at the same Winter Games and the first to capture more than two in biathlon, a demanding sport that combines high-speed cross-country skiing with rifle marksmanship and requires that the competitor slow his or her heartbeat to achieve precision while shooting.

Bjørndalen was born on Jan. 27, 1974, in Drammen, Nor., the second youngest in a family of five children. He grew up on a farm in Simostranda and became a skilled cross-country skier. He later said his older brother Dag, a biathlete, was "like a coach to me"; small wonder, then, that the younger brother followed the older into the sport. At age 16 Bjørndalen left home and entered a sports academy in Geilo. He trained in both cross-country and biathlon for a year before deciding to concentrate on the latter. Bjørndalen was on Norway's Olympic team for the 1994 Winter Games in Lillehammer. Unlike other Norwegian ski teams, however, the biathletes struggled, failing to win any medals. Bjørndalen's best individual finish was 28th in the 10-km "sprint."

With his skiing solid and swift, Bjørndalen worked to become a strong shooter. He moved to fourth in the overall World Cup standings for 1995. He dipped to ninth in 1996 but rose to second place in 1997. At the 1998 Winter Olympics in Nagano, Japan, Bjørndalen won the gold medal in the sprint and shared the silver medal with his brother and two other teammates in the 4 × 7.5-km relay. He wrapped up the season by capturing the World Cup overall title. He finished second overall in the World Cup three more times (1999–2001) and third in the 2001–02 season.

When the World Cup tour staged its pre-Olympic "test" events in 2001, Bjørndalen swept all three races. Coming into the 2002 Olympics, he was understated, as usual, but he declared his dream was to be the first person to medal in the biathlon and cross-country skiing events. In two World Cup 30-km mass-start cross-country races earlier in the season, he had been second. He was less than seven seconds off World Cup leader Per Elofsson of Sweden in the first race, then just half a second back in the other. He was a disappointing sixth, however, in the Olympic 30-km race. After catching his breath on an off day, Bjørndalen returned to form. He steamrollered all three biathlon individual races and, with the help of three teammates, added his unprecedented fourth gold in the 4 × 7.5-km relay. In Norway, where Nordic skiing was sometimes considered a birthright, Bjørndalen became the new yardstick for greatness.

(PAUL ROBBINS)

Blair, Tony

During 2002 British Prime Minister Tony Blair came to occupy a pivotal role in relations between Europe and the United States. In the aftermath of the terrorist attacks in the U.S. on Sept. 11, 2001, he underscored the U.K.'s position as the U.S.'s closest European ally, notably by publicly backing U.S. Pres. George W. Bush's "war on terrorism" and by sending British troops to join American forces in Afghanistan. As pressure mounted to strip Iraq of weapons of mass destruction, Blair fought to prevent a potentially disastrous division between the U.S. and Europe over the conditions under which military action against Iraq could take place. Blair's critics, however, claimed that the prime minister had tied the U.K. too closely to U.S. foreign policy.

Anthony Charles Lynton Blair was born in Edinburgh on May 6, 1953. He was elected to Parliament for the safe Labour Party constituency of Sedgefield in the general election of 1983, when Labour sustained its heaviest defeat since 1935. He was selected for the shadow cabinet in 1988, and when John Smith, then leader of the Labour Party, died suddenly in 1994, Blair easily won the contest to succeed him. In 1997 Blair led Labour to its greatest victory, ending 18 years in opposition, with a 179-seat majority in the 659-seat House of Commons. As prime minister he reestablished good relations between the U.K. and the rest of the European Union (EU) following years of tension under the previous Conservative Party administrations. In 1998 he led the negotiations that produced the Good Friday Agreement, which brought a cease-fire to Northern Ireland. He faced criticism in 2000 when blockades of oil refineries by truckers briefly interrupted the supply of gasoline, and his administration was accused of mishandling the 2001 foot-and-mouth epidemic. Nevertheless, the continuing strength of the economy and the feeble state of the Conservative opposition enabled Blair to lead Labour to its second successive landslide victory in June 2001.

In 2002 Blair promised to accelerate the pace of domestic reform. On the one hand, he pleased the left by explicitly embracing an economic policy of redistribution to the less well-off. On the other hand, he insisted on big changes to the organization of public services, including the greater use of private companies. For the time being, his commanding majority in the House of Commons and his continuing strength in the opinion polls enabled him to quell internal party criticism. On the international front, Blair's role was less certain, especially after a public dispute in October with French Pres. Jacques Chirac over EU farm subsidies.   (PETER KELLNER)

Bono

On May 20, 2002, Irish rock singer and songwriter Bono and U.S. Secretary of the Treasury Paul O'Neill embarked on an 11-day economic mission to Africa, visiting Ghana, South Africa, Uganda, and Ethiopia. Although the pairing might seem unlikely, Bono had for many years been a strong advocate of aid to less-developed countries, and he had gained considerable knowledge on the subject. The men were not in harmony on the best use of aid money in Africa, however. O'Neill favoured investments in African enterprises, while Bono preferred debt relief and aid given directly to organizations and individuals.

Bono was born Paul Hewson on May 10, 1960, in Dublin. In 1976 he and two high-school classmates, Dave Evans and Adam Clayton, answered an ad tacked to a bulletin board by Larry Mullen, Jr., who was seeking to form a garage band. At first they toured the local Irish club circuit, where they developed a distinctive blend of punk rock and classic rock mixed with Gaelic influences. In 1978 the band, U2, was signed by Island Records, and a series of successful albums soon followed. Marked by lyrics with social and religious references and by music that was sometimes brooding and sometimes anthemic, they included *Boy* (1980), *October* (1981), *War* (1983), *The Unforgettable Fire* (1984), and the band's international breakthrough *The Joshua Tree* (1987).

U2's music won both critical and popular acclaim. By the early 1990s the band had won several Grammy Awards and had sold more than 40 million albums. Then, describing themselves as suffocating under the image they had created, they began experimenting with electronic and dance music, often featuring heavy drumbeats, amplified guitar wails, and warped vocals. Successful albums in this mode included *Achtung Baby* (1991), *Zooropa* (1993), and *Pop* (1997). In *All That You Can't Leave Behind* (2000), U2 changed course once again, returning to the more classic rock and roll of their early years.

It was at this time that Bono developed his interest in political and social activism. In the 1980s, inspired by the Live Aid concerts that raised money for Ethiopian famine victims, he went to Ethiopia and worked with relief agencies there. In 1999 he became involved with Jubilee 2000, later known as Drop the Debt, a London-based group that considered the debt owed by less-developed countries to be a form of slavery. At this time Bono met with national leaders and Pope John Paul II to promote the group's agenda. In expressing his thoughts on the relationship between his music and his social and political activism, Bono said, "I still think that rock music is the only music that can still get you to that eternal place where you want to start a revolution."

(DAVID R. CALHOUN)

Bryant, Kobe

In 2002, for the third year in a row, Los Angeles Lakers guard Kobe Bryant helped to lead his team to the National Basketball Association (NBA) championship. Bryant staged impressive fourth-quarter performances in each of the last two games of the series, lifting his team to victories after 30-year-old centre Shaquille O'Neal, the Lakers' leading scorer, had been worn down and contained by the swarming inside defense of the New Jersey Nets. At 23 Bryant had already played a major role in winning three championships.

Bryant was born on Aug. 23, 1978, in Philadelphia. His father, Joe ("Jelly Bean") Bryant, was a basketball player who logged eight seasons in the NBA and eight more as a professional in Italy, where Kobe went to school and learned to speak fluent Italian. While attending Lower Merion High School in Ardmore, Pa., Bryant scored 2,883 points, breaking the southeastern Pennsylvania record set by Wilt Chamberlain, and he led his team to a Class AAAA title in his senior year. He received several national Player of the Year awards. Bryant's next move was part of what many considered an alarming trend in basketball: high-school players' skipping college and declaring themselves eligible for the NBA draft. Although Bryant's decision was criticized even by NBA officials—who believed that playing in college would better prepare young players for the rigours of the pro game—the Charlotte Hornets chose him on the 13th pick in the 1996 draft; he was traded to the Lakers shortly thereafter. At 18 years 2 months of age, Bryant (2.01 m; 97.5 kg [6 ft 7 in; 215 lb]) became the second youngest NBA player in history when the 1996–97 season opened, and before he had played a single game as a pro, he had signed an endorsement contract with the footwear maker Adidas.

Bryant did not wait long to prove skeptics wrong. He played well enough to be selected for the NBA All-Star game in his second season, making him the youngest all-star ever. He steadily improved his play, increasing his scoring average from 7.6 points per game in his first year to 28.5 in his fifth, the year the Lakers won their second of three titles with Bryant.

One of Bryant's biggest concerns as a pro was his uneasy relationship with O'Neal. The star in Bryant seemed reluctant to share the limelight with his popular, talented teammate, yet the more he could accept the number two position, the better he—and the Lakers—became. O'Neal won the Most Valuable Player award in the finals, but Bryant's statistics in the series rivaled those of previous MVPs. His shooting percentage of 63% in the series fourth quarters stood as ample proof that, even with O'Neal, the Lakers depended on Bryant to finish big games.   (ANTHONY G. CRAINE)

Chihuly, Dale

On July 6, 2002, Tacoma, Wash., unveiled a special public art commission: a 152.4-m (500-ft)-long pedestrian bridge adorned with dramatic glass sculptural forms. The bridge was created by Tacoma native Dale Chihuly, a glass sculptor who developed and refined the technique of glassblowing into an important contemporary art form. Co-designed by architect Arthur Andersson, the Chihuly Bridge of Glass provides a geographic as well as a cultural link, physically connecting two areas of the city and two museums—the Museum of Glass (which commissioned the project) and the Washington State History Museum. Meanwhile, the exhibition "Chihuly in the Park: A Garden of Glass," which opened in November 2001 at Chicago's Garfield Park Conservatory, was extended twice in 2002 to accommodate the public demand.

Chihuly was born in Tacoma on Sept. 20, 1941. He studied interior design at the University of Washington (B.A., 1965), sculpture

Glass artist Dale Chihuly under his
Seaform Ceiling

AP/Wide World Photos

at the University of Wisconsin (M.S., 1967), and ceramics at the Rhode Island School of Design (RISD; M.F.A., 1968), where he later held teaching positions. In 1968 he traveled to Italy on a Fulbright fellowship and worked at Venini Fabrica, the renowned glassblowing workshop in Murano, near Venice. During his time at Venini, he learned Venetian glassblowing techniques, as well as the importance of teamwork. (The latter proved especially important after a car accident in 1976 left him blind in one eye.) Returning to the U.S. in 1969, he established the RISD glassblowing program and founded (1971) the Pilchuck Glass School in Stanwood, Wash., where he created his first environmental installation—a group of clear glass bulbs floating on Pilchuck Pond. In 1996 he completed "Chihuly over Venice," a collaborative international undertaking involving glassblowers from Finland, Ireland, and Mexico. That project included "Chandeliers" installed around the city and numerous glass forms that were set out to float freely along the Venetian canals.

Although Chihuly was dependent on assistant gaffers (glassblowers), his vibrantly coloured glass creations were immediately recognizable as his own. The shapes were often organically derived forms that curved and undulated, and his technical innovations allowed for a tremendous range of patterns, colours, and textures. Chihuly's extended series, through which he explored all creative possibilities of a formal or thematic concept, included Blankets (cylindrical forms covered with patterns derived from Native American blankets), Seaforms (shapes evoking sea urchins, shells, and other marine life), and

Chandeliers (large-scale hanging sculptures illuminated by natural light sources). Variations in scale made it possible for onlookers to experience his pieces as intimate, personal objects or to be completely immersed in them, as in his prismatic interior installations in museums, public spaces, and hotels. Notable among the latter category were Chihuly's ceiling sculpture (made of more than 2,000 handblown floral shapes) in the lobby of the Bellagio Resort in Las Vegas, Nev., and the Light of Jerusalem project (1999–2000), a large-scale piece in the courtyard of the Tower of David Museum that dramatically juxtaposes over a dozen of Chihuly's glass pieces with the rough-textured stone of the ancient site.

(MEGHAN DAILEY)

Clark, Dick

Five decades after he began shaping the viewing and listening habits of music fans with *American Bandstand,* Dick Clark, the "world's oldest teenager," was still profiting from the marriage of television and rock and roll as the executive producer of *American Dreams,* a nostalgic dramatic series that premiered in 2002. Set in the early 1960s, it focused on a family whose daughter dances on *American Bandstand* and featured vintage musical performances from the show.

Richard Wagstaff Clark was born on Nov. 30, 1929, in Mount Vernon, N.Y. He was a disc jockey at the student radio station at Syracuse (N.Y.) University, from which he graduated in 1951. Clark also worked at radio and television stations in Syracuse and Utica, N.Y., before moving in 1952 to WFIL radio in Philadelphia. His career skyrocketed in 1956 when he took over as the host of *Bandstand,* a popular afternoon program on WFIL-TV on which teenagers danced to records. Largely through Clark's initiative, *Bandstand* was picked up by

A durable Dick Clark celebrates 50 years of American Bandstand.

AP/Wide World Photos

ABC as *American Bandstand* for nationwide distribution, beginning on Aug. 5, 1957. The program's mix of lip-synched performances, interviews, and its famous "Rate-a-Record" segment captivated teenagers, who rushed home weekday afternoons to learn the newest dances, pick up fashion cues, and speculate on the romances between *American Bandstand's* regulars. Overnight, Clark became one of pop music's most important tastemakers as exposure on *American Bandstand* or his prime-time program, *The Dick Clark Show,* generated countless hits. Meanwhile, Clark's vertically integrated business interests grew to include record companies, song publishing, and artist management. When the record industry's payola scandal (involving payment in return for airplay) broke in 1959, Clark told a congressional committee that he was unaware that performers in whom he had interests had received disproportionate play on his programs. He emerged from the investigation largely unscathed, partly because his clean-cut image contrasted with the rebelliousness of payola's most famous fall guy, disc jockey Alan Freed.

In 1963 *American Bandstand* moved to Saturdays and to Los Angeles, both to follow the shifting centre of the music industry and to allow Clark to broaden the scope of his involvement in television production. His Dick Clark Productions began presenting game shows, made-for-TV movies, and variety programs, most successfully *The $25,000 Pyramid* and *TV's Bloopers & Practical Jokes.* Among the many awards programs the company produced was the American Music Awards, which Clark created. While Clark's behind-the-scenes business acumen had much to do with the fortune he amassed, he was better remembered for the charming on-air personality and ageless look that allowed him to remain one of television's most popular hosts and pitchmen even after *American Bandstand* went off the air for good in 1989. At the turn of the 21st century, he remained a fixture as the host of ABC's *New Year's Rockin' Eve* and was one of the hosts of *The Other Half,* a talk show about men geared for a female audience.

(JEFF WALLENFELDT)

Clark, Helen

New Zealand Prime Minister Helen Clark faced a big challenge when she called a general election for July 27, 2002. Clark's Labour Party was under pressure from both ends of the political spectrum, and Deputy Prime Minister Jim Anderton resigned as head of the Alliance, the junior partner in the governing coalition, shortly before the election. When the ballots were counted, however, Labour had won 41.3% of the vote and 52 seats in the 120-seat House of Representatives, up slightly from 49 seats. Though this left Clark without an absolute majority, she quickly reached agreement with Anderton, whose new party, Progressive Coalition, took two seats, and the liberal United Future party (nine seats), to form a minority coalition government.

Helen Elizabeth Clark was born in provincial Hamilton on Feb. 26, 1950. She was the oldest in a family of four girls growing up on a sheep and cattle farm in the middle of New

Zealand's North Island. Clark was also an asthmatic and a homebound reader until her parents sent her to boarding school at Epsom Girls Grammar School in Auckland. She would later recall that the headmistress had told the boarders that they were country girls who would go back to where they came from—that educationally there was not much that could be done for them.

Clark, however, went on to receive an M.A. with honours (1974) in political science at the University of Auckland. It was a time when left-wing politics were verging on the rampant, and Clark protested against the Vietnam War and against foreign military bases in New Zealand. She became a junior lecturer in political studies in 1973 and a senior lecturer from 1977 and wrote a Ph.D. thesis on rural politics. Clark joined the Labour Party in 1971 and became president of the Labour Youth Council. By the end of the decade she had risen to the party's executive committee, and in 1981 she was elected to Parliament for the left-leaning Mount Albert (Auckland) electorate. That same year she married Peter Davis, later a professor of public health.

Clark joined the cabinet in 1987 and served as minister of conservation (1987–89), housing (1987–89), health (1989–90), and labour (1989–90). As health minister she gained a reputation for her unyielding antitobacco campaign. In 1989 she was the first woman elected deputy prime minister. When Labour was voted out of power in 1990, Clark became deputy to the leader of the opposition, Mike Moore. She succeeded him as Labour leader in a caucus uprising in December 1993.

In the general election on Nov. 27, 1999, she confronted Prime Minister Jenny Shipley, who had been appointed to head the ruling National Party in 1997. In a big upset the Labour-Alliance coalition secured enough seats (59) to form a minority government, and Clark was sworn in on December 10 as New Zealand's first elected woman prime minister.

(JOHN A. KELLEHER)

Couric, Katie

In 2002 NBC's *Today* show marked its 50th anniversary, but it was coanchor Katie Couric who had reason to celebrate. To millions of Americans, the preternaturally perky Couric had become as indispensable in the morning as coffee. With her folksy manner and ability to cover diverse topics, she was credited with making *Today,* a news and entertainment show, the most-watched morning program in the U.S. Her immense popularity was underscored in 2001, when there was a heated bidding war for her services. Couric ultimately signed a five-year contract extension with NBC believed to be worth $65 million, which made her one of the highest-paid news personalities. Couric's strong connection with Americans also proved invaluable in her role as national spokeswoman for colon cancer research and detection, a cause she had concentrated on since her husband, attorney Jay Monahan, died from the illness in 1998.

Katherine Anne Couric was born on Jan. 7, 1957, in Arlington, Va. After graduating from the University of Virginia in 1979, she decided to pursue a career in broadcasting. She briefly worked as a desk assistant at ABC News in Washington, D.C., before joining the Cable News Network (CNN) as an assignment editor for its Washington bureau. The post required some reporting, but Couric's high-pitched voice led the network's president to ban her from the air; she later corrected the problem by taking voice lessons. In the early 1980s she moved to CNN's Atlanta, Ga., base, where she held a number of positions, including on-air political correspondent during the 1984 elections. After CNN failed to offer her a full-time job as a reporter, however, Couric accepted a reporting position at WTVJ in Miami, Fla.

In 1986 Couric returned to Washington and joined WRC, an NBC affiliate, where she won an Associated Press Award. Three years later she became a deputy Pentagon correspondent for NBC, and her reporting during the U.S. invasion of Panama caught the attention of news executives. In late 1989 she began filling in as a weekend anchor on *NBC Nightly News,* and in 1990 she started appearing on *Today.* In February 1991 *Today* coanchor Deborah Norville went on maternity leave, and Couric was named her substitute. At the time, *Today* was struggling in the ratings, but Couric's cheerful personality soon had viewers returning. She also displayed great versatility—from covering breaking news stories to interviewing celebrities. Ratings rose sharply, and when Norville opted not to return, Couric was named her replacement. Alongside Bryant Gumbel she helped make *Today* the top-rated morning show. When Gumbel left the program in 1997, she quickly established rapport with his successor, Matt Lauer. In addition to her *Today* duties, Couric was also a contributing anchor for the television news magazine *Dateline NBC.* She won several Emmys, and her series on colon cancer, in which she underwent a colonoscopy on camera, earned her a George Foster Peabody award in 2001.

(AMY TIKKANEN)

Darwīsh, Maḥmūd

Maḥmūd Darwīsh, perhaps the most acclaimed poet of the Arab world, continued in 2002 to give voice to the plight of the Palestinian people, some of whom, like himself, had endured the painful experience of exile, while others lived under Israeli occupation. In his single-poem volume *Ḥālat Ḥiṣār* (2002; "A State of Siege"), Darwīsh explored the multiple reoccupations of the town of Ram Allah in the West Bank north of Jerusalem and described the magnitude of the ordeal and the resulting sense of Palestinian isolation. At the same time, he foresaw a future of peace and coexistence between Israelis and Palestinians that could be achieved through the dialogue of cultures. In 2000 the Israeli education minister made plans to include Darwīsh's poems of reconciliation in the school curriculum, but the prime minister vetoed the plan.

Darwīsh was born on March 13, 1942, in Birwa, Palestine (now Israel), six years before the *nakbah* ("catastrophe") of 1948 that resulted in the establishment of Israel. He witnessed massacres in his village that forced his family to escape to Lebanon. A year later their clandestine return to their homeland put them in limbo as they were declared "present-absent aliens." Darwīsh left his village a second time in 1970 and traveled to Moscow to complete his education. Before his return to Ram Allah in 1996, he lived in Cairo, Beirut, London, Paris, and Tunis, Tunisia. It was Darwīsh's conviction that his painful life in exile inspired his creative work. Since 1981 he had served as editor of the literary journal *Al-Karmel.* In addition, he authored 7 books of prose and 21 collections of poetry.

The gripping power of Darwīsh's poetry could be explained by the sincerity of his emotions, the originality of his poetic images, and the universal appeal of his work. The poet spoke with the voice of his people but not as a guiding prophet. He borrowed from the Old and New Testaments, classical Arabic literature, Arab-Islamic history, and Greek and Roman mythology to construct his metaphors. He preserved the memory of his elusive homeland in his writing, in which Palestine was often personified as a mother or a cruel beloved.

Darwīsh diverged from the political in some of his poems, relying on symbolism to relate personal experience. He devoted an entire collection, *Jidāriyya* (2002; "Mural,"), to a painful personal experience—his brush with death following heart surgery in 1998.

Darwīsh's work was translated into more than 22 languages. In November 2001 he was awarded the Lannan Foundation Prize for Cultural Freedom, which carried a $350,000 award. In addition, a translation of his work from Arabic into English was to be funded by the foundation and published by the University of California Press. Among his many international awards were the Lotus Prize (1969), the Lenin Peace Prize (1983), the French medal of Knight of Arts and Belles Letters (1997), and the *wisām* (order) of intellectual merit in 2000 from Moroccan King Muhammad VI.

(AIDA A. BAMIA)

Elizabeth II

On Feb. 6, 2002, Queen Elizabeth II marked the 50th anniversary of her accession to the throne of the United Kingdom. The occasion should have signaled the beginning of nationwide celebrations of her golden jubilee. Instead, the anniversary was soon overshadowed by two family deaths in quick succession. Her younger sister, Princess Margaret, died just three days later of a stroke, and on March 30 Queen Elizabeth, the Queen Mother, died in her sleep at the age of 101. Neither death was wholly unexpected, but they cast a pall over the buildup to the planned jubilee celebrations. Fortunately, the festivities were scheduled for May through August, to take advantage of the summer weather, and the initial grieving was over by the time that they were due to begin. The highlight of the summer, the Golden Jubilee Weekend (June 1–4), included concerts, fireworks, and a ceremonial procession to St. Paul's Cathedral (for a service of thanksgiving) with Elizabeth and her husband, Philip, duke of Edinburgh, riding in the Gold State Coach. A massive public party on the Mall ensued. The queen's nationwide tour went ahead as planned, beginning

Queen Elizabeth II launches her Jubilee.

on May 1, and she was greeted warmly in all parts of the United Kingdom. The queen also visited Jamaica, New Zealand, Australia, and Canada—all members of the Commonwealth and former British colonies.

Elizabeth Alexandra Mary was born in London on April 21, 1926, the elder daughter of Albert, duke of York. Her uncle became King Edward VIII in January 1936, but when he abdicated just 11 months later, Albert became King George VI and Elizabeth became heir presumptive. George occupied the throne for 15 years before his death in 1952. The 25-year-old Elizabeth, who was on an official visit to Kenya at the time, flew back to London to be greeted as the new queen.

Like her father, but unlike her uncle, Elizabeth became noted for her devotion to public service above all other considerations. As the head of a constitutional monarchy, she had few powers and was expected always to remain aloof from public controversies. She nevertheless managed to create a role—and to uphold values—that succeeded in retaining public confidence in an era of rapid social change and intense media scrutiny. She became identified in particular with the causes of the Commonwealth and racial tolerance. She took manifest pleasure in the return of South Africa, under Nelson Mandela's presidency, to the Commonwealth. During the late 1990s she struggled with questions about the royal finances as well as adverse publicity surrounding the divorces of her sons Charles, prince of Wales, and Andrew, duke of York. When Diana, princess of Wales, was killed in August 1997, the queen came under criticism for her delayed response. In November 2002 theft charges against Paul Burrell, Diana's former butler, had to be dropped after the queen belatedly disclosed that Burrell had told her

that he was looking after some of the princess's effects. Despite the continuing debate about the future of the British monarchy, Elizabeth seemed to be secure in her role.

(PETER KELLNER)

Enwezor, Okwui

Nigerian-born Okwui Enwezor followed a short and nontraditional path to the peaks of the art world; the part-time poet and art critic began curating important art shows in 2002 without ever having studied art history formally. In February he mounted his first major show, "The Short Century: Independence and Liberation Movements in Africa, 1945–1994," at P.S. 1 Contemporary Art Center in Queens, New York City. Just a few months later, in June, Enwezor put into practice his theory of art as an expression of social change when he became the artistic director of Documenta 11, the international exhibition held in Kassel, Ger. Ambitious in size and scope, the three-month show, held about every five years, was often likened to "the Olympics of contemporary art."

Enwezor, the first non-European to host the Documenta exhibition, took a decidedly unconventional and global approach; he prepared for the show with a series of seminars on international issues. He eschewed the trendiness of many art shows. He did not shy away from political issues, including globalization, and was understandably comfortable looking beyond American and European traditions into African arts. His emphasis on ideas over the veneration of objects "art for art's sake" was evident in his development of the "The Short Century" exhibit, which appeared first as a book in Munich, Ger., a full year before becoming a gallery show in New York City.

Enwezor was born in 1963 in Calabar, a Nigerian town bordering Cameroon. He was raised in Enugu in eastern Nigeria, but he relocated to the United States in the early 1980s to attend Jersey City State College (now New

Okwui Enwezor, world art curator

Jersey City University) in Jersey City, where he earned a B.A. in political science. His foray into the art world began as an observer. At various exhibits Enwezor noticed the absence of artists from Africa and started critiquing the shows. He began writing widely for art magazines and even launched one of his own—*Nka: Journal of Contemporary African Art*—published from 1994 in concert with the Africans Studies and Research Center at Cornell University, Ithaca, N.Y. As a curator, he became known for his work on an exhibit of African photography at the Guggenheim Museum in SoHo, New York City, in 1996; at the "Africus" Second Johannesburg Biennale in 1997; and as an adjunct curator (1998–2000) of contemporary art at the Art Institute of Chicago. Later exhibits included a group show that traveled through Europe and Canada and a showing of South African photographer David Goldblatt at the Equitable Gallery, New York City, in 2000. A frequent lecturer and member of many art juries, Enwezor also coedited, along with Olu Oguibe, *Reading the Contemporary: African Art from Theory to the Marketplace* (1999). His most recent undertaking was the drafting of a book entitled *Structural Adjustment*, a discourse on contemporary African artists.

(TOM MICHAEL)

Essy, Amara

On July 9, 2002, Amara Essy of Côte d' Ivoire became secretary-general of the newly established 53-country African Union (AU), which replaced the 39-year-old Organization of African Unity (OAU). Essy, a career diplomat, was charged with leading the new body, a difficult task given the continent's ethnic, religious, economic, and political differences and the fact that the AU was granted dramatically enhanced powers in comparison with the OAU. Whereas the OAU had been required to respect each member's territorial sovereignty, the AU could intervene in the internal affairs of countries to stop crimes against humanity, violations of human rights, and genocide. In general, the AU was modeled after the European Union, and its creators envisioned that the AU would eventually have peacekeeping troops, a regional court, a central bank, a legislature, a security council, and a single currency, similar to that of the EU's euro. Nevertheless, the principal aim of the AU was to promote economic growth to ease poverty throughout Africa.

Essy was born on Dec. 20, 1944, in Bouaké, Côte d'Ivoire. He studied in Asia, Europe, and South America, earning a degree in public law from the University of Poitiers, France. He was fluent in several languages, including English, French, and Portuguese—Africa's three most-common European languages. A practicing Muslim, Essy married a Roman Catholic, despite the fact that interfaith marriages were quite uncommon in Côte d'Ivoire.

Essy's diplomatic career began in the early 1970s. After serving as a counselor in the Côte d'Ivoire embassy in Brazil, he became a counselor at Côte d'Ivoire's mission to the United Nations. In 1975 he was appointed ambassador to Switzerland, where he also served as Côte d'Ivoire's European representative to the UN and as president of the Group of 77 (an organization of nonaligned less-developed countries).

In 1981 Essy was appointed Côte d'Ivoire's representative to the UN in New York, and during that decade he served as ambassador extraordinary and plenipotentiary for Argentina and Cuba. Gaining great respect for his diplomatic capabilities, he went on to serve as vice president of the UN General Assembly (1988–89) and as its president (1994–95). He also served as president of the UN Security Council in January 1990. That year he was appointed Côte d'Ivoire's minister of foreign affairs, a position that he continued to hold until shortly after a coup against the government in 1999.

In 1997, following the decision by the U.S. to block the reselection of Boutros Boutros-Ghali as UN secretary-general, Essy was the favoured candidate of the French, who threatened to veto the U.S.-backed Kofi Annan. That year Essy also launched a challenge against Tanzanian Salim Ahmed Salim (who was backed by Libyan leader Muammar al-Qaddafi) for head of the OAU, but Essy withdrew before its annual summit, claiming that he did not want to divide Africa. In 2000 he was Annan's special envoy to the Central African Republic. In July 2001, after eight rounds of voting in Lusaka, Zambia, Essy was elected to a four-year term as head of the OAU (and thus the AU from 2002).   (MICHAEL I. LEVY)

Fiorina, Carly

On May 3, 2002, Hewlett-Packard Co. (HP), the second largest computer company in the U.S., merged with Compaq Computer Corp., the third largest. The revenues of the newly unified company, which retained the Hewlett-Packard name, were expected to rival those of computer giant IBM Corp. That the merger took place at all, however, was mainly due to the strength and resilience of Carly Fiorina, HP's chairman and CEO.

Fiorina was born Cara Carleton Sneed in Austin, Texas, on Sept. 6, 1954, the daughter of Joseph Sneed, a judge and law professor, and artist Madelon Sneed. Her family moved often, and she attended school in Ghana, the U.K., North Carolina, and California. She graduated from Stanford University in 1976 with a bachelor's degree in medieval history and philosophy but dropped out of law school at the University of California, Los Angeles, after only one semester. She later matriculated at the University of Maryland, College Park (M.B.A., 1980), and at the Massachusetts Institute of Technology's Sloan School (M.S., 1989).

At age 25 she started in an entry-level position at AT&T Corp. (she later married Frank Fiorina, an AT&T executive). Within 10 years she had been named the company's first female officer, and at the age of 40 she became head of AT&T's North American operations. In 1996 Fiorina engineered the successful spin-off of AT&T's research division as Lucent Technologies, Inc., and two years later she was promoted to president of Lucent's Global Service Provider Business, in charge of sales

to the world's largest telecommunications companies.

On July 19, 1999, Hewlett-Packard unexpectedly announced that the then-44-year-old Fiorina would become its new chief executive—the first outsider to lead HP in its 60-year history and the first woman to head a company listed in the Dow Jones 30 Industrials. Fiorina encountered some resistance from employees as she updated the "HP Way" of working, a traditional, consensus-based system that she felt had become slow and bureaucratic. After failed talks with PricewaterhouseCoopers about acquiring that firm's consulting business, Fiorina turned her attention to Compaq. Her plan to merge HP with Compaq, announced in September 2001, was contested by Walter Hewlett and David Packard, the sons of HP's cofounders. Packard was opposed to the layoff of 15,000 staff that the merger would entail, while Hewlett expressed concern that the assimilation of Compaq would be as difficult for HP as Compaq's takeover of Digital Equipment Corp. and Tandem Computers, Inc., had been in the late 1990s. Fiorina led a strong campaign against this opposition, however, and, after a grueling eight-month proxy battle and an unsuccessful lawsuit by Hewlett, she won the support of shareholders, albeit by a slim margin of 51.4% of the votes cast.
           (ALAN STEWART)

Francisco, Don

In August 2002 Chilean television host Don Francisco celebrated the 40th anniversary of his hugely popular TV show *Sábado gigante*, which the *Guinness Book of World Records* had already recognized in 1993 as the longest-running program with the same host.

He was born Mario Kreutzberger on Dec. 28, 1940, in Talca, Chile, to German-Jewish parents who arrived in Latin America just prior to World War II. His mother, a classical singer, gave him singing lessons, and when he was a teenager, he found some success onstage as an actor. It was during this time that he formulated the character of Don Francisco, a funny emcee with a somewhat lecherous personality.

Though he was sent by his father to New York City in 1961 to study tailoring, he became enamoured of television there. He launched *Sábado gigante* in Santiago in 1962, the year that television came to Chile. Originally eight hours long, the program was a *cazuela* ("stew") or mix, of music, dance, comedy, travelog, games, news, and interviews. He proved skilled in avoiding political influences in his programming. In 1973, when Augusto Pinochet Ugarte overthrew Chilean Pres. Salvador Allende Gossens, Don Francisco convinced authorities that his comic character should not read on nationwide TV Pinochet's proclamation creating a military junta. The production of *Sábado* was moved to Miami in 1986, and the show was tailored to the Hispanic immigrant community in North America. Nonetheless, the program was shown in 42 countries for three hours every Saturday on Univision's Channel 30.

Don Francisco was also active in charitable work. As national vice president of the Muscular Dystrophy Association, he spear-

headed the MDA's 2001 landmark outreach to Hispanic Americans, *Un futuro con ezperanza*. In 1978 he had begun the telethon *Logremos un milagro* to raise money to construct hospitals for Chile's disabled children. By the end of 2000, the telethon had benefitted children in 14 countries. He also led *Los Hispanos se dan la mano* to help Florida rebuild after Hurricane Andrew. UNICEF named him its first Hispanic ambassador of goodwill. In 2001 Don Francisco became the first Latin American to be recognized with a star on the Hollywood Walk of Fame.

Despite talk of retirement—his daughter Vivi, herself a Chilean TV announcer, was being groomed to be his successor on *Sábado*—Don Francisco had a new weekly talk show, *Don Francisco presenta*. He also hosted the Chilean version of *Who Wants to Be a Millionaire?* In his autobiography, titled *Don Francisco entre la espada y la TV* (2001; *Don Francisco: Life, Camera, Action!*, 2002), he described in part the anti-Semitism he encountered while growing up in Chile, where the book became a best-seller.
           (RAMONA MONETTE SARGAN FLORES)

Friedman, Thomas L.

With fighting between Israelis and Palestinians, as well as U.S. efforts to combat terrorism, dominating the news in 2002, newspaper readers were searching out the insights of Thomas L. Friedman, the foreign affairs columnist for the *New York Times*. He had spent the first decade of his career largely in Lebanon and Israel and was known for his understanding of, and opinions on, Middle Eastern affairs. His columns in 2002 focused on the Israeli-Palestinian conflict, Arab governments and Islam, and U.S. policy toward the region. He could be outspoken, and his judgments—for example, criticism of Israeli settlements in the West Bank or of Egyptian and Saudi suppression of dissent—sometimes displeased both sides. During the year he also published *Longitudes and Attitudes: Exploring the World After September 11*, a collection of columns, supplemented by personal responses, on the Sept. 11, 2001, terrorist attacks in the U.S.

Thomas Loren Friedman was born on July 20, 1953, in Minneapolis, Minn. His interest in the Middle East was first sparked when he went to Israel in 1968 to visit his sister, who was studying at Tel Aviv University. He gained a B.A. in Mediterranean studies from Brandeis University, Waltham, Mass., in 1975, having spent a semester at Hebrew University in Jerusalem and another at American University in Cairo. In 1978 he earned an M.Phil. in modern Middle Eastern studies from the University of Oxford. Friedman then took a position with United Press International, which sent him to Beirut, Lebanon, in 1979. Beginning in 1981, he worked as a reporter for the *New York Times*, primarily covering oil and other business stories, before being sent in 1982 to Beirut as bureau chief. While there, he covered the Israeli invasion of Lebanon, including the massacre of Palestinians in the Sabra and Shatila refugee camps. In 1984 he moved to Jerusalem as bureau chief. During this time he won two Pulitzer Prizes, in 1983 for reporting from Lebanon and in 1988 for reporting from Israel. In 1989 he published *From Beirut to Jerusalem*, a memoir and analysis that won the National Book Award for nonfiction.

From 1989 to 1995 Friedman held positions in the Washington, D.C., bureau of the *New York Times*. When he became the newspaper's foreign affairs columnist in 1995, he announced that he intended to concentrate on developments in Asia, where he believed the most profound changes would take place over the following years, but he also wrote about countries such as Russia and Mexico as well as those of the Middle East. In 1999 he then published *The Lexus and the Olive Tree: Understanding Globalization*. In 2001–02, however, Friedman once again turned his attention to the region where he had first made his mark as a journalist. He collected his third Pulitzer Prize, this one for distinguished commentary, in 2002. The Pulitzer Board cited Friedman for his "clarity of vision . . . in commenting on the worldwide impact of the terrorist threat." (ROBERT RAUCH)

Fukuyama, Francis

Biotechnology and bioethics remained leading topics of talk in both the mainstream and academic press during 2002. With the publication in April of *Our Posthuman Future: Consequences of the Biotechnology Revolution*, the voice of American political theorist Francis Fukuyama echoed throughout both arenas. *Our Posthuman Future* undressed cutting-edge science, revealing the hidden dangers of preselecting human traits, extending average life spans, and relying too much on mood-altering drugs. He concluded that genetic engineering requires greater federal regulation, such as a ban on human cloning. Accustomed to being read in both popular and scholarly circles, Fukuyama was no stranger to the levers of influence, and as a member of the President's Council on Bioethics, he was in a unique position to make his opinions matter.

Fukuyama was born on Oct. 27, 1952, in Chicago. He studied classics at Cornell University, Ithaca, N.Y. (B.A., 1974), and political science at Harvard University (Ph.D., 1981). In 1979 he began a long-term association with the research organization RAND Corporation, in Santa Monica, Calif., and Washington, D.C. In 1981–82 he helped shape foreign policy for the U.S. Department of State, specializing in Middle East affairs and serving as a delegate to an Egyptian-Israeli conference on Palestinian autonomy. In 1987 he coedited *The Soviet Union and the Third World: The Last Three Decades*, and two years later he rejoined the State Department to focus on European political and military issues. As a professor he held chairs at George Mason University, Fairfax, Va., from 1996 to 2001 and at the School of Advanced International Studies at Johns Hopkins University, Washington, D.C., from 2001.

Fukuyama's first major work, *The End of History and the Last Man* (1992), earned international acclaim and made best-seller lists in the U.S., France, Japan, and Chile. His the-

sis—introduced as a magazine article in 1989, when communism in Eastern Europe was collapsing—posited that Western-style liberal democracy not only was the victor of the Cold War but marked the last ideological stage in the long march of history. Among the scholars who challenged him was Samuel P. Huntington in *The Clash of Civilizations and the Remaking of World Order* (1996), which foretold fractious cultural battles that would splinter the dominance of liberal democracy as the unrivaled political ideal. The terrorist attacks on Sept. 11, 2001, indicated to some that Islamic fundamentalism was indeed threatening the hegemony of the West. Fukuyama, however, dismissed the attacks as part of "a series of rearguard actions" against what he believed was the prevailing political philosophy of the new globalism.

Fukuyama traced parallel tracks in his follow-up books: *Trust: The Social Virtues and the Creation of Prosperity* (1995) was popular in the business market, and *The Great Disruption: Human Nature and the Reconstitution of Social Order* (1999) took a conservative look at American society in the second half of the 20th century. Critics downgraded his books for seeking too-tidy explanations of broad world movements rife with complexities, while supporters greeted each new volume

with the fanfare befitting a formidable public intellectual. (TOM MICHAEL)

Gergiev, Valery

When conductor Valery Gergiev and the Kirov Opera appeared at the Kennedy Center for the Performing Arts in Washington, D.C., in February 2002, it marked the opening of a 10-year collaboration that he had engineered between the two institutions. In its way that collaboration symbolized Gergiev's leadership of the Kirov (which he had assumed in 1988) and the broader role of artistic director of St. Petersburg's Mariinsky Theatre, to which he was named in 1996. During his tenure Gergiev virtually restored the company's artistic reputation and, in the process, took it back to the international stage, where it currently enjoyed the status of one of the world's preeminent opera houses.

Gergiev was born in Moscow on May 2, 1953. The son of Ossetian parents, he spent much of his youth in the Caucasus. He went on to study conducting with Ilya Musin at the Leningrad Conservatory and at age 23 won the Herbert von Karajan Conductors' Competition in Berlin. He made his debut with the Kirov Opera in 1978, leading a production of Sergey Prokofiev's *War and Peace* as assistant to Yury Temirkanov, the company's principal conduc-

In Valencia, Spain, Valery Gergiev puts Russia's Kirov Orchestra back on the map.

EFE Photos

tor. From 1981 to 1985 he was the chief conductor of the Armenian State Orchestra, and during that period he led performances by many of the major orchestras of the former Soviet Union.

Upon taking the helm of the Kirov in 1988, Gergiev began to establish a reputation for charismatic, intensely personal performances. In 1991 he made his European opera debut conducting Modest Mussorgsky's *Boris Godunov* with the Bayerische Staatsoper and made his first opera appearance in the U.S. leading the San Francisco Opera's production of *War and Peace*. From there the honours and international acclaim mounted. In 1993 he was named Conductor of the Year at the Classical Music Awards in London. He was also invited to be a guest conductor with many of the world's leading orchestras, including the London Symphony, Amsterdam's Royal Concertgebouw, the Berlin Philharmonic, Rome's Accademia de Santa Cecilia, and Tokyo's NHK Symphony.

Known for keeping a demanding work schedule, Gergiev devoted more than 250 days per year to the Mariinsky Theatre, where his control extended even to personally picking the singers in its productions. Over the years he founded the St. Petersburg White Nights Festival (1993) and the Mikkeli International Music Festival in Finland (1994); from 1996 he led the Rotterdam Festival and Israel's Red Sea International Music Festival. In 1997 he was named principal guest conductor at New York's Metropolitan Opera, where he remained an active participant in the company's activities.

Gergiev's activities and honours continued apace in 2002. At Moscow's Golden Mask Festival, he was named Best Conductor for his version of Wagner's *Die Walküre*, and the Kirov won three of five awards in the event's opera categories. Gergiev also released compact discs featuring works by Sofia Gubaidulina and Giya Kancheli with violist Yury Bashmet and the Orchestra of the Mariinsky Theatre and a performance of Mussorgsky's *Pictures at an Exhibition* with the Vienna Philharmonic, both of which were endowed with Gergiev's signature intensity and passion.

(HARRY SUMRALL)

Grammer, Kelsey

As the 2001–02 television season drew to a close, American actor Kelsey Grammer finished his 18th straight year of playing pompous, acerbic, but somehow lovable psychiatrist Dr. Frasier Crane. His longevity put him two years away from tying the record for consecutive years of appearing as the same character on prime-time TV, a mark set by James Arness as Marshal Matt Dillon on *Gunsmoke*. Grammer played Crane on three different shows, *Cheers*, its spin-off series, *Frasier*, and the sitcom *Wings*. In describing his feelings about his longtime character, Grammer commented, "By now, Frasier lives in my subconscious. We discover life on kind of the same terms."

Grammer was born on St. Thomas in the U.S. Virgin Islands on Feb. 21, 1955. He grew up in New Jersey and Florida and began act-

Linda Rich FRPS Dance Picture Library

The exquisite line of Sylvie Guillem

ing in high school. Encouraged by his teachers to consider acting as a career, he enrolled in the Juilliard School in New York City. After two years there, Grammer joined the Old Globe Theatre company in San Diego, Calif., where he acted in plays by William Shakespeare and George Bernard Shaw. He also performed in regional theatres throughout the U.S. and in Off-Broadway productions of *Plenty*, *Sunday in the Park with George*, *A Month in the Country*, and *Quartermaine's Terms*. On Broadway he appeared in *Macbeth* and *Othello*.

Before joining the cast of *Cheers* in 1984, Grammer acted in the television daytime dramas *Another World*, *One Life to Live*, and *Guiding Light* and in the miniseries *Kennedy*. His career was threatened in 1988 when he was arrested for drunken driving and possession of cocaine. He eventually served a short jail stint and later spent time in a drug rehabilitation clinic. *Cheers* aired until 1993, and *Frasier* debuted the following season. For his acting on *Frasier*, Grammer won the Emmy Award for outstanding lead actor in a comedy series in 1994, 1995, and 1998. He won Golden Globe Awards for best actor in a television series (musical or comedy) in 1995 and 2000. Other honours for Grammer included American Comedy Awards for funniest male performer in a television series in 1994 and 1995 and a Screen Actors Guild Award for outstanding performance by an ensemble in a television comedy series, shared with his fellow cast members. When questioned about the length of time he had played Frasier Crane, Grammer responded, "I have never been visited by the fear that he's stale. Through him, I get to bring to light a lot of things I think about myself."

Grammer also served as executive producer of *Frasier* and of the television series *In-Laws*, *Girlfriends*, and *Fired Up*. In 2000 he produced the animated Internet series *Gary the Rat* and

provided the voice of the title character. He also directed several episodes of *Frasier*.

(DAVID R. CALHOUN)

Guillem, Sylvie

When Sylvie Guillem was first seen on the ballet stage, it was her extraordinary, and seemingly effortless, extension that caught the public's attention. By 2002, however, it was widely accepted that she had developed into a multifaceted dramatic dancer with intelligence and depth, shining in both classical ballets, such as *Romeo and Juliet*, *La Bayadère*, and *The Sleeping Beauty*, and modern works, including *In the Middle, Somewhat Elevated* and *Herman Schmerman*, and winning a number of awards internationally. She was a welcome guest at companies throughout the world and also had branched out into choreography.

Guillem was born on Feb. 23, 1965, in Paris. When she was very young, she began receiving gymnastics training under the supervision of her mother, a gymnastics teacher. Early on, it was apparent that she had natural ability and astonishing flexibility, and she soon was enjoying success on the competition circuit. She came to the attention of the director of the Paris Opéra Ballet School, however, and was offered a place at the school. She studied there from 1977 to 1980 and in 1981, at the age of 16, entered the company's corps de ballet. She advanced rapidly through the ranks and, her reputation buoyed by a gold-medal win at the Varna (Bulg.) International Ballet Competition in 1983, was featured later that year in her first solo appearance, dancing the Queen of the Driads in the version of *Don Quixote* staged by Rudolf Nureyev. As artistic director of the company, Nureyev gave Guillem the opportunity to expand her range by dancing solo and principal roles both in his stagings of the classics and in ballets by contemporary choreographers, including George Balanchine, Jerome Robbins, William Forsythe, Roland Petit, and

Rudi van Dantzig. In addition, following her performance in Nureyev's *Swan Lake* in December 1984, she was promoted to the company's highest rank for a female, *étoile*, the youngest in the company's history. Nureyev frequently chose her to dance as his partner, and in 1988, when Britain's Royal Ballet celebrated Nureyev's 50th birthday by having him dance in a production of *Giselle*, Guillem was given the title role. She was an overwhelming success, and the following year, after she had left the Paris Opéra Ballet, she became a permanent guest artist with the Royal Ballet, a status that allowed her to accept engagements with other companies.

In 1995 Guillem was commissioned to create a dance program for television. The result of her efforts was *Evidentia*, which included five modern works as well as archival footage, and the program and its individual ballets were honoured with a number of international awards. In 1998 she created her own staging of *Giselle* for the Finnish National Ballet, increasing the storytelling aspects of the first act and giving the characters in both acts defined personalities, and in 2001 she restaged the ballet, with new sets and costumes, for La Scala Ballet in Milan. In 2002 she added Swedish choreographer Mats Ek's *Carmen* to her repertoire.   (BARBARA WHITNEY)

Gyanendra

The Nepalese royal family was plunged into crisis on June 1, 2001, by the assassination of King Birendra by Crown Prince Dipendra and Dipendra's death by suicide the following day. Gyanendra, the younger brother of King Birendra, was thus unexpectedly called to ascend the throne on June 4, taking the name and title Gyanendra Bir Bikram Shah Dev. Many wondered whether he was adequately prepared for the job, especially amid such turmoil. By mid-2002 the intense rivalry between several major political parties and periodic flare-ups of the bloody insurrection that had been launched in 1996 in some areas of the country by a radical "Maoist" faction contributed to the confusion and disorder.

Gyanendra was born in Kathmandu, Nepal, on July 7, 1947, the second son of King Mahendra. He was educated at St. Joseph's College in Darjeeling, India, and graduated in 1969 from Tribhuvan University in Kathmandu. As the younger son, he was not directly involved in politics or governmental activities during the reigns of King Mahendra (1955–72) and King Birendra (1972–2001), but he was active in several environmental and conservationist organizations as well as some business firms. He traveled abroad frequently, visiting most of the major Asian and European countries, the United States, the Soviet Union, Australia, and New Zealand.

Nepal's 1991 constitution had established a constitutional monarchy and a democratic parliamentary system, but there were some questions raised at that time about Gyanendra's acceptance of the democratic political system. In the first year of his reign, however, he abided strictly by the principles of a constitutional monarch.

In September 2002 Prime Minister S.B.

© AFP 2002, by Prakash Singh

Nepal's King Gyanendra prays.

Deuba of the Nepali Congress Party decided to dissolve Parliament and also to postpone for one year the parliamentary elections scheduled for November. After consultations with most of the major party leaders, King Gyanendra on October 4 dismissed the Deuba government and assumed full executive powers under Article 127 of the constitution. Two days later the leaders of the six major political parties met and recommended to the king that he appoint an "all-party" government. Gyanendra, however, selected Lokendra Bahadur Chand as prime minister to head a cabinet that had no affiliation with any of the political parties. An all-party meeting was held on October 21 and pledged to fight all "regressive steps" against multiparty democracy. Negotiations between Gyanendra and the party leaders continued until the end of the year but without any agreement's having been reached.   (LEO E. ROSE)

Hayami, Masaru

By 2002 Masaru Hayami, the governor of the Bank of Japan (BOJ), had become so alarmed at his country's faltering economy and its sluggish pace of reform that in September he announced an unprecedented move. Japan's central bank would buy some $24 billion in stock holdings directly from more than a dozen of the country's largest commercial banks, bypassing the market to provide the ailing institutions with enough capital that they could dispose of trillions of yen in bad loans. Hayami's decision, according to one observer, was the equivalent of "[tossing] a hand grenade into the financial system." Given the severity of the ongoing banking cri-

sis, drastic measures were perhaps necessary. According to official figures, Japanese bank debt had soared by 29% in the previous fiscal year. Hayami's announcement ignited a brief rally on the Nikkei 225 stock index, though it remained to be seen what long-term effect the stock purchase might have.

Hayami was born on March 24, 1925, in Kobe, Japan. After graduating from the Tokyo University of Commerce, he joined the BOJ in 1947. He remained with the central bank for the next 34 years. In 1967 Hayami was named manager of the bank's Ooita branch, and four years later he became the BOJ's chief representative in Europe. He was appointed director of the foreign department in 1975. After another stint as a branch manager—this time in Nagoya from 1976 to 1978—he was named an executive director, a position he held for three years.

In 1981 Hayami left the BOJ to take a position as senior managing director at the trading firm Nissho Iwai Corp. He rose to become president of the corporation in 1984 and served as its chairman from 1987 to 1994. During his tenure at Nissho Iwai, he also headed the Japanese Institute of Corporate Executives, one of the country's most prominent business organizations. From 1992 until his appointment as BOJ governor in 1998, he served as chairman of the board of trustees at Tokyo Women's Christian University.

As the new governor of the BOJ, Hayami was charged with restoring the institution's prestige; his predecessor, Yasuo Matsushita, had resigned over a bribery scandal. Along with his sterling credentials as a banker, Hayami brought to the job a market-oriented philosophy and a reformist agenda. In particular, he stressed the need for starting the process of corporate restructuring and helping banks rid themselves of their nonperforming loans. By 2002 it was obvious that he was losing patience with the slow pace of reform. "If you guys don't hurry up, my life will run out soon," he reportedly told one group assigned to tackle the country's financial problems. Prime Minister Junichiro Koizumi, who had come into office promising banking reform, publicly expressed his approval of Hayami's stock-purchase plan, although some considered the plan too risky. Despite rumours that he would step down before his term as BOJ governor expired in March 2003, Hayami insisted that he would serve as long as his health allowed.

(SHERMAN HOLLAR)

Hewitt, Lleyton

Lleyton Hewitt ruled as the best male tennis player in the world in 2001 and 2002, displaying a match-playing maturity well beyond his years, earning a reputation as a competitor of the highest order, and exploiting his opportunities with uncanny regularity. The scrappy Australian moved past his premier rivals to the top of the game with his astonishing court speed, fierce determination, outstanding return of serve, and unrelenting ground strokes. In September 2001 he upended the formidable Pete Sampras of the U.S. 7–6 (4), 6–1, 6–1 on the hard courts at the U.S. Open in New York City to capture his first Grand Slam title. Ten months later Hewitt came through confidently on the grass courts of the All England Club, ousting Argentina's David Nalbandian 6–1, 6–3, 6–2 in the final at Wimbledon. At the 2002 U.S. Open, however, he failed to retain his title, losing in the semifinal to American Andre Agassi.

In 2001 Hewitt was the most prolific winner on the ATP (Association of Tennis Professionals) circuit, claiming 80 match victories and becoming the youngest man to have finished a year at number one since the official ATP world rankings were introduced in 1973. He was the first Australian male to achieve preeminent status in that nearly 30-year span. Hewitt underlined his supremacy when he claimed the 2001 season-ending Tennis Masters Cup in Sydney, Australia. Moreover, he was rewarded handsomely, earning $4,045,618 for the year. Hewitt stayed at the top of the rankings all through 2002 despite sporadic health problems, including chicken pox early in the year and viruses that forced him to pull out of some tournaments later in the season. He managed to win five tournaments in 2002, including a successful defense of his Tennis Master's Cup crown. He earned $4,619,386 in prize money.

Hewitt was born Feb. 24, 1981, in Adelaide, the same city where he grew up. His father, uncle, and grandfather distinguished themselves as players in Australian Rules football, and his mother was a physical education teacher who played netball. Hewitt played Australian Rules football until he was 13, when he dedicated himself to tennis. He became the leading Australian junior tennis player in 1996. Early in 1998, at age 16, he secured his first professional singles title. By the end of 1999, he had advanced to number 22 in the world and had helped Australia to win the Davis Cup. He concluded 2000 ranked number seven in the world after having swept 61 of 80 matches he contested that season, establishing himself as the first teenager since Sampras in 1990 to garner four singles titles in a year. Hewitt's impressive range of victories in 2000 fueled the intense Australian to record his major triumphs of the next two years. Hewitt did not dominate the game as had some of his predecessors, but his consistency and mental toughness were the twin motors driving his greatness.　(STEVE FLINK)

Howard, Ron

At the 2002 Academy Awards ceremony, Ron Howard received one of the most coveted of American film honours, the Oscar for best director. A short while later that evening, he, along with fellow producer Brian Grazer, picked up a second Oscar, for best picture, and his film—*A Beautiful Mind*, an adaptation of Sylvia Nasar's book about Nobel Prize-winning mathematical genius John Nash and his struggle with schizophrenia—had already garnered two others: best actress in a supporting role (Jennifer Connelly) and best screenplay based on material previously produced or published (Akiva Goldman). Although Howard had previously won several prestigious awards, including two from the Directors Guild of America, and had been nominated

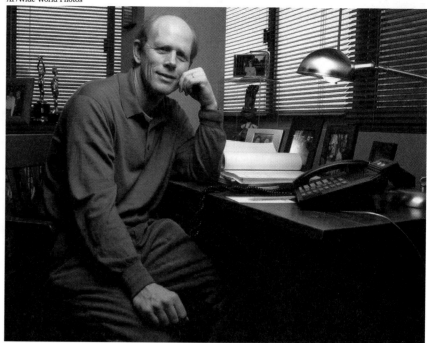

Oscar-winning director Ron Howard in his Beverly Hills office

for a number of others, Oscar nominations had eluded him, and many thought that the best director honour was long overdue.

Ronald William Howard was born on March 1, 1954, in Duncan, Okla. His parents were in show business, and he made his first screen appearance, in *Frontier Woman* (1955), at the age of 18 months. His first onstage appearance came at age two in a summer-stock production of *The Seven Year Itch*, and, as Ronny Howard, he soon was appearing on various television series, including *Playhouse 90*, *General Electric Theatre*, *The Danny Thomas Show*, *The Fugitive*, and *Dr. Kildare*, as well as the film *The Journey* (1959). In 1960 Howard began portraying one of his best-known characters, Opie Taylor, on *The Andy Griffith Show*, which ran for eight years. He was also featured in such films as *The Music Man* (1962), *The Courtship of Eddie's Father* (1963), and *The Wild Country* (1971) and made numerous appearances in TV series episodes. In 1973 Howard experienced his first big film hit, *American Graffiti*, and the following year saw the beginning of another of his best-known characters, Richie Cunningham on the series *Happy Days*, which ran until 1980. Howard had already developed an interest in directing, however, and after high school he spent two years in the University of Southern California's film program. He made his directorial debut with *Grand Theft Auto* (1977), and its financial success led to further opportunities. Among the many successes that followed were *Night Shift* (1982), *Splash* (1984), *Cocoon* (1985), *Parenthood* (1989), *Backdraft* (1991), *Apollo 13* (1995), and *Ransom* (1996). Howard often gave his brother, Clint, roles in his films, and his wife, Cheryl, and other family members also occasionally made appearances.

Howard also amassed numerous credits as a motion picture and television producer or ex-

ecutive producer, among them—besides *A Beautiful Mind*—the movie *Clean and Sober* (1988) and the TV series *Sports Night, Felicity,* and *24*. In mid-2002 his movie company, Image Entertainment, in partnership with Universal Pictures, purchased the rights to *Playboy* magazine's archives for its wealth of possible source material. Future plans included the film *The Alamo*, which was scheduled for release in 2003.

(BARBARA WHITNEY)

Hu Jintao

By 2002 Hu Jintao, the vice president of China since 1998, had emerged as the heir apparent to Pres. Jiang Zemin. Hu took over from Jiang as general secretary of the Communist Party of China (CPC) at the 16th CPC Congress in November and was widely expected to succeed him as president in early 2003. A series of high-profile trips abroad undertaken earlier by the vice president clearly pointed to him as the next leader of the world's most populous nation. In May he made his first visit to the U.S., where he met with Pres. George W. Bush at the White House for what was described as a "get-acquainted" session. The two had met for the first time in February during Bush's visit to China. In late 1999 Hu had also paid visits to Russia, Britain, France, Spain, and Germany.

Hu was born into a merchant family in December 1942 in Shanghai and grew up in Taizhou, Jiangsu province, China. As a youth he distinguished himself academically, testing into a prestigious high school and then going on to earn an engineering degree from Tsinghua University, Beijing, in 1965. He was recruited to join the CPC while still a student at the university. After graduation he served as an assistant instructor at the school before being sent to work for a year as a construction worker in Gansu province during the Cultural Revolution. He later held several technical and political posts in the province.

It was in Gansu province that Hu met Song Ping, a party elder and fellow Tsinghua graduate who became Hu's mentor. By 1982 Song had appointed him to a series of posts and introduced him to the CPC general secretary, Hu Yaobang. Within the next two years the younger Hu had moved to Beijing and risen to the top post of the Chinese Communist Youth League (CCYL), of which the elder Hu was a former general secretary. The younger Hu was named a member of the CPC Central Committee in 1987. Dispatched to Tibet a year later as a provincial party secretary, he presided over the suppression of Tibetan unrest in 1989. When Song retired as one of the seven standing members of the Political Bureau in 1992, he successfully lobbied for Hu to succeed him.

At the 1992 CPC Congress, Hu was appointed party secretariat, a key responsibility that enabled him to establish networks throughout the party. A year after his election as vice president in 1998, Hu added the vice chairmanship of the CPC Central Military Commission to his resumé—a title that solidified his status as leader-in-waiting. From that time, Hu was often noticeably patriotic in his public remarks, including his strong condemnation of the American bombing of the Chinese embassy in Belgrade in 1999. While no one could predict how he would lead China in the years to come, Hu's apparent political skills and his reported support for economic liberalization made him one of the more intriguing new figures on the world stage. (XIAOBO HU)

Im Kwon-taek

In May 2002 South Korean motion-picture director Im Kwon-taek won the best director award at the Cannes International Film Festival for *Chihwaseon* (2002), a masterly depiction of the life of legendary 19th-century Korean artist Jang Seung-up. Despite having made nearly 100 films over the course of four decades and having earned a reputation as the "father of Korean cinema," Im was relatively unknown to most filmgoers in the West; *Time* magazine described him as "the most famous director you've never heard of." His triumph at Cannes—which marked the first time that a Korean director had received the award—brought him much-deserved recognition as well as helped garner the often overlooked Korean film industry worldwide attention.

Im was born May 2, 1936, in Jansung, Cholla province, Korea. His father's death forced him to drop out of middle school, after which he eventually found work as a production assistant for a film company in Seoul. In 1962 he made his directorial debut with *Farewell to the Duman River*. Over the next 10 years, Im turned out some 50 movies, most of them B movies such as *The Two Revengeful Hunchbacks* (1971) and *Don't Torture Me Anymore* (1971).

Although his original ambition had been to direct Hollywood-style action films and comedies, Im came to realize that he would always

be hampered in this pursuit by limited financial and technical resources. Instead of trying to "compete with Hollywood," he decided to focus on creating films that were uniquely Korean, exploring the country's history and traditional culture. The movies that followed were not often great box-office successes, but they consistently earned critical praise. These included *Genealogy* (1978), a historical drama that dealt with the Japanese occupation of Korea; *Daughter of the Flames* (1983), which portrayed the shamanistic folk religion Donghak; *Sopyonje* (1993), about a family of *pansori* (folk opera) singers; and the Korean War epic *Taebaek Mountains* (1994).

Critics praised *Chihwaseon* for its imaginative re-creation of the turbulent life of Jang Seung-up, an amazingly gifted but self-destructive painter, and for the film's richly detailed look at the last years of the Choson dynasty. After Im took the best director award at Cannes, another honour came his way later in the year. At a ceremony in Paris on November 25, he was presented the UNESCO Fellini Gold Medal, awarded annually to directors whose films focused on peace and culture. Im's other awards included the 1997 Fukuoka Asian Culture Prize for arts and culture and the San Francisco International Film Festival's 1998 Akira Kurosawa Award.

(SHERMAN HOLLAR)

Kahn, Oliver

By his own admission, German goalkeeper and team captain Oliver Kahn made only one mistake in the 2002 World Cup finals—a fumble in the final against Brazil—and it cost Germany the trophy. Shot stoppers in association football (soccer), unlike more orthodox goalkeepers, block most attempts at goal but are vulnerable when failing to hold onto the ball. The irony of the occasion was not lost on Germany's captain. Before the final, Kahn had been handed the Lev Yashin Award as the best goalkeeper of the tournament, and after the game, he became the first goalkeeper to receive the Golden Ball as the best player of the finals. Kahn offered no excuses in the aftermath of the loss to Brazil, despite having sustained a hand injury just before halftime. Such disappointments did not linger long in the mind of this tall (1.88-m [6 ft 2 in]), craggy-faced German, who was playing in his 52nd international match.

Kahn was born in the industrial town of Karlsruhe, W. Ger., on June 15, 1969. He began playing as a seven-year-old with his local football club, made his first-team debut with Karlsruhe SC in 1987–88, and became a regular choice in 1990–91. He progressed so well that in 1994 Bayern Munich of the Bundesliga (Germany's top league) signed him in a £1.6 million (about $2.5 million) transfer, which in 2002 still ranked as the highest transfer fee for a German goalkeeper. In his initial season with Bayern, however, he sustained a serious knee injury that sidelined him for five months.

Variously nicknamed "King Kahn," "Kung Fu Kahn," "Sheer Kahn," and "Genghis Kahn" (but mostly just plain Ollie), the Teutonic titan became a formidable figure for opposing forwards to face. Brave, quick, athletic, and

with excellent reflexes—especially in one-on-one situations with opponents—he became a brilliant defense organizer. Kahn received able guidance from Bayern's legendary goalkeeper Sepp Maier, and after Kahn's arrival the team collected four straight Bundesliga championships (1997–2000) and two German cups (1998 and 2000), as well as the 1996 Union des Associations Européenes de Football (UEFA) Cup and the 2001 UEFA Champions League.

Despite his early diligence, Kahn did not make either the German youth or intermediate-level national teams. He played his first international match against Switzerland in 1995 and was Germany's second-string goalkeeper at the 1998 World Cup finals. From then on, however, he was Germany's number one choice. The 2002 World Cup gave Kahn his first real opportunity on the world stage. He suffered a humiliating experience in the qualifying competition when he conceded five goals to England, but he recovered with typical resilience. Though in his earlier days Kahn was considered to be rather short-tempered, by 2002 he had moderated his fiery approach, learned to curb his headstrong tendencies, and freely admitted to being inconsolable after his one mistake cost Germany the World Cup title.

(JACK ROLLIN)

Kamen, Dean

In 2002 nearly half the U.S. states changed their laws so that inventor Dean Kamen's high-tech Segway Human Transporter could be legally ridden on sidewalks and cycle paths. After months of rumours, the invention, codenamed Ginger, had finally been unveiled on Dec. 3, 2001, as a kind of superscooter. Kamen claimed the Segway, with its built-in gyroscopes, computer chips, and tilt sensors, would make getting around cities so easy that automobiles there would become not only undesirable but also unnecessary. Although the device's champions saw it as an environmentally friendly way to ease traffic and increase productivity for some businesses, the Segway's detractors warned of potential collisions and injuries. In 2002 the U.S. Postal Service was one of several companies running pilot tests of the Segway, which was not yet available to the public. Meanwhile, Kamen continued to work on developing a compact, nonpolluting Stirling engine capable of generating portable electricity or purifying water.

Kamen was born in Rockville Centre, N.Y., in 1951, the son of Jack Kamen, a comic-book artist, and Evelyn Kamen, a high-school teacher. As an undergraduate at Worcester (Mass.) Polytechnic Institute, Kamen invented a portable infusion pump, for which he was awarded the first of more than 150 patents he held in the U.S. and other countries. In 1976 he founded AutoSyringe, Inc., a medical device company, to manufacture and market the pump, and he later sold the company to Baxter International Corp. In 1982 he founded DEKA Research & Development Corp., where he built a team to create innovative products both internally and for outside clients. One such product was a 10-kg (22-lb) portable kidney dialysis machine, which *Design News* magazine in 1993 selected as its medical product of the year. In 1999 Kamen introduced the IBOT, a wheelchairlike device that he described as "wearable," which could climb stairs and stand upright on two wheels. It was his use of gyroscopic stabilizers on the IBOT that led Kamen to develop the Segway.

During 1985 Kamen established Science Enrichment Encounters, a hands-on science museum for children in Manchester, N.H., which he hoped would help young people see science and technology as fun, exciting, accessible, and rewarding. This was a forerunner of the U.S. FIRST (For Inspiration and Recognition of Science and Technology) organization, which he founded in 1989. FIRST sought to turn scientists and engineers into role models for the next generation by uniting engineering teams from business and universities with high-school students in an annual robot design and construction contest.

Kamen received numerous honours, including several honorary doctorates. In 1997 he was elected to the National Academy of Engineering, and the following year he received the Heinz Award in Technology, the Economy and Employment. Kamen was awarded a National Medal of Technology by Pres. Bill Clinton in 2000, and in 2002 he received the $500,000 Lemelson-MIT prize for inventors, which he donated to FIRST.

(ALAN STEWART)

Kidjo, Angélique

In early 2002 Beninese singer Angélique Kidjo enhanced her reputation as an international pop diva with the release of her sixth solo album—*Black Ivory Soul*—a dazzling excursion into Brazilian musical forms that deftly blended a Latin sound sensibility with traces of traditional West African rhythms. The success of this particular fusion came as no surprise to those who, on her previous albums, had witnessed Kidjo's remarkable marriage of diverse genres—including jazz, hip-hop, *zouk*, Zairean rumba, samba, salsa, funk, gospel, and Cameroonian *makossa*—to the sounds of her native Benin.

Kidjo was born on July 14, 1960, in Ouidah, Dahomey, French West Africa (now Benin). Her father was a musician, and her mother worked as a choreographer–theatre director. Kidjo began performing in her mother's theatre troupe at the age of six and as a teenager sang with her brothers in their rock–rhythm-and-blues band. By age 20 she was a professional singer, and in 1988 she recorded her first album, *Pretty*. In 1983 Kidjo had moved to Paris, where she found a veritable melting pot of artists and a number of musical influences with which to experiment; she also met French producer, composer, and bassist Jean Hebrail, whom she later married. Her first years in Paris were spent studying jazz and performing with various local groups. After teaming with Dutch pianist Jasper Van't Hof, she sang with and co-wrote songs for his jazz group, Pili-Pili.

After several years Kidjo left Pili-Pili and recorded *Logozo* (1991), which was produced by Miami Sound Machine's Joe Galdo and featured jazz musician Branford Marsalis and African artists Manu Dibango and Ray Lema. *Logozo* was an international success and gar-

© Youri Lenquette/Alamo/Corbis Sygma

Benin's genre-fusing Angélique Kidjo

nered Kidjo airplay on commercial radio stations in the U.S. The lyrics to her songs were universal, however; they dealt with homelessness, the environment, freedom, and integration. Her following album, *Ayé* (1993), was produced by Prince associate David Z and Will Mowat of the rhythm-and-blues group Soul II Soul and helped to further expand Kidjo's fan base. On *Fifa* (1995) Kidjo enlisted the aid of more than 100 musicians and performed some

of the songs in English instead of in Fon, her native language and customary singing language of choice. (She also sang in Yoruba and French.) Her album *Oremi* (1998) featured a reinterpretation of Jimi Hendrix's "Voodoo Child (Slight Return)" and guest spots by jazz singer Cassandra Wilson and rhythm-and-blues singer Kelly Price.

Kidjo spent much of 2002 on tour after the release of *Black Ivory Soul*. In addition to her recording career, Kidjo was an outspoken advocate of the need for an education, and in July UNICEF named her one of its special ambassadors.

(SHANDA SILER)

Kostelic, Janica

Demonstrating why she was called the "Croatian Sensation," Janica Kostelic overcame injury and adversity to make history at the 2002 Winter Olympics. In Salt Lake City, Utah, she became the first Croatian to win a Winter Games medal and the first skier to win four Alpine skiing medals at a single Olympics. She earned a medal in every event in which she competed—gold in the slalom, the giant slalom, and the combined event and silver in the supergiant slalom. Kostelic's achievement was all the more remarkable considering that she had spent much of 2001 undergoing operations on her left knee and rehabilitation, and she had arrived at the Games having failed to win a race during the 2001–02 World Cup season. Her record-setting performances were cheered in Croatia, where Kostelic was a national hero, and some 200,000 fans welcomed her triumphant return home.

Kostelic was born in Zagreb, Yugos. (now Croatia), on Jan. 5, 1982. Encouraged by her father, who later became her coach, she put on her first pair of skis at age three. Though there were few training facilities and ski courses in the country, Kostelic displayed promise, and at age nine she began compet-

"Croatian Sensation" Janica Kostelic

AP/Wide World Photos

ing in races throughout Europe. The family—including her older brother, Ivica, who was also a skier—drove to the events, often sleeping in the car or a tent owing to a shortage of money. In the 1996–97 season, Kostelic won all 22 events she entered and claimed the top junior titles in the slalom and giant slalom. In 1998 at Nagano, Japan, she competed in her first Winter Games, and though she did not earn a medal, her eighth-place finish in the combined event was then the highest finish by a Croatian Winter Olympian.

During the 1998–99 World Cup season, her first year on the tour, Kostelic began to receive international attention. After several strong showings, she claimed her first World Cup victory in the combined event held in St. Anton, Austria. The following season she won two World Cup slaloms, then crashed during training, tearing ligaments in her right knee. Some wondered whether she would ever compete again, but Kostelic displayed her trademark resilience. After surgery she underwent a quick rehabilitation, returning for the 2000–01 season. She did poorly at the 2001 world championships but won eight consecutive slalom races en route to claiming her first World Cup overall title. In March 2001 she injured her left knee and had to endure three more operations. A lengthy recovery followed, but she was ready for the start of the 2001–02 season. Several weeks after making history in Salt Lake, she triumphed in the slalom in Flachau, Austria, the final event of the World Cup season. Joining her on the podium was Ivica, who had won the men's giant slalom.   (AMY TIKKANEN)

Law, Bernard Cardinal

When 2002 began, Boston's Bernard Cardinal Law was the senior Roman Catholic cardinal in the U.S. and the chairman of the bishops' Committee on International Policy, but as the year drew to a close, he had resigned his position as head of his archdiocese and apologized for what he called his "shortcomings and mistakes" in response to allegations of sexual misconduct against priests. The conviction and sentencing of Rev. John Geoghan for having molested a 10-year-old boy spurred lawsuits against the cardinal for his failure to discipline the priest. When documents were released in April showing that he had also ignored warnings for years about such conduct by another priest, Rev. Paul Shanley, prominent Catholics began to call for Law's resignation. In November, after meeting with some victims of clergy sexual abuse, he said that he had acquired a "far deeper awareness of this terrible evil." He stepped down in December after lawyers released 3,000 pages of files showing how Law had routinely transferred accused clergy to other parishes without disciplining them. Pope John Paul II appointed Auxiliary Bishop Richard G. Lennon as temporary administrator of the archdiocese.

Law was born on Nov. 4, 1931, in Torreón, Mex., to a U.S. Army colonel and a concert pianist. He attended high school in the U.S. Virgin Islands. After graduating from Harvard University with a degree in history, he studied for the priesthood and was ordained in 1961. His initial assignment was in Natchez, Miss.,

in the poorest diocese in the U.S. He became an outspoken supporter of civil rights and used his position as editor of the weekly newspaper of the diocese of Natchez-Jackson as a forum for his views. This led to threats on his life. In 1968 Law went to Washington, D.C., to serve as executive director of the American bishops' Committee on Ecumenical and Interreligious Affairs. Five years later he was named bishop of the diocese of Springfield-Cape Girardeau in southern Missouri. As head of the diocese, he opened the first home for battered women in Springfield and set up a centre for Vietnamese refugees that became a national model.

In 1984 Law succeeded Humberto Cardinal Medeiros as head of the archdiocese of Boston, and he soon became a figure of national prominence when he denounced Democratic vice presidential nominee Geraldine Ferraro for her support of abortion rights. He was elevated to the College of Cardinals in 1985. On a visit to Cuba in 1990, Law met with Pres. Fidel Castro for more than two hours. It was the first of several conversations they had and gave the cardinal a role in helping to pave the way for the pope's visit to Cuba in 1998.

(DARRELL J. TURNER)

Lee, Stan

On May 3, 2002, the motion picture *Spider-Man* opened on 3,600 screens in the U.S. By the end of May 5, the movie—about a shy teenager given superhero powers when bitten by a radioactive spider—had set an American record for opening-weekend box-office receipts by grossing $114,894,116. For American cartoonist Stan Lee, the creator of Spider-Man, the movie's triumph was the capstone in a career that had begun more than 60 years earlier.

Lee was born Stanley Lieber in New York City in 1922. At the age of 17, he became an assistant editor for the Timely comics group, and in 1942 he was promoted to editor. During the 1940s and '50s, while the group—later named Atlas—struggled financially, Lee created several comic-book series, including *The Witness, The Destroyer, Jack Frost, Whizzer,* and *Black Marvel.*

In 1961 Atlas was renamed Marvel Group, and one year later Lee created *Spider-Man.* It joined a roster of increasingly successful series that included Lee's *The Fantastic Four* and *The Incredible Hulk.* Lee added another winner to the group when he created *The X-Men* in 1963. Marvel continued to prosper, and in 1972 Lee became publisher and editorial director of the group. He published a book, *Origins of Marvel Comics,* in 1974.

A distinctive feature of Lee's comic-book heroes, typified by Spider-Man, was that they combined superhuman powers with human insecurities and emotions. In commenting on Spider-Man, Lee said, "Most of the young readers could identify with him because he had all the hang-ups that they did and that I used to have when I was a kid."

Lee suffered a personal and financial setback in 2001 when Stan Lee Media, an Internet entertainment company built around Lee's creations, went bankrupt. Formed in 1999, the firm enjoyed early success with its first project, an animated on-line series called *7th Portal* featuring aliens who enter Earth through the Internet. Late in 2000 the company's stock price fell 49% in one day to $3 per share. By mid-December most of the staff of 150 had been laid off, and the firm filed for bankruptcy in February 2001. In November

Movie marvel Spider-Man (and his creator, Stan Lee)

2002 Lee filed a $10 million lawsuit against Marvel after failing to receive any profits from *Spider-Man*. Big-screen adaptations of two of his comic series, *The Incredible Hulk* and *Daredevil*, were set for release in 2003.

(DAVID R. CALHOUN)

Lubchenco, Jane

"Think globally and act locally" was a popular catchphrase that gained currency during the environmental movement of the late 20th century. American marine ecologist Jane Lubchenco was among the few who were in the position to both think *and* act globally. From the vantage point of the many national

© Joel W. Rogers

Jane Lubchenco, international science policy adviser

and international advisory panels on which she sat, she had made a career of informing public policy on environmental issues. In 2002, for example, she became the president of the International Council for Science, which promoted interdisciplinary science. Recognizing that environmental change did not come about without mass participation, she sought ways to better inform the public of scientific issues and to bridge the gulf between researchers and the rest of the world. In a 1997 speech, while she was president of the American Association for the Advancement of Science, she proposed the idea of a social contract between scientists and society. "The environment is not a marginal issue," she cautioned. Lubchenco also argued that the unseen benefits, or services, of nature—such as decomposition of wastes, protection from ultraviolet rays, and flood control—ought to be considered in the projected cost accounting for large-scale man-made projects. In addition to her work as an outspoken science administrator, Lubchenco served as a professor of marine biology in the department of zo-

ology at Oregon State University. Her husband, Bruce Menge, shared a laboratory with her there.

Lubchenco was born on Dec. 4, 1947, in Denver, Colo. She was educated at Colorado College (B.A., 1969), the University of Washington (M.S., 1971), and Harvard University (Ph.D., 1975), and her thesis work focused on community structure in coastal rockpools. In 1977 she began teaching marine biology at Oregon State University, and the following year she became a research associate at the Smithsonian Institution. Her areas of research interest included algal ecology, plant-herbivore and predator-prey interactions, global change community structure, and the evolutionary ecology of individuals.

In 1996 she was elected to the National Academy of Sciences, where she became a council member in 1999. She was also a member of the American Philosophical Society (1998), the Association for Women in Science (1997), and the American Academy of Arts and Sciences (1990). She had been the chair of the task force on the environment at the National Science Board and an adviser to Religion, Science, and the Environment, a cross-disciplinary partnership of scientists and religious leaders. In addition, she won numerous grants and awards, and her research was widely reported in academic journals, science magazines, and scholarly books.

(TOM MICHAEL)

Lula

On Oct. 27, 2002—Lula's 57th birthday—voters in Brazil handed him a landslide victory in his fourth attempt at the presidency. The election capped the remarkable rise of a former lathe operator and union leader to the nation's top political post and put a left-wing leader in power in Brazil for the first time in four decades.

Born in 1945 to sharecropping parents in Garanhuns, Pernambuco state, Braz., Luiz Inácio da Silva ("Lula" was a nickname that he added to his legal name for campaign purposes) worked as a shoeshine boy and street vendor to help supplement the family income. After his mother separated from his father and moved the family to the city of São Paulo in 1956, Lula found work at a screw-manufacturing plant and trained to operate a lathe. He lost the little finger of his left hand in an accident at age 18. During the recession that followed the military coup of 1964, Lula was laid off but eventually found employment with the Villares Metalworks in São Bernardo do Campo, an industrial suburb of São Paulo. At Villares, his brother Chico encouraged him to join the Metalworkers' Union. In 1972 Lula left the factory to work for the union full-time, heading its legal section until 1975, when he was elected union president.

Lula soon gained national fame. He launched a movement for wage increases in opposition to the military regime's economic policy. The campaign was highlighted by a series of strikes from 1978 to 1980 and culminated in Lula's arrest and indictment for violations of the National Security Law. Although he was convicted and sentenced to a prison term of three

and a half years, the Military Supreme Court absolved him of the charges.

A founding member of the Workers' Party (PT), Lula first ran for political office as the PT candidate for governor of the state of São Paulo in 1982, finishing fourth. He later led national efforts in favour of direct elections for president, organizing mass demonstrations in state capitals in 1983 and 1984. Buoyed by popularity and charisma, Lula was elected to the national Chamber of Deputies in 1986 as a federal deputy from São Paulo. The PT ran Lula as its candidate for president in 1989, but he lost to Fernando Collor de Mello. Lula continued as his party's presidential candidate in the elections of 1994 and 1998, both times finishing second to Fernando Henrique Cardoso. While he never attained more than 40% of the valid votes during his first three presidential campaigns, Lula won the presidency in 2002 with 61.5% of the ballots to government-backed candidate José Serra's 38.5%.

Lula owed his victory in part to his adoption of a more pragmatic platform than he had previously offered. While he remained committed to encouraging grassroots participation in the political process, he also took pains to court business leaders and promised to work with the International Monetary Fund to meet fiscal targets. Lula's inauguration was set for Jan. 1, 2003.

(JOHN CHARLES CUTTINO)

Manley, John

After Canadian Foreign Minister John Manley was appointed deputy prime minister in January 2002 and minister of finance in June, he emerged as the most powerful minister in the Liberal government of Prime Minister Jean Chrétien. Manley replaced longtime Finance Minister Paul Martin and was seen by many as Chrétien's logical successor.

Manley's spectacular rise in government was attributed to the decisive stand that he took after the Sept. 11, 2001, terrorist attacks in the United States. As foreign minister, Manley formulated Canada's response to the terrorist threat and immediately tightened controls on Canada's long land border with the U.S. Working with American officials concerned with homeland security, he explored the concept of a North American security perimeter. He piloted antiterrorist legislation through the Canadian Parliament and took an active part in the decision in January 2002 to send a Canadian combat mission to Afghanistan to operate beside U.S. forces there. Through these efforts he helped to dispel a degree of coolness that had developed in Canadian-American security cooperation.

As deputy prime minister, Manley presided over the cabinet when Chrétien was out of the country and served as chair of the two most important cabinet committees, those dealing with economic and social policy. He was given supervision over a long list of Crown (public) corporations and agencies. He was also named political minister for Ontario, a responsibility that enabled him to control federal grants and appointments in Canada's most populated province.

In June, when Manley moved from foreign affairs to replace Martin at finance, Manley retained his other duties to become, in effect, the chief operating officer of the Chrétien administration. Manley became Chrétien's right-hand man and the prime minister's closest colleague in the cabinet.

Manley was born on Jan. 5, 1950, in Ottawa. He was educated there at Carleton University (B.A., 1971) and the University of Ottawa, where he earned a degree in law in 1976. He entered Parliament in 1988 and five years later, when the Liberals came to power, was appointed minister of industry. In that capacity he worked to promote the adoption of new technology and innovation in Canadian industry to meet global competition. He was also responsible for strengthening economic development in regions of Canada with special problems, such as the Atlantic provinces, the four Western provinces, and Quebec. His performance in this post was unspectacular but gave him a solid grounding in Canadian economic and social affairs that would serve him well in his new broader responsibilities. Though some of Manley's responsibilities were redistributed in August, including the oversight of Canada's infrastructure program, he remained one of the most prominent politicians in the country.   (DAVID M.L. FARR)

Martínez, Tomás Eloy

In the spring of 2002, the announcement in Madrid that Argentine writer and journalist Tomás Eloy Martínez had been awarded the Alfaguara Prize for his novel *El vuelo de la reina* meant that his work, chosen from among 433 manuscripts, would be published by Alfaguara in 18 countries. In addition, Eloy Martínez would receive a cash prize of $175,000. *El vuelo de la reina* tells the story, loosely based on a real incident that took place in Brazil, of the decadent world of the editor of an important newspaper in Buenos Aires and how his erotic obsession with a journalist half his age leads to deception and murder. The action takes place in an Argentina suffering from economic and moral bankruptcy, poverty, and despair.

Martínez was best known as the author of two classics of Argentine and Latin American literature: *La novela de Perón* (1985, *The Perón Novel*, 1988) and *Santa Evita* (1995, Eng. trans., 1995); the latter was translated into 30 languages and sold more than 10 million copies. His other novels included *Sagrado* (1969) and *La mano del amo* (1991). In addition, he wrote essays, most notably *Los testigos de afuera* (1978) and *Retrato del artista enmascarado* (1982); a collection of short stories entitled *Lugar común la muerte* (1979); and 10 screenplays. He was also a prolific journalist, working as a columnist for *La nación* in Buenos Aires, *El país* in Spain, and for the New York Times Syndicate, which published his articles in 200 newspapers in Latin America and Europe.

Martínez was born on July 16, 1934, in Tucumán, Arg. He obtained a degree in Spanish and Latin American literature from the Universidad de Tucumán and went on to earn a doctorate at the Université de Paris VII. From 1957 to 1961 he was a film critic in Buenos Aires for *La nación*, and he then was

editor in chief (1962–69) of the magazine *Primera plana*. From 1969 to 1970 he served as a reporter in Paris, and from 1970 to 1972 he was the director of the magazine *Panorama*. For three years (1972–75) Martínez was in charge of the cultural supplement of *La nación*, after which he lived in exile (1975–83) in Caracas, Venez., where he remained active as a journalist, founding the newspaper *El diario de Caracas*. He subsequently started the newspaper *Siglo 21* in Guadalajara, Mex., and created the literary supplement *Primer plano* for the newspaper *Página/12* in Buenos Aires.

In addition to his literary and journalistic accomplishments and his passionate advocacy of victims of human rights abuses, Martínez enjoyed an active academic career, lecturing extensively throughout the Americas and Europe. He was a professor (1984–87) at the University of Maryland and from 1995 was a distinguished professor at Rutgers University, New Brunswick, N.J., and director of its Latin American studies program.   (JOHN BARRY)

McEwan, Ian

The publication of Ian McEwan's ninth novel, *Atonement* (2001), helped cement his reputation on both sides of the Atlantic by 2002 as one of Great Britain's premier writers of fiction. The novel failed to win the 2001 Booker Prize, but it was judged by the BBC as the "People's Booker" and was nominated for the 2003 International IMPAC Dublin Literary Award. Its sales outstripped those of the winning *True History of the Kelly Gang* (2000) by Australian author Peter Carey. A deft and luminous story of love, guilt, and redemption told over six decades, *Atonement* describes how a terrible lie, told by a 13-year-old girl in 1935, reverberates over time until the close of the century. *The Observer* (London) hailed the work as "impressive, engrossing, deep and surprising," while the *New York Times* called it "the author's most deeply felt novel yet" with "a larger, tragic vision" than McEwan's 1998 Booker winner, *Amsterdam*.

Ian Russell McEwan was born on June 21, 1948, in Aldershot, Eng. His father was an army officer, and McEwan wove his experiences at Dunkirk during World War II into *Atonement*. After earning a B.A. (1970) from the University of Sussex, in Brighton, McEwan gained an M.A. (1971) in creative writing after studying in novelist Malcolm Bradbury's literary-star-producing department at the University of East Anglia, in Norwich. The course of study exposed him to the best of American fiction, which he said galvanized him to eschew what was "polite and dull" in English writing and made him "wild" and wanting "to shock." His first publication, a short-story collection titled *First Love, Last Rites* (1975), won him the 1976 Somerset Maugham Award. The stories at once enthralled and appalled readers; the outré and the horrific were delivered in tight packages of elegant measured prose, often comic in effect. The spine-tingling style became a hallmark, earning McEwan the nickname "Ian Macabre."

Several novels, screenplays, and stories about love, death, and obsessive behaviour fol-

lowed. Childhood, often not innocent, collided with adult worlds brimming with violence and sexuality. *The Cement Garden* (1978) depicted four children's descent into bestiality, while *The Comfort of Strangers* (1981; adapted by Harold Pinter into a film starring Rupert Everett and Natasha Richardson) was a grisly murder story set in Venice. Some reviewers found his tales contrived and gratuitously shocking; others applauded his mastery of the incredible. With the birth of his two children, McEwan claimed to experience an extension of his "emotional range." The passions, actions, and events of *Atonement* also confirmed him as a master of the credible. When McEwan first revealed *Atonement*'s surprising coda to his wife, she reportedly burst into tears. He wrote it as he had recounted it to her, and it became what one reviewer hailed as a "perfect close."   (SIOBHAN DOWD)

McPartland, Marian

The format of Marian McPartland's *Piano Jazz* program, on National Public Radio, was simple: for an hour each week two jazz artists, the elegant pianist McPartland and a guest, played duets and chatted about music. Part of the program's appeal was McPartland's own playing, for she had a famously huge repertoire of jazz and popular songs, and she was a fluent, basically romantic improviser who adapted readily to many different styles. She was also an ever-gracious interviewer with a knack for putting others at ease. Her guests included a veritable who's who of jazz, from swing-band stars to avant-gardists and even the occasional pop singer. Along with famous names, her hundreds of guests also included top-notch but little-known artists, such as a Kyrgyz-born teenaged pianist from Kansas City, Kan., named Eldar Djangirov. McPartland's warmth and versatility made *Piano Jazz* the longest-running jazz program on National Public Radio and one of the longest-running network jazz shows in history; in 2002 she began her 23rd year on the air.

She was born Margaret Marian Turner on March 20, 1918, in Slough, Eng., and began playing the piano when she was three or four. She attended private schools and studied classical music at the Guildhall School of Music, London. When she was 20, she horrified her "upper-middle-class and conservative" parents by joining a touring piano quartet that played popular music. During World War II she volunteered for ENSA, England's equivalent of the USO; she then went to Europe as a USO entertainer, where she lived in tents, dodged German bullets, and met and married American jazz cornetist Jimmy McPartland. After the war the couple moved to the U.S., and she became the pianist in his Dixieland band. Soon, however, the siren sounds of bebop and cool jazz lured her into playing a more modern style. In 1951 she began leading her own trio; the next year she launched what became a 10-year-long gig at New York City's Hickory House nightclub. She was a favourite in concerts and elegant nightclubs from then on. Although she divorced her husband, they remained friends and remarried just weeks before his death in 1991.

Besides touring the world as a performer, McPartland was a prominent jazz promoter. For most of her career, beginning in 1956, she taught jazz in American grade schools, high schools, and colleges: "I couldn't fight rock and roll but I wanted kids to know there's another music." In the 1970s she ran her own record label, Halcyon, which issued albums by noted jazz pianists. It was on Oct. 8, 1978, that she began taping the *Piano Jazz* broadcasts, with fellow pianists as guests; her very first guest was Mary Lou Williams, "my role model forever." Soon she began inviting nonpianists too, such as trumpeters Dizzy Gillespie and Roy Eldridge, saxophonists Branford Marsalis and Benny Carter, and singers Rosemary Clooney and Willie Nelson. Ever the generous jazz advocate, she also found time to write occasional articles about her favourite jazz musicians; they were collected in her 1987 book *All in Good Time.* (JOHN LITWEILER)

Messier, Jean-Marie

The spectacular rise of French businessman Jean-Marie Messier ended in July 2002 when he was forced to resign as chairman and CEO of Vivendi Universal. Beginning in the mid-1990s, he had transformed a domestic French utility company into a global conglomerate centred on media and communications. In doing so, however, he had brought together a number of ill-fitting businesses, and as a promoter of global enterprises without due respect to French cultural traditions, he offended the sensibilities of fellow Frenchmen. What finally brought him down, however, were old-fashioned problems—plummeting stock values, record losses, and enormous debt.

Messier was born on Dec. 13, 1956, in Grenoble, France. He was educated at the École Polytechnique (1976–79) and the École Nationale d'Administration (1980–82) and from 1982 to 1988 held positions in the Ministry of Economy and Finance. He joined the investment bank Lazard Frères in 1989, the youngest partner in the firm's history. In 1994 he moved to Compagnie Générale des Eaux, originally a water utility company that had come to include businesses such as waste management and construction. Messier became head of the company in 1996, restructured the business, and in 1998 renamed it Vivendi, to suggest revivification. By 1999 he had a controlling interest in Canal Plus, Europe's largest pay television service and by law a source of financing for the French film industry. In 2000 Vivendi bought Seagram, which included Universal Pictures and Polygram Records. Changing the company's name to Vivendi Universal, Messier placed the nonmedia businesses in a division called Vivendi Environnement. He changed the name of Polygram to Universal Music Group and took over other media businesses, including the American publisher Houghton Mifflin, cable and production company USA Networks, and on-line music service MP3.com. Other businesses included phone companies, Internet services, computer software, and amusement parks. He was made a chevalier of the French Legion of Honour in 2001. The same year, Messier moved to New York City, which became the base of his media operations.

A flamboyant American-style capitalist, Messier referred to himself as *moi-même, maître du monde* ("myself, master of the world"), or J6M. (The title of his 2000 autobiography was *J6M.com.*) As with other media conglomerates, however, Vivendi Universal began to struggle, and the company had a record loss in 2001 of €13.6 billion (about $12.4 billion). In the first six months of 2002 alone, the stock lost more than 60% of its value, while the company found itself threatened with a debt of €33.3 billion (about $32.3 billion). When in early 2002 Messier sacked the head of Canal Plus for poor financial performance, the action became an issue in the French elections, and by July Messier had lost the backing of the French as well as the North American members of the board. Following his resignation, Messier began writing an account of his rise and downfall at Vivendi. The book, *Mon vrai journal*, was published in November. (ROBERT RAUCH)

Mistry, Rohinton

In 2002 Indian-born Canadian writer Rohinton Mistry's latest novel, *Family Matters,* joined its predecessor, *A Fine Balance* (1995), on the bestseller lists. Set in a tiny two-room flat in Mumbai (Bombay), *Family Matters* presented a compelling portrayal of a family of Parsis (descendants from Persian Zoroastrians) living in exigent circumstances in modern-day India; the story was in turns poignant, stark, and humourous—elements that had become a trademark of Mistry's work.

Of Parsi origin himself, Mistry was born in Bombay on July 3, 1952, and, after obtaining a degree in mathematics and economics from the University of Bombay (now the University of Mumbai), moved to Canada in 1975. Despite his education, he was at first unable to find work and at one point even applied—unsuccessfully—for a job at a McDonald's restaurant before eventually landing a position as a bank clerk. In the early 1980s he enrolled at the University of Toronto to pursue a degree in English and philosophy. He began writing short stories and won the university's literary competition two years in a row. Mistry attracted wider attention when in 1985 he won *Canadian Fiction Magazine*'s annual Contributors Prize. His collection of short stories, *Tales from Firozsha Baag,* published in 1987, was warmly greeted by critics and general readers alike for its insights into the complex lives of the Parsi inhabitants of an apartment block in Mumbai.

Mistry's debut novel, *Such a Long Journey,* an intricate tale of the triumphs and disasters of the friends and family of kindhearted Gustad Noble in a time of war and turbulence in India, garnered even more praise when it appeared in 1991. The book received the Governor-General's Award, the W.H. Smith/*Books in Canada* First Novel Award, and the Commonwealth Writers Prize for Best Book, as well as making the shortlist for the Booker Prize and the Trillium Award. The novel was translated into Danish, German, Japanese, Norwegian, and Swedish and in 1998 was made into a feature film directed by Sturla Gunnarsson.

A Fine Balance, Mistry's second novel, was another study of Parsis living at close quarters in varying degrees of harmony during difficult times. This novel was even more widely acclaimed than his first, winning the *Los Angeles Times* Book Prize, the Giller Prize, the Commonwealth Writers Prize for Best Book, and the Royal Society of Literature's Winifred Holtby Award. In addition, it was short-listed for the Booker Prize, the International IMPAC Dublin Literary Award, and the *Irish Times* International Fiction Prize. Sales of the novel shot up dramatically when it became a choice of Oprah's Book Club in 2001.

(ELIZABETH RHETT WOODS)

Miyazaki, Hayao

In 2002 international acclaim came at last for Japanese animation director Hayao Miyazaki. His *Sen to Chihiro no kamikakushi* (released in English as *Spirited Away*) captured the top prize at the Berlin International Film Festival, won best Asian film at the Hong Kong Film Awards, and generated considerable Oscar buzz after its October release in the U.S. In his native Japan it had already won best picture at the Japanese Academy Awards and replaced *Titanic* as the top grossing film in Japanese history.

Miyazaki was born in Tokyo on Jan. 5, 1941. His father was the director of Miyazaki Airplane, a manufacturing concern that built parts for Zero fighter planes. The family business instilled in Miyazaki a love of flying that became apparent in virtually all of his work. After having completed studies in economics at Gakushuin University, Tokyo, in 1963, he took a position as an entry-level animator at Toei Doga, Asia's largest animation studio. While at Toei Doga, he met fellow animators Isao Takahata and Akemi Ota. The first became a lifelong friend, collaborator, and business partner. The second, after a one-year courtship, became his wife. Miyazaki moved through the ranks at Toei, working on such projects as the television series *Wolf Boy Ken* and Takahata's feature directorial debut, *The Great Adventure of Hols, Prince of the Sun* (1968). After leaving Toei in 1971, Miyazaki, accompanied by Takahata, continued to work for various studios throughout the 1970s. Highlights from this period included the *Panda & Child* film shorts and, in 1979, Miyazaki's first full-length film, *Lupin III: Castle of Cagliostro.*

Miyazaki's individual style became more apparent in *Nausicaä of the Valley of the Winds,* a monthly *manga* (Japanese cartoon) strip he wrote for *Animage* magazine. Its success inspired a film of the same name (released in 1984) and encouraged Miyazaki and Takahata to undertake a more permanent partnership arrangement. Together they launched Studio Ghibli in 1985. The following year Miyazaki's film *Castle in the Sky* was released in Japan and *Nausicaä* was released in the U.S. as *Warriors of the Wind*. Confusing edits and poor dubbing rendered the American version virtually unwatchable, and more than a decade would pass before Miyazaki would consider another Western release. He and Studio Ghibli continued to produce works for the domestic market, however. Miyazaki's *My Neighbor Totoro* debuted alongside Takahata's *Grave of the Fireflies* in 1988. While both films were well received critically, the financial success of the studio was secured by the phenomenal sale of *Totoro* merchandise. Miyazaki followed with *Kiki's Delivery Service* (1989) and *Porco Rosso* (1992), which became the year's top-grossing film. This set the stage for 1997's *Mononoke Hime* (*Princess Mononoke*), a blockbuster that shattered Japanese box-office records. (MICHAEL RAY)

Murcutt, Glenn

Australian architect Glenn Murcutt won the 2002 Pritzker Architecture Prize, though unlike the majority of the previous 25 Pritzker laureates, he had designed few large-scale projects. Instead he had spent most of his career designing innovative climate-sensitive private houses. Working alone out of his office in Sydney, Murcutt had a long list of prospective clients who were content to wait for him to give their projects the personal attention that characterized his work. Drawing from influences that ranged from Ludwig Mies van der Rohe to common Australian wool sheds, Murcutt developed a style that attempted to strike a balance with nature yet maintain a distinctly modernist look.

Murcutt was born on July 25, 1936, in London while his Australian parents were en route to the Olympic Games in Berlin. His father found success as a gold prospector in New Guinea, and Murcutt spent the first five years of his life there. The family's home was constructed of corrugated iron and set on top of stilts to keep water and animals out; the design of the house, and of other houses built by his father, would later inform much of Murcutt's own choices as a planner of homes.

After earning a degree in architecture from the University of New South Wales Technical College in 1961, Murcutt spent eight years with a Sydney architectural firm before founding his own practice. He traveled extensively in Europe and North America, marveling at the works of Mies, Alvar Aalto, Luis Barragan, Frank Lloyd Wright, and Louis Sullivan. In 1970 Murcutt began a nine-year stint as a design tutor at the University of Sydney. After teaching at the University of New South Wales in 1985 and at the University of Melbourne from 1989 to 1997, he embarked on a series of visiting professorships at universities in the U.S., Papua New Guinea, Finland, and Denmark.

Murcutt's buildings reflected his desire to maintain harmony with the environment. His houses often featured corrugated iron with the ribs laid horizontally, creating a linearity that he felt responded to the landscape instead of

competing with it. Few of his designs called for air-conditioning. The flow of air was controlled through the implementation of slatted roofs, screens, and blinds; wide eaves provided shelter from the sun. Although most of his buildings were not spectacular attention-seeking projects, Murcutt was not averse to being in the spotlight. In 1998 he took a strong public stand against a $66 million plan to refurbish the Sydney Opera House. The plan was later canceled. (ANTHONY G. CRAINE)

Mwanawasa, Levy Patrick

Levy Mwanawasa was sworn in as president of Zambia on Jan. 2, 2002. His victory in the election held in December 2001 had been a narrow one—he polled only 28.69% of the votes cast, while the nearest of the other 10 candidates polled 26.76%—and the result was initially challenged by his opponents.

A member of the Lenje tribe, Mwanawasa was born in Mufulira, Northern Rhodesia, on Sept. 3, 1948. He was educated at Chiwala Secondary School in Ndola and then read law at the University of Zambia in Lusaka from 1970 to 1973. Mwanawasa became an assistant in a law firm in Ndola in 1974 and qualified for the bar in 1975. He formed his own law company in 1978 and became vice-chairman of the Law Association of Zambia in 1982. In 1985–86 he served as solicitor general of Zambia.

When Pres. Kenneth Kaunda reluctantly approved the creation of opposition parties in Zambia in December 1990, Mwanawasa joined Frederick Chiluba's new Movement for Multiparty Democracy (MMD). In the elections that followed in October 1991, he became a member of the National Assembly for the Ndola constituency. He was then appointed vice president and leader of the Assembly in President Chiluba's government, which took over from Kaunda's United National Independence Party (UNIP).

Mwanawasa resigned office in July 1994, claiming that he had been increasingly sidelined by the president to the point that his position had become irrelevant. He also accused the government of condoning irresponsibility and greed. Subsequently, Mwanawasa devoted himself primarily to his legal practice until, with Chiluba's impending retirement, he was unexpectedly adopted in August 2001 as the MMD candidate for president.

Although the opposition soon abandoned its protest against President Mwanawasa, his position was weakened by two other factors. First, the MMD, which had lost considerable support because of Chiluba's policies, had performed only modestly in the legislative elections and was unable to command an overall majority in the National Assembly. Second, although Chiluba insisted at the inauguration ceremony that Mwanawasa would formulate his own policies, the new president was widely

believed to be Chiluba's man. Because Chiluba had tried hard but unsuccessfully to change the constitution so that he could stand for a third term and he still retained the MMD presidency, many thought that he would try to control events from the wings.

Mwanawasa, however, moved quickly to establish his authority and to launch a campaign against the corruption that had brought the MMD into disrepute. He abolished the Ministry of Defense and took over that portfolio himself and also retired 10 senior military officers. In March he dismissed a number of officeholders thought to be disloyal to the government, and at about the same time, Chiluba relinquished the leadership of the MMD. In July, Foreign Minister Katele Kalumba resigned amid allegations of corruption, and any further doubts about Mwanawasa's relationship to Chiluba were dispelled when the National Assembly voted unanimously to withdraw the former president's parliamentary immunity.

(KENNETH INGHAM)

Nair, Mira

Early 2002 was a busy time for film director-producer-writer Mira Nair. On Sept. 8, 2001, *Monsoon Wedding* captured the Golden Lion for best picture at the Venice Film Festival. It was a rare honour, as she was only the second Indian, after Satyajit Ray in 1957, to win the award. For independent filmmakers Nair's win was a cause for jubilation—*Monsoon Wedding* was shot in little over a month for her own Mirabai Films, Inc., using handheld cameras and an ensemble cast that boasted only one big name. Furniture and costumes—including silk saris and traditional gold wedding jewelry—were borrowed from her family. *Monsoon Wedding*, an exuberant look at four days leading up to a Punjabi wedding set against the backdrop of modern urban India, was the latest achievement in Nair's offbeat oeuvre, much of which revolved around the themes of exile and cultural identity. In January 2002 the movie was a nominee for best foreign film at the Golden Globe Awards. At the same time, Nair's latest effort, *Hysterical Blindness*, a mainstream Hollywood

© AFP 2002, by Claudio Onorati

Director Mira Nair won kudos for her **Monsoon Wedding.**

film with no Indian actors, had its premiere at the Sundance Film Festival in Park City, Utah, before being broadcast on HBO. The filmmaker traveled to Germany in February to serve as head of the Berlin Film Festival jury. Less than a month later she was back in New York City to give the 2002 Zora Neale Hurston lecture for Columbia University's Institute for Research in African-American Studies.

Nair's unique take on expatriate life stemmed from her own identity as a global citizen. She was born on Oct. 15, 1957, in Bhubaneswar, Orissa, India, and was educated at the University of Delhi. She moved to the U.S. in 1976 for postgraduate studies in sociology at Harvard University, but she soon developed an interest in cinema. Her debut film, *India Cabaret* (1985), was a documentary about "dance bars," or strip joints, in Mumbai (Bombay). This was followed two years later by *Children of Desired Sex*.

Nair's first feature film, *Salaam Bombay!* (1988)—a documentary-style account of urban street children—was nominated for an Academy Award for best foreign-language film and won the Camera d'Or (best first feature) and the Prix du Publique (most popular entry) at the 1988 Cannes Film Festival. *Mississippi Masala* (1991), a cross-cultural, interracial romance that won three awards at the Venice Film Festival, explored the lives of Indian refugees from Uganda resettled in the U.S., while *The Perez Family* (1995), traced the lives of Cuban immigrants in the U.S. *Kama Sutra: A Tale of Love* (1996) was a controversial look at female sexuality in ancient India, but the movie bombed. With *My Own Country* (1998), a real-life account of a young Indian doctor tackling the start of the AIDS epidemic in the American South, Nair returned to familiar ground, capturing the expatriate experience on celluloid. She followed with another documentary, *The Laughing Club of India* (1999).

When not making movies, Nair was an adjunct assistant professor at Columbia University in New York City, where she lived with her second husband, Ugandan-born political scientist Mahmood Mamdani, and their son.

(SHALAKA PARADKAR)

Osbourne, Ozzy

On April 12, 2002, Ozzy Osbourne, rock singer and protagonist of the television reality show *The Osbournes*, gained his star on Hollywood's Walk of Fame. Although he had enjoyed a successful career of more than 30 years as a heavy metal vocalist, it was not until the triumph of MTV's *The Osbournes* during the 2001–02 television season that Osbourne achieved Hollywood recognition. In less than two months on the air, the show had become the third-highest-rated offering on cable TV and had the highest-rated series premiere in MTV's 20-year history.

John Osbourne was born on Dec. 3, 1948, in Birmingham, Eng. Raised in a working-class family, he dropped out of school at 15 and held several low-paying jobs. He also engaged in petty crime and at 17 was imprisoned for two months for burglary. After his release, he sang in a number of local rock groups, eventually forming the rock band Earth with guitarist

© Reuters 2002

Superstars of heavy metal and popular TV, the Osbournes

Tony Iommi. To avoid confusion with another band of the same name, the group changed its name to Black Sabbath—after an old Boris Karloff movie. The group developed a grinding, ominous sound, based on the blues but intensely amplified, and drew attention with its tendency to reference the occult in its lyrics. In February 1970 Black Sabbath released its self-titled first album and quickly developed a following in both Britain and the U.S.

The band released albums each year, except 1974, through the mid-1970s. After the tour for *Never Say Die* (1978), Osbourne left the band. A period of despair and drug abuse led to Osbourne's divorce from his first wife, Thelma Mayfair. He then met and married Sharon Arden, who encouraged him to start a career as a solo artist. His first effort, achieved with the primary help of guitarist Randy Rhoads, was *Blizzard of Ozz* (1980). A multiplatinum success, it was followed by the equally popular *Diary of a Madman* (1981), which sold more than five million copies. On the tour for the album, thinking that someone in the audience had thrown him a rubber toy, Osbourne bit into the head of a live bat, after which he was vaccinated for rabies.

Osbourne broadened his fan base with *No More Tears* (1991); one of the album's songs, "Mama, I'm Coming Home," became his first solo top 40 hit. In 1993 he won a Grammy Award for best metal performance for the song "I Don't Want to Change the World." Despite announcing his retirement in 1992, he continued recording through the decade. By the end of the 1990s, Osbourne had reunited the original members of Black Sabbath for a new album and tour, and in 1999 the band won a Grammy for best metal performance for the song "Iron Man."

The success of *The Osbournes* gained more than the Hollywood star for Ozzy and his family. In May the family sold world rights to two books for more than $3 million, and in June Epic Records released *The Osbourne Family Album*, which featured the favourite songs of each family member. Eager to retain its most popular show, MTV signed a reported $20 million contract with the family for another 20 episodes.

(DAVID R. CALHOUN)

Patchett, Ann

The novel *Bel Canto* (2001) won two awards in 2002 for American writer Ann Patchett. The book was chosen for the PEN/Faulkner Award, honouring works of fiction by contemporary writers, and it received the Orange Prize for Fiction, given to a work by a woman published in the U.K. It had also been a finalist for the National Book Critics Circle Award in 2001. The novel, which was set in a Latin American country, explores relationships between terrorists and hostages who, shut off from the rest of the world, find unexpected bonds. Like the author's previous three novels, *Bel Canto* was well received by both readers and critics, and it confirmed Patchett's prominence among contemporary writers.

Patchett was born on Dec. 2, 1963, in Los Angeles. When she was six years old, she and her mother and sister moved to Nashville, Tenn., where she grew up and where she made her home. She obtained a B.A. degree (1984) from Sarah Lawrence College, Bronxville, N.Y., and an M.F.A. (1987) from the University of Iowa. Her first fiction was published while she was an undergraduate. She held appointments at colleges and universities, including the position of Tennessee Williams fellow in creative writing at the University of the South in Nashville in 1997. From the beginning of her career, she won numerous awards for her writing, and in 1994 she received a Guggenheim fellowship.

Although Patchett published many stories and short pieces of nonfiction, it was for her novels that she became best known. Her first novel, *The Patron Saint of Liars* (1992), tells the story of a young pregnant woman who leaves the husband she does not love to travel to a home for unwed mothers. There, as her feelings change and she creates a new family, so do her plans for the future. The novel was adapted as a television movie in 1997. In *Taft* (1994) the black manager of a blues bar who is mourning the loss of his son finds a new family when he hires a young white woman, Fay Taft, and becomes involved in the problems of her brother, Carl. The author also wrote a screen adaptation of the novel. *The Magician's Assistant* (1997) tells of the discoveries of the widow of a homosexual magician named Parsifal. The woman, who also had been her husband's assistant, visits the family he had never told her of and learns about his past. One of the hostages in *Bel Canto* is a renowned operatic diva, and music becomes the medium by which the people of the novel communicate. As in Patchett's earlier novels, the characters are surprised to discover friendship, and even love, for one another.

(ROBERT RAUCH)

Pechstein, Claudia

When the Winter Olympics in Salt Lake City, Utah, ended on Feb. 24, 2002, Claudia Pechstein of Germany had carved out a remarkable place for herself in the history of long-track speed skating. Pechstein took the gold medal in the 3,000-m and 5,000-m finals, 13 days apart, winning both with world-record performances. She thus raised her career total to four golds among seven Olympic medals.

By capturing the 5,000-m Olympic gold for the third time in succession, Pechstein also

Speedy skater Claudia Pechstein pauses to acknowledge the gold.

became only the second skater in history (after American Bonnie Blair) to make a successful defense of an Olympic title twice. She did so with rare consistency, posting lap times within a narrow range of 32.05–32.48 sec on all 11 laps of the 400-m track after the first 600 m of the race. Pechstein finished off a brilliant effort in 6 min 46.91 sec—a 5½-second improvement on the former world standard.

In the 3,000-m final, she hit the finish line in 3 min 57.70 sec, taking 1½ seconds off the former world record she had set 11 months earlier in Nagano, Japan. Pechstein was the only skater in the field who covered each lap of the race faster than 32 seconds and the first skater ever to cover 3,000 m in less than 4 minutes. Her victory in Salt Lake City marked the second time that she had beaten the 4-minute barrier and the fifth world-record performance of her career.

Pechstein had taken home at least one medal from each of the four Winter Olympics in which she participated, starting with the 5,000-m bronze in Albertville, France, in 1992. She won her first Olympic gold two years later, finishing first in the 5,000 m in Lillehammer, Nor., where she also won her second bronze, for the 3,000 m. At the 1998 Winter Olympics in Nagano, Pechstein repeated her gold-medal performance at the 5,000 m and took silver in the 3,000 m.

Pechstein was born in East Berlin on Feb. 22, 1972. She began figure skating at age three and switched to speed skating at age nine. She first came on the international scene at 16, when she finished second overall in the 1988 world junior speed-skating championships in Seoul, S.Kor. During much of her career, she skated in the shadow of her teammate Gunda Niemann-Stirnemann, whom she beat for the gold by 0.04 sec in Nagano, in the closest women's 5,000 m in Olympic history. In 2000 Pechstein won the overall world speed-skating championship, having finished second to her compatriot in each of the previous four years. She finished second to an-

other teammate, Anni Friesinger, in 2001 and third behind Friesinger and Canadian Cindy Klassen in 2002, but in Salt Lake City Pechstein was unquestionably number one.

(RON REID)

Pitt, Harvey

As corporate accounting scandals emerged on an alarmingly frequent basis in the U.S. during much of 2002, Harvey Pitt, chairman of the Securities and Exchange Commission (SEC), found himself the target of withering criticism. Prominent leaders on both sides of the political aisle claimed that Pitt had been lax in enforcing SEC rules and questioned whether, as a former securities lawyer who had performed work for virtually all of the nation's major accounting firms, Pitt enjoyed too cozy of a relationship with the subjects of his agency's oversight. In a widely publicized op-ed column for the *New York Times* that appeared in early July, U.S. Sen. John McCain described the chairman's response to the accounting abuses as "slow and tepid" and joined the chorus of those calling for his resignation. Pitt hardly helped his own cause when he later asked Congress to elevate his office to a cabinet-level post and to grant him a pay raise of more than 20%. His request for a promotion and raise was denied, though the White House steadfastly refused to criticize the chairman, an appointee of Pres. George W. Bush. For his part, Pitt maintained that the SEC was the most effective ever in ensuring corporate responsibility. He pointed specifically to new SEC measures that required top executives to certify personally their companies' financial results; executives who failed to do so faced criminal as well as civil liability.

Pitt was born on Feb. 28, 1945, in Brooklyn, N.Y. He earned a B.A. from the City University of New York in 1965 and a J.D. from St. John's University School of Law, Jamaica, N.Y., in 1968. For the next 10 years, he worked as an attorney for the SEC. In 1975, at the age of 29, he was named the SEC's youngest-ever general counsel, a post he held until 1978, when he left the commission to enter private practice.

Over the next two decades, Pitt built a reputation as one of the most capable securities lawyers in the nation. At the Washington, D.C., law firm of Fried, Frank, Harris, Shriver and Jacobson—where he eventually rose to become partner—he had a client list of more than 100 firms and individuals. Some of those clients, most notably the giant accounting firm Arthur Andersen, would later come under SEC investigation. After President Bush tapped him to become SEC chairman in August 2001, Pitt made it a policy to recuse himself from cases involving former law clients. Although intended to avoid conflicts of interest, this policy left the chairman open to questions regarding his ability to crack down on corporate abuses. Pitt reversed course in 2002, deciding that he would participate in SEC cases even if they involved former clients. He also led the charge to create a comprehensive new oversight board to help regulate the accounting industry, but his appointment of former Central Intelligence Agency director William

Webster to head this board ultimately proved disastrous. Pitt resigned his SEC post on November 5 after it was revealed that Webster had served as chief of the audit committee for a small public company, U.S. Technologies Inc., accused by its investors of fraud.

(SHERMAN HOLLAR)

Polkinghorne, John

When British physicist John Polkinghorne resigned one of the most prestigious academic positions in his field to become an Anglican priest, many of his colleagues were taken by surprise. The move, however, reflected his long-standing interest in matters of science and of faith. His contributions to these two worlds were recognized when he was awarded the 2002 Templeton Prize for Progress Toward Research or Discoveries About Spiritual Realities. Science and religion are "complementary to each other," Polkinghorne said in accepting the honour. "The most important thing that they have in common is that both believe that there is a truth to be sought and found, a truth whose attainment comes through the pursuit of well-motivated belief."

John Charlton Polkinghorne was born on Oct. 16, 1930, in Weston-super-Mare, Somerset, Eng., to a quietly devout Church of England family. His mathematical ability was evident as a youngster. He earned a B.A. in mathematics as well as doctorates in quantum field theory and theoretical elementary particle physics from Trinity College, Cambridge. He was appointed lecturer in mathematical physics at the University of Edinburgh in 1956. He took the same position at Cambridge two years later and in 1968 was elevated to professor of mathematical physics.

Polkinghorne's creation of mathematical models to calculate the paths of quantum particles was recognized in 1974 with his selection as a fellow of the Royal Society. Five years later Polkinghorne concluded that "I had done my little bit for science, and it was time to do something different." He resigned his post at Cambridge and began theological studies. He was ordained in 1982 and assigned to a parish in South Bristol. He became vicar of a parish in Blean in 1984 and two years later was appointed fellow, dean, and chaplain of Trinity Hall, Cambridge. In 1989 he was appointed president of Queens' College, Cambridge, from which he retired in 1996.

In 1983 Polkinghorne published *The Way the World Is*, in which he explained how a thinking person can be a Christian. It was the first of several works on the relationship between science and religion. *The Faith of a Physicist: Reflections of a Bottom-Up Thinker* appeared in 1994 and *Faith, Science and Understanding* in 2000. Polkinghorne was one of the founders of the Society of Ordained Scientists, a preaching order of the Anglican Communion. He was also a member of the Science Research Council, the Doctrine Commission of the Church of England, and the Human Genetics Advisory Commission. Polkinghorne was knighted by Queen Elizabeth II in 1997 for distinguished service to science, religion, learning, and medical ethics.

(DARRELL J. TURNER)

Prada, Miuccia

Though retail analysts predicted a plunge in the sale of luxury goods following the Sept. 11, 2001, terrorist attacks in the U.S., Italian designer Miuccia Prada confounded the fashion industry by forging ahead in 2002 with a three-year expansion plan that had begun with the 2001 opening of her company's new flagship megashop, in a retail zone that had been hit the hardest—downtown Manhattan. Prada's sweeping retail space was designed by the Rotterdam, Neth.-based Office for Metropolitan Architecture, headed by Dutch architect Rem Koolhaas. Prada's $40-million self-described "epicentre" was a futuristic temple to the brand. Its floors were made of zebrawood; a circular glass elevator doubled as a space to display Prada merchandise; and glass fitting rooms became private (opaque) or public (translucent) with the flip of a switch. Meanwhile, inside the dressing room a computer could educate the customer with facts about Prada's merchandise—which included a mix of new clothes for the season, items from past collections, and vintage Prada. The merchandise was housed in the basement of the shop, which was designed to replicate the atmosphere of a stockroom. As a result, Prada's megashop could be utilized in the evening for artistic endeavours—showcasing performance art, screening independent films, and staging theatrical productions. Though Prada insisted that sales were not the focal point of her space, her Manhattan shop took in $500,000 on its first day of business.

Prada was born in 1949 in Milan. She obtained a doctorate in political science from the Università degli Studi, Milan, flirted briefly with communism, and studied mime for five years at Milan's Teatro Piccolo before in 1978 reluctantly taking the helm of Fratelli Prada with her husband, Patrizio Bertelli. The company had been founded in 1913 by her grandfather, Mario Prada. It had sold expensive luggage to European aristocrats but had lost its clientele.

As the creative force behind the revival of the company, Prada produced unique styles in clothing, footwear, and accessories. For one of her first designs, she fashioned a handbag out of an unconventional fabric combination—she blended expensive leather with Pocono, an industrial nylon fabric that was used to make military tents. In 1989 she produced a line of ready-to-wear, fashioning skirts and jackets using Pocono. Prada's concept of casual luxury caught on, and in the early 1990s the Prada brand developed a cult fashion following. Its products, emblazoned with the Prada-embossed silver triangle, were instantly recognizable. By 2001 Prada's sales had swelled to $1.5 billion.

The success of the company was a collaborative effort, however. Prada drew on the talents of several technical designers as well as those of Bertelli. She and her team also designed the spin-off lines Miu Miu, Granello, and Prada Sport. In 1999 Prada acquired Jil Sander, Helmut Lang, a stake in British shoe manufacturer Church & Co., Azzedine Alaia, and part of Fendi (the latter was sold to LVMH Moët Hennessy Louis Vuitton in 2001). Though

the company continued to make plans for expansion, the economic downturn forced Prada to postpone its planned initial public offering.

(BRONWYN COSGRAVE)

Radcliffe, Paula

In October 2002 British distance runner Paula Radcliffe cut 89 seconds from the women's world record for the marathon, the biggest improvement in the event in more than 17 years. Radcliffe's historic 2-hr 17-min 18-sec performance at the Chicago Marathon followed her first-ever marathon in April in London, where her winning time of 2 hr 18 min 56 sec was a debut record, just 9 seconds shy of the world record set by Kenyan Catherine Ndereba in Chicago in 2001. In 2002 Ndereba finished a distant second.

Radcliffe was born on Dec. 17, 1973, in Northwich, Cheshire. Her great-aunt Charlotte Radcliffe had won an Olympic swimming silver medal in the 4 × 100-m freestyle relay in 1920, and Paula cheered on her recreational runner father at the 1985 London Marathon, in which Norwegian Ingrid Kristiansen won the woman's race in a then world record 2 hr 21 min 6 sec.

Radcliffe soon emerged as a teenage running talent. She won the world junior cross-country title in 1992 and then entered a period of steady but sometimes frustrating progress in global track championships. Seventh in the world championships 3,000 m in 1993, she moved up to fifth in the 5,000 m in the 1995 world championships and the 1996 Olympic Games. In 1997 she advanced to fourth in the 5,000 m. In 1998 she ran a debut-record track 10,000 m of 30 min 48.58 sec. The next year, with her characteristic head-bobbing gait and eyes rolling back with the effort, she set the pace in the world championships 10,000 m in Seville, Spain. She was passed on the last lap by Gete Wami of Ethiopia and finished second in 30 min 27.13 sec. She pushed the pace again in the 2000 Olympic 10,000 m, setting up an Olympic record for winner Derartu Tulu of Ethiopia but finishing fourth herself. Later that year Radcliffe won the world half-marathon title, which signaled that her future might lie in the longer distances.

Radcliffe won a world cross-country long-course gold in March 2001, a title she successfully defended in early 2002. She again finished fourth in the 2001 track world championships 10,000 m; she then charted a course toward the marathon, training in the Pyrenees, where she logged up to 225-km (about 140-mi) per week in training. After the London Marathon, she won two gold medals within 10 days at the 2002 Commonwealth Games (5,000 m) and European championships (where she ran history's second fastest women's 10,000 m in drenching rain). An outspoken opponent of doping in sport, Radcliffe two days before the Chicago race insisted on being administered her fifth out-of-competition drug test of the year. Radcliffe was named female athlete of the year by the International Association of Athletics Federations, *Track & Field News*, and the British Athletics Writers Association, and on November 5 she was awarded an MBE for services to athletics.

(SIEG LINDSTROM)

Raffarin, Jean-Pierre

When newly re-elected Pres. Jacques Chirac named Jean-Pierre Raffarin prime minister of France on May 6, 2002, fewer than half the French people knew who the latter was. That, of course, was the Gaullist president's point.

After five years of having to share power with the Socialists, Chirac wanted a premier who not only would not eclipse him but also would be as far re-moved as possible from the traditional arrogant Parisian image of past prime ministers. In short, the president was looking for a modest provincial, and he appeared to find him in Raffarin, a man of rumpled suits and little swagger who had a political base in western France. Raffarin's only previous national ministerial experience was looking after small business in 1995–97, and the only mark he had left was legislation that made it harder for big supermarkets to expand at the expense of small corner shops.

In his first months as prime minister, Raffarin cultivated the image of being open to, and part of, *la France d'en bas*—the France of ordinary people—and of being guilelessly determined to improve their lot. The reality of his background was slightly different. He was born on Aug. 3, 1948, at Poitiers. His father had been a member of the National Assembly and a government minister, responsible for agriculture.

Raffarin was educated in Poitiers and Paris, with law studies followed by a business school diploma. He became a product manager for the Jacques Vabre coffee business, but he was quickly attracted into centre-right politics by Pres. Valéry Giscard d'Estaing and spent five years (1976–81) as a political appointee in the Labour Ministry. After the Socialist victory in 1981, Raffarin returned to marketing with the Bernard Krief management consultants, where his speciality was development strategies for towns and local authorities. He had entered local politics in Poitiers in the late 1970s, and by 1988 he was president of the regional council for the Poitou-Charentes region.

Until elevated into the premiership, Raffarin had little experience of national elections. His election in 1989 to the European Parliament was through a system that depended more on a candidate's position on his party list than on individual merit, while the French Senate, to which he was elected in 1995 and 1997, used indirect voting. Raffarin placed himself in the middle of the fragmented political world of the French right. He rose through the centre-right Union for French Democracy, but after the first round of the 2002 presidential election, he was quick to support Chirac's new Union for Presidential Majority.

As prime minister, Raffarin proved a pragmatic number two to Chirac. He cut income tax and restrained growth in the minimum wage, but moved very cautiously on partial privatization of state utilities, pension reform, and civil service cuts. Similarly, Raffarin would not let his former Europeanism prevent his government from opposing reforms to European Union farming and fishing regulations.

(DAVID BUCHAN)

Ravalomanana, Marc

Throughout 2002 the African island nation of Madagascar continued to reel from the disputed presidential elections of December 2001. A court-ordered recount was required for decision to be reached on the close contest between challenger Marc Ravalomanana, mayor of the capital city of Antananarivo, and Didier Ratsiraka, the sitting president for more than two decades. In the first round of voting, Ravalomanana's lead over Ratsiraka appeared narrow enough to require a runoff vote (required when neither candidate wins a majority), but Ravalomanana refused and declared outright victory. Outside the country observers cried foul, while inside the country two men established presidencies on parallel tracks.

Ravalomanana, a self-made millionaire whose political experience was short, had gained the reputation as a bold manager while mayor of Antananarivo. Though he was remembered for having bulldozed inhabited houses during a massive urban-restoration project, he had the backing of the capital city, where followers launched a general strike in January 2002. By March it still was not clear who was in charge of Madagascar; Ravalomanana proceeded to name a cabinet, and Ratsiraka imposed martial law. Ordering a recount in April, the Supreme Court ruled that Ravalomanana had indeed won more than 50% of the vote. Supporters of each candidate continued to clash for several months, though, as the country teetered on the cusp of civil war. Defenders of Ratsiraka, concentrated in the city of Tamatave, attempted to blockade Antananarivo, and fears loomed that political fighting would devolve into ethnic conflict.

Midway through the year, however, Ravalomanana slowly consolidated his control outside Antananarivo, particularly in rural areas, where his appeal was low. After Ravalomanana's administration was recognized by France and the United States, Ratsiraka went into exile in July. Later that month, however, the African Union (AU) declared the 2001 elections "unconstitutional" and placed Madagascar in suspension. Hoping to appease the AU and bring greater stability to the country, Ravalomanana announced his intentions to stem corruption by vastly raising the salaries of his ministers and by dissolving the parliament in anticipation of new elections to the National Assembly in December. With these changes, it was hoped that the AU would readmit Madagascar in January 2003 at its extraordinary summit.

Ravalomanana was born in 1949 near Antananarivo, Madagascar, French Union. He had a Protestant education, first by missionaries in his native village of Imerikasina and then at a Protestant school in Sweden. Returning to Antananarivo, he launched a family venture selling homemade yogurt, which quickly grew into a booming business. In less than two years, with assistance from the Protestant church, he secured a loan from the World Bank to purchase his first factory, and he soon had a monopoly of dairy and oil products. Just prior to his presidential bid, he had developed the company, TIKO, into the largest domestically owned business in Madagascar, with some 3,000 employees. (TOM MICHAEL)

Reich-Ranicki, Marcel

Marcel Reich-Ranicki, Polish-born German literary critic, capped a brilliant career in August 2002 when he was handed the Goethe Prize for literary achievement. Just prior to celebrating his 80th birthday, the outspoken critic found himself in a literary maelstrom not of his own making. Newspaper editor Frank Schirrmacher had begun a bookman's donnybrook by lobbing charges of anti-Semitism at author Martin Walser for his roman à clef *Tod eines Kritikers*, about a disgruntled author who seeks to assassinate a critic widely believed to have been modeled on Reich-Ranicki. The real-life critic, who later echoed Schirrmacher's assessment of Walser, was accustomed to being at the centre of literary debate. He was the confrontational host of the popular television show *Das literarische Quartett* and in 1999 had published an autobiography, *Mein Leben*, that remained a best-seller in Germany for more than a year. An English translation of the book, entitled *The Author of Himself*, appeared to wide acclaim at the end of 2001.

Imagine a Harold Bloom with the clout of Oprah Winfrey; Reich-Ranicki had an enormous effect on the reading public in the German-speaking areas. This was a critic who praised and denounced with equal verve, ending as well as launching writing careers. *Das literarische Quartett* pitted the plain-speaking host in debate with guest editors and critics rather than writers, whom Reich-Ranicki preferred to let speak through their books.

One of Reich-Ranicki's ongoing complaints was the abstruse seriousness of German literature, and few authors were immune to his acidic commentary. Even Günter Grass, the dominant voice in German literature of the past half century, endured his stinging censure. In 1995 Reich-Ranicki appeared on the cover of the Germany news weekly *Der Spiegel* literally tearing apart a copy of Grass's novel on German reunification, *Ein weites Feld* (1995), which he derided as "miserable." Nevertheless, Reich-Ranicki, who preferred Grass's *Katz und Maus* (1961) to his debut masterwork *Die Blechtrommel* (1959), thought him most deserving of the Nobel Prize for Literature in 1999.

Reich-Ranicki was born on June 2, 1920, in Wloclawek, Pol., and was raised in Berlin by Jewish parents who, during the Nazi persecution of Jews in World War II, were confined to the Warsaw ghetto and then killed in the concentration camp at Treblinka. With his wife, whom he had met in the ghetto, Reich-Ranicki evaded the Nazis by hiding with a sympathetic family outside the city. After the war he worked for Polish intelligence in London before returning to communist Warsaw, where he contributed to the counterculture journal *Nowa kultura* (later *Kultura*). In 1958 he resettled in West Germany, and he wrote columns for the moderate news weekly *Die Zeit* in Hamburg from 1960 until 1973, when he became the literary editor of the conservative news daily *Frankfurter Allgemeine Zeitung*. In 1988 he launched his television program, which later boasted almost a million viewers. (*Das literarische Quartett* was canceled in December 2001 after a 13-year run.) Reich-Ranicki wrote many critical books on German and Polish literature; among those translated into English was *Thomas Mann and His Family* (1987).   (TOM MICHAEL)

Rice, Condoleezza

Developments between Russia and the U.S. in 2002 bore the mark of Condoleezza Rice, national security adviser to Pres. George W. Bush. This was particularly evident in June when, with only minor protests from the Russian government, the U.S. formally withdrew from the 1972 Antiballistic Missile Treaty, which would have prohibited the development of a missile defense system. Rice had begun to prepare the way for the U.S. action with a visit to Moscow in August 2001, the first high-ranking member of the Bush administration to travel to Russia. The quick and relatively smooth U.S. withdrawal from the treaty, unthinkable only a few years before, was taken as a measure of her skill and influence. Opposed to U.S. participation in peacekeeping missions and a public supporter of the proposal to overthrow Iraqi Pres. Saddam Hussein, she was considered to be aligned with the hard-liners on the Bush foreign policy and defense staffs.

Rice was born on Nov. 14, 1954, in Birmingham, Ala. Her father was a minister and college administrator and her mother a pianist and teacher. The family later moved to Denver, Colo., and at age 15 Rice entered the University of Denver. Although she had earlier

Condoleezza Rice, the most powerful woman in the U.S.

considered a career as a concert pianist, in college she turned to the study of international relations, earning a bachelor's degree in the field in 1974. She obtained a master's degree in economics from the University of Notre Dame in 1975 and a doctorate in international studies from the University of Denver in 1981, where her speciality was Eastern and Central Europe and the Soviet Union, including military and security affairs. Rice joined the faculty of Stanford University in 1981 and in 1984 received an award for her teaching. In 1986 she served as an assistant to the Joint Chiefs of Staff on nuclear strategy, and during the administration of Pres. George H.W. Bush she was director for Soviet and Eastern European affairs for the National Security Council (NSC) and a special assistant to the president.

In 1991 Rice returned to Stanford, and in 1993 she was again honoured with an award for teaching. In 1993 she began a six-year tenure as provost, during which time she balanced the university's budget and revamped the curriculum for undergraduates. She was a fellow of the Hoover Institution and a member of the American Academy of Arts and Sciences. Writings included the book *Germany Unified and Europe Transformed* (1995; with Philip Zelikow) and many articles. In 1999 she left Stanford to become foreign policy adviser to the Bush campaign, and upon his election she was named head of the NSC, the first woman to hold the position. Though Rice seemed largely out of view following the 2001 terrorist attacks in the U.S., by 2002 she was playing a prominent role in foreign policy and frequently traveling with the president.
          (ROBERT RAUCH)

Richter, Gerhard

German artist Gerhard Richter had long been an influential and respected figure in Europe, but his work and reputation was not as well known in the U.S.—that is, until a major retrospective of his work, representing 40 years of his output, opened at the Museum of Modern Art, New York City, in February 2002. In Berlin "Gerhard Richter: Acht Grau" was on exhibit from October to January 2003 at the Deutsche Guggenheim.

Richter was born in Dresden, Ger., on Feb. 9, 1932. His father and two uncles served in the German army during World War II, and Richter himself participated in the Hitler Youth; the national struggles of this period would deeply impact Richter personally and artistically. In 1952 he began four years of study at the Dresden Art Academy; in 1961 he managed to move from Soviet-occupied East Berlin to Düsseldorf, where he continued his art studies. His years in Düsseldorf coincided with the rise of Pop art, a style that had begun to eclipse Abstract Expressionism on the international scene. In 1962 Richter abandoned abstraction (though he would make abstract works again at later points in his career) in favour of representational paintings based on photographs and rendered in gray, black, and white. This brand of German Pop art—or "Capitalist Realism," as it came to be called by Richter and fellow Düsseldorf artists Konrad Lueg and Sigmar Polke—was less

Artist-philosopher Gerhard Richter

buoyant, colourful, and cartoonish than American or British Pop art.

Richter courted controversy when he took one of the most divisive events of postwar Germany as the subject of a series of works begun in 1988. His *October 18, 1977* series consisted of 15 paintings based on forensic photographs of a group of German radicals who had died under mysterious circumstances in a Stuttgart prison. The works, which featured multiple images of corpses, were among the most complex and affecting of Richter's oeuvre.

Richter was described as an artist-philosopher who confronted the nature of perception and the fundamental questions of representation in general. His innovation and originality resided in his contribution to painting—a medium that had been pronounced "dead" as many times as it had been stirred into "revival." Never completely abandoning it, the artist consistently sought ways of keeping the medium relevant. His combination of various tropes of painting and photography created a kind of representational problem to be worked out: how and when does the eye sense the difference between a painted surface and the photographically recorded? His paintings were referred to as models of perception, and, indeed, Richter's work is as much about the act of looking and the apprehension of images as any other subject; in fact, perception might be his subject.   (MEGHAN DAILEY)

Rifbjerg, Klaus

Denmark's literary bel esprit, Klaus Rifbjerg, responded to the terrorist attacks of Sept. 11, 2001, in the U.S. and the pivotal Danish general election of Nov. 20, 2001, with a political commentary, "Tidsmaskinen. En rutsjebaneførers bekendelser" (2002). Rifbjerg's essay covered a brief span of time—the four months after the attacks until Jan. 7, 2002—and addressed what had changed, what had not, and where Denmark might be headed. In a Feb. 17, 2002, essay that appeared in the newspaper *Politiken*, he took the pulse of Danish society again with "Hvordan har vi det?".

Rifbjerg, who adeptly alternated between

fantasy and realistic forms of writing, marked his 70th birthday in 2001 with a novel, *Regnvejr*, and a collection of prose poems, *70 epifanier*. In addition, that year new editions of his work were published—*Den søde kløe*, a volume of journal commentaries from *Information* and *Politiken; Rifbjergs digte*, and *Oven over alting—og andre noveller*, a collection that illustrated Rifbjerg's talent for capturing moments at the heart of memory. In 2001 Rifbjerg also edited an anthology of essays, *Den kulturradikale udfordring—en antologi*, and he claimed the prize from the Mother Tongue Society. Ever energetic, creative, and prolific, Rifbjerg added *Nansen og Johansen. Et vintereventyr* (2002) to his impressive oeuvre that encompassed all genres and spanned nearly 50 years.

Klaus Thorvald Rifbjerg was born on Dec. 15, 1931, on Amager, an island-suburb of Copenhagen. He attended Vestre Borgerdydskole, where he wrote plays and revues. In 1950 he received a scholarship to attend Princeton University; his one-year stay there led to an appreciation of American literature and influenced his decision to become a writer. Thereafter he worked as a reviewer for *Information* and *Politiken*.

Rifbjerg made his mark as a poet with *Under vejr med mig selv: en utidig selvbiografi* (1956); the impulsive and innovative poems of the collection focused on life passages. Rifbjerg's first novel, *Den kroniske uskyld* (1958), dealt with puberty and became a modern classic. Later works included poetry, plays, short stories, journal articles, and novels, one of which, *Anna (jeg) Anna* (1969, *Anna (I) Anna* [1982]), won the 1970 Nordic Council Literature Prize. In the 1970s and '80s, he penned several romans à clef that were replete with abundant humour and irony. He explored his own life in poetry and prose in *Huset, eller hvad der gjorde størst indtryk på mig i det tyvende århundrede* (2000). Other literary awards included the Grand Prize of the Danish Academy and the Golden Laurels of the Danish Booksellers' Association. In 1967 he became a member of the Danish Academy. From 1984 to 1992 Rifbjerg served as literary director for Gyldendal Publishers. Though he and his wife resided in Málaga, Spain, they maintained a summer home in Kandestederne, Den. (LANAE HJORTSVANG ISAACSON)

Roh Moo Hyun

South Koreans went to the polls on Dec. 19, 2002, and handed Roh Moo Hyun, a former opposition party leader, a narrow victory over Lee Hoi Chang in a tightly contested presidential race. Roh's campaign had been championed by the outgoing president, Kim Dae Jung, who had also been a prominent opposition leader before his election to the country's top political post in 1997. Roh, who favoured negotiations with—rather than the isolation of—North Korea and who

had shown a willingness to criticize U.S. foreign policy, benefited from a sharp rise in anti-American sentiment in South Korea. He garnered 48.9% of the vote to Lee's 46.6%. Roh would serve a nonrenewable five-year term; his inauguration was set for February 2003.

Roh was born on Aug. 6, 1946, in rural Kimhae county, just west of the city of Pusan, in southeastern Korea. His family was poor, and he had to work as a night watchman in high school. He did not attend college, yet he studied for the bar exam on his own. He passed the bar and was appointed a judge. Later he became a highly respected human rights lawyer defending student protesters accused of being pro-communist.

In the late 1980s Roh entered politics at the invitation of then opposition leader Kim Young Sam. He won a seat in the National Assembly in 1988 and impressed his countrymen with his criticism of the military regime of Pres. Chun Doo Hwan. In 1990 he split with his party when Kim Young Sam made an alliance with general-turned-president Roh Tae Woo. The alliance led to Kim's election as president, and Roh's political fortunes seemed to crumble. He lost his seat in the National Assembly in 1992 and failed to regain it in 1996. He also lost a bid to become mayor of Pusan in 1995. Nevertheless, Roh held onto his pro-democracy principles and refused to compromise with the pro-military party. He eventually led a small opposition party into an alliance with Kim Dae Jung, and when Kim came to power in 1997, Roh served in his cabinet.

Keys to Roh's successful campaign were his appeal to young voters, his position of openness toward North Korea, and his criticism of U.S. policy toward the Korean peninsula. In

particular, Roh's rejection of U.S. Pres. George W. Bush's designation of North Korea as part of an "axis of evil" along with Iran and Iraq found resonance with many voters. Days after his election victory, Roh reiterated his call for the use of diplomacy in persuading North Korea to abandon its nuclear weapons program. (MARK PETERSON)

Ronaldo

One of the greatest comebacks in association football (soccer) history was achieved by Brazilian forward Ronaldo in the 2002 Fédération Internationale de Football Association (FIFA) World Cup. Ronaldo, who had been named FIFA's Player of the Year in 1996 and 1997, had played poorly in the 1998 World Cup final (which Brazil lost 3–0 to France) when he was not fully fit following a never properly explained prematch illness. Then he had two knee operations that kept him out of the game for almost two years, and it was feared that his career was over. He was back on the Brazilian team for the 2002 World Cup, however, and scored both goals in the 2–0 final victory over Germany. Ronaldo was awarded the Golden Boot as the tournament's top scorer, with eight goals. In 1998 he had scored four goals in the World Cup finals; in 1994, although he was picked for the World Cup squad, he did not play.

Ronaldo Luiz Nazario de Lima was born Sept. 22, 1976, in Itaguai, Braz., and grew up in the poor Rio de Janeiro suburb of Bento Ribeiro. He began playing football as a junior for the neighbourhood Social Ramos Club at age 12 and two years later joined São Cristovão in the Carioca League. By 1992 he was playing in the Brazilian championship for Cruzeiro. Ronaldo joined the national side in

It feels like flying to Ronaldo, victorious in the World Cup.

AP/Wide World Photos

1994, and by 2002 he had scored 45 goals in 65 international appearances for his country.

Ronaldo was transferred in 1994 from Cruzeiro to PSV Eindhoven of The Netherlands, where he scored 55 goals in 56 games and won the 1995 league championship and the 1996 Dutch Cup. During only one season with Barcelona (1996–97), he scored 34 goals, captured the Spanish Super Cup, and scored the only goal in Barcelona's 1–0 defeat of Paris Saint-Germain in the European Cup-Winners Cup. In 1997 Internazionale (Inter Milan) paid a then-record $27 million to move Ronaldo to Italy, despite an unsuccessful petition by Barcelona that claimed the transfer violated FIFA rules. At Inter his infectious gap-toothed smile and knack for scoring goals earned him the nickname "Il Fenomeno" until the career-threatening knee injury in 1999 left him on the sidelines. Shortly after the 2002 World Cup, Ronaldo announced that he was abandoning Inter for Real Madrid. After much wrangling, Real agreed to pay a transfer fee of €47 million (about $46.3 million). A muscle pull Ronaldo suffered in early September delayed his debut with his new team, but in his first appearance in early October, the talented striker scored two goals. In December Ronaldo gained double honours when he was named European Footballer of the Year (an award he also had received in 1997), and, once again, FIFA Player of the Year. (ERIC WEIL)

Rumsfeld, Donald

U.S. Secretary of Defense Donald Rumsfeld was no stranger to controversy in 2002. Besides overseeing the largest buildup in U.S. defense spending since the presidency of Ronald Reagan, he presided over the short life and the death of the Pentagon's Office of Strategic Information (OSI), which was created following the terrorist attacks of Sept. 11, 2001. Although the OSI's purpose was to create a favourable view of the U.S. military in foreign countries, concerns grew in Congress and the media that the office might initiate propaganda campaigns. In February 2002 Rumsfeld stated that such criticism was "off the mark" but that he was closing the OSI anyway because of the damage done to its credibility. Then, in May, he announced he was canceling the $11 billion Crusader artillery program because the self-propelled gun was far too heavy to airlift easily to distant theatres of war. The Crusader was a major acquisition program for the army and had been eight years in development. In June Rumsfeld undertook a diplomatic mission to South Asia to avert a possible war between nuclear-armed India and Pakistan. During the trip he infuriated Pakistani officials by claiming that al-Qaeda terrorists were active in the disputed Kashmir region between the two countries. Later he publicly acknowledged that his claim was speculative.

Donald Henry Rumsfeld was born in Chicago on July 9, 1932. After graduating from Princeton University (A.B., 1954), he served three years as an aviator in the U.S. Navy. He was elected to the U.S. House of Representatives in 1962 and was subsequently reelected three times. He resigned from Congress in 1969 to head Pres. Richard Nixon's Office of Economic Opportunity. In 1973–74 Rumsfeld was Nixon's ambassador to NATO.

Under Pres. Gerald R. Ford, Rumsfeld served first as White House chief of staff (1974–75), then as secretary of defense (1975–77), the youngest person ever to hold that post. As defense secretary, Rumsfeld established the B-1 strategic bomber, the Trident ballistic missile submarine, and MX (Peacekeeper) intercontinental ballistic missile (ICBM) programs.

From 1977 to 1985 Rumsfeld was CEO, president, and then chairman of G.D. Searle & Co., a pharmaceutical firm. He was chairman and CEO of General Instrument Corp. from 1990 to 1993 and later served as chairman of Gilead Sciences, Inc. Before returning to the defense secretary's post in 2001 under Pres. George W. Bush, Rumsfeld chaired the Commission to Assess the Ballistic Missile Threat to the United States. That commission's findings were released in 1998 in a document commonly known as the "Rumsfeld report." His report, which claimed that a so-called rogue state such as North Korea or Iran could—but not necessarily would—build a ballistic missile capable of striking the continental U.S. within five years, spurred debate over proposals to build a national missile defense system. (PETER SARACINO)

Salé, Jamie, and Pelletier, David

The ever-controversial world of figure-skating judging became even more so during the 2002 Winter Olympic Games in Salt Lake City, Utah. When Canadian pairs skaters Jamie Salé and David Pelletier skated a technically and emotionally compelling and nearly flawless long-program routine to the theme music from the movie Love Story, a gold medal seemed a certainty. When the scores were posted, however, their scores for presentation were lower than those of the Russian pair, Yelena Berezhnaya and Anton Sikharulidze, despite errors by the Russians. Moreover, five of the nine judges had awarded first-place ordinals to the Russians, so the Canadians would get only a silver medal. The audience was outraged, and Salé and Pelletier were stunned and mystified. Soon, though, the news media were abuzz with the rumour that the French judge, Marie-Reine Le Gougne, had been pressured to vote for the Russians by the president of the French skating federation, Didier Gailhaguet, in a vote-swapping arrangement designed to guarantee a gold medal for the French ice dancers. After five days of investigation and speculation, the decision was made to declare a tie, and Salé and Pelletier were awarded a second set of gold medals in a ceremony on February 17.

Salé was born on April 21, 1977, in Calgary, Alta., and grew up north of there in Red Deer. She began skating when she was three years old, began training in both skating and gymnastics at age five, and by age seven had chosen to concentrate on skating. Teamed with Jason Turner, she competed in the 1994 Olympics, with a 12th-place finish, and later that year in the world championships, where they finished 16th. They ended their partnership that summer, and Salé embarked on a singles career. She and Pelletier first considered working together in 1996, but it was not until 1998 that they paired up. Pelletier was born on Nov. 22, 1974, in Sayabec, Que. His mother encouraged him and his two brothers to follow her skating dream, and at age 15—realizing he did not have much hope of becoming an elite hockey player and also wanting to please his mother—he chose to concentrate on figure skating. He competed with three other partners before teaming up with Salé.

Salé and Pelletier found success almost immediately, winning bronze medals in Grand Prix events their first season together and placing second in 1999's Canadian championships. The year 2000 saw them win a number of gold medals, including the Canadian championship, and in 2001 they took gold at all their events, including the world championships. The flurry of events following the 2002 Olympics kept Salé and Pelletier from participating in the world championships the following month, and in late April they announced that they were retiring from amateur skating and joining the professional ranks. Pelletier also planned to play in a recreational hockey league.

(BARBARA WHITNEY)

Sanz, Alejandro

Spanish pop singer-songwriter Alejandro Sanz continued to figure prominently at the forefront of Latin music in 2002 with the success of his album Alejandro Sanz–MTV Unplugged (2001), which garnered him Latin Grammy awards for best album, best song, and best record of the year in September. The gravelly voiced Sanz had also won these same three awards at the previous year's ceremony in addition to the award for best male pop vocal album for his critically acclaimed El alma al aire (2000). These achievements testified to

Spanish super-singer-songwriter Alejandro Sanz

AP/Wide World Photos

the continuing ascendancy of the "flamenco-pop" artist whose 1997 effort *Más* had become the best-selling pop recording of all time in his native Spain.

Alejandro Sánchez Pizarro was born on Dec. 18, 1968, in Madrid and raised in Cádiz, a city in the Andalusia region. His father was a professional guitarist who had worked with the likes of Spanish stars Manolo Escobar and Lola Flores. Sanz took up guitar when he was seven years old and began composing songs a few years later. He left trade school at the age of 16 in order to pursue music as a career and recorded his first solo record, "Los chulos son pa' cuidarlos," in 1989.

Teenybopper pop star status came in 1991 with the release of Sanz's first album, *Viviendo deprisa*, and continued with *Si tú me miras* (1993) and *3* (1995). His next album was the record-breaking *Más*, which showcased a burgeoning maturity in lyrical content and sensibility that appealed to a broader audience base; this was in part evidenced by the whopping five million copies that were sold of "Corazón partío," a hit song from the album. *Básico*, which had previously been released in a limited edition and featured selected songs from his past albums, followed a year later; the eagerly anticipated *El alma al aire* was released in 2000. *Alejandro Sanz–MTV Unplugged* was the first Unplugged album ever to have been recorded by a Spanish artist.

An ever-evolving artist, Sanz also enjoyed working with a different medium for self-expression—painting. A collection of his works was scheduled to be on display in Madrid in October and November.   (SHANDA SILER)

Selig, Bud

At times during 2002 Bud Selig, commissioner of Major League Baseball, seemed to some observers to be vying to become the most unpopular man in the sport. Before the season began, he stirred anger among many fans with his proposal to cut two of the league's 30 teams—widely believed to be the Minnesota Twins and Montreal Expos—because of the teams' financial difficulties. Then on July 9 at the All-Star Game in Milwaukee, Wis., Selig made another controversial decision: to let the game end in a 7–7 tie at the end of 11 innings, despite boisterous chants of "Let them play!" from the sellout crowd of 41,871. Later in the season the commissioner faced additional criticism from some quarters as an August 30 deadline for a strike by players loomed. Selig and the league owners had pushed for a luxury tax on team payrolls—something that the players union had resisted but finally agreed to as part of a new collective-bargaining agreement hammered out just hours before the deadline. The agreement delayed by at least four years Selig's plan to eliminate two teams.

Allan H. Selig was born on July 30, 1934, in Milwaukee. After earning a bachelor's degree in history and political science from the University of Wisconsin at Madison in 1956, he served two years in the military before returning to Milwaukee to work as a car dealer. An avid baseball fan, he eventually became the largest public stockholder in the old Milwaukee Braves franchise, and when the team moved to Atlanta, Ga., in 1965, he organized a group of investors to bring a major league baseball team back to Milwaukee. His group failed in an attempt to buy the Chicago White Sox in 1969 but the following year succeeded in acquiring—for $10.8 million—the bankrupt Seattle Pilots, which the group renamed the Milwaukee Brewers. With Selig as club president, the Brewers grew into a successful franchise, making it to the World Series in 1982.

After baseball commissioner Fay Vincent resigned his post in 1992, Selig became the de facto commissioner when his fellow owners selected him to be chairman of the Major League Executive Council. In this capacity he presided over the contentious 234-day strike by players in 1994–95 that led to a precipitous drop in game attendance and the cancellation of the World Series for the first time since 1904. He formally assumed the title of baseball commissioner in 1998 after league owners unanimously voted to give him a five-year term. This marked the first time that a team owner had been chosen for the commissioner's post.

While some accused Selig of looking after the owners' interests at the players' expense, others praised him for the changes he was able to bring about in the sport, including the introduction of interleague play and three-division leagues and increased revenue sharing between large- and small-market franchises.
(SHERMAN HOLLAR)

Shea, Jim, Jr.

Seventy years after his grandfather, Jack Shea, won two Olympic gold medals in speed skating, American skeleton slider Jim Shea, Jr., added another gold to the family collection when he claimed first place in his event at the 2002 Winter Olympics in Salt Lake City, Utah. Despite trailing defending world champion Martin Rettl of Austria during most of his final heat, Shea sped down the skeleton track at 126.6 km/hr (78.7 mph) to finish with a time of 1 min 41.96 sec—edging Rettl by a razor-thin 0.05-sec margin. Shea had hoped that his 91-year-old grandfather would attend the Games, but only days before the opening ceremonies, Jack Shea died of injuries sustained in an automobile accident. (*See* OBITUARIES.) One of the most memorable moments of the Games came when, immediately after his gold-medal-winning performance, Jim, Jr., revealed that he had carried his grandfather's funeral card inside his helmet; he then brandished it for the cameras as fans around him erupted into chants of "U-S-Shea! U-S-Shea!"

Shea was born on June 10, 1968, in Hartford, Conn. His grandfather had become the first double gold medalist in the Winter Olympics when he won the 500- and 1,500-m speed-skating races at the 1932 Games in Lake Placid, N.Y. His father, Jim, Sr., was also an Olympic athlete, having competed in Nordic combined and cross-country skiing at the 1964 Winter Games in Innsbruck, Austria. In 1988 Shea moved with his family to Lake Placid, where he soon began to participate in sliding sports. He tried bobsledding and lugeing but eventually became fascinated with skeleton sledding, in which competitors ride a low-lying sled in a headfirst, prone position. By 1995 Shea had joined the U.S. national skeleton team.

Determined to rise to the top in his sport,

Skeleton gold winner Jim Shea with a photo of his Olympian grandfather

Shea spent two months hitchhiking across Europe to compete in World Cup events. In 1998 he became the first American to win a World Cup race, and the following year he became the first American to win a world skeleton championship. Back on his home track in Lake Placid in 2000, he won the gold medal in skeleton at the inaugural Winter Goodwill Games. When Shea qualified for the Salt Lake City Games, it marked the first time that an American family had produced three generations of Winter Olympians.

Skeleton sledding had returned as an Olympic event in 2002 after a 54-year hiatus, thanks in part to international lobbying by Shea on the sport's behalf. After winning the gold, Shea said, "My grandpa was with me the whole way. I think he had some unfinished business before he went up to heaven. I think now he can go." (SHERMAN HOLLAR)

Smith, Emmitt

With an 11-yd run in the fourth quarter of a game against the Seattle Seahawks on Oct. 28, 2002, Dallas Cowboys running back Emmitt Smith eclipsed the National Football League (NFL) career rushing record of 16,726 yd that had been set 15 years earlier by Chicago Bears great Walter Payton. The record had been a goal for Smith ever since he entered the NFL in 1990. Because of his relatively small size—he stood only 1.75 m (5 ft 9 in) tall and weighed 96 kg (212 lb)—and lack of great foot speed, however, some experts had initially doubted whether Smith could survive in the NFL. Like Payton—another undersized back who lacked breakaway speed—Smith relied on his strength, doggedness, and superb conditioning to help him succeed. He ultimately proved himself to be one of the NFL's most durable players at any position; in 13 seasons he had failed to start in only two games. "Walter Payton is the best running back of all time," Smith declared after breaking the record of the player he had modeled himself after. "That's why, for me, the record is such a tremendous opportunity to do something no man has ever done."

Emmitt James Smith III was born in Pensacola, Fla., on May 15, 1969. He excelled early in football, starring in youth leagues and, by the time he had finished high school, earning Player of the Year honours from *Parade* magazine, among other publications. He played three years (1987–89) at the University of Florida, racking up 58 school records before entering the NFL draft. The Cowboys selected him in the draft's first round, and Smith soon established himself as one of the league's premier running backs. He was named NFL Offensive Rookie of the Year in 1990 and the following season ran for 1,563 yd to capture the first of his NFL rushing titles.

Smith went on to win rushing titles in both 1992 and 1993, becoming only the fourth player in NFL history to win three consecutive rushing crowns. More important, in those two seasons he led the Cowboys to back-to-back Super Bowl wins. Against the Buffalo Bills in Super Bowl XXVII, Smith ran for 108 yd. Dallas faced Buffalo again in Super Bowl

XXVIII, in which Smith ran for 132 yd and was named Super Bowl Most Valuable Player. He also claimed league MVP honours that season. In 1995 Smith set a single-season NFL record with 25 rushing touchdowns, won his fourth league rushing title with 1,773 yd, and capped the season by powering the Cowboys to victory over the Pittsburgh Steelers in Super Bowl XXX. By the end of 1999, he not only had become the Cowboys' all-time leading rusher but was also the NFL's all-time leader in both postseason rushing yards and postseason rushing touchdowns.

In 2001, after Smith had surpassed Detroit Lions running back Barry Sanders for the number two spot on the NFL's all-time rushing list, experts and fans alike began to speculate on how long it might take him to break Payton's record. After finally having accomplished his goal in 2002, Smith announced that he was setting his sights on a once-unimaginable feat—reaching 20,000 yd before his retirement from the sport.

(SHERMAN HOLLAR)

Spears, Britney

In 2002 American pop phenomenon Britney Spears made her big-screen debut in *Crossroads;* though many speculated that the singer's foray into movies would be more "oops" than a success, the coming-of-age film was a modest hit, and she followed that with a cameo in the hugely popular *Austin Powers in Goldmember.* Soon afterward Spears formed her own production company and announced that she was developing a film about NASCAR. Her numerous ventures—as a singer, actress, commercial spokesperson, and restaurateur—helped make Spears the world's most powerful celebrity, according to *Forbes* magazine. Her exhausting schedule, however, as well as public scrutiny (especially tabloid coverage of her breakup with Justin Timberlake of the boy band *NSYNC) led Spears to announce at midyear that she was taking a six-month sabbatical.

Britney Jean Spears was born on Dec. 2, 1981, in Kentwood, La. She began singing and dancing at age two and was soon competing in talent shows. At age eight she auditioned for Disney's television show *The All New Mickey Mouse Club* but was deemed too young for the program. The impressed producers did, however, encourage her to get an agent in New York City, and she began spending her summers there, attending the Professional Performing Arts School. During this time she started making television commercials and in 1991 appeared in *Ruthless,* an Off-Broadway play. At age 11 Spears finally became a cast member of *The All New Mickey Mouse Club,* joining such fellow Mouseketeers as Timberlake and Christina Aguilera.

After the show's cancellation in 1993, Spears returned home, but she was soon eager to resume her career. At age 15 she made a demo tape that earned her a development deal with Jive Records. Two years later she released her first single, ". . . Baby One More Time." The song soon became the subject of controversy, both for its lyrics ("Hit me baby one more time") as well as for its Lolita-like video, in

Britney Spears, "the world's most powerful celebrity"

which Spears appeared as a provocative schoolgirl. The attention, however, only helped the song, and when the album (. . . *Baby One More Time*) was released in 1999, it quickly went to number one on the charts, eventually selling more than 11 million copies. Her success produced a number of imitators and helped spark the teen-pop phenomenon. In 2000 she released her second album, *Oops! . . . I Did It Again.* It sold 1.3 million copies in its first week of release, setting a record for first-week sales by a solo artist. Although Spears drew criticism for her revealing attire—often imitated by her female fans—she was able to convey a wholesomeness that proved highly profitable. In 2001 she signed a multimillion-dollar deal to be a spokesperson for Pepsi and released her third album, *Britney.* Although none of the singles from *Britney* made the Top Ten, the album sold more than four million copies. (AMY TIKKANEN)

Stanley, Ralph

Though bluegrass festivals seemed to sprout like mountain wildflowers across the United States, bluegrass music had never been one of the most popular country music idioms. It therefore came as a surprise to many when bluegrass pioneer Ralph Stanley beat out such country stars as Lyle Lovett, Tim McGraw, and Johnny Cash to capture the 2002 Grammy Award for best male country vocal performance. The vivid winning recording—the song "O Death," an unaccompanied vocal in Stanley's high, wavery tenor voice—was a highlight of the sound-track album from the film *O Brother, Where Art Thou?* After six Grammy nominations, it was the first time that Stanley—at the age of 75—had won top honours.

Ralph Edmond Stanley was born on Feb. 25, 1927, in Stratton, in the mountains of far southwestern Virginia. His mother taught him to play the banjo, and he and his guitar-

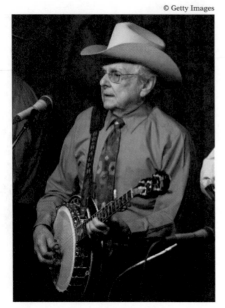

Bluegrass legend Ralph Stanley

playing older brother, Carter, became a singing team as teenagers. After service in World War II, the Stanley brothers began their career in earnest, forming the Clinch Mountain Boys, one of the first bands to play in the new bluegrass style. Their sound was distinctive—as the five-piece string band played, Carter sang lead, and Ralph sang tenor harmony. The two brothers both wrote songs, all in stark, ancient Appalachian mountain modes. For years their career was a busy round of touring, regular broadcasts over a series of Appalachian and Southern radio stations, and frequent recording sessions. The 1960s folk music revival brought the Stanleys widespread popularity—even European tours—but in 1966 Carter died suddenly. After a few weeks of silence, Ralph reorganized the Clinch Mountain Boys and returned to his extensive performing schedule.

Ralph played at the inaugurations of U.S. Presidents Jimmy Carter and Bill Clinton, and Pres. Ronald Reagan named him a National Heritage Fellow. His celebrity was recounted in the book *Traveling the High Way Home: Ralph Stanley and the World of Traditional Bluegrass Music* (1993) by John Wright. Nonetheless, Stanley continued to live in Coeburn, near where he grew up. He played about 150 dates a year, and, as usual, he spent most of 2002 on tour, appearing at bluegrass festivals, county fairs, parks, city nightclubs, and small-town high-school auditoriums. The majority of his shows were within a day's drive of Coeburn, where he again starred at the 32-year-old Hills of Home Bluegrass Festival. The prolific recording artist of some 185 albums released 2 more albums in 2002— *Live at McCabe's Guitar Shop* and *Ralph Stanley*. Though he did not entertain thoughts of retirement, his legacy was already continuing—his son, Ralph Stanley II, was the lead singer and rhythm guitarist for the Clinch Mountain Boys.   (JOHN LITWEILER)

Stoiber, Edmund

Although he had led in opinion polls throughout the entire campaign in his quest to become Germany's first Bavarian chancellor, Edmund Stoiber lost his bid on Sept. 22, 2002, when incumbent Social Democrat Gerhard Schröder narrowly defeated him. Stoiber's promise to reform Germany's stagnant economy and alleviate its stubborn unemployment problem by deregulating the labour market, cutting taxes, and creating jobs had struck a chord with voters. At the same time, he made clear that he would not touch what he called the Germans' "fundamental securities of life," including health, pensions, and unemployment benefits.

Ultimately, however, issues other than the economy decided the election. A month before the elections took place, Germany was hit by the worst floods in a century, and the telegenic Chancellor Schröder projected the better image as the candidates went before the media to console victims and promise aid. Schröder also courted voters with a pledge that Germany would not participate in a war against Iraq, regardless of the circumstances. Stoiber, who did not agree with his opponent but also did not want to look like a warmonger, ended up waffling. In the end, Schröder simply proved more attractive than Stoiber, whose stiff manner and sharp rhetoric had once earned him the nickname "the blond guillotine."

Stoiber was born on Sept. 28, 1941, in Oberaudorf, a picturesque Bavarian village near the Austrian border. He finished law school at age 30 and joined the Christian Social Union (CSU), the Bavarian partner of the federal Christian Democratic Union (CDU). Three years later he was elected to the Bavarian state legislature. There he caught the eye of Bavaria's political boss, Franz Josef Strauss, and served as his right-hand man when Strauss was elected Bavarian premier in 1979 and made a run for federal chancellor the following year. In 1993, after stints as CSU general secretary and Bavarian interior minister, Stoiber became premier himself. He was elected chairman of the CSU in 1999.

State premiers play a key role on the national level in Germany's federalist system, and Stoiber's ascendancy established him as the country's leading conservative politician. A staunch supporter of traditional and Roman Catholic values, he fought, for example, to keep crucifixes in Bavarian public-school classrooms and publicly prided himself on his healthy marriage and trouble-free children. As premier, Stoiber also promoted law and order, favoured a cautious immigration policy, and exhibited skepticism toward the European Union—especially plans for a single European currency and EU enlargement into Eastern Europe.

One of Stoiber's victories as premier came when Germany's top court ruled in 1999 that wealthy Bavaria could keep half of its tax revenues rather than continuing to hand over 80% to poorer states. A second triumph occurred in early 2002 when Stoiber effected the withdrawal of the CDU chairwoman, Angela Merkel, from the race for the chancellorship— even though for years Stoiber had denied any

ambitions for the top job in Berlin. Though he lost the election, Stoiber revived Germany's conservatives after years of scandal and infighting, putting them back on an equal footing with the country's other large party, the Social Democrats.   (CECILIE ROHWEDDER)

Sugimoto, Hiroshi

In 2002 Japanese photographer Hiroshi Sugimoto had his first major solo exhibition in the U.K. as part of the annual Edinburgh International Festival. "The Architecture of Time" was presented at the Fruitmarket Gallery, Scotland's highly regarded contemporary art space, and the Stills Gallery, the country's leading centre for photography and digital media, from August 3 to September 21. The exhibition incorporated more than 30 large-scale images from Sugimoto's "Seascapes" and "Architecture" series and a new work, "Pinetrees," a multipaneled piece he created specifically for the festival. "Time exposed" was the phrase Sugimoto used to describe his artistic effort, referring to the length of exposure (sometimes as long as an hour and a half or more) during which each image slowly burned onto the film. Photographed with a 19th-century large-format camera, long exposures, and 8 × 10-in (20 × 25-cm) negatives, Sugimoto's work had the meditative quality of Japanese art.

Sugimoto was born in Tokyo in 1948 and received a B.A. in sociology and politics from St. Paul's University in Tokyo in 1970. In 1972 he obtained a B.F.A. in photography from the Art Center College of Design in Los Angeles. He conceived his first body of work, "Dioramas," in 1976, two years after he had moved from California to New York. Photographing exhibits inside natural history museums, Sugimoto's images brought to life extinct creatures and prehistoric situations. The photographs took on a sense of authenticity that the museum dioramas themselves did not possess. In his next series, begun in 1978, he photographed movie theatres and drive-ins with an exposure the length of the film's duration. All that appeared visible in the photographs was the luminescent rectangular screen in the centre of the theatre and the surrounding architectural details.

In December 1995 Sugimoto had a pivotal three-part exhibition of more than 120 photographs at the Metropolitan Museum of Art in New York City. Two years later the Museum of Contemporary Art in Los Angeles commissioned him to take architectural portraits of the world's iconic landmarks and buildings for an exhibition called "At the End of the Century: One Hundred Years of Architecture." The exhibition debuted in Tokyo in 1998 and traveled to Mexico City, Cologne, Ger., and Chicago before it arrived in Los Angeles in April 2000. Also in the spring of 2000, the Deutsche Guggenheim Berlin presented "Sugimoto: Portraits," which traveled to New York City in 2001. Sugimoto's life-sized black-and-white images of figures from wax museums were photographed in the spirit of Renaissance portraiture. In many "Portraits" the subjects look as if they actually sat for the photographer.

Sugimoto received the International Center

of Photography's Infinity Award in 1999. In 2001 he won the Hasselblad Foundation International Award in Photography. The award was accompanied by a retrospective exhibition of his work at the Hasselblad Center in the Göteberg (Swed.) Museum of Art and celebrated Sugimoto as one of the most respected photographers of the age for his combination of "Eastern meditative ideas with Western cultural motifs." (MARLA CAPLAN)

Thomson, Robert

In February 2002 *The Times* (London) received its first non-British editor. Australian Robert Thomson, formerly the managing editor of the U.S. edition of the *Financial Times* (*FT*), was appointed to lead one of the world's oldest and most distinguished daily newspapers. Thomson took over at a challenging time. Under Peter Stothard, his predecessor, *The Times* had pursued an aggressive price-cutting strategy, which had seen the paper's circulation almost double at one point to nearly 800,000 copies a day. By early 2002, however, sales had slipped to around 700,000, while the paper's main rival, the *Daily Telegraph*, continued to sell 1,000,000 copies daily. Sharp reductions in advertising revenue—common to many media organizations following the terrorist attacks in the U.S. in September 2001—also had increased pressure on *The Times*'s finances.

Thomson was born on March 11, 1961, in Echuca, 200 km (125 mi) north of Melbourne, Australia. He was the son of a bar owner who later became a newspaper proofreader. The young Thomson entered journalism at the age of 17, working as a copy boy and then cadet on the *Herald* (Melbourne) and later at the *Sydney Morning Herald*. In 1985, when he was 24, he was appointed the *Herald*'s Beijing correspondent. In China he started working freelance for the *FT*. He also met his future wife, Ping Wang, a local computer worker. Three years later he moved to Japan as the *FT*'s Tokyo correspondent. In addition to his orthodox journalistic strengths, Thomson's ability to embrace the culture of others rather than impose his own values (by his late 20s he had become fluent in both Mandarin and Japanese) attracted the attention of the senior management at the *FT*, which was seeking to establish itself as a global business daily. In 1994 Thomson was sent to London to run the *FT*'s large foreign desk. Two years later he was appointed editor of the paper's Weekend features section. In 1998 he moved to New York City as managing editor of the *FT*'s U.S. edition, and in three years he increased daily circulation from 32,000 to 123,000.

Thomson had hoped to succeed to the editorship of the *FT* in London when Richard Lambert departed in 2001, but he was passed over in favour of another candidate. Thomson then was approached by fellow Australian Rupert Murdoch to become editor of *The Times*. *The Times*, however, was one of the U.K.'s toughest newspaper critics of the European Union, and Thomson arrived there from the *FT*, one of the strongest pro-Europe newspapers, without any personal record of sharing his new proprietor's hostility to European integration. His appointment was

widely seen as an indication that Murdoch would allow the U.K. papers in his News International group—which also included *The Sunday Times* and the downmarket tabloids the *Sun* (daily) and *News of the World* (Sundays)—to follow different editorial policies in this highly charged area. (PETER KELLNER)

Touré, Amadou Toumani

Observers were not surprised to find that Amadou Toumani Touré (affectionately known as ATT) had won Mali's May 2002 presidential elections. As only the second elected president since Mali became independent in 1960, and as one of the few African leaders voluntarily to have relinquished power, he had not lost the goodwill of the people, although he had been away from the political limelight for almost 10 years.

Touré was born in Mopti, French Sudan (now in eastern Mali), in 1948. Educated first to be a teacher, he joined the army in 1969 and received military training in France and the U.S.S.R. At one time he was a member of the Presidential Guard in Mali, but he had a falling out with the president, Gen. Moussa Traoré, and lost this position.

Touré first came to international prominence in 1991 as the leader of a coup that toppled Traoré (who had himself come to power in 1968 in a coup against Modibo Keita). Touré's coup was generally welcomed owing to Traoré's repressive policies, which had led to popular unrest in the early 1990s. It seemed to many that ATT had acted in the name of the people and brought democracy to the country. Be this as it may, the pro-democracy forces in the country lost little time in removing Touré. Presidential elections were held, and ATT was retired as president on June 8, 1992.

For the next decade ATT occupied himself with nonmilitary activities, mostly concerned with public health. In 1992 he became the head of Mali's Intersectoral Committee for Guinea Worm Eradication, and he was also associated with campaigns to eliminate polio and other childhood diseases as well as working for the control of AIDS in Africa, often collaborating with the Carter Center, the nonprofit humanitarian organization run by former U.S. president Jimmy Carter. ATT also was active in trying to resolve the disputes in the Great Lakes region (Rwanda, Burundi, and the Democratic Republic of the Congo).

In preparation for the presidential elections, Touré resigned from the armed forces in September 2001. In order to take his message to all parts of Mali, he—like the other major candidates, all former government officials—spent millions of dollars to travel by air to campaign stops. Ultimately, Touré, running as an independent, prevailed in the second round of elections. Democracy seemed to be working well in Mali, but ATT would have his hands full trying to retain his popularity when he was forced to make the tough decisions that face a democratically elected president. (PAMELA L. SMITH-IROWA)

Uribe Vélez, Álvaro

On Aug. 7, 2002, the day that Álvaro Uribe Vélez formally took office as president of

Colombia, explosions rocked the centre of the nation's capital, Bogotá. Just blocks from the site of Uribe's inauguration ceremony, bombs claimed the lives of 19 persons and injured at least 60. Although no one claimed responsibility for the attack, authorities blamed the Revolutionary Armed Forces of Colombia (FARC) guerrilla group. The attack came on the heels of Uribe's announcement that his government would negotiate with armed groups only after they had abandoned "terrorist" activities and ceased hostilities. Soon after his inauguration, Uribe declared a state of emergency and invoked powers to expand the nation's military and police forces.

In his campaign for president, Uribe had split from the traditionally dominant Liberal Party and run as an independent. He established the Colombia First electoral movement and adopted the campaign slogan "Firm Hand, Big Heart." Uribe promised a tougher line against guerrillas, paramilitaries, and drug traffickers after the failure of the previous administration to negotiate a settlement with any of these armed groups. He also stressed the need for sweeping political reforms to make the government more efficient and to reduce corruption. The success of his campaign strategy garnered him 53.1% of the votes cast when Colombians went to the polls on May 26.

Uribe was born in Medellín, Colom., on July 4, 1952. He earned a law degree from the University of Antioquia, Medellín, and later studied management and administration in the U.S. at Harvard University. In the mid-1970s he worked in the state government of Antioquia before serving as secretary-general in the Ministry of Labour in Medellín and as a director of civil aeronautics at the national level. He was mayor of Medellín from 1982 to 1984. During this time his father, a cattle rancher, was slain by FARC guerrillas during a botched kidnapping. Uribe served consecutive terms as a national senator between 1986 and 1994 and was governor of Antioquia from 1995 to 1997.

As president, Uribe promised to keep bureaucracy in check and to run an austere administration. He made clear his intent to reduce the number of government ministries, and he nominated a single minister of justice and interior—a de facto merging of the two entities. He also proposed eliminating several posts at the state and local levels. On his first day in office, he sent to Congress a large package of proposals, including the establishment of a single legislative chamber, the use of roll-call vote procedures to make decision making transparent, the elimination of "substitute" legislators, reform of congressional resources and financial management, a list of reasons for which legislators could be removed from office, and a process by which early elections could be called. His ambitious proposals were sure to strain the postelectoral congressional coalition, and his success would be dependent on his continued public popularity. (BRIAN F. CRISP)

West, Cornel

In April 2002 American intellectual Cornel West created even more media speculation as to the status of Harvard University's top-ranked African American studies department when he announced both his resignation from his position there as Alphonse Fletcher, Jr., University Professor and his plans to join the faculty of Princeton University. His decision followed months of controversy surrounding Harvard president Lawrence Summers's disapproval of West's recent publications and extracurricular activities, which Summers had deemed to be of questionable academic merit. Other prominent members of the department at Harvard threatened to defect to Princeton also, owing to their dissatisfaction with Summers's perceived ambivalence toward such issues as affirmative action; K. Anthony Appiah joined Princeton in September.

Cornel Ronald West was born on June 2, 1953, in Tulsa, Okla. His father (a civilian air force administrator) and his mother (a teacher and school administrator) instilled in him a progressive idealism and a strong practical morality rooted in the Christian faith, considerations that informed both his political orientation (democratic socialism) and his future choice of career. He entered Harvard at the age of 17 and graduated magna cum laude with a degree in Near Eastern languages and literature just three years later. He earned a Ph.D. (1980) in philosophy from Princeton. West served as assistant professor of philosophy of religion at Union Theological Seminary in New York City for several years before joining the faculty at Yale Divinity School in 1984. He briefly returned to Union in 1988 but left again to become professor of religion and director of the African American studies program at Princeton. In 1994 West returned to Harvard as professor of religion and African American studies; he was later made a university professor, an honour granted to fewer than 25 members of the entire faculty. As he grew in prominence, West became known and appreciated by many for his engaging Baptist-minister inflection and oratorical style, and his audience and influence soon extended well beyond the world of academia into intellectual circles and the public at large.

West's somewhat circular pattern of institutional wanderings was mirrored by his closely related yet also wide-ranging book topics. He wrote over a dozen volumes, including *The American Evasion of Philosophy* (1989), in which he developed his own brand of pragmatism; *Breaking Bread* (1991), which was coau-

© AFP 2002, by Boris Roessler

Willem-Alexander and Máxima

thored by feminist intellectual bell hooks and featured essays seeking to reconcile gender relations within the black community; *Race Matters* (1993), the best-seller that greatly increased West's public visibility; and *The War Against Parents* (1998), which was coauthored by economist Sylvia Ann Hewlett and presented a critique of U.S. government policies that thwarted parents' efforts to raise their children. His compact disc project, *Sketches of My Culture* (2001), included hip-hop performances and spoken word poetry.　　(SHANDA SILER)

Willem-Alexander, Crown Prince, and Princess Máxima

On Feb. 2, 2002, Crown Prince Willem-Alexander of The Netherlands and Argentine-born Máxima Zorreguieta married in Amsterdam. Their many guests included foreign royals, other friends and family members, and some Dutch political leaders (who had secured official approval for the marriage) but not the bride's father. He did not attend because of concerns in The Netherlands about his association, as a former minister of agriculture, with the Argentine military dictatorship of Jorge Videla. Security in Amsterdam was tight for fear of international terrorism after the Sept. 11, 2001, attacks in the U.S. While some acts of peaceful protest occurred in the city, the occasion was a festive one. Thousands of well-wishers celebrated in public, with many displaying items in orange, the royal colour.

Willem-Alexander was born in Utrecht on April 27, 1967, to then Princess Beatrix and Prince Claus. First in the line of succession since his mother's accession to the throne on April 30, 1980, he bears the title prince of Orange. The crown prince received most of his education in The Netherlands and in 1985 completed an international baccalaureate at Atlantic College, near Llantwit Major, Wales. After military service in the Royal Dutch Navy, he studied history at the University of Leiden from 1987 to 1993. The crown prince was responsible for performing various official duties; he represented the royal family at national and international events, accompanied the queen on state visits, and had paid working visits to the Netherlands Antilles and Aruba. He served on the International Olympic Committee and had run the New York City Marathon and completed the Elfstedentocht (Eleven-Cities Tour) skating marathon. An avid pilot, he had flown as a volunteer for charitable organizations in Africa.

Máxima was born on May 17, 1971, in Buenos Aires to Jorge Horacio Zorreguieta and María del Carmen Cerruti de Zorreguieta. She earned a degree in economics from the Universidad Católica Argentina in 1995 and later worked for international companies in Buenos Aires, New York City, and Brussels. The announcement of her engagement to the crown prince was made on March 30, 2001. She received Dutch nationality on May 17 of that year, and the Plenary Session of the States-General granted consent for the marriage the following July. Princess Máxima has made mastering Dutch and the history and constitutional law of The Netherlands a high priority. She was to take up a seat in the Council of State

Anglican leader Rowan Williams

and join her husband in performing other official duties.　　(JOLANDA VANDERWAL TAYLOR)

Williams, Rowan

In selecting Welsh Archbishop Rowan Williams to serve as the spiritual head of the world's 70 million Anglicans, British officials chose a man with a reputation as an intellectual who could relate to popular culture. When his appointment as the 104th archbishop of Canterbury was announced in July 2002, he was widely hailed as a leader who had the potential for giving Christianity a voice that would be respected in modern society. At a news conference, Williams said, "If there is one thing I long for above all else, it is that the years to come may see Christianity in this country able again to capture the imagination of our culture, to draw the strongest energies of our thinking and feeling into the exploration of what our creeds put before us."

Williams's stands on political and theological issues made him a figure of controversy in the Church of England and the wider Anglican Communion. He had criticized the 2001 bombing of Afghanistan as "morally tainted" and said an invasion of Iraq would be "immoral and illegal" unless it was approved by the United Nations. He favoured the consecration of women bishops and acknowledged having ordained a man who was an open and active homosexual. While lecturing in Australia in May, he said, "I am not convinced that a homosexual has to be celibate in every imaginable circumstance."

At age 52, Williams was the youngest man to be appointed archbishop of Canterbury since Charles Manners Sutton in 1805. A native of Wales, at his enthronement in 2003 he would become the first leader of the Anglican Communion from outside England since the 16th century.

Williams was born on June 14, 1950, as the only child of a couple in Swansea, Wales. His parents were Presbyterians at the time, and the family joined the Anglican Church in Wales when he was in his early teens. He earned his bachelor of arts and master's degrees in theology from the University of

Cambridge and his doctorates in philosophy and theology from the University of Oxford. Williams was ordained to the priesthood in 1978 and spent nine years at Cambridge as a tutor, dean, and chaplain before becoming professor of theology at Oxford in 1986. The Oxford appointment made him the youngest person ever to hold such a position there and the only person to have been a professor of theology at both Oxford and Cambridge. He became bishop of Monmouth, Wales, in 1992 and archbishop of Wales in 2000. Williams was married and the father of two children.

(DARRELL J. TURNER)

Wolfram, Stephen

With the publication in 2002 of his 1,263-page self-published book *A New Kind of Science*, British-born physicist Stephen Wolfram attempted to establish just what the title suggested. After having conducted nearly 10 years of tireless research in seclusion, Wolfram unleashed on the scientific community his conclusions about the inadequacy of math-based science as a means of unlocking the secrets of the natural world. Instead, Wolfram posited that the complexity of nature could be better understood through the study of models developed by computer programs that executed simple instructions repeatedly on a grid of black and white squares and thus created intricate patterns that replicated the way natural processes progress. Wolfram believed that this approach—known as cellular automata—could be applied to all sorts of scientific endeavours, such as predicting the weather, growing artificial organisms, explaining stock market behaviour, and understanding the very origins of the universe. Nature, Wolfram argued, operates like a computer.

Wolfram was born on Aug. 29, 1959, in London. His father was a novelist, and his mother taught philosophy at the University of Oxford. He studied at Oxford and the California Institute of Technology, where he earned a Ph.D. (1979) in theoretical physics. In 1981 he became the youngest recipient of a MacArthur Foundation "genius grant" and later that year he set his sights on an explanation of the complexity of nature. Through the 1980s Wolfram published a series of celebrated papers on what he dubbed "complex systems research."

A brash—some would say arrogant—proponent of his own work, Wolfram soon grew unhappy with the way that his peers tried to build upon his findings. Determined to articulate his theories in full, Wolfram dropped out of academia and created his own firm, Wolfram Research Inc., which sold a computer program Wolfram had devised that allowed anyone to perform complex mathematics on a personal computer. Software sales made Wolfram a millionaire and thereby allowed him to finance his own research and, eventually, the publication of his book. Beginning in 1991, Wolfram began to divide his time between the management of his company and his attempt to devise his new science.

Reaction to *A New Kind of Science* was, understandably, mixed. From a purely scientific standpoint, observers' responses covered a wide range. Some already engaged in the field of cellular automata welcomed the spotlight the book created and Wolfram's new body of evidence; others suggested that much of what Wolfram offered in his book was nothing new. The perception of Wolfram among some academics as a corporate sellout and a self-promoter surely affected the reception of the new work. In any event, it appeared that the full impact of Wolfram's radical ideas would not be realized for years.

(ANTHONY G. CRAINE)

Zerhouni, Elias

U.S. Pres. George W. Bush in 2002 tapped Algerian-born radiologist Elias Zerhouni to be the 15th director of the National Institutes of Health (NIH), the world's largest medical research facility. Though closely grilled on the question of whether he would support the president's opposition to cloning and human embryonic stem cell research, Zerhouni managed to avoid making a definitive position statement. Still, Zerhouni had helped create the Institute for Cell Engineering at the Johns Hopkins University School of Medicine, Baltimore, Md., and Johns Hopkins researchers pioneered embryonic stem cell research. The institute was established with the goal of applying that knowledge to related work in adult stem cells, which the president endorsed.

Elias Adam Zerhouni was born on April 1, 1951, in Nedroma, Alg., one of eight children. His father was a math professor. The family moved two years later to Algiers, where Zerhouni earned Algerian and French baccalaureates before studying at the University of Algiers School of Medicine. Influenced by his maternal uncle, a well-known radiologist, Zerhouni chose radiology as his field, and after receiving his medical degree in 1975, he moved to the United States. Barely able to speak English, Zerhouni nonetheless earned a position as radiology resident at Johns Hopkins's School of Medicine, rising to chief resident in 1978 and joining the faculty a short time later.

At Johns Hopkins, Zerhouni participated in research on computed tomography that led to a technique that allowed radiologists to identify benign and malignant nodules in the lungs. In 1981 he became vice chairman of the radiology department at Eastern Virginia Medical School, where he pioneered further scanning techniques. He returned to Johns Hopkins in 1985 and, as co-director of a new magnetic resonance imaging (MRI) division, invented a revolutionary MRI cardiac tagging technology and later, as director of the MRI division, helped devise an image-directed replacement for invasive methods for breast cancer diagnosis. Zerhouni rose to the post of chairman of the department of radiology at Johns Hopkins in 1992 and executive vice dean in 1996.

Peers hailed Zerhouni as a solid administrator who had the ability to find solutions where others saw only obstacles.

Zerhouni served as a consultant to the Reagan White House in 1985 and the World Health Organization in 1988. He became a naturalized U.S. citizen in 1990. He became a member of the Institute of Medicine, an arm of the National Research Council complex, in 2000.

(ANTHONY G. CRAINE)

Zimmerman, Mary

On June 2, 2002, the Tony Award for best direction of a play was presented to Mary Zimmerman for *Metamorphoses*. Although the central feature of *Metamorphoses*—Zimmerman's adaptation of tales of mythology from the Roman poet Ovid's classic epic poem of the same name—was an onstage pool in and around which the stories were enacted, Zimmerman had made her own splash in the theatre world some years earlier. Such original adaptations as *The Arabian Nights* (first produced in 1992), *The Notebooks of Leonardo da Vinci* (1994), *Journey to the West* (1995), *Eleven Rooms of Proust* (1998), and *The Odyssey* (1999) had already gone far toward illustrating her inventiveness and sealing her reputation as a creative artist of distinction, and *Metamorphoses* itself had already been performed to great acclaim around the country before it moved to Broadway in early 2002.

Zimmerman was born on Aug. 23, 1960, in Lincoln, Neb., and she was educated at Northwestern University, Evanston, Ill. (B.S., 1982; M.A., 1985; Ph.D., 1994). She joined the staff of Northwestern as an adjunct assistant in 1984 and went on to serve as teaching assistant (1985–87), instructor (1987–90), and assistant professor (1994–99) before becoming (1999) a full professor in the department of performance studies. In addition, she was an ensemble member of Lookingglass Theatre in Chicago and served as an artistic associate of the Goodman Theatre in Chicago and the Seattle Repertory Theatre. Among her numerous honours were 10 Chicago-area Joseph Jefferson Awards and, in 1998, a MacArthur Foundation "genius grant."

Shortly after Zimmerman's win at the Tonys, she was at work readying her next project—*Galileo Galilei*, a new opera by Philip Glass—for its premiere at the Goodman Theatre in late June. Zimmerman was one of the writers of the libretto and served as director of the production, which—in order to give the story a happy ending—traced the life of Galileo in reverse, from his last days as a lonely old man back through his years of scientific study and finally to his childhood. Following its run at the Goodman, the opera was presented at the Next Wave Festival at the Brooklyn (N.Y.) Academy of Music in October and then, in November, in the Barbican International Theatre Events in London.

(BARBARA WHITNEY)

Obituaries

In 2002 **THE WORLD LOST** many leaders, **PATHFINDERS**, newsmakers, **HEROES**, cultural icons, and **ROGUES**. The pages below **RECAPTURE** the **LIVES** and accomplishments of those we **REMEMBER** best.

Abu Nidal (SABRI AL-BANNA), Palestinian militant (b. 1937, Jaffa, Palestine—d. Aug. 16?, 2002, Baghdad, Iraq), was believed to have masterminded countless deadly attacks for nearly two decades, from the early 1970s to the 1990s. Abu Nidal (he took the nom de guerre in the early 1960s) was originally a member of Yasir Arafat's Palestine Liberation Organization, but he broke with the PLO in 1974 to form the more radical Fatah Revolutionary Council. Among the many attacks attributed to Fatah were the bombing of a TWA flight in 1974 that killed 88 and the 1982 shooting of Israel's ambassador to London, which triggered Israel's invasion of Lebanon that year. Abu Nidal reportedly became a fanatic gunman for hire, working in Libya, Syria, and Iraq. The PLO sentenced him to death in absentia for plotting to assassinate Arafat. Abu Nidal was reported dead numerous times, and the circumstances surrounding the most recent reports of his death remained mysterious, though Iraq officially declared that he had committed suicide.

Agar, John, American actor (b. Jan. 31, 1921, Chicago, Ill.—d. April 7, 2002, Burbank, Calif.), first achieved fame when he married (1945) Shirley Temple but then became an actor and appeared with her in two films. After they divorced in 1949, he continued working in movies, at first appearing especially in westerns and war movies.

Álvarez Bravo, Manuel, Mexican photographer (b. Feb. 4, 1902, Mexico City, Mex.—d. Oct. 19, 2002, Mexico City), was influenced by international developments, particularly Surrealism, but his art remained profoundly Mexican. His photography was part of the renaissance that occurred in the period following the Mexican Revolution of 1910–20, and his work depicted both urban scenes and rural areas, with folkways, industrial development, and politics among the subjects. Among his best-known photographs were *Striking Worker Assassinated* (1934), showing a blood-smeared body, and *The Good Reputation Sleeping* (1939), a bandaged nude lying amid cactus buds, the latter done at the request of the French Surrealist André Breton. He was largely self-taught, with other photographers playing a major role in his artistic development. When he was 21, he met the German photographer Hugo Brehme, who introduced him to Wilhelm Kahlo, a prominent Mexican photographer. Through the Italian photographer Tina Modotti, Álvarez Bravo was able to

get a review of his work from the American Edward Weston, and Modotti helped him find employment with the magazine *Mexican Folkways*. In 1932 Álvarez Bravo had his first one-man show. He then met French photographer Henri Cartier-Bresson and in 1935 participated in an exhibition with Cartier-Bresson and American Walker Evans in New York City. Álvarez Bravo was included in the 1940 exhibition *Twenty Centuries of Mexican Art* at the Museum of Modern Art (MoMA), New York City, and in Edward Steichen's 1955 traveling exhibition *Family of Man*. Among major retrospectives was a 1997 show at MoMA. Álvarez Bravo worked in the film industry, including serving as a cameraman for Sergey Eisenstein's *Que viva Mexico!* (1932), and he taught and published his work in a number of books.

Ambani, Dhirubhai (DHIRAJLAL HIRACHAND AMBANI), Indian industrialist (b. Dec. 28, 1932, Chorwad, Gujarat, India—d. July 6, 2002, Mumbai [Bombay], India), was the founder of Reliance Industries, a $13.5 billion

Robert Nickelsberg/TimePix

Indian mogul Dhirubhai Ambani

petrochemicals, communications, power, and textiles conglomerate and the only privately owned Indian company in the *Fortune* 500. Ambani migrated to the British colony of Aden at age 16 to join his brother. He worked as a gas station attendant and later as manager with Burmah-Shell Oil Co. In 1958 he returned to Bombay. Ambani's first business enterprise involved the melting of Aden currency for its silver. He became a commodities and textiles trader and set up the first Reliance textile mill in 1966, earning the sobriquet "the Prince of Polyester." He later shaped Reliance into a petrochemicals megalith, despite a stodgy economy and crippling government regulations and bureaucracy. In

1977 Ambani took Reliance public after nationalized banks refused to finance him. Despite allegations of political manipulation, corruption, and engineered raids on competitors, investor confidence in Reliance was unshaken—owing in part to the handsome dividends the company offered, as well as the founder's charisma and vision. Ambani was credited with introducing the stock market to the average investor. Share prices collapsed in 1995 amid serious accusations of crony capitalism and accounting irregularities but rebounded after an inquiry cleared the group. Ambani handed over the day-to-day running of the company to his sons in 1986.

Ambrose, Stephen Edward, American biographer and historian (b. Jan. 10, 1936, Decatur, Ill.—d. Oct. 13, 2002, Bay St. Louis, Miss.), wrote some three dozen books on U.S. history. His later works were populist in tone, celebrating the achievements of ordinary people. In 2002 he was accused of plagiarism, but in his defense he argued that he had cited sources for his material. Ambrose earned a B.S. degree in history from the University of Wisconsin at Madison (1957), an M.A. from Louisiana State University at Baton Rouge (1958), and a Ph.D. from Wisconsin (1963). He taught at several schools and from 1971 to 1995 was professor of history at the University of New Orleans. His book *Halleck: Lincoln's Chief of Staff* (1962) caught the attention of former president Dwight D. Eisenhower, who asked Ambrose to edit his papers. The two volumes of Ambrose's biography of Eisenhower appeared in 1983 and 1984, and his three-volume biography of Richard M. Nixon was published between 1987 and 1991. It was the 1994 work *D-Day, June 6, 1944,* incorporating veterans' recollections, that brought Ambrose popular success. Among his other best-sellers were *Undaunted Courage* (1996), on the expedition of Meriwether Lewis and William Clark; *Citizen Soldiers* (1997), an account of combat from D-Day to the German surrender; and *Nothing like It in the World* (2000), on the building of the transcontinental railroad. *To America: Personal Reflections of an Historian* was published in 2002 as a valedictory. Ambrose served as a commentator for the Ken Burns 1997 television documentary on Lewis and Clark, and he was a consultant on the 1998 film *Saving Private Ryan*. His 1992 book *Band of Brothers,* which followed a company of U.S. paratroopers, was adapted as a television miniseries in 2001. Ambrose conducted historical tours and founded the Eisenhower

Center for American Studies and the National D-Day Museum, both in New Orleans.

Annenberg, Walter Hubert, American publisher and philanthropist (b. March 13, 1908, Milwaukee, Wis.—d. Oct. 1, 2002, Wynnewood, Pa.), used his wealth to promote conservative political causes and to support education and the arts. He was the son of an immigrant, Moses L. Annenberg, whose businesses included the *Philadelphia Inquirer,* horse racing publications, and wire betting services. The father, as well as his son and two associates, was indicted in 1939 for tax evasion and bribery and served two years in prison after having made a settlement that included having charges against the others dropped. When his father died in 1942, the son took over the business, Triangle Publications, Inc. He bought radio and television stations, began *Seventeen* magazine in 1944, and in 1953 launched *TV Guide,* which gained the largest circulation of any American publication. As publisher and editor of the *Philadelphia Inquirer,* he promoted local reforms but also used the paper to advance partisan causes. In 1969 he sold the paper, along with the *Philadelphia Daily News,* which he had bought in 1944, and in 1988 he sold the remainder of his businesses for an estimated $3.2 billion. A supporter of Richard M. Nixon and Ronald Reagan, he was ambassador to Britain from 1969 to 1974 under President Nixon. Although the appointment was criticized, he endeared himself to many British, partly through his philanthropic projects, and in 1976 Queen Elizabeth II made him an honorary knight. Through the Annenberg Foundation he supported a number of enterprises and institutions. He established the Annenberg School for Communication at the University of Pennsylvania (1958) and at the University of Southern California (1971).

Arledge, Roone Pinckney, American television executive (b. July 8, 1931, Forest Hills, N.Y.—d. Dec. 5, 2002, New York, N.Y.), transformed television sports broadcasting in the 1960s and '70s by introducing an array of technical innovations and by creating such popular programs as *Wide World of Sports* and *Monday Night Football;* later in his career he became one of the most influential figures in television news. After graduating from Columbia University, New York City, in 1952 and serving (1953–55) in the U.S. Army, Arledge worked for five years as a producer and director for the National Broadcasting Company. In 1960 he joined the American Broadcasting Company as a producer for ABC Sports. He was named president of the division eight years later. Among other innovations, Arledge introduced instant replay, freeze frames, and slow-motion replays and used isolated cameras to record action from several angles. He launched *Wide World of Sports* in 1961 and *Monday Night Football* in 1970, and between 1964 and 1988 he supervised the coverage of 10 Olympic Games. In 1977 Arledge became president of ABC News, and he soon turned it into a top-rated division, in part by expanding news into prime time with shows

such as *20/20* and creating the highly regarded late-night news show *Nightline.* He stepped down as head of ABC News in 1998.

Armitage, (William) Kenneth, British sculptor (b. July 18, 1916, Leeds, Eng.—d. Jan. 22, 2002, London, Eng.), created semiabstract bronzes, many of which displayed quirky humour, that put him at the forefront of post–World War II British art. Armitage was the head of sculpture at the Bath Academy of Art (1946–56) and was Britain's first university artist in residence (at the University of Leeds, 1953–56). He was selected to exhibit at the Venice Biennale in 1952 and in 1958, when he won the prize for best international sculptor under age 45. During the 1960s and beyond, he adapted to changing art styles, sometimes incorporating plastic or spray paint. His mature bronzes were often first formed in clay and then cast in monumental size. Armitage was made CBE in 1969 and was elected to the Royal Academy in 1994.

Ashley, Ted (THEODORE ASSOFSKY), American business executive (b. Aug. 3, 1922, New York, N.Y.—d. Aug. 24, 2002, New York City), revived Warner Brothers studios during his tenure as chairman and CEO (1969–80) with such films as *A Clockwork Orange* (1971), *The Exorcist* (1973), *Blazing Saddles* (1974), *All the President's Men* (1976), and *Superman* (1978). In 1969 he acquired Warner Brothers with businessman Steven J. Ross. Ashley was also the force behind many hit television series of the 1970s, as well as the creation of the TV miniseries.

Augstein, Rudolf Karl, German magazine publisher (b. Nov. 5, 1923, Hanover, Ger.—d. Nov. 7, 2002, Hamburg, Ger.), was the publisher, editor (until 1995), and chief editorial writer of *Der Spiegel,* the influential weekly newsmagazine that he founded in January 1947 and guided until the day of his death. Augstein, who imbued *Der Spiegel* with a strong political viewpoint, supported

Der Spiegel's *Rudolf Karl Augstein*

© AFP 2002

Ostpolitik (West German Chancellor Willy Brandt's policy of improved relations with East Germany), as well as reunification. In 1962 he was arrested and jailed for more than 100 days after *Der Spiegel* published an article critical of Defense Minister Franz-Josef Strauss. By the time the "Speigel affair" was over, however, Augstein had been reinstated and Strauss had been forced to resign.

Azmi, Kaifi (ATHAR HUSAIN RIZVI), Indian poet and lyricist (b. about 1920, Mijwan, United Provinces [now Uttar Pradesh], India—d. May 10, 2002, Mumbai [Bombay], India), sought to inspire social change through his passionate Urdu-language verse, as well as through the lyrics (and occasional dialogue) he wrote for numerous popular Bollywood motion pictures. He was only the second Urdu poet chosen to be a fellow of the Sahitya Academy.

Badawi, Abdel Rahman ('ABD AL-RAHMAN BADAWI), Egyptian philosopher and academic (b. Feb. 17, 1917, Sharabass, Egypt—d. July 25, 2002, Cairo, Egypt), was generally regarded as Egypt's first and foremost existential philosopher. Badawi received much of his education in French and earned a Ph.D. from King Fuad University (later Cairo University) in 1944. His thesis was later edited and published under the title *Le Problème de la mort dans la philosophie existentielle* (1964). In the early 1950s he helped draft a new Egyptian constitution, which was ultimately discarded. Badawi taught at Ibrahim Pasha University (1950–71) and at universities in Lebanon (1947–49), Libya (1967–73), Iran (1973–74), and Kuwait (1975–82). His works included *Al-Zamān al-wūjudī* (1945; "Existentialist Time"), studies on Aristotle, Friedrich Nietzsche, Arthur Schopenhauer, and Oswald Spengler, and a two-volume autobiography.

Balaguer Ricardo, Joaquín, Dominican lawyer, politician, and writer (b. Sept. 1, 1906, Villa Navarrete [now Villa Bisonó], Dom.Rep.—d. July 14, 2002, Santo Domingo, Dom.Rep.), held office for 22 years as the country's elected president. He was an autocrat who had the support of businessmen and whose paternalism endeared him to the poor. With leftist opponent Juan Bosch, he dominated Dominican politics for a generation. In 1929 Balaguer gained a law degree from the University of Santo Domingo, where he later taught, and in 1934 he received a doctorate in law and political economy from the University of Paris. He entered politics in 1932, becoming a protégé of dictator Rafael Trujillo, and held diplomatic and ministerial positions. In 1960 he was appointed president, then a largely figurehead position. Upon Trujillo's assassination in 1961, Balaguer attempted to liberalize the government, but in the following year he was driven from office and into exile in the U.S. When the U.S. sent military forces in 1965 to prevent a leftist takeover, Balaguer returned. He was elected president of the Dominican Republic in 1966 and reelected in 1970 and 1974. His government was brutally repressive, with hundreds of people disappearing or fleeing the country. The economy strengthened, however, and a middle class began to develop. Balaguer lost the 1978 election, but he returned to power in 1986, by which time he was virtually blind. He was reelected in 1990 and 1994 amid charges of fraud and was forced to agree to step down in 1996. His second period as elected president was less harsh, although the economy suffered, partly from falling sugar exports. Among his extensive public works projects, the most widely criticized was an enormous lighthouse completed in 1992 to celebrate the 500th anniversary of the voyage of Christopher Columbus. Balaguer's writings included poetry and books on Latin American history, politics, and literature.

Bánzer Suárez, Hugo, Bolivian president (b. May 10, 1926, Concepción, Bol.—d. May 5, 2002, Santa Cruz, Bol.), headed a military regime in the 1970s and a democratically elected government in the late 1990s. Defenders credited him with having helped move Bolivia toward democratic government, but detractors saw him as a dictator. He entered the Colegio Militar in La Paz at the age of 14 and later studied at the Argentine staff college, at the School of the Americas in Panama, which was run by the U.S. Army, and at Fort Hood, Texas. He was a cavalry officer before serving as minister of education in 1964–66, being appointed a military attaché, which included a period of duty in Washington, D.C., and becoming head of the Colegio Militar in 1969. After leading a failed coup against Gen. Juan José Torres Gonzáles, the Bolivian president, Bánzer was exiled in January 1971, but he secretly returned later in the year and in August overthrew the government. His rule was brutally oppressive, with the news media censored and political activity forbidden. It was estimated that 15,000 citizens were arrested on political charges and that 19,000 sought asylum in other countries; several hundred people were killed. Bánzer survived 13 coup attempts before being overthrown in 1978. He then formed Nationalist Democratic Action and ran in all six presidential elections in the 1980s and 1990s. Although he won a plurality in the 1985 election, he stood aside when Congress chose another candidate as president. Under the same situation in the 1997 election, Congress picked Bánzer, and he began his second term as president. With prodding from the U.S., he effectively eliminated the country's cocaine production, but his administration was characterized by corruption and instability. He resigned the presidency in August 2001 because of poor health.

Bauer of Market Ward in the City of Cambridge, Peter Thomas Bauer, Baron (PÉTER TAMÁS BAUER), Hungarian-born British economist (b. Nov. 6, 1915, Budapest, Hung., Austria-Hungary—d. May 3, 2002, London, Eng.), fiercely opposed all developmental aid to less-developed countries because he said that it discouraged local initiative and was too often misused by corrupt leaders; he contended that economic de-

velopment was possible only through private enterprise, the unrestricted exchange of ideas, free trade, and unregulated market forces. Though Bauer spoke little English when he arrived in England in 1934, he nonetheless was accepted at Gonville and Caius College, Cambridge, and earned a first-class degree in economics (1937). He briefly worked for a rubber-trading company, then taught at the University of London (1947–48) and at Cambridge from 1948 until 1960, when he was named a professor at the London School of Economics. He retired in 1983, a year after he had been granted a life peerage on the recommendation of Prime Minister Margaret Thatcher, who applauded his conservative economic theories.

Beach, Edward Latimer, Jr., American submariner and writer (b. April 20, 1918, New York, N.Y.—d. Dec. 1, 2002, Washington, D.C.), was awarded a number of decorations for service during World War II that resulted in the sinking or damaging of 45 enemy vessels and in 1960 was commander of the nuclear-powered *Triton*, at the time the world's largest and most powerful submarine, when it made the first underwater circumnavigation of the globe. To the general public, though, he was better known as the author of the war novel *Run Silent, Run Deep* (1955), which won the National Book Award in 1956 and was filmed in 1958.

Belaúnde Terry, Fernando, Peruvian politician (b. Oct. 7, 1912, Lima, Peru—d. June 4, 2002, Lima), served two terms as president, from 1963 to 1968 and from 1980 to 1985. A reformer, he was often called the "father of democracy" in Peru, but his attempts to modernize the economy were not considered successful. When Belaúnde was 12, his family was forced into exile, and he was subsequently educated in Paris and in the U.S., where he earned (1935) a degree in architecture from the University of Texas. He then returned to Peru and practiced and taught architecture; from 1955 to 1960 he was dean of architecture at the National Engineering University in Lima. First elected to Congress in 1945, he ran unsuccessfully for president in 1956. That same year he founded Acción Popular (AP). Although he led in the voting in the 1962 election, the army nullified the results, but the following year, when he again took a plurality, the army allowed him to assume office. Although he began road-building and other projects to open up the interior of Peru, his plans for agrarian reform were blocked. The country also suffered from economic problems, including deficits and a currency devaluation, and Belaúnde was overthrown by the army in October 1968. He went into exile in Argentina and then the U.S., where he taught at several universities, including Harvard and Columbia. He returned to Peru in

the late 1970s, and in 1980 AP, in a coalition with the Partido Popular Cristiano, won both houses of Congress. His second term as president was also marked by economic problems, including high unemployment and crippling inflation, in addition to threats from terrorists such as the Sendero Luminoso (Shining Path). Nonetheless, Belaúnde served his full term and transferred power in 1985 to an elected successor. From 1985 to 1992 he sat in Congress as senator for life.

Bell, (George) Derek Fleetwood, Irish musician and composer (b. Oct. 21, 1935, Belfast, N.Ire.—d. Oct. 17, 2002, Phoenix, Ariz.), brought a classical music background to the popular Irish folk group the Chieftains when he joined them as harpist in 1972. Having already mastered a variety of instruments, including the piano, oboe, and horn, Bell took up the harp in the 1960s while he was managing the Belfast Symphony Orchestra. In 1974 he left a job with the BBC Northern Ireland Orchestra to tour full time with the Chieftains. Bell's academic training was an influence on the group's traditional music on more than 30 albums, as well as on the film sound tracks for *Barry Lyndon* (1975) and *Far and Away* (1992). In addition to his work with the Chieftains, he recorded solo albums, many of which were more classical in tone. He was appointed MBE in 2000.

Benson, Mildred Augustine Wirt, American writer (b. July 10, 1905, Ladora, Iowa—d. May 28, 2002, Toledo, Ohio), as the original author of the Nancy Drew mysteries, abandoned the stereotypical view of the heroine then common and created a teenage female who was brainy, spirited, and independent. Under the name Carolyn Keene, she wrote 23 of the first 30 books, from 1930 to 1953, but she was not publicly known as the author until a court case involving the publisher revealed that fact in 1980.

Berg, David, American cartoonist and writer (b. June 12, 1920, Brooklyn, N.Y.—d. May 16, 2002, Marina del Rey, Calif.), began contributing to *Mad* magazine in 1956 and in 1961 introduced the monthly "The Lighter Side of . . ." strip, which in 365 issues featured his own self-caricature (named Roger Kaputnik) in humorous observations of the foibles of contemporary life and its issues. His 17 books sold over 10 million copies.

Berle, Milton (MENDEL BERLINGER), American comedian, actor, and songwriter (b. July 12, 1908, New York, N.Y.—d. March 27, 2002, Los Angeles, Calif.), came to be known as "Mr. Television" after he pioneered the TV variety show in 1948, and his flamboyant antics inspired hundreds of thousands of Americans to purchase their first TV sets so they could watch his show, *Texaco Star Theater*. The number of sets grew from 136,000 in 1947 to 700,000 in 1948, and restaurants and entertainment venues arranged their schedules around his Tuesday-evening broadcast. Berle began his show business career when he was five years old and won a Charlie Chaplin im-

Milton Berle in full comic regalia

personation contest. His mother saw an opportunity and began making the rounds of agents' offices, and she and her children soon were appearing in silent films. Among Berle's silents were *The Perils of Pauline* (1914), his debut, and *The Mark of Zorro* (1920). He made his Broadway debut in *The Floradora Girl* (1920), joined the vaudeville circuit with a partner, and in late 1924 made his first appearance as a solo act. Around that time Berle began to incorporate into his act what would later become one of his trademarks—dressing in women's clothes. He also "borrowed" jokes from other comics, something that earned him the nickname "the Thief of Bad Gags." In addition to vaudeville, Berle added Broadway appearances in a few shows, including *Earl Carroll's Vanities* (1932) and *The Ziegfeld Follies* (1936), and roles in such motion pictures as *New Faces of 1937* (1937) and *Sun Valley Serenade* (1941) to his credits, and he performed on several radio shows. He also began writing what would eventually total some 400 songs (including "Sam, You Made the Pants Too Long"). It was television, however, that made the uninhibited "Uncle Miltie" a household name. Berle won an Emmy Award in 1949, and *Texaco Star Theater* was such a hit that in 1951 NBC gave him a 30-year "lifetime" contract. The show became the *Buick-Berle Show* in 1953 and ended in 1955. *The Milton Berle Show* followed but, losing ratings to ever-increasing competition, went off the air in 1956. Berle thereafter made numerous TV guest appearances, performed in nightclubs, was a staple of celebrity roasts, and continued to appear on Broadway (*Goodbye People* [1968]) and in movies, among them *It's a Mad Mad Mad Mad World* (1963) and *Broadway Danny Rose* (1984). He also was the coauthor of seven books. In 1984 Berle became one of the original inductees into the Academy of Television Arts and Sciences Hall of Fame.

Berrigan, Philip Francis, American peace activist and former Roman Catholic priest (b. Oct. 5, 1923, Two Harbors, Minn.—d. Dec. 6, 2002, Baltimore, Md.), saw combat duty during World War II but later, after having been ordained a priest in 1955 and become active in the civil rights movement, came to be one of the 20th century's most militant pacifists. During the Vietnam War he and his brother, the Rev. Daniel J. Berrigan, engaged in numerous protest activities, were repeatedly imprisoned for their deeds, and served as inspiration for the peace activists of the era. In 1968, in perhaps their most famous incident, the brothers and seven others—the "Catonsville Nine," as they came to be known—carried out a raid on the office of the Catonsville, Md., draft board and used homemade napalm to burn its files in the parking lot. Berrigan and Elizabeth McAlister, a nun, were married in 1973, whereupon both were excommunicated. They founded Jonah House in Baltimore, and in 1980 Berrigan helped found the Plowshares movement, through which he continued his activism.

Bilandic, Michael Anthony, American politician and judge (b. Feb. 13, 1923, Chicago, Ill.—d. Jan. 15, 2002, Chicago), succeeded (1976) Richard J. Daley as mayor of Chicago and later served as chief justice of the Illinois Supreme Court. The City Council chose Bilandic as a temporary successor, and six months later he won a special election to serve the remainder of Daley's term. His poor handling of snow removal following record-setting blizzards in 1979 contributed to his loss that year to Jane Byrne in the Democratic primary.

Billingham, Rupert Everett, British-born American immunologist and transplant researcher (b. Oct. 15, 1921, Warminster, Eng.—d. Nov. 16, 2002, Boston, Mass.), was a pioneer in the field of immunologic theory and transplant science. Under his mentor, zoologist Peter B. Medawar, Billingham helped conduct a series of groundbreaking experiments involving skin grafts on animals in the late 1940s and early '50s that proved the theory of acquired immunologic tolerance—the concept on which tissue transplantation was founded. These experiments led to ultimately successful attempts at organ transplantation in humans. Medawar was awarded the Nobel Prize for Physiology or Medicine in 1960 and shared the prize money with Billingham. From 1965 to 1971 Billingham served as chairman of the department of medical genetics at the University of Pennsylvania School of Medicine. He went on to chair the department of cell Biology and anatomy at the Southwestern Medical School, University of Texas, from 1971 to 1986.

Bin Salman, Prince Ahmed (PRINCE AHMED IBN SALMAN IBN 'ABD AL-AZIZ), Saudi businessman and racehorse owner (b. Nov. 17, 1958, Riyadh, Saudi Arabia—d. July 22, 2002, Riyadh), fulfilled a lifelong goal when his recently purchased horse War Emblem won the 2002 Kentucky Derby; he lost his bid for a Triple Crown, however, when War Emblem captured the Preakness Stakes but failed in the Belmont Stakes. A nephew of Saudi Arabia's King Fahd, Bin Salman became interested in horse racing while attending the University of California, Irvine, in the early 1980s. After assuming the chairmanship of Saudi Research and Marketing in 1989, he turned the company into the largest publishing empire in the Arab world. Bin Salman returned to horse racing in the late 1990s and made many successful acquisitions.

Bjørnson, Maria (MARIA ELENA PRODEN), British costume and set designer (b. Feb. 16, 1949, Paris, France—d. Dec. 13, 2002, London, Eng.), created imaginative and innovative designs for more than 125 opera, ballet, and theatre productions in a career that spanned 32 years. She was most acclaimed for her work on Andrew Lloyd Webber's *Phantom of the Opera* (1986), for which she was honoured with two Tony, two Outer Critics Circle, and two Los Angeles Drama Critics awards.

Blackwell, Otis, American singer and songwriter (b. Feb. 16, 1931/32, Brooklyn, N.Y.—d. May 6, 2002, Nashville, Tenn.), began as a singer but saw that career overshadowed by his writing of more than 1,000 songs, which hugely influenced the development of the sound of rock and roll. Among his hits were Elvis Presley's "Don't Be Cruel" and "All Shook Up" and Jerry Lee Lewis's "Great Balls of Fire" and "Breathless," and he collaborated on Peggy Lee's signature song, "Fever."

Blackwood, James, American gospel singer (b. Aug. 4, 1919, Choctaw county, Miss.—d. Feb. 3, 2002, Memphis, Tenn.), was a founding member and leader of the Blackwood Brothers Quartet, the first gospel group to sell one million records. Blackwood was also a well-known solo performer and was a lifelong friend and early mentor to Elvis Presley. The group released more than 200 albums and won nine Grammy Awards over the years. Blackwood was twice inducted into the Gospel Music Hall of Fame, first as a solo performer in 1974 and then with his quartet in 1998.

Blass, William Ralph ("BILL"), American fashion designer (b. June 22, 1922, Fort Wayne, Ind.—d. June 12, 2002, New Preston, Conn.), became an icon in the fashion world not only by designing "wearable" clothing with an understated, comfortable elegance that was popular with members of high society but also by moving in that social circle and becoming a celebrity himself. In addition, he was the first American designer of women's fashions to branch out into the field of men's designer wear, introducing options to the serious "gray flannel" look then prevalent, and he increased his renown by licensing his name to a wide range of moderately priced products—including perfume, chocolates, flight attendant uniforms, and jeans—and by making substantial donations to the New York Public

© AFP 2002, by Stan Honda

Superdesigner Bill Blass

Library and supporting and raising funds for AIDS programs. While still in high school, Blass began to sell designs to New York City clothing manufacturers. Following graduation he moved to New York, where he studied for a short time and worked as a sketch artist before enlisting (1943) in the army. When he returned to New York, Blass worked first for Anne Klein and then for Anna Miller, and after Miller retired (1959) and her firm merged with the fashion house of her brother, Maurice Rentner, Blass began to gain recognition. His name soon appeared on the label, and in 1970 he bought the company and renamed it Bill Blass Ltd. Blass ensured his success by paying attention to what his clients really wanted to wear for both everyday activities and social occasions and by expanding into sportswear and thereby paving the way for his large number of licensing deals. In 1999 he sold his $700-million-a-year business for a reported $50 million. Among Blass's numerous honours were Coty American Fashion Critics Awards (1961, 1963, and 1970), Coty Awards for men's wear (1968 [the first such award], 1971, 1982, and 1983), the Lifetime Achievement Award from the Council of Fashion Designers of America (1987), the council's first Humanitarian Leadership Award (1996), and the Fashion Institute of Technology's Lifetime Achievement Award (1999).

Bohlin, Nils, Swedish aerospace engineer and inventor (b. July 17, 1920, Härnösand, Swed.—d. Sept. 21, 2002, Tranas, Swed.), developed the revolutionary three-point seat belt, which greatly improved automotive safety and saved countless lives. After having designed aviation ejector seats, Bohlin was hired in 1958 by the Volvo Car Corp. as its

first chief safety engineer. His new seat belt was introduced in Volvo cars the following year. Unlike previous belts, Bohlin's creation secured both the upper and the lower body by means of two straps that joined at the hip and buckled into an anchor point. The three-point seat belt greatly reduced the risk of injury and became standard on cars worldwide; it was required on all new American vehicles from 1968. Bohlin was inducted into the National Inventors Hall of Fame in Akron, Ohio, on the day he died.

Bonanno, Joseph ("JOE BANANAS"), Italian-born American organized crime figure (b. Jan. 18, 1905, Castellammare del Golfo, Sicily, Italy—d. May 11, 2002, Tucson, Ariz.), was the founder of one of the five crime families that were the heart of the Commission, which united feuding Sicilian gangs. Although he guided the Bonanno family's underworld activities from 1931 until the mid-1960s, he avoided imprisonment until the 1980s, when he twice served time—once for a year for obstruction of justice and later for 14 months for contempt of court.

Borkenstein, Robert, American inventor (b. Aug. 31, 1912, Fort Wayne, Ind.—d. Aug. 10, 2002, Bloomington, Ind.), patented the Breathalyzer, the groundbreaking device used for decades by police to determine a driver's level of intoxication. In the 1960s Borkenstein led a research project that recommended a blood alcohol level of .08 as the level at which driving was impaired, a standard that was rapidly adopted.

Borst, Lyle Benjamin, American nuclear physicist (b. Nov. 24, 1912, Chicago, Ill. —d. July 30, 2002, Williamsville, N.Y.), supervised the construction of the nation's largest atomic reactor at the Brookhaven National Laboratory, Upton, N.Y., in 1950. Among his successes at the facility were improvements in how the reactor was cooled, the discovery of a radioactive iodine used to treat thyroid cancer, and evidence that explained how a supernova is created. Borst also worked on the Manhattan Project at Oak Ridge, Tenn. At the dawn of the atomic age, he organized scientists and lobbied the U.S. Congress to stress civilian rather than military uses of atomic energy; he was a founder in 1945 of the Federation of Atomic (later American) Scientists.

Bourdieu, Pierre, French sociologist (b. Aug. 1, 1930, Denguin, France—d. Jan. 23, 2002, Paris, France), was a public intellectual in the tradition of Émile Zola and Jean-Paul Sartre. Bourdieu's concept of *habitus* (socially acquired dispositions) was influential in recent postmodernist humanities and social sciences. He taught at a lycée in Moulins (1955–58), the University of Algiers (1958–60), the University of Paris (1960–64), and the École des Hautes Études en Sciences Sociales (from 1964)—where he established the Centre for the Sociology of Education and Culture—and the Collège de France (from 1982). Bourdieu's experience in Algeria resulted in *Sociologie de l'Algérie* (1958; *The Algerians,* 1962), which es-

tablished his reputation. His works—*La Distinction* (1979; *Distinction,* 1984), *Le Sens pratique* (1980; *The Logic of Practice,* 1990), *La Noblesse d'état* (1989; *The State Nobility,* 1996), and *Sur la télévision* (1996; *On Television,* 1998)—criticized neoliberal economics, globalization, the intellectual elite, and television. Bourdieu was editor of the journal *Actes de la recherche en sciences sociales,* and in 1989 he founded the review *Liber.*

Bracken, Edward Vincent ("EDDIE"), American stage and film comedian and character actor (b. Feb. 7, 1915/20, Astoria, N.Y.—d. Nov. 14, 2002, Montclair, N.J.), had a 70-year career highlighted by roles in two 1944 Preston Sturges movies, *The Miracle of Morgan's Creek* and *Hail the Conquering Hero,* and by his Tony Award-nominated role as Horace Vandergelder opposite Carol Channing in a Broadway revival of *Hello, Dolly!* (1978).

Brown, Claude, American author (b. Feb. 23, 1937, New York, N.Y.—d. Feb. 2, 2002, New York City), wrote a landmark work in African American literature, *Manchild in the Promised Land* (1965), which chronicled his poverty-stricken childhood in the Harlem district of New York City. Brown published the memoir the same year he graduated from Howard University, Washington, D.C. The book was both a critical and a commercial success. Brown followed up this effort with a novel, *The Children of Ham* (1976).

Brown, Dorris Alexander ("DEE"), American writer and academic (b. Feb. 29, 1908, near Alberta, La.—d. Dec. 12, 2002, Little Rock, Ark.), while serving as a librarian at the University of Illinois, began writing books—a number of them for children—and ultimately published some 30, including 11 novels. His best-known work was *Bury My Heart at Wounded Knee* (1970), a chronicle of the brutal treatment and conquest of Native Americans that ended in the massacre of 300 Sioux at Wounded Knee Creek in South Dakota in 1890. By 2002 the book, which essentially wiped out the then prevailing mythology regarding the settling of the American West, had sold more than five million copies and been translated into at least 15 languages.

Brown, Earle, American composer (b. Dec. 26, 1926, Lunenburg, Mass.—d. July 2, 2002, Rye, N.Y.), used graphic notation to convey the sense of the passage of sounds through time and open form to give musicians latitude in the performance of a work. His music was particularly influential among European composers such as Krzysztof Penderecki. From 1946 to 1950 he studied at the Schillinger House (now Berklee College) of Music in

Boston. He then became associated with the so-called New York school, which included John Cage and other avant-garde composers, and in 1953 he contributed *Octet I,* a work for eight loudspeakers reproducing musical sounds and noise, to Cage's "Project for Music for Magnetic Tape." The score for Brown's *December 1952* showed the influence of Cage's ideas on indeterminacy. In *Twenty-five Pages* (1953), the performers arranged the pages of the score in any order, and in the two orchestral works *Available Forms I* (1961) and *Available Forms II* (1961–62), the conductor ordered the sections at his own discretion. *Calder Piece* (1963–66), for percussion, was written to be performed on a sculpture especially created by Alexander Calder. Brown's music eventually came to incorporate a balance between open form and fixed notation, as in *Tracking Pierrot* (1992), one of his better-known later works.

Brown, James Richard ("BUSTER"), American dancer and teacher (b. March 17, 1913, Baltimore, Md.—d. May 7, 2002, New York, N.Y.), was one of the last of the legendary tap dancers known as the Copasetics. He toured with Duke Ellington, Dizzy Gillespie, Count Basie, and Cab Calloway; performed on Broadway in *Bubbling Brown Sugar* and *Black and Blue;* danced in the films *Something to Shout About* (1943), *The Cotton Club* (1984), and *Tap* (1989) and on television.

Brown, J(ohn) Carter, American museum director (b. Oct. 8, 1934, Providence, R.I.—d. June 17, 2002, Boston, Mass.), transformed the National Gallery of Art in Washington, D.C., into one of the world's major museums. He was credited with creating so-called blockbuster exhibitions, multimedia events that drew hundreds of thousands of visitors. Brown was a descendent of Roger Williams, founder of Rhode Island, and of Nicholas Brown, who endowed Brown University. He enrolled in the Institute of Fine Arts at New York University, where he received an M.A. degree in 1962. He took a position at the National Gallery of Art in 1961 and from 1969 to 1992 was its director. Brown was skillful in raising money from both public and private sources, and under his leadership the museum vastly broadened its holdings—acquiring more than 20,000 works—and expanded its activities. In 1978 the addition known as the East Building, designed by I.M. Pei, was opened. Among the museum's blockbuster exhibitions were "The Treasures of Tutankhamen" (1976–77), "The Treasure Houses of Britain" (1985–86), and "Circa 1492: Art in the Age of Exploration" (1991–92). As chair of the U.S. Commission of Fine Arts from 1971 to 2002, Brown influenced the design and placement of a number of structures in Washington's Mall, including the Vietnam Veterans Memorial. One of his most important achievements was persuading Congress to indemnify artworks on loan from other countries, which thus made it possible for American museums to afford international exhibitions. He helped create the cable arts network Ovation. Brown

was an honorary CBE and a member of the French Legion of Honour.

Brown, Norman Oliver, American philosopher and critic (b. Sept. 25, 1913, El Oro, Mex.—d. Oct. 2, 2002, Santa Cruz, Calif.), was educated in the classics, but his thought drew on psychoanalysis, literature, and other fields. A Marxist early in his career, he taught at a number of schools, including the University of California, Santa Cruz. He was best known for the book *Life Against Death* (1959), history as interpreted through Freudian thought, in which he argued that Western civilization was essentially repressive. A later book, *Love's Body* (1966), took the same stance, juxtaposing erotic love and civilization. Both works became cult books in the counterculture of the 1960s and '70s.

Brown, Raymond Matthews ("RAY"), American jazz musician (b. Oct. 13, 1926, Pittsburgh, Pa.—d. July 2, 2002, Indianapolis, Ind.), played bass with a long parade of swing- and bop-era greats on more than 2,000 recordings, on worldwide Jazz at the Philharmonic (JATP) concert tours, as a member of the Oscar Peterson Trio, and then as leader or coleader of small and large ensembles. His harmonic ingenuity, strong bass tone, and brilliant technique even at the most difficult tempos combined to provide a stimulating rhythmic foundation, and he was a fluent, skillful soloist even on his first recordings. Brown was just 19 years old when he joined the pioneering bebop big band that trumpet great Dizzy Gillespie formed in 1946; Gillespie featured him in the recordings "One Bass Hit" and "Two Bass Hit." Brown joined JATP in 1947 and toured with the show for 18 years, which included his marriage (1948) to and divorce (1952) from JATP singer Ella Fitzgerald. For

Jazz great Ray Brown

15 of those years he performed with Oscar Peterson, at first in a duo and then, from 1952, in a trio. The Oscar Peterson Trio accompanied stars ranging from Louis Armstrong to the modernists Charlie Parker and Stan Getz. He tired of constant touring and in 1966 settled in Los Angeles, where he became active in film and television studios and in the music business as an artists' manager and songwriter—his tune "Gravy Waltz" had won a Grammy in 1963. By the mid-1970s he was touring again, this time with the L.A. Four, a group of top West Coast-style veterans. He then coled groups with vibraphonist Milt Jackson, and in the 1980s he began leading his own trios.

Brown, Robert Hanbury, British astronomer (b. Aug. 31, 1916, Aravankadu, India—d. Jan. 16, 2002, Andover, Hampshire, Eng.), overcame scientific hurdles and the skepticism of his colleagues in the 1950s to invent the optical intensity spectrometer, a telescopic instrument that measures the sizes of stars. After showing how to determine the angular diameter of radio-emitting stars by collecting their signals at two widely separated dish antennas and combining them properly, he reapplied the technique to light from the star Sirius, using two handmade optical telescopes. He then constructed a more powerful optical intensity spectrometer, with R.Q. Twiss, in Narrabri, N.S.W., Australia, where he measured some 30 stars between 1963 and 1972. Brown recounted his pioneering work in his autobiography, *Boffin: A Personal Story of the Early Days of Radar, Radio Astronomy and Quantum Optics* (1991). After graduating from the University of London in 1935, Brown assisted in secret work to perfect military uses for radar, which continued through World War II. In 1949 he began studying under Sir Bernard Lovell of Manchester University at the Jodrell Bank Observatory. It was there, with several colleagues, that Brown achieved his first successes with his radio and optical measurements of stars. The opportunity to construct a larger optical intensity spectrometer led him to leave his professorship at Manchester (1960–63) for one at the University of Sydney (1964–81).

Buck, John Francis ("JACK"), American sports broadcaster (b. Aug. 21, 1924, Holyoke, Mass.—d. June 18, 2002, St. Louis, Mo.), was considered the voice of baseball's St. Louis Cardinals for nearly half a century. First as Harry Caray's sidekick and from 1969 the lead announcer, he became a St. Louis institution, and with his broadcasting of National Football League, World Series, and professional bowling games on network television and radio, he achieved national renown. In 1987 Buck was inducted into the broadcasters' wing of the Baseball Hall of Fame, and in 2000 he was honoured with an Emmy Award for lifetime achievement.

Bumpus, Dean, American oceanographer (b. May 11, 1912, Newburyport, Mass.—d. March 14, 2002, Woods Hole, Mass.), conducted one of the most comprehensive studies of ocean currents ever undertaken. The unusual method by which Bumpus—a researcher at the Woods Hole Oceanographic Institution from 1937 to 1979—carried out his study attracted widespread attention. He recruited colleagues, friends, and even strangers to dump thousands of bottles at sea, each one containing a note that promised any finder 50 cents for informing Bumpus when and where a bottle had turned up. Bumpus was thus able to measure the flow of the Atlantic Ocean over the eastern continental shelf and help scientists track weather patterns as well as nutrient flows and corresponding fish movements.

Buono, Angelo, Jr., American crime figure (b. Oct. 5, 1934, Rochester, N.Y.—d. Sept. 22, 2002, Sacramento, Calif.), was convicted in 1983 of the murder of nine women in Los Angeles during a four-month period from 1977 to 1978. He disposed of their naked bodies on area hillsides and thereby earned the nickname the "Hillside Strangler." He was found guilty in 1983 and was sentenced to life in prison.

Burton, Charles Robert, British explorer (b. Dec. 13, 1942, Cape Town, S.Af.—d. July 15, 2002, Framfield, East Sussex, Eng.), was part of the first team to circumnavigate the globe from pole to pole along the Greenwich meridian. The Transglobe Expedition, led by Sir Ranulph Fiennes and funded by Charles, prince of Wales, began on Sept. 2, 1979, and ended on Aug. 29, 1982. During the 84,000-km (52,000-mi) expedition, the explorers survived a polar bear attack, the loss of crucial supplies, and three months of being marooned on a drifting ice floe. Upon his return, Burton was awarded the Polar Medal.

Carroll, Vinnette, American stage director and actress (b. March 11, 1922, New York, N.Y.—d. Nov. 5, 2002, Lauderhill, Fla.), was the first African American woman to direct on Broadway. Although she was educated in psychology and worked as a clinical psychologist, she left the field for the theatre. In 1962 she won an Obie Award for *Moon on a Rainbow Shawl*, and in 1964 she received an Emmy Award for *Beyond the Blues*. The hit gospel review *Don't Bother Me, I Can't Cope* opened on Broadway in 1972 and was nominated for a Tony Award. Her adaptation of the Gospel According to Matthew, *Your Arms Too Short to Box with God*, opened on Broadway in 1976 and was nominated for two Tonys. As an actress she appeared in the films *Up the Down Staircase* (1967) and *Alice's Restaurant* (1969).

Castiglioni, Achille, Italian architect and interior designer (b. Feb. 16, 1918, Milan, Italy—d. Dec. 2, 2002, Milan), produced modern furnishings and accessories that were noted for their functional nature and witty styling. After graduating from the Polytechnic Institute of Milan in 1944, Castiglioni went to work with his brothers Livio and Pier Giacomo. Livio quit in 1952, but Achille and Pier Giacomo continued to collaborate. In addition to architectural projects, the brothers created signature interior pieces that included the Mezzadro, a stool topped with a tractor

seat, and the Arco lamp, a ball-shaped shade attached to a steel arch, which could replace an overhead light. After Pier Giacomo's death in 1968, Achille continued as a solo designer and urban planner. Castiglioni won the Golden Compass, Italy's top prize for industrial design, nine times.

Castle of Blackburn, Barbara Anne Castle, Baroness, British politician (b. Oct. 6, 1910, Chesterfield, Derbyshire, Eng.—d. May 3, 2002, Ibstone, Buckinghamshire, Eng.), was a staunch socialist and longtime Labour MP (1945–79) who fought for and won a series of social reforms, but her attempt to legislate sweeping changes to the powerful trade unions ended in ignominious defeat in 1969 and helped to split the Labour Party. Castle was born Barbara Betts, the daughter of a socialist tax inspector. While studying at St. Hugh's College, Oxford, on a scholarship, she became active in Labour Party politics. After graduating with a disappointing third-class degree, she worked as a journalist on the left-wing weekly *Tribune* and on the *Daily Mirror*, whose night editor, Ted Castle, she later married. Barbara Castle was elected to Parliament in 1945; she quickly became a force in the socialist wing of the Labour Party and gained a new nickname, the "Red Queen" (for both her red hair and her fiery speeches). As a cabinet minister in Prime Minister Harold Wilson's government, her triumphs far outnumbered her defeats. As minister of transport (1965–68), she expanded road building, deflected a railway strike, and introduced mandatory seat belts and the Breathalyzer to test for drunk drivers; as secretary of state for employment and productivity (1968–70), she pushed through the Equal Pay Act; and as secretary of state for social services (1974–76), she instituted a plan to tie state pensions to income and ensured that child benefits would be paid directly to the mother rather than being included in the father's paycheck. In 1969 she issued a devastating White Paper, *In Place of Strife*, which called for the modernization of trade unions. Union leadership fiercely opposed any changes (even some Castle considered pro-labour), and union power within the Labour Party prevailed. Prime Minister James Callaghan, a longtime Labour opponent, dismissed her from the cabinet in 1976. Three years later, despite having opposed Britain's entry into the Common Market, Castle was elected to the European Parliament, where she remained a leading socialist until her retirement in 1989. She was granted a life peerage in 1990.

Cela (Trulock), Camilo José, Spanish writer (b. May 11, 1916, Iria Flavia, Spain—d. Jan. 17, 2002, Madrid, Spain), won the Nobel Prize for Literature in 1989 "for a rich and intensive prose, which with restrained compassion forms a challenging vision of man's vulnerability."

Cela's literary output included novels, short stories, essays, and travel diaries and was characterized by caustic wit and experimentation in both form and content. He also championed the Spanish language, and beginning in 1968 he published *Diccionario secreto*, a multivolume compilation of colloquial vulgarities. As a young man, Cela fought in Francisco Franco's army; later, as the editor (1956–79) of the literary monthly *Papeles de son armadans*, he often published works by critics of Franco's regime. Cela's most celebrated novels, *La familia de Pascual Duarte* (1942; *Pascual Duarte's Family*, 1946) and *La colmena* (1951; *The Hive*, 1953), were banned in Spain for a time. He later received numerous honours, including election to the Spanish Royal Academy in 1957 and the Cervantes Prize in 1995. Cela was appointed to the Spanish Senate in 1977.

Chauncey, Henry, American educator (b. Feb. 9, 1905, New York, N.Y.—d. Dec. 3, 2002, Shelburne, Vt.), was an assistant dean at Harvard University when he began the quest for a meritocratic means of assessing applicants for admission to the university. In 1947, with Harvard president James Bryant Conant, he founded the Educational Testing Service (ETS) to encourage standardized testing in college admissions. Until his retirement in 1970, Chauncey served as president of ETS, which promoted the use of the Scholastic Aptitude (from 1994, Assessment) Test (SAT). Thousands of American universities adopted the SAT as part of their admissions process.

Chillida Juantegui, Eduardo, Spanish Basque sculptor (b. Jan. 10, 1924, San Sebastián, Spain—d. Aug. 19, 2002, San Sebastián), crafted monumental abstract pieces, many of which were installed in public spaces in cities throughout Europe and the U.S. Although Chillida occasionally worked in wood, alabaster, or terra-cotta, the majority of his significant sculptures were in iron, steel, concrete, or granite and displayed a use of elemental forms and open space that reflected both his architectural training and his essentially ascetic vision. His most popular and admired work, *Peines del viento* ("Wind Combs"), consists of a series of three massive sculptures of twisted iron jutting out from the rocks overlooking the coast near San Sebastián. Chillida studied architecture at the University of Madrid (1943–47) and art in Paris (1948–50) before returning to his Basque homeland to settle permanently. He had his first one-man show in Madrid in 1954 and in 1958 was awarded the sculpture prize at the Venice Biennale. Many other international honours soon followed, notably the Carnegie International Prize in 1964 and the Andrew Mellon Prize in 1979. In the 1970s Chillida campaigned for the release of Basque prisoners, but he never endorsed violent separatism. The Museum Chillida-Leku opened in Zabalaga near San Sebastián in 2000.

Cho Choong Hoon, South Korean businessman (b. Feb. 11, 1920, Seoul, Korea—d. Nov. 17, 2002, Seoul, S.Kor.), founded the Hanjin Group, which became the eighth largest conglomerate in the country and included 21 companies, including Korean Air Lines, for which he served as chairman from 1969 to 1999. Cho, who aggressively expanded Korean Air Lines and tripled revenues during the 1980s and '90s, was forced to resign as chairman of the airline following a series of plane crashes that claimed the lives of more than 800 people between 1983 and 1999.

Choi Hong Hi, Korean army officer and martial artist (b. Nov. 9, 1918, Myong Chun district, Kor. [now in North Korea]—d. June 15, 2002, Pyongyang, N.Kor.), was credited with having developed tae kwon do in the 1940s by combining elements of other Asian martial arts forms and with having helped it to spread to more than 120 countries and 40 million practitioners. He also was a founder (1946) of the South Korean army and rose in it to the rank of major general, but he went into exile in Canada in 1971 in protest against the politicizing of tae kwon do.

Clark, J(ohn) Desmond, British archaeologist and anthropologist (b. April 10, 1916, London, Eng.—d. Feb. 14, 2002, Oakland, Calif.), was a world-renowned authority on ancient Africa and the leader of archaeological expeditions that opened dramatic new windows on human prehistory. A year after graduating from the University of Cambridge in 1937, Clark became director of the Rhodes-Livingstone Museum in Northern Rhodesia (now Zambia), a position he held until 1961. During this time, while developing the museum, he conducted archaeological research and published his findings in *The Prehistoric Cultures of the Horn of Africa* (1954); he also helped found the Pan-African Congress on Prehistory, the first organization to bring together archaeologists from across the continent. As professor of anthropology at the University of California, Berkeley, from 1961 to 1986, Clark led a number of important expeditions in Africa. In Ethiopia with colleague Tim White in 1981, he unearthed a four-million-year-old skull and femur fragments; the fossils belonged to the oldest human ancestor known at that time and helped scientists establish that bipedalism had evolved independently of brain size. In 1991 a Clark-led team excavated in the Nihewan Basin near Beijing—the first team of foreign archaeologists to work inside China in 40 years.

Claus, Prince (CLAUS GEORG WILHELM OTTO FRIEDRICH GERD VON AMSBERG), German-born Dutch royal (b. Sept. 6, 1926, Dötzingen, Ger.—d. Oct. 6, 2002, Amsterdam, Neth.), was the consort of Queen Beatrix of The Netherlands. When Claus married then crown princess Beatrix in March 1966, he faced public protests and official misgivings over his boyhood membership in the Hitler Youth and his World War II service in the Wehrmacht, but he ultimately proved to be a popular and respected member of the Dutch royal family. Upon his marriage Claus was granted the title prince of the Netherlands and the designation Jonkheer van Amsberg. The birth in 1967 of Prince Willem-Alexander, the first male heir born to a Dutch monarch in more than a century, was the occasion for national rejoicing, and by the time Beatrix assumed the throne (1980), Claus had won over his critics. As prince consort he worked for development and regional planning, historic preservation, and environmental conservation.

Clooney, Rosemary, American singer (b. May 23, 1928, Maysville, Ky.—d. June 29, 2002, Beverly Hills, Calif.), employed her warm vocals to popularize such 1950s hit novelty songs as "This Ole House" and "Mambo Italiano" as well as the love songs "Tenderly," "Half as Much," and "Hey There." While living with their grandfather in Cincinnati, Ohio, 16-year-old Clooney and her younger sister, Betty, sang duets on the radio, which led to three years of tours with Tony Pastor's dance band. On her own by 1949, Clooney soared to fame with the million-selling "Come On-a My House" (1951). She had roles in several films, most notably *White Christmas* (1954) with Bing Crosby, and served as the host of The

Popular vocalist Rosemary Clooney

Rosemary Clooney Show (1956–57), a television variety show. By this time she had married (1953) actor José Ferrer, with whom she had five children, but the marriage was stormy; the couple divorced but remarried in 1961 before divorcing with finality in 1967. The next year, addicted to prescription drugs, she suffered a mental breakdown; confinement in a psychiatric ward in a Santa Monica, Calif., hospital was followed by four years of intensive therapy. Her return to performing was gradual—first in Holiday Inn hotels and television commercials, then on Crosby's 50th anniversary tour, and, beginning in 1977, with a long string of critically praised albums on the Concord Jazz label. Her autobiography was made into the 1982 television movie *Rosie: The Rosemary Clooney Story,* starring Sondra Locke as Clooney. In the 1980s and '90s, she sang in concerts and nightclubs. In 2002 Clooney was honoured with a Grammy Award for lifetime achievement.

Coburn, James, American actor (b. Aug. 31, 1928, Laurel, Neb.—d. Nov. 18, 2002, Beverly Hills, Calif.), had a powerful screen presence that was made more commanding by his deep voice, wry delivery, toothy grin, and satanic laugh. His more than 70 films ranged from the one that brought him public attention, *The Magnificent Seven* (1960), to *The Great Escape* (1963), *Charade* (1963), the James Bond spoofs *Our Man Flint* (1966) and *In like Flint* (1967), the satiric *The President's Analyst* (1967), and *Pat Garrett and Billy the Kid* (1973). He won a best supporting actor Oscar for his role in *Affliction* (1997).

Coloane, Francisco, Chilean author (b. July 19, 1910, Quemchi, Chile—d. Aug. 5, 2002, Santiago, Chile), penned seafaring adventure tales that were wildly popular and critically praised. His stories drew on local legends and reflected the landscape of the harsh Chilean coast, particularly Tierra del Fuego, which had an unforgiving climate with which Coloane was intimately familiar. His first published works were *Cabo de Hornes* (1941; *Cape Horn and Other Stories from the End of the World,* 1991), a short-story collection, and *El último grumete de "La Baquedano"* (1941). Another work, *Golfo de penas* (1945), won the Chilean Book of the Year award. His most recent works included an autobiography, *Los pasos del hombre* (2000), and *Naufragios* (2001), a long-awaited history of shipwrecks.

Conniff, Ray, American arranger, composer, and bandleader (b. Nov. 6, 1916, Attleboro, Mass.—d. Oct. 12, 2002, Escondido, Calif.), became identified with easy listening pop. He began his career in the 1930s playing trombone in big bands and in the '50s did arrangements for a number of pop stars. He also experimented with the use of voices as instruments, and *S' Wonderful* (1956), the debut recording of the Ray Conniff Orchestra and Singers, with wordless vocals and spare orchestral accompaniment, was the first of a long string of hits. He won a Grammy Award in 1966 for "Somewhere My Love." In all he recorded more than 100 albums.

Cronje, Wessel Johannes ("HANSIE"), South African cricketer (b. Sept. 25, 1969, Bloemfontein, S.Af.—d. June 1, 2002, Outeniqua Mountains, near George, S.Af.), was his country's most successful cricket captain and a national icon, admired by his players, respected by opponents, and idolized by South African fans, but his professional career was ultimately overshadowed—and his reputation destroyed—by a bookmaking scandal in 2000. He consistently denied that he had thrown any matches, but in October 2000 the United Cricket Board of South Africa banned him from the sport for life; he lost his appeal in late 2001. Cronje made his first-class debut for Orange Free State in 1987–88 and played his maiden Test match in 1991–92 against India. He became the official captain of South Africa's national side in 1994–95 and led his country to an impressive record of 27 wins, 15 draws, and only 11 losses in 53 Test matches, as well as 99 victories in 138 one-day internationals. As a player, Cronje scored 12,103 first-class runs (average 43.69) and 32 hundreds, including 3,714 runs (average 36.41) and six hundreds in 68 Tests, and took 116 first-class wickets (average 34.43), including 43 Test wickets (average 29.95), as a medium-pace bowler.

Crosby, John O'Hea, American impresario (b. July 12, 1926, New York, N.Y.—d. Dec. 15, 2002, Rancho Mirage, Calif.), was the founder, in 1957, of the Santa Fe (N.M.) Opera and served as its general director until he stepped down in 2000. The company gained international renown after Igor Stravinsky participated in the 1957–63 seasons. Crosby was also known for introducing new and little-performed works and for occasionally taking up the baton himself.

Cuadra, Pablo Antonio, Nicaraguan poet (b. Nov. 4, 1912, Managua, Nic.—d. Jan. 2, 2002, Managua), was a leading exponent of the *vanguardia,* a literary movement that emerged in the early 1930s and sought to foster the native literary traditions of Nicaragua while at the same time incorporating them into the international literary vanguard. His *Poemas nicaragüenses, 1930–1933* (1934) affirmed the customs, speech, and daily life of Nicaraguans and was the first book of verse dedicated to the new movement. Besides writing poetry, Cuadra edited several important literary journals, notably *El pez y la serpiente* from 1961, and from 1954 he served with Pedro Joaquín Chamorro Cardenal as coeditor of the influential newspaper *La prensa.* Cuadra became sole editor of the paper after Chamorro was assassinated in 1978, and he continued to espouse his political beliefs in verse, essays, and plays.

Dahl, Ole-Johan, Norwegian computer scientist (b. Oct. 12, 1931, Mandal, Nor.—d. June

29, 2002), was cocreator of the first "object-oriented" computer programming language, SIMULA, with his longtime colleague Kristen Nygaard (*q.v.*).

Davenport, Willie, American athlete (b. June 8, 1943, Troy, Ala.—d. June 17, 2002, Chicago, Ill.), competed in four Summer (1964, 1968, 1972, and 1976, as a hurdler) and one Winter (1980, on the four-man bobsled team) Olympic Games and had his best moment in 1968 when he won the gold medal in the 110-m high hurdles in an Olympic record-equaling 13.3 seconds. Davenport was named to the USA Track and Field Hall of Fame in 1982 and the U.S. Olympic Hall of Fame in 1990.

Davidson, Norman Ralph, American biochemist (b. April 5, 1916, Chicago, Ill.—d. Feb. 14, 2002, Pasadena, Calif.), conducted ground-breaking research in molecular biology that contributed to a fuller understanding of the genetic blueprint of human life. His research greatly influenced the study of genomic structure. Davidson developed new methods in electron microscopy and physical chemistry that aided genetic mapping and investigations of the information properties of DNA and RNA. Davidson was a founding member of the advisory council to the Human Genome Project. He received a National Medal of Science in 1996.

Davies, Derek Gwyn, British journalist (b. March 9, 1931, London, Eng.—d. Sept. 15, 2002, Antibes, France), revitalized the *Far Eastern Economic Review,* turning it from a single-sheet paper with a tiny readership into a prestigious magazine with a weekly circulation of 75,000. He joined the *Review* as a freelance journalist after moving to Hong Kong in 1962 and became its editor two years later. A bold and sometimes stubborn leader, Davies was noted for his journalistic integrity. He was fearless and tenacious in his coverage of regional governments, and as a result, the *Review* was often banned, pages were torn out, and reporters were fined or jailed. Davies retired in 1989 after Dow Jones & Co. took control of the *Review* and began moving the periodical toward more conservative, traditional coverage.

Davis, Benjamin Oliver, Jr., general (ret.), U.S. Air Force (b. Dec. 18, 1912, Washington, D.C.—d. July 4, 2002, Washington, D.C.), became the first African American general in the U.S. Air Force and in World War II led the 332nd Fighter Group—the Tuskegee Airmen—an all-black combat squadron. Davis also served in the Korean and Vietnam wars, reaching the rank of lieutenant general (a three-star general) in 1965; after retirement in 1998 he was awarded a fourth star, which designated the highest military order. His father, Benjamin O. Davis, Sr., was the first African American colonel (1930) and general (1940) in the U.S. Army. At the U.S. Military Academy at West Point, N.Y., he was shunned by white students. Despite graduating near the top of his class in 1936, he was not admitted to pilot training with the U.S. Army Air Corps (later Air Force)

Air Force Gen. Benjamin Oliver Davis, Jr.

until 1941. Promoted to lieutenant colonel, he organized the 99th Pursuit Squadron, and in 1943 he began leading the 332nd Fighter Group, which distinguished itself in European missions. After the war Davis was instrumental in desegregating the air force (1948). Following retirement in 1970 he was named national director of civil aviation security.

de Hartog, Jan Dutch-American novelist and playwright (b. April 22, 1914, Haarlem, Neth.—d. Sept. 22, 2002, Houston, Texas), was the author of adventure tales and works for the theatre, including the long-running hit *The Fourposter,* as well as of nonfiction. Twice as a boy, at the age of 10 and again when he was 12, he ran away to sea. He studied at the Amsterdam Naval College in 1930–31 before going to sea again, and from 1932 to 1937 he was on the staff of the Amsterdam Municipal Theatre. In the 1930s, under the pseudonym F.R. Eckmar, he wrote several detective novels. His first major novel was *Hollands glorie: roman van de zeesleepvaart* (1940; *Captain Jan: A Story of Ocean Tugboats,* 1976). The story of a boy in the merchant navy, the book became associated with the Dutch resistance, and it was banned by the Nazis. The author was forced into hiding and by 1943 had escaped to England. His first novel written and published in English was *The Lost Sea* (1951), the story of a young boy who runs away to sea. *The Fourposter,* a two-character play of a long marriage that he had written while in hiding in The Netherlands, premiered in London in 1950, opened in New York City in 1951, and won a Tony Award in 1952. It was made into a film and then into the stage musical *I Do! I Do!,* which opened in 1966. Hartog wrote additional stage works, and other films made from his novels included *The Spiral Road* (1962; from *Gods geuzen,* 1948) and *Lisa* (1962; from *De inspecteur,* 1958). *The*

Hospital, an exposé based on volunteer work he and his wife had done at a charity hospital in Houston, was published in 1964.

de León Carpio, Ramiro, Guatemalan politician (b. Jan. 12, 1942, Guatemala City, Guat.—found dead April 16, 2002, Miami, Fla.), as a longtime opponent of racial oppression, helped draft his country's constitution in 1984 and in 1989 was elected human rights ombudsman. When Pres. Jorge Serrano Elías was ousted from office in 1993 after trying to achieve dictatorial control, de León was named president; he served until early 1996.

De Toth, André (ENDRE ANTAL MIHALY SASVRAI FARKASFALVI TOTHFALUSI TOTH), Hungarian-born film and television director (b. May 15, 1913?, Mako, Austria-Hungary—d. Oct. 27, 2002, Burbank, Calif.), made a number of raw, violent, and psychologically disturbing B movies, including *Ramrod* (1947), *Pitfall* (1948), and *Crime Wave* (1954), that gained him a cult following, but he became best known to the general public for the 3-D film *House of Wax* (1953).

Decker, Alonzo Galloway, Jr., American business executive (b. Jan. 18, 1908, Orangeville, Md.—d. March 18, 2002, Earleville, Md.), transformed Black & Decker, a power-tool company cofounded by his father, into a corporate giant. Decker went to work at the company after graduating from Cornell University in Ithaca, N.Y. (1929). Under Decker's leadership the company began marketing power tools for home as well as industrial use; sales climbed dramatically, from $100 million to $650 million per year, and Black & Decker became a household name. Decker was chairman of the board from 1968 to 1979 and remained a board member until 2000.

DeLay, Dorothy, American violin teacher (b. March 31, 1917, Medicine Lodge, Kan.—d. March 24, 2002, Upper Nyack, N.Y.), was a master teacher who trained some of the world's leading violinists, including Itzhak Perlman, Sarah Chang, Midori, and Nigel Kennedy. After studying music at Oberlin (Ohio) College, and Michigan State University, DeLay toured as a concert violinist but did not like performing. She resumed her studies at the Juilliard School of Music, New York City, where she began to teach in 1948. DeLay remained associated with Juilliard for the rest of her life. She also taught at Sarah Lawrence College, Bronxville, N.Y., from 1947 to 1987. By the 1980s DeLay had established an international reputation, and she offered master classes around the world. In 1994 she was awarded the National Medal of Arts, and in 1995 she received the National Music Council's American Eagle Award.

Delvaux, André, Belgian filmmaker (b. March 21, 1926, Heverlee, Belg.—d. Oct. 4, 2002, Valencia, Spain), was widely regarded as the founder of the Belgian national cinema. A musician and teacher, Delvaux made his first short film, *Nous étions treize* (1955), with his students. Its success led him to make a series of television documentaries, and in 1962 he helped found a national film school. Delvaux's first international success came with the Flemish-language *De man die zijn haar kort liet knippen* (1965). This was the first movie to feature Delvaux's distinctive style of magic realism, which he expanded in his later films, notably the French-language *Un Soir, un train* (1968) and *Belle* (1973). In 1980 Delvaux stepped out of character to make a documentary on American filmmaker Woody Allen, and in 1988 he released *L'Oeuvre au noir,* his first big-budget film, at the Cannes Film Festival. In 1991 Delvaux received the Plateau Life Achievement Award at the International Film Festival in Ghent.

Demme, Edward ("TED"), American film director (b. Oct. 26, 1964, New York, N.Y.—d. Jan. 13, 2002, Santa Monica, Calif.), counted among his credits such films as *Beautiful Girls* (1996), *Life* (1999), and *Blow* (2001), as well as episodes of the television series *Homicide: Life on the Street* and *Action.* He also served as a co-producer of the film *Tumbleweeds* and the Emmy Award-winning TV movie *A Lesson Before Dying* (both 1999).

Deutsch, Martin, Austrian-born American physicist (b. Jan. 29, 1917, Vienna, Austria—d. Aug. 16, 2002, Cambridge, Mass.), discovered positronium, a fleeting hydrogen-like atom that contains a particle of antimatter. Building on the work of Paul Dirac and Carl Anderson, Deutsch showed in 1951 that during the encounter of a negatively charged electron and its positively charged antimatter counterpart, a positron, the two particles orbit around a common centre for less than a billionth of a second before annihilating each other in a burst of gamma rays. This confirmed Einstein's theory that matter could be converted entirely into energy and further substantiated the theory of quantum electrodynamics for a two-particle system.

Díaz, Jesús, Cuban writer and filmmaker (b. July 10, 1941, Havana, Cuba—d. May 2, 2002, Madrid, Spain), supported the Cuban Revolution with his creative efforts, editing the magazines *Pensamiento crítico* and *El caimán barbudo,* publishing the short-story collection *Los años duros* (1966), which won the Casa de las Américas prize, and making such films about the revolution as *Polvo rojo* (1980). Nevertheless, his independent thinking, as reflected in works dealing with Cuban exiles—the films *55 Hermanos* (1978) and *Lejanía* (1985)—and in the book *Las iniciales de la tierra* (1987), caused him trouble with hard-line government officials. In 1991 he went into exile in Spain, founded the literary quarterly *Encuentro de la cultura cubana,* and became an outspoken critic of Cuban Pres. Fidel Castro.

Dijkstra, Edsger Wybe, Dutch computer scientist (b. May 11, 1930, Rotterdam, Neth.—d. Aug. 6, 2002, Nuenen, Neth.), provided the mathematical foundation for "structured programming"; his idea, which came to be called Dijkstra's algorithm, established the "shortest-path" concept of logically structured sets and subsets of computer commands in place of the excessively complex and disorganized commands often written by early programmers. This concept later found application in everything from electronic circuit design to graphic image processing to voice recognition. His other work included the first version of AL-GOL60, an algorithmic language used in one of the earliest compiler programs, and Dijkstra's semaphore, a technique of organizing data to minimize computer system freezes. In 1972 he received the A.M. Turing Award, his field's highest honour.

Donegan, Anthony James ("LONNIE"), Scottish musician (b. April 29, 1931, Glasgow, Scot.—d. Nov. 3, 2002, Peterborough, Cambridgeshire, Eng.), became known as the king of skiffle—a blend of music styles that encompassed folk, country, jazz, blues, and jug band—and in the process served as the inspiration for the British rock and roll musicians who followed in the 1960s, including Paul McCartney, John Lennon, Pete Townshend, and Van Morrison. Among his hits were the Leadbelly classic "Rock Island Line" (1956), which sold some three million singles, and the million-selling "Does Your Chewing Gum Lose Its Flavour (on the Bedpost Overnight)?" (1959). Donegan was made MBE in 2000.

Dönhoff, Marion (MARION HEDDA ILSE GRÄFIN [COUNTESS] DÖNHOFF), German journalist (b. Dec. 2, 1909, Castle Friedrichstein, near Königsberg, East Prussia [now Kaliningrad, Russia]—d. March 11, 2002, Berlin, Ger.), was known as the doyenne of German journalism for her nearly 60-year association with the liberal weekly *Die Zeit* as a founding staff member (1946–55), political editor (1955–68), editor in chief (1968–72), and co-publisher (1972–2002). Dönhoff, who also wrote several books, supported reunification with East Germany and was highly critical of the Allied reluctance to recognize the resistance movement within Nazi Germany.

Duarte Cancino, Isaias, Colombian cleric (b. Feb. 15, 1939, San Gil, Colom.—d. March 16, 2002, Cali, Colom.), was archbishop of Cali from 1995 and an outspoken critic of Colombian guerrillas and drug traffickers. Duarte was slain by two gunmen outside a church where he had just presided over a wedding ceremony. After serving as a parish priest, Duarte was appointed bishop of Germania de Numidia in 1985 and three years later became bishop of Apartadó. After his elevation to archbishop, he fiercely condemned the country's two major guerrilla groups, the Revolutionary Armed Forces of Colombia and the National Liberation Army (ELN). After the ELN kidnapped more than 150 persons from a Cali church in 1999, Duarte publicly excommunicated all ELN members.

Eban, Abba (AUBREY SOLOMON MEIR), South African-born Israeli politician and diplomat (b. Feb. 2, 1915, Cape Town, S.Af.—d. Nov. 17, 2002, Jerusalem, Israel), was a key figure in the founding of the state of Israel and served as that country's first permanent representative to the UN (1949–59), first ambassador to the U.S. (1950–59), and longest serving foreign minister (1966–74). Eban was educated in England and studied the classics and Oriental languages at Queens' College, Cambridge. While serving in the British army during World War II, he worked for the Middle East Arab Centre in Jerusalem. After the war he was a political information officer with the Jewish Agency in Palestine, liaison officer with the UN Special Committee on Palestine, and a member of the delegation that lobbied the UN for the partition of Palestine and Israel. Eban was a member of the Israeli Knesset (parliament) from 1959 to 1988, and before being named foreign minister he served as minister of education and culture (1960–63) and deputy prime minister (1963–66). A resolute dove, he supported peace with the Palestinians, though he publicly championed Israel's military actions during the Six-Day War. Eban was an eloquent public speaker and wrote several highly regarded books, notably *The Tide of Nationalism* (1959) and *Heritage: Civilization and the Jews* (1984), which was based on the nine-part documentary he wrote and narrated for American public television.

Egal, Muhammad Ibrahim, Somali politician (b. Aug. 15, 1928, Odweyne, British Somaliland Protectorate—d. May 3, 2002, Pretoria, S.Af.), as president (from 1993) of the self-proclaimed Republic of Somaliland, established an island of relative stability in the war-torn Horn of Africa but failed to win international recognition for his homeland as an independent state. In June 1960 Egal was prime minister of the newly independent Somaliland Republic, which merged five days later with the former Italian Trust Territory to form Somalia. He served as Somalia's defense minister (1960–62), education minister (1962–63), prime minister (1967–69), and ambassador to India (1976–78), although he was imprisoned twice for insurgency. When the Somali Republic collapsed in 1991, Somaliland unilaterally declared a resumption of its independent status; two years later Egal was elected president by a council of elders.

Elizabeth, the Queen Mother, Queen (LADY ELIZABETH ANGELA MARGUERITE BOWES-LYON; "QUEEN MUM"), British royal (b. Aug. 4, 1900, London, Eng.—d. March 30, 2002, Windsor, Berkshire, Eng.), in a life that spanned three centuries, was the daughter of a Scottish nobleman, the queen consort of King George VI, the mother of Queen Elizabeth II and Princess Margaret, countess of Snowdon (*q.v.*), and an almost universally beloved symbol of British tradition and fortitude. Lady Elizabeth Bowes-Lyon was the 9th child (of 10) of Claude George Bowes-Lyon, Lord Glamis and (from 1904) the 14th earl of Strathmore and Kinghorne. On April 26, 1923, after a two-year courtship, she married Prince

Ken Goff/TimePix

Queen Elizabeth, the "Queen Mum"

Albert, duke of York, the second son of King George V. When her shy husband was officially proclaimed King George VI on Dec. 11, 1936, following the abdication of his brother Edward VIII, she was thrust unexpectedly into the public eye. She proved to be an able consort, and her personal charm helped to cement public support for the monarchy, which had been badly damaged by the abdication. The new queen's refusal to leave London during World War II and her extensive wartime activities further endeared her to the nation, as did her reported response in September 1940 when Buckingham Palace was damaged in the Blitz: "I'm glad we've been bombed. It makes me feel I can look the East End in the face." In 1952 the king died, and their daughter Elizabeth ascended the throne. Thereafter, the widowed Queen Mother served as an unofficial ambassador, traveling extensively until advancing age curtailed her movements. She continued to make public appearances, however, owned a string of thoroughbred racehorses, and survived several surgeries. She celebrated her 100th birthday in 2000.

Entwistle, John Alec, British bass guitarist (b. Oct. 9, 1944, London, Eng.—found dead June 27, 2002, Las Vegas, Nev.), anchored the talented but volatile rock band the Who with his steady demeanour and superb musicianship. His bass lines in songs such as "The Real Me" and "My Generation" combined dazzling dexterity with a lead guitarist's sense of melody and aggression. Instructed in piano and a variety of brass instruments, Entwistle played in jazz bands while in grammar school but was lured to rock and roll by the loud, wild sound of Duane Eddy. He joined singer Roger Daltrey in a band called the Detours in 1962; the band's lack of a rhythm guitarist required Entwistle to play louder and more prominently than most bass players of the day. This led to the development of Entwistle's signature sound. The Detours recruited guitarist Pete Townshend and drummer Keith Moon and became the High Numbers before taking

the name the Who in 1964. Whereas his fellow band members became known for smashing equipment on stage, Entwistle, nicknamed "the Ox," maintained a more stoic presence during concerts. Entwistle wrote some of the Who's darker, more humorous numbers, including "Boris the Spider" and "Cousin Kevin." Entwistle began touring and recording with his own band in 1971 but continued to perform with the Who, which disbanded in 1982, for reunion tours in 1989 and 1996–97.

Erickson, John, British military historian (b. April 17, 1929, Newcastle, Eng.—d. Feb. 10, 2002, Edinburgh, Scot.), was widely regarded as the West's foremost authority on the Soviet Union's military development, in particular the role the Red Army played in World War II. His vast knowledge and insightful judgments were most apparent in his two-volume magnum opus—*The Road to Stalingrad* (1975) and *The Road to Berlin* (1982).

Esquivel, Juan García, Mexican composer and bandleader (b. Jan. 20, 1918, Tampico, Mex.—d. Jan. 3, 2002, Jiutepec, Mex.), won international fame with eccentric instrumental pop recordings in the 1950s and '60s; late in Esquivel's life, the release of two compact disc compilations of his work, *Space-Age Bachelor Pad Music* (1994) and *Cabaret Mañana* (1995), sparked a revival of interest in his music. Esquivel was a bandleader from the age of 17, and by the 1940s he had made a name for himself in Mexico as the leader of a 22-piece orchestra that performed regularly on radio and television. His first album, *Las tandas de Juan García Esquivel* (1956), caught the attention of American producers, and RCA Victor Records took him to the U.S. in 1957. A string of popular albums followed, including *Other Worlds, Other Sounds* (1958) and *Latin-Esque* (1962), which showcased his wildly dissonant and technically innovative arrangements. Esquivel returned to Mexico in 1979; he had retired by 1990.

Esslin, Martin Julius (JULIUS PERESZLENYI), Hungarian-born British broadcaster, critic, and scholar (b. June 8, 1918, Budapest, Austria-Hungary—d. Feb. 24, 2002, London, Eng.), coined the term *theatre of the absurd* (in his 1962 book of that title) to describe post-World War II drama by playwrights he felt reflected existential philosophy and who used poetic metaphor "to convey their sense of bewilderment, anxiety, and wonder in the face of an inexplicable universe." After the Nazi takeover of Austria, Esslin settled in England, where he became a scriptwriter and producer for the BBC. He served as the head of BBC Radio Drama (1963–77) and was later professor of drama (1977–88) at Stanford University.

Estey, Willard Zebedee, Canadian attorney and judge (b. Oct. 10, 1919, Saskatoon, Sask.—d. Jan. 25, 2002, Toronto, Ont.), served as a justice on the Supreme Court of Canada from 1977 to 1988. Estey was educated at the University of Saskatchewan (B.A., 1940; LL.B., 1942) and Harvard Law School (LL.M., 1946). As an attorney in private practice in Toronto from 1947 to 1972, he was recognized for his expertise in commercial and tax law. Estey was appointed to the Ontario Court of Appeal in 1973 and became the chief justice of the Supreme Court of Ontario three years later. As a justice of the Supreme Court of Canada, he was best known for heading the Estey Commission, which in 1985 the federal government charged with investigating the collapse of the Canadian Commercial Bank and the Northland Bank. Estey was named a Companion to the Order of Canada in 1990.

Ewald, Manfred, East German sports official (b. May 17, 1926, Podejuch, Ger. [now Podjuchy, Pol.]—d. Oct. 21, 2002, Damsdorf, Ger.), formed a powerhouse Olympic team but was discredited when it was discovered that his athletes' success was based in part on the use of performance-enhancing drugs. Ewald was a member of the Nazi Party and then joined the East German Communist Party after Germany was divided. He was appointed secretary of the German Sports Committee in 1948 and sports minister in 1961; by 1973 he was head of his country's Olympic committee. Ewald's program (which administered anabolic steroids and other drugs to an estimated 10,000 athletes) was highly successful from a medal standpoint—in 1976 East Germans won 11 of the 13 women's swimming events. Despite suspicions throughout the Olympic community, he was awarded (1985) the Olympic Order. After German reunification, Ewald's activities were brought to light, and former athletes testified to serious health problems. In 2000 he was convicted of having caused bodily harm to 142 female athletes and received a 22-month suspended sentence.

Ewen, (William) Paterson, Canadian artist (b. April 7, 1925, Montreal, Que.—d. Feb. 17, 2002, London, Ont.), was a relentlessly innovative artist whose expressionistic paintings of the 1970s and '80s attracted widespread interest. His earliest paintings were representational, but from the mid-1950s his work became ever more abstract. In 1971 Ewen began painting on plywood sheets instead of on canvas and using hand tools to gouge out images of meteorologic and cosmological phenomena. He was elected to the Royal Canadian Academy in 1975, and in 1982 he represented Canada at the Venice Biennale.

Fadiman, Annalee Whitmore, American screenwriter and journalist (b. May 27, 1916, Price, Utah—d. Feb. 5, 2002, Captiva, Fla.), was working as a secretary in the typing pool at MGM when she co-wrote *Andy Hardy Meets Debutante* (1940), a vehicle for Judy Garland and Mickey Rooney, and although she produced several other screenplays and MGM offered her a seven-year contract, she was intent on reporting on the war raging in China. Though the War Department barred women from serving as foreign correspondents, she took a job as a representative of a relief agency in Chungking. There she began writing speeches for Madame Chiang Kai-shek and landed a job as a reporter with *Liberty* magazine. Later, author Theodore H. White, a

friend of her late husband, Melville Jacoby, arranged for her to join him in Chungking, where they penned the best-selling *Thunder Out of China* (1946). Following the war she married book critic and radio quiz show host Clifton Fadiman.

Farrell, Eileen, American singer (b. Feb. 13, 1920, Willimantic, Conn.—d. March 23, 2002, Park Ridge, N.J.), was considered one of the world's most outstanding dramatic sopranos. Refusing to confine herself to any particular category, she gained success in popular music, jazz, blues, and opera. By the time she was 20, she was performing a wide range of musical selections on her own weekly radio program on CBS, *Eileen Farrell Presents,* and through that show she became one of the best-known singers in the U.S. Farrell's concert career began in 1947, and in 1949 she made her first of dozens of appearances as a soloist with the New York Philharmonic Orchestra. She also provided Eleanor Parker's singing voice for the role of opera star Marjorie Lawrence in the motion picture *Interrupted Melody* (1955). Farrell's debut on the opera stage came in Tampa, Fla., in 1956, in the role of Santuzza in *Cavalleria rusticana,* and later that year she performed the role of Leonora in the San Francisco Opera's *Il trovatore.* It was not until December 1960 that she first appeared on the stage of New York City's Metropolitan Opera—in the title role of *Alceste*—and in her five seasons with that company she sang only six roles, reportedly as a result of differences with the Met's general manager, Rudolf Bing. Farrell's career and popularity flourished, however. In 1999 her autobiography, *Can't Help Singing* (co-written with Brian Kellow), was published.

Fauvet, Jacques-Jules-Pierre-Constant, French journalist (b. June 9, 1914, Paris, France—d. June 1, 2002, Paris), was a driving force at *Le Monde,* one of France's most influential and respected daily newspapers, for more than 50 years. Fauvet retained the paper's austere look and leftist stance while expanding its coverage of the arts. He also published several political books, including *La Paysans et les politique dans la France contemporaine* (1953) and *Histoire du Parti communiste français* (1964). After retiring from *Le Monde,* Fauvet was president of the National Committee for Information and Liberty (1984–94). He was elected to the Legion of Honour in January 2002.

Félix, María (MARÍA DE LOS ÁNGELES FÉLIX GUEREÑA), Mexican actress (b. May 4, 1914, Álamos, Sonora, Mex.—d. April 8, 2002, Mexico City, Mex.), used her extraordinary looks and fiery personality to propel herself from unknown to overnight star to icon of

beauty in Spanish-speaking countries. Her succession of husbands, one of them the composer Agustín Lara, and famous lovers, including the artist Diego Rivera, gave her an offscreen life that rivaled that of the strong, fierce, and glamorous on-screen characters she portrayed in her 47 films. After she moved to Mexico City, a movie director spotted her, and this paved the way for her first role, in *El peñón de las ánimas* (1942). Her film *Doña Bárbara* (1943) thoroughly established her stardom, so much so that she was thereafter often called "La Doña." For some three

Allan Grant/TimePix

Fiery Mexican actress Mária Félix

decades Félix was a major box-office draw, not only with Mexican films, including *Enamorada* (1946) and *Río escondido* (1948), but also with Argentine, French, Italian, and Spanish movies, such as *French Cancan* (1955), *La cucaracha* (1958), and *La Fièvre monte à El Pao* (1959).

Findley, Timothy Irving Frederick, Canadian writer (b. Oct. 30, 1930, Toronto, Ont.—d. June 20, 2002, south of France), was best known for his novels, although he also wrote a number of dramatic works. The novels, which tended to be complex works dealing with themes such as the loneliness of the outsider, politics and art, and madness, were written in various styles and encompassed a range of settings and eras. Known throughout his life as Tiff, an acronym formed from his initials, Findley suffered from frequent illnesses during his childhood, and he early on turned to reading and writing. His formal education ended with the ninth grade. He worked as an actor for 15 years and in 1953 became a charter member of the Stratford (Ont.) Shakespeare Festival. It was on the advice of Thornton Wilder and the actress Ruth Gordon, with whom he was appearing in Wilder's *The Matchmaker,* that he turned to writing. His first two novels were not particularly well received, but his third, *The Wars* (1977), dealing with the experiences of a soldier during World War I, was a success and won the Governor-General's Award for fiction. This was followed by another popular and critical success, *Famous Last Words* (1981). Later novels included *Headhunter* (1993) and *Pilgrim* (1999). In all, he published 12 novels. His play *Elizabeth Rex* (2000) won the Governor-General's Award for drama. France made him Chevalier de l'Ordre des Arts et des Lettres.

Firth, Sir Raymond William, New Zealand-born anthropologist (b. March 25, 1901, Auckland, N.Z.—d. Feb. 22, 2002, London, Eng.), applied his early education in economics in Auckland and at the London School of Economics (LSE), as well as his belief in rigorous scientific observation, to social anthropological research. Firth's first book, *Primitive Economics of the New Zealand Maori* (1929), was based on his study of the aboriginal people in his native New Zealand. He later wrote on subjects ranging from the economy of Malay fishermen to kinship patterns in Britain and the U.S.; he often collaborated with his wife, anthropologist Rosemary Upcott. Firth's most extensive and lasting field work was on the tiny Polynesian island of Tikopia, an atoll in the Solomon Islands he visited frequently from 1929. He wrote nine books on the people of Tikopia, beginning with *We, the Tikopia* (1936). Firth taught at the LSE from 1932 until 1968. He was elected a fellow of the British Academy in 1949 and served as secretary (1946–51), chairman (1958–61), and life president (from 1975) of the Association of Social Anthropologists. Firth was knighted in 1973 and made a Companion of the New Zealand Order of Merit in 2001.

Ford, Charles Henri (CHARLES HENRY FORD), American poet, writer, and artist (b. Feb. 10, 1908, Hazelhurst, Miss.—d. Sept. 27, 2002, New York, N.Y.), lived and worked among the bohemian avant-garde. His poems first appeared in print while he was a teenager, and in all he published 16 books of poetry, most of it in a Surrealist vein. In 1929 he founded *Blues: A Magazine of New Rhythms*, which in its eight issues included contributions by some of the most celebrated writers of the day. In 1933, with Parker Tyler, he wrote *The Young and Evil*, which was considered to be the first gay novel and was banned in the U.S. and Britain until the 1960s. He founded the journal *View* in 1940 and during its seven-year history introduced a number of European artists and writers to American audiences. His artwork included paintings, drawings, collages, and photographs.

Fortuyn, Wilhelmus Simon Petrus ("PIM"), Dutch sociologist and politician (b. Feb. 19, 1948, Velsen, Neth.—d. May 6, 2002, Hilversum, Neth.), was the headline-grabbing leader of the Lijst Pim Fortuyn, the populist anti-immigration political party he established in 2002; his assassination while campaigning for the parliament triggered a national crisis in his peace-loving homeland. The flamboyant Fortuyn supported business deregulation and abortion rights and was open about both his homosexuality and his fondness for the high life. Known for his sardonic wit, he aimed his harshest vitriol at Islam, which he denounced as "backward," and at Muslim immigrants, who, he said, were intolerant of the liberal, open-minded society that had long been a Dutch hallmark. Although he disliked being linked with right-wing anti-immigrant parties in other European countries, his calls to close The Netherlands to immigration made such comparisons inevitable. He taught before formally entering politics in 2001. After a falling out with Leefbaar Nederland ("Livable Netherlands"), a populist coalition of ultra-nationalist right-wingers and disillusioned leftists, he formed his own party in Rotterdam, where it won a majority in city elections.

Forward, Robert Lull, American physicist and science-fiction writer (b. Aug. 15, 1932, Geneva, N.Y.—d. Sept. 21, 2002, Seattle, Wash.), utilized his knowledge of gravitational physics and advanced space propulsion to create finely crafted, scientifically feasible worlds for his readers. From 1955 to 1987 he worked at the Corporate Research Laboratories of Hughes Aircraft Co., in Malibu, Calif., and became a noted inventor, designing a new type of satellite and patenting numerous inventions, including instruments to measure gravity. He went on to found his own companies, Forward Unlimited (1987), a consulting firm, and Tethers Unlimited (1994), which created space equipment for NASA. Forward was better known, however, as the author of 11 novels. His first, *Dragon's Egg* (1980), depicted an alien species that inhabits a neutron star and lives for only 45 minutes.

Frank, John Paul, American lawyer (b. Nov. 10, 1917, Appleton, Wis.—d. Sept. 7, 2002, Scottsdale, Ariz.), was involved in two of the most important U.S. Supreme Court cases of the second half of the 20th century: *Brown* v. *Board of Education of Topeka* (1954), in which school segregation was declared unconstitutional, and *Miranda* v. *Arizona* (1966), which established police procedures for handling criminal suspects. He was an adviser to Thurgood Marshall, who argued the segregation case before the court, and he represented Ernesto Miranda, who had not been advised of his rights by the police.

Frankenheimer, John Michael, American television and film director (b. Feb. 19, 1930, Queens, N.Y.—d. July 6, 2002, Los Angeles, Calif.), was considered one of the most important and creatively gifted directors of the 1950s and early '60s and enjoyed a second surge of success in the 1990s when he produced a number of outstanding films for cable TV. His body of works included more than 150 live TV dramas and such classic films as *The Manchurian Candidate* and *The Birdman of Alcatraz*. After making training films for the air force during the Korean War, he was hired by CBS in 1953, and his directing assignments quickly progressed from weather and news broadcasts to shows that included *Person to Person, See It Now,* and *You Are There.* From

Loomis Dean/TimePix

Director John Frankenheimer

1954 to 1960 he averaged one live drama every two weeks on such outstanding series as *Playhouse 90* (42 shows, including *The Days of Wine and Roses* and *The Turn of the Screw*) and *Studio One.* Frankenheimer began his film-directing career with *The Young Stranger* in 1957 but preferred directing for television and did not return to motion pictures until 1961, with *The Young Savages.* Among the movies that followed were *Seven Days in May* (1964), *The Train* (1964), and *Seconds* (1966). Personal problems—exacerbated by the assassination (1968) of his close friend Robert Kennedy—began to take their toll, however, and he counted few real successes among his films of the next several years. Frankenheimer resurrected his career and his reputation, though, with a return to television. The made-for-cable movies *Against the Wall* (1994), *The Burning Season* (1994), *Andersonville* (1996), and *George Wallace* (1997) all won Emmy Awards.

Gabreski, Francis Stanley, American fighter pilot (b. Jan. 28, 1919, Oil City, Pa.—d. Jan. 31, 2002, Huntington, N.Y.), shot down more than three dozen enemy planes as an ace fighter pilot in both World War II and the Korean War. Gabreski, who joined the Army Air Corps in 1941, was credited with 31 "kills" in Europe during World War II, and he added 6 more kills and shared credit for another one during the Korean War. He retired from the air force as a colonel in 1967. He later worked in the aviation and railroad industries.

Gadamer, Hans-Georg, German philosopher (b. Feb. 11, 1900, Marburg, Ger.—d. March 14, 2002, Heidelberg, Ger.), was a principal figure in 20th-century philosophical hermeneutics. His conception of language as a historical phenomenon had great influence in postmodernist and poststructuralist thought. Gadamer studied philosophy in Breslau (now Wrocław, Pol.), Munich, and Marburg, where he completed a doctorate (1922) on Plato under the Neo-Kantian Paul Natorp. While recovering from polio in 1923, Gadamer came under the influence of Martin Heidegger, under whom he completed a second doctorate in 1929. He served as *Privatdozent* (private lecturer) in Marburg and taught at the University of Kiel (1934) before accepting professorships at Marburg (1937) and then Leipzig (1939). He attempted to remain politically neutral during the Nazi period, though he did attend a political reeducation camp near Danzig (now Gdansk, Pol.). After the war the Soviet authorities appointed him rector of the University of Leipzig, but after being briefly detained he left the eastern zone in 1947 for a professorship at the University of Frankfurt. In 1949 he moved to Heidelberg, where he remained until his retirement in 1968. In his major work, *Wahrheit und Methode* (1960; *Truth and Method*, 1975), Gadamer argued that historically conditioned human existence makes complete objectivity and the elimination of prejudice impossible.

Gal, Uziel, Israeli army officer and inventor (b. Dec. 15, 1923, Germany—d. Sept. 7, 2002, Philadelphia, Pa.), designed the Uzi submachine gun, a compact automatic weapon used throughout the world as a police and special-forces firearm.

Garba, Joseph Nanven, Nigerian military officer and diplomat (b. July 17, 1943, Langtang, Nigeria—d. June 1, 2002, Abuja, Nigeria), participated in the 1975 bloodless coup that deposed Gen. Yakubu Gowon as head of state, then served as external affairs commissioner (foreign minister) until 1978 and as Nigeria's ambassador to the UN (1984–89). Garba studied public administration at Harvard University (1982–83). A committed pan-Africanist, he held prominent positions in several international organizations, notably as president of a foreign ministers meeting sponsored by the Organization of African Unity in 1976, leader of the 1976 summit conference of nonaligned nations, and chairman of the UN's Special Committee Against Apartheid (1984–89).

Gardner, John William, American social and political activist (b.

Oct. 8, 1912, Los Angeles, Calif.—d. Feb. 16, 2002, Palo Alto, Calif.), had a more than half-century-long career of public service highlighted by his influence on education through his presidency of the philanthropic Carnegie Corporation of New York, by the introduction of Medicare during his years as secretary of health, education, and welfare, and by his efforts to reform the political system by increasing citizens' participation in government. To help bring about the latter, he founded (1970) and became the first chairman of Common Cause, a citizens' lobby that opposed the Vietnam War and promoted civil rights, campaign finance reform, and government accountability. After earning a Ph.D. (1938) from the University of California, Berkeley, he taught psychology at Connecticut College and Mount Holyoke College, South Hadley, Mass.; served in the marines during World War II; and went to work for the Carnegie Corporation, becoming its chairman in 1955. In that post he was able to exert enormous influence over American educational policy by guiding the choice of the country's top educators. He was awarded the Presidential Medal of Freedom, the highest civilian award given in the U.S., in 1964. Impressed by Gardner's accomplishments, Pres. Lyndon B. Johnson in 1965 named him secretary of health, education, and welfare, a position he held until 1968. Gardner then served as chairman of the Urban Coalition to address racial problems in the cities, but he soon came to realize that the best way to effect change was to reform the political system from within and thus founded Common Cause. Gardner left the chairmanship of Common Cause in 1977.

Ginzburg, Aleksandr Ilich, Russian journalist, dissident, and human rights advocate (b. Nov. 21, 1936, Moscow, U.S.S.R.—d. July 19, 2002, Paris, France), edited the literary journal *Syntaksis* ("Syntax"), often said to have been the first samizdat—a self-published underground work that circulated among opponents of the Soviet government. He was repeatedly arrested and jailed and became a symbol in the West of resistance to Soviet rule. As a boy he took his mother's name in protest against Joseph Stalin's persecution of Jews. A student in journalism at Moscow University from 1956 to 1960, Ginzburg published three issues of *Syntaksis* in 1959 before being arrested in 1960 and given a two-year prison sentence. In 1966 he issued a compilation of materials on the trial of two writers, published in English in the West as *On Trial: The Case of Sinyavsky and Daniel*. He was arrested again in 1967 and given a five-year prison term. During this period he converted to Orthodox Christianity and became an advocate of the right of religious freedom. In 1974 Ginzburg became the administrator of a fund established by the exiled writer Aleksandr Solzhenitsyn to assist the families of political prisoners. He also was active in the monitoring of Soviet compliance with the Helsinki Accords of 1975. He was arrested again in 1977 and sentenced the following year to an eight-year prison term. In 1979 he was stripped of his citizenship and, along with four other writers, sent to the U.S. in exchange for two Soviet spies. Ginzburg was distressed over banishment from his homeland and settled in France, where he worked on the Russian émigré journal *Russkaya Mysl* ("Russian Thought"). After the breakup of the Soviet Union, he remained critical of the new Russian government, and he became a French citizen in 1998.

Gorton, Sir John Grey, Australian politician (b. Sept. 9, 1911, Melbourne, Australia—d. May 19, 2002, Sydney, Australia), was a colourful, nationalistic Australian prime minister (1968–71) who expanded the role of the federal government at the expense of the states, sponsored increased opportunities for Aboriginals, endorsed protectionist trade policies, and maintained Australia's commitment to the Vietnam War while complaining about insufficient access to U.S. intelligence. Gorton was educated at Brasenose College, Oxford, and took over his father's fruit farm when he returned to Australia in 1936. As a fighter pilot in the Royal Australian Air Force during World War II, he survived several crashes, sustaining disfiguring facial injuries in the first of them. After the war Gorton entered politics, winning a Senate seat for the newly created Liberal Party in 1949. He held several minor cabinet posts and was minister of education in December 1967 when Prime Minister Harry Holt disappeared while swimming and was presumed drowned. Gorton was the surprise choice to succeed Holt, but his emphasis on a strong central government, his aggressive reforms, and his abrasive personal style led to a no-confidence vote within the Liberal Party in March 1971. He was made a Companion of Honour in 1971, knighted in 1977, and named to the Order of Australia in 1988.

Gotti, John Joseph, American organized

crime leader (b. Oct. 27, 1940, South Bronx, N.Y.—d. June 10, 2002, Springfield, Mo.), arranged the murder of the head of the Gambino crime family in 1985 and took power, becoming famous both for his ability to escape successful prosecution, which earned him the nickname "the Teflon Don," and for his flamboyant attire and expensive lifestyle, for which he became known as "the Dapper Don." In 1992 he finally was convicted on racketeering and murder charges—including the murder that brought him to power—and he spent the rest of his life in prison.

Gould, Stephen Jay, American paleontologist, evolutionary biologist, and writer (b. Sept. 10, 1941, New York, N.Y.—d. May 20, 2002, New York, N.Y.), was the author of over a dozen books in addition to 300 consecutive monthly "This View of Life" essays in *Natural History* magazine (1974–2001), in which he made scientific discussion accessible and entertaining to the common reader without diluting its content. He was best known for a theory of evolution he and his colleague Niles Eldredge developed in 1972, known as punctuated equilibrium, that contradicted conventional thinking on the subject. Whereas in the theories of Charles Darwin evolution was a slow, steady process, Gould and Eldredge proposed that change came to species relatively rapidly between long periods of constancy.

Evolution expert Stephen Jay Gould

Gould earned a doctorate in paleontology at Columbia University, New York City, in 1967. In the same year he joined the faculty of Harvard University, where he would spend the rest of his career. He became a full professor in 1973. Among Gould's diverse works were an exploration of the relationship between evolution and the development of individual organisms, *Ontogeny and Phylogeny* (1977); a discussion of intelligence testing and a refutation of claims for the intellectual superiority of some races, *The Mismeasure of Man* (1981), which won the National Book Critics Circle Award in 1982; and what was considered his magnum opus, the 1,433-page summary of his life's work, *The Structure of Evolutionary Theory* (2002). His volumes of collected *Natural History* essays included *Ever Since Darwin* (1977), *The Panda's Thumb* (1980), for which he received the National Book Award in 1981, *Hen's Teeth and Horse's Toes* (1983), and *I Have Landed: The End of a Beginning in Natural History* (2002). Gould became a member of the American Academy of Arts and Sciences in 1983 and the National Academy of Sciences in 1989.

Gray, Dolores, American singer and actress (b. June 7, 1924, Chicago, Ill.—d. June 26, 2002, New York, N.Y.), had a rich contralto voice that gained her success in motion pictures and, especially, stage musicals. Her first, and perhaps greatest, triumph came in the London production of *Annie Get Your Gun*, which opened in 1947 and ran for nearly three years, playing to an audience that totaled more than 2.5 million. She followed that with other stage musicals

and cabaret acts, winning a Tony Award in 1954 for the short-lived Broadway musical *Carnival in Flanders* (1953); starred in such films as *Kismet* (1955), *It's Always Fair Weather* (1955), and *Designing Woman* (1957); and, after several years away from show business, returned to the stage for the London productions of *Gypsy* (1973) and *Follies* (1987) and Broadway's *42nd Street* (1986).

Green, Adolph, American lyricist, screenwriter, and actor (b. Dec. 2, 1915, Bronx, N.Y.—d. Oct. 23, 2002, New York, N.Y.), enjoyed a six-decade-long creative collaboration with Betty Comden that resulted in not only a number of joyously enduring stage and screen musicals but so close a working and performing relationship that they were often mistakenly thought of as a married couple. They wrote the book and lyrics for such Broadway hits as *On the Town* (1944; filmed 1949), *Wonderful Town* (1953), *Peter Pan* (1954), and *Bells Are Ringing* (1956; filmed 1960), and their screenplays included those for *Singin' in the Rain* (1952), *The Band Wagon* (1953), *It's Always Fair Weather* (1955), and *Auntie Mame* (1958). Comden and Green first met at New York University, and in 1938 with some friends (including Judy Tuvim, who later became the actress Judy Holliday), they formed a cabaret act, the Revuers. To save money Comden and Green wrote their material. Leonard Bernstein sometimes joined them onstage at the piano, and when he was writing the score for a Broadway musical to be based on the Jerome Robbins ballet *Fancy Free*, for which he had written the

music, he turned to Comden and Green for the book and lyrics. *On the Town* was a huge hit, and the pair's reputation was firmly established. A number of their songs become popular standards, among them "Make Someone Happy," "Just in Time," "The Party's Over," and "New York, New York." Green acted in the film comedies *My Favorite Year* (1982) and *I Want to Go Home* (1989). Comden and Green won Tony Awards for five of their shows—*Wonderful Town, Hallelujah, Baby!* (1967), *Applause* (1970), *On the Twentieth Century* (1978), and *The Will Rogers Follies* (1991)—and in 1991 Green and Comden were recipients of the Kennedy Center Honors.

Gueï, Robert, Ivorian military leader (b. March 16, 1941, Kabakouma, French West Africa—d. Sept. 19, 2002, Abidjan, Côte d'Ivoire), mounted in 1999 the first successful coup d'état in his native country. His rule lasted only 10 months, but it marked the beginning of years of conflict in Côte d'Ivoire, which had previously been known as a haven of stability in West Africa. Gueï became chief of staff of the army in 1990 under Pres. Félix Houphouët-Boigny. In 1996 Houphouët-Boigny's successor, Henri Konan Bédié, fired Gueï on unproven charges of fomenting a rebellion. On Dec. 24, 1999, following a mutiny by soldiers who were demanding back wages and improved living conditions, Gueï staged a bloodless military coup that toppled Bédié. Although he claimed to have come to power reluctantly, Gueï entered the October 2000 presidential elections, which he lost by a wide margin to Laurent Gbagbo; some 200 people were killed in the clashes that ensued. Gueï was found dead in Abidjan during an army mutiny.

Guggenheim, Charles Eli, American film producer and director (b. March 31, 1924, Cincinnati, Ohio—d. Oct. 9, 2002, Washington, D.C.), made more than 100 documentaries during a half-century-long career. He was nominated for 12 Academy Awards and won 4—for *Nine from Little Rock* (1964), *Robert Kennedy Remembered* (1968), *The Johnstown Flood* (1989), and *A Time for Justice* (1994).

Guy, Billy (FRANK PHILLIPS, JR.), American pop singer (b. June 20, 1936, Itasca, Texas—d. Nov. 12, 2002, Las Vegas, Nev.), was one of the original members of the Coasters, a rock and roll group popular in the late 1950s. A baritone, he sang the lead on one of the quartet's biggest hits, "Searchin'" (1957), about looking for love. He also wrote some of the songs the group performed. He later tried a solo career but met with mixed success.

Gzowski, Peter, Canadian broadcaster (b. July 13, 1934, Toronto, Ont.—d. Jan. 24, 2002, Toronto), was the inimitable gravelly voiced host of the national radio show *This Country in the Morning* (1971–74) and the three-hour radio program *Morningside* (1982–97); he infused warmth, intimacy, and passion into his programs, which featured an eclectic blend of interviews and commentary. Gzowski was a household name in English-speaking Canada

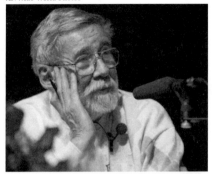

AP/Wide World Photos

Peter Gzowski, Canada's morning voice

and was beloved among listeners for the genuine regard that he showed them when they talked over the airwaves.

Hamilton, Virginia, American children's author (b. March 12, 1936, Yellow Springs, Ohio—d. Feb. 19, 2002, Dayton, Ohio), was a master storyteller who preserved black oral tradition following intensive research that uncovered long-forgotten riddles, stories, and traditions, many of which she resurrected in such books as *The People Could Fly* (1985) and *Many Thousand Gone: African Americans from Slavery to Freedom* (1993). Her first work, *Zeely* (1967), appeared at a time when most books devoted to the African American experience dealt with issues such as racial segregation and poverty. Her novels, which she termed "liberation literature," moved away from "problem" story lines; instead, her tales underscored the experiences of ordinary African Americans. Among her more than 35 works were picture books, folk tales, science-fiction stories, realistic novels, biographies, and mysteries. Hamilton's children's novel *M.C. Higgins, the Great* won a National Book Award and a Newbery Medal in 1975, and she was the recipient of a MacArthur Foundation grant in 1995.

Hampton, Lionel Leo ("HAMP"; "KING OF THE VIBES"), American musician (b. April 20, 1908, Louisville, Ky.—d. Aug. 31, 2002, New York, N.Y.), was one of the first jazz vibraphonists; he became a star during the swing era and then led bands with endless, infec-

AP/Wide World Photos

The King of the Vibes

tious energy for over 50 years. Hampton played vibes with a percussive, swinging style that excited audiences; he also improvised lyric melodies at slower tempos and composed the popular ballad "Midnight Sun." Most of all, Hampton was famous as a showman who entertained crowds by singing, drumming, and playing two-finger piano solos; leaping and tap dancing atop tom-toms; dressing his bands in outrageous costumes and parading them through theatres and nightclubs; and performing shows that ran past closing time. His bands were loud and raucous. A parade of top modern jazz musicians began their careers with Hampton. In the late 1920s he moved to Los Angeles, where he began playing the recently invented vibraphone and soon was leading a band. From 1936 to 1940 he made history as one of two African Americans to play in the first racially integrated concert jazz group, the Benny Goodman Quartet; during those years he also led a series of classic recordings (including "Sweethearts on Parade," "When Lights Are Low," and "Sunny Side of the Street") that featured great swing musicians. Despite the decline of the big-band business, Hampton's 1940–65 big band was an ongoing success, scoring hits such as "Flying Home" and "Hamp's Boogie Woogie" and touring the world; in later decades Hampton led small and large bands, including the all-star Golden Men of Jazz in the 1990s.

Handler, Ruth Mosko, American entrepreneur and businesswoman (b. Nov. 4, 1916, Denver, Colo.—d. April 27, 2002, Los Angeles, Calif.), was a cofounder of Mattel and created the Barbie doll, which in 1959 became the first mass-produced toy doll in the U.S. with adult features. Barbie, joined by several family members and friends and appearing in numerous career versions, soon was helping the company earn $100 million a year but later also became an object of controversy because of the unrealistic body image she was seen to promote. In the late 1970s Handler founded the Ruthton Corp. to manufacture the Nearly Me prosthetic breasts for women who had had mastectomies; she ran that company until she sold it to Kimberly-Clark in 1991.

Hanna, Sir Roland Pembroke American jazz pianist (b. Feb. 10, 1932, Detroit, Mich.—d. Nov. 13, 2002, Harris, N.Y.), fused classical music bravura and bop-era sophistication as a versatile accompanist, leader, and soloist. While attending the Juilliard School in New York City (M.A., 1960), Hanna toured with swing clarinet king Benny Goodman; he worked with stars such as tenor saxophonist Coleman Hawkins, singer Sarah Vaughan, and bassist-composer Charles Mingus and played in the Thad Jones–Mel Lewis big band (1966–74). He performed for the 1989 debut of Mingus's *Epitaph* and played in the Lincoln Center and Smithsonian jazz orchestras. He also led his own trio, formed the New York Jazz Sextet (which became the New York Jazz Quartet in the 1970s), and played outstanding solo piano concerts. Besides serving as a Queens College (New York City) music teacher, he composed both jazz and classical

works, including *Oasis* for piano and orchestra; in 1970, during a benefit concert tour, he was knighted by the government of Liberia.

Hannum, Alex, American basketball coach (b. July 19, 1923, Los Angeles, Calif.—d. Jan. 18, 2002, San Diego, Calif.), was the first coach to win championships in both the National Basketball Association (NBA) and the American Basketball Association (ABA); he was also one of only two coaches ever to win NBA titles with two different teams. Hannum played professional basketball from 1948 to 1957. He then became the head coach of the St. Louis Hawks of the NBA and led the team to triumph over the Boston Celtics to claim the 1958 NBA championship. Hannum later led the Philadelphia 76ers to an NBA title in 1967. Hannum also coached the Oakland Oaks to an ABA title in 1968. He retired in 1974. Hannum was elected to the Basketball Hall of Fame in 1998.

Harding, Warren, American rock climber (b. June 18, 1924, Oakland, Calif.—d. Feb. 27, 2002, Happy Valley, Calif.), was the first climber to scale El Capitan, the 1,098-m (3,604-ft) granite monolith in Yosemite National Park. Daring and charismatic, Harding brought unprecedented attention to rock climbing and helped transform it from the relatively exclusive pursuit of a few climbers into a popular sport.

Hare, R(ichard) M(ervyn), British philosopher (b. March 21, 1919, Backwell, Somerset, Eng.—d. Jan. 29, 2002, Ewelme, Oxfordshire, Eng.), attempted to provide a rational understanding of moral beliefs. His moral theory, called prescriptivism, drew on Immanuel Kant's moral philosophy and the linguistic analysis of Hare's predecessor at the University of Oxford, J.L. Austin; Hare's theory was first presented in *The Language of Morals* (1952). In opposition to the prevailing emotivism, which maintained that moral statements were merely expressions of individual preference, Hare claimed that they were prescriptions, guides to conduct, which were universalizable—that is, they applied to everyone.

Harkarvy, Benjamin, American dance teacher, choreographer, and artistic director (b. Dec. 16, 1930, New York, N.Y.—d. March 30, 2002, New York City), had an international reputation for his eclectic approach to dance education and for his leadership of a number of renowned dance companies. At the Juilliard School of Music's dance division, whose faculty he joined in 1990 and headed from 1992, he expanded the already existing emphasis on both ballet and modern technique and created new programs that provided students with increased choreographic and performing opportunities. From 1951 to 1955 he taught at Michel Fokine's school in New York City, and in 1955 he opened his own school. Harkarvy's guidance of dance companies began in 1957 with the Royal Winnipeg (Man.) Ballet, and the following year he was named ballet master of the Dutch National Ballet. Unhappy with problems in the latter company, he and a number of the dancers broke away and formed (1959) Nederlands Dans Theater, which he and Hans van Manen co-directed for a decade and whose image he formed not only by his own choreography but also by the notable modern dancers—including Anna Sokolow, Glen Tetley, and John Butler—he engaged to create works. In 1969 Harkarvy became co-director, with Lawrence Rhodes, of another troubled company, the Harkness Ballet, which was disbanded the following year. Harkarvy returned to the Dutch National Ballet for a year, and from 1973 to 1982 he was affiliated with the Pennsylvania Ballet, serving first as associate director and then as director and guiding it to increased regard and prominence.

Harris, Richard St. John, Irish actor (b. Oct. 1, 1930, Limerick, Ire.—d. Oct. 25, 2002, London, Eng.), had a sometimes-uneven career notable not only for his formidable talent in portraying the intense, volatile, and rebellious hell-raising characters that established his image but also for conducting his real life in a similar manner for a number of years. Near the end of his life, though, he became known as the lovable though curmudgeonly Professor Albus Dumbledore in the first two Harry Potter movies. Harris played rugby football while in school, but his hopes for a future in sports ended when he contracted tuberculosis and had to endure a long convalescence. Desiring to become a director, he thereafter moved to England but, unable to find suitable directing classes, instead studied acting at the London Academy of Music and Dramatic Art, and in 1956 he made his professional debut with the Theatre Workshop company of Joan Littlewood (*q.v.*) in Brendan Behan's *The Quare Fellow*. He also made an impressive television appearance in 1958 in

Richard Harris as King Arthur

The Kobal Collection/Warner Bros.

The Iron Harp. At about that same time, Harris began his motion picture career, appearing first in *Alive and Kicking* (1959) and then in such films as *Shake Hands with the Devil* (1959), *The Wreck of the Mary Deare* (1959), and *The Guns of Navarone* (1961). His breakthrough role was that of an aggressive rugby player in *This Sporting Life* (1963), for which he won the best actor award at the Cannes Film Festival. Notable films that followed included *Major Dundee* (1965), *Camelot* (1967), in which he portrayed King Arthur, and *A Man Called Horse* (1970) and its two sequels. In general, though, Harris's career had gone into a slump by that time, in part because of serious problems with alcohol abuse, but in the early 1980s he quit drinking and went on a long tour with a stage production of *Camelot*. The 1990s were more successful, with an Academy Award nomination for *The Field* (1990), a notable stage role in Luigi Pirandello's *Henry IV* (1991), and the role of Marcus Aurelius in the film *Gladiator* (2000).

Hay, Harry (HENRY HAY, JR.), American gay rights activist (b. April 7, 1912, Worthing, Eng.—d. Oct. 24, 2002, San Francisco, Calif.), believed that homosexuals should see themselves as an oppressed minority entitled to equal rights. He acted on his convictions and in large measure prompted the dramatic changes in the status of homosexuals that took place in the U.S. in the second half of the 20th century. A member of the Communist Party, he participated in labour actions in the 1930s. In 1950 he founded the first sustained gay rights organization, the Mattachine Society, a support network for homosexuals that for a time had to remain secret. When during the 1950s he was called before the House Un-American Activities Committee, both the Communist Party and the Mattachine Society forced him from their ranks as a risk. The biography *The Trouble with Harry Hay: Founder of the Modern Gay Movement*, by Stuart Timmons, was published in 1990.

Hayes, Robert Lee ("BOB"), American sprinter and football player (b. Dec. 20, 1942, Jacksonville, Fla.—d. Sept. 18, 2002, Jacksonville), commanded an incredible speed that not only helped him set records in track and field but also fundamentally changed professional football when opposing teams, finding that they could not match his speed man-to-man, adopted defensive zone coverages to contain him. He was a two-sport standout at Florida A&M University, with an unorthodox pigeon-toed running style and outsized musculature for a track star. By 1963 he was becoming one of the all-time greatest runners when he set the world record over 100 yd in 9.1 sec and matched the world indoor records over 60 yd four times in four weeks. Hayes capped a brilliant career in athletics by winning two gold medals at the 1964 Tokyo Olympics. On a soft cinder track, he won the 100-m dash by a wide margin, tying the world-record time (10.0 sec), and in the world-record (39.06) 4 × 100-m relay, he led a thrilling come-from-behind victory on an anchor leg that was clocked at 8.6 sec. Later that year he

was drafted by the Dallas Cowboys as a wide receiver, and in 10 seasons he averaged 20 yd per catch and helped the team to reach the Super Bowl in 1972. Hayes, christened the "fastest man alive," was the only athlete to win both an Olympic gold medal and a Super Bowl ring. He was inducted into the Track and Field Hall of Fame in 1976.

Hearn, Francis Dayle ("CHICK"), American sports broadcaster (b. Nov. 27, 1916, Buda, Ill.—d. Aug. 5, 2002, Los Angeles, Calif.), was for more than 40 years the play-by-play radio and television announcer for the Los Angeles Lakers of the National Basketball Association. Witty and sincere, he was

credited with the coining of several sporting terms, including *air ball* and *slam dunk*. He enjoyed nine championship seasons with the team, and in the 1970s he even served as its assistant general manager. From 1965 to 2001 he broadcast a streak of 3,338 consecutive games, and he called his final game when the Lakers clinched the NBA championship in June 2002. He was inducted into the Basketball Hall of Fame in 1991 and the American Sportscasters Hall of Fame in 1995.

Heineken, Alfred Henry, Dutch brewer (b. Nov. 4, 1923, Amsterdam, Neth.—d. Jan. 3, 2002, Noordwijk, Neth.), during a lifetime at the brewery incorporated by his grandfather in 1873, used aggressive and innovative marketing to build Heineken NV into the world's third largest beer company; he was also credited with designing Heineken beer's familiar green bottle and distinctive black-and-red logo. "Freddy" Heineken joined the firm in 1942, the same year that his family lost controlling interest. By 1948 he had personally created a market share for Heineken beer in the U.S., and in 1954 he reacquired a majority of the company stock. He served as Heineken NV's chairman of the executive board (1971–89) and remained chairman of the supervisory board until 1995.

Helms, Richard McGarrah, American intelligence official and diplomat (b. March 30, 1913, Saint Davids, Pa.—d. Oct. 22, 2002, Washington, D.C.), headed the Central Intelligence Agency from 1966 to 1973. To supporters he was a patriot who upheld the security of the country above all else, while to critics he typified the worst faults of the CIA. Helms graduated from Williams College, Williamstown, Mass., in 1935 and for several years worked in journalism. Called to military duty in 1942, he was assigned to the Office of Strategic Services (which was later reorganized into the CIA). Although he tried journalism again after the war, he soon returned to the CIA, where he undertook espionage work. In 1955 he supervised the digging of a tunnel from West to East Berlin that allowed the U.S. to listen to Soviet telephone conversations for nearly a year. In the early 1960s he was involved in intelligence on Cuba, and he was in Vietnam at the time a CIA-engineered coup against Ngo Dinh Diem resulted in the death of the Vietnamese president in 1963. Helms was appointed head of the CIA in 1966, the first career officer to gain the position. In 1973 he refused Pres. Richard M. Nixon's request that he intervene in the investigation of the Watergate scandal. Forced to resign, Helms was appointed ambassador to Iran, where he remained until 1977. In that year he pleaded no contest to charges that he had failed to disclose to Congress the CIA's involvement in attempts to assassinate Cuban Pres. Fidel Castro and in funneling money to opponents of Chilean Pres. Salvador Allende, who was deposed in a 1973 military coup.

Hern, Maj. William Richard ("Dick"; "The Major"), British racehorse trainer (b. Jan. 20, 1921, Holford, Somerset, Eng.—d. May 22, 2002, Oxford, Eng.), saddled the winners of 26 classic thoroughbred races in England and abroad. Hern was named Trainer of the Year four times (1962, 1972, 1980, and 1983) and was chief trainer for Queen Elizabeth II in the 1970s and '80s. The Horse of the Year champions he trained included Brigadier Gerard (1972), Troy (1979), Henbit (1980), and Nashwan (1989). Hern broke his neck in a hunting accident in 1984 and spent the remainder of his life a quadriplegic confined to a wheelchair, but he continued working until his official retirement in 1997. He was made CBE in 1998.

Hewett, Dorothy Coade, Australian writer (b. May 21, 1923, Perth, Australia—d. Aug. 25, 2002, Springwood, N.S.W., Australia), rebelled against the comforts of a conventional lifestyle to embrace progressivist causes in her life and her work. A self-styled "modern Romantic," Hewett crossed genres, composing poetry, plays, novels, and stories. Her first novel, the social realist *Bobbin Up* (1959), drew on her experience as a textile worker and a member of the Communist Party. With her second husband, Merv Lilley, she wrote the verse collection *What About the People!* (1962), which contains some of her greatest poetry. Amazingly prolific, Hewett also composed more than 20 plays, including *This Old Man Comes Rolling Home* (first produced in 1966) and *The Chapel Perilous* (1972). She was appointed a Member of the Order of Australia in 1986.

Heyerdahl, Thor, Norwegian anthropologist, explorer, and writer (b. Oct. 6, 1914, Larvik, Nor.—d. April 18, 2002, near Colla Michari, Italy), attempted to prove his unconventional ideas about prehistoric exploration and migration by re-creating those voyages himself. Although his theories about parallels between ancient cultures far from each other and the possibility that they may have had common origins did not gain acceptance in the scientific community, his exploits and his books about them captured the imagination of the

AP/Wide World Photos

Norwegian anthropologist-adventurer Thor Heyerdahl

general public. Heyerdahl studied zoology and geography at the University of Oslo and in 1937 traveled to Polynesia to live under primitive conditions while studying life there and its origins. It was there that he began to think that just as plant and animal life had traveled from its origins to new sites in the direction of ocean currents, so might humans have sailed from the east in ancient times and populated distant lands. Following service in the free Norwegian forces during World War II, Heyerdahl in 1947 made a 101-day balsa-raft voyage with a five-man crew to demonstrate that the original Polynesians might have traveled from South America instead of from Southeast Asia, which most scholars believed. He told the story of this trip in his book *Kon-Tiki* (1950) and documentary film of the same name, which won an Academy Award in 1951. Heyerdahl's next trip (1952–53) was to the Galápagos Islands, where he found what he considered evidence that South American travelers had visited there. He followed that in 1955 with another of his most famous voyages—to Easter Island, which he also thought had been visited by South Americans. He wrote about that trip and his thoughts about the island's huge stone figures in *Aku-Aku* (1958). Heyerdahl's attention later was directed at Egypt and what he saw as parallels between its ancient culture and that in the Americas, notably pyramid building. In 1969 he set out from Egypt in a reed boat, the *Ra*, but he had to abandon ship short of his destination in Barbados. The following year, in *Ra II*, he was successful. During that voyage Heyerdahl witnessed distressing amounts of pollution in the oceans, and he became an outspoken environmentalist. Subsequent trips included his final epic journey, a 1977–78 voyage in another reed ship, *Tigris*, down the Euphrates and Tigris rivers and the Persian

Gulf and across the Indian Ocean. Political conflicts in the area cut the trip short, however, and Heyerdahl burned the ship in protest.

Hierro, José, Spanish poet (b. April 3, 1922, Madrid, Spain—d. Dec. 20, 2002, Madrid), was one of Spain's most recognizable and beloved contemporary literary figures. Although Hierro was not a prolific poet, his intense, concise verse drew critical and commercial attention. After being jailed by Gen. Francisco Franco's government for five years (1939–44), Hierro turned to writing, publishing his first collection of poetry, *Tierra sin nosotros*, in 1947. A host of awards followed—notably the National Literature Prize in 1990 and the Cervantes Prize, Spain's highest literary honour, for his 1998 work *Cuaderno de Nueva York*—yet he remained self-effacing about his own talent. In 1999 he was elected to the Spanish Royal Academy. Hierro also had a long career as an art critic with Spanish National Radio, a post he held until 1987.

Hill, George Roy, American director, writer, and actor (b. Dec. 20, 1922, Minneapolis, Minn.—d. Dec. 27, 2002, New York, N.Y.), enjoyed for a time the distinction of being the only director to have two films on the list of the top 10 moneymakers—*Butch Cassidy and the Sundance Kid* (1969) and *The Sting* (1973), the latter of which counted best picture and best director awards among its Oscars. He included the writing, producing, and directing of the Emmy Award-winning *A Night to Remember* (1956) and the directing of *Judgment at Nuremberg* (1959) among his television credits—and the direction of such Broadway plays as *Look Homeward, Angel* (1957) and *Period of Adjustment* (1960), whose film version (1962) marked his debut as a motion picture director.

Hindley, Myra, British serial killer (b. July 23, 1942, Manchester, Eng.—d. Nov. 15, 2002, Bury St. Edmunds, Suffolk, Eng.), was convicted in 1966 of the torture and murder of two children and of having been the accessory in the murder of a third. The "Moors Murderers," as Hindley and Ian Brady came to be called because the victims' bodies were found buried on the Pennine Moors, were both sentenced to life in prison. The pair later acknowledged having killed at least two other children. As England's first convicted female serial killer, Hindley became a cause célèbre—considered a sadistic murderer by some but seen by others as a weak young woman brutalized into helping her homicidal lover.

Hnatyshyn, Ramon John ("RAY"), Canadian politician (b. March 16, 1934, Saskatoon, Sask.—d. Dec. 18, 2002, Ottawa, Ont.), served as a Conservative in the House of Commons for 14 years (1974–88) before being named governor-general of Canada, a post he held from 1990 to 1995.

Hobeika, Elie (ELIAS JOSEPH HOBEIKA), Lebanese militia leader (b. 1956, Kleiat, Lebanon—d. Jan. 24, 2002, Hazmiyeh, Lebanon), was the ruthless head of the Maronite Christian Lebanese militia (Phalangist) military intelligence and was reportedly commander of the forces who in September 1982 slaughtered hundreds of Palestinian men, women, and children in Beirut's Sabra and Shatila refugee camps. The incident triggered international condemnation of the Phalangists and of Israel, which had intervened in the Lebanese civil war and had failed to stop the massacre. Hobeika later switched his allegiance to Syria and went into exile in Paris; after the civil war ended (1990), he was appointed a Lebanese government minister. Hobeika was assassinated by a car bomb shortly after he had agreed to testify against Israeli Prime Minister Ariel Sharon, who, as Israel's defense minister in 1982, was accused of having condoned the massacre.

Hoyte, (Hugh) Desmond, Guyanese politician (b. March 9, 1929, Georgetown, Guyana—d. Dec. 22, 2002, Georgetown), became president of Guyana after the death of Forbes Burnham in 1985 and soon thereafter began dismantling Burnham's socialist framework. As leader of the People's National Congress (PNC) and president with expanded powers under the 1980 constitution, Hoyte wielded immense power. He angered many within the PNC when he began courting foreign investors and making peace with the International Monetary Fund in order to stanch rising poverty and the national debt. He helped launch the Guyana literary prizes and was instrumental in helping to create the Iwokrama project, a conservation area in the

Guyana forests. After losing the 1992 presidential election, the first to be termed fair since 1964, Hoyte remained a formidable force in opposition and blocked attempts by the People's Progressive Party to make constitutional changes.

Hunter, Kim (JANET COLE), American actress (b. Nov. 12, 1922, Detroit, Mich.—d. Sept. 11, 2002, New York, N.Y.), had a more than 60-year stage, screen, and television career highlighted by two extremely varied roles: Stella, Stanley Kowalski's anguished wife, both on Broadway (1947) and in the film version (1951) of *A Streetcar Named Desire*, and the sympathetic chimpanzee psychiatrist Dr. Zira in three *Planet of the Apes* movies (1968, 1970, and 1971). She won a best supporting actress Academy Award for her performance in *Streetcar*. Hunter's first movie role came in 1943 with *The Seventh Victim*, and that same

© John Springer Collection/Corbis

Kim Hunter: from Stella to Dr. Zira

year she appeared in *Tender Comrade*. One of her most notable roles was in the British film *A Matter of Life and Death* (1946; U.S. title, *Stairway to Heaven*), and upon her return to the U.S. she was cast in *A Streetcar Named Desire*. While performing in that play, she took the opportunity to study at the Actors' Studio. Because Hunter had helped sponsor a world peace symposium in 1949 and because some considered *Tender Comrade* pro-Soviet, Hunter was listed as a communist sympathizer in the pamphlet *Red Channels*, which led to her being blacklisted for a few years in the 1950s. In 1962 in the New York Supreme Court, her testimony against the publishers of that pamphlet helped clear the names of several actors.

Hussain, Nasir, Indian motion picture writer, director, and producer (b. 1931, Bhopal, Madhya Pradesh, India—d. March 12, 2002, Mumbai [Bombay], India), made a score of lighthearted Bollywood films, beginning with *Tumsa nahin dekha* (1957, "Never Seen Anyone Like You"). Although some critics dis-

missed Hussain as repetitive (a charge he never denied), the breezy style, lively plots, and catchy music that filled his movies made most of them box-office hits. In later years he also wrote and produced movies directed by his son, Mansoor Khan. Hussain received a lifetime achievement award from the Hindi-language film industry in 1997.

Hyakutake, Yuji, Japanese amateur astronomer (b. 1951, Japan—d. April 10, 2002, Kokubu, Japan), discovered the comet that came to be named after him, Comet Hyakutake. On Jan. 30, 1996—attempting to photograph a comet he had discovered the previous month but finding its location obscured by cloud—he began scanning the skies near where he had made his original discovery and found a second comet, one of the most spectacular of modern times.

Ienaga, Saburo, Japanese historian (b. Sept. 3, 1913, Nagoya, Japan—d. Nov. 29, 2002, Tokyo, Japan), waged a long-running battle with the Japanese Ministry of Education over his depiction in history textbooks of wartime atrocities committed by the Japanese. After having fought government censorship for more than three decades, Ienaga triumphed in a high-profile court case in 1997 when the Japanese Supreme Court ruled that the ministry had acted illegally when it suppressed descriptions in one textbook of the Japanese army's biological warfare experiments in China during World War II. He was nominated for the 2001 Nobel Prize for Peace.

Jackson, John, American blues guitarist (b. Feb. 25, 1924, Woodville, Va.—d. Jan. 20, 2002, Fairfax, Va.), was considered a master of the Piedmont blues tradition. From 1965 to 1999 Jackson recorded nine albums, including *Blues and Country Dance Songs from Virginia* (1965), *Step It Up and Go* (1979), *Deep in the Bottom* (1982), and *Country Blues and Ditties* (1999).

Jam Master Jay (JASON MIZELL), American rap musician and producer (b. Jan. 21, 1965, New York, N.Y.—d. Oct. 30, 2002, New York City), was a member of Run-D.M.C., the first rap group to attract a worldwide audience. Jam Master Jay teamed with Joe ("Run") Simmons and Darryl ("D.M.C.") McDaniels to form the group in the early 1980s. The trio's debut album, *Run-D.M.C.* (1984), featuring the hit singles "It's like That" and "Sucker MCs," became the first rap album to attain gold status (sales of 500,000 copies). The band's follow-up effort, *King of Rock* (1985), also went gold. Jam Master Jay provided the hard, pounding beats and scratching of records on his turntable that were an integral part of the stripped-down sound pioneered by the group. Run-D.M.C. was also credited with being the first group to fuse rap and rock-and-roll melodies. The trio's third album, *Raising Hell* (1986), included a wildly successful remake of rock band Aerosmith's 1975 hit "Walk This Way"; the video for the remake became one of the most-played music videos in the history of MTV. *Raising Hell* sold more than three million copies worldwide, but Run-D.M.C.'s popularity dropped off significantly thereafter. Jam Master Jay later made a name for himself as a producer of young hip-hop acts. Jam Master Jay was shot dead at his recording studio in New York City, and authorities were still investigating the case at year's end.

Jennings, Waylon, American country music singer and songwriter (b. June 15, 1937, Littlefield, Texas—d. Feb. 13, 2002, Chandler, Ariz.), recorded some 60 albums and 16 number one country hits and sold more than 40 million records worldwide; in the 1970s he spearheaded, with Willie Nelson, a movement known as "outlaw music," which blended folk lyrics, rock rhythms, and honky-tonk-style instrumentation. Jennings, who performed professionally from the age of 12, first toured as a bassist for Buddy Holly. Chet Atkins eventually signed Jennings to a contract with RCA Records and took him to Nashville in 1964. Four years later Jennings recorded his first number one song, "Only Daddy That'll Walk the Line." Other hits included "Good Hearted Woman" (1972) and "(I'm a) Ramblin' Man" (1974). Frustrated by what he saw as the increasingly bland sound of country music, Jennings teamed with Nelson in 1976 to produce their own album, *Wanted: The Outlaws*, which launched the outlaw music movement and became the first Nashville album to sell a million copies. A later duet with Nelson, "Mammas Don't Let Your Babies Grow Up to Be Cowboys," earned the two a Grammy Award in 1978. Jennings wrote the theme song and provided narration for the popular 1980s

AP/Wide World Photos

Country music outlaw Waylon Jennings

television series *The Dukes of Hazzard.* In the 1980s, with Nelson, Johnny Cash, and Kris Kristofferson, he formed the Highwaymen. Jennings was inducted into the Country Music Hall of Fame in 2001.

Jones, Charles Martin ("CHUCK"), American animator (b. Sept. 21, 1912, Spokane, Wash.—d. Feb. 22, 2002, Corona del Mar, Calif.), created some of the world's most famous and most loved cartoon characters during a 70-year career. His more than 300 films were peopled by such Looney Tunes and Merrie Melodies animated beings as Bugs Bunny, Daffy Duck, Porky Pig, Elmer Fudd, Pepe Le Pew, Marvin Martian, Road Runner, and Wile E. Coyote. Despite his lack of a high-school diploma, he studied at the Chouinard Art Institute (now the California Institute of the Arts), graduating in 1930. Jones's first job was as a cel washer for Ub Iwerks' Celebrity Productions. He worked his way up to assistant animator before going (1933) to Leon Schlesinger's studio—affectionately known as Termite Terrace to those who worked there—which produced cartoons for Warner Brothers. By 1938 he had become a director, with *The Night Watchman* his first cartoon. Bugs Bunny made a small appearance, his first, later that year in *Porky's Hare Hunt*, and in 1940 Jones began his more than 50 years of featuring Bugs in his own cartoons. During World War II, Jones collaborated with Theodor Geisel ("Dr. Seuss") on army training films that featured Private Snafu, whose name originated in a popular military acronym. They later revisited their partnership for television productions of *Dr. Seuss' How the Grinch Stole Christmas!* (1966), which won a Peabody Award, and *Horton Hears a Who!* (1970). In the meantime, Jones had created such cartoon classics as *Duck Amuck* (1953) and *What's Opera, Doc?* (1957), had won Academy Awards in 1950 for *So Much for So Little* and *Scentimental Reasons* and in 1965 for *The Dot and the Line*, and had begun (1962) working at MGM on Tom and Jerry cartoons. In 1996 Jones was honoured with an Academy Award for lifetime achievement.

Jordan, June, American writer, political activist, and scholar (b. July 9, 1936, Harlem, N.Y.—d. June 14, 2002, Berkeley, Calif.), tirelessly spoke out against the injustices and oppressions suffered by the socially marginalized. During her career she authored more than two dozen books that included volumes of poetry, essay collections, and novels, which made her one of the most prolific African American writers in history. Though Jordan credited her father with having fostered within her a love of literature, their relationship was strained by his violent temper. She attended Barnard College in New York City and became active on the political and literary scenes during the late 1960s, advocating for women, the poor, and the disenfranchised. Jordan began teaching at the City Colleges of New York in 1966. Her first book, *Who Look at Me* (1969), was a children's book, and it was followed by the poetry collection *Some Changes* (1971). *Civil Wars* (1981), a collection of political essays, also provided autobiographical material that chronicled her troubled interracial marriage, her experience as a mother, and her devotion to the black community. Other notable works by Jordan in-

Activist and author June Jordan

cluded the novel *His Own Where* (1971) and the essay collections *On Call* (1985) and *Technical Difficulties: African-American Notes on the State of the Union* (1992). She was presented with a lifetime achievement award by the National Black Writers' Conference in 1998. Jordan was a professor of African-American Studies at the University of California, Berkeley, from 1989. *Some of Us Did Not Die*, a collection of essays, was published posthumously.

Junge, Traudl (GERTRAUD HUMPS JUNGE), German secretary (b. March 16, 1920, Munich, Ger.—d. Feb. 10/11, 2002, Munich), was Adolf Hitler's private secretary from December 1942 until he dictated his last will and testament to her shortly before his suicide in April 1945. Junge was hired originally for the German chancellery typing pool. Her professional notes and intimate knowledge of life in Hitler's bunker during the final days of the war in Europe provided much information for investigators and scholars after World War II. She denied having known anything about the Holocaust until after the war and later expressed remorse over her ignorance. She spent six months in prison after the war and then later became a journalist. Junge published an autobiography, *Bis zur letzten Stunde*, in 2002.

Jurado, Katy (MARÍA CRISTINA ESTELLA MARCELLA JURADO GARCÍA), Mexican actress (b. Jan. 16, 1924, Guadalajara, Mex.—d. July 5, 2002, Cuernavaca, Mex.), projected a smoldering sensuality and vitality that captured audiences' attention first in Mexico and later in the U.S.—where she was one of the first Latina actresses to find success in Hollywood—and Europe. Among her most notable films were *El bruto* (1952), *High Noon* (1952), *Broken Lance* (1954), and *One-Eyed Jacks* (1961).

Kamen, Martin David, Canadian-born chemist (b. Aug. 27, 1913, Toronto, Ont.—d. Aug. 31, 2002, Santa Barbara, Calif.), discovered (1940), with Samuel Ruben, radioactive carbon-14. Kamen was later shunned by the scientific community, however, owing to false suspicions that he was a Soviet agent. After earning a Ph.D. from the University of Chicago, Kamen worked at the radiation laboratory at the University of California, Berkeley. While seeking a long-lived radioac-

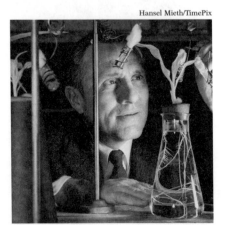

Hansel Mieth/TimePix

Canadian chemist Martin David Kamen

tive carbon tracer for photosynthesis research, Kamen and Ruben bombarded graphite in a cyclotron. Their result was the isotope carbon-14, with a half-life of 5,730 years. The availability of the isotope paved the way for key advances in biochemistry, and the later discovery of naturally occurring carbon-14 revolutionized archaeology through the use of radiocarbon dating. In 1995 Kamen was honoured with the Enrico Fermi Award for his lifetime achievements in energy research.

Kant, Krishan, Indian politician (b. Feb. 28, 1927, Kot Mohammad Khan, Punjab, India—d. July 27, 2002, New Delhi, India), devoted his entire life to Indian freedom, social welfare, and civil liberties and rose to become vice president in 1997. Kant, who came from a family of devout followers of Mohandas Gandhi, plunged into active politics while still a student and was imprisoned for his involvement in the anti-British Quit India movement of 1942. He rose in the Congress Party, identifying himself with the socialist group, and was elected to the Rajya Sabha (upper house) in 1966. In 1975 Kant was expelled from the Congress Party for his opposition to the state of emergency declared by then prime minister Indira Gandhi. He joined the Janata Party and in 1977 was elected to the Lok Sabha (lower house). He was appointed governor of Andhra Pradesh in 1990.

Karsh, Yousuf, Turkish-born Canadian photographer (b. Dec. 23, 1908, Mardin, Turkey—d. July 13, 2002, Boston, Mass.), achieved international renown for his portraits of political, military, artistic, and business leaders, as well as other celebrities—all carrying his

studio's signature, Karsh of Ottawa. What was arguably his most famous photograph was the one that initially brought him acclaim—that of a defiant Winston Churchill early in World War II. Published on the cover of *Life* magazine, it became emblematic of the indomitable British spirit and was reproduced on numerous posters and on the postage stamps of at least seven countries. Karsh, the son of Armenian parents, fled to Syria with his family in 1922 to escape the massacres of Armenians that had been taking place in Turkey, and in 1924 he moved to Canada to live with an uncle, who was a photographer in Quebec. His uncle taught him the basics of photography, and he then spent three years (1928–31) in Boston as an apprentice to John H. Garo. Returning to Canada, Karsh set up his own studio in 1932. Through his membership in the Ottawa Little Theatre, he mastered the use of artificial light that would distinguish his portraits, and he also made important contacts who led to his gaining a number of prominent political figures as clients. The picture of Churchill came about when Karsh was told that he could take only one photograph and had two minutes in which to do so. Preferring to get a shot without Churchill's ever-present cigar, Karsh uttered a quick "Sir, forgive me," snatched away the cigar, and captured Churchill's glowering reaction. Among Karsh's subsequent works were definitive portraits of Ernest Hemingway, Albert Einstein, Georgia O'Keeffe, Nikita S. Khrushchev, and Pablo Casals. He lived in Boston following his retirement in 1992. Karsh's work was featured in the permanent collections of numerous venues and in such books of his portraits as *Faces of Destiny* (1946), *Portraits of Greatness* (1959), *Faces of Our Time* (1971), and *Karsh: A Sixty-Year Retrospective* (1996). He was made a Companion of the Order of Canada in 1990.

Kawakami, Genichi, Japanese businessman (b. Jan. 30, 1912, Hamakita, Shizuoka prefecture, Japan—d. May 25, 2002, near Hamamatsu, Shizuoka prefecture, Japan), was the visionary president of the Yamaha Corp. for three decades (1950–77 and 1980–83). The company, which had been founded in the late 19th century by Torakusu Yamaha, an organ builder, as Nippon Gakki, was long an obscure domestic manufacturer. Kawakami, an innovative technical leader as well as a savvy marketing strategist, turned it into an international conglomerate. Interested in Western classical music from a young age, he studied business at the Takachiho College of Commerce and then joined the company, which was headed by his father at the time. Kawakami became president in 1950. In 1964, following trips to Europe and the U.S., where he observed the widespread interest in music instruction, he founded the first overseas Yamaha Music School, in Los Angeles; its branches offered lessons and thereby promoted Yamaha pianos and string, wind, and other instruments. Within 20 years the company had become the world's largest manufacturer of pianos. In 1966 Kawakami created the Yamaha Music Foundation to promote

Yamaha visionary Genichi Kawakami

competitions. The Electone, an electronic organ that appeared in 1959, as well as the company's digital keyboards, came to be widely used by pop musicians. The company made the first Yamaha motorcycle in 1955. Motorcycles and other sporting goods subsequently became a major part of its business. Kawakami retired as president of Yamaha in 1977, turning the company over to his son, but after family disagreements he assumed the presidency again in 1980. In 1983 he once more retired in favour of his son and took the title supreme adviser.

Kelly, Thomas Joseph, American aerospace engineer (b. June 14, 1929, New York, N.Y.—d. March 23, 2002, Cutchogue, N.Y.), led the team of engineers that designed the Lunar Excursion Module *Eagle*, in which Apollo 11 astronauts Neil Armstrong and Edwin ("Buzz") Aldrin, Jr., landed on the Moon on July 20, 1969. Kelly spent virtually his entire career as an engineer for the Grumman Aircraft Corp. In 1962 NASA contracted Grumman to develop the Lunar Module, and Kelly was given charge of the project. The result of his team's work was a spiderlike two-stage landing vehicle that ultimately proved successful in descending to the Moon's surface and then returning the astronauts to the Apollo Command Module for the flight back to Earth. In 1972 NASA bestowed its Distinguished Public Service Medal on Kelly, and he was elected to the National Academy of Engineering in 1991.

Kimball, Ward, American animator (b. March 4, 1914, Minneapolis, Minn.—d. July 8, 2002, Arcadia, Calif.), was among the "Nine Old Men" who made Walt Disney Studios the leader of film cartoons by drawing or directing the animation of classic features and shorts (including *Dumbo, Fantasia, Peter Pan, Alice in Wonderland, Cinderella,* and *The Three Caballeros*) and creating television shows for Disney for 39 years. He joined the company in 1934 and worked on *Snow White and the Seven Dwarfs* before developing the character of Jiminy Cricket for *Pinocchio* (1940) and then becoming an animation supervisor. He won Academy Awards for directing the first CinemaScope cartoon, *Toot, Whistle, Plunk, and Boom* (1953), and *It's Tough to Be a Bird* (1969). Among his most notable television productions were three 1950s programs on space exploration, *Man in Space, Man on the Moon,* and *Mars and Beyond,* which he wrote and directed while consulting with German engineer Wernher von Braun and others.

Kipnis, Igor, German-born American harpsichordist, teacher, and critic (b. Sept. 27, 1930, Berlin, Ger.—d. Jan. 23, 2002, Redding, Conn.), was perhaps the most eminent harpsichord player of his generation and made more than 80 recordings. He was the son of Alexander Kipnis, a well-known operatic bass. In addition to his mastery of the Baroque literature for his instrument, Kipnis was a great popularizer of the harpsichord, often including jazz and pop tunes in his concerts.

Knef, Hildegard Frieda Albertine, German actress and singer (b. Dec. 28, 1925, Ulm, Ger.—d. Feb. 1, 2002, Berlin, Ger.), had a versatile stage and screen career that took her back and forth between post-World War II Europe and the U.S., where she triumphed as the Soviet commissar Ninotchka in Cole Porter's Broadway musical *Silk Stockings* (1955). Knef starred as a former concentration camp prisoner in *Die Mörder sind unter uns* (1946; *Murderers Among Us*), scandalized Germany with a brief nude scene in *Die Sünderin* (1950; *The Sinner*), and played Pirate Jenny in *Die Dreigroschenoper* (1963; *The Threepenny Opera*). Her Hollywood films, in most of which she was billed as Hildegard Neff to downplay her German origins, included *Decision Before Dawn* (1951) and *The Snows of Kilimanjaro* (1952). In the 1960s she developed a cabaret act.

Knott, Frederick Major Paul, British playwright (b. Aug. 28, 1916, Hankou, China—d. Dec. 17, 2002, New York, N.Y.), wrote only three plays, but two of them met with enormous success. Seven London producers rejected his first, *Dial M for Murder,* before the BBC agreed to televise it (1952); it went on to a 552-performance run in the West End, production in 30 countries over the following five years, and a 1954 film version directed by Alfred Hitchcock. Knott's last play, *Wait Until Dark* (1966), was filmed in 1967.

Koch, Kenneth Jay, American poet, writer, and teacher (b. Feb. 27, 1925, Cincinnati, Ohio—d. July 6, 2002, New York, N.Y.), was known for verse that combined modernism with lyricism and that conveyed a sense of enthusiasm and fun. The subject matter was wide in range and included ordinary objects and references to popular culture. At the same time, Koch's poetry could be learned and technically sophisticated, reflecting his thorough academic training. He had a poem published in *Poetry* magazine when he was 18. He gained

an A.B. degree (1948) from Harvard University and M.A. (1953) and Ph.D. (1959) degrees from Columbia University, New York City. It was at Harvard that Koch met John Ashbery and Frank O'Hara, with whom he formed the so-called New York school in reaction against the poetics of the time. Major volumes included *Sleeping with Women* (1969), *The Burning Mystery of Anna in 1951* (1979), and *On the Great Atlantic Rainway: Selected Poems 1950–1988* (1994). In addition, he published two volumes of epic poetry in ottava rima in the style of Lord Byron—*Ko; or, A Season on Earth* (1959) and *The Duplications* (1977)—which later appeared together as *Seasons on Earth* (1987). Koch also wrote extensively for the theatre, primarily short plays and librettos for musical works. Other publications included a novel, short stories, books on the teaching of poetry, and, as editor, anthologies of modern poetry.

Kolar, Jiri, Czech artist and writer (b. Sept.

24, 1914, Protivin, Bohemia, Austria-Hungary—d. Aug. 11, 2002, Prague, Czech Rep.), excelled in both poetry and collage, but his works embodied independence and originality at a time when communist cultural repression made such qualities liabilities, and he suffered oppression and imprisonment in his native country. Kolar began exhibiting his art in 1937 and published his first poetry collection, *Birth Certificate,* in 1941. Communist authorities banned his writing in 1949 and again in the 1960s, and he was imprisoned for nine months in the early 1950s. Beginning in the early 1960s, Kolar focused more on visual art and became increasing experimental, eventually earning a place as one of the masters of the collage form.

Kuharic, Franjo Cardinal, Croatian Roman Catholic cleric (b. April 15, 1919, Pribic, Yugos.—d. March 11, 2002, Zagreb, Croatia), served as a strong nationalist symbol for his countrymen during Croatia's 1991 secession from Yugoslavia and the war that ensued (1991–95). In his role as archbishop of Zagreb (1970–97) and, thus, Roman Catholic primate of Croatia, Kuharic condemned religious intolerance and violence against Serbs and Muslims. He was made a cardinal in 1983.

Kyprianou, Spyros, Greek Cypriot nationalist leader and politician (b. Oct. 28, 1932, Limassol, Cyprus—d. March 12, 2002, Nicosia, Cyprus), succeeded independent Cyprus's founder, Archbishop Makarios, as president in 1977. Having served as the country's first foreign minister (1960–72), he was appointed president when Makarios died in office, and he went on to win reelection in 1978 and 1983. Beginning in 1979 Kyprianou negotiated on several occasions with the leader of the breakaway Turkish enclave in

northern Cyprus, but reunification talks between the two sides failed. He had some success in revitalizing the Cypriot economy but was voted out of office in 1988.

Lamphere, Robert Joseph, American government agent (b. Feb. 14, 1918, Wardner, Idaho—d. Jan. 7, 2002, Tucson, Ariz.), as a counterintelligence specialist for the FBI, supervised investigations into several major Soviet espionage cases from the end of World War II to the mid-1950s. In 1947 Lamphere began work on the bureau's Soviet espionage squad. He used deciphered Soviet cables to build cases against numerous spies, most notably Klaus Fuchs—a German-born British physicist who was convicted in 1950 for having given vital atomic-research secrets to the Soviet Union—and Julius and Ethel Rosenberg, who were found guilty of having passed military secrets to the Soviets and executed in 1953. He left the FBI in 1955. His memoir, *The FBI-KGB War: A Special Agent's Story,* appeared in 1986.

Landers, Ann (Esther ["Eppie"] Pauline Friedman Lederer), American advice columnist (b. July 4, 1918, Sioux City, Iowa—d. June 22, 2002, Chicago, Ill.), gave down-to-earth commonsense—and sometimes wisecracking—counsel to readers with a variety of problems that ranged from everyday family, friendship, and neighbourhood concerns to such serious health issues as depression, alcoholism, and AIDS. In so doing, she gained a readership of some 90 million people in more than 1,200 newspapers worldwide. Eppie and her younger (by 17 minutes) twin sister, Pauline ("Popo") Esther, both attended Morningside College in Sioux City but dropped out in their senior year to get married in a double wedding. With her husband, Jules Lederer, she moved to Eau Claire, Wis., where she became active in local politics and made a number of connections that would later prove valuable in her career. The couple moved to Chicago in 1955; at about that same

Chief American adviser Ann Landers

time, the *Chicago Sun-Times* was holding a contest to find someone to take over its Ask Ann Landers column, whose writer had died. Lederer was given some letters to answer and contacted such acquaintances as Supreme Court Justice William O. Douglas and the president of Notre Dame University, Theodore M. Hesburgh, to help her formulate expert replies. Before long, her column was being syndicated. Soon after that, her sister began writing her own column, using the name Abigail Van Buren and titling the column Dear Abby, and the two became intense rivals and stopped speaking to each other. They reconciled after five years, however. Landers moved to the *Chicago Tribune* in 1987 and remained at that paper for the rest of her life.

Lane, Dick ("NIGHT TRAIN"), American professional football player (b. April 16, 1928, Austin, Texas—d. Jan. 29, 2002, Austin), was one of the leading defensive backs of the National Football League (NFL) in the 1950s and '60s. As a rookie for the Los Angeles Rams in 1952, he made 14 interceptions—a single-season record that still stood at the time of his death. In 14 seasons in the NFL, Lane played for the Rams, the Chicago Cardinals, and the Detroit Lions and was a six-time Pro Bowl choice. After retiring as a player in 1966, Lane coached at Central State University, Wilberforce, Ohio, and Southern University, Baton Rouge, La. He was unanimously elected to the Pro Football Hall of Fame in 1974.

Lebed, Aleksandr Ivanovich, Soviet general and politician (b. April 20, 1950, Novocherkassk, near Rostov, Russian S.F.S.R., U.S.S.R.— d. April 28, 2002, Abakan, Russia), was a decorated military hero who made headlines in 1991 when he refused to lead troops against Russian Pres. Boris Yeltsin in the aborted coup against Soviet Pres. Mikhail Gorbachev; in 1996 he unsuccessfully ran against Yeltsin in the Russian Federation's presidential election. Lebed graduated (1973) as a paratrooper and in 1981–82 commanded a paratroop battalion in Afghanistan. Having reached the rank of general by 1991, he led troops in support of ethnic Russians in Moldova in 1992, but three years later he clashed with superiors and was forcibly retired from the army. In 1996 he ran a strong law-and-order presidential campaign and finished third with 15% of the first-round vote before offering his support to Yeltsin in the second round. Lebed was appointed national security adviser and later that year brokered a temporarily successful deal with ethnic separatists in the breakaway province of Chechnya. He was elected governor of Krasnoyarsk *kray* (region) in 1998. Lebed died from injuries he sustained in a helicopter crash in Siberia.

Lee, Peggy (NORMA DELORES EGSTROM), American singer, songwriter, and actress (b. May 26, 1920, Jamestown, N.D.—d. Jan. 21, 2002, Los Angeles, Calif.), sang in a quiet, intimate voice, with swing and subtle accenting that conveyed intelligence as well as sex appeal. She also won success as an actress and

© Reuters 2002

Chanteuse Peggy Lee

songwriter, most notably in the Walt Disney film *Lady and the Tramp* (1955), for which she co-wrote songs (with Sonny Burke) and created the voices for several animated characters. As a teenager she began singing on a Fargo, N.D., radio station, where she was renamed Peggy Lee. Benny Goodman hired her to sing with his band during 1941–43; her first hit record with Goodman was a version of Lil Green's "Why Don't You Do Right?" She married Goodman's guitarist Dave Barbour and with him wrote several songs, most notably the 1948 hit "Manana." Her film career was brief but singularly successful. Among the highlights were her costarring role in a remake of *The Jazz Singer* (1953) and her nomination for an Oscar for her portrayal of a hard-drinking singer in *Pete Kelly's Blues* (1955). Many years after her work on *Lady and the Tramp*, she won a lawsuit that gave her $2.3 million in videocassette royalties from the Disney Corp. She also wrote movie theme songs, including ones for *Johnny Guitar* (1954) and *The Heart Is a Lonely Hunter* (1968). Even as rock and roll dominated the music industry, Lee scored two of her biggest hits in simple, jazzlike versions of "Fever" (1958) and "Is That All There Is?" (1969); altogether she recorded over 600 songs. After a lifetime of performing success and four failed marriages, Lee created *Peg*, an autobiographical one-woman Broadway show, but it closed after a few performances in 1984. In later years her health was precarious—she was diabetic, and she endured two severe falls, a stroke, and, in 1985, four angioplasties and double-bypass heart surgery. Two of her later albums, *Miss Peggy Lee Sings the Blues* (1989) and *The Peggy Lee Songbook: There'll Be Another Spring* (1991), were nominated for Grammy Awards.

Lemarque, Francis (NATHAN KORB), French singer and songwriter (b. Nov. 25, 1917, Paris, France—d. April 20, 2002, La Varenne-Saint-Hilaire, France), during a nearly 70-year career, wrote some 1,000 chansons, notably *À Paris, Marjolaine, Bal petit bal,* and the ardent pacifist anthem *Quand un soldat.* He also composed for radio, television, and motion pictures and formed a music publishing company. During World War II he changed his name to Lemarque and joined the Resistance in Marseille. In 1946 the aspiring songwriter finagled an introduction to actor-singer Yves Montand, and the two formed a long and successful collaboration. Lemarque won the Charles Cros Prize for his third record album in 1951. Many of his recordings were re-released in the 1990s. Lemarque was named to the Legion of Honour in 1992.

Lewis, Flora, American journalist (b. July 29, 1922, Los Angeles, Calif.—d. June 2, 2002, Paris, France), was a top-notch reporter and columnist who specialized in international affairs. From 1945 she lived mostly in Europe, and she became known for her lucid analyses of developments on the Continent during the second half of the 20th century. Among other things, she reported on the communist takeover of Eastern Europe after World War II, the upheavals in Poland and Hungary in 1956, and the fall of communist governments at the end of the 1980s. Graduating early from high school, she earned (1941) a B.A. degree with honours from the University of California, Los Angeles, and a master's degree (1942) from the School of Journalism of Columbia University, New York City. Lewis then took a job with the Associated Press, working in both New York and Washington, D.C., before being sent to London in 1945. There she married Sydney Gruson, who worked for the *New York Times.* Being prevented by company policy from also being employed by the paper, she worked for a number of other newspapers and then, in 1956, was hired by the *Washington Post.* In 1967 she began writing a column for *Newsday,* and in 1972, after she and her husband had separated, she became the Paris bureau chief for the *New York Times.* Four years later the newspaper made her its European diplomatic correspondent. From 1980 to 1990 she was the foreign affairs columnist for the *New York Times,* and from 1990 to 1994 she was its senior columnist. Beginning in 1994 and continuing until her death, she worked as a syndicated columnist. Among her books was *Europe: Road to Unity,* published in 1992.

Lewis, R(ichard) W(arrington) B(aldwin), American literary critic (b. Nov. 1, 1917, Chicago, Ill.—d. June 13, 2002, Bethany, Conn.), helped originate the field of American studies and over his nearly half-century-long career as a scholar made significant contributions to the knowledge of American culture. His *Edith Wharton: A Biography* (1975) won a Pulitzer Prize as well as the Bancroft Prize and the first National Book Critics Circle Award for nonfiction. Among his other acclaimed titles were *The American Adam*

(1955), *The Jameses: A Family Narrative* (1991), and *Dante* (2001).

Lindgren, Astrid Anna Emilia Ericsson, Swedish children's writer (b. Nov. 14, 1907, Vimmerby, Swed.—d. Jan. 28, 2002, Stockholm, Swed.), delighted youngsters around the world with more than 70 books, but her greatest creation was the indomitable Pippi Longstocking, a freckle-faced, red-haired nine-year-old character that Lindgren had conceived in 1941 to entertain her sick daughter. The anarchic Pippilotta Delicatessa Windowshade Mackrelmint Efraim's Daughter Longstocking first appeared in print in *Pippi Långstrump* (1945; *Pippi Longstocking*, 1950); the novel and its sequels sold millions of copies and inspired both Swedish- and English-language films. Lindgren created several other popular characters, notably master detective Bill Bergson, the six Bullerby chil-

Children's favourite Astrid Lindgren

dren, the mischievous five-year-old farm boy Emil, and Ronja, the robber's daughter. She also wrote poetry collections, songs, plays, screenplays, and serials for radio and television. Her books were translated into more than 60 languages.

Littlewood, Joan Maud, British theatre director and writer (b. Oct. 5/6, 1914, London, Eng.—d. Sept. 20, 2002, London), was a pioneer of radical theatre whose experimental productions, often performed by and devoted to the working class, helped bring about a revolution on the British stage in the 1950s and '60s. She combined improvisational technique with political content to examine social issues of the day, and her innovative direction brought prominence to the works of such playwrights as Brendan Behan and Shelagh Delaney. Littlewood won a scholarship to the Royal Academy of Dramatic Art but dropped out and began making her way to Liverpool, hoping to go from there to the U.S. She got only as far as Manchester, however. There she joined (1934) the Theatre of Action, founded by writer and poet Jimmie Miller, who was later known as Ewan McColl and whom Littlewood married; that company was suc-

ceeded (1936) by Theatre Union and reestablished as the touring Theatre Workshop after World War II. Littlewood's marriage failed, and she began a relationship with the new company's administrator, Gerry Raffles, which lasted until his death in 1975. In 1953 Theatre Workshop took over the run-down Theatre Royal in a poor area of London known as Stratford East and began restoring it. With productions that included Jaroslav Hasek's *The Good Soldier Schweik* (1955), Behan's *The Quare Fellow* (1956) and *The Hostage* (1958), Delaney's *A Taste of Honey* (1958), Frank Norman and Lionel Bart's *Fings Ain't Wot They Used T'Be* (1959), and *Sparrers Can't Sing* (1960; filmed 1962, with Littlewood as director), the theatre attracted attention and ever-growing audiences, and many productions made successful transfers to the West End. Littlewood scored her greatest success with the satiric *Oh, What a Lovely War* (1963). It was translated into several languages and, in 1969, filmed. Littlewood's later successes included *Mrs. Wilson's Diary* (1967), *The Marie Lloyd Story* (1967), *The Projector* (1970), and *So You Want to Be in Pictures* (1973).

Lobanovsky, Valery Vasilevich, Ukrainian association football (soccer) player and coach (b. Jan. 6, 1939, Kiev, Ukrainian S.S.R., U.S.S.R.—d. May 13, 2002, Zaporizhya, Ukraine), as the legendary coach of Dynamo Kiev (1973–90, 1996–2001), guided that football club to eight Soviet league championships, six Soviet Cups, five straight Ukrainian league titles (1997–2001), two European Cup–Winners' Cups (1975 and 1986), the 1975 Union des Associations Européennes de Football (UEFA) Super Cup title, and the semifinal of the UEFA Champions League in 1999. Lobanovsky, who was known for his unusually strong emphasis on physical fitness and diet, also coached the Soviet national team, leading it to the second round in the 1986 World Cup finals and to the final of the 1988 European championship. After the breakup of the U.S.S.R. in 1990, he coached the U.A.E., Kuwait, and Ukraine national squads. As a player in the Soviet league for 10 years, Lobanovsky had scored 71 goals in 257 matches and led Dynamo to the 1961 championship.

Lomax, Alan, American ethnomusicologist (b. Jan. 15, 1915, Austin, Texas—d. July 19, 2002, Safety Harbor, Fla.), spent a lifetime crisscrossing the American countryside to document the nation's traditional songs and singers—the 17th-, 18th-, and 19th-century music that might otherwise have been forgotten amid the rising flood of 20th-century technology and popular music. Some of the major folk music and blues singers he discovered included Leadbelly (Huddie Ledbetter), Woody Guthrie, Muddy Waters, Josh White, and Burl Ives; Lomax also produced many record albums, concerts, and television and radio broadcasts and was an important figure in the postwar folk music revival that climaxed in the 1960s. He went on to collect hundreds more folk songs in Europe and the West Indies and to analyze singing styles. In 1933, together with his fa-

Ethnomusicologist Alan Lomax

ther, folk-song scholar John Lomax, he began making folk music field trips—carrying bulky recording equipment—to the American South for the Library of Congress. The next year they first heard Leadbelly in the Angola, La., state prison and also published the collection *American Ballads and Folksongs,* the first of their five books together. Besides comprising folk songs gathered in the South, New England, the Midwest, and the Caribbean from 1933 to 1942, Alan Lomax's Library of Congress recordings included more than eight hours of reminiscences and songs by the great jazz pianist Jelly Roll Morton; these sessions became the basis of Lomax's much-acclaimed biography *Mister Jelly Roll* (1950). During 1950–58 he lived in England, and he recorded folk music of the British Isles, Italy, and Spain before returning to the U.S. With Victor Grauer, Lomax developed cantometrics, the statistical analysis of singing styles correlated with anthropological data; his cantometrics work was the most comprehensive study of folk song undertaken. He videotaped performances of traditional music for the PBS series *American Patchwork* (1990) and developed the Global Jukebox, an interactive software project presenting world folk song and dance.

Longford, Elizabeth Harman Pakenham, Countess of, British historian and biographer (b. Aug. 30, 1906, London, Eng.—d. Oct. 23, 2002, Hurst Green, East Sussex, Eng.), was an acclaimed author and the matriarch of one of England's most brilliant literary families—her eight children included biographer Lady Antonia Fraser, writer Thomas Pakenham, novelist Rachel Billington, and poet Judith Kazantzis. Longford published her first history, *Jameson's Raid,* in 1960. *Victoria RI* (1964), a popular yet scholarly best-seller recounting Queen Victoria's life, was followed by a two-volume biography of the duke of Wellington. She was made CBE in 1974.

Lopes, Lisa Nicole ("LEFT EYE"), American rap singer and songwriter (b. May 27, 1971, Philadelphia, Pa.—d. April 25, 2002, near La Ceiba, Honduras), was a member of the ultra-successful female rhythm-and-blues group

© Laura Walters/Liaison/Getty Images

Lisa Lopes of TLC

TLC, which had sales in the multimillions and whose albums *CrazySexyCool* (1994) and *Fanmail* (1999) each won two Grammy Awards. Also well known for her volatile off-stage behaviour, she once set fire to her boyfriend's mansion after an argument. She died in an automobile accident.

Lord, (John) Walter, Jr., American writer (b. Oct. 8, 1917, Baltimore, Md.—d. May 19, 2002, New York, N.Y.), reignited public interest in the 1912 sinking of the *Titanic* with his riveting minute-by-minute account of the ship's final night in the best-seller *A Night to Remember* (1955). He followed that book with other historical narratives, including *Day of Infamy* (1957); *Incredible Victory* (1967), about the Battle of Midway; and *The Miracle of Dunkirk* (1982).

Lord Pretender (ALDRIC FARRELL), Trinidadian calypso singer (b. Sept. 8, 1917, Tobago island, British colony of Trinidad and Tobago—d. Jan. 22, 2002, Port of Spain, Trinidad and Tobago), during a 72-year career, was a master of "extempo" calypso, in which the performer spontaneously devises songs filled with intricate lyrics and rhymes, usually in response to suggested subjects shouted from the audience. Some musicologists considered extempo a forerunner of modern rap music.

Lovelace, Linda (LINDA BOREMAN), American actress (b. Jan. 10, 1949, Bronx, N.Y.—d. April 22, 2002, Denver, Colo.), starred in the classic feature-length pornographic movie *Deep Throat* (1972), which ended up being shown in mainstream theatres and earned some $600 million. She later revealed that her husband at the time had forced her to perform in that and other porno films, and she became an antipornography activist.

Lucentini, Franco, Italian novelist (b. Dec. 24, 1920, Rome, Italy—d. Aug. 5, 2002, Turin, Italy), achieved fame with Carlo Fruttero in a remarkable, if unconventional, literary partnership. After being imprisoned in 1941 for distributing anti-Fascist leaflets, Lucentini began his literary career as a news correspondent and editor. He met Fruttero in 1953 in Paris. The two worked together as translators and journalists but were best known for their mystery thrillers, which were composed in a strangely businesslike manner. After choosing a subject, they worked in ping-pong fashion, one composing, the other editing and recomposing, until a novel was complete. Their most popular works were *La donna della domenica* (1972; *The Sunday Woman*, 1973), which was filmed in 1976, and *La verità sul caso D* (1992; *The D Case*, 1993).

Luisetti, Angelo Enrico ("HANK"), American collegiate basketball player (b. June 16, 1916, San Francisco, Calif.—d. Dec. 17, 2002, San Mateo, Calif.), revolutionized the sport of basketball by introducing the running one-handed shot. Luisetti popularized his new style of shooting while starring on the basketball team at Stanford University in 1935–38. He led Stanford to three Pacific Conference championships and in 1938 became the first collegiate player to score 50 points in a single game. Luisetti was elected to the Basketball Hall of Fame in 1959.

Luns, Joseph Marie Antoine Hubert, Dutch politician (b. Aug. 28, 1911, Rotterdam, Neth.—d. July 17, 2002, Brussels, Belg.), served for 19 years as foreign minister of The Netherlands before being appointed (1971) secretary-general of NATO, a position he held until 1984. Throughout his tenure at NATO, Luns, a conservative, was committed to ties with the U.S. and the U.K. and was cautiously skeptical of Soviet policy. He pushed European governments to increase military spending and endorsed plans to install ballistic missiles in Western Europe.

Marcus, (Harold) Stanley, American businessman (b. April 20, 1905, Dallas, Texas—d. Jan. 22, 2002, Dallas), worked his way up to president (1950–72) and chairman of the board (1972–75) of the family department store, Neiman Marcus, and turned it into a retailing giant, with over 30 stores across the U.S. Among his innovations were personalized gift wrapping, weekly on-site fashion shows, and extravagant his-and-hers holiday gifts.

Margaret, Princess (PRINCESS MARGARET ROSE WINDSOR, COUNTESS OF SNOWDON), British royal (b. Aug. 21, 1930, Glamis Castle, Scot.—d. Feb. 9, 2002, London, Eng.), the second daughter of King George VI and Queen Elizabeth (from 1952 Queen Elizabeth, the Queen Mother; *q.v.*) and the younger sister of Queen Elizabeth II, was a glamorous beauty who struggled throughout her life to balance an independent spirit and artistic temperament with her duties as a member of Britain's royal family. Margaret, who displayed an early love for nightlife and the arts, gained world-

wide sympathy in 1955 when she publicly renounced Group Capt. Peter Townsend, the royal equerry she loved but could not marry because he was divorced. She married photographer Antony Armstrong-Jones (later earl of Snowdon) in 1960 and had two children, David, Viscount Linley, and Lady Sarah. By the 1970s, however, times had changed; both of the Snowdons engaged in public love affairs, and the volatile marriage finally ended in divorce (1978), the first in the British royal family in 400 years. The princess scandalized

© Hulton-Deutsch Collection/Corbis

Britain's Princess Margaret

conservative monarchists, cultivating friendships and romances among actors, writers, ballet dancers, and artists, notably Roddy Llewellyn, a landscape gardener 17 years her junior with whom she had a prolonged romance in the 1970s. She also spent much of her time on the Caribbean island of Mustique. Eventually her extensive charitable work, combined with a new, more modern sympathy for the restricted options she faced, gained her public respect.

Marmarosa, Michael ("DODO"), American jazz pianist (b. Dec. 12, 1925, Pittsburgh, Pa.—d. Sept. 17, 2002, Pittsburgh), was a teenaged musician in top swing bands (Gene Krupa, Charlie Barnet, and Artie Shaw) before he became one of the first pianists to master the complexities of bebop; he played modern harmonies and fluent melodies in classic recordings by Lester Young and Charlie Parker, and he also led his own trios; a technically gifted, lyrical soloist with a bright, clear touch, he was nationally noted in the 1940s but played primarily in the Pittsburgh area after 1954 and made his last records in 1961–62.

Martin, Archer John Porter, British biochemist (b. March 1, 1910, London, Eng.—d. July 28, 2002, Llangarron, Herefordshire, Eng.), shared with Richard L.M. Synge the Nobel Prize for Chemistry in 1952 for their joint work in the development of partition chromatography, a sophisticated analytic technique by which samples of a mixture of closely related chemicals such as amino acids can be separated for identification and further study. Martin gained a Ph.D. (1936) in biochemistry from the University of Cambridge before joining the staff at the Wool Industries Research Association (WIRA) in 1938. At WIRA he and Synge initially used a liquid-liquid system in which chloroform was percolated through a column of water-saturated silica gel. They published a paper describing the breakthrough technique in the *Biochemical Journal* in 1941. Three years later Martin, working with R. Consden and A.H. Gordon, developed paper partition chromatography, an even simpler method using a thin column of paper to hold one liquid stationary while a second liquid flowed over it. After leaving WIRA in 1946, Martin worked at the Boots Pure Drug Co. (1946–48), the Medical Research Council (1948–52), and the National Institute of Medical Research (1952–56), where he supervised A.T. James's work in gas-liquid chromatography. He later served as director of Abbotsbury Laboratories (1959–70), was a consultant at Wellcome Research Laboratories (1970–73), and taught chemistry at the University of Sussex, Brighton (1973–78), and the University of Houston, Texas (1974–79). Martin was elected a fellow of the Royal Society in 1950 and was made CBE in 1980.

Martin, James Slattin, Jr., American aeronautical engineer (b. June 21, 1920, Washington, D.C.—d. April 14, 2002, Rising Sun, Md.), was project manager for NASA's Viking 1 and 2 missions, which in 1975 sent the two unmanned orbiter-lander pairs to Mars, from which the first close-up pictures and detailed maps of that planet were relayed back to Earth the following year.

Matsuda, Kohei, Japanese corporate executive (b. Jan. 28, 1922, Hiroshima, Japan—d. July 10, 2002, Tokyo, Japan), served as president (1970–77) and chairman (1977–80) of the Mazda Motor Corp. and from 1970 owned and managed the Hiroshima Toyo Carp professional baseball team. His grandfather, Jujiro Matsuda, founded Mazda (then known as Toyo Kogyo), and his father, Tsuneji Matsuda, was the company's president until his death in 1970. Matsuda began his career as a trainee in Cincinnati, Ohio, and in 1961 became Mazda's vice president. In 1967 Matsuda helped Mazda introduce the Cosmo 110S, which had a rotary engine that was less fuel-efficient than other models. The oil crisis of the 1970s led to major losses for Mazda, and in 1977 Matsuda was forced to relinquish his presidency.

Matta, Roberto (ROBERTO SEBASTIÁN ANTONIO MATTA ECHUARREN), Chilean-born artist (b. Nov. 11, 1911, Santiago, Chile—d. Nov. 23, 2002, Civitavecchia, Italy), lived his adult life outside his homeland and became identified with the international Surrealist movement. He referred to his paintings, which were huge, often mural-like works, as "inscapes," the transferal of psychic states to canvas—hence, the description of his art as hallucinatory, nightmarish, and fantastic.

Beginning in the mid-1940s, his paintings included humanlike figures, with suggestions of insects and machines, and some critics called his later art visual science fiction. He worked quickly and spontaneously, in what was termed "automatic drawing." Matta was born into an aristocratic family. He received a diploma in architecture from the Catholic University in Santiago in 1931 and left Chile for Europe two years later. He worked for Le Corbusier in Paris in the mid-1930s, and he traveled throughout the Continent, meeting André Breton and others in the Surrealist movement. By the time he moved to New York City in 1939, he had begun to draw and paint, and in the 1940s he had a significant influence on the Abstract Expressionists. He returned to Europe in 1948, living alternately in Paris and Rome, but from 1969 on his primary home was Italy. A leftist, he was blacklisted in the U.S. in the 1950s, and as a supporter of Pres. Salvador Allende in Chile, he was equally unwelcome in his native country after the military government of Augusto Pinochet came to power in 1973. Among Matta's public works was a mural done in 1956, *Three Constellation Beings Facing the Fire,* for the UNESCO building in Paris.

McCalla, Val Irvine, Jamaican-born British publisher (b. Oct. 3, 1943, Kingston, Jam.—d. Aug. 22, 2002, Seaford, East Sussex, Eng.), founded *The Voice,* a highly successful British newspaper centred on black issues and interests. After working as editor of the Black Voices pages for the *East End News* in the late 1970s, McCalla established *The Voice* in 1982, when race issues were at the forefront of British consciousness. Semitabloid in style, the paper targeted racism in all its forms and courted controversy, a stance that led some to criticize it as sensationalist and irresponsible. Its influence, however, was undisputed, and it became a training ground for leading journalists. McCalla also owned *Chic* and *Pride* magazines.

McCrone, Walter C., Jr., American scientist (b. June 9, 1916, Wilmington, Del.—d. July 10, 2002, Chicago, Ill.), used chemical microscopy to debunk historical myths and forgeries. By examining samples of hair, he ascertained that

Professional demystifier Walter C. McCrone, Jr.

J. Barabe for McCrone Associates, Inc.

Napoleon Bonaparte did not die from poisoning but that Ludwig van Beethoven did contract lead poisoning. McCrone also found that the Vinland Map of Yale University Library, thought to show that contemporaries of Christopher Columbus were already aware of the New World, was a modern forgery—20th-century ink on medieval parchment. His biggest discovery came in 1978 when he concluded that the Shroud of Turin dated back only to the Middle Ages and thus could not have been the burial cloth of Jesus of Nazareth. McCrone attended Cornell University, Ithaca, N.Y., before moving to Chicago, where he was credited with having revolutionized the design and use of light and electron microscopes and with having led his research institute to world renown.

McGrath, Kathleen, captain (ret.), U.S. Navy (b. June 4, 1952, Columbus, Ohio—d. Sept. 26, 2002, Bethesda, Md.), was appointed captain of the guided-missile frigate USS *Jarrett* in 1998 and thereby became the first woman to command a navy warship. In 2000 she became the first woman to command a warship at sea when the *Jarrett,* with a crew of 262 members, carried out a six-month mission in the Persian Gulf to search for boats smuggling oil from Iraq, and she later led the ship on search-and-rescue missions.

McIntire, Carl Curtis, American evangelist and radio broadcaster (b. May 17, 1906, Ypsilanti, Mich.—d. March 19, 2002, Voorhees, N.J.), was a firebrand fundamentalist preacher whose radio show, *20th Century Reformation Hour,* was broadcast daily on more than 600 radio stations during the 1960s. The son of missionaries, McIntire helped found the Bible Presbyterian Church in 1937. Under his leadership the church grew into a multimillion-dollar ministry that owned radio stations and operated a publishing division. McIntire's radio show gradually lost its audience, however, after the Federal Communications Commission ruled in 1971 that a station run by the church violated a "fairness doctrine" by failing to provide free time for opposing viewpoints to be presented. The show went off the air in 1973.

McKern, Leo (REGINALD MCKERN), Australian-born character actor (b. March 16, 1920, Sydney, Australia—d. July 23, 2002, Bath, Eng.), gained international recognition as the irascible henpecked, claret-swilling, deceptively crafty English barrister Horace P. Rumpole in *Rumpole of the Bailey,* a series of 44 television dramas written by British barrister-writer John Mortimer that were originally broadcast between 1975 and 1992. McKern, a stout man with a bulbous nose and a glass eye (acquired after an accident when he was a 15-year-old engineering apprentice), was initially discouraged from acting. He moved to England in 1946 and soon joined the Old Vic Theatre in London and the Shakespeare Memorial Theatre in Stratford-upon-Avon. His distinctive appearance and resonant voice were assets in a tremendous variety of roles, including Iago in *Othello,* Big

Daddy in *Cat on a Hot Tin Roof,* Toad in *Toad of Toad Hall,* the high priest Clang in the Beatles movie *Help!,* and Number 2 in the TV cult hit *The Prisoner.* In 1960 McKern played the Common Man in the West End staging of *A Man for All Seasons;* he was recast as the menacing Thomas Cromwell for the 1966 movie version. His last screen appearance was as Bishop Maigret in *Molokai: The Story of Father Damien* (1999). In 1983 he was made an Officer of the Order of Australia.

McNally, David Arthur, ("DAVE"), American professional baseball player (b. Oct. 31, 1942, Billings, Mont.—d. Dec. 1, 2002, Billings), was a phenomenal left-handed pitcher for the Baltimore Orioles; he completed four consecutive 20-win seasons between 1968 and 1971, appeared in three All-Star games (1969, 1970, and 1972), and helped his team win World Series titles in 1966 and 1970. McNally also took part in the landmark 1975 arbitration case that ended baseball's "reserve clause"—a contractual obligation that kept players bound to one team in perpetuity—and created the free-agent system, in which players could sell their talents to the highest bidder.

Miller, Neal Elgar, American psychologist (b. Aug. 3, 1909, Milwaukee, Wis.—d. March 23, 2002, Hamden, Conn.), conducted pioneering research on biofeedback—a technique by which unconscious or involuntary bodily processes may be manipulated by conscious mental control. His theory that the autonomic (involuntary) nervous system could be susceptible to training was initially greeted with skepticism but gradually gained acceptance. Eventually biofeedback was used in the treatment of a range of medical conditions, including migraines, high blood pressure, epilepsy, and heart arrhythmia.

Milligan, Terence Alan Patrick Sean ("SPIKE"), Irish writer and comedian (b. April 16, 1918, Ahmadnagar, India—d. Feb. 27, 2002, Rye, East Sussex, Eng.), was the leader and the last surviving member of the zany band of comedians who created and presented the 1950s BBC radio hit *The Goon Show.* His anarchic sense of absurdity and unique comic genius made him a model for succeeding generations of comedians and paved the way for the Monty Python brand of alternative comedy. Milligan was raised in India and Burma (now Myanmar), where his father was in the British army, and moved to England with his family in 1933. He himself served in the army during World War II and, when he was wounded in combat, began a struggle with manic-depressive illness that lasted the rest of his life. Toward the end of the war, Milligan met Harry Secombe, and the two worked together entertaining the troops. After the war they, along with Peter Sellers and Michael Bentine, began hanging out at the Grafton Arms pub and working on comedy routines. BBC radio began broadcasting the group's work in 1951, as *Crazy People,* and in 1952 it was renamed *The Goon Show.* As such it continued until early 1960 (though Bentine soon left the show) and became a cult classic.

Tim Graham/Corbis Sygma

Zany comedian Spike Milligan (seated) with colleague Harry Secombe

Milligan later acted onstage and in small parts in movies—including *Monty Python's Life of Brian* (1979)—and wrote numerous books of poems, war memoirs, the play *The Bedsitting Room* (with John Antrobus; first performed 1962), and a number of television series. He also supported a multitude of causes, especially environmental ones. Because Milligan's father was Irish and Milligan was born in India—and despite Milligan's years of military service—the British government did not consider him a citizen; rather than take an oath of allegiance, he took Irish citizenship. Nonetheless, he was made an honorary CBE in 1992 and was given an honorary knighthood in 2000.

Milstein, César, Argentine-born British immunologist (b. Oct. 8, 1927, Bahía Blanca, Arg.—d. March 24, 2002, Cambridge, Eng.), was awarded the Nobel Prize for Physiology or Medicine in 1984 for his work in the development of a technique for producing monoclonal antibodies; Milstein shared the prize with Georges Köhler and Niels K. Jerne. Milstein was educated in Argentina and England. He worked at the National Institute of Microbiology in Buenos Aires from 1957 to 1963 and thereafter conducted research as a member of the Medical Research Council Laboratory of Molecular Biology, Cambridge. He specialized in the study of antibodies—a class of proteins that help the body eliminate infectious organisms and toxic materials. In 1975, working with Köhler, Milstein developed a method that allowed researchers to create great quantities of identical, or monoclonal, antibodies. The procedure involved fusing short-lived B cells (a type of specialized white blood cell) that produced specific antibodies with long-lived myeloma cells (cancerous B cells) that did not produce antibodies. The resulting hybrid cells, called hybridomas, com-

bined the longevity of cancer cells with the ability to produce antibodies that scientists desired. In addition to the Nobel Prize, Milstein received the Royal Medal from the Royal Society of London in 1982 and was made a Companion of Honour in 1995.

Mink, Patsy Takemoto, American politician (b. Dec. 6, 1927, Paia, Hawaii—d. Sept. 28, 2002, Honolulu, Hawaii), was the first Asian-American woman elected to the U.S. Congress. A 1951 graduate of the University of Chicago Law School, she was the first Japanese-American to practice law in Hawaii. She was elected to the Hawaii Territorial Legislature in 1956 and the Hawaii Senate in 1958. In 1964 she won election to the U.S. House of Representatives, where she remained until 1977. She lost a bid for a U.S. Senate seat in 1976, but as the result of a special election in 1990, she returned to the House of Representatives, where she served until her death. A liberal Democrat, she opposed the Vietnam War and promoted measures supporting civil rights, education, and labour. She was one of the authors of Title IX, which in 1972 mandated equal funding for women's academic and athletic programs in institutions receiving federal money.

Moore, Dudley Stuart John, British actor, comedian, and musician (b. April 19, 1935, Dagenham, Essex, Eng.—d. March 27, 2002, Plainfield, N.J.), was a versatile, multitalented performer whose career ranged from jazz and classical musician and composer to satiric comedian to Hollywood movie star. He first became known for his partnership with Peter Cook in stage revues, in films, and on television and later gained further renown for his roles in two blockbuster motion pictures—as a musician seeking the perfect woman in *10* (1979) and a lovable millionaire drunk in *Arthur* (1981). He was also an accomplished musician; he attended Magdalen College, Oxford, on a music scholarship, earning a bachelor's degree in 1957 and another in 1958, and then toured as a jazz pianist. In 1960 Moore, Cook, Jonathan Miller, and Alan Bennett created the satiric revue *Beyond the Fringe* for the Edinburgh Festival. The show thereafter was performed in London and on Broadway, where it won its creators a special Tony Award in 1963. Cook and Moore then teamed up for the television sketch comedy series *Not Only . . . but Also* (1965–66; 1970); the films *The Wrong Box* (1966), *Bedazzled* (1967), and *The Hound of the Baskervilles* (1977); three "Derek and Clive" comedy record albums in the 1970s; and, beginning in 1971, a follow-up to *Beyond the Fringe.* At first called *Behind the Fridge,* it toured Australia before being presented in London and then, retitled *Good Evening,* in the U.S., where it won Cook and Moore a special Tony

Dudley Moore as Arthur

Award in 1974. Moore also composed film scores, including those for *Bedazzled* and *Inadmissible Evidence* (1968), and starred on the London stage in the comedy *Play It Again, Sam* (1969). Following the end of his partnership with Cook, Moore made his Hollywood debut in 1978 in *Foul Play*. Moore was created CBE in 2001.

Moyola of Castledawson, Baron (MAJOR JAMES DAWSON CHICHESTER-CLARK), Northern Irish politician (b. Feb. 12, 1923, Moyola Park, Castledawson, County Londonderry, N.Ire.—d. May 17, 2002, London, Eng.), was the moderate Unionist prime minister of Northern Ireland who, in August 1969, reluctantly called in the first British troops in an attempt to stem rising sectarian violence. He was a member of the Protestant landed gentry and was elected to the Northern Ireland Parliament in 1960. He was serving as minister of agriculture (1967–69) when in May 1969 he was unexpectedly chosen to succeed reformist Prime Minister Terence O'Neill, who had been forced out in a crisis of confidence. As prime minister, Chichester-Clark released all political prisoners and ordered an amnesty for those charged with political offenses. He was unable to broker peace between the Protestants and Roman Catholics, however, and when the sectarian rioting escalated, he turned to the British military for help. He was made a life peer shortly after his resignation on March 20, 1971.

Nakamura, Kazuo, Canadian artist (b. Oct. 13, 1926, Vancouver, B.C.—d. April 9, 2002, Toronto, Ont.), was a prominent member of Painters Eleven, a group of Toronto-based avant-garde artists who championed abstract art in the 1950s and '60s; Nakamura was highly regarded for geometric paintings that were among the most distinctive abstract works in 20th-century Canadian art. During World War II Nakamura, a second-generation

Japanese in Canada, was interned at a camp near Hope, B.C. The camp and its surroundings became the subject of some of his earliest paintings. After the war Nakamura settled with his family in Ontario. He accepted an invitation by artist William Ronald to join Painters Eleven, with whom he was associated from 1953 to 1960. He exhibited with the group but also held a number of notable one-man exhibitions. Nakamura's paintings tended to be simpler in structure and more quietly introspective than those of his Painters Eleven colleagues. One work, *Infinite Waves* (1957), consisted only of white oil paint over parallel strings glued to a canvas. In later years Nakamura became interested in a field of mathematics known as number structure and, abandoning painting altogether, produced abstract works that often featured rows of numbers on large sheets of white paper.

Ne Win, U (SHU MAUNG), Burmese general and dictator (b. May 24, 1911, Paungdale, Burma [now Myanmar]—d. Dec. 5, 2002, Yangon [Rangoon], Myanmar), ruled at the head of a repressive dictatorship from March 1962, when he overthrew the elected government of Prime Minister U Nu, until he resigned in 1988. He took the nom de guerre Ne Win ("brilliant light") during Burma's struggle for independence from Great Britain, received his military training in Japan with Aung San's Thirty Comrades in the early 1940s, and served in the Japanese-sponsored Burma National Army until that group switched sides at the very end of World War II. In 1958 Ne Win was appointed the head of a caretaker government to replace Prime Minister U Nu, whose administration had failed to control ethnic insurgencies. After U Nu won the 1960 general election, Ne Win stepped down, but two years later he staged a coup and established himself at the head of a military revolutionary council. In 1964 Ne Win made

Burma a one-party state under the army-backed Burmese Socialist Program Party (BSPP). He served as prime minister (1965–74), president (1974–81), and chairman of the BSPP (1973–88). His extreme socialist and isolationist policies, however, combined with official corruption, mismanagement, and personal idiosyncrasies, turned Burma into one of the world's least-developed countries. Ne Win resigned in July 1988 after food shortages and the demonetization of some 80% of Burma's currency triggered riots.

Nelsova, Zara (SARA NELSON), Canadian-born American cellist (b. Dec. 24, 1917, Winnipeg, Man.—d. Oct. 10, 2002, New York, N.Y.), had a long career, beginning as a child prodigy. Called the "queen of cellists," she was known particularly for performing contemporary works, including *Schelomo* and other music by Ernest Bloch. When she was only 10, she formed the Canadian Trio with her sisters, a pianist and a violinist. In 1929 her parents moved the family to London to give her greater opportunities for study, and the following year she appeared as a soloist with the London Symphony Orchestra. Nelsova returned to Canada in 1939, where she became principal cellist in the Toronto Symphony Orchestra, and she made her New York debut in 1942. In 1955 she became a U.S. citizen, and from 1963 to 1973 she performed frequently with pianist Grant Johannesen, her husband at the time.

Neves, Lucas Moreira Cardinal, Brazilian-born Roman Catholic prelate (b. Sept. 16, 1925, São Joao del Rei, Braz.—d. Sept. 8, 2002, Rome, Italy), served in key Vatican posts (1974–87) and as archbishop (1987–98) of São Salvador da Bahia, where he spurred construction of a refuge for children and supported

the Landless Workers Movement. He was a close friend of Pope John Paul II, with whom he shared a common background and a conservative view of church theology. At one time Neves was considered the leading Latin American contender for the papacy. He was ordained a priest in 1950 and appointed bishop in the archdiocese of São Paulo in 1967. He was made a cardinal in 1988, and in 1998 he was named prefect of the Congregation of Bishops and president of the Pontifical Commission for Latin America, posts he held until his health began to fail in 2000.

Newbury, Milton Sim ("MICKEY"), American songwriter and musician (b. May 19, 1940, Houston, Texas—d. Sept. 29, 2002, Springfield, Ore.), wrote more than 500 songs. His most productive period was the late 1960s, when he wrote songs such as "Funny, Familiar, Forgotten Feelings" (1967) and "Just Dropped In (To See What Condition My Condition Was In)" (1968).

Nguyen Van Thuan, François Xavier Cardinal, Vietnamese Roman Catholic prelate (b. April 17, 1928, Phu Cam, French Indochina—d. Sept. 16, 2002, Rome, Italy), maintained his strong faith during 13 years of imprisonment in his homeland. Ordained a priest in 1953, he taught in Nha Trang and was appointed bishop of that diocese in 1967; Pope Paul VI named him coadjutor archbishop of Saigon in 1975. When Saigon fell to the communist Viet Cong shortly after his appointment, Thuan, a nephew of slain South Vietnamese president Ngo Dinh Diem, was imprisoned. Upon his release in 1988, he was barred from visiting Vietnam and took up residence in Rome. In 1998 Thuan was named president of the Pontifical Commission for Justice and Peace, and in 2001 he was appointed cardinal.

Norfolk, Miles Francis Stapleton Fitzalan-Howard, 17th duke of, British peer and public servant (b. July 21, 1915, London, Eng.—d. June 24, 2002, Hambleden, Buckinghamshire, Eng.), inherited (1975) the oldest dukedom in Britain (created by King Richard II in 1397) and with it the ceremonial role of hereditary Earl Marshall of England. He was an outspoken Roman Catholic member of the House of Lords. When the Lords was reformed in 1999, Norfolk was one of only two hereditary peers to retain his seat without having to seek election. In 2000 he relinquished the position of Earl Marshall to his son, Edward, who succeeded to the dukedom on his death.

Nozick, Robert, American political philosopher (b. Nov. 16, 1938, New York, N.Y.—d. Jan. 23, 2002, Cambridge, Mass.), was a highly influential champion of libertarianism; in his first and best-known book, *Anarchy, State, and Utopia* (1974), he advocated the "minimal state"—a government whose role is limited to protecting citizens from violence, theft, and breach of contract. After earning advanced degrees from Princeton University (M.A., 1961; Ph.D., 1963), Nozick embarked on a long career in academia. He was a full professor of philosophy at Harvard University from 1969 until his death. Initially associated with socialist organizations, Nozick eventually came to defend capitalism and offer pointed criticism of the modern welfare state. In *Anarchy, State, and Utopia,* he argued that the state could not redistribute wealth without violating the rights of the individual; the book won a National Book Award in 1975.

Nygaard, Kristen, Norwegian mathematician and computer scientist (b. Aug. 27, 1926, Oslo, Nor.—d. Aug. 10, 2002, Oslo), invented, with his co-worker Ole-Johan Dahl (*q.v.*), the computer programming language SIMULA, which used modules of data, called "objects," to process data more efficiently than was possible with previous complex software instructions. SIMULA, which the pair developed while working at the Norwegian Computing Centre (NCC) in the 1960s, provided a foundation for all other "object-oriented" programming, including computer languages such as C++ and Java and graphic user inter-

faces such as Microsoft's Windows and Apple Computer's Mac OS. Nygaard was on the staff of the Norwegian Defense Research Establishment (1948–60) before joining the NCC and later taught at the University of Oslo (1976–96), where Dahl was professor of informatics from 1968. In 1990 Nygaard won the Norbert Weiner Prize for his contributions to the "Scandinavian School" of participatory technical design. He was also active in the leftist Venstre political party and in the early 1990s led the opposition to Norway's entry into the European Union. Nygaard and Dahl were both created Commanders of the Order of St. Olav in 2000, and they shared both the 2001 A.M. Turing Award, the computing field's highest honour, and the Institute for Electrical and Electronics Engineers 2002 John von Neumann Medal.

Oberoi, Mohan Singh, Indian hotelier (b. Aug. 15, 1898, Bhaun, Punjab, India [now in Pakistan]—d. May 3, 2002, New Delhi, India), built an international chain of luxury hotels; he was the first Indian hotel owner to introduce such modern innovations as the employment of chambermaids. Oberoi was born in a tiny village in what later became Pakistan. In 1922 he took a job as a hotel clerk in the British government town of Simla, India, and in 1934 he bought his first hotel from his employer. Oberoi later specialized in buying run-down or undervalued properties and renovating them, with meticulous attention to detail, into luxury accommodations. He took control of Associated Hotels of India, Ltd., in 1944; by 2002 the Oberoi Group held some three dozen hotels in a half dozen countries.

Ocloo, Esther Afua, Ghanaian entrepreneur (b. April 18, 1919, Peki-Dzake, Gold Coast [now in Ghana]—d. Feb. 8, 2002, Accra, Ghana), as cofounder (1979) and head of Women's World Banking, pioneered the practice of microlending, providing tiny loans (often as little as $50) to small home-based businesses, usually those run by women in less-developed countries. Ocloo began as a street vendor of homemade orange marmalade and gradually expanded her business to form Nkulenu Industries. She studied in Accra and later went to the U.K. to study agriculture, food technology, and useful handicrafts. In 1990 Ocloo was corecipient (with Olusegun Obasanjo of Nigeria) of the $100,000 Africa Prize.

Odum, Eugene Pleasants, American ecologist (b. Sept. 17, 1913, Lake Sunapee, N.H.—d. Aug. 10, 2002, Athens, Ga.), brought prestige to the little-known field of ecology, helping to transform it from a subdivision of biology into a widely taught discipline of its own. He was educated at the University of North Carolina (A.B., 1934) and the University of Illinois (Ph.D., 1939) and then took a job as a naturalist in Rensselaerville, N.Y. In 1940 he joined the faculty of the University of Georgia. There he served as professor of zoology (1940–57) and created two major research foundations—the Institute of Ecology,

which he founded in 1961 and served as director until his retirement in 1984, and the Marine Science Institute on Sapelo Island. He also led the Savannah River Ecology Laboratory in Aiken, Ga., one of the largest in the world, which he established in 1951 to study the effects of a nuclear weapons plant on the surrounding environment. Odum championed modern ecology in his pioneering academic textbook on ecosystems, *Fundamentals of Ecology* (1953). He was the winner of the Tyler Ecological Award (1977) and, with his younger brother, Howard (*q.v.*), of the Crafoord Prize (1987).

Odum, Howard Thomas, American ecologist (b. Sept. 1, 1924, Durham, N.C.—d. Sept. 11, 2002, Gainesville, Fla.), often collaborated with his better-known older brother, Eugene (*q.v.*), who died a month earlier. After earning his doctorate from Yale University, he taught widely, notably at the University of Florida, where he founded the Center for Wetlands. His research and advocacy in southern Florida were a boost to the preservation of the Everglades. His work often looked outside ecology to incorporate disciplines such as economics and engineering. He was the author of *Environment, Power and Society* (1971). In 1987 he and his brother were awarded the Crafoord Prize.

Olayan, Suliman Saleh, Saudi businessman (b. Nov. 5, 1918, Unayzah, [Saudi] Arabia—d. July 4, 2002, New York, N.Y.), founded the Olayan Group, one of the largest and most successful corporations in Saudi Arabia, with offices and interests around the world. After attending an American school in Bahrain, he went to work for various oil companies before founding General Contracting Co. in the late 1940s. One of its first ventures was funding the Saudi oil pipeline, Tapline. Olayan helped develop much of Saudi Arabia's infrastructure, including the King Khalid International Airport in Riyadh and the Saudi British Bank, while his food and consumer distribution enterprise introduced to the region goods from major American companies. In 2001 Olayan was included on *Forbes* magazine's list of the world's richest people, with an estimated $8 billion fortune.

Olson, Carl ("BOBO"), American boxer (b. July 11, 1928, Honolulu, Hawaii—d. Jan. 16, 2002, Honolulu), was middleweight champion of the world from 1953 to 1955; his most notable fights, however, were four losses to the legendary Sugar Ray Robinson. Olson won the middleweight title by scoring a unanimous decision over Randy Turpin of Britain in October 1953 and went on to three successful title defenses. He lost the title when he was knocked out by Robinson in December 1955. Robinson had defeated Olson twice previously, in 1950 and 1952. Olson returned for a fourth fight with Robinson, in May 1956, but again was knocked out. Olson fought for another 10 years, mostly in the light heavyweight and heavyweight divisions, but never fought another title match. He left the ring with a career record of 99 wins, 16 losses, and 2 draws.

Olson was inducted into the International Boxing Hall of Fame in 2000.

Ortega Spottorno, José, Spanish journalist and publisher (b. Nov. 13, 1916, Madrid, Spain—d. Feb. 18, 2002, Madrid), founded Alianza Editorial (1966), Spain's major publisher of affordable quality paperback books, and *El País* (1976), which grew to become the country's best-selling newspaper. Ortega Spottorno also relaunched *Revista de Occidente*, a cultural periodical originally founded in 1923 by his father, the Spanish philosopher José Ortega y Gasset, and wrote a family memoir, *Los Ortega* (2002).

Palkhivala, Nani Adeshir, Indian jurist and civil rights activist (b. Jan. 16, 1920, Bombay [now Mumbai], India—d. Dec. 11, 2002, Mumbai), was revered in India as a top authority on constitutional law and government finance. In 1958 Palkhivala, a lawyer and private businessman, began an annual tradition of publicly expounding on the country's budget; these speeches brought him renown as an expert on taxation and as a gifted orator. Although he opposed Prime Minister Indira Gandhi's policies, Palkhivala in 1975 agreed to defend her when she was charged with corruption. When Gandhi declared a state of emergency and suspended the constitution, however, he resigned. After Gandhi's defeat in the 1977 general elections, Palkhivala was named ambassador to the U.S., a position he held until 1979.

Paltrow, Bruce, American producer and director (b. Nov. 26, 1943, Brooklyn, N.Y.—d. Oct. 3, 2002, Rome, Italy), earned critical acclaim as the genius behind the 1980s hit medical TV series *St. Elsewhere*. Previously, he had directed, written, and produced *The White Shadow*, a TV show about a professional basketball player coaching at an inner-city school. Paltrow, who got his start as a writer in the early 1970s, was married to actress Blythe Danner and was the father of actress Gwyneth Paltrow. In 2000 he directed his daughter in the film *Duets*.

Patchett, Jean, American model (b. Feb. 16, 1926, Preston, Md.—d. Jan. 22, 2002, La Quinta, Calif.), became a photographic icon during the 1950s and appeared on over 40 magazine covers. Her defining images were the ones in which Irving Penn captured her seated in a café chewing pensively on a string of pearls and the Erwin Blumenfeld Jan. 1, 1950, *Vogue* cover, which featured her perfectly penciled left eye, pouty red lips, and a trademark natural beauty mark. She ended her modeling career in 1963.

Pearl, Daniel, American journalist (b. Oct. 10, 1963, Princeton, N.J.—d. late January? 2002, Pakistan), went to work for *The Wall Street Journal* in 1990 and by 2000 had become the paper's South Asia bureau chief. On Jan. 23, 2002, thinking he was being taken to interview a radical Islamic leader, he was kidnapped in Karachi, and four days later an e-mailed photograph of him in chains and with

a gun to his head was released. His death was confirmed on February 21 after a videotape showing his execution was received by American officials.

Peet, Bill (WILLIAM BARTLETT PEED), American animator, screenwriter, and author-illustrator (b. Jan. 29, 1915, Grandview, Ind.—d. May 11, 2002, Studio City, Calif.), worked for Walt Disney for 27 years, during which he earned a reputation as a storyteller on a par with Disney himself. His work for Disney ranged from drawing sketches for the title character of *Dumbo* (1941) to contributing to character and story development for features including *Fantasia* (1940), *Cinderella* (1950), and *Sleeping Beauty* (1959) to writing the screenplay for *101 Dalmatians* (1961) and *The Sword in the Stone* (1963). After leaving Disney, Peet became one of the most popular writers and illustrators of children's books in the U.S., with more than 30 titles to his credit, among them *Chester the Worldly Pig* (1965) and *The Whingdingdilly* (1970).

Perlemuter, Vladislas ("VLADO"), Polish-born French pianist (b. May 26, 1904, Kovno, Russian Empire [now Kaunas, Lithuania]—d. Sept. 4, 2002, Paris, France), became one of the 20th century's foremost interpreters of the works of Ravel and Chopin, avoiding grandiose showmanship and theatrics for tonal sonority and rhythmic subtlety. Perlemuter was admitted to the Paris Conservatory at the age of 13 and went on to teach there (1950–77). Arguably the definitive voice on Ravel, he performed the entire oeuvre in two recitals in Paris in 1929; the composer attended and provided personal tutoring. He recorded countless works in the 1980s and '90s, including the entire works of Chopin. Perlemuter was appointed a grand officer of the Legion of Honour in 1993.

Perutz, Max Ferdinand, Austrian-born British biochemist (b. May 19, 1914, Vienna, Austria—d. Feb. 6, 2002, Cambridge, Eng.), shared the 1962 Nobel Prize for Chemistry with colleague John C. Kendrew and helped launch the field of molecular biology. With Kendrew, Perutz succeeded in determining the molecular structure of hemoglobin, the protein that transports oxygen and carbon dioxide throughout the body. Perutz studied at the University of Vienna and at the University of Cambridge, where he earned his Ph.D. in 1940. At Cambridge he took the first X-ray diffraction pictures of hemoglobin crystals. Although World War II interrupted his research, he later resumed work at Cambridge, and in 1947 he and Kendrew founded the university's Medical Research Council Unit for Molecular Biology. Perutz served as director of the unit until 1962, when it became the MRC's Laboratory for Molecular Biology. He was chairman of that establishment from 1962 until his retirement in 1979. Perutz's Nobel Prize-winning achievement was largely in showing that the hemoglobin molecule is composed of four separate polypeptide chains and that in oxygenated hemoglobin these four chains are rearranged, a discovery that led to the full de-

termination of the molecular mechanism of oxygen transport and release by hemoglobin.

Phillips, Julia Miller, American film producer and writer (b. April 7, 1944, New York, N.Y.—d. Jan. 1, 2002, West Hollywood, Calif.), in the 1970s became one of the very few women to have attained a position of power in the world of Hollywood filmmaking, was a co-producer of several of the decade's most successful motion pictures, and for one of those movies—*The Sting*—became the first woman to win a best-picture Academy Award. Her fame turned to notoriety in 1991, however, when—no longer powerful—she published her no-holds-barred memoir *You'll Never Eat Lunch in This Town Again*, which viciously blasted both the movie business and many Hollywood personalities. Phillips was educated at Mount

The Everett Collection

Hollywood powerhouse Julia Phillips

Holyoke College, South Hadley, Mass. (B.A., 1965), and worked in publishing before becoming (1969) a story editor for Paramount Pictures in New York City. She went on to be head of Mirisch Productions and then a creative executive for First Artist Productions. Along with her husband, investment banker Michael Phillips, and actor Tony Bill, Phillips formed (1970) Bill/Phillips Productions and moved to Los Angeles. Their films included *Steelyard Blues* (1972), *The Sting* (1973), which won seven Oscars, *Taxi Driver* (1976), which won the Cannes Film Festival's Palme d'Or, and *Close Encounters of the Third Kind* (1977). By this time, however, Phillips, who also had become president of her own company, Ruthless Productions, was suffering the effects of drug and alcohol dependency. Even though she underwent rehabilitation therapy, she was unable to regain her former status.

Phillips, William, American editor (b. Nov. 14, 1907, New York, N.Y.—d. Sept. 13, 2002, New York City), was the cofounder of *Partisan Review*, an influential magazine of politics, literature, and culture. Phillips was educated at the City College (now University) of New York (B.S., 1928) and at New York University (M.A., 1930). In 1934 he joined the John Reed Club, which was associated with the Communist Party, and, with Philip Rahv, founded *Partisan Review* as its official organ. The two men quickly became dissatisfied with the club's dogma, and in 1937 they severed their ties with it. Although *Partisan Review* continued to be identified with left-wing politics, the emphasis gradually shifted to literature and the arts. Phillips was interested in modernism and the avant-garde, and under his leadership the magazine introduced new intellectual movements—including Existentialism and Abstract Expressionism—to its readers, and it featured works by newly discovered authors as well as leading writers and critics of the period. Phillips was made editor in chief in 1965, which led to Rahv's departure. The magazine came under the auspices of Rutgers University, New Brunswick, N.J., in 1969 and Boston University in 1978. Phillips continued to be active in the magazine, although his second wife, Edith Kurzweil, assumed the editorial duties in the 1990s. Phillips taught at a number of universities, and he edited several books, including the anthology *60 Years of Great Fiction from Partisan Review* (1996).

Phipps, Ogden, American racehorse owner and breeder (b. Nov. 26, 1908, New York, N.Y.—d. April 22, 2002, West Palm Beach, Fla.), was one of the dominant figures in Thoroughbred horse racing in the 20th century. Phipps owned or bred numerous stakes winners, including Buckpasser, the 1966 Horse of the Year, and Personal Ensign, which in 1988 retired undefeated after winning the Breeders' Cup Distaff. A wealthy financier whose grandfather had been the business partner of steel magnate Andrew Carnegie, Phipps became a racehorse owner in 1932. He served as chairman of the Jockey Club, Thoroughbred racing's regulatory agency, from 1964 to 1974. He won Eclipse Awards as the sport's outstanding owner and breeder in 1988 and as the outstanding owner in 1989.

Pierce, John Robinson, American engineer (b. March 27, 1910, Des Moines, Iowa—d. April 2, 2002, Sunnyvale, Calif.), was recognized as the father of satellite communications. After earning a Ph.D. from the

California Institute of Technology (Caltech) in 1936, Pierce worked for Bell Telephone Laboratories in New York City. During World War II he helped develop the reflex klystron, a low-voltage vacuum tube used in radar receivers. In the late 1940s he coined the term *transistor* to describe a groundbreaking invention by colleagues—a solid-state device that amplified electronic signals. After becoming director of electronics research at the New Jersey division of Bell Laboratories in 1952, Pierce wrote numerous papers detailing the advantages of using satellites to relay radio communications. He eventually persuaded NASA to convert its 30-m (100-ft) Echo balloon satellite into a radio-wave reflector. Echo I was launched on Aug. 12, 1960. The success of the communications experiments carried out with Echo I provided the impetus to develop Telstar, a satellite designed to amplify signals from one Earth station and relay the signals back to another Earth station. These early satellites marked the beginning of efficient worldwide radio and television communications. After retiring from Bell Laboratories in 1971, Pierce returned to Caltech to become a professor of engineering. In 1979 he was named chief technologist at the Jet Propulsion Laboratory in Pasadena, Calif.

Porter, Roy Sydney, British historian (b. Dec. 31, 1946, Hitchin, Hertfordshire, Eng.—d. March 3, 2002, St. Leonards, East Sussex, Eng.), wrote scores of scholarly books and papers on a vast array of subjects, most notably British social history and the history of medicine. His best-known works included *English Society in the Eighteenth Century* (1982), *Health for Sale: Quackery in England 1660–1850* (1989), *London: A Social History* (1994), and *Enlightenment: Britain and the Creation of the Modern World* (2000), which won the 2001 Wolfson Prize for History. *Madness: A Brief History* was published in early 2002. Porter was named a fellow of the British Academy in 1994.

Porter of Luddenham, George Porter, Baron, British chemist (b. Dec. 6, 1920, Stainforth, Yorkshire, Eng.—d. Aug. 31, 2002, Canterbury, Eng.), was corecipient with Ronald G.W. Norrish, his colleague and mentor at the University of Cambridge, and West German physicist Manfred Eigen of the 1967 Nobel Prize for Chemistry for their studies in flash photolysis, a technique for observing the intermediate stages of very fast chemical reactions by subjecting a gas or liquid to short bursts of light that disturb its molecular equilibrium and allow the resulting intermediates to be analyzed spectroscopically. After matriculating at the University of Leeds (1938–41) and serving in the Royal Navy (1941–45), Porter went to Emmanuel College, Cambridge, and studied under Norrish. Their collaboration lasted until the mid-1950s. Porter was on the faculty of the University of Sheffield (1955–66). He held numerous other appointments, including director of the Royal Institution of Great Britain (1966–85), president of the Royal Society (1985–90), chancellor of the University of Leicester (1986–95), and chairman of the Centre for Photomolecular Sciences (1990–2002). He was knighted in 1972, appointed to the Order of Merit in 1989, and granted a life peerage in 1990.

Potok, Chaim (HERMAN HAROLD POTOK), American writer (b. Feb. 17, 1929, New York, N.Y.—d. July 23, 2002, Merion, Pa.), explored the conflict between Hasidic Jewish religious traditions and the secular world. He was the son of Polish immigrants and was educated in Orthodox schools. As a youth he was interested in painting, but when his parents objected to art, he turned to literature. In 1950 he graduated from Yeshiva University in New York City with a B.A. degree in English. Upon receiving a master's degree in Hebrew literature in 1954 from the Jewish Theological Seminary of America in New York City, he was ordained a Conservative rabbi. He was a U.S. Army chaplain in Korea from 1955 to 1957. Potok served as managing editor (1964–75) of *Conservative Judaism* and editor in chief (1965–74) of the Jewish Publication Society of America. In 1965 he earned a Ph.D. degree in philosophy from the University of Pennsylvania, and he taught at a number of colleges and universities. His first novel, *The Chosen* (1967; filmed 1981), explores the friendship between two young Jewish men, one leading a more secular life and the other trying to reconcile his Orthodox Jewish heritage with his longing to participate in modern life. A sequel, *The Promise*, which took the characters into adulthood, appeared in 1969. The protagonist of *My Name Is Asher Lev* (1972) and *The Gift of Asher Lev* (1990) is a young man whose desire to be an artist brings him into conflict with his family. In addition, he wrote short stories, plays, and children's books.

Prokhorov, Aleksandr Mikhaylovich, Russian physicist (b. July 11, 1916, Atherton, Queensland, Australia—d. Jan. 8, 2002, Moscow, Russia), was corecipient of the Nobel Prize for Physics in 1964 with Nikolay G.

John Pierce, the father of satellite communications

$$V = H_n(x/a)H_m(y$$

$$r = a_o\left(1 + \frac{3^2}{\beta_o^2 a_o^4}\right)^{1/}$$

Basov, his colleague at the P.N. Lebedev Physical Institute in Moscow, and American Charles H. Townes. The award was given for fundamental research in quantum electronics that led to the development of the maser and the laser, which produce parallel monochromatic coherent beams of microwaves and light, respectively. In 1923 Prokhorov's antitsarist family returned from exile in Australia to the Soviet Union, where he studied physics at Leningrad State University (B.S., 1939) and the Lebedev Institute (Ph.D., 1951). He worked closely with Basov from 1950 on the concept for a device that would emit microwave radiation of a single wavelength. By the time they published their findings in 1954, Townes's team at Columbia University, New York City, had independently built such a device, which they called a maser (microwave amplification by stimulated emission of radiation). Prokhorov later proposed the modification of a maser to emit visible-light or infrared wavelengths, an idea that led to the laser (light amplification by stimulated emission of radiation). Prokhorov was head (from 1954) of the Lebedev's Oscillation Laboratory, professor (from 1959) at Moscow State University, and founding director (1983–98) of the Soviet Academy of Science's General Physics Institute. He also was editor in chief (1969–78) of the *Great Soviet Encyclopedia*.

Qadir, Abdul, Afghan warlord and political official (b. 1954?, Sorkh Rod, Afg.—d. July 6, 2002, Kabul, Afg.), was one of the few Pashtun leaders in the Tajik-dominated government of Pres. Hamid Karzai. Qadir's power base lay in eastern Afghanistan, where he was a powerful warlord and governor of Nangarhar province, a post he assumed in 1992 after he had earned a reputation by leading mujahideen forces following the 1979 Soviet invasion. He fled the country when the Taliban took control and was one of a handful of Pashtun leaders to fight with the anti-Taliban Northern Alliance. In October 2001 his younger brother, a guerrilla leader known as Abdul Haq, was executed by the Taliban government. Qadir, a controversial figure with many enemies, nonetheless wielded enormous influence among eastern Pashtuns, and there were rumours that he was involved in the opium trade. He was shot dead by unknown assailants less than three weeks after he had assumed his post as one of Afghanistan's new vice presidents.

Radkowsky, Alvin, American-born Israeli nuclear physicist (b. June 30, 1915, Elizabeth, N.J.—d. Feb. 17, 2002, Tel Aviv, Israel), helped build the world's first nuclear-powered submarine, the USS *Nautilus*, in the early 1950s and, later in his career, worked on developing a nuclear reactor fuel that would produce a minimal amount of radioactive waste. In 1938

he went to work for the Department of the Navy as a civilian nuclear physicist. Radkowsky lived in Israel from 1972. While teaching at Tel Aviv University, he proposed using thorium to replace much of the uranium in nuclear reactors as a way to limit the creation of harmful waste; his thorium theory was being tested at the time of his death.

Ramone, Dee Dee (DOUGLAS GLENN COLVIN), American musician and songwriter (b. Sept. 18, 1952, Fort Lee, Va.—d. June 5, 2002, Hollywood, Calif.), was a founder and the principal songwriter of the punk rock pioneers the Ramones and was a member of that group from 1974 until 1989, when he embarked on a solo career. The Ramones were inducted into the Rock and Roll Hall of Fame in Cleveland, Ohio, 11 weeks before his death.

Rawls, John Bordley, American philosopher (b. Feb. 21, 1921, Baltimore, Md.—d. Nov. 24, 2002, Lexington, Mass.), was among the most influential political thinkers of the 20th century. Rawls, who obtained a B.A. from Princeton University in 1943, spent two years in the Pacific with the U.S. Army before returning to Princeton, where he earned a Ph.D. (1950) in philosophy. He taught at Princeton (1950–52), Cornell University, Ithaca, N.Y. (1953–59), the Massachusetts Institute of Technology (1960–62), and Harvard University (1962–91), where he was James Bryant Conant University Professor from 1979. In 1953 Rawls was a Fulbright fellow at the University of Oxford, where he came under the influence of Isaiah Berlin and H.L.A. Hart. Rawls's book *A Theory of Justice* (1971) was instrumental in changing the emphasis of political philosophy from the analysis of political language to substantive inquiry into issues such as justice, liberty, and equality. Rawls's theory of justice was a response to utilitarianism, the theory that defines the just act as that which produces the greatest good for the greatest number of people. In Rawls's opinion, utilitarianism could not provide a foundation for the rights of the individual within society. Rather, Rawls reached back to the social contract theories of Thomas Hobbes, Immanuel Kant, and Jean-Jacques Rousseau to develop a theory in which social justice was compatible with individual rights. Rawls inquired into the conditions under which individuals would agree to a given set of political and social arrangements. He maintained that they would have to be ignorant of the outcomes of a particular arrangement, for no one would agree to an arrangement under which he or she would come out a loser. Hence, for Rawls such agreement would have to take place under what he called a "veil of ignorance." Under such conditions, according to Rawls, people

would act in a risk-averse manner and would follow Rawls's two principles of justice—first, that each person should have the most liberty compatible with like liberty for others and, second, that social inequalities should be organized so as to advantage the worst-off.

Reber, Grote, American astronomer and radio engineer (b. Dec. 22, 1911, Wheaton, Ill.—d. Dec. 20, 2002, Tasmania, Australia), was widely regarded as the father of radio astronomy. After learning of engineer Karl Jansky's discovery in 1932 of interstellar radio signals, Reber began attempts to detect such signals with various receivers; ultimately, in 1937, he constructed the world's first radio telescope—

Thomas D. McAvoy/TimePix

Grote Reber, father of radio astronomy

a bowl-shaped antenna 9.4 m (31 ft) in diameter—in the backyard of his home in Wheaton. Reber spent the next few years identifying different sources of radio signals and by 1942 had created the first radio maps of the sky. He moved his radio telescope to Sterling, Va., in 1947 and later worked as a radio physicist for the National Bureau of Standards in Washington, D.C. Reber installed a new radio telescope in Hawaii in 1951. Three years later he moved to Tasmania, where he worked with the Commonwealth Scientific and Industrial Research Organization and focused his research on low-frequency cosmic radio waves. Reber won the Astronomical Society of the Pacific's highest honour—the Catherine Wolf Bruce Gold Medal—in 1962 and the Royal Astronomical Society's Jackson-Gwilt Medal in 1983.

Reisz, Karel, Czech-born British film and stage director (b. July 21, 1926, Ostrava,

Czech.—d. Nov. 25, 2002, London, Eng.), made only 11 movies during his career but was instrumental in the creation of British new wave cinema in the 1960s. After working on the film journal *Sequence* and authoring a book on film editing, Reisz began making documentaries on working-class life. His first feature, *Saturday Night and Sunday Morning* (1960), the story of a jaded young factory worker, brought fame to him and his star, Albert Finney. Reisz's Hollywood ventures included *The Gambler* (1974) and *The French Lieutenant's Woman* (1981).

Riboud, Antoine-Amédée-Paul, French industrialist (b. Dec. 25, 1918, Lyon, France—d. May 5, 2002, Paris, France), joined a small family-owned glass-making business, Souchon-Neuvesel, in 1942 and through a series of mergers, acquisitions, and hostile takeovers eventually turned it into a global food empire. In 1966 Riboud engineered a merger with another glass manufacturer, Boussois, to form BSN SA. He expanded relentlessly, acquiring the manufacturers of a wide range of food products, including Danone (Dannon) yogurt, Evian mineral water, Kronenbourg beer, Lea & Perrin bottled sauces, and baked goods from Nabisco's European operations. Riboud generated controversy in 1972 when he publicly encouraged all French companies to be socially responsible toward their employees. He changed the corporation's name to Danone in 1994, and two years later he turned over control of the $13 billion food giant to his son Franck.

Rickey, George, American sculptor (b. June 6, 1907, South Bend, Ind.—d. July 17, 2002, St. Paul, Minn.), fashioned mobile geometric forms and claimed that movement was his main medium. With a combination of engineered exactness and visual minimalism, he created nonmotorized stainless-steel forms that, fueled only by gravitation and natural wind patterns, teetered between equilibrium and motion. These slow-moving changeable displays were often composed of planes of bladelike forms anchored to centre posts. Rickey was educated in humanities and art at Trinity College, Glenalmond, Scot., where his father, an engineer, had been relocated. Rickey also attended the University of Oxford and extended his art studies in Paris (where he began an apprenticeship). The first solo exhibition of his paintings was mounted in New York City in 1933. With brief interruption for service in World War II, he taught widely at various universities. In the late 1940s, he switched his focus from painting to kinetic sculptural art. In the 1960s he relocated to East Chatham, N.Y. By this time he was earning comparisons to Alexander Calder, as well as growing acclaim, particularly in Europe. In 1967 he published *Constructivism: Origins and Evolution.* In the 1970s his forms began to follow conical patterns along a fixed path, not just through planar motion, and later he experimented with separate moving elements, jointed together. He traveled widely, and he began producing increasingly larger, complex works, culminating with a nearly

17.5-m (about 57-ft) sculpture that was installed at the Hyogo Prefectural Museum of Art in Kobe, Japan, in 2002.

Riggin, Aileen (AILEEN RIGGIN SOULE), American swimmer and diver (b. May 2, 1906, Newport, R.I.—d. Oct. 17, 2002, Honolulu, Hawaii), was the youngest American to win an Olympic gold medal and the first Olympic competitor to win medals in both swimming and diving at the same Games. After placing first in springboard diving at the 1920 Games in Antwerp, Belg., when she was only 14, Riggin was a member of both the diving and swimming teams at the 1924 Games in Paris, where she won a silver medal in springboard diving and a bronze in the 100-m backstroke. She went on to appear in films and continued to push the boundaries for women by becoming a sportswriter. Riggin was inducted into the International Swimming Hall of Fame in 1967 and set six world records at the masters level during the 1980s.

Rinser, Luise, German writer (b. April 30, 1911, Pitzling, Bavaria, Ger.—d. March 17, 2002, Unterhaching, Bavaria, Ger.), was a political activist and a prolific author of best-selling novels, essays, short stories, diaries, plays, travel journals, and children's books. She qualified as a teacher in 1934 but lost her job in 1939 because she refused to join the National Socialist (Nazi) Party. She also was barred from writing after the publication of her first novel, *Die gläsernen Ringe* (1940; *Rings of Glass,* 1958). Imprisoned for treason in 1944, she was freed by the Allies, who gave her a job on the newspaper *Neue Zeitung.*

Gefängnistagebuch (1946; *A Woman's Prison Journal: Germany, 1944,* 1987), based on a journal she secretly kept in prison as she awaited execution, was one of the few published accounts of a Nazi prison from a woman's point of view. Rinser was an outspoken critic of the arms race and supported German reunification and abortion rights; she ran for president of West Germany on the Green Party ticket in 1984.

Riopelle, Jean-Paul, Canadian artist (b. Oct. 7?, 1923, Montreal, Que.—d. March 12, 2002, Ile-aux-Grues, Que.), was widely regarded as Canada's most important modern artist; his work, much of which was done in the Abstract Expressionist style, was often compared to that of American artist Jackson Pollock. Riopelle became a founding member of the Automatistes, the first group of abstract painters in Canada. He eventually settled in Paris, where he associated with Surrealists such as André Breton and Marcel Duchamp and where his work first gained international recognition. Riopelle represented Canada at the Venice Biennale in 1954 and 1962. In 1963 the National Gallery of Canada, Ottawa, exhibited 82 of his paintings and sculptures; at the age of 40, Riopelle was the youngest artist ever to be given a retrospective exhibition at the gallery. He spent most of his time in Paris but returned to Canada in the early 1990s, settling permanently in Quebec. In 2000 his last major work, *L'Hommage à Rosa Luxemburg,* a narrative fresco of 30 paintings that was more than 40 m (130 ft) long, was acquired by the Museum of Quebec.

Jean-Paul Riopelle, artist and collector of Bugatti automobiles

Loomis Dean/TimePix

Ritts, Herbert, Jr. ("HERB"), American photographer (b. August 1952, Los Angeles, Calif.—d. Dec. 26, 2002, Los Angeles), excelled in capturing images that celebrated the beauty of the human body—especially the male body—and in creating stylish, unorthodox portraits of celebrities; his efforts gained

© Brian Snyder/Reuters 2002

Portrait photographer Herb Ritts

him such renown that he achieved nearly as much fame as his subjects. His work graced not only the covers of such magazines as *Vogue, Vanity Fair, Rolling Stone, Elle,* and *Harper's Bazaar* and fashion spreads in those publications but also album covers, advertisements, television commercials, and music videos; two of Ritts's music videos won MTV Video Music Awards in 1991. Ritts claimed that his success in black-and-white photography stemmed from a photograph he happened to take of his friend Richard Gere while they were waiting for a tire to be changed in the California desert. That photo was ultimately used for publicity when Gere starred in *American Gigolo* (1980), and both men's careers received an enormous boost. Several anthologies of Ritts's works were published, including *Men/Women* (1989), *Notorious* (1992), *Africa* (1994), *Work* (1997), and *Herb Ritts* (2000).

Rivers, Larry (YITZROCH LOIZA GROSSBERG), American artist (b. Aug. 17, 1923, New York, N.Y.—d. Aug. 14, 2002, Southampton, N.Y), had a comic sense, penchant for self-promotion, and libertine lifestyle that prefigured the irony, iconography, and celebrity of the Pop art movement. He was educated at the Juilliard School of Music, New York City, and performed as a saxophonist in bebop jazz bands of the 1940s before finding that he had an interest in and facility for painting. Breaking early from Abstract Expressionism, he became known for wry, figurative works based on historic paintings, including *The Burial* (1951) and *Washington Crossing the Delaware* (1953). He was a keen draftsman with a regard for the Old Masters. Rivers exhibited in New York City at the Tibor de Nagy Gallery throughout the 1950s before switching over to the Marlborough Gallery in the early '60s. From that period his work incorporated elements of Pop art, mixing commercial packaging and everyday objects, notably in *The History of the Russian Revolution* (1965). Restlessly moving between different mediums and disciplines (painting, sculpture, film, video, performance, and design), he experimented constantly, allowing the quality of his work to fluctuate. Shortly before his death, a retrospective appeared at the Corcoran Gallery of Art in Washington, D.C.

Rol-Tanguy, Henri (HENRI TANGUY), French World War II Resistance leader (b. June 12, 1908, Morlaix, France—d. Sept. 8, 2002, Monteaux?, France), commanded the Resistance forces during the Parisian uprising against German occupation; he helped liberate Paris in August 1944 and was one of those who signed the document accepting Germany's surrender of the city. Originally a metallurgical worker, he joined the Communist Party in 1925 and fought with the International Brigades in Spain in 1937 (he later added Rol to his birth name, Tanguy, to honour a friend killed in Spain). An early leader in the underground, Rol-Tanguy was named commander of the French Forces of the Interior just before the Normandy landing in June 1944. After the war he served in the French army until 1962, but he never relinquished his communist affiliations. Rol-Tanguy received the Grand Cross of the Legion of Honour in 1994 and was awarded honorary Spanish citizenship in 1996.

Rosenberg, William, American entrepreneur (b. June 10, 1916, Boston, Mass.—d. Sept. 20, 2002, Mashpee, Mass.), founded the iconic Dunkin' Donuts chain, the largest coffee and pastry chain in the world. He started out providing business lunches, delivering sandwiches and snacks to offices in Boston. Noticing that coffee and pastries were his best-sellers, he opened his first Dunkin' Donuts (originally named Open Kettle) in 1950. His success was due to higher-quality coffee and an astonishing variety of doughnuts. The chain spread rapidly, and by 2002 there were 5,000 outlets in 37 countries. Rosenberg's skills as a businessman were legendary, and in 1959 he helped create the International Franchise Association.

Rowell, Galen, American landscape photographer (b. Aug. 23, 1940, Berkeley, Calif.—d. Aug. 11, 2002, Bishop, Calif.), captured breathtaking images of some of the remotest parts of the world. Galen was an avid mountain climber and traveler; his photography was a natural extension of his love for the ever-decreasing wilderness around him. In turn, he used his work to further conservation awareness in an attempt to preserve the delicate regions he photographed. His work appeared in such magazines as *National Geographic, Life,* and *Outdoor Photographer.* In addition, he published 18 books of photography, including *My Tibet* (1990), with text written by the Dalai Lama. *Rainbow over Potala Palace, Lhasa,* arguably his most famous image, captured the dramatic moment when a rainbow touched and illuminated the Dalai Lama's palace. In 1984 Rowell was honoured with the Ansel Adams Award, and in 1992 he received a National Science Foundation Award to photograph Antarctica. He and his wife Barbara—an acclaimed writer, photographer, and pilot—died in a plane crash.

Rukavishnikov, Nikolay Nikolayevich, Russian cosmonaut (b. Sept. 18, 1932, Tomsk, Siberia, U.S.S.R.—d. Oct. 19, 2002, Moscow, Russia), on his third trip into space, became the first cosmonaut to land a spacecraft manually. He was test engineer on the Soyuz 10 spacecraft (April 23–25, 1971), which had to return to Earth ahead of schedule after a docking hatch failed on the Salyut 1 space station, and flight engineer on Soyuz 16 during its successful U.S.-Soviet joint mission (Dec. 2–8, 1974). On his final mission (April 10–12, 1979), Rukavishnikov was commander of Soyuz 33. When the main engine suddenly shut down, he powered up a faulty reserve engine and maneuvered the spacecraft into a reentry along a ballistic trajectory and a parachute-assisted soft landing.

Runyan, Paul, American golfer (b. July 12, 1908, Hot Springs, Ark.—d. March 17, 2002, Palm Springs, Calif.), was one of the most accomplished golfers ever at irons play and putting. Runyan won more than 50 tournaments, including the Professional Golfers' Association of America (PGA) championship in 1934 and 1938. Runyan's most notable victory came when he demolished the heavily favoured Sam Snead (*q.v.*), closing him out after 29 holes to capture the PGA championship in 1938. Runyan was inducted into the World Golf Hall of Fame in 1990.

Russell, Harold John, Canadian-born American actor (b. Jan. 14, 1914, North Sydney, N.S.—d. Jan. 29, 2002, Needham, Mass.), was the only actor ever to win two Academy Awards for the same role; for his sensitive portrayal of World War II veteran Homer Parrish in *The Best Years of Our Lives* (1946), who, like Russell, had lost both hands in military service and had them replaced with hooks, he received both the best supporting actor Oscar and a special award for "bringing aid and comfort to disabled veterans through the medium of motion pictures."

Saint Phalle, Catherine Marie-Agnès Fal de ("NIKI"), French-born artist (b. Oct. 29, 1930, Neuilly-sur-Seine, France—d. May 21, 2002, La Jolla, Calif.), first gained public attention with her artworks at which darts were thrown or guns fired. Her best-known works, however, were her "Nanas"—large, colourful papier-mâché sculptures of the female form—and her 22-piece Tarot Garden in Tuscany, Italy.

Savimbi, Jonas Malheiro, Angolan nationalist guerrilla leader (b. Aug. 3, 1934, Munhango, Portuguese Angola—d. Feb. 22, 2002, near Lucuse, Angola), was the charismatic and fiercely ambitious leader of the National Union for the Total Independence of Angola (UNITA). Savimbi originally fought alongside the Marxist-oriented Popular Movement for the Liberation of Angola (MPLA) and the U.S.-backed National Front for the Liberation of Angola (FNLA) in the war for liberation from Portugal, but he later turned against his erstwhile allies and waged war on the MPLA-led postindependence government. Savimbi was a member of the Ovimbundu tribe. He studied medicine in Lisbon, Port., where he met MPLA founder Agostinho Neto and joined the independence movement; some reports indicated that he studied political science in Switzerland. In 1965 Savimbi accepted funding and military training from China; the next year he founded UNITA and returned home with a small militia, which quickly gained popular support in eastern Angola. After independence was granted in 1975, civil war broke out between the liberation groups. Savimbi sought U.S. and South African aid to fight the MPLA, which was backed by Cuba and the Soviet Union. A peace agreement led to elections in 1992, but when the MPLA won the vote, Savimbi refused to accept the results. Thereafter, despite peace talks, occasional cease-fires, and dwindling support, he continued the guerrilla war. Savimbi was killed in a gun battle with government troops.

Schapiro, Boris, British contract bridge player (b. Aug. 22 [Aug. 9, old style], 1909, Riga, Latvia, Russian Empire—d. Dec. 1, 2002, Long Crendon, Buckinghamshire, Eng.), represented Great Britain in numerous international contract bridge tournaments and was a member of the national team that was victorious at the 1955 Bermuda Bowl world championship. At the 1965 Bermuda Bowl, however, Schapiro and Terence Reese, his partner since 1948, were accused by the World Bridge Federation (WBF) of "using illegal hand signals." After a year-long investigation, the British Bridge League found the pair not guilty of cheating. The WBF nonetheless suspended them from international competition (they were eventually reinstated), and Great Britain withdrew its team from the 1968 bridge Olympiad in protest. Schapiro captured his first title, the world pairs championship with American Oswald Jacoby, in 1932, and his last, the senior pairs world championship with Irving Gordon, in 1998, at age 89. He wrote the contract bridge column for *The Sunday Times* from 1966.

Scholl, William Howard, British businessman and shoe designer (b. Sept. 24, 1920, London, Eng.—d. March 15, 2002, Douglas, Isle of Man), developed an orthopedic wooden sandal in the late 1950s, but young women, charmed by the shoe's deceptively simple looks and the distinctive clip-clop sound it made when they walked, turned the Dr. Scholl sandal into a fashion rage in the 1960s and '70s. Scholl also expanded the Dr. Scholl footcare product line. He took the family company public in 1971, sold it to Schering-Plough HealthCare Corp. in 1979, and was president of Schering-Plough's International Consumer Products division until retiring in 1984. Scholl was appointed CBE in 1998.

Schwartz, Laurent-Moïse, French mathematician (b. March 5, 1915, Paris, France—d. July 4, 2002, Paris), was awarded the Fields Medal in 1950 for his work on the theory of distributions. In the 1920s physicist Paul Dirac introduced his "delta function" to simplify the mathematical treatment of certain point items—that is, actions highly localized, or "spiked," in space or time (e.g., point charges, masses, and spins)—in quantum mechanical problems. In a series of papers beginning in 1945, Schwartz developed a theory of generalized functions, or distributions, that rigorously brought the Dirac delta function within the mathematical framework of functional analysis. His most significant work, *Théorie des distributions,* first published in 1950–51, elaborated his work. Schwartz studied mathematics at the École Normale Superieure (later part of the Universities of Paris). Schwartz stood as a Trotskyist in the 1945 and 1946 general elections; although he ended his political allegiance with Trotskyism in 1947, he was barred from the U.S. and was unable to collect his Fields Medal in person. A signatory of the "Manifeste des 121," which endorsed the moral right of French youth who refused to fight against Algerian independence, Schwartz was fired from the École Polytechnique, where he began teaching in 1959, in 1960 for his stand on Algeria, but he returned to work in 1963. He was also outspoken in his opposition to the Vietnam War and the Soviet invasion of Afghanistan. He was elected to the Paris Academy of Sciences in 1975.

Shapey, Ralph, American composer and teacher (b. March 12, 1921, Philadelphia, Pa.—d. June 13, 2002, Chicago, Ill.), combined atonality with lyricism in his works. He composed some 200 pieces in a number of forms, including works for the voice and for orchestra and various combinations of instruments. Influenced by the serialism of Arnold Schoenberg, his music was at times dissonant and complex, but it also could be warmly expressive and romantic. Shapey began violin studies at the age of seven, and while still in his teens, he began conducting a youth orchestra in Philadelphia. His formal education ended with graduation from high school. For a number of years, he supported himself as a violinist in New York City, where he also studied composition with Stefan Wolpe, who had

been a pupil of Schoenberg. He was on the faculty of the University of Chicago for nearly all of the period from 1964 until his retirement in 1991. In 1964 he formed the Contemporary Chamber Players, a group that became widely known for its performances of modern music. He was a guest conductor of a number of major orchestras. From 1969 to 1976, as a protest against what he felt was neglect of his music, he asked that it not be performed. Among his commissions was *Concerto fantastique* for the Chicago Symphony Orchestra, which in 1992 was chosen by the music jury to receive that year's Pulitzer Prize; the Pulitzer board overturned the choice, however.

Shea, Jack (JOHN AMOS SHEA), American speed skater (b. Sept. 10, 1910, Lake Placid, N.Y.—d. Jan. 22, 2002, Saranac Lake, N.Y.), became the first double gold medalist in the Winter Olympics when he won the 500- and 1,500-m speed-skating races at the 1932 Games in Lake Placid; he was also the patriarch of the first family with three generations of Olympians. Before competing in the Olympics, Shea had won the North American overall speed-skating championship in 1929 and the U.S. national overall title in 1930. He declined to skate in the 1936 Winter Games in Garmisch-Partenkirchen, Ger., in part to protest the politics of Adolf Hitler. Shea was instrumental in persuading the International Olympic Committee to hold the Winter Games in Lake Placid in 1980. His son Jim competed in three skiing events at the 1964 Winter Games in Innsbruck, Austria. Shea's grandson, Jim, Jr., won a gold medal in the skeleton event at the 2002 Winter Games in Salt Lake City, Utah. Just days before the 2002 Games began, Shea died of injuries sustained in an automobile accident.

Shehada, Salah Mustafa, Palestinian guerrilla leader (b. 1953, Beit Hanoun, Gaza Strip—d. July 22, 2002, Gaza City, Gaza Strip), was the commander of Izz al-Din al-Qassam, the military wing of the anti-Israeli Hamas (Islamic Resistance Movement). Shehada openly endorsed armed attacks and suicide bombings. Nevertheless, many Palestinians admired him as an Islamic hero, and his charisma was responsible in part for increasing Hamas's ranks and support among the Palestinian populace. He was one of the original founders of Hamas in the early 1980s and was jailed twice by the Israeli government, which considered him the mastermind behind several bloody attacks, including a bombing at a religious school in March 2002 that left five Israeli students dead. Shehada, his wife, and a daughter were killed in an Israeli air strike against their home.

Shuster, Frank, Canadian comedian and writer (b. Sept. 5, 1916, Toronto, Ont.—d. Jan. 13, 2002, Toronto), along with his high-school friend Johnny Wayne, formed the Wayne and Shuster comedy team and performed together for some 50 years, first on Canadian Broadcasting Corp. radio and then on television, including 67 appearances on *The Ed*

Sullivan Show. Shuster was made an Officer of the Order of Canada in 1997, and the team was inducted into the Canadian Comedy Hall of Fame in 2000.

Slaughter, Enos Bradsher ("COUNTRY"),

American baseball player (b. April 27, 1916, Roxboro, N.C.— d. Aug. 12, 2002, Durham, N.C.), had a lifetime .300 batting average and was a hero of the St. Louis Cardinals, for whom he played 13 of his 19 major league seasons. He was a hard-hitting outfielder who led the National League in hits in 1942 and in runs batted in 1946; played in 10 All-Star games, and was elected in 1985 to the Baseball Hall of Fame.

Slavenska, Mia (MIA CORAK), Croatian-born American ballerina and teacher (b. Feb. 20, 1914/16, Brod-na Savi [now Slavonski Brod], Croatia—d. Oct. 5, 2002, Westwood, Calif.), was celebrated for her powerful stage presence, enhanced by her dazzling virtuoso technique and dramatic flair, as well as the beauty of her face and red hair. She later made an equally strong impression as a much-respected teacher. Slavenska began her ballet studies in Zagreb, Croatia, and later also studied in Vienna and Paris. At the age of 17, she became prima ballerina of Zagreb opera house's ballet company. In 1937 she was one of the stars of the film *La Mort du cygne* (U.S. title, *Ballerina*). In 1938 Slavenska joined the Ballet Russe de Monte Carlo, and for the next several years she traveled with that company internationally, dancing the principal roles in such classical ballets as *Giselle*, *Swan Lake*, and *Coppélia* as well as 20th-century works by Michel Fokine and Léonide Massine. She eventually settled in the United States, where she became a citizen in 1947. Slavenska formed a succession of touring groups, including Ballet Variante and, with Frederic Franklin, the Slavenska-Franklin Ballet. It was with the latter company that she danced one of her most noted roles, Blanche in *A Streetcar Named Desire* (1952).

Smith, Howard Kingsbury, Jr., American journalist and broadcaster (b. May 12, 1914, Ferriday, La.—d. Feb. 15, 2002, Bethesda, Md.), was a longtime radio and television newscaster who remained true to his convictions and was willing to take a stand on important issues despite the fact that news reporters were traditionally neutral and despite the difficulties his outspokenness caused him in his career. He was also noted for having served (1960) as the moderator of the first televised debate between presidential candidates—John F. Kennedy and Richard M. Nixon. Following graduation from Tulane University, New Orleans, in 1936 and studies at Heidelberg (Ger.) University, Smith worked as a reporter for the *New Orleans Item-Tribune*

before going (1937) to the University of Oxford as a Rhodes scholar. He went to work for United Press in London in 1939, was sent to Berlin in 1940, and in 1941 joined CBS. His refusal to follow Nazi officials' orders regarding the content of his scripts led to his expulsion, however, and on Dec. 6, 1941, he left for Switzerland. Smith covered the war as part of the "Murrow boys"—the team put together by Edward R. Murrow—and in 1946 took over Murrow's post as CBS's chief European correspondent, a position he held for 11 years. In 1957 he moved to Washington, D.C., to be a correspondent and commentator for the CBS nightly news. In 1961, greatly disturbed by the injustices taking place in the civil rights struggle, Smith wanted to end the documentary "Who Speaks for Birmingham?" with a quote from Edmund Burke—"The only thing necessary for the triumph of evil is for good men to do nothing." When the network cut the line, he left and went to ABC, where he stayed until he retired in 1979.

Snead, Samuel Jackson ("SAM"; "SLAMMIN' SAM"), American golfer (b. May 27, 1912, near Hot Springs, Va.—d. May 23, 2002, Hot Springs), won a record 81 Professional Golfers' Association of America (PGA) Tour events as well as some 70 other tournaments. Snead was renowned for his elegant yet powerful swing; he was the first golfer regularly to drive a ball some 250 m (270 yd). He taught himself to play while caddying at a country club in Hot Springs and turned professional in 1936. Success came quickly; Snead earned victories in the Oakland (Calif.) Open and the West Virginia Closed Pro in 1937. Except for

© Bettmann/Corbis

"Slammin' Sam" Snead

the U.S. Open—in which he placed second four times—he won every major golfing championship. His major victories included the Masters (1949, 1952, 1954), the PGA championship (1942, 1949, 1951), and the British Open (1946). He was a seven-time member of

the U.S. Ryder Cup team and played on the winning World Cup teams in 1956, 1960, and 1961. At the age of 52, he became the oldest golfer to have won a PGA event when he triumphed at the 1965 Greater Greensboro (N.C.) Open. He went on to win the PGA Seniors tournament six times (1964–65, 1967, 1970, 1972–73). Snead was elected to the PGA Hall of Fame in 1953.

Staley, Layne Thomas, American singer and songwriter (b. Aug. 22, 1967, Kirkland, Wash.—found dead April 19, 2002, Seattle, Wash.), was the lead singer and guitarist for the grunge band Alice in Chains, whose albums during its prominence in the early and mid-1990s included *Dirt* (1992), with songs such as "God Smack" and "Junkhead" that reflected Staley's problems with drugs.

Steiger, Rodney Stephen ("ROD"), American

actor (b. April 14, 1925, Westhampton, N.Y.—d. July 9, 2002, Los Angeles, Calif.), used the techniques of method acting—enhanced by his powerful delivery and intensity—to inhabit a wide variety of complex characters during a half-century-long career as a performer. He was nominated for an Academy Award three times and won it once, for best actor, for his role as a racist Southern sheriff in *In the Heat of the Night* (1967). Steiger dropped out of high school at age 16, lied about his age so he could join the navy, and spent most of World War II as a torpedo man on a destroyer in the Pacific. Following his discharge he took a job in Newark, N.J., and joined a theatre group. Steiger studied acting at a succession of schools in New York City, ending up at the Actors Studio. His stage debut came in 1947 with a small part in *The Trial of Mary Dugan*, and in 1951 he made his Broadway debut in a revival of *Night Music*. His film debut was also in 1951, in *Teresa*. Most of Steiger's work between 1948 and 1953 was in live television dramas, however; he appeared in more than 250 productions, most notably as the title character in the original TV version of *Marty*. That performance made him a TV star and helped him land one of his most memorable film parts—Charley Malloy, Marlon Brando's character's older brother, in *On the Waterfront* (1954)—and his first Oscar nomination, for best supporting actor. Among the roles that followed were Jud Fry in *Oklahoma!* (1955); a tyrannical film producer in *The Big Knife* (1955); a haunted survivor of the Holocaust in *The Pawnbroker* (1964), the role he considered his finest and one that gained him a second Oscar nomination, this time for best actor; the outrageous undertaker Mr. Joyboy in *The Loved One* (1965); and a serial killer with a flair for disguise in *No Way to Treat a Lady* (1968). Most of Steiger's later work was not considered to have been as accomplished or as successful, however.

Stone, W(illiam) Clement, American businessman and philanthropist (b. May 4, 1902, Chicago, Ill.—d. Sept. 3, 2002, Evanston, Ill.), made a fortune in insurance but became better known for promoting his philosophy of success and for his support of political and social causes. He espoused what he called P.M.A. (positive mental attitude) as the key to achievement and wealth. A major contributor to the 1968 and 1972 presidential campaigns of Richard M. Nixon, he also supported philanthropic causes such as mental health and youth welfare. Following the Watergate Scandal (1972–75), Stone's large contributions to Nixon were sometimes cited as an example of the need for campaign finance reform. Stone's father died when he was three years old, leaving the family impoverished, and at the age of six the boy began selling newspapers. By age 13 he had his own newsstand, and three years later he moved to Detroit to help his mother in an insurance agency. He dropped out of school, although he later received a diploma from a YMCA high school. In 1922 he opened his own agency in Chicago, the Combined Insurance Company of America, selling accident and life insurance, and by 1930 he had employed some 1,000 agents across the U.S. Over the years he bought additional companies, merging them with Combined, and in 1982 he merged his company with the Ryan Insurance Group, renaming the new firm Aon Corp. in 1987. With Napoleon Hill he developed a lecture series and the magazine *Success Unlimited*, and the two also wrote the book *Success Through a Positive Mental Attitude* (1960).

Strummer, Joe (JOHN GRAHAM MELLOR), British punk rock star (b. Aug. 21, 1952, Ankara, Turkey—d. Dec. 22, 2002, Broomfield, Somerset, Eng.), gave voice to a generation of unrest as leader of the Clash, and the band's passionate, politicized sounds were due in large part to Strummer's commitment to a populist ideology. He formed his first rhythm and blues band, the 101ers, in 1974. Influenced by the Sex Pistols, Strummer converted to punk, and in 1976 he joined Mick Jones, Paul Simonon, and Terry Chimes to form the

© Ian Hodgson/Reuters 2002

Joe Strummer of the Clash

Clash. Their debut single, "White Riot," and eponymous first album (released in the U.K. in 1977) were tinny and cranked-up in volume and tempo, and their stage shows were spearheaded by Strummer's teeth-clenched, rawthroated singing. *London Calling* (1979) earned them a reputation as masters of a sophisticated, eclectic sound and was later named the best album of the 1980s by *Rolling Stone* magazine. *Combat Rock* (1982) featured the popular anthem "Rock the Casbah," but it was the beginning of the end for the group, which disbanded in 1985. In 1999 Strummer formed a new band, the Mescaleros. The Clash was slated to be inducted into the Rock and Roll Hall of Fame in 2003.

Svetlanov, Yevgeny Fyodorovich, Russian conductor, composer, and pianist (b. Sept. 6, 1928, Moscow, U.S.S.R.—d. May 3, 2002, Moscow, Russia), as artistic director and principal conductor of his country's State Symphony Orchestra for 35 years (1965–2000), was renowned for his sensitive interpretations of Russian/Soviet symphonic composers such as Tchaikovsky, Rachmaninoff, Mussorgsky, Scriabin, Prokofiev, Shostakovich, and Khachaturyan; he also championed Jewish and lesser-known contemporary composers, notably Nikolay Myaskovsky. He recorded extensively and in 1987 was the subject of a documentary film, *Dirizhor* ("The Conductor"). Svetlanov was awarded the Order of Lenin in 1978. In April 2000 he was dismissed from the State Symphony by the culture minister, reportedly for spending too much time performing abroad.

Sylbert, Richard, American motion picture production designer (b. April 16, 1928, Brooklyn, N.Y.—d. March 23, 2002, Woodland Hills, Calif.), won two Academy Awards for his design work on *Who's Afraid of Virginia Woolf?* (1966) and *Dick Tracy* (1990) and received Academy Award nominations for his work on four other films, *Chinatown* (1974), *Shampoo* (1975), *Reds* (1981), and *The Cotton Club* (1984). From 1975 to 1978 he was the head of film production at Paramount Pictures—the first production designer ever to hold that position at a major Hollywood studio.

Talmadge, Herman Eugene, American politician (b. Aug. 9, 1913, McRae, Ga.—d. March 21, 2002, Hampton, Ga.), as governor of Georgia from 1948 to 1955 and U.S. senator from 1957 to 1981, evolved from an ardent foe of desegregation to a politician whose efforts to help expand school-lunch and food-stamp programs drew strong support from rural African Americans in his home state. Talmadge's entry into politics was a tumultuous one. His father, Eugene, was a three-term governor of Georgia who died after being reelected in 1946. In a highly controversial move, Talmadge persuaded the state legislature to allow him to succeed his father, but the State Supreme Court ruled that the office should go to Lieut. Gov. M.E. Thompson. Two years later Talmadge defeated Thompson in a special election, and he went on to win a full four-year term in 1950. He

vociferously opposed the 1954 U.S. Supreme Court ruling that outlawed school segregation, but his opposition to racial integration gradually waned over the years. As chairman of the Senate Agriculture Committee, Talmadge engineered passage of the Rural Development Act of 1972, which brought jobs and much-needed infrastructure to rural areas. Talmadge's political career ended in disgrace, however, after the Senate denounced him for financial irregularities that included pocketing cash from supporters. He lost his bid for reelection in 1980.

Tam, Roman (TAM PAK-SIN), Chinese pop musician (b. 1949, Guangxi Zhuang, China—d. Oct. 18, 2002, Hong Kong), was a flamboyant showman with an androgynous persona and a campy style who was a star for three decades; because of his influence on younger musicians, he became known as the "godfather" of Hong Kong music. He founded the band Roman and the Four Steps, which made its debut in 1967 and whose hits included "The Price of Love," and his 1970s recording of theme music from Hong Kong television programs was enormously popular. Although he originally sang in English, after a period in Japan in the mid-1970s he began performing in Cantonese, in what was called "Canto-pop." In all, he made 56 albums.

Taylor, Fred, American basketball coach (b. Dec. 3, 1924, Zanesville, Ohio—d. Jan. 6, 2002, Hilliard, Ohio), was the longtime head basketball coach at Ohio State University; during his tenure at the university from 1958 to 1976, Ohio State won the National Collegiate Athletic Association championship in 1960 and reached the title game the following two seasons. Taylor was named Collegiate Coach of the Year twice, in 1961 and 1962. His Ohio State teams won seven Big Ten championships and compiled a 297–158 record. Taylor was elected to the National Basketball Hall of Fame in 1986.

Thaw, John Edward, British actor (b. Jan. 3, 1942, Manchester, Eng.—d. Feb. 21, 2002, Luckington, Wiltshire, Eng.), was a respected actor who starred in several British television series but achieved international recognition for one of his roles—the crusty, cerebral Chief Inspector Morse, the title character in a series of 33 two-part dramas based on the novels of British detective writer Colin Dexter. Thaw trained at the Royal Academy of Dramatic Arts and made his professional stage debut in 1960 at the Liverpool Playhouse. He played a police sergeant on the TV series *Redcap* in the 1960s and became a star in the '70s as the tough Detective Inspector Jack Regan on *The Sweeney*. *Inspector Morse* dramas were broadcast intermittently starting with "The Dead of Jericho" in January 1987 (first broadcast in the U.S. in 1988). The final episode, "Remorseful Day," which featured Morse's death, aired in 2000. Thaw's other popular TV roles included a divorced father in the comedy series *Home to Roost* (1985–89), a sympathetic barrister in *Kavanaugh QC* (1994–99), and a Roman Catholic priest in Nazi-

TV's popular Inspector Morse, John Thaw

occupied France in *Monsignor Renard* (1999). He won two BAFTAs for best actor (1989 and 1992) and was nominated for best supporting actor for the 1986 film *Cry Freedom*. Thaw was made CBE in 1993 and was awarded a BAFTA for lifetime achievement in 2001.

Thom, René Frédéric, French mathematical philosopher (b. Sept. 2, 1923, Montbéliard, France—d. Oct. 25, 2002, Bures-sur-Yvette, France), was awarded the Fields Medal in 1958 for his work in topology, notably for his introduction of the concept of cobordism for classifying differentiable manifolds. He was better known, however, for his development of catastrophe theory, which he introduced in 1972 to explain biological growth and differentiation—in particular, how slow, continuous growth may lead to a sudden ("catastrophic") change in form. Catastrophe theory became something of a fad as others tried to apply the concept to different disciplines, such as sociology and economics. Thom wrote on topology, linguistics, philosophy, and theoretical biology, as well as catastrophe theory. He was elected to the French Academy of Sciences and was made a knight in the Legion of Honour.

Thomas, (Rex) David ("Dave"), American businessman (b. July 2, 1932, Atlantic City, N.J.—d. Jan. 8, 2002, Fort Lauderdale, Fla.), was the founder (1969) of the Wendy's fast-food restaurants and built the company into the world's third largest hamburger

chain, with more than 6,000 locations; to the general public, however, he was the folksy, avuncular Wendy's pitchman in more than 800 TV commercials. An adoptee himself, Thomas sought to help find homes and families for children without them and created the non-profit Dave Thomas Foundation for Adoption.

Thompson, Benjamin C., American architect (b. July 3, 1918, St. Paul, Minn.—d. Aug. 17, 2002, Cambridge, Mass.), was best known for having created the marketplace at Faneuil Hall (1976) in Boston and similar vibrant public spaces in Baltimore, Md., and Washington, D.C. A lover of cities and the spaces in which people gather, he designed his first "festival marketplace" in an effort to revitalize the urban landscape. Although criticized as conservative and homogenous by detractors, the style became immensely popular and was often repeated. Thompson's approach to architecture carried over to interior design in the offerings found at his Design Research International stores. He won the Gold Medal of the American Institute of Architects in 1992.

Thompson, J(ohn) Lee, British-born film director (b. Aug. 1, 1914, Bristol, Gloucestershire, Eng.—d. Aug. 30, 2002, Sooke, B.C.), achieved international fame with *The Guns of Navarone* (1961), which exemplified his acute visual style and use of suspenseful narrative. Thompson, who was sometimes billed as J. Lee-Thompson, began his film career as an actor and screenwriter, and the first movie he directed, *Murder Without Crime* (1950), was based on his own play. He made a succession of films in Britain, including the thriller *Tiger Bay* (1959). *The Guns of Navarone* brought him to the attention of Hollywood, and he was nominated for an Academy Award. His first Hollywood production, *Cape Fear* (1962), was considered by many to be his last great work.

Thyssen-Bornemisza de Kaszon, Hans Heinrich, Baron, Dutch-born Swiss industrialist and art collector (b. April 13, 1921, Scheveningen, Neth.—d. April 27, 2002, Sant Feliu de Guixols, Spain), amassed one of the world's most extensive and valuable private art collections while expanding his family's World War II-ravaged business conglomerate into a multibillion-dollar global empire. Thyssen-Bornemisza was put in charge of his father's German-based companies in 1944. When his father died (1947), Thyssen-Bornemisza inherited the title (derived from his maternal grandfather), the badly damaged business holdings, and a share of his father's art collection, much of which had been acquired for bargain prices during the Depression. Thyssen-Bornemisza quickly gained a reputation as a sharp businessman, a society jet-setter, and a voracious collector. When the Swiss government refused to finance expansion of the family's private museum at Villa Favorita on Lake Lugano, he sought a new home for his vast accumulation, which ranged from medieval tapestries to modern sculpture and included hundreds of priceless paintings by diverse artists. In 1988, despite heated bids

from several other countries, he negotiated a controversial deal with Spain (the homeland of his fifth wife). The Spanish government agreed to purchase the majority of the collection for a reported $350 million, a fraction of its true value. In 1992 the Thyssen-Bornemisza Museum, housing more than 800 artworks, opened to the public in Madrid.

Tjapaltjarri, Clifford Possum, Australian Aboriginal artist (b. 1932?, Napperby Station, outside Alice Springs, Northern Territory, Australia—d. June 21, 2002, Alice Springs), painted some of the earliest and most admired acrylic dot paintings in the modern Aboriginal art movement; most of his powerful, richly coloured art was inspired by Aboriginal mythology known as the Dreaming, or Dreamtime. Tjapaltjarri worked as a cattle stockman from the age of 12, wood carving in his free time, until he joined an art program at the Papunya mission in the 1960s. In 1972 the students there formed a company, Papunya Tula Artists, and Tjapaltjarri's intricate paintings gained attention. In 1983 he was awarded the Alice Springs Art Prize, and the National Gallery of Australia purchased his massive 3.7×2.4-m (12×8-ft) painting *Honey Ant Eater*. Five years later the Institute of Contemporary Arts in London mounted a retrospective of his works. Tjapaltjarri was made an Officer of the Order of Australia just days before his death.

To Huu (Nguyen Kim Thanh), Vietnamese poet and politician (b. 1920, Hue, Vietnam, French Indochina—d. Dec. 9, 2002, Hanoi, Vietnam), was hailed as North Vietnam's poet laureate and inspired generations of fellow Communist Party members with his popular propagandistic verse. An early convert to communism, he was arrested in 1939 for his political activities but escaped from prison in 1942 and joined the Viet Minh. To Huu was already known as a gifted lyricist when Vietnam was split in 1954, and he was appointed deputy culture minister in North Vietnam, in charge of ensuring that artists stayed in line with party beliefs. He was quickly named to the Central Committee of the Vietnamese Communist Party, and in the ensuing years he penned many verses exhorting people to rise up and embrace violence for the communist cause. To Huu became deputy prime minister in 1980 but fell from grace when he was blamed for the ill-fated economic reforms of 1985; he stepped down the following year.

Tobin, James, American economist (b. March 5, 1918, Champaign, Ill.—d. March 11, 2002, New Haven, Conn.), was awarded the Nobel Prize for Economics in 1981 for his portfolio selection theory—a theoretical formulation of investment behaviour that offered valuable insight into financial markets. After serving in the U.S. Navy during World War II, Tobin taught economics at Harvard University from 1946 to 1950 and earned a Ph.D. there in 1947. In 1950 he joined the faculty of Yale University, where he was appointed professor in 1955; he worked at Yale until his retirement in 1988. Tobin, perhaps the most prominent American supporter of the theories of British economist John Maynard Keynes, argued that monetary policy was particularly effective in the area of capital investment and that interest rates were an important factor in capital investment but not the only one. His portfolio selection theory explained the tendency of individuals to distribute their wealth among different investments. Tobin served for two years on the Council of Economic Advisers under Pres. John F. Kennedy. He also served as an adviser to Democratic presidential candidate George McGovern in 1972. That year his proposal for a tax on foreign-exchange transactions attracted wide attention; the "Tobin tax" was later championed by antiglobalization activists, though Tobin himself, an ardent supporter of free trade, repudiated them.

Todd, Sir (Reginald Stephen) Garfield, New Zealand-born politician (b. July 13, 1908, Invercargill, N.Z.—d. Oct. 13, 2002, Bulawayo, Zimb.), served from 1953 to 1958 as prime minister of the Federation of Rhodesia and Nyasaland (now divided into Zimbabwe, Zambia, and Malawi). In 1934 Todd went as a missionary to Southern Rhodesia, where he ran a mission and helped build clinics and schools, among them a teaching school for blacks where many of Zimbabwe's future leaders were educated. Todd was first elected to Parliament in 1946. He was elected prime minister in 1953 and supported independence from Great Britain. Although he opposed giving the vote to all people, his push to grant suffrage to educated blacks provoked his cabinet to resign, and he failed to secure a second term. In the 1960s Todd joined forces with black nationalists against Prime Minister Ian Smith, and he was repeatedly placed under house arrest. When Mugabe came to power in 1980, he appointed Todd to the Senate, but the elder statesman eventually spoke out against the corruption in his former ally's administration and left the post five years later. Todd was knighted in 1986. Just before the 2002 elections, he was stripped of his Zimbabwean citizenship.

Took, Barry, British stand-up comic and comedy writer (b. June 19, 1928, London, Eng.—d. March 31, 2002, London), wrote zany, anarchic comedy shows for BBC radio and television—including *Round the Horne, Educating Archie, The Army Game, Bootsie and Snudge,* and *The Goodies*—often in collaboration with his longtime partner, comedian Marty Feldman; in 1969 Took persuaded the BBC to hire six young comedy writers for a new show he had originally conceived as Baron Von Took's Flying Circus but that was ultimately dubbed *Monty Python's Flying Circus.*

Torres, Beatriz Mariana ("LOLITA"), Argentine actress (b. March 26, 1930,

Avellaneda, Arg.—d. Sept. 14, 2002, Buenos Aires, Arg.), gained renown and the admiration of international audiences for her roles in musical comedies, which showcased her fine singing voice. Her popularity was due in part to the balance of tradition and independence her roles offered to a changing Argentine society. Her first film, *La danza de la fortuna* (1944), was followed by starring roles in 16 other productions, including *La edad del amor* (1954), which enjoyed immense popularity in the Soviet Union. She retired from film in 1972.

Trigère, Pauline, French-born American fashion designer (b. 1908, Paris, France—d. Feb. 13, 2002, New York, N.Y.), was prominent in the world of fashion for some half a century and had a celebrity-laden list of clients. She was noted both for her elegant designs and for her outspokenness, and she was the first major designer to employ an African American model. Trigère won numerous fashion awards during her career and in December 2001 received the French Legion of Honour.

Tshwete, Stephen Vukile, South African activist and politician (b. Nov. 12, 1938, Springs, S.Af.—d. April 26, 2002, Pretoria, S.Af.), was political commissioner of Umkhonto we Sizwe ("Spear of the Nation"), the military wing of the antiapartheid African National Congress, and a member of the ANC national executive committee; he later held cabinet posts under Presidents Nelson Mandela and Thabo Mbeki. Tshwete spent 15 years (1964–79) in prison and 5 years (1985–90) in exile before being named (1994) minister of sports and recreation in Mandela's first postapartheid administration. Tshwete's success in developing sports opportunities for young blacks brought him considerable attention, and in 1999 Mbeki appointed him minister of safety and security, with responsibility for reforming the national police force.

Tutte, William Thomas, British-born Canadian mathematician (b. May 14, 1917, Newmarket, Suffolk, Eng.—d. May 2, 2002, Waterloo, Ont.), deciphered a crucial clue to the Nazis' so-called Tunny code as a member of the secret code-breaking team at Britain's Bletchley Park during World War II. Tutte studied chemistry at Trinity College, Cambridge, where, as a member of the Trinity Mathematical Society, he helped solve the long-standing mathematical puzzle of how to subdivide a square into smaller, unequally sized squares. Working at Bletchley Park from May 1941, Tutte applied a new idea on graph theory to work out on paper the fundamental pattern behind Tunny; this breakthrough and other complex algorithms he devised eventually contributed to the code-breaking Colossus computer. He was a fellow of the British Royal Society and the Canadian Royal Society and was awarded the Order of Canada in 2001.

Unitas, John Constantine ("JOHNNY"), American football player (b. May 7, 1933, Pittsburgh, Pa.—d. Sept. 11, 2002, Towson, Md.), was considered one of the greatest

NFL superhero Johnny Unitas

quarterbacks in the National Football League. Starting as a sandlot player in Pittsburgh, he was rejected for a scholarship to the University of Notre Dame owing to his small size, but he developed as a player at the University of Louisville, Ky. He was drafted by the Pittsburgh Steelers in 1955 but was released before playing a single game. He worked odd jobs and played semiprofessional football until 1957, when he took the position of backup quarterback with the Baltimore Colts, where he began his storied 18-year career, finishing it with the San Diego Chargers in 1972–74. His impressive career statistics (2,830 of 5,186 passing completions for 40,239 yd and 290 touchdowns) signaled the beginning of a new era in football as the focus switched from running to passing. Perhaps the highlight of his career was his 1958 championship overtime victory against the New York Giants in a game that reached legendary status. The Colts repeated the win the following year after Unitas threw for a single-season record of 32 touchdown passes. Distinguished by his close-cropped hair, high-top shoes, and stiff throwing style, he made his mark in the 1950s and '60s, once throwing touchdown passes in 47 consecutive games. Though the Colts lost the 1969 Super Bowl to the New York Jets in an upset led by quarterback Joe Namath, in 1971 Unitas returned to the title game with a victory over the Dallas Cowboys. A natural leader on the field who called his own plays, he was named Most Valuable Player three times, earned 10 Pro Bowl appearances, and was inducted into the Pro Football Hall of Fame in 1979. Though football injuries plagued him after retirement, he remained in the game as a mentor for younger players.

Unseld, Siegfried, German publisher (b. Sept. 28, 1924, Ulm, Ger.—d. Oct. 26, 2002, Frankfurt, Ger.), headed the literary giant Suhrkamp Verlag. Unseld took control of the publishing house when the founder died in 1959 and focused his energies on recruiting new talent, such as Uwe Johnson, as well as publishing the elite of German writers and philosophers, including Hesse, Bertolt Brecht, Theodor Adorno, and Jürgen Habermas. Unseld also published international authors in translation, notably Jacques Derrida, James Joyce, Marcel Proust, and Isabel Allende.

Urich, Robert, American actor (b. Dec. 19, 1946, Toronto, Ohio—d. April 16, 2002, Thousand Oaks, Calif.), was best remembered as the engaging star of the television series *Vega$* (1978–81) and *Spenser: For Hire* (1985–88). He also appeared in movies and TV miniseries, including *Lonesome Dove* (1989), and in 1992 won an Emmy Award for his narration of the documentary *U-Boats: Terror on Our Shores.*

Valentin, Barbara (USCHI LEDERSTEGER), German film actress (b. Dec. 15, 1940, Vienna, Austria—d. Feb. 22, 2002, Munich, Ger.), was dubbed the German Jayne Mansfield for her sexpot roles, beginning with the erotic thriller *Ein Toter hing im Netz* (1960; *A Corpse Hangs in the Web*, 1960). In the 1970s, however, she established a new career in character parts under the wing of director Rainer Werner Fassbinder. Valentin became involved in AIDS activism in the 1980s and was living with British rock singer Freddie Mercury at the time of his death from AIDS in 1991, after which she retired from public life.

Vallone, Raffaele, ("RAF"), Italian actor (b. Feb. 17, 1916, Tropea, Italy—d. Oct. 31, 2002, Rome, Italy), was one of the leading stars of Italian Neorealist films of the 1940s. Though an association football (soccer) player in his youth, he became a journalist and was discovered while researching *Riso amaro* (1949; *Bitter Rice*) for director Giuseppe De Santis, who offered him a part. Vallone became one of Italy's top draws, but when the Neorealist movement faded, he moved to France. He played the lead in a 1958 Parisian stage production of Arthur Miller's *A View from the Bridge,* for which he won great acclaim; he reprised the role in director Sidney Lumet's 1961 film version. A supporting role in *El Cid* (1961) landed Vallone a number of Hollywood jobs, in which he most often was typecast as a rugged Mediterranean. He continued to act until late in life—onstage, in movies, and in many Italian TV films.

Van Tien Dung, North Vietnamese general (b. May 1, 1917, Co Nhue, French Indochina—d. March 17, 2002, Hanoi, Vietnam), was one of North Vietnam's greatest war heroes—a peas-

ant soldier who rose to become commander in chief of the North Vietnamese army and lead the final Ho Chi Minh Campaign that captured and occupied Saigon, South Vietnam, in 1975. As a young man, Dung was arrested by French colonial authorities for his Communist Party activities, but he escaped from prison and in 1947 joined Gen. Vo Nguyen Giap's High Command staff. Despite his lack of military training and limited battlefield experience, Dung proved to be an able logistic planner. He was named chief of staff of the People's Army of Vietnam in 1953 and succeeded Giap as commander in chief in 1975. After the reunification of Vietnam, he served (1980–87) as defense minister.

Vance, Cyrus Roberts, American lawyer and statesman (b. March 27, 1917, Clarksburg, W.Va.—d. Jan. 12, 2002, New York, N.Y.), served as U.S. secretary of state from 1977 to 1980 during the administration of Pres. Jimmy Carter; in part to protest ill-fated plans

AP/Wide World Photos

American statesman Cyrus Vance

to rescue American hostages in Iran, Vance resigned his post, becoming only the third U.S. secretary of state to have done so. After graduating from Yale Law School in 1942 and serving in the navy during World War II, Vance practiced law in New York City. In 1957 he was appointed counsel for a Senate armed services subcommittee, and three years later he was named general counsel for the Department of Defense. He became secretary of the army in 1962, and a year later Pres. Lyndon B. Johnson named him deputy secretary of defense. Though initially a supporter of Johnson's escalation of the Vietnam War, Vance urged the president in 1968 to stop the bombing of North Vietnam. That year he helped prepare the first Vietnamese peace negotiations in Paris. After another stint in private law practice, he reentered public life when Carter selected him to head the State Department. Vance was an ardent advocate of détente with the Soviet Union, and he helped engineer the Camp David Accords between Egypt and Israel in 1978. He failed to negotiate the release of captive U.S. diplomats in

Iran in 1979–80, then resigned from the cabinet after Carter ignored his opposition to plans for a rescue mission that ultimately proved futile. Vance returned once again to private practice but in the early 1990s agreed to UN Secretary-General Javier Pérez de Cuéllar's request that he serve as a special envoy. He successfully brokered a cease-fire between Serbs and Croats in Croatia, but after his joint plan with European Union negotiator David Owen for a decentralized Bosnian federation was rejected, Vance retired.

Vavá (EDVALDO IZIDIO NETO), Brazilian footballer (b. Nov. 12, 1934, Recife, Braz.—d. Jan. 19, 2002, Rio de Janeiro, Braz.), was a powerful centre-forward, a pivotal member of Brazil's national team, and one of only three association football (soccer) players to score in two World Cup finals. In 22 international matches for Brazil, he scored 14 goals, including 5 in the 1958 World Cup (2 in the final against Sweden) and 4 in the 1962 World Cup (one in the final against Czechoslovakia). Vavá played professionally in Brazil, Spain, Mexico, and the U.S. After retiring as a player, he became a professional manager; he was Brazil's assistant coach at the 1982 World Cup.

Villas Bôas, Orlando, Brazilian explorer and Indian rights activist (b. Jan. 12, 1914, near Botucatu, Braz.—d. Dec. 12, 2002, São Paulo, Braz.), was a leading advocate of the rights of indigenous Brazilians. In the early 1940s Villas Bôas, along with three of his brothers, joined a government expedition to chart areas for future development in the Amazon and central-western Brazil. Over the next two decades, the brothers established Western civilization's first contact with numerous indigenous tribes. In 1961 Villas Bôas helped found Xingu National Park, a preserve for Brazil's Indians, including the Tchikao, who were threatened with extinction. He served as the park's first director. With his brother Claudio, Villas Bôas wrote 12 books, and the two were twice nominated for the Nobel Prize for Peace, in 1971 and again in 1975.

Voulkos, Peter, American ceramics artist (b. Jan. 29, 1924, Bozeman, Mont.—d. Feb. 16, 2002, Bowling Green, Ohio), helped the craft of pottery gain acceptance as an art form through his creation of ceramic works that were highly esteemed for their originality. His ceramic pieces—many of which were created spontaneously—were often tall, craggy forms whose rough-edged surfaces had been torn, punctured, or slashed. Voulkos taught at the Los Angeles County Art Institute from 1954 to 1959 and at the University of California, Berkeley, from 1959 to 1985; he established ceramics departments at both institutions. He won the Rodin Museum Prize at the first Paris Biennale in 1959 and was the winner of a Guggenheim fellowship in 1984.

Vu Ngoc Nha, Vietnamese spy (b. 1924, Thai Binh, French Indochina—d. Aug. 7, 2002, Ho Chi Minh City, Vietnam), served as a trusted adviser to two presidents of South Vietnam while simultaneously leaking information to the Viet Cong and their communist allies in the north. Nha was initially instructed to infiltrate South Vietnam in 1955, and he became a top aide to Presidents Ngo Dinh Diem and Nguyen Van Thieu. He was arrested in 1969 after a U.S. Central Intelligence Agency probe and was sentenced to life in prison, along with South Vietnam's political affairs assistant, Huynh Van Trong, who had been one of his major sources of information. Maj. Gen. Nha was returned to North Vietnam in 1973 in a prisoner exchange and released.

Waldron, Malcolm Earl ("MAL"), American jazz musician (b. Aug. 16, 1925, New York, N.Y.—d. Dec. 2, 2002, Brussels, Belg.), played piano in a rhythmically intense style that focused tightly on subtle thematic development, using spare, blues-oriented harmonies and ingeniously spaced phrases. He accompanied John Coltrane, Gene Ammons, Jackie McLean, and other stars on many recordings and played in important Billie Holiday, Charles Mingus, and Eric Dolphy groups before moving to Europe in 1965. He then enjoyed a unique freelance career as soloist and also worked with a parade of American and European improvisers, for his provocative interplay was suited to both bop and free jazz.

Walter, Fritz, German association football (soccer) player (b. Oct. 31, 1920, Kaiserslautern, Ger.—d. June 17, 2002, Enkenbach-Alsenborn, Ger.), was the captain and chief playmaker of West Germany's victorious World Cup side in 1954; it was the first time that a German team had won that trophy, and

German footballer Fritz Walter

© Hulton Getty/Getty Images

138

the triumphant players were feted as national heroes. He was recalled again, at age 37, for the 1958 World Cup finals, but West Germany lost in the semifinals. Walter made his league debut in 1938 with FC Kaiserslautern and first played for Germany in 1940. During World War II he served as a paratrooper and spent time in a Soviet labour camp. After the war he twice led his old team to the West German championship (1951 and 1953). When he retired in 1959, Walter had scored 33 goals in 61 appearances for his country, as well as 306 goals in 379 matches for Kaiserslautern. In 1985 the stadium in Kaiserslautern was named after him, and in 1999 he was voted a member of Germany's Team of the Century.

Walters, Vernon Anthony, American diplomat and military officer (b. Jan. 3, 1917, New York, N.Y.—d. Feb. 10, 2002, West Palm Beach, Fla.), served as U.S. ambassador to the UN from 1985 to 1988 and as U.S. ambassador to West Germany from 1989 to 1991; fluent in numerous languages, he also served as an interpreter to five U.S. presidents. Walters began a 35-year military career when he joined the U.S. Army in 1941. After working as an interpreter for Pres. Harry Truman at several post–World War II summits, Walters was frequently used in that capacity during top-level diplomatic meetings for the remainder of his career. From 1956 to 1960 he was a staff aide to Pres. Dwight Eisenhower. During Richard Nixon's administration, Walters helped Secretary of State Henry Kissinger conduct secret negotiations with the North Vietnamese prior to the U.S. withdrawal from Vietnam. As deputy director of the Central Intelligence Agency from 1972 to 1976, Walters reportedly refused repeated White House requests to use CIA funds to pay off Watergate burglars. Although Walters retired from the army with the rank of lieutenant general in 1976 and for a time worked as a private security consultant, he was called back into public service during the administration of Ronald Reagan. He was ambassador at large before succeeding Jeane Kirkpatrick as ambassador to the UN.

Wand, Günter, German conductor (b. Jan. 7, 1912, Elberfeld, Ger.—d. Feb. 14, 2002, Ulmiz, Switz.), was notable for his rigorous rehearsals and his strong interpretations of the Austro-German Romantic repertory, notably the symphonies of Beethoven, Brahms, Bruckner, and Schubert. Wand spent most of his career in Cologne, as principal conductor of the Cologne Opera from 1938 until 1944, when the opera house was destroyed in an Allied bombing raid, and again from 1945 to 1948 and as music director of the Gürzenich Orchestra from 1947 until he officially retired in 1974. He was also the city's general music

director and, from 1982, director of the North German Radio Symphony Orchestra.

Warfield, William Caesar, American concert and opera singer (b. Jan. 22, 1920, West Helena, Ark.—d. Aug. 25, 2002, Chicago, Ill.), had a powerful warm and elegant bass-baritone voice that he employed to dramatic effect in the concert hall, on the opera and

AP/Wide World Photos

Distinguished bass-baritone William Warfield

musical theatre stage, on recordings, on television, and in film. He was best known for his portrayal of Porgy in countless productions of *Porgy and Bess* and for his heartfelt rendition of "Ol' Man River" in the film *Show Boat* (1951), a song that became his trademark. Warfield, having won (1938) first prize—and thus a scholarship to any American university—in a competition held by the National Music Educators League, earned (1942) a bachelor's degree at the Eastman School of Music, Rochester, N.Y. He then saw service in World War II as an intelligence officer in the army. Because concert and opera career opportunities for black singers were limited, Warfield originally planned to be a music teacher. Warfield toured with the road company of *Call Me Mister* in 1946–47 and made his first Broadway appearances in the drama *Set My People Free* (1947) and the opera *Regina* (1948–49), but it was the acclaim following his recital debut (1950) at New York City's Town Hall that really launched his career, gaining him a concert tour of Australia in 1950 and then the role of Joe in *Show Boat.* His career highlights included a multitude of performances as a soloist in concerts, on television and radio, and with symphonies; his portrayal of De Lawd in a 1957 TV production of *Green Pastures;* several stage productions of *Show Boat;* and narration of Aaron Copland's *A Lincoln Portrait,* a recording of which won him a Grammy Award in 1984.

center: Dmitri Kessel/TimePix

Warhaftig, Zerach, Israeli rabbi, lawyer, and politician (b. Feb. 2, 1906, Volkovysk, Russian Empire (now in Belarus)—d. Sept. 26, 2002, Jerusalem, Israel), was one of the 37 signatories to the Israeli Declaration of Independence in 1948 and founder (1956) of the National Religious Party. He was an influential member of the Knesset (parliament) from 1949 to 1981. As deputy minister (in the 1950s) and then minister (1961–74) of religious affairs, Warhaftig created Israel's rabbinical court system, established legislation making the observance of Jewish holidays and dietary laws compulsory, and provided exemption from military service for Talmudic religious students. He supported rights for non-Jewish Israelis, however, and in 1967 he drafted an edict providing for religious autonomy and protecting Muslim and Christian as well as Jewish holy sites.

Wasserman, Lewis Robert ("Lew"), American film and record company executive (b. March 15, 1913, Cleveland, Ohio—d. June 3, 2002, Beverly Hills, Calif.), exerted enormous power and influence in the entertainment industry for more than four decades and was said to have been the last of the movie moguls. As president and then chairman of his company, Music Corporation of America, from a talent agency into a complex empire that encompassed film, television, radio, and record production and thereby revolutionized the industry. Wasserman was honoured with the Jean Hersholt Humanitarian Award in 1973 and the Presidential Medal of Freedom in 1995.

Weaver, Sylvester Laflin, Jr. ("Pat"), American television executive (b. Dec. 21, 1908, Los Angeles, Calif.—d. March 15, 2002, Santa Barbara, Calif.), revolutionized television programming by shifting the production of shows from the sponsors to the networks, with commercial time then sold to sponsors. He served as president of NBC from 1949 to 1955, during which time he created the *Today* and *Tonight* shows and commissioned live TV specials, including *Peter Pan* and *Amahl and the Night Visitors*, before being "kicked upstairs" in a power struggle. Weaver, the father of actress Sigourney Weaver, won two Emmy Awards (1967 and 1983) and was inducted into the Television Academy of Arts and Sciences Hall of Fame (1985).

Webster, Michael Lewis ("Mike"), American football player (b. March 18, 1952, Tomahawk, Wis.—d. Sept. 24, 2002, Pittsburgh, Pa.), anchored a formidable offensive line that helped the Pittsburgh Steelers win four Super Bowl championships in the 1970s. A graduate of the University of Wisconsin whose smallish stature belied his strength, he was regarded as one of the best centres in the game. He was elected to the Pro Bowl nine times with the Steelers (1974–88), but he completed his career with the Kansas City Chiefs (1989–90). The relentless beating he received without complaint during his playing days was believed to have left him brain damaged, and following his retirement he suffered many health and personal problems. Webster was inducted into the Pro Football Hall of Fame in 1997.

Weinstock of Bowden, Arnold Weinstock, Baron, British industrialist (b. July 29, 1924, London, Eng.—d. July 23, 2002, Bowden Hill, Wiltshire, Eng.), led the U.K.'s General Electric Co. (GEC) as managing director for more than three decades (1963–96); his stern management and conservative tactics evoked strong praise as well as fierce criticism. Before his tenure at GEC, Weinstock was managing director of Radio and Allied Industries (later Radio and Allied Holdings), his father-in-law's radio and television business. In 1961 he became a director of GEC, of which he and his father-in-law were the highest shareholders. Known as an uncompromising but honest leader, Weinstock turned GEC into the largest industrial conglomerate in Britain. Critics deemed him overly careful, however, citing his failure to invest shareholders' money in newer developments as evidence of out-of-date strategies. Weinstock was knighted in 1970 and made a life peer in 1980.

Weisskopf, Victor Frederick, Austrian-born American physicist (b. Sept. 19, 1908, Vienna, Austria—d. April 21, 2002, Newton, Mass.), worked on the Manhattan Project to develop the atomic bomb during World War II; he later became a noted campaigner against the prolifer-

ation of nuclear weapons. After earning a Ph.D. in physics from the University of Göttingen, Ger., in 1931, Weisskopf studied under Niels Bohr at the University of Copenhagen. In 1937 he moved to the U.S. to escape Nazism. He went to work at the Los Alamos (N.M.) National Laboratory, where he served on the Manhattan Project as associate head of the theory division. After the war he helped found the Federation of Atomic Scientists, which advocated arms control and warned of the dangers of nuclear war. In 1946 Weisskopf was named professor of physics at the Massachusetts Institute of Technology (MIT), where he worked until 1960. Much of his postwar research involved the study of the behaviour of atomic nuclei. From 1961 to 1965 Weisskopf was director general of CERN (the European Organization for Nuclear Research). He returned to MIT in 1965 and served as head of the physics department until he retired from the university in 1973.

Weitz, John (Hans Werner Weitz), German-born American fashion designer, novelist, and historian (b. May 25, 1923, Berlin, Ger.—d. Oct. 3, 2002, Bridgehampton, N.Y.), enhanced his renown as a menswear designer—and greatly increased his income—when he became one of the first to lend his name to the licensing of products. The wide variety of items sold under his name included men's cologne, neckties, umbrellas, sunglasses, sweaters, and socks—especially the John Weitz Classic Men's Sock 12-pack.

Wellstone, Paul David, American teacher and politician (b. July 21, 1944, Washington, D.C.—d. Oct. 25, 2002, near Eveleth, Minn.), was a U.S. senator from Minnesota from 1991 to his death. Often referred to as the most liberal member of the Senate, he was respected as a man of principle who did not forsake his convictions for political expediency. Wellstone's father was an immigrant Russian Jew, and his mother was the daughter of Russian immigrants. He was educated in political science at the University of North Carolina at Chapel Hill (B.A., 1965; Ph.D., 1969) and then began teaching at Carleton College, Northfield, Minn., where his involvement in political causes sometimes created problems with the school administration. In 1990 he was the candidate of the Democratic-Farmer-Labor Party for the U.S. Senate and, with only a small amount of money, pulled off a surprise victory over the incumbent. Over the years he worked with senators whose views were far to the right of his, but he consistently championed the interests of the poor, farmers, and union workers against large banks, agribusinesses, and multinational corporations. Among other things, he advocated increases in the minimum wage, protections for consumers, the strengthening of Social Security, and the expansion of Medicare to include drug benefits, and he pushed for mental health coverage by insurance companies. In 1990–91 Wellstone opposed the Persian Gulf War, and he was one of a small minority of senators who in 2002 voted against giving Pres. George W. Bush authorization for military action against Iraq. Along with his wife, daughter, three campaign aides, and two pilots, he was killed in a plane crash 11 days before the 2002 election.

Werner, Pierre, Luxembourgian politician (b. Dec. 29, 1913, near Lille, France—d. June 24, 2002, Luxembourg), was hailed as the "father of the euro"; he used his position as prime minister of Luxembourg from 1959 to 1974 and again from 1979 to 1984 to lead the campaign for a single European currency, which he dubbed the "euror" and first publicly advocated in 1960. In 1970 he was chairman of the European Economic Community committee that presented the Werner Report, an official blueprint for a monetary union of the EEC's six members. A single monetary system finally took effect in 11 of the 15 members of the European Union in 1999, and a new currency, the euro, was introduced to the general public in 12 member states in January 2002. Werner, who was a member of the centre-right

© Reuters Raymond/Corbis Sygma

The father of the euro, Pierre Werner

Christian Social People's Party, also built Luxembourg into one of Europe's most successful financial centres.

Weston, Garfield Howard ("GARRY"), Canadian-born entrepreneur and philanthropist (b. April 28, 1927, Canada—d. Feb. 15, 2002, London, Eng.), took control of his family's multinational business, Associated British Foods PLC (ABF), upon his father's retirement in 1967 and turned it into a vast international conglomerate with annual sales of £4.4 billion (about $6.4 billion). Weston's grandfather, the son of British immigrants to Canada, built a thriving bakery business there; his father, Willard Garfield Weston, returned (1931) the family to England, where he introduced presliced packaged bread and eventually expanded the company to include Twinings tea, Loblaws supermarkets (in Canada), and Fortnum & Mason's department stores. Garry Weston joined the firm in 1951, founded and was managing director (1954–67) of an Australian subsidiary, the Weston Biscuit Co., and then served as ABF chairman from 1967 until his own retirement in 2000.

Whalen, Philip Glenn, American poet, writer, and Buddhist monk (b. Oct. 20, 1923, Portland, Ore.—d. June 26, 2002, San Francisco, Calif.), was a member of the Beat movement of the 1950s and '60s. With Jack Kerouac, Allen Ginsberg, and others, he participated in the reading in 1955 at Six Gallery that came to be considered the beginning of the so-called San Francisco renaissance. Like the other Beats, Whalen favoured a free-flowing style and had an interest in Asian religions. His poetry was rarely political but rather dealt with aspects of everyday life, often with a light, whimsical touch. Whalen served in the U.S. Army Air Corps from 1943 to 1946 and then studied at Reed College, Portland, Ore., where he obtained a B.A. degree (1951) in literature and languages. At Reed he met the poets Gary Snyder and Lew Welch and began to pursue writing seriously. For much of the time between 1958 and 1971, Whalen lived in Japan, and in 1973 he was ordained a Zen Buddhist priest, taking the name Zenshin Ryufu. He spent most of the rest of his life in Buddhist centres in California and

New Mexico, with his work including care for AIDS patients. By the late 1980s he had lost his eyesight and had stopped writing. Among his early volumes were *Like I Say* and *Memoirs of an Interglacial Age,* both published in 1960 and both reflecting Beat life. These were followed by *Every Day* (1965), *On Bear's Head* (1969) and the collection *Decompressions: Selected Poems* (1978).

White, Byron Raymond ("WHIZZER"), American jurist and professional football player (b. June 8, 1917, Fort Collins, Colo.—d. April 15, 2002, Denver, Colo.), served as associate justice of the United States Supreme Court from 1962 to 1993. White achieved early fame on the gridiron—and acquired the nickname "Whizzer"—as a speedy halfback on the University of Colorado football team. After earning his bachelor's degree in 1938, he played one season for the Pittsburgh Pirates (now the Steelers), during which he led the National Football League in rushing. He then spent a year at the University of Oxford as a Rhodes scholar before returning to the U.S. to play two seasons with the Detroit Lions while attending Yale Law School. White graduated from Yale with a law degree in 1946. He clerked at the Supreme Court for Chief Justice Fred M. Vinson in 1946–47 and then worked as a corporate lawyer in Denver. In 1960 he was active in the presidential campaign of John F. Kennedy, with whom he had forged a close friendship years earlier, and in 1961 he was named deputy attorney general under the president's brother Robert Kennedy. The following year White became President Kennedy's first appointee to the Supreme Court. On civil rights issues White was generally viewed as liberal, though on social issues he was one of the court's more

Byron ("Whizzer") White

© Corbis

conservative voices. In two notable cases during his tenure—*Miranda* v. *Arizona* (1966), which required police officers to read criminal suspects their rights, and *Roe* v. *Wade* (1973), which established the constitutional right to abortion—White cast dissenting votes. He retired in 1993 and was replaced by Justice Ruth Bader Ginsberg.

Whitehead, Robert, Canadian-born theatrical producer (b. March 3, 1916, Montreal, Que.—d. June 15, 2002, Pound Ridge, N.Y.), was honoured with a special Tony Award in 2002 for his nearly 60 years of presenting serious dramas—works by modern playwrights in addition to the classics—on the Broadway stage and making them both artistically and financially successful. Among his more than 50 productions were a revival of *Medea* (1947), Carson McCullers's *The Member of the Wedding* (1950), William Inge's *Bus Stop* (1955), a revival of Arthur Miller's *Death of a Salesman* (1984), and Terrence McNally's *Master Class* (1996).

Wilder, Billy (SAMUEL WILDER), Austrian-born American film director and screenwriter (b. June 22, 1906, Sucha, Austria-Hungary [now in Poland]—d. March 27, 2002, Beverly Hills, Calif.), brought his wit and his cynical, satiric sensibility to more than 50 motion pictures in a number of genres, including film noir, drama, melodrama, slapstick, and black comedy. He counted six Academy Awards—three of them for one film, *The Apartment,* a unique achievement—among his numerous honours, and a number of his films came to be considered classics. Wilder attended the University of Vienna to study law but left after a short time and became a journalist, first in Vienna and then in Berlin. He branched out into ghostwriting silent-film scripts, gained his first credit as screenwriter for *Der Teufelsreporter* (1929), and found his first success with the semidocumentary *Menschen am Sonntag* (1929; *People on Sunday*). The rise to power of Adolf Hitler prompted Wilder, a Jew, to flee Germany and go to France, where he made his debut as a director with *Mauvaise graine* (1933; *Bad Blood,* or *Bad Seed,* 1934), and then to the U.S. Although Wilder knew only a few words of English when he first arrived in Hollywood, he persevered, and by 1938 he had begun a collaboration with Charles Brackett. Films they wrote during this partnership, which lasted until 1950, included *Ninotchka* (1939); *The Major and the Minor* (1942), Wilder's first Hollywood directorial effort; the film noir classic *Double Indemnity* (1944); *The Lost Weekend* (1945), for which Wilder won two Oscars; and *Sunset Boulevard* (1950), for which he won another Oscar. Following such films as *Stalag 17* (1953), *Sabrina* (1954), *The Seven Year Itch* (1955), and *Witness for the Prosecution* (1957). Wilder began a collaboration with I.A.L. ("Izzy") Diamond that endured from 1957 until 1981. Among the films they wrote together was one that many people think of as the all-time best comedy movie, the farce *Some Like It Hot* (1959); films that followed

Billy Wilder, "the director's director"

included *The Apartment* (1960), *One, Two, Three* (1961), *The Fortune Cookie* (1966), *The Private Life of Sherlock Holmes* (1970), and *Buddy Buddy* (1981). Among Wilder's honours were the American Film Institute Life Achievement Award (1986) and the Academy of Motion Picture Arts and Sciences' Irving G. Thalberg Memorial Award (1988).

Wilhelm, (James) Hoyt, American baseball player (b. July 26, 1923, Huntersville, N.C.—d. Aug. 23, 2002, Sarasota, Fla.), pitched knuckleballs that fluttered over the plate, baffling major league batters for 21 seasons. Unfortunately, his dancing pitch sometimes baffled his own catchers too, until Baltimore Orioles manager Paul Richards designed an oversized catcher's mitt to handle it. Altogether he pitched in 1,070 games—a record when he retired at the age of 48—and had an outstanding lifetime 2.52 earned run average, with 143 wins, 122 losses, and 227 saves. He pitched for nine teams but spent most of his years with the New York Giants, the Orioles, and the Chicago White Sox. In 1985 he became the first relief pitcher to be elected to the Baseball Hall of Fame.

Willey, Gordon Randolph, American archaeologist and writer (b. March 7, 1913, Chariton, Iowa—d. April 28, 2002, Cambridge, Mass.), expanded the study of ancient societies to include not only excavations of the tombs of the elite but also artifacts from the households of ordinary people. His field research on pre-Colombian societies, as well as such books as *Archeology of the Florida Gulf Coast* (1949), the two-volume *An Introduction to American Archaeology* (1966, 1971), and *A History of American Archaeology* (1974; with Jeremy Sabloff), established him as one of the most influential American archaeologists of his time.

Williams, Theodore Samuel ("TED"; "THE SPLENDID SPLINTER"), American baseball player (b. Aug. 30, 1918, San Diego, Calif.—d. July 5, 2002, Inverness, Fla.), was the last player in the 20th century to hit over .400 for a season. Williams burst into the American League in 1939, hitting .327 and leading the league with 145 runs batted in (RBIs); he went on to terrorize pitchers for 18 more full seasons while he played outfield for the Boston Red Sox. Sometimes called "the greatest hitter who ever lived," Williams was noted for his power and his clutch hitting—altogether he batted in a total of 1,839 runs—as well as for his irascibility; he spit at fans, refused to tip his cap to acknowledge applause, and maintained long feuds with Boston sportswriters. He had an intense rivalry with Yankees slugger Joe DiMaggio during the 1940s. Williams had a .406 average in 1941, but DiMaggio, who had a record 56-game hitting streak that year, was voted Most Valuable Player (MVP) instead; six years later DiMaggio again beat Williams for MVP, this time by one vote; nevertheless, DiMaggio called Williams "the best pure hitter I ever saw." Williams was raised by his mother, a Salvation Army worker, played sandlot baseball in San Diego, and at age 19 was signed by Red Sox general manager Eddie Collins, who admired Williams's smooth and powerful left-handed swing. By 1942 Williams led the league in the three major batting categories—average, home runs, and RBIs—a feat he repeated in 1947. He was a navy flight

Ted Williams, "The Splendid Splinter"

instructor during World War II and returned to baseball in 1946, when he led the Red Sox to an American League pennant. During the Korean War he flew combat missions as a marine pilot and was decorated for bravery. Williams had a lifetime batting average of .344, slugged 521 home runs, and had a .483 on-base average, the highest of any major-league player; he led the league in hitting six seasons, the last of them in 1958, when he was 40. Williams retired from playing in 1960. In

1969 he became manager of the Washington Senators, and he was named American League Manager of the Year in his first season; he continued to manage Washington for three more years. He wrote several books, including his autobiography, *My Turn at Bat* (1969; with John Underwood), and *The Science of Hitting* (1971; with John Underwood). After his death his heirs disputed in court whether to cremate his body, as his will directed, or to freeze it, as his son, John Henry Williams, requested.

Wilson, Sir Robert, British astrophysicist (b. April 16, 1927, South Shields, Durham, Eng.—d. Sept. 2, 2002, Chelmsford, Essex, Eng.), was the guiding force behind the International Ultraviolet Explorer (IUE) satellite, an Earth-orbiting astronomical observatory that was the forerunner of the Hubble Space Telescope. Wilson already was well known for his research in the optical spectroscopy of stars and solar plasma spectroscopy when in 1964 he was put in charge of a British team of scientists designing what came to be called the Ultraviolet Astronomical Satellite for the European Space Research Organization. When the project was abandoned in 1967, he submitted the idea to NASA, which spearheaded a collaborative project. The IUE satellite was launched in January 1978 for a three-year mission but collected valuable data for more than 18 years. Wilson served as head of spectroscopy (1962–68) and director of astrophysics research (1968–72) at Culham Laboratory (the U.K.'s atomic-energy research centre) and was Perren Professor of Astronomy at University College, London (1972–94). In 1987 he was granted the Science Award by the International Academy of Astronautics, and the next year he became the first non-American to receive a U.S. Presidential Award for Design Excellence. Wilson was a fellow of the Royal Society from 1975 and was knighted in 1989.

Winbergh, Gösta, Swedish opera singer (b. Dec. 30, 1943, Stockholm, Swed.—d. March 18, 2002, Vienna, Austria), abandoned a career in structural engineering for one in music and for almost 30 years was a leading tenor in most of the major opera houses across Europe and the U.S. Winbergh worked for his father's construction firm and sang part-time in a rock band before he entered the Stockholm Opera School at age 24. After making his professional debut in 1972, he was a principal tenor (1973–81) with the Royal Opera in Stockholm; he made his U.S. debut in 1974. As a young man, Winbergh specialized in lyrical roles, but he carefully nurtured his mature voice, and in the 1990s he excelled at powerful dramatic roles, including Wagner's Tristan and Parsifal.

Winship, Thomas, American newspaper editor (b. July 1, 1920, Cambridge, Mass.—d. March 14, 2002, Boston, Mass.), took over the post of *Boston Globe* editor from his father, Laurence Winship, in 1965 and served until 1984, raising the paper to the highest ranks and guiding it to 12 Pulitzer Prizes. As a result of his leadership of the *Globe*'s opposition to the Vietnam War and its coverage of school desegregation in the 1970s, the paper became renowned for outstanding international and investigative reporting.

Winterbottom, Sir Walter, British association football (soccer) manager and coach (b. March 31, 1913, Oldham, Lancashire, Eng.—d. Feb. 16, 2002, Guildford, Surrey, Eng.), was from 1946 to 1962 the first and longest-serving full-time manager of England's national football team as well as the Football Association's director of coaching. Winterbottom appeared in 25 matches for Manchester United (1934–37) until a spinal injury ended his playing career. After World War II service in the Royal Air Force, he was invited to become England's team manager despite having no managing experience. England qualified for all four World Cups held during Winterbottom's tenure but failed to advance past the quarterfinals. He retired in 1962 with an overall record of 79 wins, 28 losses, and 32 draws. He was made OBE in 1963, advanced to CBE in 1972, and knighted in 1978.

Wolde, Mamo (DEGAGA WOLDE), Ethiopian long-distance runner (b. June 12, 1932, Dirre Jille, Eth.—d. May 26, 2002, Addis Ababa, Eth.), became a national hero at the 1968 Olympic Games in Mexico City, where he unexpectedly captured the gold medal in the marathon and the silver in the 10,000 m. Wolde, who was participating in his third Olympics, won the marathon by more than two minutes in a time of 2 hr 20 min 26.4 sec. In the Munich, Ger., Games four years later, he won the bronze in the marathon at the record age of 40. Wolde, a former army sergeant, was arrested in 1993 on charges that in 1978 he had participated in the killing of a 15-year-old boy. He vehemently proclaimed his innocence, and his case drew

worldwide support from fellow Olympians and from the International Olympic Committee. Wolde finally was tried and convicted in early 2002, sentenced to six years, and released because he had already been in prison for nine years.

Wolstenholme, Kenneth, British sports commentator (b. July 17, 1920, Worsley, Lancashire [now in Greater Manchester], Eng.—d. March 25, 2002, Torquay, Devon, Eng.), covered more than 2,000 association football (soccer) matches, 23 FA Cup finals, and five World Cups between 1948 and 1971, when he was replaced as the BBC's chief commentator. He is best remembered, however, for having uttered one of the sport's most famous quotes; in the 1966 World Cup final match at Wembley Stadium, as English fans began to rush onto the field just as Geoff Hurst prepared to kick the final goal in England's 4–2 triumph over West Germany, Wolstenholme cried out, "Some people are on the pitch. They think it's all over. . . .It is now."

Worth, Irene (HARRIET ELIZABETH ABRAMS), American actress (b. June 23, 1915/16, Lincoln, Neb.—d. March 10, 2002, New York, N.Y.), had a distinguished half-century-long international career, especially on the New York City and London stages. Known for her elegance, her rich contralto voice, and her intelligent interpretation of roles, she shone in both classical and modern works. Worth spent five years as a teacher before moving to New York City and landing a part in the touring company of *Escape Me Never*. She made her Broadway debut in 1943 in *The Two Mrs. Carrolls* and then went to London to hone her acting skills. Worth first appeared in fringe theatres and found her breakthrough role in *The Cocktail Party*, first at the Edinburgh

Eliot Elisofon/TimePix

Grande dame of the theatre Irene Worth

Festival in 1949, returning with it to Broadway in 1950, and later that year taking over from the West End star. She then (1951) joined the Old Vic Company, where her early roles included Helena in *A Midsummer Night's Dream* (1951), Desdemona in *Othello* (1951), Portia in *The Merchant of Venice* (1953), and Lady Macbeth in *Macbeth* (1953), and became (1953) a founding member of the Shakespeare Festival Theatre at Stratford, Ont., and (1962) a member of England's Royal Shakespeare Company. On Broadway, Worth was especially celebrated for her Tony Award-winning roles in *Tiny Alice* (best actress, 1965), *Sweet Bird of Youth* (best actress, 1976), and *Lost in Yonkers* (best featured actress, 1991). Although Worth was primarily noted for her stage appearances, she also gained acclaim for her performances in a number of television productions and motion pictures, among them the films *Orders to Kill* (1958), *Nicholas and Alexandra* (1971), *Deathtrap* (1982), and *Lost in Yonkers* (1993). Worth was made an honorary CBE in 1975.

Wu Cheng-chung, Cardinal John Baptist, Chinese-born Roman Catholic prelate (b. March 26, 1925, Ho Hau, China—d. Sept. 23, 2002, Hong Kong), capably maneuvered the Roman Catholic Church through the transition period when Hong Kong was handed from British to Chinese control in 1997. Although Hong Kong's Chinese clergy balked at his appointment, his discretion and dedication aided the church's independence from Beijing authorities. Wu was ordained in 1952 and worked in the U.S. prior to being named bishop of Hong Kong in 1975. Sometimes criticized for failing to speak out openly on issues of social import, Wu did denounce the Tiananmen Square massacre and defended the rights of displaced children in Hong Kong.

Yampolsky, Mariana, American-born Mexican photographer (b. Sept. 6, 1925, Chicago,

Ethiopian marathoner Mamo Wolde

www.sporting-heros.net

Alicia Ahumada, author's personal collection

Photographer Mariana Yampolsky (right) with some Ecuadoran subjects

Ill.—d. May 3, 2002, Mexico City, Mex.), moved to Mexico as a young woman and spent half a century capturing idyllic, elegiac images of that country, its people, and its daily life. Her work was exhibited all over the world and included in a number of compilations.

Yanovsky, Zalman ("ZAL"), Canadian musician (b. Dec. 19, 1944, Toronto, Ont.—d. Dec. 13, 2002, Kingston, Ont.), was the extroverted lead guitarist of the popular 1960s rock group the Lovin' Spoonful, whose hits included "Do You Believe in Magic" (1965) and "Summer in the City" (1966). Controversy surrounding the aftermath of a marijuana-possession arrest, however, caused him to leave the band in 1967, and he eventually opened a restaurant and a bakery in Kingston. The Lovin' Spoonful was inducted into the Rock and Roll Hall of Fame in 2000.

Young of Dartington, Michael Dunlop Young, Baron, British lawyer, sociologist, and social reformer (b. Aug. 9, 1915, Manchester, Eng.—d. Jan. 14, 2002, London, Eng.), was best known for having written the Labour Party's 1945 social-welfare manifesto and for having coined the pejorative term *meritocracy* (in his 1958 satire *The Rise of the Meritocracy, 1870–2033*) to denounce the political and economic elite that he alleged used their own academic test-based success as justification for their treatment of the economic underclass, who did not have access to equivalent education. Young also founded (1956) the Consumers' Association, established the forerunner of the Open University (launched in 1964), and wrote influential sociological treatises, notably *Family and Kinship in East London* (1957; with Peter Willmott). He was created a baron in 1978.

Young of Farnworth, Janet Mary Baker Young, Baroness, British politician (b. Oct. 23, 1926, Widnes, Lancashire, Eng.—d. Sept.

6, 2002, Oxford, Eng.), was the first woman to serve as leader of the House of Lords; a committed conservative, she was perhaps best known for her zealous dedication to traditional family values and sexual morality, a stance that brought her heated criticism, especially from gay rights groups, late in her career. Young was a member of the Oxford City Council for 15 years, beginning in 1957. In 1971 she was awarded a life peerage by Prime Minister Edward Heath, and the following year she was made a Lords junior whip. In 1979 Young became minister of state at the Department of Education and Science; two years later Prime Minister Margaret Thatcher appointed her chancellor of the Duchy of Lancaster and leader of the House of Lords. Although Young became Lord Privy Seal in 1982, her tenure lasted only another year, after which Thatcher replaced her. Young was a deputy foreign minister from 1983 to 1987.

Zaid ibn Shaker, Jordanian military officer and government official (b. Sept. 4, 1934,

Jordanian official Zaid ibn Shaker

Thomas Hartwell/TimePix

Amman, Jordan—d. Aug. 30, 2002, Amman), held the top three appointed posts in his country—commander of the armed forces (1976–88), chief of the royal court (1988, 1989, and 1993), and prime minister (1989, 1991–93, and 1995–96). A lifelong adviser of King Hussein, Zaid was entrusted with commanding troops in the Six-Day War against Israel in 1967 and helped drive Yasir Arafat's Palestine Liberation Organization from Jordan in 1970. Many were skeptical of his conservative tendencies upon his appointment as prime minister, but Zaid proved to be a liberalizing force, implementing democratic elections, abolishing censorship, and lifting martial law. He also made amends with old foes, pushing for restoration of Palestinian rights and signing a cooperation agreement with Arafat in 1995. Zaid differed with Hussein on his support for Iraq, however, and was forced into a position as emir, which barred him from any further political posts.

Zildjian, Armand, American businessman (b. 1921, Milton, Mass.—d. Dec. 26, 2002, Scottsdale, Ariz.), headed Avedis Zildjian Co., the world's most famous cymbal company. He was heir to a remarkable musical and business legacy—his family had been making cymbals from a se-

cret alloy since 1623, when Avedis Zildjian, a metallurgist in Turkey, discovered the technique. Armand Zildjian, whose father inherited the business from his uncle and in 1929 moved the company from Turkey to Massachusetts, joined the firm at a young age. He learned the family's secret technique and rose through the company ranks to become president in 1977 and chairman upon his father's death two years later. Zildjian cymbals were used the world over, and Zildjian personally tested and hand-selected cymbals for some of the most famous drummers of the 20th century, including Buddy Rich and Max Roach.

Zimmerman, John Gerald, American sports photographer (b. Oct. 30, 1927, Pacoima, Calif.—d. Aug. 3, 2002, Monterey, Calif.), helped develop modern sports photojournalism. He was a pioneer in the use of lighting at indoor arenas and was the first to use remote-controlled cameras to capture the action of a sporting event. Zimmerman was a navy photographer during World War II before working his way through the ranks of Time-Life and other publishers. In 1956 he was hired as one of the first photographers for *Sports Illustrated*, for which he eventually shot 107 covers. His most famous works included an image of Wilt Chamberlain that Zimmerman shot from the backboard and a 1980 photo of Olympic diver Jennifer Chandler that was taken underwater.

Events of 2002

Association football (soccer) fans at a European Champions League match in Barcelona.

Agriculture and Food Supplies

DROUGHTS, drops in grain **HARVESTS**, and looming **FAMINES** again topped the list of agricultural problems in 2002. Some countries expressed concerns about the safety of **GENETICALLY MODIFIED FOODS**, while the U.S. inaugurated labeling for **ORGANIC** products. The world **FISH CATCH** rose slightly.

NATIONAL AND INTERNATIONAL ISSUES

Food Production. The year 2002 saw mounting concerns over global food supplies as harvests declined in many areas of the world. North America, Africa, and Australia experienced drought that significantly reduced crop output. Also contributing to the production decline in Africa was continued political instability. Total grain output in the United States fell 25,900,000 metric tons, or 8%, owing to drought. Output in other countries fell 52,070,000 metric tons, or 2.6%. With global consumption nearly constant, ending stocks fell owing to the lower output. World output of oilseeds fell slightly, less than 1%, because the reduction in U.S. output was offset by increases elsewhere. World meat output rose 2.9% in 2002. The

In the village of Ramosothoane, Lesotho, a farmer and his sons prepare their land for seeds promised by the government; Lesotho was one of several African countries threatened by famine.

© AFP 2002, by Alexander Joe

tightening global supply-and-demand balance caused strong price increases for major agricultural commodities.

Food Aid. By the early summer of 2002, concerns about the possibility of famine for over 14 million people in southern Africa had emerged. The countries most seriously affected included Zambia, Zimbabwe, Malawi, Lesotho, Swaziland, and Mozambique. By fall 2002 roughly nine million more people in Ethiopia and Eritrea were forecast to need food assistance from external sources. While drought was a factor in all countries, other forces contributed. In much of the region, a shortage of land had led to overuse and degradation of the soil. While fertilizer could compensate for the loss in soil productivity, most small farmers could not afford to buy fertilizer at commercial prices, and international donors had reduced their donations of fertilizer in recent years. Political issues often magnified the food crisis. In Zimbabwe land reform directed at large commercial white-owned farms contributed to the decline in production, while restricted access to food by members of the political opposition worsened the food crisis. Malawi's government was accused of having sold its national emergency grain stock prior to the crisis. Poor transportation and marketing systems compounded the effects of drought by slowing delivery of food aid and, over the

longer run, critical agricultural inputs such as seed and fertilizers.

Food assistance was also slowed in southern Africa by concerns that American grain offered for food relief contained genetically modified (GM) corn (maize). Thousands of tons of aid were initially rejected or locked away from the starving population. Recipient countries were further concerned that GM corn would be retained for seed and thereby introduce manipulated genes into future crops, a situation that would hamper exports to Europe, where there was resistance to importing GM corn. Eventually, Mozambique and Zimbabwe accepted offers by donor countries to grind the corn before distribution so that it could not be used as seed, but Zambia continued to resist the aid on the grounds that GM corn jeopardized the safety of the population. In Angola continued internal strife threatened an estimated half million people as refugees were forced to abandon their fields.

Other countries faced famine as well. North Korea continued to require food assistance despite domestic reforms to raise prices and salaries sharply. The World Food Programme had been feeding six million people in North Korea and generally enjoyed access to most regions of the country. Especially toward the end of the year, concerns over North Korea's nuclear-weapons-development program increased the reluctance of donor agencies to provide food aid. U.S. pursuit of its "war on terrorism" on the territory of Afghanistan affected the return to normalcy of agricultural production, so the country still had to rely on food assistance from the international community.

International Organizations. The World Food Summit organized by the United Nations Food and Agriculture Organization (FAO) was held in Rome, June 10–13, with the purpose of renewing the world's commitment to reduce hunger. Delegates approved a measure reaffirming a 1996 resolution to cut the number of hungry in the world by more than half by 2015. Delegates from less-developed countries were critical of subsidization of farmers in developed countries for depressing world commodity prices. Developed countries also came under fire for maintaining import barriers on agricultural products that denied farmers in less-developed areas access to richer markets. Calls were made to increase agricultural aid from the existing $11 billion to $24 billion. Another criticism that was voiced was that most industrialized countries had not sent top leaders to the summit (only Spain and host Italy were represented by their prime ministers) and did not seem to take the meeting very seriously.

Multilateral trade liberalization negotiations launched in Doha, Qatar, in November 2001 continued through 2002, and some progress was registered. In August the U.S. Congress granted Pres. George W. Bush trade promotion authority (TPA). The president was again given the go-ahead to negotiate trade deals subject to a "yes-no" vote in Congress. The president's TPA had expired eight years earlier, and the U.S. negotiating position was weakened because other states were reluctant to negotiate with the president when Congress could subsequently change any agreement he approved.

During 2002 several countries presented their initial negotiating positions for the Doha Round. The U.S. proposed cutting tariffs on agricultural products to an average of 15%, expanding market access commitments by 20%, and reducing domestic farm subsidies to no more than 5% of the value of production. The U.S. also sought elimination of export subsidies. The Cairns Group, a coalition of 17 agricultural exporting countries with little governmental farm support, introduced a proposal that asked for larger tariff cuts and greater market access plus elimination of trade-distorting domestic support. Proposals by less-developed countries focused on more access to developed-country markets. The Japanese proposal called for less-ambitious changes from existing WTO trade rules. The European Union (EU) did not formally make a proposal in 2002 but was judged likely to oppose ending export subsidies and domestic support in its position statement in 2003. The EU sought to restrict imports of GM foods until they were shown to be safe for consumers and the environment. The exporting states, notably the U.S., opposed restrictions on the movement of GM foods.

Agricultural Policy. Several important changes in agricultural policy occurred in 2002. The U.S. adopted new multiyear agricultural legislation formalizing the countercycle payments to farm support that had been used to supplement governmental support to American farmers since world commodity prices fell in the late 1990s. Earlier, Congress had enacted annual supplemental farm spending. The new legislation set formulas for calculating levels of support through 2007. New environmental programs were authorized in which farmers would qualify for additional subsidies for adopting environmentally friendly farming practices. Because the forecasted expenditure in support of the new laws was higher than in the past (not taking the supplemental payments into account), the new U.S. laws were seen by many to be expanding subsidy payments to American farmers and thus inconsistent with the position stated to the WTO. The U.S. came in for heavy criticism abroad.

The U.S. government also continued to promote regional trade agreements. In December a free-trade agreement was signed with Chile, the first step on a path to expand the North American Free Trade Agreement (NAFTA) into a Free Trade Area of the Americas (FTAA). Approximately three-quarters of U.S.-Chilean agricultural trade would be tariff-free in 4 years, with all barriers gone after 12 years.

In July cuts in EU farm subsidies were proposed, and it was suggested that remaining subsidies be changed to production-neutral payments and tied to environmental objectives. That proposal generated intense resistance from farm groups. During the fall Germany and France agreed on multiyear funding of agricultural policy at current levels, an agreement that paved the way for the EU to offer membership to 10 candidate states from Central Europe in December. EU environmental ministers also hammered out rules for trade in GM foods, agreeing that at point of departure shippers must provide a list of all GM organisms in the food. Products containing more than 0.9% genetically modified material would require labels. Extensive traceability rules for food products containing GM material were also proposed. The proposals were forwarded to the European Parliament for approval.

Food Quality, Safety, and Labeling. Bipartisan legislation aimed at protecting the country's food supply that had been quickly drawn up following the terrorist attacks and anthrax outbreaks in the U.S. in 2001 was apparently bogged down in House-Senate committee in 2002. The proposals would have increased the government inspections of food imports, required American food manufacturers to register with the federal government, given the FDA powers to halt and inspect food shipments, and allowed federal agents to inspect food company records. Not surprisingly, food manufacturers and retailers groups opposed such provisions, claiming that guaranteeing the security of the country's food supply from terrorist tampering could be accomplished more efficiently in other ways that did not involve huge increases in federal power.

Capping a 12-year campaign, environmentalists, organic farmers, chefs, and grocers succeeded in enacting national standards for organic foods in October. The U.S. Department of Agriculture adopted new regulations and labeling criteria, including a USDA Organic Seal of Approval (see graphic). According to the USDA, "organic" means the product is free of artificial flavours, colours, and preservatives, artificial fertilizers and sewage sludge, synthetic pesticides, irradiation, and genetically engineered ingredients. "Organic" is a more rigorous designation than "Natural," which does not exclude pesticides, irradiation, and GM processes. Three levels of organic labels were instituted. For a product to be labeled "100% Organic," every ingredient (except water and salt) must be organic. "Organic" means that 95% of the ingredients must be organic. A product labeled "Made with organic ingredients" must have at least 70% organic components, but the "USDA Organic" seal may not be used.

Earlier in the year Sen. Tom Harkin, a Democrat from Iowa and chair of the Senate Agriculture Committee, had inserted language into the Senate's version of the farm bill that would, as he said, "more clearly define pasteurization," the process that destroys bacteria in food, traditionally through heating. Henceforth, "pasteurization" would be understood to include irradiation, notably of beef, a process that was called "cold pasteurization." Sale of irradiated foods, including meats, had been approved by the FDA in 2000, but various public interest groups were resisting implementation and expansion of food irradiation. It was not clear if Harkin's proposals would also enjoin the federal government from banning irradiated foods in school lunch programs and similar public projects.

The McDonald's Corp. announced in March that it planned to settle a series of lawsuits brought by vegetarian and religious organizations. These groups claimed that their members had been misled by McDonald's announcement that in 1990 they had switched to using vegetable oils in the preparation of their french fries, when in fact the fry oils still contained some beef tallow. The fast-food giant said it would pay out $6 million to vegetarian groups and another $4 million to organizations of Hindus and Sikhs, who do not eat beef, as well as make individual monetary settlements with other claimants. In February the U.S. Drug Enforcement Agency extended the grace period given to food manufacturers to dispose of any of their products that included hemp. In October 2001 the DEA had banned food products containing tetrahydrocannabinol (THC), the active ingredient in hemp (and its relative, marijuana). THC is found in hemp seed oil, which is used in the preparation of snack foods.

Greece won a significant concession when the EU Commission ruled in October that henceforth only the raw-milk sheep's cheese made in Greece could be labeled and sold as "feta." A number of other producers in southeastern Europe and elsewhere—notably Denmark—also marketed locally made cheese as "feta," and these countries had hoped that "feta" would be ruled a generic product name, such as "cheddar" and "brie." Ironically, although Greece was the world's largest producer of feta, nearly all of its output was consumed within Greece.

GLOBAL MARKETS IN 2002

Grains, Oilseeds, and Livestock. World supplies of grain and oilseed crops fell in 2002 owing to dryness in many regions. As a result, commodity prices were higher than they had been in recent years. World crop production in the 2002 crop year was 1,810,000,000 metric tons, compared with 1,864,000,000 metric tons for crop year 2001.

World wheat production fell by more than 10 million metric tons to 569 million. Drought in the U.S. and Canada plus increasing crop area devoted to corn and oilseeds caused a 17.4% drop in U.S. and 23.8% in Canadian wheat output. Dryness also affected Southern Hemisphere wheat crops, with production in Argentina 13% less than the previous year and Australian output down more than 56%. EU output increased from 92 million to 104 million metric tons, the greatest growth in any area. World wheat trade in the 2002 crop year was 5% lower, the increase in demand being satisfied by reductions in ending stocks. The tighter global supply generated higher prices, and crop year 2002 wheat prices soared 37% above 2001 prices.

World output of coarse grains fell from 887.5 million to 861 million metric tons. Most of that decrease was attributable to the 6.3% drop in the U.S. crop, 16.7 million metric tons. By weight the Canadian crop fell less—2.8 million metric tons—but this represented a decline of 12.5%. China and the countries of the former Soviet Union showed improved production, 11 million and 26 million metric tons, respectively. Coarse grains were planted late in the year in the Southern Hemisphere and harvested early in the following year. Low precipitation reduced expectations for the 2003 harvest; forecasts for Australia were halved. World trade in coarse grains remained nearly unchanged by balancing demand and ending stocks, which totaled 144 million metric tons, compared with 174 million for crop year 2001. World prices rose 22% as supplies fell.

World rice output was about 17 million metric tons (milled basis)—or 4.2%—lower for the year. Most of the decline—14 million metric tons—occurred in India, where a below-normal crop followed an above-average 2001 crop. World trade rose by 1.6%. Global use fell less than 1%, so ending stocks adjusted by falling from 132 million metric tons to 105 million. Prices remained steady compared with the previous year.

Global oilseed production was slightly lower in crop year 2002, owing largely to a 7% reduction in the U.S. soybean crop. Increased foreign output, especially in South America, offset the decline in U.S. production. Ending stock reduction for oilseeds allowed slightly expanded meal and vegetable oil production and trade. The average annual soybean price strengthened by about 24%.

Global beef and pork output rose slightly—2.8%—while trade increased to allow a 7.4% increase in consumption. Beginning in late 2001 Japan, the world's major beef importer, experienced outbreaks of bovine spongiform encephalopathy (BSE) in four animals, and consumers reacted by sharply reducing beef consumption. During 2002, when the "mad-cow" disease did not spread, the government removed the infected cattle; efforts to convince Japanese consumers of the safety of imported beef met with some success, and beef consumption again began to rise. Meanwhile, under threat of punitive fines, France lifted the ban on purchases of British beef that it had imposed in 1996 during the BSE crisis in Great Britain. The U.K. was also declared free of foot-and-mouth disease in January, and exports of British sheep and goats resumed in February.

Poultry meat output was up 3% for the year, although trade in poultry meat reversed its recent growth trend and fell to six million tons, a drop of 3.3%. World milk production rose by 1.4%.

Tropical Products. World sugar production in 2002–03 was 139 million metric tons, 5 million above 2001–02. Brazilian output continued to expand, and EU output recovered from the previous year's low. China and Russia, both major import markets, enjoyed increased production. World trade was 3.4 million metric tons—7.8%—greater, with Brazil, the EU, and Thailand the largest exporting countries. Because of the increased output from China and Russia, exports grew notably in Africa, the Middle East, and Asia. Consumption continued to expand as it had for the past decade. Sugar prices were weaker than in 2001; the lowest prices were registered early in 2002 but recovered somewhat later.

World coffee production in 2002–03 was 125 million bags, up 12% from the 2001–02 season, mostly owing to increased output in Brazil. World trade was up roughly 4%, with Brazilian exports 15% above year-earlier levels. The weakness of the Brazilian currency aided the competitiveness of its coffee in international markets. With consumption only 1% greater, coffee prices continued to be low in 2002. A report in September from the U.K.-based charitable organization Oxfam expressed concern about the growing discrepancy between the income of the world's coffee farmers, who received on average 53 cents per kilogram (1 kg = 2.2 lb) for their coffee beans, and the revenues of the coffee companies—especially the five leading multinationals: Procter & Gamble Co., Nestlé, Kraft Foods, Sara Lee Corp., and Tchibo Holding AG—which sold the coffee for an average of $7.92 per kilogram. The problem had been magnified, the report said, by a glut of coffee in the past five years and a corresponding drop of some $4 billion in the value of coffee exports.

Investors' anxieties over the violence and civil war in Côte d'Ivoire, which grew about 40% of the world's cocoa, were reflected in a rise in prices of more than 60% over the year, reaching levels not seen since 1986. (PHILIP L. PAARLBERG)

FISHERIES

Figures produced by the UN Food and Agriculture Organization indicated that in 2000, the latest year for which figures were available, total production for the world's capture fisheries registered a rise of 1.76% over 1999 to 94,848,674 metric tons. Inland-water production increased by 3.59% to 8,801,070 metric tons, while marine output rose by 1.58% to record a total of 86,047,604 metric tons landed. Aquaculture production rose by 6.39% during the same period to 35,585,111 metric tons.

The leading catching nation was again China, with 16,987,325 metric tons, although this was a 1.47% reduction from the 1999 total of 17,240,032 metric tons caught. Peru, the second largest producer, with 10,658,620 metric tons, reaped the rewards of improved anchoveta (Peruvian anchovy) stocks to achieve a 26.46% increase in landings over the previous year.

Anchoveta remained the world's top species in terms of volume, recording a 29.27% overall increase to 11,276,357 metric tons landed. (See TABLE.) Capelin, which rose from 13th place in 1999 to 9th in 2000, showed an increase of 60.9% in landings and helped to boost the Icelandic catch to about 1,980,000 metric tons in 2000, a significant 14.2% increase over 1999 that pushed Iceland up to 11th place among catching nations. Problems with the Alaska pollock (walleye pollock) resource in the North Pacific was reflected in a 10% drop in landings during 2000, although it still maintained its place as the second most numerous commercial fish species landed, with 3,024,796 metric tons.

Total global exports of fish and fish products increased in 2000 to $55.2 billion, a gain of almost 4.5% over 1999. Thailand continued to be the main fish-exporting country, with $4.4 billion in exports. China rose to number two, with $3.6 billion in fish-related exports, an impressive growth of nearly 22% from 1999. The fisheries exporting industry in China specialized in importing raw material and reprocessing it for export at increased value.

Fish imports reached a new record of $60 billion in 2000. Developed countries accounted for about 80% of total imports in value terms. Japan, which had experienced a decline in imports during 1998 and 1999, was the largest importer of fishery products, responsible for some 26% of the worldwide total. The

European Union again relied heavily on imports for its fish supply. Most euro zone countries, however, reported a lower value of fishery imports in 2000, with the exception of Spain, the world's third leading importer. The United States, the fourth largest exporter, also was the second biggest importer of fishery products. Expanding shrimp imports accounted for much of the increase in imports of fishery products to the U.S. in 2000.   (MARTIN J. GILL)

Production Trends for the Top 10 Catching Nations, 1991–2000
(in metric tons)

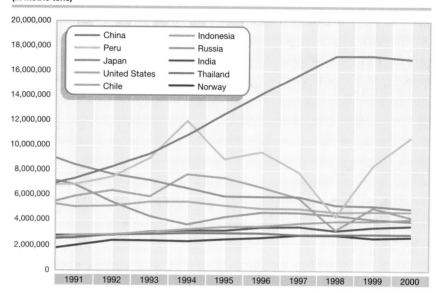

Total World Production (Aquaculture and Capture Fisheries)
(in metric tons)

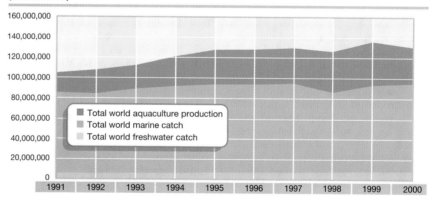

Catch Trends for the Top 10 Caught Species in 2000
(in metric tons)

	1998	1999	2000	Percent change from 1999
Anchoveta (Peruvian anchovy)	1,729,064	8,723,265	11,276,357	29.27
Alaska pollock (walleye pollock)	4,049,223	3,362,473	3,024,796	−10.04
Atlantic herring	2,422,136	2,403,835	2,370,020	−1.41
Skipjack tuna	1,888,856	1,988,276	1,890,133	−4.94
Japanese anchovy	2,093,888	1,820,259	1,725,685	−5.20
Chilean jack mackerel	2,025,758	1,423,447	1,540,494	8.22
Largehead hairtail	1,436,303	1,419,404	1,479,848	4.26
Chub mackerel	1,924,623	1,946,268	1,455,796	−25.20
Capelin	985,498	904,799	1,455,795	60.90
Blue whiting (poutassou)	1,185,003	1,318,628	1,419,911	7.68

Source: Food and Agriculture Organization.

Anthropology and Archaeology

Exciting finds of very old **HOMINID REMAINS** in Chad and a *Homo ergaster* skull in the Transcaucasus; the appearance of an **OSSUARY** thought to have been that of **JESUS' BROTHER** James; relics from the **INCA, MAYA,** and **HOPEWELL MOUNDS** cultures in the Americas; and **POST-SEPTEMBER 11** studies of **VIOLENCE** in complex societies were the **HOT-BUTTON ISSUES** in archaeology and anthropology in 2002.

ANTHROPOLOGY

Physical Anthropology. In 2002 an international paleoanthropological research team announced a monumental discovery: the remains of the earliest hominid (or hominin) in the fossil record. Both the date and the location of the finds astonished experts. The associated fauna suggested that the fossils found in Chad, central Africa, were between six million and seven million years old. The six specimens included a cranium, a mandibular fragment, and two isolated teeth (an incisor and a molar) collected during 2001, as well as a partial right mandible containing a premolar and three molars and an isolated canine collected in 2002. The nearly complete cranium exhibited a heretofore unknown mix of apelike and hominid features. This specimen was formally named *Sahelanthropus tchadensis* and dubbed Toumai, which means "hope of life" in the local Goran language. *Sahelanthropus's* unique combination of primitive and derived traits was exemplified by the large continuous and extremely thick browridge (exceeding even the gorilla's in thickness) coupled with small, hominid-like canines. The braincase was also relatively small for a hominid, with an estimated cranial capacity of 320–380 cc (1 cc = about 0.06 cu in), similar to that of a chimpanzee. The back of the skull was shaped like that of an ape, and the widely spaced eyes resembled the gorilla's. More derived hominid traits included the short, vertical face with the lower face showing less prognathism (forward protrusion) than that in the chronologically later aus-

tralopithecines; the dentition (especially the small canines and lack of a space between the upper second incisor and canine); and the basicranium (base of the skull). The cranium probably was that of a chimpanzee-sized male who lived near a lake but not far from a sandy desert in the Late Miocene Epoch. Thus, *Sahelanthropus* flourished close to the ancestral split between the evolutionary lines that eventually led to modern chimpanzees and humans, respectively. As the oldest and most primitive known member of the hominid (hominin) clade, *Sahelanthropus* may have been the sister group of *Ardipithecus,* the Ethiopian genus that in 2001 was discovered to date to as early as 5.2 million–5.8 million years ago.

A second astonishing hominid (hominin) discovery was a superbly preserved skull from the fossil-rich approximately 1.75-million-year-old deposits from Dmanisi, Georgia. The Transcaucasian site had previously yielded two partial crania provisionally assigned to *Homo ergaster* (also called *H. erectus* by many experts) with estimated cranial capacities of 780 cc and 650 cc, respectively. The new, far more complete skull represented the smallest-brained (600-cc cranial capacity), most primitive hominid (hominin) ever found outside Africa. Although the international research team led by Georgian

paleoanthropologists assigned the new specimen to *H. erectus* (= *ergaster*), numerous craniofacial features resembled the earlier taxon *H. habilis.* The skull carried four maxillary teeth and eight mandibular teeth. Ten isolated teeth were also recovered, of which six easily fit into the maxilla. This specimen was that of a young individual—perhaps female, but the relatively massive canines cautioned against making a definitive sex designation. The rather diminutive face was surmounted by thin but well-defined browridges. The palate was shallow, while the rear of the braincase displayed a low and transversely flattened appearance characteristic of *H. erectus* specimens. The extreme morphological variation evidenced among the finds at Dmanisi caused experts to call for the reassessment of both the sex and existing taxonomic designations of the early *Homo* fossils from other localities. It was now deemed possible that a relatively small-brained population with simple flake and chopper tools exited Africa soon after the first appearance of the genus *Homo,* a theory that ran counter to earlier expectations. Indeed, one iconoclastic proposal that would upset orthodox scenarios had *H. erectus*

A fossil skull found in Chad and nicknamed Toumai is an estimated six million to seven million years old—older than any other hominid fossil found to date.

deriving from this primitive Dmanisi stock somewhere in Asia and *H. erectus* (= *ergaster*) subsequently moving back to Africa. This scenario also raised the possibility of multiple hominid (hominin) migrations back and forth between Asia and Africa beginning about 1.75 million years ago.

Recently published genetic evidence from mitochrondrial DNA, the Y chromosome, the X chromosome, and six autosomal regions supported a model of multiple out-of-Africa migrations to Eurasia dating back 1.7 million years by members of the genus *Homo*. Both the Y-chromosome and the ß-hemoglobin locus also suggested hominid movements from Asia back to Africa later than the proposed origin of *H. sapiens*. These results came from the application of a novel methodology known as nested clade phylogeographic analysis devised by the geneticist Alan Templeton and implemented with the GEODIS computer program written by Templeton and his associates. This method distinguished statistically significant associations between patterns of genetic variation and geography in terms of underlying causal mechanisms such as population structure processes (i.e., recurrent gene flow restricted by isolation by distance) and population history events (for example, contiguous range expansions, long-distance colonizations, or genetic fragmentation into two or more populations). The most ancient genetic signals were all recurrent gene-flow episodes that followed the Dmanisi expansion to Georgia but predated the first genetic-based signal for an out-of-Africa expansion that occurred between 420,000 and 840,000 years ago. A second genetically defined expansion from Africa took place between 80,000 and 150,000 years ago and most probably marked the initial colonization by *H. sapiens* of non-African locales. Templeton's major conclusion was that humans expanded from Africa on multiple occasions, but these expansions resulted in interbreeding (gene flow) rather than population replacement, which thereby makes suspect any model of human origins that demands complete replacement without any interbreeding (the traditional out-of-Africa replacement model).

(STEPHEN L. ZEGURA)

Cultural Anthropology. In 2002 much was written about the events of Sept. 11, 2001, in popular and academic literature alike. These events prompted cultural anthropologists to bring their

Doug Kapustin, *The Baltimore Sun*

Floyd Graff of Stanley, N.D., a survivor of the Japanese attack on Pearl Harbor, wears his USMC uniform—the one he was married in—every year on Memorial Day. War and violence in the U.S. were top subjects for anthropologists in 2002.

talents to bear on contemporary problems of violence and globalization and to look at these problems in new ways. The anthropological study of violence was not new. The relationship between violence and human evolution, both biological and cultural, had long generated heated debate in the four fields of anthropology: sociocultural, linguistic, physical, and archaeological. While classical anthropological treatises on violence and war had focused largely on the exotic violence of "the other" in the form of small-scale tribal societies (for example, Napoleon Chagnon's 1968 study, *Yanomamö, the Fierce People*), scholars were increasingly turning their attention to the problems of violence in so-called complex societies.

The dramatic scholarly response to September 11 pointed to lines of research that had been percolating within anthropology for at least a decade. Rigorous and nuanced inquiries into the cultural and structural dimensions of violence, war, and peacemaking in the postcolonial, globally connected, industrialized, and/or urbanized regions of the globe led to the formation of what some had termed an "anthropology of violence." Groundbreaking anthropological work in the 1990s complicated and broadened definitions of violence to include structural violence caused by

economic deprivation and inequality, genocide, state terror, and social suffering. It also raised important questions about the sociocultural conditions of peacemaking. New, post-September 11 inquiries into the basic structural conditions that give rise to terrorism were expected to build on these seminal works.

Despite the fact that some scholars questioned the ability or legitimacy of anthropological comment on the events of September 11, the program of the 2002 annual meetings of the American Anthropological Association included dozens of sessions on violence and globalization or the globalization of violence—for example, the AAA public policy forum "Violences Legitimate and Illegitimate: Playing with 'Terrorism,' the Word" and other presentations entitled "Memories of Terror: Dialogue on Public Issues," "New York City (and Beyond): Before and After 9/11," "Bioterrorism, Epidemics, and the Future of Public Health: Anthropological Perspectives," and "Violence, Terrorism and the New World (Dis)Order."

In September 2002 the professional journal *American Anthropologist* dedicated a special issue to anthropological work on September 11. The articles ranged from discussions of the history of factionalism and war in Afghanistan to the impact of global violence in Indonesia. In her article "Making War at Home in the United States: Militarization and the Current Crisis," Catherine Lutz argued that war and terrorism are not abnormal states of crisis but indicative of a highly militarized U.S. population. She also analyzed the trend in American media toward the commodification of tragedy and violence in a "brand name" such as "September 11" or "9/11." These brands are metonymic, allowing a single word or phrase to encapsulate the incomprehensible destruction, violence, and subsequent nationalism produced by the events. Lutz argued that brand names of violence circulate as commodities and nationalist rallying cries.

Karin Andriolo's article, "Murder by Suicide: Episodes from Muslim History," attempted to trace the history of the idea "Muslim terrorist" beginning with the historical figures of the 13th-century assassins. While there is much to be gained from interrogating the terminology "Muslim terrorist," several problems arise with this type of "archeology of knowledge." Using the assassins as a starting point seems arbitrary, given that their goals were not global in scope, not part of a transnational production of terror. The terror generated by the assassins lay in their anonymity. The fear generated by modern terrorists is international in scope and resides in the virulence of circulated images of destruction. If anthropologists conceptualize terrorism as the ritualized production of power, the power of the terrorist acts of September 11 rests in the spectacle that could be broadcast live from the scene of the violence to the rest of the world.

In contrast to Andriolo, Mahmood Mamdani argued in the same issue of *American Anthropologist* that terrorism is a unique product of the modern world system and should not be conflated with Islam. He questioned the connection between Islam and terrorism based on a detailed analysis of the effects of the Cold War on Afghanistan. In a similar vein, Lila Abu-Lughod confronted the question "Do Muslim Women Really Need Saving?. . ." Like Mamdani, Abu-Lughod took anthropologists to task for "complicity in the reification of cultural difference." She questioned the "rhetoric of salvation" in which women of colour, in this case Afghanis, are protected from men of colour by violent intervention. She placed this rhetoric in the context of a long history of colonial rule in which colonizers justified their actions in the name of saving women.

While Lutz lamented the use of the date September 11 as a symbolic partition of history into before and after, the events of that date provided an opportunity for cultural anthropologists to reflect on important developments in the anthropological study of violence, terrorism, war, and peace. The discipline as a whole would have to continue to confront these issues if it was to remain relevant for the 21st century.

(KIMBERLY L. MILLS)

ARCHAEOLOGY

Eastern Hemisphere. The year 2002 yielded a number of stunning archaeological discoveries. A 50-cm (20-in)-long limestone ossuary, or box for storage of bones, bearing a text in Aramaic, was hailed as the first archaeological evidence for the historical Jesus. The ossuary, found near Jerusalem, was carved with a single line of text reading, "Ya'akov bar Yosef akhui diYeshua," or "James, son of Joseph, brother of Jesus." Although James (Jacob or Ya'akov), Joseph (Yosef), and Jesus (Yeshua) were common names at that time, scholars noted that the appearance of that particular combination of names and kinship order would have been rare. If the inscription proved authentic and did indeed refer to Jesus of Nazareth, said French epigrapher André Lemaire of the Sorbonne, who analyzed the inscription and dated it to c. AD 63, it would be the first documentation of the founder of Christianity outside the Bible. Until this discovery the earliest-known mention of Jesus had been that found on a papyrus containing a fragment of the Gospel of John, written in Greek and dated to c. AD 125. Unfortunately, the ossuary was damaged while being transported from Israel to Canada, where it was to go on exhibition.

Considered the oldest-known art in the world, two 77,000-year-old pieces of decorated red ochre found in a South African cave prompted a major rethinking of the emergence of "modern behaviour" in the human line, according to an international research team led by the Iziko Museums of Cape Town, S.Af. Discovered at Blombos Cave on the southern Cape, the ochre pieces had been ground down to produce a smooth work surface and then engraved with an intricate crosshatch design. Scientists had been unclear as

This limestone ossuary found near Jerusalem was among the important archaeological topics of the year; its Aramaic inscription was believed by some scholars to be the earliest archaeological reference to Jesus of Nazareth.

to just when "modern behaviour" emerged—that is, the development of the cognitive abilities necessary to create art, to modify objects beyond a pure utilitarian function. The earliest heretofore known art comprised depictions of an animal and a humanlike creature executed in red ochre on several stone slabs dated to between 32,000 and 36,000 years ago, discovered near Verona, Italy.

A 2,600-year-old Etruscan settlement found near the shores of Lake Accesa on Italy's Tuscan plain, the largest found to date, was expected to provide a window on Etruscan civic life in the late 7th to early 6th century BC. The town, spread over some 30 ha (75 ac), yielded the well-preserved remains of stone house foundations, streets, and tombs. The town was believed to have been a mining community, with the iron, copper, and tin it produced exported to Greece in exchange for polychromed ceramics found in abundance in Etruscan tombs.

What was believed to be the richest Bronze Age burial ever found in Great Britain was discovered at Amesbury, near Stonehenge. There a team recovered the 4,300-year-old remains of an archer buried with nearly 100 artifacts, including three copper knives, gold earrings, beaker pots, numerous stone arrowheads, and stone wrist guards. A Roman iron factory found near Brayford in southwestern England included furnaces, slag, and smelting equipment and apparently had been used to supply markets throughout the Roman Empire during the 2nd and 3rd centuries AD. A hoard of 4th-century AD Roman coins buried in Somerset and found by an off-duty policeman wielding a metal detector proved that counterfeiting had been alive and well in the ancient world; 56 of the 670 coins were forgeries. An early 6th-century AD trading post discovered in 2001 at the mouth of the River Avon in the south of England revised thinking about the commercial relationship between Britain and the Late Roman Empire. The site yielded abundant remains of Eastern Mediterranean amphorae and North African tableware among shards of Cornish gabbroic coarseware. The intermingling of finds suggested that trade with these distant regions had continued well after the Romans' withdrawal from the British Isles in AD 410.

A Danish National Museum team was excavating the manor house and outbuildings at that country's most important archaeological site, the Viking complex at Lake Tissoe, west of Copenhagen, where some 10,000 high-quality artifacts had already been removed. The Swedish navy discovered the well-preserved remains of an 18th-century brig sitting upright on the seafloor in 90 m (300 ft) of water in the Baltic Sea. The identity of the ship and the reason it sank remained a mystery.

In China the analysis of a suite of 20,000 newly discovered bamboo strips bearing some 200,000 characters was expected to shed light on the evolution of Chinese calligraphy. The strips, excavated in June at Liye village, Hunan province, appeared to be court documents of the Qin dynasty (221–206 BC). Qin Shi Huangdi, founder of the Qin dynasty and China's first emperor, standardized the country's many writing styles, demanding that his subjects write in Xiaozhuan, or the Lesser Seal Style. According to Li Jiahao of Beijing University, the newly discovered documents were drafted in Qin Li, a derivative of Xiaozhuan valued for its simplicity and clarity. Some 75 km (45 mi) to the south, archaeologists unearthed the tomb of an early Ming dynasty (AD 1368–1644) tribal leader. Discovered in Hunan province, the tomb was composed of a long passage lined with stone statues of lions, horses, and human figures and a large main hall. The tomb's occupant was believed to have been a Tusi, or minority ethnic administrator. Other recent Chinese finds included the 2,000-year-old remains of 30 beacon towers, two fortified castles, two ancillary defensive buildings, and a series of deep trenches situated just east of Jiuquan in northwestern Gansu province. According to the archaeologists working on the site, trenches 3–4 m (10–15 ft) deep rather than walls were the preferred defensive structure of the Han dynasty (ruled 206 BC–AD 220).

Two sandstone slabs, recovered during excavations in the east Indian state of Orissa, were expected to shed light on the life of the warrior-king Ashoka (c. 269–c. 232 BC), who took the Mauryan empire to its apogee only to renounce the violence of conquest in favour of Buddhism and a more liberal code of conduct that espoused human dignity and encouraged socioreligious harmony. One slab bore what was believed to be the first known portrait of the king; the other showed a royal figure embraced by two women, perhaps his queens.

(ANGELA M.H. SCHUSTER)

Western Hemisphere. New archaeological discoveries in 2002 ranged over the entire spectrum of American history. The redevelopment of downtown Tucson, Ariz., involved large-scale archaeological excavations on the Santa Cruz River floodplain. Excavations revealed a number of irrigation canals constructed over at least 2,500 years as well as corn (maize) fragments dating to about 2000 BC—the earliest yet found in the American Southwest. The same settlement also contained storage pits and pit houses.

Even older, well-investigated sites sometimes yielded surprises. In 2001 two students from Ohio State University, using a fluxgate gradiometer (an instrument that identifies fluctuations in the Earth's magnetic field), discovered a hitherto unknown circular shallow ditch about 27 m (90 ft) in diameter inside the great D-shaped enclosure at the Hopewell Mound Group near Chillicothe, Ohio. Their discovery was detailed in 2002 in *American Archaeology*. Spiro in eastern Oklahoma was a major religious centre for the Mississippian culture between about AD 1100 and 1450. In 1935 in a tunnel dug into Craig Mound, the largest at the site, amateur archaeologist J.G. Braeklein unearthed a stone scraper made of a green obsidian (volcanic glass). Every obsidian source contains its own distinctive trace elements, and these can be identified by using spectrographic analysis. Alex Barker of the Milwaukee (Wis.) Public Museum found that the trace elements in the Spiro flake were virtually identical to those from a source at Pachuca in central Mexico. Pachuca obsidian was greatly prized by many Central American civilizations and was traded as far south as Guatemala. The discovery at Spiro was the first find of Pachuca obsidian north of the Rio Grande. For many years archaeologists speculated about contacts between the great Mississippian centres and Mexican civilizations, and now they had the first firm, if tenuous, link.

A beautiful Maya mural dating to about AD 100 was found in a small room by a 25-m (80-ft)-tall pyramid at San Bartolo in the Petén region of northern Guatemala. The frieze depicts a mythical scene known as the dressing of the Corn God. A male figure, perhaps the Corn God, looks over his shoulder at two kneeling women who may be dressing him before he leaves the Underworld. Only an estimated 10% of the mural was exposed, but once fully excavated, the frieze would likely extend more than 18 m (60 ft) around the room. It would be the most important early Maya painting ever found.

Working 4,250 m (14,000 ft) up Pico de Orizaba, Mexico's highest mountain, Polish and Mexican archaeologists unearthed an Aztec stone shrine that served as an astronomical observatory. The lines formed by the observatory and two nearby peaks point to the rising Sun on February 9 and 10 and November 1 and 2. It was thought that Aztec priests built the shrine to the rain god Tlaloc, who was honoured on mountain peaks.

The Inca empire extended far beyond its Andean homeland to the arid Pacific coast of present-day Peru, one of the driest environments on Earth. Little was known about life in the outlying Inca provinces, but a recent discovery on the outskirts of Lima, Peru, shed new light on the subject. The Puruchuco-Huaquerones cemetery, which dates to Inca times (AD 1438–1532), lies under the Tupac Amaru shantytown on the outskirts of the city. Over the years, shantytown inhabitants had unearthed a number of Inca mummies but burned them for fear that the squatters would be relocated. Guillermo Cock of Peru's Institute of Culture started work in the cemetery in 1999 and in three seasons recovered more than 2,200 mummies of all social ranks, buried within a 75-year span. Interred in graves sealed with sand, rubble, and potsherds, the funereal bundles survived virtually intact in the arid soil. Many bore false heads of textiles and cotton, and some were adorned with magnificent woven garments or elaborate headdresses of bird feathers with ear flaps and a long panel draped down the back of the neck. Sometimes as many as seven people were wrapped in one bundle. Nearly half the burials in the cemetery were those of children who had died from anemia. One spectacular mummy bundle, wrapped with more than 135 kg (300 lb) of cotton, contained the bodies of a man and a baby, perhaps one of his children. They were buried with

food and 170 exotic and everyday artifacts, together with a mace and sandals of a type worn by the Inca elite. Exotic *spondylus* shells from distant Ecuadoran waters lay with the bodies, eloquent testimony to their social status.

The wreck of what might prove to be one of Christopher Columbus's lesser

EFE Photos

At an exhibition in Madrid in May, Peruvian archaeologist Guillermo Cock poses with one of the Incan mummies discovered in the Puruchuco-Huaquerones cemetery near Lima.

ships was discovered near Portobello, on the coast of eastern Panama. The vessel lay close to where Columbus scuttled the *Vizcaina* in 1503. Preliminary excavations recovered cannon similar to those used on Columbus's vessels, and the hull of this vessel was held together with wooden pegs and not lead sheathed, as was common practice after 1508. The wreck was not

positively identified as the *Vizcaina*, however, and could also be that of one of conquistador Francisco Pizarro's ships, wrecked a quarter century after the *Vizcaina*.

One hundred fifty years ago, a forest of derelict sailing ships lined the San Francisco waterfront, abandoned by their crews during the Gold Rush. One was the triple-masted *General Harrison*. The merchantman was converted into a floating warehouse in 1850 but burned to the waterline during the great San Francisco fire of 1851. The *General Harrison* lay in landfill under San Francisco's financial district, where she was unearthed during foundation work for a new hotel. Excavator Alan Pastron found that the ship was buried still holding numerous crates of imported red wine and bolts of cloth. Nearly a dozen bottles of wine were still intact, likely the last survivors of the Bordeaux or Burgundy vintage of 1849. The cargo also included quantities of tacks, nails, and other hardware; wheat; and large numbers of Italian trade beads aimed at the Indian trade. The *General Harrison*'s cargo was sure to provide archaeologists with valuable information on life during the Gold Rush days.

Excavations under a car wash at the corner of Front and Parliament streets in Toronto revealed Upper Canada's original Parliament building. Built in the late 1790s and burned down by invading U.S. troops during the War of 1812, the structure was not rebuilt. Some years later the Parliament of a unified Upper and Lower Canada moved to Ottawa. A prison and a gas-processing facility occupied the site during the 19th century. Recent excavations by Ron Williamson based on an early 19th-century map uncovered ceramics and a siltstone floor and even intact bricks from the historic building; further digging might reveal more of the foundations. Hopes for a museum on the site were voiced, but a Porsche dealership was currently planned for that location.   (BRIAN FAGAN)

Architecture and Civil Engineering

PLANS to fill the **VOID** in the New York City **SKYLINE** created by the loss of the **TWIN TOWERS** of the World Trade Center in 2001, the **CONSTRUCTION** of a mammoth **CATHEDRAL** in Los Angeles, and differing opinions on **PRESERVATION** were hot topics in architecture in 2002.

ARCHITECTURE

The aftermath of the Sept. 11, 2001, terrorist attacks that obliterated the World Trade Center (WTC) towers continued to dominate much of the news in architecture in 2002. In January the Max Protetch Gallery in New York City sponsored an exhibition to which more than 50 architects worldwide sent in designs for the site, some of them serious, some purely symbolic. In March came the "Tribute in Light," a temporary memorial, in which two powerful shafts of blue light rose into the sky every night to mark the location of the former towers. (*See* photograph on page 17.) A new government agency for the state of New York, the Lower Manhattan Development Corporation (LMDC), was created to decide future plans for the site. Many architects also worked in volunteer organizations, such as the New York New Visions and the Civic Alliance, to help develop ideas and guidelines for the redevelopment of the area, including proposals for improving the rest of Lower Manhattan. In July the Civic Alliance sponsored a public symposium at which 5,000 people responded to preliminary LMDC plans, finding them for the most part unimaginative. As a result, in September the LMDC hired six teams of architects and planners, chosen from more than 400 applicants and including a number of internationally known figures, to come up with more inspiring ideas. The plans would probably include a mixture of office space, shopping, hotels, a transit station, a park, and a permanent memorial. The WTC disaster also stimulated fresh thinking about the engineering of tall buildings. It was expected that there would be changes in the building codes to strengthen buildings and also to create safer ways for tenants to evacuate them in emergencies. Security too became a concern of architects everywhere after September 11. In Washington, D.C., for example, consideration was being given to new underground visitor entrances to the Washington Monument and the U.S. Capitol.

Awards. The world's top award for lifetime achievement, the Pritzker Prize, went to Australian architect Glenn Murcutt (*see* BIOGRAPHIES); unlike most other prominent architects, he works alone and without an office staff. He does not have a computer, and he makes all of his drawings by hand. Murcutt has a five-year waiting list of people who want him to design a house for them. He designs only in Australia, where he understands the climate and the culture. He was influenced by Australian Aboriginal architecture and has been best known for modest houses in a modern style, which are responsive to climate and which "touch this earth lightly"—an Aboriginal phrase he likes to quote. The Gold Medal of the American Institute of Architects, for lifetime achievement, was not awarded in 2002 because no candidate received the necessary three-fourths vote from the AIA board of directors. The AIA's 25-Year Award, given to a building of quality that had stood the test of time, went to the Fundació Joan Miró in Barcelona, Spain. The structure—a museum that housed the work of the 20th-century Catalan artist Miró—was designed by the late architect Josep Lluís Sert, dean of the Harvard Design School and a childhood friend of the artist. The AIA also bestowed its annual Honor Awards for good design for individual buildings.

Among the most notable recipients were the Rose Center for Earth and Space, a planetarium at the American Museum of Natural History in New York City, by Polshek Partnership; the Sandra Day O'Connor U.S. District Courthouse in Phoenix, Ariz., by Richard Meier; and the Sony Center in Berlin, by Helmut Jahn of Murphy/Jahn. The Gold Medal of the Royal Institute of British Architects was awarded to Archigram, a group of architects active since the 1960s, known for a subversive "pop" mentality.

Cultural and Civic Buildings. One of the most ambitious religious buildings of modern times was the Cathedral of Our Lady of the Angels in Los Angeles, by Spanish architect José Rafael Moneo. The structure, which was larger than St. Patrick's Cathedral in New York City, cost $195 million. (*See* photograph on page 305.) Following the mandates of the second Vatican Council (1962–65), the cathedral was designed to be a place in which the public would feel

German architect Helmut Jahn's Sony Center in Berlin—a seven-building complex comprising an office tower, residences, and a public square covered by a giant glass cupola—received one of the American Institute of Architects' Honor Awards in 2002.

(Top) Visitors to the Swiss National Expo, held in Yverdon-les-Baines, approach the Blur Building, a cluster of metal platforms suspended over a lake and perpetually shrouded in man-made fog. (Above) An aerial view of the Blur Building.

comfortable—a "town square" rather than a place of awe or mystery. It occupied a city block and included an underground garage, an outdoor café, and a residence for the cardinal and church offices. Modern in style, the cathedral nevertheless featured a traditional nave and was entered through a long ambulatory lined with chapels. The cathedral was built of pinkish beige concrete, with translucent windows of alabaster.

In Switzerland the Swiss National Expo in Yverdon-les-Baines included a number of experimental buildings. The most unusual was the Blur Building by New York architects Elizabeth Diller and Ricardo Scofidio. The Blur Building was a cluster of platforms hovering above the water of a lake, entirely enveloped in a white mist produced by a system of pumps and nozzles. New York saw the opening of the American Folk Art Museum by Tod Williams and Billie Tsien. Despite being built be-

tween other buildings on a narrow midtown lot, it featured a variety of daylight spaces inside. It was also notable, in an era when much architecture was light and glassy, for the use of solid heavy materials, such as rough-surfaced concrete and, at the main entrance, tall dark panels of tombasil, an alloy of bronze. Another New York debut was the Austrian Cultural Forum, by Raimond Abraham, a tall thin building that sloped back from the street as it rose and rather resembled a totem pole. In Manchester, Eng., the Imperial War Museum North was designed by Daniel Libeskind, the architect of Berlin's Jewish Museum. It was a free-form pile of big curvy shapes sheathed in metal. Much of the interior was given over to media displays rather than to objects. The displays projected images and sounds against the walls in order to re-create various aspects of war. In Sapporo, Japan, a stadium by

Hiroshi Hara, used for the World Cup Association Football (soccer) finals, invented a new principle. Instead of a retractable roof to let sun and rain onto the grass field, the field itself glided smoothly outdoors whenever necessary. Also in Japan, a young British firm called Foreign Office Architects designed the Yokohama International Port Terminal, a cruise-ship facility. It looked like a natural land formation poking out into the harbour, with a sloping roof of wood and grass and with dramatic interior spaces under a steel plate ceiling that resembled traditional Japanese origami folded paper. In Tokyo the Gallery of Horyuji Treasures opened; it contained a collection of ancient Japanese art in a severe, elegant building by Yoshio Taniguchi, the architect whose competition-winning addition to the Museum of Modern Art in New York was under construction. MoMA, meanwhile, moved some of its collection to a temporary building in Queens, designed by Los Angeles architect Michael Maltzen and New Yorker Jaquelin Robertson.

Commercial Buildings. In New York's SoHo district, a new store for Prada clothiers by Dutch architect Rem Koolhaas, became a much-visited destination, thanks to such features as a dramatic swooping floor—called the "wave"—of zebrawood (an endangered species) and changing rooms with clear glass walls that turned translucent at the press of a button. The store embodied Koolhaas's belief, expressed in his book *The Harvard Design School Guide to Shopping*, which appeared in March, that the world had become so commercial that the only remaining important public spaces were shopping areas. Hanover, Ger., was the site of the North German Regional Clearing Bank by Behnisch, Behnisch and Partner. The structure looked like two buildings; a 17-story tower seemed to float above a six-story building that wrapped around it, with public shops and cafés on the ground floor. As was typical in this group's work, a great effort was made to reduce energy consumption, and it was claimed that the building produced 1,920 fewer tons of carbon-dioxide emission annually than a conventional building of the same size. In London the Lloyd's Register of Shipping, by Richard Rogers, was an elegant glass tower that seemed to be delicately inserted among older stone buildings, including a carefully restored historic churchyard. Also debuting in London was a housing estate by British-born Swedish architect Ralph Erskine, a brightly coloured, endlessly varied cluster of apartments. It was the first stage in redevelopment of land around the Millennium Dome in Greenwich on the River Thames.

Future Buildings, Competitions, and Controversies. In London a proposal for what would be the tallest building in Europe, London Bridge Tower, by Italian architect Renzo Piano, received planning approval but was opposed by those who thought it would mar views of St. Paul's Cathedral. The tower sloped to a sharp point at the top and was to be 310 m (1,016 ft) tall. A final design for the New York Times headquarters in New York, also by Piano, was announced in late December 2001. It was a 52-story glass tower covered with a lacy skin of white ceramic tubes. Piano was also chosen to design an addition to Richard Meier's High Museum in Atlanta, Ga. A design by American landscape architect Kathryn Gustafson won a competition for a memorial fountain to honour Diana, princess of Wales. The Los Angeles County Museum of Art selected Koolhaas for a $200 million renovation and expansion. Santiago Calatrava was picked to design a $240 million hall for the Atlanta Symphony. An innovative design by Diller + Scofidio, with floors that curved up to become walls and ceilings, was chosen for Eyebeam company headquarters in New York City, and that firm's design for a new Institute of Contemporary Art in Boston was unveiled in September. London's Sir Norman Foster unveiled a design for the expansion of Boston's Museum of Fine Arts in which the museum's open courtyards would be covered with glass and turned into sculpture gardens and social spaces. Frank O. Gehry's design for a new wing for the Corcoran Gallery in Washington, D.C., a characteristic Gehry building of colliding curved panels and dramatic interior spaces, won approval from the Commission of Fine Arts in late 2001. In Berlin the Ameri-

can embassy seemed at last to be on the road to construction after the settlement of a long controversy between the U.S. government and the city about how best to make it secure from terrorism. The California firm of Moore Ruble Yudell Architects & Planners had won a competition in 1996 for the building, which would be sited next door to the historic Brandenburg Gate.

Preservation. The Museum of Contemporary Arts and Design (formerly the American Craft Museum) announced plans to renovate the former Huntington Hartford Gallery on Columbus Circle, a quirky modernist New York City landmark by Edward Durrell Stone. The museum hired Oregon architect Brad Cloepfil to produce a plan, but many in the preservation community felt that the building should not be tampered with. The National Trust for Historic Preservation issued its annual list of 11 endangered buildings, including the Guthrie Theater in Minneapolis, Minn., by Ralph Rapson; the Hackensack Water Works in Oradell, N.J.; sacred sites at Indian Pass, Imperial county, Calif.; and "Teardowns in Historic Neighborhoods," a term that referred to cases in which older houses were demolished and replaced by larger new ones. One such case in 2002 was the loss of the Maslon House in California, a 1962 modernist landmark by Richard Neutra. By way of contrast, a house designed by John Hejduk in 1973 for a site in Connecticut, which never was built at that time, had been constructed in 2001 exactly as designed, on a site in The Netherlands. Called Wall House 2 by the architect, the house was a design well known and influential among architects. The Trans World Airlines Terminal at the John F. Kennedy International Airport in New York City, a 1962 masterpiece by Eero Saarinen that was no longer considered useful for air traffic, continued to deteriorate without any decision's being reached about its future. The Bronx Developmental Center, a controversial 1977 building by Meier, was gutted and clad in new facades by a new owner. A 1914 landmark mansion in Manhattan was successfully converted by architect Anabelle Selldorf into a museum for the Neue Gallerie, a collection of Austrian and German art. Lever House in New York, a modernist landmark of 1952, was stripped of its entire glass facade, which was deteriorating. The glass was replaced with new glass that looked identical to the old and thus raised a philosophical question among preservationists: was Lever pre-

served or rebuilt? The most famous house of the 20th century, Frank Lloyd Wright's Fallingwater in Mill Run, Pa., underwent an elaborate restoration effort aimed at reversing the sagging of its cantilevered balconies.

Exhibitions. The eighth Architecture Biennale in Venice was by far the largest exhibit of the year, showing more than 150 buildings worldwide, most of them not yet built, in the form of scale models and images. The theme of the Biennale was one word, "Next," and the goal of the exhibition was to preview what would be built in the coming years. More than 100,000 people attended during the Biennale's eight-week run. At the National Building Museum in Washington, D.C., "Cesar Pelli: Connections" showcased the work of the American architect. A retrospective of Danish modernist Arne Jacobsen appeared at the Louisiana Museum of Modern Art in Humlebæk, Den. The Art Institute of Chicago mounted a show of the drawings of Helmut Jacoby, the leading architectural renderer of the 1960s and '70s.

Deaths. Samuel Mockbee, a former winner of the MacArthur Foundation "genius award," died in December 2001. He was best known as the founder of the Rural Studio, where architectural students designed and built homes and other structures for low-income people in rural Hale county, Ala., often making them out of salvaged wood or even tires, hay bales, and automobile windows. J. Carter Brown, long a major figure in architecture, died in June. During his tenure as director of the National Gallery in Washington, D.C., the gallery's East Building by architect I.M. Pei was built. As chair of the Washington Fine Arts Commission, he provided crucial support to the Vietnam Veterans Memorial, and as chair of the Pritzker Prize jury, he exercised a great influence on the careers of major architects. Boston architect Benjamin Thompson died in August. He was best known for his series of "festival marketplaces," including the Faneuil Hall Marketplace in Boston, Harborplace in Baltimore, Md., and South Street Seaport in New York City. Earlier in his career, Thompson was a founder, with Walter Gropius and others, of the Architects Collaborative. He also started a chain of stores called Design Research, selling modern fabrics and furnishings, and designed the chain's flagship building in Harvard Square. (*See* OBITUARIES.)

(ROBERT CAMPBELL)

Notable Civil Engineering Projects (in work or completed, 2002)

Name	Location		Year of completion	Notes
Airports		**Terminal area (sq m)**		
Detroit Metro (new McNamara Terminal)	Romulus, Mich.	610,000	2002	Hub for Northwest Airlines; opened February 24
Dallas/Fort Worth Int'l (new Terminal D)	Irving, Texas	610,000	2005	New international terminal
Suvarnabhumi ("Golden Land")	near Bangkok, Thai.	563,000	2005	To replace Don Muang Airport—Southeast Asia's busiest airport
Pearson International	Toronto, Ont.	332,000	2003	New horseshoe-shaped terminal at Canada's busiest airport
Baiyun ("White Cloud") Int'l (replacement)	near Guangzhou (Canton), China	300,000	2003	Main hub airport of south China (excluding Hong Kong)
Munich Int'l (new Terminal 2)	northeast of Munich, Ger.	260,000	2003	Germany's busiest domestic passenger airport as of 2001
Bridges		**Length (main span; m)**		
I-95 (Woodrow Wilson #2)	Alexandria, Va.–Md. suburbs of D.C.	1,852[1]	2007	2 bascule spans forming higher inverted v-shape for ships; begun 2000
Nancha (1 bridge of 2-section Runyang)	Zhenjiang, China (across the Chang Jiang [Yangtze])	1,490	2005	To be world's third largest suspension bridge
Alfred Zampa Memorial (Carquinez #3)	Crockett, Calif.–Vallejo, Calif.	728	2003	Begun 2000; first major U.S. suspension bridge since 1973
Rion–Antirion	near Patrai, Greece (across Gulf of Corinth)	560	2004	To be world's longest cable-stayed bridge (incl. all spans)
Lupu	Shanghai, China (across the Huangpu)	550	2003	World's longest steel-arch bridge; spans linked October 7
new US 82 (Greenville #2)	Greenville, Miss.–Lake Village, Ark.	420	2006	To be longest cable-stayed bridge in U.S.
San Francisco–Oakland Bay (East Span)	Yerba Buena Is., Calif.–Oakland, Calif.	385	2006	2-km causeway + world's largest suspension bridge hung from single tower
William Natcher	Rockport, Ind.–near Owensboro, Ky.	366	2002	Longest cable-stayed bridge over U.S. inland waterway; opened October 21
Rosario–Victoria	Rosario to Victoria, Arg.	350	2003	Bridges/viaducts across 59-km-wide Paraná wetlands
Millau Viaduct	Tarn Gorge, west of Millau, France	342	2005	7 cable-stayed spans; world's highest (270 m) road viaduct
Leonard P. Zakim Bunker Hill	Boston, Mass.	227	2002	Widest (56 m) cable-stayed bridge in world; dedicated October 3–6
Buildings		**Height (m)**		
Taipei 101 (Taipei Financial Center)	Taipei, Taiwan	448	2004	Begun 1999; will be world's second tallest building to rooftop (+ spire, 508 m)
Two International Finance Centre	Hong Kong	412	2003	Begun 2000; to be world's fourth tallest building
Kingdom Centre	Riyadh, Saudi Arabia	296	2002	Tallest building in Saudi Arabia; #29 in the world
Mok-dong Hyperion Tower A	Seoul, S.Kor.	256	2003	Will be tallest building in South Korea; #3 all-residential in world
Torre Generali	Panama City, Panama	250	2003	Begun mid-2000; will be Latin America's tallest building (+ spire, 318 m)
Torre Mayor	Mexico City, Mex.	225	2003	Will be tallest building in Mexico
Esplanade—Theatres on the Bay	Singapore		2002	Has 2 unique spiked domes; opened October 12
Dams and Hydrological Projects		**Crest length (m)**		
Three Gorges	west of Yichang, China	1,983	2009	World's largest hydroelectric project; third (final) phase from November 2002
San Roque Multipurpose	Agno River, Luzon, Phil.	1,100	2003	Irrigation and flood control; tallest earth-and-rock fill dam in Asia
Bakun Dam	Balui River, Sarawak, Borneo, Malaysia	740	2007	Hydroelectricity to peninsular Malaysia via world's longest submarine cable
Mohale (Lesotho Highlands Water Project, Leso. to S.Af. water transfer)	Senqunyane River, 100 km SE of Maseru, Lesotho	700	2003	Filling of Mohale Reservoir began October 29
Sardar Sarovar Project	Narmada River, Madhya Pradesh, India	?	?	Largest dam of controversial 30-dam project; to benefit Gujarat state
Alqueva Dam	Guadiana River, 180 km SE of Lisbon, Port.	?	2002	Creates Europe's largest (250 sq km) reservoir; gates closed February 8
Sheikh Zayed	into bedrock of Lake Nasser, Egypt (72 km)	NA[2]	2002	To feed irrigation systems for southern desert valleys; opened December
Davis (holding) Pond	near Mississippi R., New Orleans, La. (36 sq km)	NA[2]	2002	World's largest freshwater diversion project; replenishes 31,000 sq km wetlands area with controlled seasonal flooding; opened March 26
Highways		**Length (km)**		
Golden Quadrilateral superhighway	Mumbai–Chennai–Kolkata–Delhi, India	5,846	2004	Upgraded to 4 or 6 lanes; includes town bypasses and service roads
Indus Highway	Karachi–Peshawar, Pak.	1,265	2003	59% complete as of September 2001
Highway 1	Kabul–Kandahar–Herat, Afg.	1,000	2005	Reconstruction paid for by U.S., Saudi Arabia, and Japan; begun November
Egnatia Motorway	Igoumenitsa–Thessaloniki, Greece	680	2006	First Greek highway at modern int'l standards; 69 tunnels
Croatian Motorway (Section III)	Bosiljevo–Sveti Rok, Croatia	145	2004	Built through mountainous terrain with unstable slopes, caverns, and unexploded ordnance
Railways (Heavy)		**Length (km)**		
Alice Springs–Darwin ("ADrail")	Alice Springs–Darwin, Australia	1,420	2004	Completes north-south rail link ("Darwin to Adelaide"); begun 2001
Qinghai–Tibet	Golmud, Qinghai, China–Lhasa, Tibet	1,118	2007	Highest world railway (5,072 m at summit); half of the line travels across permafrost
Xi'an–Hefei	Xi'an–Hefei, China	954	2005	To promote economic growth in interior provinces; begun 2000
Ferronorte (extension to Cuiabá)	Alto Taquari–Cuiabá, Braz.	525	2005	To promote exports from Mato Grosso (Brazilian interior)
Alameda Corridor (incl. 16-km trench)	Long Beach/L.A. ports–downtown L.A., Calif.	32	2002	Consolidated corridor for streamlined cargo handling; begun 1997
Railways (High Speed)		**Length (km)**		
Spanish High Speed (second line)	Madrid–Barcelona, Spain (extension to Figueras)	855	2005	Madrid–Lleida corridor to be completed in 2003
Taiwan High Speed	Taipei–Kaohsiung, Taiwan	326	2005	Links Taiwan's two largest cities along west coast
Kyongbu (phase 1)	Seoul–Taegu, S.Kor.	323	2004	Connects largest and third largest cities
Italian High Speed (second line)	Rome–Naples, Italy	222	2004	Begun 1994; part of planned 1,300-km high-speed network
German High Speed (third line)	Frankfurt–Cologne, Ger.	219	2002	Connects Cologne to Frankfurt International Airport; opened August 1
Shanghai maglev ("magnetic levitation")	Pudong International Airport–financial district, Shanghai, China	29.9	2003	World's first maglev train for public use; 430 km/hr on metro line 2
Subways/Metros/Light Rails		**Length (km)**		
Oporto Light Rail	Oporto, Port.	70.0	2002–04	Europe's largest total rail system project; some regular service from December 7
Hong Kong Railway (West Rail, phase 1)	Western New Territories to Kowloon, Hong Kong	30.3	2003	11.5 km in tunnels and 13.4 km on viaducts
Guangzhou (Canton) Metro (line 2)	Guangzhou, China (north-south line)	23.2	2003	Begun 1999; 34.7-km line 3 to be built 2003–07
Los Angeles Metro (Gold Line)	L.A. Union Station to Pasadena, Calif.	22.0	2003	
Copenhagen Metro	Copenhagen, Den.	21.0	2002–07	Line 1: opened October 19; largest driverless system in world
Hiawatha Light Rail	Downtown Minneapolis–Bloomington, Minn.	18.7	2004	Difficult tunneling under M/SP airport in unstable limestone; begun 2001
Tren Urbano (phase 1)	San Juan, P.R.	17.2	2003	Service links Bayamón (western suburbs) to north San Juan; 60% elevated
New York Airtrain (light rail)	N.Y. Kennedy Airport–subways + L.I. Railroad	13.5	2003	Enables direct links between Kennedy terminals and Manhattan
Tunnels		**Length (m)**		
Apennine Range tunnels (9)	Bologna–Florence, Italy (high-speed railway)	73,400	2007	Begun 1996; longest tunnel, 18.6 km; tunnels to cover 93% of railway
Lötschberg #2	Frutigen–Raron, Switz.	34,800	2007	To be world's 3rd longest rail tunnel; France–Italy link
Iwate Ichinohe	Morioka–Hachinohe, Japan	25,810	2002	World's 3rd longest rail tunnel; used by bullet train from Dec. 1
A86 Ring Road	around Paris, France	17,700	2004–08	Two tunnels (to east [10,100 m], to west [7,600 m])
Södra Länken ("Southern Link")	part of Stockholm, Sweden, ring road	16,600	2004	Complex underground interchanges
Hsüeh-shan ("Snow Mountain")	near Taipei, Taiwan	12,900	2004	To be world's 4th longest road tunnel; Taipei-I-lan expressway link
Westerscheldetunnel ("Western Schelde")	Terneuzen to Ellewoutsdijk, Neth.	6,600	2003	Longest world tunnel in "bored weak soil"
Vestmannasund Subsea Tunnel	Streym (Streymoy) and Vágar islands, Faroe Is.	4,940	2002	First subsea tunnel in the Faroe Islands

1 m=3.28 ft; 1 km=0.62 mi; 1 ha=2.47 ac   [1]Length of each span.   [2]Not applicable.

Art, Antiques, and Collections

In 2002 major exhibitions such as **DOCUMENTA 11** reflected the **DIVERSE NATURE OF CONTEMPORARY ART:** artists from a variety of cultures received widespread recognition for work ranging from installation to video to painting. More **TRADITIONAL ART** remained in demand, as major auction houses set **RECORD PRICES FOR ARTISTS** such as Peter Paul Rubens and Alberto Giacometti.

ART

Organized by Nigerian-born curator and critic Okwui Enwezor (*see* BIOGRAPHIES) and his curatorial team, Documenta 11, held in Kassel, Ger., was met with much acclaim. The exhibition featured several established artists, such as Joan Jonas, Louise Bourgeois, Dieter Roth, Adrian Piper, Leon Golub, and Alfredo Jaar, many of whom contributed new works made specifically for Documenta. Given the political predilections of Enwezor, much of the work by both established and emerging artists was politically oriented in some way. Significant among these was Swiss artist Thomas Hirschhorn's *Bataille Monument*, a multipart installation set up not in the confines of a gallery or any readily legible art context, but rather in a working-class neighbourhood in Kassel. The installation consisted of spray-painted Mercedes-Benz taxis, various plywood constructions (e.g., a TV studio and a snack bar), and a large treelike sculpture, all made by local residents under Hirschhorn's guidance. Also notable was British artist Yinka Shonibare's *Gallantry and Criminal Conversation*, an elaborate tableau of headless, mannequinlike figures in 18th-century dress meant to evoke white Europeans taking the colonialist "grand tour" of "exotic" lands. There was also photography, including examples by Bernd and Hilla Becher and Jeff Wall, but film and video dominated, with new works by Steve McQueen, Rénee Green, Fiona Tan, Issac Julien, and Pierre Huyghe, among many others.

While painting was not a strong presence at Documenta, it asserted itself elsewhere. (See *Art Exhibitions*, below.) A painter of some controversy was British artist Glenn Brown, who essentially remade the works of renowned artists—including Rembrandt, Jean-Honoré Fragonard, and Willem de Kooning—but repainted the images flatly and eliminated any trace of texture or brushwork. Although this strategy of appropriation can be traced back at least to the 1980s, Brown was a vexing figure for many observers, who considered his "interventions" subversions of traditional notions of artistic integrity. A painter with a wholly different sensibility was American Brian Calvin, who populated his canvases with androgynous long-haired figures who confined their activities mostly to smoking, strolling, or staring vacantly. These pictures functioned as a kind of social record of Calvin's youthful milieu and could perhaps be considered the "slacker" equivalent to Alex Katz's large-scale figural groupings. Figurative painting continued to be notable in part because of American John Currin, who, along with British artist Lucien Freud, remained one of the most significant contemporary painters of the human form. Currin's subject matter could be something as banal as suburban housewives having coffee or as seemingly straightforward as a portrait, but his work was complicated by various art-historical references (from traditional iconography to the work of Gustave Courbet and Andrea Mantegna), an anxious line, and, especially, a distorted, almost grotesque treatment of the female figure.

Many artists were still mining the possibilities of work that self-consciously bridged the gap between painting and other media. American James Hyde combined aspects of sculpture, painting, and décor in diverse synthetic forms. His "Pillows" resembled giant inflated abstractions: the constructions of nylon webbing arranged in colourful tangles on the wall seemed like painterly gestures that have been released from an abstract painting. British artist Jim Lambie became known for his use of vinyl tape to cover gallery floors in geometric patterns, often extending the edges of these pieces beyond the exhibition spaces—a kind of metaphor for an extended definition of the painting as a medium.

In *Cosmic Thing* (first installed at the Institute of Contemporary Art, Philadelphia), Mexico City-based Damián Ortega took an actual Volkswagen Beetle and carefully disassembled each piece—frame, doors, engine, wheels, even interior upholstery—and suspended the parts from the gallery's ceiling by aircraft cables. The car appeared to have been blown apart but not destroyed, reconfigured into a schematic, three-dimensional rendering of a whole. Ortega's piece was a commentary on the pervasive economic and social presence of the VW in Mexico—it was the car millions of Mexicans drove, and the VW manufacturing plant in Puebla, outside Mexico City, was one of the largest employers in the country.

Like Ortega, Swiss artist Christoph Büchel made use of everyday materials, but to very different ends. Büchel was an artist for whom there seemed to be little distinction between construction and deconstruction. In late 2001, for the inaugural show at Maccarone, Inc., a New York City gallery, Büchel was told he could do whatever he wanted to the then-unrenovated two-story gallery space. He created a new set of spaces by hacking through floors and walls and hauling in bundles of newspaper, street detritus, desks, television sets, a shopping cart, and a tremendous quantity of cigarette butts. To experience this contemporary *Merzbau*, viewers had to traverse through holes in the walls and floors, crawl through cramped spaces, scale ladders, and crawl through windows.

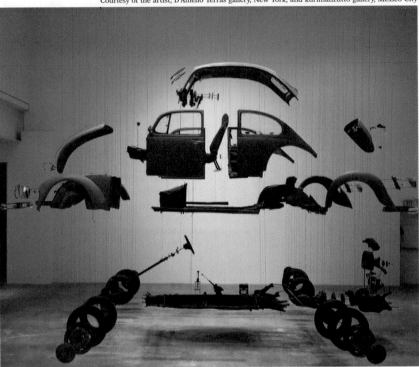

Damián Ortega's installation Cosmic Thing, *a sculptural decomposition of a Volkswagen Beetle, was on display at the Institute of Contemporary Art, Philadelphia, during the year.*

Known as a provocateur, Italian artist Maurizio Cattelan remained true to that designation with *Frank and Jamie*, two life-size wax figures of police officers from the New York City Housing Authority presented standing on their heads. These upside-down figures were controversial, and many interpreted Cattelan's image of neutralized power as a deliberate and inappropriate parody of the New York City Police Department. For the artist, however, it was a commentary on a moment of crisis in authority and a continuation of his ongoing critical examination of revered figures in contemporary culture.

More informed by personal experience was American artist Sanford Biggers's *La Racine de mémoire*. In this piece old Super-8 home movies of the artist's family at birthday parties and other gatherings were projected inside a small barnlike shed. Installed outdoors in a tree at the Aldrich Museum of Contemporary Art, Ridgefield, Conn., the shed had one side decorated with glass bottles, evoking both Southern vernacular traditions as well as the African custom of creating altars in trees or caves in memory of the dead.

In the past the Whitney Biennial had been criticized for focusing on art that was produced, exhibited, and critically favoured in New York City rather than presenting a broad survey of the contemporary American scene. Curator and organizer Lawrence Rinder and his colleagues aimed for something more inclusive in 2002, and so they traveled extensively and chose a group of 113 diverse artists and collaborative teams whose work represented a variety of media: installation, photography, painting, sculpture, film and video projections, Internet-art projects, architecture, sound and performance art, and works that, as Rinder noted, "fall outside of any conventional aesthetic definition." The latter category might have included Rosie Lee Tompkins's expressive vernacular quilts or even Robert Lazzarini's wildly distorted, almost rubberlike pay phone. Installed in nearby Central Park were Brian Tolle's series of unexpected "splashes"—Tolles used an invisible system of underwater air valves in the park's many ponds to simulate the splashes made by skipping a rock across the water's surface—and Keith Edmier's monument honouring his two grandfathers' service in World War II. (*See* Special Report.)

Works based solely on sound rather than visual components were among the most interesting contributions to the Whitney and elsewhere. At the bi-ennial, visitors could experience sound pieces ranging from Minimalist compositions to narratives and stories and instrumental works by wearing one of many pairs of headphones in a specially designed "surround sound" installation room. Among these were the "audio collages" of Gregor Asch (DJ Olive the Audio Janitor), which combined the sounds of the city with samples of existing music; Miranda July's sound track of conversation and sound effects, which played in the museum's elevator; and Stephen Vitiello's audio piece based on recordings made from his 91st-floor studio in the World Trade Center in 1999. (MEGHAN DAILEY)

ART EXHIBITIONS

Numerous important exhibitions featuring women artists took place in 2002. One of the most anticipated shows was a retrospective of Eve Hesse at the San Francisco Museum of Modern Art. During her brief career, Hesse created a significant group of sculptures that were among the most important works of postminimalism. She used unconventional materials such as latex, fibreglass, and resin to make her evocative, often corporeally suggestive work. The Whitney Museum of American Art, New York City, held an exhibition of the work of Abstract Expressionist painter Joan Mitchell, showing 59 of her works from the early 1950s onward. This show offered an opportunity to reassess Mitchell's powerful abstractions and her success as a woman artist in the male-dominated New York school. Two exhibitions focused on Judy Chicago, a key figure in the feminist art movement. The National Museum of Women in the Arts, Washington, D.C., examined examples of Chicago's early projects, including the establishment (with artist Miriam Schapiro) of the art and performance space Womanhouse in Los Angeles in 1972. Her signature work, the iconic and monumental *Dinner Party* (1979), was presented at the Brooklyn (N.Y.) Museum of Art (it was to be given its own gallery there in 2004).

In addition to these contemporary women, Artemisia Gentileschi, a compelling 17th-century Italian painter, also received recognition in 2002. Gentileschi's artistic achievements had often been obscured by the lurid details of her life; however, despite her tribulations—or, as had been suggested by feminist scholars, perhaps because of them—she developed an artistic style that rivaled that of her renowned father, Orazio. In an exhibition of both artists' work, the Metropolitan Museum of Art, New York City, explored the relationship between father and daughter in depth, presenting their individual achievements and mutual influences.

Nineteenth-century art was the subject of several exhibitions. Landscape paintings, including those by the Hudson River school, were gathered in "American Sublime," organized by the Tate Britain, London. These quintessentially American paintings focus on the majesty of nature and the transcendental philosophies that were so pervasive in the young republic in the 19th century. The Tate Britain turned a critical eye toward 19th-century British art in "The Victorian Nude," which offered a different perspective of the supposedly staid Victorians by revealing a taste for frolicking nymphs, nubile youths, and goddesses cloaked in nothing but the guise of Classicism.

Early 20th-century art attracted large audiences at several major exhibitions, notably the blockbuster Matisse/Picasso exhibition at the Tate Modern, London, which considered the work of these two

modern masters and their sustained artistic dialogue with one another. Like Picasso and Matisse, Surrealism consistently fascinated museum audiences. The Metropolitan Museum of Art exhibited "Surrealism: Desire Unbound" (organized by the Tate Modern), which focused on eroticism and sexuality—dominant Surrealist themes—and included early paintings by Marcel Duchamp, Salvador Dalí's ubiquitous dreamscapes, and Hans Bellmer's disturbing photographic tableaux of dolls and mannequins from the 1930s. In Paris, the birthplace of Surrealism, the Centre Pompidou presented "The Surrealist Revolution," an exhibition that included hundreds of objects and presented an essential overview of the movement.

At the turn of the 21st century, the art world began to engage in a retrospective consideration of important artists from the mid-20th century. Barnett Newman created expansive, richly coloured, large-scale paintings that defined the "heroic" art of the New York school in the 1950s. The Philadelphia Museum of Art displayed nearly 100 of his works, including examples of his fa-

mous "zip" paintings. From the same era as Newman, Larry Rivers broke away from the New York school's seriousness to create lighter, more representational, and often parodic work. His deadpan neo-Pop pastiche of Emanuel Leutze's *Washington Crossing the Delaware* and over 50 other works were shown in a retrospective at the Corcoran Gallery of Art, Washington, D.C., that opened just a few months before Rivers died in August. (*See* OBITUARIES.) The Tate Modern presented a major retrospective of Pop artist Andy Warhol. The show featured such iconic works as Warhol's series depicting Campbell's soup cans and Marilyn Monroe; it went on to draw a record number of visitors when it traveled to the Museum of Contemporary Art, Los Angeles, its only American venue.

Later 20th-century figures also received recognition. "Gerhard Richter: Forty Years of Painting," organized by the Museum of Modern Art, New York City, chronicled the work of this influential German artist. (*See* BIOGRAPHIES.) The exhibition featured 180 paintings, including the photo-based works Richter began in the 1960s, abstractions, landscapes, his remarkable "October 18, 1977" series, and intimate portraits. The Institute of Contemporary Art, Boston, presented a selection of sculptures by Chinese artist Chen Zhen, the first exhibition of his work since his death in 2000. The exhibition featured his last work, *Zen Garden* (2000). A model for a public garden, this piece contained sculpted representations of organs pierced by medical instruments, representing themes present in much of Chen's work: the collision of Chinese and Western art, medicine, and metaphoric representations of the human body.

Major exhibitions demonstrated the tremendous range of contemporary artistic practices. In New York City the Studio Museum in Harlem presented "Black Romantic," an eclectic show of figurative painting and sculpture by artists whose work was widely collected in the African American community. The exhibition, curated by rising star Thelma Golden, served as a reminder that there were many vital, diverse "art worlds" that coexisted but did not always intersect. Two major international exhibitions—Documenta 11 in Kassel, Ger. (see *Art*, above), and the São Paulo Bienal in Brazil—revealed the increasingly global nature of the art world. Documenta was actually the fifth and

(continued on page 166)

Judy Chicago's **The Dinner Party** *(1979), presented at the Brooklyn (N.Y.) Museum of Art in 2002, is emblazoned with the names of important women in history.*

Redefining

T hough French artist Marcel Duchamp was credited early in the 20th century with having broken down the boundaries between works of art and everyday objects, by the year 2002 the traditional meaning of the word *art* had vastly expanded. Art at the beginning of the 21st century was not limited to paintings and sculpture but encompassed a variety of media, including video, performance, installation, digital Internet work, and sound. Some art exhibitions were even devoid of what many considered any art in the traditional sense. A show held in England in 2001, entitled "Exhibition To Be Constructed in Your Head," featured only what artists called "negative space," written captions that challenged visitors to imagine the missing artworks. Later that year an installation work by British artist Damien Hirst, consisting of ashtrays brimming with cigarette butts, empty beer bottles, candy wrappers, and art supplies, was disassembled by a well-meaning custodian who mistook the collection for garbage. The action sparked a lively discussion of what is art and what is not, which Mayfair gallery spokesperson Alison Smith declared was "always healthy."

Even more controversial was an anatomic exhibition that opened in March 2002 at the Atlantis Gallery in East London. There, several human corpses were on display—including those of a pole vaulter, a dancer, a pregnant woman, a basketball player, and a cyclist. The forms were preserved by a technique called plastination, and some of them were fashioned to simulate motion.

A kaleidoscope of cutting-edge art forms—or what some considered outrageous imposters—was featured in galleries throughout the world in 2002 and also at a number of high-profile venues, including the Sydney (Australia) Biennale; Documenta 11, held in Germany; Expo.02, in Switzerland; and the 2002 Whitney Biennial, New York City. It was anyone's guess what new direction art would be taking.

by Karen J. Sparks

Karen J. Sparks is Editor of Britannica Book of the Year.

(Clockwise from top left) Bill Viola's The Crossing *(1996), a life-size video installation that utilizes intense stereo sound to amplify the viewing experience; an installation from Daniel Burden's restrospective "The Museum Which Did Not Exist," held at the Pompidou Centre, Paris, in 2002. Here Burden covered the gallery walls with striped cloth that was uniformly 3.4 in (8.7 cm) wide; Nam June Paik's* SysCop *(1994), a "video sculpture" in which an original video by Paik is played amidst various-sized television sets, neon stop lights, and a robotlike steel frame covered with chassis; Theo Jansen's* Animaris Currens Ventosa *(1992), an animal-like form constructed of yellow plastic tubes that is made to move—and seemingly come to life—with the wind; Vanessa Beecroft's* VB 35 *("Show") (1997), a performance at the Guggenheim Museum, New York City, in which 20 models, some wearing Gucci bikinis and some nude, were "installed" in the rotunda of the museum.*

(Left) A production photograph from Matthew Barney's film Cremaster 4 *(1994), part of Barney's cycle of elaborately produced Cremaster films. Here Barney portrays a satyr character. (Above) Corine Borgnet's* Tower of Babel *(2002), a structure erected from used Post-it notes and Styrofoam. (Opposite page, clockwise from top left) Sarah Sze's* Every Thing in Its Right Place *(2002), an installation, stretching up through three floors of a São Paulo, Braz., atrium, made of boxes, artificial plants, a ladder, lamps, foam, funnels, water bottles, clamps, string, Q-tips, fans, and cords; Yayoi Kusama's* Dots Obsession—New Century *(2000), a room installation made of vinyl dots and balloons; a detail of Thomas Hirschhorn's* Cavemanman *(2002), a cavelike installation of tape, cardboard, wood, assorted plastic, paper, neon bulbs, aluminum foil, integrated videos, electrical wires, assorted printed matter, aluminum cans, gold foil, photocopies, and spray paint; Tracey Emin's* Everyone I Have Ever Slept With 1963–1995 *(1995), a tent in which the artist hand-appliquéd the names of her past lovers; Mariko Mori's* Birth of a Star *(1995), a three-dimensional photograph made in part from a lightbox and accompanied by an audio CD playing pop music. Mori herself portrays the pop star character.*

(continued from page 161)
final program of "Platforms," a year-long series of lectures, symposia, films, and art in different international cities (Vienna, New Delhi, the Caribbean island of St. Lucia, Lagos, and finally Kassel). The São Paulo Bienal featured 150 artists and took "Metropolitan Iconographies" as its overarching theme. To this end, many of the works centred on representations of the city, including Alexander Brodsky's sculpted miniature city built inside large, rusty trash receptacles, Fabrice Gygi's observation tower with a mechanized elevator, and Frank Thiel's and Michael Wesely's large-scale photographs of Berlin.

Other exhibitions focused on major trends in contemporary art, often featuring more photography-based work, such as film and video, than painting. At the Whitney Biennial in New York City (see Art, above), pieces ranging from sound-based installations and digital works to live performances to paintings were on display. Still, amid declarations of the death of painting, the exhibition "Cher peintre," at the Centre Pompidou, proved the power of figurative painting in the contemporary scene. The show featured a group of very savvy contemporary painters who practiced figuration with a conceptual twist—Brian Calvin, John Currin, Kurt Kauper, and Elizabeth Peyton among them. These artists cheerfully owed a debt to precursors Martin Kippenberger (the show took its title from one of his works), Alex Katz, Sigmar Polke, and Bernard Buffett, all of whom were included in this zeitgeist-defining show.

(MEGHAN DAILEY)

PHOTOGRAPHY

The most prominent photography exhibitions and awards in 2002 reflected the diversity of the medium as it continued to expand its scope, influence, and technology.

The Dallas (Texas) Museum of Art organized the first retrospective exhibition of contemporary German photographer Thomas Struth. The exhibition consisted of 80 photographs spanning the 1970s through the present, including early black-and-white images of monumental architectural icons in international cities, depictions of cultural and spiritual meccas from the "museum" series, and large-format colour photographs of the jungles of Asia and South America.

Renowned German photographer Andreas Gursky, whose work was often compared to that of Struth, followed his highly acclaimed retrospective debut in 2001 at the Museum of Modern Art, New York City, with a traveling tour that was exhibited at the Centre Pompidou, Paris; the Museo Nacional Centro de Arte Reina Sofía, Madrid; and the Museum of Contemporary Art, Chicago. The show presented 45 images, with an emphasis on works completed in the 1990s, when Gursky began to photograph the iconography of the contemporary global market, using saturated colour, unsurpassed detail, and grand scale (his photographs were as large as [4.9 m] 16 ft wide). Also, late in 2001, Gursky's Paris, Montparnasse (1993) sold for $600,000 at Christie's, a world record for a contemporary photograph bought at auction.

Contemporary artist Lorna Simpson's film installation 31 chronicled the life of a woman over a period of 31 days, presented on 31 video monitors. After it premiered at Documenta 11 (an exhibition of international art held in Kassel, Ger.; see Art Exhibitions, above), 31 was presented with three earlier film pieces by Simpson (Call Waiting, Recollection, and Duet), as well as an exhibition of her recent photographic works in two concurrent shows at the Whitney Museum of American Art, New York City. In her art Simpson used traditional narrative devices to examine the politics of gender and race from an African American woman's perspective. Chrissie Iles, Whitney curator of film and video, explained: "The work of Lorna Simpson engages one of the defining principles of cinema: the relationship between image and language."

"Twilight," the most recent in a series of exhibitions by Gregory Crewdson, was shown at the Luhring Augustine Gallery, New York City; the Gagosian Gallery, Los Angeles; and the White Cube Gallery, London. Crewdson's elaborately staged photographs employed cinematic effects and digital enhancements, presenting a surreal tale about ordinary suburban life made extraordinary.

The first survey show of the work of British photographer Adam Fuss premiered at the Museum of Fine Arts, Boston. The exhibition was organized by Kunsthalle Bielefeld (Ger.) and was scheduled to travel across Europe after the Boston show. Fuss's cameraless photograms used traditional photographic methods and depended on the most basic elements of photography—objects as they react to light—to express the evanescent nature of the passing of time.

Irving Penn had two simultaneous museum shows in New York City. "Dancer: 1999 Nudes" was an exhibition of Penn's recent nudes shown at the Whitney Museum of American Art (in conjunction with the Museum of Fine Arts, Houston, Texas). "Earthly Bodies," a look at Penn's nudes from 1949 to 1950, premiered at the Metropolitan Museum of Art. Both shows were celebrations of Penn's brilliant ability to capture soft light bouncing off the voluptuous female form. Penn's contemporary Richard Avedon also received recognition when "Richard Avedon: Portraits" was exhibited at the Metropolitan Museum of Art. The show presented approximately 180 portraits of many celebrated artistic, intellectual, and political figures.

Photographers from past eras were also featured in major exhibitions. The J. Paul Getty Museum, Los Angeles, exhibited the work of the 19th-century French photographer Gustave Le Gray, the largest exhibition of his work ever shown in the United States. The show was selected from a survey of Le Gray's photographs at the Bibliothèque Nationale de France. "Alfred Stieglitz: Known and Unknown" was exhibited at the National Gallery of Art, Washington, D.C. The show presented more than 100 prints spanning this early 20th-century artist's career, with an emphasis on many lesser-known works, some of which had never before been exhibited or published. The show was accompanied by a scholarly catalog of the Alfred Stieglitz Collection that reproduced all 1,642 photographs held by the gallery.

At its annual Infinity awards ceremony, the International Center of Photography presented the Cornell Capa Award to the organizers of "Here Is New York," an acclaimed project featuring thousands of images, taken by both professional and amateur photographers, of the World Trade Center tragedy. The ICP Infinity award for art was given to Iranian artist Shirin Neshat, who had gained recognition for her photography, film, and video installations exploring the complex philosophical ideas behind contemporary Islam. Neshat also had a solo exhibition at the Castello di Rivoli Museum of Contemporary Art, Turin, Italy. Tyler Hicks received the ICP Infinity award for photojournalism. Hicks had won numerous awards from the National Press Photographers Association. As a New York Times contract photographer, he covered the war in Kosovo, the spread of the Ebola virus in Uganda, the Ethiopian-Eritrean war, the conflict in Sierra Leone, and the war in Afghanistan.

Other major awards presented in 2002 included the Getty Images Lifetime Achievement Award, which was presented posthumously to Michael Hoffman, the former executive director and publisher of the Aperture Foundation. During Hoffman's tenure he was directly involved in the creation and production of over 450 books and more than 100 issues of *Aperture* magazine. At the 59th Annual Pictures of the Year International Awards and Exhibition, Brian Plonka was named Newspaper Photographer of the Year, and James Nachtwey was acknowledged as Magazine Photographer of the Year. The 2002 Pulitzer Prize for breaking news photography was awarded to the *New York Times* for its outstanding coverage of the terrorist attacks in New York City and their aftermath. The Pulitzer Prize for feature photography also went to the *New York Times* for its photographs chronicling the people of war-torn Afghanistan.

On Feb. 28, 2002, nearly 100 of the world's top photojournalists were given 24 hours to capture the people and places of modern-day Africa. Their photographs were assembled in the book *A Day in the Life of Africa*, the proceeds from which funded AIDS education in Africa. (*See* photographs on pages 378–379 and 412).

Among the technological advances and product news in photography was the debut of Adobe's Photoshop 7, which featured the "Healing Brush," a new tool for photo retouching. Other remarkable advances in digital media included Kodak's digital back, an attachment that translated film images created with medium-format cameras into high-resolution digital images, and Contax's N digital SLR (single-lens reflex) camera, the first digital camera with a full-frame 35mm image sensor. The new N digital had the same basic operational characteris-

tics as the film SLR camera, using the same lenses and accessories. The N digital could write in several formats, including JPEG, RGB-TIFF, and RAW, and it was equipped with a computer interface for reliable high-speed image transfer. Equally impressive were the advances in Epson printing technology, namely the Stylus Pro 7600 and Stylus

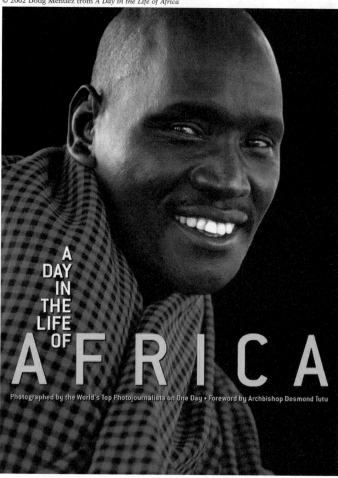

© 2002 Doug Menuez from *A Day in the Life of Africa*

Doug Menuez's image of a Tanzanian man graced the cover of A Day in the Life of Africa, *which included some 250 photographs taken in 53 African countries during a 24-hour period.*

Pro 9600, which allowed for the production of large-format grayscale prints with an archival life up to 200 years.

Notable members of the photographic community who died during the year included Canadian portrait photographer Yousuf Karsh, Mexican photographer Manuel Álvarez Bravo, celebrity photographer Herb Ritts, landscape photographer Galen Rowell, sports photographer John Zimmerman (*see* OBITUARIES), and Magnum photographer Inge Morath.

(MARLA CAPLAN)

ART AUCTIONS AND SALES

The art and auction market of 2002 continued to surprise both Sotheby's and Christie's with its resilience amid a declining economy. Buyers did not stray from intense competition over works of art and over single-owner collections of extraordinary quality and provenance.

An unexpected number of artist records were set on the auction block in 2002. Christie's and Sotheby's realized dramatically strong results for their evening sales of contemporary, Impressionist, and modern art, completely outperforming any of their auction competitors in these important markets.

As the first important fine art sales of the year, the Old Master paintings sales in New York did not disappoint at either auction house. Sotheby's sales of Old Master paintings achieved a formidable total of $33,032,000. The highlight of this event was the $3,140,750 paid for Sir Anthony Van Dyck's *Bust of the Apostle Peter*, which set a record for the artist at auction. Another record was set when François Gérard's *Portrait of Catherine Worlée, Princesse de Talleyrand-Périgord* sold for $1,875,-750. Christie's Old Master paintings sale totaled $9,287,575, yielding two auction records for major artists: Pier Francesco Mola's *An Artist and a Youth* fetched $3,086,000, while *A Landscape with the Conversion of Saint Paul on the Road to Damascus*, by Herri met de Bles (Il Civetta), was purchased for $732,000.

At the January Old Master drawings sales in New York, Christie's sales totaled $6,439,365. Rousing major interest from bidders and collectors was the sale of the previously undiscovered *Head of a Young Man Looking Up* by Parmigianino, which sold for $765,000. The sales at Sotheby's totaled $2,979,-740 and were highlighted by Giorgio Vasari's *St. Jerome and the Lion*, which soared past its high estimate of $70,000, ultimately selling for $236,750.

AP/Wide World Photos

Peter Paul Rubens's Massacre of the Innocents *was part of a record auction at Sotheby's London during the year.*

At Sotheby's London in July, the Old Master paintings sale attained historic proportions when it totaled $111,183,035, the highest total ever in this category. The sale set world auction records for five artists, the unqualified highlight of which was Peter Paul Rubens's masterpiece *Massacre of the Innocents*, which sold for $76,730,703.

The most prominent of the year's art sales were the May Impressionist and modern art sales; these were often seen as an indicator of the overall health of the marketplace. At Sotheby's New York the series totaled $149,083,878. The undisputed star there was Paul Cézanne's *Pichet et assiette de poires* from the Sandblom Collection, which sold for $16.8 million. The most intense fervour, however, was realized in the saleroom when Alberto Giacometti's *Grand tête de Diego,* from the collection of Samuel and Luella Maslon, flew past its high estimate of $7,000,000 to a staggering price of $13,759,500.

The May evening sale at Christie's reached an impressive total of $97,647,000. Constantin Brancusi's *Danaïde* sold for $18,159,500, setting a world record at auction for the artist as well as for any piece of sculpture offered through public auction. The top painting of the evening was René Magritte's *L'Empire des lumières,* which sold for $12,659,500, nearly doubling the previously established record for the artist.

These series were equally strong in London, with Christie's June Impressionist and modern art evening sale totaling $59,910,233. The highest lot of the evening was Pablo Picasso's *Nu au collier,* which reached $23,919,018. Selling for $3,225,323, and setting a world record for the artist at auction, was Emil Nolde's *Blumengarten.* The June sales at Sotheby's in London of the same category attained results of $71,196,472. The highest price paid for a painting was for Claude Monet's *Nymphéas (Water Lilies),* which brought $20,194,203.

The May postwar and contemporary art sale at Christie's in New York had a two-day total of $55,149,025. The top lot of the sale was Jean-Michel's Basquiat's *Profit I,* which sold for $5,509,500, while Donald Judd's stainless steel and Plexiglas sculpture *Untitled* brought in $4,629,500. Sotheby's spring contemporary art sale in New York garnered a result of $57,233,199. Top prices were achieved for masterworks by Gerhard Richter (*see* BIOGRAPHIES), with *180 Farben* and *Kerze* each fetching $3,969,500. Among the successful sales of Andy Warhol's work was *Five Deaths,* from the artist's *Death and Disaster* series of 1963, which brought $3,749,500.

A lucrative contemporary art evening sale at Sotheby's in London on June 26 brought $21,507,106, the highest total in London since 1990, with four works selling for more than £1,000,000 (about

$1,500,000). The top lot was Gerhard Richter's *Wolkenstudie, Grün-Blau (Study for Clouds, Green-Blue),* which earned $3,029,815. Christie's London contemporary art evening sale in June earned $13,335,180, with Basquiat's *Untitled (Saint)* reaching $2,100,100.

The Sotheby's American paintings sale in New York reached $32,732,448. Norman Rockwell's iconic image *Rosie the Riveter* established a new record for the artist at auction when it sold for $4,959,500. Christie's New York American paintings sale in April brought $12,551,515. The star of the sale was the painting by Georgia O'Keeffe entitled *Ram's Head, Blue Morning Glory,* which sold for $3,419,500.

The November sales of Impressionist and modern art underlined the health of the market at both auction houses. The evening sale at Sotheby's New York totaled $81,453,500 and culminated with the spectacular sale of Monet's *Nymphéas,* another treatment of the water lilies theme, which fetched $18,709,500. The Impressionist and modern sales were similarly strong at Christie's New York, where a total of $87,643,055 was reached. As in the spring series, the top lot of this sale was a Picasso, a bronze sculpture entitled *La Geunon et son petit,* which sold for $6,719,500.

At Sotheby's New York in November, the evening sale of contemporary art achieved its highest total since 1989, reaching $78,287,775 and setting individual records for six artists. The top lot of the evening, from a private American collection, was Willem de Kooning's *Orestes,* which surpassed its $10,000,000 estimate to sell for $13,209,500. At the postwar and contemporary art evening sale at Christie's New York on November 13, individual artist records were set in a sale that fetched a total of $66,921,785. The star of the sale was *0 Through 9* by Jasper Johns, which sparked an aggressive bidding war and ultimately sold for $9,909,500.

The jewelry market also maintained the equilibrium of years past at both houses. Christie's New York achieved a total of $12,858,163 in its April magnificent jewels sale. The highlight of the sale was a magnificent pair of Art Deco cushion-cut diamond ear pendants that went for $2,041,000. In a separate sale in April, Christie's also sold the Winter Egg by Peter Carl Fabergé for a staggering $9,579,500. At Sotheby's New York, the April magnificent jewels sales were highlighted by a collection of jewels from the estate of Janice H. Levin, which fetched a total of $8,150,033. A rare pair of pear-shaped diamond pendants by Van Cleef & Arpels sold for $1,659,500.   (AMY TODD MIDDLETON)

ANTIQUES AND COLLECTIBLES

The antiques and collectibles market was influenced by several different factors in 2002. Uncertainties in the stock market led some people to spend more money on antiques and collectibles than on traditional investment opportunities. The slowed economy stopped others from buying simply because they had less money to spend. In the early part of the year, antique shows, malls, flea markets, and small shops reported poor sales, but by the fall large flea markets and shows were seeing stronger attendance and better sales. Rare and top-quality items in particular sold for strong prices, while more common items sold about 20% lower than they had the previous year.

Different pressures affected Internet sales. Because many sellers used the Internet, the supply of some collectibles increased beyond demand and caused prices to soften. Some items once considered rare, such as World's Fair souvenirs and old books and bottles, were offered for sale on the Internet at sites such as eBay in large numbers. Traditional auction houses did not do well conducting major auctions on-line, even when they sold collectibles rather than fine art. As a result, some auction houses abandoned the Internet, merged, or went out of business. Foreign buyers helped raise Internet prices on some items, however, such as vintage sportswear, Nippon ceramics, and perfume bottles.

New television shows about collecting, such as *The Incurable Collector* and *Flea Market Finds with the Kovels*, appeared on cable and public television, and the media reported on antiques, collecting, and prices for items from the 20th century. This created a new group of younger collectors looking for items dating from the 1950s to the '70s.

Some collectibles rose in price during the year, notably items from the American West, ranging from Molesworth furniture to cowgirl clothing; sewing paraphernalia, including needle cases and sewing boxes; late 20th-century Italian art glass; American-made sets of stemware; and horror and science-fiction movie posters. While there were fewer record prices than in previous

Guitars that once belonged to Jerry Garcia, leader of the rock band the Grateful Dead, are auctioned off at Studio 54 in New York City on May 8.

years, more than 20 different auction houses in more than 15 different cities set records, several for 20th-century pieces. Among the record-setting prices were $310,500 for a 178.2-cm-tall (1 cm = 0.39 in) Honduras mahogany chiffonier—inlaid with mother-of-pearl, wood, and metal in a tree-of-life design—designed about 1908 by Charles and Henry Greene; $273,500 for a 1904 oak chest of drawers, with landscapes painted on its panel doors, made at the Byrdcliffe Arts and Crafts Colony near Woodstock, N.Y.; $36,750 for a reproduction of a Goddard-Townsend nineshell block-front Chippendale secretary, made by Wallace Nutting about 1930; and $106,400 for a 3-m (10-ft)-tall Horner mahogany grandfather clock with carved figures and a nine-tube Westminster chime.

A few glass and pottery pieces also sold for record prices. An aqua opalescent Carnival glass master ice cream bowl in the Peacock and Urn pattern with butterscotch and pink iridescence auctioned for $22,000. Tiffany glass, particularly lamps, sold well all year, but the only record was for a 1913 Favrile aquamarine goldfish vase with a solid bottom depicting a marine scene, which brought $532,000. Two pottery records were set: a 30.5-cm-square Grueby tile decorated with a seven-colour Viking ship sold for $73,700, and a 1902 English Moorcroft

Hesperian jardiniere and stand decorated with carp, seaweed, plants, and shells sold for $48,230.

Sports collectibles records included $7,820 for a Fennimore canvasback drake decoy; $82,599 for a bat used by Babe Ruth from the 1920s, complete with 11 home-run notches; and $99,445 for the red crushed-velvet boxing trunks worn by Muhammad Ali in 1971 when he lost a world championship.

Two dolls were record breakers: a 1916 Albert Marque French bisque doll with a socket head and red mohair wig auctioned for $215,000, and a Schmitt & Fils French bisque bébé with brown glass eyes and blonde hair brought $48,000. Although no other toys set records in 2002, several auctions sold metal toys for extremely high prices.

Other records set during the year included a 1930s Roy Rogers parade saddle with gold and silver trim decorated with rubies, which sold for $412,500; a Nutting photograph entitled *Old Mother Hubbard* (19.3 × 24.4 cm), which brought $8,910; a German poster advertising Orville Wright's 1909 flying exhibition in Berlin, which went for $19,550; and two custom guitars made by Doug Irwin and used by the Grateful Dead's Jerry Garcia. One of the guitars, called "Wolf," sold for $789,500, and the other, called "Tiger," brought a record $957,500.

(RALPH AND TERRY KOVEL)

Computers and Information Systems

The spread of **WIRELESS TECHNOLOGY REVOLUTIONIZED** the information services sectors in 2002, as did growing concerns about **COMPUTER SECURITY** measures. The merger of Hewlett-Packard and Compaq Computer and the **BANKRUPTCIES** of Global Crossing and WorldCom dominated corporate news, while the recording and movie industries fought back against the **ABUSE OF FILE-SHARING** Web sites.

The year 2002 was not a good one for computer technology companies. The recession sharply reduced sales; thousands of information technology (IT) workers lost their jobs; and technology-related stocks were battered on Wall Street. Even in hard times, however, the technology world seethed with activity. The legal battle over the future of on-line music continued, and there was no resolution in sight. Enthusiasm for broadband Internet access cooled, but the battle for on-line customers between AOL Time Warner, Inc., and Microsoft Corp. heated up. Hewlett-Packard Co. (HP) acquired Compaq Computer Corp. for $19 billion, despite a hard-fought battle by some shareholders to prevent the deal.

Music and Film on the Internet. The legal issue that drew the most attention was the battle between the music-recording industry and various unauthorized Web sites that distributed music for free over the Internet. The recording industry managed to drive Napster, the high-profile Web service that had popularized free music downloads, off the Internet with a court order. (Napster later filed for bankruptcy after it failed to raise capital in order to become a for-pay music service.) Other Web organizations, however, took Napster's place and attracted millions of consumers. These new organizations appeared to be harder to shut down, since they used peer-to-peer network sharing, in which a central Web site like Napster's was not necessary for individuals to trade files.

The Recording Industry Association of America (RIAA) pressed ahead with more lawsuits, sometimes in concert with the Motion Picture Association of America (MPAA), which was concerned because some of the free Internet music services also distributed free unauthorized copies of Hollywood films. (Only about 10% of U.S. households had the high-speed broadband Internet connection that was needed to make downloading a movie practical.) In October 2001 the RIAA and the MPAA filed suit against Napster successors Kazaa BV, Grokster Ltd., and StreamCast Networks, Inc., all of which distributed software created by Amsterdam-based Consumer Empowerment BV, or FastTrack. A Dutch court ordered the owners of the Kazaa software to stop distributing the music-sharing software over the Internet, but in March 2002 the Amsterdam Court of Justice ruled on appeal that the Kazaa software owners were not liable for abuse of their file-sharing program, which had other uses besides downloading copyrighted music and films.

Internet service providers (ISPs) also became a legal target. In August 13 record labels sued four ISPs—AT&T Broadband, Cable and Wireless, Sprint PCS, and WorldCom, Inc.'s UUNet Technologies—in an effort to stop them from providing access to a Chinese Web site, Listen4ever.com, from which unauthorized music files could be downloaded. The suit was withdrawn once the Web site had gone off-line. In July the RIAA claimed in U.S. federal court that the 1998 Digital Millennium Copyright Act required Verizon Communications to reveal the identity of one of its Internet access customers who allegedly had downloaded music. Verizon, backed by Yahoo! and other Internet firms, opposed the move, claiming the RIAA sought to put ISPs in the role of policing music copyrights.

The recording and movie industries also issued warnings to groups that operated high-speed networks. About 2,300 colleges received letters urging them to curb student downloading of free music; the letters were signed by the RIAA, the National Music Publishers' Association, the Songwriters Guild of America, and the MPAA. The same groups also warned top corporate executives not to let their employees use high-speed company networks to download copyrighted material for free.

Informally, the recording industry let it be known that it would use technology to disrupt the free music services; it hired software companies to flood the free on-line services with fake copies of popular songs. The recording industry helped create authorized, for-pay music Web sites to combat the free services, but restrictions placed on consumers' ability to download music and copy it to compact discs (CDs) or other devices, such as MP3 players, limited the appeal of the authorized music sites. As a result, the authorized music Web sites did not attract the millions of consumers that flocked to the free music services.

There was debate inside and outside the recording industry about whether the availability of free music on the Internet was contributing to a drop in sales of music CDs at retail stores. The International Federation of the Phonographic Industry reported that worldwide music sales fell 5% in 2001, to $33.7 billion, and analysts confirmed that sales continued to drop in 2002. Representatives of the recording industry insisted that free music was undercutting sales of legal CDs, but some observers suggested that allowing consumers to sample free music on the Internet actually contributed to CD sales and that the sales slump was related to the economy rather than to Internet file trading. Still others said that CD sales and authorized on-line music sites suffered because the recording industry was not willing to satisfy consumer demand for unlimited usage of one song at a time, a capability that was offered by the free music services. The debate occurred at the same time that several major record labels and music retailers agreed to pay $67.3 million to settle a two-year-old CD price-fixing antitrust lawsuit brought by 43 U.S. states.

The music industry experimented with copy-proof music CDs that were sold in retail stores, but either the copy protection made the CDs difficult to play or purchasers soon found simple ways to overcome the protections. One side effect of the copy-proof technology was that it prevented a CD from being played on some personal computer (PC) CD-ROM drives and DVD players.

The Internet. The adoption rate for broadband Internet access—primarily cable modem and digital subscriber line (DSL)—slowed, largely as a result of the depressed economy. A study by PricewaterhouseCoopers in June predicted that it would be 2006 before broadband Internet access was used extensively enough to create demand for broadband-only services, which would offer such great amounts of data that a dial-up Internet connection would not be fast enough. The report projected that by 2006 there would be 35.3 million U.S. broadband subscribers, up from 9.4 million in 2001, and that the number of broadband Internet access customers would nearly equal the number of customers using slower dial-up Internet access (about 38.2 million).

AOL Time Warner and Microsoft's MSN service continued to battle for Internet access customers—both broadband and dial-up—by introducing new versions of their software that offered features to combat junk e-mail and foster a sense of on-line community. AOL, which with some 34 million customers remained the world leader in Internet access, was profitable, while MSN had about 8.7 million customers and was not profitable.

America Online, a part of AOL Time Warner, reexamined the idea of creating original Internet content, a strategy it had departed from five years earlier when it chose to lease space on its service to other content developers. Faced with a sharp drop in Internet advertising and a desire to attract and retain customers who had broadband Internet access, AOL said it would sell directly to its own customers, using formats such as text-only chats with celebrities, movie trailers, and videos of vacation destinations. It was believed that AOL would make money selling tickets and merchandise and that customers with high-speed Inter-

net access might pay extra for broadband-only on-line services.

One of the Internet's larger broadband access services, AT&T Broadband, changed ownership as Comcast Corp. combined AT&T's cable business—which included Internet access, cable television, and telephone services—with its own cable operation. The $45 billion stock deal was approved by shareholders in July but would not be completed until 2003.

Microsoft conceded that its .Net plan to make computer applications more available over the Internet had been slow to take off. The company said it would try to accelerate adoption with new .Net-related versions of its Windows operating system (OS) and server software. The .Net effort was best known for its Web services, a form of distributed computing that was expected to make linking different computer systems and applications easier than it was in 2002. Market research firm IDC indicated that widespread adoption of Web services was still years away.

In September the U.S. Department of Commerce (DOC) gave the nonprofit Internet Corporation for Assigned Names and Numbers (ICANN) one year to improve its performance. The DOC reported that there had been numerous complaints about ICANN, which was established in 1998 to manage, under government contract, the system that translates familiar Internet addresses into the numbers used by the Internet to route requests for information. The DOC also said that ICANN's attempts to reform itself were promising. The one-year contract extension required ICANN to be more open about how it made decisions and more responsive to Internet users and to create an advisory role for national governments.

A study by the Pew Internet & American Life Project found that 86% of college students had gone on-line, compared with 59% of the general population. The study also showed that nearly three-fourths of college students in the U.S. used the Internet more than they used conventional libraries. A large majority of those students said the Internet had been a big help in their education. The study was based in part on more than 2,000 responses from undergraduate students at 27 American colleges and universities. Elsewhere, there were concerns that some students were misusing the Internet to cheat. (See EDUCATION: Special Report.)

Worries about the "digital divide," the idea that people who did not have on-

line access were at a disadvantage compared with those who did, subsided a bit in the U.S. in 2002. Recent figures demonstrated that Internet access was growing the fastest among households earning less than $15,000 a year and that the use of the Internet was more equal than before among different racial and ethnic groups. The figures also showed that households with incomes above $50,000 were three times more likely to have Internet access at home than households with incomes under $25,000. The United Nations concluded, however, that the international digital divide was growing. According to the International Telecommunications Union, much of the world suffered from a lack of computerized information and more than 80 countries had fewer than 10 telephone lines for every 100 inhabitants. In 60% of countries, fewer than 1% of citizens used the Internet.

Unsolicited commercial e-mail, or spam, increased to the point that it annoyed virtually anyone with an e-mail account. Many of the unwanted e-mails offered pitches for pornography and low-cost loans. By some estimates the volume of spam increased from 8% of all e-mail in late 2001 to 35% by mid-2002. Those who sent spam apparently were encouraged by its low cost as an advertising medium. On the basis of the cost of buying mailing lists, each spam message cost only a fraction of a cent to send. As a result, a single message could feasibly be sent to thousands or millions of people.

Public libraries in the U.S. were freed from the federal requirement that they use Internet filters to block pornography from being viewed on library PCs. In May a federal appeals court overturned the Children's Internet Protection Act, signed into law in 2000, because the act also would have forced libraries to block access to Web sites that contained free speech that was protected under the law.

The biggest Internet traffic slowdown in several years occurred in October when a software upgrade by UUNet caused problems. UUNet, which handled as much as half of all U.S. Internet traffic, slowed communications for most of a day. While the Internet was built to withstand the failure of even a major provider of high-speed communications, rerouting Internet traffic to follow other pathways required using smaller lines with less capacity, which resulted in slowdowns for Internet users.

Companies. Hewlett-Packard's $19 billion acquisition of Compaq Computer was completed in 2002, despite the opposition of a group of stockholders led by Walter Hewlett, son of one of HP's founders. Hewlett, who had favoured the acquisition as a company director, said in late 2001 he would fight the deal instead. He was joined by David W. Packard, the son of HP's other founder, and they later were joined by the David and Lucile Packard Foundation. Collectively, the family members controlled about 18% of HP's shares. The hard-fought and very public battle culminated on March 19 at a Hewlett-Packard shareholders meeting at which the acquisition was narrowly approved. Soon afterward, Hewlett filed a lawsuit in Delaware Chancery Court alleging that HP had unfairly influenced the shareholder vote of Deutsche Bank and had not disclosed problems encountered during the planning on how to combine HP and Compaq. A Delaware court judge dismissed the lawsuit, ending the family's challenge to the acquisition, which had been championed by HP's chairman and CEO, Carly Fiorina. (See BIOGRAPHIES.)

IBM Corp. agreed to buy the consulting arm of PricewaterhouseCoopers for an estimated $3.5 billion. The agreement was expected to augment IBM's computer consulting business, which already was a major force in that market. IBM sold its hard-disk-drive business to Hitachi Ltd. for $2.05 billion. IBM disclosed in government regulatory filings that the disk-drive business had been losing money and that it had a pretax loss of $423 million in 2001. Hitachi was to own 70% of the disk-drive business initially and through a series of payments would gain full ownership after three years. The Internet auction business eBay Inc. paid $1.3 billion to acquire PayPal, a provider of on-line payment services between individuals and businesses.

In November U.S. District Judge Colleen Kollar-Kotelly gave her approval to most details of the antitrust settlement reached earlier between Microsoft and the U.S. Department of Justice (DOJ). The settlement for the most part ended the opposition of nine states and the District of Columbia that had pushed for stronger penalties for the software industry giant. By December Massachusetts and West Virginia had said that they would appeal. Among other requirements, the court held that Microsoft had to reveal some of its technical information to competitors

months ahead of schedule. The judge said that a corporate compliance committee made up of members of Microsoft's board of directors would ensure that Microsoft met the requirements of the settlement.

Microsoft previously said that it was making progress under the proposed settlement it reached in 2001 with the DOJ and nine states. In August 2002 Microsoft listed the technical ways in which it was complying with the proposed settlement. The compliance involved application programming interfaces that enabled third-party software firms to make their products work smoothly with Microsoft's Windows OS software. Microsoft released details of the communications protocols that linked desktop Windows to Microsoft's server version of Windows and revealed how it would allow computer makers and consumers to conceal Microsoft's Web browsing, media player, instant messaging, e-mail, and Java-related software in the Windows XP and Windows 2000 versions of its desktop OS. Microsoft also explained how it had created a more evenhanded system of licensing Windows. In December Microsoft was ordered to include Java in its Windows operating system.

The DOJ and Microsoft made minor changes in the wording of the proposed settlement in February, and in July they got the approval of Judge Kollar-Kotelly for properly disclosing their discussions about the settlement. Until November the judge had continued to review the proposed settlement and to consider a request for stiffer penalties against Microsoft that was submitted by the nine dissenting states and the District of Columbia. The dissenting states originally were part of a group of 18 states that were co-plaintiffs in the federal government's antitrust suit.

In June Microsoft resolved a dispute with the Securities and Exchange Commission (SEC) in which the company said that it would not use reserve accounts to make up for shortfalls in revenues during tough economic times. The SEC alleged that at least part of the reserves did not comply with generally accepted accounting principles and claimed that Microsoft was deliberately understating its revenues. Microsoft consented to a cease-and-desist order without admitting or denying allegations that it had maintained such reserve accounts from 1994 through 1998. In August the company settled charges by the Federal Trade Commission (FTC) that it had overstated the se-

curity and privacy aspects of its Passport Internet identification service. The service stored user passwords and credit card numbers on Microsoft servers as a way to simplify Web surfing and on-line purchases. The FTC complained that Microsoft had exaggerated the safety of transactions made through its service.

Microsoft irritated many of its corporate customers by changing the way it licensed its software, but it appeared to have retained most of those customers. The licensing plan forced corporate customers to switch from paying when they upgraded their software to paying annually for upgrades under a two- or three-year contract called Software Assurance. Customers complained that this resulted in sharp increases in licensing costs. Microsoft said the new plan would help customers spread out the cost of software upgrades over several years rather than force them to pay a lump sum when an upgrade occurred.

AOL Time Warner also was investigated by the SEC, which probed AOL's practice of trading on-line advertising for stock in Internet companies or for equipment or services from other firms. Questions were raised about whether the trades reflected the true value of transactions, and there were concerns that the value of advertisements might be inflated or that supplier companies might be expected to return some money in the form of advertising purchases. AOL Time Warner said in August that $49 million might have been inappropriately treated as AOL revenue over an 18-month period; in October the company raised that figure to $190 million over a two-year period.

The SEC investigation came at the same time that stockholders were complaining that the 2001 merger of AOL and Time Warner had not produced the dominant company they expected. Analysts said that the expected synergy between Time Warner's TV, film, and magazine media and AOL's on-line information packaging never materialized. In addition, economic conditions lowered AOL's on-line advertising revenues and caused a slowdown in the rate at which AOL's on-line subscriber base grew. In September the company said AOL's on-line advertising for the year would be $100 million less than previously forecast.

The economy plagued computer technology companies, nearly all of which suffered from reduced IT spending by customers. Many were forced to lay off workers, including Electronic Data Systems Corp., data storage firm EMC Corp., and Quantum Corp., a data protection and storage firm. Industry giant IBM announced job reductions, but some analysts expected that many more would occur later. IBM layoffs totaling more than 15,600 took place in the second quarter. In October IBM cut 3,700 full-time and independent contractor jobs when it closed a hard-disk-drive plant in Hungary, citing weak demand. Analysts suggested that IBM was doing better during bad economic times than many other technology companies, largely because it had begun emphasizing services, an area where customers could more easily realize benefits from their spending. HP, in a consolidation move growing out of its acquisition of Compaq, announced that it planned to cut at least 15,000 jobs from its 150,000-employee workforce.

The IT hiring market stabilized. The Information Technology Association of America in December reported that more than 1.1 million jobs were filled in 2002, and a third-quarter report indicated that layoffs had declined.

Global Crossing Ltd., a telecommunications firm that spent $15 billion to build a worldwide network to serve high-speed Internet and telephone customers, filed for bankruptcy in January. When WorldCom in July became the largest Chapter 11 bankruptcy ever, a large chunk of the Internet itself was involved because UUNET provided a large part of the Internet's "backbone," the long-distance segment of the Internet. The Internet backbone operated by UUNET continued to function despite the parent company's bankruptcy.

E-Commerce. Privacy was a major concern of those monitoring e-commerce practices. DoubleClick Inc., which provided advertising services to Internet marketers and Web sites, paid settlements in two privacy-related cases. DoubleClick placed on consumers' computers "cookie" files that tracked Web surfing; the firm then showed advertising that was aimed at the shopping and Web-surfing preferences each consumer had exhibited.

In connection with that practice, DoubleClick settled consolidated class-action lawsuits from several states that claimed that DoubleClick violated state and federal laws by tracking consumers' Web-surfing habits and combining that information with personally identifiable data to create profiles. DoubleClick agreed to pay legal expenses of up to $1.8 million, to tell consumers about its data-collection ac-

tivities in its on-line privacy policy, and to get permission before combining a consumer's personally identifiable data with his or her Web-surfing history. In another case DoubleClick agreed to pay $450,000 to settle differences with attorneys general from 10 states who were investigating its information gathering. Privacy advocates said DoubleClick and other on-line advertisers would not be greatly hindered by the settlements because it was still feasible to match ads to consumer Web-surfing preferences without collecting personally identifiable information.

Meanwhile, some traditional businesses also found Internet marketing useful. Major League Baseball began experimenting with for-pay Webcasts of its games, although the audience was limited to consumers who had high-speed Internet connections and who were willing to accept a lower-quality picture than television provided. The first Webcast game was offered for free on the league's official Web site (mlb.com) in August and attracted 30,000 viewers. The Web continued to be important to car sales as a way to acquaint customers with what was available long before they visited an auto showroom. As a result, automobile manufacturers and dealers tended to advertise on the Internet, particularly on car-related Web sites.

On-line education—colleges and universities offering courses over the Internet—did not prosper, and investment in it sharply declined. University officials said that they had underestimated the costs and overestimated the demand for on-line learning. While commercial on-line learning faded, however, the U.S. government pressed ahead with its eArmyU program, which was intended to boost army retention by offering on-line college degree programs. Only soldiers with at least three years of army service ahead of them were eligible to participate.

Selling digital subscriptions of magazines and newspapers over the Internet was tried, but the results were not clear. The idea was to sell a digital version of the entire print publication rather than merely provide part of it free on a Web site, as was widely done by newspapers. About 60 newspapers, including the *New York Times*, offered the full digital copies. Subscribers to such services were highly valued because they could be counted in a publication's paid-circulation figures, which were used to determine what advertisers could be charged.

The MGM Mirage casino announced plans to start an Internet casino, be-

coming the first American casino to join what was said to be a $3.5 billion annual market for on-line betting. However, the MGM on-line casino would not be allowed to accept bets from residents of the U.S., where on-line gambling was illegal. The on-line casino's computer operations were to be based outside the U.S. on Britain's Isle of Man.

Personal Computers. PC market penetration leveled off in the U.S. in 2001 after having reached about 60% of the nation's households, and penetration seemed unlikely to grow in 2002 because of the economy and because, according to some analysts, consumers did not believe new PCs offered significant new benefits. In September IDC forecast that worldwide PC sales would grow 1.1% in 2002; that was a sharp reduction from IDC's June prediction of 4.7% growth.

The handwriting-recognition feature of Microsoft Corp.'s new Tablet PC is demonstrated at the product's unveiling in November in New York City.

IDC said the lowered prediction reflected slowed consumer spending and the decision of many corporations to postpone buying new PCs. Apple Computer Corp. said it did not expect a recovery in sales in the near future. Despite slow sales, the industry continued to offer ever-faster new PCs. Processor speeds of 3 GHz (gigahertz) were expected by year's end, even though there were few consumer PC applications that required that much speed. Despite the bad news in PC sales, the phenomenal two-decade rise of the PC as an essential mainstream tool passed another milestone. It was estimated that in April the one billionth PC had been shipped. If all those computers were still in use—which was doubtful—there would be about one PC for every six people on Earth.

A new type of device, the portable Tablet PC, which used a special version of the Windows XP operating system, was introduced by several manufacturers in November. The Tablet PC used a touch-sensitive screen that allowed users to use plain handwriting, which the PC would recognize and, if desired, convert into conventional text. Some wireless telephone service providers upgraded their networks to handle data at the speed of a dial-up modem in a desktop computer and announced future plans to build third-generation (3G) networks that would have enough capacity to handle streaming video and audio rates of two million bits per second or more. (*See* Special Report.)

There was continued adoption of the Linux open-source OS. Linux was a competitor of Microsoft's Windows that, unlike Windows, could be modified because its underlying structure, or source code, was freely available. Versions of Linux that had been modified for consumers typically were offered free or sold at a much lower price than that charged for Windows. Microsoft acknowledged that Linux was a serious competitor but said it would compete on the basis of what it perceived to be the additional value of Windows and would not compete on price. Linux also became more popular in science and industry. Los Alamos (N.M.) National Laboratory reported that it would buy a $6 million Linux supercomputer to run its nuclear weapons simulation software. IBM said Linux would be the main OS on its new line of supercomputers, which would be introduced in 2005 or 2006.

On-line gaming on PCs got some competition from specialized videogame consoles when Sony Corp. began its on-line service for the PlayStation 2 console in August. Initially the on-line gaming service was free, but customers had to provide their own Internet connection and had to purchase a $39.99 connector that allowed the PlayStation 2 to be attached to the Internet. Microsoft launched a for-pay on-line service for its Xbox video-game console in November. Sales of traditional off-line computer games and video games appeared recession-proof for most of the year, but by late fall analysts had begun to lower their expectations for the fourth-quarter holiday period that was critical to the game industry. By some estimates game and hardware sales would total $10.5 billion in 2002, still above the $9.4 billion in sales for 2001.

Computer Security. In the year following the terrorist attacks in the U.S. on Sept. 11, 2001, there were concerns about the

White House senior cybersecurity adviser Richard A. Clarke details the nation's computer security policy, which was introduced in September in Stanford, Calif.

security of the Internet. Because of poor economic conditions, little corporate money was spent on new security efforts, and many companies cut their spending on information technology. The U.S. government, however, boosted IT spending 64%, to $4.5 billion, for the fiscal year begun in October 2002.

In August Richard A. Clarke, who headed the Office of Cyberspace Security in U.S. Pres. George W. Bush's administration, said the biggest threat to computer security might be other nations rather than terrorists. The administration said foreign governments might have been responsible for computer intrusions at U.S. government laboratories in 1999 and 2000 and for the 2001 attack of the Code Red worm, which initially was aimed at the White House. In addition, the federal government reported that it had detected electronic attacks in August against U.S.-based ISPs; the government suggested that the attacks might have originated in Western Europe.

In October the federal government investigated whether terrorists or hackers were responsible for a "distributed denial of service attack" aimed at 13 Internet servers that handled the Internet's Domain Name System (DNS). (The DNS translates the Web addresses typed into Web browsers into the numerical codes that identify computers on the Internet.) The distributed denial of service attack attempted to overwhelm the 13 servers by flooding them

with phony communications, but it slowed Internet traffic only briefly.

Other government computers were found to be vulnerable. A computer security firm said that it had cracked U.S. military and government computers as part of a test and had learned that thousands of machines containing sensitive data were accessible. The information obtained included techniques of military data encryption, Social Security numbers, and credit card numbers. In another case some detailed engineering plans for NASA space vehicles were obtained by a Latin American hacker, who passed them on to a magazine reporter in August.

There also was interest in a new form of computer security, which involved using computers to recognize the faces of terrorists from their images on video cameras installed in public places. Recognizing faces posed a difficult computing problem in what was called "signal processing." While it was possible to recognize faces—even those disguised by beards or glasses—there was a problem with doing it in "real time," or at the moment that thousands of people passed the cameras. To do so would require huge amounts of computer processing power. In addition, some champions of civil liberties worried that scanning faces in public locations created the potential for tracking the movements of individual citizens, since the information could be retained in a database. (*See* SOCIAL PROTECTION: Special Report.)

The U.S. Department of Defense gave Carnegie Mellon University a $35.5 million, five-year grant to develop ways of fighting "cyberterrorism." Research was said to involve different means of identifying people who used computers, which thus would make it harder for hackers or terrorists to remain anonymous. Electronic signatures, fingerprints, eye patterns, face-recognition technology, and voice scans were among the methods under consideration. The centre also was researching how computer components could be made to shut down automatically if a computer attack occurred.

Computer Crime. Computer crime took many forms, including industrial espionage. In April three Chinese citizens who in 2001 had been accused of the theft of trade secrets from Lucent Technologies also were said to have taken information from four other firms that had licensed portions of their software to Lucent or that sold circuit boards to Lucent. The charges included conspiracy, possession of trade secrets, and wire fraud. The men were accused of planning to steal the ideas behind Lucent's PathStar system for data and voice transmission and to provide them to Internet service organizations in China.

Old-fashioned fraud also made news. A man and a woman received 12-year prison sentences for auction fraud after they sold items on Internet auction sites run by eBay and Yahoo!; the pair took money from buyers but did not ship the items purchased. The two were caught as part of a cooperative effort by U.S. federal and state law-enforcement agencies, and the sentences they received were believed to be among the longest ever for Internet-related fraud. The FTC said that on-line auction fraud accounted for most of the Internet-related complaints it received.

In the United Kingdom a 21-year-old man was arrested and accused of having written a piece of software called T0rnkit that helped an intruder conceal his or her presence after gaining access to a computer running the Linux OS. Civil libertarians were upset over the arrest because it appeared to equate the creation of a program that had malicious potential with the creation of a destructive program such as a virus that had actually caused damage. Unlike a virus, T0rnkit did not spread itself, and the T0rnkit author was not accused of having used it to break into any computers. However, T0rnkit was said to have been found on several hacked Linux machines over the past two years.

In another case David L. Smith, the author of the Melissa virus, was sentenced to 20 months in U.S. federal prison and ordered to pay a $5,000 fine. The Melissa virus caused major problems on the Internet in 1999; although not damaging to PCs, it replicated itself so quickly that it brought some corporate e-mail systems to a halt.

Some existing computer viruses continued to plague the Internet, although their threat was diminished. Klez.E, a virus that deleted or destroyed a variety of PC file types, including Microsoft Word and Excel, video, image, and Internet files, became one of the most common computer viruses in the world, but by late in the year the publicity about it had served as a warning to users, and damage from it declined. Meanwhile, a nondestructive variant called Klez.H—which nonetheless could cause trouble by e-mailing a recipient's personal documents to others—continued to spread itself across the Internet.

In March U.S. officials arrested 90 people said to be members of a nationwide Internet child-pornography ring. Those arrested were charged with crimes that included possession, production, and distribution of child pornography. The Federal Bureau of Investigation said 27 of those arrested admitted to having molested children. In a murder case a 25-year-old man was arrested on federal charges of having used an interstate device—the Internet—to entice a child into sexual activity. The man helped police find the body of a 13-year-old Connecticut girl whom he had met over the Internet.

Spying by using the Internet became an issue when Princeton University officials accessed student admissions information at rival Yale University. Princeton's president, Shirley Tilghman, apologized and admitted that basic principles of privacy and confidentiality had been violated when Princeton tried to learn whether some students had been admitted to Yale. A Yale report said that 14 breaches of its admissions Web site had originated from Princeton's admission office.

When the Chinese government began using its influence over China's ISPs to block citizen access to the search engine Google, some computer enthusiasts in the U.S. responded by providing the Chinese with ways to circumvent their government's actions. Chinese computer users were allowed to reach Google through a second, specially constructed Web site that was not blocked by China's government. Those close to

the effort said there was a widespread hacker effort to aid computer users in a variety of nations that engaged in censorship or electronic surveillance of Internet users.

New Technology. Scientists at IBM designed a miniature computer circuit that covered less than one-trillionth of a square inch. Rather than being made of silicon, the ultratiny circuit was composed of individual molecules of carbon monoxide on a copper surface. It was said that an equivalent silicon transistor circuit would be 260,000 times larger. The technique, however, worked only at the incredibly low temperature of a few degrees above absolute zero.

IBM also said that its researchers had created carbon nanotube transistors that performed much better than advanced silicon chip transistors while using the same design parameters. Nanotubes are tiny tube-shaped carbon molecules that are thousands of times thinner than a human hair; it was hoped that they could be used to make circuits out of strings of carbon atoms rather than out of wires. Ultimately nanotubes might result in chips that were smaller, faster, and less expensive, but IBM said commercial use of them was probably years away. Hewlett-Packard scientists said they had developed a way of manufacturing molecular-sized circuits. The circuits could make it possible to pack billions or trillions of switches into an area smaller than a fingernail. That could result in powerful and cheap computers, although the scientists said practical use of the technology was at least five years in the future.

One purported breakthrough turned out to be a fake. In September an in-house review committee ruled that advances in physics claimed by scientists at Lucent's Bell Labs—including claims that the group had created molecular-scale transistors—were based on fraudulent data. The committee said the data in research published from 1998 to 2001 had either been manipulated or made up. The blame was placed on Bell Labs scientist J. Hendrik Schön, whom Bell Labs fired.   (STEVE ALEXANDER)

MICROELECTRONICS

In 2002 the global semiconductor industry made a slight recovery from its worst-ever year, with worldwide sales projected to rise by 1.8% to $141 billion, according to the U.S.-based Semiconductor Industry Association (SIA). Much bigger increases, of 19.8% (to $169 billion) and 21.7% (to $206 billion), were anticipated in 2003 and 2004, respectively. The association believed that recovery was under way and that growth would be steady over the next few years, with global sales in 2004 expected to be higher than those in the peak year of 2000.

Asia-Pacific continued to be the world's largest semiconductor market and the only one of the four major world markets to grow in 2002 (by 30% to $52 billion). The SIA predicted 24% growth in 2003 to $64 billion and a 25% increase in 2004 to $80 billion. The Americas market, which fell 12% to $31 billion in 2002, was expected to increase in 2003 by 14% to $36 billion and in 2004 by another 14% to $43 billion. For Europe, down by 9% to $27 billion, increases of 18% (to $32 billion) and 19% (to $39 billion) were forecast for 2003 and 2004, respectively. The Japanese market, which declined 7.5% to $31 billion, was expected to rebound 22% (to $37 billion) in 2003 and 18% (to $44 billion) in 2004.

Sales of dynamic random-access memory (DRAM) rose by 35% to $15 billion in 2002. DRAM chips, which had previously been used almost exclusively in computers, were by 2002 found in a variety of consumer and communications devices. The SIA predicted that the DRAM market would grow by another 35% to $20 billion in 2003 and by 43% to $29 billion in 2004. The market for digital signal processors, which were used in both wired and wireless communications equipment, grew by 15% to $4.9 billion in 2002 and was projected to increase 33% to $6.5 billion in 2003 and another 29% to $8.4 billion in 2004. The application-specific standard products (ASSP) market—which included consumer, computer and related peripheral, communications, automotive, and industrial markets—grew by 5.7% to $15 billion in 2002, despite a decline of 27% in 2001. The SIA predicted increases in the ASSP market of 18% to $17 billion in 2003 and 21% to $21 billion in 2004. Sales of flash memory, used in communications and digital-photography applications, grew by a mere 0.7% to $7.7 billion in 2002 after a huge rise of 133% in 2000 and a sharp drop of 27% in 2001. The SIA forecast a hike of 39% to $11 billion in 2003, however, and a 28% rise to $14 billion in 2004. Other semiconductor categories—including discrete components (such as power transistors and radio-frequency solutions for wireless consumer products), analog products (required for upgraded networks for Internet and digital telecommunications technologies), microprocessors (used in

Prototypes of the Sony SDR-4X perform at a press preview in Tokyo on March 19; the bipedal 60-cm (2-ft)-tall entertainment robots used sophisticated microelectronics and sensors to enable them to communicate with people.

© AFP 2002, by Kazuhiro Nogi

personal computers), optoelectronics (including lasers and image sensors), metallic oxide semiconductor programmable logic devices, and microcontrollers (used in consumer and automotive applications)—experienced either slow growth or a slight decline in 2002, but sales were expected to climb in 2003 and 2004.

In July 2002 the global top 10 semiconductor suppliers were listed by the American market-research company IC Insights, Inc. (on the basis of sales in the first half of 2002). Although the U.S.-based companies Intel Corp. and Texas Instruments, Inc., remained in first and third place, respectively, the South Korean supplier Samsung Electronics Co. Ltd. rose from fifth to second place. Taiwan Semiconductor Manufacturing Co., the world's largest manufacturer of semiconductors on a contract basis, jumped from the 15th to the 9th position.

During 2002 some consolidation of the microelectronics industry took place. In June, Infineon Technologies AG (the sixth largest semiconductor supplier and a subsidiary of Siemens AG of Germany) bought the microelectronics unit of the Swedish telecommunications supplier Telefonaktieabolaget LM Ericsson for €400 million (€1 = about $1). In the same month, French telecommunications supplier Compagnie Financière Alcatel completed the sale of its semiconductor business to the French-Italian company STMicroelectronics (ST) for €390 million. Toward the end of the year, ST (the fourth largest supplier) was engaged in talks with seventh-place Motorola, Inc., of the U.S. with a view to a possible merger in early 2003.

Over the past few years, consumers worldwide had become increasingly dependent on wireless products, including a vast array of mobile phones, laptop computers, and personal digital assistants. (*See* Special Report.) In May IBM Corp. reported that it had shipped its 100 millionth silicon-germanium microchip, which was introduced in 1998 and had become widely used in mobile phones and other wireless devices. In October IBM revealed that research was progressing on carbon-based electronic circuits, which could eventually replace silicon semiconductors. Also in October, Intel announced that it would invest $150 million in companies developing wireless technology. The company expected as many as 30 million laptops with wireless connectivity by late 2005, with its own Banias mobile computing technology available in the first half of 2003.   (ALAN STEWART)

TELECOMMUNICATIONS

Financially, 2002 was even worse for the global telecommunications industry than the previous year had been. In Sweden, The Netherlands, the U.K., and Germany, Telefonaktieabolaget LM Ericsson, Royal KPN NV, Vodafone Group PLC, and Deutsche Telekom AG, respectively, experienced the biggest losses in corporate history. The telecommunications sector's problems brought bankruptcies, criminal investigations, and job losses and led to changes in the leadership of a number of major companies.

The first of the year's major collapses was that of the Bermuda-based international fibre-optic communications company Global Crossing Ltd., once valued at nearly $50 billion. In January the company filed for Chapter 11 bankruptcy protection, owing its creditors more than $12 billion. Global Crossing's problems were dwarfed, however, by those of WorldCom, Inc., owner of the long-distance carrier business MCI and the Internet backbone provider UUNET. At the end of April, under pressure from his board of directors, Canadian-born Bernie Ebbers stepped down as chief executive of the company, which he and three friends had founded in 1983 in Hattiesburg, Miss. In June 1999 WorldCom was valued at $180 billion, but its worth had dropped to $7 billion by the time Ebbers resigned. In June WorldCom's chief financial officer, Scott Sullivan, was fired after the discovery that $3.8 billion of operating expenses in 2001 and 2002 had been improperly recorded. In the same month, the company announced that it was laying off 17,000 people, one-fifth of its worldwide workforce. The following month, owing its creditors more than $30 billion, WorldCom filed for Chapter 11 protection in the biggest bankruptcy in U.S. history—twice as large as that of Enron Corp. in December 2001. In early August, when WorldCom reviewed its accounts for 1999 and 2000, an additional accounting error of $3.3 billion was uncovered. In November Michael Capellas, formerly president of Hewlett-Packard Co. (HP), became chairman and CEO of WorldCom. Before HP's merger with Compaq Computer Corp. in March, Capellas had held the same posts at the latter firm. In December six WorldCom directors resigned.

Criminal investigations were launched into the business affairs of WorldCom and Global Crossing, as well as those of Qwest Communications International, Inc., which was already being investigated by the U.S. Securities and Exchange Commission for its use of "swaps" of network capacity with other operators. In late August Sullivan and Buford Yates, WorldCom's director of general accounting, were indicted by a grand jury on securities fraud charges.

WorldCom was not the only telecommunications company to acquire a new face at the top in 2002. In January Patricia Russo returned to American equipment supplier Lucent Technologies, Inc., her former employer, as chief executive after less than nine months

with Eastman Kodak Co. as president and chief operating officer. Dutch-born Ben Verwaayen, previously with Lucent and KPN, replaced Sir Peter Bonfield in February as CEO of British Telecommunications PLC. Joseph Nacchio, chief executive of Qwest, was replaced in June by Richard Notebaert, previously chairman of telecommunications equipment supplier Tellabs Operations, Inc. In July David Dorman was announced as the new chief executive of AT&T Corp., to replace C. Michael Armstrong after the latter became chairman of the newly merged AT&T Comcast Corp. Ron Sommer, chief executive of Germany's largely state-owned carrier Deutsche Telekom AG (DT), resigned under pres-

© Eriko Sugita/Reuters 2002

An NTT DoCoMo employee smiles for the camera built into the Japanese company's FOMA third-generation (3G) mobile telephone.

sure in July from the German government. Sommer was replaced in November by Kai-Uwe Ricke, director of DT's mobile and on-line businesses and chairman of T-Mobile International, DT's mobile phone division. Michel Bon, executive chairman of France Télécom (also mainly state-owned), resigned as a result of disagreements with the French government. Bon was replaced in September by Thierry Breton, who had been executive chairman of the French electronics group Thomson Multimedia. In March Telia AB of Sweden and Sonera Corp. of Finland became the first two partially state-owned telecommunications companies to agree to a cross-border merger. The combined company, TeliaSonera, would have its headquarters in Stockholm. In May the

largest Chinese fixed-line company, China Telecommunications Corp., was split into two. One of the successor companies retained the trading name China Telecom, while the other merged with data communications company China Netcom Corp. Ltd. to form China Netcom Group.

The major U.K. telecommunications equipment supplier Marconi Corp. PLC, which had been worth £35 billion (£1 = about $1.58) in September 2000, avoided bankruptcy by restructuring its debt in August so that bondholders and banks owed £4 billion by the company received stock in exchange. Existing Marconi shareholders, however, were left owning only 0.5% of the company. In July the alternative communications carrier Energis Communications Ltd.—carrier of nearly 50% of the U.K.'s Internet traffic—was also saved from bankruptcy by a cash injection of £150 million from its bankers. Archie Norman, a Conservative Party MP and former chairman of the British supermarket chain Asda, became chairman of Energis, while John Pluthero, chief executive of the U.K.'s largest Internet service provider, Freeserve.com PLC (Energis's biggest customer), took over as CEO.

New products, including third-generation (3G) phones, were altering the telecommunications industry. (*See* Special Report.) In October software company Microsoft Corp. entered the mobile-phone market by providing software for a new "smartphone" launched in the U.K. by Orange SA. This device combined a cellular phone, a handheld computer with colour screen, and a camera, and it incorporated Microsoft's Outlook e-mail program, as well as Media Player to play music and show video clips. In the same month, Vodafone launched its Vodafone live! service, which the company intended to use as the platform for its 3G services in 2003. Like the Orange smartphone, Vodafone's new colour-screen handsets provided picture messaging, arcade games, and e-mail services. In late 2002 Hutchison 3G UK Ltd. was planning to launch its third-generation Internet, videoconferencing, and voice service in Italy and the U.K., the first consumer 3G service in Europe. Manx Telecom Ltd. (a subsidiary of mmO2 PLC) and Sonera had launched 3G services in late 2001 on the Isle of Man and in early 2002 in Finland, respectively, but at the end of 2002, these services were still running in test mode owing to a shortage of handsets.

(ALAN STEWART)

The Wireless Revolution

by Fiona Harvey

In Helsinki, Fin., gamblers are getting their national lottery tickets by mobile telephone. In Hull, Eng., drivers are paying for their parking spaces with their mobile phones. In Tokyo people are using their phones to make home movies. In Toronto ads for Fido cell phones show students using instant text messaging to cheat on an exam. Welcome to the wireless revolution.

The mobile phone has truly taken hold of consumers in the past few years, and in most wealthy nations the technology is virtually ubiquitous. There are now about a billion mobile phones in the world, and the increase in users shows little sign of abating as the technology gathers pace in less-developed countries too. Not only are more people getting mobile connections but as the phones themselves become more advanced people are using them for much more than mere phone calls.

The simple usefulness of the mobile phone has been the secret of its success. People are no longer tethered to fixed telephone lines or left scrabbling for loose change to feed public phones. Being able to communicate with friends, family, or business colleagues at any time from any place frees individuals to work or plan their social lives while on the move. Mobile phones can increase safety, as people monitor each other by staying in touch or phone for help from the scene of an accident. Emergency services can even use phones to trace the whereabouts of those calling for help. Indeed, a survey in the U.K. found that 7 out of 10 people would rather lose their wallet than their mobile phone.

A survey in the U.K. found that seven out of ten people would rather lose their wallet than their mobile phone.

Phones, however, are only part of the wireless revolution. Laptop and hand-held computers with wireless connections, as well as the increasingly common personal digital assistants (PDAs), have given rise to a generation of mobile workers. The average office worker is estimated to have about 15 m (1 m = about 3.3 ft) of cabling in his or her desk area. All of that could be eliminated with two technologies: Bluetooth and 802.11, sometimes known as Wi-Fi (for wireless fidelity). These two standards allow data to be sent across short distances without wires. In the U.K. Bluetooth networks are being set up in railway stations so that passengers can read their e-mail while waiting for the train. In the U.S. Wi-Fi networks are appearing in cafes, allowing patrons to log on while they drink their coffee.

Radio and television are also being reinvigorated by new digital wireless technologies that will allow radios to convert binary data into text and pictures that appear on tiny screens and enable viewers to "talk back" to the TV with interactive programs. (Interactive programming already enables viewers to change the camera angle in broadcasts of some sports matches.) Wireless technology can also be used to generate broadband Internet connections, which allow surfers to send and receive large quantities of data from their personal computers, such as live full-motion video broadcasts, and could potentially turn PCs into TVs.

The wireless revolution already has reached the farthest corners of the globe—where global positioning system (GPS) devices guide soldiers, mountaineers, sailors, and even drivers. These devices can communicate with the network of 24 global positioning satellites placed in the sky by the U.S. government, triangulating between the GPS satellites to work out the device's exact location to within about five metres in good conditions. The revolution is even reaching inside our bodies; Medtronic, Inc., for example, has developed technology that allows information from a patient's pacemaker to be transmitted to a physician over the Internet.

Two factors have been central to the success of wireless technology: the digitization of data and the increasing understanding of how to make use of the electromagnetic spectrum. When modern mobile phones were first introduced in the 1970s, they used analog technology, in which a modulated wave is transmitted across the airwaves. Analog phones, however, can be used only for making voice calls. With digital phone technology, which renders data into binary form and transmits a discrete series of zeros and ones, it is possible to squeeze much more usage from the electromagnetic spectrum. This enables mobile phone operators to take on far more users and charge them less, allows the sending and receiving of text messages, and makes possible much more advanced services, such as Internet access through phones.

These advanced services will become even more ubiquitous with so-called third-generation (3G) mobile-phone networks. Most digital mobile phones can send and receive about 9.6 Kbps (kilobits per second), which is enough for calls and exchanging text messages. Using 3G, it will be possible to send and receive perhaps 144 Kbps or 344 Kbps, enough for sending and receiving video clips, Web pages, e-mails, and more. Consumers in Japan technology raises privacy issues, as bosses will be able to keep tabs on employees, parents monitor children, and suspicious spouses spy on one another. In light of increased security following the terrorist attacks in the U.S. on Sept. 11, 2001, law-enforcement agencies may employ these capabilities to increase their surveillance of citizens, which thus raises concerns over civil liberties. (*See* SOCIAL PROTECTION: *Special Report.*)

To take advantage of these new services, very different phone handsets will be developed, and the distinction between phones and PDAs will likely blur or disappear. Handsets will need much bigger screens and may have keyboards or handwriting recognition. Some may have voice-recognition software, which will turn speech into text. Using Bluetooth technology, the handset can be separated from the headset, so a user can wear a tiny microphone in his or her ear while tapping on the handset's screen.

For less-developed countries, wireless technology holds out a tantalizing possibility. Huge swathes of the globe lack telephone lines, and this inhibits economic growth. According to the International Telecommunications Union, many of these countries are abandoning the idea of fixed phone lines and moving straight to wireless technology, which is easier to introduce, as it requires the setting up of widely spaced base stations rather than extensive cabling. Already, less-developed nations are catching up. In 2001 China overtook the U.S. and now boasts more than 120 million mobile phone users.

Fiona Harvey is a technology writer for the Financial Times.

can send each other animations with NTT DoCoMo Inc.'s i-mode phone, which was introduced in 1999 and boasts 3G-like features. T-Mobile and Vodafone, among others, offer European consumers camera phones that can take and exchange snapshots with compatible mobiles. With 3G, mobile phones will become even more like PCs, combining the ability to take digital pictures and video, send and receive e-mail, surf the Internet, and download music. The only question is how many of these services the network operators choose to provide. In most developed countries, 3G networks are expected to go into opera-

tion within the next three years or so, though ongoing problems in the telecommunications industry and the high cost of buying spectrum licenses were delaying their introduction in some areas.

One of the most intriguing features of 3G phones will be more precise location-finding capabilities. In 2002 the Pinpoint Co., based in Hong Kong, already allowed subscribing companies to track employees to within about 200 m through their company-issued phones. One technology built into 3G handsets and networks, however, will make it possible to trace the position of the handsets to within about five metres or less. This

Artwork: Ricco

Earth Sciences

The **UN** warned that a vast haze of **POLLUTION** over **SOUTH ASIA** was **DAMAGING CROPS** and **CHANGING RAINFALL PATTERNS.** Scientists recorded the **LARGEST VOLCANIC ERUPTION** ever seen— not with a seismograph but with a telescope. The **NOAH'S FLOOD HYPOTHESIS** describing the sudden filling of the Black Sea 7,500 years ago was **STRONGLY CHALLENGED.**

GEOLOGY AND GEOCHEMISTRY

A comprehensive 2002 publication by Ali Aksu of the Memorial University of Newfoundland with six coauthors (from the U.K., Canada, the U.S., and Turkey) contradicted the popular Noah's Flood Hypothesis. In 1996 William Ryan, Walter Pitman, and co-workers (Columbia University, New York City) had discovered that mollusk shells from the Mediterranean Sea suddenly appeared on the shelves of the Black Sea about 7,500 years ago. They developed the case—the Flood Hypothesis—that while the connecting channels between the Mediterranean and Black seas were closed, with bedrock bottoms exposed to the atmosphere during glacial periods, the isolated Black Sea had evaporated down to about 150 m (1 m = 3.28 ft) lower than modern sea level. About 7,500 years ago, they surmised, water broke through, causing a catastrophic flood of Mediterranean waters that refilled the Black Sea in about two years and washed in the Mediterranean mollusks that then settled on the Black Sea shelves. They suggested that this event could be the historical basis for Noah's Flood.

Aksu and coauthors reported on geologic and geochemical results from sedimentary cores drilled beneath the Sea of Marmara, a gateway that connects the Black Sea with the Mediterranean. They compiled a history of the water flowing through the Sea of Marmara during the past 10,000–25,000 years on the basis of seismic profiles of the submarine sediments and the geochemistry and sequential contents (sediment types, carbon isotopes, salinity, fossils, and pollen) of the one–two-metre-long cores drilled from the sediments. They found no evidence for a catastrophic flood and were convinced that the evidence rather supported an outflow hypothesis, which involved continuous overflow of water from the Black Sea into the Mediterranean over almost 10,000 years. The sudden appearance of Mediterranean fossils in the Black Sea was explained, they suggested, by changes in salinity 7,500 years ago that permitted the opportunistic mollusks to populate the shallow Black Sea shelves.

In 2002 a controversy over interpretation of rocks famous for evidence of early life drew attention to the continuing importance of classical geology in these days of near-magical geochemical instruments. Efforts to decipher the origin of life have often focused on the investigation of ancient rocks in southwestern Greenland, in particular the banded-iron formation (BIF) rocks of the Isua greenstone belt. These were originally sedimentary rocks formed beneath water. Tectonic activity altered their original structure and mineralogy, but their origin as sedimentary rocks is not disputed. In 1996 Stephen J. Mojzsis (then a graduate student at Scripps Institution of Oceanography, La Jolla, Calif.) and colleagues had reported that rocks from nearby Akilia island were also BIFs, with crosscutting veins of an igneous rock that yielded an age of 3.85 billion years. The researchers concluded that the values of carbon isotopes measured in small inclusions of graphite were a signature for the existence of 3.85-billion-year-old life in the original sediments. Christopher M. Fedo of George Washington University, Washington, D.C., and Martin J. Whitehouse of the Swedish Museum of Natural History, while engaged in a multiscientist investigation of the Isua belt, also visited Akilia. The rocks there did not look like the metamorphosed BIFs with which they were familiar. The researchers' geochemical analyses, published in 2002, together with the field relationships, satisfied them that the rocks were igneous, not sedimentary BIFs. Such rocks would have formed at a temperature much too high for the graphite inclusions to represent original life. Resolution of the controversy would require a satisfactory explanation for the presence of the iron oxide mineral magnetite in quartz-rich layers, which would involve traditional detailed tectonic, petrographic, and mineralogical investigation of the rocks in addition to geochemical analyses.

In a 2002 review of metamorphism, Michael Brown of the University of Maryland wrote that excitement remained focused on the extreme conditions of pressure and temperature to which some crustal rocks have been subjected. The conventional diagrams for metamorphic facies have extended to 10 kilobars (1 kilobar = 1,000 atmospheres) for rocks metamorphosed at a depth of 25–30 km (1 km = 0.62 mi) and temperatures up to about 850 °C (1,500 °F). The discovery of crustal rocks containing minerals such as coesite and diamond indicated that these rocks reached depths of 100 km (and corresponding pressures of 30 kilobars) or more in ultrahigh-pressure metamorphism (UHPM). The mineralogy of some other rocks indicated the attainment of 1,100 °C (2,000 °F) in ultrahigh temperature metamorphism (UHTM). UHPM rocks provide information about the subduction of crustal rocks to extreme depths, and UHTM rocks provide information about the involvement of crustal rocks with hot, shallow asthenospheric mantle, perhaps through the breaking off and sinking of crustal rocks. The oldest-known UHPM rocks are dated at about 620 million years, and the oldest-known UHTM rocks are about 2.5 billion years old. Brown noted that these dates correspond roughly to boundaries between the three eras—the Archean, the Proterozoic, and the Phanerozoic— that have always been recognized as distinctive. Further documentation of UHPM and UHTM rocks through time may indicate whether these three geologic eras are characterized by different styles of global geodynamics, a possibility that has been much debated.

The Autonomous Benthic Explorer, an untethered undersea robot vehicle, participated in a 12-day mission to reinvestigate the Galapagos Rift, where hydrothermal vents were first discovered in 1977.

Woods Hole Oceanographic Institution

In 2002 Ethan F. Baxter, Donald J. De-Paolo, and Paul R. Renne of the University of California, Berkeley, published a significant advance in the interpretation of mineralogical ages based on argon isotopes. Biotites sampled across the boundary between an amphibolite and a contemporaneous pelitic rock in the Alps yielded different apparent ages. The biotite ages in the pelite averaged 12 million years—consistent with known geology—but those in the amphibolite ranged from 15 million to 18 million years. The anomaly of the greater ages in the amphibolite was ascribed to "excess argon." The origin of excess argon was poorly understood, but it was a bane for geochronologists because frequently the only way to confirm its presence was to make independent age determinations. As a rock cools, $argon_{40}$ produced or incorporated within minerals at high temperatures is able to diffuse away until "closure" occurs, at a temperature where diffusivity slows effectively to zero. Subsequently, additional $argon_{40}$ is produced from potassium at a known rate and remains trapped in the mineral. Measuring the ratio of $argon_{40}$ to potassium provides the time at which closure occurred—that is, the "closure age" of the mineral; the presence of excess argon indicates exceptions to the assumptions. Baxter and his co-workers established equations that took into account not only the diffusive properties of the minerals but also the characteristics of the intergranular medium (typically a fluid) through which argon must diffuse after exiting the minerals. Numerical modeling showed that excess argon is dependent on "bulk rock argon diffusivity," a factor not included in standard geochronological thinking. Quantitative

modeling provides numerical limits for this diffusivity and suggests that it decreased rapidly about 15 million years ago in the amphibolite, which corresponds to the geologically known onset of rapid exhumation and rheological changes of the rocks. In the pelite, with its different mineralogy and texture, the bulk rock diffusivity was not affected by the tectonic uplift, and diffusive escape of argon continued until the closure temperature was reached 12 million years ago. With this kind of understanding, patterns of excess argon may be exploited to learn more about the properties and history of geologic systems.

The Galapagos Rift 2002 Expedition reported via satellite from the research ship *Atlantis* to journalists at the May meeting of the American Geophysical Union. The expedition marked the 25th anniversary of the discovery of submarine hydrothermal vents, those fascinating localities on the oceanic ridges where water circulates through the crust, is heated, and emerges as hot springs. The hot water contains material dissolved from the ocean crust, and as it encounters the cold ocean water, it precipitates sulfide-rich chimneys and provides chemical sustenance for bacterial mats and oases of exotic fauna. This expedition was continuing long-term investigations in the Galapagos Rift region that aimed to reconstruct the history of the formation of vents and the population of submarine oases, which are intermittently destroyed by lava flows. The scientists used a remarkable instrument, the Autonomous Benthic Explorer (ABE), a deep-swimming robot not attached to the surface ship. Following a pre-planned path, the ABE mapped the

seafloor by using sonar and made other measurements. Very detailed maps were produced, with vertical resolution of one metre. In 25 years of study in this region, no chimney vents had been found, but with its sensitive thermometry the ABE discovered and tracked a trail of water only 0.02 °C (0.036 °F) warmer than the surrounding ocean water. This trail led to two extinct sulfide-bearing chimneys that must have required water of at least 200 °C (392 °F)—the first evidence of high-temperature vents along the Galapagos Ridge. The "Rose Garden" oasis with its spectacular tube worms, discovered in 1979, had provided the foundation for understanding the biological communities associated with vents, but the expedition found that this site had been covered by recent lava flows. These submarine oases of life in total darkness represent a most remarkable interplay between geology, geochemistry, and biology.   (PETER J. WYLLIE)

GEOPHYSICS

Earthquakes occur mainly because of the constant movement of Earth's lithospheric plates, which include the crust. For instance, most seismic activity in Alaska results from the interaction of the northwestwardly moving Pacific Plate with the corner of the North American Plate that comprises Alaska. On November 3 one of the largest recorded earthquakes to strike North America hit central Alaska. The epicentre of this M_w (moment magnitude) 7.9 earthquake was 120 km (75 mi) south of Fairbanks. The event was preceded by a foreshock of M_w6.7 on October 23, which ruptured a 300-km (190-mi) segment of the Denali Fault, east of the Parks Highway and community of Cantwell. Although some support structures of the Trans-Alaska Pipeline were displaced, their earthquake-resistant features allowed the pipeline itself to remain intact. No casualties were recorded for either Alaskan earthquake. The Denali Fault, a bow-shaped strike-slip fault transecting Alaska, is perhaps the most significant crustal fault in the state and is seismically active. It experiences infrequent large earthquakes similar to those recorded along the northern and southern segments of the San Andreas Fault in California.

Earthquakes of 2002 with high human casualties included separate M_w 6.1 and 7.4 shocks in the Hindu Kush region of Afghanistan in March, which together killed more than 1,000, and a M_w6.5 event in northwestern Iran in June, which killed more than 200.

The most significant volcanic eruption in terms of human impact was that of Mt. Nyiragongo in the Democratic Republic of the Congo, commencing in January. Lava flowed southward at a rate of about 1–2 km (0.6–1.2 mi) per hour and entered the city of Goma. About 400,000 people in Goma were evacuated, and 14 villages were damaged by lava flows. The eruption killed at least 45 people and left about 12,000 families homeless.

Beginning late April, Mauna Loa on the island of Hawaii showed signs of renewed activity after an 18-year period of repose. Global Positioning System (GPS) stations and tiltmeters positioned around the volcano recorded the equivalent of as much as 5–6 cm (2–2.4 in) per year of deformation, interpreted as a reinflation of Mauna Loa's magma chamber caused by injection of additional material at a depth of 5 km (3 mi) beneath the summit.

Images of Jupiter's moon Io reveal what was reported in 2002 as the most energetic volcanic eruption ever seen in the solar system. Near-infrared views of Io obtained with the Keck II telescope in Hawaii on Feb. 20 and 22, 2001 (left, top and bottom), follow the growth of the hot lava outflow, which spread over an area larger than the size of London. The same views derived from Galileo satellite data are shown for orientation (right, top and bottom), with the eruption site circled.

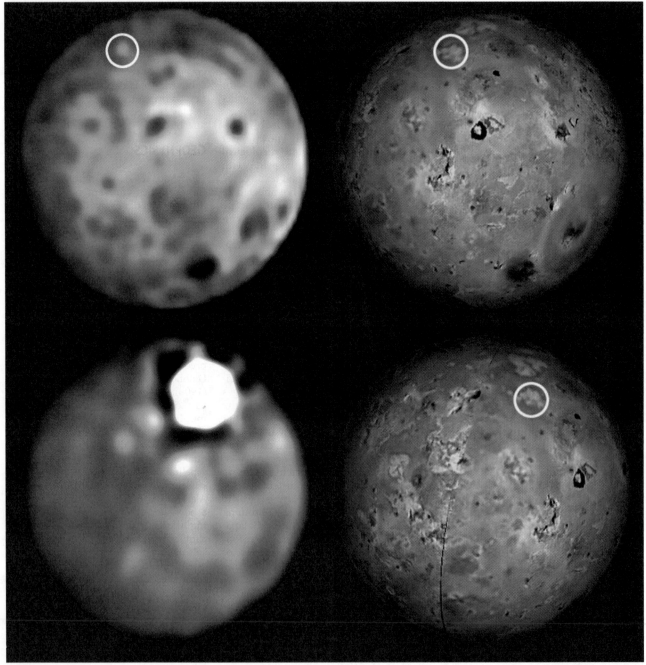

F. Marchis, University of California, Berkeley

Among persistent active volcanoes, Sicily's Mt. Etna resumed its pattern of frequent summit eruptions in October, following the large flank event of July–August 2001. On October 27 Etna spewed a column of volcanic ash, blackening skies over Sicily and as far away as North Africa, 560 km (350 mi) south. Rivers of lava flowed halfway down the mountain's slopes, setting forests afire.

In November astronomers reported what they described as the most energetic eruption ever seen in the solar system on the highly volcanic moon Io, one of the four Galilean satellites of the planet Jupiter. Working at the Keck Observatory on Mauna Kea, Hawaii, Franck Marchis and Imke de Pater of the University of California, Berkeley, and collaborators captured near-infrared images of the same side of Io two days apart, on Feb. 20 and 22, 2001. (Analysis of the images was not completed until 2002.) The earlier image showed a brightening near Surt volcano, the site of a large eruption in 1979 that had been identified from the flybys of the Voyager 1 and 2 spacecraft. Over the following two days, the hot spot grew "into an extremely bright volcanic outburst," according to the researchers. They estimated that the emitting area of the eruption was larger than the entire base of Mt. Etna. The lower limit of the interpreted temperature of the hot spot—1,400 K (2,000 °F)—was consistent with the temperature of basaltic eruptions on Earth.

Scientists had monitored changes in Earth's oblateness—a slight bulge around the Equator caused by axial rotation—by means of satellite laser ranging techniques since the 1970s. During the year Christopher Cox of Raytheon Information Technology and Scientific Services and Benjamin Chao of NASA Goddard Space Flight Center reported that, whereas the oblateness had been slowly decreasing over the past quarter century, it abruptly reversed that trend around 1998. The continually decreasing oblateness had been attributed mainly to rebound in the mantle after the last glacial period, when massive polar caps had covered the high latitudes in the north and south. The exact causes of the trend reversal were uncertain, but a possible reason was a large-scale mass redistribution in Earth's deep interior—specifically, a flow of material driven from high altitudes to the equatorial regions by Earth's dynamo in the liquid outer core and along the core-mantle boundary (located at a depth of 2,900 km [1,800

mi]). This explanation was consistent with a significant geomagnetic jerk (a sudden shift in the trend of the long-term variation of Earth's magnetic field) recorded in 1999, probably caused by the same material flow. A second possible cause examined by Cox and Chao was a large-mass redistribution in the oceans. In a subsequent report, Jean O. Dickey of the California Institute of Technology and collaborators made a case for glacial melting as yet another major factor in the trend reversal.

Seismic tomography (imaging of the structure of Earth's interior by seismic velocity differences), three-dimensional global seismicity, and detailed GPS measurements of the surface were enabling geophysicists to improve their understanding of plate motions. As two plates collide, one is forced beneath the other and sinks into the less-dense upper mantle—a process called subduction. The descent of the subducted portions of the plates, called slabs, was thought to drive the motions of the plates on Earth's surface, but the exact mechanism by which the slabs and plates interact was not yet well understood. Clinton Conrad and Carolina Lithgow-Bertelloni of the University of Michigan showed that the present-day observed plate motions could be best modeled if the slabs that are sinking into the upper mantle are still mechanically attached to their source plates and thus generate a direct pull on the plates. In contrast, by the time the slabs reach the lower mantle (at about a 700-km [430-mi] depth), they are no longer well attached and instead draw plates via a suction force created by their sinking.

The core-mantle boundary represents the most prominent discontinuity in Earth's interior with respect to chemistry and properties of deformation and flow. There the solid lower mantle, composed of silicates, meets the fluid outer core, composed of molten iron-nickel alloy. Using seismic-wave data from earthquakes in the Tonga-Fiji region in the South Pacific Ocean, Sebastian Rost and Justin Revenaugh of the University of California, Santa Cruz, detected rigid zones lying just within the top boundary of the outer core. Normally, seismic waves called shear waves cannot propagate through a fluid; when they encounter the core-mantle boundary, they reflect sharply from the molten alloy. Within the core-rigidity zones, however, the waves propagated at a very low velocity. The investigators interpreted these zones as being thin (0.12–0.18-km [400–600-ft])

patches of molten iron mixed with solid material having a small shear-wave velocity, which enables the shear waves to travel in the outermost core. Such zones at the top of the outer core had been previously detected as topographic highs of the core-mantle boundary.   (MURLI H. MANGHNANI)

METEOROLOGY AND CLIMATE

On June 24 the Moderate Resolution Imaging Spectroradiometer (MODIS) instrument aboard NASA's Aqua satellite began looking at Earth from about 700 km (435 mi) in space. Aqua, launched May 4, was a complement to NASA's Terra satellite, which had gone into orbit in 1999 carrying a twin MODIS instrument. MODIS viewed Earth's surface in 36 spectral bands ranging from visible to thermal infrared wavelengths. Combining data from the two instruments allowed a comprehensive daily examination of Earth that would help scientists study water evaporation, the movements of water vapour throughout the atmosphere, and cloud formation as well as various characteristics of the land and oceans.

Also on June 24, NASA and the National Oceanic and Atmospheric Administration (NOAA) launched NOAA-17. The spacecraft was the third in a series of five Polar-orbiting Operational Environmental Satellites (POES) that had improved imaging and sounding capabilities and that would operate over the next 10 years. The satellite was expected to improve weather forecasting and monitor environmental phenomena around the world such as El Niño events, droughts, fires, and floods. The data would be used primarily by NOAA's National Weather Service for its weather and climate forecasts. Longer-term data records from the NOAA satellites would contribute to scientists' understanding of climate change.

A new three-dimensional weather computer model from NOAA, covering the continental U.S., became operational in April. Called the RUC20 (for Rapid Update Cycle and the model's 20-km [12-mi] horizontal grid increments), it improved the accuracy and timeliness of the most immediate predictive information widely used for aviation, severe-weather forecasting, and general weather forecasting. Combining the latest observations from commercial aircraft, wind profilers, Doppler radar, weather balloons, satellites, and surface stations, the model produced new analyses and short-range

This single true-colour image of the Gulf of Oman and Persian Gulf region on Sept. 16, 2002, was synthesized from spectro-radiometer data acquired during separate overpasses of the Terra and Aqua Earth-observation satellites three hours apart.

forecasts on an hourly basis, with forecasts as far as 12 hours into the future every three hours—the most frequent updating of any NOAA forecast model. Maps and other products from the model were available on the Internet at <http://ruc.fsl.noaa.gov>.

Late in the year, drought experts from the U.S., Canada, and Mexico neared the end of their preparations to launch a new program of continental-scale drought monitoring for North America. The existing Drought Monitor program, begun in 1999, provided weekly updates in the form of maps and text reports of the status of drought in the 50 U.S. states (available on the Internet at <http://www.drought.unl.edu/dm/index.html>). The expanded program, which was to be called the North American Drought Monitor and which would initially issue monthly assessments, was a cooperative arrangement between specialists currently producing the U.S. Drought Monitor and meteorologists from Mexico and Canada.

A report issued in August by the UN Environment Programme indicated that a vast blanket of pollution stretching across South Asia, dubbed the Asian Brown Cloud, was damaging agriculture and modifying rainfall patterns. Estimated to be about three kilometres (two miles) thick, the constant haze was thought to result from forest fires, the burning of agricultural wastes, emissions from inefficient cookers, and the burning of fossil fuels in vehicles, industries, and power stations. The blanket of pollution reduced the amount of sunlight reaching Earth's surface by as much as 10–15%. The resulting combination of surface cooling and lower-atmosphere heating may be altering rainfall patterns, leading to a reduction in winter rainfall over northwestern India, Pakistan, and Afghanistan.

Paleoclimatologists reported that they had found century-scale trends for Asia's southwest monsoon, a climate system of vital importance to nearly half the world's population. A climate reconstruction for the past millennium based on the relative abundance of a certain type of fossils in sediment cores from the Arabian Sea suggested that monsoon wind strength had increased during the past four centuries as the Northern Hemisphere warmed. The finding supported an observed link between Eurasian snow cover and the southwest monsoon. The researchers predicted that southwest monsoon intensity could increase further during the 21st century if greenhouse gases continued to rise and northern latitudes continued to warm.

The rapid melting of Alaskan glaciers was contributing to a rise in sea level, according to a team of scientists who used airborne laser altimetry to estimate the volume changes of 67 glaciers in Alaska. They found that the glaciers' thicknesses had diminished at an average annual rate of 0.5 m (1.6 ft) from the mid-1950s to the mid-1990s. Repeat measurements of 28 glaciers from the mid-1990s to 2000–01 showed that the average rate of melting had increased to 1.8 m (5.9 ft) per year. Extrapolating these rates to all Alaskan glaciers yielded an annual loss of volume of 96 cu km (23 cu mi), equivalent to a 0.27-mm (0.01-in) rise in sea level per year during the past decade. These losses were nearly double the estimated annual loss from the entire Greenland Ice Sheet during the same period.

In contrast, temperatures over large parts of the interior of Antarctica exhibited a small cooling trend during the past several decades. The cooling could be related to linkages between the troposphere—the lowest layer of the atmosphere—and the stratosphere above it. Researchers presented evidence during the year that ozone losses over the southern polar region, embodied in the formation of the annual Antarctic ozone hole, were leading to a cooling of the lower stratosphere, which in turn was affecting the circulation in the troposphere so as to contribute to the observed temperature trends. Because chemical pollutants affected the formation of the yearly ozone hole, the evidence suggested that pollutants were having an impact on Antarctic climate.

(DOUGLAS LE COMTE)

Economic Affairs

Despite some **GOOD** economic **NEWS** in 2002, most international **STOCK MARKETS** fell. Five of the biggest **BANKRUPTCIES** in U.S. history occurred, and a string of financial **IRREGULARITIES**, beginning with **ENRON** in 2001, led to the **COLLAPSE** of several companies.

In early 2002 there were signs of recovery. The downturn in the world economy and fears of a global recession generated by the terrorist attacks in the U.S. on Sept. 11, 2001, ended around the turn of the year. Growth in 2002, however, was below trend, with economic momentum undermined by the relentless decline in share prices and an erosion of wealth, as well as by the likelihood of military confrontation between the U.S. and its allies and Iraq. The recovery in early 2002 was led by the U.S. and Asia, where economic turnarounds were stronger than expected. In the U.S. output rose strongly; household spending proved resilient, and businesses rebuilt stocks, reversing the upward trend in unemployment that began in November 2000. At the same time, U.S. output of information technology (IT) goods started to increase.

Although growth weakened after the first quarter, the economy continued to recover from the sharp slowdown in 2001, when world output rose by only 2.2%, down from a 15-year high of 4.7% in 2000. The International Monetary Fund (IMF) projection for 2002 was for an acceleration in growth to 2.8%, despite the continuing weakness of world financial markets. Global equities were volatile and fell by an average 24% in the year to early October, down 42% from their April 2000 peak. The latter decline reflected the erasure of $14 trillion of wealth, or the equivalent of more than 40% of annual world economic output—the largest loss of wealth since World War II. The decline reflected the lowering of profit forecasts in the industrialized countries and widespread concerns about accounting and auditing practices, particularly in the U.S.

The advanced countries (up 1.7%) grew more slowly than the less-developed countries (LDCs), which rose 4.2% in 2002. Among the major industrialized countries, much of the impetus from trade was coming from the U.S., where growth was sustained by government spending and strong levels of personal consumption. Low interest rates in many other industrialized countries were boosting demand, particularly for housing. Fortunes in the 12 euro-zone countries were more mixed. In contrast to other countries where inflation was well under control and deflationary trends were a concern—in Japan falling prices had become the norm—prices in the euro-zone countries were rising at different rates, and national governments had no power to influence them. The European Central Bank (ECB) controlled interest rates and was mandated to keep the overall inflation rate below 2.5%. Wide-ranging inflation rates were exacerbating wage and other disparities and defeating the "level playing field" objective of the European Union (EU). The countries in transition (also called the former centrally planned economies) expanded by 3.5%, with most countries continuing to make progress with reforms. Rural areas, however, still lagged well behind urban areas, with poverty and stagnating living standards affecting many of the 134 million rural poor.

In the industrialized countries the need for transparency and improved corporate governance took on a new importance in 2002. The loss of confidence in global financial markets that had been sparked by the events of Sept. 11, 2001, as well as by a correction from excessive stock valuations, was briefly restored at the beginning of 2002 before deepening and spreading. Subsequent scandals involving aggressive accounting practices and poor internal governance at some companies further dented investor confidence. Worldwide, people's faith in financial reporting, corporate leadership, and the integrity of markets was being undermined. The collapse of Enron Corp., the American energy trading company, in late 2001 and the subsequent shredding of documents by its auditors, Arthur Andersen

Inflation Rate
(percentage change from December to December)

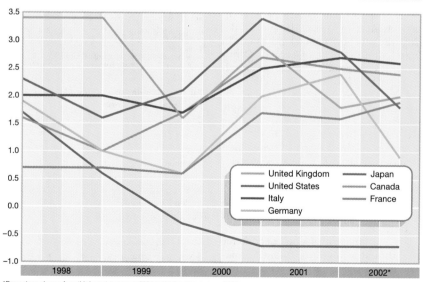

*Percentage change from third quarter average 2001 to third quarter average 2002.
Source: International Monetary Fund, *International Financial Statistics*.

LLP, had brought into question the reliability of corporate financial statements. (*See* Sidebar, page 193.) In March 2002 several high-profile technology firms were under scrutiny by the U.S. Securities and Exchange Commission (SEC), and the practices of Wall Street analysts were being investigated. Perhaps the most significant event was a $3.8 billion restatement by the large American telecommunications firm WorldCom, Inc., on June 25. Within days this was followed by reports of inflated profits by other companies, including the American photocopier giant Xerox Corp. and the French media company Vivendi Universal. The erosion of confidence triggered by these and other scandals was reflected in the volatility of stock markets worldwide.

The U.S. government was quick to respond to the scandals and reported irregularities with measures to strengthen corporate governance and auditing. On July 30 the Sarbanes-Oxley Act became law in the U.S., replacing the accountancy profession's self-regulation with a public oversight body. It made far-reaching changes to existing legislation in order to ensure the provision of timely corporate information to investors, improve accountability of corporate offers, and promote the independence of auditors. In the U.K. the Institute of Chartered Accountants also adopted measures to strengthen auditor independence.

In emerging countries the global effects of the financial problems were in some cases compounded by local events. Political concerns in Brazil, exacerbated by the national debt, were temporarily eased by the announcement of a $30 billion IMF package in early August. In Turkey the sudden departure of senior cabinet ministers in June led to a flight of capital. Confidence was boosted there, however, following the November 3 election, in which a single party achieved an absolute majority. China was increasingly embracing capitalism and making progress in becoming the next Asian superpower. The transfer of production facilities from other Asian countries was making China a major export centre. In the first nine months of 2002, China received 22.5% more foreign direct investment (FDI) than it had in the same 2001 period.

The combination of slower economic growth and a failure of financial markets to recover had a dampening effect on FDI. The largest falls were in developed countries as transnational corporations (TNCs) responded to recession and cross-border mergers and acquisitions decreased in number and value. Nevertheless, sales of foreign affiliates of TNCs rose by 9%, and the number of employees increased by 7% to 54 million. Global FDI in 2001 declined sharply following strong increases in the 1990s. This trend persisted in 2002, although there were rises in individual countries. China was a notable exception, with FDI expected to continue to increase as a result of Beijing's recent entry to membership in the World Trade Organization (WTO). At $735 billion in 2001, global inflows of FDI were 51% less than in 2000, and the $621 billion outflow was down 55%. These were the first drops since 1991 and 1992, respectively, and the largest for 30 years. Most affected by the decline were the developed countries, where inflow had halved since the year before, bringing their share down from 80% to 68%. This was largely due to the slowdown, particularly in the EU, in cross-border mergers and acquisitions, which had been the main vehicle for FDI. By contrast, inflows to LDCs fell only 14% to $205 billion.

NATIONAL ECONOMIC POLICIES

The IMF projected a 1.7% rise in gross domestic product (GDP) of the advanced economies. In the last quarter of 2002, a slowdown in the recovery occurred, and there was uncertainty about the downside risks associated with the situation in Iraq and oil prices.

United States. Although the U.S. made the widely feared "hard landing" after the Sept. 11, 2001, attacks, it recovered much more quickly than expected. In 2002 performance was uneven, and although there were signs of a slowdown toward year's end, output was predicted to rise by 2.2%. This followed a 0.3% increase in 2001, which brought to an end a decade of continuous expansion. Inflation was not an issue, and there was little risk of deflation, as falling prices for goods were being offset by services inflation. While the recession had been short-lived and mild by historical standards, it differed in two ways. The downturn was precipitated by a fall in corporate profits between the June 2000 peak and September 2001, which in turn generated job losses, and inventories had been less

Table I. Real Gross Domestic Products of Selected Developed Countries
% annual change

Country	1998	1999	2000	2001	2002[1]
United States	4.3	4.1	3.8	−0.3	2.2
Japan	−1.2	0.8	2.4	0.3	−0.5
Germany	2.0	2.0	2.9	0.6	0.5
France	3.5	3.2	4.2	1.8	1.2
Italy	1.8	1.6	2.9	1.8	0.7
United Kingdom	2.9	2.4	3.1	1.9	1.7
Canada	4.1	5.4	4.5	1.5	3.4
All developed countries	2.7	3.4	3.8	0.8	1.7
Seven major countries above	2.8	3.0	3.4	0.6	1.4
European Union	2.9	2.8	3.5	1.6	1.1

[1]Estimated.
Note: Seasonally adjusted at annual rates.
Source: OECD, *IMF World Economic Outlook,* September 2002.

Table II. Standardized Unemployment Rates in Selected Developed Countries
% of total labour force

Country	1998	1999	2000	2001	2002[1]
United States	4.5	4.2	4.0	4.8	5.8
Japan	4.1	4.7	4.7	5.0	5.5
Germany	8.7	8.0	7.3	7.3	7.8
France	11.5	10.7	9.4	8.7	9.0
Italy	11.9	11.5	10.7	9.6	9.2
United Kingdom	6.3	5.9	5.4	5.1	5.2
Canada	8.3	7.6	6.8	7.2	7.6
All developed countries	6.7	6.6	6.1	6.4	6.8
Seven major countries above	6.3	6.1	5.7	6.0	6.6
European Union	9.4	8.7	7.7	7.3	7.6

[1]Projected.
Source: OECD, *Economic Outlook,* November 2002.

run down than in earlier recessions, which left less scope for increasing output when demand recovered.

The U.S. wasted little time in reestablishing its position as the driver of world growth. Domestic demand was strong relative to the rest of the world. Household spending, which contributed three-quarters of GDP, remained buoyant and was helped by well-timed tax cuts and access to the lowest interest rates in 40 years. The latter had encouraged the refinancing of $1 trillion of mortgage debt in 2001, freeing up finance for other spending. In the summer there was strong demand for homes, and automobile sales were boosted by incentives and zero-interest-rate offers from automakers. Given that stocks accounted for only about 20% of Americans' personal wealth, the fall in share prices did little to detract from household spending. In October real personal disposable income was increasing at more than 3% a year. Third-quarter GDP growth accelerated to an annual rate of 4% from 1.3% in the second quarter. Much of the strong demand was met by imports, which rose 3.4% in volume terms, compared with a 1% decline in exports.

There was a strong deterioration in public finances. The fiscal-year budget that ended on Sept. 30, 2002, registered a deficit of $159 billion, the equivalent

of around 1.5% of GDP. It was the first deficit since 1997 and was in sharp contrast to the $313 billion surplus (3% of GDP) that had been estimated in January. Several factors contributed to the reversal of fortunes: the extra spending that followed the September 11 attacks, the tax reductions introduced to support demand, and the increased cost of defense and security. The budget plan envisaged a fall in the deficit to $81 billion in fiscal 2003 (based on a growth rate of 3.6%) and a return to surplus in 2005. The growth rate for 2003 looked optimistic, however, and tax revenues were likely to be below target, especially if additional tax cuts were forthcoming.

United Kingdom. The U.K. proved its resilience once again and, aside from the North American members, grew faster than the other Group of Seven (G-7) countries. Although U.K. output was below trend and was likely to fall marginally short of the projected 1.7%, it was nevertheless robust in comparison with the large euro-zone countries. This followed a 2001 rise of 1.9%, which had outpaced the growth rates of all other G-7 countries. Output of manufacturing, services, and the construction industry remained positive, with some of the impetus coming from public-sector demand. Agricultural output was recovering following the end of the outbreak of foot-and-mouth disease

© AFP 2002, by Tim Sloan

U.S. Federal Reserve Chairman Alan Greenspan testifies on Capitol Hill in November about the state of the American economy.

in 2001, although exports of live cattle had not yet returned to earlier levels. Other agricultural output was under pressure from cheap imports.

Economic growth was led by domestic demand. The sharp falls in equities and weak global economy did little to dampen consumer confidence. The lowest mortgage rates in 37 years and annual house-price rises of 25–30% pushed household debt as a proportion of income to record levels. Retail sales in October were running at 6% above year-earlier levels. In the summer the association football (soccer) World Cup and Queen Elizabeth II's Golden Jubilee celebration temporarily boosted sales of electronic and other goods, while overseas holiday bookings were strengthened by poor weather at home. Trends in the labour market were mainly positive, with the unemployment rate expected to rise only slightly to 5.3% (from 5.1% in 2001). There were layoffs in manufacturing, despite the slow recovery in output, and capacity contracted as multinationals rationalized their production, often moving factories to China or Eastern Europe. Professional services companies also were cutting jobs, and many companies had imposed a freeze on recruitment. An easing in the tight labour market was reflected in lower voluntary turnover rates and more applications for advertised jobs. A shortage of low-skilled labour was being eased by immigrant labour, and labourers having special skills were being recruited from abroad.

Increasing dissatisfaction of workers in the expanding public sector was of growing concern for the government. In the last week of November, teachers and firefighters took strike action

Industrial Production
semiannual averages: 1995 = 100

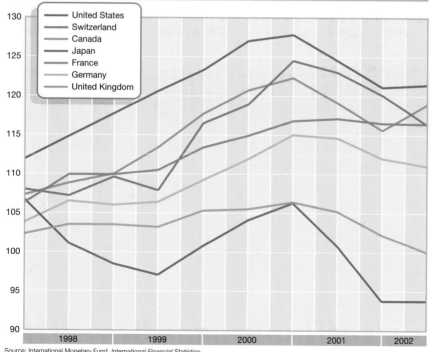

Source: International Monetary Fund, *International Financial Statistics*.

for more pay. The government was rejecting their demands on the grounds that meeting them would erode the spending required for improving public services. Increases in resources to modernize the health, education, and transport systems were rising faster than total government spending. In November Chancellor of the Exchequer Gordon Brown announced that because of a weaker-than-expected surplus in fiscal 2001–02 and falling tax revenues, public-sector borrowing was to nearly double to £20 billion (about $32 billion) in 2002–03.

Japan. At the beginning of the year, the outlook for the Japanese economy was pessimistic following three quarters of declining output, a phenomenon not experienced in Japan since the end of World War II. It was quickly followed by guarded optimism when signs emerged that the economy had at last bottomed out. The recovery that followed proved unsustainable, however, and output was expected to decline by 0.7%, following a 0.3% decline in 2001.

Nevertheless, Japan was well positioned to take advantage of the recovery in world trade, particularly in IT, and needed to rebuild its inventories. Buoyed by the weaker yen, which had depreciated 17% over the previous 18 months, exports rose 6.4% in the first quarter. Output continued to rise through the second quarter but slackened in the third quarter, not helped by a 0.7% appreciation of the yen, which increased it to 1.5% over the same year-earlier period. For a brief period, consumer spending rose modestly, reflecting the increase in confidence, but as the year ended, most indicators reflected the deflationary environment.

A major concern of policy makers was the health of the banking system and the size of its bad loans. A new classification system for bank loans was put in place that resulted in a more than fourfold increase in the estimate of nonperforming loans to ¥43 trillion (about $362 billion). This was the equivalent of 8% of GDP, and it was feared that even this was an understatement and that the true size of the debt could be double that amount. The problem was compounded by the fact that the value of the banks' shareholdings, which had been falling, could be included for capital adequacy purposes. In September the Bank of Japan (BOJ), under the direction of its governor, Masaru Hayami (*see* BIOGRAPHIES), purchased some of the banks' shares before the midyear financial results,

and additional injections of public funds were likely. In the meantime, "zombie" companies, which the banks failed to foreclose on, continued to produce goods and services at a loss. This was perpetuating the deflationary pressures and undermining the profitability of more viable companies.

Euro Zone. On Jan. 1, 2002, euro notes and coins were introduced in the euro zone. The member countries had already adopted a fixed euro rate for their national currencies, and the main rationale for the introduction of notes

and coins was political—to create a European identity. The abolition of national currencies nevertheless increased transparency and competition within the zone and helped businesses and other consumers compare prices and select competitive suppliers more easily. While some retailers took advantage of the changeover to increase prices, in general the introduction went smoothly and was an administrative success. An increase of 0.9% in GDP was projected for 2002, compared with 1.5% in 2001. The political preoccupation with gain-

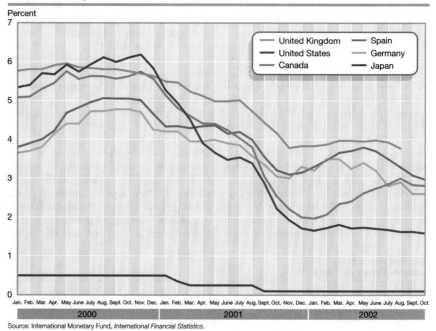

Interest Rates: Short-term
three-month money market rates

Source: International Monetary Fund, *International Financial Statistics.*

Interest Rates: Long-term

Source: International Monetary Fund, *International Financial Statistics.*

AP/Wide World Photos

Fireworks over the European Central Bank in Frankfurt, Ger., at the New Year mark the historic introduction of euro bills and coins in 12 European counries.

ing wide acceptance for the euro, particularly in France and Germany, was in stark contrast to the lack of attention given to structural reforms in product and labour markets. It also partly obscured the economic frailty of the euro zone, where activity had slowed more than expected in 2001 following a 0.2% decline in the final quarter. Although Europe had the advantage of a weak currency and less exposure to falling equity prices, the ECB underestimated the impact of the U.S. downturn. It did not take into account the euro zone's huge increase in investment exposure to the U.S., which had taken place since the mid-1990s. The lower earnings of European companies' affiliates in the U.S. were adversely affecting business income and confidence.

Structural differences between the 12 countries in the European Monetary Union (EMU) were reflected in a wide range of growth rates and prospects. In several countries budget deficits were a major concern. Under the Stability and Growth Pact, they were limited to 3% of GDP. Portugal had breached this limit in 2001 and was expected to do so again in 2002, while Germany, the architect of the pact, was extremely close, as were France and Italy. The need for governments to exercise spending restraint was causing political problems. The lack of confidence in the euro was a mixed blessing; its weakness helped exports to provide much of the impetus from growth. Germany, which had once spearheaded growth in mainland Europe, was in recession, with weak domestic demand, declining in-

dustrial output, and sluggish retail sales. The German banking sector was in crisis, with major banks either taking losses or suffering a huge decline in profits.

Relative to the U.S., most labour markets in mainland Europe were inflexible and productivity was lower. Employment grew only 0.4%. Unemployment was high and rose gradually over the year to the third quarter from 8% in 2001 to 8.3% in 2002, at which time the unemployment rate for the under-25s was 16.4%. Employment was declining in agriculture and industry, except for the construction sector, which was booming in several countries. The strong growth in service-sector jobs moderated to a 1.5% year-on-year rate.

The Countries in Transition. Growth in the countries in transition slowed from 5% in 2001 to 3.9% in 2002. Central and Eastern Europe (up 2.7%) was growing more slowly than the Commonwealth of Independent States (CIS) and Mongolia (both up 4.6%) and Russia (4.4%), since that region was most affected by the slowdown in the euro zone. In the CIS countries reforms continued to be implemented, while in Russia progress was made in strengthening financial discipline and improving standards of corporate governance. Strong domestic demand was driving growth in Russia, and privatized firms were becoming more efficient despite high labour and other cost pressures on competitiveness.

Less-Developed Countries. The IMF projection was for an acceleration in output in the LDCs to 4.2% from 3.9% in 2001. Regional and country disparities were wide, with Latin America making a negative contribution.

In Africa GDP was expected to increase by 3.1% following a 3.5% rise in 2001. Across the region political and economic problems persisted, compounded by civil unrest and armed conflicts, the HIV/AIDS pandemic, and other diseases. The World Health Organization reported that some 29.4 million people in sub-Saharan Africa were living with HIV/AIDS in 2002. Nevertheless, economic and social progress was being made. The nature of FDI was changing, with a growing share destined for the services industry, the financial and banking sector, and the transportation sector. Of the major countries, South Africa was expected to grow by 5.2%, little changed from 2001. South African industrial output in September was rising 8.6% year on year, and consumer prices were up 14.5%, which largely reflected the depreciation of the rand in 2001. The currency had recovered in 2002, however, and the inflation rate was easing. In Nigeria political instability and cutbacks in oil production contributed to a contraction of around 2%.

In much of Asia there was a marked recovery from the start of the year as countries responded quickly to the upturn in the U.S., on which many of

Table III. Changes in Output in Less-Developed Countries
% annual change in real gross domestic product

Area	1998	1999	2000	2001	2002[1]
All less-developed countries	3.5	4.0	5.7	3.9	4.2
Regional groups					
Africa	3.4	2.8	3.0	3.5	3.1
Asia	4.0	6.1	6.7	5.6	6.1
Middle East, Europe, Malta, and Turkey	3.6	1.2	6.1	1.5	3.6
Western Hemisphere	2.3	0.2	4.0	0.6	−0.6
Countries in transition	−0.7	3.7	6.6	5.0	3.9

[1]Projected.
Source: International Monetary Fund, *World Economic Outlook,* September 2002.

Table IV. Changes in Consumer Prices in Less-Developed Countries
% change from preceding year

Area	1998	1999	2000	2001	2002[1]
All less-developed countries	10.5	6.9	6.1	5.7	5.6
Regional groups					
Africa	10.9	12.3	14.3	13.1	9.6
Asia	7.7	2.5	1.9	2.6	2.1
Middle East, Europe, Malta, and Turkey	27.6	23.6	19.6	17.2	17.1
Western Hemisphere	9.8	8.9	8.1	6.4	8.6

[1]Projected.
Source: International Monetary Fund, *World Economic Outlook,* September 2002.

their exports depended, and to the improvement in the IT market. Inflation rates, a modest 2.1% on average, ranged from 15% in Myanmar (Burma) and 12% in Indonesia to a slight fall in prices in China following a rise of only 0.7% in 2001.

Output of the newly industrialized countries (NICs), including Hong Kong, South Korea, Singapore, and Taiwan, grew 4.9%. They were led by South Korea, where increased exports, combined with strong domestic demand, pushed the annual growth rate to above 6%. Unemployment was stable at 3%, and consumer prices rose more slowly despite inflationary pressures. Singapore recovered from its deepest recession in 37 years, and its GDP rose 3.9% in the year to June. Taiwan's recovery was narrowly based on exports, which were outpaced in the second quarter by high imports. Falling prices gave cause for concern—in October they were 1.7% down from a year earlier. Hong Kong's growth was marginal as the former colony struggled with a weak property market, which had fallen by 60% since 1997, but there were some positive indicators, including a fall in the rate of unemployment in August.

The Association of Southeast Asian Nations' "group of four" (Indonesia, Malaysia, the Philippines, and Thailand) expanded 3.6%. Indonesia's expansion was driven by domestic consumption, with fixed investment and exports in the second quarter running below year-earlier levels. Recovery in Malaysia was broad based and was helped by strong government consumption and fixed investment, but the economy remained highly dependent on electronics exports. In the Philippines exports were strong, but a major concern was the hefty budget deficit.

China's economy gathered more momentum, with output accelerating to 7.4% from 7.2% in 2001. In the year to August, exports rose 25% in U.S. dollar terms. While the export industries had effective management and the advantage of foreign investment and technology, however, most of China's industry remained inefficient and overmanned. India's GDP growth rate accelerated to 5%, despite the poor monsoon's adverse effect on agriculture.

The Latin American economy was contracting after a negligible rise in 2001. Although growth in Argentina was expected to fall by 15% over the year, in the second half the high rate of inflation was decelerating and the exchange rate was steadying. Confidence was boosted when the IMF agreed on November 20 to a one-year extension for repayment of a $140 million loan. The financial crisis in Argentina had been sparked by the government's inability to fund its debt at the end of 2001. Initially, the effects were contained, but in 2002 trouble spread throughout the area and most currencies lost value. Uncertainty in the run-up to the October election in Argentina caused the peso to depreciate by 40%, but stability was returning by year's end. The IMF projected growth of 3.6% in the Middle East. The region was heavily influenced by factors relating to security as well as oil-price movements and the global economy. Output in Israel was declining, and most indicators were negative. Most rapid growth was occurring in Bahrain, Iran, Jordan, and Saudi Arabia.

INTERNATIONAL TRADE, EXCHANGE, AND PAYMENTS

International Trade and Payments. World trade in 2002 began to recover from the second quarter, and the IMF predicted that it would rise in volume terms by 2.1% over the year. Recovery was from the worst growth performance in two decades in 2001, when the value of world merchandise exports declined 4% and global exports of services fell 1%. After two decades in which trade growth had outpaced production, it was the second consecutive year in which the rate lagged the increase in world output. In value terms the rise was 3.1% to a projected $7.7 billion, of which $6.2 billion was merchandise rather than services. Momentum in the market once again came from the LDCs and countries in transition, which provided the strongest growth markets for world exports. In volume terms their imports were projected to rise by 3.8% and 6.9%, respectively, in contrast to 1.7% for the advanced economies. There was a similar picture on the supply side, with LDC exports up 3.2% and countries in transition up 5.3%, while those of advanced countries rose only 1.2%.

Recovery was strongest in the U.S. and among IT producers in East Asian countries, which had experienced the fastest slowdowns in 2001. In the EU and Japan, exports rose more strongly than imports. The opposite was true in the U.S., where merchandise imports in the first half of the year rose at an annual rate of 7.2% from the second half

Table V. U.S. Trade Balance with Major Trading Partners[1] (in $000,000)	
European Union	−76,088
China	−95,829
Japan	−67,408
Canada	−49,329
Mexico	−36,075
Africa	−10,550
Rest of world	−107,688
World total	−442,967

[1]Oct. 31, 2001, to Oct. 31, 2002.
Source: <http://www.ita.gov>.

of 2001, a pace exceeded by services imports. Trade increased at an annual rate of 6% between the fourth quarter of 2001 and the second quarter of 2002. Despite this, global merchandise trade in the first half of the year was running at 4% below the same year-earlier period. Exchange rates, prices, and volume changes contributed to this decline. In dollar terms imports by the EU, the U.S., Japan, and Latin America fell. Trade in Asian LDCs was extremely buoyant and was being boosted by the strength of China's market.

The balance of trade continued its relentless shift toward the LDCs, with a 3.2% rise in the value of exports (excluding services) following a fall of 3.2% in 2001. Merchandise exports were projected at almost $1.32 trillion, of which nearly half was from Asian LDCs, while imports rose marginally to $1.19 trillion, leaving a slight increase in the trade balance compared with the year before. After taking into account trade in services and other transactions, for the third successive year LDCs returned a surplus on current account, although at $18.9 billion it was less than half the $39.6 billion achieved in 2001. Much of the momentum once again came from LDCs in Asia, where exports rose 7.4% to a record $638 billion. Increased imports contributed to a drop in the current-account surplus from $39.4 billion in 2001 to $33.5 billion. This was despite the strength of the Chinese economy, which produced a $19.6 billion surplus on current account. A growing trade surplus in India resulted from the rapid increase in exports, which outpaced imports.

Among the other less-developed regions, the Middle East (including Turkey) maintained a current-account surplus ($25 billion) for the third straight year. Latin America achieved a trade surplus after many years of deficit, but other current-account transactions resulted in a deficit of $32.6 billion. In Africa stagnating exports and rising imports contributed to a $7.2 billion deficit.

The overall current account of the advanced countries was projected to remain in deficit for the fourth straight year, rising from $188 billion to $210 billion. In value terms exports and imports rose only marginally, and the trade deficit increased from $179 billion to $188 billion. Once again the burgeoning U.S. current-account deficit exceeded the total surplus of the other advanced countries. At $480 billion, it was well up on 2001's $393 billion deficit, and no decline was expected in the near future. As was customary, the only other G-7 country to have a deficit was the U.K., with $32 billion, up from $30 billion in 2001. By contrast, the traditionally large surplus of Japan surged from $88 billion in 2001 to $119 billion. Most of the non-G-7 advanced countries maintained current-account surpluses. Notable exceptions were Spain, where the deficit fell from $15 billion to $11 billion, and Australia, where it rose from $9 billion to $15 billion. The euro-zone surplus jumped from $22 billion in 2001 to $71 billion in 2002. In Germany and France, where import demand was weak, deficits of $39 billion and $27 billion, respectively, contributed strongly to the euro-zone surplus.

The $58 billion surplus of the Asian NICs was almost unchanged from 2001. The current account of countries in transition moved back into deficit (down $1.4 billion) following two years of surplus. Of these, the Central and Eastern European deficit was more than offset by the surplus in the CIS.

Exchange and Interest Rates. Interest rates in the industrialized countries were stable in 2002 compared with the previous year. Attention continued to focus on Alan Greenspan, chairman of the U.S. Federal Reserve (Fed), following an unprecedented 11 cuts in the

Fed funds interest rate in 2001. The rate started 2002 at the 40-year low of 1.75%, and, contrary to the expectations and second guesses of the financial markets, it remained there until November 6.

Despite evidence that the U.S. and global economic outlook had improved in the first quarter, the Federal Open Market Committee (FOMC) took the view in March that "the degree of strengthening in final demand over coming quarters . . . is still uncertain." By contrast, financial markets were of the opinion that the global monetary cycle was at an end and that the Fed would raise interest rates shortly. Some central banks, including those of Sweden and New Zealand, raised their rates in expectation. It was not to be so. Growth in the second quarter faltered, and in the third quarter the signals were mixed. On September 24 the FOMC stated, "Against the background of its long-run goals of price stability and sustainable economic growth and of the information currently available, the Committee believes that the risks continue to be weighted mainly toward conditions that may generate economic weakness in the foreseeable future." In the meantime, the Bank of England and the ECB held fast, as did the BOJ. In Australia in May and June, the Reserve Bank raised its target cash rate in two moves by a total of 50 basis points (0.5%) to avert the risk of inflation and prevent the economy from overheating. The Bank of New Zealand again raised its rates.

Throughout the year exchange-rate attention focused on the dollar. At the start of the year, the launch of euro notes and coins generated some debate as to whether the U.K. might enter the EMU and adopt the euro. Despite the fact that most financial market participants believed that if British sterling did

go ahead, it would be at a much lower rate, sterling continued to appreciate against the euro. Exchange movements generally were linked to the perceived strength or weakness of the U.S. economy. It was this that determined euro movements. In the first weeks of the year, the dollar continued to make modest gains against the yen and even larger gains against the euro. Against sterling the dollar was unchanged.

From the middle of February, however, the picture changed, and the dollar came under pressure for several reasons. The growing concern about the sustainability of the U.S. deficit was given credence by Greenspan in the middle of March, when he said that the deficit would have to be restrained. U.S. equity markets were weak, and U.S. equities were seen as overvalued. There was also the threat that the U.S. would impose tariffs on some foreign steel products, which was seen as protectionist because of the strength of the dollar. Heavy selling of the dollar over the ensuing months produced a 5.5% depreciation against the euro and the yen and 1.9% against sterling. By June all the major currencies, including the Swiss franc and the Canadian, Australian, and New Zealand dollars, had appreciated against the U.S. dollar. In July sterling bounced and appreciated against all currencies, particularly the euro and the dollar, against which it reached a 27-month high. In August, however, economic news sent sterling sliding, and in September selling pressure on the dollar declined.

On November 6 the Fed cut official interest rates by half a percentage point, but the official rates of other major economies were left unchanged until December 5, when the ECB announced a similar cut, to 2.75%. The U.K., however, left its rate unchanged.

(IEIS)

Exchange rates of major currencies to U.S.$, 2002

European Union – euro – €

United Kingdom – pound – £

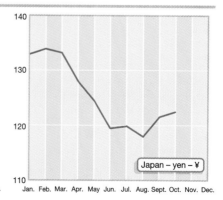

Japan – yen – ¥

Source: International Monetary Fund, *International Financial Statistics.*

STOCK MARKETS

Those who forecast stock market recovery beginning in the second half of 2002 reckoned without the impact of successive corporate scandals and profit warnings from major companies in all developed markets. In the event, hopes of a sustained stock market recovery died in the summer, along with investors' faith in the honesty of company accounts, and 2002 ended as the third year of a global bear market that had proved to be the longest in post-World War II stock market history. Early in the year Enron Corp., the world's largest and most successful energy-trading company, collapsed amid debts of more than $1 billion, the combined result of fraud and creative accounting. (See Sidebar.) With it went accounting firm Arthur Andersen LLP, the auditor that had signed off on Enron's accounts, and some $60 billion of investors' money. As the Enron debacle unfolded came news of questionable accounting by many other world-class companies struggling to present themselves in the best possible light to investors. The news in July that giant telecommunications company WorldCom, Inc., had overstated its earnings by more than $3.8 billion (a figure that WorldCom later almost doubled) shook markets worldwide.

Sleaze was not the only factor keeping stock markets depressed and volatile. Political risk throughout the world also weighed heavily on investors' minds. Throughout the year stock markets continued to weaken, even against a trend of improving economic fundamentals in the United States, where share prices fell despite the beginning of economic recovery at the start of the year, something that had not happened since 1912.

By late November the consensus among market watchers was that a global rally, begun in October, would be sustained as the threat of a "double dip" recession in the U.S. receded; companies benefited from cost cutting and restructuring; South American and Asian markets stabilized. The price of oil also stabilized at about $30 a barrel, having jumped 4% in early December when general strikes in Venezuela halted shipments. Most analysts expected equity stock prices to end 2003 higher than in 2002.   (IEIS)

United States. The year 2002 marked the third consecutive year of falling U.S. stock prices, the first time this had happened since 1941. The decline was driven by a still-sluggish economy, national security concerns, and a widespread loss of faith in corporations and their financial practices. A string of corporate accounting scandals uncovered an epidemic of misleading accounting practices, aided by crippling conflicts of interest among the outside auditors who inspected the financial statements of publicly traded companies. Congress responded with sweeping legislation, and the Securities and Exchange Commission (SEC) introduced a wave of new regulations. The possibility of war in Iraq, the continued threat of terrorism, and the lack of satisfactory insurance against future terrorist acts had a negative impact on stocks and the economy and contributed to the overall climate of uncertainty. Unemployment reached an eight-year high of 6% in April and again in November, and the prospect of recovery from the previous year's economic recession became doubtful.

The year's financial news was dominated by corporate scandal and the ensuing legislative and regulatory response. With the accounting troubles and subsequent bankruptcy of Enron fresh in their memory, investors dumped stocks of companies with hints of accounting irregularities. As the year progressed, a growing number of corporate scandals emerged. Bernard Ebbers, the CEO of WorldCom, resigned under pressure in April, and in July the company filed the largest U.S. bankruptcy claim in history, surpassing the previous record set by Enron. (Four former WorldCom executives, though not Ebbers, pleaded guilty to fraud charges in the case.) In May fraudulent accounting practices by energy company and Enron rival Dynegy, Inc., came to light, ultimately resulting in a $3 million fine, assessed by the SEC in September, and a stock price of less than a dollar per share, down from $26.11 in January. Shares of manufacturer Tyco International Ltd. fell nearly 90% after its CEO resigned in June amid accusations of concealing multimillion-dollar loans he took from the company; he was indicted for tax

(continued on page 194)

Table VI. Selected Major World Stock Market Indexes[1]

Country and Index	2002 range[2] High	Low	Year-end close	Percent change from 12/31/2001
Australia, Sydney All Ordinaries	3440	2856	2976	−11
Belgium, Brussels BEL20	2900	1774	2025	−27
Brazil, Bovespa	14,471	8371	11,268	−17
Canada, Toronto Composite	7958	5695	6615	−14
Denmark, KFX	279	187	199	−27
Finland, HEX General	9036	4820	5775	−34
France, Paris CAC 40	4688	2656	3064	−34
Germany, Frankfurt Xetra DAX	5463	2598	2893	−44
Hong Kong, Hang Seng	11,975	8859	9321	−18
Ireland, ISEQ Overall	5665	3620	3995	−30
Italy, Milan Banca Comm. Ital.	1513	974	1092	−24
Japan, Nikkei Average	11,980	8303	8579	−19
Mexico, IPC	7574	5534	6127	−4
Netherlands, The, CBS All Share	745	424	462	−35
Philippines, Manila Composite	1469	998	1018	−13
Singapore, SES All-Singapore	478	346	349	−18
South Africa, Johannesburg All Share	11,653	8871	9277	−11
South Korea, Composite Index	938	584	628	−10
Spain, Madrid Stock Exchange	848	569	634	−23
Switzerland, SPI General	4615	3096	3246	−26
Taiwan, Weighted Price	6462	3850	4452	−20
Thailand, Bangkok SET	426	305	356	17
United Kingdom, FTSE 100	5324	3671	3940	−24
United States, Dow Jones Industrials	10,635	7286	8342	−17
United States, Nasdaq Composite	2059	1114	1336	−31
United States, NYSE Composite	610	421	473	−20
United States, Russell 2000	523	327	383	−22
United States, S&P 500	1173	777	880	−23
World, MS Capital International	1031	704	784	−22

[1]Index numbers are rounded. [2]Based on daily closing price.
Sources: Financial Times, The Wall Street Journal.

Enron—What Happened?

As 2002 began, energy trader Enron Corp. found itself at the centre of one of corporate America's biggest scandals. In less than a year, Enron had gone from being considered one of the most innovative companies of the late 20th century to being deemed a byword for corruption and mismanagement.

Enron was formed in July 1985 when Texas-based Houston Natural Gas merged with InterNorth, a Nebraska-based natural gas company. In its first few years, the new company was simply a natural gas provider, but by 1989 it had begun trading natural gas commodities, and in 1994 it began trading electricity.

The company introduced a number of revolutionary changes to energy trading, abetted by the changing nature of the energy markets, which were being deregulated in the 1990s and thus opening the door for new power traders and suppliers. Enron tailored electricity and natural gas contracts to reflect the cost of delivery to a specific destination—creating in essence, for the first time, a nationwide (and ultimately global) energy-trading network. In 1999 the company launched Enron Online, an Internet-based system, and by 2001 it was executing on-line trades worth about $2.5 billion a day.

By century's end Enron had become one of the most successful companies in the world, having posted a 57% increase in sales between 1996 and 2000. At its peak the company controlled more than 25% of the "over the counter" energy-trading market—that is, trades conducted party-to-party rather than over an exchange, such as the New York Mercantile Exchange. Enron shares hit a 52-week high of $84.87 per share in the last week of 2000.

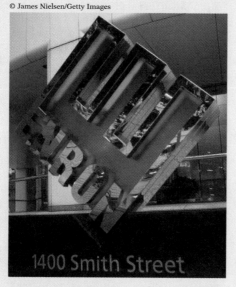

© James Nielsen/Getty Images

1400 Smith Street

Much of Enron's balance sheet, however, did not make sense to analysts. By the late 1990s, Enron had begun shuffling much of its debt obligations into offshore partnerships—many created by Chief Financial Officer Andrew Fastow. At the same time, the company was reporting inaccurate trading revenues. Some of the schemes traders used included serving as a middleman on a contract trade, linking up a buyer and a seller for a future contract, and then booking the entire sale as Enron revenue. Enron was also using its partnerships to sell contracts back and forth to itself and booking revenue each time.

In February 2001 Jeffrey Skilling, the president and chief operating officer, took over as Enron's chief executive officer, while former CEO Kenneth Lay stayed on as chairman. In August, however, Skilling abruptly resigned, and Lay resumed the CEO role. By this point Lay had received an anonymous memo from Sherron Watkins, an Enron vice president who had become worried about the Fastow partnerships and who warned of possible accounting scandals.

As rumours about Enron's troubles abounded, the firm shocked investors on October 16 when it announced that it was going to post a $638 million loss for the third quarter and take a $1.2 billion reduction in shareholder equity owing in part to Fastow's partnerships. At the same time, some officials at Arthur Andersen LLP, Enron's accountant, began shredding documents related to Enron audits.

By October 22 the Securities and Exchange Commission had begun an inquiry into Enron and the partnerships; a week later the inquiry had become a full investigation. Fastow was forced out, while Lay began calling government officials, including Federal Reserve Chairman Alan Greenspan, Treasury Secretary Paul O'Neill, and Commerce Secretary Donald Evans. In some cases, officials said, Lay was simply informing them of Enron's troubles, but Lay reportedly asked for Evans to intervene with Moody's Investors Service, which was considering downgrading Enron bonds to noninvestment-grade status. Evans declined.

On November 8 Enron revised its financial statements for the previous five years, acknowledging that instead of taking profits, it actually had posted $586 million in losses. Its stock value began to crater—it fell below $1 per share by the end of November and was delisted on Jan. 16, 2002.

On Nov. 9, 2001, rival energy trader Dynegy Inc. said it would purchase the company for $8 billion in stock. By the end of the month, however, Dynegy had backed out of the deal, citing Enron's downgrade to "junk bond" status and continuing financial irregularities—Enron had just disclosed that it was trying to restructure a $690 million obligation, for which it was running the risk of defaulting.

On December 2 Enron, which a year before had been touted as the seventh largest company in the U.S., filed for Chapter 11 bankruptcy protection and sued Dynegy for wrongful termination of the failed acquisition. A month later Lay resigned, and the White House announced that the Department of Justice had begun a criminal investigation of Enron.

By mid-2002 the once-mighty company was in tatters. Enron's energy-trading business had been sold off to the European bank UBS Warburg in January. Throughout the spring top Enron officials were subpoenaed to testify before congressional hearings. The majority of Enron's employees were unemployed, and their stock plans had become almost worthless. In June Arthur Anderson was convicted in federal court of obstruction of justice, while many other American companies scrambled to reexamine or explain their own accounting practices. As investigations continued into Enron's financial dealings, government connections, and possible involvement in California's energy problems, it appeared likely that the political and economic fallout would be making headlines for some time.

(CHRISTOPHER O'LEARY)

Martha Stewart and her stockbroker, Peter Bacanovic, are seen in happier days before Stewart came under investigation for possible insider trading of her ImClone holdings.

(continued from page 192)

evasion in the scheme. Samuel Waksal, the former CEO of ImClone Systems Inc., was arrested in June on insider-trading charges in a case that also implicated media icon Martha Stewart; Waksal pleaded guilty in October. Im-Clone's stock fell by 93%, and stock in Martha Stewart Living Omnimedia, Inc., lost as much as 75% of its value. In May executives of cable television operator Adelphia Communications Corp. resigned their posts as accounting irregularities at the firm came to light. The company went bankrupt in late June, and five former top executives were indicted on fraud charges in September. The stock was trading for pennies a share, down from $33 in January.

Arthur Andersen, one of the "Big Five" accounting firms, was convicted in June of obstruction of justice for having destroyed documents relevant to the 2001 investigation of its client Enron. The company was sentenced to five years' probation and fined $500,-000, the maximum criminal penalty under federal law, and was closed for business by the end of the year. These scandals tainted the entire stock market and were a principal reason stock prices overall fell sharply between mid-May and late July. Stock prices recovered some lost ground in October and November but finished the year in negative territory.

Congress responded to the wave of corporate accounting scandals in July, passing sweeping legislation known as the Sarbanes-Oxley Act. The act created a new regulatory board to oversee the accounting industry, particularly its au-

diting of publicly traded corporations. The act also provided broad new grounds on which to prosecute corporations and their executives for fraud, prohibited accounting firms from offering certain consulting services to companies they audited, forbade companies to extend certain types of loans to their executives, and protected research analysts from being punished by their employers for making negative statements about client companies, among other provisions. The act required the SEC to create a new accounting oversight board, and it charged the agency with adopting many of the new rules outlined in the act.

The act also authorized a massive increase in the budget and staff of the SEC. This expanded budget remained in doubt at the end of the year, however, as Pres. George W. Bush requested a smaller increase. The agency, widely considered to be overworked and underfunded, struggled to meet the requirements of the act while increasing its pace of enforcement, bringing a record 598 cases in its fiscal year 2002, which ended on September 30. This pace was up 24% from the previous year; it resulted in recovery of $1.33 billion in illegal gains, more than twice the amount recovered in the previous year. As part of the act, the SEC required CEOs of all publicly traded companies to personally sign off on the companies' financial statements.

After a short but controversial tenure, SEC Chairman Harvey Pitt (*see* BI-OGRAPHIES) resigned on November 5. The resignation followed the appointment of William Webster to head the new regulatory board to oversee the accounting industry; Webster resigned shortly thereafter. On December 10 Wall Street executive William Donaldson was named to replace Pitt. The accounting oversight board remained leaderless through the end of the year.

Stock prices were also dogged by continuing revelations of conflict of interest between research analysts and brokerages. Several major firms, including Citigroup's Salomon Smith Barney and Merrill Lynch, were subjected to fines for making conflicted recommendations. These concerns created a crisis of confidence in stock investing that helped to take share prices to new lows for the year in September and early October.

At the same time, aggressive enforcement actions by New York Attorney General Eliot Spitzer brought the nation's major brokerage firms and regu-

lators to agreement on a major restructuring of analyst research. The plan, announced on December 20, included a fine of $900 million to be shared by 10 brokerage firms, created a new system whereby the firms would purchase independent stock research to provide to their investors (at a cost of roughly $450 million over five years), and set aside $85 million for investor education.

As the year began, the economy seemed poised for recovery. The broadest overall measure of the size of the economy, gross domestic product (GDP), was rising, as were consumer spending and home sales. Corporate earnings estimates were optimistic. Jobless claims were falling, and manufacturing output was on the rise. The recession that had begun in March 2001 seemed to be coming to an end. Corporate profits and business investment, however, were still declining. By midyear the recovery appeared weak at best. Earnings proved much lower than expected, and unemployment was near an eight-year high of 6% in April. Consumer confidence and spending were flagging, and business investment was improving only modestly. Stock prices had fallen sharply through the spring, a reflection of a lack of confidence in the economy and the health of corporations.

Falling stock prices led to a growing crisis in the funding of many company pension plans. As companies experienced lower-than-expected investment returns, they were forced to dip further into earnings to shore up weakened pension funds to help meet plan obligations. A new regulation proposed by the Bush administration would allow these companies to convert traditional pension plans to another type of plan known as cash balance plans. Analysts said this would save companies money at the expense of older workers.

In November unemployment once again crept up to 6%. Worries over a possible war with Iraq sent consumer confidence sharply lower, and manufacturing slipped back into decline after seven months of growth. Announced layoffs reached 1.5 million for the year, according to outplacement firm Challenger, Gray, and Christmas. Not all signals were negative, however. GDP grew in all three quarters—5% annualized in the first quarter, 1.3% in the second, and 4% in the third. Productivity (which measures output per hour worked and is considered important to long-term economic growth) rose sharply in the first and third quarters.

Despite a seven-week rally in October and November, by year's end it was clear that investors were generally unimpressed with whatever positive signals the economy had to offer. Stock prices fell in 9 of 12 months.

Venture capital investment fell sharply, reaching only $16.9 billion by the close of the third quarter, less than half the level of the same period of 2001 and down from more than $100 billion in 2000. Mergers and acquisitions activity was down more than 40% for the year.

On December 6 U.S. Secretary of the Treasury Paul O'Neill and White House economic adviser Lawrence Lindsey resigned. The resignations of the two top economic officials came at the request of the White House and were thought to be connected to the economy's poor performance. Railroad industry executive John Snow was named to replace O'Neill. Stephen Friedman, formerly of investment banking firm Goldman Sachs, was named to replace Lindsey.

The Federal Reserve (Fed), having cut interest rates a record 11 times in 2001, chose to leave the federal funds rate, the rate charged on overnight loans between banks, at 1.75% for much of the year before lowering it by one-half percentage point on November 6. The federal funds rate ended the year at 1.25%, its lowest point since July 1961. The Fed's action underscored the weakness of the recovery. It also reflected a lack of concern over inflation, which remained quite low throughout the year.

All 10 stock sectors tracked by Dow Jones declined over the year. Utilities (−28.6%), telecommunications (−36.3%), and technology (−38.8%) stocks fared worst, while consumer noncyclicals (−6.3%), basic materials (−10.6%), and financial (−14.4%) stocks fared least poorly.

The year was especially hard on telecommunications firms. WorldCom's accounting scandal and record-breaking bankruptcy was the largest failure of a telecommunications firm in 2002. Global Crossing and Adelphia Communications also filed high-profile bankruptcies, while Qwest Communications, Inc., narrowly escaped bankruptcy but did not escape a stock collapse that brought its price down nearly to the one-dollar mark in August, from a high of $14.93 in January. The sector's collapse was due in large part to excessive speculative investment in previous years.

Energy and utilities stocks suffered as well, as the fraudulent accounting practices of Enron proved to have been more widespread than previously believed, and allegations of price manipulation in California's energy crisis of 2000 gained credence. Dynegy stock traded above $25 per share at the start of the year but fell to as low as 51 cents. Stock in El Paso Corp., a major energy company, fell by 84%.

Financial stocks on the whole did less poorly than other sectors. While the bear market squeezed brokerage firms, many of which responded by laying off workers, regional banks' traditional lending business benefited from low interest rates and increased deposits. Regional banks benefited from a wider-than-usual difference between the rates they paid to depositors and the rates they charged borrowers. By contrast, the nation's largest banks, known as money centre banks, were hurt by their dependence on investment banking, trading, and venture capital, as well as weak commercial credit quality. Stocks of consumer goods manu-

New York Stock Exchange Common Stock Index Closing Prices
stock prices (Dec. 31, 1965 = 50)

Number of shares sold
In billions of shares

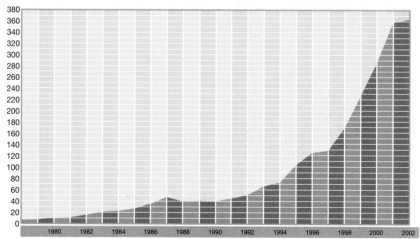

Sources: *Barron's National Business and Financial Weekly; The Wall Street Journal.*

facturers also did less poorly than others as consumers continued to spend throughout the economic slump.

The slow recovery in businesses' capital spending had a disproportionate impact on technology firms as companies held off on making upgrades to computer systems and other technology purchases. Litigation against Microsoft drew closer to resolution when the judge in charge of the case approved, with minimal alterations, a settlement agreement reached between the company and the federal government. The agreement restricted certain anticompetitive actions by the firm but stopped short of more extensive changes sought by some states. The judgment was a victory for Microsoft, but it could not keep the software giant's stock from losing more than 20% for the year.

The New York Stock Exchange (NYSE) showed average daily trading of 1.44 billion shares, up 16% from 2001, for a value of $40.9 billion, down 3.4%. There were 3,579 issues listed on the NYSE, nearly unchanged from 2001, and 151 new listings, up from 144 for the previous year. A total of 1,793 issues advanced on the year, 2,118 declined, and 45 were unchanged. The most actively traded issues on the exchange were, in sequence, Lucent Technologies, Tyco, General Electric Co., AOL Time Warner, and Nortel Networks.

Several seats on the NYSE changed hands in 2002. The last sale took place on November 25, at a price of $2 million, down from $2.55 million, fetched on June 5. Short selling—wherein investors bet that a stock will decline—was up. Short interest on the exchange was 7.8 billion shares as of December 13, up from 6.4 billion shares as of mid-December 2001. The risky practice of margin borrowing continued to fall; in November 2002 margin debt on the

exchange stood at $133.1 billion, down from a recent peak of $150.9 billion in April and an overall peak of $278.5 billion in March 2000.

The National Association of Securities Dealers automated quotations (Nasdaq) showed average daily trading of 1.5 billion shares through September, down slightly from 2 billion in 2001. Dollar volume averaged roughly $30.2 billion daily through September, down sharply from $33.9 billion daily in 2001. In 2002, 141 companies were added to the exchange. A total of 4,471 issues were listed on the Nasdaq, down somewhat from 2001, with 1,648 issues advancing on the year, 2,797 declining, and 26 unchanged. The most actively traded Nasdaq issues were, in sequence, WorldCom, Cisco Systems, Sun Microsystems, Intel Corp., and Oracle Corp.

The American Stock Exchange (Amex) listed a total of 1,160 issues, virtually unchanged from the previous year. Trading was down through September, with 12.5 billion shares traded, compared with 11.6 billion in the same period of 2001. The most actively traded issue on the Amex continued to be the Nasdaq 100 index.

Electronic communications networks (ECNs), continued to gain market share in Nasdaq trading, handling up to half of shares of Nasdaq-listed stocks through August. Nasdaq's own systems handled less than 25% of transactions. The rest were handled by private brokers. On October 14 Nasdaq introduced its new trading platform called Super-Montage, which was expected to create tough competition for ECNs. By December all Nasdaq-listed stocks were trading on the new platform.

There were a total of 83 initial public offerings (IPOs) of stocks on U.S. markets, valued at a total of $22.6 million,

compared with 85 IPOs in 2001. By contrast, 451 IPOs took place in 2000.

Through November, 7,087 arbitration cases were filed with the National Association of Securities Dealers, up 12% from the same period of the previous year, and 5,400 such cases were resolved, a rise of 7%.

In 2002 the three major stock indexes all declined for the third straight year. The Dow Jones Industrial Average (DJIA) of 30 blue-chip stocks fell 16.8% in 2002. (For a list of the 30 Dow components, see TABLE VII.) The Standard & Poor's index of 500 large-company stocks (S&P 500) was down 23.4%, and the Nasdaq composite index plunged 31.5%. (See GRAPH.) The Russell 2000, which represented small-capitalization stocks, ended the year down 21.6% after having eked out a tiny 1% gain in 2001, while the Wilshire 5000, the market's broadest measure, fell 22.1%.

The performance of the Dow's traditional blue-chip companies' stocks was disappointing, with only 4 of the 30 components ending the year up: AT&T (up nearly 44% for the year, from $18.14 to $26.11), Eastman Kodak (which opened at $29.43 and rose to $35.04 at year's end), Procter & Gamble (up from $79.13 to $85.94), and 3M (up from $118.21 to $123.30). Closing down for the year were American Express (down from $35.69 to $35.35), Philip Morris ($45.85 to $40.53), General Motors ($48.60 to $36.86), Walt Disney ($20.72 to $16.31), Merck & Co. ($58.80 to $56.61), IBM ($120.96 to $77.50), ExxonMobil ($39.30 to $34.94), Intel ($31.45 to $15.57), Johnson & Johnson ($59.10 to $53.71), Coca-Cola ($47.15 to $43.84), Caterpillar ($52.25 to $45.72), Wal-Mart Stores ($57.55 to $50.51), and General Electric ($40.08 to $24.35).

Mixed signals on the economy and a disappointing stock market kept mutual

Selected U.S. Stock Market Indexes Closing Prices, 2002

Sources: [1]Dow Jones, [2]National Association of Securities Dealers, [3]Standard & Poor's.

Table VII. Component Stocks of Dow Jones Industrial Index[1] (as of December 2002)

Company	Year added
3M Co.	1976[2]
Alcoa, Inc.	1999[2]
American Express Co.	1982
AT&T Corp.	1994[2]
Boeing Co.	1987
Caterpillar, Inc.	1991
CitiGroup, Inc.	1998
Coca-Cola Co.	1987[2]
E.I. du Pont De Nemours & Co.	1935
Eastman Kodak Co.	1930
ExxonMobil Corp.	1972[2]
General Electric Co.	1928
General Motors Corp.	1928
Hewlett-Packard Co.	1997
Home Depot, Inc.	1999
Honeywell International, Inc.	1999[2]
Intel Corp.	1999
International Business Machines Corp.	1979
International Paper Co.	1956
J.P. Morgan Chase & Co.	1991[2]
Johnson & Johnson	1997
McDonald's Corp.	1985
Merck & Co., Inc.	1979
Microsoft Corp.	1999
Philip Morris Companies, Inc.	1985
Procter & Gamble Co.	1932
SBC Communications, Inc.	1999
United Technologies Corp.	1975
Wal-Mart Stores, Inc.	1997
Walt Disney Co.	1991

[1]Index has consisted of 30 stocks since 1928.
[2]Earlier listing under predecessor company name.
Sources: <http://indexes.dowjones.com>;
<http://stocksquest.thinkquest.org>;
<http://www.thebullandbear.com>.

fund investors guessing. Money flowed into stock mutual funds in the first five months of the year and out from June to October, reversing course again in November. Investors were especially panicked in July after a wave of corporate accounting scandals came to light. Investors pulled a record $40.9 billion out of stock funds that month, far exceeding even the $23.7 billion outflow in the catastrophic month of September 2001. Through the month of November, investors moved a net total of $16.2 billion into stock mutual funds, compared with an inflow of $38.7 billion the previous year.

Large-cap stock mutual funds lost an average of 23.21%, according to fund tracker Morningstar. Small-cap funds did marginally better, losing 21.13%. The two largest U.S. stock funds, Vanguard's 500 Index Fund and Fidelity's Magellan Fund, lost 22.15% and 23.66%, respectively.

The market's plunge had a profound effect on the retirement prospects of American workers. More than 65% of the assets held by over 40 million Americans in 401(k) retirement plans were invested in stocks and stock mutual funds, and many workers had to postpone their retirement owing to declines in the value of their 401(k) plans.

Bonds played their standard role as foil to a declining stock market and a sluggish economy. Treasuries returned 11.79%, according to the Lehman Brothers U.S. Treasuries Composite index. Corporate bonds returned somewhat less, 10.52%, according to Lehman's U.S. Credit index. This reflected investors' desire for the security of government bonds and their lack of faith in corporate debt.

Mutual fund investors fled stock funds in favour of bond funds, which contributed to the decline of stock prices and boosted bond prices. In the third quarter, investors plunged a record $43.5 billion into taxable bond funds, mostly government bond funds. Through November, investors moved $103 billion into taxable bond funds, compared with the previous year's inflow of $86 billion. They were largely rewarded. According to Morningstar, long-term government bond funds returned 13.15% in 2002, and short-term government bond funds returned 6.61%. An important indication of the move from stock funds to bond funds was the fact that PIMCO Total Return, a bond fund, surpassed Fidelity Magellan and Vanguard 500 Index, both stock funds, to become the largest mutual fund in September. Vanguard 500 Index ended the year as the largest fund, however, followed by PIMCO Total Return.

Ten-year Treasuries yielded less than 4% at year's end, reflecting the uncertain economy and poor stock market returns. (As demand for bonds increases, prices rise and yields fall.) Yields on high-yield corporate bonds, also known as junk bonds, however, soared as uneasiness over the business climate grew. The spread between the yields of junk bonds and similar maturity treasuries reached 10.63% in October, breaking the previous record set in 1991. This spread reflected concern over the risk of default among troubled firms.

Canada. Despite a relatively strong economy in Canada, stock prices fell considerably in 2002 for the second year in a row. Market indexes were brought down in part by the struggling computer network manufacturer Nortel Networks and by banks, which suffered from bad loans made to U.S. telecommunications companies. The market also suffered from worries about the possible effect of the flagging U.S. economy.

The TSX Group, formed by the 2001 merger of the Toronto Stock Exchange (TSE), Canada's largest share-trading forum, and the Canadian Venture Stock Exchange (CDNX), announced several branding changes in April. The CDNX became the TSX Venture Exchange; the TSE 300 index, which measured the overall performance of the TSE, became the S&P/TSX Composite index; the TSE 60 index of blue-chip stocks became the S&P/TSX 60 index; and the S&P/CDNX Composite index became the S&P/TSX Venture Composite index. There were no related changes in the values of the indexes.

The broadest measure of the Canadian stock market, the S&P/TSX Composite index, fell 13.87% in 2002, while the S&P/TSX 60 dropped 15.68%. The Dow Jones Global index for Canada declined 12.96% in U.S. dollar terms.

The TSE reported that average daily trading was 184.3 million shares, up 23.9% from the same period of the previous year. The dollar value of these trades, however, averaged $2.5 billion per day, down 11% from the previous year, reflecting lower share prices. All told, 1,654 issues were listed on the exchange, up from 1,645 in 2001. IPOs were up at 75, compared with 56 for the same period of the previous year.

The Royal Bank of Canada, the largest TSE stock by market capitalization, gained 11.6% to close the year at $57.85. Nortel Networks, which ended its run as the largest stock on the TSE, lost 79% of its value to close at $2.52. The most actively traded TSE stocks were Nortel Networks, Bombardier, Kinross Gold Corp., Placer Dome, and BCE.

The three-year-old TSX Venture Exchange (formerly CDNX) rose 2.9% as measured by the S&P/TSX Venture Composite index. Through November, 24 companies graduated from this exchange to the larger TSE. There were 77 new companies listed on the exchange through November, down 53% from the same period of the previous year. Through November, average daily trading on the exchange was 33.9 million shares, down 3.1% from the previous year, and was valued at $12.8 million, down 13.4%. Average market capitalization remained roughly constant at $3.8 million.

Standard & Poor's on July 9 announced that the S&P 500, its blue-chip index, would no longer include non-U.S. stocks. This affected five Canadian issues: Nortel Networks, Alcan Inc., Barrick Gold, Placer Dome, and Inco Ltd., all of which suffered temporary losses as a result of the delisting.

Corporate profits were up approximately 8% through the third quarter. Foreign investment in Canadian stocks continued to fall, showing a net withdrawal of $3.8 billion through the third quarter, compared with a net investment of $3.8 billion in the same period of the previous year. Canadians also withdrew $13.5 billion from foreign stocks, continuing the trend of previous years.

The Canadian central bank, the Bank of Canada, cut its key overnight interest rate once, on January 15, and raised it three times, on April 16, June 4, and July 16. All changes were in quarter-point increments. The rate began the year at 2.25% and ended it at 2.75%. Unemployment remained fairly high, at 7.5% in November. Overall, however, the economy performed well, as 502,000 jobs were added through November, and GDP grew 5.7% annualized in the first quarter, 4.4% in the second, and 3.1% in the third.   (BETH KOBLINER)

Western Europe. Corporate governance was less an issue with European investors, according to the European Commission (EC), although the markets appeared to react in concert with the U.S. to each piece of bad corporate news wherever it arose. Between May 21 and July 23, when negative news flow was at its height, the S&P 500 fell 26%, the U.K.'s *Financial Times* Stock Exchange index of 100 stocks (FTSE 100) also was down 26%, and Germany's Xetra DAX dropped 30% (all in local currencies). Tough trading conditions and corporate governance worries left firms more concerned with cleaning up their balance sheets than with planning new investments. In its autumn economic forecast for 2002–04, the EC predicted that business investment in almost all member states would continue to contract for another year.

Some of the world's largest companies shrank dramatically. Although Enron's implosion was the most notorious, the biggest failure was ABB, a Swiss-Swedish engineering conglomerate, which dropped 300 places in the FT 500 index of the world's largest companies by capitalization.

The overall stock market decline raised the cost and cut the availability of capital, eroded household wealth, and undermined the financial structure of insurance companies and pension funds. July's share price falls indicated more strongly than ever before a loss of confidence in the financial sector as a whole, the Bank for International Settlements reported in September. In July share prices of European insurers had dipped below the levels to which they had fallen immediately after the terrorist attacks of Sept. 11, 2001. Many insurers around the world were placed under extreme pressure by their high exposure to equity markets. By year-end 2002 Europe's biggest insurer, Standard Life, had cut policy bonus payments, while troubled U.K. insurer Equitable Life had cut stock market exposure to 5% from 25% in May. Germany's banks, which were heavily invested in domestic industry, were badly hit by collapsing stock markets. In the three months to the end of October, shares in the country's biggest bank, Deutsche Bank AG, fell by 28%. The share prices of Commerzbank, HVB Group, and Allianz were all down more than 40%.

Across Europe the stock exchanges were themselves in a state of flux. In the two years to the end of September, the S&P Euro index lost half its market value. Trading volumes shrank dramatically, and competition squeezed margins. As much as 30% of business was being lost to big investment banks that matched buy and sell orders in-house rather than through exchanges. In Germany the Deutsche Börse closed down the Neuer Markt spin-off that it had set up to serve "new economy" companies. The strongest exchanges were offering new, mainly electronic, products and services as fees from traditional sources dried up and thus became data vendors, systems providers, and transaction processors. Alliances and mergers proliferated, and a paper written for the Organisation for Economic Co-operation and Development proclaimed an irresistible trend toward a single global market through the interlinkage of national equity markets.

European markets reacted badly to the threat of war in Iraq, and sentiment was further undermined by the reelection in September of German Chancellor Gerhard Schröder, who had been judged, particularly by foreign investors, to have been dragging his feet over imposing necessary economic reform. Most European markets tracked the U.S. trend and hit their lows in October before edging up slightly at year's end. Germany's DAX remained the region's worst performer, plunging 43.9% for the year, followed by Sweden, The Netherlands, Finland, and France's CAC 40, all of which dropped more than 30%. The FTSE 100 ended the year down 24.5%. Only Austria was in positive territory, with a gain of less than 1%.

Other Countries. Global equity markets established a long-term trend of increasing correlation as markets became more integrated and investors tended to choose industry sectors globally, rather than by region or country. A rise in global risk aversion added to the domestic economic and political problems of many emerging markets. Worst punished by investors were Latin American countries, such as Brazil and Argentina, that combined political instability with huge debt burdens that also undermined their financial stability. Over the year Brazil's market fell some 46% and Argentina's dropped nearly 50% (in U.S. dollars), though measured in the heavily devalued local currency the Argentine Merval index peaked at almost 78% and ended the year up 60% over 12 months.

Although the S&P/International Finance Corporation Investible Asia regional indexes ended the third quarter around 5% down year-to-date, stock markets in some countries outperformed strongly. Thailand's market entered the fourth quarter up by more than 21%; Indonesia's was up 13.7%; and South Korea's was up more than 12%, in dollar values. The most consistently strong performer was Australia, where the S&P/ASX All Ordinaries index peaked in March and subsequently dropped around 10% over the next six months. In the third quarter the market was up 4% over three years, compared with an 18% drop by the S&P Asia Pacific 100 index over the same period. Australian companies generally met earnings expectations, and the economy showed 4% growth, but there were signs that the prolonged drought was beginning to affect that growth. The Australia (All Ordinaries) index ended the year down 2.6% in U.S. dollar terms.

The star performer was Russia, where the stock market entered the final quarter 37% up in dollar terms and held on. China's top-down approach to building a market economy disconcerted some foreign investors, and the country's economic statistics were widely doubted. The Chinese stock market ended the year down 16.1% (per the Morgan Stanley Capital International [MSCI] China index) in U.S. dollars. Of the main Asian markets, only Taiwan recorded a marginally weaker performance, with the MSCI Taiwan index ending the year 25.3% down.

Although warnings about terrorist attacks and rising political tension between India and Pakistan led to a sell-off in the U.S. and European stock markets in early summer, Japan's markets held up well until mid-summer, when technology stocks fell further and investors' continuing doubts about government commitment to reform of the country's financial sector kept the market depressed. Sentiment was improved, though, by the Tokyo Stock Exchange's announcement in late summer of new delisting rules. Under these changes, a company would be delisted if its market capitalization fell below ¥1 billion (about $8.5 million) for more than nine months or it recorded a negative net worth for two successive years. The new plan aimed to end the problem of disconcertingly sudden bankruptcies among apparently well-capitalized companies and the fact that share prices might not reflect their state of near bankruptcy. In October the Bank of Japan, led by Masaru Hayami (*see* BIOGRAPHIES), launched a program of buying shares from banks in a move to break a cycle of falling markets and lower financial sector capital adequacy ratios. A similar course of action by Hong Kong, begun in 1998, was nearing what looked to be a successful conclusion, but views on Japan's experiment were mixed. The broad MSCI World index entered the final month of the year down just 0.6% over 12 months.

Commodity Prices. While stock markets struggled, commodity markets performed well overall. The Economist Commodity Index (U.S. dollars) for All Items recorded a rise of more than 15% over the year ended November 30. Food commodities rose 17.1%, narrowly beating gold's 16.4% increase, but gold climbed higher in December. The most spectacular rise over the year was in oil, up 57.3%.

Oil prices increased to close to $30 per barrel in the third quarter of 2002 amid high tension in the Middle East, fell back by November to $26 a barrel as the immediate threat of war with Iraq receded, and then spiked to more than $31 a barrel after a strike by oil workers in Venezuela cut off that country's exports. The continuing uncertainty and the determination of OPEC to keep the world price above $18 dollars a barrel boosted oil industry investment in other parts of the world. Beneficiaries included West Africa, where some potential was found for offshore development, Mexico, Brazil, and Russia. By the beginning of 2002, Russia's output

of 7.1 million bbl a day rivaled that of the U.S. (7.7 million) and the world's biggest producer, Saudi Arabia (8.8 million). Yet the OPEC countries, of which Saudi Arabia was the most prominent, controlled 75% of the world's oil reserves, and Russia controlled just 5%.

Over the year, gold's popularity as a safe investment in times of uncertainty raised the price per ounce to $324 in May from its 20-year low of $252 in August 1999 and then sent it up to $348 at year's end. There was a marked increase in demand for gold jewelry on the Indian subcontinent, particularly at the height of tensions between India and Pakistan. Figures released by the World Gold Council in November showed that the rates of decline in the demand for gold had slowed sharply from 14% in the first half of 2002 to just 7% year-on-year. A glut of reserves held down the prices of silver and most base metals. (IEIS)

BANKING

The global banking industry, which was challenged by generally weak market conditions for its products and services in 2002, also grappled with broad new requirements to combat money laundering and the financing of terrorism while at the same time having to deal with the fallout from the collapse of Enron Corp. and WorldCom, Inc., and other corporate and accounting

scandals. (*See* Sidebar, page 193.) In other developments, the year saw the smooth changeover to euro banknotes and coins at the beginning of the year in the 12 European Union countries constituting the Economic and Monetary Union. Meanwhile, a number of countries continued to modernize the regulatory structure governing their financial markets.

The repercussions from Enron and similar cases of corporate malfeasance reverberated throughout much of the banking industry during the year. The Sarbanes-Oxley Act was signed into law on July 30 by Pres. George W. Bush. The act included provisions that, among other things, created a new regulatory board to oversee the accounting industry, prohibited public companies from making personal loans to their directors and executive officers, and prohibited investment banking firms from punishing research analysts who issued negative reports on firm clients. Concerns were raised outside the U.S. about the extraterritorial reach of the act, particularly with regard to the prohibition on loans to directors and executive officers. Notably, an exemption in the statute that allowed American banks insured by the Federal Deposit Insurance Corporation to continue to make such loans under applicable banking regulations was not applied to non-American banks that were also subject to their home country's super-

Enron whistleblower Sherron Watkins listens as former CEO and president Jeffrey Skilling testifies before the U.S. Senate; corporate malfeasance such as that of Enron led to strict new regulations in the banking industry.

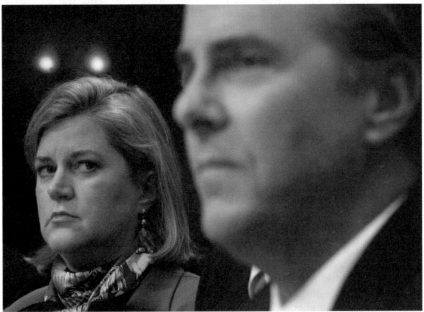

Mark Wilson/Getty Images

vision of insider trading. At the same time, other countries undertook their own initiatives in response to the collapse of Enron. In the U.K., for example, a variety of precautionary measures were taken, focusing on issues of corporate governance, auditor relationships, and financial reporting.

U.S. congressional inquiries into Enron, WorldCom, and other corporate meltdowns—and the possible role of their banks in having facilitated some of the alleged abuses—led some observers to suggest a need to revisit the Gramm-Leach-Bliley Act of 1999, which repealed provisions of the Depression-era Glass-Steagall Act that separated commercial from investment banking. Others pointed out that the potential conflicts of interest and related problems also applied to stand-alone securities firms that were not affiliated with banks and bank holding companies.

In addition to having influenced the creation of new anti-money-laundering initiatives, the terrorist attacks of Sept. 11, 2001, focused the attention of the financial-services industry and regulatory authorities on disaster-recovery/business-continuity issues, including the risk of having operations concentrated in one area. In August 2002 a draft White Paper on "sound practices" was issued jointly by the U.S. Federal Reserve, the Office of the Comptroller of the Currency, the Securities and Exchange Commission, and the New York State Banking Department. This draft paper emphasized the need for major banks and securities firms to consider establishing "out-of-region" back-up sites. The New York Stock Exchange, which had been forced to shut down for several days in September 2001 following the attacks, was looking into building a back-up trading floor outside Manhattan.

On June 6 the House Financial Services Committee passed on to Congress the Financial Services Regulatory Relief Act of 2002 bill, which would, among other things, ease restrictions on interstate branching and clarify merchant-banking provisions of the Gramm-Leach-Bliley Act to ease cross-marketing restrictions. The bill also included an amendment proposed by the comptroller of the currency that would eliminate the mandatory 5% capital equivalency deposit requirement applicable to federally licensed American branches and agencies of international banks in favour of a risk-focused approach under which the comptroller would have the discretionary authority

to impose such a requirement in appropriate circumstances. Ultimately, no action was taken on regulatory-relief legislation before Congress adjourned for the year, but the measure was expected to be taken up again early in 2003. The New York State Banking Department revised its asset-pledge requirement, greatly reducing the approximately $35 billion of collateral currently pledged by New York-licensed branches and agencies of international banks. Asset-pledge reform initiatives were also completed in Connecticut, which lowered the requirement to 2% of third-party liabilities from 3% and capped the maximum requirement for qualified institutions at $100 million. Other than the U.S., only Canada applied asset-pledge requirements to branches of nondomestic banking organizations.

A number of countries implemented sweeping regulatory-reorganization measures in 2002. On April 1 the Austrian Financial Market Authority assumed its powers and responsibilities under the Financial Market Supervision Act. The Austrian approach to financial-system supervision concentrated on the core functions performed by the financial system, rather than on institutions or sectors, and was in line with a functional approach to supervision.

Bahrain in April announced the creation of a single integrated financial-sector regulator within the Bahrain Monetary Agency, the central bank of Bahrain. Responsibilities for the regulation and supervision of the stock exchange and the insurance sector were in the process of being transferred to the agency. Banking supervision had been a key function of the agency since its creation in 1973.

In the spring the German Bundestag (parliament) passed the Act on the Integrated Supervision of Financial Services, which radically reformed the institutional framework for financial-services supervision in Germany. Germany's three separate supervisory offices for banking, insurance, and securities trading were combined on May 1, 2002, into a single agency, the Federal Financial Supervisory Agency, which was overseen by the Ministry of Finance. The restructuring mirrored changes made in several other European countries to establish single financial-supervisory authorities.

The Central Bank and Financial Services Authority of Ireland Bill was published in April. The bill allowed for the restructuring of the Central Bank of

Ireland to include a new regulatory authority with extended supervisory responsibilities that included control over the insurance sector. The measure was aimed at ensuring that the system of prudential regulation and coordination of financial stability enhanced the regulatory system. The considerable role given to consumer issues in the new measures was also designed to increase protection to the customers of financial services and to promote greater consumer awareness and education. An interim board has been appointed to manage the transition to the new regulatory arrangements.

Under new financial-sector reform measures in Canada, regulated, non-operating holding companies were permitted for the first time, offering financial institutions the potential for greater operational efficiency and lighter regulation. The holding-company structure allowed banks the choice of moving certain activities that had been conducted in-house to an outside entity that would be subject to lighter regulation than the bank. A broader range of investments were permitted for both the holding company and the parent-subsidiary structures and included expanded opportunities for investment in the area of e-commerce. As a general principle, any activity carried out by a financial institution could be carried out through a subsidiary of the financial institution or of its holding company. This gave banks and insurance companies in Canada greater choice and flexibility in the way they structured their operations. Trust companies could also have a broader range of investments.

[*This article is based in part on the Global Survey 2002 of the Institute of International Bankers.*]

(LAWRENCE R. UHLICK)

BUSINESS OVERVIEW

The year 2002 was a strange, tumultuous one that held few moments of rest for weary investors and companies. The recession seemed to continue unabated; many sectors were rife with bankruptcies; and executives were hauled before judges and congressional investigators. Behind the chaos lurked the possibility of a war with Iraq.

The technology-fueled stock market boom that defined the 1990s was a fading memory. Signs of hope that the worst was over were matched by fears that poor conditions would extend for another year. The Consumer Confidence Index hit 79.4 in October, its lowest standing since 1993. Nevertheless, U.S. gross domestic product expanded by a rate of 4% in third-quarter 2002, an improvement over the previous year's performance.

There was no ambiguity about the poor shape of many industries. Sectors ranging from energy to steel to textiles had appalling years, owing in part to the aftereffects of the terrorist attacks of Sept. 11, 2001, and also to evidence of mismanagement and fraud at some companies. The airline industry was perhaps the most visibly distraught sector, and many airlines bled losses throughout the year. The overall American airline industry lost $1.4 billion in the second quarter of 2002 alone and was expected to post more than $7.7 billion in losses for the year.

In August U.S. Airways filed for Chapter 11 bankruptcy protection, listing assets of roughly $7.81 billion, compared with liabilities of $7.83 billion. The airline, which was one of the carriers most affected by the September 11 attacks owing to its business concentration on the East Coast, had lost $2 billion between August 2001 and August 2002. It arranged financing to keep some of its flights going while it reorganized, but it also gutted its staff and canceled many of its routes. United Airlines followed suit, filing for bankruptcy protection on December 9 after a long, fruitless bid for billions of dollars in federal loan guarantees. UAL Corp., United's parent company, had lost $3 billion over 18 months, posted an $889 million loss for the third quarter alone, and slashed more than 1,250 jobs. UAL's more than $1 billion in debt obligations, which were due before year's end and which it ultimately could not pay, made bankruptcy the only route possible. The only American airlines that kept above water were low-cost regional companies such as Southwest Airlines and JetBlue.

These companies showed increased ambition; Southwest planned its first nonstop coast-to-coast route, which would put it in direct competition with the major carriers.

The airline industry in Europe showed some improvement early in the year. In the spring Swiss Air Lines, Ltd., launched a new airline to be called swiss to replace the bankrupt Swissair. British Airways, Air France, and Lufthansa revealed better-than-expected profits for the first half of 2002. As in the U.S., however, low-cost airlines such as Ireland's Ryanair and the U.K.'s easy-Jet, which completed its £374 million (about $590 million) takeover of budget rival Go, showed the strongest growth. Air Afrique, which officially went bankrupt in February, was replaced by two new, privately financed airlines in Africa: Uganda-based AfricaOne and Afrinat International Airlines, which expected to fly between New York City and several West African countries.

The woes afflicting aircraft carriers spread to aircraft manufacturing. Boeing Co., the world's largest aircraft maker, said it would greatly reduce its jet production through 2004. Boeing planned to deliver 380 planes in 2002, a 28% drop from the previous year, and in 2003 it would likely deliver between 275 and 285 planes, even fewer if more carriers declared bankruptcy. This opened a door for Boeing's most aggressive European rival, Airbus, which said that it would likely deliver more airplanes in 2003 than Boeing. If so, this would be the first time that Airbus had surpassed Boeing in aircraft production.

Another woebegone sector was energy production. In this case many of the industry's problems were due to one prime culprit; Enron Corp., a company that had once symbolized the sector's ambitions for the 21st century, poisoned the well for many of its competitors in 2002. (See Sidebar, page 193.) The size

and scope of the ongoing Enron scandals soon enmeshed other companies and industries, most notably Enron's accounting firm, Arthur Andersen, which was virtually destroyed after its conviction on charges of obstruction of justice.

The investigation into the 2000–01 California power crisis hit other West Coast players. El Paso Corp. was charged by a federal administrative judge with having distorted California energy prices, and one by one many of the energy producers that had attempted to match Enron's massive trading operations of the late 1990s began bailing out of the market. CMS Energy Corp. admitted to $4.4 billion in fraudulent trades and halted its trading operation. Dynegy Inc., which had almost bought Enron in late 2001, closed down its energy-trading operation after it also faced allegations of fraudulent trades. Many other American energy producers, including TXU Corp., Mirant Corp., Calpine Corp., and Williams Companies Inc., experienced stock-value depreciation and in some cases severe earnings losses.

In addition to experiencing financial difficulties stemming from the Enron fallout, energy companies suffered from not receiving a boost from oil prices, which stayed relatively flat despite rumours of war with Iraq. Crude oil hovered in the $25–$30-per-barrel range all year, though a strike by oil workers in Venezuela pushed prices up at year's end, and average monthly gasoline prices in the U.S. increased just two cents a gallon from April through September. One reason for the relative stability was an increase in European gasoline exports to the U.S. Flat oil prices for much of the year squeezed even the top global oil superpowers, such as ExxonMobil Corp., Chevron-Texaco Corp., BP Amoco PLC, and Royal Dutch/Shell Group. Chevron had its net income fall 75% to $1.13 billion for the first half of 2002 compared with the first half of 2001. Exxon's third-quarter net income fell by 17% compared with the previous year's period.

Another in the queue of battered industries was steel manufacturing, a sector that inspired Pres. George W. Bush's controversial decision in March 2002 to introduce tariffs on foreign steel imports. The tariffs, which ranged from 8% to 30%, were to be a short-term measure meant to buy the American steel industry time to recover and improve market share and would be phased out in 2005. The tariffs sparked

The 10 Largest U.S. Bankruptcies Filed Since 1980

Company	Date Filed	Prebankruptcy Assets
WorldCom, Inc.	July 21, 2002	$103.9 billion
Enron Corp.	Dec. 2, 2001	$63.4 billion
Conseco, Inc.	Dec. 18, 2002	$61.4 billion
Texaco, Inc.	April 12, 1987	$35.9 billion
Financial Corp. of America	Sept. 9, 1988	$33.9 billion
Global Crossing Ltd.	Jan. 28, 2002	$30.2 billion
UAL Corp.	Dec. 9, 2002	$25.2 billion
Adelphia Communications Corp.	June 25, 2002	$21.5 billion
Pacific Gas and Electric Co.	April 6, 2001	$21.5 billion
MCorp	March 31, 1989	$20.2 billion

Source: <http://www.BankruptcyData.com>.

Aircraft belonging to United Airlines, which filed for bankruptcy protection on December 9, wait at the terminal at Chicago's O'Hare Airport.

© Reuters 2002

protests from the country's trading partners, however, and the European Union for a time considered retaliating with duties of its own. As the year went on, the Bush administration began watering down its decision. The number of product categories hit with tariffs soon narrowed until by year's end more than half of European steel exports were exempt. American steelmakers also lost a bid to increase the tariffs when the U.S. International Trade Commission in August slapped down their request to impose duties on cold-rolled steel. The tariffs had a quick impact on pricing. The U.S. price for hot-rolled steel (which had a 30% tariff) jumped to $350 a ton at midyear from $210 a ton in late 2001. A counterbalance for higher pricing was the increasing amount of supply from international producers. Brazil, for example, produced 36% more steel in July 2002 than in the same month the year before—indicative of a worldwide glut in production. Even with the tariffs, steel imports by the U.S. boomed. Total steel imports, as of the end of the third quarter, were 8.2% higher than in the same period in 2001, and 2002 was expected to be the fourth highest steel-import year in U.S. history.

There were signs of recovery, however, in the American steel industry. U.S. Steel posted two profitable quarters in a row; in third-quarter 2002 it posted $106 million in earnings, compared with a loss of $23 million in the same period in 2001. This was its best quarterly performance in more than four years. U.S. Steel's recovery was due in part to higher prices, which helped the

company run its mills at nearly 94% capacity, compared with the 65–70% capacity at which many domestic mills had run in the late 1990s. In October U.S. Steel sold its coke mills, iron mines, and transportation holdings to a new company formed by Apollo Management, a New York City-based private equity firm, for $500 million, and the company also planned to sell off its coal business. Meanwhile, bankrupt Bethlehem Steel Corp. said that it would likely take a charge of $1.5 billion at the end of the year to cover its burgeoning pension costs and reported a third-quarter loss of $54 million. The rise of "minimills"—smaller steel-producing operations with higher efficiency rates and lower employee payrolls than traditional manufacturers—also presented a challenge to the traditional producers. Minimill operators such as Nucor Corp. and Steel Dynamics Inc. both prospered in 2002.

It was a mixed year for aluminum producers. Prices declined, and there was idle capacity for producers. Year-to-date American aluminum shipments as of September were up 4.7%, but foreign imports overwhelmed exports. Total American exports of aluminum ingot and mill products were 818 million kg (1.8 billion lb) year-to-date as of September, down 2.3% from the 841 million kg (1.85 billion lb) in the same period in 2001, while imports were up 15% for the year. The leading worldwide aluminum producer, Alcoa Inc., had a down year. For the first nine months of 2002, Alcoa's net income was $643 million, compared with $1 billion in the same period in 2001. Anglo-Dutch steelmaker Corus Group began pulling out of the aluminum market during the year. In August Corus sold its stake in a Quebec aluminum smelter to Alcan of Canada, and in October the French metals giant Pechiney bought two of Corus's remaining aluminum businesses. Corus, which announced a loss of some $364 million in the first six months of 2002, intended to sell its remaining aluminum business to focus on steel.

Gold, a traditional haven during tough market conditions, had a solid year. Gold prices sustained long runs above $300 per ounce throughout the year, which it had not done since the mid-1990s, and in June gold hit its highest per-ounce price since 1997. Analysts credited the pricing improvements to the weakening U.S. dollar and dismal stock market. Some top producers indicated that they expected gold's improvement to continue. Barrick Gold

Corp., which had been a major proponent of using hedging as a protection against falling prices, said that it would cut back on hedging devices, such as options. Top producers such as Barrick and Placer Dome Inc. instead would put much of their production on the spot market (where prices were always in flux), rather than trying to get a predetermined price via futures contracts. In May Placer announced plans to buy AurionGold of Australia. The takeover would make Placer the world's fifth largest gold-mining company.

The lodging industry was hammered by the poor economy. The hotel occupancy rate in 2002 was roughly 60%, one of the lowest levels in the industry's history. Business travel and convention business, which historically made up about 75% of the overall lodging demand, seriously slowed throughout 2002, and whatever business there was tended to go to lower-end hotels. Leisure travel, a crucial business for higher-end operators, was at much lower levels than those of the pre-September 11 environment. The lodging industry also faced a glut of supply. In the period between 1996 and 2000, new room construction rose by roughly 19%. Demand did not nearly match that pace, however, and hotel operators found that whatever revenues they earned were diluted by excess room capacity. PricewaterhouseCoopers LLP estimated that revenue per available room would decline by 2.3% in 2002 to $49.68, down from $50.83 in 2001. These factors drained many of the top American hotel operators. Marriott International Inc. reported a slight increase in earnings for third-quarter 2002, mainly on its nonlodging businesses, but was fighting a brutal court battle with some of its hotel owners and contending with reports that its most recent earnings releases obscured key information.

In order to keep revenues up during a difficult environment, auto manufacturers turned to severe price reductions that, for the short term at least, translated into improved performances. Critics believed that automakers were setting up for serious losses in the years to come. Total American light-vehicle sales for the January–September period were 12.87 million vehicles sold, up 0.8% from the 12.76 million posted in the same period in 2001. Sales were expected to wind up in the 16.8 million range overall in 2002, which would be one of the best performances in the market's history. The key reason that sales held steady was the continued prevalence of 0% financing plans, which inspired many buyers to make purchases that they normally might have put off for years. The 0% plans, however, also ate away at the auto industry's profitability. General Motors Corp. gave customers as much as $2,600 off per vehicle, which translated into the squeezing out of more than $1 billion from overall revenues in 2002, according to analysts. When GM suspended its program in September, it experienced a sharp 13% sales drop, and the company swiftly reinstituted the program the following month.

Despite such issues, GM's market share rose to 28.2%, and its productivity improved—it had shaved its vehicle-construction time by 20% over the previous four years and cut its materials expenses substantially. Perhaps most important, GM increased sales of its high-profit vehicles. Sales of full-size pickup trucks were up 4.6% at midyear, and researchers said that 2002 could be the first year that trucks outsold cars in the U.S. Italian car company Fiat, which was 20% owned by GM, announced huge losses for the year, however, and proved to be a drag on the American automaker.

Ford Motor Co. spent much of the year under the gun, burdened with a heavy debt load—roughly $170 billion—that showed no signs of lessening. Ford's worldwide automotive operations had a loss of $243 million in the third quarter, despite a 14% increase in revenues. The company struggled to control costs, which ran higher than most of its major rivals. The push to reduce costs caused companies such as Ford to begin exploiting their alliances with foreign automakers and essentially outsource their development and engineering departments overseas. Daimler-Chrysler AG's revenues for the year were expected to fall slightly, although its net income fell 22% in the third quarter alone, and officials indicated that they expected 2003 to be worse should consumer demand lessen. DaimlerChrysler moved to buy a stake in Mitsubishi's truck division. DaimlerChrysler sold fewer than 1% of trucks on the road in Asia, a major truck market, while Mitsubishi had a 24% share of the total Asian truck market.

For all their hustle, the Big Three American automakers continued in 2002 to lose ground to foreign imports. GM, Ford, and Chrysler's total market share for cars and light trucks was 61.7% of the total American market, compared with more than 80% 20 years

earlier. There was also a pricing imbalance between American and foreign car manufacturers. The Big Three spent an average of $3,764 a vehicle, or 14% of the selling price, on selling incentives, and Japanese and South Korean manufacturers spent about half that figure. Worse, studies found that consumers were replacing American cars with foreign counterparts at much greater margins than they were replacing foreign cars with American vehicles. Toyota Motor Corp., which sold about 1.8 million vehicles a year in the U.S., wanted to boost that number to 2 million by 2005 and expand its 10% market share to 15% market share by 2010. BMW also announced increased sales in the U.S., especially of its redesigned Mini Cooper.

Tobacco manufacturing was another American industry facing a pricing conundrum. The major producers—R.J. Reynolds Tobacco Co., Philip Morris Companies, and Brown & Williamson Tobacco Corp.—had grown used to raising prices when it suited them and had raised them often. The average retail price in 2002 was $3.58 per pack for premium cigarettes, up 90% since 1997. As increased taxes hit such major markets as New York City—and increased the price of a premium-brand pack of cigarettes to more than $7—consumers began turning to the generic markets for price relief. By 2002 cut-rate cigarette manufacturers owned about 10% of the overall market, compared with 3% only four years earlier. As a way to fight back, the major cigarette companies began to offer their own incentives, including two-for-one deals and other short-term promotions. This in turn helped to dilute profits. Philip Morris's domestic tobacco unit was expected to have its profit per thousand cigarettes fall by more than 50% in fourth-quarter 2002 compared with fourth-quarter 2001; Reynolds's tobacco unit's profit was expected to fall by 70% in the same period. The wild card for tobacco companies continued to be the possibility of consumer lawsuits. While the drain caused by the $206 billion legal agreement many companies signed in 1998 had lessened, cigarette companies remained frequent courtroom visitors.

Other traditional industries continued to experience hard times. The textiles sector endured Depression-era conditions as several major American players were swept off the board and more than 30 mills closed. Guilford Mills Inc. filed for bankruptcy in March, but the

company emerged six months later after having cut its senior debt substantially, laid off thousands of workers, and vowed to concentrate on core business areas such as technical textiles and select apparel. Top denim producer Galey & Lord was not so lucky—it remained under bankruptcy protection at year's end. The Bush administration said that it was stepping up plans to help domestic textile manufacturers by trying to reduce foreign nations' reliance on cheap imports, which had flooded the U.S. Total American imports for the year as of August were up 12% over the same period in 2001.

The Bush administration also played a key role in the pharmaceutical industry in 2002, as its decision to try to bring generic drugs more quickly to market had the potential to further increase the power of generic manufacturers over premium-brand players. The battle between generics and premium manufacturers had come to define the industry, and the generics appeared to be winning. According to the Federal Trade Commission, about 47% of all prescriptions filled were generics, compared with 19% in 1984. After raking in profits for a decade, thanks to exclusive patents, many drug manufacturers were watching their former market shares wither in the face of generic competition. A generic alternative to Prozac, for example, received eight times as many new prescriptions as the formerly exclusive drug did. Eli Lilly & Co., which saw its net income fall by 11% and worldwide sales decline by 7% for the first nine months of 2002, blamed much of the decline on lower Prozac sales. British drugmaker Glaxo-SmithKline faced a similar problem after a U.S. court ruled in May that the patents on its antibiotic Augmentin were invalid and thus opened the door to generic competition. In July Pfizer Inc., the world's biggest pharmaceutical company, with such best-selling drugs as Viagra, announced that it would acquire Pharmacia Corp., maker of Rogaine and Celebrex among other popular products, in a $60 billion deal.

The retail industry experienced some of the most extreme variations in 2002. Kmart Corp., the nation's second largest discount retailer, filed for Chapter 11 bankruptcy protection in January and spent most of the year trying to regroup. Meanwhile, industry giant Wal-Mart displaced ExxonMobil in the number one spot on *Fortune* magazine's list of the top 500 companies in the world. (CHRISTOPHER O'LEARY)

Education

Nationwide achievement **TESTING** in the U.S., controversies over the relationship between governments and **RELIGIOUS SCHOOLS**, attempts to reduce the school **DROPOUT RATE**, efforts to recruit more qualified teachers, an increase in **PROFIT-MAKING** higher-education programs, concern over the quality of university instruction, the **ASSESSMENT** of higher education in **ARAB NATIONS**, and more educational uses of the **INTERNET** were some of the educational issues scrutinized in 2002.

PRIMARY AND SECONDARY EDUCATION

On Jan. 8, 2002, U.S. Pres. George W. Bush signed into law his administration's education reform plan titled No Child Left Behind. The plan was based on four principles—stronger statewide accountability for students' proficiency, increased flexibility for state and local control in the use of government education funds, expanded school options for parents, and an emphasis on proven teaching methods. The legislation's provisions included mandatory nationwide achievement testing, funds for parents to transfer their child from a "failing school" to a better one, money to finance charter schools, and extra after-school help for students in reading, language arts, and mathematics. The testing portion of the plan required states to set standards for what every child should learn in reading, mathematics, and science in elementary and secondary schools. Beginning in 2002 all schools were to administer reading and math tests in three grade spans—grades 3–5, 6–9, and 10–12. Beginning in 2005 annual testing would be required in grades three through eight, and in 2007 science tests would be added. This high-stakes testing enlarged the industry of producing test-preparation materials from a negligible level to a $50 million business during 1999–2002. Critics, however, charged that standardized tests encouraged teachers to "teach for the tests" in reading, math, and science and therefore neglect other areas of the curriculum

such as history, citizenship education, art, music, vocational studies, and foreign languages. Among the difficulties the testing program faced was the need to create exams that accurately evaluated students' knowledge and quickly returned test results to teachers. One solution to the problem was the development of computerized tests that adapted questions to each student's current level of knowledge and furnished test results the following day. In 2002 Idaho became the first state to replace traditional tests with computerized versions.

Two educational issues resolved by the U.S. Supreme Court in 2002 concerned drug testing and the practice of having students evaluate their classmates' written assignments. On the issue of drug testing, the justices in a 5–4 decision ruled not only that schools could require members of athletic teams to be tested for the use of illegal substances but also that testing could be extended to include students who participated in other extracurricular activities, such as a photography club, chess contest, or cheerleading squad. The assignment-evaluation case involved the question of whether a student's privacy rights were violated when a teacher directed class members to mark each other's tests or homework assignments while the teacher read aloud the correct answers. In a unanimous decision the judges declared that "we do not think [federal law] prohibits these educational techniques."

Controversies over the relationship between government and religious education appeared in several countries. Two midyear court decisions in the U.S. bore important consequences for the nation's

traditional policy of separating government from religion. By a vote of 5–4, the U.S. Supreme Court approved of government agencies' funding vouchers that families could use to pay for their children to attend private schools, including schools sponsored by religious groups. The decision, praised by President Bush and many church leaders, was expected to be of greatest benefit to the nation's Roman Catholic schools, which played a major role in educating inner-city children. Roman Catholic schools made up 30% of the nation's private schools and enrolled 2,610,000 of the 5,300,000 students who attended nonpublic schools. The court's decision, however, was condemned by opponents who predicted that the voucher policy would weaken public schools' financial support and result in the use of tax money for teaching religious beliefs. In a public-opinion poll, respondents by a five-to-four margin favoured vouchers for sending children to private schools, but, by a two-to-one margin, they opposed voucher plans that would reduce the funds available to public schools. Whether voucher programs would be widely adopted depended, however, on decisions made in state legislatures and local school districts. The second court case concerned the Pledge of Allegiance, which nearly all public-school pupils were obliged to recite. The 9th Circuit Court in San Francisco ruled, by a two-to-one vote, that the phrase "under God," which had been inserted into the pledge in 1954, violated the U.S. Constitution's prohibition against the government's endorsing particular religious beliefs. In England and Wales, where church-sponsored "faith schools" were supported by public tax funds, the ruling Labour government recommended a substantial increase in the number of such schools on the belief that they offered a better quality of education than did secular schools. Strong opposition to the plan was voiced by members of Parliament and by teachers unions, which charged that faith schools fomented antagonism between religious groups, accepted only students who subscribed to the school's faith, employed only staff members of the school's faith, and did not offer a superior level of education. An opinion poll in Scotland reported that respondents, by a four-to-one margin, supported a government proposal to abolish the traditional policy of segregating pupils at age five into schools sponsored by their parents' church affiliation. A coalition of Roman Catholic parents vigorously objected, however, to their children's mixing in school with students from other religious backgrounds, on the belief that such integration would be morally damaging to the 130,000 pupils attending Scotland's 416 Roman Catholic secondary and primary schools. A spokesman for the Roman Catholic church said, "There is no evidence that Catholic schools provoke bigotry. Scotland's sectarianism is a real problem, but it is not caused by schooling."

In Afghanistan, where only boys had been permitted to attend school under the former Taliban government, girls returned to schools in large numbers for the first time in five years. The 1.8 million students attending the 3,000 primary and secondary schools represented the largest enrollment in the nation's history. Instructional innovations included the distribution of nearly 10 million textbooks as part of a $6.7 million program funded by the U.S. government to give teachers educational materials that did not focus on war, in contrast to the emphasis of textbooks used during the Taliban regime. The new books, in both the Dari (Persian) and the Pashto languages, included pictures of women, a rarity in the days of the Taliban.

A law drafted by the Pakistan government to influence the conduct of the nation's 8,000 *madrasah*s (Muslim schools) was strongly opposed by the schools' headmasters, who objected to the state's meddling with the schools' curricula, funding, enrollments, and teachers. The move to control *madrasah*s was urged by American and other Western officials who viewed educational reform in Pakistan as crucial to changing anti-Western attitudes and creating a more moderate state.

Truancy was a concern in Japan, where a panel of experts was appointed to investigate the alarming increase in elementary and junior-high students' unexcused absences from school. A record 138,696 students missed school for at least 30 days without good reason—a 10-fold increase since 1990. An estimated 90% of the absentees were spending their time out of school at home. To help stem this trend, the Ministry of Education planned to provide home tutors and improve community networks to aid truants and their families. Efforts to retain teenagers longer in secondary education were mounted in Britain, Australia, and New Zealand. The results of a British pilot study in 56 districts encouraged the government to expand a program to keep students in school beyond age 16 by paying families between £5 (about $7.50) and £40 (about $60) a week, depending on the income of the family. In the pilot districts, an average of 5% more students continued in school beyond age 16 than in comparable regions. A law passed in Queensland, Australia, was designed to retain students in secondary school for a longer period of time by raising the compulsory-schooling age from 15 to 17. Officials in New Zealand, distressed by the dismal prospects of employment for youths under age 19, maintained the school-leaving age at 16 but planned special programs that would persuade young people to continue in some sort of schooling through age 18.

German Chancellor Gerhard Schröder, speaking to the Bundestag (parliament), declared that the nation's "soft" educational policy of recent years was an "embarrassment" and should be replaced. Past policy, founded on a belief that children should not be burdened with excessive study at too young an age, had resulted in the closing of schools at midday and the watering down of subject matter in early grades. One apparent cause for Schröder's alarm was German 15-year-olds' weak showing on an international test, in which Germany ranked 25th out of 32 countries in reading, math, and scientific literacy.

In Vietnam the country's first nationwide assessment of grade-five primary-school pupils' reading and mathematics skills revealed that the highest test scores were achieved in schools where teachers assigned and corrected homework, teachers had a greater knowledge of subject matter, pupils had access to reading materials beyond the basic textbooks, and a larger percentage of teachers were women. Government officials in the state of Goa, India, launched a program to furnish computers in the homes of secondary-school students for a nominal fee that would be reduced for low-income families. The plan began with students majoring in science and would gradually be extended to those in other subjects.

A shortage of properly qualified teachers impaired schooling in a variety of countries. In Britain, John Dunford, general secretary of the Secondary Heads Association, announced that 300,000 experienced teachers under age 60 (many of whom had elected for early retirement) were no longer in the education system, while 83,400 people held teaching certificates that they had never used. According to Dunford, reasons for the dearth of competent teachers included heavy workloads, poor pay, badly behaved pupils, and the low esteem in which the profession was held. As a modest emergency effort toward easing the shortfall of 40,000 primary-school teachers in Thailand, officials in 120 schools in Nonthaburi province recruited monks to teach a range of classes. Meanwhile, the national government sought to appoint 10,000 new

(continued on page 208)

AP/Wide World Photos

A Buddhist monk supervises students as they practice meditation at a school in Nonthaburi province, Thai. A shortage of teachers in Thailand led officials there to enlist the help of monks in 2002.

New Frontiers in
Cheating

by R. Murray Thomas

A number of high-profile instances involving plagiarism and résumé padding that were reported in 2001 continued to capture headlines in 2002 and to bring increased scrutiny to the methodology of cheating. Though historian Doris Kearns Goodwin maintained that the cribbing in her book *The Fitzgeralds and the Kennedys* (1987) was unintentional, her reputation was severely damaged, and in June she resigned her post on the Pulitzer Prize board. Fellow historian Stephen Ambrose apologized in January for having failed to acknowledge his source material in at least six books. (*See* OBITUARIES.) After Piper (Kan.) High School teacher Christine Pelton accused some students of having taken material from the Internet for a botany project, gave them all failing grades in 2001, and had her decision overruled by the school board in December, she resigned in February 2002; other teachers were inspired to follow suit as well, and the handling of the incident sparked a national uproar. Pulitzer Prize-winning historian Joseph Ellis lost his credibility and was suspended in 2001 for one year from teaching at Mount Holyoke College, South Hadley, Mass., after it became known that he had fabricated stories about military exploits in Vietnam and subsequent activity in the peace and civil rights movements. Football coach George O'Leary lost his dream job in 2002 at the University of Notre Dame a few days after signing his contract when "inaccuracies" sprang up in his résumé.

As a result of technological advances in recent years, cheating in educational and academic circles has become more sophisticated. At the same time, however, the ability of school personnel (and journalists) to catch cheaters has also been enhanced. Inventions contributing to such progress include photocopying equipment, computers, the Internet, scanners, optical-character-recognition software, language-translation programs, cell phones, and pagers, among others. Three of the most common forms of cheating affected by these trends are plagiarism, fake credentials, and unauthorized test assistance.

Plagiarism. Plagiarism is the act of claiming to be the author of material that someone else actually wrote. Students have plagiarized book reports, term papers, essays, projects, and graduate-degree theses. Teachers—including college professors—have plagiarized journal articles, course materials, and textbooks. Researchers have plagiarized reports, articles, and book chapters. Although academic plagiarism is not new, what is new since the latter years of the 20th century is the ease with which writings on virtually any topic can be misappropriated with little risk of detection. The principal instrument responsible for the recent rapid rise in academic plagiarism has been the Internet, which John Barrie, a developer of software for detecting Web plagiarism, called "a 1.5 billion-page searchable, cut-and-pasteable encyclopedia."

Especially popular are the on-line "paper mills" or cheat sites—companies that sell students completed essays, book reports, projects, or theses that can be submitted in school under the students' own names. At least 150 cyber paper mills have been operating over the past three years. Those available on the World Wide Web bear such names as Evil House of Cheat (more than 8,000 essays), Genius Papers, Research Assistance, Cheat Factory Essay Warehouse, School Sucks, Superior Term Papers, and 12,000 Papers.com. In Germany, <cheatweb.de> advertised high-scoring essays, term papers, stories, interpretations, book reports, and other types of homework. The site reported having between 3,000 and 5,000 high-school and college users daily.

Just as the Internet has greatly expanded students' opportunities to plagiarize, however, it has also increased teachers' ability to discover sources from which students have lifted material. This new ability to discover plagiarism is attributed to Web-plagiarism checkers or verifiers.

The typical Web checker is an Internet service that works in the following way. A student's paper is entered into the checker's Web site. That Web site is programmed to compare the contents of the paper with the contents of thousands of documents on the World Wide Web. A report showing how much of the student's paper is identical to, or highly similar to, documents on the Web is sent back to the teacher, and the report identifies what those original documents were.

Web checkers usually charge for their services, either a flat annual fee or a stated amount for each paper processed. One popular plagiarism checker is <turnitin.com>. In 2001 the operators of the site claimed 20,000 subscribers worldwide. Another much-used checker is the Essay Verification Engine (EVE), which between February 2000 and late August 2002 conducted 45,840,495 assessments. Educators who have used Web-plagiarism checkers report that telling students that their papers will be Web-checked reduces the incidence of Internet plagiarism.

Fake Credentials. Besides the simple inflation of credentials on a résumé, an increasingly popular method of faking credentials involves obtaining a

> . . . virtually any topic can be misappropriated with little risk of detection.

Sarah St.Claire

legitimate certificate that someone has earned, erasing the original recipient's name, printing a photocopy of the certificate, and inserting one's own name as the beneficiary. Modern photocopy machines produce such accurate copies of documents that only an expert can distinguish between a copy and its original. The Internet too has rapidly improved people's access to fake credentials. A Liverpool, Eng.-based company that advertises on the Web as "the largest degree template library available in the world" is prepared to sell "impressive authentic looking certificates" of graduation from universities based in Australia, New Zealand, the United Kingdom, and the United States. Two sources in Australia have marketed fake degrees throughout Asia over the Internet, selling verifiable degrees ("original certificate and transcript . . .

with valid serial number and student ID") or nonverifiable degrees (the certificate itself without a serial number). An administrator of Australia's Internet system, while trying to discover if the fake-degree scheme was popular, managed to intercept more than 1,000 potential customers' e-mail inquiries in response to the on-line advertisements. The universities for which fake degrees could be provided totaled eight in Australia; seven in Great Britain, including the University of Cambridge; and four in the United States, including Harvard University and the Massachusetts Institute of Technology.

With no international agency in control of Internet traffic, education officials have been unable to shut down fake-degree operations.

Unauthorized Test Assistance. As teachers and test makers develop computer

skills, they increasingly store test items in computers rather than in traditional file cabinets. The convenience of storing items in computers, however, has been accompanied by the danger that hackers can break into test-question files and distribute the questions to students prior to the test period. Educators' attempts to guard test items now involve devising complex passwords for accessing computer files, strictly limiting the number of people who know those passwords, and equipping computers with firewall software. A typical example of present-day test-security practice is the policy adopted by Sunway College near Kuala Lumpur, Malaysia, where information about exams and test questions is never sent over the college's network of computers or sent in the form of e-mail because of fears that it may be hacked by dishonest students.

During test sessions, present-day students continue to use a variety of traditional ploys to gain an advantage—crib notes hidden in a shoe, mathematical formulas written on an arm, and notes passed to neighbouring test takers. Those ruses have now been joined by schemes made possible by wireless communication devices known as personal digital assistants (PDAs), which include cell phones, pagers, and handheld computers. From inside or outside the classroom, students can communicate with each other during a test session by means of PDAs. Thus, it is becoming common practice for teachers to confiscate all such devices prior to administering tests.

If the pattern and pace of cybernetic development over the past decade are accurate predictors of the future, the contest between academic cheaters and cheat preventers can be expected to become ever more complex as the years advance.

R. Murray Thomas is Professor Emeritus of Education at the University of California, Santa Barbara, and the author of Folk Psychologies Across Cultures *(2001).*

(continued from page 205)

permanent teachers in addition to the 10,000 teachers hired in 2001. Difficulty finding substitute teachers in Australia resulted in the periodic cancellation of classes. Among 250 schools surveyed, nearly 60% reported problems finding relief teachers, while principals made up to 30 phone calls every morning in an attempt to hire extra staff. One school in Sydney was forced to cancel 41 classes within a single 10-day period. The government of Jamaica forbade New York agencies to conduct unauthorized seminars designed to lure Jamaicans to teach in New York City schools. The ban was imposed following the news that in 2001 New York had attracted more than 500 teachers from the Caribbean, 320 of them math and science teachers from Jamaica. In the U.S. a nationwide survey of 16,000 teachers revealed that nearly 25% of secondary-school classes in English, math, science, and social studies were staffed by teachers who lacked a college major or minor in the subject matter being taught. A continuing decline in the number of men entering the teaching profession in the U.S. caused the nation's largest teachers union, the National Education Association, to launch a campaign to recruit more men. According to analysts, low pay and low prestige were two key reasons that fewer men were choosing teaching as a career.

HIGHER EDUCATION

The number of profit-making degree-granting higher-education campuses in the U.S. more than doubled from about 350 in 1990 to more than 750 in 2002, when over 300,000 students were enrolled. The largest of the for-profit institutions was the University of Phoenix, with 95,000 students pursuing degree programs in such fields as education, business administration, and nursing on 105 campuses in 19 states. Another of the country's largest for-profit companies was DeVry University, with an enrollment of more than 80,000.

The Russian government adopted a variety of institutional reforms intended to promote the nation's economic de-

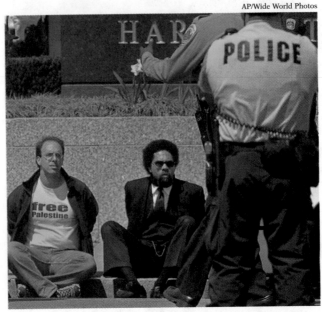

On April 11 Cornel West (centre) sits after being arrested in Washington, D.C., during a protest against the U.S. government's response to Israeli military operations in the West Bank. Under pressure from Harvard University president Lawrence Summers for his extra-academic activities, the black-studies professor later left Harvard for Princeton.

velopment. The country's research centres would be revised in an effort to reward disciplines that contributed to the nation's wealth in a free-market economy. Money would be channeled into nine areas of research and several dozen types of technology. Over the past decade, 200,000 Russian scientists had left the country for more favourable opportunities elsewhere. To help slow the flow of professionals from the country, the government planned to raise the salaries of scientists under age 35 and to increase the pensions for senior scientists in order to replace older personnel with a new generation of experts.

Education officials in Russia and China expressed concern over the quality of instruction in their countries' tertiary institutions. An apparent deterioration in teachers' effectiveness in Russian universities prompted the Ministry of Education to establish 10 teams of "quality police," with each team composed of 15 specialists assigned to conduct unannounced assessments of instruction in the nation's higher-learning institutions. Primary targets of the visits were classes in the most popular subject areas—law, economics, psychology, and foreign languages. Though college and university enrollments in China nearly doubled between 1998 and 2002, standards of instruction declined, according to Ma Luting, a Ministry of Ed-

ucation spokesperson. Much of the rapid growth in the number of students entering higher-learning institutions resulted from the nation's unemployment problem, which the government hoped to alleviate by sending more young people to college, a practice that would also increase the number of graduates with the skills required in a technologically advanced economy. The sudden growth of enrollments, coupled with a history of the underfundingofeducation,led to the apparent decline in instructional quality. The funding problem was reflected in the fact that China devoted less than 3% of its gross domestic product to education, compared with 4.8% in Brazil, 6.4% in the U.S., and 7.4% in South Korea.

Representatives from Arab nations met in Morocco to assess the condition of higher education in their countries and to recommend changes needed for raising the quality of their institutions to the level of the best universities in the rest of the world. Among the most serious shortcomings of Arab institutions described by conference speakers were a shortage of research, inadequate information technology, and the practice of teaching dogma rather than guiding students in critical inquiry. Another target of criticism was the low percentage (12.4%) of college-age women enrolled in higher education compared with the world average of 16.4%. Two factors cited as causes of such conditions were a lack of official concern for education in some countries and a lack of funds in many.

To provide more higher-education opportunities for Brazil's blacks, who made up nearly half of the country's 170 million people, the state of Rio de Janeiro passed a law requiring its two public universities to reserve 40% of their freshman class openings for black students. As a result, university admissions officers were faced with the problem of deciding which applicants qualified as blacks—people of pure African descent were rare in Brazil. Police in Kenya arrested 21 people for producing and selling fake diplomas that bore the official seals of prominent Kenyan universities. The accused included several high-level ministry officials. In addition to the fake diplomas, police found hundreds of false elementary- and secondary-school certificates, academic transcripts, passports, and property deeds.

During 2002 the Web site <degree info.com> was periodically overwhelmed by a flood of messages that rose to 65,000 in a single day and thereby forced the site to close down temporarily. The purpose of the Web site was to disseminate information about degree-granting institutions, especially ones offering distance education. Because <degreeinfo.com> often exposed purveyors of fraudulent degrees, the site's officials suspected that the "mail bomb attack" had been launched by persons who ran diploma mills and hoped to prevent Internet users from discovering the true nature of their illicit operations.

More American universities developed courses that combined in-class teaching with lessons over the Internet. Advocates of this hybrid instructional approach claimed that it offered students the convenience of Internet instruction that could be accessed whenever they chose and also furnished them periodic in-class face-to-face lectures and discussions with their professors. Fairleigh Dickinson University at Madison, N.J., adopted a policy of requiring students to take at least one course a year via the Internet, a plan that some officials believed would become increasingly widespread. On the other hand, the Internet was also among the technologies used heavily by students as a source to help them cheat on homework assignments. (*See* Special Report.)

A survey of alcohol consumption in American colleges revealed that 44% of students engaged in binge drinking, a percentage constant over the 1993–2002 period despite authorities' efforts to discourage the habit. The term *binge drinkers* was defined as men who had had five or more drinks on one occasion in the previous two weeks and women who had had four or more. Underage college students were found to drink nearly half of all the alcohol consumed by undergraduates. More than half of Northern Ireland's college and university students took illegal drugs, according to a study by the Union of Students in Ireland. The most popular substance was cannabis, used by 89% of the survey respondents, followed by Ecstasy (9%) and cocaine (2%). Two-thirds of the participants in the study had first tried drugs in secondary school, and 58% wanted cannabis decriminalized.

(R. MURRAY THOMAS)

The Environment

SUSTAINABLE DEVELOPMENT, implementation of the Kyoto Protocol, and the **DISPOSAL** of electronic, chemical, and **NUCLEAR WASTE** were among the environmental issues in 2002. Conservation efforts included plans to **CLONE** the extinct **TASMANIAN TIGER** and the endangered **BANTENG**. More than two million people attended The Netherlands' **FLORIADE**, the World's Fair of horticulture.

INTERNATIONAL ACTIVITIES

The World Summit on Sustainable Development, which opened on Aug. 26, 2002, in Johannesburg, S.Af., was attended by delegates from 192 countries, the European Union (EU), and a number of intergovernmental institutions. Participants reviewed the implementation of the Agenda 21 plan agreed to at the 1992 Rio Summit, with a particular emphasis on social and economic issues. Though agreement was reached on a plan of action, environmental groups staged a walkout to protest what they saw as U.S. obstruction of a stronger final plan, and some opponents jeered and heckled U.S. Secretary of State Colin Powell when he addressed the conference.

The official four-page declaration supported the leadership role of the UN in promoting sustainable development and committed governments to the action plan as well as regular monitoring of progress. There was no agreement on targets for the proportion of energy that should come from renewable sources, nor was there a clear commitment to introduce rules on corporate social and environmental responsibility.

The action plan set out a number of objectives. It sought to halve by 2015 the proportion of the world's population living on less than $1 per day, suffering from hunger, or having no access to safe drinking water or improved sanitation. In the same time period, participating governments would aim to reduce child-mortality rates by two-thirds and maternal-mortality rates by three-quarters, compared with 2000.

The scheme called for increased investment in cleaner technologies and greater efficiency, especially in energy supply, which would become more diverse; reiterated commitment to the Kyoto Protocol; and urged states that had not ratified it to do so. Adverse health and environmental effects of chemical use should be minimized by 2020. Children's exposure to lead was to be reduced by phasing out lead in gasoline and lead-based paint.

The blueprint of a plan to prevent illegal fishing was scheduled to be implemented by 2004, with a UN Food and Agriculture Organization (FAO) strategy for managing fishing capacity to be in place by 2005. The aim was to maintain fish stocks at maximum sustainable yields, or restore depleted stocks to that level by 2015.

The plan called on developed countries to try to reach the target of 0.7% of gross national product for overseas development aid, to consider measures for mitigating the volatility of short-term capital flows, and to reduce unsustainable debt burdens through such measures as debt relief. Tariffs on nonagricultural products were to be reduced or eliminated. Countries were asked to formulate national strategies to implement the plan by 2005. The plan would be integrated into the policies of UN agencies.

Global Environment Outlook-3 was published in May by the UN Environment Programme (UNEP). The work of

Workers inspect a section of the Three Gorges Dam in Hubei province, China, on October 22.

1,000 authors, it recorded improvements in air and water quality in North America and Europe since the 1972 UN Conference on the Human Environment and applauded the steps taken to reduce damage to the ozone layer. Overall, however, the study found that generally there had been a steady environmental deterioration, especially in less-developed countries. The report divided the world into 17 regions and set out four possible environmental scenarios—markets-first, policy-first, security-first, and sustainability-first—extending over 30 years. Markets-first represented the current situation. Policy-first included stronger environmental legislation. Security-first envisaged conflicts and inequalities, with the rich withdrawing into protected enclaves. Sustainability-first assumed a global consensus on dealing with environmental issues. Even under the sustainability-first scenario, however, environmental improvements would take decades to emerge. The UNEP picture was repudiated by many scientists, particularly Bjørn Lomborg, head of the newly created Environmental Assessment Institute. (See *European Union,* below.)

In May delegates attending a meeting in Washington, D.C., of donor nations to the Global Environment Facility (GEF) failed to agree on a budget. The U.S., which owed the GEF $220 million, resisted a proposal to increase funding from $2.2 billion to $3.2 billion over four years to cover the widening of the GEF mandate to include desertification and persistent organic pollutants. The U.S. felt that GEF monitoring was inadequate, and there was no assurance that the money was being spent wisely. The GEF was established in 1992 to fund the UN Conventions on Biological Diversity and Climate Change.

NATIONAL DEVELOPMENTS

Angola. In late June Angolan authorities imposed a fine of $2 million on ChevronTexaco Corp. for an oil spill earlier in the month that was caused by leaks from poorly maintained pipes being used to transport crude oil. It was the first time that an African nation had fined a foreign company operating in its waters.

Bangladesh. In January the government began enforcing a complete ban on the sale and use of polythene bags in the capital, Dhaka. Environment Minister Shahajahan Siraj said the action aimed to avert an imminent disaster caused by the clogging of the city's drainage system. Polythene bags replaced jute bags in the 1980s, and nearly 10 million were disposed of in Dhaka every day.

China. In January the government announced an $84 billion, five-year program to combat air and water pollution. The director of the State Environmental Protection Agency (SEPA) said SEPA would also monitor closely the Three Gorges Dam project on the Chang Jiang (Yangtze River). According to the World Bank, millions of tons of waste were being dumped into the dam every year.

It was reported in May that the government planned a 10-year, $12 billion program to plant trees over almost 500,000 sq km (193,000 sq mi), an area larger than Germany. The deputy chief of the state forestry administration claimed that the plan would help reverse years of environmental degradation during which large areas of forest had been cleared. Deforestation was blamed for increased flooding on the Chang Jiang and for causing severe spring sandstorms.

European Union. In February the right-of-centre government elected in Denmark in November 2001 appointed Bjørn Lomborg, a professor of statistics at the University of Århus, to head the Environmental Assessment Institute, which had a €1,300,000 (about $1,282,000) budget. The new institute aimed to improve environmental policy by obtaining the best value for money. Lomborg maintained that environmental problems were exaggerated and could not be solved until poverty had been greatly reduced, because very poor people could not afford to protect the environment. He was the author of *The Skeptical Environmentalist*, a controversial best-selling book that criticized and challenged what he saw as exaggerated claims of impending environmental catastrophe. His appointment outraged most environmentalists.

Following a landslide win for the right in the June 16 general elections in France, Roselyne Bachelot, an outspoken advocate of nuclear power, became the new environment minister. Her predecessor, Dominique Voynet, lost her seat in the election, while the Green Party dropped from seven seats to three in the National Assembly. In the German federal election on September 22, the Green Party increased its share of the vote from the 6.7% it won in 1998 to 8.6%. The Greens' number of seats in the Bundestag (lower house of parliament) increased from 47 to 55.

Planning permission was granted on January 11 for a scheme to build what could become the biggest offshore wind farm in the world on the 27-km (1 km = about 0.62 mi) Arklow sandbank in the Irish Sea. Construction by the developer, Eirtricity, of the first 60 MW of capacity was scheduled to commence in 2002 and would rise to 520 MW, from 200 80-m (1 m = about 3.3 ft) turbines. The total cost of the project would be about €700 million (about $630 million), and it would supply nearly 10% of Ireland's generating capacity. It also was reported in January that BP PLC and ChevronTexaco had proposed installing a 22.5-MW array of wind turbines at a jointly owned oil refinery near Rotterdam,

Neth. This would be the world's biggest wind farm to be built on an industrial site.

South Africa. In September, 16 families living in Steel Valley, close to a large steel works at Vanderbijlpark in southwestern Johannesburg, took Iscor Corp., owners of the plant, to court, claiming the plant had polluted their water. In what was described as one of the most important environmental battles in the country's history, the families said the factory had polluted boreholes on their smallholdings, degraded their environment, and caused illness and suffering. The suit contended that the soil was contaminated, crops had failed, animals had died, and no one would buy the farms. The company denied responsibility, but the Department of Water Affairs said that it would close down the plant if the company failed to comply with the law.

United States. In April the Senate rejected a plan, supported by Pres. George W. Bush's administration, to drill for oil in 810 ha (1 ha = about 2.5 ac) of the Arctic National Wildlife Refuge in Alaska.

ENVIRONMENTAL ISSUES

Climate Change. On April 19 Robert Watson was replaced as chairman of the Intergovernmental Panel on Climate Change (IPCC) after the U.S. had failed to nominate him for reelection. His replacement was Rajendra Pachauri of India, director of the nonprofit Tata Energy Research Institute and vice-chairman of the IPCC.

The European Parliament voted in early February (540–4 with 10 abstentions) to support EU ratification of the Kyoto Protocol. On March 4, environment ministers unanimously adopted a legal instrument that would oblige each member state to ratify the protocol, and representatives from all EU governments and the European Commission formally ratified the protocol in New York City on May 31.

In June Australian Prime Minister John Howard said his country would not ratify the protocol because it would "cost jobs and damage our industry." Russian Prime Minister Mikhail Kasyanov confirmed at the Johannesburg summit that Russia would soon be ready to ratify the Kyoto Protocol. Chinese Premier Zhu Rongji also expressed support for the measure and said his government had completed the steps needed for its adoption. Although as a less-developed country China was not

required to agree to the protocol, Zhu announced that Beijing had ratified it.

President Bush on February 14 introduced an alternative plan based on tax breaks to encourage industry to make voluntary reductions in American greenhouse-gas emissions. The aim was to achieve an 18% reduction in "emissions intensity"—the amount of emissions relative to economic growth—between 2002 and 2012. Critics—including the EU, many Democratic politicians, and environmentalist groups—claimed this scheme would allow American emissions to increase in absolute terms. The plan also included two scientific initiatives included in the 2003 budget request to Congress that would increase research spending by $80 million. The Climate Change Technology Initiative would encourage research into such areas as carbon sequestration. The Climate Change Research Initiative would augment the existing Global Change Research Program, aimed at discovering whether regulation was required. The Climate Change Research Initiative would study the carbon cycle and aerosols and their climatic influence, bolster climate observations in less-developed countries, and strengthen U.S. climate modeling.

In its report on the world energy outlook, published in September, the International Energy Agency (IEA) said countries in the Organisation for Economic Co-operation and Development (OECD) would fail to meet their Kyoto targets for carbon dioxide reduction even if all the policies currently being considered were implemented. The IEA calculated that with all policies enacted, OECD aggregate emissions would stabilize by 2030 rather than falling by 5.2% between 2008 and 2012, as required by the Kyoto Protocol.

Carbon Sequestration. It was reported in June that opposition from environmentalists had led an international consortium to withdraw its application to the U.S. Environmental Protection Agency (EPA) for permission to conduct a $5 million experiment in carbon sequestration off the coast of Hawaii. The experiment, supported by Japan, the U.S., and Norway, would have injected 60 metric tons (1 metric ton = about 2,205 lb) of liquefied carbon dioxide into the deep ocean. On the basis of an assessment made for the EPA, researchers said there were no environmental reasons for abandoning the plan, but local objectors claimed the experiment would acidify fishing grounds.

The consortium decided to transfer the experiment to Norway, using less carbon dioxide. Although it received a license from the Norwegian pollution-control agency on July 5, the license was rescinded, and on August 22 Environment Minister Børge Brende announced that the project would be abandoned. Echoing the opinion of Greenpeace and the Worldwide Fund for Nature, Brende said the project might conflict with international rules on the marine environment and that it should first be discussed internationally and its legality clarified. Environmentalists feared the carbon dioxide would damage marine organisms and might eventually leak back into the atmosphere. The experiment was intended to determine whether such fears were justified.

The success of an experiment in carbon sequestration that had been running in the North Sea since 1996 was reported in September. Instead of being vented to the atmosphere, carbon dioxide separated from methane extracted from the Sleipner Field was made into a fluid slightly lighter than water and pumped into a layer of porous sandstone 800 m deep. The experiment, run under the direction of the Norwegian company Statoil, had returned five million tons of carbon dioxide. Seismic imaging showed that the carbon dioxide had formed a bubble, about 1.7 km wide, that had reached the top of the reservoir but was not leaking from it.

Air Pollution. The Indian Ocean Experiment, the results of which were released by UNEP in August, found a brown haze, extending to a height of three kilometres and covering much of southern Asia. A similar haze also covered parts of southeastern and eastern Asia. The haze was caused by forest fires, the burning of agricultural wastes, an increase in the burning of fossil fuels, and emissions from millions of inefficient cookers burning wood, cow dung, and other "biofuels." The report suggested that by reflecting sunlight, the haze might cool and dry the area beneath it, reducing monsoon rainfall by 40% in some parts of central Asia while increasing rainfall in southeastern Asia.

In June it was reported that standard statistical software used to estimate the health risk from very small (2.5 parts per million) soot particles had introduced an error that elevated the reputed risk. Researchers at Johns Hopkins University, Baltimore, Md., and at Health Canada, Ottawa, revised the risk downward by 20–50%.

Marine Pollution. On May 7 the Finnish environment institute warned of the widespread growth of toxic algae during the summer, especially in the Gulf of Finland, southern parts of the Archipelago Sea, and the waters off southeastern Sweden. The forecast, which was based on measurements of nutrient levels throughout the Baltic Sea, proved correct. Dense blooms formed, and many swimmers reported skin irritation. In August mild weather triggered a surge in *Nodularia spumigena* around islands off the Swedish coast, forcing the authorities to ban swimming in some areas. (The blue-green algae *N. spumigena* feeds on nutrients found in sewage, especially effluent from St. Petersburg, which enters the Baltic untreated. It can cause liver damage.)

On September 10 a fire broke out on the *Jolly Rubino*, an Italian-registered freighter bound from Durban, S.Af., to Mombasa, Kenya, forcing its crew of 22 to abandon ship. The vessel then ran aground about 11 km south of the Saint Lucia Wetland, an internationally important site. Some 400 metric tons of heavy fuel oil leaked through a 20-m crack in the ship's side. Booms placed across the mouth of the Umfolozi River and sand dunes built on top of sandbars contained the slick. Attempts to refloat the ship were abandoned on September 18 owing to bad weather. The remaining 800 metric tons of fuel oil were pumped from the ship's tanks.

In mid-November the Bahamian-registered oil tanker *Prestige* broke in two during a storm and sank a few days

A helicopter evacuates a crew member of the Jolly Rubino *after the ship ran aground near the Santa Lucia Wetland.*

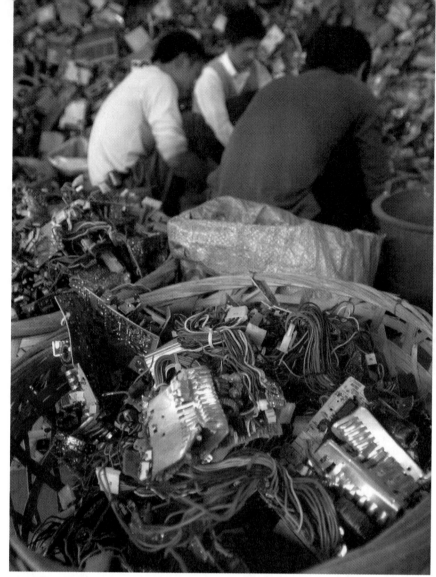

Piles of junk computer parts fill a recycling centre near Guiyu, Guangdong province, China.

dockside, where the material covered two hectares, contaminating soil and threatening a warehouse containing food aid.

On July 9 the U.S. Senate authorized the building of the nuclear-waste-storage facility at Yucca Mountain, Nevada, and President Bush signed the congressional resolution. This prepared the way for a further technical investigation by the Department of Energy (DOE), which had to produce convincing data on hundreds of issues, including 293 separate topics raised by the Nuclear Regulatory Commission, before construction could begin. The DOE hoped to file its application by 2004. Nevada opposed the scheme and was taking legal action in the hope of preventing it. After studies conducted over nearly 20 years and costing about $7 billion, work building the facility would commence no sooner than 2008. It was due to open in 2010 and would hold about 77,000 metric tons of waste from 103 nuclear power plants, which was currently stored at 131 temporary sites in 39 states. The waste would remain in the facility for 10,000 years.

(MICHAEL ALLABY)

WILDLIFE CONSERVATION

In 2002 the bombing campaign in Afghanistan was exacerbating the environmental catastrophe that had been initiated by years of ongoing civil conflict and drought. The country's remaining forests were being bombed or burned in the search for terrorists, and refugees were clearing forests for farming and fuel. The number of birds crossing eastern Afghanistan on one of the world's major migratory routes was down by 85%. Afghanistan's mountains—home to leopards, gazelles, bears, and Marco Polo sheep—also were at risk. Some refugees were reported to be hunting rare snow leopards to buy a safe passage across the border.

Elsewhere, marine conservation issues were prominent. In January the U.S. Navy admitted that its use of a high-intensity sonar system had most likely caused whale strandings and deaths in The Bahamas in March 2000—it was the first time that such strandings had been definitely linked to these commonly used systems. Research using satellite tags to track white sharks (*Carcharodon carcharias*) revealed that they ranged more widely and could tolerate a broader temperature range than was thought previously.

later some 210 km off the coast of Galicia, Spain. The tanker was carrying twice the amount of fuel that had been spilled in 1989 from the *Exxon Valdez,* and environmentalists braced for a major ecological disaster.

Toxic Waste. A report issued in February said that several villages on the outskirts of Guiyu, in China's Guangdong province, had been turned into heavily polluted recycling centres for Western electronic scrap. The director of the Seattle, Wash.-based Basel Action Network, the main group behind the report, said the ground was saturated in lead and acid by-products and that pollutant levels were hundreds to thousands of times higher than those deemed safe in developed countries. A former recycling director for the state of Massachusetts calculated that about 100 shipping containers of used elec-

tronic equipment were being exported weekly from the U.S.

It was reported in March that the FAO had recommended that chemical waste at the port of Djibouti should be cleaned up and returned to the U.K., where it originated, and that the company responsible for shipping it should bear the cost, possibly exceeding $1 million. The waste consisted of plastic drums containing chromated copper arsenate, a wood preservative, on its way from CSI Wood Protection of Widnes, a subsidiary of the American conglomerate Rockwood Specialties, to Ethiopia, where it was to be used to treat wooden pylons owned by the Ethiopian Electric Power Corp. The drums, held inside 10 shipping containers, began to spill during unloading in mid-January. By late February, 200 metric tons had leaked onto the

This snakehead fish was caught in a crab net at the Inner Harbor in Baltimore, Md., in September.

In February tropical coral reefs were reported to be endangered by rising ocean temperatures (which causes bleaching), and reefs in the northeastern Atlantic Ocean were being irreparably damaged by unregulated deep-sea bottom trawling. In June an aerial survey confirmed that Australia's Great Barrier Reef was suffering one of the worst coral bleaching episodes on record. The first global study of the dugong (sea cow, an aquatic mammal) found that it was disappearing or extinct in most of its 37 range countries. Only one viable population remained in East Africa, while in much of the tropics, the seagrass beds where dugong fed were being cleared for shrimp farming and saltpans or were smothered by silt. The UN Environment Programme launched an action plan to preserve seagrass habitats.

In March the secretary-general of the Convention on International Trade in Endangered Species reversed a 2001 ban on trade in caviar from sturgeon caught in the Caspian Sea, after the countries involved produced a plan to raise and release young sturgeon. Biologists objected because the problem of illegal harvests, which took 10 times more fish than the legal quotas, had not been solved.

Introduced species continued to threaten native wildlife in many places. In Tasmania 77 Australian species, including some that had been eradicated on the mainland, were potentially at risk after foxes were introduced, perhaps deliberately by individuals who wanted new game to hunt. Wildlife managers were trying to devise ways of killing the foxes without harming native species. A threat to native freshwater species in the eastern U.S. was feared when northern snakehead fish (*Channa argus*)—a species that can survive out of water for several days and travel over land—were found in a pond in Maryland. A local man evidently had released two of these voracious predatory fish from China, and they were breeding. In September Maryland wildlife officials sprayed poison into the pond where the snakeheads had been found.

After four Iberian lynx (*Lynx pardinus*) died in two weeks—two in road accidents—Spain in March announced an emergency $6.8 million plan to save the species. In three decades the population had declined from 1,000 to around 200 in the Doñana and Sierra Morena national parks. The new plan would augment rabbit populations (the lynx's main prey), protect scrubland refuges, and connect isolated habitats.

Illegal logging threatened the Tesso Nilo forest in Sumatra, which the World Wildlife Fund had identified as biologically the world's richest lowland forest. It was Indonesia's most important remaining elephant habitat. As the forest was being surveyed, it was being felled at a rate that, if continued, would destroy it completely by 2005.

On the Hawaiian island of Maui, an attempt to bring together a pair of the world's rarest birds failed in May when a female po'ouli (*Melamprosops phaeosoma*), after being transferred to the territory of the only male, flew back to her own home range without encountering the male. There were only three surviving birds. Efforts to save the kakapo (*Strigops habroptilus*), New Zealand's giant ground-nesting parrot, met with more success. The last surviving birds, brought together on one island that was free of predatory rats, produced 24 chicks, more than in the whole of the previous two decades. This brought the world total to 86 kakapo, compared with 50 in 1995. Conservationists claimed that Australian plans to build a refugee camp on Christmas Island would jeopardize the last breeding colony of Abbott's booby, one of the world's most endangered birds.

On May 9 two adult female mountain gorillas were shot by poachers and a young gorilla taken for illegal sale. Fourteen people were arrested in connection with the incident. The animals were part of a group habituated for tourism in the Volcanoes National Park in Rwanda and had been monitored daily for 20 years. This was the first gorilla-poaching incident since 1985 in Rwanda, which held about 350 of the 650 mountain gorillas left in the world.

On October 8 the World Conservation Union published an updated Red List of Threatened Species. It listed 11,167 species, an increase of 121 since the year 2000. Notable changes included some East Asian species, such as the saiga (*Saiga tatarica*), a medium-sized hoofed mammal, and the Bactrian camel (*Camelus bactrianus*), which were classified as critically endangered for the first time.

A new epidemic of phocine distemper started in May in Denmark and by August had spread to Dutch, Belgian, Swedish, Norwegian, French, German, and British coasts, killing an estimated 19,000 seals. The last epidemic, in 1988, had killed 18,000 seals.

Australian scientists embarked on an attempt to resurrect the Tasmanian tiger (*Thylacinus cynocephalus*), which had become extinct in 1936. They successfully amplified DNA extracted from three Tasmanian tigers preserved in alcohol more than 100 years ago. The next steps would include assembling a DNA library for the species, building chromosomes and cell nuclei, inserting genetic material into the egg of a Tasmanian devil, a closely related species, and

Whale sharks swim at the newly opened Churaumi Aquarium on Okinawa island, Japan.

placing a fertilized egg into a surrogate mother. Some biologists argued that it would be better to spend the money on conservation efforts for extant species.

New species described during the year included a new species of gerbil (*Gerbillus rupicola*) found in rocky outcrops in the Inner Delta of the Niger River in Mali and a new Congo shrew (*Congosorex verheyeni*) from three localities north of the Congo River. A new species of green parrot, bald and with an intensely orange head (*Pionopsitta aurantiocephala*), was described from the vicinity of the Tapajós and Lower Madeira rivers in Brazil, where its forest home was disappearing at the hands of loggers and ranchers.

(JACQUI M. MORRIS)

ZOOS

Despite a tough year, accredited zoos and aquariums in North America continued to garner large attendance numbers in 2002, attracting over 134 million visitors—more than professional baseball, basketball, football, and ice hockey combined. Innovative new experiences such as the Philadelphia Zoo's Zooballoon ride, a hot-air balloon tour over the zoo's 1,800 animals, attracted repeat and first-time visitors alike.

International attention focused on the plight of the troubled Kabul Zoo in Afghanistan. The North Carolina Zoo spearheaded a fund to aid the zoo that raised more than $530,000. In April a group of veterinarians, funded by the donations, traveled to Afghanistan to continue the work to aid the zoo. Medical treatment was administered to an injured bear, but, unfortunately, the zoo's most famous resident, Marjan, a lion blinded during the Afghan civil war, had died only a few weeks after supplies of fresh food had been made available. A freshwater supply was established, and preparations were made for drilling a borehole on the zoo grounds to secure a long-term water supply. The struggling zoo continued to be supported through the efforts of the World Association of Zoos and Aquariums (WAZA) as well as the North Carolina Zoo.

The bushmeat (hunting of wild animals for food) crisis in Africa, which was leading to the unsustainable loss of wildlife due to overhunting, was brought to Americans' attention in July when the House Subcommittee on Fisheries Conservation, Wildlife and Oceans held an oversight hearing on the issue. Bushmeat was a long-term concern of the zoo community, addressed through its Bushmeat Crisis Taskforce (BCTF). Michael Hutchins, director of conservation and science for the American Zoo and Aquarium Association (AZA) and steering committee chair for the BCTF, testified, urging an international collaborative effort to provide sustainable financing for a system of protected areas in Africa and advocating for the establishment of a Congressional Bushmeat Caucus to identify actions the U.S. government could take to address the crisis.

Summer flooding in Germany and the Czech Republic affected several zoos and wildlife parks. The Prague Zoo was the most severely flooded. More than half the zoo was submerged, the roofs of some pavilions no longer visible. The zoo staff stayed long after the city had been evacuated, risking their lives to rescue more than 1,000 animals. Unfortunately, 90 animals drowned, and an Asian elephant and a hippopotamus had to be destroyed because rescue was impossible. WAZA organized a fund to help rebuild the zoo and replace the lost animals.

Tracey McNamara of the Bronx Zoo (New York City) and Dominic Travis of the Lincoln Park Zoo (Chicago) headed up a study of the effect of the West Nile virus on zoo species. WNV swept westward across the country in 2002, particularly affecting bird populations. Nationally, zoo officials worked to administer an equine vaccine to those mammal and bird populations it could protect, and to identify additional methods of protection for other species in their care. In September a promising breakthrough surfaced. Clinical trials of a bird vaccine developed by the American Bird Conservancy in partnership with the AZA showed a 60% increase in survival rates over unvaccinated birds.

Marking a major advent in the science of protecting endangered species, the San Diego (Calif.) Zoo's scientists fused cow eggs with the DNA of the endangered banteng (a Southeast Asian ox). The DNA came from the "frozen zoo," a collection of tissue samples that the San Diego Zoo had maintained since 1977. Scientists expected at least six cloned banteng births in March 2003.

In November the U.S. Fish and Wildlife Service called upon the North American zoo community to place six polar bears seized from the Suárez Brothers Circus in Puerto Rico. Another bear from the circus was taken in by the Baltimore (Md.) Zoo in March 2002. The rescued bears, accompanied by Diana Weinhardt, the Houston (Texas) Zoo's curator of large mammals, were flown to the Point Defiance (Wash.) Zoo, the Detroit Zoo, and the North Carolina Zoo, where they received professional husbandry and veterinary care.

While Colorado's Ocean Journey Aquarium declared bankruptcy during the year, several other aquariums began large expansion projects, including the National Aquarium in Baltimore and the John G. Shedd Aquarium in Chicago. Several new aquariums, including one in Tulsa, Okla., planned 2003 openings. On November 1 the Churaumi Aquarium opened on the Japanese island of Okinawa. The second largest aquarium in the world, Churaumi featured a wealth of exhibits centring on aquatic life at all depths of the Kuroshio Current, which passes by Okinawa. (HILLARY A. WALKER)

GARDENING

In 2002 drought again played a major role in gardening. A drought throughout Europe, especially in Italy, affected horticultural crops, while in the U.S. a shortage of rainfall was reported in portions of all 48 contiguous states. Nearly half of the U.S. reported below-average rainfall at some point during the year. In Santa Fe, N.M., the water shortage became severe enough to allow outdoor watering only once a week; many residents turned to artificial flowers to brighten their homes and businesses.

Despite the drought, sales of plant material continued their five-year climb (up 42% over that period), the only exception being sales of trees and shrubs, which showed a continuing decline. Urban nurseries saw patrons lining up to buy exotic plant varieties with little attention to frugality. "Boutique dirt" was also increasingly popular; Scotts and Miracle-Gro led the trend toward branded specialty mixes, as opposed to unbranded topsoil.

Harsh weather and pollution continued to take their toll on street trees in the U.S. In Washington, D.C., a survey by the Casey Trees Endowment Fund showed that only 32% of the 106,000 city-owned street trees were completely healthy, and more than 10,000 were dead. That figure conformed with national statistics that showed a 25% decline in the "urban forest" of America over the past 30 years. The U.S. government unveiled a program to plant more trees. Secretary of Agriculture Ann Veneman announced the awarding of $933,000 in grants to plant memorial groves and healing gardens in New York, New Jersey, Pennsylvania, Connecticut, and Washington, D.C., to honour victims of the Sept. 11, 2001, attacks. The Lower Manhattan Development Corp. unveiled prospective plans for a memorial garden at the site of the World Trade Center.

The year brought changes at two venerable horticultural institutions in New England. The 98-year-old Horticulture magazine was sold by Primedia to F&W Publications of Cincinnati, Ohio. F&W planned to keep the 200,000-circulation publication in its Boston offices. Gardener's Supply Co., which specialized in organic products, purchased the bulb company Dutch Gardens and moved its operation from New Jersey to Vermont.

There were also major changes on the set of PBS's The Victory Garden, the most recognizable television program in American home gardening for 27 years. In the spring of 2002, the network announced that both producer Russ Morash and host Roger Swain were leaving the show. Michael Weishan replaced Swain, and the bulk of the filming was scheduled for Weishan's garden. Swain signed on to cohost a new program, People, Places & Plants, The Gardening Show, which was seeking sponsors and affiliates.

The Missouri Botanical Garden received the largest private gift ever to an American botanical garden, $30 million from the Jack Taylor family. The endowment would be used to identify and preserve plant species before they became extinct. The New York Botanical Garden got a $100 million face-lift to its facilities, adding an International Plant Science Center and herbarium and restoring its Beaux-Arts Library Rotunda. At Hanbury Hall, Droitwich, Worcestershire, Eng., a nine-year project to restore the 18th-century parterre gardens was completed.

In 2002 Fleuroselect, the organization that recognized outstanding advances in plant breeding, announced five gold medal winners for 2003: Petunia Blue Wave, a deep blue spreading petunia with good weather tolerance; Salvia superba Merleau, a perennial species that produces bright purplish blue spikes the first year after sowing; Rudbeckia hirta Prairie Sun, an annual with striking two-tone golden blossoms; Viola cornuta Sorbet Orange Duet, selected for its remarkable colour combination of orange and purple, the first ever in a viola cultivar; and Dianthus caryophyllus Can Can Scarlet, a brilliant red carnation that was bred to perform well in the home garden, especially in containers and pots.

The All-America Selections (AAS) announced its winners for 2003, including three honoured by Fleuroselect: Blue Wave, Prairie Sun, and Can Can Scarlet. Also designated AAS winners were: Agastache foeniculum Golden Ju-

Floriade, a Fusion of Nature and Art

Floriade, the "world's fair" of horticulture, was held in Haarlemmermeer, Neth., in 2002. Occurring only once every 10 years, Floriade celebrated all things horticultural with displays, exhibits, classes, and competitions. More than two million visitors attended the fifth Floriade, which ran from April to October.

"Feel the Art of Nature" was the event's theme, and exhibits covered more than 64.8 ha (160 ac). The master plan, which was developed by landscape designer Niek Roozen, included three distinct areas—designated "Near the Roof," "By the Hill," and "On the Lake." Notable features included Big Spotters' Hill, a pyramid constructed of 500,000 cu m (654,000 cu yd) of sand, and several man-made lakes on which floated 10 artificial islands. Each of the islands incorporated its own unique environment, with pasture, woodlands, and water features. Near the lake section, paths wound through a landscape with more than 60,000 plants, including rare flower bulbs and wild orchids.

The three dozen indoor exhibitions changed with the seasons, from spring bulbs in April to autumn foliage in October. Scores of countries sponsored displays, including the U.S., Germany, France, Russia, Canada, Pakistan, India, China, and Japan. For the National Day of France, Alain Meilland of Meilland International, a French rose-breeding company, introduced a new variety of rose called Les Quatre Saisons.

Among the thousands of plants on display at the 2002 Floriade was a new variety of rose, Les Quatre Saisons.

photo Floriade

The Floriade Keurings Commissie awarded the model garden prize to Harry Esselink for his "Verstaalde Eenvoud" (Steeled Simplicity) in the Green City, constructed on one of the man-made islands. The futuristic garden consisted solely of steel structures and patches of different species of grass with their varying textures and shades of green.

Perhaps more spectacular than the displays themselves was the structure that housed them. *Guinness World Records* recognized the solar roof over Floriade as the world's largest. The 30,000-sq-m (35,900-sq-yd) roof contained nearly 20,000 solar panels, providing enough electricity to power the entire exhibit. The panels were to continue to operate after Floriade's conclusion, providing electricity to the remaining permanent exhibits as well to nearby homes. *Guinness* also recognized the exhibition of summer flowers, which included a massive display, as the bouquet with the greatest number of cultivars ever—more than 1,000.

photo Floriade

Visitors to the Floriade make their way to and from the top of Big Spotters' Hill, a spectacular 40-m (130-ft) high pyramid.

(WARREN SCHULTZ)

bilee, a symmetrical branching annual ornamental with pale green fragrant leaves and lavender-blue flower spikes; *Dianthus* Corona Cherry Magic, a bicolor dianthus with five-centimetre (two-inch) blooms of red and lavender; *Eustoma* Forever White, with large blooms on compact branching plants, good for containers; *Gaillardia pulchella* Sundance Bicolor, with globe-shaped mahogany and yellow blooms; *Petunia* Merlin Blue Morn, with blue and white blooms on a tall spreading plant; and *Vinca* Jaio Dark Red, a red and white vinca. The AAS awarded its highest honour, a gold medal, to the ornamental millet Purple Majesty. The 1.5-m (5-ft)-tall purple-leafed cornlike plants produce long flower spikes that were used for floral arrangements. The AAS also honoured two new vegetable varieties—melon Angel, a very sweet white-fleshed melon, and summer squash Papaya Pear, a yellow squash with a squat, bulbous shape that grows on a semibush plant.

All-America Rose Selections winners for 2003 were Hot Cocoa, a unique brownish orange Floribunda, bred by Tom Carruth; Whisper, a pure white Hybrid Tea Rose with glossy green foliage developed in Ireland by Colin Dickson; Cherry Parfait, a bicolour white and red Grandiflora from the house of Meilland; and Eureka, an apricot yellow floribunda hybridized by the Kordes Co.

The All-American Daylily Selection Council winners were: Frankly Scarlet, a vibrant red, and Plum Perfect, a deep purple. *Hedera helix* Golden Ingot was chosen Ivy of the Year 2003 by the American Ivy Society. This variegated ivy, bred in Denmark, has bright-yellow leaves edged with dark green and vibrant green and gray centres.

More than two million people attended Floriade, the World's Fair of horticulture, which was held in Haarlemmermeer, Neth. (*See* Sidebar.)

(WARREN SCHULTZ)

Fashions

Luxurious apparel, **RELAXED STYLES**, architecturally **STUNNING NEW CLOTHING STORES**, and **ATTRACTIVE MATERNITY CLOTHES** brightened the fashion scene in 2002.

Feel-good fashion was the predominant style delivered by international designers in 2002. Colour and comfort were the bywords for women's wear in summer. Rainbow-bright shades of orange and yellow were popular, as were vibrant prints—notably Celine's flower-power pattern, which appeared on bikinis, skirts, and ruffled blouses. Paul Smith, Mui Mui, and Dolce & Gabanna featured floral-printed dress shirts for men.

Delicate floral embroidery (seen first on white folkloric-inspired coats and knee-high leather boots at Marc Jacobs's 2002 spring-summer collection for Louis Vuitton) and exotic butterfly appliqués (seen on skirts and chiffon tops by Matthew Williamson and on Christian Dior handbags) were looks that were later copied by a slew of lower-priced fashion labels. Fresh white became the alternative to basic black. Several designers, including Viktor & Rolf, Bally, Calvin Klein, and Strenesse, presented white trouser and skirt suits on their runways.

Relaxed styles, including loose peasant and ethnic-inspired tops and layered skirts, flooded boutiques. Prada delivered burnished-gold pajama-style tops, and one of the most popular items on Tom Ford's Yves Saint Laurent catwalk was a floaty, roomy caftan, made of hand-embroidered jaguar print on silk muslin, which was later worn by singer Alicia Keys. With a price tag of £22,285 (about $32,425), it was reportedly the most expensive caftan in the world. Less-expensive variations were produced by Allegra Hicks, Dries Van Noten, and Marni.

High-profile celebrities such as Madonna, Elle Macpherson, Sadie Frost, Kate Winslet, and Kate Beckinsale opted for casual-chic clothing. All were captured by the paparazzi sporting plush velour tracksuits by Juicy Couture—a Los Angeles fashion brand designed by two friends, Pamela Skaist-Levy and Gela Nash-Taylor. Meanwhile, the most popular footwear for women for summer included Prada's low kitten heels (which appeared in suede and brocade) and for men and women stylish sneakers that designers made by collaborating with sportswear brands. Comme des Garcons designed a few styles with Nike, and Yohji Yamamoto collaborated with Adidas. Vintage Adidas nylon-striped tracksuits became cult fashion items after actor Ben Stiller and his two film sons sported them in Wes Anderson's *The Royal Tenenbaums;* Gwyneth Paltrow's Lacoste dresses for that film repopularized the early 1980s preppy style.

Elizabeth Hurley—who appeared on the August cover of *Harper's Bazaar* cuddling her newborn baby boy—was at the forefront of a new generation of stylish new mothers and mothers-to-be, including Sarah Jessica Parker, Brandy, Macpherson, Frost, Claudia Schiffer, and Kate Moss, who transformed the notion of maternity clothes by wearing high heels and oversized designer fashion for public appearances. As a result, a number of designers, including Anna Sui and Diane von Furstenberg (who launched a maternity wrap dress), introduced some plus-size versions of their traditional styles; the denim label Earl debuted a style of jeans with a comfortable elasticized waist.

Chanel designer Karl Lagerfeld—recipient of the Council of Fashion Designers of America 2002 Lifetime Achievement Award—further translated the look-good, feel-good idea by having shed some 40 kg (90 lb) since 2000. In October he published a low-calorie cookbook with the French doctor whose diet he followed.

Ethnic accessories, particularly those inspired by Africa—such as Yves Saint Laurent's Mombasa bag, a chunky dark leather, bone-handled handbag, and items by Anna Trzebinski, such as bags, shawls, and suede coats that were inspired by the Masai and Samburu tribes of Kenya—came to be sought after by women. The accessories that typified fashion's feel-good factor, however, were necklaces, bracelets, and belts made of stones such as rock crystal and Navajo Indian-inspired turquoise and coral, which were thought to be infused with healing properties.

The fashion retail sector experienced a sharp decline in sales in 2002, however, after the global economy faltered and the U.S. went to war in Afghanistan and then hovered on the brink of war with Iraq. The Gucci Group announced in June that its net income had fallen by 42%. Despite the efforts of Prada designer Miuccia Prada (*see* BIOGRAPHIES), the company reportedly incurred over $1 billion in

Television actress Sarah Jessica Parker represented the mothers-to-be who made fashion statements with trendy outfits that belied the notion of frumpy maternity wear.

Mark Mainz/Getty Images

debt. Layoffs in American textile mills reflected that the industry had been hard hit by the lean economy. Luxury analysts predicted that the sale of Valentino to the Marzotto apparel group in late March could be one of the last in a long line of luxury takeovers that had begun in the late 1990s.

Nevertheless, some fashion labels attempted to modernize their look to attract new customers. In April Christian Lacroix was appointed artistic director of the Florentine fashion label Pucci by LVMH (which also owned his personal fashion label), and Parisian designer Christophe Lemaire filled the same post at Lacoste. British designer Lizzy Disney presented her collection for Jacques Fath; Indian designer Ritu Beri displayed her redeveloped look for Jean-Louis Scherrer; and Laetitia Hecht unveiled a new ready-to-wear collection for Guy Laroche. Their new work met with mixed reviews, however.

Despite the gloomy outlook, there was positive fashion news. Rose Marie Bravo, chief executive of the British luxury label Burberry Ltd., successfully floated 25% of the company's shares on the London Stock Exchange in July. During Bravo's five-year tenure, the company had experienced a fivefold increase in value, and she was rewarded with $15 million in compensation. Marc Jacobs proved to be another fashion success story; sales for his personal labels totaled $50 million. His eponymous label, his diffusion line, Marc, and his designs for Louis Vuitton all proved popular with customers, despite his tendency to reinterpret 1970s styles for men and women. Designer Stephen Burrows, whose signature look—sleek lettuce-edged bias-cut dresses and separates—was revived in collections produced by Jacobs and von Furstenberg, also relaunched his label and opened a boutique at the upscale New York department store Henri Bendel.

Zac Posen—a 21-year-old New York designer—debuted his first collection on the New York 2002 spring-summer catwalk; his 1940s-inspired dresses proved so popular that in September his work appeared in every window of

Mike Segar/Reuters/TimePix

A champagne-coloured bell top and snap skirt, worn by model Rie Rasmussen, was one of the highlights of the spring 2003 collection of 21-year-old New York City designer Zac Posen.

Bloomingdale's department store in New York City.

Marks & Spencer, Britain's largest fashion retailer, reported a growth of more than 8% in clothing sales for the three months to September 2001. In addition, French luxury brand Hermès reported a 15.3% rise in net income for

2001 and announced plans to open seven new shops. Prada, Burberry, Donna Karan, Escada, Chanel, and Louis Vuitton all spent millions of dollars opening huge architecturally designed retail flagship stores in New York in 2002. In May, Kuwaiti Prince Majed al-Sabah hosted a lavish party to open Villa Moda, a 9,000-sq-m (100,000-sq-ft) luxury fashion store in Kuwait City. His posh store would feature designs by Stella McCartney, Consuela Castiglioni (of Marni's), and Carla Fendi. Upscale boutiques opened during the Paris couture shows in July—including Bottega Veneta (as a showcase for its new designer, Tomas Maier), Manolo Blahnik, and Dolce & Gabbana. Giorgio Armani opened his first boutique in Moscow.

Though sales in the U.S. had reportedly dropped 5% in 2001, luxury items were still selling. Saks Fifth Avenue claimed that the store's top luxury sellers included an $11,200 patchwork coat by Oscar de la Renta. Conspicuous consumption, however, had lost its allure. Sales of handbags and accessories embossed with designer logos by Chanel, Fendi, Gucci, Ferragamo, Hermès, and Prada declined sharply. Retail analysts explained that consumers wanted a change—the new trend was individuality.

Excessive luxury dominated many of the autumn-winter ready-to-wear catwalks, even though it seemed out of sync with the leaner economic times. The flat shoes seen in the summer were replaced by extremely high heels, some of which featured grosgrain and velvet ribbon ankle straps. A soft round-toe shoe emerged to replace the pointy styles seen in past seasons. Expensive exotic skins such as crocodile, python, and eel were used to make accessories as well as clothing items such as skirts and trousers.

Fur also experienced a new popularity. French *Vogue's* entire September issue was dedicated to fur. Supermodel Gisele Bündchen became the face of Blackglama mink's "What becomes a legend most?" advertising campaign. Early in the year, mink-lined jean jackets were popular streetwear items. At the autumn-winter couture shows, sable was used as trimming at Valentino and Balmain. Carolina Herrera produced sable cuffs in her ready-to-wear collection; Bottega Veneta introduced a sable stole; and Jean Paul Gaultier and Gucci used it to make sweaters. Michael Kors used coyote to create vests and gaiters, and Jacobs trimmed a wool and cashmere tunic in coyote for Louis Vuitton. Kors delivered coyote-trimmed parkas for his autumn-winter women's ready to wear, and Alberta Ferretti made duffle coats with rabbit-lined hoods. Rabbit fur coats were a less-expensive alternative offered by Allesandro Dell'Acqua and MaxMara. Model Iman, meanwhile, became the ambassador and consultant for De Beers LV, a new jewelry line launched by LVMH in collaboration with the South African diamond company De Beers.

Some designers merged practicality with luxury. The dominant trend for autumn-winter menswear was what British *GQ* labeled "expensive scruff," a look that blended luxury and casual wear—a pin-striped suit jacket mixed with denim jeans or a crewneck sweater worn with a pair of Converse athletic shoes. Reliable black dresses dominated the catwalks. Long chunky knit scarves by Jacobs, Missoni, and Dolce & Gabanna were affordable items that could update an old look. Staples such as trousers—in a variety of styles from super tight to cropped short above the ankle—and pencil skirts proliferated. Reappearing on the autumn-winter catwalks were folk-inspired ethnic looks and mini-skirts by Chloé and Chanel as well as designer denim. Alexander McQueen

produced sweeping jean skirts. Skinny jeans produced by Karl Lagerfeld and Diesel for the Lagerfeld Gallery line were highly desired.

AP/Wide World Photos

A patterned wool coat was paired with a colourful dress for the debut of the 2002–03 Missoni fall-winter fashion collection in Milan.

Collaborations between artists and designers increased the desirability of fashion items. A new term, *fashion/art* was coined to explain the phenomenon. Illustrator Julie Verhoeven was commissioned by Jacobs to produce a

fairy-tale-style collage for a Louis Vuitton handbag, which became known as its Dreamscape bag. Painter Gary Hume's line drawings were reproduced on T-shirts and dresses in Stella McCartney's spring-summer collection. McCartney utilized pencil drawings of the model Tetyana produced by painter David Remfry for her autumn-winter advertising campaign. Belgian menswear designer Raf Simons produced transparent ponchos with the British artist Simon Periton. Illustrator Tanya Ling presented her autumn-winter collection in an installation designed by artist Gavin Turk.

A number of fashion-inspired exhibitions dominated some of London's leading galleries during the year. Mario Testino's photographs were the subject in February–June of a retrospective at the National Portrait Gallery; fashion historian Anne Hollander curated "Fabric of Vision: Dress and Drapery in Painting," which opened in June at the National Gallery; and "When Philip Met Isabella" opened in July at the Design Museum. The latter displayed hats that Irish milliner Philip Treacy had created for his muse, British stylist Isabella Blow. Two fashion exhibitions opened in London in October. At the Barbican, "Rapture: Art's Seduction by Fashion Since 1970" explored fashion's relationship with art, and a major retrospective featuring the works of Gianni Versace appeared at the Victoria and Albert Museum.

Other major events that rocked the fashion world included the retirement of Yves Saint Laurent and the deaths of American designers Bill Blass and John Weitz; American model Jean Patchett; and French-born American fashion designer Pauline Trigère. (See OBITUARIES.) Celebrity makeup artist Kevyn Aucoin also died during the year.

(BRONWYN COSGRAVE)

Health and Disease

Continued **BIOTERRORISM** concerns prompted the U.S. to launch a **SMALLPOX-VACCINATION PROGRAM** for select military personnel and civilian workers. Doctors halted a major study of **POSTMENOPAUSAL HORMONE REPLACEMENT THERAPY** once the treatment's **SERIOUS HEALTH RISKS** became clear.

Bioterrorism preparedness became a national priority in many countries in 2002 in the wake of the previous year's September 11 terrorist attacks and subsequent anthrax mailings in the U.S. The possibility that terrorists would use deadly pathogens as weapons underscored the need for new drugs to treat and prevent infectious diseases. The Pharmaceutical Research and Manufacturers of America reported in April that more than 100 companies, predominantly American firms, were developing 256 such medicines, which included vaccines, antibiotics, and antiviral agents. At the same time, the pharmaceutical industry was identifying existing antibiotics that could be used to counter bacterial agents, among them anthrax, tularemia, and plague, if they were used as weapons.

By far the major focus of bioterrorism planning was on smallpox, which was eradicated from the planet in 1980 and for which routine vaccination in the U.S. ceased in 1972. Only two high-security laboratories—at the Centers for Disease Control and Prevention (CDC), Atlanta, Ga., and the State Research Center of Virology and Biotechnology, Koltsovo, Russia—were known to have live samples of the smallpox virus. Government security officials, however, had good reason to suspect that clandestine samples could be in the hands of potential terrorists.

In late October the Food and Drug Administration (FDA) licensed the use of the U.S. government's 30-year-old stockpile of smallpox vaccine—15.4 million doses. The government also possessed 75 million doses that the French vaccine maker Aventis Pasteur discovered in its storage facilities during the year, and it ordered a further 209 million new doses from the British company Acambis, to be pre-

pared by means of modern cell-culture techniques.

Securing an ample vaccine supply to protect the entire U.S. population proved easier than determining who should be vaccinated, especially because smallpox vaccine has significant risks. For every million persons vaccinated, hundreds would be likely to develop severe rashes or other non-life-threatening illnesses, 15 would likely have life-threatening complications, and 1 or 2 would die. Furthermore, for every million receiving the vaccine, the live vaccinia virus from which the vaccine is made could spread by contact to as many as 27 others who had not been vaccinated and who then would be at risk for various adverse effects. Because

A specialist demonstrates use of a biohazard suit in a Biosafety-Level-4 (highest-security) laboratory at the Centers for Disease Control and Prevention, Atlanta, Ga.—one of two research centres in the world known to have live samples of smallpox virus.

AP/Wide World Photos

of these risks a federal advisory panel on immunizations specified that certain groups should not be vaccinated against smallpox. They included people with current or past eczema, atopic dermatitis, or similar skin diseases, as well as people living with someone who has such a skin disease; people with HIV; people with impaired immunity; pregnant women; and women trying to become pregnant.

On December 13 U.S. Pres. George Bush announced his long-awaited smallpox-vaccination plan. Its first phase called for about 500,000 military and other personnel serving in high-risk areas to be immunized immediately. In addition, civilian health-care and emergency workers who would be likely to come in contact with the initial victims of a smallpox attack on the U.S. would be asked to volunteer for immunizations. Subsequently the vaccine would be offered to more traditional first responders such as fire, police, and emergency medical service personnel. At the time, Bush recommended against vaccination for the general public. (Well before the December announcement, more than 15,000 soldiers and health-care workers in Israel had received smallpox vaccine on a voluntary basis, with relatively few adverse effects.)

In July American scientists reported having successfully created a poliovirus from scratch—that is, from only its genome sequence, which was available in the public domain, and genetic material provided by a scientific mail-order supplier. J. Craig Venter, one of the geneticists instrumental in the sequencing of the human genome—an accomplishment announced in 2000—called the work, which had been financed in part by the Pentagon, "inflammatory without scientific justification" and "irresponsible." The relative ease with which the experiment was completed led many scientists to wonder whether other, potentially more lethal viruses such as smallpox or Ebola virus could also be synthesized.

Infectious Diseases. The dreaded Ebola hemorrhagic fever, called one of the "most virulent viral diseases known to humankind," struck Gabon in late 2001 and quickly spread to neighbouring villages in the Republic of the Congo. By March 2002 about 100 persons had been infected, and 80% of them had died. The speedy arrival of international health teams helped curtail the outbreak and undoubtedly saved many lives. In May the U.S. National Institutes of Health (NIH) contracted with Crucell, a small Dutch biotechnology company, to develop the first human vaccine against Ebola hemorrhagic fever; the collaborators hoped to have a product ready to test in humans within two years.

An alarming rise in the number of cases of gonorrhea resistant to the first-line drugs used to treat the sexually transmitted disease (STD) was seen in California. Strains of *Neisseria gonorrhoeae* resistant to antibiotics known as fluoroquinolones had migrated from East Asia to Hawaii and then to California. In response, the state issued new guidelines for treating gonorrhea, specifying that another drug group, cephalosporins, should replace fluoroquinolones. Late in the year two new vaccines against STD were reported to be highly effective—one against human papillomavirus type 16, which is responsible for half of all cervical cancers, and other against genital herpes (herpes simplex viruses types 1 and 2) in women. Neither vaccine would be on the market until considerable further testing was completed.

The mosquitoborne disease West Nile virus (WNV) made its fourth annual late-summer appearance in the U.S., striking with a vengeance. As of mid-December, 3,829 human cases had been reported in 39 states and the District of Columbia, with 225 deaths. The virus was found in 29 species of mosquitoes, at least 120 species of birds, and many mammals, including squirrels, dogs, horses, mules, goats, and rabbits. A number of exotic species housed in zoos had also been infected, including penguins, cormorants, and flamingos. During the year evidence emerged that WNV could be transmitted between humans via blood transfusion and organ transplantation and possibly by infected mothers to infants through breast milk.

The U.S. National Institute of Allergy and Infectious Diseases continued to sponsor research on several potential WNV vaccines, with hopes that one might be ready for trials in 2003. The FDA was developing a blood-screening process for WNV, which could be in use by mid-2003.

Following the first outbreak of WNV in the New York City area in the summer of 1999, health authorities in Canada had begun to plan for its possible arrival in that country. In the summer of 2001, WNV was confirmed in mosquitoes and

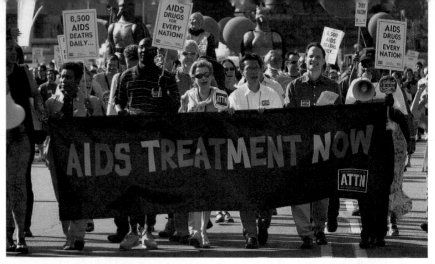

Demonstrators march in Barcelona, Spain, on July 7 to urge making drugs for the treatment of HIV/AIDS available to less-developed countries.

AP/Wide World Photos

birds in southern Ontario. The first human cases occurred in 2002; from August through October there were 79 probable cases and 31 confirmed cases.

HIV and AIDS. Some 17,000 participants from 124 countries gathered in Barcelona, Spain, in July for the 14th—and largest—International AIDS Conference. Twenty-one years after the first cases of a new deadly disease were diagnosed in the U.S., the AIDS pandemic had become one of the most virulent scourges in human history. Worldwide, 40 million people were infected with HIV, and new infections were occurring at a rate of 15,000 a day. The lethal virus had taken 20 million lives and created at least 14 million "AIDS orphans," defined as children under age 15 who had lost one or both parents to AIDS. In seven countries in sub-Saharan Africa, more than 20% of adults were infected with HIV, and life expectancy had been reduced to less than 40 years.

A major report prepared by a team of public health experts, clinicians, research scientists, and people affected by HIV/AIDS was released just prior to the conference and largely set the tone of the weeklong meeting. Entitled "Global Mobilization for HIV Prevention: A Blueprint for Action," it argued that massive expansion of the HIV/AIDS epidemic was not inevitable. Rather, if significantly scaled-up and appropriately targeted prevention efforts were initiated without delay, they could reverse the course of the pandemic by 2010 and prevent about 28 million new infections. According to the report, despite the "immense resources" at the global community's disposal, prevention efforts were reaching fewer than 20% of those at risk. Cited were dozens of examples of prevention strategies, such as school sex education

and programs to increase condom use, that had curbed the spread of HIV in high-risk groups. Many of the successes were in less-developed countries.

The report's view that prevention and treatment were "natural partners in the global fight against HIV/AIDS" was echoed by the World Health Organization (WHO), which acknowledged that the battle against AIDS would never be won as long as drugs remained unavailable to nearly six million HIV-infected people in less-developed countries. WHO took several important steps toward changing that situation. For the first time, it issued guidelines on the various combinations of three drugs—so-called AIDS drug cocktails—that were known to work best, and it stressed that they should be made available to people in poor countries. It also outlined the minimal acceptable laboratory tests both for diagnosing HIV infection and for monitoring treatment. Furthermore, WHO added a dozen antiretroviral drugs to its essential-drugs list in an effort to encourage generic companies to increase their output of inexpensive effective drugs for treating HIV infection.

An alarming report released in September by the National Intelligence Council, an advisory group for the U.S. Central Intelligence Agency, predicted that the growth of AIDS in five countries—India, China, Nigeria, Russia, and Ethiopia—would pose economic, social, and political security threats to the respective regions as well as to the U.S. HIV epidemics in each of the countries were in their infancy but were poised for explosion. The report estimated that by 2010 the number of cases in those five countries, which together represented 40% of the world's population, would be 50 million to 75 million.

On the clinical front, there was considerable excitement about a new class of antiretroviral drugs called fusion inhibitors, which act by preventing HIV's entry into host cells. (The other classes of antiretroviral drugs act by preventing replication of HIV after entry.) Trials in the U.S., Europe, Australia, and South America, involving people whose HIV infections were partially or wholly resistant to existing drugs, were focused on an experimental drug called T-20 (or enfuvirtide), which would be marketed under the trade name Fuzeon. Study participants who received T-20 in combination with customized AIDS drug cocktails experienced significant reductions in the amount of virus in their systems as well as increases in their healthy immune cells. It was expected that the FDA would approve the drug by early 2003.

Cardiovascular Disease. In the hundreds of thousands of balloon angioplasty procedures performed each year to open blocked coronary arteries, it was common practice to place tiny mesh coils, called stents, in the treated artery to help keep it open. In up to 20% of cases, however, scar tissue formed at the stent site, causing reblockage (restenosis). During the year, investigators reported promising results from trials that had tested the ability of stents coated with an immunosuppressive drug to inhibit restenosis. The coated stents prevented renarrowing of the artery in 96–100% of recipients. They were expected to receive FDA approval and be available in the U.S. in 2003.

Another approach to staving off restenosis after angioplasty was investigated by Swiss and American researchers. Previous studies had shown that high blood levels of the amino acid homocysteine were highly predictive of restenosis following angioplasty. It was also known that a group of B vitamins lowered homocysteine levels. Accordingly, the researchers gave patients who had undergone angioplasty a combination of the B vitamin folic acid and vitamins B_{12} and B_6, in dosages considerably higher than those in standard multivitamins, for a period of six months. Compared with angioplasty patients who were not given the vitamin regimen, those receiving vitamins had a significantly decreased incidence of restenosis and other adverse cardiac events—outcomes that lasted well beyond the time they took the vitamins.

Cancer. In mid-August the FDA approved the drug oxaliplatin (Eloxatin) for patients with advanced colon cancer that had failed to respond to existing drugs. The approval, which occurred in the record time of seven weeks, was based on a trial that found that oxaliplatin used in conjunction with two other chemotherapeutic drugs, 5-fluorouracil and leucovorin, shrank tumours by at least 30% in about 9% of patients and prevented tumours from growing again for several months. At the time oxaliplatin was approved in the U.S., it was already in use in more than 55 countries.

Cancer death rates for African Americans, compared with those for whites, had been disproportionately high ever since statistics on cancer were first collected. Some scientists thought the difference had a biological basis. In 2002 a team of researchers published a review of data on nearly 190,000 whites and 32,000 blacks with 14 different types of cancer. Rather than identifying any biological differences between the two groups, the review found that blacks received less-optimal care than whites and were generally diagnosed at a later, less-curable stage of the disease. The researchers believed that it was time to abandon the biological trail and focus on remedying the underlying socioeconomic causes of elevated cancer mortality among blacks.

Obesity. The latest data from an ongoing government-sponsored survey of the health and nutrition of the U.S. population indicated that nearly 65% of American adults were overweight and more than 30% were obese. The most disquieting finding was that more than 80% of all black women over age 40 were overweight and half were obese. In a separate report focusing on children and adolescents, 15% of those aged 6–19 were overweight, with the highest prevalences in Mexican American and black adolescents.

CDC researchers published the disturbing results of a 20-year study that analyzed hospital-discharge records of children. They found that overweight children were increasingly being diagnosed with illnesses formerly seen mainly in overweight or obese adults. These included type II (non-insulin-dependent) diabetes, gallbladder disease, and sleep apnea. Although the overall numbers of children with these serious conditions remained relatively low, the increases over the period 1979–99 were striking. For example, the diagnosis of gallbladder disease in 6–17-year-olds rose 228%.

A report on obesity among children worldwide by the London-based International Obesity Task Force was presented in May at the annual meeting of the World Health Assembly, WHO's decision-making body. The task force estimated that 22 million children under age five were overweight or obese. Among 10-year-olds, the U.S. had the third highest prevalence of overweight children, after Malta and Italy. Much to the surprise of many health professionals, obesity was found to be a growing problem in less-developed countries. In Morocco and Zambia, for example, more children were overweight than malnourished. In Egypt, Chile, Mexico, and Peru, as many as 25% of children aged 4–10 were overweight or obese.

Two hormones associated with appetite and weight gain were identified during the year. One appeared to stimulate appetite and the other to suppress it. Ghrelin, a hormone secreted by cells in the stomach and small intestine, was shown to increase hunger, slow metabolism, and decrease the body's fat-burning capacity. Researchers found that people who had lost significant weight produced large quantities of ghrelin, which helped explain why maintaining weight loss was so difficult. On the other hand, extremely obese people who had undergone gastric bypass surgery, which reduces the size of the stomach as well as the ability of the small intestine to absorb nutrients, had low levels of ghrelin and decreased appetites. This finding helped explain why those who had received the surgery tended to be successful at keeping weight off. Whether these findings would lead to new treatments for obesity, such as a drug that turns off ghrelin production, remained unclear.

Scientists had known about the substance called peptide YY_{3-36} for years but did not know what role it played in controlling appetite. Recently they found that the hormone was directly linked to the feeling of fullness that tells a person to stop eating. When it was given to study subjects two hours before a buffet meal, they consumed about 33% fewer calories than they did when they were not given the hormone. The appetite suppression lasted about 12 hours. Even after the hormone's effects had worn off, subjects did not overeat to make up for their reduced caloric intake. Although further research was needed, obesity specialists were enthusiastic about the possibility of using the hormone to help people lose weight. It appeared to have no adverse effects and was relatively easy and inexpensive to synthesize.

Women's Health. The medical story that probably received the most attention

Botox: Quick Fix, Serious Medicine

On April 15, 2002, the U.S. Food and Drug Administration (FDA) approved injections of botulinum toxin type A (trademarked Botox) for the treatment of facial wrinkles. The manufacturer, Allergan Inc., wasted no time in launching a $50 million advertising blitz to promote its already overwhelmingly popular product. In fact, doctors had been using the drug "off-label" to relieve patients of their wrinkles long before it was officially sanctioned for that purpose.

The FDA approved Botox for just one type of wrinkle—frown lines. These vertical creases between the eyebrows result from lifelong use of particular facial muscles. When tiny amounts of a highly dilute, purified solution of botulinum toxin are injected into the muscles, they become temporarily paralyzed and can no longer cause the brow to furrow. As a result, the unwanted facial lines begin to soften and fade. The desired effect becomes apparent 3–10 days after the injections and lasts three to five months.

Botox injections work best for frown lines but are also used for crow's-feet (laugh lines around the eyes), horizontal forehead lines, and neck creases. Ironically, the "wrinkle wonder drug," as it has been called, is derived from one of the most poisonous substances known, the bacterial toxin responsible for botulism food poisoning. During the year its popularity was evidenced by the proliferation of Botox parties—group Botox treatments in casual social settings rather than a controlled medical environment. Professional medical societies in the U.S. and the U.K. considered such venues inappropriate and risky because individuals may not have been properly screened as suitable candidates for Botox or fully informed

© Reuters 2002

A cosmetic surgeon administers Botox to select facial muscles of a patient; the drug surged in popularity after being approved for treating facial wrinkles.

of potential side effects—e.g., headache, droopy eyelids, and redness. Furthermore, if alcohol is consumed, as it often is at Botox parties, the likelihood of bruising is increased.

Botox is much more than a quick fix for wrinkles. In the 1970s doctors found that injections of botulinum toxin into overactive eye muscles alleviated strabismus (cross-eye) and blepharospasm (involuntary blinking). It was for these two conditions that the FDA originally approved Botox in 1989. In the early 1980s a Canadian couple—Jean Carruthers, an ophthalmologist, and her husband, Alastair Carruthers, a dermatologist—noticed the wrinkle-alleviating side effect of Botox and went on to pioneer its cosmetic use. Serendipity played a part again when an American physician who used Botox to treat wrinkles heard from several of his patients that they were having fewer headaches. Since then, more than a dozen studies have shown promising results for treating both chronic tension and migraine headaches with the drug.

In December 2000 the FDA approved the related botulinum toxin type B (Myobloc) as well as Botox for treating cervical dystonia, which causes muscle contractions in the neck and shoulders and an abnormal head position. With these two products available, medical researchers were investigating them as promising treatments for a variety of other afflictions, including urinary incontinence, anal fissures, excessive perspiration, pain following hemorrhoid surgery, and physical disabilities caused by stroke and cerebral palsy.

(ELLEN BERNSTEIN)

during the year was the discontinuation of a major study of postmenopausal hormone replacement therapy (HRT) three years earlier than planned. The study was part of the Women's Health Initiative (WHI), a long-term project to study diseases that affect women. It involved more than 16,000 healthy women between the ages of 50 and 79 who took either estrogen plus progestin or a placebo. When it became clear a little over five years into the study that women taking the hormones were developing breast cancer as well as heart disease, stroke, and blood clots more often than placebo takers, the investigators decided that risks of HRT exceeded any health benefits.

The news about these previously unknown risks was a source of great concern not only for the millions of women on HRT but also for the doctors who had been enthusiastically prescribing it. Its wide use had been encouraged by long-term observational studies of large groups of women, the results of which had suggested multiple benefits. HRT not only eased the hot flushes, night sweats, and vaginal dryness of menopause but also appeared to lower the risk of osteoporosis, heart disease, Alzheimer disease, incontinence, and even depression. In speculating on how doctors and patients drew false assurance from these observations, surgeon and breast cancer specialist Susan Love, in an op-ed article in the *New York Times* (July 16), wrote that "medical practice . . . got ahead of medical science" and that although the observations of HRT's benefits led to hypotheses, "observation . . . can't prove cause

and effect." Only a large randomized placebo-controlled study could do that.

In October the NIH convened a meeting at which experts offered guidance to clinicians on key HRT questions. On the whole, they agreed that no healthy woman should take HRT to prevent heart disease or other chronic conditions. For women using hormones to prevent osteoporosis, there were better options, such as calcium and vitamin D supplements, weight-bearing exercise, and the nonhormonal prescription drugs alendronate (Fosamax) and raloxifene (Evista). For women suffering from acute menopausal symptoms, alternatives should be considered first, but for some, HRT might be appropriate at the lowest-possible dosage for the shortest-possible time.

(ELLEN BERNSTEIN)

Law, Crime, and Law Enforcement

The formal establishment of the **INTERNATIONAL CRIMINAL COURT**, Supreme Court rulings on **CAPITAL PUNISHMENT** and **FREEDOM OF SPEECH** cases, the continued hunt for **AL-QAEDA** operatives, and a congressional inquiry into **INTELLIGENCE FAILURES** before September 11 were among the legal and criminal issues attracting attention in 2002.

INTERNATIONAL LAW

In the most significant development in international law during 2002, the International Criminal Court (ICC) came into force on July 1. Despite objections by the U.S., the ICC garnered the requisite 60 ratifications among United Nations member states and opened its permanent headquarters in The Hague. As of October, the ICC had obtained 81 ratifications. Citing concern that Americans abroad would be the victims of false allegations, the U.S. in May submitted a formal renunciation of the American signature to the ICC treaty; the U.S. had signed the treaty in December 2001 but never ratified it. Israel submitted a similar letter in August. Following the withdrawal of several U.S. military observers from the UN mission in East Timor and American threats to veto a continuation of the peacekeeping missions in Bosnia and Herzegovina and Croatia, the Security Council guaranteed a one-year amnesty from ICC prosecution to nationals who were from countries that had not ratified the treaty and who were serving in official UN peacekeeping operations. Included in this group were American, Russian, and Chinese personnel. The Security Council indicated that it would renew this exemption on a yearly basis.

Despite the formal announcement regarding its position on the ICC, the U.S. continued to be concerned about the reach of international law as represented by the court. The U.S. launched a full-scale diplomatic effort to reach bilateral agreements with more than 150 countries that would promise to provide immunity from ICC prosecution to Americans abroad. As of October, about a dozen countries had signed such agreements with the U.S. In late September the European Union (EU) gave its member states permission to negotiate such accords but only for U.S. soldiers and officials—and only if the agreements specified that the U.S. would agree to prosecute the accused in American courts instead. These conditions met with dissatisfaction in the U.S., where the administration of Pres. George W. Bush continued to argue that unconditional immunity was needed to protect Americans from "politically motivated" prosecutions. In January Britain had negotiated a similar agreement with the Afghan interim government. That agreement protected the troops from several nations working with the International Security Assistance Force stationed in Afghanistan from prosecution by international tribunals.

The International Court of Justice. The International Court of Justice (ICJ) issued two rulings of importance to international law in 2002. In October the ICJ decided a territorial dispute between Nigeria and Cameroon in favour of the latter state. The Bakassi peninsula, rich in natural gas and oil reserves, was the disputed territory. Nigeria's claims rested on self-determination, as most of the inhabitants of the territory were Nigerian. Cameroon's claims stemmed from a 1913 treaty between colonial rulers Britain and Germany, which gave the territory to Cameroon.

In February the ICJ had ruled in a case pitting the Democratic Republic of the Congo (DRC, formerly Zaire) against Belgium. The DRC had instituted proceedings against Belgium following the latter's issuance of an arrest warrant in 2000 for Abdulaye Yerodia Ndombasi, foreign minister of the DRC at that time. Yerodia was accused of crimes against humanity for his role in inciting a massacre of Tutsi in Kinshasa, the capital of Zaire in 1998. The warrant was issued under Belgium's law that established universal jurisdiction of the Belgian courts over grave violations of humanitarian law regardless of where, by whom, or against whom they were committed. The DRC contended, and the ICJ agreed, that Belgium had failed to respect customary international law regarding the immunity of incumbent heads of state and, by extension, official representatives of that position such as a foreign minister. Although initially the DRC's position challenged the legality of the entire Belgian law, the DRC changed its claim to focus only on the issue of ministerial immunity. The ICJ found that the issuance of the warrant, even though it was never executed, violated Yerodia's immunity because, by exposing him to arrest abroad, it interfered with his ability to conduct his official duties. This ruling forced Belgian courts to reconsider a similar warrant that the government had issued against Israeli Prime Minister Ariel Sharon.

International Criminal Tribunals. The trial of former Yugoslav president Slobodan Milosevic began in February at The Hague. He stood accused of crimes against humanity and war crimes in Kosovo, genocide in Bosnia, and crimes against humanity in Croatia. The International Criminal Tribunal for the Former Yugoslavia (ICTY) heard testimony during the year from dozens of witnesses, including Croatian Pres. Stipe Mesic, who had served as the last president of the Yugoslav federation before its collapse in 1991. In a heated exchange in October, Milosevic, who had opted to defend himself at trial, accused Mesic of murder and betrayal of Yugoslavia. Mesic, who sternly denied those charges, had testified that Milosevic intentionally ignited ethnic violence in Croatia. The trial was ongoing at year's end.

Former Bosnian Serb president Biljana Plavsic pleaded guilty to crimes against humanity. Though her sentencing hearing began in December, the judges could take several months to reach a decision. Other charges against

Former Bosnian Serb president Biljana Plavsic, the highest-ranking figure to plead guilty to war crimes before the International Criminal Tribunal for the Former Yugoslavia, awaited sentencing in 2002.

her, including genocide, were dropped. Plavsic, who apologized and expressed remorse for her crimes, could be compelled to testify against other defendants, including Momcilo Krajisnik, her co-defendant and a former high-level adviser to Bosnian Serb Pres. Radovan Karadzic. Karadzic and Bosnian military leader Gen. Ratko Mladic remained at large in 2002.

Also at the ICTY, the trial of Radoslav Brdjanin, a former Bosnian Serb deputy prime minister, produced an ancillary case focusing on the rights of journalists. The case, for which initial arguments were heard in September, focused on an article written by *Washington Post* correspondent Jonathan Randal. Defense attorneys for Brdjanin wanted to question Randal regarding the accuracy of an article he wrote that had been presented as evidence against Brdjanin. More than 30 media organizations joined in the case supporting Randal and arguing for journalistic privilege. Given the interest in and attention to the case, defense attorneys indicated that they might drop the request to force Randal to testify, keeping the ICTY from issuing a ruling on what many perceived as a test case for journalists' rights.

Fifty-three suspects continued to await their trials at the International Criminal Tribunal for Rwanda (ICTR). Following a reward offer of five million dollars,

nine more genocide suspects were arrested in early August. Primary among them was Augustin Bizimungu, former chief of staff of the Rwandan army, who was arrested in Angola. Because of the backlog of cases, Bizimungu, who was charged with 10 counts of genocide, conspiracy to commit genocide, and crimes against humanity, would not go to trial for another year.

Thousands of Cambodians took to the streets in October to call for an international tribunal to bring members of the Khmer Rouge to justice for the atrocities that occurred during their reign in the 1970s. In February, however, the five-year-long talks between the Cambodian government and the UN to establish a tribunal on the models of the ICTY and ICTR broke down. In December the UN General Assembly began considering a UN committee resolution to resume talks.

U.S. Court Decisions Relating to International Law. Basing their claims on the Alien Tort Claims Act and the Torture Victim Protection Act, citizens of Zimbabwe brought a class-action suit in a federal court in New York against Zimbabwe Pres. Robert Mugabe and his foreign minister, Stan Mudenge, individually and as officers of the Zimbabwe African National Union–Patriotic Front (ZANU-PF). Mugabe, Mudenge, and ZANU-PF were accused of having orchestrated a campaign of violence against their political opposition, the Movement for Democratic Change. Mugabe and Mudenge were served while they were in New York City for a UN conference. Backed by the U.S. Department of State, the men requested dismissal of the case.

In February the U.S. District Court for the Southern District of New York agreed to dismiss charges against Mugabe and Mudenge on the basis of diplomatic and sovereign immunity. The court stated that it had to consider the potential harm to diplomatic relations and the request of the State Department in making its determination. The court allowed the charges against ZANU-PF to stand, arguing that there was a difference between suing a head of state and suing a group with which he was associated. The court rejected the U.S. government's claim that there was absolute inviolability for the leaders under international law that would extend to whether they could be served process as representatives of a group such as the ZANU-PF. The court specified that the purpose of diplomatic and head-of-state immunity was not to protect those who

abused human rights but rather to protect diplomatic relations, and diplomatic relations were jeopardized less by the case against ZANU-PF. The court did, however, recognize the continuing interest of the U.S. government in the case in allowing it to appeal the final judgment. (VICTORIA WILLIAMS)

COURT DECISIONS

The 2001–02 term of the United States Supreme Court was notable for many reasons. The year marked the 30th anniversary—and arguably the most influential year—of Chief Justice William Rehnquist's tenure on the bench. The composition and character of the court were far different from those of the court he had joined during the twilight of the Earl Warren era. The year also marked the longest period of personnel continuity since the early 19th century, with no member of the bench possessing fewer than eight years of service. Moreover, seven of the nine justices had been appointed by Republican presidents, so the stability of the court had been favourable to conservative issues. Rehnquist, originally a frequent dissenter, had emerged as the leader of both the institution and the conservative bloc that had secured victories, many of them narrow (28% of all cases in the 2001–02 session were decided by 5–4 margins), in a number of important areas of constitutional law.

Perhaps the most significant ruling of the term was in the case of *Zelman* v. *Simmons-Harris*. The case pertained to a movement in a number of states to consider alternatives to "failing" public educational institutions. The issue that gave rise to the case was the city of Cleveland's policy of providing "school vouchers," financial assistance for students to attend schools of their choice. An estimated 96% of the recipients of vouchers elected to use them in private religious institutions. The implications for the establishment clause (the First Amendment prohibition on the government's making law on the establishment of religion) were abundantly clear; indeed, the prevailing wisdom among opponents of the law had been that the policy blatantly violated the separation of church and state. The present court, however, considered "accommodationist" on freedom of religion, upheld the school-voucher program. The pivotal element of the law—and the court's opinion—was neutrality. Rehnquist wrote for the majority that because the program provided benefits to a "wide spectrum of individuals, defined only by financial need and residence in a particular school district," it constituted "a genuine choice among options public and private, secular and religious."

In a second education-related case, *Board of Education* v. *Earls,* the court upheld the right of schools to administer drug tests randomly to students involved in extracurricular activities. Turning back a claim that the privacy rights of students would be surrendered under such a policy, Justice Clarence Thomas distinguished between the rights of adults and those of minors and championed the broad authority of schools to undertake measures designed to create a disciplined, safe, and healthy learning environment for students. Citing the "custodial responsibility" of the schools, he persuaded a bare majority that such initiatives justified "greater controls [for students] than those appropriate for adults."

The court's interest in protecting minors from another vice—pornography—was addressed in the case of *Ashcroft* v. *Free Speech Coalition.* By a vote of 6–3, the court struck down the Child Pornography Prevention Act of 1996, which criminalized the creation, distribution, and possession of digitally created or manipulated ("virtual") child pornography. In his majority opinion, Justice Anthony Kennedy did not question the government's interest in halting the proliferation of child pornography but noted that the virtual format at issue here distinguished the medium from pornography per se. On that distinction in particular, and artistic expression in general, he wrote that "the Constitution gives significant protection from over-broad laws that chill speech within the First Amendment's vast and privileged sphere."

In a more limited ruling concerning the proliferation of "harmful" materials via the Internet, the court decided in *Ashcroft* v. *ACLU* that the Child Online Protection Act of 1998's dependence on community standards in a global digital domain, though inherently questionable, did not "by itself render the statute substantially overbroad" and therefore unconstitutional. The substantive elements of the law neglected by the intermediate appellate court would, by this ruling, be reexamined by the federal appeals court in Philadelphia and almost certainly serve as a foundation for further scrutiny by the Supreme Court during its 2002–03 term.

A third major freedom of speech case involved the scope of protection afforded commercial speech. In *Thompson* v. *Western States Medical Center,* Justice Sandra Day O'Connor led a bare majority in declaring unconstitutional a federal ban on the advertisement of compounded pharmaceuticals (medications designed by pharmacists to treat the specific needs of a patient). Because the medications are created by pharmacists, they are not subjected to standard drug approval processes. The ban was exacted to protect consumers from the effects of such drugs in the absence of information common to ordinary prescriptions. Reasoning that "regulating speech must be a last—not first—resort," O'Connor found such broad a priori legal remedies to be a violation of speech rights.

In *Rush Prudential HMO Inc.* v. *Moran,* the court sided with patients in claims against managed-care companies. In a 5–4 ruling joined by Justices Stephen Breyer, Ruth Bader Ginsburg, O'Connor, and John Paul Stevens, Justice David Souter held that Employee Retirement Income Security Act rules did not apply to cases in which patients were denied medically recommended treatments. State laws mandating independent medical reviews of denied-treatment claims were therefore upheld.

In the area of criminal law, the court decided four important cases—two involving capital punishment and two involving the constitutional rights of sex offenders. The death penalty cases raised both substantive and procedural questions.

Substantively, the court ruled in *Atkins* v. *Virginia* that the imposition of the death penalty in cases involving mentally retarded defendants violated the Eighth Amendment's protection against cruel and unusual punishment. On the basis of "evolving standards of decency," the majority, led by Justice Stevens, held that mentally retarded persons "do not act with the level of moral culpability that characterizes the most serious adult criminal conduct" and that to impose the same lethal sentence would compromise the principle of fairness in capital cases. Procedurally, the court struck down protocol in five states that allowed judges, rather than juries, to determine whether the prosecution had successfully demonstrated the aggravating circumstances necessary for imposition of the death penalty in capital cases. Without questioning the constitutional validity of capital punishment itself, the court ruled 7–2 in *Ring* v. *Arizona* that fair trials required jury involvement in the

fact-finding process relevant to death penalty cases. (*See* Special Report.)

Both sex offense cases involved Kansas laws, one of which was designed to protect citizens and the other of which was intended to rehabilitate perpetrators. In *Kansas* v. *Crane,* the court clarified the rules governing postdetention civil confinement. In a 7–2 ruling the court held that civil confinement could be imposed only if it could be proved that a convicted sexual offender was still dangerous, likely to repeat the crime, and experiencing "serious difficulty in controlling behavior." In *McKune* v. *Lile,* a sharply divided court upheld the state's Sexual Abuse Treatment Program. The act penalized inmates who refused to participate in a program that required them to reveal (and potentially stand accountable for) other crimes they had committed prior to their current conviction. To Justice Kennedy both the means and the ends (both geared toward reducing recidivism) were legitimate and the therapy designed to cure the problem did not amount to coerced self-incrimination, as the dissenters contended.

The Supreme Court also continued its interest in cases involving Americans with disabilities. In three separate cases the court sided with employers and limited the recourse of workers. In the case of *Toyota Motor Manufacturing Inc.* v. *Williams,* the court clarified the qualifications for claiming a disability, deciding unanimously that disabilities had to limit not only specific job-performance activity but also general abilities "central to daily life." In *US Airways* v. *Barnett,* the court limited the breadth of requirements designed to accommodate disabled worker job transfers in light of governing seniority rules; arguing that the law would treat unfairly employees whose security depends on company seniority plans, the court ruled that such transfers do not constitute a "reasonable accommodation" of disabled workers under the Americans with Disabilities Act. In *Chevron USA* v. *Echazabal,* the court ruled unanimously that the Americans with Disabilities Act could not be interpreted as requiring potential employees to hire individuals whose existing health status might be jeopardized by job requirements.

Despite the significance of the year's Supreme Court rulings, the one case that emerged as perhaps the most salient and controversial came from the U.S. Court of Appeals in San Francisco. On the eve of the Fourth of July, the court decided

Kindergartners recite the Pledge of Allegiance in Elk Grove, Calif., a day after a federal appeals court ruled that reciting the pledge in public schools was an unconstitutional "endorsement of religion."

AP/Wide World Photos

a case questioning the constitutionality of the phrase "under God" in the Pledge of Allegiance. In a ruling that earned front-page coverage coast-to-coast the following day, the court declared that the utterance of those words by teachers in their classrooms amounted to an unconstitutional interference with students' freedom of religion.

(BRIAN SMENTKOWSKI)

CRIME

Terrorism. Throughout the year a relentless international hunt continued to bring to justice those responsible for the Sept. 11, 2001, terrorist attacks in the U.S. In September Pakistani authorities arrested a key al-Qaeda operative, 30-year-old Yemen native Ramzi Binalshibh, in Karachi. Binalshibh was believed to have been designated as the 20th hijacker on September 11, but he had failed in his attempts to gain a visa for entry into the U.S. in order to participate in the attacks. Until his capture, Binalshibh had last been seen in Hamburg, Ger., where he reportedly had been a roommate of Mohammed Atta, believed to have been the leader of the September 11 hijackers. By his own admission, Binalshibh provided logistic support to the hijackers. He was soon handed over to U.S. authorities and moved out of Pakistan to an undisclosed location for further interrogation.

Some successes were also claimed by U.S. officials in striking against suspected terrorist plots while they were still in their embryonic stages. A total of at least 15 persons, many of them American citizens, were arrested by federal officials in separate terrorism cases in Lackawanna, N.Y.; Detroit, Mich.; Seattle, Wash.; and Portland, Ore. In early October U.S. federal courts dealt with two highly publicized prosecutions. In Alexandria, Va., John Walker Lindh, a 21-year-old American citizen, received a 20-year prison sentence after pleading guilty to the charges of having aided the Taliban in Afghanistan and carried explosives. In Boston, Richard C. Reid, a British citizen who admitted membership in al-Qaeda, pleaded guilty to charges of having attempted to blow up a trans-Atlantic flight in December 2001 with explosives hidden in his shoes.

Despite these successes, there were ominous indications that al-Qaeda was far from being a spent force. On October 12 two powerful bomb explosions ripped apart a packed nightclub and its surrounding area at Kuta Beach, a popular tourist resort on the Indonesian island of Bali. The blast and ensuing fire claimed the lives of at least 180 people and injured more than 300. The majority of those killed or injured were Australians, but the death toll also included other foreign tourists as well as many Balinese. This was by far the worst international terrorist atrocity since September 11; according to CIA Director George Tenet, it represented a regrouping by al-Qaeda and a determination to execute new attacks against targets in the U.S. and overseas.

In May the U.S. Department of State reported that during 2001, despite the horrific events of September 11, the number of international terrorist attacks declined to 346, down from 426 the previous year. A total of 3,547 persons were killed in these attacks, the highest annual death toll ever recorded. Ninety percent of the fatalities were the result of the events of September 11. In August 2002 one of the world's most dangerous and sought-after terrorists, Abu Nidal, died in Baghdad, the Iraqi capital, where he had been granted sanctuary. (*See* OBITUARIES.)

Drug and Human Trafficking. In February the International Narcotics Control Board (INCB) warned governments that they needed to address the challenges that new technologies posed to drug-law enforcement in an era of increasing globalization. The INCB urged the development of a UN Convention on Cybercrime to combat organized criminal groups that were exploiting the Internet to facilitate their drug-trafficking activities. The INCB also confirmed that in 2001 opium poppy production in Afghanistan fell by more than 90% following a ban by the Taliban on the cultivation of this crop. With the fall of the Taliban regime, poppy growing was believed to have resumed on a large scale despite the best efforts of the new interim government to eradicate opium production.

Experts on both sides of the U.S.-Mexican border warned that drug smuggling was becoming a much easier mission after a shift of focus in law-enforcement priorities as a result of September 11. With the FBI and other agencies involved almost exclusively in combating terrorism in 2002, it was estimated that as few as 10% of the personnel once devoted to interdicting the flow of drugs remained in place.

At an international conference on child trafficking held in Rome in July, charitable organizations reported that a growing number of adolescent girls from Eastern Europe were being sold into sex slavery. Each year more than 6,000 children between the ages of 12 and 16 were being smuggled into Western Europe. According to a UNICEF report given at the conference, the victims of human traffickers were in general becoming younger, and the criminal gangs were using more sophisticated techniques to prevent apprehension. The UNICEF report suggested that it was time to devote more effort to prosecuting traffickers rather than simply returning victims to their countries of origin.

Murder and Other Violence. Preliminary figures released in June from the FBI's Uniform Crime Reporting Program indicated that in 2001 the Crime Index, comprising murder, forcible rape, robbery, aggravated assault, burglary, larceny theft, and motor vehicle theft, increased by 2%. The increase, which was the first of its kind in almost a decade, came after steady inroads had been made against serious crime during the 1990s. While criminologists cautioned against drawing sweeping conclusions about crime trends on the basis of a single year, they emphasized that local police departments were now facing severe resource constraints as they confronted new and complex demands of fighting terrorism together with routine crime. The FBI figures, which excluded offenses arising directly from the events of September 11, showed that among violent crimes robbery had the greatest increase, rising by nearly 4%.

In Europe a spate of mass shootings and other gun-related crimes caused widespread concern that a problem that had long been viewed mainly as one afflicting only the U.S. was spreading across the Atlantic. On March 27 in the Paris suburb of Nanterre, a disturbed 33-year-old man walked into a municipal council meeting wielding a pair of automatic pistols and shot dead eight councillors and wounded more than a dozen other people. The man was arrested but subsequently jumped to his death while in police custody. On April 26, in one of the worst school shootings ever, 18 people were killed at a school in Erfurt, Ger. The gunman, a 19-year-old student who had recently been expelled, roamed the corridors of the school on a killing spree before taking his own life as police commandos closed in to apprehend him.

Sniper attacks over a roughly three-week span in October brought normal life to a halt in Washington, D.C., and its surrounding suburbs. Authorities eventually arrested two suspects—41-year-old John Allen Muhammad and his 17-year-old companion, John Lee Malvo—for a shooting spree that claimed the lives of 10 persons and wounded 3 others. The arrests came after a series of critical breaks in the case, which reportedly included a reference that one of the snipers made to police about an earlier crime, a robbery-murder in Montgomery, Ala., in September. The attacks had baffled investigators. Each of the victims had been selected seemingly at random and shot from long range with a high-pow-

Sniper suspects John Lee Malvo (left) and John Allen Muhammad were arrested in the early morning of October 24 at an interstate rest stop in Maryland.

ered rifle. Several eyewitness accounts proved misleading, and a motive for the crimes was not immediately clear. Muhammad faced a number of federal charges as well as murder prosecutions in Maryland, Virginia, and Alabama. Malvo, though a juvenile, could be executed if found guilty of capital murder in Virginia, where he and Muhammad were to be tried first.

White-Collar Crime, Corruption, and Fraud. Throughout much of the year, a seemingly endless stream of scandals continued to be uncovered involving some of the largest corporations in the U.S. The scandals shook public confidence in Wall Street and prompted calls for tougher measures to prevent executives from falsifying accounts and plundering company coffers at the expense of shareholders. In an attempt to assuage critics and shame those involved, regulators paraded an array of handcuffed white-collar defendants to the courthouse. These included Andrew S. Fastow, the former chief financial officer of Enron, a firm once ranked as the seventh largest in the U.S. In October Fastow was charged before a federal court in Houston with having engaged in a vast scheme to use off-the-books partnerships fraudulently to disguise the company's financial performance while enriching himself with millions in Enron funds. In a display of bipartisanship in August, the U.S. Congress gave overwhelming support to broad new regulatory measures for businesses and their auditors and enacted stiffer penalties for those who committed financial fraud.

In April, A. Alfred Taubman, the principal owner and former chairman of Sotheby's, an international auction house, was sentenced by a federal court in New York City to one year in prison and a fine of $7.5 million. Taubman had been convicted in December 2001 of

having conducted a price-fixing scheme with rival auction house Christie's and its former head Anthony Tennant. Tennant, who was also indicted for his role in the scheme, refused to leave England in order to face trial in the U.S. In separate proceedings Sotheby's pleaded guilty to price fixing and paid a $45 million fine while both Sotheby's and Christie's also settled a civil suit brought by duped customers by agreeing to pay them more than $512 million. In December American financier George Soros was convicted in a French court of insider trading and fined $2.2 million.

Law Enforcement. In the aftermath of September 11, U.S. law-enforcement and intelligence agencies came under intense scrutiny to determine whether lapses in their counterterrorism activities had allowed al-Qaeda to launch its deadly attack. Hearings were held as part of an aggressive congressional inquiry into intelligence failures, and many concluded that both the FBI and the CIA had missed warning signals of the attack and had focused too much attention on threats overseas rather than upon a terrorist assault on U.S. soil. To prevent failures of this type from occurring in the future, radical changes began to be implemented in the structure, mission, and powers of the FBI and other key law-enforcement bodies in the U.S. In May U.S. Attorney General John Ashcroft (*see* BIOGRAPHIES) announced comprehensive revisions to the FBI's investigative guidelines. Ashcroft stated that in the future the war against terrorism would represent the central mission and highest priority of the FBI and that there would be early and aggressive investigation where information existed to suggest a possible terrorist threat.

In June U.S. Pres. George W. Bush, outlining the most ambitious reorganization of the government's national security structure in half a century, urged Congress to create a Department of Homeland Security to coordinate intelligence about terrorism and tighten the nation's domestic defenses. More than a dozen existing federal entities, including the Immigration and Naturalization Service, the Customs Service, and the Coast Guard, were to be amalgamated into this new department, whose employee strength would be exceeded only by the Department of Defense and the Department of Veteran Affairs. The president's proposal at first received enthusiastic bipartisan support, but congressional approval was (continued on page 232)

The Death Penalty on Trial

by Andrew Rutherford

An electric chair in which 315 convicts met their death is dismantled at the Southern Ohio Correctional Facility, Lucasville, in February 2002.

AP/Wide World Photos

Along with the report in 2002 that the number of executions carried out worldwide in 2001—3,048—was more than double the 1,457 known to have taken place in 2000 came the news that more than 90% of them had occurred in just four countries—China, Iran, Saudi Arabia, and the United States. This dramatic increase has been attributed to the Chinese government's "strike hard" anticrime campaign, during which 1,781 people were executed in only four months. Internationally, however, the trend has moved toward abolishing the death penalty. At the end of 2001, according to Amnesty International, 84 countries were retentionist, while 111 countries were abolitionist in law or practice—a considerable increase from the 63 at the end of 1981. In fact, every year since 1997 the United Nations Commission on Human Rights has adopted a resolution on the death penalty that calls on all retentionist states to, among other things, establish a moratorium on executions with a view to eventual abolition. Following the adoption of the resolution at the commission's annual session in Geneva in April 2001, however, 60 states—mostly African, Middle Eastern, and Asian countries but also the U.S.—issued a joint statement disassociating themselves from the resolution.

In the U.S., 38 of the 50 states provide for the death penalty in law. Since January 1977— when Gary Gilmore became the first person to be executed after the Supreme Court's lifting of the moratorium it had imposed on the death penalty five years earlier— 820 people have been executed in the country, 677 of them since 1991. During the past 25 years, though, as many as 100 persons have also been exonerated after having received a death sentence.

Fueling the questions regarding the possibility that innocent persons have been executed in the U.S. was a study published in 2002 by James Liebman and colleagues at Columbia University, New York City, that found that the overall rate of prejudicial error—an error so serious that it would normally require a new trial—in the American capital punishment system was 68%. The research also found that 82% of defendants whose capital judgments were overturned owing to serious error were given a sentence less than death after the errors were corrected on retrial, and a further 7% were found not to be guilty of a capital offense. The study thus claimed to have revealed "a death penalty system collapsing under the weight of its own mistakes."

In October 2001 Gerald Mitchell was executed by lethal injection for a murder he committed when he was 17. Mitchell was the 18th person in the U.S. to be executed during the modern era for a crime committed as a juvenile. His execution took place in spite of international pleas for clemency. Only seven countries are known to have put juvenile offenders to death since 1990. While Mitchell was only the 13th juvenile offender to have been executed worldwide since 1997, nine of these executions took place in the U.S.

Similar pleas for clemency were also made for Alexander Williams, who had been scheduled to be executed in February 2002. Williams was 17 when, in 1986, he kidnapped, raped, and murdered Aleta Carol Bunch. He also had a history of childhood abuse and suffered from schizophrenia and paranoid delusions. The Georgia Board of Pardons and Paroles, citing the exceptional circumstances of the case, granted clemency. The question of whether the mentally ill should face the death penalty was raised again a month later by the highly publicized case of Andrea Yates, a Texas mother who had struggled with mental illness for a number of years before drowning her five children in a bathtub. Prosecutors in Houston uncharacteristically stopped short of asking for a death sentence, and the jury—consisting of four men and eight women—took just 35 minutes to decide on life imprisonment rather than the death penalty for Yates.

In 1989 the Supreme Court decided in *Penry* v. *Lynaugh* that, since only two of the states with the death penalty explicitly outlawed execution of the mentally retarded, "there [was] insufficient evidence of a national consensus" for an Eighth Amendment argument that the practice amounted to "cruel and unusual punishment." By accepting in 2002 the case of Daryl Atkins, who was an 18-year-old high-school dropout with an IQ of 59 when he abducted and murdered Eric Nesbitt, the court took the opportunity to reconsider this finding.

Executions by country in 2001	
China	2,468
Iran	139
Saudi Arabia	79
United States	66
Other countries	296
TOTAL	3,048

THE DEATH PENALTY IN THE UNITED STATES

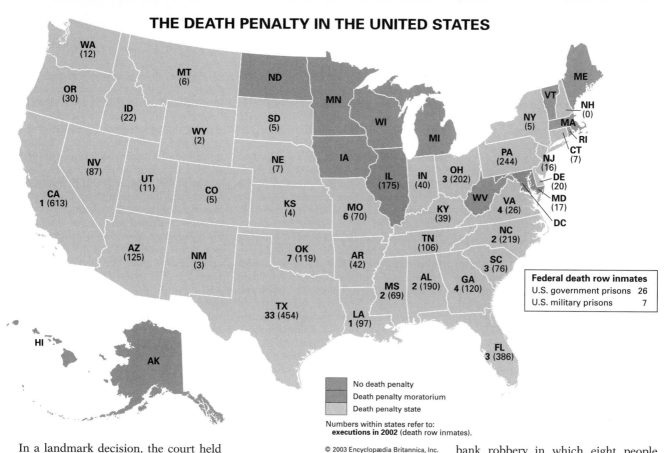

Federal death row inmates
U.S. government prisons	26
U.S. military prisons	7

No death penalty
Death penalty moratorium
Death penalty state

Numbers within states refer to:
executions in 2002 (death row inmates).

© 2003 Encyclopædia Britannica, Inc.

In a landmark decision, the court held by a 6–3 majority that executing mentally retarded persons did indeed constitute cruel and unusual punishment.

The issue of racial bias in the American capital punishment system was raised in a 2001 study undertaken by researchers at the University of North Carolina at Chapel Hill. The study found that of all homicide cases before the courts in North Carolina between 1993 and 1997, the odds of being sentenced to death increased three and a half times if the victim was white rather than black. In the U.S. whites account for approximately half of all murder victims, yet 83% of all capital cases involve white victims, and while during the modern era only 12 whites have been executed for murdering blacks, 170 black people have been put to death for murdering whites.

In 2000 Illinois Gov. George Ryan declared an indefinite death penalty moratorium in his state after the release of 13 death row inmates whose convictions were flawed. He also set up a commission, which completed a two-year study of the death penalty in April 2002. While the commission did not go so far as to call for the abolition of capital punishment, it did propose measures such as reducing the number of crimes eligible for the death penalty from 20 to 5, improving the mechanism for appointing competent attorneys in capital cases, and eliminating the death penalty when convictions are based solely on the word of jailhouse informants. In 2002 Maryland Gov. Parris Glendening declared a moratorium in his state.

Over the past 25 years, the international climate on the death penalty has changed dramatically. An estimated 50 countries abolished the death penalty for all offenses during this period, and a further 12 abolished it for all ordinary crimes. By contrast, only four abolitionist countries have reintroduced the death penalty since 1985, and one of these (Nepal) has since abolished it again, while two of the others (Gambia and Papua New Guinea) have not yet carried out any executions. The trend toward abolition continued in 2002: the Serbian parliament abolished the death penalty in February; the Cuban government applied a de facto moratorium on executions; and Taiwan and Kyrgyzstan took steps toward abolition. Furthermore, a decision of the U.K. Privy Council in March held that mandatory death penalty laws constituted "inhuman and degrading punishment or other treatment" and so violated the constitutions of Belize and six other Caribbean states.

In the midst of this movement toward abolition, calls were still being made for capital punishment. In May 2002 outgoing Hungarian Prime Minister Viktor Orban, in response to a violent bank robbery in which eight people were killed, called for the country to reconsider its ban of the death penalty. In Russia the State Council and National Assembly of Dagestan approved an appeal to Pres. Vladimir Putin to reinstate the death penalty following a bombing during a World War II Victory Day parade that killed 42 people. In the U.S. the first federal executions in 38 years were carried out when terrorist bomber Timothy McVeigh and, a few days later, Juan Raul Garza died by lethal injection in June 2001.

One leading law scholar, Roger Hood of the University of Oxford, concluded that while the pace for abolition has increased over the past 35 years, notably in Europe, any immediate prospects that retentionist countries are likely to change course seem remote. Antiterrorist proposals—including expansion of the death penalty—were made in several U.S. states following the events of Sept. 11, 2001, and overall the consequential international unease has made the apparent trend toward abolition highly problematic. In many regions of the globe, at least for the foreseeable future, the death penalty appears likely to remain an instrument of criminal policy.

Andrew Rutherford is a Professor of Law and Criminal Policy at the University of Southampton, Eng., and the author of Transforming Criminal Policy *(1996).*

(continued from page 229)
delayed until November. On November 25 President Bush signed the homeland security bill and named Tom Ridge, the White House domestic security adviser, head of the new Department of Homeland Security.

In May Robert P. Hanssen, considered one of the most damaging spies in U.S. history, was sentenced by a federal court in Alexandria, Va., to life imprisonment without the possibility of parole. Hanssen, who was a 25-year veteran counterintelligence agent of the FBI, apologized for 21 years of spying for Moscow. His sentence followed a plea agreement in July 2001 that spared him the death penalty in exchange for his cooperation.

In July a public inquiry in Britain concluded that Harold Shipman, a family doctor convicted in January 2000 of having killed 15 elderly patients with lethal injections of diamorphine, was in fact responsible for the deaths of at least 215 of his patients. The inquiry, conducted by British High Court Justice Dame Janet Smith, found that Shipman had murdered 171 women and 44 men over a period of 23 years. Smith said that it was deeply disturbing that Shipman's actions did not arouse suspicion for so many years and that the public health and legal systems that should have safeguarded his patients against his misconduct failed to operate satisfactorily. In a second and ongoing phase of the inquiry, a proposal was made to examine how one of the world's most prolific serial killers was able to avoid detection by law-enforcement agencies and what measures could prevent this from happening again.

(DUNCAN CHAPPELL)

PRISONS AND PENOLOGY

The global prison population in 2002 exceeded 8.75 million, with approximately half of these prisoners held in Russia, China, and the U.S. Prison populations rose in 69% of the world's countries, but the prison population rate in China remained stable at 110 per 100,000 inhabitants, while in Russia it was 665, despite the amnesties of more than 100,000 prisoners in recent years. The highest prison population rate in the world was in the U.S.—700 per 100,000 residents—although the 1.1% increase in the prison population during 2001 was the lowest annual increase recorded since 1972. This was due in part to the efforts of Texas, Louisiana, and Mississippi, the states with the highest rates of incarceration, to limit the growth of their prison populations. In Europe the highest prison population rate for any country was 130 in Portugal, slightly higher than the rate of 125 in Britain, while the Scandinavian countries of Finland (50), Denmark (60), and Sweden (65) had the lowest rates.

Human rights groups objected to the treatment of al-Qaeda and Taliban detainees at Camp X-Ray at the U.S. naval base at Guantánamo Bay, Cuba, after photographs surfaced of blindfolded and shackled detainees kneeling inside wire cages. The U.S. government maintained that the photos were taken as prisoners were being processed and insisted that they were being treated humanely. Prisoners in Turkey continued to protest their conditions; about 50 prisoners starved to death in hunger strikes during these protests. In Sri Lanka 400 prisoners seized control of Tangalla prison for two days, taking at least 10 staff members hostage, to demand better conditions and quicker bail applications. More than 400 prisoners rioted in a juvenile detention centre in Thailand when a protest over conditions at the jail turned violent.

Violence also occurred in Urso Branco prison in northern Brazil, where at least 27 inmates were killed during fighting between rival gangs within the prison. In Haiti armed supporters of a local leader drove a bulldozer through a prison wall, freeing him and some 150 other inmates. In Scotland a standoff occurred at Shotts prison, during which prisoners caused significant damage after an electrical storm caused a power outage in the prison. Inmates in a high-security jail in Algiers set fire to their mattresses, starting a blaze that killed 14 prisoners.

DEATH PENALTY

The gradual movement toward worldwide abolition of the death penalty continued during the year. (See SPECIAL REPORT.) A World Coalition Against the Death Penalty, representing many national and international anti-capital punishment organizations, was formally constituted, and the Council of Europe adopted Protocol 13 to the European Convention on Human Rights—the first legally binding international treaty to abolish the death penalty in all circumstances with no exceptions.

The two republic parliaments of Serbia and Montenegro abolished capital punishment in 2002 to clear the way for Yugoslavia's admittance to the Council of Europe. To increase its chances of joining the EU, Turkey replaced capital punishment with life imprisonment without parole for all peacetime offenses. Taiwan's legislature reduced the scope of the mandatory death penalty, and the Tanzanian president commuted to life imprisonment the death sentences of 100 people. The U.S. Supreme Court held that executing the mentally retarded and any form of sentencing by a judge in capital cases were both unconstitutional. Nearly 800 of the 3,700 death row inmates in the U.S. had been sentenced without the protections extended by the latter decision.

In contrast to this global trend, the outgoing Hungarian prime minister called for his country to reconsider its ban on capital punishment. In addition, the events of Sept. 11, 2001, led to antiterrorist proposals, including expansion of the death penalty, in several U.S. states, with legislators in two states, Iowa and Wisconsin, proposing the reintroduction of capital punishment. Elsewhere, death penalties were imposed for nonviolent offenses; in Saudi Arabia three men were publicly beheaded following convictions for homosexual acts, and in Nigeria a young mother was sentenced to death by stoning for having committed adultery and given birth to a child out of wedlock.

(ANDREW RUTHERFORD)

A 30-year-old Nigerian Muslim woman, Amina Lawal, shown here with her eight-month-old daughter, Wasila, faced death by stoning after her conviction on adultery charges.

Libraries and Museums

FUNDING PROBLEMS, damage to structures by man-made and natural disasters, and questions about the preservation of **CIVIL LIBERTIES** were some of the issues that overshadowed the jubilation over the construction in 2002 of **EXTRAVAGANT NEW LIBRARIES AND MUSEUMS.**

LIBRARIES

By early 2002 libraries in Afghanistan—which had been devastated by fighting or shuttered by the Taliban— had reopened. Though the facilities had little to offer readers, not even light to read by, children returned. Female staff resumed work, and men visited without fear of conscription. To Afghanis the symbolism of the reopenings was profound.

In the aftermath of the Sept. 11, 2001, terrorist attacks in the U.S., alarms were raised concerning the perceived threat to long-standing American library freedoms. The USA PATRIOT Act, passed with virtually no congressional debate just six weeks after the attacks, overrode laws in nearly every state that had made library records confidential. Law-enforcement officials investigating terrorism or national security could demand information on what a person had read or where an Internet search had taken them. Library workers who revealed such a demand to a co-worker or supervisor were guilty of a crime.

By May 2002 Attorney General John Ashcroft (*see* BIOGRAPHIES) had given the FBI new powers to monitor individuals in libraries, churches, political gatherings, and other public places and had thereby rescinded restrictions enacted in the 1970s. Associations of librarians and booksellers and members of Congress protested the threat to civil liberties. Throughout the year American library workers wrestled to balance compliance with professional ethics. (*See* SOCIAL PROTECTION: *Special Report.*)

Other procedures also changed. At the Library of Congress (LC), which received 22,000 pieces of mail daily, irradiation of mail following the anthrax attacks damaged or destroyed many documents, tapes, photos, and other media. An indeterminate number of the damaged materials had been sent by authors or publishers to secure copyright.

American libraries also faced other legal challenges. A federal district court struck down the Children's Internet Pornography Act (CIPA) in May. CIPA denied federal funds to libraries that had not installed Internet filtering software. The American Library Association, one of the plaintiffs, successfully argued that filters block constitutionally protected speech while failing to block pornography effectively. The Justice Department later announced that it would appeal the decision to the Supreme Court. In April the European Parliament voted 460–0, with three abstentions, against installing filters.

Conflicts in other regions also afflicted libraries. The dedication of the Bibliotheca Alexandrina, the much-publicized successor to the fabled Library of Alexandria, had been postponed from April by Egyptian Pres. Hosni Mubarak in light of Palestinian-Israeli hostilities but finally took place with some 3,000 foreign dignitaries in attendance on October 17.

Library-funding problems were grave in 2002. Many German cities sold public hospital clinics, libraries, and swimming pools to cut deficits. Employee strikes over compensation affected the British Library and libraries at the University of California, Berkeley. Plummeting stock prices eroded the endowments of libraries that had such assets. Public libraries in South Africa reduced services and struggled to forestall closing. In Washington, the Seattle Public Library closed for two weeks owing to operating budget shortfalls. Nevertheless, a new $160 million public library for the city was under construction. A number of other closures were barely averted, and many libraries reduced hours and services.

Even as many libraries struggled financially, others looked forward to expansive new facilities. Construction of a 46,450-sq-m (500,000-sq-ft) Parliament Library neared completion in New Delhi. A $90.6 million library was being built in the heart of Montreal that would serve as a centrepiece of Quebec culture.

Information technology offered libraries stunning opportunities to disseminate information. A 700-year-old Qur'an, written in gold, had been digitized by the British Library. An audio commentary was added to explain important parts of the book. The LC digitized high-resolution images of the Gutenberg Bible. Print historians believed that the images might force a reevaluation of Gutenberg's technique. Both projects would be Web accessible. The LC also debuted the "Portals to the World" Web site <http://www.loc.gov/rr/international/portals.html>, which featured up-to-date information on more than 80 countries, including links to digital information in the countries themselves. All nations were expected to be included by 2003. Library consortiums continued to develop 24-hour-a-day online reference services in New Jersey; Cleveland, Ohio; Southern California; Chicago; and other areas. In Zimbabwe donkey-drawn carts were taking e-mail, Internet, fax, and book services to remote areas. The Nkayi District in northwestern Zimbabwe had an 86% literacy rate that an International Federation of Library Associations' report attributed primarily to those mobile libraries.

China's ongoing love-hate relationship with the Web continued. Even as a $20 million Sino-U.S. Digital Library was under construction at Zhejiang University, Hangzhou, the government blocked access to the Google and AltaVista search engines in late August. Speculation about the motive centred on the Communist Party's annual congress, scheduled for November. Chinese state media quoted Pres. Jiang Zemin in August as telling propaganda officials to create a "sound atmosphere" for the gathering. Access to Google reappeared without explanation on September 12, but some content was blocked. AltaVista remained blocked, however.

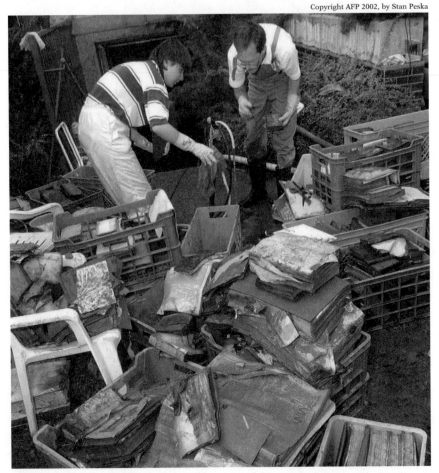

Workers at the Prague Municipal Library attempt to salvage books damaged in the flooding that wreaked havoc across much of Central Europe in August.

Natural and man-made disasters also affected libraries. Floods in Central Europe in August caused damage to libraries in Germany and the Czech Republic. Hardest hit was the Prague Municipal Library. Among the hundreds of damaged books was a 1488 Prague Bible, one of only 12 extant copies. In March welding in a subbasement of the National Library of Canada activated a sprinkler system. Among the materials damaged were government documents, children's books, videotapes, and valuable prints. The NLC had suffered some 72 material-damaging incidents in just 10 years. For the third consecutive year, scores of langur monkeys overran the library at Loreto College in Darjeeling, India. Some 6,000 books were destroyed; furniture was broken; and library users were routed. Speculation about the causes of the attacks focused on deforestation and the possibility that perfumes and plastic bags used by students might have provoked the onslaughts. (THOMAS M. GAUGHAN)

MUSEUMS

On Dec. 9, 2002, the Egyptian Museum in Cairo celebrated its centenary anniversary. To commemorate the occasion, the museum opened its basement vault and displayed some 40 artifacts from its King Tutankhamen collection, including jewelry from his tomb, never before seen by the public. Egypt also announced an architectural competition for a "Great Egyptian Museum" that would be sited near Cairo's pyramids. When completed in about five years, the new museum would house many of the Egyptian Museum's treasures.

A number of museums funded striking architectural statements, continuing a trend toward dramatic, attention-getting museum designs. At the new $40 million Imperial War Museum North in Manchester, Eng., architect Daniel Libeskind's bold forms represented the war zones of land, air, and sea. The Royal Ontario Museum also chose a Libeskind design, a prismatic glass "Crystal," for its approximately $124 million addition. Meanwhile, the Art Gallery of Ontario planned an addition designed by Frank Gehry. In Madrid the Prado Museum prepared for a modern cubelike addition to open in 2004. The National Gallery of Ireland's Millennium Wing, designed by Benson & Forsyth, was praised for its lofty interior spaces and integration with surrounding Irish Georgian buildings.

The Pinakothek der Moderne, devoted to 20th- and 21st-century visual arts, opened in September in Munich, Ger. The 12,000-sq-m (129,000-sq-ft) space held paintings, sculptures, video installations, photographs, drawings, prints, design objects, and architectural models. The Sakip Sabanci Museum, a mansion that opened in Emirgan (a suburb of Istanbul), contained antiques, Islamic calligraphy, and Turkish paintings. In Washington, D.C., the $40 million International Spy Museum opened its doors in July. Visitors could choose a cover identity and subject themselves to a mock interrogation. (*See* photo, page 34.) In Santa Rosa, Calif., the Charles M. Schulz Museum opened, delighting fans of the comic strip *Peanuts*.

In Long Island City, Queens, the Museum of Modern Art (MoMA) moved accessible exhibits—including Van Goghs and exquisite cars—for display in a new temporary space, dubbed MoMAQNS, while its Manhattan site closed for expansion. The renovation was scheduled for completion in late 2004. In Moscow, at the Pushkin State Museum of Fine Arts, previously uncataloged Egyptian collections went on display. A raging fire in the Abdul Rauf Hasan Khalil Museum in Jeddah, Saudi Arabia, completely destroyed one of the three buildings that held some 13,5000 works of art; the museum sustained an estimated $27 million in damages.

Funding bedeviled several museums. In Germany, Peter-Klaus Schuster, secretary-general of the 17 state museums in Berlin, sought $1 billion in government aid to renovate the institutions, aging propaganda tools of the Cold War. The British Museum introduced budget cuts of £6 million (about $9 million), including partial gallery closings, and French national museums estimated a loss of €5.5 million (about $5.4 million) for 2002. Illinois public museums sought $400 million over 10 years in government funds for unglamorous yet much-needed projects, such as replacing zoo sewers.

Underscoring the fact that corporations were among the most powerful museum benefactors and art collectors, the firm UBS PaineWebber promised to give MoMA 37 artworks from its distinctive collection, including *Cagney*, a 1962 Andy Warhol silk screen of the movie star. In Barcelona, Spain's largest savings bank, la Caixa, opened the CaixaForum to display its collection of more than 800 contemporary artworks, including a mural by American artist Sol LeWitt.

A $36.5 million proposed gift—to create a hall of fame of American achievers at the Smithsonian Institution's National Museum of American History—was withdrawn after scholars objected that the donor, Catherine B. Reynolds, wanted popular celebrities to be included in the exhibit and had too much control. Though Smithsonian director Lawrence M. Small had made fundraising a top priority, it was felt that the museum should retain ultimate authority over exhibits.

In London, Charles Saumarez Smith, who during his tenure as director of the National Portrait Gallery saw the number of visitors double to 1.3 million, moved next door to become director of the National Gallery. That museum's di-rector, Neil MacGregor, left to head the British Museum. At the age of 37, Miguel Zugaza became the Prado's youngest director ever, and Serge Lemoine became director of the Musée d'Orsay, Paris. J. Carter Brown, the widely admired former director of the National Gallery of Art in Washington, D.C., for 23 years, died in June. (*See* OBITUARIES.)

The Jewish Museum in New York City sparked outrage with its exhibit of artworks seen as trivializing the Holocaust. The exhibit—which included empty boxes for a mock Lego concentration camp set and a photograph of emaciated Buchenwald concentration camp inmates altered to include the artist raising a can of Diet Coke—was defended by the museum, as signalling to the public that a new generation of artists was drawing on Holocaust and Nazi images in a new way.

Efforts continued to identify artworks in museum collections that had been stolen by Nazis. Twelve museums in Europe and North America faced claims for drawings by Albrecht Dürer that were allegedly stolen during World War II from the Lubomirski Museum in Lvov, Poland (now Lviv, Ukraine). A federal judge granted the U.S. government permission to seek to confiscate a painting lent to MoMA by the Leopold Museum in Vienna, allegedly stolen by a Nazi from a Jew.

A number of museums dealt with foreign claims to antiquities. Egypt demanded the return of a granite relief from the Virginia Museum of Fine Arts in Richmond. The Michael C. Carlos Museum in Atlanta, Ga., announced that it was returning to Egypt an unwrapped royal mummy, allegedly the body of Ramses I. The Princeton University Art Museum returned an ancient Roman relief that had wrongly left Italy. The British Museum declined to return 10 "tabots," sacred wooden images taken by British troops in 1868 and sought by the Ethiopian Orthodox Church. The British Museum also refused to lend the Parthenon (Elgin) Marbles—prized monuments from ancient Greece that had been viewed by millions since the museum acquired them in 1816—to the New Acropolis Museum, scheduled to open in conjunction with the 2004 Olympic Games in Athens.   (MARTHA LUFKIN)

Bold forms characterize the main exhibition space of the newly opened Imperial War Museum North in Manchester, Eng.

Life Sciences

A major **SURPRISE** emerging from **STEM CELL** studies in 2002 was that cells derived from **ADULT DONORS** could develop into more kinds of tissues than previously thought. New findings suggested that the proportion of the world's **PLANTS FACING EXTINCTION** has been greatly underestimated. **SEEDS** were identified in the stomach of a **FOSSIL BIRD** more than 100 million years old.

ZOOLOGY

Insects, the most abundant and diverse group of animals on Earth, were a major focus of research in 2002. An understanding of their evolutionary relationships is based on fossil records dating back more than 390 million years; nevertheless, the first 60 million years of insect evolution derived from paleontological data have remained poorly understood. To examine very early relationships between five insect orders, Michael W. Gaunt and Michael A. Miles of the London School of Hygiene and Tropical Medicine developed a molecular clock based on selected amino acid and DNA data from the proteins and genes of existing insects to trace their origins back to approximately 430 million years ago. A molecular clock dates evolutionary divergence by determining the rate of DNA or amino acid mutations from a known evolutionary time, or calibration point, such as a major group of fossils. In a very slowly evolving gene, for example, a change of a single amino acid in the gene's protein product may occur on average every four million years.

From their molecular clock Gaunt and Miles concluded that insects and fairy shrimps (order Anostraca) were derived from a common ancestor about 430 million years ago, during the transition from the Ordovician to the Silurian Period. Thus, insects emerged as a separate line at the same time that the earliest land plants appeared. The investigators also found that a major group of bloodsucking insects, the triatomines in the order Hemiptera (true bugs), became isolated in South America around

95 million years ago during the breakup of the supercontinent Gondwanaland. All of the findings were consistent with, and augment, earlier interpretations based on the fossil record. Such molecular dating also provided time points for additional studies of more recent evolutionary divergences, such as insect families and genera.

Krill are tiny planktonic crustaceans that are a major prey item for birds, fish, and several whale species. During the year Andrew S. Brierley of the University of St. Andrews, Scot., and colleagues reported the results of a study in which echo sounding from a battery-powered robot submarine was used to survey the distribution and abundance of Antarctic krill (*Euphausia superba*) beneath sea ice and open water. The researchers determined that krill densities were significantly higher under sea ice than in the open ocean. The underwater vehicle continuously recorded under-ice densities of krill for as far inward as 27 km (17 mi) from the ice edge, the highest densities being between 1 and 13 km from the ice edge. The under-ice habitat serves as protection from predators; it is also a favourable habitat for krill because they feed on algae in the melt zone of the ice, where primary productivity is high. The findings helped to explain why krill-eating whales often congregate along the edges of sea ice and to determine how krill distribution and abundance patterns may be affected by anticipated climate changes that could alter ice patterns in the Antarctic.

Does the glow that some bird feathers give off under ultraviolet light have a biological function or merely represent a by-product of pigment structure?

Kathryn E. Arnold of the University of Glasgow, Scot., Ian P.F. Owens of Imperial College at Silwood Park, Eng., and N. Justin Marshall of the University of Queensland, Australia, gained insight into this question after conducting tests on the common shell parakeet, or budgerigar (*Melopsittacus undulatus*), to determine if its fluorescent head plumage is used as a signal. Both sexes have fluorescent yellow plumage on parts of the head that is used for display during courtship. The investigators applied sunblock to key areas of the heads of birds to reduce the amount of ultraviolet light reaching the feathers and stimulating fluorescence. They also treated the heads of a control group of birds with petroleum jelly alone, which does not reduce fluorescence. In subsequent mate-choice trials, both male and female parakeets showed a sexual preference for members of the opposite sex exhibiting strong fluorescence. Neither sex showed a social preference for members of the same sex whether fluorescence was normal or artificially subdued. The investigators suggested that the biochemical pathways that produce fluorescence may be so energetically costly that brightly fluorescent plumage would serve as a true indicator of an individual bird's good health and overall quality to the opposite sex.

Analyses of isotopic ratios figured in two independent studies on New World migrant songbirds. In one, Dustin R. Rubenstein of Dartmouth College, Hanover, N.H., and colleagues used ratios of naturally occurring stable isotopes of carbon and hydrogen in feathers of black-throated blue warblers (*Dendroica caerulescens*) to determine the degree to which birds from different breeding populations in continental North America mix in their Caribbean wintering quarters. The isotope ratios in the feathers become fixed at molting, which in this case was at or near the breeding site, and they reflect the diet of the birds at the time. Thus, the ratios can be used to indicate the breeding origins of birds whose feathers are analyzed. The researchers found that birds wintering on western Caribbean islands migrate from northern areas of North America, whereas those on eastern islands are from more southern regions. Such studies can help assess

Photographs by Justin Marshall, University of Queensland, Australia

Rear and front views of the head of a shell parakeet are compared under white and ultraviolet light (top and bottom, respectively). Researchers from the U.K. and Australia showed that both female and male birds prefer members of the opposite sex whose head feathers have strongly fluorescent patches.

how the loss of wintering habitat affects the size of breeding populations. For example, observed declines in southern breeding populations of black-throated blue warblers could be explained by severe deforestation in Haiti, on the island of Hispaniola, where the southern populations spend the winter.

In an extension of the previous study, Gary R. Graves of the Smithsonian Institution, Washington, D.C., and Christopher S. Romanek and Alejandro Rodriguez Navarro of the Savannah River Ecology Laboratory, Aiken, S.C., used patterns in the ratios of stable carbon and nitrogen isotopes in the warblers' feathers to study their preference for breeding territory in southern Appalachian Mountains. The investigators found that, on their return in spring from their wintering grounds, yearling

males in their first breeding season showed no preference for the altitude of their breeding territory, whereas adult males were strongly inclined to seek altitudes they had occupied the previous year.

Owing to negative public attitudes about snakes, limited research funding, and the secretive nature of the animals themselves, the conservation status and population trends of most snake species are poorly known. Robert N. Reed and Richard Shine of the University of Sydney, Australia, examined Australian snakes to address the question of why some species decline rapidly when disturbed by human activity whereas others readily exploit disturbed habitats. One purpose of the study was to identify ways to predict the vulnerability of a species. The investigators examined more than 18,000 specimens of snakes

of the cobra family (Elapidae) in museums to identify common traits among threatened and nonthreatened species. Most traits that typically correlate with endangerment, such as large body size, low number of offspring, and specialization for particular habitats or prey, were judged to be inapplicable to Australian snakes. Instead, threatened species were characterized by two primary traits related to foraging behaviour and mating systems. Threatened species were generally ambush predators, rather than wide-ranging active foragers, and they did not engage in male-male combat for females. A plausible explanation for the first relationship is that ambush predators do not move long distances in search of prey; consequently, they may be more dramatically affected when habitat disturbance reduces the density of prey. The explanation for the second relationship may be that, because females grow appreciably larger in species without male-male combat, they may be more obvious to humans and therefore more likely to be killed. Once humans alter the habitats of these species, the added impact of the loss of the reproductively important large females may result in rapid population declines. Understanding how specific biological traits may make some species more susceptible to human-caused changes could help identify potentially vulnerable species not currently protected.

Determining the actual number of living species within a region or taxonomic group continued to be a challenging task in efforts to characterize biodiversity. An unsettled question was how closely the number of known species in a phylum represents the actual number in existence. Mollusks in the world's oceans have the highest-known diversity of any animal group, a diversity that is especially high in the tropical Indo-Pacific region. Philippe Bouchet of the National Museum of Natural History, Paris, and colleagues conducted an intensive survey of mollusk species within a 30,000-ha (74,000-ac) site on the west coast of New Caledonia, collecting more than 127,000 specimens of 2,738 species of mollusks—numbers that exceeded any previous surveys. Rare species, represented by single specimens, made up 20% of the species collected. When the data were projected beyond the actual captures by means of a species accumulation curve, the estimated total species ranged from 3,358 to 3,971. The results suggested that current estimates of global biodiversity of mollusks were greatly undercalculated.

(J. WHITFIELD GIBBONS)

BOTANY

The potential dangers of genetically modified (GM) plants continued to be debated in 2002. New research suggested that it would be impossible to avoid interbreeding between GM crops and neighbouring plants, despite the efforts of many governments to impose safety limits around fields of GM plants. Mary Rieger of the University of Adelaide, Australia, monitored the spread of genes from canola (oilseed rape) that had been bred for herbicide resistance and found that the pollen could reach up to three kilometres (almost two miles) away and fertilize small numbers of nonresistant plants.

For the first time, it was shown that weedy relatives can be strengthened considerably by genes passed from nearby GM crops. Researchers found that a gene engineered into sunflower crops to repel moth and butterfly larvae also migrated into closely related weeds and made them more pest-resistant and, surprisingly, more productive. "Weeds are already hardy plants; the addition of transgenes [i.e., artificially inserted genes] could just make them tougher," said Allison Snow, one of the investigators at Ohio State University involved in the study.

The idea that GM crops can provide a powerful weapon against pests received a setback when it was discovered that potato plants that had been genetically engineered to resist sap-sucking insects turned out to be vulnerable to other kinds of pests. Nicholas Birch and his team at the Scottish Crop Research Institute near Dundee examined plants that had been modified to produce lectins, which sap suckers find distasteful. They found that the plants also had lower levels of glycoalkaloids, which repel many other insects.

The debate over the safety of GM crops grew more heated when the science journal *Nature* took the highly unusual step of criticizing in an editorial note (April 11, 2002, issue) a report that it had published the previous November about the leakage of foreign genes from GM corn (maize) into traditional corn crops in Mexico. The note accompanied scientific challenges to the paper that focused primarily on what happened to the genes once they had invaded the native corn. Nevertheless, the original researchers, David

Termites cluster at the pitcher rim of the carnivorous plant Nepenthes albomarginata, *which was found to lure the insects with edible hairs.*

Dennis & Marlis Merbach

Quist and Ignacio Chapela of the University of California, Berkeley, stood by their contention that transgenes had entered traditional strains of corn in Mexico, a development that was accepted as likely by their critics. In addition, a survey of native corn samples in Mexico revealed that as many as 25% in some regions contained GM corn, despite a four-year-old moratorium on planting GM crops in Mexico.

That foreign genes are not always needed to modify a plant genetically was demonstrated by Peter Horton and colleagues at the University of Sheffield, Eng. The researchers developed an ingenious technique that allowed them to make extra copies of a plant gene involved in the production of xanthophyll, a substance that protects plants from intense heat and light, and then reinsert them into the same plant. The result was a plant in which the pool of substances that participate in xanthophyll production are increased, which thus enables the plant to withstand a far harsher climate.

A powerful new herbicide was discovered when scientists identified the biochemical weapon unleashed by spotted knapweed (*Centaurea maculosa*), an aggressive weed that had spread over large areas of the northwestern U.S. Jorge Vivanco of Colorado State University found that the plant's roots secrete catechin into the soil, killing most other plants in the immediate vicinity, apart from grasses. Scientists hoped to exploit catechin as a powerful natural weed killer that leaves grasses and cereal crops, such as wheat and rice, unharmed.

Carnivorous pitcher plants have unusual tubular leaves shaped like urns or small pitchers that collect rainwater in their bases. Insects that walk around the pitcher mouth tend to slip and fall into the pitcher, where they drown and are broken down by digestive enzymes. During the year a carnivorous pitcher plant, *Nepenthes albomarginata*, was reported to use a unique trick to lure termites to its traps. The pitcher rim grows hairs that mimic a favourite food of the termites; once one termite has fed on the hairs, it calls on others to join in, many of which then end up being caught. This degree of specialization on a particular prey was unprecedented for a carnivorous plant.

The oldest seed ever observed to sprout into a fully grown plant was reported by a team headed by Jane Shen-Miller of the University of California, Los Angeles, which succeeded in germinating a 500-year-old lotus seed. Interestingly, the lotus plant showed abnormal growth, which was attributed to prolonged exposure to low-level radiation in the soil in which it had been buried—possibly the world's longest-running radiation experiment. In another experiment on seed longevity, the seeds of two common plants, moth mullein (*Verbascum blattaria*) and common mallow (*Malva rotundifolia*), kept in a bottle of soil since 1879 were also found to be viable, the longest-running test of seed dormancy in soil.

In contrast, a global survey of seeds stored in seed banks revealed that much of the plant material was deteriorating and needed replanting to stay viable, a laborious and costly process at a time when many seed banks were suffering budget cuts and staff shortages. In August the UN Food and Agriculture Organization sanctioned a new international fund, the Global Conservation Trust, with the aim of raising $260 million to help rescue these stocks. Seed banks around the world held some two million varieties of crop plants, an invaluable repository of plant genes vital for agricultural breeding.

At least 22% of the world's plant species could be facing extinction, almost double the rate that had been assumed previously. Peter Jorgensen of the Missouri Botanic Garden, St. Louis, and Nigel Pitman of Duke University, Durham, N.C., based their assessment on the numbers of plant species endemic to each country, which they used as a rough guide to the number threatened. This approach gave a better estimate of endangered species in the tropics, where most of the world's plants grow.

A new national park on the Kitulo Plateau in the southern highlands of Tanzania was established to protect scores of terrestrial orchid species, many of them unique to the region and under threat of extinction from being harvested for their edible tubers. This was the first protected area in tropical Africa set aside primarily to preserve its plant life.

Scientists were heartened when a new and unusual conifer tree was discovered in Vietnam. The mature tree is highly distinctive in bearing two different types of leaves, needles and scale leaves, and it formed a new genus, *Xanthocyparis*. This was only the second new conifer species to be found in the past 50 years. (PAUL SIMONS)

MOLECULAR BIOLOGY

Stem Cell Research. Once of interest mainly to developmental biologists, stem cells stood definitely at centre stage in 2002 in a debate of international proportions involving scientists, healthcare professionals, politicians, theologians, and many others. At stake was the future of a new and potentially very powerful technology that could one day offer treatment, if not cure, for many serious medical conditions such as diabetes, stroke, spinal cord injury, and neurodegenerative disorders such as Parkinson's disease.

At the core of the debate lay the fact that this technology was not entirely artificial—it involved the use of specialized cells called stem cells that are, at least in some cases, of human fetal origin. Whether it was just for any society to use fetal stem cells for biomedical application in living adults or children was clearly a complex question; it was, in essence, the abortion debate reincarnated with a biomedical twist. Nevertheless, not all stem cells are of fetal origin, and new research suggested that with some modification stem cells derived from nonfetal sources, such as adult donors, could prove to be as useful as, or even more useful than, previously studied fetal cell lines.

The term *stem cell* is applied to any living cell that retains the ability not only to replicate itself indefinitely but also to give rise to distinct differentiated cell types. Some stem cells are already somewhat specialized—in addition to replenishing themselves, they can also give rise to only one differentiated cell type or, at most, a small number of related types. These cells typically are referred to in terms of the differentiated tissue they represent—for example, myogenic (muscle) stem cells or hematopoietic (blood) stem cells. In contrast, other stem cells can give rise to a variety of distinct cell types; these are typically called multipotent or pluripotent cells. Finally, some stem cells remain competent to give rise to every possible cell type; these are called totipotent cells.

Although specialized stem cells have been known for many years to exist in the accessible tissues (e.g., blood or bone marrow) of living adults and children, multipotent stem cells historically have been derived only from adult cancers or from embryonic or fetal cells. (In this context, *embryonic* refers to the earliest stages of prenatal development; *fetal* refers to the later stages.) Indeed, until recently only three different types of multipotent mammalian stem cell lines had been isolated: embryonal carcinoma cells, which are embryonic-like cells derived from testicular tumours in adult males; embryonic stem cells, derived from preimplantation embryos (embryos not yet implanted in the lining of the uterus); and embryonic germ cells, derived from primordial germ cells of postimplantation embryos. During 2002, researchers reported that they had derived additional multipotent stem cells from adult bone marrow, offering hope not only to ethicists opposed to the use of fetal cells but also to the biomedical community at large, because using such cells derived from patients themselves might circumvent the problems of host-graft rejection so often seen with cells donated by a second individual. Theoretically at least, multipotent stem cells harvested from a patient could be used to grow any replacement tissue needed by that individual, from new spinal cord neurons to a new heart. Furthermore, if those stem cells could be genetically modified before they were induced to differentiate, then a long list of genetic disorders previously considered incurable or treatable only with high-risk therapies would become reasonable targets for application.

Studies of hematopoietic stem cells (HSCs) from both mice and humans revealed some important statistics about the potential of these cells for proliferation and differentiation and about the success of their subsequent engraftment into a host. In brief, all of these properties vary with the age of the donor, with the youngest cells faring best. For example, HSCs from fetal mouse liver have a greater proliferation potential than do their counterparts harvested from the bone marrow of either younger or older postnatal donors. Furthermore, the proportion of "more specialized" HSCs that can give rise to only red or white cells, but not to both, goes up with age. Finally, stem cells derived from human umbilical-cord blood engraft 10–50 times better than do stem cells derived from adult bone marrow. Although none of these observations precludes the successful use of adult-derived stem cells, each represents a technical hurdle to be overcome if these cells are to become a reliable clinical tool.

Stem cells derived from adult tissues had been believed to be competent only to differentiate into additional cells of the tissue of origin. Thus, adult-derived hematopoietic stem cells could give rise only to blood cells, not to liver or nerve cells. Given that many genetic or degenerative diseases affect tissues (e.g., the brain) that cannot easily be accessed for stem cell harvesting, this limitation of stem cell potential represented a significant problem. In 2002 several reports suggested that stem cells derived from adult bone marrow can, albeit by some as yet poorly understood process, become other types of cells, including skeletal-muscle, cardiac-muscle, lung, skin, liver, and even neuronal cells.

In one major study, Catherine Verfaillie of the University of Minnesota's Stem Cell Institute and colleagues identified a rare cell type within adult human bone-marrow mesenchymal stem cell cultures that could be expanded through more than 80 population doublings and also differentiated in culture into many distinct cell types. Switching to a mouse model to enable further manipulation, the researchers identified similar cells from mouse bone marrow. These cells were cultured and manipulated in the laboratory and then injected back into early blastocyst mouse embryos and followed. Although they were derived originally from adult bone marrow, the descendents of these cells turned up in the injected host embryos in a multitude of different tissue types, including blood and the epithelia of the liver, lung, and gut. Given that these cells, called MAPCs, for multipotent adult progenitor cells, were capable of extended if not indefinite culture in the laboratory and could differentiate and engraft into a multitude of different tissue types in the recipient, they represented a nearly ideal source for therapy of inherited or degenerative diseases. Whether this success in mouse embryos could be duplicated in adult human hosts remained to be determined.

Applications and Issues of Stem Cell Technology. The potential medical applications of human stem cells, especially if they are host-derived, were enormous. For example, for a patient with spinal cord injury, rare multipotent stem cells could be harvested from a sample of bone marrow, expanded in culture, and then returned to the site of the injury to engraft and differentiate into new neurons. For a patient with diabetes, multipotent stem cells could be returned to the appropriate location in the pancreas to engraft and differentiate into insulin-secreting beta cells. Indeed, given that diabetes is an autoimmune disease and that the new beta cells could eventually become depleted as did their predecessors, some of the extracted stem cells could be frozen and the engraftment procedure repeated on an as-needed basis. For a patient with a recessive genetic disorder

Researcher Catherine Verfaillie identified a type of adult stem cell that can differentiate into many cell types.

such as cystic fibrosis (CF), multipotent stem cells could be harvested from bone marrow, genetically engineered in culture to express functional CFTR, the protein defective in CF, and then expanded in culture and returned to the patient's airway epithelium (lungs) and pancreas, the two major organs affected by CF. Such examples represented just the tip of the iceberg.

As with any powerful new technology, myriad political, social, and ethical issues surrounded stem cell research. Perhaps the most obvious ones dealt with human embryo- or fetal-derived stem cells, owing to ethical or religious concerns. To date, different communities and countries had addressed these concerns in their own way, each attempting to balance the desire for new

clinical treatments with the desire to preserve and protect all forms of human life. For example, by late 2000 authorities in Great Britain had allowed for the laboratory creation and use of human embryos up to 14 days old, subject to a government license and strict guidelines. Similar standards had been enacted in Singapore as of 2002. In contrast, Pres. George W. Bush in 2001 decided to restrict the use of federal funds for embryonic stem cell research in the U.S. to work with embryonic cell lines that already existed. The question of how embryonic stem cells may be derived, and how their use will be funded and regulated in different countries, remained unclear. Nonetheless, the great promise of stem cell technology was certain to keep it a topic of hot discussion for years to come.

(JUDITH L. FRIDOVICH-KEIL)

The Origin of Organelles. Cells of eukaryotic organisms—that is, humans and other animals, plants, fungi, and protists—contain membrane-enclosed structures called organelles in which certain specialized activities take place. Mitochondria and chloroplasts, two kinds of organelles that are intimately involved in cellular energy production, possess their own DNA, which encodes a fraction of their own proteins. Mitochondria and chloroplasts also contain the machinery needed to transcribe that DNA into RNA and to translate the RNA into the corresponding proteins. This retained autonomy of protein synthesis, as well as many other similarities between these organelles and free-living prokaryotes—single-celled organisms, such as bacteria, that lack a nuclear membrane and many other components of eukaryotic cells—has led to the view that mitochondria and chloroplasts are descendants of symbiotic prokaryotes that took up residence within primitive eukaryotic cells. During the year this well-accepted hypothesis gained support and insight from two reports that contributed additional details about the mechanism by which these organelles divide. One, by Janet Shaw of the University of Utah and Jodi Nunnari of the University of California, focused on budding yeast; the other, by Shin-ichi Arimura and Nobuhiro Tsutsumi of the University of Tokyo, focused on the green plant *Arabidopsis*.

In prokaryotic cells the binary division that follows replication of the DNA occurs by the pinching of the mother cell into two daughter cells. The contractile protein that causes this pinching is called FtsZ. During division FtsZ assembles into a ring around the equator of the cell; the ring then draws chemical energy from the hydrolysis of the energy-rich molecule guanosine triphosphate (GTP) to power constriction. The chloroplasts of green plants also use FtsZ to carry out binary division. Experimentally inhibiting the production of FtsZ inhibits this division, which ultimately results in the presence of one or only a few giant chloroplasts per cell. In the mitochondria of algae, which are eukaryotic protists, FtsZ is also the motor of binary division and has been observed to assemble into a ring at the site of pinching.

On the other hand, the mitochondria of two other eukaryotes, yeasts and nematodes (roundworms), have been found not to use FtsZ. In its place they use another protein related to a class of proteins called dynamins, which also use the energy of GTP hydrolysis to drive constriction. Likewise, the mitochondria of higher plants such as *Arabidopsis* have been shown to employ the dynamin-related protein. One can thus envision that in primitive mitochondria, division was carried out by FtsZ, as is still the case in bacteria, but at some point in the coevolution of mitochondria and their host eukaryotic cells, the job of constriction was taken over by the dynamin-related protein.

One possible scenario of how this could have happened is based on a postulated intermediate stage of mitochondrial evolution in which both FtsZ and the dynamin-related protein functioned together. Consistent with this hypothesis, FtsZ has been found to form a constricting ring on the inner surface of the inner membrane of gram-negative bacteria, the chloroplasts of green plants, and the mitochondria of red algae. In contrast, the dynamin-like protein forms a similar ring, but on the outer surface of the inner membrane, in green-plant mitochondria. From this evidence one can visualize a transition organism in which both proteins acted together, one on the inner surface of the inner membrane and the other on the outer surface. The existence of such redundancy could then have allowed the loss of FtsZ from the mitochondria in higher plants without loss of constriction function. There may exist as-yet-undiscovered organisms in which mitochondrial division depends on both FtsZ and the dynamin-related protein acting in concert, and their identification would strongly support the evolutionary scenario described above.

Intracellular Rail Transport. A substance made in one part of a cell may be quickly needed in another part of the cell, or it may have to be sent through the cell to be secreted for use elsewhere in the body. In the case of large cells, simple diffusion is far too slow to meet these intracellular-transport requirements. An example is a motor neuron that must transmit signals to a muscle fibre in the lower leg. That neuron has a projecting extension, the axon, that may be more than a metre (3.3 feet) long, yet the nucleus that contains the DNA encoding all the proteins made in that neuron is at one end. How are the proteins, made in the vicinity of the nucleus, moved efficiently to the rest of the cell?

Microscopy reveals an array of thin fibres aligned in the axon and, in addition, numerous membrane-enclosed vesicles, or organelles, attached to and moving along those fibres, much like railroad cars moving along a track. The fibres are called microtubules. Each is a hollow bundle of 13 strands that are composed of a protein called tubulin. Various organelles, some of which may be filled with proteins or neurotransmitters, move along the microtubule tracks, some in one direction and others in the opposite direction. The tiny "locomotive engines" carrying out this movement are proteins called kinesins and dyneins. Kinesins travel in one direction and dyneins in the other. Directed movement requires energy, which the proteins obtain from the hydrolysis of the energy-currency molecule of the cell, adenosine triphosphate (ATP). During the year, David Hackney of Carnegie Mellon University, Pittsburgh, Pa., reported new details regarding the interaction of kinesins and microtubules.

To comprehend the scale involved, it is helpful to know that a microtubule is only 25 billionths of a metre (25 nm [nanometres], or about a millionth of an inch) in diameter. Kinesin is 80 nm long, and it moves along the microtubule in steps of 8 nm, using the energy of one ATP molecule per step. The rate of this movement is about 640 nm per second. Hence, the kinesin protein makes 80 steps per second while pulling along its burden. Because there are several kinds of organelles requiring transport and because each must be recognized by, and bound to, its own specific kinesin or dynein, it is not surprising that there are multiple kinesins and dyneins. The kinesin molecule has two globular head groups, which bind to microtubules, and a stalklike tail. It is possible that kinesin pulls itself along the microtubule in hand-over-hand fashion, using its head groups, while the tail remains tethered to the vesicle being transported. The details of that mechanism were among the many unanswered mysteries about intracellular transport to be addressed by future research.   (IRWIN FRIDOVICH)

PALEONTOLOGY

Highlighting the year 2002 in paleontology were several spectacular fossil discoveries reported from China, including that of a nonavian theropod dinosaur covered with primitive feathers. According to a number of paleontologists, of the previous finds of the past few years that had been first described as representing feathered dinosaurs, at least some, such as *Caudipteryx* and *Protarchaeopteryx*, were actually flightless birds. During the year, however, a specimen that was clearly a dromaeosaur—one of a family of nonavian theropods thought to share a common ancestry with birds—from the Early Cretaceous Jiufotang Formation. The investigators who described the approximately 120-million-year-old specimen claimed that the discovery finally proved that modern feathers evolved in theropod dinosaurs prior to the emergence of birds and flight.

Sinovenator changii, a second Chinese dinosaur described during the year, represented a very early basal troodontid, a primitive member of another nonavian theropod family believed to share an ancestor with birds. From the Cretaceous Yixian Formation and more than 130 million years old, the fossil has several features found in both dromaeosaurs and birds that are not typical of the more advanced troodontids. No feathers were identified, although they may have been present on the animal but not preserved in the fossil. The study concluded that several principal avian structures had developed earlier than previously thought but were then lost in some later theropod lineages.

An Early Cretaceous fossil from Liaoning province, China, *Jeholornis prima*, was described as a turkey-sized bird that lived between 110 million and 125 million years ago. Its remains included several dozen well-preserved seeds in the stomach, the first direct evidence of seed eating in a bird. Unlike other Cretaceous birds, the animal retained a long skeletal tail resembling the tail of dromaeosaurid theropods.

This specimen provided yet another strong link between birds and nonavian theropod dinosaurs. *Eomaia scansoria*, a small animal found in the same deposits in Liaoning province, was established to lie at the very base of the lineage leading to placental mammals. The find pushed the origin of the placentals back to 125 million years ago.

Yet another discovery from the Liaoning area was hailed as one of the most significant flowering-plant fossils ever found. The well-preserved 125-million-year-old specimen of *Archaefructus sinensis* suggested that the ancestors of the modern flowering plants, or angiosperms, may have been aquatic weedy plants. The closest-known living relatives of the flowering plants, the gymnosperms, are all woody plants. Hence, before this discovery paleobotanists had generally agreed that the angiosperms arose from woody plants similar to the magnolia tree.

Among other Chinese fossils was an important new invertebrate animal species from the Early Cambrian Chengjiang Lagerstätte near Kunming. *Didazoon haoae* represented an entirely new phylum of metazoans (multicellular animals), the phylum Vetulicolia. The specimen has a series of gill slits, which suggested that this new group illustrates an early stage in the diversification of the deuterostomes, one of the major animal divisions. Other deuterostome groups are the chordates (which includes the vertebrates), hemichordates, and echinoderms. Also reported was a Devonian Chinese fossil fish, *Styloichthys changae*, that has features linking the lungfish to tetrapods (four-legged vertebrates).

Biomechanical studies to determine the traveling speeds of ichthyosaurs in water and large theropod dinosaurs on land were concluded during the year. The ichthyosaur study, carried out by scientists from the Royal Ontario Museum, Toronto, estimated that the aquatic reptiles swam at speeds similar to those of large modern fish such as the tuna. A U.S.-based project used estimates of extensor muscle mass to measure maximum running speeds for some dinosaurs. They concluded that huge bipedal theropods such as *Tyrannosaurus rex* were not capable of running very fast.

Paleontological discoveries from other parts of the world during the year included a new candidate for the oldest land-walking tetrapod, from Scotland. With an estimated age of 344 million–354 million years, *Pederpes finneyae* filled in what previously had been a 20-million-year gap in the early evolution of the land vertebrates. A new species of placental mammal from the Bissekty Formation of Uzbekistan pushed the known fossil record of the primitive zalambdalestid mammal group back 10 million years. With a mid-Cretaceous age of 90 million years, this animal became one of the oldest-known placental mammals. A new statistical analysis of the primate fossil record arrived at a postulated age of 81.5 million years for the oldest common ancestor of the primate order. The study also estimated that no more than 7% of all primate species that ever existed were known from the fossil record.

In central Colorado a highly diverse fossil leaf site from the early Tertiary Period was dated to an age only 1.4 million years younger than the Cretaceous-Tertiary extinction event 65 million years ago. The existence of such a high-diversity tropical rainforest had been unexpected because most other known Paleocene plant assemblages showed a very low variety of species, particularly those that were close to the extinction event.

A second analysis of the wormlike Silurian invertebrate *Acaenoplax hayae* concluded that this animal, from 425-million-year-old deposits in England, does not represent the oldest-known aplacophoran mollusk, as had been reported in early 2001. The new study contended that the fossil exhibits more characteristics of polychaetes than of mollusks and hence should be placed in the class of marine worms, Polychaeta. A reanalysis of what had been described in 1998 as the world's oldest-known worm tracks, at 1.1 billion years old, suggested that the groove-shaped structures are actually 1.6 billion years old. Because this age predates that of the earliest accepted trace fossil of a metazoan by almost a billion years, the study also questioned whether the structures are actually fossils. The authors argued that one would not expect a billion years to pass without similar fossils being preserved.

Microscopic traces in approximately 3.5-billion-year-old Australian chert that were reported in 1993 to be of bacterial origin and to represent the oldest-known fossils also came under question. A paper published in March contended that the squiggle-shaped structures were formed chemically in an ancient hot spring and hence were not fossils. Another project, which examined fossils of single-celled eukaryotic algae from Roper Group rocks in northern Australia, found structural evidence that complex processes already were present in these cells; thus, eukaryotes must have evolved much earlier than the 1.5-billion-year age of the specimens. This added support to previous studies suggesting that eukaryotes originated at a much earlier time than the age of the oldest preserved cells. On the basis of molecular and geochemical evidence, the researchers estimated that eukaryotic cells first appeared between 2.5 billion and 2.7 billion years ago, in the late Archean Eon.

(WILLIAM R. HAMMER)

Sinovenator changii, *a birdlike dinosaur depicted here with feathers, was reported from China.*

Michael W. Skrepnick © 2002

Literature

The year's big literary **PRIZES** went to writers relatively unknown on the international scene. **IMRE KERTÉSZ** won the **NOBEL**, and the **BOOKER** went to **YANN MARTEL**. **WOMEN WRITERS** dominated the Arabic literary scene and carried away several prizes in the U.S. **JULIA GLASS'S** first novel won the **NATIONAL BOOK AWARD**, while **POLITICS** seized Russian literature.

ENGLISH

United Kingdom. Martyn Goff, chairman of the Booker Prize committee, aroused debate in literary circles in 2002 when he suggested that by 2004 titles by writers from the United States should be eligible for the prize, which was open only to British, Irish, and Commonwealth writers. The chairman of judges, Lisa Jardine, countered that American authors such as Philip Roth would overwhelm the rest of the competition. "With someone like Roth at his best," she said, "I can't see how an [Martin] Amis or a [Ian] McEwan could touch him. The American novelists paint on a much bigger canvas. If you look at Pulitzer Prize winners, every book there is on a majestic scale." Other Britons agreed, despite the ambitious breadth of much recent British fiction. In November, Booker Prize organizers announced that the prize would remain closed to American writers, however, they were contemplating the establishment of a second prize for lifetime achievement, and for that prize Americans might be able to compete. The Booker also had a modern makeover. The main award was increased from £20,000 to £50,000 (about $29,000 to $72,000), and a new five-year sponsorship partner was found in the Man Group, a global provider of alternative investment funds.

The year's judges read 130 titles, from which the original list of 20 novels was chosen. Young stars such as Zadie Smith, with her novel *The Autograph Man*, were pitted against seasoned authors such as Anita Brookner, whose elegant *The Next Big Thing* was a compassionate story of a lonely 73-year-old man. The shortlist, comprising six novels, contained few surprises. *Family Matters* by Rohinton Mistry (*see* BIOGRAPHIES), a dark Mumbai (Bombay)-based story about a 79-year-old widower, was a favourite with many critics, as was William Trevor's *The Story of Lucy Gault*, which featured Protestants living in Ireland's County

© AFP 2002, by Toby Melville

Ian McEwan, the 1998 Booker Prize laureate, won praise again with his Atonement.

Cork during the independence struggle in 1921. Carol Shields's offering, *Unless*, was an admired depiction of the bonds between mothers and daughters. *The Sunday Times* promised that it would resound in readers' minds "for years, perhaps for a lifetime." (Both Shields and

Mistry were Canadian contenders.) An Australian possibility was Tim Winton's *Dirt Music* (2001), about a woman stranded in a remote fishing community with a husband she does not love and two stepchildren. The only British finalist was Sarah Waters. Her fast-paced Victorian-world *Fingersmith* was a popular success but was perhaps deemed too conventional in form to win.

The judges' decision was rendered more transparent by the broadcasting of some of their debate on BBC Television. The unexpected winner, possibly a compromise choice, was Yann Martel's *Life of Pi* (Canadian-U.S. edition 2001), published in Edinburgh by Canongate, a small independent press. A lively and readable fable, with Noah's Ark resonances, the novel charts the voyage of a young boy, Pi, who emigrates from India to Canada with animals from his family's zoo. Lisa Jardine hailed it as an "audacious book in which inventiveness explores belief. It is, as the author says, 'a novel which will make you believe in God—or ask yourself why you don't.'" Martel, who lives in Montreal, said that his book "was the luckiest" and that accepting the prize was like "winning the lottery." Canongate immediately began reprinting 50,000 copies, and its managing director, David Graham, said the win was a "quantum leap" for his press, although it had enjoyed another popular success with the bawdy *The Crimson Petal and the White*, an 864-page Dickensian-style epic by Michel Faber.

The Booker Prize, although the most famous of British literary awards, was not the most lucrative. The new Northern Rock Foundation Writer Award, worth £60,000 (about $87,000) was established by a Newcastle-based bank for writers living in England's northeast. The first winner was Anne Stevenson, a poet from Durham. Her award, she said, was a challenge to those who "imagine that London is and will always be the only city of culture." The much praised novel *Atonement* (2001) by Ian McEwan (*see* BIOGRAPHIES), which had been hotly tipped for the 2001 Booker Prize, was a popular winner of the 2002 WH Smith literary prize, worth £5,000 (about $7,200). Meanwhile, American writer Ann Patchett (*see* BIOGRAPHIES) won the Orange Prize for Fiction, aimed at women writers and worth £30,000. Her topical novel *Bel Canto* (2001), about terrorists in Latin America who take hostage an American opera diva and a Japanese CEO, was praised for its attractive simplicity. On receiving the money, she said, "Hopefully I'll give it away. If I can find it in my character." The Whitbread Book of the Year, also worth £30,000 (about $43,000), went for the first time to a children's author, Philip Pullman. The third volume in the *His Dark Materials* trilogy, *The Amber Spyglass* (2000), was deemed "exceptional" by the judges and was enjoyed as much by adults as by children; the author insisted that the sharp divide between writing for children and writing for adults was over.

The robustness of the children's market continued. Terry Pratchett, another best-selling author who crossed the child-adult divide, won the year's Carnegie Medal. His *The Amazing Maurice and His Educated Rodents* (2001) was a dark but humorous take on the Pied Piper tale and was praised by the chair of the judges' panel for its deft questioning of "our society's attitudes and behaviour" and its ability to be at once "funny and irreverent." On receiving the award, the prolific author castigated J.R.R. Tolkien's *Lord of the Rings* for its insistence on war as a remedy to evil, saying he preferred to explore the possibility "that peace. . .can be maintained by careful diplomacy." The international Hans Christian Andersen Children's Author of the Year was Aidan Chambers, the first British writer to win the title since Eleanor Farjeon in 1956. The Carnegie Medal winner in 1999, Chambers was admired for his nonpatronizing handling of complex issues such as war, homosexuality, and death.

There was critical approval when W.G. Sebald, a German writer who had settled in East Anglia and had died in a car crash in December 2001, posthumously won both the National Book Critics Circle fiction prize in the U.S. and the U.K.'s Independent Foreign Fiction Prize. The awards confirmed him as a literary giant whose international reputation was rapidly increasing. Sebald's works were compared to those of Franz Kafka, Jorge Luis Borges, Italo Calvino, and Vladimir Nabokov, and the judges of the British award hailed his novel *Austerlitz* (2001), a story told in a single 415-page paragraph, as a "novel of the first magnitude." His 1988 prose poem, *After Nature*, was published in English in 2002

and was applauded as a haunting and sublime interweaving of memory, migration, and identity.

Notable fiction that was omitted from the prize lists included A.S. Byatt's *A Whistling Woman*, her fourth tale in an engaging series about the lives of post-World War II women, and Linda Grant's *Still Here*, a Liverpool-set portrayal of family, love, and loss that was autobiographical in tone. John Banville's *Shroud*, a story about an aging academic, was also praised, for its exceptional fluency, but it made only the Booker long list, while Maggie Gee's *The White Family*, a gritty drama of a contemporary North London family, reached the Orange shortlist. Tim Lott's *Rumours of a Hurricane*, about a worker in a printing concern who goes on the picket line, was another deserving offering, with its deft portrait of politics and working-class culture in Margaret Thatcher's Britain.

In nonfiction, themes of insecurity, war, and shifting identities threaded many titles as if echoing larger global trends. Philip Bobbitt's 922-page *The Shield of Achilles: War, Peace and the Course of History* was a reflection of the growing anxiety that history might be "ending." Charting 500 years of conflict, it claimed that the nation-state was dying, that a new constitutional order was emerging, and that politicians had to grasp the new reality if further warfare was to be prevented. Past wars remained under the historian's lens. Michael Howard's *The First World War* was a terse summation of that conflict and its aftermath, while Ian Ousby rendered a dense microcosm of one bloody battle in *The Road to Verdun: France, Nationalism and the First World War*. Paul Preston's *Doves of War: Four Women of Spain* followed the fortunes of two English and two Spanish women caught up in the Spanish Civil War. The Oxford historian Robert Gildea offered a thought-provoking study of France under the Nazis in *Marianne in Chains: In Search of the German Occupation, 1940–1945*. More provocative was Martin Amis's reappraisal of Stalin. His *Koba the Dread: Laughter and the Twenty Million* was criticized for what some deemed a simplistic equation of Hitler and Stalin, although others welcomed its reappraisal of a regime that killed millions. Richard Fletcher went back farther in time in his *Bloodfeud: Murder and Revenge in Anglo-Saxon England*, an ingenious early history that used anthropology to illuminate scanty historical sources.

History as it illuminates identity—particularly English identity—was a preoccupation of many writers, perhaps in response to the Queen's celebration of her Golden Jubilee. William Shawcross rendered an upbeat 50-year account of her reign in *Queen and Country*, while Richard Weight's *Patriots: National Identity in Britain, 1940–2000* optimistically expected another 100 years of British Union, despite the increasing resentment of England in Wales and Scotland. Peter Ackroyd pondered English identity across a larger canvas. His 516-page *Albion: The Origins of the English Imagination* concluded that although the English vision "tended towards the local and the circumstantial," it had made possible a vast creative achievement across many fields. Robert Colls's *Identity of England* probed the more elusive nature of national definition. Examining imperial expansion and immigration and how these affected what it was to be English or British, he pointed to history as the "first act of recognition" in the process of building a sense of identity. Maurice Cowling, a retired Cambridge historian, delivered the third and final volume of his immense *Religion and Public Doctrine in Modern England* (2001). Subtitled *Accommodations*, it asked "whether the modern mind can escape religion" and analyzed, often with barbed invective, the basis on which British leaders and thinkers assumed their authority. Eric Hobsbawn's memoir *Interesting Times: A Twentieth-Century Life* also illuminated England's intellectual life, while *The Victorians* by A.N. Wilson, a survey of 724 pages, examined the previous century and what its author termed "the period of the most radical transformation ever seen by the world." Another history on the broad scale was T.C.W. Blanning's *The Culture of Power and the Power of Culture: Old Regime Europe, 1660–1789*, a broadly interpretative vision of the Age of Enlightenment.

Controversy followed when three politicians produced memoirs. Edwina Currie's *Diaries 1987–1992* covered her time in the House of Commons and shocked many with its revelation of her love affair with former prime minister John Major. The imprisoned former politician and blockbuster writer Jeffrey Archer broke prison regulations with the publication of his prison diaries, which berated the state of the penal system; the prison authorities decided not to punish him so long as he

(continued on page 246)

WORLD LITERARY PRIZES 2002

All prizes are annual and were awarded in 2002 unless otherwise stated

Nobel Prize for Literature

Awarded since 1901; included in the behest of Alfred Nobel, who specified a prize for those who "shall have produced in the field of literature the most outstanding work in an ideal direction." The prizewinners are selected in October by the Swedish Academy and receive the award on December 10 in Stockholm. Prize: a gold medal and an award that varies from year to year; in 2002 the award was SKr 10 million (about $1 million).
Imre Kertész (Hungary)

International IMPAC Dublin Literary Award

First awarded in 1996; the largest and most international prize of its kind and is open to books written in any language, the award is a joint initiative of Dublin City Council, the Municipal Government of Dublin City, and the productivity-improvement company IMPAC. It is administered by Dublin City Public Libraries. Prize: €100,000 (about $100,000), of which 25% goes to the translator if the book was not written in English, and a Waterford Crystal trophy. The awards are given at Dublin Castle by the president of Ireland in May or June.
Atomised by Michel Houellebecq (France), translated from the French by Frank Wynne

Neustadt International Prize for Literature

Established in 1969 and awarded biennially by the University of Oklahoma and World Literature Today. Novelists, poets, and dramatists are equally eligible. Prize: $50,000, a replica of an eagle feather cast in silver, and a certificate.
Álvaro Mutis (Colombia)

Commonwealth Writers Prize

Established in 1987 by the Commonwealth Foundation. In 2002 there was one award of £10,000 (about $15,725) for the best book submitted and an award of £3,000 (about $4,725) for the best first book. In each of the four regions of the Commonwealth, two prizes of £1,000 (about $1,575) are awarded: one for the best book and one for the best first book.

Best Book	Gould's Book of Fish by Richard Flanagan (Australia)
Best First Book	Ama: A Story of the Atlantic Slave Trade by Manu Herbstein (South Africa—an electronic book)
Regional winners—Best Book	
Africa	The Pickup by Nadine Gordimer (South Africa)
Caribbean & Canada	Hateship, Friendship, Courtship, Loveship, Marriage by Alice Munro (Canada)
Eurasia	Atonement by Ian McEwan (British)
Southeast Asia & South Pacific	Gould's Book of Fish by Richard Flanagan (Australia)

Booker Prize

Established in 1969 and sponsored by Booker McConnell Ltd. and, beginning in 2002, the Man Group; administered by the National Book League in the U.K. Awarded to the best full-length novel written by a citizen of the U.K., Ireland, Pakistan, or the Commonwealth and published in the U.K. during the 12 months ended September 30. Prize: £50,000 (about $78,750) for the winner; £2,500 (almost $4,000) for each author on the shortlist.
Life of Pi by Yann Martel (Canada)

Whitbread Book of the Year

Established in 1971. The winners of the Whitbread Book Awards for Poetry, Biography, Novel, and First Novel as well as the Whitbread Children's Book of the Year, in addition to winning £5,000 (about $7,875) apiece, are eligible for the £25,000 (about $39,375) Whitbread Book of the Year prize.
The Amber Spyglass by Philip Pullman (2001 award)

Orange Prize for Fiction

Established in 1996. Awarded to a work of published fiction written by a woman in English and published in the U.K. during the 12 months ended March 31. Prize: £30,000 (about $47,250).
Bel Canto by Ann Patchett

PEN/Faulkner Award

The PEN/Faulkner Foundation each year recognizes the best published works of fiction by contemporary American writers. Named for William Faulkner, the PEN/Faulkner Award was founded in 1980 to honour their peers and is now the largest juried award for fiction in the U.S. Prize: $15,000 for the winner; $5,000 for each finalist.
Bel Canto by Ann Patchett

Pulitzer Prizes in Letters and Drama

Begun in 1917 and awarded by Columbia University, New York City, on the recommendation of the Pulitzer Prize Board for books published in the previous year. Five categories in Letters are honoured: Fiction, Biography, and General Non-fiction (authors of works in these categories must be American citizens); History (the subject must be American history); and Poetry (for original verse by an American author). The Drama prize is for "a distinguished play by an American author, preferably original in its source and dealing with American life." Prize: $7,500 in each category.

Fiction	Empire Falls by Richard Russo
Biography	John Adams by David McCullough
Poetry	Practical Gods by Carl Dennis
History	The Metaphysical Club: A Story of Ideas in America by Louis Menand
General Non-fiction	Carry Me Home: Birmingham, Alabama, the Climactic Battle of the Civil Rights Revolution by Diane McWhorter
Drama	Topdog/Underdog by Suzan-Lori Parks

National Book Awards

Awarded since 1950 by the National Book Foundation, a consortium of American publishing groups. Categories have varied, beginning with 3—Fiction, Nonfiction, and Poetry—swelling to 22 awards in 1983, and returning to 4 (the initial 3 plus Young People's Literature) in 2001. Prize: $10,000 and a crystal sculpture for the winner; $1,000 for each finalist.

Fiction	Three Junes by Julia Glass
Nonfiction	Lyndon Johnson: Master of the Senate by Robert A. Caro
Poetry	In the Next Galaxy by Ruth Stone

Frost Medal

Awarded annually since 1930 by the Poetry Society of America for distinguished lifetime service to American poetry.
Galway Kinnell

Governor General's Literary Awards

Canada's premier literary awards. Prizes are given in 14 categories altogether: Fiction, Poetry, Drama, Translation, Non-fiction, and Children's Literature (Text and Illustration), each in English and French. Established in 1937. Prize: Can$15,000 (about US$9,650).

Fiction (English)	A Song for Nettie Johnson by Gloria Sawai
Fiction (French)	La gloire de Cassiodore by Monique LaRue
Poetry (English)	Surrender by Roy Miki
Poetry (French)	Humains paysages en temps de paix relative by Robert Dickson

Griffin Poetry Prize

Established in 2001 and administered by the Griffin Trust for Excellence in Poetry, the award honours first-edition books of poetry published in the preceding year. Prize: Can$40,000 (about US$25,700) each for the two awards—one for a living Canadian poet and one for a living poet of any nationality.

Canadian Award	Eunoia by Christian Bök
International Award	Disobedience by Alice Notley (United States)

Büchner Prize

Georg-Büchner-Preis. Awarded for a body of literary work in the German language. First awarded in 1923; now administered by the German Academy for Language and Literature. Prize: €40,000 (about $40,000).
Wolfgang Hilbig (Germany)

Hooft Prize

P.C. Hooftprijs. The Dutch national prize for literature, established in 1947. Prize: €35,000 (about $35,000).
Sem Dresden, for his literary studies

Nordic Council Literary Prize

Established in 1961. Selections are made by a 10-member jury from among original works first published in Danish, Norwegian, or Swedish during the previous two years or other Nordic languages (Finnish, Faroese, Sami, etc.) during the previous four years. Prize: DKr 350,000 (about $48,000)
Halvbroren by Lars Saabye Christensen (Norway)

Prix Goncourt

Prix de l'Académie Goncourt, first awarded in 1903 from the estate of the French literary figure Edmond Huot de Goncourt to memorialize him and his brother, Jules. Prize: €10 (about $10).
Les Ombres errantes by Pascal Quignard

Prix Femina

Established in 1904. The awards for works "of imagination" are announced by an all-woman jury in the categories of French fiction, fiction in translation, and nonfiction. Announced in October or November together with the Prix Médicis. The prize in 2001 was €782 (about $690).

French Fiction	Les Adieux à la reine by Chantal Thomas

Cervantes Prize for Hispanic Literature

Premio Cervantes. Established in 1976 and awarded for a body of work in the Spanish language. Announced in December and awarded the following April. Prize: €90,000 (about $90,000).
José Jiménez Lozano (Spain)

Planeta Prize

Premio Planeta de Novela. Established in 1951 by the Planeta Publishing House for the best unpublished original novel in Spanish. Awarded in Barcelona in October. Prize: €600,000 (about $600,000) and publication by Planeta.
El huerto de mi amada by Alfredo Bryce Echenique (Peru)

Camões Prize

Premio Luis da Camões da Literatura. Established in 1988 by the governments of Portugal and Brazil to honour a "representatative" author writing in the Portuguese language. Prize $100,000.
Maria Velho de Costa (Portugal)

Russian Booker Prize

Awarded since 1992, the Russian Booker Prize has sometimes carried the names of various sponsors—e.g., Smirnoff in 1997–2001. In 2002 it was underwritten in part by the Yukos Oil Co. and called the Booker/Open Russia Literary Prize. Awards: $12,500 for the winner; $1,000 for each finalist.
Karagandinskiye devyatiny ("Karaganda Nines") by Oleg Pavlov

Naguib Mahfouz Medal for Literature

Established in 1996 and awarded for the best contemporary novel published in Arabic. The winning work is translated into English and published in Cairo, London, and New York. Prize: $1,000 and a silver medal.
Al-'Allamah (2001; "The Erudite") by Ben Salem Himmich

Jun'icherō Tanizaki Prize

Tanizaki Jun'icherō Shō. Established in 1965 to honour the memory of novelist Jun'ichirō Tanizaki. Awarded annually to a Japanese author for an exemplary literary work. Prize: ¥1,000,000 (about $8,000) and a trophy.
No prize awarded in 2002

Ryūnosuke Akutagawa Prize

Akutagawa Ryūnosuke Shō. Established in 1935 and now sponsored by the Association for the Promotion of Japanese Literature, the prize is awarded in January and June for the best serious work of fiction by a promising new Japanese writer published in a magazine or journal. Prize: ¥1,000,000 (about $8,000) and a commemorative gift.
"Mōsupiido de haha wa" ("Mom, at Full Speed") by Yū Nagashima
"Paaku raifu" ("Park Life") by Shūichi Yoshida

Mao Dun Literary Award

Established in 1981 to honour contemporary Chinese novels and named after novelist Shen Yanbing (1896–1981), whose nom de plume was Mao Dun; awarded every four years. Latest awards were announced on Oct. 12, 2000 (the same day as the Nobel Prize for Literature):
Jueze ("Hard Choice") by Zhang Ping
Chang hen ge (2000; "Song of Everlasting Sorrow") by Wang Anyi
Chen'ai luo ding (1999; "When Dust Settles") by Ah Lai
Nanfang you jiamu ("Fine Tree Possessed in the Southland") and Buye zhi hou (Delightful Marquis to Break Drowsiness"), from Charen sanbuqu ("Trilogy of Tea Men") by Wang Xufeng

(continued from page 244)
promised to publish no more memoirs until his release. A third Thatcherite, former defense minister John Nott, published *Here Today, Gone Tomorrow: Recollections of an Errant Politician*, a memoir containing revelatory inside information, especially on the handling of the 1982 Falkland Islands War.

Well-received biographies included Rosemary Ashton's *Thomas and Jane Carlyle: Portrait of a Marriage*, which provided the domestic context behind the development of Carlyle's thought, and Vanessa Collingridge's *Captain Cook*, an adventurous study of the explorer's life. The fourth and penultimate volume in John Grigg's biography of Lloyd George covered his war years, but Grigg's untimely death in the last days of 2001 begged the question of who would complete the study. Claire Tomalin's *Samuel Pepys: The Unequalled Self* showed Tomalin as mistress of her craft with its sure sense of period and multifaceted portrait of her subject. *Wilfred Owen: A New Biography* by Dominic Hibberd was only the second study of arguably World War I's most famous poet; it captured Owen's shy charm and thoughtful morality. David Gilmour demonstrated similar shrewd perception in his *The Long Recessional: The Imperial Life of Rudyard Kipling*.

Comedian Spike Milligan, a beloved radio and television personality as well as poet, died at 83. A former member of the radio quartet the Goons, he also authored several volumes of hilarious war memoirs and nonsense poetry, rejoicing in such titles as *Floored Masterpieces with Worse Verse*, which he penned with Tracey Boyd. Lady Elizabeth Longford, the biographer of figures such as Queen Victoria and the duke of Wellington, also passed away. (*See* OBITUARIES.)

(SIOBHAN DOWD)

United States. Most serious readers of American fiction would have to say that 2002 was an unusual year because the novel that dominated the best-seller list from late spring on was a first novel— California writer Alice Sebold's *The Lovely Bones*—and the National Book Award (NBA) nominees in fiction, some of them first books, were all by writers unknown to a general audience. The winner was Julia Glass's first novel, *Three Junes*, a family tale taking place on three continents.

Which was not to say that some known quantities had not published fiction of value and interest. Novelist William Kennedy weighed in early in the year with *Roscoe*, an addition to his Albany, N.Y., cycle that celebrates both the comedy and the pathos of urban American politics. Its eponymous hero cavorts through the thicket of time and competing interests that make up a city alive with pols and entrepreneurs, madames and lovers, mayors and thugs. After a 10-year hiatus, Thomas McGuane brought out a novel, *The Cadence of Grass*, with a smart if damned protagonist ("Good looking, quick-witted, a soul rented to darkness"), which won him some critical praise. Among other master veterans who published fiction were Gilbert Sorrentino with *Little Casino*, Ann Beattie with *The Doctor's House*, Howard Norman with *The Haunting of L.*, and Bharati Mukherjee with *Desirable Daughters*.

Kathryn Harrison, famous for her incest memoir *The Kiss*, published a novel, *The Seal Wife*, interesting both for its unusual presentation of her usual themes—passion and history— and for its exotic far north setting. In spare but telling prose, the story carves in ice a portrait of a young American present at the creation of modern meteorology. (Bigelow, the main character, "records ephemera: clouds, a fall of rain or of snow; hailstones, that after their furious clatter, melt silently into the ground. Like recounting a sigh. . . . He is recording a narrative that unfolds invisibly to most people, events that, even if noted, are soon forgotten.")

A hard act to imagine—let alone follow—was the Bausch brothers, Richard and Robert, identical twins and both of them novelists, and both of them with well-received novels published in 2002. In *Hello to the Cannibals*, Richard Bausch produced an imaginative hybrid of a book, with a contemporary narrative about a young woman doing the research for a play about 19th-century British explorer and eccentric Mary Kingsley, whose story Bausch interweaves into the modern tale. Robert Bausch chose rural Virginia for his story of intrigue and retribution titled *The Gypsy Man*. Tennessee-born-and-raised novelist Madison Smartt Bell also went south in *Anything Goes*, his novel about a young rock musician on the American road. Robert Hellenga's *Blues Lessons* (2001) took the reader into the world of contemporary music as he told the story of a young Michigan man and his love of the blues guitar and a girl from his childhood.

Less successful in execution was *The Incantation of Frida K.*, Kate Braverman's lyrical reconstruction of the life of 20th-century Mexican painter Frida Kahlo. Oscar Hijuelos had a bit more success with the life of a Cuban composer in *A Simple Habana Melody (from When the World Was Good)*. For his second novel, *Walk Through Darkness*, David Anthony Durham went to the history of slavery for an intense narrative about love and escape. In *Big If*, Mark Costello chose to make subtle comedy out of the material usually reserved for genre books. Spy novelist Robert Littell outdid himself with *The Company*, an 892-page novel recounting the birth and life of the Central Intelligence Agency. Craig Nova went to science fiction to produce *Wetware*, a story about two androids on the run and, in his competent hands, a study of the nature of what it is to be human.

Alice Sebold's first novel, **The Lovely Bones,** *dominated the U.S. best-seller lists in 2002.*

With *Rapture,* her book-length story of an act of coitus, Susan Minot stumbled badly. A fantasy writer with a literary bent (or a literary writer with a fantasy bent?), Jonathan Carroll produced *White Apples.* The late William Gaddis came to life again, with a posthumous short novel titled *Agapē Agape.*

One of the fine first books of 2002 was Berkeley novelist David Masiel's *2182 kHz,* the recounting of a rudderless Alaska tugboat crewman and his hope for a life beyond the ice and cold, a story told in lively, sensual language evoking a particular place: "The smell of the barge, with its mix of oil and grease and fuel, and its outdoor wind filled with diesel exhaust. . . . The patterned ground of the tundra . . . like a geometric field reaching to forever. The incongruity of a land that was at once desert and frozen marsh, the smell of the sea when it finally thawed, the sound of a lone seal." Another great first book was Daniel Mason's extremely well-reviewed novel about a late 19th-century London music technician traveling in eastern Burma—*The Piano Tuner.* Montana writer Debra Magpie Earling's first novel, *Perma Red,* beautifully evoked the loneliness and solitude of a young woman's life on a remote Indian reservation. Brad Watson's first novel, *The Heaven of Mercury,* the thickly painted portrait of a small Southern town, was nominated for a National Book Award.

Among short-story collections, some masters of the form were at work during the year. Richard Ford came out with *A Multitude of Sins* (first published in London in 2001). Ron Carlson offered *At the Jim Bridger;* the late Alice Adams was represented by *The Stories of Alice Adams;* and the genre-busting Ursula K. Le Guin signed in with *The Birthday of the World and Other Stories.* Rick Bass published a new collection called *The Hermit's Story,* and MacArthur Award winner Andrea Barrett delivered *Servants of the Map. Tell Me,* Mary Robinson's collected stories, also came out. New writer Maile Meloy made her debut with *Half in Love,* and first-time book writer Adam Haslett's collection *You Are Not a Stranger Here* was nominated for a National Book Award.

The value of some of the book-length essays and critical works for the year was readily apparent. Former U.S. poet laureate Robert Pinsky spoke strongly and well on one of his favourite themes—the role of poetry in an entertainment culture—in *Democracy, Culture, and the Voice of Poetry.* William

Gaddis was represented once again by a posthumous volume, in this case the sharp-eyed (and sharp-tongued) essays on art and contemporary culture in *The Rush for Second Place.* Prize-winning novelist Jonathan Franzen approached the same subject in many of the essays and articles in *How to Be Alone.*

New Yorker Morris Dickstein took a traditional critical approach to post-World War II American fiction in *Leopards in the Temple: The Transformation of American Fiction, 1945–1970.* Louis Menand, also a mainstay of New York criticism and winner of a Pulitzer for his work on American intellectual history, looked at writing and other aspects of contemporary culture in *American Studies.* Peter Gay went to bourgeois European culture, his traditional stamping grounds, in *Savage Reprisals,* an analysis of the novels of Charles Dickens, Gustave Flaubert, and Thomas Mann.

Poet Edward Hirsch, the recently appointed head of the Guggenheim Foundation, looked mainly to poetry for his subject in the lively *The Demon and the Angel: Searching for the Source of Artistic Inspiration.* Arguing for a broad synthesis of modernist art and the work of American jazz geniuses such as Duke Ellington and Louis Armstrong, the literary critic Alfred Appel, Jr., made *Jazz Modernism: From Ellington and Armstrong to Matisse and Joyce* one of the most interesting critical works of the year. Russell Martin focused on the painting *Guernica* in his well-argued study *Picasso's War.*

"Norma Olivia Walgren met Winfield Sprague Harrison in 1933 at the River Gardens, a dance hall just north of Big Rapids, Mich., on the banks of the Muskegon River." Thus novelist and poet Jim Harrison's memoir *Off to the Side* opens, rather conventionally, but Harrison manages before it is over to offer discourse on childhood, outdoor sports, food, writing, Hollywood, the American landscape, and philosophy in a spare and unpretentious voice. Writers Anne Bernays and Justin Kaplan, a couple for many decades, jointly composed *Back Then: Two Lives in 1950s New York,* in which family, the literary life, and indoor sports are recalled and scrutinized with great charm.

Some younger writers revealed themselves in memoirs such as *Teacher* by Mark Edmundson, an insightful glimpse into the intellectual (and nonintellectual) life of a Boston-area high school in the late 1960s; *The Black Veil,* in which novelist and storyteller Rick

Moody assays his own moods and airs; and *My Sky Blue Trades,* in which one of the U.S.'s best young literary critics, Sven Birkerts, depicts his early life. Poet Gregory Orr wrote of a tumultuous event in childhood in *The Blessing.* Kim Stafford chronicled life with his father, the Oregon poet William Stafford, in *Early Morning.*

The third volume in Robert A. Caro's massive biography of Lyndon Johnson appeared (and won an NBA)—*The Years of Lyndon Johnson: Master of the Senate*—while scholar Stanley P. Hirshson published *General Patton* and Edmund S. Morgan added *Benjamin Franklin* to the bookshelves. In *Sinclair Lewis, Rebel from Main Street,* Richard Lingeman turned the light on an American writer being reevaluated by critics and readers. *May Sarton: Selected Letters, 1955–1995* was edited by Susan Sherman.

For poets, the year never lost its lustre, though it was dimmed somewhat by the death in late 2001 of Agha Shahid Ali ("A night of ghazals comes to an end. The singer/ departs through her chosen mirror, her one diamond/ cut on her countless necks. I, as ever, linger/ till chandeliers dim to the blue of Samarkand domes and I've again lost everyone"). The poet's *Rooms Are Never Finished* made him seem quite alive still. Maxine Kumin in *The Long Marriage* (2001) went "Skinnydipping with William Wordsworth." Among other senior poets, 87-year-old Ruth Stone's *In the Next Galaxy* won the poetry NBA, Grace Schulman presented *Days of Wonder: New and Selected Poems,* and Mona Van Duyn offered *Selected Poems.*

"Call it a field where the animals/ who were forgotten by the Ark/ come to graze under the evening clouds./ Or a cistern where the rain that fell/ Before history trickles over a concrete lip./ However you see it,/ this is no place to set up/ the three-legged easel of realism": so U.S. poet laureate Billy Collins displayed his off-hand manner and Frost-driven plain style in *Nine Horses.* J.D. McClatchy put out *Hazmat;* Elizabeth Spires published *Now the Green Blade Rises;* and C.D. Wright signed in with *Steal Away: Selected and New Poems* ("In the space of an ear/ she told him the uncut version/ in all but inaudible detail/ without motors without phones/ he gathered round her/ like books like chairs/ her warmth her terrible warmth/ flooded the tone").

Among the other many fine poets with books out in 2002 were Alan Shapiro

(*Song and Dance*), Frank Bidart (*Music like Dirt*), Gerald Stern (*American Sonnets*), Donald Hall (*The Painted Bed*), Charles Wright (*A Short History of the Shadow*), Jorie Graham (*Never*), Stephen Sandy (with a long poem *Surface Impressions*), Joy Harjo (*How We Became Human: New and Selected Poems*), and John Koethe (*North Point North: New and Selected Poems*). In addition, Robert Sward signed in with *Heavenly Sex* ("Hello wife, hello world, hello God./ I love you. Hello certain monsters,/ ghosts, office buildings, I love you. Dog,/ dog-dogs, cat, cat-cats, I love you./ Hello Things-in-Themselves, Things Not Quite/ in Themselves [but trying], I love you.") The debut volume by Santa Cruz poet Tilly Washburn Shaw, *Swimming Closer to Shore*, was met with serious pleasure. Among translations were Anne Carson's *If Not, Winter: Fragments of Sappho* and Mark Strand's renditions from the Quechua and from Carlos Drummond de Andrade and Rafael Alberti in *Looking for Poetry*.

Ann Patchett (*see* BIOGRAPHIES) won the 2002 PEN/Faulkner Prize for her novel *Bel Canto* (2001), and the Pulitzer committee chose Richard Russo in fiction for his novel *Empire Falls* (2001), Carl Dennis in poetry for *Practical Gods* (2001), Suzan-Lori Parks in drama for *Topdog/Underdog* (2001), and Louis Menand in history for *The Metaphysical Club* (2001).   (ALAN CHEUSE)

Canada. In Canadian novels of 2002, the family—the importance of, the saving of, the destructiveness of, the hopes for—was a persistent theme. It

In Crow Lake, *Canadian author Mary Lawson chronicled a family of four orphans.*

CP Aaron Harris

was often explored from the viewpoint of a child, as in Mary Lawson's *Crow Lake*, in which four orphans struggle to raise each other under the fierce, protective leadership of the oldest brother. In *Lures*, Sue Goyette studied temptation in the lives of two families, using their respective daughters as lenses. Donna Morrissey, in *Downhill Chance*, presented successive generations attempting to unravel the past in their search for a future. In *Family Matters*, Rohinton Mistry (*see* BIOGRAPHIES), wove the unpromising strands of poverty, age, and estrangement with those of love, forbearance, and luck into a tapestry of life in modern Mumbai (Bombay). In *Unless*, Carol Shields investigated the meaning of goodness by portraying a mother's efforts to understand her daughter's decision to live on the streets. Nino Ricci approached similar themes from radical new angles in *Testament*. Cynthia Flood employed the metaphor of a calcified fetus in *Making a Stone of the Heart* to examine how love can die but remain unburied.

Escape from one's family was a significant subtheme. In Christy Ann Conlin's *Heave*, the bride flees the altar in order to come to terms with her life; in Marnie Woodrow's *Spelling Mississippi*, two women inform each other's search for love and independence. Also on the run, in this instance from the consequences of political activism, was the protagonist of Ann Ireland's *Exile*. In contrast, the search for one's family, one's origins, was the core of Wayne Johnston's *The Navigator of New York* and, in a different way, at the heart of Lori Lansens's *Rush Home Road*, the story of a black woman's de facto adoption of a mixed-race child. Nightlong reminiscences were the thread on which Austin Clarke, in *The Polished Hoe*, and Neil Bissoondath, in *Doing the Heart Good*, hung their tales of murder, mayhem, regret, and reconciliation, while David Bergen, in *The Case of Lena S.*, strung up the myths of adolescent relationships with a fine noose of humour.

Short stories also covered familiar terrain. In *The Broken Record Technique*, Lee Henderson presented families who have lied so often to themselves and others that they no longer know what the truth is. Nancy Lee, in *Dead Girls*, dissected the lives of women in peril, whether in their homes or on the streets, and in *Real Life: Short Stories*, Sharon Butala deftly depicted how the uneven contours of dailiness

can trip up even the wariest. Bill Gaston's *Mount Appetite* studied the nature of the hungers, spiritual and physical, that drive us, often away from ourselves. Lisa Moore's *Open* lifted the lid on young people looking for a way out, and Diane Schoemperlen's *Red Plaid Shirt: Stories New and Selected* focused on the lives of lonely single small-town women. In *Silent Cruise and Other Stories*, Timothy Taylor explored the fates of people caught in the nets of their own elaborate plots.

Poetry went its usual idiosyncratic way, whether in Lorna Crozier's *Apocrypha of Light*, in which women of the Bible were newly illuminated; Stephanie Bolster's *Pavilion*, a metaphoric stroll through a garden of elemental images; Colin Browne's lyrical fusion of war, conquest, and sacrifice in *Ground Water;* or Erin Mouré's explorations of the nuances of citizenship and feminism in *O Cidadan.* Games also figured, from *Take Me Out to the Ballgame*, Raymond Souster's playful musings on that enduring summer pastime, to bill bissett's *peter among th towring boxes, text bites*, in which the excesses of vernacular were subtly disciplined, to Kathleen McConnell's satiric sporting with modernity in *Nail Builders Plan for Strength and Growth*, Douglas Barbour's experiments with sound in *Breath Takes* (2001), and Linda Rogers's examination of how people resist the pressures of modern life in *The Bursting Test*. Michael Crummey picked gems of insight from the wrack of loneliness, death, and broken pride in *Salvage;* Marilyn Bowering mixed emotions in transformative moments in *The Alchemy of Happiness;* and P.K. Page circumnavigated humanity in *Planet Earth*.

(ELIZABETH RHETT WOODS)

Other Literature in English. In 2002 literature in English from Africa, Australia, and New Zealand was distinguished by the number of international, regional, and national awards received as well as by new releases from major writers. Nigeria's Wole Soyinka, the first African Nobel laureate in literature (1986), became the first black and African recipient of Italy's Vita di Poeta Prize. His new verse collection, *Samarkand & Other Markets I Have Known*, was published at year's end, and his 2001 play *King Baabu*, a satire on the dictatorship of Nigeria's Gen. Sani Abacha, appeared in print. Two nonfiction works that focused on the subject of African dictatorship were David Blair's *Degrees in Violence: Robert Mugabe and the Struggle for Power in*

Zimbabwe and Martin Meredith's volume *Our Votes, Our Guns: Robert Mugabe and the Tragedy of Zimbabwe*. On a lighter note, Nigerian fiction writer Femi Ojo-Ade provided unpredictable twists of fate in his short-story collection *Black Gods*, while countryman Chimalum Nwankwo offered lyrical virtuosity with *The Womb in the Heart & Other Poems*.

In South Africa, J.M. Coetzee, twice winner of the Booker Prize, brought out *Youth: Scenes from Provincial Life II*, his much-anticipated second volume of serialized memoirs, in which he offers a self-portrait as a young artist whose eventual success is born out of misery. Talented 44-year-old novelist Ivan Vladislavic garnered South Africa's 2002 *Sunday Times* Fiction Award with *The Restless Supermarket* (2001). Jack Mapanje was the recipient of the 2002 Fonlon-Nichols Award conferred by the African Literature Association (U.S.) for his contribution to African poetry and civil rights. Nobelist Nadine Gordimer won the Africa regional competition for the Commonwealth Writers Prize for best book with her novel *The Pickup* (2001), and Manu Herbstein won the Commonwealth best first book award with *Ama: A Story of the Atlantic Slave Trade* (2000).

Best-selling Australian novelist Colleen McCullough completed her Roman series by re-creating Julius Caesar in *The October Horse: A Novel About Caesar and Cleopatra*. Veteran author Thomas Keneally brought out *American Scoundrel*, his biography of the infamous politician, American Civil War general, and murderer Daniel Sickles, while Australia's finest living poet, Les Murray, saw the publication of two new works: *Poems the Size of Photographs* and *Collected Poems 1961–2002*. Tim Winton's novel *Dirt Music* (2001) won the 2002 Miles Franklin Award. Winner of the 2002 Commonwealth Writers Prize was Richard Flanagan's entertaining *Gould's Book of Fish: A Novel in Twelve Fish* (2001).

In neighbouring New Zealand, notable recipients of the Montana New Zealand Book Awards were Lynley Hood for *A City Possessed: The Christchurch Civic Crèche Case* (winner in three categories: reader's choice, nonfiction, and history), Craig Marriner for his provocative *Stonedogs* (fiction), and Hone Tuwhare for his collection *Piggy-Back Moon* (poetry).

One of Australia's most distinguished authors of children's books, Elyne Mitchell, died on March 4. Mitchell, a writer for more than 60 years, was best known for her *Silver Brumby* series.

(DAVID DRAPER CLARK)

GERMANIC

German. Günter Grass, who turned 75 on Oct.16, 2002, published *Im Krebsgang*, a novel about the destruction of the German refugee ship *Wilhelm Gustloff* in January 1945, during the final months of World War II; this catastrophe, which killed thousands, many of them women and children, was probably the most horrendous passenger-ship disaster in history, far surpassing the sinking of the *Titanic*. The survivor-mother of the novel's fictional narrator was pregnant with him at the time of the catastrophe and gives birth to him shortly thereafter. The novel addresses the difficult moral and political question of whether it is permissible or appropriate for Germans to explore their status as victims, not just as perpetrators. *Im Krebsgang* initiated a major discussion in Germany about the expulsion of ethnic Germans from East Prussia, Silesia, Pomerania, and Czechoslovakia at the end of World War II and afterward. Grass's position, in the novel and elsewhere, is that the topic of German victimization should not be left to the right wing.

Christa Wolf published *Leibhaftig*, an extended narrative about an elderly woman fighting a near-fatal disease during the final crisis of the German Democratic Republic. In interior monologues the woman explores the borderline between life and death and the one between body and soul; she comes to the therapeutic realization that the differences between these poles are not as well defined as she had previously believed. In her novel *Endmoränen*, Monika Maron, like Wolf a writer from the former German Democratic Republic, also explored a woman's experience of aging and her terrifying realization that the most important part of her life has passed and that she faces an indeterminate, but possibly very long, period of decline and decay.

The most controversial novel of the year was Martin Walser's *Tod eines Kritikers*, a ferocious, barely hidden attack on Marcel Reich-Ranicki (*see* BIOGRAPHIES), Germany's most popular literary critic. In this roman à clef, a famous critic who strongly resembles Reich-Ranicki, and who is portrayed as unscrupulous and scheming, is believed to have been murdered by an author

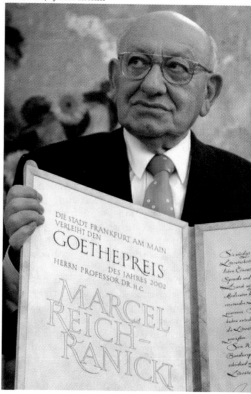

Very much alive and well, German critic Marcel Reich-Ranicki accepts the Goethe Prize in August.

whom he had previously criticized. (In the end it turns out that the critic is alive and well.) The novel, originally scheduled for serialized publication in the *Frankfurter Allgemeine Zeitung*, was rejected by that newspaper's editor, Frank Schirrmacher, in an open letter on the front page of the newspaper; this very public rejection by a former defender of the controversial Walser was accompanied by accusations that the novel was anti-Semitic. After a hefty controversy, the Suhrkamp publishing company decided to stand behind Walser and rejected the accusations of anti-Semitism. Bodo Kirchhoff's *Schundroman* was another satire on Germany's frequently overheated literary world; in it a critic who also strongly resembles Reich-Ranicki actually is killed. Kirchhoff's novel, however, did not stir up the kind of controversy that Walser's did.

Liane Dirks's autobiographical novel *Vier Arten meinen Vater zu beerdigen* was about a woman and the father who abuses her sexually and ultimately disappears from her life, winding up as a master chef on the island of Barbados, where his daughter rushes, too late, to see him on his deathbed. As an old

Caribbean woman tells the daughter, one of the four ways of burying her father is to tell his story, and it is this final method of coming to terms with the past that results in the narrative itself.

Martin Z. Schröder's *Allgemeine Geschäftsbedingungen* was a novel about everyday life in the criminal underworld of a major German city. The novel's protagonist Savio is a young man who embarks on a downward spiral of criminality; his encounters with German bureaucracy fail to improve his, or society's, problems. André Kubiczek's novel *Junge Talente* portrays a young man from the East German countryside who goes to Berlin at the end of the 1980s, just as the state is collapsing, and lives the life of a bohemian.

In her novel *Eden Plaza*, Dagmar Leupold depicted a romantic triangle involving an unhappily married woman, her prosaic husband, and her romantic lover. Christoph D. Brumme's novel *Süchtig nach Lügen* also dealt with a romantic relationship, one between two people who can hardly stand each other; they seem to take pleasure in inflicting pain. In contrast, Hans Pleschinski's autobiographical novel *Bildnis eines Unsichtbaren* was about a gay man mourning but also celebrating the memory of his longtime partner, who has died of AIDS. Arno Geiger's novel *Schöne Freunde* related the fantastic tale of a small boy living in a world entirely determined by literature and the imagination. In his short-story collection *Von den Deutschen*, Georg Klein sought to explore the roots of German identity even in a world of globalization. (STEPHEN BROCKMANN)

Netherlandic. The year 2002 saw the publication of novels by several second-generation immigrants to The Netherlands whose initial entries had catapulted them into prominence and thereby launched them into the role of sought-after lecturers and authors of opinion pieces. Among them Naima El Bezaz and Abdelkader Benali demonstrated again their right to such prominence. In *Minnares van de duivel*, El Bezaz, a Moroccan-Dutch lawyer, retold folktales of Arabic origin in a deceptively simple style and with minimal literary artifice. Benali, in *De langverwachte*, offered a tangle of stories, with frequent references to other texts. The work illustrated—and sometimes questioned—a variety of approaches to Moroccan-Dutch identity.

Robert Anker received the Libris Literatuur Prijs for his novel *Een soort Engeland* (2001). It was praised for presenting "passionately, intelligently, with irony and self-mockery" both the life of an actor and the Dutch theatre world in the second half of the 20th century. Allard Schröder was awarded the AKO Literatuur Prijs for his historical novel *De hydrograaf*, a love story about a German hydrographer as well as a "novel of ideas on a European scale."

One theme of several major novels in 2002 was the importance of imagination in life and literature. The protagonist in Maria Stahlie's *De lijfarts*, a hypochondriac, indulges in exasperating magical thinking. That she is not destroyed by her strange approach to the truth is due only to another's remarkable act of imagination and grace. In Nelleke Noordervliet's *Pelican Bay*, a novelist travels to Curaçao to solve a family mystery—the 18th-century murder of a slaveholder's wife—and perhaps to reunite with her vanished brother. She finds that imagination is a necessary requirement for a return to the past. With *Boze tongen*, Tom Lanoye's "monster" trilogy ended without revealing the "truth," although the reader understands that the main character is destroyed by others' fantasies. The trilogy offered an incisive social and political critique dressed up as grotesque soap opera. Leon de Winter's *God's Gym* dared to imagine alternative chains of events even as it spun a virtuosic tale in a world of surprises.

(JOLANDA VANDERWAL TAYLOR)

Danish. In 2002 Danish writers often looked to the past. Maria Helleberg's novel about Princess Louise Augusta (1771–1843), *Kærlighedsbarn*, portrayed the love affair between the princess and her husband and the one between the princess's parents, the traitor Johann Friedrich Struensee and Queen Caroline Matilda. Peter Fogtdal's *Lystrejsen* also depicted regal romance, between Frederik IV and someone he met long ago in Italy. Italy also figured importantly in Adda Lykkeboe's *Balladen om Antonie* (2001). In *Fortællinger til Abram* (2001), Janina Katz focused on the love affair of two Polish Jews. *Nansen og Johansen: et vintereventyr*, the well-received novel by Klaus Rifbjerg (see BIOGRAPHIES) about Fram-expedition polar explorers, sparked controversy in Norway. Both Jane Aamund (*Vesten for måne*) and Hans Edvard Nørregård-Nielsen (*Riber ret: et tidsbillede*) created family chronicles of life in Jutland. The poet Henrik Nordbrandt explored his troubled past in

Novelist Klaus Rifbjerg was branching out into political commentary on the Danish and international scenes.

© Georg Oddner

Døden fra Lübeck. Mogens Lehmann created a fictional portrait of 17th-century scientist Ole Rømer in *Lysets tøven*, while Kirsten Rask focused on the founder of comparative linguistics in her biography *Rasmus Rask: store tanker i et lille land*.

Misfits also figured in Danish fiction in 2002. In Mads Brenøe's *Bjerget* (2001), recipes punctuated the travails of portly Jens, who planned a reunion for all his childhood tormenters. In *Nordkraft*, Jakob Ejersbo depicted a group of ne'er-do-wells in 1990s Aalborg. Kim Fupz Aakeson focused on the boxing gym in *Mellemvægt*. Helle Helle's novella *Forestillingen om et ukompliceret liv med en mand* introduced a curious ménage à trois. Ib Michael's *Kejserens atlas* (2001) centred on two sets of twins: two wildly dissimilar Danes and a Japanese shogun and his gardener-brother. Leif Davidsen presented a tale of family secrets in *De gode søstre* (2001). In Bjarne Reuter's *Barolo Kvartetten*, casual thoughts of murder became reality. F.P. Jac's *Numse-Kajs otier på de græske øer* (2001) depicted the mishaps of a retired school principal during a holiday on Crete. Niels Jørgensen's poems in the brief but glorious *Gilliaps store tid* (2001) harmoniously melded love and nature. In *Det værste og det bedste*, Søren Ulrik Thomsen's poems traversed life's triumphs and tragedies. The journalist

Poul Blak ranged far in *En ø i galaksen: ekspanderende essays.*

Hans Edvard Nørregård-Nielsen was named an honorary member of the Royal Danish Academy of Fine Arts in 2002 and received the Golden Laurels for *Riber ret*, while Bo Lidegaard garnered the Søren Gyldendal Prize for *Jens Otto Krag*, his biography of the former prime minister.

(LANAE HJORTSVANG ISAACSON)

Norwegian. The year 2002 was a successful one for Norway's recently established authors, who shared a compassionate interest in portraying the abused and wounded child. Niels Fredrik Dahl was awarded the Brage Literary Prize for his second novel, *På vei til en venn*, which portrayed the effects of abuse on a young boy. Others who addressed the vulnerable child in acclaimed novels included Lars Amund Vaage (nominated for the Brage Prize for *Kunsten å gå*), Merethe Lindstrøm (*Natthjem*), MiRee Abrahamsen (*BOLS: en fortelling fra landet*), Håvard Syvertsen (*I lyset*), and Sylvelin Vatle (*Mørket bak Gemini*). Synne Sun Løes tackled youth and depression in *Å spise blomster til frokost*, which was awarded the Brage Literary Prize for Youth Literature.

Bror Hagemann's *De blyges hus* won acclaim for its unsentimental depiction of an institution for mentally disabled children and for its brave and beautiful portrayal of the love between a patient and a teacher. Linn Ullmann addressed euthanasia, heightening awareness and increasing dialogue on the subject with her third novel, *Nåde*, which was commended for its graceful tone and humour.

Among well-established authors, Jostein Gaarder was awarded the Brage Honorary Prize for his comprehensive work—from children's literature to philosophy—in the previous 10 years; his works had been translated into 48 languages. Lars Saabye Christensen was awarded the 2002 Nordic Council Literature Prize for his widely praised *Halvbroren* (2001), and Liv Køltzow was nominated for the following year's prize for her acclaimed *Det avbrutte bildet*, about a woman's maturing into an artist after a broken relationship. Køltzow's work offered perceptive reflections on not only art but also the dynamics between women and men. The latter subject, especially the topic of unfaithfulness, was a popular theme during the year and was lustfully described by Hans Petter Blad, who debuted with the critically

applauded *I skyggen av små menn midt på dagen.*

Among other debuts, Heidi Linde's *Under bordet*, about the lives of young urbanites in Oslo, received most of the acclaim and attention. Erik Honoré probed the uses and abuses of the Internet by pedophiles and pornographers in his critically commended *Orakelveggen.*

Treasured poet Jan Erik Vold delighted with his characteristic talent in making the everyday poetic in *Tolv meditasjoner*. Time-honoured Stein Mehren plumbed the existential experience of time in *Den siste ildlender*. Newlyweds Princess Märtha Louise and Ari Behn's book of collected meditations on love and spirituality, *Fra hjerte til hjerte*, raised eyebrows for its atypical format. Journalist Åsne Seierstad's *Bokhandleren i Kabul: et familiedrama*, a documentary about an Afghan family after the fall of the Taliban regime, became an award-winning bestseller.

(ANNE G. SABO)

Swedish. There was a touch of pastiche to many novels published in Sweden during 2002. Some—such as Stewe Claeson's *Rönndruvan glöder*, Ernst Brunner's *Fukta din aska*, and Monica Braw's *Främling*—were based on careful studies of a historical epoch, focusing on a great figure of the time. In other novels—such as Carl-Johan Vallgren's *Den vidunderliga kärlekens historia*, Gabriella Håkansson's *Fallet Sandemann*, Torbjörn Elensky's *Döda vinklar*, Aris Fioretos's *Sanningen om Sasha Knisch*, Mons Kallentoft's *Marbella Club*, and Jerker Virdborg's *Svart krabba*—genres with a mystifying potential (gothic fiction, crime novels, or thrillers) were used, both out of sheer fascination with their characteristics and, it seemed, in order to portray strong, basic human feelings in our ironical time.

Long-established authors Kerstin Ekman, with *Sista rompan*, and Torgny Lindgren, with *Pölsan*, used their skilled craftsmanship to display an interest in history. Their depictions of the hardships of Swedish rural life in the not-too-distant past were on the surface simple and realistic but turned out to be burgeoning with symbolic possibilities and narrative inventiveness. The same was true for Elisabeth Rynell's *Till Mervas* and Lotta Lotass's *Band II: Från Gabbro till Löväng*, the latter using the short-story cycle rather than the full-length novel form.

Among younger writers, the trend toward shorter fiction kept its grip. Cecilia Davidsson and Ninni Holmqvist,

trendsetters in the mid-1990s, appeared with new minimalist collections, *Vänta på vind* and *Biroller*, respectively. Karl Johan Nilsson worked with separate stories thematically interlinked in *Korsakovs syndrom*. Helena Ljungström's *Kring en trädgård*, Åsa Ericsdotter's *Kräklek*, and Sara Villius's first book, *Nej, det är en snöklump*, could be read either as fragmented novels or as collections of poetry devoted to the roving experience of young love. Daniel Sjölin's *Oron bror* and Johannes Sjögren's *Backabo* used the flickering possibilities of short fiction to cast uneasy light on childhood in the 1970s, while Henrik Kullander's *Elfenbenssvart* and Oscar Danielson's *Siljans konditori* could be the start of a new type of clearly nostalgic stories about prolonged boyhood.

(IMMI LUNDIN)

FRENCH

France. One of the themes most prevalent in French literature of 2002 was the empty isolation felt to be characteristic of modern life. In *Mon petit garçon*, Richard Morgiève explored this theme on the personal level in the post-divorce misery of his separation from his son. The title, endlessly repeated, became a refrain of paternal longing. In Danièle Sallenave's *D'amour*, the author considered two suicides disastrous for her, her aunt's and her lover's, in an attempt to understand how two people so different could have committed the same lonely act and whether she might have done something to stop them.

On a larger scale, the idea of modern capitalistic times as empty in contrast to the poetic idealism of the more revolutionary 1960s and '70s suffused Patrick Raynal's *Ex*, in which a man who in 1968 joined a Marxist group aiming at revolution by 2001 receives an unexpected visit in 2001 from the leader of his long-disbanded group. Olivier Rolin told a similar, if more autobiographical tale in his *Tigre en papier* through his alter ego, Martin, who relives the violence of the 1970s when he, like the author, had belonged to the armed branch of the revolutionary "cause." As Martin portrays the activists, gone now or absorbed into the society they once combated, he resurrects not only the youthful beauty of their devotion but also their surrounding crowd of pseudo-Marxists, hangers-on, and police informants.

Modern-day blandness as the victory of image over substance was the subject of Nicolas Fargues's satiric *One*

Olivier Rolin's remembrances of the 1970s revolutionaries in France were well received.

Man Show, in which a writer, tired of being a "good guy," decides to explore his Machiavellian side and enter the world of television, where illusion reigns supreme. The struggle between illusion and reality also dominated Eric-Emmanuel Schmitt's *Lorsque j'étais une œuvre d'art*, the story of a man on the brink of suicide who sells his soul to an artist. The artist then turns him into a human sculpture, a piece of merchandise exposed to the multitudes; but when the sculpture falls in love it is only a matter of time until its buried human reality resurfaces.

Isolation pushed to the extreme of sexual predation was at the heart of Nicolas Jones-Gorlin's scandalous *Rose bonbon*, which brings the reader into the mind of a pedophile murderer, a novel that reaches such levels of violence that the French government briefly threatened to prohibit the book's sale to minors.

In Christian Gailly's *Un Soir au club* (2001), however, hope for escape from loneliness was found in the love of another. A man saved from a downward spiral of alcohol and sex, but at the price of his music, learns to live again when by accident he steps into a jazz club, where a piano and a woman invite rebirth. It is also a chance meeting, this time on a train, that offers the protagonist of Christian Oster's *Dans le train* a chance for happiness: neurotic and alone, Franck offers to carry Anne's absurdly heavy baggage, and their subsequent train adventure opens the way to love.

In two of the year's novels, happiness could be found only by eliminating society altogether. In Pierre Senges's *Ruines-de-Rome*, a geometer, inspired by the Bible he reads backward, from the Apocalypse to the Garden of Eden, tries to speed the coming of paradise by sowing, in the cracks of the city, any plant that will crumble the steel and concrete

monstrosity mankind has built. In a more intimate project, Philippe Sollers's *L'Étoile des amants* shows a man and a woman, stranded alone after a shipwreck on a deserted isle, who learn to truly live, as they had been unable to do in society, by reawakening their dulled senses and sensuality.

Two historical novels stood out by their exuberance in an often laconic, even gloomy literary landscape: Gilles Lapouge's *La Mission des frontières* offered a fictional account of an 18th-century mission sent from Portugal to drag a massive monolith through the mountains of newly conquered Brazil to mark its border with the neighbouring Spanish territory. When the absurd task fails, the men descend into an insane trip through the jungles to São Luis, where their adventures with paganized priests and prostitutes are interrupted by a thundering bishop come to call his flock back to order. The Martinique-born Patrick Chamoiseau's *Biblique des derniers gestes* (2001), destined to become a classic of *francophonie* (French-language literature produced outside France), displays the vast panorama of 20th-century armed resistance to colonialism through the imaginary biography of a fictional revolutionary, Balthazar Bodule-Jules, who on his deathbed reflects on his fight for freedom, which took him from his native Caribbean to countries as distant as Vietnam, Algeria, and the Congo.

Pascal Quignard won the 2002 Prix Goncourt for *Les Ombres errantes*, less a novel than a series of reflections on mythology from across the globe and on the passage of time in history. Gérard de Cortanze won the Prix Renaudot for *Assam*, a historical novel about his ancestor Aventino di Cortanze, who traveled to India in search of the legendary Assam tea. Chantal Thomas was awarded the Prix Femina for *Les Adieux à la reine*, a fictionalized account of Marie-Antoinette's downfall in July 1789, and Anne F. Garréta won the Prix Médicis for *Pas un jour*, in which she describes 12 women she has desired or who have desired her.

(VINCENT AURORA)

Canada. French Canadian literature displayed its usual variety in 2002, both cleaving to its favourites and following global trends. The literary scene in Quebec, the Canadian province in which virtually all French writing and publishing were located, evinced a flair for mixing politics and culture. At the book fair in Montreal, the Salon du Livre de

Montréal—the year's main literary event—fairgoers discovered a large exhibit extolling the joys of the French language in Canada, including the art of blasphemy. The exhibit underscored the 25th anniversary of the Charter of the French Language in the province of Quebec. Also at the fair, the Union des Écrivaines et des Écrivains Québécois, or Quebec Writers' Union, celebrated its 25th year of existence. (First organized as a promoter of Quebec independence, the union passed through a period of reflection as support for that political option waned.) Another event of note was the Blue Metropolis International Literary Festival, which celebrated its fourth year. Mixing readings and discussions in French and English, and sometimes in Spanish, the festival billed itself as an alternative to the segregation by language that often plagued cultural events in Montreal, the literary capital of French Canada.

Louis Gauthier won the Grand Prix du Livre de Montréal for his prose work *Voyage au Portugal avec un Allemand*. Having written in the shadows for decades, Gauthier was finally rewarded for his work. Academic-based literature got a boost when Monique LaRue won the Governor-General's Award, the country's top prize, for her novel about a college teacher, *La Gloire de Cassiodore*. At the cash registers, Monique Proulx triumphed with *Le Cœur est un muscle involontaire*, a novel whose main character could not stand writers. As for up-and-comers, Guillaume Vigneault showed that men could attract their share of the glory with *Chercher le vent* (2001). Vigneault's father, Gilles, was one of French Canada's best-loved poets and singers.

French Canada is a territory where writers cross genres with no self-consciousness at all; for example, in 2002 playwright Larry Tremblay produced a novel, *Le Mangeur de bicyclette*. His work was part of the general resurgence of the Leméac publishing firm, which reentered the marketplace after a period of difficulty. (DAVID HOMEL)

ITALIAN

The Sept. 11, 2001, terrorist attacks in the U.S., had quantitative and qualitative repercussions on the Italian literary scene in 2002. Book sales had begun to increase considerably during the last quarter of 2001. Readers showed a pronounced preference for essays, perhaps in an attempt to find a rational explanation for the traumatic

events. Breaking 10 years of self-imposed silence, Oriana Fallaci, one of the most influential Italian opinion makers of all time (and a resident of New York City), produced a hugely successful and controversial volume. Published in December 2001, *La rabbia e l'orgoglio* expanded an inflammatory newspaper article written in the weeks following September 11. It combined a passionate defense of democracy and pluralism with an affirmation of the superiority of the Western and Judeo-Christian world that many found offensive and untimely. Soon translated into several languages, *La rabbia e l'orgoglio* enjoyed considerable popularity abroad while continuing to spark controversy. After an unsuccessful attempt to prevent the distribution of the volume in France, human rights groups brought legal charges against Fallaci, who was accused of inciting racial hatred.

A competent account of the war in Afghanistan was provided by Gino Strada's *Buskashì: viaggio dentro la guerra*. The author's knowledge of the country predated the September 11 attacks and was linked to the personal and professional interests that had led him, as a surgeon, to found Emergency, a humanitarian association for the treatment of civilian victims of war.

Another successful polemical essay, Giorgio Bocca's *Piccolo Cesare*, dealt with the unique Italian political situation. The country's billionaire prime minister, Silvio Berlusconi, also served as minister of foreign affairs for almost a year and controlled a multimedia empire that included television channels, a major publishing house, and an influential newspaper. Bocca saw Berlusconi's success as a prime example of the degeneration of capitalism, resulting from blind faith in market laws, and he examined its significance in an international context.

This strong tendency toward reflection could be noticed too in books that were not directly inspired by the news, such as Michele Serra's *Cerimonie*. The volume's 12 pieces brought a combination of essay and fiction to bear on the secular practices of the 21st century, from "happy hour" to public gatherings. Elegant and lucid, this remarkable book explored the need to elaborate new rituals for expressing joy and sorrow in a world that had lost faith in religious and political ideologies.

Giuseppe Pontiggia's analysis of contemporary phenomena alternated with

more detached cultural and literary considerations in *Prima persona*, a collection of articles he had written for the newspaper *Il sole 24 ore*. A strong ethical vein ran throughout the collection, especially in the reflections on the link between responsibility, justice, crime, and punishment.

Two prominent artists produced autobiographical works: Dario Fo, recipient of the 1997 Nobel Prize for Literature, gave a tender and ironic account of his childhood in *Il paese dei Mezaràt: i miei primi sette anni (e qualcuno in più)*. Dacia Maraini's *La nave per Kobe: diari giapponesi di mia madre*, published in

Jerry Bauer

The Italian writer Dacia Maraini's novel again stops "on the verge of the forest."

late 2001, drew inspiration from the journals in which the writer's mother described the family's long journey from Italy to Japan and its experiences in the latter country. Memories from a distant past were juxtaposed with remarks on the author's present life and with reflections on the travels that would lead Maraini, as an adult, to revisit the same cities her mother had written about. Maraini had fashioned other works based on her life but had always refrained from describing the time spent in Japan, which ended tragically with the deportation of the entire family to a concentration camp because of the parents' refusal to swear allegiance to the Republic of Salò. Even in this book, only a few pages were devoted to that experience. In the conclusion, Maraini talked about her decision to stop, once again, "al limitare del bosco" ("on the verge of the forest") before venturing into the painful memories of the concentration camp.

Compared with this intense activity of critical reflection, the year's novels seemed to be somewhat less intense and vibrant, less capable of retaining readers' interest. Marta Morazzoni and Alessandro Baricco enjoyed a predictable but limited success among their followers with their latest works, *Una lezione di stile* and *Senza sangue*, respectively. Margaret Mazzantini won the Strega Prize with *Non ti muovere* (2001), a novel in which a man, awaiting news of his 15-year-old daughter who is undergoing a difficult surgery, remembers the events that led him to become a distant, indifferent father.

Andrea Camilleri confirmed his success with six new adventures of his hero, police inspector Montalbano, in *La paura di Montalbano*. Far more important, however, was the publication by Mondadori of a volume devoted entirely to Camilleri in the prestigious *Meridiani* series. The volume included the totality of Montalbano's adventures, other works by Camilleri, and relevant criticism. Apart from being a tribute to the author, it acknowledged the new status reached by the *giallo* (detective story), a genre traditionally deemed inferior by Italian literary criticism.

The publication of the first volume of Anna Maria Ortese's collected works (*Romanzi*, vol. 1) by Adelphi constituted a milestone in the critical recognition of one of the most original—and long-neglected—voices of 20th-century Italian narrative.   (LAURA BENEDETTI)

SPANISH

Spain. The main themes of the fiction published in Spain in 2002 had to do with emotions: pain, solitude, treason, passion, disaffection, and jealousy. Arturo Pérez-Reverte's best-selling novel *La reina del sur*, popular in both Spain and Latin America, explored the life of a Mexican drug dealer whose total lack of moral restraint goes hand in hand with an infinite capacity for cruelty. Josefina Aldecoa's *El enigma* was a story about love, the failure of love, and the difficulties of building a relationship. Manuel Rivas offered the reader a broad human landscape in the 25 short

stories found in *Las llamadas perdidas;* much of their strength lay in the author's synthetic style and power of suggestion. The characters of Antonio Gala's *Los invitados al jardín* are not afraid to show what they have hitherto hidden—their desire to love and be loved. In *Dos mujeres en Praga* by Juan José Millás, the reader is introduced to a mysterious and lonely middle-aged woman who decides to attend a writing workshop in order to look for a professional to write the story of her life. Javier Marías reflected on the importance of both speech and silence as he depicted treason and betrayal in his new novel, *Tu rostro mañana*. Luis Landero's *El guitarrista* told the story of Emilio, an adolescent who learns to play the guitar, hoping to be able to escape from his depressing job as a mechanic and from his evening classes. Pain, absence, and solitude are the three constant features of Eugenia Rico's *La muerte blanca*, in which the author recalls the death of her brother. The 26-year-old writer of *La matriz y la sombra*, Ana Prieto Nadal, described the fervour of a loving passion that runs away from its object in order to avoid its decay in time.

The winner of the Cervantes Prize was José Jiménez Lozano, a Spanish fiction writer, mystic, and journalist. His most recent work was the novel *El viaje de Jonás* (2002). Two of the publishing world's most renowned literary prizes were awarded to Latin American writers in 2002: the Alfaguara prize to the Argentine Tomás Eloy Martínez (*see* BIOGRAPHIES) and the Planeta prize to Peruvian Alfredo Bryce Echenique. The National Prize for Narrative was given to a novel written in Basque, *SP rako tranbia*, ("A Tram in SP") by Unai Elorriaga. The National Prize for Poetry was awarded to Carlos Marzal for his book *Metales pesados* (2001), where, in the words of the poet, "I explore humanity divided between the most excessive vitality and the anguish of solitude." José Álvarez Junco was honoured with the National Prize for Essay for his work *Mater dolorosa* (2001), which explores the question of Spanish identity in terms of the progressive nationalism of the 19th century. In Mexico Juan Goytisolo was granted the Octavio Paz Prize for Poetry and Essay for lifetime achievement. During the year Spain lost Nobel Prize winner Camilo José Cela (*see* OBITUARIES), author of *La colmena*.
(VERÓNICA ESTEBAN)

Latin America. As in years past, literary news from Latin America in 2002 cen-

tred on novels, but also noteworthy were memoirs and essays published by some of Latin America's best-known writers. The first volume of the much-anticipated memoirs of Gabriel García Márquez, *Vivir para contarla*, came out in October and became an instant bestseller throughout the Spanish-speaking world. In a narrative style and language familiar to his readers, García Márquez depicted his early years in Colombia before the publishing of *Cien años de soledad*. Fellow novelist Carlos Fuentes of Mexico constructed an intellectual autobiography of social, political, and personal reflections in *En esto creo*, a dictionary of brief essays based on the letters of the alphabet: *amistad* (friendship), *belleza* (beauty), *celos* (jealousy), *dios* (God), *educación*, and so on. Guatemalan writer Augusto Monterroso published *Pájaros de Hispanoamérica*, in which he related anecdotes and experiences he had shared with some of Latin America's most important writers. Another nonfiction work making news in Latin America was *Los Bioy*, a book on the lives of the famous Argentine literary couple Adolfo Bioy Casares and Silvina Ocampo written by the journalist Silvia Arias and Jovita Iglesias, a Spanish woman who worked for the couple for 50 years. From Uruguay, Mario Benedetti offered a series of reflections on contemporary life and its problems in the prose poems of *Insomnios y duermevelas*.

Several important prizes were awarded to Latin American writers in 2002. Argentine novelist and journalist Tomás Eloy Martínez (*see* BIOGRAPHIES) won the Alfaguara Prize in Spain for his novel *El vuelo de la reina*, which told the story of a newspaper editor's erotic obsession with a woman half his age against the backdrop of an Argentina suffering from economic and moral bankruptcy. The Planeta Prize was given to Peruvian novelist Alfredo Bryce Echenique for *El huerto de mi amada*, a tale of passionate love between a young man of 17 and an attractive woman in her 30s. The Emecé 2002 Prize went to the Argentine writer Ángela Pradelli for her novel *Amigas mías*, about the lives of four friends—their daily lives, their husbands, their children, and their jobs, as well as their desires, passions, and tragedies. Finally, Peruvian Mario Vargas Llosa won the PEN/Nabokov Award 2002 from the PEN American Center.

Other novels published in 2002 included, from Chile, Isabel Allende's *La ciudad de las bestias*, about a young man sent to New York to live with his grandmother, who turns out to be a travel writer and who then takes her grandson on a magical journey to the Amazon in search of a giant creature. The life of Cleopatra was fictionalized in *De un salto descabalga la reina* by Carmen Boullosa of Mexico. Also coming out of Mexico was Hugo Hiriart's *El agua grande*, a novel presenting an elaborate metafictional dialogue between a teacher and his student on the origin and meaning of narrative. Mayra Montero wrote *El capitán de los dormidos*, a story of love and betrayal written against the background of Puerto Rican politics and history. Peruvian journalist Jaime Bayly published the novel *La mujer de mi hermano*, which portrayed the love triangle between a meticulous banker, his wife, and his artistic and seductive younger brother.

The accomplished short-story writer Juan Carlos Botero, son of internationally known Colombian painter Fernando Botero, published his first novel, *La sentencia*. It tells the story of Francisco Rayo, an adventurer who spends half his time studying archives of Spanish history in search of information on sunken treasure and the rest of his time in the Caribbean searching for it. Also coming out of Colombia was *Comandante Paraíso*, by novelist Gustavo Álvarez Gardeazábal, a novel that

painted a broad picture of drug trafficking in his country. It fictionalizes the lives of the great drug lords and the social and political consequences of their actions. *Los impostores* by the Colombian Santiago Gamboa tells the tale of three characters—impostors longing to be what they are not—who meet by chance in Beijing as they search for a mysterious manuscript. Gamboa's novel avoids the references to Colombia's violence prevalent in much of the country's current narrative and employs humour and a variety of literary styles. Further evidence of the current vitality of Colombian prose fiction comes from Mario Mendoza and his collection of stories, *Satanás*, which are brought together through the historical personnage Campo Elías, a Vietnam veteran who killed dozens of people in a restaurant in Bogotá in the 1980s.

The Argentine novelist Federico Andahazi wrote a unique mystery story, *El secreto de los flamencos*, which takes place in Renaissance Flanders, where Florentine masters hide mathematical secrets on perspective and Flemish masters protect secrets about pigmentation and colour. A disciple of one of the great painters turns up murdered and a beautiful Portuguese woman complicates the painter's rivalries.

(JOHN BARRY)

PORTUGUESE

Portugal. One of the most distinguished Portuguese authors, Agustina Bessa Luís, was awarded the fiction prize of the Association of Portuguese Writers for her novel *Jóia de família*. This was the first volume of a proposed trilogy known as *The Uncertainty Principle*. It was remarkable that such a prize, the most coveted by any Portuguese fiction writer, was awarded for a second time to one author.

The novels of Bessa Luís, all of which were set in the northern part of Portugal, had tangled plots. They examined the problems of great families living in a small area. This circumscribed society, hitherto quite stable, begins to be shaken by waves of economic change, and Bessa Luís spun her narrative in a way that captured the new moods and the psychological makeup of her characters. Bessa Luís was particularly good at detecting the nature of the conflicts, unclear to the characters themselves, and she challenged the reader to follow her in her inquiry. Her style was rich and ornate, overly allusive and visually impressive, and it was fluent in its evocation of passions and situations, showing a descriptive quality that translated well into the film adaptations of her novels. *Jóia de família* was made into a film by the acclaimed Portuguese director Manoel de Oliveira.

Portuguese fiction was flourishing. The number of titles published was on the increase, which provided a better opportunity for works of quality to appear. Short narratives were taking the place of the long novel, but literary experimentation was still the preserve of well-established names. Júlio Moreira, one of the most innovative authors of fiction, published a new novel, *Dentro de cinco minutos*, in which he addressed the conflict of the big corporations in their relations with the society they were supposed to serve. Relying mainly on the art of the dialogue, he succeeded in showing the elusiveness of intentions in a complex game of interests that swamps everything.

One of Portugal's most prolific writers, Urbano Tavares Rodrigues, who had been writing fiction for more than 50 years, was honoured for his work. Its main themes were solitude, the pain of living and loving, and the injustice of social conditions. The human variety of his characters was impressive, and his engaging style made the reading of his novels a real joy. (L.S. REBELO)

The Argentine writer Tomás Eloy Martínez receives the Alfaguara Prize.

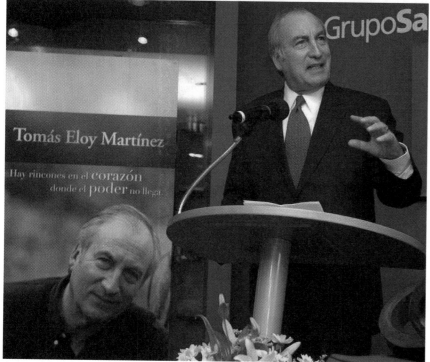

AP/Wide World Photos

Brazil. João Ubaldo Ribeiro's new novel *Diário do farol* was a best-seller during 2002, perhaps in part owing to the worldwide scandals within the Roman Catholic Church. (*See* RELIGION: *Sidebar.*) The protagonist is a morally corrupt priest whose confessions take the form of a rambling memoir. (Ribeiro's distinguished artistic career was examined by Zilá Bernd and Francis Utéza in *O caminho do meio: uma leitura da obra de João Ubaldo Ribeiro* [2001].)

The 2002 collections of short fiction included Rubem Fonseca's *Pequenas criaturas*, which focused on both the common and the extreme psychological dilemmas of daily living. For example, in one story a young fellow's girlfriend urges him to tattoo her name on his penis.

Several new works of theatre graced the Brazilian stage in 2002. Among them were *Astro por um dia*, João Bethencourt's latest light comedy about the show-business world, and Matheus Nachtergaele's co-production of a version of Georg Büchner's *Woyzeck*, called *Woyzeck, o brasileiro*. Büchner's play was adapted to contemporary proletarian Brazil, a nation that, coincidentally, in 2002 elected Latin America's first president to rise from the proletariat: "Lula" (Luiz Inácio da Silva; *see* BIOGRAPHIES).

In late 2001 Christopher Dunn published a new study of the Brazilian Tropicália countercultural movement of the late 1960s, *Brutality Garden: Tropicália and the Emergence of a Brazilian Counterculture*. In 2002 the *Revista do livro*, a leading journal of intellectual debate in Brazil between 1956 and 1970, was relaunched by the Biblioteca Nacional with an orientation similar to that of the original but with a mission to incorporate technology into the Brazilian intellectual panorama. Zélia Gattai was inducted into the Brazilian Academy of Letters and occupied the chair held by Jorge Amado, her recently deceased husband.

Several Internet sites dedicated to broadening the appeal of Brazilian literature and culture gained large audiences. Jaime Leibovitch founded "Projeto poesia brasileira" <http://www.geocities.com/SoHo/6705/poesiabr/apres.html> to stimulate a wider interest in Brazilian poetry. João Cézar de Castro Rocha, in conjunction with the Advanced Program in Contemporary Culture at the Federal University of Rio de Janeiro and other organizations, further enhanced his site, "Crítica literária brasileira: pólo de pesquisa e infor-mação" <http://acd.ufrj.br/pacc/literaria/index.html>, which sought to make its audience aware of recent Brazilian literary trends within an international context.   (IRWIN STERN)

RUSSIAN

The year 2002 in Russian literature was marked by a series of literary scandals with distinctly political overtones. For one, the conservatively oriented youth group Idushchiye Vmeste ("Forward Together") organized a campaign against two of Russia's most popular writers of the 1990s, Viktor Pelevin and Vladimir Sorokin. In Sorokin's case Idushchiye Vmeste managed to have an official criminal investigation launched into Sorokin's allegedly "pornographic" writings. A criminal investigation was also initiated against Bayan Shiryanov (pseudonym of Kirill Vorobyov), whose novels depicted the underworld of drug users. Even more seriously, the trial of Eduard Limonov, the famous writer and leader of the extremist National Bolshevik Party, began. Limonov, who had been in jail for almost two years, was charged with having plotted antigovernment violence. Finally, there was the uproar associated with the awarding of the 2002 National Best-Seller Prize to Aleksandr Prokhanov, editor in chief of the nationalistic daily newspaper *Zavtra* ("Tomorrow"), for his novel *Gospodin Geksogen* ("Mr. Geksogen"). Rather pedestrian as a literary work, *Gospodin Geksogen* nevertheless drew widespread attention for its depiction of the Moscow apartment bombings of late 1999 as the work of the Russian government and secret police. The scandals associated with these works, most of which had little literary value, bore witness to the continuing social importance of the writer and literature in Russia.

Several books by younger writers depicting the experiences of their genera-

Viktor Pelevin and other popular authors found themselves under attack by conservatives.

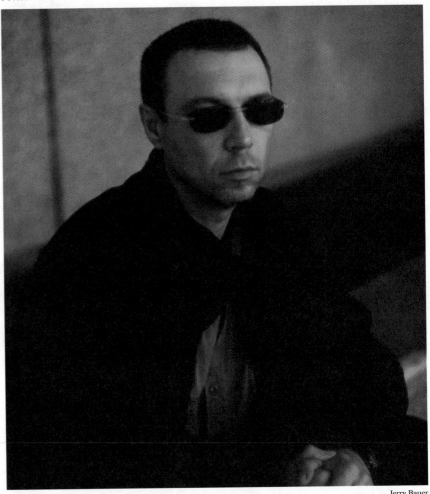

Jerry Bauer

tion garnered critical acclaim and commercial success. The two most significant among them were Ilya Stogov's *Macho ne plachut* (2001; "Macho Men Don't Cry") and Irina Denezhkina's *Day mne!—Song for Lovers*. The former, stylistically reminiscent of Henry Miller and Charles Bukowski, grittily portrayed Russian bohemian life. *Day mne!*, which placed second to Prokhanov's novel for the National Best-Seller Prize, told the story of a group of Russian teenagers.

Russia's literary establishment still took little notice of the younger generation. The Apollon Grigoryev Prize was awarded to the 78-year-old playwright Leonid Zorin for his novel *Trezvennik* ("The Teetotaler"), which follows several members of the liberal Soviet intelligentsia as they attempt to adapt to post-Soviet life. The poet Sergey Gandlevsky's *Nrzb* ("Indeciph."), a finalist for the Russian Booker Prize, essentially took up the same subject. Among the other Booker finalists was Vladimir Sorokin's *Lyod* ("Ice"). The political significance of Sorokin's nomination did not go unnoticed. He had never before been a Booker Prize finalist, and the work itself was generally thought of as one of his weaker literary performances. The winner, however, was Oleg Pavlov for *Karagandinskiye devyatiny* ("Karagarnda Nines"), the final book of his *Povest poslednikh dney: trilogiya* (2001, "A Tale of Recent Days: Trilogy").

Poets Aleksey Tsvetkov, Nikolay Kononov, and Oleg Yuryev published prose in 2002. Tsvetkov, prominent in the 1970s and '80s poetry group Moscow Time, released a novel and selection of other prose under the title *Prosto golos* ("The Voice Itself"). Kononov, in a collection of short stories entitled *Magichesky bestiariy* ("A Magical Bestiary"), continued his explorations of sexual deviance and high literary style. Yuryev brought out the second in a series of novels, *Novy golem, ili voyna starikov i detei* ("The New Golem, or the War of the Old Folk and the Children"), in part based on Gustav Meyrink's classic novel *Der Golem;* it presented a highly subjective and grotesque panorama of Russia, Europe, and the U.S. in the mid-1990s. Oleg Postnov's novel *Strakh* (2001; "Fear") combined a Nabokovian style with late- and post-Soviet subject matter and stirred some debate. Another novelist of the Nabokov school, Leonid Girshovich, published *Subbota navsegda* (2001; "Saturday Forever"). Asar

Eppel, a well-known poet and translator as well as one of Russia's finest living prose stylists, released a collection of stories, *Tri povestvovaniya* ("Three Narratives"). Vasil Bykov, the famed bilingual—Russian and Belarusian—author, also published a new book during the year, *Korotokaya pesnya* ("A Brief Song"). Vladimir Sharov's *Voskreseniye Lazarya* ("The Resurrection of Lazarus") was the most accomplished of many works that continued to explore fictionally the meaning of Russia's political and intellectual history.

The most important single book of poetry published in 2002 was Yelena Shvarts's two-volume selected works. Other important poets publishing new collections were Bella Akhmadulina, Aleksandr Kushner, Timur Kibirov, Sergey Wolf, Aleksandr Mironov, Mariya Stepanova, and Svetlana Ivanova. The writer and postmodern critic Vyacheslav Kuritsyn, who in September shut down his influential Web site *Kuritsyn-Weekly*, conducted a poll of Russian writers to "rate" Russia's poets. The winner was Gandlevsky. Kibirov, Shvarts, and Dmitry Prigov followed close behind. Since the poll illustrated the makeup of contemporary Russia's literary groups and the power relations among them, its results might be of interest to future historians of Russian literature.

The deaths of several beloved figures of the Soviet era occurred: Viktor Astafyev (who died at the end of 2001), the greatest of the "Country Prose" writers; historical novelist Yury Davydov; poet and science-fiction writer Vadim Shefner; adventure writer Viktor Konetsky; and playwright Aleksandr Volodin (who also died at the end of 2001).

(VALERY SHUBINSKY)

JEWISH

Hebrew. By 2002 the autobiographical novel had become one of the leading genres in contemporary Hebrew fiction. Perhaps the best one in 2002 was Ory Bernstein's *Safek hayim* ("A Dubious Life"). Others included Amos Oz's *Sipur 'al ahavah ve-ḥoshekh* ("Tale of Love and Darkness"), Ioram Melcer's *Ḥibat tsiyon* ("The Lure of Zion"), and Jacob Buchan's *Naḥal ḥalav ve-tapuz dam* ("Flowing Milk and Blood Orange").

David Grossman chose to focus on family matters in *Ba-guf ani mevinah* ("In Another Life"). Michal Govrin, on the other hand, dealt directly with the complicated political situation in

Jerry Bauer

Established author Meir Shalev scored again in 2002 with the family drama **Fontanelle.**

Hevzeḳim ("Snapshots"), and so did Orly Castel-Bloom in *Ḥalaḳim enoshiyim* ("Human Parts"). Other works by veteran writers included Aharon Appelfeld's *Lailah ve-'od lailah* (2000; "Night After Night"), Meir Shalev's *Fontanelle*, Savion Liebrecht's *Makon tov lalaila* ("A Good Place for the Night"), and Dan Tsalka's *Besiman halotus* ("Under the Sign of the Lotus"). Hanna Bat Shahar departed from the short-story form in her first novel, *Hana'ara me'agan Michigan* ("The Girl from Lake Michigan"). Works by younger writers included Edgar Keret's *Anihu* ("Cheap Moon"), Aleks Epshṭain's *Matkone ḥalomot* ("Dream Recipes"), and Shoham Smith's collection of short stories *Homsenṭer* ("Homecenter").

Veteran poet Haim Gouri published a new collection of poems (*Me'uḥarim* ["Late Poems"]), as did Arieh Sivan (*Hashlamah* ["Reconciliation"]) and Nurit Zarchi (*ha-Tiḳrah 'afah* [2001; "The Ceiling Flew"]). Yitzchak Laor's *Shirim, 1974–1992* ("Poems, 1974–1992") and Rachel Chalfi's *Miḳla'at ha-shemesh* ("Solar Plexus)," poems from 1975 to 1999, were collections of early poems. Aharon Shabtai published *Artseinu* ("Our Land"), poems from 1987 to 2002. The most interesting first collection of poetry was Anna Herman's *Ḥad-ḳeren* ("Unicorn"), rich in imagery and sound patterns. The veteran dramatist Yoram Levy Porat published his first book of poetry, *Oniyot ha-teh* (2001; "Tea Boats").

The most comprehensive literary study was Yael S. Feldman's *Lelo heder mishlaḥen* ("No Room of Their Own," translated from the English edition of 1999), which examined gender and nation in Israeli women's fiction. Avner Holtzman published *Temunah le-neged 'enai* ("Image Before My Eyes"), with essays on Micah Joseph Berdichevsky, Uri Nissan Gnessin, and Joseph Ḥayyim Brenner. (AVRAHAM BALABAN)

Yiddish. During 2002 autobiography was important in Yiddish literature. Yoysef Gubrin's *In shotn fun umkum: zikhroynes* ("In the Shadow of the Holocaust: Reminiscences") portrayed his childhood in Transnistria, his stay in the ghetto of Mogilev, and his journey by ship to Israel. Avrom Meyerkevitsh's *Oyfn veg tsu dem tsugezogtn land* ("On the Way to the Promised Land") vividly recounted his sojourn in Russia and homecoming to Israel.

Aaron Spiro's *Mentshn un goyrl* ("Men and Fate") provided an absorbing account of the war period and the post-Holocaust scene in Eastern Europe.

Jeremy Cahn wrote a masterful study of the Jew as reflected by Christians in the Middle Ages in *Vi a blinder in a shpigl* ("Like a Blind Man in a Mirror"). In his *Der bal-khaloymes fun Manhetn* ("The Dreamer from Manhetn"), Yakov Belek fashioned an intriguing mixture of historical boundaries and authorial fantasy to effect the transformation of Jesus of Nazareth into an Israeli Jew.

In his collection *Reportazshn un eseyen* ("Reportage and Essays"), Dovid Sh. Katz described a variety of Eastern European Jewish communities.

The 37,000-word *Dos naye yidish-frantseyzishe verterbukh* ("The New Yiddish-French Dictionary") was compiled by Berl Vaysbrot and Yitskhak Ni-

borski. Yoysef Guri issued a valuable anthology of picturesque Yiddish expressions, *Vos darft ir mer?* ("What More Do You Need?").

December saw the appearance of the second volume of Emanuel S. Goldsmith's monumental collection *Di Yidishe literatur in Amerike 1870–2000*. Yekhiel Shayntukh published a reconstruction of writer Aaron Zeitlin's polemics in a collection of letters titled *Bereshus harabim uvirshus hayokhed: Aaron Tseytlin vesifrus yidish* ("In the Public Domain and the Private Domain: Aaron Zeitlin in Yiddish Literature"). Aleksandr Shpiglblat issued a highly acclaimed study of Itsik Manger in *Bloe vinklen: Itsik Manger—lebn, lid, un balade* ("Blue Corners: Itsik Manger—His Life, Poems, and Ballads"). It included a selection of the poet's work.

Troim Katz Handler's *Simkhe* (2001; "Celebration") was a rich gathering of love letters in poem form. Beyle Schaechter-Gottesman pursued her lyrical muse in *Perpl shlengt zikh der veg* ("The Purple Winding Road").

(THOMAS E. BIRD)

TURKISH

For poetry, usually strong in Turkey, the year 2002 was meagre. An exceptionally fine new book entitled *Şeyler kitaby* ("Book of Things") came from the perennially innovative poet İlhan Berk, who won top honours at the Istanbul Book Fair. Noteworthy collections included Ataol Behramoğlu's *Yeni aşka gazel* ("Ode to New Love"), which marked the poet's coming to terms with the aesthetics of classical Ottoman poetry; Süreyya Berfe's *Seni seviyorum* ("I Love You"), highly polished neoromantic lyrics; and İzzet Yasar's *Dil oyunları* ("Language Games"), which Berk characterized as "obscure, difficult, imprecated."

UNESCO proclaimed 2002 International Nazım Hikmet Year. The centennial of Hikmet's birth was observed by many activities in Turkey and abroad (London, Paris, and New York, for example). Literary circles were impressed, too, that Özdemir İnce was elected to membership in the European Poetry Academy.

The year basically belonged to fiction. Two eminent novelists, Adalet Ağaoğlu and Yaşar Kemal, were honoured at major symposia—the former at Boğaziçi University in Istanbul and the latter at Ankara's Bilkent University, which also gave him an honorary doc-

torate (first ever to a novelist by a leading Turkish university).

Orhan Pamuk's *Kar* ("Snow"), with its potent political comments, was a runaway best-seller, although its critical reception was cool, sometimes hostile. It marked a new age in American-type book promotions and called forth opinions about aggressive campaigns distorting literary values.

Important novels included Kemal's *Karıncanın su içtiği* ("Where the Ant Drank Water"), Murathan Mungan's *Yüksek topuklar* ("High Heels"), Tahsin Yücel's *Yalan* ("The Lie"), Erendiz Atasü's *Bir yaşdönümü rüyası* ("A Mid-Life Dream"), Zülfü Livaneli's *Mutluluk* ("Joy"), Şebnem İşigüzel's *Sarmaşık* ("Ivy"), and Mehmet Eroğlu's *Zamanın manzarası* ("Panorama of Time"). Two best-sellers stirring extensive debate were Perihan Mağden's *İki genç kızın romanı* ("A Novel of Two Young Girls"), depicting a lesbian love affair, and Ahmet Altan's *Aldatmak* ("To Deceive"), about types of deception.

Among the significant collections of essays and critical articles were *Budalalığın keşfi* ("The Discovery of Stupidity") by Hilmi Yavuz and *Güzel yazı defteri* ("Lovely Notebook") by Tomris Uyar.

Turkey mourned the loss of two prominent literary figures in 2002: Melih Cevdet Anday, poet, novelist, essayist, playwright, and translator, and Memet Fuat, literary critic.

(TALAT SAIT HALMAN)

PERSIAN

Thanks to the more culturally tolerant atmosphere in Iran brought about by the reform movement led by Pres. Mohammad Khatami, Persian-language literary activity in 2002 was more abundant and more diffuse, if not higher in artistic quality than in recent years. The year's best-selling book was a biography of Sha'bān Ja'farī, a low-level functionary of the monarchical state who was thought to have organized the 1953 coup. Written by Los Angeles-based journalist Humā Sarshār and published in Los Angeles in March, the book appeared in Tehran by May in pirated editions, sometimes heavily censored. By year's end it had gone through at least 12 printings (about 50,000 copies), a phenomenal achievement in the context of Iran's recent history. The situation gave rise to renewed political controversy and also to heated debates over Iran's refusal to join the Berne conventions on copyright.

The proliferation of literary prizes in Iran and the establishment of similar awards in Tajikistan and Afghanistan brought lesser-known authors to the fore. In Iran the Mehregan Prize went to Zūyā Pīrzād for *Chirāghhā rā man khāmūsh mīkunam* ("I'll Turn Off the Lights"), which told the story of an Armenian-Iranian family in the oil boomtown of Abadan in the early 1960s; the novel shed much-needed light on this important ethnic and religious minority. A better-known and pioneer woman writer, octogenarian Simin Daneshvar, published the novel *Sariban-i sargardan* ("Wandering Caravan Master").

Among expatriate Iranians too, women dominated the fiction scene, led by two California-based writers. Veteran novelist Shahrnush Parsipur and the younger Mihrnūsh Mazārī'i made new strides with, respectively, *Bar bal-i bad nishastan* ("Riding on the Wind's Wing") and *Khākistarī* ("Gray").

The year marked the death of several literary figures, most notably that of Ahmad A'ta, who was associated with the leftist Tudeh Party and wrote under the pen name Ahmad Mahmud. His death marked the end of a generation of political fiction writers whose work typified the middle decades of the 20th century. The new dominant trend appeared to be writing from a conservative Islamic point of view.

(AHMAD KARIMI-HAKKAK)

ARABIC

An outflow of fiction by women writers characterized Arabic literary pro-

Palestinian poet Maḥmūd Darwīsh performs at a reading in Beirut in April.

duction in 2002. This literature distinguished itself from past contributions by the absence of a confrontational tone and by the extension of feminist themes to an interest in national and global affairs. Dealing with mainstream social issues, these works portrayed female characters whose strong voices lacked the apologetic or defensive tone of earlier writings. An outstanding novel in this category is Mayy al-Ṣāyigh's *Fī intiẓār al-qamar* ("Waiting for the Moon"), which chronicled the story of the 1948 *Nakba* ("Disaster," as the Palestinians refer to the events attending the first Arab-Israeli War). The novel, set in Lebanon, reveals the strength of Palestinian women as they assume responsibility in exile when men falter or are busy resisting the occupation. Al-Ṣayigh softened the harshness of her topic with a flowing poetic prose. In *Bustān aḥmar* ("A Red Garden"), Lebanese writer Hādyah Sa'īd examined the lives of political refugees in exile. Moving between Baghdad, Iraq; Beirut, Lebanon; Rabat, Morocco; and London, her novel depicted the refugees' failure to find meaning in their lives.

Egyptian Mīrāl al-Ṭaḥāwī established herself as an innovative writer with a well-defined technique in her third novel, *Naqarāt al-ẓibā'* ("The Hoofbeats of Gazelles"). Her subject was the changing world of the Bedouins, which she had previously evoked in *Al-khibā'* (1996; *The Tent*). *Naqarāt al-ẓibā'* focuses on the desperate efforts of an aging man to maintain tradition, to which he sacrifices the happiness of his three daughters. Al-Ṭaḥāwī has a distinctive style and a solid knowledge of Bedouin dialect, reinforced by her familiarity with classical Arabic literature. Egyptian novelist Najwā Sha'bān moved into new territory for women when she set her novel *Nawwat al-Karm* ("Al-Karm Gales") in the world of sailors.

Leila Aboulela published her collection of short stories *Coloured Lights* at the end of 2001, transporting the reader to her native Sudan as she depicted both its conflict of cultures and the strength of its traditions. "The Museum," a story from that collection, won the Caine Prize 2000. In Syria, Nādra Barakāt al-Ḥaffār pursued more traditional themes of love and betrayal in her latest novel, *Qulūb mansiyyah* ("Forgotten Hearts").

The young Tunisian Rashīdah al-Shārnī continued to make her mark with a collection of short stories, *Ṣahīl al-as'ilah* ("The Neighing of Questions"), which in 2000 received the first prize for women's creativity in the short story awarded by young women's clubs in Sharja. Another prizewinner was the Egyptian-born Francophone writer Yasmine Khlat, who received the Prize of Five Francophone Continents for her novel *Le Désespoir est un péché* ("Despair Is a Sin") in November 2001. Commemorating the centenary of the death of the Egyptian poet and woman of letters 'A'ishah Taymūr, the Egyptian Forum of Women and Memory reedited her 1892 book *Mir'āt al-ta'ammul fī al-umūr* ("The Mirror to Contemplate Matters"). Both Dār al-Mar'ah al-'Arabiyyah (The Institute of the Arab Woman) and its journal *Nūr* played similar roles.

Two male novelists portrayed city life, 'Alā' al-Aswānī in *'Imārat Ya'qūbiyyān* ("Ya'qūbiyān Building"), which centres on the life of some of the inhabitants of an old downtown building in Cairo, and Muḥammad Jibrīl in *Madd al-mawj* ("The Rising of the Waves"), which takes place in Alexandria.

Poetry was recognized in November 2001 through the awarding of the Lannan Foundation Prize for Cultural Freedom to Palestinian Maḥmūd Darwīsh. (*See* BIOGRAPHIES.) His latest collection, *Ḥālat ḥiṣār* ("A State of Siege"), revolved, as did poetry in many Arab countries, around the events of the second *intifāḍah*. Young poets were recognized in the fifth Tangiers poetry award festival, named after Iraqi poet Nāzik al-Malā'ikah. The first prize was shared by Syrian Ghāliyyah Khujah, for her collection *Unshūdat al-dhanni* ("The Song of Suspicion"), and Moroccan 'Abd al-Karīm al-'Ammārī, for *Al-Awā'il* ("The First Ones"). The Naguib Mahfouz Medal for Literature was awarded to the Moroccan Ben Salem Himmich for his novel *Al-'Allamah* (1997 and 2001; "The Erudite"), which features the renowned sociologist Ibn Khaldun.

Egypt lost its well-known literary critic 'Abd al-Qādr al-Qutt in June 2002. A professor of Arabic literature at Ayn Shams University, al-Qutt had centred his attention on modern Arabic poetry and contributed to the translation into Arabic of established English writers. Jordanian novelist Mu'nis al-Razzāz also died during the year.

(AIDA A. BAMIA)

CHINESE

The year 2002 was one of poor harvest in the literary fields of China. Although more than 500 novels and 400 collections of short stories and essays were published, critics commonly felt that the year brought no outstanding new book of literature.

Like print literature, electronic or Internet literature was in the doldrums in 2002. The biggest of the literary Web sites in mainland China, Rongshu.com, was sold at a very low price and lost its appeal to both authors and readers. Other like-minded Web sites, such as Wenxue.com, one by one curtailed their activities and narrowed their scope, mainly for lack of financial support.

Nonetheless, a bright spot was provided by Yang Chunguang, a ferocious poet whose verses and essays on poetry could be seen only on the Internet. As a former officer and an activist during the Tiananmen Square pro-democracy movement of 1989, Yang developed a powerful poetic style that since 1990 had combined linguistic experiment with political protest. By his own account, he deliberately "deconstructed" his straightforward narration by cutting the links between scenes. This unusual style gave a shocking power to most of his recent poems, especially his suites of poems entitled *Mengma* ("Mammoth"), *Wo xiang dengshang Tiananmen* ("I Want to Mount the Tiananmen"), and *Pige waitao* ("Leather Overcoat"), which were widely read on the Internet in 2002.

Two novels of 2002 were also worthy of mention. One was *Anshi* ("Hint") by Han Shaogong, one of the leading contemporary novelists in China. In contrast to Han's last novel, *Maqiao ci dian* (1996; "Dictionary of Maqiao"), which stressed the language's decisive power to transform human life, *Anshi* tried to expose the limits of language. Having no coherent plot and no central character, the novel consisted of 113 independent chapters, some of which were short essays while others seemed to be theoretical analyses. This odd structure caused some critics to treat *Anshi* as nonfiction, although Han insisted that the book was a novel.

The other novel of interest was *Tao li* ("Disciples"), a first novel by reporter Zhang Zhe. Using his well-developed reportorial skills, Zhang described vividly a series of ugly incidents in the lives of a famous law professor and his students and lovers, some of which were based on actual events of the 1990s. With its calm narration and black humour, the novel presented a satire view of corruption on campus, which could be seen as a microcosm of society at large. (WANG XIAO MING)

JAPANESE

In September 2002 the Supreme Court ruled that Miri Yū's *Ishi ni oyogu sakana* ("Fish Swimming in Stones"), published in the September 1994 issue of *Shinchō*), could not be published in book form, since Yū portrayed as a friend of the heroine a Korean-Japanese girl who resembled one of Yū's friends in her physical features (including a conspicuous tumour on her face) and in her personal history. The girl's family relationships also resembled those of Yū's friend. This decision by the Supreme Court marked the first instance in which the court had prohibited publication on the basis of an individual's right to privacy and dignity. The court said that the damage to the real person could well be greater than any damage suffered by Yū as a fiction writer. This misfortune did not extend to Yū's former work *Gōrudo rasshu* (1998; *Gold Rush*), translated into English in 2002. *Gold Rush* fared well in the United States as well as in Asian countries. Furthermore, a movie based upon Yū's nonfiction work *Inochi* (2000; "Life") became one of the most popular Japanese films of 2002.

In the first half of 2002, the Akutagawa Prize, awarded semiannually to the most promising new Japanese writer of fiction, went to Yu Nagashima's "Mō supiido de haha wa" ("Mom, at Full Speed"), published in the November 2001 issue of *Bungakukai*. Nagashima told the story of a divorced mother from the viewpoint of her only son, who found her attitudes toward him sometimes cold-blooded, sometimes too sweet. The story depicted sensitively the emotional ups and downs and maternal love of a middle-aged woman. In the second half of the year, the Akutagawa Prize went to Shūichi Yoshida's "Paaku raifu" ("Park Life," from the June 2002 *Bungakukai*). Setting his story in a central Tokyo park, Yoshida portrayed the present-day life led by urban adolescents.

Haruki Murakami published a new novel, *Umibe no Kafuka* ("Kafka on the

Jerry Bauer

Haruki Murakami found literary success in both Japan and the United States in 2002.

Shore"), in which a 15-year-old boy trips through the world of concepts in the quiet of a library. Murakami's collection of short stories *Kami no kodomotachi wa mina odoru* (2000; "All God's Children Can Dance"), which was translated into English in 2002 as *After the Quake: Stories*, received good reviews in the United States. In Kenzaburō Ōe's new novel, *Ureigao no dōji* ("A Child's Sorrow on His Face"), the Nobel Prize winner depicted the comical adventure befalling an old novelist seeking the truth about his dead mother and a disappearing friend. Keiichirō Hirano, four years after his sensational debut with *Nisshoku* ("Solar Eclipse"), told a story of great Parisian artists of the 19th century in *Maisō* ("Burial").

The Yomiuri Prize for Literature went to Anna Ogino's *Horafuki Anri no boken* ("The Adventures of Henri, a Boaster"), about a girl searching for her father's roots. The Kawabata Prize was awarded to Taeko Kōno's *Han shoyūsha* (2001; "A Half Owner") and to Kō Machida's *Gongen no odoriko* ("A Dancer of Incarnation"). Best-selling literary works that appeared during the year included Kaori Ekuni's *Oyogu no ni anzen de mo tekisetsu de mo arimasen* ("It's Not Safe or Suitable for Swim"), Yasutaka Tsutsui's *Ai no hidarigawa* ("The Left Side of Love"), and Hiromi Kawakami's *Ryūgū* ("The Palace of the Dragon King").

(YOSHIHIKO KAZAMARU)

Mathematics and Physical Sciences

Scientists made a novel **TUNGSTEN STRUCTURE** that promised **MORE-EFFICIENT LIGHTBULBS** and moved closer to explaining the **LACK OF ANTIMATTER** in the universe. Six **AMERICANS** and one **ISRAELI** died tragically on the **COLUMBIA** in February 2003.

MATHEMATICS

Mathematics in 2002 was marked by two discoveries in number theory. The first may have practical implications; the second satisfied a 150-year-old curiosity.

Computer scientist Manindra Agrawal of the Indian Institute of Technology in Kanpur, together with two of his students, Neeraj Kayal and Nitin Saxena, found a surprisingly efficient algorithm that will always determine whether a positive integer is a prime number.

Since a prime is divisible only by 1 and itself, primality can, of course, be determined simply by dividing a candidate n in turn by successive primes 2, 3, 5, . . . up to $\sqrt{n}$ (larger divisors would require a corresponding smaller divisor, which would already have been tested). As the size of a candidate increases, however—for example, contemporary cryptography utilizes numbers with hundreds of digits—such a brute-force method becomes impractical; the number of possible trial divisions increases exponentially with the number of digits in a candidate.

For centuries mathematicians sought a primality test that executes in polynomial time—that is, such that the maximum number of necessary operations is a power of the number of digits of the candidate. Several primality tests start from the "little theorem" discovered in 1640 by the French mathematician Pierre de Fermat: "For every prime p and any smaller integer a, the quantity $a^{p-1} - 1$ is divisible by p." Hence, for a given number n, choose a and check whether the relation is satisfied. If not, then n is not prime (i.e., is composite). While passing this test is necessary for primality, it is not sufficient; some composites (called pseudoprimes) pass the test for at least one a, and some (called Carmichael numbers, the smallest of which is 561) even pass the test for every a.

Two alternative approaches are conditional tests and probabilistic (or randomized) tests. Conditional tests require additional assumptions. In 1976 the American computer scientist Gary L. Miller obtained the first deterministic, polynomial-time algorithm by assuming the extended Riemann hypothesis about the distribution of primes. Later that year the Israeli computer scientist Michael O. Rabin modified this algorithm to obtain an unconditional, but randomized (rather than deterministic), polynomial-time test. Randomization refers to his method of randomly choosing a number a between 1 and $n - 1$ inclusive to test the primality of n. If n is composite, the probability that it passes is at most one-fourth. Tests with different values of a are independent, so the multiplication rule for probabilities applies (the product of the individual probabilities equals the overall probability). Hence, the test can be repeated until n fails a test or its probability of being composite is as small as desired.

Although such randomized tests suffice for practical purposes, Agrawal's algorithm excited theoreticians by showing that a deterministic, unconditional primality test can run in polynomial time. In particular, it runs in time proportional to slightly more than the 12th power of the number of digits, or to the 6th power if a certain conjecture about the distribution of primes is true. While the new algorithm is slower than the best randomized tests, its existence may spur the discovery of faster deterministic algorithms.

While these primality tests can tell if an integer is composite, they often do not yield any factors. Still unknown— and a crucial question for cryptography—is whether a polynomial-time algorithm is possible for the companion problem of factoring integers.

Another famous problem in number theory, without far-reaching consequences, was apparently solved in 2002. The Belgian mathematician Eugène Charles Catalan conjectured in 1844 that the only solution to $x^m - y^n = 1$ in which x, y, m, and n are integers all greater than or equal to 2 is $3^2 - 2^3 = 1$. In 1976 the Dutch mathematician Robert Tijdeman showed that there could not be an infinite number of solutions. Then in 1999 the French mathematician Maurice Mignotte showed that $m < 7.15 \times 10^{11}$ and $n < 7.78 \times 10^{16}$. This still left too many numbers to check, but in 2002 the Romanian mathematician Preda Mihailescu announced a proof narrowing the possible candidates to certain extremely rare numbers, known as double Wieferich primes.   (PAUL J. CAMPBELL)

CHEMISTRY

Inorganic Chemistry. In 2002 two groups of U.S. researchers working together reported the serendipitous synthesis of compounds of uranium and the noble gases argon, krypton, and xenon. Despite more than 40 years of effort, chemists had been able to make only a handful of compounds from the noble gases. These gases are the six elements helium, neon, argon, krypton, xenon, and radon. All have an oxidation number of 0 and the maximum possible number of electrons in their outer shell (2 for helium, 8 for the others). Those traits are hallmarks of chemical stability, which means that the noble gases resist combining with other elements to form compounds. Indeed, until the 1960s chemists had regarded these elements as completely inert, incapable of forming the bonds that link atoms together to make compounds.

Lester Andrews and co-workers of the University of Virginia were studying reactions involving CUO, a molecule of carbon, uranium, and oxygen atoms bonded together in a linear fashion. In order to preserve the CUO, they protected it in frozen neon chilled to –270 °C (–450 °F). When they repeated the reactions by using argon as the protectant, however, the results were totally different, which suggested that new compounds had formed. Xenon and krypton also gave unanticipated results. Bruce Bursten and associates at Ohio State University then performed theoretical calculations on supercomputers to confirm the findings. Andrews and Bursten speculated that other metals also might bond to noble gases under the same ultracold conditions.

For nearly 200 years chemists had tried to decipher the structure of the complex molecules in the solutions called molybdenum blues. Scientists knew that the elements molybdenum and oxygen form large molecules that impart a blue colour to the solutions. The first of these so-called polyoxomolybdate (POM) molecules were identified in 1826. No one, however, had been able to explain the compounds' molecular structure in solution. During the year Tianbo Liu, a physicist at Brookhaven National Laboratory, Upton, N.Y., reported the presence of giant clusterlike structures in molybdenum blue solutions that resemble the surface of a blackberry. Unlike other water-soluble inorganic compounds, POM molecules apparently do not exist as single ions in solution; rather, they cluster together by the hundreds in bunches. Liu said the "blackberry" structures in molybdenum blue may represent a heretofore unobserved stable state for solute molecules.

Carbon Chemistry. Scientists continued their search for commercial and industrial applications of the tiny elongated molecular structures known as carbon nanotubes. Discovered in 1991, nanotubes consist of carbon atoms bonded together into graphitelike sheets that are rolled into tubes 10,000 times thinner than a human hair. Their potential applications range from tiny wires in a new generation of ultrasmall computer chips to biological probes small enough to be implanted into individual cells. Many of those uses, however, require attaching other molecules to nanotubes to make nanotube derivatives. In general, methods for making small amounts of derivatives for laboratory experimentation have required high temperatures and other extreme conditions that would be too expensive for industrial-scale production.

During the year chemists from Rice University, Houston, Texas, and associates from the Russian Academy of Sciences, Moscow, described groundbreaking work that could simplify the production of nanotube derivatives.

Rice's John Margrave, who led the team, reported that the key procedure involved fluorination of the nanotubes—i.e., attaching atoms of fluorine, the most chemically reactive element—an approach developed at Rice over the previous several years. Fluorination made it easier for nanotubes to undergo subsequent chemical reactions essential for developing commercial and industrial products. Among the derivatives reported by the researchers were hexyl, methoxy, and amido nanotubes; nanotube polymers similar to nylon; and hydrogen-bonded nylon analogs.

Organic Chemistry. Antiaromatic molecules are organic chemistry's will-o'-the-wisps. Like aromatic molecules, they have atoms arranged in flat rings and joined by two different kinds of covalent bonds. Unlike aromatic molecules, however, they are highly unstable and reactive and do not remain long in existence. Chemistry textbooks have used the cyclopentadienyl cation—the pentagonal-ring hydrocarbon molecule C_5H_5 deficient one electron and thus having a positive charge—as the classic example of the antiaromatics' disappearing act.

Joseph B. Lambert and graduate student Lijun Lin of Northwestern University, Evanston, Ill., reported a discovery that may rewrite the textbooks. While trying to synthesize other organic cations (molecules with one or more positive charges), they produced a cyclopentadienyl analog in which methyl (CH_3) groups replace the hydrogen atoms and found that it did not behave like the elusive entity of textbook fame. Rather, it remained stable for weeks in the solid state at room temperature. Lambert proposed that cyclopentadienyl be reclassified as a nonaromatic material.

Physical Chemistry. Gold has been treasured throughout history partly because of its great chemical stability. Resistant to attack by oxygen, which rusts or tarnishes other metals, gold remains bright and beautiful under ordinary environmental conditions for centuries. Gold, however, does oxidize, forming Au_2O_3, when exposed to environments containing a highly reactive form of oxygen—e.g., atomic oxygen or ozone. Hans-Gerd Boyen of the University of Ulm, Ger., led a German-Swiss team that announced the discovery of a more oxidation-resistant form of gold. The material, called Au_{55}, consists of gold nanoparticles; each nanoparticle is a tiny cluster comprising exactly 55 gold atoms and measuring about 1.4 nm (nanometres). Boyen's group reported

that Au_{55} resisted corrosion under conditions that corroded bulk gold and gold nanoparticles consisting of either larger or smaller numbers of atoms. The researchers speculated that the chemical stability is conferred by special properties of the cluster's 55-atom structure and that Au_{55} may be useful as a catalyst for reactions that convert carbon monoxide to carbon dioxide.

Incandescent tungsten-filament light-bulbs, the world's main source of artificial light, are noted for inefficiency. About 95% of the electricity flowing through an incandescent bulb is transformed into unwanted heat rather than the desired entity, light. In some homes and large offices illuminated by many lights, the energy waste multiplies when additional electricity must be used for air conditioning to remove the unwanted heat from electric lighting.

Shawn Lin and Jim Fleming of Sandia National Laboratories, Albuquerque, N.M., developed a microscopic tungsten structure that, if it could be incorporated into a filament, might improve a lightbulb's efficiency. The new material consists of tungsten fabricated to have an artificial micrometre-scale crystalline pattern, called a photonic lattice, that traps infrared energy—radiant heat—emitted by the electrically excited tungsten atoms and converts it into frequencies of visible light, to which the lattice is transparent. The artificial lattice, in effect, repartitions the excitation energy between heat and visible light, favouring the latter. Lin and Fleming believed that the tungsten material could eventually raise the efficiency of incandescent bulbs to more than 60%.

Applied Chemistry. Zeolites are crystalline solid materials having a basic framework made typically from the elements silicon, aluminum, and oxygen. Their internal structure is riddled with microscopic interconnecting cavities that provide active sites for catalyzing desirable chemical reactions. Zeolites thus have become key industrial catalysts, selectively fostering reactions that otherwise would go slowly, especially in petroleum refining. About 40 zeolites occur naturally as minerals such as analcime, chabazite, and clinoptilolite. To date, chemists had synthesized more than 150 others, and they were on a constant quest to make better zeolites.

Avelino Corma and colleagues of the Polytechnic University of Valencia, Spain, and the Institute of Materials Science, Barcelona, reported synthesis of a new zeolite that allows molecules enhanced access to large internal cavities suitable for petroleum refining. Dubbed ITQ-21, it incorporates germanium atoms rather than aluminum atoms in its framework, and it possesses six "windows" that allow large molecules in crude oil to diffuse into the cavities to be broken down, or cracked, into smaller molecules. In contrast, the zeolite most widely used in petroleum refining has just four such windows, which limits its efficiency.

Chemists at Oregon State University reported an advance that could reduce the costs of making crystalline oxide films. The films are widely used in flat-panel displays, semiconductor chips, and many other electronic products. They can conduct electricity or act as insulators, and they have desirable optical properties.

To achieve the necessary crystallinity with current manufacturing processes, the films must be deposited under high-vacuum conditions and temperatures of about 1,000 °C (1,800 °F). Creating those conditions requires sophisticated and expensive processing equipment. Douglas Keszler, who headed the research group, reported that the new process can deposit and crystallize oxide films of such elements as zinc, silicon, and manganese with simple water-based chemistry at atmospheric pressure and at temperatures of about 120 °C (250 °F). The method involved a slow dehydration of the materials that compose crystalline oxide films. In addition to reducing manufacturing costs, the process could allow the deposition of electronic thin films on new materials. Among them were plastics, which would melt at the high temperatures needed in conventional deposition and crystallization processes.

(MICHAEL WOODS)

PHYSICS

Particle Physics. In 2002 scientists took a step closer to explaining a major mystery—why the observed universe is made almost exclusively of matter rather than antimatter. The everyday world consists of atoms built up from a small number of stable elementary particles—protons, neutrons, and electrons. It has long

been known that antiparticles also exist, with properties that are apparently identical mirror images of their "normal" matter counterparts—for example, the antiproton, which possesses a negative electric charge (rather than the positive charge of the proton). When matter and antimatter meet, as when a proton and an antiproton collide, both particles are annihilated. Antiparticles are very rare in nature. On Earth they can be produced only with great difficulty under high vacuum conditions and, unless maintained in special magnetic traps, they survive for a very short time before colliding with normal matter.

If matter and antimatter are mirror images, why does the vast majority of the universe appear to be made up of normal matter? In other words, what asymmetry manifested itself during the big bang to produce a universe of matter rather than of antimatter? The simplest suggestion is that matter and antimatter particles are not completely symmetrical. During the year physicists working at the Stanford Linear Accelerator Center (SLAC) in California confirmed the existence of such an asymmetry, although their experiments raised other questions. The huge research team, comprising scientists from more than 70 institutions around the world, studied very short-lived

particles known as B mesons and their antiparticles, which were produced in collisions between electrons and positrons (the antimatter counterpart of electrons). A new detector dubbed BaBar enabled them to measure tiny differences in the decay rates of B mesons and anti-B mesons, a manifestation of a phenomenon known as charge-parity (CP) violation. From these measurements they calculated a parameter called $\sin 2\beta$ (sine two beta) to a precision of better than 10%, which confirmed the asymmetry. Although the BaBar results were consistent with the generally accepted standard model of fundamental particles and interactions, the size of the calculated asymmetry was not large enough to fit present cosmological models and account for the observed matter-antimatter imbalance in the universe. SLAC physicists planned to examine rare processes and more subtle effects, which they expected might give them further clues.

Researchers from Brookhaven National Laboratory, Upton, N.Y., confirmed previous work showing a nagging discrepancy between the measured value and the theoretical prediction of the magnetic moment of particles known as muons, which are similar to electrons but heavier and unstable. The magnetic moment of a particle is a measure of its propensity to twist itself into alignment with an external magnetic field. The new value, measured to a precision of seven parts per million, remained inconsistent with values calculated by using the standard model and the results of experiments on other particles. It was unclear, however, whether the discrepancy was an experimental one or pointed to a flaw in the standard model.

Lasers and Light. One region of the electromagnetic spectrum that had been unavailable for exploitation until 2002 was the so-called terahertz (THz) region, between frequencies of 0.3 and 30 THz. (A terahertz is one trillion, or 10^{12}, hertz.) This gap lay between the high end of the microwave region, where radiation could be produced by high-frequency transis-

A collaborating physicist stands on a ladder at one end of the BaBar detector, where an asymmetry was measured in the way B mesons and their antiparticles decay.

tors, and the far-infrared region, where radiation could be supplied by lasers. In 2002 Rüdeger Köhler, working with an Italian-British team at the nanoelectronics-nanotechnology research centre NEST-INFM, Pisa, Italy, succeeded in producing a semiconductor laser that bridged the gap, emitting intense coherent pulses at 4.4 THz. The device used a so-called superlattice, a stack of periodic layers of different semiconductor materials, and produced the radiation by a process of quantum cascade.

Claire Gmachl and co-workers of Lucent Technologies' Bell Laboratories, Murray Hill, N.J., fabricated a similar multilayered configuration of materials to produce a semiconductor laser that emitted light continuously at wavelengths of six to eight micrometres, in the infrared region of the spectrum. Unlike typical semiconductor lasers, which give off coherent radiation of a single wavelength, the new device represented a true broadband laser system having many possible applications, including atmospheric pollution detectors and medical diagnostic tools. In principle, the same approach could be used to fabricate devices with different wavelength ranges or much narrower or wider ranges.

Condensed-Matter Physics. Since 1995, when it was first made in the laboratory, the state of matter known as a Bose-Einstein condensate (BEC) has provided one of the most active fields of physical research. At first the mere production of such a state represented a triumph, garnering for the scientists who first achieved a BEC the 2001 Nobel Prize for Physics. By 2002 detailed investigations of the properties of such states and specific uses for them were coming to the fore. Bose-Einstein condensation involves the cooling of gaseous atoms whose nuclei have zero or integral-number spin states (and therefore are classified as bosons) so near to a temperature of absolute zero that they "condense"—rather than existing as independent particles, they become one "superatom" described by a single set of quantum state functions. In such a state the atoms can flow without friction, making the condensate a superfluid.

During the year Markus Greiner and co-workers of the Max Planck Institute for Quantum Optics, Garching, Ger., and Ludwig Maximilian University, Munich, Ger., demonstrated the dynamics of a BEC experimentally. To manipulate the condensate, they formed an "optical lattice," using a number of crisscrossed laser beams; the result was a standing-wave light field having a regular three-dimensional pattern of energy maxima and minima. When the researchers caught and held the BEC in this lattice, its constituent atoms were described not by a single quantum state function but by a superposition of states. Over time, this superposition carried the atoms between coherent and incoherent states in the lattice, an oscillating pattern that could be observed and that provided a clear demonstration of basic quantum theory. The researchers also showed that, by increasing the intensity of the laser beams, the gas could be forced out of its superfluid phase into an insulating phase, a behaviour that suggested a possible switching device for future quantum computers.

BECs were also being used to produce atom lasers. In an optical laser the emitted light beam is coherent—the light is of a single frequency or colour, and all the components of the waves are in step with each other. In an atom laser the output is a beam of atoms that are in an analogous state of coherence, the condition that obtains in a BEC. The first atom beams could be achieved only by allowing bursts of atoms to escape from the trap of magnetic and optical fields that confined the BEC—the analogue of a pulsed laser. During the year Wolfgang Ketterle (one of the 2001 Nobel physics laureates) and co-workers at the Massachusetts Institute of Technology succeeded in producing a continuous source of coherent atoms for an atom laser. They employed a conceptually simple, though technically difficult, process of building up a BEC in a "production" trap and then moving it with the electric field of a focused laser beam into a second, "reservoir" trap while replenishing the first trap. The researchers likened the method to collecting drops of water in a bucket, from which the water could then be drawn in a steady stream. Making a hole in the bucket—i.e., allowing the BEC to flow as a beam from the reservoir—would produce a continuous atom laser. The work offered a foretaste of how the production, transfer, and manipulation of BECs could become an everyday technique in the laboratory.

Solid-State Physics. The study of systems containing only a few atoms not only gives new insights into the nature of matter but also points the way toward faster communications and computing devices. One approach has been the development and investigation of so-called quantum dots, tiny isolated clumps of semiconductor atoms with dimensions in the nanometre (billionth of a metre) range, sandwiched between nonconducting barrier layers. The small dimensions mean that charge carriers—electrons and holes (traveling electron vacancies)—in the dots are restricted to just a few energy states. Because of this, the dots can be thought of as artificial atoms, and they exhibit useful atomlike electronic and optical properties.

Toshimasa Fujisawa and co-workers of the NTT Basic Research Laboratories, Atsugi, Japan, studied electron transitions in such dots involving just one or two electrons (which acted as artificial atoms analogous to hydrogen and helium, respectively). Their encouraging results gave support to the idea of using spin-based electron states in quantum dots for storage of information. Other researchers continued to investigate the potential of employing coupled electron-hole pairs (known as excitons) in quantum dots for information storage. Artur Zrenner and co-workers at the Technical University of Munich, Ger., demonstrated the possibility of making such a device. Although technological problems remained to be solved, it appeared that quantum dots were among the most promising devices to serve as the basis of storage in future quantum computers.

(DAVID G.C. JONES)

ASTRONOMY

Solar System. The question of whether Pluto should be regarded as a full-fledged planet was highlighted in late 2002 with the announcement of a discovery by astronomers from the California Institute of Technology. In October Michael Brown and Chad Trujillo reported an object beyond the orbits of Neptune and Pluto some 6.3 billion km (4 billion mi) from the Sun. Designated 2002 LM60 and tentatively named Quaoar by its discoverers, the object falls into the class of bodies called trans-Neptunian objects, whose count has grown into the hundreds since the first one was identified in 1992. Quaoar was first spotted in June with a telescope on Mt. Palomar and subsequently observed with the Earth-orbiting Hubble Space Telescope, which resolved its image. It appeared to be about 1,300 km (800 mi) in diameter, about half the size of Pluto.

Quaoar was the largest object found in the solar system since the discovery of Pluto in 1930. Although it is about 100 million times more massive than a typical comet, the object—like Pluto and the other bodies orbiting beyond Neptune—was thought to be part of the Kuiper belt, a region in the outer solar system believed to contain myriad icy bodies and to be the source of most short-period comets. The latest discovery was certain to provoke further debate about the planetary nature of the larger trans-Neptunian objects and the inclusion of Pluto among them.

After NASA's 2001 Mars Odyssey spacecraft reached the planet Mars in October 2001, it spent the next few months lowering and reshaping its orbit for its science mapping mission. Throughout 2002 the probe imaged the Martian surface and took a variety of measurements. Its instruments included a neutron detector designed to map the location of intermediate-energy neutrons knocked off the Martian surface by incoming cosmic rays. The maps revealed low neutron levels in the high latitudes, which was interpreted to indicate the presence of high levels of hydrogen. The hydrogen enrichment, in turn, suggested that the polar regions above latitude 60° contain huge subsurface reservoirs of frozen water ice. The total amount of water detected was estimated to be 10,000 cu km (2,400 cu mi), nearly the amount of water in Lake Superior. Odyssey's instruments, however, could not detect water

lying at depths much greater than a metre (3.3 ft), so the total amount could be vastly larger. Such information would be vitally important if human exploration of Mars was ever to be undertaken in the future.

In line with the accelerating rate of discoveries of new moons for the giant planets, astronomers reported finding still more moons for Jupiter. After combining the results of telescopic observations in December 2001 and May 2002 from Mauna Kea, Hawaii, a team led by Scott S. Sheppard and David C. Jewitt of the University of Hawaii announced the detection of 11 new Jovian moons, bringing the total number known to 39. In view of the latest discoveries, the team proposed that there might be as many as 100 Jovian moons. The new objects are tiny—no more than 2–4 km (1.25–2.5 mi) in diameter—and have large elliptical orbits inclined with respect to the orbits of the four large Galilean moons. They also revolve around Jupiter in a direction opposite to its rotation. Together these properties suggested that the small moons are objects captured by Jupiter's gravity early in its history.

Stars. The rate of discovery of planets orbiting other stars, like that of moons in the solar system, continued to accelerate. Extrasolar planets were first reported in 1995; by the end of 2002,

more than 100 had been reported, roughly a third of them in that year alone. Among the latest discoveries was a planetary system somewhat similar to the Sun's own. In 1996, 55 Cancri—a star lying in the constellation Cancer—had been found to have a planet with about the mass of Jupiter orbiting it about every 14.6 days. That period placed the planet at about one-tenth the Earth-Sun distance from its central star. In 2002 Geoffrey Marcy and Debra A. Fisher of the University of California, Berkeley, R. Paul Butler of the Carnegie Institution of Washington, D.C., and co-workers announced their finding of a second planet with a mass of three to five times that of Jupiter revolving around 55 Cancri in an orbit comparable to Jupiter's orbit around the Sun. The Marcy team also described the likely presence of yet a third planet in the system having an orbital period of about 44 days. Although the known companions of 55 Cancri did not make the system an exact analogue of the Sun's, their discovery offered hope that more closely similar systems would be found.

Pulsars—rapidly rotating, radio-emitting, highly magnetized neutron stars—were first detected in 1967. By 2002 more than 1,000 were known. Pulsars arise as the by-product of supernova explosions, which are the final event in

This global map of Mars in intermediate-energy (epithermal) neutrons was created from measurements made by the 2001 Mars Odyssey spacecraft. Deep blue areas indicate the lowest levels of neutrons, suggestive of water ice below the surface.

NASA/JPL/University of Arizona/Los Alamos National Laboratories

the life cycle of massive stars. During the past millennium, only a half dozen supernova explosions in the Milky Way Galaxy have been preserved in historical records—in the years 1006, 1054, 1181, 1572, 1604, and 1680. The explosion leading to the famous Crab Nebula, for example, occurred on July 4, 1054. This supernova remnant has long been known to contain a pulsar.

In 2002 discovery of the youngest radio pulsar found to date was reported. It lies within an extended radio source known as 3C 58, the remnant of the supernova explosion of 1181. To detect it radio astronomers began with the 2001 observation of a point X-ray source, dubbed RXJ 1856-3754, made with NASA's Earth-orbiting Chandra X-Ray Observatory. Fernando Camilo of Columbia University, New York City, and

Earth Perihelion and Aphelion, 2003

Jan. 4	Perihelion, 147,102,650 km (91,405,350 mi) from the Sun
July 4	Aphelion, 152,100,360 km (94,510,780 mi) from the Sun

Equinoxes and Solstices, 2003

March 21	Vernal equinox, 01:00[1]
June 21	Summer solstice, 19:10[1]
Sept. 23	Autumnal equinox, 10:47[1]
Dec. 22	Winter solstice, 07:04[1]

Eclipses, 2003

May 16	Moon, total (begins 01:05[1]), the beginning visible in Europe, southern Greenland, eastern North America, Central and South America, Africa, the western Middle East; the end visible in southern Greenland, North America (except extreme northwest), Central and South America, western Africa, southwestern Europe, part of New Zealand.
May 31	Sun, annular (begins 01:46[1]), the beginning visible in northwestern North America, central Greenland, Iceland, most of Europe, central and northern Asia, the Arabian Peninsula; the end visible in extreme northeastern Africa, southwestern Asia, central Europe, Greenland, northern North America.
Nov. 8–9	Moon, total (begins 22:15[1]), the beginning visible in Africa, Europe, western and central Asia, Greenland, eastern North America, Central and South America (except the southern tip); the end visible in Europe, northwestern Asia, Greenland, North America, Central and South America, Africa (except extreme eastern part), the western Middle East.
Nov. 23–24	Sun, total (begins 20:46[1]), the beginning visible in the extreme southern tip of South America, Australia, New Zealand; the end visible in southern Indonesia, western Australia, the southern Indian Ocean, the southern Atlantic Ocean.

[1] Universal time.
Source: *The Astronomical Almanac for the Year 2003* (2002).

collaborators then used the 100 × 110-m (328 × 361-ft) Robert C. Byrd Green Bank Telescope to detect the X-ray source by its radio pulses. The radio pulsar was found to be rotating at about 15 times per second, in agreement with the previously reported X-ray source. X-ray data from the Chandra Observatory, combined with the young age of the pulsar, implied that the pulsar might be cooler or smaller (or both) than it should be if it was made up mainly of neutrons. Some theoretical interpretations suggested that the pulsar may consist of quarks, pions, or other exotic form of matter.

Galaxies and Cosmology. Although astronomers can study distant galaxies in great detail, it is very difficult to peer into the centre of Earth's own Galaxy by using optical telescopes. The plane of the Milky Way contains a great deal of dust, which strongly obscures what lies within it. Infrared radiation emitted by objects at the Galaxy's core, however, can penetrate the dust. Using near-infrared telescopes, an international team of astronomers led by Rainer Schödel of the Max Planck Institute for Extraterrestrial Physics, Garching, Ger., managed to penetrate to the heart of the Milky Way to track the motion of stars in the vicinity of the compact radio source—and black hole candidate—called Sagittarius (Sgr) A*. Over a period of 10 years, they watched the motion of a star (designated S2) that lies close to Sgr A*. They found that S2 orbits the galactic centre in about 15.2 years with a nearest approach to Sgr A* of only about 17 light-hours. This corresponds to such a small orbit that only a black hole having a mass equal to three million to five million Suns can fit within it. These observations provided the best evidence to date that black holes exist.

The hot big-bang model proposes that the universe began with an explosive expansion of matter and energy that subsequently cooled, leading to its present state. As optical observations have revealed, the universe contains visible galaxies that are receding from one another. It also contains a nearly uniform background of microwave radiation, which currently has a temperature of about 3 K (three degrees above absolute zero). New studies in 2002 of distant galaxies and of the microwave background radiation continued to clarify and solidify the validity of the big-bang evolutionary picture.

By year's end as many as 26 separate experiments had measured fluctuations

in the intensity of the background radiation. Details of the measurements provided valuable information about the expansion of the universe some 400,000 years after its inception. The most startling conclusion from these studies was that the universe consists of about 5% ordinary matter (the luminous matter seen in galaxies) and about 25% dark (nonluminous) matter, which is probably cold but whose composition is unknown. The other 70% comprises a kind of repulsive force that was proposed originally by Albert Einstein, who called it the *cosmological constant*, and that more recently was being termed *dark energy* or *quintessence*, although it does not have the character of what is usually called energy. Together these constituents add up to just what is needed to make the spatial geometry of the universe "flat" on cosmic scales. One implication of this flatness is that the universe will continue to expand forever rather than eventually collapsing in a "big crunch."

(KENNETH BRECHER)

SPACE EXPLORATION

Manned Spaceflight. Assembly of the International Space Station (ISS) continued to dominate manned space operations in 2002. Construction was delayed several months, however, when in June a sharp-eyed ground inspector spotted tiny cracks in the metal liner of a main-engine propellant line of the space shuttle orbiter *Atlantis*. Similar cracks, which had the potential to destroy both vehicle and crew, turned up in the fuel or oxygen lines of the orbiter *Discovery* and subsequently *Columbia* and *Endeavour*. NASA halted shuttle missions until October while a welding fix was developed, tested, and implemented.

On Feb. 1, 2003, a shocked world learned the news that the shuttle orbiter *Columbia* had broken up catastrophically over north-central Texas at an altitude of about 60 km (40 mi) as it was returning to Cape Canaveral, Florida, from a non-ISS mission. All seven crew members—five men and two women—died; among them was Ilan Ramon, the first Israeli astronaut to fly in space. One focus of the investigation into the cause of the disaster was on *Columbia*'s left wing, which had been struck by a piece of insulation from the external tank during launch and which had been the first part of the orbiter to cease supplying sensor data during its descent.

The ISS grew during 2002 with the attachment of the first three segments of the primary truss, the station's structural backbone. The central S0 segment, carried up by shuttle in April, was placed atop the Destiny laboratory module delivered the previous year. The rest of the truss would extend to port and starboard from the station. S1 (starboard) and P1 (port) segments, added in October and November, respectively, would hold radiators for eliminating waste heat generated by the crew and the station's systems. They would also support electrical cables supplying power to the ISS modules from the solar-panel arrays that would eventually be attached to the ends of the completed main truss. In addition, the truss segments had rails to allow the Canadian-built robot arm Canadarm2, delivered to the ISS in 2001, to travel the length of the truss and help attach new elements.

On a separate shuttle mission in June, the reusable Leonardo Multi-Purpose Logistics Module carried supplies and gear to outfit the station. A significant piece of that cargo was the Microgravity Science Glovebox, which would allow astronauts to conduct a wide range of experiments in materials science, combustion, fluids, and other space-research fields. In September, NASA

named biochemist-astronaut Peggy Whitson, then aboard the ISS, as the station's first science officer, a new position intended to emphasize the position of science on the ISS.

Space tourism received a boost with the flight of South African businessman Mark Shuttleworth to the ISS aboard a Russian Soyuz TM in April. In contrast to the controversy surrounding Dennis Tito's similar flight in 2001, Shuttleworth's sortie received some support from NASA, and Shuttleworth carried experiments developed by South African students. Another Soyuz mission, launched to the station in October, served as a test flight for an improved version of the TM design, designated Soyuz TMA.

A non-ISS shuttle mission in March was devoted to servicing the Hubble Space Telescope (HST) for the fourth time. The crew replaced the Faint Object Camera, the last of the HST's original science instruments, with a new Advanced Camera for Surveys, which soon provided stunning images of the universe. The crew also installed improved solar arrays and other equipment.

China carried on in its methodical quest to place a human in space with the third and fourth unmanned test flights (launched March 25 and De-

cember 30, respectively) of its Shenzhou spacecraft, which was based on the Soviet-Russian Soyuz design. The latest flights incorporated tests of escape and life-support systems. The first human flight could come as early as 2003. China also began expressing interest in participating in the ISS program even as Russia was voicing doubts that it had the resources to continue meeting its commitments.

Space Probes. An important deep-space mission, NASA's Comet Nucleus Tour (CONTOUR), was lost as it was being boosted from Earth orbit on August 15. CONTOUR had been placed in a parking orbit on July 3 to await the proper moment to begin the planned trajectory that would take it within 100 km (60 mi) of comet nuclei in 2003 and 2006. After its upper stage fired, ground controllers were unable to regain contact, and tracking stations soon found debris near the planned trajectory. A preliminary investigation indicated that the stage failed and destroyed the craft.

After reaching Mars in late 2001, NASA's 2001 Mars Odyssey spacecraft spent three months using atmospheric braking techniques to settle into the orbit selected for its science mapping mission, which began February 18. In addition to returning high-quality images of the Martian surface, Odyssey's instruments mapped the distribution of surface and near-surface elements. Some of these data suggested the presence of subsurface frozen water in large areas surrounding the poles. (See *Astronomy,* above.)

Launched in February 1999, NASA's Stardust spacecraft opened its ultra-pure collector arrays between August and December 2002 to capture interstellar dust particles. On November 2 it flew within 3,000 km (1,900 mi) of asteroid Annefrank, returning images and other data. This was a dress rehearsal of its planned Jan. 2, 2004, flight through the tail of Comet Wild 2, when it would gather comet dust particles. The spacecraft was to return to Earth with its collection of extraterrestrial materials in January 2006.

Unmanned Satellites. A unique Earth-mapping mission began on March 17 with the orbiting of the U.S.-German twin Gravity Recovery and Climate Experiment spacecraft (GRACE 1 and 2, nicknamed Tom and Jerry after the cartoon characters). By tracking the precise distance between the two spacecraft and their exact altitude and path over Earth, scientists could measure subtle variations in Earth's gravitational field

European Space Agency astronaut Frank De Winne demonstrates the Microgravity Science Glovebox before its delivery to the International Space Station in June.

ESA 2002

and detect mass movements due to such natural activity as sea-level changes, glacial motions, and ice melting.

Other environmental satellites sent into space in 2002 included the U.S. Aqua, launched May 4 as a complement to Terra (launched 1999), and the European Space Agency's Envisat 1, launched March 1. Aqua was designed to study the global water cycle in the oceans, ice caps, land masses, and atmosphere. Its six instruments were provided by the U.S., Japan, and Brazil. (*See* EARTH SCIENCES: *Meteorology and Climate.*) Envisat carried an array of 10 instruments to investigate global warming, the ozone hole, and desertification. China orbited its Fengyun ("Wind and Cloud") 1D and Haiyang ("Marine") 1 satellites on May 15. Fengyun employed

a digital imager to observe clouds and monitor for floods and sandstorms. Haiyang had an ocean imager to observe chlorophyll concentration, temperatures, and other aspects of the seas. On May 4 France launched its SPOT 5 Earth-observation satellite, which carried cameras for producing high-resolution colour and black-and-white images in conventional and stereo versions. Applications of SPOT imagery ranged from specialized map products and agricultural management to defense and natural-hazard assessment.

NASA's High Energy Solar Spectroscopic Imager (HESSI) was launched on February 5 in a successful bid to replace an earlier version lost during launch in 1999. HESSI monitored X-ray and gamma-ray energy released by

solar flares. Its instruments measured the energy levels and intensity of flares across a map of the Sun's disk.

In September NASA awarded a contract to TRW to design and build the Next Generation Space Telescope. The instrument would orbit the Sun at a gravitationally stable point about 1.5 million km (930,000 mi) from Earth on the planet's night side, and it would be named after James Webb, NASA's second administrator, who led the Apollo program and pursued a strong U.S. program of space science. Since its launch was not expected before 2010, Congress asked NASA to ensure that the HST operated as long as possible.

Launch Vehicles. The quest to develop safer, more cost-effective replacements for the space shuttle continued as the U.S. refocused efforts in its Space Launch Initiative. While a clear winner had yet to emerge, NASA turned its attention to multistage systems rather than the single-stage-to-orbit approach exemplified by the VentureStar project, which was canceled in 2001. Engine-design work was refined to concentrate on kerosene as a fuel rather than liquid hydrogen. Although liquid hydrogen is a more efficient source of energy than kerosene, it is also less dense and so requires larger vehicles. NASA also initiated programs to upgrade the space shuttle system and keep it flying through the year 2020 (almost 40 years after its first flight) and to develop a small Atlas- or Delta-launched spaceplane to ferry crews to and from the ISS and serve as a lifeboat for the station.

Two new U.S. commercial launch systems made their debut. The Atlas 5, combining technologies evolved from U.S. and former Soviet ballistic missiles, made its first flight on August 21, with the Hot Bird 6 satellite as payload. The Delta IV, using the new RS-68 hydrogen-oxygen liquid-fueled engine derived from the space shuttle main engine, was delayed by a series of small problems but finally made a successful first flight November 20 carrying the Eutelsat W5 spacecraft. On September 10 Japan's H-2A rocket made its third flight, in which it placed a twin payload into orbit. The vehicle's first flight, in August 2001, went smoothly, but during the second launch on February 4, one of its two payloads, a $4.5 million reentry technology demonstrator, failed to separate and was lost. Continued success of the H-2A was deemed crucial to Japan's hopes of competing in the commercial launch market.

(DAVE DOOLING)

Launches in support of human spaceflight, 2002

Country	Flight	Crew[1]	Dates[2]	Mission/payload
U.S.	STS-109, *Columbia*	Scott Altma Duane Carey John Grunsfeld Nancy Currie James Newman Richard Linnehan Michael Massimino	March 1–12	repairs and upgrades to Hubble Space Telescope
Russia	Progress	—	March 21	ISS supplies
China	Shenzhou 3	—	March 25	third unmanned test flight of China's first manned spacecraft
U.S.	STS-110, *Atlantis*	Michael Bloomfield Stephen Frick Jerry Ross Steven Smith Ellen Ochoa Lee Morin Rex Walheim	April 8–19	delivery of S0 truss segment to ISS
Russia	Soyuz TM-34	Yury Gidzenko Roberto Vittori Mark Shuttleworth[3]	April 25–May 4	exchange of Soyuz return craft for ISS crew (TM-33 with TM-34)
U.S.	STS-111, *Endeavour*	Kenneth Cockrell Paul Lockhart Franklin Chang-Diaz Philippe Perrin Valery Korzun (u) Peggy Whitson (u) Sergey Treshchev (u) Yury Onufriyenko (d) Carl Walz (d) Daniel Bursch (d)	June 5–19	repairs and equipment delivery to ISS; station crew exchange
Russia	Progress	—	June 26	ISS supplies
Russia	Progress	—	September 25	ISS supplies
U.S.	STS-112, *Atlantis*	Jeffrey Ashby Pamela Melroy David Wolf Piers Sellers Sandra Magnus Fyodor Yurchikhin	October 7–18	delivery of S1 truss segment to ISS
Russia	Soyuz TMA-1	Sergey Zalyotin Yury Lonchakov Frank De Winne	October 29–November 9	exchange of Soyuz return craft for ISS crew (TM-34 with TMA-1); first flight of upgraded Soyuz
U.S.	STS-113, *Endeavour*	James Wetherbee Paul Lockhart Michael Lopez-Alegria John Herrington Ken Bowersox (u) Nikolay Budarin (u) Donald Pettit (u) Valery Korzun (d) Peggy Whitson (d) Sergey Treshchev (d)	November 23–December 7	delivery of P1 truss segment to ISS; station crew exchange
China	Shenzhou 4	—	December 30	fourth unmanned test flight of China's first manned spacecraft

[1] Commander and pilot (or flight engineer for Soyuz) are listed first.
[2] Launch date for unmanned missions; launch and return dates for manned missions.
[3] Flew as paying passenger.
u = ISS crew member transported to station (ISS commander listed first).
d = ISS crew member returned to Earth (ISS commander listed first).

Media and Publishing

TURBULENCE at the top of such global media giants as **VIVENDI** and **BERTELSMANN,** growing dissatisfaction with American **NEWSCASTING,** and a surge in **SPANISH-LANGUAGE** programming in the U.S. were the top stories in broadcasting in 2002. The pressures of **ELECTRONIC MEDIA** on magazines and newspapers as well as **FREEDOM OF THE PRESS** issues were of topmost concern to ink-and-paper publishers.

TELEVISION

Organization. The international television news of the year 2002 centred on the corporate maneuverings of European media giants. At Vivendi Universal, Jean-Marie Messier (*see* BIOGRAPHIES) had grown the company into a global multimedia empire—but with a €20 billion (€1 = about $1) debt. In restructuring the company after his departure, new CEO Jean-René Fourtou sold off Italian pay-TV Telepiù and broke up pay-TV Canal Plus. In Germany, Bertelsmann AG's Thomas Middlehoff departed too, and in his wake the TV group RTL was to be expanded. Bankrupt KirchGruppe offered international investors its TV- and film-rights catalog and control of Germany's biggest commercial broadcaster, ProSiebenSat.1. Kirch's sports rights were sold separately from the pay-TV company Premiere.

News Corp. and Telecom Italia paid €900 million for Telepiù, which, after combining with rival Stream, became pay-TV Sky Italia and dominated the market. BSkyB partnered with the BBC and transmitter Crown Castle International to broadcast Freeview, a 30-channel digital TV service. Liberty Media-controlled OpenTV purchased both rival ACTV and Liberty's Wink Communications to centralize the development of interactive applications for TV. Granada, the U.K.'s largest commercial TV group, merged with rival Carlton Communications and acquired majority control of 15 ITV regional TV licenses, including two in London. Granada also doubled its stake in independent Irish TV3 to 90% for €50 million.

The Chinese government required dominant free-to-air Television Broadcasts Ltd. to reduce its 50% stake in pay-TV Galaxy Satellite Broadcasting Ltd. In August China allowed ATV, Hong Kong's second largest TV network, to broadcast its ATV World and ATV Home channels to the Pearl River Delta area of southern China. Former People's Liberation Army propaganda officer Liu Changle, chairman of Phoenix Satellite TV, the first nonmainland network to broadcast in China, acquired a 46% controlling share of ATV.

In contrast to the flurry of international events, the business side of American television was relatively calm for much of the year. NBC in November purchased the arts-themed cable channel Bravo, with its few but affluent viewers, from Cablevision Systems for $1.25 billion. Bravo's signature series was *Inside the Actors Studio*, a program featuring one-on-one interviews with famous and sometimes talented actors taped at the storied New York acting school.

Consolidation continued, however, in the cable world, as the Federal Communications Commission approved the acquisition of the No. 1 cable company, AT&T Broadband, by the No. 3 company, Comcast. The new behemoth would serve some 27 million homes in 17 of the 20 largest U.S. cities. As a condition of the deal, AT&T had to put its minority ownership stake in the second largest cable company, Time Warner Cable, into a trust for sale within five years.

The U.S. Department of Justice, however, announced its opposition to the planned merger of the two leading satellite-television-distribution systems,

DirecTV and Dish Network, on the grounds that the consolidation would leave insufficient competition in the direct-broadcast satellite (DBS) market. In the department's suit to block the merger, each DBS was seen as an important competitor to cable television. The two services had a combined 18.4 million customers, and the government's opposition was seen as a likely deal killer.

Programming. By the end of 2002, American television was rebounding from the advertising slump caused by the Sept. 11, 2001, terrorist attacks—and the recession. Ad sales at the May "upfront" markets, at which much of the network TV time is sold for the coming season starting in September, reached a record $8.2 billion. That was more than a 14% increase over the previous, sluggish May. The trade publication *Advertising Age* reported an industry forecast that ad spending during the second half of the year would be up 6.2% over the previous year.

Despite network TV's outperforming most other ad-based media in a still-soft economy and demonstrating its continued power as an aggregator of audience, all was not well in TV land. For the first time, the number of people watching the basic cable channels in prime time was larger than the number watching the six broadcast networks—NBC, CBS, ABC, Fox, the WB, and UPN.

One of the key Emmy Awards, for best actor in a dramatic series, went to Michael Chiklis, the star of *The Shield*, a new police drama on a little-known cable channel, FX. A leading network, ABC, was in desperate trouble, having bet too much of its future on the one-time hit game show *Who Wants to Be a Millionaire*, which it had been running up to four times per week. When that show's audience disappeared and the series ended its prime-time run, ABC was caught without much of a succession plan. It took the unprecedented step of airing in prime time repeats of a series that had first run on cable, the detective series *Monk*.

As a further sign of the rise of cable relative to the old-line networks, for much of the year ABC was reported to be in talks with CNN about the two companies' combining their news operations. Both sides were said to be attracted by the potential for saving money and reaching new viewers, although by year's end no deal had been struck.

In another gesture of disrespect toward its news division, ABC got caught in 2002 trying to woo late-night comedy star David Letterman over from his longtime home, CBS. To make way for Letterman, ABC was prepared to cancel *Nightline*, the weeknight half-hour news program that had been a beacon of quality television and responsible reportage since it began during the Iranian hostage crisis. Letterman ultimately opted to stay at CBS, while ABC instead canceled *Politically Incorrect*, the topical talk show airing after *Nightline*. ABC announced plans to replace *Politically Incorrect* in early 2003 with an hour-long late-night comedy talk show starring the comic Jimmy Kimmel, best known as the host of an unapologetically sexist cable curiosity called *The Man Show*.

The *Politically Incorrect* cancellation was brought about, in large measure, by controversial remarks host Bill Maher had made after the September 11 attacks to the effect that the U.S. military's penchant for bombing targets from safe remove was more "cowardly" than the deeds of the suicide bombers who had piloted planes into the World Trade Center and the Pentagon. In other ways, though, television coped admirably with the September 11 aftermath. Two of 2002's most watched and critically lauded documentaries relived the day, CBS's *9/11* in March and HBO's *In Memoriam: New York City, 9/11/01* in May. Each was an Emmy Award winner. On the one-year anniversary of the attacks, much of television paid respectful attention to the daylong commemorations. The attacks had brought about a boost in news viewing that continued well past the one-year anniversary. Taking most advantage of the increased audience was Rupert Murdoch's upstart Fox News Channel, which early in the year surpassed CNN as the country's most popular cable news channel. CNN was also openly struggling with a slight format change that saw it focusing more on the personalities of its news presenters. Shows hosted by news "stars" such as Connie Chung took centre stage, and the CNN founding credo that "the news is the star" was sent to the wings.

All of the news channels, however, continued to draw fire for their tendency to provide "wall-to-wall" coverage of hot-button topics, regardless of their relative newsworthiness. Critics suggested that such coverage choices turned molehills into mountains and fueled illogical public fears of such relatively rare phenomena as child abduction. The channels responded that they were only serving public demand, as viewership always tended to spike during such sagas as the Washington, D.C.-area sniper manhunt.

On the network news front, NBC became the first of the "Big Three" networks to announce an official heir to one of their trio of aging news anchors—NBC's Tom Brokaw, ABC's Peter Jennings, and CBS's Dan Rather. NBC said that Brian Williams, the lead anchor on the network's cable station MSNBC, would take over for Brokaw in 2004.

The November elections demonstrated continuing problems with network coverage of American voting. During the 2000 presidential election, Voter News Service (VNS), a multinetwork consortium, had dropped the ball, causing the networks to call both Democrat Al Gore and Republican George W. Bush winners in the critical state of Florida. In fact, neither would be a clear winner there on election night. The result was public outcry, a congressional inquiry, and a promise to reform the VNS. Nonetheless, in the 2002 midterm elections, VNS exit-polling information was declared unreliable and was not released, so the networks' principal method of determining why people voted the way they did was still unusable.

The most popular prime-time series during the 2001–02 season ended in May was the long-running NBC comedy *Friends*, about six pals who live near each other in New York City. By the following fall, however, the top series spot had been taken by the CBS forensics drama *CSI: Crime Scene Investigation*. Both programs were exemplars of a trend that had begun after the September 11 attacks toward audiences' favouring more traditional programming. *Friends* also won its first-ever Emmy Award for top comedy series. Best drama honours went, for the third year running, to *The West Wing*, NBC's look at a fictionalized and idealized White House. As the 2002–03 season got under way, a weakened NBC and a strengthened CBS battled for the title of most popular network, but few new series struck a powerful chord with critics or viewers. Meanwhile, Public Broadcasting Service, the nation's public-television programmer, continued to grapple publicly with declining and aging viewership as many of its former niches—animal programming, biographies, British imports, and history—had been turned into separate cable channels by private companies.

Much of the year's programming buzz was generated not by in-season network programs but by reality programming, a genre that continued to prove its viability, if not its good taste. The year's most-discussed series was undoubtedly MTV's *The Osbournes*, chronicling the lives in Los Angeles of addled patriarch Ozzy (*see* BIOGRAPHIES), the former lead singer of the heavy-metal band Black Sabbath, his shrewd manager-wife, Sharon, and their two almost-grown children. The show's clever conceit was to edit such domestic moments as Ozzy's being unable to work the television remote device so that they played like a 1950s sitcom, albeit a 1950s sitcom spiced up by frequent bleeped-out expletives.

During the summer the Fox network had a breakout hit with *American Idol*, an American version of the British singing-talent-contest series *Pop Idol*. Week after week a large call-in vote narrowed a group of finalists performing popular songs down to one eventual winner, Texan Kelly Clarkson. After the show ended, her first single, performed several times on the series itself, shot to number one. Fox, of course, readied a sequel, and other networks rushed to air their own talent-contest series.

Reality and game shows went global—with mixed results. *The Weakest Link* in Thailand upset contestants and viewers. The National Youth Bureau protested its promotion of "fierce competition and selfishness . . . which contravenes Thai generosity." A contestant on the Philippine version of the show died of a heart attack while waiting to go on, and another who was booted out as the "weakest link" tried to commit suicide; immediately after his aborted attempt, he fell to his death. *Who Wants to Be a Millionaire* spin-offs in Argentina and in Germany awarded jobs to weekly winners chosen by phoned-in votes.

Program content continued to be an issue. The research group of the advertising agency McCann-Erickson in the Philippines advised sponsors to withdraw their ads unless changes were made in popular noontime shows filled with distasteful visual materials and language and subjecting "game contestants to ridicule." The French audiovisual watchdog group CSA recommended banning pornography, particularly during early-morning viewing hours. Russian Deputy Press Minister Valery Sirozhenko announced special monitoring of all TV channels in his country; the

ITAR-TASS news agency reported that an estimated one-fifth of programs contained subliminal messages inserted in extra frames. The Japanese Diet (parliament) debated a human rights protection bill that would create a committee to advise crime victims and families of suspects hounded by media. The banned quasi-religious Falun Gong organization interrupted state broadcasts in northeastern China on March 5 with a TV spot alleging that the self-immolation of demonstrators in Tiananmen Square in 2001 had been staged by the government.

Freedom of speech had its ups and downs, too. On nationwide TV, Cuban Pres. Fidel Castro repeatedly called Mexican counterpart Vicente Fox a liar for denying that he had pressured Castro to leave a UN aid summit in Mexico before U.S. Pres. George W. Bush arrived. Venezuela's Pres. Hugo Chávez claimed the coup in April in which he was ousted temporarily was abetted by private TV stations promoting an anti-Chávez demonstration at Venezuela's oil

Twenty-year-old Kelly Clarkson (left), winner of **American Idol**—*a hugely popular reality television series on which contestants competed in a singing contest—is congratulated by fellow contestant Nikki McKibbin.*

company headquarters. State-run Iraqi TV did not carry President Bush's speech to the UN General Assembly seeking a resolution on Iraqi arms, but it ran a commentary labeling his remarks ignorant prattle that reflected "his irresponsible attitude to humanity." During Ramadan one-year-old Dream TV, Egypt's first privately owned satellite network, ran 41 episodes of *Horseman Without a Horse,* a story set in the Middle East between 1855 and 1917 and based in part on the discredited anti-Jewish "Protocols of the Elders of Zion." Kabul (Afg.) TV and Radio's decision to ban all TV screenings of Indian movies and female singers was upheld by the country's highest court, but the ban was lifted on September 17. In Qatar, TV cameras were allowed for the first time to film the ruler's wife, a mother of seven in her early 40s, who opened Cornell University's medical college in Doha. Mexico's government and broadcasters agreed in October to overhaul the secretive frequency-licensing process in the 41-year-old Federal Radio and Television Law and create a public registry for concessions.

The Spanish-language Univision's *Sábado gigante* celebrated 40 years on TV with the same comedic host, Don Francisco. (*See* BIOGRAPHIES.) Meanwhile, NBC's *Today* show marked its 50th anniversary on the air, and that show's cohost, Katie Couric, made headlines with her generous new contract. (*See* BIOGRAPHIES.)

Technology. Digital personal video recorders (PVRs) continued to fail to emerge at more than a snail's pace. Industry experts contended that the devices, the best-known example of which went by the trade name TiVo, would revolutionize television because their digital recording capacities allowed consumers to rearrange TV schedules, including skipping over commercials, quickly and conveniently. Despite reams of positive pub-

Don Francisco, host of the Spanish-language variety show **Sábado gigante,** *signs copies of his autobiography at a Los Angeles bookstore.*

licity, PVRs were forecast to be in only 1.8 million homes by the end of 2002—less than a 2% market penetration.

SONICBlue's ReplayTV came under fire from major TV and film companies that claimed that the system, which recorded TV shows on PC hard drives and allowed users to skip over commercials, violated copyright laws. A portable version was being developed, using Intel's XScale processors for mobile devices. Cable operators predicted that their video-on-demand service would add PVR capabilities after testing PVRs built into cable boxes. In response, television networks started integrating ads into their programs themselves. Scripps Networks' Fine Living cable channel incorporated various forms of advertising to foil PVRs.

Sony Corp. unveiled a new Wega lineup of flat TV monitors that ranged from a 32-in (1 inch = 2.54 cm) liquid crystal display (LCD) TV to 42-in and 50-in plasma sets. Sanyo Electric introduced a new range of flat plasma display panel-based TVs with higher contrast and luminance.

RADIO

Good Morning Afghanistan was inaugurated on state-run radio early in 2002 to provide an up-to-the-minute look at changes in that country. The anchors

Radio announcer Ghani Mudaqiq (left) and reporter Shakeeb Hasrati work on a news segment for Good Morning Afghanistan *in their studio in Kabul on February 26.*

Paula Bronstein/Getty Images

adopted a freewheeling style but remained mindful of cultural and religious taboos. Supported by Baltic Media Center in Denmark and financed by the European Commission with $10,000 monthly, the show's advisers came from the BBC and the Voice of America. *Good Evening Afghanistan* debuted in September.

In October Russian Pres. Vladimir Putin revoked the 1991 decree that gave special permission to the Prague-based U.S.-funded surrogate broadcaster Radio Liberty to maintain a bureau in Moscow. The station had often been at odds with Russian officialdom for its "tendentious" reporting, especially on Chechnya and Ukraine.

India's broadcasting deregulation triggered a boom in sales of car and pocket radios, but FM broadcasters worried that hefty license fees could prove burdensome in a limited market. Five stations started in April in Mumbai (Bombay), where there used to be only the state-owned All India Radio.

On June 20 the U.S. Copyright Office's Copyright Arbitration Royalty Panel (CARP) set a royalty for Internet radio rate of seven hundredths of a cent per song per listener for simulcasts and Internet-only materials. Payments retroactive to 1998 were due October 20. This resulted in the shutting down of hundreds of stations, with most of the 10,000 Webcasters expected to follow suit. Broadcasters claimed the rate was too high, while recording-industry representatives said that the expansion of broadcast services to an Internet audience was unfair to artists and record labels. In November CARP called for further comments and proposals to be discussed in 2003.

Like the television broadcasters, American radio joined in an ad-sales recovery after a weak 2001. Some of the industry's major companies boasted of year-to-year third-quarter sales gains on the order of 10–15%, according to the trade journal *Mediaweek*, which said radio was helped by "trickle-down" from the tight TV ad market but also cautioned that the economy remained volatile. At the same time, radio ad buying, traditionally focused on the 25–54-year-old demographic group, began aiming slightly younger. This boosted the popularity of younger-skewing formats and personalities, including ABC's Tom Joyner and Doug Banks.

In another growth area, leading Spanish-language television network Univision was expecting to complete its $3.5 billion purchase of Hispanic Broadcasting by the end of the year; the deal had been announced in June. Hispanic, the leading Spanish-language radio group, said its third-quarter net profits were up 50% over the previous year on revenue that was up just 7%.

Two companies, XM Satellite Radio Holdings and Sirius Satellite Radio, competed aggressively against each other even while trying to sell the public on the new category of satellite radio. The services, which, except in some new cars, required new receiver-unit purchases and a monthly fee of $10–13, were pitched as commercial-free and providing better sound and far more formats than did the increasingly homogenized AM or FM radio. After little more than a year of business, XM had a commanding market lead, with an estimated 400,000 customers expected by year's end, compared with Sirius' 30,000. Neither number was over-

whelming for businesses that took an estimated $2 billion to launch, however. XM and auto parts maker Delphi Corp. presented a pocket-sized device that tuned into XM's service outside cars.

Sound capabilities such as these, aimed at 16–23-year-olds, could add to potential driver distraction, according to the insurance industry. The U.S. National Highway Traffic Safety Administration had estimated that driver distractions—talking, eating, reading, and changing radio stations—were a factor in 20–30% of all auto crashes. The distractions that such devices as radios, cellular phones, e-mail- and Internet-accessing devices, navigation systems, and automatic collision notification were the subject of a five-year study in Detroit by Wayne State University's Brain and Behavior Institute and the General Motors Corp.

Some of the radio formats that the satellite providers marketed themselves against were losing market share. Country radio failed to break out of its ongoing slump, and the relatively new all-1980s music format was losing steam across the country, according to the radio ratings service Arbitron, but classic rock, urban, and "contemporary hits" formats were doing well.

Conservative radio personality Rush Limbaugh was also doing well. In 2001 Limbaugh stunned his fans by announcing that he was nearly deaf. The bombastic talk host received a cochlear implant in December of that year, however, and began bragging on air about his "bionic ear." It seemed to be working; his audience in 2002 was claimed to be 20 million listeners on some 600 stations, and a Milwaukee critic, comparing the Limbaugh shows before and after the implant, wrote that "the old Rush is back."

CBS/Viacom in November announced that it would begin simulcasting David Letterman's CBS *Late Show* on some of Viacom's Infinity Broadcasting radio stations to see how a TV comedy show might go over on the picture-free medium.

(RAMONA MONETTE SARGAN FLORES; STEVE JOHNSON)

NEWSPAPERS

A prolonged advertising recession and new fears of reader and advertiser flights to digital options prompted newspapers in 2002 to make structural cuts in staffing, reduce the number of pages printed, and begin strategic preparations for evolving news operations to

Blogs Mix Up the Media

Web logs were not new, but as a forum for personal expression they sprouted prodigiously on the Internet, captured new audiences, and drew intensified attention in the media in 2002. Web logs (usually abbreviated to "blogs") originated in the U.S. in 1997 as a few on-line journals, often with links to news items on the World Wide Web plus brief, personal comments on those items by the originators-editors ("bloggers"), as well as responses from readers. By mid-2002 the number of blogs had grown from only 23 (by one count) at the start of 1999 to as many as 500,000 globally. This growth was fueled by the spread of free blog-creation software (such as Blogger, Pitas, Movable Type, and Radio UserLand), which removed the need for the blogger to be skilled in computer programming.

In the wake of the terrorist attacks in the U.S. on Sept. 11, 2001, a new type of Web log was born: the "war blog." The generally better quality of writing and the political stance of the blogger (often right-wing) distinguished the war blogs from the on-line diaries. War bloggers included Andrew Sullivan, former editor of *The New Republic,* whose blog reportedly received more than 800,000 visits in one month from more than 200,000 individual readers. Glenn Reynolds, a University of Tennessee law professor, drew around 43,000 visits in a single day to his *InstaPundit* site. The *Jerusalem Post* also reported in 2002 that Israeli and Palestinian bloggers were writing Web logs as a way to let the outside world see

their respective sides of the ongoing Middle East conflict.

Alex Beam, a columnist at the *Boston Globe,* scathingly referred to blogs as an "infinite echo chamber of self-regard." Web logs' high site-visit figures made the mainstream media jumpy, however, especially as some of the new bloggers carried on their sites detailed criticism of stories in newspapers, such as the *New York Times* and the *Los Angeles Times.* A number of mainstream media outlets even added blogs to their Web sites, notably the British daily *The Guardian,* which ran a competition for the U.K.'s best blog. The on-line magazine *Slate* embraced a preexisting blog by Mickey Kaus, a former *Newsweek* magazine reporter.

In 2001 John Robb, president and chief operating officer of blogging software developer UserLand, put forward a business use for Web logs, in which workers would use blogs as a collaborative medium to record and disseminate their thoughts. In 2002, however, the Web log came of age; the University of California, Berkeley, Graduate School of Journalism began offering a class in blogging, in which students created a blog on copyright issues. The course tutors were John Battelle, a cofounder of *Wired* magazine, and Paul Grabowicz, media program director at the school.

While veteran bloggers might object to the new, more politicized Web logs, blogging as an expanding form of on-line communication seemed to be here to stay.

(ALAN STEWART)

ing one-half of the on-line employment advertising market.

Meanwhile, the local retail advertising sector remained weak for newspapers, though losses were not as severe as in employment advertising. In the U.S. retail advertising growth in newspapers had been at or below inflationary levels for nearly two decades. As low-advertising national chains continued to overshadow and put out of business high-advertising local retailers, the fundamentals of the newspaper's advertising base continued in neutral gear with little hope for growth.

Newspapers spent much of 2001 adjusting to the new economic environment with layoffs, early retirements, and employee buyouts, affecting profit-and-loss statements yet freeing up space in the budget in 2002. Companies that delayed cutbacks in 2001 were forced to act in 2002, including several notable newspapers in Europe. Despite a 2% revenue decline, publicly traded American newspaper companies improved operating profits by 24% in the first half of 2002, thanks to cutbacks and efficiencies.

At least 55 free commuter newspapers representing 10.1 million in daily distribution were being circulated in Europe, Latin America, North America, and Asia/Pacific—a publishing phenomenon that did not exist prior to 1995. Approximately 70% of the commuter newspaper circulation was in Europe. Commuter newspapers, started by Stockholm-based Metro International, were typically advertising-rich free tabloids handed out to subway riders. Metro's success prompted traditional publishers such as Associated Newspapers in England, Bonnier in Sweden, De Telegraaf in The Netherlands, Schibsted in Norway, and News Ltd. in Australia to launch commuter titles, in some cases to fend off competitive threats and in other cases to test the market. In the 12 euro-area countries in which commuter newspapers were distributed, free newspapers distributed in public transportation systems represented 11% of total daily newspaper circulation.

While paid daily newspapers fretted over economic declines, innovators aiming new newspapers at the 18- to 34-year-old urban demographic disrupted trends and sent traditional publishers searching for competitive answers. The concept behind the free commuter newspapers spawned new publishing initiatives in Chicago and Copenhagen. In Chicago the Tribune Co. launched

multimedia delivery. Before the Sept. 11, 2001, terrorist attacks in the United States, 2002 was expected to be a year of economic recovery, a point critical to the success of the advertising industry in general and newspapers specifically. Though the recovery never materialized, double-digit revenue declines leveled off to single-digit declines late in the year.

Particularly hard hit was classified employment advertising, the fastest-growing category in the 1990s, which plummeted 35% and 43% in the United States and Germany, respectively, in 2001—trends that moderated in 2002 yet still pointed downward. In 2000 em-

ployment advertising represented 18% of an American newspaper's advertising base; one year later that percentage dropped to 10%. Globally, newspaper executives wondered about the degree to which employment advertising's decline was cyclical versus structural. At the heart of worries was the haphazard way in which Internet classifieds, led by digital powerhouse Monster.com, were growing market share during recessionary times. Though employment advertising in American newspapers declined 35% to $5.7 billion, American revenues from on-line job sites increased 38% to $727 million, with Monster.com captur-

RedEye, and its rival *Chicago Sun-Times* debuted *Red Streak,* colourful daily tabloids sold at a low price. In Copenhagen a 32-page tabloid titled *Dagen* focused on longer articles and lifestyle features. All three new titles were aimed at the young upscale urban audience that traditional newspapers had failed to capture in sufficient numbers.

In Latin America newspapers continued to experiment with "popular" tabloids to reach audiences that upmarket newspapers were unable to reach. In Lima, Peru, for example, publisher EPENSA became the market leader in daily newspaper circulation as its two-year-old *Correo* overtook its lead title, *Diario OJO,* in circulation. With 4 of Lima's 18 daily newspapers, EPENSA achieved its goal of market leadership even as rival El Comercio mounted a counteroffensive.

Circulations of paid daily newspapers continued to decline less than 1% annually in Western countries, with traditional newspaper powerhouse countries such as the United Kingdom and Germany leading the declines in 2000–01. Spain and Portugal, on the other hand, experienced increases in paid circulations. While newspapers, especially in the United States, saw strong sales after the September 11 terrorist attacks, readership waned to normal levels afterward. Critically important for newspapers was that circulation penetration (the percentage of paid newspaper copies sold to the general population), which had slowly declined during the past half century, appeared to be dropping faster. This development emerged even as national press associations and other industry bodies argued that "readership," a broader measure of the audience that included pass-along copies, was a better measurement and a better story for newspapers.

Publishers continued to watch survey after survey indicate that younger people were turning to digital options for news and information. Newspapers responded with higher-quality local-news Web sites, rich with advertising, and several notable companies reported that these business ventures were profitable for the first time in 2002. In the United States, newspapers dominated local markets in terms of Web-site hits. In the United Kingdom, newspapers experimented with streaming headlines and promotional messages via cellular telephones. (*See* COMPUTERS: Special Report.)

As traditional publishers ventured into niche publishing—multiple Web-site

*Two new daily tabloids aimed at 18- to 34-year-olds—***RedEye** *and* **Red Streak**—*debuted in Chicago during the year.*

management, e-mail newsletter delivery, cellular telephone "publishing," and digital versions of the print newspaper—industry chief executives talked openly of publishing companies as "information mills" with many delivery platforms and the print newspaper as its core product.

Notable management developments included the *Washington Post*'s agreement to sell its 50% ownership stake in the *International Herald Tribune* to the *New York Times,* which became sole owner of the entire business enterprise. In the United Kingdom, Johnston Press continued its growth by acquiring Regional Independent Media and becoming the fourth largest newspaper publisher in the country. In the United

States, Midwestern publisher Lee Enterprises bought Howard Publications for $694 million. The number of ownership changes—which had been brisk in the 1990s in countries such as Australia, Canada, the United Kingdom, and the United States—ground to a halt in 2001–02 owing to the poor economy. Speculation was constant, however, about mergers and acquisitions related to Australia's four major publishers: News Ltd., John Fairfax Ltd., Rural Press Ltd., and Australian Provincial Newspapers. Meanwhile, analysts talked openly of ownership "swap" possibilities in the United States, especially if the Federal Communication's Commission removed a ban on local cross-media ownership, presumably to cluster newspapers and television stations in the same market for news gathering and advertising sales purposes.

Elsewhere, for the second time in a decade, U.K. national newspapers engaged each other in a circulation price-cutting war that depleted coffers during a recession and little else. Germany's venerable broadsheet titles, *Frankfurter Allgemeine Zeitung* and *Süddeutsche Zeitung,* implemented cutbacks in the face of the advertising recession. In Latin America deteriorating economies in Argentina, Brazil, and Uruguay hurt newspapers as depressed currencies caused economic distress via newsprint purchases made in U.S. dollar denominations. A legendary newspaper name, the *New York Sun,* resurfaced after several decades of extinction to inject Manhattan with a politically conservative view on the world.

In the context of information glut, publishers, editors, and academics engaged each other in new debates about the role of traditional journalism in an emerging multimedia world. Increasingly, executives agreed that an increase in the quality and quantity of local news—including nontraditional concepts of content development such as Web logs ("blogs")—were vital to the future of journalism within publishing companies. (*See* Sidebar.)

(EARL J. WILKINSON)

MAGAZINES

The economic downturn continued to batter American magazines in 2002, although some positive signs toward year's end pointed toward recovery. Magazine advertising revenue for September 2002 was up 9% over September 2001, while ad revenue for the first nine months of 2002 was up 1.5% over the same period in 2001.

The recession claimed one of its most glamorous magazine victims when *Talk* magazine was abruptly halted on Jan. 18, 2002. Staff members were told that day about the closure in a meeting with editor Tina Brown and publisher Ron Galotti, who revealed that the decision had been reached within "the last 24 hours." Brown, editor of *Vanity Fair* in the 1980s, had left *The New Yorker* some 18 months earlier to become *Talk*'s founding editor.

After giving up her television program in May, Rosie O'Donnell quit the magazine *Rosie* in September following a bitter dispute over editorial control with publisher Gruner + Jahr USA. The last issue was published in December 2002. The 125-year-old *McCall's* title was changed to *Rosie* in early 2001 after O'Donnell and the company invested $10 million each to launch the joint venture. The magazine's 3.5 million circulation in June 2002 was a 12.5% decline from the 4 million of a year earlier; single-copy sales of some issues had fallen by more than 50%. In October the company filed suit for damages in New York State Superior Court, claiming that O'Donnell had breached "duties of good faith and fair dealing and of fiduciary duty." Time Inc. closed down two publications in October: *Sports Illustrated Women* and *Mutual Funds*, a personal-finance magazine.

Several Muslim nations banned the Feb. 11, 2002, issue of *Newsweek International* after the magazine published an undated Turkish manuscript depicting the Prophet Muhammad with the angel Gabriel in an article comparing Islamic and Christian scriptures. Islam forbade the display of any image of the prophet. *Newsweek International* was pulled from the newsstands amid fears of widespread protests. Malaysia's deputy prime minister told the BBC, "Normally if publications contain photographs . . . of the Prophet Muhammad, the law of the country would have been violated. As such we will not allow the edition to be circulated." Earlier, Indonesia and Bangladesh had banned that issue of the magazine, and the Egyptian parliament had declared that the magazine's depiction of the prophet was blasphemous. In May *Newsweek* won the American Society of Magazine Editors top award for "general excellence" for magazines with a circulation of over two million.

Magazine circulation in the U.S. continued to surpass that of any other country. The 10 highest-circulation magazines in the U.S. at the end of June 2002 were as follows:

Magazine	Circulation
Modern Maturity	17.5 million
Reader's Digest	12.2 million
TV Guide	9.1 million
Better Homes and Gardens	7.6 million
National Geographic	6.9 million
Good Housekeeping	4.7 million
Family Circle	4.7 million
Woman's Day	4.2 million
Time	4.1 million
Ladies' Home Journal	4.1 million

The number of subscribers, however, did not necessarily translate into revenue; the top 10 magazines in total revenue were: *People, TV Guide, Time, Sports Illustrated, Better Homes and Gardens, Reader's Digest, Parade, Newsweek, Business Week,* and *Good Housekeeping.* Among other nations, the highest-circulation magazine was China's *Reader* magazine, with 5 million subscribers. France's weekly *TV Magazine* had 4.5 million readers, while the United Kingdom's *Sky Customer,* also a TV magazine, led there with 3.9 million. Germany's leading magazine was *TV Movie,* with 2.5 million readers, and Italy's TV magazine, *Sorrisi e canzoni TV,* had 1.6 million readers.

A study by the Blue Dolphin Group found that among American households subscribing to magazines, 11% subscribed on-line in the last quarter of 2001. That figure increased steadily throughout 2002 from 5.7% during the first quarter of 2001. According to a study from Insight Express, however, most Americans preferred a traditional print magazine over an on-line magazine, according to a study from Insight Express. The study also found that only 32% read any magazines on-line, 22% preferred reading magazines on-line, and 73% said that they would not give up their print magazine for an on-line alternative—even for half the price.

In a major victory for press freedom in Latin America, Costa Rica eliminated the crime of *desacato* ("insult") and voided this restriction on press scrutiny of public officials. More than a dozen countries in the region still had similar laws. Pres. Miguel Ángel Rodríguez Echeverría signed the bill into law in May after Costa Rica's legislature voted in March to eliminate references to *desacato* from Article 309 of the Criminal Code.

In Kenya the Law Society of Kenya chairman, Raychelle Omamo, called for her country's magazines to portray a more positive image of women. "Inculcate a new image of women as workers, mothers, leaders, and politicians . . . if you engage women positively, the country will change," she said at a Nairobi hotel during the launch of the magazine *Eve,* whose slogan was "the essence of Africa's new woman."

(DAVID E. SUMNER)

BOOK PUBLISHING

United States. Notwithstanding lamentations by some insiders that the publishing industry was in a "death spiral," the reports of the industry's demise were greatly exaggerated. Though modest in growth, overall book sales were projected to rise 2.8% in 2002. Consumer purchases of adult trade books in the first six months of the year increased 1.6% over the same period in 2001, and spending on books ($5.3 billion) was 3% higher than in 2001. Publishers' sales of adult hardbound consumer books reportedly rose 21.1% over 200l; paperback consumer book sales increased 14.6%. Despite the absence of a new Harry Potter title in 2002, sales of juvenile hardbound books still rose 17.6% through August, and juvenile paperbound registered a 10.6% increase.

A major development in the consumer books segment was the growing demand for Spanish-language books and for English books geared to the Latino market. Reflecting the increasing importance of this market segment, the Association of American Publishers created a special task force to spearhead industry efforts to serve this market.

Though a number of e-book-only imprints—including AtRandom, iPublish, and MightyWords—shut down, the market continued to exhibit steady if unspectacular growth. A survey conducted by the Open e-Book Forum revealed double-digit sales growth (10% to 15% annually) and an even greater increase in the number of consumers downloading e-book readers (a 70% increase in downloads of the Adobe Acrobat e-book readers and more than five million copies of the Microsoft Reader). Estimates for 2002 indicated that one million e-books would be sold, double the number sold in 2001.

Oprah Winfrey's decision to deemphasize her book club proved less catastrophic than publishers had feared; *Good Morning America, The Today Show, Regis & Kelly,* and *USA Today* rushed into the breach with book clubs of their own. Book clubs generally were experiencing a nationwide resurgence.

Amazon.com's practice of offering used books for sale on the same page as the new edition drew the wrath of authors (and some publishers). The Authors Guild sent Amazon a letter of protest and urged its members to "de-link" their own Web pages from Amazon's.

Contributing to the industry's unease was an announcement in mid-August that—despite earlier assurances to the contrary—the financially troubled Vivendi Universal SA (which had realized a €12.3 billion [about $12 billion] loss for the first half of 2002) was putting its American publishing arm, Houghton Mifflin, on the block. The fate of the venerable publishing house was still unresolved at year's end.

Intellectual property rights were a major concern for the industry, and much attention was focused on two pending court cases. In *Random House* v. *RosettaBooks*, Random House sought to enjoin the distribution by e-book publisher RosettaBooks of eight electronic books by Random House authors, claiming that it held the e-book rights by virtue of contracts granting it exclusive rights to

In April former Washington Post *correspondent Jonathan C. Randal (left) escorts Turkish publisher Abdullah Keskin outside the State Security Court in Istanbul, where Keskin was being tried for "spreading separatist propaganda" for publishing Randal's 1997 book about the Kurds,* After Such Knowledge, What Forgiveness.

publish the works in book form. In October 2002 the U.S. Supreme Court heard arguments in *Eldred* v. *Ashcroft*, a constitutional challenge to the 1998 Copyright Term Extension Act, which added 20 years to existing and future copyright terms.　　(PATRICIA S. SCHROEDER)

International. During 2002 the European Union (EU) Council of Ministers ignored pressure from the U.S. government to abandon plans to insist that non-EU suppliers of digital products, including e-books, charge value-added tax (VAT) at the rate applicable to the buyer's country of residence.

The Dutch Ministry of Economics set out to abolish resale price maintenance (RPM) for educational books. In March, however, the European Commission and the German publishing industry agreed to keep German RPM intact but exempted foreign on-line book retailers that sold books to consumers in Germany. Collective embargoes were outlawed other than to prevent deliberate abuse—for example, reimports specifically designed to circumvent RPM. The Buchpreisbindung covering RPM would come into force in October. Meanwhile, the European Parliament's legal committee ruled that imports of books into EU member states with fixed-price regimes should be subject to the same controls as locally published books as part of a proposed EU directive on book pricing. No member state would be forced to introduce RPM, but the goal was to achieve a harmonization of practices across the EU.

In February the European Commission called on Belgium to adopt the EU law on public lending right (PLR) into national law; Belgium had not made payments since 1994. The Danish government announced in March that a 15% reduction in PLR payments would be effected by making no payments to any author entitled to less than about $600 a year. This would affect 15,000 of the 19,660 people registered for PLR. In February 2002 the new Danish minister of culture reneged on a longstanding promise to reduce the VAT on books, keeping it at 25%—the highest in the EU. Although the rate had been lowered to 6% in Sweden, the minister argued that an equivalent move would have almost no effect upon total sales.

After two years of discussion, amendments to laws governing the relationship between authors and publishers were finally passed by the German government. The German Copyright Contract Act was designed to guarantee "appropriate" payment to authors, translators,

and other freelance writers by those who commissioned them. In addition, a special "best-seller" provision increased royalties when sales were unexpectedly large. The law was not retroactive, however. The World Intellectual Property Organization's long-awaited digital copyright treaty, which supplemented the Berne Convention for the Protection of Literary and Artistic Works (1886, revised 1971), came into force in March after the 13th country signed the treaty.

Antipiracy raids in India continued to root out the endemic abuse of copyright, which involved half of all fiction and academic titles. These took place in December 2001 in Lucknow and New Delhi and in 2002 in Mumbai (Bombay)—where the haul was the largest ever—and Hyderabad and Kerala state.

There were a number of insolvencies and takeovers involving German companies. Könemann of Cologne, the fastest-growing publisher in Germany, called in the administrators in January 2002 with debts of $140 million. This had a severe trickle-down effect for the U.K.'s Quarto Group, which was owed $1.8 million. Meanwhile, travel publisher Mairs Geographischer Verlag acquired bankrupt Swiss publisher Kümmerly + Frey, and Random House sold imprints Falken and Bassermann to Gräfe und Unzer, subject to regulatory approval, as well as announcing the shutdown of Mosaik Verlag and Orbis by the end of 2002 and the sale of Frederking & Thaler back to its founders.

David & Charles parent F&W Publications was sold to private equity firm Providence Equity Partners for $130 million. Taylor & Francis tabled a bid worth approximately £300 million (about $450 million) for Blackwell Publishing and subsequently expressed interest in buying the academic division of Wolters Kluwer. By August a queue of bidders, including other trade publishers and private equity firms, had formed for both ventures as well as the academic publishing units of BertelsmannSpringer, which were put up for sale in June.

U.K. publishers' exports overtook those of the U.S., which was seen as evidence of both the anglicization of the EU and the failure of American exporters to take advantage of the opening up of the Australian market. Internet retailing in Europe was increasingly dominated by Amazon.com. In July 2002 Bol.com, Bertelsmann's Internet retailer in the U.K., was converted into a book club with fewer titles but lower prices.　　(PETER CURWEN)

Military Affairs

The spectre of **NUCLEAR WEAPONS** reappeared on the world stage in 2002 even as the Cold War superpowers withdrew from the nuclear **ARMS CONTROL TREATIES** of the past. Governments began to act decisively to control international **TERRORISM**. **NATO EXPANDED** right up to Russia's borders. Armed conflict continued in **AFGHANISTAN**, **COLOMBIA**, **ISRAEL**, the **CAUCASUS** region, and elsewhere—and a U.S. attack on **IRAQ** seemed inevitable for much of the year. Conflicts wound down in **AFRICA** and **SRI LANKA**.

NUCLEAR WEAPONS, ARMS CONTROL, AND DISARMAMENT

After having given the required six months' notice, the United States formally withdrew from the 1972 Anti-Ballistic Missile (ABM) Treaty with Russia in June in order to pursue the development of a ballistic missile defense system. Construction of six underground silos to house missile interceptors began in Alaska. Under the ABM Treaty such construction was prohibited. In response, Russia withdrew from the 1993 Strategic Arms Reduction Talks II (START II) treaty with the U.S. Although never implemented, START II would have reduced the number of nuclear warheads in each side's arsenal to between 3,000 and 3,500.

Pres. George W. Bush and his Russian counterpart, Vladimir Putin, signed an agreement in May to reduce each side's stockpile of nuclear weapons by two-thirds over 10 years. The remarkably brief 475-word document, dubbed the Treaty of Moscow, required that each side reduce its arsenal to between 1,700 and 2,200 nuclear warheads but did not define how the numbers should be counted or how each side's nuclear force should be structured.

In November more than 90 countries signed the International Code of Conduct Against Ballistic Missile Proliferation (ICOC). Although the code lacked the legal force of an international treaty, it sought to restrict the export of ballistic missiles and their related technologies to countries of concern by requiring signatories to conduct their affairs more openly. The ICOC built on the 1987 Missile Technology Control Regime, which was supported by 33 countries.

In March the U.S. Nuclear Posture Review (NPR), a confidential document, was leaked to journalists. The document revealed the willingness of the government to break a long-standing commitment that the U.S. would abstain from using nuclear weapons against nonnuclear states. The NPR suggested that nuclear weapons could be used in retribution for attacks against the U.S. using biological or chemical weapons and that small accurate "mininukes" could be used against well-protected underground bunkers. Britain's defense minister, Geoff Hoon, announced that his government too reserved the right to use nuclear weapons if Britain or British troops were threatened by biological or chemical weapons.

North Korea allegedly admitted that it had nuclear weapons but later claimed that it was merely reasserting its "right" to possess them. The Pyongyang government rejected calls for United Nations inspectors to be allowed to verify that there were no such weapons or a program to develop them in the country. Israel was reported to be arming three of its new diesel-electric submarines with nuclear-armed cruise missiles as a means of enhancing its deterrent against foreign aggression.

GLOBAL TERRORISM

The number of terrorist incidents remained high in many places throughout the world. Although some were isolated criminal acts, others were the work of international terrorist organizations.

Several states began taking tough measures to eradicate terrorist groups. In response to the terrorist attacks of

Tom Ridge, director of the U.S. Office of Homeland Security, introduces the colour-coded threat advisory system on March 12 in Washington, D.C.

Sept. 11, 2001, U.S. President Bush signed into law in November the Homeland Security Act, the most sweeping change in the U.S.'s security infrastructure since the 1940s. The act created the Department of Homeland Security, which was to have about 170,000 employees and merge the functions of 22 existing agencies, including the U.S. Coast Guard, the Secret Service, and the Border Patrol. Bush announced in June that because of the growing threat of global terrorism, the United States reserved the right to launch preemptive strikes without warning against terrorist states or groups suspected of plotting to use weapons of mass destruction against American targets. Similarly, following the mass hostage-taking incident in Moscow in October (*see* below), the Kremlin announced that it was prepared to strike preemptively across international borders in order to stop terrorist actions. In December, Australian Prime Minister John Howard angered several Asian countries when he announced that he was prepared to order preemptive strikes against terrorists anywhere in the region. Nearly 200 people, including many foreign tourists, had been killed when a nightclub on the Indonesian island of Bali was bombed by terrorists. Australia, which counted about 90 of its citizens among the dead, put its security forces on a high state of alert after the attack. (*See* photograph on page 444.)

Other incidents of terror included a suicide bombing in Karachi, Pak., in May that killed 14 people, including 11 French defense consultants helping Pakistan build submarines. In October a French oil tanker, the *Limburg*, was crippled by a blast off the coast of Yemen that killed one crewman. Government officials in both France and Yemen believed that the blast was the result of a suicide attack by a small boat. On November 28 terrorists made two attacks on targets in Mombasa, Kenya. In one, two shoulder-launched surface-to-air missiles were fired at an Israeli jet flying tourists home from Kenya, but the missiles missed their target. At nearly the same time, 16 people died when suicide bombers attacked an Israeli-owned hotel in the Kenyan capital. (*See* photograph on page 455.)

In October the Pentagon agreed to deploy several RC-7 Airborne Reconnaissance Low aircraft to help federal, state, and local law-enforcement officials capture a sniper terrorizing the Washington, D.C., area. More than 1,000 personnel were engaged in the hunt for the culprits in a three-week shooting spree that left 10 people dead and 3 wounded.

OTHER CONFLICTS

Former Soviet Union. In April the first of 150 U.S. Special Operations Forces troops arrived in Georgia to train local forces in antiterrorist operations. Georgia had requested American help in defeating guerrilla forces entrenched in the Pankisi Gorge region, which borders Russia's rebellious republic of Chechnya. U.S. officials believed that the Georgian guerrillas could be linked to al-Qaeda.

In the same month, Russia's intelligence agency, the FSB, announced that it had assassinated a Saudi-born Chechen field commander known as Khattab. Chechen forces acknowledged the death, saying that Khattab had received a poisoned letter. In November a Chechen ambush killed Russia's Lieut. Gen. Igor Shifrin, commander of the army's Chief Special Construction Directorate.

A Chechen suicide squad of more than 40 guerrillas seized control of a Moscow theatre in October and held hostage nearly 700 members of the audience and performers for three days. The incident came to a tragic conclusion when Russian security forces used a powerful opium-based narcotic gas to incapacitate the guerrillas: at least 119 hostages were killed and more than 245 hospitalized, most as a result of inhaling the gas. Following the incident, Russia canceled plans to recall some of the 80,000 troops that it had stationed in Chechnya and instead stepped up military operations in the republic.

Latin America. Colombia's 38-year-old civil war intensified despite hopes that peace talks would lead to an early cease-fire. Pres. Andrés Pastrana Arango ended the talks in February after FARC (Revolutionary Armed Forces of Colombia) guerrillas hijacked a civilian airliner. Pastrana then launched a major military offensive against FARC strongholds. The U.S. was drawn deeper into the war and deployed army special forces (Green Berets) to train government troops in counterinsurgency operations. Previous U.S. military aid had been restricted to the war on drugs. The number of American troops in Colombia grew to an estimated 400.

Elements of Venezuela's armed forces attempted to stage a coup against elected Pres. Hugo Chávez Frias in April. After being deposed for a mere two days, however, Chávez staged a surprising comeback with the support of loyal officers and many ordinary citizens. Chávez announced in October that another coup attempt had been thwarted.

Middle East. Following a wave of Palestinian suicide bombings that killed scores of citizens, Israel mounted a six-week offensive in the West Bank in March. The Israel Defense Forces (IDF) rounded up thousands of suspected militants and carried out dozens of "targeted killings" of what it considered leading militants. The IDF also destroyed Palestinian leader Yasir Arafat's headquarters in Ram Allah. Following more suicide bombings it conducted a similar offensive in June and July. Palestinian agencies and some international organizations accused the IDF of numerous human rights abuses.

British and U.S. aircraft patrolled the northern and southern "no-fly zones" over Iraq throughout the year. In the first 10 months of 2002, coalition aircraft attacked Iraqi air-defense sites nearly 60 times, and the number of incidents increased as speculation grew that a war to topple the Iraqi regime was forthcoming. In October the U.S. Air Force announced that it had begun using armed unmanned aerial vehicles (UAVs) to strike targets in the "no-fly zone" over southern Iraq. Inspectors from the United Nations Monitoring, Verification and Inspection Commission (UNMOVIC) began arriving in Iraq in November on a mission to assess whether the country was in compliance with a series of UN Security Council resolutions that required Iraq to dismantle its weapons of mass destruction programs and eliminate its stockpiles of ballistic missiles with a range longer than 150 km (1 km = 0.6 mi).

South Asia. For several weeks during the year, a nuclear confrontation between India and Pakistan seemed a possibility, and several countries advised their citizens to leave the region. Tensions soared in May following a guerrilla attack on an Indian military base in the disputed region of Kashmir. India said that the attackers were based in Pakistan, but the government in Islamabad denied the accusation. Indian and Pakistani troops exchanged mortar, artillery, and machine-gun fire across their international border for weeks afterward, and the two sides deployed up to a million troops in total along the border. Dozens of civilians and soldiers on both sides were killed during the exchanges, and thousands of civilians were forced to flee.

The two nuclear rivals each tested new missile systems in 2002. In April India fired a supersonic cruise missile that it had developed jointly with Russia. Named Brahmos, the missile was claimed to be capable of delivering a 200-kg (440-lb) conventional warhead to ranges of 300 km. Over a span of several days in May, Pakistan tested three types of new ballistic missile. The Ghaznavi had a range of 290 km and had not been test-launched before. The 1,500-km-range Ghauri and 2,900-km-range Shaheen were also fired during the tests. The three types—all named after medieval Afghan Muslim warriors who had invaded India—gave Pakistan the ability to strike targets anywhere on the subcontinent.

Nepal's six-year war against Maoist rebels intensified. Hundreds of government troops and guerrillas, as well as hundreds of civilians, were killed.

Nineteen countries contributed approximately 4,500 troops to the International Security Assistance Force (ISAF) in Afghanistan. ISAF was mandated by the UN Security Council to assist the interim government in Afghanistan in bringing security and stability to Kabul. During the year ISAF mounted thousands of joint patrols with Afghan security forces in and around the Afghan capital. It also disposed of millions of unexploded munitions, helped rebuild local infrastructure, and trained elements of the new Afghan National Guard. The biggest U.S. ground offensive of the war took place in March. Dubbed Operation Anaconda, the two-week campaign to eliminate al-Qaeda and Taliban forces in the Shah-e Kot Valley left eight U.S. soldiers dead, plus a disputed number of enemy casualties. At year's end the United States still maintained about 9,000 troops in Afghanistan, and continued factional fighting in the country did not augur well for their early withdrawal.

The government of Sri Lanka and rebels of the Liberation Tigers of Tamil Eelam agreed to a permanent cease-fire in February as a step toward ending the 19-year civil war. During peace talks in September, the Tamil Tigers dropped their demand for full independence, and additional talks occurred in October and December.

East and Southeast Asia. In June U.S. marines engaged Muslim guerrillas in

Women troops, part of the International Security Assistance Force assigned to Afghanistan, sit alongside Afghani women at an International Women's Day seminar in Kabul on March 8.

combat in the Philippines for the first time. About 1,200 U.S. troops were in the country to train government forces to combat indigenous guerrilla movements and were given permission to assist Philippine troops in front-line operations against groups such as Abu Sayyaf.

Nearly 800 people were killed in the first six months of 2002 in fighting between Indonesian troops and the rebel Free Aceh Movement. The number of human rights abuses committed by both sides was reported to have soared.

A South Korean patrol boat was sunk in a naval clash with North Korea in June. The incident took place in a disputed part of the Yellow Sea and left 4 South Korean sailors dead and 19 wounded. More than 100 South Korean fishing boats operating in the area were evacuated. Following a period of increased tension between North Korea and the U.S., both sides announced the end of the 1994 agreed framework that saw North Korea forgo its efforts to acquire nuclear weapons in exchange for annual supplies of fuel oil and the construction of two modern nuclear power plants.

Africa. Hundreds of people were killed in fighting between Algerian government forces and Islamist rebel groups during the year. The government announced in February that it had killed Antar Zouabri, the leader of the Armed Islamic Group. Dozens of citizens were killed in bombings in July during cele-

brations of Algeria's 40th anniversary of independence. In April the Permanent Court of Arbitration in The Hague delimited a 1,000-km stretch of border between Ethiopia and Eritrea that the two countries had fought over in 1998–2000.

Angolan army troops killed longtime UNITA rebel leader Jonas Savimbi in February, a move that led to the signing of a peace accord between the two sides in April. (*See* OBITUARIES.) The 27-year conflict was Africa's longest civil war.

The Democratic Republic of the Congo (DRC) and Rwanda signed a peace agreement in July to end the four-year war that had left an estimated two million people dead. Although there were outbreaks of fighting between local groups afterward, Rwandan and most Ugandan troops (who had supported rebels inside the country) pulled out of the DRC in October. Troops sent by Angola, Namibia, and Zimbabwe to aid the Congolese army were also repatriated under the arrangement. UN peacekeepers and about 1,000 Ugandan troops remained in the DRC to prevent fighting between local militia groups.

Uganda sent thousands of troops into southern Sudan in March in an attempt to wipe out the Lord's Resistance Army rebel group. At least 67 rebels were killed during a later raid, in June, which had the approval of the *(continued on page 282)*

(continued on page 282)

Warfare
in the 21st Century

by Peter Saracino

Unmanned aerial vehicles, such as this $15 million Global Hawk, have played a prominent role in the war in Afghanistan.

U.S. Air Force photo

The war that began in Afghanistan on Oct. 7, 2001, demonstrated both the capabilities and the limitations of modern military technology. It should have come as no surprise that the U.S.-led 17-member coalition toppled the Taliban regime in only a few weeks. In conventional terms, the Taliban were a pushover; they possessed no air force, had very limited air defenses, and were an unpopular and weak regime. It must be remembered, however, that in 1979 the Soviet Union controlled Afghanistan's capital, Kabul, within a week of beginning its invasion and then spent the next decade trying to defeat the mujahideen guerrillas. The coalition faced a similar challenge in 2002 against widely dispersed and tenacious al-Qaeda forces operating in rugged and inhospitable terrain. Consequently, the coalition has yet to eliminate al-Qaeda's terrorist infrastructure or determine the fate of its leader, Osama bin Laden.

New Weapons. Shortly after the war began, an American bomb designed to destroy underground tunnels and bunkers was rushed into service. The BLU-118/B thermobaric bomb was dropped on a suspected enemy cave in the eastern part of the country in March 2002. Although the device detonated as intended, a problem with its laser guidance caused it to land far enough away from the cave entrance to negate its effect. Thermobaric weapons work in two stages; first they release a fine cloud of high-explosive fuel, and then the fuel is detonated, creating a large fireball and a devastating shockwave. These weapons are most effective in confined spaces, because there the immense overpressures they create are contained and magnified. Ironically, the Soviets employed thermobaric bombs in Afghanistan in the 1980s. Research on thermobaric bombs continues in the U.S., Great Britain, and other countries as a means of destroying deep underground bunkers and hidden supplies of biological or chemical weapons without having to resort to the use of tactical nuclear weapons.

Another 21st-century device, the laser-guided bomb, now used by many countries, has two main disadvantages: the laser beam marking the target has to be aimed by someone on the ground or in an aircraft, and smoke and bad weather can degrade the laser beam such that it can no longer guide the falling bomb. In Afghanistan such problems have been overcome through the use of the new Global Positioning System (GPS) Aided Munition. A computer mounted in the bomb is programmed with the coordinates of the intended target and uses GPS guidance to strike with a reported accuracy of 12–18 m (40–60 ft). Since the 1990–91 Persian Gulf War, special forces troops have been using handheld GPS receivers, laser designators, and satellite radios to help artillery and aircraft attack targets with minimal delay. This capability has assumed a greater importance in Afghanistan, where reducing the "sensor to shooter" loop to just a few minutes has helped pin down and destroy small groups of guerrillas on the move.

The Afghan war will also be remembered as the first in which armed unmanned aerial vehicles (UAVs) were used to attack targets. UAVs have been in service for more than 40 years as drones for target practice and to gather intelligence with onboard sensors, but the CIA used a specially adapted Predator UAV to fire a Hellfire antitank missile at a group of three men believed to be al-Qaeda leaders. All were killed, but it later turned out that they were local villagers. Although expensive (the price of a Global Hawk UAV is over $15 million, and a Predator costs over $3.3 million), they have the advantage of being able to overfly enemy territory without risking the lives of pilots and can remain on patrol longer than most manned aircraft. UAVs are, however, vulnerable to ground fire, bad weather, ice buildup on their wings, and operator

Joe Raedle/Getty Images

Coalition troops use explosives to blast away at a rock wall in the Tora Bora region of Afghanistan on May 5.

Assisting special forces troops is among the primary missions of the HH-60G Pave Hawk helicopter, shown here during a training mission near the Golden Gate Bridge, north of San Francisco.

U.S. Air Force photo by Tech. Sgt. Lance Cheung

error. At least five Predators and one Global Hawk have crashed or been shot down during the war.

Logistic Challenges. What sets the U.S. military apart from all others is its ability to dispatch thousands of troops and their weapons, vehicles, and supplies to any point on Earth and to sustain them there. No other country could wage war in a landlocked country by supplying its forces almost entirely by air. By the end of September 2001, nearly the entire active-duty fleet of C-5 Galaxy and C-17 Globemaster III transport aircraft—a total of about 140—was dedicated to the war effort. The 30-year-old C-5 can carry 122,000 kg (270,000 lb) of cargo, but it requires a runway at least 1,495 m (4,900 ft) long for landing. Conversely, the C-17 can land on runways as short as 915 m (3,000 ft), which makes it much better suited to the primitive or war-damaged airfields in Afghanistan. At the height of the war in early 2002, coalition troops each month consumed 7.9 million litres (2.1 million gal) of fuel, 13.6 million litres (3.6 million gal) of water, and the equivalent of 72 18-wheel transport trucks of food. Meeting such a demand for supplies does not come cheap, however. For example, the price of delivering fuel to remote war zones can exceed $1,500 per litre.

The Role of Special Forces. The elimination of remaining al-Qaeda and Taliban members from their isolated mountain caves and village hideouts has remained problematic for the coalition and is a major reason why up to 2,000 special forces troops have been committed to the campaign. Although much of their work has been kept secret, several coalition members have admitted that they have deployed such forces, including Australia, Canada, Denmark, Germany, Norway, Turkey, the U.K., and the U.S. What sets special operations forces apart from regular troops is that they tend to be organized in groups of fewer than a dozen soldiers and are trained in specialties such as mountain, desert, and jungle warfare, counterterrorism, combat search-and-rescue operations, and covert reconnaissance. Special forces troops are also highly mobile and take advantage of specialized equipment that permits them to travel at night and in most weather conditions. For example, the MH-53J Pave Low III heavy-lift helicopter (based on the 1960s-era CH-53 Sea Stallion) has sophisticated radar and a forward-looking infrared sensor to enable its crew to avoid obstacles and fly just above the ground at night. The Pave

Low is equipped with armour plating and machine guns and can transport up to 38 troops.

Command and Information. For the most part, the war in Afghanistan has been managed from U.S. Central Command headquarters in Florida, more than 11,260 km (7,000 mi) and 10 time zones away. Commanders have for the first time been able to watch battles live via TV cameras mounted in UAVs. Although a technical achievement, this has led to complaints that the attention of headquarters staff is diverted and that troops in the field are being micromanaged. The large volume of data moving between commanders and troops in the field has been a mixed blessing for coalition forces. On one hand it has allowed commanders to deploy forces quickly and effectively to where they are needed most, but on the other hand information overload has created the requirement for new positions, such as that of "knowledge management officer" to filter out minor details and ensure that commanders get only the information they need in order to make decisions.

Peter Saracino is a freelance defense journalist and a contributor to PEJ News *based in Victoria, B.C.*

(continued from page 279)
Sudanese government under an agreement signed in March.

Fighting broke out between government forces and rebels in Côte d'Ivoire in September. The civil war began when government forces crushed an attempted mutiny by elements of the army. Gen. Robert Gueï, the Ivoirian former military leader, was killed during the attempted mutiny. (*See* OBITUARIES.) Hundreds of soldiers and civilians were subsequently killed on both sides. France sent several hundred troops to the capital, Yamoussoukro, and the main city of Abidjan in order to protect French and other foreign nationals.

MILITARY TECHNOLOGY

For the first time ever, the U.S. Army shot down an artillery shell in flight by using a high-powered laser. The Mobile Tactical High Energy Laser, a joint project with Israel, was test-fired in November. An earlier version of the system had been used to shoot down Russian Katyusha rockets in 2000. A modified Boeing 747-400 jet carrying a laser capable of shooting down ballistic missiles in flight was flight-tested for the first time in July. The U.S. Airborne Laser (ABL) program envisioned a fleet of seven such aircraft to be part of the country's defenses against ballistic missile attack. The test flight marked the beginning of the accelerated development of a national missile-defense system that became possible once the constraints of the ABM Treaty had been removed. (*See* Special Report.)

The X-45A unmanned combat aerial vehicle (UCAV) made its first flight in May, reaching a maximum airspeed of 360 km/hr (195 knots) and an altitude of 2,275 m (7,500 ft). The UCAV would preclude the need to send manned aircraft on a range of combat missions. Advances in military capabilities were sometimes little more than new applications of an existing technology; for example, in August Colombian troops seized nine remote-control model airplanes that rebel FARC troops were planning to fill with explosives.

The requirement for troops to fight for many hours and perhaps even days without a normal rest was seen as a key to success in future conflicts. The U.S. Defense Advanced Research Projects Agency (DARPA) was developing drugs to help troops manage stress and sleep deprivation. The Continuous Assisted Performance program included research into areas such as altering the body's metabolism so that it could use lipids as a source of energy rather than the normal carbohydrates.

Britain announced that its Defence Science and Technology Laboratory had developed an electrically charged hull to protect armoured vehicles against antitank grenades and shells. Known as the Pulsed Power System, the new armour used a highly charged capacitor to create a force field that would vaporize incoming metal objects before they could penetrate the vehicle's hull.

MILITARY AND SOCIETY

History caught up with a number of war criminals in 2002. In July a Florida court found two retired Salvadoran generals guilty of having been responsible for the torture of civilians during El Salvador's civil war more than two decades earlier. The court ordered the generals, who were residing in the U.S., to pay $54.6 million in damages to three of the victims. Gen. Leopoldo Galtieri, the former Argentine military dictator, was arrested in July and charged with offenses relating to the kidnapping and murder of domestic opponents during the so-called Dirty War of the 1980s. Warrants were also issued for the arrest of more than 30 other members of Galtieri's military administration. At least 9,000 and possibly as many as 30,000 people had "disappeared" during the Dirty War. A Chilean judge sentenced 11 former members of the military services and one civilian to prison terms for their role in the murder of a union leader in 1982 during the dictatorship of Augusto Pinochet Ugarte.

In July the head of the Ukrainian air force was arrested, the chief of staff of the armed forces fired, and the defense minister asked to resign as a consequence of the world's worst-ever airshow disaster, the crash of an Su-27 jet fighter in Lviv that killed 83 people and injured nearly 200. (*See* DISASTERS.)

ARMED FORCES, POLITICS, AND THE ENVIRONMENT

In August NATO scrapped its main rapid-reaction unit, the Allied Command Europe Mobile Force, after Britain withdrew its contribution to ensure that troops would be available to support any U.S. attack on Iraq. Then, at its November summit in Prague, NATO announced that it was creating a new rapid-reaction unit called the NATO Response Force that would be able to deploy up to 20,000 troops within 7–10 days. The summit was also used to announce the extension of NATO membership to seven more European countries (Bulgaria, Estonia, Latvia, Lithuania, Romania, Slovakia, and Slovenia). The move brought to 26 the number of NATO member states and for the first time brought the alliance into direct geographic contact with Russia's borders. In May, before it expanded its membership eastward, NATO had formalized its relationship with its former Cold War enemy by forming the new NATO-Russia Council. The arrangement was aimed at fostering greater cooperation in areas such as crisis management, peacekeeping, and search-and-rescue operations.

Germany undertook its largest naval deployment since World War II when it took command of a multinational antiterror operation in the Horn of Africa. Twelve warships from Germany and other European countries conducted surveillance and intelligence-gathering activities around the Red Sea, the Somali coast, and the Gulf of Aden in search of evidence of activity by members of al-Qaeda or the Taliban.

The dispute over the U.S. Navy's continued use of a bombing range on the Puerto Rican island of Vieques continued. Protesters attempted to disrupt a military exercise on the island in September, even though the navy had agreed to use only inert ordnance.

A UN Environment Programme task force found evidence of contamination from depleted uranium (DU) ammunition in Bosnia and Herzegovina. During its 1995 bombing campaign against Serb forces in Bosnia, NATO used armour-piercing munitions that contained DU, a slightly radioactive heavy metal. The UN task force identified three sites that it judged potential health hazards to people living nearby.

On the 60th anniversary of the World War II Battle of El-Alamein, the Egyptian government claimed that there were still approximately 20 million pieces of unexploded ordnance—of which 5 million were land mines—in the area around the site of the famous clash, which had pitted the forces of German Field Marshal Erwin Rommel against British Lieut. Gen. Bernard Montgomery's 8th Army.

(PETER SARACINO)

Performing Arts

CHANGES IN ARTISTIC DIRECTION at several theatre and dance companies; the **EMERGENCE OF SEVERAL NEW STARS,** including jazz singer **NORAH JONES** and Spanish pop singer-songwriter **ALEJANDRO SANZ;** the attempted **REBOUND BY SEVERAL ORCHESTRAS AND BROADWAY** following the 2001 terrorist attacks in the U.S., and the unexpected popularity of a romantic comedy, *MY BIG FAT GREEK WEDDING,* were some of the **TOP STORIES** in entertainment news in 2002.

MUSIC

Classical Music. Classical music, by its very definition, concerns itself with universal verities that transcend the moment. In 2002, however, the music and the artists who created it were often drawn in by world events that made it suddenly relevant as an expression and a reflection of the turmoil of its time.

At 8:46 AM local time on Sept. 11, 2002, 51 snowbound scientists at the Amundsen-Scott South Pole Station in Antarctica played a recording of Mozart's *Requiem* and sang along to commemorate the terrorist attacks in the U.S. on that day a year earlier. Their performance was the opening round of an international event, dubbed the Rolling Requiem, that saw choral ensembles from around the world performing the work at exactly the same moment in 20 time zones (the time was chosen to coincide with the minute when the first airliner hit the World Trade Center in New York City). While the idea for the event originated with a choral group in Seattle, Wash., it soon took on a life of its own, eventually encompassing more than 15,000 singers on every continent.

That event was mirrored by countless others around the world in which classical music became a universal means of expressing a sense of sorrow and remembrance. In the United States, Samuel Barber's *Adagio for Strings* became an unofficial national anthem of mourning, performed by orchestras and chamber ensembles across the country. The spirit of that work was up-dated and tied specifically to the tragedy by composer John Adams, who was commissioned by the New York Philharmonic to commemorate September 11 with a new work that was premiered at Lincoln Center on September 19. The piece, *On the Transmigration of Souls,* featured taped recitations of the victims' names and other sounds from that day set against an evocative orchestral background. At the Great Hall of the Moscow Conservatory, a concert devoted to a remembrance of September 11 was given by the Russian Chamber Choir. One of the most unusual tribute events featured cellist-conductor Mstislav Rostropovich leading the Hanover Radio Philharmonie from Germany and various Russian and British musicians in a peace concert at the former Nazi rocket base of Peenemünde on the Baltic Sea.

The impact of current events on classical music was felt not only in the artistic sphere, however. Israeli conductor-pianist Daniel Barenboim—who had created a firestorm of controversy in 2001 when he defied an unofficial ban and performed music by Richard Wagner at the Israel Festival—generated international headlines in March when he attempted to perform a concert for Middle East understanding and reconciliation in the West Bank city of Ram Allah at the height of the Palestinian suicide bombings. Israeli authorities refused him permission to travel to the Palestinian city, but in September he tried again, that time successfully. At the city's Friends School, Barenboim played Beethoven's *Moonlight Sonata* for about 100 Palestinian music students and conducted a master class. A few days later right-wing Israelis attacked him and his wife in a Jerusalem café and called him a traitor. Undeterred, he and U.S.-based Palestinian scholar Edward Said coauthored the book *Parallels and Paradoxes,* the stated purpose of which was to dispel cultural myths and misconceptions about Israel and Palestine.

World economic events also intruded on classical music during the year. With attendance and ticket revenues slumping in the wake of the terrorist attacks of 2001—and with their endowments falling along with the stock market—many orchestras and other performing arts companies were increasingly beset by budget deficits that threatened their existence. The San Jose (Calif.) Symphony was forced to shut down owing to a financial shortfall, and other major North American orchestras, including those in Philadelphia and Pittsburgh, Pa.; Cleveland, Ohio; Dallas, Texas; and Calgary, Alta., announced that their annual budgets were in the red. The San Francisco Opera reported a deficit of $7.7 million, while Chicago's Lyric Opera was forced to end its nationally syndicated radio broadcasts because of lack of funds.

Global financial difficulties notwithstanding, classical music continued to flourish. In London the annual BBC Promenade Concerts (the Proms) marked their biggest season ever, selling a record £33.6 million (about $53 million) in tickets. Similarly, the Salzburg (Austria) Festival set a new attendance record with 212,000 visitors. The China Philharmonic announced that its debut season had been a smashing success and offered an expanded second season that included the first performances in that country of the complete Beethoven symphonies and concertos. After a two-year hiatus, the production of Verdi's *Aida* returned to the Pyramids of Giza near Cairo. In addition, a production of Bizet's *Carmen* on the Boston Common, which was offered free to the public, drew audiences of 135,000 over a two-day period.

Where it counted most—in the creation of new pieces of music—classical music also continued to prosper. In addition to Adams, composer and violinist Mark O'Connor completed work on his *Folk Mass* (based on books of the Old Testament), which also paid tribute to the victims of September 11. In the prevailing atmosphere of national fervour following the tragedy, composer George Crumb went back home—literally and figuratively—with . . . *Unto the Hills* (*Appalachian Songs of Sadness, Yearning and Innocence*) for folk singer, percussion quartet, and amplified piano, which quoted Appalachian folk songs he had first heard in his youth.

Works unrelated to September 11 were also unveiled. In October the San Francisco-based Kronos Quartet premiered Terry Riley's *Sun Rings*, which incorporated interstellar sounds recorded on NASA space missions. Based on the life of contemporary German politician Angela Merkel and premiering in Berlin on August 18, the opera *Angela*, by composer Frank Schwemmer and librettist Michael Frowin, created a stir. Chinese-American composer Bright Sheng announced that he had begun work on an opera based on the life of the wife of Mao Zedong, and in the U.S., Garrison Keillor (host of the popular radio program *A Prairie Home Companion*) unveiled his opera, *Mr. and Mrs. Olson*, about two people who fall in love on the Internet. In each of these works and myriad others, classical music demonstrated its continuing vitality as a creative and expressive form.

If sheer activity connotes vitality, the year in classical music was filled with just that, from the sublime to the ridiculous, with all points covered in between. The sublime unfolded in September when Benjamin Britten's *War Requiem* was performed on the 40th anniversary of its creation in Coventry England's St. Michael's Cathedral, which had been destroyed during a Nazi air attack in 1940 and was later rebuilt. Not far away, the ridiculous took the form of an English National Opera production of Verdi's *A Masked Ball*, which raised the ire of critics and turned away the public in droves with its graphic depictions of a homosexual rape, transvestism, and, at one point, a chorus that gave the Nazi salute. The furor caused by the production (and a similarly scandalous interpretation of Mozart's *Don Giovanni* in 2001) led to the ouster of the company's director, Nicholas Payne. The points in between included a billboard ad campaign for the El Paso (Texas) Opera production of Donizetti's *Lucia di Lammermoor* in which the bloody images frightened the local populace; an unscheduled cameo appearance by a bull snake on the stage of the Santa Fe (N.M.) Opera, which caused a power outage that interrupted

a performance; and the Los Angeles Philharmonic's decision to institute "Casual Friday" concerts in which audiences and musicians turned out in, among other things, jeans and sneakers. Pranksters wreaked havoc in Paris when the opening night at the Paris Opéra's Palais Garnier was sabotaged by a recording of the dress rehearsal for Handel's *Giulio Cesare* that was played through concealed speakers as the actual production was unfolding on stage. Down Under, a computer hacker somehow infiltrated a promotional compact disc (CD) by the New Zealand Symphony Orchestra and inserted pornographic texts in place of the disc's track title listings. All these hijinks paled, however, in comparison with a surreal court case that was brought against British composer Mike Batt by the estate of composer John Cage. It seems that on a CD Batt recorded with his group, the Planets, he included a minute of silence in tribute to the composer of the famous conceptual work *4' 33"*, which featured a pianist sitting at a keyboard in silence for that allotted time period. Cage's estate sued Batt for infringement of copyright—on silence.

A number of world-famous conductors played musical chairs, in some cases ending long-standing musical relationships. Seiji Ozawa said farewell to the Boston Symphony Orchestra after 29 years as its music director; in September he took over his new post at the Vienna Staatsoper. Britain's Sir Simon Rattle made his long-awaited debut as director of the Berlin Philharmonic, the start of a 10-year collaboration. Franz Welser-Möst made his debut as the

music director of the Cleveland Orchestra, while Kurt Masur departed from the New York Philharmonic. Finally, in one of the more controversial episodes of the year, Charles Dutoit—months before what would have been the start of his 25th anniversary season with the orchestra—abruptly resigned from his post as music director with the Montreal Symphony following an acrimonious dispute with the head of the local musicians' union. Major soloists, including Rostropovich, Yo-Yo Ma, and Vladimir Ashkenazy promptly canceled scheduled performances with the orchestra in protest.

World-famous tenor Luciano Pavarotti was the focus of speculation throughout much of 2002, with many sources suggesting that he was on the verge of retirement. Rumours ran rampant that his scheduled appearance in the Metropolitan Opera's production of *Tosca* in May would be his last on an operatic stage. When he canceled his two performances at the last moment owing to illness—the latter performance generating nonrefundable ticket prices of up to $1,875—fans were outraged, but Pavarotti was unrepentant. Later in the year he announced that he would indeed retire from opera productions—but not solo performances—when he turned 70 in 2005. Equally famous soprano Dame Kiri Te Kanawa made headlines as well when she announced in mid-September that her appearance with the Washington (D.C.) Opera in October could be her last on an operatic stage.

In January the classical music world lost its most acclaimed harpsichordist

British conductor Sir Simon Rattle acknowledges applause at the end of his debut performance on September 7 as director of the Berlin Philharmonic.

when Igor Kipnis died at age 71 after a brief battle with cancer. During his long career Kipnis championed the works of contemporary composers and was also a noted music critic. In March the Juilliard School's illustrious violin teacher Dorothy DeLay, whose students had included Itzhak Perlman, Midori, Nigel Kennedy, Gil Shaham, and Nadia Salerno-Sonnenberg, died at age 84. (*See* OBITUARIES.)

The death of another musical titan was also the basis of one of the year's most remarkable recordings. To mark the 20th anniversary of the death of pianist Glenn Gould, the Sony label released the CD *A State of Wonder*, which featured his legendary 1955 debut recording of Bach's *Goldberg Variations* accompanied by his final 1981 recording of the same work made shortly before his death at age 50. In the former version his youthful impetuosity and interpretative innovations were on full display, while on the latter his brilliantly layered and deeply introspective playing revealed the rich textures of a musical mind still in ferment even as it yielded to deeper thoughts and emotions sculpted by the passage of time. In its way the CD encapsulated all that classical music is and has ever been about: genius giving voice to genius, for one time, for all time.　　(HARRY SUMRALL)

Jazz. Though no new trends or fads appeared and only one new star emerged, jazz and related musics at last crossed a final frontier in 2002. The jazz idiom, originally created by African Americans, had been played on six of the world's seven continents, but in 2001–02 guitarist Henry Kaiser spent two months in Antarctica, the last continent. Kaiser, with extensive experience playing free improvisations and jazz-rock fusion music, was a guest of the National Science Foundation's Artists and Writers Program. He recorded himself playing slide guitar at the South Pole while the temperature dipped to –40 °C (–40 °F).

The new star was singer Norah Jones, and like other recent jazz stars she was noted for her youth and beauty as well as for her talent. The daughter of sitarist Ravi Shankar, the 22-year-old Jones accompanied herself on piano and recorded *Come Away with Me* for a major label, Blue Note. The content of her first full album was unusual for a jazz singer; it featured mostly original songs. Four other singers also rejected the conventional repertoire in favour of music that had more personal meaning. Mississippi-born Cas-

sandra Wilson recorded *Belly of the Sun* in the Clarksdale, Miss., train station, Nnenna Freelon sang Stevie Wonder songs in *Tales of Wonder*, and Patricia Barber composed all the songs in *Verse*. Susanne Abbuehl wrote lyrics for Carla Bley songs and set E.E. Cummings poems to music; she sang them all in *April*.

This dissatisfaction with standard songs, which were mostly composed before these singers were born, was a tendency that stood out in the present, postmodern phase of jazz, a long-standing, developmentally static period. A

Jazz singer Norah Jones earned high praise for her first album, Come Away with Me.

similar frustration led jazz artists such as pianists Jason Moran, Uri Caine, and Mal Waldron to turn to Robert Schumann, Gustav Mahler, and Johannes Brahms for material more meaningful than the traditional song forms and narrow range of harmonic structures. Stefon Harris (marimba and vibes), Kenny Barron (piano), Ron Carter (bass), Lewis Nash (drums), and Bob Belden (arranger) offered *The Classical Jazz Quartet Plays Bach* in 2002.

Robert Harth, the new executive and artistic director of Carnegie Hall, denied that the declining economy was the reason for discontinuing the Carnegie Hall Jazz Band, the 10-year-old repertory band conducted by trum-

peter Jon Faddis. Verve Records cut its roster of jazz artists to 30–35, and the chief executive officer, Ron Goldstein, announced that the company would hereafter focus on crossover acts. Independent record companies remained the leading sources of jazz, and saxophonist Branford Marsalis founded Marsalis Music, which released his CD *Footsteps of Our Fathers*. After soprano saxophonist Steve Lacy, a major artist, had spent 32 years in Paris, the decline of jazz opportunities there led him to return to the U.S. and accept a teaching position at the New England Conservatory of Music, Boston. In 2000 jazz flutist James Newton had sued the Beastie Boys for sampling six seconds of his 1980 recording "Choir" without his permission; Newton lost his suit in a federal district court in 2002 but appealed. On the brighter side, Queen Elizabeth II made jazz guitarist Martin Taylor MBE. A hit in concerts and festivals, if less successful musically, was saxophonist Wayne Shorter's jazz quartet, which recorded *Footprints Live!*

The free-jazz underground remained the music's healthiest aspect in 2002. George Lewis—a trombonist, composer, and electronic music explorer who invented the improvising-keyboards computer program Voyager—became the latest jazz artist to receive a John D. and Catherine T. MacArthur Foundation "genius" grant. As the Chicago Jazz Festival's first artist in residence, Lewis conducted the NOW Orchestra in his own works; the Vancouver, B.C.-based NOW was one of the few repertory ensembles to specialize in free jazz. By contrast, composition was banished at Freedom of the City 2002, the second annual festival in London to celebrate the city's lively free improvisation scene. A wildly diverse lot of jazz, classical, and pop musicians found common ground in improvising together, and the London Improvisers Orchestra was again the festival's centrepiece.

It was a good year for recordings. Pianist-composer Simon Nabatov and his quintet offered remarkable jazz impressions of Mikhail Bulgakov's novel *The Master and Margarita*. Two of Lewis's saxophonist colleagues offered important new albums. Roscoe Mitchell led his Note Factory in *Song for My Sister*. Another veteran free-jazz saxophonist, Jemeel Moondoc, was joined by bassist and double-reed player William Parker and drummer Hamid Drake in *New World Pygmies Volume 2*. Andrew Hill led a big band at New

York's Birdland and in the compact disc *A Beautiful Day*, while Hill's former tenor saxophonist Von Freeman offered *The Improviser* and, on his 80th birthday, had part of 75th Street in Chicago officially renamed Von Freeman Way. Two major British free improvisers offered retrospectives: soprano saxophonist Lol Coxhill (*Spectral Soprano*) and solo trombonist Paul Rutherford (*Trombolenium*).

A new discovery, *Norman Granz' J.A.T.P. Carnegie Hall, 1949*, brought Charlie Parker, Fats Navarro, and the inspired Coleman Hawkins together. Among the year's reissues, Albert Ayler's *Lörrach, Paris 1966* and two volumes of *Ornette Coleman Trio Live at the Golden Circle* stood out, as did several boxed sets from Mosaic, especially *Classic Columbia and OKeh Recordings of Joe Venuti and Eddie Lang* and *The Complete OKeh and Brunswick Recordings of Bix Beiderbecke, Frank Trumbauer, and Jack Teagarden 1924–1936*. Among the deaths during the year were those of swing giant Lionel Hampton, legendary bassist Ray Brown, singers Peggy Lee and Rosemary Clooney, pianist Michael ("Dodo") Marmarosa, and Dixieland bandleader Ward Kimball. (*See* OBITUARIES.) Other notable deaths included those of pianist Russ Freeman, baritone saxophonist Nick Brignola, German bassist Peter Kowald, and organists Shirley Scott and John Patton. (JOHN LITWEILER)

Popular. The year 2002 was a classic one for African music, and arguably the finest of a batch of great new albums came from the celebrated Malian singer Salif Keita. His recent work had included excursions into jazz-rock and funk, but the album *Moffou* was very different—an acoustic set that marked a return to his African roots. The relaxed, gently rhythmic backing was provided by guitar, percussion, and traditional West African instruments, and against this Keita demonstrated his intimate, delicate, and soulful vocals on an album that reestablished his reputation as one of the greatest vocalists in the world.

Across the border in Senegal, there was also a return to more gentle and reflective styles from another internationally acclaimed singer, Youssou N'Dour. In his earlier work N'Dour had matched African rhythms and styles with Western pop, but on his new album, *Nothing's in Vain* (*Coono du reer*), he was backed by traditional Senegalese instruments such as the kora and balafon on a set of gently passionate or thoughtful ballads that were matched with echoes of French chanson. N'Dour also acted as co-producer on the much-praised comeback album by Orchestra Baobab, a band that had dominated the music of Senegal in the 1970s with its lively blend of Cuban dance songs and West African influences. *Specialists in All Styles*, its first new recording in 15 years, included appearances from N'Dour and the Cuban star Ibrahim Ferrer, of Buena Vista Social Club fame, and proved that the band was still as energetic and versatile as ever.

From along the coast in Guinea, there was another rousing and stylish comeback from a second legendary West African big band, Bembeya Jazz. The group's album *Bembeya* was its first new release in 14 years. Beninese pop singer Angélique Kidjo solidified her reputation as an international star with the release of *Black Ivory Soul*. (*See* BIOGRAPHIES.) There were also impressive albums from African newcomers. Pape and Cheikh's *Mariama* was an exhilarating blend of Western pop and Senegalese influences from a duo who strummed acoustic guitars like Western folk singers and initially modeled themselves on Simon and Garfunkel. Mali's Issa Bagayogo also created an unusual fusion by matching instruments such as his *kamele ngoni* (the hunter's lute) against Western dance beats and dub effects on his album *Timbuktu*. From across the Sahara there was more impressive fusion work from the Algerian-born Souad Massi, with her thoughtful blend of Arabic songs and ballads influenced by the popular music of France, where she resided. African and Arabic influences continued to transform French popular music, with the new French multiethnic community represented by the neorealist movement of bands such as Lo'Jo. A compilation of its songs was released on the album *Cuisine Non-Stop: Introduction to the French Nouvelle Generation*.

As European music began to win a wider audience (owing partly to the continued success of Manu Chao), artists such as Mariza, the young and striking new fado star from Portugal, benefited from greater exposure to their works. In the U.K., enthusiasts of the new African music scene included Damon Albarn, the singer-songwriter best known for his work with Blur and his highly successful anonymous band Gorillaz (who performed hidden behind a giant screen showing cartoons and graphics). Albarn released an album, *Mali Music*, that consisted of recordings he had made in West Africa along with collaborations with Malian musicians. He was joined for a concert in London by members of Gorillaz and Malian singer Afel Bocoum. Elsewhere in Britain it was a good year for Coldplay, with its best-selling album *A Rush of Blood to the Head*, and for the 21-year-old London rap artist Ms Dynamite, winner of the Mercury Music Prize. Among those also nominated was veteran star David Bowie, whose new album *Heathen* was widely praised as his finest work in many years. It was also a good year for British veteran Peter Gabriel, who delighted his record company by at last releasing a new album, *Up*, after a nine-year wait.

In Latin America there were further experiments in mixing musical styles. Susana Baca, the leading exponent of Afro-Peruvian music, was joined by jazz keyboard player John Medeski and guitarist Marc Ribot on her new album *Espiritu vivo*, which included everything from French chanson to a song by Icelandic star Björk. From Mexico there was a lively new set from Los de Abajo, mixing local *jarocho* styles with ska and dub effects. (ROBIN DENSELOW)

Hip-hop artist Eminem—Detroit native Marshall Mathers III—in 2002 further advanced his standing as a pop-culture favourite with the release of his third album, *The Eminem Show,* and a starring role in the movie *8 Mile,* about a white rap artist trying to establish himself in the black-dominated idiom. *The Eminem Show* debuted at number one on *Billboard*'s Top 200 album chart in June after having been rushed to stores a week early to thwart piracy. Six months after its release, the compact disc (CD) had sold more than six and a half million copies. In November the *8 Mile* sound track, with contributions from Eminem, Nas, and Jay-Z, also debuted at number one on *Billboard*'s album chart. The movie grossed $54.5 million in its opening weekend.

Rapper Nelly (Cornell Haynes, Jr.) released a funk-rooted CD, *Nellyville,* including the hits "Hot in Herre" and "Dilemma." With first-week sales of 714,000, he held the top slot on several *Billboard* album, single, and radio airplay charts at once. Ashanti, a 21-year-old rhythm-and-blues artist, sold 502,000 copies of her self-titled debut CD in its first week of release, a record for a female artist's debut. The album later received double-platinum certification, for shipments of two million copies. Ashanti's first three entries on the *Billboard* pop singles chart—collaborations with Ja Rule and Fat Joe and her own "Foolish"—were in the top 10 at the same time in March. Only the Beatles had accomplished the feat before.

Overall, album sales were down 9.8% at midyear compared with the first half of 2001. Sales stood at 311.1 million units, compared with 344.8 million units in the first half of 2001, as counted by Nielsen SoundScan. The bleak picture was attributed to CD burning, computer file sharing, bootlegging, and a lack of hit albums.

Bruce Springsteen & the E Street Band released *The Rising*, a CD interlaced with songs about the events of Sept. 11, 2001, and its aftereffects. Critics hailed *The Rising* as a return to form for Springsteen. The Rolling Stones' albums from 1964–1970 were reissued on CD, and a selection of their work, including four new songs, was gathered on the anthology *Forty Licks*, also the name of their international tour. Also making successful U.S. tours were Paul McCartney; Billy Joel and Elton John; Crosby, Stills, Nash & Young; *NSYNC; the Dave Matthews Band; Britney Spears (see BIOGRAPHIES); the Eagles, Cher, Creed, Kenny Chesney, Kid Rock, and Brooks & Dunn.

Alicia Keys won five Grammys, including best new artist and song of the year for "Fallin'." *O Brother, Where Art Thou?* was album of the year. The sound track sold more than six million albums and gave rise to the Down from the Mountain tour, which featured Alison Krauss + Union Station, Emmylou Harris, and Ralph Stanley (see BIOGRAPHIES), among others. Isaac Hayes, Brenda Lee, Tom Petty and the Heartbreakers, Gene Pitney, the Ramones, and Talking Heads joined the Rock and Roll Hall of Fame; Porter Wagoner and Bill Carlisle were elected to the Country Music Hall of Fame. At the Latin Grammys, Spanish pop singer-songwriter Alejandro Sanz (see BIOGRAPHIES) dominated the awards.

Country singer Alan Jackson released *Drive* with live and studio versions of "Where Were You (When the World Stopped Turning)," a song inspired by the events of September 11. *Drive* was named album of the year by the Country Music Association; Jackson won five awards in all. The Dixie Chicks released *Home*, an acoustic CD with songs by Patty Griffin and Stevie Nicks. Faith Hill issued the pop-leaning *Cry*, and Shania Twain released *UP!*, her first album in five years; it included two discs,

Canadian singer-songwriter Avril Lavigne shows off her award for best new artist at the MTV Video Music Awards on August 29 in New York City.

one with pop versions of her songs and the other with country treatments.

Neo-garage bands such as the Strokes, White Stripes, the Hives, and the Vines featured a rock sound and stance that recalled the anticorporate mid-1960s. Avril Lavigne, an 18-year-old singer-songwriter from Canada, played guitar and wrote every song on her successful debut album, *Let Go*. Critics cast Lavigne, Michelle Branch, and Vanessa Carlton as alternatives to the teen-oriented pop of Spears and Christina Aguilera.

Among the music figures who died during the year were Lisa ("Left Eye") Lopes of the rhythm-and-blues trio TLC, pop singer Peggy Lee, Country Music Hall of Fame members Waylon Jennings and Harlan Howard, punk pioneer Dee Dee Ramone (Douglas Colvin), Layne Staley of the rock group Alice in Chains, songwriter Otis Blackwell, John Entwistle of the Who, Rosemary Clooney, and rapper Jam Master Jay (Jason Mizell). (*See* OBITUARIES.)

(JAY ORR)

DANCE

North America. Despite the vicissitudes of living in an awakened world following the 2001 terrorist attacks in the U.S., most plans in place for dance

went forward in 2002. Though American Ballet Theatre (ABT) was forced for budgetary reasons to cancel plans for an all-Stravinsky program—featuring *Firebird*, a work created by James Kudelka for his National Ballet of Canada (NBC)—ABT managed to present two new stagings of classic works by British choreographer Sir Frederick Ashton: *The Dream* and *La Fille mal gardée*. Both *The Dream*, a one-act work that was set to Felix Mendelssohn's *A Midsummer Night's Dream*, and *La Fille mal gardée*, a two-act production based on Jean Dauberval's 1789 ballet about love in a rustic setting, won eager approval from audiences and the press. Each provided stellar showcases for the company's dancers, especially its strong male contingent. The radiant Cuban-born dancer Carlos Acosta, who made his ABT debut during the season, the mercurial Ethan Stiefel, and the brilliant Angel Corella reached new plateaus of their already splendid artistry. Elsewhere in the same season, two young comers, Gillian Murphy and Marcelo Gomes—both recently promoted to principal dancer—stood out; Murphy made a grand debut as Lise in *La Fille mal gardée*, and Gomes gave a memorable accounting of the title role in *Onegin*, the Aleksandr Pushkin-inspired John Cranko ballet that the company acquired in 2001. ABT ballerina Susan Jaffe retired from the stage after 22 years with the company; later in the year she joined the troupe's administrative staff and planned to pursue an acting career.

New York City Ballet (NYCB) completed its winter season with little of major note except *Telemann Overture Suite in E-Minor*, a charming new work by novice choreographer Melissa Barak; the work served as an antidote to the less-than-impressive new works offered by ballet master in chief Peter Martins. In the spring NYCB celebrated the 10th anniversary of the Diamond Project, the new-ballet showcase named for the Irene Diamond Fund, its principal donor. Little in NYCB's spring program—which included selections from past Diamond Project ballets—gave much cause for celebration, with the exception of two works that had their premiere in June: Barak's *If by Chance* (set to Dmitry Shostakovich's *Sonata for Cello and Piano in D minor*) and Christopher Wheeldon's *Morphoses* (set to the music of Gyorgy Ligeti). Wheeldon is the company's resident choreographer and one of the world's leading classical dancemakers. NYCB ballerina Heléne Alexopoulos took her final bow in May, ending her career with George Balanchine's challenging *The Prodigal Son.* A mostly lacklustre selection of some eight works associated with the new-ballet project was nationally televised. The rare dance offering by the Public Broadcasting System, *Live from Lincoln Center,* achieved a dubious impact and low ratings.

In the realm of modern dance, the Merce Cunningham Dance Company (MCDC) launched its 50th-anniversary year. Helping cap the Lincoln Center Festival (LCF), MCDC offered an array of Cunningham works that spanned the company's history—one work each from the 1950s and '60s and two from the '80s, as well as a brand new work by Cunningham, *Loose Time,* which involved design elements by contemporary artist Terry Winters. In striking contrast, the Martha Graham Dance Company (MGDC) barely existed. Though the troupe's operations remained suspended owing to both financial difficulties and ligation problems with Ronald Protas, Graham's legal heir, over the ownership of copyright to Gra-

ham's dances and to the use of her name, MGDC gave one newsworthy performance in New York City in midyear, for which the participants donated their services. In late summer the troupe learned that a court ruling had been made in its favour. The Martha Graham Center of Contemporary Dance, which was taken to court by Protas, was granted the copyrights to most of Graham's dances, and MGDC was thereby allowed to resume presenting its founder's work without constraint.

Highlighting the Paul Taylor Dance Company's New York City season was the amusingly jittery *Antique Valentine* (set to music-box recordings) and the world premiere of the grandly scaled *Promethean Fire* (set to Bach) at the American Dance Festival. Mark Morris's partly elegiac and partly ecstatic *V* (set to Robert Schumann) helped cap his first Brooklyn Academy of Music (BAM) season since he moved into his specially built headquarters across the street. The Alvin Ailey American Dance Theater featured an array of dances by women choreographers for its annual month-long New York City winter season.

Highlighting the season were visits by various Russian ballet troupes. St. Petersburg's Mariinsky Ballet played the Kennedy Center for the Performing Arts (KC) in Washington, D.C., in the winter with its historic 1999 revival of *The Sleeping Beauty* (1890) and its equally historic staging of George Balanchine's *Jewels,* the world's first multi-act "abstract" ballet. For the first time under its new artistic director, Boris Akimov, the Bolshoi Ballet appeared at the KC in *Swan Lake* and *La Bayadère,* productions of its ousted artistic director Yury Grigorovich. Both productions then returned to the U.S. for a national tour in the fall; KC finished off its year with Grigorovich's *The Nutcracker.* By year's end, KC's opera house had closed for renovations. The Mariinsky also opened the LCF with its new "old" staging of *La Bayadère,* in a production based on historical research conducted both in Russia and at the Harvard Theatre Collection. The same New York City season also offered *Swan Lake, Don Quixote,* and the first local performances by a Russian company of *Jewels.* St. Petersburg's Eifman Ballet

Dancers with the Alvin Ailey American Dance Theater perform a scene from Lynne Taylor-Corbett's ballet Prayers from the Edge *on December 4 at New York's City Center.*

celebrated its 25th anniversary while appearing in New York City.

BAM's annual Next Wave Festival featured France's Angelin Preljocaj, including his recent rendering of Stravinsky's *The Rite of Spring*, which featured nudity. In the same festival, making a local debut was Sasha Waltz, who presented *Körper* ("Bodies"), which offered more bare skin. Japan's Sankai Juku and the Mark Morris Dance Group helped cap the BAM festival, the latter with Morris's comic-book take on *The Nutcracker*, called *The Hard Nut*. Mikhail Baryshnikov's White Oak Dance Project (WODP) helped open the festivities to mark the 70th anniversary of the Jacob's Pillow dance seasons. The WODP also toured a good deal nationally and internationally. In December, however, Baryshnikov announced that WODP would disband and that the Baryshnikov Center for Dance, a dance studio and space for creating new works, would open in 2004. On a grander scale, Dance Theater Workshop held the grand opening in New York City of its newly refurbished state-of-the-art quarters.

In Florida, Miami City Ballet's Edward Villella finished *The Neighborhood Ballroom*, his multiact work based on ballroom dancing. The San Francisco Ballet presented its first staging of *Jewels* and played an ambitious three-program, one-week season at New York City's City Center. Pacific Northwest Ballet presented the world premiere of Donald Byrd's *Seven Deadly Sins*, after which Byrd announced the closure of his own ensemble, Donald Byrd/The Group. Houston (Texas) Ballet (HB) offered *Peter Pan*, a charming and original ballet by Trey McIntyre. HB's longtime artistic director Ben Stevenson announced his impending retirement from the Houston troupe. Oregon Ballet Theater's James Canfield announced his decision to leave his position. Mikko Nissinen launched his first season as director of Boston Ballet with a repertory that would include Ashton's *La Fille mal gardée*.

The 28-year-old Southern Ballet Theatre announced its name change to Orlando Ballet. Cincinnati (Ohio) Ballet and the Cincinnati Art Museum teamed up to help salute Ballet Russe de Monte Carlo (BRDMC) octogenarian Frederic Franklin with a ballet gala and a longer-running show of BRDMC visual designs. In June an offshoot of Dance/USA, a national service organization, was formed; Dance/NYC was established with the prominent Web

site <http://www.dancenyc.org>. NBC's Kudelka convened a symposium for fellow artistic directors to address and discuss aspects of running a ballet company in the 21st century. His newest work, *The Contract*, inspired in part by *The Pied Piper*, represented his first multiact original creation and earned welcoming reviews but weak ticket sales. The Royal Winnipeg (Man.) Ballet closed its spring season with Mauricio Wainrot's *Carmina Burana* and opened its fall season with Andre Prokovsky's *Anna Karenina*. John Alleyne, the artistic director of Ballet British Columbia, presented the world premiere of *Orpheus*. A new ballet company, the Atlantic Ballet Theatre of Canada, directed by Igor Dobrovolskiy, was launched in May in New Brunswick. In late summer the Toronto area hosted another sprawling version of the fringe Festival of Independent Dance Artists.

Deaths during the year included those of dance preservationist Barbara Barker, historical dance teacher Wendy Hilton, dance critic Laurie Horn, dance promoter Stephanie Reinhart, dancers Mia Slavenska, Jackie Raven, Florence Lessing, and William Marrié, and dancer-teacher-choreographers Benjamin Harkarvy (*see* OBITUARIES), Rod Rodgers, David Wood, Pauline Tish, James Richard ("Buster") Brown (*see* OBITUARIES), Beverly Brown, Meredith Baylis, Duncan Noble, and Pepsi Bethel.   (ROBERT GRESKOVIC)

Europe. Though some distinguished new work was seen in Europe in 2002, as in previous years the main news was made by changes in the artistic direction of companies all over the continent. The most publicized resignations were those of Ross Stretton at the Royal Ballet and American choreographer William Forsythe in Frankfurt, Ger.

In the London ballet world, the Royal Ballet's first season under director Ross Stretton had aroused both interest and controversy. He introduced several short works by choreographers new to the company, including Stephen Baynes, Nacho Duato, Mats Ek, and Mark Morris. Some of these works were panned by the critics, and questions were asked about the direction in which Stretton was taking the company. Fortunately, the only world premiere provided the hit of the season; *Tryst*, a complex pure-dance piece by British-born choreographer Christopher Wheeldon, was acclaimed as one of the best new ballets seen from this company in years. Just before the start

of the 2002–03 season, however, Stretton resigned, saying that he was not happy with the rate at which he was being allowed to introduce new work. Assistant director Monica Mason took over the management of the company until a new appointment could be made. English National Ballet also had a success with Christopher Hampson's *Double Concerto*, and Hampson also made a new version of the company's signature piece, *Nutcracker*, with designs by cartoonist Gerald Scarfe. Birmingham Royal Ballet moved back into its refurbished home theatre, where it presented a program to mark the centenary of the birth of composer William Walton.

Scottish Ballet announced the appointment of Royal Ballet dancer and choreographer Ashley Page to replace Robert North as artistic director. Page was charged with helping to "redefine the company as a modern ballet company," and his appointment ended speculation that the troupe would abandon ballet for contemporary dance. The company produced Sir Frederick Ashton's *Two Pigeons* for its spring tour, with former Royal Ballet star Sarah Wildor as guest artist. Northern Ballet Theatre had a successful year under its new director, David Nixon, who introduced *I Got Rhythm* (set to the music of George and Ira Gershwin) and his own version of *Madame Butterfly* and made his first piece especially for the company; it was based on Emily Brontë's novel *Wuthering Heights*.

Christopher Bruce retired after eight years as artistic director of the Rambert Dance Company, and he was succeeded by choreographer Mark Baldwin. Another former Royal Ballet star, Bruce Sansom, became the company's head of development after two years spent in management training first with the San Francisco Ballet and then as one of the first fellows of the Vilar Institute of Arts Management at the Kennedy Center for the Performing Arts in Washington, D.C. The Siobhan Davies Dance Company resumed operations after a year-long absence with *Plants and Ghosts*, a new work designed to be shown in non-dance venues, including a disused aircraft hanger and a former cotton mill. In October the Royal Academy of Dance hosted a conference to mark the 10th anniversary of the death of choreographer Sir Kenneth MacMillan.

Visits by American troupes to London included the long-awaited return of both the Alvin Ailey Dance Company and Dance Theatre of Harlem and a

Northern Ballet Theatre dancers Chiaki Nagao and Neil Westmoreland perform in choreographer David Nixon's version of Madame Butterfly *in London.*

first appearance by the Hubbard Street Dance Company of Chicago. The Lithuanian National Ballet mounted an unusual *Romeo and Juliet* in a semi-staged performance choreographed by Vladimir Vasiliev. The orchestra was conducted by Mstislav Rostropovich, who left the podium in the closing scene to join the action.

The Mariinsky Ballet of St. Petersburg followed its re-creation of the original *Sleeping Beauty* by attempting a similar reconstruction of Marius Petipa's *La Bayadère*. The new production was based on the version used in 1900 but also included some later additions that had become widely accepted as part of the ballet. *La Bayadère* was generally perceived as less satisfying than the *Sleeping Beauty* experiment, partly because the ballet contained so much more mime than modern audiences expected. Also in repertory were a triple bill of ballets by John Neumeier and a new *Cinderella* by Aleksey Ratmansky. The Bolshoi Ballet scored a great success with the first Russian production of Ashton's *La Fille mal gardée*, some 40 years after plans for this acquisition were first discussed.

The dance scene in Germany was dominated by the decision of William Forsythe to leave the Ballett Frankfurt, which under his leadership had become one of the world's best-known companies. Threats of cuts in the funding provided by the city of Frankfurt and a reported desire by the city council to see a company providing more

accessible work were believed to be behind Forsythe's departure. A worldwide outcry had greeted the original announcement of the city's plans, but the clamour failed to influence the outcome. Another unhappy situation unfolded in Berlin, where Bianca Li resigned as director of the ballet of the Komische Oper after only nine months on the job, citing difficult working conditions as her reason for quitting. Neumeier's Hamburg Ballet had a more successful year, including the premiere of Neumeier's latest work, *The Seagull*, a two-act ballet based on Anton Chekov's play.

In France the most important new work for the Paris Opéra Ballet was another *Wuthering Heights* piece. *Hurlevent*, with choreography by company étoile Kader Belarbi and music by Philippe Hersant, was a nonliteral treatment of the novel; it was designed as a modern commentary on the traditional romantic ballet as well as a retelling of the famous story. Other programs during the year included an all-Stravinsky evening and a revival of Maurice Béjart's full-evening ballet *Le Concours*, which was based on a ballet competition. Leading soloist Laetitia Pujol was promoted to étoile during the year. The Ballet de Lorraine, based in Nancy, France, presented an evening of three new works inspired by American dancer Loie Fuller. Almost 30 different companies from Latin America were featured in Terra Latina, the 2002 Lyon Biennale de la Danse.

A change of management at the Dutch National Ballet saw Wayne Eagling replaced as artistic director by his former assistant, Ted Brandsen. In Belgium choreographer Anne Teresa de Keersmaeker celebrated 20 years as director of her company, Rosas, and the Royal Ballet of Flanders mounted a controversial new production of *Swan Lake*, with choreography by Jan Fabre. The latter was also shown later in the season at the Edinburgh International Festival, and it aroused strong reactions both for and against its reworking of the Petipa/Lev Ivanov original. Ireland held its first International Dance Festival in May and imported a number of distinguished overseas companies, including Merce Cunningham's, as well as providing a new showcase for Irish artists.

After a long period of discussion, the Royal Swedish Ballet replaced Petter Jacobsen as artistic director with former company dancer Madeleine Onne. The Swedish dance company in Göteborg—formerly ballet-based but now a modern dance troupe—also lost its director when Anders Hellstrom resigned. Johan Inger, a dancer in Forsythe's Frankfurt company, took over as director of the Cullberg Ballet, Sweden's premier dance company. The Peter Schaufuss company, based in Århus, Den., premiered *Diana—the Princess*. Choreographed by Schaufuss himself, it was based on the life of Diana, princess of Wales. The Royal Danish Ballet showed the first performance of another Neumeier ballet, this one entitled *The Odyssey*.

Two different companies in Italy based programs on ballets from, or inspired by, Sergey Diaghilev's Ballet Russes. The company of the Teatro Massimo in Palermo, Sicily, revived two pieces by Léonide Massine: *Parade* and *Le Chant du rossignol*, and the Aterballetto company premiered versions by director Mauro Bigonzetti of *Petrushka* and *Les Noces*. The Rome Opera Ballet saw August Bournonville's *La Sylphide* restaged by Carla Fracci and Niels Kehlet, and the ballet of La Scala, Milan, took its revival of Luigi Manzotti's *Excelsior* on tour to Paris.

A number of dance luminaries died during the year, including South African choreographer and dancer Alfred Rodrigues, British teacher and author Joan Lawson, Russian-born French ballet critic and writer Irène Lidova, and Dutch dancer and choreographer Dirk Sanders.   (JANE SIMPSON)

World Dance. Popular folk dance troupes from the former Soviet Union toured the United States and Europe in 2002 and showed that they had lost none of their verve or attraction. Remarkably, the companies were headed by legendary figures active into their 90s. The Moiseyev Dance Company was created in 1937 by choreographer Igor Moiseyev, and in 2002, aged 95, he was still involved with the company. The Moiseyev dancers thrilled a new generation of Americans in East Coast and West Coast venues in their portrayals of athletes, Argentine horsemen, American countryfolk, and Russian peasants. Moiseyev's brilliant and colourful choreography in *Gopak* and his signature *Partisans,* where dancers donned long cloaks that hid their foot movements to skim smoothly over the stage as if rolling on wheels, continued as staples of the repertoire. After its tour in the U.S., the company traveled to the U.K.

The Georgian State Dance Company—founded in 1945 by Iliko Sukhishvili and his wife, Nino Ramishvili, who led the company until her death in 2000 at age 90—performed their strenuous Transcaucasian dances with virtuosity, mainly in American college theatres. Another touring group that was seen in many college towns was the Red Army Chorus and Dance Ensemble; its 60 singers and dancers, directed by Col. Boris Gastev, presented *The Sky of Russia,* a dazzling spectacle.

Perhaps as an echo of the current Western fascination with Indian film and music, the colourful dances of the Asian subcontinent were featured prominently. A festival in New Delhi attracted artists from all parts of India and some from London, while Toronto-based dancer Rina Singha introduced *Am I My Sister's Keeper?* At

Clarita Filgueiras of the Spanish dance company Flamenco Vivo performs in Bailaor/Bailaora, *choreographer Antonio Hidalgo's portrayal of the evolution of flamenco dance.*

© Carol Rosegg

the Edinburgh Festival, the six major Indian dance styles were performed— *kathak, odissi, manipuri, kuchipudi, bharatnatyam,* and *mohini attam.* Among the prominent dancers were Birju Maharaj and Madhavi Mudgal. The Lincoln Center for the Performing Arts in New York City presented Indian dancer Swati Bhise in *Emotions in Indian Dance.* Indian classical dance companies were active in Chicago and other cities as well.

From Burkina Faso came the Compagnie Salia nï Seydou, which performed ritual dances in Canada and five American cities. The principal presentation was a piece titled *Figninto,* a tale about being open to love, friendship, and the real values of life. A more traditional African company that had toured North America every season since 1998 was the National Song and Dance Company of Mozambique; in 2002 its American tour director, Julio Armando Matlombe, arranged a program of war dances.

Spanish troupes remained popular. Noche Flamenca appeared in New York, and the Gitanos de Granada—featuring Juan Andros Maya of the Maya clan, which lives in the caves of Granada—was seen in London. Flamenco Vivo was on tour; an American flamenco festival was staged in New York City; and the New World Flamenco Festival was held in Irvine, Calif. Joaquín Cortés, meanwhile, took Europe by storm and titillated the haut monde with his stylish flamenco interpretations.

The Thunderbird Dancers, who performed at American Indian powwows and gave workshops for non-Indians, aimed to educate the public. Their programs included the Robin Dance of the Iroquois, the Rabbit Dance of the Sioux, a War Dance by men, and a Shawl Dance by women. Hawaiians, unhappy that their traditional dance was constantly shown in false imitations, held a

World Conference on Hula in Hilo on July 29–Aug. 4, 2001, that drew 1,000 enthusiasts.

Currently in its 12th season, Chicago's Human Rhythm Project, directed by Lane Alexander, presented some 20 performances with tap-dancing greats Gregory Hines and Savion Glover as well as picturesque veterans such as Reggie the Hoofer. Tap virtuoso Alexander danced his own choreography to Morton Gould's *Tap Dance Concerto* with a full orchestra. Jazz dance achieved renewed recognition through the efforts of the Jazz Dance World Congress, held in Chicago in August and organized by jazz authority Gus Giordano.

Preservation of folklore was the concern of the 47th International Festival of Folklore, held in August in Licata, Sicily. The Bayanihan Philippine National Dance company was awarded the highest prize, and secondary awards were given to groups from Taiwan and Macedonia. In France the Lyon Dance Biennial hosted 27 companies from South America that harkened back to their native Indian roots. In addition, French choreographer Maguy Marin's *Applause Is Not Edible,* an abstract work about power, made its debut.

(ANN BARZEL)

THEATRE

Great Britain and Ireland. The Royal Shakespeare Company (RSC) was plunged into turmoil again when its artistic director, Adrian Noble, resigned on April 24, 2002. Noble's announcement came the week after his West End production of *Chitty Chitty Bang Bang,* a new musical based on the 1968 movie, opened to good reviews and a healthy advance at the box office at the London Palladium. Cynics saw *Chitty's* flying car and future success bearing Noble conveniently away from a mess not necessarily all of his own making.

No one knew what would happen to Noble's plan for the proposed demolition of the main Stratford theatre, the so-called "Shakespeare village" by the River Avon, or indeed where future London seasons would be presented— now that the company had torn up its contract with the Barbican Theatre, where it had enjoyed special rates and terms of employment for staff. In addition, Noble's intention to operate as a player in the West End seemed fraught with danger, especially since most theatregoing taxpayers saw the government-funded RSC as an idealist alternative to the commercial imperatives of

Shaftesbury Avenue, the heart of London's theatre district.

How the RSC would recover from this debacle was not clear. Debts mounted with an economically disastrous season of late romances—*The Tempest, The Winter's Tale,* and *Pericles*—at the Roundhouse in North London. In July, Michael Boyd, an RSC associate director, was named to succeed Noble when his contract expired in March 2003. Boyd promptly gave an unfortunate press interview in which he said that theatre was no longer all that important, that Shakespeare was "horny," and that he hoped to employ Hollywood actors, such as Nicole Kidman.

Productions of *Much Ado About Nothing* and *Antony and Cleopatra* moved from Stratford to the Haymarket in the West End. Harriet Walter and Nicholas Le Prevost were delightful as a middle-aged Beatrice and Benedick drenched in vituperation and Sicilian sunshine, and Sinead Cusack was a skittish and sensual Cleopatra opposite Stuart Wilson's grizzled Antony. Back in Stratford, the Swan had a critically approved season of Elizabethan and Jacobean rarities supervised brilliantly by Gregory Doran, another RSC associate director. The company was led by Sir Antony Sher, who tore a passion to tatters in both Philip Massinger's *The Roman Actor* and John Marston's *The Malcontent.*

Change was in the air all over the British theatre. Sam Mendes announced that he would leave his post as artistic director at the Donmar Warehouse after 10 years and presented a season of new American plays: Kenneth Lonergan's *Lobby Hero,* David Auburn's *Proof* (starring a luminous Gwyneth Paltrow), and the world premiere of *Take Me Out,* Richard Greenberg's stunning drama of sexual confusions and rivalries at the baseball diamond. Mendes himself bowed out after directing and bagging the *Evening Standard* best director

award for Chekhov's *Uncle Vanya* and Shakespeare's *Twelfth Night* with a handpicked company led by Simon Russell Beale, Emily Watson, Helen McCrory, and Mark Strong.

Michael Grandage was named Mendes's successor and had as his first production a revival at year's end of Noël Coward's *The Vortex,* starring

A scene from director Steven Pimlott's musical Bombay Dreams, *which became one of the biggest hits in London's West End during the year.*

Francesca Annis and Chiwetel Ejiofor. Grandage would continue to be responsible for programming at the Sheffield Crucible in Yorkshire, where he enjoyed another outstanding year; he had enticed Kenneth Branagh back to the stage in an electrifying *Richard III.*

New directors were also named at the Almeida Theatre in London (Michael Attenborough), the Hampstead Theatre (Anthony Clark), the West Yorkshire

Playhouse in Leeds (Ian Brown), and the Chichester Festival Theatre, where a panel of three—directors Steven Pimlott and Martin Duncan, with administrator Ruth Mackenzie—were charged with halting the theatre's financial slide. Whether they could win back the aging Chichester audience was another matter. Outgoing director Andrew Welch had done sterling work with new directors, and his summer season boasted a fine revival of the Broadway classic *The Front Page,* with Michael Pennington as the irascible editor Walter Burns.

Pimlott directed one of the West End's biggest hits, the new musical *Bombay Dreams,* a colourful satire of Bollywood movies with a vibrant score by A.R. Rahman ("the Asian Mozart"). Andrew Lloyd Webber was the producer, which was some consolation for him; the composer's *Starlight Express* closed after 17 years, and his trailblazing blockbuster *Cats* drew in its claws on its 21st anniversary, May 11.

The other big musical hit was *We Will Rock You,* a show scripted by Ben Elton around the songs of the rock group Queen. As with *Mamma Mia!,* which featured the music of Abba, the audience for the music found its way to the theatre, although unlike *Mamma Mia!,* the show was harshly received by the critics. The mania for making musicals out of pop music's back catalogs continued with *Our House,* which used the songs of the 1980s ska group Madness.

Boy George, a flamboyant pop star of 20 years earlier, recreated a vanished pop era in his likable new musical *Taboo,* which featured some excellent new songs that bolstered a couple of his more familiar hits. *Taboo* opened a new West End venue just off Leicester Square and featured an ever-changing roster of guest stars, rather like the long-running *Art,* which closed with popular television comedy trio League of Gentlemen occupying roles first taken by Albert Finney, Tom Courtenay, and Ken Stott.

The hit Broadway musical version of the British movie *The Full Monty* was warmly welcomed but struggled to attract full houses. Madonna had no such problem when she appeared in *Up for Grabs*, by Australian playwright David Williamson, though her performance as an unscrupulous art dealer was notable only for the attention she generated offstage. The play was dire, too, and added more fuel to the debate about Hollywood stars performing on the London stage and the question of "can they really act?" The answer this year was—they certainly can—except for Madonna.

Three young Hollywood stars—Hayden Christensen, Anna Paquin, and Jake Gyllenhaal—were outstanding in Kenneth Lonergan's *This Is Our Youth*, and Matt Damon, Summer Phoenix, and Casey Affleck served as their able and charismatic replacements (though Damon was too old for the role of a spoiled brat and minor drug runner). Woody Harrelson and Kyle MacLachlan were positively mesmerizing in Canadian playwright John Kolvenbach's *On an Average Day*, which was only an average play, with too many obvious echoes of Sam Shepard and David Mamet; two brothers meet up after a long period apart and unravel family problems.

Still, in comparison with these transatlantic imports, much of the West End seemed dull, even a revival of Oscar Wilde's *Lady Windermere's Fan*, which starred Vanessa Redgrave paired with her own daughter, Joely Richardson, as an onstage mother and daughter. West End long-running hits of yesteryear, Anthony Shaffer's *Sleuth* (1970s) and Denise Deegan's *Daisy Pulls It Off* (1980s), were dusted down to contrasting, but not devastating, effect. *Sleuth*, with Peter Bowles adding to his gallery of smooth rogues, was given a chic, antiseptic setting and a patina of homoeroticism that would have surprised original audiences; *Daisy*, on the other hand, was just the same old jolly hockey sticks schoolgirl fun, with nothing much new to say to anyone.

Sir Alan Ayckbourn and Sir Tom Stoppard came through with ambitious trilogies—three new plays each in a year when most of the other brand-name dramatists were also represented. Ayckbourn's *Damsels in Distress*—which originated in his Scarborough, Yorkshire, home theatre—arrived in the West End with the original cast of seven actors in three unrelated plays in an identical London Docklands apartment. This event marked a return to Ayckbourn's top form, though none of the plays was as good as his *Bedroom Farce*, which was gorgeously revived with Richard Briers and June Whitfield giving a master class in understated comedy and timing. Stoppard's *The Coast of Utopia* trilogy followed the fortunes of a group of mid-19th-century Russian radicals and was sumptuously staged at the Royal National Theatre (RNT) by Sir Trevor Nunn. Most felt that the three three-hour-long plays (*Voyage, Shipwreck,* and *Salvage*) could have been trimmed or compressed, but Nunn had assembled a crack acting ensemble led by Stephen Dillane as the heroic, pragmatic Aleksandr Herzen, Douglas Henshall as the tempestuous Mikhail Bakunin, and rising star Eve Best as a woman worth changing the world for. Karl Marx was a walk-on funny turn.

At the National, Nunn instigated a "Transformations" season in an attempt to attract younger audiences, but the artistic results were mixed. A series of mundane "pub theatre" plays were not all that impressive, but Matthew Bourne, choreographer of Nunn's still-running *My Fair Lady* revival, came up with a gem, *Play Without Words*, in the reconfigured Lyttelton Theatre. The work was a virtually wordless dance drama based on British movies of the 1960s such as *The Servant* and *Darling*. Each character was played-danced in triplicate to the intricate, seductive jazz score—played live—by Terry Davies. It was the most unusual and original piece of the year.

A strong contender for the best play of the year also emerged at the National. *Vincent in Brixton* by Nicholas Wright used some recently established information about Vincent van Gogh's residency in South London to create a compelling drama about awakening love and creative impulses. Jochum Ten Haaf was the wonderful young Dutch actor playing van Gogh, and Clare Higgins gave one of the performances of the year as his widowed landlady, a woman whose recharged sexuality corresponded with van Gogh's realization of his destiny. The play was directed with dedicated intensity by Sir Richard Eyre.

Other notable events at the RNT were Bryony Lavery's *Frozen*, in which Anita Dobson gave a performance to rival Higgins's as the mother of a murdered 10-year-old girl; Glenn Close as Blanche Du Bois in Nunn's production of *A Streetcar Named Desire;* and Sir Ian Holm and Ralph Fiennes appearing, respectively, in new plays by Shelagh Stephenson (*Mappa Mundi*) and Christopher Hampton (*The Talking Cure*).

In Sir David Hare's *A Breath of Life,* old friends Dame Maggie Smith and Dame Judi Dench appeared together onstage for the first time since they shared a dressing room in 1960 at the Old Vic. At the Young Vic, David Lan directed two superb productions: Jude Law in Christopher Marlowe's *Doctor Faustus* and Ann-Marie Duff, Marjorie Yates, and Paul Hilton in D.H. Lawrence's 1912 masterpiece *The Daughter-in-Law*. The best new plays at the Royal Court were *The York Realist* by Peter Gill and *A Number* by Caryl Churchill, with Michael Gambon and Daniel Craig playing out a dense duet about cloning.

In Dublin, Brian Friel created an afterlife in *Afterplay* for two Chekhov characters—Sonya from *Uncle Vanya* and Andrey from *Three Sisters*. The two meet in a Moscow cafe in the 1920s, and their catch-up, cross play, and burgeoning companionship—there is never any real companionship in Chekhov— was a joy to behold in the perfect performances of Penelope Wilton and John Hurt at the Gate Theatre. Also at the Gate was Frank McGuinness's *Gates of Gold,* a speculative and beautiful coda for the real-life founders of the Gate, Michael McLiammoir and Hilton Edwards. Again, this was an occasion for a brace of unforgettable performances, this time by Alan Howard and Richard Johnson.

The 45th Dublin Theatre Festival offered a notable program of new plays, including Ronald Harwood's adaptation of a French farce, *Le Dîner de cons* (also a successful film), and Marina Carr's *Ariel*. The latter was an exploration of power and corruption in contemporary Irish society and a poetic com- panion piece to Sebastian Barry's *Hinterland,* one of the most underrated plays of the year, in which Patrick Malahide gave a momentous performance as a character not totally dissimilar to Charles Haughey, the disgraced politician. (MICHAEL COVENEY)

U.S. and Canada. It was a year of economic and creative recuperation for the American theatre in 2002, and both the commercial and the not-for-profit sectors of the field seemed willing to accept a little help from their friends across the Atlantic in order to get by. The British influence was palpable on Broadway and beyond during this unsettled post-September 11 period. London-originated shows such as

Trevor Nunn's "realistic" version of *Oklahoma!* (about which one critic quipped, "There's a dark fetid smog on the medder") and a nonmusical adaptation of Mike Nichols's film *The Graduate*, with a briefly nude Kathleen Turner as Mrs. Robinson, helped boost the bottom line on Broadway—which turned out to be surprisingly healthy for the year, considering the entertainment industry's vulnerability in times of national stress and early misgivings about the loss of New York City tourism. On the artistic front, British directors seemed to be spotting and introducing new American writing talent far more aggressively than were their counterparts in the U.S.

This was especially true at London's innovative Donmar Warehouse, where artistic director Sam Mendes scheduled a full slate of American works (including the U.K. premiere of David Auburn's *Proof*, with Gwyneth Paltrow) for his company's 10th anniversary and his final season. Several of the new plays on the Donmar roster—Stephen Adly Guirgis's tough-talking urban drama *Jesus Hopped the A Train;* Keith Reddin's *Frame 312*, about the John F. Kennedy assassination investigation; and Richard Greenberg's witty, tack-sharp morality play about media and major league baseball, *Take Me Out*—found their way back to American theatres, in one incarnation or another, before the year ended.

The same London-first pattern marked the debut of 27-year-old playwright Christopher Shinn, whose raw dramas *Four* and *Where Do We Live* (which touches on the impact of September 11) were successes at the Royal Court before American. theatres realized that attention must be paid. Manhattan Theatre Club mounted a well-acted production of *Four* in early 2002, and Playwrights Horizons followed with *What Didn't Happen*, a play about the imaginative lives of three writers, Shinn's first premiere on his home turf.

There was even a British connection to the American season's most talked-about Shakespeare, Seattle, Wash.-based director Bartlett Sher's eclectic *Cymbeline*—which gleefully mixed a Wild West ambiance with kabuki-style orientalia—for New York's Theatre for a New Audience. Prior to its sold-out run Off Broadway, the crowd-pleasing production had been the first American staging ever to visit the Royal Shakespeare Company.

Other accomplishments of the season were as all-American as could be—most markedly in their treatment of such themes as racial attitudes, celebrity, and the power of the media. Suzan-Lori Parks's seriocomic two-hander about racial anger and sublimation, *Topdog/Underdog*, made an unlikely transfer from the Public Theater to Broadway, but neither George C. Wolfe's taut production nor a Pulitzer Prize for Parks's play could sustain audience interest for a long run. Just as unlikely but far more popular was Second Stage's transfer of *Metamorphoses*, a sexy and lyrical adaptation of Ovid, performed mostly in an onstage pool. The show's creator, Chicago-based visual-theatre specialist Mary Zimmerman (*see* BIOGRAPHIES), followed up later in the year with an intriguing experimental opera, *Galileo Galilei*, a collaboration with composer Philip Glass that presented events from the Renaissance scientist's life in reverse order. It debuted at the Goodman Theatre in Chicago and later played at Brooklyn (N.Y.) Academy of Music and the Barbican in London.

Two disturbing true American stories—the famous abduction of the Lindbergh baby in 1932 and the more

A stage version of film director John Waters's 1988 movie Hairspray *became an instant hit on Broadway in 2002.*

recent tragedy of Susan Smith, who drove a car into a South Carolina lake with her two young boys in the back seat and then claimed that a black man had made off with them—served as templates for adventurous new musical-theatre works. Michael Ogborn's *Baby Case*, developed by the Arden Theatre Company of Philadelphia and directed by Terrence J. Nolen, posited that Bruno Hauptmann, who was executed for the Lindbergh kidnapping, was framed and perhaps even noble; its disturbing libretto featured newshound Walter Winchell gleefully reporting one gruesome development after another. In the jazz-inflected *Brutal Imagination*, poet Cornelius Eady's imaginative take on the Smith killings and their media aftermath, staged at New York's Vineyard Theatre, the black man invented by Smith materialized to offer his own perspective.

At the other end of the musical-theatre spectrum, the relentlessly mainstream *Hairspray*, adapted for the stage from John Waters's campy 1988 movie, took Broadway by storm, owing in no small part to the inspired casting of onetime drag queen (and successful playwright) Harvey Fierstein in the role originated by the late Divine. With its themes of the triumphant underdog and racial harmony, *Hairspray* took its place beside *The Producers* as a sure bet—one likely to outlast such tepid competition as the revamped Rodgers and Hammerstein's *Flower Drum Song* (imported from Los Angeles's Mark Taper Forum with a new book by David Henry Hwang) and even the Tony-winning *Thoroughly Modern Millie*, an expertly turned-out $10 million compilation of musical comedy tropes and clichés.

Joining *Millie* as the most-honoured shows of the year were *The Goat, or Who Is Sylvia?*, Edward Albee's dark comedy of human aberration, which won the best play Tony virtually by default; and the smart tongue-in-cheek musical *Urinetown*, which began as a penniless production in the downtown New York Fringe Festival. Once past these venturesome choices, commercial theatre audiences had to settle for stars: Liam Neeson and Laura Linney in Arthur Miller's warhorse *The Crucible;* Alan Bates and Frank Langella in a rare Ivan Turgenev, *Fortune's Fool;* and Billy Crudup as *The Elephant Man,* among others.

In Canada two major forces from the Quebec performing arts scene paired up for the first time; the proliferating Cirque du Soleil hired auteur Robert Lepage to create a new show that was scheduled to premiere at the MGM Grand Hotel in Las Vegas, Nev., in 2004. Lepage's performance spectacle *Zulu Time*, a collaboration with composer Peter Gabriel that includes scenes of airport terrorism, premiered in Montreal in June after a planned September 2001 opening in New York was canceled in the wake of the terrorist attacks.

Among the significant productions of the Canadian season was the Factory Theater of Toronto's strong revival of *Belle*, Florence Gibson's poetic study of black-white relations in the years after the American Civil War. Critics remarked that the Reconstruction-era drama should be well received by American audiences, but thus far no south-of-the-border theatres had taken the cue. The venerable Stratford Festival, located two hours outside Toronto, celebrated its 50th anniversary season with a burst of stardust as Christopher Plummer, 73, returned to the scene of his early Shakespearean triumphs to play Lear, under Jonathan Miller's direction. In October fraud charges were filed against Livent Inc. founders Garth Drabinsky and Myron Gottlieb, who were charged with having defrauded investors of $325 million; Livent was one of North America's largest theatre companies.

Those passing from the scene in 2002 included Adolph Green (*see* OBITUARIES), the musical comedy legend whose name is inseparable from that of his surviving collaborator, Betty Comden; Vinnette Carroll (*see* OBITUARIES), a pioneering director of gospel-inflected musicals; Jan Kott, Polish-born critic and author of *Shakespeare Our Contemporary;* actress and director Rosetta LeNoire, who appeared in Orson Welles's landmark *Voodoo Macbeth* in the 1930s and went on to found Amas Repertory Company; Nobu McCarthy, the former Hollywood starlet and Miss Tokyo who became the longtime artistic director of East West Players, the U.S.'s first Asian-American theatre company; Robert Whitehead (*see* OBITUARIES), one of Broadway's most prolific producers of serious drama; and the great Nebraska-born, London-trained actress Irene Worth (*see* OBITUARIES).

(JIM O'QUINN)

MOTION PICTURES

United States. As the year 2002 ended, Peter Jackson's virtuoso adaptation of J.R.R. Tolkien's *The Lord of the Rings: The Two Towers* and Chris Columbus's interpretation of J.K. Rowling's *Harry Potter and the Chamber of Secrets* promised to surpass their predecessors, the worldwide box-office winners of Christmas 2001, to take their place among the highest-earning films in history. Though their magical-mythical atmospheres had evidently special appeal, other film series were also profitably revived, with George Lucas's *Star Wars Episode II—Attack of the Clones* and Brett Ratner's *Red Dragon* (based on Thomas Harris's novel that was earlier [1986] filmed as *Manhunter*), which chronicled the earliest exploits of the cannibalistic killer Hannibal Lecter. Meanwhile, Sam Raimi's *Spider-Man*, adapted from the Marvel Comics adventures, promised to initiate an entire new series.

Of the individualists of the American cinema, Martin Scorsese made a historical epic of the New York underworld in the years before the Civil War, *Gangs of New York*. Steven Spielberg's *Minority Report* forecast a future United States with new technology but old-fashioned crime, while his *Catch Me if You Can* was a biopic on the life of 1960s confidence trickster Frank Abagnale, Jr. With *25th Hour*, Spike Lee exceptionally directed a drama about white characters—tracing a convicted drug dealer's final day and night before imprisonment. Clint Eastwood directed *Blood Work* and played a veteran cop who investigates the murder of the woman whose heart he received in a transplant.

Of newer talents the writer-director team of Charlie Kaufman and Spike Jonze followed *Being John Malkovich* (1999) with *Adaptation*, another inventive fantasy on the creative process. Todd Haynes's *Far from Heaven* used a stylish pastiche of 1950s melodramas to look at two kinds of prejudice—racial and sexual. Alexander Payne directed veteran actor Jack Nicholson in *About Schmidt*. Several star actors made effective debuts as directors: Nicolas Cage (*Sonny*); John Malkovich (*The Dancer Upstairs*, made in Spain with a Spanish cast); Matt Dillon (*City of Ghosts*); Denzel Washington (*Antwone Fisher*, based on the true story of the psychiatric reclamation of a young serviceman), and George Clooney (*Confessions of a Dangerous Mind*, a subtly skeptical adaptation of the "reminiscences" of Chuck Barris's double life as television producer and CIA agent).

Lavish adaptations of period novels were in vogue: Kevin Reynolds directed *The Count of Monte Cristo;* Douglas

McGrath, *Nicholas Nickleby;* Pakistan-born Shekhar Kapur, *The Four Feathers;* and Simon Wells, great-grandson of the author H.G. Wells, *The Time Machine.* The scarcity of good scripts encouraged remakes; Jonathan Demme successfully refurbished Stanley Donen's 1963 *Charade* as *The Truth About Charlie,* while Philip Noyce's remake of *The Quiet American* was more faithful to Graham Greene's novel than Joseph L. Mankiewicz's 1958 version. Adrian Lyne's *Unfaithful* was a polished and precise adaptation of Claude Chabrol's 1969 *Une Femme infidèle,* though Steven Soderbergh's version of Stanislaw Lem's science-fiction novel *Solaris* missed the mystical fascination of Andrey Tarkovsky's 1972 original.

In *Real Women Have Curves,* Colombian-born Patricia Cardoso dealt with the coming-of-age problems of a Mexican-American teenager striving to break out of the narrow expectations of her blue-collar background. Julie Taymor directed *Frida,* a star vehicle for Mexican actress Salma Hayek that was based on the complicated relationships of painters Frida Kahlo and Diego Rivera and their friends. Rebecca Miller won the dramatic competition at the Sundance Festival with *Personal Velocity,* from her own script about three women in crisis. Meanwhile, *My Big Fat Greek Wedding,* directed by Joel Zwick and written by and starring Nia Vardalos, opened quietly in the spring and gained such momentum during the year that by December it had become the biggest-

ever indie hit and top-grossing romantic comedy in history. Stephen Daldry and a trio of leading women—Meryl Streep, Julianne Moore, and Nicole Kidman—won critical acclaim for *The Hours,* which looked at the lives of Virginia Woolf and two women united with Woolf across time and space by the effects of her works on them.

Movie musicals were ably represented by Rob Marshall's adaptation, *Chicago,* with a star-studded cast in a tale of music and murder. Animation continued its renaissance. The Disney studios' *Lilo and Stitch,* directed and written by Chris Sanders and Dean DeBlois, related the story of an obstreperous little alien exiled from his native planet to Hawaii. Cathy Malkasian and Jeff McGrath's *The Wild Thornberrys Movie* offered an ecological message for younger people. The October U.S. release of the latest film from Japan's Hayao Miyazake (*see* BIOGRAPHIES), *Spirited Away* (*Sen to Chihiro no kamikakushi*), further fueled the American passion for animé.

Britain. The biggest-earning British film of the year was inevitably the 20th James Bond film, *Die Another Day,* with Pierce Brosnan as Bond and 2002 Oscar-laureate Halle Berry (*see* BIOGRAPHIES) as Jinx. Roman Polanski's *The Pianist,* about the Polish musician Wladislaw Szpilman's flight from Nazi persecution, won the Palme d'Or at the Cannes Film Festival.

Some of the best films of the year exemplified the national taste for social

realism: Ken Loach's *Sweet Sixteen,* about a Glasgow boy sucked into the drug trade; Mike Leigh's *All or Nothing,* about London housing-estate dwellers; and Gillies MacKinnon's *Pure,* a study of deprived and drug-wrecked London lives. Britain's ethnic communities featured in Gurinder Chadha's exuberant comedy *Bend It like Beckham* and in Metin Hüseyin's *Anita and Me,* about a young Punjabi girl growing up in a depressed provincial township in the 1970s. Stephen Frears's *Dirty Pretty Things* was the first British film to treat sympathetically the problems of illegal immigrants and asylum seekers existing in a London half-world. The Northern Ireland conflict was recalled in Paul Greengrass's powerful dramatization of a catastrophic incident, *Bloody Sunday.* Peter Mullan's *The Magdalene Sisters,* which won the Golden Lion at the Venice Film Festival, exposed the brutal laundry-reformatories to which the Irish Catholic Church condemned unmarried mothers from the mid-19th century right up to the late 1990s.

Canada. Unusually, one of the most highly profiled North American films of the year was a documentary, Michael Moore's devastating study of American gun culture, *Bowling for Columbine.* With *Ararat,* Atom Egoyan investigated the Turkish genocide of the Armenians in 1915 through the eyes of a filmmaker (played by Charles Aznavour) researching a film. In *Spider,* David Cronenberg abandoned his familiar special-effects horrors to portray a deeply disturbed man and his warped perceptions of a working-class world.

Australia. Several directors looked critically at the recent history of Aboriginal Australians. Philip Noyce's *Rabbit-Proof Fence* recalled the true story of three young girls who fled from incarceration under the official policy of the first three-quarters of the 20th century of seizing quarter- and half-caste children from their Aboriginal families so they could be "civilized" in white institutions. Craig Lahiff's *Black and White* dramatized a real case of 1959 in which an Aboriginal was charged with the rape and murder of a nine-year-old girl. In *One Night the Moon,* Aboriginal director Rachel Perkins told a story, set in the 1930s, about the alliance of a farmer's wife and an Aboriginal tracker to find a lost child.

European Union. With the funding facilities of the European Union's MEDIA

(continued on page 298)

John Corbett and Nia Vardalos starred in My Big Fat Greek Wedding, *a surprise hit that became the top-grossing romantic comedy of all time.*

The Kobal Collection/IFC Films/Giraud, Sophie

INTERNATIONAL FILM AWARDS 2002

American Film Institute Awards, awarded in Beverly Hills, California, in January 2002

Movie of the Year	The Lord of the Rings: The Fellowship of the Ring (New Zealand/U.S.; director, Peter Jackson)
Actor of the Year—Male	Denzel Washington (Training Day, U.S.)
Actor of the Year—Female	Sissy Spacek (In the Bedroom, U.S.)
Featured Actor of the Year—Male	Gene Hackman (The Royal Tenenbaums, U.S.)
Featured Actor of the Year—Female	Jennifer Connelly (A Beautiful Mind, U.S.)
Director of the Year	Robert Altman (Gosford Park, Italy/U.K./U.S./Germany)

Golden Globes, awarded in Beverly Hills, California, in January 2002

Best motion picture drama	A Beautiful Mind (U.S.; director, Ron Howard)
Best musical or comedy	Moulin Rouge! (Australia/U.S.; director, Baz Luhrmann)
Best director	Robert Altman (Gosford Park, Italy/U.K./U.S./Germany)
Best actress, drama	Sissy Spacek (In the Bedroom, U.S.)
Best actor, drama	Russell Crowe (A Beautiful Mind, U.S.)
Best actress, musical or comedy	Nicole Kidman (Moulin Rouge!, Australia/U.S.)
Best actor, musical or comedy	Gene Hackman (The Royal Tenenbaums, U.S.)
Best foreign-language film	No Man's Land (Bosnia and Herzegovina/Slovenia/Italy/France/U.K./Belgium; director, Danis Tanovic)

Sundance Film Festival, awarded in Park City, Utah, in January 2002

Grand Jury Prize, dramatic film	Personal Velocity: Three Portraits (U.S.; director, Rebecca Miller)
Grand Jury Prize, documentary	Daughter from Danang (U.S.; directors, Gail Dolgin and Vicente Franco)
Audience Award, dramatic film	Real Women Have Curves (U.S.; director, Patricia Cardoso)
Audience Award, documentary	Amandla! A Revolution in Four Part Harmony (South Africa/U.S.; director, Lee Hirsch)
Audience Award, world cinema	Bloody Sunday (U.K./Ireland; director, Paul Greengrass); L'ultimo bacio (The Last Kiss) (Italy; director, Gabriele Muccino)
Best director, dramatic film	Gary Winick (Tadpole, U.S.)
Best director, documentary	Rob Fruchtman and Rebecca Cammisa (Sister Helen, U.S.)
Special Jury Prize, dramatic film	Secretary (U.S.; director, Steven Shainberg)
Special Jury Prize, documentary	How to Draw a Bunny (U.S.; director, John W. Walter); Señorita extraviada (Mexico; director, Lourdes Portillo)

Berlin International Film Festival, awarded in February 2002

Golden Bear (ex aequo)	Sen to Chihiro no kamikakushi (Spirited Away) (Japan; director, Hayao Miyazaki); Bloody Sunday (U.K./Ireland; director, Paul Greengrass)
Silver Bear, Grand Jury Prize	Halbe Treppe (Grill Point) (Germany; director, Andreas Dresen)
Best director	Otar Iosseliani (Lundi Matin [Monday Morning], France)
Best actress	Halle Berry (Monster's Ball, U.S.)
Best actor	Jacques Gamblin (Laissez-passer, France)

British Academy of Film and Television Arts, awarded in London in February 2002

Best film	The Lord of the Rings: The Fellowship of the Ring (New Zealand/U.S.; director, Peter Jackson)
Best director	Peter Jackson (The Lord of the Rings: The Fellowship of the Ring, New Zealand/U.S.)
Best actress	Judi Dench (Iris, U.K./U.S.)
Best actor	Russell Crowe (A Beautiful Mind, U.S.)
Best supporting actress	Jennifer Connelly (A Beautiful Mind, U.S.)
Best supporting actor	Jim Broadbent (Moulin Rouge!, Australia/U.S.)
Best foreign-language film	Amores perros (Love's a Bitch) (Mexico; director, Alejandro González Iñárritu

Césars (France), awarded in March 2002

Best film	Le Fabuleux Destin d'Amélie Poulain (Amélie) (France/Germany; director, Jean-Pierre Jeunet)
Best director	Jean-Pierre Jeunet (Le Fabuleux Destin d'Amélie Poulain [Amélie], France/Germany)
Best actress	Emmanuelle Devos (Sur mes lèvres [Read My Lips], France)
Best actor	Michel Bouquet (Comment j'ai tué mon père, France/Spain)
Best first film	No Man's Land (Bosnia and Herzegovina/Slovenia/Italy/France/U.K./Belgium; director, Danis Tanovic)

Academy of Motion Picture Arts and Sciences (Oscars, U.S.), awarded in Los Angeles in March 2002

Best film	A Beautiful Mind (U.S.; director, Ron Howard)
Best director	Ron Howard (A Beautiful Mind, U.S.)
Best actress	Halle Berry (Monster's Ball, U.S.)
Best actor	Denzel Washington (Training Day, U.S.)
Best supporting actress	Jennifer Connelly (A Beautiful Mind, U.S.)
Best supporting actor	Jim Broadbent (Iris, U.K./U.S.)
Best foreign-language film	No Man's Land (Bosnia and Herzegovina/Slovenia/Italy/France/U.K./Belgium; director, Danis Tanovic)

Cannes International Film Festival, France, awarded in May 2002

Palme d'Or	The Pianist (France/Poland/Germany/U.K.; director, Roman Polanski)
Grand Prix	Mies vailla menneisyyttä (The Man Without a Past) (Finland/Germany/France; director, Aki Kaurismäki)
Special Jury Prize	Yadon ilaheyya (Chronicle of Love and Pain) (France/Palestine/Morocco/Germany; director, Elia Suleiman)
Best director (ex aequo)	Paul Thomas Anderson (Punch-Drunk Love, U.S.); Im Kwon Taek (Chihwaseon, South Korea)
Best actress	Kati Outinen (Mies vailla menneisyyttä [The Man Without a Past], Finland/Germany/France)
Best actor	Olivier Gourmet (Le Fils [The Son], Belgium/France)
Caméra d'or	Bord de mer (Seaside) (France; director, Julie Lopes-Curval)

Locarno International Film festival, awarded in August 2002

Golden Leopard	Das Verlangen (The Longing) (Germany; director, Iain Dilthey)
Silver Leopard	Tan de repente (Suddenly) (Argentina; director, Diego Lerman); Szép napok (Pleasant Days) (Hungary; director, Kornél Mundruczó)
Special Jury Prize	Man, taraneh, panzdah sal daram (I Am Taraneh, I Am 15 Years Old) (Iran; director, Rassul Sadrameli)
Best actress	Taraneh Allidousti (Man, taraneh, panzdah sal daram [I Am Taraneh, I Am 15 Years Old], Iran)
Best actor	Giorgos Karayannis (Diskoli apocheretismi: o babas mou [Hard Goodbyes: My Father], Greece/Germany)

Montreal World Film Festival, awarded in September 2002

Best film (Grand Prix of the Americas)	Il piu bel giorno della mia vita (The Best Day of My Life) (Italy; director, Cristina Comencini)
Best actress (ex aequo)	Maria Bonnevie (I Am Dina, Norway/Sweden/Denmark/Germany/France); Leila Hatami (Istgah-e Matrouk [The Deserted Station], Iran)
Best actor	Aleksey Chadov (Voyna [War], Russia)
Best director	Sophie Marceau (Parlez-moi d'amour [Speak to Me of Love], France)
Grand Prix of the Jury	Hiçbiryerde (Innowhereland) (Turkey; director, Tayfun Pirselimoglu)
Best screenplay	Corazón de fuego (The Last Train) (Spain/Argentina/Uruguay; writers, Diego Arsuaga, Beda Docampo Feijóo, and Fernando León de Aranoa)
International cinema press award	Cofralandes, Chilean Rhapsody (Chile; director, Raul Ruiz)

Toronto International Film Festival, awarded in September 2002

Best Canadian feature film	Spider (director, David Cronenberg)
Best Canadian first feature	Marion Bridge (director, Wiebke von Carolsfeld)
Best Canadian short film	Blue Skies (director, Ann Marie Fleming)
International cinematographic press award	Les Chemins de l'oued (Under Another Sky) (France; director, Gaël Morel)
People's Choice Award	Whale Rider (New Zealand/Germany; director, Niki Caro)

Venice Film Festival, Italy, awarded in September 2002

Golden Lion	The Magdalene Sisters (U.K./Ireland; director, Peter Mullan)
Grand Jury Prize	Dom Durakov (Russia/France; director, Andrey Konchalovsky)
Volpi Cup, best actress	Julianne Moore (Far from Heaven, U.S./France)
Volpi Cup, best actor	Stefano Accorsi (Un viaggio chiamato amore, Italy)
Special Director's Award	Lee Chang Dong (Oasis, South Korea)
Marcello Mastroianni Prize for acting newcomer	Moon So Ri (Oasis, South Korea)
Prize for outstanding individual contribution	Ed Lachman (for photography, Far from Heaven, U.S./France)

San Sebastian International Film Festival, Spain, awarded in September 2002

Best film	Los lunes al sol (Mondays in the Sun) (Spain/France/Italy; director, Fernando León de Aranoa)
Special Jury Prize	Historias mínimas (Minimal Stories) (Argentina/Spain; director, Carlos Sorín)
Best director	Kaige Chen (He ni zai yiqi [Together], China)
Best actress	Mercedes Sampietro (Lugares comunes, Spain/Argentina)
Best actor	Peiqi Liu (He ni zai yiqi [Together], China)
Best Photography	Sergey Mikhalchuk (Lyubovnik [The Lover], Russia)
New Directors Prize	Alice Nellis (Výlet [Some Secrets], Czech Republic/Slovakia)
International Critics' Award	Los lunes al sol (Mondays in the Sun) (Spain/France/Italy; director, Fernando León de Aranoa)

Chicago International Film Festival, awarded in October 2002

Best feature film	Madame Satã (Brazil/France; director, Karim Ainouz)
Special Jury Prize	Yadon ilaheyya (Chronicle of Love and Pain) (France/Palestine/Morocco/Germany; director, Elia Suleiman)
Best director	Andreas Dresen (Halbe Treppe [Grill Point], Germany)
Best Ensemble Playing	Steffi Kühnert, Thorsten Merten, Axel Prahl, Gabriela Maria Schmeide (Halbe Treppe [Grill Point], Germany)
Best actor	Vincent Rottiers (Les Diables [The Devils], France/Spain)
Gold Plaque	Avazhayé sarzaminé madariyam (Marooned in Iraq) (Iran; director, Bahman Ghobadi)
International Film Critics' Prize	El bonaerense (Argentina/Chile/France/Netherlands; director, Pablo Trapero)

(DAVID ROBINSON)

(continued from page 296)
program, possibilities for co-production, and the formation of a European Film Promotion organization, a clear grouping of national film industries developed, linking the member countries of the European Union along with "candidate countries" and Iceland, Norway, and Switzerland—countries that, though outside the EU, had cooperation contracts with the MEDIA program.

France. World War II was recalled in several films. In *Laissez-passer*, his *film à clef*, Bertrand Tavernier re-created the atmosphere of filmmaking in occupied France. Gérard Jugnot directed and starred in the accomplished *Monsieur Batignole*, about a Gentile butcher who saves a Jewish boy from the Gestapo. The American documentarist Frederick Wiseman filmed Catherine Samie's stage monologue in the character of a woman in a condemned Ukrainian ghetto and released it as *La Dernière Lettre*. Costa-Gavras's *Amen* re-created the story of Kurt Gerstein, an SS officer who vainly pleaded with the Vatican to oppose the Nazi extermination of the Jews. Michel Deville's exquisite *Un Monde presque paisible* (*Almost Peaceful*) chronicled a Parisian Jewish community trying to settle back to normality in the aftermath of the war and all its depredations. Notable commercial success was enjoyed by *Astérix & Obélix: Mission Cléopâtre*, a live-action version of the comic-book characters, reportedly the most costly French film ever. François Ozon's comedy-thriller *8 femmes* attracted worldwide distribution mainly by its cast, which united several generations of French movie divas.

Other distinctive talents active during the year included the Georgian-born Otar Iosseliani, with a characteristically idiosyncratic work, *Lundi matin*, the saga of a factory worker who impetuously abandons everything to see the world.

The prolific Patrice Leconte made two films, *Rue des plaisirs*, a kindly tale of the selfless adoration of a prostitute by the brothel's diminutive man-of-all-work and *L'Homme du train*, chronicling the unlikely encounter of a retired schoolteacher and a veteran bank robber.

Italy. The most costly Italian production to date, Roberto Benigni's adaptation of the children's classic *Pinocchio* failed disastrously to win the international popularity of his Oscar-winning

1997 *Life Is Beautiful*. Among the most notable productions of the year were Marco Bellocchio's *L'ora di religione (Il sorriso di mia madre)* (*The Religion Hour [My Mother's Smile]*), a fierce satire about an agnostic painter's reaction to a campaign to make his mother a saint. Giuseppe Farrara's *I banchieri di Dio* (*God's Bankers*) presented an unsparing exposé of the sinister links between the Vatican, the secret service, freemasonry, and Opus Dei and the financial machinations that led to the murder of Roberto Calvi in London in 1982. Literary adaptations included Emidio Greco's lively and intelligent interpretation of Leonardo Sciascia's historical novel *Il consiglio d'Egitto*. In the genre of biography, Franco Zeffirelli offered an impressionistic portrait of his late friend and collaborator Maria Callas in *Callas Forever*, with Fanny Ardant in the title role.

Germany. Two notable films in a generally undistinguished year were Winfried Bonengel's *Führer Ex*, a dramatic investigation of contemporary neo-Nazism, seen as a legacy of communist oppression in the former East Germany, and Eoin Moore's *Pigs Will Fly*, a battered-wife story that observed the unhappy relationship through the psychology of the husband, himself a painfully troubled character. Director Leni Riefenstahl celebrated her 100th birthday in August and brought out a

documentary, *Impressionen unter Wasser* (*Underwater Impressions*).

Iberia. Spain's major international success was Pedro Almodóvar's *Hable con ella* (*Talk to Her*), an idiosyncratic reflection on solitude and communication. Spanish directors showed a new concern for social subjects, exemplified in Chus Gutiérrez's *Poniente*, about the exploitation of immigrant agricultural workers, and Fernando León de Aranoa's *Los lunes al sol* (*Mondays in the Sun*), a Ken Loach-inspired group portrait of unemployed men. The 93-year-old Portuguese Manoel de Oliveira created a witty and complex adaptation of Agustina Bessa-Luis's tangled tale of marital life and cruelties, *O princípio da incerteza* (*The Uncertainty Principle*).

Nordic Countries. Finland's Aki Kaurismaki looked, with characteristic wry humour, at the deprived of modern society through the eyes of a man suffering amnesia after a ferocious mugging in *Mies vailla menneisyyttä* (*The Man Without a Past*). From Sweden, Lukas Moodysson's *Lilja 4-ever* was a harrowing portrayal of a young girl, as much abused by the "benefactor" who takes her away to Sweden as she is in her native Russia. Joel Bergvall and Simon Sandquist's *Den osynlige* (*The Invisible*) related an original story of a young boy who, following a brutal beating, finds himself in a state of invisibility, be-

A scene from Finnish director Aki Kaurismaki's film Mies vailla menneisyyttä (The Man Without a Past).

tween life and death. The newest product of the stern aesthetic of Denmark's "Dogme" school was Susanne Bier's *Elsker dig for evigt* (*Open Hearts*), about the complex relationships that result when a young husband is paralyzed following a motor accident. Nils Malmros's *At kende sandheden* (*Facing the Truth*) re-created a medical controversy in which a surgeon who saved a child's life is charged, more than 40 years later, with having used a chemical preparation that subsequently produced harmful side-effects.

Eastern and Southeastern Europe. One of the most original and most perfectly achieved films of the year, Aleksandr Sokurov's *Russky kovcheg* (*Russian Ark*) used digital resources to make a 96-minute film in a single shot as the camera explored the endless galleries of St. Petersburg's Hermitage Museum. Pavel Lungin's *Oligarkh* (*Tycoon*) was a ferocious portrayal of corruption that instilled and linked big business, organized crime, and the Kremlin. Andrey Konchalovsky's *Dom durakov* (*House of Fools*) set its action in a mental hospital on the Chechen border. The gifted Valery Todorovsky's *Lyubovnik* (*The Lover*) related the working out of the jealous passions of a man who discovers upon the death of his beloved wife that for 15 years she has had a lover. Aleksey Muradov's debut feature *Zmey* (*The Kite*) was an intimate, often painful study of the external and internal problems of a prison officer, his wife, and their disabled child, whose joy is the kite of the title.

In Poland, Krzysztof Zanussi's *Suplement*, a characteristically acute observation of modern relationships, was complementary to his 2001 film, *Life as a Fatal Sexually Transmitted Disease*, involving the same characters. From the Czech Republic came Zdenek Tyc's *Smradi* (*Brats*), which told the disturbing story of a family that suffers the hostility of neighbours to their adopted Roma (Gypsy) children. Alice Nellis's *Výlet* (*Some Secrets*) unfolded a socially revealing family comedy-drama in the course of a journey to carry the ashes of the beloved paterfamilias to Slovakia. The year's most original Hungarian films were György Pálfi's *Hukkle*, a wordless entomological view of the life of a small village, and Kornél Mundruczó's inappropriately titled *Szép napok* (*Pleasant Days*).

An outstanding first film by Penny Panayotopoulou, *Diskoli apocheretismi: o babas mou* (*Hard Goodbyes: My Father*),

won the Locarno Festival Best Actor award for 10-year-old Yorgos Karayannis. Following successful commercial release and nomination as Turkey's Oscar contender, Handan Ipekçi's 2001 production *Hejar* (also released as *Büyük adam küçük ask*), the story of an old judge who shelters a Kurdish orphan, was banned at the request of the police. Sinan Cetin achieved an effective mix of absurdism and pathos in *Komser Sekspir* (*Sergeant Shakespeare*).

Iran. Iran's major filmmaker Abbas Kiarostami made headlines worldwide in September when he was denied a U.S. visa, ostensibly on security grounds, to attend the screening at the New York Film Festival of his boldly experimental *Ten*, which explored the special characteristics of digital video cameras to create an absorbing social drama through the minimalist means of close-ups of car drivers and passengers. Rasul Sadrameli's *Man, taraneh, panzdah sal daram* (*I Am Taraneh, 15 Years Old*) described the problems and prejudices facing a teenage single mother who has extricated herself from an unhappy marriage. The veteran Dariush Mehrjui looked at the harsh fates of a number of despairing young women in *Bemani* (*Staying Alive*). Manijeh Hekmat's *Zendan-e zanan* (*Women's Prison*), suppressed for more than a year, was finally seen at international festivals, though not at home. *Ravaryete makdush* (*Black Tape: A Tehran Diary—the Videotape Fariborz Kambari Found in the Garbage*) was ingeniously presented as if it were a home video record made by the 18-year-old "trophy wife" of an Iranian. A lighter approach to women's life was Nasser Refaie's *Emtehan* (*The Exam*).

India. With the rise of an international taste for "Bollywood"—Indian commercial cinema—two spectacular all-star films vied for the claim to be the most costly films in Indian history; *Devdas* was directed by Sanjay Leela Bhansali from a much-filmed early 20th-century novel with a Romeo and Juliet theme, and Karan Johar's *Kabhi khushi kabhie gham . . .* (2001; *Sometimes Happiness, Sometimes Sorrow*), a family saga, shrewdly cast several generations of favourite Indian stars. Other notable films were the veteran Keralan director Adoor Gopalakrishnan's *Nizhalkkuthu* (*Shadow Kill*), about the anxieties of an old hangman during British occupation, and Buddhadev Dasgupta's *Manda meyer upakhyan* (*A Tale of a Naughty Girl*), which

portrayed Bengali village life in the 1960s.

Far East. A few Japanese films stood out from the commercial run. In *Dolls*, Takeshi Kitano linked three contemporary love stories inspired by the traditional *bunraku* doll theatre. Kitano's own early career in vaudeville was imaginatively chronicled by Makoto Shinozaki in *Asakusa Kid*. Akira Kurosawa's former assistant Takashi Koizumi adapted a novel by Keishi Nagi and fashioned it into *Amida-do dayori* (*Letter from the Mountain*).

Chinese cinema moved markedly toward greater concern with personal stories, as was exemplified in Zhang Yuan's *Wo ai nin* (*I Love You*), the sad chronicle of a doomed love affair; Chen Kaige's *Han ni zai yiki* (*Together*), the story of a talented teenage musician struggling in contemporary Beijing for education and integrity; and a promising first feature by Lu Chuan, *The Missing Gun*, which related the escalating anxieties of a small-town cop when his gun goes missing after a drunken revelry. Tian Zhuangzhuang, after a decade of officially enforced inactivity, returned with an admirable remake of a 1948 film, *Xiao cheng zhi chun* (*Springtime in a Small Town*), a love story set in the immediate post-World War II years in a war-devastated place.

The biggest South Korean box-office success of the year, Jeong Heung Sun's comedy *Gamunui yeonggwang* (*Married to the Mafia*), about a young businessman forced into a shotgun marriage with the daughter of a gang boss, was instantly bought by Warner Brothers for a Hollywood remake. Im Kwon-taek (see BIOGRAPHIES) won the best director prize at the Cannes Film Festival for *Chihwaseon* (*Strokes of Fire*), the story of Jang Seung-up (1843–97), also known as Ohwon, an inspired but uncouth and rebellious natural painter. Lee Chang Dong's remarkable *Oasis* fearlessly portrayed a love affair between two handicapped people—a boy with slight mental disturbance and a criminal past and a girl with cerebral palsy.

Latin America. Brazilian Fernando Meirelles's *Cidade de Deus* (*City of God*) was an unsparing study of the drug trade and gang wars in the favelas of Rio de Janeiro over two decades, based on the firsthand evidence of Paulo Lins's novel. In *Madame Satã*, Karim Ainouz chronicled the life of a real-life figure of the 1930s, a legendary flamboyant gay gangster, killer, and street fighter.

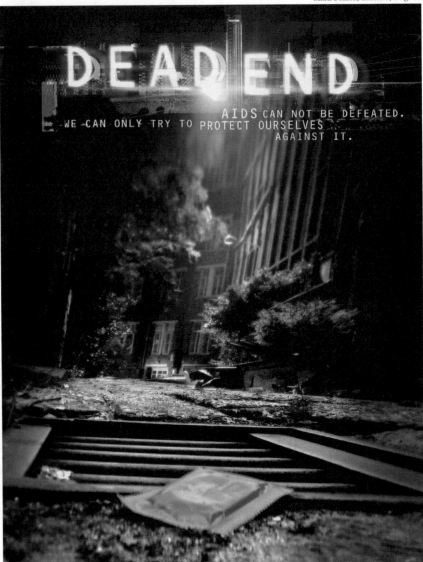

Mark Damen, Emblem, Belgium

DEAD END

AIDS CAN NOT BE DEFEATED. WE CAN ONLY TRY TO PROTECT OURSELVES AGAINST IT.

Belgian director Mark Damen's nontheatrical film Dead End *delivered a strong message about AIDS and the danger posed by unprotected sex.*

Generally thanks to Spanish co-production, Argentine cinema survived the country's economic disasters to produce a lively variety of works ranging from Carlos Sorín's minimalist *Historias mínimas* (*Minimal Stories*), the stories of three people in different quests across the steppes of Patagonia, to Diego Lerman's literate and witty first film *Tan de repente* (*Suddenly*), a road movie about the diverse emotional adventures of a young woman hijacked by two punk lesbians. Pablo Trapero's *El Bonaerense* told the story of a provincial boy who is forced into crime and then recruited into a corrupt Buenos Aires police service. Actor-director Federico León's *Todo juntos* (*Everything Together*) was a delicately observed portrait of the prolonged process of a couple's breakup. Marcelo Piñeyro's *Kamchatka* was a strong drama of the military dictatorship, seen through the experience of one tight-knit family. Mexico's major box-office hit—immeasurably helped by the condemnation of the Roman Catholic Church—was *El crimen del padre Amaro*, directed by Carlos Carrera and updating a scandalous 1975 novel of corruption and illicit sexuality in a provincial parish. In *La virgen de la lujuria* (*The Virgin of Lust*), star director Arturo Ripstein concocted a fable of *amour fou*, the domination of an introverted waiter by a sadistic hooker.

Africa. In Senegal, Joseph Gaï Ramaka's *Karmen Geï* translated Prosper Merimée's *Carmen* to modern Africa and a sexually more complex society, while Moussa Sene Absa's *Madame Brouette* was a lively music-driven story of independent women in revolt against feckless and self-serving men. From Chad, Mahamet Saleh Haroun's *Abouna* (*Our Father*) related the optimistic saga of two young boys in search of the father who deserted his family. Mauritania produced Abderrahmane Sissako's *Heremakono* (*Waiting for Happiness*), an exquisite impression of life, with all its frustrations and pleasures, in a small isolated coastal village. From Algeria, Yamina Bachir's *Rachida* was a harrowing story of a young woman victim of Algeria's worst era of terrorism and of women's role in combating the violence.

(DAVID ROBINSON)

Nontheatrical Films. Creators of nontheatrical films continued to explore historical and contemporary landscapes in 2002. *Dead End* (2001), an imaginative science-fiction film aimed at young Belgian soldiers, won five Grand Prix awards. Made for the Belgian Defense Ministry by Mark Damen, the film

tackled the subject of AIDS in a realistic, modern, and fast-paced fashion.

The Academy Award-winning documentary *Un Coupable idéal* (2001; *Murder on a Sunday Morning*), directed by Jean-Xavier de Lestrade, told the story of Brenton Butler, a 15-year-old falsely accused of murder who confessed to the crime after being beaten by police.

Wit compassionately portrayed an independent intellectual coming to terms with her life while battling ovarian cancer. The film, an HBO/Avenue Pictures production directed by Mike Nichols, won CINE Golden Eagle, CINE Masters Series, and Peabody awards, among others.

Florida State University's Greg Marcks reaped eight awards for his film *Lector*,

including top prize at the Angelus Awards. Set in a factory in the 1920s, it explored progress and the dehumanization of industry. The story centred around a man employed to read to cigar rollers and the threat to his job posed by the advent of radio.

The Tower of Babble, written and directed by University of Southern California student Jeff Wadlow, with opening narration by Kevin Spacey, featured three vastly different tales woven together in a commentary on language and expression. It put Wadlow in competition with 500 other students in the Chrysler Million Dollar Film Festival, which he won, earning him a $1 million film production deal.

(THOMAS W. HOPE)

Religion

STRIFE marked the world of religion in 2002 as faith groups found themselves targeted for sometimes **VIOLENT ATTACKS** by adherents of other faiths. Sexual-abuse **SCANDALS** rocked churches around the world, while **SAME-SEX RELATIONSHIPS** continued to be a source of controversy. Some groups found themselves reexamining some of their key doctrines, particularly on **SALVATION**.

Sectarian and Political Violence. Violence marked the relationships between religious groups in several areas of the world in 2002. The Christian minority in Pakistan was attacked several times during the year, including a grenade attack on a church on Christmas Day in which three young girls were killed. In January, Pres. Pervez Musharraf banned five militant Islamic organizations, outlined new measures regulating Islamic religious schools, and accused Muslim leaders of stirring up religious extremism. Relations between Muslims and Hindus in South Asia were not much improved. In late February a Muslim mob in Godhra, India, burned a train car carrying Hindu activists and killed 58 people. The incident touched off three weeks of Hindu-Muslim upheavals in western Gujarat state and eventually resulted in the killing of more than 1,000 people. In late March attackers who were suspected of being Islamic militants set off grenades and exchanged gunfire with police at a Hindu temple in Jammu, and 10 people were killed. An attack on a Hindu temple in Gandhinagar in September killed 32 people. Prime Minister Atal Bihari Vajpayee called for an end to the cycle of violence, in which one incident touched off others in what he called mindless revenge.

The Church of the Nativity in Bethlehem, West Bank, was the site of a five-week standoff between Israeli troops and more than 200 armed Palestinians who took refuge in it in April. Twelve se-

AP/Wide World Photos

A Muslim girl swims in a pool in Kuala Lumpur, Malaysia. Requiring Muslim girls to wear—or not to wear—headscarves in public continued to be an issue in many countries in Asia and Europe in 2002.

curity force members were killed in Hebron in November when Palestinians ambushed armed guards for a group of Jewish worshippers walking home from a prayer service. In response to worldwide protests from Christians, the Israeli government announced in March that it was withdrawing permission for the construction of a mosque next to the Basilica of the Annunciation in Nazareth. The continuing strife in the Middle East was cited as a factor in a worldwide outbreak of anti-Jewish attacks in places including Tunisia, Russia, Ukraine, Canada, England, and France, where authorities said 360 crimes were committed against Jews and Jewish institutions in the first half of April alone. Leaders of the World Jewish Congress said the level of such attacks in Europe was the worst since World War II. The violence spurred seven leaders of Christian and conservative organizations in the United States to urge Pres. George W. Bush to "actively confront all leaders, countries, and movements that finance or propagate the lie of anti-Semitism." In Colombia, Catholic clergy were the victims of kidnappings and killings that included the assassination in March of Archbishop Isaías Duarte Cancino of Cali, who had often been critical of leftist rebels. (*See* OBITUARIES.) In November Bishop Jorge Enrique Jiménez, president of the Latin American bishops conference, and a priest were rescued by army troops four days after they were kidnapped by rebels.

Verbal Violence. The Rev. Jerry Vines of Jacksonville, Fla., past president of the 16-million-member Southern Baptist Convention, the largest Protestant denomination in the U.S., was criticized by Muslims and some Jewish leaders when he said in St. Louis, Mo., in June that the Prophet Muhammad was a "demon-possessed pedophile." In response to Vines's comments, the denomination's newly elected president, the Rev. Jack Graham of Plano, Texas, said that Southern Baptists loved Muslims and wanted to share their faith with them. Another prominent Southern Baptist, the Rev. Jerry Falwell of Lynchburg, Va., touched off protests from Muslims in several countries in October when he said in a televised interview that the Prophet Muhammad was a terrorist. Falwell later apologized and said he intended no disrespect to any sincere, law-abiding Muslim. Jewish leaders voiced dismay when the National Archives released a 1972 conversation between evangelist Billy Graham and Pres. Richard Nixon in which the evangelist agreed that Jews had a stranglehold on the media in the U.S. Graham issued a statement of apology and met with Jewish leaders in Cincinnati, Ohio, in June to further express his regrets.

Interfaith Relations. Despite these setbacks, interfaith relations saw some positive developments in 2002. In January the Anglican archbishop of Canterbury, George Carey, hosted a two-day international conference between Christians and Muslims at Lambeth Palace and later joined with the grand imam of Cairo's University of al-Azhar al-Sharif in launching a process for dialogues between Anglicans and Sunni Muslims. Also in January about 200 leaders of 12 faith groups attended a daylong retreat in Assisi, Italy, at the invitation of Pope John Paul II, who told the gathering that "there is no religious goal that could possibly justify the use of violence by man against man." In the U.S. the National Council of Churches asked congregations in its 36 member denominations to host open houses for Muslims in the days surrounding the first anniversary of the terrorist attacks of Sept. 11, 2001.

Christians found themselves in disagreement on how to relate to members of other faiths. The Rev. David Benke, president of the Atlantic District of the Lutheran Church–Missouri Synod, was suspended from his duties for having taken part in an interfaith prayer service in New York in the wake of the Sept. 11, 2001, attacks. The suspension was issued by the Rev. Wallace Schulz, the denomination's second vice president, who said that Benke's participation in a service with "pagans" gave the impression that there might be more than one God. Schulz was subsequently removed from his position as speaker on *The Lutheran Hour* radio broadcast for his involvement in the controversy. In January the Vatican issued a docu-

ment stating that Jews and Christians shared their wait for the Messiah, although Jews were waiting for the first coming and Christians for the second. A joint task force of American Catholic bishops and Jewish rabbis released a statement in August saying that targeting Jews for conversion was "no longer theologically acceptable to the Catholic Church because Jews already dwell in a saving covenant with God." Jim Sibley, the Southern Baptist Convention's coordinator of Jewish ministries, said the statement demonstrated that "the bishops have abandoned any semblance of biblical authority," but a few weeks later 21 Catholic and Protestant scholars said Jews need not believe in Jesus Christ for salvation and denounced "missionary efforts directed at converting Jews." The annual General Assembly of the Presbyterian Church (USA) approved a statement in June in Columbus, Ohio, declaring that "Jesus Christ is the only Savior and Lord, and all people everywhere are called to place their faith, hope, and love in him."

In the area of ecumenical relations between Christians, the Central Committee of the World Council of Churches (WCC) responded to concerns voiced by some Orthodox churches by replacing its parliamentary voting procedure with a consensus model of decision making. The change, approved by a vote at WCC headquarters in Geneva in September, led to the resignation from the committee of Lutheran Bishop Margot Kässmann of Germany, who said it would be "no longer possible to celebrate ecumenical worship" at WCC events. The church council also announced plans to reduce spending sharply because of the failure of many of its 342 members to make financial contributions.

A new organization called Christian Churches Together in the USA was organized in Chicago in April by 34 leaders of the National Council of Churches, the Salvation Army, the U.S. Conference of Catholic Bishops, and the evangelical Call to Renewal coalition. In a statement the group said that no existing ecumenical organization represented the full spectrum of Christian belief in the United States.

The Vatican's decision in February to upgrade four Catholic apostolic administrations in Russia to full dioceses led to protests by the Russian Orthodox Church, whose Holy Synod called it an unprecedented move and a challenge to Orthodoxy. In April Russian Roman Catholic Archbishop Tadeusz Kondrusiewicz denounced what he called a

"large-scale anti-Catholic campaign" that included the denial of the visas of five foreign-born priests. In contrast, a visit to Bulgaria in May by Pope John Paul II helped to improve relations between Catholics and Orthodox Christians there. The pontiff had earlier visited Azerbaijan, an almost completely Muslim country. In July John Paul traveled to Toronto for the weeklong World Youth Day festival, which he addressed on July 25. The Polish-born pontiff made an emotional return to his home country, where he spent three days and celebrated an enormous open-air mass in Krakow on August 18. On November 14 he addressed the Italian Parliament, a first for any pope and an especially significant gesture for the first non-Italian pontiff in four and a half centuries.

The Antiochian Orthodox Christian Archdiocese of America announced in June that it had been granted autonomous status by its mother church in Syria. The biennial Clergy-Laity Congress of the Greek Orthodox Archdiocese, which had been seeking more autonomy from the Ecumenical Patriarchate of Constantinople, approved provisions for appointing local bishops and nominating candidates for archbishop. Bishops of the Orthodox Church in America, which has a predominantly Russian heritage, appointed Archbishop Herman of Philadelphia in July to succeed Metropolitan Theodosius as the church's North American primate.

The Clergy. The year 2002 saw an explosion of scandals involving accusations of sexual abuse and cover-ups in the Roman Catholic Church in countries including Australia, Ireland, Poland, and the U.S. (*See* Sidebar.) The developments spurred resignations and expulsions of some prominent church leaders and led the pope to say in April that there was "no place in the priesthood and religious life for those who would harm the young." Five people were expelled from the Jehovah's Witnesses in the United States after they accused leaders of covering up the sexual abuse of children by members.

The Anglican diocese of New Westminster, B.C., stirred a storm in the worldwide Anglican Communion when it voted in June to permit the blessing of same-sex unions. The action led 13 of the nation's 41 Anglican bishops to ask the diocese not to implement the rite and spurred Archbishop Carey to tell the Anglican Consultative Council meeting in Hong Kong in September that unilateral actions by dioceses and bishops could lead to the formation of two or more distinct Anglican bodies. A majority of the 173 regional bodies of the Presbyterian Church (USA) defeated a move to rescind a five-year-old ban on noncelibate gay clergy. In June, Matthew J. Smucker became the first openly gay person to be ordained by the Church of the Brethren. His status was unclear, however, after the denomination's annual conference, meeting in July in Louisville, Ky., reaffirmed its stance against ordaining "any persons known to be engaging in homosexual practices."

In August the Vatican excommunicated seven women who claimed to have been ordained to the priesthood in June, saying their actions had "wounded" the Roman Catholic Church. The Southern Baptist Convention, reflecting a revision of its faith statement in 2000 to oppose the ordination of women, announced in February that it would no longer endorse ordained women's serving as chaplains. In Thailand Varanggana Vanavichayen, a Buddhist nun, was ordained as a monk in February, the first female to join that country's all-male clergy. She was ordained by a female monk from Sri Lanka, where women had been allowed in the clergy since 1998.

A revision of the New International Version of the Bible that replaced some masculine pronouns with gender-neutral language drew criticism from 100 Christian leaders and the annual meeting of the Southern Baptist Convention. The Forum of Bible Agencies, made up of several leading translation and distribution organizations, said in a statement, however, that the revision, the Today's New International Version (TNIV) New Testament, "falls within the forum's translation principles and procedures." In another controversy among evangelical Christians, Wayne Pederson resigned as the new president of National Religious Broadcasters just before his installation in February. Glenn Plummer, chairman of the organization of 1,400 broadcasters, said Pederson had touched off a "firestorm" a few weeks earlier when he said that he was concerned that evangelicals "are identified politically more than theologically."

Church-State Relations. In a landmark case on church-state separation, the U.S. Supreme Court ruled in June that government may give financial aid to parents to enable them to send their children to religious schools. The 5–4

ruling upheld a school-voucher program in Ohio and said the program "is entirely neutral with respect to religion." Justice David Souter wrote in a dissenting opinion, however, that the ruling would force citizens to subsidize faiths they did not share. In August a Florida judge ruled against that state's voucher program because it gave money directly to religious schools. A federal appeals court in California ruled in June that the Pledge of Allegiance violates the U.S. Constitution because it describes the country as "one nation, under God." In the 2–1 ruling, the Court of Appeals for the 9th Circuit said the 1954 law that added those words to the pledge violated the First Amendment ban on a government establishment of religion. The decision stirred so much controversy, however, that Judge Alfred Goodwin blocked it from taking effect while the case was being appealed.

Israel's Orthodox Jewish religious establishment faced several challenges to its influence during 2002. When Rabbi Uri Regev in January became the first Israeli-born rabbi to serve as head of the Reform movement's World Union for Progressive Judaism, he decried the chief rabbinate's refusal to meet with Reform or Conservative rabbis or to allow any non-Orthodox prayer services at the Western Wall in Jerusalem. In

February, Israel's High Court ruled that the Interior Ministry must register residents who convert to Judaism in procedures used by the Reform or Conservative movements. The decision marked the first time such conversions had been put on a par with Orthodox conversions for the purpose of listing people as Jews in the population registry. In the landmark case the court president, Aharon Barak, said Israel is a pluralistic state of the Jewish people rather than a monolithic religious community. Orthodox Jews won a victory in July when Israeli's Knesset (parliament) legalized the tradition of exempting thousands of religious men from having to serve in the military.

In May, a U.S. federal appeals court upheld a lower court's ruling that New York state's standards for kosher food violate the First Amendment. The three-judge panel said that the state's enforcement of these laws "confers a substantial benefit on Orthodox Jews and not on others." A German federal court in Berlin ruled in October that teachers in government-operated schools must refrain from openly displaying religious symbols in class. The landmark ruling involved a Muslim teacher who wore a head scarf in class, but some observers said it could also apply to Christians wearing crosses as

(continued on page 305)

Pope John Paul II, on a visit to his native Poland in August, approaches the altar during a celebration of an open-air mass at Krakow's Blonie Park.

© Vincenzo Pinto/Reuters 2002

Roman Catholic Church Scandal

The Roman Catholic Church was rocked by accusations of sexual abuse and cover-ups around the world during 2002. The scandal spurred the resignations of Bernard Cardinal Law (*see* BIOGRAPHIES) of Boston and other bishops in Australia, Ireland, Poland, and the United States as Catholics and other commentators accused the hierarchy of gross negligence in its failure to take action against priests accused of abuse. By year's end more than 300 of the 46,000 Catholic priests in the United States had either resigned or been removed from duty in response to claims of sexual abuse, hundreds of civil suits seeking millions of dollars in damages were pending, and more than a dozen criminal grand juries were investigating whether church leaders had violated the law by failing to report crimes committed by priests.

The storm of controversy erupted in the U.S. in January when John Geoghan, a defrocked priest, was convicted of having fondled a boy 10 years earlier. Soon more than 130 people claimed that he had abused them at one time or another over a period of three decades, and 118 people sued Law for his failure to discipline or remove Geoghan even after allegations had been made against the priest. The cardinal was later accused of similar inaction against the Rev. Paul Shanley, a retired priest who was accused of having molested at least 26 children over three decades. After Geoghan was sentenced to 10 years in prison in February, a wave of reports of similar misconduct and inaction by church officials surfaced. The Roman Catholic Church in Ireland agreed to pay $110 million to settle cases involving hundreds of people who said that they were abused by clergy over several decades. In Australia the church acknowledged having paid some victims of clergy sexual abuse to stay silent.

In April, Pope John Paul II called the sexual abuse of children a crime and "an appalling sin in the eyes of God." He said that there was "no place in the priesthood and religious life for those who would harm the young" and expressed "solidarity and concern" for the victims. His remarks came during a Vatican meeting with American Catholic bishops, who were considering what steps to take as a body in response to the scandal. Two months later the bishops met in Dallas, Texas, and heard testimony from victims of abuse. Bishop Wilton Gregory of Belleville, Ill., who headed the American bishops' conference, acknowledged that the prelates had not reported the allegations to civil authorities because they were "worried more about the possibility of scandal than in bringing about the kind of openness that helps prevent abuse."

The bishops drafted a policy urging prelates in all 194 American dioceses to report all allegations of sexual abuse of minors to civil authorities and expel offenders from public ministry. They also created a national lay review board to name publicly each year those dioceses that failed to comply with the policy. The Vatican and some experts in church law, however, said that the draft policy would vio-

Getty Images

late the rights of priests in an effort to show concern for victims of abuse. Following consultations with the Vatican, the American bishops met in Washington in November and approved a compromise policy that allowed each bishop to conduct an inquiry to determine whether a molestation claim was credible. If the claim was deemed plausible, the priest would be put on leave and appear before a clerical tribunal to determine his guilt or innocence. Victims would have to come forward with accusations by age 28, although bishops could ask the Vatican for a waiver. The prelates pledged to report all allegations involving children to civil authorities and sent the policy to the Vatican, where it was approved in December.

In December lawyers representing plaintiffs in civil suits against the archdiocese of Boston released 3,000 pages of files documenting how priests had sexually abused both children and adults and used illegal drugs. The files also showed a pattern in which Law and other church leaders had routinely transferred accused clergy to other parishes without disciplining them. The cardinal went to Rome to consult with Pope John Paul II and other Vatican officials while reports indicated that a grand jury was preparing to question Law and seven bishops who had been under his authority. The new revelations spurred Law's resignation.

Law was not the only high-profile Catholic to be brought down by the scandal. In Wisconsin, Milwaukee's Archbishop Rembert Weakland, who had taken an aggressive stand against sexual misconduct by priests, resigned in May following the disclosure that his archdiocese had reached a $450,000 settlement in 1998 with a man who had accused the prelate of having sexually abused him more than two decades earlier. Archbishop Juliusz Paetz of Poznan, Pol., an appointee and longtime acquaintance of John Paul II, stepped down in March as the Vatican began investigating accusations that he had made sexual advances on priests. Bishop Brendan Comiskey of Ferns, Ire., resigned in April following criticism of his failure to act on abuse complaints in his diocese, and the nation's bishops acknowledged what they called the "justifiable anger and distress" that had caused "great pain and shame" to the Catholic Church in Ireland. Archbishop George Pell of Sydney, Australia, stepped down from his post for two months until an inquiry cleared him of charges of having abused a 12-year-old boy four decades earlier.

As the year drew to a close, the diocese of Manchester, N.H., reached a settlement giving state prosecutors oversight of its policies on how to handle abuse claims in the wake of threats of possible criminal charges against the diocese. Officials of the archdiocese of Boston considered a declaration of bankruptcy after having settled lawsuits for about $50 million, and legislatures in at least three states passed legislation waiving or extending the statute of limitations for civil cases involving child sexual abuse.

(DARRELL J. TURNER)

(continued from page 303)

jewelry. A panel from the Norwegian Church Council recommended in March that the government end its official relationship with the Evangelical Lutheran Church of Norway, which had been the state church for 465 years; the church had been chafing at the government's involvement in the hiring of clergy.

The parliament in Belarus passed a law in October giving privileged status to the Russian Orthodox Church, imposing censorship on religious publications, and barring religious groups that had not been in the country for at least 20 years from distributing literature or establishing missions. In June China announced that it was undertaking a large-scale restoration of sacred buildings in Tibet, including the Potala Palace, the Norbuglinkha, and the Sagya Lamasery. Addressing a gathering of university students in Beijing in February, U.S. Pres. George W. Bush expressed the hope that all religious persecution would end in China. In his address, which was broad-cast across China, he said that 95% of Americans believe in God and called his country "a nation guided by faith." A survey released in March by the Pew Research Center for the People & the Press, however, found that 52% of Americans who were asked said that they thought the influence of religion was in decline. The finding represented a reversal of the increase of religious expression after the attacks of Sept. 11, 2001. In early November about 2,000 atheists, agnostics, freethinkers, and secular humanists conducted the Godless Americans March on Washington to draw attention to what they described as the 14% of the U.S. population made up of nonbelievers.

Church Membership. For the first time, the 5.2-million-member Church of Jesus Christ of Latter-day Saints was listed among the country's five largest denominations in the *Yearbook of American and Canadian Churches*. The LDS church dedicated a new Nauvoo Temple in Illinois in late June to replace the original temple, which had been de-stroyed 156 years earlier when the Mormon community was forced to flee the town. The Catholic Church retained its position as the largest U.S. church body, with 63.6 million members. In September the $189.5 million Cathedral of Our Lady of the Angels was dedicated in Los Angeles in a four-hour service attended by 3,000 people. It was the first major American cathedral to be built in three decades and replaced a structure that had been severely damaged in an earthquake in 1994. (*See* ARCHITECTURE AND CIVIL ENGINEERING.)

An ossuary, or container for burial or storage of bones, with the inscription "James, son of Joseph, brother of Jesus," was made public. If authentic, it would represent the first appearance of Jesus in the archaeological record and the earliest known non-Biblical reference to his existence. (*See* ARCHAEOLOGY AND ANTHROPOLOGY: Archaeology.)

Personalities. All of Central America's heads of state attended a ceremony in Guatemala City, Guat., in which Pope John Paul II canonized Pedro de San

The Cathedral of Our Lady of the Angels opened in Los Angeles on September 2.

José Betancur, a 17th-century Spanish missionary, as the region's first saint. A day later, on July 31, in Mexico City, the pope canonized Juan Diego, an Aztec farmer who reportedly saw a vision of the Virgin Mary in 1531, as the Catholic Church's first Indian saint. The attendance of Pres. Vicente Fox at the ceremony marked the first time that a Mexican president had attended a papal

mass. Other canonizations during the year included, in May, Amabile Lucia Visintainer, known as Mother Paulina, the first Brazilian saint; in June the popular Italian stigmatic Padre Pio da Pietrelcina, who died in 1968; and in October, Josemaría Escrivá, the founder of the secretive and influential Roman Catholic organization Opus Dei. Since his accession in 1979 John Paul canon-

ized 468 persons, more than any other pope. Also in October John Paul made the first major changes in the rosary since the 16th century. He added "five mysteries of light," or meditations, to the three previous sets in the series of Roman Catholic prayers in order to focus on Christ's public ministry.

In July, Welsh Archbishop Rowan Williams was selected to succeed Carey

Worldwide Adherents of All Religions by Six Continental Areas, Mid-2002

	Africa	Asia	Europe	Latin America	Northern America	Oceania	World	%	Number of Countries
Christians	376,453,000	322,753,000	559,083,000	492,148,000	262,884,000	25,580,000	2,038,905,000	32.9	238
Affiliated Christians	350,719,000	317,161,000	536,351,000	486,673,000	213,913,000	21,829,000	1,926,649,000	31.1	238
Roman Catholics	126,631,000	113,718,000	285,133,000	471,291,000	71,749,000	8,427,000	1,076,951,000	17.4	235
Protestants	93,028,000	51,480,000	77,466,000	49,901,000	70,350,000	7,566,000	349,792,000	5.6	232
Orthodox	36,790,000	14,326,000	158,648,000	571,000	6,458,000	730,000	217,522,000	3.5	134
Anglicans	44,531,000	742,000	26,619,000	1,106,000	3,217,000	5,447,000	81,663,000	1.3	163
Independents	87,150,000	160,535,000	25,978,000	41,020,000	81,834,000	1,567,000	398,085,000	6.4	221
Marginal Christians	2,581,000	2,557,000	3,649,000	6,968,000	10,966,000	479,000	27,199,000	0.4	215
Unaffiliated Christians	25,544,000	5,572,000	22,634,000	5,391,000	48,967,000	3,743,000	111,851,000	1.8	232
Baha'is	1,826,000	3,603,000	134,000	914,000	813,000	116,000	7,406,000	0.1	218
Buddhists	143,000	358,437,000	1,593,000	674,000	2,855,000	312,000	364,014,000	5.9	126
Chinese folk religionists	33,800	388,123,000	262,000	199,000	861,000	65,000	389,543,000	6.3	89
Confucianists	260	6,291,000	10,900	450	0	24,200	6,327,000	0.1	15
Ethnic religionists	98,734,000	129,718,000	1,253,000	1,287,000	448,000	267,000	231,708,000	3.7	140
Hindus	2,417,000	821,759,000	1,435,000	782,000	1,373,000	364,000	828,130,000	13.3	114
Jains	67,800	4,270,000	0	0	7,000	0	4,345,000	0.1	10
Jews	215,000	4,523,000	2,485,000	1,148,000	6,065,000	98,200	14,535,000	0.2	134
Muslims	329,869,000	858,018,000	31,883,000	1,732,000	4,587,000	313,000	1,226,403,000	19.8	204
New-Religionists	29,300	101,494,000	162,000	645,000	851,000	67,300	103,249,000	1.7	60
Shintoists	0	2,639,000	0	7,000	57,200	0	2,703,000	0.0	8
Sikhs	55,800	22,961,000	242,000	0	543,000	18,900	23,821,000	0.4	34
Spiritists	2,600	2,000	135,000	12,300,000	154,000	7,100	12,601,000	0.2	55
Taoists	0	2,673,000	0	0	11,300	0	2,685,000	0.0	5
Zoroastrians	930	2,575,000	680	0	80,600	1,400	2,659,000	0.0	22
Other religionists	69,000	64,100	240,000	101,000	613,000	9,500	1,096,000	0.0	78
Nonreligious	5,320,000	615,192,000	104,669,000	16,507,000	29,526,000	3,401,000	774,615,000	12.5	236
Atheists	445,000	122,877,000	22,201,000	2,817,000	1,720,000	374,000	150,434,000	2.4	161
Total population	**820,222,000**	**3,777,193,000**	**728,047,000**	**533,601,000**	**314,195,000**	**30,527,000**	**6,203,789,000**	**100.0**	**238**

Continents. These follow current UN demographic terminology, which now divides the world into the six major areas shown above. See United Nations, *World Population Prospects: The 1998 Revision* (New York: UN, 1999), with populations of all continents, regions, and countries covering the period 1950–2050. Note that "Asia" includes the former Soviet Central Asian states and "Europe" includes all of Russia extending eastward to Vladivostok, the Sea of Japan, and the Bering Strait.

Countries. The last column enumerates sovereign and nonsovereign countries in which each religion or religious grouping has a numerically significant and organized following.

Adherents. As defined in the 1948 Universal Declaration of Human Rights, a person's religion is what he or she says it is. Totals are enumerated for each of the world's 238 countries following the methodology of the *World Christian Encyclopedia*, 2nd ed. (2001), and *World Christian Trends* (2001), using recent censuses, polls, surveys, reports, Web sites, literature, and other data.

Christians. Followers of Jesus Christ affiliated with churches (church members, including children: 1,907,363,000, shown divided among the six standardized ecclesiastical megablocs), plus persons professing in censuses or polls to be Christians though not so affiliated. Figures for the subgroups of Christians do not add up to the totals in the first line because some Christians adhere to more than one denomination.

Independents. This term here denotes members of churches and networks that regard themselves as postdenominationalist and neo-apostolic and thus independent of historic, organized, institutionalized, denominationalist Christianity.

Marginal Christians. Members of denominations on the margins of organized mainstream Christianity (e.g., Church of Jesus Christ of Latter-day Saints, Jehovah's Witnesses, and Christian Science).

Buddhists. 56% Mahayana, 38% Theravada (Hinayana), 6% Tantrayana (Lamaism).

Chinese folk religionists. Followers of traditional Chinese religion (local deities, ancestor veneration, Confucian ethics, universism, divination, and some Buddhist and Taoist elements).

Confucianists. Non-Chinese followers of Confucius and Confucianism, mostly Koreans in Korea.

Ethnic religionists. Followers of local, tribal, animistic, or shamanistic religions, with members restricted to one ethnic group.

Hindus. 70% Vaishnavites, 25% Shaivites, 2% neo-Hindus and reform Hindus.

Jews. Adherents of Judaism. For detailed data on "core" Jewish population, see the annual "World Jewish Populations" article in the American Jewish Committee's *American Jewish Year Book*.

Muslims. 83% Sunnites, 16% Shi'ites, 1% other schools.

New-Religionists. Followers of Asian 20th-century New Religions, New Religious movements, radical new crisis religions, and non-Christian syncretistic mass religions, all founded since 1800 and most since 1945.

Other religionists. Including a handful of religions, quasi-religions, pseudoreligions, parareligions, religious or mystic systems, and religious and semireligious brotherhoods of numerous varieties.

Nonreligious. Persons professing no religion, nonbelievers, agnostics, freethinkers, uninterested, or dereligionized secularists indifferent to all religion but not militantly so.

Atheists. Persons professing atheism, skepticism, disbelief, or irreligion, including the militantly antireligious (opposed to all religion).

Total population. UN medium variant figures for mid-2001, as given in *World Population Prospects: The 1998 Revision*.

in 2003 as the 104th archbishop of Canterbury and spiritual head of the world's 70 million Anglicans. (*See* BIOGRAPHIES.) The Rev. John C. Polkinghorne, a mathematical physicist and Anglican priest, was the 2002 recipient of the Templeton Prize for Progress Toward Research or Discoveries About Spiritual Realities. (*See* BIOGRAPHIES.) Apart from Colombian Archbishop Duarte, religious leaders who died during the year included W.A. Criswell, pastor of the First Baptist Church of Dallas, Texas, the largest Southern Baptist congregation in the U.S.; Carl McIntire, a firebrand fundamentalist preacher whose radio show, *20th Century Reformation Hour*, was heard throughout the U.S. in the 1960s; Franjo Cardinal Kuharic, archbishop of Zagreb, Croatia, and a nationalist icon for his people; Lucas Cardinal Moreira Neves, archbishop of São Salvador da Bahia, Braz., and close friend of Pope John Paul II; and John Baptist Cardinal Wu, bishop of Hong Kong, who helped that territory's Roman Catholics make the transition from British to Chinese rule. (*See* OBITUARIES.)

(DARRELL J. TURNER)

Religious Adherents in the United States of America, AD 1900–2000

	Year 1900	%	mid-1970	%	mid-1990	%	Annual Change, 1990–2000 Natural	Conversion	Total	Rate (%)	mid-1995	%	mid-2000	%
Christians	73,270,000	96.4	191,182,000	91.0	217,719,000	85.7	2,081,000	−278,000	1,802,000	0.80	227,586,000	85.2	235,742,000	84.7
Affiliated Christians	54,425,000	71.6	153,299,000	73.0	175,820,000	69.2	1,680,000	−79,500	1,601,000	0.88	184,244,000	69.0	191,828,000	68.9
Protestants	35,000,000	46.1	58,568,000	27.9	60,216,000	23.7	575,000	−140,000	435,000	0.70	62,525,000	23.4	64,570,000	23.2
Roman Catholics	10,775,000	14.2	48,305,000	23.0	56,500,000	22.2	540,000	−390,000	150,000	0.26	56,715,000	21.2	58,000,000	20.8
Anglicans	1,600,000	2.1	3,196,000	1.5	2,450,000	1.0	23,400	−28,400	−5,000	−0.21	2,445,000	0.9	2,400,000	0.9
Orthodox	400,000	0.5	4,163,000	2.0	5,150,000	2.0	49,200	12,000	61,200	1.13	5,472,000	2.1	5,762,000	2.1
Multiple affiliation	0	0.0	−2,704,000	−1.3	−24,336,000	−9.6	−233,000	−87,300	−320,000	1.24	−25,360,000	−9.5	−27,534,000	−9.9
Independents	5,850,000	7.7	35,645,000	17.0	66,900,000	26.3	639,000	526,000	1,165,000	1.62	72,943,000	27.3	78,550,000	28.2
Marginal Christians	800,000	1.1	6,126,000	2.9	8,940,000	3.5	85,400	28,600	114,000	1.21	9,502,000	3.6	10,080,000	3.6
Evangelicals	*32,068,000*	*42.2*	*31,516,000*	*15.0*	*37,349,000*	*14.7*	*357,000*	*−27,800*	*329,000*	*0.85*	*39,314,000*	*14.7*	*40,640,000*	*14.6*
evangelicals	*11,000,000*	*14.5*	*45,500,000*	*21.7*	*87,656,000*	*34.5*	*838,000*	*263,000*	*1,101,000*	*1.19*	*93,457,000*	*35.0*	*98,662,000*	*35.4*
Unaffiliated Christians	18,845,000	24.8	37,883,000	18.0	41,899,000	16.5	400,000	−199,000	202,000	0.47	43,342,000	16.2	43,914,000	15.8
Baha'is	2,800	0.0	138,000	0.1	600,000	0.2	5,700	9,600	15,300	2.30	682,000	0.3	753,000	0.3
Buddhists	30,000	0.0	200,000	0.1	1,880,000	0.7	18,000	39,000	57,000	2.68	2,150,000	0.8	2,450,000	0.9
Chinese folk religionists	70,000	0.1	90,000	0.0	76,000	0.0	730	−480	250	0.32	77,000	0.0	78,500	0.0
Ethnic religionists	100,000	0.1	70,000	0.0	280,000	0.1	2,700	12,800	15,500	4.50	387,000	0.1	435,000	0.2
Hindus	1,000	0.0	100,000	0.1	750,000	0.3	7,200	21,000	28,200	3.24	930,000	0.4	1,032,000	0.4
Jains	0	0.0	0	0.0	5,000	0.0	48	150	200	3.36	6,000	0.0	7,000	0.0
Jews	1,500,000	2.0	6,700,000	3.2	5,535,000	2.2	52,900	−44,300	8,600	0.15	5,600,000	2.1	5,621,000	2.0
Muslims	10,000	0.0	800,000	0.4	3,560,000	1.4	34,000	23,200	57,200	1.50	3,825,000	1.4	4,132,000	1.5
Black Muslims	0	0.0	200,000	0.1	1,250,000	0.5	12,700	17,300	30,000	2.29	1,400,000	0.5	1,650,000	0.6
New-Religionists	0	0.0	110,000	0.1	575,000	0.2	5,500	18,100	23,600	3.50	690,000	0.3	811,000	0.3
Shintoists	0	0.0	0	0.0	50,000	0.0	480	140	620	1.18	53,900	0.0	56,200	0.0
Sikhs	0	0.0	1,000	0.0	160,000	0.1	1,500	5,900	7,400	3.87	192,000	0.1	234,000	0.1
Spiritists	0	0.0	0	0.0	120,000	0.1	1,100	690	1,800	1.44	133,000	0.1	138,000	0.1
Taoists	0	0.0	0	0.0	10,000	0.0	96	17	110	1.08	10,600	0.0	11,100	0.0
Zoroastrians	0	0.0	0	0.0	42,400	0.0	410	630	1,000	2.20	47,500	0.0	52,700	0.0
Other religionists	10,000	0.0	450,000	0.2	530,000	0.2	5,100	−390	4,700	0.85	550,000	0.2	577,000	0.2
Nonreligious	1,000,000	1.3	10,070,000	4.8	21,414,000	8.4	205,000	162,000	366,000	1.59	23,150,000	8.7	25,078,000	9.0
Atheists	1,000	0.0	200,000	0.1	770,000	0.3	7,400	30,600	37,900	4.09	950,000	0.4	1,149,000	0.4
Total population	75,995,000	100.0	210,111,000	100.0	254,076,000	100.0	2,428,000	0	2,428,000	0.92	267,020,000	100.0	278,357,000	100.0

Methodology. This table extracts and analyzes a microcosm of the world religion table. It depicts the United States, the country with the largest number of adherents to Christianity, the world's largest religion. Statistics at five points in time across the 20th century are presented. Each religion's *Annual Change* for 1990–2000 is also analyzed by *Natural* increase (births minus deaths, plus immigrants minus emigrants) per year and *Conversion* increase (new converts minus new defectors) per year, which together constitute the *Total* increase per year. *Rate* increase is then computed as percentage per year.

Structure. Vertically the table lists 30 major religious categories. The major religions (including nonreligion) in the U.S. are listed with largest (Christians) first. Indented names of groups in the "Adherents" column are subcategories of the groups above them and are also counted in these unindented totals, so they should not be added twice into the column total. Figures in italics draw adherents from all categories of Christians above and so cannot be added together with them. Figures for Christians are built upon detailed head counts by churches, often to the last digit. Totals are then rounded to the nearest 1,000. Because of rounding, the corresponding percentage figures may sometimes not total exactly 100%.

Christians. All persons who profess publicly to follow Jesus Christ as Lord and Saviour. This category is subdivided into **Affiliated Christians** (church members) and **Unaffiliated** (nominal) **Christians** (professing Christians not affiliated with any church). *See also* the note on Christians to the world religion table.

Evangelicals/evangelicals. These two designations—italicized and enumerated separately here—cut across all of the six Christian traditions or ecclesiastical megablocs listed above and should be considered separately from them. **Evangelicals** are mainly Protestant churches, agencies, and individuals that call themselves by this term (for example, members of the National Association of Evangelicals); they usually emphasize 5 or more of 7, 9, or 21 fundamental doctrines (salvation by faith, personal acceptance, verbal inspiration of Scripture, depravity of man, Virgin Birth, miracles of Christ, atonement, evangelism, Second Advent, et al). The **evangelicals** are Christians of evangelical conviction from all traditions who are committed to the evangel (gospel) and involved in personal witness and mission in the world; alternatively termed Great Commission Christians.

Jews. Core Jewish population relating to Judaism, excluding Jewish persons professing a different religion.

Other categories. Definitions are as given under the world religion table.

(DAVID B. BARRETT; TODD M. JOHNSON)

Social Protection

Governments made newfound efforts to preserve social protection programs, an **INTERNATIONAL CRIMINAL COURT** was established, massive numbers of **AFGHAN REFUGEES** returned home, and more than 81,000 **LIBERIANS WERE DISPLACED** as war escalated in that country.

BENEFITS AND PROGRAMS

With economic downturn or crisis prevailing worldwide, concern was voiced in 2002 over the financial viability of social protection programs. Reform proposals and actual reforms were guided by this concern. Oftentimes simply increasing the responsibility of the programs' beneficiaries was regarded as a solution, especially if people were offered more flexibility and greater choice.

North America. Even as reports showed a rise in poverty in the United States, social welfare activity was generally pushed to the back burner by budgetary concerns, election-year politics, and the nation's overriding focus on terrorism and Iraq. The lack of action was most apparent in Congress in the area of welfare, where the landmark 1996 reform legislation was scheduled to expire on September 30. That overhaul had transformed the U.S. approach to financial aid for the poor, establishing time limits and work requirements for welfare recipients and giving states greater power to experiment with their own versions of assistance. In the period since 1996, welfare rolls in the United States had dropped by more than 50%, from 12.2 million to 5.3 million. A majority of lawmakers in both political parties viewed the reform as a success, and the year began with strong expectations that a new welfare law would be passed.

Difficulties arose, however, when Congress got down to the details. Pres. George W. Bush, who made rewriting the welfare law a major part of his social agenda, outlined the administration's view with a proposal for more stringent work requirements, increased flexibility for states to design their own programs, and money for an experimental plan to promote marriage and encourage teenagers to abstain from sex. In May, on what was essentially a party-line vote, the Republican-controlled House of Representatives approved an extension bill much along the lines that Bush had requested. The battle then moved to the Senate, where Democrats came up with a much different version. One of the most significant points of conflict was over money for child care. President Bush did not propose any increase in the $2.7 billion states had been getting in block grants from Washington. The House bill increased grants by $1 billion over five years, compared with the Senate bill's $5.5 billion rise. Another sticking point was work requirements. The House measure increased the number of hours welfare recipients would have to work from 30 to 40 a week and said vocational training would not count as work. The Senate kept the current work requirement and added vocational training to the work category. In the 1996 overhaul of welfare, most legal immigrants were denied federal cash welfare benefits. The House voted to continue this ban, while the Senate gave states the option of restoring federal benefits to legal immigrants and extending health insurance benefits to some. After being approved by the Finance Committee, welfare legislation bogged down in the Senate when lawmakers and the White House could not hammer out a compromise. Backers of the Senate bill said it offered welfare recipients the best chance of becoming self-sufficient. President Bush complained that work requirements in the measure were weakened by loopholes. With the expiration date approaching and no agreement in sight, Congress voted to extend the 1996 law for three months, until December 31.

Those who felt that Congress should increase spending on social programs for the needy pointed to a number of reports. The Census Bureau, for example, said that in 2001, for the first time in eight years, the number of people living

An unemployed and permanently disabled man exhibits some of his prescription drugs, which cost $1,100 a month, only half of which was paid by Medicaid; new state plans to hold down costs could reduce Medicaid's contribution to his medical regimen.

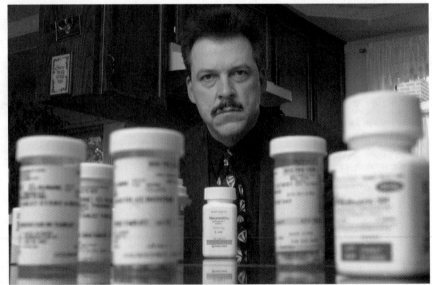

in poverty in the U.S. had risen—to 32.9 million, including 11.7 million under the age of 18. That was a 1.3% increase over 2000 and meant that 11.7% of the population was by definition poor, compared with 11.3% the previous year. The greatest increases in poverty were found in the suburbs, the South, and among non-Hispanic whites.

According to studies by the Center for Law and Social Policy, many of the people who had moved off welfare to work held low-paying jobs that did not provide health benefits. Another study found that the number of child-only welfare cases had increased and that there was a high rate of hunger and hardship among those children.

Partisan political squabbling also undercut reform efforts for Medicare, although there was widespread agreement that change was needed to provide the 40 million recipients with some form of prescription-drug coverage, which Medicare had never included. During and after the 2000 election campaign, politicians from both parties had promised help with soaring drug costs. Ideological differences, however, undercut efforts to compromise. Republicans favoured a private-sector approach in which insurance companies would receive government subsidies and offer packages that could vary from region to region. Democrats wanted to provide uniform coverage through Medicare. Although about two-thirds of the elderly had some type of private insurance coverage for prescription drugs, the Kaiser Family Foundation, a health research group, said that the average Medicare beneficiary spent $928 on those drugs in 2001, and the figure was expected to rise to $1,051 in 2002.

Failure to reach agreement on drug benefits jeopardized another piece of legislation in Congress involving Medicare—"provider givebacks." These would give hospitals, doctors, and other health care providers more money for treating Medicare patients. Medicare suffered a further jolt when the trade association for the managed-care industry reported that health maintenance organizations (HMOs) serving 200,000 elderly and disabled persons would withdraw from Medicare in 2003. That increased the number of beneficiaries who had been dropped by HMOs to 2.5 million.

Another of President Bush's social programs—his faith-based initiative—also languished in Congress. The plan would provide federal money to religious organizations so that they could get more involved in activities for the poor and disabled, such as homeless shelters, drug treatment, and other programs. The major stumbling block was the question of whether the religious groups would be allowed to give preference to members of their own faith in hiring. A bill passed by the House of Representatives in 2001 gave them leeway, but opponents argued that it violated church-state separation and could foster religious discrimination. What eventually emerged was a watered-down part of the original Bush plan that would allow a limited charitable tax deduction for people who did not itemize deductions on their returns.

Although the future of Social Security had been a major concern for years, the sense of urgency diminished in 2002. Part of the reason for this was an announcement by the Social Security trustees that the program's financial outlook had improved. Instead of running out of money in 2038, as had been predicted in 2001, the trustees said that the date would be 2041 if no changes were made in the current law. The expected tipping point for Medicare was extended one year, from 2029 to 2030. The main reason for the brighter outlook, according to the trustees, was an expected increase in the productivity of American workers during the next 75 years. Nevertheless, Social Security still faced a substantial financial challenge because vast numbers of baby boomers would reach retirement age in the years between 2011 and 2029, putting new pressures on the system. Debate over Social Security continued to focus on President Bush's effort to allow workers to invest part of their payroll tax in private savings accounts that could be used to buy stocks. Proponents of the idea argued that it would generate greater earnings, but in the face of a reeling stock market, the plan appeared to lose steam.

Outside Washington many states were forced to cut back their social protection services owing to steep drops in revenues, along with increases in unemployment and poverty. Especially hard hit was Medicaid, the federal-state health care program that covered 47 million poor and disabled persons. Medicaid costs had been growing at the rate of 13% a year, much faster than overall state spending. As a result, Medicaid accounted for one-fifth of the average state budget in 2002. A survey by the *Washington Post* found that all but nine states were taking, or planning, steps to hold down Medicaid spending, a turnaround after nearly a decade of increases in the U.S.'s largest public health insurance program. Cost-cutting strategies included dropping certain groups of patients, reducing some services, requiring patients to help pay for their own care, and limiting their access to high-priced drugs.

In Canada a major concern during the year was the national health system. A Senate committee report revealed that the system needed a major overhaul that could require more than Can$3 billion (about $2 billion) in new funding. In addition, a report prepared for health ministers warned that the public-health infrastructure was so fragile that the system could be overwhelmed by a crisis such as local contamination of drinking water. Among the problems cited by the study were shortages of funds, staffing difficulties, political interference, and a lack of planning.

Maclean's magazine, in its fourth annual ranking of health centres across the country, found that communities with medical schools led the way, while largely rural regions, which did not have easy access to the newest equipment and well-trained specialists, were generally at the bottom. Although Canadians spent Can$102.5 billion (about $67.5 billion) on public and private medical services, one-eighth of them said their health care needs had not been met in fiscal year 2000–01.

Europe. European countries took various measures aimed at ensuring the long-term stability of their old-age schemes. In June Greece's Parliament enacted a pension reform that included a change in the benefit formula that, over time, would result in a reduction in the maximum retirement benefit from 80% to 70% of final average salary and to 60% for those who entered the labour market after 1993. The retirement age was also boosted from 60 to 65.

In Spain the social security law was amended, effective retroactively from Jan. 1, 2002. Incentives were given to people to work past the age of 65—for example, they would receive their old-age pension in addition to their employment earnings. Finland also took measures to encourage people to work longer. A flexible retirement age—between age 62 and 68—would be introduced in 2005 as part of an agreement between the government, the pension institutions, and the social partners (employers' and workers' organizations). In addition, Finland's part-time pensions were made less attractive and starting in 2003 would be available only from age 58 instead of 56.

The new French prime minister, Jean-Pierre Raffarin (*see* BIOGRAPHIES), announced that the government would introduce tax incentives for retirement savings in 2003. In the fall Ireland began the approval process for providers of Personal Retirement Savings Accounts, which were intended to encourage more people to take out private pension coverage. In October the Swiss government announced a reduction in the guaranteed interest rate for mandatory occupational pensions from 4% to 3.25%, following pressure by the insurance industry, which claimed that because of the currently low investment earnings, it could not meet the guaranteed rate without touching its reserves.

Russia's new state pension system became effective in January. The plan included a flat-rate basic pension; an "insured labour pension," with benefits based on earnings and length of service; and a mandatory "funded labour pension" that was essentially based on investments. The Slovak parliament approved parts of a pension reform that would apply to all workers under the age of 40 and create a three-tiered system. The first and third pillar were enacted, but no agreement could be reached on the second tier, which would be financed through individual retirement accounts. Similarly, in May the Lithuanian parliament voted against a second pillar in the form of a mandatory funded system of pensions. In January Hungary began reducing the role of private pensions by eliminating the obligation for employees and self-employed persons to become members of a mandatory private pension scheme and by abolishing the minimum state guarantee under mandatory private pension schemes.

Rising costs triggered a range of options for disability plans and health care. The United Kingdom introduced new rules to encourage the disabled to return to work by allowing them to retain their disability benefits even if they returned to the workforce. Previously, the disabled had to show that the work would be beneficial to their medical condition. Beginning in April the costs of medicines and dental treatment under Britain's National Health Service were increased. The Norwegian government proposed to tighten the eligibility criteria for disability pensions by introducing a requalification mechanism for people younger than 50 years receiving disability benefits; heretofore they had been granted a pension for life. The government in The Nether-

lands, in an effort to create strong incentives for employers to reintegrate disabled people, tabled a law that would require employers to continue salary payments for sick employees for up to two years; the existing law required a one-year payment. In Austria the National Council approved the cross-subsidizing of health funds. Financially better-off funds had to make payments into an equalization fund, and the recipients of the subsidy were obliged to repay by December 2009.

Various measures were adopted throughout Europe to deal with increased unemployment. German Chancellor Gerhard Schröder announced that his government would implement proposals made by the Hartz Commission, including a restructuring of the labour market. Efforts would be made to improve job-matching and placement procedures, and unemployment assistance and social assistance would be brought more into line. In Belgium, in an effort to stimulate the employment of older workers, the employer contribution to social security was reduced for workers over the age of 58, effective in April. Starting in September Belgian companies were required to pay for outplacement services—including psychological guidance and job-search assistance—for dismissed employees over age 45. Beginning in February France no longer prevented a person from registering on the list of jobless if that person had started a business. Spain increased public spend-

ing on active labour-market policies and tightened the eligibility criteria for the receipt of unemployment benefits. In addition, a system of unemployment protection for temporary workers in the agricultural sector was established. Estonia introduced a new unemployment insurance that would become effective in January 2003.

Throughout the European Union (EU) the social protection of home-based employees and other "teleworkers" was improved. Thanks to an agreement between EU employer and trade-union organizations, they were granted equal rights in terms of health and safety measures, training, work time, and the right to belong to a trade union.

Industrialized Asia and the Pacific. In September Singapore launched a long-term care insurance called "Elder-Shield" for Singaporean nationals and permanent residents. Enrollment was automatic at age 40, but those eligible could elect not to join. Premiums would be deducted from Medisave (the Central Provident Fund's medical savings plan) accounts. Some 400,000 eligible persons opted out of the program, owing to the annual cost. In addition, a means-tested program was set up to cover people between 40 and 69 years old with preexisting disabilities, as well as persons age 70 or older.

Japan further revised its health insurance system, essentially by introducing higher co-payments and premiums that would take effect in April 2003. The

People walk past a homeless man in downtown Tokyo in November; because of the bad economy, Japan was experiencing a tremendous increase in homelessness, which was occurring on a scale not seen since the period immediately following World War II.

Japanese Ministry of Health, Labor and Welfare made initial proposals for the next pension reform. It suggested that older workers might postpone their "special early retirement pension" (available to people between 60 and 64 years old). The ministry also proposed to permit temporarily unemployed persons to remain covered by the Employees' Pension Insurance Program, which was for private-sector employees, instead of having to switch to the National Pension Program, designed mainly for self-employed persons.

In Australia discussions were under way on how to increase competition and efficiency in the superannuation (mandatory occupational pensions) industry. A bill was presented that would allow superannuation fund members to choose the fund that would hold their Superannuation Guarantee Accounts. Another bill provided for government assistance to low-income earners in the payment of superannuation contributions.

New Zealand introduced a new paid parental leave that would be financed from general tax revenue. The legislation applied to those becoming parents on or after July 1. They received the right to 12 weeks of paid leave at a rate of 100% of previous earnings, subject to a maximum that slightly exceeded the minimum wage. Employers were required to keep the job position open, except in unusual circumstances.

Emerging and Less-Developed Countries. The Philippines established a health care scheme for the poorest families, which was implemented through a partnership between local governments and the Philippine Health Insurance Corp.

In Nigeria work was under way to establish a national health insurance scheme, with five programs to cover various groups of people across the country (employees of the public and organized private sector, urban self-employed people, permanently disabled persons, children under five, and people in rural communities). In Tunisia a law adopted in March created a special social protection scheme for low-income people, such as domestic workers, small-scale craftsmen, and small fishermen and farmers, giving them access to old-age, survivors, and illness benefits. The National Social Security Authority in Zimbabwe published plans to extend social security coverage to domestic workers. In South Africa a committee of inquiry published a report recommending a move away from

an employment-centred concept of social protection and the adoption of a more comprehensive approach. Among the proposals were the introduction of a basic income grant, extension of unemployment insurance coverage, and a better appreciation for the role of informal social protection.

Argentina's economic crisis prompted the government to cut public-sector salaries and pensions by 13%, a move that was reversed in August when the Supreme Court declared it unconstitutional. The legislature approved a pension-reform bill, which, contrary to earlier regulations, permitted employees to switch from a private to a public pension plan. New employees who did not choose a fund would be placed automatically in the public system.

The national commission that regulated the system of personal pension accounts in Mexico announced new procedures to simplify the transfer of retirement accounts from one fund (Afore) to another. Starting in August Chilean pension-management companies were required to offer at least four types of investment funds with varying percentages of assets to be invested in equities. (CHRISTIANE KUPTSCH; DAVID M. MAZIE)

HUMAN RIGHTS

The campaign for human rights moved in some dramatic new directions during 2002, particularly in promoting the attachment of criminal penalties to human rights abusers and increasing attention to the long-overlooked economic, social, and developmental elements of the status of human rights. Another factor affecting human rights was the threat posed by terrorism and antiterrorism activities.

Criminal Accountability. For the first time since the post-World War II war crimes trials in Japan, a head of state—Slobodan Milosevic, former president of Yugoslavia—was brought before an international court to face criminal charges based on major human rights violations that took place under his regime. Milosevic's war crimes trial before the International Criminal Tribunal for the Former Yugoslavia (ICTY) began on February 12. He was charged with genocide and crimes against humanity based on officially sanctioned policies of ethnic cleansing, forced migration, and the use of rape to punish and intimidate Muslim and Croat civilians in connection with Serbia's military and paramilitary operations in Bosnia and Kosovo.

Another innovative step in the expanding effort to apply criminal sanctions to human rights abusers was the establishment on July 1 of the International Criminal Court (ICC), a permanent international tribunal that would prosecute a wide variety of crimes wherever they might occur, including war crimes, genocide, crimes against humanity, and torture. By the end of the year, 87 governments had ratified and become parties to the ICC. One highly contentious aspect of the establishment of the ICC was the decision by the U.S. government to withdraw from the ICC process to seek special agreements with individual governments that would exempt U.S. citizens from the jurisdiction of the tribunal. The basis for these actions was the desire to prevent potential criminal prosecutions by the ICC of U.S. peacekeepers and other U.S. citizens as well as military personnel engaged in operations around the world. Critics were concerned that the U.S. position would undermine future efforts to hold accountable nationals from other countries who committed grave human rights abuses and other crimes against humanity.

Economic and Social Rights and the Right to Development. The important emphasis on the principle of "universality" in applying human rights standards was signaled by several events. The World Summit on Sustainable Development, held in August and September in Johannesburg, S.Af., brought international attention to such concerns as land reform, environmental pollution, unrestricted population growth, protection of the world's natural resources, and the problems faced by the poorest people. The plan of implementation drafted and approved at the official summit, which was submitted for approval to more than 100 world leaders attending the conference (U.S. Pres. George W. Bush did not attend), called for governments to act "with a sense of urgency" to work toward several goals, among them a substantial increase in the use of renewable sources of energy (such as solar power), a great improvement in the accessibility of clean water and sanitary facilities, and the phasing out of the use and production of chemicals harmful to humans and the environment. The plan was sharply criticized, however, for not setting binding timetables for compliance. An "antisummit" gathering of farmers, squatters, and the unemployed organized by the Landless People's Movement *(continued on page 314)*

Security vs. Civil Liberties

by Stephen J. Phillips

Technology was at the forefront of international efforts to fight terrorism and bolster security in 2002 in the wake of the terrorist attacks in the U.S. on Sept. 11, 2001. The rush to deploy new technologies and to give law-enforcement officials new investigative powers in cyberspace sparked concerns for the civil liberties of law-abiding citizens. For other observers, however, the threat posed by religious extremists and other shadowy groups bent on mass destruction gave security precedence over freedom.

In the U.S. debate continued on the implications of the antiterrorist USA PATRIOT Act enacted in October 2001. The new law, aimed at empowering authorities to move more nimbly against terrorist threats, relaxed legal checks on surveillance, granting the Central Intelligence Agency (CIA) and the Federal Bureau of Investigation (FBI) a freer hand to gather data electronically on citizens and resident foreigners. The legislation, approved by a sweeping majority in Congress, reduced the need for subpoenas, court orders, or warrants for eavesdropping on Internet communications, monitoring financial transactions, and obtaining individuals' electronic records. As part of criminal investigations, law-enforcement and intelligence agencies were authorized to track the Web sites that suspects visited and identify those to whom they sent e-mail. Internet service providers were required to turn over data on customers' Web-surfing habits to authorities on demand.

Many of the measures were hailed as necessary revisions of surveillance laws to keep increasingly sophisticated and determined terrorists at bay. Civil liberties advocates, however, worried that the PATRIOT Act's easing of judicial oversight and vague definition of legitimate subjects for electronic surveillance

opened it to abuse and could cast the legal dragnet too wide in the search for incriminating evidence. The legislation paved the way for wider deployment of the controversial FBI program formerly known as Carnivore—renamed, less menacingly, DCS 1000—which sifts e-mail for particular addresses or specific text strings (sequences of characters). In December 2001 it was reported that the FBI had developed "Magic Lantern," a so-called Trojan horse program designed to crack encrypted files and e-mails. The program could implant itself

surreptitiously in a suspect's computer via an e-mail message and then record keystrokes to obtain the user's passwords. In mid-2002 the Department of Justice (DOJ) announced Operation TIPS (Terrorism Information and Prevention System), a plan to recruit workers such as mail carriers and utility meter readers as informants to spot and report "suspicious activity."

Concerns about government access to personal information were not limited to the U.S. In June the British government, amid a public outcry,

Illustration by Mirko Ilić Corp.

posals, however, based on cards bearing unique biological identifiers—such as an iris scan or a digitized thumbprint—known as biometrics, as well as a microchip programmed with additional personal details. In September 2001 Malaysia mandated such a "smart card," dubbed the Mykad, for all citizens over the age of 12. Hong Kong geared up to overhaul its compulsory ID system with smart cards for its 6.8 million inhabitants in 2003. Officials hoped to crack down on illegal immigrants while easing bottlenecks at the territory's border with China. Border crossers would have their thumbprint scanned by an optical reader and could pass through the checkpoint in a matter of seconds if the print matched the digital replica on their card.

In July 2002 British ministers began a six-month public consultation to determine how an ID card scheme could be administered. The measure faced opposition from various quarters, ranging from civil libertarians to individuals concerned about bureaucratic overheads. Such a scheme would not come cheap either. The cost of issuing biometrics cards to the 60.2 million population was put at £3.1 billion (about $4.8 billion). Belgium planned to issue ID cards with embedded digital signatures.

Identity-authentication schemes were also contentious in the U.S. As an alternative to building an infrastructure from scratch, driver's licenses—held by more than 87% of the adult population—offered an obvious starting point for a de facto national scheme. The Driver's License Modernization Act of 2002, proposed in May, sought to set nationwide standards for licenses issued by each of the 50 states that would include embedded chips and biometrics data. The cards would be linked to networked databases, allowing officials to check out any suspicious activity.

Others feared that cards linked to databases would turn into internal passports to monitor citizens' movements. Privacy groups called for the U.S. government at the very least to spell out the uses to which data gleaned from credential checks could be put—anticipating "function creep," the tendency for information to be used for purposes beyond those originally envisaged. Public support for a national identity scheme appeared to cool as the memory of September 11 receded. A Pew Research Center poll conducted right after the attacks returned a 70% approval rating for such

a scheme, but support had dwindled to 26% by March 2002, according to a survey by Gartner Group.

The Enhanced Border Security and Visa Entry Reform Act mandated that by Oct. 26, 2003, all U.S. visas, as well as passports issued by visa-waiver countries, such as Australia, had to be machine-readable and tamper-resistant and had to incorporate biometric identifiers. In October 2002, the Immigration and Naturalization Service began fingerprinting tens of thousands of foreign visitors on arrival from designated, mainly Middle Eastern, countries.

Other technologies under consideration included scanners—tested at Orlando (Fla.) International Airport—that deployed low-level X-rays to subject airline passengers to virtual strip searches. Supporters said such drastic measures were necessary to deal with terrorists prepared to conceal explosives in body cavities, but critics branded them invasive. Another biometrics application was facial-recognition cameras, or "facecams." Such technology uses software to map facial characteristics, sounding an alarm if a certain proportion of features picked up by a camera match those of police mugshots. It has been used in London to collar criminals since 1998. In 2002 such cameras were installed in several American cities and airports. The systems, also condemned by civil libertarians, proved unreliable. Cameras tested at Palm Beach (Fla.) International Airport failed more than half the time to identify employees whose features were programmed into the database, while a trial in nearby Tampa did not make a single match in six months of use. Moreover, biometrics are only as effective as the comprehensiveness of the background information archives they scrutinize. Technologically sophisticated face scans or thumbprint matching probably would not have identified, much less foiled, the September 11 hijackers, as only 2 of the 19 were on the CIA's "watch list."

While no security panacea, technology puts some powerful counterterrorism tools at the disposal of governments, but the debate in 2002 showed that leaders must plot a judicious path to ensure that new techniques do not undermine the freedoms they are intended to protect.

Stephen J. Phillips is a freelance journalist and a U.S.-based information technology writer for the Financial Times.

shelved plans to give local government units and other administrative bodies the right to access an individual's telephone and e-mail records. Such privileges were given only to police, tax authorities, and security agencies. Across the world, debate raged over national identity cards to verify people's identity and to screen access to potential terrorist targets. Compulsory identification schemes, based on laminated ID cards, had been long-standing in countries as diverse as China, Argentina, and Spain. The latest pro-

Children sing before a backdrop of an enormous globe at the welcoming ceremony of the World Summit on Sustainable Development in Johannesburg, S.Af., on August 25.

AP/Wide World Photos

(continued from page 311)
and the Anti-Privatization Forum—held 32 km (20 mi) from the site of the official meetings—focused on the need to provide land and jobs to the homeless and unemployed in South Africa as well as to needy people elsewhere. Those in attendance condemned the global plan of action proposed by the official representatives at the summit as too weak and a "sell-out to business interests."

The antiglobalization movement—critical of how the restrictive-credit, loan-repayment, trade, and financial-assistance policies of developed nations and the international monetary institutions, such as the World Bank and the International Monetary Fund (IMF), were harming efforts by less-developed countries to meet the needs of their poorer citizens—mounted protests in September at the World Bank–IMF meetings in Washington, D.C. The demonstrators called for a reduction or forgiveness of loan repayments by less-developed countries, the elimination of trade barriers, broader access to global markets, and a greater focus on human rights concerns in the planning and administration of projects funded by the international monetary agencies.

Protestors gave special emphasis to the demand that debts owed by African nations suffering high rates of HIV-AIDS be canceled so that additional funds could be allocated to provide improved access to drug treatment in those countries. More than 600 demonstrators were arrested. The IMF reportedly agreed to move the issue of relieving the Third World's debt burdens to the top of its agenda, in what was described as "a dramatic new approach to resolving debt crises."

Antiterrorism Concerns. In the aftermath of the Sept. 11, 2001, terrorist attacks, the U.S. government instituted a variety of measures to deal with suspected terrorists that drew concerns from the international human rights community because of the restrictions these measures might place on civil liberties. (*See* Special Report.) Immediately after the attacks more than 1,200 aliens residing in the U.S. were arrested as suspected terrorists, placed in detention, and subjected to secret deportation proceedings without access to lawyers. More than 600 suspected al-Qaeda supporters who were captured during the fighting in Afghanistan were transported to a U.S. military base at Guantánamo Bay,

Cuba, where they were placed in indefinite detention under military control without access to lawyers or to the U.S. courts; they were treated as "unlawful enemy combatants" and therefore were not entitled to the usual protections afforded to prisoners of war. Two of these captives, John Walker Lindh and Yasar Esam Hamdi, were later found to have been born in the U.S. Because they were U.S. citizens, they were transferred to the U.S. for criminal trial in U.S. courts. Lindh entered into a plea agreement and received a 20-year sentence. Hamdi's case was pending, but questions continued to be raised about his status as a military prisoner and his being denied access to legal assistance.

Additional concerns about the human rights implications of U.S. treatment of alleged terrorists were raised in connection with the issuance by President Bush of a presidential order, shortly followed by regulations from the U.S. Department of Defense, authorizing the trial of alleged terrorists by specially constituted military tribunals that were designed to operate in secret with considerably reduced due-process protections. No military tribunal trials took place, however, nor were any scheduled.

A number of governments cited terrorism as a basis for limiting dissent or for punishing "separatists" and other minority groups. China labeled its Uighur minority, which had been seeking self-determination and independence, as linked to "international terrorism." Russia renewed its crackdown on rebels in Chechnya, particularly in the aftermath of the takeover of a Moscow theatre by Chechen terrorists, resulting in the death of at least 127 civilian hostages. South Korea introduced an "antiterrorism" bill criticized by human rights groups as unduly limiting free speech and assembly. India passed an ordinance giving police wide powers to arrest and detain suspected terrorists for up to six months without charge. Jordan amended its penal code to expand the definition of *terrorism* to cover a broad range of loosely defined offenses. Australia—already under criticism for having abruptly turned away some 430 mainly Afghan asylum seekers rescued by the Norwegian freighter *Tampa* and ordering the ship to leave Australian waters—used the September 11 attacks to justify a policy of keeping refugees in detention and to further tighten its immigration policies. (*See* WORLD AFFAIRS: *Australia:* Special Report.) The United Kingdom passed emergency legislation authorizing the detention of aliens without legal proceedings.

Individual Country Problems. Nigeria was condemned for the application of particularly severe punishments, such as execution by stoning and burial alive under the Shari'ah legal code that was adopted in the Muslim-dominated states. Particular attention was paid to the case of Amina Lawal, a 30-year-old woman who had been condemned to death by stoning by a Shari'ah court in Katsina state, for being in an adulterous relationship and bearing a child. (*See* photograph on page 232.) Zimbabwe forcefully expropriated the property of nearly 5,000 white farmers, ordering them to surrender their land to landless war veterans. More than 130 property owners who refused to give up their land were imprisoned. This policy was described by Australian Foreign Minister Alexander Downer as "ethnic cleansing on the farms."

In Myanmar (Burma) opposition leader Daw Aung San Suu Kyi was released from long-term house arrest, but most of the other 1,600 political prisoners remained in jail; widespread abuses such as forced labour, arbitrary arrests, and unlawful executions continued.

Human rights abuses and repressive policies continued in Aceh and Papua, two Indonesian provinces seeking greater independence, and a massive terrorist attack in Bali in October—also generally viewed as an act of international terrorism—raised fears about the imposition of restrictions on additional civil liberties and human rights. The human rights court established in East Timor to apply criminal sanctions to those participating in the ethnic cleansing that was instituted in response to the 1999 independence movement was roundly criticized by human rights advocates after many of the first 18 defendants subjected to trial on March 20 were acquitted or given lenient sentences.   (MORTON SKLAR)

REFUGEES AND INTERNATIONAL MIGRATION

At the beginning of 2002, the number of people of concern to the United Nations High Commissioner for Refugees (UNHCR) worldwide was 19.8 million—roughly one out of every 300 persons on Earth—compared with about 21.8 million at the beginning of 2001. This figure included some 12 million refugees, as well as several other categories of displaced or needy persons, notably asylum seekers (940,000); refugees who had returned home but still needed help in rebuilding their lives (460,000); local communities that were directly affected by the refugee movements; and some 5.3 million internally displaced persons (IDPs). Unlike refugees, IDPs are not protected by international law and are ineligible to receive certain types of aid. Though they did not fall within UNHCR's original mandate, certain specific IDP groups were given UNHCR protection in recent years following requests by the UN Secretary-General or the General Assembly. With a rising number of internal conflicts replacing interstate wars, the number of IDPs has increased significantly. According to UN estimates in 2002, there were between 20 million and 25 million IDPs worldwide, with major concentrations in The Sudan, Angola, Colombia, the Democratic Republic of the Congo, Afghanistan, Sri Lanka, Bosnia and Herzegovina, and countries of the former Soviet Union.

An estimated 3.9 million Palestinians were not included in UNHCR's mandate of responsibility as they were covered by a separate mandate of the United Nations Relief and Works Agency for Palestine Refugees in the Near East (UNRWA). Palestinians outside the UN-

RWA area of operations, however—such as those in Iraq, Libya, or Egypt—were considered to be of concern to the organization. At the beginning of 2002, they numbered almost 350,000.

The Search for Durable Solutions. UNHCR encourages voluntary repatriation as the best solution for displaced persons and often provides transportation and a start-up package, which might include cash grants and practical assistance such as farm tools and seeds. Field staff monitor the well-being of returnees in cases where their security might be at risk. The duration of such activities varies but rarely lasts more than two years when longer-term development support from other organizations is more appropriate. Keenly aware of the importance of such multilateral development support to ensure the sustainability of voluntary repatriation, UNHCR undertook new initiatives in 2002 to strengthen the transition from emergency humanitarian relief to longer-term development. An integrated approach described as the "4-Rs"—repatriation, reintegration, rehabilitation, and reconstruction—was proposed in partnership with governments and other international agencies.

Some refugees, however, cannot or are unwilling to return home, usually because they would face continued persecution if they did. In such circumstances UNHCR helps to find them new homes, either in the asylum country where they are living or in a third country where they can be permanently resettled. The last option continued to occupy an important place within UNHCR's global protection strategy, both as a durable solution and as a means of protecting individual refugees whose safety was in jeopardy. Although many countries agreed to accept refugees on a temporary basis during the early phases of a crisis, only some 20 states worldwide participate in official resettlement programs and accept quotas of refugees on an annual basis. In 2002 renewed efforts were made to expand the resettlement base and to encourage receiving countries to diversify their resettlement intake, increase the level of their quotas, and allow for flexible allocation of their quotas by region, country, or population.

Main Achievements in 2002. The conclusion of the process of Global Consultations on International Protection, which involved states, legal experts, nongovernmental organizations, regional bodies, and refugees themselves, was a notable milestone for UNHCR. The outcome of these consultations was the Agenda for Protection, a framework document that outlined a series of goals and objectives for addressing and managing contemporary refugee-protection challenges confronting individuals, states, and UNHCR. The Global Consultations helped revitalize the international protection regime, and the next challenge will be to sustain this momentum.

Another highlight of 2002 was the massive return movement of Afghan refugees and displaced persons following the establishment of the new Transitional Authority in Afghanistan. Significant headway was also made in a number of countries toward conflict resolution, political and social stabilization, and reintegration of refugees and displaced persons. Despite a fall in the number of returnees recorded in 2001—some 460,000 as opposed to 786,000 the previous year—in 2002 there was a sharp increase. In the first six months alone, 1.4 million Afghans repatriated from Pakistan, Iran, and Tajikistan. Other significant groups who returned to their countries of origin were 20,000 East Timorese who repatriated from Indonesia, 17,000 Croatian refugees from Yugoslavia, 15,000 Burundians from camps in Tanzania, 11,000 Somali refugees from Ethiopia, and 10,000 Angolans from Zambia.

Following East Timor's accession to independence in May and the return of the majority (some 222,000) of the East Timorese refugees who had fled in 1999, UNHCR announced that refugee status for East Timorese would cease on Dec. 31, 2002. Cessation of refugee status for Eritrean refugees was also scheduled to take effect on that date, and UNHCR informed those remaining outside the country—an estimated 325,000—of their options.

The development of the peace process in Sri Lanka and subsequent confidence-building measures prompted the spontaneous movement of tens of thousands of IDPs to their home villages. By the end of August, more than 183,000 IDPs had returned to their homes and another 1,000 refugees had returned from India. As a result, UNHCR was able to reorient its programs in Sri Lanka toward finding effective ways to address the protection and humanitarian needs of the remaining 620,000 IDPs and to create conditions conducive to sustainable reintegration, including that of some 64,000 refugees in India.

Main Challenges in 2002. The largest new refugee displacement in 2002 was recorded in Liberia, where civil conflict intensified in the course of the year. By September more than 81,000 new Liberian refugees had fled the country. More than 24,000 crossed into Sierra Leone, quadrupling the number of Liberian refugees in that country, which was itself struggling to reintegrate its own returning refugees. The second largest new displacement concerned some 11,000 refugees from the Democratic Republic of the Congo who fled to Tanzania. Other major new outflows concerned Sudanese refugees who arrived in Kenya (4,300), Uganda (4,300), and Ethiopia (2,000); Somali refugees who entered Yemen (5,300) and Kenya (3,200); and Angolan refugees who fled to Zambia (4,600). In Colombia the humanitarian crisis deteriorated further in 2002; according to official estimates, there were more than one million registered IDPs, and other sources suggested that the actual figure could be double that.

Largely as a result of the events of Sept. 11, 2001, in the United States, there were delays and a fall in the level of resettlement in a number of

countries in 2002. It was anticipated, however, that levels for 2003 would be brought back into line with those of previous years. During the first six months of 2002, UNHCR resettled 9,300 refugees of 43 different nationalities. The following accounted for 94% of the total number resettled: Afghanistan (2,440), Iran (1,170), Iraq (940), The Sudan (920), Bosnia and Herzegovina (700), Somalia (660), Vietnam (570), Croatia (420), Ethiopia (380), and Myanmar (170).

The number of pending asylum applications at the beginning of 2002 was 940,000, compared with 902,000 at the start of 2001. According to findings issued by the United Nations Population Division in October 2002, the number of migrants worldwide had more than doubled since 1975, with most living in Europe (56 million), Asia (50 million), and North America (41 million). The sociological changes that such movements have brought, coupled with the continued growth in human smuggling and trafficking, were undoubtedly motives for the intensified preoccupation with migration control demonstrated by many governments during the year. (*See* WORLD AFFAIRS: *Australia:* Special Report.) This inevitably affected attitudes toward asylum seekers, and the reactions of shock and outrage following the September 2001 terrorist attacks served to further exacerbate these restrictive tendencies. In a few countries anti-immigrant sentiments ran high during election campaigns, with some populist political leaders having indulged in negative stereotyping and denigration of asylum seekers. Recognition rates decreased, and UNHCR was obliged to devote considerable time and resources to communication and information campaigns to counter such xenophobia and intolerance.

For UNHCR, efforts to find solutions for refugees and others of concern remained firmly entrenched in the principle of sustainability in order to rebuild a stable social, political, and economic environment for refugees who repatriate or find local settlement opportunities in their host country. It became even clearer in 2002 that effective solutions to global displacement problems would be found only by addressing the whole chain of movement. The management of complex flows of refugees, asylum seekers, economic migrants, and other people on the move requires coherent and coordinated strategies and responses by the entire international community. (UNHCR)

An Eritrean at a refugee camp in The Sudan in June; at year's end Eritreans in The Sudan lost their status as refugees by order of UNHCR.

Sports and Games

The **WINTER OLYMPIC GAMES** in Salt Lake City, Utah, the association football (soccer) **WORLD CUP** in Japan and South Korea, and the **COMMONWEALTH GAMES** in Manchester, Eng., were the highlights of the world of sports in 2002.

ARCHERY

There were two world field archery championships in 2002. The International Field Archery Association (IFAA) held its biennial championship on extremely difficult terrain in Dollar, Scot., on August 4–9, while the Fédération Internationale de Tir à l'Arc (FITA) held its championship in Canberra, Australia, on moderate terrain, on September 10–14.

In the IFAA event, after five complete daily rounds with no rain (a small miracle), Jeff Button of the U.S. won the gold medal in the men's professional unlimited division with a total score of 2,752 out of 2,800 possible points. The silver went to Chris Deston and the bronze to Larry Wise, both also Americans. Carolyn Elder won the women's professional limited gold medal over fellow American Judy McCutcheon. In the hotly contested men's amateur unlimited division, England swept the medals. Chris White had a winning total score of 2,768. Second place went to Tim Mundon and third to Ben Jones.

At the five-day FITA championship, the top eight participants in each division shot five final targets apiece to determine the medal winners. The women's barebow champion was Reingild Linhart of Austria over Monika Jentges of Germany, while the bronze went to Britain's Patricia Lovell. The men's gold was won by Martin Ottosson of Sweden over Twan Cleven of The Netherlands and Italy's Danielle Bellotti. Laure Barczynski of France captured the women's recurve division 52–51 (out of 60) over silver medalist Cristina Loriatt of Italy. Another Italian, Irene Franchini, won the bronze. The men's recurve gold medal went to Italy's Michele Frangilli, who shot an outstanding 57 to beat German Sebastian Rohrberg's 55. Alan Wils of Great Britain won the bronze. In the men's compound bow division, American David Cousins beat Britain's Chris White 60–58, while Stephane Dardenne of France secured the bronze. The women's champion was France's Catherine Pellen over Sweden's Karin Teghammer. Third place went to Anne Laurila of Finland.

In the FITA team competition, Sweden captured both the men's and women's gold medals. Austria won the women's silver, and Australia took the bronze. The men's silver was won by Germany, with Italy finishing third.

(LARRY WISE)

AUTOMOBILE RACING

Grand Prix Racing. Michael Schumacher of Germany and the Ferrari team rewrote the Formula 1 (F1) record book with such alarming intensity during the 2002 F1 Grand Prix season that by the end of the year the Fédération Internationale de l'Automobile (FIA), the sport's governing body, had to force through a package of rule changes in a bid to spice up the racing going into 2003.

The metronomic consistency of Schumacher and his Ferrari F2002 made it look as though the famous Italian cars were running in an event that was totally separate from the remainder of the field, and if Schumacher was not winning, then Brazilian teammate Rubens Barrichello was usually taking the top spot on the winner's rostrum. Of 17 races, Schumacher won 11—a new record for wins in a single season—while Barrichello won 4. That left the remaining two race wins to be shared by the opposition—Ralf Schumacher (Michael's younger brother) triumphed for Williams/BMW in the Malaysian Grand Prix at Kuala Lumpur's Sepang circuit in March, and Scottish driver David Coulthard (McLaren/Mercedes) won the Monaco Grand Prix on the streets of Monte Carlo in May.

With his victory in the French Grand Prix at Magny-Cours in July, the elder Schumacher locked up his fifth driver's title with five races to go. This finally brought him level with Juan Manuel Fangio's record of five world championships and marked yet another significant milestone in the career of a German champion whose relentless precision was matched only by his unyielding determination. Beating the Argentine legend's record, however, was only one of Schumacher's achievements in a remarkable year in which his opposition appeared to have psychologically capitulated to his anticipated domination prior to the first race. He also helped Ferrari amass a record points total of 221 in the constructors' championship stakes—a tally that equaled the combined total of all the other teams on the circuit.

Most seasonal reviews of Grand Prix racing traditionally measure the achievements of the leading drivers against those of their closest rivals. In 2002, however, Schumacher stood above such comparisons. Other competitors might have had the basic driving talent to equal him, but few, if any, could match his application to behind-the-scenes development or the manner in which he gathered up and motivated the entire Ferrari team.

Barrichello, to his credit, drove superbly in what was cast as a supporting role from the start, and it was unfortunate that a season of such singular domination was spoiled by the controversy surrounding the Ferrari team's performance in the Austrian Grand Prix in May. In that race Barrichello appeared to have the measure of Schumacher and led from the start, but the Brazilian was told by the Ferrari team to relinquish the lead to his senior colleague. He did so just short of the finish line. The furor that enveloped the sport after what many people regarded as a "fixed" result led the FIA to introduce a rule that would ban team orders from influencing the outcome of a race. Ferrari vowed it would keep its team orders system, however.

The two acknowledged rising stars in the Grand Prix firmament both had patchy seasons. Colombian Juan Pablo Montoya, the winner of the 2000 Indi-

317

anapolis 500, had made the switch to F1 a year later as a member of the Williams/BMW team, but he did not manage to string things together as expected. Montoya smoked his way to seven pole positions but never managed to parlay any of them into race wins. In the McLaren camp Coulthard's young teammate Kimi Raikkonen of Finland made terrific progress in only his second year of F1 racing. If it had not been for a brief skid on a patch of oil at Magny-Cours, Raikkonen would have finished the French Grand Prix ahead of Schumacher.

It was not the merits of the drivers, however, but the shortage of sponsorship income that was holding everyone's attention by the end of the season. The year had started with the Prost team, which went into receivership in November 2001, going bankrupt only about a month before the start of the 2002 season. By the end of November 2002, the Arrows team was struggling to keep its head above water, while both Jordan and Minardi were finding it extremely difficult to raise what they considered to be adequate budgets for 2003. Jordan, together with British American Racing and Jaguar, had shed jobs during the year in a bid to keep costs under control. Yet as the season ended, there were signs that more economies were likely to be needed as television viewers across the globe reached for the off switch.

Arrows was dropped from the 2003 championship by the FIA authorities in early December. A week earlier the Jaguar F1 team had dismissed veteran Niki Lauda as team principal.

(ALAN HENRY)

U.S. Auto Racing. A constricting U.S. economy and escalating prize money helped shape an exciting but unsettling 2002 season in the many phases of American auto racing. While the National Association for Stock Car Auto Racing (NASCAR) remained the country's dominant sanctioning body, the Indianapolis (Ind.) Motor Speedway's Indianapolis 500, the oldest and richest auto race in the world, was one of the year's most controversial races. The 2001 winner, Helio Castroneves of Brazil, driving a Roger Penske Dallara-Chevrolet, was finally certified in July as the repeat winner of the May classic, withstanding a protest from second-place Paul Tracy in a Team Green Dallara. Tracy believed that he had passed Castroneves before the yellow caution was displayed in the 198th lap following a crash. The race ended

under yellow. Castroneves earned $1,606,215 to Tracy's $489,315. Brazilian Felipe Giaffone in a G-Force was third, and fourth-place Alex Barron shared rookie honours with Thomas Sheckter in a Dallara-Infiniti. Fifth place went to Eddie Cheever, Jr., also in a Dallara-Infiniti. Infiniti, which powered 7 of the 33 entries in the race, announced that it was retiring from the Indy Racing League (IRL), just as Toyota and Honda were switching major sponsorship to the IRL from Championship Auto Racing Team (CART) competition.

The depth of driving talent in the Indy 500, an IRL event, signaled that the IRL had achieved primacy in American single-seater racing. CART, in fact, had added more international and street events after losing established stars, while the IRL raced only on American ovals, many of them capable of accommodating more than 200,000 spectators. Despite the switch, IRL TV ratings and team support money declined. Sam Hornish, Jr., in a Dallara-Chevrolet won his second straight season IRL championship ahead of former CART drivers Castroneves and his Penske teammate Gil de Ferran of Brazil. Eight of the 15 IRL contests had margins of victory of less than a second.

Helio Castroneves of Brazil celebrates his second straight Indianapolis 500 victory in May.

The Speedway's major race, NASCAR's Brickyard 400 in August, was won by Bill Elliott in a Dodge. Elliott earned $449,056, besting a trio of Fords led by Rusty Wallace. Matt Kenseth finished third, and Ryan Newman ran fourth. Elliott had won the Pennsylvania 500 the previous week at Pocono. Thirty of the 43 entries in the Brickyard finished on the lead lap. The race was also notable because it was the first NASCAR event run on a track equipped with Steel and Foam Energy Reduction (SAFER) "soft wall" barriers at the corners, which were designed to mitigate crashes. NASCAR declared that the technology improved driver safety but that research was needed on a track-by-track basis. In early October SAFER barriers were installed at the Talladega (Ala.) Superspeedway. The organization also mandated other safety-related changes, including the use of head-and-neck restraint systems.

NASCAR operated three major national series and sanctioned points races for local tracks. NASCAR's Daytona 500, the marquee race of a 36-event Winston Cup season, offered $12.31 million in prize money. Winner Ward Burton (Dodge Intrepid), who took home $1,383,017, came from the 19th starting position and led for only the last five laps, just three of them under a green flag. He bested three Fords—driven by Elliott Sadler, Geoffrey Bodine, and Kurt Busch—and the Chevy of defending champion Michael Waltrip. After an earlier crash had taken out 18 cars, the survivors were halted for 20 minutes approximately 12.5 mi from the finish when race leaders Sterling Marlin (Dodge) and Jeff Gordon (Chevy) collided.

Marlin's season ended with an injured neck in September after he had led the standings for much of the season. In the end the NASCAR champion was Tony Stewart, Pontiac's star. After finishing last at Daytona, Stewart scored consistent high finishes, including victories at Atlanta, Richmond, and Watkin's Glen. He beat Ford's Mark Martin in the final standings by 38 points. Stewart won

$9,163,761. The top 34 Winston Cup drivers won over $2 million each. Mike Bliss won the Craftsman Truck series. In the Busch Grand National Series, Greg Biffle won easily over Jason Keller.

In contrast, the CART series title was won early. Cristiano da Matta of Brazil in a Lola-Toyota dominated the series with seven victories and seven pole starts in 19 events. He clinched the title at the Miami, Fla., street race in October, with three events left. In second place, 73 points back, was fellow Brazilian Bruno Junquera. In November da Matta left CART and signed a two-year deal with Toyota's Formula One team. CART signed a two-year pact to make Ford-Cosworth its official engine.

(ROBERT J. FENDELL)

Rallies and Other Races. Two organizations continued to compete for American sports racing supremacy. The American LeMans Series (ALMS) classic Sebring 12-hour race, held in part on the old Florida airport course at Sebring International Raceway, was won by Britain's Johnny Herbert in an Audi R8. Another Audi R8 driver, Tom Kristensen of Denmark, won the ALMS season's driver crown. Cadillac announced that it was retiring its Northstar racing prototype after it finished third and fourth behind two Audi R8s at the ALMS finale, the Petit LeMans at Road Atlanta.

In the sparsely attended Rolex 24 Hours of Daytona, sanctioned by the Grand American Road Racing Association, Didier Theys, Mauro Baldi, Max Papis, and Freddy Lienhard circled the Daytona road course a record 716 times in a Kevin Doran V-10–powered Dallara, six laps ahead of a Riley and Scott Mk IIIc driven by Scott Sharp, Robby Gordon, Jim Matthews, and Guy Smith. The Grand American series, in an attempt to change from a venue of rich privateers to cars more commercially attractive, announced rules meant to chop racing costs radically.

Marcus Grönholm (Peugeot) of Finland won five races in the 14-event world rally circuit and secured his second world championship in three years with 77 points. Despite having been stripped of his victory in the Rally of Argentina in May on a rules violation, Grönholm wrapped up the title with a win in New Zealand in October and then took the Rally Australia a month later. Petter Solberg (Subaru) of Norway won the final race of the season, the Rally of Great Britain. It was Solberg's first victory on the circuit, but it gave him enough points to finish sec-

ond in the final standings with 37 points, just ahead of Carlos Sainz (Ford) of Spain. In his first year driving for Subaru, four-time world champion Tommi Mäkinen of Finland was awarded his fourth consecutive Monte Carlo Rally (and a record 24th career victory) after the initial winner, Sébastien Loeb (Citroën) of France, was disqualified.

(ROBERT J. FENDELL;
MELINDA C. SHEPHERD)

BADMINTON

The temporary retirement of reigning Olympic badminton gold medalist Gong Zhichao opened the door for Denmark's Camilla Martin at the All England championships in Birmingham, Eng., in March 2002. Nevertheless, Martin had to overcome four formidable Chinese opponents on her way to her first All England title, including a semifinal victory over Dai Yun and a final-round win over world champion Gong Ruina. China fared better in other events, as the 2001 men's singles runner-up, Chen Hong, won his first title against Indonesian Budi Santoso. In women's doubles all four semifinal teams were Chinese, with Gao Ling and Huang Sui, the world number one team, emerging victorious. South Korea's Kim Dong Moon captured the men's doubles title with Ha Tae Kwon and the mixed doubles with Ra Kyung Min.

The Thomas Cup and the Uber Cup, team events for men and women, respectively, were held in Guangzhou, China, in May. As expected, the Indonesian men advanced to the Thomas Cup finals with a semifinal win over Denmark. In the other semifinal Malaysia staged a stunning upset of China, owing in large part to Malaysian Hafiz Hashim's comeback against Bao Chunlai. In the final it was Indonesian Hendrawan's turn to be the hero, clinching the deciding point against Malaysia's Roslin Hashim and securing his team's fourth Thomas Cup title in a row. In women's Uber Cup competition, China earned its third straight title and eighth overall by defeating South Korea in the final.

South Korea's Ra and Lee Kyung Won captured the Japan Open women's doubles by defeating Gao and Huang. At the Indonesian Open, Taufik Hidayat thrilled the home crowd with his men's singles win over Chen Hong, while Gong Ruina took the women's singles. Denmark's Peter Gade, a former world number one, marked his return to the

sport after an almost yearlong injury layoff with a victory at the U.S. Open in September. The Asian Games featured South Korean victories in all three doubles events, while Hidayat won the men's singles. In the Copenhagen Masters, China's Zhang Ning outplayed Martin, while the Indonesian men's doubles team of Sigit Budiarto and Candra Wijaya defeated Martin Lundgaard and Jens Eriksen. Gade dispatched Peter Rasmussen in an all-Danish men's singles final.

(DONN GOBBIE)

BASEBALL

North America. Although the 2002 season proceeded without interruption after management and labour agreed on a new contract late in the summer, Major League Baseball was affected by the threat of another job action and the proposal by Commissioner Bud Selig (see BIOGRAPHIES) to cut two franchises. As a result, overall attendance dropped 6.1% from the previous year, the biggest decrease since the season after the last strike ended in 1995. The average game attendance in 2002 was 28,168, the lowest since 1996 and down from 30,013 in 2001.

World Series. The Anaheim Angels won the World Series by defeating the San Francisco Giants four games to three in a series that featured a record for total runs, 85, and home runs, 21. The Angels, who finished 41 games out of first place in 2001, won game seven at Edison Field in Anaheim, Calif., on October 27 by a score of 4–1. Angels outfielder Garret Anderson hit a three-run double off Giants pitcher Livan Hernandez, and John Lackey earned the victory for Anaheim in a series that featured two wildcard (second-place) teams. Troy Glaus of the Angels was voted World Series Most Valuable Player (MVP).

In the series opener on October 19 in Anaheim, Giants slugger Barry Bonds hit a home run in his first-ever World Series and led his team to a 4–3 victory over Anaheim. Reggie Sanders and J.T. Snow also hit home runs for the Giants, while Glaus homered twice for the Angels. Pitcher Jason Schmidt recorded the victory, with 3⅓ innings of hitless relief by the Giants' bullpen.

In game two the following night, Anaheim rebounded to win 11–10. Tim Salmon hit a two-run home run in the bottom of the eighth to break a 9–9 tie, and the Angels then withstood another Bonds home run in the ninth. The

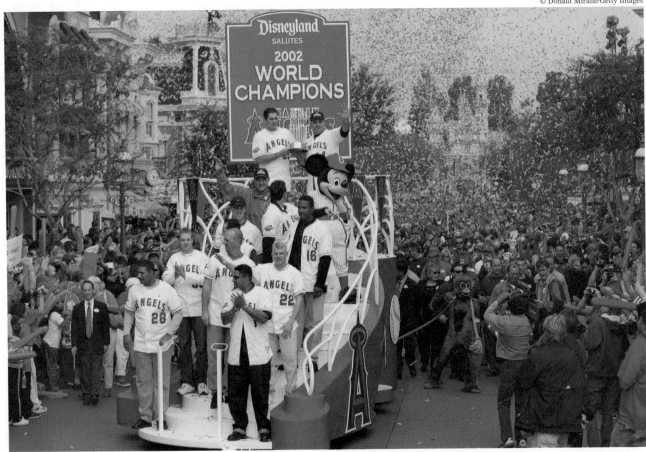

Disneyland, in Anaheim, Calif., holds a victory parade on October 29 to honour the World Series-winning Anaheim Angels.

Angels had jumped to a 5–0 lead in the first but then had fallen behind 9–7 in the highest-scoring World Series game since Florida beat Cleveland 14–11 in 1997. Francisco Rodriguez, a 20-year-old pitching sensation from Venezuela, recorded his fifth postseason victory, tying a mark established by Arizona's Randy Johnson in 2001.

When the series moved to Pac Bell Park in San Francisco on October 22, the Angels routed Giants starter Hernandez and romped to a 10–4 conquest. Hernandez incurred his first postseason defeat ever as the Angels accumulated 16 hits. Bonds hit another home run for the Giants.

In game four on October 23, David Bell singled in the winning run in the eighth inning to provide the Giants a 4–3 victory. The Angels took a 3–0 lead after three innings, but San Francisco tied the game in the fifth inning and then scored an unearned run in the eighth.

In game five on October 24, the Giants clobbered the Angels 16–4 to move within one victory of the championship. Jeff Kent hit two home runs and the Giants amassed 16 hits off four

pitchers, including the starter—and loser—Jarrod Washburn.

When the series returned to Anaheim on October 26, the Giants seemed poised to clinch the title when they jumped to a 5–0 lead with the help of Bonds's fourth home run and a two-run homer by Shawon Dunston. Scott Spiezio, however, hit a three-run homer for Anaheim in the seventh inning, and Glaus's two-run double in the eighth culminated the rally that brought the Angels a stunning 6–5 triumph in game six.

Play-offs. Adam Kennedy hit three home runs in game five of the best-of-seven American League Championship Series to lead the Angels to a 13–5 rout of the Minnesota Twins. The victory clinched the ALCS for the Angels four games to one and propelled them to their first World Series, in the 42nd year of the franchise. Kennedy became only the fifth player in major league history to hit three home runs in a postseason game. The Angels, who had been frustrated on several occasions in their pursuit of a pennant, exploded for 10 runs in the seventh inning before a

raucous home crowd of 44,835. Minnesota had won the first game of the series at home but then lost game two in Minneapolis. When the series moved to Anaheim, the Angels won games three, four, and five. Kennedy was voted MVP of the ALCS.

In the National League Championship Series, the Giants vanquished the St. Louis Cardinals four games to one. The clinching victory was by a score of 2–1 in San Francisco. The Cardinals took a 1–0 lead in game five, but the Giants tied the score in the bottom of the eighth inning on a sacrifice fly by Bonds and then won in the bottom of the ninth on a run-scoring single by Kenny Lofton. The Giants had won the first two games of the series in St. Louis. The Cardinals prevailed in game three at San Francisco despite a three-run home run by Bonds, but the Giants came back to win game four 4–3.

Despite a deep and experienced pitching staff, the New York Yankees were defeated by the Angels three games to one in the American League best-of-five Division Series. The Yankees rallied to win the opener at home 8–5, but

Anaheim took the second game at Yankee Stadium by a score of 8–6. In game three in Anaheim, the Angels pounded the Yankees 9–6. Then the Angels clinched their first victory in a play-off series since the team's inception by scoring eight runs in the fifth inning to eliminate New York.

Meanwhile, the Diamondbacks, who won the 2001 World Series against the Yankees, were also beaten in the best-of-five National League Division Series by the St. Louis Cardinals three games to none. In doing so, the Cardinals survived the formidable duo of Johnson and Curt Schilling, generally considered the best two starting pitchers on any major league rotation. Facing Johnson in the opener at Phoenix, the Cardinals rolled to a 12–2 conquest. Then, against Schilling in game two, the Cardinals prevailed. St. Louis completed its sweep at home by winning 6–3.

The Twins advanced by downing the favoured Oakland A's three games to two in the other American League Division Series. Minnesota came from a 5–1 deficit in game one to take a 7–5 decision and then lost game two at Oakland 9–1. Oakland won game three in Minneapolis 6–3 but lost game four by a score of 11–2. In the deciding contest at Oakland, the Twins scored three runs in the ninth and then withstood a three-run outburst by the A's to win 5–4.

The Giants took a similar path, winning game one of their National League Division Series at Atlanta. San Francisco lost game two in Atlanta and game three at home before registering an 8–3 triumph in game four. In the decisive game five in Atlanta, Bonds smacked a fourth-inning home run that proved to be the winning run in a 3–1 victory.

Individual Accomplishments. Bonds enjoyed a banner season, winning the National League (NL) batting title with a .370 average, hitting 46 home runs, and taking home a record fifth MVP award. The 38-year-old slugger smashed his 600th career home run on August 9 and thereby became only the fourth player in major league history, and the first in 31 years, to reach that mark, lagging only Hank Aaron (755 home runs), Babe Ruth (714), and Willie Mays (660). Bonds also walked a record 198 times—68 on intentional passes—and thus recorded an on-base average of .582, bettering the mark of .553 established by Ted Williams in 1941. Sammy Sosa of the Chicago Cubs led the NL in home runs with 49. Arizona's outstanding pitching tandem led the league in

victories—Johnson was 24–5 and Schilling 23–7.

Atlanta's John Smoltz led in saves with 55. Manny Ramirez of the Boston Red Sox led the American League (AL) in batting average with .349. Alex Rodriguez of the Texas Rangers had the most home runs in the AL, 57, and most runs batted in, 142. The top starting pitchers were Barry Zito of Oakland (23–5), Derek Lowe of Boston (21–8) and Pedro Martinez, also of the Red Sox (20–4). Lowe also pitched a no-hitter against Tampa Bay. In a game against the Chicago White Sox, Mike Cameron of the Seattle Mariners hit four home runs in one game, only the 13th player in history to do so. Shawn Green of the Los Angeles Dodgers, in a game against the Milwaukee Brewers, became the 14th player to mark that achievement. He also doubled and singled for 19 total bases, breaking the major league record of 18 established by Joe Adcock of the Milwaukee Braves in 1954. Luis Castillo of the Florida Marlins authored a consecutive-game hitting streak of 35, the longest since Paul Molitor's 39 with the Brewers in 1987.

Commissioner Bud Selig declared the 73rd All-Star Game a 7–7 tie after 11 innings because both the NL and AL teams had run out of pitchers.

Collective Bargaining Agreement. Under the threat of another work stoppage, management and labour settled on a new collective bargaining agreement (CBA) on August 30, the same date that the Major League Players Association had established as a strike deadline. The settlement came early in the morning, only hours before an afternoon game scheduled for Wrigley Field in Chicago stood to be the first cancellation. The four-year deal, which extended through Dec. 19, 2006, was hailed by Selig and union chief Donald Fehr as a breakthrough in a contentious relationship that had existed between ownership and the players since 1972. During that time, baseball had endured eight job actions, the most damaging of which resulted in cancellation of the 1994 World Series. Under terms of the new deal, in 2003 teams with payrolls over $117 million would be subject to a luxury tax; in 2004 the cutoff figure would be $120.5 million, and so on up to $136.5 million in 2006. The tax rate would start at 17.5% and could grow to as much as 40%.

The agreement also provided for increased revenue sharing, a system whereby the most profitable franchises

would contribute money to a pool designated for less-profitable teams. The union also agreed to testing for illegal steroids beginning in 2003. The CBA was seen as a victory for the owners, although the powerful union did delay by at least four years Selig's professed intent to eliminate 2 of the 30 teams—presumed to be the Minnesota Twins and Montreal Expos—because of their financial difficulties.

Little League World Series. Louisville, Ky., won the Little League World Series by defeating a team from Sendai, Japan, by a score of 1–0 before 41,000 spectators at Howard J. Lamade Stadium in Williamsport, Pa., on August 25. The star for Louisville was Aaron Alvey, who not only accounted for the only run with a first-inning home run but pitched a brilliant game, allowing just three hits and striking out 11. Alvey recorded 44 strikeouts in three starts and one inning of relief, breaking a tournament record. He also extended his string to 21 consecutive scoreless innings, another tournament record. Louisville became the first team ever from Kentucky to win the Little League World Series. Louisville also became the first American team to win the title since 1998, when Toms River, N.J., defeated Kashima, Japan. (ROBERT VERDI)

Latin America. The 2002 Caribbean Series was held in Caracas, Venez., on February 2–8. The Culiacán Tomato Growers (Tomateros), representing Mexico, compiled a 5–1 record to win the title. The Dominican Republic, represented by the Cibao Eagles (Águilas Cibaeñas), handed Mexico its only defeat and came in second with a 3–3 record. Venezuela (Magallanes Navigators [Navegantes]) and Puerto Rico (Bayamon Cowboys [Vaqueros]) tied for third place with 2–4 marks.

In Cuba Holguín defeated Sancti Spiritus four games to three to win the 41st Serie Nacional (National Series) championship. It was Holguín's first Cuban league title. Holguín had defeated Camagüey in the quarterfinals and Villa Clara in the semifinals to advance. Three-time defending champion Santiago de Cuba was eliminated by Villa Clara in the quarterfinals. The victory for Holguín capped off a dream season—it had won its four-team division with a 55–35 record after having finished in last place only a year earlier.

Five players who had been the core of the Cuban national team for 15 years were not on the 2002 squad. After the Serie Nacional, third baseman Omar Linares, first baseman Orestes Kinde-

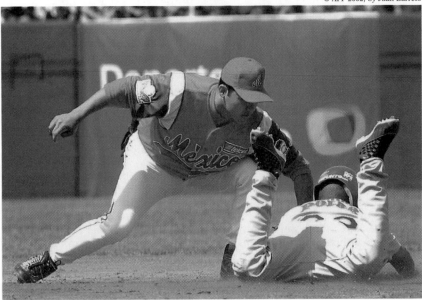

Mexican second baseman Alfredo Amézaga tags the runner out in the Caribbean Series on February 3; Mexico won the game and the series.

lan, second baseman Antonio Pacheco, shortstop German Mesa, and outfielder Luis Ulacia were allowed to go to Japan. Linares was going to play for the Chunichi Dragons in the Japanese Central League, while the others were to play for and coach amateur teams.

The Mexico City Red Devils defeated the Mexico Tigers (who had recently moved from Mexico City to Puebla) four games to three to win the Mexican League championship series. It was the Red Devils' 13th league title.

(MILTON JAMAIL)

Japan. The Yomiuri Giants won the 2002 Japan Series by completing a four-game sweep over the Seibu Lions. The Giants claimed their 20th Japan Series title, the most in Japanese baseball history, and their first since 2000. Tomohiro Nioka, who belted a decisive grand slam in game three and had three hits in each of the first three games, was named series Most Valuable Player (MVP).

Hideki ("Godzilla") Matsui, Yomiuri's cleanup hitter, just missed winning the triple crown during the 140-game regular season. Matsui, the Central League MVP, led the league with 50 home runs and 107 runs batted in, but his .334 batting average was second to Kosuke Fukudome of the Chunichi Dragons, who had a .343 average. Matsui became a free agent and announced shortly after the Japan Series his intention to play in the North American major leagues. Yomiuri hurler Koji Uehara, with a 17–5 record, won his second

Sawamura Award as the best starting pitcher of the year.

Seibu cleanup batter Alex Cabrera, formerly of the Arizona Diamondbacks, was named the MVP of the Pacific League as he tied Japan's single-season record of 55 home runs, set by Japanese baseball legend Sadaharu Oh in 1964 and tied by Osaka Kintetsu Buffaloes slugger Karl ("Tuffy") Rhodes in 2001. Cabrera, along with his teammates, Kazuo Matsui (with a .332 batting average and 36 home runs) and closer Kiyoshi Toyoda (38 saves and a 0.78 earned run average), led the Lions to dominate opponents with a regular-season record of 90–49.

(HIROKI NODA)

BASKETBALL

Professional. The Los Angeles Lakers, coached masterfully by Phil Jackson, won their third straight National Basketball Association (NBA) championship in 2002, leaving no doubt that another dynasty had emerged to claim its place among the pro game's all-time great teams. With two superstars, Shaquille O'Neal and Kobe Bryant (*see* BIOGRAPHIES), abetted by an able cast of extras, the Lakers proved potent in the clutch.

Their season, however, had teetered on the brink of disaster in the Western Conference play-off finals with the talent-laden Sacramento Kings. Trailing 3–2 in the best-of-seven series, the Lakers beat back the Kings to take

Game 6. Then they captured the winner-take-all showdown to keep their championship run alive.

After that emotional escape, rolling to a "three-peat" in the NBA finals proved easy. The upstart New Jersey Nets had survived the Eastern Conference play-offs but were no match for a Shaq attack, going down in the finals in a 4–0 sweep. O'Neal averaged a whopping 36.3 points and 12.3 rebounds in those four games. Battering and bullying his way through would-be defenders, he scored 145 points, shattering the NBA's individual scoring record for a four-game final series.

Understandably, O'Neal was named Most Valuable Player in the championship round, taking that honour for the third straight time. Only Michael Jordan had accomplished that feat before, doing it twice with the Chicago Bulls (in 1991–93 and 1996–98). A cloud of doubt arrived to hang over the Lakers' "four-peat" aspirations, however, when O'Neal subsequently pulled out of the world championship tournament. The towering veteran elected to have surgery on a painfully arthritic big toe and faced the prospect of missing training camp and perhaps the early part of the 2002–03 season.

Despite the players' heroics, it was coach Jackson who emerged as the main history maker when the Lakers ended the series and the season with a 113–107 victory over the Nets. It was his 156th play-off win, eclipsing Miami Heat coach Pat Riley's record. Jackson also tied legendary Boston Celtics coach Red Auerbach's mark of nine NBA crowns.

Robert Johnson, the founder of Black Entertainment Television, won a bid on December 18 for an NBA-franchised team in Charlotte, N.C., and thus became the first African American NBA team owner.

A dramatic 3-point basket by rookie guard Nikki Teasley in the final seconds gave the Los Angeles Sparks their second straight Women's National Basketball Association title with a 69–66 victory over the New York Liberty. The win sealed a 2–0 finals sweep for the Sparks, led by Lisa Leslie, the most valuable player of the championship series.

College. Mike Davis, the unheralded coach of Indiana University's overachieving basketball team, just missed capturing his first National Collegiate Athletic Association (NCAA) tournament title. The Hoosiers fell to Maryland 64–52 in the tourney final at the Georgia Dome in Atlanta. Many basketball experts and even some Indiana fans had ticketed the young coach—Davis turned 42 in September—for failure in the daunting task of succeeding the legendary Bobby Knight. Knight, who had resumed his coaching career at Texas Tech, found himself on the sidelines early in the 2002 NCAA tournament. Davis and the Hoosiers just kept rolling, right into the Final Four.

The Hoosiers astonished everyone by storming through the South Regional as a number five seed, knocking top-seeded Duke, the defending national champion, off its perch. Then it was on to Atlanta to continue the parade of upsets in Indiana's first Final Four appearance since 1992. The Hoosiers sent number four seed Oklahoma home to

Lisa Leslie of the Los Angeles Sparks goes to block a shot in game two of the WNBA finals; the Sparks beat the New York Liberty two games to none.

reach the winner-take-all showdown with Maryland.

Maryland, however, was eager to ease the sting of having lost a big lead—and the game—to Duke a year earlier. Juan Dixon, Maryland's senior all-American guard, tallied a game-high 18 points in the championship clash. His clutch three-point basket snuffed out a second-half Indiana rally and put the Terrapins back in front to stay.

Behind for most of the game, the Hoosiers grabbed a short-lived lead midway through the final half, but Dixon's accurate outside shooting down the stretch sealed the victory for Maryland.

In a bid to avoid NCAA sanctions and ostracism by rival teams, the University of Michigan imposed stiff penalties on its basketball team after acknowledging that several players had accepted illegal payments totalling some $616,000 from a fan. The university agreed to repay postseason receipts, give up scores for about five years of games (including four team championships), and be ineligible for 2003 NCAA and NIT tournaments.

In women's college basketball, Connecticut was the whole show in 2001–02, with the kind of year undreamed of on any level of competition. The Huskies defeated Oklahoma 82–70 in the NCAA tournament final to capture their third national championship in seven years and their second in three. The victory sealed an incredible 39–0 season record for the team, which rolled up an average victory margin of 35.4 points per game. Surrounded by a cast of talented seniors, Connecticut's charismatic coach Geno Auriemma was able to play his entire roster most nights. That provided valuable experience for the younger Huskies, boding well for their bid to keep Auriemma's domination rolling into the 2003 season. Along with senior captain Sue Bird, who was hailed as one of the nation's top guards, the

Huskies lost starters Swin Cash, Tamika Williams, and Asjha Jones. Although Bird (the number one pick; chosen by the Seattle Storm), Cash (number two), Jones (number four), and Williams (number six) were chosen by different teams, most observers labeled them the best-ever group of WNBA recruits from the same school in the same year. (ROBERT G. LOGAN)

International. The basketball calendar in 2002 was dominated by the 14th Fédération Internationale de Basketball (FIBA) men's world championships, held in Indianapolis, Ind., August 29 to September 8. Yugoslavia defied all expectation by winning its fifth world crown in the spiritual home of the sport, the United States. The tournament was likely to be remembered as the most extraordinary in the event's 52-year history, because the National Basketball Association (NBA) players representing the U.S. did not even contest a medal.

The preliminary rounds in Indianapolis were expected to shuffle the pack to produce a final between the U.S. and Yugoslavia, but the tournament soon departed from the script. The U.S. won its preliminary group unbeaten, but Yugoslavia finished second in its group after losing 71–69 to Spain. In the next round Yugoslavia lost 85–83 to Puerto Rico, and the U.S. was beaten 87–80 by Argentina. Suddenly, instead of playing for gold, Yugoslavia and the U.S. faced a sudden-death quarterfinal. Ironically, NBA Sacramento Kings teammates Vlade Divac and Peja Stojakovic combined for 36 points for Yugoslavia as their homeland held on for an 81–78 win. In the semifinals Argentina outscored Germany 6–2 in the final 45 seconds for an 86–80 win, while Yugoslavia recovered from being down 48–39 at halftime to beat New Zealand 89–78. The final was a triumph for Yugoslavia's Dejan Bodiroga, who scored nine consecutive points in the final 2 min 16 sec of regulation play to force overtime, in which Argentina finally fell 84–77. Germany defeated New Zealand 117–94 for third place, and the U.S. lost 81–75 against Spain to finish sixth.

The U.S. drew some consolation from the women's national team, which retained its title by beating Russia 79–74 in the world championship final in Nanking, China, on September 25. Women's National Basketball Association duo Sheryl Swoopes of the Houston Comets and Lisa Leslie of the L.A. Sparks led the U.S. scorers with 18 and 17 points, respectively.

AP/Wide World Photos

Houston Rockets centre Yao Ming towers over the Los Angeles Lakers' Samaki Walker. The 2.26-m (7-ft 5-in) Yao needed permission from the China Basketball Association and the Fédération Internationale de Basketball to join the NBA.

European club basketball continued to be split between the world governing body, FIBA, and the breakaway Union des Ligues Européennes de Basket-Ball (ULEB), which attracted the leading clubs and sponsors, major marketing deals, and television coverage. Greek club Panathinaikos won the ULEB's Euroleague title by defeating Kinder Bologna of Italy 89–83 in the 2002 final in Bologna on May 5. Meanwhile, FIBA reorganized its men's competitions, merging the Korac and Saporta cups into the Champions Cup, which in its initial stages featured three conferences: North, South, and West.   (RICHARD TAYLOR)

BILLIARD GAMES

Carom Billiards. Swedish carom billiards star Torbjörn Blomdahl ended 2001 with his ninth Billiards Worldcup Association title, scoring 325 points and winning four of seven tournaments during the year. He was trailed by Semih Sayginer of Turkey, with 277 points and two tournament titles, and Dick Jaspers of The Netherlands, with 240 points and one title. Blomdahl racked up points by capturing the Oosterhout, Neth., and Lugo, Spain, tournaments in late 2001. He also led the world rankings (calculated separately on a 12-month basis) going into 2002. In February Blomdahl defeated Belgian legend Raymond Ceulemans, the 2001 Union Mondiale de Billard (UMB) champion, for the world three-cushion Supercup. In the summer it was announced that Ceulemans was to be knighted by King Albert II of Belgium for his contributions to the international sports scene.

Frédéric Caudron of Belgium began 2002 with a strong challenge, taking the Dutch Open Grand Prix in January with an impressive 1.721 average and then following with a win and a 1.670 average in Oporto, Port., in March. Blomdahl managed only an unfamiliar third place in Portugal despite having a 1.909 average. In June Jaspers won his fourth Crystal Kelly tournament with a record-setting grand average of 2.536. The ninth edition of this lavish invitational event brought eight of the top three-cushion specialists together for 50-point round-robin competition. Sayginer and Caudron tied for second place.

Sang Chun Lee's 12-year reign as U.S. national champion came to an end in February as his fellow American Pedro Piedrabuena was named 2002 champion. Piedrabuena averaged 2.083 in the title match with Lee, toppling the former champion 50–25 with a high run of 12.

In October Italy's Marco Zanetti won his first UMB world championship, besting Dion Nelin of Denmark in the final with an average of 2.360. Zanetti had defeated Jaspers in the semifinal, while Blomdahl, Sayginer, and Caudron all fell in the quarterfinals.

Pocket Billiards. Organizations rather than competition made the biggest news in the pocket billiards world in 2002. A new professional men's organization continued to develop in the U.S., and a new international tour organization took shape in Japan. The Billiard Congress of America (BCA) took steps toward becoming an Olympic governing body. The manufacturer-dominated BCA approved a bylaw change that added significant player representation to its board of directors and brought its structure into line with U.S. Olympic Committee requirements.

The United Poolplayers Association (UPA) became a legal entity composed of most of the top male players. The UPA was launched by American player Charlie Williams and a handful of supporters in an attempt to fill the gap left when the R.J. Reynolds Tobacco Co. discontinued its Camel Pro Billiards Series after the 1999 season. By mid-2002 the UPA had established standards and scheduled its first three self-promoted tournaments.

The International Billiard Council (IBC) made big news in late 2001 with its ¥100,000,000 (about $800,000) tournament in Tokyo, won by Efren Reyes of the Philippines. The 2002 IBC Tour got under way in May at the Nanki Classic in Shirahama, Japan. American Cory Deuel won $14,000 for first place, in contrast to Reyes's $163,000 for first place in the 2001 kick-off event in Tokyo. As the season proceeded, the top prize settled at around $7,000. In Munich, Ger., in early June, Filipino Francisco Bustamante pocketed $6,000 for first place. At the Holland Open in July, Ralf Souquet of Germany defeated 2001 world champion Mika Immonen of Finland to take the $7,000 prize; then in September he took home another $7,000 for beating American Johnny Archer at the U.S. championship in Nashville, Tenn. In November Souquet lost the season-ending Tokyo 9-Ball International (and the $10,000 top prize) to Bustamante, but the German earned enough points to be named the overall IBC Tour champion.

The Women's Professional Billiard Association (WPBA) marked its 25th year

Carla Bonner

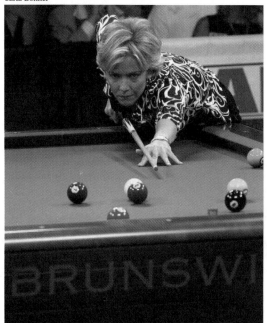

England's Allison Fisher lines up a shot en route to winning the WPBA Midwest Classic in August.

by expanding the field of its Classic Tour events from 48 to 64. The WPBA tour continued to be dominated by two former snooker players, England's Allison Fisher and Northern Ireland's Karen Corr. Corr had swept the entire 2001 season, but Fisher battled back and took the 2002 season's first title in March at Valley Forge, Pa., and the Amway Cup in Taiwan in April. Corr came back to win the Spring Classic in Viejas, Calif., and the BCA Open in Las Vegas, Nev., in May, but she lost to Fisher at the Fall Classic in New York City in October. Sweden's Helena Thornfeldt, who resided in the U.S., upset the status quo with a win in September at the U.S. Open in Albuquerque, N.M. It was her first WPBA title since 1997.

Perhaps pocket billiards' most-watched event, the World Pool–Billiard Association (WPA) men's world pool championship, held in Cardiff, Wales, in July, was televised in over 70 countries. In the U.K., viewers were treated to more than 60 hours of live coverage, including American Earl Strickland's nail-biting 17–15 victory over Busta-mante for the $65,000 top prize. Earlier in the month, Liu Shin-mei of Taiwan bested Corr for the women's WPA title, worth $12,000.

In September live televised pool coverage returned in the U.S. after a decade-long hiatus with Billiard Club TV's presentation of the finals of the U.S. Open 9-Ball Championship live on pay-per-view satellite television. Souquet defeated Filipino-born Canadian Alex Pagulayan 13–11 in the exciting final just three minutes before the broadcast was scheduled to end.

Snooker. The 2002 men's professional snooker season ended with a thrilling world championship title in May at the Crucible Theatre in Sheffield, Eng. The tournament produced a new champion, a new rankings leader, and remarkable television ratings. In a 35th-frame victory, England's Peter Ebdon defeated Stephen Hendry 18–17 to deny the Scotsman his eighth world championship title. The suspenseful final drew 7.5 million viewers for a 60% share of the TV audience. Ebdon entered the season finale ranked number seven in the world and moved up to number three, while 2001 champ Ronnie O'Sullivan of England consoled himself over the loss of his title with the number one ranking.

Despite hours of TV coverage and loyal audiences, the loss of tobacco-company sponsors loomed large. Tobacco sponsorship was due to begin phasing out in Europe in 2003, much as it had in the U.S. in the late 1990s. In July the players, who controlled the game through the World Professional Billiards and Snooker Association (WPBSA), held a vote to choose from the companies proposing to take over management of the professional tour. None of the three companies received a majority of the vote, however, and after one of the companies withdrew its proposal, the WPBSA decided to appoint World Snooker Enterprises as its new commercial management team.

(KIRSTIN PIRES)

BOBSLEIGH, SKELETON, AND LUGE

Bobsleigh. American bobsleigh driver Todd Hays and his crew began the 2001–02 season with three consecutive gold medals on the World Cup circuit before returning to the U.S. to prepare for the Winter Olympics in Salt Lake City, Utah. Taking full advantage of the Americans' absence, Swiss teams led by Martin Annen went on to clinch both the two- and four-man World Cup season titles decisively.

At the Winter Games, the Germans won gold in both the two- and four-man competitions. Christoph Langen and teammate Markus Zimmermann took the two-man gold, while André Lange drove his four-man sled to victory. In four-man action, the U.S. men broke their 46-year Olympic medal drought by claiming the silver and bronze medals. Hays led his team to the silver, and five-time Olympian Brian Shimer's team took the bronze.

In women's action, German drivers dominated World Cup competition, with Susi Erdmann edging out Sandra Prokoff for the season title. American driver Jean Racine finished in third place in the drivers' standings.

With all eyes on the inaugural women's bobsleigh competition at the Winter Games, Americans Jill Bakken and Vonetta Flowers surprised the field and broke the track record on their way to the gold medal. Prokoff and Ulrike Holzner broke the push record and took the silver medal. Erdmann and Nicole Herschmann captured the bronze.

Skeleton. The 2001–02 men's skeleton season was dominated by Gregor Stähli of Switzerland. He went undefeated in the first four of five total World Cup races and finished first in season standings. American Chris Soule edged Stähli in the season finale in Switzerland; it was Soule's first career World Cup win. Soule ranked second for the season, and Martin Rettl of Austria took third place overall.

In women's skeleton, each World Cup race produced a different winner. The most consistent slider was Great Britain's Alex Coomber, who was eventually crowned World Cup season champion.

At the Winter Games, American sliders dominated the two-heat races, collecting three of the six medals in the sport, which returned to Olympic competition after a 54-year hiatus. Third-generation Olympian Jim Shea, Jr., slid to victory in heavy snow. (*See* BIOGRAPHIES.) Tristan Gale and Lea Ann Parsley went 1–2 in the women's race.

(JULIE URBANSKY)

Luge. The 2001–02 World Cup season proved to be a remarkable one for the German team. In women's singles action, Germany dominated every race, with Silke Kraushaar capturing the overall World Cup gold medal. Another German slider, Sylke Otto, placed second overall. Barbara Niedernhuber finished the World Cup competition in third place, completing the sweep for

Jill Bakken and Vonetta Flowers of the U.S. cheer after capturing the women's bobsleigh gold medal at the Winter Olympics in Salt Lake City, Utah.

the German team. Germany also swept the women's singles podium at the Winter Olympics in Salt Lake City, Utah. Otto led the way, followed by Niedernhuber and Kraushaar, who won the silver and bronze, respectively.

In men's action, Austria's Markus Prock won the overall World Cup gold medal, followed by Italy's Armin Zöggeler and Germany's Georg Hackl. The Olympic competition was a showdown of these top three sliders. Hackl fell to Zöggeler in an action-packed men's singles race but became the first Winter Olympian ever to win five consecutive Olympic medals. Prock slid to the bronze medal.

In doubles action, Patric Leitner and Alexander Resch of Germany raced to the Olympic gold. Americans Mark Grimmette and Brian Martin, the defending 1998 Olympic bronze medal-

ists, blazed the last run to take the silver medal. Fellow Americans Chris Thorpe and Clay Ives won the bronze. (JANELE M. HINMAN)

BOWLING

World Tenpins. The annual increase in the number of countries participating in the World Tenpin Bowling Association (WTBA) Bowling World Cup had been the hallmark of the tournament's 37-year history, and in November 2001, players from a record 88 nations were on the lanes in Pattaya, Thai. In the men's two-game grand final, Norwegian Kim Haugen defeated Ahmed Shaheen of Qatar 528–402. Japan's Nachimi Itakura won over Liza del Rosario of the Philippines 504–448 for the women's title.

The first major event of 2002, the World Ranking Masters, took place in Ålborg, Den., in May, with the top eight women and eight men from each of the three WTBA geographic zones. The men's final was a duplicate of the 2001 European championship, which Gery Verbruggen of Belgium lost to Anders Öhman of Sweden. This time, Verbruggen had his revenge and defeated Öhman. In the women's final Jesmine Ho, the 2001 victor, had a chance to repeat, but fellow Singaporean Jennifer Tan put an end to her dreams.

Two major European events were held in July. At the European Cup teams event in Mülheim, Ger., for the fourth time in a row, the Finnish women secured the gold medal, beating the Germans in the final match 382–366. In the men's division Norway continued its golden year, besting Sweden 439–337 in the final.

Later in the month the British girls dominated the European youth championships in Rome, capturing four gold, three silver, and two bronze medals. All three qualifiers for the grand final were from England. In the last match Holly Towersey, the all-events champion, outclassed teammate Jemma Smith 403–357. On the boys' side Sweden was on top with two golds, one silver, and a bronze. The all-events king was Peter Smits of The Netherlands.

Less than two weeks later, the world youth tenpin championships were held in Pattaya. Angkana Netruiseth of Thailand won the girls' singles, but England captured the girls' doubles and team event. In the boys' competition the singles winner was Yannaphon Larpapharat of Thailand, the best duo came from South Korea, and the best team was from Sweden. (YRJÖ SARAHETE)

U.S. Tenpins. The reorganized Professional Bowlers Association (PBA) put its show on the road in 2001–02 in the form of a 19-tournament schedule on ESPN cable television. The PBA president, Steve Miller, reported an 18% increase in TV ratings over the previous season, a 34% jump in PBA membership, and a 35% increase in tournament entries. The renewed interest was attributed largely to the fact that the prize fund went from $1.8 million to $4.3 million.

In March 2000 the PBA had been rescued from bankruptcy and converted from a nonprofit into a potentially for-profit corporation. In 2002, 70 top bowlers were given stock options, believed to be a first for any sports organization. One TV event, the PBA Tournament of Champions, had to be dropped because of a cancellation by its sponsor. During the summer, however, the tournament was reinstated as the first major event of the 2002–03 season. It was held in Uncasville, Conn., in December and was won by Jason Couch.

The 22-event schedule for 2002–03 included two tournaments in Japan. In the Dream Bowl 2002, members of the Japanese PBA and the South Korean PBA, as well as Japanese and Chinese amateurs, competed. Hugh Miller of Seattle, Wash., defeated Japan's Yukio Yamazaki 431–427 in a two-game match for the $40,000 prize. In the Oronamin C Japan Cup, Robert Smith of Simi Valley, Calif., won $50,000 by topping Chris Barnes of Dallas, Texas, 224–222.

The plan to consolidate the four major nonprofessional bowling groups into a single-membership organization was stalled when delegates to the Women's International Bowling Congress (WIBC) delayed their vote until 2004. The consolidation had been approved by the men's American Bowling Congress (ABC), the Young American Bowling Alliance (YABA), and USA Bowling, which oversaw American participation in international events.

In 2002 membership in the ABC slipped 5.3%, to 1,866,023, while the WIBC fell 7.3%, to 1,481,163. YABA membership rose 3,599, to 409,465. High scores, however, were slightly ahead of the previous season—41,303 ABC-sanctioned 300 games were bowled by men, 915 by women, and 1,213 by youngsters in YABA leagues. Karen Rosenburg of Rolla, Mo., rolled the highest three-game series in WIBC history, 878, in a league match in Rolla. (JOHN J. ARCHIBALD)

BOXING

The much-anticipated match between World Boxing Council (WBC) and International Boxing Federation (IBF) heavyweight champion Lennox Lewis (U.K.) and former heavyweight champion Mike Tyson (U.S.) took place in Memphis, Tenn., on June 8, 2002. While the fight itself was a one-sided affair that ended with Lewis's scoring an eighth-round knockout, the bout was a financial blockbuster. Approximately 1.8 million homes purchased the pay-per-view telecast, setting a new all-time revenue record of $103 million. The live gate of $17.5 million, contributed by a crowd of 15,327, also established a new all-time record.

Tyson made a promising start in the first round but soon fell prey to Lewis's left jabs and right-hand counters. In the eighth round a bleeding Tyson was dropped by a right uppercut. He regained his feet, but the fight was stopped when Lewis knocked him down again with a right to the side of the jaw. The emphatic victory over Tyson further secured Lewis's status as the best heavyweight in the world.

John Ruiz (U.S.) defended the World Boxing Association (WBA) heavyweight title against Kirk Johnson (Can.) on July 27 in Las Vegas, Nev. The unappealing bout was filled with clinches and fouls, with Johnson being disqualified in the 10th round for repeatedly hitting Ruiz below the belt. When Lewis relinquished the IBF title in September, former champion Evander Holyfield (U.S.) and Chris Byrd (U.S.) were matched for the vacant title. The bout was held in Atlantic City on December 14, with the skillful Byrd boxing his way to a 12-round decision over the 40-year-old Holyfield.

Ukrainian Wladimir Klitschko became a major force in the heavyweight division in 2002, scoring knockout victories over former IBF titleholder Frans Botha (S.Af.), former Olympic gold medalist Ray Mercer (U.S.), and high-ranking contender Jameel McCline (U.S.). Klitschko was expected to challenge Lewis in 2003.

Roy Jones, Jr. (U.S.), defended the WBA, WBC, and IBF light heavyweight titles twice in 2002. On February 2 he knocked out Glen Kelly (Australia) in the seventh round of a bout held in Miami, Fla. Then on September 7 Jones knocked out Clinton Woods (U.K.) in the sixth round of a match held in Portland, Ore.

Bernard Hopkins (U.S.), holder of the WBA, WBC, and IBF middleweight titles, set a new division record for successful defenses by knocking out Carl Daniels (U.S.) in the 10th round on February 2 in Reading, Pa. Hopkins's 15th defense eclipsed the mark established by Carlos Monzón (Arg.) in 1977.

In a high-profile title-unification bout, WBC super welterweight (junior middleweight) champion Oscar de La Hoya (U.S.) knocked out WBA titleholder Fernando Vargas (U.S.) in the 11th round of a grudge match held in Las Vegas. An intense personal rivalry between the fighters created much interest, and approximately 900,000 homes purchased the pay-per-view telecast, which generated an estimated $45.6 million and thereby made it the second richest nonheavyweight fight in history. Vargas's postfight urinalysis revealed anabolic steroids in his system. He was fined $100,000 and suspended for nine months by the Nevada State Athletic Commission.

In the biggest upset of the year, Vernon Forrest (U.S.) captured the WBC welterweight title by winning a unanimous 12-round decision over previously undefeated Shane Mosley (U.S.) on January 26 in New York City. Forrest emphasized his superiority over Mosley by winning another 12-round decision in the rematch on July 20 in Indianapolis, Ind. Neither fight was particularly entertaining, and both featured almost as much holding as punching.

Unified WBA, WBC, and IBF super lightweight (junior welterweight) titleholder Kostya Tszyu (Australia) made only one defense in 2002, winning a unanimous 12-round decision over Ben Tackie (Ghana) on May 18 in Las Vegas. Tszyu, usually considered more of a puncher than a boxer, impressed observers with a flawless exhibition of technical craftsmanship against Tackie.

In the year's most celebrated fight, Micky Ward (U.S.) won a 10-round majority decision over Arturo Gatti (Can.) on May 18 in Uncasville, Conn. The super lightweight nontitle bout was a savage give-and-take brawl that evoked comparisons with many of the great fights of the past. The highly anticipated rematch between Ward and Gatti took place in Atlantic City, N.J., on November 23, with Gatti winning a unanimous 10-round decision. After Ward suffered a knockdown in the third round, Gatti, employing far more defensive skills than normally, dominated the suspenseful but ultimately one-sided contest.

Major featherweight action centred on Marco Antonio Barrera (Mex.) and Erik Morales (Mex.), who had outpointed Barrera in the best action fight of 2000. They fought a rematch on June 22 in Las Vegas, with Barrera winning a close 12-round decision. Barrera followed with an impressive 12-round

Mike Tyson of the U.S. (left) staggers after a punch from British WBC and IBF heavyweight champion Lennox Lewis in their title bout in Memphis, Tenn., on June 8.

AP/Wide World Photos

decision over Johnny Tapia (U.S.) on November 2 in Las Vegas. Although Barrera was widely considered the best featherweight in the world, no alphabet title was on the line in his bout with Tapia. Barrera declined to fight for the WBC belt, which he had technically acquired when he defeated Morales, because he did not want to pay the sanctioning fee. Tapia was stripped of the IBF featherweight title for accepting the lucrative bout with Barrera. Morales kept pace, winning an equally imposing 12-round decision over Paulie Ayala (U.S.) on November 16 in Las Vegas to win the vacant WBC featherweight title. Barrera and Morales were expected to fight a third time in 2003 to settle supremacy at 126 lb.   (NIGEL COLLINS)

CHESS

The first concerted effort to heal the schism in world chess took place in early 2002 and culminated in a historic agreement signed on May 6 in Prague. The schism dated from 1993, when Russian Garry Kasparov, then the world chess champion, and his official challenger, Nigel Short of England, set up the short-lived Professional Chess Association to facilitate their title match in London outside the aegis of the Fédération Internationale des Échecs (FIDE). Kasparov maintained his distance from FIDE from that time.

Kasparov was also hostile to the FIDE innovation of arranging annual knock-out tournaments and giving the winner the title of world champion, which broke with hallowed tradition; since the initial match between Wilhelm Steinitz and Johann Zukertort in 1886, the title had changed hands only as a result of single combat over a large number of games at a slow time limit (except in 1946 after the death of Alexander Alekhine had removed the titleholder from consideration).

The third FIDE knockout title event began in November 2001 in Moscow. Zhu Chen of China defeated Aleksandra Kostenyuk of Russia for the women's title in December, and the men's final between two Ukrainians, Vasyl Ivanchuk and 18-year-old Ruslan Ponomaryov, followed in January 2002. The younger man won the first and fifth games, securing the scheduled eight-game match at a quick time limit by the overwhelming score of 4.5 to 2.5, with no need to play the scheduled final game. The quality of the seven games played left much to be desired. *British Chess Magazine* did not publish all of them,

an eloquent gesture in view of the tradition of publishing all the previous championship games back to 1886.

Ponomaryov crossed swords with Kasparov at the Linares, Spain, tournament, held February 22 to March 10, and performed creditably, drawing the first game and losing the second. (*See* game diagram.) In the double-round event, Kasparov was undefeated (8 points out of 12 games). Ponomaryov (6.5) finished in second place, followed by Ivanchuk, Viswanathan Anand of India, and Michael Adams of England (all 6). The final scores left no doubt about the quality of the young Ukrainian's game, but he could hardly be considered Kasparov's superior.

This result, combined with the refusal of Russian Vladimir Kramnik to grant Kasparov a return match for the world title in 2001 or 2002 and the realization that the claims of rival world champions were a cause of skepticism and even ridicule (as well as being counterproductive in the search for sponsors), led the rival parties to Prague in May and thus ended the boycott by Kasparov and Kramnik.

Credit for breaking the deadlock went to American grandmaster Yasser Seirawan, who lobbied untiringly for his project of a "new start." FIDE Pres. Kirsan Ilyumzhinov had already announced that the knockout championships would be held only every two years in the future owing to financial strains, so the scene was set for compromise. The Prague Unity Plan was

In round 13 at the 2002 tournament in Linares, Spain, Garry Kasparov, playing White in a French Defense, enforced the win by a neat switchback move: 36 Be2 and the game ended 36 . . . Qf6 37 Bh5+ Ke7 38 Rxe6+ and reigning FIDE champion Ruslan Ponomaryov, playing Black, resigned, as he loses the queen after 38 . . . Kxe6 39 Rd6+, or 38 . . . Qxe6 39 Qg7+ and mate next move.

signed by six interested parties— Ilyumzhinov; the head of Czech Telecom, Bessel Kok; Kasparov; Kramnik; Seirawan; and Aleksey Orlov, president of the World Chess Foundation.

The unification plan accepted the main principle that FIDE would be the custodian and owner of the world championship title, something that FIDE's founders had been unable to stipulate at the time of its formation in 1924 or at its reconstitution in 1946–47. Kok was to draw up a business plan that envisaged issuing a license to the World Chess Foundation to run a single unified title contest in the future. The existing contractual rights between Kramnik and the Einstein Group would be taken care of by arranging a match in spring 2003 between Kramnik and the winner of the 2002 Dortmund, Ger., tournament. The winner of that contest would play a unification match in late 2003 with the winner of a Kasparov-Ponomaryov match. A "normal" cycle of events would start in 2004 to provide a challenger to a universally recognized world titleholder in 2005.

Certain logical challengers for the title, however, such as Anand and Ivanchuk, did not wish to participate at Dortmund. The winner was 22-year-old Hungarian Peter Leko, who played in more dynamic style than had been his practice in earlier years. Leko already had a near-level record against Kramnik in previous contests and was widely judged to be a worthy challenger.

The traditionally strong Wijk aan Zee, Neth., tournament, held Jan. 12–27, 2002, lacked Kasparov because of illness and was won by the Russian Yevgeny Bareyev (9 points out of 13), ahead of teenage star Aleksandr Grishchuk of Russia (8.5). The strongest and most interesting team match of the year was the China-U.S. contest in Shanghai on July 10–15. China repeated its victory of the previous year in Seattle, Wash., this time by 20.5–19.5.

In October the long-awaited eight-game match between Kramnik and the Deep Fritz computer program was held in Bahrain. After drawing game one, Kramnik decisively won games two and three. Fritz came back to win game five, after a Kramnik blunder, and game six, which Kramnik resigned in a position many observers believed was still tenable. Two more drawn games left the duel in a final 4–4 draw, for which Kramnik earned $800,000.

The FIDE world chess Olympiad was held in Bled, Slovenia, from October 25 to November 11, with teams from 140 countries taking part. In the men's (open) event, the mainly young Russian team, reinforced by the return of Kasparov, took the gold medal (38.5 game points out of 54), followed by Hungary (37.5), which fielded the world's best woman player, Judit Polgar, Armenia (35), and Georgia (34). In the women's section, Georgia collapsed in the last 4 rounds of the 14-round event, leaving China (29.5 points out of 42) to edge Russia (29) for the title, with Poland (28) third and Georgia (27.5) fourth.

(BERNARD CAFFERTY)

CONTRACT BRIDGE

The world championship competition, the major international tournament of the year, was held in Montreal Aug. 16–31, 2002. In the team competition for the Power Rosenblum Cup, the Italians (Norberto Bocchi, Giorgio Duboin, Lorenzo Lauria, Alfredo Versace, Maria Teresa Lavazza, and Guido Ferraro) took first place, with Indonesia finishing second and Poland third. The world women's teams competition for the McConnell Cup was won by a U.S. team (Lynn Deas, Irina Levitina, Jill Meyers, Randi Montin, Beth Palmer, and Kerri Sanborn), with a second U.S. team as runners-up and France claiming third. In the world open pairs, Fulvio Fantoni–Claudio Nunes (Italy) took first, followed by Michael Rosenberg–Zia Mahmood (U.S.) and Gabriel Chagas–Diego Brenner (Brazil) in second and third. The world women's pairs results were led by Karen McCallum–Debbie Rosenberg (U.S.), with Blandine de Hérédia–Anne-Frédérique Levy (France) in second place and Irina Levitina–Kerri Sanborn (U.S.) in third. The world mixed pairs competition ended with Becky Rogers–Jeff Meckstroth (U.S.) on top, followed by Babette Hugon–Jean-Jacques Palau (France) and Sabine and Jens Auken (Denmark). Finally, the world senior teams victors were Canada/U.S.A. (Diana Holt, Boris Baran, Joe Godefrin, George Mittelman, and Ed Schulte), trailed by a U.S. team and one from The Netherlands.

Because no one could earn a living from bridge tournaments, some professionals played for pay, "bought" by wealthy clients who wished to compete with top partners. The Conditions of Contest stated that in the Rosenblum Cup and the McConnell Cup, "individuals making up any...team...must be members of the same NBO [National Bridge Organization]." In 2002 in the Rosenblum Cup, however, one Italian pair played with four Poles, and two Americans competed together with four Swedes, purely for financial reasons. There was also some debate about players who were born in one country and lived in another; which country should they be allowed to represent? No one seemed quite sure of the regulations, and the World Bridge Federation (WBF) turned a blind eye to the irregularities, believing that the players preferred to have the flexibility to play for nonnational teams.

Bridge players had been trying to gain a berth in the Winter Olympics. A demonstration event was held before the 2002 Games in Salt Lake City, Utah, but the International Olympic Committee (IOC) was expected to reject contract bridge. Even so, the WBF continued with drug tests of participants, as required by the IOC. Two players in Montreal failed (perhaps only for excess caffeine consumption), while another refused the test, stating that she was taking a banned substance for a back condition. She was stripped of the silver medal she won in the McConnell.

The first world university bridge championship took place in Brugge, Belg., August 4–14. Team winners were, first, Denmark (Michael Askgaard, Gregers Bjarnarson, Anders Hagen, and Kasper Konow), second Italy, and third The Netherlands.

The 16th worldwide pairs championships took place on June 7–8. Playing in 320 clubs in 41 countries, a total of 5,870 pairs competed the first day. The highest percentage score (76.06%, and 139,804.67 match points) was achieved by Ken Barbour and Markland Jones of the United States. On the second day, 5,219 pairs competed in 260 clubs in 40 countries. The winners were Luo Jianchao and Luo Ming of China, with 80.55% (130,890.75 match points).

(PHILLIP ALDER)

CRICKET

The power struggle within cricket reached new levels in 2001–02. In November 2001 former England captain Mike Denness, the match referee for the South Africa–India series, suspended one Indian player, Virender Sehwag (for excessive appealing), and disciplined five others, including Indian hero Sachin Tendulkar (for ball tampering), after an ill-tempered second Test in Port Elizabeth, S.Af. The Indian team was outraged by the accusations and demanded the removal of Denness as match referee for the third Test. The International Cricket Council (ICC) refused, and with the support of the United Cricket Board in South Africa, which was worried about

---

One of the most enjoyable aspects of bridge—especially if you are on the winning side, of course—is the way that apparently guaranteed tricks can evaporate out the window. In this deal West seemed destined to win four tricks—three hearts and one club—against 4♥, but it did not work out that way.

```
                    North
                    ♠ A Q 10 8
                    ♥ 9 5 4
                    ♦ K Q 5 4 3
                    ♣ 10
West                                East
♠ K 4 3                             ♠ J 9 7
♥ A Q J                             ♥ 7 2
♦ J 7 6             South           ♦ A 10 9 8 2
♣ A 5 4 2           ♠ 6 5 2         ♣ 7 6 3
                    ♥ K 10 8 6 3
                    ♦ ...
                    ♣ K Q J 9 8
```

Dealer: West
Vulnerable: North–South

South	West	North	East
...	1NT	Pass	Pass
2♥	Pass	4♥	All Pass

Opening lead: ♠3

West's 1NT opening showed 15–17 high-card points, and South's two-heart overcall promised hearts and either minor. The declarer was Sebastian Kristensen from Denmark, who had been playing the game for only two and a half years when this deal occurred during a Danish tournament.

West led the ♠3. Kristensen finessed dummy's ♠Q successfully, then led the ♣10, overtaking with his queen. After winning with his ♣A, West continued with the ♠4 to dummy's ace. Declarer called for the ♦K to be led, ruffing away East's ace.

East was marked with the ♠J from West's low-spade continuation. (If West had started with the ♠K–J–x or ♠K–J–x–x, he would have led the ♠K at trick three.) East had produced the ♦A, so West must have had the ♥A–Q–J for his opening bid.

Kristensen ruffed a club in the dummy, cashed the ♦Q for a spade discard, ruffed a spade in hand, trumped another club, and ruffed a diamond to give this position:

```
                    North
                    ♠ 10
                    ♥ 9
                    ♦ 5 4
                    ♣ ...
West                                East
♠ ...                               ♠ ...
♥ A Q J            South            ♥ 7 2
♦ ...              ♠ ...            ♦ 10 9
♣ 5               ♥ K 10            ♣ ...
                    ♦ ...
                    ♣ K J
```

Kristensen ruffed a club in the dummy, then called for any card from the dummy and discarded his last club. West was forced to ruff with the ♥J and lead away from the ♥A–Q around to South's ♥K–10, and South made his 4♥ bid. Kristensen won the 2002 Digital Fountain Best-Played Deal Award from the International Bridge Press Association for this performance, during which he ruffed three winning clubs in the dummy and West lost a "guaranteed" trump trick.

offending India, the third "test" was declared "unofficial" and went ahead without the sanction of the game's authorities. When the Indian authorities threatened to play the banned Sehwag in the first Test against England, it seemed possible that England's tour of India would be canceled, but the tour went ahead. In May New Zealand cut short its tour of Pakistan and canceled the second Test in Karachi after a bomb exploded outside the team's hotel; Australia threatened to cancel its October tour of Pakistan unless the matches were played elsewhere.

On the field three explosive double centuries in the space of three weeks rewrote the record books. In February, in the first Test in Johannesburg, S.Af., Adam Gilchrist of Australia flailed the South African attack for an unbeaten 204 scored off 212 balls, the fastest in history. Less than a month later, in the first Test against England in Christchurch, N.Z., Nathan Astle of New Zealand broke Gilchrist's record by scoring 222 from 168 balls, an astonishing innings that eclipsed England's Graham Thorpe's score of 200 off 231 balls in the same match.

The outbreak of sustained hitting was indicative of the year's Test cricket, which saw only 14 of 51 official Tests end in a draw. Following the lead of the Australians, who ended the year as undisputed champions again, and influenced by the quick tempo of one-day international cricket, Test sides looked to score their runs at a breakneck pace and give their bowlers time to complete the victory. The exception was England's winter tour of India, which ended in a 1–0 victory for the home side and heavy criticism for the negative bowling tactics of England captain Nasser Hussain. The same countries fought out a 1–1 drawn series in the summer in England, notable for the exceptional batting of Michael Vaughan for England and Rahul Dravid for India. In the last match of that series, Tendulkar reached the milestone of his 100th Test.

In March England's tour of New Zealand was marred by the news of the death of 24-year-old Ben Hollioake, one of England's most talented young players, in a car crash near Perth, Australia. On June 1 the entire cricket world was stunned by the death of former South African captain Wessel Johannes ("Hansie") Cronje (see OBITUARIES) in a small-plane crash.

In the defining home and away Test series of the year, Australia routed South Africa 5–1. Australia, led by Steve Waugh, had surprisingly failed to beat New Zealand in a home series, but with Matthew Hayden and Justin Langer forming a formidable opening partnership and bowlers Glenn McGrath and Shane Warne recovering their poise, the Aussies proved far too strong for a disappointing South African side. Warne marked his 100th Test by bowling a marathon 98 overs and taking 8 for 231. He also became only the fourth player—after Richard Hadlee of New Zealand, Kapil Dev of India, and Pakistan's Wasim Akram—to complete the double of 2,000 runs and 400 wickets in Test cricket.

West Indies had a disappointing year, losing heavily to Sri Lanka and Pakistan—a series exiled to Sharjah in the United Arab Emirates because of the political situation in Pakistan—before returning home to beat India. Defeat at home by New Zealand, a result utterly unthinkable a decade earlier, merely reflected the decline of a once-dominant cricketing nation. In contrast, Sri Lanka confirmed its rise to prominence with convincing victories over Zimbabwe and West Indies. Muttiah Muralitharan, the unorthodox Sri Lankan spinner, took 30 wickets in three Tests against Zimbabwe at an average of 9.8 runs conceded, becoming only the second spinner—and at 29 the youngest—to reach 400 wickets.

In the ICC one-day Champions Trophy in September, Pakistan's Shoaib Malik became the first batsman to be dismissed leg before wicket on the basis of a television replay and the adjudication of the third umpire. Many thought it merely a matter of time before the influence of the camera on umpires' decision making became more widespread, and an experiment in Test cricket was expected before the end of the 2002–03 season.

In domestic cricket Surrey won the county championship in England for the third time in four years, Yorkshire won the one-day C&G Cup. In Australia, Queensland won the Pura Cup final for the third time in succession, while Guyana drew with Jamaica in the final of the Busta International Shield, winning the trophy on first innings. In South Africa, KwaZulu/Natal did the double, winning the SuperSport series final and the one-day Standard Bank Cup. Australia beat South Africa in the final of the Under-19 World Cup, and a new international cricket venue was unveiled in Tangier, Mor.   (ANDREW LONGMORE)

CURLING

Curling received a huge boost in its Scottish birthplace and across the U.K. in 2002. First, Rhona Martin of Dunlop, Scot., claimed Great Britain's first Winter Olympic gold medal in 18 years when she won the women's curling side at the Salt Lake City, Utah, Games in February. Jackie Lockhart of Aberdeen followed with Scotland's first women's

Scottish skip Rhona Martin (centre) releases the stone in the women's curling final at the Winter Olympics in Salt Lake City, Utah; the U.K. beat Switzerland 4–3 for the gold.

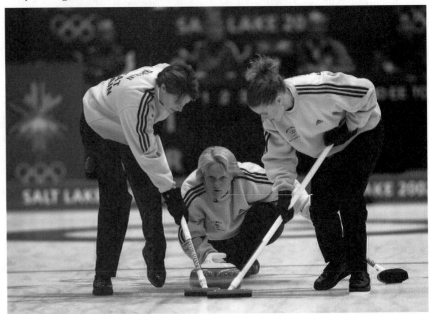

world curling title at the championships in Bismarck, N.D., in April. Lockhart had earned her berth in the world championship by defeating Martin at the Scottish nationals just two weeks after the Olympic Games.

In Salt Lake City, Martin finished round-robin play in the middle of the pack, won two tiebreakers to advance to the semifinals, and narrowly beat the tournament-leading Canadians to gain entry to the medal round. The Scots went on to edge Switzerland's Luzia Ebnoether 4–3 for the gold, while Canada's Kelley Law claimed bronze by beating Kari Erickson of the U.S.

Norway's Pål Trulsen won the Olympic men's gold medal, also at the expense of a Canadian side that had led the tournament. Trulsen upset Kevin Martin 6–5 in the final when the favoured Canadian overthrew his final stone, allowing Norway to steal a point and the game. Andreas Schwaller of Switzerland beat defending world champion Peter Lindholm of Sweden for the bronze.

In Bismarck, Lockhart's foursome was the class of the field, finishing first in the round-robin, knocking off defending champion Colleen Jones of Canada in the semifinal, and defeating Margaretha Sigfridsson of Sweden 6–5 for the title. While Scotland had three previous men's world championships, it was the first for Scottish women. Norway finished third, beating Canada.

Trulsen's bid for a double-gold-medal year fell short, however, when Randy Ferbey of Canada defeated the Norwegian skip 10–5 for the 2002 world men's title. Scotland defeated the U.S. for the bronze.   (BRUCE CHEADLE)

CYCLING

In 2002 cycling's premier road event, the Tour de France, was won by American Lance Armstrong, who became the fourth rider to win the race in four successive years since it was first held in 1903. Armstrong joined Jacques Anquetil (1961–64), Eddy Merckx (1969–72), and Miguel Indurain (1991–95) when he finished 7 min 17 sec clear of his nearest challenger, Joseba Beloki of Spain, in the 3,277.5-km (1 km = about 0.62 mi) race, which began in Luxembourg and finished three weeks later on the Champs-Élysées in Paris. Armstrong won the opening prologue time trial but suffered his first defeat in a place-to-place individual time-trial stage in four years when Colombian Santiago Botero beat him by 11 seconds in the 52-km leg between Lanester

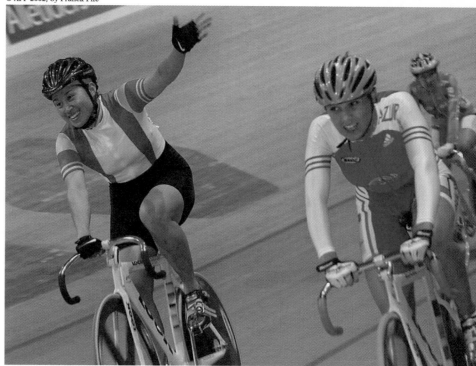

China's Na Li (left) is all smiles after winning the women's keirin at the cycling world track championships in Copenhagen in September.

and Lorient. Armstrong later won the 50-km time trial to Mâcon after wins on successive days in the first major mountain stages of the race had given him a clear overall lead. Botero went on to secure Colombia's first world road title when he won the individual time trial at the road world championships in Zolder, Belg., in October.

Doping again affected the Tour of Italy (Giro d'Italia). Stefano Garzelli of Italy tested positive for probenecid (a diuretic used as a masking agent to hide traces of steroids in urine) after he won the second stage on May 13; he was later disqualified and suspended for two years after a second analysis of his sample gave the same result. The morning after Garzelli left the race, 2001 winner Gilberto Simoni of Italy was revealed to have registered a positive result for cocaine in a World Anti-Doping Agency (WADA) test on April 24; he was also disqualified and suspended. Another favourite, Italian Francesco Casagrande, was disqualified for dangerous riding. The race was won by Italy's Paolo Savoldelli, who took the lead in the final week through his performances in the Dolomites. Mario Cipollini of Italy won six stages to equal Alfredo Binda's overall record of 41. German rider Jan Ullrich, the winner of the 1997 Tour de France and a

former world and Olympic champion, missed the entire road season with a knee injury and was handed a six-month suspension for amphetamine use following a random out-of-competition test by the WADA.

Australia set a new world record of 3 min 59.583 sec for the men's 4,000-m team pursuit when it won the gold medal at the Commonwealth Games in Manchester, Eng. Na Li became the first Chinese woman to win a world track title with her victory in the keirin at the world track championships held in Copenhagen in September.

(JOHN R. WILKINSON)

EQUESTRIAN SPORTS

Thoroughbred Racing. *United States.* A breach of pari-mutuel wagering security that placed the integrity of the burgeoning simulcast and phone account wagering industry in jeopardy rocked American horse racing in October 2002 when a plot was uncovered to collect fraudulently more than $3.1 million in winning wagers on the Breeders' Cup World Thoroughbred Championships, held on October 26 at Arlington Park outside Chicago. The Breeders' Cup was held at Arlington Park for the first time in the 19-year history of the competition, and worldwide wagering on the 11-race program was a Breeders' Cup record $116,367,198.

Suspicions of irregularities were aroused when it was revealed that one man held all six winning tickets (worth $428,392 each) and 108 of 186 winning consolation tickets (worth $4,606 each) among all bets placed nationwide on a wager called the Ultra Pick Six. The winning tickets became objects of closer scrutiny when it was revealed that only one horse, the winner, had been selected in each of the first four Ultra Pick Six races, while all of the horses in each of the last two races had

ation (NTRA), announced the formation of the NTRA Wagering Technology Working Group to recommend security measures and to ensure that the system was protected from any further abuse. Individual measures also were being taken by Catskill OTB and by tracks in other horse-racing jurisdictions around the country.

On May 4 War Emblem stunned the racing world with a front-running victory in the 2002 Kentucky Derby. The colt won the Preakness Stakes two weeks later but was stymied in his bid to become the 12th U.S. Triple Crown

Emblem won the Kentucky Derby, Reineman claimed that he and not Bin Salman was entitled to the entire bonus. The decision was in the hands of the courts when Bin Salman died of a heart attack in July. (*See* OBITUARIES.) War Emblem was sold in September for $17 million and was to be put to stud in Japan in 2003.

It was announced in August that Sportsman's Park would cease operations. The National Jockey Club, owner and operator of the venerable Chicago-area track, entered into a 99-year lease agreement with Hawthorne Race Course, where racing operations would continue. The two tracks had coexisted on adjacent properties as separate family-owned and operated organizations for seven decades.

Jockey Chris McCarron surprised the racing world by announcing his retirement in June. During his 28-year career, the two-time Eclipse Award winner won 7,139 races (sixth on the all-time list). On August 10 Pat Day guided With Anticipation to victory in the Sword Dancer Invitational Handicap. The triumph gave Day $264,580,968 in career purse earnings and thereby vaulted him ahead of McCarron as the leading purse-winning jockey of all time. On October 26 Russell Baze, age 44, reached the 8,000-career-victory plateau. Laffit Pincay, Jr., Bill Shoemaker, and Day were the only other members of the exclusive "8,000" club. Jockey Jerry D. Bailey ended the year with purse earnings of more than $22,800,000, breaking the single-season record he set in 2001.

Veteran owner and breeder Ogden Phipps died on April 22 at age 93. (*See* OBITUARIES.) John Mabee, who was prominent for 45 years as a breeder, owner, and track executive, died two days later. On May 7 the last living U.S. Triple Crown winner, Seattle Slew, died of old age at 28. Seattle Slew, which won the Triple Crown in 1977, was retired undefeated to stud in 1979 and went on to a successful career as a stallion. His passing left the sport without a living Triple Crown winner for the first time in 83 years. Sunday Silence, the 1989 Horse of the Year and the world's all-time leading sire by earnings, died from the complications of an infection on August 19. Spend a Buck, the 1985 Horse of the Year, died on November 24.   (JOHN G. BROKOPP)

AP/Wide World Photos

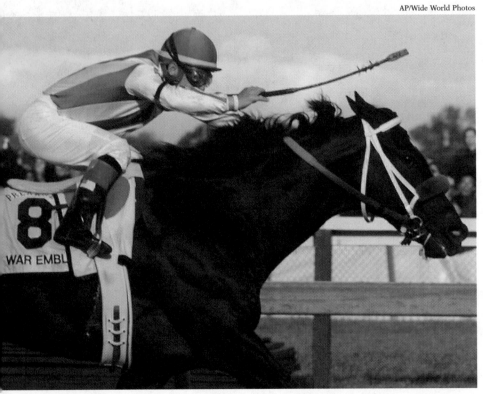

Kentucky Derby winner War Emblem, with jockey Victor Espinoza on board, races down the stretch to victory in the Preakness Stakes on May 18.

been selected, a highly unusual betting pattern. Three former college fraternity brothers appeared before a federal magistrate on November 12, charged with conspiracy to commit wire fraud in connection with a wager that had been placed by means of an automated telephone betting account with the Catskill Regional Off Track Betting Corp. Further investigation revealed that the trio may have successfully cashed fraudulent winning bets at other tracks during "test runs" in the weeks leading up to Breeders' Cup Day.

Tim Smith, the commissioner of the National Thoroughbred Racing Associ-

winner when he stumbled at the start of the Belmont Stakes and finished eighth behind the astonishing victor, 70–1 long shot Sarava.

National attention had been drawn to War Emblem when he won the April 6 Illinois Derby at Sportsman's Park (in Cicero, Ill.), which advertised a $1 million insured cash bonus to the owner of a three-year-old that won the Illinois Derby and any one of the three Triple Crown races. Trainer Bob Baffert encouraged Saudi Prince Ahmed bin Salman to purchase a 90% interest in the colt from Chicago-based industrialist Russell L. Reineman. When War

Thoroughbred Racing. *International.* On Oct. 6, 2002, BBC television broadcast a *Panorama* program dealing with corruption in horse racing, and the repercussions were likely to have a lasting effect on the sport in Britain. The program included accusations by Roger Buffham, former head of security for the Jockey Club, one of British racing's key regulatory organizations, that the sport was "institutionally corrupt." Jeremy Phipps, who had succeeded Buffham as the club's chief security officer in 2001, resigned a few days after the broadcast, which contained covert film of him making disparaging remarks about the club. In the longer term, the scandal was likely to result in the loss of the club's disciplinary responsibilities to the British Horseracing Board, although Minister for Sport Richard Caborn left it to the Jockey Club to propose improved ways of discharging its responsibilities.

Aidan O'Brien was champion trainer for the second consecutive year in Britain and for the sixth time in succession at home in Ireland. He gained seven Group 1 (G1) victories in Britain, four in France, three in Ireland, and two in Italy. He also scored with High Chaparral, winner of both the English and Irish Derbys, in the Breeders' Cup Turf and with Ballingarry in the Canadian International Stakes. O'Brien extended Rock of Gibraltar's sequence of G1 victories to seven, five of them in 2002, but he was disappointed when that colt beat the favourite, Hawk Wing (which he also had trained) by a neck in the Two Thousand Guineas. O'Brien would have been even more dominant during the year if his stable had not been afflicted by a respiratory infection for most of August. Rock of Gibraltar was named Horse of the Year in November, two days after being retired to stud.

Johannesburg was another disappointment for O'Brien, both in the Kentucky Derby, where he finished eighth, and in the newly created Golden Jubilee Stakes at Royal Ascot, after which he was retired. The royal meeting was extended to five days because of Queen Elizabeth II's Golden Jubilee celebration, an experiment that was to be repeated in 2003. O'Brien had almost ceased to train for steeplechase, where he gained his early success, but he retained Istabraq. The 10-year-old champion was retired in 2002 as the winner of 23 of his 29 races over hurdles.

Jockey Michael Kinane, who rode for O'Brien, was champion rider in Ireland for the 12th time. Kieren Fallon claimed his fifth British riding title in six years, while Dominique Boeuf headed the list in France for the fourth time. André Fabre was the leading French trainer for the 16th time, although he was pressed by Pascal Bary for most of the season.

Although Coolmore (and O'Brien) won the battle with rival Godolphin for the 2002 European Thoroughbred season, Godolphin gained a notable success with Marienbard in the Prix de l'Arc de Triomphe in Paris. Marienbard was then retired to stud in Japan. Marienbard was one of 12 English- or Irish-trained winners in the 26 G1 races in France. Foreign horses were also active at lower levels, winning 18 Group 2 and Group 3 events there. Italian horses had their best year in some time, highlighted when Rakti became the first home-trained winner of the Derby Italiano since Tisserand in 1988 and Falbrav won the Japan Cup. Nevertheless, German horses, forced abroad by poor domestic prize money, continued to dominate many Italian prizes. Boreal, winner of the 2001 Deutsches Derby, gained a significant success in the Coronation Cup at Britain's Epsom Downs on the same day that Kazzia, bought by Godolphin in Germany, won the Oaks.

In Canada, T J's Lucky Moon, an 82–1 long shot, scored an upset in the Queen's Plate on June 23, giving his trainer, Vito Armata, and jockey, Steven Bahen, their biggest career victories. His time was the slowest since 1986, and he finished 10th behind la Cinquieme Essai in the Prince of Wales Stakes on July 21. Portcullis won the Breeders' Stakes, the final leg of the Triple Crown, in a poor year for Canadian three-year-olds.

Ireland's Dermot Weld, the first trainer from the Northern Hemisphere to win a Melbourne Cup (with Vintage Crop in 1993), added a second victory in Australia's greatest race with Media Puzzle. Northerly won the Cox Plate and the Caulfield Cup but was not risked over the 3.2-km (2-mi) Melbourne Cup. Godolphin's Grandera ran third in the Cox Plate, one length in front of the great New Zealand mare Sunline, which was retired immediately after failing in her attempt to win a 14th G1 race. In 2003 Northerly was likely to be groomed for the Dubai World Cup, which Godolphin won in 2002 with Street Cry.

The British breeding industry lost both Nashwan and Unfuwain during the year, as well as their former trainer, Dick Hern, who died in May. (See OBITUARIES.) The stallions were to be replaced at Shadwell Stud by the 2001 Arc winner, Sakhee, and Act One, which lost his unbeaten record when he finished second to Sulamani in the Prix du Jockey-Club in June. Act One's

breeder, Gerald Leigh, who also gained G1 success with Irish One Thousand Guineas winner Gossamer, died that same month.   (ROBERT W. CARTER)

Harness Racing. The year 2002 was a decisive one for Karin and Blair Burgess and their champion pacer Real Desire. At the end of the 2001 racing season, the Burgesses and Blair's father, Bob, had a decision to make. Should they retire their prize three-year-old to a lucrative life of breeding or race him another year? Their partners were breeders who believed that Real Desire had done enough. In two seasons on the track, he had won 15 of 27 races and more than $2 million.

The Burgesses, who had cared for and trained Real Desire his entire career, decided to race him, and they were absolutely right. As a four-year-old in 2002, Real Desire won 10 of 13 starts and added another $1 million to his career bankroll. Probably his most impressive victory came in late July when he started from the extreme outside number 10 post position in the $500,000 Breeders Crown at the Meadowlands Racetrack in East Rutherford, N.J. He raced on the outside for much of the mile and still had the speed and courage to pull away from some of the best pacers in the world in the homestretch. Real Desire retired in early October and was scheduled to begin breeding duties in 2003 at a fee of $10,000.

The most heralded American trotter of the year was Kadabra, whose magical speed carried him from humble beginnings to the heights of harness racing. Kadabra was a winner from the time he started racing. In his 14 starts as a two-year-old in 2001, the Illinois-born colt won a dozen times and finished second twice. Those accomplishments prompted a group of American and Canadian investors to purchase Kadabra for $800,000 in early 2002. The new owners formed the Abra Kadabra Stable and sat back and enjoyed the magic show of their talented trotter. Kadabra was not eligible to race in the Hambletonian, the biggest event for three-year-old trotters, because he was not nominated in time, but he won virtually everything else, including the Breeders Crown, the Canadian Trotting Classic, and the Stanley Dancer. He earned over $1 million in 2002.

The pony-sized colt Chip Chip Hooray trotted to an upset win in the $1 million Hambletonian at the Meadowlands on August 3. On the same race card, seven-year-old Swedish import Victory Tilly set a world trotting record for one mile of 1 min 50.4 sec in the $500,000 Nat Ray.

The best trotter on the European continent remained the Italian sensation Varenne. In 2002 he won both the Prix d'Amerique, the French endurance classic, in Paris in January, and the Elitlopp, the Swedish sprint test, in Stockholm in May. Varenne's only North American appearance in 2002 came as the defending champion in the Trot Mondial in Montreal in September. After repulsing a brave challenge by the American seven-year-old Fool's Goal, Varenne was passed just before the wire by the French mare Fan Idole. The taste of defeat was made even more bitter after Varenne was disqualified and placed last for having cut the final turn too sharply and left the course.

In Australia Smooth Satin scored a major upset in March as he nipped Shakamaker to win the Inter-Dominion Grand Final at Harold Park in Sydney. Courage Under Fire and Shakamaker were the favourites and engaged in a speed duel before Smooth Satin's come-from-behind win. (DEAN A. HOFFMAN)

Steeplechasing. Tony ("AP") McCoy became the most successful jump jockey ever, riding his 1,700th career winner on Aug. 27, 2002. He was British champion for the seventh time and finished the 2001–02 season with a season-record 289 wins (plus one in Ireland). McCoy was the stable jockey for Martin Pipe, who was the top trainer for the 12th time.

Meanwhile, Jim Culloty rode the winners of both the Cheltenham Gold Cup, Best Mate, and the Grand National, Bindaree. Irish-trained Florida Pearl beat Best Mate by three-quarters of a length in the King George VI Chase but finished well behind him in the Gold Cup. French-bred Hors La Loi III took the Champion Hurdle in March. Double Car won the Grand Steeple-Chase de Paris in May, but later he was disqualified for failing a drug test; after an appeal failed, El Paso III was awarded the race. Five European horses and the U.S.-trained All Gong challenged for the Nakayama Grand Jump in Japan in April, but none of them finished closer than fifth behind the New Zealand-trained St. Steven.

(ROBERT W. CARTER)

Show Jumping and Dressage. Dermott Lennon of Ireland won the individual gold medal for show jumping at the World Equestrian Games in Jérez de la Frontera, Spain, in September 2002. Riding Liscalgot, he beat Eric Navet of France, American Peter Wylde, and

Helena Lundback of Sweden in a final that required each competitor to ride all four horses. Navet was also a member of the quartet that won the jumping team gold medal for France.

Nadine Capellman, riding Farbenfroh, defeated Beatriz Ferrer-Salat of Spain on Beauvalais and fellow German Ulla Salzgeber on Rusty in the individual dressage championship. Germany won the team gold, ahead of the U.S. and Spain.

The U.S. triumphed in the three-day eventing team competition, beating France, Great Britain, and Australia. Jean Teulere of France captured the individual eventing gold on Espoir de la Mare. (ROBERT W. CARTER)

Polo. A record 15 teams participated in the 2002 high-handicap season in Palm Beach, Fla., where Jedi, led by Argentines Adolfo Cambiaso and Marcos Heguy, won the first of the three 26-goal tournaments, the Gold Cup of Americas, defeating White Birch in the final. Venezuelan Víctor Vargas's La Lechuza Caracas, with brothers Sebastián and Juan Ignacio ("Pite") Merlos as its outstanding players, gained the CV Whitney Cup. Gillian Johnston was the first woman to win the U.S. Open as a patron; her team, Coca Cola, was led by Miguel Novillo Astrada and Adam Snow. In the American summer season, brothers Agustín and Sebastián Merlos triumphed with Mercedes Benz in the Mercedes Benz Challenge Cup, held in Long Island, N.Y. Windsor Capital won the Pacific Coast Open, played in Santa Barbara, Calif.

In the English high-handicap season, Urs Schwatzenbach's Black Bears, with brothers Eduardo, Miguel, and Alejandro Novillo Astrada, bested Emerging—led by Milo Fernández Araujo—in the final to capture the British Gold Cup. Emerging won the Queen's Cup, while Foxcote White gained the prestigious Warwickshire Cup. In the Spanish high-handicap season in Sotogrande, Ciguinuelas defeated local Santa María in the Gold Cup, Scapa John-Smith won the Silver Cup, and La Margarita triumphed in the Bronze. Edouard Carmignac's Talandracas overcame Royal Berrière in the final of the Gold Cup, played in Deauville, France. In Gstaad, Switz., Swissca Polo Team gained the Silver Cup.

La Dolfina, comprising Adolfo Cambiaso, Sebastián and Pite Merlos, and Bartolomé ("Lolo") Castagnola, showed itself to be the best team in the world after winning its first Argentine Open and third consecutive Hurlingham

Open. In both finals La Dolfina downed Indios Chapaleufú II, with brothers Alberto ("Pepe"), Ignacio, and Eduardo Heguy and Milo Fernández Araujo. Indios Chapaleufú II won the Tortugas Open, where the Merlos brothers did not play for Cambiaso's quartet because they were playing in the U.S. Colorado won the São Paulo Open in Brazil.

(JORGE ADRIÁN ANDRADES)

FENCING

The most important issue to confront world fencing during 2002 was that of the qualifying system for the 2004 Olympic Games in Athens. Women's sabre had become established, and the International Olympic Committee (IOC) had accepted its inclusion for the first time for the Athens Olympics. This would result in 12 events (6 individual and 6 team), but the IOC confirmed that, whatever the format, only 200 fencers would be allowed to compete for 10 sets of medals. This impasse lasted most of the year, while officials of the Fédération Internationale d'Escrime (FIE), pressured by the leading international fencers and national governing bodies, struggled for an acceptable formula and lobbied for additional medals and an increase in athlete numbers. Finally, with no movement from the IOC, at a special congress at the senior world championships in Lisbon in August, the FIE decided to replace women's team foil with individual women's sabre and omit women's team sabre for the Athens Games.

The senior world championships saw the traditionally strong nations under pressure, especially from China and South Korea, both of which won medals. China ended 7th in the overall championship rankings, with South Korea 8th and the U.S. 10th. The clear overall winner, however, was Russia, followed by France and Germany. Hungary, Italy, Poland, and Romania rounded out the top 10. At the junior/cadet world championships in Antalya, Turkey, in April, China and South Korea again won medals, along with the U.S., Great Britain, Canada, and Venezuela.

In 2002 the world's oldest national fencing federation, the British Fencing Association, celebrated its centenary with a dinner and a special match against Hungary in London in September. The British federation was established two years earlier than the French federation, while the FIE was founded in 1913. (GRAHAM MORRISON)

FIELD HOCKEY

The 10th men's field hockey World Cup was held in Kuala Lumpur, Malaysia, Feb. 24–March 9, 2002. Germany, led by the 2001 Player of the Year, Florian Kunz, beat Australia 2–1 on a match-winning goal by Oliver Domke to secure its first men's World Cup. The Netherlands sank South Korea 2–1 with a golden goal for third place. The tournament featured 16 teams, for the first time in two pools of eight each. The Fédération Internationale de Hockey (FIH) format of four groups of four was unacceptable to Malaysia, which argued that a defeat for the home team in the early rounds would hurt spectator interest.

China captured the women's Champions Trophy at Macau on September 1, beating Argentina 3–1 in the final tiebreaker after a 2–2 draw, despite extra-time play. The Netherlands defeated Australia 4–3 for the bronze. A week later, The Netherlands won the men's Champions Trophy at Cologne, Ger., in a 3–2 tiebreaker against Germany after a goalless final. Pakistan placed third, beating India 4–3.

The FIH plan for a four-nation event involving Ireland, Lithuania, India, and the U.S. to identify the sixth and seventh women's World Cup qualifiers was rejected by the Court of Arbitration, which upheld Ireland's place as the sixth. The FIH scheduled a three-Test series in New Delhi between India and the U.S., which had missed its qualifier after the terrorist strikes on Sept. 11, 2001. The U.S. team, citing security concerns relating to the threat of war in Kashmir, left New Delhi and forced the FIH to shift the venue to Cannock, Eng., in June. The U.S. won the deciding third match 3–1 after drawing the earlier two matches by identical margins (1–1), making it the seventh qualifier and the last of the 16 World Cup teams.

Argentina won the women's World Cup, beating The Netherlands 4–3 in a sudden-death tiebreaker after having been deadlocked 1–1 in regulation time. China finished third, followed by Australia.

The 2002 men's and women's Players of the Year were, respectively, Michael Green of Germany and Cecilia Rognoni of Argentina.   (S. THYAGARAJAN)

FOOTBALL

Association Football (Soccer). *Europe.* In the summer of 2002, Japan and South Korea served as joint hosts of the Fédération Internationale de Football

© AFP 2002, by Patrick Hertzog

Brazil's Ronaldo kicks the ball past German goalkeeper Oliver Kahn to score the first of his two goals in the World Cup final, which Brazil won 2–0.

Association (FIFA) World Cup finals. (*See* Sidebar.) In the final match, in Yokohama, Japan, on June 30, Brazil, led by a resurgent Ronaldo (*see* BIOGRAPHIES), defeated Germany 2–0, despite the efforts of German goalkeeper and captain Oliver Kahn (*see* BIOGRAPHIES), who won the Golden Ball award as the tournament's top player. It was Brazil's record fifth World Cup title. At year's end Ronaldo was named European Player of the Year and, for a record third time, FIFA World Player of the Year.

While the main thrust of attention was centred on the events in South Korea and Japan, there was considerable speculation over the future of FIFA's president Joseph S. Blatter. Despite concerns over the financial situation that affected the world's governing body of football and a strong challenge for Blatter's position from Issa Hayatou, FIFA vice president and African Football Confederation president, the incumbent received enough votes to secure another four years in office with a 139–56 endorsement from member countries.

Unease of a different nature affected Europe, with the growth of the Union des Associations Européennes de Football (UEFA) Champions League (formerly the European Champion Clubs' Cup) and the UEFA Cup making excessive demand upon domestic football schedules and causing concern over the fitness of leading players for international duty. On May 15 Real Madrid, the Spanish champions, returned to Hampden Park in Glasgow, Scot., the scene of the club's 1960 European Champion Clubs' Cup triumph, to register its ninth championship by defeating Bayer 04 Leverkusen of Germany 2–1. The German team, which already had snatched defeat from the jaws of victory in the German Bundesliga and had similarly thrown away its chances in the domestic cup competition, lost a goal in the ninth minute to a well-directed strike from Real's Raúl (Raúl González Blanco). A firmly headed goal for Leverkusen by the Brazilian Lucio (Lucimar da Silva Ferreira) from a free kick by Bernd Schneider leveled the score only five minutes later.

On the stroke of halftime, the French international player Zinedine Zidane restored Real's advantage with a classic goal. A ball centred from the left wing by Roberto Carlos (da Silva) found Zidane just outside the penalty area. His left-foot volley was of such precision and power that German goalkeeper Hans-Jörg Butt had no chance of stopping it. A succession of injuries in the second half extended normal time by seven minutes, during which Real's replacement goalkeeper, Iker Casillas Fernández, made three breathtaking saves to deny Leverkusen an equalizer. The Germans had committed everyone into attack, including Butt, who had a header attempt of his own.

Seven days earlier, in the UEFA Cup final in Rotterdam, Neth., there had been disappointment for Germany's Borussia Dortmund, which was beaten

World Cup 2002

On June 30, 2002—with some 69,000 spectators in the stands and an estimated billion fans watching on televisions around the world—Brazil won a record fifth association football (soccer) World Cup title, beating Germany 2–0 in an evenly contested final in Yokohama, Japan. In its early stages the tournament had been one of unexpected shocks, with several unfancied teams causing major upsets. France, the defending champion, lost to Senegal in the opening match in Seoul, S.Kor., and failed to qualify from its group matches. Argentina, Portugal, and Poland also failed to advance.

In contrast, during the first dual hosting of a World Cup, home teams South Korea and Japan each headed its group. The surprises continued in the round of 16 as Korea stunned Italy in overtime, the U.S. upset Mexico to merit a quarterfinal place, and Senegal became only the second African nation to reach the last eight. Yet stripped of such episodes, the overall standard of play in the monthlong tournament disappointed.

It was the Brazilians, patchy but potentially a threat, and the dogged, persistent Germans who survived the mayhem around them to reach the final. Germany might have taken the lead in the 49th minute, but Oliver Neuville's blistering long-range freekick was brilliantly fingertipped onto a post by Brazilian goalkeeper Marcos (Roberto Silveira Reis). Gradually Brazil assumed control, and in the 67th minute Ronaldo (see BIOGRAPHIES) side-footed the ball in after Oliver Kahn (see BIOGRAPHIES), voted Goalkeeper of the Tournament, had spilled a shot by Rivaldo (Vitor Borba Ferreira) into his path. Ronaldo added his second goal 12 minutes later after Rivaldo cleverly feinted to allow the ball to run

© AFP 2002

2002
FIFA WORLD CUP
KOREA JAPAN

to his teammate. It confirmed Ronaldo as the tournament's leading scorer, with eight goals in seven games.

Overall attendance at the 64 matches was 2,705,566 (1,438,637 in Japan and 1,266,929 in South Korea). While organization was generally satisfactory, high prices and poor ticket distribution kept crowds down. Statistically, 272 yellow cards, including 16 in one game (both records), and 17 red cards were shown. Hakan Unsal of Turkey became the 100th player sent off in a final tournament. Among the 161 goals scored, Hakan Sukur hit the fastest in any finals—just 10.8 seconds into Turkey's 3–2 third-place triumph over South Korea.

The estimated worldwide television audience was a record 45 billion; Italy's Paolo Maldini completed a record 2,100 minutes of play over four World Cup finals; and Bora Milutinovic of Yugoslavia became the first man to have coached five different countries: Mexico (in 1986), Costa Rica (1990), the U.S. (1994), Nigeria (1998), and China (2002). Cafu (Marcos Evangelista de Moraes), Brazil's captain, became the first player to have appeared in three World Cup final matches.

While Belgium won the Fair Play award, there was a general increase in discipline in penalty areas, with players engaging in shirt pulling and wrestling while awaiting corners and free kicks. There also was criticism of the refereeing and poor interpretation by touchline officials—Spain had two apparently legitimate goals ruled out in its quarterfinal loss to South Korea. The final itself, however, was superbly controlled by the Italian referee, Pierluigi Collina.

(JACK ROLLIN)

3–2 by the local Dutch team Feyenoord. (Ironically, Borussia had won the German championship ahead of Leverkusen.) Pierre van Hooijdonk put Feyenoord ahead from a 33rd-minute penalty after Jon Dahl Tomasson had been pulled down in the penalty area by Jürgen Kohler. For this indiscretion 36-year-old Kohler was sent off in his last competitive match. Reduced to 10 players, Dortmund had more problems when van Hooijdonk doubled Feyenoord's lead with a 40th-minute free kick. Within two minutes of the restart following halftime, Marcio Amoroso converted a penalty after he had been shoved off the ball by Patrick Paauwe. The respite lasted barely three minutes before Tomasson restored Feyenoord's two-goal lead by taking advantage of a deflected through ball. Back came Dortmund, and in the 58th minute Jan

Koller scored with a dipping half-volley to make it 3–2. This led to a frantic finale, but the Germans were unable to save the match.

Domestically, Ajax achieved the Dutch League and Cup double, taking its number of such titles to 28 and 15, respectively. In Italy, Juventus won its 26th championship. Olympique Lyonnais, the most steadily improved team in France over the past six years, captured its first national title. Sporting Lisbon's title in Portugal owed much to Europe's leading scorer, Brazilian Mario Jardel, who had made 42 of the team's 74 league goals.

Celtic and Rangers, which between them had accounted for all but 19 of Scotland's championships since 1891, were at loggerheads with the rest of the Scottish Premier League clubs over voting rights and were threatening to

break away to play in a new European league or to make an unprecedented move to the English league.

Shakhtyor Donetsk was the unbeaten champion in Ukraine, winning 20 and drawing just 6 of its 26 matches. Kazakhstan, another former Soviet constituent, was transferred from Asia to Europe and thereby brought UEFA's membership to 52 out of a global total of 204 under the overall control of FIFA.

The dominance of European clubs was evident at the World Cup, where countries from around the world featured players based in Europe, notably Ronaldo, who transferred from Internazionale (Inter Milan) to Real Madrid for the 2002–03 season. The majority of Africa's more gifted players played for European clubs. Senegal recruited all but 2 of its 23-man World Cup squad from French clubs, while Cameroon had players who were based in eight different countries. Ireland's contingent was drawn almost entirely from English clubs, while Spain, Italy, and England each had just one player based abroad. English teams provided 101 World Cup players from 21 nations and several others who had been loaned to English clubs. The attraction of the English Premier League helped to boost overall local attendance figures with those of the three Football League divisions to 27,756,977, a level last achieved 30 years earlier. In 2001–02 the Premier League's average crowd of 34,324 was Europe's highest. (JACK ROLLIN)

The Americas. Brazil returned to the number one spot in the FIFA ranking of teams in 2002, mainly as a result of its World Cup win, its fifth. Paraguay's Olimpia celebrated its 100th anniversary in style by winning South America's premier club competition, the Libertadores de América Cup, for the third time, beating small-town Brazilian club São Caetano on penalties after scores of 0–1 and 2–1 in the two-legged final. Olimpia could not regain the Intercontinental Cup for South America, however, losing 2–0 to Real Madrid. Following the cancellation of the Mercosur and Merconorte cups for financial reasons, a proposed Pan-American Cup, for leading clubs from the Americas, had to be postponed. In its place a South American Cup, without Brazilian clubs, was played and won by Argentina's San Lorenzo, which had qualified by winning the previous year's Mercosur Cup. In the final San Lorenzo beat Colombia's Atlético Nacional (4–0, 0–0).

On the domestic scene most clubs continued to experience financial difficulties and owed their players between two and five months' salaries. This resulted in a three-week strike by all clubs in Chile and by clubs in Uruguay, Bolivia, and Peru; in the latter two countries, players even complained of not having enough food and of lacking money for transport to training sessions and matches. Some clubs could continue playing only with amateur youngsters from time to time. Fan interest in the game was as high as ever, and clubs' financial problems were primarily due to bad administration, in spite of the continual exodus of leading South American players, mostly to European clubs, for good transfer fees.

In league action Santos won its first Brazilian national title since 1984. Santos had collected numerous trophies in

the 1950s and '60s when Pelé was the team star, in the days before the national championship (dating from 1971) was played. In 2002 the cash-strapped team relied on youngsters, with Diego, age 17, and Robinho, 18, among the continent's brightest stars and worthy heirs of Pelé. Meanwhile, striker Joaquín Botero, of Bolivian champion Bolívar, set a professional world record by scoring 49 league goals during the season. On December 21, however, Paraguayan José Saturnino Cardozo scored his 50th league goal of the season for Toluca as it won the Mexican winter tournament in the second leg of the final.

In the MLS Cup, held in Foxboro, Mass., on October 20, the Los Angeles Galaxy defeated the New England Revolution 1–0 on a golden goal by rookie Carlos Ruiz in sudden-death overtime to capture its first Major League Soccer title. Los Angeles, which finished the regular season with a league-best record of 16 wins, 9 losses, and 3 ties, had lost in the championship match in 1996, 1999, and 2001. In the second full season of the Women's United Soccer Association, the Carolina Courage beat the Washington Freedom 3–2 in Founders Cup II on August 24. (ERIC WEIL)

Africa and Asia. In 2002 the association football world was focused on Asia as Japan and South Korea served as joint hosts of the 17th FIFA World Cup finals. It was the first time that the quadrennial tournament had been held in Asia and the first time that two countries had shared the honour. In the final match, held in Yokohama, Japan, on June 30, Brazil defeated Germany 2–0 in front of an appreciative crowd of some 69,000. South Korea lost 3–2 to Turkey in the semifinals for its best finish in six World Cup appearances, while Japan reached the round of 16 in only its second World Cup. China, playing in its first World Cup, lost all three games in its group. In May, however, Chinese defender Fan Zhiyi was named Asian Football Confederation (AFC) Player of the Year for 2001.

In Bamako, Mali, on February 10, Cameroon won its second consecutive African Cup of Nations, despite the absence from the semifinal and the final of injured striker Patrick Mboma. The Indomitable Lions defeated Senegal 3–2 on penalties after a scoreless final match. Senegal unexpectedly outdid Cameroon in the World Cup, however, upsetting defending champion France in the opening game and reaching the quarterfinals for the best finish of any African team. In April Senegal's El

Hadji Diouf was named African Football Confederation (CAF) Player of the Year for 2001, and in December he was selected as a finalist for the 2002 title, which was expected to be awarded in spring 2003.

In club football Al Hilal of Riyadh, Saudi Arabia, won the final AFC Cup Winners' Cup, defeating Chonbuk Hyundai of South Korea 2–1 in the final, held in Doha, Qatar, in March. In 2003 the Cup Winners' Cup, the Asian Super Cup, and the Asian Club Championship would be replaced by the AFC Champions League. Wydad Casablanca narrowly won the CAF Cup Winners' Cup 2–2 on aggregate over Asante Kotoko of Ghana. It was the first Cup Winners' Cup title for a Moroccan club. A few days later Zamalek of Egypt captured the CAF Champions League, beating Morocco's Raja Casablanca (0–0, 1–0) in the two-leg final.

(MELINDA C. SHEPHERD)

U.S. Football. *College.* The 2002 college football season ended on a high as Ohio State University won its first national football championship since 1968 by defeating the University of Miami (Fla.) 31–24 in double overtime in the Fiesta Bowl at Tempe, Ariz., on Jan. 3, 2003. Big Ten cochampion Ohio State (14–0) won for the seventh time in the season by seven points or less when it stopped heavily favoured Big East champion Miami (12–1) at its one-yard line on the last three plays of the game, breaking Miami's 34-game winning streak. The teams had finished the regular season with the only two undefeated records in Division I-A of the National Collegiate Athletic Association (NCAA)—Miami scoring the third most points per game and Ohio State allowing the second fewest. The Buckeyes were the eighth different national champion in eight years, which had not happened since 1963.

Southeastern Conference and Sugar Bowl winner Georgia (13–1) ranked third in both the media reporters' and coaches' polls, followed by Orange Bowl winner Southern California (12–2) and Big 12 and Rose Bowl winner Oklahoma (12–2). The coaches ranked Kansas State (11–2) ahead of Texas (11–2) for sixth, with the reporters reversing the order, and the polls each rounded out the top 10 with Big Ten cochampion Iowa (11–2), Michigan (10–3), and Pacific-10 champion Washington State. Other Division I-A conference champions were Boise State (12–1) in the Western Athletic, Marshall (11–2) in the Mid-American,

Texas Christian (10–2) in Conference USA, Colorado State (10–3) in the Mountain West, Florida State (9–5) in the Atlantic Coast, and North Texas (8–5) in the Sunbelt.

Southern Cal senior quarterback Carson Palmer was honoured as Player of the Year with the Heisman Trophy, as were Iowa senior quarterback Brad Banks, who was named the Associated Press's top player, and Penn State senior tailback Larry Johnson, winner of the Walter Camp Award and the Maxwell Trophy. Johnson led the division with 2,015 yd rushing, 8 yd per carry, and 2,575 all-purpose yards and won the Doak Walker Award for running backs. Banks won the Davey O'Brien Award for quarterbacks and led all passers with 166.1 efficiency-rating points, 8.2 yd per attempt, a 9.7 touchdown percentage, and a 1.55 interception percentage with just four passes picked off. Iowa's Kirk Ferentz and Notre Dame's Tyrone Willingham won top awards for Coach of the Year.

Other passing leaders were Brian Jones of Toledo with 70.2% of his passes completed and Kliff Kingsbury of Texas Tech, who made 45 touchdowns, 5,017 yd passing, and 4,903 yd total offense, including losses on sacks, as his team led Division I-A with 388.9 yd passing per game. Marshall quarterback Byron Leftwich had the most total offense per game, 355.6 yd in 12 games. Receiving leaders were Nate Burleson with 138 catches for Nevada, J.R. Tolver with 1,785 yd for San Diego State, and Rashaun Woods with 17 touchdowns for Oklahoma State, while Michigan State's Charles Rogers won the Fred Biletnikoff Award for the best receiver. Willis McGahee had the most rushing touchdowns with 27 for Miami, and Brock Forsey scored the most total touchdowns with 29 for Boise State, which ranked first with both 516.8 yd per game and 46.6 points per game. Air Force led all teams in rushing with 314.5 yd per game.

Kansas State led all defenses by allowing only 249 yd and 11.8 points per game, along with a second-ranked offensive output of 44.8 points per game. Texas Christian allowed the fewest rushing yards per game yield, 62.6, and Miami led pass defenses by allowing both 119.5 yd per game and a passer efficiency rating of 85.2. Arizona State defensive end Terrell Suggs set a Division I-A record with 22 sacks and won the Vince Lombardi Trophy for all linemen and the Bronko Nagurski Award, one of two honours for the top defensive player. The other, the Chuck Bednarik Award, went to Maryland linebacker E.J. Henderson, who also won the top linebacker award, named for Dick Butkus. Washington defensive tackle Rien Long was awarded the Outland Trophy for interior linemen; Kansas State's Terence Newman won the Jim Thorpe Award for defensive backs; and Wisconsin's Jim Leonhard was the interception leader with 11.

Ohio State's Mike Nugent had the most field goals and the best percentage, .923 (24 for 26 attempts), just ahead of Lou Groza Award winner Iowa's Nate Kaeding's .909. Colorado's Mark Mariscal won the Ray Guy Award with a 47.55-yd punting average that was only 0.04 yd behind that of leader Matt Payne for Brigham Young.

Among schools with smaller football budgets, 12–3 Western Kentucky won the Division I-AA championship game over 13–2 McNeese State (La.), 14–0 Grand Valley State (Mich.) defeated 14–1 Valdosta State (Ga.) for the Division II championship, 14–0 Mount Union (Ohio) won its sixth Division III title in seven years (and 96th game out of 97) by beating 14–1 Trinity (Texas), and 12–2 Carroll (Mont.) won the National Association of Intercollegiate Athletics (NAIA) championship game over 12–2 Georgetown (Ky.). Players of the Year were Sioux Falls (S.D.) running back Nick Kortan in the NAIA, Eastern Illinois quarterback Tony Romo on offense and Bethune-Cookman safety Rashean Mathis on defense in Division I-AA, Grand Valley State quarterback Curt Anes in Division II, and Mount Union running back Dan Pugh in Division III, where the trophy was named for St. John's (Minn.) coach John Gagliardi, who ended the season with 400 victories, eight short of the all-division record.

Professional. The old adage "A good defense beats a good offense" rang true on Jan. 26, 2003, when the National Football Conference (NFC) Tampa Bay Buccaneers routed the American Football Conference (AFC) Oakland Raiders 48–21 in Super Bowl XXXVII in San Diego, Calif. The Bucs' number one-ranked defense sacked Oakland's veteran quarterback Rich Gannon five times and made five interceptions as the 27-year-old franchise captured the National Football League (NFL) championship in its first Super Bowl appearance. Tampa Bay safety Dexter Jackson became only the seventh defensive player to be named Super Bowl Most Valuable Player (MVP). The win was a vindication for the Bucs' 39-year-old head coach, Jon Gruden, who had been acquired from the Raiders in March for what many thought was an outrageous price (two first-round draft picks, two second-round picks, and $8 million). In the playoffs Tampa Bay crushed the San Francisco 49ers 31–6 and then upset the Philadelphia Eagles 27–10 for the NFC title. Oakland beat the New York Jets 30–10 and defeated the Tennessee Titans 41–24 in the AFC championship

Dallas Cowboys running back Emmitt Smith (22) evades a tackle by the Seattle Seahawks on October 27; during the game Smith broke the all-time rushing record.

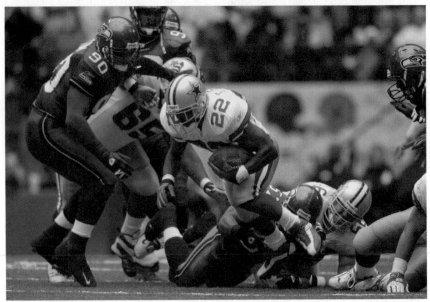

game for the Raiders' first trip to the Super Bowl since 1984.

In the regular season the AFC West champion Raiders had the league's best offense, with Gannon winning the MVP award. Oakland led the league with 389.8 yd total and 279.7 yd passing per game and finished second to the Kansas City Chiefs' league-high 29.2 points per game. Gannon, in his 15th season, set NFL records with 418 completions, 21 consecutive completions in a game, and 10 games of at least 300 yd passing. He led the league with 4,689 yd passing, ranked second to Chad Pennington's 104.2 passer rating for the Jets, and was only two touchdown passes behind league leader New England's Tom Brady, who had 28. Pennington tied Tampa Bay's Brad Johnson for fewest interceptions at six, with Johnson's .013 percentage the lowest, and the Chiefs' Trent Green led the league with 7.9 yd per pass attempt.

NFC South champion Tampa Bay's defense was the most statistically dominating in 17 years, its per-game yield of 252.8 yd leading the second-ranked Carolina Panthers by more than the Panthers led the 16th-ranked team. The Bucs also allowed NFL lows of 155.6 yd passing and 12.2 points per game and tied the Green Bay Packers for best turnover differential at plus-17.

The league realigned from six divisions into eight, each with four teams, as the expansion Houston Texans became the 32nd NFL team. Three teams repeated as champions after only two had done so in the previous four seasons. They were the Eagles in the NFC East, the Pittsburgh Steelers in the AFC North, and the Raiders, which won a third consecutive division title. The 49ers won the NFC West, and the Packers took the NFC North.

Other division winners were the Jets in the AFC East and the Titans in the AFC South. "Wild-card" play-off berths to the two best division runners-up in each conference went to the Colts and Cleveland Browns in the AFC and the New York Giants and Atlanta Falcons in the NFC. After having last qualified in 1994, the Browns had moved to Baltimore in 1996 and rejoined the league as an expansion team in 1999. The Panthers improved their record the most, by six games, and the biggest declines were by the Chicago Bears at nine games and the St. Louis Rams at seven.

The Dallas Cowboys' Emmitt Smith (see BIOGRAPHIES) broke Walter Payton's career records with 17,162 yd rushing and 4,052 carries after the sea-

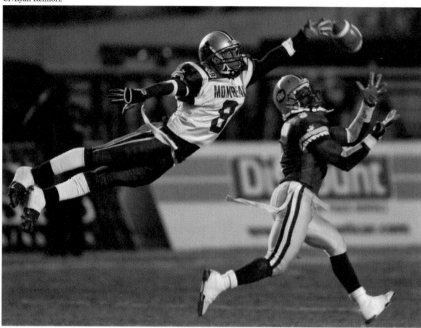

Reggie Durden of the champion Montreal Alouettes makes an unsuccessful attempt to intercept a pass thrown during the CFL Grey Cup game on November 24.

son, his 13th. NFL rushing leader Ricky Williams's 1,853 yd for the Miami Dolphins brought his team within five total yards of the league-leading Minnesota Vikings' 156.7 per game. The Denver Broncos' Clinton Portis led with 5.5 yd per carry, as did the Chiefs' Priest Holmes with 2,297 yd from scrimmage, 144 points, and 24 touchdowns (21 by rushing). Pittsburgh's league-best rushing defense allowed 85.9 yd per game.

Marvin Harrison's 143 catches for Indianapolis broke the previous record by 20, and his 1,722 yd receiving also led the league. San Francisco's Terrell Owens led receivers with 13 touchdowns, while Oakland's Jerry Rice became the first player with more than 200 touchdowns in his career and broke Payton's career record for yards from scrimmage with 22,242.

Defensive leaders were Miami's Jason Taylor with 18.5 sacks, Oakland's Rod Woodson and Tampa Bay's Brian Kelly with 8 interceptions each, and Chicago's Brian Urlacher with 116 official tackles, in which assists count for half. Leaders in the kicking game were Atlanta's Jay Feely with 138 points, New England's Adam Vinatieri with a .900 field-goal percentage (27 for 30), Carolina's Todd Sauerbrun with 45.5 gross yards per punt, San Francisco's Jimmy Williams with 16.8 yd per punt return, and the Arizona Cardinals' MarTay Jenkins with 28 yd per kickoff return.

(KEVIN M. LAMB)

Canadian Football. The Montreal Alouettes won the Canadian Football League (CFL) championship by defeating the Edmonton Eskimos 25–16 in the Grey Cup on Nov. 24, 2002, at Edmonton, Alta. Quarterback Anthony Calvillo was the game's Most Valuable Player for Montreal, which won its first Grey Cup in 25 years. East Division champion Montreal (13–5) led the league with 32.1 points and 398.3 yd per game behind Calvillo's league-high 8.8 yd per pass.

West Division winner Edmonton (13–5) featured league rushing leader John Avery with 1,448 yd and 6.3 yd per attempt, passing efficiency leader Ricky Ray, with 101.3 rating points, and Elfrid Payton, who had 16 sacks and was voted the league's most outstanding defensive player. The Saskatchewan Roughriders (8–10) led the league defensively with per-game yields of 21.8 points and 218.7 yd passing while leading CFL offenses with 139.9 yd rushing per game.

Most Outstanding Player Milt Stegall set CFL records with 23 touchdowns, both total and receiving, for the Winnipeg Blue Bombers (12–6). The slotback also led the league with 106 catches and 1,896 yd receiving as Winnipeg led with 308 yd passing per game. Bombers quarterback Khari Jones led league passers with 5,334 yd and 46 touchdowns, while the team's defense led the league by allowing

293.5 total yards and 84 yd rushing per game. Other individual honours went to Sean Millington with 14 rushing touchdowns for the British Columbia Lions (10–8), BC slotback Jason Clermont as outstanding rookie, Saskatchewan's Corey Holmes as outstanding special teams player, Montreal centre Brian Chiu as outstanding offensive lineman, and Montreal slotback Ben Cahoon as outstanding Canadian. The CFL added a team in Canada's capital after a six-year absence by expanding to nine teams with the Ottawa Renegades (4–14).   (KEVIN M. LAMB)

Australian Football. On a rainy Sept. 28, 2002, the Brisbane Lions established themselves as one of the greatest clubs in Australian Football League (AFL) history by winning the AFL Grand Final for the second successive year. A crowd of 91,817 packed into the Melbourne Cricket Ground to see the Lions beat Collingwood, one of footy's most famous clubs, by nine points, for a final score of 10.15 (75) to 9.12 (66). The Lions became the first club since the Adelaide Crows in 1997–98 to win back-to-back premierships. Before the game many tipsters had predicted a huge Lions win, but Collingwood played brilliantly and made Brisbane call on all its reserves to win. The star of the match was Collingwood captain Nathan Buckley, who, as best man on the ground, won the Norm Smith Medal.

Brisbane's Simon Black won the 2002 Brownlow Medal as the season's fairest and best player, and Brisbane captain Michael Voss was selected captain of the All-Australian team. Melbourne captain David Neitz won the Coleman Medal as the AFL's top goalkicker, while St. Kilda's Nick Riewoldt won the AFL Rising Star award as the best young player.
(GREG HOBBS)

Rugby Football. The year 2002 would be remembered as the 12 months in Rugby Union's history in which the New Zealand All Blacks returned to the top of the game's roll of honour. Fourth place in the 1999 Rugby World Cup was far below the expectations of the world's most famous Rugby Union team, and since then a top-to-bottom review of the game in New Zealand had been undertaken.

That review eventually resulted in a new team headed by coach John Mitchell that led New Zealand back to the top of the world rankings and to an impressive victory in the Tri-Nations championship in August 2002. The All Blacks won three of their four games, including a crucial 30–23 victory over South Africa.

The 2003 World Cup would have some new entrants after Georgia secured its place in the tournament with a close win over Russia in qualifying competition. Levan Tsabadze scored the try that sealed the victory for Georgia, which would be drawn against England as the World Cup opened.

England once again went into the Six Nations championship as the clear favourite but failed to achieve that elusive grand slam (victories against all five of the other nations). France emerged triumphant from the championship, its 20–15 victory over England in Paris proving the decisive result. Italy stayed at the bottom, conceding 183 points while Ireland emerged from the Celtic pack to take third, with wins over Wales, Scotland, and Italy.

It was a big year for the women's game, with the World Cup being staged in Barcelona, Spain, and the final in the city's Olympic Stadium. The tournament revolved around the two teams that had dominated the women's game in recent years, New Zealand and England. Unfortunately for England, the team showed its best form in the semifinals, where it thrashed Canada 53–10. New Zealand prevailed over England in the final by a score of 19–9 to retain the trophy it had won in 1998.

The Super 12 championship (contested by the best sides in New Zealand, Australia, and South Africa) also went to New Zealand as the Canterbury Crusaders defeated Australia's ACT Brumbies 31–13 in the final. In Europe Leicester continued to be the dominant club, capturing its second consecutive Heineken European Cup and its fourth consecutive English title.

In Rugby League, St. Helens won the English grand final, clinching a nerve-wracking 19–18 victory over the Bradford Bulls with a late kick from halfback Sean Long before 61,138 fans—a grand final record. In Australia the Sydney Roosters ended a 27-year title drought with a 30–8 victory over the New Zealand Warriors in a bruising National Rugby League grand final.
(PAUL MORGAN)

GOLF

Eldrick ("Tiger") Woods continued to leave his mark on golf in 2002. A third victory in the Masters at the Augusta (Ga.) National Golf Club and a second win in the U.S. Open at Bethpage State Park's Black Course on Long Island, N.Y., gave Woods the opportunity to become the first player to capture all four of the game's major championships in one season.

The magnitude of that feat might have daunted others, but the four trophies had already been in Woods's possession for a brief time following his 2001 Masters triumph. He had ended 2000 by winning the U.S. Open, British Open, and Professional Golfers' Association of America (PGA) championship.

As it turned out, the Grand Slam remained an elusive dream. In the British Open at Muirfield, Scot., Woods was forced to play during a freakish storm and recorded his highest score as a professional—81 in the third round. In the PGA championship he finished with four successive birdies but failed to overtake fellow American Rich Beem. For consistency, however, there was nobody to touch Woods, and as the only other golfer besides Tom Watson to top the PGA Tour money list four years in a row (Woods won $6,912,625 in 2002 to boost his career earnings on the circuit to $33 million), he remained the sport's dominant force.

At the Masters Woods faced a course that had been lengthened considerably since the 2001 tournament. Previously only Jack Nicklaus and Nick Faldo had been able to make a successful defense of the Masters title, but Woods joined them by shooting a closing round of 71 and a 12-under-par total of 276, three better than South Africa's Retief Goosen. The buildup to his attempt to win again in 2003, however, was overshadowed by a row over the absence of any women members at Augusta National.

At the U.S. Open, Woods shot a two-over-par 72 on the last round to finish with a three-under 277 and win again by three strokes, this time over American Phil Mickelson. The rain and high winds that hampered Woods's play during the British Open also spelled trouble for Colin Montgomerie of Scotland, who shot an 84 just 24 hours after he had scored a 64. South African Ernie Els enjoyed a two-shot lead going into the last day of the tournament, but the two-time U.S. Open champion had to struggle for the third major title of his career. The event went into a four-hole play-off between Els, Australians Steve Elkington and Stuart Appleby, and France's Thomas Levet, who all tied at 278, and then into sudden death between Els and Levet before the former prevailed.

The PGA championship was staged at Hazeltine National Golf Club in Chaska, Minn., and Beem admitted that he was stunned to be the victor. In 1995 the Arizona native had quit the game, but his interest in golf eventually returned. In only his fourth appearance at a major tournament, Beem held off Woods to win by one with a 10-under 278.

Despite Woods's dominance, there was one stage on which he had yet to impose his personality and genius—the Ryder Cup event. The cup was returned to European hands during the year after their dramatic 15½–12½ victory over the U.S. team at the De Vere Belfry in Sutton Coldfield, Eng. Postponed for 12 months because of the Sept. 11, 2001, terrorist attacks in the U.S., the Ryder Cup was played amid unprecedented security for a golf event. The competition was successful in restoring dignity and decorum to an occasion that had in 1999 witnessed some unsavoury crowd scenes and unsportsmanlike behaviour from members of the U.S. squad.

The lead story of the 2002 Ryder Cup was a controversial decision by U.S. captain Curtis Strange that backfired badly for the Americans. With the competition tied 8–8 going into the concluding 12 singles matches, Sam Torrance, captain of the European team, packed the top of his order with his strongest players in the hope of building an unstoppable momentum. Strange, in contrast, put world number two Mickelson in the 11th spot and Woods last. Mickelson, however, lost to Ryder Cup newcomer Phillip Price, who was ranked only 119th in the world, and Woods's clash with Swedish player Jesper Parnevik was too late to be relevant. A 3-m (10-ft) par putt by Ireland's Paul McGinley to halve with American Jim Furyk had already sealed the victory for Europe. Montgomerie led the European team with a top score of 4½ out of a possible 5 points.

Woods had gone into the contest on the back of another victory, the World Golf Championships–American Express Championship at Mount Juliet in Thomastown, County Kilkenny, Ire., but his comment that he would rather win that event—with its million-dollar first prize—than the Ryder Cup sparked a debate about his priorities. Strange's successor as captain, Hal Sutton, made it his mission for 2004 to have a team displaying the same passion as the Europeans.

There were two surprise winners in the World Golf Championships series.

In the Accenture match play in Carlsbad, Calif., Kevin Sutherland was ranked 62nd of the 64 players taking part and had not won a PGA Tour title in 183 attempts, but a last-green success over fellow Californian Scott McCarron gave him the million-dollar prize. Then, in the NEC Invitational at Sahalee Country Club in Sammamish, Wash., Australian Craig Parry achieved his first PGA Tour success at the 236th try. He became a million dollars richer as well, winning by four strokes. In the EMC–World Cup at Vista Vallarta in Puerto Vallarta, Mex., Japan's Shigeki Maruyama and Toshimitsu Izawa outplayed the U.S.'s Mickelson and David Toms to give Japan its first victory since 1957.

Masters runner-up Goosen topped the European money list for the second successive season, with Ireland's Padraig Harrington again second, while a spectacular 11 wins—and 13 worldwide—made Sweden's Annika Sörenstam the all-conquering performer on the Ladies Professional Golf Association (LPGA) Tour once more. In the women's majors, Sörenstam took the Kraft Nabisco title, South Korean Se Ri Pak the McDonald's LPGA championship, American Juli Inkster the U.S. Women's Open, and Australian Karrie Webb the Weetabix Women's British Open. Inkster then led the U.S. team as it regained the Solheim Cup, defeating Europe 15½–12½ at the Interlachen Country Club in Edina, Minn.

The Australian women's team and the U.S. men's team were the winners of the world amateur team championships at Saujana Golf and Country Club outside Kuala Lumpur, Malaysia. In the women's competition, Australia won the Espirito Santo Trophy by tiebreaker over Thailand. A week later France led the men's tournament with a round to play, but a 66 from American College Player of the Year D.J. Trahan helped the U.S. to a successful defense of the Eisenhower Trophy.

The year saw the passing of the player who had won more professional golf titles than anyone else. American legend Sam Snead, owner of what was generally considered to be the sweetest swing ever, died four days short of his 90th birthday. (*See* OBITUARIES.)

(MARK GARROD)

Ireland's Paul McGinley jumps for joy after sinking the putt that sealed Europe's victory over the United States in the Ryder Cup in September.

GYMNASTICS

The 2002 artistic gymnastics world championships took place in Debrecen, Hung., on November 20–24. On the women's side Yelena Zamolodchikova of Russia, the 2000 Olympic champion in vault, once again earned the vault title, winning gold with a score of 9.443. Zamolodchikova was followed by teammate Natalya Ziganshina, who earned the silver medal, and bronze medal winner Oksana Chusovitina of Uzbekistan. American Courtney Kupets upset two-time Olympic gold medalist Svetlana Khorkina of Russia for the uneven bars title, scoring a 9.550. Romania's Ioana Petrovschi earned the silver medal, and Russia's Lyudmila Eyova won bronze. Khorkina fell twice and finished in seventh place. Ashley Postell, a new face from the U.S. at international competitions, balanced her way to gold on the beam, scoring 9.537. Oana Mihaela Ban of Romania won the silver medal, and Irina Yarotska of Ukraine took the bronze. Spain's Elena Gómez scored a 9.487 on floor exercise to win the gold, followed by Verona Van Der Leur of The Netherlands and Samantha Sheehan of the U.S.

On the men's side Marian Dragulescu of Romania won the floor event with a score of 9.712, followed by Spain's Gervasio Deferr in second and Bulgaria's Jordan Jovtchev in third. Marius Daniel Urzica of Romania, the 2000 Olympic pommel horse champion, earned the gold medal in that event with a score of 9.787. Xiao Qin of China took the silver and Takehiro Kashima of Japan the bronze. On still rings Hungary's Szilveszter Csollany finished first with a score of 9.725. Jovtchev was second, and Italy's Matteo Morandi was third. China took first and third on vault, with Li Xiaopeng winning gold with a score of 9.818 and Yang Wei claiming the bronze. Poland's Leszek Blanik earned the silver. Li also won the parallel bars with a score of 9.812, followed by Mitja Petkovsek of Slovakia in second and Aleksey Sinkevich of Belarus in third. Vlasios Maras of Greece earned a 9.725 on the horizontal bar to win the gold, followed by Belarus's Ivan Ivankov and Slovakia's Aljaz Pegan.

The rhythmic world championships were held on July 12–14 in New Orleans, La. The Russians performed to near perfection to win the team gold medal with a score of 49.050. This made the fourth title for Russia at a rhythmic world championships. The Belarus team, which had medaled consistently at the worlds, including a second-place finish in 1999, performed a high-energy routine and showed excellent execution to finish second, followed by Greece in third.

At the Trampoline and Tumbling World Cup finals, France's Nicolas Fournials earned the men's tumbling title, and Russia's Anna Korobeynikova won the women's. In the men's trampoline competition, France's David Martin took top honours, while Russia's Irina Karavayeva won the women's title. In synchronized trampoline France earned gold on the men's side, and Great Britain won gold on the women's.　　　(LUAN PESZEK)

ICE HOCKEY

North America. The Detroit Red Wings dominated the National Hockey League (NHL) from start to finish during 2001–02, highlighting a high-pressure season by winning the Stanley Cup for the third time in six years. With a $64.4 million payroll and a star-studded roster, Detroit was derided by some as "the best team money can buy." The Red Wings were the oldest team in the league as well, with an average player age of about 31. None of those factors, however, prevented the team from storming through a season in which failure was never an option. The Red Wings were validated on June 13, 2002, when they beat the Carolina Hurricanes 3–1 to take the Stanley Cup finals four games to one.

The victory brought Detroit its 10th Stanley Cup and stood as a milestone in the careers of Dominik Hasek, the Czech goalie signed by the Red Wings in June 2001, and head coach Scotty Bowman. It ended a prolonged quest for Hasek, an Olympic champion and six-time Vézina Trophy winner, who had played 678 games, including playoffs, before he won his first NHL title. Hasek had taken a pay cut to sign with Detroit, but it was offset considerably by the $1 million bonus he earned when Detroit defeated the Hurricanes, who scored only seven goals off Hasek in the five-game series. The victory gave Bowman his ninth Stanley Cup, one better than the former NHL record he shared with Toe Blake, his mentor at Montreal. Bowman announced his retirement moments after the game was over, then put on his skates to take one last victory lap with the Cup held high above his head. His résumé also included 1,224 regular-season victories, the highest total in NHL history.

Bowman's coaching proficiency was evident in the superb teamwork he got all season long, from young players and veterans alike. Blessed with superior talent and a wealth of experience, the Red Wings put ego and nationality issues aside to blend into a team that played tough on defense and never lost its focus. Nicklas Lidstrom, a defenseman from Sweden who had played on Detroit's Stanley Cup championship teams in 1996–97 and

Luc Robitaille of the Detroit Red Wings advances the puck past the Carolina Hurricanes defense in the decisive fifth game of the Stanley Cup finals in June.

1997–98, was awarded the Conn Smythe Trophy as the most valuable player (MVP) of the 2002 play-offs—the first European so honoured. Lidstrom scored five goals, including two game winners, and had 11 assists for 16 points in 23 play-off games.

Lost in the outcome was the Carolina achievement of becoming the first 16th-seeded team in the play-offs to advance to the final series. It was an ironic success for a franchise that had compiled only three winning seasons in its 18-year existence as the Hartford Whalers before moving to Raleigh, N.C., in 1997. A frustrating close-checking Carolina defense limited Detroit to 14 goals in the series and sent all five games into the third period with the score tied or with one team leading by only one goal. It helped the Hurricanes win the opening game of the series 3–2 in overtime, but Detroit came back to capture game two 3–1. Game three ended in a 3–2 Detroit victory in triple overtime on Carolina's home ice, with 41-year-old Igor Larionov scoring the winning goal. It was a psychological blow the Hurricanes never overcame. A 3–0 Hasek shutout followed, and in game five Carolina had no answer for Brendan Shanahan, who scored two goals, or Steve Yzerman, the Red Wings captain, who battled through every play-off game on a damaged right knee. Hasek posted a record six shutouts during Detroit's 23-game play-off run to become the first European goalie to lead his team to the title.

Among the 30 teams that contested the 82-game regular season, Detroit led the NHL in victories (51) and points (116) to win its division by an eight-point margin over the runner-up St. Louis Blues (43 wins). Boston (101 points), Colorado and San Jose (99 each), Philadelphia (97), and Carolina (91) were the other division champions that advanced to the 16-team play-offs. Carolina made the Stanley Cup finals by beating New Jersey and Montreal, each by four games to two, before taking the Eastern Conference final series over Toronto by the same margin. Detroit returned to the final series by beating Vancouver four games to two and St. Louis four games to one as a prelude to defeating Colorado four games to three for the Western Conference championship. In that dramatic series the Red Wings took the final game 7–0.

In the 52nd NHL All-Star game in Los Angeles on Feb. 2, 2002, the World team scored five goals in the third period to defeat the North Americans 8–5. The 13 goals were half as many as the All-Star game had produced one year earlier, thanks to Tampa Bay's Nikolai Khabibulin, the World goalie from Russia. He stopped 20 shots to shut out North America in the third period, only the fourth All-Star goalie in 14 years to post a shutout period. In his first All-Star appearance, Eric Daze of Chicago was voted MVP, with two goals and an assist for North America.

International. The golden moment of the international ice hockey season occurred in Salt Lake City, Utah, on Feb. 24, 2002, when the Canadian men's team beat the U.S. 5–2 to win the Olympic ice hockey gold medal for the first time in 50 years. The long-awaited triumph set off a huge celebration throughout Canada, where thousands of ecstatic fans took to the streets for impromptu parades, joyous flag-waving, and unbridled revelry. The moment was doubly sweet for fans from Vancouver to the Maritime provinces because the Canadian victory over the U.S. came only three days after the Canadian women's team had upset the Americans 3–2 in their gold-medal game.

With the runner-up finish, the U.S. men earned their first Olympic ice hockey medal since the 1980 team won the gold in the Lake Placid, N.Y., Games. The silver medal brought little joy to either American team, however. Over the first 10 days of the men's Olympic tournament, the U.S. had played better than any of its rivals. The U.S. women's team had beaten Canada eight times in eight pre-Olympic meetings and was favoured to make a successful defense of the Olympic title it had won in Nagano, Japan, in 1998. With 14 players from the 1998 team on the 2002 roster, the U.S. forged a 31-game win streak against pre-Olympics opposition.

The U.S. men traveled a tougher road to the gold medal game than did the Canadians, and it showed when they squared off in a superb show of skill and intensity. On February 22 Canada beat a weak Belarus team 7–1 in a stress-free semifinal, while the U.S. eked out a 3–2 win over Russia in a semifinal that was physically and emotionally draining.

The Canadian men began to dominate the final contest in the second period and would have turned it into a rout but for American Mike Richter, who was named the Olympics' best goaltender. Richter had 34 saves and held off Canada on a five-against-three power play before Joe Sakic sent the go-ahead goal past him late in the second period. Canada put it away in the third period after Sakic assisted on a goal by Jarome Iginla and then scored his second goal of the game with 80 seconds left. Russia crushed Belarus 7–2 in the bronze-medal matchup.

The women's gold-medal game lived up to its billing. Canada, playing with visible confidence, outshot the U.S. 8–3 in the first 10 minutes and stuck with an aggressive style of offense throughout. Caroline Ouellette put Canada ahead before the game was two minutes old, and, with one second left in the second period, Jayna Hefford scored on a breakaway to give Canada a 3–1 lead that proved insurmountable. Sweden edged past Finland 2–1 for the bronze.

Slovakia won the 66th International Ice Hockey Federation (IIHF) men's world championship in Göteborg, Swed., on May 11 by beating Russia 4–3. Peter Bondra, a forward with the NHL Washington Capitals, scored his game-winning second goal with 1 minute 40 seconds left. It brought Slovakia its first-ever ice hockey gold medal in international play. Miroslav Satan of Slovakia and the NHL Buffalo Sabres led all scorers with 13 points and was named tournament MVP. The bronze medal went to Sweden.

The U.S. won its first IIHF world under-18 championship gold medal with a 3–1 victory over Russia on April 21 in Piestany, Slovakia. The Americans got a 35-save effort from goalkeeper James Howard and posted a 7–1 record for the tournament. (RON REID)

ICE SKATING

Figure Skating. On Feb. 21, 2002, Sarah Hughes, at 16 the youngest member of the U.S. Winter Olympics team, pulled off one of the most startling upsets in figure-skating history when she captured the gold medal in Salt Lake City, Utah, with the performance of a lifetime. Hughes held fourth place in the ladies competition after the short program. In the longer free skate, she delivered a go-for-broke effort fueled by dazzling athleticism and landed an unprecedented seven triple jumps, five in combination, during one of the most technically demanding programs ever skated in Olympic competition. Neither the silver medalist, Irina Slutskaya of Russia, nor bronze medalist Michelle Kwan, the six-time U.S. champion and overwhelming pre-Games favourite,

(continued on page 346)

The XIX Olympic Winter Games

by Melinda C. Shepherd

(Above) Opening Ceremony; (right) Closing Ceremony.

For 17 days, Feb. 8–24, 2002, Salt Lake City, Utah, played host to the XIX Olympic Winter Games. In the years leading up to the event, the scandal-ridden Salt Lake Olympic Committee had faced allegations of official bribery, corruption, and misused funds as well as a change in leadership. The terrorist attacks in the U.S. on Sept. 11, 2001, and the subsequent "war on terrorism" had also increased the need for additional costly security measures. Initially, some observers raised concerns that the event would become little more than a display of U.S. strength and patriotism, and some criticized the introduction in the Opening Ceremony of a U.S. flag from New York City's "ground zero," where the destroyed World Trade Center had stood. At the Closing Ceremony, however, International Olympic Committee Pres. Jacques Rogge praised Salt Lake, the largest city ever to host the Winter Olympics, for the "superb games."

Some 2,400 athletes representing 77 national Olympic committees from places as far away (and unlikely) as Cameroon, Kenya, India, Brazil, Iran, Thailand, and Fiji competed for 234 medals in 78 events. Athletes from 25 countries, including Australia and Estonia, took home medals, led by Germany's record 35 (12 gold). The U.S. finished with 34 (10 gold), far exceeding the 13 earned at the 1998 Winter Games in Nagano, Japan. Norway finished third with 24 (11 gold). Fifty-three competitors won more than one medal, notably Norwegian Ole Einar Bjørndalen (*see* BIOGRAPHIES), who swept all four golds in men's biathlon; Croatian Janica Kostelic (*see* BIOGRAPHIES), who captured three golds and a silver in Alpine skiing; Samppa Lajunen of Finland, who won all three Nordic

combined events; and Swiss sensation Simon Ammann, who upset the favourites to win both the 90-m and 120-m individual ski jumps. Eight speed-skating world records were broken, including two by Jochem Uytdehaage of The Netherlands and two by Germany's Claudia Pechstein (*see* BIOGRAPHIES). Men's skeleton, which returned to the Olympics after a 54-year absence, was won by third-generation U.S. Olympian Jim Shea, Jr. (*see* BIOGRAPHIES), just a month after the death of his grandfather, champion speed skater Jack Shea (*see* OBITUARIES). Two women's events made their

Olympic Champions, XIX Winter Games, Salt Lake City

ALPINE SKIING		
Men		
Downhill	Fritz Strobl (AUT)	1 min 39.13 sec
Slalom	Jean-Pierre Vidal (FRA)	1 min 41.06 sec
Giant slalom	Stephan Eberharter (AUT)	2 min 23.28 sec
Super G	Kjetil Andre Aamodt (NOR)	1 min 21.58 sec
Combined event	Kjetil Andre Aamodt (NOR)	3 min 17.56 sec
Women		
Downhill	Carole Montillet (FRA)	1 min 39.56 sec
Slalom	Janica Kostelic (CRO)	1 min 46.10 sec
Giant slalom	Janica Kostelic (CRO)	2 min 30.01 sec
Super G	Daniela Ceccarelli (ITA)	1 min 13.59 sec
Combined event	Janica Kostelic (CRO)	2 min 43.28 sec
NORDIC SKIING		
Men		
1.5-km sprint	Tor Arne Hetland (NOR)	2 min 56.9 sec
10-km freestyle pursuit	Johann Mühlegg (ESP)	49 min 20.4 sec
15-km classical	Andrus Veerpalu (EST)	37 min 7.4 sec
30-km freestyle mass start	Johann Mühlegg (ESP)	1 hr 9 min 28.9 sec
50-km classical	Mikhail Ivanov (RUS)	2 hr 6 min 20.8 sec
4 × 10-km relay	Norway	1 hr 32 min 45.5 sec
90-m ski jump	Simon Ammann (SUI)	269.0 pt
120-m ski jump	Simon Ammann (SUI)	281.4 pt
120-m team ski jump	Germany	974.1 pt
Nordic combined sprint (7.5-km)	Samppa Lajunen (FIN)	16 min 40.1 sec
Nordic combined 15-km	Samppa Lajunen (FIN)	39 min 11.7sec
Nordic combined team relay	Finland	48 min 42.2 sec
Women		
1.5-km sprint	Yuliya Chepalova (RUS)	3 min 10.6 sec
5-km freestyle pursuit	Olga Danilova (RUS)	24 min 52.1 sec

NORDIC SKIING		
Women (continued)		
10-km classical	Bente Skari (NOR)	28 min 5.6 sec
15-km freestyle mass start	Stefania Belmondo (ITA)	39 min 54.4 sec
30-km classical	Gabriella Paruzzi (ITA)	1 hr 30 min 57.1 sec
4 × 5-km relay	Germany	49 min 30.6 sec
BIATHLON		
Men		
10-km sprint	Ole Einar Björndalen (NOR)	24 min 51.3 sec
12.5-km pursuit	Ole Einar Björndalen (NOR)	32 min 34.6 sec
20 km	Ole Einar Björndalen (NOR)	51 min 3.3 sec
4 × 7.5-km relay	Norway	1 hr 23 min 42.3 sec
Women		
7.5-km sprint	Kati Wilhelm (GER)	20 min 41.4 sec
10-km pursuit	Olga Pyleva (RUS)	31 min 7.7 sec
15 km	Andrea Henkel (GER)	47 min 29.1 sec
4 × 7.5-km relay	Germany	1 hr 27 min 55.0 sec
FREESTYLE SKIING		
Men		
Moguls	Janne Lahtela (FIN)	27.97 pt
Aerials	Ales Valenta (CZE)	257.02 pt
Women		
Moguls	Kari Traa (NOR)	25.94 pt
Aerials	Alisa Camplin (AUS)	193.47 pt
SNOWBOARDING		
Men		
Parallel giant slalom	Philipp Schoch (SUI)	
Halfpipe	Ross Powers (USA)	46.1 pt

(Page 344) AP/Wide World Photos; (above) © Wolfgang Rattay/Reuters 2002

first appearance—skeleton and bobsleigh, which was won in an upset by Americans Jill Bakken and Vonetta Flowers, the first black Winter Olympic gold medalist.

Once again, a judging scandal in figure skating captured world headlines.

In the pairs competition a French judge initially claimed that she had been pressured to vote for gold medal winners Yelena Berezhnaya and Anton Sikharulidze of Russia over the second-place Canadian pair, Jamie Salé and David Pelletier (*see* BIOGRAPHIES).

Although the judge later recanted her story, after four days of discussions Salé and Pelletier were awarded a second pair of gold medals.

Melinda C. Shepherd is Associate Editor of Encyclopædia Britannica Yearbooks.

SNOWBOARDING (continued)		
Women		
Parallel giant slalom	Isabelle Blanc (FRA)	
Halfpipe	Kelly Clark (USA)	47.9 pt
FIGURE SKATING		
Men	Aleksey Yagudin (RUS)	1.5 pt
Women	Sarah Hughes (USA)	3.0 pt
Pairs	Yelena Berezhnaya, Anton Sikharulidze (RUS)*; Jamie Salé, David Pelletier (CAN)*	
Ice dancing	Marina Anissina, Gwendal Peizerat (FRA)	2.0 pt
SPEED SKATING		
Men		
500 m	Casey FitzRandolph (USA)	1 min 9.23 sec
1,000 m	Gerard van Velde (NED)	1 min 7.18 sec†
1,500 m	Derek Parra (USA)	1 min 43.95 sec†
5,000 m	Jochem Uytdehaage (NED)	6 min 14.66 sec†
10,000 m	Jochem Uytdehaage (NED)	12 min 58.92 sec†
Women		
500 m	Catriona LeMay Doan (CAN)	1 min 14.75 sec
1,000 m	Chris Witty (USA)	1 min 13.83 sec†
1,500 m	Anni Friesinger (GER)	1 min 54.02 sec†
3,000 m	Claudia Pechstein (GER)	3 min 57.70 sec†
5,000 m	Claudia Pechstein (GER)	6 min 46.91 sec†
SHORT-TRACK SPEED SKATING		
Men		
500 m	Marc Gagnon (CAN)	41.802 sec‡
1,000 m	Steven Bradbury (AUS)	1 min 29.109 sec

SHORT-TRACK SPEED SKATING		
Men (continued)		
1,500 m	Apolo Anton Ohno (USA)	2 min 18.541 sec
5,000-m relay	Canada	6 min 51.579 sec
Women		
500 m	Yang Yang (A) (CHN)	44.187 sec
1,000 m	Yang Yang (A) (CHN)	1 min 36.391 sec
1,500 m	Ko Gi Hyun (KOR)	2 min 31.581 sec
3,000-m relay	South Korea	4 min 12.793 sec†
ICE HOCKEY		
Men (winning team)	Canada	4–1–1
Women (winning team)	Canada	5–0–0
CURLING		
Men (winning team)	Norway	9–2–0
Women (winning team)	Great Britain	9–4–0
BOBSLEIGH (BOBSLED)		
Two man	Christoph Langen, Markus Zimmermann (GER 1)	3 min 10.11 sec
Four man	Germany 2	3 min 7.51 sec
Women	Jill Bakken, Vonetta Flowers (USA 2)	1 min 37.76 sec
LUGE		
Men (singles)	Armin Zöggeler (ITA)	2 min 57.941 sec
Men (doubles)	Patric-Fritz Leitner, Alexander Resch (GER)	1 min 26.082 sec
Women (singles)	Sylke Otto (GER)	2 min 52.464 sec
SKELETON		
Men	Jim Shea, Jr. (USA)	1 min 41.96 sec
Women	Tristan Gale (USA)	1 min 45.11 sec

*Two gold medals awarded. †World record. ‡Olympic record.

345

(continued from page 343)

came close to matching Hughes, who radiated joy.

Hughes's upset victory helped to return respect to a sport that had suffered a judging scandal in the pairs competition when the French judge, Marie Reine Le Gougne, cast the decisive vote that gave the gold medal to Yelena Berezhnaya and Anton Sikharulidze of Russia, despite six flaws in their program. The Canadian team of Jamie Salé and David Pelletier (see BIOGRAPHIES) had skated an error-free program earlier, hitting all of their elements and thrilling an appreciative crowd. When the marks were posted for presentation, however, the Canadians were outscored by the Russians 5–2 (with two tie votes.) The vote left Salé in tears and Pelletier in stunned disbelief moments before the crowd of 16,000 spectators sent up an angry chorus of booing.

During the investigation launched by the International Skating Union (ISU), Le Gougne initially claimed that she had been coerced into voting for the Russian pair by Didier Gailhaguet, the president of the French skating federation. Gailhaguet denied the charge, amid allegations that Le Gougne's vote was a trade-off for the Russian vote in favour of the French team in ice dancing. Five days later the ISU, bowing to pressure from both the International Olympic Committee and the public, awarded a second set of gold medals to the Canadians while allowing the Russians to keep theirs. In April both Le Gougne and Gailhaguet were given three-year suspensions by the ISU and were banned from the 2006 Winter Olympics in Turin, Italy.

No such controversy sullied the men's competition, thanks to a flawless performance by Aleksey Yagudin of Russia. The reigning European champion landed two quadruple jumps and won four perfect 6s from the judges. Russia's Yevgeny Plushchenko took the silver medal, while the bronze went to American Timothy Goebel in his first Olympic competition.

In ice dancing Marina Anissina and Gwendal Peizerat of France won the gold medal. The silver medal went to Irina Lobachyova and Ilya Averbukh of Russia, while Barbara Fusar Poli and Maurizio Margaglio of Italy won the bronze, despite a fall.

Yagudin followed his Olympic success with another gold-medal performance on March 21 at Nagano, Japan, where he won the world championship

Canada's Jamie Salé and David Pelletier and Russia's Yelena Berezhnaya and Anton Sikharulidze show off their joint Olympic figure-skating gold medals. The Canadian pair was upgraded from the silver after a judging scandal.

for the fourth time in five years. After skating a difficult program that included two quadruple and six triple jumps, Yagudin was rewarded with seven 5.9 marks and two 6s for presentation. Goebel also skated a strong program to win the silver medal, while the bronze went to Japan's Takeshi Honda, despite a fall.

All of the other Olympic winners skipped the world championships. Slutskaya beat Kwan for the eighth time in their last 10 meetings and thus prevented the defending champion from taking her fifth world title. In pairs competition Shen Xue and Zhao Hongbo, the bronze medalists in Salt Lake City, survived a fall to become the first Chinese duo to win at the world championships. The ice-dancing gold medal went to Lobachyova and Averbukh.

Speed Skating. Eight world records fell on the ultrahard ice of the Utah Olympic Oval during the Games' long-track competition. Jochem Uytdehaage of The Netherlands captured two gold medals with world-record performances in the 5,000-m and 10,000-m finals and took the 1,500-m silver medal behind American Derek Parra. Germany's Claudia Pechstein (see BIOGRAPHIES) ruled the women's long track, striking gold in world-record time at 3,000 m and 5,000 m.

At the long-track world championships, held in Heerenveen, Neth., on March 15–17, Uytdehaage took the men's all-around title. Germany's Anni Friesinger, winner of the 1,500 m in Salt Lake City, captured her second consecutive women's all-around title.

In short-track competition China's Yang Yang (A) became the first athlete from her nation to capture a Winter Olympics gold medal when she won the women's 500-m final; she struck gold again in the 1,000 m. Australia won its first Winter Games gold medal by accident when Steven Bradbury was the last man standing in the five-man 1,000-m final. China's Li Jiajun had run into American Apolo Anton Ohno on the final turn, and the crash knocked down every skater except Bradbury. Ohno, who dived across the finish line for the silver medal, won a gold four nights later in the 1,500 m, thanks to the disqualification of South Korea's Kim Dong Sung.

At the short-track world championships in Montreal in April, Yang took the women's overall title for the sixth straight year, while Kim swept all four individual events to win the men's overall title.   (RON REID)

JUDO

Among the most notable judo events of 2002 were the world championships by team of nations, held on August 31–September 1 in Basel, Switz., and the junior world championships, held on September 12–15 in Jeju, S.Kor. Japan dominated the former event. In a dramatic finale to the women's competition, heavyweight Midori Shintani, a silver medalist at the 2001 world championships and a fast-rising star in the sport, scored an *ippon* (full-point) victory over Daima Beltran of Cuba to give the Japanese women the team title. Cuba's women's team finished in second place, and Italy and China tied for third. In the men's competition Japan again came out on top, sweeping France in the semifinals by a score of 7–0 and posting another 7–0 victory over Georgia in the finals. Even more impressive was the fact that in 11 of those 14 matches, the Japanese men won by *ippon*. Georgia went home with the silver medal, while France and Italy shared the bronze.

Japanese fighters also stood out at the junior world championships. Yoshie Ueno, the women's under-63-kg gold medalist, won both the Best Judoka award for best overall performance and the Ippon Trophy for most victories by *ippon*. On the men's side, under-90-kg champion Toshihiro Takesawa was the Best Judoka award winner, while heavyweight gold medalist Young Hwan Choi of South Korea earned the Ippon Trophy. Together the Japanese men's and women's teams won six golds, one silver, and three bronze medals, followed by Brazil with two golds and two bronzes. (FRANÇOIS BESSON)

RODEO

Validating his bold initiatives to modernize the century-old sport, Commissioner Steve Hatchell of the Professional Rodeo Cowboys Association (PRCA) announced numerous changes in December 2002 designed to further showcase top athletes in televised competitions. The ProRodeo Tour, established in 2000, would encompass 20 regular-season rodeos plus three finale events to be held in Las Vegas, Nev., Omaha, Neb., and Dallas, Texas. Significantly, the tour realized Hatchell's goal of separating the elite athletes from the rank-and-file competitors of the 8,500-member sports organization.

Other announcements included expanded television agreements promising to deliver 211 hours of coverage split between ESPN, the Outdoor Life Network, and, most notably, CBS. According to the commissioner, 23 million fans attended PRCA-sanctioned rodeos in 2002, placing pro rodeo seventh among all American sports in overall attendance.

Pro rodeo's world champions were crowned at the $4.8 million Wrangler National Finals Rodeo (NFR), December 6–15 in Las Vegas. Charmayne James of Athens, Texas, claimed her 11th world barrel-racing title, a record. The victory broke an eight-year dry spell that had followed her 10 consecutive championships (1984–93) earned with her now-retired horse Scamper.

Trevor Brazile of Anson, Texas, claimed the title of world all-around champion cowboy, with earnings of $273,998; world championships in professional rodeo were based on money earned over the yearlong season in addition to money earned at the season-ending NFR. Brazile earned money in calf roping, steer roping, and team roping.

Team ropers Speed Williams of Jacksonville, Fla., and Rich Skelton of Llano, Texas, claimed their sixth-straight world titles to set a record for consecutive wins. They remained one championship short of the all-time record of seven world titles set by Pro-Rodeo Hall of Famers Jake Barnes and Clay O'Brien Cooper.

In the saddle-bronc riding event, Glen O'Neill of Didsbury, Alta., became the first cowboy ever to win the PRCA world title in addition to national titles in Australia and Canada. Bull rider Blue Stone of Ogden, Utah, defended his 2001 title, becoming the first cowboy since 1981 to win back-to-back championships in that event. Other rodeo world champions for 2002 were Bobby Mote of Redmond, Ore., bareback riding, $174,377, and Sid Steiner of Bastrop, Texas, steer wrestling, $162,516.

In the Professional Bull Riders (PBR), Brazilian Ednei Caminhas of Palves, São Paolo, captured the PBR championship held in October in Las Vegas. Caminhas earned $291,921 for the year. His win marked the third time in the association's 10-year history that a Brazilian had claimed the PBR championship. The PBR was scheduled to make the jump to network television in 2003 with competitions to be shown on NBC and CBS. (GAVIN FORBES EHRINGER)

ROWING

World rowing moved forward in 2002 by clearly defining the path of progress from junior to full senior status following promotion by the Fédération In-

All-around champion cowboy Trevor Brazile competes in the calf-roping event at the National Finals Rodeo.

AP/Wide World Photos

ternationale des Sociétés d'Aviron (FISA) of the World Under 23 Regatta to world championship status.

The high standard of racing at the FISA world championships in Seville, Spain, in September indicated the strength being developed for the 2004 Olympic Games in Athens. Thirteen of the 53 nations racing in Seville shared the 24 gold medals. Three titles were decided by less than one second in men's events. Germany secured the closest verdict when it defeated Great Britain, the titleholder, in coxless fours by only 0.25 sec, but the British coxed four crew avenged this setback, winning by 2.18 sec. Germany was hard pressed by Poland to retain the quadruple sculls by 0.86 sec and finished clear of the U.S. in coxed pairs. The fourth German men's gold was won by Marcel Hacker in single sculls.

After an earlier defeat by Australia in the World Cup series, the British coxless pair—Matthew Pinsent and James Cracknell—led all the way to beat South Africa by 1.33 sec to retain their title. In eights Canada also went ahead from the start and opened up a clear lead before denying Germany another title by 1.24 sec. Hungary retained the double sculls. Italy dominated the men's lightweight events with three victories; Chile, Denmark, and Ireland were the other men's lightweight winners.

Australia won three of the 10 women's events but lost narrowly by 0.85 sec to the United States in eights. Bulgaria won both titles in open and lightweight single sculls. The other gold medalists were Germany (quadruple sculls), Great Britain (lightweight coxless pairs), New Zealand (double sculls), and Romania (coxless pairs).

Germany continued its unbroken supremacy in the World Cup, the sixth series of which was held in Hazewinkel, Belg.; Lucerne, Switz.; and Munich, Ger. The top nations in 2002 were Germany (67 points), Australia (50), Great Britain (28), Italy (27), and Denmark (21). Overall, Germany (209 points) led Great Britain (103) and Italy (74).

The World Under 23 Regatta, held in Genoa, Italy, in July, was a triumph for the host nation, which captured four gold medals. Australia and Germany each won three, and there were double successes for Canada and France. The five other gold medals went to the Czech Republic, Great Britain, Romania, Spain, and the United States.

Italy was in the forefront with eight medals, three of them gold, at the FISA world junior championships in Trakai,

Lithuania, in August. Romania also earned three golds, while Australia and the Czech Republic each won twice. The other gold medalists were Belarus, France, Germany, and Latvia.

At the 153rd Henley Royal Regatta in England, overseas entries from five countries won seven trophies. The U.S. reached its 100th victory when three Harvard University crews won the Ladies Plate (eights), Temple Cup (eights), and Britannia Cup (coxed fours). Canada triumphed for the first time in the Grand Challenge Cup (eights); Denmark took the Stewards Cup (coxless fours); and the Double Sculls cup went to France. A month later, at the Commonwealth rowing championships in Nottingham, Eng., the principal honours went to Australia, Canada, and England, which shared 18 titles.

In the 148th University Boat Race, the crews overlapped, with Cambridge always less than one length ahead, for nearly 6.4 km (4 mi). Oxford forged ahead in the last three minutes, however, to win a memorable encounter by only ⅔ of a length, which reduced the Cambridge lead in the series to 77–70.

(KEITH L. OSBORNE)

SAILING (YACHTING)

In 2002 the sailing world was still reeling from the loss of Sir Peter Blake—winner of the America's Cup for New Zealand in 1995—who was killed in December 2001 during a robbery aboard his research vessel on the Amazon River.

Meanwhile, technology continued its expensive quest for speed under sail. New designs featured streamlined lead bulbs on long carbon-fibre struts suspended beneath space-age composite hulls that sported lofty rigs of similar light material. In some designs a larger righting moment at minimum weight was afforded by keel structures that pivoted at the hull to move the bulb outward toward the wind, while water ballast was pumped to tanks on the windward side of the boat to offset the heeling moment of the sails. The results were spectacular, producing large boats that planed off the wind like dinghies at speeds very nearly equal to the speed of the wind driving them. These monohulls and similarly constructed large catamarans were shattering long-held sailing speed records—and then breaking the new records again. One unfortunate side effect of this remarkable resistance to heeling was a decided reduction in what sailors called "sea kindliness."

Pyewacket crosses the finish line in the Newport–Bermuda Race in a time of 53 hr 39 min 22 sec, breaking the old record by 3 hr 52 min 28 sec.

These boats banged and lurched through the sea, responding immediately with a quick snap back to the vertical and demanding that those onboard hold on tight. This characteristic of power may have been responsible for an increasing number of crew overboard incidents that occurred in 2002. Sailing authorities were urging that safety gear be worn under heavy air conditions, when these very stiff boats might behave "unkindly" toward their crews.

The Volvo Around the World Race between eight "Open 60" class monohulls was won by the superbly prepared German entry, *Illbruck*, which established a new monohull 24-hour distance record on the North Atlantic passage, achieving 484 nm (nautical miles; 1 nm = 1.85 km). The Cruising Club of America's Newport–Bermuda Race in June featured a long southerly meander of the Gulf Stream and a strong southwesterly airflow that produced fast but hard sailing. The big boats relished the conditions, slamming into the breaking seas and free-falling into the succeeding troughs. Corrected-time winners were *Zaraffa* (St. David's Lighthouse trophy) and *Blue Yankee* (Gibb's Hill Lighthouse trophy). *Pyewacket* trimmed nearly four hours off the previous course record set by *Boomerang* in 1996 and was then shipped to the Great Lakes, where it broke the course record for the Chicago–Mackinac Race, finishing the 333 nm in just under 24 hours.

In quiet conditions the 27.4-m (90-ft) *Alfa Romeo* recorded the second fastest time—2 days 4 hr 58 min 52 sec—in the 2002 Australian Sydney–Hobart Race.

The new 33.5-m (110-ft) catamaran *Maiden II* set a multihull 24-hour speed record, achieving 695 nm, with one burst to 44 knots, and surpassing *Playstation*'s 2001 record of 687 nm.

Nor were small boats immune from technology's appeal. An International 14 dinghy flew across the water on lifting foils added to its rudder and keel. A foil-equipped catamaran was aiming for 50 knots under sail at year's end. Several new planing dinghies appeared with obvious ancestry in the high-performance Australian 18s. Even the venerable Stars class voted to reduce the overall weight allowance of crews, which would improve the power-weight ratio of the boats. The Olympic catamaran Tornado class added an asymmetrical spinnaker for more downwind power, and the Laser class voted the first significant changes in its rigging in some 30 years.

The 2002 International Sailing Federation Sailors of the Year were the team of Sofia Bekatorou and Emilia Tsoulfa of Greece and Britain's Ben Ainslie, who became the first person to win the award twice. At year's end *Orack* of San Francisco was to take on the Swiss *Alinghi* for the right to contest the America's Cup in February 2003. *Orack*'s onboard radar system had been challenged and found illegal, but cup officials chose to invite other teams to adopt the technology in the future.

(JOHN B. BONDS)

SKIING

Alpine Skiing. In 2002 the Austrian men's team did not miss a beat when Hermann Maier, who had won four World Cup titles in each of the two previous seasons, was sidelined with a broken leg from a preseason motorcycle accident. Stephan Eberharter, who had built a large following for the classy way in which he had gone from world champion to national team castoff after a couple of knee surgeries and then returned to the team, stepped out of Maier's immense shadow during the year. He captured three World Cup titles (men's overall, downhill, and supergiant slalom [super G])—and scored an Olympic hat trick with gold

in giant slalom (GS), silver in super G, and bronze in downhill at the Winter Games in Salt Lake City, Utah.

Eberharter, second to Maier in 2001, overwhelmed the opposition in 2002. He won 10 races—six downhills, three super Gs, and a giant slalom—in grabbing the overall title with 1,702 points. He finished 606 points ahead of Norwegian runner-up Kjetil Andre Aamodt, which meant that even if Aamodt had won six races (100 points for first) in which Eberharter did not compete, he could not have caught him.

Slalom and GS, the so-called technical events, were more competitive. Frenchman Frederic Covili won the 2001–02 season-opening GS en route to claiming the World Cup crown, narrowly beating Benjamin Raich of Austria (with Eberharter third). Slalom was a duel between Croatian Ivica Kostelic and American Bode Miller, who went from turning in no World Cup slalom finishes in the previous two seasons to giving the best U.S. performance in slalom and GS since Phil Mahre in 1983. Kostelic finished 51 points ahead of Miller (611–560). Miller's storybook season—three slalom wins and another in GS—saw him finish not only second in slalom but fourth overall.

In Salt Lake City Janica Kostelic, Ivica's sister, became the first competitor to earn four Alpine skiing medals at a single Games. (*See* BIOGRAPHIES.) She won gold in the slalom, the GS, and the combined event and silver in the super G. Michaela Dorfmeister of Austria was the women's overall World Cup champion. She won five races during the year, compiling 1,271 points to second-place finisher and teammate Renate Goetschl's 931. Strangely, Dorfmeister did not win a title in any single event. Her consistency, with 15 top-six results, gave her the overall crown, however. She was second to Italy's Isolde Kostner in downhill, third behind German Hilde Gerg in super G, and second to Sonja Nef of Switzerland in GS. The slalom title went to Laure Pequegnot of France, whose first World Cup win came at Copper Mountain, Colorado, with American Kristina Koznick second in the final slalom points.

Nordic Skiing. Standouts in Nordic skiing at the Winter Games included Samppa Lajunen of Finland, who took home three gold medals after placing first in the Nordic combined and Nordic combined sprint events and helping the Finnish squad take the

team combined competition. Swiss ski jumper and Harry Potter look-alike Simon Ammann became one of the biggest stars of the Games after he came out of nowhere to win both the 90-m and 120-m individual events. In relay competition the Norwegian men dominated the 40-km race, while Germany's women's team captured the 20-km gold.

Three Nordic skiers—Johann Mühlegg of Spain and two Russians, Larisa Lazutina and Olga Danilova—were ejected from the Games on the last day when they tested positive for darbepoetin (a drug designed to increase the production of red blood cells); Mühlegg and Lazutina (who had been barred from an earlier race when a blood test showed elevated hemoglobin levels) were stripped of the medals they had won that day.

Sweden's Per Elofsson claimed his second straight World Cup cross-country title, holding off fast-closing Thomas Alsgaard of Norway by three points after 20 races. Norwegian Bente Skari started fast and finished fast with seven victories as she earned her third World Cup crown in four years. With the top Russian women skipping the final month of the season, keeping their heads down in the aftermath of the Olympic doping scandal (and missing six races), Skari was unstoppable.

Norway's Thomas Alsgaard (bottom) stretches out to tie teammate Frode Estil for the silver medal in the men's 10-km cross-country freestyle pursuit at the Winter Olympics.

AP/Wide World Photos

Thumb-sized ski jumper Adam Malysz of Poland rolled to his second straight World Cup title, winning seven events and finishing in the top three in 14 of 20 meets. German Sven Hannawald became the first skier to win all four meets in the renowned Springertournee held in Germany and Austria, but he could not keep up with Malysz.

Ronny Ackermann of Germany won five Nordic combined events and was second or third in 10 others as he earned his first combined title. Austrian Felix Gottwald ran out of steam after the Olympics and could not hold off Ackermann, who finished with 2,110 points to 1,986 for Gottwald, the 2001 combined king. For the first time in history, two American skiers finished in the top 10, with Todd Lodwick placing 6th and Bill Demong 10th.

Freestyle Skiing. The American "Killer B's"—aerialist Eric Bergoust and moguls skier Jeremy Bloom—entered the 2002 season at different levels. Bergoust, the 1998 Olympic champion and 2001 World Cup title winner, was the poster boy for aerials success. Bloom, meanwhile, had put a football scholarship to the University of Colorado on hold to chase his Olympic dream.

By season's end Bergoust had won three more contests to clinch his second straight World Cup crown. Bloom finished ninth at the Winter Games but rebounded to win the World Cup moguls title, notching a victory in the World Cup competition at Lake Placid, N.Y. Kari Traa of Norway, winner of the Olympic gold in women's moguls in 2002, later breezed to the World Cup title, with Americans Hannah Hardaway, Shannon Bahrke, and Ann Battelle finishing second, third, and fourth, respectively. In dual moguls Richard Gay of France won the men's title, while Christine Gerg of Germany was the women's champion.

Snowboarding. The snowboarding competition at the Winter Olympics was staged at Utah's Park City Mountain Resort. Americans dominated the halfpipe event, with Ross Powers taking the men's gold over teammate Danny Kass and Kelly Clark winning the women's gold over Doriane Vidal of France. Philipp Schoch of Switzerland was the gold medalist in the men's GS, while France's Isabelle Blanc won the women's GS.

Canadian Jasey Jay Anderson and Karine Ruby of France were the World Cup overall champions. Anderson also captured the Fédération Internationale de Ski World Cup snowboardcross title, while Austrian Doresia Krings won the women's snowboardcross. In the halfpipe competition Nicola Pederzolli of Austria was the top woman, and Germany's Jan Michaelis claimed the men's title.

(PAUL ROBBINS)

SQUASH

With most of the world's top squash players participating at the Commonwealth Games, held on July 25–August 4 in Manchester, Eng., the singles events became something of an unofficial world championships. The men's final saw another duel between the number one and number two players, Peter Nicol of England and Jonathon Power of Canada. Nicol had taken the title four years previously in Malaysia while competing under the Scottish flag, but this time he was dominated by the Canadian in a final in which Nicol appeared tired after an arduous semifinal against David Palmer of Australia. On the women's side another Australian, Sarah Fitz-Gerald, was the favourite to win the singles title—the only title in the women's game to have eluded her. The 33-year-old Fitz-Gerald did not disappoint, beating New Zealander Carol Owens in the final. In doubles competition Owens and Leilani Rorani secured the gold for New Zealand. Rorani also teamed with Glen Wilson to snatch the mixed doubles title, and in men's doubles Nicol made up for his failure in the singles final by winning gold with Lee Beachill.

The Commonwealth Games were closely followed by the Pan American championships in Quito, Ecuador. The men's title went to Argentine Jorge Gutiérrez, who beat Eric Gálvez of Mexico in the final. Samantha Teran of Mexico was the women's winner; she took the title by defeating Marnie Baizley of Canada.

Next came the Asian Games in Busan, S.Kor., in September and October. Ong Beng Hee of Malaysia topped Mansoor Zaman of Pakistan to win the men's gold, and Rebecca Chiu of Hong Kong upset top-seeded Nicol David of Malaysia for the women's title.

It was in late August that word emerged that squash had come tantalizingly close to making the shortlist of three possible Olympic additions for 2008 in Beijing but had missed out yet again despite a concerted campaign and positive signs from within the International Olympic Committee.

In November at the Women's World Open in Doha, Qatar, Fitz-Gerald stretched her unbeaten streak into a 13th month and overcame Natalie Pohrer of England in a close final. It was Fitz-Gerald's fifth World Open title. December saw more world titles being contested. In Chennai, India, the previously postponed men's World Junior championship saw an all-English final with James Willstrop beating Peter Barker, but they failed to return home with the team title as England lost to Pakistan in the final. Meanwhile, in his adopted base of Antwerp, Belg., David Palmer won his first World Open title when he beat fellow Australian John White in a five-game final in which he saved two match balls in the fourth game.

(ANDREW SHELLEY)

SWIMMING

The year 2002 was a busy one in swimming; 12 long-course (50-m pool) and an amazing 22 short-course (25-m pool) world records were broken—some more than once—as swimmers took advantage of several high-profile international meets. In long-course competition the U.S. regained its spot as the world's swimming superpower, firmly displacing Australia from its number one spot after the Americans triumphed at the Pan Pacific (Pan Pac) championships in Yokohama, Japan, August 24–29. Other major meets included the European championships (held July 29–August 4 in Berlin), the Commonwealth Games (July 25–August 4 in Manchester, Eng.), and the Asian Games (in Busan, S.Kor., September 29–October 14). In short-course competition the world championships, held in Moscow on April 3–7, and the Fédération Internationale de Natation Amateur (FINA) World Cup tour provided the most spectacular fireworks. At year's end swimmers from 11 different countries were newly inscribed in the world record book.

Two 19-year-olds were anointed by *Swimming World* magazine as the male and female "Swimmers of the Year." Australia's Ian Thorpe—the "Thorpedo"—confirmed his status as the world's greatest male swimmer, winning a record six gold medals at the Commonwealth Games, where he lowered his own world record in the 400-m freestyle to 3 min 40.08 sec, and adding five more golds at the Pan Pacs less than a month later.

American Natalie Coughlin was equally spectacular, winning five gold medals at the U.S. championships (a feat achieved only once before, by

Tracy Caulkins in 1978). Coughlin's 59.58-sec world record in the 100-m backstroke made her the first woman to crack the one-minute barrier in the event. At the Pan Pacs Coughlin demonstrated her remarkable versatility by winning four golds, including the 100-m freestyle, backstroke, and butterfly races. She went on to set three short-course world records (100-m backstroke, butterfly, and individual medley) at a World Cup meet in November.

American Michael Phelps, 17, who had set his first world record in the 200-m butterfly at age 15, broke the world record in the 400-m individual medley (4 min 11.09 sec) at the U.S. nationals. The longest-standing men's record finally fell when Kosuke Kitajima won the 200-m breaststroke in 2 min 9.97 sec at the Asian Games. Kitajima was the first Japanese man to set a world mark in swimming in 30 years.

At the European championships Franziska van Almsick of Germany lowered her own world record (set in 1994) in the 200-m freestyle to 1 min 56.64 sec. Van Almsick also had a hand in a second world record in Berlin, joining with teammates Kathrin Meissner, Petra Dallmann, and Sandra Völker to break the standard in the 4 × 100-m freestyle relay with a 3-min 36.00-sec effort. Sweden's Anna-Karin Kammerling blazed a 25.57-sec swim in the 50-m butterfly. Otylia Jedrzejczak, with a sparkling time of 2 min 5.78 sec in the 200-m butterfly, became the first Polish woman to set a world record in swimming. On the men's side, Ukraine's Oleg Lisogor erased American Ed Moses's name from the long-course record book with a 27.18-sec swim for the 50-m breaststroke.

Three other long-course records fell in 2002. At the Commonwealth Games, England's Zoe Baker swam the 50-m breaststroke in 30.57 sec. Eighteen-year-old Aaron Peirsol clocked 1 min 55.15 sec in the 200-m backstroke at the U.S. spring nationals. In the final event of the Pan Pacs, the U.S. men's 4 × 100-m medley relay team (Peirsol, Brendan Hansen, Phelps, and Jason Lezak) lit up the scoreboard in 3 min 33.48 sec.

American Jenny Thompson—the most bemedaled female Olympic swimmer in history—made a comeback in 2002 at age 29 and reestablished herself as one of the world's premier aquatic aces. At the Commonwealth Games, South African Natalie du Toit, 18, finished a distant eighth in the 800-m freestyle but made sporting history by becoming

Franziska van Almsick of Germany races for the gold medal and a new world record in the 200-m freestyle at the European swimming championships.

the first amputee to contest a final of a major championship against able-bodied swimmers.

In short-course competition, Moses and Sweden's Emma Igelström set world records in breaststroke. On the World Cup tour, Moses clocked 57.47 sec for 100 m and an astonishing 2 min 3.17 sec for 200 m, lowering his own standard three times in the longer distance. Igelström knocked off the 50- and 100-m records for women, winding up the holder of the 50-m mark at 29.96 sec, after she had taken turns with Baker and Luo Xuejuan of China in reducing it, and setting a 100-m record of 1 min 5.38 sec.

Germany's Thomas Rupprath broke the 100-m backstroke short-course record and lowered the 100-m butterfly mark to 50.10 sec, which led to expectations that the first sub-50-second 100-m time might not be far off. Peirsol smashed the 200-m backstroke with his 1-min 51.17-sec performance, while Lisogor took the 50-m breaststroke down to 26.20 sec. Four men's short-course records were set by Australians: Grant Hackett in the 400-m freestyle (3 min 34.58 sec), Matt Welsh in the 50-m backstroke (23.31 sec), Geoff Huegill in the 50-m butterfly (22.74 sec), and the men's 4 × 100-m medley relay (3 min 28.12 sec).

At the short-course world championships, American Lindsay Benko broke the 200-m freestyle mark with a

time of 1 min 54.04 sec, and Ukrainian Olympic champion Yana Klochkova lowered the 400-m individual medley record to 4 min 27.83 sec. Two women's relay marks were set in Moscow; Sweden went 3 min 55.78 sec in the 4 × 100-m medley, and China touched in 7 min 46.30 sec in the 4 × 200-m freestyle.

Sachiko Yamada raced to a global mark in the 800-m freestyle in 8 min 14.35 sec at the Japanese national championships, while Slovakia's Martina Moravcova took the 100-m butterfly record down to 56.55 sec at the Berlin World Cup stop, a record she held until November. At the end of the 2001–02 World Cup tour, Moravcova was named the tour's top female performer for the third year in a row. Moses was named the outstanding male swimmer.

Performance-enhancing drugs continued to plague the sport. Several high-profile athletes tested positive for drugs during the year, while others retired suddenly and without explanation. Among the dozen swimmers receiving suspensions for drug offenses were two of China's top female swimmers—sprinter Shan Ying and Zhou Jiawei. World record holder Wu Yanyan of China retired suddenly on the eve of the Asian Games, while her teammate Luo Nan, ranked second in the world in the 200-m breaststroke, withdrew from the regional games just before they began.

In the most shocking development, Costa Rica's Claudia Poll—who had won medals at the 1996 and 2000 Olympic Games—tested positive for steroids in out-of-competition testing. The four-year suspension she received was under appeal owing to a large number of procedural irregularities on the part of the testing authorities.

Diving. The 13th FINA diving World Cup, held June 25–29 in Seville, Spain, was the premier international diving competition of 2002. Among a record 300 of the world's top competitors from 29 nations gathered in Seville, Chinese divers won 8 of the 10 events contested, the same feat they had accomplished at the 2001 world championships. Only Russian Olympic champion Dmitry Sautin and the Russian synchronized-diving duo of Vera Ilyina and Yuliya Pakhalina deprived China of a complete sweep.

In the men's events, China's Xu Xiang captured the gold medal in the 1-m springboard. Sautin reprised his Olympic and world championship victories in the 3-m springboard, but his score was only 1.59 points more than China's Peng Bo. Tian Liang led a one-two sweep for China in the 10-m platform, with Hu Jia second. In the men's synchronized events, China's Wang Tianling and Wang Feng handily defeated Australia's Robert Newberry and Steven Barnett for the 3-m springboard title. The 10-m platform synchro crown went to China's Tian and Luo Yutong, ahead of the Cuban duo of Erik Fornaris and José Guerra.

Guo Jingjing, a three-time Olympian, won the women's 1-m springboard. She earned a second individual gold in the 3-m springboard, well ahead of her teammate Wu Minxia. Lao Lishi breezed to victory in the 10-m platform, with the U.S.'s Kimiko Soldati the surprising silver medalist. Lao teamed with Li Ting to win the 10-m platform synchro event ahead of the Russian duo of Yevgeniya Olshevskaya and Svetlana Timoshinina. Russia eked out its sole women's victory by a minuscule two-thirds of a point in the 3-m springboard synchro event when Ilyina and Pakhalina deprived Guo and Wu of another gold.

Not surprisingly, China topped the women's team trophy contest with an overwhelming 288 points. Russia was second with 140, and the U.S. finished third with 132.

Synchronized Swimming. The most important international synchronized swimming competition of 2002 was the 10th FINA World Cup, held in Zürich, Switz., September 12–15. In her fifth year on the international stage, France's Virginie Dedieu won her first world-level title when she took the solo crown with six perfect scores of 10. Japan's Miya Tachibana, the bronze medalist at the 2001 world championships, moved up to second, and Russia's Anastasiya Davydova finished third.

Davydova and Anastasiya Yermakova won gold in the duet competition, dethroning Tachibana and Miho Takeda, the 2001 world champions. Paced by Davydova, Russia reconfirmed its global dominance by winning the team competition. Japan was second, and the U.S. nipped Canada for third. In the overall standings, the teams finished in the same order: Russia, Japan, and the U.S.

(PHILLIP WHITTEN)

TABLE TENNIS

China dominated singles play at the 2002 table tennis Pro Tour grand finals, held Dec. 12–15, 2002, in Stockholm. Chuan Chi-yuan won the men's title from Kalinikos Kreanga of Greece. In the women's competition China's Zhang Yining triumphed over her countrywoman Guo Yue. Germany's Timo Boll had the best individual year. He defeated Vladimir Samsonov of Belarus for the Europe Top 12 championship in Rotterdam, Neth., in February, secured the European men's championship in Zagreb, Croatia, in April, and captured his first World Cup title over China's Kong Linghui in Jinan, China, in November. Croatia's Tamara Boros earned her Europe Top 12 title by beating Nicole Struse of Germany. Former European women's champion Ni Xia Lian of Luxembourg won that title again with a victory over Hungary's Krisztina Toth. Zhang successfully defended her women's World Cup over countrywoman Li Nan in Singapore in September.

In 2002 the International Table Tennis Federation (ITTF) instituted a new service rule to ensure that a serve could not be hidden by any part of the server's body and always had to be visible to the receiver. The ITTF also launched a junior tour, the World Junior Circuit, similar to the Pro Tour. In addition, the first World Cadet Challenge, a new competition between continental teams, was held in Tiszaujvaros, Hung., in June, and all singles and doubles titles were won by China.

(TIM BOGGAN)

TENNIS

Tennis fans were rewarded on a multitude of levels in 2002. They witnessed the extraordinary ascendancy of Serena Williams, who captured three of the four major championships. They appreciated the style and grace of Venus Williams, who had the misfortune to be beaten by her sister in the finals of the French Open, Wimbledon, and the U.S. Open. They admired the temerity of Jennifer Capriati, who claimed her second straight Australian Open title.

While tennis aficionados could almost always anticipate what might happen in the women's game, they were hard pressed to predict the eventual champions in the men's Grand Slam tournaments. The highly charged Australian Lleyton Hewitt (see BIOGRAPHIES) celebrated his second year in a row as the best player in the world, cementing his status at the top by winning Wimbledon for the first time and securing a second Tennis Masters Cup title. The other three major events all produced surprising outcomes, however.

Not only were Serena Williams and Hewitt the top-ranked players in the game, but they were also the most highly paid. Hewitt garnered $4,619,-386 to set the pace among the men. Williams made $3,935,668 to establish herself as the women's leader.

Australian Open. Battling three-time former champion Martina Hingis in the final, Capriati somehow survived on an oppressive afternoon with the courtside temperature at 41 °C (107 °F). The 25-year-old American overcame her Swiss adversary despite dropping the opening set and trailing 4–0 in the second. On her way to a remarkable 4–6, 7–6 (9–7), 6–2 victory, Capriati set a record for a women's Grand Slam final by saving no fewer than four match points. No woman had rescued herself from match point down in a title match at a Grand Slam event since 1962. With this stirring stand Capriati won her third career Grand Slam title. In another milestone match four-time former Australian Open victor Monica Seles toppled number two seed Venus Williams 6–7 (4), 6–2, 6–3 in the quarterfinals, achieving her first win over Williams in seven career meetings.

Sweden's Thomas Johansson was the number 16 seed but took full advantage of an excellent draw to reach his first major final. Number nine seed Marat Safin—the 2000 U.S. Open winner—was heavily favoured to take apart Johansson in the title match, but the talented yet immature Russian was way out of sorts. Johansson returned serve superbly in surging to a 3–6, 6–4, 6–4, 7–6 (7–4) win. It had been a decade since a Swede (Stefan Edberg at the 1992 U.S. Open) had won a major title.

French Open. Not since 1999 had Spain's Albert Costa won a tournament, but his fluid shot making helped carry him to his first major title. The number 20 seed stopped defending champion Gustavo Kuerten of Brazil in the quarterfinals, two-time finalist Alex Corretja of Spain in the semis, and another Spaniard, heavily favoured Juan Carlos Ferrero, in the final. The 26-year-old Costa sparkled at the outset of the final match. Ferrero gradually found his range, but Costa came through for a 6–1, 6–0, 4–6, 6–3 triumph.

Neither Serena nor Venus Williams had appeared previously in the final at Roland Garros, but the two prodigiously gifted sisters set up a final-round appointment this time around. Number two seed Venus never came close to conceding a set on her way to the championship match, but Serena, the number three seed, found herself in an ominous position during her crackling semifinal encounter with Capriati. The defending champion took the first set from Williams and led 6–5 on serve in the second. At that propitious moment Capriati surrendered her authority, and Williams not atypically elevated her game decidedly, pulling through 3–6, 7–6 (7–2), 6–2.

In the final Serena defeated Venus 7–5, 6–3. Venus had built a 5–3 first-set lead before her younger sibling's superior court craft ruled the day. Venus was broken in 8 of 11 service games. Serena was sturdier from the backcourt. With her impressive win she garnered the second major title of her career, and her first since the 1999 U.S. Open.

Wimbledon. After one favourite after another had been ushered out of the tournament in a startling stream of upsets, the top-seeded Hewitt restored order in the end. The 21-year-old became the first Australian man to rule at the All-England Club since Pat Cash in 1987. Hewitt ousted number four seed Tim Henman of the U.K. 7–5, 6–1, 7–5 in the semifinals and then crushed number 28 seed David Nalbandian of Argentina 6–1, 6–3, 6–2 in the final.

On the tumultuous third day of the event, Pete Sampras, Andre Agassi, and Safin were all eliminated in second-round matches. The seven-time Wimbledon champion Sampras lost to George Bastl of Switzerland in five sets; Agassi fell in straight sets to the rapidly

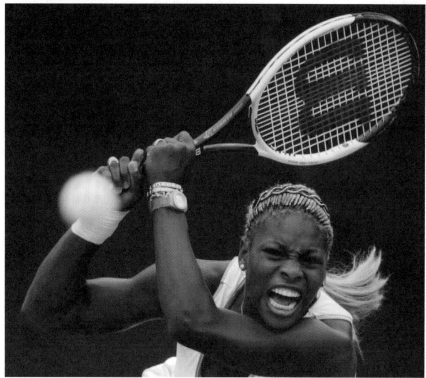

Serena Williams of the U.S. demonstrates her power at the Wimbledon tennis championships, the second of three Grand Slam events she won in 2002.

improving Paradorn Srichaphan of Thailand; and Safin bowed in four sets against Belgium's Olivier Rochus.

Serena and Venus Williams marched commandingly into the final, and their clash was the best tennis they would offer in 2002. Serena made good on 67% of her first serves, while Venus succeeded with 70%. Venus, however, could not keep up with Serena in this ferocious battle of big hitters. Serena prevailed in a tiebreaker and then glided through the second set, winning her first singles title on the fabled grass courts 7–6 (7–4), 6–3. Venus's bid to become the first woman since Steffi Graf in 1991–93 to win Wimbledon three years in a row thus fell short.

U.S. Open. Heading into the last Grand Slam event of the season, Sampras had not taken a tournament title since winning his record-breaking 13th major title at Wimbledon two years earlier. He arrived at Flushing Meadows, N.Y., as the number 17 seed, with most observers in the media dismissing his chances; he left with perhaps the most gratifying victory of his career. On his way to a final round meeting with Agassi—his oldest and most revered rival—Sampras defeated number three seed Tommy Haas and his U.S. Davis Cup teammate, Andy Roddick.

Sampras had overcome Agassi in their three previous meetings at the U.S. Open and had won three of their four finals at the majors. Now, 12 years after beating Agassi in the 1990 Open final, Sampras did it again. Serving stupendously, attacking Agassi's second serve with vigour, and volleying with supreme touch and creativity, Sampras mastered Agassi 6–3, 6–4, 5–7, 6–4 to win his fifth U.S. Open. At the age of 31, he was the oldest men's champion since Ken Rosewall in 1970, and he became the first man since Rosewall to win majors in his teens, 20s, and 30s. During the Open, Sampras had lost his booming serve only six times in seven matches. Agassi, meanwhile, had compensated in some ways for his 20th defeat in 34 career duels with Sampras by striking down the top-ranked Hewitt in a four-set semifinal.

The women's final was once more an All-American, all-Williams family affair between Serena and Venus. When the chips were on the line in this prime-time Saturday-night final, Serena was a level above her sister in every facet of the game. Victorious for the fourth straight time over Venus in 2002, Serena bested Venus in a third consecutive major final, winning convincingly 6–4, 6–3. After missing the Australian Open with an injury, Serena had won every subsequent Grand Slam event, demonstrating her all-surface prowess with triumphs on clay, grass, and hard courts.

A resurgent Lindsay Davenport—unable to compete in the first three majors of the season following knee surgery—gave Serena a tussle in the semifinals before bowing 6–3, 7–5, while Amélie Mauresmo—a quarterfinal victor over Capriati—pressed Venus even harder, losing their riveting battle 6–3, 5–7, 6–4.

Other Events. Hewitt and his girlfriend, Kim Clijsters of Belgium, took the season-ending events in style. Hewitt defeated Ferrero in a five-set final at the Tennis Masters Cup in Shanghai. Clijsters handed Serena Williams only her fifth defeat of the year when she crafted a 7–5, 6–3 win in the final of the Home Depot Championships in Los Angeles.

For the first time in history, Russia won the Davis Cup—and became the 11th country to have enjoyed the honour. With former Russian president Boris Yeltsin on hand to offer support from the stands, the Russian players held back defending champion France 3–2 in the Cup final in Paris. Slovakia secured its first Fed Cup title with a 3–1 win over Spain.

Arantxa Sánchez-Vicario—the winner of four Grand Slam singles titles during her stellar career—retired from the game at the end of the year, one month before she turned 31. The former world number one from Spain had won 29 singles titles altogether and another 67 championships in doubles. Sampras became a father on November 21 when his wife—actress Bridgette Wilson—gave birth to a son, Christian Charles.

(STEVE FLINK)

TRACK AND FIELD SPORTS (ATHLETICS)

In 2002 the men's and women's world records in the longest standard running event, the marathon, and a men's record in the shortest, the 100 m, stood out in a season in which the absence of a global title meet focused the efforts of many top competitors on the Golden League series.

Golden League. The format of the Golden League circuit of super-elite outdoor track competitions remained in flux in its fifth season, as the International Association of Athletics Federations (IAAF) had mandated that in 2002 athletes had to win at all seven meets in the series (Oslo, Paris, Rome,

Monaco, Zürich, Switz., Brussels, and Berlin) in order to share in the jackpot of 50 kg (110 lb) of gold. Seven of the 12 winners in Oslo fell from contention before the meet in Monaco, and in Zürich 100-m hurdler Gail Devers of the U.S. lost, which whittled the field to four contenders, who retained clean slates through Berlin. The final four—Moroccan Hicham El Guerrouj (1,500 m), Mexico's Ana Guevara (400 m), American Marion Jones (100 m), and Felix Sánchez (400-m hurdles) of the Dominican Republic—each won gold worth about $100,000. In addition, each victory in the series brought €15,000 (about $15,660) for "premium event" competitors El Guerrouj, Jones, and Sánchez and €7,500 (about $7,800) for "classic event" runner Guevara. Substantial appearance fees negotiated on an individual basis imparted further financial lustre, but El Guerrouj and Jones, citing fatigue, said that they doubted they would contest the entire Golden League in 2003. At season's end the IAAF pared the 2003 series to six meets, with Monaco withdrawing to host a new two-day version of the Grand Prix final, the World Athletics Gala, in the coming season.

World Cup. At the quadrennial World Cup, held in Madrid on September 20–21, the African men's squad (134 points) won for a record fourth straight time, with the U.S. (119) as the runner-up. The women's title went to Russia 126–123 over Europe. The outstanding individual men's performance belonged to discus thrower Robert Fazekas of Hungary, who established a World Cup record of 71.25 m (233 ft 9 in). Guevara won the women's 400 m in 49.56 sec, and Jones took the 100 m on a rain-soaked track in 10.90 sec. Maria Mutola of Mozambique won the 800 m (1 min 58.60 sec), her fourth at a World Cup.

Men's International Competition. American 100-m sprinter Tim Montgomery began the season as a man frustrated by a narrow loss to teammate Maurice Greene in the 2001 IAAF world championships. Over the course of the 1997–2001 seasons, Greene had won Olympic gold medals and three world titles in his specialty and had set the world record (9.79 sec). Montgomery announced in May 2002 that he wanted what Greene had, and by season's end he had taken Greene's world record.

Greene won the U.S. championship, running a wind-aided 9.88 sec to best Montgomery by 0.01 sec. Briton Dwain Chambers won in Oslo and at the Grand Prix in Sheffield, Eng., before

Greene came roaring back in July with three fast Golden League wins in Paris, Rome, and Monaco. The stage was set for a Chambers-Greene showdown in Zürich in August, but it was Montgomery who sped across the line first, in 9.98. Chambers stole back the spotlight momentarily with a win at the London Grand Prix, but Montgomery triumphed in 9.91 sec in Brussels, where Greene managed only sixth place. At the Grand Prix final in Paris on September 14, everything went Montgomery's way. He reacted to the gun in 0.104 sec, less than an eye blink from triggering an automatic recall. The wind at his back blew at exactly the legal limit, and Montgomery flew down the track in 9.78 sec, clipping 0.01 sec from Greene's record.

El Guerrouj remained unassailable in the 1,500-m and mile runs. Undefeated in 12 races, the Moroccan ran 1,500-m times of 3 min 26.89 sec and 3 min 26.96 sec in Zürich and Rieti, Italy, respectively. Only El Guerrouj himself (in 2001) had previously matched the depth of quality exhibited in six sub-3-min-30-sec 1,500-m times. Sánchez, unbeaten in nine top-level 400-m hurdles races, ran his best in Zürich (47.35 sec). In two meets thereafter, he added the flat 400-m to his workload, winning a double in London with times of 48.08 over the hurdles and 45.14 on the flat. At the Grand Prix final, Sánchez placed fifth in the 400 m. Going into the Grand Prix final, El Guerrouj and Sánchez had been tied atop the men's standings, but the bonus points Montgomery scored for his record catapulted him from sixth in the standings to first and $250,000—including a $100,000 bonus.

In the field events, all-time performance lists were altered notably by throwers. In Szombathely, Hung., on July 14, Fazekas, who won 16 of his 18 meets, threw the discus 71.70 m (235 ft 2 in). He also won the European title and became just the third man ever to have thrown beyond 71 m at two meets in a season. At the Sheffield Grand Prix on June 30, Sergey Makarov of Russia launched his javelin 92.61 m (303 ft 10 in), defeating Britain's Steve Backley and Jan Zelezny of the Czech Republic. Backley captured his fourth consecutive European title, knocking Makarov into second place with an 88.54-m (290-ft 6-in) throw. Makarov rebounded to win at the World Cup. Shotputter Adam Nelson of the U.S. threw 22.51 m (73 ft 10¼ in), the longest throw since 1990, at the Portland, Ore., Grand Prix on

May 18. He lost his next meet, the Eugene, Ore., Grand Prix, as fellow American Kevin Toth reached 22.19 m (72 ft 9¾ in). Three-time world champion John Godina threw near his career best in Eugene and at the USA Track & Field (USATF) championships in Palo Alto, Calif., in June, but he could not defeat Nelson, who also won at the World Cup.

Triple jumpers clashed intensely all season. American Walter Davis eliminated British world record holder Jonathan Edwards from Golden League contention in Rome, and Christian Olsson of Sweden triumphed over Edwards at the European championships and the Grand Prix final. At the Commonwealth Games in Manchester, Eng., on July 25–August 4, however, the graying 36-year-old Edwards leaped 17.86 m (58 ft 7¼ in) to defeat countryman Phillips Idowu. Edwards also won at the World Cup.

Moroccan steeplechaser Brahim Boulami's apparent improvement of his world record (by more than two seconds) in Zürich was erased when his prerace-drug-test results, released two weeks later, showed the presence of banned synthetic erythropoietin.

Women's International Competition. British distance runner Paula Radcliffe (*see* BIOGRAPHIES) hoped after many near misses to win gold at a major track championship and sandwiched races at the Commonwealth Games (5,000 m) and the European championships (10,000 m) between the London and Chicago marathons. In Manchester Radcliffe tore away from her competition to win the 5,000 m by more than 100 m in 14 min 31.42 sec. At the European championships Radcliffe aimed to break Norwegian Ingrid Kristiansen's 10,000-m European record of 30 min 13.74 sec. She did, but drenching rain slowed her just enough to prevent her from becoming the second woman ever to run the distance in under 30 min. She crossed the line in 30 min 1.09 sec, leaving defending champion Sonia O'Sullivan of Ireland almost a lap behind. Radcliffe's time was the second fastest in history, inferior only to Wang Junxia's 29 min 31.78 sec at the Chinese national games of 1993, a meet that produced so many anomalous performances that the legality of the marks had since been questioned by most experts.

Svetlana Feofanova of Russia soared to the top in the women's pole vault, breaking the indoor world record three times in a single February week and culminating with a clearance of 4.73 m (15 ft 6¼ in) in Ghent, Belg. She added another centimetre to the record in Liévin, France, two weeks later, and then in March she won the European indoor championship with her fifth record of the season, 4.75 m (15 ft 7 in). Although Feofanova missed American Stacy Dragila's outdoor world record of 4.81 m (15 ft 9¼ in) and lost twice during the year, she won the European title and amassed a perfect record against Dragila in their nine meetings.

Golden League co-winners Guevara and Jones capped undefeated seasons at the World Cup. Jones's first perfect campaign at the elite level was largely attributable to her not having participated in the long jump—the only event in which she lost in 1998—since the 2000 Olympics. At the London Grand Prix, Jones avenged her 2001 world championships 100-m loss to Zhanna Pintusevich-Block of Ukraine. In London the American, timed in 10.97 sec, left her rival more than a metre behind. Pintusevich-Block false-started at the Grand Prix final, where Jones won the women's overall Grand Prix crown.

Cross Country and Marathon Running. The London Marathon, in April, and the Chicago Marathon, in October, were arguably the two greatest marathons ever. Khalid Khannouchi of the U.S. and Radcliffe each won twice, and each set a world record. Although he had held the world record since 1999, Khannouchi received little attention before London, as the meeting of Ethiopia's Haile Gebrselassie and Kenyan Paul Tergat, the two fastest 10,000-m runners of all time, drew the spotlight. Khannouchi's powerful low stride, however, carried him to the line first in 2 hr 5 min 38 sec and made him the first male marathoner since Derek Clayton in 1969 to break his own world record. Tergat (2 hr 5 min 48 sec) became history's second fastest marathoner. At Chicago, the first-ever marathon in which five men broke 2 hr 7 min, Khannouchi won in 2 hr 5 min 56 sec, and at year's end he held three of the four fastest times in history.

In her marathon debut in London, Radcliffe ran a near-record 2 hr 18 min 56 sec. In Chicago she finished in 2 hr 17 min 18 sec, cutting a whopping 89 sec from Kenyan Catherine Ndereba's world record, set at the same venue in 2001. Ndereba placed second in 2 hr 19 min 26 sec in the first marathon with two women under 2 hr 20 min.

At the world cross country championships in Dublin, 19-year-old Kenenisa Bekele of Ethiopia became the

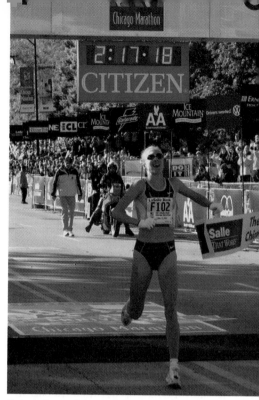

Britain's Paula Radcliffe sets a new world record at the Chicago Marathon in only her second race at that distance.

© Jonathan Daniel/Getty Images

first man ever to win both short- and long-course titles. Radcliffe defended her women's long-course crown, while Kenya's Edith Masai won the women's short-course race. Kenya scooped up four of the six team titles, with Ethiopia taking the women's short-course and long-course team victories.

(SIEG LINDSTROM)

VOLLEYBALL

In men's volleyball Brazil and Russia proved that they were the world's best with gold-medal performances at the Fédération Internationale de Volleyball (FIVB) world championships and World League, respectively. At the world championships, in Buenos Aires, Arg., in October, Brazil rallied to defeat Russia in five sets to capture the title. France downed Yugoslavia for the bronze. Argentina's Marcos Milinkovic was named the tournament's Most Valuable Player. In the $15 million World League, Russia had proved too powerful for Brazil and charged to a 3–1 victory over the host country in the final match on August 18 in Belo Horizonte. It was the Russian team's first World League title. Yugoslavia won the bronze medal over eight-time World League winner Italy. Ivan Miljkovic of Yugoslavia won the best scorer award,

Martin Conde of Argentina watches his partner, Mariano Baracetti, spike the ball past an airborne Marcio Araujo of Brazil at the beach volleyball Swiss Open in June.

FIVB Photo Gallery

and Russia's Aleksey Kuleshov was tabbed the best blocker.

Italy rewrote the history books when it took home the 2002 women's FIVB world championship title by defeating the U.S. for its best-ever performance in women's international competition. Russia claimed the bronze medal with a triumph over China. Danielle Scott of the U.S. was voted top blocker, and Yumilka Ruiz Luaces of Cuba was the tournament's top scorer. In the FIVB World Grand Prix, Russia triumphed over China to claim its third title in the $1 million volleyball tournament.

In beach volleyball the U.S. pair of Kerri Walsh and Misty May won five tournament crowns and the overall title in the 11-event World Tour. Brazil's two-time world champions, Adriana Behar and Shelda Bruno Bede, and Australians Natalie Cook and Kerri Pottharst placed second and third, respectively. On the men's tour Argentina's duo of Mariano Baracetti and Martin Conde captured the world title over two teams from Brazil.

(RICHARD S. WANNINGER)

WEIGHT LIFTING

Warsaw was the site of the 2002 world weight lifting championships, held on November 18–26. A total of 285 athletes entered the competition, 170 men representing 47 countries in eight body-weight classes and 115 women representing 37 countries in seven body-weight classes.

In the women's division China topped the medal rankings with 18 (9 gold, 8 silver, and 1 bronze), followed by Russia (5 gold, 2 silver, and 3 bronze), Thailand (2 gold, 3 silver, and 3 bronze), and Poland and South Korea (2 gold and 1 silver each). Agata Wrobel of Poland won the superheavyweight category with a 287.5-kg (633.9-lb) overall total. Superheavyweight Cheryl Haworth of the U.S. won two bronze medals, one in the snatch and one in the clean and jerk—the only medals won by an American athlete at these championships. Chinese athletes broke 13 world records, South Korean and Greek competitors one each.

China topped the men's rankings with 13 medals (8 gold, 4 silver, and 1 bronze), followed by Bulgaria (4 gold, 8 silver, and 3 bronze), Iran (3 gold and 3 bronze), Russia (2 gold, 1 silver, and 1 bronze), and Azerbaijan (2 gold and 1 silver). Superheavyweight Hosein Rezazadeh of Iran, the reigning Olympic champion, won the overall world champion title with a 472.5-kg (1041.9-lb) total result. He broke the world record in the clean and jerk with a lift of 263 kg (580 lb). Two-time Olympic champion Andrey Chemerkin of Russia was eliminated from the competition after he missed all three attempts in the clean and jerk at 245 kg (540.2 lb). Rezazadeh's world record was the only one set in the men's competition.

(DRAGOMIR CIOROSLAN)

WRESTLING

Freestyle and Greco-Roman. In the freestyle world championships, held in Tehran on Sept. 5–7, 2002, host Iran claimed the team gold medal—its fourth team title, previous wins having occurred in 1961, 1965, and 1998. Iran earned four individual medals and the team gold with 43 points, followed by Russia with 42 points and Cuba with 34. Top wrestlers from more than 40 countries took part in the event; the U.S. team withdrew, however, after Iranian officials indicated that it would be "out of our control" to protect American wrestlers from possible anti-U.S. demonstrators.

The Greco-Roman championships were held in Moscow on September 19–22. Russia took the team crown with 45 points, followed by Georgia with 27 points and Cuba with 26. The U.S. placed fifth in competition but came away with one gold medal when Dremiel Byers won the 120-kg (264.5-lb) event to become only the fourth American wrestler to have captured a world Greco-Roman title.

Milan Ercegan resigned as president of the Fédération Internationale de Lutte Amateur (FILA; International Federation of Associated Wrestling Styles) on September 19. Ercegan had served as FILA's president for 30 years and had been instrumental in organizing the first World Cup in 1973 and in developing women's wrestling, set to become an Olympic sport in 2004 in Athens. Succeeding Ercegan was Raphael Martinetti, who was elected FILA's sixth president.

History was made at the 2002 U.S. collegiate championships held in Albany, N.Y., on March 21–24, when Cael Sanderson of Iowa State University won his 159th consecutive match to finish his four-year collegiate career undefeated. Sanderson was only the second college wrestler in history to have won four Division I championships. Defending team champion Minnesota won its second straight title. (ANDRÉ REDDINGTON)

Sumo. The year 2002 began with freshly promoted *ozeki* (champion) Tochiazuma winning the New Year's tournament (Hatsu Basho), defeating *ozeki* Chiyotaikai in a play-off. Chiyotaikai took the *yusho* (tournament championship) in July, while *yokozuna* (grand champion) Musashimaru won in March and May. Newly promoted *ozeki* Asashoryu won his first *yusho* in November's Kyushu Basho, the first Mongolian to do so.

After an unprecedented seven-basho absence, *yokozuna* Takanohana returned for September's Aki Basho. Contending for the championship until the final day, he lost to Musashimaru. Takanohana, the dominant *rikishi* of the 1990s, had injured his right knee in May 2001 and required extensive recuperation. He was ordered to fight well or retire, and the drama of his comeback was a remedy for the malaise that afflicted sumo's popularity.

There were several significant retirements during 2002. Terao, whose career spanned three decades, called it quits at the age of 39. Takatoriki, winner of the March 2000 *yusho*, was to take over for sumo legend Taiho at his training facility. Tomonohana, Daishi, Asanosho, and Minatofuji also exited during what was seen as a "changing of the guard" from the Chiyonofuji era. (KEN COLLER)

Sporting Record

ARCHERY

FITA Outdoor World Target Archery Championships*

Year	Men's individual			Men's team	
	Winner	**Points**		**Winner**	**Points**
1997	Kim Kyung Ho (S.Kor.)	108		South Korea	254
1999	Hong Sung Chil (S.Kor.)	115		Italy	252
2001	Yeon Jung Ki (S.Kor.)	115		South Korea	247

Year	Women's individual			Women's team	
	Winner	**Points**		**Winner**	**Points**
1997	Kim Du Ri (S.Kor.)	105		South Korea	242
1999	Lee Eun Kyung (S.Kor.)	115		Italy	240
2001	Park Sung Hyun (S.Kor.)	111		China	232

*Olympic (recurve) division.

Daytona 500 winner Ward Burton.

AUTOMOBILE RACING

Formula One Grand Prix Race Results, 2002

Race	Driver	Winner's time (hr:min:sec)
Australian GP	M. Schumacher	1:35:36.792
Malaysian GP	R. Schumacher	1:34:12.912
Brazilian GP	M. Schumacher	1:31:43.663
San Marino GP	M. Schumacher	1:29:10.789
Spanish GP	M. Schumacher	1:30:29.981
Austrian GP	M. Schumacher	1:33:51.562
Monaco GP	D. Coulthard	1:45:39.055
Canadian GP	M. Schumacher	1:33:36.111
European GP	R. Barrichello	1:35:07.426
British GP	M. Schumacher	1:31:45.015
French GP	M. Schumacher	1:32:09.837
German GP	M. Schumacher	1:27:52.078
Hungarian GP	R. Barrichello	1:41:49.001
Belgian GP	M. Schumacher	1:21:20.634
Italian GP	R. Barrichello	1:16:19.982
United States GP	R. Barrichello	1:31:07.934
Japanese GP	M. Schumacher	1:26:59.698

WORLD DRIVERS' CHAMPIONSHIP: M. Schumacher 144 points, Barrichello 77 points, Montoya 50 points. CONSTRUCTORS' CHAMPIONSHIP: Ferrari 221 points, Williams/BMW 92 points, McLaren/Mercedes 65 points.

International Cup for Formula One Manufacturers

Year	Car	Year	Car
1997	Williams/Renault	2000	Ferrari
1998	McLaren/Mercedes	2001	Ferrari
1999	Ferrari	**2002**	**Ferrari**

National Association for Stock Car Auto Racing (NASCAR) Winston Cup Champions

Year	Winner
2000	B. Labonte
2001	J. Gordon
2002	**T. Stewart**

Indy Car Champions*

Year	Driver
2000	G. de Ferran (Braz.)
2001	G. de Ferran (Braz.)
2002	**C. da Matta (Braz.)**

*CART champion.

World Championship of Drivers

Year	Winner	Car
2000	M. Schumacher (Ger.)	Ferrari
2001	M. Schumacher (Ger.)	Ferrari
2002	**M. Schumacher (Ger.)**	**Ferrari**

Daytona 500

Year	Winner	Avg. speed in mph
2000	D. Jarrett	155.669
2001	M. Waltrip	161.783
2002	**W. Burton**	**142.971**

Indianapolis 500

Year	Winner	Avg. speed in mph
2000	J. Montoya	167.607
2001	H. Castroneves	153.601
2002	**H. Castroneves**	**166.499**

Le Mans 24-Hour Grand Prix d'Endurance

Year	Car	Drivers
2000	Audi R8	F. Biela, T. Kristensen, E. Pirro
2001	Audi R8	F. Biela, T. Kristensen, E. Pirro
2002	**Audi R8**	**F. Biela, T. Kristensen, E. Pirro**

Monte-Carlo Rally

Year	Car	Driver
2000	Mitsubishi Lancer	T. Mäkinen (Fin.)
2001	Mitsubishi Lancer	T. Mäkinen (Fin.)
2002	**Subaru**	**T. Mäkinen (Fin.)**

BADMINTON

All-England Championships—Singles

Year	Men	Women
2000	Xia Xuanze (China)	Gong Zhichao (China)
2001	P. Gopichand (India)	Gong Zhichao (China)
2002	**Chen Hong (China)**	**C. Martin (Den.)**

Uber Cup (women)

Year	Winner	Runner-up
1997–98	China	Indonesia
1999–2000	China	Denmark
2001–02	**China**	**South Korea**

Thomas Cup (men)

Year	Winner	Runner-up
1997–98	Indonesia	Malaysia
1999–2000	Indonesia	China
2001–02	**Indonesia**	**Malaysia**

World Badminton Championships

Year	Men's singles	Women's singles	Men's doubles	Women's doubles
1997	P. Rasmussen (Den.)	Ye Zhaoying (China)	B. Sigit, C. Wijaya (Indon.)	Ge Fei, Gu Jun (China)
1999	Sun Jun (China)	C. Martin (Den.)	Kim Dong Moon, Ha Tae Kwon (S.Kor.)	Ge Fei, Gu Jun (China)
2001	Hendrawan (Indon.)	Gong Ruina (China)	T. Gunawan, H. Haryanto (Indon.)	Gao Ling, Huang Sui (China)

BASEBALL

Final Major League Standings, 2002

AMERICAN LEAGUE

East Division

Club	W.	L.	G.B.
*New York	103	58	—
Boston	93	69	10½
Toronto	78	84	25½
Baltimore	67	95	36½
Tampa Bay	55	106	48

Central Division

Club	W.	L.	G.B.
*Minnesota	94	67	—
Chicago	81	81	13½
Cleveland	74	88	20½
Kansas City	62	100	32½
Detroit	55	106	39

West Division

Club	W.	L.	G.B.
*Oakland	103	59	—
*Anaheim	99	63	4
Seattle	93	69	10
Texas	72	90	31

NATIONAL LEAGUE

East Division

Club	W.	L.	G.B.
*Atlanta	101	59	—
Montreal	83	79	19
Philadelphia	80	81	21½
Florida	79	83	23
New York	75	86	26½

Central Division

Club	W.	L.	G.B.
*St. Louis	97	65	—
Houston	84	78	13
Cincinnati	78	84	19
Pittsburgh	72	89	24½
Chicago	67	95	30
Milwaukee	56	106	41

West Division

Club	W.	L.	G.B.
*Arizona	98	64	—
*San Francisco	95	66	2½
Los Angeles	92	70	6
Colorado	73	89	25
San Diego	66	96	32

*Gained play-off berth.

Caribbean Series

Year	Winning team	Country
2000	Santurce Crabbers	Puerto Rico
2001	Cibao Eagles	Dominican Republic
2002	**Culiacán Tomato Growers**	**Mexico**

World Series*

Year	Winning team	Losing team	Results
2000	New York Yankees (AL)	New York Mets (NL)	4–1
2001	Arizona Diamondbacks (NL)	New York Yankees (AL)	4–3
2002	**Anaheim Angels (AL)**	**San Francisco Giants (NL)**	**4–3**

*AL—American League; NL—National League.

Japan Series*

Year	Winning team	Losing team	Results
2000	Yomiuri Giants (CL)	Fukuoka Daiei Hawks (PL)	4–2
2001	Yakult Swallows (CL)	Osaka Kintetsu Buffaloes (PL)	4–1
2002	**Yomiuri Giants (CL)**	**Seibu Lions (PL)**	**4–0**

*CL—Central League; PL—Pacific League.

BASKETBALL

NBA Final Standings, 2001–02

EASTERN CONFERENCE

Atlantic Division

Team	Won	Lost	G.B.
*New Jersey	52	30	—
*Boston	49	33	3
*Orlando	44	38	8
*Philadelphia	43	39	9
Washington	37	45	15
Miami	36	46	16
New York	30	52	22

Central Division

Team	Won	Lost	G.B.
*Detroit	50	32	—
*Charlotte	44	38	6
*Toronto	42	40	8
*Indiana	42	40	8
Milwaukee	41	41	9
Atlanta	33	49	17
Cleveland	29	53	21
Chicago	21	61	29

WESTERN CONFERENCE

Midwest Division

Team	Won	Lost	G.B.
*San Antonio	58	24	—
*Dallas	57	25	1
*Minnesota	50	32	8
*Utah	44	38	14
Houston	28	54	30
Denver	27	55	31
Memphis	23	59	35

Pacific Division

Team	Won	Lost	G.B.
*Sacramento	61	21	—
*L.A. Lakers	58	24	3
*Portland	49	33	12
*Seattle	45	37	16
L.A. Clippers	39	43	22
Phoenix	36	46	25
Golden State	21	61	40

*Gained play-off berth.

National Basketball Association (NBA) Championship

Season	Winner	Runner-up	Results
1999–2000	Los Angeles Lakers	Indiana Pacers	4–2
2000–01	Los Angeles Lakers	Philadelphia 76ers	4–1
2001–02	**Los Angeles Lakers**	**New Jersey Nets**	**4–0**

Women's National Basketball Association (WNBA) Championship

Season	Winner	Runner-up	Results
2000	Houston Comets	New York Liberty	2–0
2001	Los Angeles Sparks	Charlotte Sting	2–0
2002	**Los Angeles Sparks**	**New York Liberty**	**2–0**

Division I National Collegiate Athletic Association (NCAA) Championship—Men

Year	Winner	Runner-up	Score
2000	Michigan State	Florida	89–76
2001	Duke	Arizona	82–72
2002	**Maryland**	**Indiana**	**64–52**

Division I National Collegiate Athletic Association (NCAA) Championship—Women

Year	Winner	Runner-up	Score
2000	Connecticut	Tennessee	71–52
2001	Notre Dame	Purdue	68–66
2002	**Connecticut**	**Oklahoma**	**82–70**

World Basketball Championship—Men

Year	Winner	Runner-up
1998	Yugoslavia	Russia
2000	United States	France
2002	**Yugoslavia**	**Argentina**

World Basketball Championship—Women

Year	Winner	Runner-up
1998	United States	Russia
2000	United States	Australia
2002	**United States**	**Russia**

BILLIARD GAMES

World Three-Cushion Championship*

Year	Winner
2000	D. Jaspers (Neth.)
2001	R. Ceulemans (Belg.)
2002	**M. Zanetti (Italy)**

*Union Mondiale de Billard champion.

WPA World Nine-Ball Championships

Year	Men's champion
2000	Chao Fong-pang (Taiwan)
2001	M. Immonen (Fin.)
2002	**E. Strickland (U.S.)**

Year	Women's champion
2000	J. Kelly (Ire.)
2001	A. Fisher (U.K.)
2002	**Liu Shin-mei (Taiwan)**

World Professional Snooker Championship

Year	Winner	Year	Winner
1997	K. Doherty	2000	M. Williams
1998	J. Higgins	2001	R. O'Sullivan
1999	S. Hendry	**2002**	**P. Ebdon**

BOBSLEIGH AND LUGE

Bobsleigh and Skeleton World Championships

Year	Two-man bobsleigh	Four-man	Women's bobsleigh	Men's skeleton	Women's skeleton
2000	C. Langen, M. Zimmerman (Ger.)	Germany	G. Kohlisch, K. Hering (Ger.)	A. Böhme (Ger.)	S. Hanzlik (Ger.)
2001	C. Langen, M. Jakobs (Ger.)	Germany	F. Burdet, K. Sutter (Switz.)	M. Rettl (Austria)	M. Pedersen (Switz.)
2002*	**C. Langen, M. Zimmerman (Ger.)**	**Germany**	**J. Bakken, V. Flowers (U.S.)**	**J. Shea, Jr. (U.S.)**	**T. Gale (U.S.)**

*Olympic champions.

Luge World Championships*

Year	Men	Women	Doubles	Team
2000	J. Müller (Ger.)	S. Otto (Ger.)	P. Leitner, A. Resch (Ger.)	Germany
2001	A. Zöggeler (Italy)	S. Otto (Ger.)	A. Florschütz, T. Wustlich (Ger.)	Germany
2002†	**A. Zöggeler (Italy)**	**S. Otto (Ger.)**	**P. Leitner, A. Resch (Ger.)**	

*Artificial track.   †Olympic champions.

BOWLING

ABC Bowling Championships—Regular Divisions

Year	Singles	Score	All-events	Score
2000	G. Hein	811	R. Daniels	2,181
2001	N. Hoagland	798	D.J. Archer	2,219
2002	**M. Millsap**	**823**	**S.A. Hardy**	**2,279**

WIBC Bowling Championships—Classic Division

Year	Singles	Score	All-events	Score
2000	C. Krasner	729	C. Dorin-Ballard	2,147
2001	L. Wagner	756	J. Armon	2,044
2002	**T. Smith**	**752**	**C. Honeychurch**	**2,150**

Professional Bowlers Association (PBA) Tournament of Champions

Year	Champion
2000	J. Couch
2001	not held
2002–03	**J. Couch**

FIQ World Bowling Championships—Men

Year	Singles	Pairs	Triples	Team (fives)
1991	Ying Chieh Ma (Taiwan)	United States	United States	Taiwan
1995	M. Doi (Can.)	Sweden	Netherlands	Netherlands
1999	G. Verbruggen (Belg.)	Sweden	Finland	Sweden

FIQ World Bowling Championships—Women

Year	Singles	Pairs	Triples	Team (fives)
1991	M. Beckel (Ger.)	Japan	Canada	South Korea
1995	D. Ship (Can.)	Thailand	Australia	Finland
1999	K. Kulick (U.S.)	Australia	South Korea	South Korea

BOXING

World Heavyweight Champions
No Weight Limit

WBA

John Ruiz (U.S.; 3/3/01)

WBC

Lennox Lewis (U.K.; 11/17/01)

IBF

Lennox Lewis (U.K.; 11/17/01)
  gave up title in 2002
Chris Byrd (U.S.; 12/14/02)

World Cruiserweight Champions
Top Weight 195 Pounds

WBA

Virgil Hill (U.S.; 12/9/00)
Jean-Marc Mormeck (Fr.; 2/23/02)

WBC

Juan Carlos Gómez (Ger.; 2/21/98)
  gave up title in 2002
Wayne Braithwaite (U.S.; 10/11/02)

IBF

Vassily Jirov (Kazak.; 6/5/99)

World Light Heavyweight Champions
Top Weight 175 Pounds

WBA

Roy Jones, Jr. (U.S.; 7/18/98)
  declared super champion in 2001
Bruno Girard (Fr.; 12/22/01)

WBC

Roy Jones, Jr. (U.S.; 8/7/97)

IBF

Roy Jones, Jr. (U.S.; 6/5/99)
  stripped of title in 2002

BOXING (continued)

World Super Middleweight Champions
Top Weight 168 Pounds

WBA

Byron Mitchell (U.S.; 3/3/01)

WBC

Eric Lucas (Can.; 7/10/01)

IBF

Sven Ottke (Ger.; 10/24/98)

World Middleweight Champions
Top Weight 160 Pounds

WBA

Bernard Hopkins (U.S.; 9/29/01)
  declared super champion in 2001
William Joppy (U.S.; 11/17/01)

WBC

Bernard Hopkins (U.S.; 4/14/01)

IBF

Bernard Hopkins (U.S.; 4/29/95)

World Junior Middleweight Champions
Top Weight 154 Pounds
(also called super welterweight)

WBA

Fernando Vargas (U.S.; 9/22/01)
Oscar de la Hoya (U.S.; 9/14/02)
  declared super champion in 2002
Santiago Samaniego (Pan.; 8/10/02)

WBC

Oscar de la Hoya (U.S.; 6/23/01)

IBF

Ronald Wright (U.S.; 10/12/01)

World Welterweight Champions
Top Weight 147 Pounds

WBA

Andrew Lewis (Guyana; 2/17/01)
Ricardo Mayorga (Nic.; 3/30/02)

WBC

Shane Mosley (U.S.; 6/17/00)
Vernon Forrest (U.S.; 1/26/02)

IBF

Vernon Forrest (U.S.; 5/12/01)
  stripped of title in 2001
Michele Piccirillo (Italy; 4/13/02)

World Junior Welterweight Champions
Top Weight 140 Pounds
(also called super lightweight)

WBA

Kostya Tszyu (Austl.; 2/3/01)
  declared super champion in 2001
Diobelys Hurtado (Cuba; 5/11/02)
Vivian Harris (Guyana; 10/19/02)

WBC

Kostya Tszyu (Austl.; 8/21/99)

IBF

Kostya Tszyu (Austl.; 11/3/01)

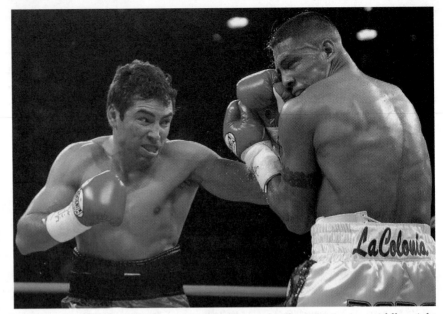

Oscar de la Hoya (left) defeats Fernando Vargas for the WBA junior middleweight championship in Las Vegas, Nev., on September 14.

AP/Wide World Photos

World Lightweight Champions
Top Weight 135 Pounds

WBA

Raul Balbi (Arg.; 10/8/01)
Leonard Dorin (Can.; 1/5/02)

WBC

José Luis Castillo (Mex.; 6/17/00)
Floyd Mayweather, Jr. (U.S.; 4/20/02)

IBF

Paul Spadafora (U.S.; 8/20/99)

World Junior Lightweight Champions
Top Weight 130 Pounds
(also called super featherweight)

WBA

Joel Casamayor (Cuba; 5/21/00)
Acelino Freitas (Braz.; 1/12/02)
  declared super champion in 2002
Yodsanan Nanthachai (Thai.; 4/13/02)

WBC

Floyd Mayweather, Jr. (U.S.; 10/3/98)
  gave up title in 2002
Sirimongkol Singmanassuk (Thai.; 8/24/02)

IBF

Steve Forbes (U.S.; 12/3/00)
  stripped of title in 2002

World Featherweight Champions
Top Weight 126 Pounds

WBA

Derrick Gainer (U.S.; 9/9/00)

WBC

Erik Morales (Mex.; 2/17/01)
Marco Antonio Barrera (Mex.; 6/22/02)
  declined title; declared vacant
Erik Morales (Mex.; 11/16/02)

IBF

Manuel Medina (Mex.; 11/16/01)
Johnny Tapia (U.S.; 4/27/02)
  stripped of title in 2002

World Junior Featherweight Champions
Top Weight 122 Pounds
(also called super bantamweight)

WBA

Yober Ortega (Venez.; 11/17/01)
Yoddamrong Sithyodthong (Thai.; 2/21/02)
Osamu Sato (Japan; 5/18/02)
Salim Medjkoune (Fr.; 10/9/02)

WBC

Willie Jorrin (U.S.; 9/9/00)
Oscar Larios (Mex.; 11/1/02)

IBF

Manny Pacquiao (Phil.; 6/23/01)

World Bantamweight Champions
Top Weight 118 Pounds

WBA

Eidy Moya (Venez.; 10/14/01)
Johnny Bredahl (Den.; 4/19/02)

WBC

Veeraphol Sahaprom (Thai.; 12/29/98)

IBF

Tim Austin (U.S.; 7/19/97)

World Junior Bantamweight Champions
Top Weight 115 Pounds
(also called super flyweight)

WBA

Shoji Kobayashi (Japan; 3/11/01)
Alexander Muñoz (Venez.; 3/9/02)

WBC

Masanori Tokuyama (Japan; 8/27/00)

IBF

Félix Machado (Venez.; 7/22/00)

BOXING (continued)

World Flyweight Champions
Top Weight 112 Pounds

WBA

Eric Morel (P.R.; 8/5/00)

WBC

Pongsaklek Wongjongkam (Thai.; 3/2/01)

IBF

Irene Pacheco (Colom.; 4/10/99)

World Junior Flyweight Champions
Top Weight 108 Pounds

WBA

Rosendo Alvarez (Nic.; 3/3/01)

WBC

Choi Yo Sam (S.Kor.; 10/17/99)
Jorge Arce (Mex.; 7/6/02)

IBF

Ricardo López (Mex.; 10/2/99)

World Mini-flyweight Champions
Top Weight 105 Pounds
(also called strawweight)

WBA

Yutaka Niida (Japan; 8/25/01)
  gave up title in 2001
Keitaro Hoshino (Japan; 1/29/02)
Noel Arambulet (Venez.; 7/29/02)

WBC

José Antonio Aguirre (Mex.; 2/11/00)

IBF

Roberto Leyva (Mex.; 4/29/01)
Miguel Barrera (Colom.; 8/9/02)

CHESS

FIDE Chess Championship—Men

Year	Winner	Runner-up
1999	A. Khalifman (Russia)	V. Akopyan (Arm.)
2000	V. Anand (India)	A. Shirov (Spain)
2002	**R. Ponomaryov (Ukr.)**	**V. Ivanchuk (Ukr.)**

FIDE Chess Championship—Women

Year	Winner	Runner-up
1999	Xie Jun (China)	A. Galyamova (Russia)
2000	Xie Jun (China)	Qin Karying (China)
2001	Zhu Chen (China)	A. Kostenyuk (Russia)

FIDE Olympiad—Men

Year	Winner	Runner-up
1998	Russia	United States
2000	Russia	Germany
2002	**Russia**	**Hungary**

FIDE Olympiad—Women

Year	Winner	Runner-up
1998	China	Russia
2000	China	Georgia
2002	**China**	**Russia**

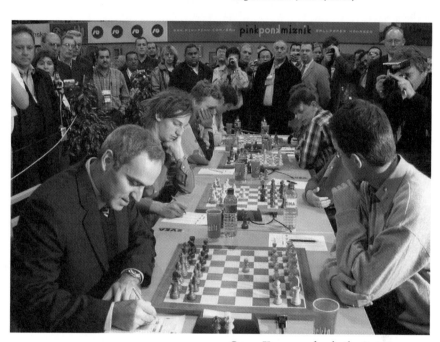

Garry Kasparov leads the Russian team to victory at the 35th Chess Olympiad in Bled, Slovenia.

© Eugeny Atarov

CONTRACT BRIDGE

World Team Olympiad

Year	Open winner	Open runner-up	Women's winner	Women's runner-up
1992	France	United States	Austria	United Kingdom
1996	France	Indonesia	United States	China
2000	Italy	Poland	United States	Canada

World Contract Bridge Pair Championship

Year	Open winners	Women's winners	Mixed winners
1994	Marcin Lesniewski, Marek Szymanowski (Pol.)	Carla Arnolds, Bep Vriend (Neth.)	Danuta Hocheker, Apolinare Kowalski (Pol.)
1998	Michal Kwiecien, Jacek Pszczola (Pol.)	Jill Meyers, Shawn Quinn (U.S.)	Enza Rossano, Antonio Vivaldi (Italy)
2002	**Fulvio Fantoni, Claudio Nunes (Italy)**	**Karen McCallum, Debbie Rosenberg (U.S.)**	**Becky Rogers, Jeff Meckstroth (U.S.)**

World Contract Bridge Zonal Team Championships

Year	Bermuda Bowl (open)		Venice Cup (women)	
	Winner	Runner-up	Winner	Runner-up
1997	France	United States	United States	China
2000	United States	Brazil	Netherlands	United States
2001	United States	Norway	Germany	France

CRICKET

Cricket World Cup

Year	Result			
1992	Pakistan	249–6	England	227
1996	Sri Lanka	245–3	Australia	241
1999	Australia	133–2	Pakistan	132

CRICKET (continued)

Test Match Results, October 2001–September 2002

Host/Ground	Date	Scores	Result
South Africa/Bloemfontein	Nov. 3–6	India 379 and 237; S.Af. 563 and 54 for 1	S.Af. won by 9 wickets
South Africa/Port Elizabeth	Nov. 16–20	S.Af. 362 and 233 for 5 dec; India 201 and 206 for 3	Match drawn
South Africa/Centurion (unofficial "Test")	Nov. 23–27	India 232 and 261; S.Af. 566 for 8 dec	S.Af. won by an innings and 73 runs; S.Af. won series 2–0
Australia/Brisbane	Nov. 8–12	Austl. 486 for 9 dec and 84 for 2 dec; N.Z. 287 for 8 dec and 274 for 6	Match drawn
Australia/Hobart	Nov. 22–26	Austl. 558 for 8 dec; N.Z. 243 for 7	Match drawn
Australia/Perth	Nov. 30–Dec. 4	N.Z. 534 for 9 dec and 256 for 9 dec; Austl. 351 and 381 for 7	Match drawn; series drawn 0–0
Bangladesh/Dhaka	Nov. 8–12	Bangl. 107 and 125 for 3; Zimb. 431	Match drawn
Bangladesh/Chittagong	Nov. 15–19	Zimb. 542 for 7 dec and 11 for 2; Bangl. 251 and 301	Zimb. won by 8 wickets; Zimb. won series 1–0
Sri Lanka/Galle	Nov. 13–17	W.Ind. 448 and 144; SriL. 590 for 9 dec and 6 for 0	SriL. won by 10 wickets
Sri Lanka/Kandy	Nov. 21–25	SriL. 288 and 224 for 6 dec; W.Ind. 191 and 190	SriL. won by 131 runs
Sri Lanka/Colombo	Nov. 29–Dec. 3	W.Ind. 390 and 262; SriL. 627 for 9 dec and 27 for 0	SriL. won by 10 wickets; SriL. won series 3–0
India/Mohali	Dec. 3–6	Eng. 238 and 235; India 469 and 5 for 0	India won by 10 wickets
India/Ahmedabad	Dec. 11–15	Eng. 407 and 257; India 291 and 198 for 3	Match drawn
India/Bangalore	Dec. 19–23	Eng. 336 and 33 for 0; India 238	Match drawn; India won series 1–0
Australia/Adelaide	Dec. 14–18	Austl. 439 and 309 for 7 dec; S.Af. 374 and 128	Austl. won by 246 runs
Australia/Melbourne	Dec. 26–29	S.Af. 277 and 219; Austl. 487 and 10 for 1	Austl. won by 9 wickets
Australia/Sydney	Jan. 2–5	Austl. 554 and 54 for 0; S.Af. 154 and 452	Austl. won by 10 wickets; Austl. won series 3–0
New Zealand/Hamilton	Dec. 18–22	N.Z. 365 for 9 dec; Bangl. 205 and 108	N.Z. won by an innings and 52 runs
New Zealand/Wellington	Dec. 26–29	Bangl. 132 and 135; N.Z. 341 for 6 dec	N.Z. won by an innings and 74 runs; N.Z. won series 2–0
Sri Lanka/Colombo	Dec. 27–31	SriL. 586 for 6 dec; Zimb. 184 and 236	SriL. won by an innings and 166 runs
Sri Lanka/Kandy	Jan. 4–7	Zimb. 236 and 175; SriL. 505	SriL. won by an innings and 94 runs
Sri Lanka/Galle	Jan. 12–15	SriL. 418 and 212 for 2 dec; Zimb. 236 and 79	SriL. won by 315 runs; SriL. won series 3–0
Bangladesh/Dhaka	Jan. 9–11	Bangl. 160 and 152; Pak. 490 for 9 dec	Pak. won by an innings and 178 runs
Bangladesh/Chittagong	Jan. 16–18	Bangl. 148 and 148; Pak. 465 for 9 dec	Pak. won by an innings and 169 runs; Pak. won series 2–0
Pakistan/Sharjah (U.A.E.)	Jan. 31–Feb. 4	Pak. 493 and 214 for 6 dec; W.Ind. 366 and 171	Pak. won by 170 runs
Pakistan/Sharjah (U.A.E.)	Feb. 7–10	Pak. 472 and 225 for 5 dec; W.Ind. 264 and 189	Pak. won by 244 runs; Pak. won series 2–0
India/Nagpur	Feb. 21–25	Zimb. 287 and 182; India 570 for 7 dec	India won by an innings and 101 runs
India/Delhi	Feb. 28–March 4	Zimb. 329 and 146; India 354 and 126 for 6	India won by 4 wickets; India won series 2–0
South Africa/Johannesburg	Feb. 22–24	Austl. 652 for 7 dec; S.Af. 159 and 133	Austl. won by an innings and 360 runs
South Africa/Cape Town	March 8–12	S.Af. 239 and 473; Austl. 382 and 334 for 6	Austl. won by 4 wickets
South Africa/Durban	March 15–18	Austl. 315 and 186; S.Af. 167 and 340 for 5	S.Af. won by 5 wickets; Austl. won series 2–1
Pakistan/Lahore	March 6–10	Pak. 234 and 325; SriL. 528 and 33 for 2	SriL. won by 8 wickets; SriL. won Asian Test championship final
New Zealand/Christchurch	March 13–16	Eng. 228 and 468 for 6 dec; N.Z. 147 and 451	Eng. won by 98 runs
New Zealand/Wellington	March 21–25	Eng. 280 and 293 for 4 dec; N.Z. 218 and 158 for 4	Match drawn
New Zealand/Auckland	March 30–April 3	N.Z. 202 and 269 for 9 dec; Eng. 160 and 233	N.Z. won by 78 runs; series drawn 1–1
West Indies/Guyana	April 11–15	W.Ind. 501; India 395 for 7	Match drawn
West Indies/Trinidad	April 19–23	India 339 and 218; W.Ind. 245 and 275	India won by 37 runs
West Indies/Barbados	May 2–5	India 102 and 296; W.Ind. 394 and 5 for 0	W.Ind. won by 10 wickets
West Indies/Antigua	May 10–14	India 513 for 9 dec; W.Ind. 629 for 9 dec	Match drawn
West Indies/Jamaica	May 18–22	W.Ind. 422 and 197; India 212 and 252	W.Ind. won by 155 runs; W.Ind. won series 2–1
Pakistan/Lahore	May 1–3	Pak. 643; N.Z. 73 and 246	Pak. won by an innings and 324 runs
Pakistan/Karachi	May 8	Match canceled	Pak. won series 1–0
England/London (Lord's)	May 16–20	SriL. 555 for 8 dec and 42 for 1; Eng. 275 and 529 for 5 dec	Match drawn
England/Birmingham	May 30–June 2	SriL. 162 and 272; Eng. 545	Eng. won by an innings and 111 runs
England/Manchester	June 13–17	Eng. 512 and 50 for 0; SriL. 253 and 308	Eng. won by 10 wickets; Eng. won series 2–0
West Indies/Barbados	June 21–24	N.Z. 337 and 243; W.Ind. 107 and 269	N.Z. won by 204 runs
West Indies/Grenada	June 28–July 2	N.Z. 373 and 256 for 5; W.Ind. 470	Match drawn; N.Z. won series 1–0
Sri Lanka/Colombo	July 21–23	Bangl. 161 and 184; SriL. 541 for 9 dec	SriL. won by an innings and 196 runs
Sri Lanka/Colombo	July 28–31	SriL. 373 and 263 for 2 dec; Bangl. 164 and 184	SriL. won by 288 runs; SriL. won series 2–0
England/London (Lord's)	July 25–29	Eng. 487 and 301 for 6 dec; India 221 and 397	Eng. won by 170 runs
England/Nottingham	Aug. 8–12	India 357 and 424 for 8 dec; Eng. 617	Match drawn
England/Leeds	Aug. 22–26	India 628 for 8 dec; Eng. 273 and 309	India won by an innings and 46 runs
England/London (The Oval)	Sept. 5–9	Eng. 515 and 114 for 0; India 508	Match drawn; series drawn 1–1

CURLING

World Curling Championship—Men		
Year	Winner	Runner-up
2000	Canada	Sweden
2001	Sweden	Switzerland
2002	**Canada**	**Norway**

World Curling Championship—Women		
Year	Winner	Runner-up
2000	Canada	Switzerland
2001	Canada	Sweden
2002	**Scotland**	**Sweden**

CYCLING

Cycling Champions, 2002

Event	Winner	Country
WORLD CHAMPIONS—TRACK		
Men		
Sprint	S. Eadie	Australia
Individual pursuit	B. McGee	Australia
Kilometre time trial	C. Hoy	Great Britain
30-km points	C. Newton	Great Britain
Team pursuit	P. Dawson, B. Lancaster, L. Roberts, S. Wooldridge	Australia
Keirin	J. Dajka	Australia
Team sprint	C. Hoy, C. MacLean, J. Staff	Great Britain
50-km Madison	J. Neuville, F. Perque	France
15-km scratch	F. Marvulli	Switzerland
Women		
Sprint	N. Tsylinskaya	Belarus
Individual pursuit	L. Zijlaard-van Moorsel	Netherlands
500-m time trial	N. Tsylinskaya	Belarus
25-km points	O. Slyusareva	Russia
10-km scratch	L. Kozlikova	Czech Republic
Keirin	Na Li	China
WORLD CHAMPIONS—ROAD		
Men		
Individual road race	M. Cipollini	Italy
Individual time trial	S. Botero	Colombia
Women		
Individual road race	S. Ljungskog	Sweden
Individual time trial	Z. Zabirova	Russia
WORLD CHAMPION—CYCLO-CROSS		
Men	M. De Clercq	Belgium
Women	L. Leboucher	France

Event	Winner	Country
WORLD CHAMPIONS—MOUNTAIN BIKES		
Men		
Cross-country	R. Green	Canada
Downhill	N. Vouilloz	France
Women		
Cross-country	G.-R. Dahle	Norway
Downhill	A.-C. Chausson	France
MAJOR ELITE ROAD-RACE WINNERS		
Tour de France	L. Armstrong	United States
Tour of Italy	P. Savoldelli	Italy
Tour of Spain	A. González	Spain
Tour of Switzerland	A. Zülle	Switzerland
Milan–San Remo	M. Cipollini	Italy
Tour of Flanders	A. Tafi	Italy
Paris–Roubaix	J. Museeuw	Belgium
Liège–Bastogne–Liège	P. Bettini	Italy
Amstel Gold	M. Bartoli	Italy
HEW–Cyclassics Cup	J. Museeuw	Belgium
San Sebastian Classic	L. Jalabert	France
Zürich championship	D. Frigo	Italy
Paris–Tours	J. Piil	Denmark
Tour of Lombardy	M. Bartoli	Italy
Paris–Nice	A. Vinokourov	Kazakhstan
Ghent–Wevelgem	M. Cipollini	Italy
Flèche Wallonne	M. Aerts	Belgium
Tour of Romandie	D. Frigo	Italy
Dauphiné Libéré	L. Armstrong	United States
Tirreno–Adriatico	E. Dekker	Netherlands

Tour de France		
Year	Winner	Kilometres
2000	L. Armstrong (U.S.)	3,663
2001	L. Armstrong (U.S.)	3,454
2002	**L. Armstrong (U.S.)**	**3,778**

EQUESTRIAN SPORTS

The Kentucky Derby		
Year	Horse	Jockey
2000	Fusaichi Pegasus	K. Desormeaux
2001	Monarchos	J. Chavez
2002	**War Emblem**	**V. Espinoza**

The Preakness Stakes		
Year	Horse	Jockey
2000	Red Bullet	J. Bailey
2001	Point Given	G. Stevens
2002	**War Emblem**	**V. Espinoza**

The Belmont Stakes		
Year	Horse	Jockey
2000	Commendable	P. Day
2001	Point Given	G. Stevens
2002	**Sarava**	**E. Prado**

2,000 Guineas		
Year	Horse	Jockey
2000	King's Best	K. Fallon
2001	Golan	K. Fallon
2002	**Rock of Gibraltar**	**J. Murtagh**

The Derby		
Year	Horse	Jockey
2000	Sinndar	J. Murtagh
2001	Galileo	M. Kinane
2002	**High Chaparral**	**J. Murtagh**

The St. Leger		
Year	Horse	Jockey
2000	Millenary	R. Quinn
2001	Milan	M. Kinane
2002	**Bollin Eric**	**K. Darley**

EQUESTRIAN SPORTS (continued)

Triple Crown Champions—U.S.		Triple Crown Champions—British		Melbourne Cup			The Hambletonian Trot		
Year	Horse	Year	Winner	Year	Horse	Jockey	Year	Horse	Driver
1973	Secretariat	1918	Gainsborough	2000	Brew	K. McEvoy	2000	Yankee Paco	T. Ritchie
1977	Seattle Slew	1935	Bahram	2001	Ethereal	S. Seamer	2001	Scarlet Knight	S. Melander
1978	Affirmed	1970	Nijinsky	**2002**	**Media Puzzle**	**D. Oliver**	**2002**	**Chip Chip Hooray**	**E. Ledford**

Major Thoroughbred Race Winners, 2002

Race	Won by	Jockey
United States		
Acorn	You	J. Bailey
Alabama Stakes	Farda Amiga	P. Day
Apple Blossom	Azeri	M. Smith
Arlington Million	Beat Hollow	J. Bailey
Ashland Stakes	Take Charge Lady	A. D'Amico
Beldame	Imperial Gesture	J. Bailey
Belmont	Sarava	E. Prado
Beverly D.	Golden Apples	P. Valenzuela
Blue Grass Stakes	Harlan's Holiday	E. Prado
Breeders' Cup Juvenile	Vindication	M. Smith
Breeders' Cup Juvenile Fillies	Storm Flag Flying	J. Velazquez
Breeders' Cup Sprint	Orientate	J. Bailey
Breeders' Cup Mile	Domedriver	T. Thulliez
Breeders' Cup Distaff	Azeri	M. Smith
Breeders' Cup Turf	High Chaparral	M. Kinane
Breeders' Cup Filly and Mare Turf	Starine	J. Velazquez
Breeders' Cup Classic	Volponi	J. Santos
Champagne	Toccet	J. Chavez
Charles Wittingham Memorial	Denon	G. Gomez
Cigar Mile Handicap	Congaree	J. Bailey
Coaching Club American Oaks	Jilbab	M. Luzzi
Donn Handicap	Mongoose	E. Prado
Eddie Read	Sarafan	C. Nakatani
Florida Derby	Harlan's Holiday	E. Prado
Flower Bowl Invitational	Kazzia	J. Chavez
Fountain of Youth	Booklet	J. Chavez
Futurity Stakes	Whywhywhy	E. Prado
Gulfstream Park Handicap	Hal's Hope	R. Velez
Haskell Invitational	War Emblem	V. Espinoza
Hollywood Derby	Johar	A. Solis
Hollywood Futurity	Toccet	J. Chavez
Hollywood Gold Cup	Sky Jack	L. Pincay, Jr.
Hollywood Starlet	Elloluv	P. Valenzuela
Hollywood Turf Cup	Sligo Bay	L. Pincay, Jr.
Hopeful Stakes	Sky Mesa	E. Prado
Jockey Club Gold Cup	Evening Attire	S. Bridgmohan
Kentucky Derby	War Emblem	V. Espinoza
Kentucky Oaks	Farda Amiga	C. McCarron
Man o' War	With Anticipation	P. Day
Matriarch Stakes	Dress To Thrill	P. Smullen
Matron Stakes	Storm Flag Flying	J. Velazquez
Metropolitan	Swept Overboard	J. Chavez
Mother Goose	Nonsuch Bay	J. Bailey
Oaklawn Handicap	Kudos	E. Delahoussaye
Pacific Classic	Came Home	M. Smith
Preakness	War Emblem	V. Espinoza
Queen Elizabeth II Challenge Cup	Riskaverse	M. Guidry
Santa Anita Derby	Came Home	C. McCarron
Santa Anita Handicap	Milwaukee Brew	K. Desormeaux
Secretariat Stakes	Chiselling	K. Desormeaux
Spinaway Stakes	Awesome Humor	P. Day
Spinster Stakes	Take Charge Lady	E. Prado
Stephen Foster Handicap	Street Cry	J. Bailey
Travers	Medaglia d'Oro	J. Bailey
Turf Classic Invitational	Denon	E. Prado
Turf Classic Stakes	Beat Hollow	A. Solis
United Nations Handicap	With Anticipation	P. Day
Whitney	Left Bank	J. Velazquez
Wood Memorial	Buddha	P. Day
Woodward	Lido Palace	J. Chavez
Yellow Ribbon Stakes	Golden Apples	P. Valenzuela

Race	Won by	Jockey
England		
One Thousand Guineas	Kazzia	L. Dettori
Two Thousand Guineas	Rock of Gibraltar	J. Murtagh
Derby	High Chaparral	J. Murtagh
Oaks	Kazzia	L. Dettori
St. Leger	Bollin Eric	K. Darley
Coronation Cup	Boreal	K. Fallon
Ascot Gold Cup	Royal Rebel	J. Murtagh
Coral-Eclipse Stakes	Hawk Wing	M. Kinane
King George VI and Queen Elizabeth Diamond Stakes	Golan	K. Fallon
Sussex Stakes	Rock of Gibraltar	M. Kinane
Juddmonte International Stakes	Nayef	R. Hills
Champion Stakes	Storming Home	M. Hills
France		
Poule d'Essai des Poulains	Landseer	M. Kinane
Poule d'Essai des Pouliches	Zenda	R. Hughes
Prix du Jockey-Club	Sulamani	T. Thulliez
Prix de Diane	Bright Sky	D. Boeuf
Prix Royal-Oak	Mr Dinos	D. Boeuf
Prix Ganay	Aquarelliste	D. Boeuf
Prix Jacques Le Marois	Banks Hill	O. Peslier
Grand Prix de Paris	Khalkevi	C. Soumillon
Grand Prix de Saint-Cloud	Ange Gabriel	T. Jarnet
Prix Vermeille	Pearly Shells	C. Soumillon
Prix de l'Arc de Triomphe	Marienbard	L. Dettori
Grand Criterium	Hold That Tiger	K. Fallon
Ireland		
Irish Two Thousand Guineas	Rock of Gibraltar	M. Kinane
Irish One Thousand Guineas	Gossamer	J. Spencer
Irish Derby	High Chaparral	M. Kinane
Irish Oaks	Margarula	K. Manning
Irish St. Leger	Vinnie Roe	P. Smullen
Irish Champion Stakes	Grandera	L. Dettori
Italy		
Derby Italiano	Rakti	M. Demuro
Gran Premio del Jockey Club	Black Sam Bellamy	M. Kinane
Germany		
Deutsches Derby	Next Desert	A. Starke
Grosser Preis von Baden	Marienbard	L. Dettori
Preis von Europa	Well Made	T. Hellier
Australia		
Melbourne Cup	Media Puzzle	D. Oliver
Cox Plate	Northerly	P. Payne
Caulfield Cup	Northerly	G. Childs
United Arab Emirates		
Dubai World Cup	Street Cry	J. Bailey
Asia		
Japan Cup	Falbrav	L. Dettori
Singapore Cup	Grandera	L. Dettori
Canada		
Queen's Plate Stakes	T J's Lucky Moon	S. Bahen
Prince of Wales Stakes	Le Cinquieme Essai	B. Bochinski
Breeders' Stakes	Portcullis	S. Callaghan

FENCING

World Fencing Championships—Men

Year	Individual			Team		
	Foil	Épée	Sabre	Foil	Épée	Sabre
2000	Kim Young Ho (S.Kor.)	P. Kolobkov (Russia)	M.C. Covaliu (Rom.)	France	Italy	Russia
2001	S. Sanzo (Italy)	P. Milanoli (Italy)	S. Pozdnyakov (Russia)	France	Hungary	Russia
2002	**S. Vanni (Italy)**	**P. Kolobkov (Russia)**	**S. Pozdnyakov (Russia)**	**Germany**	**France**	**Russia**

World Fencing Championships—Women

Year	Individual			Team		
	Foil	Épée	Sabre	Foil	Épée	Sabre
2000	V. Vezzali (Italy)	T. Nagy (Hung.)	E. Jemaeva (Azer.)	Italy	Russia	United States
2001	V. Vezzali (Italy)	C. Bokel (Ger.)	A.-L. Touya (Fr.)	Italy	Russia	Russia
2002	**S. Bojko (Russia)**	**Hyun Hee (S.Kor.)**	**Tan Xue (China)**	**Russia**	**Hungary**	**Russia**

FOOTBALL

FIFA World Cup—Men

Year	Result			
1994	Brazil*	0	Italy	0
1998	France	3	Brazil	0
2002	**Brazil**	**2**	**Germany**	**0**

*Won on penalty kicks.

FIFA World Cup—Women

Year	Result			
1991	United States	2	Norway	1
1995	Norway	2	Germany	0
1999	United States*	0	China	0

*Won on penalty kicks.

FIELD HOCKEY

World Cup Field Hockey Championship—Men

Year	Winner	Runner-up
1994	Pakistan	Netherlands
1998	Netherlands	Spain
2002	**Germany**	**Australia**

World Cup Field Hockey Championship—Women

Year	Winner	Runner-up
1994	Australia	Argentina
1998	Australia	Netherlands
2002	**Argentina**	**Netherlands**

Association Football National Champions, 2002

Nation	League Champions	Cup Winners	Nation	League Champions	Cup Winners
Argentina	Independiente (Opening)	River Plate (Closing)	Mexico	América (summer)	Toluca (winter)
Australia	Olympic Sharks		Morocco	Hassania	
Austria	Tirol Innsbruck	Graz AK	Nigeria	Enyimba	Dolphin
Belgium	Genk	FC Brugge	Northern Ireland	Portadown	Linfield
Bolivia	Bolívar		Norway	Rosenborg	Viking
Brazil	Santos	Corinthians	Paraguay	Libertad	
Bulgaria	Levski	Levski	Peru	Sporting Cristal	
Cameroon	Cotonsport	Fovu	Poland	Legia	Wisla
Chile	Universidad Catolica (Opening)	Colo Colo (Closing)	Portugal	Sporting	Sporting
China	Dalian Shide	Dalian Shide	Romania	Dinamo	Rapid
Colombia	América (Opening)	Independiente Medellín (Closing)	Russia	Spartak Moscow	CSKA Moscow
Costa Rica	Alajuelense		Saudi Arabia	Al-Hilal	Al-Ahli
Croatia	Zagreb	Dynamo Zagreb	Scotland	Celtic	Rangers
Czech Republic	Slovan Liberec	Slavia Prague	Senegal	Jeanne d'Arc	AS Douanes
Denmark	Brondby	Odense	Slovakia	Zilina	Koba
Ecuador	Emelec		Slovenia	Maribor	Gorica
England	Arsenal	Arsenal	South Africa	Santos	
Finland	Tampere U	Atlantis	South Korea	Songnam	Taejon Citizens
France	Lyon	Lorient	Spain	Valencia	La Coruna
Georgia	Torpedo Kutaisi	Lokomotivi	Sweden	Hammarby	
Germany	Borussia Dortmund	Schalke	Switzerland	Basle	Basle
Greece	Olympiakos	AEK Athens	Tunisia	Esperance	Hammam-Lif
Holland	Ajax	Ajax	Turkey	Galatasaray	Kocaeli
Hungary	Zalaegerszeg	Ujpest	Ukraine	Shakhtjor Donetsk	Shakhtjor Donetsk
Ireland	Shelbourne	Dundalk	Uruguay	Nacional	
Israel	Maccabi Haifa	Maccabi Tel Aviv	United States (MLS)	Los Angeles Galaxy	
Italy	Juventus	Parma	Venezuela	Nacional Táchira	
Japan	Kashima Antlers	Shimizu S-Pulse	Yugoslavia	Partizan Belgrade	Red Star Belgrade

UEFA Champions League*

Season	Result				
1999–2000	Real Madrid (Spain)	3	Valencia (Spain)		0
2000–01	Bayern Munich (Ger.)†	1	Valencia (Spain)		1
2001–02	**Real Madrid (Spain)**	**2**	**Bayer 04 Leverkusen (Ger.)**		**1**

*Called European Cup of Champion Clubs until 1992–93.   †Won on penalty kicks.

UEFA Cup

Season	Result				
1999–2000	Galatasaray (Tur.)*	0	Arsenal (Eng.)		0
2000–01	Liverpool (Eng.)	5	Alavés (Spain)		4
2001–02	**Feyenoord (Neth.)**	**3**	**Borussia Dortmund (Ger.)**		**2**

*Won on penalty kicks.

FOOTBALL (continued)

Libertadores de América Cup

Year	Winner (country)	Runner-up (country)	Scores
2000	Boca Juniors (Arg.)	Palmeiras (Braz.)	2–2, 0–0, 4–2*
2001	Boca Juniors (Arg.)	Cruz Azul (Mex.)	1–0, 0–1, 3–1*
2002	**Olimpia (Par.)**	**São Caetano (Braz.)**	**0–1, 2–1, 4–2***

*Winner determined in penalty shootout.

Copa América

Year	Result			
1997	Brazil	3	Bolivia	1
1999	Brazil	3	Uruguay	1
2001	**Colombia**	**1**	**Mexico**	**0**

MLS Cup

Year	Result			
2000	Kansas City Wizards	1	Chicago Fire	0
2001	San Jose Earthquakes	2	Los Angeles Galaxy	1
2002	**Los Angeles Galaxy**	**1**	**New England Revolution**	**0**

U.S. College Football National Champions

Season	Champion
2000–01	Oklahoma
2001–02	Miami
2002–03	**Ohio State**

Rose Bowl

Season	Result			
2000–01	Washington	34	Purdue	24
2001–02	Miami	37	Nebraska	14
2002–03	**Oklahoma**	**34**	**Washington State**	**14**

Orange Bowl

Season	Result			
2000–01	Oklahoma	13	Florida State	2
2001–02	Florida	56	Maryland	23
2002–03	**Southern California**	**38**	**Iowa**	**17**

Fiesta Bowl

Season	Result			
2000–01	Oregon State	41	Notre Dame	9
2001–02	Oregon	38	Colorado	16
2002–03	**Ohio State**	**31**	**Miami**	**24**

Sugar Bowl

Season	Result			
2000–01	Miami	37	Florida	20
2001–02	Louisiana State	47	Illinois	34
2002–03	**Georgia**	**26**	**Florida State**	**13**

NFL Final Standings, 2002–03

AMERICAN CONFERENCE

East Division	W	L	T	North Division	W	L	T	South Division	W	L	T	West Division	W	L	T
*New York Jets	9	7	0	*Pittsburgh	10	5	1	*Tennessee	11	5	0	*Oakland	11	5	0
New England	9	7	0	*Cleveland	9	7	0	*Indianapolis	10	6	0	Denver	9	7	0
Miami	9	7	0	Baltimore	7	9	0	Jacksonville	6	10	0	San Diego	8	8	0
Buffalo	8	8	0	Cincinnati	2	14	0	Houston	4	12	0	Kansas City	8	8	0

NATIONAL CONFERENCE

East Division	W	L	T	North Division	W	L	T	South Division	W	L	T	West Division	W	L	T
*Philadelphia	12	4	0	*Green Bay	12	4	0	*Tampa Bay	12	4	0	*San Francisco	10	6	0
*New York Giants	10	6	0	Minnesota	6	10	0	*Atlanta	9	6	1	St. Louis	7	9	0
Washington	7	9	0	Chicago	4	12	0	New Orleans	9	7	0	Seattle	7	9	0
Dallas	5	11	0	Detroit	3	13	0	Carolina	7	9	0	Arizona	5	11	0

*Qualified for play-offs.

Super Bowl

	Season	Result			
XXXV	2000–01	Baltimore Ravens (AFC)	34	New York Giants (NFC)	7
XXXVI	2001–02	New England Patriots (AFC)	20	St. Louis Rams (NFC)	17
XXXVII	**2002–03**	**Tampa Bay Buccaneers (NFC)**	**48**	**Oakland Raiders (AFC)**	**21**

Grey Cup*

Year	Result			
2000	British Columbia Lions (WD)	28	Montreal Alouettes (ED)	26
2001	Calgary Stampeders (WD)	27	Winnipeg Blue Bombers (ED)	19
2002	**Montreal Alouettes (ED)**	**25**	**Edmonton Eskimos (WD)**	**16**

*ED—Eastern Division; WD—Western Division.

FOOTBALL (continued)

AFL Grand Final

Year	Result			
2000	Essendon	19.21 (135)	Melbourne	11.9 (75)
2001	Brisbane Lions	15.18 (108)	Essendon	12.10 (82)
2002	**Brisbane Lions**	**10.15 (75)**	**Collingwood**	**9.12 (66)**

Rugby League World Cup

Year	Result			
1992	Australia	10	Great Britain	6
1995	Australia	16	England	8
2000	Australia	40	New Zealand	12

Rugby Union World Cup

Year	Result			
1991	Australia	12	England	6
1995	South Africa	15	New Zealand	12
1999	Australia	35	France	12

Six Nations Championship*

Year	Result
2000	England
2001	England
2002	**France†**

*Five Nations until 2000.   †Grand Slam winner.

GOLF

Masters Tournament

Year	Winner
2000	V. Singh (Fiji)
2001	T. Woods (U.S.)
2002	**T. Woods (U.S.)**

British Open Tournament (men)

Year	Winner
2000	T. Woods (U.S.)
2001	D. Duval (U.S.)
2002	**E. Els (S.Af.)**

United States Amateur Championship (men)

Year	Winner
2000	J. Quinney (U.S.)
2001	B. Dickerson (U.S.)
2002	**R. Barnes (U.S.)**

United States Women's Open Championship

Year	Winner
2000	K. Webb (Austl.)
2001	K. Webb (Austl.)
2002	**J. Inkster (U.S.)**

Ladies Professional Golf Association (LPGA) Championship

Year	Winner
2000	J. Inkster (U.S.)
2001	K. Webb (Austl.)
2002	**Pak Se Ri (S.Kor.)**

Ladies' British Amateur Championship

Year	Winner
2000	R. Hudson (U.K.)
2001	M. Prieto (Spain)
2002	**R. Hudson (U.K.)**

United States Open Championship (men)

Year	Winner
2000	T. Woods (U.S.)
2001	R. Goosen (S.Af.)
2002	**T. Woods (U.S.)**

U.S. Professional Golfers' Association (PGA) Championship

Year	Winner
2000	T. Woods (U.S.)
2001	D. Toms (U.S.)
2002	**R. Beem (U.S.)**

British Amateur Championship (men)

Year	Winner
2000	M. Ilonen (Fin.)
2001	M. Hoey (Ire.)
2002	**A. Larrazabal (Spain)**

Women's British Open Championship

Year	Winner
2000	S. Gustafson (Swed.)
2001	Pak Se Ri (S.Kor.)
2002	**K. Webb (Austl.)**

United States Women's Amateur Championship

Year	Winner
2000	M. Newton (U.S.)
2001	M. Duncan (U.S.)
2002	**B. Lucidi (U.S.)**

World Cup (men; professional)

Year	Winner
2000	United States (T. Woods and D. Duval)
2001	South Africa (E. Els and R. Goosen)
2002	**Japan (T. Izawa and S. Maruyama)**

Solheim Cup (women; professional)

Year	Result
1998	United States 16, Europe 12
2000	Europe 14½, United States 11½
2002	**United States 15½, Europe 12½**

Ryder Cup (men; professional)

Year	Result
1999	United States 14½, Europe 13½
2001	postponed until 2002
2002	**Europe 15½, United States 12½**

AP/Wide World Photos

Pak Se Ri on her way to winning the LPGA championship on June 9.

GYMNASTICS

World Gymnastics Championships—Men

Year	All-around team	All-around individual	Horizontal bar	Parallel bars
2000	China	A. Nemov (Russia)	A. Nemov (Russia)	Li Xiaopeng (China)
2001	Belarus	Feng Jing (China)	V. Maras (Greece)	S. Townsend (U.S.)
2002	**not held**	**not held**	**V. Maras (Greece)**	**Li Xiaopeng (China)**

Year	Pommel horse	Rings	Vault	Floor exercise
2000	M. Urzica (Rom.)	S. Csollany (Hung.)	G. Deferr (Spain)	I. Vihrovs (Latvia)
2001	M. Urzica (Rom.)	J. Jovtchev (Bulg.)	M. Dragulescu (Rom.)	J. Jovtchev (Bulg.)* M. Dragulescu (Rom.)*
2002	**M. Urzica (Rom.)**	**S. Csollany (Hung.)**	**Li Xiaopeng (China)**	**M. Dragulescu (Rom.)**

* Tied.

World Gymnastics Championships—Women

Year	All-around team	All-around individual	Balance beam
2000	Romania	S. Amanar (Rom.)	Liu Xuan (China)
2001	Romania	S. Khorkina (Russia)	A. Raducan (Rom.)
2002	**not held**	**not held**	**A. Postell (U.S.)**

Year	Uneven parallel bars	Vault	Floor exercise
2000	S. Khorkina (Russia)	Ye. Zamolodchikova (Russia)	Ye. Zamolodchikova (Russia)
2001	S. Khorkina (Russia)	S. Khorkina (Russia)	A. Raducan (Rom.)
2002	**C. Kupets (U.S.)**	**Ye. Zamolodchikova (Russia)**	**E. Gómez (Spain)**

AP/Wide World Photos

Gold medalist Ashley Postell soars above the balance beam.

ICE HOCKEY

NHL Final Standings, 2002

EASTERN CONFERENCE

Northeast Division

	W	L	T	OTL*
†Boston	43	24	6	9
†Toronto	43	25	10	4
†Ottawa	39	27	9	7
†Montreal	36	31	12	3
Buffalo	35	35	11	1

Atlantic Division

	W	L	T	OTL*
†Philadelphia	42	27	10	3
†New York Islanders	42	28	8	4
†New Jersey	41	28	9	4
New York Rangers	36	38	4	4
Pittsburgh	28	41	8	5

Southeast Division

	W	L	T	OTL*
†Carolina	35	26	16	5
Washington	36	33	11	2
Tampa Bay	27	40	11	4
Florida	22	44	10	6
Atlanta	19	47	11	5

WESTERN CONFERENCE

Central Division

	W	L	T	OTL*
†Detroit	51	17	10	4
†St. Louis	43	27	8	4
†Chicago	41	27	13	1
Nashville	28	41	13	0
Columbus	22	47	8	5

Northwest Division

	W	L	T	OTL*
†Colorado	45	28	8	1
†Vancouver	42	30	7	3
Edmonton	38	28	12	4
Calgary	32	35	12	3
Minnesota	26	35	12	9

Pacific Division

	W	L	T	OTL*
†San Jose	44	27	8	3
†Los Angeles	40	27	11	4
†Phoenix	40	27	9	6
Dallas	36	28	13	5
Anaheim	29	42	8	3

*Overtime losses, worth one point. †Qualified for play-offs.

The Stanley Cup

Season	Winner	Runner-up	Games
1999–2000	New Jersey Devils	Dallas Stars	4–2
2000–01	Colorado Avalanche	New Jersey Devils	4–3
2001–02	**Detroit Red Wings**	**Carolina Hurricanes**	**4–1**

World Ice Hockey Championship—Men

Year	Winner
2000	Czech Republic
2001	Czech Republic
2002	**Slovakia**

World Ice Hockey Championship—Women

Year	Winner
2000	Canada
2001	Canada
2002	**not held**

ICE SKATING

World Figure Skating Champions—Men

Year	Winner
2000	A. Yagudin (Russia)
2001	Ye. Plushchenko (Russia)
2002	**A. Yagudin (Russia)**

World Figure Skating Champions—Women

Year	Winner
2000	M. Kwan (U.S.)
2001	M. Kwan (U.S.)
2002	**I. Slutskaya (Russia)**

World Figure Skating Champions—Pairs

Year	Winners
2000	M. Petrova, A. Tikhonov (Russia)
2001	J. Salé, D. Pelletier (Can.)
2002	**Shen Xue, Zhao Hongbo (China)**

World Ice Dancing Champions

Year	Winners
2000	M. Anissina, G. Peizarat (Fr.)
2001	B. Fusar Poli, M. Margaglio (Italy)
2002	**I. Lobacheva, I. Averbukh (Russia)**

Aleksey Yagudin of Russia wins the men's world figure-skating championship in Nagano, Japan.

© Allsport UK/Getty Images

ICE SKATING (continued)

World Ice Speed-Skating Records Set in 2002 on Major Tracks*

Event	Name	Country	Time
MEN			
1,000 m	Gerard van Velde	Netherlands	1 min 7.18 sec
1,500 m	Derek Parra	United States	1 min 43.95 sec
5,000 m	Jochem Uytdehaage	Netherlands	6 min 14.66 sec
10,000 m	Jochem Uytdehaage	Netherlands	12 min 58.92 sec
WOMEN			
1,000 m	Christine Witty	United States	1 min 13.83 sec
1,500 m	Anni Friesinger	Germany	1 min 54.02 sec
3,000 m	Claudia Pechstein	Germany	3 min 57.70 sec
5,000 m	Claudia Pechstein	Germany	6 min 46.91 sec

*May include records awaiting ISU ratification at year's end.

World Ice Speed-Skating Records Set in 2002 on Short Tracks*

Event	Name	Country	Time
MEN			
1,500 m	Steve Robillard	Canada	2 min 12.234 sec
3,000 m	Steve Robillard	Canada	4 min 38.061 sec
WOMEN			
1,000 m	Yang Yang (A)	China	1 min 31.191 sec
1,500 m	Choi Eun Kyung	South Korea	2 min 21.069 sec
3,000-m relay	South Korea National Team	South Korea	4 min 12.793 sec

*May include records awaiting ISU ratification at year's end.

World Speed-Skating Sprint Championships

Year	Men	Women
2000	J. Wotherspoon (Can.)	M. Garbrecht (Ger.)
2001	M. Ireland (Can.)	M. Garbrecht-Enfeldt (Ger.)
2002	**J. Wotherspoon (Can.)**	**C. LeMay Doan (Can.)**

World All-Around Speed-Skating Champions

Year	Men	Women
2000	G. Romme (Neth.)	C. Pechstein (Ger.)
2001	R. Ritsma (Neth.)	A. Friesinger (Ger.)
2002	**J. Uytdehaage (Neth.)**	**A. Friesinger (Ger.)**

World Short-Track Speed-Skating Championships—Overall Winners

Year	Men	Women
2000	Ryoung Min (S.Kor.)	Yang Yang (A) (China)
2001	Li Jianjun (China)	Yang Yang (A) (China)
2002	**Kim Dong Sung (S.Kor.)**	**Yang Yang (A) (China)**

JUDO

World Judo Championships—Men*

Year	Open weights	60 kg	65 kg (66 kg)	71 kg (73 kg)
1997	R. Kubacki (Pol.)	T. Nomura (Japan)	Kim Hyuk (S.Kor.)	K. Nakamura (Japan)
1999	S. Shinohara (Japan)	M. Poulot (Cuba)	L. Benboudaoud (Fr.)	J. Pedro (U.S.)
2001	A. Mikhaylin (Russia)	A. Lounifi (Tun.)	A. Miresmaeili (Iran)	V. Makarov (Russia)

Year	78 kg (81 kg)	86 kg (90 kg)	95 kg (100 kg)	+95 kg (+100 kg)
1997	Cho In Chul (S.Kor.)	Jeon Ki Young (S.Kor.)	P. Nastula (Pol.)	D. Douillet (Fr.)
1999	G. Randall (U.K.)	H. Yoshida (Japan)	K. Inoue (Japan)	S. Shinohara (Japan)
2001	Cho In Chul (S.Kor.)	F. Demontfaucon (Fr.)	K. Inoue (Japan)	A. Mikhaylin (Russia)

*Figures in parentheses represent new weight classes established in 1999.

World Judo Championships—Women*

Year	Open weights	48 kg	52 kg	56 kg (57 kg)
1997	D. Beltran (Cuba)	R. Tamura (Japan)	M.-C. Restoux (Fr.)	I. Fernández (Spain)
1999	D. Beltran (Cuba)	R. Tamura (Japan)	N. Narasaki (Japan)	D. González (Cuba)
2001	C. Lebrun (Fr.)	R. Tamura (Japan)	Kye Sun Hui (N.Kor.)	Y. Lupetry (Cuba)

Year	61 kg (63 kg)	66 kg (70 kg)	72 kg (78 kg)	+72 kg (+78 kg)
1997	S. Vandenhende (Fr.)	K. Howey (U.K.)	N. Anno (Japan)	C. Cicot (Fr.)
1999	K. Maeda (Japan)	S. Veranes (Cuba)	N. Anno (Japan)	B. Maksymow (Pol.)
2001	G. Vandecaveye (Belg.)	M. Ueno (Japan)	N. Anno (Japan)	Yuan Hua (China)

*Figures in parentheses represent new weight classes established in 1999.

RODEO

Men's World All-Around Rodeo Championship

Year	Winner	Year	Winner
1997	D. Mortensen	2000	J. Beaver
1998	T. Murray	2001	C. Ohl
1999	F. Whitfield	**2002**	**T. Brazile**

ROWING

World Rowing Championships—Men

Year	Single sculls	Min:sec	Double sculls	Min:sec	Quadruple sculls	Min:sec	Coxed pairs	Min:sec
2000	R. Waddell (N.Z.)	6:48.90	L. Spik, I. Cop (Slvn.)	6:16.63	Italy	5:45.56	K. Borcherding, M. Guerrieri (U.S.)	7:07.15
2001	O. Tufte (Nor.)	6:43.04	A. Haller, T. Peto (Hung.)	6:14.16	Germany	5:40.89	J. Cracknell, M. Pinsent (Gr.Brit.)	6:49.33
2002	**M. Hacker (Ger.)**	**6:36.33**	**A. Haller, T. Peto (Hung.)**	**6:05.74**	**Germany**	**5:39.57**	**L. Krisch, A. Werner (Ger.)**	**6:47.93**

Year	Coxless pairs	Min:sec	Coxed fours	Min:sec	Coxless fours	Min:sec	Eights	Min:sec
2000	M. Andrieux, J.-C. Rolland (Fr.)	6:32.97	Great Britain	6:16.82	Great Britain	5:56.24	Great Britain	5:33.08
2001	J. Cracknell, M. Pinsent (Gr.Brit.)	6:27.57	France	6:08.25	Great Britain	5:48.98	Romania	5:27.48
2002	**J. Cracknell, M. Pinsent (Gr.Brit.)**	**6:14.27**	**Great Britain**	**6:06.70**	**Germany**	**5:41.35**	**Canada**	**5:26.92**

World Rowing Championships—Women

Year	Single sculls	Min:sec	Coxless pairs	Min:sec
2000	Ye. Karsten (Bela.)	7:28.14	G. Damian, D. Ignat (Rom.)	7:11.00
2001	K. Rutschow-Stomporowski (Ger.)	7:19.25	G. Damian, V. Susanu (Rom.)	7:01.27
2002	**R. Neykova (Bulg.)**	**7:07.71**	**G. Andrunache, V. Susanu (Rom.)**	**6:53.80**

Year	Double sculls	Min:sec	Coxless fours	Min:sec
2000	J. Thieme, K. Boron (Ger.)	6:55.44	Belarus	6:44.90
2001	K. Boron, K. Kowalski (Ger.)	6:50.20	Australia	6:27.23
2002	**G. Evers-Swindell, C. Evers-Swindell (N.Z.)**	**6:38.78**	**Australia**	**6:26.11**

Year	Quadruple sculls	Min:sec	Eights	Min:sec
2000	Germany	6:19.58	Romania	6:06.44
2001	Germany	6:12.95	Australia	6:03.66
2002	**Germany**	**6:15.66**	**United States**	**6:04.25**

Marcel Hacker of Germany celebrates his win in the world rowing championships single sculls event.

© Marcelo del Pozo/Reuters 2002

SAILING (YACHTING)

America's Cup

Year	Winning yacht	Owner	Skipper	Losing yacht	Owner
1992	*America³* (U.S.)	America³ Foundation	B. Koch	*Il Moro di Venezia* (Italy)	Compagnia della Vela di Venezia
1995	*Black Magic* (N.Z.)	P. Blake and Team New Zealand	R. Coutts	*Young America* (U.S.)	Pact 95 syndicate
2000	*Black Magic* (N.Z.)	Team New Zealand	R. Coutts	*Luna Rossa* (Italy)	Prada Challenge

World Class Boat Champions, 2002

Class	Winner	Country
Etchells 22	S. Childerly	Great Britain
Europe dinghy	S. Blanck	Australia
Finn dinghy	B. Ainslie	Great Britain
2.4 Metre	S. Berlin	Sweden
470 (men)	S. Cooke/P. Nicholas	New Zealand
470 (women)	S. Bekatorou/E. Tsoulfa	Greece
49er	I. Martínez/X. Fernández	Spain
Laser	R. Scheidt	Brazil
Mistral (men)	G. Fridman	Israel
Mistral (women)	B. Kendall	New Zealand
J/24	B. Read	United States
Optimist	F. Matika	Croatia
Star	I. Percy/S. Mitchell	Great Britain
Tornado	D. Bundock/J. Forbes	Australia
Yngling (women)	M. Azon	Spain

Admiral's Cup

Year	Winning team
1997	United States
1999	Netherlands
2001	canceled

Transpacific Race

Year	Winning yacht	Owner
1997	*Ralphie*	J. Montgomery
1999	*Grand Illusion*	J. McDowell
2001	*Bull*	S. Radow

Bermuda Race

Year	Winning yacht	Owner
1998	*Kodiak*	L. Ecclestone
2000	*Restless*	E. Crawford
2002	***Zaraffa***	**S. Sheldon**

SKIING

World Alpine Skiing Championships—Slalom

Year	Men's slalom	Men's giant slalom	Men's supergiant	Women's slalom	Women's giant slalom	Women's supergiant
1999	K. Palander (Fin.)	L. Kjus (Nor.)	L. Kjus (Nor.)* H. Maier (Austria)*	Z. Steggall (Austl.)	A. Meissnitzer (Austria)	A. Meissnitzer (Austria)
2001	M. Matt (Austria)	M. von Grünigen (Switz.)	D. Rahlves (U.S.)	A. Paerson (Swed.)	S. Nef (Switz.)	R. Cavagnoud (Fr.)
2002†	**J.-P. Vidal (Fr.)**	**S. Eberharter (Austria)**	**K.A. Aamodt (Nor.)**	**J. Kostelic (Cro.)**	**J. Kostelic (Cro.)**	**D. Ceccarelli (Italy)**

*Tie.   †Olympic champions.

World Alpine Skiing Championships—Downhill

Year	Men	Women
1999	H. Maier (Austria)	R. Götschl (Austria)
2001	H. Trinkl (Austria)	M. Dorfmeister (Austria)
2002*	**F. Strobl (Austria)**	**C. Montillet (Fr.)**

*Olympic champions.

World Alpine Skiing Championships—Combined

Year	Men	Women
1999	K.A. Aamodt (Nor.)	P. Wiberg (Swed.)
2001	K.A. Aamodt (Nor.)	M. Ertl (Ger.)
2002*	**K.A. Aamodt (Nor.)**	**J. Kostelic (Cro.)**

*Olympic champions.

World Nordic Skiing Championships—Men

Year	Sprint	10-km	15-km	30-km	50-km	Relay
1999		M. Myllylä (Fin.)	T. Alsgaard (Nor.)	M. Myllylä (Fin.)	M. Myllylä (Fin.)	Austria
2001	T.A. Hetland (Nor.)	P. Elofsson (Swed.)	P. Elofsson (Swed.)	A. Veerpalu (Est.)	J. Mühlegg (Spain)	Norway
2002*	**T.A. Hetland (Nor.)**	**J. Mühlegg (Spain)**	**A. Veerpalu (Est.)**	**J. Mühlegg (Spain)**	**M. Ivanov (Russia)**	**Norway**

*Olympic champions.

World Nordic Skiing Championships—Women

Year	Sprint	5-km	10-km	15-km	30-km	Relay
1999		B. Martinsen (Nor.)	S. Belmondo (Italy)	S. Belmondo (Italy)	L. Lazutina (Russia)	Russia
2001	P. Manninen (Fin.)	V. Kuitunen (Fin.)	B. Skari Martinsen (Nor.)	B. Skari Martinsen (Nor.)	canceled	Russia
2002*	**Yu. Chepalova (Russia)**	**O. Danilova (Russia)**	**B. Skari (Nor.)**	**S. Belmondo (Italy)**	**G. Paruzzi (Italy)**	**Germany**

*Olympic champions.

World Nordic Skiing Championships—Ski Jump

Year	Normal hill (90 m)	Large hill (120 m)*	Team jump (normal hill)	Team jump (large hill)	Nordic Combined (7.5-km)	Nordic Combined (15-km)	Nordic Combined Team
1999	K. Funaki (Japan)	M. Schmitt (Ger.)		Germany	B.E. Vik (Nor.)	B.E. Vik (Nor.)	Finland
2001	A. Malysz (Pol.)	M. Schmitt (Ger.)	Austria	Germany	M. Baacke (Ger.)	B.E. Vik (Nor.)	Norway
2002†	**S. Ammann (Switz.)**	**S. Ammann (Switz.)**		**Germany**	**S. Lajunen (Fin.)**	**S. Lajunen (Fin.)**	**Finland**

*116 m in 2001.   †Olympic champions.

Alpine World Cup

Year	Men	Women
2000	H. Maier (Austria)	R. Götschl (Austria)
2001	H. Maier (Austria)	J. Kostelic (Cro.)
2002	**S. Eberharter (Austria)**	**M. Dorfmeister (Austria)**

Nordic World Cup

Year	Men	Women
2000	J. Mühlegg (Spain)	B. Martinsen (Nor.)
2001	P. Elofsson (Swed.)	Yu. Chepalova (Russia)
2002	**P. Elofsson (Swed.)**	**B. Skari Martinsen (Nor.)**

Freestyle Skiing World Cup

Year	Men	Women
2000	J. Lahtela (Fin.)	J. Cooper (Austl.)
2001	M. Ronkainen (Fin.)	J. Cooper (Austl.)
2002	**E. Bergoust (U.S.)**	**K. Traa (Nor.)**

Snowboard World Cup

Year	Men	Women
2000	M. Bozzetto (Fr.)	M. Riegler (Austria)
2001	J.J. Anderson (Can.)	K. Ruby (Fr.)
2002	**J.J. Anderson (Can.)**	**K. Ruby (Fr.)**

SQUASH

British Open Championship—Men

Year	Winner
1999–2000	D. Evans (Wales)
2000–01	D. Palmer (Austl.)
2001–02	**P. Nicol (Eng.)**

British Open Championship—Women

Year	Winner
1999–2000	L. Joyce (N.Z.)
2000–01	S. Fitz-Gerald (Austl.)
2001–02	**S. Fitz-Gerald (Austl.)**

World Open Championship—Men

Year	Winner
2000	not held
2001	canceled
2002	**D. Palmer (Austl.)**

World Open Championship—Women

Year	Winner
2000	C. Owens (Austl.)
2001	S. Fitz-Gerald (Austl.)
2002	**S. Fitz-Gerald (Austl.)**

Sarah Fitz-Gerald (left) defeats Linda Charman in the semifinals en route to winning the women's World Open squash championship.

SquashPics.com

SWIMMING

World Swimming Records Set in 2002 in 25-m Pools*

Event	Name	Country	Time
MEN			
400-m freestyle	Grant Hackett	Australia	3 min 34.58 sec
50-m backstroke	Matt Welsh	Australia	23.31 sec
100-m backstroke	Thomas Rupprath	Germany	50.58 sec
200-m backstroke	Aaron Peirsol	United States	1 min 51.17 sec
50-m breaststroke	Ed Moses	United States	26.28 sec
	Oleg Lisogor	Ukraine	26.20 sec
100-m breaststroke	Ed Moses	United States	57.47 sec
200-m breaststroke	Ed Moses	United States	2 min 4.37 sec
	Ed Moses	United States	2 min 3.28 sec
	Ed Moses	United States	2 min 3.17 sec
50-m butterfly	Geoff Huegill	Australia	22.74 sec
100-m butterfly	Thomas Rupprath	Germany	50.10 sec
200-m butterfly	Frank Esposito	France	1 min 50.73 sec
4 × 100-m medley relay	United States National Team	United States	3 min 29.00 sec
	Australia National Team	Australia	3 min 28.12 sec
WOMEN			
200-m freestyle	Lindsay Benko	United States	1 min 54.04 sec
800-m freestyle	Sachiko Yamada	Japan	8 min 14.35 sec
100-m backstroke	Natalie Coughlin	United States	56.71 sec
50-m breaststroke	Zoe Baker	United Kingdom	30.53 sec
	Zoe Baker	United Kingdom	30.51 sec
	Luo Xuejuan	China	30.47 sec
	Emma Igelström	Sweden	30.43 sec
	Zoe Baker	United Kingdom	30.31 sec
	Emma Igelström	Sweden	30.24 sec
	Emma Igelström	Sweden	29.96 sec
100-m breaststroke	Emma Igelström	Sweden	1 min 5.38 sec
200-m breaststroke	Qi Hui	China	2 min 18.86 sec
100-m butterfly	Martina Moravcova	Slovakia	56.55 sec
	Natalie Coughlin	United States	56.34 sec
100-m individual medley	Natalie Coughlin	United States	58.80 sec
400-m individual medley	Yana Klochkova	Ukraine	4 min 27.83 sec
4 × 100-m medley relay	Sweden National Team	Sweden	3 min 55.78 sec
4 × 200-m free relay	China National Team	China	7 min 46.30 sec

*May include records awaiting FINA ratification at year's end.

World Swimming Records Set in 2002 in 50-m Pools*

Event	Name	Country	Time
MEN			
400-m freestyle	Ian Thorpe	Australia	3 min 40.08 sec
200-m backstroke	Aaron Peirsol	United States	1 min 55.15 sec
50-m breaststroke	Oleg Lisogor	Ukraine	27.18 sec
200-m breaststroke	Kosuke Kitajima	Japan	2 min 9.97 sec
400-m individual medley	Michael Phelps	United States	4 min 11.09 sec
4 × 100-m medley relay	United States National Team	United States	3 min 33.48 sec
WOMEN			
200-m freestyle	Franziska van Almsick	Germany	1 min 56.64 sec
100-m backstroke	Natalie Coughlin	United States	59.58 sec
50-m breaststroke	Zoe Baker	United Kingdom	30.57 sec
50-m butterfly	Anna-Karin Kammerling	Sweden	25.57 sec
200-m butterfly	Otylia Jedrzejczak	Poland	2 min 5.78 sec
4 × 100-m freestyle relay	German National Team	Germany	3 min 36.00 sec

*May include records awaiting FINA ratification at year's end.

World Swimming and Diving Championships (50-m pool)—Men

	Freestyle					
Year	50 m	100 m	200 m	400 m	800 m	1,500 m
1994	A. Popov (Russia)	A. Popov (Russia)	A. Kasvio (Fin.)	K. Perkins (Austl.)		K. Perkins (Austl.)
1998	B. Pilczuk (U.S.)	A. Popov (Russia)	M. Klim (Austl.)	I. Thorpe (Austl.)		G. Hackett (Austl.)
2001	A. Ervin (U.S.)	A. Ervin (U.S.)	I. Thorpe (Austl.)	I. Thorpe (Austl.)	I. Thorpe (Austl.)	G. Hackett (Austl.)

	Backstroke			**Breaststroke**		
	50 m	100 m	200 m	50 m	100 m	200 m
1994		M. López Zubero (Spain)	V. Selkov (Russia)		N. Rozsa (Hung.)	N. Rozsa (Hung.)
1998		L. Krayzelburg (U.S.)	L. Krayzelburg (U.S.)		F. De Burghgraeve (Belg.)	K. Grote (U.S.)
2001	R. Bal (U.S.)	M. Welsh (Austl.)	A. Peirsol (U.S.)	O. Lisogor (Ukr.)	R. Sludnov (Russia)	B. Hansen (U.S.)

	Butterfly			**Individual medley**		**Team relays**
	50 m	100 m	200 m	200 m	400 m	4 × 100-m freestyle
1994		R. Szukala (Pol.)	D. Pankratov (Russia)	J. Sievinen (Fin.)	T. Dolan (U.S.)	United States
1998		M. Klim (Austl.)	D. Silantyev (Ukr.)	M. Wouda (Neth.)	T. Dolan (U.S.)	United States
2001	G. Huegill (Austl.)	L. Frölander (Swed.)	M. Phelps (U.S.)	M. Rosolino (Italy)	A. Boggiatto (Italy)	Australia

	4 × 200-m freestyle	4 × 100-m medley	**Diving**				
			1-m springboard	3-m springboard	Platform	3-m synchronized	10-m synchronized
1994	Sweden	United States	E. Stewart (Zimb.)	Yu Zhuocheng (China)	D. Sautin (Russia)		
1998	Australia	Australia	Yu Zhuocheng (China)	D. Sautin (Russia)	D. Sautin (Russia)	China	China
2001	Australia	Australia	Wang Feng (China)	D. Sautin (Russia)	Tian Liang (China)	China	China

SWIMMING (continued)

World Swimming and Diving Championships (50-m pool)—Women

	Freestyle					
Year	50 m	100 m	200 m	400 m	800 m	1,500 m
1994	Le Jingyi (China)	Le Jingyi (China)	F. van Almsick (Ger.)	Yang Aihua (China)	J. Evans (U.S.)	
1998	A. Van Dyken (U.S.)	J. Thompson (U.S.)	C. Poll (C.Rica)	Chen Yan (China)	B. Bennett (U.S.)	
2001	I. de Bruijn (Neth.)	I. de Bruijn (Neth.)	G. Rooney (Austl.)	Ya. Klochkova (Ukr.)	H. Stockbauer (Ger.)	H. Stockbauer (Ger.)

	Backstroke			Breaststroke		
	50 m	100 m	200 m	50 m	100 m	200 m
1994		He Cihong (China)	He Cihong (China)		S. Riley (Austl.)	S. Riley (Austl.)
1998		L. Maurer (U.S.)	R. Maracineanu (Fr.)		K. Kowal (U.S.)	A. Kovacs (Hung.)
2001	H. Cope (U.S.)	N. Coughlin (U.S.)	D. Mocanu (Rom.)	Luo Xuejuan (China)	Luo Xuejuan (China)	A. Kovacs (Hung.)

	Butterfly			Individual medley		Team relays
	50 m	100 m	200 m	200 m	400 m	4 × 100-m freestyle
1994		Liu Limin (China)	Liu Limin (China)	Lu Bin (China)	Dai Guohong (China)	China
1998		J. Thompson (U.S.)	S. O'Neill (Austl.)	Wu Yanyan (China)	Chen Yan (China)	United States
2001	I. de Bruijn (Neth.)	P. Thomas (Austl.)	P. Thomas (Austl.)	M. Bowen (U.S.)	Ya. Klochkova (Ukr.)	Germany

			Diving				
	4 × 200-m freestyle	4 × 100-m medley	1-m springboard	3-m springboard	Platform	3-m synchronized	10-m synchronized
1994	China	China	Chen Lixia (China)	Tan Shuping (China)	Fu Mingxia (China)		
1998	Germany	United States	I. Lashko (Russia)	Y. Pakhalina (Russia)	O. Zhupina (Ukr.)	Russia	Ukraine
2001	United Kingdom	Australia	B. Hartley (Can.)	Guo Jingjing (China)	Xu Mian (China)	China	China

TABLE TENNIS

World Table Tennis Championships—Men

Year	St. Bride's Vase (singles)	Iran Cup (doubles)
1997	J.-O. Waldner (Swed.)	Kong Linghui, Liu Guoliang (China)
1999	Liu Guoliang (China)	Kong Linghui, Liu Guoliang (China)
2001	Wang Liqin (China)	Wang Liqin, Yan Sen (China)

World Table Tennis Championships—Women

Year	G. Geist Prize (singles)	W.J. Pope Trophy (doubles)
1997	Deng Yaping (China)	Deng Yaping, Yang Ying (China)
1999	Wang Nan (China)	Wang Nan, Li Ju (China)
2001	Wang Nan (China)	Wang Nan, Li Ju (China)

World Table Tennis Championships—Mixed

Year	Heydusek Prize
1997	Liu Guoliang, Wu Na (China)
1999	Ma Lin, Zhang Yingying (China)
2001	Qin Zhijian, Yang Ying (China)

World Table Tennis Championships—Team

Year	Swaythling Cup (men)	Corbillon Cup (women)
1997	China	China
2000	Sweden	China
2001	China	China

2002 Table Tennis World Rankings*

Men	Women
1. Wang Liqin (China)	1. Wang Nan (China)
2. Ma Lin (China)	2. Zhang Yining (China)
3. Vladimir Samsonov (Bela.)	3. Tamara Boros (Cro.)
4. Werner Schlager (Austria)	4. Lin Ling (Hong Kong)
5. Timo Boll (Ger.)	5. Li Nan (China)

*ITTF ranking as of September 2002.

Table Tennis World Cup

Year	Men
2000	Ma Lin (China)
2001	V. Samsonov (Bela.)
2002	**T. Boll (Ger.)**

Year	Women
2000	Li Ju (China)
2001	Zhang Yining (China)
2002	**Zhang Yining (China)**

TENNIS

Australian Open Tennis Championships—Singles

Year	Men	Women
2000	A. Agassi (U.S.)	L. Davenport (U.S.)
2001	A. Agassi (U.S.)	J. Capriati (U.S.)
2002	**T. Johansson (Swed.)**	**J. Capriati (U.S.)**

Australian Open Tennis Championships—Doubles

Year	Men	Women
2000	E. Ferreira, R. Leach	L. Raymond, R. Stubbs
2001	J. Bjorkman, T. Woodbridge	S. Williams, V. Williams
2002	**M. Knowles, D. Nestor**	**M. Hingis, A. Kournikova**

TENNIS (continued)

French Open Tennis Championships—Singles

Year	Men	Women
2000	G. Kuerten (Braz.)	M. Pierce (Fr.)
2001	G. Kuerten (Braz.)	J. Capriati (U.S.)
2002	**A. Costa (Spain)**	**S. Williams (U.S.)**

All-England (Wimbledon) Tennis Championships—Singles

Year	Men	Women
2000	P. Sampras (U.S.)	V. Williams (U.S.)
2001	G. Ivanisevic (Cro.)	V. Williams (U.S.)
2002	**L. Hewitt (Austl.)**	**S. Williams (U.S.)**

United States Open Tennis Championships—Singles

Year	Men	Women
2000	M. Safin (Russia)	V. Williams (U.S.)
2001	L. Hewitt (Austl.)	V. Williams (U.S.)
2002	**P. Sampras (U.S.)**	**S. Williams (U.S.)**

Davis Cup (men)

Year	Winner	Runner-up	Results
2000	Spain	Australia	3–1
2001	France	Australia	3–2
2002	**Russia**	**France**	**3–2**

Fed Cup (women)

Year	Winner	Runner-up	Results
2000	United States	Spain	5–0
2001	Belgium	Russia	2–1
2002	**Slovakia**	**Spain**	**3–1**

French Open Tennis Championships—Doubles

Year	Men	Women
2000	T. Woodbridge, M. Woodforde	M. Hingis, M. Pierce
2001	M. Bhupathi, L. Paes	V. Ruano Pascual, P. Suarez
2002	**P. Haarhuis, Ye. Kafelnikov**	**V. Ruano Pascual, P. Suarez**

All-England (Wimbledon) Tennis Championships—Doubles

Year	Men	Women
2000	T. Woodbridge, M. Woodforde	S. Williams, V. Williams
2001	D. Johnson, J. Palmer	L. Raymond, R. Stubbs
2002	**J. Bjorkman, T. Woodbridge**	**S. Williams, V. Williams**

United States Open Tennis Championships—Doubles

Year	Men	Women
2000	L. Hewitt, M. Mirnyi	J. Halard Decugis, A. Sugiyama
2001	W. Black, K. Ullyet	L. Raymond, R. Stubbs
2002	**M. Bhupathi, M. Mirnyi**	**V. Ruano Pascual, P. Suarez**

TRACK AND FIELD SPORTS (ATHLETICS)

World Outdoor Track and Field Championships—Men

Event	1999	2001
100 m	M. Greene (U.S.)	M. Greene (U.S.)
200 m	M. Greene (U.S.)	K. Kederis (Greece)
400 m	M. Johnson (U.S.)	A. Moncur (Bahamas)
800 m	W. Kipketer (Den.)	A. Bucher (Switz.)
1,500 m	H. El Guerrouj (Mor.)	H. El Guerrouj (Mor.)
5,000 m	S. Hissou (Mor.)	R. Limo (Kenya)
10,000 m	H. Gebrselassie (Eth.)	C. Kamathi (Kenya)
steeplechase	C. Koskei (Kenya)	R. Kosgei (Kenya)
110-m hurdles	C. Jackson (U.K.)	A. Johnson (U.S.)
400-m hurdles	F. Mori (Italy)	F. Sánchez (Dom.Rep.)
marathon	A. Antón (Spain)	G. Abera (Eth.)
20-km walk	I. Markov (Russia)	R. Rasskazov (Russia)
50-km walk	G. Skurygin (Russia)	R. Korzeniowski (Pol.)
4 × 100-m relay	United States (J. Drummond, T. Montgomery, B. Lewis, M. Greene)	United States (M. Grimes, B. Williams, D. Mitchell, T. Montgomery)
4 × 400-m relay	United States (J. Davis, A. Pettigrew, A. Taylor, M. Johnson)	United States (L. Byrd, A. Pettigrew, D. Brew, A. Taylor)
high jump	V. Voronin (Russia)	M. Buss (Ger.)
pole vault	M. Tarasov (Russia)	D. Markov (Austl.)
long jump	I. Pedroso (Cuba)	I. Pedroso (Cuba)
triple jump	C.M. Friedek (Ger.)	J. Edwards (U.K.)
shot put	C.J. Hunter (U.S.)	J. Godina (U.S.)
discus throw	A. Washington (U.S.)	L. Riedel (Ger.)
hammer throw	K. Kobs (Ger.)	S. Ziolkowski (Pol.)
javelin throw	A. Parviainen (Fin.)	J. Zelezny (Cz.Rep.)
decathlon	T. Dvorak (Cz.Rep.)	T. Dvorak (Cz.Rep.)

World Outdoor Track and Field Championships—Women

Event	1999	2001
100 m	M. Jones (U.S.)	Z. Pintusevich-Block (Ukr.)
200 m	I. Miller (U.S.)	M. Jones (U.S.)
400 m	C. Freeman (Austl.)	A. Mbacke Thiam (Senegal)
800 m	L. Formanova (Cz.Rep.)	M. Mutola (Mozam.)
1,500 m	S. Masterkova (Russia)	G. Szabo (Rom.)
5,000 m	G. Szabo (Rom.)	O. Yegorova (Russia)
10,000 m	G. Wami (Eth.)	D. Tulu (Eth.)
100-m hurdles	G. Devers (U.S.)	A. Kirkland (U.S.)
400-m hurdles	D. Pernía (Cuba)	N. Bidouane (Mor.)
marathon	Jong Song Ok (N.Kor.)	L. Simon (Rom.)
20-km walk	Liu Hongyu (China)	O. Ivanova (Russia)
4 × 100-m relay	Bahamas (S. Fynes, C. Sturrup, P. Davis, D. Ferguson)	United States (K. White, C. Gaines, I. Miller, M. Jones)
4 × 400-m relay	Russia (T. Chebykina, S. Goncharenko, O. Kotlyarova, N. Nazarova)	Jamaica (S. Richards, C. Scott, D.-A. Parris, L. Fenton)
high jump	I. Babakova (Ukr.)	H. Cloete (S.Afr.)
pole vault	S. Dragila (U.S.)	S. Dragila (U.S.)
long jump	N. Montalvo (Spain)	F. May (Italy)
triple jump	P. Tsiamita (Greece)	T. Lebedeva (Russia)
shot put	A. Kumbernuss (Ger.)	Y. Korolchik (Bela.)
discus throw	F. Dietzsch (Ger.)	N. Sadova (Russia)
hammer throw	M. Melinte (Rom.)	Y. Moreno (Cuba)
javelin throw	M. Tzelili (Greece)	O. Menéndez (Cuba)
heptathlon	E. Barber (Fr.)	Ye. Prokhorova (Russia)

TRACK AND FIELD SPORTS (ATHLETICS) (continued)

World Indoor Track and Field Championships—Men

Event	1999	2001
60 m	M. Greene (U.S.)	T. Harden (U.S.)
200 m	F. Fredericks (Nam.)	S. Crawford (U.S.)
400 m	J. Baulch (Gr.Brit.)	D. Caines (Gr.Brit.)
800 m	J. Botha (S.Af.)	Yu. Borzakovskiy (Russia)
1,500 m	H. Gebrselassie (Eth.)	R. Silva (Port.)
3,000 m	H. Gebrselassie (Eth.)	H. El Guerrouj (Mor.)
60-m hurdles	C. Jackson (Gr.Brit.)	T. Trammell (U.S.)
4 × 400-m relay	United States (A. Morris, D. Johnson, D. Minor, M. Campbell)	Poland (P. Rysiukiewicz, P. Haczek, J. Bocian, R. Mackowiak)
high jump	J. Sotomayor (Cuba)	S. Holm (Swed.)
pole vault	J. Galfione (Fr.)	L. Johnson (U.S.)
long jump	I. Pedroso (Cuba)	I. Pedroso (Cuba)
triple jump	C.M. Friedek (Ger.)	P. Camossi (Italy)
shot put	A. Bagach (Ukr.)	J. Godina (U.S.)
heptathlon	S. Chmara (Pol.)	R. Sebrle (Cz.Rep.)

World Indoor Track and Field Championships—Women

Event	1999	2001
60 m	E. Thanou (Greece)	C. Sturrup (Bah.)
200 m	I. Tirlea (Rom.)	J. Campbell (Jam.)
400 m	G. Breuer (Ger.)	S. Richards (Jam.)
800 m	L. Formanova (Cz.Rep.)	M. Mutola (Mozam.)
1,500 m	G. Szabo (Rom.)	H. Benhassi (Mor.)
3,000 m	G. Szabo (Rom.)	O. Yegorova (Russia)
60-m hurdles	O. Shishigina (Kazak.)	A. Kirkland (U.S.)
4 × 400-m relay	Russia (T. Chebykina, S. Goncharenko, O. Kotlyarova, N. Nazarova)	Russia (Yu. Nosova, O. Zykina, Yu. Sotnikova, O. Kotlyarova)
high jump	K. Kalcheva (Bulg.)	K. Bergqvist (Swed.)
pole vault	N. Ryshich (Ger.)	P. Hamackova (Cz.Rep.)
long jump	T. Kotova (Russia)	D. Burrell (U.S.)
triple jump	A. Hansen (Gr.Brit.)	T. Marinova (Bulg.)
shot put	S. Krivelyova (Russia)	L. Peleshenko (Russia)
pentathlon	L. Nathan (U.S.)	N. Sazanovich (Bela.)

2002 World Indoor Records—Men*

Event	Competitor and country	Performance
10,000 m†	Mark Bett (Kenya)	27 min 50.29 sec

*May include records awaiting IAAF ratification at year's end. †Not an officially ratified event; best performance on record.

2002 World Outdoor Records—Men*

Event	Competitor and country	Performance
100 m	Tim Montgomery (U.S.)	9.78 sec
300-m hurdles†	Chris Rawlinson (U.K.)	34.48 sec
marathon†	Khalid Khannouchi (U.S.)	2 hr 5 min 38 sec
20-km walk	Francisco Fernández (Spain)	1 hr 17 min 22 sec
50-km walk	Robert Korzeniowski (Pol.)	3 hr 36 min 39 sec

*May include records awaiting IAAF ratification at year's end. †Not an officially ratified event; best performance on record.

2002 World Indoor Records—Women*

Event	Competitor and country	Performance
800 m	Jolanda Ceplak (Slovenia)	1 min 55.82 sec
3,000 m	Berhane Adere (Eth.)	8 min 29.15 sec
pole vault	Svetlana Feofanova (Russia)	4.71 m (15 ft 5½ in)
	Svetlana Feofanova (Russia)	4.72 m (15 ft 5¾ in)
	Svetlana Feofanova (Russia)	4.73 m (15 ft 6¼ in)
	Svetlana Feofanova (Russia)	4.74 m (15 ft 6½ in)
	Svetlana Feofanova (Russia)	4.75 m (15 ft 7 in)

*May include records awaiting IAAF ratification at year's end.

2002 World Outdoor Records—Women*

Event	Competitor and country	Performance
steeplechase	Justyna Bak (Pol.)	9 min 22.29 sec
	Alesya Turova (Bela.)	9 min 21.72 sec
	Alesya Turova (Bela.)	9 min 16.51 sec
25,000 m	Tegla Loroupe (Kenya)	1 hr 27 min 5.9 sec
marathon†	Paula Radcliffe (U.K.)	2 hr 17 min 18 sec
5,000-m walk	Gillian O'Sullivan (Ire.)	20 min 2.60 sec

*May include records awaiting IAAF ratification at year's end. †Not an officially ratified event; best performance on record.

© Getty Images

American sprinter Tim Montgomery celebrates his new world record set in the men's 100-m race on September 14 in Paris.

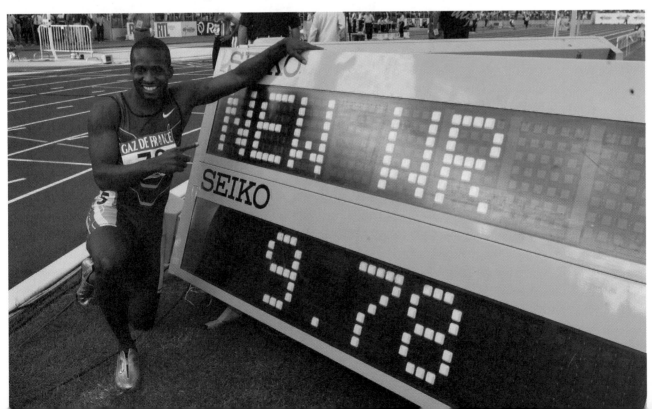

TRACK AND FIELD SPORTS (ATHLETICS) (continued)

World Cross Country Championships—Men

Year	Individual	Team
2000	M. Mourhit (Belg.)	Kenya
2001	M. Mourhit (Belg.)	Kenya
2002	**K. Bekele (Eth.)**	**Kenya**

World Cross Country Championships—Women

Year	Individual	Team
2000	D. Tulu (Eth.)	Ethiopia
2001	P. Radcliffe (U.K.)	Kenya
2002	**P. Radcliffe (U.K.)**	**Ethiopia**

Boston Marathon

Year	Men	h:min:s
2000	E. Lagat (Kenya)	2:09:47
2001	Lee Bong Ju (S.Kor.)	2:09:43
2002	**R. Rop (Kenya)**	**2:09:02**

Year	Women	h:min:s
2000	C. Ndereba (Kenya)	2:26:11
2001	C. Ndereba (Kenya)	2:23:53
2002	**M. Okayo (Kenya)**	**2:20:43**

Chicago Marathon

Year	Men	h:min:s
2000	K. Khannouchi (U.S.)	2:07:01
2001	B. Kimondiu (Kenya)	2:08:52
2002	**K. Khannouchi (U.S.)**	**2:05:56**

Year	Women	h:min:s
2000	C. Ndereba (Kenya)	2:21:33
2001	C. Ndereba (Kenya)	2:18:47
2002	**P. Radcliffe (U.K.)**	**2:17:18**

London Marathon

Year	Men	h:min:s
2000	A. Pinto (Port.)	2:06:36
2001	A. El Mouaziz (Mor.)	2:07:11
2002	**K. Khannouchi (U.S.)**	**2:05:38**

Year	Women	h:min:s
2000	T. Loroupe (Kenya)	2:24:33
2001	D. Tulu (Eth.)	2:23:57
2002	**P. Radcliffe (U.K.)**	**2:18:55**

New York City Marathon

Year	Men	h:min:s
2000	A. El Mouaziz (Mor.)	2:10:09
2001	T. Jifar (Eth.)	2:07:43
2002	**R. Rop (Kenya)**	**2:08:07**

Year	Women	h:min:s
2000	L. Petrova (Russia)	2:25:45
2001	M. Okayo (Kenya)	2:24:21
2002	**J. Chepchumba (Kenya)**	**2:25:56**

VOLLEYBALL

Beach Volleyball World Championships

Year	Men	Women
1998	D. Blanton, E. Fonoimoana (U.S.)	N. Cook, K. Pottharst (Austl.)
1999	E. Scheffer, J. Loiola (Braz.)	A. Behar, Shelda (Braz.)
2001	M. Baracetti, M. Conde (Arg.)	A. Behar, Shelda (Braz.)

World Volleyball Championships

Year	Men	Women
1998	Italy	Cuba
2000	Yugoslavia	Cuba
2002	**Brazil**	**Italy**

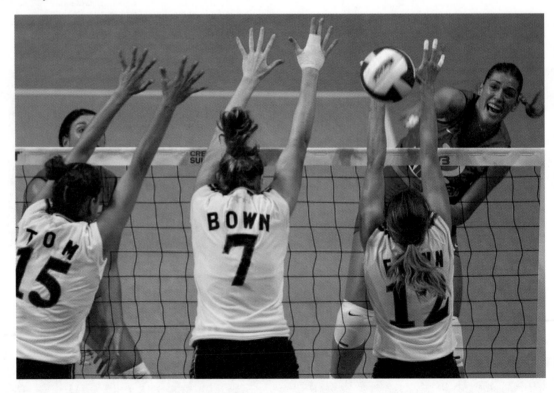

Italy's Francesca Piccinini drives the ball past the U.S. team as she helps Italy win the world championship in volleyball.

AP/Wide World Photos

WEIGHT LIFTING

World Weight Lifting Champions, 2002

MEN			WOMEN		
Weight class	Winner and country	Performance	Weight class	Winner and country	Performance
56 kg (123 lb)	Wu Meijin (China)	287.5 kg (633.9 lb)	48 kg (105.5 lb)	Wang Mingjuan (China)	207.5 kg (457.5 lb)
62 kg (136.5 lb)	Im Yong Su (N.Kor.)	315 kg (694.6 lb)	53 kg (116.5 lb)	Ri Song Hui (N.Kor.)	225 kg (496.1 lb)
69 kg (152 lb)	Zhang Gouzheng (China)	347.5 kg (766.2 lb)	58 kg (127.5 lb)	Song Zhijuan (China)	230 kg (507.2 lb)
77 kg (169.5 lb)	Georgi Markov (Bulg.)	370 kg (815.9 lb)	63 kg (138.5 lb)	Liu Xia (China)	242.5 kg (534.7 lb)
85 kg (187 lb)	Zlatan Vassilev (Bulg.)	385 kg (848.9 lb)	69 kg (152 lb)	Pawina Thongsuk (Thai.)	260 kg (573.3 lb)
94 kg (207 lb)	Nizami Pashaev (Azer.)	392.5 kg (865.5 lb)	75 kg (165 lb)	Svetlana Khabirova (Russia)	262.5 kg (578.8 lb)
105 kg (231 lb)	Denys Gotfrid (Ukr.)	420 kg (926.1 lb)	+75 kg (+165 lb)	Agata Wrobel (Pol.)	287.5 kg (633.9 lb)
105 kg (231 lb)	Hossein Rezazadeh (Iran)	472.5 kg (1,041.9 lb)			

WRESTLING

World Wrestling Championships—Freestyle*

Year	54 kg (55 kg)	58 kg (60 kg)	63 kg (66 kg)	69 kg
2000	N. Abdullayev (Azer.)	A.R. Dabier (Iran)	M. Umakhanov (Russia)	D. Igali (Can.)
2001	H. Kantoyeu (Bela.)	G. Sissaouri (Can.)	S. Barzakov (Bulg.)	N. Paslar (Bulg.)
2002	**R. Montero (Cuba)**	**H. Dogan (Tur.)**	**E. Tedeyev (Ukr.)**	

Year	76 kg (74 kg)	85 kg (84 kg)	97 kg (96 kg)	130 kg (120 kg)
2000	B. Slay (U.S.)	A. Saytyev (Russia)	S. Murtasaliyev (Russia)	D. Musulbes (Russia)
2001	B. Saytyev (Russia)	K. Magomedov (Russia)	G. Gogchelidze (Russia)	D. Musulbes (Russia)
2002	**M. Hajizadeh (Iran)**	**A. Saytyev (Russia)**	**E. Kurtanidze (Georgia)**	**D. Musulbes (Russia)**

*Figures in parentheses represent new weight classes established in 2002.

World Wrestling Championships—Greco-Roman Style*

Year	54 kg (55 kg)	58 kg (60 kg)	63 kg (66 kg)	69 kg
2000	Sim Kwon Ho (S.Kor.)	A. Nazaryan (Bulg.)	V. Samurgashev (Russia)	F. Azcuy (Cuba)
2001	H. Rangraz (Iran)	D. Aripov (Uzbek.)	V. Galustyan (Arm.)	F. Azcuy (Cuba)
2002	**G. Mamedaliyev (Russia)**	**A. Nazaryan (Bulg.)**	**J. Samuelsson (Swed.)**	

Year	76 kg (74 kg)	85 kg (84 kg)	97 kg (96 kg)	130 kg (120 kg)
2000	M. Kardanov (Russia)	H. Yerlikaya (Tur.)	M. Ljungberg (Swed.)	R. Gardner (U.S.)
2001	A. Abrahamian (Swed.)	M. Vakhrangadze (Georgia)	A. Bezruchkin (Russia)	R. Gardner (U.S.)
2002	**V. Samurgashev (Russia)**	**A. Abrahamian (Swed.)**	**M. Ozal (Tur.)**	**D. Byers (U.S.)**

*Figures in parentheses represent new weight classes established in 2002.

Sumo Tournament Champions, 2002

Tournament	Location	Winner	Winner's record
Hatsu Basho (New Year's tournament)	Tokyo	Tochiazuma	13–2
Haru Basho (spring tournament)	Osaka	Musashimaru	13–2
Natsu Basho (summer tournament)	Tokyo	Musashimaru	13–2
Nagoya Basho (Nagoya tournament)	Nagoya	Chiyotaikai	14–1
Aki Basho (autumn tournament)	Tokyo	Musashimaru	13–2
Kyushu Basho (Kyushu tournament)	Fukuoka	Asashoryu	14–1

Musashimaru (left) intimidates his opponent en route to winning the Aki Basho in September, his third championship of the year.

Kyodo News

The World in 2002

World Affairs

A **NEW** country emerged, **EAST TIMOR** (Timor-Leste), during 2002 and was **WELCOMED** into the **UNITED NATIONS**, as was **SWITZERLAND**. **NATO** looked to **EXPAND** its **MEMBERSHIP** to **26** by 2004 and invited **7 EUROPEAN COUNTRIES** to join its ranks. The **EUROPEAN UNION** introduced colourful **NEW** euro **BILLS AND COINS** and also **APPROVED** the applications of **10** new members by 2004.

UNITED NATIONS

In 2002 the United Nations continued to refocus its overall mission as one of comprehensively promoting human security rather than separately promoting peace and security, economic and social well-being, sustainable development, human rights, or a variety of other goals. As a result, a somewhat greater sense of coherence was brought to the world body's vast agenda. A new high-level UN Commission on Human Security had been formed in June 2001 and co-chaired by two highly visible figures, former UN high commissioner for refugees Sadako Ogata of Japan and Nobel Prize-winning economist Amartya Sen of India. On Sept. 11, 2001, the United Nations was preparing for the opening of the 56th General Assembly at its headquarters in New York City when terrorists attacked the World Trade Center, just a few kilometres away. Although the action was targeted against just one UN member state, representatives of all member states witnessed the tragedy, and the experience served to reinforce the growing consensus in the international community that making people secure meant more than protecting them from armed conflict between states and their agents.

Terrorism. Following the September 11 events, the UN Security Council in its landmark Resolution 1373 (2001) called on all member states to take immediate actions to suppress terrorism. The resolution set forth a program of state action and called for members to conform to a score of laws to deny safe haven to terrorists, block funding of terrorism, freeze assets of terrorist groups, bring suspected terrorists to justice, and suppress recruitment of terrorists on their soil. A Counter-terrorism Committee was established and charged with ascertaining the extent to which member states were complying with this program. At the end of six months, the committee reported that three-quarters of the member states had responded favourably. The bombing in Bali, Indon., in October 2002 underscored the fact that the perceived threat to peace and human security was a real one. The UN Security Council responded by unanimously condemning the act and again calling on member states to take necessary action.

International Law. The UN's evolving focus on human security represented a not-so-subtle challenge to the international legal principle of sovereignty that underpinned the very foundations of the United Nations and other international organizations. The actions—and inactions—of states themselves had often been among the most significant factors underlying violations of human security. Challenges to sovereignty lay at the core of UN debates over critical issues such as humanitarian intervention in response to gross violations of human rights and retaliatory and preemptive military strikes in dealing with terrorism. One clear case was the declaration by U.S. Pres. George W. Bush after the attacks of September 11 that the United States had the right to resort to military force against any state that aided, harboured, or supported international terrorists, regardless of sovereignty. Other world leaders made similar declarations. (*See* MILITARY AFFAIRS.) In early December 2002, Australian Prime Minister John Howard called for review of the UN Charter to consider new international legal norms to deal preemptively with terrorist attacks.

The International Criminal Court (ICC) entered into force on July 1, 2002, and as the year came to a close, more than 85 states had become parties to the convention. The ICC was to deal exclusively with matters related to war crimes, crimes against humanity, and genocide committed after July 1, 2002. The U.S., however, refused to accede to the court's jurisdiction or even to acknowledge the competency of the international judicial body. (*See* LAW, CRIME, AND LAW ENFORCEMENT.)

War Crimes Tribunals. In the case of both the International Criminal Tribunal for the Former Yugoslavia (ICTY) and the International Criminal Tribunal for Rwanda (ICTR), officials were frustrated by the lack of cooperation of the governments involved. The situation was so bad in the case of Rwanda that UN officials had to remind the Rwandan government of its legal obligation to cooperate. The most important case for the ICTY to date was that against former Yugoslav president Slobodan Milosevic. Because of Milosevic's health, however, the trial was put on hold. In early December the government of Yugoslavia announced that it would no longer turn over suspected war criminals to the ICTY.

Iraq. Iraq was one of the most important issues occupying the attention of the UN Security Council. In his address to the 57th General Assembly, President Bush laid out his indictment against Iraq and challenged UN member states to deal with the situation immediately, making it clear that unless the UN responded, the U.S. was prepared to do so alone. Thus prodded, the Security Council passed Resolution 1441 (2002), demanding that Iraq unconditionally submit to weapons inspections and do so under a strict timetable.

The government of Saddam Hussein continued to refuse entry to UN arms inspectors for most of the year. On November 27, however, the UN Monitoring, Verification and Inspections Commission (UNMOVIC) and the International Atomic Energy Agency (IAEA) inspection teams resumed inspections. The following week the Security Council unanimously agreed to extend its oil-for-food program in Iraq

Under the auspices of the United Nations, the search for evidence of the production of weapons of mass destruction resumed in Iraq; here, on December 22, UN inspectors enter the military research centre at Al-Nahrwan, near Baghdad.

James Hill/Getty Images

for six months. Shortly thereafter, in keeping with the timetable specified in Resolution 1441, the Iraqi government presented the UN with a 12,000-page declaration of its production programs for weapons of mass destruction. The face-off between the U.S. and Iraq was still going on at year's end.

Refugees. Nearly 20 million persons fell under the purview of the UN High Commissioner for Refugees, and many others—mostly persons displaced within their own countries—occupied the attention of the UN and its agencies. Of the international refugees, almost nine million were in Asia, five million in Europe, and four million in Africa.

Human Rights. The deliberations of the spring 2002 session of the UN Commission on Human Rights were characterized by an especially high degree of politicization and controversy. Many alleged cases of systematic abuses and gross rights violations went without condemnation or other action because of the absence of the United States, which was for the first time not re-elected to membership. A draft resolution proposed by Mexico that states' actions against terrorism be compatible with international human rights norms and laws was withdrawn.

Development. Under the authorization of the UN General Assembly, the World Summit on Sustainable Development was held in Johannesburg, S.Af., on August 26–September 4. Coming 10 years after the 1992 Earth Summit in Rio de Janeiro, the "Johannesburg Summit 2002" represented an attempt to reinvigorate sustainable development activities in the wake of deepening poverty and environmental degradation. New targets were set, timetables established,

and commitments agreed upon. Yet, as the UN Web site for the meeting made clear, "there were no silver bullet solutions . . . no magic and no miracle—only the realization that practical and sustained steps were needed to address many of the world's most pressing problems." The summit reflected a new approach to sustainable development. Instead of concentrating primarily on the production of treaties and other outcome documents, the conferees focused on the creation of new partnerships for bringing additional resources to bear to support and enhance implementation of sustainable development initiatives.

Health. The Joint United Nations Programme on HIV/AIDS (UNAIDS) released its AIDS Epidemic Update December 2002, presenting the latest statistics on what had now become the worst pandemic in human history. According to the report, more than 3.1 million people died as a result of HIV/AIDS during 2002, and there were more than 5 million new cases. Some 42 million persons were currently living with the disease, and UNAIDS predicted that another 45 million would be infected in the next eight years. Africa, the former Soviet Union, Central Asia, India, and China were among the worst-affected areas, while Estonia, Latvia, Russia, and Ukraine led in new incidences reported. In Africa alone 29.4 million were already infected, or about 70% of the worldwide total.

A special Global Fund to Fight AIDS, Tuberculosis and Malaria was established after Secretary-General Annan's call in April 2001. The European Union, the World Bank, and the U.S. pledged major contributions.

Children. In February an international agreement banning the use of children in combat roles entered into force. The UN General Assembly held a special session in May devoted to children's issues and adopted by consensus an action plan for promoting children's health and education and fighting child abuse and exploitation. The 57th General Assembly's Committee on Social and Humanitarian Affairs passed a detailed resolution that called for the elimination of child labour and the protection of children against torture, sexual abuse, and slavery. The U.S., alone (except for Somalia, which had no central government) in not having signed the Convention on the Rights of the Child, was also the only member state to vote against the resolution, which passed overwhelmingly 164–1.

Peacekeeping. As 2002 drew to a close, the Security Council closed shop on two of its missions in the Balkans; only the UN mission in Kosovo remained. The European Union Police Mission took over from UNMIBH, the UN Mission in Bosnia and Herzegovina. A joint Croatian-Yugoslav force was to administer the Prevlaka Peninsula. UNMIK, the UN Mission in Kosovo, oversaw the provincial elections held in November 2001, although it was not until March 2002 that a coalition government could be formed and brought into power.

The UN Transitional Administration in East Timor (UNTAET) successfully completed its mandate and turned over constitutional authority to the local government. In April the UN oversaw its last Timorese election, which brought to power East Timor's first independently elected president, and on May 20 full independence was confirmed. A new UN mission was established, the UN Mission of Support in East Timor (UNMISET), with a two-year mandate to support the development of civil, political, judicial, and security infrastructures.

Agreement was reached in December 2001 at the UN-brokered conference in Bonn, Ger., for a peace-building exercise aimed at establishing self-determination for the people of Afghanistan. The UN Assistance Mission in Afghanistan (UNAMA) was mandated to oversee capacity building, reconstruction, recovery, and relief as well as vouchsafe judicial and human rights. UNAMA began supervising disarmament in northern Afghanistan beginning in late November 2002. The Bonn Agreement also called for the establishment of an International Assistance Force (ISAF) in Afghanistan to facilitate the transition to peace. On November 27 the Security Council adopted a resolution extending ISAF authority for one year. Germany and The Netherlands assumed joint leadership of the force from Turkey.

In his November report to the General Assembly and the Security Council on the peaceful settlement of the question of Palestine, Secretary-General Annan cautioned that the situation had deteriorated, undermining many of the past achievements of the peace process. A self-proclaimed "quartet" of parties—the United Nations, the United States, the European Union, and the Russian Federation—was working to broker a permanent solution to the Palestinian-Israeli conflict. On September 17 the group released a "road map" that laid out a three-phase strategy for reaching a final peace accord by 2005.

The UN Mission in Sierra Leone (UN-AMSIL) was actively engaged in disarming former combatants in the West African country's 10-year civil war, and the focus of UN efforts began shifting from peacekeeping to humanitarian relief and development. On December 4 the Security Council extended for another six months the ban on export of rough diamonds by all parties except the government. In addition, an ad hoc war crimes tribunal was established.

In late November the Security Council accused Liberia of violating the embargo on importing weapons and extended sanctions, including a ban on diamond exports. At year's end the government of Liberian Pres. Charles Taylor continued to violate UN sanctions.

Also in late November the transitional government of Burundi and its development assistance partners held a roundtable conference focused on acquiring support for its Social Emergency Program to provide assistance to the Burundi population. In his report on the country, the secretary-general noted that the humanitarian situation remained dire after eight years of civil war, and nearly one-sixth of the population was internally displaced.

In response to Security Council requests and other factors, direct foreign engagement in the civil war in the Democratic Republic of the Congo (DRC) had lessened dramatically. The UN Observer Mission in Congo (MONUC) moved to consolidate gains and drive for complete withdrawal of all foreign forces. The mission was also tasked with the job of disarming tens of thousands of rebel forces. In support of this effort,

the Security Council moved on December 4 to double the troop strength of the UN mission. Moreover, the secretary-general's special representative for the DRC in late November reached an understanding with the various parties to the conflict on general principles for a transitional government.

In August the Security Council created a UN mission in Angola to replace the UN office there. This mission was to assist parties in implementing the Lusaka Protocol by clearing land mines, providing humanitarian and election assistance, promoting human rights, and reintegrating rebel forces into society.

Budget and Membership. For the second year in a row, the UN budgetary situation appeared to be in better health, although it remained on shaky grounds because of nonpayment and slow payment of dues. At times as many as one-half of member states could not or would not pay their assessed contributions. The biggest problem in this regard over the past two decades was the United States. The situation was complicated by the fact that member states of UN agencies often seemed to prefer funding disaster-relief efforts—short-term commitments that grabbed public attention—rather than regular, long-term programs. In the case of the World Health Organization, for example, regular budgetary funds had been declining in real terms for more than a decade and a half.

The United Nations inaugurated two new members in 2002. Switzerland, the European centre of UN activities and the seat of many international agencies, joined on September 10, and East Timor, the world's youngest state, was welcomed on September 27.

In his address to the 57th General Assembly in September, President Bush stated that as a demonstration of its commitment to multilateralism, the United States would rejoin UNESCO, from which it had withdrawn 18 years earlier.   (ROGER A. COATE)

COMMONWEALTH OF NATIONS

The Commonwealth of Nations was the only worldwide political grouping of states besides the United Nations. It had no constitution and membership was voluntary. The organization had evolved from the British Empire but long ago ceased to be British. Even though the position of Queen Elizabeth II (see BIOGRAPHIES) as head of the Commonwealth was symbolic, her long

reign and her personal informal network of contacts with leaders of nations and states elevated her stature within the body. For her golden jubilee the queen traveled in 2002 from one end of the Commonwealth to the other—from Iqaluit, Nunavut, northernmost Canada, to Coolum, northern Queensland, Australia.

The biennial Commonwealth Heads of Government Meeting (CHOGM), delayed following the Sept. 11, 2001, terrorist attacks in the U.S., was hosted in Coolum in March. Politically, it was a difficult meeting, particularly because of events in Zimbabwe, which many in the organization believed was in violation of the 1991 Declaration of Commonwealth Principles and had not complied with the Abuja agreement of 2001 on land reform. Elections were about to be held there, and Commonwealth observers were monitoring the event; they represented the only international body present. Australia, New Zealand, and the U.K. initially wanted Zimbabwe expelled, but with the election imminent CHOGM instead established a troika of leaders (Presidents Thabo Mbeki of South Africa and Olusegun Obasanjo of Nigeria and Prime Minister John Howard of Australia) to act on its behalf after the election observers reported their findings. Zimbabwean Pres. Robert Mugabe boycotted the meeting but sent his foreign minister.

The observer group found that conditions in Zimbabwe did not adequately allow for a free expression of will by the electorate. After a tense meeting in London on March 19, the troika suspended Zimbabwe for a year from the councils of the Commonwealth (two stages from expulsion). African members resisted tougher measures against Mugabe, but when the troika invited him to meet with them in Abuja, Nigeria, on September 23, he failed to appear. Howard wanted Zimbabwe fully suspended, but Mbeki and Obasanjo said that the one-year suspension agreed to in March should stand. In Pakistan, which was also under suspension, Commonwealth observers found the October elections flawed, and the watchdog Commonwealth Ministerial Action Group decided to maintain Pakistan's suspension until a democratic government was in place.

Nevertheless, the Commonwealth was making headway elsewhere in the pursuit of good governance and democracy. Peace came to Sierra Leone, and elections were held with Commonwealth technical help. Lesotho introduced a new voting system and produced a more representative parliament. Technical aid and advice in the Fiji Islands, Solomon Islands, and Swaziland were helping enhance stability. Fiji had been readmitted as a full member in December 2001. On August 19–20 a Commonwealth roundtable in Fiji's Denarau Island was attended by the leaders of 10 countries. They explored ways in which Pacific states might adapt their democracy to reflect regional cultures better.

When Commonwealth Finance Ministers met in London in September, nongovernmental organizations (NGOs) from six regions presented proposals for the reduction of global poverty. It was the first time that NGOs had participated in such a meeting, a fact that highlighted the growing influence of the nearly 100 specifically Commonwealth NGOs. Another Commonwealth innovation was a meeting of foreign ministers held in New York City at the same time that the UN General Assembly was convening. The 37 ministers present decided that it should be an annual event.

The nonpolitical activities of the Commonwealth were flourishing as never before. The Commonwealth Games, held in Manchester, Eng., July 25–August 4, were a major success—smoothly organized and financially profitable. (DEREK INGRAM)

EUROPEAN UNION

As people across the continent greeted the arrival of 2002, a new era was born in the European Union (EU). At a few seconds past midnight, crisp and colourful euro notes appeared from cash machines in 12 EU countries. The ambitions of Europe's integrationists to unite their continent with a single currency had finally been partially realized after more than 30 years of effort. German Chancellor Gerhard Schröder bade a fond farewell to the Deutsche Mark that had symbolized his country's postwar recovery. At the same time, he welcomed its successor as the badge of a confident new epoch. "We are witnessing the dawn of an age that the people of Europe have dreamed of for centuries: borderless travel and payment in a common currency," he said. Many had predicted that the arrival of euro notes and coins would be chaotic, leaving consumers and shopkeepers confused. Detractors said that the banking system would be unable to cope and that the EU's 300 million citizens would be so unfamiliar with their new money

that they would be susceptible to fraud. The introduction and distribution of six billion euro notes and 37 billion coins in 12 countries—and the withdrawal of a dozen national currencies—amounted to the largest peacetime operation ever carried out in Europe. The changeover, however, occurred almost without a hitch. Apart from a few complaints, Europeans seemed to enjoy the novelty of using euros. Counterfeiters were deterred by the sophisticated security features that adorned the new notes, and police reported little trouble. Polls showed that Sweden, Denmark, and the U.K., the three EU states that chose not to adopt the euro, might soon do so. It was a truly optimistic—and unexpectedly smooth—start to 2002.

European integrationists never pause long for breath, however, and they began concentrating on the next daunting challenge—to adapt the EU's institutions and alter its decision-making processes to ensure that it could function with an expanded membership of 25–30 countries. There were 13 states, including 10 from former communist Central and Eastern Europe, that were knocking on the EU's door asking for entry. The existing 15, members keen to bind those applicants with strong economies and functioning democracies into their Western club, knew that their existing structures, designed for the six founding members, were woefully ill-equipped to serve a membership five times as high.

At the end of February, a historic Convention on the Future of Europe was launched under the chairmanship of former French president Valéry Giscard d'Estaing. The goal of the meeting, modeled on the U.S. 1787 Constitutional Convention, was to prepare the EU for a first wave of enlargement in 2004 and further expansions in the years to come. In addition, Giscard made it clear that the convention's task was to define once and for all the levels of power sharing between European institutions and national and regional ones. "In order to avoid any disagreement over semantics," he said "let us agree now to call it a constitutional treaty for Europe." A final report from the convention would be drawn up in the summer of 2003, demarcating the relative roles of the European Commission, the European Parliament, and the European Court of Justice. Europe's institutions would be recast in line with the ambition to turn Europe into a "superpower" with its own military arm, police functions, and currency.

In October Giscard floated some initial ideas, many of them radical. He suggested that the European Union could be renamed the United States of Europe. The British government, however—eager not to inflame Euroskeptic opinion at home as it prepared for battle to win public approval for the euro—shot down the idea immediately. Euroskeptics had long claimed that Europe's integrationists had a secret agenda to abolish nation states and create one European superstate on a federal model similar to that of the United States. Giscard seemed to be playing into their hands.

As this high-minded debate over institutional architecture raged, the European dream was being aggressively challenged on the streets by populist political forces from the far right. The spring of 2002 was dominated by the unexpected successes of two right-wing politicians in The Netherlands and France. Taking into account that parties from the hard right were already in power in Italy, Denmark, and Austria—and the anti-immigrant Vlaams Blok was thriving in parts of Belgium—the alarm bells began ringing loudly. Were right-wing, anti-integration, and anti-immigration politics sweeping the continent? In March it appeared to be true. Pim Fortuyn (see OBITUARIES), a maverick who headed an anti-immigration party in The Netherlands, won 35% of the vote in local elections in Rotterdam and set his sights on national elections the following May. Then, in April, the leader of France's extreme right-wing National Front, Jean-Marie Le Pen—who was fervently anti-EU and called for France to abandon the euro—astonished the French and European political establishments when he beat Socialist Prime Minister Lionel Jospin and finished in second place in the first round of the French presidential elections. The result threw mainstream politicians in France into a state of shock, and Le Pen's success was condemned across Europe.

The fears about a rightward, anti-EU shift subsided, however, after Le Pen was crushed in the second round by Pres. Jacques Chirac, who won 82% of the vote, compared with Le Pen's 18%. (See France: Sidebar, below.) The centre-right's hold on power in France was consolidated a few weeks later in the general election when the parties backing Chirac gained 399 of the 577 seats in the National Assembly. In The Netherlands Fortuyn's rise came to a shocking end when he was shot dead nine days before the country's general election. His death was met by a national outpouring of grief, and in the election his party was propelled to power with 26 of the lower house's 150 seats—enough to assure it a role in a new coalition government. It was a short-run victory, however. In October Fortuyn followers fell out among themselves so spectacularly that the entire coalition government fell, and new elections were called for 2003.

The rise of far-right parties, while alarming centrist parties, also focused leaders' attention on the issue of immigration. In June a summit in Seville, Spain, saw EU heads of government arguing over how to stem the flow of illegal immigrants and asylum seekers. With the EU about to expand eastward, the concerns about illegal immigration into a borderless Europe had become all the greater. By year's end few solutions had been found, however. (See *Australia:* Special Report, below.)

These disturbing events coincided with a gathering economic gloom in many parts of Europe—most of all in Germany, the EU's largest economy. There was also rising concern that the euro had been used by shopkeepers and businesses to hike up their prices. Suddenly the currency that had seemed so popular was losing its appeal as it became associated increasingly with rises in the cost of living. In Germany it had earned the nickname "the teuro" after the German word *teuer* ("expensive"). The Bundesbank, Germany's central bank, said that there was evidence that the currency had increased prices, although the European Commission and the European Central Bank maintained the impact had been minimal at most.

In September attention became focused on elections in Germany. With the national economy flagging and unemployment nearing 10%, it appeared that Schröder's centre-left government might lose to the centre-right. In the event, Schröder warded off the challenge from Bavarian Prime Minister Edmund Stoiber (*see* BIOGRAPHIES), having courted German voters with a promise not to support a U.S.-led war on Iraq. The pledge appealed to the pacifist majority in Germany and, while it did serious damage to U.S.-German relations, ensured that Germany would buck the EU trend toward centre-right governments.

A month later the European Commission formally announced that 10 applicant states could join the community in 2004. Although many were not fully fit for entry either economically or in terms of the way that they ran their democracies, the historic opportunity of a "big-bang" expansion was seen as too good to miss. Cyprus, the Czech Republic, Estonia, Hungary, Latvia, Lithuania, Malta, Poland, Slovakia, and Slovenia were all approved as potential members. Together they would add another 75 million people to the EU population.

One further cloud hovered on the horizon, however, threatening to scupper the entire enlargement process. The Irish—who 18 months earlier had rejected in a referendum the Nice Treaty, which prepared the community for expansion—were voting again on the same issues. The Irish had feared that the EU's ambition to develop its own defense identity would threaten Irish neutrality. Were the Irish to vote "no" a second time, the entire enlargement process would be thrown into doubt. With Europe on tenterhooks and the Irish receiving reassurances that Ireland could opt out of military operations, 63% voted in favour of the measure. The way was clear for expansion.

The remaining months saw EU countries squabbling over how to pay the bills for enlargement. At a meeting in Brussels in October, France and Germany settled a long-running dispute over farm spending by agreeing to keep the total outlay from the Common Agricultural Policy at around its current level until 2013, excluding the 1% annual increase provided for inflation. The agreement gave the EU a financial framework within which to negotiate the precise terms of entry for the applicant countries. With just a year to go before the 10 new entrants took their place as permanent members in the councils of Brussels, there was still plenty of haggling to be done.   (EMMA TUCKER)

MULTINATIONAL AND REGIONAL ORGANIZATIONS

Nontraditional threats to security and terrorism dominated the agendas of many multinational and regional organizations in 2002. At a special ministerial meeting of the Association of Southeast Asian Nations (ASEAN) in May, members focused on enhancing law enforcement and other cooperation. In August they pledged to work with the United States in combating terrorism. At the eighth summit, on November 4–5 in Phnom Penh, Cam-

bodia, following the attacks in Bali, Indon., and the Philippines, ASEAN leaders vowed to intensify efforts to prevent and suppress terrorist group activities in the region. In addition, they established a Regional Counter-terrorism Centre in Kuala Lumpur, Malaysia. On November 4, ASEAN members issued joint declarations with China on a proposed code of conduct for the South China Sea and on nontraditional threats to regional security such as drug trafficking, people smuggling, and sea piracy. The summit also concluded a framework agreement for a free-trade area with China, a Comprehensive Economic Partnership with Japan, and, following the first-ever summit with India, agreement to advance cooperation on common challenges.

In an unprecedented step, the March 27–28 Arab League summit in Beirut approved a proposal by Saudi Crown Prince Abdullah (*see* BIOGRAPHIES) to normalize relations between Israel and

For the inaugural ceremonies for the new African Union, posters with pictures of some of the 40 African presidents and monarchs expected to attend are held aloft on July 9 at a stadium in Durban, S.Af.

all Arab countries in exchange for Palestinian independence and borders based on 1967 boundaries. Members pledged to work with the U.S., Russia, the European Union, the UN General Assembly, and the UN Security Council to end bloodshed between Israelis and Palestinians. A November 10 extraordinary session of the Arab League Council endorsed UN Security Council Resolution 1441, concerning the resumption of weapons inspections in Iraq, and called on Iraq to cooperate with inspectors. Representatives urged that more Arab inspectors be added to inspection teams and stated that the resolution should serve as a means of avoiding, not legitimizing, war with Iraq.

Unlike the 2001 summit in Genoa, Italy, which was marred by violent demonstrations, Group of Seven/Eight leaders met in secluded Kananaskis, Alta., on June 26–27 and focused on strengthening global economic growth, building a partnership for Africa's development, and fighting terrorism. The presidents of four African states and the UN secretary-general were invited—the first time that non-G8 leaders had participated in such a meeting. In addition to giving impetus to the Africa Action Plan, leaders agreed to call on the IMF, the World Bank, and other multilateral institutions to increase participation in the initiative to reduce debts of heavily indebted poor countries. They also launched a Global Partnership against the Spread of Weapons and Materials of Mass Destruction, with particular attention to preventing terrorists or those harbouring them from acquiring or developing such weapons. They pledged $20 billion over 10 years to support projects, first in Russia, involving nuclear safety and nonproliferation. On August 8, G7 finance ministers endorsed the agreement between Brazil and the IMF to help restore market confidence, and on September 27 they endorsed IMF support for Argentina, combating terrorist financing, and increased development assistance, particularly for Africa.

On June 28 the African Union officially came into existence in Durban, S.Af., as the successor to the 39-year-old Organization of African Unity. Earlier in June the second Organization for African Union–Civil Society conference had convened in Addis Ababa, Eth., to establish a framework for interactions between civil society groups and the new union, particularly its Economic and Social Council (ECOSOC). This

© Anton Meres/Reuters 2002

Gibraltar's Chief Minister Peter Caruana waves to crowds gathered on March 18 to protest talks between Spain and the United Kingdom over the sovereignty of the territory.

conference also agreed on the framework for the Conference on Security, Stability, Development, and Cooperation in Africa. During October the African Union established the African Economic Council to increase economic integration on the continent and drafted the Nuclear Weapon-Free Zone Treaty to prohibit nuclear weapons in Africa.

On June 3 the General Assembly of the Organization of American States (OAS) adopted the Inter-American Convention Against Terrorism at its regular session in Bridgetown, Barbados. The convention committed parties to preventing, punishing, and eliminating terrorism and to making necessary changes in banking and other laws to address financing, money laundering, and border controls. The OAS and the Caribbean Community (CARICOM) both focused on threats to democracy in Venezuela and Haiti. On January 15 the OAS Permanent Council met in special session to discuss political violence in Haiti. The council established a mission of inquiry and later allocated funds for a joint OAS-CARICOM Special Mission to Strengthen Democracy in Haiti. The OAS Permanent Council condemned the April 11–14 coup in Venezuela and called for the restoration of democracy. The chairman of CARICOM, Guyanan Pres. Bharrat Jagdeo, announced in December that Haiti pledged to hold legislative elections soon.   (MARGARET P. KARNS)

DEPENDENT STATES

Europe and the Atlantic. On April 2, 2002, Argentine officials and war veterans commemorated the 20th anniversary of their country's invasion of the Falkland Islands/Islas Malvinas. Pres. Eduardo Duhalde declared his intention to negotiate with the U.K. for the island group's eventual return to Argentina. On June 14, however, a ceremony and parade in Stanley, the Falklands' capital, celebrated the 20th anniversary of the islands' liberation from Argentine occupation. Adam Ingram, the U.K. minister of state for the armed forces, represented the British government at the June ceremony and reiterated "the Falkland Islanders' right to self-determination."

Halfway around the world, Gibraltarians watched with increasing bitterness and fear as London and Madrid continued to discuss joint British-Spanish sovereignty over Gibraltar. Protest marches in May and September drew more than 20,000 of the dependency's 30,000 residents, and U.K. Foreign Minister Jack Straw was jeered when he arrived in Gibraltar for talks in May. Straw reported in July that an agreement with Spain had been reached "in principle." On November 8 Gibraltar's chief minister, Peter Caruana, announced the results of a referendum held the previous day—17,900 (98.48%) of the 18,176 Gibraltarians who cast ballots (an 87.9% turnout) voted "no" on the question of joint Spanish sovereignty, with only 187 (1.03%) voting "yes" and 72 ballots left blank. Straw dismissed the unofficial referendum as "eccentric" and meaningless.

In December voters in Greenland gave a majority of seats to parties advocating independence from Denmark. The ruling Siumut party, with 28.7% of the vote and 10 seats in the 31-seat parliament, formed a coalition government with the Inuit Brotherhood (25.5% and 8 seats). The new government, headed by Siumut leader Hans Enoksen, pledged to push for greater autonomy and to hold a referendum on independence in 2005. In April elections pro-independence parties in the Faroe Islands captured 17 of 32 legislative seats and formed a coalition government, although the Union Party, which opposed independence from Denmark, received the largest number of votes (26%).

Caribbean and Bermuda. The handling of government contracts by officials in the British Virgin Islands became the subject of a review that commenced in March 2002 against the background of the arrest of the territory's financial secretary, L. Allen Wheatley, for misconduct and conspiracy to defraud in connection with construction of the Terrance B.

Lettsome International Airport. The chief auditor had expressed "concern" about a number of other contracts in which required procedures had not been followed. In April the British Virgin Islands joined other Caribbean offshore financial centres by making a commitment to improve the transparency of its tax and regulatory systems and to exchange information on criminal tax matters with the Organisation for Economic Co-operation and Development (OECD). From July 1 it became mandatory for local auditing firms to sign off on the accounts of Cayman Islands-registered mutual funds, a policy designed to ensure that firms issuing auditing opinions were subject to the jurisdiction of the Cayman Islands Monetary Authority.

The Netherlands Antilles signaled its willingness to cooperate in criminal tax investigations by signing a Tax Information Exchange Agreement with the U.S. in April. The provisions of the agreement were similar to those previously signed with other offshore centres. The Netherlands Antilles government indicated in October that tougher visa restrictions on nationals of Colombia, Haiti, and the Dominican Republic were being implemented following 26 execution-style murders that had taken place in Curaçao since January. The killings were blamed on professional assassins from the countries concerned, particularly Colombia.

The U.S. Navy resumed target practice off the coast of Puerto Rico on Vieques Island in April, and the inevitable protests followed. Puerto Rican authorities reiterated their conviction that U.S. Pres. George W. Bush would stick to his pledge to halt the bombing and close the Vieques naval base by May 2003. A poll of Puerto Rican opinions in April, however, found that as many as 43.8% of those surveyed wanted the navy to retain a presence in Puerto Rico.

A sharp rise in crime in the U.S. Virgin Islands and the effect this could have on tourism prompted Gov. Charles Turnbull to announce the introduction in May of a string of unprecedented measures, including a reduction in the age at which a minor could be prosecuted as an adult for murder (from 14 to 13 years) and the enforcement of curfews obliging minors to be off the streets by 10 PM. Funds were also made available for additional police personnel and vehicles. In June Carnival Cruise Lines blamed crime for its decision to cancel calls to the islands by its ships during the 2002–03 winter season.

A new threat from the Soufrière Hills volcano, which had been disrupting the

lives of Montserrat's inhabitants since 1995, forced the evacuation of five areas on the island's northern side in October. Shortly after the evacuation had been completed, mudflows from the buildup of debris on the outside of the volcano, activated by heavy rain, buried cars and buildings.

Pacific Ocean. French Polynesia Pres. Gaston Flosse continued to pursue constitutional changes that would increase French Polynesia's autonomy while retaining its connection to France. In October agreement was reached on France's financial assistance to the territory, with the provision of €150 million (about $155.6 million) for 2003. The new Economic Restructuring Fund replaced grants made in 1996 as compensation for the loss of spending following the closure of France's nuclear-testing facilities at Moruroa.

In New Caledonia, with a quarter of the world's nickel reserves, there were several proposals for new nickel ventures under consideration. With regional governments acting as partners in joint ventures, there were concerns over internal competition and the viability of some projects. A major venture at Goro in the south, which was proceeding with the support of the South Province government, was deferred because of cost escalations. Indigenous Kanak groups opposed this proposed development and another at nearby Prony because of environmental concerns and the low financial returns to New Caledonia. Despite assurances that France would respect the territory's wishes on future constitutional status, France's overseas minister, Brigitte Girardin, was greeted in December by widespread protests, especially on mining issues, social security, and the employment of foreign workers.

In April Niue held the world's smallest national election, with some 800 voters taking part from a resident population of 1,800. All 20 sitting Assembly members were returned, but Premier Sani Lakatani lost his office to former premier Young Vivian. In May Niue joined French Polynesia, the Cook Islands, and several other South Pacific countries and territories in declaring its Exclusive Economic Zone to be a whale sanctuary. In October Niue was removed from the OECD's blacklist of money-laundering states in recognition of steps taken to counter the illegal practice.

The Cook Islands, on the other hand, remained blacklisted and, despite some reform, would remain so, at least until 2003, when an inspection visit from the International Monetary Fund was

Dependent States[1]

Australia	United Kingdom
Christmas Island	Anguilla
Cocos (Keeling) Islands	Bermuda
Norfolk Island	British Virgin Islands
Denmark	Cayman Islands
Faroe Islands	Falkland Islands
Greenland	Gibraltar
	Guernsey
France	Isle of Man
French Guiana	Jersey
French Polynesia	Montserrat
Guadeloupe	Pitcairn Island
Martinique	Saint Helena
Mayotte	Tristan da Cunha
New Caledonia	Turks and Caicos
Réunion	Islands
Saint Pierre and	
Miquelon	**United States**
Wallis and Futuna	American Samoa
	Guam
Netherlands, The	Northern Mariana
Aruba	Islands
Netherlands Antilles	Puerto Rico
	Virgin Islands
New Zealand	(of the U.S.)
Cook Islands	
Niue	
Tokelau	

[1]Excludes territories (1) to which Antarctic Treaty is applicable in whole or in part, (2) without permanent civilian population, (3) without internationally recognized civilian government (Western Sahara), or (4) representing unadjudicated unilateral or multilateral territorial claims.

expected. In February, Prime Minister Terepai Maoate was replaced by his former deputy, Robert Woonton. In its July budget the new government announced increased spending on welfare and raised the lower threshold for the payment of income tax.

In the Commonwealth of the Northern Marianas, garment manufacturers reached a major legal settlement and agreed to compensation payments for as many as 30,000 Asian workers who allegedly had been made to work under "sweatshop" conditions in Saipan. Nearly half of Saipan's population of some 64,000 were migrants, mostly Filipinos and Chinese working in the garment industry. During October the government reached agreement with the U.S. on a $120 million financial-assistance package over 11 years to be introduced when the current agreement expired in 2003.

In January the UN General Assembly removed American Samoa from the list of colonial territories, accepting that it was a U.S. territory with no desire to seek independence. The U.S. Department of the Interior approved a fiscal-reform package of $4.3 million. Meanwhile, Eni Faleomavaega, the delegate representing American Samoa in the U.S. House of Representatives, continued a campaign for the renewal of a U.S. tax law allowing concessions to major fish canneries operating in American Samoa. In this context, one of the canneries StarKist, announced a $2.5 million expansion.

Indian Ocean. On May 20, 2002, East Timor (Timor-Leste) officially celebrated its independence. The new country had been under UN administration for three years. (See *East Timor,* below.)

The development of "renewable energy" (including biomass, solar, and wind power) was the order of the day in Réunion, where these sources represented 42% of total energy production in 2002. Air transport, however, was in a serious crisis, faced with privatization and competition between national carrier Air France and other companies, financial difficulties, and trade union resistance. The situation risked compromising the Principle of Territorial Continuity, to which the French government had been committed for so long. According to this principle, air service to the islands of the French Republic—including Réunion and other overseas departments and territories—had to be guaranteed at comparable prices to all citizens, regardless of the distance involved.

Mayotte, which was also affected by the air-service problems, hoped for an improvement of its department collectivity status with the next Overseas Law, announced for the end of 2002 by the newly elected conservative government in France. Mayotte's geographic (and geopolitical) location halfway between the Comoros Islands and Madagascar once more exposed the island in 2002 to the social and political instabilities of its surroundings. The island of Anjouan in the Comoros continued its secessionist tendencies, and Antsiranana remained one of the six traditional provinces of Madagascar that expressed a desire for greater autonomy, even independence.

The American naval base on Diego Garcia in the Chagos Archipelago, or British Indian Ocean Territory (BIOT), was preparing for another Gulf War against Iraq. As of October, approximately 1,900 troops were stationed on the island, as well as material for two brigades (of ground troops and marines) and 10 B-2 stealth bombers. Meanwhile, the Ilois, who were evicted from the BIOT between 1967 and 1973, continued their legal battle for compensation and the right of return. The Australian government, which expressed increasing concern over the threat of international terrorism, announced that an additional detention centre for illegal immigrants would be constructed on Christmas Island.

(CHARLES CADOUX; BARRIE MACDONALD; DAVID RENWICK; MELINDA C. SHEPHERD)

ANTARCTICA

Ice averaging 2,160 m (7,085 ft) in thickness covers about 98% of the continent of Antarctica, which has an area of 14 million sq km (5.4 million sq mi). There is no indigenous human population, and there is no land-based industry. Human activity consists mainly of scientific research. The 45-nation Antarctic Treaty is the managerial mechanism for the region south of latitude 60° S, which includes all of Antarctica. The treaty reserves the area for peaceful purposes, encourages cooperation in science, prescribes environmental protection, allows inspections to verify adherence, and defers the issue of territorial sovereignty.

Antarctica's Larsen B ice shelf collapsed in February 2002. (*See* Map.) The shelf, 3,265 sq km (1,260 sq mi—about the size of Rhode Island) in size, had existed as long as 12,000 years ago. The collapse was caused by water from surface melting that ran down into crevasses, refroze, and wedged the shelf into pieces. The surface melting had increased because in the last 50 years the Antarctic Peninsula region, where the ice shelf had been, had warmed by

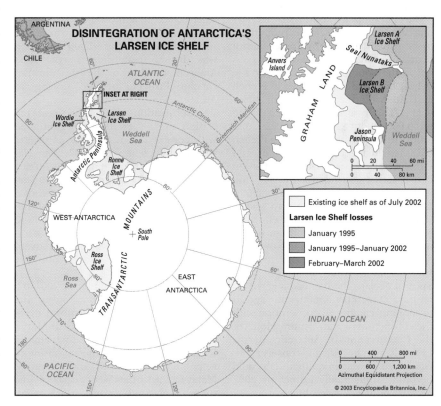

DISINTEGRATION OF ANTARCTICA'S LARSEN ICE SHELF

Existing ice shelf as of July 2002

Larsen Ice Shelf losses

January 1995

January 1995–January 2002

February–March 2002

© 2003 Encyclopædia Britannica, Inc.

2.5 °C (4.5 °F). Some researchers, however, saw little evidence that global warming had caused this local rise in temperature, while others linked it at least partially to human-induced worldwide climate change. The collapse did not raise the sea level, since the shelf, 200 m (650 ft) thick before its collapse, had already been floating on the ocean. The collapse took just 35 days.

Just two months later, two huge icebergs calved from the Ross Ice Shelf, returning the shelf's edge to its position in the early 1900s. The larger of the two icebergs, called C-19 and measuring some 5,200 sq km (about 2,000 sq mi) in area, was still in the western Ross Sea in late 2002, but the other had moved north and was breaking up.

While the iceberg calvings seemed to suggest warming, scientists reported in May that Antarctica as a whole had been cooling over the past 35 years. The scientists had studied data from weather stations across the continent and acknowledged that the Antarctic Peninsula was warming but said that the continent overall was cooling. This cooling was unique among the Earth's continents and contrasted with the global average increase in air temperature of 0.6 °C (1.1 °F) during the 20th century. The finding also seemed to contradict the generally accepted prediction that polar regions would respond first and most rapidly to an increase in global temperature.

The Patagonian toothfish (usually marketed as Chilean sea bass) continued to be caught illegally. A French patrol boat seized the Spanish longliner *Eternal* in the Southern Ocean in July; the fishing boat had been a target of French and Australian authorities for three years. The fine was expected to be €150,000 (about $150,000) for the ship's failure to declare its presence in a French EEZ (exclusive economic zone) and €75,000 for every metric ton of fish on board. Earlier, an Australian navy ship had seized the Russian-flagged longliner *Lena*. The arrests were said to underscore the failure of diplomatic efforts to halt the pirate trade, which ran to $90 million annually. Australia in November dropped a bid to have the Convention on International Trade in Endangered Species declare the fish endangered after the 160-member organization agreed to monitor catches in cooperation with the 24-member-state Commission for the Conservation of Antarctic Marine Living Resources. Marine conservationists said the Patagonian toothfish could become commercially extinct by 2007 because of illegal overfishing.

Intense commercial squid fishing was blamed for a die-off of penguins in the Falkland Islands/Islas Malvinas, where the population of the birds was said to have crashed from six million to one million in recent years. The penguins died of starvation.

Japanese whaling continued to generate controversy. An Australian Antarctic vessel found three Japanese ships off the West Ice Shelf on New Year's Day and asked them to leave. Japan's whaling under its self-issued "scientific permit" provided for it to take up to 440 minke whales annually, but Australian law forbade the killing of whales. A U.S. recommendation at a late-2001 meeting of the International Whaling Commission resulted in a resolution expressing concern that the minke whale population may have declined over the past decade to less than half the 1990 estimate of 760,000. The commission urged Japan to halt its take until its scientific committee could report impacts.

The Antarctic ozone hole in September 2002 was much smaller than in 2000 and in 2001, and it was split in two. Peculiar stratospheric weather was said to be the cause, so available evidence was not conclusive that the ozone layer was yet recovering. Rather, higher-than-normal temperatures around the polar vortex that forms annually over Antarctica suppressed the usual formation of polar stratospheric clouds, where chlorine and bromine from man-made chemicals destroy the ozone.

Ice believed to be 530,000 years old was drilled from deep in the East Antarctic ice sheet by the 10-nation European Project for Ice Coring in Antarctica.

Modernization of the U.S. research station at the South Pole continued with completion of the first of several new buildings in late 2002. The National Science Foundation in August approved a $17 million microwave telescope for the station, offering a novel approach to mapping the distribution of matter in the universe. The 8-m (315-in) scope would join other astronomical instruments that take advantage of the extremely clear and dry atmosphere at the site.

Tourism declined slightly in 2001–02, with 11,588 tourists landing in the Antarctic on privately organized expeditions. Indonesian scientists in March reached Antarctica for the first time in what was hoped to be the beginning of a polar program for that country. Malaysian scientists were guests of Australia on a similar voyage. A Russian expedition led by State Duma Deputy Chairman Artur Chilingarov flew to the South Pole in January, but its plane broke down, and the U.S. Antarctic Program, which operated a research station there, flew the chairman out of Antarctica. Britain's Princess Anne visited U.S. and New Zealand stations on Ross Island to commemorate the 100th anniversary of Robert Scott's first Antarctic expedition, part of an international appeal by the Antarctic Heritage Trust to raise funds to restore "heroic age" explorers' huts.

(GUY G. GUTHRIDGE)

ARCTIC REGIONS

The Arctic regions may be defined in physical terms (astronomical [north of the Arctic Circle, latitude 66° 30′ N], climatic [above the 10 °C (50 °F) July isotherm], or vegetational [above the northern limit of the tree line]) or in human terms (the territory inhabited by the circumpolar cultures—Inuit [Eskimo] and Aleut in North America and Russia, Sami [Lapp] in northern Scandinavia and Russia, and 29 other peoples of the Russian North, Siberia, and East Asia). No single national sovereignty or treaty regime governs the region, which includes portions of eight countries: Canada, the United States, Russia, Finland, Sweden, Norway, Iceland, and Greenland (part of Denmark). The Arctic Ocean, 14.09 million sq km (5.44 million sq mi) in area, constitutes about two-thirds of the region. The land area consists of permanent ice cap, tundra, or taiga. The population (2002 est.) of peoples belonging to the circumpolar cultures is about 375,000. International organizations concerned with the Arctic include the Arctic Council, institutions of the Barents Region, the Inuit Circumpolar Conference, and the Indigenous Peoples' Secretariat. International scientific cooperation of the Arctic is the focus of the International Arctic Research Center of the University of Alaska at Fairbanks.

At the beginning of the year 2002, it appeared that natural gas producers were in a frenzy to propose and then build multibillion-dollar natural gas pipelines from the North Slope of Alaska and the Mackenzie Delta in the Canadian Northwest Territories. Although there had been a sharp decline in gas prices from 2001, industry observers agreed that it was not a matter of whether a northern pipeline would be built but when. Production from other gas basins on the continent was rapidly declining, and by 2015 demand for gas was expected to climb to 885.8 million cu m (1 cu m = 35.3 cu ft) a year from the present demand level of 679.2 billion cu m. Alaska's North Slope and the Mackenzie Delta

An oil derrick stands on the frozen tundra near the Russian petroleum-export terminal at Varandey, on the Barents Sea. Russian and international oil companies were developing facilities in this remote far-northern area.

AP/Wide World Photos

were estimated to hold 2.8 billion and 707.9 million cu m, respectively, and the exploration potential was even larger. These huge gas reserves constituted the major proven untapped and secure supply of natural gas for North America.

Three main pipeline options were being considered. The Alaska pipeline route, estimated to cost $17.2 billion, would carry gas from the vast reserves at Prudhoe Bay south along the Alaska Highway through the Yukon and across British Columbia and Alberta to the U.S. markets. A second, so-called over-the-top route would transport Prudhoe Bay gas along the Beaufort Sea coast to Inuvik, N.W.Terr., where it would be combined with gas from the Mackenzie Delta. A single pipeline carrying gas from both Alaskan and Delta reserves would then continue down the Mackenzie Valley to southern markets. The preliminary cost estimate of this route was $15 billion.

In Canada a consortium of four gas producers proposed a stand-alone pipeline from Inuvik to transport up to 42 million cu m of gas a day south down the Mackenzie Valley to northern Alberta to hook up with existing Canadian pipeline systems. The cost was estimated at $3 billion, with another $1 billion needed for the drilling and exploration infrastructure to support the operations. In addition, the government of the Northwest Territories requested $133 million to establish an infrastructure that would facilitate the building of the pipeline. The territorial government also wanted revenue generated from resource development to be shared among the federal, territorial, and aboriginal governments.

Whichever route was chosen, any northern pipeline would face the most extensive and complex regulatory exercises ever held in Canada and the United States before a final decision was made to proceed with the construction. The politics of the various pipeline projects became mired in conflicting interests between the various federal, state, and territorial governments and industry, environmentalist, and aboriginal organizations. In April the U.S. Senate approved some $10 billion in loan guarantees and potentially billions more in tax credits aimed at supporting a $3.25-per-thousand-cubic-feet floor price of gas sold by Alaskan gas producers. The legislation also contained language that would eliminate all pipeline routes that bypassed the Alaskan heartland, including the proposed route along the North Slope of Alaska. By midyear, industry spokespersons were indicating that the cost projections for the Alaskan pipeline project had increased to $19.4 billion after larger start-up expenses and increased pipeline capacity were factored in, which made, the project uneconomical. Proponents suggested that the decision to build the pipeline would likely be delayed until 2003, citing fiscal uncertainty in Alaska and the need to await outcomes of negotiations concerning energy legislation being considered by the U.S. Congress.

Meanwhile, in Canada the Mackenzie Valley pipeline proponents announced that they had concluded their project-feasibility study and intended to go on to the next stage of pipeline development with the expectation that delta gas could be onstream in six to eight years. There was pressure on the Canadian government to provide subsidies for the building of roads and other infrastructure to support construction and to move quickly to deal with aboriginal land claims on the pipeline route.

In May the U.S. Geological Survey reported that National Petroleum Reserve—Alaska likely contained a mean amount of 1.5 billion cu m (9.3 billion bbl) of recoverable oil, up to four times the amount reported in 1980. The reserve, located west of Prudhoe Bay on Alaska's North Slope and created specifically for development before World War II, had been partly opened for drilling, with stringent environmental restrictions, in 1998. Washington had made developing the oil reserve an energy priority but had not announced specific plans for exploiting its potential.

In March U.S. Navy scientists predicted that routine commercial shipping would flow across the Arctic Ocean within 10 years. The Arctic ice cap was reported to be shrinking 4% a decade, and submarine sonar information suggested that ice cover had decreased by as much as 40% since 1970. The political consequences could be considerable for Canada's Northwest Passage and Russia's Northern Sea Route. Both Canada and Russia considered these passages to be their territorial waters, while the United States considered them international waters.

Frustrated by a number of unfavourable decisions against it by the International Whaling Commission, Japan led a successful drive to deny Alaskan and Siberian native peoples a renewal of permission to hunt whales. This was the first time in the 56-year history of the commission that quotas allowing subsistence whaling had been rejected. A group of privately funded Japanese scientists developed a plan to create an Ice Age wildlife park in Siberia that eventually could feature a genetic hybrid of the extinct mammoth and modern-day elephants. The scientists were conducting excavations in Siberia in the hope of discovering a frozen mammoth specimen preserved well enough in the permafrost for its sperm to be used to impregnate an elephant.

In August Inuit from across the North met at the general assembly of the Inuit Circumpolar Conference in Kuujjuaq, Arctic Quebec, to discuss many Inuit issues, including the idea of a single alphabet for Inuktitut, the Inuit language. The Inuit currently used the Roman and Cyrillic alphabets, syllabic symbols, and a half dozen spelling variations within those writing systems.

(KENNETH DE LA BARRE)

AFGHANISTAN

Area: 652,225 sq km (251,825 sq mi)
Population (2002 est.): 27,756,000 (including Afghan refugees estimated to number about 1,100,000 in Pakistan and about 1,400,000 in Iran)
Capital: Kabul
Chief of state and head of government: Chairman of the Interim Administration and, from June 19, President Hamid Karzai

Warlordism and ethnic rivalry were prominent in Afghanistan throughout 2002, yet important steps were taken toward building a stable, democratic social structure based on traditional Afghan values. Hamid Karzai, who was picked to head an Interim Authority in Afghanistan by a UN-sponsored international conference in Bonn, Ger., in December 2001, sought to maintain balance among the country's ethnic and tribal groups while laying a foundation for national institutions. Although he was a Pashtun tribal leader, Karzai had no armed group of his own. Security in Kabul was maintained by an Inter-national Security Assistance Force (ISAF) of 4,000 to 5,000 troops whose command was rotated among various participating countries.

U.S. troops did not participate in the ISAF, but they operated throughout the country in an attempt to root out fighters loyal to the ousted Islamist Taliban regime and Osama bin Laden's al-Qaeda terrorist organization. U.S. military reports of a large-scale operation in March near the Pakistani border claimed that hundreds of holdouts had been killed, but the fate of Bin Laden as well as that of Taliban leader Muhammad Omar remained unclear even at year's end. Most Afghans did not view U.S. forces in Afghanistan as invaders, however, and many constructive results of their intervention were welcomed. Still, as the year progressed, growing numbers of Afghan civilian casualties from American military activity provoked criticism from some who opposed Karzai's friendly relations with the U.S.

In March Karzai took initial steps toward the creation of a national army not dependent on tribal or ethnic loyalties. The projected strength of the new army was 50,000, but only a few hundred recruits could be found for the first unit to be trained. In an effort to unify the country's economy, Karzai announced in September that the national currency, the afghani, would be renumerated with one new afghani replacing 1,000 old ones. Afghanistan's monetary integrity had been compromised by uncontrolled printing of money by various regimes.

Beyond Kabul, Karzai's government depended for support on Tajik militias, sometimes called Panjshiris, led by Karzai's defense minister, Muhammad Qasim Fahim; tough Uzbek fighters in northern Afghanistan commanded by Abdul Rashid Dostam; and the powerful governor of Herat, Ismail Khan, also a Tajik. In the southern and eastern provinces, home to many Pashtun tribes from which the Taliban had drawn the core of its strength, support for the central government was uneven. Many Pashtuns, who constituted more than half of the country's population, expressed dissatisfaction with their share in the government, and there was often ill feeling expressed toward Pashtuns in areas where they constituted only a minority.

In April the country's former king, Mohammed Zahir Shah, returned to Kabul after an exile of 29 years. Many hoped that the king's return would lead to the reestablishment of Afghanistan's Pashtun monarchy, but Zahir Shah himself ruled this out. In June the former king officially opened an emergency Loya Jirga, as prescribed by the Bonn agreement. An assembly of the most important leaders from across Afghanistan, the Loya Jirga embodied supreme authority in Afghanistan's political life. The Loya Jirga's most important task was to choose a president of the Transitional Authority that, according to the Bonn agreement, should replace the Interim Authority. Karzai was expected to be elected, and challenges from former president Burhaneddin Rabbani, a Tajik, and from supporters of the former king were avoided when both men withdrew in a demonstration of national unity. The Loya Jirga then approved Karzai and 13 members of his cabinet. An additional 16 ministers were named by Karzai only after the Loya Jirga had adjourned. By late June Karzai's administration had been expanded to include four vice presidents, one each from Afghanistan's Pashtun, Tajik, Uzbek, and Hazara ethnic groups.

Still, violence persisted throughout the year. On February 14 Aviation and Tourism Minister Abdul Rahman was killed at Kabul's airport. On July 6 the Pashtun vice president, Haji Abdul Qadir, was assassinated outside his office in Kabul (*see* OBITUARIES). Three

The slain Northern Alliance military leader Ahmad Shah Masoud is remembered at a gathering near his burial site in the Panshir Valley on September 9, the one-year anniversary of his death.

Tyler Hicks/The New York Times

weeks later a car loaded with explosives was discovered in downtown Kabul before the vehicle could be detonated. On September 5 a car bomb in Kabul killed more than two dozen Afghans, and on the same day in Kandahar, Karzai narrowly escaped the bullets of a gunman who attacked his car. These and other incidents during the year demonstrated the government's continued vulnerability to breakdowns in public security.   (STEPHEN SEGO)

ALBANIA

Area: 28,703 sq km (11,082 sq mi)
Population (2002 est.): 3,108,000 (not including Albanians living abroad)
Capital: Tirana
Chief of state: Presidents Rexhep Meidani and, from July 24, Alfred Moisiu
Head of government: Prime Ministers Ilir Meta, Pandeli Majko from February 22, and, from July 31, Fatos Nano

The major development in Albania in 2002 was the return in July of Socialist Party (PS) Chairman Fatos Nano as prime minister. His appointment marked the end of a power struggle between the party leader and his two younger challengers, Ilir Meta and Pandeli Majko, both of whom had served as prime minister since Nano resigned the post during a period of civil unrest in 1998. Nano's return followed a government crisis in February 2002, during which Majko had succeeded Meta and had begun his second short-lived term as prime minister on February 22. Meta was named foreign minister and Majko defense minister in the new cabinet.

Media analysis suggested that Nano had elbowed Meta and Majko aside in a grab for power after realizing that he was too controversial a figure to aspire to the presidency. The European Parliament had urged Albanian legislators to elect a president who would be acceptable to both the governing coalition and the opposition. Moreover, Meta and the outgoing president, Rexhep Meidani, both openly opposed Nano's candidacy for the presidency. The election of Alfred Moisiu on July 24 essentially sealed the PS legislators' compromise with the opposition, led by the Democratic Party (PD).

Nano and PD Chairman Sali Berisha said that the deal signaled that the two rival party leaders had put years of fighting behind them. Moisiu, a 73-year-old retired general, had served as president of the Albanian North Atlantic Treaty Association and was considered friendly by the opposition.

Albania's relations with neighbouring countries were dominated by efforts to increase cross-border cooperation within the framework of the Stability Pact for Southeastern Europe. In 2002 Albania was working to conclude free-trade agreements with Macedonia, Yugoslavia, Bosnia and Herzegovina, and Croatia. The Organization for Security and Co-operation in Europe's chief of mission, Geert-Hinrich Ahrens, praised Albania in his end-of-mission address to the OSCE Permanent Council on August 29, reporting that the country was "in the forefront of reform in the region" and adding that recent achievements had "brought Albania to the threshold of opening negotiations for a Stabilisation and Association Agreement with the European Union." Finnish diplomat Osmo Lipponen succeeded Ahrens on September 1.

The Albanian economy suffered a slight setback in 2002. The budget deficit reached 8.5% of gross domestic product (GDP), according to September Finance Ministry estimates. Ministry officials said they expected to reduce the deficit to 6.2% in 2003. Unemployment remained at 13.5% but continued to creep up during the year. A United Nations Development Project report estimated that one-third of the population lived in poverty, earning less than $1 per capita per day. Large segments of the population lived from subsistence agriculture and did not receive unemployment benefits. The expected growth of GDP was 6%, and it was estimated that the inflation rate would reach about 4% by the end of the year.

(FABIAN SCHMIDT)

ALGERIA

Area: 2,381,741 sq km (919,595 sq mi)
Population (2002 est.): 31,261,000
Capital: Algiers
Chief of state: President Abdelaziz Bouteflika
Head of government: Prime Minister Ali Benflis

Despite major efforts by the Algerian army throughout 2002, violence continued to erupt in many parts of the country, including the capital. By October at least 1,200 persons had died. Algiers faced the reintroduction of security barriers, removed two years

In March, after having taken over the headquarters of the local gendarmerie in the town of Azazga in Algeria's Kabylia region, Berber protesters stage an antigovernment demonstration.

AP/Wide World Photos

earlier, despite the dismantling of a major terrorist cell in August. Although Antar Zouabri—the head of the Armed Islamic Group—was killed in February, Hassan Hattab's Islamist guerrilla group, Salafist Group for Call and Combat, extended its control over parts of Kabylia and the Skikda region.

Algerians continued to protest poor living conditions. In the central and eastern parts of the country, riots ensued over water supplies and poor administration. In addition, only 46.7% of the electorate voted in the May 30 legislative elections; it was the lowest turnout in any election since independence. The elections produced a dramatic turnaround in the fortunes of the former single party, the National Liberation Front (FLN), which trounced its rival, the National Democratic Rally (RND), to become the largest party by far in the Popular National Assembly, with 199 of the 389 seats. The event was marred, however, by a boycott in Kabylia by both Berber parties, the Socialist Forces Front (FFS) and the Rally for Culture and Democracy (RCD); there the turnout was only 2%.

In the local elections held on October 10, however, the FFS participated. The "citizens movement"—created from the local groups that had reacted to government oppression in 2001—promised to fight for the boycott to continue. The group sought government concessions as outlined in the May 2001 El Kseur Platform. These involved the granting of regional autonomy, the recognition of Tamazight as an official language, the removal of the gendarmerie—held responsible for oppression that had involved up to 100 deaths—from Kabylia, and the punishment of those officials directly responsible. The government had partially conceded by registering Tamazight in the constitution as a national language and withdrawing the gendarmerie from Kabylia in April.

Nonetheless, election day was marked by riots, and in many communities in Kabylia, voting did not take place. The FLN was the overall victor, winning control of 668 of the country's 1,541 town councils and 43 of 48 provincial councils. The Islamic parties suffered a decline in support except for El-Islah, which won control of 39 councils. The RCD again did badly, as did the FFS, because of the boycott in Kabylia, where the turnout was about 2%, compared with a national average of 52%.

In June, Gen. Khaled Nezzar—former defense minister and a key figure in the 1992 army-backed coup—sued Habib Souaidia, a former sublieutenant and author of *La Sale Guerre* (2001), in a Paris court for defamation. Souaidia asserted that during the war against Islamic extremists Algerian troops tortured rebels and killed them in cold blood while disguising themselves as rebels. The trial judge reserved judgment in the case and warned that there could be no penalty "because this touches upon history"—to the regime's embarrassment. Relations with the United States continued to improve. In April, Algeria signed an association agreement with the European Union. Foreign currency reserves rose to nearly $22.5 billion for the year as a result of buoyant oil prices and Algerian overproduction of almost 46% by year's end.

(GEORGE JOFFÉ)

ANDORRA

Area: 468 sq km (181 sq mi)
Population (2002 est.): 66,500
Capital: Andorra la Vella
Chiefs of state: Co-princes of Andorra, the president of France and the bishop of Urgell, Spain
Head of government: Chief Executive Marc Forné Molné

Andorra's banking sector came under fire for its secrecy laws as the international search to uncover terrorist funds intensified in 2002. On April 18 the Organisation for Economic Co-operation and Development named seven territories as uncooperative tax havens—Andorra, Liberia, Liechtenstein, the Marshall Islands, Monaco, Nauru, and Vanuatu—and threatened sanctions against them. Gabriel Makhlouf, a member of the OECD's Committee on Fiscal Affairs, stated, "The globalised economy of the 21st century is going to rely on greater openness."

The Andorran police had earlier established a Money Laundering Prevention Unit to centralize information about money laundering, whether from drug trafficking, organized crime, or terrorism. The unit scored a major success on July 17 when the Andorran prosecutor's office ordered the preventive freezing of a €2 million (about $2 million) bank account that was suspected of belonging to a terrorist group.

An ongoing investigation begun in 2000 was concluded in March when police in Spain and Andorra arrested nine members of a money-laundering ring involved in drug trafficking. The joint police action resulted in the arrests of seven people in Andorra and two in Spain; the suspects were accused of having laundered €6 million (about $5.2 million) through front companies and banks in both countries.

(ANNE ROBY)

ANGOLA

Area: 1,246,700 sq km (481,354 sq mi)
Population (2002 est.): 10,593,000 (excluding more than 400,000 refugees in the Democratic Republic of the Congo and Zambia)
Capital: Luanda
Chief of state and head of government: President José Eduardo dos Santos

The death of Jonas Savimbi (*see* OBITUARIES), longtime leader of the rebel National Union for the Total Independence of Angola (UNITA), in a military skirmish on Feb. 22, 2002, raised hopes of an end to the civil war that had raged since Angola achieved independence in 1975. Initially, spokesmen for UNITA insisted that the struggle would go on. Government forces also tried to press home their tactical advantage by continuing to destroy crops to force the rebels to surrender. On March 15 the government offered a cease-fire, accompanied by the blanket amnesty demanded by UNITA to all fighters who laid down their arms and by a plan to rebuild the lives of the displaced civilian population, numbering more than 180,000. In return, 50,000 rebel soldiers would surrender, and many of them would be integrated into the Angolan armed forces. Appeals from UN Secretary-General Kofi Annan and from the leaders of South Africa, the U.S., and Portugal resulted in the signing of a cease-fire agreement in Luanda on April 4.

Numerous problems still remained before the country could return to normal, however. The restoration of the infrastructure, virtually all of which had been destroyed during the war, was an urgent task. Encouraged by the prospect of

AP/Wide World Photos

Angolans line up to receive medical attention at a Médecins sans Frontières (Doctors Without Borders) station in Ndele in June.

increased international investment in oil exploration as a result of the end of hostilities—and stimulated by the perceived need to find alternative supplies to those from the troubled Persian Gulf region—the government promised to use its oil revenues, hitherto swallowed up in military expenditure, to restore the road system. In August, however, the director general of Angola's National Institute of Roads announced that funding was lacking for the $270 million project. In June plans were also announced to rebuild the 1,609-km (1,000-mi)-long Benguela Railway, which had formerly been part of a rail link between the west and east coasts of the continent.

The rehabilitation of the agricultural sector, for which an initial fund of $6 million was made available, was complicated by the presence of thousands of land mines that were scattered indiscriminately during the fighting and made farming impossible over a considerable part of the country. The fact that the government ratified the 1997 Ottawa Convention banning the use of land mines had little impact on the existing problem.

Underlying these various endeavours was a problem that had a devastating effect upon plans for regenerating the economy. Two years of drought, interspersed with floods and coupled with the ravages of civil war, had danger-

ously depleted the country's food stocks. By the middle of the year, the UN World Food Programme estimated that half a million people in Angola were suffering from starvation and a million others were entirely dependent upon food aid for their survival. A UN spokesman estimated that in spite of the efforts of aid workers, up to three million people would require some form of assistance in the months ahead. In addition, UNITA's participation in the recovery program was hampered by divisions within the movement.

(KENNETH INGHAM)

ANTIGUA AND BARBUDA

Area: 442 sq km (171 sq mi)
Population (2002 est.): 76,400
Capital: Saint John's
Chief of state: Queen Elizabeth II, represented by Governor-General James Carlisle
Head of government: Prime Minister Lester Bird

In February 2002 Antigua and Barbuda joined other Caribbean states that had

been fingered by the Paris-based Organisation for Economic Co-operation and Development (OECD) as indulging in "harmful" tax competition and yielded to demands for transparency and the "effective exchange of information in criminal tax matters" with OECD countries. This concession saved the country from being included in a definitive OECD blacklist of offshore tax havens, which would have attracted unspecified sanctions.

Although never on the Financial Action Task Force's list of states deemed "uncooperative" in the fight against money laundering, Antigua and Barbuda faced scrutiny on the issue during the year. Its legal and regulatory defenses against money laundering were questioned by the U.K., among others.

In August the U.K. provided two fraud specialists and a special prosecutor to determine whether any of the 14 people named in Antigua and Barbuda's Medical Benefits Scheme (MBS) investigation could be charged with criminal offenses. A commission of inquiry into how millions of dollars in public funds disappeared from the MBS had recommended that the government take action in the matter.   (DAVID RENWICK)

ARGENTINA

Area: 2,780,092 sq km (1,073,400 sq mi)
Population (2002 est.): 36,446,000
Capital: Buenos Aires
Head of state: Presidents Eduardo Camaño (acting) and, from January 2, Eduardo Duhalde

In 2002 Argentina experienced an economic collapse of proportions nearly unheard-of when a war or major natural disaster was not involved. The country's gross domestic product fell by 15% (for a cumulative drop of 21% since the current recession began in 1998). Inflation increased from an average annual rate of 1% during the previous eight years to nearly 50% in 2002. The country's currency (the peso), which between 1991 and 2001 had been equal in value to the U.S. dollar (under the country's Convertibility Law, which pegged the peso to the dollar), was by October worth only 27 cents. The

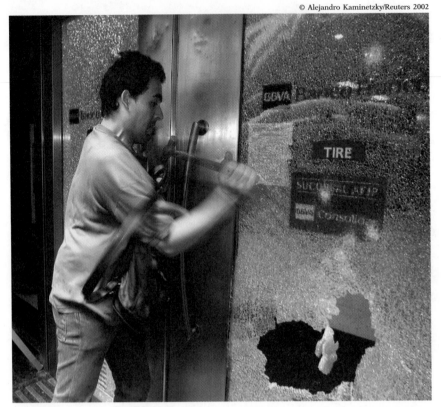

An Argentine man hammers through a window of a bank during a protest in the financial district of Buenos Aires in February.

percentage of the population that was unemployed reached a record 22%; the percentage that was underemployed totaled 19%. By September more than half of the country's population (53%) was living below the poverty line.

Following Pres. Fernando de la Rúa's resignation in December 2001 and the subsequent resignation of interim president Adolfo Rodríguez Saá, Eduardo Duhalde was elected president on January 1 by a joint session of the Chamber of Deputies and the Senate to complete the remainder of de la Rúa's term, which was to run until Dec. 10, 2003. At the time of his election, Duhalde was a senator from the province of Buenos Aires. He had been governor of the province of Buenos Aires between 1991 and 1999 and was the Justicialist (Peronist) Party (PJ) candidate for president in 1999 (finishing second behind de la Rúa).

Upon assuming office on January 2, Duhalde was faced with the unenviable tasks of reducing the considerable social tensions that had brought about de la Rúa's resignation, restoring investor and consumer confidence, and in general repairing the massive damage to the economy that had occurred during the disastrous tenure of de la

Rúa's final economy minister, Domingo Cavallo.

The most important policy change implemented during Duhalde's first three months in office was the forced conversion of all dollar bank accounts into peso accounts (at a rate of 1.4 pesos to the dollar) combined with a nearly complete freeze on bank accounts (which prevented most withdrawals). Second in importance was the end of the Convertibility Law and the ensuing devaluation of the peso (which by October was trading at 3.7 to the dollar).

A consequence of these two policy changes was that nearly one million Argentines with savings accounts or certificates of deposit saw the value of their money drop by between 60% and 70%, while all citizens and companies with dollar-dominated debt abroad faced the nearly impossible task of repaying that debt. At the same time, owing to the country's unilateral default on its debt (declared during the brief Rodríguez Saá administration in December 2001) and the collapse of the country's banking system, the government as well as most companies and individuals found it nearly impossible to obtain credit at anything other than exorbitant interest

rates (if credit was even to be found). On December 2 the freeze on most bank accounts was lifted.

Throughout 2002 the Duhalde administration and the International Monetary Fund (IMF) held a series of meetings in an attempt to reach a new agreement that would allow Argentina to restructure its debt with the IMF as well as to receive new funds for economic and political restructuring. By year's end no agreement had been reached, but the Group of Seven gave its backing to Argentina in late December in an effort to help stimulate the resumption of IMF aid. In November Argentina defaulted on its $805 million loan with the World Bank.

Experiencing little success during his first six months in office and faced with stubborn economic and social difficulties, in July Duhalde called for new presidential elections on March 30, 2003, with the new president to assume office on May 25, 2003 (six and a half months prior to the originally scheduled date).

There was no clear front-runner for the March 2003 presidential election, however. The most noteworthy result of a review of six public opinion surveys in September–October was that over one-third of all citizens supported none of the candidates running for the office. Furthermore, the person most highly regarded by the electorate, Carlos Reutemann (governor of Santa Fe), adamantly refused to run for president.

Another noteworthy result gleaned from these surveys was the low percentages of prospective votes for even the most prominent candidates. The front-runner was Adolfo Rodríguez Saá (governor of San Luis between 1983 and 2001 and president for a week in 2001) with 18%, followed by former president Carlos Menem (1989–99) with 12% and national deputy Elisa Carrio with 11%. The remaining relevant candidates were Néstor Kirchner (governor of Santa Cruz) with 9% and Ricardo López Murphy (a government minister during much of the de la Rúa administration) with 7%.

Though the PJ had tentatively scheduled its presidential primary for Jan. 19, 2003, by December 2002 bitter PJ infighting over the proposed date had resulted in the matter's being sent to the courts. It remained unclear if all the PJ candidates (Rodríguez Saá, Menem, and Kirchner, along with the governor of Córdoba, José Manuel de la Sota) would participate in the primary.

(MARK P. JONES)

ARMENIA

Area: 29,743 sq km (11,484 sq mi). About 14% of neighbouring Azerbaijan (including the 4,400-sq-km [1,700-sq-mi] disputed region of Nagorno-Karabakh [Armenian: Artsakh]) has been under Armenian control since 1993.
Population (2002 est.): 3,800,000; actually present 3,008,000 (plus 140,000 in Nagorno-Karabakh)
Capital: Yerevan
Chief of state: President Robert Kocharyan
Head of government: Prime Minister Andranik Markaryan

Armenian opposition forces continued to cooperate increasingly closely in 2002 with the aim of ousting Pres. Robert Kocharyan. Outraged by a controversial tender that stripped the country's most respected independent TV station, A1+, of its broadcast frequency, 13 opposition parties aligned and staged weekly demonstrations in April and May to demand Kocharyan's impeachment for allegedly having violated the constitution and having failed to improve economic and social conditions. They failed, however, to garner support in the parliament for a debate on the issue during either the spring or the fall session. In early September, 16 opposition parties signed a declaration of intent to remove Kocharyan from power and to prevent his supporters from rigging the presidential election scheduled for Feb. 19, 2003, in order to ensure his reelection. They further vowed to field a single candidate for that election. Within weeks, however, the Communist and National Unity parties were threatening to back out of that alliance and nominate their own presidential candidates. Former president Levon Ter-Petrossyan decided not to run despite rumours that he might do so, but several small parties that had split in the late 1990s from the former ruling Armenian Pan-National Movement realigned in preparation for contesting the May 2003 parliamentary ballot. In the October 2002 local elections, Prime Minister Andranik Markaryan's Republican Party of Armenia scored an impressive victory. In February a Yerevan court handed down a suspended sentence to a member of Kocharyan's bodyguard accused of having beaten a man

to death in a café brawl in 2001. Despite persistent pressure from the Council of Europe, Armenia refused to annul a loophole in the criminal code adopted in June that would permit a court to sentence to death the five gunmen responsible for parliament shootings that resulted in eight deaths in 1999.

Armenia's economic recovery continued. Gross domestic product grew by 10.1% during the first half of the year to reach approximately $771 million; industrial output over that period increased by 12.1%. In July Armenia and Russia finally signed an agreement whereby Yerevan ceded ownership of at least four major enterprises in payment of its outstanding $98 million debt, and the deal was ratified by the parliament in December. In late August the Armenian energy-distribution network was sold to a little-known offshore company.

(ELIZABETH FULLER)

AUSTRALIA

Area: 7,692,030 sq km (2,969,910 sq mi)
Population (2002 est.): 19,702,000
Capital: Canberra
Chief of state: Queen Elizabeth II, represented by Governor-General the Right Rev. Peter Hollingworth
Head of government: Prime Minister John Howard

Domestic Affairs. Australians were shocked when a terrorist bomb attack on Oct. 12, 2002, killed nearly 100 Australians on holiday in the resort town of Kuta on the Indonesian island of Bali. Prime Minister John Howard declared that "our nation has been changed by this event" and wept when he visited the blackened bomb site where two popular night spots had once stood.

After having won a historic third term in office in the 2001 general elections, Howard and his Liberal Party of Australia (LPA) faced weak federal opposition parties in 2002. Despite the fact that all Australian states had Australian Labor Party (ALP) premiers, the national ALP was unable to transform itself and recover its appeal to the wider community. The leader of the federal opposition, Simon Crean, endorsed a plan to shift the ALP's internal power balance by adopting

a scheme for reform devised by former ALP prime minister Bob Hawke and former ALP New South Wales premier Neville Wran. Hawke and Wran repudiated the claim that the ALP's traditional close links with the trade union movement were an electoral liability and produced a blueprint that gave less power to factional chiefs and union members. Crean called for a rank-and-file revival to give "ownership and involvement back to the community."

The LPA's other major opponent, the Australian Democrats (AD), was damaged as a political force when Sen. Meg Lees resigned from the party in July. Members of the ALP and the AD were shaken when the Australian Green Party (AG) defeated both of their parties and rocked the political establishment by winning their first lower house seat in the federal Parliament at a by-election in Cunningham. While not "finger pointing," as he put it, AG leader Sen. Bob Brown commented that there was a strong feeling that among the Cunningham electorate many voters did not want Australians sent to Iraq. Public opinion in Australia was quick to blame Howard for the bombing on Bali. Many people believed that Howard had made Australians a target for Muslim extremists by his overenthusiastic support for U.S. foreign policy.

The prime minister's high public standing on matters of immigration allowed him to remain firmly defiant regarding the treatment of asylum seekers in Australia. (*See* Special Report.) Throughout the year Immigration Minister Philip Ruddock defended Australia's Pacific Solution against local and overseas condemnation. On March 29 a razor-wire fence at the Woomera Detention Centre was torn down, which allowed several detainees to escape and triggered violent local protests. Forty-two Iraqi asylum seekers, who were being held on Papua New Guinea's Manus Island, were eventually accepted as refugees in Australia, but almost all of the asylum seekers claiming to be Afghans were rejected. In order to provide a more humane form of detention, the government built the new Baxter detention centre on 28 ha (69 ac) of the El Alamein Army Base near Port Augusta.

The Economy. The Australian economy was adversely affected by the worldwide downturn in 2002. Growth stalled in midyear as the Australian economy slowed to its lowest level in 18 months. Gross domestic product grew by 0.6%

(continued on page 398)

Strangers at the Gates
The Immigration Backlash

by Bob Birrell

By 2002 immigration had emerged as a key issue in many developed nations of the world. The determination of governments to control the flow of immigrants to their nations' shores was the focus of intense debate and, increasingly, the subject of controversy. In an incident that captured worldwide attention in August 2001, Australian authorities intercepted the Norwegian freighter *Tampa* and refused to allow the 433 asylum seekers who had been picked up by the vessel to set foot on Australian soil. These asylum seekers—mostly Afghans and Iraqis—were subsequently transported to Nauru while their claims for refugee status were processed. Meanwhile, the Australian government hastened to pass legislation toughening the country's asylum laws, and the United Nations High Commissioner for Refugees (UNHCR) eventually ruled that most of the asylum seekers did not qualify for refugee protection visas.

Despite international protests over the treatment of the *Tampa* "boat people," the hard-line stance taken by the government of Australian Prime Minister John Howard was consistent with a recent trend toward the tightening of immigration policies around the globe. This trend was particularly evident in Europe during 2002. Under new rules announced in Britain, for example, immigrants could be deported even before their appeals regarding refugee status had been heard. Legislation was introduced in the Italian Parliament that would facilitate expulsions from the country and impose stiff fines and prison sentences on those involved in human trafficking. It was Denmark, however, that enacted the strictest

asylum laws on the continent; a new immigration package that went into effect in July denied immigrants a residence permit until they had lived in the country for at least seven years and curbed the rights of immigrants to bring their families into the country.

While foreign workers often play vital roles in helping developed nations maintain their economies, illegal immigration and the difficulty in reconciling cultural differences between various ethnic groups can pose major problems. By 2002, an estimated 300,000 to 500,000 illegal immigrants were believed to be arriving in Europe each year. Tightening border controls was a response that appealed to many voters, as evidenced by the recent rise in popularity of anti-immigrant political groups. In Austria the far-right Freedom Party—led by Jörg Haider, who virulently denounced immigration—joined the country's ruling coalition in 2000. In Portugal a right-wing coalition that included the anti-immigrant Popular Party came into power in 2002, while in France, Norway, Switzerland, and The Netherlands, anti-immigrant parties began to exert considerable influence on mainstream politics.

In Australia evidence that many citizens were prepared to vote on the basis of immigration issues was made clear when Pauline Hanson's One Nation party won 8% of first preference votes in the House of Representatives in the 1998 federal election, primarily owing to the party's strident anti-immigration and antimulticultural platform. Hanson had rapidly raised her party's profile by warning that the country was in danger of being overrun by Asian immigrants—who, she claimed, took jobs from Australian citizens and made no

effort to assimilate into Australian society—and by calling for a short-term halt to Asian immigration.

This atmosphere shaped the response of Howard's government to the *Tampa's* arrival in Australian waters. At the time, the country's detention camps were bulging. The government could not even return the minority of claimants who had been denied refugee status to their countries of origin because most states would not accept them. There had been dramatic protests within these camps, including hunger strikes and riots; in one incident 58 detainees at a remote camp north of Adelaide sewed up their lips to protest delays in processing their visa applications. These protests polarized public opinion. For liberals detention was a deep stain on Australia's reputation. Although the country had no tradition of welcoming "tired and huddled masses," it had witnessed the relatively trouble-free settlement of a large influx of people from Southern and Eastern Europe in the 1950s and '60s and from Asia and the Middle East during the 1980s and much of the '90s. In 1999–2000, however, the arrival of unauthorized boat people—most of them Muslims from Afghanistan, Iraq, and Iran—increased fourfold from the year before, to 4,175. This led to widespread frustration over the government's apparent inability to stop an unwelcome influx.

The government was in a difficult situation because, once they were in Australia, most unauthorized claimants were being determined to be refugees according to the requirements of the 1951 UN Convention Relating to the Status of Refugees. As outlined by the convention, a person is considered a

Immigration—A Global Concern

Off the coast of Sicily on March 18, a freighter carries some 1,000 refugees seeking asylum on the island.

Passports confiscated by U.S. Immigration and Naturalization inspectors at Miami (Fla.) International Airport are displayed at a news conference on July 2.

Asylum seekers sit in custody on September 23 after being arrested while attempting to reach the coast of Spain.

Illegal immigrants scale a fence to escape from the detention centre in Woomera, S.Aus., on March 29 as demonstrators protest the government's treatment of the detainees.

refugee who, "owing to a well-founded fear of being persecuted for reasons of race, religion, nationality, membership in a particular social group, or political opinion, is outside the country of his nationality, and is unable or, owing to such fear, is unwilling to avail himself of the protection of that country." In many cases it was not possible to put asylum claims to any empirical test, because there was a lack of access to relevant information in states where the alleged persecution occurred. Nevertheless, the various review tribunals, as well as the Australian federal and high court judges hearing the appeals of those rejected, tended to give claimants the benefit of the doubt. The government feared that Australia was turning itself into a beacon, virtually inviting human traffickers to look to it as a destination for their clients.

The *Tampa* incident brought these matters to a head. A federal election campaign was in progress at the time, with neither major party assured of victory. The coalition government's decisive actions, which, besides transporting the asylum seekers to Nauru, also included denying the Australian courts any jurisdiction over their cases, effectively prevented any further unauthorized boat people from making asylum claims in the country. These actions were condemned by many observers as violations of the spirit of the 1951 convention, to which Australia is a signatory. The political consequence in Australia, however, was a surge in Howard's popularity, which carried through to an electoral victory in November 2001.

The problem remains of what to do with those asylum seekers who fail in their refugee claims. Many who have been denied Australian visas have resisted repatriation and languish in processing camps at considerable expense to taxpayers. Still, most voters continue to support the government's tough control measures. Meanwhile, other countries appeared to be moving toward the adoption of common policies for the treatment of asylum seekers. In June 2002 leaders of the 15 European Union nations grappled with immigration issues at a summit held in Seville, Spain. The leaders agreed to work on visa regulations that would apply in every EU country, to speed up the repatriations of those immigrants who do not qualify, and to ensure closer cooperation on border controls.

Bob Birrell is Director of the Centre for Population and Urban Research at Monash University, Clayton, Victoria, Australia.

Authorities in Spain carry the body of a drowning victim on October 8 after at least seven refugees died while attempting to enter the country illegally.

Marchers in Lewiston, Maine, in October show their support for Somali immigrants to the city.

397

(continued from page 395)

in the June quarter, putting annual economic growth at 3.8% for fiscal 2001–02. Treasurer Peter Costello stressed that the greatest threat to the economy was the uncertain international scene. In his seventh budget, Costello provided for $A 2.1 billion ($A 1 = about U.S. $0.55) to be spent on the "war on terrorism" and allocated $A 2.9 billion for border protection. The budget papers showed a loss of $A 1.2 billion for 2001–02, bringing to an end the treasurer's run of four successive

the collapse of telecommunications company One.Tel, which cost shareholders $A 5 billion.

The government continued to wrestle with the difficult issues of privatizing Telstra. Telstra's status as an Australian telecommunications icon—and resistance from residents who thought that they would suffer reduced services in a wholly privatized telecommunications system—stopped progress on the government's eventual full-sale strategy while the matter was debated by Parliament and by the public. The gov-

July, offered strong backing to the Bush government. After the bombing on Bali and the Cunningham by-election, Downer watered down his support for a war in Iraq, saying Australia "had an overwhelming focus on [its] own region and [its] own environment." President Bush telephoned Howard to express American sympathy, and a wattle tree was planted in the U.S. embassy in Canberra as a mark of solidarity.

Trade considerations were behind the new warmth in relations with China, and both countries benefited from co-operative economic treaties. Howard took a major role in securing for Australia a 25-year, $A 25-billion-liquid-gas supply contract with China and led six Australian companies in the plan to provide clean energy to China's Guang-dong province. Price and reliability were factors in China's decision to favour Australia LNG, as the new consortium was called, over a rival British-Indonesian bid. Chinese Premier Zhu Rongji was also influenced by a determination to move relations into a new phase in which Australia partly guaranteed China's energy security.

In February Howard visited Indonesia and signed a joint memorandum of understanding on sharing intelligence between Indonesia and Australia. Subsequently, Defense Minister Robert Hill visited Jakarta as part of Canberra's efforts to counter terrorism. After talks with his Indonesian counterpart, Matori Adul Jalil, as well as Foreign Minister Hassan Wirayuda and Security Minister Susilo Bambang, Hill announced that Australia was discussing maritime surveillance exchanges and had offered Indonesian cadets places at Australia's military academy. The Australian and Indonesian governments moved closer together in the aftermath of the Bali bombing. Indonesian Pres. Megawati Sukarnoputri and Howard set up Operation Alliance to investigate the bomb blast. Many of the Indonesian victims were flown to Australia for medical treatment.

Australia faced pressure from East Timor when Prime Minister Mari Alkatiri made it clear that East Timor claimed an area that extended 200 nautical miles from its coastline. This area included the Greater Sunrise gas fields, 80% of which were in Australian waters. The relationship between trade and diplomacy was also illustrated when Iraq threatened to cancel wheat purchases unless Australia dropped its belligerent stand toward Iraq.

© AFP 2002, by Torsten Blackwood

On October 20 members of the Coogee Dolphins rugby football club mourn six of their teammates who were among the nearly 100 Australians killed in a bomb attack in Bali.

years in surplus. Costello maintained that the deficit was a good result, given the recessions into which most developed countries had plunged.

Australian investor confidence was shaken by financial scandals. Howard followed U.S. Pres. George W. Bush in campaigning to restore consumer faith in publicly listed companies. The prime minister warned Australian companies that unless they improved corporate behaviour, pressure for more government regulation would become irresistible. He also observed that there had been an inevitable reaction to spectacular business failures in Australia and the U.S. and justifiable criticism of some entrepreneurs. In Australia Lachlan Murdoch and James Packer were criticized for "not giving it their best shot." Murdoch was asked to explain why he did not do more to stop

ernment acted decisively to reject a QANTAS airline submission for legislation to lift the 49% threshold on total foreign ownership. QANTAS officials argued that the 49% cap on foreign ownership increased the cost of capital, depressed its share prices, and made it difficult to fund a multibillion-dollar investment in new aircraft. QANTAS chairman Margaret Jackson remarked that the airline was disappointed that its two-year campaign to end the ownership restrictions had been caught up in the politics surrounding Telstra.

Foreign Affairs. The Australian government strengthened ties with the U.S., Indonesia, and China during 2002. Howard said that he would commit troops to a U.S.-led military strike against Saddam Hussein's regime in Iraq. Foreign Minister Alexander Downer, who held talks in Washington, D.C., in

(A.R.G. GRIFFITHS)

AUSTRIA

Area: 83,858 sq km (32,378 sq mi)
Population (2002 est.): 8,077,000
Capital: Vienna
Chief of state: President Thomas Klestil
Head of government: Chancellor Wolfgang Schüssel

The beginning of 2002 saw the second anniversary of the formation of Austria's controversial coalition government, comprising the centre-right People's Party (ÖVP) and the populist, sometimes xenophobic Freedom Party (FPÖ). This coincided with the beginning of a series of crises within the fractious FPÖ that broke out intermittently in the first half of the year as moderates in the cabinet clashed with more extreme elements led by the party's erstwhile leader Jörg Haider.

In an attempt to boost his own profile and the party's flagging support, Haider launched a number of headline-grabbing campaigns, caring little whether these were at variance with his own government's positions. Playing on widespread fears about a Soviet-era nuclear power station in the Czech Republic only 50 km (30 mi) from the Austrian border, for example, he demanded that the government use every means at its disposal to pressure the Czechs into shutting down the plant. Most controversially, this included Haider's advocating the use of Austria's membership in the European Union to veto Czech endeavours to join the organization. Relations with Prague deteriorated further when Haider again advocated the use of Austria's EU veto on Czech membership unless it repealed laws still on the books that allowed the expulsion of German-speakers after World War II.

By midyear it was clearly only a matter of time before the FPÖ would fall apart. The final sign came from the heavens; in August persistent heavy rainfall caused the worst flooding in half a century. The cleanup and rebuilding costs took their toll on the public finances, forcing the government to abandon promised tax cuts. Refusing to accept this, Haider led an intraparty revolt, effectively deposing the FPÖ leader and vice-chancellor, Susanne Riess-Passer. Her resignation from both positions in turn led the ÖVP

to declare the coalition arrangement with the FPÖ unworkable and call an early general election.

In the voting on November 24, the Freedom Party saw its support plummet from 27% in the most recent general election (1999) to a mere 10%. Voters abandoned the party for a number of reasons. Austrians traditionally tended to punish any party that failed to see out its four-year term in office. More significant, though, was the party's poor record in government. Having swept to power in 1999 on a wave of popular discontent with the two largest parties, which had cornered power for decades, the FPÖ saw its failure to implement change, for ill or good, prompted supporters to desert in droves.

The big winner in the election was the senior coalition partner, the ÖVP. By taking 42% of the vote, up from 27% in 1999, it leapfrogged its nearest rivals, the Social Democrats (SPÖ), to become the largest party for the first time in more than three decades. This gave its leader, Chancellor Wolfgang Schüssel, the choice of making a coalition with any one of the other three parties represented in the Federal Assembly—the FPÖ, SPÖ, or the environmentalist Greens. Talks on the formation of a new coalition continued into the final month of the year.

As in the rest of Europe, and indeed much of the world, the Austrian economy faltered in 2002. The export sector stagnated as foreign demand dried up, consumers curtailed their spending, and businesses took a gloomy view of future prospects and slashed investments. The result was a sharp uptick in employment, though with 5.5% of the labour force out of work, Austria continued to enjoy one of the lowest levels of joblessness in Europe. (DAN O'BRIEN)

AZERBAIJAN

Area: 86,600 sq km (33,400 sq mi), including the 5,500-sq-km (2,100-sq-mi) exclave of Nakhichevan and the 4,400-sq-km (1,700-sq-mi) disputed region (with Armenia) of Nagorno-Karabakh
Population (2002 est.): 8,176,000
Capital: Baku
Head of state and government: President Heydar Aliyev, assisted by Prime Minister Artur Rasizade

Pres. Heydar Aliyev's four-week hospitalization in the U.S. in February 2002 for prostate surgery fueled speculation that failing health would ultimately compel him to abandon his stated intention of seeking a third presidential term in 2003. In July Aliyev announced a nationwide referendum for August 24 on sweeping constitutional changes apparently intended to facilitate the election of his son Ilham to succeed him. Opposition parties staged a series of demonstrations in the spring and summer, some of them brutally dispersed by police, to demand Aliyev's resignation. The parties joined forces to monitor the August referendum, however. They registered widespread procedural violations that officials of the U.S., the Council of Europe, and the Organization for Security and Co-operation in Europe (OSCE) condemned, and they called for the annulment of the official referendum results, according to which 88% of the electorate participated and overwhelmingly endorsed the proposed changes.

Popular anger over unemployment and the lack of basic facilities triggered protests in the village of Nardaran in January–February and again in early June, when one resident was killed in clashes with police. Similar protests disrupted Aliyev's visit to Gyandja in September. Also in September 2,000 military cadets staged a protest against mediocre instruction and conditions of service.

Bowing to Council of Europe pressure, the Azerbaijani authorities agreed to retry three prominent political prisoners. President Aliyev pardoned 43 more political prisoners in May.

In August Azerbaijan's state oil company and seven foreign oil companies established a company to build and operate the Baku-Tbilisi-Ceyhan pipeline to export Azerbaijan's Caspian oil. Ground was broken for the project at a ceremony in Baku on September 18.

Aliyev visited Moscow twice, in January to sign an agreement permitting Russia to lease the Gabala radar station for 10 years and in September to agree on a delineation of the Caspian seabed. No major accords were signed, however, during his oft-postponed visit to Iran, which finally took place in May. Pope John Paul II made a brief visit to Azerbaijan in May. Despite visits to Armenia and Azerbaijan by the OSCE Minsk Group cochairmen in March and late September, two rounds of talks in Prague in May and July between Armenian and Azerbaijani deputy foreign ministers, and face-to-face talks in late August between Aliyev and Armenian Pres. Robert Kocharyan, no progress was registered toward resolving the Karabakh conflict. Arkady Ghukasyan was reelected as the enclave's president on August 11 with 89% of the vote. (ELIZABETH FULLER)

BAHAMAS, THE

Area: 13,939 sq km (5,382 sq mi)
Population (2002 est.): 309,000
Capital: Nassau
Chief of state: Queen Elizabeth II, represented by Governor-General Ivy Dumont
Head of government: Prime Ministers Hubert Ingraham and, from May 3, Perry Christie

In a referendum in February 2002 organized by the Free National Movement (FNM) government, Bahamians voted against a package of proposals that included ending all discrimination against women in the country's constitution and creating an independent Electoral Boundaries Commission. The long-standing commitment to a tax-free environment in The Bahamas was reaffirmed even as the country bowed to pressure from the Organisation for Economic Co-operation and Development and agreed to improve the trans-

parency of the tax system and exchange information with OECD members on criminal tax matters if required.

The Progressive Liberal Party, led by lawyer Perry Christie, returned to power in an impressive 29–11-seat victory over the FNM in the May general election. The FNM, which had governed The Bahamas under Hubert Ingraham for 10 years, lost 28 of the 35 seats it had held before the poll. Independents obtained four seats. As prime minister, Christie was not expected to alter fundamentally the country's tried and tested development strategy of focusing on financial services, tourism, and ship registration.

Privatization of state assets remained on the agenda. The new government announced in July that the state airline, Bahamasair, would be sold off, as would 49% of The Bahamas Telecommunications Corp.   (DAVID RENWICK)

BAHRAIN

Area: 694 sq km (268 sq mi)
Population (2002 est.): 672,000
Capital: Manama
Chief of state: King Hamad ibn Isa al-Khalifah
Head of government: Prime Minister Khalifah ibn Sulman al-Khalifah

On Feb. 14, 2002, Bahrain was officially transformed from an emirate into a kingdom as Emir Hamad ibn Isa al-Khalifah assumed the title of king. The new king immediately announced political reforms, calling for general elections for a municipal council and a new parliament and giving both men and women the right to vote. The government also approved a modification of its 1973 constitution; major articles of that constitution had been suspended in 1975. Under these modifications the new parliament was to be bicameral. A chamber, appointed by King Hamad, would have legislative powers on a par with the elected chamber, a matter that was criticized by the opposition.

Municipal elections were held on May 9, but voters failed to elect any of the women candidates. Parliamentary elections were held in October, the first since the body was dissolved 27 years earlier. The Bahraini government also allowed the establishment of "political associations" but not political parties. In response to long-standing popular demand, the government granted Bahraini nationality to more than 10,000 stateless persons, some of them Shi'ites of Persian origin.

On August 17 King Hamad made a historic two-day visit to Iran and met with top Iranian officials. The visit represented an improvement in relations between the two countries, which had been tense since the 1990s, when Bahrain had accused Iran of supporting the Shi'ite popular protest movement that sought reform of the Sunnite-led government.   (LOUAY BAHRY)

BANGLADESH

Area: 147,570 sq km (56,977 sq mi)
Population (2002 est.): 133,377,000
Capital: Dhaka
Chief of state: Presidents A.Q.M. Badruddoza Chowdhury, Jamiruddin Sircar (acting) from June 21, and, from September 6, Iajuddin Ahmed
Head of government: Prime Minister Khaleda Zia

The year 2002 was marked by the continued standoff between the ruling four-party alliance government, led by the Bangladesh Nationalist Party (BNP),

Supporters of Perry Christie, leader of the Progressive Liberal Party, celebrate the PLP's victory in the Bahamian general election on May 2.

AP/Wide World Photos

© Rafiqur Rahman/Reuters 2002

Bangladeshi children await the arrival of a government-supplied mobile water tank in Dhaka; a drought affected much of the country in early 2002.

and the opposition Awami League. Arbitrary arrests, detention without charges, torture in custody, and police raids of the homes of opposition leaders continued. In response, the opposition staged occasional *hartals* (country-wide general strikes) and boycotted Parliament for most of the year.

The most dramatic political event of the year was the forced resignation on June 21 of Pres. A.Q.M. Badruddoza Chowdhury, who was accused of having neglected to pay homage to BNP founder Ziaur Rahman on the anniversary of his death. In a move that some viewed as unconstitutional, the parliamentary wing of the BNP passed a resolution that removed him from office. It was the first time in the country's history that a ruling party had forced its own nominated president to resign. Parliament Speaker Jamiruddin Sircar served as interim president until Iajuddin Ahmed, a highly respected scientist from the University of Dhaka, replaced him on September 6.

Some tough new laws were enacted during the year. On March 13 a law was passed that provided for capital punishment for the crime of throwing acid on women. Parliament passed a law on April 9 that would speed the sluggish judicial process; some cases had taken

years to resolve. In the environmental sector, the government banned the production and use of highly damaging polyethylene bags and wrapping material and decided to phase out the air-polluting two-stroke auto rickshaws (three-wheeled scooters); they would be replaced with compressed-natural-gas-driven vehicles. Millions of television viewers bemoaned the closing of the country's first and most successful private television station after the high court ruled that the issuance of its license had been faulty.

On the economic front, the government-owned Adamjee Jute Mills—which employed 36,000 workers—was shut down following losses totaling $171 million over the past three decades. Though many feared that the closure would result in serious social and political repercussions, their worries proved unfounded. Economic indicators were mixed. Bangladesh's gross domestic product growth rate fell to 4.2% from 6.04% a year earlier; industrial growth was stalled at 4.1%; and export earnings slipped to $5.98 billion, a 7.44% reduction. By August the foreign-exchange reserve had risen significantly from $1.05 billion to $1.82 billion, helped by the 38.9% increase in remittances from Bangladeshi workers

abroad. Inflation jumped from 1.59% to 2.39%, and agricultural growth decreased (from 2.6% to 1.9%), most likely as a result of the drought in the early months of the year and the severe flooding that later submerged nearly half the country. The fiscal deficit—more than 6% of GDP in 2001—was reduced to 4.3% in 2002.

On the international scene, the most delicate issue facing the government was whether to export gas. Two government committees suggested that priority be given to domestic use, but the government remained under considerable international pressure, especially from the U.S., to export.

(MAHFUZ ANAM)

BARBADOS

Area: 430 sq km (166 sq mi)
Population (2002 est.): 270,000
Capital: Bridgetown
Chief of state: Queen Elizabeth II, represented by Governor-General Sir Clifford Husbands
Head of government: Prime Minister Owen Arthur

Barbados's hope of finding offshore oil was dashed in January 2002 when petroleum giant Conoco's exploratory well 112 km (70 mi) off the island's southwestern coast failed to find hydrocarbons in commercial quantities. Better results continued to come from the traditional land production areas; an exploratory well near the town of Flat Rock in St. George parish identified new sources of oil in February. The state-owned Barbados National Oil Co. was responsible for all land activity.

Barbados was removed during the year from the Organisation for Economic Co-operation and Development's list of countries offering "harmful tax competition." Barbados agreed to enter into tax information exchange agreements with OECD members, though government spokesmen stressed that Barbados had made no "concessions" to the OECD and stood by the integrity of its system.

The 2002–03 national budget, presented in March, provided for the equivalent of $1.15 billion in current and capital spending, with an emphasis

AP/Wide World Photos

A woman walks past the newly opened United Nations building in Christ Church, Barbados, on January 2; the regional centre will serve 10 eastern Carribean nations.

on new educational infrastructure. In an effort to help turn Bridgetown into a premier world cruise destination, the government in April announced plans to give the city's port a $5.5 million face-lift. (DAVID RENWICK)

BELARUS

Area: 207,595 sq km (80,153 sq mi)
Population (2002 est.): 9,933,000
Capital: Minsk
Head of state and government: President Alyaksandr G. Lukashenka, assisted by Prime Minister Henadz Navitski

The year 2002 was most uncomfortable for Pres. Alyaksandr Lukashenka (who was reelected in September 2001) as a result of his differences with Russian Pres. Vladimir V. Putin. Their disputes centred on the Russia-Belarus Union, the establishment of which had long been a goal of Lukashenka's.

In June Putin publicly condemned the "Soviet" (i.e., federal) model for the union, pointing out that, because the Belarusian economy was only 3% the size of Russia's, the two sides could hardly be regarded as equals. Two months later Putin proposed either a unified state or a union formed according to the principles of the European Union. He suggested a timetable for the former option that included a referendum in May 2003, elections to a unified parliament in December 2003, and a presidential election in March 2004. Lukashenka, however, sought an agreement based on the Union State Treaty that he and Russian Pres. Boris Yeltsin had signed in 1999 that would preserve the sovereignty of both states. The Belarusians also rejected a Russian proposal for a single currency that would have been issued and controlled in Moscow. Putin, however, stood pat.

Internationally, Belarus was still under fire for its continuing repressions of members of the political opposition and for its apparent attempts to evict from Minsk the Advisory and Monitoring Group of the Organization for Security and Co-operation in Europe (OSCE). On July 11 the OSCE Parliamentary Assembly meeting in Berlin sharply criticized Belarusian policies, calling for the introduction of free and fair elections and an end to Belarus's international isolation and voicing its concern over alleged assassinations of political opposition members and the funneling of weapons to terrorists.

During the 2001 presidential election campaign, Belarusian Trade Union Federation leader Uladzimir Hancharyk had mounted a credible challenge to Lukashenka, the incumbent. Following an extraordinary trade union congress on Sept. 18–19, 2002, the president brought the federation under government control, changed its name to Trade Union Federation of Belarus, and

installed as its new head Leanid Kozyk, formerly the deputy chairman of the presidential administration. In similar fashion Mikhail Myasnikovich, former head of the same administration, was made rector of the Belarusian Academy of Sciences. Belarus's cycle of public protests and harsh official retribution continued, most notably on April 20, when about 85 people were detained after an opposition rally in central Minsk.

In 2002 the government arbitrarily raised the minimum wage to an average of $100 per month, even while more than 40% of factories were reported to be operating at a loss (the comparable figure in 2001 was 35.6%). Moreover, it was estimated that the number of unemployed would reach 230,000 by 2003 as a result of the laying off of managers, skilled personnel, and schoolteachers in a drive for austerity. Gross domestic product grew by 4.7% in the first half of the year (the target was 7–7.5%), but inflation remained higher than in neighbouring states, and it was feared that it could reach 40% for the year.

(DAVID R. MARPLES)

BELGIUM

Area: 30,528 sq km (11,787 sq mi)
Population (2002 est.): 10,280,000
Capital: Brussels
Chief of state: King Albert II
Head of government: Prime Minister Guy Verhofstadt

Belgium's coalition government of Liberals, Socialists, and Greens successfully weathered various political storms during 2002 and looked set to remain in power until the general election scheduled for June 15, 2003—four years after it had entered office. Internal disputes over immigrants' voting rights, ecotaxes, and the closure of nuclear power stations were successfully defused. The most serious crisis, however, occurred in August after the government had agreed to the controversial sale a month earlier of 5,500 machine guns to Nepal. Opponents argued that this violated a 1991 law banning the sale of weapons to countries involved in civil wars. The government easily defeated an opposition-sponsored no-confidence vote tabled in an emergency debate by 87 votes to 38.

Belgium became the second country in the world, after The Netherlands, to legalize euthanasia. The legislation came into force in September despite heavy criticism from the Roman Catholic Church and the opposition Christian Democrats. In a further sign of changing societal values, a law passed in May made the private use of cannabis no longer a criminal offense, although penalties for causing a nuisance in a public place when smoking the drug were increased.

A Brussels appeals court rejected attempts to try Israeli Prime Minister Ariel Sharon in Belgium for his role in alleged war crimes committed against Palestinian refugees 20 years earlier. The case had been brought by 23 Palestinians under a controversial 1993 law, modified in 1999. This law gave Belgian courts universal jurisdiction to try genocide cases and war crimes, irrespective of the location of the alleged offenses or the nationality of those involved. The appeals court dismissed the case by referring to the Belgian criminal code, which states that alleged crimes committed outside the country may be pursued only "when the suspect is found in Belgium."

Despite the poor economic climate, which saw growth in Belgium fall to 1.1% in 2001 from 4% the previous year, the country entered 2002 with a slight budget surplus, equivalent to 0.2% of its gross domestic product. Although tax revenue fell, this was offset by increased income from the social security system, reduced administrative expenditures, lower public-debt interest payments, and the proceeds from several one-off sales, such as mobile telephone licenses. Several months after the collapse of Sabena, Belgium's national airline, its successor, SN Brussels Airlines, was launched in February.

Belgium's Royal Museum for Central Africa established an investigation into claims that up to 10 million Congolese had been either murdered or worked to death by the private army of King Leopold II. A committee of eminent historians was due to complete its study of the allegations—the first serious inquiry into the events of more than a century earlier—in 2004, the centenary of the death of explorer Henry Morton Stanley, who secured the colony for Leopold in 1885. The decision in July to set up the committee followed a formal apology from Belgian Foreign Minister Louis Michel for the death in 1961 of Patrice Lumumba, the first prime minister of the Democratic Republic of the Congo, the country's former colony. A Belgian parliamentary inquiry found that Belgium bore "moral responsibility" for Lumumba's death after he was overthrown in a military coup by the head of the armed forces, Mobutu Sese Seko.

(RORY WATSON)

BELIZE

Area: 22,965 sq km (8,867 sq mi)
Population (2002 est.): 251,000
Capital: Belmopan
Chief of state: Queen Elizabeth II, represented by Governor-General Colville Young
Head of government: Prime Minister Said Musa

In early 2002 Belize was still reeling from the tremendous devastation caused by Hurricane Iris, which had struck the southern third of the country in October 2001. The damages—which were estimated at more than $150 million—included the substantial devastation of the banana industry, Belize's fifth largest source of exports. Inevitably, the unexpected outlay toward reconstruction created a dent in the national economy and augmented the public debt, which climbed to almost $1 billion, or a little under 59% of the country's gross domestic product.

In response to a rise in violent crimes, the government embarked on an ambitious initiative to work on youth development programs. In a rare demonstration of bipartisan consensus, the National Assembly passed a constitutional amendment that would allow all appeals on capital offenses to be settled by the national Appeals Court rather than the British Privy Council.

A major breakthrough toward settling the more-than-century-old territorial dispute between Belize and Guatemala occurred during the year. With the Organization of American States acting as an intermediary, a comprehensive proposal that could form the framework of a treaty was presented to both Belize and Guatemala. National referenda to decide the fate of the proposal, which was introduced with much fanfare in September, would be held simultaneously in both countries in early 2003.

(JOSEPH O. PALACIO)

BENIN

Area: 112,622 sq km (43,484 sq mi)
Population (2002 est.): 6,788,000
Capital: Porto-Novo (executive and ministerial offices remain in Cotonou)
Head of state and government: President Mathieu Kérékou

The decision to introduce merit pay for Benin's civil servants in 2002 led to a series of strikes that paralyzed the government for much of January and February. An agreement with six of the seven main public service unions was reached on March 7, after the government agreed to reinstate the old system temporarily, to pay salary arrears, and to reconsider the entire question of replacing the automatic wage system with one based on merit. Periodic strikes continued, however, in the education sector. Students at the University of Abomey Calavi, near Porto-Novo, went on strike in February, protesting the expulsion of five of their leaders. On March 21 security forces used tear gas to disperse a demonstration, injuring several students and arresting more than a dozen.

A demonstration on April 25 by members of the main opposition party, Benin Renaissance, who supported former president Nicéphore Soglo, was broken up by police using truncheons and tear gas. Nineteen members of the National Electoral Commission were named on August 19 to supervise local and regional polls scheduled for December.

UNICEF and the Benin Health Ministry began a mass vaccination program on March 1 aimed at eliminating preventable childhood diseases. On June 29 the International Monetary Fund and the African Development Fund Agency agreed to provide $20 million for the upgrading of local fishing industries. The U.S. announced on August 8 that it would provide over $16 million for improvements in education, health, and local government. A week later the European Commission made it known that €275 million (about $270 million) would be made available over five years to fight poverty in Benin through sustainable economic and social development programs.

(NANCY ELLEN LAWLER)

BHUTAN

Area: 47,000 sq km (18,150 sq mi)
Population (2002 est.): 721,000 (excluding more than 100,000 refugees in Nepal)
Capital: Thimphu
Head of state: Druk Gyalpo (King) Jigme Singye Wangchuk
Head of government: Chairmen of Council of Ministers Lyonpo Khandu Wangchuk and, from August 14, Lyonpo Kinzang Dorji

The political situation in Bhutan continued to be stable at both the national and the district levels in 2002. In mid-August Lyonpo Kinzang Dorji replaced Lyonpo Khandu Wangchuk as prime minister, but the rest of the cabinet remained intact. The king stated that the cabinet's primary tasks would continue to be to expel the three Indian local political forces from Assam and West Bengal from the bases they had established in southern Bhutan, to complete the draft of the new constitution by the end of October, and to implement the ninth economic development plan.

Several rounds of talks had been held with the Assamese (ULFA) and the BODO militants since 1998. Though both groups had agreed to close down the bases that they had established on Bhutanese territory, as of mid-2002 several of these camps were still functioning. In addition, a new Indian group, the Kamatapur Liberation Organisation, based in West Bengal, established camps on Bhutanese territory. Bhutan continued its talks with India on this issue, and agreement was reached that this was an issue of concern to both governments and that India "was fully behind" the Bhutan government.

Bhutan's discussions with Nepal on the Bhutanese in "refugee camps" in southeastern Nepal continued, and some progress was made in resolving this dispute. Bhutan also held meetings with China, Australia, and Singapore. Bhutan's economy continued to flourish in 2001–02.   (LEO E. ROSE)

BOLIVIA

Area: 1,098,581 sq km (424,164 sq mi)
Population (2002 est.): 8,401,000
Capitals: La Paz (administrative) and Sucre (judicial)
Head of state and government: Presidents Jorge Quiroga Ramírez and, from August 6, Gonzalo Sánchez de Lozada

Hundreds of coca growers from the Chapare region of Bolivia face off with riot police near Cochabamba on January 16.

The social unrest that had been brewing in Bolivia for several years left its imprint on the June 2002 elections, in which Evo Morales Ayma, leader of the union representing growers of illegal coca crops, staged a surprising second-place finish. Morales drew support from voters disillusioned with the failure of market-oriented economic policies to ease the poverty afflicting more than 60% of Bolivians and with the continuing influence of the United States in Bolivian affairs. Gonzalo Sánchez de Lozada, a mining magnate and former president, claimed 22.4% of the vote against 20.9% for Morales. The Bolivian Congress, which chooses the president if no candidate wins a majority, picked Sánchez de Lozada after he unexpectedly reached a coalition agreement with former president Jaime Paz Zamora. The new cabinet included seven ministers from Paz Zamora's Movement of the Revolutionary Left. Acknowledging the appeal of Morales and other rival candidates, Sánchez de Lozada promised a "social pact to get Bolivia out of this terrible economic crisis." He pledged to double public investment and to improve public education with profits from Pacific LNG, a huge project to export natural gas to Mexico and the U.S.

Controversy continued over the U.S.-supported program to eradicate coca plantations. Clashes involving coca growers, police, and soldiers claimed 14 lives between August 2001 and March 2002, and an elite U.S.-financed Bolivian army unit supporting eradication efforts was accused of committing human rights abuses. During the presidential campaign Morales called for the expulsion of U.S. Drug Enforcement Administration agents from Bolivia. U.S. Ambassador Manuel Rocha then warned that U.S. aid would be threatened if "those who want Bolivia again to be a cocaine exporter" were elected. His statement led leading candidates to protest against interference in Bolivian affairs.

In the Chapare coca-growing region, where the average income had fallen by two-thirds since 1998, about 20,000 farmers were receiving international aid. The eradication campaign was accompanied by incentives to switch to bananas, black pepper, and palm hearts, but farmers complained that the alternative crops were far harder than coca to grow and market. Sánchez de Lozada and Morales held meetings in September to explore solutions to the coca problem, but Interior Minister

Alberto Gasser Vargas said the eradication program was not negotiable.

The Pacific LNG project revived landlocked Bolivia's dream of recovering permanent access to the sea, which it had lost to Chile in the 19th century. Bolivian gas was to be piped to a Pacific Ocean port and liquefied there for export. The government faced a choice between port sites in Chile and Peru. The British-Spanish-American consortium promoting the scheme said the cheapest route lay through Chile, but support for a Peruvian port grew stronger after the Peruvian government offered a renewable 99-year lease on a coastal site where Bolivia could enforce its own laws and tax regimes. There were reports that Chile and Bolivia were discussing a similar proposal.

(PAUL KNOX)

BOSNIA AND HERZEGOVINA

Area: 51,129 sq km (19,741 sq mi)
Population (2002 est.): 3,964,000
Capital: Sarajevo
Heads of state: Nominally a tripartite presidency chaired by Jozo Krizanovic, Beriz Belkic, from February 14 and, from October 28, Mirko Sarovic; final authority resides in the Office of the High Representative, Wolfgang Petritsch (Austria) and, from May 27, Paddy Ashdown, Baron Ashdown (U.K.)
Head of government: Prime Ministers Zlatko Lagumdzija, Dragan Mikerevic from March 15, and, from December 23, Adnan Terzic

Despite the political efforts of the international community and the more than $5 billion that had flowed into the country over the previous six years, Bosnia and Herzegovina in 2002 remained enmeshed in a profound economic and social crisis. In October nationalist parties won in general elections organized without international supervision for the first time since war broke out in 1992. The elections were held for the multiethnic three-member presidency, the legislatures for the Croat-Muslim Federation and the Bosnian Serb Republic entities, the president and vice president of the Bosnian Serb Republic, and the cantonal governments. Electoral turnout was low. According to High Commissioner Paddy Ashdown, the elections

met international standards, and the results suggested a backlash against reforms by moderates over the previous two years rather than a victory for nationalists.

The nationalist-oriented parties—the Muslim Party of Democratic Action, the Serbian Democratic Party, and the Croatian Democratic Union—had little room to maneuver, because of new election laws and constitutional changes handed down in April by then high commissioner Wolfgang Petritsch. Muslims, Serbs, and Croats were now politically equal throughout the federation, and government positions were expected to be filled more equitably. The newly elected government representatives would also rule for four years rather than two, as they had previously. In keeping with an ethnic-quota system based on the 1991 census, the changes attempted to undercut the foundations of the ethnic-oriented political entities. After the election, however, nationalists quickly made it clear that they would not be intimidated. Bosnian Serb leaders reiterated that the Bosnian Serb Republic had to remain Serb.

Ashdown also issued a series of decrees after the elections aimed at improving the country's business climate and at strengthening his own powers. In keeping with the constitutional changes, his approval would henceforth be required for many ministerial appointments and decrees on the formation of governments. The move also anticipated the formal withdrawal of the United Nations peacekeeping mission at the end of the year.

The situation remained bleak in both entities as the economy continued its downward spiral amid frequent labour and civil unrest. Almost 50% of the active labour force remained unemployed, and the average monthly wage of workers stood at about $250. Foreign capital investment was lacking because of the region's political instability, rampant corruption, and confusing tax codes and business regulations that forced much economic activity underground.

Reforms had also so far failed to unite the separate and antagonistic educational systems, and widespread ethnic distrust remained. In July, when several thousand people gathered in Srebrenica to mark the seventh anniversary of the massacre of as many as 8,000 Muslim males by Bosnian Serb forces, none of the invited leaders of the Bosnian Serb Republic attended, and local Serbs reportedly jeered the mourners and held up pictures of in-

dicted war criminals Gen. Ratko Mladic (who had commanded the Srebrenica forces) and Radovan Karadzic.

(MILAN ANDREJEVICH)

BOTSWANA

Area: 582,356 sq km (224,848 sq mi)
Population (2002 est.): 1,679,000
Capital: Gaborone
Head of state and government: President Festus Mogae

In June 2002 it was confirmed that Botswana's international credit rating had risen higher than that of Japan. Relative standards of living were indicated by the fact that there were 22 cell phones for every 100 people, but 23% of adults were undernourished. Because of the increasing grip of HIV/AIDS, the country slipped farther down the United Nations Development Programme human development index, but Botswana was the only country in the region that provided antiretroviral therapy through its public health service.

Transparency International found low levels of corruption in Botswana, but the international nongovernmental organization was critical of secrecy in government bureaucracy. National debate on the political representation and land rights of ethnic minorities continued. Pres. Festus Mogae periodically toured the country during the year seeking opinions on this question in open assemblies.

After February 1 the government no longer trucked in water supplies for people living in the Central Kalahari Game Reserve. Khoe and San Bushmen were directed to settlements elsewhere for government-provided services, including water. Possibly as many as 60 people who made their living by hunting elected to stay within the reserve but were threatened by antipoaching measures. An estimated 65,000 Khoe and San continued to live elsewhere in Botswana, some in destitution. Wildlife tourism in Chobe and Okavango suffered from a downturn in tourism because of events in neighbouring Zimbabwe.

English-born Lady Khama, the former Ruth Williams, died at her home near Gaborone on May 23. In 1948 her marriage to Seretse Khama, later Botswana's president, had aroused racist ire around the world.   (NEIL PARSONS)

BRAZIL

Area: 8,514,047 sq km (3,287,292 sq mi)
Population (2002 est.): 174,619,000
Capital: Brasília
Head of state and government: President Fernando Henrique Cardoso

With his wife, Marisa, at his side, Brazilian President-elect Lula waves to supporters during his victory speech on October 27.
AP/Wide World Photos

The October 2002 elections for president, the legislature (Federal Senate and Chamber of Deputies), governorships, and state assemblies dominated the year's events in Brazil. Unable to stand for reelection, Pres. Fernando Henrique Cardoso would in January 2003 oversee the first transition of a democratically elected president to a democratically elected successor in Brazil in more than 40 years.

Entering 2002 the three front-runners for the presidency were "Lula" (Luiz Inácio da Silva; *see* BIOGRAPHIES) of the leftist Workers' Party (PT), Roseana Sarney of the centre-right Liberal Front Party (PFL), and government-backed candidate José Serra of the Brazilian Social Democratic Party (PSDB). The spectre of political violence emerged early on. On January 20 the body of Celso Augusto Daniel, mayor of Santo Andre, was discovered riddled with bullets on a dirt road outside São Paulo. Daniel, who had been kidnapped two days earlier, had been a moderate voice in the PT and was responsible for preparing the government program for Lula. This was the second murder of a PT mayor in São Paulo state in six months, the first having been the September 2001 assassination of Campinas Mayor Antônio da Costa Santos. Responding to the killings, Cardoso stated, "Violence has surpassed all reasonable limits in Brazil....We need a war against organized crime, against banditry in Brazil, and against impunity." Adding to the terror, on February 2 the headquarters of Unified Labour Central, a PT-influenced labour union, was broken into and robbed. Claiming responsibility for the mayoral murders was an unknown group, the Brazilian Revolutionary Action Front.

On March 1 a federal circuit court judge issued an order for federal police to conduct a search-and-seizure operation in São Luis, Maranhão state, at the offices of the Lunus consultancy, owned by PFL presidential candidate and the governor of Maranhão, Roseana Sarney, and her husband, State Planning Secretary Jorge Murad. Finding about $570,000 in cash at the offices, authorities alleged that Lunus had benefited from a corruption scheme involving the defunct Superintendency for Development of the Amazon. The federal Supreme Court quashed the investigation, however, ruling that only it was imbued with powers to judge governors accused of crimes. Viewing the allegations as a political maneuver by the government to bring down the ascending candidacy of Sarney, the PFL formally broke its seven-year alliance with the PSDB. On March 4 four PFL cabinet ministers resigned their posts. Sarney withdrew her candidacy for president on April 13, though she decided to run for the Senate in Maranhão.

On September 13 Lula addressed the Superior War College and the Air Force Club, which included the leaders of the high command of three branches of the armed forces. In an effort to assuage military fears of his candidacy, Lula gave his views on foreign policy, national defense, and the role of the armed forces, stressing compulsory military service, investments in defense, and a review of Brazil's participation in the Nuclear Non-proliferation Treaty and agreement with the U.S. concerning use of the Alcântara satellite base.

On October 6 more than 94 million Brazilians went to the polls in first-round elections. With no candidate receiving a majority of the valid votes cast for president, Lula (46.4%) and Serra (23.2%) competed in a second-round runoff election on October 27. During the lead-up to the second round, the third- and fourth-place finishers, Anthony Garotinho of the Brazilian Socialist Party and Ciro Ferreira Gomes of the Popular Socialist Party, threw their support behind Lula. With an overwhelming 62% of the valid votes, Lula was elected president on October 27. On his coattails the PT became the largest party in the 513-seat lower house, increasing its numbers from 58 to 91 seats, followed by the PFL (84), the Brazilian Democratic Movement Party (74), and the PSDB (71). The gubernatorial landscape was markedly different, however, with a number of parties winning states; the PSDB led the way with seven states, the PT claiming only three.

President-elect Lula named the mayor of Ribeirão Prêto, Antônio Palocci, to lead his transition team. To facilitate the transfer of power, Cardoso created a transition team with ministerial status. The PT platform, launched on June 23 and titled "Change Without Rupture," stressed, among other provisions, an end to hunger, more job creation, economic growth of 5% per annum, and a reduction in the workweek from 44 to 40 hours. The PT also promised to continue to maintain a floating exchange rate with inflation targets and to honour the privatizations concluded and under way.

Beset with political uncertainty, Brazil faced volatile foreign exchange markets in 2002. The Brazilian real lost ground against the U.S. dollar, beginning the year at R$2.30 and topping R$4 in trading on October 10. By mid-November the real had strengthened to R$3.50 to the dollar. To mitigate damage caused by a weak currency, the central bank on October 11 implemented several measures to remove the real from the market, increasing the reserve requirement from 48% to 53% on checking deposits and from 23% to 30% for savings deposits. Banks were limited to using only their own funds on the exchange market, which could not exceed 30% of their net assets, and on October 14 the monetary policy committee raised its benchmark interest rate from 18%—where it had been for most of the year—to 21%.

The official expanded consumer price index (IPCA), which the government used for its inflation targets with the International Monetary Fund, revealed inflation to have been 7.67% in 2001. In the 12 months leading up to October 2002, the IPCA had accumulated inflation of 7.4%. In 2001 the Brazilian Census Bureau reported weak industrial growth of gross domestic product of 1.5%.

On June 30, led by star Ronaldo (*see* BIOGRAPHIES) and coach Felipão, Brazil won its fifth World Cup association football (soccer) championship by defeating Germany 2–0. The national team returned to Brasília on July 2 to a record assembly of 400,000 fans in the streets. The victory complemented World Cups from 1958, 1962, 1970, and 1994 and gave Brazil more World Cup titles than any other country.

(JOHN CHARLES CUTTINO)

BRUNEI

Area: 5,765 sq km (2,226 sq mi)
Population (2002 est.): 351,000
Capital: Bandar Seri Begawan
Head of state and government: Sultan and Prime Minister Haji Hassanal Bolkiah Mu'izzaddin Waddaulah

In 2002 Brunei recovered somewhat from the adverse international publicity and the multibillion-dollar financial loss that had been brought about by the 1998 collapse of the Amedeo Development Corp. Prince Jeffri Bolkiah, the sultan's youngest brother, had been sued by the state in 2001 for squandering public funds on Amedeo projects. The affair generated what by Brunei standards was a high volume of insolvency-oriented litigation. The cases were largely settled out of court, however, and the government was thus left room to focus on domestic development.

Sluggish economic growth and rising unemployment were the main causes of concern in Brunei. Measures aimed at jump starting the economy included the establishment of a national oil company, the creation of two new territorial sectors for oil and gas exploration, the establishment of the Brunei Economic Development Board to develop strategies for attracting foreign investment, and the reduction of car tariffs to a flat 20% from a variable rate that had ranged from 20% to 200%.

Two new cabinet ministers, one for development and the other for health, were named during the year, and new appointments were made at the deputy ministers' and permanent secretaries' levels. In August Brunei hosted another high-profile international meeting, the 9th ASEAN (Association of Southeast Asian Nations) Regional Forum, which was chaired by Brunei Foreign Minister Prince Mohammed. The meeting was attended by U.S. Secretary of State Colin Powell, who signed a U.S.-ASEAN antiterrorism pact.

(B.A. HUSSAINMIYA)

BULGARIA

Area: 110,971 sq km (42,846 sq mi)
Population (2002 est.): 7,890,000
Capital: Sofia
Chief of state: Presidents Petar Stoyanov and, from January 22, Georgi Purvanov
Head of government: Prime Minister Simeon Saxecoburggotski

Bulgarian political life in 2002 was influenced by the need for national unity pending decisions on the country's applications to join NATO and the European Union (EU). This meant that a number of confrontations were softened, though not eliminated.

There were considerable differences between the prime minister and the new, socialist president, Georgi Purvanov, who assumed office on January 22, but both men played them down for the appearance of national unity. There were also tensions between the prime minister's main supporters in the National Movement Simeon II (NDSV); in April the NSDV reorganized itself as a political party with the prime minister (and former king) as its leader.

Crime and corruption remained visible. A serious embarrassment occurred on March 21 when a newspaper published the minutes of an October 2001 cabinet meeting. The minutes appeared to show that in awarding a contract for the reform of Bulgaria's customs authorities, the government had evaded the Public Procurement Act; the question was who had arranged or paid for such a leak from which only the illegal smuggling groups could profit. During the summer suspicions were also rife about favouritism in the privatization of the large tobacco concern, Bulgartabak.

The government pursued tight economic policies, which intensified some social tensions. The most notable protest came in mid-February when the largely Roma (Gypsy) population of the Plovdiv suburb of Stolipinovo rioted for three days after the electricity company cut off their supplies because of nonpayment of bills. Another provincial protest was staged in August by people living near Stara Zagora who feared that their health would be endangered by the decommissioning of Bulgaria's stockpile of SS-23 missiles stationed near the town. There was also anger at the end of May when the European Union commissioner for enlargement appeared to dictate when the Bulgarian government had to close two further reactors at the Kozloduy nuclear power complex. In November Bulgaria was invited to join NATO along with six other European nations.

In February the long-awaited trial of six Bulgarian medical workers accused of having deliberately infected 393 children with HIV—begun in 2001 but then postponed—recommenced in Libya. The case was referred to a lower court, but hopes for a final decision had not been fulfilled at year's end.

On May 23 Pope John Paul II arrived for a four-day visit during which he expressed his conviction that there had been no Bulgarian involvement in the attempt to assassinate him in 1981.

(RICHARD J. CRAMPTON)

BURKINA FASO

Area: 274,400 sq km (105,946 sq mi)
Population (2002 est.): 12,603,000
Capital: Ouagadougou
Chief of state: President Blaise Compaoré
Head of government: Prime Minister Ernest Paramanga Yonli

In Burkina Faso's parliamentary elections, held on May 5, 2002, Pres. Blaise Compaoré's Congress for Democracy and Progress barely maintained its majority, winning 57 of 111 seats—44 fewer than in the previous parliament. The Alliance for Democracy and Federation/African Democratic Rally became the major opposition party after securing 17 seats; the remaining seats were distributed among 11 other parties.

In February human rights campaigners accused the government of carrying out extrajudicial killings in its campaign against a recent upsurge of armed robberies. Despite the government's swift denial of the allegations, Amnesty International called for an official investigation. On March 4 Burkina Faso announced that it would allocate $7.75 million to compensate families and victims of past human rights abuses.

The economic picture was mixed. In 2001 cotton had constituted some 60% of Burkina Faso's total exports and had been a major factor behind the achievement of a 5.7% growth in gross domestic product. In 2002, however, despite a 36% increase in production, cotton growers faced a crisis as world prices continued to drop. The International Monetary Fund, the World Bank, and the African Development Bank granted Burkina Faso more than $1 billion in debt relief as well as substantial amounts of development aid. In April and again in July, the capital was hit by a wave of strikes as thousands of workers demonstrated against low wages and plans for continued privatization.

(NANCY ELLEN LAWLER)

BURUNDI

Area: 27,816 sq km (10,740 sq mi)
Population (2002 est.): 6,373,000 (including 350,000 refugees in Tanzania)
Capital: Bujumbura
Head of state and government: President Pierre Buyoya

Heavy fighting between Burundi government forces and rebel groups continued throughout 2002 amid several attempts to broker cease-fire agreements. In November 2001, a transitional government headed by Pres. Pierre Buyoya, a minority Tutsi, was created to share power with the majority Hutu after 39 years of Tutsi political dominance. Two Hutu rebel groups, the National Liberation Front (FNL) and the Forces for Defense of Democracy (FDD), refused to participate in the power-sharing government, however, and entered into peace negotiations with the transitional government. Peace talks scheduled to begin on July 18 between the government and the three main Hutu-led rebel groups were stalled owing to heavy fighting between rebels and the army in Bujumbura. The Burundi defense minister accused Tanzania of aiding the rebels in the fighting that had broken out earlier that month. The Tanzanian government, which had hosted the peace negotiations, flatly denied the accusations.

In the ongoing effort to end Burundi's nine-year civil war, South African Deputy Pres. Jacob Zuma chaired cease-fire negotiations in Tanzania between the Bujumbura government and the main rebel groups. Government officials and Col. Jean-Bosco Ndayikengurukiye, the head of the FDD rebel group, signed a draft peace accord in late August, with a resumption of talks scheduled for September 16. Attempts to start peace talks between the FNL and the government failed. Thirty civilians were reportedly killed and 1,500 others displaced when fighting broke out on August 27 between government troops and rebels in the hills surrounding Bujumbura. Government officials denied the civilian casualties, but witnesses fleeing the violence said at least 17 women and 7 children had been killed. The September talks were suspended when the FDD walked out after the government admitted that its forces had killed 173 civilians in Gitega province during an intense firefight with FDD rebels earlier in the month.

Repatriation of Burundi refugees living in Tanzania began in March. By the end of May, more than 12,000 refugees had returned home, and another 58,000 had signed up with the United Nations High Commissioner for Refugees to return home.

(MARY F.E. EBELING)

(Seated, from left to right) Burundian Pres. Pierre Buyoya and rebel leaders Jean-Bosco Ndayikengurukiye and Alain Mugarabona sign a cease-fire agreement in October.

CAMBODIA

Area: 181,035 sq km (69,898 sq mi)
Population (2002 est.): 13,414,000
Capital: Phnom Penh
Chief of state: King Norodom Sihanouk
Head of government: Prime Minister Hun Sen

On Feb. 8, 2002, after five years of discussions about establishing an international tribunal to try perpetrators of Khmer Rouge atrocities in the 1970s, UN Secretary-General Kofi Annan abandoned the effort and blamed the intransigence of Cambodian Prime Minister Hun Sen. For his part, Hun Sen, faced with inevitable political destabilization if he capitulated to the demands of Western nations, allowed the matter to lapse until the end of the year, when he referred vaguely to finding a new formula. In September, however, two former Khmer Rouge commanders were convicted of the 1994 murder of three Western travelers. UN High Commissioner for Human Rights Mary Robinson visited Phnom Penh in August and strongly criticized corruption and nepotism in the government and the judiciary. Earlier, the U.S. Immigration and Naturalization Service, unhappy with transparency issues, had ended American adoption of Cambodian infants.

The February 3 elections for 1,621 local communes were observed by thousands of neutral international and local poll watchers. Credible cases of intimidation were reported, but the result, a resounding victory for Hun Sen's Cambodian People's Party, was not in doubt. The opposition Sam Rainsy Party, named for its leader, captured only 13 councils, while the royalist Funcinpec Party (FP), which had won 45% of the vote in the 1993 UN-run polls, scored only 22% and took control of just 10 councils. This dealt a blow to party leader Prince Norodom Ranariddh, son of King Norodom Sihanouk. All parties began preparations for the 2003 National Assembly elections, but internal divisions during the FP March annual congress further marginalized the once-dominant royalists. You Hokry, its all-powerful cominister of the interior, appeared isolated from the party mainstream. The National Election Committee, widely criticized for a perceived pro-government stance, was marked for reform, and in July Hun Sen announced that he preferred nonpolitical outsiders, putting himself at odds with the other parties, who feared he would dominate selections.

As King Sihanouk approached his 80th birthday, questions arose about the succession. The UN-brokered 1993 constitution stipulated that a Throne Council, made up of legislative leaders, should nominate any suitable descendant of three related 19th-century kings. Hun Sen clearly favoured choosing a successor who would keep out of politics. This seemed to rule out Prince Ranariddh. The mercurial monarch himself weighed in with a threat (not his first) to abdicate and throw the country into constitutional turmoil. The king, ailing for decades, clearly wished to influence the succession, even proposing that Queen Monineath be appointed regent, but Hun Sen seemed unwilling to discuss the matter.

The World Bank twice—in June and September—delayed payment of the structural adjustment credit upon which the government relied for general expenditures, including civil service salaries. Phnom Penh blamed slow progress in legal reforms, but inability to satisfy the World Bank on accounting seemed a more probable cause. In September, however, the bank announced support for demobilization of surplus soldiers. The brightest star on the economic horizon was the continuing growth of tourism, especially at Angkor Wat, where privately funded infrastructure and hotel building showed no sign of diminishing.

(ROBERT WOODROW)

CAMEROON

Area: 475,442 sq km (183,569 sq mi)
Population (2002 est.): 16,185,000
Capital: Yaoundé
Chief of state: President Paul Biya
Head of government: Prime Minister Peter Mafany Musonge

Pres. Paul Biya's Cameroon People's Democratic Movement crushed the opposition in the country's June 30, 2002, legislative elections, increasing its majority of the 180 seats from 116 to 133. Despite opposition charges of widespread fraud, observers representing the Commonwealth and the United Nations declared the elections to have been generally fair, although marred by poor preparation and disorganization at the polls. The Supreme Court still voided the results in 9 districts (17 seats) owing to voting irregularities and set new elections for September 15. John Fru Ndi's Social Democratic Front did poorly in the elections, retaining only 21 of its 43 seats and managing to hold on to control of 10 municipal councils. Ndi's brief threat to boycott the parliament and the municipal councils was rescinded, however, on July 12. The new government, announced on August 25, contained a sprinkling of opposition members, and 20 ministers would be serving in the cabinet for the first time.

In mid-February the International Court of Justice began hearings on the long-standing dispute between Nigeria and Cameroon over ownership of the Bakassi peninsula. The court awarded the oil-rich peninsula to Cameroon in October.

Oil company officials announced on April 8 that construction of infrastructure for the Chad-Cameroon pipeline had begun and that they anticipated production in Chad to be under way by 2004. The controversial undertaking, opposed by many environmental groups in both countries, was expected to bring Cameroon $500 million in transit fees and taxes over the projected 25–30-year life of the scheme.

The government on March 26 inaugurated a $6 million, three-year program to combat AIDS. Its goal was to reduce the national HIV infection rate to less than 10%.

(NANCY ELLEN LAWLER)

CANADA

Area: 9,984,670 sq km (3,855,103 sq mi)
Population (2002 est.): 31,244,000
Capital: Ottawa
Chief of state: Queen Elizabeth II, represented by Governor-General Adrienne Clarkson
Head of government: Prime Minister Jean Chrétien

Domestic Affairs. National politics in Canada in 2002 were dominated by questions of party leadership. The differences were not confined to the opposition parties, however, and emerged in the governing Liberal Party. Prime Minister Jean Chrétien faced a revolt against his continuation as party chief. Many Liberals believed that it was time for Chrétien to step down. At age 68, he had been a member of Parliament, with a short break, since 1963, but he showed little vision for the country. His style of governance also had become increasingly authoritarian.

Disaffection in the Liberal Party gathered around Minister of Finance Paul Martin. He and Chrétien had been rivals in the contest to head the party in 1990, and, although Martin had been a mainstay of the Chrétien administration, there was bitter animosity between them. Besides the bitterness left from their 1990 rivalry, Chrétien believed that Martin was soft when it came to facing the threat posed by nationalists in Quebec. Martin barely concealed his ambition to succeed Chrétien. On June 2, citing "irreconcilable differences," Chrétien dropped Martin from his cabinet. Martin remained in Parliament and immediately mustered support for his leadership bid.

The Liberals had planned to hold a convention to review Chrétien's position as leader in February 2003. By the end of the summer, however, evidence had emerged that Martin's supporters had won over a majority of Liberal MPs. At a closed-door caucus of the party on August 21, Chrétien dramatically announced that he would retire by February 2004. The 18-month period would give him time to fulfill his personal agenda, including the reform of the health care system, alleviation of child poverty, and protection of the environment. His plan was intended to avoid a divisive battle over his leadership and allow potential successors to come forward. The move might also damage Martin's bid, however, for he would reach the age of 65 in the early months of 2004.

Although Chrétien's decision resulted in a truce, it did not guarantee harmony beyond the short term. A contest between senior ministers might divert them from the task of carrying out the government's agenda, a program that Chrétien said would constitute his legacy. The agenda items were costly for a government facing a shrinking surplus. Having balanced the budget five years earlier, the Chrétien adminis-

tration prided itself on its ability to maintain fiscal discipline.

Chrétien's own favourite successor emerged through a number of cabinet shuffles beginning on January 15, when 30 ministers were moved or replaced. John Manley (*see* BIOGRAPHIES), minister for foreign affairs since October 2000, was promoted to deputy prime minister with a long list of executive responsibilities. Bill Graham, a backbencher who had chaired the standing committee on international affairs in the House of Commons, replaced Manley as foreign minister. Following

During a ceremony at Rideau Hall in Ottawa on June 2, John Manley is sworn in as Canada's minister of finance as Prime Minister Jean Chrétien (background) looks on.

Martin's dismissal Manley also was given the finance minister's post—an action that showed clearly that he possessed Chrétien's confidence. The Liberals, with 169 seats in the 301-seat Commons, possessed a comfortable majority. Public opinion polls also showed that the Liberals held only slightly less support across the country than did the combined fragmented opposition.

Leadership changes occurred or were pending in Canada's other political groupings. The official opposition—the Western-based Canadian Alliance—had been damaged severely in 2001 by a bit-

ter dispute over the performance of its chief, Stockwell Day, who was challenged by several contenders, including former party strategist Stephen Harper. Harper, who believed in smaller government, strict fiscal management, and policies that treated Quebec on the same basis as other provinces, won 55% of the votes of Alliance members in a mail-in ballot. After replacing Day, Harper went on to win a parliamentary seat in Calgary on May 13, and eight days later he was sworn in as leader of the opposition. Although the Alliance's 63 Commons seats made it the largest opposition party, polls showed that its national support stood at only 14%. Harper sought to remain true to the party's founding principles, which were strongly endorsed in the West, but he needed to broaden the Alliance's appeal. He also had to grapple with the split among conservative voters. Harper had long pressed for cooperation with the historic Progressive Conservative Party, but the PCP rejected the Alliance's overtures.

The PCP, with 14 members of Parliament, was faced with selecting a new leader when former prime minister Joe Clark, who had led the party since 1998, announced his retirement on August 6. At 63, with 30 years of parliamentary and ministerial experience, Clark was a veteran of Canadian politics. In spite of strenuous efforts to rebuild the party after its disastrous defeat in 1993, the PCP commanded the support of only 15% of the electorate. Clark believed that it was time for him to give up the struggle.

With the parties of the centre and right facing leadership choices, Canada's New Democratic Party (NDP) also moved to elect a new leader. Through the 1990s the party had struggled to define its role. In 1995 the NDP had turned to Alexa McDonough to serve as its leader. McDonough had sought to move the party to a more middle-of-the-road position. In 2002 the NDP held 14 seats in the Commons, but its popular vote across the country was stalled at 12%. Faced with these discouraging facts, McDonough tendered her resignation. Canada's fourth opposition party, the Bloc Québécois (BQ), the federalist arm of the Quebec separatist movement, seemed a spent force in 2002. As Quebec's push for independence declined, the 37 BQ members seemed unsure of their purpose.

The fractured political opposition in Canada worked to the clear advantage of Chrétien and the Liberals. Despite ministerial scandal and financial irregularities, the Liberal government remained impregnable. Although opposition parties had regularly demanded an accounting from the Liberal government, they found difficulty in defining political positions for themselves.

The Economy. The economy moved forward steadily in 2002. The turmoil on the stock markets brought down the value of many Canadian equities but did not interrupt the economy's growth. The proportion of Canadians who held stocks was half that in the United States, and there were no corporate scandals in Canadian business. Job creation was strong, with the unemployment rate hovering above 7%. The consumer price index stood at 3.2% in October, pushed upward by energy costs. For the economy on the whole, the increase in gross domestic product was expected to rise 3–4% to the end of 2003. This upsurge gave Canada the strongest rate of growth among the Group of Seven industrialized nations. Canada regained the Triple-A credit rating that it had lost in 1993–94, when the federal operating deficit had stood at $42 billion. Since 1998 Ottawa's budget had enjoyed a surplus.

A severe drought, reminiscent of the dust-bowl conditions of the 1930s, settled over the Western prairies in 2002. Overall wheat production was expected to decline 40% from 2001, which in itself was considered an off year. To add to the farmers' misery, an infestation of grasshoppers consumed surviving crops. The federal and provincial governments stepped in to help, but the most heartening assistance came from farmers in Eastern Canada, who sent several hundred railcars of surplus hay to distressed farmers in the west.

Foreign Affairs. Reverberations from the 2001 terrorist attacks in the United States spurred the government of Canada to strengthen the country's security and join in the international coalition against global terrorism. Canada took swift steps to make a contribution to the international effort. In January 850 troops were prepared for service in Afghanistan to work under U.S. Army command in the search for al-Qaeda fighters. This was the largest deployment of Canadian combat forces since the Korean War. The troops, who were stationed in the Kandahar area of southern Afghanistan, were sent to guard the Kandahar airport and to investigate sites taken from the Taliban. A naval detachment of six vessels to patrol the Arabian Sea and a small group of transport and surveillance aircraft brought

another 1,700 personnel to the troubled region. The overall size of Canadian defense forces, combined with the earlier commitment of 2,000 peacekeepers to Bosnia and Herzegovina, made it difficult for Canada to continue its military involvement in Afghanistan. The force was withdrawn in August.

Satisfaction with the mission was marred by an unfortunate incident on April 17, when four Canadian soldiers were killed by a 227-kg (500-lb) bomb dropped by a U.S. Air National Guard F-16 pilot. The Canadians were on a night-training exercise near Kandahar. The two countries set up boards of inquiry to investigate the accident, which apparently resulted from the failure of the U.S. pilot to observe his force's rules of engagement.

Canada did not adopt a firm position on a possible United States strike on Iraq to topple Saddam Hussein and stop his alleged accumulation of weapons of mass destruction. At the United Nations, Canada had long criticized Iraq for its refusal, after 1998, to accept UN weapons inspectors. Foreign Minister Graham declared that Iraq's barring of the inspectors suggested that it had something to hide. Graham cautioned that the United States should not intervene unilaterally but should seek UN approval for any action taken. It was also important that the United States present evidence of Hussein's stockpile of weapons. Chrétien made it clear that Canada would not participate

in military action against Iraq unless it were carried out under UN auspices.

Canada played host to the Group of Eight summit of leading industrialized nations on June 26–27. The meeting, in Kananaskis, Alta., deep in the Canadian Rockies, was undisturbed by the violent demonstrations that had taken place at past summits. About 200 demonstrators gathered outside a security checkpoint, however, and blocked the admission of U.S. and Japanese delegates. Chrétien, who chaired the meeting, hoped to focus on assistance to Africa contingent upon African states' maintaining democratic political systems and protecting human rights. Earlier it had been proposed that wealthy nations pledge an additional $12 billion in development assistance annually, of which half would go to Africa. At the Kananaskis summit this objective was reaffirmed but with the crucial qualification that the new aid could go to Africa. Canada and several other countries at the meeting agreed to open their domestic markets to most African products. U.S. Pres. George W. Bush then proposed to raise $20 billion over the next 10 years to decommission nuclear arms and place strict security around nuclear, biological, and chemical weapons storage sites. Bush's plan proved contentious, and no firm commitment was made by the leaders.

Canada's declaration that it would ratify the Kyoto Protocol to reduce the emission of greenhouse gases in 2002 proved controversial but was achieved

Vehicles driven by demonstrators protesting the Group of Eight summit meeting in Kananaskis, Alta., line a road outside a security checkpoint on June 26.

AP/Wide World Photos

by a parliamentary vote on December 10. There were sharp disagreements between the provinces regarding the costs of approving Kyoto. The most vociferous opposition came from Ralph Klein, premier of oil-and-gas-rich Alberta. The province's energy production had been hurt by federal regulation in the 1980s, and Klein had no intention of allowing Ottawa to impose controls on his province again. Since the Canadian provinces owned the natural resources within their boundaries, their cooperation with federal regulation appeared vital for the implementation of the accord.

Trade relations between Canada and the U.S. remained troubled in 2002. The chief issue was the U.S. Department of Commerce's decision to impose final duties averaging 27% on $10 billion worth of Canadian construction lumber exported to the U.S. Canadian lumber exports to the U.S. in June, the first full month after the duties were confirmed, fell by 40%.

Canada also was unhappy, as were many other countries, with the U.S. approval of $190 billion in agricultural subsidies over 10 years, a plan signed by President Bush on May 13. Canadian grain exports would be hurt by this form of protection.

(DAVID M.L. FARR)

CAPE VERDE

Area: 4,033 sq km (1,557 sq mi)
Population (2002 est.): 453,000
Capital: Praia
Chief of state: President Pedro Pires
Head of government: Prime Minister José Maria Neves

In his 2002 New Year's message to the island nation, Pres. Pedro Pires praised workers for not demanding higher wages in a difficult economic climate and appealed to the large number of Cape Verdeans living abroad to help their country. When in January he promulgated the general state budget without having secured the necessary two-thirds in the parliament, the main opposition party, the Movement for Democracy (MPD) reacted with outrage. Claiming that Pires had no respect for the democratic process and had become a de facto dictator, the

Fans surround Mandatta (centre)—the Central African Republic's top recording star—during a performance at a nightclub in Bangui.

© 2002 Nick Kelsh/from *A Day in the Life of Africa*

MPD organized a protest march in the capital and said that it would appeal to the Supreme Tribunal of Justice to test the constitutionality of the president's action. Pires claimed that he had no choice but to act because projects could not be delayed; in addition, pledges had been made to international financial institutions and development partners.

Though South African Airways continued to use Sal Island as a refueling stop for planes en route to the United States, the fragile Cape Verdean economy faced many problems. The country produced only about 10% of its annual food requirements, and a particularly dry season had much reduced the corn (maize) crop. As a result, the government requested help from the UN World Food Programme, which in June launched a $1.3 million emergency food operation to help feed some 30,000 Cape Verdeans on the islands of Santiago and Santo Antão. Meanwhile, HIV/AIDS was spreading rapidly.

(CHRISTOPHER SAUNDERS)

CENTRAL AFRICAN REPUBLIC

Area: 622,436 sq km (240,324 sq mi)
Population (2002 est.): 3,643,000
Capital: Bangui
Chief of state: President Ange-Félix Patassé
Head of government: Prime Minister Martin Ziguélé

The aftermath of an abortive coup attempt on May 28, 2001, continued to dominate the political scene in the Central African Republic in 2002. On February 15 the oft-postponed trials of 85 of the nearly 700 people accused of complicity in the coup began with the case against former defense minister Jean-Jacques Demafouth. Most of the defendants had already fled the country, although 69 were present in court. Former president André Kolingba, who was in Uganda while seeking asylum in another country, was the most notable absentee. On August 26 the court passed sentence on 600 people tried in absentia. Kolingba was sentenced to death, as were 21 coconspirators, including three of Kolingba's sons. Demafouth was acquitted in October.

In February the Organization of African Unity announced that it had petitioned the UN Security Council to send an international peacekeeping force to the Central African Republic once again. On February 12 a national disarmament campaign was launched in an attempt to reduce violence in the country. A nationwide curfew that had been enforced since the coup attempt was lifted on May 9. The killing of 11 Chadian herdsmen on the border between Chad and the Central African Republic in March heightened tensions between the two countries. In early August a clash left at least 20 soldiers dead, with each country accusing the other of having instigated the attack. A commission composed of UN officials and representatives from both countries toured the border area on August

21 to investigate the incidents. New clashes were reported in September.

(NANCY ELLEN LAWLER)

CHAD

Area: 1,284,000 sq km (495,755 sq mi)
Population (2002 est.): 8,997,000
Capital: N'Djamena
Chief of state: President Lieut. Gen. Idriss Déby
Head of government: Prime Ministers Nagoum Yamassoum and, from June 12, Haroun Kabadi

In January 2002, after mediation by Libya, the government of Chad signed a peace agreement with the Movement for Democracy and Justice in Chad (MDJT), which had been fighting since 1998 in the northern Tibesti region of the country, bordering Libya. The agreement provided for a cease-fire and amnesty for rebel fighters, and in February the Chad parliament passed the necessary amnesty legislation. The peace process moved slowly, but with the death of Youssouf Togoimi, the leader and founder of the MDJT (*see* OBITUARIES), in September of wounds received in a land-mine accident, the peace process was expected to gather momentum.

In April, when Pres. Idriss Déby met his Central African Republic counterpart in N'Djamena, the two agreed to the immediate reopening of their common border and called for a bilateral commission of experts and parliamentarians to address outstanding issues causing tension between the two countries.

The building of the pipeline from the Doba oil fields in southern Chad to the coast in Cameroon went ahead, though an inspection panel set up by the World Bank raised serious concerns over the project. The inspection team's report, which was leaked to critics of the project before the World Summit on Sustainable Development in Johannesburg, S.Af., suggested that the project might cause environmental damage, destroy the livelihood of people in the area affected, and fail to meet the bank's social and economic goals. The bank itself, however, seemed satisfied with the Chad government's

commitment to spending 80% of its oil revenues on the priority sectors of health, education, rural development, infrastructure, environment, and water.

The most spectacular news from Chad in 2002 was the report of the discovery of hominid fossil remains much older than any previously known—and far distant from earlier finds in the Rift Valley of Eastern Africa. (*See* ARCHAEOLOGY AND ANTHROPOLOGY: *Physical Anthropology.*)

(CHRISTOPHER SAUNDERS)

CHILE

Area: 756,096 sq km (291,930 sq mi)
Population (2002 est.): 15,082,000
Capitals: Santiago (national) and Valparaíso (legislative)
Head of state and government: President Ricardo Lagos Escobar

The end of 2002 marked the midway point of Chilean Pres. Ricardo Lagos Escobar's administration. Among its notable accomplishments was the continuing stability of Chile's economy, especially at a time of growing regional economic turbulence. In his annual address to the National Congress in May, Lagos highlighted the three top priorities for his government: fostering economic growth and achieving greater social justice and a fuller democracy.

The economic picture was mixed. Although Chile had avoided some of the deep economic problems that had plagued its neighbours, it had not avoided the fallout altogether. Economic growth, estimated to reach 2.8% for the year, still lagged behind the 6–7% growth rate of the 1990s, and, although the government had combated unemployment with significant job creation, the jobless rate remained stubbornly high at 9%. The region's economic problems had adversely affected foreign investment in Chile. There were, however, important positive economic signs. The continuing devaluation of the Chilean peso against the dollar helped the export sector. Inflation remained low at 2.6%, and the country's trade balance was positive. In May the government finalized a free-trade agreement with the European

Union (EU). The agreement helped protect Chile's crucial export sector at a time when other regions with which Chile traded, especially Latin America, were in an economic slump. Although Chilean trade was diversified, the European Union had become the country's top export destination. However, it also looked as if Chile might finally sign a free-trade agreement with the U.S. after eight years of discussion. Talks between the two countries were scheduled to continue through the end of the year in hopes of settling all outstanding concerns, such as labour and environmental issues and conflict-resolution mechanisms.

In terms of social justice, the Lagos administration continued to press for reforms to help reduce extreme poverty and improve public education and health care. One of the more controversial proposals had been Plan Auge, designed to correct problems in the health care system by guaranteeing universal health coverage for treatment of the 56 most common diseases. The plan was to be funded by tax increases. The Senate was debating another controversial bill that would legalize divorce.

Lagos also continued to press for reforms to eliminate undemocratic features of the 1980 Pinochet-era constitution, even threatening in September to call a plebiscite on the outstanding issues. These included eliminating an electoral system viewed as biased as well as nonelected senators. In November, however, the Lagos government's credibility was undercut by political corruption charges against six of its legislators.

In early July the Supreme Court reaffirmed that former president Gen. Augusto Pinochet was not fit to stand trial for human rights abuses. Even though Pinochet gave up his lifetime senatorial status, it was small consolation to human rights activists and victims' families; more than 250 cases against him were left unresolved. The Supreme Court also refused to extradite five Chilean military men, as requested by an Argentine judge, to stand trial for the 1974 murder of Chilean Gen. Carlos Prats and his wife in a car bombing in Buenos Aires. A group of 12 military men were found responsible for the 1982 murder of labour leader Tucapel Jiménez, however, and they were sentenced in criminal court. Continuing controversy over a secret Air Force death squad forced Air Force head Patricia Rios to resign in October.

(LOIS HECHT OPPENHEIM)

CHINA

Area: 9,572,900 sq km (3,696,100 sq mi), including Tibet and excluding Taiwan and the special autonomous regions of Hong Kong and Macau

Population (2002 est., excluding Taiwan, Hong Kong, and Macau): 1,284,211,000

Capital: Beijing

Chief of state: President Jiang Zemin

Head of government: Premier Zhu Rongji

The year 2002 was a critical one for China. Domestically, it was a year of political transition to a new generation of leaders; internationally, significant changes in geopolitical alignments had major repercussions for the country. The 16th Congress of the Communist Party of China (CPC), after some delay, was convened in early November. China's "Three Represents" doctrine was affirmed, and the recruitment of private business owners into the party gained acceptance. Three Represents referred to the CPC's stated mission to represent three essential concerns: the development needs of the country, China's advanced culture, and the fundamental interests of the vast majority of the Chinese people. In February, U.S. Pres. George W. Bush traveled to Beijing—his second trip to China within four months. His visit marked the 30th anniversary of the first U.S. presidential visit to China, which had begun the normalization of relations between the two countries. China reciprocated with two heavyweight visits to the U.S., first by Vice Pres. Hu Jintao (*see* BIOGRAPHIES) and then by Pres. Jiang Zemin.

Politics and the Economy. The months before the start of the 16th Congress were filled with speculation regarding the anticipated political transition in China. Three officials were considered as possible successors to Jiang: Hu, Zeng Qinghong, and Li Ruihuan. Hu was considered the preeminent figure among the next generation of Chinese leaders. He had been promoted by legendary paramount leader Deng Xiaoping (who had also promoted Jiang to the top leadership position in the wake of the military crackdown on the 1989 student-led pro-democracy movement). Hu held three pivotal positions; he was a standing member of the CPC Political Bureau and the first vice-chairman of the CPC Central Military Affairs Commission as well as the Chinese vice president. Like Hu, Zeng was seen as one of Jiang's political protégés, but he held only an alternate membership in the Political Bureau—two ranks below the standing members. Li had been chairman of the Chinese People's Political Consultative Conference and was a longtime standing member of the Political Bureau. In terms of his background, Li belonged to Jiang's generation of leaders, but he was "young enough"—69 years of age—to serve for another term in office. A factor working against Li, however, was his reported opposition to some of Jiang's major policies.

Chinese Vice Pres. Hu Jintao (far left) acknowledges applause after being elected on November 15 in Beijing to succeed Pres. Jiang Zemin as general-secretary of the Communist Party of China.

Although Hu was widely regarded as Jiang's designated successor, a rumour circulated at the beginning of the year that Jiang would not, in fact, step down at the upcoming Congress. Apparently as a prelude to taking control upon Jiang's retirement, Hu had inserted followers in top positions in Shanghai and Guangdong. Upon learning of this maneuver, Jiang was reportedly upset and told his close aides that he would not step down that year.

The party Congress, usually scheduled every five years and held in September, was postponed until early November in part because of the difficulties that the top leaders had in reaching a consensus on succession. As November approached, there was a strange absence of public promotion of Hu's leadership.

The result of the party Congress surprised some but not others. Jiang ensured that the Congress's proceedings were carefully scripted to focus on his achievements in the 13 years since he became party chief. As Jiang stepped down from the position of party general secretary, Hu was elected to succeed him. The new Political Bureau consisted of only those younger than 70 years old and was dominated by technocrats—18 of 25 full and alternate members were engineers and 5 of them had received degrees from China's premier scientific and technological institution, Tsinghua University. Li retired from the party's Central Committee. The standing committee of the Political Bureau was expanded from seven members to nine, and Hu was the only remaining member of the previous standing committee. Among the eight new standing members, six were believed to be Jiang's protégés, including Zeng.

More important, Jiang maintained his position as the chairman of the CPC Central Military Affairs Commission. During the 1980s Deng had been able to exercise his power over the party's general secretary by holding just this position after he had given up all his other official titles. Such a decision clearly pointed more toward continuity than toward change. If changes were to be made, they would fall within Jiang's framework.

Though not all expectations were met, fundamental changes did take place at the Congress. The Three Represents doctrine was included in the party constitution, and some liberal programs were initiated at lower levels within the party structure. The pronouncements issued during the Congress suggested that the party indeed remained committed to a middle-class agenda: maintaining high growth and social stability, encouraging private enterprises, breaking up government monopolies, and respecting private rights. The party was expected to be ever more pro-private business.

In 1997 the 15th Congress of the CPC had concluded with expectations that the 16th Congress would be much more open-minded in regard to political and economic reform. The new leadership that emerged in 2002, however, would be cautious in its transformation of Chinese politics because it first had to consolidate its power base before launching any substantial programs. Nonetheless, the new leaders were presented with a historic opportunity to pursue further political and economic reform at home and engage in promoting international peace abroad.

Along with a changing of the guard in the party leadership, the CPC itself continued to search for what it stood for. Responding to a mounting identity crisis that had swept through its ranks in the past few years, the CPC had begun searching aggressively for a new set of principles to define its future and for reforms to ensure its relevance and survival in an increasingly market-oriented, pluralistic society.

Encouraging private business ranked high among those reforms. The number of private enterprises in China had reached more than two million by the beginning of 2002. At the annual People's Political Consultative Conference in March, China's Chamber of Commerce reiterated its call for the constitutional protection of private properties. The Three Represents doctrine justified the inclusion of capitalists—private owners—in the CPC.

Efforts continued at all levels of government to crack down on corruption and on the activities of the outlawed spiritual movement Falun Gong. Institutional corruption was considered a threat to party rule from the inside, while Falun Gong was viewed as a threat from the outside. In the first six months of 2002, according to one Chinese newspaper, 555 government officials were arrested on corruption charges, including one banking chief suspected of having laundered some $730 million—the largest amount in any single money-laundering case in China's history. A new campaign to discredit Falun Gong also got under way, with authorities accusing it of being an "evil cult" that posed a challenge to "modern civilization." Authorities were particularly incensed by an incident on March 5 in which Falun Gong members hijacked state television broadcasts to air antigovernment messages. Fifteen members were charged in the incident and received prison sentences of between 4 and 20 years.

China's economy enjoyed another year of strong growth, with the gross domestic product rate surpassing government forecasts to reach 7.9% after the first three quarters. Chinese exports were up nearly 20% at that time, while foreign investment was up 22.6%. These numbers helped confirm China as Asia's fastest-growing economy. On the negative side, however, economic reforms had produced more than six million laid-off workers, and it was estimated that—following China's accession to the World Trade Organization—there would be another five million workers terminated from their jobs in five years. As a control mechanism over the macro economy, the state limited the freedom of newly privatized enterprises to lay off workers. This was a new paradox for China. On the one hand, without such state intervention, the new enterprises would improve their productivity by firing surplus labour, which could increase the chance of social unrest—which in turn would worsen the environment for investment and development. On the other hand, such intervention rendered privatization incomplete; private owners and investors wondered how far the state would go in order to maintain a "healthy environment" for investment at the expense of a sound property rights system.

Foreign Relations. China began the year with active diplomacy. Within the first month of 2002, Chinese Premier Zhu Rongji visited two countries, while President Jiang had talks with the heads of an additional six states. Aside from his visit to the U.S., Jiang also visited six more countries in June, and Li Peng, chairman of the National People's Congress, made visits to multiple foreign countries as well.

Contrary to the rocky relationship the previous year between China and the U.S., the two countries seemed to find some common ground amid mutual suspicion in 2002. While the post-September 11 American economy continued its downward slide, U.S. investment in China remained the largest among all foreign direct investments. Some 300 of the 500 largest American

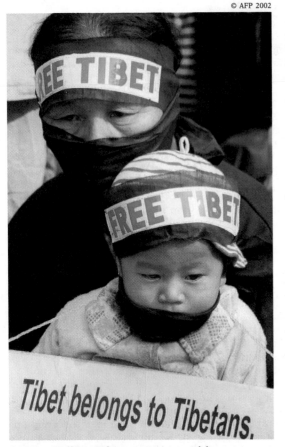

© AFP 2002

In New Delhi a Tibetan woman and boy participate in a demonstration staged by Tibetan refugees during a January visit to India by Chinese Premier Zhu Rongji.

companies had investments in China. The two-way trade between China and the U.S. surged 11.7% during the first half of the year.

With an extensive national border and 15 neighbouring countries, China had been long afraid of encirclement by other powers. Such a fear was reinforced by the reaction of the U.S. to the events of Sept. 11, 2001. American efforts against terrorism had included the establishment of bases in several Central Asian states adjacent to Afghanistan. China worried that these temporary bases might stretch into a long-term presence that would prevent China from normalizing relations with these states. Beijing's uneasiness was compounded when the Bush administration announced that the war against terrorism would be expanded to such countries as North Korea, the Philippines, and Indonesia.

Perceptions that the post-September 11 campaign against terrorism was being used as an excuse for imposing American hegemony worldwide were exacerbated by a classified U.S. Department of Defense document leaked to the *Los Angeles Times* in March. The document recommended a contingency plan for nuclear strikes in which seven countries, including China, were possible targets. Another irritant was the visit of Taiwan's defense minister to a conference in Florida, again in March, where he met with the U.S. deputy secretary of defense. As far as was publicly known, this constituted the highest-level defense contact between the U.S. and Taiwan since Washington broke formal relations with Taipei in 1979. In addition, the media reported on the likelihood of increased U.S. arms sales to Taiwan. Shortly after assuming office in 2001, President Bush had stated that he would do "whatever it took" to help the island repel an invasion by the mainland. China remained determined on reunification with Taiwan.

China had indicated to the U.S. that, in the campaign against international terrorism, the best way for China to contribute was to fight on its own domestic front—i.e., against Muslim separatists in its northwestern regions. Washington downplayed the threat from Chinese Muslim separatists at first but later added the group to its list of foreign terrorist organizations.

Japanese Prime Minister Junichiro Koizumi's April 21 visit to the Yasukuni Shrine in Tokyo—the site dedicated to more than two million military personnel lost since the 1850s—infuriated Beijing. China's Foreign Ministry issued a statement vehemently denouncing the visit to the shrine, "which honours Class A war criminals" and was "a symbol of militarism." It was Koizumi's second visit to the Yasukuni Shrine in a year. Beijing promptly summoned Japan's ambassador to China to criticize "the erroneous action that damages ties" between the two nations. The incident alone could prevent the two neighbouring countries from developing a closer, more productive relationship. The fact that Japan was talking about participating in a joint missile defense program with the U.S. also aroused suspicion. China worried that these developments pointed to a revival of Japanese militarism.

Later in the year there were signs of a possible settlement between Beijing and the Dalai Lama regarding the latter's relationship with Tibet. Representatives of the exiled leader made a visit to Beijing in September; the trip marked the first formal contact between the two sides since 1993. There was no immediate word on whether the subject of reopening official ties had been broached during the visit.   (XIAOBO HU)

COLOMBIA

Area: 1,141,568 sq km (440,762 sq mi)
Population (2002 est.): 41,008,000
Capital: Bogotá
Head of state and government: Presidents Andrés Pastrana Arango and, from August 7, Álvaro Uribe Vélez

In 2002 the outgoing administration of Pres. Andrés Pastrana Arango was unable to make headway on peace talks with the Revolutionary Armed Forces of Colombia (FARC), the country's major guerrilla group. After the guerrillas hijacked an airplane carrying the president of the Senate's peace commission, the government broke off negotiations on February 21 and began bombing the rebel-held demilitarized zone. Repeated failed attempts to push forward either peace talks with the guerrillas or political and economic reform with Congress left the administration with little popular support and heightened the mood in the country that dramatic changes were needed.

Promising such changes, Álvaro Uribe Vélez was elected president of Colombia on May 26. (*See* BIOGRAPHIES.) Despite his long career as a Liberal politician, Uribe split from the traditionally dominant party, establishing the Colombia First electoral vehicle and adopting the slogan "Firm Hand, Big Heart." He promised a tougher line against guerrillas, paramilitaries, and drug traffickers and stressed the need for sweeping political reforms to make the government more efficient and reduce corruption. By winning more than 53.1% of the votes cast, Uribe avoided the need for a second round of voting.

Uribe's convincing victory was taken as evidence of support for that tougher line regarding armed groups on both the left and the right. He called on the U.S. for military aid to combat narcotics trafficking and to prevent guerrilla groups from obtaining more arms. He asked the United Nations for assistance in negotiating with left-wing rebels as well as right-wing paramilitaries. He also established networks of citizen informants. While governor of Antioquia, Uribe had successfully used anonymous civilian watchdog groups to curb kidnappings between 1995 and 1997, and as president he sought to replicate the strategy at the national level. In August the president declared a national state of emergency. A subsequent cabinet meeting resulted in the suspension of civil liberties in the face of threats to the country's security, and the government established an emergency tax that would allow it to direct approximately $778 million toward military expenditures.

On the political front Uribe sought to address public concerns regarding corruption, vote buying, and the general excess of politicians. Immediately after taking office, the administration called for a referendum on several proposals, including downsizing Congress and eliminating legislators' access to funds for relatively unmonitored spending in their districts. Despite the government's repeated claim that the text of the referendum was nonnegotiable, the bill was bogged down in committee when legislators divided primarily over reforming the country's electoral bureaucracy. Congress had to approve the use of a referendum before the proposals could be submitted to the public, and the government's legislative majority could prove to be fragile.

Economic growth was less than 1.5% in 2002, but a predicted improvement in domestic and external conditions could allow gross domestic product growth of 2.5% in 2003. Weak domestic demand served as a check on inflationary pressures, but planned increases in military spending could stress public finances. In response, the government sought to increase revenues and cut expenditures. Cost-cutting measures included purging the payroll of bureaucracy and merging state institutions, but with unemployment at 17.5%, extensive public job cuts were likely to generate serious opposition. The administration also sought to counter deficit projections by pushing Congress to enact pension and fiscal reforms. Internationally, the government sought a standby agreement with the International Monetary Fund to cover the country's large external-financing requirement.

(BRIAN F. CRISP)

COMOROS

Area: 1,862 sq km (719 sq mi), excluding the 375-sq-km (145-sq-mi) island of Mayotte, a de facto dependency of France since 1976
Population (2002 est.): 583,000 (excluding 165,000 on Mayotte)
Capital: Moroni
Chief of state and head of government: Heads of State Col. Azali Assoumani and, from January 21 to May 26, Hamada Madi; President from May 26, Col. Azali Assoumani

A referendum passed on Dec. 23, 2001, granted the three islands of the Comoros more autonomy and renamed the Federal Islamic Republic of the Comoros as the new Union of the Comoros. Accordingly, a series of elections were held in the first five months of 2002. Violence and protests over the first round of voting for union president in April resulted in the voiding of Col. Azali Assoumani's unopposed victory, but he went on to win in a fresh round and was sworn in as union president on May 26. Under the new constitution, each island had its own president and parliament. Voters on Anjouan elected Col. Mohammed Bacar, Mohamed Said Fazul was elected president for Mohéli, and Abdou Soule Elbak was voted president of Grande Comore (Njazidja). By mid-December 2002, parliaments for each autonomous island as well as for the Union of the Comoros were in place.

The new political structure was threatened in June when a struggle erupted between Union President Assoumani and Grande Comore President Elbak on how power should be shared. The military briefly occupied parts of Moroni, and in August soldiers shot demonstrators protesting against Assoumani. Owing to political uncertainty, the International Monetary Fund postponed plans for economic reform until the country had stabilized.

(MARY F.E. EBELING)

Colombians in Bogotá on June 12 have themselves buried up to their necks as a way to protest government hikes in fees for public services.

CONGO, DEMOCRATIC REPUBLIC OF THE

Area: 2,344,858 sq km (905,354 sq mi)
Population (2002 est.): 52,557,000 (adjusted for 1998–2001 war deaths of 2.5 million in eastern DRC [mostly from starvation, disease, and deprivation])
Capital: Kinshasa
Head of state and government: President Joseph Kabila

The year 2002 in the Congo began in tragedy and grief. The eruption of Mt. Nyiragongo near Lake Kivu in eastern Congo in mid-January destroyed more than a third of the town of Goma as well as several villages.

British Foreign Secretary Jack Straw and his French counterpart, Hubert Védrine, arrived in late January to launch a new diplomatic initiative to end the war that had raged in Congo for more than three years. The European Commission approved $45 million in immediate emergency aid for the stricken region, but local authorities, while acknowledging the generosity of the offer, complained that the aid was slow to reach the areas of need.

Talks sponsored by South Africa's president, Thabo Mbeki, and aimed at reaching a peace settlement began in Sun City, S.Af., on January 28 but broke down in April without having reached a comprehensive agreement. Congolese Pres. Joseph Kabila, had, however, privately arranged with Jean-Pierre Bemba, leader of the rebel movement that controlled much of northern Congo, that he himself should remain president of a transitional government while Bemba could become prime minister. The deal was flatly rejected by the Congolese Rally for Democracy (RCD), the Rwanda-backed rebel group, which wanted a significant role in any interim government and in any case objected to Kabila's remaining in office.

Prospects for peace looked even bleaker when the rebels killed about 180 people in reaction to calls for an uprising against the Rwandan invaders. Two more promising developments soon followed. On July 30 the presidents of Rwanda and Congo, under considerable pressure from President Mbeki and the UN but against the wishes of some of Kabila's officials (for-

mer supporters of the late president Mobutu Sese Seko), signed a peace agreement in Pretoria, S.Af. Rwanda was to withdraw its troops from Congo as soon as Kabila's government had disarmed and repatriated the Hutu who had taken refuge in Congo after their part in the massacre in Rwanda in 1994. Encouraged by this measure, on September 6 Ugandan Pres. Yoweri Museveni also signed a peace accord with Kabila, brokered by Pres. José dos Santos of Angola, in Luanda, the Angolan capital. Uganda, which had already withdrawn many of its troops from Congo, promised to complete the process, and in return Kabila agreed to take action against any rebels threatening Uganda's western border.

There were grounds for concern about these agreements, however. First, neither of the main rebel movements had been party to the deals. Second, it was doubtful that the Congo government had the ability to restrain, let alone to disarm and repatriate, the forces deemed to be threatening either Rwanda or Uganda. Third, the benefits accruing to senior officers of the foreign armies occupying the mineral-rich region of Congo might prompt hardliners to find pretexts for defying the agreements. In spite of these uncertainties, Zimbabwe, Congo's staunchest ally, also began to withdraw its troops.

On February 5 the long-awaited official apology for the Belgian government's role in the death in 1981 of Patrice Lumumba, Congo's first elected prime minister, arrived from Brussels, but it failed to impress the Congo government.

(KENNETH INGHAM)

CONGO, REPUBLIC OF THE

Area: 342,000 sq km (132,047 sq mi)
Population (2002 est.): 2,899,000
Capital: Brazzaville
Head of state and government: President Denis Sassou-Nguesso

Pres. Denis Sassou-Nguesso took 89% of the vote in the Republic of the Congo's March 10, 2002, presidential election, defeating seven little-known candidates. An estimated 75% of the electorate turned out for the vote. His major opponent, former prime minister

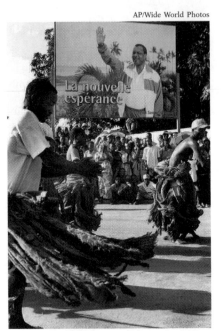

In Brazzaville, Republic of the Congo, on March 7, dancers perform at an election rally for Pres. Denis Sassou-Nguesso, whose image appears on a poster in the background.

André Milongo, had withdrawn two days earlier, claiming that the election was already rigged. On March 29, 16 opposition parties formed a new alliance, the Convention for Democracy and Salvation (CODESA), to prepare for legislative and municipal elections; it was to be led by Milongo. Parties supporting former president Pascal Lissouba and former prime minister Bernard Kolélas opted not to join CODESA.

Widespread violence and charges of fraud in Brazzaville, Pointe-Noire, and Gamboma disrupted the first round of the legislative elections on May 26. Attacks by "Ninja" militia, loyal to Kolélas, severely affected voting in the southern Pool region of the country. The second round, held on June 23, saw parties supporting Sassou-Nguesso win an absolute majority in the new parliament. A new National Assembly replaced the appointed National Transition Council that, having governed since 1998, was officially dissolved on August 9. Fighting continued throughout the summer as guerrilla groups in Pool attacked trains and government positions and extended their activities to Brazzaville in June. An estimated 50,000 Congolese were displaced by the new outbreak of fighting.

Despite rising oil revenues, the economy remained under stress, with 70%

of its citizens living below the poverty line. The non-oil sector appeared to be recovering, although serious difficulties resulting from the prolonged civil unrest continued to hinder substantial economic growth. Civil servants demanded full payment of salary arrears, while Congolese university students studying in Brazzaville, Gabon, and Mali staged strikes and sit-downs in July and August to protest delays, for some as long as 26 months, in the disbursement of grants.

(NANCY ELLEN LAWLER)

COSTA RICA

Area: 51,100 sq km (19,730 sq mi)
Population (2002 est.): 3,960,000
Capital: San José
Head of state and government: Presidents Miguel Ángel Rodríguez Echeverría and, from May 8, Abel Pacheco de la Espriella

Costa Rica's national election, held on Feb. 3, 2002, proved to be one of the country's most unusual. For decades Costa Rica had enjoyed a stable two-party system in which the parties regularly alternated in power. In this election, however, the incumbent Social Christian Unity Party (PUSC) succeeded itself in office—something that had happened only occasionally in the past—and, for the first time ever, no party achieved the necessary 40% plurality. A strong third-party movement siphoned away votes from the PUSC and its rival, the National Liberation Party (PLN); although in the past third parties had won no more than 8% of the vote, they garnered nearly 28% in 2002. A runoff election took place on April 7.

PUSC candidate Abel Pacheco de la Espriella emerged as the victor in the presidential race. The 68-year-old Pacheco, a nationally known psychiatrist and television personality, overcame opposition from the entrenched elite of his own party to claim 58% of the vote against Rolando Araya of the PLN.

In office Pacheco was faced with a divided 57-seat legislature, in which his party won only 19 seats. Observers expected him to try to form a coalition with other parties; in the election the PLN secured 17 seats and the upstart Citizen Action Party 14 seats. Two other

parties together won a total of 7 seats. The economic challenges confronting the new government were formidable, especially with respect to reducing Costa Rica's fiscal deficit and overcoming sluggish growth, made all the more difficult by the post-Sept. 11, 2001, economic slowdown in the U.S.

(MITCHELL A. SELIGSON)

CÔTE D'IVOIRE

Area: 320,803 sq km (123,863 sq mi)
Population (2002 est.): 16,805,000
De facto capital: Abidjan
Chief of state: President Laurent Gbagbo
Head of government: Prime Minister Affi N'Guessan

On Sept. 19, 2002, Gen. Robert Guëï (*see* OBITUARIES), the apparent mastermind behind an attempted coup in which at least 20 soldiers and civilians (including Côte d'Ivoire's interior minister) lost their lives, was killed by loyalist government troops. The uprising, which involved about 750 soldiers who mutinied in Bouaké, Abidjan, and Korhogo, occurred during Pres. Laurent Gbagbo's state visit to Italy.

In January Gbagbo met his three major rivals—former prime minister Alassane Ouattara, Guëï, and former president Henri Konan Bédié, who had been ousted by Guëï in the December 1999 military coup—for the first time in a fence-mending gathering. Though he had been banned from standing in the 2000 election on the grounds that he was a Burkinabe, Ouattara's Ivorian citizenship was confirmed on July 1, 2002, by the issuing of a certificate of nationality. In local elections held on July 7, Bédié's Democratic Party of Côte d'Ivoire (PDCI) rebounded strongly and took control of 18 of the country's 58 departments.

A cabinet reshuffle announced on August 5 brought in ministers from all of the major opposition parties. The ruling Ivorian Popular Front secured 20 portfolios; the PDCI, 7; Ouattara's Rally of Republicans, 4; and the Ivorian Workers' Party, 2. Guëï's Union for Democracy and Peace in Côte d'Ivoire (UDPCI) lost one but retained one position in the new government.

On May 30 six men on trial for involvement in the January 2001 attempt to overthrow President Gbagbo were sentenced to terms of up to 20 years; the court acquitted seven other defendants. Balla Keïta—a longtime PDCI supporter and frequent cabinet minister in the governments of founding president Félix Houphouët-Boigny—was murdered on August 1 in Ouagadougou,

Government supporters flood the streets of Abidjan, Côte d'Ivoire, on October 2, days after a bloody coup attempt was put down.

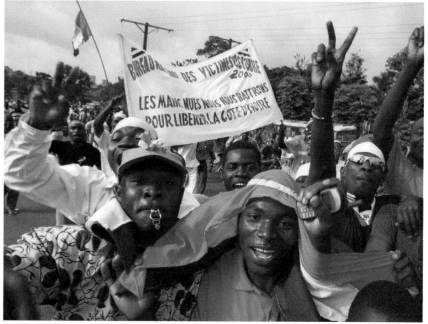

Burkina Faso, where he had lived in exile since March 2001. Keïta had been a strong supporter of Guëi's 1999 military coup (Guëi lost power in 2000, however), claiming that it would restore "orthodox Houphouëtism," and had been named secretary-general of the UDPCI in May. Burkina Faso's Justice Department announced on August 20 that it believed the assassination to have been politically motivated.

In February, following the government's payment of $44.5 million in debt arrears, the World Bank resumed full economic participation in the development of Côte d'Ivoire. On March 28 the International Monetary Fund (IMF) agreed to loan the country $365 million for poverty-reduction programs. The loan was tied to the government's pledge to keep wage increases in the civil service under control. On April 11 the Paris Club of wealthy donor nations restructured $2.26 billion of Côte d'Ivoire's external debt and immediately canceled $911 million of debt. Following recommendations by the IMF, the government increased export taxes on cocoa beans on August 22.

(NANCY ELLEN LAWLER)

CROATIA

Area: 56,542 sq km (21,831 sq mi)
Population (2002 est.): 4,405,000
Capital: Zagreb
Chief of state: President Stipe Mesic
Head of government: Prime Minister Ivica Racan

In 2002 Croatia continued to see its political landscape fragment and the broad-based ruling coalition split further amid slow economic recovery. On July 5 the five-party coalition government of Prime Minister Ivica Racan resigned, only to reconstitute itself absent the second largest party in the coalition, the Croatian Social Liberal Party (HSLS), following the latter's refusal to support ratification of a Croatia-Slovenia agreement concerning joint custodianship of the Krsko nuclear power plant. The break between Racan's Social Democratic Party (SDP) and the HSLS, led by Deputy Prime Minister Drazen Budisa, reflected long-brewing ideological differences over ba-

sic policy decisions made by the SDP-led government. Disaffected deputies from the HSLS, led by Defense Minister Jozo Rados, who had been soundly defeated by Budisa for party president on February 2, rebelled in support of the SDP and founded a new party, Libra.

The flap over Krsko, however, was just one of many disputes between the two neighbours. In August and September a squabble over territorial boundaries in the Bay of Piran that pitted Slovenian against Croatian fishermen turned into a full-fledged diplomatic crisis. These and other serious border disputes with Slovenia, Bosnia and Herzegovina, and Serbia highlighted the country's inability to extricate itself from unresolved postsecessionist problems stemming from the breakup of Yugoslavia more than a decade earlier. Though Croatia was admitted into NATO's Membership Action Plan and initialed its formal application for full membership on May 14, it was apparent by year's end that the government would fail to deliver on its major electoral promise of securing Croatia's early admission into NATO and the European Union—essential steps in the country's integration into Western Europe. The end of the United Nations' monitoring mission in the strategic Prelavka Peninsula on December 15 restored Croatia's sovereignty over its full territory, however.

With hopes for early integration dashed, public confidence in the government's ability to resolve the many pressing economic problems—especially an unemployment rate of 22% and the need to face further painful cuts in social welfare spending—also lessened. Revenues expected from the privatization of major energy state enterprises did not materialize, and the foreign investment needed to boost job creation remained weak. The important tourist trade proved resilient, however, increasing 4% and helping the government to register a modest 4% growth in gross domestic product.

The truncated SDP-led coalition still enjoyed a comfortable parliamentary majority after the split with the HSLS. Growing public dissatisfaction with its performance at home and abroad, however, coupled with the reemergence of the Croatian Democratic Union (HDZ), the party that previously had governed the country, as a viable centre-right alternative to the centre-left coalition, raised speculation about early elections. Moderate nationalist Ivo Sanader, a former deputy foreign min-

ister, was elected president of the HDZ on April 22, and the expulsion of the HDZ's hard-line wing a few months later gave new shape and vitality to the Croatian political scene. The prospect of an HDZ-led centre-right coalition with participation by the HSLS and other like-minded smaller parties invigorated the country's political scene.

Croatian politicians were of a single mind on one issue, however. On September 27 Parliament unanimously backed the government's legal challenge to the International Criminal Tribunal for the Former Yugoslavia, which had indicted retired general Janko Bobetko, a wartime commander and Croatian hero, as a war criminal. This rare broad-based political consensus reflected frustration with recent indictments by the tribunal in The Hague that seemed implicitly to revise and even criminalize Croatia's homeland war for independence.

Croatia's skiing sensation Janica Kostelic became a national icon in February after winning a record four medals at the Winter Olympics in Salt Lake City, Utah. (See BIOGRAPHIES.) On March 11 Franjo Cardinal Kuharic, one of Croatia's most influential post-World War II religious leaders, died. (See OBITUARIES.) Kuharic was a symbol of the nation's resistance to communism and an advocate of ethnic and political tolerance.

(MAX PRIMORAC)

CUBA

Area: 110,861 sq km (42,804 sq mi)
Population (2002 est.): 11,267,000
Capital: Havana
Head of state and government: President of the Council of State and President of the Council of Ministers Fidel Castro Ruz

In 2002 Cuba's constitution was amended to declare the socialist revolution irreversible, despite increasing evidence of new and serious challenges to the Cuban system. Leading Cuban dissident Osvaldo Payá collected an unprecedented 11,200 signatures as part of the Varela Project, which proposed a constitutional amendment to allow greater political and economic freedoms. This initiative was neutralized by a counterpetition organized by the government of Fidel Castro. More than

On May 17, the final day of his high-profile trip to Cuba, former U.S. president Jimmy Carter appears with Pres. Fidel Castro at the airport in Havana.

eight million Cubans—about 99% of registered adults—signed a proposal calling for a constitutional change rendering the Cuban system "untouchable," which was subsequently ratified by the National Assembly.

A mix of official hostility, increased trade, and high-profile visits characterized U.S.-Cuban relations in 2002. In May the George W. Bush administration accused Cuba of having the capacity to develop an offensive bioweapons program; in September the State Department further implied that Cuba was intentionally trying to obstruct the American "war on terrorism." Meanwhile, quiet cooperation continued in areas such as counternarcotics operations, migration, and security regarding several hundred alleged al-Qaeda operatives captured in Afghanistan and transferred to the U.S. naval base at Guantánamo Bay. In May former president Jimmy Carter became the highest-ranking former U.S. official to have visited Cuba since the 1959 revolution and the first U.S. president to visit since Calvin Coolidge in 1928. In addition to meeting with Castro, other top government officials, and human rights groups, Carter gave a speech broadcast live throughout the island that criticized both U.S. policy and human rights in Cuba. Bush responded by announcing the "Initiative for a New Cuba" designed to maintain the trade embargo until Cuba undertakes democratic reform. Meanwhile, American farmers continued to sell agricultural products to Cuba in all-cash trades

made permissible under a law passed in October 2000. In September nearly 300 American companies gathered in Cuba for the largest U.S. Food and Agribusiness Exhibition ever to have occurred on the island. Cuba was expected to make $165 million in food purchases from the U.S. by the end of the year and to become the 45th biggest export market for American agricultural exports.

Cuba's relations with several other Latin American countries exhibited increased tension. At a United Nations conference in Monterrey, Mex., Castro attacked the world financial system as a "gigantic casino" and then abruptly left, prompting widespread speculation that Mexican Pres. Vicente Fox had engineered his exit. When Mexico later joined countries including Argentina, Canada, Chile, Peru, and Uruguay in passing a UN resolution condemning the human rights situation in Cuba, Castro released tape recordings of private conversations with Fox, sinking Cuban-Mexican relations to their lowest point in decades. Similarly rebuked, Uruguay broke off diplomatic relations with Cuba. In April, Castro ally Pres. Hugo Chávez Frias of Venezuela was temporarily removed from power, which resulted in the suspension of Venezuelan oil shipments under preferential financial terms. Ties with Europe were also strained; Cuba's arbitrary handling of foreign investment prompted the European Union to submit a document to Cuba of investors' complaints. The Cuban government responded by promising to cut red tape.

The Cuban economy continued to struggle in the aftermath of the Sept. 11, 2001, attacks, which decreased revenues from both tourism and remittances. The island's dual currency system remained intact, but peso stores became increasingly empty while dollar stores raised their prices. Euros were allowed to circulate alongside dollars in major resorts. In June the government announced the decision to close an estimated 71 of the island's 156 sugar mills. Official estimates of gross domestic product were lowered to 3% in 2001, and further decline seemed likely. Foreign direct investment dropped dramatically in 2001, to slightly less than $40 million—far below the estimated $488 million in 2000. This trend was expected to continue in 2002. According to the Cuban central bank, the island owed nearly $11 billion in foreign debt.

International human rights groups continued to condemn the lack of freedom of expression and the treatment of political prisoners in Cuba. The UN Development Programme's Human Development Index ranked Cuba 55th out of 173 nations in terms of life expectancy, educational attainment, adjusted real income, and governance. Although the adult literacy rate was estimated at 96.7% and the average life expectancy in Cuba was 76 years, Cuba was given the lowest possible score for civil liberties and political rights. Cuba's increasing informal economy and expanded dissident activities, however, indicated that the island's government needed to contend with a growing domestic constituency for political and economic change.

(DANIEL P. ERIKSON)

CYPRUS

Area: 9,251 sq km (3,572 sq mi) for the entire island; the area of the Turkish Republic of Northern Cyprus (TRNC), proclaimed unilaterally (1983) in the occupied northern third of the island, 3,355 sq km (1,295 sq mi)

Population (2002 est.): island 907,000; TRNC only, 215,000 (including Turkish settlers and Turkish military)

Capital: Lefkosia/Lefkosa (also known as Nicosia)

Head(s) of state and government: President Glafcos Clerides; of the TRNC, President Rauf Denktash

Greek-Cypriot women, participating in a march within the UN buffer zone in Cyprus, hold photographs of relatives missing since the Turkish invasion in 1974.

In 2002 political events in Cyprus were dominated by the vision of European Union (EU) membership and direct talks between the leaders of the two republics. Greek Cyprus completed virtually all the requirements for EU membership. The EU was prepared to accept Greek Cyprus in the hope that the island's future could be resolved, but Turkish Cyprus and the metropolitan Turks made dire threats should that take place. Greek Cyprus continued to maintain that it was the island's legal government, with Turkish Cyprus a rogue breakaway regime. The Cyprus Turks insisted that any settlement contain recognition of their sovereignty. Despite some 60 meetings during the year between Greek-Cypriot Pres. Glafcos Clerides and Turkish-Cypriot Pres. Rauf Denktash, no settlement of the issue was reached.

Other problems continued. Greek Cyprus protested Turkish overflights, while the Cyprus Turks protested Greek Cyprus's taking over search-and-rescue operations on the island from Britain. The economy felt the global economic distress and uncertainty. Per capita gross national product growth of about 2% was expected in Greek Cyprus, while the Turkish side of the line was much less prosperous.

Nicosia was such a treasure house of archaeology that it was difficult for Greek Cyprus to find an unhistorical site for a new parliament house. Aridity was a constant, and Turkish Cyprus planned to complete a pipeline to transport water from Turkey by 2004.

(GEORGE H. KELLING)

CZECH REPUBLIC

Area: 78,866 sq km (30,450 sq mi)
Population (2002 est.): 10,210,000
Capital: Prague
Chief of state: President Vaclav Havel
Head of government: Prime Ministers Milos Zeman and, from July 12, Vladimir Spidla

The year 2002 was a difficult one for the Czech Republic, as massive floods in August wreaked havoc on Prague and other important centres of tourism and industry. The flooding inflicted tremendous damage on the country and complicated the already strained fiscal situation.

The political left scored a victory in 2002, winning a parliamentary majority for the first time since the fall of communism in 1989. The Czech Social Democratic Party (CSSD), which had ruled since 1998 in a power-sharing opposition agreement with the right-wing Civic Democratic Party (ODS), emerged victorious in the lower-house elections on June 14–15, winning 30.2% of the vote and 70 seats in the 200-member parliament. The ODS finished a somewhat distant second, and the only other groups that surpassed the 5% threshold needed for entry into the parliament were the Communists and the Coalition. Voter turnout was disappointingly low.

The CSSD would have had considerable leeway in forming leftist-oriented policy had it created a minority government with tacit support from the Communists, particularly given the two parties' relatively strong parliamentary majority. The ongoing negotiations on accession to the European Union and the EU's upcoming decision on enlargement, however, led the CSSD to choose instead the centre-right Coalition, which later broke down into its separate parts: the Christian Democrats (KDU-CSL) and the Freedom Union. Pres. Vaclav Havel appointed CSSD Chairman Vladimir Spidla prime minister on July 12, and the rest of the cabinet was installed on July 15. The ruling coalition had a parliamentary majority of just one seat.

The KDU-CSL and the Freedom Union had little influence on policy making, with the CSSD filling 11 of the 17 cabinet positions, including most of the important ones. In entering the new cabinet, the KDU-CSL and the Freedom Union wanted both to confirm their reliability as negotiating partners and to prevent other alternatives that could damage the country's interests. Nonetheless, the situation remained precarious, as demonstrated most notably on September 13, when the parliament narrowly defeated the government's proposed tax measures that were designed to funnel new revenues toward flood relief in 2003 and 2004. The bill failed when former Freedom Union chairwoman Hana Marvanova voted with the opposition forces, throwing the government into a crisis. A government collapse was averted five days later when the leaders of the three ruling parties signed an addendum to the coalition agreement guaranteeing that their parliamentary deputies would unanimously back key government legislation. In Senate elections in November, the CSSD lost 10 seats, reducing its total number in the 81-seat chamber to 36; the ODS picked up 4 seats to raise its total to 26.

The biggest economic concerns in 2002 related to fiscal and exchange-rate policy. The country's budget deficit was mounting owing to the high cost of bank restructuring and increasing mandatory payments for pensions and social benefits. The CSSD was reluctant to heed calls for reforms. The new coalition parties vowed that the public finance deficit would not surpass 4.9–5.4% of gross domestic product by the end of their term in 2006. That was far above the 3% limit set in the Maastricht criteria for accession to the European Monetary Union and meant that the Czech Republic's entry into the euro zone would likely be delayed, possibly until as late as 2010. Currency traders were undeterred by the government's lack of fiscal responsibility, and the Czech koruna reached new heights against the euro in 2002. With exporters expressing anxiety that the stronger currency was hindering sales abroad, the Czech National Bank cut interest rates several times and intervened against the koruna in an effort to halt its appreciation.

Foreign affairs were somewhat steamy for the Czechs in 2002, particularly in the months prior to the parliamentary elections. The post-World War II Benes decrees that led to the expulsion of ethnic Germans from Czechoslovakia were the subject of considerable debate with Germany and Austria, and some argued that the Czech Republic should be kept out of the EU unless the decrees were canceled. (SHARON FISHER)

DENMARK

Area: 43,098 sq km (16,640 sq mi)
Population (2002 est.): 5,377,000
Capital: Copenhagen
Chief of state: Queen Margrethe II
Head of government: Prime Minister Anders Fogh Rasmussen

In 2002, after storming to power in November 2001 following the biggest swing to the right in Danish politics since the 1920s, the Liberal-Conservative coalition government of Prime Minister Anders Fogh Rasmussen—with backing from the populist, nationalist Danish People's Party—introduced tighter immigration controls and sweeping expenditure cuts, denting Denmark's image abroad as a bastion of tolerance and humanitarianism. Budgets for overseas development aid were trimmed; expenditures for cultural activities were slashed; and more than 100 government think tanks, advisory committees, and similar bodies were axed, rationalized, or merged. One of the most significant cuts was that of the Board for Ethnic Equality, a forum for communication with ethnic minority groups.

On the issue of asylum, the government abolished the concept of de facto refugees, stipulating that only individuals entitled to protection under international conventions were to be allowed to live in Denmark. Refugees

and immigrants would receive 30% less in social benefits than native Danes; family-reunification rules were tightened: young people could not marry and bring in foreigners under the age of 24, and access to family reunions with parents over the age of 60 was abolished (unless the child was under 18 years of age); permanent-residence permits could be obtained by foreigners only after seven years (previously three); permits would be denied to foreigners guilty of serious crime; and stringent tests in the Danish language and culture were imposed, coupled with a program of incentives to gain employment and integrate into society. The government's package—which came under heavy criticism from the United Nations High Commissioner for Refugees—reflected a crisis of national identity in a small country fearful of becoming a multiethnic society in an ever-more-globalized world.

In 2001, 12,512 asylum seekers entered the country, mainly from Iraq, Afghanistan, Bosnia and Herzegovina, and Yugoslavia; just over half were granted asylum, but the influx fell sharply in 2002. Foreign citizens accounted for barely 5% of the population in homogenous Denmark (only 1.7% were of non-European extraction)—a lower percentage than that in most European countries. (See *Australia: Special Report,* above.)

Denmark held the six-month rotating presidency of the European Union in the second half of the year. Topping the list of priorities was EU enlargement—an epic task for Copenhagen. After an intense two-day summit in Copenhagen on December 12–13, EU leaders agreed on a landmark accord opening the union's doors to 10 mostly Eastern European countries and paving the way for the largest expansion in the bloc's 45-year history.

In early December the diplomatic atmosphere between Copenhagen and Moscow plummeted to the freezing point when Denmark's Justice Ministry released Akhmed Zakayev, a leading Chechen separatist, while Russia sought his extradition. The ministry said that evidence received from the Russian authorities was insufficient. At the request of the Russian prosecutor general, Zakayev had been taken into custody by Danish police on October 30, only days after Chechen gunmen took hundreds of hostages in a Moscow theatre. Moscow wanted Zakayev to be extradited to stand trial for crimes he

allegedly committed in the late 1990s in connection with the war in Chechnya.

Meanwhile, the transformation of Copenhagen into a modern metropolis and economic hub continued with the opening of a new Italian-designed state-of-the-art driverless underground railway system. To the south of the city centre, near the airport, a new town—dubbed Ørestad—mushroomed; the University of Copenhagen, the Danish Broadcasting Corporation (including a stunning new concert hall designed by French architect Jean Nouvel), and a huge shopping mall were to become part of the city.

(CHRISTOPHER FOLLETT)

DJIBOUTI

Area: 23,200 sq km (8,950 sq mi)
Population (2002 est.): 473,000 (excluding 25,000 refugees from Somalia)
Capital: Djibouti
Chief of state and head of government: President Ismail Omar Guelleh, assisted by Prime Minister Dileita Muhammad Dileita

Djibouti's proximity to Yemen and Somalia, two countries cited by the U.S. government as possible terrorist havens, became the dominant factor affecting the country's foreign relations in 2002. In late January German naval forces began to arrive in Djibouti to stage patrols of the regional maritime traffic, searching for terrorist suspects possibly fleeing Afghanistan. The U.S. also assembled a military presence at a French base in the country. Pres. Ismael Omar Guelleh met with Gen. Tommy Franks of the U.S. Central Command in March and July to discuss Djibouti's role in the antiterrorism campaign. U.S. and Djibouti officials also signed an agreement in June to allow the U.S. to set up radio relays for Arabic-language broadcasts to eastern Africa and the Arabian Peninsula.

In July the UN High Commissioner for Refugees and its partner agencies instituted a voluntary repatriation program for Somali refugees in Djibouti, most of whom had, beginning in the late 1980s, fled the Somalian civil war. The repatriation project had been delayed somewhat owing to a shortage in food aid.

On June 27 Djibouti celebrated 25 years of independence from France. Another anniversary came on September 4, marking 10 years since the adoption of Djibouti's present constitution. President Guelleh chose the occasion to announce the approval of multiparty politics.

(ANDREW EISENBERG)

DOMINICA

Area: 750 sq km (290 sq mi)
Population (2002 est.): 71,700
Capital: Roseau
Chief of state: President Vernon Shaw
Head of government: Prime Minister Pierre Charles

In common with most other Caribbean states, Dominica agreed in March 2002 to improve the transparency of its tax-regulatory systems in order to secure its removal from the list of countries allegedly posing "harmful tax competition" to member states of the Organisation for Economic Co-operation and Development. In May Dominica also agreed to liberalize its telecommunications industry to permit competition for the first time. It took the action in concert with other members of the Organisation of Eastern Caribbean States.

A controversial "economic citizenship" program was reinstated in July that essentially allowed foreigners to purchase Dominican citizenship; for example, a family of four could obtain citizenship at a cost of $150,000. The program was revived despite criticism from countries such as Canada, which had imposed visa restrictions on Dominican passport holders on the grounds that the system lent itself to abuse by human traffickers and other criminals.

Dominica's economic situation deteriorated sharply toward year's end, mainly as a result of low banana production and prices and a decline in tourist arrivals following the Sept. 11, 2001, attacks in the U.S. The government was forced to cut spending by 15% and slap higher fees on fuel and telephone usage, as well as a highly un-

popular 4% special tax on nationals who earned the equivalent of more than $3,308 annually.

(DAVID RENWICK)

DOMINICAN REPUBLIC

Area: 48,671 sq km (18,792 sq mi)
Population (2002 est.): 8,833,000
Capital: Santo Domingo
Head of state and government: President Hipólito Mejía Domínguez

Competing as the two most important events in the Dominican Republic in 2002 were the country's legislative elections and the death of seven-time president Joaquín Balaguer. Balaguer, who had dominated political life in the Dominican Republic even when out of power, died on July 14. (*See* OBITUARIES.)

Legislative elections were held on May 16. The overwhelming victory of Pres. Hipólito Mejía's Dominican Revolutionary Party (PRD) was as much a surprise to PRD members as to local pundits. The party secured a majority in both legislative chambers and won 104 of 125 municipalities. Exhilarated by its success, the PRD, with Mejía's acquiescence, pushed through a constitutional change permitting the reelection of a

sitting president to a second term. The change provoked widespread unease, as it rolled back a key provision of the reforms enacted in the aftermath of the 1994 presidential contest, which had been marred by charges of electoral fraud. Mejía asserted that he would not stand for reelection.

The PRD's victory was attributed to Mejía's skills in communicating at the popular level and to a partial rebound of the economy from the troubles of 2001. Gross domestic product growth rose by 1% to a projected 3.2% for the year, notwithstanding a decline in tourism revenue.

Mejía received Haitian Pres. Jean-Bertrand Aristide in mid-January and continued to give priority to improving relations with his neighbour, recognizing that major environmental challenges could be addressed only through cross-border collaboration.

(JOHN W. GRAHAM)

EAST TIMOR (TIMOR-LESTE)

Area: 14,604 sq km (5,639 sq mi)
Population 797,000
Capital: Dili
Chief of state: President (from May 20) Xanana Gusmão
Head of government: Prime Minister (from May 20) Mari Alkatiri

East Timorese children hold candles during the country's independence celebration in Dili, the capital, on May 19.

On May 20, 2002, in the presence of international officials who included the president of Indonesia, East Timor officially celebrated its independence, and on September 27 Timor-Leste (the Portuguese spelling of its name) became the 191st member of the United Nations. These events marked the end of almost five centuries of foreign domination: Portuguese colonization, occupation by the Indonesian military, and, for the preceding three years, United Nations administration. In April 2002 the UN Security Council proposed a two-year mission of support (UNMISET) to assist with the orderly transfer of authority to the new government.

East Timor adopted a liberal form of government. Parliament was the sovereign body, with 88 deputies elected for five-year terms. The president was head of state, elected by direct universal suffrage to a five-year term (with a two-term limit). The government was led by the prime minister, who was designated by the majority party and nominated by the president.

The new nation faced enormous difficulties. East Timor was one of the poorest countries in Asia, with 41% of the population living below the poverty line. In addition, some 250,000 Timorese had been removed to West Timor (Indonesia) during the war of independence and were attempting to return.

Indonesia remained the focus of East Timor's external relations. In February a commission was put in place with a two-year mission of establishing the truth about crimes committed against the population between 1974 and 1999. The following month a special Indonesian court heard accusations against 18 Indonesian military, militia, and civilian leaders, and the former Indonesian governor-general of East Timor was being sought for crimes against humanity.

(CHARLES CADOUX)

ECUADOR

Area: 272,045 sq km (105,037 sq mi), including the 8,010-sq-km (3,093-sq-mi) Galápagos Islands
Population (2002 est.): 13,095,000 (Galápagos Islands, about 20,000)
Capital: Quito
Chief of state and head of government: President Gustavo Noboa Bejarano

Ecuadoran presidential candidate Álvaro Noboa Pontón is surrounded by supporters after casting his ballot at a school in Guayaquil on November 24.

Lucio Gutiérrez Borbúa was elected to a four-year term as president in a runoff vote in late November 2002, defeating Álvaro Noboa Pontón. He was to take office on Jan. 15, 2003. Gutiérrez, a former army colonel who had participated in an antigovernment uprising in January 2000, had the support of leftist groups and the Indian movement Pachakutik. Noboa, the owner of extensive banana plantations and the richest man in Ecuador, ran as an independent. The election was interpreted as a rejection of traditional political parties, whose candidates trailed both men in first-round voting in October. Both Gutiérrez and Noboa promised to retain the U.S. dollar as Ecuador's currency and renegotiate the $16 billion foreign debt.

Despite widespread poverty, the economy was one of the stronger performers in Latin America, with 3.5% growth forecast for the year. Pressure from environmentalists dogged construction of a new $1.3 billion Ecuadoran pipeline to carry crude oil from the Amazon region to the Pacific coast, scheduled for completion in 2003. Activists said it would threaten the ecotourism industry and the habitat of endangered bird species. Dozens of people were arrested after they staged protests against the pipeline, but by November it was 70% complete. The pipeline's economic impact would be considerably less than initially anticipated, as the foreign consortium building it lowered estimates of the amount of oil to be pumped. Some oil firms threatened to withhold further investment because of a quarrel with the government over tax refunds, and Ecuador agreed to submit the dispute to arbitration.

The banana industry, Ecuador's second largest foreign exchange earner, also faced political difficulties. In April the U.S.-based Human Rights Watch issued a report criticizing labour conditions, alleging that children were subjected to working long hours in pesticide-laden fields and earning an average of $3.50 a day. Workers on seven of Álvaro Noboa's plantations went on strike in May to support demands for higher wages, payment of legally mandated benefits, and union recognition. Armed gangs descended on the strikers' homes, and witnesses reported that some of them were beaten and shot. Noboa's company promised to improve conditions after a major American banana distributor expressed concern.

The armed conflict in Colombia continued to worry Ecuadorans, and military patrols along the northern border were beefed up. Temporary relief from the country's problems came in June when Ecuadorans rejoiced as the national soccer team competed for the first time in the World Cup finals.

(PAUL KNOX)

EGYPT

Area: 997,690 sq km (385,210 sq mi)
Population (2002 est.): 66,341,000
Capital: Cairo
Chief of state: President Hosni Mubarak
Head of government: Prime Minister Atef Ebeid

Egypt began the year 2002 with a devalued currency. On Dec. 13, 2001, the government devalued the Egyptian pound 7.8%—to E£ 4.50 to the U.S. dollar—in an effort to boost the economy and help the tourist industry, which had been hit hard in the aftermath of the Sept. 11, 2001, attacks in the U.S.

Pres. Hosni Mubarak visited the U.S. and met Pres. George W. Bush on March 5. In a joint news conference, Mubarak proposed holding a summit in Egypt between Israeli Prime Minister Ariel Sharon and Palestinian leader Yasir Arafat. Mubarak urged the U.S. to play a more active role in Israeli-Palestinian peace efforts, and he also supported the peace initiative proposed by Saudi Crown Prince Abdullah. (*See* BIOGRAPHIES.)

President Mubarak was active in conferring with his Arab allies. He met Jordanian King Abdullah II on April 21 and again on June 19, the Saudi crown prince on May 11 in the Egyptian resort Sharm al-Shaykh, and Syrian Pres. Bashar al-Assad on May 11, June 19, and September 30. All these deliberations focused primarily on the revival of the dormant Israeli-Palestinian peace process.

To show Egypt's support for the Palestinians, Egyptian Minister of Information Safwat al-Sharif announced on April 3 that Egypt had suspended all contacts with Israel with the exception of diplomatic communications needed to help the Palestinians. When U.S. Secretary of State Colin Powell visited Egypt on April 9, large demonstrations in support of the Palestinians were sanctioned by the Egyptian government to send a message to the Bush administration.

On June 7–8 President Mubarak met President Bush at Camp David, Maryland, and pressed him to set a timetable for the establishment of a Palestinian state. Mubarak stated that he did not expect that "anti-Israeli violence" could be stopped until some tangible progress had been made toward Palestinian statehood. Mubarak expressed the urgency of the matter by saying, "We have to exert or make the maximum effort to solve the Palestinian problem, to calm down the situation." Without that, he warned, expanding the war on terrorism to Iraq would be "very dangerous."

The case of Sa'd al-Din Ibrahim—a professor at the American University in Cairo who had been sentenced in May 2001 to seven years' hard labour for having accepted money from overseas without obtaining government approval—continued to capture the limelight. His

Sa'd al-Din Ibrahim (centre), who had been convicted of "defaming Egypt's image" and of receiving foreign funding without official permission, is escorted by police officers on December 3 after an Egyptian appeals court granted him a retrial.

retrial and that of 27 staff members from his Ibn Khaldun Center for Development Studies began on April 27, 2002. On July 29 the 27 members were convicted of bribery and fraud charges and were sentenced to varying terms of one to three years in jail. Ibrahim was again sentenced to seven years of hard labour for having defamed Egypt and accepted foreign research funds without government approval. The U.S. Department of State expressed its deep disappointment, but its reaction was mild and ineffective. Leading foreign-affairs *New York Times* analyst Thomas Friedman (*see* BIOGRAPHIES) took the Department of State to task and stated that it should have expressed its "outrage" for the Egyptian government's jailing of an innocent academic, human rights activist, and American citizen. Though Egypt was dependent on the U.S. for $2 billion in military and economic aid, the government's conviction of Ibrahim seemed intended to show the Egyptian people that their government was not subservient to the U.S. It appeared that President Mubarak was basking in this defiance. His foreign minister, Ahmad Maher, stated that the U.S. protest would not alter the verdict against Ibrahim, and he proudly announced, "Egypt . . . will not bow to pressure."

A new TV show, a 41-part series called *Horseman Without a Horse*, began airing in November. It told the story of an Egyptian journalist who struggled against British occupation and Zionism in the late 19th and early 20th centuries. Although the series was partly inspired by the forged "Protocols of the Elders of Zion," Mubarak's spokesman, Nabil Osman, insisted that it was not anti-Jewish. The Egyptian Organization for Human Rights, however, declared that a disclaimer should appear before the airing of the show, making it clear that the Protocols were forged and that "different forms of expression should not be abused to propagate events that might incite hatred." It was the first time that a domestic group had leveled criticism against the government.

(MARIUS K. DEEB)

EL SALVADOR

Area: 21,041 sq km (8,124 sq mi)
Population (2002 est.): 6,354,000
Capital: San Salvador
Head of state and government: President Francisco Flores Pérez

Although there was criticism about converting El Salvador's currency to the U.S. dollar, especially as the U.S. dollar declined in value during the year, Pres. Francisco Flores Pérez—who took credit for implementing dollarization—nonetheless enjoyed high approval ratings as he completed his third year in office in June 2002. Flores was also responsible for the expansion of manufacturing in the country's free-trade zones, the negotiation of free-trade agreements with other countries in the region, and the construction of schools and housing following the 2001 earthquake. Economic difficulties remained, however, with continued low coffee prices and a serious transportation strike in February slowing economic recovery. El Salvador also was suffering a serious drought and an epidemic of dengue fever, which was especially serious in

San Salvador. There was also major opposition from labour to the government's efforts to privatize the country's health care system.

El Salvador welcomed U.S. Pres. George W. Bush's initiatives to expand free trade. Bush visited El Salvador in March and praised the country as a model for economic development in Latin America, even though it was one of the poorest countries in the Western Hemisphere. The farm bill passed by the U.S. Congress in May, however, threatened to hurt Salvadoran agricultural interests.

The leading opposition to the ruling National Republican Alliance suffered a serious split in March as reformist members of the socialist Farabundo Martí Front for National Liberation broke away to form the Renovator Movement Party, which then sought to form a coalition with other parties—notably the Christian Democrats and Social Democrats—in the Legislative Assembly and in municipal elections.

In July a U.S. federal court in Florida ordered former Salvadoran minister of defense José Guillermo García and former National Guard chief Carlos Eugenio Vides Casanova, a resident of Florida, to pay $54.6 million to three Salvadoran civilians who had been tortured by state security forces during the bitter civil war of the 1980s. The case was tried under the U.S. Torture Victims Protection Act of 1992.

In September El Salvador filed an appeal with the International Court of Justice challenging the 1992 resolution of its border dispute with Honduras. The appeal charged that a map submitted by Honduras in the proceedings had been significantly altered from the original.

(RALPH LEE WOODWARD, JR.)

EQUATORIAL GUINEA

Area: 28,051 sq km (10,831 sq mi)
Population (2002 est.): 498,000
Capital: Malabo
Chief of state: President Brig. Gen. Teodoro Obiang Nguema Mbasogo
Head of government: Prime Minister Cándido Muatetema Rivas

The discovery in 2002 of new offshore oil fields made Equatorial Guinea one of the most exciting countries anywhere for new oil production. Western oil companies increased production to over 200,000 bbl per day. While 70% of the population remained illiterate, the vast new wealth allowed the government to commit itself to providing basic education for all.

The country remained notorious for its poor human rights record, however. The year was marked by mass arrests and numerous allegations of torture and mistreatment of political opponents of Pres. Teodoro Obiang Nguema Mbasogo and the ruling Democratic Party of Equatorial Guinea. Those arrested for an alleged conspiracy against Obiang included two founder-members of a clandestine opposition party, the Fuerza Democrática Republicana, a leader of the Popular Union (UP), and senior army officers from the president's home region. In April Fabian Nsue Nguema Obono, a lawyer and UP member, was charged with having slandered the president in a statement published by a UP exile in Spain. After allegedly having been severely tortured, Obono was tried and sentenced. Another opposition political activist died in jail in July, apparently from injuries inflicted during police torture, and an international outcry ensued. Some urged Spain to put pressure on Equatorial Guinea, but the government continued to deny that detainees were subjected to any ill treatment. (CHRISTOPHER SAUNDERS)

One year after a powerful earthquake in January 2001 left some 200,000 persons homeless in El Salvador, a woman in the town of Comasagua totes water past houses newly constructed by the government.

AP/Wide World Photos

ERITREA

Area: 121,144 sq km (46,774 sq mi)
Population (2002 est.): 3,981,000
Capital: Asmara
Head of state and government: President Isaias Afwerki

The year 2002 began with good prospects for postwar recovery and normalization of Eritrea's regional and international relations. Strained relations with the European Commission were patched up, allowing the disbursement during the year of some €25 million (about $25 million). The refugee repatriation program, which had been mired in disagreements about procedures and budgets since the early 1990s, successfully oversaw the return of hundreds of Eritreans from The Sudan to their homeland, signaling a rapprochement between Asmara and Khartoum. The scaling back of development aid by European countries, which was intended to

The body of Philipos I, the first patriarch of the Eritrean Orthodox Church, lies in state at St. Mary's Church in Asmara on September 20.

AP/Wide World Photos

bring about a constructive dialogue between the government of Eritrea and its jailed dissidents, nevertheless underscored the potential for future discord.

The second quarter began with a resolution by the Permanent Court of Arbitration in The Hague that delimited the border between Ethiopia and Eritrea, which both sides immediately accepted and thereby ended a dispute that had led to war in 1998–2000. Warning came of an impending drought, which placed 1.4 million inhabitants in danger of famine. In June the cabinet announced a new national campaign, called Wefri Warsay Yi'Kaalo, that was designed to transform existing policies and structures and to redress flaws in governance. Major points in it were a recognition of the failure of state-sponsored collective farming, an acknowledgement of the ineffectiveness of the post-1991 secondary-education curricula, the elimination of low-level administrative positions in local government, and the introduction of direct local elections at the city and village levels. The education and local-administration reforms were undertaken quickly. The Ministry of Education announced the return to the conventional four-year secondary school curriculum, and local elections at the village level were successfully carried out in the Debub region, with Mae'kel elections scheduled in the near future. It was noteworthy, however, that in the flurry of reforms, no changes to the 1994 Land Proclamation, under which the state was given ownership of all lands, were proposed.

New ambassadors were exchanged between Italy and Eritrea, healing the rift caused by the expulsion of the Italian envoy in the fallout over the arrests in September 2001 of 11 parliamentarians. Nonetheless, in the last months of the year, a crisis of legitimacy for the ruling People's Front for Democracy and Justice seemed to be looming. Most telling was the sensational escape to Ethiopia of a jailed student dissident, Semere Kesete, in August. Unprecedented international criticism of the regime was heard from the U.S. Department of State and former envoy Anthony Lake. Italian parliamentarians also protested the involuntary repatriation of some Eritrean refugees. Eritrea's international image reached its lowest point since independence, when it had been portrayed as a "new hope" for democratizing African nations. (RUTH IYOB)

ESTONIA

Area: 45,227 sq km (17,462 sq mi)
Population (2002 est.): 1,359,000
Capital: Tallinn
Chief of state: President Arnold Rüütel
Head of government: Prime Ministers Mart Laar and, from January 28, Siim Kallas

At the end of January, Siim Kallas, head of the Reform Party, was approved as prime minister of a new coalition government with the Center Party. Although the two parties commanded only 46 seats in the 101-member parliament, they were usually supported by two small groups—the People's Union and the Estonian United People's Party. In domestic affairs the coalition members sought to strengthen their position for the parliamentary elections scheduled for March 2003 and emphasized the principle of continuity in Estonia's foreign policy. The results of local elections, held on October 20, provided a vote of confidence for the national coalition. Edgar Savisaar's Center Party captured an outright majority of seats in Tallinn, and the Reform Party was the overwhelming winner in Tartu, Estonia's second city. Res Publica, a new party that ran on an anticorruption platform while also reaching out to non-Estonians, performed surprisingly well throughout the country.

The closing months of 2002 brought to fruition two of Estonia's long-standing foreign policy goals: invitations for membership in NATO at the Prague summit in November and in the European Union at the Copenhagen summit in December. Formal induction into both organizations was expected in 2004, following a ratification process in the case of NATO and a referendum, scheduled for September 2003, in the case of the EU. Opinion polls in Estonia indicated increasing support for membership in both organizations.

The Kallas government adopted a policy of more active engagement with Russia and showed a willingness to resolve certain issues of interest to Moscow, including official registration of the Orthodox Church in Estonia associated with the Moscow patriarchate and continued state support for Russian-language secondary schools. Responding to these gestures, various

Russian officials suggested that ratification of the long-stalled border agreement and an end to double tariffs on Estonian imports would likely occur soon. (TOIVO U. RAUN)

ETHIOPIA

Area: 1,133,882 sq km (437,794 sq mi)
Population (2002 est.): 67,673,000
Capital: Addis Ababa
Chief of state: President Girma Wolde-Giyorgis
Head of government: Prime Minister Meles Zenawi

Foreign affairs dominated politics in Ethiopia in 2002. In April the border demarcation between Ethiopia and Eritrea was finalized. The Ethiopian government was not completely satisfied, because the decision placed the town of Badme in Eritrea. An interpretation was requested, but the petition was dismissed. Popular dissatisfaction was manifested in a large street demonstration organized by the Ethiopian Democratic Party. The United Nations Mission in Ethiopia and Eritrea was to remain in place along the border between the two states until de-mining could be accomplished and the border was properly marked. Prisoners still held from the war by both sides remained a point of contention between the two states. In May there was an apparent incursion into Somali territory by Ethiopian troops, though the Ethiopian government denied the charges.

Several outbreaks of violence in the south of the country left more than 100 people dead. Clashes broke out in March between the Sheko and Mezhenger (Majang) people and other ethnic communities that had settled in the area over control of the local administration. The Sheko-Mezhenger party believed that it had won more seats than it was allocated following the December 2001 elections. After a demonstration in Tepi, violence broke out, which led to a month of reprisal killings against the Sheko and Mezhenger people in which the death toll of all parties reached at least 128. At least 15 people, including two policemen, were killed in Awasa in May when police opened fire on demonstrators protesting a decision to move the re-gional capital of the Southern region elsewhere. Sporadic violence also occurred throughout the year in the Oromo region owing to rebel activity by the Oromo Liberation Front. On September 12 the Tigray Hotel was bombed for a second time, killing 5 people and injuring 38.

Taye Wolde-Semayat, former president of the Ethiopian Teachers' Association, who was jailed on charges of armed conspiracy in 1996, was released in May. Amnesty International considered him to have been a prisoner of conscience.

International coffee prices fell to a 40-year low in the first part of 2002. Coffee was Ethiopia's largest export, and this was bad news for an economy that had been growing at a rate of only about 2% for a few years. Drought affected the grain harvest in the highlands, and by year's end famine was looming in the northeastern Afar region, where rains failed for a second year. The drought, in combination with ethnic clashes between the Afar, Kereyu, Ittu, and Issa peoples, had left 500,000 people displaced, while an estimated 8,000,000 people were reported to be in need of food aid, a number that was expected to almost double by early 2003. Both the Ethiopian government and the UN World Food Programme made pleas for international food aid in response to the crisis. (SANDRA F. JOIREMAN)

FIJI

Area: 18,272 sq km (7,055 sq mi)
Population (2002 est.): 824,000
Capital: Suva
Chief of state: President Ratu Josefa Iloilo
Head of government: Prime Minister Laisenia Qarase

The aftereffects of the May 2000 coup continued to dominate Fijian politics in 2002. Former prime minister Sitiveni Rabuka was implicated as one of the instigators of the rebellion, and a paramount Fijian chief was charged with conspiracy for similar involvement.

Prime Minister Laisenia Qarase, an ethnic Fijian, appealed to the Supreme Court in defense of his decision to ignore a constitutional stipulation that he include in his cabinet representatives of

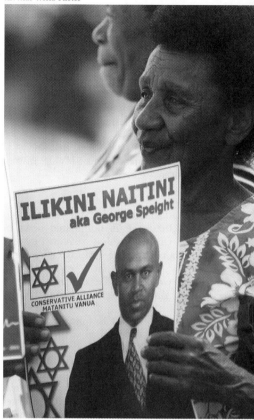

The grandmother of George Speight, leader of the May 2000 coup attempt in Fiji, holds a sign in support of her grandson outside the court in Suva where he faced treason charges in February.

the main opposition party, the Indian-dominated Labour Party. The government also came under scrutiny by the auditor general, who reported widespread abuse of government funds through fraud, waste, and mismanagement. As part of its Twenty Year Development Plan released in September, the government proposed affirmative action policies that would give tax relief to businesses owned and managed by indigenous Fijians and grant greater protection to indigenous land and fisheries rights.

Fiji's sugar industry was threatened with legal action. European Union subsidies, which had allowed the purchase of sugar at 1.5–2 times those of international prices, were challenged as excessive by Australia and Brazil.

An important archaeological discovery on Moturiki Island suggested that human settlement in Fiji first took place about 2,600–2,900 years ago, much earlier than previously thought. (BARRIE MACDONALD)

FINLAND

Area: 338,145 sq km (130,559 sq mi)
Population (2002 est.): 5,201,000
Capital: Helsinki
Chief of state: President Tarja Halonen
Head of government: Prime Minister Paavo Lipponen

Finland's historically edgy relationship with Russia again dominated news in 2002. During his July visit to Finland, Russian Defense Minister Sergey Ivanov declared that Moscow's NATO links would not be damaged if the other Baltic states—Estonia, Latvia, and Lithuania—joined NATO, but Russia would not be pleased if NATO bases were established within 200 km (124 mi) of its borders. Prior to his visit, a newspaper had quoted Ivanov as saying that it was up to Finland to define its own security policy; Moscow, however, thought that NATO enlargement was contrary to regional and global security. Finnish leaders said that Finland was not about to join NATO but that the option would be kept open. National polls since the Sept. 11, 2001, terrorist attacks in the United States had shown that a majority of Finns favoured nonalliance. In an effort to lessen its reliance on Russia for its energy needs, in May Parliament approved the construction of another nuclear reactor, the country's fifth.

The diaries of Urho Kekkonen were made public during the year. Kekkonen, who was president from 1956 to 1981 and died in 1986, was associated with "finlandization," or, as he called it, "national realism," a policy that allowed a small country like Finland to coexist with a superpower. He wrote that he was deeply shocked by the Soviet occupation of Czechoslovakia in 1968 and that he had not believed Moscow's reassurances; if the Soviet Union had invaded Finland, Kekkonen wrote, he would not have expected help from the West.

In another echo of the Cold War, Alpo Rusi, a foreign policy adviser (1994–99) to former president Martti Ahtisaari, came under investigation by security police on suspicion that he had spied for former East Germany. Rusi denied the charge but acknowledged that he was under investigation and scrapped plans to enter politics and run for a par-

Finnish Prime Minister Paavo Lipponen fields questions from reporters at the World Economic Forum in New York City on February 1.

liamentary seat in March 2003. *Helsingin Sanomat*, the leading Finnish daily, reported in 2001 that it had obtained records showing that a large number of Finns supplied information to the Stasi, East Germany's intelligence agency, but it did not list their names.

Prime Minister Paavo Lipponen, a proponent of the "northern dimension" of the European Union, sought EU funding to help underwrite a prospective health program among the Baltic states. Finnish men were crossing into Russia to purchase sex services, and HIV, a rarity in Finland, was rife there.

(EDWARD M. SUMMERHILL)

FRANCE

Area: 543,965 sq km (210,026 sq mi)
Population (2002 est.): 59,440,000
Capital: Paris
Chief of state: President Jacques Chirac
Head of government: Prime Ministers Lionel Jospin and, from May 6, Jean-Pierre Raffarin

Elections, both presidential and parliamentary, dominated France in 2002. The surprise success of the far-right National Front's Jean-Marie Le Pen, who beat Socialist Prime Minister Lionel Jospin for a place in the second-round runoff against Pres. Jacques Chirac, gave the country (and its neighbours and partners abroad) a bad fright. This also gave Chirac a record victory margin in his reelection as president in May and helped ensure a resounding majority for his centre-right forces in the June parliamentary election, which marked the end of five years of uneasy cohabitation between a Gaullist president and a Socialist-led government. (*See* Sidebar.)

France also faced a slowdown in the country's export-led growth at a time when Chirac and the new prime minister, Jean-Pierre Raffarin (*see* BIOGRAPHIES), were starting to carry out Chirac's election promise to cut taxes. The economic slowdown reduced government revenues and threw the president's plans to cut the budget deficit off course. This, in turn, brought some tension with France's partners in the euro zone because of the commitment by euro zone countries to aim for balanced budgets.

The end of cohabitation brought renewed vigour and apparent success to French foreign policy. In the European Union (EU), Chirac safeguarded the interests of France's powerful farm lobby by securing an agreement to maintain the level of EU farm spending to 2013, despite the likelihood that the anticipated entry of new member states from Eastern Europe would strengthen the case for radical agricultural reform. After the French elections, Chirac set out to be more conciliatory toward the U.S. Over Iraq, however, Chirac bargained hard at the UN with the U.S. over the latter's wish for a tough Security Council resolution on weapons inspections in Iraq, backed with the threat of force.

Politics. The presidential election had been widely expected to be a rerun of the Chirac-Jospin contest of 1995. It was therefore the shock of the year when Le Pen outscored Jospin in the first round. After his double victory in the runoff and the subsequent parliamentary vote, Chirac plucked Raffarin out of relative obscurity to be prime minister. Of the 27 other ministers in the new government, only 6 had previously held office. The most senior political novice was Finance and Economy Minister Francis Mer, a veteran steel industrialist. The intent clearly was to signal a break with the Parisian political clique that had dominated past governments.

The French Elections

France's 2002 presidential election campaign started in lacklustre fashion. The two presumed main rivals—Pres. Jacques Chirac and Prime Minister Lionel Jospin—declared their candidacies in February and were joined by a record 14 other contenders for the Élysée Palace. Many voters appeared bored by what seemed to be just a rerun of the Chirac-Jospin contest of 1995 and bemused by the plethora of candidates in a campaign that focused more on crime and immigration than broader economic or foreign policy issues. The upshot was record apathy for a presidential election—a 28.4% abstention rate in the first round of voting on April 21—and the shocking success of Jean-Marie Le Pen, leader of the far-right National Front.

The April 21 poll was close, with Chirac polling 19.88% of the vote, Le Pen 16.86%, and Jospin 16.18%. Only the top-two vote getters moved to the second round, and a stunned Jospin was thus left out of the runoff. Le Pen had received only 230,000 more votes than he had in 1995, but he was helped by the low turnout, the poorer-than-expected showing by Jospin (whose schoolmasterly approach attracted few outside his own Socialist Party), and the fragmentation of the vote.

Chirac refused to hold the customary TV debate with his opponent, saying he did not want to give Le Pen any more of a platform than he already had. The president also may have feared that Le Pen would air the accusations of corruption that swirled around Chirac from his nearly 20 years as mayor of Paris. In the May 5 second round, the left voted reluctantly but massively for Chirac, who gained 82.05% of the vote, against 17.95% for Le Pen. Chirac thereby broke two records for a Fifth Republic president, winning the lowest score in the first round and the highest in the second.

Jospin immediately resigned as prime minister, and the president replaced him with Jean-Pierre Raffarin. (*See* BIOGRAPHIES.) The result of the parliamentary elections, which began on June 9, was almost a foregone conclusion. The demoralized Socialist Party swung to the left with a manifesto calling for an end to privatization and a rise in the minimum wage. On the right there was a historic closing of ranks between the Gaullists and much of the centre-right, which formed the Union for Presidential Majority (UMP). In the second round of voting, on June 16, the UMP won 353 seats in the 577-seat National Assembly. The centre-right Union for French Democracy won 27 seats. The Socialist Party lost over 100 seats to end up with 140. Among the casualties were several prominent Socialists, including Martine Aubry, the creator of the 35-hour workweek. The Communist Party won less than 5% of the vote, which left it with 22 seats, and Communist Party leader Robert Hue lost his seat. Dominique Voynet, leader of the Greens, also was defeated, as was former interior minister Jean-Pierre Chevenement, who lost the seat he had held for 29 years.   (DAVID BUCHAN)

Corsican autonomy had been opposed by Chirac and by former interior minister Jean-Pierre Chevenement, who in 2000 had resigned over the issue. Raffarin therefore caused some surprise when he joined Sarkozy on a visit to Corsica in July 2002, apparently endorsing the need for some autonomy and special concessions for France's troubled Mediterranean island.

Economy. The weakening of the world economy helped to depress France's export-led growth, lowering the growth in national output for the year to 1.5% and raising the overall public-sector deficit to nearly 2% of gross domestic product. The economy barely figured in the presidential election campaign, and Chirac did little to spell out what economic policy he and his new government would pursue, apart from a promise to cut income tax by 30% over five years. Raffarin made a start on this by getting a 5% tax reduction through Parliament in July. The prime minister also tackled—against union opposition—structural reforms to reduce France's outsize civil service, amend the Socialists' flagship measure of the 35-hour workweek to allow more flexible overtime, and pursue privatization of the state electricity and gas monopolies.

For the private sector the dramatic event of the year was the failure of Jean-Marie Messier to turn Vivendi Universal into an enduring transatlantic media group. Vivendi reported a net loss of €12.3 billion (€1 = about $1) for the first half of 2002, on top of a net debt of €35 billion. In July the company replaced Messier with Jean-René Fourtou, who set about selling many of the group's assets. In September Michel Bon was forced to resign as chairman of France Télécom, which had run up debts of more than €70 billion.

Foreign Policy. Chirac used the end of cohabitation with the Socialists to appoint his longtime chief of staff, Dominique de Villepin, foreign minister with the mission of improving France's relations with its most important partners. When Gerhard Schröder narrowly won reelection in September, Chirac sought to improve relations with the German chancellor. In late October he persuaded Schröder to agree to maintain future EU farm spending as France's price for agreeing to enlarge the EU. British Prime Minister Tony Blair sharply criticized Chirac for preempting any meaningful farm budget cuts but went along with the deal for the sake of enlargement.

Nicolas Sarkozy, the new interior minister, launched a drive to recruit more police, gendarmes, and magistrates as several dramatic incidents highlighted the law-and-order issue. In March a man opened fire on a town council meeting at Nanterre, a Paris suburb, killing 8 people and wounding 19 others; a day later he killed himself by jumping out a police station window. At the July 14 Bastille Day parade in Paris, 25-year-old Maxime Brunerie shot at Chirac's car before being overpowered. Brunerie had been associated with Unité Radicale, a small extremist party that campaigned against immigration, Israel, and glo-balization. The party was formally banned by the French government in August. More widespread was the spate of anti-Jewish incidents, including attacks on a kosher butcher in Toulouse, a Jewish school bus in Paris, and synagogues in Marseilles, Lyon, and Strasbourg.

Violence of a more habitual kind persisted in Corsica. In January the Constitutional Council (France's highest court) ruled that the 2001 devolution of certain legislative powers to the Corsican assembly was unconstitutional and that school courses in the Corsican language had to be voluntary. The Jospin government's bill on

On April 21 in Paris, supporters of French Prime Minister and presidential candidate Lionel Jospin react to early first-round poll results showing Jospin running behind Pres. Jacques Chirac as well as far-right National Front leader Jean-Marie Le Pen.

De Villepin, a former press attaché in the French embassy in Washington, D.C., also set out to be more positive about Bush, who visited Paris in late May. The new foreign minister conceded that the status quo in Iraq was not acceptable, even if France felt that removing Iraqi leader Saddam Hussein should be a last resort. France strongly pursued this argument in the UN Security Council debate over a resolution on Iraq. Chirac, however, moved to improve France's military potential. He instructed the Raffarin government to raise defense spending over the 2003–08 period and to order a second aircraft carrier.

(DAVID BUCHAN)

GABON

Area: 267,667 sq km (103,347 sq mi)
Population (2002 est.): 1,233,000
Capital: Libreville
Chief of state: President Omar Bongo
Head of government: Prime Minister Jean-François Ntoutoume-Emane

In January, following his Gabonese Democratic Party's victory in the December legislative elections, Pres. Omar Bongo pledged that his new gov-ernment would be an open one. He invited opposition parties to participate in the collective management of the state. Father Paul Mba Abessole, leader of the opposition National Rally of Woodcutters, told his members that they should join the new government to help solve the nation's economic and social problems. On January 27 Prime Minister Jean-François Ntoutoume-Emane was asked by President Bongo to form a new cabinet. It was the first government since multiparty elections began in 1990 that included members of the opposition.

On August 13 the Council of Ministers adopted a revised electoral code designed to simplify the process of voter registration. Despite fierce arguments, opposition parties were unable to achieve their primary goal of having a single-ballot system rather than the existing system with separate ballots for each party. The reformed code would be in effect for municipal elections scheduled for late December.

On May 6, the Ministry of Public Health announced that the outbreak of Ebola fever had ended. It was known to have taken at least 53 lives in northeastern Gabon alone, but no new cases were reported after March 19, when the last death occurred. On July 19, in an effort to cut communication costs drastically, the government banned the use of mobile phones for all civil servants, claiming they were being used mainly for personal purposes. Security forces bull-dozed four fishing villages near Libreville on July 24, leaving hundreds homeless. According to the government, these villages were being used as bases by drug traffickers and were destroyed as part of the ongoing war against crime.

(NANCY ELLEN LAWLER)

GAMBIA, THE

Area: 10,689 sq km (4,127 sq mi)
Population (2002 est.): 1,418,000
Capital: Banjul
Head of state and government: President Col. Yahya Jammeh

In February 2002 Senegalese Pres. Abdoulaye Wade visited The Gambia for celebrations to mark the anniversary of independence from Britain, and in April Pres. Yahya Jammeh was guest of honour in Dakar at the celebrations to mark Senegal's independence from France. Jammeh's efforts to mediate in the ongoing conflict in the southern Senegalese region of Casamance achieved little, and refugees from the conflict continued to enter The Gambia. In June relations with Guinea-Bissau suddenly deteriorated after Pres. Kumba Ialá of that country threatened to "crush The Gambia in two minutes" if it did not deal with alleged coup plotters based there. After Jammeh denounced this threat, UN Secretary-General Kofi Annan sent a special peace envoy to defuse the tension.

Internal controversy in 2002 focused on increased threats to freedom of expression, seen especially in the arrest of a number of journalists and in the passage through the National Assembly of the harsh Media Commission bill. It proposed a body that would register all reporters, enforce the disclosure of sources, be able to impose fines for the publication of "unauthorized stories," and close down papers for noncompliance with its orders. Following some negotiations between the president and the National Assembly, the bill was signed into law. The Gambia Press Union threatened to take the measure to the high court, however, claiming that it violated the 1997 constitution.

(CHRISTOPHER SAUNDERS)

GEORGIA

Area: 69,700 sq km (26,911 sq mi)
Population (2002 est.): 4,961,000
Capital: T'bilisi
Head of state and government: President Eduard Shevardnadze, assisted by Minister of State Avtandil Djorbenadze

Three new opposition parties—the New Rights, former justice minister Mikhail Saakashvili's National Movement, and former Parliament speaker Zurab Zhvania's United Democrats—made a strong showing in the June 2, 2002, local elections, thrashing the former ruling Union of Citizens of Georgia (SMK) in T'bilisi. Disputes over alleged fraud, however, necessitated a recount in T'bilisi, which dragged on until November 4, when Saakashvilis' supporters elected him chairman of the T'bilisi City Council. Pres. Eduard Shevardnadze sought to revive the SMK at a mid-June congress at which most government ministers joined its ruling board and Shevardnadze endorsed Minister of State Avtandil Djorbenadze as a candidate for the 2005 presidential elections. Shevardnadze was not eligible to run again.

On October 11, 80 deputies from five opposition factions, including the New Rights, National Movement, and United Democrats, walked out of Parliament to protest the fact that the new development plan, including sweeping government reforms, unveiled by Shevardnadze in his annual address to the legislature contained no new solutions to social and economic problems.

Gross domestic product increased by 4% during the first nine months of the year, but revenue shortfalls and a European Union decision to withhold two grants totaling $23.5 million to protest the abduction in June of British adviser Peter Shaw necessitated the slashing of budget spending. Shaw was released under mysterious circumstances on November 6.

Accusing Georgia of reneging on a promise to withdraw its troops from the Kodori Gorge, the leadership of the secessionist Abkhaz region refused to attend any talks on resolving its long-standing conflict with T'bilisi. On October 10 the Georgian Parliament voted to amend the constitution to designate Abkhazia an autonomous republic.

The February revelation by the U.S. chargé d'affaires, Philip Remler, that Afghan militants had joined forces with Chechen fighters ensconced in the Pankisi Gorge in northeastern Georgia prompted the United States to launch a $64 million program named Train and Equip to improve the Georgian army's ability to combat terrorism. Georgia repeatedly rejected Russian officials' proposals to launch a joint military operation against Chechen fighters and international mercenaries in Pankisi, however. In late August one man was killed when unidentified aircraft bombed Pankisi, and on September 11 Russian Pres. Vladimir Putin threatened a military strike in Pankisi if Georgia failed to capture and extradite all militants still on its territory. Meeting on October 6, Shevardnadze and Putin succeeded in defusing tensions and reached agreement on joint border patrols and closer cooperation between the two countries' security services. At the November NATO summit in Prague, Georgia formally announced its intention to seek membership of that alliance.

(ELIZABETH FULLER)

GERMANY

Area: 357,021 sq km (137,847 sq mi)
Population (2002 est.): 82,506,000
Capital: Berlin; some ministries remain in Bonn
Chief of state: President Johannes Rau
Head of government: Chancellor Gerhard Schröder

A worsening economy and stubbornly high unemployment were the dominant issues for most of 2002 in Germany. Gerhard Schröder was reelected chancellor nonetheless, eking out a narrow victory that was perhaps due more to his personal popularity than to his political successes. He also benefited from his handling of the worst floods in over a century and his countrymen's fear of a war with Iraq.

While the year was marked by a stream of bad economic news—ranging from slow growth to corporate bankruptcies and a growing budget deficit—the campaign also showed that voters had little interest in attacking the structural causes of Germany's economic problems. In the run-up to the national election in September, neither of the two main candidates proposed the deep reforms that Europe's most populous nation would have needed to rekindle its economy. In an apparent effort to shift the focus of his campaign away from economic issues, Chancellor Schröder made an unprecedented move in foreign relations: he publicly and forcefully ruled out any German involvement in an American-led military campaign against Iraq, regardless of whether the United Nations and U.S. allies supported such a venture. His categorical rejection of a military engagement angered the U.S. government and marked the first time in post-World War II history that Germany had parted ways with its allies and the UN. Schröder's step led election-time Germany into controversy and international isolation, which the government tried to redress after the balloting. Schröder's reelection chances also benefited from his personal popularity. Throughout his first four-year term, his personal approval ratings remained far higher than those of his conservative challenger, the archconservative premier of Bavaria, Edmund Stoiber (*see* BIOGRAPHIES), whose stiff manner and sharp rhetoric put off many voters. In an intensely personalized campaign, Stoiber continued to lose support and eventually, the election.

Domestic Affairs. On September 22, 62.5 million voters reelected Germany's incumbent coalition government of the centre-left Social Democratic Party (SPD), led by Chancellor Schröder, and the environmentalist Greens under Foreign Minister Joschka Fischer. Election night was a thriller, keeping Germans glued to their television sets until the wee hours of the morning. In the end the Social Democrats and the conservative Christian Democratic Union–Christian Social Union (CDU-CSU) tied at 38.5% of the vote each.

The small parties decided the election. The Greens, Schröder's coalition partner, scored higher than Stoiber's potential coalition partner, the business-friendly Free Democrats. Before the September ballot the Greens had been largely dismissed as a phenomenon of an earlier generation whose main issues—pacifism and the environment—were now passé or had been absorbed into the programs of the mainstream parties. The devastating floods that destroyed large parts of eastern Germany in early August revived the environment as a political is-

Christian Social Union leader Edmund Stoiber, who lost to German Chancellor Gerhard Schröder in the September elections, holds up a postcard bearing Schröder's image—and the words "Ha-ha, fooled you!"—at the CSU party congress in Munich on November 22.

sue, however. Similarly, American sabre rattling awakened the long-standing Green supporters in the peace movement. Nor did it hurt that Foreign Minister Fischer was the most popular politician in Germany. On campaign billboards voters were urged to cast a "Joschka-vote." The Free Democrats lost ground for reasons of their own making. The problems began in May, when, with an eye to the three million Muslim voters in Germany, party vice-chairman Jürgen Möllemann sharply criticized Israel and accused Michel Friedman, a Jewish leader and popular television personality, of provoking anti-Semitism through his behaviour. Möllemann also supported a Syrian-born critic of Israel as a new member of the Free Democratic faction in a state parliament. Politicians, including his own party leaders, were quick to distance themselves from Möllemann but not before the election campaign had acquired an ugly tinge of anti-Semitism.

The principal loser was the Party of Democratic Socialism, the renamed communist party of the former East Germany. For the first time in years, the neocommunists failed to muster the 5% of all votes required for the party to be represented in the Bundestag (lower house of parliament). One problem was that, 13 years after the fall of the Berlin

Wall, the party had become irrelevant, and eastern Germans stopped voting for it. Others were the resignation of party figurehead Gregor Gysi and the fact that Schröder trumped the neocommunists' traditional antimilitarism with his strong opposition to military intervention in Iraq.

For Germany's conservatives the ballot was a setback but not a disaster. The race was closer than many Germans had initially predicted. The CDU had not entirely recovered from its thundering defeat in 1998, when a 16-year run of conservative rule under Helmut Kohl was terminated. Since then it had offered few new faces or policies. In 1999 the Christian Democrats had also endured a crippling party-financing scandal that disgraced Kohl, followed by a spell of divisive infighting among its new leadership. These internal battles ended only when party chair Angela Merkel ceded the nomination for the election to Stoiber in January 2002.

Election day marked a comeback for Schröder from a lag in the polls and a tough year. The government suffered through two food scandals, in January and July, that threatened its "agricultural turnaround" aimed at boosting organic farming and consumer protection. The Social Democrats were at the centre of a large financial scandal in

Cologne in March, which cost the party some of its moral high ground vis-à-vis the scandal-ridden CDU. Partly as a result, the SPD was defeated in the April election in the eastern state of Saxony-Anhalt, its share of the vote falling by 16% from four years earlier. Voters punished Schröder for Germany's economic problems, which were even more pronounced in the depressed east. Another incident that shook public confidence in the government in April was the shooting spree by a 19-year-old student at a high school in Erfurt that left 17 people dead in 10 minutes. Shocked Germans feared a wave of American-style school massacres.

Summer brought hardly better news for Schröder. In June Germany lost in the World Cup soccer final to Brazil, which further dampened the country's mood. In July the chancellor was forced to fire Defense Minister Rudolf Scharping, who was implicated in a corruption scandal that subsequently cost the jobs of several other Social Democrats and Greens. Relief for Schröder—if not for people living along the Elbe—came only when the river rose and flooded towns and vast areas of land. The flood focused public attention away from economic performance and political scandals and onto the chancellor himself. His compassionate and decisive demeanour on television consoling victims and promising state aid to the damaged region surely gained back a number of voters, especially in the east.

The Economy. The year started on a sour note with the introduction of the euro, Europe's common currency. Germans already disliked the new money before it arrived. In opinion polls a majority said they wanted to keep their old currency, the Deutsche Mark. With the exception of a few money truck robberies, the gigantic currency swap just after New Year's went smoothly, but when the euro bills and coins went into circulation, they quickly became even more unpopular. Many retailers, restaurants, and other businesses used the switch to raise their prices. Public outrage was so strong that Germans dubbed the euro the *teuro*, a play on the German word *teuer*, "expensive."

March saw several high-profile bankruptcies, starting with the collapse of construction giant Philipp Holzmann AG. After years of extending the company's credit lines, the banks finally balked. The episode was particularly embarrassing for Schröder because, in a grand gesture almost three years earlier, he had promised to save Holzmann by

With the dome of the Reichstag in the background, the Quadriga of Victory atop the Brandenburg Gate in Berlin is illuminated on October 3—Unification Day in Germany.

pressuring banks and pledging government aid. In April, just before the vote in Saxony-Anhalt, Schröder tried the same trick by rescuing a manufacturer of train cars near the eastern town of Halle. Neither was Stoiber immune from such embarrassments. In April the conservative Bavarian media magnate Leo Kirch went bankrupt after years of financial cliff-hanging. Kirch had long been receiving oversized loans from Bavarian banks, including public banks under Stoiber's sway. The insolvency wave also swept away Babcock Borsig AG, an old industrial group in Germany's Ruhr valley, and nearly drowned MobilCom AG, a newer telecommunications operator. Days before the election in September, the chancellor mounted yet another rescue mission by organizing a large financial package for the company. The plan preserved MobilCom's sizable long-distance business as well as 5,500 jobs at the company, but it did not ensure MobilCom's long-term survival and further undercut Schröder's reputation as an economic reformer.

That reputation had largely vanished already. In the first two years of his tenure, Chancellor Schröder had embarked on a series of tax-cutting reforms, launched an austerity program, encouraged Germans to buy private pensions, and published a policy plan jointly written with British Prime Minister Tony Blair for economic liberalization.

His reformist zeal slowed in the middle of his term, and in some areas, such as labour law, he even backtracked.

Economic indicators were dire. Growth was close to zero in 2002, a worse showing than the year before, and Germany registered the lowest growth rate in the European Union. By election time, unemployment stood at 10% of the labour force and had reached close to 20% in some depressed regions of eastern Germany. Business investment had fallen for seven consecutive quarters, and consumer spending was flat. Germany's share of world trade was falling and its international competitiveness was sinking. The country also came close to breaching the EU's budget-deficit limit for members of the euro zone. In February Germany received its first warning letter from Brussels, telling Berlin to rein in the deficit. Even German schools and universities, long the country's pride, were failing: in January it was reported that in an international study German secondary-school students ranked a mere 25th out of 32 countries in reading, math, and scientific literacy. (*See* EDUCATION.)

Stoiber went on the attack in April, after the Saxony-Anhalt election, with an economic recovery plan he called "3 × 40," which would lower the top tax rate to 40%, social welfare contributions to 40%, and public spending to 40% of gross domestic product. His govern-

ment team included, as minister for economics, labour, and eastern Germany, Lothar Späth, a former state governor and chief executive of the eastern technology group Jenoptik. In comparison, the chancellor's team looked spent and unexciting. Stoiber's problem, though, was that most Germans did not feel any need for change. Generous welfare payments and long-term unemployment compensation—along with union-negotiated job security, salaries, and benefits—still shielded Germans from true economic hardship. Gauging this mindset, Stoiber did not propose changes that anyone found very meaningful.

In July Schröder began again to talk of the economy. The chief executive of communications colossus Deutsche Telekom resigned under heavy pressure from the government, which feared it was losing the votes of small shareholders in the partly privatized company. In the same month, the chancellor created a commission to reform the rigid labour market. The group, known as the Hartz Commission after the Volkswagen executive who chaired it, offered several proposals in August on improving job-seeking and job-offering procedures, especially at the bureaucratic unemployment offices. The report did not, however, touch on the deeper issues: German industry's overprotected and inflexible workforce, high labour costs, and stifling red tape.

435

Foreign Relations. Perhaps the most significant development in 2002 happened in the realm of foreign relations. In an apparent effort to revive his faltering election campaign, Chancellor Schröder proposed "a German way" in August. The slogan was mainly directed against U.S.-style capitalism—what many Germans saw as a "hire and fire" culture—but it was also a criticism of U.S. policy toward Iraq. After U.S. Vice Pres. Dick Cheney outlined the case for a military strike in a televised speech in late August, the chancellor went a step farther by declaring that Germany would not engage in military adventures against the Arab state. Encouraged by a surge in SPD ratings, Schröder sharpened his rhetoric further. In the second of two television debates with Stoiber in early September, he said Germany would say "no" to military intervention even if a strike had blessing from the UN. He put Stoiber on the spot by asking whether he supported war in Iraq—"yes or no?" Stoiber, who was opposed to the chancellor's stance but did not want to come off as a hawk, appeared helpless. He replied that he opposed the use of force in general but that one could not exclude any theoretical possibility. That ambivalence may have cost Stoiber the election.

Beyond Germany's borders, Schröder's words hit like a bombshell. The U.S. government was outraged. Just as it was beginning to build international support for a war, one of its closest allies was publicly thwarting its efforts. Suddenly, a decade of cozy U.S.–German relations seemed empty. Observers agreed that Schröder's move was a slap in the face of the UN, a shock to Germany's European allies, and a shot in the arm for Iraqi dictator Saddam Hussein. Schröder's position surprised even France, Germany's closest friend in Europe, which had not been consulted beforehand and distanced itself from the German view. The government's stance was something of a watershed for Germany itself. No postwar German leader had ever risked his friendship with the U.S. or publicly opposed an American strategic imperative. No other leader had put Germany on an isolationist course, at odds with its allies and the UN (where Germany was still seeking a permanent seat on the Security Council). No leader had ever questioned the country's postwar policy of international integration and cautious rhetoric.

A further blow to German-American relations came days before the election when Minister of Justice Herta Däubler-Gmelin compared the tactics of U.S. Pres. George W. Bush with regards to Iraq to those of Adolf Hitler. Schröder quickly apologized for her remarks in a letter to Washington, but senior American officials said relations had been "poisoned" and did not congratulate Schröder on his reelection soon afterward. Earlier in 2002 Germans themselves had been the victims of international terrorism. An explosion in April at a synagogue in Djerba, Tun., killed 16 people, including 11 German tourists. During the year, it also became increasingly clear that much of the planning for the Sept. 11, 2001, terrorist attacks in the U.S. had taken place on German soil, notably in an important terrorist cell in Hamburg. Many Germans would probably agree with the American newspaper that wrote that Schröder "traded allies for votes."   (CECILIE ROHWEDDER)

GHANA

Area: 238,533 sq km (92,098 sq mi)
Population (2002 est.): 20,244,000
Capital: Accra
Head of state and government: President John Agyekum Kufuor

Ghana had, until recently, generally avoided the ethnic tensions that plagued other West African nations. In March 2002, however, fighting between rival clans and ethnic groups broke out in the Northern Region, the largest administrative area of the country. Different clans claimed the right to certain chieftainships, and several ethnic groups—all minorities within Ghana itself—clashed over reportedly unfair treatment and discrimination in the region and the nation generally. Despite the national government's declaration of a state of emergency, including curfews and press censorship, the conflicts continued. More than 30 people were killed during the month of March, and another 20 were reported killed in April. In mid-May the government extended the state of emergency, sealing off the Northern Region from the rest of the country. Conflicts continued sporadically throughout the year, with more than 100 people killed. The rest of Ghana remained calm.

Severe flooding disrupted life in Accra, the capital, in early June. The flash floods had become a yearly occurrence, owing to poor drainage and overpopulation. Mud slides contributed to the devastation. Thousands were affected, with many losing their homes. At least 10 people drowned.

In mid-September an army mutiny in neighbouring Côte d'Ivoire disrupted cocoa production in that country, the world's leading producer of the crop. The global market price of cocoa, one of Ghana's chief exports, rose dramatically, which helped the national economy.

                (ANDREW F. CLARK)

Women in Accra, Ghana, leave their flooded homes on June 14; thousands of people in the Ghanaian capital were affected by the heavy flooding.

GREECE

Area: 131,957 sq km (50,949 sq mi)
Population (2002 est.): 10,994,000
Capital: Athens
Chief of state: President Konstantinos Stephanopoulos
Head of government: Prime Minister Konstantinos Simitis

In 2002 Greek security forces managed to crack down on the elusive left-wing terrorist group November 17. Heretofore, not a single suspected member of the group believed to have been responsible for 23 killings since 1975 had been arrested. The breakthrough came when on June 29 an explosive device went off in the hands of Savvas Xiros, who also carried a weapon stolen from a policeman killed in a November 17 attack. On the basis of his confessions—and subsequently those of other suspects—police arrested more than a dozen alleged members of the group, among them Alexandros Giotopoulos, believed to be one of the cofounders and the head of November 17. On September 5 Dimitris Koufodinas, the last suspected leading figure still at large, turned himself in, ending the largest manhunt in recent Greek history. Though Giotopoulos denied all charges against him, Koufodinas assumed "political responsibility" for his actions.

Lawmakers had a busy year. On June 20 Parliament passed the controversial social security bill, which restructured the social security and pension systems. The bill had been put on hold in 2001 owing to large-scale protests and strikes. A law against gambling that went into effect in August had to be "clarified" through government guidelines in September since it also effectively prohibited computer games of all kinds. A new law banning smoking in public buildings and restricting it in other places took effect on October 1.

The Special Supreme Court ruled on September 18 that victims of Nazis could not seek compensation from Germany through the Greek legal system. This decision overturned a 2000 Supreme Court ruling in which victims of the 1944 Distomo massacre were awarded $27 million in compensation.

In April a group of 12 British and two Dutch "plane spotters" who had been arrested in November 2001 while taking pictures of military aircraft at an air show were tried for espionage. Eight of them were given three-year prison sentences; the others received one-year suspended sentences. All were released and allowed to return home, however, pending their appeals; 13 of the 14 defendants were acquitted in November.

Outgoing Athens Mayor Dimitris Avramopoulos announced on June 11 that his Movement of Free Citizens, launched in March 2001, would "suspend operations" owing to financial problems and the "suffocating frame of polarization" in Greek politics. On October 13 and 20, local elections were held at the municipal and prefecture levels. As expected, most races for mayors and prefects were decided between the ruling Panhellenic Socialist Movement (PASOK) and the centre-right New Democracy (ND), although smaller leftist parties and independent candidates also managed to win several contests. ND candidates carried the majority of prefectures and the plurality of major municipalities, including the three biggest cities—Athens (where Dora Bakoyanni was elected the city's first female mayor), Thessaloniki, and Piraeus. PASOK, however, won several important municipalities and prefectures and the crucial supraprefecture of Athens-Piraeus.

Large infrastructure works continued in and around Athens in preparation for the 2004 Olympic Summer Games. The International Olympic Committee said that it was largely satisfied with preparations but cautioned that no further delays were permissible.

The Greek economy continued to grow in 2002, with the government expecting 3.8% growth in gross domestic product and 9.5% in investments. Unemployment dropped to 9.6% in the second quarter of 2002, from 10.2% a year earlier. The Athens Stock Exchange continued its downward slide, however; the index fell from 2,592 points at the end of 2001 to 1,838 on Sept. 30, 2002, the lowest figure in more than four years. The introduction of the euro as the new currency proceeded smoothly. Officials figures put inflation at 3.3%, but the public complained that there were price hikes related to the new currency. In September consumer groups organized a successful one-day nationwide boycott of stores and markets.

A statue of Greek marathoner and 1896 Olympic gold medalist Spyridon Louis stands before the massive sports complex being constructed in Athens, where the 2004 Olympic Summer Games would be held.

Greek foreign policy remained unchanged. Greece continued to engage in peacekeeping missions but maintained that any action against Iraq should come within the framework of the United Nations, and Prime Minister Konstantinos ("Kostas") Simitis warned against "unilateral action." No resolution to the dispute with Macedonia over the latter's name was found, but the 1996 interim agreement regulating relations between the two countries was extended on September 12. In relations with Turkey, both sides agreed to install direct phone lines linking their defense ministries. On the issue of European Union expansion, Greece maintained its position that unless Cyprus was included in the first wave of expansion, the Greek Parliament would not ratify the measure.   (STEFAN KRAUSE)

GRENADA

Area: 344 sq km (133 sq mi)
Population (2002 est.): 101,000
Capital: Saint George's
Chief of state: Queen Elizabeth II, represented by Governor-General Daniel Williams
Head of government: Prime Minister Keith Mitchell

In February 2002 Grenada was removed from the Organisation for Economic Co-operation and Development's (OECD's) list of "uncooperative" tax havens after it had made a commitment to transparency in the regulation of its offshore banking system and agreed to "effective exchange of information" on tax matters.

A major initiative toward advancing the fortunes of Grenada's cruise industry was taken in June when the Port Authority entered into an agreement with a Swiss company to participate in the establishment of a new cruise complex in the capital, St. George's. Switzerland's Zueblin Group agreed to spend up to $125 million on commercial facilities associated with the complex, while the Port Authority would contribute $25 million for the port itself. In the same month, the European Union announced an $8 million loan to boost tourism in Grenada and develop a marketing plan for small hotels.

Four questionable offshore banks were shut down in September as the government strove to improve the image of an industry that had been under attack in recent years not only by the OECD but by the Financial Action Task Force. Grenada had revoked the licenses of 36 offshore banks since February 2001, and only 9 remained in operation in 2002.   (DAVID RENWICK)

GUATEMALA

Area: 109,117 sq km (42,130 sq mi)
Population (2002 est.): 11,987,000
Capital: Guatemala City
Head of state and government: President Alfonso Portillo Cabrera

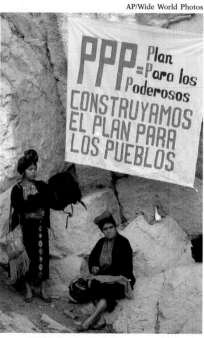

On a road along the Mexican-Guatemalan border in October, two indigenous Guatemalan women participate in a blockade to protest a massive development project known as the Puebla-Panama Plan.

During 2002 Guatemala suffered from serious economic difficulties and widespread crime. Low coffee prices contributed to the country's declining export revenues, as did a serious drought on the Pacific coast. Declining investments and unemployment exacerbated widespread poverty and social injustice. Pres. Alfonso Portillo was implicated in multimillion-dollar corruption schemes, but he resisted demands from civic organizations that he resign, citing improvements in health, education, road construction, and housing programs and a declining inflation rate during his tenure. Worker discontent was reflected in peasant seizures of land and massive protests, to which Portillo responded with land distributions to 38,000 farmers and increases in the minimum wage and other benefits for urban workers. Nevertheless, a *Vox Latina* poll showed that only 8% of respondents had any confidence in Portillo and 41.2% regarded him as the worst president in Guatemalan history.

Guatemala joined other Central American countries in responding favourably to U.S. Pres. George W. Bush's support for a proposed Free Trade Area of the Americas. In March Bush promised to speed up negotiations for a free-trade agreement while recommending that Central American states pass legislation to make the agreement work.

Political assassinations and human rights violations continued to plague Guatemala, but the 30-year prison sentence given during the year to Col. Juan Valencia Osorio for having ordered the 1990 murder of sociologist Myrna Mack marked the first time that a high-ranking Guatemalan military officer had been brought to justice for human rights abuses. There were accusations that Efraín Ríos Montt, president of the Congress and head of the ruling Guatemalan Republican Front party, directed secret forces threatening human rights advocates and labour leaders and that the government was failing to implement the 1996 peace accord.

Thousands welcomed Pope John Paul II to Guatemala on July 29, and on the following day the pope canonized Pedro de Betancur (1619–67), a former shepherd who founded the international Bethlehemite Order. Although born in the Canary Islands, Betancur spent his career in Guatemala helping the poor and ill. He was Central America's first saint.   (RALPH LEE WOODWARD, JR.)

GUINEA

Area: 245,857 sq km (94,926 sq mi)
Population (2002 est.): 7,775,000
Capital: Conakry
Head of state and government: President Gen. Lansana Conté, assisted by Prime Minister Lamine Sidimé

Tensions along Guinea's borders with Liberia and Sierra Leone in 2002 prompted the three nations to seek a common solution to the general insecurity in the area. On March 7, cabinet ministers from the three governments agreed to revive the Mano River Union, a long-moribund economic group, and create a joint security commission under its umbrella. The body proposed, on April 1, that each country expel armed dissident groups from its territories and that joint border patrols be formed to prevent the smuggling of weapons. Despite efforts to end border skirmishes, the Liberian government continued to accuse Guinea of supporting the rebel Liberians United for Reconciliation and Democracy by allowing the group to operate from within its borders. Guinea alleged that in September Liberian troops had crossed its frontier to carry out two raids. ECOWAS, the economic community of 16 West African states, met in emergency session in Nigeria on September 16 to try to defuse the situations. In August the UN estimated that 90,000 Sierra Leonean and Liberian refugees remained in camps in Guinea, with another 60,000 Liberians scattered throughout the country.

After two years of postponements, parliamentary elections were finally held on June 30. Turnout was low, partly a result of calls for a boycott by the main opposition parties. Pres. Lansana Conté's Party for Unity and Progress took 85 of the 114 seats. Indicating its general dissatisfaction with the electoral procedures, the European Union refused to send observers and rejected government requests to help finance the election.

Illegal fishing remained a problem in West Africa. European trawlers were able to breach the 1995 UN Food and Agricultural Organization fishing agreement with impunity, as there were few surveillance airplanes available to spot them. On April 10 the FAO announced a new program to combat illegal fishing off the shores of Guinea, Guinea-Bissau, Senegal, and Sierra Leone. The European Commission planned to grant Guinea €221 million (about $216 million) to facilitate a new five-year program to upgrade roads, promote rural-development projects, and finance a part of the country's budget deficit.

(NANCY ELLEN LAWLER)

GUINEA-BISSAU

Area: 36,125 sq km (13,948 sq mi)
Population (2002 est.): 1,345,000
Capital: Bissau
Chief of state: President Kumba Ialá (Yalla)
Head of government: Prime Minister Alamara Nhassé

Guinea-Bissau remained tense in 2002 after the failed coup attempt against Pres. Kumba Ialá in December 2001. In May the government claimed that there had been another coup attempt from within the military. Under pressure from the UN, President Ialá in June

made a gesture of national reconciliation by proposing an amnesty for soldiers who had been involved in the coup attempts, but he also threatened to invade The Gambia, accusing it of supporting those plotting against him. After mediation by a UN envoy, The Gambia handed over three alleged coup plotters, and relations between the two countries began to calm. In October Ialá visited The Gambia and declared that relations were cordial.

In July the UN Security Council called on Ialá to speed up the demobilization and reintegration of former combatants, and by October the process of demobilization had been declared complete. The UN also appealed to the executive and legislative branches to agree to compromise on the issue of separation of powers. New tensions between Ialá and Prime Minister Alamara Nhassé arose after the president dismissed a number of cabinet ministers.

(CHRISTOPHER SAUNDERS)

GUYANA

Area: 215,083 sq km (83,044 sq mi)
Population (2002 est.): 775,000
Capital: Georgetown
Chief of state: President Bharrat Jagdeo
Head of government: Prime Minister Sam Hinds

For most of 2002 Guyana was in the grip of a crime wave following the breakout from jail of five hardened criminals in February. Eight police officers were killed in clashes with the gang during the year, and several businessmen were murdered. Three of the escapees were also killed. In August gunmen sprayed the office of the Customs Anti-Narcotics Unit with bullets and lobbed four hand grenades into the building. Even the country's director of public prosecutions was wounded in an attack in September. The ruling People's Progressive Party/Civic alliance set up a new unit in midyear to combat what the government described as "domestic terrorism."

Lawlessness in the country took a new turn when in July antigovernment demonstrators stormed the presidential compound in Georgetown to protest what they alleged to be racial discrimination practiced by the government, which had traditionally been supported by those of East Indian descent. At the time, leaders of Caribbean Community and Common Market (Caricom) states were holding their annual summit in Georgetown. Some of the demonstrators were said to have threatened presidential staff members with knives. Two people were shot dead by the police.

The government agreed in June to relinquish its hold on the money-losing Linden Mining Enterprise bauxite operator through the formation of a joint-venture company, in which the government would hold 20% of the shares and the Canadian firm Cambior the majority 80%.   (DAVID RENWICK)

Soldiers patrol the streets of Buxton, Guyana, following the announcement by Pres. Bharrat Jagdeo of new anticrime measures in June.

HAITI

Area: 27,700 sq km (10,695 sq mi)
Population (2002 est.): 7,064,000
Capital: Port-au-Prince
Chief of state and government: President Jean-Bertrand Aristide, assisted by Prime Ministers Jean-Marie Chérestal and, from March 15, Yvon Neptune

The Haitian government's tenuous grasp on the economy and political institutions continued to weaken in 2002. It was unable to provide basic security, health care, education, or enough food and jobs for its citizens. The country lingered near the bottom of the United Nation's annual survey of living conditions. Life expectancy was less than 53 years. At least 23% of children aged five and under suffered from malnutrition, and only 39% of Haitians had clean water available to them. Preventable diseases went untreated. Roughly one out of every 12 Haitians had HIV/AIDS. According to the Centers for Disease Control and Prevention, 44,000 new HIV/AIDS cases would occur in Haiti in 2002—at least 4,000 more than the projected number for the U.S. It was feared that the number of children orphaned by AIDS

would soar from 163,000 to between 323,000 and 393,000 in the next decade.

A study by the World Bank concluded that 15 years of aid through 2001 had not had a noticeable effect on the reduction of poverty in Haiti, since projects had been implemented in a disorganized manner and government officials had not continued improvements. Direct aid to Haiti had been suspended in 2001 owing to irregularities in the May 2000 elections. The Haitian government publicly declared that the $18 million it owed would not be paid until international agencies released additional funds to the country.

Pres. Jean-Bertrand Aristide remained Haiti's most popular figure, but the breadth and depth of that popularity were increasingly coming into question. A large amount of his domestic and foreign support had evaporated. In addition, allegations circulated widely that an attack on the national palace that took place on Dec. 17, 2001, had been staged to allow government supporters to launch violent reprisals against offices and homes of opposition leaders. An Organization of American States (OAS) report supported these allegations. In August, for the first time since Aristide appeared on the political stage in the early 1990s, some of his own loyal followers revolted against him, and for a while they controlled Gonaïves, the country's fourth largest city. The possibility that the political situation was

getting out of hand prompted the U.S. and the OAS to reconsider their aid embargo. In a significant shift of policy, they resolved in September to support Haiti's proposal that foreign aid be unblocked. In return the OAS called for the Haitian government to establish an electoral council, improve justice and public security, and keep the door open for a role for the opposition.

(JEAN-CLAUDE GARCIA-ZAMOR)

HONDURAS

Area: 112,492 sq km (43,433 sq mi)
Population (2002 est.): 6,561,000
Capital: Tegucigalpa
Head of state and government: Presidents Carlos Roberto Flores Facussé and, from January 27, Ricardo Maduro

On Jan. 27, 2002, in the third peaceful transition between parties in Honduras since democratic rule began in 1982, Pres. Carlos Flores of the Liberal Party handed over power to Ricardo Maduro of the National Party. The new administration was the first to govern without a majority in the congress. The National Party held 61 seats, 4 shy of a majority.

Crime was a major issue in 2002. Historically low compared with neighbouring countries, the rate of violent crime—often gang-related—had in two years grown to levels that affected the quality of life of all sectors of society. Acting on campaign pledges, President Maduro immediately sent army troops on joint patrols with the local police in the major cities. Particularly in Tegucigalpa, results were quickly felt, with a dramatic reduction in crime and a popular feeling of reclaiming the streets. Questions remained, however, about how long the government would have the finances to maintain this program and whether it would lead to human rights violations or a militarized police force. Roots of the crime problem, such as inadequate job opportunities for youth and police corruption, persisted.

While Honduras's economy had largely rebounded from the widespread destruction caused by Hurricane Mitch in 1998, economic performance was depressed in 2002 owing to low world

A television image shows some of the estimated 200 illegal immigrants from Haiti who waded ashore in Key Biscayne, Fla., on October 29 after the small wooden freighter that had transported them ran aground.

AP/Wide World Photos

Honduran Pres. Ricardo Maduro poses with his new bride, the Spanish-born Aguas Ocaña, after their marriage on October 10 in Tegucigalpa. Maduro was the first-ever Honduran president to wed while in office.

market prices for Honduras's main exports (coffee, bananas, sugar). In addition, the *monilia* fungus ravaged the cacao crop, which had a strong market, and farmers lacked funds for new plants.

In a final act the Flores administration reopened diplomatic relations with Cuba after a 40-year lapse. On May 1 the U.S. government extended temporary protection status to 105,000 Hondurans living in the U.S.

(MICHELLE M. TAYLOR-ROBINSON)

HUNGARY

Area: 93,030 sq km (35,919 sq mi)
Population (2002 est.): 10,162,000
Capital: Budapest
Chief of state: President Ferenc Madl
Head of government: Prime Ministers Viktor Orban and, from May 27, Peter Medgyessy

The elections of 2002 were the most heated Hungary had experienced in more than a decade. The patriotic propaganda of the conservative government led by Fidesz–Hungarian Civic Party stirred emotions among both its supporters and its opponents and caused an unprecedented cultural-political division in the country. In the event, Prime Minister Viktor Orban's group lost the April parliamentary elections to the opposition Hungarian Socialist Party, which set up a coalition with its longtime ally, the liberal Alliance of Free Democrats. Turnout was a record high of 73.5%.

Beyond these parties, only deputies of the Hungarian Democratic Forum made it into the National Assembly. The populist Independent Smallholders Party and the extreme-right Hungarian Justice and Life Party (MIEP) lost all their seats. The number of political parties in the new assembly was therefore reduced from six to four.

For their part, the MIEP and Fidesz challenged the government's legitimacy, demanded a recount, complained of election fraud, and generally kept the country in election mode until the October municipal elections. The Central Elections Committee ruled that a recount was unnecessary, however, a position supported by observers from the Organization for Security and Cooperation in Europe, whose only substantive criticism of the election conduct was that the state television carried a consistent bias in favour of Fidesz.

Under the leadership of Peter Medgyessy, an economist and former banker, the new centre-left coalition's first priority was to deliver on its main campaign promises—that is, raising pensions and public service salaries, especially in the health and education sectors. During its first 100 days, the government also tried to create a new scheme to lure foreign investment. In recent years investors had found other Central European countries more attractive in this regard.

In June, Medgyessy was caught up in a major scandal after it was revealed that he had been a counterintelligence agent in the communist period. He admitted having acted as an agent while working for the Finance Ministry in 1977–82, but he insisted he was only protecting economic secrets and trying to prevent the Soviet KGB from disrupting Hungary's application to join the International Monetary Fund. Public concern abated after an investigation found that 10 of 24 postcommunist Hungarian ministers had been involved in similar counterintelligence activities. One surprise conclusion of the much-publicized parliamentary investigation that ensued was that the conservative, strongly anticommunist opposition was implicated equally with the left-wing officials. Polls of politicians' personal approval ratings revealed that Medgyessy's popularity had not been affected by the affair.

The Medgyessy government inherited an economy on the downturn. Following a record 5.1% growth in gross domestic product in 2000, a slowdown was generated by the weakness in the export markets within the European Union, a slump in foreign investments, and excessive state spending during Prime Minister Orban's tenure. The country's 3.7% GDP growth was still higher than the Organisation for European Co-operation and Development average of 1.9%. Inflation was reduced dramatically during the year, from 9% in 2001 to just over 5%.

In August thousands of people were affected by major flooding that raged through all of Central Europe, but, compared with Germany and the Czech Republic, damage was limited in Hungary. Before the October municipal elections, Orban put forward a controversial request to carve up Hungary's public service broadcasting between the two political blocs, but the government turned him down. Nor did the plan help Orban's campaign: the opposition came in second with only 32.9% of the votes. Gabor Demszky of the Free Democrats was returned for a fourth term as mayor of Budapest.

(ZSOFIA SZILAGYI)

ICELAND

Area: 102,819 sq km (39,699 sq mi)
Population (2002 est.): 288,000
Capital: Reykjavík
Chief of state: President Ólafur Ragnar Grímsson
Head of government: Prime Minister Davíd Oddsson

Though the Icelandic economy had entered into a mild recession late in 2001, when economic growth slowed and inflation rose to about 9%, by early 2002 inflation had eased. This was partly due to pressure on the government by the unions, which threatened to ask for wage increases unless inflation could be brought under control. By year's end 2002, inflation stood at 1–2%, and the exchange rate had partially recovered from a sharp dip early in the year. Economic growth for the year was close to zero, however, owing to sluggish domestic demand.

Plans were back under active consideration for the construction of a hydroelectric dam complex at Kárahnjúkar, in the northeastern part of the country, as well as for an aluminium plant at Reyðarfjörður. Despite concerns by environmental groups, an administrative appellate verdict ruled that construction could forge ahead. The government was in the process of negotiating a deal with the American company Alcoa, Inc. The $3 billion project equaled nearly one-third of Iceland's gross domestic product. Plans to establish a reservoir for hydropower stations at Norðlingaalda, in southern Iceland, ignited strong protests from environmentalists. The reservoir would touch the periphery of an important wetland area and bird refuge.

On the question of applying for membership in the European Union, the government hesitated, primarily because Iceland would have to share its ocean fish resources with other member states and would run the risk of partly losing its independence. This was likely to be one of the main issues in parliamentary elections in spring 2003.

Chinese Pres. Jiang Zemin paid an official visit to Iceland in the middle of June. He received a frosty greeting from the public, and several hundred Falun Gong members traveled to Iceland to stage a protest during his visit. Icelandic authorities banned a large number of foreigners who planned to participate in the demonstrations.

(BJÖRN MATTHÍASSON)

INDIA

Area: 3,166,414 sq km (1,222,559 sq mi)
Population (2002 est.): 1,047,671,000
Capital: New Delhi
Chief of state: Presidents Kocheril Raman Narayanan and, from July 25, A.P.J. Abdul Kalam
Head of government: Prime Minister Atal Bihari Vajpayee

An Indian soldier guards his post in a mountainous area near Doda in Jammu and Kashmir state one day before local elections on October 8.

© Pawel Kopczynski/Reuters 2002

India's major preoccupations in 2002 were continuing infiltration of terrorists and an outbreak of violent Hindu-Muslim riots in the state of Gujarat. On the positive side was the fact that elections were held for the state assembly of Jammu and Kashmir in spite of frantic efforts by militants to frighten voters and disrupt polling.

On February 27 a train carrying Hindu pilgrims was attacked and set on fire by a Muslim mob in Godhra, Gujarat state, resulting in 58 deaths. This ignited a widespread counterattack on Muslims in Ahmedabad, Vadodara, and other towns and villages throughout the state. Hundreds were stabbed to death or burned alive; Muslim-owned shops and properties were looted; and houses were destroyed. More than 100,000 Muslims were forced to take shelter in relief camps. There were widespread complaints that the state government—led by the Bharatiya Janata Party (BJP)—did not exert itself to enforce order and provide relief to the sufferers. The number of deaths was placed between 1,000 and 2,000. The National Human Rights Commission held the state government guilty of having failed in its duty, and the opposition parties demanded the resignation of the chief minister, Narendra Modi, but the BJP rejected the demand. The government instead decided to call new elections in the state a year ahead of schedule, and the governor dissolved the state assembly in July. The Election Commission, however, felt that conditions were not suitable for immediate elections.

The forces of Hindu militancy received fresh impetus when Muslim terrorists attacked Akshardham, a Hindu temple in Gandhinagar, in September and killed 28 worshipers. Eventually elections were held on December 12. The BJP, which campaigned on a plank of Hindu assertiveness and cultural nationalism, won a resounding victory, securing 126 seats in the 182-member house and 51% of the vote. The Congress (I) party won only 51 seats.

Militants kept up a steady pressure throughout the year on security personnel as well as on the civilian population in Jammu and Kashmir. Hardly a day passed in which there was no violent incident, but there were also clear signs that the people of the state yearned for a return to peace. The government made a bold decision to hold elections to the state assembly. At one stage it looked likely that the All Party Hurriyat Conference, an alliance of groups hostile to Indian rule, might participate in the elections, but its leaders decided not to do so. Polling was spread over four phases between September 14 and October 8, in full view of diplomats and the international media. No party won a clear majority, but the People's Democratic Party, which secured 16 seats in the 87-member house, and the Congress (I), with 20 seats, formed a coalition with the support of two minor parties and independents.

In February, elections to four state assemblies were held. The Congress (I) party won by large margins in Punjab and Uttaranchal. In Uttar Pradesh no party captured a clear lead, and after a period of presidential rule, a coalition of the Bahujan Samaj Party (BSP) and the BJP was formed in May. Manipur also had a coalition government, led by the Congress (I). The country acquired a new president and vice president, and the Lok Sabha (lower house) obtained a new speaker. All three officials were nominees of the ruling National Democratic Alliance (NDA). A.P.J. Abdul Kalam (*see* BIOGRAPHIES) was elected president and succeeded K.R. Narayanan, whose five-year term ended on July 25. Vice Pres. Krishan Kant (*see* OBITUARIES) died in office on July 27, and a veteran BJP leader, Bhairon Singh Shekhawat, was elected to the post. Shekhawat was sworn in on August 19. The speaker of the Lok Sabha, G.M.C. Balayogi, died in an air crash in March, and Manohar Joshi of the Shiv Sena was elected to succeed him in May. Toward the end of June, the home minister, L.K. Advani, was designated deputy prime minister. In a cabinet reshuffle in July, the foreign minister, Jaswant Singh, and the finance minister, Yashwant Sinha, swapped their portfolios, and M. Venkiah Naidu left the cabinet to assume the presidency of the BJP. Unexpected differences arose between the BJP and the Hindu organizations that were its traditional supporters, Rashtriya Swayamsevak Sangh and the Vishwa Hindu Parishad.

The Economy. There was a marked fall in India's economic growth rate in 2002 and a general belief that economic reform and liberalization had slowed because of increasing opposition within the BJP. A major decision to sell key petroleum companies was held over until the end of the year. There was some progress in disinvestment, however. Tatas, India's largest corporate conglomerate, acquired from the government the controlling stake in Videsh Sanchar Nigam Ltd., an international telecommunications carrier. Several state-owned hotels were also sold off. Restrictions on the storage and movement of food grains as well as price controls on gasoline (petrol) and diesel fuel were ended. The ban on direct foreign investment in newspapers and journals was lifted.

The government's budget for 2002–03, presented on February 28, slashed subsidies on fertilizers, kerosene, and liquefied natural gas. It introduced a service charge in the insurance and several other industries in addition to an across-the-board national security surcharge. Nonresident Indians were given the facility of complete capital account convertibility. The government's rev-

enue expenditure stood at Rs 4.1 trillion (about $84 billion), with a budget deficit of 3.9%. Taking capital expenditure also into account, the overall fiscal deficit worked out to 5.3% of gross domestic product. The allocation for defense was Rs 650 billion (about $13.3 billion).

Foreign Relations. In order to de-escalate tension with Pakistan, India withdrew troops from the international border in October and also announced that it would be willing to hold talks with the new Pakistani government provided that infiltration of terrorists was ended. Pakistan turned down India's demand to hand over 20 terrorists and criminals as well as a proposal made by the Indian prime minister for joint patrolling of the Line of Control. In spite of the feeling in India that the U.S. should have put greater pressure on Pakistan to check infiltration of militants into Jammu and Kashmir, relations with the U.S. were better than ever before. Prime Minister Vajpayee was in close touch with Pres. George W. Bush. The two met in September when Vajpayee went to New York to address the UN General Assembly. Secretary of State Colin Powell paid three visits to India, and National Security Adviser Condoleezza Rice and Secretary of Defense Donald Rumsfeld were among other senior officials to visit New Delhi. India expressed reservations about American plans to launch military operations against Iraq. In November Vajpayee attended a meeting of the Association of Southeast Asian Nations and broached a plan for a free trade area between India and ASEAN members. Russian Pres. Vladimir Putin paid a three-day visit to New Delhi in December during which a number of agreements were signed between the two countries. Other important visitors to India included Prime Minister Zhu Rongji of China, King Gyanendra (*see* BIOGRAPHIES) of Nepal, and Pres. Chandrika Kumaratunga of Sri Lanka.

(H.Y. SHARADA PRASAD)

INDONESIA

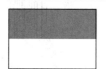

Area: 1,922,570 sq km (742,308 sq mi)
Population (2002 est.): 211,023,000
Capital: Jakarta
Head of state and government: President Megawati Sukarnoputri

Megawati Sukarnoputri celebrated her first anniversary as president in July 2002 but received mixed assessments of her and her government's performance. On the one hand, she had returned a measure of political stability to Indonesian politics after the tumultuous presidency of Abdurrahman Wahid. On the other hand, she had had only limited success in managing the country's internal conflict and economic problems. She had also drawn fire for her cautious and reticent presidential style and for resisting political reforms. Despite such criticisms, opinion polls consistently showed her to be the country's most popular political leader, and she was the clear favourite in the race for the presidency in 2004.

Megawati's leadership style proved more conservative and reserved than many observers had expected. She had yet to give a single interview to the press, and most of her public speeches were carefully scripted and banal. Rarely did she take a lead in the public debate on controversial issues. She appeared to relish the ceremonial aspects of the presidency over the exercise of political decision making, which prompted one commentator to write that she was more interested in "reigning than ruling."

The performance of her government was uneven. Some progress was made on resolving the bloody religious conflicts in the eastern provinces of Central Sulawesi and Maluku when government ministers brokered peace agreements between warring Christian and Muslim groups. The agreements, which were signed in December 2001 and February 2002, respectively, brought an uneasy calm for a short time, but sporadic violence returned to both areas, and the peace process was placed in jeopardy.

The situation in the restive provinces of Aceh and Papua was also little improved, despite the fact that both had been granted special autonomy in the past year. Successive central governments had seen the bestowal of extensive autonomy as their primary means of undercutting separatist sentiment. Under the autonomy laws, each province stood to gain at least a threefold increase in revenue and far greater local authority over political and economic affairs. In Aceh the level of violence remained high, with more than 500 people losing their lives in separatist violence since January 2002. Peace negotiations between the central government and the Free Aceh Movement

(GAM) were proceeding fitfully, but the Indonesian military (TNI) had stepped up its campaign in recent months, believing that GAM insurgents were in disarray and retreating farther into hinterland areas. Conditions in Papua had arguably deteriorated in the past year. Many Papuans initially welcomed special autonomy, but attitudes toward the central government and especially the TNI hardened following the murder of Theys Eluay, chairman of the Papua Presidium Council, in November 2001. Twelve Special Forces soldiers were charged in the killing. The real motives for Eluay's assassination remained open to dispute, but his death clearly undermined confidence in the special autonomy process and could encourage some Papuan leaders to renew their demands for independence.

The Megawati government also came under close scrutiny over its handling of the terrorism issue. U.S. officials as well as the Singaporean and Malaysian governments claimed that Indonesia had become a major regional base for international terrorist groups. Particular attention was given to the leadership role that a small number of Indonesians had played in the Jemaah Islamiyah (JI) network, a major cell of which was uncovered by the Singaporean authorities in December 2001. Initially the Megawati government was criticized for being tardy in acting against terrorism, but Indonesian officials in 2002 were cooperating closely with the CIA and other regional intelligence forces in investigating and apprehending suspected terrorists.

Events took a dramatic and tragic turn on October 12, when a massive bomb blast at a nightclub on the resort island of Bali killed 184 people, the majority of whom were Western tourists. This was the worst terrorist attack since Sept. 11, 2001. The Indonesian government allowed several hundred foreign police and intelligence officials to join the investigation into the bombing. By year's end authorities had taken more than 20 suspects into custody. Under intense international pressure, the Megawati government supported a United Nations motion to ban JI and faced growing demands to arrest suspected terrorists and act against radical Muslim groups.

Indonesia's economy proved surprisingly resilient during the year. Annual growth was 3.5%, down slightly from the budget estimate of 4% but still stronger than many other countries in the region. To a large extent, this growth was driven by strong domestic consumption as well as higher prices for oil, gas, and agricultural exports. The performance of Megawati's economic team had been lacklustre, but the government did gain credit for taking a number of unpopular but fiscally sound measures. Chief among them was a sharp reduction in fuel subsidies, which had the effect of cutting the short-term budget deficit in half. The longer-term prognosis was less rosy. Foreign investment had slowed to a trickle; there had been little new investment in infrastructure since the 1997 financial crisis; restructuring of the battered financial sector had been desultory; and a steady rise in real wages was reducing Indonesia's competitive advantage with other cheap-labour countries such as Vietnam and Bangladesh.

The Megawati government's record on political reform was patchy. The president's own party was implicated in a succession of corruption scandals, only a small number of which were effectively dealt with. The burgeoning business activities and political string pulling of Megawati's husband, Taufik Kiemas, also became a matter of public debate. The TNI continued to consolidate itself as a force in Indonesian politics, particularly on issues relating to security policy, though its influence over broader government and parliamentary decision making remained limited.

Although the government had been halfhearted in its approach to reform, other political forces pushed through significant changes, the most salient of which was the passage of major constitutional revisions. In August the country's supreme decision-making body, the People's Consultative Assembly (MPR), agreed to the introduction

On October 12, in what was described as the worst-ever terrorist attack in Indonesia, a powerful bomb blast destroyed a popular nightclub and claimed at least 180 lives on the island of Bali.

of direct presidential elections and the restructuring of the MPR, both of which were to take effect in 2004. The MPR would no longer have appointed military, police, and community group representatives but would be fully elected for the first time since its establishment in 1960. The Assembly would comprise the House of People's Representatives, as in the past, as well as a new Regional Representative Council. Other reforms included the setting up of a constitutional court and a constitutional commission to advise on further reforms. These reforms strengthened the system of checks and balances between the executive, the legislature, and the judiciary and were a further step to consolidating democracy.

The judicial system was also showing signs of greater effectiveness. In July the youngest son of former president Suharto was found guilty of complicity in the murder of a judge and sentenced to 15 years in jail. Shortly afterward Akbar Tandjung, the parliamentary speaker and chairman of the second largest party, Golkar, was given a three-year sentence for corruption. Although Indonesia's legal system remained riddled with graft, such verdicts went some way toward restoring public confidence. Other prominent figures in the Suharto regime were under investigation and would likely stand trial in 2003.

(GREG FEALY)

IRAN

Area: 1,629,918 sq km (629,315 sq mi)
Population (2002 est.): 65,457,000 (excluding roughly 1,400,000 Afghan refugees and about 220,000 Iraqi refugees)
Capital: Tehran
Supreme political and religious authority: *Rahbar* (Spiritual Leader) Ayatollah Sayyed Ali Khamenei
Head of state and government: President Mohammad Khatami

Iran was deeply affected by the state of the union address by Pres. George W. Bush on Jan. 29, 2002, in which he denounced Iran's leading role in an "axis of evil" that also included Iraq and North Korea. Senior officials in the Bush administration alleged that the Iranian government was sympathetic to the Taliban regime in Afghanistan and supportive of the al-Qaeda movement. For the rest of 2002, the president and other key U.S. representatives continued to list Iran as a "rogue state" that supported terrorism, persisted in developing weapons of mass destruction, and deliberately impeded the Middle East peace process.

Under the threat of an attack by the U.S. once the Afghan and Iraqi campaigns had been completed, the Iranian regime was forced into a change in foreign policy. The established pattern of anti-American propaganda came to a temporary halt, and efforts were made to appease the U.S. For example, the government shut the offices in Tehran of the head of the Afghan Hezb-i-Islami.

In response to alarm at allegations that Iran was developing weapons of mass destruction, it was announced that an advanced ballistic missile program would be curtailed, though other missile developments continued. Iran also rounded up al-Qaeda suspects, some of whom were handed over to Turkish authorities. Support for terrorist groups, as defined by the U.S., caused more difficulty in Tehran, where open links with such groups as Hezbollah and Hamas continued on the grounds that they were Islamic independence organizations. Nonetheless, the Ministry of Foreign Affairs for the first time publicly asserted that Iran would support any plan that would bring justice and peace to the Middle East arena.

The impact of the strong U.S. policies in respect to terrorism brought about a polarization of opinion within the Islamic regime. Until that stage, how to come to terms with the U.S. had been an area taboo for public debate. All but the extreme hard-line Islamists took the view that talks with the U.S. had to be a priority, and even former leaders of the conservative Islamic factions within the regime, such as Hashemi Rafsanjani, took the view that Iran could no longer ignore the U.S. A softening in the stance against negotiations with the U.S. assisted the reformist and liberal tendencies within the regime to publish their own support for a detente with Washington. The extreme Islamists, rather than giving ground, became even more entrenched in their determination to exclude the U.S. and, indeed, resisted the domestic political reform and economic modernization programs implicit in Iran's coming to terms with the Bush administration. Thus, the deadlock between the Khatami government and the extreme hard-liners became more intense in the second half of the year and made the country unable to act decisively at home or abroad.

U.S. pressure was offset somewhat by Iran's strengthening of links with Russia. The Russian minister of nuclear energy, Aleksandr Rumyantsev, emphasized in March that Russia would continue to supply Iran with conventional weapons and maintain its support for the completion of the Bushehr nuclear power plant—and would also examine construction of a second power plant, with possibly more reactors in the future—despite U.S. protests. One cloud over Irano-Russian relations arose from the outcome of the February conference on Caspian Sea resources, in which Iran was left with a mere 13% of the resources against its claim for 20%. Iran refused to endorse the apportionment.

Relations with Great Britain were adversely affected during the year by an argument that erupted over the appointment of ambassadors. Iran refused to accept a British nominee, and in retaliation the Iranian minister to London was demoted; the matter was resolved only in September. Iran's connections with Turkey were strained by a dispute over pipeline facilities, in which Turkey was alleged to have reneged on its commitments to off-take Iranian gas on the grounds that supplies were substandard. There was also some uneasiness in Tehran about Turkey's supportive role for the proposed U.S. attack on Iraq.

Iran's economic performance during the year was sound, with oil revenues easily outstripping government forecasts of $14.9 billion. Nonoil exports of goods and services rose to more than $5 billion. Growth in the construction sector ran at 35% against an average for the economy as a whole of 6%. Agriculture gradually recovered from the impact of drought after better-than-average rain in most areas. Unfortunately, structural progress by way of privatization and modernization lagged behind as a result of the political impasse. In social affairs the regime itself recognized that major problems were developing from increasing youth unemployment and severe social tensions, a situation that was acknowledged by Ayatollah Ebrahim Amini in May when he warned of a potential "social explosion" as popular discontent deepened.

(KEITH S. MCLACHLAN)

IRAQ

Area: 435,052 sq km (167,975 sq mi)
Population (2002 est.): 24,002,000
Capital: Baghdad
Head of state and government: President and Prime Minister Saddam Hussein

On October 17, two days after winning 100% of the vote in a presidential referendum, Iraqi Pres. Saddam Hussein brandishes a sword as he is sworn in for another seven-year term.

The hard-line policy of the United States toward Iraq escalated dramatically after Jan. 29, 2002, when Pres. George W. Bush, addressing Congress in the annual state of the union speech, accused Iraq—along with Iran and North Korea—of being part of an "axis of evil." Bush charged Iraq with being hostile toward the U.S. and supporting terrorism. Early in the year, President Bush adopted the notion of replacing Pres. Saddam Hussein with a democratic regime by any means, including the use of U.S. military force. Iraqi officials vowed to fight this change. The war of words continued throughout the year.

In preparation for a possible invasion, the U.S. increased its military presence at its bases in the Middle East and pressured Arab and European countries to join in an anti-Iraq political and military alliance. Among the countries approached by the U.S., Great Britain evinced the most support for military action against Iraq, while German Chancellor Gerhard Schröder was outspoken in his opposition. France and Russia objected to U.S. unilateralism, claiming that punitive action could be taken only within the framework of the United Nations and only in the event that Iraq continued to defy UN resolutions.

By the summer, international attention was focusing on the return of UN inspectors to Iraq to search for weapons of mass destruction, including biological and chemical weapons, and to destroy any that were found. Iraq had agreed in 1991 to accept weapons inspections as part of the cease-fire agreement (UN Security Council Resolution 687) imposed on it after its defeat in the Persian Gulf War. Obdurate Iraqi refusal to cooperate had obliged the UN inspectors to leave in December 1998; their return became the pivotal demand of the international community. Iraq objected to the return of inspectors, claiming that they had finished their work and that in any event Iraq no longer possessed chemical, biological, or nuclear weapons or proscribed long-range missiles. During 2002 three rounds of talks over the resumption of inspections were held between Iraq and the UN in New York and Vienna. All of these talks failed as Iraq continued to object to an unconditional return of inspectors.

Faced with U.S. threats and international pressure, Baghdad suddenly changed its policy and, on September 16, announced that it would accept a new round of weapons inspections. This move succeeded in dividing the members of the UN Security Council over how to proceed. France, Russia, and China declared that they were satisfied with Iraq's acquiescence; the U.S. and Britain believed that this was merely a tactical move, and they continued to work for a tough UN resolution on weapons inspections. These two countries repeated their wish for a regime change in Iraq, even by the use of force if necessary, and they tried to show that Iraq had links with international terrorist groups such as al-Qaeda. By the end of September, the Bush administration had proposed giving Iraq a seven-day deadline to accept a new UN resolution with stiff conditions for weapons inspections. Iraqi leaders said that they would not abide by such a resolution, however. In October, Congress gave the president the right to use force in Iraq. In late November the first UN weapons inspectors arrived, and in December Iraq submitted a 12,000-page declaration on the status of its weapons program, which indicated that in the past it had secretly attempted to get equipment from a number of countries for nuclear weapons.

After several months of discussion, on May 14 the Security Council adopted a new resolution easing UN economic sanctions on Iraq, imposed after Iraq's invasion of Kuwait in 1990. According to the new resolution, Iraq would be permitted, without seeking advanced approval, to import all products needed for nonmilitary civilian use.

The year saw an improvement in Iraq's diplomatic status. On March 26, at an Arab summit conference in Beirut, Iraq officially reconciled differences with both Saudi Arabia and Kuwait. Relations with both had badly deteriorated after Iraq's failed occupation of Kuwait. Iraq also improved political and economic ties with Syria and Egypt. Relations with Iran remained uneasy, however.

In August the Revolutionary Command Council, with the approval of the National Assembly, nominated Hussein as the sole candidate for a new seven-year term as president. A national plebiscite on his leadership took place on October 15 and gave Hussein a massive 100% vote.

The central government in Baghdad attempted to strengthen its control over the Kurdish area of northern Iraq, lost after the rebellion of 1991, by distributing more than four million textbooks to pupils in preparation for the 2002–03 school year. The books included literature and grammar in Kurdish and Arabic, and Kurdish-Arabic dictionaries were printed for the first time.

(LOUAY BAHRY)

IRELAND

Area: 70,273 sq km (27,133 sq mi)
Population (2002 est.): 3,926,000
Capital: Dublin
Chief of state: President Mary McAleese
Head of government: Prime Minister Bertie Ahern

The Irish economic boom that peaked in 1999–2000 finally petered out in 2002, which would be remembered as the year in which readjustments had to be made in light of new realities. Budget surpluses became a memory; spending for health and education was cut back; and infrastructure developments were scaled down or deferred. It became clear that in framing a budget for 2003, the government would face a choice between borrowing, raising taxes, or making further cuts in spending in order to stay within the guidelines of the European Union's (EU's) Growth and Stability Pact.

Double-digit growth, a healthy tax base, moderate inflation, and extremely low unemployment had earned Ireland the soubriquet "the Celtic Tiger." By international standards 2002 would still be good. The Department of Finance, usually conservative in its estimates, forecast in September that growth for the year would be 3.6%, down from its earlier estimate of 3.9%. As a result, Prime Minister Bertie Ahern and Finance Minister Charlie McCreevy came under criticism, especially since prior to the May general election they had assured voters that public finances were healthy.

By May the coalition of Fianna Fail and the smaller Progressive Democrats, led by Mary Harney, had held power for five years. As the Dail (parliament) approached its constitutional time limit, the government parties claimed that the economy was sound, taxes would not be raised, and services would not be cut. On May 17 voters returned Fianna Fail and the Progressive Democrats with an overall majority, and the Progressive Democrats doubled their seats from four to eight. The main opposition party, Fine Gael, suffered a rout, losing almost half of its Dail seats. Fine Gael leader Michael Noonan resigned and was replaced by Enda Kenny. Ruairi Quinn, the leader of the smaller opposition Labour Party, also resigned; he was succeeded by Pat Rabbitte.

By September McCreevy was calling on ministers to find savings in their budgets. Orders for new Sikorsky helicopters for the army were canceled; health boards were instructed to shed hundreds of jobs; and educational-opportunity programs for disadvantaged children were scrapped. It was even suggested that Ireland's free universities should once again start charging fees. McCreevy refused to rule out changes in taxation. Ireland's inflation rate was the highest in the EU, and prices for goods and services in Dublin were found to be second only to those in Helsinki, Fin. The most dramatic manifestation of the deterioration in public finances was the government's decision in September not to proceed with public funding for a state-of-the-art sports complex and stadium near Dublin, the pet project of Prime Minister Ahern.

In September Ahern faced more troubles following the publication of a judicial inquiry into planning corruption in Dublin. Judge Fergus Flood found that former minister Ray Burke, an Ahern cabinet appointee in 1997, was deeply involved in corruption and had accepted large sums of money from builders and developers. Ahern steadfastly denied knowledge of Burke's shady activities.

On October 19 the electorate said "yes" to a second referendum on the Treaty of Nice. The 63–37% vote cleared the way for reform of the EU and for the admission of 10 new member states. In an earlier referendum held in June 2001, the electorate had rejected the treaty by a small majority but with a low turnout. Since any treaty of the EU had to be ratified by all member states, the rejection had sidelined prospects for EU enlargement. At that time the government sustained intense criticism at home and abroad for alleged complacency.

The government's relief over the success of the second Nice referendum was somewhat overshadowed, however, by the suspension in October of the political institutions established in Northern Ireland under the 1998 Good Friday Agreement. Tensions rose during the year as the Ulster Unionist Party demanded the expulsion of Sinn Fein ministers from the administration owing to the continued activities of the Irish Republican Army (IRA). When security forces announced the discovery of an IRA espionage operation within

In Ballacolla, Ire., on September 26, Irish Prime Minister Bertie Ahern pauses to look at a sign urging people to vote "yes" in the October referendum on the Treaty of Nice.

the government's offices, direct rule was reimposed from London. Fresh elections in the spring of 2003 might lead to a restoration of local democracy. On the positive side, the ceasefires by the main paramilitary groups appeared secure.

In October a bitter controversy developed after a television program revealed that Dublin's Roman Catholic cardinal, Desmond Connell, had failed to act properly in dealing with revelations involving sexual abuse of children by priests of the archdiocese. There were calls for the cardinal's resignation, and the government announced a state inquiry. (*See* RELIGION: *Sidebar.*)

(CONOR BRADY)

ISRAEL

Area: 21,671 sq km (8,367 sq mi), including the Golan Heights and disputed East Jerusalem, excluding the Emerging Palestinian Autonomous Areas
Population (2002 est.): 6,394,000
Capital: Jerusalem is the proclaimed capital of Israel (since Jan. 23, 1950) and the actual seat of government, but recognition has generally been withheld by the international community
Chief of state: President Moshe Katzav
Head of government: Prime Minister Ariel Sharon

The Emerging Palestinian Autonomous Areas (the West Bank and the Gaza Strip)
Total area: West Bank 5,900 sq km (2,270 sq mi), of which (prior to September 2000) 342 sq km is under Palestinian administration, 3,369 sq km under Israeli administration, and 2,189 sq km under joint administration; Gaza Strip 363 sq km (140 sq mi), of which (prior to September 2000) about 236 sq km is under Palestinian administration and about 127 sq km under Israeli administration
Population (2002 est.): West Bank 2,414,000, including 2,204,000 Arabs and 210,000 Jews; Gaza Strip 1,269,000, including 1,262,000 Arabs and 7,000 Jews
Principal administrative centres: Ram Allah and Gaza
Head of government: President Yasir Arafat

The ongoing Israeli-Palestinian conflict and efforts to break out of the cycle of violence continued to dominate the

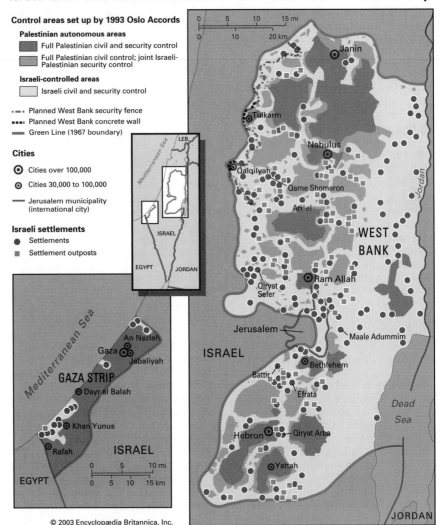

Israeli and Palestinian Settlements in the West Bank and Gaza Strip

Control areas set up by 1993 Oslo Accords
Palestinian autonomous areas
Full Palestinian civil and security control
Full Palestinian civil control; joint Israeli-Palestinian security control
Israeli-controlled areas
Israeli civil and security control
Planned West Bank security fence
Planned West Bank concrete wall
Green Line (1967 boundary)
Cities
Cities over 100,000
Cities 30,000 to 100,000
Jerusalem municipality (international city)
Israeli settlements
Settlements
Settlement outposts

© 2003 Encyclopædia Britannica, Inc.

Middle East agenda in 2002. Perhaps the most significant political development was the American disaffection with Yasir Arafat as leader of the Palestinians and the attempt to create an alternative Palestinian leadership that would be able reach a peaceful modus vivendi with Israel. Arafat was seen by both the Americans and the Israelis as deeply involved in Palestinian terror and an obstacle to peace.

The shift in the American attitude toward Arafat occurred after the Israeli seizure on January 3 of the *Karine A*, a ship owned by the Palestinians and filled with arms acquired in Iran. Initially the U.S. was uncertain that the arms had been purchased (reportedly for $15 million) on Arafat's authority; he had repeatedly denied any involvement. Israel was able to document, however, that the contraband had been bought by Fuad Shubaki, a close associate of Arafat whom he often used as a finan-

cial go-between. On January 13 the CIA announced that it was convinced of Arafat's direct involvement in the controversial shipment and of his links with Tehran. A few weeks later President Bush suspended the U.S. mediation mission headed by Gen. Anthony Zinni and declared that he "was disappointed in Arafat." On February 5 Secretary of State Colin Powell told the Senate Foreign Relations Committee that Arafat "must . . . confront . . . terror and choose . . . peace over violence. He cannot have it both ways."

In early April, during a major ground operation, Israeli forces discovered documents in Arafat's Ram Allah-based headquarters that appeared to show his personal involvement in terror, especially his links to the Tanzim-al-Aqsa Brigades, the young militant cadres affiliated with his Fatah faction. In a major policy speech on June 24, Bush called for the Arafat era to be ended and implored the Palestinians to elect new leaders who were "not compromised by terror."

Bush's speech was supported immediately by a joint Israeli-American statement insisting on reform of Palestinian political, financial, and military institutions. "Reform" was seen, at least partly, as a euphemism for sidelining Arafat. From the Israeli perspective another key demand was reform of the Palestinian security services, in the hope that once this reform had been implemented, the Palestinians would be able to control terrorist attacks. The demands for reform and Israel's tightening military grip on the Palestinian territories sparked a debate among leading Palestinian politicians and intellectuals on whether violence was serving their cause.

The international community made clear its willingness to support Palestinian claims to statehood if the violence stopped. On March 12 the UN Security Council passed Resolution 1397, "affirming a vision of a region where two states, Israel and Palestine, live side by side within secure and recognized borders." President Bush reaffirmed his commitment to Palestinian statehood in his June 24 policy statement, and on July 16 the "quartet"—made up of the U.S., the European Union, Russia, and the UN—endorsed Bush's vision of a Palestinian state within three years of a cease-fire and meaningful Palestinian reform.

Regional developments also seemed to push toward Israeli-Palestinian accommodation. In late February, Saudi Arabia announced a peace plan by which Israel would withdraw from all occupied Arab land in return for normal ties with all the Arab states and a formal end to the Arab-Israeli conflict. The Saudi plan was unanimously endorsed at an Arab League summit in Beirut, Lebanon, on March 28, but continued Israeli-Palestinian fighting kept it on the back burner. In the run-up to the anticipated U.S. attack on Iraq in the late summer and autumn, the U.S. constrained Israeli military actions against the Palestinians.

Though the year began with one of the few periods of relative quiet in the uprising between Palestine and Israel—known as the second *intifadah*—Israel's targeted killing on January 14 of Riad Karmi, head of Arafat's Fatah-Tanzim in Tul Karm, shattered a six-week lull and sparked a ferocious 10-week wave of violence. It started with a deadly Fatah-Tanzim attack on a 13-year-old

girl's bat mitzvah celebration in Hadera in mid-January and culminated in a Fundamentalist Hamas suicide bombing in late March, in which nearly 30 mostly elderly Jews sitting down to a Passover meal at a hotel in the seaside resort of Netanya were killed. Israel responded by launching Operation Defensive Shield, by far its biggest ground operation since the eruption of hostilities in September 2000. The Israel Defense Forces (IDF) moved into West Bank cities, towns, villages, and refugee camps, killing and capturing wanted men and destroying weapons and explosives. After a week of fighting, the U.S. began pressing Israel to withdraw, and a few weeks later it complied.

When Israel launched Operation Determined Path in mid-June, however, and reoccupied virtually the entire West Bank, there was no such American pressure. After President Bush's censure of Arafat, Israel seemed to have been given a free hand to act against Palestinian violence. Indeed, Israel persisted with its controversial targeted killings of terrorist activists. In late July, Hamas military chief Salah Shehadeh (*see* OBITUARIES) was assassinated when an Israeli F-16 fighter-bomber dropped a one-ton bomb on his Gaza apartment, killing 16 civilians, including nine children. The assassination sparked a new round of Hamas suicide attacks and undermined European efforts to arrange a cease-fire.

Despite increasing American support, Israel faced great international criticism, notably from Europe, for its handling of the *intifadah*. The most heated criticism came after the IDF's action in early April in the Jenin refugee camp, in which Palestinians claimed that a massacre had taken place. A UN report in late July disputed these claims but criticized the Israelis for having not allowed humanitarian aid to reach Palestinians for several days. Though calls for a boycott of Israeli goods were made in some parts of Europe, they had little impact.

The *intifadah* took a tremendous toll financially on both Israel and the Palestinians. For the Palestinians, economic activity essentially ceased and food supplies were strained after Israel imposed curfews on Palestinian cities to halt terrorist movements. The effects on the Israelis were also serious: investments declined; gross domestic product per capita decreased 6% compared with figures for 2000–01; fewer than 400,000 tourists visited Israel in the first half of 2002; and the percentage of Israelis unemployed topped 10%,

breaking previous record levels. The government introduced a number of austerity programs but failed to reinvigorate the economy or restore public confidence in its economic policies.

In late October the Labor Party, led by Defense Minister Binyamin Ben-Eliezer, withdrew from the national unity government on the grounds that the state budget did not address the acute economic problems that the country was facing. On November 5, after an attempt to set up an alternative coalition with the far right failed, Prime Minister Ariel Sharon decided to hold new elections within 90 days. Two weeks later, Haifa Mayor Amram Mitzna won the Labor leadership primary and defeated Ben-Eliezer and Haim Ramon, chairman of the Knesset's foreign affairs and defense committee. On November 28 Sharon easily staved off a challenge from former prime minister Benjamin Netanyahu for the Likud leadership. A general election was scheduled for January 2003.   (LESLIE D. SUSSER)

ITALY

Area: 301,337 sq km (116,347 sq mi)
Population (2002 est.): 57,988,000
Capital: Rome
Chief of state: President Carlo Azeglio Ciampi
Head of government: Prime Minister Silvio Berlusconi

In Italy the ruling centre-right coalition led by billionaire media magnate Silvio Berlusconi entered its second year in office in 2002 and encountered major street protests against its policies as well as a centre-left opposition slipping further into disarray.

The government experienced an early setback in January when Foreign Minister Renato Ruggiero, after only eight months in office, was forced to resign after he protested what he perceived as an increasingly anti-European stance taken by his fellow cabinet ministers and by Berlusconi himself. Ruggiero was particularly bothered by the government's lukewarm response to the introduction of the euro. Berlusconi assumed the foreign affairs portfolio on an interim basis, taking pains to characterize government policy as "convincingly and intrinsically pro-European."

In February award-winning film director Nanni Moretti administered a sharp knock to squabbling opposition parties in the so-called Olive Tree alliance headed by Francesco Rutelli. At a political rally in Rome, he caused an uproar by vociferously denouncing alliance leaders in their presence. "With these leaders, we will never win, not for three or more generations!" the director said during a tirade that prompted at least one prominent Olive Tree member, former prime minister Massimo D'Alema, to leave the stage.

By far the largest protests of 2002, however, were mounted by organized labour. Near the end of March, an estimated two million to three million demonstrators marched in Rome against labour-law reforms supported by the government but decried by its enemies as harmful to job security. In April Italy's three main union federations staged the first daylong nationwide general strike in 20 years. The strike paralyzed the country for the day, with the unions claiming that some 90% of the labourers in 21 cities—or 13 million workers in all—had walked off the job; employers placed the figure at around 60%. The government responded by quickly signing a compromise reform pact with two of the three main unions.

Just days before the massive demonstration in late March, economist Marco Biagi, who had helped draft the labour-law reforms that were the target of the protest, was gunned down outside his home in Bologna. A letter claiming responsibility for the killing was posted on

the Internet by a group calling itself an offshoot of the Red Brigades, a militant left-wing organization that had gained notoriety in the 1970s for terrorist acts in Italy. The day of the attack, a newspaper editorial by Biagi had appeared in which he criticized the unions for opposing labour reform. In the wake of the murder, Berlusconi vowed to "continue on the road to reform" and to "stand firm against street movements and pistol shots."

Another target of mass protests during the year was the Cirami bill—named after its author, Melchiorre Cirami, a senator—which gave defendants a "legitimate suspicion" as to a judge's impartiality the right to request that their trials be transferred elsewhere. The bill was denounced by its opponents as the latest of a series of measures aimed at helping rescue Berlusconi and his associates from pending court cases. Moretti lead thousands in a grassroots protest demonstration in September that gave voice to the frustration felt by many on the left not only over Berlusconi's agenda but also over the internal bickering that threatened to cripple the opposition. Protests broke out in the Senate in July when the bill survived a first reading, and further rowdiness erupted in the Lower House in October. After further tumult during debates, it was signed into law by Pres. Carlo Azeglio Ciampi in November.

In the same month, a severe earthquake shook the mountainous Molise region northeast of Naples, and in the small town of San Giuliano di Puglia,

26 children and a teacher were killed when their school collapsed, the only building to do so. Two women were also killed and some 11,000 in surrounding areas were left homeless. (*See* DISASTERS.)

Fear of terrorism briefly flared in April when a single-engine plane piloted by a 68-year-old Swiss citizen, Luigi Fasulo, crashed into the 26th story of a skyscraper in Milan. Three people, including the pilot, were killed, but Interior Minister Claudio Scajola quickly pronounced it an accident on the basis of tapes suggesting the pilot's failure to grasp orders from the Milan air traffic control tower.

In two-stage elections for 28 city and 10 provincial councils in May and June, the frayed Olive Tree alliance managed to make some modest gains, winning control in 15 cities—a pickup of 4 cities from the previous election cycle. One of those cities was Verona, where victory for Berlusconi's House of Freedoms alliance had been expected. The House of Freedoms prevailed in 10 cities.

Despite fractious disagreements, both alliances did agree on one matter during the year—the return to Italy of the male heirs of the former Italian monarchy after more than 50 years in exile that had been imposed on them under Italy's 1948 constitution. The exile of the male descendants of the house of Savoy had followed the abolition of the monarchy in a bitterly contested referendum in 1946. Paving the way for their return was a written statement circulated in February 2002 by Vittorio Emanuele, the son of Italy's last king, and his son, Emanuele Filiberto, in which they renounced any claim to the throne and formally pledged loyalty to Italy's Republican constitution and to its president.

Emblematic of a slowdown of the economy in 2002 was a decision in October by Italy's biggest automaker, Fiat, to lay off some 8,100 workers, nearly a fifth of the company's total employees. The overall jobless rate for the country stood at 9.1% in September. Also that month, Italy's inflation rate hit a 12-month high, and the official index of consumer confidence dropped to its lowest level in more than five years. By the second quarter of the year, the economic growth rate of the country had risen just 0.2% from the previous quarter.

The flow of illegal immigrants into Italy continued to cause problems and spark controversy. By the end of September, some 14,000 illegal immigrants

Gondolas fill the Grand Canal in Venice on May 30 during a strike by gondoliers to protest illegal immigrant street vendors in the city.

had landed on Italy's coasts, and at least 85 had drowned while attempting to do so. After heated debate, the Italian Parliament approved some of the strictest immigration laws in Europe, including measures that would facilitate expulsions from the country and require immigrants to show proof of employment before being granted residence permits. (See *Australia:* Special Report, above.) (DEREK WILSON)

JAMAICA

Area: 10,991 sq km (4,244 sq mi)
Population (2002 est.): 2,630,000
Capital: Kingston
Chief of state: Queen Elizabeth II, represented by Governor-General Sir Howard Cooke
Head of government: Prime Minister Percival J. Patterson

In March 2002 the Jamaican government announced that it would join the growing list of countries opting for liquefied natural gas (LNG) as the preferred fuel for power generation. Japanese and South Korean investors indicated an interest in funding LNG-importation facilities, and the Japanese government was approached to support a feasibility study.

The leaders of the two main political parties—Prime Minister Percival J. Patterson of the People's National Party (PNP) and opposition leader Edward Seaga of the Jamaica Labour Party (JLP)—signed a political code of conduct in June, pledging to discourage their followers from resorting to violence during the election campaign. Nonetheless, about 60 persons were killed in political violence. In the general election held on October 16, the PNP won 35 seats in the 60-seat House of Representatives, and the JLP captured 25. As a result, the PNP clinched its fourth successive term in office, and Patterson would remain in office for a record third consecutive term.

Despite strenuous efforts by international human rights bodies, particularly Amnesty International, to persuade the government to abandon the death penalty for the crime of murder, the government responded that it was considering a constitutional change that would make it easier to enforce the death penalty, including eliminating the right of final appeal to the judges of the Privy Council in London, a holdover from Jamaica's colonial days.

(DAVID RENWICK)

JAPAN

Area: 377,873 sq km (145,898 sq mi)
Population (2002 est.): 127,347,000
Capital: Tokyo
Symbol of state: Emperor Akihito
Head of government: Prime Minister Junichiro Koizumi

Domestic Affairs. By April 2002 Japanese Prime Minister Junichiro Koizumi had spent one year in office. Already, however, he had encountered opposition by conservative factions within his Liberal Democratic Party (LDP). They were led by party bosses entrenched in the postal service, construction and retail trade, and rice farming. As Koizumi wryly admitted, his popular victory may have been a product of the nation's penchant for mass political fads. His campaign had stressed the need for economic reform, including deregulation and privatization. Over the year, reality had set in.

Japan's economy, the second largest in the world, remained enmeshed in its fourth recession in a decade. A government report noted that property values had declined 5.9% in 2001, the sharpest fall in nine years. In October 2002 the Nikkei 225 stock index fell to 8,439, its lowest level since June 1983. Two days before the anniversary of Koizumi's election, an *Asahi shimbun* poll revealed that 72% of its respondents believed that there had been "little or no improvement" in the economy.

Meanwhile, the prime minister had felt the force of opposition within his cabinet. On January 29 he dismissed Makiko Tanaka, the first woman to have served as Japan's foreign minister. He felt that she had been too vigorous in attacking conservative leaders in the Foreign Ministry. Koizumi was unable to recruit Sadako Ogata, another woman, who had become well known as UN High Commissioner for Refugees, and on February 1 appointed Yoriko Kawaguchi to be foreign minister. She had previously served as environment minister.

On April 16 the cabinet adopted measures designed to assign a role for the military in domestic defense. The step was a reaction to the attacks on Sept. 11, 2001, in the U.S. Tokyo would instruct local governments to control airports and harbours the moment a threat was detected. Under Japan's constitution the Self Defense Forces continued to be barred from taking offensive military actions abroad.

One remarkable domestic development was the spread of Web-capable phones. In late April the number of cell phones equipped for e-mail totaled 50 million (in the hands of about 40% of the population). Nippon Telegraph & Telephone, formerly a state monopoly, operated NTT DoCoMo, which controlled 60% of the cellular market. Nonetheless, by May sales of Web phones had plunged because of sheer saturation, falling 28% lower than the level of sales in the same month of 2001.

On August 5 the government unveiled a plan for a national computer registry of all citizens. It would record basic data—name, address, sex, and birthdate—but would not place this information on the Internet. Yokohama, the nation's second largest municipality, and six other cities opted out of the registry, leaving four million residents outside the system. A bill protecting personal information died in the Diet (parliament) as legislators went on summer vacation.

The Economy. In March the government reported that in the fourth quarter of 2001, the economy had contracted sharply (by 1.2%), the third consecutive losing quarter. For the year it was down 0.5%, and unemployment was near a postwar high. Public debt reached a level of 130% of gross domestic product, the highest among the seven major industrial nations. In an interview the prime minister admitted he did not know why the economy had shown no sign of recovery.

Heretofore almost 90% of Japanese considered themselves members of the middle class. This class had not yet disappeared, but there were signs it was dwindling. In half a decade (1995–2000), income disparities grew by almost 50%. With the fastest-aging population in the world, Japan faced the dilemma of a shrinking workforce to support the growing sector of retired persons. Most obvious, in 10 years the unemployment rate had climbed to a record 5.5%. At the other extreme were a relatively small number of wealthy Japanese, who had spawned a building boom for luxury

Japanese Prime Minister Junichiro Koizumi (left) appears with his newly appointed economic minister, Heizo Takenaka, at a meeting in Tokyo in November.

apartments in the big cities. Gerald Curtis of Columbia University, New York City, noted the "strong trend of emerging class differences" in Japan.

The nation's central bank had long provided a useful instrument for surveying the economy—a quarterly report (*tankan*) on the state of business. On February 8 the Bank of Japan stated that the economy was "broadly worsening" and left monetary policy unchanged. It kept ¥15 trillion ($114 billion) available for money markets. By the end of the month, the bank had promised to buy ¥1 trillion ($7.6 billion) in government bonds every month.

On March 30 two of the largest banks (UFJ Holdings and Bank of Tokyo–Mitsubishi) stated that they would slash interest rates to 0.001%. Many Japanese began to hoard gold rather than use savings accounts; the first quarter saw sales of gold nearly quadruple from the same period the previous year.

The *tankan* released on July 16 claimed that the economy was "bottoming out" and moving to firmer ground. Exports and corporate profits continued to expand, but capital and consumer spending (representing 70% of the economy) remained weak. By September the Nikkei index had fallen for seven consecutive sessions, giving up more than 8% of its value. Banks were especially vulnerable to the slide, since they held large portfolios and depended on stocks for much of their capital. The bank's *tankan* of September indicated that the economy could soon slip back into recession.

In 2001 the merchandise trade surplus had reached an 18-year low (38% below the 2000 level), with the U.S. recession cutting imports of electronic and high-tech equipment from Japan. The surplus expanded slightly in January 2002 but again fell off about 11% in February. For the first time, Japan would be earning more from investments overseas than from trade. The population was shifting from producers to coupon clippers. Meanwhile, China was on the verge of displacing Japan as the biggest exporter to the U.S. In April Japan's trade surplus grew by over 26.6% to ¥837 billion ($6.7 billion). The surplus with the U.S., however, slipped 3.5% because of Washington's trade action on imports of steel. In June the current account surplus nearly doubled (from June 2001). Exports increased (over 8%), but imports tailed off (–4.6%) because of the weak domestic economy. For a fifth straight month, the surplus grew (8.9%) in July. In September, however, export growth slowed and the surplus grew by only 1.1%.

In many different ways Japan's production of automobiles had become an essential element in the economy. Honda, for example, recorded robust sales and profits in the last quarter of 2001 and the first quarter of 2002. The company enjoyed wide circulation of low-priced models at home and in the U.S. It passed Nissan in volume of sales to become the nation's second leading automaker, behind Toyota.

In record sales, operations profit, and net income, Toyota strengthened its position as leader by commanding a 43% market share in Japan. The company, the world's third largest producer of autos, earned about $2.9 billion in the April–June quarter. Meanwhile, in April Toyota's production overseas increased by 37%.

Aside from the Bank of Japan, the nation's private banks and investment firms had also played a vital role in the economy. In March, however, Merrill Lynch and Morgan Stanley Dean Witter moved to abandon all retail finance in Japan. In August deflation led the government to consider savings interest rates below zero. These would be, however, guaranteed settlement accounts. On September 30 the prime minister, declaring an "emergency," appointed a 51-year-old academic, Heizo Takenaka, to be an "economic czar." Takenaka moved swiftly to try to solve the banks' bad-loan problems but encountered stiff resistance from bankers, cabinet members, and even conservative critics in the LDP. Eventually he backed down, allowing an 11-member task force to design modest reforms.

Foreign Affairs. Early in the year Japan was prominently represented in two important conferences. After a tour of five Southeast Asian nations, on January 14 Prime Minister Koizumi made a major address at a meeting in Singapore, held to promote the expansion of the Association of Southeast Asian Nations to countries such as Japan, South Korea, Australia, and New Zealand. He proposed a broad East Asian economic bloc. At the time, however, he was hampered by a falling yen, which meant a loss of competitiveness for Japan's neighbours. Earlier he had assured Asian leaders, "Japan will never again walk the path of a military power."

A week later Tokyo hosted a gathering of delegates from more than 50 nations to discuss the rebuilding of Afghanistan. The prime minister pledged $250 million for the first year and a like amount to be paid later.

On February 17 U.S. Pres. George W. Bush began a delayed trip to Japan and South Korea. In Tokyo he faced the dilemma of discussing the gravity of Japan's deflationary crisis without appearing to exert unwelcome pressure on Japan. On the eve of the visit, to show that he was indeed in charge, Koizumi ordered increased inspections of the troubled banks.

Bush addressed the (upper) House of Councillors on February 19, turning to shared problems of foreign relations. He praised Japan for its indirect support of American actions in Afghanistan. He denounced North Korea as a member of an "axis of evil" and pledged support to South Korea (ignoring Tokyo's support of Seoul's effort to normalize relations with the North). After the speech, with wife Laura Bush, the president had lunch with Emperor Akihito and Empress Michiko.

During the year Tokyo and Washington faced policy problems with regard to whaling. On February 22 Japan notified the International Whaling Commission

(IWC) that it planned to double its catch for the purpose of "scientific research." American officials charged that Japan was actually engaging in commercial whaling, as the whale meat it used for "research" ultimately was sold for human consumption. In May the commission met in Shimonoseki, Japan's whaling port, and forbad Japan's return to commercial whaling. Tokyo tried several maneuvers, but in November, in a meeting in Chile, delegates to a convention on endangered species limited trade in products from minke and Bryde's whales, favoured by the Japanese.

In January 2001 an American air force sergeant stationed in Okinawa had been charged with the rape of a local woman. He claimed that the encounter was consensual, and the U.S. military hesitated for days before handing him over to the local court. An immediate Japanese reaction included demands for the reduction of American forces on the island. (Some 47,000 military personnel were based on Okinawa.) In March 2002 a district court in Naha sentenced the airman to 32 months in jail. The protest continued, however, and some officials called for a renegotiation of the status of forces agreement governing the U.S. military presence in Japan.

Another issue inherited from the previous year was resolved in Japan's favour. In February 2001 an American nuclear submarine in a surface drill off Hawaii had collided with a Japanese fishing trawler, the *Ehime-maru*. In March 2002 the U.S. Navy pledged $10 million to the vessel's home port.

Relations between Japan and the two regimes on the peninsula of Korea remained strained because of history. Indeed, attempts to normalize relations with North Korea were stalled over Pyongyang's insistence that Tokyo publicly apologize and compensate for Japan's wartime record. Equally disruptive was Tokyo's demand that the North account for, and return, 11 Japanese citizens abducted in the 1970s. In December 2001 a vessel disguised as a fishing boat (and later determined to have come from North Korea) exchanged fire with the Japanese Coast Guard. The vessel fled and sank in waters in the Chinese economic zone. In April 2002 the New China News Agency announced that after some delay Beijing had given Japan permission to recover the ship. Japanese crews salvaged the vessel in September. The incident marked a low point in the relations between Pyongyang and Tokyo.

The possibility of a breakthrough, however, came on September 17 when Koizumi became the first Japanese prime minister to visit Pyongyang. He won an accounting for the kidnapped Japanese (eight had died) and an agreement to continue dialogue toward normal relations. For their part the North Koreans received a public apology for Japan's colonial record and assurance that they would receive monetary aid. At first praised for the visit to Pyongyang, Koizumi encountered increasing criticism as more details about the abductees emerged. Moreover when, in October, the North Koreans confessed to an American official that they were, in violation of agreements, involved in work on nuclear weapons, the Japanese announced that normalization was on hold. Indeed, on October 23 at a meeting in Mexico, Japan joined the U.S. and South Korea in a warning to Pyongyang.

The year 2002 witnessed an unusual cooperation between Japan and South Korea; the two countries served as the first cohosts of the World Cup association football (soccer) tournament—the world's biggest sporting event. On March 22 Koizumi visited Seoul to promote goodwill before the competition. It was the first time that the World Cup had been held in Asia. (*See* SPORTS AND GAMES: *Football:* Sidebar.)

As to its largest neighbour to the west, Japan had expressed support for the American statement of policy: there was but one China, but Taiwan must not be integrated by force. With Beijing, however, a different and sensitive issue emerged. In 2001 Koizumi had become the first prime minister in five years to go to the Yasukuni Shrine in Tokyo, the site dedicated to more than two million military personnel lost since the 1850s. On April 21, 2002 (carefully avoiding the August anniversary of Japan's surrender in 1945), he made a surprise, "private" visit to the sanctuary. Known for his nationalist leanings, Japan's leader sparked regional outrage over the visit. Beijing immediately summoned Japan's ambassador to China to denounce "the erroneous action that damages ties" between the two nations. China's Foreign Ministry in a statement expressed vehement disapproval of the visit to the Yasukuni Shrine, "which honors Class A war criminals" and "is a symbol of militarism." In South Korea members of the governing and opposition parties jointly condemned the Japanese prime

Thousands of demonstrators march in Tokyo on May 9 to urge the International Whaling Commission to lift its ban on commercial whaling.

© Toshiyuki Aizawa/Reuters 2002

minister. The issue was further expanded by Tokyo's refusal to revise strongly nationalistic school textbooks.

On May 8 a slightly less-inflammatory incident further disturbed relations between Tokyo and Beijing. In Japan, Koizumi met with China's Ambassador Wu Dawei to inform him that he believed China had violated the Vienna Convention governing diplomatic relations. Videotape aired on television clearly showed how Chinese police had seized five North Korean refugees from Japan's consulate in Shenyang. After lengthy ministerial negotiations, the refugees were released via South Korea.

Contacts between Tokyo and Moscow were struck on what appeared to be a minor territorial issue. Since 1945 the Russians had occupied several tiny islands between Japan's Hokkaido and Russia's Kuril Islands. Failure to recover the islets—Tokyo referred to them as the "Northern Territories," historically Japanese—blocked negotiations toward a final peace treaty to end World War II. Ministers representing the two nations met informally at international conferences and had often promised to settle the dispute, but it dragged on through 2002.   (ARDATH W. BURKS)

JORDAN

Area: 89,342 sq km (34,495 sq mi)
Population (2002 est.): 5,260,000 (including about 1,675,000 Palestinian refugees, most of whom hold Jordanian citizenship)
Capital: Amman
Head of state and government: King Abdullah II, assisted by Prime Minister 'Ali Abu al-Raghib

Following the Jan. 14, 2002, cabinet reshuffle, 7 new ministers joined the 27-member cabinet. The most important change was in the post of foreign minister. Marwan Muasher, the Jordanian ambassador to the United States, replaced foreign minister 'Abd al-Ilah al-Katib.

On February 11 the State Security Court sentenced to death Raed Hijazi, a U.S.-born Islamic militant, who had been found guilty of possessing arms and explosives and of plotting attacks on U.S. and Israeli targets on Jordanian territory during the 2000 millennium celebrations.

King Abdullah II did not attend the Arab League meeting held in Beirut, Lebanon, in March because Palestinian leader Yasir Arafat was unable to attend. The Jordanian king, however, fully supported the Saudi peace initiative that was publicly announced by Saudi Crown Prince Abdullah (see BIOGRAPHIES) and was subsequently endorsed by the Arab League.

Toujan Faisal, who had made history as the first woman ever elected to the Jordanian parliament and who had served from 1993 to 1997, was arrested on March 16, 10 days after having published an open letter addressed to King Abdullah II in which she accused Prime Minister 'Ali Abu al-Raghib of corruption by having benefited from the doubling of car insurance rates. She also criticized the Jordanian judiciary as "unjust." On May 16 she was sentenced to 18 months in jail for having disseminated "lies that damage the Jordanian state's integrity and honour."

King Abdullah II, accompanied by Queen Rania, visited France and met Pres. Jacques Chiraq on July 26. In October he traveled to Germany, where he emphasized the importance of Jordan's association agreement with the European Union, which came into effect in May. During his summit meeting with U.S. Pres. George W. Bush on August 1, Abdullah discussed the ongoing Israeli-Palestinian conflict. The following month, on the anniversary of the terrorist attacks, the king sent a message to President Bush reiterating his strong support of U.S. efforts against terrorism. On October 28 the director of the USAID office in Amman was assassinated. The incident had all the characteristics of a terrorist operation. In early November the southern city of Ma'an was put under a curfew as police made a house-to-house search for armed Islamic militants believed to be involved in arms and drug smuggling, killings, fires on university campuses, assaults, and robberies. Dozens were arrested in the sweep, and five persons were killed.

There remained strong opposition among Islamists and leftists to normalization with Israel, especially in the wake of the second Palestinian *intifadah*. The first antinormalization conference was convened on January 27. 'Abd al-Latif 'Arabeyat, one of the speakers representing an antinormalization movement, called for jihad rather than normalization.

A new law on information technology went into effect on March 19. The Posts and Telecommunications Ministry was renamed the Information and Communications Technology Ministry, and it was given autonomy in drawing up government policies concerning information technology.   (MARIUS K. DEEB)

KAZAKHSTAN

Area: 2,724,900 sq km (1,052,090 sq mi)
Population (2002 est.): 14,888,000
Capital: Astana
Head of state and government: President Nursultan Nazarbayev, assisted by Prime Ministers Kasymzhomart Tokayev and, from January 28, Imangali Tasmagambetov

While Kazakhstan's economy continued to perform relatively well in 2002, particularly in the petroleum sector, concerns were increasingly being expressed both inside and outside the country that the deteriorating political situation could discourage the international investors so vital to furthering economic growth. Pres. Nursultan Nazarbayev charged the new government installed in January with providing fresh ideas on economic management and ensuring annual gross domestic product growth of 7–8%. Sixty percent of the state budget was supposed to be spent on social improvements.

Undermining Kazakhstan's reputation as a country well on the road to democracy were pressures on the independent media and the adoption of a law on political parties that would effectively exclude the opposition from participation in the political life of the country. The attacks—including physical assaults on journalists, firebombing, and sabotage of the equipment of independent media—were generally assumed by the targets to be the work of the authorities, although government officials claimed the actions were perpetrated by criminals. The savage beating in August of well-known journalist Sergey Duvanov moved the head of Kazakhstan's Journalists' Union to describe 2002 as the darkest year for the media in Kazakhstan since the country gained its independence.

The political opposition received a major blow at the end of March when former minister of energy Mukhtar Ablyazov, one of the founders in 2001 of the new political grouping Democratic

Choice of Kazakhstan, was arrested on fraud charges. An arrest warrant was issued for another leading member of the party who took refuge in the French embassy and thereby drew international attention to the tribulations of the political opposition.

In June Parliament approved a law requiring that political parties have at least 50,000 members, instead of the previously required 3,000, in order to register with the authorities. The law drew sharp criticism from abroad, and the domestic opposition described it as putting an end to their activities. By September, however, a number of opposition parties were considering merging in order to meet the requirements.

Kazakhstan's status as a major oil producer was enhanced when an Italian-led consortium announced that the Kashagan field in the Caspian Sea was proving to be as oil-rich as the Persian Gulf. In order to overcome limitations on oil development caused by the unresolved status of the Caspian, in May Kazakhstan and Russia agreed on a division of their share of the sea.

(BESS BROWN)

KENYA

Area: 582,646 sq km (224,961 sq mi)
Population (2002 est.): 31,139,000
Capital: Nairobi
Head of state and government: President Daniel arap Moi and, from December 30, Mwai Kibaki

With half of Kenya's population living below the poverty line, there was urgent need for action in 2002, but Parliament's decision to award its members a major increase in pay and benefits showed scant evidence of any concern about the crisis. Corruption and indifference were not the only problems, however. Climatic vagaries and a failure to appreciate the impact of human activities upon the environment were also at the root of some of the country's difficulties. On the one hand, floods and landslides in central and western districts early in the year forced 150,000 people to leave their homes, while in September it was reported that there were water shortages on Mt. Kenya that were affecting the lives of 7,000,000

people, a problem that had arisen for a variety of preventable reasons. The destruction of forests to make possible the illegal sale of timber, to make charcoal, and to create space to grow marijuana was a major factor. So too were overgrazing and the overextraction of water for irrigation purposes, though this latter development was in part the result of Kenya's success in having become the leading horticultural exporter to European markets.

The announcement in March that the coalition between the ruling party, the Kenya African National Union (KANU), and the hitherto prominent opposition National Development Party (NDP) had become a merger appeared at the time to have consolidated Pres. Daniel arap Moi's hold on power. Sharp divisions began to appear within the newly merged party, however, when Moi, without consulting any of his KANU associates, came out in favour of Uhuru Kenyatta, son of former president Jomo Kenyatta, as his candidate to succeed him upon his resignation, which was due, under the terms of the constitution, on Jan. 4, 2003. Kenyatta had been appointed to the National Assembly as recently as October 2001 and was raised to cabinet rank only in November, and there were fears that Moi, who was continuing as president of KANU, would try to control events through his young protégé or at least ensure his own immunity from legal action by those who might wish to accuse him of corruption. At the same time, several of Moi's cabinet members, including long-serving Vice Pres. George Saitoti and Raila Odinga, a former leader of the NDP, were eager to promote their own claims to become KANU's candidate.

Early in August a group of these dis-

gruntled aspirants for office, together with their supporters, formed what became known as the KANU Rainbow Alliance to press for a democratic vote to choose the party's candidate for the presidency. Moi countered by dismissing Saitoti from the vice presidency; in turn the Rainbow Alliance threatened to form an independent party if KANU did not hold a secret ballot to select a candidate. Kenyatta was duly chosen in mid-October, and KANU was split in two.

Meanwhile, the numerous opposition parties had not been inactive. Twelve of the parties, including three of the most powerful, agreed on September 18 to combine to form the National Rainbow Coalition (NARC) and put forward one presidential candidate, Mwai Kibaki, to challenge KANU's official nominee. The KANU dissidents agreed to support Kibaki. In September too the Constitutional Review Commission made known its draft recommendations, which included the creation of the post of executive prime minister to be elected by a national assembly consisting of two chambers. The president would then be left with responsibility for safeguarding the constitution and for promoting national unity.

In the December presidential elections, Kibaki won in a landslide, with 62.3% of the vote, while KANU candidate Kenyatta garnered just 31.2%. Kibaki, the first opposition leader to take power since Kenya gained independence in 1963, was sworn on December 30. In parliamentary elections NARC won 125 of the 210 seats, KANU took 64, and the remaining seats were split among five smaller parties. Voter turnout was about 56%, down from the 68% registered in the 1997 elections. (KENNETH INGHAM)

A Kenyan soldier stands before the wreckage at the Israeli-owned Paradise Hotel near Mombasa, where suicide bombers detonated explosives that killed themselves and at least 12 others on November 28.

KIRIBATI

Area: 811 sq km (313 sq mi)
Population (2002 est.): 90,600
Capital: Bairiki, on Tarawa
Head of state and government: President Teburoro Tito

Pres. Teburoro Tito's Maneaban Te Mauri Party retained a comfortable majority in the House of Assembly in 2002. With general elections slated for December and the presidential election due in early 2003, the government made changes to the electoral laws in regard to bribery and allowing traditional gifts to be made and celebrations to occur. The government also pushed through controversial legislation that established a commission to hear complaints against the news media. Critics claimed that the measure was aimed at the newspaper owned by the main opposition leader, former president Ieremia Tabai.

In his address in September at the World Summit on Sustainable Development in Johannesburg, S.Af., Tito suggested that international development plans focus on social and environmental issues as well as economic concerns. Kiribati, comprised of low-lying coral islands and atolls, was threatened by rising sea levels and increased cyclonic storms as a result of global warming.

Kiribati's economy remained heavily dependent on revenue from a trust fund created with proceeds from phosphate mining, which was discontinued in 1979, and remittances from nationals working overseas. The government also received $A2.5 million (about $1.4 million) from the sale of passports and residence permits. In new ventures, trial pearl farms were funded, as were infrastructure and educational developments. A survey by the Asian Development Bank highlighted the poor living conditions in South Tarawa and concluded that at least half of the population was living in poverty. (BARRIE MACDONALD)

KOREA, DEMOCRATIC PEOPLE'S REPUBLIC OF

Area: 122,762 sq km (47,399 sq mi)
Population (2002 est.): 22,224,000
Capital: Pyongyang
Chief of state: Chairman of the National Defense Commission Kim Jong Il
Head of government: Chairman of the Council of Ministers (Premier) Hong Sang Nam

North Korea in the year 2002 saw its domestic economy improve slightly, while on the international scene its standing rose and fell sharply in a series of dramatic events in relations with South Korea, Japan, and the U.S.

For several years the highly secretive state had had a severe problem producing enough food for its people. In 2002 the economy grew at a rate reported to be about 3.7%, but another disastrous season of floods in August ruined crops and threatened continued food shortages. The floods also killed several dozen people. The regime had relied on external food aid provided by South Korea, the U.S., and Japan, but Japan halted its donations after a diplomatic breakdown. Early in the year North Korea announced reforms of the economy that would permit some market transactions, and by the end of the year, it had been announced that an economic free zone, where capitalist enterprises would be welcome, would open in Kaesong, near the South Korean border.

Relations with Japan took a dramatic turn in September when, on the heels of a historic visit to Pyongyang by Japanese Prime Minister Junichiro Koizumi, North Korea admitted that it had abducted as many as 13 Japanese during the 1970s and '80s. The abductions were apparently for the purpose of stealing identities for espionage purposes in some cases and for obtaining Japanese-language instructors in others. In admitting the crime, chief of state Kim Jung Il said that misguided elements within the government had carried out the scheme and that they would be punished.

North Korea's relations with China were dominated by the issue of Korean refugees' asylum in foreign embassies in Beijing and eventually passage to South Korea. In March, 25 North Koreans who had slipped into China stormed into the Spanish embassy, while smaller groups rushed into other embassies in Beijing. Relations with South Korea were marred when on June 29 a naval firefight broke out on the Yellow Sea. A North Korean ship fired first, leaving four South Korean sailors dead; 13 North Koreans were killed when South Korean forces returned fire. The incident was quickly defused, however, after North Korea issued a statement of regret and South Korea accepted the statement as an apology.

North Korea vigorously protested U.S. Pres. George W. Bush's characterization of the regime as part of an "axis of evil," along with Iran and Iraq, and announced that planned talks with the U.S. would be

Working near the demilitarized zone dividing North and South Korea, labourers in Onjungri, N.Kor., reconstruct a railway link between the two countries in September.

AP/Wide World Photos

called off until the criticism was withdrawn. This was followed later in the year by a threat to deal the U.S. "merciless blows" should armed forces ever land in North Korea. Nonetheless, an American delegation visited Pyongyang in October. Any hopes of improved relations between the two countries were dashed when North Korea admitted that it was still attempting to develop nuclear weapons. Some analysts believed that the cash-strapped country was placing nuclear weapons on the bargaining table in hopes of getting economic aid in exchange for abandoning the project.

(MARK PETERSON)

KOREA, REPUBLIC OF

Area: 99,461 sq km (38,402 sq mi)
Population (2002 est.): 47,640,000
Capital: Seoul
Head of state and government: President Kim Dae Jung

As South Korea prepared for a presidential election on Dec. 19, 2002, three candidates emerged. The president, Kim Dae Jung, was limited by the constitution to a single five-year term so could not run for reelection. Kim threw his support behind Roh Moo Hyun (*see* BIOGRAPHIES), a lawyer and former maritime affairs and fisheries minister. The lead opposition candidate was Lee Hoi Chang, who had run against Pres. Kim Dae Jung in 1997. In the event Roh, of the ruling Millennium Democratic Party, narrowly defeated Lee, with 49% of the vote to Lee's 46.5%. Roh would take office in February 2003.

Aside from the election, the biggest stories in South Korea for 2002 were in sports. In June the country cohosted, with Japan, the World Cup association football championships, and in September and October it played host to the Asian Games. The World Cup was a remarkable, even historic event, and the Asian Games, held in Pusan, were a huge success. For the World Cup, South Korea built or remodeled 10 stadiums around the country. This was the first time that South Korea had hosted the event. On the field the home team had its best result ever, reaching the semifinal round. Off the field the cele-

brants who flooded the streets of Seoul numbered in the millions. Photographs of the throngs filled the Korean newspapers and appeared in media around the world.

Teams from all over the continent, including North Korea, participated in the Asian Games. As in the 2000 Olympic Games in Sydney, Australia, the two Korean teams entered the field together, bearing a single white flag with the silhouette of the Korean peninsula in blue. The teams competed separately, however. Throughout, the South Korean fans rooted for the North Korean teams in a positive show of reconciliation toward their northern rivals.

While President Kim could bask in the success of the World Cup and Asian Games, he did suffer several political setbacks during the year. Two of his sons were arrested and charged with taking bribes. In midyear he suggested a new prime minister, Chang Sang—the nation's first female candidate for the position—but the National Assembly rejected the nomination. A month later, on August 8, in the elections for the National Assembly, Kim's party suffered a huge defeat that further weakened the president's ability to pass new legislation. Public opinion polls placed support for Kim at less than 10%.

Relations with North Korea were up and down. On the positive side, April saw the fourth reunion in three years of families separated by the political division of the Korean peninsula. One hundred elderly South Koreans visited relatives in the North. On the negative side, there was a firefight on the Yellow Sea involving naval ships of both countries. Even more troubling to relations was the admission by the North Koreans in October that they were, in violation of agreements, involved in work on nuclear weapons. At a meeting in Mexico on October 23, South Korea joined the U.S. and Japan in a warning to Pyongyang.

Toward the end of the year, tensions on the peninsula were lessened when North Korea indicated that it was going to experiment with a new economic

On August 14 North Korean negotiator Kim Ryong Song (right) walks hand-in-hand with South Korean Unification Minister Jeong Se Hyun following talks in Seoul during which both sides signaled their willingness to resume their reconciliation process after months of tension.

policy. Following the model of the Chinese, North Korea announced that it was going to open a special economic zone where capitalist enterprises could operate without interference from the central government. Pyongyang first stated that the location of the economic zone would be near the Chinese border to the north but later indicated that Kaesong, a city near the South Korean border, would be home to the new zone. Officials hoped to attract South Korean as well as international investors to provide capital and expertise for the endeavour.

(MARK PETERSON)

KUWAIT

Area: 17,818 sq km (6,880 sq mi)
Population (2002 est.): 2,253,000
Capital: Kuwait City
Head of state and government: Emir Sheikh Jabir al-Ahmad al-Jabir al-Sabah, assisted by Prime Minister Crown Prince Sheikh Saad al-Abdullah al-Salim al-Sabah

The political situation in Kuwait was clouded in 2002 by the comeback of "movement Islamists" (those associated with organizations such as the Islamic Constitution Movement, which in turn was linked to the Muslim Brotherhood). Following revelations after Sept. 11, 2001, about Kuwaiti involvement in Osama bin Laden's operations, the Islamists were subjected to rare public criticism, and there were even calls for government supervision of Islamist-run "charities" that solicited money from the population. By the spring of 2002, however, reports of civilian casualties from U.S. bombing in Afghanistan and the staunchly pro-Israel stance of U.S. Pres. George W. Bush had helped restore Islamist credibility and popularity. October saw two attacks by Kuwaitis on American servicemen who were training in the country for a possible attack on Iraq. The government quickly reaffirmed support for U.S. goals in the region, but the attacks reflected popular resentment of U.S. Middle East policy. On the other hand, Kuwait shut down the local office of the Arabic satellite TV channel al-Jazeera, citing its lack of objectivity.

Stock prices in Kuwait were strong through most of the year, while fears about a U.S. attack on Iraq pushed oil and gas prices higher. Another boost to national income came from reparation payments flowing from the United Nations Compensation Committee for damage incurred during the Iraqi occupation. At the same time, lower world interest rates and declining corporate revenues reduced government income from the overseas investments that made up most of the assets in the Reserve Fund for Future Generations, a repository comprising 10% of annual state revenues.

Not all was well in Kuwait's petroleum industry in 2002, and some disturbing problems threatened the sector that provided 84% of the country's budgeted revenues. Project Kuwait, a plan to include foreign investors in the expansion of production capacity in the northern oil fields, had been stalled for well over a year. A run of oil-industry accidents dating back several years was topped by a spectacular explosion on Jan. 31, 2002, at a gathering centre in the north. The explosion killed four people, destroyed the most technically advanced parts of the gathering centre, damaged several production installations, and led to the resignation of the oil minister.   (MARY ANN TÉTREAULT)

KYRGYZSTAN

Area: 199,900 sq km (77,200 sq mi), including about 1,250 sq km (480 sq mi) ceded to China in May 2002
Population (2002 est.): 5,002,000
Capital: Bishkek
Head of state and government: President Askar Akayev, assisted by Prime Ministers Kurmanbek Bakiyev and, from May 22 (acting until May 30), Nikolay Tanayev

Kyrgyzstan in 2002 continued to host a large international military presence, mostly American and French, at Bishkek's Manas International Airport in support of the antiterrorist coalition. Opposition parliamentarians questioned the existence of a foreign air base on Kyrgyz soil, but government leaders asserted that it was to the country's benefit to help crush international terrorism. Although there were no assaults by extremist groups on Kyrgyzstan such as had occurred in previous years, the security services warned that the danger was still there. Some officials explained that restrictions on the media were motivated at least in part by the fact that extremist literature was being published in Kyrgyzstan for distribution in the rest of Central Asia.

It was unclear whether official references to the existence in Kyrgyzstan of groups such as Hezb-e Tahrir, an international movement that hoped to establish a medieval-style Islamic caliphate in Central Asia, or the extremist Islamic Movement of Uzbekistan were motivated by genuine fear of religious extremism's spreading, particularly in the south of the country, or were intended to discredit the political opposition. Opposition parties, human rights activists, and citizens disgusted by the government's inability to improve living conditions for most of the country's popula-

tion were more vocal and active in 2002 than ever before. The authorities reacted with repression on the independent media. Civil disobedience spread throughout the society, which led to warnings that the country was in danger of civil war.

The trigger for much of the unrest was the arrest in January of parliamentarian Azimbek Beknazarov, apparently for his criticism of an unpopular border agreement with China that transferred some 1,250 sq km (480 sq mi) to Chinese sovereignty. Opposition members of the parliament protested the arrest, and activists began picketing and demonstrating in Bishkek and elsewhere. In February human rights activist Sheraly Nazarkulov died after a hunger strike, which intensified the popular unrest. On March 17 five people were killed and many were wounded in a clash between police and

Policemen in Bishkek, Kyrgyzstan, drag away one of the demonstrators who had turned out on November 16 to demand punishment for those responsible for five civilian deaths during a protest in March.

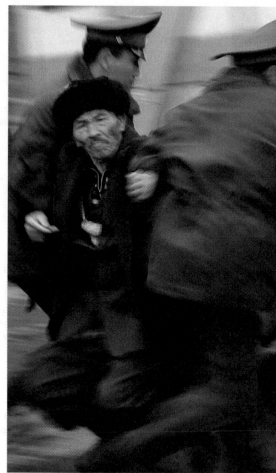

protesters in the southern district of Aksy. Recriminations between the government and the opposition over the punishment of those responsible dominated political life for the rest of the year.

The government resigned about two months after the Aksy shootings; an official commission was formed to investigate what had happened; and several police officers were arrested. Nevertheless, popular anger continued to run high amid charges that the top officials responsible for the tragedy were not being held to account. There were even calls for the resignation of Pres. Askar Akayev.   (BESS BROWN)

LAOS

Area: 236,800 sq km (91,429 sq mi)
Population (2002 est.): 5,777,000
Capital: Vientiane (Viangchan)
Chief of state: President Khamtai Siphandon
Head of government: Prime Minister Boungnang Vorachith

The elections on Feb. 24, 2002, for the 109-seat National Assembly returned many members of the ruling Central Committee of the Lao People's Revolutionary Party, as well as one noncommunist among the 166 candidates—Justice Minister Khamouane Boupha, a confidant of Pres. Khamtai Siphandon. In April the Assembly met to reelect the 78-year-old Khamtai unanimously for another five years. Prime Minister Boungnang Vorachith, promoted from finance minister in 2001, was reappointed, which thereby confounded predictions that Khamtai would turn instead to foreign-investment-friendly Thongloun Sisoulith, deputy prime minister and president of the Committee for Planning and Cooperation. In September the Assembly met again to hear typically rosy economic predictions for 2003. Boungnang visited Indonesia and the Philippines in April, while Khamtai was received in the Vietnamese capital the following month.

Soubanh Sritthirath, chairman of the Lao National Commission for Drug Supervision and Control, claimed in June that in four years opium poppy cultivation in the country had been reduced by 50% to 14,000 ha (34,600 ac).

In August Laotian and Thai drug-eradication forces swapped names of known drug traders. A lingering dispute with Bangkok over the repatriation of Laotians involved in the July 2000 storming of a border post remained unresolved. Thai Defense Minister Chavalit Yongchaiyudh told his Laotian counterpart, Douangchai Phichit, that the matter would have to await a court decision. By September Laos had dropped its objection to the repatriation from Thailand of Hmong refugees but insisted that troublemakers first be weeded out. In July London-based Amnesty International accused Vientiane of using torture and arbitrary detention. Laos asked Thailand in May to give its citizens preferential treatment for foreign-labour permits in view of close language and cultural ties.

Ambitious plans for a highway from China through Laos to the Thai road network and port systems seemed likely to get a green light by the year's end. Vientiane revived a plan to lease its allotted communications-satellite position to Western media companies. A Thai-French-Laotian consortium in October agreed upon a long-stalled hydroelectricity project to sell power to Thailand. Malaysian investors discussed building a railroad network. In October the National Assembly set an optimistic goal for gross domestic product growth of 6–7% for 2003, partly encouraged by an International Monetary Fund report praising Laos's efforts in fighting inflation, stabilizing the economy, rekindling interest from foreign investors, reducing dependence on electricity exports, and encouraging tourism.   (ROBERT WOODROW)

LATVIA

Area: 64,589 sq km (24,938 sq mi)
Population (2002 est.): 2,331,000
Capital: Riga
Chief of state: President Vaira Vike-Freiberga
Head of government: Prime Ministers Andris Berzins and, from November 7, Einars Repse

If the first half of the year 2002 was characterized by stability and preparations for change, then the second half saw those changes, both in Latvia's in-

ternational status and in its domestic political life, come about. The parliamentary elections in October altered the composition of the Saeima (parliament) and led to the formation of a four-party centre-right coalition government. In November Latvia received the long-awaited invitation to begin membership negotiations with NATO, and in December came the bid to join the European Union.

Manifesting lack of faith in the ruling parties, the voters returned only 33 of the 100 deputies of the previous parliament. The voter turnout was about 72%. The most conspicuous loser was Latvia's Way, heretofore represented in all of the parliaments and governments since 1993. Despite the popularity of Prime Minister Andris Berzins and other Latvia's Way members, the party received only 4.87% of the ballots cast, just under the 5% minimum for getting into the Saeima. The winners were centre-right newcomers (New Era—26 seats; Green and Farmers' Party—12 seats; and Latvia's First Party—10 seats) and two opposition parties (the left-wing For Human Rights in a United Latvia [FHRUL] of former foreign minister Janis Jurkans—25 seats; and the centre-right People's Party of former prime minister Andris Skele—20 seats). Noteworthy was the success of FHRUL, the strongest left-wing party, which cultivated Latvia's Russian-

Einars Repse, the newly elected prime minister of Latvia, carries flowers presented to him after he formally assumed office in Riga on November 7.

AP/Wide World Photos

speaking population and good relations with Moscow.

The new prime minister, Einars Repse, was a former governor of the Bank of Latvia and the leader of New Era. He and his coalition government sought to maintain Latvia's westward political orientation and prudent economic policies, which had ensured a GNP growth rate of about 5% in 2002.

(DZINTRA BUNGS)

LEBANON

Area: 10,400 sq km (4,016 sq mi)
Population (2002 est.): 3,678,000 (excluding Palestinian refugees estimated to number about 375,000)
Capital: Beirut
Chief of state: President Gen. Émile Lahoud
Head of government: Prime Minister Rafiq al-Hariri

Two major world meetings took place in Lebanon in 2002—the Arab summit on March 27–28 and the 9th Francophone summit (which had been postponed a year because of the Sept. 11, 2001, events) on October 18–20. The Arab summit adopted a Saudi Arabian peace plan and transformed it into an Arab peace initiative that called upon Israel to withdraw from the Palestinian and Syrian lands occupied since 1967 and promised an Arab normalization of relations with Israel in return. French Pres. Jacques Chirac opened the Francophone summit, which later elected former Senegalese president Abdou Diouf as secretary-general, replacing the Egyptian Boutros Boutros-Ghali. The meeting concentrated on cultural matters but also signaled its resistance to threatened U.S. moves against Iraq.

Following a visit to Lebanon in July, U.S. Sen. Bob Graham accused Lebanon and Syria of harbouring training facilities for "a new generation of terrorists." The local press was furious and suggested that the Lebanese had been betrayed by an ungrateful guest who might at least have brought up the issue with his official hosts. The U.S. government asked Israel to put an end to aerial patrolling of Lebanon because it both contravened UN Resolution 425 and gave

Hezbollah, the main Lebanese resistance force in the south, a reason not to lay down its arms.

A pro-Syrian bloc of Christian parliamentarians took shape in August to counter the Qornet Shehwan Gathering of anti-Syrian Christian politicians. The new group was expected to throw its support behind the Syrian presence in the country as guarantor of "sovereignty and independence," according to its organizers.

The year 2002 witnessed the introduction of the new value-added tax. Although foreign debt was still about 180% of gross domestic product, the anticipated 40% budget deficit dropped to 35%. A study published in February found that 36% of Lebanon's 13,616 government employees were redundant and represented a burden on the state treasury. Prime Minister Rafiq al-Hariri sought to reduce spending on the army and intelligence services but met resistance from Pres. Émile Lahoud.

After weeks of infighting the government reached an interim deal with the two mobile-phone companies whose contracts were scheduled to expire at the end of August. The companies would continue to run the sector for another five months, while all mobile phone revenues—estimated at $50 million a month—would go to the state. The two companies would receive $15 million a month as a fee for managing the networks, which served 800,000 users, and the government would re-

ceive a net revenue of $175 million until the end of January 2003, when an auction for two or more new licenses would take place. Middle East Airlines, Lebanon's national flag carrier, was almost in the black, having posted no operating losses in 2002 and having purchased six new Airbus planes.

(MAHMOUD HADDAD)

LESOTHO

Area: 30,355 sq km (11,720 sq mi)
Population (2002 est.): 2,208,000
Capital: Maseru
Chief of state: King Letsie III
Head of government: Prime Minister Bathuel Pakalitha Mosisili

After years of delay, general elections were held in Lesotho on May 25, 2002. Many feared a repetition of problems that had plagued the 1998 elections, which were marred by claims of voting fraud, but South Africa and the Southern African Development Community worked with the Lesotho government, the Interim Political Authority, and the Independent Electoral Commission to try to prevent this. The many observer missions found the elections free and fair. The

© Mike Hutchings/Reuters 2002

Voters in Maseru, Lesotho's capital, wait to cast their ballots in the country's general elections held on May 25.

ruling Lesotho Congress for Democracy (LCD) retained its majority in Parliament, winning 77 seats in all. The opposition Basotho National Party secured 21 seats, and though the party disputed the final results, there were no violent protests against them.

The new LCD government faced very serious problems. Half of Lesotho's population lived in poverty. The country had one of the highest rates of HIV infection in the world, with an estimated 31% prevalence rate, and because of poor harvests, Prime Minister Bathuel Pakalitha Mosisili had to declare a state of food emergency in April and appeal for international assistance. The unemployment rate continued to rise, though Lesotho did take advantage of the African Growth and Opportunity Act, and exports to the U.S. doubled in value.

The long trial of Masupha Ephraim Sole, the former chief executive of the Lesotho Highlands Development Authority, came to an end when the Lesotho High Court found him guilty of having accepted bribes from foreign companies and sentenced him to an effective 18 years in jail.

(CHRISTOPHER SAUNDERS)

LIBERIA

Area: 97,754 sq km (37,743 sq mi)
Population (2002 est.): 3,288,000 (including about 250,000 refugees in neighbouring countries)
Capital: Monrovia
Head of state and government: President Charles Taylor

The civil war between the Liberian armed forces and the rebel movement of the Liberians United for Reconciliation and Democracy continued throughout 2002. On February 8, as rebel forces advanced from the north toward Monrovia, Pres. Charles Taylor declared a state of emergency. Armed troops patrolled the capital's streets. Fighting intensified throughout late February and early March. Hundreds of people were killed, and more than 20,000 were displaced internally. Several thousand fled into refugee camps in neighbouring Sierra Leone and Guinea. Peace talks scheduled for early March collapsed because rebel leaders refused to negotiate with Taylor. April and May were marked by increased fighting, which displaced tens of thousands both internally and externally, and in April Taylor ordered a ban on political rallies. The government extended the state of emergency for six more months. Renewed fighting occurred in June in western areas of the country.

On August 24 Taylor called a peace conference, which was again boycotted by the rebels and opposition politicians. The president criticized United Nations sanctions imposed in 2001 against his government for supporting rebels in Sierra Leone. On September 14, claiming advances against rebel forces, Taylor lifted the state of emergency. He also reiterated his opposition to an international peacekeeping force. Fighting continued throughout the final months of the year. No peacekeeping force intervened, and the UN sanctions—including a worldwide ban on Liberian diamonds, travel restrictions on senior government officials, and a ban on arms sales to the Liberian government—continued.

The deteriorating situation throughout the country, sporadic fighting in different areas, and mounting insecurity hindered relief agencies' efforts throughout 2002. Some agencies withdrew from Liberia and instead focused their efforts on the swelling refugee camps in neighbouring countries.

(ANDREW F. CLARK)

LIBYA

Area: 1,759,540 sq km (679,362 sq mi)
Population (2002 est.): 5,369,000
Capital: Tripoli (policy-making body intermittently meets in Surt)
Chief of state: (de facto) Col. Muammar al-Qaddafi; (nominal) Secretary of the General People's Congress Zentani Muhammad al-Zentani
Head of government: Secretary of the General People's Committee (Prime Minister) Mubarak Abdallah al-Shamikh

The Libyan leadership continued to seek improved international relations with the United States and European Union countries. Diplomatic relations had been restored with all except the United States by the beginning of 2002. The outcome of the Lockerbie trial in January 2001 was unconvincing internationally, unsatisfactory from the point of view of the families of the American victims, and unhelpful in advancing the Libyan campaign. The U.S. remained unyielding on the issue that Libya should accept responsibility for the Lockerbie event. By the end of the year and despite serious efforts by U.K. officials and other intermediaries to find a form of words acceptable to both sides regarding "responsibility," no agreement had been reached. Libya was prepared to pay the families of the victims substantial sums out of funds frozen in American bank accounts, but this did not satisfy the U.S. government in its post-Sept. 11, 2001, determination to punish international terrorism.

Muammar al-Qaddafi adopted a low profile regarding the major Middle East flash points of Palestine-Israel, the aftermath of Afghanistan, and Iraq. In the past, for example, such aggressive behaviour on the part of the United States would have evoked very trenchant condemnation from Qaddafi. The Libyan leader reinforced his concern with the affairs of Africa, assisting Zimbabwe with oil in return for property (although the arrangement fell through in late November). Libya looked at a number of ambitious hydraulic projects, notably a massive project to pump water from the Congo River into Lake Chad.

The Libyan economy prospered during the year as a consequence of relatively high world oil prices. Confidence among those queuing to invest in Libya was enhanced by the promise of even higher oil and gas prices as a result of the disruptions of a Gulf conflict. The domestic economy continued to be afflicted by high levels of unemployment and its unresponsiveness to decades of central direction. The country was locked in a deal made by Qaddafi with his people during the era of austerity imposed by UN and U.S. trade sanctions and low oil prices (the U.S. sanctions remained in place). The deal was over wages and staple commodity prices. High subsidies were introduced nationally on staples and energy, and salaries were fixed at an equivalent low level. The disincentives to enterprise seriously inhibited effective response to Qaddafi's calls for local economic enterprise.

(J.A. ALLAN)

LIECHTENSTEIN

Area: 160 sq km (62 sq mi)
Population (2002 est.): 33,300
Capital: Vaduz
Chief of state: Prince Hans Adam II
Head of government: Otmar Hasler

Prince Hans Adam II's welcoming speech at the Aug. 15, 2002, celebration of Liechtenstein's national holiday again centred on the country's decades-long constitutional dispute. On August 2 the prince had proposed a petition allowing citizens to vote directly on changes that would increase his power and reiterated his threat to move to Vienna if the proposed changes were not made.

In 2002 Liechtenstein pressed forward in its suit against Germany at the International Court of Justice in The Hague, seeking compensation for the property of Liechtenstein citizens seized by Czechoslovakia from Germany after World War II. A German court had earlier ruled that the artworks and other items had been taken legally by the Czechs and that Germany was not liable for their return.

Although in June 2001 a task force of the Organisation for Economic Co-operation and Development (OECD) had removed Liechtenstein from its list of countries that were not doing enough to combat money laundering, in April 2002 the OECD added the country to its list of uncooperative tax havens. In July Liechtenstein signed a treaty with the U.S. that allowed U.S. prosecutors to obtain from Liechtenstein banks information for criminal investigations into money laundering, terrorist financing, and major fraud.

(ANNE ROBY)

LITHUANIA

Area: 65,300 sq km (25,212 sq mi)
Population (2002 est.): 3,473,000
Capital: Vilnius
Chief of state: President Valdas Adamkus
Head of government: Prime Minister Algirdas Brazauskas

Energy—including its impact on foreign relations—was a top issue in Lithuania in 2002. In August a series of negotiations resulted in the Lithuanian energy giant, the Mazeikiu Nafta oil refinery, coming under the control of a Russian company, which raised economic and political concerns in the country. An American corporation, Williams International, controlled 27% of the refinery and sold its shares to a YUKOS Oil Co. subsidiary, which emerged with a 54% stake in Lithuania's largest producer of gasoline—and a company that represented some 10% of the country's gross domestic product.

Otherwise, the economy showed positive trends: a growth in foreign trade of about 1% a month and a GDP approaching 7%, but prosperity eluded the population, the standard of living remained low, and the average annual wage was stuck at about $3,350.

The invitation of Lithuania to join NATO, made at the Prague Summit in November, constituted the most important international event in Lithuania since the withdrawal of Russian troops in 1993. To celebrate the event and Lithuania's leadership in the "Vilnius-10" process, George W. Bush stopped in Vilnius on November 22–23, the first U.S. president to visit Lithuania. He was awarded the Order of Vytautas the Great for his dedication to a united and free Europe and for his effective leadership toward this goal. An invitation for Lithuania to join the European Union was received in mid-December.

In the latter part of the year, the country geared up for elections on December 22. For the first time, local council elections were held at the same time as the presidential balloting; the Social

Democrats won 332 seats. In the presidential race, the political right gathered around popular Pres. Valdas Adamkus, and Andrius Kubilius of the conservative Homeland Union bowed out on September 9 so as not to split the vote. The first round gave Adamkus 35.5% and former prime minister Rolandas Paksas, a populist from the Liberal Democratic Party 19.7%. A runoff election was scheduled for Jan. 5, 2003. By the end of the year, most political parties had endorsed Adamkus, who looked certain to remain in office.

(DARIUS FURMONAVIČIUS)

LUXEMBOURG

Area: 2,586 sq km (999 sq mi)
Population (2002 est.): 447,000
Capital: Luxembourg
Chief of state: Grand Duke Henri
Head of government: Prime Minister Jean-Claude Juncker

A bomb threat was called in to local police during a meeting of European Union foreign ministers in the Kirchberg cultural centre in Luxembourg on Oct. 22, 2002. Although no explosives were found during the search, the phone call was traced, and two men were arrested.

A peace march of about 1,000 demonstrators—large for Luxembourg—was held on October 19 to protest the potential war with Iraq. The demonstra-

On October 19 demonstrators march in front of the British and American embassies in Luxembourg to protest possible war in Iraq.

AP/Wide World Photos

tion was held around the British and American embassies.

Amid concerns about recession and the global economy, Luxembourg released a balanced budget plan for 2003 that called for a 7.72% increase in expenditures. Almost half of the allotment, some €2.8 billion (€1 = about $1) was designated for such social projects as pensions and geriatric health care, while €873 million was earmarked for new infrastructure developments.

Luxembourg mourned the death of Pierre Werner, who had served for 20 years as the country's prime minister (1959–74; 1979–84) and whose plan for a common European currency led to the creation of the euro. (*See* OBITUARIES.)

Luxembourg suffered its first fatal airplane crash on November 6 when a Luxair flight from Berlin crashed near Luxembourg's international airport. (*See* DISASTERS.)   (ANNE ROBY)

MACEDONIA

Area: 25,713 sq km (9,928 sq mi)
Population (2002 est.): 2,036,000
Capital: Skopje
Chief of state: President Boris Trajkovski
Head of government: Prime Ministers Ljubco Georgievski and, from November 1, Branko Crvenkovski

In 2002 Macedonia tried to overcome the consequences of the previous year's armed conflict between the ethnic-Albanian National Liberation Army (UCK) and state security forces. Implementing the August 2001 Ohrid agreement, the parliament passed several key pieces of legislation aimed at improving relations between Macedonia's two largest ethnic communities. These included a new law in January on local self-government that transferred some powers from the central government to the municipal level, an amnesty law in March, and a package of language laws in June that established Albanian as the second official language.

Throughout the first half of 2002, ethnically mixed police units accompanied by international monitors returned to villages previously held by the UCK. The last nighttime curfew was lifted on July 11. Although violent incidents continued throughout the year, ethnic-Albanian politicians and NATO rejected allegations by government officials that a new Albanian guerrilla organization was responsible.

In June the parliament adopted a new election law based on proportional representation. In the September 15 parliamentary elections, the coalition For Macedonia Together, which united the Social Democratic Union of Macedonia (SDSM), the Liberal Democratic Party (LDP), and several parties representing smaller national minorities, won half of the 120 seats. The coalition of the ruling Internal Macedonian Revolutionary Organization–Democratic Party for Macedonian National Unity received 33 seats and the Socialist Party of Macedonia one. Of the Albanian parties, the newly formed Democratic Union for Integration (BDI), led by former UCK political commander Ali Ahmeti, won 16 seats, the governing Democratic Party of Albanians 7, and other Albanian parties 3. Previous attempts to form an electoral alliance of the ethnic-Albanian parties had failed. In its first session on October 3, the new parliament elected Nikola Popovski (SDSM) as its speaker. A new government led by SDSM Chairman Branko Crvenkovski and made up of the SDSM, LDP, and BDI was approved by Parliament on November 1.

NATO's Amber Fox peacekeeping mission was extended until December 15; attempts to replace it with a mission led by the European Union had failed.

While Skopje and Athens failed to resolve their dispute over Macedonia's name, they extended the interim agreement regulating bilateral relations on September 12. On May 23 both sides signed a military cooperation agreement. In late July Greece pledged $73.6 million in financial aid. On March 12 an international donors' conference had pledged $515 million in aid. Macedonia failed to reach agreement with the IMF on a new standby agreement, however. In October Macedonia joined the World Trade Organization.

Macedonia's Orthodox Church faced a crisis. A proposed agreement with the Serbian Orthodox Church that would have subordinated the Macedonian to the Serbian church caused a split in the Holy Synod. Bishop Jovan of Veles-Povardarie, dismissed by the Macedonian church in July after placing himself under the authority of the Serbian church, was later named exarch of the Serbian Orthodox Church for Macedonia.   (STEFAN KRAUSE)

MADAGASCAR

Area: 587,041 sq km (226,658 sq mi)
Population (2002 est.): 16,473,000
Capital: Antananarivo
Chief of state and head of government: Presidents Didier Ratsiraka and, from May 6, Marc Ravalomanana

In 2002 Madagascar was plunged into its most serious crisis since independence. Official results for the December 2001 presidential election, announced in January, gave incumbent Pres. Didier Ratsiraka 40% of the vote and challenger Marc Ravalomanana, the wealthy mayor of Antananarivo, 46%. (*See* BIOGRAPHIES.) The High Constitutional Court ruled that because Ravalomanana had not obtained at least 50% of the vote, a runoff should be held, but Ravalomanana insisted that he had won a majority of votes and alleged that the results had been rigged. Hundreds of thousands of people took to the streets of Antananarivo in Ravalomanana's support, but Ratsiraka refused to give way. Ravalomanana then declared himself president and installed his own cabinet, while Ratsiraka's administration fled to Tamatave, the country's main

Pres. Marc Ravalomanana waves to the crowd at an official ceremony in Antananarivo on June 26, a day after the U.S. formally recognized him as Madagascar's president.

© AFP 2002, by Alexander Joe

port. The Organization of African Unity (OAU) brokered an agreement between the two men, who were brought together in Dakar, Senegal, and consented to a recount. In April the Constitutional Court found that Ravalomanana had indeed won 51% of the vote, to Ratsiraka's 36%. Before the verdict was announced, however, Ratsiraka alleged that the court had not been appointed legally and said that he would not accept its recount. The OAU also refused to accept Ravalomanana as the legitimate president and maintained that a referendum should be held. Ravalomanana, whose support base lay in the capital, saw no need for delay and was officially sworn in as president on May 6.

Ravalomanana soon won recognition from the U.S., though not from most other African governments. There were threats of secession from provinces loyal to Ratsiraka, but after France recognized the new president, Ratsiraka suddenly left the island. Though he had won the struggle for power, Ravalomanana continued to be cold-shouldered by most other African states and was not invited to the African Union summit in Durban, S.Af., in July. The political crisis had a negative effect on the economy of a country where some 75% of the population lived below the government's official poverty line and 55% were illiterate. The country owed $4.4 billion by 2002, yet the per capita income was only $250 a year.

(CHRISTOPHER SAUNDERS)

MALAWI

Area: 118,484 sq km (45,747 sq mi)
Population (2002 est.): 10,520,000
Capital: Lilongwe; judiciary meets in Blantyre
Head of state and government: President Bakili Muluzi

In February 2002, with hundreds of people dying of starvation as a result of floods followed by a season of drought, the government of Malawi made an international appeal for food aid. Responding to accusations of mismanagement and corruption, the government claimed that it had sold off reserves of corn (maize) on the advice of the World Bank and International

Monetary Fund (IMF), though there was no trace of the proceeds of the sale. Disclaiming responsibility for the action, the IMF announced in May that it would withhold $47 million in aid until the government cut overspending and introduced a new budget. Denmark, normally a consistent donor, also suspended aid, having been further dismayed by an attempt by Pres. Bakili Muluzi to amend the constitution in order to allow himself to stand for election for a third term of office. On June 3 the High Court ruled that Muluzi had no authority to ban demonstrations against his proposal, and a private member's bill promoting the president's plan failed in the National Assembly on July 4, but this did not stop Muluzi's campaign.

Apparently bowing to external and internal pressures, the government issued a budget statement aimed at living within its means, but food aid agencies still estimated that more than three million people in the country would need food aid until March 2003.

(KENNETH INGHAM)

MALAYSIA

Area: 329,847 sq km (127,355 sq mi)
Population (2002 est.): 24,370,000
Capital: Kuala Lumpur; head of government office in Putrajaya (the future planned capital) from 1999
Chief of state: *Yang di-Pertuan Agong* (Paramount Ruler) Tuanku Syed Sirajuddin ibni al-Marhum Tuanku Syed Putra Jamalullail
Head of government: Prime Minister Datuk Seri Mahathir bin Mohamad

Malaysia's long-awaited political transition was under way in 2002. Prime Minister Datuk Seri Mahathir bin Mohamad, in his closing address to the United Malays National Organization (UMNO) General Assembly in June, announced his intention to retire. Soon after, he outlined a 16-month transition scenario. Leadership of the politically dominant UMNO and the governing National Front coalition would pass to his deputy prime minister, Datuk Seri Abdullah Ahmad Badawi.

Transition scenarios had been the popular leitmotif of the latter part of

Mahathir's two-decade-long leadership. The first collapsed in the brutal fallout in 1998 between Mahathir and his previous deputy, Datuk Seri Anwar Ibrahim, who was subsequently imprisoned on dubious charges of corruption and sexual misconduct. Electoral setbacks followed in 1999 for the National Front and especially for the UMNO. Mahathir continued to seek an opportune time to begin the transition process but did not wish to withdraw at the bottom of a political down cycle.

By mid-2002 Mahathir had largely restored his authority. He had shattered the broad opposition coalition that had united against him in 1999; curbed the ardour of the judiciary to challenge executive domination; offered himself, before Sept. 11, 2001, and even more forcefully thereafter, as a leading Muslim moderate in the worldwide struggle against regressive Islamism; moved against some of the unpopular but previously UMNO-cosseted Malay corporate barons; and survived politically until his "contrarian" anti-International Monetary Fund policies—denounced by international and domestic critics alike—were vindicated by a Malaysian economic recovery. His reputation rehabilitated and legacy assured, Mahathir found it possible to trigger the succession scenario.

Some questioned whether Abdullah Ahmad Badawi would have the guile and will to dominate the unruly UMNO organization as the sometimes-criticized but always-feared Mahathir did. Yet Badawi was not to be underestimated. He had been centrally involved in Malaysian politics since he served as a key civil servant in the early 1970s; he had survived a falling-out with Mahathir during the traumatic UMNO split of the mid-1980s and had quietly worked his way back to the centre; and he enjoyed a reputation for Islamic piety and knowledge that could make him a more credible opponent of the fundamentalist Islamic Party of Malaysia (PAS) than Mahathir had ever managed to be.

Malaysia's economic outlook remained positive. Foreign investment continued to pour into the country, and the stock index had gained more than 5% by August. In what was interpreted as a particularly bright economic sign, Standard & Poor's upgraded Malaysia's long-term foreign-currency debt rating—a move prompted in part by the government's success in debt restructuring. Since the height of the Asian

© AFP 2002

In a tearful address to the ruling United Malays National Organization General Assembly in June, Malaysian Prime Minister Datuk Seri Mahathir bin Mohamad (centre) announces his intention to retire.

financial crisis in 1998, some \$12 billion in Malaysian corporate debts had been resolved. A controversial shift from Malay- to English-language education, especially in the areas of science and mathematics, was intended to help the country become more competitive internationally in technically complex economic sectors but met with fierce resistance from Malay nationalists during the year.   (CLIVE S. KESSLER)

MALDIVES

Area: 298 sq km (115 sq mi)
Population (2002 est.): 281,000
Capital: Male
Head of state and government: President Maumoon Abdul Gayoom

The development policy for 2002, outlined by Maldives Pres. Maumoon Abdul Gayoom in his address at the opening session of the Majlis (parliament) on February 19, placed emphasis on diversification and revitalization of the country's economy, which had grown only slowly in 2001 owing to a

slump in the tourism industry. Development of human resources, improvement of child welfare, and preservation of the environment were also given priority. About 35% of the total budget was earmarked for social development and general services. Aimed at strengthening the institutions of governance, three parliamentary standing committees—on economy and environment, social affairs, and public administration—were established by the cabinet. In tune with the government policy of empowering women, a Gender Equality Council with advisory status was also established. On April 29 the Majlis enacted comprehensive legislation on the use, allocation, lease, and ownership of land.

A four-day visit in September by Indian Prime Minister Atal Bihari Vajpayee strengthened diplomatic ties between India and Maldives. India offered to train and equip the Maldivian security forces in coastal defense and cooperate in areas such as information technology, tourism, and agriculture. Christina Rocca, U.S. assistant secretary of state for South Asia, was another foreign dignitary who visited Maldives, on March 13. President Gayoom served as vice president of the World Summit on Sustainable Development in Johannesburg, S.Af.
          (PONMONI SAHADEVAN)

MALI

Area: 1,248,574 sq km (482,077 sq mi)
Population (2002 est.): 11,340,000
Capital: Bamako
Chief of state: Presidents Alpha Oumar Konaré and, from June 8, Amadou Toumani Touré
Head of government: Prime Ministers Mande Sidibe, Modibo Keita from March 18, and, from June 9, Ahmed Mohamed Ag Hamani

In the presidential elections held on April 28, 2002, voters had a choice of 24 candidates, but none of them secured more than 50% of the vote. As a result, the two leading candidates—former head of state Amadou Toumani Touré (*see* BIOGRAPHIES), popularly known as ATT, and Soumaïla Cissé of the ruling Alliance for Democracy in Mali (ADEMA)—faced each other in a runoff election on May 12. ATT won easily, taking 65% of the vote.

A fairly low turnout marred the first round of parliamentary elections, held on July 14. Voters were apparently affected by widespread allegations of fraud in the presidential elections and by the mysterious disappearance of 50,000 voting cards just before the polls opened. In the second round even fewer voted, with only 14% of those eligible casting votes in Bamako. After provisional results showed ADEMA the leader with 57 of the 147 seats, the Constitutional Court on August 9 reversed the outcome, citing fraud. ADEMA immediately entered into negotiations with smaller parties and independents to try to form a coalition government with an absolute parliamentary majority. The final results gave the Rally for Mali 66, ADEMA 51, and the National Congress for Democratic Initiative 13; numerous other parties and alliances took the rest.

Another poor rainy season caused consumer prices of staples to rise sharply. To ameliorate the situation, the government announced it would suspend the value-added tax on salt and rice, distribute free grain, import emergency supplies of rice, and grant a 30% salary increase to civil servants. There were also grave concerns about the final size of the cotton crop, Mali's primary export product, which, it was estimated, would be down 20% from earlier predictions.   (NANCY ELLEN LAWLER)

MALTA

Area: 316 sq km (122 sq mi)
Population (2002 est.): 386,000
Capital: Valletta
Chief of state: President Guido de Marco
Head of government: Prime Minister Eddie Fenech Adami

The Maltese government registered further progress in 2002 in preparing for European Union (EU) accession, and Malta was identified as one of the 10 countries eligible for the next enlargement, due in 2004. Negotiations were completed in December 2002. The political divide over EU membership, however, continued unabated. Though the government would hold a referendum on the issue in 2003, the opposition claimed that it would accept the outcome only in light of a general election, also due in 2003.

In January in Malta 20 Mediterranean countries signed an agreement that was aimed at reducing pollution in the sea from all sources. In February, Transend Worldwide Ltd., a subsidiary of New Zealand Post, bought 35% of the shares in Maltapost, with an undertaking to manage Maltapost for two years. Later a 40% stake in Malta International Airport was sold to a consortium in which Vienna International Airport of Austria was a majority shareholder.

As part of a plan to restore the shipyards to viability and phase out state subsidies by 2008, about 700 workers left Malta Drydocks and Malta Shipbuilding under an early-retirement and voluntary-resignation scheme. As a result of the Sept. 11, 2001, terrorist attacks in the U.S., tourist arrivals were the lowest in six years. Under a governmental scheme to register overseas currency, more than $450 million held by Maltese abroad was declared in the first half of 2002. The government allowed ENI, the Italian petroleum company, to lay a gas pipeline across Malta's continental shelf on its route from Libya to Sicily.

On February 4 former president Agatha Barbara died in Zabbar at age 78. Barbara, a longtime Labour Party member, was Malta's first woman MP (1947–82) and third president (1982–87). (ALBERT GANADO)

MARSHALL ISLANDS

Area: 181 sq km (70 sq mi)
Population (2002 est.): 56,600
Capital: Majuro
Head of state and government: President Kessai Note

Negotiations on an amended Compact of Free Association between the Marshall Islands and the U.S. continued for much of 2002. The Marshall Islands sought more than $1 billion over the proposed 20-year term of the amended agreement. Funding, which would include ongoing compensation to the peoples of four islands affected by nuclear testing—Bikini, Enewetak, Utirik, and Rongelap—would likely fall in the range of $40 million–$50 million a year. The Marshalls continued to seek to broaden its funding base through international aid; it had become eligible for development assistance through the European Union and secured the release of loans from the Asian Development Bank for financial stabilization and outer islands infrastructure.

In October the Organisation for Economic Co-operation and Development removed the Marshall Islands from its blacklist of money-laundering states in recognition of the progress that the islands had made on appropriate reforms. At the World Summit on Sustainable Development in Johannesburg, S.Af., Marshall Islands Pres. Kessai Note emphasized the commitment of Pacific Island states to environmental protection and sustainable development. Note also made a state visit to Taiwan, which is recognized by the Marshall Islands. (BARRIE MACDONALD)

MAURITANIA

Area: 1,030,700 sq km (398,000 sq mi)
Population (2002 est.): 2,656,000
Capital: Nouakchott
Chief of state: President Col. Maaouya Ould Sidi Ahmad Taya
Head of government: Prime Minister Cheikh El Afia Ould Mohamed Khouna

On Jan. 3, 2002, the government banned the opposition Action for Change (AC) party, claiming that it advocated racism and violence. The AC, which promoted the rights of black Mauritanians and descendents of slaves, would, however, be permitted to retain the four seats in the National Assembly that it had won in the October 2001 elections.

Heavy rains and extremely cold weather in January killed at least 25 people and an estimated 80,000 head of livestock. On January 28 the United Nations World Food Programme (WFP) put an emergency food-distribution plan into action to help approximately 5,500 families affected in the northwest of the country. Drought, which had plagued the region since 2001, returned after the adverse weather, and on April 3 the WFP appealed for $7.5 million in addition to the $22 million already earmarked for famine relief. International donors were slow to respond, and the WFP announced on June 4 that purchase and distribution of staple foodstuffs to a quarter of a million people had been delayed owing to lack of funding. The government reported that by September the lack of rainfall had seriously affected 9 of the country's 13 regions. On September 17 the Christian charity World Vision revealed plans to open 181 feeding centres in the Tagant and Assaba regions, calling the situation one of near famine.

The Paris Club of creditor nations accepted Mauritania's pledge to initiate further economic reforms and on July 8 announced it would reduce its debt by $188 million. On July 17 the African Development Bank approved further debt relief in the amount of $72.8 million. (NANCY ELLEN LAWLER)

MAURITIUS

Area: 2,040 sq km (788 sq mi)
Population (2002 est.): 1,211,000
Capital: Port Louis
Chief of state: Presidents Cassam Uteem, Angidi Chettiar (acting) from February 15, Ariranga Pillay (acting) from February 18, and, from February 25, Karl Offmann
Head of government: Prime Minister Sir Anerood Jugnauth

On Jan. 21–22, 2002, cyclone Dina skirted Mauritius, causing extensive

AP/Wide World Photos

In Port Louis, Mauritius's capital, in October, a girl helps her mother surf the Internet inside a "cyberbus" run by the country's National Computer Board; the board aims to increase computer literacy in the island nation.

infrastructure damage estimated at over $50 million. Throughout the year, farmers implored the government for compensation and subsidy aid to help them recover in the wake of the storm.

In February Mauritius's presidency, a largely ceremonial position, changed hands three times. In a move that surprised and confused many in the government and civilian population, Pres. Cassam Uteem decided to resign rather than approve a controversial antiterrorism bill that would limit the rights of persons accused of terror-related crimes. His successor, Vice Pres. Angidi Chettiar, soon followed suit. On February 19 Supreme Court Chief Justice Ariranga Pillay, the acting president, signed the bill into law. Prime Minister Anerood Jugnauth, a staunch supporter of the legislation, continually rejected the claims of Uteem and the opposition in the parliament that the antiterror act could open the door to an abuse of police power. On February 25 the parliament elected Karl Offmann of the Militant Socialist Movement as the new president and Raouf Bundhun as vice president.

In June Mauritius raised its value-added-tax rate 3% to 15%. According to Deputy Prime Minister and Finance Minister Paul Bérenger, the increase was designed to reduce the national debt and allow for increased spending on education and other aspects of the nation's critical infrastructure.

(ANDREW EISENBERG)

MEXICO

Area: 1,964,375 sq km (758,449 sq mi)
Population (2002 est.): 100,977,000
Capital: Mexico City
Head of state and government: President Vicente Fox Quesada

The year 2002 was one of uncertainty for Mexico in both economic and political terms.

The Mexican economy recovered somewhat from its disappointing performance in 2001, when there was a 0.2% decline in the country's inflation-adjusted gross domestic product. Analysts expected the economy to grow by 1.6% in real terms during 2002, and the official target for inflation was a low 4.5%. Nevertheless, the key variable—future economic trends in the U.S., the recipient of nearly 90% of Mexico's exports—remained outside policy makers' control.

The future of the *maquiladora* industry (manufacturing plants that import and assemble duty-free components for export) remained especially uncertain. The industry, concentrated principally along the northern border with the U.S., had been the most rapidly growing segment of the manufacturing sec-

tor throughout the 1990s, but it suffered a 9% drop in output during 2001 and showed slow signs of recovery during 2002. Many observers feared that factories that had suspended production during the 2001 economic slowdown would not reopen, opting instead to transfer their activities to lower-wage locations in Central America, the Caribbean, or Southeast Asia.

Mexico did, however, weather the regional wave of financial instability that resulted from Argentina's economic collapse in 2001–02. The peso–U.S. dollar exchange rate slipped somewhat, but foreign-investment flows into the country were strong. The government remained firmly committed to maintaining macroeconomic discipline, and it held very substantial foreign-exchange reserves. In early 2002 Mexican government loans received a highly sought "investment grade" rating from Wall Street. Financial analysts noted that Mexico's membership in the North American Free Trade Agreement also helped insulate the country from regional disturbances by encouraging foreign financial analysts to differentiate between Mexico and other Latin American nations.

In domestic politics, the administration of Pres. Vicente Fox appeared to be losing momentum on some fronts, though Fox's personal popularity remained high. Indeed, after declining in early 2002, public approval of the president's performance rose after March to the 60% range. The administration also won a victory when the Supreme Court rejected a constitutional challenge by supporters of the rebel Zapatista National Liberation Army (EZLN) to the 2001 Law on Indigenous Rights and Culture.

However, divisions within the government and its lack of a legislative majority in the Congress severely hindered major legislative initiatives. In April the government's efforts to expand private investment in the generation of electrical power suffered a setback when the Supreme Court ruled that an executive decree on this matter was unconstitutional. The administration subsequently worked to build multiparty support for constitutional amendments that would encourage increased private investment but without privatizing the public enterprises that dominated the sector. Nevertheless, both the Party of the Democratic Revolution (PRD) and the Institutional Revolutionary Party (PRI) remained on record against proposed constitutional reforms.

Two campaign-finance-related scandals drew much attention during the year. President Fox was placed on the defensive by allegations that "Friends of Fox," the nonparty organization that he employed so successfully in his presidential campaign, had violated federal electoral law by accepting substantial contributions from foreign sources. The second controversy involved the federal comptroller's investigation into charges that PRI candidate Francisco Labastida's 1999–2000 presidential campaign had illegally received large transfers of funds from the state-owned oil company, PEMEX, via the PRI-allied Mexican Petroleum Workers' Union. The case tested the Fox administration's public commitment to rooting out corruption. Some observers also feared that successful prosecution of the union leaders involved in the scandal might further complicate efforts to enact significant labour law reform.

In foreign policy terms as well, the prospects for key Mexican initiatives remained decidedly mixed. In 2002 Mexico assumed one of the 10 rotating seats on the UN Security Council, and in March in Monterrey the government hosted the UN International Conference on Financing for Development. In early September the Mexican government formally withdrew from the 1947 Inter-American Treaty of Reciprocal Assistance (known as the Rio Treaty), which a government spokesperson characterized as "a relic of the Cold War."

Mexico proved unsuccessful, however, at moving forward its negotiations with the administration of Pres. George W. Bush over U.S. immigration reforms. Although the Fox administration continued to seek U.S. legislative changes that would safeguard the rights of undocumented Mexican workers already resident in the U.S., as well as increase the availability of visas for Mexican citizens seeking temporary employment there, American concerns remained focused on the "war on terrorism" and heightened border controls. Admitting publicly that negotiations on the subject were "stalled," Fox expressed some frustration with the Bush administration's inability to follow through on its stated commitment to addressing the status of Mexican immigrants. Nevertheless, the prospect in late 2002 of armed conflict with Iraq suggested that it might prove difficult to draw U.S. attention back to bilateral issues.

Certainly the most sensational foreign policy development during 2002 concerned Mexico's diplomatic relations with Cuba. In an effort to remain consistent with the pro-human rights image that the democratically elected Fox administration wished to project, the Ministry of Foreign Relations signaled that Mexico would vote in favour of the UN Human Rights Commission's critical statement on the Castro government's human rights record. (In preceding years Mexico had abstained when this evaluation was made.) In retaliation, in late April, Cuban Pres. Fidel Castro released a secretly recorded tape of a March 19 telephone conversation between Fox and Castro, in which Fox indirectly suggested that Castro might shorten his participation in the Monterrey summit and not appear at the forum at the same time as President Bush.

Castro's revelation unleashed a storm of criticism from the PRD and the PRI. The parties strongly denounced the Fox government's alignment with the U.S. and its "betrayal" of Mexico's historic ties with the Cuban Revolution, and they acted together to deny Fox congressional approval for a scheduled trip to the U.S. and Canada. This background may have contributed to Fox's decision in August to cancel a trip to Texas in order to protest that state's execution of a Mexican prisoner who had been arrested for murder without being allowed access to Mexican consular authorities. His decision won applause from across the political spectrum.

(KEVIN J. MIDDLEBROOK)

MICRONESIA, FEDERATED STATES OF

Area: 701 sq km (271 sq mi)
Population (2002 est.): 109,000
Capital: Palikir, on Pohnpei
Head of state and government: President Leo A. Falcam

Negotiations over the renewal of the Federated States of Micronesia's (FSM's) Compact of Free Association with the U.S. continued in 2002. The FSM was seeking an extension of the present levels of funding, with inflation adjustments. In August the electorate voted on 14 proposed constitutional amendments, which included the establishment of national educational standards with appropriate funding for implementation, the direct election of the president and vice president, and the allowance of dual citizenship. None of the proposals secured the required 75% of the vote needed for approval. Fewer than a quarter of the FSM's 67,000 eligible voters went to the polls.

In October a national symposium undertook an overview of the economic prospects and development plans for the FSM. The symposium supported the development of proposals for tax reform and the establishment of an independent tax and customs authority. It also addressed concerns over the relationship between national and state governments. The FSM joined the countries entitled to assistance from the European Union (EU) under the Cotonou Agreement, through which the EU assisted less-developed countries. Projects in renewable energy and private-sector development were anticipated. In early July Tropical Storm Chata'an caused 47 deaths and widespread damage in Chuuk state. (*See* DISASTERS.) (BARRIE MACDONALD)

MOLDOVA

Area: 33,843 sq km (13,066 sq mi)
Population (2002 est.): 3,621,000 (excluding some 600,000 persons working abroad)
Capital: Chisinau
Chief of state: President Vladimir Voronin
Head of government: Prime Minister Vasile Tarlev

On Jan. 9, 2002, Moldova's opposition Christian Democratic Popular Party (PPCD) began a marathon of protests in downtown Chisinau against the incumbent Communists' Russification policies: the planned introduction of compulsory Russian courses in primary schools, the proclamation of Russian as an official language, and the replacement of courses in the history of the Romanian people with the Soviet-style version of the history of Moldova. Although the government later backed off somewhat, it adopted a hard line against the protest organizers, suspending the PPCD on January 22. The move sparked criticism from European organizations, and the suspension was eventually annulled on February 8. On

March 21 PPCD deputy chairman Vlad Cubreacov disappeared under murky circumstances and was held or remained incognito for more than two months. The anticommunist demonstrations peaked on March 31, when as many as 80,000 people demanded that the Communists step down. In a resolution on April 24, the Parliamentary Assembly of the Council of Europe (PACE) pressed the Communists to make concessions. On September 1, when progress seemed mired down, the Christian Democrats staged a further mass protest. A second PACE resolution on September 26, however, was less critical of the Communists' policies.

In early July the Organization for Security and Co-operation in Europe (OSCE) presented the draft of a project to resolve the Transdniester conflict through the federalization of Moldova, which caused an immediate political uproar. Russia failed to keep its pledge to withdraw its military from eastern Moldova fully by the end of 2002, although efforts were accelerated after late September. Moldova strengthened its relations with Russia and the Commonwealth of Independent States, which held a summit in Chisinau on October 6–7. On December 7 an OSCE foreign ministers conference in Porto, Port., had to extend by one year the deadline for Russia's withdrawal from Transdniestria.   (DAN IONESCU)

MONACO

Area: 1.96 sq km (0.76 sq mi)
Population (2002 est.): 32,000
Chief of state: Prince Rainier III
Head of government: Minister of State Patrick Leclercq

On April 2, 2002, concerns about the health of Prince Rainier III led Monaco to define the ranks of succession in the principality. Prince Albert remained first in line to succeed his father, but if Albert died without children, Princess Caroline would be next in line, followed by her eldest son, Prince Andrea.

The Port Condamine harbour upgrade was completed in 2002. Pontoon-type sea walls were erected outside the existing harbour, and a floating dock enclosed 8,000 sq m (9,568 sq yd) of re-

claimed land at Fort Antoine. Half of the floating breakwater was intended to provide parking, while the other half was designed to hold boat stores.

In mid-April the Organisation for Economic Co-operation and Development named Monaco one of seven uncooperative tax havens, although the government said it had taken steps to increase the exchange of tax information. The banking-secrecy laws came under further scrutiny in October when British banker Stephen Troth confessed to having embezzled approximately €20 million (about $19.6 million) while working at the private bank HSBC Republic in Monaco.   (ANNE ROBY)

MONGOLIA

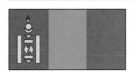

Area: 1,564,116 sq km (603,909 sq mi)
Population (2002 est.): 2,457,000
Capital: Ulaanbaatar
Chief of state: President Natsagiyn Bagabandi
Head of government: Prime Minister Nambaryn Enkhbayar

In 2002 Prime Minister Nambaryn Enkhbayar faced a number of economic challenges as he entered his third

year in office as head of the ruling Mongolian People's Revolutionary Party (MPRP). The budget deficit had soared to $72 million in 2002 before he reduced it to $66 million in August. The foreign-trade deficit, $170 million for 2001, was still hovering at $141 million by mid-2002. Enkhbayar had also pledged to raise pensions and state employees' wages. Opposition Democratic Party member Gündalay in the Great Hural (parliament) attacked the administration in April for having secretly handed out the equivalent of $8,930 to each of the MPRP's 72 Great Hural members in 2001 to spend in their constituencies and for planning to repeat the action in 2002. Opposition parties also continued to campaign against the MPRP's undemocratic practices and restriction of the media.

In June the Great Hural adopted the Law on Land and the Law on Land Privatization, due to come into force in 2003. The area to be privatized was limited, however, to 1% of Mongolia's total territory. As a result of two years of autumn drought and severe winters, 2.7 million livestock perished in early 2002.

Russian Prime Minister Mikhail Kasyanov's March visit to Ulaanbaatar ended in confusion after the Russian press reported that Mongolia had agreed to pay at par with the U.S. dollar its Soviet aid debt of 11.5 billion "transferable rubles" (used for international accounting during the Soviet period). Prime Minister Enkhbayar said

A Mongolian woman rounds up livestock near Ulaanbaatar on November 3. Drought and severe winter weather in Mongolia claimed the lives of millions of livestock during the year.

AP/Wide World Photos

methods of debt repayment had been discussed with Russia, but without agreement on the dollar equivalent. In June the Chinese foreign trade and economic cooperation minister, Shi Guangsheng, signed a 10 million yuan (about $1.2 million) economic-cooperation pact in Ulaanbaatar and agreed to defer Mongolia's debt of 28.3 million transferable rubles to China. At the July meeting in Ulaanbaatar of the Consultative Group on aid to Mongolia, agreement was reached on a one-year aid package of $333 million.

(ALAN J.K. SANDERS)

MOROCCO

Area: 710,850 sq km (274,461 sq mi), including the 252,120-sq-km (97,344-sq-mi) area of the disputed Western Sahara annexation
Population (2002 est.): 29,632,000, of which Western Sahara 256,000
Capital: Rabat
Head of state and government: King Muhammad VI, assisted by Prime Ministers 'Abd al-Rahman Youssoufi and, from October 9, Driss Jettou

King Muhammad VI appears with his new bride, Princess Lalla Salma, in Rabat on July 13, breaking a tradition in Morocco of keeping royal wives hidden.

Moroccans went to the polls on Sept. 27, 2002, to elect a new 325-member House of Representatives. For the first time, 10% of the seats were reserved for women and the immigrant population was excluded from the vote. Twenty-six parties took part in the election. The turnout was low—only 52% of the electorate voted. The Socialist Union of Popular Forces won 50 seats, followed by the former independence party, Istiqlal (48 seats). The surprise result was that the Islamist Party of Justice and Development (42 seats) edged past the conservative National Assembly of Independents (41 seats). In a move that was highly criticized, King Mohammed VI did not call upon the leader of the largest party to form the new government but instead turned to former interior minister and technocrat Driss Jettou, who had no party affiliation.

Relations with Spain—which had been poor since 2001—were further strained in July. After Morocco sent soldiers to the disputed though unoccupied islet of Leila/Perejil, Spain invaded the islet (near Ceuta in the Strait of Gibraltar) and expelled the six gendarmes. Though the U.S. brokered an agreement to leave the islet unoccupied, relations between the two countries remained at a low level for the remainder of the year.

The longtime territorial dispute between Morocco and the Polisario Front over the Western Sahara was raised at the UN Security Council in January and again in July. At the January meeting, the peace plan put forward in 2001 by special UN envoy James Baker was discussed, and the secretary-general offered four alternative approaches. The Security Council renewed the UN Mission for the Referendum in Western Sahara (MINURSO) mandate for six months. In July Baker agreed to reformulate his plan, and the MINURSO mandate was renewed for an additional six months, albeit in an atmosphere of generalized frustration.

In the Western Sahara itself, protests continued over Morocco's occupation of the region. Attacks on a police station in El Aaiun in June resulted in a series of arrests, as did protests over persons who had disappeared from the Western Sahara. Human rights organizations continued to point to the Western Sahara situation as the one remaining area where

doubt remained about Morocco's human rights record.   (GEORGE JOFFÉ)

MOZAMBIQUE

Area: 812,379 sq km (313,661 sq mi)
Population (2002 est.): 18,083,000
Capital: Maputo
Head of state and government: President Joaquim Chissano, assisted by Prime Minister Pascoal Mocumbi

During the eighth annual congress of the ruling Mozambique Liberation Front (Frelimo), held in Matola on June 13–17, 2002, Armado Emilio Guebuza, former minister of transport and communication, was elected secretary-general of the party. It was announced that he would be Frelimo's candidate in the 2004 presidential elections, and the decision was later endorsed by Pres. Joaquim Chissano in a televised address. While the congress was taking place, Antonio Palanje announced the formation of the Congress of United Democrats, a new party that would promote economic freedom and interethnic understanding.

In mid-January the government signed a deal with Spoornet, South Africa's public railways, that would allow Spoornet to run its trains from the South African border to Maputo for a payment of $67.7 million; Spoornet would also invest an additional $17.2 million in Mozambique's railways. After the devastating impact of civil war and serious flooding on the country's communications, it was hoped that the agreement would encourage tourism in Mozambique as well as the completion of the Maputo Development Corridor scheme to improve the economy, infrastructure, and general living conditions in the southern part of the country.

Any optimism was soon muted when severe drought resulted in serious crop shortages; the UN World Food Programme estimated that at least 515,000 people would need food aid until the end of the year. Italy's decision to can-

cel Mozambique's debt, amounting to $524 million, came as a timely gesture. There was another setback on May 25 when 196 people were killed in the worst rail crash in the country's history. (*See* DISASTERS.) In August the managers of the Maragra sugar plantation complained that the heavy subsidies received by their European competitors made it difficult for the managers to sell their produce and forced them to cut back on employee wages.

Although Mozambique offered 50-year land leases to a limited number of white farmers who had been expelled from their landholdings in Zimbabwe, President Chissano voiced his full support for Pres. Robert Mugabe's land-reform program while visiting Zimbabwe in September. In December Chissano welcomed Mugabe and South African Pres. Thabo Mbeki to Maputo to sign the treaty officially launching the Great Limpopo Transfrontier Park, which linked game reserves in all three countries.   (KENNETH INGHAM)

MYANMAR (BURMA)

Area: 676,577 sq km (261,228 sq mi)
Population (2002 est.): 42,238,000
Capital: Yangon (Rangoon)
Head of state and government: Chairman of the State Peace and Development Council Gen. Than Shwe

The major event in Myanmar in 2002 was the release on May 6 of Aung San Suu Kyi, the National League for Democracy (NLD) leader, from a 19-month-long house arrest. The State Peace and Development Council (SPDC) apparently buckled under the threat of tougher economic sanctions. In April the European Union (EU) extended its economic embargo by six months, and the U.S. Congress was

GREAT LIMPOPO TRANSFRONTIER PARK

Beira

Sofala Bay

Masvingo

GREAT ZIMBABWE NAT'L MONUMENT

Save

Save

Mwenezi

Runde

GONAREZHOU NAT'L PARK

ZINAVE NAT'L PARK

BAZARUTO NAT'L PARK

ZIMBABWE

Limpopo

Changane

MOZAMBIQUE

KRUGER NAT'L PARK

BANHINE NAT'L PARK

Tropic of Capricorn

Seshego

Olifants

SOUTH AFRICA

Incomati

COUTADA 16*

Limpopo

Inhambane

Xai-Xai

INDIAN OCEAN

Maputo

Matola

SWAZILAND

— International boundary

— Core area of Great Limpopo Transfrontier Park (GLTF)

National parks and conservation area* within GLTF

National parks and monuments outside GLTF

0   25   50   75   100 mi

0   50   100   150 km

AFRICA

© 2003 Encyclopædia Britannica, Inc.

Members of a village near the Thai border in Myanmar take refuge in a forest in late February after learning of a possible clash between army troops and rebel insurgents in the area.

considering tightening its ban on imports from Myanmar, in addition to existing economic and travel restrictions.

The decision to release Suu Kyi had apparently created rifts within the military. In April the SPDC charged four relatives of former dictator Ne Win with treason for their role in a failed coup in early March. The news of the coup was greeted with skepticism and widely interpreted as a move against factions of the military opposed to a deal with the NLD and as a way to bring an end to the Ne Win family-business empire. Ne Win, who had been under house arrest since March, died suddenly in December. (*See* OBITUARIES.)

While welcoming the release of Suu Kyi, the U.S. and the EU refused to lift economic sanctions until all the estimated 1,500 political prisoners had been freed and restrictions on political activities lifted. Japan and Australia, however, agreed to provide financial support for targeted developmental programs and dispatched their foreign ministers to Yangon after almost two decades. Tokyo began releasing part of a $28 million aid package for a hydroelectric dam. In April 2002 the foreign ministers of India, Myanmar, and Thailand agreed to link a highway between the three countries.

In May and June border tensions escalated between Thailand and Myanmar as army troops and ethnic minority rebel insurgents engaged in sporadic armed clashes that led to a worsening military and diplomatic row.

Besides a 40% growth in military expenditures, the only other growth was in the illicit trade in drugs (opium production reportedly netted $150 million annually), gemstones, and timber. Many investors withdrew, including 18 Australian companies, and Britain's Premier Oil pulled out of its controversial $650 million investment in Myanmar.

The World Health Organization ranked the health services in the country the second worst among 191 countries. Inflation shot up from 21% to 34.2%; the government foreign-exchange reserves were less than $25 million; and market prices for basic foods rose by more than 20%. Gas exports expanded rapidly, however, a slowdown in overall gross domestic product growth was expected in 2002–03.

(MOHAN MALIK)

NAMIBIA

Area: 825,118 sq km (318,580 sq mi)
Population (2002 est.): 1,837,000
Capital: Windhoek
Chief of state and head of government: President Sam Nujoma, assisted by Prime Ministers Hage Geingob and, from August 28, Theo-Ben Gurirab

The November 2001 announcement by the South West Africa People's Organization that Sam Nujoma, SWAPO's president since the formation of the party, would not seek another term as president of the country heightened speculation in 2002 regarding the identity of his successor after his term ended in March 2005. In August 2002, after denouncing "factions" within SWAPO, Nujoma unexpectedly reshuffled his cabinet, presumably with his succession in mind. He replaced Hage Geingob, prime minister since independence, with another Damara speaker, long-term Foreign Minister Theo-Ben Gurirab. Nujoma's closest Ovambo colleagues, Hidipo Hamutenya and Hifikepunye Pohamba, became foreign minister and SWAPO vice president, respectively. Nujoma himself took charge of the Ministry of Information and Broadcasting and soon insisted that the Namibian Broadcasting Corp. replace foreign television programs with ones containing local content. His increasingly authoritarian style was coupled with a strong defense of Pres. Robert Mugabe's land policies in Zimbabwe. As in Zimbabwe, the Namibian government employed North Koreans to build the expensive Heroes' Acre—a memorial burial place outside Windhoek—and a large new presidential complex.

In August the SWAPO Congress determined that 192 farms belonging to foreign absentee landlords should be expropriated within the framework of the law and directed the government to increase the annual budget for land resettlement from about $1.9 million to about $9.5 million. Though whites made up less than 5% of the Namibian population, they owned more than 70% of the 360,000 sq km (139,000 sq mi) of farmland.

The Caprivi region was affected by drought, but peace returned to the north, and many of those exiled in Botswana returned. Despite the peace in Angola, 78 alleged National Union for the Total Independence of Angola supporters continued to be held at Dordabis without trial, and efforts to secure their release from detention failed.　　　(CHRISTOPHER SAUNDERS)

NAURU

Area: 21.2 sq km (8.2 sq mi)
Population (2002 est.): 12,300, excluding asylum seekers
Capital: Government offices in Yaren district
Head of state and government: President René Harris

Nauru received economic assistance in 2002 in the form of A$30 million (about $16 million) in Australian goods and services for its role in housing refugees who had been denied access to Australia. What started out as Australia's "Pacific solution" and a bonus for Nauru turned into a source of antagonism toward Australia and its policy makers when it took more than 12 months to process asylum seekers. In late October 2002, 871 people were being held in Nauru, which placed great strains on infrastructure and created a political dilemma for Nauruan Pres. René Harris.

The Australian government and the UN High Commissioner for Refugees categorized most people detained on Nauru as Afghans. By mid-September, however, only 133 Afghans had been determined to be genuine refugees and thus eligible for resettlement in Australia. The remaining asylum seekers waited for possible voluntary repatriation to Afghanistan with a grant of A$2,000 (about $1,100) per person for resettlement or forcible removal if they refused to go. As a result of this standoff

and the time taken to process refugee applications, relationships deteriorated between the asylum seekers and Nauruans. In President Harris's view, the camp in Nauru demonstrated that the "Pacific solution" had become a "Pacific nightmare." (See also *Australia:* Special Report, above.)　　　(A.R.G. GRIFFITHS)

NEPAL

Area: 147,181 sq km (56,827 sq mi)
Population (2002 est.): 23,692,000
Capital: Kathmandu
Head of state: King Gyanendra Bir Bikram Shah Dev
Head of government: Prime Ministers Sher Bahadur Deuba and, from October 11, Lokendra Bahadur Chand

Political crises at both the central and the regional level were the norm in Nepal throughout most of 2002. Conflicts within and between major political parties, including the ruling Nepali Congress Party, were critical. Prime Minister Sher Bahadur Deuba decided in September to dissolve the parliament and to postpone the elections scheduled for November. The negative response from the major political factions led King Gyanendra Bir Bikram Shah Dev (*see* BIOGRAPHIES) to use his constitutional powers to dismiss the Deuba government. Party leaders then recommended to the king that he appoint a multiparty government, but instead Gyanendra decided to install a government headed by Lokendra Bahadur Chand, which took office in early November without obtaining a support vote from the parliament. In December Chand stated that a parliamentary election "could be held" within six months, but no arrangements had been made by year's end.

The Nepalese army had not yet demonstrated the capacity to crush the Maoist insurrection in the country's western hill area, but it had been able to confine the insurgents. This conflict promised to continue to divide the country politically and to undermine most economic and social development programs. India, China, and the U.S. supported the central government and continued to provide substantial economic and military aid.　　　(LEO E. ROSE)

NETHERLANDS, THE

Area: 41,528 sq km (16,034 sq mi)
Population (2002 est.): 16,142,000
Capital: Amsterdam; seat of government, The Hague
Chief of state: Queen Beatrix
Head of government: Prime Ministers Wim Kok and, from July 22, Jan Peter Balkenende

The year 2002 was an eventful one in The Netherlands. On February 2 Crown Prince Willem-Alexander married Argentine Máxima Zorreguieta (*see* BIOGRAPHIES) in a civil ceremony in the old Berlage Stock Exchange building in Amsterdam, followed by a church blessing in the Nieuwe Kerk (New Church). The newlyweds were driven through the city in the Golden Coach, and they waved to the crowds from the balcony of the Palace on Dam Square.

On April 10 the Netherlands Institute for War Documentation published its report following five years of research into the massacre that took place in Srebrenica, Bosnia, in July 1995, when more than 7,000 Islamic men and boys were murdered while the area was under the protection of a Dutch battalion of the UN Protection Force. The independent report held the UN and the Dutch government partially responsible for the fiasco, stating that while they had acted out of humanitarian ideals, they had put Dutch forces in an impossible position by not providing proper armaments and a clear mandate. In response, the Dutch government, led by Prime Minister Wim Kok, tendered its resignation. Kok asserted that while the report had laid the blame for the deaths squarely on Bosnian Serbs, it had also attributed mistakes to the international community, including Dutch leaders. Kok stated, "The international community is anonymous and cannot take responsibility in a visible way vis-à-vis the victims and survivors of the events in Srebrenica. I can—and do—take that responsibility." Many praised Kok's integrity, while regretting that his successful political career in The Netherlands had ended on this sombre note.

In the subsequent election campaign, immigration and integration, crime,

At a lying-in-state ceremony for slain Dutch politician Pim Fortuyn in Rotterdam on May 9, some of the thousands of mourners in attendance hold up images of Fortuyn, who had been gunned down outside a radio station three days earlier.

health care, and the economy were central issues. A relatively new political party achieved national prominence. Pim Fortuyn (*see* OBITUARIES), a flamboyant political outsider, criticized Dutch political culture as too cautious and consensus-oriented, and he proceeded to express his opinions less neutrally. He argued, for instance, that The Netherlands should tighten its immigration policies and, referring to the Dutch tradition of gay rights, that essential Dutch values were being challenged by the presence of Islamic residents and citizens. The nation was deeply shocked when Fortuyn was killed on May 6. The motives of the alleged gunman, who was apprehended immediately, were unclear. Although subsequent political debates and campaigning were canceled, elections were nevertheless held on May 15. The List Pim Fortuyn became the second largest party, after the Christian Democrats—a dramatic shift from the previous right-left "purple coalition." The formation of the government and the first months in power were fraught with dissent and upheaval, however, and on October 16 the coalition government collapsed. New elections were scheduled for January 2003.

Prince Claus, the husband of Queen Beatrix, died on October 6, after years of poor health. (*See* OBITUARIES.)

(JOLANDA VANDERWAL TAYLOR)

NEW ZEALAND

Area: 270,534 sq km (104,454 sq mi)
Population (2002 est.): 3,893,000
Capital: Wellington
Chief of state: Queen Elizabeth II, represented by Governor-General Dame Silvia Cartwright
Head of government: Prime Minister Helen Clark

In 2002, her first full year in office, Gov.-Gen. Dame Silvia Cartwright was able to add her touch to the prominence of women in New Zealand affairs. The speech from the throne she read on August 27 to open Parliament bore the touch of Prime Minister Helen Clark (*see* BIOGRAPHIES), who had spent the last parliamentary term cementing her grip on power. Clark, as leader of the Labour Party, had seen her team come from behind in the general election in July. Neither Labour, which won 41.3% of the votes and a total of 52 seats in the 120-seat House, nor the once mighty National Party (NP), with 20.9% and 27 seats, won a clear majority. The real victor was mixed member proportional (MMP) voting, which distributed some seats on the basis of proportional representation. New Zealand First took 10.4% and 13 seats, 12 from its MMP list. Labour, however, had become skilled at negotiating with the smaller parties, notably the Greens (7% and 9 seats).

Under its swashbuckling new leader, Bill English, the NP, which had lost seats since the last election, found itself defending its right to be seated as the official parliamentary opposition. What might have been a coup for National, in better times, was that the Reserve Bank's governor, Don Brash, a widely respected curtailer of inflation, had resigned the bank post, had won a National Party seat, and would have been posted to the front benches if the NP had prevailed. Clark also lost her deputy prime minister, former Alliance leader Jim Anderton, who in June launched a new party, the Progressive Coalition (1.7% and 2 seats). She substituted Finance Minister Michael Cullen as her new deputy prime minister in August. Against this background, it was remarkable that the official speech from the throne indicated a continuing unruffled program of initiatives.

Some strain was evident between Australia and New Zealand when Canberra moved to limit the access of New Zealanders to Australian government benefits. New Zealanders too were critical of visitors to the larger country living like residents without joining in any payment for resettlement. New Zealanders were not far behind Australians, however, in deploying Special Air Service forces alongside American troops in Afghanistan. The old ANZAC spirit, a remnant of the World War I combined Australia and New Zealand Army Corps, was to be seen in combined peacekeeping forces in East Timor. For New Zealand air and navy forces, there was radical change in the balance of defense spending at home.

Leaky buildings became a concern in New Zealand when a pattern was uncovered involving poor design, construction, and materials used in new domestic housing that left buildings vulnerable to rot and, in wet weather, internal and structural leaks. The problems were seen to plague near-new apartment blocks and subdivisions built mainly with monolithic cladding and untreated timber. The situation rated a summit in September in Wellington, which was attended by local government representatives, building inspectors, and other industry leaders, to deal with a repair problem that was already estimated to cost from NZ$36 million to NZ$240 million (about U.S. $17.5 million to U.S. $117 million). Questions were raised about the lack of strict building standards and the responsibilities of the government-appointed Building Industry Authority. In November a parliamentary select committee began hearings on the issue.

(JOHN A. KELLEHER)

NICARAGUA

Area: 130,373 sq km (50,337 sq mi)
Population (2002 est.): 5,024,000
Capital: Managua
Head of state and government: Presidents Arnoldo Alemán Lacayo and, from January 10, Enrique Bolaños Geyer

Nicaraguan Pres. Enrique Bolaños Geyer, inaugurated in January 2002 af-

A Nicaraguan mother and her children sit at a landfill in Managua where they go to collect salvageable items. The per capita income in Nicaragua is the second lowest in the hemisphere.

ter promising a "New Era," asked the legislature to strip former president Arnoldo Alemán Lacayo's immunity to prosecute him for having allegedly stolen $100 million from the public treasury and laundered it through domestic and foreign accounts. This followed arrests of officials who had profited from bank collapses costing the government $300 million and of Byron Jerez, head of the country's revenue department. The prosecutions represented a political showdown between Bolaños and Alemán for control of the Constitutionalist Liberal Party. In September the National Assembly removed Alemán from its presidency; in December they voted 47–45 to remove his immunity, and he was placed under house arrest in anticipation of criminal prosecution.

Per capita income, second lowest in the hemisphere, fell for the second consecutive year, ending the modest recovery (1994–2000) that followed the end of the Contra insurgency against the Sandinista government. The recovery had been fueled by foreign aid, debt forgiveness, and family remittances from Nicaraguans abroad. Adverse weather and collapsed world coffee prices crippled the agricultural sector, spurring protests by coffee growers demanding support. With 11% official unemployment and 36% underemployment, the government was squeezed between popular protests and International Monetary Fund demands for fiscal austerity.

Continuing Nicaragua's embrace of world markets since the 1990 Sandinista electoral defeat, President Bolaños opened bidding for exploration of newfound oil and natural gas deposits. The legislature approved concessions for a $2.6 billion, 40-year "dry canal" involving high-speed railroads, an oil pipeline, and two deepwater ports. These initiatives were opposed by Atlantic coast indigenous and community groups concerned about environmental impact, land speculation, and violation of regional rights under the 1987 Atlantic Coast Autonomy Bill.

The Sandinista party congress re-elected thrice-defeated presidential candidate Daniel Ortega Saavedra as its general secretary, despite party dissidents' demands for democratization. Ortega's stepdaughter asked the Supreme Court to overturn a statute of limitations ruling on her sexual abuse charges against the former president.

(RICHARD STAHLER-SHOLK)

NIGER

Area: 1,267,000 sq km (489,000 sq mi)
Population (2002 est.): 10,640,000
Capital: Niamey
Head of state and government: President Tandja Mamadou, assisted by Prime Minister Hama Amadou

On July 31, 2002, soldiers demanding higher pay and better conditions of service mutinied in Diffa, N'Guigmi, and N'Gourti in southeastern Niger. Several army officers and government officials, including Diffa's prefect, were taken hostage. Another mutiny in the capital on August 5 was quashed by troops loyal to the government who, responding quickly, overran the last of the rebel garrisons on August 9. The president of the Nigérien League for the Rights of Man, Bagnou Bonkoukou, was arrested on August 15 for having publicly questioned the official toll of those killed and injured in the mutinies. He was sentenced to one year in prison. On August 28 opposition parties denounced the imposition of two presidential decrees that effectively put a communications blackout on all reports from the affected region in the southeast. The Constitutional Court, however, certified the legality of the decrees. The government announced on September 23 that, as peace had been restored, the tight security measures imposed by the decrees would be eased.

After two weeks of strikes, on March 12 thousands of students called for the release of two leaders of the University of Niamey's Students Union, who had been arrested following violent protests in 2001. Citing a severe drop in revenue, Prime Minister Hama Amadou announced in early August that civil service salaries would be paid 10 days in arrears for the next four months. The decision triggered strikes by the two largest unions, which closed banks and the airport on August 28 and 29. New austerity measures were announced on September 23.

The severe drought continued, with 70% of villages reporting insufficient water supplies. The former sultan of Zinder, Aboubacar Sanda, deposed by the government in 2001 on fraud charges, was sentenced to two years in prison on September 11.

(NANCY ELLEN LAWLER)

NIGERIA

Area: 923,768 sq km (356,669 sq mi)
Population (2002 est.): 129,935,000
Capital: Abuja
Head of state and government: President Olusegun Obasanjo

Throughout 2002 Nigeria suffered from violence of many kinds, including communal clashes and religious, ethnic, or land disputes. Ethnic conflicts in Lagos in early February killed more than 100 people. In mid-March, disputes over land in southeastern Nigeria resulted in more than 40 deaths. Ethnic and religious clashes broke out periodically in northern states. Clashes between rival university cult groups at the University of Nigeria in southeastern Enugu state in mid-June left at least 12 students dead. Sporadic violence occurred here and there throughout the year, with a total death toll approaching 1,000. Some government officials blamed the

disturbances on former military officers seeking to undermine democracy and prove that a civilian administration was incapable of providing security.

In mid-March the federal government declared some of the most severe sentences imposed under Shari'ah, or Islamic law, unconstitutional. Twelve of 19 northern and central states had extended jurisdiction of Shari'ah to criminal matters and moral offenses, and these areas rejected the central government's declaration. Several people were to have been executed under Islamic law, but only one execution, the hanging of a man convicted of murder, actually took place in 2002. In Katsina state the execution of Amina Lawal, who had been condemned to death by stoning for adultery, was postponed after her trial and sentence drew international outrage. (*See* CRIME AND LAW ENFORCEMENT: Special Report.) A second appeal in Lawal's case was pending.

In April and again in August, because of ethnic violence and vigilantism the central government postponed local elections, which were finally set for spring of 2003. The House of Representatives called for the immediate resignation of Pres. Olusegun

Obasanjo in August and, when he did not resign, issued a list of 17 charges against him, including corruption, breach of the constitution, and "inability to steer the ship of state"; he refuted all the allegations. Disturbances broke out, and troops were deployed, which resulted in hundreds of fatalities. Obasanjo announced that presidential elections would be held as scheduled in 2003.

The oil-producing Niger delta region was again the focus of political protests in 2002. In April the Supreme Court awarded all offshore oil revenues to the central administration; this angered state governors in the region, who threatened to revolt and warned of potential violence throughout the country. A bill passed in October, however, stipulated that all oil-producing states would receive their 13% share of the oil revenues paid to the federal government. This placated the governors, but local residents protested that their share of the deal was only the industrial pollution, with none of the benefits. Rights groups also criticized the government for destroying the environment, crushing dissent, and avoiding sharing the profits with local residents. Disruptions of oil production and transport were common. For more than two weeks in July, two groups of women attracted international attention by blockading and occupying oil pumping stations and terminals.

On January 27 a fire and explosions at a large munitions dump at the Ikeja Military Cantonment north of Lagos killed more than 1,000 people, a number of whom drowned in a nearby canal while trying to escape the blasts. Many unexploded munitions remained. Despite government efforts to clean up the area, dozens of people were injured or killed over the following few months.

Another aspect of the violence besetting the country was the activity of vigilante groups. These gangs operated openly—frequently with government support—engaging in extrajudicial killings, public burnings, mutilations, torture, and unlawful detention. Particularly noted for their brutality were the Bakassi Boys, who operated in the southeastern states and subjected those they caught to torture and mutilation, often killing suspected criminals rather than turning them over to the authorities. In August and September, under criticism from international groups and some government officials, the police tried to crack down on the Bakassi Boys in their strongholds of Abia and Anambra states. The federal

A Nigerian soldier stands guard on November 17 as contestants in the Miss World pageant attend a boat regatta in the town of Calabar. The pageant was later moved from the Nigerian capital, Abuja, to London after deadly rioting erupted over a front-page article in a Lagos daily newspaper suggesting that the prophet Muhammad would have approved of the pageant and chosen a wife from among its contestants.

AP/Wide World Photos

government outlawed the group, but many vigilantes continued to act clandestinely. (ANDREW F. CLARK)

NORWAY

Area: 323,758 sq km (125,004 sq mi)
Population (2002 est.): 4,537,000
Capital: Oslo
Chief of state: King Harald V
Head of government: Prime Minister Kjell Magne Bondevik

In 2002 the coalition government of Prime Minister Kjell Magne Bondevik met with considerable resistance in its attempt to persuade Norwegians to accept tighter economic policies despite the fact that, as a major oil and gas producer, Norway ranked among the most prosperous countries of the world. The government cited the risk of economic overheating in the near future and the long-term need to secure pensions for the country's growing elder population in its call to limit spending of Norway's huge oil income and to reduce the number of state-owned enterprises. The Progress Party, whose support in opinion polls jumped to nearly 30% during the year, wanted to spend more generously on social programs—an attitude strongly opposed by the Conservatives, who held the majority in the government. In order to secure passage of its budget for 2003, the government was forced to negotiate, first with the Progress Party, then with the formerly dominant Labour Party and the Socialist Left. An agreement was finally obtained toward the end of November. The new budget included some tax reductions as well as allocations for such popular measures as better old-age pensions for married couples and cheaper spirits.

The Storting (parliament) had decided in 2001 that Norway should join the war against terrorism in Afghanistan, sending soldiers trained in mine clearing and high-mountain winter warfare. As one of the rotating members of the United Nations Security Council for 2001–02, Norway insisted that the UN have a say in any decision regarding Iraq. In September 2002 Norwegian Foreign Minister Jan Petersen called a British intelligence report on Iraq's weapons program "disturbing" and voiced support for a new UN resolution outlining demands on Saddam Hussein's regime.

The Bank of Norway, having maintained since December 2001 the reduction of its interest rate to 6.5%, in July 2002 raised this rate to 7%, the highest in Western Europe. The raise was intended to help keep the inflation rate at around 2.5% per year. The high interest rate also meant a strong Norwegian currency. In fact, since the beginning of 2002, the value of the krone had grown by 10%, which made imports easier to afford but resulted in considerable market difficulties for Norwegian export industries. In any case, unemployment remained low, at 3.8%.

In May, less than a year after Crown Prince Haakon married commoner Mette-Marit Tjessem Høiby, Princess Märtha Louise, older sister to the crown prince and the second heiress to the throne, followed his lead, marrying writer Ari Behn in Nidaros Cathedral in Trondheim. Behn, the author of a 1999 short-story collection titled *Trist som faen*, was pilloried in some media outlets, though the princess herself remained immensely popular. In a break with tradition, she decided to keep her maiden name and would still be known as Princess Märtha Louise.

(GUDMUND SANDVIK)

OMAN

Area: 309,500 sq km (119,500 sq mi)
Population (2002 est.): 2,522,000
Capital: Muscat
Head of state and government: Sultan and Prime Minister Qabus ibn Sa'id

Throughout 2002 Oman—as chair of the Supreme Council of the six-member Gulf Cooperation Council—carried an international burden greater than most of its neighbouring states. As American war drums favouring an invasion of Iraq mounted steadily, Oman remained at the forefront of Arab and Islamic countries cautioning that any and all international action relating to Iraq should take place solely within the framework of the United Nations.

On the domestic front, Oman continued to suffer economically owing to the decline in international air transporta-

U.S. Vice Pres. Dick Cheney (right), accompanied by Omani officials, tours the Sultan Qabus Grand Mosque in Muscat during his mission to the Middle East early in the year to build support for Pres. George W. Bush's antiterrorism campaign.

tion and tourism following the Sept. 11, 2001, attacks in the U.S. Oman had invested heavily in tourism in hopes of diversifying the economy and attracting much-needed foreign investment. Offsetting these downturns were continued higher-than-expected oil revenues and ongoing strong demand for the country's liquefied natural gas exports.

Oman continued to face the twofold challenge of mounting unemployment and limited job opportunities for its increasingly educated youth. To address these challenges, there was heightened emphasis placed on the acceleration of more market-centred education and training for the present and future generations, the reduction of the traditional significant reliance on imported labour, and the continuing implementation of the several previous bold moves to encourage foreign and domestic direct investment as well as private ownership. Among the more notable achievements in this regard were the further streamlining and regulation of the country's securities exchange as well as its banking and financial sectors and the ongoing promotion of Oman's extraordinary favourable geographic location as a regional hub for corporate headquarters and the transshipment of goods.

(JOHN DUKE ANTHONY)

PAKISTAN

Area: 796,095 sq km (307,374 sq mi), excluding the 84,159-sq-km Pakistani-administered portion of Jammu and Kashmir
Population (2002 est.): 145,960,000 (excluding 4.3 million residents of Pakistani-administered Jammu and Kashmir as well as 1.1 million Afghan refugees)
Capital: Islamabad
Head of state and government: President and Chief Executive Gen. Pervez Musharraf

On Jan. 12, 2002, Pres. Pervez Musharraf, addressing the Pakistani people, declared that his government's highest priority was the eradication of extremism, violence, and terrorism. He said that he had decided to join the international coalition against terrorism because it was in Pakistan's interest and that it pained him when religious parties opposed his action. Musharraf asserted that the mosque was no place for the preaching of hatred. He banned five militant Islamist organizations and placed mosques under surveillance. Musharraf ignored opposition protests, and the government subsequently announced the closing of 254 offices and the arrests of more than a thousand activists.

In late January, Daniel Pearl, an American journalist for the *Wall Street Journal*, was kidnapped while pursuing a lead related to the war on terrorism. All efforts to trace his whereabouts failed, and several weeks passed before a video surfaced graphically detailing Pearl's death. (*See* OBITUARIES.) The Pearl case tested Musharraf's resolve, and by early February the major culprits in the kidnapping and killing were in custody and had been placed on trial. All were found guilty. In late February the Pakistani government issued a warning that other Americans could become targets. U.S. diplomatic installations were placed on high alert, and American firms doing business in

Pakistan were also told to examine their security measures.

Musharraf ordered the army, police, and intelligence services to act more aggressively in ferreting out terrorist cells. In late February four such groups were exposed in Karachi and quickly linked with religious and sectarian killings. On March 8 the government announced that it intended to expel thousands of Arab and other foreign students. Terrorist cells, however, continued their orgy of blood. A Protestant church frequented by American diplomats and their families in Islamabad was attacked by grenade-wielding militants, and a number of worshippers were killed. Subsequently, Washington ordered all nonessential diplomats in Pakistan to leave the country. On March 19 gunmen on motorcycles took the lives of a Sunni scholar and a Shi'ite leader in Lahore. Again the government's response was an expressed determination to identify and eliminate the terrorists, but, as one government official put it, "Every inch of the country's land cannot be monitored." With U.S. assistance, Abu Zubaydah, a member of Osama bin Laden's inner circle, was captured and turned over to the Americans. Another arrest of a high-ranking al-Qaeda member occurred in September when Ramzi Binalshibh was arrested in Karachi.

For a brief period in April, terrorism took a backseat to politics. Insisting on holding to his multiple roles and already having given himself an extended term as chief of the army staff, Musharraf called for a confirmation of his status as the country's principal leader. He announced that a national referendum would be held to determine whether he should be given an additional five-year term as president and chief executive. Challenged by criticism from every quarter, the general deflected all opposition to his plan, arguing that the country needed his brand of leadership. Despite protests and petitions calling for the rescinding of the referendum it was held on schedule on April 30, and those casting ballots gave Musharraf the expected resounding victory. According to official returns, he won 98% of the 43.4 million votes cast. Musharraf's new term began in October.

Observers concluded that Pakistan was home to the largest number of terrorists in the world, but that was not Islamabad's only concern. An estimated one million Indian troops remained massed on Pakistan's frontier. More than Pakistan's nuclear deterrent, however, it was the presence of U.S. forces

in Pakistan that kept India from engaging in another war with its neighbour. New Delhi pointed to the almost daily terrorist attacks in Kashmir and attributed all of them to Islamabad's policies.

In October, India agreed to withdraw thousands of its forces that had been poised for war on the Pakistani border for almost a year. Receiving even more attention, however, was the first national election held during Musharraf's tenure. Musharraf's party, the Pakistan Muslim League (Q), won the most seats, 118 in the 342-seat Parliament, but not nearly enough to form a government. Moreover, there seemed to be little interest among the other parties in forming a government with the PML (Q). By mid-November discussion had begun to focus on the calling of a new election.

(LAWRENCE ZIRING)

PALAU

Area: 488 sq km (188 sq mi)
Population (2002 est.): 19,900
Provisional capital: Koror; new capital buildings at Melekeok (on Babelthuap) to be completed in 2003
Head of state and government: President Tommy Remengesau, Jr.

Palau improved its relationships with both the United States and Taiwan in 2002. House Speaker Mario S. Guilbert led a nine-member delegation from Palau on a five-day visit to Taiwan to support its mission to join the United Nations. During his visit Guilbert thanked Taiwan for its long-term assistance in the areas of tourism, agriculture, education, and cultural and medical services. Taiwanese Pres. Chen Shui-bian particularly thanked Guilbert for his personal contribution to maintaining bilateral ties and especially noted Guilbert's role in guiding through the Palau legislature a resolution that called for China to remove its missiles aimed at Taiwan.

Palau was sympathetic to the major diplomatic drive by the United States to exempt U.S. troops from prosecution by the International Criminal Court, and it became one of a group of signatories to an agreement not to extradite U.S. soldiers for prosecution to the Hague-based court. Palau moved closer to trade integration with the Pacific Island Countries Trade Agreement group of nations, set up to establish a free-trade area. (A.R.G. GRIFFITHS)

PANAMA

Area: 74,979 sq km (28,950 sq mi)
Population (2002 est.): 2,915,000
Capital: Panama City
Head of state and government: President Mireya Moscoso

The year 2002 saw increasing attention to corruption involving all three branches of the Panamanian government. Pres. Mireya Moscoso was repeatedly accused of nepotism for appointing to government offices relatives and members of various prominent families who supported her political party. The legislative assembly was embroiled in a major scandal involving accusations of vote buying in the approval of Supreme Court justices and of a transportation and industrial development project known as CEMIS. The investigation against members of the legislature, however, had been thwarted by their immunity from legal prosecution. A battle to remove their immunity ensued, with no resolution by year's end. The attorney general refused to investigate the allegations fully until the immunity issue had been resolved. Public opinion polls indicated that more than 90% of Panamanians opposed legislative immunity.

Panama's first significant transparency law came into effect during the year. The law gave individuals the right to see most public documents but contained exceptions to protect individuals' privacy and other specified sensitive data. A controversial provision restricted requests for information to those who were "personally and immediately affected" by the information. The provision had been used to deny a series of requests by various groups for information regarding expenditures in the executive and legislative branches.

The governments of Panama and the U.S. announced agreement on an amendment to an existing antidrug accord that would allow U.S. military forces and law-enforcement agencies to pursue and arrest drug traffickers in Panamanian territory. Moscoso put Panama's National Police on heightened alert after peace negotiations between Colombia's government and guerrilla groups broke down.

(ORLANDO J. PÉREZ)

Upon her arrival in Bogotá, Colom., for an official visit in December, Panamanian Pres. Mireya Moscoso is welcomed by Colombian Pres. Álvaro Uribe Vélez.

© Eliana Aponte/Reuters 2002

PAPUA NEW GUINEA

Area: 462,840 sq km (178,704 sq mi)
Population (2002 est.): 5,426,000
Capital: Port Moresby
Chief of state: Queen Elizabeth II, represented by Governor-General Sir Silas Atopare
Head of government: Prime Ministers Sir Mekere Morauta and, from August 5, Sir Michael Somare

Sir Michael Somare was elected—88 votes to 0—prime minister of Papua New Guinea on Aug. 5, 2002. It was his third term as prime minister, and he had also served as chief minister (1972–75) prior to independence. In a surprise move, incumbent Prime Minister Sir Mekere Morauta announced that he would not contest the general election, and he also resigned as party leader of the People's Democratic Movement. Former prime minister Bill Skate took up the position of speaker in the new Parliament.

Upon taking office, Somare was urged to act soon to deal with the sharply declining economy. The president of the country's Chamber of Commerce and Industry pointed out that the kina (worth about 25 cents) was close to its lowest-ever level, company income and investment were way down, and economic activity was sluggish. As a result of the new Organic Law on the Integrity of Political Parties and Candidates, which outlawed the MPs' traditional practice of switching political allegiance after an election, Somare's position was secure.

(A.R.G. GRIFFITHS)

PARAGUAY

Area: 406,752 sq km (157,048 sq mi)
Population (2002 est.): 5,774,000
Capital: Asunción
Head of state and government: President Luis Ángel González Macchi

The year 2002 in Paraguay ended much where it had begun, mired in a

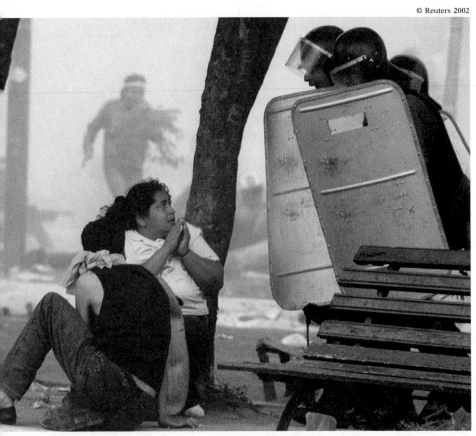

© Reuters 2002

On September 17 riot police in Asunción disperse protesting supporters of the exiled former general Lino Oviedo, who was thought to have been behind a 1996 coup attempt in Paraguay.

cycle of economic recession, social protest, corruption, and political paralysis. Nearly bankrupt, the Paraguayan government began the year hoping to raise $400 million from the privatization of several state enterprises, specifically the state water and sanitation company and the Paraguayan Communications Corp. (COPACO), the public telecommunications firm. In March the government fell behind on debt repayments and found itself unable to pay public-sector wages. The International Monetary Fund (IMF) pressed the government of Pres. Luis Ángel González Macchi to accelerate the sale of COPACO; however, González's unpopularity and dispute with a divided Congress delayed much of the government's state reform program until June. During the first six months of the year, the government faced recurring protests from peasant and labour groups demanding an end to free-market policies, namely privatization. In June, after police clashed with hundreds of protesters, the president suspended the privatization of COPACO indefinitely.

In March, Lino Oviedo, a former general living in asylum in Brazil who was suspected of having masterminded an attempted coup in 1996 and of having arranged the murder of Vice Pres. Luis María Argaña in 1999, announced that the National Union of Ethical Citizens (UNACE)—a faction he controlled within Paraguay's ruling Colorado Party—was breaking away. Subsequently, Oviedo formed a political alliance with a faction within the opposition Authentic Radical Liberal Party, headed by Vice Pres. Julio César Franco. The alliance, known as the National Patriotic Front, sought to impeach the president while supporting peasant and labour organizations in their effort to pressure the government to scrap an unpopular fiscal-adjustment package that the IMF had called for in return for a $200 million rescue loan.

In July González decreed a state of emergency after nationwide protests against his economic policies led to riots and violent confrontations with police that resulted in the shooting of four people. In September and October

the government resorted to violent suppression of demonstrations allegedly organized and financed by the Oviedo-Franco alliance. More than 250 protesters were taken into custody during a three-day demonstration in September. A general feeling of despair and frustration was exacerbated when Transparency International, a global organization that monitors corruption, rated Paraguay as the nation perceived to be the most corrupt in Latin America and the third worst in the world. Contributing to a climate of political uncertainty, Franco, in accordance with the constitution, resigned his post on October 16, six months before the deadline to qualify for the April 2003 presidential election.

By the end of the year, Paraguay's economy had contracted by nearly 3%. Buffeted by neighbouring Argentina's worst-ever economic crisis and Brazil's slumping currency, Paraguay's currency depreciated by nearly 35%.

(FRANK O. MORA)

PERU

Area: 1,285,216 sq km (496,225 sq mi)
Population (2002 est.): 26,749,000
Capital: Lima
Head of state and government: President Alejandro Toledo

Peru went through 2002 with its rather fragile democracy intact under Pres. Alejandro Toledo, but the year had more than its share of disruptions and worries. Toledo had been inaugurated in July 2001 with probably unrealistic expectations. In the elections called to replace Alberto Fujimori—who had resigned in late 2000 in the wake of a corruption scandal—Toledo had campaigned as a champion of the poor, especially of the country's impoverished indigenous masses, and his pledges were taken seriously, since he had come from such a background. For some years Peru had been mired in a deep recession that had left more than half of the country's population in poverty and pushed many into the informal sector in Peru's major cities. Toledo had pledged that he would create a million new jobs, but such promises had not been kept, and his public approval ratings fell steadily after he took office, hovering around an abysmal 20% for much of 2002.

Other factors contributed to the president's unpopularity. Although during his campaign he had consistently pledged not to privatize state enterprises, Toledo named a centrist cabinet that was inclined toward neoliberal economic policies, including downsizing of the state in general and privatization in particular. Such inconsistencies came to a head in June in the southern city of Arequipa, where a weeklong citywide strike against the sale of two regional power companies led to broad-scale public mobilizations that resulted in hundreds of casualties, including two fatalities. Nationwide regional and municipal elections were held on November 17. The opposition American Popular Revolutionary Alliance won 12 regional elections and finished far ahead of Toledo's party and all others, likely meaning that Toledo will face increased opposition during his next three years in office.

In addition, Toledo had been pursued by a scandal that he was the father of an illegitimate 14-year-old girl; after denying the allegation for years—the girl's mother had filed a paternity suit in Peruvian courts a decade earlier—he admitted in October that he was indeed the girl's father and reportedly agreed to a financial settlement in the case. Toledo also was accused of leading a lavish personal lifestyle, and a series of intemperate remarks by his Belgian-born wife added fuel to the fire.

The spectre of terrorism in Peru resurfaced during the year. A car bombing near the U.S. embassy in Lima on March 21 claimed the lives of 9 people and wounded at least 30 others. The blast came just days before a visit by U.S. Pres. George W. Bush—the first to Peru by a sitting American head of state. Although no one claimed responsibility for the attack, Interior Minister Fernando Rospigliosi maintained that the bombing was "connected to the events of September 11 and the presence of President Bush." While in Lima, Bush met with Toledo to discuss cooperation in the fight against drug trafficking and terrorism. Bush also promised increased development assistance for Peru over the next three years. In his private meeting with Toledo, Bush reportedly raised the case of Lori Berenson, an American whose 20-year prison term for collaboration with a Marxist rebel group was upheld by Peru's Supreme Court in February. According to a White House spokesman, Bush called for humane treatment of Berenson but did not push for her release.

Of worldwide interest was the announcement in March that a group of Peruvian and British scholars and explorers had discovered the ruins of a large Inca settlement atop a mountain peak in the Andes about 40 km (25 mi) from Machu Picchu. According to expedition leader Peter Frost, the site—in an area that served as a place of resistance against Spanish conquerors—could "yield a record of Inca civilization from the very beginning to the very end, undisturbed by European contact." (HENRY A. DIETZ)

PHILIPPINES

Area: 300,076 sq km (115,860 sq mi)
Population (2002 est.): 79,882,000
Capital: Quezon City (designated national government centre and the location of the lower house of the legislature and some ministries); many government offices are in Manila or other suburbs
Head of state and government: President Gloria Macapagal Arroyo

Kidnappings and bombings plagued the Philippines during much of 2002. Pres. Gloria Macapagal Arroyo appealed for "grassroots vigilance" and improved police and military work. Most trouble occurred in the southern islands, where the Abu Sayyaf group claimed to be fighting for a separate Muslim state. Intelligence reports linked the guerrilla organization to the al-Qaeda terrorist network. Abu Sayyaf had kidnapped three Americans in May 2001 and beheaded one of them. After its army failed to catch the kidnappers, the Philippines requested American military advice, training, and equipment; some 4,000 personnel began arriving in January 2002 with orders to fight only if attacked. On June 7 a Philippine Ranger unit working with U.S. assistance caught up with a 50-man Abu Sayyaf unit in jungle terrain. One kidnapped American, missionary Martin Burnham, and a Filipino nurse were killed in a brief firefight. Burnham's wife, Gracia, was wounded

On July 26 near the government palace in Lima, 14-year-old Zaraí Orozco leads others in washing diapers as a way to symbolize her demand that Peruvian Pres. Alejandro Toledo recognize her as his daughter.

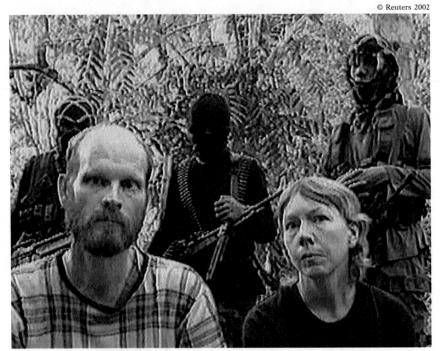

© Reuters 2002

In video footage released in March, American missionaries Martin and Gracia Burnham are held hostage by Abu Sayyaf guerrillas in the Philippines; Martin Burnham was later killed during a rescue attempt.

in the rescue. Two weeks later a guerrilla leader was reported killed in a U.S.-aided ambush at sea. Most American military advisers left in July, but the U.S. offered a $5 million reward for the capture of five other Abu Sayyaf leaders.

Bombings occurred in several cities of predominately Christian inhabitants living in mostly Muslim southern islands. Two bombings on April 21 killed 15 and wounded 45 in General Santos City. Five bombings within a few weeks in September–October killed 12 people, including an American soldier in Zamboanga. Police arrested five men who they said belonged to Abu Sayyaf.

Kidnappings for ransom were a problem in Manila. Some 20 gangs specialized in kidnapping wealthy businessmen and their families. This deterred investment and caused some businessmen to emigrate. One gang was on a U.S. terrorist list. A leader of the gang was caught in February but escaped in June from the police, who were popularly regarded as corrupt and incompetent. The leader was killed in August when authorities raided his hideout. One of the gang members turned out to be a policeman.

In a state of the nation address before the Philippines Congress on July 22, President Arroyo announced that American-trained troops would be used to break up organized crime gangs and drug syndicates. She said the nation had to lower its high crime rate in order to attract foreign investment needed to create jobs and reduce widespread poverty. Drugs were "a national security problem and no longer just a police problem," she said.

American military help was controversial, however. The Philippines had obtained independence from the U.S. in 1946 and closed American bases in the 1990s. Vice Pres. Teofisto Guingona protested U.S. assistance by resigning his second job as foreign minister.

Arroyo announced on December 30 that she would not seek reelection as president when her term expired in 2004. The trial on corruption charges of her predecessor, imprisoned former president Joseph Estrada, dragged inconclusively throughout 2002. In a television interview on February 25, he admitted having signed bank documents with a false name, a key accusation against him, but insisted he was innocent of corruption.

The government's budget deficit ballooned as projects such as new irrigation systems were hurried in expectation of drought. The economy expanded, however, partly because of increased exports of electronics and greater demand for domestic vehicles.

(HENRY S. BRADSHER)

POLAND

Area: 312,685 sq km (120,728 sq mi)
Population (2002 est.): 38,644,000
Capital: Warsaw
Chief of state: President Aleksander Kwasniewski
Head of government: Prime Minister Leszek Miller

Despite Prime Minister Leszek Miller's pledge of continuity with the policies of the previous Polish government, the first months of 2002 saw a series of dismissals followed by often controversial appointments to midlevel public service and administrative positions. The turnover was described as necessary to bring in more competent staff. A series of actions by the new ministers, such as the recall of the new secondary-school final examination and the decision to liquidate regional funds for treatment of medical patients, seemed to suggest that the government sought primarily to undo what had previously been achieved—even when its own decisions, apparently made in haste, were often subsequently modified or left unimplemented. There were worries that the government's actions were threatening the efficiency of public services and, perhaps worse, jeopardizing Poland's implementation of the Public Service Law of 1998, which was a criterion for the country's accession to the European Union (EU).

Legislation to stimulate corporate economic growth was addressed mainly to small and mid-sized businesses. These bills foresaw the elimination of bureaucratic barriers, certain tax exemptions, simplification of tax regulations and procedures, transparent legislation, anticorruption measures, and amendments to the labour code. The latter were strongly opposed by the Solidarity Trade Union and the leftist National Trade Unions Alliance but were eventually passed in August.

Seeing high interest rates as an obstacle to business activity, the government started a battle with the Monetary Policy Council (RPP), demanding a more relaxed monetary policy. The RPP, which had succeeded in cutting the inflation rate to 3.5% by January and then to a record 1.9% in May, rejected these demands for lacking any sound economic grounds. Political pressure and attempts to reduce the RPP's independence continued into the summer months, however, possibly influencing the objectivity of the central bank and thus weakening Poland's chances of meeting the requirements of EU membership.

Another blow came in June when the privatized Szczecin shipyard, Europe's third largest shipbuilder, in which the state treasury held a 10% stake, filed for bankruptcy with debts of over $400 million. Industrial output was rising, however, and in June it went up by 2.2% year-on-year and 3.3% month-on-month. Exports grew 0.2% year-on-year in the period January to May to almost $15 billion, while imports were unchanged at $20.8 billion.

Meanwhile, opinion surveys showed that the level of public frustration was growing. Perhaps this was not surprising, considering that the unemployment rate—which topped 17%—was the highest in more than a decade and in June almost one million young people under 24 were reported to be out of work—more than double the number in the corresponding period in 1998.

In July Finance Minister Marek Belka resigned unexpectedly, declaring himself "burnt out," but many believed his actions had to do with the 2002 budget deficit. His successor, Grzegorz Kolodko (another rather controversial appointment), accepted a deficit of 40 billion zlotys (about $10 billion)—5% of gross domestic product—but pledged early improvements. The cabinet adopted his "anticrisis package," which focused on help for ailing companies, redemption of selected companies' debts to the state, corporate restructuring, tax loans, and a broad system of credit guarantees. The personnel reshuffling continued with two other sudden dismissals in ministerial positions—the minister of justice (appointed only a few months earlier) and the minister of culture.

The visit by Pope John Paul II in August, always a special and much-awaited event, helped to divert attention from Poland's economic worries. The pontiff's homecoming was also important to the government, which, determined to lead the country into the EU, recognized the influence of the Roman Catholic Church and its potential for impact upon the results of a referendum planned for spring 2003. John Paul eventually expressed his support for EU accession, but tensions continued within the government coalition, especially over agricultural issues and

privatization. When the EU Commission report was published in early October, the issue of restructuring Polish steelworks, which was to be settled by the end of the year, still remained unresolved. In local elections on October 27, village chiefs, city mayors, and municipal counsellors were directly elected for the first time in democratic Poland, using a variation of the Italian system. (IWONA GRENDA)

PORTUGAL

Area: 92,365 sq km (35,662 sq mi)
Population (2002 est.): 10,384,000
Capital: Lisbon
Chief of state: President Jorge Sampaio
Head of government: Prime Minister António Guterres and, from April 6, José Manuel Durão Barroso

The year 2002 was not a very good one for Portugal. Economic stagnation, political turmoil, an embarrassing reprimand from the European Union (EU), and a feeble showing at the association football (soccer) World Cup all brought clouds of pessimism and a sense that after more than a decade of robust growth and modernization, the country had lost its way.

In December 2001 the Socialist-led government, headed by Prime Minister António Guterres, ran into trouble after losing ground in key municipal elections. Two major cities—Lisbon and Oporto—saw Socialist mayors ousted in favour of candidates from the Social Democratic Party (PSD). The political shift to the right, as well as slow economic growth, forced Guterres—in power since 1995—to call early elections. In the March vote the Socialists lost to the right-leaning PSD, led by José Manuel Durão Barroso, who fell short of an absolute majority in the parliament but was able to form a coalition government with the more conservative Partido Popular (PP).

Durão Barroso, a foreign minister in the previous PSD government, campaigned on a platform that included a "fiscal shock"—cutting taxes while tightening government spending in an effort both to reduce Portugal's budget deficit and to jump-start the faltering economy. A midyear audit of the public finances

by the Bank of Portugal and the National Statistics Institute revealed that the combination of a sharp downturn and spending overruns by the previous government reversed seven straight years of deficit reduction and left the gap at a whopping 4.1% of gross domestic product in 2001. That figure was well above the forecast deficit of 1.1% of GDP and also breached the EU's limit of 3%, which forced the EU to reprimand Portugal and initiate—for the first time ever—its excessive-deficit procedure, which could eventually lead to a fine.

The incoming prime minister was forced to delay his tax-cut plans and hike value-added taxes (VAT). The government also sold some of its real-estate holdings and curtailed state spending in order to restore finances. In October the government published a draft budget for 2003, targeting a deficit of 2.4% of GDP and cutting operating expenses at most ministries by 10%. In an effort to stimulate the flagging economy, Durão Barroso's 2003 budget sought to boost public investment and lower the corporate tax burden for companies that invested in capital goods and infrastructure, among other measures. Straightforward income and corporate tax cuts were delayed, however, and the VAT hike remained in place. The 2003 budget was expected to clear the parliament when the final vote came in mid-November, as the PSD-PP coalition controlled a majority of seats.

Meanwhile, growth slowed to a forecast 0–1% for 2002 and was expected to recover only modestly in 2003, by 1.25–2.25%. The austerity measures sparked labour unrest, with the main unions threatening strikes over the public-sector wage containment planned for 2003. As in other parts of the euro zone, inflation also crept higher, above 3%, though unemployment remained relatively muted. The main opposition party, the Socialists, headed by former infrastructure minister Eduardo Ferro Rodrigues, chastized Durão Barroso for having created a "climate of crisis" around the deficit troubles, though the PSD remained firm in stressing the need for Portugal to toe the line and restore credibility within the EU and among international investors.

At the 2002 World Cup in South Korea and Japan, Portugal lost its debut game in a shocker to the underdog U.S. team and then suffered elimination after another loss in the first round—a poor showing for what was heralded at home and abroad as a team of "golden boys." (ERIK T. BURNS)

QATAR

Area: 11,427 sq km (4,412 sq mi)
Population (2002 est.): 606,000
Capital: Doha
Head of state and government: Emir Sheikh Hamad ibn Khalifah al-Thani, assisted by Prime Minister Sheikh Abdullah ibn Khalifah al-Thani

In 2002 Qatar continued to figure prominently in regional and international news, largely as a result of its ongoing chairmanship of the Organization of the Islamic Conference and its 57 member countries. Qatar was a prominent interlocutor with international and regional organizations and, in particular, with the United Nations, the United States, and other allied governments engaged in the global campaign against terrorism.

Three developments advanced Qatar closer to its potential role as a prominent player in Gulf Cooperation Council (GCC) region integration: the scheduled launch of the pan-GCC common external tariff (5%) and customs union, which was expected to increase trade between Qatar and the rest of the GCC region; the provision in the future of low-cost gas supplies to Bahrain, Dubai, and Kuwait; and the selection of Qatar to chair the GCC's Supreme Council for 2003.

The country's phenomenal economic success continued to validate the government's earlier pathbreaking role in amassing immense foreign and domestic investment to build its state-of-the-art gas infrastructure. Qatar owned the world's third largest natural gas reserves and was on its way to becoming the leading exporter of liquefied natural gas within the next five years.

Qatar's constitutional process also proceeded apace. Building on the experience of the 1999 municipal elections, in which women voted and stood as candidates, Qatar continued to prepare for its first national parliamentary elections in 2003.   (JOHN DUKE ANTHONY)

ROMANIA

Area: 237,500 sq km (91,699 sq mi)
Population (2002 est.): 21,667,000
Capital: Bucharest
Chief of state: President Ion Iliescu
Head of government: Prime Minister Adrian Nastase

Romania obtained a major foreign policy success when it was invited to open negotiations to join NATO at the Atlantic Alliance's summit in Prague on Nov. 22, 2002. The next day, U.S. Pres. George W. Bush paid an official visit to Bucharest to show his approval for the active backing provided by the government of Adrian Nastase not only in the war against terrorism but in the mounting confrontation with Iraq. The Sept. 11, 2001, terrorist attacks transformed Romania's strategic importance in Washington's eyes. Romania's willingness to act as a bridgehead in the event of U.S. military operations in the Middle East meant that the daunting economic and political handicaps that had seemed to make early NATO membership a remote possibility no longer counted against it.

In January 2002 U.S. Ambassador Michael Guest warned that "corruption has become endemic in Romanian society" and that confidence in the justice system was collapsing because of it. Fears that the ruling Social Democratic Party (PSD) was trying to obtain a political monopoly were reinforced by the passage in September of a law that declared that a political party could enjoy a legal existence only if it had at least 50,000 members.

On October 9 the European Union (EU) announced that it hoped Romania might be in a position to join its ranks by 2007, but, in a report critical of corruption and political influence over the legal system, it singled out Romania as the only candidate country that lacked a properly functioning market economy.

In fact, entry into the EU was not expected before 2010 because of foot-dragging in Bucharest about key reform issues. Incidents in 2002 involving allegations that the intelligence services might have bugged the telephone of the head of the EU delegation in Bucharest and the attempted embezzlement of funds from an EU aid program, worth about €250,000 (about $250,000), apparently with the involvement of local PSD officials, were not helpful either. The sharpest difference with the EU arose after Romania became the first country to sign a bilateral agreement with the U.S., on August 1, giving American soldiers and diplomats on its territory immunity from prosecution by the International Criminal Court. The EU condemned Romania for breaking ranks in a gesture that strengthened suspicions that it would not be a reliable partner as the EU sought to put together a common foreign and security policy.

Nonetheless, Romania appeared ready to overlook international conventions as long as its security partnership with the U.S. shielded it from adverse reac-

Romanian Pres. Ion Iliescu and U.S. Pres. George W. Bush address a crowd of thousands gathered in Revolution Square in Bucharest on November 23.

tions. The minister of tourism rejected a report from UNESCO expressing alarm about a proposal to build a large theme park dedicated to Count Dracula close to the medieval centre of Sighisoara, a UNESCO World Heritage Site. The government also brushed aside the World Bank's repudiation of a scheme to exploit the biggest remaining gold deposits in Europe, which a coalition of local and international environmentalists said threatened ecological disaster in the Danube basin.

(TOM GALLAGHER)

RUSSIA

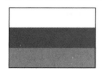

Area: 17,075,400 sq km (6,592,800 sq mi)
Population (2002 est.): 143,673,000
Capital: Moscow
Chief of state: President Vladimir Putin
Head of government: Prime Minister Mikhail Kasyanov

Domestic Policy. Russian Pres. Vladimir Putin's popularity remained high in 2002 and, in the year that he celebrated his 50th birthday, his political position continued to be strong. Russia's regions remained compliant, many of them repudiating the idiosyncratic power-sharing treaties they had signed during the Boris Yeltsin period. The most independent-minded of Russia's republics, Tatarstan and Bashkortostan, reluctantly brought their constitutions into accord with that of the Russian Federation.

The mass media were made to toe the line. In January TV6, Russia's last independent TV station, was forced off the air by a court order. As exiled tycoon Boris Berezovsky lost control of the company, the station's managers accused the presidential administration of concentrating control of the media in the hands of the state; the Kremlin denied the charge. In November, however, Putin vetoed the parliament's attempt to introduce new media curbs following a three-day hostage-taking drama in central Moscow; Putin explained his action by saying that the restrictions would introduce media censorship.

Others of Russia's "oligarchs" came to heel as well, abandoning the overtly political roles they had adopted during

the Yeltsin years and confining themselves to the serious business of making money. Putin assured them that, as long as they did not challenge the state's authority, there would be no review of the often questionable deals that had made them rich. Above all, the tycoons were told, they had to stop trying to manipulate the media. Instead, they formed themselves into a business lobby and began to diversify their interests. Analysts calculated that eight major Russian business groups controlled 85% of the Russian economy.

A coalition of Kremlin-oriented parties headed by United Russia—a centre-right coalition set up at the end of 2001—dominated the parliament and ensured legislative enactment of presidential and governmental initiatives. With the coalition's support, important reforms of taxation, property rights in agricultural land, the judicial system, and the bankruptcy law were enacted, all directed at achieving a more level playing field. Reforms included legislation aimed at protecting companies from spurious bankruptcy proceedings by preventing corporate raiders from seizing the assets of rivals and wrecking their businesses. Implementation of reform legislation remained uneven, however.

A new Labour Code came into force in February, replacing the one adopted in the 1970s. It established a 40-hour workweek and specified for the first time that the minimum wage was not to fall below the official state-determined subsistence minimum. In June a law was passed allowing the free sale and purchase of agricultural land. Marking the first step since 1917 toward the creation of a nationwide market in farmland, the law represented a significant legal and psychological departure not only from the Soviet period but also from centuries of serfdom. It was adopted in the face of strong opposition from rural constituencies backed by Communist members of the parliament. Opponents were not mollified by provisions allowing regional governments to set the pace of privatization locally and barring foreigners from owning farmland (though they might lease it). The Kremlin ignored the Communist Party's call for a national referendum on the sale of agricultural land.

As part of a larger reform of the judicial system, a new Code of Criminal Procedure came into force in July, replacing that adopted in 1960 and aiming to protect citizens against the abuses of the Soviet past. The presumption of

innocence was enshrined in Russian law, and suspects were promised a fair trial. They would be entitled to immediate access to a lawyer and could be remanded in custody for no longer than 48 hours without an extension approved by a judge. Serious crimes would be tried by jury. State prosecutors lost the power to authorize arrests; in the future this right would be exercised only by judges. New rules of evidence were instituted to help defendants in criminal cases challenge evidence produced by the prosecution. At the same time, a law against extremism was adopted in a bid

© Sergei Karpukhin/Reuters 2002

On February 22—the eve of Defender of the Fatherland Day in Russia—Pres. Vladimir Putin delivers an address at the Great Kremlin Palace in Moscow.

to combat a perceived rise in racist and neofascist activity. It empowered the Interior Ministry, without a court decision, to suspend any organization considered to be extremist and to freeze its assets. This provoked protests from human rights lobbyists, who saw it as a potential threat to free speech.

In June military journalist Grigory Pasko lost his appeal against his 2001 conviction for espionage and high treason. Pasko had been arrested in 1997 after he revealed the Pacific Fleet's practice of dumping nuclear waste at sea. Human rights groups in Russia and abroad expressed concern over this case and others brought by the security services against journalists and scientists. In July the government confirmed that it was leaky torpedo fuel, not a foreign submarine, that caused the explosion that sank the nuclear submarine *Kursk* in August 2000.

In March, Russia's Constitutional Court overturned rulings by lower courts that banned the Salvation Army from operating in Russia as a religious organization and charity. Russia's relations with the Vatican became strained when the Roman Catholic Church announced its intention of setting up four dioceses in Russia; the Russian Orthodox Church accused Rome of trying to poach converts in traditionally Orthodox lands. In August, Russia refused the Dalai Lama a visa to visit his followers in Russian regions with substantial Buddhist populations and close to the border with China.

Economy. The Russian economy saw its fourth consecutive year of growth since the prolonged output collapse of 1989–98. Gross domestic product (GDP) growth slowed in 2002 to around 4% from the annual average rate of 6% recorded in 1999–2001. Growth was expected to continue at this relatively healthy pace into 2003, even though the outlook for most of the rest of the world was highly uncertain.

This growth translated into gains in material well-being for much of the population. In the first half of 2002, real wages were running 8% above the same period of the previous year. The economy had stuttered in late 2001 and the first quarter of 2002, depressing some social indicators; by the autumn of 2002, however, unemployment (as measured by the International Labour Organization) had fallen below 8%, while the proportion of the population estimated to be living below the subsistence level was less than 30%—still a high proportion but one that was tending to decline.

The continuing economic recovery was driven by domestic demand and, in particular, by consumption. Investment growth was lower than forecast, growing in the first seven months of 2002 by only 2.5% year on year, but this reflected influences that might prove transient. Changes in taxation reduced incentives to report the reinvestment of profits, but that too might prove a one-off phenomenon. The fall in world oil prices in late 2001 and early 2002 had a dampening effect on profits and therefore on investment, but from spring 2002 oil prices began to see growth again.

The business environment tended to improve, and a survey of Russian firms found that a majority of the business community expected output to continue to grow. Their fortunes made, Russian tycoons began to work on their images, adopting international accounting standards and codes of corporate governance. Several said they were ready to sell out to foreign strategic investors and move on—a significant departure from the recent past. Several members of the business elite appeared also to support a real opening up of the economy as part of the requirement for Russia to join the World Trade Organization. Most telling of all, capital flight fell sharply, from around $20 billion a year to an expected $10 billion in 200, although an exact figure remained subject to debate.

Deep structural problems remained, however. Plans for the reform of electricity and gas production and supply proved highly contentious. Meanwhile, domestic users—households as well as companies—continued to obtain gas and electricity at far below world prices and below cost. Eliminating this implicit subsidy to producers remained on the government agenda but politically was extremely sensitive, and Putin signaled that it would not be rushed before the presidential election in 2002. The same was true of housing reform; the great majority of Russians, rich as well as poor, continued to pay well below cost for the maintenance of the housing stock and the domestic supply of gas and water as well as electricity.

The direction of institutional change was nonetheless toward better-functioning markets. At the same time, the government and central bank were keeping public-sector finances in good order. Foreign and domestic debt was being serviced without the need for significant new borrowing; the budget stayed in surplus; and inflation was around 15% a year and falling.

The most immediate source of concern was Russia's sensitivity to changes in world oil prices. Exports in 2002 of crude oil, oil products, and natural gas were equivalent to around 16% of GDP. War in the Middle East could send oil prices very high and be followed—especially if Iraqi oil was released onto the market—by a sharp fall. Insulating the Russian budget and money supply from such fluctuations would not be easy.

Signs of improving economic health left some underlying social problems untouched. In particular, the popula-

tion continued to decline by nearly one million people per year. That is to say, deaths plus emigration continued to exceed the sum of the births and immigration. Premature deaths among males, often linked to excessive alcohol consumption, remained common. The incidence of tuberculosis and of HIV/AIDS increased.

A nationwide census was held in October 2002, the first since 1989, and a new law on citizenship came into effect in July. The new regulations made it considerably harder than it had previously been for people from the other former Soviet states to acquire Russian citizenship; they made no exception for those who were ethnic Russians. Meanwhile, recognizing that Russia needed immigrants, the government tried to assert more control over who those immigrants would be and for the first time made plans to introduce quotas for foreign workers.

Foreign and Defense Policy. The year saw the continuation of the trend toward warmer relations with the West that began with President Putin's election to office and that received a further boost when Russia joined the U.S.-led antiterror coalition after Sept. 11, 2001. Putin told foreign ambassadors in Moscow in July that for Russia the period of confrontation in international relations was past. Russia, he said, wanted to be seen by the rest of the world not just as a partner but as an ally. Moscow reacted calmly not only when the U.S. abandoned the 1972 Anti-Ballistic Missile Treaty but also when it established temporary military bases in several of the former Soviet states in Central Asia and dispatched special forces on a training mission to Georgia. While Moscow continued to express unhappiness at the prospect that the three Baltic states would be invited to join NATO at the alliance's meeting in Prague in November, Russian leaders publicly acknowledged the right of those states to decide for themselves which international alliances they should join.

Analysts spoke of a fundamental shift in Russian foreign policy when, at a NATO summit in Rome in late May, East-West rapprochement was cemented by the establishment of the NATO-Russia Council. The new body, on which Russia was to sit as an equal alongside NATO's 19 member-states, gave Moscow a voice in NATO security matters without granting it a veto over NATO decisions. The council would focus on issues ranging from counter-

An elderly man peers out through a window at a centre for refugees in the Chechen capital of Grozny on December 11.

© Viktor Korotayev/Reuters 2002

terrorism to nonproliferation and civil emergencies. Also in May, Putin and U.S. Pres. George W. Bush signed the Moscow Treaty, according to which Russia and the U.S. would both, by the end of 2012, cut the number of operationally deployed strategic nuclear warheads by two-thirds (that is, to between 1,700 and 2,200 warheads from current levels of between 5,000 and 6,000). Each side retained the right to hold warheads in reserve and to continue to produce nuclear weapons. A bilateral commission was established to ensure a transparent inspection process, including on-site inspections.

Putin made it clear that Russia would remain in the U.S.-led antiterror coalition, since it saw participation as in its own interests. On the other hand, he expressed Russia's disquiet with Washington's switch of focus from Afghanistan to three other countries—Iran, Iraq, and North Korea—with which Russia had close relations. Moscow warned that it would oppose any move made by Washington to oust Iraqi Pres. Saddam Hussein without UN sanction. Among broader concerns, Russia was eager both to ensure that Iraq repaid the billions of dollars it owed to Russia and to protect its substantial investments in Iran's oil industry. Russia's relations with Iran were, as in previous years, another source of tension between Moscow and Washington. Russia continued to help Iran to build a nuclear reactor at Bushehr. Russia was unwilling to cut its ties with Iran, seeing the country as an important market and a reliable ally against the threat of militant

Islamism from Russia's south. Russia expressed concern throughout the year that the anticipated enlargement of the European Union (EU) to include Poland and Lithuania would cut off the population of Russia's Baltic exclave, Kaliningrad, from the rest of Russia. A compromise was worked out in November that satisfied both sides by introducing controls over travelers between Kaliningrad and mainland Russia but avoiding the use of the term "visa regime." Putin had the opportunity to size up China's new leadership when, in December, he was the first major world leader to visit Beijing and meet new Chinese Communist Party General Secretary Hu Jintao.

Russia continued its efforts to pacify its breakaway republic, Chechnya. Moscow declared that the military phase of the campaign was over, but casualties remained high. The ranks of the rebels were much weakened, yet they refused to give up the fight. Human rights groups complained about the violation of human rights by Russian forces, but Moscow continued to insist that it would not negotiate with the rebels and would accept only their surrender. Opinion polls indicated that 90% of the Russian population supported this position and that one-third favoured even tougher methods. The Moscow-installed government worked on a new constitution for the ravaged republic. The seizure of more than 800 hostages in a Moscow theatre by a group of armed Chechens on October 23–26 led many to predict an even tougher Russian policy toward Chechnya. Of the hostages, 129 died

during the incident, 5 from gunfire and the rest as a result of inhaling gas released by the security forces in order to subdue the terrorists. The authorities' initial refusal to identify what turned out to have been a potentially lethal gas provoked controversy. The authorities said 50 hostage-takers—18 of them women—were killed during the storming of the building.

Tension rose between Russia and Georgia following Russian complaints that Georgia was sheltering Chechen guerrillas in the Pankisi Gorge, a mountainous area in northeastern Georgia adjoining the border with Chechnya. Moscow called on Tbilisi to crack down on the rebels. Tempers cooled in October after Moscow and Tbilisi agreed jointly to monitor their common border.

In November, Defense Minister Sergey Ivanov promised to relaunch reforms of the armed forces that had run aground amid strong opposition within the military establishment. Though precise figures were elusive, the Russian army remained somewhere in excess of one million soldiers. Senior officers argued against a hasty transition to a professional army, claiming that such a transition would be prohibitively expensive. Some limited experiments were launched, however, including the transfer of one airborne division to a professional-contract basis. If successful, the measure was expected to speed the transformation of other army units. June saw the adoption for the first time in Russia of a law on alternative military service. This allowed conscripts to opt for civilian service in hospitals, prisons, or orphanages in place of the normally obligatory military service. The law was criticized by the military establishment, which considered it too lenient, and by the human rights lobby, which viewed the conditions for alternative service as too harsh.

(ELIZABETH TEAGUE)

RWANDA

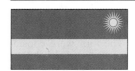

Area: 26,338 sq km (10,169 sq mi)
Population (2002 est.): 7,398,000
Capital: Kigali
Head of state and government: President Maj. Gen. Paul Kagame, assisted by Prime Minister Bernard Makuza

© AFP 2002, by Marco Longari

A survivor of the 1994 Rwandan genocide is restrained by family members and a policeman at a stadium in Butare, where some 2,000 prisoners suspected of involvement in the massacre were made to face their victims in September.

At the end of January 2002, the Rwandan government convened *gacacas* ("traditional courts") to help alleviate the backlog of cases involving the 1994 genocide. Some 5,000 cases had been heard since the trials began in Arusha, Tanz., in 1996, but owing to the size of the caseload—there were 115,000 suspects awaiting trial in Rwandan prisons—it would take the International Criminal Tribunal for Rwanda (ICTR) 200 years to complete all the hearings. The *gacaca* system tried minor crimes, such as arson, as well as capital crimes. The 10,000 suspects accused of having orchestrated the genocide, however, would continue to be tried by the ICTR. In February a government report on the genocide revealed that the estimated number of victims—500,000–800,000—was low; a more accurate figure was estimated at more than one million. Four senior military officers accused of genocide, including Col. Theoneste Bagosora, boycotted their trial in early April claiming that their rights to a fair trial had been violated. The trial was postponed until September. The ICTR alleged that Bagosora had begun planning the genocide as early as 1992, and it also charged that all four had trained the militias that killed Tutsi and moderate Hutu. The four were considered responsible for the murders of 10 UN peacekeepers, as well as the murder of the prime minister, Agathe Uwilingiyimana, in 1994. In late September Tharcisse Renzaho, a leading suspect in the genocide and the former governor of Kigali, was arrested in the Democratic Republic of the Congo (DRC).

The French UN envoy in the DRC told the UN in March that 10,000 Rwandan troops had launched an offensive in southeastern DRC, threatening fragile peace negotiations between the two countries. Rwanda flatly denied the allegations. A peace accord between Rwanda and the DRC was signed in July, four years after Rwandan troops had entered the country to track down militias accused of genocide. On September 17 Rwanda began withdrawing its troops from South Kivu province, and by mid-October 15,000 troops had been evacuated; the several thousand remaining troops were scheduled to leave by the end of the month. On October 18 the brokered peace was put in jeopardy when fighting erupted between a Congolese militia and rebels supported by Rwanda, who were left vulnerable when the troops withdrew.

(MARY F.E. EBELING)

SAINT KITTS AND NEVIS

Area: 269 sq km (104 sq mi)
Population (2002 est.): 46,200
Capital: Basseterre
Chief of state: Queen Elizabeth II, represented by Governor-General Sir Cuthbert Montraville Sebastian
Head of government: Prime Minister Denzil Douglas

Prime Minister Denzil Douglas pledged in April 2002 to readjust the focus of Saint Kitts and Nevis's offshore financial services policy away from an emphasis on tax exemption to other attractions that a "reputable" offshore location could offer. That same month the country was removed from the Organisation for Economic Co-operation and Development's blacklist of centres posing "harmful tax competition." In June the country, having agreed to pass all the necessary legislation to facilitate the prevention of money laundering, was also removed from the Financial Action Task Force's (FATF's) blacklist.

In May Saint Kitts and Nevis joined those countries, led by Japan, that wanted the International Whaling Commission to allow the full resumption of commercial whaling and added its name to a statement that accused antiwhaling countries such as the U.S. and the U.K. of "intolerance" to different cultures.

Along with four of its fellow smaller Caribbean Community and Common Market countries, Saint Kitts and Nevis moved a step closer in May to the liberalization of its telecommunications market when it agreed to revoke the exclusive rights to landline telephony held by the U.K.'s Cable and Wireless.

The premier of Nevis, Vance Amory, revived the subject of greater autonomy for his part of the federation when he held discussions with a broad spectrum of the community in September.

(DAVID RENWICK)

SAINT LUCIA

Area: 617 sq km (238 sq mi)
Population (2002 est.): 160,000
Capital: Castries
Chief of state: Queen Elizabeth II, represented by Governor-General Dame Pearlette Louisy
Head of government: Prime Minister Kenny Anthony

Saint Lucia, normally among the most buoyant of the smaller Caribbean economies, faced severe economic problems during the year; banana exports were stagnant, and tourism declined by about 8%, primarily because of the effects of the Sept. 11, 2001, attacks in the U.S. In addition, in September Tropical

Storm Lili destroyed almost 50% of the banana crop. Real growth in 2002 was considered unlikely.

Saint Lucia moved closer to becoming one of the air-transport hubs of the southeastern Caribbean in February when it signed an agreement with Saint Vincent and the Grenadines for preclearance to its Hewanorra Airport.

Like other Caribbean Community and Common Market states, Saint Lucia was moving to establish a Caribbean Court of Justice as the final-appeal court in an effort to abolish appeals to the London-based Privy Council. Prime Minister Kenny Anthony and opposition leader Marius Wilson sought common ground on the matter during discussions in August.

Walter François, the minister of planning, development, environment, and housing, resigned in July after admitting that his claim to holding a doctoral degree was untrue.   (DAVID RENWICK)

SAINT VINCENT AND THE GRENADINES

Area: 389 sq km (150 sq mi)
Population (2002 est.): 113,000
Capital: Kingstown
Chief of state: Queen Elizabeth II, represented by Governors-General Sir Charles Antrobus, Monica Dacon (acting) from June 3, and, from September 2, Frederick Ballantyne
Head of government: Prime Minister Ralph Gonsalves

In February 2002 Saint Vincent and the Grenadines, along with some of its fellow offshore centres, was removed from the blacklist of countries considered "uncooperative" in matters of tax investigation after it took steps that satisfied the Organisation for Economic Co-operation and Development. In May the parliament repealed the Confidential Relationships Preservation (International Finance) Act and replaced it with an act that allowed the sharing of information on suspect bank accounts with regulators in other countries.

The country received a boost to its flagging tourism industry in midyear when American real-estate tycoon Donald Trump took over management of the $300 million Carenage Beach Resort on the Vincentian island of Canouan. The government expected that the Trump name would be a magnet for other investors.

Kuwait agreed in June to provide $8 million in assistance for the expansion of the country's international airport. The soft loan was negotiated by Prime Minister Ralph Gonsalves during a visit to Kuwait.

Governor-General Sir Charles Antrobus died in June while in Canada for treatment of leukemia. He was 69.

(DAVID RENWICK)

SAMOA

Area: 2,831 sq km (1,093 sq mi)
Population (2002 est.): 178,000
Capital: Apia
Chief of state: *O le Ao o le Malo* (Head of State) Malietoa Tanumafili II
Head of government: Prime Minister Tuila'epa Sa'ilele Malielegaoi

In June 2002 Samoa celebrated 40 years of independence. Among the leaders in the region who traveled there to mark the anniversary were New Zealand Prime Minister Helen Clark (*see* BIOGRAPHIES), who, to the surprise of observers in both countries, made a formal apology for acts committed by the New Zealand government against a nationalist movement in the 1920s and '30s during its rule of Samoa under a League of Nations mandate.

In 2001 economic growth was 10%, and growth for 2002 was projected at 5%. Tourism dominated the economy in 2001, with earnings of more than $40 million. Remittances from Samoans living overseas and exports were the other main contributors to the economy. In March 2002 the government released its economic development strategy for 2002–04 with an emphasis on stabilizing economic conditions, improving social services, strengthening infrastructure, and increasing efficiency in the public sector. In September Samoa hosted the third annual Pacific Regional Trade Fair.

During his address to the UN General Assembly in September, Prime Minister Tuila'epa Sa'ilele Malielegaoi deplored the increase in weapons of mass destruction and reminded delegates of the testing and use of nuclear weapons in the Pacific region. In May, Samoa declared its 124,000-sq-km (48,000-sq-mi) exclusive economic zone to be a whale, turtle, and shark sanctuary.

(BARRIE MACDONALD)

SAN MARINO

Area: 61.2 sq km (23.6 sq mi)
Population (2002 est.): 27,700
Capital: San Marino
Heads of state and government: The republic is governed by two *capitani reggenti,* or coregents, appointed every six months by a popularly elected Great and General Council.

In 2002 San Marino continued to redefine its role in the world economy. Concern focused in particular on pressure from international agencies to bring its banking practices into alignment with those of major industrialized nations. San Marino, along with about a dozen other microstates, had come under close scrutiny as a suspected fiscal haven. Thousands of Italians responded to the banking inspections by withdrawing their hidden savings from San Marino.

The small republic also attempted to ensure its future security by aligning itself with other European nations. The government took steps to explore eventual membership in the European Union. San Marino, although landlocked, also became a member of the International Maritime Organization, a group of countries dedicated to maritime safety and pollution regulation.

(GREGORY O. SMITH)

SÃO TOMÉ AND PRÍNCIPE

Area: 1,001 sq km (386 sq mi)
Population (2002 est.): 147,000
Capital: São Tomé
Chief of state: President Fradique de Menezes
Head of government: Prime Ministers Evaristo de Carvalho, Gabriel Costa from March 26, and, from October 7, Maria das Neves

The year 2002 opened in São Tomé and Príncipe with the promise of new legislative elections. Pres. Fradique de Menezes had dissolved the National Assembly in December 2001 with the agreement that he would call new elections in an effort to form a more broad-based government. As a result, de Menezes called legislative elections for March 3. In the campaign each side accused the other of receiving financial backing from outside—the Movement for the Liberation of São Tomé and Príncipe (MLSTP) from Angola's ruling party and its opponents from Taiwan and Nigeria. The MLSTP won 24 seats, the Democratic Movement Force for Change/Party of Democratic Governance (MDFM/PCD) 23 seats, and the Ue-Kedadji coalition 8. Without a majority in the legislature, the president appointed Gabriel Costa, the ambassador to Portugal, to head a coalition government. At the end of September, however, de Menezes dissolved the government after complaints from the army over Costa's promotion of two officers to the rank of lieutenant colonel. One of them had been defense minister, and regular officers complained that they had been sidelined. The Costa government continued in office while the president held discussions to find a new prime minister. In October de Menezes asked Maria das Neves, the minister for trade, industry, and tourism, to form a government. The archipelago's first woman prime minister, she was proposed for the post by the MLSTP. She began consultations to form a unity government from parties in the 55-member parliament.

(CHRISTOPHER SAUNDERS)

SAUDI ARABIA

Area: 2,149,690 sq km (830,000 sq mi)
Population (2002 est.): 23,370,000
Capital: Riyadh
Head of state and government: King Fahd

As part of a diplomatic effort aimed at improving Saudi-U.S. relations, Crown Prince Abdullah, Saudi Arabia's de facto leader, launched a comprehensive peace initiative toward Israel early in 2002. (*See* BIOGRAPHIES.) The initiative, which called for an Israeli with-

AP/Wide World Photos

Saudi Crown Prince Abdullah poses with U.S. Pres. George W. Bush at the president's ranch near Crawford, Texas, on April 25.

drawal from Palestinian territories in exchange for full Arab normalization of relations with the Jewish state, was accepted at an Arab summit meeting in Beirut, Lebanon, in March. The crown prince traveled to the U.S. to meet with Pres. George W. Bush in April, and while there were points of disagreement between the Saudi and U.S. plans for peace in the Middle East, the White House described Abdullah's proposal as "constructive."

Relations were strained again, however, after Saudi Arabia made clear its unwillingness to support any attack on Iraq. An especially tense time ensued after the publication of a study by the RAND Corporation, a California-based think tank, that described Saudi Arabia as "an enemy disguised as a friend" and "active in every level of terrorism." The study, which had been commissioned by a defense advisory panel for the Pentagon, recommended that the U.S. seize Saudi oil fields and financial assets if Saudi Arabia did not do more to fight terrorism. The study was quickly dismissed by Crown Prince Abdullah, who stressed his country's "solid historical" relations with the U.S., and Washington later dissociated itself from the report. When RAND analyst and study author Laurent Murawiec repeated the same views in an interview, however—and after families of September 11 victims joined in a lawsuit against "the financial sponsors of terrorism," among them three Saudi princes—the Saudi media returned fire. "This is pure blackmail," one newspa-

per wrote, adding that "it would be more appropriate for the families of the victims of September 11 to sue the American government itself." Tempers had cooled somewhat by year's end. Although Riyadh reiterated that Saudi airfields would not be used in an attack on Iraq, it pledged its support of U.S. efforts to dismantle the al-Qaeda terrorist network.

Although Saudi Arabia had projected a $12 billion budget deficit for 2002, by fall it was instead expected to boast a small surplus as a result of a rise in oil prices. Revenues from oil exports, projected at around $30 billion, shot up to more than $40 billion. Negotiations progressed on a long-awaited $25 billion gas scheme, though a large gap remained between the government's position and the position of the large Western oil companies interested in the project. While the former wanted the companies to explore for gas in relatively virgin areas, the companies wanted to take an easier route and invest in producing from already proven gas reserves, especially in the huge Ghawar oil and gas field in the eastern region of the country.

According to a new report by the United Nations Industrial Development Organization (UNIDO), Saudi Arabia had not kept up with world industrial development over the past two decades. It lost rank in industrial competitiveness between 1985 and 1998 and ranked lowest in UNIDO's technological effort and inventiveness index for 1998.

(MAHMOUD HADDAD)

SENEGAL

Area: 196,712 sq km (75,951 sq mi)
Population (2002 est.): 9,905,000
Capital: Dakar
Chief of state: President Abdoulaye Wade, assisted by Prime Ministers Mame Madior Boye and, from November 4, Idrissa Seck

More than 1,000 people drowned when the ferry *Le Joola* capsized in a violent storm off the coast of The Gambia on Sept. 26, 2002. (*See* DISASTERS.) The vessel, en route from Ziguinchor to Dakar, had become a main transport link since the ongoing rebellion in the Casamance area had made land travel dangerous. On October 2 the ministers of transport and the armed forces accepted responsibility for the tragedy and resigned. Pres. Abdoulaye Wade fired the commander of the navy, Ousseynou Combo, and later Prime Minister Mame Madior Boye as well.

Despite a series of peace meetings between representatives of the government and leaders of the Movement of Democratic Forces of the Casamance, a solution to the rebellion remained elusive. A succession of armed clashes added to the death toll on both sides. Thousands had been killed in the 20-year-long conflict.

Although heavy unseasonable rains and unusually cold weather brought se-rious flooding to northern Senegal in January, overall the two-year drought continued. On August 9 Pape Diouf, minister of agriculture, appealed for international aid to counter the threat of rural famine. After touring the areas most affected by the drought, however, President Wade claimed that his advisers had misled him by alleging that five million people were at risk of starvation. On August 29 he fired his communications adviser and apologized to international donors.

(NANCY ELLEN LAWLER)

SEYCHELLES

Area: 455 sq km (176 sq mi)
Population (2002 est.): 83,400
Capital: Victoria
Head of state and government: President France-Albert René

In January 2002 the Seychelles National Party's (SNP's) petition to void the previous year's presidential election owing to alleged irregularities was denied by the Constitutional Court. SNP candidate Wavel Ramkalawan had won 45% in a close race against Pres. France-Albert René.

Parliament was dissolved in October and elections held in December. The president's Seychelles People's Progressive Front won 54.3% of the vote and 23 seats.

The international press-freedom organization Reporters sans Frontières protested the government's libel suit against the independent paper *Regar* for an article alleging that Vice Pres. James Alix Michel had benefited from corrupt real-estate deals. Reporters sans Frontières claimed that the latest suit was part of a series of targeted actions against one of the few independent media organizations in the country.

The slump in the global economy adversely affected Seychelles, which relied heavily on tourism. In March, President René refused to implement economic reforms recommended by the International Monetary Fund. René also denied allegations that members of the al-Qaeda terrorist network had fled Afghanistan and found refuge in Seychelles. The former president of Madagascar, Didier Ratsiraka, was granted passage to Paris via Seychelles in July following the election crisis in his country. (MARY F.E. EBELING)

SIERRA LEONE

Area: 71,740 sq km (27,699 sq mi)
Population (2002 est.): 4,823,000
Capital: Freetown
Head of state and government: President Ahmad Tejan Kabbah

Weapons turned in by rebels in Sierra Leone are burned at a ceremony marking the end of the country's civil war. A sign thanks the United Nations and the Economic Community of West African States (ECOWAS) for their help in resolving the conflict.

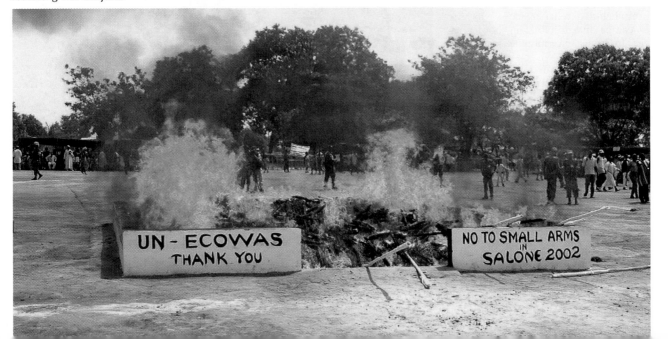

An official end to the civil war that had plagued the country since 1991 was declared on Jan. 5, 2002, with a symbolic weapons-burning ceremony in Freetown. More than 45,000 rebels belonging to the Revolutionary United Front turned in their weapons. With the declaration of peace, the United Nations Security Council lifted the ban on the trade in rough diamonds from Sierra Leone.

In April the opposition Revolutionary United Front Party nominated Pallo Bangura, the party's secretary-general, as its candidate for the May 14 presidential elections. The ruling Sierra Leone's People Party nominated incumbent Pres. Ahmad Tejan Kabbah. International observers declared the campaign and election free and fair. Kabbah won nearly 71% of the vote, and his party won 83 of the 112 parliamentary seats up for election. A new electoral system was devised for the latter elections. Each of the country's 12 administrative districts was set up as an electoral district with eight seats and two supplementary districts were established in the Western Area (to account for the dense population there) and awarded eight seats each.

In early July riots broke out in Freetown between youth gangs and Nigerian businessmen. Several people were killed, and businesses were looted. Calm was quickly restored by the armed forces. In general, however, throughout 2002 the security situation improved, and the nation began a slow recovery from its long civil war. Areas near the Liberian border remained unstable as a result of numerous border incursions by Liberian armed forces and rebels of the Liberians United for Reconciliation and Democracy. Sierra Leone also had to cope with tens of thousands of refugees fleeing into the country from Liberia, overwhelming relief agencies working in camps and destabilizing border areas. In August, in reply to a request by President Kabbah, who claimed that the war in Liberia was destabilizing the region, the United Nations sent 17,000 peacekeepers to Sierra Leone. In light of the continuation of the Liberian war and the ongoing influx of refugees into Sierra Leone, the mandate of the United Nations Mission in Sierra Leone was eventually extended to early 2003. The peacekeeping mission would gradually be downsized before the security apparatus was handed over to government forces. Lack of progress in resolving the Liberian conflict had delayed the downsizing of the peacekeeping force.

A Truth and Reconciliation Committee was established on July 5, with public hearings scheduled to begin in October. On December 2 eight judges who were to constitute a United Nations special tribunal on the civil war were sworn in. The court was expected to begin work in 2003.

(ANDREW F. CLARK)

SINGAPORE

Area: 683 sq km (264 sq mi)
Population (2001 est.): 3,322,000 (excluding 808,000 newly arrived nonresidents)
Chief of state: President S.R. Nathan
Head of government: Prime Minister Goh Chok Tong

A year after suffering its worst-ever recession, Singapore experienced a modest economic comeback in 2002. The economy had witnessed double-digit percentage falls throughout the last half of 2001, but 3.9% growth was achieved in the second quarter of 2002—the first expansion in five quarters. The boost was attributed in part to an increase in electronics exports, which had been in a steep slump. While most forecasters were predicting an overall growth rate of between 2% and 4% for Singapore for the year, unemployment was expected to worsen. In fact, the government warned that the jobless rate could rise as high as 6% before the economy made a full recovery.

Many of Singapore's woes were externally induced. The weakened demand for imports in American and Asian markets posed serious problems for a country whose manufacturing sector was heavily geared toward exports. Singapore was also worried about losing foreign investment to such regional competitors as China and Malaysia. A number of major companies—including shipping giant Maersk Sealand and such prominent investment firms as Merrill Lynch and Goldman, Sachs—had either partially or entirely relocated out of Singapore. In order to ensure that the country remained competitive in the global marketplace, an Economic Review Committee, comprising some 100 business and government leaders, was established in October 2001 and charged with examining how Singapore might restructure its economy. The committee presented its first set of recommendations to Parliament in April 2002. Recommendations included reducing the corporate income tax rate from 24.5% to 20% within three years, reducing personal income tax rates significantly, and offering a broad range of sector-specific tax incentives to help make doing business in Singapore more attractive to companies.

Chee Soon Juan, leader of the opposition Singapore Democratic Party and a vocal critic of the government, is arrested at a rally of supporters outside the presidential palace on May 1.

AP/Wide World Photos

Hockey fans turn out by the thousands in Bratislava, Slovakia, to welcome home the national team and celebrate its win in the world ice hockey championships, held in Sweden in May.

© Joe Klamar/Reuters 2002

Some officials blamed the sluggish economy for a surge in crime during the first half of the year, when the overall crime rate increased by 10.4%. Terrorism was also a growing concern. In January the government announced the arrest of 15 persons with suspected links to the al-Qaeda terrorist network and accused them of targeting foreign embassies and military installations. These developments were especially alarming to a country that prided itself on its reputation for law and order.

By 2002, as part of a general strategy to foster the study of life sciences, Singapore was actively promoting human stem-cell research at a time when the U.S. and other countries were restricting government funding for such research. Singapore's regulatory "open door" to stem-cell research had helped attract some of the world's top scientists to the island and had thereby boosted hopes that Singapore would become one of the global leaders in biotechnology.   (LINDA LOW)

SLOVAKIA

Area: 49,035 sq km (18,933 sq mi)
Population (2002 est.): 5,383,000
Capital: Bratislava
Chief of state: President Rudolf Schuster
Head of government: Prime Minister Mikulas Dzurinda

Parliamentary elections held on September 20–21 were the major event of 2002 in Slovakia. The outcome was considered crucial for the future direction of the country, particularly in light of the upcoming decisions on the enlargement of NATO and the European Union (EU). Many feared that Slovaks would turn away from the reformist, pro-Western government that had held office since 1998 and would instead support the return of populist and nationalist forces that could lead the country to international isolation.

Much to the surprise of everyone (including the parties themselves), four centre-right parties managed to win a majority in the elections, with 78 of 150 parliamentary seats. Three of the four had worked together in government over the previous four years, and within just two weeks they had set up the new cabinet and agreed on the basic policies they would like to pursue. Mikulas Dzurinda was reappointed prime minister on October 15, and the remaining ministers were installed the following day. In addition to Dzurinda, a number of other key players were retained, marking a sign of continuity. Foreign policy was arguably the most important impetus behind voters' decisions. Turnout at the polls was 70%, boosted by a Western-funded get-out-the-vote campaign.

The new government promised to push forward rapidly with economic and social reforms. Unlike the previous Dzurinda cabinet, the new ruling coalition did not include the left-wing parties that had blocked many of the

changes proposed in 1998–2002. Key issues that the new government vowed to address included reforms in the areas of health care, education, pensions, social welfare, police, and the judiciary.

Slovakia enjoyed one of the highest economic growth rates in the region in 2002. Moreover, low inflation helped to boost real wages substantially, giving consumers more leeway to spend. On a negative note, the country continued to struggle with high fiscal and current-account deficits; however, the reforms proposed by the new cabinet were expected to alleviate those problems in the medium term.

Slovaks were rewarded for their voting behaviour by gaining invitations from both NATO and the EU.

(SHARON FISHER)

SLOVENIA

Area: 20,273 sq km (7,827 sq mi)
Population (2002 est.): 1,948,000
Capital: Ljubljana
Chief of state: Presidents Milan Kucan and, from December 23, Janez Drnovsek
Head of government: Prime Ministers Janez Drnovsek and, from December 11, Anton Rop

Janez Drnovsek, Slovenia's prime minister for most of its 11 years of inde-

Slovenian Prime Minister Janez Drnovsek, the leading candidate in the country's presidential election, casts his ballot at a polling place in Ljubljana on November 10.

pendence, was elected the country's president on December 1. Drnovsek, leader of the Liberal Democrat Party, Slovenia's largest, began his five-year term on December 23. He succeeded Milan Kucan, the former head of Slovenia's Communist Party, who was limited by the constitution to two consecutive five-year terms. With his election as president, Drnovsek resigned both as prime minister and as president of the Liberal Democrats.

The four parties constituting the country's left-of-centre coalition government chose Anton Rop, also a Liberal Democrat, to form a new government. The legislature confirmed Rop's election by a two-thirds vote, indicating that there would be no substantive changes in policy until Slovenia's next parliamentary elections in the fall of 2004.

Slovenia achieved a long-sought foreign policy objective on November 21 when it was among seven Central and Eastern European countries invited to become a member of NATO in 2004. Slovenia's government pledged to do everything necessary to fulfill the remaining membership requirements, a decision supported by all the country's major political parties. Public opinion polls reflected strong skepticism toward NATO membership, however, with opposition totals in the 40% range. This attitude led to consensus among the parties represented in legis-

lature for a binding national referendum on the issue, to be held most likely in the first three months of 2003.

On December 13 Slovenia achieved a second key foreign and economic policy goal, an invitation to join the European Union. While it had long expected to be among the 10 countries receiving an invitation to join, there remained some issues open in the negotiations between Slovene and EU representatives, particularly in agriculture. Slovenia's membership would mean that its southern border would also become the EU's border. This would impose special financial and security obligations on the small country, and it remained a concern for Slovenia and for the EU. It was complicated by the inability—despite continuing negotiations during 2002—of Slovenia and its southern neighbour, Croatia, to reach a definitive settlement of the land and sea border between them. Slovenia's political parties agreed to hold in 2003 the required national referendum on joining the EU, but polls showed the public strongly in favour of membership.

At the close of 2002, Slovenia was chosen to preside over the Organization for Security and Co-operation in Europe in 2005. (RUDOLPH M. SUSEL)

SOLOMON ISLANDS

Area: 28,370 sq km (10,954 sq mi)
Population (2002 est.): 439,000
Capital: Honiara
Chief of state: Queen Elizabeth II, represented by Governor-General Sir John Lapli
Head of government: Prime Minister Sir Allan Kemakeza

Solomon Islands remained in a state of crisis in 2002 in regard to both public order and the economy. Two years after the Townsville Peace Agreement nominally ended ethnic conflict, many had still not surrendered their weapons. Skirmishes between militias and government attempts to capture militant leaders led to a number of deaths. Some alleged that compensation payments for property damage and personal injury were inconsistent and affected by political considerations and nepotism; strikes

and disorder ensued when payments were curtailed partway through the distribution process.

The disruption of export industries, destruction of infrastructure, and reduced employment meant that government was able to meet only 60% of recurrent costs. In April the minister of finance was sacked when he announced a 25% currency devaluation, and the Solomon Islands dollar was restored to its former value. The IMF advised against the proposed adoption of Australian currency, because reserves were insufficient to purchase the foreign currency required for covering government debt. Taiwan supported the Solomon Islands' budget with some $7 million over the year.

Cyclone Zoe, with winds of over 300 km/hr (186 mph) and 10-m (33-ft) waves, struck the Solomon Islands on December 29. The extent of the massive damage would not be known for weeks. (BARRIE MACDONALD)

SOMALIA

Area: 637,000 sq km (246,000 sq mi), including the 176,000-sq-km (68,000-sq-mi) area of the unilaterally declared (in 1991) and unrecognized Republic of Somaliland
Population (2002 est.): 7,753,000 (including Somaliland); about 250,000 refugees are registered in neighbouring countries
Capital: Mogadishu; Hargeysa is the capital of Somaliland
Head of state and government: Somalia's government under President Abdiqassim Salad Hassan was barely functioning in 2002, with opposition forces controlling parts of the country.

By 2002 the Transitional National Government (TNG) set up in 2000 had failed to bring unity to the country and had little effective power. In effect it represented one alliance of clans, which was opposed by a counteralliance, the Somali Reconciliation and Restoration Council (SRRC). The SRRC's main political leader was Hussein Aydid, and its military leader was Gen. Muhammad Sayid Hersi, known as "Morgan." Even in the former capital of Mogadishu, the TNG struggled for control with other factions. Acts of banditry and kidnapping continued there in spite of the attempts by the TNG to form a police force and enforce a weapons ban, and in May and again in July there was bloody factional fighting. Violence continued to break out from time to time over local disputes in different parts of the country.

By contrast, the self-declared Republic of Somaliland in the north remained stable. In June Britain made moves toward some form of recognition, and it seemed that the U.S. and the Scandinavian countries might follow suit. Somaliland's president, Muhammad Ibrahim Egal, died in May (*see* OBITUARIES); he was succeeded by the vice president, Dahir Riyale Kahin.

In the self-declared Autonomous Region of Puntland in the northeast, hostilities continued between Jama Ali Jama, elected president by a council of elders in 2001, and the former leader, Col. Abdullahi Yusuf Ahmed. On May 8 Abdullahi captured Bosaso, the port town and commercial capital, and thus effectively established control of the region.

In April the Rahanweyn Resistance Army (RRA), which controlled much of the southwest, set up a new regional administration to be known as the State of South-western Somalia, reportedly with support from Ethiopia. Its president was Col. Hassan Muhammad Nur Shatigadud, the chairman of the RRA. The valley of the Jubba River continued to be disputed between the Jubba Valley Alliance (JVA), which supported the TNG, and the SRRC, led by Morgan, who threatened to recapture the port of Kismayo from the JVA.

On October 15 a reconciliation conference between the TNG and the SRRC, sponsored by the Intergovernmental Authority on Development (IGAD—the regional alliance of Djibouti, Eritrea, Ethiopia, Kenya, The Sudan, Uganda, and, nominally, Somalia), finally opened in Eldoret, Kenya, after repeated postponements.

The major food crisis feared by humanitarian agencies did not develop in 2002, although economic hardship continued owing to drought, warfare, and the continued closure of the Saudi Arabian market to Somali livestock exports. Suspicion that extremist Islamic groups had training bases in Somalia (though not overtly supported by any of the factions) led to fears among Somalis that their country would be targeted in an antiterrorist campaign, but this did not occur.

(VIRGINIA LULING)

SOUTH AFRICA

Area: 1,219,090 sq km (470,693 sq mi)
Population (2002 est.): 45,172,000
Capitals (de facto): Pretoria/Tshwane (executive); Bloemfontein/Mangaung (judicial); Cape Town (legislative)
Head of state and government: President Thabo Mbeki

In his 2002 annual address to Parliament, South African Pres. Thabo Mbeki of the African National Congress (ANC) detailed the progress made in land reform and in the provision of water, electricity, and housing; he defined as national goals black economic empowerment, poverty eradication, and nation building driven by volunteerism. During the year a mining charter was enacted, requiring that 15% of the industry be black owned within 5 years and 26% within 10 years; similar goals were set for the oil industry. The black presence on the Johannesburg Stock Exchange was estimated at a mere 2.2% in February 2002.

The 34% collapse of the rand against the dollar in the second half of 2001 shook the country. Following allegations by the CEO of the South African Chamber of Business that the fall had been caused by speculative collusion between foreign banks and local corporations, Mbeki established a commission of inquiry. A majority report of this commission gave a variety of reasons for the fall, including weak export performance and the outflow of portfolio capital, but conceded that the spirit of foreign-exchange control had been broken. The minority report, however, maintained that the inquiry had been superficial and that at least one foreign bank should be investigated further.

The government's policy on HIV/AIDS continued to be controversial. In March an ANC document portrayed AIDS as a conspiracy theory with the aim of dehumanizing Africans. In the same month, the AIDS-activist organization the Treatment Action Campaign won a court action that declared that the government had to supply nevirapine (an antiretroviral drug) to HIV-positive pregnant women in public hospitals. The government appealed the ruling, which was upheld by

the constitutional court in early July. By October the government was promising to widen access to antiretrovirals.

As a result of the breakup of the Democratic Alliance (DA) and the subsequent alliance between the New National Party (NNP) and the ANC in late 2001, Western Cape DA premier Gerald Morkel was replaced by former NNP Cape Town mayor Peter Marais. Morkel then became mayor of Cape Town. In 2002, however, both Marais and Morkel came under criticism. In April Jurgen Harksen, a German businessman and fugitive from justice claimed that he had donated money to Morkel, personally and for the DA. Morkel admitted to the Desai Commission, which was set up to investigate possible internal political spying in the Cape, that he had a close relationship with Harksen but denied having received money from him. The DA declared that the commission was a "kangaroo court." Harksen, citing threats against his life, withdrew his evidence in October. These events harmed the "clean" image previously presented by the DA. At the end of May, Marais resigned after he was accused of sexual harassment, but the state declined to prosecute him; he was replaced by Marthinus van Schalkwyk, leader of the NNP.

Legislation was passed by Parliament allowing elected representatives a short

Kami, a Muppet "living with HIV," debuted on Takalani Sesame, *the South African version of* Sesame Street, *during the year. Nearly five million South Africans were HIV-positive or had developed AIDS by 2002.*

"window period" in which they could defect to other political parties. The constitutional court subsequently approved this legislation for municipal councillors but rejected it on technical grounds for provincial and national representatives. Defections from the DA to the NNP meant that the ANC-NNP coalition took control of the city of Cape Town and other councils in the Western Cape.

There was considerable controversy within the "Triple Alliance"—the ANC, the South African Communist Party (SACP), and the Congress of South African Trade Unions (COSATU). At the SACP's conference in July, two ministers in Mbeki's government were voted off the central committee to protest the government's economic policy. The conference also criticized the emergence of a new black elite that sought to enrich itself. Shortly before a two-day general strike called by COSATU on October 1–2 to protest the government policy of privatization, unemployment, and increases in food prices and interest rates, President Mbeki accused the alliance of harbouring ultraleft elements. COSATU's general secretary cautioned that unemployment was a "ticking time bomb."

In April, at the end of a 300-day showcase trial for alleged apartheid offenses, Wouter Basson—a cardiologist accused of having masterminded Nazi-like

atrocities—was acquitted of the remaining 46 charges against him, including murder, fraud, and theft. Desmond Tutu, former archbishop and head of the Truth and Reconciliation Commission, criticized the verdict as "shocking." State authorities launched an appeal.

The Inkatha Freedom Party (IFP) went to court to try to stop publication of the final report of the Truth and Reconciliation Commission because it alleged that the IFP had committed gross violations of human rights. The Jali Commission's investigation of inhuman prison conditions revealed evidence of endemic corruption and maladministration. In September the 10 white right-wingers accused of plotting to overthrow the government were indicted for treason. At the end of October eight bombs were set off in Soweto, probably by members of the white ultra-right wing.

The remains of Sarah Baartman, a Khoisan woman first taken abroad for exhibit as a sexual freak some 200 years ago, were returned to South Africa from France and reburied in August in the Eastern Cape. South African billionaire Mark Shuttleworth became the first African astronaut after he completed a 10-day trip in space.

Economy. The economy grew by 2.9% in the first quarter of 2002, by 3.9% in

the second quarter, and 3% in the third quarter, rates that were considered good in view of the world slowdown. The unemployment rate continued to be troubling; it fell only slightly, from an estimated 29.5% in September 2001 to 26.4% in February 2002. Some encouragement could be drawn, however, from growth in the manufacturing sector, which rose from 3.1% in 2001 to 5.1% by the end of July 2002; in addition, by the end of July manufacturing exports had risen 21% year-on-year.

By September, interest rates had been raised 4% in attempts to curb inflation. Consumer price inflation (excluding mortgages) rose from 5.8% in September 2001 to 12.5%% by October 2002, owing largely to the fall in the rand's value. The value of the rand to the U.S. dollar fell dramatically from January 2001 from about 7.5–1 to about 12–1 in January 2002 before recovering slightly in November to 9–1.

The 2002–03 budget projected a 9.6% increase in spending and a 6.7% rise in revenue. The 2002–03 deficit was estimated at 2.1% of gross domestic product, up from 1.4% in 2001–02. Tax cuts amounting to R 15.2 billion (about $1.3 billion) were announced, and social grants for the elderly, the disabled, and veterans as well as child-support grants were increased above the level of inflation. Nevertheless, three million households continued to live below the poverty level.

Foreign Affairs. President Mbeki continued as a resolute advocate of the New Partnership for Africa's Development, a plan for the economic development of Africa that was adopted by the World Economic Forum held in Durban, S.Af., in June; by the African Union (AU), launched in Durban in July; and by the UN General Assembly in September. The UN World Summit on Sustainable Development was also held in South Africa—in Johannesburg—in August.

The South African government brokered eight weeks of peace talks on the civil war in the Democratic Republic of the Congo (DRC) in March and April and was involved in other efforts to secure peace in Central Africa. Rwanda and the DRC signed a peace agreement in Pretoria at the end of July.

Following presidential elections in Zimbabwe, Mbeki failed in his efforts to help in the formation of a "national unity" government. He played a role, however, in softening the stance of the Commonwealth toward Zimbabwean Pres. Robert Mugabe.

(MARTIN LEGASSICK)

A billboard in Johannesburg displays the names of world leaders scheduled to attend the Earth Summit in South Africa in late August. Many participants were disappointed by the low turnout of Western leaders.

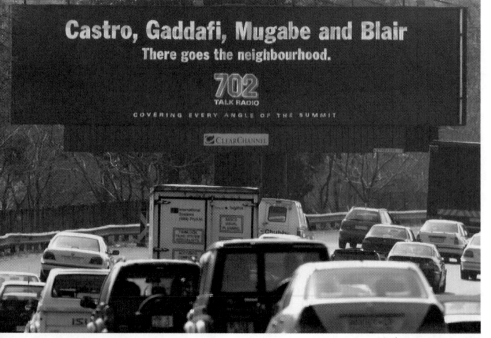

© Juda Ngwenya/Reuters 2002

SPAIN

Area: 506,030 sq km (195,379 sq mi)
Population (2002 est.): 40,998,000
Capital: Madrid
Chief of state: King Juan Carlos I
Head of government: Prime Minister José María Aznar López

Though still outperforming most of its European Union (EU) partners, Spain failed to escape the global economic downturn in 2002. Falling exports, near 4% inflation, declining domestic consumption, and a sharp drop in tourist revenue helped bring annual gross domestic product growth down to an estimated 2%, the lowest level since 1996.

In addition, rising crime rates and soaring house prices (up almost 50% since 1998) were the object of widespread public concern, providing the opposition parties with powerful ammunition against Prime Minister José María Aznar's Popular Party (PP) government.

The centre-right majority government ran into even deeper trouble in its attempt to reform the unemployment benefit system. A controversial decree-law issued on May 27 introduced new restrictions on entitlement to benefits, made it harder for those receiving welfare to turn down jobs offered by the public employment agency, and phased out the special subsidy for agricultural workers in the south. The labour unions reacted by calling a 24-hour general strike on June 20, embarrassing the government on the eve of the EU summit in Seville. The stoppage proved a largely unexpected success. Government spokesman Pío Cabañillas, who had initially dismissed the impact of the strike, and Labour Minister Juan Carlos Aparicio lost their jobs in a cabinet reshuffle in early July. On October 7, just two days after a major national demonstration in Madrid to protest the law, new Labour Minister Eduardo Zaplana announced an abrupt U-turn, accepting nearly all of the unions' demands and leaving only the reform of the subsidy for farm labourers on the statute book.

A major secondary-education bill also proved controversial. Intended to raise educational standards, the proposed Law of Quality lowered the age at which students were streamed into different educational tracks, allowed special schools in the state sector to select on merit, and introduced a new secondary-school-leaving exam. Opposition to the bill's allegedly socially divisive effects and inadequate funding for the public educational system brought student organizations, trade unions, and left-wing parties into the streets as the bill was being debated in the parliament in October.

In November Spain suffered the ecological repercussions of the breaking in two and sinking of the oil tanker *Prestige*, which was carrying twice the amount of fuel that spilled in 1989 from the *Exxon Valdez*. The new spill, which occurred some 210 km (130 mi) off the coast of Galicia, created an oil slick about 240 km (150 mi) long by 24 km (15 mi) wide and threatened fishing and related industries.

Once again, however, it was the Basque country that dominated national politics in 2002. With the support of the Socialist opposition, the PP government intensified its fight against terrorism, combining successful police operations against the armed Basque separatists in Euskadi Ta Askatasuna (ETA) with legal action against the organization's political wing, Batasuna. At the end of June, the parliament passed a new Law of Political Parties that enabled the Supreme Court to ban organizations that defended the use of violence; it was clearly drafted with Batasuna in mind. Two months later the PP and the Socialists again united to pass a motion calling on the government to initiate the procedure to have Batasuna banned. Meanwhile, "Superjudge" Balthasar Garzón used existing antiterrorist legislation to suspend the organization for three years. Though this two-pronged legal assault on Batasuna enjoyed broad political and popular support in Spain as a whole, opinion was much more divided in the Basque country. There the Basque Nationalist Party (PNV)-dominated regional government denounced Garzón's ruling and the new law as counterproductive if not actually illegal, and it announced that it would challenge both measures in the courts.

The rift between Basque nationalists and nonnationalist forces deepened in the fall when Basque Regional Pres. Juan José Ibarretxe unveiled plans to call a referendum on self-determination and convert the Basque country into a "freely associated state" with Spain. The nonnationalist parties and population rallied in defense of the region's

AP/Wide World Photos

Volunteers working along the Spanish coast near the town of Bayona haul away oil that was spilled when the tanker Prestige *broke in two and sank in November.*

existing Autonomy Statute and denounced Ibarretxe's proposals as anticonstitutional and divisive, arguing that ongoing terrorist violence and intimidation of nonnationalist opinion would condition the outcome of any ballot or peace process.

The Spanish presidency of the EU dominated the international agenda during the first six months of the year. The final balance for Spain was mixed. Government satisfaction with the successful introduction of the euro, agreements on energy liberalization, and the Galileo satellite-navigation system contrasted with frustration over the watering down of Spain's hard-line proposals on illegal immigration and the limited progress made toward EU enlargement.

On July 11, just days after the end of Spain's EU presidency, rumbling tensions with Morocco flared up when a small detachment of Moroccan armed police landed on Leila/Perejil, a barren rock a few hundred metres off the North African mainland over which both countries claimed sovereignty. After a weeklong standoff, on July 17 Spanish troops seized the islet without encountering resistance from the six Moroccan soldiers there. The Spanish forces withdrew three days later after the two countries reached an agreement, brokered by the U.S., to return to the status quo and initiate talks on the various issues souring bilateral relations (including fishing rights, immigration, territorial claims, and the Western Sahara). Despite continued tension, the message sent by Morocco's King Muhammed VI to King Juan Carlos I on October 12, the Spanish National Holiday, raised hopes of a thaw in relations between these two mutually important neighbours.

(JUSTIN BYRNE)

Women troops belonging to the secessionist Liberation Tigers of Tamil Eelam march inside the rebel-held city of Kilinochchi, Sri Lanka, on October 10.
© AFP 2002

SRI LANKA

Area: 65,610 sq km (25,332 sq mi)
Population (2002 est.): 18,870,000
Capitals: Sri Jayawardenepura Kotte (legislative and judicial); Colombo (executive)
Head of state and government: President Chandrika Kumaratunga, assisted by Prime Minister Ranil Wickremesinghe

In 2002 hope of ending Sri Lanka's long-standing civil war, which had raged since 1983 and cost more than 60,000 lives, at last emerged. Following the return to parliamentary control of the United National Party (UNP) in December 2001 and weakened international support for the secessionist Liberation Tigers of Tamil Eelam (LTTE), Norwegian mediators negotiated an indefinite cease-fire in February. Internal political opposition delayed the start of peace talks, but in September the ban on the LTTE was lifted and talks began at a naval base in Thailand.

Profound war weariness on both sides seemed to have motivated serious negotiations. Following the initial round of talks, the LTTE unexpectedly dropped its claim for independence, saying it would accept "genuine autonomy and self-determination" in place of a separate state. The two sides agreed to cooperate on such matters as clearing land mines and resettling displaced persons.

After the initial talks, Pres. Chandrika Kumaratunga, leader of the opposition People's Alliance, repeated earlier demands for the LTTE to disarm. Although seven people were killed in a brief clash on Sri Lanka's east coast in mid-October, efforts to incite opposition to the negotiations among southern Sinhalese made little headway. Additional negotiations occurred in October and December. Though many details were still unresolved, at year's end it seemed likely that peace would finally be achieved.

Sri Lanka's economy contracted in 2001, but slow economic growth resumed in 2002, and tourism began to recover. The UNP government was committed to deregulation and privatization. Much needed to be done, however, to refurbish neglected infrastructure and restore business confidence. Population growth slowed to 1%, and the population was aging rapidly.   (DONALD SNODGRASS)

SUDAN, THE

Area: 2,503,890 sq km (966,757 sq mi)
Population (2002 est.): 37,090,000
Capitals: Khartoum (executive and ministerial) and Omdurman (legislative)
Head of state and government: President and Prime Minister Lieut. Gen. Omar Hassan Ahmad al-Bashir

On Jan. 19, 2002, the U.S. special envoy to The Sudan, John Danforth, brokered a six-month cease-fire between the Sudanese government and the rebel Sudanese People's Liberation Army (SPLA). The agreement covered only a limited area of the Nuba mountains of south-central Sudan but proved sufficiently successful for it to be renewed for a further six months on July 20. The U.S. had briefly suspended contact with Sudanese authorities in February after government helicopter gunships attacked and killed 17 civilians at a United Nations aid-distribution point. Though discussions were renewed, there seemed little immediate prospect of ending the nearly 20-year-old civil war.

The rebels' position had been strengthened when two of the leading factions were reconciled in January and proceeded to pose a growing threat to the security of the oil fields in the centre of the country. That threat, together with international pressure to disinvest in The Sudan, caused the Lundin Petroleum company to suspend operations. Both sides recognized that control of the oil industry had become an increasingly important factor in any future settlement. With that in view, the SPLA captured the strategic town of Kapoeta in early June.

On July 20, after five weeks of peace talks under the aegis of Kenyan Pres. Daniel arap Moi, the two sides signed the Machakos Protocol, named after the town outside Nairobi where negotiations took place. Under terms of the deal, after a six-year "interim" period—during which the rebel-dominated

South would have its own legislature within a united Sudan under a constitution acceptable to both parties—there would be an internationally monitored referendum to allow the southerners to vote either for a continuation of the interim arrangement or for secession.

No provision was made in the agreement for a cease-fire, and on July 31 the government launched a large-scale attack on SPLA positions. Ten weeks later the rival combatants agreed to a total cessation of hostilities with effect from October 17 to allow for discussions aimed at achieving a political settlement. The U.S. government then legislated to authorize sanctions against the Sudanese government if the president believed that it was not taking the peace talks seriously. The Sudan's first vice president roundly condemned the U.S. action. (KENNETH INGHAM)

SURINAME

Area: 163,820 sq km (63,251 sq mi)
Population (2002 est.): 436,000
Capital: Paramaribo
Head of state and government: President Ronald Venetiaan, assisted by Prime Minister Jules Rattankoemar Ajodhia

The modest successes that had characterized Pres. Ronald Venetiaan's first two years in office became mostly wistful memories in 2002. Key to a disquieting range of political and economic difficulties was the government's failure to curb a sharply rising fiscal deficit. Substantial pay increases fueled inflation, increased depreciation of the Suriname guilder, and apparently provoked the IMF into seeking the preparation of a revised government budget. Agriculture—traditionally important for both employment and foreign exchange—suffered owing to the closure of the commercial banana industry and the loss of the key Jamaican market for rice. The vast informal economy of narcotics smuggling and ecologically corrosive mining, fish poaching, and timber cutting continued to resist government control measures while creating hazards for potentially productive new industrial-scale bauxite and gold projects.

Although Venetiaan's faltering stewardship shook the confidence of citizens and members of his four-party New Front Coalition, the coalition's parliamentary majority appeared solid and almost attractive when viewed against the mismanagement of former president Jules Wijdenbosch and former military dictator Dési Bouterse.

Though bright spots were few, positive signs included mining and palm-oil enterprises, continuing and significant disbursements by major donors, and slow but ongoing discussions with Guyana to open up joint exploration for oil and gas. (JOHN W. GRAHAM)

SWAZILAND

Area: 17,364 sq km (6,704 sq mi)
Population (2002 est.): 1,124,000
Capitals: Mbabane (administrative and judicial); Lozitha and Ludzidzini (royal); Lobamba (legislative)
Chief of state: King Mswati III, with much power shared by his mother, Queen Mother Ntombi Latfwala
Head of government: Prime Minister Barnabas Sibusiso Dlamini

The detention and trial of Mario Masuku, president of the People's United Democratic Movement, drew widespread attention in 2002. Masuku had been arrested in late 2000 after he made an allegedly seditious statement about King Mswati III. The high court released Masuku in August 2002 after the state failed to prove its claim.

The Constitution Drafting Committee (CDC), headed by Prince David Dlamini, built on the findings of the Constitutional Review Commission released in 2001. In February King Mswati expressed reservations about the pace at which the CDC was working and the economic vision it was reflecting. Despite concerns, the king expected a draft constitution in October. He extended the submission date to February 2003, however, as he went into ritual seclusion in preparation for the annual Incwala (Kingship) ceremony.

Throughout the year Prime Minister Barnabas Sibusiso Dlamini and his cabinet made repeated political and economic blunders that strengthened the pro-democracy movement. In September the parliament rejected financing for a 450 million emalangeni (about $45 million) jet for the king. Dlamini claimed sole responsibility for the decision to purchase the executive jet; local and international critics argued that the money could be better spent fighting rampant poverty and the HIV/AIDS epidemic.

Pro-democracy protests intensified when Mswati chose three high-school-age women as his intended brides despite his 2001 decree that young women should not engage in sexual activity for the next five years. The mother of one of the girls filed suit in an unprecedented legal dispute with the king to get her daughter back, but she dropped the suit after her daughter's engagement became official.

(ACKSON M. KANDUZA)

SWEDEN

Area: 449,964 sq km (173,732 sq mi)
Population (2002 est.): 8,925,000
Capital: Stockholm
Chief of state: King Carl XVI Gustaf
Head of government: Prime Minister Göran Persson

The centre-left Social Democratic Party (SDP), under the leadership of Prime Minister Göran Persson, was returned to power in the 2002 general election but faced the challenge of convincing Swedes that they should abandon the krona and adopt the single European currency, the euro. The results of the September election were seen as a foregone conclusion. Against a backdrop of low unemployment and with tax cuts and reduced fees for key public services boosting household consumption, the SDP was able to portray itself as the party of economic competence. Persson's unequivocal support of the U.S. and its "war on terrorism" in the aftermath of the attacks of Sept. 11, 2001, also hit a chord with voters. In the weeks before the vote, however, opinion polls indicated that the contest was much closer than had been predicted. Instead of focusing on the upbeat economic news, voters turned their attention to the problems of integrating the country's sizable immigrant community. Sweden had by far the largest number of immigrants in the Nordic region, with about 22% of the

Swedish Prime Minister Göran Persson, flanked by Swedish Trade Union Confederation Chairman Vanja Lundby Wedin (left) and Foreign Minister Anna Lindh (right), exults on September 15 after having led the Social Democrats to victory in the general elections.

population born outside the country or with a parent born abroad. (See *Australia: Special Report,* above.)

Unlike neighbouring Denmark and Norway, Sweden had no credible populist or anti-immigrant party. Instead, the Liberal Party tapped into the unease over immigration after its leader, Lars Leijonborg, demanded that immigrants pass a Swedish-language test before they became citizens. In the end the Liberal Party almost tripled its support from the 1998 election, gaining over 13% of the vote. The Liberal Party's success came largely at the expense of its opposition partner, the conservative Moderate Party, which lost support following a lacklustre campaign in which its promises to lower taxes and improve public services failed to convince voters. The Social Democrats won just under 40% of the vote, and after some tough negotiations, Persson reached an agreement with the Left and Green parties to ensure that his minority government would have a stable parliamentary majority. In power for all but 9 of the previous 70 years, the SDP even managed to regain control of the capital, Stockholm.

Persson would not be able to rely on his allies for support over the single-currency issue, however. Both the Left and the Green parties opposed membership, fearing that the country's cherished welfare state and high employment would have to be sacrificed inside the euro zone. Supporters of membership contended that Sweden would benefit from lower interest rates and cheaper prices if the krona was abandoned. Although the major nonsocialist opposition parties as well as business organizations and key labour unions would campaign hard for the "yes" side, opinion was divided within the SDP itself, and the eventual vote, set for Sept. 14, 2003, was likely to be tight.

Away from politics, the excesses of the Internet and telecommunications investment bubbles continued to batter the economy. The most high-profile victim, Ericsson, the world's largest producer of wireless telecom systems, was forced to fire thousands of staff and raise about $3 billion from its shareholders. The consumer, rather than industry, appeared to be keeping the economy going. Estimated gross domestic product growth was forecast at about 2% for 2003. (NICHOLAS GEORGE)

SWITZERLAND

Area: 41,284 sq km (15,940 sq mi)
Population (2002 est.): 7,282,000
Capitals: Bern (administrative) and Lausanne (judicial)
Head of state and government: President Kaspar Villiger

Switzerland eased away from self-imposed isolation when it joined the United Nations on Sept. 10, 2002, following a referendum in March in which 55% of the electorate voted in favour of UN membership. Pres. Kaspar Villiger and other government members argued that rejection would be disastrous for the country's international standing and that membership was compatible with Swiss neutrality. An overwhelming majority had voted against UN membership in 1986 out of fears that national sovereignty would be weakened. Switzerland had long been an active member of specialized international agencies such as the World Health Organization, and Geneva served as the UN European headquarters.

Switzerland showed little inclination, however, to follow the 10 other countries accepted for accession negotiations with the European Union. Anti-EU sentiment was heightened as a result of British-led pressure to relax banking secrecy and crack down on tax evasion—which was not an offense in Switzerland. The EU wanted to impose a tax on income earned on savings and investments abroad, which necessitated the introduction of an information-swapping system. Switzerland offered to withhold taxes on interest and dividend payments to EU residents and give it to the EU—but without identifying the depositors. Swiss banks said even that concession would hurt them and warned that abolition of banking secrecy would put 20,000 jobs at risk. Switzerland had earned praise from the U.S. for lifting banking secrecy in the hunt for assets linked to the al-Qaeda terrorist network—although it only found negligible sums.

The government was embarrassed when voters killed its plan to set up a Swiss Solidarity Foundation using "excess" gold. The aim was to invest an expected 20 billion Swiss francs (about $13.5 billion) from the sale of gold reserves and spend the interest, with one-third of the money going to the Swiss social security program, a third to the foundation to help cantonal (state) governments, and a third to people in need at home or abroad. Billionaire industrialist Christoph Blocher, the country's leading nationalist, slammed the foundation as the product of foreign "blackmail" because it had been conceived in 1997 to calm international accusations that Switzerland had profited from the Holocaust. In the September 22 referendum, 52% voted against the plan, with many saying that, given the international economic climate, it would be better to keep the gold.

Martin Ebner, Switzerland's best-known financier, was the most prominent victim of the stock-market downturn. In July he was forced to sell the controlling interest in four publicly traded investment companies as part of a restructuring of his debt-laden BZ Group. Lukas Mühlemann, the chairman and chief executive of Credit Suisse Group, the country's second largest bank, also announced that he would stand down because of its poor performance. Swiss-Swedish engineering conglomerate ABB forced out its chief, Jörgen Centerman, and

© Andreas Meier/Reuters 2002

An aerial view of the Swiss Alpine village of Rueun shows the course of a mud slide that brought heavy damage—but no reported deaths—to the area after torrential rains in November.

then witnessed its share price collapse by about 75% in the space of a few days in late October as a result of bankruptcy fears.

The new national airline—swiss—took to the air March 31, combining the services of the defunct Swissair and regional carrier Crossair. Federal and cantonal governments and companies led by Nestlé raised 2.75 billion francs (about $1.7 billion) to get it aloft. Swiss precision was thrown into question after its air traffic controllers admitted to being at least partly to blame for the midair collision of a Russian charter jet and a cargo plane in Swiss airspace over Germany. The crash killed 71 people, many of them school students heading for a beach vacation in Spain.

In the closest outcome on record, a referendum on November 24 rejected by a majority of just 3,422 votes a proposal by the nationalist Swiss People's Party to keep out all but a trickle of asylum seekers. The government urged cantonal authorities to do a manual recount to ward off potential legal challenges.   (CLARE KAPP)

SYRIA

Area: 185,180 sq km (71,498 sq mi)
Population (2002 est.): 17,156,000
Capital: Damascus
Head of state and government: President Bashar al-Assad, assisted by Prime Minister Muhammad Mustafa Mero

Spontaneous popular demonstrations in defense of Palestinian rights became a regular occurrence in Damascus in the spring of 2002. Such protests reflected not only the public's antipathy toward Israeli policies in the occupied territories but also growing impatience over the glacial pace of political and economic reform inside Syria. Ostensibly pro-Palestinian marches soon exhibited the symbols and slogans of a wide range of organizations excluded from the Ba'th Party-dominated National Pro-

gressive Front. Dissidents took advantage of the rallies to distribute handbills that urged the authorities to release political detainees, end martial law, and relax restrictions on permissible debate. The potentially subversive character of the demonstrations became clear in mid-April when a crowd of protesters gathered outside the State Security Court to cheer the historic leader of the Syrian Communist Party Political Bureau, Riyad al-Turk, as he emerged from his trial for treason.

Meanwhile, allies of Pres. Bashar al-Assad continued to purge the top levels of the armed forces and security services. Moves to replace long-serving commanders with younger officers loyal to the new president were facilitated by the promulgation of guidelines requiring all military officers to retire at age 60. The minister of the interior ordered the immediate resignation of a number of senior figures in the political and military intelligence apparatus in July and promoted other high-ranking commanders to advisory posts in the state bureaucracy. These moves complemented efforts to fight pervasive corruption in the civilian administration. The director-general of the state-run Commercial Bank of Syria was taken into custody in March after squandering some $5 million in risky investments; the head of Syrian Airlines was dismissed the same month. Dozens of mid-level government bureaucrats were dismissed on charges of mismanagement and misconduct throughout the spring and summer. The anticorruption campaign redoubled after a structurally defective and overburdened dam across the Orontes River north of Hama burst in early June, inundating the rich farmlands of the Ghab. (*See* DISASTERS.)

Syria served on the UN Security Council, but its term brought only unpalatable choices. Syria's representative abstained from voting on a March resolution that for the first time referred explicitly to a Palestinian state and walked out before the vote on an April resolution that demanded the withdrawal of Israeli troops from Palestinian-administered towns in the West Bank. Despite Damascus's long-standing opposition to U.S. military intervention in the region, Syria voted in favour of the U.S.-sponsored resolution on Iraq passed by the UN Security Council on November 8. Syria originally opposed the resolution, which allowed weapons inspectors unfettered access to all Iraqi sites. It agreed to endorse the measure only after language was added to the resolution preventing the immediate use of force if Iraq failed to comply. The U.S. government had credited Syria with forwarding information that enabled it to thwart an al-Qaeda attack on U.S. military personnel in April. Syrian troops also undertook the delicate task of restraining, but tolerating, Hezbollah operations against Israel's continued occupation of the disputed border between Lebanon and the Golan Heights.

(FRED H. LAWSON)

TAIWAN

Area: 36,188 sq km (13,972 sq mi)
Population (2002 est.): 22,457,000
Capital: Taipei
Chief of state: President Chen Shui-bian
Head of government: Presidents of the Executive Yuan (Premiers) Chang Chun-hsiung and, from February 1, Yu Shyi-kun

In Taiwan the year 2002 began with a major cabinet reshuffle that was widely perceived to be part of an effort by Pres. Chen Shui-bian to lay the groundwork for reelection in 2004. More than half of the cabinet ministers were replaced. Yu Shyi-kun, secretary-general to the president, was named the new premier. Minister of Economic Affairs Lin Hsin-i was promoted to vice-premier. Experienced business managers were handed the finance and economics portfolios. Chen appeared in complete control of the changes, and his protégés dominated the new cabinet. Many of those who had served in the Taipei municipal government when Chen was mayor of the capital received promotions, while those who could not see eye to eye with the president were removed from leadership positions.

In an effort to maintain its independence from China, as well as to consolidate American support, Chen's administration dispatched a number of high-ranking officials to the U.S. during the year. They included the premier, the vice minister of defense, the chairwoman of the Mainland Affairs Council, and first lady Wu Shu-chen. Taiwan also made plans to purchase four state-of-the-art Aegis-class destroyers from the U.S., which was expected to formally announce the sale in 2003. The proposed arms sale was estimated at $5.7 billion.

Early in 2002 China extended an invitation to members of Taiwan's governing Democratic Progressive Party (DPP) to visit the mainland, apparently signaling a more conciliatory approach toward the disputed island. In the past, Chinese leaders had made general invitations to party officials from Taiwan, but this was the first offer expressly issued to the officially pro-independence DPP.

Chinese Vice-Premier Qian Qichen made another diplomatic overture later in the year when he called for negotiations with Taiwan on the establishment of direct cross-strait transportation operations. Although a survey conducted by the Mainland Affairs Council found that more than 72% of Taiwanese supported such operations—provided that Taiwanese authority and national security were assured—comments by Chen clearly indicated his reluctance to develop closer economic ties with China. The president further rankled the Chinese leadership by expressing at different times his view regarding the status of

Taiwan. In a May interview with *Newsweek* magazine, Chen called Taiwan "already an independent state." In August Chen's speech about "one country on each side [of the Taiwan Strait]" drew immediate criticism from the opposition parties in Taiwan and the governments of China, the U.S., and Japan, among others.

Taiwan's economy grew only 0.9% in the first months of 2002, which was even lower than experts had forecast. Statistics showed continual weak domestic demand. In August Taiwan's imports and exports increased by 18.8% and 15.5%, respectively, compared with the same period the previous year. Total exports from January to August had increased by just 2.7%, however—a sign of weak recovery from the economic downtown that hit Taiwan in 2001. Real economic recovery was not in sight by the end of the year.

The Ministry of Finance planned to speed up its pace in resolving nonperforming loan problems, although many experts had questioned whether tax money should be used to help failing financial institutions. According to official figures, the total amount of nonperforming loans stood at $40.3 billion, though private-sector commentators estimated an amount close to $86.3 billion.

In November President Chen announced a five-year plan to address economic woes, vowing to bring the jobless rate down by one percentage point to 4.5% in 2003. Four days after the announcement, some 120,000 demonstrators took to the streets of Taipei to protest the proposed financial reforms, which included abolishing agricultural cooperatives that provided funding to poor farmers and fishermen. In the wake of the protests, Premier Yu and his finance minister submitted their resignations, though Yu later announced that he would stay in office.

(XIAOBO HU)

TAJIKISTAN

Area: 143,100 sq km (55,300 sq mi)
Population (2002 est.): 6,327,000
Capital: Dushanbe
Chief of state: President Imomali Rakhmonov
Head of government: Prime Minister Akil Akilov

In 2002 Tajikistan was able to benefit from its participation in the international antiterrorism coalition to forge closer ties with a number of countries, including the U.S., France, the U.K., China, and Iran. These states, as well as international financial institutions, promised their assistance in overcoming the legacy of widespread poverty and lagging economic development that was left by Tajikistan's civil war in the first years of independence. In March the Asian Development Bank announced a $2.9 million program to reduce rural poverty, and later in the year the World Bank offered $26.4 million worth of credits to build a power plant in the Pamirs. Development of hydropower was high on the Tajik government's agenda for stimulating economic growth. Not only could it be used as the basis for domestic industry, but it could also readily be exported to neighbouring countries. Consequently, Tajik officials placed special emphasis on finding foreign investors to help complete Soviet-era hydroelectric projects, in particular that at Rogun.

Despite its own difficult economic situation, Tajikistan promised such assistance as it was able to provide for the reconstruction of Afghanistan. In particular, the Tajiks offered training in various skills, notably for the Afghan military. The improving ties between the two countries were symbolized by the starting of weekly flights between Kabul and Dushanbe.

Although in 2002 there was little evidence that Islamic extremists were entering Tajikistan from outside, the government asserted that there were plenty of the homegrown variety operating in the northern part of the country. The international movement Hizb-ut Tahrir, which sought to create a medieval-style caliphate in the Fergana Valley, had already gained a foothold in the northern, Tajik portion of the valley and was reported to be stepping up distribution of its literature. In July, embarrassed by the fact that there were a few Tajiks among al-Qaeda supporters held in the U.S. camp at Guantánamo Bay, Cuba, Pres. Imomali Rakhmonov warned of increasing militancy in the north and accused the Islamic Renaissance Party, a partner in the governing coalition, of encouraging extremism—a charge that the head of the party hotly denied. In August Rakhmonov warned the Muslim clergy to stay out of politics because international press reports of extremism in Tajikistan were undermining efforts

to attract foreign investment. Between August and October, 33 of the 152 mosques in the Isfara district in the north were reported to have been closed—Rakhmonov had asserted that there were too many of them—and a number of imams were removed from their posts. (BESS BROWN)

TANZANIA

Area: 945,090 sq km (364,901 sq mi)
Population (2002 est.): 34,902,000
De facto capital: Dar es Salaam; the legislature meets in Dodoma, the pending capital
Chief of state and head of government: President Benjamin William Mkapa, assisted by Prime Minister Frederick Tulway Sumaye

In January 2002 a new deal was made between the ruling Chama Cha Mapinduzi (CCM) party and the leading opposition party, the Civic United Front (CUF). The arrangement restored working relations that had been disrupted in 2001 and called for the implementation of the peace accord signed in October of that year. It was strongly endorsed by the secretary-general of the CUF, Seif Shariff Hamad. Hamad said that the CUF no longer disputed the outcome of the 2000 elections but simply wanted to ensure that the mechanics of the constitution were wholly apparent.

On March 3 Pres. Benjamin William Mkapa announced that he would defy the World Bank and implement an air traffic control system supplied by the British aerospace company BAE Systems. British Prime Minister Tony Blair had authorized the transaction in December 2001 against the advice of Chancellor of the Exchequer Gordon Brown. Brown argued that Tanzania, one of the world's poorest countries, should not invest in such an unnecessarily expensive system. The British secretary of state for international development, Clare Short, agreed with Brown and initially suspended £10 million (about $15.5 million) in aid in protest. Short also voiced her suspicions that the deal had been corrupt, though she admitted that she had no evidence to prove it so.

The corporate privatization program encouraged by the World Bank and the

IMF continued to make steady progress in 2002. The Presidential Parastatal Sector Reform Commission (PSRC), however, came under increasing attack from CCM critics who feared that the country's assets were being sold to foreigners. Although the government denied the charge, CCM MPs threatened to bring a motion calling for an investigation into the conduct of the PSRC. In September their case gained substance when, in response to the government's attempt to dispose of 75% of Air Tanzania shares, South African Airways emerged as the only bidder for a 49% holding in the failing company. The government had already encountered a serious setback on June 24 when the Tanzania Railways Corp., one of the largest entities scheduled for privatization, reported that more than 280 people had been killed in a crash near Dodoma. (*See* DISASTERS.)

The task of creating a customs union with Kenya and Uganda within the East African Community also proved difficult. Government officials and businessmen feared that freeing the regional market would benefit only the stronger economy of Kenya.

(KENNETH INGHAM)

THAILAND

Area: 513,115 sq km (198,115 sq mi)
Population (2002 est.): 63,430,000
Capital: Bangkok
Chief of state: King Bhumibol Adulyadej
Head of government: Prime Minister Thaksin Shinawatra

Prime Minister Thaksin Shinawatra's ambition to dominate politics in Thailand was evident throughout 2002. His Thai Rak Thai Party merged with two smaller coalition members to secure a huge parliamentary majority, leaving the Democrats—led by former prime minister Chuan Leekpai—virtually alone in opposition. A far-reaching reorganization of the cabinet, state bureaucracy, and military hierarchy was enacted in October, but not before King Bhumibol Adulyadej had unexpectedly used his constitutional prerogative to delay royal assent for several days. Six new ministries were created, bringing the total number to 20. Six deputy prime ministers were also appointed, including former prime minister Chavalit Yongchaiyudh, who relinquished his post as defense minister. Gen. Somdhat Attanand was tapped as army chief. Interior Minister Purachai Piemsombun, whose "social order" crackdown on nightlife had upset the entertainment industry, was moved to Justice and replaced by former transport minister Wan Muhamad Nor Matha, one of the few Muslims active in the government. Finance Minister Somkid Jatusripitak and Foreign Minister Surakiart Sathirathai kept their jobs.

Thaksin faced criticism during the year for spending too much time on overseas trips, including one to India for reasons critics claimed had more to do with protecting his family's vast personal fortune in telecommunications than with statecraft. There were also allegations that old-style patronage, nepotism, and cronyism were very much alive. Thaksin had appointed two of his cousins to top army posts, while his sister controlled a leading faction in his party. In addition, the wife of his chief adviser was appointed to the cabinet and took charge of the new Culture Ministry, and many of the prime minister's former military academy classmates were promoted in the police and armed forces. Nevertheless, anticorruption reforms implemented under the 1997 constitution snared several of the country's leading figures in 2002. A member of the National Assembly was sentenced to six years' imprisonment for having received kickbacks from drug companies in exchange for helping authorize sales to hospitals at inflated prices. A former health minister faced a likely prison sentence after the National Counter Corruption Commission ruled that he had no feasible explanation for his wealth. By year's end the commission was closing in on several other leading politicians and high-ranking bureaucrats. Meanwhile, efforts continued to impeach four Constitutional Court judges who had sided with Thaksin in an 8–7 ruling over the prime minister's mandatory assets declaration the year before. The judges had acquitted the prime minister, despite having convicted other politicians in similar cases.

Relations with neighbouring Myanmar (Burma) deteriorated steadily, as Yangon (Rangoon) accused Bangkok of siding with the Shan States Army, an ethnic Thai rebel group active in Myanmar. Thailand in turn accused Myanmar of border encroachments. A

series of newspaper articles critical of the Thai monarchy appeared in Myanmar and enraged the Thais.

As Thailand emerged from a five-year recession, economic growth of 4–6% was predicted for the year. Interest rates and inflation remained low. Privatization of state enterprises faltered, but massive infrastructure projects—including railways, highways, city subways, bridges, and ports—were revitalized.   (ROBERT WOODROW)

TOGO

Area: 56,785 sq km (21,925 sq mi)
Population (2002 est.): 5,286,000
Capital: Lomé
Chief of state: President Gen. Gnassingbé Eyadéma
Head of government: Prime Ministers Gabriel Agbéyomé Kodjo and, from June 29, Koffi Sama

Modifications to Togo's electoral code were introduced early in 2002. These included new residency requirements and exclusive Togolese nationality for all candidates, measures clearly designed to prevent participation in the political process of certain high-profile opponents of the regime, most notably the exile Gilchrist Olympio. National and international protests over these changes to the code—which were approved by the National Assembly on February 8—led to the cancellation of the March 10 legislative elections. Opposition party members refused to sit on the reconstituted National Electoral Commission, which was reduced to 10 members—half of whom represented the ruling Rally of the Togolese People (RPT).

On June 27 Pres. Gnassingbé Eyadéma fired Prime Minister Agbéyomé Kodjo. Kodjo fled the country immediately afterward. On August 7 he was ousted from the RPT, and on September 17 the government issued an international warrant for his arrest. Major opposition parties boycotted the legislative elections, held on October 27. As a result, the RPT took 72 of the 81 seats.

The government issued a statement on August 15 strongly protesting allegations brought by Amnesty International that it engaged in systematic repression

of political opponents. On October 22 a delegation of Togolese officials testified before the United Nations Human Rights Committee, denying such abuses as torture, extrajudicial executions, and illegal detention of prisoners.

(NANCY ELLEN LAWLER)

TONGA

Area: 750 sq km (290 sq mi)
Population (2002 est.): 101,000
Capital: Nuku'alofa
Head of state and government: King Taufa'ahau Tupou IV, assisted by Prime Minister of Privy Council Prince 'Ulukalala Lavaka Ata

Parliamentary elections in March 2002 attracted 52 candidates competing for the nine seats available to commoners; seven of the nine seats were won by the Tonga Human Rights and Democracy Movement (THRDM), and the other two went to independents. The balance

American J.D. Bogdonoff, the former financial adviser and court jester to Tongan King Taufa'ahau Tupou IV, poses in a costume shop in Penngrove, Calif. Tongan authorities alleged that Bogdonoff defrauded the country of millions.

AP/Wide World Photos

of the 30-member Legislative Assembly comprised 9 members elected by and from the group of 30 nobles and 12 ministers nominated by the king. Later in the year, the THRDM unsuccessfully proposed a constitutional change that would have removed the king's legislative and executive powers, established a bicameral legislature, and shifted the balance of power to elected members. In June, American J.D. Bogdonoff, onetime financial adviser and court jester to King Taufa'ahau Tupou IV, was sued in a U.S. district court for having defrauded the Tonga Trust Fund of $25 million.

Tonga's ship registry caused international embarrassment and was closed when Israeli forces boarded a Tongan-registered vessel carrying 50 tons of weapons, allegedly earmarked for a Palestinian organization. Later in the year, a group of Pakistanis identified as having links to al-Qaeda were arrested in Italy on terrorism charges after they landed in Sicily from a Tongan-flagged vessel. Tonga was represented by Deputy Prime Minister James Cocker at the World Summit on Sustainable Development in Johannesburg, S.Af. In September, Prime Minister Prince 'Ulukalala Lavaka Ata addressed the UN General Assembly, emphasizing the environmental challenges to small less-developed Pacific Island states. On Jan. 1, 2002, the Vava'u islands in the north of Tonga were struck by Cyclone Waka, which caused over $50 million in damages but no loss of life.

(BARRIE MACDONALD)

TRINIDAD AND TOBAGO

Area: 5,128 sq km (1,980 sq mi)
Population (2002 est.): 1,304,000
Capital: Port of Spain
Chief of state: President Arthur Napoleon Raymond Robinson
Head of government: Prime Minister Patrick Manning

Parliament failed to elect a speaker at its first meeting of 2002 in April. The opposition United National Congress (UNC) party declined to cooperate in the process, even voting against its own nominees. A second attempt was made at another sitting in August and pro-

duced the same result, which left Prime Minister Patrick Manning with no option but to advise the president to dissolve Parliament and call a fresh election. This was duly held on October 7, and Manning's People's National Movement emerged clearly victorious, with 20 seats in the House of Representatives to the UNC's 16.

Manning, who assumed the portfolio of finance minister as well as prime minister, presented the first budget of his new term later that month. The budget provided for $3.3 billion in public expenditure during fiscal year 2002–03.

Prior to the election, the authorities had charged former prime minister Basdeo Panday with having failed to declare money held in a London bank account. Panday had been obliged to declare assets under local integrity legislation.

(DAVID RENWICK)

TUNISIA

Area: 164,150 sq km (63,378 sq mi)
Population (2002 est.): 9,764,000
Capital: Tunis
Chief of state: President Gen. Zine al-Abidine Ben Ali
Head of government: Prime Minister Mohamed Ghannouchi

In Tunisia the year 2002 was dominated by the explosion of a bomb placed outside the El-Ghriba synagogue in Jarbah (Djerba) on April 11. A group of tourists was visiting the synagogue when an oil tanker parked next to the building exploded, killing 19 people, including 14 Germans from a tourist party. The incident was believed to be the first successful al-Qaeda assault since the Sept. 11, 2001, attacks in the U.S. The perpetrator, Nizar Nawar, a local man who had been trained in Afghanistan, died in the explosion. In November several arrests were made in connection with the bombing.

Pres. Zine al-Abidine Ben Ali's government continued its harsh treatment of internal dissidents after the bombing. Amnesty International visited Tunisia in late September and subsequently called for the immediate liberation of prisoners of conscience and the review of all trials of political prisoners,

which it estimated numbered 1,000. Political prisoners also staged a collective hunger strike in August to commemorate the 10th anniversary of the 1992 Bab Saadoun and Bouchoucha military trials, which resulted in the imprisonment of 265 persons on charges of threatening state security.

At the end of January, 34 people were sentenced—31 of them in absentia—to long terms of imprisonment for their involvement with a terrorist organization based abroad. The trials took place before a military tribunal, which thus prevented the accused individuals from appealing the ruling.

In early February journalist Hama Hammami was imprisoned on charges of subversion for his work with the Tunisian Communist Workers' Party. He and two of his associates had been in hiding for four years. Hammami's wife, the noted attorney and human rights advocate Radhia Nasraoui, went on a hunger strike following her husband's imprisonment in an attempt to draw attention to his plight and to other human rights abuses in Tunisia. Hammami was released conditionally from jail in early September owing to health problems.

Despite a significant decline in tourism, the Tunisian economy continued to grow at a rate of approximately 5% annually, earning praise from the IMF. Controversy continued to rage over the president's plan to seek a fourth term in 2004, a move prohibited by Tunisia's constitution.

(GEORGE JOFFÉ)

TURKEY

Area: 779,452 sq km (300,948 sq mi)
Population (2002 est.): 69,359,000
Capital: Ankara
Chief of state: President Ahmet Necdet Sezer
Head of government: Prime Minister Bulent Ecevit and, from November 19, Abdullah Gul

The collapse of the three-party coalition headed by 77-year-old Bulent Ecevit, leader of the centre-left Democratic Left Party (DSP), precipitated early elections that transformed the Turkish political scene in 2002. The first serious rift occurred on February 6 when a set of democratization measures designed to bring Turkish legislation in line with European Union (EU) standards was opposed by the Nationalist Action Party (MHP), the second strongest party in the coalition, and was passed only with the help of the opposition in the Turkish Grand National Assembly. Confidence was further eroded when Ecevit refused to name an acting prime minister during a protracted illness that began in May. The decision taken on July 1 by Ecevit and his two coalition partners, Devlet Bahceli, leader of the MHP, and Mesut Yilmaz, leader of the centre-right Motherland Party (ANAP), to continue in office until the end of the parliamentary term in April 2004 failed to calm the still-unsteady markets. A few days later, fearing that he would be supplanted in the coalition by Tansu Ciller's more liberal centre-right True Path Party (DYP), Bahceli demanded early elections in November. Mesut Yilmaz agreed, and the fate of the coalition was sealed when between July 8 and 11 seven ministers resigned from the DSP; more than half of the party's parliamentary group followed over the next few months. On July 31, the parliament voted overwhelmingly to bring elections forward to November 3, against Ecevit's wishes. On August 3 a wide-ranging set of amendments to the constitution and penal laws that would abolish the death penalty and allow instruction and broadcasting in minority languages was endorsed by the parliament, once again over the opposition of the MHP. As a result, the death sentence on the Kurdish rebel leader Abdullah Ocalan was commuted to life imprisonment on October 3.

On August 10 Ecevit's economic supremo, Kemal Dervis, resigned, and soon after that he joined the opposition centre-left Republican People's Party (CHP), led by Deniz Baykal. Attempts to lower the threshold of 10% of the countrywide poll, which parties had to pass in order to qualify for representation in the parliament, failed. As public opinion surveys predicted a massive win by the Justice and Development Party (AKP), the more moderate of the two successors to the banned Virtue Party (FP) of Islamic inspiration, the judiciary moved against the AKP leader, former Istanbul mayor Recep Tayyip Erdogan. In September the High Electoral Board ruled that a previous conviction disqualified him from standing for the parliament and, therefore, from becoming prime minister. On October 23 the chief prosecutor

Turkish Deputy Prime Minister Mesut Yilmaz welds as other officials look on during a groundbreaking ceremony on September 26 for the construction of an oil pipeline from Baku, Azerbaijan, to Ceyhan in southern Turkey.

asked the Constitutional Court to ban the AKP for maintaining Erdogan in the leadership, but no ruling on the question occurred before the election.

On November 3 the AKP won 363 seats in the 550-member Turkish Grand National Assembly on 34.3% of the total vote and was thus able to form a single-party government after more than a decade of fissiparous coalitions. Only one other party, the CHP, crossed the 10% barrier, winning 178 seats on 19.4% of the poll. With only 6.2% of the poll, the Democratic People's Party (DEHAP), the legal vehicle for Kurdish nationalism, failed to enter the parliament. The new government formed by Abdullah Gul, deputy leader of the AKP, was confirmed by the parliament on November 28. On December 27 the parliament voted through a constitutional amendment that would clear the way for Erdogan to run for prime minister.

At its meeting in Copenhagen on December 12, the EU Council of Ministers noted the democratization measures approved by the outgoing parliament and decided that a firm date should be set to begin negotiations on Turkey's entry.

At the end of October, Gen. Tommy Franks, chief of U.S. Central Command, and the NATO supreme allied

commander Europe, Gen. Joseph Ralston, visited Ankara. After his party's election victory, Erdogan echoed Ecevit and other party leaders in asking for UN authorization of any military action against Saddam Hussein in Iraq. On June 20 Turkey took over from Britain the command of the International Security Assistance Force in Afghanistan.

Economic growth resumed and inflation fell, but the consequences of the 2001 economic crisis were still felt in low investment and high unemployment. The Blue Stream pipeline, the deepest underwater pipeline in the world, which would transport Russian natural gas under the Black Sea to Turkey, was completed on October 20.

(ANDREW MANGO)

TURKMENISTAN

Area: 488,100 sq km (188,500 sq mi)
Population (2002 est.): 4,946,000
Capital: Ashgabat
Head of state and government: President Saparmurad Niyazov

Throughout 2002 Turkmen Pres. Saparmurad Niyazov continued to destabilize his own government through an increasingly rapid turnover of top officials and the concentration of progressively more tasks in the hands of fewer and fewer ministries. Early in the year, Muhammet Nazarov, head of the National Security Committee (KNB), to whom Niyazov had handed control of the country's security, military, and foreign affairs in 2001, was sharply attacked and then arrested on a variety of charges, including drug trafficking and murder, along with his two deputies, the minister of defense, and other security officials. Later in the year Niyazov transferred the fire service and traffic police from the Ministry of Internal Affairs to the Defense Ministry, and expanded the authority of the Ministry of the Economy and Finance to include a number of control functions previously carried out by other agencies. These transfers appeared to be related to the president's degree of personal trust in the individual ministers rather than in any rational plan of workload distribution.

In May Niyazov fired the head of the central bank, Seyitbay Gandymov, who was also the deputy prime minister responsible for foreign economic relations, accusing him of embezzlement and other crimes. In September the president fired Gandymov's successor after a central bank official made an allegedly unauthorized transfer of $41.5 million to foreign accounts; Niyazov decreed that in future no such transfers could take place without his personal permission. At the end of December, a former foreign minister, Boris Shikhmuradov, was convicted and sentenced to life in prison after he confessed to responsibility for an armed attack on Niyazov's motorcade on November 25.

In April Niyazov announced a reform of higher education that reduced the number of years of classroom study to two—the rest to be spent in practical work—and harnessed education to training for specific jobs. Study of Niyazov's own eccentric account of Turkmen history and traditions, the *Ruhnama*, was made the basis for all levels of education in the country.

A summit of leaders of the Caspian littoral states held in Ashgabat in April failed to agree on the division of the sea. Niyazov actively sought to revive a project to build a pipeline from Turkmenistan across Afghanistan to Pakistan. While the other two countries were enthusiastic about the project, potential investors were cautious. The Asian Development Bank offered to finance a project study, however, and Russian gas companies expressed some interest in taking part in the construction.

(BESS BROWN)

TUVALU

Area: 25.6 sq km (9.9 sq mi)
Population (2002 est.): 10,900
Capital: Government offices in Vaiaku, Fongafale islet, of Funafuti atoll
Chief of state: Queen Elizabeth II, represented by Governor-General Sir Tomasi Puapua
Head of government: Prime Ministers Koloa Talake and, from August 2, Saufatu Sopoaga

In the July 2002 elections, 39 candidates, including 2 women, vied for seats in the 15-member Parliament; six sitting members, including Prime Minister Koloa Talake, lost their seats. The new prime minister was Saufatu Sopoaga, the former minister of finance. In August Sopoaga announced plans for a referendum to determine whether Tuvalu should become a republic, with the head of government directly elected, rather

Turkmen elders listen to the national anthem prior to the start of an Independence Day parade in Ashgabat on October 27.

than the current parliamentary democracy system with the British sovereign as head of state.

At the World Summit on Sustainable Development, in Johannesburg, S.Af., Tuvalu highlighted the environmental vulnerability of its coral islands to global warming, rising sea levels, and cyclonic storms. It particularly attacked the position of the U.S. (the world's largest producer of greenhouse gases) and Australia (which produced the highest levels of greenhouse gases on a per capita basis). Tuvalu threatened to take legal action in international courts. Australia rejected the claims and announced an aid package for improved meteorological services and projects that would allow Pacific Island countries to adapt to changing climatic conditions.

The Asian Development Bank approved financial assistance for Tuvalu Maritime Training Institute, which prepared young men for employment in the international merchant marine. Though overseas workers contributed some \$A 5 million (U.S. \$2.6 million) to the Tuvalu economy through remittances, the main source of government revenue during the year came from Tuvalu's .tv Internet franchise.

(BARRIE MACDONALD)

UGANDA

Area: 241,038 sq km (93,065 sq mi)
Population (2002 est.): 24,378,000
Capital: Kampala
Head of state and government: President Yoweri Museveni, assisted by Prime Minister Apolo Nsibambi

On Jan. 12, 2002, a public meeting arranged in Kampala by the Uganda People's Congress (UPC) without the government's consent was broken up by police using tear gas and live ammunition. A student journalist was killed, and several other people were injured. In April the government threatened to ban the UPC, but on May 9 Parliament instead passed a bill restricting the activities of political parties. Concerned international donor agencies said that the new law did not appear to advance the process of transition to democracy and urged the government to hold a more positive dialogue with those advocating greater freedom for political parties. Nevertheless, Pres. Yoweri Museveni gave his assent to the bill on June 2.

On two later occasions Museveni challenged donor agencies. Speaking at a meeting of the Commonwealth Parliamentary Association in Kampala on August 6, he accused the agencies of undue interference in the affairs of African states, and at the Earth Summit meeting in Johannesburg, S.Af., in September, he charged the IMF and nongovernmental organizations with inhibiting environmental improvements to Uganda.

These attempts to assert his country's sovereignty came at a time of difficulty for Uganda. The world price for coffee, the country's chief export commodity, had fallen so low that it was estimated that earnings from that source fell from about \$400 million in 1994–95 to \$90 million in 2001–02. Many farmers abandoned coffee in favour of the more profitable cocoa or vanilla, while many local exporters went out of business, the trade falling into the hands of foreigners. The Neumann Kaffee Gruppe began to plant a 2,512-ha (6,280-ac) coffee farm that would employ 6,000 workers. Attempts were made to increase profits from coffee sales by processing the beans before export and by seeking new markets in China and the Middle East. To boost cocoa production the government provided planting materials to farmers.

Operations by the rebel Lord's Resistance Army (LRA) in the north caused grave concern. In March the government launched Operation Iron Fist, aimed at putting an end to the rebellion. After The Sudan had given Uganda permission for its troops to pursue the LRA into southern Sudan, the two countries agreed that neither government would support rebels against the other. By the middle of the year, however, the LRA was once more operating in strength inside Uganda, and the need to divert troops to resist the incursion meant that cattle raiders in the northeastern district of Karamoja were able to range freely.

Uganda's military operations against the Democratic Republic of the Congo, already considerably reduced, came nearer to a conclusion when Pres. José Eduardo dos Santos of Angola chaired discussions between the presidents of Uganda and Congo. In September Uganda withdrew more than 2,000 of its troops, with the rest—1,000 in all—remaining until its western border was secure.

An appeal by the family and friends of Idi Amin for the former president to be allowed to return in peace to Uganda was flatly rejected by the government in May. (KENNETH INGHAM)

UKRAINE

Area: 603,700 sq km (233,100 sq mi)
Population (2002 est.): 48,120,000
Capital: Kiev
Chief of state: President Leonid Kuchma
Head of government: Prime Ministers Anatoly Kinakh and, from November 21, Viktor Yanukovich

The year 2002 in Ukraine was notable for a political impasse that followed the parliamentary election of March 31. Voting took part in two stages: the election of 225 deputies based on party lists by proportional representation and the election of a further 225 in one-seat constituencies. In the former, Our Ukraine, a democratic coalition led by former prime minister Viktor Yushchenko, won 23.6% of the vote (70 seats), the Communists 20% (59 seats), and For a United Ukraine, the party endorsed by Pres. Leonid Kuchma, 11.8% (36 seats). Three other parties received more than 6% of the vote: the Yuliya Tymoshenko Bloc, the Socialist Party, and the Social Democratic Party.

In single-mandate constituencies, however, For a United Ukraine, bolstered by the official media, won 66 seats, and 18 independent deputies were persuaded to join its ranks. Our Ukraine won 42 seats, the Communists 7, and the Social Democratic Party 5. Ultimately then, For a United Ukraine had 119 deputies and Our Ukraine 113, with 66 Communist deputies, 23 for the Tymoshenko Bloc, and 23 for the Socialists. The U.S. criticized the elections and the favouritism shown to progovernment parties through the use of official facilities and the media.

Four blocs—Our Ukraine, Tymoshenko, the Socialist, and Communist parties—protested what they saw as the government's manipulation of the election results and the use of bribery and intimidation by the government during the election. Volodymyr Lytvyn, leader

© AFP 2002, by Sergei Supinsky

An antigovernment demonstrator in Kiev punches at an effigy of Ukrainian Pres. Leonid Kuchma on September 24.

Lviv air show on July 27, when a fighter jet crashed shortly after takeoff, killing 76 people and injuring more than 100. (*See* DISASTERS.)

(DAVID R. MARPLES)

UNITED ARAB EMIRATES

Area: 83,600 sq km (32,280 sq mi)
Population (2002 est.): 3,550,000
Capital: Abu Dhabi
Chief of state: President Sheikh Zayid ibn Sultan Al Nahyan
Head of government: Prime Minister Sheikh Maktum ibn Rashid al-Maktum

of For a United Ukraine, maintained that his party had won the election. The outcome initially was the virtual equal division of the new legislature into two blocs: pro-government and the opposition.

The opposition grew even more incensed at the election of Lytvyn as speaker and two other pro-Kuchma candidates—Hennady Vasilyev (For a United Ukraine) and Oleksandr Zinchenko (Social Democratic Party)— as his deputies. Also controversial was the president's appointment in mid-June of well-known oligarch Viktor Medvedchuk as the new head of the presidential administration.

The opposition staged major antigovernment demonstrations on September 16 and 24, but Kuchma made it clear to opposition leaders that he planned to step down as president in 2004. On October 8 Lytvyn announced a majority bloc of pro-government deputies in the legislature (231 members), but demonstrations continued on October 12 and 19. The opposition put forward a motion to impeach the president should he refuse to step down.

Revelations from the incident in which tapes made in 2000 by former presidential bodyguard Mykola Melnychenko allegedly caught President Kuchma agreeing to the elimination of Georgy Gongadze, a dissident journalist, continued to have repercussions in 2002. On September 14 the prosecutor general declared that Gongadze's mur-

der was politically motivated and that an investigation would be carried out together with international experts. In the spring the parliamentary commission investigating the tapes declared that it had uncovered a conversation between Kuchma and the head of a state arms-exporting company in which the president agreed to sell $100 million worth of weapons to Iraq in contravention of the 1990 UN Security Council resolution banning such sales. Accusations broadened in April to include Kuchma's alleged approval of the sale to Iraq of Kolchuga radar systems (which could detect stealth bombers). The Ukrainian government denied these allegations.

Ukraine continued to show impressive economic growth. Industrial output was reportedly up by 14.2% in 2001, and gross domestic product grew by 4.1% in 2002. On the other hand, a government report of August indicated that some 13 million people (about 27%) were living below an official poverty line of $33 per month. This poverty was particularly acute in the western region of Transcarpathia and in Crimea, where the Tatar population had resettled in large numbers in recent years.

The year was marked by industrial and military accidents, especially in the Donets Basin coal mines, perhaps the most dangerous workplace in the world. World attention also focused on Ukraine following a disaster at the

Sheikh Hamdan ibn Zayid Al Nahyan, the United Arab Emirates (U.A.E.) minister of state for foreign affairs and son of the president, made an official visit to Tehran on May 26–27, 2002, seeking to ameliorate the tension that existed between his country and Iran. Relations had been tense for more than a decade, partly because of a dispute over control of three small islands in the Persian Gulf. This visit helped clear the air between the two Gulf neighbours. The islands dispute was not resolved, but it was not mentioned publicly during the visit. In June a 70-member delegation of Dubai businessmen visited Tehran to discuss increased U.A.E.-Iranian trade.

The U.A.E. government worked closely with the United States to combat terrorism by taking steps in banking and law enforcement designed to help close channels that might be used by al-Qaeda and other international terrorists. The U.A.E. president, however, expressed opposition to U.S. use of force against Iraq, saying in an October 2002 interview that "war never solves a problem." The government also expressed its dismay at Israeli incursions against Palestinians in the West Bank and called on the U.S. to help resolve the situation. The year saw informal boycotts of American products to protest U.S. support of Israel.

In May 2002 the U.A.E. selected Occidental Petroleum and a French company as new partners in the huge Dolphin gas project, which would involve an international pipeline from Qatar to the U.A.E.

(WILLIAM A. RUGH)

UNITED KINGDOM

Area: 244,101 sq km (94,248 sq mi)
Population (2002 est.): 60,178,000
Capital: London
Chief of state: Queen Elizabeth II
Head of government: Prime Minister Tony Blair

Domestic Affairs. The year 2002 was noteworthy as the Golden Jubilee of Queen Elizabeth II (*see* BIOGRAPHIES), who had ascended to the throne in 1952. The two months of official celebrations, however, were preceded by the deaths of her sister, Princess Margaret, and their mother, Queen Elizabeth, the Queen Mother (*see* OBITUARIES), and were followed by a controversial court case toward year's end.

In November the queen faced criticism for having held back evidence in the trial of Paul Burrell, a former butler to Diana, princess of Wales, the queen's former daughter-in-law who had died in 1997. Burrell had been charged with the theft of some of Diana's possessions after her death. Shortly before he was to give evidence at his trial—evidence that was widely expected to be embarrassing to the royal family—the queen disclosed that Burrell had told her at the time that he was looking after some of Diana's effects. Once this information had been made known to the court, the trial collapsed. Although the queen was largely absolved from personal criticism, the event triggered a national debate about whether British monarchs should continue to be beyond the reach of the courts and police inquiries. After a series of controversies in previous years, this one added pressure on the monarchy to make further accommodation to the modern age.

The year was no less turbulent for Prime Minister Tony Blair. (*See* BIOGRAPHIES.) He remained the commanding figure in British politics, but he faced economic difficulties, troubles inside his own government, tensions with the Labour Party's traditional trade union allies, and a widespread popular perception that public services such as health, education, and transport had not improved since he took office in 1997.

Two cabinet ministers resigned following intense criticism of their performance in office. On May 28 Stephen Byers stood down as secretary of state for transport, local government, and the regions. He was blamed for continuing troubles on Britain's railways, which most travelers regarded as having deteriorated since they were privatized in 1996. Events came to a head when Byers's former press secretary alleged that Byers had misled the House of Commons. Although Byers refuted the allegations, he eventually resigned, admitting that he would "damage the government" if he stayed in office. In the reshuffle that followed, Blair appointed Paul Boateng as Britain's first black cabinet minister. Boateng became chief secretary to the treasury—in effect, the deputy of Gordon Brown, the chancellor of the Exchequer.

On October 23 Estelle Morris resigned as education secretary. Like Byers, she had faced weeks of pressure, in her case

Queen Elizabeth II and her husband, Prince Philip, ride in the State Carriage during celebrations in June marking the queen's Golden Jubilee.

over a variety of specific problems ranging from errors in the marking of A-level examinations (the tests used to allocate university places) to severe delays in criminal records checks on school employees. (The checks had been ordered following the deaths of two young girls and the arrest of a part-time teacher and school janitor for their murder.) When Morris, herself a former teacher, resigned, she made the unusual admission for a front-rank politician that she was "not good at dealing with the modern media" and, more generally, "not as effective as I should be, or as effective as you [Blair] need me to be."

Internal Labour Party matters caused Blair some concern through the year. Against a backdrop of declining membership—down by almost a third since 1997, from 405,000 to 280,000 in 2002—the party suffered severe financial problems. On January 2 the General, Municipal and Boilermakers' Union, one of the largest trade unions (traditionally Labour's biggest sources of income), announced that it would reduce its donations to the party by £2 million (£1 = about $1.58) over five years, in protest against the increasing use of private management in the public sector. Other large unions followed suit. Labour's attempts to compensate by seeking money from the private sector backfired when, on May 12, it was disclosed that the party had received money from Richard Desmond, the proprietor of the *Daily Express* tabloid newspaper and publisher of a number of pornographic magazines.

Against this backdrop, the Conservatives might have expected strong advances as Britain's main opposition party. In fact, the party remained well behind in the opinion polls, and its leader, Iain Duncan Smith, found it difficult to make headway. Opinion polls asking who would make the best prime minister found that he trailed far behind Blair and even behind Charles Kennedy, the leader of the Liberal Democrats. On July 23 Duncan Smith sacked David Davis as Conservative Party chairman and replaced him with Theresa May, the first woman to hold the post, in an attempt to revive the party's fortunes.

May and Duncan Smith sought to assert their authority over a party increasingly divided between modernizers and traditionalists. The modernizers wanted an active strategy to secure more women and ethnic minority Conservative MPs and to end the party's hostility toward unmarried and gay couples and single parents; traditionalists largely opposed

these plans. The leader and the chairman appeared to side with the modernizers when, on July 29, they welcomed the acknowledgement by Alan Duncan, the deputy foreign affairs spokesman, that he was gay. He was the first Conservative MP ever to volunteer such a statement. At the party's annual conference, May said that the Conservatives had to shed their image as the "nasty" party; Duncan Smith said the party needed to come to terms with "the way life in Britain is lived today, and not the way it was lived 20 years ago."

Less than a month later, however, Duncan Smith upset the modernizers when he committed his party to opposing government plans to allow unmarried and gay couples to apply to adopt children. One member of Duncan Smith's shadow cabinet resigned, and one in four Conservative MPs failed to support the party line in a vote in Parliament on November 4. The following day Duncan Smith delivered a short speech to the media in which he said, "A small group of my parliamentary colleagues have decided consciously to undermine my leadership." He concluded, "My message is simple: unite or die."

One major piece of social reform was unveiled on July 10 when Home Secretary David Blunkett announced that cannabis (marijuana) would be downgraded from a "class B" to a "class C" drug. Although possession of the drug would technically remain a criminal offense, in practice those in possession of small quantities would no longer be prosecuted. Blunkett announced that this change would free police forces to devote more resources to fighting drug dealers and the users of "hard" drugs such as heroin and cocaine.

Economic Affairs. For the second successive year, growth in the British economy slowed, declining to less than 2%, but fears of a recession, prompted by weaknesses in the global economy, did not materialize. Unemployment remained broadly stable throughout 2002, at just over 5% (according to the definition set by the International Labour Organization), while inflation remained subdued at around 2%. The Bank of England maintained its main "repo" rate at 4% throughout the year. This historically low rate contributed to a sharp rise in house prices, which at the end of 2002 were on average almost 30% higher than a year earlier.

London's stock market fared less well, reflecting both the low rate of economic growth and turbulence on Wall Street.

For the third successive year, share prices on December 31 were lower than those of 12 months earlier. This in turn put pressure on pension funds. A number of large companies dropped their commitment to link pensions to retiring employees to their final salary; henceforth, pensions would depend on the value of the underlying fund.

For the government the clearest negative impact of the economic slowdown was on the public finances. In his annual budget Brown forecast that the government deficit would reach £11 billion in the fiscal year ending March 2003. By November he had raised this forecast to £20 billion. He also said that the strength of Britain's underlying public finances meant that he would be able to fill the gap by borrowing more rather than by raising taxes further.

In his budget speech Brown did announce future tax increases totaling £8.3 billion a year, mainly to pay for increased spending on the National Health Service (NHS). At the general election in 2001, Labour had promised to raise the budget of the NHS, as a percentage of national income, to the average European level. After leading a debate on the alternatives, Brown rejected a greater reliance on private medical care or new forms of social insurance. He argued that a nationally funded service, free at the point of use, remained the fairest and most efficient means of funding and organizing the NHS, notwithstanding criticisms that the NHS had become one of the worst health services in the developed world. Brown linked the injection of extra money to a program of reforms designed to correct the NHS's organizational weaknesses.

Foreign Affairs. Throughout 2002 Blair worked closely with U.S. Pres. George W. Bush on strategy regarding Iraq. In part, this represented a continuation of a partnership between the two countries that had begun in the 1990s with British aircraft help in patrolling the "no-fly" zone in Iraq south of the 33rd parallel. During 2002 the prime minister expressed his willingness to commit British troops to fight alongside American troops in a possible military action in Iraq—if necessary without UN approval. Blair, however, made clear his own strong preference for any such action to be authorized by the UN Security Council—a case he put strongly to Bush when the two men met in Washington on September 7. On September 24 Blair published a 50-page dossier setting out evidence of Iraq's accumulation of weapons of mass destruction. The report argued that Iraq had "military plans" for the use of chemical and biological weapons, even against its own population. It also said that Iraqi leader Saddam Hussein could have a nuclear weapon within two years if he could obtain weapons-grade material from abroad.

Britain's relations with France deteriorated in October following a deal between French Pres. Jacques Chirac and German Chancellor Gerhard Schröder over the future of the European Union's (EU's) Common Agricultural Policy (CAP). Blair blamed Chirac for insisting on only limited reforms to the CAP, which, Blair argued, would continue to mean that around half the EU's budget would continue to be spent on agriculture and that poorer countries would continue to be denied free access to European markets. At an angry exchange between the two men in Brussels on October 25, Blair accused Chirac of reneging on previous commitments to reform the CAP and open Europe up to global food markets. Chirac retorted by calling Blair "very rude" and by postponing a summit meeting that the two men had planned to hold in December.

One reason for Blair's anger was that he had set great store by free trade in helping to alleviate poverty, especially in Africa. He wanted to open Europe's markets to more food imports from the Third World. At the Group of Eight (G-8) summit meeting in Canada in June, Blair was one of the prime movers in an agreement to support the New Partnership for Africa's Development. He also announced at the G-8 summit that British aid to Africa would rise from £632 million to £1 billion by 2006.

Northern Ireland. On October 14 Northern Ireland's government and Assembly were suspended for the fourth time since their establishment in 1998. John Reid, the U.K.'s Northern Ireland secretary, announced the suspension in the wake of police raids on the offices at Stormont (the home of the Assembly in Belfast) of Sinn Fein, the republican party with close links to the Irish Republican Army (IRA).

The raids, which took place on October 4, led to Sinn Fein's head of administration being charged with having documents likely to be of use to terrorists. The police said that computer disks obtained during the raids contained large amounts of sensitive information, including the personal details of the senior British army officer in Northern Ireland, Lieut. Gen. Sir Alistair Irwin. First Minister David Trimble, of the Ulster Unionist Party, threatened to withdraw his ministers from the Assembly unless action was taken against Sinn Fein. Reid's decision to suspend the administration was designed in part to forestall the collapse of the Assembly and to allow time for tempers to cool.

The suspension brought to a head tensions that had been simmering for some months. On March 18 the police disclosed that a break-in had taken place at the Castlereagh Police Station in Belfast, which had been regarded as one of the most secure police stations in the world. The police accused Sinn Fein of being responsible for the break-in. With Sinn Fein on the defensive, its IRA allies sought to regain the initiative. On April 8 the IRA announced that it had placed a second tranche of arms "beyond use." Although no details were given, Gen. John de Chastelain, the independent international arms inspector, described the event as "substantial."

Five days later Gerry Adams, the head of Sinn Fein, told a rally of 2,500 republicans in Dublin that they had to "reach out to make peace with those we have hurt and with those who have hurt us." This paved the way for an IRA statement on July 17 apologizing to the "noncombatant" victims of its 30-year terrorist campaign against British rule. Trimble, however, accused Sinn Fein and the IRA of hypocrisy, pretending to embrace the peace process but continuing to retain the means to return to violence.

Although the five-year-old cease-fire by the main paramilitary groups remained in force, 2002 saw a number of local sectarian clashes. In January 500 Protestants rioted in north Belfast against Roman Catholic families walking through their streets to take their children to the Catholic Holy Cross school. In April a group of loyalists attacked the police in Belfast with gasoline bombs. Later that month dissident republicans took the blame for a bomb blast at Northern Ireland's police training college. In May and June rioting moved to east Belfast. It took negotiations between two historic enemies—Adams and David Ervine, leader of the Progressive Unionist Party—to cool tempers.

Following the suspension of the Executive and the Assembly in October, Blair made it clear that further progress toward peaceful, devolved politics in Northern Ireland would require the IRA to disband. Adams responded by saying that he could envisage a time when the IRA did not exist, but it would not be forced to meet a deadline imposed by London. On October 30 the IRA announced that it had broken off contacts with Chastelain, as a protest against Blair's stance. On October 24, however, Blair had appointed Paul Murphy to succeed Reid as Northern Ireland secretary. Murphy had been a more junior Northern Ireland minister between 1997 and 1999 and had played a leading role in the negotiations that led to the Good Friday Agreement in 1998.

(PETER KELLNER)

A masked gunman is among the group of loyalists that gathered in central Belfast, N. Ire., on July 12 to commemorate King William III's victory over former king James II, a Roman Catholic, in the Battle of the Boyne on July 11, 1690.

UNITED STATES

Area: 9,363,364 sq km (3,615,215 sq mi), including 204,446 sq km of inland water but excluding the 155,534 sq km of the Great Lakes that lie within U.S. boundaries

Population (2002 est.): 287,602,000; based on 2000 unadjusted census results

Capital: Washington, D.C.

Head of state and government: President George W. Bush

In the decade following the collapse of the Soviet Union, the reign of the United States as the world's sole superpower was largely positive, with little apparent downside. The U.S. military created a Pax Americana, its might virtually unchallenged, complementing a dependable U.S. economic engine that seemed to pull the global economy through good times and bad. In 2002, however, Americans came to understand that leadership was costly and often involved disquieting risk.

The year started with the U.S. determinedly addressing fallout from the Sept. 11, 2001, terrorist attacks and apparently emerging from a mild economic recession. By year-end, however, both external and internal problems appeared far more complicated. Confrontation with the al-Qaeda terrorist network produced modest progress, but the overall terrorism conflict actually expanded; the U.S. was preparing for a potential military assault on Iraq and attempting to defuse a nuclear crisis with North Korea. The national economy, plagued by war jitters and corporate accounting irregularities, stalled in midrecovery, with stock prices plunging and unemployment edging upward, which threw the federal budget back into long-term deficit.

Contributing to the national malaise were a series of crises suffered by major American institutions. Virtually unprecedented revelations of dishonesty in corporate executive suites, accompanied by a wave of major business bankruptcies, shook confidence in the foundations of U.S. economic prosperity. A sexual-abuse scandal rocked the Roman Catholic Church. (*See* RELIGION: *Sidebar.*) In addition, the competency of the CIA and the FBI was questioned during inquiries into intelligence lapses before September 11.

Nevertheless, Pres. George W. Bush managed to solidify his position with the American people, in large part owing to his purposeful handling of the "war on terrorism." He announced a new policy favouring preemptive strikes against increased terrorist threats, expanding the national right of self-defense, and his allies steered several measures through Congress that increased U.S. preparedness. The U.S. Senate, however, controlled by Democrats, delayed approval of several administration initiatives, including terrorism-related bills. Bush took the issue into the midterm election in November, and his party regained total control of Congress. (*See* Sidebar.)

War on Terrorism. In his January state of the union address, President Bush effectively broadened the antiterrorist struggle by declaring that nations attempting to produce "weapons of mass destruction" were part of the world terrorist threat. He specifically named Iraq, Iran, and North Korea as "an axis of evil" developing nuclear, chemical, or biological weaponry, and he challenged other governments to confront these states as well. The speech set the tone for a year in which the new terrorist threat dominated foreign relations as well as U.S. domestic politics.

Dramatic developments in the war on terrorism were rare during 2002. U.S. forces led a successful March coalition military effort in Afghanistan, dubbed Operation Anaconda, that claimed an estimated 500 Taliban and al-Qaeda

dead. The top al-Qaeda and Taliban leaders, Osama bin Laden and Mullah Mohammad Omar, remained at large throughout the year, however, and rumours of Bin Laden's death were never confirmed. Despite plentiful warnings and alarms, there were no new terrorist attacks on American soil. The perpetrator of anthrax attacks through U.S. postal facilities, which killed five Americans in late 2001, was never identified, nor was any connection with the September 11 events established. Nonetheless, a political consensus developed behind the main elements of the president's drive to increase domestic precautions against terrorist attacks—to beef up military preparedness and to lead the world response to the threat.

Bush proposed a 14% increase—to $379 billion annually—for defense spending, the largest increase in two decades, and he sought a doubling of expenditures for homeland security, to $37.7 billion. Some proposals became entangled in politics. Numerous U.S. allies, including top officials of the European Union and France, faulted Bush's approach as excessively unilateral and jingoistic. Two key parts of Bush's antiterrorism legislative package—establishment of a new federal Department of Homeland Security and the provision of federal terrorism reinsurance—became stalled in the U.S. Senate owing to objections from labour unions and trial lawyers. They were belatedly approved only after the

In the opening ceremony of the Winter Olympic Games in Salt Lake City, Utah, in February, American athletes and police officers and firefighters from New York City carry the American flag that was flying at the World Trade Center on Sept. 11, 2001, into the stadium.

AP/Wide World Photos

November election, along with a measure creating a bipartisan commission to study intelligence failures prior to the September 11 attacks. Most administration initiatives, however, including a major bioterrorism defense bill that increased vaccine stockpiles and protected water and food supplies, were swiftly put into place.

Congress also accepted Bush's expanded definition of the war on terrorism, including his call for a "regime change" in Iraq. In October, only days before national elections, both chambers overwhelmingly approved a resolution authorizing the use of force against Saddam Hussein and Iraq. After an extended delay led by Russia, France, and other countries, the United Nations also agreed to demand Iraqi compliance with inspections to ensure that weapons prohibited in the 1991 peace agreement were not being developed. The inspectors were not scheduled to report their findings until early 2003, but by year's end a U.S.-dominated coalition had more than 100,000 troops deployed or en route to the region.

Domestic Issues. Election-year maneuvering had always had an impact on U.S. federal legislation, but the close division in the U.S. House and Senate made 2002 notable for bills that failed to become law. Only 2 of 13 final appropriation bills were cleared by year's end, for example, and partisan gridlock became a major issue in November balloting.

Both chambers of Congress approved separate energy bills during the year, but conference negotiators failed to agree on a compromise; the Republican-controlled House insisted on oil exploration in Alaska's Arctic National Wildlife Refuge, a measure opposed by environmentalists. A major bankruptcy reform measure, approved by both the House and the Senate in 2001, also died over a partisan argument on the treatment of bankrupt abortion protesters. Congress also failed to agree on prescription drug benefits for Medicare recipients, on denying tax benefits to companies incorporating in offshore tax havens, on reforming medical malpractice liability, and on

reauthorizing a successful 1996 welfare-reform law.

Political considerations were apparent in legislation affecting corporate fraud and farm subsidies. Early in the year, amid early indications that Republicans would suffer from the 2001 Enron bankruptcy and other corporate malfeasance, Democrats pressed for punitive measures to address business accounting problems, corporate governance, and securities-law fraud. Public opinion polls showed, however, that neither political party had an advantage on the issue of corporate dishonesty; Congress easily approved a compromise bill tightening securities regulation and establishing an oversight board for the accounting industry. In renewing farm legislation, Republicans initially resisted a proposal to increase agricultural subsidies dramatically. A $248 billion, six-year bill was approved, however, after party strategists noted that most federal payments would go to states that had voted for Bush in 2000.

Two measures regulating elections also became law, but their impact was in doubt. A campaign finance reform bill was approved that banned unrestricted "soft-money" donations from corporations and labour unions to national political parties and regulated campaign advertising by outside groups. The bill was quickly challenged in federal court, however, as violative of First Amendment free-speech protections. Critics noted that the law continued to allow soft-money donations to other groups, including state politi-

cal parties, and reform supporters complained that Federal Election Commission members had begun watering down the reform via regulations. Congress later approved a long-delayed reform law, inspired by year 2000 problems in Florida and elsewhere, setting national standards for voting rules and equipment. The law envisioned $3.9 billion in federal aid to states to meet the standards, but Congress failed to appropriate those funds.

After Republicans made unexpected gains in November, Democratic House Minority Leader Richard Gephardt of Missouri, a moderate who had sided with the president on national security issues, resigned his leadership post. Gephardt later announced his candidacy for president in 2004. He was replaced by Democratic Rep. Nancy Pelosi of California. The Senate Republican leader, Trent Lott of Mississippi, was forced to resign his post in a bizarre controversy that started at a 100th birthday party in December for Republican Sen. Strom Thurmond of South Carolina. Lott implied to the crowd that the U.S. might have been better off if Thurmond, who had run as an archsegregationist, had been elected president in 1948 instead of Harry S. Truman. Criticism of Lott's remarks started slowly but snowballed, and he resigned as presumptive Senate majority leader two weeks later.

FBI statistics indicated that the incidence of serious crime in the U.S. began inching up again in 2002 following nine years of decline. The figures showed that while violent crimes dropped during the first six months of the year, crimes against property rose significantly, and the result was an overall 1.3% increase in seven index crimes. The body of former intern Chandra Levy, victim of the most notorious crime of 2001, was found in a Washington, D.C., park in May. She had apparently been strangled, but authorities brought no charges in the case. The U.S. congressman from her Modesto, Calif., district, Gary Condit, who had admitted to a relationship with Levy, was defeated in his reelection bid in the Democratic primary.

Rep. Nancy Pelosi of California celebrates her election in November as Democratic leader in the House of Representatives with Rep. Richard Gephardt of Missouri, whom she is replacing.

AP/Wide World Photos

The national capital area was again traumatized during 2002 by apparently random sniper shooting attacks that killed 10 people and wounded 3 in Maryland, Virginia, and Washington, D.C., over a 20-day period. The crime spree ended on October 24 with the arrest of John Allen Muhammad, a former army infantryman, and his teenage companion, John Lee Malvo. The pair, later named suspects in other crimes in Alabama, Louisiana, Arizona, and Georgia, apparently operated out of a 1990 Chevrolet Caprice that had been modified to allow rifle shots from a hiding place in the car's trunk. (*See* LAW, CRIME, AND LAW ENFORCEMENT: *Crime.*)

The Economy. For most of the previous decade, while other countries were suffering economic hard times, the U.S. economy had continued to expand, providing a market and needed economic activity that benefited global economic health. In 2002, however, the U.S. economic beacon flickered markedly, the strain aggravated by a declining stock market, fears over war and terrorism, government uncertainty, a historic wave of corporate dishonesty, and a near breakdown in the system of regulation that framed American economic success.

The economic landscape was littered with casualties. Technically, the U.S. economy continued to expand during 2002, although anemically, but in little more than a year, 6 of the 10 largest corporate bankruptcies in U.S. history were recorded. Widespread accounting irregularities were reported, and Arthur Andersen LLP, one of the "Big Five" accounting firms, went out of business after its criminal conviction on obstruction of justice charges regarding the Enron investigation. (*See* ECONOMIC AFFAIRS: *Business Overview:* Sidebar.) Some 250 companies, a record by far, were forced to restate their earnings. Prominent businessmen were arrested, and some were led off in handcuffs, doing the "perp walk" for news cameras. The nation's stock markets declined for the third consecutive demoralizing year. At year's end, as problems mounted, President Bush replaced his economic team leadership, including the chairman of the Securities and Exchange Commission, Harvey Pitt (*see* BIOGRAPHIES), in search of a fresh start.

Some analysts blamed the debacle on a hangover from the 10-year expansion, the longest in U.S. history, that ended in March 2001 shortly after the technology-dominated dot-com bubble was

British Prime Minister Tony Blair and U.S. Pres. George W. Bush appear together at a press conference in Crawford, Texas, in April.

deflated. Alan Greenspan, chairman of the Board of Governors of the Federal Reserve System, however, attributed the stock decline to "infectious greed" that corrupted even those who should police it: analysts, credit-rating agencies, and auditors. Others placed the blame on the rise of incentives for managers, especially stock options.

As the year began, the national economy appeared to be rebounding smartly from a short-lived recession and adverse consequences of the September 2001 terrorist assault. Both interest rates and inflation remained low, and the economy expanded at a healthy 5% rate in the first quarter. Although business investment contracted, consumer spending, especially for homes and automobiles, remained vigorous, spurred by low interest rates. In April, however, the continuing wave of devastating corporate business news sent equity markets reeling. The Dow Jones Industrial average dropped from 10,600 to 7,200 over the next six months.

Because the U.S. economy had proved so resilient in the past, government response was muted. The recession helped produce a federal deficit for fiscal 2002 of $159 billion, the first government red ink in four years. Federal Reserve officials had little room to maneuver: they had lowered interest rates 11 times in 2001, and they dropped the key federal funds rate another one-half point, to 1.25%, as markets deteriorated. Following extensive discussion, Congress approved a corporate fraud reform law, known as the Sarbanes-Oxley bill, that provided for accounting standard oversight, banned auditors from supplying other services, and required audit committee board members to be independent company directors. The law also required corporate chief executive and financial officers to attest personally, with their signature, to the accuracy of their financial reports. For his part President Bush replaced his treasury secretary and his top economic adviser.

Foreign Policy. U.S. allies overwhelmingly supported the 2001 incursion into Afghanistan, but the Bush administration's stepped-up aggressiveness toward perceived terrorist threats in 2002, targeted initially at Iraq, attracted numerous skeptics. Especially in Europe, critics complained about U.S. arrogance and unilateralism. The new U.S. line was formalized in September in a document, "National Security Strategy of the United States—2002," that promised U.S. preemptive removal of weapons of mass destruction from those deemed to be a national enemy. "The gravest danger our nation faces lies at the crossroads of radicalism and technology....In the new world we have entered, the only path to peace and security is the path of action," the Bush administration declared.

Only a handful of countries, including Britain and Australia, endorsed the preemption policy openly. Reaction in France and Germany was hostile. German Chancellor Gerhard Schröder, running for reelection, repeatedly promised that his administration would never join any U.S. war effort against Iraq. President Bush early on demanded "regime change" in Iraq, but following domestic and international criticism, he appeared before the United Nations in September to urge multilateral support for merely disarming Iraq in accordance with agreements made following the 1991 Persian Gulf War. After an uncomfortable delay, the UN Security Council unanimously approved a strong resolution demanding that Saddam Hussein admit UN weapons inspectors with intrusive authority. Both France and Russia made it clear, however, that their involvement in any potential military action against Iraq would require specific UN approval.

Hussein's government eventually agreed to—and did—provide a catalog of facilities, products, and scientists and submit to an inspection regime. At year's end the U.S.-Iraqi face-off intensified as inspectors examined Iraqi sites. Meanwhile, both sides worked a clamorous public relations strategy, with U.S. authorities proclaiming that Iraqis were violating their obligations by resisting enforcement of U.S.-led no-fly zones and Iraqis insisting that inspections had found nothing incriminating.

A decade-old border conflict between India and Pakistan, two nuclear powers, threatened to escalate into open combat at midyear. At one point the two populous countries had one million troops massed on their common border. Top Bush administration officials, including Secretary of Defense Donald Rumsfeld (see BIOGRAPHIES), led an international mediation effort that defused the immediate crisis.

The Bush administration's tilt toward Israel in its half-century conflict with Palestinian interests—another issue dividing the U.S. from much of Europe—became more pronounced during the year. After a particularly bloody series of terrorist bombings that killed more than 30 Israelis in three days, the government of Ariel Sharon mounted a determined incursion into Palestinian territory. President Bush urged moderation on Israel but pointedly continued to refuse to meet with Palestinian leader Yasir Arafat or to intervene decisively to stop the Israeli action.

U.S. relations with Russia under Pres. Vladimir Putin continued to improve. The two countries finally signed a delayed nuclear arms treaty reducing warheads on both sides. Nevertheless, U.S. exhortations failed to dissuade Russia from assisting Iran in weapons-capable nuclear-power projects.

In early fall, even as the U.S. was focusing diplomatic and military efforts on Iraq, the third axis of evil country lurched again into world headlines. Confronted with evidence that its scientists had been working on a uranium-enrichment program in apparent violation of a 1994 promise, North Korean officials freely admitted the violation and implied that they were working on nuclear weapons as well. Under the 1994 pact, negotiated in part by former U.S. president Jimmy Carter, North Korea had agreed to accept two light-water reactors and 500,000 tons of heavy fuel oil annually in exchange for a freeze on weapons-capable nuclear power. North Korean officials followed the admission with further breaches, expelling International Atomic Energy Agency inspectors, removing surveillance cameras and seals from key sites, and restarting a nuclear plant using plutonium-generating spent fuel rods.

Some analysts suggested that North Korean strongman Kim Jong Il was using a renewed nuclear threat to extort additional concessions from the West. North Korea, a land of scant resources, in recent years had devoted most of them to military purposes and depended on outside assistance in recent years to thwart famine, power shortages, and hardship for its 22 million citizens. Other analysts suggested that Kim, sensing that North Korea would be the next target of President Bush's campaign against the axis of evil, was arming himself with a nuclear deterrent. In any event, the Bush administration refused to negotiate with the North Koreans, and Rumsfeld pointedly warned that the Pentagon was prepared to fight a second war if Kim felt "emboldened" because of the world's preoccupation with Iraq.

North Korea had 500 Scud missiles, plus additional Nodong and Taepodong-2 ballistic missiles capable of reaching Japan, Alaska, and eastern Russia. Since signing the 1994 agreement, according to Western intelligence reports, North Korea had gained the capability of producing both chemical and biological weapons. In December former president Carter was awarded the Nobel Prize for Peace, in part for his work on the North Korea situation. (See NOBEL PRIZES.)

(DAVID C. BECKWITH)

DEVELOPMENTS IN THE STATES

A decade-long revenue boom for state governments came to an abrupt halt in 2002 after events conspired to produce the most drastic state fiscal crisis in a half century. After having expanded spending programs freely and cut taxes in sunny economic times, officials were forced to reverse course sharply during the year, raising revenue and reducing services on even essential programs across the board.

The hard economic times were exacerbated by continuing state struggles with the federal government, usually over which level should fund expensive initiatives such as those covering low-income persons' health coverage, election reform, education mandates, homeland security, and prescription drug costs. Although public education traditionally had been the purview of states, the year saw enactment of a significant new federal law addressing K–12 education, and federal courts approved state tax support for private schools. Those courts also banned state execution of the mentally impaired.

Forty-four states held regular legislative sessions during the year, and more than two dozen held special sessions, often to deal with budget problems.

Party Strengths. Republicans made notable gains in state legislative elections and edged ahead of Democrats in total state legislative seats for the first time in five decades. Democrats, however, continued to erode a recent GOP advantage in governorships, particularly in larger states. The net result was that the two major parties were at virtual parity nationwide at year's end.

After the new Congress assumed office in January 2003, Republicans would hold both state legislative chambers in 21 states, up from 17 before the election. Democrats would have control in 16 states, down from 18 in 2002. Twelve states were split, with neither party organizing both chambers. Nebraska had a nonpartisan legislature.

The incumbent party was turned out in half of the 36 gubernatorial elections

Sen. Paul Wellstone of Minnesota and his wife, Sheila, were killed when his campaign plane crashed on October 25.

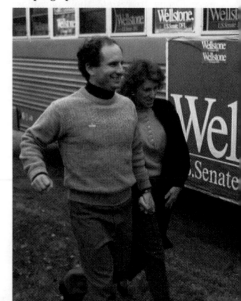

The U.S. 2002 Midterm Elections

The 2002 midterm elections proved that no generality in American politics was absolute. Although a first-term president's party had not gained ground in midterm elections since 1934, Republicans in 2002 increased their narrow margins in the U.S. House and regained control of the U.S. Senate with Pres. George W. Bush taking the point.

Though Democrats were perceived to have had the advantage early in the year as concerns over the sluggish national economy and a declining stock market unsettled voters, Bush's conduct regarding the "war on terrorism" was widely supported. Democrats were generally supportive of that effort and had attempted to remove security as an issue by focusing public attention on domestic issues, such as the establishment of a prescription drug benefit for senior citizens, the provision of additional federal help for education, and a slower phase-in period for Bush's 2001 tax-cut plan.

With control of the White House "bully pulpit," however, Republicans kept the focus on support for the popular president. During the year the Republican-controlled House passed dozens of Bush-approved bills, only to see them die in the Senate. When Bush attempted to set up a new umbrella Department of Homeland Security to coordinate domestic antiterrorism efforts, Democrats objected because the proposal allowed the administration to bypass civil-service protections for department employees. By accident or design the controversy was not settled before the election, and Democrats were widely criticized for blocking security efforts.

At one point Republicans appeared poised to replace a rising Democratic star, Sen. Robert Torricelli of New Jersey, who was admonished by his Senate colleagues following an ethics investigation into his campaign contributions and acceptance of personal gifts. Torricelli fell more than 10 points behind an inexperienced GOP challenger and abruptly quit the race only five weeks before the election. Democrats, however, were able to replace him with former senator Frank Lautenberg, 78, who won the seat handily.

Then, in late October, Sen. Paul Wellstone, a liberal Democrat who was expected to win a third term, was killed when his light plane crashed in northern Minnesota. (*See* OBITUARIES.) Democrats quickly settled on replacement candidate Walter Mondale, 74, a popular former senator and U.S. vice president. A nationally televised memorial service for Wellstone turned ugly, however, when Wellstone partisans booed conservative politicians in attendance, and Democrats were perceived to have turned the occasion into a political rally. As a result, support for Republican Norm Coleman surged.

Bush was unusually active on the campaign trail, barnstorming the country and effectively transforming local elections into referenda on his stewardship. By contrast, Democrats had difficulty settling on a common message. A notable split developed among prominent Democrats over scrapping the tax cuts to balance the federal budget; another appeared over challenging Bush's aggressive stance against Iraq.

On election day Republicans picked up six seats in the House, expanding their advantage to 229–206. More important, the GOP recorded a net gain of two Senate slots, including the Minnesota seat, to take control of that body. Sen. Mary Landrieu of Louisiana won a competitive runoff in December to retain her seat, which allowed Democrats to finish the year on an upbeat note. As a practical matter, however, the two parties would be at parity across the country when the new Congress was sworn in in 2003, but Republicans would enjoy control of the White House and both chambers of Congress.

(DAVID C. BECKWITH)

nationwide, and Democrats made modest gains overall. Republicans had a 27–21 advantage (with two independents) prior to November balloting. In 2003 the party lineup would be 26 Republicans and 24 Democrats. (*See* Sidebar.)

Government Structures, Powers. Efforts to limit the service of state officials, a popular cause in the 1990s, suffered setbacks during the year. Idaho voters endorsed a legislative initiative, and the state became the first to repeal a term-limit law. Oregon failed to overturn a late 2001 court decision invalidating that state's term limits.

Rhode Island and North Dakota reduced the size of their legislatures. In Rhode Island the House saw a reduction of 25% (from 100 to 75), while the Senate was reduced from 50 members to 38. The reduction in North Dakota was smaller, the number in the House moving from 98 to 94 and that in the Senate from 49 to 47.

Government Relations. Controversy over the appropriate balance of responsibilities between states and the federal government, always fluid in the U.S. federalist system, escalated during 2002. States continued to protest unfunded mandates from Washington and complained that promises of added federal funding had been broken. State officials also campaigned specifically for additional U.S. funds to combat the state fiscal crisis. They noted that, in the absence of federal help, state budget-cutting efforts—raising taxes and cutting spending—would actually aggravate problems caused by the lagging national economy. A measure to provide temporary assistance to states was approved by the U.S. Senate but died owing to opposition from the administration of Pres. George W. Bush.

States continued to complain about federal foot-dragging in homeland security reimbursement. President Bush proposed spending $3.5 billion to train local first responders, but Congress failed to appropriate the funds. Though Congress approved a law to clean up election procedures nationwide, no money was sent to states for new election machinery or for training the workers at the polls in compliance with the law.

Nevada Gov. Kenny C. Guinn became the first state chief executive to veto a U.S. presidential decision, having turned down an executive order to establish a nuclear-waste repository at Yucca Mountain, near Las Vegas, Nev. After Congress reversed the state action and reinstated the executive order, the repository battle moved to federal courts. In another federalism struggle, a federal judge enjoined efforts by the U.S. Department of Justice to overturn Oregon's unique assisted-suicide law, which had been approved by state voters twice in the 1990s.

Finances. Long-term trends and cyclic events combined to thrust states into

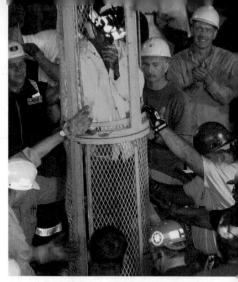

their most dramatic budget crisis since World War II. Revenues plunged as the national economy remained sluggish, and structural problems with state tax sources belatedly surfaced. Even as officials rushed to trim outlays, expenditures continued to rise owing to the escalating costs of medical, security, education, and other programs. The situation was aggravated by actions taken during the 1990s, when an economic bonanza allowed states to reduce tax rates and increase spending extensively.

Several tax sources continued to deteriorate during the year. States, having found it difficult to tax services—which played a growing role in the modern U.S. economy—experienced a lag in sales-tax revenue. In addition, corporate income taxes dropped owing to the increasingly sophisticated measures used by corporations to move profits to low-tax jurisdictions. Income taxes garnered from capital gains and the exercise of stock options dried up as capital markets edged lower. A survey by the National Governors Association in late 2002 declared that "nearly every state is in fiscal crisis," with a cumulative budget shortfall for the year of more than $40 billion.

With 49 states required to balance their budgets, officials moved to stanch the red ink mainly by cutting costs—freezing employee salaries, laying off employees, and cutting Medicaid. Twelve states increased higher-education tuition. Though some 30 states had created a "rainy-day fund" to weather economic hard times, those savings were used to cushion the immediate impact of the downturn. States also tapped funds from the 1998 settlement with tobacco companies to shore up revenues.

Most states resisted significant politically unpopular tax increases during the election year, although 19 states boosted cigarette levies. At year's end, however, the budget shortfalls in many states continued to accelerate, and fiscal experts predicted that tax-increase legislation was inevitable in many jurisdictions. In late December, California Gov. Gray Davis announced that the state's two-year deficit projection had been raised to just under $35 billion. State workers vowed to resist pay cuts and job losses, and conservative legislators declared that the shortfall was the result of profligate spending and promised to stop tax increases.

Health and Welfare. As state finances deteriorated, officials increasingly looked to Medicaid for savings. Outlays for the program, targeted at low-income individuals, rose more than 13%

owing to rising medical costs and additional enrollees, even as increasing numbers of middle-class Americans lost their health coverage. Many states responded by reducing medical reimbursements and tightening eligibility, measures that further roiled an embattled health care system.

Proposals for major reform were debated in several states, but progress was slow as states awaited relief from the federal government. Oregon voters turned down a referendum that would have established the nation's first universal health care program.

Education. A historic federal education law, which was titled No Child Left Behind, dramatically increased accountability requirements for states and their local school districts. The U.S. Education Department issued the regulations late in the year, however, and some states complained about inadequate direction and funding from Washington. At year's end several states were seeking temporary waivers from federal requirements, but critics viewed the law as a major step forward in improving public education. (*See* EDUCATION.)

In a landmark 5–4 decision, the U.S. Supreme Court declared that it was constitutional to utilize public funds to assist elementary and secondary students in private and even parochial schools. The ruling upheld a pilot "voucher" program in Cleveland, Ohio, and appeared to settle a key issue in providing additional choice in education. No new states joined Florida, Ohio, and Wisconsin in allowing private school assistance during the year, but the high-court ruling ensured that the idea would be widely considered in 2003.

Massachusetts voters joined California and Arizona in banning bilingual education, but Colorado rejected a similar measure. In Florida voters approved a measure limiting the number of pupils in a classroom. California endorsed funding for a new after-school enrichment program.

Law and Justice. Responding to perceived abuses, West Virginia, Pennsylvania, Mississippi, and Nevada approved new measures to reform their civil liability systems. Critics claimed that sizable jury awards in lawsuits brought by plaintiffs' trial lawyers were creating "jackpot justice" that distorted the economy, caused bankruptcies, and drove some lawsuit targets, including physicians, out of business. The new laws brought to 17 the number of states that had established a limit on punitive,

Three days after a wall leading into a flooded abandoned mine was breached, trapping nine miners in a coal mine near Quecreek, Pa., the ninth and final miner is safely rescued.

AP/Wide World Photos

or noneconomic, damage awards and boosted standards of proof in order to stabilize lawsuit risks. Voters in Arizona, Ohio, and Nevada rejected marijuana-liberalization proposals. The Nevada measure would have allowed possession of three ounces of the substance for personal use. A federal judge endorsed an antitrust suit settlement between the Bush administration, the Department of Justice, and Microsoft Corp., but intervening attorneys general in Massachusetts and West Virginia vowed to appeal, saying that the deal did not adequately address the software giant's alleged monopolistic practices.

In a controversial ruling, the U.S. Supreme Court told 20 states that they could no longer execute mentally retarded convicts. The court cited changing public standards, including action by several state legislatures to eliminate the death penalty for those with low IQs.

The high court decision did not quiet controversy over capital punishment. Maryland joined Illinois in imposing a moratorium on all executions pending a review of procedures. (*See* LAW, CRIME, AND LAW ENFORCEMENT: *Special Report.*)

Energy and Environment. The bankruptcy of energy giant Enron Corp., a politically active backer of deregulatory policies, helped stall the spread of electricity deregulation in state legislatures. No new states were added in 2002 to the 26 that had initiated a free market for electricity in previous years. (*See* ECONOMIC AFFAIRS: *Sidebar.*) Oregon voters rejected a proposal to require labeling of genetically modified foods.

(DAVID C. BECKWITH)

URUGUAY

Area: 176,215 sq km (68,037 sq mi)
Population (2002 est.): 3,383,000
Capital: Montevideo
Head of state and government: President
Jorge Batlle Ibáñez

Unfortunately, 2002 was a year of worsening economic crisis for Uruguay. The most negative effect on the economy was produced by a freeze on deposits in Argentina following the collapse of the Argentine peso when that government abandoned its convertibility plan, which pegged its currency one-to-one with the U.S. dollar. This forced many Argentines to withdraw dollars from their bank accounts in the traditionally safe haven of Montevideo. The subsequent collapse of two banks in Uruguay had many Uruguayans fearing for the safety of their banking system. The result was that in the first seven months of the year, Uruguay lost about 80% of its foreign reserves. The country's sovereign debt had abruptly declined from investment grade to junk status by the beginning of May. Gross domestic product fell 7.8% in the first half of the year and was expected to contract 11% for the year as a whole. Uruguay's GDP had declined some 20% since 1999. Unemployment climbed to a record 19%. Inflation, which had been a mere 3.59% in 2001, hit 24% by September and was expected to increase to about 40% by the end of the year.

Pres. Jorge Batlle Ibáñez tried to contain the damage but was obliged to accept the resignation of his minister of the economy, Alberto Bensión, and replace him with the more highly respected Alejandro Atchugarry. The goodwill Batlle enjoyed in Washington helped him obtain a $1.5 billion bridge loan from the U.S. to keep the banking system solvent until more than $3 billion in funds could arrive from the International Monetary Fund, the World Bank, and the Inter-American Development Bank.

Politically, the left appeared to be gaining strength as a result of the economic crisis. By October, Tabaré Vázquez Rosas, leader of the leftist Broad Front coalition, had seen his approval rating in public opinion polls increase to 50%, though the next presidential election was not scheduled until 2004.

(MARTIN WEINSTEIN)

UZBEKISTAN

Area: 447,400 sq km (172,700 sq mi)
Population (2002 est.): 25,484,000
Capital: Tashkent
Chief of state and head of government:
President Islam Karimov, assisted by Prime Minister Otkir Sultonov

During 2002 Uzbekistan sought to strengthen and solidify the relationship it had established with the United States as one of the main partners in the international antiterrorist coalition. Although some questions were raised on the U.S. side about the depth of Uzbek Pres. Islam Karimov's commitment to economic reform and improving his country's human rights record, Uzbekistan appeared to be doing well out of the relationship. For 2002 the U.S. provided $193 million to promote democracy, market reform, and security projects, with the largest amount going for humanitarian aid. In March Karimov visited Washington, where he was promised that economic and military relations would continue to be close even after the departure of the U.S. military presence in Uzbekistan when operations ceased in Afghanistan.

Human rights activists in Uzbekistan and abroad warned that Karimov would use Washington's overall support as an excuse to avoid reducing human rights abuses, a concern that seemed to be justified as the banned opposition political party Erk reported increased police harassment of its members and larger numbers of women were detained for what the authorities considered religious extremism. There were some improvements in human rights practices in the course of the year, however. In January four police officers were tried and sentenced for having tortured suspects, the first time law-enforcement officials had been known to have been held to account for such behaviour. In March the Independent Human Rights Organization of Uzbekistan was registered by the authorities after a multiyear struggle; the human rights monitoring group promised that it would continue its very vocal defense of persons whose rights had been abused. Censorship, which was specifically prohibited in the Uzbek constitution, was officially abolished in May, but the announcement was greeted with skepticism by journalists and human rights activists.

In October limitations on access to the Internet were lifted, and high tariffs on imports by small private traders were reduced after widespread complaints were voiced that the bazaars were empty because people could not afford the prices resulting from the high duties. Nor could Uzbekistan produce substitutes for the imported goods. The affected merchants were ambivalent about the reductions, saying that they were too small.

In late September the International Monetary Fund criticized Uzbekistan for its failure to implement promised economic reforms and to liberalize the

© Andres Stapff/Reuters 2002
On a board in Montevideo, an update is posted of the Uruguayan peso's collapsing exchange rate against the U.S. dollar on July 11, some three weeks after the government decided to allow the national currency to float.

foreign currency exchange system. Earlier in the year the World Bank president, James Wolfensohn, warned the country that if it did not accelerate economic reform, living standards would continue to fall and its problems would increase.   (BESS BROWN)

VANUATU

Area: 12,190 sq km (4,707 sq mi)
Population (2002 est.): 207,000
Capital: Vila
Chief of state: President John Bernard Bani
Head of government: Prime Minister Edward Natapei

In the May 2002 elections, Prime Minister Edward Natapei's Vanua'aku Party and its coalition partner, the Union of Moderate Parties, won 14 and 15 seats, respectively, in the 52-member Parliament. With additional support from independent members, Natapei was returned as prime minister. The election was monitored by Transparency International observers, who found fundamental flaws with the electoral roll and noted delays, discrepancies, and errors in counting and reporting of results.

In July former prime minister Barak Sopé was jailed for fraud in connection with his signing of unauthorized government guarantees worth millions of dollars, but Pres. John Bernard Bani later pardoned and released him on medical grounds. The fragility of governance in Vanuatu was further demonstrated following the controversial appointment in August of Mael Apisai to the position of police commissioner and his subsequent arrest by police. Though the Supreme Court later ruled that the appointment and the arrest were invalid, the police paramilitary wing arrested the police who had arrested Apisai. After a customary reconciliation ceremony, involving presentations of pigs, the 26 charged agreed to appear in court; charges against 18 of the 26 were subsequently withdrawn. The eight remaining senior officers were charged with mutiny and incitement to mutiny; if convicted of the latter, they could face life imprisonment.

Development assistance of $6 million–$9 million over three years from the Asian Development Bank was approved for infrastructure, agriculture, and private-sector projects. The economy suffered from the international downturn and especially from the continuing decline in copra prices and reduced tourism.

Vanuatu remained a strong supporter of West Papua independence from Indonesia; it offered West Papua separatists the opportunity to establish an office in Port Vila.

(BARRIE MACDONALD)

VATICAN CITY STATE

Area: 44 ha (109 ac)
Population (2002 est.): 900
Chief of state: (sovereign pontiff) Pope John Paul II
Head of administration: Secretary of State Angelo Cardinal Sodano, who heads a pontifical commission of five cardinals

On Jan. 24, 2002, Pope John Paul II, joined by more than 200 religious leaders representing Judaism, Islam, Buddhism, Hinduism, and traditional African religions, gathered in Assisi, Italy, for a day of prayer denouncing violence and terror perpetrated under any auspices, especially in the name of religion. In an effort to reaffirm its role as the universal defender of human dignity, the Vatican summoned all the tools required, including the Internet, to disseminate its message of peace. The value of modern telecommunications technology in facilitating the Vatican's apostolic mission was witnessed when the aging pontiff, in his 24th year of office, made his first virtual visit to Moscow to pray the rosary with the Roman Catholic faithful.

On a more explicitly political front, the restructuring of the Roman Church in Russia occupied a prominent position in the year's activities, although Vatican officials were quick to point out that this was hardly the case of converting the Orthodox faithful to Catholicism but rather a case of restoring the Roman Church to the status it occupied in the precommunist era. (*See also* RELIGION and WORLD AFFAIRS: *Russia.*)

The pope offered words of exhortation to the Argentine faithful beset by mighty economic woes, reminding them that the way to economic recovery should start with the cultivation of moral values. On November 14 Pope John Paul II addressed the Italian Parliament, the first time a pontiff had done so, and urged a continuing important role for Christianity in the European Union. The modernity of the church's position was expressed in its various calls for sustainable economic development, declaring that human beings had a God-given "ecological vocation."   (GREGORY O. SMITH)

VENEZUELA

Area: 916,445 sq km (353,841 sq mi)
Population (2002 est.): 25,093,000
Capital: Caracas
Head of state and government: President Hugo Chávez Frías

Loyalist military officers restored Venezuelan Pres. Hugo Chávez Frías to the presidency on the morning of April 14, 2002, just 48 hours after he had been removed from office. The overthrow followed a massive protest march by Chávez's opponents that ended in the death of at least 17 demonstrators. The protest was organized by the National Business Federation, the National Labour Federation, and the Democratic Coordinating Committee—a mixture of political party leaders and middle-class groups from civil society. The demonstrators had hoped to convince Chávez that his high-handed efforts to implement leftist policies had destroyed his government's legitimacy and that he should resign.

Accusations that the president had authorized supporters to fire on the demonstrators emboldened the armed forces, whose high command had long opposed Chávez. The military installed businessman Pedro Carmona Estanga as interim president. Instead of seeking approval for his government from the National Assembly and Supreme Court, as anticipated, Carmona dissolved both institutions, suspended civil liberties, and annulled recently passed land-reform legislation. This unleashed a clash between right-wing and moderate opponents of Chávez. Concurrently, the senior military fell to squabbling among

Tens of thousands of people march in a rally in Caracas on the 28th day of a nationwide general strike that began in early December in an attempt to force Venezuelan Pres. Hugo Chávez to call early elections.

themselves over how to distribute positions within the interim government. These divisions encouraged supporters of the ousted president. Violence escalated during the afternoon of April 13, and middle-level military officers, the core of Chávez's support, rallied. By midnight the coup had collapsed.

The role of the U.S. government in the events of April 11–14 remained murky. Opponents of the Chávez government met with the assistant secretary of state for Western Hemisphere affairs, Otto Reich, in the weeks prior to the coup. On February 5, in testimony before the Senate Foreign Relations Committee, Secretary of State Colin Powell expressed concern that Chávez did not understand "what a democratic system was all about." Director of Central Intelligence George Tenet made similar

remarks on February 6. The cumulative impact of these signals from Washington was to convince opponents of Chávez that the administration of Pres. George W. Bush would not oppose his ouster. After the coup failed, however, the U.S. ambassador to Venezuela, Charles Shapiro, distanced the administration from the coup plotters.

At the beginning of 2002, Venezuela remained the sixth largest oil producer in the world, but overall the economic news was bad. As of the end of September, the petroleum sector had experienced a 16.7% contraction, largely as a result of adhering to reductions in the OPEC production quota. Also, gross domestic product declined by 9.9% in the second quarter, and as of September the national currency—the bolívar—had lost 46% of its value against the dollar. Inflation picked up and was expected to reach 30% by the end of the year. Nevertheless, the bolívar remained overvalued, and as a result, businesses that could not compete with cheap imports were wiped out. Venezuela's ranking by the World Economic Forum fell to 68th (from 62nd in 2001), and a third-quarter report by the central bank stated that it did not expect growth in 2003.

As of mid-November the conflict between opponents and supporters of President Chávez remained at an impasse. A general strike by the opposition paralyzed much of the country on October 21, and several days later disgruntled military officers called for the overthrow of the government. On November 4 the opposition delivered two million signatures demanding a referendum (deemed unconstitutional by the government) on whether President Chávez should remain in office. A defiant Chávez took control of the Caracas Metropolitan Police Force on November 16. This force had been controlled by Alfredo Peña, the metropolitan mayor, who was a vocal critic of the president. Protests against federal intervention were met with riot troops and tear gas. This confrontation undermined negotiations sponsored by the Organization of American States, the United Nations Development Programme, and the Carter Center—institutions that were seeking to craft a peaceful solution to the crisis. It also gave credence to a warning by former presidential candidate Eduardo Fernández: "It is starting to look much like what led to the Spanish Civil War....We are tempting the devil." The crisis deepened in December when opposition forces (labour unions, busi-

ness federations, and a coordinating committee of democratic political parties) declared a general strike for the purpose of forcing Chávez to resign or call early elections. When the strike spread to the petroleum sector, oil production was drastically curtailed, and Chávez threatened to impose a state of emergency.   (DAVID J. MYERS)

VIETNAM

Area: 332,501 sq km (128,379 sq mi)
Population (2002 est.): 79,939,000
Capital: Hanoi
Chief of state: President Tran Duc Luong
Head of government: Prime Minister Phan Van Khai

The December 2001 arrest of Nam Cam—a Ho Chi Minh City-based crime boss, whose criminal network was found to implicate more than 150 persons, including police, party cadres, and government officials—attracted such widespread media and public interest that in June 2002 a senior party leader ordered the media to curb its coverage to prevent further leaks and damaging speculation about the identity of others who might be involved.

The Vietnam Communist Party's (VCP) top decision-making body, the Central Committee, met in executive session three times during the year. At its first meeting in February–March, the fifth plenum (numbered consecutively from the last national party congress) adopted policies to boost the role of the private sector and to permit party members to engage in private business for the first time.

On May 19 Vietnamese voters went to the polls to elect deputies to the 11th legislature of the National Assembly. A record 759 candidates were certified as eligible to contest 498 seats. Election proceedings were marred when three candidates were disqualified for corruption, including Tran Mai Hanh, who was head of Voice of Vietnam Radio, secretary-general of the Vietnam Journalists' Association, and a member of the VCP Central Committee. At the Central Committee's sixth plenum in July, Hanh and a deputy minister of public security were expelled for involvement in the Nam Cam scandal.

The Central Committee also adopted a number of policy initiatives designed to spur the information technology sector.

The new National Assembly convened immediately after the plenum. Nearly 90% of the deputies were VCP members. The National Assembly reelected Tran Duc Luong and Phan Van Khai for another five-year term as president and prime minister, respectively. Deputies also endorsed Nguyen Van An as chairman of the National Assembly Standing Committee, but not before 99 legislators had taken the unprecedented step of voting against An. On the eve of the vote, rumours circulated that members of An's family had accepted gifts from Nam Cam. National Assembly deputies unsuccessfully challenged the prime minister's proposal to create three new ministries, and they rejected his candidate for minister of public security. The deputies chose instead to bring in an outsider to head this corruption-tainted body. All other ministerial nominations were approved.

In November the Central Committee's seventh plenum adopted an economic development plan for 2003 that included two controversial projects, the Son La hydroelectric power plant and the Cau Mau fertilizer complex.

During the year Vietnam hosted visits by China's president and party leader (February), the prime ministers of South Korea (April) and Japan (April), and the president of the Philippines (November). All of these visits focused on trade, investment, and business and technology cooperation. In May Russia completed its withdrawal from Cam Ranh Bay and turned over its naval facilities to Vietnam.

Prime Minister Phan Van Khai attended the Asia-Europe Meeting in Denmark in September, the APEC forum in Mexico with a side trip to Cuba and Chile in October, and the eighth ASEAN summit in Cambodia in November. Party Secretary-General Nong Duc Manh ventured abroad in October to visit Japan, Belarus, and Russia. Pres. Tran Duc Luong traveled to Myanmar (Burma) in May and attended the Francophone summit in Beirut, Lebanon, in October, after which he visited France, Iran, and several African countries.

Vietnam's relations with the United States underwent strains as American lobby groups charged Vietnam with dumping catfish and shrimp on the American market. Vietnam's human rights and religious practices also attracted official criticism.

(CARLYLE A. THAYER)

YEMEN

Area: 555,000 sq km (214,300 sq mi)
Population (2002 est.): 19,495,000
Capital: Sanaa
Chief of state: President Maj. Gen. 'Ali 'Abdallah Salih
Head of government: Prime Minister, 'Abd al-Qadir al-Ba Jamal

During 2002 international attention focused on Yemen's role in antiterrorism. Following the Sept. 11, 2001, terrorist attacks in the United States, the Yemeni and U.S. governments substantially increased their cooperation in combating terrorism, quietly exchanging information and working together to identify possible supporters of Osama bin Laden's al-Qaeda network. Though authorities of the Yemeni central government did not have full control over the entire country, they made new efforts to expand their reach into the southeastern part of the country and provide greater security. Yemen also closed a number of Koranic schools and instructed mosque preachers to use moderation in their sermons. U.S. Vice Pres. Dick Cheney met Pres. 'Ali 'Abdallah Salih in Yemen in March to discuss joint security.

In early October 2002, however, a terrorist-related explosion and fire erupted on the large French-flagged oil tanker *Limburg*, near the Yemeni port of Al-Mukalla. On November 3 the CIA and Yemen coordinated a missile attack that claimed the lives of six alleged al-Qaeda operatives in Yemen, including its top leader in the country. The missile was launched from a pilotless aircraft and signaled that the war on terrorism would be unconventional. (*See* MILITARY AFFAIRS: Special Report.) On December 30 three Baptist missionaries were gunned down in a hospital in Jibla by a man believed to have links to an Islamist cell. (WILLIAM A. RUGH)

YUGOSLAVIA

Area: 102,173 sq km (39,449 sq mi)
Population (2002 est.): 10,664,000
Capital: Belgrade
Chief of state: President Vojislav Kostunica
Head of government: Prime Minister Dragisa Pesic

Despite intense international pressure to keep the processes of democratization and reform moving, stubbornness among the leadership prevented basic solutions to the catastrophic economic and social situation in Yugoslavia.

Spanish sailors board an unflagged cargo vessel off the coast of Yemen on December 9; the ship had a hidden cargo of Scud missiles that Yemen had purchased from North Korea, and the U.S., which had ordered the interception, reluctantly agreed to release the cargo to Yemen two days later.

Elections were held on the republican level as well as in Serbia's internationally administered province of Kosovo, where the predominantly ethnic Albanians succeeded in electing officials amid a Serb boycott. Amid great confusion and voter apathy, Serbia failed to elect a new president in three attempts.

In March the parliaments of Serbia and Montenegro, Yugoslavia's two constituent republics, voted on an agreement regarding the future status of the federation. After intense international pressure, the framework of the agreement gave both republics broad autonomy. Each would operate a separate economic, currency, and customs system while sharing a common defense structure and foreign policy. There would be a single, federal presidency. In addition, each republic was awarded the right to hold a referendum on independence three years after the new state, to be called Serbia and Montenegro, came into being on Jan. 1, 2003.

The new arrangement was designed to placate Montenegrins who for 10 years had mulled over whether to declare full independence or keep some sort of union with Serbia. The European Union feared that if Montenegro was to secede, other groups in the region, namely the Albanians in Kosovo and Macedonia and Serbs and Croats in Bosnia and Herzegovina, might feel encouraged to make similar moves and thereby again touch off violence.

Reforms to alleviate the dire situation in Yugoslavia's economic, health, education, and media sectors were obstructed by squabbles among political elites and chaos in public-sector institutions headed by political appointees. Amid concerns of an ultranationalist backlash among voters in the run-up to the December 8 presidential balloting, in early November two bitter rivals, Serbian Premier Zoran Djindjic and Yugoslav Pres. Vojislav Kostunica, agreed to end their political feud in an attempt to get the country back on the reform track. Their agreement did not convince the electorate, however, and only 45% of eligible voters cast ballots. According to election law, a 50% minimum was required for validating the balloting. Kostunica won the majority of votes, with ultranationalist Vojislav Seselj finishing a strong second. Montenegrin balloting on December 22 also failed to elect a president because of low voter turnout.

Voter apathy in Serbia was largely attributed to the government's failure to improve living standards as well as to allegations of corruption and mismanagement. Industrial production fell by 0.8% compared with the previous year, and exports were up only 10%, while imports jumped by 30%. Almost 60,000 companies employing 1.2 million workers were on the brink of bankruptcy. The average monthly salary was $130—barely enough to live on. More than a third of the population continued to live at or below the poverty line, and 18% lived in absolute destitution. In such a situation, the demand by lawmakers in January that frosted cakes be added to the Serbian parliament restaurant menu understandably caused a public outcry. Belgrade media responded by publishing articles and photos contrasting the politicians' call for confectionery delights with soup kitchens and homeless shelters.

In late October elections were held in 30 municipalities in Kosovo, and most outside observers hailed the balloting as fair and successful. The election was also regarded as crucial in laying the foundations for local government, but the poor turnout by the Serb population troubled international observers. Voter participation was high in five enclaves where Serbs constituted a majority, and of the 82 seats won by Serbs, 68 were in these five municipalities.

No solution was found to the problem of the final status of Kosovo. In November, Kosovo's Albanian-dominated assembly approved a resolution denouncing the preamble of the draft constitution for the new union between Serbia and Montenegro as proof of Belgrade's intention to annex Kosovo. The Albanian deputies threatened to declare unilateral independence if the offending passage was not deleted. UN representatives affirmed that neither Belgrade nor the Kosovo parliament could unilaterally decide the future of the region.

The Serbian government in October officially admitted that Yugoimport, a state-owned arms dealer, had violated United Nations weapons-trade bans by overhauling MiG jet engines and providing other unspecified military services to Iraq. The scandal also included several Bosnian Serb companies and led to the firing of several key officials in Sarajevo and in Belgrade. In late November, U.S. weapons experts arrived in Yugoslavia to determine whether Belgrade had stopped all arms trade with Iraq and what benefit Saddam Hussein's military had derived from the massive arms-for-cash trade since 1999. In December the govern-

ments of Croatia and Yugoslavia signed an interim solution ending a decade of dispute over the strategic and commercially important Prevlaka Peninsula on the Adriatic coast.

(MILAN ANDREJEVICH)

ZAMBIA

Area: 752,612 sq km (290,585 sq mi)
Population (2002 est.): 9,959,000
Capital: Lusaka
Head of state and government: Presidents Frederick Chiluba and, from January 2, Levy Mwanawasa

The results of the presidential and legislative elections in late December 2001 had been so close that the defeated parties took to the streets in early January 2002 to protest the outcome. Levy Mwanawasa, the successful Movement for Multiparty Democracy (MMD) candidate who polled only 28.69% of the votes cast, was sworn in as president on January 2. He immediately acted with firmness, and the protest died down. Although his party could not command an overall majority in the National Assembly, Mwanawasa demonstrated that he would not countenance the corruption and mismanagement that had tarnished the reputation of the MMD under former president Frederick Chiluba. He dismissed a number of senior military personnel, became his own minister of defense, and on March 11 sacked one of his ministers, Vernon Mwaanga, for disloyalty.

On July 11 Foreign Minister Katele Kalumba resigned amid allegations of corruption. Five days later Chiluba, who had already been stripped of his retirement benefits because of his continued involvement in politics, had his immunity from prosecution lifted by the National Assembly in response to an appeal from Mwanawasa. Other senior officials were also charged with having mishandled public finances, but the president's campaign began to falter when evidence emerged later in July that suggested he might have acted too precipitately in leveling some of his accusations.

These political maneuvers were carried out against a background of economic uncertainty. Toward the end of

January, Anglo American PLC gave notice of its intention to pull out of its activities in Konkola Copper Mines. Various offers of assistance, pending the discovery of another international buyer, came from the U.K., the European Union, and other organizations, and the situation appeared to improve when, with copper production recovering and a slight increase in world prices, Anglo American offered the government $30 million in compensation, together with a loan of $26.5 million and a payment of an additional $25.4 million to each of two other shareholders. Sun International Hotels also threatened to pull out after harassment by government officials but later relented.

On a more optimistic note, a report indicated that the Non-ferrous Metal Industries of China had invested more than $59 million in the Chambishi Copper Mines since the company bought it in 1998. In February Celtel-Zambia established a new cell-phone site, primarily to serve Sun International Hotels.

In May, however, Mwanawasa was forced to declare a national disaster and appeal for international aid when food shortages threatened more than 2.5 million Zambians with starvation. The U.S. offered to make up 50% of the deficit, but the government refused to accept food containing genetically modified organisms.   (KENNETH INGHAM)

ZIMBABWE

Area: 390,757 sq km (150,872 sq mi)
Population (2002 est.): 11,377,000
Capital: Harare
Head of state and government: President Robert Mugabe

The early months of 2002 were dominated by preparations for the presidential elections, which were held on March 9–11. Western nations were highly skeptical about the conduct of the elections, and the U.K., already angered by the forcible eviction of white farmers as a result of Pres. Robert Mugabe's land-reform program, took the lead in urging Commonwealth and European Union (EU) countries to take action against him.

The U.K. government's concern over the land issue enabled Mugabe to depict the West as attempting to reintroduce colonialism. Mugabe claimed that he was defending his country's sovereignty and argued that the opposition Movement for Democratic Change (MDC) was wholly financed by Western capital. In taking this stance, he won the sympathy of other African leaders and diverted attention from the violent attacks by his party's activists on black Zimbabwean opponents. Though the EU agreed on February 18 to impose limited sanctions on the president and his closest associates, African and Asian leaders of Commonwealth countries who attended a summit meeting in Australia on March 3 rejected the U.K.'s proposal to suspend Zimbabwe from membership. (See *Commonwealth of Nations,* above.)

On January 8 a law was enacted that banned all correspondents working for foreign newspapers and required all Zimbabwean journalists to seek an annual license from the information minister. On January 30 another law gave the president draconian powers to suppress opposition. A month later Morgan Tsvangirai, leader of the MDC, was charged with treason, and on March 7 Didymus Mutasa, foreign affairs spokesman for the ruling Zimbabwe African National UnionPatriotic Front (ZANU-PF) said that his party would stage a coup if the MDC candidate was victorious. On March 13, however, it was announced that Mugabe had triumphed, gaining 54% of the vote to his opponent's 40%. Six days later Zimbabwe was suspended from membership in the Commonwealth in response to an adverse report on the conduct of the elections by the Commonwealth's monitoring team.

Hopes that there might be some accommodation between Zimbabwe's two main political parties, mediated by South Africa and Nigeria, were quickly extinguished when ZANU withdrew from the discussions. Mugabe renewed his criticisms of the West, winning further support from African leaders at a World Food Summit in Rome in June and again at the World Summit on Sustainable Development in Johannesburg, S.Af., in September. Later in the month an attempt by the Commonwealth to negotiate a working arrangement with Zimbabwe through the agency of Nigeria, South Africa, and Australia broke down when Mugabe boycotted a planned meeting in Nigeria. Meanwhile, the land-reform program was relaunched in June; 2,900 white farmers were told to leave their land by August 8. Attacks on black opponents of the government grew steadily more violent.

On a number of occasions, members of the judiciary challenged government actions on legal grounds, but their rulings were often reversed by the Supreme Court or ignored by the government. The judges concerned were often forced from office. These political struggles occurred against a background of acute food shortages, which Mugabe attributed to the West's failure to give appropriate assistance, while the West claimed that the shortages were the result of the president's land-reform program.   (KENNETH INGHAM)

Zimbabwean farmer Alain Faydherbe stands in his sugarcane fields in Chiredze on July 26, only days before most of his farm would be taken over by the Zimbabwe government as part of its land-redistribution program.

Photo by Lori Waselchuk

Alder, Phillip. Syndicated Bridge Columnist. Associate Editor, *The Bridge World.* Author of *Get Smarter at Bridge.* •SPORTS AND GAMES: *Contract Bridge*

Alexander, Steve. Freelance Technology Writer. •COMPUTERS AND INFORMATION SYSTEMS

Allaby, Michael. Freelance Writer. Author of *Encyclopedia of Weather and Climate* and *Basics of Environmental Science.* •THE ENVIRONMENT: *Environmental Issues; International Activities*

Allan, J.A. Professor of Geography, School of Oriental and African Studies, University of London. Author of *The Middle East Water Question: Hydropolitics and the Global Economy.* •WORLD AFFAIRS: *Libya*

Anam, Mahfuz. Editor and Publisher, *The Daily Star,* Bangladesh. •WORLD AFFAIRS: *Bangladesh*

Andrades, Jorge Adrián. Freelance Journalist. •SPORTS AND GAMES: *Equestrian Sports:* Polo

Andrejevich, Milan. Adjunct Professor of Communications and History, Valparaiso University and Indiana University Northwest. Team Leader, Scholars Initiative on the Former Yugoslavia. Author of *The Sandžak: A Perspective of Serb-Muslim Relations.* •WORLD AFFAIRS: *Bosnia and Herzegovina; Yugoslavia*

Anthony, John Duke. President and CEO, National Council on U.S.-Arab Relations; Secretary, U.S. Gulf Cooperation Council Corporate Cooperation Committee; Consultant to U.S. Departments of Defense and State. •WORLD AFFAIRS: *Oman; Qatar*

Archibald, John J. Retired Feature Writer, *St. Louis* (Mo.) *Post-Dispatch.* Member of the American Bowling Congress Hall of Fame. •SPORTS AND GAMES: *Bowling:* U.S. Tenpins

Aurora, Vincent. Lecturer in French and Romance Philology, Columbia University, New York City. Author of *Michel Leiris' Failles: immobile in mobili.* •LITERATURE: *French:* France

Bahry, Louay. Adjunct Professor of Political Science, University of Tennessee. Author of *The Baghdad Bahn.* •WORLD AFFAIRS: *Bahrain; Iraq*

Balaban, Avraham. Professor of Modern Hebrew Literature, University of Florida. Author of *Shiv'ah.* •LITERATURE: *Jewish:* Hebrew

Bamia, Aida A. Professor of Arabic Language and Literature, University of Florida. Author of *The Graying of the Raven: Cultural and Sociopolitical Significance of Algerian Folk Poetry.* •BIOGRAPHIES *(in part);* LITERATURE: *Arabic*

Barrett, David B. Research Professor of Missiometrics, Regent University, Virginia Beach, Va. Author of *World Christian Encyclopedia* and *Schism and Renewal in Africa.* •RELIGION: *Tables (in part)*

Barry, John. Professor of Spanish, Roosevelt University, Chicago. Editor, *Voces en el viento: nuevas ficciones desde Chicago.* •BIOGRAPHIES *(in part);* LITERATURE: *Spanish:* Latin America

Barzel, Ann. Senior Editor, *Dance Magazine.* •PERFORMING ARTS: *Dance:* World

Beckwith, David C. Vice President, National Cable Television Association. •WORLD AFFAIRS: *United States; United States:* Sidebar; *United States:* State and Local Affairs

Benedetti, Laura. Laura and Gaetano De Sole Associate Professor of Italian Contemporary Culture, Georgetown University, Washington, D.C. Author of *La sconfitta di Diana: un percorso per la Gerusalemme liberata.* •LITERATURE: *Italian*

Bernstein, Ellen. Freelance Writer and Editor, specializing in health and medicine, Chicago. •HEALTH AND DISEASE; HEALTH AND DISEASE: Sidebar

Besson, François. Sports Director, International Judo Federation; Cabinet Member, French Sport Ministry. Coauthor of *Judo.* •SPORTS AND GAMES: *Judo*

Bird, Thomas E. Professor of European Languages, the Jewish Studies Program, Queens College, City University of New York. Coeditor of *Hryhorij Savyč Skovoroda: An Anthology of Critical Articles.* •LITERATURE: *Jewish:* Yiddish

Birrell, Bob. Director, Centre for Population and Urban Research, Monash University, Clayton, Australia. Author of *Federation: The Secret Story.* •WORLD AFFAIRS: *Australia; Special Report:* Strangers at the Gates: The Immigration Backlash

Boggan, Tim. Historian, U.S.A. Table Tennis Association (USATT). Author of *Winning Table Tennis* and *History of U.S. Table Tennis,* vol 1. •SPORTS AND GAMES: *Table Tennis*

Bonds, John B. Adjunct Professor of History, The Citadel, Charleston, S.C. Author of *Bipartisan Strategy: Selling the Marshall Plan.* •SPORTS AND GAMES: *Sailing (Yachting)*

Bradsher, Henry S. Foreign Affairs Analyst. Author of *Afghan Communism and Soviet Intervention.* •WORLD AFFAIRS: *Philippines*

Brady, Conor. Editor Emeritus, *The Irish Times,* Dublin. •WORLD AFFAIRS: *Ireland*

Brecher, Kenneth. Professor of Astronomy and Physics; Director, Science and Mathematics Education Center, Boston University. •MATHEMATICS AND PHYSICAL SCIENCES: *Astronomy*

Brockmann, Stephen. Associate Professor of German, Carnegie Mellon University, Pittsburgh, Pa. Author of *Literature and German Reunification.* •LITERATURE: *German*

Brokopp, John G. Director of Public Relations, National Jockey Club; Syndicated casino gambling columnist. Author of *Thrifty Gambling* and *Insider's Guide to Internet Gambling: Your Sourcebook for Safe and Profitable Gambling.* •SPORTS AND GAMES: *Equestrian Sports:* Thoroughbred Racing: *United States*

Brown, Bess. Political Officer, OSCE Centre, Ashgabat, Turkmenistan. Author of *Authoritarianism in the New States of Central Asia.* •WORLD AFFAIRS: *Kazakhstan; Kyrgyzstan; Tajikistan; Turkmenistan; Uzbekistan*

Buchan, David. Foreign Editorial Writer, *Financial Times,* London. Author of *The Single Market and Tomorrow's Europe: A Progress Report from the European Commission.* •BIOGRAPHIES *(in part);* WORLD AFFAIRS: *France; France:* Sidebar

Bungs, Dzintra. Senior Research Fellow, Latvian Institute of International Affairs, Riga. Author of *The Baltic States: Problems and Prospects of Membership of the European Union.* •WORLD AFFAIRS: *Latvia*

Burks, Ardath W. Professor Emeritus of Asian Studies, Rutgers University, New Brunswick, N.J. Author of *Japan: A Postindustrial Power.* •WORLD AFFAIRS: *Japan*

Burns, Erik T. Bureau Chief, Dow Jones Newswires, Lisbon. •WORLD AFFAIRS: *Portugal*

Byrne, Justin. Researcher, Center for Advanced Study in the Social Sciences, Instituto Juan March de Estudios e Investigaciones, Madrid. •WORLD AFFAIRS: *Spain*

Cadoux, Charles. Professor of Public Law, University of Aix-Marseille III, Aix-en-Provence, France. •WORLD AFFAIRS: *Dependent States:* Indian Ocean and Southeast Asia; *East Timor*

Cafferty, Bernard. Associate Editor, *British Chess Magazine.* Author of *The Soviet Championships.* •SPORTS AND GAMES: *Chess*

Calhoun, David R. Freelance Editor and Writer. •BIOGRAPHIES *(in part)*

Campbell, Paul J. Professor of Mathematics and Computer Science, Beloit (Wis.) College. Coauthor of *For All Practical Purposes.* •MATHEMATICS AND PHYSICAL SCIENCES: *Mathematics*

Campbell, Robert. Architect and Architecture Critic. Author of *Cityscapes of Boston: An American City Through Time.* •ARCHITECTURE AND CIVIL ENGINEERING: *Architecture*

Caplan, Marla. Graduate Education Assistant, International Center of Photography, New York City. •BIOGRAPHIES *(in part);* ART, ANTIQUES, AND COLLECTIONS: *Photography*

Carter, Robert W. Journalist. •SPORTS AND GAMES: *Equestrian Sports:* Show Jumping and Dressage; Steeplechasing; Thoroughbred Racing: *International*

Chappell, Duncan. President, Mental Health Review Tribunal, Sydney, Australia. Author of *Violence at Work.* •LAW, CRIME, AND LAW ENFORCEMENT: *Crime*

Cheadle, Bruce. Journalist, Canadian Press news agency. •SPORTS AND GAMES: *Curling*

Cheuse, Alan. Writing Faculty, English Department, George Mason University, Fairfax, Va.; Book Commentator, National Public Radio. Author of *The Light Possessed* and *Listening to the Page: Adventures in Reading and Writing.* •LITERATURE: *English:* United States

Cioroslan, Dragomir. National Team Coach, U.S.A. Weightlifting, Inc.; Executive Board Member, International Weightlifting Federation. Coauthor of *Banish Your Belly.* •SPORTS AND GAMES: *Weight Lifting*

Clark, Andrew F. Professor of African and Global History, University of North Carolina at Wilmington. Author of *From Frontier to Backwater: Economy and Society in the Upper Senegal Valley, 1850–1920.* •WORLD AFFAIRS: *Ghana; Liberia; Nigeria; Sierra Leone*

Clark, David Draper. Editor, *World Literature Today.* •LITERATURE: *English:* Other Literature in English

Clark, Janet H. Editor, Standard & Poor's, London. •NOBEL PRIZES *(in part)*

Coate, Roger A. Professor of International Organization; Director, Walker Institute of International Studies, University of South Carolina. Coauthor of *The United Nations and Changing World Politics.* •WORLD AFFAIRS: *United Nations*

Coller, Ken. President, West Seattle Productions. •SPORTS AND GAMES: *Wrestling:* Sumo

Collins, Nigel. Editor in Chief, *The Ring, KO, World Boxing,* and *Boxing 2003.* •SPORTS AND GAMES: *Boxing*

Cosgrave, Bronwyn. Editor, *Harvey Nichols* magazine. Author of *Costume and Fashion: A Complete History.* •BIOGRAPHIES *(in part);* FASHIONS

Coveney, Michael. Theatre Critic, *The Daily Mail.* Author of *The Andrew Lloyd Webber Story* and others. •PERFORMING ARTS: *Theatre:* Great Britain and Ireland

Craine, Anthony G. Writer. •BIOGRAPHIES *(in part);* OBITUARIES *(in part)*

Crampton, Richard J. Professor of East European History, University of Oxford. Author of *A Concise History of Bulgaria* and *The Balkans Since the Second World War.* •WORLD AFFAIRS: *Bulgaria*

Crisp, Brian F. Associate Professor of Political Science, University of Arizona. Author of *Democratic Institutional Design.* •BIOGRAPHIES *(in part);* WORLD AFFAIRS: *Colombia*

Curwen, Peter. Professor of Business and Management, Sheffield Hallam University, Sheffield, Eng. Author of *The U.K. Publishing Industry* and others. •MEDIA AND PUBLISHING: *Book Publishing* (international)

Cuttino, John Charles. Lyndon B. Johnson School of Public Affairs, University of Texas at Austin. Coauthor of *The Impacts of U.S.-Latin American Trade on the Southwest's Economy and Transportation System: An Assessment of Impact Methodologies.* •BIOGRAPHIES *(in part);* WORLD AFFAIRS: *Brazil*

Dailey, Meghan. Art Historian and Critic, New York City. •ART, ANTIQUES, AND COLLECTIONS: *Art; Art Exhibitions;* BIOGRAPHIES *(in part)*

Deeb, Marius K. Professor of Middle East Studies, SAIS, Johns Hopkins University, Washington, D.C. Author of *Syria's Terrorist War on Lebanon and the Peace Process 1974–2002* and others. •WORLD AFFAIRS: *Egypt; Jordan*

de la Barre, Kenneth. Fellow, Arctic Institute of North America; Research Associate, Yukon College, Northern Research Institute. •WORLD AFFAIRS: *Arctic Regions*

Denselow, Robin. Correspondent, BBC Television's *Newsnight.* Author of *When the Music's Over: The Story of Political Pop.* •PERFORMING ARTS: *Music:* Popular (international)

Dietz, Henry A. Professor, Department of Government, University of Texas at Austin. Author of *Urban Poverty, Political Participation and the State: Lima 1970–1990.* •WORLD AFFAIRS: *Peru*

Dooling, Dave. Outreach Education Officer, National Solar Observatory, Sacramento Peak, New Mexico. Coauthor of *Engineering Tomorrow.* •MATHEMATICS AND PHYSICAL SCIENCES: *Space Exploration; Space Exploration:* Sidebar

Dowd, Siobhan. Columnist, *Literary Review* (London); *Glimmer Train* (U.S.). Author of *This Prison Where I Live* and *Roads of the Roma*. •BIOGRAPHIES *(in part)*; LITERATURE: *English:* United Kingdom

Ebeling, Mary F.E. Department of Sociology, University of Surrey, Guildford, Eng. •WORLD AFFAIRS: *Burundi; Comoros; Rwanda; Seychelles*

Ehringer, Gavin Forbes. Sports Columnist, *Rocky Mountain News* and *Western Horseman*. Coauthor of *Rodeo in America: Wranglers, Roughstock, and Paydirt*. •SPORTS AND GAMES: *Rodeo*

Eisenberg, Andrew. Department of Music, Ethnomusicology Program, Columbia University, New York City. •WORLD AFFAIRS: *Djibouti; Mauritius*

Erikson, Daniel P. Director, the Cuba Program, Inter-American Dialogue, Washington, D.C. •WORLD AFFAIRS: *Cuba*

Esteban, Verónica. Journalist and Bilingual Editor. •LITERATURE: *Spanish:* Spain

Fagan, Brian. Professor of Anthropology, University of California, Santa Barbara. Author of *The Little Ice Age: How Climate Made History, 1300–1850* and *Floods, Famines, and Emperors: El Niño and the Collapse of Civilizations*. •ANTHROPOLOGY AND ARCHAEOLOGY: *Archaeology:* Western Hemisphere

Farr, David M.L. Professor Emeritus of History, Carleton University, Ottawa. •BIOGRAPHIES *(in part)*; WORLD AFFAIRS: *Canada*

Fealy, Greg. Research Fellow in Indonesian History, Research School of Pacific and Asian Studies, Australian National University, Canberra. Author of *The Release of Indonesia's Political Prisoners: Domestic Versus Foreign Policy, 1975–1979*. •WORLD AFFAIRS: *Indonesia*

Fendell, Robert J. Freelance Writer on automobiles and racing. Author of *The Encyclopedia of Auto Racing Greats*. •SPORTS AND GAMES: *Automobile Racing:* U.S. Auto Racing *(in part)*

Fisher, Sharon. Central European Specialist, Global Insight, Inc., Washington, D.C. •WORLD AFFAIRS: *Czech Republic; Slovakia*

Flink, Steve. Senior Correspondent, *Tennis Week*. Author of *The Greatest Tennis Matches of the Twentieth Century*. •BIOGRAPHIES *(in part)*; SPORTS AND GAMES: *Tennis*

Flores, Ramona Monette Sargan. Professor, Department of Speech Communication and Theatre Arts, University of the Philippines, Quezon City; Program Director, Asia Business Consultants, Inc. •BIOGRAPHIES *(in part)*; MEDIA AND PUBLISHING: *Radio* (international); *Television* (international)

Follett, Christopher. Denmark Correspondent, *The Times*; Editor, *Copenhagen This Week*. Author of *Fodspor paa Cypern*. •WORLD AFFAIRS: *Denmark*

Fridovich, Irwin. James B. Duke Professor of Biochemistry, Emeritus, Duke University Medical Center, Durham, N.C. •LIFE SCIENCES: *Molecular Biology (in part)*

Fridovich-Keil, Judith L. Associate Professor, Department of Human Genetics, Emory University School of Medicine, Atlanta, Ga. •LIFE SCIENCES: *Molecular Biology (in part)*

Fuller, Elizabeth. Editor, *Newsline*, Radio Free Europe/Radio Liberty, Prague. •WORLD AFFAIRS: *Armenia; Azerbaijan; Georgia*

Furmonavičius, Darius. Research Associate, Baltic Research Unit, Department of European Studies, University of Bradford, Eng. •WORLD AFFAIRS: *Lithuania*

Gallagher, Tom. Professor of European Peace Studies, University of Bradford, Eng. Author of *Outcast Europe: The Balkans 1789–1989*. •WORLD AFFAIRS: *Romania*

Ganado, Albert. Lawyer; Chairman, Malta National Archives Advisory Committee; President, Malta Historical Society. Coauthor of *A Study in Depth of 143 Maps Representing the Great Siege of Malta of 1565* and others. •WORLD AFFAIRS: *Malta*

Garcia-Zamor, Jean-Claude. Professor of Public Administration, Florida International University. •WORLD AFFAIRS: *Haiti*

Garrod, Mark. Golf Correspondent, PA Sport, U.K. •SPORTS AND GAMES: *Golf*

Gaughan, Thomas. Library Director, Muhlenberg College, Allentown, Pa. •LIBRARIES AND MUSEUMS: *Libraries*

George, Nicholas. Stockholm Correspondent, *Financial Times*. •WORLD AFFAIRS: *Sweden*

Gibbons, J. Whitfield. Professor of Ecology, Savannah River Ecology Laboratory, University of Georgia. Coauthor of *Ecoviews: Snakes, Snails and Environmental Tales*. •LIFE SCIENCES: *Zoology*

Gill, Martin J. Executive Director, Food Certification (Scotland) Ltd. •AGRICULTURE AND FOOD SUPPLIES: *Fisheries*

Gobbie, Donn. CEO, American Badminton League. •SPORTS AND GAMES: *Badminton*

Graham, John W. Chair, Canadian Foundation for the Americas; Former Canadian Ambassador. •WORLD AFFAIRS: *Dominican Republic; Suriname*

Grenda, Iwona. Senior Lecturer, English Faculty of Law and Administration, Adam Mickiewicz University, Poznan, Pol. •WORLD AFFAIRS: *Poland*

Greskovic, Robert. Dance Writer, *The Wall Street Journal*. Author of *Ballet 101*. •PERFORMING ARTS: *Dance:* North America

Griffiths, A.R.G. Associate Professor in History, Flinders University of South Australia. Author of *Contemporary Australia* and *Beautiful Lies*. •WORLD AFFAIRS: *Australia; Nauru; Palau; Papua New Guinea*

Guthridge, Guy G. Manager, Antarctic Information Program, U.S. National Science Foundation. •WORLD AFFAIRS: *Antarctica*

Haddad, Mahmoud. Associate Professor of History, the University of Balamand, Lebanon. •BIOGRAPHIES *(in part)*; WORLD AFFAIRS: *Lebanon; Saudi Arabia*

Halman, Talat Sait. Professor and Chairman, Department of Turkish Literature, Bilkent University, Ankara, Turkey. Author of *Doğrusu*. •LITERATURE: *Turkish*

Hammer, William R. Professor and Chair, Department of Geology, Augustana College, Rock Island, Ill. Author of *Gondwana Dinosaurs from the Jurassic of Antarctica*. •LIFE SCIENCES: *Paleontology*

Harvey, Fiona. Technology Writer, *Financial Times*, London. •COMPUTERS AND INFORMATION SYSTEMS: *Special Report:* The Wireless Revolution

Henry, Alan. Grand Prix Editor, *Autocar* (London). Motor Racing Correspondent, *The Guardian*. Author of *50 Years of World Championship Grand Prix Motor Racing* and *Four Seasons at Ferrari: The Lauda Years*. •SPORTS AND GAMES: *Automobile Racing:* Grand Prix Racing

Hinman, Janele M. Former Marketing Assistant, USA Luge. •SPORTS AND GAMES: *Bobsleigh, Skeleton, and Luge:* Luge

Hobbs, Greg. Senior Writer, *AFL Record*. Author of *One Hundred and Twenty-Five Years of the Melbourne Demons*. •SPORTS AND GAMES: *Football:* Australian

Hoffman, Dean A. Executive Editor, *Hoof Beats*. Author of *The Hambletonian: America's Trotting Classic*. •SPORTS AND GAMES: *Equestrian Sports:* Harness Racing

Hollar, Sherman. Assistant Editor, Encyclopædia Britannica. •BIOGRAPHIES *(in part)*; DISASTERS; OBITUARIES *(in part)*

Homel, David. Freelance Writer; Lecturer, Concordia University, Montreal. Author of *Get on Top* and others. •LITERATURE: *French:* Canada

Hope, Thomas W. Owner, Hope Reports, Inc.; Former Film Producer. Author of *Large Screen Presentation Systems*. •PERFORMING ARTS: *Motion Pictures:* Nontheatrical Films

Hu, Xiaobo. Assistant Professor of Political Science, Clemson (S.C.) University. Coeditor of *Transition Towards Post-Deng China*. •BIOGRAPHIES *(in part)*; WORLD AFFAIRS: *China; Taiwan*

Hussainmiya, B.A. Senior Lecturer, Department of History, University of Brunei Darussalam. Author of *The Brunei Constitution of 1959: An Inside History*. •WORLD AFFAIRS: *Brunei*

IEIS. International Economic Information Services. •ECONOMIC AFFAIRS: *World Economy; Stock Markets* (international)

Ingham, Kenneth. Emeritus Professor of History, University of Bristol, Eng. Author of *Politics in Modern Africa: The Uneven Tribal Dimension* and others. •BIOGRAPHIES *(in part)*; WORLD AFFAIRS: *Angola; Congo, Democratic Republic of the; Kenya; Malawi; Mozambique; Sudan, The; Tanzania; Uganda; Zambia; Zimbabwe*

Ingram, Derek. President Emeritus, Commonwealth Journalists Association; Contributor to *The Round Table*. Author of *A Much-Too-Timid Commonwealth* and others. •WORLD AFFAIRS: *Commonwealth of Nations*

Ionescu, Dan. Broadcaster/Editor, Radio Free Europe/Radio Liberty. Contributor to *Transition*. •WORLD AFFAIRS: *Moldova*

Isaacson, Lanae Hjortsvang. Editor, *Nordic Women Writers*. •BIOGRAPHIES *(in part)*; LITERATURE: *Danish*

Iyob, Ruth. Associate Professor of Political Science, University of Missouri at St. Louis. •WORLD AFFAIRS: *Eritrea*

Jamail, Milton. Lecturer, Department of Government, University of Texas at Austin. Author of *Full Count: Inside Cuban Baseball*. •SPORTS AND GAMES: *Baseball:* Latin America

Joffé, George. Director, Centre of North African Studies, University of Cambridge. Editor, *Perspectives on Development: The Euro-Mediterranean Partnership*. •WORLD AFFAIRS: *Algeria; Morocco; Tunisia*

Johnson, Steve. Television Critic, *Chicago Tribune*. •MEDIA AND PUBLISHING: *Radio* (U.S.); *Television* (U.S.)

Johnson, Todd M. Director, Center for the Study of Global Christianity. Coauthor of *World Christian Encyclopedia*. •RELIGION: *Tables (in part)*

Joireman, Sandra F. Associate Professor of Politics and International Relations, Wheaton (Ill.) College. Author of *Property Rights and Political Development in Ethiopia and Eritrea*. •WORLD AFFAIRS: *Ethiopia*

Jones, David G.C. Tutor, Department of Continuing Education, University of Aberystwyth, Wales. Author of *Atomic Physics*. •MATHEMATICS AND PHYSICAL SCIENCES: *Physics*

Jones, Mark P. Associate Professor of Political Science, Michigan State University. Author of *Electoral Laws and the Survival of Presidential Democracies*. •WORLD AFFAIRS: *Argentina*

Kanduza, Ackson M. Associate Professor and Chair, Department of History, University of Swaziland. Author of *Political Economy of Democratisation in Swaziland*. •WORLD AFFAIRS: *Swaziland*

Kapp, Clare. Freelance Journalist; Contributor to *The Lancet*. •WORLD AFFAIRS: *Switzerland*

Karimi-Hakkak, Ahmad. Professor of Persian Languages and Literature, University of Washington. Author of *Recasting Persian Poetry: Scenarios of Poetic Modernity in Iran*. •LITERATURE: *Persian*

Karns, Margaret P. Professor of Political Science, University of Dayton, Ohio. Coauthor of *The United Nations in the Post-Cold War Era*. •WORLD AFFAIRS: *Multinational and Regional Organizations*

Kazamaru, Yoshihiko. Literary Critic. •LITERATURE: *Japanese*

Kelleher, John A. Journalist and Editorial Consultant; Former Editor, *Dominion* and *Dominion Sunday Times* (Wellington, N.Z.). •BIOGRAPHIES *(in part)*; WORLD AFFAIRS: *New Zealand*

Kelling, George H. Lieutenant Colonel, U.S. Army (ret.). Author of *Countdown to Rebellion: British Policy in Cyprus 1939–1955*. •WORLD AFFAIRS: *Cyprus*

Kellner, Peter. Chairman, YouGov Ltd. Journalist, *London Evening Standard*. Author of *The New Mutualism* and others. •BIOGRAPHIES *(in part)*; WORLD AFFAIRS: *United Kingdom*

Kessler, Clive S. Professor of Sociology, University of New South Wales, Sydney, Australia. •WORLD AFFAIRS: *Malaysia*

Knox, Paul. International Affairs Columnist, *The Globe and Mail*, Toronto. •WORLD AFFAIRS: *Bolivia; Ecuador*

Kobliner, Beth. Journalist. Author of *Get a Financial Life*. •ECONOMIC AFFAIRS: *Stock Markets:* Canada, U.S.

Kovel, Ralph and Terry. Publishers. Authors of *Kovels on Antiques and Collectibles.* •ART, ANTIQUES, AND COLLECTIONS: *Antiques and Collectibles*

Krause, Stefan. Freelance Political Analyst, Athens. •WORLD AFFAIRS: *Greece; Macedonia*

Kuptsch, Christiane. Research Officer, International Institute for Labour Studies, International Labour Office. Coeditor of *Social Security at the Dawn of the 21st Century.* •SOCIAL PROTECTION (international)

Lamb, Kevin M. Health and Medical Writer, *Dayton* (Ohio) *Daily News.* Author of *Quarterbacks, Nickelbacks & Other Loose Change.* •SPORTS AND GAMES: *Football:* Canadian, U.S.

Lawler, Nancy Ellen. Professor Emeritus, Oakton Community College, Des Plaines, Ill. Author of *Soldiers, Airmen, Spies, and Whisperers: The Gold Coast in World War II* and others. •WORLD AFFAIRS: *Benin; Burkina Faso; Cameroon; Central African Republic; Congo, Republic of the; Côte d'Ivoire; Gabon; Guinea; Mali; Mauritania; Niger; Senegal; Togo*

Lawson, Fred H. Professor of Government, Mills College, Oakland, Calif. Author of *Why Syria Goes to War.* •WORLD AFFAIRS: *Syria*

Le Comte, Douglas. Meteorologist, Climate Prediction Center, National Oceanic and Atmospheric Administration. •EARTH SCIENCES: *Meteorology and Climate*

Legassick, Martin. Professor of History, University of the Western Cape, Bellville, S.Af. Author of *Skeletons in the Cupboard: South African Museums and the Trade in Human Remains 1907–1917.* •WORLD AFFAIRS: *South Africa*

Levy, Michael I. Associate Editor, Encyclopædia Britannica. •BIOGRAPHIES *(in part)*

Lindstrom, Sieg. Managing Editor, *Track & Field News.* •BIOGRAPHIES *(in part);* SPORTS AND GAMES: *Track and Field Sports (Athletics)*

Litweiler, John. Jazz Critic. Author of *The Freedom Principle: Jazz After 1958* and *Ornette Coleman: A Harmolodic Life.* •BIOGRAPHIES *(in part);* OBITUARIES *(in part);* PERFORMING ARTS: *Music:* Jazz

Logan, Robert G. Sports Journalist. Author of *Bob Logan's Tales from Chicago Sports: Cubs, Bulls, Bears, and Other Animals* and others. •SPORTS AND GAMES: *Basketball:* United States

Longmore, Andrew. Chief Sports Feature Writer, *The Independent;* Former Assistant Editor, *The Cricketer.* Author of *The Complete Guide to Cycling.* •SPORTS AND GAMES: *Cricket*

Low, Linda. Associate Professor, Department of Business Policy, National University of Singapore. •WORLD AFFAIRS: *Singapore*

Lufkin, Martha. Legal Correspondent, *The Art Newspaper;* Attorney at Law, Lincoln, Mass. •LIBRARIES AND MUSEUMS: *Museums*

Luling, Virginia. Independent Researcher. Author of *Somali Sultanate: The Geledi City-State over 150 Years.* •WORLD AFFAIRS: *Somalia*

Lundin, Immi. Freelance Journalist and Literary Critic. •LITERATURE: *Swedish*

Macdonald, Barrie. Professor of History, Massey University, Palmerston, N.Z. •WORLD AFFAIRS: *Dependent States: Pacific; Fiji; Kiribati; Marshall Islands; Micronesia, Federated States of; Samoa; Solomon Islands; Tonga; Tuvalu; Vanuatu*

Malik, Mohan. Associate Professor, Asia-Pacific Center for Security Studies, Honolulu. •WORLD AFFAIRS: *Myanmar (Burma)*

Manghnani, Murli H. Professor of Geophysics, University of Hawaii at Manoa, Honolulu. •EARTH SCIENCES: *Geophysics*

Mango, Andrew. Foreign Affairs Analyst. Author of *Atatürk: The Biography of the Founder of Modern Turkey* and *Turkey: The Challenge of a New Role.* •WORLD AFFAIRS: *Turkey*

Marples, David R. Professor of History, University of Alberta. Author of *Belarus: A Denationalized Nation* and *Lenin's Revolution: Russia, 1917–1921.* •WORLD AFFAIRS: *Belarus; Ukraine*

Matthíasson, Björn. Economist, Ministry of Finance, Iceland. •WORLD AFFAIRS: *Iceland*

Mazie, David M. Freelance Journalist. •SOCIAL PROTECTION (U.S.)

McLachlan, Keith S. Professor Emeritus, School of Oriental and African Studies, University of London. Coeditor of *Landlocked States of Africa and Asia.* Author of *Boundaries of Modern Iran.* •WORLD AFFAIRS: *Iran*

Michael, Tom. Editor, Encyclopædia Britannica. •BIOGRAPHIES *(in part);* OBITUARIES *(in part)*

Middlebrook, Kevin J. Lecturer in Politics, Institute of Latin American Studies, University of London. Coeditor of *Confronting Development: Assessing Mexico's Economic and Social Policy Challenges.* •WORLD AFFAIRS: *Mexico*

Mills, Kimberly L. Instructor, Department of Anthropology, Beloit (Wis.) College. •ANTHROPOLOGY AND ARCHAEOLOGY: *Anthropology:* Cultural

Mora, Frank O. Associate Professor and Chair of International Studies, Rhodes College, Memphis, Tenn. •WORLD AFFAIRS: *Paraguay*

Morgan, Paul. Editor, *Rugby World.* •SPORTS AND GAMES: *Football:* Rugby Football

Morris, Jacqui M. Freelance Editor; Lecturer, University of Sussex, Brighton, Eng. •THE ENVIRONMENT: *Wildlife Conservation*

Morrison, Graham. Press Officer, British Fencing Association; Correspondent, *Daily Telegraph; Country Life.* •SPORTS AND GAMES: *Fencing*

Myers, David J. Professor of Political Science, Pennsylvania State University. Coauthor of *Capital City Politics in Latin America: Democratization and Empowerment.* •WORLD AFFAIRS: *Venezuela*

Noda, Hiroki. Staff Reporter, *Jiji Press Ltd.,* Japan. •SPORTS AND GAMES: *Baseball:* Japan

O'Brien, Dan. Senior Editor/Economist (Europe), Economist Intelligence Unit. •WORLD AFFAIRS: *Austria*

O'Leary, Christopher. Senior Editor, *Investment Dealers Digest.* •ECONOMIC AFFAIRS: *Business Overview;* Sidebar

Oppenheim, Lois Hecht. Professor of Political Science and Vice President for Academic Affairs, University of Judaism, Los Angeles. Author of *Politics in Chile: Democracy, Authoritarianism and the Search for Development.* •WORLD AFFAIRS: *Chile*

O'Quinn, Jim. Editor in Chief, *American Theatre.* •PERFORMING ARTS: *Theatre:* U.S. and Canada

Orr, Jay. Senior Museum Editor, Country Music Hall of Fame. •BIOGRAPHIES *(in part);* PERFORMING ARTS: *Music:* Popular (U.S.)

Osborne, Keith L. Editor, *British Rowing Almanack.* Author of *Berlin or Bust, Boat Racing in Britain, 1715–1975,* and *One Man Went to Row.* •SPORTS AND GAMES: *Rowing*

Paarlberg, Philip L. Professor of Agricultural Economics, Purdue University, West Lafayette, Ind. •AGRICULTURE AND FOOD SUPPLIES: *Agriculture*

Palacio, Joseph O. Resident Tutor and Head, University Centre, University of the West Indies School of Continuing Studies. Author of *Development in Belize, 1960–1980: Initiatives at the State and Community Levels.* •WORLD AFFAIRS: *Belize*

Paradkar, Shalaka. Content Manager, Magic Software. •BIOGRAPHIES *(in part);* OBITUARIES *(in part)*

Parsons, Neil. Professor of History, University of Botswana. Author of *King Khama, Emperor Joe, and the Great White Queen.* •WORLD AFFAIRS: *Botswana*

Pérez, Orlando J. Associate Professor of Political Science, Central Michigan University. Editor of *Post-Invasion Panama: The Challenges of Democratization in the New World Order* and others. •WORLD AFFAIRS: *Panama*

Peszek, Luan. Publications Director and Editor, *U.S.A. Gymnastics.* Author of *Gymnastics Almanac.* •SPORTS AND GAMES: *Gymnastics*

Peterson, Mark. Associate Professor of Korean Studies, Brigham Young University, Provo, Utah. Author of *Korean Adoption and Inheritance* and others. •BIOGRAPHIES *(in part);* WORLD AFFAIRS: *Korea, Democratic People's Republic of; Korea, Republic of*

Phillips, Stephen J. Freelance Journalist; U.S. Correspondent, *The London Times Education Supplement;* Information Technology Writer, *Financial Times,* London. •SOCIAL PROTECTION: *Special Report:* Security vs. Civil Liberties

Pires, Kirstin. Former Editor, *Billiards Digest.* •SPORTS AND GAMES: *Billiard Games*

Ponmoni Sahadevan. Associate Professor, Jawaharlal Nehru University, New Delhi. Author of *Conflict and Peacemaking in South Asia.* •WORLD AFFAIRS: *Maldives*

Prasad, H.Y. Sharada. Vice President, Indian Council for Cultural Relations; Former Information Adviser to the Prime Minister of India. •BIOGRAPHIES *(in part);* OBITUARIES *(in part);* WORLD AFFAIRS: *India*

Primorac, Max. Executive Director, Institute of World Affairs, Zagreb, Croatia. •WORLD AFFAIRS: *Croatia*

Rauch, Robert. Freelance Editor and Writer. •BIOGRAPHIES *(in part);* NOBEL PRIZES *(in part);* OBITUARIES *(in part)*

Raun, Toivo U. Professor of Central Eurasian Studies, Indiana University. Author of *Estonia and the Estonians.* •WORLD AFFAIRS: *Estonia*

Ray, Michael. Freelance Writer; Contributor to *Trimtab* (the newsletter of the Buckminster Fuller Institute). •BIOGRAPHIES *(in part)*

Rebelo, L.S. Professor Emeritus, Department of Portuguese Studies, King's College, University of London. •LITERATURE: *Portuguese:* Portugal

Reddington, André. Assistant Editor, *Amateur Wrestling News.* •SPORTS AND GAMES: *Wrestling:* Freestyle and Greco-Roman

Reid, Ron. Staff Writer, *Philadelphia Inquirer.* •BIOGRAPHIES *(in part);* SPORTS AND GAMES: *Ice Hockey; Ice Skating*

Renwick, David. Freelance Journalist. •WORLD AFFAIRS: *Antigua and Barbuda; Bahamas, The; Barbados; Dependent States: Caribbean and Bermuda; Dominica; Grenada; Guyana; Jamaica; Saint Kitts and Nevis; Saint Lucia; Saint Vincent and the Grenadines; Trinidad and Tobago*

Robbins, Paul. Freelance Writer. Correspondent, *Ski Trax* and *Ski Racing.* •BIOGRAPHIES *(in part);* SPORTS AND GAMES: *Skiing*

Robinson, David. Film Critic and Historian. Author of *A History of World Cinema* and others. •PERFORMING ARTS: *Motion Pictures*

Roby, Anne. Freelance Journalist. •WORLD AFFAIRS: *Andorra; Liechtenstein; Luxembourg; Monaco*

Rohwedder, Cecilie. Staff Reporter, *The Wall Street Journal Europe.* •BIOGRAPHIES *(in part);* WORLD AFFAIRS: *Germany*

Rollin, Jack. Editor, *Rothmans Football Yearbook* and *Playfair Football Annual.* Author of *The World Cup 1930–1990: Sixty Glorious Years of Soccer's Premier Event* and others. •BIOGRAPHIES *(in part);* SPORTS AND GAMES: *Football:* Association Football (Soccer); *Football:* Sidebar

Rose, Leo E. Professor Emeritus of Political Science, University of California, Berkeley. •BIOGRAPHIES *(in part);* WORLD AFFAIRS: *Bhutan; Nepal*

Rugh, William A. President and CEO, AMIDEAST; Former U.S. Ambassador to Yemen and the United Arab Emirates. Author of *The Arab Press.* •WORLD AFFAIRS: *United Arab Emirates; Yemen*

Rutherford, Andrew. Professor of Law and Criminal Policy, University of Southampton, Eng. Author of *Transforming Criminal Policy* and others. •LAW, CRIME, AND LAW ENFORCEMENT: *Death Penalty; Prisons and Penology; Special Report:* The Death Penalty on Trial

Sabo, Anne G. Assistant Professor of Norwegian, St. Olaf College, Northfield, Minn. •LITERATURE: *Norwegian*

Sanders, Alan J.K. Former Lecturer in Mongolian Studies, School of Oriental and African Studies, University of London. Author of *Historical Dictionary of Mongolia;* Coauthor of *Colloquial Mongolian.* •WORLD AFFAIRS: *Mongolia*

Sandvik, Gudmund. Professor Emeritus of Legal History, Faculty of Law, University of Oslo. •WORLD AFFAIRS: *Norway*

Saracino, Peter. Freelance Defense Journalist; Contributor to *PEJ News,* Victoria, B.C. •BIOGRAPHIES *(in part);* MILITARY AFFAIRS: *Special Report:* Warfare in the 21st Century

Sarahete, Yrjö. Secretary Emeritus, Fédération Internationale des Quilleurs. •SPORTS AND GAMES: *Bowling:* World Tenpins

Contributors

Saunders, Christopher. Professor of Historical Studies, University of Cape Town. Coauthor of *Historical Dictionary of South Africa* and *South Africa: A Modern History.* •WORLD AFFAIRS: *Cape Verde; Chad; Equatorial Guinea; Gambia, The; Guinea-Bissau; Lesotho; Madagascar; Namibia; São Tomé and Príncipe*

Schmidt, Fabian. Head of the Bosnian Program, Deutsche Welle. •WORLD AFFAIRS: *Albania*

Schroeder, Patricia S. President and CEO, Association of American Publishers. Author of *24 Years of House Work . . . and the Place Is Still a Mess.* •MEDIA AND PUBLISHING: *Book Publishing* (U.S.)

Schultz, Warren. Freelance Writer; Contributing Editor, *Organic Style.* Author of *A Man's Garden.* •THE ENVIRONMENT: *Gardening; Gardening:* Sidebar

Schuster, Angela M.H. Director of Publications, World Monuments Fund; Contributing Editor, *Archaeology;* Editor, *The Explorers Journal* and *ICON.* •ANTHROPOLOGY AND ARCHAEOLOGY: *Archaeology:* Eastern Hemisphere

Sego, Stephen. Freelance Journalist; Former Director, Radio Free Afghanistan. •BIOGRAPHIES (*in part*); WORLD AFFAIRS: *Afghanistan*

Seligson, Mitchell A. Daniel H. Wallace Professor of Political Science, University of Pittsburgh, Pa. Editor of *Elections and Democracy in Central America, Revisited.* •WORLD AFFAIRS: *Costa Rica*

Serafin, Steven R. Director, Writing Center, Hunter College, City University of New York. Coeditor of *Encyclopedia of American Literature* and *The Continuum Encyclopedia of British Literature.* •NOBEL PRIZES (*in part*)

Shelley, Andrew. Director, Women's International Squash Players Association; Technical Director, World Squash Federation. Author of *Squash Rules: A Players Guide.* •SPORTS AND GAMES: *Squash*

Shepherd, Melinda C. Associate Editor, Encyclopædia Britannica. •OBITUARIES (*in part*); SPORTS AND GAMES: *Automobile Racing:* U.S. Auto Racing (*in part*); *Football:* Association Football (Soccer): *Africa and Asia; Special Report:* The XIX Olympic Winter Games; WORLD AFFAIRS: *Dependent States:* Europe and the Atlantic

Shubinsky, Valery. Freelance Critic and Journalist. •LITERATURE: *Russian*

Siler, Shanda. Editorial Assistant, Encyclopædia Britannica. •BIOGRAPHIES (*in part*); OBITUARIES (*in part*)

Simons, Paul. Freelance Journalist. Author of *The Action Plant.* •LIFE SCIENCES: *Botany*

Simpson, Jane. Freelance Writer. •PERFORMING ARTS: *Dance:* European

Sklar, Morton. Executive Director, World Organization Against Torture USA; Judge, Administrative Labor Tribunal, Organization of American States; Member of the Board of Directors, Amnesty International USA. Editor, *The Status of Human Rights in the United States* and *Torture in the U.S.* Author of *The Right to Travel* and others. •SOCIAL PROTECTION: *Human Rights*

Smentkowski, Brian. Associate Professor of Political Science, Southeast Missouri State University. (*The author acknowledges research assistance of Benjamin Lowrance.*) •LAW, CRIME, AND LAW ENFORCEMENT: *Court Decisions*

Smith, Gregory O. Academic Director, European School of Economics. •WORLD AFFAIRS: *San Marino; Vatican City State*

Smith-Irowa, Pamela L. Freelance Writer. •BIOGRAPHIES (*in part*)

Snodgrass, Donald. Institute Fellow Emeritus, Harvard University. Coauthor of *Economics of Development,* 5th ed. •WORLD AFFAIRS: *Sri Lanka*

Sparks, Karen J. Editor, Encyclopædia Britannica. •OBITUARIES (*in part*); ART, ANTIQUES, AND COLLECTIONS: *Special Report:* Redefining Art

Stahler-Sholk, Richard. Associate Professor of Political Science, Eastern Michigan University. •WORLD AFFAIRS: *Nicaragua*

Stern, Irwin. Lecturer in Foreign Languages, North Carolina State University. Editor of *Dictionary of Brazilian Literature.* •LITERATURE: *Portuguese:* Brazil

Stewart, Alan. Freelance Journalist. Author of *How to Make It in IT.* •BIOGRAPHIES (*in part*); COMPUTERS AND INFORMATION SYSTEMS: *Microelectronics; Telecommunications;* MEDIA AND PUBLISHING: *Sidebar*

Summerhill, Edward M. Lead Editor of the News Bulletin, Finnish News Agency. •WORLD AFFAIRS: *Finland*

Sumner, David E. Professor of Journalism and Head of the Magazine Program, Ball State University, Muncie, Ind. •MEDIA AND PUBLISHING: *Magazines*

Sumrall, Harry. Editor in Chief, RedLudwig.com. •BIOGRAPHIES (*in part*); PERFORMING ARTS: *Music:* Classical

Susel, Rudolph M. Editor, *American Home.* •WORLD AFFAIRS: *Slovenia*

Susser, Leslie D. Diplomatic Correspondent, *The Jerusalem Report.* Coauthor of *Shalom Friend: The Life and Legacy of Yitzhak Rabin.* •WORLD AFFAIRS: *Israel*

Szilagyi, Zsofia. Freelance Writer. •WORLD AFFAIRS: *Hungary*

Taylor, Jolanda Vanderwal. Associate Professor of Dutch and German, University of Wisconsin at Madison. Author of *A Family Occupation: Children of the War and the Memory of World War II in Dutch Literature of the 1980s.* •BIOGRAPHIES (*in part*); LITERATURE: *Netherlandic;* WORLD AFFAIRS: *The Netherlands*

Taylor, Richard. Freelance Journalist; Basketball Columnist, *The Independent.* •BIOGRAPHIES (*in part*)

Taylor-Robinson, Michelle M. Associate Professor of Political Science, Texas A&M University. Coauthor of *Negotiating Democracy: Transitions from Authoritarian Rule.* •WORLD AFFAIRS: *Honduras*

Teague, Elizabeth. Ministry of Defence, London. (The opinions expressed are personal and do not necessarily represent those of the British government.) •WORLD AFFAIRS: *Russia*

Tétreault, Mary Ann. Una Chapman Cox Distinguished Professor of International Affairs, Trinity University, San Antonio, Texas. Author of *Stories of Democracy: Politics and Society in Contemporary Kuwait* and others. •WORLD AFFAIRS: *Kuwait*

Thayer, Carlyle A. Professor of Politics, Australian Defence Force Academy, Canberra. Author of *The Vietnam People's Army Under Doi Moi.* •WORLD AFFAIRS: *Vietnam*

Thomas, R. Murray. Professor Emeritus of Education, University of California, Santa Barbara. Author of *Recent Theories of Human Development* and *Folk Psychologies Across Cultures.* •EDUCATION; EDUCATION: *Special Report:* New Frontiers in Cheating

Thyagarajan, S. Deputy Editor and Hockey Correspondent, *The Hindu.* •SPORTS AND GAMES: *Field Hockey*

Tikkanen, Amy. Freelance Writer and Editor. •BIOGRAPHIES (*in part*)

Todd Middleton, Amy. Vice President, Sotheby's. •ART, ANTIQUES, AND COLLECTIONS: *Art Auctions and Sales*

Tucker, Emma. Correspondent, *Financial Times,* London. •WORLD AFFAIRS: *European Union*

Turner, Darrell J. Freelance Writer; Former Religion Writer, *The Journal Gazette* (Fort Wayne, Ind.); Former Associate Editor, Religion News Service. •BIOGRAPHIES (*in part*); RELIGION; RELIGION: *Sidebar*

Uhlick, Lawrence R. Executive Director and General Counsel, Institute of International Bankers. •ECONOMIC AFFAIRS: *Banking*

UNHCR. The Office of the United Nations High Commissioner for Refugees. •SOCIAL PROTECTION: *Refugees and International Migration*

Urbansky, Julie. Media and Public Relations Director, U.S. Bobsled and Skeleton Federation. •SPORTS AND GAMES: *Bobsleigh, Skeleton, and Luge:* Bobsleigh; Skeleton

Verdi, Robert. Senior Writer, *Golf Digest, Golf World;* Contributing Columnist, *Chicago Tribune.* •SPORTS AND GAMES: *Baseball* (U.S. and Canada)

Walker, Hillary. Public Affairs Program Assistant, American Zoo and Aquarium Association. •THE ENVIRONMENT: *Zoos*

Wallenfeldt, Jeff. Senior Editor, Encyclopædia Britannica. •BIOGRAPHIES (*in part*)

Wang Xiao Ming. Professor of Modern Chinese Literature; Director, Center for Contemporary Culture Studies, Shanghai University. Author of *The Cold Face of Reality: A Biography of Lu Xun.* •LITERATURE: *Chinese*

Wanninger, Richard S. Freelance Journalist. •SPORTS AND GAMES: *Volleyball*

Watson, Rory. Freelance Journalist specializing in European Union affairs. Coauthor of *The American Express Guide to Brussels.* •WORLD AFFAIRS: *Belgium*

Weil, Eric. Sports Editor, *Buenos Aires Herald;* South America Correspondent, *World Soccer Magazine.* •BIOGRAPHIES (*in part*); SPORTS AND GAMES: *Football:* Association Football (Soccer): *The Americas*

Weinstein, Martin. Professor of Political Science, William Paterson University of New Jersey. Author of *Uruguay: Democracy at the Crossroads.* •WORLD AFFAIRS: *Uruguay*

White, Martin L. Freelance Writer, Chicago. •OBITUARIES (*in part*)

Whitney, Barbara. Copy Supervisor, Encyclopædia Britannica. •BIOGRAPHIES (*in part*); OBITUARIES (*in part*)

Whitten, Phillip. Editor in Chief, Swiminfo.com, *Swimming World, Swim,* and *Swimming Technique* magazines. Author of *The Complete Book of Swimming* and others. •SPORTS AND GAMES: *Swimming*

Wilkinson, Earl J. Executive Director and Chief Executive Officer, International Newspaper Marketing Association. Author of *Branding and the Newspaper Consumer.* •MEDIA AND PUBLISHING: *Newspapers*

Wilkinson, John R. Sportswriter, Coventry Newspapers. •SPORTS AND GAMES: *Cycling*

Williams, Victoria C. Assistant Professor of the Humanities, Alvernia College, Reading, Pa.; Independent Consultant on International Affairs. •LAW, CRIME, AND LAW ENFORCEMENT: *International Law*

Wilson, Derek. Former Correspondent, BBC, Rome. Author of *Rome, Umbria and Tuscany.* •WORLD AFFAIRS: *Italy*

Wise, Larry. Freelance Writer; Former World Champion Archer and Professional Coach. Author of *On Target for Tuning Your Compound Bow* and others. •SPORTS AND GAMES: *Archery*

Wittbrodt, Beth. Assistant Editor, Encyclopædia Britannica. •OBITUARIES (*in part*)

Woodrow, Robert. Former Assistant Managing Editor, *Asiaweek.* •WORLD AFFAIRS: *Cambodia; Laos; Thailand*

Woods, Elizabeth Rhett. Writer. Author of *Family Fictions, If Only Things Were Different (I): A Model for a Sustainable Society, Bird Salad,* and others. •BIOGRAPHIES (*in part*); LITERATURE: *English:* Canada

Woods, Michael. Science Editor, *The Toledo* (Ohio) *Blade.* Author of *Ancient Technology.* •MATHEMATICS AND PHYSICAL SCIENCES: *Chemistry;* NOBEL PRIZES (*in part*)

Woodward, Ralph Lee, Jr. Neville G. Penrose Professor of Latin American Studies, Texas Christian University. Author of *Central America, a Nation Divided.* •WORLD AFFAIRS: *El Salvador; Guatemala*

Wyllie, Peter J. Emeritus Professor of Geology, California Institute of Technology. Author of *The Dynamic Earth* and *The Way the Earth Works.* •EARTH SCIENCES: *Geology and Geochemistry*

Zegura, Stephen L. Professor of Anthropology, University of Arizona. •ANTHROPOLOGY AND ARCHAEOLOGY: *Anthropology:* Physical

Ziring, Lawrence. Arnold E. Schnieder Professor of Political Science, Western Michigan University. Author of *Pakistan in the Twentieth Century: A Political History.* •WORLD AFFAIRS: *Pakistan*

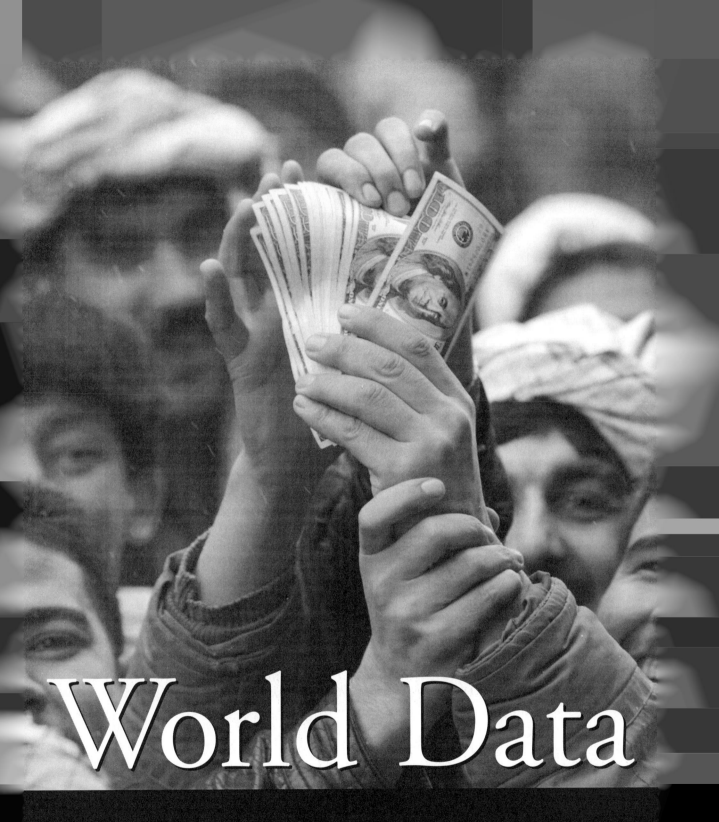

World Data

The afghani (the Afghan national currency) has dramatically declined in value since 1980. The U.S. dollar or Pakistan rupee are the currencies

CONTENTS

531

INTRODUCTION

Britannica World Data provides a statistical portrait of some 217 countries and dependencies of the world, at a level appropriate to the significance of each. It contains 213 country statements (the "Nations of the World" section), ranging in length from one to seven pages, and permits, in the 20 major thematic tables (the "Comparative National Statistics" [CNS] section), comparisons among these larger countries and 4 other states.

Updated annually, *Britannica World Data* is particularly intended as direct, structured support for many of Britannica's other reference works—encyclopaedias, yearbooks, atlases—at a level of detail that their editorial style or design do not permit.

Like the textual, graphic, or cartographic modes of expression of these other products, statistics possess their own inherent editorial virtues and weaknesses. Two principal goals in the creation of *Britannica World Data* were up-to-dateness and comparability, each possible to maximize separately, but not always possible to combine. If, for example, research on some subject is completed during a particular year (x), figures may be available for 100 countries for the preceding year ($x - 1$), for 140 countries for the year before that ($x - 2$), and for 180 countries for the year before that ($x - 3$).

Which year should be the basis of a thematic compilation for 217 countries so as to give the best combination of up-to-dateness and comparability? And, should $x - 1$ be adopted for the thematic table, ought up-to-dateness in the country table (for which year x is already available) be sacrificed for agreement with the thematic table? In general, the editors have opted for maximum up-to-dateness in the country statistical boxes and maximum comparability in the thematic tables.

Comparability, however, also resides in the meaning of the numbers compiled, which may differ greatly from country to country. The headnotes to the thematic tables explain many of these methodological problems; the Glossary serves the same purpose for the country statistical pages. Published data do not always provide the researcher or editor with a neat, unambiguous choice between a datum compiled on two different bases (say, railroad track length, or route length), one of which is wanted and the other not. More often a choice must be made among a variety of official, private, and external intergovernmental (UN, FAO, IMF) sources, each reporting its best data but each representing a set of problems: (1) of methodological variance from (or among) international conventions; (2) of analytical completeness (data for a single year may, successively, be projected [based on 10 months' data], preliminary [for 12 months], final, revised or adjusted, etc.); (3) of time frame, or accounting interval (data may represent a full Gregorian calendar year [preferred], a fiscal year, an Islamic or other national or religious year, a multiyear period or average [when a one-year statement would contain unrepresentative results]); (4) of continuity with previous data; and the like. Finally, published data on a

particular subject may be complete and final but impossible to summarize in a simple manner. The education system of a single country may include, for example, public and private sectors; local, state, or national systems; varying grades, tracks, or forms within a single system; or opportunities for double-counting or fractional counting of a student, teacher, or institution. When no recent official data exist, or they exist, but may be suspect, the tables may show unofficial estimates, a range (of published opinion), analogous data, or no data at all.

The published basis of the information compiled is the statistical collections of Encyclopædia Britannica, Inc., some of the principal elements of which are enumerated in the Bibliography. Holdings for a given country may include any of the following: the national statistical abstract; the constitution; the most recent censuses of population; periodic or occasional reports on vital statistics, social indicators, agriculture, mining, labour, manufacturing, domestic and foreign trade, finance and banking, transportation, and communications. Further information is received in a variety of formats—telephone, letter, fax, microfilm and microfiche, and most recently, in electronic formats such as computer disks, CD-ROMs, and the Internet. So substantial has the resources of the Internet become that it was decided to add uniform resource locators (URLs) to the great majority of country pages and a number of the CNS tables (summary world sites with data on all countries still being somewhat of a rarity) so as to apprise the reader of the possibility and means to access current information on these subjects year-round.

The recommendations offered are usually to official sites (national statistical offices, general national governments, central banks, embassies, intergovernmental organizations [especially the UN Development Programme], and the like). Though often dissimilar in content, they will usually be updated year-round, expanded as opportunity permits, and lead on to related sites, such as parliamentary offices, information offices, diplomatic and consular sites, news agencies and newspapers, and, beyond, to the myriad academic, commercial, and private sites now accessible from the personal computer. While these URLs were correct and current at the time of writing, they may be subject to change.

The great majority of the social, economic, and financial data contained in this work should not be interpreted in isolation. Interpretive text of long perspective, such as that of the *Encyclopædia Britannica* itself; political, geographic, and topical maps, such as those in the *Britannica Atlas;* and recent analysis of political events and economic trends, such as that contained in the articles of the *Book of the Year,* will all help to supply analytic focus that numbers alone cannot. By the same token, study of those sources will be made more concrete by use of *Britannica World Data* to supply up-to-date geographic, demographic, and economic detail.

GLOSSARY

A number of terms that are used to classify and report data in the "Nations of the World" section require some explanation.

Those italicized terms that are used regularly in the country compilations to introduce specific categories of information (*e.g., birth rate, budget*) appear in this glossary in italic boldface type, followed by a description of the precise kind of information being offered and how it has been edited and presented.

All other terms are printed here in roman boldface type. Many terms have quite specific meanings in statistical reporting, and they are so defined here. Other terms have less specific application as they are used by different countries or organizations. Data in the country compilations based on definitions markedly different from those below will usually be footnoted.

Terms that appear in small capitals in certain definitions are themselves defined at their respective alphabetical locations.

Terms whose definitions are marked by an asterisk (*) refer to data supplied only in the larger two- to four-page country compilations.

access to services, a group of measures indicating a population's level of access to public services, including electrical power, treated public drinking water, sewage removal, and fire protection.*

activity rate, *see* participation/activity rates.

age breakdown, the distribution of a given population by age, usually reported here as percentages of total population in 15-year age brackets. When substantial numbers of persons do not know, or state, their exact age, distributions may not total 100.0%.

area, the total surface area of a country or its administrative subdivisions, including both land and inland (nontidal) water area. Land area is usually calculated from "mean low water" on a "plane table," or flat, basis.

area and population, a tabulation usually including the first-order administrative subdivisions of the country (such as the states of the United States), with capital (headquarters, or administrative seat), area, and population. When these subdivisions are especially numerous or, occasionally, nonexistent, a planning, electoral, census, or other nonadministrative scheme of regional subdivisions has been substituted.

associated state, *see* state.

atheist, in statements of religious affiliation, one who professes active opposition to religion; "nonreligious" refers to those professing only no religion, nonbelief, or doubt.

balance of payments, a financial statement for a country for a given period showing the balance among: (1) transactions in goods, services, and income between that country and the rest of the world, (2) changes in ownership or valuation of that country's monetary gold, SPECIAL DRAWING RIGHTS, and claims on and liabilities to the rest of the world, and (3) unrequited transfers and counterpart entries needed (in an accounting sense) to balance transactions and changes among any of the foregoing types of exchange that are not mutually offsetting. Detail of national law as to what constitutes a transaction, the basis of its valuation, and the size of a transaction visible to fiscal authorities

all result in differences in the meaning of a particular national statement.*

balance of trade, the net value of all international goods trade of a country, usually excluding reexports (goods received only for transshipment), and the percentage that this net represents of total trade.

Balance of trade refers only to the "visible" international trade of goods as recorded by customs authorities and is thus a segment of a country's BALANCE OF PAYMENTS, which takes all visible and invisible trade with other countries into account. (Invisible trade refers to imports and exports of money, financial instruments, and services such as transport, tourism, and insurance.) A country has a favourable, or positive (+), balance of trade when the value

of exports exceeds that of imports and negative (–) when imports exceed exports.

barrel (bbl), a unit of liquid measure. The barrel conventionally used for reporting crude petroleum and petroleum products is equal to 42 U.S. gallons, or 159 litres. The number of barrels of crude petroleum per metric ton, ranging typically from 6.20 to 8.13, depends upon the specific gravity of the petroleum. The world average is roughly 7.33 barrels per ton.

birth rate, the number of live births annually per 1,000 of midyear population. Birth rates for individual countries may be compared with the estimated world annual average of 22.5 births per 1,000 population in 2000.

budget, the annual receipts and expenditures—of a central government for its activities only;

Abbreviations

Measurements

cu m	cubic metre(s)	U.S.	United States
kg	kilograms(s)	U.S.S.R.	Union of Soviet Socialist
km	kilometre(s)		Republics
kW	kilowatt(s)		
kW-hr	kilowatt-hour(s)	**Months**	
metric ton-km	metric ton-kilometre(s)	Jan.	January	Oct.	October
mi	mile(s)	Feb.	February	Nov.	November
passenger-km	passenger-kilometre(s)	Aug.	August	Dec.	December
passenger-mi	passenger-mile(s)	Sept.	September		
short ton-mi	short ton-mile(s)		
sq km	square kilometre(s)		
sq m	square metre(s)	**Miscellaneous**	
sq mi	square mile(s)		
troy oz	troy ounce(s)	AIDS	Acquired Immune
yr	year(s)		Deficiency Syndrome
		avg.	average
		c.i.f.	cost, insurance, and

Political Units and International Organizations

CACM	Central American Common Market	commun.	communications
		CPI	consumer price index
Caricom	Caribbean Community and Common Market	est.	estimate(d)
		excl.	excluding
CFA	Communauté Financière Africaine	f.o.b.	free on board
		GDP	gross domestic product
CFP	Comptoirs Françaises du Pacifique	GNP	gross national product
		govt.	government
CIS	Commonwealth of Independent States	incl.	including
		mo.	month(s)
CUSA	Customs Union of Southern Africa	n.a.	not available (in text)
		n.e.s.	not elsewhere specified
EC	European Communities	no.	number
ESCWA	Economic and Social Commission for Western Asia	pl.	plural
		pos.	position
		pub. admin.	public administration
		PVC	Polyvinyl Chloride
EU	European Union	SDR	Special Drawing Right
FAO	United Nations Food and Agriculture Organization	SITC	Standard International Trade Classification
IMF	International Monetary Fund	svcs.	services
OECD	Organization for Economic Cooperation and Development	teacher tr.	teacher training
		transp.	transportation
		voc.	vocational
OECS	Organization of Eastern Caribbean States	$	dollar (of any currency area)
U.A.E.	United Arab Emirates	£	pound (of any currency area)
U.K.	United Kingdom	…	not available (in tables)
UNDP	United Nations Development Programme	—	none, less than half the smallest unit shown, or not applicable (in tables)

does not include state, provincial, or local governments or semipublic (parastatal, quasi-nongovernmental) corporations unless otherwise specified. Figures for budgets are limited to ordinary (recurrent) receipts and expenditures, wherever possible, and exclude capital expenditures—*i.e.,* funds for development and other special projects originating as foreign-aid grants or loans.

When both a recurrent and a capital budget exist for a single country, the former is the budget funded entirely from national resources (taxes, duties, excises, etc.) that would recur (be generated by economic activity) every year. It funds the most basic governmental services, those least able to suffer interruption. The capital budget is usually funded by external aid and may change its size considerably from year to year.

capital, usually, the actual seat of government and administration of a state. When more than one capital exists, each is identified by kind; when interim arrangements exist during the creation or movement of a national capital, the de facto situation is described.

Anomalous cases are annotated, such as those in which (1) the de jure designation under the country's laws differs from actual local practice (*e.g.,* Benin's designation of one capital in constitutional law, but another in actual practice), (2) international recognition does not validate a country's claim (as with the proclamation by Israel of a capital on territory not internationally recognized as part of Israel), or (3) both a state and a capital have been proclaimed on territory recognized as part of another state (as with the Turkish Republic of Northern Cyprus).

capital budget, *see* budget.

causes of death, as defined by the World Health Organization (WHO), "the disease or injury which initiated the train of morbid events leading directly to death, or the circumstances of accident or violence which produced the fatal injury." This principle, the "underlying cause of death," is the basis of the medical judgment as to cause; the statistical classification system according to which these causes are grouped and named is the *International List of Causes of Death,* the latest revision of which is the Tenth. Reporting is usually in terms of events per 100,000 population. When data on actual causes of death are unavailable, information on morbidity, or illness rate, usually given as reported cases per 100,000 of infectious diseases (notifiable to WHO as a matter of international agreement), may be substituted.

chief of state/head of government, paramount national governmental officer(s) exercising the highest executive and/or ceremonial roles of a country's government. In general usage, the chief of state is the formal head of a national state. The primary responsibilities of the chief of state may range from the purely ceremonial—convening legislatures and greeting foreign officials—to the exercise of complete national executive authority. The head of government, when this function exists separately, is the officer nominally charged (by the constitution) with the majority of actual executive powers, though they may not in practice be exercised, especially in military or single-party regimes in which effective power may reside entirely outside the executive governmental machinery provided by the constitution. A prime minister, for example, usually the actual head of government, may in practice exercise only Cabinet-level authority.

In communist countries an official identified as the chief of state may be the chairman of the policy-making organ, and the official given as the head of government the chairman of the nominal administrative/executive organ.

c.i.f. (trade valuation): *see* imports.

colony, an area annexed to, or controlled by, an independent state but not an integral part of it; a non-self-governing territory. A colony has a charter and may have a degree of self-government. A crown colony is a colony originally chartered by the British government.

commonwealth (U.K. and U.S.), a self-governing political entity that has regard to the common weal, or good; usually associated with the United Kingdom or United States. Examples include the Commonwealth of Nations (composed of independent states [from 1931 onward]), Puerto Rico since 1952, and the Northern Marianas since 1979.

communications, collectively, the means available for the public transmission of information within a country. Data are tabulated for: daily newspapers and their total circulation; radio and television as total numbers of receivers; telephone data as "main lines," or the number of subscriber lines (not receivers) having access to the public switched network; cellular telephones as number of subscribers; and facsimile machines and personal computers as number of units. For each, a rate per 1,000 persons is given.

constant prices, an adjustment to the members of a financial time series to eliminate the effect of inflation year by year. It consists of referring all data in the series to a single year so that "real" change may be seen.

constitutional monarchy, *see* monarchy.

consumer price index (CPI), also known as the retail price index, or the cost-of-living index, a series of index numbers assigned to the price of a selected "basket," or assortment, of basic consumer goods and services in a country, region, city, or type of household in order to measure changes over time in prices paid by a typical household for those goods and services. Items included in the CPI are ordinarily determined by governmental surveys of typical household expenditures and are assigned weights relative to their proportion of those expenditures. Index values are period averages unless otherwise noted.

coprincipality, *see* monarchy.

current prices, the valuation of a financial aggregate as of the year reported.

daily per capita caloric intake (supply), the calories equivalent to the known average daily supply of foodstuffs for human consumption in a given country divided by the population of the country (and the proportion of that supply provided, respectively, by vegetable and animal sources). The daily per capita caloric intake of a country may be compared with the corresponding recommended minimum daily requirement. The latter is calculated by the Food and Agriculture Organization of the United Nations from the age and sex distributions, average body weights, and environmental temperatures in a given region to determine the calories needed to sustain a person there at normal levels of activity and health. The daily per capita caloric requirement ranges from 2,200 to 2,500.

de facto population, for a given area, the population composed of those actually present at a particular time, including temporary residents and visitors (such as immigrants not yet granted permanent status, "guest" or expatriate workers, refugees, or tourists), but excluding legal residents temporarily absent.

de jure population, for a given area, the population composed only of those legally resident at a particular time, excluding temporary residents and visitors (such as "guest" or expatriate workers, refugees, or tourists), but including legal residents temporarily absent.

deadweight tonnage, the maximum weight of cargo, fuel, fresh water, stores, and persons that may safely by carried by a ship. It is customarily measured in long tons of 2,240 pounds each, equivalent to 1.016 metric tons. Deadweight tonnage is the difference between the tonnage of a fully loaded ship and the fully unloaded tonnage of that ship. *See also* gross ton.

death rate, the number of deaths annually per 1,000 of midyear population. Death rates for individual countries may be compared with the estimated world annual average of 9.0 deaths per 1,000 population in 2000.

density (of population), usually, the DE FACTO POPULATION of a country divided by its total area. Special adjustment is made for large areas of inland water, desert, or other uninhabitable areas—*e.g.,* excluding the ice cap of Greenland.

dependent state, constitutionally or statutorily organized political entity outside of and under the jurisdiction of an independent state (or a federal element of such a state) but not formally annexed to it (*see* Table).

Dependent states[1]

Australia	**United Kingdom**
Christmas Island	Anguilla
Cocos (Keeling) Islands	Bermuda
Norfolk Island	British Virgin Islands
	Cayman Islands
Denmark	Falkland Islands
Faroe Islands	Gibraltar
Greenland	Guernsey
	Isle of Man
France	Jersey
French Guiana	Montserrat
French Polynesia	Pitcairn Island
Guadeloupe	Saint Helena and Dependencies
Martinique	Turks and Caicos Islands
Mayotte	
New Caledonia	**United States**
Réunion	American Samoa
Saint Pierre and Miquelon	Guam
Wallis and Futuna	Northern Mariana Islands
	Puerto Rico
Netherlands, The	Virgin Islands (of the U.S.)
Aruba	
Netherlands Antilles	
New Zealand	
Cook Islands	
Niue	
Tokelau	

[1]Excludes territories (1) to which Antarctic Treaty is applicable in whole or in part, (2) without permanent civilian population, (3) without internationally recognized civilian government (Western Sahara, Gaza Strip), or (4) representing unadjudicated unilateral or multilateral territorial claims.

direct taxes, taxes levied directly on firms and individuals, such as taxes on income, profits, and capital gains. The *immediate* incidence, or burden, of direct taxes is on the firms and individuals thus taxed; direct taxes on firms may, however, be passed on to consumers and other economic units in the form of higher prices for goods and services, blurring the distinction between direct and indirect taxation.

distribution of income/wealth, the portion of personal income or wealth accruing to households or individuals constituting each respective decile (tenth) or quintile (fifth) of a country's households or individuals.*

divorce rate, the number of legal, civilly recognized divorces annually per 1,000 population.

doubling time, the number of complete years required for a country to double its population at its current rate of natural increase.

earnings index, a series of index numbers comparing average wages in a collective industrial sample for a country or region with the same industries at a previous period to measure changes over time in those wages. It is most commonly reported for wages paid on a daily, weekly, or monthly basis; annual figures may represent total income or averages of these shorter periods. The scope of the earnings index varies from country to country. The index is often limited to earnings in manufacturing industries. The index for each country applies to all wage earners in a designated group and ordinarily takes into account basic wages (overtime is normally distinguished), bonuses, cost-of-living allowances, and contributions toward social security. Some countries include payments in kind. Contributions toward social security by employers are usually excluded, as are social security benefits received by wage earners.

economically active population, *see* population economically active.

education, tabulation of the principal elements of a country's educational establishment, classified as far as possible according to the country's own system of primary, secondary, and higher levels (the usual age limits for these levels being identified in parentheses), with total number of schools (physical facilities) and of teachers and students (whether full- or part-time). The student-teacher ratio is calculated whenever available data permit.

educational attainment, the distribution of the population age 25 and over with completed educations by the highest level of formal education attained or completed; it must sometimes be reported, however, for age groups still in school or for the economically active only.

emirate, *see* monarchy.

enterprise, a legal entity formed to conduct a business, which it may do from more than one establishment (place of business or service point).

ethnic/linguistic composition, ethnic, racial, or linguistic composition of a national population, reported here according to the most reliable breakdown available, whether published in official sources (such as a census) or in external analysis (when the subject is not addressed in national sources).

exchange rate, the value of one currency compared with another, or with a standardized unit of account such as the SPECIAL DRAWING RIGHT, or as mandated by local statute when one currency is "tied" by a par value to another. Rates given usually refer to free market values when the currency has no, or very limited, restrictions on its convertibility into other currencies.

exports, material goods legally leaving a country (or customs area) and subject to customs regulations. The total value and distribution by percentage of the major items (in preference to groups of goods) exported are given, together with the distribution of trade among major

trading partners (usually single countries or trading blocs). Valuation of goods exported is free on board (f.o.b.) unless otherwise specified. The value of goods exported and imported f.o.b. is calculated from the cost of production and excludes the cost of transport.

external debt, public and publicly guaranteed debt with a maturity of more than one year owed to nonnationals of a country and repayable in foreign currency, goods, or services. The debt may be an obligation of a national or subnational governmental body (or an agency of either), of an autonomous public body, or of a private debtor that is guaranteed by a public entity. The debt is usually either outstanding (contracted) or disbursed (drawn).

external territory (Australia), *see* territory.

federal, consisting of first-order political subdivisions that are prior to and independent of the central government in certain functions.

federal republic, *see* republic.

federation, union of coequal, preexisting political entities that retain some degree of autonomy and (usually) right of secession within the union.

fertility rate, *see* total fertility rate.

financial aggregates, tabulation of seven-year time series, providing principal measures of the financial condition of a country, including: (1) the exchange rate of the national crurency against the U.S. dollar, the pound sterling, and the International Monetary Fund's SPECIAL DRAWING RIGHT (SDR), (2) the amount and kind of international reserves (holdings of SDRs, gold, and foreign currencies) and reserve position of the country in the IMF, and (3) principal economic rates and prices (central bank discount rate, government bond yields, and industrial stock [share] prices). For BALANCE OF PAYMENTS, the origin in terms of component balance of trade items and balance of invisibles (net) is given.*

fish catch, the live-weight equivalent of the aquatic animals (including fish, crustaceans, mollusks, etc., but excluding whales, seals, and other aquatic mammals) caught in freshwater or marine areas by national fleets and landed in domestic or foreign harbours for commercial, industrial, or subsistence purposes.

f.o.b. (trade valuation), *see* exports.

food, see daily per capita caloric intake.

form of government/political status, the type of administration provided for by a country's constitution—whether or not suspended by extralegal military or civil action, although such de facto administrations are identified—together with the number of members (elected, appointed, and ex officio) for each legislative house, named according to its English rendering. Dependent states (*see* Table) are classified according to the status of their political association with the administering country.

gross domestic product (GDP), the total value of the final goods and services produced by residents and nonresidents within a given country during a given accounting period, usually a year. Unless otherwise noted, the value is given in current prices of the year indicated. The *System of National Accounts* (SNA, published under the joint auspices of the UN, IMF, OECD, EC, and World Bank) provides a framework for international comparability in classifying domestic accounting aggregates and international transactions comprising "net factor income from abroad," the measure that distinguishes GDP and GNP.

gross national product (GNP), the total value of final goods and services produced both from within a given country *and* from external (foreign) transactions in a given accounting period, usually a year. Unless otherwise noted, the value is given in current prices of the year indicated. GNP is equal to GROSS DOMESTIC PRODUCT (*q.v.*) adjusted by net factor income from abroad, which is the income residents

receive from abroad for factor services (labour, investment, and interest) less similar payments made to nonresidents who contribute to the domestic economy.

gross ton, volumetric unit of measure (equaling 100 cubic feet [2.83 cu m]) of the permanently enclosed volume of a ship, above and below decks available for cargo, stores, or passenger accommodation. Net, or register, tonnage exempts certain nonrevenue spaces—such as those devoted to machinery, bunkers, crew accommodations, and ballast—from the gross tonnage. *See also* deadweight tonnage.

head of government, see chief of state/head of government.

health, a group of measures including number of accredited physicians currently practicing or employed and their ratio to the total population; total hospital beds and their ratio; and INFANT MORTALITY RATE.

household, economically autonomous individual or group of individuals living in a single dwelling unit. A family household is one composed principally of individuals related by blood or marriage.

household income and expenditure, data for average size of a HOUSEHOLD (by number of individuals) and median household income. Sources of income and expenditures for major items of consumption are given as percentages.

In general, household income is the amount of funds, usually measured in monetary units, received by the members (generally those 14 years old and over) of a household in a given time period. The income can be derived from (1) wages or salaries, (2) nonfarm or farm SELF-EMPLOYMENT, (3) transfer payments, such as pensions, public assistance, unemployment benefits, etc., and (4) other income, including interest and dividends, rent, royalties, etc. The income of a household is expressed as a gross amount before deductions for taxes. Data on expenditure refer to consumption of personal or household goods and services; they normally exclude savings, taxes, and insurance; practice with regard to inclusion of credit purchases differs markedly.

immigration, usually, the number and origin of those immigrants admitted to a nation in a legal status that would eventually permit the granting of the right to settle permanently or to acquire citizenship.*

imports, material goods legally entering a country (or customs area) and subject to customs regulations; excludes financial movements. The total value and distribution by percentage of the major items (in preference to groups of goods) imported are given, together with the direction of trade among major trading partners (usually single countries), trading blocs (such as the European Union), or customs areas (such as Belgium-Luxembourg). The value of goods imported is given free on board (f.o.b.) unless otherwise specified; f.o.b. is defined above under EXPORTS.

The principal alternate basis for valuation of goods in international trade is that of cost, insurance, and freight (c.i.f.); its use is restricted to imports, as it comprises the principal charges needed to bring the goods to the customs house in the country of destination. Because it inflates the value of imports relative to exports, more countries have, latterly, been estimating imports on an f.o.b. basis as well.

incorporated territory (U.S.), *see* territory.

independent, of a state, autonomous and controlling both its internal and external affairs. Its date usually refers to the date from which the country was in effective control of these affairs within its present boundaries, rather than the date independence was proclaimed or the date recognized as a de jure act by the former administering power.

indirect taxes, taxes levied on sales or transfers of selected intermediate goods and services, including excises, value-added taxes, and tariffs, that are ordinarily passed on to the ultimate consumers of the goods and services. Figures given for individual countries are limited to indirect taxes levied by their respective central governments unless otherwise specified.

infant mortality rate, the number of children per 1,000 live births who die before their first birthday. Total infant mortality includes neonatal mortality, which is deaths of children within one month of birth.

invisibles (invisible trade), *see* balance of trade.

kingdom, *see* monarchy.

labour force, portion of the POPULATION ECONOMICALLY ACTIVE (PEA) comprising those most fully employed or attached to the labour market (the unemployed are considered to be "attached" in that they usually represent persons previously employed seeking to be reemployed), particularly as viewed from a short-term perspective. It normally includes those who are self-employed, employed by others (whether full-time, part-time, seasonally, or on some other less than full-time, basis), and, as noted above, the unemployed (both those previously employed and those seeking work for the first time). In the "gross domestic product and labour force" table, the majority of the labour data provided refer to population economically active, since PEA represents the longer-term view of working population and, thus, subsumes more of the marginal workers who are often missed by shorter-term surveys.

land use, distribution by classes of vegetational cover or economic use of the land area only (excluding inland water, for example, but not marshland), reported as percentages. The principal categories utilized include: (1) forest, which includes natural and planted tracts, (2) meadows and pastures, which includes land in temporary or permanent use whose principal purpose is the growing of animal fodder, (3) agricultural and under permanent cultivation, which includes temporary and permanent cropland, as well as land left fallow less than five years, but capable of being returned to production without special preparation, and (4) other, which includes built-up, wasteland, watercourses, and the like.

leisure, the principal monetary expenditures, uses, or reported preferences in the use of the individual's free time for recreation, rest, or self-improvement.*

life expectancy, the number of years a person born within a particular population group (age cohort) would be expected to live, based on actuarial calculations.

literacy, the ability to read and write a language with some degree of competence; the precise degree constituting the basis of a particular national statement is usually defined by the national census and is often tested by the census enumerator. Elsewhere, particularly where much adult literacy may be the result of literacy campaigns rather than passage through a formal educational system, definition and testing of literacy may be better standardized.

major cities, usually the five largest cities proper (national capitals are always given, regardless of size); fewer cities may be listed if there are fewer urban localities in the country. For multipage tables, 10 or more may be listed.* Populations for cities will usually refer to the city proper—*i.e.,* the legally bounded corporate entity, or the most compact, contiguous, demographically urban portion of the entity defined by the local authorities. Occasionally figures for METROPOLITAN AREAS are cited when the relevant civil entity at the core of a major agglomeration had an unrepresentatively small population.

manufacturing, mining, and construction enterprises/retail sales and service enterprises, a detailed tabulation of the principal industries in these sectors, showing for each industry the number of enterprises and employees, wages in that industry as a percentage of the general average wage, and the value of that industry's output in terms of value added or turnover.*

marriage rate, the number of legal, civilly recognized marriages annually per 1,000 population.

material well-being, a group of measures indicating the percentage of households or dwellings possessing certain goods or appliances, including automobiles, telephones, television receivers, refrigerators, air conditioners, and washing machines.*

merchant marine, the privately or publicly owned ships registered with the maritime authority of a nation (limited to those in Lloyd's of London statistical reporting of 100 or more GROSS TONS) that are employed in commerce, whether or not owned or operated by nationals of the country.

metropolitan area, a city and the region of dense, predominantly urban, settlement around the city; the population of the whole usually has strong economic and cultural affinities with the central city.

military expenditure, the apparent value of all identifiable military expenditure by the central government on hardware, personnel, pensions, research and development, etc., reported here both as a percentage of the GNP, with a comparison to the world average, and as a per capita value in U.S. dollars.

military personnel, see total active duty personnel.

mobility, the rate at which individuals or households change dwellings, usually measured between censuses and including international as well as domestic migration.*

monarchy, a government in which the CHIEF OF STATE holds office, usually hereditarily and for life, but sometimes electively for a term. The state may be a coprincipality, emirate, kingdom, principality, sheikhdom, or sultanate. The powers of the monarch may range from absolute (*i.e.,* the monarch both reigns and rules) through various degrees of limitation of authority to nominal, as in a constitutional monarchy, in which the titular monarch reigns but others, as elected officials, effectively rule.

monetary unit, currency of issue, or that in official use in a given country; name, spelling, and abbreviation in English according to International Monetary Fund recommendations or local practice; name of the lesser, usually decimal, monetary unit constituting the main currency; and valuation in U.S. dollars and U.K. pounds sterling, usually according to free-market or commercial rates.

    See also exchange rate.

natural increase, also called natural growth, or the balance of births and deaths, the excess of births over deaths in a population; the rate of natural increase is the difference between the BIRTH RATE and the DEATH RATE of a given population. The estimated world average during 2000 was 13.5 per 1,000 population, or 1.35% annually. Natural increase is added to the balance of migration to calculate the total growth of that population.

net material product, *see* material product.

nonreligious, *see* atheist.

official language(s), that (or those) prescribed by the national constitution for day-to-day conduct and publication of a country's official business or, when no explicit constitutional provision exists, that of the constitution itself, the national gazette (record of legislative activity), or like official documents. Other languages may have local protection, may be permitted in parliamentary debate or legal action (such as a trial), or may be "national languages," for the protection of which special provisions have been made, but these are not deemed official. The United States, for example, does not yet formally identify English as "official," though it uses it for virtually all official purposes.

official name, the local official form(s), short or long, of a country's legal name(s) taken from the country's constitution or from other official documents. The English-language form is usually the protocol form in use by the country, the U.S. Department of State, and the United Nations.

official religion, generally, any religion prescribed or given special status or protection by the constitution or legal system of a country. Identification as such is not confined to constitutional documents utilizing the term explicitly.

organized territory (U.S.), *see* territory.

overseas department (France), *see* department.

overseas territory (France), *see* territory.

parliamentary state, *see* state.

part of a realm, a dependent Dutch political entity with some degree of self-government and having a special status above that of a colony (*e.g.,* the prerogative of rejecting for local application any law enacted by The Netherlands).

participation/activity rates, measures defining differential rates of economic activity within a population. Participation rate refers to the percentage of those employed or economically active who possess a particular characteristic (sex, age, etc.); activity rate refers to the fraction of the total population who *are* economically active.

passenger-miles, or **passenger-kilometres,** aggregate measure of passenger carriage by a specified means of transportation, equal to the number of passengers carried multiplied by the number of miles (or kilometres) each is transported. Figures given for countries are often calculated from ticket sales and ordinarily exclude passengers carried free of charge.

people's republic, *see* republic.

place of birth/national origin, if the former, numbers of native- and foreign-born population of a country by actual place of birth; if the latter, any of several classifications, including those based on origin of passport at original admission to country, on cultural heritage of family name, on self-designated (often multiple) origin of (some) ancestors, and on other systems for assigning national origin.*

political status, *see* form of government/political status.

population, the number of persons present within a country, city, or other civil entity at the date of a census of population, survey, cumulation of a civil register, or other enumeration. Unless otherwise specified, populations given are DE FACTO, referring to those actually present, rather than DE JURE, those legally resident but not necessarily present on the referent date. If a time series, noncensus year, or per capita ratio referring to a country's total population is cited, it will usually refer to midyear of the calendar year indicated.

population economically active, the total number of persons (above a set age for economic labour, usually 10–15 years) in all employment statuses—self-employed, wage- or salary-earning, part-time, seasonal, unemployed, etc. The International Labour Organisation defines the economically active as "all persons of either sex who furnish the supply of labour for the production of economic goods and services." National practices vary as regards the treatment of such groups as armed forces, inmates of institutions, persons seeking their first job, unpaid family workers, seasonal workers and persons engaged in part-time economic activities. In some countries, all or part of these groups may be included among the economically active, while in other countries the same groups may be treated as inactive. In general, however, the data on economically active population do not include students, persons occupied solely in family or household work, retired persons, persons living entirely on their own means, and persons wholly dependent upon others.

See also labour force.

population projection, the expected population in the years 2010 and 2020, embodying the country's own projections wherever possible. Estimates of the future size of a population are usually based on assumed levels of fertility, mortality, and migration. Projections in the tables, unless otherwise specified, are medium (*i.e.,* most likely) variants, whether based on external estimates by the United Nations, World Bank, or U.S. Department of Commerce or on those of the country itself.

price and earnings indexes, tabulation comparing the change in the CONSUMER PRICE INDEX over a period of seven years with the change in the general labour force's EARNINGS INDEX for the same period.

principality, *see* monarchy.

production, the physical quantity or monetary value of the output of an industry, usually tabulated here as the most important items or groups of items (depending on the available detail) of primary (extractive) and secondary (manufactured) production, including construction. When a single consistent measure of value, such as VALUE ADDED, can be obtained, this is given, ranked by value; otherwise, and more usually, quantity of production is given.

public debt, the current outstanding debt of all periods of maturity for which the central government and its organs are obligated. Publicly guaranteed private debt is excluded. For countries that report debt under the World Bank Debtor Reporting System (DRS), figures for outstanding, long-term EXTERNAL DEBT are given.

quality of working life, a group of measures including weekly hours of work (including overtime); rates per 100,000 for job-connected injury, illness, and mortality; coverage of labour force by insurance for injury, permanent disability, and death; workdays lost to labour strikes and stoppages; and commuting patterns (length of journey to work in minutes and usual method of transportation).*

railroads, mode of transportation by self-driven or locomotive-drawn cars over fixed rails. Length-of-track figures include all mainline and spurline running track but exclude switching sidings and yard track. Route length, when given, does not compound multiple running tracks laid on the same trackbed.

recurrent budget, *see* budget.

religious affiliation, distribution of nominal religionists, whether practicing or not, as a percentage of total population. This usually assigns to children the religion of their parents.

republic, a state with elected leaders and a centralized presidential form of government, local subdivisions being subordinate to the national government. A *federal republic* (as distinguished from a unitary republic) is a republic in which power is divided between the central government and the constituent subnational administrative divisions (*e.g.,* states, provinces, or cantons) in whom the central government itself is held to originate, the division of power being defined in a written constitution and jurisdictional disputes usually being settled in a court; sovereignty usually rests with the authority that has the power to amend the constitution. A *unitary republic* (as distinguished from a federal republic) is a republic in which power originates in a central authority and is not derived from constituent subdivisions. A *people's republic,* in the dialectics of Communism, is the first stage of development toward a communist state, the second stage being a *socialist republic.* An *Islamic republic* is structured around social, ethical, legal, and religious precepts central to the Islamic faith.

retail price index, *see* consumer price index.

retail sales and service enterprises, *see* manufacturing, mining, and construction enterprises/retail sales and service enterprises.

roundwood, wood obtained from removals from forests, felled or harvested (with or without bark), in all forms.

rural, see urban-rural.

self-employment, work in which income derives from direct employment in one's own business, trade, or profession, as opposed to work in which salary or wages are earned from an employer.

self-governing, of a state, in control of its internal affairs in degrees ranging from control of most internal affairs (though perhaps not of public order or of internal security) to complete control of all internal affairs (*i.e.,* the state is autonomous) but having no control of external affairs or defense. In this work the term self-governing refers to the final stage in the successive stages of increasing self-government that generally precede independence.

service/trade enterprises, see manufacturing, mining, and construction enterprises/retail sales and service enterprises.

sex distribution, ratios, calculated as percentages, of male and female population to total population.

sheikhdom, *see* monarchy.

social deviance, a group of measures, usually reported as rates per 100,000 for principal categories of socially deviant behaviour, including specified crimes, alcoholism, drug abuse, and suicide.*

social participation, a group of measures indicative of the degree of social engagement displayed by a particular population, including rates of participation in such activities as elections, voluntary work or memberships, trade unions, and religion.*

social security, public programs designed to protect individuals and families from loss of income owing to unemployment, old age, sickness or disability, or death and to provide other services such as medical care, health and welfare programs, or income maintenance.

socialist republic, *see* republic.

sources of income, *see* household income and expenditure.

Special Drawing Right (SDR), a unit of account utilized by the International Monetary Fund (IMF) to denominate monetary reserves available under a quota system to IMF members to maintain the value of their national currency unit in international transactions.*

state, in international law, a political entity possessing the attributes of: territory, permanent civilian population, government, and the capacity to conduct relations with other states. Though the term is sometimes limited in meaning to fully independent and internationally recognized states, the more general sense of an entity possessing a *preponderance* of these characteristics is intended here. It is, thus, also a first-order civil administrative subdivision, especially of a federated union. An associated state is an autonomous state in free association with another that conducts its external affairs and defense; the association may be terminated in full independence at the instance of the autonomous state in consultation with the administering power. A *parliamentary state* is an independent state of the Commonwealth that is governed by a parliament and that may recognize the British monarch as its titular head.

structure of gross domestic product and labour force, tabulation of the principal elements of the national economy, according to standard industrial categories, together with the corresponding distribution of the labour force (when possible POPULATION ECONOMICALLY ACTIVE) that generates the GROSS DOMESTIC PRODUCT.

sultanate, *see* monarchy.

territory, a noncategorized political dependency; a first-order administrative subdivision; a dependent political entity with some degree of self-government, but with fewer rights and less autonomy than a colony because there is no charter. An *external territory* (Australia) is a territory situated outside the area of the country. An *organized territory* (U.S.) is a territory for which a system of laws and a settled government have been provided by an act of the United States Congress. An *overseas territory* (France) is an overseas subdivision of the French Republic with elected representation in the French Parliament, having individual statutes, laws, and internal organization adapted to local conditions.

ton-miles, or **ton-kilometres,** aggregate measure of freight hauled by a specified means of transportation, equal to tons of freight multiplied by the miles (or kilometres) each ton is transported. Figures are compiled from waybills (nationally) and ordinarily exclude mail, specie, passengers' baggage, the fuel and stores of the conveyance, and goods carried free.

total active duty personnel, full-time active duty military personnel (excluding militias and part-time, informal, or other paramilitary elements), with their distribution by percentages among the major services.

total fertility rate, the sum of the current age-specific birth rates for each of the child-bearing years (usually 15–49). It is the probable number of births, given present fertility data, that would occur during the lifetime of each woman should she live to the end of her child-bearing years.

tourism, service industry comprising activities connected with domestic and international travel for pleasure or recreation; confined here to international travel and reported as expenditures in U.S. dollars by tourists of all nationalities visiting a particular country and, conversely, the estimated expenditures of that country's nationals in all countries of destination.

transfer payments, *see* household income and expenditure.

transport, all mechanical methods of moving persons or goods. Data reported for national establishments include: for railroads, length of track and volume of traffic for passengers and cargo (but excluding mail, etc.); for roads, length of network and numbers of passenger cars and of commercial vehicles (*i.e.,* trucks and buses); for merchant marine, the number of vessels of more than 100 gross tons and their total deadweight tonnage; for air transport, traffic data for passengers and cargo and the number of airports with scheduled flights.

unincorporated territory (U.S.), *see* territory.

unitary republic, see republic.

urban-rural, social characteristic of local or national populations, defined by predominant economic activities, "urban" referring to a group of largely nonagricultural pursuits, "rural" to agriculturally oriented employment patterns. The distinction is usually based on the country's own definition of urban, which may depend only upon the size (population) of a place or upon factors like employment, administrative status, density of housing, etc.

value added, also called value added by manufacture, the gross output value of a firm or industry minus the cost of inputs—raw materials, supplies, and payments to other firms—required to produce it. Value added is the portion of the sales value or gross output value that is actually created by the firm or industry. Value added generally includes labour costs, administrative costs, and operating profits.

The Nations of the World

Afghanistan

Official name: Islamic State of Afghanistan[1] (Dowlat-e Eslāmī-ye Afghānestān [Persian]; Pashto long-form name, n.a.).
Form of government: transitional government[2].
Head of state and government: President.
Capital: Kabul.
Official languages: Dari (Persian); Pashto.
Official religion: Islam.
Monetary unit: 1 (old) afghani (Af) = 100 puls (puli); valuation (Sept. 23, 2002) 1 U.S.$ = Af 4,750; 1 £ = Af 7,382[3].

Arabian Sea

Area and population[4]

Geographic regions	Principal cities	area sq mi	area sq km	population 1993 estimate
Central	Kabul	11,657	30,192	3,481,400
East	Jalālābād	9,802	25,386	1,567,500
East-central	Bāmiān	21,739	56,304	685,600
North	Mazār-e Sharīf	29,520	76,457	2,421,900
North-east	Kondūz	30,233	78,304	2,518,300
South	Gardeyz	19,525	50,569	1,659,600
South-west	Kandahār (Qandahār)	77,000	199,430	2,188,700
West	Herāt	46,187	119,624	1,497,500
TOTAL		251,825[5]	652,255[5]	16,020,500

Demography

Population (2002): 27,756,000[6].
Density (2002): persons per sq mi 110.2, persons per sq km 42.6.
Urban-rural (2001): urban 22.3%; rural 77.7%.
Sex distribution (2000): male 51.31%; female 48.69%.
Age breakdown (2000): under 15, 43.8%; 15–29, 25.4%; 30–44, 16.8%; 45–59, 9.1%; 60–74, 4.2%; 75 and over, 0.7%.
Population projection: (2010) 33,864,000; (2020) 41,735,000.
Doubling time: 29 years.
Ethnolinguistic composition (early 1990s[6]): Pashtun 52.4%; Tajik 20.4%; Hazāra 8.8%; Uzbek 8.8%; Chahar Aimak 2.8%; Turkmen 1.9%; other 4.9%.
Religious affiliation (2000): Sunnī Muslim 89.2%; Shīʿī Muslim 8.9%; Zoroastrian 1.4%; Hindu 0.4%; other 0.1%.
Major cities (1988): Kabul 2,602,000[7]; Kandahār (Qandahār) 225,500; Herāt 177,300; Mazār-e Sharīf 130,600; Jalālābād 55,000.

Vital statistics

Birth rate per 1,000 population (2000): 41.8 (world avg. 22.5).
Death rate per 1,000 population (2000): 18.0 (world avg. 9.0).
Natural increase rate per 1,000 population (2000): 23.8 (world avg. 13.5).
Total fertility rate (avg. births per childbearing woman; 2000): 5.9.
Life expectancy at birth (2000): male 46.6 years; female 45.1 years.

National economy

Budget (1997–98). Revenue: primarily from narcotics trade. Expenditures: more than 90% of revenue used to finance war effort.
Gross national product (1999): U.S.$21,000,000,000 (U.S.$840 per capita).

Structure of gross domestic product and labour force

	1992–93 in value Af '000,000[8]	% of total value	labour force	% of labour force
Agriculture	61,400	48.5	4,276,100	67.2
Manufacturing } Mining and public utilities }	32,800	25.9	298,900	4.7
Construction	12,400	9.8	81,400	1.3
Transp. and commun.	5,300	4.2	139,900	2.2
Trade	12,400	9.8	420,600	6.6
Pub. admin., services } Other }	2,400	1.9	929,300 214,300	14.6 3.4
TOTAL	126,700	100.0[9]	6,360,500	100.0

Public debt (external, outstanding; 1993): U.S.$5,381,000,000.
Production (metric tons except as noted). Agriculture, forestry, fishing (1999): wheat 2,834,000, rice 450,000, grapes 330,000, barley 300,000, corn (maize) 240,000, potatoes 235,000, apricots 37,500, opium poppy 4,600[10]; livestock (number of live animals) 14,300,000 sheep, 2,200,000 goats, 1,500,000 cattle, 1,160,000 asses; roundwood (1998) 8,091,000 cu m; fish catch (1997) 1,250. Mining and quarrying (1997): salt 13,000; copper (metal content) 5,000. Manufacturing (by production value in Af '000,000; 1988–89): food products 4,019; leather and fur products 2,678; textiles 1,760; printing and publishing 1,070; industrial chemicals (including fertilizers)

1,053; footwear 999. Energy production (consumption): electricity (kW-hr; 1997) 513,000,000 (613,000,000); coal (metric tons; 1997) 2,000 (2,000); petroleum products (metric tons; 1997) none (237,000); natural gas (cu m; 1997) 147,355,000 (147,355,000).
Population economically active (1994)[11]: total 5,557,000; activity rate of total population 29.4% (participation rates: female 9.0%; unemployed [1995] c. 8%).

Consumer price index (1990 = 100)

	1988	1989	1990	1991	1992	1993	1994
Consumer price index	64.3	83.1	100.0	266.0	420.8	563.9	676.7

Tourism: receipts (1997) U.S.$1,000,000; expenditures (1997) U.S.$1,000,000.
Land use (1994): forested 2.9%; meadows and pastures 46.0%; agricultural and under permanent cultivation 12.4%; other 38.7%.

Foreign trade[12]

Balance of trade (current prices)

	1993	1994	1995	1996	1997	1998
U.S.$'000,000	+263	−245	−193	−371	−376	−300
% of total	23.6%	54.6%	36.8%	59.8%	55.3%	50.0%

Imports (1997): U.S.$525,000,000 (1995; food 18.8%, machinery and transport equipment 15.2%, unspecified commodities 46.5%). *Major import sources* (1997): Singapore 19.2%; Japan 18.5%; China 6.9%; India 4.8%; Russia 4.0%.
Exports (1997): U.S.$149,000,000 (1995; carpets and rugs 54.3%, dried fruits and nuts 15.6%). *Major export destinations* (1997): Pakistan 20.1%; Belgium-Luxembourg 8.7%; France 7.4%; United States 6.7%; Japan 6.0%.

Transport and communications

Transport. Railroads (1997): length 16 mi (25 km). Roads (1996): total length 21,000 km (paved 13%). Vehicles (1996): passenger cars 31,000; trucks and buses 25,000. Merchant marine: none. Air transport[13]: passenger-km (1995) 276,000,000; metric ton-km cargo 38,000,000; airports (1996) 3.

Communications

Medium	date	unit	number	units per 1,000 persons
Daily newspapers	1996	circulation	113,000	5.0
Radio	1997	receivers	2,750,000	116
Television[14]	1997	receivers	270,000	11
Telephones	1999	main lines	29,000	1.2

Education and health

Educational attainment (1980). Population age 25 and over having: no formal schooling 88.5%; some primary education 6.8%; complete primary 0.3%; some secondary 1.2%; postsecondary 3.2%. *Literacy* (1995): total population age 15 and over literate 31.5%; males 47.2%; females 15.1%.

Education (1995–96)

	schools	teachers	students	student/ teacher ratio
Primary	2,146	21,869	1,312,197	60.0
Secondary	...	19,085	512,851	26.9
Higher	...	...	12,800	...

Health: physicians (1997) 2,555[6] (1 per 9,091 persons); hospital beds, n.a.; infant mortality rate (2000) 149.3.
Food (1999): daily per capita caloric intake 1,755 (vegetable products 79%, animal products 21%); 72% of FAO recommended minimum requirement.

Military

Total active duty personnel (2002): first 600 troops of planned 68,000-member army completed basic training in April 2002[15].

[1]Long-form name of transitional government. [2]Replaced interim government in June 2002; to be the governmental authority until early 2004. [3]Black market rate in July 2002: 1 U.S.$ = more than Af 40,000; most currency transactions are conducted with the Pakistan rupee or U.S. dollar. The afghani was re-denominated on Oct. 7, 2002; from this date 1,000 (old) afghanis equalled 1 (new) afghani. [4]A 1993 administrative reorganization created 32 provinces (wilayah); more recent detail not presented here because of a lack of space. [5]Detailed breakdown does not account for 6,162 sq mi (15,959 sq km), which is included in the total. [6]Includes Afghan refugees (estimated to number about 1.1 million in Pakistan and about 1.4 million in Iran in August 2002). [7]2001 estimate for urban agglomeration. [8]At prices of 1978–79. [9]Detail does not add to total given because of rounding. [10]Represents 75% of world production; production declined significantly in 2001. [11]Based on settled population only. [12]Exports are f.o.b. and imports are c.i.f. [13]Ariana Afghan Airlines only. [14]Officially outlawed in 1998–2001. [15]Foreign troops (June 2002): 5,000-member, 19-nation International Security Assistance Force (ISAF) and 7,000-member, non-ISAF U.S. troops searching for al-Qaeda and Taliban fighters.

Internet resources for further information:
• **UN Development Programme: Afghanistan Recovery**
  http://www.undp.org/afghanistan/index.html

Albania

Official name: Republika e Shqipërisë (Republic of Albania).
Form of government: unitary multiparty republic with one legislative house (Assembly [140]).
Chief of state: President.
Head of government: Prime Minister.
Capital: Tirana (Tiranë).
Official language: Albanian.
Official religion: none.
Monetary unit: 1 lek = 100 qindars; valuation (Sept. 23, 2002)
1 U.S.$ = 139.07 leks;
1 £ = 216.13 leks.

Area and population

Provinces	Capitals	area sq mi	area sq km	population 2001 census
Berat	Berat	353	915	128,410
Bulqizë	Bulqizë	277	718	42,985
Delvinë	Delvinë	142	367	10,859
Devoll	Bilisht	166	429	34,744
Dibër	Peshkopi	294	761	86,144
Durrës	Durrës	176	455	182,988
Elbasan	Elbasan	498	1,290	224,974
Fier	Fier	328	850	200,154
Gjirokastër	Gjirokastër	439	1,137	55,991
Gramsh	Gramsh	268	695	35,723
Has	Krumë	144	374	19,842
Kavajë	Kavajë	152	393	78,415
Kolonjë	Ersekë	311	805	17,179
Korçë	Korçë	676	1,752	143,499
Krujë	Krujë	144	372	64,357
Kuçovë	Kuçovë	43	112	35,571
Kukës	Kukës	369	956	64,054
Kurbin[1]	Laç	91	235	54,519
Lezhë	Lezhë	185	479	68,218
Librazhd	Librazhd	425	1,102	72,520
Lushnjë	Lushnjë	275	712	144,351
Malësi e Madhe	Koplik	346	897	36,770
Mallakastër	Ballsh	125	325	39,881
Mat	Burrel	397	1,028	61,906
Mirditë	Rrëshen	335	867	37,055
Peqin	Peqin	74	191	32,920
Përmet	Përmet	359	929	25,837
Pogradec	Pogradec	280	725	70,900
Pukë	Pukë	399	1,034	34,454
Sarandë	Sarandë	282	730	35,235
Shkodër	Shkodër	630	1,631	185,794
Skrapar	Çorovoda	299	775	29,874
Tepelenë	Tepelenë	315	817	32,465
Tiranë	Tirana (Tiranë)	461	1,193	523,150
Tropojë	Bajram	403	1,043	28,154
Vlorë	Vlorë	621	1,609	147,267
TOTAL		11,082	28,703	3,087,159

Demography

Population (2002): 3,108,000.
Density (2002): persons per sq mi 280.5, persons per sq km 108.3.
Urban-rural (2002): urban 43.0%; rural 57.0%.
Sex distribution (2000): male 48.90%; female 51.10%.
Age breakdown (2000): under 15, 30.2%; 15–29, 26.6%; 30–44, 19.8%; 45–59, 13.2%; 60–74, 7.9%; 75 and over, 2.3%.
Population projection: (2010) 3,248,000; (2020) 3,497,000.
Doubling time: 58 years.
Ethnic composition (2000): Albanian 91.7%; Vlach (Aromanian) 3.6%; Greek 2.3%; other 2.4%.
Religious affiliation (2000): Muslim 38.8%; Roman Catholic 16.7%; nonreligious 16.6%; Albanian Orthodox 10.4%; other Orthodox 5.7%; other 11.8%.
Major cities (1991): Tirana (Tiranë) (1999) 279,000; Durrës 86,900; Shkodër 83,700; Elbasan 83,200.

Vital statistics

Birth rate per 1,000 population (2001): 18.6 (world avg. 21.2).
Death rate per 1,000 population (2001): 6.5 (world avg. 8.9).
Natural increase rate per 1,000 population (2001): 12.1 (world avg. 13.2).
Total fertility rate (avg. births per childbearing woman; 2001): 2.3.
Marriage rate per 1,000 population (1998): 7.4.
Life expectancy at birth (2001): male 69.3 years; female 75.1 years.

National economy

Budget (2000). Revenue: 120,588,000,000 leks (taxes 86.3%, of which value-added tax 31.6%, import duties and export taxes 18.8%, income tax 11.9%, social security contributions 11.2%, other 12.8%; nontax revenue 13.7%). Expenditures: 169,423,000,000 leks (current expenditure 79.3%, of which social security 22.1%, interest on debt 17.5%, wages 15.2%, government operations 11.4%, other 13.1%; capital expenditure 20.7%).
Public debt (2000): U.S.$644,200,000.
Production (metric tons except as noted). Agriculture, forestry, fishing (2000): cereals 580,000, vegetables and melons 444,000 (mainly beans, peas, onions, tomatoes, cabbage, eggplants, and carrots), watermelons 240,000, potatoes 180,000; livestock (number of live animals) 1,941,000 sheep, 1,120,000 goats, 720,000 cattle, 4,000,000 poultry; roundwood (2000) 409,000 cu m; fish catch (1999) 3,055. Mining and quarrying (1999): chromium ore 79,000; copper ore 34,000. Manufacturing (1999): cement 106,000; bread 67,000; rolled steel 20,000; cheese 7,000; beer 91,000 hectolitres; wine 10,000 hectolitres.

Construction (1990): 12,428 units. Energy production (consumption): electricity (kW-hr; 1999) 5,396,000,000 (5,396,000,000); coal (metric tons; 1997) 80,000 (60,000); crude petroleum (barrels; 1999) 2,368,000 (2,413,000[2]); petroleum products (metric tons; 1997) 277,000 (382,000); natural gas (cu m; 1997) 17,939,000 (17,939,000).
Gross national product (2000): U.S.$3,833,000,000 (U.S.$1,120 per capita).

Structure of gross domestic product and labour force

	1999 in value '000,000 leks	1999 % of total value	1995 labour force	1995 % of labour force
Agriculture	266,270	52.6	778,000	58.7
Manufacturing, mining, public utilities	60,026	11.8	95,000	7.2
Construction	68,387	13.5	21,000	1.6
Transp. and commun.	16,531	3.3	30,000	2.3
Trade			62,000	4.7
Pub. admin., defense	94,991	18.8	...	...
Services			79,000	6.0
Other	—	—	260,000[3]	19.6[3]
TOTAL	506,205	100.0	1,325,000	100.0[4]

Population economically active (2000): total 1,940,000; activity rate of total population 57.0% (participation rates [1998]: ages 15–64, 69.9%; female 49.9%; unemployed 16.8%).

Price index (1995 = 100)

	1994	1995	1996	1997	1998	1999	2000
Consumer price index	92.8	100.0	112.7	150.1	181.1	181.8	187.0

Household income and expenditure. Average household size (1998): 3.9; annual income per rural household (1989) 80,835 leks (U.S.$ value, n.a.); sources of income: wages 53.0%, transfers from relatives abroad 21.5%, social insurance 11.4%; expenditure: n.a.
Tourism (2000): receipts U.S.$389,000,000; expenditures U.S.$272,000,000.

Foreign trade

Balance of trade (current prices)

	1994	1995	1996	1997	1998	1999	2000
U.S.$'000,000	−460	−475	−678	−535	−621	−846	−814
% of total	62.0%	53.7%	58.2%	62.8%	60.2%	60.6%	61.4%

Imports (2000): U.S.$1,070,000,000 (manufactured goods 23.8%; machinery and transport equipment 21.6%; food and beverages 19.8%; mineral fuels 9.0%; chemicals 7.0%; crude materials 1.4%). *Major import sources:* Italy 36.2%; Greece 28.0%; Germany 5.5%; Turkey 5.5%.
Exports (2000): U.S.$256,000,000 (miscellaneous manufactured articles 68.0%; manufactured goods 12.1%; crude materials 8.7%; food and beverages 6.6%). *Major export destinations:* Italy 70.3%; Greece 12.9%; Germany 6.6%.

Transport and communications

Transport. Railroads (1998): length 670 km; passenger-km 116,000,000; metric ton-km cargo 25,000. Roads (1998): total length 18,000 km (paved 30%). Vehicles (1998): passenger cars 90,766; trucks and buses 34,378. Merchant marine (1992): vessels (100 gross tons and over) 24; total deadweight tonnage 80,954. Air transport (1997): passenger-km 3,519,000; short ton-mi 223,000; metric ton-km 325,000; airports (1999) with scheduled flights 1.

Communications

Medium	date	unit	number	units per 1,000 persons
Daily newspapers	1996	circulation	116,000	37
Radio	1997	receivers	810,000	259
Television	1998	receivers	430,000	137
Telephones	2001	main lines	197,500	50
Cellular telephones	2001	subscribers	350,000	88
Internet	2001	users	10,000	3.2

Education and health

Educational attainment (1989). Population age 10 and over having: primary education 65.3%; secondary 29.1%; higher 5.6%. *Literacy* (1989): total population age 10 and over literate 91.8%; males 95.5%; females 88.0%.

Education (1996)

	schools	teachers	students	student/ teacher ratio
Primary (age 6–13)	1,782[5]	31,369	558,101	17.8
Secondary (age 14–17)	162[6]	4,147	71,391	17.2
Voc., teacher tr.	259[6]	2,174	18,504	8.5
Higher	10	2,348	34,257	14.6

Health (1995): physicians 4,848 (1 per 657 persons); hospital beds (1994) 10,200 (1 per 333 persons); infant mortality rate per 1,000 live births (2000) 41.3.
Food (1999): daily per capita caloric intake 2,717 (vegetable products 73%, animal products 27%); 113% of FAO recommended minimum requirement.

Military

Total active duty personnel (2001): 27,000 (army 74.1%, navy 9.3%, air force 16.7%). *Military expenditure as percentage of GNP* (1999): 1.3% (world 2.4%); per capita expenditure U.S.$21.

[1]Name changed from Laç to Kurbin in 1999. [2]1997. [3]Includes 171,000 undistributed unemployed. [4]Detail does not add to total given because of rounding. [5]1995. [6]1990.

Internet resources for further information:
• Albanian Economic Development Agency http://www.aeda.gov.al

Algeria

Official name: Al-Jumhūrīyah
al-Jazāʾirīyah ad-Dīmuqrāṭīyah
ash-Shaʿbīyah (Arabic) (People's
Democratic Republic of Algeria).
Form of government: multiparty
republic with two legislative bodies
(Council of the Nation [144][1]; National
People's Assembly [389]).
Chief of state: President.
Head of government: Prime Minister.
Capital: Algiers.
Official language: Arabic[2].
Official religion: Islam.
Monetary unit: 1 Algerian dinar
(DA) = 100 centimes; valuation (Sept.
23, 2002) 1 U.S.$ = DA 79.12;
1 £ = DA 122.96.

Population (1998 census)

Provinces	population	Provinces	population	Provinces	population
Adrar	313,417	El-Bayadh	172,957	Ouargla	444,683
Aïn Defla	658,897	El-Oued	525,083	Oum el-Bouaghi	529,540
Aïn Temouchent	337,570	Et-Tarf	350,789	Relizane	646,175
Alger	2,423,694	Ghardaïa	311,678	Saïda	313,351
Annaba	559,898	Guelma	444,231	Sétif	1,299,116
Batna	987,475	Illizi	34,189	Sidi bel-Abbès	535,634
Béchar	232,012	Jijel	582,865	Skikda	793,146
Bejaïa	836,301	Khenchela	345,009	Souk Ahras	365,106
Biskra	568,701	Laghouat	326,862	Tamanrasset	138,704
Blida	796,616	Mascara	651,239	Tébessa	565,125
Bordj Bou Arreridj	561,471	Médéa	859,273	Tiaret	770,194
Bouira	637,042	Mila	663,578	Tindouf	27,053
Boumerdes	608,806	Mostaganem	636,884	Tipaza	507,959
Constantine	807,371	M'Sila	835,701	Tissemsilt	274,380
Djelfa	805,298	Naâma	131,846	Tizi Ouzou	1,100,297
Ech-Cheliff	874,917	Oran	1,208,171	Tlemcen	873,039
				TOTAL	29,273,343

Demography

Area: 919,595 sq mi, 2,381,741 sq km.
Population (2002): 31,261,000.
Density (2002): persons per sq mi 34.0, persons per sq km 13.0.
Urban-rural (1998): urban 80.8%; rural 19.2%.
Sex distribution (1998): male 50.56%; female 49.44%.
Age breakdown (1998): under 15, 36.2%; 15–29, 30.6%; 30–44, 17.7%; 45–59, 8.9%; 60–74, 5.1%; 75 and over, 1.5%.
Population projection: (2010) 35,022,000; (2020) 40,365,000.
Doubling time: 49 years.
Ethnic composition (2000): Algerian Arab 59.1%; Berber 26.2%, of which Arabized Berber 3.0%; Bedouin Arab 14.5%; other 0.2%.
Religious affiliation (2000): Muslim 99.7%, of which Sunnī 99.1%, Ibāḍīyah 0.6%; Christian 0.3%.
Major cities (1998): Algiers 1,519,570; Oran 692,516; Constantine 462,187; Annaba 348,554; Batna 242,514; Blida 226,512; Sétif 211,859.

Vital statistics

Birth rate per 1,000 population (2000): 19.8 (world avg. 22.5).
Death rate per 1,000 population (2000): 5.5 (world avg. 9.0).
Natural increase rate per 1,000 population (2000): 14.3 (world avg. 13.5).
Total fertility rate (avg. births per childbearing woman; 2000): 2.8.
Marriage rate per 1,000 population (2000): 5.8.
Life expectancy at birth (2000): male 68.3 years; female 71.0 years.
Notified cases of infectious diseases per 100,000 population (1996): measles 67.8; typhoid fever 15.2; hepatitis 11.3; dysentery 10.1; meningitis 9.4.

National economy

Budget (2000). Revenue: DA 1,578,100,000,000 (taxes on hydrocarbons 76.9%, value-added taxes 8.0%). Expenditures: DA 1,178,100,000,000 (current expenditure 72.7%, development expenditure 27.3%).
Land use (1994): forested 1.6%; meadows and pastures 13.3%; agricultural and under permanent cultivation 3.4%; other (mostly desert) 81.7%.
Production (metric tons except as noted). Agriculture, forestry, fishing (1999): wheat 1,503,000, potatoes 1,100,000, tomatoes 790,000, barley 481,000, dates 427,600, onions 400,000, olives 311,200, oranges 307,300, grapes 190,300; livestock (number of live animals) 18,000,000 sheep, 3,200,000 goats; roundwood (1997) 2,735,000 cu m; fish catch (1997) 99,332. Mining and quarrying (1999): iron ore (gross weight) 2,330,000; phosphate rock (gross weight) 1,300,000; mercury 12,000 flasks. Manufacturing (value added in U.S.$'000,000; 1997): food products 463; cement, bricks, and tiles 393; iron and steel 118; tobacco products 114; paints, soaps, and related products 105; electrical machinery 79. Energy production (consumption): electricity (kW-hr; 1997) 21,489,000,000 (21,489,000,000); coal (metric tons; 1997) 23,000 (1,193,000); crude petroleum (barrels; 2000) 307,091,000 ([1997] 165,974,000); petroleum products (metric tons; 1997) 41,601,000 (8,146,000); natural gas (cu m; 2000) 89,300,000,000 (25,981,000,000).
Household income and expenditure. Average household size (1998) 7.1; income per household: n.a.; sources of income (2000): wages and salaries 41.2%, self-employment 39.3%, transfers 19.5%; expenditure (1995): food and beverages 58.5%, transportation and communications 9.5%, clothing and footwear 13.9%, health 4.4%, other 13.7%.
Gross national product (2000): U.S.$47,897,000,000 (U.S.$1,580 per capita).

Structure of gross domestic product and labour force

	1996			
	in value DA '000,000	% of total value	labour force	% of labour force
Agriculture	277,842	12.3	881,000	12.1
Petroleum and natural gas	761,084[3]	33.8[3]		
Other mining	5,216	0.2	676,000	9.3
Manufacturing	165,875[3]	7.4[3]		
Public utilities, construction	268,873	12.0	677,000	9.3
Transp. and commun.	148,886	6.6	750,000	10.3
Trade, restaurants	352,464	15.7	615,000	8.5
Pub. admin., defense	...	...	1,479,000	20.3
Services	58,950	2.6		
Other	212,300	9.4	2,200,000[4]	30.2
TOTAL	2,251,490	100.0	7,278,000	100.0

Population economically active (1994): total 6,814,000; activity rate of population 24.8% (participation rates [1987] ages 15–64, 44.3%; female 9.2%; unemployed [February 2000] 29.8%).

Price and earnings indexes (1995 = 100)

	1996	1997	1998	1999	2000	2001	2002
Consumer price index	118.7	128.7	131.7	135.2	134.4	139.1	153.4[5]
Earnings index[6]	110.0	...	...	...	...	...	...

Public debt (external, outstanding; 2000): U.S.$23,062,000,000.
Tourism: receipts from visitors (1998) U.S.$24,000,000; expenditures by nationals abroad (1997) U.S.$64,000,000.

Foreign trade[7]

Balance of trade (current prices)

	1994	1995	1996	1997	1998	1999
U.S.$'000,000	–979	–1,425	+1,994	+5,206	+435	+3,363
% of total	5.4%	6.8%	9.9%	23.1%	2.4%	15.5%

Imports (1999): U.S.$9,162,000,000 (machinery and apparatus 25.0%, food 24.3%, transport equipment 7.6%). *Major import sources:* France 22.8%; Italy 9.9%; U.S. 8.4%; Germany 7.4%; Spain 5.5%.
Exports (1999): U.S.$12,525,000,000 (natural and manufactured gas 41.7%, crude petroleum 39.7%, refined petroleum 15.0%). *Major export destinations:* Italy 23.5%; U.S. 14.0%; France 13.7%; Spain 10.6%; The Netherlands 8.2%.

Transport and communications

Transport. Railroads (1997): route length 2,451 mi, 3,945 km; (1996) passenger-km 1,826,000,000; metric ton-km cargo 2,139,000,000. Roads (1995): total length 63,643 mi, 102,424 km (paved 69%). Vehicles (1996): passenger cars 725,000; trucks and buses 780,000. Air transport (1998)[8]: passenger-km 2,901,000,000; metric ton-km cargo 18,285,000; airports (1996) 28.

Communications

Medium	date	unit	number	units per 1,000 persons
Daily newspapers	1996	circulation	1,080,000	38
Radio	1997	receivers	7,100,000	253
Television	1999	receivers	3,300,000	110
Telephones	2001	main lines	1,880,000	60
Cellular telephones	2001	subscribers	100,000	3.2
Personal computers	2001	units	220,000	7.1
Internet	2001	users	60,000	1.9

Education and health

Educational attainment (1998). Percentage of economically active population age 6 and over having: no formal schooling 30.1%; primary education 29.9%; lower secondary 20.7%; upper secondary 13.4%; higher 4.3%; other 1.6%.
Literacy (1998): total population age 10 and over literate 15,314,109 (68.1%); males literate 8,650,719 (76.3%); females literate 6,663,392 (59.7%).

Education (1996–97)

	schools	teachers	students	student/teacher ratio
Primary (age 6–11)	15,426	170,956	4,674,947	27.3
Secondary (age 12–17)	3,954[9]	151,948	2,618,242	17.2
Higher[9]	...	19,910	347,410	17.4

Health (1996): physicians 27,650 (1 per 1,015 persons); hospital beds 34,544 (1 per 812 persons); infant mortality rate per 1,000 live births (2000) 51.1.
Food (1999): daily per capita caloric intake 2,965 (vegetable products 90%, animal products 10%); 124% of FAO recommended minimum requirement.

Military

Total active duty personnel (2001): 124,000 (army 86.3%, navy 5.6%, air force 8.1%). *Military expenditure as percentage of GNP (1999):* 4.0% (world 2.4%); per capita expenditure U.S.$60.

---

[1]Includes 48 nonelected seats appointed by the president. [2]The Berber language, Tamazight, became a national language in April 2002. [3]Petroleum and natural gas includes (and Manufacturing excludes) refined petroleum and manufacture of hydrocarbons. [4]Estimated number of unemployed. [5]January. [6]Public workers only; all data based on January averages of gross income. [7]Imports c.i.f.; exports f.o.b. [8]Air Algérie. [9]1995–96.

Internet resources for further information:
• Statistiques Algérie
http://www.ons.dz/them_sta.htm

American Samoa

Official name: American Samoa (English); Amerika Samoa (Samoan).
Political status: unincorporated and unorganized territory of the United States with two legislative houses (Senate [18]; House of Representatives [20])[1].
Chief of state: President of the United States.
Head of government: Governor.
Capital: Fagatogo[2] (legislative and judicial) and Utulei (executive).
Official languages: English; Samoan.
Official religion: none.
Monetary unit: 1 dollar (U.S.$) = 100 cents; valuation (Sept. 23, 2002) 1 U.S.$ = £0.64.

Area and population	area		population
			2000
Districts and islands	sq mi	sq km	census
Eastern District	25.9	67.1	23,441
Tutuila Island (part)	25.3	65.5	21,673
Aunu'u Island	0.6	1.6	1,768
Western District	28.8	74.6	32,435
Tutuila Island (part)	28.8	74.6	32,435
Manu'a District (Manu'a Islands)	21.9	56.7	1,378
Ofu Island	2.8	7.2	289
Olosega Island	2.0	5.2	216
Ta'u Island	17.1	44.3	873
Rose Island[3]	0.1	0.3	0
Swains Island[3]	0.6	1.5	37
LAND AREA	77.3	200.2	—
INLAND WATER (HARBOUR) AREAS	7.1	18.4	—
TOTAL AREA	84.4	218.6	57,291

Demography

Population (2002)[4]: 60,000.
Density (2002): persons per sq mi 776.2, persons per sq km 299.7.
Urban-rural (1998): urban 51.5%; rural 48.5%.
Sex distribution (2000): male 48.50%; female 51.50%.
Age breakdown (2000): under 15, 38.7%; 15–29, 24.5%; 30–44, 20.5%; 45–59, 10.9%; 60–74, 4.4%; 75 and over, 1.0%.
Population projection: (2010) 70,000; (2020) 86,000.
Doubling time: 32 years.
Ethnic composition (2000): Samoan 88.2%; Tongan 2.8%; Asian 2.8%; Caucasian 1.1%; other 5.1%.
Religious affiliation (1995): 4 major Protestant groups 60.1%; Roman Catholic 19.4%; Mormon 12.5%; other 8.0%.
Major villages (2000): Tafuna 8,406; Nu'uuli 5,154; Pago Pago 4,278 (urban agglomeration [2001] 15,000); Leone 3,568; Fagatogo 2,096[2].

Vital statistics

Birth rate per 1,000 population (2001): 24.9 (world avg. 21.2); legitimate, n.a.; illegitimate, n.a.
Death rate per 1,000 population (2001): 4.3 (world avg. 8.9).
Natural increase rate per 1,000 population (2001): 20.6 (world avg. 12.3).
Total fertility rate (avg. births per childbearing woman; 2000): 3.6.
Marriage rate per 1,000 population (1999): 4.8.
Divorce rate per 1,000 population (1993): 0.5.
Life expectancy at birth (2001): male 70.9 years; female 80.0 years.
Major causes of death per 100,000 population (1999): heart diseases 70.9; malignant neoplasms (cancers) 58.5; cerebrovascular diseases 31.9; accidents 28.4; chronic obstructive pulmonary diseases 19.5; influenza and pneumonia 19.4.

National economy

Budget (1997). Revenue: U.S.$144,438,095 (U.S. government grants 67.4%; taxes 23.6%; insurance claims 4.9%; other 4.1%). Expenditures: U.S.$152,912,308 (education and culture 28.5%; health and welfare 27.3%; general government 14.1%; public works and parks 12.8%; public safety 6.9%; economic development 6.1%; capital projects 3.4%; debt 0.9%).
Gross national product (1997): U.S.$253,000,000 (U.S.$4,300 per capita).

Structure of labour force		
	2000	
	labour force	% of labour force
Agriculture, forestry, and fishing	517	2.9
Manufacturing	5,900	33.4
Construction	1,066	6.0
Transp. and commun.	1,036	5.9
Trade	1,790	10.1
Finance, real estate	311	1.8
Public administration	1,550	8.8
Services	4,548	25.7
Other	946[5]	5.4
TOTAL	17,664	100.0

Production (metric tons except as noted). Agriculture, forestry, fishing (2001): coconuts 4,700, taros 1,500, fruits (excluding melons) 1,200, bananas 750, vegetables and melons 470; livestock (number of live animals; 2001) 10,700 pigs, 37,000 chickens; forestry, n.a.; fish catch (1999) 1,000, of which tunas, bonitos, and billfish 950. Mining and quarrying: n.a. Manufacturing

(value of export in U.S.$; 1999): canned tuna 334,219,881; garments 4,598,766; other manufactures include pet food, handicrafts, soap, and alcoholic beverages. Construction (value of building permits in U.S.$; 1999) 15,209,000. Energy production (consumption): electricity (kW-hr; 1999) 158,576,000 (137,834,000); coal, none (n.a.); crude petroleum; none (n.a.); petroleum products (metric tons; 1997) none (94,000); natural gas, none (n.a.).
Public debt: n.a.
Population economically active (2000): total 17,664, activity rate of total population 30.8% (participation rates: ages 16 and over 52.0%; female 41.5%; unemployed 5.3%).

Price index (1990 = 100)							
	1990	1991	1992	1993	1994	1995	1996
Consumer price index	100.0	104.0	109.0	109.0	111.0	113.0	118.0

Household income and expenditure. Average household size (2000) 6.0; income per household (2000): U.S.$24,000; sources of income: n.a.; expenditure (1995): food and beverages 30.9%, housing and furnishings 25.8%, church donations 20.7%, transp. and commun. 9.4%, clothing 2.9%, other 10.3%.
Tourism: receipts from visitors (1997) U.S.$10,000,000; expenditures by nationals abroad (1996) U.S.$2,000,000.
Land use (1994): forested 70%; agricultural and under permanent cultivation 15%; other 15%.

Foreign trade[6]

Balance of trade (current prices)						
	1994	1995	1996	1997	1998	1999
U.S.$'000,000	−245.6	−144.2	−157.8	−104.3	−83.4	−107.5
% of total	32.7%	21.0%	20.1%	10.9%	9.1%	13.5%

Imports (1999): U.S.$452,600,000 (fish and cannery related products 57.4%, petroleum and petroleum products 10.8%, food 10.5%, manufactured goods 9.9%, transport equipment 4.3%, building materials 3.4%). *Major import sources* (1999): United States 66.5%; New Zealand 9.2%; Australia 8.6%; Fiji 5.6%; Western Samoa 2.9%; Japan 1.9%; South Korea 1.4%; Taiwan 1.1%; China 0.7%.
Exports (1999): U.S.$345,100,000 (tuna in airtight containers 96.8%, finished garments 1.3%, pet food 1.2%, fish meal 0.6%). *Major export destinations:* United States 100.0%.

Transport and communications

Transport. Railroads: none. Roads (1991): total length 217 mi, 350 km (paved, 43%). Vehicles (1999): passenger cars 5,984; trucks and buses 576. Merchant marine (1990): vessels (100 gross tons and over) 3; total deadweight tonnage 143. Air transport (1999): incoming flights 7,748; incoming passengers 92,368; incoming cargo 833 metric tons; airports (1999) with scheduled flights 3.

Communications				units per 1,000
Medium	date	unit	number	persons
Daily newspapers	1996	circulation	5,000	85
Radio	1997	receivers	57,000	929
Television	1997	receivers	14,000	221
Telephones	1999	main lines	11,919	211
Cellular telephones	1999	subscribers	2,643	47

Education and health

Educational attainment (2000). Percentage of population age 25 and over having: no formal schooling to some secondary education 33.9%; completed secondary 39.3%; some college 19.4%; undergraduate degree 4.8%; graduate degree 2.6%. *Literacy* (2000): total population age 10 and over literate 33,993 (99.4%); males literate 17,704 (99.4%); females literate 16,589 (99.5%).

Education (1999–2000)	schools	teachers	students	student/teacher ratio
Primary (age 6–14)	32	...	11,418	...
Secondary (age 14–18)	9	...	4,645	...
Vocational	...	21[7]	160[7]	7.6[7]
Higher	1	...	1,474[8]	...

Health (1991): physicians 26 (1 per 1,888 persons); hospital beds (1995) 140 (1 per 4.7 persons); infant mortality rate per 1,000 live births (2001) 10.4.
Food: daily per capita caloric intake, n.a.

Military

Military defense is the responsibility of the United States.

[1]Excludes nonvoting delegate representing Swains Island. [2]The seat of the legislature, as defined by the Constitution of American Samoa, is at Fagatogo, one of a number of villages within an urban agglomeration collectively known as Pago Pago. [3]Not within district administrative structure. Swains Island is administered by a village government and a representative of the governor. [4]Based on land area. [5]Includes 909 unemployed and 37 in military. [6]Imports c.i.f.; exports f.o.b. [7]1997–98. [8]American Samoa Community College at Mapusaga.

Internet resources for further information:
- **U.S. Department of the Interior: Pacific Web http://www.pacificweb.org**
- **Bank of Hawaii: Economics Research Center**
  http://www.boh.com/econ/pacific
- **American Samoa Government Department of Commerce**
  http://www.amsamoa.com

Andorra

Official name: Principat d'Andorra
(Principality of Andorra).
Form of government: parliamentary
coprincipality with one legislative
house (General Council [28]).
Chiefs of state: President of France;
Bishop of Urgell, Spain.
Head of government: Head of
Government.
Capital: Andorra la Vella.
Official language: Catalan.
Official religion: none[1].
Monetary unit[2]: 1 euro (€) = 100 cents;
valuation (Sept. 23, 2002)
1 U.S.$ = €1.02; 1 £ = €1.58.

Area and population

Parishes	Capitals	area sq mi	area sq km	population 2001[3] estimate
Andorra la Vella	Andorra la Vella	49[4]	127[4]	20,845
Canillo	Canillo	74	191	2,808
Encamp	Encamp			10,576
La Massana	La Massana	25	65	6,280
Les Escaldes–Engordany	—	4	4	15,397
Ordino	Ordino	33	85	2,291
Sant Julià de Lòria	Sant Julià de Lòria	4	4	7,647
TOTAL		181	468	65,844

Demography

Population (2002): 66,500.
Density (2002): persons per sq mi 367.4, persons per sq km 142.1.
Urban-rural (1999): urban 93%; rural 7%.
Sex distribution (2000): male 52.04%; female 47.96%.
Age breakdown (2000): under 15, 15.3%; 15–29, 19.8%; 30–44, 29.1%; 45–59, 19.2%; 60–74, 10.9%; 75 and over, 5.7%.
Population projection: (2010) 70,000; (2020) 74,000.
Doubling time: 74 years.
Ethnic composition (by nationality; 2000): Spanish 40.6%; Andorran 36.0%; Portuguese 10.2%; French 6.5%; British 1.4%; Moroccan 0.7%; German 0.5%; other 4.1%.
Religious affiliation (2000): Roman Catholic 89.1%; other Christian 4.3%; Muslim 0.6%; Hindu 0.5%; nonreligious 5.0%; other 0.5%.
Major urban areas (2001[3]): Andorra la Vella 20,845; Les Escaldes–Engordany 15,397; Encamp 10,576.

Vital statistics

Birth rate per 1,000 population (2000): 11.3[5] (world avg. 21.2).
Death rate per 1,000 population (2000): 3.9[5] (world avg. 8.9).
Natural increase rate per 1,000 population (2000): 7.4[5] (world avg. 12.3).
Total fertility rate (avg. births per childbearing woman; 2001): 1.2.
Marriage rate per 1,000 population (2000): 3.4.
Life expectancy at birth (2001): male 80.6 years; female 86.6 years.
Major causes of death per 100,000 population (1996–2000 avg.): cancers (neoplasms) 103.2; diseases of the circulatory system 90.0; diseases of the respiratory system 28.6; accidents and violence 24.3; diseases of the digestive system 16.9.

National economy

Budget (2001). Revenue: €234,705,780 (indirect taxes 75.2%, taxes from government enterprises 17.8%, revenue from capital 7.0%). Expenditures: €250,775,790 (current expenditures 51.5%, development expenditures 48.5%).
Public debt (1995): about U.S.$500,000,000.
Production. Agriculture (2000): tobacco 324 metric tons; other traditional crops include hay, potatoes, and grapes; livestock (number of live animals; 2000) 1,586 sheep[6], 1,181 cattle, 850 horses. Quarrying: small amounts of marble are quarried. Manufacturing (value of recorded exports in €'000; 2000): electrical machinery and apparatus 11,090; motor vehicles and parts 8,500; newspapers and periodicals 4,690; clothing 2,180; other products include furniture, cigarettes, and liqueurs. Construction (approved new building construction; 2000): 233,940 sq m. Energy production (consumption): electricity (kW-hr; 1997) 116,000,000 ([2000] 412,143,000); coal, none (n.a.); crude petroleum, none (n.a.); petroleum products, none ([2000] 201,677,000 litres); natural gas, none (n.a.).
Household expenditure (1997)[11]: food, beverages, and tobacco 25.5%, housing and energy 19.4%, transportation 17.7%, clothing and footwear 9.2%.
Land use (1994): forested 22.0%; meadows and pastures 56.0%; agricultural and under permanent cultivation 2.0%; other 20.0%.
Population economically active (2000)[7]: total 34,494; activity rate of total population 52.4% (participation rates: ages 15–64, 72.6%; female, n.a.; unemployed [2000] unofficially, none[8]).

Price and earnings indexes (1997 = 100)[9]

	1994	1995	1996	1997	1998	1999	2000
Consumer price index	...	...	...	100.0	101.6	104.3	108.8
Annual earnings index[10]	91.2	95.5	98.6	100.0	101.6	103.7	105.8

Gross national product (at current market prices; 1998): U.S.$1,110,000,000 (U.S.$16,930 per capita)[12].

Structure of labour force[7]

	2000 labour force	2000 % of labour force
Agriculture / Mining	161	0.5
Manufacturing	1,170	3.4
Construction	5,791	16.8
Public utilities	...	...
Transp. and commun.	...	...
Trade	6,673	19.3
Restaurants, hotels	6,434	18.7
Finance, real estate, insurance	1,416	4.1
Pub. admin., defense	4,275	12.4
Services	6,533	18.9
Other	2,041	5.9
TOTAL	34,494	100.0

Tourism (2000): 10,991,284 visitors; number of hotels 271.

Foreign trade

Balance of trade (current prices)

	1995	1996	1997	1998	1999	2000
€'000,000	−754.3	−778.7	−901.6	−918.2	−989.1	−1,056
% of total	88.0%	91.7%	91.4%	89.8%	92.4%	91.4%

Imports (2000): €1,106,006,000 (food, beverages, and tobacco 20.0%; machinery and apparatus 16.2%; chemicals and chemical products 10.1%; transport equipment 9.1%; textiles and wearing apparel 9.1%; photographic and optical goods and watches and clocks 5.0%). *Major import sources:* Spain 48.5%; France 26.6%; Asia 6.2%; Germany 4.4%; Italy 4.1%; U.K. 2.5%.
Exports (2000): €49,491,000 (electrical machinery and apparatus 17.2%; motor vehicles and parts 15.2%; newspapers, books, and periodicals 9.5%; chemicals 7.4%; optical and photo equipment 7.2%; tobacco 6.9%; clothing 4.4%). *Major export destinations:* Spain 60.9%; France 26.1%; Greece 1.7%; Germany 1.5%; The Netherlands 0.5%.

Transport and communications

Transport. Railroads: none; however, both French and Spanish railways stop near the border. Roads (1999): total length 167 mi, 269 km (paved 74%). Vehicles (2000): passenger cars 60,287; trucks and buses 4,400. Airports with scheduled flights: none.

Communications

Medium	date	unit	number	units per 1,000 persons
Daily newspapers	1996	circulation	4,000	62
Radio	1997	receivers	16,000	247
Television	1998	receivers	30,000	457
Telephones	2001	main lines	35,000	438
Cellular telephones	2001	subscribers	23,543	302
Internet	2001	users	7,000	88

Education and health

Educational attainment (mid-1980s). Percentage of population age 15 and over having: no formal schooling 5.5%; primary education 47.3%; secondary education 21.6%; postsecondary education 24.9%; unknown 0.7%. *Literacy:* resident population is virtually 100% literate.

Education (1998–99)

	schools	teachers	students	student/ teacher ratio
Primary/lower secondary (age 7–15)	12	...	5,960	...
Upper secondary	6	...	1,164	...
Higher	1	...	1,405	...

Health (1999): physicians 218 (1 per 303 persons); hospital beds 203 (1 per 323 persons); infant mortality rate per 1,000 live births (1999–2001 avg.) 4.1.
Food: n.a.

Military

Total active duty personnel: none. France and Spain are responsible for Andorra's external security; the police force is assisted in alternate years by either French gendarmerie or Barcelona police.

[1]Roman Catholicism enjoys special recognition in accordance with Andorran tradition. [2]The French franc and Spanish peseta were the former monetary units; on Jan. 1, 2002, F 6.56 = €1 and Pta 166.39 = €1. [3]January 1. [4]Andorra la Vella includes Les Escaldes–Engordany and Sant Julià de Lòria. [5]Official government figures. [6]Large herds of sheep and goats from Spain and France feed in Andorra in the summer. [7]Labour force receiving wages only; total population economically active equals 39,895. [8]The restricted size of the indigenous labour force has in the near past necessitated immigration to serve the tourist trade. [9]All indexes are end of year. [10]Official minimum salary. [11]Weights of consumer price index components. [12]Tourism (including winter-season sports, fairs, festivals, and income earned from low-duty imported manufactured items) and the banking system are the primary sources of GNP.

Internet resources for further information:
• Andorra National Information Centre
  http://www.andorra.ad
• Department d'Estudis i d'Estadística
  http://www.finances.ad

Angola

Official name: República de Angola (Republic of Angola).
Form of government: unitary multiparty republic with one legislative house (National Assembly [220])[1].
Head of state and government: President[2].
Capital: Luanda.
Official language: Portuguese.
Official religion: none.
Monetary unit: 1 refloated kwanza[3] = 100 lwei; valuation (Sept. 23, 2002) 1 U.S.$ = refloated kwanza 48.15; 1 £ = refloated kwanza 74.83.

Indian Ocean

Area and population

Provinces	Capitals	area sq mi	area sq km	population 2001 estimate
Bengo	Caxito	12,112	31,371	...
Benguela	Benguela	12,273	31,788	...
Bié	Kuito	27,148	70,314	...
Cabinda	Cabinda	2,807	7,270	...
Cunene	N'Giva	34,495	89,342	...
Huambo	Huambo	13,233	34,274	...
Huíla	Lubango	28,958	75,002	...
Kuando Kubango	Menongue	76,853	199,049	...
Kuanza Norte	N'Dalatando	9,340	24,190	...
Kuanza Sul	Sumbe	21,490	55,660	...
Luanda	Luanda	934	2,418	...
Lunda Norte	Lucapa	39,685	102,783	...
Lunda Sul	Saurimo	17,625	45,649	...
Malanje	Malanje	37,684	97,602	...
Moxico	Lwena	86,110	223,023	...
Namibe	Namibe	22,447	58,137	...
Uíge	Uíge	22,663	58,698	...
Zaire	M'Banza Kongo	15,494	40,130	...
TOTAL		481,354[4]	1,246,700	10,366,000

Demography

Population (2002): 10,593,000.
Density (2002): persons per sq mi 22.0, persons per sq km 8.5.
Urban-rural (2001): urban 34.9%; rural 65.1%.
Sex distribution (2000): male 50.59%; female 49.41%.
Age breakdown (2000): under 15, 43.2%; 15–29, 26.5%; 30–44, 16.9%; 45–59, 8.7%; 60 and over, 4.7%.
Population projection: (2010) 12,646,000; (2020) 15,750,000.
Doubling time: 32 years.
Ethnic composition (2000): Ovimbundu 25.2%; Kimbundu 23.1%; Kongo 12.6%; Lwena (Luvale) 8.2%; Chokwe 5.0%; Kwanyama 4.1%; Nyaneka 3.9%; Luchazi 2.3%; Ambo (Ovambo) 2.0%; Mbwela 1.7%; Nyemba 1.7%; other 10.2%.
Religious affiliation (2001): Christian 94.1%, of which Roman Catholic 62.1%, Protestant 15.0%; traditional beliefs 5.0%; other 0.9%.
Major cities (1999): Luanda 2,555,000; Huambo 400,000[5]; Benguela 155,000[6]; Lobito 150,000[6]; Lubango 105,000[7].

Vital statistics

Birth rate per 1,000 population (2000): 46.9 (world avg. 22.5).
Death rate per 1,000 population (2000): 25.0 (world avg. 9.0).
Natural increase rate per 1,000 population (2000): 21.9 (world avg. 13.5).
Total fertility rate (avg. births per childbearing woman; 2000): 6.5.
Life expectancy at birth (2000): male 37.1 years; female 39.6 years.
Major causes of death (percentage of total deaths; 1990): diarrheal diseases 25.8%; malaria 19.4%; cholera 7.3%; acute respiratory infections 6.8%.

National economy

Budget (1999). Revenue: NKz 7,540,000,000[3] (tax revenue 99.4%, of which petroleum corporate taxes 71.1%, tax on goods 20.5%, import duties 3.0%; nontax revenue 0.6%). Expenditures: NKz 8,940,000,000[3] (defense and internal security 41%; administration 16.1%; interest 10.7%; economic services 10.3%; education 4.8%; health 2.8%; other 14.3%).
Public debt (external, outstanding; 2000): U.S.$8,758,000,000.
Tourism: receipts (2000) U.S.$18,000,000; expenditures U.S.$11,000,000.
Household income and expenditure. Average household size (1998) 5.0; annual income per household: n.a.; sources of income: n.a.; expenditure: n.a.
Production (metric tons except as noted). Agriculture, forestry, fishing (2000): cassava 3,129,734, corn (maize) 428,045, sugarcane 330,000, bananas 290,000, oil palm fruit 250,000, sweet potatoes 182,050, millet 101,736, dry beans 67,509, pineapples 32,000, peanuts (groundnuts) 23,000, coffee 4,260; livestock (number of live animals) 4,042,000 cattle, 2,150,000 goats, 800,000 pigs, 350,000 sheep, 6,400,000 chickens; roundwood (2000) 6,676,000 cu m; fish catch (1999) 177,497. Mining and quarrying (1999): diamonds 1,080,000 carats. Manufacturing (1999): bread 87,500; frozen fish 57,700; wheat flour 57,500; soap 8,565; salt 7,803; leather shoes 25,000 pairs; beer 160,900 hectolitres; fabric 316,000 sq m. Construction (value in NKz '000,000[3]; 1986): residential 608; nonresidential 1,977. Energy production (consumption): electricity (kW-hr; 1998) 1,885,000,000 (1,885,000,000); coal, none (none); crude petroleum (barrels; 1999) 278,900,000 (14,100,000); petroleum products (metric tons; 1999) 1,956,000 (1,124,000); natural gas (cu m; 1997) 187,077,000 (187,077,000).
Gross national product (at current market prices; 2000): U.S.$3,847,000,000 (U.S.$290 per capita).

Structure of gross domestic product and labour force

	1999 in value NKz '000,000,000[8]	1999 % of total value	1999 labour force	1999 % of labour force
Agriculture	1,076	6.9	4,132,000	72.1
Mining	10,968	70.1		
Manufacturing	562	3.6		
Construction	529	3.4		
Finance				
Trade	1,370	8.8	1,597,000	27.9
Public utilities				
Transp. and commun.				
Pub. admin., defense	1,102	7.0		
Services				
Other	37[9]	0.2[9]	...	...
TOTAL	15,644	100.0	5,729,000	100.0

Population economically active (1999): total 5,729,000; activity rate of total population 57.7% (participation rates over age 10 [1991] 60.1%; female 38.4%; unemployed [2002] 70%).

Price and earnings indexes (1995 = 100)

	1995	1996	1997	1998	1999	2000
Consumer price index	100.0	4,245.2	13,550.1	25,327.3	43,661	61,311
Monthly earnings index	100.0	...	...	...	...	...

Land use (1995): forested 18.5%; meadows and pastures 43.3%; agricultural and under permanent cultivation 2.8%; other 35.4%.

Foreign trade

Balance of trade (current prices)

	1995	1996	1997	1998	1999
U.S.$'000,000	+1,871	+3,055	+2,529	+1,464	+2,077
% of total	33.6%	42.8%	33.9%	26.0%	24.1%

Imports (1999): U.S.$3,267,000,000 (1991; current consumption goods 50.2%, capital goods 20.2%, intermediate consumption goods 18.9%, transport equipment 6.8%). *Major import sources* (1999): Portugal 18.8%; U.S. 14.6%; South Africa 11.9%; France 8.2%; U.K. 6.2%; Spain 5.9%; Brazil 5.1%.
Exports (1999): U.S.$5,344,000,000 (mineral fuels 87.8%, diamonds 11.8%). *Major export destinations* (1999): U.S. 59.5%; China 8.2%; Taiwan 7.7%; Germany 2.4%; France 2.1%.

Transport and communications

Transport. Railroads (1998): route length 1,834 mi, 2,952 km; passenger-mi 203,000,000[10], passenger-km 326,000,000[10]; short ton-mi cargo 1,178,000,000[10], metric ton-km cargo 1,720,000,000[10]. Roads (1998): total length 45,128 mi, 72,626 km (paved 25%). Vehicles (1997): passenger cars 207,000; trucks and buses 25,000. Merchant marine (1998): vessels (100 gross tons and over) 123; total deadweight tonnage 73,907. Air transport (1997): passenger-mi 385,000,000, passenger-km 620,000,000; short ton-mi cargo 60,300,000, metric ton-km cargo 97,000,000; airports (1999) with scheduled flights 17.

Communications

Medium	date	unit	number	units per 1,000 persons
Daily newspapers	1996	circulation	128,000	14
Television	1999	receivers	190,000	19
Telephones	2001	main lines	80,000	5.9
Cellular telephones	2001	subscribers	86,500	6.4
Personal computers	2001	units	17,000	1.3
Internet	2001	users	60,000	4.4

Education and health

Educational attainment: n.a. *Literacy* (1998): percentage of population age 15 and over literate 41.7%; males literate 55.6%; females literate 28.5%.

Education (1991–92)

	schools[11]	teachers	students	student/ teacher ratio
Primary (age 7–10)	6,308	31,062	989,443	...
Secondary (age 11–16)	5,276	5,138[12]	196,099	...
Voc., teacher tr.	...	566[12]	22,888	...
Higher	1	787	6,331	8.0

Health (1997): physicians 736 (1 per 12,985 persons); hospital beds (1990) 11,857 (1 per 845 persons); infant mortality rate per 1,000 live births (2000) 195.8.
Food (2000): daily per capita caloric intake 1,903 (vegetable products 92%, animal products 8%); 81% of FAO recommended minimum requirement.

Military

Total active duty personnel (2001): 130,500 (army 92.0%, navy 1.9%, air force 6.1%). *Military expenditure as percentage of GNP* (1999): 21.2% (world 2.4%); per capita expenditure U.S.$248.

[1]Civil war begun in 1975 was officially declared over on Aug. 2, 2002. A cease-fire agreement had been signed earlier in April 2002. [2]President annulled post of Prime Minister in January 1999. [3]The refloated kwanza (or [second] new kwanza), equal to 1,000 readjusted kwanza, was introduced on Jan. 1, 2000; previously, in July 1995, the readjusted kwanza, equal to 1,000 new kwanza (NKz), was introduced. [4]Detail does not add to total given because of rounding. [5]1995. [6]1983. [7]1984. [8]In refloated kwanza. [9]Import duties. [10]1988. [11]1985–86. [12]1989–90.

Internet resources for further information:
• **Official Home Page of the Republic of Angola** http://www.angola.org
• **Bank of Angola** http://www.ebonet.net/bna/bna_blind.htm

Antigua and Barbuda

Official name: Antigua and Barbuda.
Form of government: constitutional monarchy with two legislative houses (Senate [17]; House of Representatives [17[1]]).
Chief of state: British Monarch represented by Governor-General.
Head of government: Prime Minister.
Capital: Saint John's.
Official language: English.
Official religion: none.
Monetary unit: 1 Eastern Caribbean dollar (EC$) = 100 cents; valuation (Sept. 23, 2002) 1 U.S.$ = EC$2.70; 1 £ = EC$4.20.

Area and population	area		population
			2001
Parishes (of Antigua)[2]	sq mi	sq km	census[3]
Saint George	9.3	24.1	
Saint John's	28.5	73.8	
Saint Mary	22.0	57.0	74,324
Saint Paul	18.5	47.9	
Saint Peter	12.7	32.9	
Saint Phillip	17.0	44.0	
Other islands[2]			
Barbuda	62.0	160.6	1,417
Redonda	0.5	1.3	0
TOTAL	170.5	441.6	75,741

Demography

Population (2002): 76,400.
Density (2002): persons per sq mi 448.1, persons per sq km 173.0.
Urban-rural (2001): urban 36.9%; rural 63.1%.
Sex distribution (2001): male 47.55%; female 52.45%.
Age breakdown (1991): under 15, 30.4%; 15–29, 27.8%; 30–44, 20.5%; 45–59, 10.2%; 60–74, 7.7%; 75 and over, 3.4%.
Population projection: (2010) 80,000; (2020) 84,000.
Doubling time: 50 years.
Ethnic composition (2000): black 82.4%; U.S. white 12.0%; mulatto 3.5%; British 1.3%; other 0.8%.
Religious affiliation (1991): Protestant 73.7%, of which Anglican 32.1%, Moravian 12.0%, Methodist 9.1%, Seventh-day Adventist 8.8%; Roman Catholic 10.8%; Jehovah's Witness 1.2%; Rastafarian 0.8%[4]; other religion/no religion/not stated 13.5%.
Major city (1991): Saint John's 22,342[5].

Vital statistics

Birth rate per 1,000 population (2000): 20.2 (world avg. 22.5); (1988) legitimate 23.4%; illegitimate 76.6%.
Death rate per 1,000 population (2000): 6.0 (world avg. 9.0).
Natural increase rate per 1,000 population (2000): 14.2 (world avg. 13.5).
Total fertility rate (avg. births per childbearing woman; 2000): 2.3.
Marriage rate per 1,000 population (1995): 22.1.
Divorce rate per 1,000 population (1988): 0.2.
Life expectancy at birth (2000): male 68.2 years; female 72.8 years.
Major causes of death per 100,000 population (1993–95): diseases of the circulatory system 258.1, of which cerebrovascular disease 103.3, diseases of pulmonary circulation and other forms of heart disease 76.9; malignant neoplasms (cancers) 104.9; endocrine and metabolic disorders 73.7.

National economy

Budget (1998). Revenue: EC$362,300,000 (taxes on international transactions 35.6%, of which import duties 15.8%; consumption taxes 24.9%; nontax revenue 12.5%; corporate income taxes 7.1%). Expenditures: EC$427,300,000 (current expenditures 90.1%; development expenditures 9.9%).
Public debt (external, outstanding; end of 1998): U.S.$406,400,000.
Production (metric tons except as noted). Agriculture, forestry, fishing (1999): tropical fruit (including papayas, guavas, soursops, and oranges) 6,500, mangoes 1,300, eggplants 250, lemons and limes 220, carrots 210, "Antiguan Black" pineapples 150; livestock (number of live animals) 15,700 cattle, 12,200 sheep; roundwood, n.a.; fish catch (1997) 500. Mining and quarrying: crushed stone for local use. Manufacturing (1994): beer and malt 166,000 cases; T-shirts 179,000 units; other manufactures include cement, handicrafts, and furniture, as well as electronic components for export. Construction (1998): gross value of building applications EC$323,000,000. Energy production (consumption): electricity (kW-hr; 1997) 153,700,000 (115,300,000); coal, none (none); crude petroleum, none (none); petroleum products (metric tons; 1997) negligible (110,000); natural gas, none (none).
Population economically active (1991): total 26,753; activity rate of total population 45.1% (participation rates: ages 15–64, 69.7%; female 45.6%; unemployed [end of 1999] *c.* 5%).

Price and earnings indexes (1996 = 100)						
	1995	1996	1997	1998	1999	2000
Consumer price index	96.9	100.0	98.9	103.6	104.4	104.6
Annual earnings index[6]	...	100.0	100.0	106.0	106.0	106.0

Household income and expenditure. Average household size (2001) 3.1; income per household: n.a.; sources of income: n.a.; expenditure: n.a.

Gross national product (2000): U.S.$642,000,000 (U.S.$9,440 per capita).

Structure of gross domestic product and labour force				
	1998		1991	
	in value EC$'000,000	% of total value	labour force	% of labour force
Agriculture, fishing	56.1	3.4	1,040	3.9
Quarrying	24.3	1.5	64	0.2
Manufacturing	31.7	1.9	1,444	5.4
Construction	166.5	10.0	3,109	11.6
Public utilities	42.6	2.5	435	1.6
Transp. and commun.	289.6	17.4	2,395	9.0
Trade, restaurants, and hotels	323.7	19.4	8,524	31.9
Finance, real estate	235.7	14.1	1,454	5.4
Pub. admin., defense	247.1	14.8	2,572	9.6
Services	104.4	6.3	5,207	19.5
Other	144.5[7]	8.7[7]	509	1.9
TOTAL	1,666.2	100.0	26,753	100.0

Land use (1994): forested 11.0%; meadows and pastures 9.0%; agricultural and under permanent cultivation 18.0%; other 62.0%.
Tourism: receipts from visitors (2000) U.S.$290,000,000; expenditures by nationals abroad (1997) U.S.$26,000,000.

Foreign trade[8]

Balance of trade (current prices)					
	1996	1997	1998	1999	2000
U.S.$'000,000	−302	−309	−327	−322	−307
% of total	90.0%	92.2%	91.7%	91.6%	91.1%

Imports (1998)[9]: U.S.$357,500,000 (agricultural products 11.0%, other [including petroleum products for reexport] 89%). Major import sources (1997): United States 26.3%; United Kingdom 10.0%; Caricom 7.8%.
Exports (1998): U.S.$36,200,000 (reexports [significantly, petroleum products reexported to neighbouring islands] 59.1%, domestic exports 40.9%). Major export destinations (1994)[9]: United States 40.0%; others include the United Kingdom, Canada, and Caricom.

Transport and communications

Transport. Railroad[10]. Roads (1996): total length 155 mi, 250 km (paved, n.a.). Vehicles (1995): passenger cars 13,588; trucks and buses 1,342. Merchant marine (1992): vessels (100 gross tons and over) 292; total deadweight tonnage 997,381. Air transport (1995): passenger-mi 157,000,000, passenger-km 252,000,000; (1991) short ton-mi cargo 137,000, metric ton-km cargo 200,000; airports (1996) with scheduled flights 2.

Communications				units per 1,000
Medium	date	unit	number	persons
Daily newspapers	1996	circulation	6,000	87
Radio	1997	receivers	36,000	523
Television	1997	receivers	31,000	451
Telephones	2001	main lines	37,300	474
Cellular telephones	2001	subscribers	25,000	318
Internet	2000	users	5,000	65

Education and health

Educational attainment (1991). Percentage of population age 25 and over having: no formal schooling 1.1%; primary education 50.5%; secondary 33.4%; higher (not university) 5.4%; university 6.2%; other/unknown 3.4%. *Literacy* (1995): percentage of total population age 15 and over literate, 90.0%.

Education (1996–97)	schools	teachers	students	student/ teacher ratio
Primary (age 5–11)	58	559	12,229	21.9
Secondary (age 12–16)	13	389	4,260	11.0
Higher[11]	1	16	46	2.9

Health (1996): physicians 75 (1 per 915 persons); hospital beds 255 (1 per 269 persons); infant mortality rate per 1,000 live births (2000) 23.0.
Food (1999): daily per capita caloric intake 2,396 (vegetable products 68%, animal products 32%); 102% of FAO recommended minimum requirement.

Military

Total active duty personnel (2000): a 170-member defense force (army 73.5%, navy 26.5%) is part of the Eastern Caribbean regional security system. *Military expenditure as percentage of GNP* (1998): 0.7%[9] (world 2.5%); per capita expenditure U.S.$57.

---

[1]Directly elected seats only; attorney general and speaker may serve ex officio if they are not elected to House of Representatives. [2]Community councils on Antigua and the local government council on Barbuda are the organs of local government. [3]Preliminary figures. [4]Increased to more than 3% of population by 2000. [5]Large settlements include (1991): All Saints 2,230; Liberta 1,473; Codrington 814. [6]Public sector only. [7]Net indirect taxes less imputed bank service charges. [8]Balance of trade excludes reexports; data for commodities and destinations includes reexports. [9]Estimated percentages. [10]Mostly nonoperative privately owned tracks. [11]1994–95.

Internet resources for further information:
• **Eastern Caribbean Central Bank**
  http://www.eccb-centralbank.org
• **Ministry of Foreign Affairs**
  http://www.foreignaffairs.gov.ag

Argentina

Official name: República Argentina (Argentina Republic).
Form of government: federal republic with two legislative houses (Senate [72]; Chamber of Deputies [257]).
Head of state and government: President[1].
Capital: Buenos Aires.
Official language: Spanish.
Official religion: Roman Catholicism.
Monetary unit: 1 peso (pl. pesos) (Arg$) = 100 centavos; valuation (Sept. 23, 2002) 1 U.S.$ = Arg$3.68; 1 £ = Arg$5.47.

Area and population		area		population
Provinces	**Capitals**	sq mi	sq km	2001 census[2]
Buenos Aires	La Plata	118,754	307,571	13,818,677
Catamarca	Catamarca	39,615	102,602	333,661
Chaco	Resistencia	38,469	99,633	983,087
Chubut	Rawson	86,752	224,686	413,240
Córdoba	Córdoba	63,831	165,321	3,061,611
Corrientes	Corrientes	34,054	88,199	929,236
Entre Ríos	Paraná	30,418	78,781	1,156,799
Formosa	Formosa	27,825	72,066	485,700
Jujuy	San Salvador de Jujuy	20,548	53,219	611,484
La Pampa	Santa Rosa	55,382	143,440	298,460
La Rioja	La Rioja	34,626	89,680	289,820
Mendoza	Mendoza	57,462	148,827	1,576,585
Misiones	Posadas	11,506	29,801	963,869
Neuquén	Neuquén	36,324	94,078	473,315
Río Negro	Viedma	78,384	203,013	552,677
Salta	Salta	60,034	155,488	1,079,422
San Juan	San Juan	34,614	89,651	622,094
San Luis	San Luis	29,633	76,748	366,900
Santa Cruz	Río Gallegos	94,187	243,943	197,191
Santa Fe	Santa Fe	51,354	133,007	2,997,376
Santiago del Estero	Santiago del Estero	52,645	136,351	806,347
Tierra del Fuego[3]	Ushuaia	8,210	21,263	100,960
Tucumán	San Miguel de Tucumán	8,697	22,524	1,336,664
Other federal entity				
Distrito Federal	Buenos Aires	77	200	2,768,772
TOTAL		1,073,400[4]	2,780,092	36,223,947

Demography

Population (2002): 36,446,000.
Density (2002): persons per sq mi 34.0, persons per sq km 13.1.
Urban-rural (2000): urban 89.6%; rural 10.4%.
Sex distribution (2001): male 48.77%; female 51.23%.
Age breakdown (2000): under 15, 27.7%; 15–29, 25.6%; 30–44, 18.8%; 45–59, 14.6%; 60–74, 9.6%; 75 and over, 3.7%.
Population projection: (2010) 39,904,000; (2020) 43,630,000.
Ethnic composition (2000): European extraction 86.4%; mestizo 6.5%; Amerindian 3.4%; Arab 3.3%; other 0.4%.
Religious affiliation (2000): Roman Catholic 79.8%; Protestant 5.4%; Muslim 1.9%; Jewish 1.3%; other 11.6%.
Major cities (1999): Buenos Aires 2,904,192 (12,423,000[5]); Córdoba 1,275,585; Rosario 1,000,000; Mar del Plata 579,483; La Plata 556,308.

Vital statistics

Birth rate per 1,000 population (2001): 18.2 (world avg. 21.2).
Death rate per 1,000 population (2001): 7.6 (world avg. 8.9).
Natural increase rate per 1,000 population (2001): 10.6 (world avg. 12.3).
Total fertility rate (avg. births per childbearing woman; 2001): 2.4.
Life expectancy at birth (2001): male 72.1 years; female 79.0 years.
Major causes of death per 100,000 population (1998): diseases of the circulatory system 265.8; neoplasms (cancers) 146.3; diseases of the respiratory system 91.0; accidents 30.5.

National economy

Budget (1999). Revenue: Arg$56,621,300,000 (current revenue 98.2%, of which tax revenue 90.4%, nontax revenue 7.8%; capital revenue 1.8%). Expenditure: Arg$63,662,000,000 (social security 35.3%; debt service 13.6%; general public services 8.4%; education 5.0%; health 5.0%; economic services 3.9%; defense 3.3%).
Public debt (external, outstanding; 2000): U.S.$86,599,000,000.
Tourism (2000): receipts U.S.$2,874,000,000; expenditures U.S.$4,338,000,000.
Gross national product (2002): U.S.$276,228,000,000 (U.S.$7,460 per capita).

Structure of gross domestic product and labour force				
	1999		**1996**	
	in value Arg$'000,000	% of total value	labour force	% of labour force
Agriculture	12,329	4.4	190,300[6]	1.5[6]
Mining	4,821	1.7		
Manufacturing	48,471	17.1	1,999,600	15.9
Construction	15,970	5.6	1,217,400	9.7
Public utilities	6,041	2.1	115,700	0.9
Transp. and commun.	22,614	8.0	873,300	6.9
Trade, restaurants	45,806	16.2	2,523,800	20.0
Finance, real estate	56,466	20.0	1,021,800	8.1
Pub. admin., defense	53,609	18.9	1,010,500	8.0
Services			3,573,000	28.4
Other	16,643	6.0	63,500	0.5
TOTAL	282,769[4]	100.0	12,588,900[6]	100.0[4]

Production (metric tons except as noted). Agriculture, forestry, fishing (1999): soybeans 19,500,000, sugarcane 16,700,000, wheat 14,200,000, corn (maize) 13,500,000, sunflower seeds 7,100,000, potatoes 3,450,000, grapes 2,425,000; livestock (number of live animals) 55,000,000 cattle, 14,000,000 sheep; roundwood (1998) 11,428,000 cu m; fish catch 1,012,804. Mining and quarrying (1999): silver 1,149,970 troy oz; gold 655,870 troy oz. Manufacturing (1999): cement 7,187,000; vegetable oil 5,658,000; wheat flour 3,563,000; sugar 1,578,000; paper 1,130,000; wine 12,809,000 hectolitres; beer 12,503,000 hectolitres. Energy production (consumption): electricity (kW-hr; 2001) 84,540,000,000 ([1997] 78,190,000,000); coal (1999) 336,000 ([1997] 1,258,000); crude petroleum (barrels; 2001) 277,000,000 ([1997] 191,000,000); petroleum products (metric tons; 1997) 21,923,000 (18,700,000); natural gas (cu m; 2001) 53,298,000,000 ([1997] 36,717,000,000).
Population economically active (1995): total 14,345,171; activity rate of total population 41.5% (participation rates: ages 15–64, 64.5%; female 36.9%; unemployed [1996] 17.0%).

Price and earnings indexes (1995 = 100)							
	1995	1996	1997	1998	1999	2000	2001
Consumer price index	100.0	100.2	100.7	101.6	100.4	99.5	98.4
Monthly earnings index[7]	100.0	100.7	...	...	...	...	...

Household size and expenditure. Average household size (1991) 3.8; expenditure (1985–86): food 38.2%, transportation 11.6%, housing 9.3%, energy 9.0%, clothing 8.0%, health 7.9%, recreation 7.5%, other 8.5%.

Foreign trade[8]

Balance of trade (current prices)						
	1996	1997	1998	1999	2000	2001
U.S.$'000,000	+1,621	−2,183	−3,117	−796	+4,357	+7,507
% of total	3.5%	4.0%	5.6%	1.7%	8.9%	16.4%

Imports (1999): U.S.$25,508,000,000 (machinery and transport equipment 46.5%, chemical products 19.4%, manufactured products 15.0%, food products and live animals 4.4%). *Major import sources:* Brazil 21.9%; U.S. 19.6%[9]; France 5.9%[10]; Germany 5.5%; Italy 5.3%; Japan 4.2%; Spain 3.9%.
Exports (1999): U.S.$23,333,000,000 (food products and live animals 35.1%, petroleum and petroleum products 12.1%, machinery and transport equipment 12.0%, manufactured products 10.8%, vegetable and animal oils 9.9%, crude materials 8.0%, chemical products 7.7%). *Major export destinations:* Brazil 24.4%; U.S. 11.4%; Chile 8.0%; The Netherlands 4.3%; Spain 4.1%; Uruguay 3.5%; Italy 3.0%.

Transport and communications

Transport. Railroads (1999): route length 33,958 km; passenger-km 9,102,000,000; metric ton-km cargo 9,101,852,000. Roads (1999): total length 133,890 mi, 215,471 km (paved 29%). Vehicles (1998): passenger cars 5,047,630; commercial vehicles and buses 1,496,567. Air transport (2001): passenger-km 4,575,000,000; metric ton-km cargo 105,342,000; airports (1997) 39.

Communications				units per 1,000
Medium	date	unit	number	persons
Daily newspapers	1996	circulation	4,320,000	123
Radio	1998	receivers	21,500,000	595
Television	1998	receivers	10,600,000	293
Telephones	2001	main lines	8,108,000	216
Cellular telephones	2001	subscribers	6,974,900	186
Personal computers	2001	units	3,000,000	80
Internet	2001	users	2,000,000	53

Education and health

Educational attainment (1991). Percentage of population age 25 and over having: no formal schooling 5.7%; less than primary education 22.3%; primary 34.6%; incomplete secondary 12.5%; complete secondary 12.8%; higher 12.0%. *Literacy* (1995): percentage of total population age 15 and over literate 96.2%; males literate 96.2%; females literate 96.2%.

Education (1998–99)				student/
	schools	teachers	students	teacher ratio
Primary (age 6–12)	22,395	313,764[11]	5,262,066	16.1[11]
Secondary (age 13–17)[12]	6,373	233,564[13]	2,539,740	9.6[13]
Higher	1,700	118,695[13]	1,342,565	7.8[13]

Health: physicians (1992) 88,800 (1 per 376 persons); hospital beds (1996) 115,803 (1 per 304 persons); infant mortality rate (2000) 18.3.
Food (2000): daily per capita caloric intake 3,181 (vegetable products 69%, animal products 31%); 135% of FAO recommended minimum requirement.

Military

Total active duty personnel (2001): 70,100 (army 59.1%, navy 23.1%, air force 17.8%). *Military expenditure as percentage of GNP* (1999): 1.6% (world 2.4%); per capita expenditure U.S.$118.

[1]Assisted by a ministerial coordinator who exercises general administration of the country. [2]Preliminary. [3]Area of Tierra del Fuego (province since 1991) excludes claims to British-held islands in the South Atlantic Ocean. [4]Detail does not add to total given because of rounding. [5]Urban agglomeration. [6]Based on October survey; data for agriculture and mining sectors are incomplete. [7]Manufacturing sector only. [8]Import figures are f.o.b. in balance of trade and c.i.f. in commodities and trading partners. [9]Includes Puerto Rico. [10]Includes Monaco. [11]1996. [12]Secondary includes vocational and teacher training. [13]1994–95.

Internet resources for further information:
• National Institute of Statistics and Censuses http://www.indec.mecon.ar

Armenia

Official name: Hayastani Hanrape-tut'yun (Republic of Armenia).
Form of government: unitary multiparty republic with a single legislative body (National Assembly [131]).
Head of state: President.
Head of government: Prime Minister.
Capital: Yerevan.
Official language: Armenian.
Official religion: none[1].
Monetary unit: 1 dram = 100 lumas; valuation (Sept. 23, 2002) official, 1 U.S.$ = 558.14 drams; 1 £ = 867.41 drams.

Area and population	area		population
Regions	sq mi	sq km	2000 estimate[2]
Aragatsotn	1,064	2,755	167,500
Ararat	812	2,104	310,800
Armavir	479	1,241	322,300
Gegharkunik	1,573	4,073	278,600
Lori	1,464	3,791	394,400
Kotayk	811	2,100	329,400
Shirak	1,034	2,679	362,300
Syunik	1,739	4,505	163,900
Vayots-Dzor	891	2,308	69,200
Tavush	1,043	2,702	156,800
City			
Yerevan	81	210	1,248,200
Other	493[3]	1,278[3]	
TOTAL	11,484[4]	29,743[4, 5]	3,803,400[6]

Demography

Population (2002): 3,008,000.
Density (2002): persons per sq mi 261.9, persons per sq km 101.1.
Urban-rural (2001): urban 66.6%; rural 33.4%.
Sex distribution (2001): male 48.68%; female 51.32%.
Age breakdown (2001): under 15, 23.2%; 15–29, 24.6%; 30–44, 23.3%; 45–59, 14.5%; 60–74, 11.6%; 75 and over, 2.8%.
Population projection: (2010) 3,021,000; (2020) 3,007,000.
Doubling time: n.a.; doubling time exceeds 100 years.
Ethnic composition (2000): Armenian 94.6%; Kurdish 1.7%; Russian 1.5%; Azerbaijani 0.5%; other 1.7%.
Religious affiliation (1995): Armenian Apostolic 64.5%; other Christian 1.3%; other (mostly nonreligious) 34.2%.
Major cities (2000): Yerevan 1,248,200; Gyumri 211,700[7]; Kirovakan 172,700[7].

Vital statistics

Birth rate per 1,000 population (2001): 11.3 (world avg. 21.2); (1993) legitimate 86.0%; illegitimate 14.0%.
Death rate per 1,000 population (2001): 7.9 (world avg. 8.9).
Natural increase rate per 1,000 population (2001): 3.4 (world avg. 12.3).
Total fertility rate (avg. births per childbearing woman; 2001): 1.5.
Marriage rate per 1,000 population (2000): 2.9.
Divorce rate per 1,000 population (2000): 0.4.
Life expectancy at birth (2001): male 62.1 years; female 71.1 years.
Major causes of death per 100,000 population (1999): circulatory diseases 342.1; cancers 106.0; respiratory diseases 36.2; accidents and violence 33.2.

National economy

Budget (2000). Revenue: 202,005,000,000 drams (tax revenue 96.7%, of which value-added tax 33.4%, excise tax 12.5%, payroll tax 11.6%, enterprise profit tax 10.1%, income tax 7.3%, other taxes 21.8%; grants 3.3%). Expenditures: 267,411,000,000 drams (current expenditures 79.1%, of which pensions and social welfare 24.8%, wages 13.7%, interest 6.5%, health 5.5%, education 3.3%, other 25.3%; capital expenditure and net lending 20.9%).
Public debt (external, outstanding; 2000): U.S.$677,700,000.
Tourism (2000): receipts from visitors U.S.$45,000,000; expenditures by nationals abroad U.S.$37,000,000.
Land use (1994): forest 13.4%; pasture 23.1%; agriculture 20.1%; other 43.4%.
Gross national product (2000): U.S.$1,991,000,000 (U.S.$520 per capita).

Structure of net material product and labour force				
	2000			
	in value '000,000 drams	% of total value	labour force	% of labour force
Agriculture	231,908	22.5	555,800	38.7
Manufacturing, mining } Public utilities	226,898	22.0	192,900	13.4
Construction	112,743	10.9	53,000	3.7
Transp. and commun.	71,698	6.9	47,400	3.3
Trade	94,878	9.2	107,900	7.5
Pub. admin., defense	—	—	27,900	2.0
Services	—	—	287,900	20.0
Other	294,330	28.5	164,100[8]	11.4[8]
TOTAL	1,032,455	100.0	1,436,900	100.0

Production (metric tons except as noted). Agriculture, forestry, fishing (2001): potatoes 363,834, wheat 297,791, tomatoes 173,837, grapes 116,500, barley 58,830, watermelons 54,797, apples 22,150; livestock (number of live animals) 497,306 cattle, 497,165 sheep, 68,912 pigs, 42,837 goats, 4,200,000 poultry;

roundwood (1998) 35,700 cu m; fish catch (1999) 1,730. Mining and quarrying (1999): copper 9,600,000; molybdenum 2,900; gold (metal content) 1,200 kg. Manufacturing (value in '000,000 drams; 1999): food products 109,016; jewelry 17,430; machine-building and metalworking equipment 15,286; tobacco 10,587; chemicals 8,186; metals 5,160; textiles 3,567. Construction (1999): residential 190,400 sq m. Energy production (consumption): electricity (kW-hr; 2000) 5,958,000,000 (5,958,000,000); coal (metric tons; 2000) none (5,000); crude petroleum (barrels; 1996) none (1,026,000); petroleum products (metric tons; 1997) none (139,000); natural gas (cu m; 1997) none (1,323,600).
Population economically active (2000): total 1,436,900; activity rate of total population 37.8% (participation rates: ages 16–60, 77.4%; female 49.0%; unemployed 10.7%).

Price and earnings indexes (1995 = 100)						
	1995	1996	1997	1998	1999	2000
Consumer price index	100	119	135	147	147.9	146.7
Earnings index	...	...	...	...	...	...

Household income and expenditure. Average household size (1999) 4.5; income per household (1999) 664,700 drams (U.S.$1,200); sources of income (1999): agricultural income 32.1%, wages and salaries 24.6%, transfers 19.3%, help from abroad 12.8%, self-employment 10.6%, other 0.6%; expenditure (1999): food 67.0%, beverages and tobacco 19.2%, services 12.4%, other 1.4%.

Foreign trade

Balance of trade (current prices)						
	1994	1995	1996	1997	1998	1999	2000
U.S.$'000,000	−178.3	−403.0	−469.2	−659.8	−640.0	−474.0	−592.0
% of total	29.3%	42.7%	44.7%	58.7%	47.0%	49.0%	49.1%

Imports (2000): U.S.$899,000,000 (minerals and chemicals 29.4%, food 16.6%, jewelry 12.6%, machinery and equipment 2.7%). *Major import sources:* EU countries 33.6%; former Soviet Union (FSU) 18.7%, of which Russia 14.7%; U.S. 11.5%; Iran 9.3%.
Exports (2000): U.S.$307,000,000 (jewelry 39.4%, machinery and equipment 14.3%, mineral products 12.4%, agricultural products 9.8%). *Major export destinations:* Belgium 24.5%; Russia 14.7%; U.S. 12.4%; Iran 9.1%; Georgia 4.9%.

Transport and communications

Transport. Railroads (1999): length 516 mi, 830 km; passenger-mi 28,832,000, passenger-km 46,400,000; ton-mi cargo 201,262,000, metric ton-km cargo 323,900,000. Roads (1997): length 5,238 mi, 8,431 km (paved 100%). Vehicles (1996): passenger cars 1,300; trucks and buses 4,460. Air transport (2000): passenger-mi 355,672,000, passenger-km 572,400,000; short ton-mi cargo 5,931,000, metric ton-km cargo 9,545,000; airports (2000) 1.

Communications				units per 1,000
Medium	date	unit	number	persons
Daily newspapers	1995	circulation	80,000	23
Television	1998	receivers	840,000	221
Telephones	2001	main lines	529,300	140
Cellular telephones	2001	subscribers	25,000	6.6
Personal computers	2001	units	30,000	7.9
Internet	2001	users	50,000	14.2

Education and health

Educational attainment (1999). Percentage of population age 15 and over having: primary education or no formal schooling 5.9%; some secondary 15.2%; completed secondary and some postsecondary 60.2%; higher 15.0%. *Literacy* (1999): total population age 15 and over literate 99.3%.

Education (1999–2000)				student/
	schools	teachers	students	teacher ratio
Primary (age 6–13)	1,407	60,565	583,541	9.6
Secondary (age 14–17)	1,446			
Voc., teacher tr.	63	1,809	28,048	15.5
Higher	16	4,156	39,770	9.6

Health (2000): physicians 10,029 (1 per 301 persons); hospital beds 18,800 (1 per 166 persons); infant mortality rate (2000) 15.6[9].
Food (2000): daily per capita caloric intake 1,944 (vegetable products 83%, animal products 17%); 77% of FAO recommended minimum requirement.

Military

Total active duty personnel (2001): 42,060 (army 92%, air force 8%). *Military expenditure as percentage of GNP* (1999): 5.8% (world 2.4%); per capita expenditure U.S.$170.

---

[1]The constitution provides for the right to practice the religion of one's choice. In practice, the law imposes restrictions on religious freedom. The 1991 Law on Religious Organizations establishes the separation of church and state but recognizes the Armenian Apostolic Church (the Armenian Orthodox Church) as having special status. The law requires all nonapostolic religious denominations to register with the Ministry of Justice and prohibits proselytizing. [2]De jure figure (about ¼ of Armenia's population has migrated since the demise of the Soviet Union in 1991). [3]Area of Lake Sevan. [4]In addition, about 14% of neighbouring Azerbaijan (including the 4,400-sq km geographic region of Nagorno-Karabakh [Armenian: Artsakh] has been occupied by Armenian forces since 1993. [5]Detail does not add to total given because of rounding. [6]October 2001 preliminary de facto census figure for country equals 3,020,768. [7]1999. [8]Includes 153,900 unemployed. [9]Official figure.

Internet resources for further information:
• The Embassy of the Republic of Armenia http://www.armeniaemb.org

Aruba

Official name: Aruba.
Political status: nonmetropolitan territory of The Netherlands with one legislative house (States of Aruba [21]).
Chief of state: Dutch Monarch represented by Governor.
Head of government: Prime Minister.
Capital: Oranjestad.
Official language: Dutch.
Official religion: none.
Monetary unit: 1 Aruban florin[1] (Af.) = 100 cents; valuation (Sept. 23, 2002) 1 U.S.$ = Af. 1.79; 1 £ = Af. 2.78.

Area and population	area[2]		population
Census region	sq mi	sq km	2000 census
Noord/Tanki Leendert	14	37	16,944
Oranjestad East	5	13	14,224
Oranjestad West	4	10	12,131
Paradera	10	25	9,037
San Nicolas North	9	23	10,118
San Nicolas South	4	10	5,730
Santa Cruz	18	47	12,326
Savaneta	11	28	9,996
TOTAL	75	193	90,506

Demography

Population (2002): 91,600.
Density (2002): persons per sq mi 1,221.3, persons per sq km 474.6.
Urban-rural (2000): urban 67.0%; rural 33.0%.
Sex distribution (2000): male 47.99%; female 52.01%.
Age breakdown (2000): under 15, 23.1%; 15–29, 19.3%; 30–44, 27.9%; 45–59, 18.1%; 60–74, 8.6%; 75 and over, 2.6%; unknown 0.4%.
Population projection: (2010) 95,000; (2020) 98,000.
Linguistic composition (2000): Papiamento 69.4%; Spanish 13.2%; English 8.1%; Dutch 6.1%; Portuguese 0.3%; other 2.0%; unknown 0.9%.[3]
Religious affiliation (2000): Christian 96.2%, of which Roman Catholic 81.9%, Protestant 7.3%, other Christian (Jehovah's Witness) 1.3%; Spiritist 1.0%; nonreligious 1.4%; other 1.4%.
Major urban areas (2000): Oranjestad 26,355[4]; San Nicolas 15,848[5].

Vital statistics

Birth rate per 1,000 population (2001): 13.9 (world avg. 21.2); legitimate 57.8%; illegitimate 42.2%.
Death rate per 1,000 population (2001): 5.2 (world avg. 8.9).
Natural increase rate per 1,000 population (2001): 8.7 (world avg. 12.3).
Total fertility rate (avg. births per childbearing woman; 2000): 1.8.
Marriage rate per 1,000 population (1998): 6.1.
Divorce rate per 1,000 population (1998): 3.6.
Life expectancy at birth (2000): male 70.0 years; female 76.0 years.
Major causes of death per 100,000 population (1998): diseases of the circulatory system 184.0, malignant neoplasms (cancers) 118.0, infectious and parasitic diseases/diseases of the respiratory system 61.7.

National economy

Budget (1999). Revenue: Af. 712,900,000 (tax revenue 85.4%, of which taxes on wages and income 32.1%, import duties 13.7%, taxes on profits 11.2%, excise taxes on gasoline 8.4%; nontax revenue 14.4%). Expenditures: Af. 736,900,000.
Production (metric tons except as noted). Agriculture, forestry, fishing: aloes are cultivated for export; small amounts of tomatoes, beans, cucumbers, gherkins, watermelons, and lettuce are grown on hydroponic farms; divi-divi pods, sour orange fruit, sorghum, and peanuts (groundnuts) are nonhydroponic crops of limited value; (livestock; number of live animals) Aruba has very few livestock; roundwood, n.a.; fish catch (1997) 205. Mining and quarrying: excavation of sand for local use. Manufacturing[6]: rum, cigarettes, aloe products, and soaps. Construction (value of residential and nonresidential buildings completed; 1992: Af. 16,900,000. Energy production (consumption): electricity (kW-hr; 1999) 738,000,000 ([2000] 644,000,000); coal, none (none); crude petroleum (barrels; 1997) none (2,353,000); petroleum products (metric tons; 1997) none (289,000); natural gas, none (none).
Gross domestic product (2000): U.S.$1,970,000,000 (U.S.$21,760 per capita).

Structure of gross domestic product and labour force	1994		1997	
	in value Af. '000,000	% of total value	labour force[7]	% of labour force[7]
Agriculture	12	0.5	198	0.4
Mining			—	—
Manufacturing	130	5.5	2,627	5.9
Construction	156	6.5	3,395	7.6
Public utilities	77	3.2	810	1.8
Transp. and commun.	204	8.6	3,388	7.5
Trade, restaurants	636	26.7	14,240	31.8
Finance, real estate	254	10.7	4,634	10.3
Pub. admin., defense	316	13.3	4,349	9.7
Services	277	11.6	6,404	14.3
Other	319	13.4	4,795[8]	10.7[8]
TOTAL	2,381	100.0	44,840	100.0

Population economically active (1997[7]): total 44,840; activity rate of total population 48.9% (participation rates: ages 15–64, 68.3%; female 43.8%; unemployed 7.4%).

Price and earnings indexes (1995 = 100)						
	1996	1997	1998	1999	2000	2001	2002
Consumer price index	103.0	106.0	108.0	111.0	115.0	119.0	120.0[9]
Earnings index[10]	103.1	106.6	109.5	111.9	...	...	...

Public debt (external, outstanding; December 2000): U.S.$209,800,000.
Household income and expenditure (1999): average household size 3.6; average annual income per household: Af. 39,000 (U.S.$21,800); sources of income: n.a.; expenditure (1994)[11]: transportation and communications 20.7%, food and beverages 18.4%, clothing and footwear 11.3%, household furnishings 10.4%, housing 9.8%.
Tourism: receipts from visitors (2000) U.S.$638,000,000; expenditures by nationals abroad (1999) U.S.$122,000,000.
Land use (1998): forest, negligible; meadows and pastures, negligible; agricultural and under permanent cultivation 11.0%; other (dry savanna and built-up) 89.0%.

Foreign trade

Balance of trade (current prices)						
	1995	1996	1997	1998	1999	2000
U.S.$'000,000	−425	−308	−391	−354	−594	−32
% of total	13.6%	8.1%	10.2%	13.2%	17.3%	0.6%

Imports (1999): U.S.$2,003,000,000 (petroleum [all forms] and free-zone imports 61.0%, electrical and nonelectrical machinery 8.0%, base and fabricated metals 4.3%). *Major import sources* (1999)[12]: United States 63.3%; The Netherlands 11.1%; Venezuela 3.0%; Netherlands Antilles 2.8%.
Exports (1999): U.S.$1,420,000,000 (petroleum [all forms] and free-zone exports 97.9%). *Major export destinations*[12]: United States 41.4%; Colombia 20.3%; The Netherlands 12.1%; Netherlands Antilles 8.4%.

Transport and communications

Transport. Railroads: none. Roads (1995): total length 497 mi, 800 km (paved 64%). Vehicles (1999): passenger cars 38,834; trucks and buses 990. Air transport (2001)[13]: passenger-mi 497,000,000, passenger-km 800,000,000; short ton-mi cargo, n.a., metric ton-mi cargo, n.a.; airports (1998) with scheduled flights 1.

Communications				units per 1,000 persons
Medium	date	unit	number	
Daily newspapers	1996	circulation	73,000	851
Radio	1997	receivers	50,000	558
Television	1997	receivers	20,000	223
Telephones	2001	main lines	37,100	350
Cellular telephones	2001	subscribers	53,000	500
Internet	2001	users	24,000	226

Education and health

Educational attainment (2000). Percentage of population age 25 and over having: no formal schooling or incomplete primary education 9.7%; primary education 33.9%; secondary/vocational 39.2%; advanced vocational/higher 16.2%; unknown status 1.0%. *Literacy* (2000): percentage of total population age 13 and over literate 96.3%.

Education (1998–99)	schools	teachers	students	student/teacher ratio
Primary (age 6–12)	33	397	8,456	21.3
Secondary (age 12–17) Voc., teacher tr.	15	470	7,157	15.2
Higher	2	53	394	7.4

Health (1999): physicians (1997) 103 (1 per 870 persons); hospital beds 308 (1 per 306 persons); infant mortality rate per 1,000 live births (2000) 6.5.
Food (1997): n.a.

Military

Total active duty personnel (1999): a 45-member Dutch naval/air force contingent is stationed in Aruba and the Netherlands Antilles.

[1]The Aruban florin (Af.) is pegged to the U.S. dollar at a fixed rate of Af. 1.79 = 1 U.S.$. [2]Areas for census regions are approximate. [3]Most Arubans are racially and ethnically mixed; ethnic composition (1998): Amerindian/other 80%; other (primarily Dutch, Spanish and/or black) 20%. [4]Combined population of Oranjestad East and Oranjestad West. [5]Combined population of San Nicolas North and San Nicolas South. [6]Service facilities include a free zone, offshore corporate banking facilities, casino/resort complexes, a petroleum transshipment terminal, a cruise ship terminal, and ship repair and bunkering facilities. [7]Based on labour force survey of October 1. [8]Includes 3,339 unemployed. [9]March. [10]Minimum wage in construction and manufacturing. [11]Weights of consumer price index components. [12]Excludes petroleum (all forms) and free-zone trade. [13]Air Aruba only.

Internet resources for further information:
• **Aruba Central Bureau of Statistics**
 http://www.arubastatistics.com/toc.htm
• **Centrale Bank van Aruba**
 http://www.cbaruba.org

Australia

Official name: Commonwealth of Australia.
Form of government: federal parliamentary state (formally a constitutional monarchy) with two legislative houses (Senate [76]; House of Representatives [150]).
Chief of state: British Monarch represented by Governor-General.
Head of government: Prime Minister.
Capital: Canberra.
Official language: English.
Official religion: none.
Monetary unit: 1 Australian dollar ($A) = 100 cents; valuation (Sept. 23, 2002) 1 U.S.$ = $A 1.83; 1 £ = $A 2.84.

Area and population

States	Capitals	area sq mi	area sq km	population 2001 census
New South Wales	Sydney	309,130	800,640	6,609,304
Queensland	Brisbane	668,210	1,730,650	3,635,121
South Australia	Adelaide	379,720	983,480	1,514,854
Tasmania	Hobart	26,410	68,400	472,931
Victoria	Melbourne	87,810	227,420	4,822,663
Western Australia	Perth	976,790	2,529,880	1,906,114
Territories				
Australian Capital Territory	Canberra	940	2,430	321,680
Northern Territory	Darwin	520,900	1,349,130	200,019
TOTAL		2,969,910	7,692,030	19,485,278[1,2]

Demography

Population (2002): 19,702,000.
Density (2002): persons per sq mi 6.6, persons per sq km 2.6.
Urban-rural (2002): urban 85.0%; rural 15.0%.
Sex distribution (2001): male 49.35%; female 50.65%.
Age breakdown (2001): under 15, 20.8%; 15–24, 13.7%; 25–44, 29.8%; 45–64, 23.1%; 65 and over, 12.6%.
Population projection: (2010) 21,091,000; (2020) 22,587,000.
Doubling time: over 100 years.
Ethnic composition (1999): white 91.4%; Asian 6.4%; aboriginal 1.5%; other 0.7%.
Religious affiliation (1996): Christian 70.9%, of which Roman Catholic 27.0%, Anglican Church of Australia 22.0%, other Protestant 21.9% (Uniting Church and Methodist 7.5%, Presbyterian 3.8%), Orthodox 2.8%, other Christian 2.4%; Muslim 1.1%; Buddhist 1.1%; Jewish 0.4%; Hindu 0.4%; no religion 16.6%; other 9.5%.
Metropolitan areas (2001): Sydney 3,997,321; Melbourne 3,366,542; Brisbane 1,627,535; Perth 1,339,993; Adelaide 1,072,585; Newcastle 470,610; Gold Coast 444,077; Canberra 353,149; Wollongong 257,510; Caloundra 192,397; Hobart 191,169.
Place of birth (1999): 76.4% native-born; 23.6% foreign-born, of which Europe 10.8% (United Kingdom 6.5%[3], Italy 1.3%, Greece 0.7%, Germany 0.7%, The Netherlands 0.5%, other Europe 1.1%), Asia and Middle East 2.7%, New Zealand 1.9%, Africa, the Americas, and other 8.2%.
Mobility (1995–96). Population age 15 and over living in the same residence as in 1994: 81.6%; different residence between states, regions, and neighbourhoods 18.4%.
Households (1996). Total number of households 7,100,000. Average household size 2.6; couples only 34.1%, couples with dependent children only 40.6%, couples with nondependent children 9.0%, single parent with children 9.9%, other 6.4%.
Immigration (1996): permanent immigrants admitted 96,970, from United Kingdom and Ireland 12.8%, New Zealand 11.8%, China 7.6%, Vietnam 4.8%, Hong Kong 4.6%, India 4.4%, Philippines 3.9%, South Africa 3.2%, Bosnia and Herzegovina 3.2%, Yugoslavia 3.1%, Sri Lanka 2.2%. Refugee arrivals (1998–99): 8,790.

Vital statistics

Birth rate per 1,000 population (2002): 12.8 (world avg. 21.2); (1997) legitimate 72.0%; illegitimate 28.0%.
Death rate per 1,000 population (2002): 7.4 (world avg. 8.9).
Natural increase rate per 1,000 population (2002): 5.4 (world avg. 12.3).
Total fertility rate (avg. births per childbearing woman; 2000): 1.8.
Marriage rate per 1,000 population (2001): 5.3.
Divorce rate per 1,000 population (2001): 2.8.
Life expectancy at birth (2000): male 76.6 years; female 82.0 years.
Major causes of death per 100,000 population (2000): diseases of the circulatory system 215.6; cancers 185.4; respiratory diseases 46.3; accidents, poisoning, and violence 26.7; diabetes 15.6; suicides 12.3.

Social indicators

Educational attainment (1999). Percentage of population age 15 to 64 having: no formal schooling and incomplete secondary education 38.0%; completed secondary 18.3%; postsecondary, technical, or other certificate/diploma 28.3%; university 15.4%.
Quality of working life (1999–2000). Average workweek: 35.7 hours (16.8%[4] overtime). Annual rate per 100,000 workers for: accidental injury and indus-

trial disease, 3,200[5]; death, n.a. Proportion of employed persons insured for damages or income loss resulting from: injury 100%[4]; permanent disability 100%[5]; death 100%[5]. Working days lost to industrial disputes per 1,000 employees (1999): 87. Means of transportation to work (1986): private automobile 69.4%; public transportation 10.1%; motorcycle and bicycle 3.2%; foot 6.6%; other 10.7%. Discouraged job seekers (considered by employers to be too young or too old, having language or training limitations, or no vacancies in line of work; 1999): 1.1% of labour force.

Distribution of household income (1997–98)

percentage of household income by quintile

lowest	second	third	fourth	highest
3.8%	9.0%	15.0%	23.9%	48.3%

Access to services (1976). Proportion of dwellings having access to: electricity 99.5%; bathroom 96.0%; flush toilet 92.2%; kitchen 97.9%; public sewer 73.4%.
Social participation. Eligible voters participating in last national election (1996): 95.8%; voting is compulsory. Population age 16 and over participating in voluntary work: n.a. Trade union membership in total workforce (1996): 31%.
Social deviance (1999). Offense rate per 100,000 population for: murder 1.8; sexual assault 74.2; assault 704.5; auto theft 684.8; burglary and housebreaking 2,191.6; armed robbery 49.8. Incidence per 100,000 in general population of (1996): alcoholism, n.a.; prisoners with drug offenses 539.5; suicide 13.1.
Material well-being (1995). Households possessing: automobile 85%; telephone 95%; refrigerator 99.7%; air conditioner 32.3%[6]; personal computers 54.0%[4]; washing machine 90.0%; central heating 3.9%[6]; swimming pool 10.1%[6].

National economy

Gross national product (2000): U.S.$388,252,000,000 (U.S.$20,240 per capita).

Structure of gross domestic product and labour force

	1997–98[7] in value $A '000,000	1997–98[7] % of total value	1999–2000 labour force	1999–2000 % of labour force
Agriculture	16,668	3.0	437,500	4.6
Mining	23,769	4.3	78,200	0.8
Manufacturing	65,878	11.8	1,113,100	11.6
Construction	30,003	5.4	695,400	7.3
Public utilities	14,292	2.6	64,500	0.7
Transp. and commun.	49,129	8.8	576,600	6.0
Trade[8]	110,688	19.9	2,252,300	23.5
Finance, real estate	92,060	16.5	1,316,200	13.7
Pub. admin., defense	23,185	4.2	345,800	3.6
Services	88,849	15.9	2,006,800	21.0
Other	42,402[9]	7.6[9]	691,500[10]	7.2[10]
TOTAL	556,923	100.0	9,577,900	100.0

Budget (1998–99). Revenue: $A 146,444,000,000 (income tax 70.3%, of which individual 52.4%, corporate 14.2%; excise duties and sales tax 22.1%). Expenditures: $A 140,814,000,000 (social security and welfare 37.5%; health 16.6%; economic and public services 11.2%; defense 8.0%; education 6.9%; interest on public debt 5.3%).
Public debt (2000–01): $A 69,226,000,000.
Tourism (2000): receipts from visitors U.S.$8,006,000,000; expenditures by nationals abroad U.S.$5,740,000,000.

Manufacturing, mining, and construction enterprises (2000)[11]

	no. of establishments	no. of employees	Turnover per person employed ($A '000)	annual turnover ($A '000,000)
Manufacturing[12]				
Food, beverages, and tobacco	3,912[13]	170,600	287.7	49,085
Metal products	9,348[14]	149,200	262.8	39,207
Machinery and equipment	8,988[15]	198,100	221.8	43,935
Chemical, petroleum, and coal products	3,038[13]	96,500	348.2	33,602
Printing and publishing	5,265[15]	103,800	158.0	16,402
Miscellaneous manufacturing	7,134[13]	55,600	121.0	6,727
Wood and paper products	4,218[14]	60,200	198.7	11,963
Nonmetallic mineral products	2,138[13]	35,400	280.5	9,930
Textile, clothing, footwear, and leather	6,720[13]	68,000	142.7	9,705
Mining[16]				
Coal, oil, and gas	254[15]	26,769	813.9	21,788
Metallic minerals	261[15]	24,106	645.3	15,556
Nonmetallic minerals[17]	699	8,799	254.6	2,240
Construction[18]	194,300	484,100	119.6	57,899

Production (gross value in $A '000 except as noted). Agriculture, forestry, fishing (1998–99): livestock slaughtered 7,401,400 (cattle 4,476,600, sheep and lambs 1,045,500, poultry 1,174,300, pigs 689,700); wheat 3,860,000, wool 2,139,100, seed cotton 1,353,000, grapes 1,115,600, sugarcane 1,044,000, barley 885,000, canola 638,000, potatoes 486,000, rice 332,000, apples 325,000, oranges 307,000, sorghum 285,000, bananas 264,000, lupins 244,000, tomatoes 222,000, carrots 162,000, oats 157,000, pears 114,000, sunflower seeds 74,000, peaches 65,000, corn (maize) 60,000, tobacco 40,000, pineapples 39,000; livestock (number of live animals; 1999) 115,456,000 sheep and lambs, 26,578,000 cattle, 2,626,000 pigs, 93,578,000 poultry; roundwood (1999) 22,938,000 cu m; fish catch (1998) 201,216 metric tons. Mining and quarrying (metric tons [tons of contained metal]; 1997–98): iron ore 169,568,000; bauxite 50,418,000; zinc 2,029,000; copper 1,665,000; lead 943,000; uranium oxide 5,797; gold 330,095 kg; diamonds (1998–99) 36,000,000 carats. Manufacturing (value added in U.S.$'000,000 except as noted; 1995): food products 12,239; transport equipment 5,745; printing and publishing 5,252; metal products 4,840; nonferrous metals 4,766; nonelectrical machinery 4,054. Construction (buildings completed, by value in $A '000; 1998–99): new dwellings 17,080,000; alterations and additions to dwellings 3,194,000; nonresidential 14,016,000.

Retail and service enterprises (2000)

	no. of establishments	no. of employees	total wages and salaries ($A '000,000)	annual turnover ($A '000,000)
Retail[19]				
Motor vehicle dealers, gasoline and tire dealers	37,305	220,661	2,572[20]	44,954
Food stores	53,166	406,299	2,461[20]	54,674[12]
Department and general stores	459	87,148	1,175[20]	12,367[12]
Clothing, fabric, and furniture stores	21,688	91,138	965[20]	9,636[12]
Household appliances and hardware stores	14,268	75,355	629	15,332[12]
Recreational goods	...	...	...	6,879[12]
Services				
Real estate agents[12]	7,589	52,079	1,847.5	3,902.7
Pubs, taverns, and bars[16]	4,792	81,724	...	8,253.3
Dental services[16]	5,257	24,108	568.4	1,685.2
Consulting engineering services[13]	5,514	30,736	1,242	3,233.3
Legal services[12]	10,819	73,186	2,181.0	7,034.3
Accounting services[13]	8,389	66,792	...	4,939.1
Computing services[12]	14,731	74,395	4,065.0	10,474.0
Travel agency services[18]	3,266	24,451	647.9	1,979.5
Market research services[12]	272	10,744	203.4	455.8
Private security services[12]	1,714	31,752	756.2	1,394.8

Energy production (consumption): electricity (kW-hr; 1997) 183,069,000,000 (183,069,000,000); coal (metric tons; 1997) 264,972,000 (115,424,000); crude petroleum (barrels; 1997) 153,000,000 (223,000,000); petroleum products (metric tons; 1997) 33,445,000 (31,038,000); natural gas (cu m; 1997) 31,909,000,000 (21,116,000,000).

Population economically active (1999–2000): total 9,577,900; activity rate of total population 50.5% (participation rates: over age 15, 63.4%; female 43.6%; unemployed 6.9%).

Price and earnings indexes (1995 = 100)

	1995	1996	1997	1998	1999	2000	2001
Consumer price index	100.0	102.6	102.9	103.7	105.3	110.0	114.8
Weekly earnings index	100.0	104.0	108.3	112.7	115.7	121.4	127.4

Household income and expenditure (1998–99). Average household size (1996) 2.6; average annual income per household $A 45,708 (U.S.$24,200); sources of income: wages and salaries 39.9%, self-employment 32.1%, transfer payments 10.1%, other 17.9%; expenditure: food and nonbeverages 18.2%, transportation and communications 16.9%, housing 13.9%, recreation 12.7%, household durable goods 6.0%, household services and operation 5.9%, clothing and footwear 4.6%, health 4.6%, alcoholic beverages 2.9%, energy 2.6%, other 11.7%.

Financial aggregates

	1994	1995	1996	1997	1998	1999	2000
Exchange rate, $A 1.00 per:							
U.S. dollar	0.73	0.74	0.78	0.74	0.63	0.65	0.58
£	0.48	0.47	0.50	0.45	0.38	0.40	0.38
SDR	0.53	0.50	0.55	0.48	0.44	0.48	0.43
International reserves (U.S.$)							
Total (excl. gold; '000,000)	11,285	11,896	14,485	16,845	14,641	21,212	18,118
SDRs ('000,000)	73	55	37	19	18	72	94
Reserve pos. in IMF ('000,000)	506	502	482	727	1,256	1,633	1,243
Foreign exchange ('000,000)	10,706	11,340	13,967	16,099	13,366	19,507	16,782
Gold ('000,000 fine troy oz)	7.90	7.90	7.90	2.56	2.56	2.56	2.56
% world reserves	0.9	0.9	0.9	0.3	0.3	0.3	0.3
Interest and prices							
Central bank discount (%)	5.75	5.75	5.75	...	...	...	...
Govt. bond yield (short-term; %)	8.19	8.42	7.53	6.00	5.02	5.55	6.18
Industrial share prices (1995 = 100)	100.7	100.0	112.1	125.2	131.3	145.1	156.6
Balance of payments (U.S.$'000,000)							
Balance of visible trade	–3,277	–4,223	–635	1,849	–5,367	–9,767	...
Imports, f.o.b.	50,648	57,443	61,032	63,044	61,215	65,826	...
Exports, f.o.b.	47,371	53,220	60,397	64,893	55,848	56,059	...
Balance of invisibles	–14,139	–15,431	–15,380	–14,580	–12,878	–13,408	...
Balance of payments, current account	–17,416	–19,654	–16,015	–12,731	–18,245	–23,175	...

Land use (1998): agricultural and under permanent cultivation 7.0%; other 93.0% (of which, meadows and pastures 54.0%).

Foreign trade[21]

Balance of trade (current prices)

	1996	1997	1998	1999	2000	2001
$A '000,000	–1,424	–1,423	–7,746	–14,551	–6,376	+5,307
% of total	0.9%	0.8%	4.2%	7.7%	2.8%	2.2%

Imports (1999–2000): $A 110,083,000,000 (machinery and transport equipment 46.6%, of which road motor vehicles 11.6%, office machines and automatic data-processing equipment 6.9%, telecommunications equipment 6.2%; basic manufactures 12.4%, of which textile yarn and fabrics 2.4%, paper and paperboard products 2.1%; chemicals and related products 11.4%; mineral fuels and lubricants 7.0%; food and live animals 3.6%). *Major import sources:* U.S. 20.9%; Japan 12.8%; China 6.8%; U.K. 5.8%; Germany 5.3%; New Zealand 4.0%; Singapore 4.0%.

Exports (1999–2000): $A 97,255,000,000 (crude materials excluding fuels 18.9%, of which metalliferous ores and metal scrap 11.6%, textile fibres and their waste 4.4%; mineral fuels and lubricants 18.6%, of which coal, coke, and briquettes 8.6%, petroleum, petroleum products, and natural gas 7.3%; food and live animals 17.3%, of which cereals and cereal preparations 5.1%,

meat and meat preparations 4.6%, dairy products 2.4%; basic manufactures 12.7%). *Major export destinations:* Japan 19.3%; U.S. 9.8%; South Korea 7.8%; New Zealand 6.9%; China 5.1%; Singapore 5.0%; Taiwan 4.8%.

Trade by commodity group (1999–2000)

SITC Group	imports U.S.$'000,000	%	exports U.S.$'000,000	%
00 Food and live animals	2,488	3.6	10,570	17.3
01 Beverages and tobacco	445	0.6	988	1.6
02 Crude materials, excluding fuels	1,162	1.7	11,556	18.9
03 Mineral fuels, lubricants, and related materials	4,832	7.0	11,366	18.6
04 Animal and vegetable oils, fat, and waxes	174	0.3	190	0.3
05 Chemicals and related products, n.e.s.	7,863	11.4	2,638	4.3
06 Basic manufactures	8,614	12.4	7,746	12.7
07 Machinery and transport equipment	32,305	46.6	7,302	11.9
08 Miscellaneous manufactured articles	9,759	14.1	2,409	3.9
09 Goods not classified by kind	1,614	2.3	6,421	10.5
TOTAL	69,256	100.0	61,186	100.0

Direction of trade (1999–2000)

	imports U.S.$'000,000	%	exports U.S.$'000,000	%
Africa	627	0.9	1,363	2.2
Asia	31,198	45.1	37,117	60.7
Japan	8,895	12.8	11,828	19.3
South America	403	0.6	498	0.8
North and Central America	16,018	23.1	7,020	11.5
United States	14,462	20.9	6,025	9.8
Europe	16,512	23.8	8,254	13.5
European Union	15,321	22.1	7,573	12.4
Russia	37	—	119	0.2
Other Europe	1,154	1.7	562	0.9
Oceania	4,220	6.1	5,663	9.2
New Zealand	2,750	4.0	4,235	6.9
Other	278	0.4	1,271	2.1
TOTAL	69,256	100.0	61,186	100.0

Transport and communications

Transport. Railroads (1998–99)[22]: route length 22,233 mi, 35,780 km; passengers carried 595,200,000; short ton-mi cargo 87,262,000,000, metric ton-km cargo 127,400,000,000. Roads (2000): total length 502,356 mi, 808,465 km (paved 40%). Vehicles (1999): passenger cars 9,719,900; trucks and buses 2,214,900. Merchant marine (1999): vessels (150 gross tons and over) 77; total deadweight tonnage 2,505,369. Air transport (1999)[23]: passenger-mi 46,646,591,000, passenger-km 75,070,556,000; short ton-mi cargo 1,156,331,000, metric ton-km cargo 1,688,215,000; airports (1996) with scheduled flights 400.

Communications

Medium	date	unit	number	units per 1,000 persons
Daily newspapers	1996	circulation	5,370,000	296
Radio	1997	receivers	25,500,000	1,391
Television	1999	receivers	13,400,000	706
Telephones	2001	main lines	10,060,000	520
Cellular telephones	2001	subscribers	11,169,000	578
Personal computers	2001	units	10,000,000	517
Internet	2001	users	7,200,000	372

Education and health

Literacy (1996): total population literate, virtually 100%[24].

Education (1996)

	schools	teachers	students	student/teacher ratio
Primary (age 6–12)	7,713	102,267	1,848,169	18.1
Secondary (age 13–17)	1,917	101,706	1,294,846	12.7
Vocational[25]	541	26,345	985,428	37.4
Higher	44[26]	26,920	634,094	23.6

Health: physicians (1999–2000) 55,200 (1 per 345 persons); hospital beds (1998–99) 77,631 (1 per 243 persons); infant mortality rate (2000) 6.0.
Food (1999): daily per capita caloric intake 3,150 (vegetable products 69%, animal products 31%); (1997) 118% of FAO recommended minimum requirement.

Military

Total active duty personnel (2001): 50,700 (army 47.7%, navy 24.7%, air force 27.6%). *Military expenditure as percentage of GNP* (1999): 1.8% (world 2.4%); per capita expenditure U.S.$372.

[1]Census total adjusted for underenumeration; unadjusted census total equals 18,972,350. [2]Total includes 2,592 persons in the civilian-populated Australian internal territories (Christmas Island, Cocos Islands, and Jervis Bay). [3]Includes both Northern Ireland and Republic of Ireland. [4]1994. [5]1992–93. [6]1983. [7]At 1996–97 prices. [8]Trade includes hotels and restaurants. [9]Import duties less imputed bank service charges. [10]Mostly unemployed. [11]Excludes operations of single-establishment enterprises employing fewer than four persons. [12]1998–99. [13]1995–96. [14]1994–95. [15]1993–94. [16]1997–98. [17]1990–91. [18]1996–97. [19]1991–92. [20]1985–86. [21]Exports and imports are f.o.b. in the balance of trade table. [22]Government railways only. [23]Includes Qantas and Ansett Australia. [24]A national survey conducted in 1996 put the number of persons who had very poor literacy and numeracy skills at about 17% of the total population (age 15 to 64). [25]Includes special education. [26]1991.

Internet resources for further information:
• Australian Bureau of Statistics http://www.abs.gov.au

Austria

Official name: Republik Österreich
 (Republic of Austria).
Form of government: federal state
 with two legislative houses (Federal
 Council [64]; National Council [183]).
Chief of state: President.
Head of government: Chancellor.
Capital: Vienna.
Official language: German.
Official religion: none.
Monetary unit: 1 euro (€) = 100 cents;
 valuation (Sept. 23, 2002)
 1 U.S.$ = €1.02; 1 £ = €1.58[1].

Area and population

States	Capitals	area sq mi	area sq km	population 2001 census
Burgenland	Eisenstadt	1,531	3,966	278,600
Kärnten	Klagenfurt	3,681	9,533	561,126
Niederösterreich	Sankt Pölten	7,403	19,174	1,549,658
Oberösterreich	Linz	4,626	11,980	1,381,993
Salzburg	Salzburg	2,762	7,154	518,587
Steiermark	Graz	6,327	16,388	1,186,379
Tirol	Innsbruck	4,883	12,647	675,070
Vorarlberg	Bregenz	1,004	2,601	351,570
Wien (Vienna)	—	160	415	1,562,482
TOTAL		32,378[2]	83,858	8,065,465

Demography

Population (2002): 8,077,000.
Density (2002): persons per sq mi 249.5, persons per sq km 96.3.
Urban-rural (2001): urban 67.4%; rural 32.6%.
Sex distribution (2001): male 48.44%; female 51.56%.
Age breakdown (2001): under 15, 16.8%; 15–29, 18.7%; 30–44, 24.9%; 45–59,
 18.6%; 60–74, 13.8%; 75 and over, 7.2%.
Population projection: (2010) 8,170,000; (2020) 8,265,000.
Doubling time: not applicable; population is stable.
Ethnic composition (national origin; 1998): Austrian 91.2%; citizens of former
 Yugoslavia 4.0%; Turkish 1.6%; other 3.2%.
Religious affiliation (1995): Roman Catholic 75.1%; nonreligious and atheist
 8.6%; Protestant (mostly Lutheran) 5.4%; Muslim 2.1%; Eastern Orthodox
 0.7%; Jewish 0.1%; other 1.9%; unknown 6.1%.
Major cities (2001): Vienna 1,562,482; Graz 226,892; Linz 186,266; Salzburg
 144,817; Innsbruck 113,826; Klagenfurt 90,257.

Vital statistics

Birth rate per 1,000 population (2001): 9.2 (world avg. 21.2); (2000) legitimate
 68.7%; illegitimate 31.3%.
Death rate per 1,000 population (2001): 9.2 (world avg. 8.9).
Natural increase rate per 1,000 population (2001): 0.0 (world avg. 13.2).
Total fertility rate (avg. births per childbearing woman; 2000): 1.3.
Marriage rate per 1,000 population (1999): 4.9.
Divorce rate per 1,000 population (1999): 2.3.
Life expectancy at birth (2000): male 75.4 years; female 81.2 years.
Major causes of death per 100,000 population (1998): diseases of the circula-
 tory system 527.9, of which ischemic heart diseases 217.2; malignant neo-
 plasms (cancers) 231.5.

National economy

Budget (1997). Revenue: S 950,820,000,000 (tax revenue 92.0%, of which social
 security contributions 37.7%, individual income taxes 17.3%, value-added
 taxes 16.2%). Expenditures: S 1,017,870,000 (social security and welfare
 42.0%; health 14.4%; education 9.2%; interest 9.2%; defense 2.0%).
National debt (end of year 1998): U.S.$133,897,000,000.
Production (metric tons except as noted). Agriculture, forestry, fishing (2000):
 sugar beets 2,600,000, corn (maize) 1,800,000, wheat 1,313,000, barley
 855,000, potatoes 496,000, apples 410,000, grapes 364,000, rye 183,000, rapeseed 140,000, triticale 135,000; livestock (number of live animals) 3,790,000
 pigs, 2,150,000 cattle, 13,540,000 chickens; roundwood (1999) 14,083,000 cu
 m; fish catch (1997) 3,486. Mining and quarrying (1999): iron ore 1,747,000;
 magnesite 748,600; talc 129,600. Manufacturing (value added in S '000,-
 000; 1997): nonelectrical machinery and apparatus 46.1; food and beverages 44.1; electrical machinery and apparatus 42.9; fabricated metals 36.9;
 chemicals and chemical products 28.6; transport equipment 22.0. Energy production (consumption): electricity (kW-hr; 1999) 60,348,000,000 ([1997]
 56,082,000,000); hard coal (metric tons; 1999) negligible ([1997] 4,087,000);
 lignite (metric tons; 1999) 1,137,000 ([1997] 1,287,000); crude petroleum (barrels; 1999) 7,054,000 ([1997] 66,323,000); petroleum products (metric tons;
 1997) 8,792,000 (10,760,000); natural gas (cu m; 1999) 1,833,000,000 ([1997]
 8,353,000,000).
Tourism (U.S.$'000,000; 2000): receipts U.S.$10,031; expenditures U.S.$9,291.
Population economically active (1999): total 3,909,000; activity rate of total
 population 48.3% (participation rates: ages 15–64 [1998] 70.7%; female
 43.2%; unemployed [October 1999–September 2000] 6.0%).

Price and earnings indexes (1996 = 100)

	1997	1998	1999	2000	2001	2002[3]
Consumer price index	101.8	103.0	103.6	106.1	108.9	110.6
Annual earnings index	100.5	104.0	104.6	...	...	...

Gross national product (at current market prices; 2000): U.S.$204,525,000,000
 (U.S.$25,220 per capita).

Structure of gross domestic product and labour force

	1998 in value S '000,000	1998 % of total value	1999 labour force	1999 % of labour force
Agriculture, forestry	56,750	2.2	233,900	6.0
Mining	8,760	0.3	11,600	0.3
Manufacturing	492,470	18.9	797,100	20.4
Construction	205,580	7.9	360,500	9.2
Public utilities	63,900	2.4	31,700	0.8
Transp. and commun.	184,050	7.0	261,600	6.7
Trade, restaurants	404,940	15.5	848,600	21.7
Finance, real estate	540,220	20.7	396,400	10.1
Pub. admin., defense	164,010	6.3	250,900	6.4
Services	335,520	12.9	698,600	17.9
Other	154,700[4]	5.9[4]	18,100	0.5
TOTAL	2,610,910[2]	100.0	3,909,000	100.0

Household income and expenditure. Average household size (2000) 2.5; sources
 of income (1995): wages and salaries 54.8%, transfer payments 25.9%; expenditure (1995): transportation and communications 15.4%, housing 15.4%,
 food and beverages 15.3%, cafe and hotel expenditures 12.6%.
Land use (1994): forested 39.2%; meadows and pastures 24.3%; agricultural
 and under permanent cultivation 18.3%; other 18.2%.

Foreign trade[5]

Balance of trade (current prices)

	1996	1997	1998	1999	2000	2001
€'000,000,000	−100.6[6]	−75.3[6]	−67.4[6]	−5.05	−5.25	−4.21
% of total	7.6%	5.0%	4.2%	4.0%	3.6%	2.7%

Imports (1999): €65,320,000,000 (machinery and transport equipment 41.3%,
 of which road vehicles 12.1%, electrical machinery and apparatus 7.5%;
 chemicals and related products 10.3%; food products 5.2%; clothing 4.4%).
Major import sources: Germany 41.9%; Italy 7.6%; United States 5.3%;
 France 5.0%; Switzerland 3.4%; Hungary 3.3%.
Exports (1999): €60,270,000,000 (machinery and transport equipment 43.1%,
 of which road vehicles 10.0%, electrical machinery and apparatus 8.1%;
 chemical products 9.4%; fabricated metals 4.9%; paper and paper products
 4.7%). *Major export destinations:* Germany 34.9%; Italy 8.4%; Switzerland
 6.0%; Hungary 4.9%; United States 4.6%; France 4.4%.

Transport and communications

Transport. Railroads[7]: (1999) length 5,643 km; (1998) passenger-km
 7,971,000,000; (1998) metric ton-km cargo 15,348,000,000. Roads (1997): total
 length 200,000 km (paved 100%). Vehicles (1999): passenger cars 4,009,604;
 trucks and buses 328,591. Air transport[8] (1999): passenger-km 12,460,000,000;
 metric ton-km cargo 361,348,000; airports (1999) with scheduled flights 6.

Communications

Medium	date	unit	number	units per 1,000 persons
Daily newspapers	1996	circulation	2,382,000	296
Radio	1996	receivers	6,000,000	744
Television	1998	receivers	4,200,000	520
Telephones	2001	main lines	3,810,000	468
Cellular telephones	2001	subscribers	6,565,900	807
Personal computers	2000	units	2,270,000	279
Internet	2001	users	2,600,000	319

Education and health

Educational attainment (1993). Percentage of population age 25 and over having: lower-secondary education 37.5%; vocational education ending at secondary level 44.6%; completed upper secondary 6.1%; higher vocational
 5.5%; higher 6.3%. *Literacy:* virtually 100%.

Education (1999–2000)

	schools	teachers	students	student/ teacher ratio
Primary/lower secondary (age 6–13)	4,544	68,147	655,335	9.6
Upper secondary/voc. (age 14–17)	711	41,341	315,590	7.6
Higher[9]	19	16,239	228,936	14.1

Health: physicians (2001) 25,001[10, 11] (1 per 323 persons); hospital beds (2000)
 67,964[11] (1 per 119 persons); infant mortality rate per 1,000 live births (2001)
 4.9.
Food (1998): daily per capita caloric intake 3,531 (vegetable products 65%,
 animal products 35%); 134% of FAO recommended minimum requirement.

Military

Total active duty personnel (2001): 41,100 (army 84.4%; air force 15.6%).
Military expenditure as percentage of GNP (1999): 0.8% (world 2.4%); per
 capita expenditure U.S.$208.

---

[1]The Austrian Schilling (S) was the former monetary unit; on Jan. 1, 2002, S 13.76 =
€1. [2]Detail does not add to total given because of rounding. [3]April. [4]Value-added tax
less imputed bank service charges and subsidies. [5]Imports c.i.f., exports f.o.b. [6]In
Austrian Schillings. [7]Federal railways only. [8]Austrian Airlines and Lauda Air. [9]1998–99;
universities only. [10]Excludes 5,585 doctors in training. [11]January 1.

Internet resources for further information:
• **Austrian Central Office of Statistics http://www.statistik.at**
• **Austrian Press and Information Service (Washington, D.C.)**
 http://www.austria.org/index.html

Azerbaijan

Official name: Azərbaycan Respublikası (Republic of Azerbaijan).
Form of government: unitary multiparty republic with a single legislative body (National Assembly [124[1]]).
Head of state and government:
President assisted by Prime Minister.
Capital: Baku (Azerbaijani: Bakı).
Official language: Azerbaijani.
Official religion: none.
Monetary unit: 1 manat (A.M.) = 100 gopik; valuation (Sept. 23, 2002) free rate, 1 U.S.$ = A.M. 4,886; 1 £ = A.M. 7,593.

Area and population

Economic regions	Area sq km	Population 2000 estimate
Absheron	5,400	2,182,000
Gyadza	5,400	529,000
Kazakh	7,100	568,000
Kelbadjar	7,400	259,000
Khachmas	7,000	455,000
Lenkoran	6,100	744,000
Mil-Karabakh	6,500	696,000
Mugan-Salyan	9,000	621,000
Priarak	4,300	323,000
Sheki	9,000	531,000
Shirvan	11,200	661,000
Upper-Karabakh[2]	2,700	143,000
Autonomous Regions		
Nakhchivan	5,500	363,000
TOTAL	86,600	8,075,000[3]

Demography

Population (2002): 8,176,000.
Density (2002): persons per sq mi 244.8, persons per sq km 94.4.
Urban-rural (1998): urban 56.6%; rural 43.4%.
Sex distribution (2000): male 48.94%; female 51.06%.
Age breakdown (2000): under 15, 31.8%; 15–29, 25.6%; 30–44, 24.1%; 45–59, 9.5%; 60–69, 7.6%; 70 and over, 1.4%.
Population projection: (2010) 8,545,000; (2020) 8,985,000.
Doubling time: 77 years.
Ethnic composition (1995): Azerbaijani 89.0%; Russian 3.0%; Lezgian 2.2%; Armenian 2.0%; other 3.8%.
Religious affiliation (1995): Muslim 93.4%, of which Shī'ī 65.4%, Sunnī 28.0%; Russian Orthodox 1.1%; Armenian Apostolic (Orthodox) 1.1%; other 4.4%.
Major cities (1997): Baku 1,727,200; Gäncä (formerly Kirovabad) 291,900; Sumqayıt (Sumgait) 248,500; Mingäçevir (Mingechaur) 97,200.

Vital statistics

Birth rate per 1,000 population (2001): 14.8 (world avg. 21.2); (1994) legitimate 94.8%; illegitimate 5.2%.
Death rate per 1,000 population (2001): 5.9 (world avg. 8.9).
Natural increase rate per 1,000 population (2001): 8.9 (world avg. 12.3).
Total fertility rate (avg. births per childbearing woman; 2001): 1.6.
Life expectancy at birth (2001): male 68.1 years; female 75.1 years.
Major causes of death per 100,000 population (1994): diseases of the circulatory system 336.3; accidents, poisoning, and violence 99.1; diseases of the respiratory system 98.6; malignant neoplasms (cancers) 67.6; diseases of the digestive system 31.7; infectious and parasitic diseases 29.0; endocrine and metabolic disorders 14.2; diseases of the nervous system 12.1.

National economy

Budget (2000). Revenue: A.M. 4,004,000,000,000 (tax revenue 69.3%, of which value-added tax 22.8%, social security contributions 11.4%, enterprise profits tax 11.4%, personal income tax 8.3%, excise taxes 7.3%, tax on international trade 5.8%, other taxes 2.3%; nontax revenue 30.7%). Expenditures: A.M. 3,801,000,000,000 (education 23.8%; social security 18.3%; national economy 17.8%; defense 12.8%; health 5.4%; culture 2.8%; other 19.1%).
Public debt (external, outstanding; 2000): U.S.$692,100,000.
Production (metric tons except as noted). Agriculture, forestry, fishing (2000): cereals 950,000, vegetables (except potatoes) 780,800, fruit (except grapes) 477,000, potatoes 469,000, cotton 91,500, grapes 76,800, sugar beets 45,600, tobacco leaves 17,300, tea 1,100; livestock (number of live animals) 6,086,000 sheep and goats, 2,021,600 cattle, 63,700 horses, 18,600 pigs, 14,740,500 poultry; roundwood (2000) 13,500 cu m; fish catch (1999) 4,935. Mining and quarrying (1996): iron ore 1,000,000; alunite 600,000. Manufacturing (value of production in A.M. '000,000,000; 1998): oil refinery products 2,980; electricity and gas 2,005; food products 1,972; textiles 468; chemicals 320. Construction (2000): residential 487,000 sq m. Energy production (consumption): electricity (kW-hr; 1997) 16,800,000,000 (16,800,000,000); coal (metric tons; 1997) none (1,000); crude petroleum (barrels; 2000) 102,200,000 (47,200,000); petroleum products (metric tons; 2000) 7,520,000 ([1998] 6,200,000); natural gas (cu m; 2000) 5,600,000,000 (5,600,000,000).
Household income and expenditure. Average household size (1997) 5.2; income per household: n.a.; sources of income (1993): wages and salaries 50.9%, agricultural income 24.0%, social benefits 10.2%, expenditure: food 61.2%, clothing 11.1%, services 3.0%.
Tourism (2000): receipts U.S.$63,000,000; expenditures U.S.$132,000,000.

Gross national product (2000): U.S.$4,960,000,000 (U.S.$610 per capita).

Structure of gross domestic product and labour force

	2000			
	in value A.M. '000,000[4]	% of total value[4]	labour force	% of labour force
Agriculture	4,271,000	18.9	1,567,000	42.3
Mining }			39,600	1.1
Manufacturing }	6,948,000	30.7	180,700	4.9
Public utilities	587,000	2.6	38,800	1.0
Construction	1,039,000	4.6	155,000	4.2
Transp. and commun.	3,404,000	15.0	168,600	4.6
Trade	1,444,000	6.4	685,500	18.5
Finance	250,000	1.1	15,200	0.4
Pub. admin., defense			260,200	7.0
Services }	4,688,000	20.7	593,900	16.0
Other }		—	—	—
TOTAL	22,631,000	100.0	3,704,500	100.0

Population economically active (2000): total 3,704,500, activity rate 45.8% (participation rates: ages 15–64, 73.1%; female 47.7%; unemployed 1.2%).

Price and earnings indexes (1995 = 100)

	1995	1996	1997	1998	1999	2000
Consumer price index	100.0	119.9	124.3	123.3	112.8	114.9
Earnings index	...	...	...	...	...	...

Land use (2000): forest 11.5%; pasture 25.4%; agriculture 50.0%; other 12.6%.

Foreign trade

Balance of trade (current prices)

	1997	1998	1999	2000	2001
U.S.$'000,000	−567	−1,046	−408	+573	+329
% of total	26.0%	43.5%	16.6%	19.6%	20.2%

Imports (2000): U.S.$1,172,069,000 (machinery and equipment 31.0%, food 19.0%, metals 10.5%, minerals 9.8%, vehicles 8.5%, chemicals 7.2%). *Major import sources:* Russia 21.3%; Turkey 11.0%; U.S. 8.9%; Germany 5.8%; Kazakhstan 4.9%; Iran 4.8%; Switzerland 4.8%; Ukraine 3.1%.
Exports (2000): U.S.$1,744,900,000 (petroleum products 84.0%, food 3.3%, cotton 2.1%, chemicals 2.1%, machinery and equipment 1.9%, metals 1.8%). *Major export destinations:* Italy 43.7%; France 11.8%; Israel 7.7%; Turkey 6.0%; Russia 5.6%; Georgia 4.3%; Iceland 1.8%.

Transport and communications

Transport. Railroads (2000): length 2,120 km; passenger-km 493,200,000; metric ton-km cargo 5,770,000. Roads (1999): total length 45,870 km (paved 94%). Vehicles (2000): passenger cars 332,100; trucks and buses 78,300. Merchant marine (2000): vessels (100 gross tons and over) 68; total deadweight tonnage, n.a. Air transport (1995): passenger-km 1,650,000,000; metric ton-km cargo 183,000,000; airports (2000) 3.

Communications

Medium	date	unit	number	units per 1,000 persons
Daily newspapers	1995	circulation	210,000	28
Radio	1997	receivers	175,000	23
Television	1998	receivers	1,950,000	253
Telephones	2001	main lines	865,500	111
Cellular telephones	2001	subscribers	620,000	79
Internet	2001	users	25,000	3.2

Education and health

Educational attainment (1995). Percentage of population age 15 and over having: primary education or no formal schooling 12.1%, some secondary 9.1%; completed secondary and some postsecondary 27.5%; higher 7.6%. *Literacy* (1989): percentage of total population 15 and over literate 97.3%; males literate 98.9%; females 95.9%.

Education (1995–96)

	schools	teachers	students	student/ teacher ratio
Primary (age 6–13)	4,462	34,201	697,510	20.4
Secondary (age 14–17)	...	105,656	812,660	7.7
Voc., teacher tr.	78[5]	...	26,585	...
Higher	23[5]	18,184[5]	120,870[5]	6.6

Health (2000): physicians 28,600 (1 per 283 persons); hospital beds (1998) 71,100 (1 per 110 persons); infant mortality rate per 1,000 live births (2001) 30.0.
Food (2000): daily per capita caloric intake 2,468 (vegetable products 85%, animal products 15%); 96% of FAO recommended minimum requirement.

Military

Total active duty personnel (2001): 72,100 (army 86.0%, navy 3.0%, air force 11.0%). *Military expenditure as percentage of GNP* (1999): 6.6% (world 2.4%); per capita expenditure U.S.$120.

---

[1]Excludes one vacant seat reserved for Nagorno-Karabakh representative. [2]Controlled in part by Armenian forces from 1993. [3]Sum of grossly rounded parts; beginning of year 2001 population estimate is 8,081,000. [4]At factor cost. [5]1994–95.

Internet resources for further information:
• **State Statistical Committee of Azerbaijan Republic**
  http://www.statcom.baku-az.com
• **Azerbaijan Republic** http://www.president.az/azerbaijan/azerbaijan.htm

Bahamas, The

Official name: The Commonwealth of The Bahamas.
Form of government: constitutional monarchy with two legislative houses (Senate [16]; House of Assembly [40]).
Chief of state: British Monarch represented by Governor-General.
Head of government: Prime Minister.
Capital: Nassau.
Official language: English.
Official religion: none.
Monetary unit: 1 Bahamian dollar (B$) = 100 cents; valuation (Sept. 23, 2002) 1 U.S.$ = B$1.00; 1 £ = B$1.55.

Area and population

Islands and Island Groups[2]	area[1] sq mi	area[1] sq km	population 2000 census
Abaco, Great and Little	649	1,681	13,170
Acklins	192	497	428
Andros	2,300	5,957	7,686
Berry Islands	12	31	709
Bimini Islands	9	23	1,717
Cat Island	150	388	1,647
Crooked and Long Cay	93	241	350
Eleuthera	187	484	7,999
Exuma, Great, and Exuma Cays	112	290	3,571
Grand Bahama	530	1,373	46,994
Harbour Island	3	8	1,639
Inagua, Great and Little	599	1,551	969
Long Island	230	596	2,992
Mayaguana	110	285	259
New Providence	80	207	210,832
Ragged Island	14	36	72
Rum Cay	30	78	− 80
San Salvador	63	163	970
Spanish Wells	10	26	1,527
Other uninhabited cays and rocks	9	23	—
TOTAL	5,382	13,939[3]	303,611

Demography

Population (2002): 309,000.
Density (2002)[4]: persons per sq mi 79.4, persons per sq km 30.7.
Urban-rural (2000): urban 88.3%; rural 11.7%.
Sex distribution (2000): male 49.34%; female 50.66%.
Age breakdown (2000): under 15, 29.5%; 15–29, 27.2%; 30–44, 23.3%; 45–59, 12.1%; 60–74, 5.9%; 75 and over, 2.0%.
Population projection: (2010) 325,000; (2020) 334,000.
Doubling time: 55 years.
Ethnic composition (2000): local black 67.5%; mulatto 14.2%; British 12.0%; Haitian black 3.0%; U.S. white 2.4%; other 0.9%.
Religious affiliation (1995): non-Anglican Protestant 45.4%, of which Baptist 17.5%; Roman Catholic 16.8%; Anglican 10.8%; nonreligious 5.3%; Spiritist 1.5%; other (mostly independent and unaffiliated Christian) 20.2%.
Major cities (2000): Nassau 210,832[5]; Freeport/Lucaya 35,255[6]; Marsh Harbour (1990) 3,611; Bailey Town (1990) 1,490.

Vital statistics

Birth rate per 1,000 population (2000): 19.5 (world avg. 22.5); (1995) legitimate 45.7%; illegitimate 54.3%.
Death rate per 1,000 population (2000): 6.8 (world avg. 9.0).
Natural increase rate per 1,000 population (2000): 12.7 (world avg. 13.5).
Total fertility rate (avg. births per childbearing woman; 2000): 2.3.
Marriage rate per 1,000 population (1996): 9.3.
Life expectancy at birth (2000): male 68.3 years; female 73.9 years.
Major causes of death per 100,000 population (1995)[7]: diseases of the circulatory system 160.1; endocrine and metabolic disorders 137.4; malignant neoplasms (cancers) 85.6.

National economy

Budget (1998–99). Revenue: B$730,102,000 (import taxes 45.1%, stamp taxes from imports 11.0%, business and professional licenses 7.4%, departure taxes 6.6%). Expenditures: B$748,150,000 (education 19.7%, health 15.5%, interest on public debt 13.2%, public order 11.1%, defense 3.7%).
National debt (2001): U.S.$1,483,800,000.
Production (value of production in B$'000 except as noted). Agriculture, forestry, fishing (1998): crayfish 56,500[8], poultry products 28,300, citrus and other fruit 21,300, ornamental plants and flowers 6,000, conch 4,300[8]; roundwood (1998) 117,000 cu m. Mining and quarrying (value of export production; 1996): salt 18,100; aragonite 4,900. Manufacturing (value of export production; 1996): pharmaceuticals and other chemical products (1995) 74,200; rum 5,200. Energy production (consumption): electricity (kW-hr; 2000) 1,665,000,000 ([1997] 1,414,000,000); petroleum products (metric tons; 1997) none (566,000).
Tourism (U.S.$'000,000; 2000): receipts 1,814; expenditures 293.
Household income and expenditure. Average household size (1996) 3.9; income per household (1996) B$27,252 (U.S.$27,252); sources of income: n.a.; expenditure (1995)[9]: housing 32.8%, transportation and communications 14.8%, food and beverages 13.8%, household furnishings 8.9%.
Gross national product (at current market prices; 2000): U.S.$4,533,000,000 (U.S.$14,960 per capita).

Structure of gross domestic product and labour force

	1995 in value B$'000,000	1995 % of total value	1996 labour force	1996 % of labour force
Agriculture, fishing	100	3.3	6,445	4.4
Manufacturing	80	2.6	5,400	3.7
Mining	26	0.8 }	1,665	1.1
Public utilities	116	3.8 }		
Construction	71	2.3	12,045	8.2
Transp. and commun.	295	9.6	11,475	7.8
Trade, restaurants	705	23.0	38,700	26.4
Finance, real estate	599	19.5	11,125	7.6
Pub. admin., defense	210	6.8 }	42,295	28.8
Services	301	9.8 }		
Other	568[10]	18.5[10]	17,485[11]	11.9[11]
TOTAL	3,069[3]	100.0	146,635	100.0[3]

Population economically active (1996): total 146,635; activity rate of total population 51.6% (participation rates: [1994] ages 15–64, 77.8%; female 47.5%; unemployed [1998] 9.5%).

Price and earnings indexes (1995 = 100)

	1996	1997	1998	1999	2000	2001	2002
Consumer price index	101.4	101.9	103.3	104.6	106.3	108.4	110.1[12]
Annual earnings index	...	...	...	...	...	...	...

Land use (1994): forest 32.4%; pasture 0.2%; agriculture 1.0%; other 66.4%.

Foreign trade[13]

Balance of trade (current prices)

	1996	1997	1998	1999	2000	2001
B$'000,000	−1,187	−1,441	−1,374	−1,421	−1,313	−998
% of total	76.9%	79.9%	65.4%	59.4%	44.9%	39.5%

Imports (1999): B$1,907,000,000 (machinery and transport equipment 30.8%; food products 13.7%; chemicals and chemical products 11.7%; petroleum for domestic use 8.7%). *Major import sources* (1998)[14]: U.S. 91.5%; EC 1.6%.
Exports (1999): B$486,300,000 (domestic exports 48.3%, of which crayfish 14.9%, rum 6.4%; reexports 44.2%; petroleum exports 7.5%). *Major export destinations* (1998)[14]: U.S. 56.5%; EC 31.4%; Canada 2.1%.

Transport and communications

Transport. Railroads: none. Roads (1999): total length 1,673 mi, 2,693 km (paved 57%). Vehicles (1996)[15]: passenger cars 89,263; trucks and buses 17,228. Air transport (2001)[16]: passenger-mi 232,000,000, passenger-km 374,000,000; short ton-mi cargo 1,208,000, metric ton-km cargo 1,764,000; airports (1997) with scheduled flights 22.

Communications

Medium	date	unit	number	units per 1,000 persons
Daily newspapers	1996	circulation	28,000	99
Radio	1997	receivers	215,000	744
Television	1997	receivers	67,000	232
Telephones	2001	main lines	123,300	400
Cellular telephones	2001	subscribers	60,600	197
Internet	2001	users	16,900	54

Education and health

Educational attainment (1990). Percentage of population age 25 and over having: no formal schooling 3.5%; incomplete primary education 25.4%; complete primary/incomplete secondary 57.6%; complete secondary/higher 13.5%. *Literacy* (1995): total percentage age 15 and over literate 98.2%.

Education (1996–97)

	schools	teachers	students	student/teacher ratio
Primary (age 5–10)	113	1,540	34,199	22.2
Secondary (age 11–16)[17]	...	1,352	27,970	20.7
Higher[18]	1	160	3,463	21.6

Health: physicians (1996) 419 (1 per 678 persons); hospital beds (1997) 1,119 (1 per 258 persons); infant mortality rate per 1,000 live births (2000) 17.0.
Food (1999): daily per capita caloric intake 2,500 (vegetable products 71%, animal products 29%); 103% of FAO recommended minimum requirement.

Military

Total active duty personnel (2001): 860 (paramilitary coast guard 100%). *Military expenditure as percentage of GNP* (2000): 0.6% (world, n.a.); per capita expenditure U.S.$85.

[1]Includes areas of lakes and ponds, as well as lagoons and sounds almost entirely surrounded by land; area of land only is about 3,890 sq mi (10,070 sq km). [2]For local administrative purposes, The Bahamas are divided into districts comprising parts of an island, a single island, or a group of islands. [3]Detail does not add to total given because of rounding. [4]Land area only. [5]Population cited is for New Providence Island. [6]Population cited is for the 4 central districts of Grand Bahama Island. [7]All rates include AIDS-related deaths. [8]2001. [9]Weights of retail price index components. [10]Includes net indirect taxes (B$503,000,000) and statistical discrepancy (B$65,000,000). [11]Includes 615 not adequately defined and 16,870 unemployed. [12]April. [13]Imports c.i.f.; exports f.o.b. [14]Excludes all petroleum imports/exports. [15]New Providence and Grand Bahama only. [16]Bahamasair only. [17]Public sector only. [18]College of The Bahamas only; 1997–98.

Internet resources for further information:
• **The Central Bank of The Bahamas** http://www.bahamascentralbank.com
• **The Commonwealth of The Bahamas (official site)** http://bahamas.gov.bs/bahamasweb/home.nsf

Bahrain

Official name: Mamlakat al-Baḥrayn
(Kingdom of Bahrain).
Form of government: constitutional
monarchy with a parliament comprising
two bodies (Chamber of Deputies [40];
Consultative Council [40])[1].
Chief of state: Monarch.
Head of government: Prime Minister.
Capital: Manama.
Official language: Arabic.
Official religion: Islam.
Monetary unit: 1 Bahrain dinar
(BD) = 1,000 fils; valuation (Sept. 23,
2002) 1 BD = U.S.$2.63 = £1.69.

Area and population	area		population
Regions[2]	sq mi	sq km	2001 census
Al-Gharbīyah (Western)	60.3	156.1	26,149
Al-Hadd	2.3	6.0	11,637
Jidd (Judd) Ḥafṣ	8.3	21.6	52,450
Al-Manāmah (Manama)	10.0	25.8	153,395
Al-Muharraq	6.2	16.0	91,939
Ar-Rifāʿ	112.6	291.6	79,985
Ash-Shamālīyah (Northern)	14.2	36.8	43,691
Ash-Sharqīyah (Eastern)	...	...	3,875[3]
Sitrah	11.1	28.8	43,910
Al-Wusṭā (Central)	13.6	35.2	49,969
Towns with special status			
Hammād	5.1	13.1	52,718
Madīnat ʿĪsā	4.8	12.4	36,833
Islands			
Ḥawār and other[4]	19.5	50.6	3
TOTAL	268.0	694.2[5]	650,604[6]

Demography

Population (2002): 672,000.
Density (2002): persons per sq mi 2,507.5, persons per sq km 968.0.
Urban-rural (1995): urban 90.3%; rural 9.7%.
Sex distribution (2001): male 57.43%; female 42.57%.
Age breakdown (2001): under 15, 27.9%; 15–29, 27.5%; 30–44, 29.7%; 45–59,
11.0%; 60–74, 3.2%; 75 and over, 0.7%.
Population projection: (2010) 758,000; (2020) 859,000.
Doubling time: 41 years.
Ethnic composition (1991): Bahraini Arab 63.6%; Persian, Indian, Pakistani,
and other Asians 30.3%; other Arab 3.5%; European 1.2%; other 1.4%.
Religious affiliation (1991): Muslim 81.8%, of which Shīʿī 61.3%, Sunnī 20.5%;
Christian 8.5%; other 9.7%.
Major cities (2001): Manama 153,395; Ar-Rifāʿ 79,985; Ḥammād 52,718; Al-
Muḥarraq (1991) 45,337; Madīnat ʿĪsā 36,833.

Vital statistics

Birth rate per 1,000 population (2001): 20.1 (world avg. 21.2); legitimate 100%.
Death rate per 1,000 population (2001): 3.9 (world avg. 8.9).
Natural increase rate per 1,000 population (2001): 16.2 (world avg. 12.3).
Total fertility rate (avg. births per childbearing woman; 2001): 2.8.
Marriage rate per 1,000 population (1999): 5.5.
Divorce rate per 1,000 population (1999): 1.3.
Life expectancy at birth (2001): male 70.8 years; female 75.7 years.
Major causes of death per 100,000 population (2000): diseases of the circula-
tory system 77.6; injury and poisoning 44.9; malignant neoplasms (cancers)
35.8; metabolic and immunity diseases 20.3; diseases of the respiratory sys-
tem 12.2; diseases of the digestive system 10.6; congenital anomalies 7.2.

National economy

Budget (2000). Revenue: BD 572,000,000 ([1998] entrepreneurial and property income 53.7%, social security contribution 13.1%, import duties 12.3%,
foreign grants 7.3%). Expenditures: BD 732,000,000 ([1998] general administration and public order 29.9%, defense 17.3%, education 13.2%, fuel and
energy 13.0%, health 9.0%, transportation, communications, and other services 8.6%).
Population economically active (2001): total 308,341; activity rate of total population 47.4% (participation rates: ages 15 and over 63.3%; female 21.7%;
unemployed 5.5%).

Price and earnings indexes (1995 = 100)							
	1993	1994	1995	1996	1997	1998	1999
Consumer price index	96.5	97.4	100.0	99.5	102.0	101.6	96.4
Earnings index	...	...	...	...	...	...	...

Production (metric tons except as noted). Agriculture, forestry, fishing (2000):
fruit (excluding melons) 21,500, dates 16,508, cow's milk 15,000, tomatoes
4,000, hen's eggs 3,100; livestock (number of live animals) 18,000 sheep,
16,000 goats, 11,000 cattle; fish catch (1999) 10,295. Manufacturing (barrels;
1999): gas oil 32,958,000; fuel oil 22,067,000; kerosene and jet fuel 18,520,000;
naphtha 13,554,000; gasoline 6,756,000; butane 1,440,000; aluminum (1999)
502,700 metric tons. Construction (permits issued; 1998): residential 6,105;
nonresidential 703. Energy production (consumption): electricity (kW-hr;
1999) 5,041,000,000 (5,041,000,000); crude petroleum (barrels; 1999)
13,472,000 ([1997] 85,951,000); petroleum products (metric tons; 1997)
10,990,000 (1,032,000); natural gas (cu m; 1999) 7,310,000,000 (7,310,000,000).
Gross national product (1998): U.S.$4,909,000,000 (U.S.$7,640 per capita).

Structure of gross domestic product and labour force				
	1999		1991	
	value in BD '000,000	% of total value	labour force	% of labour force
Agriculture	21.4	0.9	5,108	2.3
Mining	453.6	18.6	3,638	1.6
Manufacturing	306.7	12.6	26,618	11.8
Construction	105.6	4.3	26,738	11.6
Public utilities	44.9	1.8	2,898	1.3
Transp. and commun.	196.3	8.1	13,789	6.1
Trade	264.3	10.9	29,961	13.2
Finance	778.9	32.0	17,256	7.6
Pub. admin., defense	448.3	18.4	83,944	37.1
Services	125.1	5.1		
Other	−312.8[7]	−12.8[7]	16,498	7.3
TOTAL	2,432.3	100.0[5]	226,448	100.0[5]

Public debt (1999): BD 589,800,000 (U.S.$1,568,632,000).
Household income and expenditure. Average household size (2001) 6.2; income
per household: n.a.; sources of income: n.a.; expenditure (1984): food and
tobacco 33.3%, housing 21.2%, household durable goods 9.8%, transportation and communications 8.5%, recreation 6.4%, clothing and footwear 5.9%,
education 2.7%, health 2.3%, energy and water 2.2%.
Land use (1994): meadows and pastures 5.8%; agricultural and under permanent cultivation 2.9%; built-on and wasteland 91.3%.
Tourism (2000): receipts from visitors U.S.$469,000,000; expenditures by
nationals abroad U.S.$169,000,000.

Foreign trade[8]

Balance of trade (current prices)						
	1995	1996	1997	1998	1999	2000
BD '000,000	+149.3	+160.5	+134.6	−111.3	+188.0	+420.0
% of total	5.1%	4.8%	4.3%	4.3%	6.1%	10.8%

Imports (2000): BD 1,734,000,000 (petroleum products 44.4%, machinery and
transport equipment 11.3%, food and live animals 9.5%, chemicals 8.1%).
Major import sources[9]: Australia 10.1%; Saudi Arabia 8.8%; U.S. 7.7%;
United Kingdom 7.0%; Japan 6.8%; Germany 6.4%.
Exports (2000): BD 2,154,000,000 (petroleum products 69.7%, metal and metal
products 14.3%, textile 5.8%, mineral products 3.5%). *Major export destina-
tions*[9]: United States 22.9%; Saudi Arabia 14.1%; Taiwan 8.6%; Japan 5.7%;
South Korea 4.1%; India 3.8%.

Transport and communications

Transport. Railroads: none. Roads (1999): total length 3,224 km (paved 77%).
Vehicles (2000): passenger cars 170,161; trucks and buses 35,008. Merchant
marine (1992): vessels (100 gross tons and over) 87; total deadweight tonnage
192,487. Air transport (1999)[10]: passenger-km 2,835,900,000; metric ton-km
cargo 118,681,000; airports (2000) with scheduled flights 1.

Communications				units per 1,000
Medium	date	unit	number	persons
Daily newspapers	1996	circulation	67,000	117
Radio	1997	receivers	338,000	580
Television	1999	receivers	270,000	405
Telephones	2001	main lines	173,900	247
Cellular telephones	2001	subscribers	299,600	425
Personal computers	2001	units	100,000	142
Internet	2001	users	140,200	21,500

Education and health

Educational attainment (2001). Percentage of population age 15 and over having: no formal education 24.0%; primary education 37.1%; secondary 26.4%;
higher 12.5%. *Literacy* (2001): percentage of population age 15 and over literate 87.7%; males literate 92.5%; females literate 83.0%.

Education (1998–99)[11]	schools	teachers	students	student/teacher ratio
Primary (age 6–11)	190	3,615	68,589	19.0
Secondary (age 12–17)		2,393	36,763	15.4
Voc., teacher tr.	7	718	7,147	10.0
Higher[12]	4	772	9,665	12.5

Health (1998): physicians 709 (1 per 907 persons); hospital beds 1,832 (1 per
351 persons); infant mortality rate per 1,000 live births (2001) 19.8.

Military

Total active duty personnel (2001): 11,000 (army 77.3%, navy 9.1%, air force
13.6%)[13]. *Military expenditure as percentage of GNP* (1999): 8.1% (world
2.4%); per capita expenditure U.S.$666.

[1]Constitutional monarchy declared Feb. 14, 2002. Seats of Chamber of Deputies are
elected, and seats of the Consultative Council are appointed by the king. [2]Regions
have no administrative function; the creation of four actual administrative units was
begun in 1997. [3]Ash-Sharqīyah includes population of Ḥawār and other islands. [4]The
International Court of Justice awarded the jurisdiction of Ḥawār to Bahrain in early
2001. Jurisdiction of islets nearby to Ḥawār was to be split between Bahrain and Qatar.
[5]Detail does not add to total given because of rounding. [6]Includes 4,053 living abroad.
[7]Less imputed bank service charges. [8]Imports c.i.f. [9]Excludes trade in petroleum. [10]One-
fourth apportionment of international flights of Gulf Air (jointly administered by the
governments of Bahrain, Oman, Qatar, and the United Arab Emirates). [11]Public education only. [12]Public and private education. [13]U.S. troops in Bahrain (2002): 4,200.

Internet resources for further information:
• **State of Bahrain http://www.bahrain.gov.bh**

Bangladesh

Bay of
Bengal

Official name: Gana Prajatantri Bangladesh (People's Republic of Bangladesh).
Form of government: unitary multiparty republic with one legislative house (Parliament [330[1]]).
Chief of state: President.
Head of government: Prime Minister.
Capital: Dhaka.
Official language: Bengali (Bangla).
Official religion: Islam.
Monetary unit: 1 Bangladesh taka (Tk) = 100 paisa; valuation (Sept. 23, 2002) 1 U.S.$ = Tk 57.85; 1 £ = Tk 89.90.

Area and population

Divisions	Administrative centres	area sq mi	area sq km	population 1991 census[2]
Barisal	Barisal	5,134	13,297	7,757,334
Chittagong	Chittagong	7,906	20,476	20,823,477
Dhaka	Dhaka	12,015	31,119	33,939,848
Khulna	Khulna	8,600	22,274	13,243,054
Rajshahi	Rajshahi	13,326	34,513	27,499,727
Sylhet	Sylhet	4,863	12,596	7,149,372
Tribal region				
Chittagong Hill Tracts[3]	Rangamati	5,133	13,295	1,042,373
TOTAL		56,977[4]	147,570[4]	111,455,185

Demography

Population (2002): 133,377,000.
Density (2002)[5]: persons per sq mi 2,479.3, persons per sq km 957.2.
Urban-rural (2002): urban 26.0%; rural 74.0%.
Sex distribution (1999): male 51.44%; female 48.56%.
Age breakdown (1996): under 15, 42.0%; 15–29, 26.4%; 30–44, 17.8%; 45–59, 8.9%; 60–74, 3.8%; 75 and over, 1.1%.
Population projection: (2010) 150,392,000; (2020) 169,613,000.
Doubling time: 33 years.
Ethnic composition (1997): Bengali 97.7%; tribal 1.9%, of which Chakma 0.4%, Saontal 0.2%, Marma 0.1%; other 0.4%.
Religious affiliation (2000): Muslim 85.8%; Hindu 12.4%; Christian 0.7%; Buddhist 0.6%; other 0.5%.
Major urban agglomerations (2000): Dhaka (2001) 13,181,000; Chittagong 3,651,000; Khulna 1,442,000; Rajshahi 1,035,000.

Vital statistics

Birth rate per 1,000 population (2002): 30.1 (world avg. 21.2).
Death rate per 1,000 population (2002): 8.8 (world avg. 8.9).
Natural increase rate per 1,000 population (2002): 21.3 (world avg. 12.3).
Total fertility rate (avg. births per childbearing woman; 2002): 3.6.
Marriage rate per 1,000 population (1998): 9.2.
Divorce rate per 1,000 population (1981): 3.6.
Life expectancy at birth (2002): male 60.0 years; female 61.0 years.
Major causes of death (1990; percentage of recorded deaths): typhoid fever 19.8%; old age 14.8%; tetanus 10.1%; tuberculosis and other respiratory diseases 8.7%; diarrhea 6.4%; suicide, accidents, and poisoning 5.1%; high blood pressure and heart diseases 5.0%.

National economy

Budget (1998–99). Revenue: Tk 210,000,000,000 (value-added tax 37.4%; customs duties 24.0%; income taxes 11.7%; service charges 5.0%; public telephone enterprises 4.3%; interest receipts 2.8%). Expenditures: Tk 157,500,000,000 (goods and services 52.4%; transfer payments 28.4%; interest payments 16.3%).
Production (metric tons except as noted). Agriculture, forestry, fishing (2000): paddy rice 35,821,000, sugarcane 6,951,000, wheat 1,900,000, jute 1,852,000, bananas 562,000, pulses 500,000, oilseeds 415,000, mangoes 187,000, pineapples 146,000, tea 56,000; livestock (number of live animals) 33,800,000 goats, 23,652,000 cattle, 1,121,000 sheep, 828,000 buffalo, 139,300,000 chickens, 13,000,000 ducks; roundwood 33,629,000 cu m; fish catch (1998) 839,141. Mining and quarrying (1997–98): marine salt 350,000; industrial limestone 26,000. Manufacturing (value added in U.S.$'000,000; 1995): textiles 651; industrial chemicals 441; food products 331; wearing apparel 242; tobacco products 347; transport equipment 128; iron and steel 108. Construction: n.a. Energy production (consumption): electricity (kW-hr; 1997) 12,820,000,000 (12,820,000,000); coal (metric tons; 1997) none (646,000); crude petroleum (barrels; 1997) none (10,000,000); petroleum products (metric tons; 1997) 769,000 (2,337,000); natural gas (cu m; 1997) 8,135,000,000 (8,135,000,000).
Household income. Average household size (1995–96) 5.3; average annual income per household Tk 52,389 (U.S.$1,277); sources of income: self-employment 56.9%, wages and salaries 28.1%, transfer payments 9.1%, other 5.9%; expenditure: food and drink 57.7%, housing and rent 11.1%, clothing and footwear 6.5%, energy 5.6%, other 19.1%.
Population economically active (1995–96): total 56,014,000; activity rate of total population 46.0% (participation rates: over age 10, 64.8%; female 38.1%; unemployed 2.5%[6]).

Price and earnings indexes (1995 = 100)

	1995	1996	1997	1998	1999	2000	2001
Consumer price index	100.0	104.1	109.5	118.6	125.9	128.9	131.4
Earnings index[7]	100.0	106.0	111.0	123.0	129.5	...	...

Public debt (external, outstanding; 2000): U.S.$15,098,000,000.
Gross national product (2000): U.S.$47,864,000,000 (U.S.$370 per capita).

Structure of gross domestic product and labour force

	1997–98 in value Tk '000,000	1997–98 % of total value	1995–96 labour force	1995–96 % of labour force
Agriculture	443,560	28.6	34,530,000	61.7
Mining	149,156	9.6	23,000	—
Manufacturing			4,085,000	7.3
Construction	92,333	6.0	1,015,000	1.8
Public utilities	32,161	2.1	103,000	0.2
Transp. and commun.	173,110	11.2	2,308,000	4.1
Trade	138,256	8.9	6,060,000	10.8
Finance	30,452	2.0	213,000	0.4
Public admin., defense	92,039	5.9	7,677,000	13.7
Services and other	397,267	25.7		
TOTAL	1,548,334	100.0	56,014,000	100.0

Land use (1998): pasture 4.6%; agriculture 68.6%; forest and other 26.8%.
Tourism (2000): receipts U.S.$50,000,000; expenditures U.S.$301,000,000.

Foreign trade[8]

Balance of trade (current prices)

	1996	1997	1998	1999	2000	2001
Tk '000,000	–110,988	–99,478	–118,772	–149,493	–149,482	–144,885
% of total	28.7%	23.0%	24.8%	28.0%	23.4%	20.8%

Imports (1997–98): Tk 341,850,000,000 (textile yarn, fabrics, and made-up articles 24.6%; machinery and transport equipment 12.5%; petroleum and products 5.8%; iron and steel 5.2%; cereals and cereal preparations 3.9%). *Major import sources:* India 15.0%; Western Europe 13.0%; China 10.0%; Japan 9.0%; South Korea 7.0%; Hong Kong 6.0%; Singapore 5.0%; U.S. 5.0%.
Exports (1997–98): Tk 203,970,000,000 (ready-made garments 61.9%; fish and prawns 7.3%; jute manufactures 6.5%; hides, skins, and leather 4.0%; raw jute 2.4%; tea 1.0%). *Major export destinations:* Western Europe 49.0%; U.S. 32.0%; Hong Kong 3.0%; Japan 2.7%; Canada 2.0%; Pakistan 1.2%.

Transport and communications

Transport. Railroads (1998–99): route length 1,699 mi, 2,734 km; passenger-mi 3,094,000,000, passenger-km 4,980,000,000; short ton-mi cargo 567,000,000, metric ton-km cargo 828,000,000. Roads (1996): total length 126,773 mi, 204,022 km (paved 12%). Vehicles (1998): passenger cars 54,784; trucks and buses 69,394. Merchant marine (1992): vessels (100 gross tons and over) 301; total deadweight tonnage 566,775. Air transport (1999)[9]: passenger-mi 2,153,757,000, passenger-km 3,466,143,000; short ton-mi cargo 94,885,000, metric ton-km cargo 138,530,000; airports with scheduled flights (1997) 8.

Communications

Medium	date	unit	number	units per 1,000 persons
Daily newspapers	1996	circulation	1,117,000	9.0
Radio	1998	receivers	8,000,000	64
Television	1999	receivers	940,000	7.4
Telephones	2001	main lines	514,000	3.9
Cellular telephones	2001	subscribers	520,000	4.0
Personal computers	2001	units	250,000	1.9
Internet	2001	users	150,000	1.1

Education and health

Educational attainment (1991). Percentage of population age 25 and over having: no formal schooling 65.4%; primary education 17.1%; secondary 13.8%; postsecondary 3.7%. *Literacy* (1995): total population age 15 and over literate 38.1%; males literate 49.4%; females literate 26.1%.

Education (1996–97)

	schools	teachers	students	student/ teacher ratio
Primary (age 6–10)	61,638	249,928	17,319,000	69.3
Secondary (age 11–17)	13,087	156,137	5,957,000	38.2
Voc., teacher tr.	165	1,896[10]	41,650	16.1[10]
Higher[11]	3,123	77,644	2,573,439	33.1

Health (1997): physicians 26,608 (1 per 4,627 persons); hospital beds 39,900 (1 per 3,086 persons); infant mortality rate (2002) 68.0.
Food (1999): daily per capita caloric intake 2,201 (vegetable products 97%, animal products 3%); (1997) 95% of FAO recommended minimum requirement.

Military

Total active duty personnel (2001): 137,000 (army 87.6%, navy 7.7%, air force 4.7%). *Military expenditure as percentage of GNP* (1999): 1.4% (world 2.4%); per capita expenditure U.S.$5.

[1]Includes 30 seats reserved for women. [2]Adjusted for underenumeration. [3]Autonomous region for non-Bengali tribal people was created in December 1997 and formally established in May 1999. [4]The total area excluding the river area equals 53,797 sq mi (139,334 sq km). [5]Based on the total area excluding the river area. [6]Excluding underemployment. [7]Wage earnings in manufacturing. [8]Import figures are f.o.b. in balance of trade. [9]Bangladesh Biman only. [10]Excludes teachers' training school data. [11]Excludes professional and technical colleges.

Internet resources for further information:
• **Government of the People's Republic of Bangladesh**
  http://www.bangladeshgov.org
• **National Data Bank**
  http://www.bbsgov.org

Barbados

Official name: Barbados.
Form of government: constitutional monarchy with two legislative houses (Senate [21]; House of Assembly [28]).
Chief of state: British Monarch represented by Governor-General.
Head of government: Prime Minister.
Capital: Bridgetown.
Official language: English.
Official religion: none.
Monetary unit: 1 Barbados dollar (BDS$) = 100 cents; valuation (Sept. 23, 2002) 1 U.S.$ = BDS$1.99; 1 £ = BDS$3.09.

Area and population	area		population
Parishes[1]	sq mi	sq km	1990 census
Christ Church	22	57	47,050
St. Andrew	14	36	6,346
St. George	17	44	17,905
St. James	12	31	21,001
St. John	13	34	10,206
St. Joseph	10	26	7,619
St. Lucy	14	36	9,455
St. Michael[2]	15	39	97,516
St. Peter	13	34	11,263
St. Philip	23	60	20,540
St. Thomas	13	34	11,590
TOTAL	166	430[3]	260,491

Demography

Population (2002): 270,000.
Density (2002): persons per sq mi 1,627, persons per sq km 628.
Urban-rural (1998): urban 48.9%; rural 51.1%.
Sex distribution (2000): male 48.07%; female 51.93%.
Age breakdown (2000): under 15, 22.0%; 15–29, 24.2%; 30–44, 26.1%; 45–59, 15.7%; 60–74, 7.9%; 75 and over, 4.1%.
Population projection: (2010) 278,000; (2020) 284,000.
Doubling time: n.a.; doubling time exceeds 100 years.
Ethnic composition (2000): local black 87.1%; mulatto 6.0%; British expatriates 4.3%; U.S. white 1.2%; Indo-Pakistani 1.1%; other 0.3%.
Religious affiliation (1995): Protestant 63.0%, of which Anglican 26.3%, Pentecostal 10.6%, Methodist 5.7%; Roman Catholic 4.8%; other Christian 2.0%; nonreligious/other 30.2%.
Major cities (1990): Bridgetown 6,070 (urban agglomeration [2001] 136,000); Speightstown, c. 3,500.

Vital statistics

Birth rate per 1,000 population (2000): 13.6 (world avg. 22.5); (1979) legitimate 26.9%; illegitimate 73.1%.
Death rate per 1,000 population (2000): 8.7 (world avg. 9.0).
Natural increase rate per 1,000 population (2000): 4.9 (world avg. 13.5).
Total fertility rate (avg. births per childbearing woman; 2000): 1.6.
Marriage rate per 1,000 population (1995): 13.5.
Divorce rate per 1,000 population (1995): 1.5.
Life expectancy at birth (2000): male 70.4 years; female 75.6 years.
Major causes of death per 100,000 population (1995): diseases of the circulatory system 369.7; malignant neoplasms (cancers) 163.6; endocrine and metabolic disorders 151.3; diseases of the respiratory system 56.3; accidents, poisonings, and violence 36.4; diseases of the digestive system 34.5; infectious and parasitic diseases 27.6; diseases of the nervous system 23.0.

National economy

Budget (1997–98). Revenue: BDS$1,458,274,000[4] (tax revenue 94.7%, of which goods and services taxes 49.5%, personal income and company taxes 29.5%, import duties 8.8%; nontax revenue 5.3%). Expenditures: BDS$1,508,869,000 (current expenditure 83.2%, of which education 18.8%, economic services 11.5%, health 10.9%, social security and welfare 8.3%).
Production (metric tons except as noted). Agriculture, forestry, fishing (1999): raw sugar 48,000, sweet potatoes 5,100, yams 1,350, cucumbers and gherkins 1,300, cabbage 1,200, pumpkins, squash, and gourds 1,000, cassava 820, carrots 790, tomatoes 650, onions 480, lettuce 450; livestock (number of live animals) 41,000 sheep, 33,000 pigs, 23,000 cattle, 4,500 goats; roundwood, n.a.; fish catch (1997) 2,764. Manufacturing (value added in BDS$'000; 1995): food, beverages, and tobacco (mostly sugar, molasses, rum, beer, and cigarettes) 108,000; paper products, printing, and publishing 33,400; metal products and assembly-type goods (mostly electronic components) 28,000; textiles and wearing apparel 11,700. Energy production (consumption): electricity (kW-hr; 1997) 678,000,000 (678,000,000); crude petroleum (barrels; 1997) 328,000 (1,639,000); petroleum products (metric tons; 1997) 277,000 (307,000); natural gas (cu m; 1997) 23,372,000 (23,372,000).
Household income and expenditure. Average household size (1990) 3.5; income per household (1988) BDS$13,455 (U.S.$6,690); sources of income: n.a.; expenditure (1994): food 39.4%, housing 16.8%, transportation 10.5%, household operations 8.1%, alcohol and tobacco 6.4%, fuel and light 5.2%, clothing and footwear 5.0%, other 8.6%.
Population economically active (1997): total 135,800; activity rate of total population 51.3% (participation rates: ages 15 and over, 67.5%; female 62.1%; unemployed 14.5%).

Price and earnings indexes (1995 = 100)							
	1995	1996	1997	1998	1999	2000	2001
Consumer price index	100.0	102.4	110.3	108.9	110.6	113.3	116.2
Earnings index	...	...	...	...	...	...	...

Gross national product (2000): U.S.$2,469,000,000 (U.S.$9,250 per capita).

Structure of gross domestic product and labour force				
	1997			
	in value BDS$'000,000	% of total value	labour force	% of labour force
Agriculture, fishing	174.9	4.0	6,100	4.5
Mining	20.2[5]	0.5[5]	...	...
Manufacturing	225.8	5.2	10,700	7.8
Construction	182.9	4.2	10,200	7.5
Public utilities	127.4[5]	2.9[5]	1,500	1.1
Transp. and commun.	339.6	7.8	4,700	3.4
Trade, restaurants	1,117.6	25.6	28,200	20.7
Finance, real estate	614.3	14.1	8,100	5.9
Pub. admin., defense	611.0	14.0 }	46,900	34.4
Services	157.8	3.6 }		
Other	799.1[6]	18.3[6]	20,000[7]	14.7[7]
TOTAL	4,370.6	100.0[3]	136,400	100.0

Public debt (external, outstanding; 1999): U.S.$359,100,000.
Tourism: receipts from visitors (2000) U.S.$711,000,000; expenditures by nationals abroad (1999) U.S.$87,000,000.

Foreign trade[8]

Balance of trade (current prices)						
	1996	1997	1998	1999	2000	2001
BDS$'000,000	−1,106	−1,425	−1,510	−1,684	−1,767	−1,521
% of total	49.6%	55.7%	59.7%	61.4%	61.9%	62.6%

Imports (1997): BDS$1,991,001,000 (retained imports 92.7%, of which capital goods 20.4%, food and beverages 15.0%, construction materials 8.2%, chemicals 5.6%, fuels 3.7%; reexported imports 7.3%). *Major import sources* (2000): U.S. 41.6%[9]; Trinidad and Tobago 16.5%; U.K. 8.1%; Japan 5.2%.
Exports (1997): BDS$565,887,000 (domestic exports 74.4%, of which sugar 12.7%, chemicals 10.0%, electrical components 9.2%, rum 4.9%, margarine and lard 2.0%, clothing 1.2%; reexports 25.6%). *Major export destinations* (2000): U.S. 15.8%[9]; Trinidad and Tobago 13.2%; U.K. 13.2%; Jamaica 7.0%; bunkers and ships' stores 16.3%.

Transport and communications

Transport. Railroads: none. Roads (1999): total length 9,942 mi, 1,600 km (paved 99%). Vehicles (1999): passenger cars 60,826; trucks and buses 9,578. Merchant marine (1992): vessels (100 gross tons and over) 37; total deadweight tonnage 84,000. Air transport (1995): passenger arrivals 699,000, passenger departures 707,400; cargo unloaded 8,382 metric tons, cargo loaded 4,717 metric tons; airports (1997) with scheduled flights 1.

Communications				units per 1,000
Medium	date	unit	number	persons
Daily newspapers	1996	circulation	53,000	199
Radio	1997	receivers	237,000	888
Television	1999	receivers	78,000	292
Telephones	2001	main lines	123,800	460
Cellular telephones	2000	subscribers	28,500	106
Personal computers	2001	units	25,000	93
Internet	2000	users	10,000	37

Education and health

Educational attainment (1990). Percentage of population age 25 and over having: no formal schooling 0.4%; primary education 23.7%; secondary 60.3%[10]; higher 11.2%; other 4.4%. *Literacy* (1995): total population age 15 and over literate 97.4%; males literate 98.0%; females literate 96.8%.

Education (1995–96)	schools	teachers	students	student/ teacher ratio
Primary (age 3–11)	79	994	18,513	18.6
Secondary (age 12–16)	21	1,263	21,455	17.0
Vocational[11]	8	79	996	12.6
Higher	4	544[12]	6,622	...

Health (1992): physicians 312 (1 per 842 persons); hospital beds 1,966 (1 per 134 persons); infant mortality rate per 1,000 live births (2000) 12.4.
Food (2000): daily per capita caloric intake 3,022 (vegetable products 77%, animal products 23%); 124% of FAO recommended minimum requirement.

Military

Total active duty personnel (2001): 610 (army 82.0%, navy 18.0%). *Military expenditure as percentage of GNP* (1999): 0.5% (world 2.4%); per capita expenditure U.S.$44.

---

[1]Parishes and city of Bridgetown have no local administrative function. [2]Includes city of Bridgetown. [3]Detail does not add to total given because of rounding. [4]Current revenue only. [5]Mining excludes natural gas; Public utilities includes natural gas. [6]Net indirect taxes. [7]Unemployed. [8]Import figures are c.i.f. [9]Includes Puerto Rico. [10]Includes composite senior. [11]1987–88. [12]1984.

Internet resources for further information:
• **Barbados Statistical Services http://www.bgis.gov.bb/stats**
• **Central Bank of Barbados http://www.centralbank.org.bb**

Belarus

Official name: Respublika Belarus
(Republic of Belarus).
Form of government: republic
with two legislative bodies (Council
of the Republic [62[1]]; House of
Representatives [110[1]]).
Head of state and government:
President assisted by Prime Minister.
Capital: Minsk.
Official languages: Belarusian; Russian.
Official religion: none.
Monetary unit: rubel[2] (Rbl; plural rubli);
valuation (Sept. 23, 2002) free rate,
1 U.S.$ = (new) Rbl 1,867;
1 £ = (new) Rbl 2,902.

Area and population

Provinces	Capitals	area sq mi	area sq km	population 2001 estimate
Brest	Brest	12,700	32,800	1,481,900
Homel (Gomel)	Homel	15,600	40,400	1,535,000
Hrodno (Grodno)	Hrodno	9,700	25,100	1,173,900
Mahilyoŭ (Mogilyov)	Mahilyoŭ	11,200	29,100	1,200,900
Minsk (Mensk)	Minsk	15,500[3]	40,200[3]	1,539,300
Vitebsk	Vitebsk	15,500	40,000	1,360,300
City				
Minsk (Mensk)	—	3	3	1,699,100
TOTAL		80,200[4]	207,600[4]	9,990,400

Demography

Population (2002): 9,933,000.
Density (2002): persons per sq mi 123.9, persons per sq km 47.8.
Urban-rural (2001): urban 70.2%; rural 29.8%.
Sex distribution (2001): male 46.92%; female 53.08%.
Age breakdown (2001): under 15, 18.3%; 15–29, 22.5%; 30–44, 23.2%; 45–59, 16.9%; 60–69, 10.2%; 70 and over, 8.9%.
Population projection: (2010) 9,645,000; (2020) 9,339,000.
Doubling time: not applicable; population is declining.
Ethnic composition (1999): Belarusian 81.2%; Russian 11.4%; Polish 3.9%; Ukrainian 2.4%; Jewish 0.3%; other 0.8%.
Religious affiliation (1995): Belarusian Orthodox 31.6%; Roman Catholic 17.7%; other (mostly nonreligious) 50.7%.
Major cities (2001): Minsk 1,699,000; Homel 490,000; Mahilyoŭ 361,000; Vitebsk 349,000; Hrodno 307,000.

Vital statistics

Birth rate per 1,000 population (2000): 9.4 (world avg. 22.5); legitimate 81.4%; illegitimate 18.6%.
Death rate per 1,000 population (2000): 13.5 (world avg. 9.0).
Natural increase rate per 1,000 population (2000): –4.1 (world avg. 13.5).
Total fertility rate (avg. births per childbearing woman; 2000): 1.3.
Marriage rate per 1,000 population (2000): 6.2.
Divorce rate per 1,000 population (2000): 4.3.
Life expectancy at birth (1999): male 63.4 years; female 74.7 years.
Major causes of death per 100,000 population (2000): diseases of the circulatory system 722.6; malignant neoplasms (cancers) 195.3; accidents and violence 157.8; diseases of the respiratory system 66.7.

National economy

Budget (2000). Revenue: Rbl 3,181,000,000,000 (tax revenue 76.5%, of which value-added tax 25.7%, taxes on profits 13.8%, taxes on income 8.7%, excise taxes 8.0%, taxes on international trade 4.5%, other 15.8%; nontax revenue 23.5%). Expenditures: Rbl 3,236,000,000,000 (target budgetary fund 17.6%, education 17.4%, health 14.1%, subsidies 7.7%, capital expenditure 6.9%, other 36.3%).
Public debt (external, outstanding; 2000): U.S.$692,000,000.
Household income and expenditure. Average household size (2000) 3.4; income per household (1995) (old) Rbl 2,400,000[2]; sources of income (2000): wages and salaries 51.9%, business activities 28.3%, transfers 18.0%, property income 1.8%; expenditure (2000): food, beverages, and tobacco 64.9%; clothing 11.7%; transport 6.9%; household appliances 4.1%; rent 3.0%; health 2.2%; education 2.2%; other 5.0%.
Population economically active (2000): 4,537,000; activity rate of total population 45.4% (participation rate: ages 16–59 [male], 16–54 [female] 97.9%; female 51.3%; unemployed 2.1%).

Price and earnings indexes (1995 = 100)

	1995	1996	1997	1998
Consumer price index	100.0	152.7	204.5	246.1
Monthly earnings index	100.0	160.5	240.1	350.2

Production (metric tons except as noted). Agriculture, forestry, fishing (2000): potatoes 8,718,000, cereal 4,856,000, sugar beets 1,474,000, vegetables 1,379,000, fruit 310,000; livestock (number of live animals) 4,221,000 cattle, 3,431,000 pigs, 221,300 horses, 150,200 sheep and goats, 30,141,000 poultry; roundwood (1998) 17,745,000 cu m; fish catch (1999) 450. Mining and quarrying (2000): potash 3,400,000; peat 2,211,000. Manufacturing (value of production in [old] Rbl '000,000; 1994): machine-building equipment 1,086,650; chemical products 659,438; food products 562,438; construction materials 142,555. Construction (2000): 3,528,000 sq m. Energy production (consump-

tion): electricity (kW-hr; 1997) 26,057,000,000 (33,677,000,000); coal (1994) none (1997; 810,000); crude petroleum (barrels; 1997) 13,355,000 (86,406,000); petroleum products (1997) 9,589,000 (10,473,000); natural gas (cu m; 2000) 257,000,000 (16,402,000,000).
Gross national product (2000): U.S.$28,735,000,000 (U.S.$2,870 per capita).

Structure of gross domestic product and labour force

	2000 in value Rbl '000,000,000[5]	2000 % of total value[5]	2000 labour force	2000 % of labour force
Agriculture	1,197.5	15.3	657,600	14.5
Mining } Manufacturing	2,354.9	30.1	1,226,700	27.0
Public utilities	153.4	2.0	208,100	4.6
Construction	516.3	6.6	312,300	6.9
Transp. and commun.	1,078.1	13.8	318,300	7.0
Trade	967.3	12.4	532,300	11.7
Finance	500.3	6.4	58,400	1.3
Public admin., defense	276.2	3.5 }	912,200	20.1
Services	952.2	12.2		
Other	–177.3[6]	–2.3[6]	311,100[7]	6.9[7]
TOTAL	7,818.9	100.0	4,537,000	100.0

Tourism (2000): receipts U.S.$19,000,000; expenditures U.S.$123,000,000.
Land use (1994)[8]: forested 33.7%; meadows and pastures 14.1%; agricultural and under permanent cultivation 30.5%; other 21.7%.

Foreign trade[9]

Balance of trade (current prices)

	1995	1996	1997	1998	1999	2000
U.S.$'000,000	–761	–1,287	–1,388	–1,479	–765	–1,161
% of total	7.3%	10.2%	8.7%	9.5%	6.1%	7.3%

Imports (2000): U.S.$8,492,000,000 (mineral products 31.2%, machinery and transport equipment 18.2%, chemical products 15.3%, food and beverages 12.5%, light industry 11.4%, other 15.8%; wood and paper products 3.2%). *Major import sources:* Russia 63.4%; Germany 6.9%; Ukraine 4.0%; Poland 2.5%; Italy 1.9%; U.S. 1.6%; Czech Republic 1.6%; U.K. 1.3%.
Exports (2000): U.S.$7,331,000,000 (machinery and transport equipment 25.3%, mineral products 20.2%, chemicals and synthetic rubber 19.8%, ferrous metals 7.2%, food 6.9%, light industry 6.4%, wood and paper products 4.3%). *Major export destinations:* Russia 50.7%; Ukraine 7.6%; Latvia 6.4%; Lithuania 4.8%; Poland 3.8%; Germany 3.2%; China 2.0%.

Transport and communications

Transport. Railroads (2000): length 5,533 km; (1997) passenger-km 17,722,000,000; metric ton-km cargo 31,425,000,000. Roads (2000): total length 74,400 km (paved 89.0%). Vehicles (2000): passenger cars 1,448,461; trucks and buses 85,791. Air transport (2000): passenger-km 513,000,000; metric ton-km cargo 18,000,000; airports 1.

Communications

Medium	date	unit	number	units per 1,000 persons
Daily newspapers	1997	circulation	1,437,000	140
Radio	1998	receivers	3,021,000	296
Television	1999	receivers	3,300,000	327
Telephones	2001	main lines	2,857,900	279
Cellular telephones	2001	subscribers	138,300	8.6
Internet	2001	users	422,200	41.2

Education and health

Educational attainment: n.a.

Education (2000–01)

	schools	teachers	students	student/teacher ratio
Primary (age 6–13) } Secondary (age 14–17)	4,757	151,100	1,546,500	10.2
Voc., teacher tr.	156	8,800[10]	150,300	...
Higher	57	16,300[10]	281,700	...

Literacy (1999): total population age 15 and over literate 99.5%; males literate 99.7%; females literate 99.4%.
Health (2000): physicians 45,817 (1 per 218 persons); hospital beds 126,209 (1 per 79 persons); infant mortality rate per 1,000 live births (2000) 9.3.
Food (2000): daily per capita caloric intake 2,902 (vegetable products 72%, animal products 28%); 113% of FAO recommended minimum requirement.

Military

Total active duty personnel (2001): 82,900 (army 52.3%, air force and air defense 27.1%, other 20.6%). *Military expenditure as percentage of GNP* (1999): 1.3% (world 2.4%); per capita expenditure U.S.$89.

[1]Statutory number. [2]Rubel re-denominated Jan. 1, 2000; 1,000 (old) rubli = 1 (new) rubel. [3]Minsk province includes Minsk city. [4]Rounded area figures; exact area figures are 80,153 sq mi (207,595 sq km). [5]At factor cost. [6]Less imputed bank service charge. [7]Includes 96,000 unemployed and 215,100 undistributed employed. [8]25% of Belarusian territory severely affected by radioactive fallout from Chernobyl. [9]Imports in c.i.f. [10]1997–98.

Internet resources for further information:
• **Ministry of Statistics and Analysis**
  http://president.gov.by/Minstat/en/main.html
• **The Belarusian WWW-server for Businessmen**
  http://www.belarus.net

Belgium

Official name: Koninkrijk België (Dutch); Royaume de Belgique (French) (Kingdom of Belgium).
Form of government: federal constitutional monarchy with a Parliament composed of two legislative chambers (Senate [71[1]]; House of Representatives [150]).
Chief of state: Monarch.
Head of government: Prime Minister.
Capital: Brussels.
Official languages: Dutch; French; German.
Official religion: none.
Monetary unit: 1 euro (€) = 100 cents; valuation (Sept. 23, 2002) 1 U.S.$ = €1.02; 1£ = €1.58[2].

Area and population

Regions[3] Provinces	Capitals	area sq mi	area sq km	population 2000[4] estimate
Brussels[5]	—	62	161	964,405
Flanders	—	5,221[6]	13,522	5,952,552
Antwerp	Antwerp	1,107	2,867	1,645,652
East Flanders	Ghent	1,151	2,982	1,363,672
Flemish Brabant	Leuven	813	2,106	1,018,403
Limburg	Hasselt	935	2,422	794,785
West Flanders	Brugge	1,214	3,145	1,130,040
Wallonia		6,504[6]	16,844	3,346,457
Hainaut	Mons	1,462	3,786	1,279,823
Liège	Liège	1,491	3,862	1,020,042
Luxembourg	Arlon	1,714	4,440	248,750
Namur	Namur	1,415	3,666	445,824
Walloon Brabant	Wavre	421	1,091	352,018
TOTAL		11,787	30,528[6]	10,263,414

Demography

Population (2002): 10,280,000.
Density (2002): persons per sq mi 872.1, persons per sq km 336.7.
Urban-rural (2001)[7]: urban 97.4%; rural 2.6%.
Sex distribution (2000): male 48.89%; female 51.11%.
Age breakdown (2000): under 15, 17.5%; 15–29, 18.8%; 30–44, 22.9%; 45–59, 18.8%; 60–74, 14.8%; 75 and over, 7.2%.
Population projection: (2010) 10,318,000; (2020) 10,265,000.
Ethnic composition (2000): Flemish 53.7%; Walloon (French) 31.6%; Italian 2.6%; French 2.0%; Arab 1.8%; German 1.5%; Berber 0.9%; other 5.9%.
Religious affiliation (1995): Roman Catholic 87.9%; Muslim 2.5%; other Christian 2.4%, of which Protestant 1.0%; Jewish 0.3%; other 6.9%.
Major cities (2000[4]): Brussels 959,318[5]; Antwerp 446,525; Ghent 224,180; Charleroi 200,827; Liège 185,639.

Vital statistics

Birth rate per 1,000 population (2001): 11.2 (world avg. 21.2).
Death rate per 1,000 population (2001): 10.2 (world avg. 8.9).
Natural increase rate per 1,000 population (2001): 1.0 (world avg. 12.3).
Total fertility rate (avg. births per childbearing woman; 2000): 1.5.
Marriage rate per 1,000 population (1999): 4.3.
Divorce rate per 1,000 population (1994): 2.2.
Life expectancy at birth (2000): male 74.5 years; female 81.3 years.
Major causes of death per 100,000 population (1992): diseases of the circulatory system 383.3; malignant neoplasms (cancers) 272.6; diseases of the respiratory system 90.6; accidents and violence 40.9.

National economy

Budget (1999). Revenue: €107,764,000,000 (social security contributions 29.6%, taxes on goods and services 26.9%, income tax 26.7%). Expenditures: €109,772,000,000 (transfer payments 49.4%, interest on debt 15.1%, other 35.5%).
Public debt (1999): U.S.$250,459,000,000.
Production (metric tons except as noted). Agriculture, forestry, fishing (2000)[7]: sugar beets 6,200,000, potatoes 3,000,000, wheat 1,634,000, apples 497,075, barley 370,000, tomatoes 300,000; livestock (number of live animals) 7,671,000 pigs, 3,085,000 cattle, 152,000 sheep, 67,000 horses; roundwood (2000)[7] 4,400,000 cu m; fish catch (1999) 29,900. Mining and quarrying (1997): limestone 30,000,000; granite (Belgium bluestone) 2,115,000 cu m; marble 400 cu m. Manufacturing (value added in BF '000,000; 1996): metal products 468,894; food 263,382; chemicals 243,787; printing 89,991; textiles 66,524; furniture 58,115. Construction (1993): residential 33,063,000 cu m; nonresidential 42,864,000 cu m. Energy production (consumption): electricity (kW-hr; 1998) 83,244,000,000 ([1997] 82,209,000,000); coal (metric tons; 1997) negligible (11,255,000); crude petroleum (barrels; 1997) none (239,860,000); petroleum products (metric tons; 1997) 28,995,000 (17,516,000); natural gas (cu m; 1997) 188,556 (16,468,000,000).
Household income and expenditure. Avg. household size (1999) 2.5; sources of income (1992): wages 49.6%, transfer payments 20.7%, property income 18.8%, self-employment 10.9%; expenditure (1992): food 18.0%, housing and transp. 13.3%, health 11.8%, durable goods 10.7%, clothing 7.7%.
Land use (1994)[7]: forest 21.3%; pasture 21.0%; agriculture 24.2%; other 33.5%.
Population economically active (1999): total 3,905,500; activity rate 38.2% (participation rates: ages 15–64, 58.0%; female 42.7%; unemployed 9.6%).

Price and earnings indexes (1995 = 100)

	1994	1995	1996	1997	1998	1999	2000
Consumer price index	98.6	100.0	102.1	103.7	104.7	105.9	108.6
Earnings index	...	...	...	...	...	...	...

Gross national product (2000): U.S.$251,583,000,000 (U.S.$24,540 per capita).

Structure of gross domestic product and labour force

	1999 in value BF '000,000	1999 % of total value	1999 labour force	1999 % of labour force
Agriculture	124,128	1.4	80,900	2.1
Mining	14,080	0.2	4,400	0.1
Manufacturing	1,644,106	18.7	651,000	16.7
Construction	435,122	5.0	229,800	5.9
Public utilities	233,994	2.7	28,200	0.7
Transp. and commun.	596,727	6.8	265,500	6.8
Trade	1,180,565	13.5	613,700	15.7
Finance	2,473,438	28.2	581,200	14.9
Pub. admin., defense Services	} 2,071,216	23.6	1,450,800	37.1
Other	—	—	—	—
TOTAL	8,773,376	100.0[6]	3,905,500[8]	100.0[8]

Tourism (2000): receipts U.S.$7,422,000,000; expenditures U.S.$10,151,000,000.

Foreign trade[7]

Balance of trade (current prices)

	1995	1996	1997	1998	1999	2000
BF '000,000	+415,800	+364,000	+442,700	+562,000	+581,000	+542,822
% of total	4.2%	3.5%	3.8%	4.6%	4.4%	4.2%

Imports (1999): BF 6,237,963,000,000 (machinery and transport equipment 31.9%; basic manufactures 20.8%; chemicals 16.4%; food 7.8%; mineral fuels 5.7%, of which petroleum products 4.3%; diamonds 3.9%). *Major import sources:* Germany 17.4%; The Netherlands 16.7%; France 13.7%; U.K. 8.6%; U.S. 7.5%.
Exports (1999): BF 6,780,785,000,000 (machinery and transport equipment 30.0%; chemicals 20.3%, of which plastics 4.4%; food 8.7%; iron and steel 4.0%; textiles 3.7%; petroleum products 2.5%). *Major export destinations:* Germany 17.9%; France 17.7%; The Netherlands 12.8%; U.K. 10.0%; U.S. 5.2%.

Transport and communications

Transport. Railroads (1999): route length 3,380 km; passenger-km 7,354,000,000; metric ton-km cargo 7,392,000,000. Roads (1997): total length 143,800 km (paved 97%). Vehicles (1998): passenger cars 4,491,734; trucks and buses 453,122. Merchant marine (1992): vessels (100 gross tons and over) 232; total deadweight tonnage 218,506. Air transport (2000)[9]: passenger-km 19,378,689,000; metric ton-km cargo 568,244,000; airports (1999) 2.

Communications

Medium	date	unit	number	units per 1,000 persons
Daily newspapers	1996	circulation	1,625,000	161
Radio	1997	receivers	8,075,000	795
Television	1999	receivers	5,300,000	518
Telephones	2001	main lines	5,074,000	493
Cellular telephones	2001	subscribers	7,690,000	747
Personal computers	2001	units	3,500,000	345
Internet	2001	users	2,881,000	280

Education and health

Educational attainment (1981). Percentage of population age 15 and over having: less than secondary education 44.4%; lower secondary 26.5%; upper secondary 17.0%; vocational 2.9%; teacher's college 0.6%; university 3.5%.

Education (1999–2000)

	schools[10]	teachers	students	student/teacher ratio
Primary (age 6–12)	4,401	82,168[11]	778,000	...
Secondary (age 12–18)	1,727	115,262	779,000	...
Voc., teacher tr.[12]	304	...	155,192[10]	...
Higher	151	38,014[10]	298,000	...

Health: physicians (1998) 40,300 (1 per 253 persons); hospital beds (1994) 77,181 (1 per 131 persons); infant mortality rate (2000) 4.8.
Food (2000)[7]: daily per capita caloric intake 3,701 (vegetable products 70%, animal products 30%); 140% of FAO recommended minimum requirement.

Military

Total active duty personnel (2001): 39,420 (army 67.0%, navy 6.5%, air force 21.8%, medical service 4.7%). *Military expenditure as percentage of GNP* (1999): 1.4% (world 2.4%); per capita expenditure U.S.$352.

[1]Excludes children of the monarch serving ex officio from age 18. [2]The Belgian franc (BF) was the former monetary unit; on Jan. 1, 2002, BF 40.34 = €1. [3]Corresponding to three language-based federal community councils: Dutch (Flanders), French (Wallonia), and bilingual (Brussels) having authority in cultural affairs; a fourth (German) community council (within Wallonia; 2001 population 70,036) lacks expression as an administrative region. [4]January 1. [5]Officially, Brussels Capital Region. [6]Detail does not add to total given because of rounding. [7]Includes Luxembourg. [8]Includes 375,000 unemployed. [9]Sabena airlines only; shut down November 2001. [10]1996–97. [11]Includes preschool teachers. [12]1991–92.

Internet resources for further information:
- Belgian Federal Government On Line http://belgium.fgov.be
- National Bank of Belgium http://www.bnb.be/DQ/E/dq3/SDDS/SDDS.htm

Belize

Official name: Belize.
Form of government: constitutional monarchy with two legislative houses (Senate [8[1]]; House of Representatives [29[2]]).
Chief of state: British Monarch represented by Governor-General.
Head of government: Prime Minister.
Capital: Belmopan.
Official language: English.
Official religion: none.
Monetary unit: 1 Belize dollar (BZ$) = 100 cents; valuation (Sept. 23, 2002) 1 U.S.$ = BZ$1.97[3]; 1 £ = BZ$3.06.

Area and population

Districts	Capitals	area sq mi	area sq km	population 2000 census
Belize	Belize City	1,663	4,307	68,197
Cayo	San Ignacio/Santa Elena	2,006	5,196	52,564
Corozal	Corozal	718	1,860	32,708
Orange Walk	Orange Walk	1,790	4,636	38,890
Stann Creek	Dangriga	986	2,554	24,548
Toledo	Punta Gorda	1,704	4,413	23,297
TOTAL		8,867[4]	22,965[4, 5]	240,204

Demography

Population (2002): 251,000.
Density (2002): persons per sq mi 28.3, persons per sq km 10.9.
Urban-rural (2000): urban 47.7%; rural 52.3%.
Sex distribution (2000): male 50.49%; female 49.51%.
Age breakdown (1998): under 15, 41.2%; 15–29, 26.5%; 30–44, 16.7%; 45–59, 8.8%; 60–74, 5.0%; 75 and over, 1.8%.
Population projection: (2010) 288,000; (2020) 329,000.
Doubling time: 26 years.
Ethnic composition (2000): mestizo (Spanish-Indian) 48.7%; Creole (predominantly black) 24.9%; Mayan Indian 10.6%; Garifuna (black-Carib Indian) 6.1%; white 4.3%; East Indian 3.0%; other or not stated 2.4%.
Religious affiliation (2000): Roman Catholic 49.6%; Protestant 31.8%, of which Pentecostal 7.4%, Anglican 5.3%, Seventh-day Adventist 5.2%, Mennonite 4.1%; other Christian 1.9%; nonreligious 9.4%; other 7.3%.
Major cities (2000): Belize City 49,050; Orange Walk 13,483; San Ignacio/Santa Elena 13,260; Dangriga 8,814; Belmopan 8,130.

Vital statistics

Birth rate per 1,000 population (2000): 32.3 (world avg. 22.5); (1997) legitimate 40.3%; illegitimate 59.7%.
Death rate per 1,000 population (2000): 4.8 (world avg. 9.0).
Natural increase rate per 1,000 population (2000): 27.5 (world avg. 13.5).
Total fertility rate (avg. births per childbearing woman; 2000): 4.1.
Marriage rate per 1,000 population (1997): 6.6.
Divorce rate per 1,000 population (1997): 0.2.
Life expectancy at birth (2000): male 68.7 years; female 73.3 years.
Major causes of death per 100,000 population (1995): diseases of the circulatory system 119.8; accidents and violence 57.1; diseases of the respiratory system 47.8; malignant neoplasms 38.1; infectious and parasitic diseases 23.7.

National economy

Budget (1997). Revenue: BZ$324,600,000 (tax revenue 77.4%, of which import duties 25.7%, general sales taxes 23.6%; grants 12.7%; nontax revenue 9.2%). Expenditures: BZ$362,300,000 (education 20.5%; transportation and communication 16.7%; general admin. 11.4%; health 8.2%; defense 5.4%).
Production (metric tons except as noted). Agriculture, forestry, fishing (1998): sugarcane 1,208,000, oranges 170,000, bananas 81,000, grapefruits 41,000, corn (maize) 37,000, rice 17,000, red kidney beans 5,000, coconuts 3,000; livestock (number of live animals; 1999) 58,000 cattle, 23,000 pigs, 1,400,000 chickens; roundwood (1998) 187,600 cu m; fish catch (1998) 2,620, of which shrimp 1,682, conchs 253, lobsters 251, freshwater and marine fish 111. Mining and quarrying (1997): sand and gravel 350,000; limestone 310,000. Manufacturing (2000–01): sugar 105,500; molasses 35,000; flour 11,800; orange concentrate 187,000 hectolitres; beer 110,000 hectolitres; grapefruit concentrate 29,000 hectolitres; cigarettes (1996) 80,000,000 units; garments (1996) 2,100,000 units. Energy production (consumption): electricity (kW-hr; 1997) 167,000,000 (192,000,000); coal, none (none); crude petroleum, none (none); petroleum products (metric tons; 1997) none (127,000); natural gas, none (none).
Household income and expenditure. Average household size (2000) 4.5; average annual income of employed head of household (1993) BZ$6,450[6] (U.S.$3,225[6]); sources of income, n.a.; expenditure (1990): food, beverages, and tobacco 34.0%, transportation 13.7%, energy and water 9.1%, housing 9.0%, clothing and footwear 8.8%, household furnishings 8.0%.
Tourism (2000): receipts from visitors U.S.$121,000,000; expenditures by nationals abroad U.S.$24,000,000.
Land use (1994): forested 92.1%; meadows and pastures 2.2%; agricultural and under permanent cultivation 3.6%; other 2.1%.
Population economically active (1998): total 85,595; activity rate of total population 36.2% (participation rates: ages 14–64, 64.1%; female 34.5%; unemployed [2001] 9.3%).

Price and earnings indexes (1995 = 100)

	1995	1996	1997	1998	1999	2000	2001
Consumer price index	100.0	106.4	107.5	106.6	105.3	105.9	107.2
Monthly earnings index[7]	100.0	102.5	98.8	...	...	...	...

Gross national product (2000): U.S.$746,000,000 (U.S.$3,110 per capita).

Structure of gross domestic product and labour force

	1998 in value BZ$'000[8]	1998 % of total value[8]	2001 labour force	2001 % of labour force
Agriculture, fishing, forestry	213,600	20.1	23,610	24.7
Mining	6,200	0.6	315	0.3
Manufacturing	139,800	13.1	8,170	8.5
Construction	59,600	5.6	5,055	5.3
Public utilities	35,100	3.3	1,135	1.2
Transp. and commun.	109,400	10.3	4,685	4.9
Trade, restaurants	199,100	18.7	19,965	20.9
Finance, real estate, insurance	143,000	13.4	3,285	3.4
Pub. admin., defense	133,600	12.6	20,315	21.2
Services	68,100	6.4		
Other	−44,200[9]	−4.2[9]	9,155[10]	9.6[10]
TOTAL	1,063,300	100.0[5]	95,690	100.0

Public debt (external, outstanding; 2000): U.S.$449,000,000.

Foreign trade[11]

Balance of trade (current prices)

	1996	1997	1998	1999	2000	2001
BZ$'000,000	−175.7	−219.7	−257.4	−379.3	−480.0	−382.9
% of total	20.8%	23.8%	27.6%	33.9%	39.1%	26.2%

Imports (2001): BZ$921,100,000 (machinery and transport equipment 27.7%; food 13.5%; mineral fuels and lubricants 18.2%; chemicals and chemical products 8.0%). *Major import sources:* U.S. 47.2%; Mexico 11.2%; Caricom 5.0%; U.K. 2.7%; other EU 3.8%.
Exports (2001): BZ$538,200,000 (domestic exports 61.8%, of which citrus concentrate 16.5%, raw sugar 11.0%, shrimp 8.7%, bananas 8.0%, garments 5.6%; reexports [principally to Mexico] 38.2%). *Major export destinations[12]:* U.S. 53.8%; U.K. 23.0%; other EU 6.7%; Caricom 6.4%.

Transport and communications

Transport. Railroads: none. Roads (1999): total length 1,785 mi, 2,872 km (paved 18%). Vehicles (1998): passenger cars 9,929; trucks and buses 11,755. Merchant marine (1992): vessels (100 gross tons and over) 32; total deadweight tonnage 45,706. Air transport (1998)[13]: passenger arrivals 199,475, passenger departures 193,620; cargo loaded 166 metric tons, cargo unloaded 1,082 metric tons. Airports (1997) with scheduled flights 9.

Communications

Medium	date	unit	number	units per 1,000 persons
Daily newspapers	1996	circulation	0	0
Radio	1997	receivers	133,000	571
Television	1998	receivers	42,000	183
Telephones	2001	main lines	35,200	144
Cellular telephones	2001	subscribers	28,200	115
Personal computers	2001	units	33,000	135
Internet	2001	users	18,000	74

Education and health

Educational attainment (2000). Percentage of population age 25 and over having: no formal schooling 36.6%; primary education 40.9%; secondary 11.7%; postsecondary/advanced vocational 6.4%; university 3.8%; other/unknown 0.6%. *Literacy* (1991): total population age 14 and over literate 75,500 (70.3%).

Education (1997–98)

	schools	teachers	students	student/teacher ratio
Primary (age 5–12)	247	2,015	53,118	26.4
Secondary (age 13–16)	30	726	11,260	15.5
Higher	12	228	2,753	12.1

Health (1998): physicians 155 (1 per 1,558 persons); hospital beds 554 (1 per 435 persons); infant mortality rate per 1,000 live births (2000) 26.0.
Food (1999): daily per capita caloric intake 2,889 (vegetable products 79%, animal products 21%); 128% of FAO recommended minimum requirement.

Military

Total active duty personnel (2001): 1,050 (army 100%).[14] *Military expenditure as percentage of GNP* (1999): 1.6% (world 2.4%); per capita expenditure U.S.$47.

[1]Excludes president of the Senate, who may be elected by the Senate from outside its appointed membership. [2]Excludes speaker of the House of Representatives, who may be elected by the House from outside its elected membership. [3]The Belize dollar is officially pegged to the U.S. dollar. [4]Includes offshore cays totaling 266 sq mi (689 sq km). [5]Detail does not add to total given because of rounding. [6]Estimated figure for about 33,000 employed heads of household. [7]In manufacturing, transportation, trade, and finance. [8]At factor cost. [9]Less imputed bank service charges. [10]Includes 245 not adequately defined and 8,910 unemployed. [11]Imports c.i.f.; exports f.o.b. [12]Domestic exports only. [13]Belize international airport only. [14]Foreign forces (2001): British army 180.

Internet resources for further information:
• Government of Belize http://www.belize.gov.bz

Benin

Official name: République du Bénin (Republic of Benin).
Form of government: multiparty republic with one legislative house (National Assembly [83]).
Head of state and government: President, assisted by Prime Minister[1].
Capital[2]: Porto-Novo.
Official language: French.
Official religion: none.
Monetary unit: 1 CFA franc (CFAF) = 100 centimes; valuation (Sept. 23, 2002) 1 U.S.$ = CFAF 667.00; 1 £ = CFAF 1,037[3].

Area and population

Departments	Capitals	area sq mi	area sq km	population 1992 census
Alibori	...	9,916	25,683	355,950
Atacora	Natitingou	7,899	20,459	400,613
Atlantique	...	1,248	3,233	530,246
Borgou	Parakou	9,772	25,310	471,975
Collines	...	5,236	13,561	340,284
Couffo	Aplahoue	928	2,404	403,132
Donga	Djougou	4,128	10,691	248,693
Littoral	Cotonou	31	79	536,827
Mono	Lokossa	539	1,396	281,245
Ouémé	Porto-Novo	1,095	2,835	568,898
Plateau	Ketou	720	1,865	307,676
Zou	Abomey	1,971	5,106	478,714
TOTAL		43,483	112,622	4,924,253[4]

Demography

Population (2002): 6,788,000.
Density (2002): persons per sq mi 156.1, persons per sq km 60.3.
Urban-rural (1999): urban 41.5%; rural 58.5%.
Sex distribution (2001): male 49.26%; female 50.74%.
Age breakdown (2001): under 15, 47.3%; 15–29, 27.8%; 30–44, 13.9%; 45–59, 7.1%; 60–74, 3.1%; 75 and over, 0.8%.
Population projection: (2010) 8,411,000; (2020) 10,588,000.
Doubling time: 24 years.
Ethnic composition (1992): Fon 39.7%; Yoruba (Nago) 12.1%; Adjara 11.1%; Bariba 8.6%; Aizo 8.6%; Somba (Otomary) 6.6%; Fulani 5.6%; other 7.7%.
Religious affiliation (1992): Christian 35.4%, of which Roman Catholic 25.9%, Protestant 9.5%; traditional beliefs, including voodoo 35.0%; Muslim 20.6%; other 9.0%.
Major cities (1998): Cotonou 649,580; Porto-Novo 218,241; Djougou 132,000[5]; Parakou 128,277; Abomey 80,000.

Vital statistics

Birth rate per 1,000 population (2001): 44.2 (world avg. 21.2).
Death rate per 1,000 population (2001): 14.5 (world avg. 8.9).
Natural increase rate per 1,000 population (2001): 24.7 (world avg. 12.3).
Total fertility rate (avg. births per childbearing woman; 2001): 6.2.
Life expectancy at birth (2001): male 49.0 years; female 50.9 years.

National economy

Budget (2000). Revenue: CFAF 251,300,000,000 (1999; tax revenue 85.5%; nontax revenue 14.5%). Expenditures: CFAF 375,800,000,000 (1999; current expenditures 64.5%, of which salaries 26.8%, debt service 5.6%; development expenditure 35.5%).
Production (metric tons except as noted). Agriculture, forestry, fishing (2001): cassava 2,800,000, yams 1,773,363, corn (maize) 662,958, seed cotton 340,000, oil palm fruit 220,000, sorghum 136,371, peanuts (groundnuts) 80,670, dry beans 77,518, tomatoes 67,375, karité nuts (shea nuts) 20,000; livestock (number of live animals; 2001) 1,500,000 cattle, 1,182,527 goats, 644,997 sheep, 470,000 pigs, 23,000,000 chickens; roundwood (2000) 6,242,329 cu m; fish catch (1999) 38,542. Manufacturing (1998): cement 350,000; cotton fibre 175,000; meat 70,000; wheat flour 12,500; palm oil 11,000. Energy production (consumption): electricity (kW-hr; 1997) 7,000,000 (272,000,000); coal, none (none); crude petroleum (barrels; 1997) 426,000 (negligible); petroleum products (metric tons; 1997) none (151,000); natural gas, none (none).
Public debt (external, outstanding; 2000): U.S.$1,143,000,000.
Gross national product (2000): U.S.$2,345,000,000 (U.S.$370 per capita).

Structure of gross domestic product and labour force

	1999 in value CFAF '000,000,000	1999 % of total value	1992 labour force[6]	1992 % of labour force[6]
Agriculture	553.5	40.8	1,147,746	55.0
Mining	3.3	0.2	661	0.0
Manufacturing	120.4	8.9	160,406	7.7
Public utilities	10.9	0.8	1,176	0.1
Construction	64.4	4.8	51,655	2.5
Transp. and communications	101.2	7.5	52,837	2.5
Trade	267.2	19.7	432,501	20.7
Finance	139.1	10.3	3,106	0.1
Pub. admin., defense	95.5	7.0	164,544	7.9
Services				
Other	—	—	70,814	3.4
TOTAL	1,355.5	100.0	2,085,446	100.0[7]

Population economically active (1997): total 2,608,000; activity rate of total population 44.2% (participation rates: ages 15–64, 84.3%; female 48.3%; unemployed, n.a.).

Price and earnings indexes (1995 = 100)

	1994	1995	1996	1997	1998	1999	2000
Consumer price index	87.4	100.0	104.9	108.6	114.8	115.2	120.0
Hourly earnings index	...	...	...	...	...	...	...

Household income and expenditure. Average household size (1992) 5.9; income per household (1983) U.S.$240; sources of income; self-employement 73.7%, wages and salaries 26.3%; expenditure: n.a.
Land use (1995): agricultural and under permanent cultivation 17.0%; other 83.0% (of which [1994] forested 30.7%, meadows and pastures 4.0%).
Tourism (1998): receipts from visitors U.S.$33,000,000; expenditures by nationals abroad U.S.$7,000,000.

Foreign trade[8]

Balance of trade (current prices)

	1995	1996	1997	1998	1999	2000
CFAF '000,000,000	−162.6	0.0	0.0	−153.5	−163.1	−160.8
% of total	27.9%	—	—	23.9%	24.7%	23.1%

Imports (1999): CFAF 346,400,000,000 (1997; cotton yarn and fabric 20.2%; machinery and transport equipment 16.2%; rice 7.4%; iron and steel 4.5%). *Major import sources* (1995): France 27.1%; United Kingdom 9.6%; China 9.3%; Thailand 9.1%; Hong Kong 8.8%; The Netherlands 5.6%; United States 4.8%; Germany 4.3%.
Exports (1999): CFAF 237,200,000,000 (1997; cotton yarn 51.6%, reexport 38.5%, cotton seed 2.8%, crude petroleum 2.2%). *Major export destinations* (1997): Brazil 18.0%; Portugal 11.0%; Morocco 10.0%; India 6.5%; Libya 6.0%; Italy 4.5%; United States 4.5%.

Transport and communications

Transport. Railroads (1997): length 359 mi, 578 km; passenger-mi 75,683,000, passenger-km 121,800,000; short ton-mi cargo 193,495,000, metric ton-km cargo 311,400,000. Roads (1999): total length 4,217 mi, 6,787 km (paved 20.0%). Vehicles (1996): passenger cars 37,772; trucks and buses 8,058. Merchant marine (1992): vessels (100 gross tons and over) 12; total deadweight tonnage 210. Air transport (1998)[9]: passenger-mi 160,477,000, passenger-km 258,263,000; short ton-mi cargo 8,404,000, metric ton-km cargo 13,524,000; airports (2000) with scheduled flights 1.

Communications

Medium	date	unit	number	units per 1,000 persons
Daily newspapers	1996	circulation	12,000	2
Radio	1996	receivers	620,000	110
Television	1998	receivers	65,000	10.8
Telephones	2001	main lines	59,300	9.2
Cellular telephones	2001	subscribers	125,000	19.4
Personal computers	2001	units	11,000	1.7
Internet	2001	users	25,000	3.8

Education and health

Educational attainment (1992). Percentage of population age 25 and over having: no formal schooling 78.5%; primary education 10.8%; some secondary 8.2%; secondary 1.2%; postsecondary 1.3%. *Literacy* (1998): total percentage of population age 15 and over literate 37.7%; males literate 53.8%; females literate 22.6%.

Education (1996–97)

	schools	teachers	students	student/ teacher ratio
Primary	3,072	13,957	779,329	55.8
Secondary	145[10]	5,352	146,135	27.3
Voc., teacher tr.[10]	14	283	4,873	17.2
Higher	16[10]	962	14,085	14.6

Health: physicians (1993) 363 (1 per 14,216 persons); hospital beds (1993) 1,235 (1 per 4,182 persons); infant mortality rate (2001) 89.7.
Food (2000): daily per capita caloric intake 2,558 (vegetable products 96%, animal products 4%); 111% of FAO recommended minimum requirement.

Military

Total active duty personnel (2001): 4,750 (army 94.7%, navy 2.1%, air force 3.2%). *Military expenditure as percentage of GNP* (1999): 1.4% (world 2.4%); per capita expenditure U.S.$5.

---

[1]Office of Prime Minister vacant from May 1998. [2]Porto-Novo, the official capital established under the constitution, is the seat of the legislature, but the president and most government ministers reside in Cotonou. [3]Formerly pegged to the French franc and since Jan. 1, 2002, to the euro at the rate of €1 = CFAF 655.96. [4]Represents sum of departments' populations; reported census total is 4,915,555. [5]1994. [6]Age 10 years and over. [7]Detail does not add to total given because of rounding. [8]Import figures are c.i.f. in balance of trade and f.o.b. in commodities and trading partners. [9]Represents 1/11 of the traffic of Air Afrique, which is operated by 11 West African states. [10]1993–94.

Internet resources for further information:
- Embassy of Benin in Paris, France
  http://www.ambassade-benin.org/index1.html
- Investir en Zone Franc
  http://www.izf.net/Index.htm

Bermuda

Official name: Bermuda.
Political status: colony (United Kingdom) with two legislative houses (Senate [11]; House of Assembly [40]).
Chief of state: British Monarch, represented by Governor.
Head of government: Premier.
Capital: Hamilton.
Official language: English.
Official religion: none.
Monetary unit: 1 Bermuda dollar (Bd$) = 100 cents; valuation (Sept. 23, 2002) 1 U.S.$ = Bd$1.00[1]; 1 £ = Bd$1.55.

Atlantic Ocean

Area and population

Municipalities	area		population 1991 census
	sq mi	sq km	
Hamilton	0.3	0.8	1,100
St. George	0.5	1.3	1,648
Parishes			
Devonshire	2.0	5.1	7,371
Hamilton	2.0	5.1	4,680
Paget	2.1	5.3	4,877
Pembroke[2]	1.8	4.6	10,407
St. George's[3, 4]	3.5	8.0	2,975
Sandys	2.1	5.4	6,437
Smith's	1.8	4.7	5,261
Southampton	2.2	5.6	5,804
Warwick	2.0	5.1	7,900
TOTAL	20.5[5, 6]	53.1[5, 6]	58,460[7]

Demography

Population (2002): 63,600.
Density (2002): persons per sq mi 3,102, persons per sq km 1,198.
Urban-rural (2000): urban 100.0%; rural, none.
Sex distribution (1999): male 48.57%; female 51.43%.
Age breakdown (1999): under 15, 19.8%; 15–29, 18.3%; 30–44, 27.5%; 45–59, 19.4%; 60–74, 11.2%; 75 and over, 3.8%.
Population projection: (2010) 67,000; (2020) 69,000.
Ethnic composition (2000): black 50.4%; British expatriates 29.0%; mulatto 10.0%; U.S. white 6.0%; Portuguese 4.5%; other 0.1%.
Religious affiliation (2000): Protestant 67.2%, of which Anglican 37.2%; Roman Catholic 16.0%; unaffiliated Christian 7.0%; nonreligious 4.0%; other 5.8%.
Major cities (1991): St. George 1,648; Hamilton 1,100.

Vital statistics

Birth rate per 1,000 population (2000): 13.4 (world avg. 22.5); legitimate 64.3%; illegitimate 35.7%.
Death rate per 1,000 population (2000): 7.5 (world avg. 9.0).
Natural increase rate per 1,000 population (2000): 5.9 (world avg. 13.5).
Total fertility rate (avg. births per childbearing woman; 2000): 1.8.
Marriage rate per 1,000 population (2000): 16.3.
Divorce rate per 1,000 population (1996): 3.7.
Life expectancy at birth (2000): male 74.9 years; female 78.9 years.
Major causes of death per 100,000 population (1993): diseases of the circulatory system 318.6; malignant neoplasms (cancers) 212.4; infectious and parasitic diseases 61.4; accidents and violence 39.8.

National economy

Budget (1999). Revenue: Bd$562,200,000 (customs duty 31.3%; payroll tax 27.0%; fees, sales, recoveries, and other miscellaneous receipts 15.0%; tax on international companies 6.3%). Expenditures: Bd$545,700,000 (current expenditure 91.4%, of which public debt 2.3%; development expenditure 8.6%).
Production (value in Bd$'000 except as noted). Agriculture, forestry, fishing (1999): vegetables 3,000, milk 1,657, fruits 900, eggs 435, honey 160; livestock (number of live animals; 1999) 900 horses, 600 cattle, 45,000 chickens; roundwood, n.a.; fish catch (metric tons; 1998) 457, of which crustaceans and mollusks 38. Mining and quarrying: crushed stone for local use. Manufacturing: industries include pharmaceuticals, cosmetics, electronics, fish processing, handicrafts, and small boat building[8]. Construction (2000): residential 35,600; nonresidential 111,000. Energy production (consumption): electricity (kW-hr; 1997) 530,000,000 (530,000,000); coal, none (none); crude petroleum, none (none); petroleum products (metric tons; 1997) none (167,000); natural gas, none (none).
Land use (1988): forested 20.0%; meadows and pastures 0.9%; agricultural and under permanent cultivation 3.1%; built-on, wasteland, and other 76.0%.
Tourism: receipts from visitors (2000) U.S.$431,000,000; expenditures by nationals abroad (1997) U.S.$148,000,000.
Population economically active (1991): total 35,222; activity rate of total population 60.2%[7] (participation rates: ages 15–64, 80.9%[7]; female 47.1%[7]; unemployed [1995] 1.5%).

Price and earnings indexes (1995 = 100)

	1994	1995	1996	1997	1998	1999	2000
Consumer price index	97.5	100.0	102.5	104.6	106.7	109.3	112.3
Weekly earnings index[9]	97.1	100.0	103.2	106.5	109.8	113.1	...

Gross domestic product (1999–2000): U.S.$2,624,000,000 (U.S.$41,690 per capita).

Structure of gross domestic product and labour force

	1998–99		1997[10]	
	in value U.S.$'000	% of total value	labour force[11]	% of labour force
Agriculture, fishing	...	...	400	1.1
Quarrying	...	...	106	0.3
Manufacturing	...	...	889	2.5
Construction	...	...	2,043	5.8
Public utilities	...	...	522	1.5
Transp. and commun.	...	...	2,220	6.3
Trade, restaurants	...	...	10,914	30.9
Finance, real estate	...	...	5,240	14.8
Pub. admin., defense	...	...	4,608	13.1
Services	...	...	5,687	16.1
Other[12]	...	...	2,667	7.6
TOTAL	2,499,000	100.0	35,296	100.0

Public debt (external, outstanding; 1998): n.a.
Household income and expenditure. Average household size (1993) 2.5; average annual income per household (2001) Bd$72,500 (U.S.$72,500); sources of income (1993): wages and salaries 65.3%, imputed income from owner occupancy 10.6%, self-employment 9.0%, net rental income 4.8%, other 10.4%; expenditure (1993): housing 27.7%, household furnishings 16.6%, food and nonalcoholic beverages 14.6%, health care 7.6%, transportation 7.3%, foreign travel 6.0%, clothing and footwear 4.9%, recreation 4.8%.

Foreign trade

Balance of trade (current prices)

	1993	1994	1995	1996	1997	1998	1999
Bd$'000,000	−495	−514	−496	−514	−554	−564	−661
% of total	86.4%	87.4%	82.1%	82.4%	81.0%	80.3%	86.6%

Imports (1999): Bd$712,000,000 (machinery 21.7%; food, beverages, and tobacco 19.0%; chemicals and chemical products 10.6%; transport equipment 7.7%; clothing 5.7%). Major import sources: United States 72.8%; Canada 5.7%; United Kingdom 4.9%.
Exports (1999): Bd$51,000,000 (nearly all reexports; detail is unavailable). Major export destinations (1995): United States 49.8%; United Kingdom 6.2%; nonspecified 44.0%.

Transport and communications

Transport. Railroads: none. Roads (1997): total length 140 mi, 225 km (paved 100%)[13]. Vehicles (1996): passenger cars 21,220; trucks and buses 4,007. Air transport (2000): passenger arrivals 913,000, passenger departures 913,000; cargo loaded and unloaded 5,600 metric tons; airports (1998) with scheduled flights 1.

Communications

Medium	date	unit	number	units per 1,000 persons
Daily newspapers	1996	circulation	17,000	277
Radio	1997	receivers	82,000	1,328
Television	1997	receivers	66,000	1,069
Telephones	2001	main lines	56,300	872
Cellular telephones	2001	subscribers	13,300	206
Personal computers	2001	units	32,000	495
Internet	1999	users	25,000	390

Education and health

Educational attainment (1991). Percentage of total population age 25 and over having: no formal schooling 0.5%; incomplete or complete primary 18.2%; incomplete or complete secondary 62.9%; higher 18.4%. *Literacy* (1997): total population age 15 and over literate, 98%.

Education (1996–97)

	schools	teachers	students	student/ teacher ratio
Primary (age 5–11)	26	478	5,883	12.3
Secondary (age 12–16)	...	355	3,726	10.5
Higher	1	...	543	...

Health (1996): physicians 96 (1 per 639 persons); hospital beds 251[14] (1 per 244 persons); infant mortality rate per 1,000 live births (1998–2000 avg.) 1.6.
Food (1999): daily per capita caloric intake 2,883 (vegetable products 73%, animal products 27%); 114% of FAO recommended minimum requirement.

Military

Total active duty personnel (1997): 700; part-time defense force assists police and is drawn from Bermudian conscripts.

[1]The Bermuda dollar is at par with the U.S. dollar. [2]Excludes the area and population of the city of Hamilton. [3]Excludes the area and population of the town of St. George. [4]Includes the 2.0 sq mi (5.2 km) area of the former U.S. military base closed in 1995. [5]Includes 0.4 sq mi (1.1 sq km) of uninhabited islands. [6]Detail (including areas cited in footnote 5) does not add to total given because of rounding. [7]Excludes 12,624 short-term visitors, 2,889 on-base military personnel, and 864 institutionalized persons. [8]The economy of Bermuda is overwhelmingly based on service industries such as tourism, insurance companies, offshore financial centres, e-commerce companies, and ship repair facilities. [9]Service industry. [10]August. [11]Employed only; excludes family workers. [12]Extraterritorial organizations and bodies. [13]Excludes 138 mi (222 km) of paved private roads. [14]Excludes beds in geriatric, rehabilitation, and hospice units.

Internet resources for further information:
• Bermuda Online: Economy http://bermuda-online.org/economy.htm

Bhutan

Official name: Druk-Yul (Kingdom of Bhutan).
Form of government: constitutional[1] monarchy with one legislative house (National Assembly [150[2]]).
Chief of state: Monarch[1].
Head of government: Chairman of Council of Ministers[1].
Capital: Thimphu.
Official language: Dzongkha (a Tibetan dialect).
Official religion: Mahāyāna Buddhism.
Monetary unit: 1 ngultrum[3] (Nu) = 100 chetrum; valuation (Sept. 23, 2002) 1 U.S.$ = Nu 48.41; 1 £ = Nu 75.23.

Area and population		area		population
				1998
Districts	Capitals	sq mi	sq km	estimate
Bumthang	Jakar	1,150	2,990	...
Chirang	Damphu	310	800	...
Dagana	Dagana	540	1,400	...
Gaylegphug	Gaylegphug	1,020	2,640	...
Ha	Ha	830	2,140	...
Lhuntshi	Lhuntshi	1,120	2,910	...
Mongar	Mongar	710	1,830	...
Paro	Paro	580	1,500	...
Pema Gatsel	Pema Gatsel	150	380	...
Punakha	Punakha	2,330	6,040	...
Samchi	Samchi	830	2,140	...
Samdrup Jongkhar	Samdrup Jongkhar	900	2,340	...
Shemgang	Shemgang	980	2,540	...
Tashigang	Tashigang	1,640	4,260	...
Thimphu	Thimphu	630	1,620	...
Tongsa	Tongsa	570	1,470	...
Wangdi Phodrang	Wangdi Phodrang	1,160	3,000	...
TOTAL		18,150[4, 5]	47,000[4, 5]	633,000[6]

Demography

Population (2002): 721,000[6].
Density (2002): persons per sq mi 39.7, persons per sq km 15.3.
Urban-rural (2002): urban 8.0%; rural 92.0%.
Sex distribution (1988): male 50.97%; female 49.03%.
Age breakdown (1988): under 15, 40.3%; 15–29, 26.4%; 30–44, 16.5%; 45–59, 10.5%; 60–74, 5.2%; 75 and over, 1.1%.
Population projection: (2010) 853,000; (2020) 1,038,000.
Doubling time: 27 years.
Ethnic composition (1993): Bhutiā (Ngalops) 50.0%; Nepalese (Gurung) 35.0%; Sharchops 15.0%.
Religious affiliation (2000): Buddhist 74.0%; Hindu 20.5%; other 5.5%.
Major cities (1997 est.): Thimphu 45,000; Phuntsholing 45,000.

Vital statistics

Birth rate per 1,000 population (2002): 34.9 (world avg. 21.2).
Death rate per 1,000 population (2002): 8.7 (world avg. 8.9).
Natural increase rate per 1,000 population (2002): 26.2 (world avg. 12.3).
Total fertility rate (avg. births per childbearing woman; 2002): 5.1.
Marital status of population 15 years and over (1985): married 71.2%; single 19.7%; widowed 7.5%; divorced 1.6%.
Divorce rate per 1,000 population: n.a.
Life expectancy at birth (2002): male 62.0 years; female 64.0 years.
Major causes of death (percentage distribution; 1989): respiratory tract infections 19.5%; diarrhea/dysentery 15.2%; skin infections 12.2%; parasitic worm infestations 10.0%; malaria 9.4%.

National economy

Budget (1998–99). Revenue: Nu 6,844,000,000 (internal revenue 45.2%, grants from government of India 33.2%, grants from UN and other international agencies 21.6%). Expenditures: Nu 6,999,000,000 (capital expenditures 59.3%, current expenditures 40.7%).
Public debt (external, outstanding; 2000): U.S.$197,300,000.
Production (metric tons except as noted). Agriculture, forestry, fishing (1999): oranges 58,000, rice 50,000, corn (maize) 39,000, potatoes 34,100, sugarcane 12,800, green peppers and chilies 8,500, millet 7,000, apples 5,500, wheat 5,000, barley 4,000, pulses 1,600; livestock (number of live animals) 435,000 cattle, 74,900 pigs, 58,500 sheep, 42,100 goats, 29,900 horses; roundwood (1998) 1,702,000 cu m; fish catch (1999) 330. Mining and quarrying (1997): limestone 270,000; dolomite 250,000; gypsum 50,000. Manufacturing (value in Nu '000,000; 1994): chemical products 419.0; cement 255.1; wood board products 230.6; distillery products 178.3; processed fruits 103.0. Construction (number of buildings completed; 1977–78): residential 10; nonresidential (guest house) 1. Energy production (consumption): electricity (kW-hr; 1997) 1,838,000,000 (415,000,000); coal (metric tons; 1997) 54,000 (71,000); crude petroleum, none (n.a.); petroleum products (metric tons; 1997) none (40,000); natural gas, none (n.a.).
Household income and expenditure. Average household size (1980) 5.46; income per household: n.a.; sources of income: n.a.; expenditure (1979): food 72.3%, clothing 21.2%, energy 3.7%, household durable goods 0.7%, personal effects and other 2.1%.
Tourism (2000): receipts from visitors U.S.$10,000,000; expenditures by nationals abroad, n.a.
Gross national product (2000): U.S.$479,000,000 (U.S.$590 per capita).

Structure of gross domestic product and labour force				
	1997		1984	
	in value Nu '000,000	% of total value	labour force	% of labour force
Agriculture	5,288	38.4	303,000[7]	87.2
Mining	310	2.2		
Manufacturing	1,742	12.7		
Construction	1,206	8.8		
Trade	1,014	7.4		
Public utilities	1,732	12.6	3,000[7]	0.9
Transportation and communications	1,018	7.4		
Finance	495	3.6		
Pub. admin., defense			12,000[7]	3.4
Services	1,363	9.9	30,000[7]	8.5[8]
Other	–417[9]	–3.0[9]	...	...
TOTAL	13,751	100.0	348,000	100.0

Population economically active (1984)[6]: total 348,000; activity rate of total population 53.4% (participation rates: ages 15–64, 94.8%; female 55.0%; unemployed 6.5%).

Price and earnings indexes (1995 = 100)							
	1993	1994	1995	1996	1997	1998	1999
Consumer price index	85.4	91.3	100.0	108.8	115.9	128.1	136.8
Earnings index	...	...	...	...	...	...	...

Land use (1994): forested 66.0%; meadows and pastures 5.8%; agricultural and under permanent cultivation 2.8%; other 25.4%.

Foreign trade[10]

Balance of trade (current prices)						
	1994	1995	1996	1997	1998	1999
Nu '000,000	–793.7	–292.8	–971.4	–703.9	–1,060.8	–2,846.9
% of total	16.0%	4.2%	12.0%	7.6%	10.6%	22.2%

Imports (1997): Nu 4,978,000,000 ([11]petroleum products 4.6%, rice 4.6%, vegetable fats and oils 3.0%, steel products 2.4%, wheat 2.0%, industrial machinery 1.7%). *Major import source* (1997–98): India 70.5%.
Exports (1997): Nu 4,274,100,000 ([11]electricity 21.0%, calcium carbide 15.0%, particle board 8.0%, cement 7.1%). *Major export destination* (1997–98): India 94.5%.

Transport and communications

Transport. Railroads: none. Roads (1999): total length 2,293 mi, 3,691 km (paved 60%). Vehicles (1999): passenger cars 6,468; trucks and buses 3,273. Merchant marine: none. Air transport (1998): passenger-mi 30,000,000, passenger-km 49,000,000; short ton-mi cargo 2,700,000, metric ton-km cargo 4,000,000; airports (1997) with scheduled flights 1.

Communications				units per 1,000
Medium	date	unit	number	persons
Radio	1997	receivers	37,000	19
Television	1999	receivers	13,000	20
Telephones	2001	main lines	14,000	20
Personal computers	2001	units	4,000	5.8
Internet	2001	users	2,500	3.6

Education and health

Educational attainment: n.a. *Literacy* (1995 est.): total population age 15 and over literate 42.2%; males literate 56.2%; females literate 28.1%.

Education (1994)				student/
	schools	teachers	students	teacher ratio
Primary (age 7–11)	235[12]	1,611	60,089	37.3
Secondary (age 12–16)	31[13]	544	7,299	13.4
Voc., teacher tr.	8[13]	95	1,822[13]	12.2[13]
Higher	2[13]	57[13]	2,055	9.1[13]

Health: physicians (1994) 100 (1 per 8,000 persons); hospital beds 970 (1 per 825 persons); infant mortality rate per 1,000 live births (2002) 55.0.
Food (1975–77): daily per capita caloric intake 2,058 (vegetable products 98%, animal products 2%); 89% of FAO recommended minimum requirement.

Military

Total active duty personnel (2000): about 6,000 (army 100%).

[1]There is no formal constitution, but a form of constitutional monarchy is in place; reforms in July 1998 curtailed the powers of the monarchy and increased the powers of the Council of Ministers. [2]Includes 45 nonelective seats occupied by representatives of the King and religious groups. [3]Indian currency is also accepted legal tender; the ngultrum is at par with the Indian rupee. [4]2,700 sq mi (7,000 sq km) are not included in the estimated district area totals. [5]Three districts are not listed: Chhukha, created in 1987 from Samchi, Paro, and Thimphu districts; Gasa, created in 1992 from Punakha; and Tashi Yangtse, created in 1992 from Tashigang. [6]Excludes nearly 100,000 Bhutanese of Nepalese origin declared stateless by the Bhutanese government in late 1990. [7]Derived value. [8]Includes 6.5% with no occupation. [9]Imputed bank service charges. [10]Import figures are c.i.f. in balance of trade, commodities, and trading partners. [11]1996. [12]1993. [13]1990.

Internet resources for further information:
• **The Library of Congress Country Studies: Bhutan**
  http://memory.loc.gov/frd/cs/bttoc.html

Bolivia

Official name: República de Bolivia (Republic of Bolivia).
Form of government: unitary multiparty republic with two legislative houses (Chamber of Senators [27]; Chamber of Deputies [130]).
Head of state and government: President.
Capitals: La Paz (administrative); Sucre (judicial).
Official languages: Spanish, Aymara, Quechua.
Official religion: Roman Catholicism.
Monetary unit: 1 boliviano (Bs) = 100 centavos; valuation (Sept. 23, 2002) 1 U.S.$ = Bs 7.34; 1 £ = Bs 11.41.

Area and population

Departments	Capitals	area sq mi	area sq km	population 2001 census
Beni	Trinidad	82,458	213,564	362,521
Chuquisaca	Sucre	19,893	51,524	531,522
Cochabamba	Cochabamba	21,479	55,631	1,455,711
La Paz	La Paz	51,732	133,985	2,350,466
Oruro	Oruro	20,690	53,588	391,870
Pando	Cobija	24,644	63,827	52,525
Potosí	Potosí	45,644	118,218	709,013
Santa Cruz	Santa Cruz	143,098	370,621	2,029,471
Tarija	Tarija	14,526	37,623	391,226
TOTAL		424,164	1,098,581	8,274,325

Demography

Population (2002): 8,401,000.
Density (2002): persons per sq mi 19.8, persons per sq km 7.6.
Urban-rural (2001): urban 62.4%; rural 37.6%.
Sex distribution (2001): male 49.84%; female 50.16%.
Age breakdown (2000): under 15, 39.1%; 15–29, 28.1%; 30–44, 16.6%; 45–59, 9.9%; 60–74, 4.5%; 75 and over, 1.8%.
Population projection: (2010) 9,449,000; (2020) 10,691,654.
Doubling time: 34 years.
Ethnic composition (1996): Indian 55.0%; mestizo 30.0%; white 15.0%.
Religious affiliation (1995): Roman Catholic 88.5%; Protestant 9.0%; other 2.5%.
Major cities (2001): Santa Cruz 1,116,059; La Paz 789,585 (urban agglomeration 1,499,000); El Alto 647,350[1]; Cochabamba 516,683; Oruro 201,230; Sucre 193,873.

Vital statistics

Birth rate per 1,000 population (2000): 31.9 (world avg. 22.5).
Death rate per 1,000 population (2000): 8.6 (world avg. 9.0).
Natural increase rate per 1,000 population (2000): 23.3 (world avg. 13.5).
Total fertility rate (avg. births per childbearing woman; 2000): 3.7.
Marriage rate per 1,000 population: n.a.
Life expectancy at birth (2000): male 61.2 years; female 66.3 years.
Major causes of death (percentage of total registered deaths; 1980–81): infectious and parasitic diseases 23.9%; diseases of the circulatory system 19.5%; diseases of the respiratory system 14.0%; accidents, homicides, and violence 9.8%; diseases of the digestive system 8.6%.

National economy

Budget (1998). Revenue: Bs 11,698,500,000 (tax revenue 78.9%, of which indirect taxes 49.0%, taxes on petroleum and petroleum products 18.8%; nontax revenue 8.9%). Expenditures: Bs 13,681,300,000 (current expenditure 78.8%, of which wages and salaries 31.3%, transfers 21.9%; capital expenditure 21.2%).
Production (metric tons except as noted). Agriculture, forestry, fishing (1999): sugarcane 4,160,000, soybeans 762,000, potatoes 783,000, bananas and plantains 767,000, corn (maize) 613,000, cassava 400,000, rice 189,000, sorghum 148,000, wheat 140,000; livestock (number of live animals) 8,575,000 sheep, 6,556,000 cattle, 2,715,000 pigs, 1,500,000 goats, 631,000 asses, 322,000 horses; roundwood (1998) 1,989,000 cu m; fish catch (1998) 6,055. Mining and quarrying (metric tons of pure metal; 1998): zinc 150,709; lead 13,848; tin 10,542; silver 402; gold 14.4. Manufacturing (value added in U.S.$'000; 1994): petroleum products 375; food products 169; beverages 99; nonmetal mineral products 36; textiles 23; printing and publishing 19; nonferrous metals 18. Energy production (consumption): electricity (kW-hr; 1998) 3,771,000,000 (3,252,000,000); coal, none (none); crude petroleum (barrels; 1998) 12,628,000 (10,382,000); petroleum products (metric tons; 1997) 1,354,000 (1,514,000); natural gas (cu m; 1998) 3,106,000,000 (1,511,000,000).
Population economically active (1997): total 3,645,165; activity rate of total population 46.6% (participation rates: ages 15–64, 72.1%; female 43.7%; unemployed 2.1%).

Price and earnings indexes (1995 = 100)

	1996	1997	1998	1999	2000	2001
Consumer price index	112.4	117.7	126.8	129.5	135.5	137.6
Monthly earnings index[2]	108.8	117.1	146.3	161.0	173.2	...

Tourism (2000): receipts U.S.$160,000,000; expenditures U.S.$102,000,000.
Gross national product (at current market prices; 2000): U.S.$8,206,000,000 (U.S.$990 per capita).

Structure of gross domestic product and labour force

	1999 in value Bs '000[3]	1999 % of total value[3]	1997 labour force[4]	1997 % of labour force[4]
Agriculture	3,105,038	14.1	1,541,859	42.3
Mining	1,998,841	9.1	63,871	1.7
Manufacturing	3,649,645	16.6	393,451	10.8
Construction	824,155	3.7	187,015	5.1
Public utilities	452,631	2.1	11,029	0.3
Transp. and commun.	2,383,850	10.9	170,531	4.7
Trade	1,866,818	8.5	632,415	17.3
Finance	2,235,150	10.2	78,842	2.2
Pub. admin., defense	1,954,104	8.9	490,728	13.5
Services	1,658,209	7.6		
Other	1,820,911[5]	8.3[5]	75,424[6]	2.1[6]
TOTAL	21,949,352	100.0	3,645,165	100.0

Public debt (external, outstanding; 2000): U.S.$4,120,000,000.
Household income and expenditure. Average household size (1997): 4.4; expenditure (1988): food 35.5%, transportation and communications 17.7%, housing 14.8%, household durable goods 7.3%, clothing and footwear 5.1%, beverages and tobacco 4.5%, recreation 2.7%, health 2.1%.
Land use (1994): forested 53.5%; meadows and pastures 24.4%; agricultural and under permanent cultivation 2.2%; other 19.9%.

Foreign trade[7]

Balance of trade (current prices)

	1995	1996	1997	1998	1999	2000
U.S.$'000,000	−162.5	−313.4	−531.6	−721.0	−487.9	−375.0
% of total	6.9%	12.1%	18.6%	24.6%	18.8%	13.2%

Imports (1998): U.S.$1,983,000,000 (raw materials 42.2%, of which raw materials for industry 32.8%; capital goods 40.0%, of which transportation equipment 23.1%, capital goods for industry 15.9%; consumer goods 18.2%, of which nondurable consumer goods 9.3%, durable consumer goods 8.9%; other 0.4%). *Major import sources:* U.S. 26.3%; Japan 20.0%; Brazil 10.3%; Argentina 10.0%; Chile 6.0%; Peru 3.7%; France 1.1%.
Exports (1998): U.S.$1,104,900,000 (zinc 14.1%; soybeans 13.6%; gold 10.1%; silver 6.6%; oils 5.8%; natural gas 5.1%; tin 5.1%; timber 4.6%). *Major export destinations:* U.S. 18.4%; U.K. 17.8%; Peru 11.9%; Argentina 10.9%; Chile 2.9%; Brazil 2.4%; Germany 1.9%.

Transport and communications

Transport. Railroads (1997): route length 2,187 mi, 3,519 km; passenger-mi 84,900,000, passenger-km 136,700,000; short ton-mi cargo 358,900,000, metric ton-km cargo 524,200,000. Roads (1999): total length 32,445 mi, 52,216 km (paved 6%). Vehicles (1996): passenger cars 223,829; trucks and buses 138,536. Merchant marine (1992): vessels (100 gross tons and over) 1; total deadweight tonnage 15,765. Air transport (2000): passenger-mi 1,189,653,000, passenger-km 1,914,566,000; short ton-mi cargo 132,083,000, metric ton-km cargo 192,838,000; airports (1997) with scheduled flights 14.

Communications

Medium	date	unit	number	units per 1,000 persons
Daily newspapers	1996	circulation	420,000	55
Radio	1997	receivers	5,250,000	675
Television	1999	receivers	960,000	118
Telephones	2001	main lines	514,800	62
Cellular telephones	2001	subscribers	744,000	90
Personal computers	2001	units	170,000	21
Internet	2001	users	120,000	15

Education and health

Educational attainment (1992). Percentage of population age 25 and over having: no formal schooling 23.3%; some primary 20.3%; primary education 21.7%; some secondary 9.0%; secondary 6.5%; some higher 5.0%; higher 4.8%; not specified 9.4%. *Literacy* (1995): total population age 15 and over literate 82.3%; males literate 92.1%; females literate 79.4%.

Education (1997)

	schools	teachers	students	student/ teacher ratio
Primary (age 6–13)	9,758[8]	61,451	1,430,020	23.3
Secondary (age 14–17)	724[8]	15,178	272,584	18.0
Voc., teacher tr.	478			
Higher	10[9]	4,261[9]	160,917	25.7[9]

Health (1996): physicians 4,346 (1 per 1,747 persons); hospital beds (1998) 11,548 (1 per 689 persons); infant mortality rate (2000) 60.4.
Food (2000): daily per capita caloric intake 2,218 (vegetable products 84%, animal products 16%); 93% of FAO recommended minimum requirement.

Military

Total active duty personnel (2001): 31,500 (army 79.4%, navy 11.1%, air force 9.5%). *Military expenditure as percentage of GNP* (1998): 1.8% (world 2.4%); per capita expenditure U.S.$18.

---

[1]Within La Paz urban agglomeration. [2]December. [3]In 1990 prices. [4]Population 10 years of age and over. [5]Net import duties. [6]Unemployed. [7]Import figures are f.o.b. in balance of trade and c.i.f. for commodities and trading partners. [8]1986–87. [9]1991–92.

Internet resources for further information:
• **Instituto Nacional de Estadística http://www.ine.gov.bo**

Bosnia and Herzegovina[1]

Official name: Bosna i Hercegovina (Bosnia and Herzegovina).
Form of government: federal multiparty republic with bicameral legislature (House of Peoples [15[2]]; House of Representatives [42]).
Chiefs of state: nominally a tripartite presidency.
International authority: High Representative[1].
Head of government: Prime Minister (Chairman of the Council of Ministers).
Capital: Sarajevo.
Official language: Bosnian.
Official religion: none.
Monetary unit: 1 marka[3, 4, 5] (KM) = 100 fenning; valuation (Sept. 23, 2002) 1 U.S.$ = KM 1.99; 1 £ = KM 3.09.

Area and population

Autonomous regions Cantons	Principal cities	area sq mi	area sq km	population 2002 estimate[6]
Federation of Bosnia and Herzegovina	Sarajevo	10,081	26,110	2,312,397
Central Bosnia	Travnik	1,231	3,189	239,728
Goražde	Goražde	195	505	35,258
Neretva	Mostar	1,699	4,401	217,333
Posavina	Orašje	125	325	43,706
Sarajevo	Sarajevo	493	1,277	400,498
Tuzla-Podrinje	Tuzla	1,023	2,649	507,490
Una-Sava	Bihać	1,593	4,125	305,905
Western Bosnia	Livno	1,905	4,934	83,974
Western Herzegovina	Ljubuški	526	1,362	81,304
Zenica-Doboj	Zenica	1,291	3,343	397,201
Republika Srpska	Banja Luka	9,660	25,019	...
TOTAL		19,741	51,129	3,964,388[7]

Demography

Population (2002)[8]: 3,964,000.
Density (2002)[8]: persons per sq mi 200.8, persons per sq km 77.5.
Urban-rural (1999): urban 42.5%; rural 57.5%.
Sex distribution (2001): male 50.46%; female 49.54%.
Age breakdown (2001): under 15, 20.1%; 15–29, 22.2%; 30–44, 25.8%; 45–59, 17.4%; 60–74, 12.2%; 75 and over, 2.3%.
Population projection: (2010) 4,103,000; (2020) 4,182,000.
Ethnic composition (1999): Bosniac 44.0%; Serb 31.0%; Croat 17.0%; other 8.0%.
Religious affiliation (1999): Sunnī Muslim 43.0%; Serbian Orthodox 30.0%; Roman Catholic 18.0%; other (mostly nonreligious) 9.0%.
Major cities (1991): Sarajevo 360,000[9] (urban agglomeration [2001] 552,000); Banja Luka 160,000[9]; Zenica 96,027; Tuzla 83,770; Mostar 75,865.

Vital statistics

Birth rate per 1,000 population (2001): 12.9 (world avg. 21.2); (1993) legitimate 92.6%; illegitimate 7.4%.
Death rate per 1,000 population (2001): 8.0 (world avg. 8.9).
Natural increase rate per 1,000 population (2001): 4.9 (world avg. 12.3).
Total fertility rate (avg. births per childbearing woman; 2001): 1.7.
Marriage rate per 1,000 population (1991): 6.0.
Life expectancy at birth (2001): male 69.0 years; female 74.7 years.
Major causes of death per 100,000 population (1989): circulatory diseases 344.1; malignant neoplasms (cancers) 122.6; accidents, violence, and poisoning 47.1; digestive system diseases 29.2; respiratory diseases 29.0.

National economy

Budget (2000). Revenue: KM 1,819,600,000 (tax revenue 75.9%, of which taxes on goods and services 58.1%, customs duties 9.2%; nontax revenue 24.1%). Expenditures: KM 2,042,900,000 (defense 21.0%; disability benefits 15.7%; wages 15.1%; social funds 14.3%; transfer to state government 12.0%).
Public debt (external, outstanding; 2000): U.S.$2,575,000,000.
Gross national product (2000): U.S.$4,899,000,000 (U.S.$1,230 per capita).

Structure of gross domestic product and labour force

	2000 in value KM '000,000	2000 % of total value	1990 labour force[10]	1990 % of labour force[10]
Agriculture	1,033	11.2	39,053	3.8
Manufacturing, mining	1,164	12.6	496,190	48.3
Construction	461	5.0	74,861	7.3
Public utilities	611	6.6	22,345	2.2
Transp. and commun.	808	8.7	68,798	6.7
Trade, restaurants	958	10.3	130,914	12.8
Finance, real estate	524	5.7	38,686	3.8
Pub. admin., defense	1,114	12.0		
Services	1,115	12.0	155,411	15.1
Other	1,473[11]	15.9[11]		
TOTAL	9,261	100.0	1,026,258	100.0

Production (metric tons except as noted). Agriculture, forestry, fishing (2001): corn (maize) 640,329, potatoes 320,000, wheat 269,105, cabbages 90,000, oats

54,129, tomatoes 30,000, plums 27,000, tobacco 4,395; livestock (number of live animals) 640,000 sheep, 440,000 cattle; roundwood (1998) 40,000 cu m; fish catch (1999) 2,500. Mining (1996): iron ore (gross weight) 100,000; bauxite 75,000; kaolin 3,000; barite (concentrate) 2,000. Manufacturing (1996): cement 150,000; crude steel 115,000; pig iron 100,000. Energy production (consumption): electricity (kW-hr; 1999) 2,585,000,000 (2,684,000,000); coal (metric tons; 1997) 1,640,000 (1,640,000); petroleum products (metric tons; 1997) none (684,000); natural gas (cu m; 1997) none (115,600,000).
Population economically active (1991): total 992,000; activity rate of total population 22.7% (participation rates: ages 15–64, 35.6%; female [1990] 37.7%; unemployed [December 2000] *c.* 40%).

Price and earnings indexes (1995 = 100)

	1995	1996	1997	1998	1999	2000
Retail price index[12]	100.0	75.5	83.7	87.9	87.6	88.7
Monthly earnings index	...	...	...	...	...	...

Household income and expenditure. Average household size (1991) 3.4; income per household: n.a.; sources of income (1990): wages 53.2%, transfers 18.2%, self-employment 12.0%, other 16.6%; expenditure (1988): food 41.3%, clothing 8.3%, fuel and lighting 7.8%, housing 7.8%, transportation 6.0%, beverages and tobacco 5.7%.
Tourism (1999): receipts from visitors U.S.$21,000,000; expenditures by nationals abroad, n.a.
Land use (1994): forested 53.1%; meadows and pastures 23.5%; agricultural and under permanent cultivation 15.7%; other 7.7%.

Foreign trade[13]

Balance of trade (current prices)

	1995	1996	1997	1998	1999	2000
U.S.$'000,000	−930	+336	−1,758	−1,709	−1,415	−1,661
% of total	75.4%	100.0%	60.4%	51.1%	42.1%	46.2%

Imports (2000): U.S.$2,629,000,000. *Major import sources:* Croatia 20.6%; Italy 15.9%; Slovenia 14.2%; Germany 10.7%; Yugoslavia 5.7%.
Exports (2000): U.S.$968,000,000. *Major export destinations:* Italy 23.4%; Yugoslavia 21.6%; Switzerland 11.9%; Germany 9.2%; Croatia 7.9%.

Transport and communications

Transport. Railroads (2001)[14]: length 1,031 km; passenger-km 38,740,000; metric ton-km cargo 239,138,000. Roads (2001): total length 21,846 km (paved 64%). Vehicles (1996): passenger cars 96,182; trucks and buses 10,919. Air transport (1998)[15]: passenger-km 40,390,000; metric ton-km 430,000. Airports (1997) with scheduled flights 1.

Communications

Medium	date	unit	number	units per 1,000 persons
Daily newspapers	1995	circulation	520,000	155
Radio	1997	receivers	940,000	282
Telephones	2001	main lines	450,100	60
Cellular telephones	2001	subscribers	233,300	57
Internet	2001	users	45,000	11

Education and health

Educational attainment: n.a. *Literacy:* n.a.

Education (1990–91)

	schools	teachers	students	student/ teacher ratio
Primary (age 7–14)	2,205	23,369	539,875	23.1
Secondary (age 15–18)	238	9,030	172,063	19.1
Higher	44	2,802	37,541	13.4

Health: physicians (1998) 5,000[11] (1 per 700 persons); hospital beds (1996) 15,586 (1 per 208 persons); infant mortality rate (2001) 24.5.
Food (2000): daily per capita caloric intake 2,661 (vegetable products 86%, animal products 14%); 115% of FAO recommended minimum requirement.

Military

Total active duty personnel (2001): 38,000 (army 100%); about 19,000 troops of the NATO-commanded Stabilization Force are stationed in Bosnia and Herzegovina to assure implementation of the Dayton accords. *Military expenditure as percentage of GNP* (1999): 4.5% (world 2.4%); per capita expenditure U.S.$75.

[1]Government structure provided for by Dayton accords and constitutions of 1993 and 1994 is being implemented in stages since formal signing of peace accord on Dec. 14, 1995. [2]All seats are nonelective. [3]An interim currency, the marka (or "convertible mark"; KM), was introduced on June 22, 1998, to replace another interim currency, the Bosnian dinar (BD), at a rate of 1 KM to 100 BD. [4]The KM is pegged to the euro from Jan. 1, 2002. [5]The euro also circulates as semiofficial legal tender. [6]January 1. [7]July 1 estimate of U.S. Census Bureau International Database. [8]Excludes about 200,000 refugees in adjacent countries and Western Europe. [9]1997. [10]Excludes 28,000 workers in the private sector. [11]Taxes on products and imports less subsidies. [12]Federation of Bosnia and Herzegovina only. [13]Estimated figures. [14]1991–95 war destroyed much infrastructure; limited service resumed in 1998. [15]Air Bosna only.

Internet resources for further information:
• **Central Bank of Bosnia and Herzegovina**
  http://www.cbbh.gov.ba
• **Embassy of Bosnia and Herzegovina (Washington, D.C.)**
  http://www.bosnianembassy.org
• **NATO Stabilization Force**
  http://www.nato.int/sfor

Botswana

Official name: Republic of Botswana.
Form of government: multiparty
republic with one legislative body[1]
(National Assembly [47[2]]).
Head of state and government:
President.
Capital: Gaborone.
Official language: English[3].
Official religion: none.
Monetary unit: 1 pula (P) = 100 thebe;
valuation (Sept. 23, 2002)
1 U.S.$ = P 6.30; 1 £ = P 9.79.

Area and population		area		population
				2001 census (prelim.)
Districts	Capitals	sq mi	sq km	
Central	Serowe	57,039	147,730	499,903
Ghanzi	Ghanzi	45,525	117,910	33,775
Kgalagadi	Tsabong	41,290	106,940	42,072
Kgatleng	Mochudi	3,073	7,960	73,072
Kweneng	Molepolole	13,857	35,890	229,755
North East	Masunga	1,977	5,120	49,598
North West				
Chobe	Kasane	8,031	20,800	20,962
Ngamiland	Maun	33,359	86,400	72,197
Okavango	Orapa	8,776	22,730	49,584
South East	Ramotswa	687	1,780	61,031
Southern	Kanye	10,991	28,467	169,586
Towns				
Francistown	—	31	79	84,406
Gaborone	—	65	169	185,891
Jwaneng	—	39	100	15,179
Lobatse	—	16	42	29,747
Orapa	—	7	17	9,244
Selebi-Pikwe	—	23	60	50,012
Sowa	—	61	159	2,877
TOTAL		224,848[4]	582,356[4]	1,678,891

Demography

Population (2002): 1,679,000.
Density (2002): persons per sq mi 7.5, persons per sq km 2.9.
Urban-rural (1999): urban 29.4%; rural 70.6%.
Sex distribution (2000): male 48.58%; female 51.42%.
Age breakdown (2000): under 15, 40.6%; 15–29, 30.8%; 30–44, 15.0%; 45–59, 7.7%; 60–74, 4.3%; 75 and over, 1.6%.
Population projection: (2010) 1,585,000; (2020) 1,391,000.
Doubling time: n.a.; doubling time exceeds 100 years.
Ethnic composition (2000): Tswana 66.8%; Kalanga 14.8%; Ndebele 1.7%; Herero 1.4%; San (Bushman) 1.3%; Afrikaner 1.3%.
Religious affiliation (2000): traditional beliefs 38.8%; African Christian 30.7%; Protestant 10.9%; Roman Catholic 3.7%.
Major cities (2001): Gaborone 185,891; Francistown 84,406; Molepolole 54,124; Selebi-Pikwe 50,012; Maun 43,952.

Vital statistics

Birth rate per 1,000 population (2002): 28.0 (world avg. 21.2).
Death rate per 1,000 population (2002): 26.3 (world avg. 8.9).
Natural increase rate per 1,000 population (2002): 1.7 (world avg. 12.3).
Total fertility rate (avg. births per childbearing woman; 2002): 3.6.
Marriage rate per 1,000 population (1987): 1.6.
Life expectancy at birth (2001): male 36.8 years; female 37.5 years.

National economy

Budget (1997–98). Revenue: P 8,468,900,000 (mineral royalties 57.7%, customs and excise taxes 14.0%, property income 13.2%, non-mineral income tax 6.4%). Expenditures: P 7,616,400,000 (education 24.2%, defense 8.4%, health 5.1%, interest 1.3%).
Population economically active (1995): total 439,933; activity rate of total population 29.9% (participation rates: ages 15–64, 59.6%[5]; female 35.5%, unemployed 21.5%).

Price and earnings indexes (1995 = 100)							
	1995	1996	1997	1998	1999	2000	2001
Consumer price index	100.0	110.1	119.7	127.7	137.5	149.4	159.2
Annual earnings index	100.0	105.1	110.4	142.5	...	...	...

Tourism: receipts (2000) U.S.$313,000,000; expenditures (1999) U.S.$143,000,000.
Production (metric tons except as noted). Agriculture, forestry, fishing (1999): cereals 19,800 (of which sorghum 13,000, corn [maize] 5,000, millet 1,300), pulses 16,000, vegetables and melons 15,000, tubers 12,000, fruits 9,500; livestock (number of live animals) 2,380,000 cattle, 1,835,000 goats, 250,000 sheep, 237,500 mules and asses, 33,000 horses; roundwood (1998) 1,066,000 cu m; fish catch (1998) 2,000. Mining and quarrying (1998): nickel 19,432; copper 15,593; cobalt 352; diamonds 19,773,000 carats. Manufacturing (value added in P '000,000; 1994): food products 164.3; wearing apparel 78.9; paper and paper products 28.0; industrial chemicals 18.7; wood products 17.5. Construction (value added in P '000,000; 1995–96): 877,900. Energy production (consumption): electricity (kW-hr; 1993) 970,000,000 (970,000,000); coal (metric tons; 1992) 901,452 (n.a.); crude petroleum, none (n.a.).
Gross national product (2000): U.S.$5,280,000,000 (U.S.$3,300 per capita).

Structure of gross domestic product and labour force				
	1996–97		1995	
	in value P '000,000	% of total value	labour force	% of labour force
Agriculture	617,200	3.4	53,779	12.2
Mining	6,486,800	36.0	15,133	3.4
Manufacturing	853,300	4.7	29,530	6.7
Construction	988,000	5.5	41,025	9.3
Public utilities	314,400	1.7	2,805	0.6
Transp. and commun.	621,700	3.4	7,715	1.8
Trade[6]	3,016,800	16.7	54,156	12.3
Finance	1,885,900	10.5	4,096	0.9
Pub. admin., defense	2,998,000	16.6	102,564	23.3
Services	695,100	3.9	14,948	3.4
Other	−462,100[7]	−2.5[7]	114,182[8]	26.0[8]
TOTAL	18,015,100	100.0[4]	439,933	100.0[4]

Public debt (external, outstanding; 2000): U.S.$397,600,000.
Household income and expenditure (1991). Average household size 4.8; average annual income per household (1985–86) P 3,910 (U.S.$2,080); sources of income (1987): wages and salaries 73.3%, self-employment 15.9%, transfers 10.8%; expenditure: food 39.4%, household durable goods 14.0%, rent and services 13.3%, transportation 13.1%, clothing 5.6%, health 2.3%.
Land use (1994): forest 46.8%; pasture 45.2%; agriculture 0.7%; other 7.3%.

Foreign trade

Balance of trade (current prices)						
	1996	1997	1998	1999	2000	2001
P '000,000	2,390.5	3,049.0	−767.0	3,234.8	4,937.5	2,734.6
% of total	17.2%	12.8%	3.2%	10.7%	14.6%	29.2%

Imports (1998): P 9,513,126,000 (machinery and transport equipment 37.5%, of which transport equipment 16.3%; food, beverages, and tobacco 13.1%; metal and metal products 10.1%; chemical and rubber products 8.9%). *Major import sources:* Customs Union of Southern Africa (CUSA) 74.9%; South Korea 4.8%; Zimbabwe 3.9%; U.K. 3.4%; U.S. 1.4%.
Exports (1998): P 8,696,922,000 (diamonds 69.4%; vehicles and parts 11.1%; copper-nickel matte 5.0%; textiles 3.5%; meat products 3.4%). *Major export destinations:* U.K. 55.5%; CUSA 17.2%; Zimbabwe 2.9%; U.S. 1.0%.

Transport and communications

Transport. Railroads (1996–97): length 705 mi, 1,135 km; passenger-km 96,000,000; metric ton-km cargo 795,000. Roads (1996): total length 11,388 mi, 18,327 km (paved 25%). Vehicles (1996): passenger cars 30,517; trucks and buses 59,710. Merchant marine: none. Air transport (1998)[9]: passenger-km 56,835,000; metric ton-km cargo 211,000; airports (1998) 7.

Communications				units per 1,000
Medium	date	unit	number	persons
Daily newspapers	1996	circulation	40,000	27
Radio	1997	receivers	237,000	154
Television	1999	receivers	33,000	21
Telephones	2000	main lines	150,300	93
Cellular telephones	2001	subscribers	278,000	167
Personal computers	2001	units	65,000	39
Internet	2000	users	25,000	15

Education and health

Educational attainment (1993). Percentage of population age 25 and over having: no formal schooling 34.7%; primary education 44.1%; some secondary 19.8%; postsecondary 1.4%. *Literacy* (2000): total population over age 15 literate 934,200 (77.2%); males literate 449,200 (74.4%); females literate 485,000 (79.8%).

Education (1997)	schools	teachers	students	student/ teacher ratio
Primary (age 6–13)	714	11,454	322,268	28.1
Secondary (age 14–18)	274	6,772	116,076	17.1
Voc., teacher tr.	53	2,889	11,482	4.0
Higher	1	507[10]	8,007	10.0[10]

Health (1994): physicians 339 (1 per 4,395 persons); hospital beds (1993) 3,299 (1 per 434 persons); infant mortality rate (2002) 64.7.
Food (1998): daily per capita caloric intake 2,159 (vegetable products 82%, animal products 18%); 93% of FAO recommended minimum requirement.

Military

Total active duty personnel (2001): 9,000 (army 94.4%, navy, none [land locked], air force 5.6%). *Military expenditure as percentage of GNP* (1999): 4.7% (world 2.4%); per capita expenditure U.S.$142.

---

[1]In addition, the House of Chiefs, a 15-member body consisting of chiefs, subchiefs, and associated members, serves in an advisory capacity to the government. [2]Includes four specially elected members, the speaker elected from outside of the National Assembly, and 2 ex officio members. [3]Tswana is the national language. [4]Detail does not add to total given because of rounding. [5]1991. [6]Includes hotels. [7]Imputed bank service charge. [8]Includes 94,528 unemployed. [9]Air Botswana only. [10]1994.

Internet resources for further information:
• **Central Statistical Office** http://www.cso.gov.bw/cso
• **Republic of Botswana: The Government of Botswana Web Site** http://www.gov.bw/home.html

Brazil

Official name: República Federativa do Brasil (Federative Republic of Brazil).
Form of government: multiparty federal republic with 2 legislative houses (Federal Senate [81]; Chamber of Deputies [513]).
Chief of state and government: President.
Capital: Brasília.
Official language: Portuguese.
Official religion: none.
Monetary unit: 1 real[1] = 100 centavos; valuation (Sept. 23, 2002)
1 U.S.$ = 3.46 reais; 1 £ = 5.38 reais.

Area and population

States	Capitals	area sq mi	area sq km	population 2000 census[2]
Acre	Rio Branco	58,889	152,522	557,337
Alagoas	Maceió	10,741	27,818	2,817,903
Amapá	Macapá	55,142	142,816	475,843
Amazonas	Manaus	606,546	1,570,947	2,840,889
Bahia	Salvador	217,867	564,273	13,066,764
Ceará	Fortaleza	56,260	145,712	7,417,402
Espírito Santo	Vitória	17,779	46,047	3,093,171
Goiás	Goiânia	131,320	340,118	4,994,897
Maranhão	São Luís	128,154	331,918	5,638,381
Mato Grosso	Cuiabá	348,799	903,386	2,498,150
Mato Grosso do Sul	Campo Grande	137,893	357,140	2,075,275
Minas Gerais	Belo Horizonte	226,469	586,552	17,835,488
Pará	Belém	481,741	1,247,703	6,188,685
Paraíba	João Pessoa	21,753	56,341	3,436,718
Paraná	Curitiba	76,943	199,282	9,558,126
Pernambuco	Recife	38,041	98,527	7,910,992
Piauí	Teresina	97,032	251,312	2,840,969
Rio de Janeiro	Rio de Janeiro	16,911	43,798	14,367,225
Rio Grande do Norte	Natal	20,493	53,077	2,770,730
Rio Grande do Sul	Porto Alegre	108,778	281,734	10,178,970
Rondônia	Porto Velho	91,724	237,564	1,377,792
Roraima	Boa Vista	86,532	224,118	324,152
Santa Catarina	Florianópolis	36,790	95,285	5,333,284
São Paulo	São Paulo	95,822	248,177	36,966,527
Sergipe	Aracaju	8,480	21,962	1,779,522
Tocantins	Palmas	107,065	277,298	1,155,251
Federal District				
Distrito Federal	Brasília	2,240	5,802	2,043,169
Disputed areas[3]		1,088	2,819	—
TOTAL		3,287,292[4]	8,514,047[4, 5]	169,543,612

Demography

Population (2002): 174,619,000.
Density (2002): persons per sq mi 53.1, persons per sq km 20.5.
Urban-rural (1999): urban 79.7%; rural 20.3%.
Sex distribution (2000)[6]: male 49.26%; female 50.74%.
Age breakdown (2000)[6]: under 15, 29.0%; 15–29, 28.4%; 30–44, 22.2%; 45–59, 12.5%; 60–74, 6.3%; 75 and over, 1.6%.
Population projection: (2010) 191,662,000; (2020) 210,817,000.
Doubling time: 74 years.
Racial composition (1999)[7]: white 54.0%; mulatto and mestizo 39.9%; black and black/Amerindian 5.4%; Asian 0.5%; Amerindian 0.2%.
Religious affiliation (1995)[8]: Catholic 74.3%[9], of which Roman Catholic 72.3%[9]; Protestant 23.2%, of which Pentecostal 19.1%; other Christian 0.9%; New-Religionist 0.3%; Buddhist 0.3%; Jewish 0.2%; Muslim 0.1%; other 0.7%.
Major cities[10] *and metropolitan areas* (2000)[2]: São Paulo 9,785,640 (17,833,757); Rio de Janeiro 5,850,544 (10,871,960); Salvador 2,439,881 (3,018,326); Belo Horizonte 2,229,697 (4,208,508); Fortaleza 2,138,234 (2,843,304); Brasília 2,043,169 (2,043,169); Curitiba 1,586,898 (2,697,924); Recife 1,421,947 (3,316,451); Manaus 1,394,724 (1,403,796); Porto Alegre 1,320,069 (3,507,-624); Belém 1,271,615 (1,807,556); Goiânia 1,083,396 (1,616,370); Guarulhos 1,048,280[11]; Campinas 951,824 (1,717,410).

Other principal cities[10] (2000)[2]

	population		population		population
Aracaju	460,898	Niterói	458,465[13]	São João de	
Campo Grande	654,832	Nova Iguaçu	915,364[13]	Meriti	449,562[13]
Contagem	531,715[12]	Osasco	650,993[11]	São Jose dos	
Duque de Caxias	767,724[13]	Ribeirão Preto	502,333	Campos	532,403
Jaboatão	567,319[14]	Santo André	648,443[11]	São Luis	834,968
João Pessoa	594,922	São Bernardo		Sorocaba	487,907
Maceió	794,894	do Campo	688,161[11]	Teresina	676,596
Natal	709,422	São Gonçalo	889,828[11]	Uberlândia	487,887

Families (1996). Average family size 3.9; 1–2 persons 25.2%, 3 persons 20.3%, 4 persons 22.2%, 5–6 persons 23.3%, 7 or more persons 9.0%.
Domestic migration. Percent of population moving to different *município* between 1991 and 1996: 7.6%.
Number of emigrants/immigrants (1986–96): 2,355,057/169,303. Emigrants' most popular destinations in order of preference are the United States, Japan, and the United Kingdom.

Vital statistics

Birth rate per 1,000 population (2000): 18.8 (world avg. 22.5).
Death rate per 1,000 population (2000): 9.4 (world avg. 9.0).
Natural increase rate per 1,000 population (2000): 9.4 (world avg. 13.5).

Total fertility rate (avg. births per childbearing woman; 2000): 2.1.
Marriage rate per 1,000 population (1995): 4.7.
Divorce rate per 1,000 population (1995): 0.6.
Life expectancy at birth (2000): male 58.5 years; female 67.6 years.
Major causes of death per 100,000 population (1996)[15]: diseases of the circulatory system 225; accidents, murder, and violence 108; malignant neoplasms (cancers) 93; diseases of the respiratory system 80; infectious and parasitic diseases 47; diseases of the digestive system 35; endocrine, metabolic, and nutritional disorders 33; ill-defined conditions 124.

Social indicators

Educational attainment (1996). Percentage of population age 25 and over having: no formal schooling or less than one year of primary education 17.7%; lower primary only 19.1%; upper primary 30.7%; complete primary to some secondary 11.6%; complete secondary to some higher 13.9%; complete higher 6.2%; unknown 0.8%.

Distribution of income (1995)

percentage of national income by decile/quintile

1	2	3	4	5	6	7	8	9	10 (highest)
0.8	1.7	—5.7—		—9.9—		—17.7—		16.3	47.9

Quality of working life. Annual estimated rate per 100,000 insured workers (1990) for: on-the-job injury 2,032; industrial illness 17; death 4. Proportion of labour force participating in national social insurance system (1990): 50.1%. Proportion of formally employed population receiving minimum wage (1993): 25.0%.
Access to services (1999)[7]. Proportion of households having access to: electricity 94.8%, of which urban households having access 99.2%, rural households having access 75.4%; safe public (piped) water supply 79.8%, of which urban households having access 92.3%, rural households having access 24.9%; public (piped) sewage system 43.6%, of which urban household having access 52.5%, rural households having access 4.5%; no sewage disposal 8.5%, of which urban households having no disposal 2.9%, rural households having no disposal 32.9%.
Social participation. Voting is mandatory for national elections; abstention is punishable by a fine. Trade union membership in total workforce (1991): 16,748,155. Practicing Roman Catholic population in total affiliated Roman Catholic population (2000): large cities 10–15%; towns and rural areas 60–70%.
Social deviance. Annual murder rate per 100,000 population (1996): Brazil 23, Rio de Janeiro only 69, São Paulo only 55.
Leisure. Favourite leisure activities include: playing soccer, dancing, rehearsing all year in neighbourhood samba groups for celebrations of Carnival, and competing in water sports, volleyball, and basketball.
Material well-being (1999)[7]. Households possessing: telephone lines (1997) 27.9%, of which urban 33.2%, rural 4.9%; television receiver 87.7%, of which urban 93.2%, rural 63.8%; refrigerator 82.8%, of which urban 89.7%, rural 52.5%; washing machine 32.8%, of which urban 38.0%, rural 10.0%.

National economy

Gross national product (at current market prices; 2000): U.S.$610,058,000,000 (U.S.$3,580 per capita).

Structure of gross domestic product and labour force

	1998 in value R$'000,000[1, 16]	% of total value	labour force[7, 17]	% of labour force
Agriculture	75,764	8.4	16,338,100	21.3
Mining	5,759	0.6	} 861,600	1.1
Public utilities	24,745	2.8		
Manufacturing	182,662	20.3	8,230,600	10.7
Construction	92,321	10.3	4,980,000	6.5
Transportation and communications	50,390	5.6	2,786,600	3.6
Trade	65,236	7.2	9,417,000[18]	12.2[18]
Finance, real estate	196,879	21.9	1,308,700[19]	1.7[19]
Pub. admin., defense	139,291	15.5	26,040,500[20]	33.9[20]
Services	113,287	12.6		
Other	−46,520[21]	−5.2[21]	6,922,600[22]	9.0[22]
TOTAL	899,814	100.0	76,885,700	100.0

Budget (1995). Revenue R$320,178,000,000 (development receipts 62.6%, of which credits 58.4%; current receipts 37.4%, of which social contributions 19.3% [including social security 9.2%], taxes 13.3%). Expenditures: R$320,178,000,000 (administration and planning 59.5%; social welfare 13.9%; regional development 6.0%; health and sanitation 4.9%; agriculture 3.1%; education 2.7%; defense and public order 2.6%).
Public debt (external, outstanding; 2000): U.S.$92,590,000,000.
Production ('000 metric tons except as noted). Agriculture, forestry, fishing (2000): sugarcane 324,668, soybeans 32,687, corn (maize) 32,038, cassava 22,960, oranges 22,745, rice 11,168, bananas 6,339, tomatoes 3,043, dry beans 3,037, potatoes 2,582, seed cotton 1,915, wheat 1,895, coffee 1,824, coconuts 1,822, papayas 1,700, cashew apples 1,500, pineapples 1,353, apples 1,160, onions 1,078, grapes 978, sorghum 842, mangoes 605, tobacco 594, sweet potatoes 500, lemons and limes 480, oil palm fruit 387, maté 220, cacao beans 210, sisal 195, peanuts (groundnuts) 188, cashews 154, garlic 72, natural rubber 70, Brazil nuts 23; livestock (number of live animals) 167,471,000 cattle, 27,320,000 pigs, 18,300,000 sheep, 6,400,000 horses; roundwood (1999) 197,897,000 cu m, of which fuelwood 90,210,000 cu m, sawlogs and veneer logs 46,779,000 cu m, pulpwood 30,701,000 cu m; fish catch (1997) 820, of which freshwater fishes 267. Mining and quarrying (value of export production in U.S.$'000,000; 1998): iron ore 3,066; ferroniobium 242; silicon 135; bauxite 122; kaolin (clay) 106; ferrosilicon 101; granite (1996) 97; copper 89; manganese 52; nickel 52; gold production for both domestic use and export

1,594,000 troy oz; Brazil is also a world-leading producer of high-quality grade quartz and tantalum. Manufacturing (value added in R$'000,000; 1995): industrial chemicals 21,937; transport equipment 20,434; food products 18,117; fabricated and base metals 13,813; electrical machinery 9,563; non-electrical machinery 8,122; paper and paper products 5,667; cement, bricks, and tiles 5,125; pharmaceuticals 4,958; textiles 4,907; printing and publishing 4,807.

Land use (1994): forested 57.7%; meadows and pastures 21.9%; agricultural and under permanent cultivation 6.0%; other 14.4%.

Manufacturing enterprises (1995)

	no. of enter-prises	number of labourers[23]	wages of labourers as a % of avg. of all mfg. wages	value added in producer's prices (in R$'000,000)[1]
Industrial chemicals	1,817	218,756	164.3	21,937
Transport equipment	711	262,712	157.7	20,434
Food products	4,241	527,064	60.6	18,117
Fabricated metals, iron and steel, and nonferrous metals	2,050	325,406	114.2	13,813
Electrical machinery	1,081	191,740	126.6	9,563
Nonelectrical machinery	1,694	227,196	124.7	8,122
Paper and paper products	676	103,339	114.1	5,667
Nonmetallic mineral products	1,508	126,925	88.2	5,125
Pharmaceuticals	359	51,953	178.6	4,958
Textiles	1,192	208,857	66.8	4,907
Publishing and printing	782	105,165	132.1	4,807
Clothing and footwear	1,681	299,193	49.8	4,706
Beverages	451	76,452	87.1	4,027
Plastics	724	101,971	81.0	3,111
Paints, soaps, and perfumes	249	31,143	116.7	2,553
Rubber products	407	49,368	111.5	1,767

Population economically active (1998)[7, 17]: total 76,885,700; activity rate of total population 47.4% (participation rates: ages 15–59 [1997] 72.0%; female 40.7%; unemployed [May 1999] officially 8%).

Price and earnings indexes (1995 = 100)

	1996	1997	1998	1999	2000	2001	2002
Consumer price index	115.8	123.8	127.7	133.9	143.4	153.2	164.4[24]
Monthly earnings index[25]	118.3	128.5	138.8	146.8	161.8	…	…

Tourism (2000): receipts from visitors U.S.$4,228,000,000; expenditures by nationals abroad U.S.$3,893,000,000.

Retail trade enterprises (1996)

	no. of businesses	total no. of employees	annual wage as a % of all trade wages	annual values of sales in R$'000,000[1]
General merchandise stores (including food products)	10,382	437,452	131.2	35,766
Vehicles, new and used	9,348	202,892	229.9	30,926
Gas stations	20,388	210,250	124.7	23,199
Electronics, kitchen equipment, musical instruments	18,245	158,755	143.7	14,855
Metal products, lumber, glass, and construction materials	81,303	386,285	90.1	14,047
Vehicles, parts	55,534	252,731	110.6	10,881
Pharmaceutical and cosmetic products	50,778	240,633	94.2	9,658
Clothing and apparel	128,908	428,150	76.4	9,023
Food, beverages, and tobacco	135,672	378,102	60.7	6,900

Households. Average household size (2000) 3.8.

Family income and expenditure. Average family size (1997) 3.5[7]; annual income per family (1993) Cr$608,364 (U.S.$2,178[7, 26]); sources of income (1987–88)[27]: wages and salaries 62.4%, self-employed 14.7%, transfers 10.9%, other 12.0%; expenditure (1995–96)[28]: housing, energy, and household furnishings 28.8%, food and beverages 23.4%, transportation and communications 13.8%, health care 9.2%, education and recreation 8.4%.

Financial aggregates[29]

	1996	1997	1998	1999	2000	2001
Exchange rate, reais[1] per:						
U.S. dollar	1.039	1.116	1.209	1.789	1.955	2.320
£	1.506	1.846	2.011	2.892	2.917	3.365
SDR	1.495	1.506	1.702	2.455	2.547	2.916
International reserves (U.S.$)						
Total (excl. gold; '000,000)	58,323	50,827	42,580	34,796	32,488	35,740
SDRs ('000,000)	1	1	2	10	—	11
Reserve pos. in IMF ('000,000)	—	—	—	—	—	—
Foreign exchange ('000,000)	58,322	50,826	42,578	34,786	32,488	35,729
Gold ('000,000 fine troy oz)	3.69	3.03	4.60	3.17	1.89	0.46
% world reserves	0.41	0.34	0.48	0.44	0.20	0.05
Interest and prices						
Central bank discount (%)	25.34	45.09	39.41	21.37	18.52	21.43
Govt. bond yield (%)	…	…	…	…	…	…
Industrial share prices	…	…	…	…	…	…
Balance of payments (U.S.$'000,000)						
Balance of visible trade	−5,453	−8,372	−6,603	−1,260	−696	+2,645
Imports, f.o.b.	53,304	61,358	57,739	49,272	55,783	55,579
Exports, f.o.b.	47,851	52,986	51,136	48,012	55,087	58,224
Balance of invisibles	−17,795	−23,839	−27,226	−24,140	−23,936	−25,853
Balance of payments current account	−23,248	−30,491	−33,829	−25,400	−24,632	−23,208

Energy production (consumption): electricity (kW-hr; 1999) 332,304,000,000 ([1998] 287,864,000,000); coal (metric tons; 1999) 4,284,000 ([1997] 17,802,000); crude petroleum (barrels; 2001) 468,873,000 ([1997] 518,296,000); petroleum products (metric tons; 1997) 62,549,000 (71,404,000); natural gas (cu m; 2001) 13,999,000,000 ([1997] 5,462,000,000); carburant alcohol (barrels; 1997) 76,650,000 (76,650,000).

Foreign trade[30]

Balance of trade (current prices)

	1995	1996	1997	1998	1999	2000
U.S.$'000,000	−3,157	−5,453	−8,372	−6,603	−1,260	−697
% of total	3.3%	5.4%	7.3%	6.1%	1.4%	0.6%

Imports (2000): U.S.$55,783,000,000 (electrical machinery and apparatus 32.5%; chemicals and chemical products 16.7%; mineral fuels 13.7%; motor vehicles 8.8%; food products 3.4%). *Major import sources:* United States 23.1%; Argentina 12.3%; Germany 7.9%; Japan 5.3%; Italy 3.9%; France 3.4%; Algeria 2.7%; South Korea 2.5%; Venezuela 2.4%; United Kingdom 2.2%.

Exports (2000): U.S.$55,086,000,000 (transportation equipment 16.6%; machinery and apparatus 11.2%; fabricated metal products 10.7%; soybeans 7.6%; chemicals and chemical products 7.4%; iron ore and other ores 5.9%; paper and cellulose 4.6%; meat 3.5%). *Major export destinations:* United States 23.9%; Argentina 11.3%; The Netherlands 5.1%; Germany 4.6%; Japan 4.5%; Italy 3.9%; Belgium 3.2%; Mexico 3.1%; France 3.1%; United Kingdom 2.7%.

Transport and communications

Transport. Railroads (1998)[31]: route length (1997) 18,458 mi, 29,706 km; passenger-mi 8,676,000,000, passenger-km 12,667,000,000; short ton-mi cargo 96,741,000,000, metric ton-km cargo 141,239,000,000. Roads (1999): total length 1,071,816 mi, 1,724,924 km (paved 9%). Vehicles (1998): passenger cars 21,313,351; trucks and buses 3,743,836. Air transport (1999)[32]: passenger-mi 21,765,000,000, passenger-km 35,028,000,000; short ton-mi cargo 891,000,000, metric ton-km cargo 1,301,000,000; airports (1995) with scheduled flights 139.

Communications

Medium	date	unit	number	units per 1,000 persons
Daily newspapers	1996	circulation	6,472,000	41
Radio	1997	receivers	71,000,000	446
Television	1999	receivers	56,000,000	336
Telephones	2001	main lines	37,430,800	217
Cellular telephones	2001	subscribers	28,745,800	167
Personal computers	2001	units	10,800,000	63
Internet	2001	users	8,000,000	46

Education and health

Literacy (2000)[33]: total population age 15 and over literate 103,500,000 (85.3%); males literate 50,300,000 (85.1%); females literate 53,200,000 (85.4%).

Education (1998)

	schools	teachers	students	student/teacher ratio
Primary (age 7–14)	187,497	1,460,469	35,845,742	24.5
Secondary (age 15–17)	17,602	380,222	6,968,531	18.3
Higher[34]	900	173,705	1,948,200	11.2

Health: physicians (1997) 205,828 (1 per 774 persons); hospital beds (1999) 484,945 (1 per 343 persons); infant mortality rate per 1,000 live births (2000) 38.0.

Food (1997): daily per capita caloric intake 2,974 (vegetable products 80%, animal products 20%); 124% of FAO recommended minimum requirement.

Military

Total active duty personnel (2001): 287,600 (army 65.7%, navy 16.9%, air force 17.4%). *Military expenditure as percentage of GNP* (1999): 1.9% (world 2.4%); per capita expenditure U.S.$59.

[1]The real (R$) replaced the cruzeiro real (CR$) on July 1, 1994, at a rate of 2,750 cruzeiros reais to 1 real (a rate par to the U.S.$ on that date). Previously, the cruzeiro real replaced the cruzeiro (Cr$) at a rate of 1,000 cruzeiros to 1 cruzeiro real on Aug. 2, 1993; the cruzeiro replaced the new cruzado (NCz$) at a rate of 1 to 1 on March 16, 1990; and the new cruzado replaced the (old) cruzado (Cz$) at a rate of 1,000 (old) to 1 new on Jan. 15, 1989. [2]Preliminary figures. [3]Area in dispute between Ceará and Piauí. [4]Total area including inland water per survey of late 1990s. [5]Detail does not add to total given because of rounding. [6]Estimated figures. [7]Excludes rural population of Acre, Amapá, Amazonas, Pará, Rondônia, and Roraima. [8]Christian data include nominal Christians. [9]Includes syncretic Afro-Catholic cults having Spiritist beliefs and rituals. [10]Populations are for *municípios*, which may include adjacent urban or rural districts. [11]Within São Paulo metropolitan area. [12]Within Belo Horizonte metropolitan area. [13]Within Rio de Janeiro metropolitan area. [14]Within Recife metropolitan area. [15]Projected rates based on about 71% of total deaths. [16]At factor cost. [17]Excludes members of armed forces in barracks. [18]Excludes restaurants and hotels. [19]Includes activities not adequately defined. [20]Includes restaurants and hotels. [21]Less imputed bank service charges. [22]Unemployed. [23]End of year. [24]May. [25]Minimum wages. [26]Based on end-of-year exchange rate. [27]Based on 10,408,833 families in Brazil's nine largest metropolitan regions. [28]Based on survey of 11 metropolitan areas only. [29]End-of-period figures. [30]Imports f.o.b. in balance of trade; c.i.f. in commodities and trading partners. [31]Includes suburban services. [32]TAM Regional, TAM Meridional, VARIG, and VASP airlines only. [33]In the late 1990s, functional literacy was 30.5% of total population over age 15. [34]1997.

Internet resources for further information:
- **IBGE: Instituto Brasileiro de Geografia e Estatística**
  http://www.ibge.gov.br/english/default.php#
- **Central Bank of Brazil: Economic Data**
  http://www.bcb.gov.br/defaulti.htm

Brunei

Official name: Negara Brunei Darussalam (State of Brunei, Abode of Peace).
Form of government: monarchy (sultanate)[1].
Head of state and government: Sultan.
Capital: Bandar Seri Begawan.
Official language: Malay[2].
Official religion: Islam.
Monetary unit: 1 Brunei dollar (B$) = 100 cents; valuation (Sept. 23, 2002) 1 U.S.$ = B$1.78; 1 £ = B$2.76.

Area and population

Districts	Capitals	area sq mi	area sq km	population 1999 estimate
Belait	Kuala Belait	1,052	2,724	66,800
Brunei and Muara	Bandar Seri Begawan	220	571	218,800
Temburong	Bangar	504	1,304	9,400
Tutong	Tutong	450	1,166	35,700
TOTAL		2,226	5,765	330,700

Demography

Population (2002): 351,000.
Density (2002): persons per sq mi 157.7, persons per sq km 60.9.
Urban-rural (2002): urban 73.0%; rural 27.0%.
Sex distribution (2002): male 52.35%; female 47.65%.
Age breakdown (2002): under 15, 30.2%; 15–29, 27.0%; 30–44, 25.2%; 45–59, 13.2%; 60–74, 3.6%; 75 and over, 0.8%.
Population projection: (2010) 408,000; (2020) 475,000.
Doubling time: 42 years.
Ethnic composition (1999): Malay 67.6%; Chinese 14.9%; other indigenous 5.9%; Indian and other 11.6%.
Religious affiliation (2000): Muslim 64.4%; traditional beliefs 11.2%; Buddhist 9.1%; Christian 7.7%; other religions and nonreligious 7.6%.
Major cities (1991): Bandar Seri Begawan (1999) 85,000[3]; Kuala Belait 21,163; Seria 21,082; Tutong 13,049.

Vital statistics

Birth rate per 1,000 population (2002): 20.1 (world avg. 21.2); (1982) legitimate 99.6%; illegitimate 0.4%.
Death rate per 1,000 population (2002): 3.4 (world avg. 8.9).
Natural increase rate per 1,000 population (2002): 16.7 (world avg. 12.3).
Total fertility rate (avg. births per childbearing woman; 2002): 2.4.
Marriage rate per 1,000 population (1995): 6.1.
Divorce rate per 1,000 population (1992): 1.1.
Life expectancy at birth (2002): male 71.7 years; female 76.6 years.
Major causes of death per 100,000 population (1994): cardiovascular disease 51.8; malignant neoplasms (cancers) 41.8; accidents, poisoning, and violence 20.0; pneumonia 12.3; congenital anomalies 7.3.

National economy

Budget (1998). Revenue: B$2,775,000,000 (tax revenue 54.6%, of which corporate income tax 47.3%, import duty 7.2%; nontax revenue 45.4%, of which property income 33.8%, commercial receipts 10.9%). Expenditures: B$4,295,000,000 (current expenditure 65.5%; capital expenditure 34.5%).
Public debt (external, outstanding): none.
Tourism (1995): receipts from visitors U.S.$40,000,000; expenditures by nationals abroad U.S.$1,000,000.
Production (metric tons except as noted). Agriculture, forestry, fishing (1999): vegetables and melons 8,700, fruits (excluding melons) 5,225, cassava 1,500, pineapples 700, rice 290; livestock (number of live animals) 6,000 buffalo, 4,500 pigs, 3,302 goats, 1,924 cattle, 4,929,000 chickens; roundwood (1998) 296,000 cu m; fish catch (1997) 4,677. Mining and quarrying: other than petroleum and natural gas, none except sand and gravel for construction. Manufacturing (1998): gasoline 187,600; distillate fuel oils 147,800; kerosene 76,500. Construction (value in B$'000,000; 1989): residential 26.2; nonresidential 5.1. Energy production (consumption): electricity (kW-hr; 1997) 1,705,000,000 (1,705,000,000); coal, none (none); crude petroleum (barrels; 1997) 60,000,000 (1,400,000); petroleum products (metric tons; 1997) 861,000 (939,000); natural gas (cu m; 1997) 9,217,000,000 (1,318,000,000).
Population economically active (1991): total 111,955; activity rate of total population 43.0% (participation rates: ages 15–64, 67.6%; female 32.9%; unemployed 4.7%).

Price and earnings indexes (1998 = 100)

	1998	1999	2000	2001
Consumer price index	100.0	99.9	101.2	101.7
Earnings index	...	...	...	...

Household income and expenditure. Average household size (1991) 5.8; income per household: n.a.; sources of income: n.a.; expenditure (1990): food 38.7%, transportation and communications 19.9%, housing 18.6%, clothing 6.4%, other 16.4%.
Gross national product (at current market prices; 1998): U.S.$7,209,000,000 (U.S.$22,278 per capita).

Structure of gross domestic product and labour force

	1998 in value B$'000,000	1998 % of total value	1991 labour force	1991 % of labour force
Agriculture	231	2.8	2,162	1.9
Mining } Manufacturing }	2,975	36.7	9,397	8.4
Construction	539	6.7	14,145	12.6
Public utilities	88	1.1	2,223	2.0
Transportation and communications	351	4.3	5,392	4.8
Trade	780	9.6	15,404	13.8
Finance	520	6.4	5,807	5.2
Services	2,847	35.1	52,121	46.6
Other	−220	−2.7	5,304[4]	4.7[4]
TOTAL	8,111	100.0	111,955	100.0

Land use (1994): forested 85.4%; meadows and pastures 1.1%; agricultural and under permanent cultivation 1.3%; other 12.2%.

Foreign trade[5]

Balance of trade (current prices)

	1993	1994	1995	1996	1997	1998
B$'000,000	+577.5	+530.0	+338.0	+153.2	+819.0	+135
% of total	8.6%	8.8%	5.2%	2.1%	11.5%	2.2%

Imports (1997): B$3,154,000,000 (machinery and transport equipment 39.0%, manufactured goods 25.5%, miscellaneous manufactured articles 11.6%, food and live animals 11.1%, chemicals 6.4%, crude materials 3.4%, beverages and tobacco 1.9%). *Major import sources:* ASEAN 45.5%, of which Singapore 25.6%, Malaysia 13.6%; EEC 17.9%; Japan 11.2%; United States 10.0%.
Exports (1997): B$3,973,000,000 (natural gas 46.8%, crude petroleum 41.5%, petroleum products 2.8%). *Major export destinations:* Japan 53.1%; ASEAN 20.9%, of which Thailand 11.2%, Singapore 6.6%; South Korea 18.1%; Taiwan 2.7%.

Transport and communications

Transport. Railroads[6]: length 12 mi, 19 km. Roads (1996): total length 1,064 mi, 1,712 km (paved 75%). Vehicles (1997): passenger cars 91,047; trucks and buses 15,918. Merchant marine (1992): vessels (100 gross tons and over) 51; total deadweight tonnage 349,718. Marine transport (1998): cargo loaded 25,900,000 metric tons, cargo unloaded 1,195,200 metric tons. Air transport (1998): passenger-mi 1,742,000,000, passenger-km 2,803,000,000; short ton-mi cargo 75,020,000, metric ton-km cargo 109,527,000; airports (1996) with scheduled flights 1.

Communications

Medium	date	unit	number	units per 1,000 persons
Daily newspapers	1996	circulation	21,000	69
Radio	1997	receivers	93,000	302
Television	1999	receivers	205,000	637
Telephones	2000	main lines	80,500	245
Cellular telephones	2000	subscribers	95,000	289
Personal computers	2001	units	25,000	75
Internet	2001	users	35,000	104

Education and health

Educational attainment (1991). Percentage of population age 25 and over having: no formal schooling 17.0%; primary education 43.3%; secondary 26.3%; postsecondary and higher 12.9%; not stated 0.5%. *Literacy* (1995): percentage of total population age 15 and over literate 89.1%; males literate 93.2%; females literate 84.6%.

Education (1998)

	schools	teachers	students	student/ teacher ratio
Primary (age 5–11)[7]	184	3,858	58,548	15.2
Secondary (age 12–20)	38	2,636	30,956	11.7
Voc., teacher tr.	9	516	2,553	4.9
Higher	4	370	2,080	5.6

Health (1996): physicians 281 (1 per 1,086 persons); hospital beds 961 (1 per 317 persons); infant mortality rate per 1,000 live births (2002) 14.0.
Food (1999): daily per capita caloric intake 2,793 (vegetable products 82%, animal products 18%); (1997) 125% of FAO recommended minimum requirement.

Military

Total active duty personnel (2001): 5,900[8] (army 66.1%, navy 15.3%, air force 18.6%). British troops (a Gurkha batallion; 2000): 1,050. *Military expenditure as percentage of GNP* (1999): 4.0% (world 2.4%); per capita expenditure U.S.$897.

[1]A nonelective 21-member body advises the sultan on legislative matters. [2]All official documents that must be published by law in Malay are also required to be issued in an official English version. [3]Urban agglomeration. [4]Mostly unemployed. [5]Import data is c.i.f. [6]Privately owned. [7]Includes preprimary. [8]All services form part of the army.

Internet resources for further information:
• **Brunei Darussalam http://www.brunet.bn**
• **The Government of Brunei Darussalam http://www.brunei.gov.bn/index.htm**

Bulgaria

Official name: Republika Bŭlgaria
(Republic of Bulgaria).
Form of government: unitary multiparty
republic with one legislative body
(National Assembly [240]).
Chief of state: President.
Head of government: Prime Minister.
Capital: Sofia.
Official language: Bulgarian.
Official religion: none[1].
Monetary unit: 1 lev (Lw; leva)[2] = 100
stotinki; valuation (Sept. 23, 2002)
1 U.S.$ = 1.99 (new) leva;
1 £ = 3.09 (new) leva.

Area and population

Districts	area sq km	population 2001 census	Districts	area sq km	population 2001 census
Blagoevgrad	6,452.3	341,245	Ruse	2,791.3	266,213
Burgas	7,747.9	423,608	Shumen	3,379.8	204,395
Dobrich	4,723.2	215,232	Silistra	2,847.0	142,003
Gabrovo	2,023.0	144,150	Sliven	3,544.1	218,474
Khaskovo	5,539.0	277,483	Smolyan	3,193.9	140,067
Kurdzhali	3,208.8	164,019	Sofiya[3]	7,059.0	273,252
Kyustendil	3,051.5	162,622	Sofiya-Grad[4]	1,344.4	1,173,988
Lovech	4,128.5	169,951	Stara Zagora	5,152.0	370,665
Montana	3,627.6	182,267	Targovishte	2,560.2	137,689
Pazardzhik	4,459.3	310,741	Varna	3,818.9	462,218
Pernik	2,392.8	149,856	Veliko Turnovo	4,662.6	293,294
Pleven	4,338.0	312,018	Vidin	3,033.4	130,094
Plovdiv	5,962.2	715,904	Vratsa	3,937.6	243,039
Razgrad	2,637.6	152,417	Yambol	3,355.5	156,080
			TOTAL	110,971.4	7,932,984

Demography

Population (2002): 7,890,000.
Density (2002): persons per sq mi 184.1, persons per sq km 71.6.
Urban-rural (2001): urban 67.4%; rural 32.6%.
Sex distribution (2001): male 48.48%; female 51.52%.
Age breakdown (2000): under 15, 15.6%; 15–29, 21.8%; 30–44, 20.0%; 45–59, 20.5%; 60–74, 16.3%; 75 and over, 5.8%.
Population projection: (2010) 7,229,000; (2020) 6,528,000.
Ethnic composition (2000): Bulgarian 79.8%; Turkish 9.6%; Roma (Gypsy) 5.4%; Macedonian 2.5%; Pomak 0.9%; other 1.8%.
Religious affiliation (1995): Bulgarian Orthodox 36.5%, Protestant 1.4%, Roman Catholic 0.8%; Sunnī Muslim 13.1%; other/nonreligious 47.8%.
Major cities (2001): Sofia 1,173,988; Plovdiv 338,302; Varna 320,668.

Vital statistics

Birth rate per 1,000 population (2000): 9.0 (world avg. 21.2); legitimate 61.6%; illegitimate 38.4%.
Death rate per 1,000 population (2000): 14.1 (world avg. 8.9).
Natural increase rate per 1,000 population (2000): −5.1 (world avg. 12.3).
Total fertility rate (avg. births per childbearing woman; 2000): 1.3.
Life expectancy at birth (2000): male 68.2 years; female 75.3 years.
Major causes of death per 100,000 population (2000): diseases of the circulatory system 933.9; malignant neoplasms (cancers) 186.5; diseases of the respiratory system 55.1; accidents, poisoning, and violence 57.0.

National economy

Budget (2001). Revenue: 10,268,300,000 leva (tax revenue 74.8%, of which social insurance 24.3%, value-added tax 23.9%, income and profit tax 12.4%, excises 10.8%, customs and duties 1.9%, other 1.5%; nontax revenue 23.1%; grants 2.1%). Expenditures: 10,212,600,000 leva (social insurance 35.5%; administration and defense 13.4%; capital expenditure 10.7%; interest on debt 10.7%; health 9.6%; wages 7.6%; public safety 5.2%; education 4.5%).
Public debt (external, outstanding; 2000): U.S.$7,513,000,000.
Gross national product (2000): U.S.$12,391,000,000 (U.S.$1,520 per capita).

Structure of gross domestic product and labour force

	2001 in value '000,000 leva	2001 % of total value	2000 labour force	2000 % of labour force
Agriculture, forestry, and fishing	3,578.6	12.1	765,096	21.8
Manufacturing, mining	4,951.5	16.7	672,826	19.1
Construction	1,162.3	3.9	127,554	3.6
Transp. and commun.	3,369.7	11.4	219,453	6.2
Trade	2,204.2	7.4	437,441	12.4
Public utilities, housing	1,323.4	4.5	88,635	2.5
Finance	789.6	2.7	44,107	1.3
Pub. admin., defense }			91,700	2.6
Services }	12,233.8[5]	41.3[5]	533,296	15.2
Other }			536,700[6]	15.3[6]
TOTAL	29,613.1	100.0	3,516,808	100.0

Production (metric tons except as noted). Agriculture, forestry, fishing (2001): wheat 3,800,000, corn (maize) 1,739,969, sunflower seeds 605,832, grapes 400,000, barley 830,000, tomatoes 370,000; livestock (number of live animals) 2,286,000 sheep, 1,144,000 pigs, 970,000 goats, 640,000 cattle; roundwood (2001) 3,991,890 cu m; fish catch (1999) 18,336. Mining and quarrying (2000): copper 23,297,000; iron ore 1,002,299; lead 351,449; zinc 119,603; silver 25,000 kg, gold 1,030 kg. Manufacturing (value of production in '000,000 [old] leva;

1997): food, beverages, and tobacco 2,834,413; chemical and oil processing 1,633,583; machine and metalworking 1,460,220; metallurgy 890,614; electronic and electrical equipment 524,383. Construction (2000): residential 573,116 sq m; nonresidential 162,357. Energy production (consumption): electricity (kW-hr; 2000) 40,925,011,000 (40,925,011,000); coal (metric tons; 2000) 26,583,426 (1998; 34,200,000); crude petroleum (barrels; 1998) 232,360 (50,979,000); petroleum products (metric tons; 1997) 4,966,000 (3,626,000); natural gas (cu m; 1997) 37,210,000 (4,900,029,000).
Household income and expenditure. Average household size (2000) 3.0; income per household (2000) 4,610 leva (U.S.$2,154); sources of income: wages and salaries 36.8%, transfer payments 23.2%, self-employment in agriculture 15.8%, other 24.2%; expenditure (2000): food 42.1%, housing and energy 11.7%, transportation 4.9%, clothing 3.8%, health 3.5%, education and culture 3.1%, household durable goods 2.7%, other 28.2%.
Population economically active (2001): total 3,264,700; activity rate of total population 48.1% (participation rates: age 16–59 [male], 16–54 [female] 54.2%; female 46.4%; unemployed 16.3%).

Price and earnings indexes (1995 = 100)

	1996	1997	1998	1999	2000	2001	2002[7]
Consumer price index	221.6	2,567.0	3,047.2	3,124.8	3,447.1	3,654.0	3,736.0
Monthly earnings index	174.4	1,864.4	...	...	...	...	...

Tourism (2000): receipts U.S.$1,074,000,000; expenditures U.S.$538,000,000.

Foreign trade[8]

Balance of trade (current prices)

	1995	1996	1997	1998	1999	2000
'000,000 (new) leva	−20.3	−32.3	+12.9	−1,195	−2,740	−3,581
% of total	2.8%	1.8%	0.0%	7.3%	15.9%	14.9%

Imports (2001): U.S.$7,224,000,000 (petroleum and natural gas 22.5%; machine-building and metalworking equipment 14.0%; textile 10.9%; chemicals and plastics 6.4%; electrical and electronic equipment 4.4%; food, beverages, and tobacco 2.7%). *Major import sources:* Russia 19.9%; Germany 15.3%; Italy 9.6%; Turkey 3.8%; Ukraine 3.2%; U.S. 2.6%.
Exports (2001): U.S.$5,096,000,000 (clothing and footwear 20.0%; mineral fuels 13.5%; metals 8.3%; iron and steel 6.9%; machine-building and metalworking equipment 6.0%; food, beverages, and tobacco 5.6%). *Major export destinations:* Italy 15.0%; Germany 9.6%; Greece 8.8%; Turkey 8.1%; France 5.6%; Belgium 5.6%; U.S. 5.5%.

Transport and communications

Transport. Railroads (2000): track length 6,518 km; passenger-km 3,472,000,000; metric ton-km cargo 5,538,000,000. Roads (2000): length 37,301 km (paved 92%). Vehicles (1999): cars 1,908,392; trucks and buses 272,102. Merchant marine (2000): vessels (100 gross tons and over) 94; deadweight tonnage 1,786,149. Air transport (2000): passenger-mi 1,402,000,000, passenger-km 2,257,000,000; short ton-mi cargo 29,000,000, metric ton-km cargo 46,000,000; airports (2000) with scheduled flights 3.

Communications

Medium	date	unit	number	units per 1,000 persons
Daily newspapers	1998	circulation	2,145,000	254
Television	1998	receivers	3,400,000	418
Telephones	2001	main lines	2,913,900	359
Cellular telephones	2001	subscribers	1,550,000	191
Personal computers	2001	units	361,000	44
Internet	2001	users	605,000	74.6

Education and health

Educational attainment (1992). Percentage of population age 25 and over having: no formal schooling 4.7%; incomplete primary education 12.5%; primary 31.9%; secondary 35.7%; higher 15.0%. *Literacy* (1998): total population age 15 and over literate 98.2%; males 98.9%; females 97.6%.

Education (2000–01)

	schools	teachers	students	student/ teacher ratio
Primary (age 6–14) } Secondary (age 15–17) }	3,113	66,020	883,700	13.4
Voc., teacher tr.	384	20,274	191,246	9.4
Higher	88	23,329	247,006	10.6

Health (2001): physicians 27,526 (1 per 288 persons); hospital beds 62,272 (1 per 127 persons); infant mortality rate per 1,000 live births (2000) 13.3.
Food (2000): daily per capita caloric intake 2,467 (vegetable products 72%, animal products 28%); 99% of FAO recommended minimum requirement.

Military

Total active duty personnel (2001): 77,260 (army 54.9%, navy 6.8%, air force 23.7%, other 14.6%). *Military expenditure as percentage of GNP* (1999): 3.0% (world 2.4%); per capita expenditure U.S.$158.

[1]Bulgaria has no official religion; the 1991 constitution, however, refers to Eastern Orthodoxy as the "traditional" religion. [2]The lev was re-denominated as of July 5, 1999; as of this date 1,000 (old) leva = 1 (new) lev. [3]District nearly encircles Sofiya-Grad district on north, east, and south. [4]Sofiya-Grad includes Sofia city and immediately adjacent urban and rural areas. [5]Includes hotels, restaurants, and real estate. [6]Unemployed. [7]April. [8]Imports c.i.f.; exports f.o.b.

Internet resources for further information:
• **National Statistical Institute of the Republic of Bulgaria**
  http://www.nsi.bg
• **Bulgarian National Bank** http://www.bnb.bg

Burkina Faso

Official name: Burkina Faso
(Burkina Faso).
Form of government: multiparty
republic with one advisory body
(Chamber of Representatives [178[1]])
and one legislative body
(National Assembly [111]).
Chief of state: President.
Head of government: Prime Minister.
Capital: Ouagadougou.
Official language: French.
Official religion: none.
Monetary unit: 1 CFA franc
(CFAF) = 100 centimes; valuation
(Sept. 23, 2002) 1 U.S.$ = CFAF 667.00;
1 £ = CFAF 1,037[2].

Population[3]

Provinces	Capitals	population estimate[4]	Provinces	Capitals	population estimate[4]
Balé	Boromo	169,543	Mouhoun	Dédougou	237,048
Bam	Kongoussi	212,295	Nahouri	Pô	121,314
Banwa	Solenzo	214,234	Namentenga	Boulsa	251,909
Bazéga	Kombissiri	214,450	Nayala	Toma	136,273
Bougouriba	Diébougou	76,444	Noumbiel	Batié	51,449
Boulgou	Tenkodogo	415,414	Oubritenga	Ziniaré	198,130
Boulkiemde	Koudougou	421,083	Oudalan	Gorom-Gorom	136,583
Comoé	Banfora	240,942	Passoré	Yako	271,216
Ganzourgou	Zorgho	257,707	Poni	Gaoua	196,568
Gnagna	Bogandé	307,386	Sanguié	Réo	249,169
Gourma	Fada N'Gourma	221,956	Sanmatenga	Kaya	460,684
Houet	Bobo-Dioulasso	674,916	Séno	Dori	202,972
Ioba	Dano	159,422	Sissili	Léo	153,560
Kadiogo	Ouagadougou	976,513	Soum	Djibo	253,867
Kénédougou	Orodara	198,936	Sourou	Tougan	189,726
Komondjari	Gayéri	49,389	Tapoa	Diapaga	235,288
Kompienga	Pama	73,949	Tuy	Houndé	160,249
Kossi	Nouna	217,866	Yagha	Sebba	116,985
Koulpélogo	Ouargaye	188,760	Yatenga	Ouahigouya	443,967
Kouritenga	Koupéla	250,699	Ziro	Sapouy	117,774
Kourwéogo	Boussé	117,370	Zondoma	Gourcy	127,580
Léraba	Sindou	93,351	Zoundwéogo	Manga	196,698
Loroum	Titao	111,707	TOTAL		10,373,341

Demography

Area: 105,946 sq mi, 274,400 sq km.
Population (2002): 12,603,000.
Density (2002): persons per sq mi 119.0, persons per sq km 45.9.
Urban-rural (1999): urban 17.0%; rural 83.0%.
Sex distribution (2000): male 48.76%; female 51.24%.
Age breakdown (2000): under 15, 47.6%; 15–29, 27.5%; 30–44, 13.0%; 45–59, 7.3%; 60–74, 3.8%; 75 and over, 0.8%.
Population projection: (2010) 15,424,000; (2020) 19,402,000.
Ethnic composition (1983): Mossi 47.9%; Mande 8.8%; Fulani 8.3%; Lobi 6.9%; Bobo 6.8%; Senufo 5.3%; Grosi 5.1%; Gurma 4.8%; Tuareg 3.3%.
Religious affiliation (2000): Muslim 48.6%; traditional beliefs 34.1%; Christian 16.7%, of which Roman Catholic 9.5%.
Major cities (1996): Ouagadougou 709,736; Bobo-Dioulasso 309,736; Koudougou 72,490; Banfora 62,548; Ouahigouya 52,193.

Vital statistics

Birth rate per 1,000 population (2000): 45.3 (world avg. 22.5).
Death rate per 1,000 population (2000): 17.0 (world avg. 9.0).
Natural increase rate per 1,000 population (2000): 28.3 (world avg. 13.5).
Total fertility rate (avg. births per childbearing woman; 2000): 6.4.
Life expectancy at birth (2000): male 46.3 years; female 47.2 years.

National economy

Budget (1999). Revenue: CFAF 238,100,000,000 (tax revenue 93.4%, of which sales tax 43.3%, import duties 25.3%, personal income taxes 22.6%, other 2.2%; nontax revenue 6.6%). Expenditures: CFAF 246,900,000,000 (wages and salaries 27.5%; investment 27.3%; health and education 22.4%; transfers 17.3%; debt service 5.5%).
Public debt (external, outstanding; 2000): U.S.$1,135,000,000.
Household income and expenditure. Average household size (1985) 6.2; average annual income per household CFAF 303,000 (U.S.$640); sources of income: n.a.; expenditure (1985)[5]: food 38.7%, transportation 18.6%, electricity and fuel 13.7%, beverages 9.0%, health 5.2%, housing 5.1%.
Tourism: receipts (1998) U.S.$42,000,000; expenditures (1994) U.S.$23,000,000.
Production (metric tons except as noted). Agriculture, forestry, fishing (1999): sorghum 1,178,400, millet 945,000, corn (maize) 468,900, sugarcane 400,000, peanuts (groundnuts) 281,400, seed cotton 280,000, rice 94,200, pulses 22,000, sweet potatoes 17,300, sesame 12,600, cassava 2,000; livestock (number of live animals) 7,950,000 goats, 6,350,000 sheep, 4,550,000 cattle, 21,000,000 chickens; roundwood (1998) 10,794,000 cu m; fish catch (1998) 8,335. Mining and quarrying (1999): gold 869 kg[6]; silver 120 kg. Manufacturing (1999): sugar 29,905; flour 21,454; edible oils 11,850; soap 9,910; beer 387,000 hectolitres; soft drinks 155,000 hectolitres; printed fabric 1,462,000 sq m; bicycles 24,079 units; mopeds 17,364 units; cigarettes 60,000,000 packets. Construction (value added in CFAF; 1995): 62,400,000,000. Energy production (consumption): electricity (kW-hr; 1998) 267,000,000 (267,000,000); crude petroleum, none (n.a.); petroleum products (metric tons; 1997) none (317,000).
Gross national product (2000): U.S.$2,422,000,000 (U.S.$210 per capita).

Structure of gross domestic product and labour force

	2000		1991	
	in value CFAF '000,000	% of total value	labour force	% of labour force
Agriculture	530,700	34.0	4,293,784	91.8
Mining	187,700	12.0	2,590	0.1
Manufacturing }			51,694	1.1
Construction	55,200	3.5	11,016	0.2
Public utilities	20,900	1.3	3,844	0.1
Transp. and commun.	77,300	5.0	15,041	0.3
Trade	272,700	17.5	120,314	2.6
Finance	...	...	2,075	—
Pub. admin., defense }	392,600	25.2	111,556	2.4
Services				
Other	23,600[7]	1.5[7]	67,279[8]	1.4[8]
TOTAL	1,560,600[9]	100.0	4,679,193	100.0

Population economically active (1991): total 4,679,193; activity rate 50.9% (participation rates: over age [1988] 10, 78.1%; female 48.7%; unemployed 1.1%).

Price and earnings indexes (1995 = 100)

	1995	1996	1997	1998	1999	2000	2001
Consumer price index	100.0	106.2	108.6	114.2	112.9	112.5	118.0
Earnings index	...	...	...	...	...	...	...

Land use (1994): forest 50.5%; pasture 21.9%; agriculture 13.0%; other 14.6%.

Foreign trade

Balance of trade (current prices)

	1996	1997	1998	1999	2000	2001
CFAF '000,000	−227.2	−204.6	−231.4	−212.1	−222.4	−204.5
% of total	41.5%	38.0%	49.1%	40.4%	43.2%	37.7%

Imports (2001): CFAF 373,300,000,000 (capital equipment 30.9%, petroleum products 18.2%, food products 14.4%, raw materials 9.8%). *Major import sources* (2000): Côte d'Ivoire 22.7%; France 22.4%; Japan 5.6%; China 4.1%; United States 3.7%; Germany 3.6%; Italy 3.1%; Belgium-Luxembourg 2.8%.
Exports (2001): CFAF 168,800,000,000 (raw cotton 56.9%, live animals 11.4%, hides and skins 6.4%, gold 2.1%). *Major export destinations* (2000): France 21.6%; Côte d'Ivoire 11.5%; Belgium-Luxembourg 8.4%; Italy 7.7%; Singapore 5.6%; Mali 5.0%.

Transport and communications

Transport. Railroads (1995)[10]: route length 386 mi, 622 km; passenger-km 202,000,000; metric ton-km cargo 45,000,000. Roads (1996): total length 7,519 mi, 12,100 km (paved 16%). Vehicles (1996): passenger cars 38,220; trucks and buses 17,980. Merchant marine: none. Air transport (1993): passenger-km 217,154,000; metric ton-km cargo 34,204,000; airports (1998) 2.

Communications

Medium	date	unit	number	units per 1,000 persons
Daily newspapers	1996	circulation	14,000	1.3
Radio	1997	receivers	370,000	34.0
Television	1998	receivers	120,000	10.6
Telephones	2001	main lines	57,600	4.7
Cellular telephones	2001	subscribers	75,000	6.1
Personal computers	2001	units	17,000	1.4
Internet	2001	users	21,000	1.7

Education and health

Educational attainment (1985). Percentage of population age 10 and over having: no formal schooling 86.1%; some primary 7.3%; general secondary 2.2%; specialized secondary and postsecondary 3.8%; other 0.6%. *Literacy* (1995): percentage of total population age 15 and over literate 23.0%; males literate 31.2%; females literate 13.1%.

Education (1995–96)

	schools	teachers	students	student/ teacher ratio
Primary	3,568	14,037	702,204	50.0
Secondary	252	4,162	137,257	33.0
Vocational	41	731	9,539	13.0
Higher	9	632	9,531	15.1

Health (1991): physicians 341 (1 per 27,158 persons); hospital beds 5,041 (1 per 1,837 persons); infant mortality rate (2000) 108.5.
Food (2000): daily per capita caloric intake 2,293 (vegetable products 95%, animal products 5%); 97% of FAO recommended minimum requirement.

Military

Total active duty personnel (2001): 5,800 (army 96.6%, air force 3.4%). *Military expenditure as percentage of GNP* (1999): 1.6% (world 2.4%); per capita expenditure U.S.$4.

[1]All seats are appointed or indirectly elected. [2]Formerly pegged to the French franc and since Jan. 1, 2002, to the euro at the rate of €1 = CFAF 655.96. [3]In 1997 the number of first-order administrative subdivisions was increased from 30 to 45. [4]Actual date is unknown. Probable date is 1995–97. [5]Weights of consumer price index components; Ouagadougou only. [6]Officially marketed gold only; does not include substantial illegal production. [7]Includes indirect taxes less imputed bank service charges and subsidies. [8]Includes 49,819 unemployed. [9]Detail does not add to total given because of rounding. [10]Passenger-km and metric ton-km cargo figures are based on traffic between Abidjan, Côte d'Ivoire, and Ouagadougou.

Internet resources for further information:
• **Embassy of Burkina Faso http://www.burkinaembassy-usa.org**

Burundi

Official name: Republika y'u Burundi
(Rundi); République du Burundi
(French) (Republic of Burundi).
Form of government: transitional
regime[1] with one legislative body
(Transitional Assembly[2] [178]).
Head of state and government:
President assisted by Vice President.
Capital: Bujumbura.
Official languages: Rundi; French.
Official religion: none.
Monetary unit: 1 Burundi franc
(FBu) = 100 centimes; valuation
(Sept. 23, 2002) 1 U.S.$ = FBu 1,045;
1 £ = FBu 1,624.

Area and population

Provinces	Capitals	area sq mi	area sq km	population 1990 census
Bubanza	Bubanza	420	1,089	222,953
Bujumbura	Bujumbura	476[3]	1,232[3]	608,931[4]
Bururi	Bururi	952	2,465	385,490
Cankuzo	Cankuzo	759	1,965	142,707
Cibitoke	Cibitoke	631	1,636	279,843
Gitega	Gitega	764	1,979	565,174
Karuzi	Karuzi	563	1,457	287,905
Kayanza	Kayanza	476	1,233	443,116
Kirundo	Kirundo	658	1,703	401,103
Makamba	Makamba	757	1,960	223,799
Muramvya	Muramvya	269	696	441,653[5]
Muyinga	Muyinga	709	1,836	373,382
Mwaro	Mwaro	324	840	[5]
Ngozi	Ngozi	569	1,474	482,246
Rutana	Rutana	756	1,959	195,834
Ruyigi	Ruyigi	903	2,339	238,567
Urban Province				
Bujumbura	—	34	87	[4]
TOTAL LAND AREA		10,020	25,590	
INLAND WATER		721	1,867	
TOTAL		10,740[6]	27,816[6]	5,292,703

Demography

Population (2002): 6,373,000.
Density (2002)[7]: persons per sq mi 636.1, persons per sq km 245.6.
Urban-rural (2001): urban 9.3%; rural 90.7%.
Sex distribution (2001): male 49.58%; female 50.42%.
Age breakdown (2001): under 15, 46.7%; 15–29, 27.2%; 30–44, 14.5%; 45–59, 7.3%; 60–74, 3.2%; 75 and over, 1.1%.
Population projection: (2010) 7,669,000; (2020) 9,553,000.
Doubling time: 29 years.
Ethnic composition (1995): Rundi 98.0%, of which Hutu 82.5%, Tutsi 14.5%; Twa Pygmy 1.0%; other 2.0%.
Religious affiliation (1990): Roman Catholic 65.1%; Protestant 13.8%; Muslim 1.6%; nonreligious 18.6%; traditional beliefs 0.3%; other 0.6%.
Major cities (1990): Bujumbura (2001) 346,000; Gitega 101,827; Bururi 15,816; Ngozi 14,511; Cibitoke 8,280.

Vital statistics

Birth rate per 1,000 population (2001): 40.1 (world avg. 21.2).
Death rate per 1,000 population (2001): 16.4 (world avg. 8.9).
Natural increase rate per 1,000 population (2001): 23.7 (world avg. 12.3).
Total fertility rate (avg. births per childbearing woman; 2001): 6.2.
Life expectancy at birth (2001): male 45.2 years; female 47.0 years.
Major causes of death: n.a.; however, major health problems include malaria, influenza, diarrheal diseases, measles, and AIDS.

National economy

Budget (1999). Revenue: FBu 70,400,000,000 (tax revenue 92.9%, of which taxes on goods and services 39.3%, taxes on international trade 23.3%, income tax 13.8%, corporate tax 13.1%, administrative receipts 3.4%; non-tax revenue 7.1%). Expenditures: FBu 99,000,000,000 (wages and salaries 29.1%, goods and services 28.0%, subsidies and transfers 8.5%, public debt 6.1%).
Public debt (external, outstanding; 2000): U.S.$1,028,000,000.
Production (metric tons except as noted). Agriculture, forestry, fishing (2001): bananas 1,548,897, sweet potatoes 780,839, cassavas 712,713, dry beans 248,914, sugarcane 200,000, corn (maize) 124,395, yams and taros 94,624, sorghum 69,074, rice 60,920, potatoes 27,319, coffee 25,000, peanuts (groundnuts) 8,800, millet 8,700, wheat 8,667; livestock (number of live animals) 600,000 goats, 315,000 cattle, 230,000 sheep, 70,000 pigs, 4,700,000 chickens; roundwood (2001) 8,284,615 cu m; fish catch (1999) 9,254. Mining and quarrying (1999): peat 8,000; kaolin clay 5,000; gold 10 kg. Manufacturing (1998): beer 1,036,321 hectolitres; carbonated beverages 60,390 hectolitres; cottonseed oil 133,600 litres; cigarettes 316,820,000 units; blankets 174,407 units; footwear 76,000 pairs. Construction: n.a. Energy production (consumption): electricity (kW-hr; 1999) 99,133,000 (128,450,000); coal, none (n.a.); crude petroleum, none (n.a.); petroleum products (metric tons; 1999) none (60,667); natural gas, none (n.a.); peat (metric tons; 1997) 12,000 (12,000).
Household income and expenditure. Average household size (1998) 5.0; income per household: n.a.; sources of income: n.a.; expenditure[8]: (1990) food 59.6%, clothing and footwear 11.1%, furniture and household goods 6.0%, energy and water 5.8%, housing 4.4%, other 13.1%.

Land use (1994): forested 12.7%; meadows and pastures 38.6%; agricultural and under permanent cultivation 45.9%; other 2.8%.
Gross national product (at current market prices; 2000): U.S.$732,000,000 (U.S.$110 per capita).

Structure of gross domestic product and labour force

	1999 in value FBu '000,000	1999 % of total value	1990 labour force	1990 % of labour force
Agriculture	183,000	46.3	2,574,443	93.1
Mining			1,419	—
Public utilities }	2,900	0.7	1,672	0.1
Manufacturing	26,400	6.7	33,867	1.2
Construction	18,400	4.7	19,737	0.7
Transp. and communications	14,200	3.6	8,504	0.3
Trade	14,800	3.7	25,822	0.9
Finance	...	...	2,005	0.1
Pub. admin., defense	72,500	18.4	85,191	3.1
Services	9,600	2.4 }		
Other	53,100[9]	13.4[9]	13,270	0.5
TOTAL	394,900	100.0[6]	2,765,945[6]	100.0

Population economically active (1997): total 3,475,000; activity rate of total population 63.1% (participation rates [1991]: ages 15–64, 91.4%; female 48.9%; unemployed, n.a.).

Price and earnings indexes (1995 = 100)

	1995	1996	1997	1998	1999	2000	2001
Consumer price index	100.0	126.4	165.8	186.5	192.8	239.7	261.9
Earnings index	...	...	...	...	...	...	...

Tourism (2000): receipts from visitors U.S.$800,000; expenditures by nationals abroad U.S.$14,000,000.

Foreign trade

Balance of trade (current prices)

	1994	1995	1996	1997	1998	1999
FBu '000,000	−26,434	−24,018	−26,039	−12,482	−26,700	−23,100
% of total	30.6%	31.1%	53.6%	16.9%	31.8%	26.4%

Imports (1999): FBu 55,300,000,000 (consumption goods 31.8%, of which food and food products 8.5%; capital goods 25.5%; petroleum products 17.2%). *Major import sources* (1998): Belgium-Luxembourg 19.3%; France 9.1%; Zambia 8.0%; Germany 6.1%; Kenya 5.6%; Japan 3.8%; United States 1.5%.
Exports (1999): FBu 32,200,000,000 (coffee 78.0%, tea 18.3%, animal hides and skins 0.2%). *Major export destinations* (1998): United Kingdom 28.4%; Germany 10.4%; Belgium-Luxembourg 9.2%; United States 1.7%; The Netherlands 0.9%; Rwanda 0.8%.

Transport and communications

Transport. Railroads: none. Roads (1999): total length 8,997 mi, 14,480 km (paved 7%). Vehicles (1996): passenger cars 19,200; trucks and other vehicles 18,240. Air transport (1998)[10]: passenger arrivals 12,113, departures 11,725; cargo loaded 1,490 metric tons, unloaded 9,329 metric tons; airports (2000) 1.

Communications

Medium	date	unit	number	units per 1,000 persons
Daily newspapers	1996	circulation	20,000	3.2
Radio	1997	receivers	440,000	69
Television	1999	receivers	100,000	15.2
Telephones	2001	main lines	20,000	2.9
Cellular telephones	2001	subscribers	20,000	2.9
Internet	2001	users	6,000	0.9

Education and health

Educational attainment: n.a. *Literacy* (1995): percentage of total population age 15 and over literate 35.3%; males literate 49.7%; females literate 22.5%.

Education (1996)

	schools	teachers	students	student/ teacher ratio
Primary (age 6–11)	1,418[11]	10,400[11]	453,746	...
Secondary (age 12–18)	113[12]	2,562[12]	56,887	...
Vocational and teacher training	...	...	5,712	...
Higher	8[12]	556[11]	4,379	...

Health (1996): physicians 329 (1 per 16,507 persons); hospital beds 3,560 (1 per 1,526 persons); infant mortality rate per 1,000 live births (2001) 70.7.
Food (2000): daily per capita caloric intake 1,605 (vegetable products 98%, animal products 2%); 69% of FAO recommended minimum requirement.

Military

Total active duty personnel (2001): 40,000 (army 100%). *Military expenditure as percentage of GNP* (1999): 7.0% (world 2.4%); per capita expenditure U.S.$8.

---

[1]Transitional government following military coup of July 1996 was modified into a "new" transitional government between November 2001 and November 2004 per implementation of the Tutsi-Hutu agreement (Arusha Accords) on July 23, 2001. [2]"New" transitional body installed January 2002. [3]Unverified figure. [4]Bujumbura (province) includes Bujumbura urban province. [5]Muramvya includes Mwaro. [6]Detail does not add to total given because of rounding. [7]Based on land area. [8]Weights of consumer price index components. [9]Indirect taxes less subsidies. [10]Figures for Bujumbura airport only. [11]1992–93. [12]1990–91.

Cambodia

Official name: Preah Reach Ana Pak Kampuchea (Kingdom of Cambodia).
Form of government: constitutional monarchy with two legislative houses (Senate [61[1]]; National Assembly [122]).
Chief of state: King.
Head of government: Prime Minister[2].
Capital: Phnom Penh.
Official language: Khmer.
Official religion: Buddhism.
Monetary unit: 1 riel = 100 sen; valuation (Sept. 23, 2002) 1 U.S.$ = 3,835 riels; 1 £ = 5,960 riels.

Area and population		area		population
Provinces	**Capitals**	sq mi	sq km	1998 census
Banteay Mean Chey	...	2,579	6,679	577,772
Bat Dambang	Bat Dambang	4,518	11,702	793,129
Kampong Cham	Kampong Cham	3,783	9,799	1,608,914
Kampong Chhnang	Kampong Chhnang	2,132	5,521	417,693
Kampong Spueu	Kampong Spueu	2,709	7,017	598,882
Kampong Thum	Kampong Thum	5,334	13,814	569,060
Kampot	Kampot	1,881	4,873	528,405
Kandal	...	1,378	3,568	1,075,125
Kaoh Kong	Krong Kaoh Kong	4,309	11,160	132,106
Kracheh	Kracheh	4,283	11,094	263,175
Mondol Kiri	Senmonorom	5,517	14,288	32,407
Otdar Mean Cheay	...	2,378	6,158	68,279
Pousat	Pousat	4,900	12,692	360,445
Preah Vihear	Phum Tbeng Mean Cheay	5,324	13,788	119,261
Prey Veaeng	Prey Veaeng	1,885	4,883	946,042
Rotanak Kiri	Lumphat	4,163	10,782	94,243
Siem Reab	Siem Reab	3,976	10,299	696,164
Stueng Traeng	Stueng Traeng	4,283	11,092	81,074
Svay Rieng	Svay Rieng	1,145	2,966	478,252
Takaev	Takaev	1,376	3,563	790,168
Municipalities				
Kaeb	...	130	336	28,660
Pailin	...	310	803	22,906
Phnom Penh	...	112	290	999,804
Preah Sihanouk	...	335	868	155,690
TOTAL LAND AREA		68,740	178,035	
INLAND WATER		1,158	3,000	
TOTAL		69,898	181,035	11,437,656

Demography

Population (2002): 13,414,000.
Density (2002)[3]: persons per sq mi 195.1, persons per sq km 75.3.
Urban-rural (2002): urban 17.0%; rural 83.0%.
Sex distribution (1998): male 48.19%; female 51.81%.
Age breakdown (1998): under 15, 42.8%; 15–29, 26.1%; 30–44, 17.3%; 45–59, 8.6%; 60–74, 4.2%; 75 and over, 1.0%.
Population projection: (2010) 16,218,000; (2020) 19,870,000.
Doubling time: 28 years.
Ethnic composition (1994): Khmer 88.6%; Vietnamese 5.5%; Chinese 3.1%; Cham 2.3%; other (Thai, Lao, and Kola) 0.5%.
Religious affiliation (2000): Buddhist 84.7%; Chinese folk religionist 4.7%; traditional beliefs 4.3%; Muslim 2.3%; Christian 1.1%; other 2.9%.
Major cities (1998): Phnom Penh 999,804; Preah Sihanouk 155,690; Kaeb 28,660; Pailin 22,906.

Vital statistics

Birth rate per 1,000 population (2002): 35.2 (world avg. 21.2).
Death rate per 1,000 population (2002): 10.6 (world avg. 8.9).
Natural increase rate per 1,000 population (2002): 24.6 (world avg. 12.3).
Total fertility rate (avg. births per childbearing woman; 2002): 4.9.
Life expectancy at birth (2002): male 54.0 years; female 59.0 years.
Major causes of death per 100,000 population: n.a.; however, major health problems include tuberculosis, malaria, and pneumonia. Violence, acts of war, and military ordnance (especially unexploded mines) remain hazards.

National economy

Budget (1999). Revenue: 1,224,000,000,000 riels (taxes on international trade 36.0%; indirect taxes 27.1%, of which value-added taxes 13.7%; nontax revenue 28.2%). Expenditures: 1,485,000,000,000 riels (current expenditure 74.4%, of which civil administration 36.1%, defense and security 30.7%; development expenditure 25.6%).
Public debt (external, outstanding; 2000): U.S.$2,180,000,000.
Production (metric tons except as noted). Agriculture, forestry, fishing (1999): rice 3,800,000, bananas 145,000, sugarcane 138,000, roots and tubers 111,000 (of which cassava 67,500, sweet potatoes 25,000), oranges 63,000, corn (maize) 50,000, rubber 40,000, mangoes 33,000, soybeans 27,700, tobacco leaves 10,000; livestock (number of live animals; 1999) 2,821,000 cattle, 2,438,000 pigs, 694,000 buffalo, 16,498,000 chickens and ducks; roundwood (1998) 8,008,000 cu m; fish catch (1997) 114,600. Mining and quarrying (1995): legal mining is confined to fertilizers, salt, and construction materials. Manufacturing (value added in '000,000 riels; 1995): glass and glass products 42,659; cigarettes 1,064.5; wearing apparel 37,567; rubber products 30,114; processed meat, fish, fruits, and vegetables 24,521; sawmilling and planing of wood 18,099; tobacco products 10,163. Construction: n.a. Energy production (consumption): electricity (kW-hr; 1997) 208,000,000 (208,000,000); petroleum products (metric tons; 1997) none (167,000).

Household income and expenditure. Average household size (1998) 5.2.
Gross national product (2000): U.S.$3,150,000,000 (U.S.$260 per capita).

Structure of gross domestic product and labour force					
	1998			1996	
	in value '000,000,000 riels	% of total value		labour force	% of labour force
Agriculture	5,443	50.6		3,732,000	72.6
Mining	33	0.3			
Manufacturing	665	6.2	}		
Construction	794	7.4			
Public utilities	95	0.9			
Transp. and commun.	445	4.1	}	1,406,000	27.4
Trade	1,530	14.3			
Public admin., defense	344	3.2			
Services	1,401	13.0	}		
Other					
TOTAL	10,750	100.0		5,138,000	100.0

Population economically active (1996): total 4,904,294; activity rate of total population 47.4% (participation rates: ages 15 and over, 78.9%; female 52.7%).

Price and earnings indexes (1995 = 100)							
	1995	1996	1997	1998	1999	2000	2001
Consumer price index	100.0	110.1	113.6	130.4	135.6	134.5	133.7
Earnings index	...	...	...	...	...	...	...

Tourism (2000): receipts U.S.$228,000,000; expenditures U.S.$19,000,000.
Land use (1994): forested 69.1%; meadows and pastures 8.5%; agricultural and under permanent cultivation 21.7%; other 0.7%.

Foreign trade[4]

Balance of trade (current prices)						
	1995	1996	1997	1998	1999	2000
U.S.$'000,000	−425	−459	−264	−227	−259	−335
% of total	21.0%	26.1%	14.4%	11.6%	11.8%	10.7%

Imports (1998): U.S.$1,334,000,000 (cigarettes 11.2%; petroleum products 10.4%; motorcycles 2.8%; clothing 1.6%). *Major import sources* (1996): Singapore 34.2%; Thailand 23.9%; Vietnam 7.3%.
Exports (1998): U.S.$999,000,000 (reexports 39.6%; garments 39.0%; sawn timber and logs 17.8%; rubber 2.5%). *Major export destinations* (1996): Thailand 13.0%; Singapore 13.0%; India 9.3%.

Transport and communications

Transport. Railroads (1995): length (1999) 403 mi, 649 km; passenger-km 38,443,600; metric ton-km 7,797,600. Roads (1997): total length 22,226 mi, 35,769 km (paved 8%). Vehicles (1997): passenger cars 52,919; trucks and buses 13,574. Merchant marine (1992): vessels (100 gross tons and over) 3; total deadweight tonnage 3,839. Air transport (1977): passenger-mi 26,098,800, passenger-km 42,000,000; short ton-mi cargo 274,000, metric ton-km cargo 400,000; airports (1997) with scheduled flights 8.

Communications				units
Medium	date	unit	number	per 1,000 persons
Daily newspapers	1996	circulation	17,000	1.7
Radio	1997	receivers	1,340,000	128
Television	1999	receivers	98,000	9.0
Telephones	2001	main lines	33,500	2.5
Cellular telephones	2001	subscribers	223,500	17
Personal computers	2001	units	20,000	1.5
Internet	2001	users	10,000	0.7

Education and health

Educational attainment (1998). Percentage of population age 25 and over having: no formal schooling 2.1%; some primary education 56.6%; primary 24.7%; some secondary 11.8%; secondary and above 4.8%. *Literacy* (1998): percentage of total population age 15 and over literate 67.3%; males literate 79.5%; females literate 57.0%.

Education (1997–98)				student/
	schools	teachers	students	teacher ratio
Primary (age 6–10)	5,026	43,282	2,011,772	46.5
Secondary (age 11–16)	440[5]	16,820	302,951	18.0
Voc., teacher tr.	65[5]	2,315	9,983	4.3
Higher	9[5]	1,001	8,901	8.9

Health: physicians (1994) 1,200 (1 per 7,900 persons); hospital beds (1994) 12,098[6] (1 per 791 persons); infant mortality rate (2002) 74.0.
Food (2000): daily per capita caloric intake 2,070 (vegetable products 91%, animal products 9%); 93% of FAO recommended minimum requirement.

Military

Total active duty personnel (2001)[7]: 140,000 (army 64.3%, navy 2.1%, air force 1.4%, provincial 32.2%). *Military expenditure as percentage of GNP* (1999): 4.0% (world 2.4%); per capita expenditure U.S.$28.

[1]All seats appointed in 1999; all seats to be elected in future. [2]A single prime minister was head of government from November 1998 per the king's forced moral persuasion. [3]Based on land area. [4]Trade balance statistics indicate imports are f.o.b. [5]1992–93. [6]Public hospitals only. [7]Figures include provincial and exclude paramilitary forces.

Internet resources for further information:
• **Cambodian Information Center** http://www.cambodia.org
• **National Institute of Statistics** http://www.nis.gov.kh

Cameroon

Official name: République du Cameroun (French); Republic of Cameroon (English).
Form of government: unitary multiparty republic with one legislative house (National Assembly [180]).
Chief of state: President.
Head of government: Prime Minister.
Capital: Yaoundé.
Official languages: French; English.
Official religion: none.
Monetary unit: 1 CFA franc (CFAF) = 100 centimes; valuation (Sept. 23, 2002) 1 U.S.$ = CFAF 667.00; 1 £ = CFAF 1,036[1].

Area and population

Regions	Capitals	area sq mi	area sq km	population 1987 census
Adamaoua	Ngaoundéré	24,591	63,691	495,200
Centre	Yaoundé	26,613	68,926	1,651,600
Est	Bertoua	42,089	109,011	517,200
Extrême-Nord	Maroua	13,223	34,246	1,855,700
Littoral	Douala	7,814	20,239	1,354,800
Nord	Garoua	25,319	65,576	832,200
Nord-Ouest	Bamenda	6,877	17,810	1,237,400
Ouest	Bafoussam	5,356	13,872	1,339,800
Sud	Ebolowa	18,189	47,110	373,800
Sud-Ouest	Buea	9,448	24,471	838,000
LAND AREA		179,519	464,952	
INLAND WATER		4,051	10,492	
TOTAL		183,569[2]	475,442[2]	10,495,700

Demography

Population (2002): 16,185,000.
Density (2002)[3]: persons per sq mi 90.2, persons per sq km 34.8.
Urban-rural (2001): urban 49.7%; rural 50.3%.
Sex distribution (2001): male 50.22%; female 49.78%.
Age breakdown (2001): under 15, 42.4%; 15–29, 28.0%; 30–44, 15.6%; 45–59, 8.8%; 60–74, 4.2%; 75 and over, 1.0%.
Population projection: (2010) 19,202,000; (2020) 22,869,000.
Doubling time: 29 years.
Ethnic composition (1983): Fang 19.6%; Bamileke and Bamum 18.5%; Duala, Luanda, and Basa 14.7%; Fulani 9.6%; Tikar 7.4%; Mandara 5.7%; Maka 4.9%; Chamba 2.4%; Mbum 1.3%; Hausa 1.2%; French 0.2%; other 14.5%.
Religious affiliation (2000): Roman Catholic 26.4%; traditional beliefs 23.7%; Muslim 21.2%; Protestant 20.7%.
Major cities (1992): Douala 1,200,000; Yaoundé 800,000; Garoua 160,000; Maroua 140,000; Bafoussam 120,000.

Vital statistics

Birth rate per 1,000 population (2001): 36.1 (world avg. 21.2).
Death rate per 1,000 population (2001): 12.0 (world avg. 8.9).
Natural increase rate per 1,000 population (2001): 24.1 (world avg. 12.3).
Total fertility rate (avg. births per childbearing woman; 2001): 4.8.
Life expectancy at birth (2001): male 53.8 years; female 55.4 years.
Major causes of death per 100,000 population: n.a.; however, major health problems include measles, malaria, tuberculosis of respiratory system, anemias, meningitis, and intestinal obstruction and hernia.

National economy

Budget (1998–99). Revenue: CFAF 838,000,000,000 (taxes on goods and services 40.5%; income tax 20.8%; customs duties 16.5%; oil revenue 15.9%). Expenditures: CFAF 1,023,000,000,000 (current expenditure 80.9%, of which debt service 27.6%, wages and salaries 26.9%, goods and services 16.3%, transfers 9.8%; capital expenditure 19.1%).
Public debt (external, outstanding; 2000): U.S.$7,357,000,000.
Gross national product (2000): U.S.$8,644,000,000 (U.S.$580 per capita).

Structure of gross domestic product and labour force

	1998–99 in value CFAF '000,000,000	1998–99 % of total value	1985 labour force	1985 % of labour force
Agriculture	1,789	33.1	2,900,871	74.0
Mining	243	4.5	1,793	0.1
Manufacturing	703	13.0	174,498	4.5
Construction	157	2.9	66,684	1.7
Public utilities	119	2.2	3,522	0.1
Transp. and commun.	} 2,395	} 44.3	51,688	1.3
Trade			154,014	3.9
Finance			8,009	0.2
Services	}	}	292,922	7.5
Public admin., defense				
Other	...	...	263,634	6.7
TOTAL	5,406	100.0	3,917,635	100.0

Household income and expenditure. Average household size (1998) 5.7; average annual income per household (1983)[4] U.S.$420; sources of income: n.a.; expenditure (1993)[4]: food 49.1%, housing 18.0%, transportation and communications 13.0%, health 8.6%, clothing 7.6%, recreation 2.4%.
Population economically active (1991): total 4,740,000; activity rate of total population 40.0% (participation rates [1985]: ages 15–69, 66.3%; female 38.5%; unemployed, n.a.).

Price and earnings indexes (1995 = 100)

	1995	1996	1997	1998	1999	2000	2001
Consumer price index	100.0	103.9	108.9	112.4	114.4	115.8	116.8
Earnings index	...	...	...	...	...	...	...

Production (metric tons except as noted). Agriculture, forestry, fishing (2001): cassava 1,700,000, sugarcane 1,350,000, plantains 1,000,000, bananas 990,000, corn (maize) 850,000, sorghum 450,000, vegetables and melons 450,000, yams 260,000, seed cotton 220,000, sweet potatoes 180,000, palm oil 150,000, cacao 115,000, peanuts (groundnuts) 100,000, millet 71,000, rice 65,000, coffee 61,500, natural rubber 60,000, palm kernels 52,000; livestock (number of live animals) 5,900,000 cattle, 4,400,000 goats, 3,880,000 sheep, 1,350,000 pigs; roundwood (2001) 12,142,670 cu m; fish catch (1999) 95,067. Mining and quarrying (1996): pozzolana 100,000; aluminum 82,000; limestone 50,000; tin ore and concentrate 1. Manufacturing (value added in CFAF '000,000; 1994): beverages 49,314; wood and wood products 42,756; rubber and plastic products 38,928; food products 30,030; iron and steel products 29,424; textiles 20,113; refined petroleum products 17,888; industrial chemicals 8,559; pottery, china, and earthenware 6,773; paper products 3,652. Energy production (consumption): electricity (kW-hr; 1997) 2,758,000,000 (2,758,000,000); coal (metric tons; 1997) 1,000 (1,000); crude petroleum (barrels; 1997) 40,276,000 (4,928,000); petroleum products (metric tons; 1997) 1,045,000 (1,112,000); natural gas, none (n.a.).
Land use (1994): forested 77.1%; meadows and pastures 4.3%; agricultural and under permanent cultivation 15.1%; other 3.5%.
Tourism (1995): receipts U.S.$36,000,000; expenditures U.S.$105,000,000.

Foreign trade

Balance of trade (current prices)

	1994	1995	1996	1997	1998	1999
CFAF '000,000,000	+223.7	+398.8	+277.5	+290.6	+209.4	+112.4
% of total	15.7%	24.4%	18.1%	15.6%	10.7%	6.0%

Imports (1998–99): CFAF 881,500,000,000 (semifinished goods 15.9%, industrial equipment 13.3%, food and beverages 11.3%, minerals 10.6%, transport equipment 10.3%, unrecorded trade 6.1%). *Major import sources:* France 25.6%; Germany 6.4%; U.S. 5.7%; Japan 5.0%; Belgium-Luxembourg 4.8%; Italy 4.3%; The Netherlands 2.6%; United Kingdom 2.6%.
Exports (1998–99): CFAF 993,900,000,000 (crude petroleum 31.6%, lumber 12.1%, coffee 7.5%, cocoa 7.4%, aluminum 5.0%, cotton 4.7%). *Major export destinations:* Italy 22.4%; France 12.6%; Spain 9.4%; The Netherlands 9.4%; Portugal 3.3%; Germany 1.9%.

Transport and communications

Transport. Railroads (1997): route length 625 mi, 1,006 km; (1995) passenger-mi 197,000,000, passenger-km 317,000,000; short ton-mi cargo 556,000,000, metric ton-km cargo 812,000,000. Roads (1997): total length 30,074 mi, 48,400 km (paved 8%). Vehicles (1997): passenger cars 98,000; trucks and buses 64,350. Merchant marine (1992): vessels (100 gross tons and over) 47; total deadweight tonnage 39,797. Air transport (1996): passenger-mi 347,970,000, passenger-km 560,000,000; short ton-mi cargo 56,540,000, metric ton-km cargo 91,000,000; airports (1998) with scheduled flights 5.

Communications

Medium	date	unit	number	units per 1,000 persons
Daily newspapers	1996	circulation	91,000	6.7
Radio	1997	receivers	2,270,000	163
Television	1998	receivers	480,000	33.5
Telephones	2001	main lines	101,400	6.7
Cellular telephones	2001	subscribers	310,000	20.4
Personal computers	2001	units	60,000	3.9
Internet	2001	users	45,000	3.0

Education and health

Educational attainment (1976). Percentage of population age 15 and over having: no schooling 51.1%; primary education 41.7%; some postprimary 0.2%; secondary 5.7%; some postsecondary 0.3%; higher 0.2%; other 0.8%.
Literacy (1995): percentage of total population age 15 and over literate 63.4%; males literate 75.0%; females literate 52.1%.

Education (1994–95)

	schools	teachers	students	student/ teacher ratio
Primary (age 6–14)	6,801	40,970	1,896,722	46.3
Secondary (age 15–24)	388[5]	14,917	459,068	30.8
Vocational	220[5]	5,885	91,779	15.6
Higher[6]	5[5]	1,086	33,177	30.5

Health: physicians (1996) 1,031 (1 per 13,510 persons); hospital beds (1988) 29,285 (1 per 371 persons); infant mortality rate (2001) 69.8.
Food (2000): daily per capita caloric intake 2,255 (vegetable products 94%, animal products 6%); 97% of FAO recommended minimum requirement.

Military

Total active duty personnel (2001): 13,100 (army 87.8%, navy 9.9%, air force 2.3%). *Military expenditure as percentage of GNP* (1999): 1.8% (world 2.4%); per capita expenditure U.S.$10.

[1]Formerly pegged to the French franc and since Jan. 1, 2002, to the euro at the rate of 1 € = CFAF 655.96. [2]Detail does not add to total given because of rounding. [3]Based on land area. [4]Weights of consumer price index components. [5]1986–87. [6]1990–91.

Internet resources for further information:
• Investir en Zone Franc http://www.izf.net/izf/Index.htm

Canada

Official name: Canada.
Form of government: federal multiparty parliamentary state with two legislative houses (Senate [105]; House of Commons [301]).
Chief of state: Queen of Canada (British Monarch).
Representative of chief of state: Governor-General.
Head of government: Prime Minister.
Capital: Ottawa.
Official languages: English; French.
Official religion: none.
Monetary unit: 1 Canadian dollar (Can$) = 100 cents; valuation (Sept. 23, 2002) 1 U.S.$ = Can$1.57; 1 £ = Can$2.45.

Area and population		area		population
				2001
Provinces	Capitals	sq mi	sq km	census
Alberta	Edmonton	255,541	661,848	3,064,249
British Columbia	Victoria	364,764	944,735	4,095,934
Manitoba	Winnipeg	250,116	647,797	1,150,034
New Brunswick	Fredericton	28,150	72,908	757,077
Newfoundland and Labrador	St. John's	156,453	405,212	533,761
Nova Scotia	Halifax	21,345	55,284	942,691
Ontario	Toronto	415,599	1,076,395	11,874,436
Prince Edward Island	Charlottetown	2,185	5,660	138,514
Quebec	Quebec	595,391	1,542,056	7,410,504
Saskatchewan	Regina	251,367	651,036	1,015,783
Territories				
Northwest Territories	Yellowknife	519,735	1,346,106	40,860
Nunavut[1]	Iqaluit	808,185	2,093,190	28,159
Yukon Territory	Whitehorse	186,272	482,443	29,885
TOTAL		3,855,103	9,984,670	31,081,887[2]

Demography

Population (2002): 31,244,000.
Density (2002)[3]: persons per sq mi 8.8, persons per sq km 3.4.
Urban-rural (2001): urban 78.9%; rural 21.1%.
Sex distribution (2001): male 49.51%; female 50.49%.
Age breakdown (2001): under 15, 18.8%; 15–29, 20.3%; 30–44, 24.4%; 45–59, 19.7%; 60–74, 11.1%; 75 and over, 5.7%.
Population projection: (2010) 33,132,000; (2020) 35,187,000.
Doubling time: not applicable; doubling time exceeds 100 years.
Ethnic origin (1996): British 11.5%; French 9.4%; other European 13.1%, of which Southern European 4.8%, Western European 3.9%, Eastern European 3.0%; Asian origin 7.0%; Amerindian and Inuit (Eskimo) 1.7%; Latin American origin 1.4%; Arab origin 0.6%; African origin 0.5%; multiple origin and other 54.8%[4].
Religious affiliation (2000): Roman Catholic 41.8%; Protestant 39.7%; Eastern Orthodox 1.9%; Jewish 1.3%; Muslim 1.0%; Hindu 1.0%; Buddhist 0.8%; nonreligious 10.9%; other 1.6%.
Major metropolitan areas (2001): Toronto 4,881,400; Montreal 3,511,800; Vancouver 2,078,800; Ottawa-Hull 1,106,900; Calgary 971,500; Edmonton 956,800; Quebec 693,100; Winnipeg 684,800; Hamilton 680,600; Kitchener 431,700.

Other metropolitan areas (2001)					
	population		population		population
Chicoutimi-Jonquière	158,700	Regina	198,100	Sherbrooke	154,900
		St. Catharines–		Sudbury	156,700
Halifax	359,200	Niagara	393,100	Trois Rivières	141,500
London	426,300	St. John's	176,200	Victoria	318,800
Oshawa	305,300	Saskatoon	230,500	Windsor	313,800

Place of birth (1996): 83.4% native-born; 16.6% foreign-born, of which U.K. 2.2%, other European 4.2%, Asian countries 5.2%, U.S. 0.8%, other 4.2%.
Mobility (1996). Population living in the same residence as in 1991: 56.7%; different residence, same municipality 23.0%; same province, different municipality 3.3%; different province 13.4%; different country 3.5%.
Households (1999). Total number of households 11,553,000. Average household size 2.5; (1997) 1 person 25.2%, 2 persons 33.0%, 3 persons 16.7%, 4 persons 16.3%, 5 or more persons 8.8%. Family households (1999): 8,139,700 (70.6%), nonfamily 3,413,300 (29.4%, of which 1 person 83.6%).
Immigration (1999–2000): permanent immigrants admitted 252,088; from Asia 62.1%, of which India 11.6%, Philippines 5.6%, Vietnam 0.7%, Hong Kong 0.3%; United States 2.4%; United Kingdom 2.1%; refugee arrivals 22,899.

Vital statistics

Birth rate per 1,000 population (2000): 10.8 (world avg. 22.5); (1997) legitimate 72.3%; illegitimate 27.7%.
Death rate per 1,000 population (2000): 7.5 (world avg. 9.0).
Natural increase rate per 1,000 population (2000): 3.3 (world avg. 13.5).
Total fertility rate (avg. births per childbearing woman; 2000): 1.6.
Marriage rate per 1,000 population (2000): 5.0.
Divorce rate per 1,000 population (2000): 2.2.
Life expectancy at birth (2000): male 76.0 years; female 83.0 years.
Major causes of death per 100,000 population (1997): diseases of the circulatory system 220.8; malignant neoplasms (cancers) 181.5; diseases of the respiratory system 52.7; accidents and violence 39.7 (including suicide 12.0).

Social indicators

Educational attainment (1996). Percentage of population age 15 and over having: no formal schooling or not known 4.2%; at least primary education 12.3%; some secondary 19.6%; completed secondary 19.8%; postsecondary 30.5%; university graduates 13.6%.

Distribution of income (1996)				
percentage of household income by quintile				
1	2	3	4	5 (highest)
6.1%	11.9%	17.4%	24.0%	40.6%

Quality of working life. Average workweek (1997): 31.3 hours. Annual rate per 100,000 workers for (1997): injury, accident, or industrial illness 1,330; death 2.7. Average days lost to labour stoppages per 1,000 employee-workdays (1997): 0.9. Average duration of journey to work (1996): n.a.; mode of transportation: automobile 80.6%, public transportation 10.1%, other 9.3%. Rate per 1,000 workers of discouraged (unemployed no longer seeking work; 1983): 10.5.
Access to services (1999). Proportion of households having access to: electricity 100.0%; public water supply 99.8%[5]; public sewage collection 99.3%[5].
Social participation. Eligible voters participating in last national election (November 2000): 61.2%. Population over 18 years of age participating in voluntary work (2000): 26.7%. Union membership in total workforce (1999): 32.9%. Practicing religious population in total affiliated population (1996): 92.5%.
Social deviance (2000). Offense rate per 100,000 population for: violent crime 981, of which assault 758.9, sexual assault 78.2, homicide 1.6; property crime 4,067, of which auto theft 521, burglary 954.
Leisure (1998). Favourite leisure activities (hours weekly): television 15.4; social time 13.3; reading 2.8; sports and entertainment 1.4.
Material well-being (1998). Households possessing: automobile 78.8%, of which two or more 34.5%; telephone 98.2%; colour television 98.8%; refrigerator 99.8%; central air conditioner 33.1%; cable television 66.5%; video recorder 88.1%; microwave oven 88.7%; home computers 45.1%.

National economy

Gross national product (2000): U.S.$649,829,000,000 (U.S.$21,130 per capita).

Structure of gross domestic product and labour force				
	2000			
	in value Can$'000,000[6]	% of total value	labour force	% of labour force
Agriculture	22,862	2.5	655,700	4.1
Mining	36,125	3.9		
Manufacturing	169,471	18.2	2,344,800	14.7
Construction	48,534	5.2	866,100	5.4
Public utilities	28,234	3.0	116,400	0.7
Transportation	44,658	4.8	779,800	4.9
Trade	105,479	11.3	2,318,100	14.5
Finance	177,925	19.1	867,000	5.4
Pub. admin., defense	51,009	5.6	761,700	4.8
Services[7]	245,259	26.4	6,200,000	38.7
Other	—	—	1,089,600[8]	6.8[8]
TOTAL	929,556[9]	100.0	15,999,200	100.0

Budget (1999–2000). Revenue: Can$172,532,000,000 (individual income taxes 47.8%, value-added tax 20.3%, corporate income tax 13.0%, contributions to social security 10.8%, import duties 1.3%). Expenditures: Can$169,966,000,000 (social services 29.6%, public debt interest 24.5%, defense and social protection 10.8%, education 2.6%, health 1.0%).
National debt (1997): Can$619,710,000,000.
Tourism (2000): receipts U.S.$10,704,000,000; expenditures U.S.$12,140,000,000.

Manufacturing, mining, and construction enterprises (1999)			
	no. of estab-lishments[10]	no. of employees	weekly wages as a % of avg. of all mfg. wages	annual value added[10] (Can$'000,000)
Manufacturing				
Food and beverages	3,202	230,100	102.1	20,110
Transport equipment	1,224	246,300	148.4	19,430
Chemicals and related products	1,396	90,000	145.7	12,860
Machinery	4,000	92,100	140.1	9,130
Electrical and electronic products	1,176	129,900	142.3	8,520
Printing, publishing, and related products	4,655	150,300	107.7	8,500
Paper and related products	651	99,300	157.5	7,890
Wood	2,201	142,800	113.0	7,880
Primary metals	417	84,000	157.0	7,790
Metal fabricating	3,287	182,000	123.2	6,290
Rubber and plastic	1,394	104,000	112.8	5,900
Textiles	1,057	53,300	91.0	3,600
Nonmetallic mineral products	1,519	51,500	122.8	3,440
Wearing apparel	1,923	89,400	72.4	3,220
Petroleum and coal products	170	14,800	180.2	2,560
Furniture and fixtures	1,965	61,800	94.6	2,310
Tobacco products industries	17	4,300	211.7	1,220
Mining	13,692	169,700	182.3	29,650
Construction	203,253	524,500	114.5	28,182

Production (metric tons except as noted). Agriculture, forestry, fishing (2001): wheat 20,695,300, barley 11,103,300, rapeseed 7,778,000, corn (maize) 7,550,000, potatoes 4,568,500, oats 2,838,300, dry peas 2,175,400, vegetables 2,135,000 (of which tomatoes 670,000, carrots 278,608, onions 189,334, cabbage 167,450), soybeans 2,040,100, sugar beets 821,000, linseed 703,700, apples 580,000; livestock (number of live animals) 12,860,000 cattle, 12,600,000 pigs, 694,800 sheep, 385,000 horses; roundwood (2000) 148,871,000 cu m; fish catch (1999) 1,135,516. Mining and quarrying (1999): iron ore 33,004,000; zinc 960,099; copper 580,036; nickel 177,029; lead 156,102; uranium 9,892; molybdenum 6,293; silver 1,173 kg; gold 157,790 kg. Manufacturing (value of shipments in Can$'000,000; 1999): transportation equipment 125,034.3; food 52,-352.8; electrical machinery 36,760.6; paper products 33,150.3; wood industries 30,600.6; metal products 26,883.9; machinery 16,890.5; rubber and plastic products 16,885.0; printing and publishing 16,526.3; furniture 8,506.4; wearing apparel 6,996.3; textiles 3,683.3. Construction (value of building permits in Can$'000,000; 1999): residential 19,956.9; nonresidential 15,813.5.

Retail trade (2000)

	no. of enterprises	no. of employees[11]	weekly wages as a % of all wages	annual sales (Can$'000,000)
Motor vehicle dealers	...	79,800	143.5	73,104
Food stores	...	213,400	84.2	61,090
Service stations	...	63,700	143.5	22,364
Department stores	...	[12]	81.7	[12]
Clothing stores	...	50,200	79.4	15,278
Pharmacies	...	52,400	...	13,499
Furniture and appliance stores	...	62,100	119.2	15,159
Automotive stores	...	31,500	143.5	88,687
General merchandise	...	231,700[12]	81.7	31,297[12]
Sporting goods	...	...	...	332[13]
General stores	...	[12]	81.7	[12]
Hardware stores	...	17,300	81.7	486[13]
Shoe stores	...	18,400	79.4	1,770
Jewelry stores	...	14,000	...	315[13]
Variety stores	...	45,100	92.0	805[13]

Energy production (consumption): electricity (kW-hr; 1999) 541,900,000,000 (545,460,300,000); coal (metric tons; 2000) 69,164,000 (60,761,000); crude petroleum (barrels; 1997) 719,729,000 (608,411,000); petroleum products (metric tons; 1997) 95,026,000 (81,240,000); natural gas (cu m; 1999) 163,-384,000,000 ([1998] 89,163,000,000).

Population economically active (2000): total 15,999,200; activity rate of total population 52.0% (participation rates: ages 15 and over 65.9%; female 45.9%; unemployed [2001] 7.3%).

Price and earnings indexes (1995 = 100)

	1995	1996	1997	1998	1999	2000	2001
Consumer price index	100.0	100.4	101.3	101.2	102.9	108.1	111.7
Hourly earnings index[14]	100.0	103.2	104.1	106.3	106.4	112.3	114.8

Household income and expenditure (1999). Average household size 2.6; average annual income per family (1999) Can$63,818 (U.S.$43,413); sources of income (1995): wages and salaries 57.0%, transfer payments 20.7%, property and entrepreneurial income 13.7%, profits 8.6%; expenditure (1999): housing 27.2%, food, alcohol, and tobacco 19.3%, transportation and communications 18.2%, recreation 7.9%, utilities 6.4%, clothing 6.2%, household durable goods 3.9%, health 3.3%, education 2.0%.

Financial aggregates

	1995	1996	1997	1998	1999	2000
Exchange rate, Can$ per:						
U.S. dollar	1.37	1.37	1.42	1.53	1.44	1.50
£	2.17	2.33	2.34	2.55	2.33	2.24
SDR	2.03	1.97	1.93	2.16	1.98	1.95
International reserves (U.S.$)						
Total (excl. gold; '000,000)	15,049	20,422	17,823	23,308	28,126	31,924
SDRs ('000,000)	1,177	1,168	1,126	1,098	527	574
Reserve pos. in IMF ('000,000)	1,243	1,226	1,575	2,299	3,168	2,509
Foreign exchange ('000,000)	12,629	18,028	15,122	19,991	24,432	28,841
Gold ('000,000 fine troy oz)	3.41	3.09	3.09	2.49	1.81	1.18
% world reserves	0.38	0.34	0.35	0.26	0.18	0.12
Interest and prices						
Central bank discount (%)	5.79	3.25	4.50	5.25	5.00	6.00
Govt. bond yield (%)	8.28	7.50	6.42	5.47	5.69	5.89
Industrial share prices (1995 = 100)	100.0	118.8	145.7	152.4	159.2	216.7
Balance of payments (U.S.$'000,000)						
Balance of visible trade,	22,341	31,091	17,223	12,775	22,756	36,610
of which:						
Imports, f.o.b.	−167,513	−174,352	−200,516	−204,631	−220,064	−244,538
Exports, f.o.b.	189,854	205,443	217,739	217,406	242,820	281,148
Balance of invisibles	−31,034	−27,713	−27,288	−23,908	−25,029	−23,944
Balance of payments, current account	−8,693	−3,378	−10,065	−11,133	−2,273	+12,666

Land use (1994): forested 53.6%; meadows and pastures 3.0%; agricultural and under permanent cultivation 4.9%; built-on, wasteland, and other 38.5%.

Foreign trade

Balance of trade (current prices)

	1995	1996	1997	1998	1999	2000	2001
Can$'000,000,000	+38.7	+42.2	+25.5	+19.8	+35.1	+59.3	+58.9
% of total	7.9%	8.3%	4.5%	3.2%	5.2%	7.5%	7.9%

Imports (2000): Can$363,281,300,000 (1999; machinery and transport equipment 56.3%, of which motor vehicles 23.2%; chemical products 6.9%; food 5.4%; petroleum and energy products 3.3%; forestry products 0.8%). *Major import sources* (1999): U.S. 67.2%; Japan 4.7%; Mexico 3.0%; China 2.8%; U.K. 2.5%; Germany 2.2%; France 1.7%; Taiwan 1.4%; Italy 1.1%; South Korea 1.1%.

Exports (2000): Can$422,558,700,000 (1999; machinery and transport equipment 50.3%, of which motor vehicles 26.5%; mineral fuels 8.2%, of which crude petroleum 3.1%; food 7.1%; lumber 5.5%; newsprint and paper products 3.5%; wood pulp 1.9%). *Major export destinations* (1999): U.S. 86.8%; Japan 2.5%; U.K. 1.3%; South Korea 0.6%.

Trade by commodities (1998)

	imports		exports	
SITC Group	U.S.$'000,000	%	U.S.$'000,000	%
00 Food and live animals	9,629.6	4.8	12,443.0	5.8
01 Beverages and tobacco	1,065.2	0.5	1,039.0	0.5
02 Crude materials, excluding fuels	5,718.0	2.8	19,337.5	9.0
03 Mineral fuels, lubricants, and related materials	6,847.8	3.5	17,584.3	8.2
04 Animal and vegetable oils, fats, and waxes	...	...	...	...
05 Chemicals and related products, n.e.s.	16,363.1	8.1	11,792.8	5.5
06 Basic manufactures	27,121.9	13.5	34,591.1	16.1
07 Machinery and transport equipment	105,052.9	52.2	88,180.3	41.2
08 Miscellaneous manufactured articles	23,369.9	11.6	13,996.2	6.5
09 Goods not classified by kind	5,568.9	2.8	14,280.2	6.7
TOTAL	201,219.3[15]	100.0[15]	214,187.9[15]	100.0[15]

Direction of trade (1999)

	imports		exports	
	U.S.$'000,000	%	U.S.$'000,000	%
Africa	1,440	0.7	993	0.4
Asia	28,838	13.8	11,587	4.9[15]
China	6,017	2.9	1,673	0.7
Japan	10,104	4.8	5,254	2.2
Taiwan	3,100	1.5	740	0.3
Other	9,617	4.6	3,920	1.6
Americas	153,335	73.2	211,454	89.4
United States	143,498	68.5	208,013	88.0
Mexico	6,263	3.0	1,025	0.4
Other Americas	3,574	1.7	2,416	1.0
Europe	24,904	11.9	11,587	4.9
EU	21,524	10.3	10,427	4.4
Other Europe	3,380	1.6	1,160	0.5
Oceania	1,077	0.5	758	0.3
TOTAL	214,161[15, 16]	100.0[15, 16]	237,337[15]	100.0[15]

Transport and communications

Transport. Railroads (1998): length 65,403 km; passenger-km 1,458,000,000; metric ton-km cargo 299,508,000,000. Roads (1999): total length 901,903 km (paved 35%). Vehicles (1998): passenger cars 13,887,270; trucks and buses 3,694,125. Merchant marine (1993): vessels (100 gross tons and over) 1,049; total deadweight tonnage 1,910,000. Air transport (2000): passenger-km 68,202,000,000; metric ton-km cargo 1,786,600,000; airports (1997) with scheduled flights 269.

Communications

Medium	date	unit	number	units per 1,000 persons
Daily newspapers	1996	circulation	4,718,000	159
Radio	1997	receivers	32,300,000	1,077
Television	1998	receivers	21,450,000	715
Telephones	2001	main lines	20,319,000	655
Cellular telephones	2001	subscribers	9,923,000	320
Personal computers	2001	units	12,000,000	390
Internet	2001	users	13,500,000	435

Education and health

Literacy (1996): total population age 15 and over literate virtually 100%.

Education (1998–99)

	schools[17]	teachers	students	student/ teacher ratio
Primary (age 6–14) } Secondary (age 14–18) }	15,566	296,901	5,369,716	18.1
Postsecondary	270	65,429	494,955	7.6
Higher[17]	75	33,702	573,099	17.0

Health: physicians (2000) 60,559 (1 per 508 persons); hospital beds (1997) 161,867 (1 per 185 persons); infant mortality rate (2000) 5.1.
Food (1999): daily per capita caloric intake 3,161 (vegetable products 71%, animal products 29%); 119% of FAO recommended minimum requirement.

Military

Total active duty personnel (2001): 56,800 (army 32.7%, navy 15.8%, air force 23.7%, not identified by service 27.8%). *Military expenditure as percentage of GNP* (1999): 1.4% (world 2.4%); per capita expenditure U.S.$269.

[1]Nunavut came into existence on April 1, 1999. [2]Preliminary unadjusted 2001 census total equals 30,007,094. [3]Based on land area of 3,551,023 sq mi (9,093,507 sq km). [4]Includes 35.8% population of mixed origin. [5]1990. [6]At prices of 1997. [7]Services includes communications. [8]Unemployed. [9]GDP at current values in 2000 was Can$1,067,956,-000,000. [10]1993. [11]1984. [12]Department and General stores included with General merchandise. [13]1997. [14]Manufacturing only. [15]Detail does not add to total because of discrepancies in estimates. [16]Total for imports includes U.S.$3,299,000,000 (1.7% of total imports; mostly special transactions) not distributable by region. [17]1997–98.

Internet resources for further information:
• Statistics Canada http://www.statcan.ca

Cape Verde

Official name: República de Cabo Verde (Republic of Cape Verde).
Form of government: multiparty republic with one legislative house (National Assembly [72]).
Chief of state: President.
Head of government: Prime Minister.
Capital: Praia.
Official language: Portuguese.
Official religion: none.
Monetary unit: 1 escudo (C.V.Esc.)[1] = 100 centavos; valuation (Sept. 23, 2002) 1 U.S.$ = C.V.Esc. 119.80; 1 £ = C.V.Esc. 174.24.

Area and population

Island Groups Islands/Counties[2] Counties	Capitals	area sq mi	area sq km	population 2000 census
Leeward Islands		696[3]	1,803	287,323
Brava	Nova Sintra	26	67	6,820
Fogo				
Mosteiros[4]	...	} 184	476	9,479
São Filipe	São Filipe			27,930
Maio	Porto Inglês	104	269	6,742
Santiago		383	991	236,352
Praia	Praia	153	396	106,052
Santa Catarina	Assomada	94	243	49,970
Santa Cruz	Pedra Badejo	58	149	32,822
São Domingos[4]	...			13,296
São Miguel[4]	...	} 78	203	16,153
Tarrafal	Tarrafal			18,059
Windward Islands		861[3]	2,230	147,489
Boa Vista	Sal Rei	239	620	4,193
Sal	Santa Maria	83	216	14,792
Santo Antão		300	779	47,124
Paúl	Pombas	21	54	8,325
Porto Novo	Porto Novo	215	558	17,239
Ribeira Grande	Ponta do Sol	64	167	21,560
São Nicolau	Ribeira Brava	150	388	13,536
São Vicente[5]	Mindelo	88	227	67,844
TOTAL		1,557	4,033	434,812

Demography

Population (2002): 453,000.
Density (2002): persons per sq mi 290.9, persons per sq km 112.3.
Urban-rural (2000): urban 53.3%; rural 46.7%.
Sex distribution (2000): male 48.42%; female 51.58%.
Age breakdown (2000): under 15, 43.6%; 15–29, 24.8%; 30–44, 17.1%; 45–59, 5.8%; 60–74, 6.3%; 75 and over, 2.4%.
Population projection: (2010) 531,794; (2020) 619,410.
Doubling time: 32 years.
Ethnic composition (2000): Cape Verdean *mestico* (black-white admixture) 69.6%; Fulani 12.2%; Balanta 10.0%; Mandyako 4.6%; Portuguese white 2.0%; other 1.6%.
Religious affiliation (2000): Roman Catholic 91.4%; Muslim 2.8%; other 5.8%.
Major cities (2000): Praia 94,757; Mindelo 62,970; São Filipe 7,894.

Vital statistics

Birth rate per 1,000 population (2001): 28.7 (world avg. 21.2); (1989) legitimate 28.9%; illegitimate 71.1%.
Death rate per 1,000 population (2001): 7.2 (world avg. 8.9).
Natural increase rate per 1,000 population (2001): 21.5 (world avg. 12.3).
Total fertility rate (avg. births per childbearing woman; 2001): 4.0.
Marriage rate per 1,000 population (1990): 4.5.
Life expectancy at birth (2001): male 65.9 years; female 72.6 years.
Major causes of death per 100,000 population (1987): enteritis and other diarrheal diseases 97.4; heart disease 77.9; malignant neoplasms (cancers) 47.9; pneumonia 46.4; accidents, poisoning, and violence 44.0.

National economy

Budget (2000). Revenue: C.V.Esc. 13,228,000,000 (tax revenue 88.9%, of which taxes on international trade 52.9%, income taxes 29.8%, other taxes 6.2%; nontax revenue 11.1%). Expenditures: C.V.Esc. 29,114,000,000 (current expenditure 75.5%, of which transfers 23.5%, wages and salaries 22.1%, public debt 6.0%, goods and services 1.6%; capital expenditure 24.5%).
Public debt (external, outstanding; 2000): U.S.$314,600,000.
Production (metric tons except as noted). Agriculture, forestry, fishing (2001): corn (maize) 21,469, sugarcane 14,000, bananas 6,000, coconuts 5,500, vegetables (including melons) 5,000, fruits (except melons) 4,700, sweet potatoes 3,800, cassava 3,300, potatoes 1,500; livestock (number of live animals) 636,000 pigs, 110,000 goats, 21,500 cattle, 8,450 sheep; roundwood, n.a.; fish catch (1999) 10,371. Mining and quarrying (2000): salt 2,000. Manufacturing (1999): flour 15,901; bread 5,628[6]; soap 833; paint 628[7]; canned tuna 337[6]; cigarettes 41 kg; beer 4,104,546 litres; soft drinks 922,714[7] litres. Energy production (consumption): electricity (kW-hr; 2000) 148,783,000,000 (130,792,-000,000); coal, none (none); crude petroleum, none (none); petroleum products (metric tons; 1999) none (97,346); natural gas, none (none).
Tourism: receipts from visitors (2000) U.S.$23,000,000; expenditures by nationals abroad (1998) U.S.$24,000,000.
Land use (1994): forest 0.2%; pasture 6.2%; agriculture 11.2%; other 82.4%.
Gross national product (2000): U.S.$588,000,000 (U.S.$1,330 per capita).

Structure of gross domestic product and labour force

	2000 in value C.V.Esc. '000,000	2000 % of total value	1990 labour force	1990 % of labour force
Agriculture	7,031	10.9	29,876	24.7
Manufacturing			5,520	4.6
Public utilities	} 5,907	9.1	883	0.7
Mining			410	0.3
Construction	5,448	8.4	22,722	18.9
Transp. and commun.	11,759	18.2	6,138	5.1
Trade	14,311	22.2	12,747	10.6
Finance	7,426	11.5	821	0.7
Pub. admin., defense	7,341	11.3	} 17,358	14.4
Services	1,932	3.0		
Other	3,525[8]	5.4[8]	24,090	20.0
TOTAL	64,680	100.0	120,565	100.0

Population economically active (1997): total 160,000; activity rate of total population 41.2% (participation rates (1990): ages 15–64, 64.3%; female 39.0%; unemployed [1990] 25.8%).

Price and earnings indexes (1995 = 100)

	1994	1995	1996	1997	1998	1999	2000
Consumer price index	92.0	100.0	106.0	115.0	120.0	126.0	123.0
Monthly earnings index	87.9	100.0	...	...	...	...	...

Household income and expenditure. Average household size (2000) 4.6; income per household: n.a.; sources of income: n.a.; expenditure (1988): food 51.1%, housing, fuel, and power 13.5%, beverages and tobacco 11.8%, transportation and communications 8.8%, household durable goods 6.9%, other 7.9%.

Foreign trade

Balance of trade (current prices)

	1995	1996	1997	1998	1999	2000
U.S.$'000,000	−208.4	−176.0	−173.4	−185.2	−215.2	−193.6
% of total	80.6%	74.8%	69.7%	80.4%	93.2%	80.2%

Imports (2000): C.V.Esc. 25,212,000,000 (food 31.3%, machinery and apparatus 17.8%, nonmetallic mineral products 10.8%, transport equipment 10.4%, metal products 7.2%, chemicals 7.0%). *Major import sources* (2000): Portugal 52.4%; The Netherlands 13.0%; France 4.4%; U.S. 3.6%; Spain 2.5%.
Exports (2000): C.V.Esc. 2,774,000,000 (domestic export 45.9%, of which shoes 23.8%, clothing 16.1%, fish and fish preparations 3.4%, other 2.6%; reexports 54.1%). *Major export destinations* (2000): Portugal 80.1%; United States 11.4%; Spain 3.5%.

Transport and communications

Transport. Railroads: none. Roads (1999): total length 684 mi, 1,100 km (paved [1996] 78%). Vehicles (2000): passenger cars 13,473; trucks and buses 3,085. Air transport (2001)[9]: passenger-mi 171,000,000, passenger-km 276,000,000; short ton-mi cargo (1998) 16,200,000, metric ton-km cargo 26,000,000; airports (1997) with scheduled flights 9.

Communications

Medium	date	unit	number	units per 1,000 persons
Radio	1997	receivers	71,000	179
Television	1999	receivers	2,000	4.7
Telephones	2001	main lines	62,300	143
Cellular telephones	2001	subscribers	31,500	72
Internet	2001	users	12,000	27

Education and health

Educational attainment (1990). Percentage of population age 25 and over having: no formal schooling 47.9%; primary 40.9%; incomplete secondary 3.9%; complete secondary 1.4%; higher 1.5%; unknown 4.4%. *Literacy* (1999): total population age 15 and over literate 73.6%; males 84.5%; females 65.1%.

Education (1997–98)

	schools	teachers	students	student/teacher ratio
Primary (age 7–12)	370[10]	3,219	91,777	28.5
Secondary (age 13–17)[11]	...	1,372	31,602	23.0
Voc., teacher tr.[11]	...	...	...	...
Higher	...	...	...	...

Health (1998): physicians 165 (1 per 2,574 persons); hospital beds 792 (1 per 513 persons); infant mortality rate per 1,000 live births (2001) 53.2.
Food (2000): daily per capita caloric intake 3,278 (vegetable products 86%, animal products 14%); 141% of FAO recommended minimum requirement.

Military

Total active duty personnel (2001): 1,200 (army 83.3%, air force 8.3%, coast guard 8.4%). *Military expenditure as percentage of GNP* (1999): 0.9% (world 2.4%); per capita expenditure U.S.$13.

---

[1]Formerly pegged to the Portuguese escudo and since Jan. 1, 2002, to the euro at the rate of €1 = C.V.Esc. 110.27. [2]Island/county areas are coterminous except Fogo, Santiago, and Santo Antão islands. [3]Detail does not add to total given because of rounding. [4]Created after the 1990 census. [5]Includes Santa Luzia Island, which is uninhabited. [6]1995. [7]1996. [8]Taxes and duties on imports. [9]TACV airline only. [10]1991. [11]Includes vocational.

Internet resources for further information:
• **Instituto Nacional de Estatística de Cabo Verde** http://www.ine.cv
• **Banco de Cabo Verde** http://www.bcv.cv

Central African Republic

Official name: République Centrafricaine (Central African Republic).
Form of government: multiparty republic with one legislative body (National Assembly [109[1]]).
Chief of state: President.
Head of government: Prime Minister.
Capital: Bangui.
Official languages: French; Sango.
Official religion: none.
Monetary unit: 1 CFA franc (CFAF) = 100 centimes; valuation (Sept. 23, 2002) 1 U.S.$ = CFAF 667.00; 1 £ = CFAF 1,037[2].

Area and population

Prefectures	Capitals	area sq mi	area sq km	population 1988 census
Bamingui-Bangoran	Ndélé	22,471	58,200	28,643
Basse-Kotto	Mobaye	6,797	17,604	194,750
Haut-Mbomou	Obo	21,440	55,530	27,113
Haute-Kotto	Bria	33,456	86,650	58,838
Kemo	Sibut	6,642	17,204	82,884
Lobaye	Mbaïki	7,427	19,235	169,554
Mambéré-Kadéï	Berbérati	11,661	30,203	230,364
Mbomou	Bangassou	23,610	61,150	119,252
Nana-Gribizi	Kaga-Bandoro	7,721	19,996	95,497
Nana-Mambéré	Bouar	10,270	26,600	191,970
Ombella-M'poko	Boali	12,292	31,835	180,857
Ouaka	Bambari	19,266	49,900	208,332
Ouham	Bossangoa	19,402	50,250	262,950
Ouham-Pendé	Bozoum	12,394	32,100	287,653
Sangha-Mbaéré	Nola	7,495	19,412	65,961
Vakaga	Birao	17,954	46,500	32,118
Autonomous commune				
Bangui	Bangui	26	67	451,690
TOTAL		240,324	622,436	2,688,426

Demography

Population (2002): 3,643,000.
Density (2002): persons per sq mi 15.2, persons per sq km 5.9.
Urban-rural (2001): urban 41.7%; rural 58.3%.
Sex distribution (2001): male 49.43%; female 50.57%.
Age breakdown (2001): under 15, 43.5%; 15–29, 28.0%; 30–44, 14.9%; 45–59, 8.1%; 60–74, 4.2%; 75 and over, 1.3%.
Population projection: (2010) 4,135,000; (2020) 4,672,000.
Doubling time: 37 years.
Ethnolinguistic composition (1988): Gbaya (Baya) 23.7%; Banda 23.4%; Mandjia 14.7%; Ngbaka 7.6%; Sara 6.5%; Mbum 6.3%; Kare 2.4%; French 0.1%; other 15.3%.
Religious affiliation (2000): Christian 67.8%, of which Roman Catholic 18.4%, Protestant 14.4%, African Christian 11.6%, other Christian 23.4%; Muslim 15.6%; traditional beliefs 15.4%; other 1.2%.
Major cities (1994): Bangui 524,000; Berbérati 47,000; Bouar 43,000; Bambari 41,000; Carnot 41,000; Bossangoa 33,000.

Vital statistics

Birth rate per 1,000 population (2001): 37.1 (world avg. 21.2).
Death rate per 1,000 population (2001): 18.5 (world avg. 8.9).
Natural increase rate per 1,000 population (2001): 18.6 (world avg. 12.3).
Total fertility rate (avg. births per childbearing woman; 2001): 4.9.
Life expectancy at birth (2001): male 42.2 years; female 45.5 years.

National economy

Budget (1999). Revenue: CFAF 59,700,000,000 (taxes 88.0%, of which international trade tax 38.0%, indirect domestic tax 30.1%, taxes on income and profits 19.9%; nontax receipts 12.0%). Expenditures: CFAF 116,100,000,000 (current expenditure 49.0%, of which wages 23.3%; public investment program 51.0%).
Production (metric tons except as noted). Agriculture, forestry, fishing (2001): cassava 561,700, yams 360,000, bananas 118,000, peanuts (groundnuts) 121,900, taro 100,000, corn (maize) 107,000, sugarcane 90,000, plantains 83,000, sorghum 50,300, sesame seeds 32,400, pulses 31,000, seed cotton 30,000, paddy rice 25,300, oranges 24,000, millet 12,000, coffee 13,000; livestock (number of live animals; 2002) 3,273,000 cattle, 2,921,000 goats, 738,000 pigs, 246,000 sheep, 4,575,000 chickens; roundwood (2000) 3,011,000 cu m; fish catch (1999) 15,117. Mining and quarrying (2000): gold 38.7 kg, diamonds 460,000 carats[3]. Manufacturing (value added in U.S.$'000; 1994): food, beverages, and tobacco 19,000; chemical products 3,000; wood products 2,000; textiles, wearing apparel, and leather products 1,000; transport equipment 1,000. Construction (1992)[4]: residential 10,052 sq m; nonresidential 82,411 sq m. Energy production (consumption): electricity (kW-hr; 1998) 114,700,000 (114,700,000); coal, none (none); crude petroleum, none (none); petroleum products (metric tons; 1997) none (79,000); natural gas, none (none).
Household income and expenditure. Average household size (1998) 5.9; average annual income per household (1988) CFAF 91,985 (U.S.$435); sources of income: n.a.; expenditure (1991)[5]: food 70.5%, clothing 8.5%, other manufactured products 7.6%, energy 7.3%, services (including transportation and communications, recreation, and health) 6.1%.
Gross national product (2000): U.S.$1,031,000,000 (U.S.$280 per capita).

Structure of gross domestic product and labour force

	1999 in value CFAF '000,000	1999 % of total value	1988 labour force	1988 % of labour force
Agriculture	326,800	50.1	1,113,900	80.4
Mining	26,200	4.0	15,400	1.1
Manufacturing	54,500	8.4	22,400	1.6
Construction	29,500	4.5	7,000	0.5
Public utilities	4,600	0.7	1,500	0.1
Transp. and commun.	15,400	2.4	1,500	0.1
Trade	78,800	12.1	118,000	8.5
Services	40,100	6.1	15,600	1.1
Pub. admin., defense	35,900	5.5	91,700	6.6
Other	40,700[6]	6.2[6]	—	—
TOTAL	652,500	100.0	1,387,000	100.0

Public debt (external, outstanding; 2000): U.S.$810,100,000.
Population economically active (1988): total 1,186,972; activity rate of total population 48.2% (participation rates: ages 15–64, 78.3%; female 46.8%; unemployed 7.5%).

Price and earnings indexes (1995 = 100)

	1993	1994	1995	1996	1997	1998	1999
Consumer price index[4]	67.4	83.9	100.0	103.7	105.4	103.4	101.9
Earnings index	...	...	100.0	...	...	...	...

Land use (1994): forest 75.0%; meadows 4.8%; agriculture 3.2%; other 17.0%.
Tourism (1997): receipts U.S.$5,000,000; expenditures U.S.$39,000,000.

Foreign trade

Balance of trade (current prices)

	1995	1996	1997	1998	1999	2000
CFAF '000,000,000	+0.1	+8.3	+6.1	−6.7	−2.0	+28.7
% of total	0.1%	6.1%	3.5%	3.9%	1.2%	14.4%

Imports (2000): CFAF 85,500,000,000 (1992; food products 22.2%, transportation equipment 16.6%, chemical products 13.7%, energy products 11.0%). *Major import sources* (1999): France 33.8%; Cameroon 12.2%; Belgium-Luxembourg 7.4%; U.K. 4.1%; Germany 2.7%; United States 2.7%.
Exports (2000): CFAF 114,200,000,000 (diamonds 45.9%, wood 18.2%, cotton 10.4%, coffee 10.2%). *Major export destinations:* Belgium-Luxembourg 64.7%; Spain 6.3%; France 3.2%; Taiwan 3.2%; Italy 1.4%; Germany 1.4%.

Transport and communications

Transport. Railroads: none. Roads (1998): total length 15,104 mi, 24,307 km (paved 3%). Vehicles (1996): passenger cars 8,900; trucks and buses 7,000. Merchant marine: vessels (100 gross tons and over) none. Air transport (1998)[7]: passenger-mi 160,300,000, passenger-km 258,000,000; short ton-mi cargo 23,600,000, metric ton-km cargo 38,000,000; airports[8] (2001) 1.

Communications

Medium	date	unit	number	units per 1,000 persons
Daily newspapers	1996	circulation	6,000	1.8
Radio	1997	receivers	283,000	83.0
Television	1999	receivers	20,000	5.6
Telephones	2001	main lines	10,000	2.6
Cellular telephones	2001	subscribers	11,000	2.9
Personal computers	2001	units	7,000	1.9
Internet	2001	users	2,000	0.5

Education and health

Educational attainment (1988). Percentage of population age 10 and over having: no formal schooling 59.3%; primary education 29.6%; lower secondary 7.5%; upper secondary 2.3%; higher 1.3%. *Literacy* (1999): total population age 15 and over literate 45.4%; males literate 58.6%; females literate 33.3%.

Education (1991–92)

	schools	teachers	students	student/teacher ratio
Primary (age 6–11)	930[9]	4,004[9]	277,961	...
Secondary (age 12–18)	46[9]	845[9]	42,263	...
Vocational	10	10	1,477	...
Higher[11]	1	139	2,923	21.0

Health (1992): physicians 157 (1 per 18,660 persons); hospital beds (1991) 4,258 (1 per 672 persons); infant mortality rate (2001) 105.3.
Food (2000): daily per capita caloric intake 1,946 (vegetable products 90%, animal products 10%); 86% of FAO recommended minimum requirement.

Military

Total active duty personnel (2001): 3,150[12] (army 95.2%; navy, none; air force 4.8%). *Military expenditure as percentage of GNP* (1999): 2.8% (world 2.4%); per capita expenditure U.S.$8.

[1]Number increased as of November–December 1998 elections. [2]Formerly pegged to the French franc and since Jan. 1, 2002, to the euro at the rate of €1 = CFAF 655.96. [3]Export figure; an unknown but substantial amount is believed to be smuggled out of the country annually. [4]Bangui only. [5]Weights of consumer price index components. [6]Indirect taxes and customs duties. [7]Includes 1/11 of the traffic of Air Afrique, which is operated by 11 West African states. [8]International air service only. [9]1990–91. [10]Included with secondary. [11]University of Bangui only. [12]Excludes 1,000 gendarmerie, who are part of the armed forces.

Internet resources for further information:
• Central African Republic http://www.africa.co.uk/country/cenafrep.htm
• Investir en Zone Franc http://www.izf.net/izf/Index.htm

Chad

Official name: Jumhūrīyah Tshad
  (Arabic); République du Tchad
  (French) (Republic of Chad).
Form of government: unitary republic
  with one legislative body (National
  Assembly [155]).
Chief of state: President.
Head of government: Prime Minister.
Capital: N'Djamena.
Official languages: Arabic; French.
Official religion: none.
Monetary unit: 1 CFA franc
  (CFAF) = 100 centimes; valuation
  (Sept. 23, 2002) 1 U.S.$ = CFAF 667.00;
  1 £ = CFAF 1,037[1].

Area and population

Préfectures[2]	Capitals	area sq mi	area sq km	population 1993 census
Batha	Ati	34,285	88,800	288,458
Biltine	Biltine	18,090	46,850	184,807
Borkou-Ennedi-Tibesti	Faya Largeau	231,795	600,350	73,185
Chari-Baguirmi	N'Djamena	32,010	82,910	1,251,906
Guéra	Mongo	22,760	58,950	306,253
Kanem	Mao	44,215	114,520	279,927
Lac	Bol	8,620	22,320	252,932
Logone Occidental	Moundou	3,357	8,695	455,489
Logone Oriental	Doba	10,825	28,035	441,064
Mayo-Kebbi	Bongor	11,625	30,105	825,158
Moyen-Chari	Sarh	17,445	45,180	738,595
Ouaddaï	Abéché	29,436	76,240	543,900
Salamat	Am Timan	24,325	63,000	184,403
Tandjilé	Laï	6,965	18,045	453,854
TOTAL		495,755[3]	1,284,000	6,279,931

Demography

Population (2002): 8,997,000.
Density (2002): persons per sq mi 18.1, persons per sq km 7.0.
Urban-rural (1999): urban 23.4%; rural 76.6%.
Sex distribution (2001): male 48.56%; female 51.44%.
Age breakdown (2001): under 15, 47.7%; 15–29, 26.1%; 30–44, 14.1%; 45–59,
  7.6%; 60–74, 3.6%; 75 and over, 0.9%.
Population projection: (2010) 11,616,000; (2020) 15,772,000.
Doubling time: 22 years.
Ethnolinguistic composition (1993): Sara 27.7%; Sudanic Arab 12.3%; Mayo-
  Kebbi peoples 11.5%; Kanem-Bornu peoples 9.0%; Ouaddaï peoples 8.7%;
  Hadjeray (Hadjaraï) 6.7%; Tangale (Tandjilé) peoples 6.5%; Gorane peoples
  6.3%; Fitri-Batha peoples 4.7%; Fulani (Peul) 2.4%; other 4.2%.
Religious affiliation (1993): Muslim 53.9%; Christian 34.7%, of which Roman
  Catholic 20.3%, Protestant 14.4%; traditional beliefs 7.4%; other 4.0%.
Major cities (1993): N'Djamena 530,965; Moundou 282,103; Bongor 196,713;
  Sarh 193,753; Abéché 187,936; Doba 185,461.

Vital statistics

Birth rate per 1,000 population (2001): 48.3 (world avg. 21.2).
Death rate per 1,000 population (2001): 15.4 (world avg. 8.9).
Natural increase rate per 1,000 population (2001): 32.9 (world avg. 12.3).
Total fertility rate (avg. births per childbearing woman; 2001): 6.6.
Life expectancy at birth (2001): male 48.9 years; female 53.0 years.

National economy

Budget (2000). Revenue: CFAF 128,200,000,000 (tax revenue 53.3%, of which
  income tax 19.0%, taxes on international trade 17.0%, taxes on goods and services 14.7%, other taxes 2.6%; nontax revenue 9.3%; grants 37.4%).
  Expenditures: CFAF 203,200,000,000 (current expenditure 49.2%, of which
  government salaries 19.7%, materials and supply 10.2%, defense 7.5%, transfer payments 5.9%, debt service 5.1%, other 0.8%; capital expenditure 50.8%).
Public debt (external, outstanding; 2000): U.S.$1,009,000,000.
Tourism (1994): receipts from visitors U.S.$12,000,000; expenditures by nation-
  als abroad U.S.$26,000,000.
Production (metric tons except as noted). Agriculture, forestry, fishing (2001):
  sorghum 566,577, cassava 342,000, peanuts (groundnuts) 333,000, millet
  320,701, yams 230,000, seed cotton 170,000, corn (maize) 86,684, rice 69,140;
  livestock (number of live animals) 5,900,000 cattle, 5,250,000 goats, 2,400,000
  sheep, 725,000 camels, 5,000,000 chickens; roundwood (1998) 1,919,000 cu m;
  fish catch (1999) 84,000. Mining and quarrying (1997): aggregate (gravel)
  170,000; limited commercial production of natron (10,000) and salt; artisanal
  gold production. Manufacturing (2000): cotton fibre 86,260[4]; refined sugar
  27,000; gum arabic 3,420; woven cotton fabrics 1,000,000 metres; edible oil
  10,000,000 hectolitres; beer 78,000,000 hectolitres; cigarettes 30,000,000
  packs; bicycles 3,444 units[4]. Energy production (consumption): electricity
  (kW-hr; 2000) 86,400,000 (81,800,000); coal, none (none); crude petroleum,
  none (none); petroleum products (metric tons; 1998) none (47,057); natural
  gas, none (none).
Household income and expenditure (1993). Average household size 5.0; average annual income per household CFAF 96,806 (U.S.$458); sources of income
  (1995–96; urban): informal-sector employment and entrepreneurship 36.7%,
  transfers 24.8%, wages 23.6%, ownership of reals estate 8.6%; expenditure
  (1983)[5]: food 45.3%, health 11.9%, energy 5.8%, clothing 3.3%.
Population economically active (1997): total 3,433,000; activity rate of total
  population 47.9% (participation rates: over age 15, 72.3%; female 44.5%;
  unemployed [1993] 0.6%).

Price and earnings indexes (1995 = 100)

	1994	1995	1996	1997	1998	1999	2000
Consumer price index	91.7	100.0	112.4	118.7	133.1	124.1	128.8
Earnings index	...	...	...	...	...	...	...

Gross national product (2000): U.S.$1,541,000,000 (U.S.$200 per capita).

Structure of gross domestic product and labour force

	2000 in value CFAF '000,000	2000 % of total value	1993 labour force	1993 % of labour force
Agriculture	349,000	34.8	1,903,492	83.0
Mining	31,200	3.1	...	...
Manufacturing	108,400	10.8	33,670	1.5
Construction	19,700	2.0	10,885	0.5
Public utilities	5,900	0.6	756	—
Transp. and commun. }	244,600	24.4	13,252	0.6
Trade and finance			179,169	7.8
Pub. admin., defense	114,700	11.4	61,875	2.7
Services	96,400	9.6	79,167	3.4
Other	32,500[6]	3.2[6]	9,311	0.4
TOTAL	1,002,400	100.0[3]	2,293,603	100.0

Land use (1994): forested 25.7%; meadows and pastures 35.7%; agricultural
  and under permanent cultivation 2.6%; other 36.0%.

Foreign trade[7]

Balance of trade (current prices)

	1994	1995	1996	1997	1998	1999	2000
CFAF '000,000	−16,150	−61,127	−47,838	−56,602	−55,752	−70,385	−104.1
% of total	8.9%	20.1%	16.4%	17.0%	15.3%	22.1%	28.6%

Imports (2000): CFAF 234,300,000,000 (1995; petroleum products 17.9%;
  machinery 15.5%; transport equipment 8.3%; raw and refined sugar 7.9%;
  cereal products 7.4%; pharmaceutical and other chemical products 7.2%).
  Major import sources (1997[8]): France 41.3%; Nigeria 10.1%; Cameroon 7.2%;
  India 5.8%; Belgium-Luxembourg 5.1%; Italy 4.3%; Portugal 2.9%.
Exports (2000): CFAF 130,200,000,000 (cotton fibre 55.9%; cattle, sheep, and
  goats 16.9%; other 27.2%). *Major export destinations* (1997[8]): Portugal
  29.9%; Germany 14.2%; Thailand 7.5%; Costa Rica 6.0%; Hong Kong 4.8%;
  Taiwan 4.8%; France 3.7%.

Transport and communications

Transport. Railroads: none. Roads (1999): total length 33,400 km (paved 1%).
  Vehicles (1996): passenger cars 10,560; trucks and buses 14,550. Air transport
  (1996)[9]: passenger-km 233,000,000; metric ton-km cargo 37,000,000; airports
  (2000) with scheduled flights 1.

Communications

Medium	date	unit	number	units per 1,000 persons
Daily newspapers	1997	circulation	2,000	0.2
Radio	1997	receivers	1,310,000	205.9
Television	1999	receivers	10,300	1.4
Telephones	2001	main lines	11,000	1.4
Cellular telephones	2001	subscribers	22,000	2.7
Personal computers	2001	units	12,000	1.5
Internet	2001	users	4,000	0.5

Education and health

Educational attainment (1993). Percentage of economically active population
  age 15 and over having: no formal schooling 81.1%; Qur'anic education
  4.2%; primary education 11.2%; secondary education 2.7%; higher education 0.3%; professional education 0.5%. *Literacy* (1995): percentage of total
  population age 15 and over literate 48.1%; males literate 62.1%; females literate 34.7%.

Education (1996–97)

	schools	teachers	students	student/teacher ratio
Primary (age 6–12)	2,660	10,151	680,909	67.1
Secondary (age 13–19)	153	2,598	97,011	37.3
Voc., teacher tr.	18	194	2,778	14.5
Higher[10]	8	288	3,274	11.4

Health (2000): physicians 1,667 (1 per 4,471 persons); hospital beds (1993)
  3,962 (1 per 1,521 persons); infant mortality rate (2001) 95.1.
Food (2000): daily per capita caloric intake 2,046 (vegetable products 93%,
  animal products 7%); 86% of FAO recommended minimum requirement.

Military

Total active duty personnel (2001): 30,350[11] (army 82.4%; navy, none; air force
  1.2%; paramilitary 16.4%). *Military expenditure as percentage of GNP* (1999):
  2.4% (world 2.4%); per capita expenditure U.S.$5.

[1]Formerly pegged to the French franc and since Jan. 1, 2002, to the euro at the rate of
€1 = CFAF 655.96. [2]Chad was administratively reorganized into 28 departments in *c.*
2000; detail does not add to total given because of rounding. [3]Detail does not add to total
because of rounding. [4]1998. [5]Capital city only. [6]VAT and import taxes. [7]Import figures are c.i.f. in balance of
trade and f.o.b. in commodities and trading partners. [8]Based on direction of trade data
(analysis of reports of trading partners, rather than country's own customs data). [9]One-
eleventh portion of total traffic of Air Afrique, which is operated by 11 West African
states. [10]Universities and equivalent institutions only. [11]Excludes 900 French troops.

Internet resources for further information:
• **Embassy of Chad in the U.S. http://www.chadembassy.org**
• **Investir en Zone Franc http://www.izf.net/izf/Index.htm**

Chile

Official name: República de Chile (Republic of Chile).
Form of government: multiparty republic with two legislative houses (Senate [49[1]]; Chamber of Deputies [120]).
Head of state and government: President.
Capital: Santiago[2].
Official language: Spanish.
Official religion: none.
Monetary unit: 1 peso (Ch$) = 100 centavos; valuation (Sept. 23, 2002) 1 U.S.$ = Ch$741.95; 1 £ = Ch$1,153.

Gross national product (2000): U.S.$69,850,000,000 (U.S.$4,590 per capita).

Structure of gross domestic product and labour force

	2001		1998[7]	
	in value Ch$'000,000[8]	% of total value	labour force	% of labour force
Agriculture	2,052,900	5.6	809,000	13.8
Mining	3,050,700	8.3		
Manufacturing	5,722,100	15.7	1,015,000	17.3
Public utilities	1,214,800	3.3		
Construction	2,952,500	8.1	533,000	9.1
Transp. and commun.	2,727,900	7.5	456,000	7.8
Trade	3,904,100	10.7	1,075,000	18.4
Finance	4,557,200	12.5	437,000	7.5
Pub. admin., defense			1,478,000	25.3
Services	10,350,800[9]	28.3[9]		
Other			47,000[10]	0.8[10]
TOTAL	36,583,000[11]	100.0	5,852,000[11]	100.0

Public debt (external, outstanding; 2000): U.S.$5,210,000,000.
Household income and expenditure. Average household size (2002) 3.4; average annual income per household (1994) Ch$5,981,706 at November prices (U.S.$12,552); sources of income (1990): wages and salaries 75.1%, transfer payments 12.0%, other 12.9%; expenditure (1989): food 27.9%, clothing 22.5%, housing 15.2%, transportation 6.4%.
Tourism (2000): receipts U.S.$827,000,000; expenditures U.S.$752,000,000.

Area and population[3]

Regions	Capitals	area sq mi	area sq km	population 2002 census[4]
Aisén del General Carlos				
Ibáñez del Campo	Coihaique	41,890	108,495	86,697
Antofagasta	Antofagasta	48,668	126,049	492,846
Araucanía	Temuco	12,294	31,842	864,929
Atacama	Copiapó	29,026	75,176	252,353
Bío-Bío	Concepción	14,310	37,063	1,853,678
Coquimbo	La Serena	15,668	40,580	600,363
Libertador General				
Bernardo O'Higgins	Rancagua	6,327	16,387	773,950
Los Lagos	Puerto Montt	25,874	67,013	1,061,735
Magallanes y la				
Antártica Chilena	Punta Arenas	51,080	132,297	151,869
Maule	Talca	11,697	30,296	904,104
Santiago,				
Región Metropolitana de	Santiago	5,947	15,403	6,038,974
Tarapacá	Iquique	22,818	59,099	426,351
Valparaíso	Valparaíso	6,331	16,396	1,542,492
TOTAL		291,930[5]	756,096[5]	15,050,341

Demography

Population (2002): 15,082,000.
Density (2002): persons per sq mi 51.7, persons per sq km 19.9.
Urban-rural (2002): urban 86.7%; rural 13.3%.
Sex distribution (2002): male 49.19%; female 50.81%.
Age breakdown (2000): under 15, 28.5%; 15–29, 24.2%; 30–44, 22.9%; 45–59, 14.3%; 60–74, 7.5%; 75 and over, 2.6%.
Population projection: (2010) 16,492,000; (2020) 18,203,000.
Ethnic composition (1992): European and mestizo 89.7%; Araucanian (Mapuche) 9.6%; Aymara 0.5%; Rapa Nui Polynesian 0.2%.
Religious affiliation (1992): Roman Catholic 76.7%; Protestant 13.2%; atheist and nonreligious 5.8%; other 4.3%.
Major cities[6] (2002): Greater Santiago 4,647,444; Puente Alto 501,042; Concepción 376,043; Viña del Mar 298,828; Antofagasta 298,153; Valparaíso 270,242.

Vital statistics

Birth rate per 1,000 population (2000): 17.2 (world avg. 22.5).
Death rate per 1,000 population (2000): 5.5 (world avg. 9.0).
Natural increase rate per 1,000 population (2000): 11.7 (world avg. 13.5).
Total fertility rate (avg. births per childbearing woman; 2000): 2.2.
Life expectancy at birth (2000): male 72.4 years; female 79.2 years.
Major causes of death per 100,000 population (1994): diseases of the circulatory system 149.5; malignant neoplasms (cancers) 111.9; accidents and adverse effects 64.3; diseases of the respiratory system 61.2.

National economy

Budget (2001). Revenue: Ch$9,537,200,000,000 (income from taxes 76.2%, nontax revenue 23.5%, capital 0.3%). Expenditures: Ch$9,932,200,000,000 (pensions 29.5%, wages 19.0%, capital expenditure 15.0%, interest 2.1%).
Population economically active (1999): total 5,822,700; activity rate of total population 38.6% (participation rates [1995]: ages 15–64, 58.6%; female 32.4%; unemployed [1999] 9.7%).

Price and earnings indexes (1995 = 100)

	1995	1996	1997	1998	1999	2000	2001
Consumer price index	100.0	107.4	113.9	119.8	123.8	128.5	133.1
Hourly earnings index	100.0	114.8	124.7	134.5	142.4	149.9	157.8

Production (metric tons except as noted). Agriculture, forestry, fishing (1999): sugar beets 3,100,000, grapes 1,575,000, tomatoes 1,243,000, wheat 1,196,600, apples 1,165,000, corn (maize) 624,000, potatoes 994,694, onions (dry) 262,000, oats 201,000, barley 81,000, rice 61,000; livestock (number of live animals) 4,134,000 cattle, 4,116,000 sheep, 2,221,000 pigs; roundwood (1998) 31,670,000 cu m; fish catch (1998) 3,265,300. Mining (1998): iron 8,277,000; copper 3,843,000; zinc 26,000; molybdenum 25,000; silver 1,300,000 kg; gold 43,253 kg. Manufacturing (value added in Ch$'000,000; 1997): food products 3,810,200; metal and metal products 2,631,900; petroleum and petroleum products 1,100,200; paper and paper products 964,900; beverages 807,400; nonmetallic mineral products 593,000. Construction (1994): residential 7,049,369 sq m; nonresidential 2,875,935 sq m. Energy production (consumption): electricity (kW-hr; 1999) 38,389,000,000 (31,204,000,000); coal (metric tons; 1997) 1,080,000 (6,153,000); crude petroleum (barrels; 1997) 2,027,000 (63,163,000); petroleum products (metric tons; 1997) 8,151,000 (10,469,000); natural gas (cu m; 1997) 2,017,000,000 (2,387,000,000).

Foreign trade

Balance of trade (current prices)

	1996	1997	1998	1999	2000	2001
U.S.$'000,000	−1,091	−1,557	−2,516	+1,665	+1,482	+2,093
% of total	3.4%	4.5%	7.8%	5.6%	4.3%	6.0%

Imports (1999): U.S.$15,137,000,000 (intermediate goods 59.5%; capital goods 21.8%; consumer goods 18.7%). *Major import sources:* Argentina 13.9%; Brazil 6.7%; Japan 4.4%; Germany 4.3%; France 2.9%.
Exports (1999): U.S.$15,616,000,000 (mining products 44.4%, of which copper 37.7%; industrial products 38.5%; foodstuffs 17.1%). *Major export destinations:* U.S. 19.4%; Japan 14.3%; United Kingdom 6.8%; Argentina 4.6%; Brazil 4.3%; Germany 3.5%; Taiwan 3.2%.

Transport and communications

Transport. Railroads (1999): route length 5,410 mi, 8,707 km; passenger-km 605,900,000; metric ton-km cargo 2,329,246,000[12]. Roads (1996): total length 49,590 mi, 79,800 km (paved 14%). Vehicles (1999): passenger cars 1,323,800; trucks and buses 687,500. Air transport (1999): passenger-km 10,650,500,000; metric ton-km cargo 2,107,000,000; airports (1998) with scheduled flights 23.

Communications

Medium	date	unit	number	units per 1,000 persons
Daily newspapers	1996	circulation	1,410,000	98
Radio	1997	receivers	5,180,000	354
Television	1999	receivers	3,600,000	240
Telephones	2001	main lines	3,703,300	249
Cellular telephones	2001	subscribers	5,271,600	353
Personal computers	2001	units	1,300,000	87.2
Internet	2001	users	3,102,200	208

Education and health

Educational attainment (1992). Percentage of population age 25 and over having: no formal schooling 5.7%; primary education 44.2%; secondary 42.2%; higher 7.9%. *Literacy* (1995): total population age 15 and over literate 95.2%; males 95.4%; females 95.0%.

Education (1995)

	schools	teachers	students	student/ teacher ratio
Primary (age 6–13)	8,702	80,155	2,149,501	26.8
Secondary (age 14–17)[13]	2,956[14]	51,042	679,165	13.3
Higher	201[14]	18,084[15]	367,094	...

Health (1999): physicians 17,853 (1 per 841 persons); hospital beds (1998) 41,706 (1 per 355 persons); infant mortality rate (2000) 9.6.
Food (2000): daily per capita caloric intake 2,882 (vegetable products 78%, animal products 22%); 118% of FAO recommended minimum requirement.

Military

Total active duty personnel (2002): 87,500 (army 58.3%, navy 27.4%, air force 14.3%). *Military expenditure as percentage of GNP* (1999): 3.0% (world 2.4%); per capita expenditure U.S.$133.

[1]Includes 10 nonelective seats. General Pinochet resigned as Senator-for-life in July 2002. [2]Legislative bodies meet in Valparaíso. [3]Excludes the 480,000-sq mi (1,250,000-sq km) section of Antarctica claimed by Chile (and administered as part of Magallanes y la Antártica Chilena region) and "inland" (actually tidal) water areas. The 2002 census population of Chilean-claimed Antarctica is 130. [4]Preliminary. [5]Excludes the Laguna del Desierto region lost to Argentina in 1994 via international arbitration. [6]Preliminary census populations of single communes except Greater Santiago and Concepción, which is a total for 3 communes. [7]Excludes all or some classes or elements of the military. [8]In constant prices of 1996. [9]Less imputed bank service charges, import duties, and value-added tax on imports. [10]Includes unemployed not previously employed. [11]Detail does not add to total given because of rounding. [12]1994. [13]Includes vocational. [14]1988. [15]Universities only.

Internet resources for further information:
• **Instituto Nacional de Estadísticas http://www.ine.cl**
• **Gobierno de Chile http://www.gobiernodechile.cl**

China

Official name: Chung-hua Jen-min
Kung-ho-kuo (People's Republic
of China).
Form of government: single-party
people's republic with one legislative
house (National People's Congress
[2,989[1]]).
Chief of state: President.
Head of government: Premier.
Capital: Peking (Beijing).
Official language: Mandarin Chinese.
Official religion: none.
Monetary unit: 1 Renminbi (yuan)
(Y) = 10 jiao = 100 fen; valuation
(Sept. 23, 2002) 1 U.S.$ = Y 8.27;
1 £ = Y 12.85.

Area and population[2, 3]

Provinces	Capitals	area sq mi	area sq km	population 2000 estimate
Anhwei (Anhui)	Ho-fei (Hefei)	54,000	139,900	59,860,000
Chekiang (Zhejiang)	Hang-chou (Hangzhou)	39,300	101,800	46,770,000
Fukien (Fujian)	Fu-chou (Fuzhou)	47,500	123,100	34,710,000
Hainan (Hainan)	Hai-k'ou (Haikou)	13,200	34,300	7,870,000
Heilungkiang (Heilongjiang)	Harbin	179,000	463,600	36,890,000
Honan (Henan)	Cheng-chou (Zhengzhou)	64,500	167,000	92,560,000
Hopeh (Hebei)	Shih-chia-chuang (Shijiazhuang)	78,200	202,700	67,440,000
Hunan (Hunan)	Ch'ang-sha (Changsha)	81,300	210,500	64,400,000
Hupeh (Hubei)	Wu-han (Wuhan)	72,400	187,500	60,280,000
Kansu (Gansu)	Lan-chou (Lanzhou)	141,500	366,500	25,620,000
Kiangsi (Jiangxi)	Nan-ch'ang (Nanchang)	63,600	164,800	41,400,000
Kiangsu (Jiangsu)	Nanking (Nanjing)	39,600	102,600	74,380,000
Kirin (Jilin)	Ch'ang-ch'un (Changchun)	72,200	187,000	27,280,000
Kwangtung (Guangdong)	Canton (Guangzhou)	76,100	197,100	86,420,000
Kweichow (Guizhou)	Kuei-yang (Guiyang)	67,200	174,000	35,250,000
Liaoning (Liaoning)	Shen-yang (Shenyang)	58,300	151,000	42,380,000
Shansi (Shanxi)	T'ai-yüan (Taiyuan)	60,700	157,100	32,970,000
Shantung (Shandong)	Chi-nan (Jinan)	59,200	153,300	90,790,000
Shensi (Shaanxi)	Sian (Xi'an)	75,600	195,800	36,050,000
Szechwan (Sichuan)	Ch'eng-tu (Chengdu)	210,800	546,000	83,290,000
Tsinghai (Qinghai)	Hsi-ning (Xining)	278,400	721,000	5,180,000
Yunnan (Yunnan)	K'un-ming (Kunming)	168,400	436,200	42,880,000
Autonomous regions				
Inner Mongolia (Nei Monggol)	Hu-ho-hao-t'e (Hohhot)	454,600	1,177,500	23,760,000
Kwangsi Chuang (Guangxi Zhuang)	Nan-ning (Nanning)	85,100	220,400	44,890,000
Ningsia Hui (Ningxia Hui)	Yin-ch'uan (Yinchuan)	25,600	66,400	5,620,000
Sinkiang Uighur (Xinjiang Uygur)	Wu-lu-mu-c'hi (Urumqi)	635,900	1,646,900	19,250,000
Tibet (Xizang)	Lhasa	471,700	1,221,600	2,620,000
Municipalities				
Chungking (Chongqing)	—	8,900	23,000	30,900,000
Peking (Beijing)	—	6,500	16,800	13,820,000
Shanghai (Shanghai)	—	2,400	6,200	16,740,000
Tientsin (Tianjin)	—	4,400	11,300	10,010,000
TOTAL		3,696,100[4]	9,572,900[4]	1,262,280,000[5]

Demography

Population (2002): 1,284,211,000.
Density (2002): persons per sq mi 347.5, persons per sq km 134.2.
Urban-rural (2002): urban 33.0%; rural 67.0%.
Sex distribution (2000): male 51.63%; female 48.37%.
Age breakdown (1998): under 15, 24.3%; 15–29, 24.6%; 30–44, 24.8%; 45–59,
15.2%; 60–74, 8.8%; 75 and over, 2.3%.
Population projection: (2010) 1,357,864,000; (2020) 1,433,111,000.
Doubling time: 88 years.
Ethnic composition (1990): Han (Chinese) 91.96%; Chuang 1.37%; Manchu
0.87%; Hui 0.76%; Miao 0.65%; Uighur 0.64%; Yi 0.58%; Tuchia 0.50%;
Mongolian 0.42%; Tibetan 0.41%; Puyi 0.23%; Tung 0.22%; Yao 0.18%;
Korean 0.17%; Pai 0.14%; Hani 0.11%; Kazakh 0.10%; Tai 0.09%; Li 0.09%;
other 0.51%.
Religious affiliation (2000): nonreligious 42.1%; Chinese folk-religionist 28.5%;
Buddhist 8.4%; atheist 8.1%; Christian 7.1%; traditional beliefs 4.3%; Muslim
1.5%.
Major cities (1998): Shanghai 8,937,175; Peking 6,633,929; Tientsin 4,835,327;
Wu-han 3,911,824; Shen-yang 3,876,289; Canton 3,306,277; Chungking
3,193,889; Harbin 2,586,978; Nanking 2,388,915; Sian 2,294,790; Ch'eng-tu
2,146,126; Ch'ang-ch'un 2,072,324; Talien (Dalian) 2,000,944; T'ai-yüan
1,768,530; Chi-nan 1,713,036; Ch'ing-tao (Qingdao) 1,702,108; Cheng-chou
1,465,069; Tzu-po (Zibo) 1,458,060; Lan-chou 1,429,673; K'un-ming 1,350,640;
Hang-chou 1,346,148; Ch'ang-sha 1,334,036; Kuei-yang 1,320,566.
Households. Average rural household size (1996) 4.4; urban household size
(1998) 3.2. Family households (1990): 277,390,000 (99.4%); collective
1,671,000 (0.6%).

Vital statistics

Birth rate per 1,000 population (2001): 14.9 (world avg. 21.2).
Death rate per 1,000 population (2001): 7.0 (world avg. 8.9).
Total fertility rate (avg. births per childbearing woman; 2001): 1.8.
Marriage rate per 1,000 population (1996): 7.6.
Divorce rate per 1,000 population (1996): 0.9.

Life expectancy at birth (2002): male 69.0 years; female 73.0 years.
Major causes of death per 100,000 population (1998)[6]: diseases of the circulatory system 244.3; malignant neoplasms (cancers) 139.3; diseases of the respiratory system 86.8; accidents, violence, and intoxication 38.7; digestive diseases 18.7.

Social indicators

Educational attainment (1997). Percentage of population age 15 and over having: no schooling and incomplete primary 20.7%; completed primary 37.6%;
some secondary and complete secondary 39.2%; college and postsecondary
education 2.5%.

Distribution of urban household income (1996)

avg. per capita income by quintile (avg. Y 4,845)

first quintile	second quintile	third quintile	fourth quintile	fifth quintile
Y 2,801	Y 3,780	Y 4,580	Y 5,599	Y 8,039

Quality of working life (1991). Average workweek: 48 hours. Annual rate per
100,000 workers for: injury or accident, n.a.; industrial illness, n.a.; death, n.a.
Funds for pensions and social welfare relief (1996): Y 181,780,000,000.
Average days lost to labour stoppages per 1,000 workdays: n.a. Average duration of journey to work: n.a. Method of transport: n.a. Rate per 1,000 workers of discouraged (unemployed no longer seeking work): n.a.
Access to services. Proportion of communes having access to electricity (1979)
87.1%. Percentage of urban population with: safe public water supply (1996)
95.0%; public sewage collection, n.a.; public fire protection, n.a.
Social participation. Eligible voters participating in last national election: n.a.
Population participating in voluntary work: n.a. Trade union membership in
total labour force (1996): 14.7%. Practicing religious population in total affiliated population: n.a.
Social deviance. Annual reported arrest rate per 100,000 population (1986) for:
property violation 20.7; infringing personal rights 7.2; disruption of social
administration 3.3; endangering public security 1.07.
Leisure. Favourite leisure activities: n.a.
Material well-being. Urban families possessing (number per family; 1996): bicycles 1.9; televisions 1.2; washing machines 0.9; refrigerators 0.7; sewing machines 0.6; cameras 0.3. Rural families possessing (number per family; 1998):
bicycles 1.4; televisions 1.3; sewing machines 0.7; washing machines 0.2.

National economy

Gross national product (at current market prices; 2000): U.S.$1,062,919,000,000
(U.S.$840 per capita).

Structure of gross domestic product and labour force

	1998 in value Y '000,000,000	1998 % of total value	1998 labour force ('000)	1998 % of labour force
Agriculture	1,429.87	18.0	332,320	47.5
Mining	3,354.09	42.2	7,210	1.0
Manufacturing			83,190	11.9
Construction	560.89	7.0	33,270	4.8
Public utilities	...	...	2,830	0.4
Transp. and commun.	502.93	6.3	20,000	2.9
Trade	660.96	8.3	46,450	6.6
Finance	...	...	4,080	0.6
Pub. admin.	...	...		
Services	1,446.54	18.2	170,220[8]	24.3[8]
Other	...	...		
TOTAL	7,955.28	100.0	699,570	100.0

Budget (1997). Revenue: Y 492,650,000,000 (taxes on goods and services
66.6%; grants 12.3%; income taxes 8.2%; import duties 6.5%; nontax revenue 2.3%). Expenditures: Y 601,720,000,000 (defense 13.6%; general public services 7.5%; agriculture 6.0%; industry 2.9%; public order 2.6%; education 2.0%; utilities 1.8%; other economic affair expenditures 5.9%; non-
functional expenditures 56.3%).
Public debt (external, outstanding; 2000): U.S.$104,709,000,000.
Tourism (2000): receipts from visitors U.S.$16,224,000,000; expenditures by
nationals abroad U.S.$13,114,000,000.

Retail and catering enterprises (1996)

	no. of enter- prises	no. of employees	annual wage as a % of all wages	annual gross output value (Y '000,000)
Retail trade	13,963,162	31,892,181	...	...
Food, beverage, and tobacco	5,177,416	10,738,924	...	241,350
Articles for daily use	3,242,769	8,614,944	...	88,470
Textile goods, garments, shoes, and hats	2,018,136	4,030,888	...	125,250
Sundry goods for daily use	799,486	1,670,984	...	...
Hardwares, electrical appliances, and chemicals	583,466	1,828,788	...	...
Medicines and medical appliances	123,534	405,424	...	57,980
Books and newspapers	140,856	365,424	...	23,110
Other	1,877,499	4,236,805	...	...
Catering trade	2,587,730	7,753,108	...	...
Restaurants	1,181,732	4,321,824	...	...
Fast-food eateries	397,561	1,049,829	...	...
Other	1,008,437	2,381,455	...	...

Production (metric tons except as noted). Agriculture, forestry, fishing (2000):
grains—rice 190,168,000, corn (maize) 105,231,000, wheat 99,370,000,
sorghum 2,784,000, barley 3,940,000, millet 2,091,000; oilseeds—soybeans
15,400,000, peanuts (groundnuts) 15,067,000, rapeseed 11,350,000, sunflower
seeds 2,100,000; fruits and nuts—watermelons 38,382,000, apples 22,888,000,
pears 8,618,000, cantaloupes 6,418,000, oranges 3,508,000; other—sweet potatoes 121,024,000, sugarcane 70,205,000, potatoes 62,036,000, cabbage
20,209,000, tomatoes 19,309,000, sugar beets 7,700,000, cucumbers 17,176,000,

seed cotton 13,050,000, onions 12,176,000, eggplants 11,915,000, garlic 6,466,000, tobacco leaves 2,509,000, tea 721,000; livestock (number of live animals) 437,551,000 pigs, 148,401,000 goats, 131,095,000 sheep, 104,582,000 cattle, 22,599,000 water buffalo, 9,348,000 asses, 8,916,000 horses, 3,625,000,000 chickens, 611,899,000 ducks; roundwood (1999) 291,330,000 cu m; fish catch (1998) 17,229,957. Mining and quarrying (1998): metal concentrates—zinc 1,540,000, copper 1,150,000, lead 733,000, antimony 80,000, tin 79,000, tungsten 24,000; metal ores—iron ore 210,000,000, bauxite 8,500,000, manganese ore 6,100,000, silver 1,400, gold 178; nonmetals—salt 22,420,000, gypsum 7,900,000, soda ash 7,200,000, barite 3,200,000, fluorspar 2,550,000, magnesite 2,200,000, talc 2,200,000, asbestos 250,000. Manufacturing (1998): cement 536,000,000; rolled steel 105,180,000; chemical fertilizer 30,100,000; sulfuric acid 21,710,000; paper and paperboard 21,260,000; sugar 8,260,000; cotton yarn 5,420,000; cotton fabrics 24,100,000,000 m; colour television sets 34,970,000 units; bicycles 23,125,000 units; household washing machines 12,073,000 units; household refrigerators 10,600,000 units; motor vehicles 1,630,000 units. Construction (1996): residential 1,221,880,000 sq m; nonresidential 406,380,000 sq m. Distribution of industrial production (percentage of total value of output by sector; 1978 [1996]): state-operated enterprises 80.6% (28.5%); collectives 19.2% (39.4%); privately operated enterprises 0.2% (32.1%). Retail sales (percentage of total sales by sector; 1978 [1996]): state-operated enterprises 90.5% (27.3%); collectives 7.4% (18.4%); privately operated enterprises 2.1% (54.3%).

Manufacturing and mining enterprises (1996)

	no. of enterprises	no. of employees[9]	annual wages as a % of avg. of all wages[10]	annual gross output value (Y '000,000)
Manufacturing				
Machinery, transport equipment, and metal manufactures,	23,032	21,560	96.7	880,886
of which,				
Metal products	2,641	1,810,000	...	23,593
Industrial equipment	8,875	7,020,000	...	183,951
Transport equipment	4,303	3,540,000	...	187,581
Electronic goods	1,579	1,630,000	...	70,046
Measuring equipment	1,179	820,000	...	14,738
Textiles	4,031	6,340,000	95.5	161,949
Garments	1,177	1,680,000	...	11,359
Foodstuffs,	18,191	4,710,000	87.5	383,264
of which,				
Food processing	14,520	3,170,000	...	196,393
Beverages	3,367	1,210,000	...	70,368
Tobacco manufactures	304	330,000	...	116,503
Chemicals,	10,707	8,140,000	92.1	537,768
of which,				
Pharmaceuticals	2,044	1,020,000	...	53,749
Plastics	1,667	1,050,000	...	15,167
Secondary forest products				
(including paper and stationery)	3,664	2,310,000	96.1	51,238
Primary forest products	877	1,140,000	114.3	16,750
Mining				
Nonferrous and ferrous metals	1,163	810,000	107.6	22,711
Crude petroleum	71	1,250,000	...	149,525
Coal	2,011	5,050,000	119.8	105,946

Energy production (consumption): electricity (kW-hr; 2001) 1,421,262,000,000 ([1997] 1,127,356,000,000); coal (metric tons; 2001) 960,476,000 ([1997] 1,331,589,000); crude petroleum (barrels; 2001) 1,207,000,000 ([1997] 1,281,000,000); petroleum products (metric tons; 1997) 125,698,000 (142,635,000); natural gas (cu m; 2001) 30,252,000,000 ([1997] 22,449,000,000).

Financial aggregates[11]

	1994	1995	1996	1997	1998	1999	2000
Exchange rate, Y per:							
U.S. dollar	8.45	8.32	8.30	8.28	8.28	8.28	8.28
£	13.18	12.90	12.95	13.58	13.74	13.41	12.59
SDR	12.33	12.36	11.93	11.17	11.66	11.36	10.78
International reserves (U.S.$)							
Total (excl. gold; '000,000)	52,914	75,377	107,039	142,762	149,188	157,728	168,278
SDRs ('000,000)	539	582	614	602	676	741	798
Reserve pos. in IMF ('000,000)	755	1,216	1,396	2,270	3,553	2,312	1,905
Foreign exchange	51,620	73,579	105,029	139,890	144,959	154,675	165,574
Gold ('000,000 fine troy oz)	12.7	12.7	12.7	12.7	12.7	12.7	12.7
% world reserves	1.4	1.4	1.4	1.4	1.4	1.3	1.3
Interest and prices							
Central bank discount (%)	10.08	10.44	9.00	8.55	4.59	3.24	3.24
Govt. bond yield (%)	...	...	...	...	...	...	...
Industrial share prices	...	...	...	...	...	...	...
Balance of payments (U.S.$'000,000)							
Balance of visible trade,	+7,290	+18,050	+19,535	+46,222	+46,614	+36,207	...
of which:							
Imports, f.o.b.	−95,271	−110,060	−131,542	−136,448	−136,915	−158,509	...
Exports, f.o.b.	102,561	128,110	151,077	182,670	183,529	194,716	...
Balance of invisibles	−382	−16,432	−12,292	−9,259	−15,142	−20,540	...
Balance of payments, current account	+6,908	+1,618	+7,243	+36,963	+31,472	15,667	...

Household income and expenditure (1996). Average household size (2000) 3.4; rural household 4.4, urban household (1998) 3.2. Average annual income per household Y 13,459; rural household Y 12,406, urban household (1998) Y 17,248. Sources of income: rural household—income from household businesses 79.6%, wages 16.1%, other 4.3%; urban household—wages 80.5%, business income 5.9%, other 13.6%. Expenditure: rural household—food 56.3%, housing 13.9%, cultural activities 8.4%, clothing 7.2%, household materials 5.4%, health 3.7%, transportation 3.0%; urban household (1998)—food 44.5%, clothing 11.1%, housing 9.4%, household materials 8.2%, education 6.3%, transportation and communications 5.9%, health 4.7%.

Population economically active (1998): total 699,570,000; activity rate of total population 55.7% (participation rates: over age 15 [1996] 75.9%; female 49.7%[12]; unemployed 3.1%). Urban workforce by sector 1978 (1998): state enterprises 74,500,000 (90,580,000); collectives 20,000,000 (19,630,000); self-employment or privately run enterprises 150,000 (96,570,000).

Price and earnings indexes (1995 = 100)

	1994	1995	1996	1997	1998	1999	2000
Consumer price index	85.6	100.0	108.3	111.3	110.5	109.0	109.3
Annual earnings index[13]	82.2	100.0	112.1	116.1	114.8	...	...

Land use (1999): meadows and pastures 42.9%; agricultural and under permanent cultivation 14.5%; forested and other 42.6%.

Foreign trade[14]

Balance of trade (current prices)

	1995	1996	1997	1998	1999	2000
U.S.$'000,000	+18,050	+19,535	+46,222	+46,614	+35,982	+34,474
% of total	7.6%	6.9%	14.5%	14.5%	10.2%	7.4%

Imports (1998): U.S.$140,166,000,000 (machinery and transport equipment 40.5%; products of textile industries, rubber and metal products 22.2%; chemical and related products 14.4%; inedible raw materials 7.6%; mineral fuel and lubricants 4.8%; food and live animals 2.7%). *Major import sources:* Japan 20.1%; United States 12.1%; Taiwan 11.9%; South Korea 10.7%; Germany 5.0%; Hong Kong 4.8%; Singapore 3.0%; Russia 2.6%; France 2.3%; Australia 1.9%; Malaysia 1.9%.
Exports (1998): U.S.$183,757,000,000 (machinery and transport equipment 27.3%; products of textile industries, rubber and metal products 17.6%; food and live animals 5.8%; chemicals and allied products 5.6%; mineral fuels and lubricants 2.8%; inedible raw materials 1.9%). *Major export destinations:* Hong Kong 21.1%; United States 20.7%; Japan 16.2%; Germany 4.0%; South Korea 3.4%; The Netherlands 2.8%; United Kingdom 2.5%.

Transport and communications

Transport. Railroads (1998): length 35,781 mi, 57,584 km; passenger-mi 229,657,000,000, passenger-km 369,598,000,000; short ton-mi cargo 843,302,-000,000, metric ton-km cargo 1,231,200,000,000. Roads (1998): total length 794,405 mi, 1,278,474 km (paved 93%). Vehicles (1998): passenger cars 6,548,300; trucks and buses 6,278,900. Merchant marine (1992): vessels (100 gross tons and over) 2,390: total deadweight tonnage 20,657,996. Air transport (1998): passenger-mi 49,725,000,000, passenger-km 80,024,000,000; short ton-mi cargo 2,291,000,000, metric ton-km cargo 3,345,000,000; airports (1996) with scheduled flights 113.

Communications

Medium	date	unit	number	units per 1,000 persons
Daily newspapers	1994	circulation	27,790,000	23
Radio	1997	receivers	417,000,000	335
Television	1999	receivers	370,000,000	292
Telephones	2001	main lines	179,034,000	138
Cellular telephones	2001	subscribers	144,812,000	112
Personal computers	2001	units	25,000,000	19
Internet	2001	users	33,700,000	26

Education and health

Literacy (1995): total population age 15 and over literate 81.5%; males literate 89.9%; females literate 72.7%.

Education (1998)

	schools	teachers	students	student/teacher ratio
Primary (age 7–13)	609,626	5,819,000	139,538,000	24.0
Secondary (age 13–17)	77,888	3,697,000	63,010,000	17.0
Secondary specialized	4,109	279,000	4,981,000	17.9
Higher	1,022	407,000	3,409,000	8.4

Health (1998): physicians 1,999,500 (1 per 629 persons); hospital beds 2,913,700 (1 per 431 persons); infant mortality rate per 1,000 live births (2002) 37.0.
Food (1999): daily per capita caloric intake 3,042 (vegetable products 81%, animal products 19%); (1997) 129% of FAO recommended minimum.

Military

Total active duty personnel (2001): 2,310,000 (army 69.3%, navy 12.5%, air force 18.2%). *Military expenditure as percentage of GNP* (1999): 2.3% (world 2.4%); per capita expenditure U.S.$71.

[1]Includes 36 seats allotted to Hong Kong and 12 seats to Macau. [2]Names of the provinces, autonomous regions, and municipalities are stated in conventional form, followed by Pinyin transliteration; names of capitals are stated in conventional form or Wade-Giles transliteration, followed by Pinyin transliteration. [3]Data for Taiwan, Quemoy and Matsu (parts of Fukien province occupied by Taiwan); Hong Kong (which reverted to China from British administration on July 1, 1997) and Macau (which reverted to China from Portuguese administration on Dec. 20, 1999) are excluded. [4]Includes 4,600 sq mi (11,900 sq km) not shown separately. [5]Sum of provincial and autonomous region populations; national total may differ. [6]Based on urban sample population. [7]Excludes arrests for anti-Communist activities. [8]Includes 5,710,000 persons who are unemployed. [9]In state-owned and collective-owned industries only. [10]1979. [11]Exchange rates and international reserves are period average figures. [12]1987. [13]Average annual wage in industrial establishments in urban areas. [14]Imports and exports f.o.b.

Internet resource for further information:
• Embassy of The People's Republic of China http://www.china-embassy.org
• China Statistical Information Net http://www.stats.gov.cn/english/index.html

Colombia

Official name: República de Colombia (Republic of Colombia).
Form of government: unitary, multiparty republic with two legislative houses (Senate [102]; House of Representatives [166[1]]).
Head of state and government: President.
Capital: Bogotá.
Official language: Spanish.
Official religion: none.
Monetary unit: 1 peso (Col$) = 100 centavos; valuation (Sept. 23, 2002) 1 U.S.$ = Col$2,825; 1 £ = Col$4,391.

Area and population

Departments	Capitals	area sq mi	area sq km	population 1999 estimate
Antioquia	Medellín	24,445	63,912	5,300,000
Atlántico	Barranquilla	1,308	3,388	2,081,000
Bolívar	Cartagena	10,030	25,978	1,951,000
Boyacá	Tunja	8,953	23,189	1,355,000
Caldas	Manizales	3,046	7,888	1,094,000
Caquetá	Florencia	34,349	88,965	410,000
Cauca	Popayán	11,316	29,308	1,234,000
Cesar	Valledupar	8,844	22,905	944,000
Chocó	Quibdó	17,965	46,530	406,000
Córdoba	Montería	9,660	25,020	1,308,000
Cundinamarca	Bogotá, D.C.	8,735	22,623	2,099,000
Huila	Neiva	7,680	19,890	911,000
La Guajira	Riohacha	8,049	20,848	475,000
Magdalena	Santa Marta	8,953	23,188	1,260,000
Meta	Villavicencio	33,064	85,635	686,000
Nariño	Pasto	12,845	33,268	1,603,000
Norte de Santander	Cúcuta	8,362	21,658	1,316,000
Orinoquía-Amazonía[2]	...	186,519	483,083	1,162,000
Quindío	Armenia	712	1,845	552,000
Risaralda	Pereira	1,598	4,140	928,000
San Andrés y Providencia	San Andrés	17	44	71,000
Santander	Bucaramanga	11,790	30,537	1,939,000
Sucre	Sincelejo	4,215	10,917	779,000
Tolima	Ibagué	9,097	23,562	1,293,000
Valle	Cali	8,548	22,140	4,104,000
Capital District				
Bogotá		613	1,587	6,276,000
TOTAL		440,762[3]	1,141,568[3]	41,537,000[4]

Demography

Population (2002): 41,008,000[5].
Density (2002): persons per sq mi 93.0, persons per sq km 35.9.
Urban-rural (1999): urban 73.5%; rural 26.5%.
Sex distribution (2000): male 49.14%; female 50.86%.
Age breakdown (2000): under 15, 32.2%; 15–29, 26.6%; 30–44, 22.6%; 45–59, 11.6%; 60–74, 5.6%; 75 and over, 1.4%.
Population projection: (2010) 46,109,000; (2020) 52,199,000.
Ethnic composition (2000): mestizo 47.3%; mulatto 23.0%; white 20.0%; black 6.0%; black-Amerindian 1.0%; Amerindian/other 2.7%.
Religious affiliation (1995): Roman Catholic 91.9%; other 8.1%.
Major cities (1999): Bogotá, D.C., 6,276,428; Cali 2,110,571; Medellín 1,957,928; Barranquilla 1,226,292; Bucaramanga 520,874.

Vital statistics

Birth rate per 1,000 population (2000): 22.9 (world avg. 22.5).
Death rate per 1,000 population (2000): 5.7 (world avg. 9.0).
Natural increase rate per 1,000 population (2000): 17.2 (world avg. 13.5).
Total fertility rate (avg. births per childbearing woman; 2000): 2.7.
Life expectancy at birth (2000): male 66.4 years; female 74.3 years.
Major causes of death per 100,000 population (1994): accidents, violence, and suicides 114.5, of which homicide with firearms 73.1; malignant neoplasms (cancers) 58.3; ischemic heart disease 50.4; infectious and parasitic diseases 13.7.

National economy

Budget (1998). Revenue: Col$16,706,000,000,000 (tax revenue 70.8%, nontax revenue 25.6%, transfers 3.6%). Expenditures: Col$21,526,000,000,000 (current expenditure 77.0%, of which wages 23.9%; capital expenditure 23.0%).
Public debt (external, outstanding; 2000): U.S.$20,951,000,000.
Population economically active (1998): total 6,550,679[9]; activity rate 47.4% (participation rates: ages 15–69, 67.7%; female 45.1%; unemployed 19.7%).

Price and earnings indexes (1995 = 100)

	1995	1996	1997	1998	1999	2000	2001
Consumer price index	100.0	120.2	142.5	172.0	191.3	209.4	227.7
Earnings index	100.0	107.4	108.9	109.2	112.3	114.7	...

Production (metric tons except as noted). Agriculture, forestry, fishing (1999): sugarcane 36,900,000, plantains 2,789,000, potatoes 2,705,413, rice 2,059,374, cassava 1,956,051, bananas 1,570,000, corn 974,583, coffee 648,000; livestock (number of live animals) 25,614,200 cattle, 2,195,600 sheep, 2,764,000 pigs; roundwood (1998) 18,618,000 cu m; fish catch (1998) 167,464. Mining and quarrying (1997): iron ore 631,500; salt 560,300; gold 521,800 troy oz; silver 109,500 troy oz; emeralds 6,305,903 carats[6]. Manufacturing (value added in Col$'000,000; 1996): processed food 9,362,300; beverages 2,485,900; textiles 2,107,300; machinery and electrical apparatus 2,049,000; transport equipment

1,632,700; paper products 1,581,700. Energy production (consumption): electricity (kW-hr; 1997) 46,378,000,000 (46,577,000,000); coal (metric tons; 1997) 32,592,000 (5,069,000); crude petroleum (barrels; 2001) 243,208,000 ([1997] 111,247,000); petroleum products (metric tons; 1997) 13,092,000 (11,141,000); natural gas (cu m; 1997) 5,681,838,000 (5,681,838,000).
Gross national product (2000): U.S.$85,279,000,000 (U.S.$2,020 per capita).

Structure of gross domestic product and labour force

	1998 in value Col$'000,000	1998 % of total value	1997 labour force	1997 % of labour force
Agriculture	10,330,739	13.7	3,478,832	22.8
Mining	3,213,148	4.3	110,969	0.7
Manufacturing	10,809,494	14.4	1,996,470	13.1
Construction	3,778,973	5.0	798,739	5.2
Public utilities	[7]	[7]	132,999	0.9
Transp. and commun.	6,007,799	8.0	831,591	5.5
Trade	8,790,382	11.7	3,330,221	21.8
Finance	[7]	[7]	753,572	4.9
Pub. admin., defense	6,783,180	9.0 }	3,744,301	24.5
Services	[7]	[7] }		
Other	25,471,697[7]	33.9[7]	81,777[8]	0.6[8]
TOTAL	75,185,412	100.0	15,259,471	100.0

Household income and expenditure. Average household size (1998) 5.3; sources of income (1992): wages 45.1%, self-employment 35.4%, transfer payments 14.2%; expenditure (1992): food 34.2%, transportation 18.5%, housing 7.8%, health care 6.4%, household durable goods 5.7%, clothing 4.5%.
Tourism (2000): receipts U.S.$1,028,000,000; expenditures U.S.$1,057,000,000.

Foreign trade[10]

Balance of trade (current prices)

	1996	1997	1998	1999	2000	2001
U.S.$'000,000	−2,206.7	−2,886.5	−2,874.1	+1,586.3	+2,256.8	+247.2
% of total	9.4%	11.1%	11.7%	7.4%	9.5%	1.0%

Imports (2000): U.S.$11,538,500,000 (machinery and transport equipment 37.9%, chemicals 23.4%, food and tobacco 6.6%, textiles and leather products 6.5%, vegetable products 6.2%, metals 5.1%, paper and paper products 4.0%). *Major import sources* (2000): U.S. 33.7%; Venezuela 8.2%; Japan 4.6%; Brazil 4.4%.
Exports (2001): U.S.$13,037,400,000 (petroleum products 35.0%, chemicals 13.0%, vegetable products 8.7%, coffee 8.2%, textiles and leather products 7.3%, food and tobacco 6.7%, coal 6.1%). *Major export destinations* (2000): U.S. 50.0%; Venezuela 9.9%; Ecuador 3.5%; Germany 3.2%; Peru 2.8%.

Transport and communications

Transport. Railroads (1997): route length 2,000 mi, 3,230 km; passenger-mi 9,646,000[11], passenger-km 15,524,000[11]; metric ton-km cargo 736,247,000. Roads (1999): total length 70,200 mi, 112,988 km (paved 14%). Vehicles (1999): cars 762,000; trucks 672,000. Air transport (2000): passenger-km 7,141,973,000; metric ton-km cargo 1,023,703,000; airports (1998) 43.

Communications

Medium	date	unit	number	units per 1,000 persons
Daily newspapers	1996	circulation	1,800,000[12]	46[12]
Radio	1997	receivers	21,000,000	524
Television	1999	receivers	8,273,000	199
Telephones	2001	main lines	7,300,000	181
Cellular telephones	2001	subscribers	3,160,000	78
Personal computers	2001	units	1,800,000	45
Internet	2001	users	1,154,000	29

Education and health

Educational attainment (1985). Percentage of population age 25 and over having: no schooling 15.3%; primary education 50.1%; secondary 25.4%; higher 6.8%; not stated 2.4%. *Literacy* (1995): population age 15 and over literate 91.3%; males literate 91.2%; females literate 91.4%.

Education (1999)

	schools	teachers	students	student/ teacher ratio
Primary (6–10)	60,183	214,911	5,162,260	24.0
Secondary (11–16)	13,421	200,337	3,594,083	17.9
Higher[13]	266	75,568	673,353	8.9

Health: physicians (1997) 40,355 (1 per 1,102 persons); hospital beds 40,043 (1 per 1,000 persons); infant mortality rate (1999) 25.6.
Food (2000): daily per capita caloric intake 2,597 (vegetable products 84%, animal products 16%); 112% of FAO recommended minimum requirement.

Military

Total active duty personnel (2001): 158,000 (army 86.1%, navy 9.5%, air force 4.4%). *Military expenditure as percentage of GNP* (1999): 3.2% (world 2.4%); per capita expenditure U.S.$68.

[1]Two seats are occupied by representatives from indigenous communities. [2]Geographic designation for eight political entities in eastern Colombia elevated to departmental status in the early 1990s. [3]Detail does not add to total given because of rounding. [4]De jure. [5]Excludes at least 2,000,000 Colombians who left the country since 1997 because of the violence and high unemployment. [6]1995. [7]Services include public utilities and finance. [8]Activities not adequately described. [9]The data relate to Bogotá, Barranquilla, Medellín, Cali, Bucaramanga, Manizales, and Pasto. [10]Import figures are f.o.b. [11]1992. [12]Circulation for 26 newspapers only. [13]1996.

Internet resources for further information:
• **National Administration Department of Statistics http://www.dane.gov.co**

Comoros[1]

Official name: L'Union des Comores (French); (Union of the Comoros)[2].
Form of government: republic[3].
Head of state and government:
President assisted by Vice presidents.
Capital: Moroni.
Official languages: Comorian (Shikomor); Arabic; French.
Official religion: Islam.
Monetary unit: 1 Comorian franc[4] (CF) = 100 centimes; valuation (Sept. 23, 2002) 1 U.S.$ = CF 500.22; 1 £ = CF 777.39.

Indian Ocean

Area and population

Autonomous Islands	Capitals	area sq mi	area sq km	population 2000 estimate
Mwali (Mohéli)	Fomboni	112	290	28,600
Nzwani (Anjouan)	Mutsamudu	164	424	219,500
Ngazidja (Grande-Comore)	Moroni	443	1,148	261,100
TOTAL		719	1,862	509,200[5]

Demography

Population (2002): 583,000[6].
Density (2002): persons per sq mi 810.8, persons per sq km 313.1.
Urban-rural (1995): urban 24.1%; rural 75.9%.
Sex distribution (2000): male 49.62%; female 50.38%.
Age breakdown (2000): under 15, 42.7%; 15–29, 28.6%; 30–44, 15.9%; 45–59, 8.1%; 60–74, 3.9%; 75 and over, 0.8%.
Population projection[6]: (2010) 734,000; (2020) 950,000.
Doubling time: 23 years.
Ethnic composition (2000): Comorian (a mixture of Bantu, Arab, Malay, and Malagasy peoples) 97.1%; Makua 1.6%; French 0.4%; Arab 0.1%; other 0.8%.
Religious affiliation (2000): Sunnī Muslim 98.0%; Christian 1.2%; other 0.8%.
Major cities (1995): Moroni 34,168 (urban agglomeration [2001] 49,000); Mutsamudu (1991) 20,000; Domoni (1990) 8,000; Fomboni (1990) 5,600.

Vital statistics

Birth rate per 1,000 population (2000): 40.0 (world avg. 22.5).
Death rate per 1,000 population (2000): 9.6 (world avg. 9.0).
Natural increase rate per 1,000 population (2000) 30.4 (world avg. 13.5).
Total fertility rate (avg. births per childbearing woman; 2000): 5.4.
Marriage rate per 1,000 population: n.a.[7]
Divorce rate per 1,000 population: n.a.
Life expectancy at birth (2000): male 57.8 years; female 62.2 years.
Major causes of death per 100,000 population: n.a.; however, major diseases include malaria (afflicts 80–90% of the adult population), tuberculosis, leprosy, and kwashiorkor (a nutritional deficiency disease).

National economy

Budget (1998). Revenue: CF 14,066,000,000 (tax revenue 64.0%, grants 29.4%, nontax revenue 6.6%). Expenditures: CF 16,307,000,000 (current expenditures 85.4%, development expenditures 14.6%).
Production (metric tons except as noted). Agriculture, forestry, fishing (2000): coconuts 60,000[8], bananas 60,000[9], cassava 45,000, taro 12,000, corn (maize) 3,500, rice 3,100, cloves 1,000, vanilla 140, ylang-ylang essence 40, other export crops grown in small quantities include coffee, cinnamon, and tuberoses; livestock (number of live animals; 1998) 40,000 goats, 40,000 cattle; roundwood, n.a.; fish catch (2000) 13,200. Mining and quarrying: sand, gravel, and crushed stone from coral mining for local construction. Manufacturing: products of small-scale industries include processed vanilla and ylang-ylang, cement, handicrafts, soaps, soft drinks, woodwork, and clothing. Construction: n.a. Energy production (consumption): electricity (kW-hr; 2000) 35,200,000 ([1999] 22,000,000); coal, none (none); crude petroleum, none (none); petroleum products (metric tons; 1997) none (22,000); natural gas, none (none).
Population economically active (1991): total 215,000; activity rate of total population 44.4% (participation rates: ages 10 years and over, 57.8%; female 40.0%; unemployed [2000] 20%).

Price and earnings indexes (1995 = 100)

	1994	1995	1996	1997	1998	1999
Consumer price index	93.4	100.0	102.4	104.0	105.9	106.8
Monthly earnings index[10]	88.3	100.0	...	...	...	...

Tourism: receipts from visitors (2000) U.S.$15,000,000; expenditures by nationals abroad (1998) U.S.$3,000,000.
Household income and expenditure. Average household size (1995) 6.3[11]; average annual income per household (1995) CF 188,985 (U.S.$505)[11]; sources of income: n.a.; expenditure (1993)[12]: food and beverages 67.3%, clothing and footwear 11.6%, tobacco and cigarettes 4.1%, energy 3.8%.
Land use (1994)[8]: forested 17.9%; meadows and pastures 6.7%; agricultural and under permanent cultivation 44.9%; other 30.5%.
Gross national product (at current market prices; 2000): U.S.$212,000,000 (U.S.$380 per capita).

Structure of gross domestic product and labour force

	2000 in value CF '000,000	2000 % of total value	1980 labour force[13]	1980 % of labour force
Agriculture, fishing	44,082	40.9	53,063	53.3
Mining	...	...	62	0.1
Manufacturing	4,488	4.2	3,946	4.0
Construction	6,733	6.2	3,267	3.3
Public utilities	1,654	1.5	129	0.1
Transportation and communications	5,715	5.3	2,118	2.1
Trade, restaurants, hotels	27,155	25.2	1,873	1.9
Finance, insurance	4,648	4.3	237	0.2
Public admin., defense	15,420	14.3	2,435	2.5
Services	595	0.6	4,646	4.7
Other	−2,689[14]	−2.5[14]	27,687[15]	27.8[15]
TOTAL	107,801	100.0	99,463	100.0

Public debt (external, outstanding; 2000): U.S.$201,900,000.

Foreign trade[16]

Balance of trade (current prices)

	1995	1996	1997	1998	1999	2000
CF '000,000,000	−19.2	−22.2	−23.6	−19.6	−20.7	−16.8
% of total	69.4%	82.0%	81.8%	78.8%	70.9%	57.3%

Imports (2000): CF 23,085,000,000 (petroleum products 20.0%, rice 12.3%, vehicles 10.8%, meat and fish 7.4%, cement 5.6%). *Major import sources:* France 36.6%; Pakistan 13.7%; Kenya 10.8%; South Africa 9.0%; Belgium-Luxembourg 3.8%.
Exports (2000): CF 6,259,000,000 (vanilla 49.5%, cloves 32.1%, ylang-ylang 14.2%). *Major export destinations:* France 38.6%; United States 19.9%; Germany 6.6%.

Transport and communications

Transport. Railroads: none. Roads (1996): total length 559 mi, 900 km (paved [1995] 76%). Vehicles (1996): passenger cars 9,100; trucks and buses 4,950. Merchant marine (1992): vessels (100 gross tons and over) 6; total deadweight tonnage 3,579. Air transport (1996): passenger-mi 1,900,000, passenger-km 3,000,000; short ton-mi cargo, n.a., metric ton-mi cargo, n.a.; airports (1997) with scheduled flights 2.

Communications

Medium	date	unit	number	units per 1,000 persons
Daily newspapers	1997	circulation	0	0
Radio	1997	receivers	90,000	170
Television	1997	receivers	1,000	1.8
Telephones	2001	main lines	8,900	12
Personal computers	2001	units	4,000	5.5
Internet	2001	users	2,500	3.4

Education and health

Educational attainment (1980). Percentage of population age 25 and over having: no formal schooling 56.7%; Qur'anic school education 8.3%; primary 3.6%; secondary 2.0%; higher 0.2%; not specified 29.2%. *Literacy* (1995)[8]: total population age 15 and over literate 192,000 (57.0%); males literate 108,000 (64.0%); females literate 84,000 (50.0%).

Education (1995–96)

	schools	teachers	students	student/ teacher ratio
Primary (age 7–12)	327	1,508	78,527	52.1
Secondary (age 13–19)	...	591	21,192	35.9
Higher	...	...	348	...

Health (1995): physicians 64[17] (1 per 7,800[17] persons); hospital beds 1,450[17] (1 per 342[17] persons); infant mortality rate per 1,000 live births (2000) 86.3.
Food (1997)[8]: daily per capita caloric intake 1,800 (vegetable products 94%, animal products 6%); 77% of FAO recommended minimum requirement.

Military

Total active duty personnel (1997): 1,500. *Military expenditure as percentage of GNP:* n.a.

[1]Excludes Mayotte, an overseas possession of France, unless otherwise indicated. [2]New official name effective with the swearing in of the first president of the new union on May 26, 2002. [3]New constitution effective from mid-2002 grants each island greater powers. [4]Formerly pegged to the French franc and since Jan. 1, 2002, to the euro at the rate of €1 = CF 491.97. [5]Projection based on 1991 census. [6]Includes 100,000 to 150,000 Comorians living abroad in France or Mayotte. [7]In the early 1990s, 20% of adult men had more than one wife. [8]Includes Mayotte. [9]1998. [10]July average for government employees only. [11]Based on sample survey of 2,004 households on all three islands. [12]Weights of consumer price index components for Moroni. [13]The wage labour force was very small in 1995; total of less than 7,000 including government employees, and less than 2,000 excluding them. [14]Less imputed bank service charge. [15]Not adequately defined. [16]Imports c.i.f.; exports f.o.b. [17]Estimated figure.

Internet resources for further information:
• **Indian Ocean Commission**
   http://www.coi-info.org

Congo, Democratic Republic of the

Official name: République Democratique du Congo (Democratic Republic of the Congo).
Form of government: transitional military regime with one legislative body (Assembly [300 nonelected seats]).
Chief of state: President.
Capital: Kinshasa.
Official languages: French; English.
Official religion: none.
Monetary unit: Congolese franc (FC)[1]; valuation (Sept. 23, 2002)
1 U.S.$ = FC 366.00;
1 £ = FC 568.80.

Area and population

Provinces	Capitals	area sq mi	area sq km	population 1998 estimate
Bandundu	Bandundu	114,154	295,658	5,201,000
Bas-Congo	Matadi	20,819	53,920	2,835,000
Equateur	Mbandaka	155,712	403,292	4,820,000
Kasai-Occidental	Kananga	59,746	154,742	3,337,000
Kasai-Oriental	Mbuji-Mayi	65,754	170,302	3,830,000
Katanga	Lubumbashi	191,845	496,877	4,125,000
Maniema	Kindu	51,062	132,250	1,246,787
Nord-Kivu	Goma	22,967	59,483	3,564,434
Orientale	Kisangani	194,302	503,239	5,566,000
Sud-Kivu	Bukavu	25,147	65,130	2,837,779
City				
Kinshasa	—	3,848	9,965	4,787,000
TOTAL		905,354[2]	2,344,858	42,150,000

Demography

Population (2002): 52,557,000[3].
Density (2002): persons per sq mi 58.1, persons per sq km 22.4.
Urban-rural (2001): urban 30.6%; rural 69.3%.
Sex distribution (2000): male 49.40%; female 50.60%.
Age breakdown (2000): under 15, 48.3%; 15–29, 26.9%; 30–44, 13.8%; 45–59, 7.0%; 60–74, 3.3%; 75 and over, 0.7%.
Population projection: (2010) 66,471,000; (2020) 87,913,000.
Doubling time: 23 years.
Ethnic composition (1983): Luba 18.0%; Kongo 16.1%; Mongo 13.5%; Rwanda 10.3%; Azande 6.1%; Bangi and Ngale 5.8%; Rundi 3.8%; Teke 2.7%; Boa 2.3%; Chokwe 1.8%; Lugbara 1.6%; Banda 1.4%; other 16.6%.
Religious affiliation (1995): Roman Catholic 41.0%; Protestant 32.0%; indigenous Christian 13.4%, of which Kimbanguist 13.0%; other Christian 0.8%; Muslim 1.4%; traditional beliefs and other 11.4%.
Major cities (1994): Kinshasa 4,655,313; Lubumbashi 851,381; Mbuji-Mayi 806,475; Kolwezi 417,800; Kisangani 417,517; Kananga 393,030.

Vital statistics

Birth rate per 1,000 population (2000): 46.4 (world avg. 22.5).
Death rate per 1,000 population (2000): 15.4 (world avg. 9.0).
Natural increase rate per 1,000 population (2000): 31.0 (world avg. 13.5).
Total fertility rate (avg. births per childbearing woman; 2000): 6.9.
Life expectancy at birth (2000): male 47.6 years; female 50.8 years.

National economy

Budget (1999). Revenue: FC 2,328,600,000 (tax revenue 76.9%, of which taxes on international trade 18.5%, taxes on goods and services 13.8%, income tax 12.6%; nontax revenue 12.8%). Expenditures: FC 4,113,800,000; wages and salaries 50.5%; defense 14.6%; investment 13.5%; interest on debt 7.2%).
Public debt (external, outstanding; 2000): U.S.$7,842,000,000.
Tourism (1997): receipts U.S.$9,000,000; expenditures U.S.$7,000,000.
Production (metric tons except as noted). Agriculture, forestry, fishing (2000): cassava 15,959,000, plantains 1,800,000, sugarcane 1,669,000, corn (maize) 1,184,000, oil palm fruit 900,000, peanuts (groundnuts) 382,000, sweet potatoes 370,000, rice 337,800, bananas 312,000, yams 255,000, mangoes 216,000, papayas 213,000, pineapples 196,000, oranges 185,000, dry beans 122,000, coffee 36,000, seed cotton 28,000, natural rubber 8,000; livestock (number of live animals) 4,131,321 goats, 1,048,710 pigs, 822,355 cattle, 924,000 sheep, 21,559,000 chickens; roundwood (2000) 50,754,000 cu m; fish catch (1999) 208,862. Mining and quarrying (1999): copper (metal content) 29,600; cobalt (metal content) 1,600; zinc (metal content) 1,300; gold 207 kg; diamonds 20,100,000 carats. Manufacturing (1999): iron and steel 965,000; cement 172,900; sugar 73,400; soap 46,773; tires 41,000 units; printed fabrics 13,615,000 sq m; matches 2,500,000 packs; shoes 848,000 pairs; beer 1,398,000 hectolitres; soft drinks 738,000 hectolitres. Energy production (consumption): electricity (kW-hr; 1999) 5,087,000,000 (5,087,000,000); coal (metric tons; 1997) 95,000 (141,000); crude petroleum (barrels; 1997) 8,425,000 (520,000); petroleum products (metric tons; 1997) 49,000 (469,000); natural gas, none (none).
Household income and expenditure. Average household size (1998) 2.3; average annual income per household, n.a.; sources of income: n.a.; expenditure (1985): food 61.7%, housing and energy 11.5%, clothing and footwear 9.7%, transportation 5.9%, furniture and utensils 4.9%.
Gross national product (2000): U.S.$4,417,000,000 (U.S.$85 per capita).

Structure of gross domestic product and labour force

	1999 in value FC '000,000	1999 % of total value	1993 labour force	1993 % of labour force
Agriculture	27,138,200	53.9	9,432,000	65.0
Mining	4,120,300	8.2		
Manufacturing	2,144,000	4.3		
Construction	1,178,300	2.3	2,321,000	16.0
Public utilities	1,089,400	2.2		
Transp. and commun.	1,204,800	2.4		
Trade	8,686,900	17.2		
Pub. admin., defense	2,096,300	4.2		
Finance and services	2,589,400	5.1	2,757,000	19.0
Other	121,900	0.2		
TOTAL	50,369,500	100.0	14,510,000	100.0

Population economically active (1997): total 19,618,000; activity rate 42.0% (participation rates [1987]: over age 10, 57.4%; female 43.5%).

Price and earnings indexes (1995 = 100)

	1993	1994	1995	1996	1997
Consumer price index	0.1	15.6	100.0	758.8	2,090.7
Earnings index	...	...	...	...	...

Land use (1994): forested 76.7%; meadows and pastures 6.6%; agricultural and under permanent cultivation 3.5%; other 13.2%.

Foreign trade

Balance of trade (current prices)

	1996	1997	1998	1999	2000
U.S.$'000,000	+249	+56	−50	−175	−275
% of total	8.2%	2.2%	2.1%	8.6%	15.3%

Imports (1999): U.S.$1,108,000,000 (non-oil 95.0%; oil 5.0%). *Major import sources*[4] (1999): South Africa 22.0%; Belgium 15.8%; Nigeria 10.0%; Zambia 5.3%; France 4.6%; U.S. 3.2%; China 3.2%; Germany 2.7%; The Netherlands 2.5%.
Exports (1999): U.S.$933,000,000 (diamonds 61.3%, crude petroleum 12.4%, coffee 9.8%, cobalt 8.6%, copper 5.1%). *Major export destinations* (1999): Belgium-Luxembourg 63.8%; U.S. 19.0%; Finland 4.1%; Italy 3.0%.

Transport and communications

Transport. Railroads (1996)[5]: length 5,138 km; passenger-km 29,000,000[6]; metric ton-km cargo 176,000,000[6]. Roads (1996): total length 154,027 km (paved 2%). Vehicles (1996): passenger cars 787,000; trucks and buses 60,000. Air transport (1996): passenger-km 279,000,000; metric ton-km cargo 42,000,000; airports (1997) with scheduled flights 22.

Communications

Medium	date	unit	number	units per 1,000 persons
Daily newspapers	1996	circulation	124,000	2.7
Radio	1997	receivers	18,030,000	376.0
Television	1997	receivers	6,478,000	135.0
Telephones	2001	main lines	20,000	0.4
Cellular telephones	2001	subscribers	150,000	2.9
Internet	2001	users	6,000	—

Education and health

Educational attainment: n.a. *Literacy* (1999): percentage of total population age 15 and over literate 60.3%; (1995) males literate 86.6%; females literate 67.7%.

Education (1994–95)

	schools	teachers	students	student/ teacher ratio
Primary (age 6–11)	14,885	121,054	5,417,506	44.8
Secondary (age 12–17)	4,276[7]	59,325[7]	640,298[8]	22.6[7]
Voc., teacher tr.	7	7	701,148[8]	7
Higher	...	3,873[9]	93,266	15.9[9]

Health: physicians (1990) 2,469 (1 per 15,584 persons); hospital beds (1986) 68,508 (1 per 487 persons); infant mortality rate (2000) 101.6.
Food (2000): daily per capita caloric intake 1,514 (vegetable products 97%, animal products 3%); 68% of FAO recommended minimum requirement.

Military

Total active duty personnel (2001): 81,400 (army 97.1%, navy 1.1%, air force 1.8%); national opposition forces (2001): 41,000; foreign forces were leaving DRC in September 2002[10]. *Military expenditure as percentage of GNP* (1997): 14.4% (world 2.4%); per capita expenditure U.S.$102.

[1]The new zaïre (NZ) replaced the (old) zaïre (Z) at a rate of 3,000,000 (old) zaïres to 1 NZ on Oct. 22, 1993; the Congolese franc (FC) replaced the new zaïre (NZ) at a rate of FC 1 to NZ 100,000 on July 1, 1998. Both zaïres ceased to be legal tender on June 30, 1999. [2]Detail does not add to total given because of rounding. [3]2002 population estimate adjusted for about 2.5 million war deaths between August 1998 and May 2001. [4]DOT (Direction of Trade) valuation; the valuation as the sum of all known trading partners, by external analysis, rather than as the reported sum of the country's own trade data. [5]Traffic statistics are for services operated by the Zaire National Railways (SNCZ), which controls more than 90% of the country's total rail facility. [6]1994. [7]Secondary includes Voc., teacher tr. [8]1993–94. [9]1989. [10]UN peacekeeping force numbered 3,700 troops in May 2002.

Internet resources for further information:
• **Permanent Mission of the Democratic Republic of the Congo**
  http://www.un.int/drcongo

Congo, Republic of the

Official name: République du Congo
(Republic of the Congo).
Form of government: republic[1]
with two legislative houses (Senate[2]
[66[3]]; National Assembly [137[4]]).
Chief of state and government: President.
Capital: Brazzaville.
Official language: French[5].
Official religion: none.
Monetary unit: 1 CFA franc (CFAF) =
100 centimes; valuation (Sept. 23,
2002) 1 U.S.\$ = CFAF 667.00;
1 £ = CFAF 1,037[6].

Area and population		area		population
Regions	Capitals	sq mi	sq km	1992 estimate
Bouenza	Madingou	4,733	12,258	177,357
Cuvette Est	Owando	28,900	74,850	151,839
Cuvette Ouest	Ewo			
Kouilou	Pointe-Noire	5,270	13,650	89,296
Lékoumou	Sibiti	8,089	20,950	74,420
Likouala	Impfondo	25,500	66,044	70,675
Niari	Loubomo	10,007	25,918	120,077
Plateaux	Djambala	14,826	38,400	119,722
Pool	Kinkala	13,110	33,955	182,671
Sangha	Ouesso	21,542	55,795	35,961
Communes				
Brazzaville	—	39	100	937,579
Loubomo	—	7	18	83,605
Mossendjo	—	2	5	16,405
Nkayi	—	3	8	42,465
Ouesso	—	2	5	16,171
Pointe-Noire	—	17	44	576,206
TOTAL		132,047	342,000	2,694,449

Demography

Population (2002): 2,899,000.
Density (2002): persons per sq mi 22.0, persons per sq km 8.5.
Urban-rural (2001): urban 66.1%; rural 33.9%.
Sex distribution (2000): male 49.17%; female 50.83%.
Age breakdown (2000): under 15, 42.5%; 15–29, 28.7%; 30–44, 16.1%; 45–59,
7.7%; 60–74, 4.1%; 75 and over, 0.9%.
Population projection: (2010) 3,425,000; (2020) 4,129,000.
Doubling time: 31 years.
Ethnic composition (1983): Kongo 51.5%; Teke 17.3%; Mboshi 11.5%; Mbete
4.9%; Punu 3.0%; Sango 2.7%; Maka 1.8%; Pygmy 1.5%; other 5.8%.
Religious affiliation (2000): Roman Catholic 49.3%; Protestant 17.0%; African
Christians 12.6%; unaffiliated Christians 11.9%; traditional beliefs 4.8%;
other 4.4%.
Major cities (1992): Brazzaville 937,579; Pointe-Noire 576,206; Loubomo
83,605; Nkayi 42,465; Mossendjo 16,405.

Vital statistics

Birth rate per 1,000 population (2000): 38.6 (world avg. 22.5).
Death rate per 1,000 population (2000): 16.4 (world avg. 9.0).
Natural increase rate per 1,000 population (2000): 22.2 (world avg. 13.5).
Total fertility rate (avg. births per childbearing woman; 2000): 5.1.
Life expectancy at birth (2000): male 44.5 years; female 50.5 years.
Major causes of morbidity and mortality in the 1990s included malaria, acute
respiratory infections, diarrhea, trauma, helminthiasis, and sexually trans-
mitted diseases.

National economy

Budget (1999). Revenue: CFAF 390,600,000,000 (petroleum revenue 70.6%;
nonpetroleum receipts 27.8%; grants 1.6%). Expenditures: CFAF 475,400,-
000,000 (current expenditure 81.3%, of which debt service 35.4%, salaries
21.2%, transfers and subsidies 5.5%; capital expenditure 18.7%).
Public debt (external, outstanding; 2001): U.S.\$3,758,000,000.
Household income and expenditure. Average household size (1984) 5.2.
Gross national product (at current market prices; 2000): U.S.\$1,735,000,000
(U.S.\$570 per capita).

Structure of gross domestic product and labour force				
	1999		1991	
	in value CFAF '000,000[7]	% of total value	labour force	% of labour force
Agriculture, forestry, fishing	119,800	9.0	471,000	59.1
Petroleum	692,300	52.1		
Manufacturing, mining	79,300	6.0	101,000	12.7
Construction	26,200	2.0		
Public utilities	9,300	0.7		
Trade	116,700	8.8		
Transp. and commun.	72,000	5.4	225,000	28.2
Pub. admin., defense	122,200	9.2		
Services	91,100	6.9		
Other	36,400	2.7	—	—
TOTAL	1,328,900[8]	100.0[8]	797,000	100.0

Production (metric tons except as noted). Agriculture, forestry, fishing (2000):
cassava 790,000, sugarcane 450,000, oil palm fruit 90,000, plantains 78,000,
bananas 52,000, sweet potatoes 22,000, peanuts (groundnuts) 25,000, avocados 25,000, yams 13,500, pineapples 13,000, cacao beans 1,800, coffee 1,400,

rubber 1,000; livestock (number of live animals) 285,000 goats, 116,000 sheep,
77,000 cattle, 46,000 pigs; roundwood (2000) 3,243,000 cu m; fish catch (1999)
43,886. Mining and quarrying (1998): gold 10 kg. Manufacturing (1998): residual fuel oil 240,000; cement 110,000; distillate fuel oils 85,000; aviation gas
48,000; gasoline 45,400; kerosene 44,600; refined sugar 42,861; wheat flour
4,002; cigarettes 380,000,000 cartons; beer 342,000 hectolitres; soft drinks
165,000 hectolitres; cotton textiles (1993) 1,800,000 m; veneer sheets 50,000
cu m. Energy production (consumption): electricity (kW-hr; 1998)
408,000,000 (535,000,000); crude petroleum (barrels; 1996) 77,837,000
(11,882,000); petroleum products (metric tons; 1996) 534,000 (507,000); natural gas (cu m; 1996) 3,357,000 (3,357,000).
Population economically active (1997): total 1,110,000; activity rate of total
population 42.0% (participation rates [1984]: ages 15–64, 54.0%; female
[1997] 43.4%; unemployed[9] [1984] 2.3%).

Price and earnings indexes (1995 = 100)							
	1995	1996	1997	1998	1999	2000	2001
Consumer price index	100.0	110.0	...	124.1	130.8	129.7	129.8
Earnings index	...	...	...	...	...	...	...

Land use (1994): forested 58.3%; meadows and pastures 29.3%; agricultural
and under permanent cultivation 0.5%; other 11.9%.
Tourism (1999): receipts U.S.\$12,000,000; expenditures U.S.\$60,000,000.

Foreign trade

Balance of trade (current prices)						
	1994	1995	1996	1997	1998	1999
CFAF '000,000,000	+192.2	+251.1	+79.1	+433.1	+405.6	+644.1
% of total	22.0%	27.3%	5.2%	28.6%	33.6%	46.0%

Imports (1999): CFAF 378,100,000,000 (machinery and transport equipment
20.8%, basic manufactures 20.1%, food and live animals 20.0%, chemicals
and chemical products 14.2%, mineral fuels 12.1%). *Major import sources:*
France 23.2%; U.S. 7.8%; Italy 7.8%; Hong Kong 4.9%; Belgium 3.8%; U.K.
3.1%; The Netherlands 2.9%.
Exports (1999): CFAF 1,022,200,000,000 (petroleum and petroleum products
91.9%, wood and wood products 4.3%, other 3.8%). *Major export destinations:* Taiwan 31.5%; U.S. 22.8%; South Korea 15.3%; Germany 6.7%; France
2.6%; Italy 2.3%.

Transport and communications

Transport. Railroads: (1998) length 894 km; passenger-km 242,000,000; metric
ton-km cargo 135,000,000. Roads (1997): total length 12,800 km (paved 10%).
Vehicles (1997): passenger cars 37,240; trucks and buses 15,500. Air transport
(1998)[10]: passenger-km 258,272,000; metric ton-km cargo 13,524,000; airports
(1998) with scheduled flights 10.

Communications				units per 1,000 persons
Medium	date	unit	number	
Daily newspapers	1995	circulation	20,000	7.8
Radio	1997	receivers	341,000	126
Television	1997	receivers	33,000	12
Telephones	2001	main lines	22,000	7.1
Cellular telephones	2001	subscribers	150,000	48
Internet	1999	users	500	0.18

Education and health

Educational attainment (1984). Percentage of population age 25 and over having: no formal schooling 58.7%; primary education 21.4%; secondary education 16.9%; postsecondary 3.0%. *Literacy* (1995): total population age 15 and
over literate 80.7%; males literate 87.5%; females literate 74.4%.

Education (1996–97)				student/ teacher ratio
	schools	teachers	students	
Primary (age 6–13)	1,612	6,926	489,546	70.7
Secondary (age 14–18)	2381[11]	5,466	190,409	34.8
Voc., teacher tr.	601[11]	1,746	23,606	13.5
Higher[12]	12	1,341	16,602	12.4

Health: physicians (1995) 632 (1 per 4,083 persons); hospital beds (1989) 4,817
(1 per 446 persons); infant mortality rate per 1,000 live births (2000) 101.6.
Food (1999): daily per capita caloric intake 2,212 (vegetable products 94%,
animal products 6%); 100% of FAO recommended minimum requirement.

Military

Total active duty personnel (2001): 10,000 (army 80.0%, navy 8.0%, air force
12.0%). *Military expenditure as percentage of GNP* (1999): 3.5% (world
2.4%); per capita expenditure U.S.\$21.

[1]New constitution effective from Aug. 10, 2002. [2]First elections to new Senate held in
July 2002. [3]Includes 6 vacant seats in Pool region. [4]Includes 8 vacant seats in Pool region.
[5]"Functional" national languages are Lingala and Monokutuba. [6]Formerly pegged to
the French franc and since Jan. 1, 2002, to the euro at a rate of €1 = CFAF 655.96. [7]At
current factor cost. [8]Detail does not add to total given because of rounding. [9]Previously
employed only. [10]Represents 1/11 of the traffic of Air Afrique, which is operated by 11
African states. [11]1989. [12]1995.

Internet resources for further information:
• **Investir en Zone Franc http://www.izf.net/izf/Index.htm**

Costa Rica

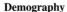

Official name: República de Costa Rica (Republic of Costa Rica).
Form of government: unitary multiparty republic with one legislative house (Legislative Assembly [57]).
Head of state and government: President.
Capital: San José.
Official language: Spanish.
Official religion: Roman Catholicism.
Monetary unit: 1 Costa Rican colón (₡) = 100 céntimos; valuation (Sept. 23, 2002) 1 U.S.$ = ₡367.78; 1 £ = ₡571.57.

Area and population

Provinces	Capitals	area sq mi	area sq km	population 2000 census
Alajuela	Alajuela	3,766	9,753	716,286
Cartago	Cartago	1,207	3,125	432,395
Guanacaste	Liberia	3,915	10,141	264,238
Heredia	Heredia	1,026	2,657	354,732
Limón	Limón	3,548	9,188	339,295
Puntarenas	Puntarenas	4,354	11,277	357,483
San José	San José	1,915	4,959	1,345,750
TOTAL		19,730[1]	51,100	3,810,179

Demography

Population (2002): 3,960,000.
Density (2002): persons per sq mi 200.7, persons per sq km 77.5.
Urban-rural (2000): urban 59.0%; rural 41.0%.
Sex distribution (2000): male 49.94%; female 50.06%.
Age breakdown (2000): under 15, 31.9%; 15–29, 27.1%; 30–44, 21.7%; 45–59, 11.4%; 60–74, 5.7%; 75 and over, 2.2%.
Population projection: (2010) 4,620,000; (2020) 5,303,000.
Doubling time: 45 years.
Ethnic composition (2000): white 77.0%; mestizo 17.0%; black/mulatto 3.0%; East Asian (mostly Chinese) 2.0%; Amerindian 1.0%.
Religious affiliation (1995): Roman Catholic 86.0%; Protestant 9.3%, of which Pentecostal 4.9%; other Christian 2.4%; other 2.3%.
Major cities (2000): San José 309,672[2] (urban agglomeration 983,000[3]); Limón 60,298[4]; Alajuela 42,889[4]; San Isidro de El General 41,221[4]; Cartago 39,958[5]; Liberia 39,242[4].

Vital statistics

Birth rate per 1,000 population (2001): 19.7 (world avg. 21.2); (1999) legitimate 51.0%; illegitimate 49.0%.
Death rate per 1,000 population (2001): 4.0 (world avg. 8.9).
Natural increase rate per 1,000 population (2001): 15.7 (world avg. 12.3).
Total fertility rate (avg. births per childbearing woman; 1999): 2.6.
Marriage rate per 1,000 population (1999): 7.3.
Divorce rate per 1,000 population (1995): 1.4.
Life expectancy at birth (1999): male 74.2 years; female 79.9 years.
Major causes of death per 100,000 population (1999): diseases of the circulatory system 127.6; malignant neoplasms (cancers) 87.2; accidents and violence 50.1; diseases of the respiratory system 44.5.

National economy

Budget (1998). Revenue: ₡459,700,000,000 (general sales tax 38.3%, selective taxes on goods and services 21.6%, income and profit taxes 19.3%, import duties 11.0%). Expenditures: ₡562,300,000,000 (current expenditures 91.3%, development expenditures 8.7%).
Public debt (external, outstanding; 2000): U.S.$3,274,000,000.
Gross national product (2000): U.S.$14,510,000,000 (U.S.$3,810 per capita).

Structure of gross domestic product and labour force

	1998 in value ₡'000,000,000	1998 % of total value	labour force	% of labour force
Agriculture, forestry, fishing	410	15.2	261,584	19.0
Mining	505	18.7	1,595	0.1
Manufacturing			203,501	14.8
Construction	67	2.5	81,176	5.9
Public utilities	82	3.0	13,103	1.0
Transp. and commun.	170	6.3	73,272	5.3
Trade, restaurants	554	20.5	251,735	18.3
Finance, real estate	312	11.6	70,119	5.1
Public administration	367	13.6	333,685	24.2
Services	229	8.5		
Other	—	—	86,770[6]	6.3[6]
TOTAL	2,696	100.0[1]	1,376,540	100.0

Production (metric tons except as noted). Agriculture, forestry, fishing (1999): sugarcane 3,950,000, bananas 2,101,000, oil palm fruit 440,000, pineapples 400,000, oranges 283,200, rice 262,200, coffee 147,000, cassava 119,500, potatoes 91,700, plantains 90,000, other products include other tropical fruits, cut flowers, and ornamental plants grown for export; livestock (number of live animals) 1,617,000 cattle, 290,000 pigs, 17,000,000 chickens; roundwood (1998) 5,311,000 cu m; fish catch (1997) 33,613, of which shrimp 5,717. Mining and quarrying (1997): limestone 1,500,000; gold 17,700 troy oz. Manufacturing (value added in ₡'000,000; 1996): food products 90,498; beverages 43,101; fertilizers and pesticides 18,360; plastic products 12,196; radio, television, and communications equipment 10,955; paper and paper products 10,589; wearing apparel 9,519. Energy production (consumption): electricity (kW-hr; 1997) 5,589,000,000 (5,714,000,000); coal, none (none); crude petroleum (barrels; 1997) none (4,955,000); petroleum products (metric tons; 1997) 625,000 (1,462,000); natural gas, none (none).
Population economically active (1998): total 1,376,540; activity rate of total population 41.2% (participation rates: ages 12–59, 59.3%; female 32.6%; unemployed [1999] 6.0%).

Price and earnings indexes (1996 = 100)

	1996	1997	1998	1999	2000	2001
Consumer price index	100.0	113.3	126.5	139.1	154.5	165.4[7]
Monthly earnings index[8]	100.0	115.3	134.6	156.5	183.7	...

Tourism (2000): receipts U.S.$1,229,000,000; expenditures U.S.$482,000,000.
Household income and expenditure. Average household size (2000) 4.1; average annual household income (1997) ₡1,468,597 (U.S.$6,314); sources of income (1987–88): wages and salaries 61.0%, self-employment 22.6%, transfers 9.6%; expenditure (1987–88): food and beverages 39.1%, housing and energy 12.1%, transportation 11.6%, household furnishings 10.9%.
Land use (1994): forested 30.8%; meadows and pastures 45.8%; agricultural and under permanent cultivation 10.4%; other 13.0%.

Foreign trade[9]

Balance of trade (current prices)[10]

	1996	1997	1998	1999	2000
U.S.$'000,000	−568	−764	−713	+289	−560
% of total	7.0%	8.3%	6.1%	2.2%	4.6%

Imports (2000): U.S.$6,380,000,000 ([11]general merchandise 68%; goods for reassembly 32%). *Major import sources*[12]: U.S. 33.5%; Mexico 8.4%; Venezuela 7.2%; Japan 4.5%; Guatemala 3.1%.
Exports (2000): U.S.$5,820,000,000 (reexports 57.1%; domestic exports 42.9%, of which bananas 9.4%, processed food and tobacco products 5.9%, coffee 4.7%, tropical fruit 3.4%). *Major export destinations*[13]: U.S. 33.9%; Nicaragua 6.9%; Guatemala 6.8%; Germany 5.3%; El Salvador 4.8%.

Transport and communications

Transport. Railroads[14]. Roads (1999): total length 22,292 mi, 35,876 km (paved 17%). Vehicles (1999): passenger cars 326,524; trucks and buses 181,272. Merchant marine (1992): vessels (100 gross tons and over) 24; total deadweight tonnage 8,368. Air transport (1999)[15]: passenger-mi 1,312,000,000, passenger-km 2,112,000,000; short-ton mi cargo 58,013,000, metric ton-km cargo 84,697,000; airports (1996) 14.

Communications

Medium	date	unit	number	units per 1,000 persons
Daily newspapers	1996	circulation	320,000	94
Radio	1997	receivers	980,000	283
Television	1999	receivers	900,000	242
Telephones	2001	main lines	945,000	230
Cellular telephones	2001	subscribers	311,300	78
Personal computers	2001	units	700,000	170
Internet	2001	users	384,000	93

Education and health

Educational attainment (1996). Percentage of population age 5 and over having: no formal schooling 11.7%; incomplete primary education 28.5%; complete primary 25.8%; incomplete secondary 16.0%; complete secondary 9.0%; higher 8.5%; other/unknown 0.5%. *Literacy* (1995): total population age 15 and over literate 2,118,000 (94.8%); males literate 1,054,000 (94.7%); females literate 1,064,000 (95.0%).

Education (1998)

	schools	teachers	students	student/teacher ratio
Primary (age 7–12)	3,711	19,235	529,637	27.5
Secondary (age 13–17)	353[16]	10,943	202,415	18.5
Higher	40[16]	...	83,106[16]	...

Health (1997): physicians 5,500 (1 per 630 persons); hospital beds 5,953 (1 per 582 persons); infant mortality rate per 1,000 live births (2001) 10.8.
Food (1999): daily per capita caloric intake 2,761 (vegetable products 82%, animal products 18%); 123% of FAO recommended minimum requirement.

Military

Paramilitary expenditure as percentage of GNP (1999): 0.5% (world 2.4%); per capita expenditure U.S.$19. The army was officially abolished in 1948. Paramilitary (police) forces had 8,400 members in 2001.

---

[1]Detail does not add to total given because of rounding. [2]Population of San José canton. [3]2001 est. [4]District population. [5]Population of three districts. [6]Includes 10,235 not adequately defined and 76,535 unemployed. [7]Average of first quarter. [8]Data for June only. [9]Imports c.i.f.; exports f.o.b. [10]Includes goods imported for reassembly and reexported. [11]Estimated figures. [12]Excludes goods imported for reassembly. [13]Excludes reexports. [14]National rail service was not in regular service from 1995 through 2000. [15]Lacsa (Costa Rican Airlines) only. [16]1997.

Internet resources for further information:
• **Central Bank of Costa Rica: Economic Indicators**
  http://websiec.bccr.fi.cr/indicadores/indice.web
• **Government of Costa Rica http://www.casapres.go.cr**

Côte d'Ivoire

Atlantic
Ocean

Gulf of
Guinea

Official name: République de Côte
d'Ivoire (Republic of Côte d'Ivoire
[Ivory Coast][1]).
Form of government[2]: republic with one
legislative house (National Assembly
[225[3]]).
Chief of state and government:
President assisted by Prime Minister.
De facto capital: Abidjan.
Official language: French.
Official religion: none.
Monetary unit: 1 CFA franc
(CFAF) = 100 centimes; valuation
(Sept. 23, 2002) 1 U.S.$ = CFAF 667.00;
1 £ = CFAF 1,036.[4]

Area and population

Regions	Capitals	area sq mi	area sq km	population 2000 estimate
Agnebi	Agboville	3,510	9,080	641,400
Bafing	Touba	3,370	8,720	158,700
Bas-Sassandra	San-Pédro	9,960	25,800	937,700
Denguélé	Odienné	7,950	20,600	246,400
Dix-huit Montagnes	Man	6,410	16,600	1,051,600
Fromager	Gagnoa	2,660	6,900	604,800
Haut-Sassandra	Daloa	5,870	15,200	1,055,600
Lacs	Yamoussoukro	3,450	8,940	531,600
Lagunes	Abidjan	5,480	14,200	3,894,300
Marahoué	Bouaflé	3,280	8,500	579,800
Moyen-Cavally	Guiglo	5,460	14,150	394,200
Moyen-Comoé	Abengourou	2,660	6,900	434,200
Nzi-Comoé	Dimbokro	7,550	19,560	809,400
Savanes	Korhogo	15,570	40,323	1,081,000
Sud-Bandama	Divo	4,110	10,650	735,100
Sud-Comoé	Aboisso	2,410	6,250	328,500
Vallée du Bandama	Bouaké	11,020	28,530	1,188,000
Worodougou	Séguéla	8,460	21,900	356,000
Zanzan	Bondoukou	14,670	38,000	746,300
TOTAL		123,863[5]	320,803	15,774,600

Demography

Population (2002): 16,805,000.
Density (2002): persons per sq mi 135.7, persons per sq km 52.4.
Urban-rural (2002): urban 44.0%; rural 56.0%.
Sex distribution (2001): male 50.79%; female 49.21%.
Age breakdown (2001): under 15, 46.2%; 15–29, 28.2%; 30–44, 14.2%; 45–59, 7.6%; 60–74, 3.0%; 75 and over, 0.8%.
Population projection: (2010) 20,003,000; (2020) 23,748,000.
Ethnolinguistic composition (1998)[6]: Akan 42.1%; Mande 26.5%; other 31.4%.
Religious affiliation (1998): Muslim 38.6%; Christian 30.4%; nonreligious 16.7%; animist 11.9%; other 2.4%.
Major cities (1995): Abidjan (1999) 3,199,000; Bouaké 330,000; Daloa 123,000; Yamoussoukro 110,000.

Vital statistics

Birth rate per 1,000 population (2001): 40.4 (world avg. 21.2).
Death rate per 1,000 population (2001): 16.6 (world avg. 8.9).
Natural increase rate per 1,000 population (2001): 23.8 (world avg. 12.3).
Total fertility rate (avg. births per childbearing woman; 2001): 5.7.
Life expectancy at birth (2001): male 43.6 years; female 46.3 years.

National economy

Budget (2000). Revenue: CFAF 1,237,100,000,000 (tax revenue 87.1%, of which import taxes and duties 29.2%, export taxes 13.2%, taxes on profits 11.6%, income tax 10.2%; nontax revenue 12.9%). Expenditures: CFAF 1,358,200,000,000 (wages and salaries 33.0%, debt service 22.7%; capital expenditure 15.4%; transfers 13.1%; other 15.8%).
Production (metric tons except as noted). Agriculture, forestry, fishing (2001): yams 3,000,000, cassava 1,900,000, plantains 1,500,000, sugarcane 1,300,000, cacao beans 1,200,000, rice 1,000,000, corn (maize) 692,749, taro 365,000, cotton seed 287,000, coffee 280,000, bananas 247,000, coconuts 230,000, pineapples 225,675, rubber 108,000; livestock (number of live animals) 1,451,000 sheep, 1,409,000 cattle, 1,134,000 goats, 336,000 pigs, 29,400,000 chickens; roundwood (2001) 11,968,000 cu m; fish catch (1999) 77,000. Mining and quarrying (1999): gold 2,706 kg; diamonds (1994) 84,300 carats. Manufacturing (value added in CFAF '000,000,000; 1997): food 156.6, of which cocoa and chocolate 72.4, vegetable oils 62.7; chemicals 60.2; wood products 55.9; refined petroleum 46.0; textiles 37.9; tobacco 27.6; fabricated metal products 25.9. Energy production (consumption): electricity (kW-hr; 1997) 2,760,-000,000 (2,760,000,000); crude petroleum (barrels; 1997) 9,267,000 (31,376,000); petroleum products (metric tons; 1997) 2,197,000 (2,165,000).
Household income and expenditure. Average household size (1998) 8.0; expenditure (1992–93)[7]: food 48.0%, transportation 12.2%, clothing 10.1%, energy and water 8.5%, housing 7.8%, household equipment 3.4%.
Population economically active (2000): total 6,531,000; activity rate of total population 40.9% (participation rates: [1994] over ages 10, 64.3%; female 33.0%; unemployed [1996] 38.8%).

Price and earnings indexes (1995 = 100)

	1995	1996	1997	1998	1999	2000	2001
Consumer price index	100.0	102.5	106.6	111.6	112.5	115.2	120.2
Minimum earnings index	100.0	102.7	108.3	...	...	...	...

Gross national product (2000): U.S.$9,591,000,000 (U.S.$600 per capita).

Structure of gross domestic product and labour force

	1999 in value CFAF '000,000,000	1999 % of total value	2000 labour force	2000 % of labour force
Agriculture	1,795.2	26.0	3,211,000	49.2
Manufacturing, mining, and public utilities	1,466.4	21.3		
Construction	352.8	5.1		
Transp. and commun.	592.8	8.6		
Trade	1,042.6	15.1	3,320,000	50.8
Public admin., defense	525.8	7.6		
Services	875.5	12.7		
Other (customs receipts)	248.6	3.6		
TOTAL	6,899.7	100.0	6,531,000	100.0

Public debt (external, outstanding; 2000): U.S.$9,063,000,000.
Tourism (2000): receipts U.S.$57,000,000; expenditures U.S.$226,000,000.

Foreign trade

Balance of trade (current prices)

	1994	1995	1996	1997	1998	1999
CFAF '000,000,000	+700	+681	+777	+777	+810	+832
% of total	28.2%	21.7%	21.6%	19.5%	19.9%	19.2%

Imports (1999): CFAF 1,739,500,000,000 (machinery and transport equipment 20.8%, food and food products 19.8%, crude and refined petroleum 18.9%, iron and steel products 4.5%, plastics 4.1%, pharmaceuticals 4.0%). *Major import sources* (1999): France 25.9%; Italy 5.6%; U.S. 5.2%; Germany 4.3%; Japan 4.3%; Spain 3.5%.
Exports (1999): CFAF 2,572,100,000,000 (cocoa beans and products 30.2%, crude petroleum and petroleum products 12.5%, fish products 6.2%, wood and wood products 6.1%, coffee beans 3.7%, cotton and cotton cloth 2.3%). *Major export destinations:* France 14.4%; The Netherlands 13.4%; United States 8.5%; Brazil 7.7%; Mali 4.7%; Italy 4.3%; Burkina Faso 4.3%; Spain 3.7%; Germany 3.2%.

Transport and communications

Transport. Railroads (1998): route length 655 km; passenger-km 118,800,000; metric ton-km cargo 529,800,000. Roads (1999): total length 50,400 km (paved 9.7%). Vehicles (1996): passenger cars 293,000; trucks and buses 163,000. Air transport (1998): passenger-km 318,000,000; metric ton-km cargo 44,000,000; airports (1999) 5.

Communications

Medium	date	unit	number	units per 1,000 persons
Daily newspapers	1996	circulation	231,000	17
Radio	1998	receivers	1,600,000	97
Television	1998	receivers	1,000,000	65
Telephones	2001	main lines	293,600	18
Cellular telephones	2001	subscribers	728,500	45
Personal computers	2001	units	100,000	6.1
Internet	2001	users	70,000	4.3

Education and health

Educational attainment (1988). Percentage of population age 6 and over having: no formal schooling 60.0%; Koranic school 3.6%; primary education 24.8%; secondary 10.7%; higher 0.9%. *Literacy* (1999): percentage of population age 15 and over literate 45.7%; males 53.8%; females 37.2%.

Education (1996–97)

	schools	teachers[8]	students	student/teacher ratio
Primary (age 7–12)	7,599	40,529	1,734,416	41.0[8]
Secondary (age 13–19)	147	15,959	534,214	30.7[8]
Vocational[9]	...	1,424	11,037	7.8
Higher[9]	7	1,657	43,147	26.0

Health: physicians (1996) 1,318 (1 per 11,111 persons); hospital beds (1993) 7,928 (1 per 1,698 persons); infant mortality rate (2001) 93.7.
Food (2000): daily per capita caloric intake 2,590 (vegetable products 96%, animal products 4%); 112% of FAO recommended minimum requirement.

Military

Total active duty personnel (2001): 13,900[10] (army 81.0%, navy 10.7%, air force 8.3%). *Military expenditure as percentage of GNP* (1999): 0.8% (world avg. 2.4%); per capita expenditure U.S.$5.

---

[1]Since 1986, Côte d'Ivoire has requested that the French form of the country's name be used as the official protocol version in all languages. [2]Referendum approving new constitution took place on July 24, 2000. Effective status of the constitution was still in question as of late September 2002. [3]Includes vacant/unoccupied seats. [4]Formerly pegged to the French franc and since Jan. 1, 2002, to the euro at the rate of €1 = CFAF 655.96. [5]Detail does not add to total given because of rounding. [6]Local population only; foreigners constitute 26% of the population and 2/3 of all foreigners are from Burkina Faso. [7]Weights of consumer price index components for a worker's family living in the capital city. [8]1995–96. [9]1994–95. [10]Excludes 680 French troops.

Internet resources for further information:
• Côte d'Ivoire—A Country Study http://lcweb2.loc.gov/frd/cs/citoc.html

Croatia

Official name: Republika Hrvatska
(Republic of Croatia).
Form of government: multiparty
republic with one legislative house
(House of Representatives [151[1]])[2].
Head of state: President.
Head of government: Prime Minister.
Capital: Zagreb.
Official language: Croatian
(Serbo-Croatian).
Official religion: none.
Monetary unit: 1 kuna (HrK; plural
kune) = 100 lipa; valuation
(Sept. 23, 2002) 1 U.S.$ = HrK 7.44;
1 £ = HrK 11.57.

Area and population

Counties	area sq km	population 2001 census	Counties	area sq km	population 2001 census
Bjelovar-Bilogora	2,638	131,343	Šibenik-Knin	2,994	112,070
Dubrovnik-Neretva	1,782	121,871	Sisak-Moslavina	4,448	183,531
Istria	2,813	205,717	Slavonski Brod-Posavina	2,027	172,993
Karlovac	3,622	140,125	Split-Dalmatia	4,524	456,967
Koprivnica-Križevci	1,734	123,736	Varaždin	1,260	183,730
Krapina-Zagorje	1,230	142,006	Virovitica-Podravina	2,021	92,381
Lika-Senj	5,350	52,221	Vukovar-Srijem	2,448	197,838
Medimurje	730	116,225	Zadar	3,643	158,936
Osijek-Baranja	4,149	326,446	Zagreb	3,078	304,186
Požega-Slavonia	1,821	84,562	**City**		
Primorje-Gorski kotar	3,590	304,410	Zagreb	640	770,058
			TOTAL	56,542	4,381,352[3]

Demography

Population (2002): 4,405,000[4].
Density (2002): persons per sq mi 201.8, persons per sq km 77.9.
Urban-rural (2000): urban 57.7%; rural 42.3%.
Sex distribution (2000): male 48.58%; female 51.42%.
Age breakdown (2000): under 15, 18.0%; 15–29, 20.1%; 30–44, 21.6%; 45–59, 19.6%; 60–74, 15.4%; 75 and over, 5.3%.
Population projection: (2010) 4,559,000; (2020) 4,615,000.
Ethnic composition (2000): Croat 82.0%; Serb 5.9%; other 12.1%.
Religious affiliation (2000): Christian 95.2%, of which Roman Catholic 88.5%, Eastern Orthodox 5.6%, Protestant 0.6%; Sunnī Muslim 2.3%; nonreligious/atheist 2.5%.
Major cities (2001): Zagreb 682,598; Split 173,692; Rijeka 147,709; Osijek 91,046; Zadar 69,239.

Vital statistics

Birth rate per 1,000 population (2001): 12.8 (world avg. 21.2); (1999) legitimate 91.8%; illegitimate 8.2%.
Death rate per 1,000 population (2001): 11.4 (world avg. 8.9).
Natural increase rate per 1,000 population (2001): 1.4 (world avg. 12.3).
Total fertility rate (avg. births per childbearing woman; 2000): 1.4.
Marriage rate per 1,000 population (1999): 5.2.
Divorce rate per 1,000 population (1999): 0.8.
Life expectancy at birth (2001): male 70.8 years; female 77.7 years.
Major causes of death per 100,000 population (1998): diseases of the circulatory system 633.7; cancers 268.6; accidents, violence, and poisoning 74.4; diseases of the digestive system 59.6; diseases of the respiratory system 51.2.

National economy

Budget (2000). Revenue: HrK 66,734,998,000 (sales tax 32.9%; extra budgetary social services 31.5%; excise taxes 11.3%; income tax 6.1%). Expenditures: HrK 74,432,276,000 (extra budgetary social services 50.7%, of which pensions 27.1%, health 18.7%; education 8.8%; defense 7.4%; public order 7.0%).
Population economically active (2000): total 1,698,829; activity rate 38.8% (participation rates: ages 15–64, 51.1%; female 46.0%; unemployed (2000) 21.1%).

Price and earnings indexes (1995 = 100)

	1995	1996	1997	1998	1999	2000	2001
Consumer price index	100.0	104.3	108.6	115.6	119.6	125.9	131.9
Annual earnings index	100.0	111.8	130.7	147.5	168.1	182.9	...

Production (metric tons except as noted). Agriculture, forestry, fishing (2001): corn (maize) 2,005,900, sugar beets 1,040,000, potatoes 663,600, wheat 1,032,000, grapes 353,541, barley 151,439, soybeans 115,529, cabbage 112,025, apples 81,339, tomatoes 69,555, sunflower seed 54,600, plums 39,857; livestock (number of live animals) 1,234,000 pigs, 529,000 sheep, 427,000 cattle, poultry 11,256,000; roundwood (1998) 3,398,000 cu m; fish catch (1999) 25,519. Mining and quarrying (2000): gypsum 100,000; ferrochromium 16,000. Manufacturing (value added in U.S.$'000,000; 1996): food products 895; transport equipment 425; electrical machinery 362; textiles 285; wearing apparel 260. Construction (value in HrK '000,000; 1998): residential 3,199; nonresidential 8,045. Energy production (consumption): electricity (kW-hr; 2000) 10,293,000,000 ([1997] 13,633,000,000,000); hard coal (metric tons; 1999) 50,839 ([1997] 286,000); lignite (metric tons; 1997) none (133,000); crude petroleum (barrels; 1999) 9,475,000 ([1997] 37,471,000); petroleum products (metric tons; 1997) 4,629,000 (3,540,000); natural gas (cu m; 2000) 1,768,000,000 ([1997] 2,679,000,000).
Gross national product (2000): U.S.$20,240,000,000 (U.S.$4,620 per capita).

Structure of gross domestic product and labour force

	1999			
	in value HrK '000,000	% of total value	labour force	% of labour force
Agriculture	10,900.5	7.9	247,400	16.6
Mining	642.5	0.5	8,800	0.6
Manufacturing	24,661.2	17.9	325,000	21.8
Construction	7,732.1	5.6	97,100	6.5
Public utilities	3,770.4	2.7	26,200	1.8
Transp. and commun.	9,777.2	7.1	101,100	6.8
Trade	17,369.0	12.6	271,200	18.2
Finance, real estate	16,387.5	11.9	91,200	6.1
Pub. admin., defense	11,684.0	8.5	105,400	7.1
Services	13,369.0	9.7	218,200	14.6
Other	21,310.3[5]	15.5[5]	—	—
TOTAL	137,603.7	100.0[6]	1,491,600[7]	100.0[6]

Public debt (external, outstanding; 2000): U.S.$7,686,000,000.
Household income and expenditure. Average household size (1999) 3.0; income per household HrK 53,534 (U.S.$8,200); sources: wages 47.7%, self-employment 19.6%, pension 19.6%, other 13.1%; expenditure (1999): food 37.9%, housing and energy 13.3%, transportation 11.0%, clothing 7.4%, household furnishings 5.9%, recreation and culture 5.7%, drink and tobacco 4.9%, health care 1.8%, education 0.7%, other 11.4%.
Tourism (2000): receipts from visitors U.S.$2,758,000,000; expenditures by nationals abroad U.S.$1,257,000,000.
Land use (1994): forest 37.1%; pasture 19.3%; agriculture 21.6%; other 22.0%.

Foreign trade[8]

Balance of trade (current prices)

	1995	1996	1997	1998	1999	2000
U.S.$'000,000	−2,877	−3,276	−4,933	−3,842	−3,496	−3,455
% of total	23.7%	26.6%	37.2%	29.7%	28.9%	28.0%

Imports (2000): U.S.$7,923,000,000 (machinery and transport equipment 32.9%; manufactured goods 29.4%; mineral fuels 14.4%; chemicals and chemical products 12.7%; food and live animals 7.0%; crude materials except fuels 2.4%). *Major import sources:* Italy 17.0%; Germany 16.3%; Russia 8.5%; Slovenia 7.9%; Austria 6.7%; France 4.3%.
Exports (2000): U.S.$4,432,000,000 (machinery and transport equipment 27.0%; manufactured goods 20.0%; chemical and chemical products 12.5%; mineral fuels and lubricants 11.0%; food 6.2%; crude materials except fuels 5.7%). *Major export destinations:* Italy 22.3%; Germany 14.3%; Bosnia and Herzegovina 11.2%; Slovenia 10.8%; Austria 6.6%.

Transport and communications

Transport. Railroads (2000): length 2,726 km; passenger-km 996,000,000; metric ton-km cargo 1,928,000,000. Roads (2000): total length 28,123 km (paved 82%). Vehicles (2000): passenger cars 1,124,825; trucks and buses 113,134. Merchant marine (1999): cargo ships 260. Air transport (2000): passenger-km 763,000,000; metric ton-km cargo 3,219,000; airports (2000) 4.

Communications

Medium	date	unit	number	units per 1,000 persons
Daily newspapers	1996	circulation	515,000	118
Radio	1999	receivers	1,110,000	261
Television	1999	receivers	1,083,000	254
Telephones	2001	main lines	1,646,000	365
Cellular telephones	2001	subscribers	1,755,000	377
Personal computers	2001	units	400,000	86
Internet	2001	users	250,000	56

Education and health

Educational attainment (1991). Percentage of population age 15 and over having: no schooling or unknown 10.1%; less than full primary education 21.2%; primary 23.4%; secondary 36.0%; postsecondary and higher 9.3%. *Literacy* (1995): population age 15 and over literate 98.3%; males 99.4%; females 97.3%.

Education (1999–2000)

	schools	teachers	students	student/ teacher ratio
Primary (age 7–14)	2,144	26,820	413,468	15.4
Secondary (age 15–18)	627	18,436	196,023	10.6
Higher	93	7,563	96,798	12.8

Health (1999): physicians 8,046 (1 per 529 persons); hospital beds 27,000 (1 per 158 persons); infant mortality rate per 1,000 live births (2001) 7.2.
Food (2000): daily per capita caloric intake 2,489 (vegetable products 79%, animal products 21%); 98% of FAO recommended minimum requirement.

Military

Total active duty personnel (2001): 58,300 (army 87.0%, navy 5.1%, air force and air defense 7.9%). *Military expenditure as percentage of GNP* (1999): 6.4% (world 2.4%); per capita expenditure U.S.$491.

[1]Includes six seats representing Croatians abroad. [2]A constitutional amendment in March 2001 abolished the former upper house (House of Counties). [3]Preliminary figure; final census figure equals 4,437,360. [4]Based on 2001 preliminary census figure. [5]Import and turnover taxes less imputed bank service charges. [6]Detail does not add to total given because of rounding. [7]Includes 321,900 unemployed. [8]Imports c.i.f.; exports f.o.b.

Internet resources for further information:
• Croatian Bureau of Statistics http://www.dzs.hr/Eng/ouraddress.htm
• Ministry of Foreign Affairs http://www.mvp.hr

Cuba

Official name: República de Cuba
(Republic of Cuba).
Form of government: unitary socialist
republic with one legislative house
(National Assembly of the People's
Power [601]).
Head of state and government:
President.
Capital: Havana.
Official language: Spanish.
Official religion: none.
Monetary unit: 1 Cuban peso (CUP) =
100 centavos; valuation (Sept. 23, 2002)
1 U.S.$ = 21.00 CUP;
1 £ = 32.64 CUP.

Area and population		area		population
				2001[1]
Provinces	**Capitals**	sq mi	sq km	estimate
Camagüey	Camagüey	6,174	15,990	789,900
Ciego de Ávila	Ciego de Ávila	2,668	6,910	410,700
Cienfuegos	Cienfuegos	1,613	4,178	396,700
Ciudad de la Habana[2]	—	281	727	2,189,700
Granma	Bayamo	3,232	8,372	832,600
Guantánamo	Guantánamo	2,388	6,186	514,100
Holguín	Holguín	3,591	9,301	1,032,700
La Habana[3]	Havana	2,213	5,731	704,800
Las Tunas	Las Tunas	2,544	6,589	530,300
Matanzas	Matanzas	4,625	11,978	661,900
Pinar del Río	Pinar del Río	4,218	10,925	737,300
Sancti Spíritus	Sancti Spíritus	2,604	6,744	462,300
Santiago de Cuba	Santiago de Cuba	2,382	6,170	1,037,700
Villa Clara	Santa Clara	3,345	8,662	836,300
Special municipality				
Isla de la Juventud	Nueva Gerona	926	2,398	80,100
TOTAL		42,804	110,861	11,217,100

Demography

Population (2002): 11,267,000.
Density (2002): persons per sq mi 263.2, persons per sq km 101.6.
Urban-rural (2001): urban 75.5%; rural 24.5%.
Sex distribution (2000): male 50.00%; female 50.00%.
Age breakdown (2000): under 15, 21.4%; 15–29, 22.7%; 30–44, 26.2%; 45–59,
16.1%; 60–74, 9.2%; 75 and over, 4.4%.
Population projection: (2010) 11,514,000; (2020) 11,721,000.
Ethnic composition (1994): mixed 51.0%; white 37.0%; black 11.0%; other
1.0%.
Religious affiliation (1995): Roman Catholic 39.5%; Protestant 2.4%; other
Christian 0.2%; other (mostly Santería) 57.9%.
Major cities (1999): Havana 2,189,716; Santiago de Cuba 441,524; Camagüey
306,049; Holguín 259,300; Santa Clara 210,100; Guantánamo 208,030.

Vital statistics

Birth rate per 1,000 population (2000): 12.7 (world avg. 22.5).
Death rate per 1,000 population (2000): 7.3 (world avg. 9.0).
Natural increase rate per 1,000 population (2000): 5.4 (world avg. 13.5).
Total fertility rate (avg. births per childbearing woman; 2000): 1.6.
Marriage rate per 1,000 population (1999): 5.1.
Divorce rate per 1,000 population (1993): 6.0.
Life expectancy at birth (2000): male 73.8 years; female 78.3 years.
Major causes of death per 100,000 population (1998): heart disease 142.6;
malignant neoplasms (cancers) 111.0; cerebrovascular disease 52.9; accidents
39.0; influenza and pneumonia 31.3; diseases of the blood vessels 21.9.

National economy

Budget (1999). Revenue: CUP 13,575,000,000. Expenditures: CUP 14,270,000,-
000 (education and health 26.5%; investment 11.9%; other 61.6%).
Public debt (external, outstanding; 1999): U.S.$11,078,000,000.
Production (metric tons except as noted). Agriculture, forestry, fishing (2000):
sugarcane 36,000,000, oranges and tangerines 447,000, rice 368,770, potatoes
344,215, plantains 329,000, grapefruit 232,879, cassava 210,000, corn (maize)
185,286, tomatoes 181,000, bananas 133,280; livestock (number of live animals) 4,700,000 cattle, 2,800,000 pigs, 15,000,000 chickens; roundwood (2000)
1,593,000 cu m; fish catch (1999) 122,425. Mining and quarrying (2000): nickel (metal content) 68,305; cobalt (metal content) 3,096. Manufacturing (value
added in U.S.$'000,000; 1990): tobacco products 2,629; food products 1,033;
beverages 358; chemical products 354; transport equipment 225; nonelectrical
machinery 176. Construction (gross value of construction in CUP '000,000;
1989): residential 227; nonresidential 872. Energy production (consumption):
electricity (kW-hr; 1997) 14,087,000,000 (14,087,000,000); coal (metric tons;
1997) none (42,000); crude petroleum (barrels; 2000) 17,380,000 ([1997]
20,772,000); petroleum products (metric tons; 1997) 2,284,000 (7,262,000);
natural gas (cu m; 1997) 21,987,966 (21,987,966).
Household income and expenditure. Average household size (1999) 3.6; average annual income per household (1982) CUP 3,680 (U.S.$4,330); sources of
income (1982): wages and salaries 57.3%, bonuses and other payments 42.7%;
personal consumption (1989): food 26.7%, other retail purchases 60.5%,
transportation services 5.4%, energy 2.7%, value of self-produced and consumed food 1.5%, household repairs 1.3%, other 1.9%.
Population economically active (1988): total 4,570,236; activity rate of total
population 43.7% (participation rates: over age 15, 56.9%; female [1998]
37.0%; unemployed [2000–01] 4.1%).

Price and earnings indexes (1994 = 100)					
	1994	1995	1996	1997	1998
Consumer price index	100.0	88.5	84.2	85.8	88.2
Monthly earnings index	...	...	...	...	...

Gross domestic product (1999): U.S.$18,600,000,000 (U.S.$1,700 per capita).

Structure of gross domestic product and labour force				
	1999		1989	
	in value CUP '000,000[4]	% of total value	labour force	% of labour force
Agriculture	1,122.9	7.2	721,100	20.4
Mining	186.0	1.2	}	
Manufacturing	4,594.9	29.3	767,500	21.8
Public utilities	430.2	2.7		
Construction	632.0	4.0	344,300	9.8
Transp. and commun.	911.7	5.8	235,900	6.7
Finance, insurance	637.0	4.1	21,700	0.6
Trade	3,370.2	21.5	395,300	11.2
Public administration			151,700	4.3
Services	3,789.5	24.2	835,700	23.7
Other	—	—	53,400	1.5
TOTAL	15,674.4	100.0	3,526,600	100.0

Tourism: receipts from visitors (2000) U.S.$1,756,000,000; expenditures by
nationals abroad (1990) U.S.$48,000,000.
Land use (1994): forested 23.7%; meadows and pastures 27.0%; agricultural
and under permanent cultivation 30.7%; other 18.6%.

Foreign trade[5]

Balance of trade (current prices)						
	1994	1995	1996	1997	1998	1999
U.S.$'000,000	−797	−1,166	−1,179	−1,200	−1,300	−1,800
% of total	24.4%	28.3%	24.4%	25.2%	25.5%	39.1%

Imports (1999): U.S.$3,200,000,000 (1996; mineral fuels and lubricants 27.9%,
food and live animals 19.8%, machinery and transport equipment 16.1%,
basic manufactures 14.9%, chemicals 8.7%, inedible crude materials 2.8%).
Major import sources (1999): Spain 19.5%; France 8.2%; Canada 8.1%; China
7.7%; Italy 7.0%; Russia 3.8%.
Exports (1999): U.S.$1,400,000,000 (1996; sugar 52.8%, minerals and concentrates
23.7%, fish products 6.8%, raw tobacco and tobacco products 5.9%, citrus and
other agricultural products 2.1%). *Major export destinations* (1999): Russia
23.3%; Canada 14.5%; The Netherlands 12.9%; Spain 8.0%; China 3.6%.

Transport and communications

Transport. Railroads (1999): length 2,987 mi, 4,807 km; (1997) passenger-km
1,962,200; metric ton-km cargo 1,074,800,000. Roads (1997): total length
37,815 mi, 60,858 km (paved 49%). Vehicles (1998): passenger cars 172,574;
trucks and buses 185,495. Air transport (1997): passenger-km 3,543,176,000;
metric ton-km cargo 56,239,000; airports with scheduled flights (1999) 14.

Communications				units
				per 1,000
Medium	date	unit	number	persons
Daily newspapers	1996	circulation	1,300,000	118
Radio	1997	receivers	3,900,000	352
Television	1999	receivers	2,750,000	246
Telephones	2001	main lines	573,000	51
Cellular telephones	2001	subscribers	8,100	0.7
Personal computers	2001	units	220,000	20
Internet	2001	users	120,000	11

Education and health

Educational attainment (1981). Percentage of population age 25 and over having: no formal schooling or some primary education 39.6%; completed primary 26.6%; secondary 29.6%; higher 4.2%. *Literacy* (1995): total population age 15 and over literate 95.7%; males 96.2%; females 95.3%.

Education (1999–2000)				student/
	schools	teachers	students	teacher ratio
Primary (age 6–11)	9,375	76,300	987,900	12.9
Secondary (age 12–17)	2,018	70,900	857,700	12.1
Voc., teacher tr.	618[6]	27,267[7]	244,253[7]	9.0[7]
Higher	37	23,500	106,500	4.5

Health (1998): physicians 63,554 (1 per 175 persons); hospital beds 80,684 (1
per 123 persons); infant mortality rate per 1,000 live births (2000) 7.5.
Food (2000): daily per capita caloric intake 2,564 (vegetable products 86%,
animal products 14%); 111% of FAO recommended minimum requirement.

Military

Total active duty personnel (2001): 46,000 (army 76.1%, navy 6.5%, air force
17.4%). *Military expenditure as percentage of GDP* (1999): 1.9% (world
2.4%); per capita expenditure: U.S.$57.

[1]January 1. [2]Province coextensive with the city of Havana. [3]Province bordering the city
of Havana on the east, south, and west. [4]At constant 1981 prices. [5]Imports c.i.f.; exports
f.o.b. [6]1989–90. [7]1995–96.

Internet resources for further information:
• Oficina Nacional de Estadísticas
http://www.cubagob.cu/otras_info/estadisticas.htm
• Naciones Unidas en Cuba
http://www.onu.org.cu/uunn/homepage/index2.html

Cyprus

Island of Cyprus

Area: 3,572 sq mi, 9,251 sq km.
Population (2002): 907,000[1].

Two de facto states currently exist on the island of Cyprus: the Republic of Cyprus (ROC), predominantly Greek in character, occupying the southern two-thirds of the island, which is the original and still the internationally recognized de jure government of the whole island; and the Turkish Republic of Northern Cyprus (TRNC), proclaimed unilaterally Nov. 15, 1983, on territory originally secured for the Turkish Cypriot population by the July 20, 1974, intervention of Turkey. Only Turkey recognizes the TRNC, and the two ethnic communities have failed to reestablish a single state. Provision of separate data below does not imply recognition of either state's claims but is necessitated by the lack of unified data.

Republic of Cyprus

Official name: Kipriakí Dhimokratía (Greek); Kıbrıs Cumhuriyeti (Turkish) (Republic of Cyprus).
Form of government: unitary multiparty republic with a unicameral legislature (House of Representatives [80[2]]).
Head of state and government: President.
Capital: Lefkosia (Nicosia).
Official languages: Greek; Turkish.
Monetary unit: 1 Cyprus pound (£C) = 100 cents; valuation (Sept. 23, 2002) 1 £C = U.S.$1.72 = £1.10.

Demography

Area[3]: 2,276 sq mi, 5,896 sq km.
Population (2002): 692,000[4].
Urban-rural (2001): urban 68.7%; rural 31.3%.
Age breakdown (1999[5]): under 15, 23.8%; 15–29, 21.5%; 30–44, 22.3%; 45–59, 17.2%; 60–74, 10.6%; 75 and over, 4.6%.
Ethnic composition (2000): Greek Cypriot 91.8%; Armenian 3.3% Arab 2.9%, of which Lebanese 2.5%; British 1.4%; other 0.6%.
Religious affiliation (1995): Greek Orthodox 93.4%; Armenian Apostolic 2.9%; Roman Catholic 1.5%; Muslim 1.0%; other 1.2%.
Urban areas (2001): Lefkosia 198,697[6]; Limassol 156,458; Larnaca 70,147.

Vital statistics

Birth rate per 1,000 population (2000): 12.4 (world avg. 22.5).
Death rate per 1,000 population (2000): 7.9 (world avg. 9.0).
Natural increase rate per 1,000 population (2000): 4.5 (world avg. 13.5).
Life expectancy at birth (1998–99): male 75.3 years; female 80.1 years.

National economy

Budget (1998). Revenue: £C 1,473,900,000 (income taxes 19.7%, value-added taxes 15.3%, social security contributions 14.9%). Expenditures: £C 1,731,500,000 (current expenditures 89.7%, development expenditures 10.3%).
Tourism (2000): receipts U.S.$1,894,000,000; expenditures U.S.$285,000,000.
Household expenditure (1994): food and beverages 23.0%, transportation and communications 14.5%, expenditures in cafes and hotels 14.5%.
Gross national product (at current market prices; 2000): U.S.$9,361,000,000 (U.S.$12,370 per capita).

Structure of gross domestic product and labour force				
	1998			
	in value £C '000,000	% of total value	labour force	% of labour force
Agriculture, fishing	204.6	4.4	29,000	9.3
Mining	13.0	0.3	600	0.2
Manufacturing	508.0	10.9	40,200	13.0
Construction	357.0	7.7	24,500	7.9
Public utilities	99.9	2.1	1,600	0.5
Transportation and communications	393.3	8.5	19,600	6.3
Trade	911.2	19.6	77,800	25.0
Finance, insurance	890.2	19.1	24,600	7.9
Pub. admin., defense	635.6	13.7 }	71,100	22.9
Services	400.9	8.6 }		
Other	236.4	5.1	21,800[7]	7.0[7]
TOTAL	4,650.1	100.0	310,800	100.0

Production. Agriculture (in '000 metric tons; 2000): potatoes 117.0, grapes 108.0, cereals 48.0, oranges 42.7, grapefruit 28.1, olives 21.0. Manufacturing (value added in £C '000,000; 1999): food 102.7; cement, bricks, and tiles 47.1; tobacco products 46.3; beverages 45.3; fabricated metal products 35.1. Energy production: electricity (kW-hr; 2001) 3,552,000,000.

Foreign trade[8]

Imports (1998): £C 1,904,700,000 (consumer goods 34.2%; transport equipment 12.9%; capital goods 11.2%; mineral fuels 6.6%). *Major import sources:* U.S. 12.5%; U.K. 11.3%; Italy 9.4%; Germany 8.5%; Greece 8.2%.

Exports (1998): £C 551,134,000 (reexports 55.6%[9]; domestic exports 38.7%, of which clothing 5.3%, chemicals 5.2%; ships' stores 5.7%). *Major export destinations:* U.K. 14.6%; Russia 10.3%; Greece 9.8%; Lebanon 5.5%; United Arab Emirates 4.9%.

Transport and communications

Transport. Roads (1999): total length 11,009 km (paved 58%). Vehicles (1999): cars 256,989; trucks and buses 113,802. Air transport (2001)[10]: passenger-km 3,017,000,000; metric ton-km cargo 39,981,000; airports (1996) 2.

Communications				units per 1,000 persons
Medium	date	unit	number	
Daily newspapers[11]	1996	circulation	84,000	111
Radio[11]	1997	receivers	310,000	406
Television	1999	receivers	120,000	180
Telephones	2001	main lines	435,000	642
Cellular telephones	2001	subscribers	314,400	464
Personal computers	2001	units	170,000	251
Internet	2001	users	150,000	222

Education and health

Educational attainment (1997). Percentage of population age 20 and over having: no formal schooling 4%; higher education 17%.

Education (1996–97)	schools	teachers	students	student/ teacher ratio
Primary (age 6–11)	376	4,159	64,761	15.6
Secondary (age 12–17) } Vocational	125	5,757	61,266	10.6
Higher	35	812	9,982	12.3

Health (2000): physicians 1,824 (1 per 372 persons); hospital beds 3,147 (1 per 216 persons); infant mortality rate per 1,000 live births (2000) 5.6.

Internet resources for further information:
• Central Bank of Cyprus http://www.centralbank.gov.cy
• Rep. of Cyprus Statistical Service http://www.pio.gov.cy/dsr

Turkish Republic of Northern Cyprus

Official name: Kuzey Kıbrıs Türk Cumhuriyeti (Turkish) (Turkish Republic of Northern Cyprus).
Capital: Lefkoşa (Nicosia).
Official language: Turkish.
Monetary unit: 1 Turkish lira (LT) = 100 kurush; valuation (Sept. 23, 2002) 1 U.S.$ = LT 1,662,000; 1 £ = LT 2,582,914.
Population (2002): 215,000[1] (Lefkoşa 39,176[12]; Gazimağusa (Famagusta) 27,637; Girne (Kyrenia) 14,205.
Ethnic composition (1996): Turkish Cypriot/Turkish 96.4%; other 3.6%.

Structure of gross domestic product and labour force				
	1998		1999	
	in value LT '000,000,000	% of total value	labour force	% of labour force
Agriculture and fishing	18,076	7.9	15,547	17.6
Mining and manufacturing	17,203	7.5	7,196	8.1
Construction	10,132	4.4	12,361	14.0
Public utilities	10,836	4.7	1,356	1.5
Transportation and communications	22,713	9.9	7,747	8.7
Trade, restaurants	36,624	16.0	9,536	10.8
Pub. admin.	49,486	21.6	17,689	20.0
Finance, real estate	25,077	10.9 }	16,083	18.2
Services	20,514	8.9 }		
Other	18,823[13]	8.2[13]	957[14]	1.1[14]
TOTAL	229,484	100.0	88,472	100.0

Budget (1998). Revenue: U.S.$406,200,000 (aid from Turkey 33.3%, direct taxes 25.2%, indirect taxes 19.8%, loans 7.3%). Expenditures: U.S.$406,200,000 (investments 13.6%, defense 10.4%, other 76.0%).
Imports (1998): U.S.$390,100,000 (transport equipment 18.6%, prepared foodstuffs 12.3%). *Major import sources:* Turkey 59.3%; U.K. 12.8%.
Exports (1998): U.S.$53,400,000 (ready-made garments 40.2%, citrus fruits 24.0%). *Major export destinations:* Turkey 50.7%; U.K. 30.9%.

Education (1998–99)	schools	teachers	students	student/ teacher ratio
Primary (age 7–11)	91	1,093	16,773	15.3
Secondary (age 12–17)	30	1,256	13,981	11.1
Vocational	10	363	1,890	5.2
Higher	8	884	21,912	24.8

Health (1998): physicians 451 (1 per 416 persons); hospital beds 1,002 (1 per 187 persons); infant mortality rate per 1,000 live births (1999) 3.7.

Internet resources for further information:
• Turkish Republic of Northern Cyprus http://www.cypnet.com/.ncyprus/root.html

---

[1]Includes 75,000 "settlers" from Turkey and 36,000 Turkish military in the TRNC; excludes 3,200 British military in the Sovereign Base Areas (SBA) in the ROC and 1,200 UN peacekeeping forces. [2]Twenty-four seats reserved for Turkish Cypriots are not occupied. [3]Area includes 99 sq mi (256 sq km) of British military SBA and c. 107 sq mi (c. 278 sq km) of the UN Buffer Zone. [4]Excludes British and UN military forces. [5]January 1. [6]ROC only. [7]Includes 10,400 unemployed. [8]Imports c.i.f.; exports f.o.b. [9]Mainly cigarettes, vehicles, and consumer electronics. [10]Cyprus Airways. [11]Island of Cyprus. [12]1996 census. [13]Import duties. [14]Unemployed.

Czech Republic

Official name: Česká Republika.
Form of government: unitary multiparty republic with two legislative houses (Senate [81]; Chamber of Deputies [200]).
Chief of state: President.
Head of government: Prime Minister.
Capital: Prague.
Official language: Czech.
Official religion: none.
Monetary unit: 1 koruna (Kč) = 100 halura; valuation (Sept. 23, 2002)
1 U.S.$ = 30.62 Kč
1 £ = 47.58 Kč

Area and population

Regions[1]	area sq km	population 2001 census[2]	Regions[1]	area sq km	population 2001 census[2]
Brno	7,067	1,133,916	Pardubice	4,519	510,079
Budejovice	10,056	630,168	Plzeň	7,560	553,741
Hradec Králové	4,757	554,348	Střed	11,014	1,129,627
Jihlava	6,925	521,212	Ústí	5,335	826,380
Karlovy Vary	3,315	306,799	Zlín	3,965	597,758
Liberec	3,163	430,789	**Capital city**[1]		
Olomouc	5,139	642,465	Prague (Praha)	496	1,178,576
Ostrava	5,555	1,277,095	TOTAL	78,866	10,292,933[2]

Demography

Population (2002): 10,210,000.
Density (2002): persons per sq mi 335.3, persons per sq km 129.5.
Urban-rural (1999): urban 74.6%; rural 25.4%.
Sex distribution (2001): male 48.76%; female 51.24%.
Age breakdown (2001): under 15, 16.2%; 15–29, 23.5%; 30–44, 20.2%; 45–59, 21.6%; 60–74, 13.0%; 75 and over, 5.5%.
Population projection: (2010) 10,101,000; (2020) 9,859,000.
Ethnic composition (2001): Czech 90.1%; Moravian 3.6%; Slovak 1.8%; Polish 0.5%; German 0.4%; Silesian 0.1%; Rom (Gypsy) 0.1%; other 3.5%.
Religious affiliation (2000): Catholic 43.8%, of which Roman Catholic 40.4%, Hussite Church of the Czech Republic 2.2%; nonreligious 31.9%; atheist 5.0%; Protestant 3.1%; Orthodox Christian 0.6%; Jewish 0.1%; other (mostly unaffiliated Christian) 15.5%.
Major cities (2001): Prague 1,178,576; Brno 379,185; Ostrava 319,293; Plzeň 166,274; Olomouc 103,293; Liberec 99,832.

Vital statistics

Birth rate per 1,000 population (2000): 8.8 (world avg. 21.2); legitimate 78.2%; illegitimate 21.8%.
Death rate per 1,000 population (2000): 10.6 (world avg. 8.9).
Natural increase rate per 1,000 population (2000): –1.8 (world avg. 12.3).
Total fertility rate (avg. births per childbearing woman; 2000): 1.0.
Marriage rate per 1,000 population (2000): 5.4.
Divorce rate per 1,000 population (2000): 2.9.
Life expectancy at birth (2000): male 71.7 years; female 78.4 years.
Major causes of death per 100,000 population (2000): diseases of the circulatory system 566.5; malignant neoplasms (cancers) 279.4; accidents, poisoning, and violence 68.8; diseases of the respiratory system 48.3.

National economy

Budget (2000). Revenue: Kč 586,208,000,000 (tax revenue 93.6%, of which social security contributions 37.1%, value-added tax 18.8%, personal income tax 13.2%, excise tax 9.2%, corporate tax 9.2%; nontax revenue 6.4%). Expenditures: Kč 632,268,000,000 (1999; social security and welfare 37.1%; health 17.5%; education 9.9%; defense 5.0%; police 4.6%).
Production (metric tons except as noted). Agriculture, forestry, fishing (2001): cereals 6,869,000 (of which wheat 4,545,729, barley 2,018,028, corn [maize] 349,951), sugar beets 3,517,570, potatoes 1,590,050, rapeseed 985,465; livestock (number of live animals) 3,593,717 pigs, 1,582,027 cattle, 90,241 sheep, 14,687,000 chickens; roundwood (2000) 14,441,000 cu m; fish catch (1999) 22,965. Mining and quarrying (1999): kaolin 3,600,000; feldspar 345,000. Manufacturing (value added in Kč '000,000,000; 1998): nonelectrical machinery and apparatus 47.0; food products 37.4; fabricated metals 35.2; motor vehicles 34.2; electrical machinery and apparatus 31.1; iron and steel 25.5. Construction (2000): 143,000,000,000 Kč. Energy production (consumption): electricity (kW-hr; 2000) 73,466,000,000 (63,449,000,000); hard coal (metric tons; 2000) 14,855,000 (14,855,000); lignite (metric tons; 2000) 50,307,000 (50,307,000); crude petroleum (barrels; 2000) 1,176,500 (39,826,000); petroleum products (metric tons; 2000) 6,132,000 (7,998,000); natural gas (cu m; 2000) 219,000,000 (9,428,000,000).
Tourism (2000): receipts from visitors U.S.$2,869,000,000; expenditures by nationals abroad U.S.$1,257,000,000.
Household income and expenditure. Average household size (2000) 2.5; disposable income per household Kč 286,920 (U.S.$8,900); sources of income (2000): wages and salaries 69.3%; transfer payments 24.2%, of which pensions 17.8%; other 6.5%; expenditure (2000): food and beverages 23.3%, housing and utilities 18.4%, transportation and communications 14.1%, recreation 10.8%, clothing and footwear 6.7%.
Population economically active (2001): total 4,663,885; activity rate of total population 45.0% (participation rates: ages 15–64, 70.1%; female 39.3%; unemployed 8.1%).

Price and earnings indexes (1995 = 100)

	1995	1996	1997	1998	1999	2000
Consumer price index	100.0	108.8	118.0	130.7	133.5	138.7
Annual earnings index	100.0	118.4	130.8	143.1	154.9	165.0

Public debt (external, outstanding; 2000): U.S.$8,132,000,000.
Gross national product (2000): U.S.$53,925,000,000 (U.S.$5,250 per capita).

Structure of gross domestic product and labour force

	2000 in value Kč '000,000	2000 % of total value	2001 labour force	2001 % of labour force
Agriculture, forestry	65,700	3.4	216,870	4.6
Mining	[3]	[3]	58,605	1.3
Manufacturing	607,700[3]	31.8[3]	1,362,052	29.2
Construction	124,000	6.5	376,565	8.1
Public utilities	[3]	[3]	72,463	1.6
Transportation and communications	164,200	8.6	346,431	7.4
Trade, hotels	253,100	13.2	841,620	18.0
Finance, real estate	279,000	14.7	496,798	10.7
Pub. admin., defense	} 252,900	13.2	182,358	3.9
Services			710,123	15.2
Other	164,000[4]	8.6[4]	—	—
TOTAL	1,910,600	100.0	4,663,885	100.0

Land use (1994): forested 33.3%; meadows and pastures 11.3%; agricultural and under permanent cultivation 43.0%; other 12.4%.

Foreign trade

Balance of trade (current prices)

	1995	1996	1997	1998	1999	2000
Kč '000,000	–99,569	–148,911	–148,221	–71,615	–68,124	–120,825
% of total	8.1%	10.9%	9.3%	3.8%	3.5%	5.1%

Imports (2000): Kč 1,241,924,000,000 (machinery and apparatus 30.9%, chemicals and chemical products 12.0%, transport equipment 9.0%, mineral fuels 9.6%). *Major import sources* (2000): Germany 34.2%; Slovakia 6.1%; Austria 5.7%; Russia 5.7%; France 5.6%; Italy 5.3%.
Exports (2000): Kč 1,121,099,000,000 (machinery and transport equipment 52.9%, basic manufactures 25.5%, chemicals and chemical products 9.3%, furniture 7.4%, iron and steel 7.1%, fabricated metals 5.2%). *Major export destinations* (2000): Germany 41.8%; Slovakia 8.5%; Austria 6.6%; Poland 5.5%; France 3.8%.

Transport and communications

Transport. Railroads (2000): length 9,444 km; passenger-km 6,884,000,000; metric ton-km cargo 17,496,000,000. Roads (1999): total length 125,905 km (paved, n.a.). Vehicles (2000): passenger cars 3,720,316; trucks and buses 442,076. Merchant marine (1993): vessels (oceangoing) 18; total deadweight tonnage 514,126. Air transport (2000): passenger-km 5,864,666,000; metric ton-km 37,788,000; airports (2000) with scheduled flights 2.

Communications

Medium	date	unit	number	units per 1,000 persons
Daily newspapers	1996	circulation	2,620,000	254
Television	2000	receivers	3,289,000	341
Telephones	2001	main lines	3,846,000	374
Cellular telephones	2001	subscribers	6,769,000	659
Personal computers	2001	units	1,400,000	136
Internet	2001	users	1,250,000	121

Education and health

Educational attainment (1991). Percentage of adult population having: no schooling through complete primary education 31.7%; secondary 58.6%; higher 8.5%; unknown 1.2%. *Literacy* (1998): 99%.

Education (2000–01)

	schools	teachers	students	student/ teacher ratio
Primary (age 6–14)	4,032	68,155	1,056,860	15.5
Secondary (age 15–18)	347	11,502	137,110	11.9
Voc., teacher tr.	1,369	10,042	190,186	18.9
Higher[5]	24	13,260	207,260	15.6

Health (2000): physicians 39,342 (1 per 261 persons); hospital beds 115,894 (1 per 89 persons); infant mortality rate per 1,000 live births (2000) 4.1.
Food (2000): daily per capita caloric intake 3,104 (vegetable products 73%, animal products 27%); 126% of FAO recommended minimum requirement.

Military

Total active duty personnel (2001): 53,600 (army 44.4%, air force 21.6%, ministry of defense 34.0%). *Military expenditure as percentage of GNP* (1999): 2.3% (world 2.4%); per capita expenditure: U.S.$292.

---

[1]New local government structure as of November 2000 elections. [2]Preliminary figure; final census figure equals 10,230,060. [3]Manufacturing includes Mining and Public utilities. [4]Taxes less subsidies and imputed bank charges. [5]Universities only.

Internet resources for further information:
• Czech Statistical Office http://www.czso.cz

Denmark

Official name: Kongeriget Danmark (Kingdom of Denmark).
Form of government: parliamentary state and constitutional monarchy with one legislative house (Folketing [179]).
Chief of state: Danish Monarch.
Head of government: Prime Minister.
Capital: Copenhagen.
Official language: Danish.
Official religion: Evangelical Lutheran.
Monetary unit: 1 Danish krone (Dkr; plural kroner) = 100 øre; valuation (Sept. 23, 2002) 1 U.S.$ = Dkr 7.56; 1 £ = Dkr 11.74.

Area and population[1]		area		population
				2001
Counties	Capitals	sq mi	sq km	estimate
Århus	Århus	1,761	4,561	640,637
Bornholm	Rønne	227	589	44,126
Frederiksborg	Hillerød	520	1,347	368,116
Fyn	Odense	1,346	3,486	472,064
København	—	204	528	615,115
Nordjylland	Ålborg	2,383	6,173	494,833
Ribe	Ribe	1,209	3,132	224,446
Ringkøbing	Ringkøbing	1,874	4,854	273,517
Roskilde	Roskilde	344	891	233,212
Sønderjylland	Åbenrå	1,521	3,939	253,249
Storstrøm	Nykøbing Falster	1,312	3,398	259,691
Vejle	Vejle	1,157	2,997	349,186
Vestsjælland	Sorø	1,152	2,984	296,875
Viborg	Viborg	1,592	4,122	233,921
Municipalities				
Copenhagen (København)	—	34	88	499,148
Frederiksberg	—	3	9	91,076
TOTAL		16,640[2]	43,098	5,349,212

Demography

Population (2002): 5,377,000.
Density (2002): persons per sq mi 323.1, persons per sq km 124.8.
Urban-rural (2001): urban 85.1%; rural 14.9%.
Sex distribution (2001): male 49.43%; female 50.57%.
Age breakdown (2001): under 15, 18.6%; 15–29, 18.5%; 30–44, 22.3%; 45–59, 20.8%; 60–74, 12.7%; 75 and over, 7.1%.
Population projection: (2010) 5,525,000; (2020) 5,706,000.
Ethnic composition (2001)[3]: Danish 95.2%; Asian 1.7%, of which Turkish 0.7%; residents of former Yugoslavia 0.7%; African 0.5%; German 0.2%; English 0.2%; other 1.5%.
Religious affiliation (1998): Christian 87.5%, of which Evangelical Lutheran 85.8%; Muslim 2.2%; other/nonreligious 10.3%.
Major urban areas (2001): Greater Copenhagen 1,081,673; Århus 218,380; Odense 144,849; Ålborg 119,996; Esbjerg 73,046.

Vital statistics

Birth rate per 1,000 population (2000): 12.6 (world avg. 22.5); (1995) legitimate 53.5%; illegitimate 46.5%.
Death rate per 1,000 population (2000): 10.9 (world avg. 9.0).
Natural increase rate per 1,000 population (2000): 1.7 (world avg. 13.5).
Total fertility rate (avg. births per childbearing woman; 2000): 1.7.
Marriage rate per 1,000 population (2000): 7.2.
Divorce rate per 1,000 population (2000): 2.7.
Life expectancy at birth (2001): male 74.3 years; female 79.1 years.
Major causes of death per 100,000 population (1995): malignant neoplasms (cancers) 296.6; ischemic heart disease 242.3; cerebrovascular disease 105.9.

National economy

Budget (1997)[4]. Revenue: Dkr 612,077,000,000 (direct taxes 52.2%, indirect taxes 30.7%). Expenditures: Dkr 626,536,000,000 (social security assistance 31.8%, education 12.2%, welfare services 10.1%, health 8.4%, defense 2.8%).
National debt (end of year; 1996): Dkr 664,128,000,000.
Tourism (2000): receipts U.S.$4,025,000,000; expenditures U.S.$5,139,000,000.
Population economically active (2000): total 2,877,000; activity rate of total population 54.0% (participation rates: ages 16–66 77.5%; female 46.5%; unemployed [May 2000–April 2001 avg.] 5.3%).

Price and earnings indexes (1995 = 100)							
	1995	1996	1997	1998	1999	2000	2001
Consumer price index	100.0	102.1	104.4	106.3	108.9	112.1	114.7
Hourly earnings index	100.0	...	...	...	...	...	...

Household income and expenditure. Average household size (2001) 2.2; income per household (1988) Dkr 199,354 (U.S.$29,613); expenditure (1993): housing 22.9%, food and beverages 17.9%, transportation and communications 15.5%, recreation 8.3%, household furnishings 6.1%, energy 6.1%.
Production (in Dkr '000,000 except as noted). Agriculture, forestry, fishing (value added; 2000): meat 21,059 (of which pork 17,032, beef 2,654); milk 11,254; cereals 7,458 (of which wheat 3,732, barley 3,214); flowers and plants 2,602, mink furs 2,118; livestock (number of live animals) 11,921,573 pigs, 1,867,937 cattle; roundwood (2000) 3,086,000 cu m; fish catch (1999) 1,447,664 metric tons. Mining and quarrying (2000): sand and gravel 23,000,000 cu m; chalk 400,000 metric tons. Manufacturing (value added in U.S.$'000,000;

1998): nonelectrical machinery and apparatus 3,874; food products 3,848; fabricated metals 2,228; printing and publishing 2,177; plastic and rubber products 1,114; furniture 1,089. Construction (completed; 2000): residential 2,184,000 sq m; nonresidential 4,284,000 sq m. Energy production (consumption): electricity (kW-hr; 2000) 35,844,000,000 ([1996] 39,582,000,000); coal (metric tons; 1997) 23,000 (11,161,000); crude petroleum (barrels; 2000) 136,095,000 ([1997] 66,971,000); petroleum products (metric tons; 1997) 8,654,000 (7,274,000); natural gas (cu m; 2000) 8,168,000,000 ([1997] 3,787,000,000).
Gross national product (2000): U.S.$172,238,000,000 (U.S.$32,280 per capita).

Structure of gross domestic product and labour force				
	1999		2000	
	in value Dkr '000,000[5]	% of total value[5]	labour force	% of labour force
Agriculture, fishing	36,258	3.1	107,900	3.7
Mining	11,430	1.0		
Manufacturing	149,842	12.8	464,300	16.1
Construction	43,598	3.7	167,600	5.8
Public utilities	20,022	1.7	16,200	0.6
Transp. and commun.	79,561	6.8	183,400	6.4
Trade, restaurants	156,035	13.3	503,000	17.5
Finance, real estate	163,052	13.9	344,200	12.0
Pub. admin., defense	217,713	18.6	962,200	33.4
Services	112,645	9.6		
Other	180,747[6]	15.4[6]	128,200[7]	4.5[7]
TOTAL	1,170,903	100.0[2]	2,877,000	100.0

Land use (1994): forested 10.5%; meadows and pastures 7.5%; agricultural and under permanent cultivation 55.9%; other 26.1%.

Foreign trade[8]

Balance of trade (current prices)						
	1995	1996	1997	1998	1999	2000
Dkr '000,000	+26,171	+32,889	+24,353	+13,776	+30,911	+42,495
% of total	4.9%	6.0%	4.0%	2.2%	4.8%	5.6%

Imports (2000): Dkr 360,790,000,000 (machinery and apparatus 14.2%, chemicals and chemical products 12.3%, food and live animals 8.2%, transport equipment and parts 7.8%, fuels 5.4%). *Major import sources:* Germany 21.0%; Sweden 12.2%; The Netherlands 8.6%; U.K. 7.6%; Norway 5.1%; France 5.1%.
Exports (2000): Dkr 403,285,000,000 (machinery and apparatus 23.5%, food and live animals 18.4%, pharmaceuticals 5.1%, mineral fuels and lubricants 4.8%, furniture 3.8%). *Major export destinations:* Germany 18.9%; Sweden 13.0%; U.K. 9.8%; Norway 5.5%; France 4.9%.

Transport and communications

Transport. Railroads (2001): route length 2,743 km; passenger-km 5,318,000,000; metric ton-km cargo 2,025,000,000. Roads (2001): total length 71,663 km (paved 100%). Vehicles (2001): passenger cars 1,854,060; trucks and buses 335,690. Air transport (2001)[9]: passenger-km 8,942,000,000; metric ton-km cargo 183,152,000; airports (1996) with scheduled flights 13.

Communications				units per 1,000
Medium	date	unit	number	persons
Daily newspapers	1998	circulation	1,613,000	284
Radio	1997	receivers	6,020,000	1,145
Television	1999	receivers	3,300,000	621
Telephones	2001	main lines	3,882,000	723
Cellular telephones	2001	subscribers	3,954,000	737
Personal computers	2001	units	2,300,000	432
Internet	2001	users	2,400,000	447

Education and health

Educational attainment (2000). Percentage of population age 25–69 having: completed lower secondary or not stated 34.6%; completed upper secondary or vocational 42.3%; undergraduate 17.6%; graduate 5.5%. *Literacy:* 100%.

Education (1998–99)				student/
	schools	teachers[10]	students	teacher ratio
Primary/lower secondary (age 7–15)	1,836	58,500	651,667	...
Upper secondary (age 16–18)	154	11,000	65,022	...
Vocational	177	12,000	180,784	...
Higher	158	8,000	170,169	...

Health: physicians (1994) 14,497 (1 per 358 persons); hospital beds (1999) 23,352 (1 per 228 persons); infant mortality rate per 1,000 live births (2001) 5.0.
Food (2000): daily per capita caloric intake 3,396 (vegetable products 62%, animal products 38%); 126% of FAO recommended minimum requirement.

Military

Total active duty personnel (2001): 21,400 (army 60.3%, navy 18.7%, air force 21.0%). *Military expenditure as percentage of GNP* (1999): 1.6% (world 2.4%); per capita expenditure U.S.$524.

[1]Excludes the Faroe Islands and Greenland. [2]Detail does not add to total given because of rounding. [3]Based on nationality. [4]Includes both central and local governments. [5]At constant 1995 prices. [6]Taxes on products less imputed bank service charges. [7]Includes 10,500 not adequately defined and 117,700 unemployed. [8]Imports c.i.f., exports f.o.b. [9]Danish share of Scandinavian Airlines System (scheduled air service only) and Maersk Air. [10]1993–94.

Internet resources for further information:
• Statistics Denmark http://www2.dst.dk/internet/startuk.htm

Djibouti

Official name: Jumhūrīyah Jībūtī
  (Arabic); République de Djibouti
  (French) (Republic of Djibouti).
Form of government: multiparty
  republic with one legislative house
  (National Assembly [65]).
Head of state and government:
  President.
Capital: Djibouti.
Official languages: Arabic; French.
Official religion: none.
Monetary unit: 1 Djibouti franc
  (DF) = 100 centimes; valuation (Sept.
  23, 2002) 1 U.S.$ = DF 164.90;
  1 £ = DF 256.27.

Area and population

Districts	Capitals	area[1] sq mi	area[1] sq km	population 1982 estimate
'Alī Sabīḥ (Ali-Sabieh)	'Alī Sabīḥ	925	2,400	15,000
Dikhil	Dikhil	2,775	7,200	30,000
Djibouti	Djibouti	225	600	200,000
Obock	Obock	2,200	5,700	15,000
Tadjoura (Tadjourah)	Tadjoura	2,825	7,300	30,000
TOTAL		8,950	23,200	335,000[2]

Demography

Population (2002): 473,000.
Density (2002): persons per sq mi 52.8, persons per sq km 20.4.
Urban-rural (1999): urban 83.1%; rural 16.9%.
Sex distribution (2001): male 51.59%; female 48.41%.
Age breakdown (2001): under 15, 42.6%; 15–29, 26.4%; 30–44, 14.3%; 45–59,
  11.5%; 60–74, 4.6%; 75 and over, 0.6%.
Population projection: (2010) 579,000; (2020) 729,000.
Doubling time: 27 years.
Ethnic composition (2000): Somali 46.0%; Afar 35.4%; Arab 11.0%; mixed
  African and European 3.0%; French 1.6%; other/unspecified 3.0%.
Religious affiliation (1995): Sunnī Muslim 97.2%; Christian 2.8%, of which
  Roman Catholic 2.2%, Orthodox 0.5%, Protestant 0.1%.
Major city and towns (1991): Djibouti 383,000[3]; 'Alī Sabīḥ 8,000; Tadjoura
  7,500; Dikhil 6,500.

Vital statistics

Birth rate per 1,000 population (2001): 40.7 (world avg. 21.2).
Death rate per 1,000 population (2001): 14.7 (world avg. 8.9).
Natural increase rate per 1,000 population (2001): 26.0 (world avg. 12.3).
Total fertility rate (avg. births per childbearing woman; 2001): 5.7.
Marriage rate per 1,000 population: n.a.
Divorce rate per 1,000 population: n.a.
Life expectancy at birth (2001): male 49.4 years; female 53.1 years.
Major causes of death (percentage of total deaths [infants and children to age
  10, district of Djibouti only]; 1984): diarrhea and acute dehydration 16.0%;
  malnutrition 16.0%; poisoning 11.0%; tuberculosis 6.0%; acute respiratory
  disease 6.0%; malaria 6.0%; anemia 6.0%; heart disease 2.0%; kidney disease 1.0%; other ailments 19.0%; no diagnosis 11.0%.

National economy

Budget (1998)[4]. Revenue: DF 23,154,000,000 (tax revenue 87.5%, of which
  domestic consumption taxes 27.1%, wages and salary tax 13.7%, surcharge
  on khat 8.9%, income and profit tax 6.1%; nontax revenue 12.5%).
  Expenditures: DF 30,427,000,000 (current expenditures 80.0%, of which general administration 26.7%, defense and mobilization 20.0%, education 8.7%,
  health 5.4%; capital expenditures 20.0%).
Tourism (1995): receipts from visitors U.S.$4,000,000; expenditures by nation-
  als abroad U.S.$4,000,000.
Production (metric tons except as noted). Agriculture, forestry, fishing (2001):
  vegetables and melons 23,060, of which tomatoes 1,100, onions 80, eggplant
  33; lemons and limes 1,800; tropical fruit 1,700; livestock (number of live animals) 513,000 goats, 465,000 sheep, 269,000 cattle, 70,000 camels, 8,700 asses;
  roundwood, n.a.; fish catch (1999) 350. Mining and quarrying: mineral production limited to locally used construction materials and evaporated salt.
  Manufacturing (2000): structural detail, n.a.; main products include furniture,
  nonalcoholic beverages, meat and hides, light electromechanical goods, and
  mineral water. Construction (1989): 53,900 sq m. Energy production (consumption): electricity (kW-hr; 1999) 180,000,000 (167,400,000); firewood and
  charcoal, n.a. (n.a.); coal, none (n.a.); crude petroleum, none (n.a.); petroleum products (metric tons; 1997) none (119,000); natural gas, none (n.a.); geothermal, wind, and solar resources are substantial but largely undeveloped.
Population economically active (1991): total 282,000; activity rate of total population 61.5% (participation rates: over age 10, 70.4%; female 40.8%; unemployed [2000] *c.* 40–50%).

Price and earnings indexes (1990 = 100)

	1990	1991	1992	1993	1994	1995	1996
Consumer price index[5]	100.0	106.8	110.4	115.3	122.8	128.8	134.2
Earnings index	...	...	...	...	...	...	...

Household income and expenditure. Average household size (1985)[6] 7.2; income per household: n.a.; sources of income: n.a.; expenditure (expatriate
  households; 1984): food 50.3%, energy 13.1%, recreation 10.4%, housing

6.4%, clothing 1.7%, personal effects 1.4%, health care 1.0%, household
  goods 0.3%, other 15.4%.
Public debt (external, outstanding; 2000): U.S.$237,900,000.
Gross national product (2000): U.S.$553,000,000 (U.S.$880 per capita).

Structure of gross domestic product and labour force

	1998 in value DF '000,000	1998 % of total value	1991 labour force	1991 % of labour force
Agriculture	2,917	3.2	212,000	75.2
Mining	—	—		
Manufacturing	4,239	4.6	31,000	11.0
Construction	6,971	7.6		
Public utilities	4,850	5.3		
Transp. and commun.	15,824	17.4		
Trade	14,481	15.9		
Finance	8,772	9.6	39,000	13.8
Pub. admin., defense	18,469	20.3		
Services	4,340	4.8		
Other	10,335	11.3	...	...
TOTAL	91,198	100.0	282,000	100.0

Land use (1994): forested 0.9%; meadows and pastures 56.1%; agricultural and
  under permanent cultivation[7]; built-on, wasteland, and other 43.0%.

Foreign trade

Balance of trade (current prices)

	1993	1994	1995	1996	1997	1998
U.S.$'000,000	−183.9	−180.7	−169.2	−161.1	−161.4	−179.7
% of total	56.4%	61.6%	69.0%	67.0%	65.3%	60.3%

Imports (1998): U.S.$238,800,000 (food, beverages, khat, and tobacco 53.2%;
  petroleum products 12.4%; machinery and electric appliances 10.9%; base
  metals and base metal products 4.9%; chemical products 4.6%; transport
  equipment 4.3%; clothing and footwear 3.7%). *Major import sources:* France
  12.5%; Ethiopia 12.0%; Italy 9.2%; U.K. 6.2%; Saudi Arabia 5.7%; Japan
  4.2%.
Exports (1998): U.S.$59,100,000 (1992; unspecified special transactions 60.0%;
  live animals [including camels] 21.3%; basic manufactures 5.2%; crude materials 4.5%). *Major export destinations:* Somalia 53.0%; Yemen 22.5%;
  Ethiopia 5.0%; Saudi Arabia 0.7%.

Transport and communications

Transport. Railroads (1997): length (1989) 66 mi, 106 km; passenger-mi
  361,000,000, passenger-km 762,000,000; short ton-mile cargo 144,000,000,
  metric ton-km cargo 232,000,000. Roads (1999): total length 1,796 mi, 2,890
  km (paved 13%). Vehicles (1996): passenger cars 9,200; trucks and buses
  2,040. Merchant marine (2000): vessels (100 gross tons and over) 13; total
  deadweight tonnage 4,356. Air transport (1998): passengers handled 107,369;
  metric tons of freight handled 7,290; airports (2000) with scheduled flights 1.

Communications

Medium	date	unit	number	units per 1,000 persons
Daily newspapers	1995	circulation	500	0.8
Radio	1997	receivers	52,000	84
Television	1999	receivers	30,000	67
Telephones	2001	main lines	9,900	15.4
Cellular telephones	2001	subscribers	3,000	4.7
Personal computers	2001	units	7,000	10.9
Internet	2001	users	3,300	5.1

Education and health

Educational attainment: n.a. *Literacy* (1998): percentage of population age 15
  and over literate 62.7%; males literate 74.0%; females literate 51.4%.

Education (1996–97)

	schools	teachers	students	student/ teacher ratio
Primary (age 6–11)	72	1,096	36,896	33.7
Secondary (age 12–18) Voc., teacher tr.	26[8]	628[9]	11,628	...
Higher	1[8]	13[8]	130[9]	...

Health (1996): physicians 60 (1 per 7,100 persons); hospital beds[10] (1989) 1,383
  (1 per 369 persons); infant mortality rate per 1,000 live births (2001) 93.2.
Food (2000): daily per capita caloric intake 2,050 (vegetable products 87%,
  animal products 13%); 88% of FAO recommended minimum requirement.

Military

Total active duty personnel (2001): 9,600[11] (army 83.3%, navy 2.1%, air force
  2.1%, paramilitary 12.5%). *Military expenditure as percentage of GNP* (1999):
  4.3% (world 2.4%); per capita expenditure U.S.$51.

---

[1]Original figures are those given in sq km; sq mi equivalent is rounded to appropriate
level of generality. [2]Includes 45,000 persons not distributed by district. [3]1995 estimate.
[4]Preliminary. [5]Based on expatriates' expenditures. [6]City of Djibouti only. [7]In 1988–89
only 1,005 acres (407 hectares) of land were cultivated. [8]1991. [9]1995–96. [10]Public health
facilities only. [11]Excludes 3,200 French troops; other military forces from mid-2002
include 1,200 German naval personnel and 800 U.S. troops.

Dominica

Official name: Commonwealth of Dominica.
Form of government: multiparty republic with one legislative house (House of Assembly [32[1]]).
Chief of state: President.
Head of government: Prime Minister.
Capital: Roseau.
Official language: English.
Official religion: none.
Monetary unit: 1 East Caribbean dollar (EC$) = 100 cents; valuation (Sept. 23, 2002) 1 U.S.$ = EC$2.70; 1 £ = EC$4.20.

Area and population	area		population
Parishes	sq mi	sq km	1991 census
St. Andrew	69.3	179.6	11,106
St. David	49.0	126.8	6,977
St. George	20.7	53.5	20,365
St. John	22.5	58.5	4,990
St. Joseph	46.4	120.1	6,183
St. Luke	4.3	11.1	1,552
St. Mark	3.8	9.9	1,943
St. Patrick	32.6	84.4	8,929
St. Paul	26.0	67.4	7,495
St. Peter	10.7	27.7	1,643
TOTAL	285.3[2]	739.0[2]	71,183[3]

Demography

Population (2002): 71,700.
Density (2002): persons per sq mi 247.2, persons per sq km 95.6.
Urban-rural (2001): urban 70.4%; rural 29.6%.
Sex distribution (2001): male 51%; female 49%.
Age breakdown (2000): under 15, 29.1%; 15–29, 27.2%; 30–44, 23.7%; 45–59, 9.6%; 60–74, 7.0%; 75 and over, 3.4%.
Population projection: (2010) 72,000; (2020) 72,000.
Doubling time: 63 years.
Ethnic composition (2000): black 88.3%; mulatto 7.3%; black-Amerindian 1.7%; British expatriates 1.0%; Indo-Pakistani 1.0%; other 0.7%.
Religious affiliation (1991): Roman Catholic 70.1%; six largest Protestant groups 17.2%, of which Seventh-day Adventist 4.6%, Pentecostal 4.3%, Methodist 4.2%; other 8.9%; nonreligious 2.9%; unknown 0.9%.
Major towns (1991): Roseau 15,853; Portsmouth 3,621; Marigot 2,919; Atkinson 2,518; Mahaut 2,372.

Vital statistics

Birth rate per 1,000 population (2000): 18.3 (world avg. 22.5); (1991) legitimate 24.1%; illegitimate 75.9%.
Death rate per 1,000 population (2000): 7.3 (world avg. 9.0).
Natural increase rate per 1,000 population (2000): 11.0 (world avg. 13.5).
Total fertility rate (avg. births per childbearing woman; 2000): 2.0.
Marriage rate per 1,000 population (1996): 3.1.
Divorce rate per 1,000 population (1996): 0.7.
Life expectancy at birth (2000): male 70.5 years; female 76.3 years.
Major causes of death per 100,000 population (1994): diseases of the circulatory system 237.8, of which hypertensive disease 93.8, diseases of pulmonary circulation and other forms of heart disease 72.0; malignant neoplasms (cancers) 125.0; endocrine and metabolic disorders 59.8; infectious and parasitic diseases 46.2; diseases of the respiratory system 38.0.

National economy

Budget (1998–99). Revenue: EC$232,700,000 (tax revenue 73.9%, of which consumption taxes on imports 26.9%, income taxes 20.9%; nontax revenue 14.7%; grants 9.2%). Expenditures: EC$260,300,000 (current expenditures 77.1%; development expenditures 22.9%).
Public debt (external, outstanding; 2000): U.S.$89,200,000.
Land use (1994): forested 66.0%; meadows and pastures 3.0%; agricultural and under permanent cultivation 23.0%; other 8.0%.
Tourism: receipts from visitors (2000) U.S.$47,000,000; expenditures by nationals abroad (1998) U.S.$8,000,000.
Gross national product (at current market prices; 1999): U.S.$238,000,000 (U.S.$3,260 per capita).

Structure of gross domestic product and labour force	1998		1991	
	in value EC$'000,000[4]	% of total value[4]	labour force[5]	% of labour force[5]
Agriculture	121.2	20.3	7,344	30.8
Mining	5.3	0.9	65	0.3
Manufacturing	52.5	8.8	1,947	8.2
Construction	46.7	7.8	2,819	11.8
Public utilities	29.9	5.0	304	1.3
Transportation and communications	100.5	16.8	1,202	5.0
Trade, hotels, restaurants	83.2	13.9	3,658	15.4
Finance, real estate	83.9	14.0	810	3.4
Services	120.8	20.2	3,446	14.5
Pub. admin., defense			1,520	6.4
Other	−45.5[6]	−7.6[6]	699	2.9
TOTAL	598.4[7]	100.0[7]	23,814	100.0

Population economically active (1991): total 26,364; activity rate of total population 38.0% (participation rates: ages 15–64, 62.4%; female 34.5%; unemployed [1994] 23%).

Price and earnings indexes (1995 = 100)							
	1995	1996	1997	1998	1999	2000	2001
Consumer price index	100.0	101.7	104.2	105.2	106.4	107.3	108.5[8]
Earnings index	...	...	...	...	...	...	...

Household income and expenditure. Average household size (1991) 3.6; income per household: n.a.; sources of income: n.a.; expenditure (1984)[9]: food and nonalcoholic beverages 43.1%, housing and utilities 16.1%, transportation 11.6%, clothing and footwear 6.5%, household furnishings 6.0%.
Production (metric tons except as noted). Agriculture, forestry, fishing (1998): bananas 28,640[10], root crops 23,168 (of which dasheens 11,903, yams 7,560, tanias 3,534), plantains 22,236, grapefruit 19,100, coconuts 8,906, oranges 7,230, limes 3,560, mangoes 1,700, pepper 340, bay oil 12; livestock (number of live animals: 1999) 13,400 cattle, 9,700 goats, 7,600 sheep; roundwood, n.a.; fish catch (1997) 855 metric tons. Mining and quarrying: pumice, limestone, and sand and gravel are quarried primarily for local consumption. Manufacturing (value of production in EC$'000; 1998): toilet soap 21,816; laundry soap 16,467; crude coconut oil 1,848; toothpaste 1,662 metric tons; other products include fruit juices, beer, garments, bottled spring water, and cardboard boxes. Energy production (consumption): electricity (kW-hr; 1996) 37,000,000 (37,000,000); coal, none (none); crude petroleum, none (none); petroleum products (metric tons; 1996) none (26,000); natural gas, none (none).

Foreign trade[11]

Balance of trade (current prices)						
	1995	1996	1997	1998	1999	2000
EC$'000,000	−194.9	−212.4	−193.3	−196.8	−196.2	−253.1
% of total	44.4%	43.4%	40.3%	36.6%	40.0%	46.9%

Imports (1999): EC$343,400,000 (food and beverages 20.8%; machinery 16.4%; transport equipment 9.3%; mineral fuels 6.4%). *Major import sources:* U.S. 30.7%; Caricom 27.0%; U.K. 8.8%; Japan 7.8%; France 5.0%.
Exports (1999): EC$147,400,000 (manufactured exports 61.7%, of which coconut-based laundry and toilet soaps 26.7%; agricultural exports 38.3%, of which bananas 27.1%). *Major export destinations:* Caricom 55.3%; U.K. 27.5%; Guadeloupe 4.9%; U.S. 4.0%.

Transport and communications

Transport. Railroads: none. Roads (1996): total length 485 mi, 780 km (paved 50%). Vehicles (1994): passenger cars 6,581; trucks and buses 2,825. Merchant marine (1992): vessels (100 gross tons and over) 7; total deadweight tonnage 3,153. Air transport: (1991) passenger arrivals 43,312, passenger departures, n.a.; (1997) cargo unloaded 575 metric tons, cargo loaded 363 metric tons; airports (1996) with scheduled flights 2.

Communications				units per 1,000
Medium	date	unit	number	persons
Radio	1997	receivers	46,000	608
Television	1997	receivers	6,000	79
Telephones	2001	main lines	23,300	291
Cellular telephones	2001	subscribers	1,200	16
Personal computers	2001	units	6,000	77
Internet	2000	users	6,000	77

Education and health

Educational attainment (1991). Percentage of population age 25 and over having: no formal schooling 4.2%; primary education 78.4%; secondary 11.0%; higher vocational 2.3%; university 2.8%; other/unknown 1.3%. *Literacy* (1994): total population age 15 and over literate, c. 44,000 (90.0%).

Education (1997–98)	schools	teachers	students	student/ teacher ratio
Primary	63	587	13,636	23.2
Secondary	15	293	5,455	18.6
Higher[12]	2	34	484	14.2

Health (1998): physicians 38 (1 per 2,007 persons); hospital beds 262 (1 per 291 persons); infant mortality rate per 1,000 live births (2000) 17.1.
Food (2000): daily per capita caloric intake 2,994 (vegetable products 77%, animal products 23%); 124% of FAO recommended minimum requirement.

Military

Total active duty personnel (1999): none[13].

[1]Includes 22 seats that are elective (including speaker if elected from outside of the House of Assembly) and 10 seats that are nonelective (including 9 appointees of the president and the attorney general serving ex officio). [2]Total area of Dominica per more recent survey is 290 sq mi (750 sq km). [3]March 2001 preliminary census total equals 71,727. [4]At current factor cost. [5]Employed persons only. [6]Less imputed banking service charge. [7]Detail does not add to total given because of rounding. [8]April. [9]Weights of consumer price index components. [10]Export production only. [11]Imports c.i.f.; exports f.o.b. [12]1992–93. [13]300-member police force includes a coast guard unit.

Internet resources for further information:
• **Eastern Caribbean Central Bank**
  http://www.eccb-centralbank.org

Dominican Republic

Official name: República Dominicana (Dominican Republic).
Form of government: multiparty republic with two legislative houses (Senate [32]; Chamber of Deputies [150]).
Head of state and government: President.
Capital: Santo Domingo.
Official language: Spanish.
Official religion: none[1].
Monetary unit: 1 Dominican peso (RD$) = 100 centavos; valuation (Sept. 23, 2002) 1 U.S.$ = RD$17.10; 1 £ = RD$26.58.

Area and population

Provinces	area sq km	population 2000 estimate	Provinces	area sq km	population 2000 estimate
Azua	2,532	243,157	Peravia	998	223,273[2]
Baoruco	1,283	124,592	Puerto Plata	1,857	302,799
Barahona	1,739	179,945	Salcedo	440	106,450
Dajabón	1,021	78,045	Samaná	854	82,135
Duarte	1,605	318,151	San Cristóbal	1,265	519,906
Elías Piña	1,424	66,267	San José de Ocoa	650	2
El Seibo (El Seybo)	1,786	105,447	San Juan	3,571	265,562
Espaillat	838	228,173	San Pedro de Macorís	1,255	260,629
Hato Mayor	1,329	87,595	Sánchez Ramírez	1,196	194,282
Independencia	2,008	41,778	Santiago	2,836	836,614
La Altagracia	3,010	128,627	Santiago Rodríguez	1,112	65,853
La Romana	654	213,628	Santo Domingo	1,296	3
La Vega	2,286	390,314	Valverde	823	198,979
María Trinidad Sánchez	1,271	142,030			
Monseñor Nouel	992	174,923	**National district**		
Monte Cristi	1,925	103,711	Santo Domingo (city)	105	2,677,055[3]
Monte Plata	2,633	174,126	TOTAL	48,671[4]	8,553,744[3]
Pedernales	2,077	19,698			

Demography

Population (2002): 8,833,000.
Density (2002): persons per sq mi 470.0, persons per sq km 181.5.
Urban-rural (2000): urban 66.0%; rural 34.0%.
Sex distribution (2000): male 50.80%; female 49.20%.
Age breakdown (2000): under 15, 34.5%; 15–29, 27.3%; 30–44, 20.3%; 45–59, 10.8%; 60–74, 5.7%; 75 and over, 1.4%.
Population projection: (2010) 9,995,000; (2020) 11,489,000.
Doubling time: 34 years.
Ethnic composition (2000): mulatto 69.5%; white 17.0%; local black 9.4%; Haitian black 2.4%; other/unknown 1.7%.
Religious affiliation (1995): Roman Catholic 81.8%; Protestant 6.4%; other Christian 0.6%; other 11.2%.
Major urban centres (1993): Santo Domingo (urban agglomeration; 2001) 2,629,000; Santiago 365,463; La Romana 140,204; San Pedro de Macorís 124,735; San Francisco de Macorís 108,485.

Vital statistics

Birth rate per 1,000 population (2000): 25.2 (world avg. 22.5).
Death rate per 1,000 population (2000): 4.7 (world avg. 9.0).
Natural increase rate per 1,000 population (2000): 20.5 (world avg. 13.5).
Total fertility rate (avg. births per childbearing woman; 2000): 3.0.
Marriage rate per 1,000 population (1994): 2.0.
Life expectancy at birth (2000): male 71.1 years; female 75.4 years.
Major causes of death per 100,000 population (1994)[5]: diseases of the circulatory system 160; accidents and violence 60; malignant neoplasms (cancers) 56; infectious and parasitic diseases 54.

National economy

Budget (1998). Revenue: RD$38,566,000,000 (tax revenue 93.8%, of which taxes on goods and services 47.7%, import duties 27.0%, income taxes 17.9%, nontax revenue 5.3%). Expenditures: RD$41,179,000,000 (current expenditures 72.2%; development expenditures 27.8%).
Public debt (external, outstanding; 2000): U.S.$3,368,000,000.
Gross national product (2000): U.S.$17,847,000,000 (U.S.$2,130 per capita).

Structure of gross domestic product and labour force

	1998 in value RD$'000,000	1998 % of total value	1997 labour force	1997 % of labour force
Agriculture	28,171	11.6	529,000	16.7
Mining	4,722	2.0	8,400	0.3
Manufacturing	40,215	16.6	483,300	15.3
Construction	29,307	12.1	153,600	4.9
Public utilities	5,105	2.1	20,300	0.6
Transp. and commun.	28,061	11.6	202,700	6.4
Trade, restaurants	48,063	19.9	647,600	20.5
Finance, real estate	21,172	8.8	34,000	1.1
Pub. admin., defense	18,839	7.8	125,400	4.0
Services	18,255	7.5	447,500	14.2
Unemployed	—	—	503,700	16.0
TOTAL	241,910	100.0	3,155,500	100.0

Production (metric tons except as noted). Agriculture, forestry, fishing (1998): sugarcane 5,097,000, rice 475,000, bananas 359,000, plantains 341,000, cacao

beans 59,000, coffee 57,000, pulses 56,000; livestock (number of live animals) 2,528,000 cattle, 960,000 pigs, 38,000,000 chickens; roundwood (2000) 562,300 cu m; fish catch (2000) 11,029. Mining (2000): nickel (metal content) 68,300; gold 40,700 troy oz[6]. Manufacturing (1998)[7]: cement 1,872,000; refined sugar 105,000; beer 2,990,000 hectolitres; rum 420,000 hectolitres. Energy production (consumption): electricity (kW-hr; 2000) 9,788,000,000 (5,777,000,000); coal (metric tons; 1996) none (128,000); crude petroleum (barrels; 1996) none (17,035,000); petroleum products (metric tons; 1996) 2,147,000 (3,671,000); natural gas, none (none).
Tourism (2000): receipts U.S.$2,860,000,000; expenditures U.S.$309,000,000.
Population economically active (1993): total 2,556,225; activity rate of total population 35.0% (participation rates: ages 15–64, 54.3%; female 24.9%; unemployed [2000] 13.9%).

Price and earnings indexes (1995 = 100)

	1995	1996	1997	1998	1999	2000	2001
Consumer price index	100.0	105.4	114.1	119.7	127.4	137.2	148.2[8]
Annual earnings index[9]	100.0	100.0	120.0	120.0	...	...	...

Household income and expenditure. Average household size (1993) 3.9; average income: n.a.; sources of income: n.a.; expenditure (1980–85): food and beverages 46.0%, housing 10.0%, household goods 8.0%.
Land use (1994): forested 12.4%; meadows and pastures 43.4%; agricultural and under permanent cultivation 30.6%; other 13.6%.

Foreign trade[10]

Balance of trade (current prices)

	1995	1996	1997	1998	1999	2000
U.S.$'000,000	−2,292	−2,635	−3,175	−4,008	−4,402	−5,450
% of total	56.8%	58.2%	61.0%	69.3%	73.2%	73.2%

Imports (1998): U.S.$4,897,000,000[11] (capital goods 22.1%, consumer durables 13.2%, crude petroleum and petroleum products 11.0%). *Major import sources* (1997)[12]: U.S. 56%; Venezuela 23%; Mexico 9%; Japan 4%.
Exports (1998): U.S.$889,000,000[13] (ships' stores 15.8%, ferronickel 15.0%, cacao and cocoa 13.6%, raw sugar 13.2%, raw coffee 7.2%). *Major export destinations* (1997): U.S. 53.9%; Belgium 11.9%; Puerto Rico 7.0%.

Transport and communications

Transport. Railroads (1997)[14]: route length 1,083 mi, 1,743 km. Roads (1996): total length 7,829 mi, 12,600 km (paved 49%). Vehicles (1996): passenger cars 224,000; trucks and buses 151,550. Air transport (1997)[15]: passenger-mi 9,823,000, passenger-km, 15,808,000; short ton-mi cargo 7,962,000, metric ton-km cargo 11,624,000; airports (2002) 6.

Communications

Medium	date	unit	number	units per 1,000 persons
Daily newspapers	1996	circulation	416,000	53
Radio	1997	receivers	1,440,000	179
Television	1997	receivers	770,000	96
Telephones	2001	main lines	939,500	108
Cellular telephones	2001	subscribers	1,073,000	124
Internet	2001	users	186,000	21

Education and health

Educational attainment: n.a. *Literacy* (1995): total population age 15 and over literate, *c.* 4,164,000 (82.1%); males literate, *c.* 2,118,000 (82.0%); females literate, *c.* 2,046,000 (82.2%).

Education (1994–95)

	schools	teachers	students	student/ teacher ratio
Primary (age 6–13)	4,001	42,135	1,462,722	34.7
Secondary (age 14–17)	...	10,757	240,441	22.4
Voc. teacher tr.	...	1,297	22,795	17.6
Higher[16]	...	9,041	176,995	19.6

Health: physicians (1997) 17,460 (1 per 460 persons); hospital beds (1996) 11,921 (1 per 662 persons); infant mortality rate per 1,000 live births (2000) 35.9.
Food (2000): daily per capita caloric intake 2,325 (vegetable products 85%, animal products 15%); 103% of FAO recommended minimum.

Military

Total active duty personnel (2001): 24,500 (army 61.2%, navy 16.3%, air force 22.4%). *Military expenditure as percentage of GNP* (1999): 0.7% (world 2.4%); per capita expenditure U.S.$15.

---

[1]Roman Catholicism is the state religion per concordat with Vatican City. [2]Peravia includes San José de Ocoa province created in January 2001. [3]Includes new province created in October 2001 bordering the more narrowly defined National District to the east, north, and west. [4]Mainland total is 48,512 sq km and offshore islands total 159 sq km. [5]Projected rates based on about 50% of total deaths. [6]The mining of gold was temporarily suspended from 1999 through late 2002. [7]Excludes free-zone sector for reexport (mostly ready-made garments) employing (1998) 195,000. [8]July. [9]Minimum wage for medium-sized businesses in private sector. [10]Excludes free zones. [11]Excludes 1998 imports of free zones equaling U.S.$2,701,000,000. [12]Estimated figures. [13]Excludes 1998 reexports of free zones equaling U.S.$4,100,000,000. [14]Most track is privately owned and serves the sugar industry only. [15]Aerochago and Dominair airlines. [16]1996–97.

Internet resources for further information:
- Banco Central de la República Dominicana
  http://www.bancentral.gov.do
- Oficina Nacional de Estadística
  http://www.one.gov.do

Ecuador

Official name: República del Ecuador (Republic of Ecuador).
Form of government: unitary multiparty republic with one legislative house (National Congress [123]).
Head of state and government: President.
Capital: Quito.
Official language: Spanish[1].
Official religion: none.
Monetary unit[2]: 1 dollar (U.S.$); valuation (Sept. 23, 2002) 1 U.S.$ = £ 0.64.

Area and population

Regions Provinces	Capitals	area sq mi	area sq km	population 2001 census[3]
Amazonica				
Morona-Santiago	Macas	13,100	33,930	113,300
Napo	Tena	} 9,918	} 25,690	79,610
Orellana	Franciscode Orellana			85,771
Pastaza	Puyo	11,496	29,774	61,412
Sucumbíos	Nueva Loja	7,076	18,327	130,095
Zamora-Chinchipe	Zamora	8,923	23,111	76,414
Costa				
El Oro	Machala	2,259	5,850	515,664
Esmeraldas	Esmeraldas	5,884	15,239	386,032
Guayas	Guayaquil	7,916	20,503	3,256,763
Los Ríos	Babahoyo	2,770	7,175	650,709
Manabí	Portoviejo	7,289	18,879	1,180,375
Insular				
Galápagos	Puerto Baquerizo Mareno	3,093	8,010	18,555
Sierra				
Azuay	Cuenca	3,137	8,125	598,504
Bolívar	Guaranda	1,521	3,940	168,874
Cañar	Azogues	1,205	3,122	206,953
Carchi	Tulcán	1,392	3,605	152,304
Chimborazo	Riobamba	2,536	6,569	403,185
Cotopaxi	Latacunga	2,344	6,072	350,450
Imbabura	Ibarra	1,760	4,559	345,781
Loja	Loja	4,257	11,026	404,085
Pichincha	Quito	4,987	12,915	2,392,409
Tungurahua	Ambato	1,288	3,335	441,389
TOTAL		105,037[4, 5]	272,045[5]	12,090,804[6]

Demography

Population (2002): 13,095,000.
Density (2002): persons per sq mi 124.7, persons per sq km 48.1.
Urban-rural (2001): urban 61.0%; rural 39.0%.
Sex distribution (2001): male 49.60%; female 50.40%.
Age breakdown (2002): under 15, 35.3%; 15–29, 28.5%; 30–44, 19.2%; 45–59, 10.5%; 60–74, 4.8%; 75 and over, 1.7%.
Population projection: (2010) 14,899,000; (2020) 16,904,000.
Ethnic composition (2000): mestizo 42.0%; Amerindian 40.8%; white 10.6%; black 5.0%; other 1.6%.
Religious affiliation (2000): Roman Catholic 94.1%; Protestant 1.9%; other 4.0%.
Major cities (2001): Guayaquil 1,952,029; Quito 1,399,814; Cuenca 276,964; Santo Domingo de los Colorados 200,421; Machala 198,123; Manta 183,166.

Vital statistics

Birth rate per 1,000 population (2000): 26.5[7] (world avg. 22.5).
Death rate per 1,000 population (2000): 5.5[7] (world avg. 9.0).
Total fertility rate (avg. births per childbearing woman; 2000): 3.2.
Marriage rate per 1,000 population (1997): 5.6[7].
Life expectancy at birth (2000): male 68.3 years; female 74.0 years.
Major causes of death per 100,000 population (1995): circulatory diseases 55.1; accidents, poisoning, and violence 29.2; pneumonia 27.2; diabetes mellitus 15.4; neoplasms (cancers) 12.7; parasitic diseases 12.2.

National economy

Budget (1996). Revenue: S/. 10,233,300,000,000 (petroleum revenue 45.9%, indirect taxes 30.9%, direct taxes 11.1%). Expenditures: S/. 11,836,700,000,000 (administration 40.8%, debt service 20.7%, subsidies 7.4%).
Public debt (external, outstanding; 2000): U.S.$11,366,000,000.
Production (metric tons except as noted). Agriculture, forestry, fishing (1999): sugarcane 6,800,000, bananas 4,563,000, rice 1,043,000, corn (maize) 688,000; livestock (live animals) 5,534,000 cattle, 2,892,000 pigs, 2,182,000 sheep, 64,736,000 chickens; roundwood (1998) 11,340,000 cu m; fish catch (2000) 592,547. Mining and quarrying (2000): limestone 3,147,000; gold 2,823 kg. Manufacturing (value added in S/. '000,000; 1996): chemical products 2,364,091; food products 1,779,894; nonmetallic mineral products 453,148; textiles 305,369. Construction (in S/.; 1992)[8]: residential 93,166,704,000; nonresidential 58,102,274,000. Energy production (consumption): electricity (kW-hr; 1997) 9,560,000,000 (9,560,000,000); crude petroleum (barrels; 2001) 146,200,000 (52,000,000[9]); petroleum products (metric tons; 1997) 7,602,000 (5,627,000); natural gas (cu m; 1997) 502,000,000 (502,000,000).
Household income and expenditure. Average household size (1990) 4.1; average annual income per household (1995) S/. 9,825,610 (U.S.$3,830); sources of income (1995): self-employment 70.9%, wages 16.0%, transfer payments 6.7%, other 6.4%; expenditure (1995): food and tobacco 37.9%, transportation and communications 15.0%, clothing 9.2%, household furnishings 6.5%.
Population economically active (1997): total 3,373,810; activity rate of total population 44.9% (participation rates: ages 15 and over, 64.2%; female 39.1%).

Price and earnings indexes (1995 = 100)

	1995	1996	1997	1998	1999	2000	2001
Consumer price index	100.0	124.4	162.5	221.1	336.7	660.2	908.9
Monthly earnings index[10]	100.0	136.4	171.8	217.0	292.7	...	...

Gross national product (2000): U.S.$15,256,000,000 (U.S.$1,210 per capita).

Structure of gross domestic product and labour force

	1998 in value S/. '000,000[11]	1998 % of total value[11]	1997 labour force	1997 % of labour force
Agriculture	39,342	17.3	520,970	15.4
Mining	30,788	13.5	11,240	0.3
Manufacturing	35,239	15.5	475,280	14.1
Construction	5,837	2.6	185,130	5.5
Public utilities	3,176	1.4	10,230	0.3
Transp. and commun.	14,236	6.2	175,580	5.2
Trade	30,784	13.5	870,900	25.8
Finance	8,083	3.6	138,550	4.1
Pub. admin., defense	15,508	6.8	} 983,140	} 29.1
Services	43,166	18.9		
Other	1,519[12]	0.7[12]	2,790[13]	0.1[13]
TOTAL	227,678	100.0	3,373,810	100.0[5]

Tourism (2000): receipts U.S.$402,000,000; expenditures U.S.$299,000,000.

Foreign trade[14]

Balance of trade (current prices)

	1996	1997	1998	1999	2000	2001
U.S.$'000,000	+1,329.0	+744.3	−809.8	+1,714.1	+1,525.6	−288.6
% of total	15.7%	7.6%	8.8%	23.8%	18.3%	3.0%

Imports (1999): U.S.$3,017,200,000 (machines and transport equipment 28.8%; chemicals and chemical products 22.0%; food and live animals 9.4%; mineral fuels 8.2%). *Major import sources:* U.S. 30.4%; Colombia 12.0%; Venezuela 6.4%; Japan 4.7%; Germany 4.2%.
Exports (1999): U.S.$4,451,100,000 (food 51.7%, of which bananas 21.4%, crustaceans 13.7%, fish 5.9%; crude petroleum 29.5%). *Major export destinations:* U.S. 38.4%; Colombia 5.1%; Panama 4.9%; South Korea 4.8%.

Transport and communications

Transport. Railroads (1999): route length 966 km; passenger-km (1998) 44,000,000; metric ton-km cargo (1996) 1,000,000. Roads (1997): total length 43,197 km (paved 19%). Vehicles (1996): passenger cars 464,902; trucks and buses 52,630. Air transport (2001)[15]: passenger-km 901,000,000; metric ton-km cargo 14,344,000.

Communications

Medium	date	unit	number	units per 1,000 persons
Daily newspapers	1996	circulation	820,000	70
Radio	1997	receivers	4,150,000	348
Television	1998	receivers	2,500,000	205
Telephones	2001	main lines	1,335,800	104
Cellular telephones	2001	subscribers	859,200	67
Personal computers	2001	units	300,000	23
Internet	2001	users	327,700	25

Education and health

Educational attainment (1990). Percentage of population age 25 and over having: no formal schooling 2.2%; incomplete primary 54.3%; primary 28.0%; postsecondary 15.5%. *Literacy* (1995): total population age 15 and over literate 90.1%; males 92.0%; females 88.2%.

Education (1996–97)

	schools	teachers	students	student/ teacher ratio
Primary (age 4–12)	17,367	74,601	1,888,172	25.3
Secondary (age 12–18) Vocational	}	62,630[16]	813,557[16]	13.0[16]
Higher	...	12,856[17]	206,541[17]	16.1[17]

Health (1997): physicians 20,243 (1 per 590 persons); hospital beds 18,510 (1 per 645 persons); infant mortality rate (2002) 33.0.
Food (2000): daily per capita caloric intake 2,693 (vegetable products 84%, animal products 16%); 118% of FAO recommended minimum requirement.

Military

Total active duty personnel (2001): 59,500 (army 84.0%, navy 9.3%, air force 6.7%). *Military expenditure as percentage of GNP* (1999): 3.7% (world 2.4%); per capita expenditure U.S.$38.

---

[1]Quechua and Shuar are also official languages for the indigenous peoples. [2]The United States dollar was formally adopted as the national currency on Sept. 9, 2000; the pegged value of the Sucre (S/.), the former national currency, to the U.S. dollar was S/. 25,000 = 1 U.S.$. [3]Preliminary and unadjusted. [4]Detail does not add to total given because of rounding. [5]Includes 884 sq mi (2,289 sq km) in nondelimited areas. [6]Total includes 72,170 persons in nondelimited areas. [7]Excluding nomadic Indian tribes. [8]Authorized construction in Cuenca, Guayaquil, and Quito only. [9]1997. [10]General minimum wage. [11]At constant 1975 prices. [12]Minus imputed bank service charges plus gross import duties. [13]Activities not adequately defined. [14]Import figures are f.o.b. in balance of trade and c.i.f. for commodities and trading partners. [15]Ecuatoviana and TAME airlines. [16]1992–93. [17]1990–91.

Internet resources for further information:
• **Instituto Nacional de Estadistica y Censos** http://www4.inec.gov.ec
• **Banco Central del Ecuador** http://www.bce.fin.ec

Egypt

Official name: Jumhūrīah Miṣr al-ʿArabīyah (Arab Republic of Egypt).
Form of government: republic with one legislative house (People's Assembly [454[1]]).
Chief of state: President.
Head of government: Prime Minister.
Capital: Cairo.
Official language: Arabic.
Official religion: Islam.
Monetary unit: 1 Egyptian pound (£E) = 100 piastres; valuation (Sept. 23, 2002) 1 U.S.$ = £E 4.65; 1 £ = £E 7.22.

Area and population

Regions		area		population
Governorates	**Capitals**	sq mi	sq km	1996 census
Frontier				
Al-Baḥr al-Aḥmar	Al-Ghurdaqah	78,643	203,685	155,695
Janūb Sīnāʾ	Aṭ-Ṭūr	12,796	33,140	54,495
Maṭrūḥ	Marsā Maṭrūḥ	81,897	212,112	211,866
Shamāl Sīnāʾ	Al-ʿArīsh	10,646	27,574	252,750
Al-Wādī al-Jadīd	Al-Kharijah	145,369	376,505	141,737
Lower Egypt				
Al-Buḥayrah	Damanhūr	3,911	10,129	3,981,209
Ad-Daqahlīyah	Al-Manṣūrah	1,340	3,471	4,223,655
Dumyāṭ	Dumyāṭ	227	589	914,614
Al-Gharbīyah	Ṭanṭā	750	1,942	3,404,827
Al-Ismāʿīlīyah (Ismailia)	—	557	1,442	715,009
Kafr ash-Shaykh	Kafr ash-Shaykh	1,327	3,437	2,222,920
Al-Minūfīyah	Shibīn al-Kawm	592	1,532	2,758,499
Al-Qalyūbīyah	Banhā	387	1,001	3,302,860
Ash-Sharqīyah	Az-Zaqāzīq	1,614	4,180	4,287,848
Upper Egypt				
Aswān	Aswān	262	679	973,671
Asyūṭ	Asyūṭ	600	1,553	2,802,185
Banī Suwayf	Banī Suwayf	510	1,322	1,860,180
Al-Fayyūm	Al-Fayyūm	705	1,827	1,989,881
Al-Jīzah	Al-Jīzah	32,859	85,105	4,779,865
Al-Minyā	Al-Minyā	873	2,262	3,308,875
Qinā	Qinā	693	1,796	2,441,420
Sawhāj	Sawhāj	597	1,547	3,125,000
Urban				
Būr Saʿīd (Port Said)	—	28	72	469,533
Al-Iskandarīyah (Alexandria)	—	1,034	2,679	3,328,196
Al-Qāhirah (Cairo)	—	83	214	6,789,497
Al-Uqṣur (Luxor)	—	21	55	360,503
As-Suways (Suez)	—	6,888	17,840	417,610
TOTAL		385,210[2]	997,690	59,274,400[3]

Demography

Population (2002): 66,341,000.
Density (2002): persons per sq mi 172.2; persons per sq km 66.5.
Urban-rural (2001): urban 42.7%; rural 57.3%.
Sex distribution (2000): male 50.50%; female 49.50%.
Age breakdown (2000): under 15, 35.1%; 15–29, 28.5%; 30–44, 19.0%; 45–59, 11.3%; 60–74, 5.0%; 75 and over, 1.0%.
Population projection: (2010) 74,986,000; (2020) 84,896,000.
Doubling time: 40 years.
Ethnic composition (2000): Egyptian Arab 84.1%; Sudanese Arab 5.5%; Arabized Berber 2.0%; Bedouin 2.0%; Rom (Gypsy) 1.6%; other 4.8%.
Religious affiliation (1997): Sunnī Muslim 89%; Christian 11%[4].
Major cities (ʾ000; 1996): Cairo 6,789 (10,345[5]); Alexandria 3,328; Al-Jīzah 2,222; Shubrā al-Khaymah 871; Port Said 470; Suez 418.

Vital statistics

Birth rate per 1,000 population (2000): 25.4 (world avg. 22.5).
Death rate per 1,000 population (2000): 7.8 (world avg. 9.0).
Natural increase rate per 1,000 population (2000): 17.6 (world avg. 13.5).
Total fertility rate (avg. births per childbearing woman; 2000): 3.2.
Life expectancy at birth (2000): male 61.3 years; female 65.5 years.

National economy

Budget (1998–99). Revenue: £E 71,295,000,000 (income and profits taxes 21.9%, sales taxes 20.1%, customs duties 14.2%, Suez Canal fees 4.1%, oil revenue 3.1%). Expenditures: £E 75,285,000,000 (current expenditure 79.1%, of which wages and pensions 31.7%, public debt interest 20.8%, defense 11.0%; capital expenditure 20.9%).
Public debt (external, outstanding; 2000): U.S.$24,279,000,000.
Population economically active (1999–2000): total 18,818,000; activity rate 29.7% (participation rates [1995]: ages 15–64, 49.8%; female 22.0%; unemployed 7.4%).

Price and earnings indexes (1995 = 100)

	1995	1996	1997	1998	1999	2000	2001
Consumer price index	100.0	108.3	112.8	114.4	120.4	123.7	126.5
Annual earnings index	100.0	...	...	...	...	...	...

Production (ʾ000; metric tons except as noted). Agriculture, forestry, fishing (2000): sugarcane 15,668, wheat 6,564, corn (maize) 6,395, rice 5,996, tomatoes 5,900, potatoes 1,784, oranges 1,550, watermelons 1,507; livestock (ʾ000; number of live animals) 4,450 sheep, 3,300 goats, 3,200 buffalo, 3,180 cattle, 88,000 chickens; roundwood 2,883,000 cu m; fish catch (1999) 606,780. Mining and quarrying (1998–99): iron ore 3,002; gypsum 2,666; salt 2,588; phosphate

rock 1,165; kaolin 314. Manufacturing (1999–2000): cement 26,000; nitrate fertilizers 1,550; sugar 1,285; cotton yarn 280; refrigerators 585,000 units; automobiles 48,167 units. Energy production (consumption): electricity (ʾ000,000 kW-hr; 1997) 54,924 (54,924); coal (ʾ000 metric tons; 1997) none (1,880); crude petroleum (ʾ000 barrels; 1999) 303,576 (210,243); petroleum products (ʾ000 metric tons; 1999) 28,538 (23,761); natural gas (ʾ000,000 cu m; 2000) 21,000 (14,897[6]).
Gross national product (2000): U.S.$95,380,000,000 (U.S.$1,490 per capita).

Structure of gross domestic product and labour force

	1998–99[7]		1995	
	in value £E ʾ000,000	% of total value	labour force	% of labour force
Agriculture	45,530	17.0	5,215,600	29.4
Mining (petroleum) }	67,401	25.1	40,700	0.2
Manufacturing			2,183,500	12.3
Construction	15,580	5.8	967,600	5.5
Public utilities	4,824	1.8	166,800	0.9
Transp. and commun.	24,874[8]	9.3[8]	907,600	5.1
Trade	50,379[9]	18.8[9]	1,587,700	9.0
Finance	16,736	6.2	282,700	1.6
Pub. admin., defense, services	22,164	8.2	3,990,800	22.5
Other	20,910	7.8	2,382,900[10]	13.5[10]
TOTAL	268,398	100.0	17,725,900	100.0

Household income and expenditure. Average household size (1986) 4.9; expenditure (1986–87)[11]: food 55.7%, clothing 10.9%, housing 10.5%.
Tourism (2000): receipts U.S.$4,345,000,000; expenditures U.S.$1,073,000,000.

Foreign trade

Balance of trade (current prices)

	1995	1996	1997	1998	1999	2000
U.S.$ʾ000,000	−7,597	−8,390	−8,632	−10,214	−9,928	−8,321
% of total	46.3%	46.7%	43.9%	53.7%	48.7%	37.4%

Imports (1999): U.S.$15,165,000,000 (machinery and transport equipment 32.7%; foodstuffs 21.2%; iron and steel products 7.7%; wood and paper 6.2%; chemical products 5.1%). *Major import sources* (1999): U.S. 14.3%; Germany 8.6%; Italy 6.6%; France 4.9%; Saudi Arabia 4.4%.
Exports (1999): U.S.$5,327,000,000 (petroleum and petroleum products 22.9%; cotton yarn, textiles, and clothing 9.7%; basic metals and manufactures 9.4%). *Major export destinations* (1999): U.S. 12.4%; Italy 10.1%; The Netherlands 7.1%; Israel 5.3%; bunkers and ships' stores 10.3%.

Transport and communications

Transport. Railroads (1999): length 4,810 km; passenger-km (1998) 56,667,000,000; metric ton-km cargo (1996) 4,117,000,000. Roads (1998): length 64,000 km (paved 78%). Vehicles (1998): passenger cars 1,154,753; trucks and buses 510,766. Inland water (1999): Suez Canal, number of transits 13,490; metric ton cargo 384,994,000. Air transport (1999): passenger-km 9,074,000,000; metric ton-km cargo 269,520,000; airports (1998) 11.

Communications

Medium	date	unit	number	units per 1,000 persons
Daily newspapers	1996	circulation	2,400,000	38.0
Radio	1997	receivers	20,500,000	330
Television	1999	receivers	11,400,000	183
Telephones	2001	main lines	6,650,000	103
Cellular telephones	2001	subscribers	2,793,800	43
Personal computers	2001	units	1,000,000	16
Internet	2001	users	600,000	9.3

Education and health

Literacy (1995): total population age 15 and over literate 51.4%; males 63.6%; females 38.8%.

Education (1998–99)

	schools	teachers	students	student/ teacher ratio
Primary (age 6–11)[12, 13]	15,566	314,528	7,351,118	23.4
Secondary (age 12–17)[12, 13]	8,887	272,687	5,394,019	19.8
Vocational	1,767	145,050	1,852,332	12.8
Higher	356	...	1,316,491[14]	...

Health: physicians (1996) 129,000 (1 per 472 persons); hospital beds (1994) 113,020 (1 per 515 persons); infant mortality rate (2000) 62.3.
Food (2000): daily per capita caloric intake 3,346 (vegetable products 92%, animal products 8%); 133% of FAO recommended minimum requirement.

Military

Total active duty personnel (2001): 443,000 (army 72.2%, navy 4.3%, air force [including air defense] 23.5%). *Military expenditure as percentage of GNP* (1999): 2.7% (world 2.4%); per capita expenditure U.S.$36.

[1]Includes 10 nonelective seats. [2]Detail does not add to total given because of rounding. [3]Excludes 2,180,000 Egyptians abroad. [4]According to the 1986 census, the Christian population of Egypt was 5.9% of the total; this figure is considered by some external authorities to understate significantly the Christian population. [5]1999 urban agglomeration. [6]1997. [7]At 1996–97 factor cost. [8]Transportation includes earnings from traffic on the Suez Canal. [9]Trade includes restaurants and hotels. [10]Unemployed and those seeking work for the first time. [11]Weight of consumer price components; urban households only. [12]Data exclude 2,655 primary and secondary schools in the Al-Azhar education system. [13]Includes preparatory. [14]1996–97.

Internet resources for further information:
• **Egypt State Information Service http://www.sis.gov.eg**
• **Ministry of Economy http://www.economy.gov.eg**

El Salvador

Official name: República de El Salvador (Republic of El Salvador).
Form of government: republic with one legislative house (Legislative Assembly [84]).
Chief of state and government: President.
Capital: San Salvador.
Official language: Spanish.
Official religion: none[1].
Monetary unit[2]: 1 colón (₡) = 100 centavos; valuation (Sept. 23, 2002) 1 U.S.$ = ₡8.75; 1 £ = ₡13.59.

Area and population

Departments	Capitals	area sq mi	area sq km	population 1998 estimate[3]
Ahuachapán	Ahuachapán	479	1,240	307,056
Cabañas	Sensuntepeque	426	1,104	151,079
Chalatenango	Chalatenango	779	2,017	193,866
Cuscatlán	Cojutepeque	292	756	198,643
La Libertad	Nueva San Salvador	638	1,653	642,159
La Paz	Zacatecoluca	473	1,224	283,209
La Unión	La Unión	801	2,074	283,246
Morazán	San Francisco	559	1,447	171,692
San Miguel	San Miguel	802	2,077	463,049
San Salvador	San Salvador	342	886	1,884,700
San Vicente	San Vicente	457	1,184	157,173
Santa Ana	Santa Ana	781	2,023	531,516
Sonsonate	Sonsonate	473	1,225	429,143
Usulután	Usulután	822	2,130	334,795
TOTAL		8,124	21,041[4]	6,031,326

Demography

Population (2002): 6,354,000.
Density (2002): persons per sq mi 782.1, persons per sq km 302.0.
Urban-rural (2001): urban 61.5%; rural 38.5%.
Sex distribution (2000): male 48.65%; female 51.35%.
Age breakdown (2000): under 15, 38.0%; 15–29, 28.7%; 30–44, 16.6%; 45–59, 9.5%; 60–74, 5.3%; 75 and over 1.9%.
Population projection: (2010) 7,293,000; (2020) 8,494,000.
Doubling time: 31 years.
Ethnic composition (2000): mestizo 88.3%; Amerindian 9.1%, of which Pipil 4.0%; white 1.6%; other/unknown 1.0%.
Religious affiliation (1995): Roman Catholic 78.2%; Protestant 17.1%, of which Pentecostal 13.3%; other Christian 1.9%; other 2.8%.
Major cities[5] (1998): San Salvador 467,004 (urban agglomeration 1,856,788); Soyapango 282,066[6]; Santa Ana 241,266; San Miguel 227,414; Mejicanos 180,775[6].

Vital statistics

Birth rate per 1,000 population (2000): 29.0 (world avg. 22.5); (1998) legitimate 27.2%; illegitimate 72.8%.
Death rate per 1,000 population (2000): 6.3 (world avg. 9.0).
Natural increase rate per 1,000 population (2000): 22.7 (world avg. 13.5).
Total fertility rate (avg. births per childbearing woman; 2000): 3.4.
Marriage rate per 1,000 population (1998): 4.4.
Life expectancy at birth (2000): male 66.1 years; female 73.5 years.
Major causes of death per 100,000 population (1998)[7]: accidents and violence 118; diseases of the circulatory system 89; diseases of the respiratory system 60; malignant neoplasms (cancers) 58; ill-defined conditions 116.

National economy

Budget. Revenue (1997): ₡11,345,000,000 (sales taxes 50.2%, corporate taxes 14.7%, individual income taxes 11.7%, import duties 11.2%). Expenditures: ₡12,027,000,000 (education 19.6%, police 16.3%, transportation and communications 12.4%, health 10.3%, defense 7.1%).
Public debt (external, outstanding; 2000): U.S.$2,775,000,000.
Production (metric tons except as noted). Agriculture, forestry, fishing (1999): sugarcane 5,500,000, corn (maize) 683,500, sorghum 181,500, coffee 143,800, dry beans 71,700, bananas 70,000, rice 60,400, yautia 53,000, tobacco 1,100; livestock (number of live animals) 1,141,000 cattle, 335,000 pigs; roundwood (1998) 5,129,000 cu m; fish catch (1997) 10,987, of which crustaceans 3,920. Mining and quarrying (1997): limestone 3,000,000 metric tons. Manufacturing (value added in U.S.$'000,000; 1998): food products 306; wearing apparel 249; drugs and medicines 128; textiles 120; beverages 112; soaps, cleansers, and cosmetics 92; nonmetallic mineral products 76. Energy production (consumption): electricity (kW-hr; 1998) 3,868,000,000 (3,906,000,000); coal, none (none); crude petroleum (barrels; 1997) none (5,703,000); petroleum products (metric tons; 1997) 722,000 (1,592,000); natural gas, none (none).
Household income and expenditure. Average household size (1992–93) 4.8; average income per household (1992–93) ₡22,930 (U.S.$2,562); expenditure (1990–91)[8]: food and beverages 37.0%, housing 12.1%, transportation and communications 10.2%, clothing and footwear 6.7%.
Land use (1994): forested 5.0%; meadows and pastures 29.5%; agricultural and under permanent cultivation 35.2%; other 30.3%.
Population economically active (1995): total 2,136,400; activity rate of total population 39.1% (participation rates: ages 15–64, 62.9%; female 37.1%; unemployed [1998] 7.5%).

Price and earnings indexes (1995 = 100)

	1996	1997	1998	1999	2000	2001	2002
Consumer price index	109.8	114.7	117.6	118.2	120.9	125.5	127.8[9]
Monthly earnings index[10]	108.5	116.7	121.9	...	...	...	...

Gross national product (at current market prices; 2000): U.S.$12,569,000,000 (U.S.$2,000 per capita).

Structure of gross domestic product and labour force

	1998 in value ₡'000,000	1998 % of total value	1997 labour force	1997 % of labour force
Agriculture	12,532	12.1	547,100	24.3
Mining	417	0.4	1,700	0.1
Manufacturing	22,591	21.8	334,100	14.8
Construction	4,389	4.2	138,700	6.1
Public utilities	1,681	1.6	15,200	0.7
Transp. and commun.	8,304	8.0	96,700	4.3
Trade	19,850	19.1	445,100	19.7
Finance, real estate	12,191	11.7	30,300	1.3
Public admin., defense	7,116	6.9 }	467,100	20.7
Services	}	14,795	14.2	180,000[11]	8.0[11]
Other				
TOTAL	103,864[4]	100.0	2,256,000	100.0

Tourism (2000): receipts U.S.$254,000,000; expenditures U.S.$171,000,000.

Foreign trade[12]

Balance of trade (current prices)

	1996	1997	1998	1999	2000	2001
U.S.$'000,000	−1,646.5	−1,607.6	−1,849.6	−1,963.9	−2,454.2	−2,652.3
% of total	44.6%	37.5%	42.3%	45.8%	47.8%	52.2%

Imports (1999): U.S.$3,128,100,000 (food 14.9%; chemicals and chemical products 14.2%; mineral fuels 11.5%; nonelectrical machinery and equipment 10.2%). *Major import sources:* U.S. 37.5%; Guatemala 11.8%; Mexico 8.4%; Japan 4.1%; Costa Rica 3.7%.
Exports (1999): U.S.$1,164,200,000 (coffee 21.0%; yarn, fabrics, made-up articles 6.9%; paper and paper products 6.3%; wearing apparel 5.4%; refined petroleum products 4.6%). *Major export destinations:* Guatemala 23.4%; U.S. 21.3%; Honduras 14.7%; Germany 9.0%; Costa Rica 7.9%.

Transport and communications

Transport. Railroads (1997): operational route length 283 km; (1997) passenger-km 7,100,000; (1996) metric ton-km cargo 17,300,000. Roads (1999): total length 10,029 km (paved 20%). Vehicles (1997): passenger cars 177,488; trucks and buses 184,859. Air transport (1999)[13]: passenger-km 5,091,000,000; metric ton-km cargo 43,636,000; airports (1997) with scheduled flights 1.

Communications

Medium	date	unit	number	units per 1,000 persons
Daily newspapers	1996	circulation	278,000	49
Radio	1997	receivers	2,750,000	475
Television	1999	receivers	1,777,000	196
Telephones	2001	main lines	598,000	93
Cellular telephones	2001	subscribers	800,000	125
Personal computers	2001	units	140,000	22
Internet	2000	users	50,000	8.0

Education and health

Educational attainment (1992). Percentage of population over age 25 having: no formal schooling 34.7%; incomplete primary education 37.6%; complete primary[14] 10.8%; secondary 9.4%; higher technical 2.4%; incomplete undergraduate 1.1%; complete undergraduate 2.9%; other/unknown 1.1%.
Literacy (1992): total population age 15 and over literate 2,326,800 (74.1%); males literate 1,141,007 (77.4%); females literate 1,185,793 (71.3%).

Education (1996)

	schools	teachers	students	student/ teacher ratio
Primary (age 7–15)	5,025	34,496	1,130,900	32.8
Secondary (age 16–18)	...	9,255	143,588	15.5
Higher	...	5,919	112,266	19.0

Health: physicians (1997) 6,177 (1 per 936 persons); hospital beds (1996) 9,571 (1 per 593 persons); infant mortality rate per 1,000 live births (2000) 29.2.
Food (1999): daily per capita caloric intake 2,503 (vegetable products 88%, animal products 12%); 109% of FAO recommended minimum requirement.

Military

Total active duty personnel (2001): 16,800 (army 89.3%, navy 4.2%, air force 6.5%). *Military expenditure as percentage of GNP* (1999): 0.9% (world 2.4%); per capita expenditure U.S.$18.

---

[1]Roman Catholicism, although not official, enjoys special recognition in the constitution. [2]The U.S. dollar was legal tender in El Salvador from Jan. 1, 2001 (along with the colón) at a pegged rate of 1 U.S.$ = ₡8.75. [3]Official projection based on 1992 census. [4]Detail does not add to total given because of rounding. [5]Populations are for *municipios* (urban centres that may include adjacent rural areas). [6]Within San Salvador urban agglomeration. [7]Projected rates based on about 78% of total deaths. [8]536,628 urban households only. [9]April. [10]Private sector only. [11]Unemployed. [12]Imports c.i.f., exports f.o.b. [13]TACA International Airlines only. [14]Education completed through ninth grade.

Internet resources for further information:
• Banco Central de Reserva de El Salvador http://www.bcr.gob.sv

Equatorial Guinea

Official name: República de Guinea
Ecuatorial (Spanish); République du
Guinée Équatoriale (French)
(Republic of Equatorial Guinea).
Form of government: republic with
one legislative house (House of
Representatives of the People [80]).
Chief of state: President.
Head of government: Prime Minister.
Capital: Malabo.
Official languages: Spanish; French.
Official religion: none.
Monetary unit: 1 CFA franc
(CFAF) = 100 centimes; valuation
(Sept. 23, 2002) 1 U.S.$ = CFAF 667.00;
1 £ = CFAF 1,037[1].

Area and population

Regions Provinces	Capitals	area sq mi	area sq km	population 1987 estimate
Insular		785[2]	2,034	70,280
Annobón	Palé	7	17	2,360
Bioko Norte	Malabo	300	776	56,600
Bioko Sur	Luba	479	1,241	11,320
Continental		10,045[2]	26,017	259,950
Centro-Sur	Evinayong	3,834	9,931	55,970
Kie-Ntem	Ebebiyin	1,522	3,943	74,050
Litoral[3]	Bata	2,573	6,665	75,640
Wele-Nzas	Mongomo	2,115	5,478	54,290
TOTAL		10,831[2]	28,051	330,230

Demography

Population (2002): 498,000.
Density (2002): persons per sq mi 46.0, persons per sq km 17.8.
Urban-rural (2001): urban 49.4%; rural 50.6%.
Sex distribution (2000): male 48.71%; female 51.29%.
Age breakdown (2000): under 15, 42.7%; 15–29, 26.8%; 30–44, 15.9%; 45–59, 8.6%; 60–74, 4.9%; 75 and over, 1.1%.
Population projection: (2010) 604,000; (2020) 755,000.
Doubling time: 28 years.
Ethnic composition (1995): Fang 82.9%; Bubi 9.6%; other 7.5%.
Religious affiliation (2000): Roman Catholic 80.1%; Muslim 4.0%; African Christian 3.7%; Protestant 3.1%; other 9.1%.
Major cities (1983): Malabo 47,500[4]; Bata 37,000[4]; Ela-Nguema 6,179; Campo Yaunde 5,199; Los Angeles 4,079.

Vital statistics

Birth rate per 1,000 population (2000): 38.1 (world avg. 22.5); legitimate, n.a.; illegitimate, n.a.
Death rate per 1,000 population (2000): 13.4 (world avg. 9.0).
Natural increase rate per 1,000 population (2000): 24.7 (world avg. 13.5).
Total fertility rate (avg. births per childbearing woman; 2000): 4.9.
Marriage rate per 1,000 population: n.a.
Divorce rate per 1,000 population: n.a.
Life expectancy at birth (2000): male 51.5 years; female 55.7 years.
Major causes of death per 100,000 population: n.a.; however, major diseases include malaria (about 24% of total mortality), respiratory infections (12% of mortality), cholera, leprosy, trypanosomiasis (sleeping sickness), and waterborne (especially gastrointestinal) diseases.

National economy

Budget (1996). Revenue: CFAF 24,637,000,000 (domestic revenue 95.1%, of which oil revenue 46.9%, tax revenue 36.8%, nontax revenue 11.4%; foreign grants 4.9%). Expenditures: CFAF 32,955,000,000 (current expenditure 60.6%, of which goods and services 23.8%, salaries 17.3%, interest on debt 15.6%, transfers 3.9%; capital expenditure 9.7%).
Public debt (external, outstanding; 2000): U.S.$198,000,000.
Gross national product (at current market prices; 2000): U.S.$363,000,000 (U.S.$800 per capita).

Structure of gross domestic product and labour force

	1998 in value CFAF '000,000	1998 % of total value	1983 labour force	1983 % of labour force
Agriculture, fishing	40,480	15.0	59,390	57.9
Forestry	17,719	6.6		
Crude petroleum	164,969	61.3	1,616	1.6
Manufacturing	1,007	0.4		
Construction	7,752	2.9	1,929	1.9
Public utilities	3,368	1.3	224	0.2
Transportation and communications	2,100	0.8	1,752	1.7
Trade	9,625	3.6	3,059	3.0
Finance, real estate	2,135	0.8	409	0.4
Pub. admin., defense	12,723	4.7	8,377	8.2
Services	4,959	1.8		
Other	2,427[5]	0.9[5]	25,809	25.2
TOTAL	269,266[2]	100.0[2]	102,565	100.0[2]

Production (metric tons except as noted). Agriculture, forestry, fishing (1999): roots and tubers 84,000 (of which cassava 49,000, sweet potatoes 35,000), bananas 15,000, coconuts 8,000, coffee 6,300, palm oil 5,000, cacao beans

5,000, palm kernels 3,000; livestock (number of live animals) 36,000 sheep, 8,100 goats, 5,300 pigs, 4,800 cattle; roundwood (1998) 811,000 cu m; fish catch (1997) 6,090. Mining and quarrying: details, n.a.; however, in addition to quarrying for construction materials, unexploited deposits of iron ore, lead, zinc, manganese, and molybdenum are present. Manufacturing (1998): sawn timber 21,500 cu m; processed timber 3,900 cu m. Construction: n.a. Energy production (consumption): electricity (kW-hr; 1999) 21,000,000 ([1997] 20,000,000); coal, none (none); crude petroleum (barrels; 2001) 66,065,000 ([1996] 37,000); petroleum products (metric tons; 1996) none (42,000); natural gas, none (none).
Population economically active (1997): total 177,000; activity rate of total population 40.0% (participation rates: ages 15–64, 74.7%; female 35.4%; unemployed [1983] 24.2%).

Price and earnings indexes (1995 = 100)

	1992	1993	1994	1995	1996	1997	1998
Consumer price index	61.3	64.1	89.7	100.0	104.5	107.7	116.2
Earnings index							

Household income and expenditure. Average household size (1980) 4.5; income per household: n.a.; sources of income (1988): wages and salaries 57.0%, business income 42.0%, other 1.0%; expenditure (1988): food and beverages 62.0%, clothing and footwear 10.0%; medical care 6.0%.
Tourism: tourism is a government priority but remains undeveloped.
Land use (1994): forested 65.2%; meadows and pastures 3.7%; agricultural and under permanent cultivation 8.2%; built-on, wasteland, and other 22.9%.

Foreign trade[6]

Balance of trade (current prices)

	1994	1995	1996	1997	1998
CFAF '000,000,000	−1.0	−5.1	−26.1	+85.0	+15.6
% of total	1.4%	5.6%	11.5%	17.1%	5.5%

Imports (1998): CFAF 256,200,000,000 (petroleum sector 83.1%; other 16.9%). *Major import sources:* United States 35.4%; France 15.0%; Spain 9.9%; Cameroon 9.9%; United Kingdom 6.2%; The Netherlands 5.7%.
Exports (1998): CFAF 271,800,000,000 (petroleum 87.6%; wood 9.2%; cocoa 1.5%). *Major export destinations:* United States 62.0%; Spain 17.3%; China 8.9%; Japan 3.4%; France 3.4%.

Transport and communications

Transport. Railroads: none. Roads (1996): total length 1,740 mi, 2,800 km (paved 13%). Vehicles (1994): passenger cars 6,500; trucks and buses 4,000. Merchant marine (1992): vessels (100 gross tons and over) 3; total deadweight tonnage 6,699. Air transport (1996): passenger-mi 4,000,000, passenger-km 7,000,000; short ton-mi cargo 700,000, metric ton-km cargo 1,000,000; airports (1998) with scheduled flights 1.

Communications

Medium	date	unit	number	units per 1,000 persons
Daily newspapers	1996	circulation	2,000	4.9
Radio	1997	receivers	180,000	428
Television	1997	receivers	4,000	9.8
Telephones	2001	main lines	6,900	14.7
Cellular telephones	2001	units	15,000	31.9
Internet	2001	users	6	0.1

Education and health

Educational attainment (1983). Percentage of population age 15 and over having: no schooling 35.4%; some primary education 46.6%; primary 13.0%; secondary 2.3%; postsecondary 1.1%; not specified 1.6%. *Literacy* (1995): percentage of total population age 15 and over literate 77.8%; males literate 89.3%; females literate 67.4%.

Education (1993–94)

	schools	teachers	students	student/ teacher ratio
Primary (age 6–11)	781	1,381	75,751	54.9
Secondary (age 12–17)	...	466	14,511	31.1
Voc., teacher tr.	...	122	2,105	17.3
Higher	...	58	578	10.0

Health: physicians (1996) 106 (1 per 4,065 persons); hospital beds (1990) 992 (1 per 350 persons); infant mortality rate per 1,000 live births (2000) 94.8.
Food: daily per capita caloric intake, n.a.

Military

Total active duty personnel (2001): 1,320 (army 75.8%, navy 9.1%, air force 7.6%). *Military expenditure as percentage of GNP* (1999): 3.2% (world 2.4%); per capita expenditure U.S.$40.

---

[1]Formerly pegged to the French franc and since January 1, 2002, to the euro at the rate of CFAF 655.96 = €1. [2]Detail does not add to total given because of rounding. [3]Includes three islets in Corisco Bay. [4]1995. [5]Import duties. [6]Imports c.i.f.; exports f.o.b.

Internet resources for further information:
• Investir en Zone Franc
  http://www.izf.net/izf/Index.htm

Eritrea

Official name: State of Eritrea.
Form of government: transitional regime with one interim legislative body (Transitional National Assembly [150][1]).
Head of state and government: President.
Capital: Asmara.
Official language: none.
Official religion: none.
Monetary unit: nakfa[2] = 100 cents; valuation (Sept. 23, 2002)
1 U.S.$ = Nfa 8.76; 1 £ = Nfa 13.62.

Area and population

Regions[4]	Capitals	area[3] sq mi	area[3] sq km	population 1997 estimate
Anseba	Keren	8,960	23,200	...
Debub	Mendefera	3,090	8,000	...
Debub-Keih-Bahri	Asseb (Aseb)	10,660	27,600	...
Gash-Barka	Barentu	12,820	33,200	...
Maekel	Asmara (Asmera)	500	1,300	...
Semien-Keih-Bahri	Massawa (Mitsiwa)	10,730	27,800	...
TOTAL		46,770[5]	121,100	3,590,000

Demography

Population (2002): 3,981,000[6].
Density (2002): persons per sq mi 85.1, persons per sq km 32.9.
Urban-rural (1998): urban 18.0%; rural 82.0%.
Sex distribution (2001): male 49.83%; female 50.17%.
Age breakdown (2001): under 15, 42.8%; 15–29, 28.8%; 30–44, 14.3%; 45–59, 9.0%; 60–74, 4.1%; 75 and over, 1.0%.
Population projection[6]: (2010) 5,097,000; (2020) 6,382,000.
Doubling time: 23 years.
Ethnolinguistic composition (2000): Tigrinya (Tigray) 51.8%; Tigré 17.9%; Afar 8.1%; Saho 4.3%; Kunama 4.1%; other 13.8%.
Religious affiliation (2000): Christian 50.5%, of which Eritrean Orthodox 46.1%; Muslim 44.7%; other 4.8%.
Major cities (2001): Asmara 503,000; Asseb 50,000[7]; Keren 40,000[7]; Massawa 40,000[7].

Vital statistics

Birth rate per 1,000 population (2001): 42.5 (world avg. 21.2).
Death rate per 1,000 population (2001): 12.1 (world avg. 8.9).
Natural increase rate per 1,000 population (2001): 30.4 (world avg. 12.3).
Total fertility rate (avg. births per childbearing woman; 2001): 5.9.
Marriage rate per 1,000 population (1992): 6.8.
Divorce rate per 1,000 population: n.a.
Life expectancy at birth (2001): male 53.7 years; female 58.7 years.
Major causes of death per 100,000 population: n.a.; morbidity (principal causes of illness) arises mainly in malaria and other infectious diseases, parasitic infections, malnutrition, diarrheal diseases, and dysenteries.

National economy

Budget (1999). Revenue: Nfa 1,822,900,000 (tax revenue 53.9%, of which direct taxes 26.1%, import duties 14.5%, indirect taxes 13.3%; nontax revenue 46.1%). Expenditures: Nfa 3,822,200,000 (current expenditure 61.1%, of which defense 38.2%, wages and salaries 14.5%; capital expenditure 38.9%).
Public debt (external, outstanding; 2000): U.S.$298,000,000.
Production (metric tons except as noted). Agriculture, forestry, fishing (2001): sorghum 86,990, roots and tubers 85,000, barley 44,633, wheat 36,418, pulses 32,000, vegetables 28,000, millet 14,788, corn (maize) 9,257, chickpeas 8,283, sesame seeds 4,000, dry beans 3,000, peanuts (groundnuts) 1,369; livestock (number of live animals) 1,570,000 sheep, 1,700,000 goats, 2,200,000 cattle, 75,000 camels; roundwood (2000) 2,246,265; fish catch (1999) 4,797, of which artisanal fisheries 941. Mining and quarrying (2000): salt 200,000; marble and granite are quarried, as are sand and aggregate (gravel) for construction. Manufacturing (gross value in Nfa '000; 1998): food production 234,700; beverages 161,300; chemicals 59,800; leather products and shoes 49,400; textile products 28,800; nonmetallic products 19,300; paper and printing products 14,800; metal products 11,500. Construction (1997): Nfa 270,794,000. Energy production (consumption): electricity (kW-hr; 1999) 207,000,000 (n.a.); crude petroleum, none (none); petroleum products, n.a. (n.a.); natural gas, none (none).
Land use (1994): forested 7.3%; agricultural and under permanent cultivation 5.1%; meadows and pastures 69.0%; other (predominantly barren land) 18.6%.
Household income and expenditure. Average household size (1998) 4.7; average annual income per household: n.a.; sources of income: n.a.; expenditure: n.a.
Population economically active (1996): 1,649,000; activity rate of total population 41.4%.

Price and earnings indexes (December 1992 = 100)

	1991	1992	1993	1994	1995
Consumer price index[8]	91.9	100.0	119.2	127.4	141.3
Earnings index	...	...	...	...	...

Gross national product (at current market prices; 2000): U.S.$696,000,000 (U.S.$170 per capita).

Structure of gross domestic product

	1999 in value Br '000,000	1999 % of total value
Agriculture	853.6	14.7
Manufacturing	741.2	12.7
Mining	4.7	0.1
Public utilities	84.0	1.4
Construction	624.9	10.7
Transp. and commun.	542.7	9.3
Trade	1,139.4	19.6
Finance	249.5	4.3
Pub. admin., defense	1,014.4	17.4
Services	66.5	1.1
Other	507.6[9]	8.7[9]
TOTAL	5,828.3[5]	100.0

Tourism (2000): receipts from visitors U.S.$26,000,000.

Foreign trade[10]

Balance of trade (current prices)

	1993	1994	1995	1996	1997	1998	1999
U.S.$'000,000	−239.0	−331.4	−323.2	−418.5	−441.1	−498.9	−480.6
% of total	58.1%	72.0%	66.7%	68.7%	80.4%	89.9%	90.2%

Imports (1999): U.S.$506,900,000 (1998; machinery and transport equipment 38.3%, manufactured goods 23.9%, food products 17.1%, chemical products 5.7%, animal and vegetable oil 2.6%). *Major import sources* (1998): Italy 17.4%; United Arab Emirates 16.2%; Germany 5.7%; United Kingdom 4.5%; United States 4.2%; Japan 4.0%.
Exports (1999): U.S.$26,300,000 (1998; raw materials 45.5%, food products 29.6%, manufactured goods 13.2%, machinery and transport equipment 2.4%, chemical products 2.1%). *Major export destinations* (1998): The Sudan 27.2%; Ethiopia 26.5%; Japan 13.2%; United Arab Emirates 7.3%; Italy 5.3%.

Transport and communications

Transport. Railroads (2000): the 190-mi (306-km) rail line that formerly connected Massawa and Agordat is currently under reconstruction; a 51-mi (82-km) section between Massawa and Embatkala was reopened in stages by 2001. Roads (1999): total length 2,491 mi, 4,010 km (paved 22%). Vehicles (1996): automobiles 5,940, trucks and buses, n.a. Merchant marine: vessels (100 gross tons and over) n.a. Air transport (1999)[11]: passenger arrivals and departures 93,007; short ton cargo handled 2,974, metric ton cargo handled 3,279; airports (2000) with scheduled flights 2.

Communications

Medium	date	unit	number	units per 1,000 persons
Radio	1995	receivers	310,000	89.6
Television	1999	receivers	60,000	15.1
Telephones	2001	main lines	32,000	8.4
Personal computers	2001	units	7,000	1.8
Internet	2001	users	10,000	2.6

Education and health

Literacy (1998): total population age 15 and over literate, 51.7%; males 65.7%; females 38.2%.

Education (1996–97)

	schools	teachers	students	student/ teacher ratio
Primary (age 7–12)	549	5,476	240,737	44.0
Secondary (age 13–18)	86[12]	1,959	88,054	44.9
Voc., teacher tr.	4[12]	112	1,145	10.2
Higher[13]	1	198	3,096	15.6

Health (1993): physicians 69 (1 per 36,000 persons); hospital beds (1986–87): 2,449 (1 per 1,100 persons); infant mortality rate per 1,000 live births (2001) 75.1.
Food (2000): daily per capita caloric intake 1,655 (vegetable 94%, animal products 6%); 71% of FAO recommended minimum requirement.

Military

Total active duty personnel (2000): estimated strength of Eritrean armed forces (predominantly former guerrillas) is between 200,000 and 250,000. UN peacekeeping force along Eritrean-Ethiopian border (May 2002): 4,200. *Military expenditure as percentage of GNP* (1999): 27.4% (world 2.4%); per capita expenditure U.S.$52.

---

[1]New constitution adopted in May 1997 was still not implemented in 2002. [2]The nakfa was introduced in July 1997 as the new national currency. [3]Approximate figures. The published total area is 46,774 sq mi (121,144 sq km); water area is 7,776 sq mi (20,140 sq km). [4]On May 20, 1995, a resolution was approved dividing the country into six administrative regions. [5]Detail does not add to total given because of rounding. [6]Estimate of the UN *World Population Prospects* (2000 revision). [7]1992. [8]Asmara only; year-end. [9]Including indirect taxes less subsidies. [10]Imports c.i.f. [11]Asmara airport only. [12]1992–93. [13]1997–98.

Estonia

Official name: Eesti Vabariik (Republic of Estonia).
Form of government: unitary multiparty republic with a single legislative body (Riigikogu[1] [101]).
Chief of state: President.
Head of government: Prime Minister.
Capital: Tallinn.
Official language: Estonian.
Official religion: none.
Monetary unit: 1 kroon (EEK) = 100 senti; valuation (Sept. 23, 2002)
1 U.S.$ = EEK 15.95;
1 £ = EEK 24.78.

Area and population

Counties	Capitals	area sq mi	area sq km	population 2000 census[2]
Harju	Tallinn	1,672	4,332	525,700
Hiiu	Kärdla	395	1,023	10,400
Ida-Viru	Jõhvi	1,299	3,364	179,700
Järva	Paide	1,013	2,623	38,800
Jõgeva	Jõgeva	1,005	2,604	38,300
Lääne	Haapsalu	920	2,383	28,600
Lääne-Viru	Rakvere	1,338	3,465	67,800
Pärnu	Pärnu	1,856	4,806	91,200
Põlva	Põlva	836	2,165	32,700
Rapla	Rapla	1,151	2,980	37,600
Saare	Kuressaare	1,128	2,922	36,000
Tartu	Tartu	1,156	2,993	149,600
Valga	Valga	789	2,044	35,800
Viljandi	Viljandi	1,321	3,422	58,000
Võru	Võru	890	2,305	39,900
TOTAL		16,769[3, 4, 5]	43,431[3, 4, 5]	1,370,100

Demography

Population (2002): 1,359,000.
Density (2001)[3]: persons per sq mi 81.0, persons per sq km 31.3.
Urban-rural (2001): urban 69.4%; rural 30.6%.
Sex distribution (2001[6]): male 46.12%; female 53.88%.
Age breakdown (2000[6]): under 15, 18.0%; 15–29, 21.9%; 30–44, 21.5%; 45–59, 18.3%; 60–74, 15.0%; 75 and over, 5.3%.
Population projection: (2010) 1,316,000; (2020) 1,279,000.
Ethnic composition (2000[6]): Estonian 65.3%; Russian 28.1%; Ukrainian 2.5%; Belarusian 1.5%; Finnish 0.9%; other 1.7%.
Religious affiliation (1995): Christian 38.1%, of which Orthodox 20.4%, Evangelical Lutheran 13.7%; other (mostly nonreligious) 61.9%.
Major cities (2001[6]): Tallinn 399,850; Tartu 101,240; Narva 68,538; Kohtla-Järve 47,484; Pärnu 44,978.

Vital statistics

Birth rate per 1,000 population (2001): 9.3 (world avg. 21.2); (2000) legitimate 45.5%; illegitimate 54.5%.
Death rate per 1,000 population (2001): 13.6 (world avg. 8.9).
Natural increase rate per 1,000 population (2001): –4.3 (world avg. 12.3).
Total fertility rate (avg. births per childbearing woman; 1999): 1.2.
Marriage rate per 1,000 population (2001): 4.1.
Divorce rate per 1,000 population (2001): 3.2.
Life expectancy at birth (1999): male 65.4 years; female 76.1 years.
Major causes of death per 100,000 population (1998): diseases of the circulatory system 732.8; malignant neoplasms (cancers) 235.1; accidents, violence and homicide 162.2; diseases of the digestive system 44.4.

National economy

Budget (1998). Revenue: EEK 24,130,000,000 (social security contributions 32.9%, value-added taxes 26.6%, excise taxes 11.6%, personal income taxes 11.4%). Expenditures: EEK 24,103,000,000 (social security and welfare 30.6%, health 16.4%, education 8.6%, police 7.3%, defense 4.0%).
Public debt (external, outstanding; 2000): U.S.$206,300,000.
Production (metric tons except as noted). Agriculture, forestry, fishing (1999): potatoes 340,000, barley 198,000, wheat 135,000, oats 85,000, rye 44,000, rapeseed 30,000; livestock (number of live animals) 326,400 pigs, 307,500 cattle; roundwood (1998) 6,061,000 cu m; (1997) fish catch 123,873. Mining and quarrying (1998): oil shale 10,913,000; peat 333,500. Manufacturing (value of production in EEK '000,000; 1999): food products 6,770; wood products (excluding furniture) 4,703; furniture 2,546; textiles 2,536; printing and publishing 2,127; fabricated metal products 2,062. Energy production (consumption): electricity (kW-hr; 2001) 8,484,000,000 ([2000] 5,422,000,000); hard coal (metric tons; 1997) none (98,000); lignite (metric tons; 1997) 14,383,000 (15,951,000); crude petroleum, none (n.a.); petroleum products (metric tons; 1997) 367,000 (1,231,000); natural gas (cu m; 1997) none (670,000,000).
Tourism (2000): receipts U.S.$506,000,000; expenditures U.S.$204,000,000.
Population economically active (1997): total 707,800[7]; activity rate of total population 48.4% (participation rates: ages 15–64, 71.3%; female 47.9%; unemployed [2001] 12.6%).

Price and earnings indexes (1995 = 100)

	1996	1997	1998	1999	2000	2001	2002
Consumer price index	123.1	136.1	147.2	152.1	158.2	167.3	174.4[8]
Annual earnings index	118.7	123.0	141.1	152.1	168.2	189.9	...

Household income and expenditure (1998). Average household size 2.3; average disposable income per household EEK 53,049 (U.S.$3,769); sources of income: wages and salaries 63.8%, transfers 24.1%, self-employment 6.2%, other 5.9%; expenditure[9]: food and beverages 35.5%, housing 14.6%, transportation 10.7%, clothing and footwear 9.0%.
Gross national product (2000): U.S.$4,894,000,000 (U.S.$3,580 per capita).

Structure of gross domestic product and labour force

	2001 in value EEK '000,000	2001 % of total value	1997 labour force[10, 11]	1997 % of labour force[10, 11]
Agriculture, fishing, forestry	5,342	5.6	60,800	8.5
Mining	915	1.0	7,600	1.1
Manufacturing	15,222	16.0	144,100	20.1
Public utilities	2,712	2.8	17,600	2.5
Construction	4,938	5.2	47,400	6.6
Trade, restaurants	13,534	14.2	105,200	14.7
Transp. and commun.	13,816	14.5	59,400	8.3
Finance, real estate	13,220	13.9	42,600	5.9
Pub. admin., defense	3,947	4.1	34,300	4.8
Services	11,529	12.1	95,800	13.3
Other	10,100[12]	10.6[12]	103,200[13]	14.4[13]
TOTAL	95,275[14]	100.0	717,800[14]	100.0[14]

Land use (1994): forest 44.7%; pasture 7.2%; agriculture 32.2%; other 15.9%.

Foreign trade[15]

Balance of trade (current prices)

	1996	1997	1998	1999	2000	2001
EEK '000,000	–13,861	–20,925	–21,812	–17,070	–18,369	–17,635
% of total	21.7%	20.4%	19.3%	16.5%	14.6%	13.3%

Imports (2000): EEK 72,246,000,000 (electrical and nonelectrical machinery 38.5%, fabricated and base metals 8.1%, textiles and apparel 7.5%). *Major import sources:* Finland 27.4%; Sweden 9.8%; Germany 9.5%; Russia 8.5%; Japan 6.1%.
Exports (2000): EEK 53,877,000,000 (electrical and nonelectrical machinery 37.5%, wood and wood products 13.4%, textiles and clothing 11.3%). *Major export destinations:* Finland 32.3%; Sweden 20.5%; Germany 8.5%; Latvia 7.0%; United Kingdom 4.4%.

Transport and communications

Transport. Railroads (2000): route length 968 km; passenger-km 263,000,000; metric ton-km cargo 8,102,000,000. Roads (2000): total length 16,430 km (paved 51%). Vehicles (1999): passenger cars 458,700; trucks and buses 87,226. Air transport (2001)[16]: passenger-km 295,000,000; metric ton-km cargo 1,412,000; airports (1997) 1.

Communications

Medium	date	unit	number	units per 1,000 persons
Daily newspapers	1996	circulation	255,000	174
Radio	1997	receivers	1,010,000	693
Television	1999	receivers	800,000	568
Telephones	2001	main lines	503,600	352
Cellular telephones	2001	subscribers	651,200	455
Personal computers	2001	units	250,000	175
Internet	2001	users	429,700	300

Education and health

Educational attainment (1989). Percentage of persons age 25 and over having: no formal schooling 2.2%; primary education 39.0%; secondary 45.1%; higher 13.7%.

Education (1995–96)

	schools	teachers	students	student/ teacher ratio
Primary (age 7–12)	727	...	125,718	...
Secondary (age 13–17)	...	9,299	95,342	10.3
Vocational	...	1,793	16,870	9.4
Higher[17]	37	...	40,621	...

Health (1998): physicians 4,471 (1 per 324 persons); hospital beds 10,509 (1 per 138 persons); infant mortality rate per 1,000 live births (2000) 8.1.
Food (1999): daily per capita caloric intake 3,154 (vegetable products 74%, animal products 26%); 123% of FAO recommended minimum requirement.

Military

Total active duty personnel (2001): 4,450 (army 90.8%, navy 6.7%, air force 2.5%). *Military expenditure as a percentage of GNP* (1999): 1.5% (world 2.4%); per capita expenditure U.S.$120.

[1]Official legislation bans translation of parliament's name. [2]March 2000 final de jure figures. [3]Area used by Estonian government to calculate population densities. [4]Total area including the Estonian portion of Lake Peipus (590 sq mi [1,529 sq km]), Lake Võrtsjärv, and Muuga harbour is 17,462 sq mi (45,227 sq km). [5]Total includes 1,596 sq mi (4,133 sq km) of Baltic Sea islands. [6]As of January 1. [7]First quarter average. [8]May. [9]For a two-adult household with one child. [10]Ages 15–69 only. [11]Annual average. [12]Includes net taxes (EEK 11,551,000,000) less imputed bank service charges (EEK 1,450,000,000). [13]Includes 33,800 not adequately defined and 69,400 unemployed. [14]Detail does not add to total given because of rounding. [15]Imports c.i.f.; exports f.o.b. [16]Estonian Air. [17]1998–99.

Internet resources for further information:
• Statistical Office of Estonia http://www.stat.ee

Ethiopia

Official name: Federal Democratic Republic of Ethiopia.
Form of government: federal republic[1] with two legislative houses (Federal Council [108]; Council of People's Representatives [546]).
Chief of state: President.
Head of government: Prime Minister.
Capital: Addis Ababa.
Official language: none[2].
Official religion: none.
Monetary unit: 1 birr (Br) = 100 cents; valuation (Sept. 23, 2002) 1 U.S.$ = Br 8.46; 1 £ = Br 13.15.

Area and population

Regional states	Capitals	area sq mi	area sq km	population 1994 census
Afar	Aysaita	...	...	1,106,383
Amhara	Bahir Dar	66,000	170,000	13,834,297
Benishangul/ Gumuz	Asosa	20,000	51,000	460,459
Gambella	Gambella	9,758	25,274	181,862
Harari	Harer (Harar)	131	340	131,139
Oromiya	Addis Ababa	136,560	353,690	18,732,525
Somali	Jijiga	116,000	300,000	3,383,165
Southern Nations, Nationalities and Peoples'	Awasa	44,000	114,000	10,377,028
Tigray	Mekele	31,000	80,000	3,136,267
Cities				
Addis Ababa	...	208	540	2,112,737
Dire Dawa	...	500	1,300	251,864
TOTAL		437,794	1,133,882	53,707,726[3]

Demography

Population (2002): 67,673,000.
Density (2002): persons per sq mi 154.6, persons per sq km 59.7.
Urban-rural (2001): urban 15.9%; rural 84.1%.
Sex distribution (2000): male 50.19%; female 49.81%.
Age breakdown (2000): under 15, 47.0%; 15–29, 26.4%; 30–44, 14.2%; 45–59, 7.9%; 60–74, 3.7%; 75 and over, 0.8%.
Population projection: (2010) 82,312,000; (2020) 103,163,000.
Ethnolinguistic composition (1994): Oromo 31.8%; Amharic 29.3%; Somali 6.2%; Tigrinya 5.9%; Walaita 4.6%; Gurage 4.2%; Sidamo 3.4%; Afar 1.9%; Hadya-Libide 1.7%; other 11.0%.
Religious affiliation (1994): Ethiopian Orthodox 50.3%; Muslim 32.9%; Protestant 10.1%; traditional beliefs 4.8%; Roman Catholic 0.6%; other 1.3%.
Major cities (1994): Addis Ababa 2,112,737; Dire Dawa 164,851; Harer 131,139; Nazret 127,842; Gonder 112,249.

Vital statistics

Birth rate per 1,000 population (2000): 45.1 (world avg. 22.5).
Death rate per 1,000 population (2000): 17.6 (world avg. 9.0).
Natural increase rate per 1,000 population (2000): 27.5 (world avg. 13.5).
Total fertility rate (avg. births per childbearing woman; 2001): 7.1.
Life expectancy at birth (2000): male 44.4 years; female 45.9 years.
Major causes of death (1987–88)[4, 5]: infectious and parasitic diseases 33.1%; respiratory diseases 15.7%; digestive system diseases 10.7%.

National economy

Budget (1997–98). Revenue: Br 9,686,000,000 (taxes 54.4%, of which import duties 21.0%, income and profit tax 17.1%, sales tax 12.2%, export duties 1.9%; nontax revenue 29.2%; grants 13.1%; privatization receipts 3.3%). Expenditures: Br 7,140,000,000 (general services 45.2%, of which defense 29.3%; social services 24.1%, of which education 15.8%, public health 5.6%; debt payment 12.3%).
Public debt (external, outstanding; 2000): U.S.$5,325,000,000.
Tourism (2000): receipts U.S.$68,000,000; expenditures U.S.$74,000,000.
Gross national product (2000): U.S.$6,737,000,000 (U.S.$100 per capita).

Structure of gross domestic product and labour force

	1997–98 in value Br '000,000[7]	1997–98 % of total value	1995[6] labour force	1995[6] % of labour force
Agriculture	6,687.0	45.7	21,605,317	88.6
Manufacturing, mining	1,055.8	7.2	401,535	1.6
Construction	412.1	2.8	61,232	0.3
Public utilities	223.1	1.5	17,066	0.1
Transp. and commun.	907.8	6.2	103,154	0.4
Trade	1,263.3	8.7	935,937	3.8
Finance	999.2	6.8	19,451	0.1
Pub. admin., defense	1,848.3	12.7	}	
Services	1,234.4	8.4	1,252,224	5.1
Other	—	—		
TOTAL	14,631.0	100.0	24,395,916	100.0

Production (metric tons except as noted). Agriculture, forestry, fishing (1999): corn (maize) 2,840,000, sugarcane 2,200,000, sorghum 1,340,000, wheat 1,150,000, barley 970,000, millet 381,486, potatoes 370,000, yams 267,000, coffee 232,020, seed cotton 45,500; livestock (number of live animals) 35,095,230 cattle, 22,000,000 sheep, 16,950,000 goats, 8,580,000 horses, mules, and asses, 1,050,000 camels; roundwood (1998) 50,148,000 cu m; fish catch (1998) 14,000. Mining and quarrying (1995): cement 400,000; limestone 200,000; salt 165,000;

gold 4,500 kg; platinum 48 troy oz. Manufacturing (gross value in Br '000; 1997): food 1,351,200; beverages 876,408; textiles 593,341; leather and shoes 483,364; cigarettes 240,371; paper and paper products 126,316; chemicals 29,688. Construction (authorized; 1987–88)[8]: residential 260,251 sq m; nonresidential 63,346 sq m, of which commercial 16,994 sq m. Energy production (consumption): electricity (kW-hr; 1997) 1,662,000,000 (1,662,000,000); coal, none (n.a.); crude petroleum (barrels; 1997) n.a. (1,187,000); petroleum products (metric tons; 1996) 139,000 (389,000); natural gas, n.a. (n.a.).
Land use (1994): forest 13.3%; pasture 20.0%; agriculture 11.0%; other 55.7%.
Population economically active (1997): total 26,408,000; activity rate of total population 44.8% (participation rates [1995]: ages 15–64, 72.2%; female [1997] 41.0%; unemployed [1994] 62.9%).

Price index (1995 = 100)

	1995	1996	1997	1998	1999	2000
Consumer price index	100.0	94.9	97.2	99.7	105.5	105.5

Household income and expenditure. Average household size (1998) 5.0; income per household (1981–82)[4] Br 1,728 (U.S.$835); sources of income (1981–82): self-employment 79.5%, wages and salaries 0.2%, other 20.3%; expenditure (1988)[4]: food 66.7%, fuel and power 15.9%, clothing and footwear 6.8%, health care 3.1%, education 2.5%, household goods 2.1%.

Foreign trade

Balance of trade (current prices)

	1993	1994	1995	1996	1997	1998
U.S.$'000,000	−507.1	−553.7	−713.7	−384.7	−430.5	−473.9
% of total	56.0%	42.7%	45.8%	27.0%	26.8%	29.4%

Imports (1997–98): Br 7,615,100,000 (consumer goods 24.9%, semifinished goods 17.2%, petroleum products 16.2%, food and live animals 13.9%, transport equipment 13.2%, machinery 13.1%, raw materials 2.1%). *Major import sources:* Japan 10.5%; Germany 9.8%; Saudi Arabia 9.7%; Italy 9.5%; U.K. 6.0%; India 5.7%; U.S. 4.7%.
Exports (1997–98): Br 3,966,000,000 (coffee 69.8%, hides 8.4%, pulses 2.5%, petroleum products 0.2%). *Major export destinations:* Germany 24.8%; Japan 12.2%; Saudi Arabia 9.9%; Italy 6.8%; U.S. 6.8%; Belgium 4.4%; France 3.6%.

Transport and communications

Transport. Railroads (1996–97)[9]: length 782 km; passenger-km 157,000,000; metric ton-km cargo 106,000,000. Roads (1996): total length 19,500 km (paved 15%). Vehicles (1997): passenger cars 52,012; trucks and buses 39,936. Air transport (1997)[10]: passenger-km 1,915,000,000; metric ton-km cargo 328,000,000; airports (1997) 31.

Communications

Medium	date	unit	number	units per 1,000 persons
Daily newspapers	1997	circulation	86,000	1.5
Radio	1997	receivers	11,750,000	202
Television	1999	receivers	350,000	6.1
Telephones	2001	main lines	310,000	4.8
Cellular telephones	2001	subscribers	27,500	0.4
Personal computers	2001	units	75,000	1.2
Internet	2001	users	25,000	0.3

Education and health

Educational attainment: n.a. *Literacy* (1995): total population age 15 and over literate 35.5%; males 45.5%; females 25.3%.

Education (1994–95)

	schools	teachers	students	student/ teacher ratio
Primary (age 7–12)	9,276	83,113	2,722,192	32.8
Secondary (age 13–18)	1,209[11]	22,779	747,142	32.8
Voc., teacher tr.	...	826	9,103	11.0
Higher	11[12]	1,937	32,671	16.9

Health: physicians (1988)[4] 1,466 (1 per 30,195 persons); hospital beds (1986–87)[4] 11,745 (1 per 3,873 persons); infant mortality rate (2000) 101.3.
Food (2000): daily per capita caloric intake 2,023 (vegetable products 95%, animal products 5%); 87% of FAO recommended minimum.

Military

Total active duty personnel (2001): 252,500 (army 99.0%, air force 1.0%); UN peacekeeping personnel along Ethiopian-Eritrean border (May 2002): 4,200. *Military expenditure as percentage of GNP* (1999): 8.8% (world 2.4%); per capita expenditure U.S.$9.

---

[1]Federal republic formally established on Aug. 22, 1995. [2]Amharic is the "working" language. [3]Represents sum of regional state populations; reported census total is 53,477,265. [4]Includes Eritrea. [5]Percentage of illnesses in a sample population of hospital outpatients. [6]For age 10 and up. [7]At 1980–81 factor cost. [8]Addis Ababa only. [9]Includes 100 km of the Chemin de Fer Djibouti-Ethiopiën (CDE) in Djibouti. [10]Ethiopian Airlines only. [11]1985–86. [12]1983–84.

Internet resources for further information:
• Ethiopian Embassy (Washington, D.C.)
http://www.ethiopianembassy.org

Faroe Islands[1]

Official name: Føroyar (Faroese);
Færøerne (Danish) (Faroe Islands).
Political status: self-governing region
of the Danish realm with a single
legislative body (Lagting [32]).
Chief of state: Danish Monarch
represented by High Commissioner.
Head of home government: Prime
Minister.
Capital: Tórshavn (Thorshavn).
Official languages: Faroese; Danish.
Official religion: Evangelical Lutheran.
Monetary unit: 1 Danish krone[2]
(Dkr) = 100 øre; valuation (Sept. 23,
2002) 1 U.S.$ = Dkr 7.56;
1£ = Dkr 11.74.

Area and population		area		population
				2002[3]
Districts	Capitals	sq mi	sq km	estimate
Klaksvík	...	4	4	5,220
Nordhara Eysturoy				
(Østerø Nordre)	...	5	5	1,599
Nordhoy (Norderøernes)	...	93[4]	241[4]	720
Sandoy (Sandø)	...	48	125	1,494
Streymoy (Strømø)	...	151[6]	392[6]	3,285
Suduroy (Suderø)	...	65	167	5,064
Sydhra Eysturoy				
(Østerø Søndre)	...	110[5]	286[5]	8,806
Tórshavn (Thorshavn)	...	6	6	18,071
Vágar (Vágø)	...	73	188	2,737
TOTAL		540	1,399	46,996

Demography

Population (2002): 47,400.
Density (2002): persons per sq mi 87.8, persons per sq km 33.9.
Urban-rural (2000): urban[7] 36.3%; rural 63.7%.
Sex distribution (2001): male 51.88%; female 48.12%.
Age breakdown (2000): under 15, 23.0%; 15–29, 21.1%; 30–44, 19.5%; 45–59, 18.4%; 60–74, 11.5%; 75 and over, 6.5%.
Population projection: (2010) 49,700; (2020) 52,300.
Ethnic composition (2000): Faroese 97.0%; Danish 2.5%; other Scandinavian 0.4%; other 0.1%.
Religious affiliation (1995): Evangelical Lutheran Church of Denmark 80.8%; Plymouth Brethren 10.1%; Roman Catholic 0.2%; other (mostly nonreligious) 8.9%.
Major towns (2002[3]): Tórshavn 18,070; Klaksvík 4,773; Runavík 2,516; Tvøroyri 1,837.

Vital statistics

Birth rate per 1,000 population (2001): 13.5 (world avg. 21.2); (1998) legitimate 62.0%; illegitimate 38.0%.
Death rate per 1,000 population (2001): 7.7 (world avg. 8.9).
Natural increase rate per 1,000 population (2001): 5.8 (world avg. 12.3).
Total fertility rate (avg. births per childbearing woman; 2000): 2.3.
Marriage rate per 1,000 population (2001): 5.9.
Divorce rate per 1,000 population (2001): 0.8.
Life expectancy at birth (2000): male 75.0 years; female 81.9 years.
Major causes of death per 100,000 population (1992): diseases of the circulatory system 354.5, of which ischemic heart disease 222.1, cerebrovascular disease 81.2; malignant neoplasms (cancers) 192.2; diseases of the respiratory system 59.8, of which pneumonia 36.3, bronchitis, emphysema, and asthma 17.1; suicides 8.5; automobile accidents 4.3.

National economy

Budget (1999). Revenue: Dkr 3,104,530,000 (income taxes 33.8%; customs and excise duties 32.4%; transfers from the Danish government 30.4%). Expenditures: Dkr 3,105,530,000 (health and social welfare 43.3%; education 16.6%; debt service 7.7%; agriculture, fishing, and commerce 7.5%; administration 6.0%).
Gross national product (at current market prices; 2000): U.S.$1,029,000,000 (U.S.$22,460 per capita).

Structure of gross domestic product and labour force				
	1999		1977	
	in value Dkr '000,000	% of total value	labour force	% of labour force
Agriculture	53	0.8	282	1.6
Fishing	1,344	20.5	3,032	17.2
Mining	18	0.3	}	
Manufacturing	744	11.4	} 3,854	21.9
Construction	321	4.9	1,952	11.1
Public utilities	150	2.3	[8]	[8]
Transp. and commun.	552	8.4	1,944	11.1
Trade, hotels	768	11.7	2,237[8]	12.7[8]
Finance and real estate	1,145	17.5	[8]	[8]
Pub. admin., defense	1,556	23.8	2,927	16.6
Services	234	3.6	796	4.5
Other	−340[9]	−5.2[9]	561[10]	3.2[10]
TOTAL	6,546[11]	100.0	17,585	100.0[11]

Production (metric tons except as noted). Agriculture, forestry, fishing (2000): potatoes 1,500, other vegetables, grass, hay, and silage are produced; live-

stock (number of live animals) 68,100 sheep, 2,000 cattle; fish catch (1999) 358,013 (of which blue whiting 105,106, mackerel 56,476, saithe 34,423, cod 33,725, capelin 24,275, prawns, shrimps, and other crustaceans 20,916, haddock 19,697). Mining and quarrying: negligible[12]. Manufacturing (value added in Dkr '000,000; 1999): processed fish 393; all other manufacturing 351; important products include handicrafts and woolen textiles and clothing. Construction (1993): completed dwellings 41. Energy production (consumption): electricity (kW-hr; 2001) 231,000,000 ([1997] 181,000,000); coal, none (none); crude petroleum, none (none); petroleum products (metric tons; 1997) none (207,000); natural gas, none (none).
Population economically active (1997): total 26,500; activity rate of total population *c.* 60% (participation rates: age 14–64, n.a.; female *c.* 46%; unemployed *c.* 10%).

Price and earnings indexes (1995 = 100)					
	1996	1997	1998	1999	2000	2001
Consumer price index	102.6	106.0	109.6	114.6	119.6	128.7
Hourly wage index	100.0	101.5	102.5	104.4	109.3	...

Public debt (to Denmark; end of 1999): U.S.$653,000,000.
Household income and expenditure. Average household size: n.a.; average annual income per household: n.a.; sources of income: n.a.; expenditure (1998)[13]: food and beverages 25.1%, transportation and communications 17.7%, housing 12.5%, recreation 11.9%, energy 7.7%.
Tourism (1987): receipts from visitors U.S.$10,000,000; expenditures by nationals abroad U.S.$42,600,000.
Land use (1994): forested, none; meadows and pastures, none; agricultural and under permanent cultivation 2.1%; other 97.9%.

Foreign trade

Balance of trade (current prices)					
	1996	1997	1998	1999	2000	2001
Dkr '000,000	+270	+198	+331	−17	−381	+132
% of total	5.9%	4.0%	6.0%	0.3%	4.8%	1.6%

Imports (2000): Dkr 4,185,000,000 (machinery and transport equipment 31.0%; goods for household consumption 22.4%; petroleum products 12.1%). *Major import sources:* Norway 27.0%; Denmark 24.9%; Germany 6.6%; United Kingdom 5.3%; Sweden 4.8%.
Exports (2000): Dkr 3,804,000,000 (fish for human consumption 92.1%, of which fresh chilled fish 28.5%, frozen fish 17.2%, dried, salted, and smoked fish 14.3%; ships 6.9%). *Major export destinations:* Denmark 31.2%; United Kingdom 19.0%; France 6.9%; Spain 6.7%; Germany 5.7%; United States 5.3%.

Transport and communications

Transport. Railroads: none. Roads (1998): total length 285 mi, 458 km (paved, n.a.). Vehicles (2000): passenger cars 14,608; trucks and buses 3,455. Merchant marine (1998): vessels (20 gross tons and over) 232; total gross tonnage 77,435. Air transport (1998): airports with scheduled flights 1.

Communications				units per 1,000
Medium	date	unit	number	persons
Daily newspapers	1996	circulation	6,000	136
Radio	1997	receivers	26,000	582
Television	1997	receivers	15,000	333
Telephones	2001	main lines	25,471	542
Cellular telephones	1999	subscribers	11,000	244
Internet	1998	users	5,000	113

Education and health

Education (1997–98)				student/
	schools	teachers	students	teacher ratio
Primary (first 7 grades) }	68	...	5,037	...
Secondary			2,750	...
Voc., teacher tr.	11	...	2,195[14]	...
Higher[15]	1	18	70[16]	...

Health (1998): physicians 83 (1 per 537 persons); hospital beds 277 (1 per 161 persons); infant mortality rate per 1,000 live births (2000) 6.9.
Food (1979–81): daily per capita caloric intake 3,195 (vegetable products 68%, animal products 32%); 120% of FAO recommended minimum requirement.

Military

Defense responsibility lies with Denmark.

[1]English-language alternative spelling is Faeroe Islands. [2]The local currency, the Faroese króna (Fkr), is equivalent to the Danish krone. Banknotes used are Faroese or Danish; coins are Danish. [3]January 1. [4]Nordhoy contains Klaksvík. [5]Sydhra Eysturoy contains Nordhara Eysturoy. [6]Streymoy contains Tórshavn. [7]Tórshavn only. [8]Trade, hotels includes Public utilities and Finance and real estate. [9]Imputed bank service charges. [10]Not adequately defined. [11]Detail does not add to total given because of rounding. [12]The maritime boundary demarcation agreement between the Shetland Islands (U.K.) and the Faroes in May 1999 allowed for the exploration of deep-sea petroleum. [13]Weight of consumer price index. [14]1996–97. [15]University of the Faroe Islands. [16]Full-time students only.

Internet resources for further information:
• **Statistics Faroe Islands**
http://www.hagstova.Fo/Welcome_uk.html
• **Danmarks Statistik**
http://www.dst.dk/665

Fiji

Official name: Republic of the Fiji Islands[1].
Form of government: multiparty republic with two legislative houses (Senate [32[2]; House of Representatives [72]).
Chief of state: President.
Head of government: Prime Minister.
Capital: Suva.
Official languages: [3].
Official religion: none.
Monetary unit: 1 Fiji dollar (F$) = 100 cents; valuation (Sept. 23, 2002) 1 U.S.$ = F$2.14; 1 £ = F$3.32.

Area and population

Divisions Provinces	Capitals	area sq mi	area sq km	population 1996 census
Central	Suva			
Naitasiri	—	643	1,666	126,641
Namosi	—	220	570	5,742
Rewa	—	105	272	101,547
Serua	—	320	830	15,461
Tailevu	—	369	955	48,216
Eastern	Levuka			
Kadavu	—	185	478	9,535
Lau	—	188	487	12,211
Lomaiviti	—	159	411	16,214
Rotuma	—	18	46	2,810
Northern	Labasa			
Bua	—	532	1,379	14,988
Cakaudrove	—	1,087	2,816	44,321
Macuata	—	774	2,004	80,207
Western	Lautoka			
Ba	—	1,017	2,634	212,197
Nadroga-Navosa	—	921	2,385	54,083
Ra	—	518	1,341	30,904
TOTAL	—	7,055[4]	18,272[4]	775,077

Demography

Population (2002): 824,000.
Density (2002): persons per sq mi 116.8, persons per sq km 45.1.
Urban-rural (1996): urban 46.4%; rural 53.6%.
Sex distribution (2000): male 50.88%; female 49.12%.
Age breakdown (2000): under 15, 32.8%; 15–29, 27.9%; 30–44, 20.9%; 45–59, 12.3%; 60–74, 5.0%; 75 and over, 1.1%.
Population projection: (2010) 872,000; (2020) 918,000.
Doubling time: 39 years.
Ethnic composition (2000): Fijian 52.0%; Indian 41.5%[5]; other 6.5%.
Religious affiliation (2000): Christian 56.8%, of which Protestant 37.1%, independent Christian 8.5%, Roman Catholic 8.4%; Hindu 33.3%; Muslim 6.9%; nonreligious 1.3%; Sikh 0.7%; other 1.0%.
Major cities (1996; "urban centres"): Suva 167,421; Lautoka 42,917; Nadi 30,791; Labasa 24,187; Nausori 21,645.

Vital statistics

Birth rate per 1,000 population (2001): 23.3 (world avg. 21.2).
Death rate per 1,000 population (2001): 5.8 (world avg. 8.9).
Natural increase rate per 1,000 population (2000): 17.5 (world avg. 12.3).
Total fertility rate (avg. births per childbearing woman; 2001): 2.9.
Life expectancy at birth (2001): male 65.8 years; female 70.8 years.
Major causes of death per 100,000 population (1987): diseases of the circulatory system 153.4; malignant neoplasms (cancers) 35.5; accidents, poisoning, and violence 32.2; diseases of the respiratory system 31.7.

National economy

Budget (2000). Revenue: F$884,337,000 (income taxes, estate taxes, and gift duties 57.0%; customs duties and port dues 26.1%; fees, royalties, and sales 4.9%; other 12.0%). Expenditures: F$920,186,000 (departmental expenditure 72.9%; public-debt charges 23.2%; pensions and gratuities 3.9%).
Production (metric tons except as noted). Agriculture, forestry, fishing (2001): sugarcane 3,500,000, coconuts 215,000, taro 37,000, cassava 32,582, paddy rice 16,131, sweet potatoes 6,600, bananas 6,500, yams 5,165, pineapples 3,662, tomatoes 2,800, okra 1,200; livestock (number of live animals) 340,000 cattle, 245,749 goats, 137,000 pigs; roundwood 486,000 cu m; fish catch (1999) 25,100. Mining and quarrying (2000): cement 87,000; gold 3,794 kg; silver 1,462 kg. Manufacturing (2000): raw sugar 335,000; flour 54,931; soap 6,142; coconut oil 5,634. Energy production (consumption): electricity (kW-hr; 2000) 687,000,000 (687,000,000); coal (metric tons; 1997) none (22,000); crude petroleum, none (n.a.); petroleum products (metric tons; 1997) none (213,000).
Tourism (2000): receipts from visitors U.S.$195,000,000; expenditures by nationals abroad U.S.$66,000,000.
Land use (1994): forested 64.9%; agricultural and under permanent cultivation 14.2%; meadows and pastures 9.5%; other 11.4%.
Population economically active (1997): total 297,800; activity rate of total population 33.8% (participation rates [1986]: ages 15–64, 56.0%; female 21.2%; unemployed [1990] 6.4%).

Price and earnings indexes (1995 = 100)

	1995	1996	1997	1998	1999	2000	2001
Consumer price index	100.0	103.1	106.5	112.6	114.8	116.1	121.1
Earnings index	...	...	...	...	...	...	...

Gross national product (2000): U.S.$1,480,000,000 (U.S.$1,820 per capita).

Structure of gross domestic product and labour force

	1999 in value F$'000[6]	1999 % of total value[6]	1986 labour force	1986 % of labour force
Agriculture	352,897	17.1	106,305	44.1
Mining	59,522	2.9	1,345	0.5
Manufacturing	317,825	15.4	18,106	7.5
Construction	99,288	4.8	11,786	4.9
Public utilities	89,826	4.4	2,154	0.9
Transp. and commun.	302,987	14.7	13,151	5.4
Trade	332,034	16.2	26,010	10.8
Finance	251,539	12.2	6,016	2.5
Pub. admin., defense } Services	367,350	17.8	36,619	15.2
Other	−114,911[7]	−5.6[7]	19,668[8]	8.2[8]
TOTAL	2,058,357	100.0[4]	241,160	100.0

Public debt (external, outstanding; 2000): U.S.$101,200,000.
Household income and expenditure. Average household size (1999) 6.1; income per household: n.a.; sources of income: n.a.; expenditure (1991[9]): food, beverages, and tobacco 41.5%, housing and energy 21.4%, transportation and communications 12.9%, household durable goods 6.5%.

Foreign trade

Balance of trade (current prices)

	1995	1996	1997	1998	1999	2000
F$'000,000	−454.45	−225.26	−334.16	−204.8	−578,181	−555,127
% of total	22.9%	10.9%	16.8%	9.2%	19.4%	18.6%

Imports (2000): F$1,758,338,000 (durable manufactures 27.3%; machinery and transport equipment 19.5%; petroleum products 16.8%; miscellaneous manufactured consumer articles 14.9%; food, beverages, and tobacco 12.5%; chemicals 6.6%). *Major import sources* (1999): Australia 41.1%; New Zealand 13.3%; United States 12.4%; Japan 6.4%; China 4.6%.
Exports (2000)[10]: F$1,057,285,000 (sugar 25.6%; clothing 25.3%; gold 7.4%; timber 5.7%; fish 5.2%; molasses 1.9%; coconut oil 0.8%). *Major export destinations*[11]: Australia 40.6%; United Kingdom 19.6%; United States 13.3%; New Zealand 4.8%; Japan 3.9%.

Transport and communications

Transport. Railroads (1999)[12]: length 370 mi, 595 km. Roads (1999): total length 2,140 mi, 3,440 km (paved 49%). Vehicles (2000): passenger cars 50,005; trucks and buses 35,038. Merchant marine (1992): vessels (100 gross tons and over) 64; total deadweight tonnage 60,444. Air transport (1999)[13]: passenger-km 1,838,264,000; metric ton-km cargo 100,124,000; airports (1997) with scheduled flights 13.

Communications

Medium	date	unit	number	units per 1,000 persons
Daily newspapers	1996	circulation	40,000	51
Radio	1997	receivers	500,000	636
Television	1999	receivers	88,908	111
Telephones	2001	main lines	90,400	84
Cellular telephones	2001	subscribers	76,000	92
Personal computers	2001	units	50,000	61
Internet	2001	users	15,000	18

Education and health

Educational attainment (1986). Percentage of population age 25 and over having: no formal schooling 28.3%; primary only 19.1%; some secondary 44.1%; secondary 4.1%; postsecondary 3.3%; other 1.1%. *Literacy* (1996): total population age 15 and over literate 92.9%; males 94.5%; females 91.4%.

Education (1998)

	schools	teachers	students	student/teacher ratio
Primary (age 5–15)	709[14]	5,054	143,863	28.5
Secondary (age 16–19)	146[14]	3,519	69,284	19.7
Voc., teacher tr.	35[14]	864	9,997	11.6
Higher[15]	1	277	7,908	28.5

Health (1998): physicians 252 (1 per 3,147 persons); hospital beds 1,797 (1 per 441 persons); infant mortality rate per 1,000 live births (2001) 14.1.
Food (2000): daily per capita caloric intake 2,861 (vegetable products 81%, animal products 19%); 125% of FAO recommended minimum requirement.

Military

Total active duty personnel (2001): 3,500 (army 91.4%, navy 8.6%, air force, none). *Military expenditure as percentage of GNP* (1999): 2.0% (world 2.4%); per capita expenditure U.S.$42.

[1]The long-form name in Fijian is Kai Vakarairai ni Fiji. [2]All seats are nonelected. [3]English, Fijian, and Hindustani (Fijian Hindi) have equal status per 1998 constitution. [4]Detail does not add to total given because of rounding. [5]The emigration of Indian population after the coup in 1987 has resulted in the reemergence of a Fijian majority. [6]Constant 1989 prices. [7]Less imputed bank service charges. [8]Not stated and unemployed. [9]Weights of consumer price index components based on 3,000 urban households. [10]Excludes reexports valued at F$159,926,000. [11]Based on exports of local products only. [12]Owned by the Fiji Sugar Corporation. [13]Air Pacific only. [14]1995. [15]1991.

Internet resources for further information:
• Fiji Islands Statistics Bureau http://www.statsfiji.gov.fj
• Fiji Government Online http://www.fiji.gov.fj
• High Commission of the Republic of Fiji to New Zealand http://www.fiji.org.nz

Finland

Official names[1]: Suomen Tasavalta (Finnish); Republiken Finland (Swedish) (Republic of Finland).
Form of government: multiparty republic with one legislative house (Parliament [200[2]]).
Chief of state: President.
Head of government: Prime Minister.
Capital: Helsinki.
Official languages: none[1].
Official religion: none.
Monetary unit: 1 euro (€) = 100 cents, valuation (Sept. 23, 2002) 1 U.S.$ = €1.02; 1 £ = €1.58[3].

Area and population

Provinces	Capitals	area		population
		sq mi	sq km	2002 estimate[4]
Eastern Finland	Mikkeli	23,444	60,720	588,106
Lapland	Rovaniemi	38,203	98,946	189,288
Oulu	Oulu	23,773	61,572	456,502
Southern Finland	Hämeenlinna	13,273	34,378	2,095,416
Western Finland	Turku	31,265	80,976	1,839,581
Autonomous Territory				
Åland (Ahvenamaa)	Mariehamn (Maarianhamina)	599	1,552	26,008
TOTAL		130,559[5, 6]	338,145[5, 6]	5,194,901

Demography

Population (2002): 5,201,000.
Density (2002)[7]: persons per sq mi 44.2, persons per sq km 17.1.
Urban-rural (2002[4]): urban 61.4%; rural 38.6%[8].
Sex distribution (2002[4]): male 48.85%; female 51.15%.
Age breakdown (2002[4]): under 15, 17.9%; 15–29, 18.6%; 30–44, 21.0%; 45–59, 22.1%; 60–74, 13.7%; 75 and over, 6.7%.
Population projection: (2010) 5,267,000; (2020) 5,317,000.
Ethnic composition (2000): Finnish 91.9%; Swedish 5.9%; Karelian 0.8%; Russian 0.2%; other 1.2%.
Religious affiliation (2000[3]): Evangelical Lutheran 85.2%; Finnish (Greek) Orthodox 1.1%; nonreligious 12.6%; other 1.1%.
Major cities (2002[4]): Helsinki 559,718 (metro area 964,953); Espoo 216,836[9]; Tampere 197,774; Vantaa 179,856[9]; Turku 173,686; Oulu 123,274.

Vital statistics

Birth rate per 1,000 population (2001): 10.8 (world avg. 21.2); (2000) legitimate 60.8%; illegitimate 39.2%.
Death rate per 1,000 population (2001): 9.4 (world avg. 8.9).
Natural increase rate per 1,000 population (2001): 1.4 (world avg. 12.3).
Total fertility rate (avg. births per childbearing woman; 2000): 1.7.
Marriage rate per 1,000 population (2000): 5.1.
Divorce rate per 1,000 population (2000): 2.7.
Life expectancy at birth (2000): male 74.1 years; female 81.0 years.
Major causes of death per 100,000 population (1997): ischemic heart diseases 245.4; malignant neoplasms (cancers) 202.7; cerebrovascular diseases 103.2; accidents and violence 83.3; diseases of the respiratory system 77.8.

National economy

Budget (2000). Revenue: Fmk 199,579,000,000 (income and property taxes 33.7%, value-added taxes 27.7%, excise duties 13.8%). Expenditures: Fmk 199,575,000,000 (social security and health 21.8%, education 14.0%, interest on state debt 13.4%, agriculture and forestry 6.6%, defense 4.9%).
National debt (2001): U.S.$86,666,000,000.
Production (metric tons except as noted). Agriculture, forestry, fishing (1999): silage 6,799,000, barley 1,568,000, sugar beets 1,172,000, oats 990,000, potatoes 791,000, wheat 254,000; livestock (number of live animals; 2000) 1,541,000 pigs, 1,101,000 cattle, (1999) 195,000 reindeer; roundwood (1999) 53,851,000 cu m; fish catch (1999) 176,018. Mining and quarrying (1998): chromite (gross weight) 498,000; gold 5,000 kilograms. Manufacturing (value added in Fmk '000,000; 1998): wood pulp, paper, and paper products 24,304; radio, television, and communications equipment 21,271; nonelectrical machinery 17,398; food and beverages 11,505; fabricated metals 9,485; printing and publishing 9,368; wood and wood products (excluding furniture) 7,498. Energy production (consumption): electricity (kW-hr; 2000) 67,278,000,000 (79,158,000,000); coal (metric tons; 1997) none (6,995,000); crude petroleum (barrels; 1997) none (70,904,000); petroleum products (metric tons; 1997) 10,721,000 (9,222,000); natural gas (cu m; 1997) none (3,509,000,000).
Population economically active (1999): total 2,557,000; activity rate of total population 49.5% (participation rates: ages 15–64, 73.6%; female 47.8%; unemployed [2001] 9.1%).

Price and earnings indexes (1995 = 100)

	1996	1997	1998	1999	2000	2001	2002
Consumer price index	100.6	101.8	103.2	104.4	108.0	110.7	112.6[10]
Hourly earnings index	102.1	101.4	103.7	104.9	...	...	...

Household income and expenditure (1998). Average household size 2.2; disposable income per household Fmk 146,400 (U.S.$27,395); sources of gross income: wages and salaries 55.4%, transfer payments 27.4%, other 17.2%; expenditure: housing and energy 27.3%, transportation and communications 18.9%, food, beverages, and tobacco 16.5%.

Gross national product (2000): U.S.$130,106,000,000 (U.S.$25,130 per capita).

Structure of gross domestic product and labour force

	1999			
	in value Fmk '000,000	% of total value	labour force	% of labour force
Agriculture, fishing	7,891	1.1	121,000	4.7
Forestry	15,202	2.1	23,000	0.9
Mining	1,743	0.2	488,000	19.1
Manufacturing	155,340	21.5		
Public utilities	12,838	1.8	...	...
Construction	35,276	4.9	149,000	5.8
Transp. and commun.	57,720	8.0	168,000	6.6
Trade, restaurants	76,872	10.6	355,000	13.9
Finance, real estate	131,859	18.2	267,000	10.4
Pub. admin., defense	112,477	15.5	116,000	4.5
Services	17,809	2.5	603,000	23.6
Other	98,587[11]	13.6[11]	267,000[12]	10.4[12]
TOTAL	723,614	100.0	2,557,000	100.0[5]

Tourism (in U.S.$'000,000; 2000): receipts 1,397; expenditures 1,836.
Land use (1994): forested 76.1%; meadows and pastures 0.4%; agricultural and under permanent cultivation 8.5%; other 15.0%.

Foreign trade[13]

Balance of trade (current prices)

	1996	1997	1998	1999	2000	2001
€'000,000	+44,164[14]	+51,845[14]	+57,750[14]	+9,615	+12,648	+11,923
% of total	13.6%	13.9%	14.3%	13.9%	14.7%	14.3%

Imports (1999): €39,306,000,000 (electrical machinery and apparatus 16.7%; nonelectrical machinery and apparatus 15.4%; mineral fuels 8.5%; automobiles 8.4%). *Major import sources:* Germany 15.3%; Sweden 11.2%; U.S. 7.9%; Russia 7.2%; U.K. 6.6%; Japan 6.2%; France 4.3%.
Exports (1999): €29,691,000,000 (electrical machinery and apparatus 23.7%; paper and paper products 20.5%; nonelectrical machinery and apparatus 11.8%; wood products and furniture 7.2%). *Major export destinations:* Germany 13.1%; Sweden 9.9%; U.K. 9.1%; U.S. 7.9%; France 5.3%; The Netherlands 4.3%; Russia 4.1%.

Transport and communications

Transport. Railroads: route length (1999) 5,836 km; passenger-km 3,415,000,000; metric ton-km cargo 9,753,000,000. Roads (2000[4, 15]): total length 77,900 km (paved 65%). Vehicles (2000[4]): passenger cars 2,069,055; trucks and buses 300,048. Air transport (1999): passenger-km 12,916,000,000; metric ton-km cargo 315,883,000; airports (1999) 27.

Communications

Medium	date	unit	number	units per 1,000 persons
Daily newspapers	1996	circulation	2,332,000	455
Radio	1997	receivers	7,700,000	1,498
Television	1997	receivers	3,200,000	623
Telephones	2001	main lines	2,845,000	548
Cellular telephones	2001	subscribers	4,044,000	778
Personal computers	2001	units	2,200,000	424
Internet	2001	users	2,235,300	430

Education and health

Educational attainment (end of 1998). Percentage of population age 25 and over having: incomplete upper-secondary education 40.7%; complete upper secondary or vocational 33.6%; higher 25.7%. *Literacy:* virtually 100%.

Education (1999–2000)

	schools	teachers	students	student/teacher ratio
Primary/Lower Secondary (age 7–15)	4,101	41,631[16]	591,272	...
Upper Secondary (age 16–18)	456	6,693 [16]	130,624	...
Voc. (incl. higher)	398	...	258,845	...
Higher[17]	20	7,252[16]	152,466	...

Health (1999): physicians 15,794[18] (1 per 327 persons); hospital beds (1998) 39,718 (1 per 130 persons); infant mortality rate per 1,000 live births 4.2.
Food (1998): daily per capita caloric intake 3,180 (vegetable products 61%, animal products 39%); 117% of FAO recommended minimum requirement.

Military

Total active duty personnel (2001): 32,250 (army 76.1%, navy 15.5%, air force 8.4%). *Military expenditure as percentage of GNP* (1999): 1.4% (world 2.4%); per capita expenditure U.S.$344.

[1]Finnish and Swedish were official languages until mid-1995 and national languages thereafter. [2]Includes one representative from Åland not taking part in the 1999 general elections. [3]The Finnish markka (Fmk) was the former monetary unit; on Jan. 1, 2002, Fmk 5.95 = €1. [4]January 1. [5]Detail does not add to total given because of rounding. [6]Total includes land area of 117,579 sq mi (304,529 sq km) and inland water area of 12,979 sq mi (33,615 sq km). [7]Based on land area only. [8]Includes semi-urban. [9]Within Helsinki metro area. [10]June. [11]Taxes less subsidies and imputed bank service charges. [12]Includes 261,000 unemployed persons not previously employed and 6,000 not adequately defined. [13]Imports c.i.f., exports f.o.b. [14]In Finnish markkas. [15]Excludes Åland Islands. [16]1998–99. [17]Universities only. [18]Registered professionals of working age.

Internet resources for further information:
• **Embassy of Finland** (Washington, D.C.) http://www.finland.org/facts.html
• **Statistics Finland** http://www.stat.fi/index_en.html

France

Official name: République Française (French Republic).
Form of government: republic with two legislative houses (Parliament; Senate [321], National Assembly [577]).
Chief of state: President.
Head of government: Prime Minister.
Capital: Paris.
Official language: French.
Official religion: none.
Monetary unit: 1 euro (€) = 100 cents; valuation (Sept. 23, 2002) 1 U.S.$ = €1.02; 1 £ = €1.58[1].

Area and population

Regions Departments	Capitals	area sq mi	area sq km	population 1999 census
Alsace	Strasbourg			1,734,145
Bas-Rhin	Strasbourg	1,836	4,755	1,026,120
Haut-Rhin	Colmar	1,361	3,525	708,025
Aquitaine	Bordeaux			2,908,359
Dordogne	Périgueux	3,498	9,060	388,293
Gironde	Bordeaux	3,861	10,000	1,287,334
Landes	Mont-de-Marsan	3,569	9,243	327,334
Lot-et-Garonne	Agen	2,070	5,361	305,380
Pyrénées-Atlantiques	Pau	2,952	7,645	600,018
Auvergne	Clermont-Ferrand			1,308,878
Allier	Moulins	2,834	7,340	344,721
Cantal	Aurillac	2,211	5,726	150,778
Haute-Loire	Le Puy	1,922	4,977	209,113
Puy-de-Dôme	Clermont-Ferrand	3,077	7,970	604,266
Basse-Normandie	Caen			1,422,193
Calvados	Caen	2,142	5,548	648,385
Manche	Saint-Lô	2,293	5,938	481,471
Orne	Alençon	2,356	6,103	292,337
Bourgogne (Burgundy)	Dijon			1,610,067
Côte-d'Or	Dijon	3,383	8,763	506,755
Nièvre	Nevers	2,632	6,817	225,198
Saône-et-Loire	Mâcon	3,311	8,575	544,893
Yonne	Auxerre	2,868	7,427	333,221
Bretagne (Brittany)	Rennes			2,906,197
Côtes-d'Armor	Saint-Brieuc	2,656	6,878	542,373
Finistère	Quimper	2,600	6,733	852,418
Ille-et-Vilaine	Rennes	2,616	6,775	867,533
Morbihan	Vannes	2,634	6,823	643,873
Centre	Orléans			2,440,329
Cher	Bourges	2,793	7,235	314,428
Eure-et-Loir	Chartres	2,270	5,880	407,665
Indre	Châteauroux	2,622	6,791	231,139
Indre-et-Loire	Tours	2,366	6,127	554,003
Loir-et-Cher	Blois	2,449	6,343	314,968
Loiret	Orléans	2,616	6,775	618,126
Champagne-Ardenne	Châlons su Marne			1,342,363
Ardemmes	Charleville-Mézières	2,019	5,229	290,130
Aube	Troyes	2,318	6,004	292,131
Haute-Marne	Chaumont	2,398	6,211	194,873
Marne	Châlons-sur-Marne	3,151	8,162	565,229
Corse[2] (Corsica)	Ajaccio			260,196
Corse-du-Sud	Ajaccio	1,550	4,014	118,593
Haute-Corse	Bastia	1,802	4,666	141,603
Franche-Comté	Besançon			1,117,059
Doubs	Besançon	2,021	5,234	499,062
Haute-Saône	Vesoul	2,070	5,360	229,732
Jura	Lons-le-Saunier	1,930	4,999	250,857
Territoire de Belfort	Belfort	235	609	137,408
Haute-Normandie	Rouen			1,780,192
Eure	Évreux	2,332	6,040	541,054
Seine-Maritime	Rouen	2,424	6,278	1,239,138
Île-de-France	Paris			10,952,011
Essonne	Évry	696	1,804	1,134,238
Hauts-de-Seine	Nanterre	68	176	1,428,881
Paris	Paris	40	105	2,125,246
Seine-et-Marne	Melun	2,284	5,915	1,193,767
Seine-Saint-Denis	Bobigny	91	236	1,382,861
Val-de-Marne	Créteil	95	245	1,227,250
Val-d'Oise	Pontoise	481	1,246	1,105,464
Yvelines	Versailles	882	2,284	1,354,304
Languedoc-Roussillon	Montpellier			2,295,648
Aude	Carcassonne	2,370	6,139	309,770
Gard	Nîmes	2,260	5,853	623,125
Hérault	Montpellier	2,356	6,101	896,441
Lozère	Mende	1,995	5,167	73,509
Pyrénées-Orientales	Perpignan	1,589	4,116	392,803
Limousin	Limoges			710,939
Corrèze	Tulle	2,261	5,857	232,576
Creuse	Guéret	2,149	5,565	124,470
Haute-Vienne	Limoges	2,131	5,520	353,893
Lorraine	Metz			2,310,376
Meurthe-et-Moselle	Nancy	2,024	5,241	713,779
Meuse	Bar-le-Duc	2,400	6,216	192,198
Moselle	Metz	2,400	6,216	1,023,447
Vosges	Épinal	2,268	5,874	380,952
Midi-Pyrénées	Toulouse			2,551,687
Ariège	Foix	1,888	4,890	137,205
Aveyron	Rodez	3,373	8,736	263,808
Gers	Auch	2,416	6,257	172,335
Haute-Garonne	Toulouse	2,436	6,309	1,046,338
Hautes-Pyrénées	Tarbes	1,724	4,464	222,368
Lot	Cahors	2,014	5,217	160,197
Tarn	Albi	2,223	5,758	343,402
Tarn-et-Garonne	Montauban	1,435	3,718	206,034
Nord-Pas-de-Calais	Lille			3,996,588
Nord	Lille	2,217	5,742	2,555,020
Pas-de-Calais	Arras	2,576	6,671	1,441,568

Area and population (continued)

		area sq mi	area sq km	population 1999 census
Pays de la Loire	Nantes			3,222,061
Loire-Atlantique	Nantes	2,631	6,815	1,134,266
Maine-et Loire	Angers	2,767	7,166	732,942
Mayenne	Laval	1,998	5,175	285,338
Sarthe	Le Mans	2,396	6,206	529,851
Vendée	La Roche-sur-Yon	2,595	6,720	539,664
Picardie (Picardy)	Amiens			1,857,834
Aisne	Laon	2,845	7,369	535,842
Oise	Beauvais	2,263	5,860	766,441
Somme	Amiens	2,382	6,170	555,551
Poitou-Charentes	Poitiers			1,640,068
Charente	Angoulême	2,300	5,956	339,628
Charente-Maritime	La Rochelle	2,650	6,864	557,024
Deux-Sèvres	Niort	2,316	5,999	344,392
Vienne	Poitiers	2,699	6,990	399,024
Provence-Alpes–Côte d'Azur	Marseille			4,506,151
Alpes-de-Haute-Provence	Digne	2,674	6,925	139,561
Alpes-Maritimes	Nice	1,660	4,299	1,011,326
Bouches-du-Rhône	Marseille	1,964	5,087	1,835,719
Hautes-Alpes	Gap	2,142	5,549	121,419
Var	Toulon	2,306	5,973	898,441
Vaucluse	Avignon	1,377	3,567	499,685
Rhône-Alpes	Lyon			5,645,407
Ain	Bourg-en-Bresse	2,225	5,762	515,270
Ardèche	Privas	2,135	5,529	286,023
Drôme	Valence	2,521	6,530	437,778
Haute-Savoie	Annecy	1,694	4,388	631,679
Isère	Grenoble	2,869	7,431	1,094,006
Loire	Saint-Étienne	1,846	4,781	728,524
Rhône	Lyon	1,254	3,249	1,578,869
Savoie	Chambéry	2,327	6,028	373,258
TOTAL		210,026	543,965	58,518,748

Demography

Population (2002): 59,440,000.
Density (2002): persons per sq mi 283.0, persons per sq km 109.3.
Urban-rural (1999): urban 75.5%; rural 24.5%.
Sex distribution (1999): male 48.56%; female 51.44%.
Age breakdown (1999): under 15, 17.9%; 15–29, 20.2%; 30–44, 21.9%; 45–59, 18.7%; 60–74, 13.6%; 75 and over, 7.7%.
Population projection: (2010) 60,596,000; (2020) 61,371,000.
Ethnic composition (2000): French 76.9%; Algerian and Moroccan Berber 2.2%; Italian 1.9%; Portuguese 1.5%; Moroccan Arab 1.5%; Fleming 1.4%; Algerian Arab 1.3%; Basque 1.3%; Jewish 1.2%; German 1.2%; Vietnamese 1.0%; Catalan 0.5%; other 8.1%.
Religious affiliation (2000): Roman Catholic 82.3%; Muslim 7.1%; atheist 4.4%; Protestant 3.7%; Orthodox 1.1%; Jewish 1.0%; other 0.4%.
Major cities (1999): Paris 2,125,246 (metropolitan area 9,644,507); Marseille 798,430 (1,349,772); Lyon 445,452 (1,348,832); Toulouse 390,350 (761,090); Nice 342,738 (888,784); Nantes 270,251 (544,932); Strasbourg 264,115 (427,245); Montpellier 225,392 (287,981); Bordeaux 215,363 (753,931); Rennes 206,229 (272,263); Le Havre 190,905 (248,547); Reims 187,206 (215,581); Lille 184,493 (1,000,900); Saint-Étienne 180,210 (291,960); Toulon 160,639 (519,640).
Mobility (1990). Population living in same residence as in 1982: 51.4%; same region 89.0%; different region 8.8%; different country 2.2%.
Households (1993). Average household size 2.6; 1 person 27.7%, 2 persons 32.0%, 3 persons 17.4%, 4 persons 14.7%, 5 persons or more 8.2%. Family households (1990): 14,118,940 (72.1%); nonfamily 5,471,460 (27.9%, of which 1-person 24.6%).
Immigration (1998): immigrants admitted 100,014 (Algeria 15.3%, Turkey 6.0%, Tunisia 4.9%, Sri Lanka 1.7%, Vietnam 1.0%).

Vital statistics

Birth rate per 1,000 population (2000): 10.8 (world avg. 22.5); (1997) legitimate 59.9%; illegitimate 40.1%.
Death rate per 1,000 population (2000): 9.1 (world avg. 9.0).
Natural increase rate per 1,000 population (2000): 1.7 (world avg. 13.5).
Total fertility rate (avg. births per childbearing woman; 2000): 1.7.
Marriage rate per 1,000 population (1998): 4.6.
Divorce rate per 1,000 population (1998): 2.0.
Life expectancy at birth (2000): male 74.8 years; female 82.9 years.
Major causes of death per 100,000 population (1997): heart disease and other circulatory diseases 291.6; malignant neoplasms (cancers) 252.2; accidents and violence 74.4; respiratory diseases 74.4; digestive tract diseases 44.8.

Social indicators

Educational attainment (1990). Percentage of population age 25 and over having: primary 22.1%; lower secondary 7.8%; higher secondary and vocational 29.4%; postsecondary 11.6%; undeclared attainment 29.1%.

Distribution of income (1984)

percentage of household income by quintile

1	2	3	4	5 (highest)
7.1%	12.3%	17.1%	23.2%	40.3%

Quality of working life. Average workweek (1994): 38.9 hours. Annual rate per 100,000 workers for: injury or accident 5,322 (deaths 0.8%); accidents in transit to work 708 (deaths 68.3). Average days lost to labour stoppages per 1,000 workers (1994): 21.0. Average length of journey to work (1990): 8.7 mi (14 km).
Access to services (1992). Proportion of dwellings having: central heating 86.0%; piped water 97.0%; indoor plumbing 95.8%.
Social participation. Eligible voters participating in last (June 2002) national election: 64.4%. Population over 15 years of age participating in voluntary associations (1997): 28.0%.

Social deviance. Offense rate per 100,000 population (1998) for: murder 1.6, rape 13.4, other assault 583.8; theft (including burglary and housebreaking) 6,107.6. Incidence per 100,000 in general population of: alcoholism, n.a. (deaths related to alcoholism; 1991) 5.0; suicide (1993) 21.1.

Leisure (1987–88). Participation rate for favourite leisure activities: watching television 82%; reading magazines 79%; listening to radio 75%; entertaining relatives 64%; visiting relatives 61%; attending fairs/expositions 56%.

Material well-being (1994). Households possessing: automobile 79.5%; colour television 92.4%; VCR 52.8%; refrigerator 99.0%; washing machine 89.4%.

National economy

Gross national product (2000): U.S.$1,438,293,000,000 (U.S.$24,090 per capita).

Structure of gross domestic product and labour force

	1998[3]			
	in value F '000,000	% of total value	labour force	% of labour force
Agriculture	242,185	3.2	986,600	3.9
Mining	[4]	[4]	246,800	1.0
Manufacturing	1,411,010[4]	18.5[4]	3,973,400	15.6
Construction	361,253	4.7	1,371,100	5.4
Public utilities	213,198	2.8	205,100	0.8
Transp. and commun.	326,007[5]	4.3[5]	1,001,600	3.9
Trade[6]	1,726,864[5]	22.7[5]	3,812,400	15.0
Finance	383,133	5.0	683,300	2.7
Pub. admin., defense	1,601,161	21.0	5,767,600	22.6
Services	1,588,888	20.9	4,381,700	17.2
Other	−235,465[7]	−3.1[7]	3,029,600[8]	11.9[8]
TOTAL	7,618,234	100.0	25,459,200	100.0

Budget (1998). Revenue: F 1,331,838,000,000 (value-added taxes 58.3%, personal income tax 22.2%, corporate income tax 16.5%). Expenditures: F 1,585,307,000,000 (education 21.1%, defense 15.0%, health and social services 4.6%, research and development 2.5%).

Manufacturing enterprises (1995)

	no. of enter- prises[9]	no. of employees	annual salaries as a % of avg. of all salaries[9]	annual value added (F '000,000)
Food products	55,197	545,900	87	208,065
Transport equipment	4,293	508,700	108	167,357
Electrical machinery	15,620	433,600	118	156,221
Iron and steel	27,847	403,800	96	131,376
Mechanical equipment	32,134	390,300	104	127,637
Petroleum refineries	180	46,200	174	117,041
Printing, publishing	30,359	231,900	125	83,083
Textiles and wearing apparel	29,701	281,500	78	63,633
Rubber products	5,875	204,200	94	57,758
Chemical products	1,442	102,100	128	51,146
Paper and paper products	1,916	101,500	102	38,585
Metal products	442	43,700	103	28,115
Glass products	1,536	52,400	104	16,638
Footwear	4,236	55,400	75	12,970

Production (metric tons except as noted). Agriculture, forestry, fishing (2000): wheat 37,559,000, sugar beets 31,454,000, corn (maize) 16,469,000, barley 9,927,000, grapes 7,627,000, potatoes 6,652,000, rapeseed 3,569,000, apples 2,157,000, dry peas 1,918,000, sunflower seeds 1,813,000, triticale 1,213,000, tomatoes 898,000, carrots 633,000, green peas 550,000, lettuce 513,000, oats 503,000, peaches 476,000, onions 361,000; livestock (number of live animals) 20,527,000 cattle, 14,635,000 pigs, 10,004,000 sheep, 1,190,000 goats; roundwood 50,170,000 cu m; fish catch (1999) 845,649. Mining and quarrying (2000): gypsum 4,500,000; potash 360,000; kaolin 330,000; gold 84,600 troy oz. Manufacturing (value added in F '000,000,000; 1998[10]): transport equipment 157.2, of which motor vehicles 75.7, aircraft 38.8; fabricated metals 83.0; non-electrical machinery 80.5; electronics, radios, and televisions 58.9; pharmaceuticals 56.6; printing and publishing 55.0, of which publishing 33.9; other electrical machinery 48.6.

Retail trade enterprises (1995)[11]

	no. of enter- prises	no. of employees	weekly wages as a % of all wages	annual turnover (F '000,000)
Large food stores	4,373	385,402	...	617,222
Clothing stores	51,873	195,535	...	126,504
Pharmacies	22,301	126,508	...	121,980
Small food stores	64,565	163,474	...	110,928
butcher shops	21,548	59,962	...	36,732
Furniture stores	7,179	53,080	...	54,390
Electrical and electronics stores	10,990	55,560	...	43,995
Department stores	736	35,074	...	27,741
Publishing and paper	15,083	40,375	...	24,591
Gas, coal, and other energy products	6,042	25,375	...	19,204

Energy production (consumption)[12]: electricity (kW-hr; 2000) 543,966,000,000 ([1997] 450,072,000,000); hard coal (metric tons; 2000) 3,168,000 ([1997] 21,527,000); lignite (metric tons; 2000) 300,000 ([1997] 852,000); crude petroleum (barrels; 2001) 11,027,000 ([1997] 651,981,000); petroleum products (metric tons; 1997) 79,634,000 (70,965,000); natural gas (cu m; 2000) 1,787,-000,000 ([1997] 37,102,600,000).

Population economically active (1998[11]): total 25,459,200; activity rate of total population 43.4% (participation rates: ages 15–64, 67.6%[13]; female 45.8%; unemployed 11.9%).

Price and earnings indexes (1995 = 100)

	1995	1996	1997	1998	1999	2000	2001
Consumer price index	100.0	102.0	103.2	103.9	104.5	106.3	108.0
Earnings index	100.0	101.9	104.7	107.6	110.0	115.0	120.2

Household income and expenditure (1995). Average household size 2.6; average annual income per household F 302,560 (U.S.$60,610); sources of income: wages and salaries 70.0%, self-employment 24.4%, social security 5.6%; expenditure (1997): housing 22.5%, food 17.9%, transportation 16.3%, health 10.3%, recreation and education 7.4%, clothing 5.2%.

Tourism (2000): receipts U.S.$29,900,000,000; expenditures U.S.$17,166,000,-000.

Public debt (1998): F 5,030,000,000,000 (U.S.$853,000,000,000).

Financial aggregates

	1996	1997	1998	1999	2000	2001
Exchange rate, F per:[14]						
U.S. dollar	5.24	5.99	5.62	1.00	1.07	1.13
£	8.90	9.90	9.35	1.62	1.60	1.65
SDR	7.53	8.08	7.92	1.37	1.40	1.43
International reserves (U.S.$)						
Total (excl. gold; '000,000)	26,796	30,927	44,312	39,701	37,039	31,749
SDRs ('000,000)	981	971	1,107	347	402	492
Reserve pos. in IMF ('000,000)	2,695	2,859	4,452	5,241	4,522	4,894
Foreign exchange	23,120	27,097	38,753	33,933	32,114	26,363
Gold ('000,000 fine troy oz)	81.85	81.89	102.37	97.24	97.25	97.25
% world reserves	9.0	9.2	10.6	10.1	10.2	10.3
Interest and prices						
Central bank discount (%)	...	...	...	...	...	...
Govt. bond yield (%)	6.39	5.63	4.72	4.69	5.45	5.05
Industrial share prices						
(1995 = 100)	113.7	149.6	201.8	249.7	337.4	270.2
Balance of payments (U.S.$'000,000)						
Balance of visible trade	+14,940	+26,900	+24,940	+17,990	+1,130	+2,850
Imports, f.o.b.	266,910	259,170	278,080	282,060	294,400	288,560
Exports, f.o.b.	281,850	286,070	303,020	300,050	295,530	291,410
Balance of invisibles	+5,620	+10,900	+12,760	+17,050	+19,300	+18,510
Balance of payments, current account	+20,560	+37,800	+37,700	+35,040	+20,430	+21,360

Land use (1994): forest 27.3%; pasture 19.3%; agriculture 35.4%; other 18.0%.

Foreign trade

Balance of trade (current prices)

	1996	1997	1998	1999[15]	2000[15]	2001[15]
F '000,000,000	+85.7	+170.4	+160.1	+18.4	+2.8	+9.1
% of total	3.0%	5.3%	4.6%	3.4%	0.9%	1.4%

Imports (1998): F 1,687,500,000,000 (machinery and transport equipment 39.1%; chemicals 12.2%; agricultural products 7.9%; fuels 5.9%). *Major import sources:* Germany 17.2%; Italy 9.9%; U.K. 8.4%; U.S. 8.2%; Belg.-Lux. 7.7%; Spain 7.1%.

Exports (1998): F 1,773,200,000,000 (machinery and transport equipment 43.8%, of which transport equipment 17.7%; chemical products 12.7%; agricultural products 12.0%; plastics 3.3%). *Major export destinations:* Germany 16.1%; U.K. 10.0%; Italy 9.2%; Spain 8.7%; Belg.-Lux. 7.7%; U.S. 7.4%.

Transport and communications

Transport. Railroads (1999): route length 32,105 km; passenger-km 66,590,-000,000; metric ton-km cargo 52,110,000,000. Roads (1999[11]): total length 893,300 km (paved 100%). Vehicles (1999): passenger cars 27,480,000; trucks and buses 5,610,000. Merchant marine (1998): vessels (100 gross tons and over) 808; total deadweight tonnage 4,850,000. Air transport (2000): passenger-km 110,270,500,000; metric ton-km cargo 15,221,900,000; airports (1996) 61.

Communications

Medium	date	unit	number	units per 1,000 persons
Daily newspapers	1996	circulation	12,725,000	218
Radio	1997	receivers	55,300,000	946
Television	1999	receivers	36,500,000	623
Telephones	2001	main lines	34,033,000	575
Cellular telephones	2001	subscribers	35,922,000	606
Personal computers	2001	units	20,000,000	338
Internet	2001	users	15,653,000	264

Education and health

Education (1996–97)

	schools	teachers	students	student/ teacher ratio
Primary (age 6–10)	35,019	211,192	4,004,704	19.0
Secondary (age 11–18)	11,212[16]	483,493	4,333,690 1,646,377	12.4
Voc., teacher tr.				
Higher	...	141,410	2,062,495	14.6

Health: physicians (1996) 171,704 (1 per 346 persons); hospital beds (1998) 651,208 (1 per 91 persons); infant mortality rate (2000) 4.5.

Food (2000): daily per capita caloric intake 3,591 (vegetable products 63%, animal products 37%); 143% of FAO recommended minimum requirement.

Military

Total active duty personnel (2002): 260,400 (army 52.6%, navy 17.5%, air force 24.6%, unallocated 5.3%). *Military expenditure as percentage of GNP* (1999): 2.7% (world 2.4%); per capita expenditure U.S.$658.

[1]The French franc was the former monetary unit; on Jan. 1, 2002, F 6.56 = €1. [2]Expect evolving autonomy from central government between 2001 and 2004. [3]Labour survey is from Jan. 1, 1998. [4]Manufacturing includes Mining. [5]Trade includes communications. [6]Includes hotels. [7]Imputed rents and imputed bank service charges. [8]Unemployed. [9]1991. [10]Data unavailable for production of food, beverages, and tobacco products. [11]January 1. [12]Consumption data includes Monaco. [13]1994. [14]Beginning in 1999 exchange rates expressed in euros. [15]In billions of euros. [16]1995–96.

Internet resources for further information:
• INSEE http://www.insee.fr/fr/home/home_page.asp

French Guiana

Official name: Département de la Guyane française (Department of French Guiana).
Political status: overseas department of France with two legislative houses (General Council [19]; Regional Council [31]).
Chief of state: President of France.
Heads of government: Prefect (for France); President of the General Council (for French Guiana); President of the Regional Council (for French Guiana).
Capital: Cayenne.
Official language: French.
Official religion: none.
Monetary unit: 1 euro (€) = 100 cents; valuation (Sept. 23, 2002) 1 U.S.$ = €1.02; 1 £ = €1.58[1].

Area and population

Arrondissements	Capitals	area sq mi	area sq km	population 1999 census
Cayenne	Cayenne	17,590	45,559	119,660
Saint-Laurent-du-Maroni	Saint-Laurent-du-Maroni	15,809	40,945	37,553
TOTAL		33,399	86,504	157,213

Demography

Population (2002): 172,000.
Density (2002): persons per sq mi 5.1, persons per sq km 2.0.
Urban-rural (2000): urban 78.2%; rural 21.8%.
Sex distribution (1999): male 50.36%; female 49.64%.
Age breakdown (1999): under 15, 34.0%; 15–29, 24.2%; 30–44, 23.3%; 45–59, 12.5%; 60–74, 4.3%; 75 and over, 1.7%.
Population projection: (2010) 220,000; (2020) 290,000.
Doubling time: 40 years.
Ethnic composition (2000): Guianese Mulatto 37.9%; French 8.0%; Haitian 8.0%; Surinamese 6.0%; Antillean 5.0%; Chinese 5.0%; Brazilian 4.9%; East Indian 4.0%; other (other West Indian, Hmong, other South American) 21.2%.
Religious affiliation (2000): Christian 84.6%, of which Roman Catholic 80.0%, Protestant 3.9%; Chinese folk-religionist 3.6%; Spiritist 3.5%; nonreligious/atheist 3.0%; traditional beliefs 1.9%; Hindu 1.6%; Muslim 0.9%; other 0.9%.
Major cities (1999)[2]: Cayenne 50,594 (urban agglomeration 84,181); Saint-Laurent-du-Maroni 19,211; Kourou 19,107; Matoury 18,032[3]; Rémire-Montjoly 15,555[3].

Vital statistics

Birth rate per 1,000 population (2000): 22.4 (world avg. 22.5); (1993) legitimate 20.0%; illegitimate 80.0%.
Death rate per 1,000 population (2000): 4.7 (world avg. 9.0).
Natural increase rate per 1,000 population (2000): 17.7 (world avg. 13.2).
Total fertility rate (avg. births per childbearing woman; 2000): 3.2.
Marriage rate per 1,000 population (1997): 4.5.
Divorce rate per 1,000 population (1993): 0.4.
Life expectancy at birth (2000): male 75.0 years; female 81.9 years.
Major causes of death per 100,000 population (1996): diseases of the circulatory system 307.0; malignant neoplasms (cancers) 225.0; violence and suicide 114.0; diseases of the respiratory system 54.0; diseases of the digestive system 52.0; infectious and parasitic diseases 40.0.

National economy

Budget (1995). Revenue: F 945,000,000 (current receipts 78.2%, of which taxes 50.8%, revenue from French central government 22.5%; development receipts 21.8%). Expenditures: F 945,000,000 (current expenditures 78.2%; capital expenditures 21.8%).
Production (metric tons except as noted). Agriculture, forestry, fishing (2000): rice 31,000, cassava 10,400, sugarcane 5,300, cabbages 4,800, taro 4,100, bananas 3,900, tomatoes 3,100, cucumbers 2,800, plantains 2,600, lemons and limes 1,300; livestock (number of live animals) 10,500 pigs, 9,000 cattle; roundwood (1998) 118,000 cu m; fish catch (1998) 7,709. Mining and quarrying: stone, sand, and gravel (1994) 1,034; gold (2000) 90,000 troy oz[4]. Manufacturing (1998): pork 1,245; chicken meat 461; finished wood products 3,172 cu m[5]; rum 2,728 hectolitres; other products include leather goods, clothing, rosewood essence, yogurt, and beer. Number of satellites launched from the Kourou Space Centre (1999): 10[6]. Construction (authorized; 1996): residential 169,400 sq m; nonresidential authorized 85,900 sq m. Energy production (consumption): electricity (kW-hr; 1998) 566,000,000 ([1997] 450,000,000); coal, none (none); crude petroleum, none (none); petroleum products (metric tons; 1997) none (284,000); natural gas, none (none).
Household income and expenditure. Average household size (1999) 3.3; income per household (1980) F 75,762 (U.S.$16,776); sources of income (1989): wages and salaries 64.4%, pensions and rents 18.0%, industrial and commercial profits 15.4%, other 2.2%; expenditure (1994)[7]: food and beverages 28.7%, housing 11.7%, energy 9.0%, clothing and footwear 6.4%, health 2.7%, other 41.5%.
Land use (1994): forested 90.6%; meadows and pastures 0.1%; agricultural and under permanent cultivation 0.2%; other 9.1%.

Gross national product (1997): U.S.$1,430,000,000 (U.S.$9,410 per capita).

Structure of gross domestic product and labour force

	1995 in value F '000,000	1995 % of total value	1990 labour force	1990 % of labour force
Agriculture, forestry, fishing	572	5.3	4,177	8.7
Mining	988	9.2	250	0.5
Manufacturing			2,477	5.1
Construction	858	8.0	4,440	9.2
Public utilities	139	1.3	403	0.8
Finance, real estate	815	7.6	408	0.8
Transp. and commun.	1,241	11.5	1,867	3.8
Trade, restaurants, hotels	1,895	17.6	3,152	6.5
Pub. admin., defense	1,492	13.8	12,068	25.0
Services	2,451	22.7	7,352	15.2
Other	323	3.0	11,722[8]	24.3[8]
TOTAL	10,772[9]	100.0	48,306	100.0[9]

Public debt (external, outstanding; 1999): n.a.
Population economically active (1998): total 61,100; activity rate of total population 39.0% (participation rates [1990]: ages 15–64, 67.3%; female 38.2%; unemployed [1998] 21.4%).

Price and earnings indexes (1990 = 100)

	1995	1996	1997	1998	1999	2000	2001
Consumer price index	110.9	111.8	112.9	113.5	113.7	115.3	117.1
Monthly earnings index[10, 11]	112.3	112.3	114.5	127.8	...	...	...

Tourism (1999): receipts U.S.$50,000,000; expenditures, n.a.

Foreign trade

Balance of trade (current prices)

	1993	1994	1995[12]	1996[12]	1997	1998
F '000,000	−2,740	−2,919	−2,983	−2,878	−2,913	−2,852
% of total	70.0%	63.8%	68.9%	64.4%	61.4%	70.9%

Imports (1998): F 3,449,000,000 (food products 21.3%; unspecified 78.7%). Major import sources (1997): France 51.6%; U.S. 14.3%; Trinidad and Tobago 6.0%.
Exports (1996): F 856,000,000 (gold 21.5%; shrimp 20.5%; parts for air and space vehicles 14.6%; rice 7.0%). Major export destinations (1997): France 61.5%; Switzerland 6.6%; U.S. 2.2%.

Transport and communications

Transport. Railroads: none. Roads (1996): total length 774 mi, 1,245 km (paved, n.a.). Vehicles (1997): passenger cars 28,200; trucks and buses 9,400. Merchant marine: n.a. Air transport (2000): passenger arrivals 215,745, passenger departures 219,676; cargo unloaded 4,117 metric tons, cargo loaded 1,935 metric tons; airports (1998) with scheduled flights 1.

Communications

Medium	date	unit	number	units per 1,000 persons
Daily newspapers	1996	circulation	2,000	14
Radio	1997	receivers	104,000	702
Television	1997	receivers	30,000	202
Telephones	1999	main lines	49,000	308
Cellular telephones	1999	subscribers	18,000	113
Personal computers	1999	units	23,000	145
Internet	1999	users	2,000	13

Education and health

Educational attainment (1990). Percentage of population age 25 and over having: incomplete primary education or no declaration 61.7%; completed primary 5.3%; some secondary 15.9%; completed secondary 8.2%; some higher 4.9%; completed higher 4.0%. Literacy (1982): total population age 16 and over literate 38,964 (82.0%); males literate 21,021 (82.5%); females literate 17,943 (81.3%).

Education (1994–95)

	schools	teachers	students	student/ teacher ratio
Primary (age 6–11)	131	1,267	27,700[13]	19.2
Secondary (age 12–18)	28	968	17,100[13]	14.3
Higher[14]	1	...	239	...

Health: physicians (1998) 223 (1 per 684 persons); hospital beds (1996) 730 (1 per 196 persons); infant mortality rate per 1,000 live births (2000) 14.0.
Food (1992): daily per capita caloric intake 2,900 (vegetable products 70%, animal products 30%); 128% of FAO recommended minimum requirement.

Military

Total active duty personnel (2001): 3,250[15].

[1]French franc replaced by euro. [2]Commune population. [3]Within Cayenne urban agglomeration. [4]Officially declared figure; unofficial total is 240,000 troy oz. [5]1996. [6]In 1991 the European Space Agency accounted for 28.7% of GDP, 28.2% of employed labour force, and 70.9% of imports. [7]Weights of consumer price index components. [8]Unemployed. [9]Detail does not add to the total given because of rounding. [10]Index based on end-of-year figures. [11]Based on minimum-level wage in public administration. [12]Excludes December. [13]1996–97. [14]Université des Antilles et de la Guyane, Cayenne campus: 1997–98. [15]Includes French Foreign Legion troops assigned to guard the Kourou Space Centre.

Internet resources for further information:
• Chambre de Commerce et l'Industrie: Guyane http://www.guyane.cci.fr

French Polynesia

Official name: Territoire de la
Polynésie française (French);
Polynesia Farani (Tahitian)
(Territory of French Polynesia).
Political status: overseas territory
(France) with one legislative house
(Territorial Assembly [49]).
Chief of state: President of France.
Head of government: High
Commissioner (for France); President
of the Council of Ministers (for
French Polynesia).
Capital: Papeete.
Official languages: French; Tahitian.
Official religion: none.
Monetary unit: 1 Franc de la Comptoirs
française du pacifique (CFPF) = 100
centimes; valuation (Sept. 23, 2002)[1]
1 U.S.$ = CFPF 121.25;
1 £ = CFPF 188.44.

Pacific
Ocean

Area and population

Circumscriptions	Capitals	area		population
		sq mi	sq km	1996 census
Austral Islands	Mataura	57	148	6,563
Leeward Islands	Uturoa	156	404	26,838
Marquesas Archipelago	Talohae	405	1,049	8,064
Tuamotu–Gambier Islands	Papeete	280	726	15,370
Windward Islands	Papeete	461	1,194	162,686
TOTAL		1,544[2]	4,000[2]	219,521

Demography

Population (2002): 242,000.
Density (2002)[3]: persons per sq mi 178.1, persons per sq km 68.7.
Urban-rural (2002): urban 53.0%; rural 47.0%.
Sex distribution (1996): male 51.92%; female 48.08%.
Age breakdown (1996): under 15, 33.7%; 15–29, 27.3%; 30–44, 21.6%; 45–59, 11.4%; 60–74, 5.0%; 75 and over, 1.0%.
Population projection: (2010) 272,000; (2020) 304,000.
Doubling time: 44 years.
Ethnic composition (1996): Polynesian and part-Polynesian 82.8%; European (mostly French) 11.9%; Asian (mostly Chinese) 4.7%; other 0.6%.
Religious affiliation (1995): Protestant 50.2%, of which Evangelical Church of French Polynesia (Presbyterian) 46.1%; Roman Catholic 39.5%; other Christian 9.9%, of which Mormon 5.9%; other 0.4%.
Major cities (1996)[4]: Faaa 25,888[5]; Papeete 25,553 (urban agglomeration [1999] 121,000); Punaauia 19,524[5]; Pirae 13,974[5]; Mahina 11,640[5].

Vital statistics

Birth rate per 1,000 population (2002): 20.5 (world avg. 21.2); (1996) legitimate 35.4%; illegitimate 64.6%.
Death rate per 1,000 population (2002): 4.8 (world avg. 8.9).
Natural increase rate per 1,000 population (2002): 15.7 (world avg. 12.3).
Total fertility rate (avg. births per childbearing woman; 2002): 2.5.
Marriage rate per 1,000 population (1996): 5.7.
Life expectancy at birth (2002): male 71.0 years; female 76.0 years.
Major causes of death per 100,000 population (1994–95): diseases of the circulatory system 123; malignant neoplasms (cancers) 104; accidents, suicide, and violence 52; respiratory diseases 47; diseases of the digestive system 17.

National economy

Budget (1998). Revenue: CFPF 85,671,000,000 (indirect taxes 60.3%, direct taxes and nontax revenue 39.7%). Expenditures: CFPF 114,143,000,000 (current expenditure 72.5%; capital expenses 27.5%).
Production (metric tons except as noted). Agriculture, forestry, fishing (1999): coconuts 85,000, copra (1998) 11,000, cassava 5,500, potatoes 5,000, pineapples 3,500, sugarcane 2,800, watermelon 1,100, tomatoes 900, cucumbers 700, bananas 650; livestock (number of live animals) 33,000 pigs, 6,500 cattle, 16,000 goats; roundwood, n.a.; fish catch (1998) 11,406; export production of black pearls (1998) 6,050 kg. Mining and quarrying: estimated annual production of phosphates ranges from 1,000,000 to 1,200,000 tons. Manufacturing (1999): coconut oil 6,386; other manufactures include *monoï* oil (primarily refined coconut and sandalwood oils), beer, printed cloth, and sandals. Construction (buildings completed; 1994): 102,305 sq m. Energy production (consumption): electricity (kW-hr; 1997) 360,000,000 (360,000,000); coal, none (none); crude petroleum, none (none); petroleum products (metric tons; 1997) none (183,000); natural gas, none (none).
Tourism (1998): number of visitors 236,000; receipts from visitors U.S.$394,000,000; number of hotel rooms 3,396; occupancy percentage 57.5%; expenditures by nationals abroad, n.a.
Household income and expenditure (1986). Average household size (1996) 4.3; average annual income per household CFPF 2,153,112 (U.S.$17,831); sources of income (1993): salaries 61.9%, self-employment 21.5%, transfer payments 16.6%; expenditure: food and beverages 32.1%, household furnishings 12.3%, transportation 12.2%, energy 8.1%, recreation and education 6.9%, clothing 6.3%.
Land use (1998): forested and other 81.4%; meadows and pastures 5.5%; agricultural and under permanent cultivation 13.1%.
Gross national product (at current market prices; 2000): U.S.$4,064,000,000 (U.S.$17,290 per capita).

Structure of gross domestic product and labour force

	1997		1996	
	in value CFPF '000,000	% of total value	labour force	% of labour force
Agriculture, fishing	15,534	4.1	10,888	12.5
Manufacturing[6]	26,360	7.0	6,424	7.4
Construction	20,104	5.3	4,777	5.5
Public utilities[6]	12,221	3.2	459	0.5
Transp. and commun.	27,832	7.4	3,788	4.4
Trade	81,854	21.6	9,357	10.7
Finance, real estate[7]	...	...	1,865	2.1
Pub. admin., defense	97,238	25.7	13,475	15.5
Services[7]	97,360	25.7	23,514	27.0
Other	—	...	12,574[8]	14.4[8]
TOTAL	378,503	100.0	87,121	100.0

Population economically active (1996): total 87,121; activity rate of total population 39.7% (participation rates: ages 14 and over, 68.3%; female 38.7%; unemployed 13.2%).

Price and earnings indexes (1990 = 100)[9]

	1995	1996	1997	1998	1999	2000	2001
Consumer price index	106.8	108.0	109.1	110.9	111.8	112.9	113.9
Monthly earnings index	106.5	...	112.7	119.6	124.6	124.6	128.4

Public debt (external, outstanding; 1999): U.S.$542,000,000.

Foreign trade[10]

Balance of trade (current prices)

	1996	1997	1998	1999	2000	2001
CFPF '000,000	−71,118	−82,819	−82,685	−75,512	−97,491	−114,948
% of total	60.3%	71.5%	61.0%	57.1%	62.9%	68.9%

Imports (1997): CFPF 99,300,000,000 (machinery and appliances 16.3%, food products 6.8%, pharmaceutical products 3.1%, metal manufactures 2.6%). *Major import sources* (2000): France 35.9%; United States 13.9%; Australia 9.3%; New Zealand 7.4%; Germany 4.8%.
Exports (1997): CFPF 16,481,000,000 (black cultured pearls 61.6%, coconut oil 1.6%, mother-of-pearl 1.4%, vanilla 0.5%[11]). *Major export destinations* (2000): Japan 36.9%; Hong Kong 20.9%; France 14.5%; United States 12.1%; New Caledonia 5.0%.

Transport and communications

Transport. Railroads: none. Roads (1996): total length 549 mi, 884 km (paved 44%). Motor vehicles: passenger cars (1996) 47,300; trucks and buses (1993) 15,300. Air transport (1998): passengers carried 1,219,907; freight handled 9,542 metric tons; airports (1994) with scheduled flights 17.

Communications

Medium	date	unit	number	units per 1,000 persons
Daily newspapers	1996	circulation	24,000	110
Radio	1997	receivers	128,000	574
Television	1999	receivers	43,000	186
Telephones	2001	main lines	52,600	222
Cellular telephones	2001	subscribers	67,000	283
Personal computers	1995	units	20,000	1.2
Internet	2001	users	16,000	68

Education and health

Educational attainment (1996). Percentage of population age 15 and over having: no formal schooling 4.9%; primary education 37.4%; secondary 49.0%; higher 8.7%. *Literacy* (1983): total population age 15 and over literate 98,314 (95.0%); males literate 51,910 (94.9%); females literate 46,404 (95.0%).

Education (1996–97)

	schools	teachers	students	student/teacher ratio
Primary (age 6–10)	170	2,811	29,415	10.5
Secondary (age 11–17)	32[12]	1,897	28,438	15.0
Vocational[13]	[14]	316	3,730	11.8
Higher[15]	4	70	701	10.0

Health (1996): physicians 384 (1 per 175 persons); hospital beds 981 (1 per 447 persons); infant mortality rate per 1,000 live births (2002) 9.0.
Food (1999): daily per capita caloric intake 2,969 (vegetable products 72%, animal products 28%); (1997) 130% of FAO recommended minimum.

Military

Total active duty personnel (2001): 3,100 French military personnel. *Military expenditure as percentage of GNP:* n.a.

---

[1]Pegged to the euro on Jan. 1, 2002, at the rate of €1 = CFPF 119.25. [2]Approximate total area including inland water; total land area is 1,359 sq mi (3,521 sq km). [3]Based on land area. [4]Populations cited are for communes. [5]Part of Papeete urban agglomeration. [6]The manufacture of energy-generating products is included in public utilities. [7]Services includes Finance, Real estate. [8]Includes not adequately defined and unemployed. [9]All end-of-year. [10]Imports c.i.f.; exports f.o.b. [11]Remaining exports are primarily professional goods including military and aeronautical equipment and parts. [12]1989–90. [13]1991–92. [14]Included with secondary schools. [15]1988–89.

Internet resources for further information:
• **Polynésie française**
  http://www.ciral.ulaval.ca/alx/amlxmonde/pacifique/polfr.htm
  http://www.outre-mer.gouv.fr/domtom/polynesie/index.htm
• **Institut de la Statistique de la Polynésie Francaise**
  http://www.ispf.pf

Gabon

Official name: République Gabonaise (Gabonese Republic).
Form of government: unitary multiparty republic with a Parliament comprising two legislative houses (Senate [91]; National Assembly [120]).
Chief of state: President.
Head of government: Prime Minister.
Capital: Libreville.
Official language: French.
Official religion: none.
Monetary unit: 1 CFA franc (CFAF) = 100 centimes; valuation (Sept. 23, 2002) 1 U.S.$ = CFAF 667.00; 1 £ = CFAF 1,036[1].

Area and population

Provinces	Capitals	area sq mi	area sq km	population 1993 census[2]
Estuaire	Libreville	8,008	20,740	463,187
Haut-Ogooué	Franceville	14,111	36,547	104,301
Moyen-Ogooué	Lambaréné	7,156	18,535	42,316
Ngounié	Mouila	14,575	37,750	77,781
Nyanga	Tchibanga	8,218	21,285	39,430
Ogooué-Ivindo	Makokou	17,790	46,075	48,862
Ogooué-Lolo	Koulamoutou	9,799	25,380	43,915
Ogooué-Maritime	Port-Gentil	8,838	22,890	97,913
Woleu-Ntem	Oyem	14,851	38,465	97,271
TOTAL		103,347[3]	267,667	1,014,976

Demography

Population (2002): 1,233,000.
Density (2002): persons per sq mi 11.9, persons per sq km 4.6.
Urban-rural (1998): urban 46.9%; rural 53.1%.
Sex distribution (2001): male 49.77%; female 50.23%.
Age breakdown (1999): under 15, 33.3%; 15–29, 25.7%; 30–44, 15.3%; 45–59, 16.2%; 60–74, 8.0%; 75 and over, 1.4%.
Population projection: (2010) 1,309,000; (2020) 1,386,000.
Doubling time: 68 years.
Ethnic composition (1983): Fang 35.5%; Punu, Sira, and Nzebi 16.9%; Mpongwe 15.1%; Mbete 14.2%; other 18.3%.
Religious affiliation (2000): Christian 90.6%, of which Roman Catholic 56.6%, Protestant 17.7%; Muslim 3.1%; traditional beliefs 1.7%.
Major cities (1993); Libreville 362,386; Port-Gentil 80,841; Franceville 30,246; Oyem 22,669; Moanda 21,921.

Vital statistics

Birth rate per 1,000 population (2001): 27.4 (world avg. 21.2).
Death rate per 1,000 population (2001): 17.2 (world avg. 8.9).
Natural increase rate per 1,000 population (2001): 10.2 (world avg. 12.3).
Total fertility rate (avg. births per childbearing woman; 2001): 3.7.
Life expectancy at birth (2001): male 48.5 years; females 50.8 years.
Major causes of death per 100,000 population: n.a.; however, in the 1990s major causes of morbidity and mortality included malaria, shigellosis (infection with dysentery), tetanus, cardiovascular diseases, trypanosomiasis, and tuberculosis.

National economy

Budget (1997). Revenue: CFAF 914,700,000,000 (oil revenues 62.4%; taxes on international trade 18.8%; customs duties 10.7%; other revenues 8.1%). Expenditures: CFAF 756,100,000,000 (current expenditure 71.5%, of which wages and salaries 25.0%, service on public debt 23.5%; capital expenditure 28.5%).
Public debt (external, outstanding; 2000): U.S.$3,512,000,000.
Tourism (2000): receipts from visitors U.S.$7,000,000; expenditures by nationals abroad U.S.$174,000,000.
Production (metric tons except as noted). Agriculture, forestry, fishing (1999): roots and tubers 436,300 (of which cassava 225,000, yams 150,000, taro 58,500), plantains 280,000, sugarcane 175,000, corn (maize) 31,000, peanuts (groundnuts) 17,000, bananas 11,500, natural rubber 11,000, palm oil 3,000, cacao beans 700; livestock (number of live animals) 212,000 pigs, 195,000 sheep, 90,000 goats, 35,000 cattle, 3,100,000 chickens; roundwood (2000) 3,099,000 cu m; fish catch (2000) 47,470. Mining and quarrying (2000): manganese ore 1,700,000; gold 2,250 troy oz[4]. Manufacturing (1995): fuel oil 295,000; diesel and gas oil 274,000; cement 130,000; kerosene 88,000; wheat flour 27,000; refined sugar 15,000; beer 816,419 hectolitres; soft drinks 415,613 hectolitres; plywood 52,500,000 cu m; textiles are also significant. Energy production (consumption): electricity (kW-hr; 1997) 1,257,000,000 (1,257,000,000); crude petroleum (barrels; 2001) 110,230,000 ([1997] 6,201,000); petroleum products (metric tons; 1997) 701,000 (520,000); natural gas (cu m; 1997) 1,020,000,000 (1,020,000,000).
Population economically active (1997): total 542,000; activity rate of total population 45.5% (participation rates [1985]: ages 15–64, 68.2%; female 44.5%; unemployed [1996] 20%).

Price and earnings indexes (1995 = 100)

	1996	1997	1998	1999	2000	2001
Consumer price index	100.7	104.7	108.4	107.7	108.3	110.5
Earnings index	103.6	102.5	101.2	...	...	...

Gross national product (2000): U.S.$3,928,000,000 (U.S.$3,190 per capita).

Structure of gross domestic product and labour force

	1997 in value CFAF '000,000	1997 % of total value	1993 labour force	1993 % of labour force
Agriculture, forestry, fishing	224,500	7.4	156,000[5]	41.6
Mining	1,306,100	43.3		
Manufacturing	167,100	5.5	43,000[5]	11.5
Construction	116,300	3.9		
Public utilities	36,400	1.2		
Transp. and commun.	143,400	4.8		
Trade	245,800	8.2		
Finance	13,000	0.4	115,000[5]	30.7
Services	345,400	11.5		
Pub. admin., defense	267,100	8.9	61,000[5]	16.2
Other	148,600[6]	4.9[6]	...	...
TOTAL	3,013,700	100.0	376,000[3]	100.0

Household income and expenditure. Average household size (1998) 6.1; income per household: n.a.; sources of income (1983): private sector 73.4%, public sector 26.6%; expenditure: n.a.
Land use (1994): forested 77.2%; meadows and pastures 18.2%; agricultural and under permanent cultivation 1.8%; other 2.8%.

Foreign trade

Balance of trade (current prices)

	1992	1993	1994	1995	1996	1997
CFAF '000,000	+362,800	+419,400	+882,000	+870,800	+1,095,800	+1,198,200
% of total	43.6%	46.7%	50.6%	49.3%	52.5%	50.9%

Imports (1997): CFAF 578,100,000,000 (machinery and mechanical equipment 26.4%, food and agricultural products 23.1%, consumer products 15.5%, transport equipment 11.5%, metals 6.2%). *Major import sources:* France 39.1%; Belgium 9.7%; U.S. 8.1%; U.K. 4.3%; Japan 4.0%.
Exports (1997): CFAF 1,776,300,000,000 (crude petroleum and petroleum products 77.1%, wood 14.5%, manganese ore and concentrate 5.0%, uranium ore and concentrate 0.7%). *Major export destinations:* U.S. 68.2%; France 8.1%; other EU 4.4%; Japan 3.2%; Africa 1.6%.

Transport and communications

Transport. Railroads (1998): route length 506 mi, 814 km; passenger-km 85,000,000[7]; metric ton-km cargo carried 503,000,000[8]. Roads (1996): total length 4,760 mi, 7,670 km (paved 8.2%). Vehicles (1997): passenger cars 24,750; trucks and buses 16,490. Merchant marine (1992): vessels (100 gross tons and over) 29; total deadweight tonnage 30,186. Air transport (1996): passenger-mi 452,000,000, passenger-km 728,000,000; short ton-mi cargo 62,100,000, metric ton-km cargo 100,000,000; airports (1997) 17.

Communications

Medium	date	unit	number	units per 1,000 persons
Daily newspapers	1997	circulation	33,000	30
Radio	1997	receivers	195,000	16
Television	1999	receivers	300,000	251
Telephones	2000	main lines	39,000	32
Cellular telephones	2000	subscribers	120,000	98
Personal computers	2001	units	15,000	12
Internet	2000	users	15,000	12

Education and health

Educational attainment of economically active population (1993): none, or incomplete primary 37.7%; complete primary 32.1%; complete secondary 16.4%; postsecondary certificate or degree 13.8%. *Literacy* (1995): total population age 15 and over literate 63.2%; males literate 73.7%; females literate 53.3%.

Education (1995–96)

	schools	teachers	students	student/ teacher ratio
Primary	1,147	4,944	250,606	50.7
Secondary	88	2,683	72,888	27.2
Voc., teacher tr.	11	411	7,664	18.6
Higher[9, 10]	2	299	3,000	10.0

Health: physicians (1989) 448 (1 per 2,377 persons); hospital beds (1988) 5,329 (1 per 199 persons); infant mortality rate per 1,000 live births (1998) 83.1.
Food (2000): daily per capita caloric intake 2,564 (vegetable products 86%, animal products 14%); 109% of FAO recommended minimum requirement.

Military

Total active duty personnel (2001): 4,700 (army 68.1%, navy 10.6%, air force 21.3%), excluding 700 French troops. *Military expenditure as percentage of GNP* (1999): 2.4% (world 2.4%); per capita expenditure U.S.$78.

[1]Formerly pegged to the French franc and since Jan. 1, 2002, to the euro at the rate of 1 € = CFAF 655.96. [2]De jure; excludes nonnationals numbering 100,000 to 150,000 (mainly West African) prior to their large-scale expulsion in February 1995. [3]Detail does not add to total given because of rounding. [4]Excludes about 13,000 troy oz of illegally mined gold smuggled out of Gabon. Uranium mining ceased in 1999. [5]Derived values. [6]Import duties. [7]1996. [8]1995. [9]Universities only. [10]1991–92.

Internet resources for further information:
• **Gabon: 1998 U.N. Report**
  http://mirror.undp.org/gabon/dc98.htm
• **Investir en Zone Franc**
  http://www.izf.net/izf/Index.htm

Gambia, The

Official name: The Republic of the Gambia.
Form of government: multiparty republic with one legislative house (National Assembly [53[1]]).
Head of state and government: President.
Capital: Banjul.
Official language: English.
Official religion: none.
Monetary unit: 1 dalasi (D) = 100 butut; valuation (Sept. 23, 2002) 1 U.S.$ = D 22.25; 1 £ = D 34.58.

Atlantic Ocean

Gulf of Guinea

Area and population

		area		population
Divisions	Capitals	sq mi	sq km	2002 estimate
Basse	Basse	799	2,069	211,800
Brikama	Brikama	681	1,764	320,700
Janjanbureh	Janjanbureh	493	1,280	120,500
Kanifing[2, 3]	Kanifing	29	76	311,700
Kerewan	Kerewan	871	2,256	213,700
Kuntaur	Kuntaur	623	1,614	92,600
Mansakonko	Mansakonko	625	1,618	89,000
City				
Banjul[3]	—	5	12	57,800
TOTAL		4,127[4, 5]	10,689[5]	1,417,800

Demography

Population (2002): 1,418,000.
Density (2002)[6]: persons per sq mi 426.5, persons per sq km 164.7.
Urban-rural (1999): urban 36.8%; rural 63.2%.
Sex distribution (2001): male 49.96%; female 50.04%.
Age breakdown (2001): under 15, 45.2%; 15–29, 26.2%; 30–44, 15.6%; 45–59, 8.7%; 60–74, 3.5%; 75 and over, 0.8%.
Population projection: (2010) 1,833,000; (2020) 2,365,000.
Doubling time: 23 years.
Ethnic composition (1993): Malinke 34.1%; Fulani 16.2%; Wolof 12.6%; Diola 9.2%; Soninke 7.7%; other 20.2%.
Religious affiliation (1993): Muslim 95.0%; Christian 4.1%; traditional beliefs and other 0.9%.
Major cities/urban areas (1993): Serekunda 151,450[2]; Brikama 42,480; Banjul 42,326 (Greater Banjul 270,540[3]); Bakau 38,062[2]; Farafenni 21,142.

Vital statistics

Birth rate per 1,000 population (2001): 41.8 (world avg. 21.2).
Death rate per 1,000 population (2001): 12.9 (world avg. 8.9).
Natural increase rate per 1,000 population (2001): 28.9 (world avg. 12.3).
Total fertility rate (avg. births per childbearing woman; 2001): 5.7.
Marriage rate per 1,000 population: n.a.
Life expectancy at birth (2001): male 51.7 years; female 55.6 years.
Major causes of death per 100,000 population: n.a.; however, major infectious diseases include malaria, gastroenteritis and dysentery, pneumonia and bronchitis, measles, schistosomiasis, and whooping cough.

National economy

Budget (1999). Revenue: D 944,500,000 (tax revenue 81.9%, of which import duties and excises 29.0%, income taxes 19.4%, sales tax 6.9%; nontax revenue 11.1%; grants 7.0%). Expenditures: D 1,118,200,000 (wages and salaries 26.9%; interest payments 22.2%; goods and services 16.9%; education and culture 13.1%; health 7.9%; defense 3.6%).
Production (metric tons except as noted). Agriculture, forestry, fishing (2001): peanuts (groundnuts) 153,000, millet 105,000, paddy rice 33,000, sorghum 29,000, corn (maize) 23,000, cassava 7,500, seed cotton 5,500, pulses (mostly beans) 5,500, palm oil 3,000, palm kernels 2,000; livestock (number of live animals) 365,000 cattle, 145,000 goats, 106,000 sheep; roundwood (1998) 661,000 cu m; fish catch (1998) 29,002, of which Atlantic Ocean 26,702, inland water 2,300. Mining and quarrying: sand and gravel are excavated for local use. Manufacturing (value of production in D '000; 1982): processed food, including peanut and palm-kernel oil 62,878; beverages 10,546; textiles 3,253; chemicals and related products 1,031; nonmetals 922; printing and publishing 358; leather 150. Construction: n.a. Energy production (consumption): electricity (kW-hr; 1998) 122,187,000 (122,187,000); coal, none (none); crude petroleum, none (none); petroleum products (metric tons; 1998) none (44,000); natural gas, none (none).
Population economically active (1998): total 575,140; activity rate of total population 47.3% (participation rates: [1983] ages 15–64, 78.2%; female 46.3%; unemployed, n.a.).

Price and earnings indexes (1995 = 100)

	1994	1995	1996	1997	1998	1999	2000
Consumer price index	93.5	100.0	101.1	103.9	105.1	109.1	110.0
Earnings index	...	...	...	...	...	...	...

Tourism (1998): receipts from visitors U.S.$33,000,000; expenditures by nationals abroad (1997) U.S.$16,000,000.
Household income and expenditure. Average household size (1998) 9.4; income per household: n.a.; sources of income: n.a.; expenditure (1991)[7]: food and beverages 58.0%, clothing and footwear 17.5%, energy and water 5.4%, hous-

ing 5.1%, education, health, transportation and communications, recreation, and other 14.0%.
Public debt (external, outstanding; 2000): U.S.$425,200,000.
Gross national product (at current market prices; 2000): U.S.$440,000,000 (U.S.$340 per capita).

Structure of gross domestic product and labour force

	1999		1983	
	in value D '000,000	% of total value	labour force	% of labour force
Agriculture	1,466.5	29.6	239,940	73.7
Mining	8	8	66	0.0
Manufacturing	234.6	4.7	8,144	2.5
Construction	236.2[8]	4.8[8]	4,373	1.3
Public utilities	82.0	1.7	1,233	0.4
Transp. and commun.	717.6	14.5	8,014	2.5
Trade	735.0	14.8	16,551	5.1
Finance	299.8	6.0	4,577	1.4
Public administration	421.6	8.5	8,295	2.5
Services	204.4	4.1	9,381	2.9
Other	557.9[9]	11.3[9]	25,049[10]	7.7[10]
TOTAL	4,955.6	100.0	325,623	100.0

Land use (1994): forested 10.0%; meadows and pastures 19.0%; agricultural and under permanent cultivation 17.2%; built-on area, wasteland, and other 53.8%.

Foreign trade[11]

Balance of trade (current prices)

	1994	1995	1996	1997	1998	1999
D '000,000	−1,695.0	−1,586.0	−2,318.5	−1,624.0	−2,319.4	−2,106.2
% of total	71.5%	83.6%	84.7%	84.4%	80.2%	96.3%

Imports (1999): D 2,186,820,000 (food 32.9%; basic manufactures 23.9%; machinery and transport equipment 20.7%; chemicals and related products 7.3%; mineral fuels and lubricants 7.2%; vegetable oils 3.0%). *Major import sources:* China 17.2%; Hong Kong 10.6%; U.K. 8.7%; The Netherlands 7.3%; Senegal 5.2%; France 4.7%; Côte d'Ivoire 4.3%; Thailand 1.0%.
Exports (1999): D 80,600,000 (domestic exports 13.3%, of which peanuts (groundnuts) 8.3%, fish products 2.2%; reexports 86.7%). *Major export destinations:* Belgium-Luxembourg 61.0%; Japan 19.4%; U.K. 6.8%; Spain 1.8%.

Transport and communications

Transport. Railroads: none. Roads (1999): total length 1,678 mi, 2,700 km (paved 35%). Vehicles (1997): passenger cars 7,267; trucks and buses (1996) 9,000. Merchant marine (1992): vessels (100 gross tons and over) 11; total deadweight tonnage 2,029. Air transport (1994): passenger-mi 31,100,000, passenger-km 50,000,000; cargo 3,107,000 short ton-mi, metric ton-km 5,000,000; airports (2000) with scheduled flights 1.

Communications

Medium	date	unit	number	units per 1,000 persons
Daily newspapers	1996	circulation	2,000	1.7
Radio	1997	receivers	196,000	165
Television	1999	receivers	4,000	3.1
Telephones	2001	main lines	35,000	26
Cellular telephones	2001	subscribers	43,000	32
Personal computers	2001	units	17,000	13
Internet	2001	users	18,000	14

Education and health

Educational attainment: n.a. *Literacy* (1998): total population age 15 and over literate 34.6%; males literate 41.9%; females literate 27.5%.

Education (1998–99)

	schools	teachers	students	student/ teacher ratio
Primary (age 8–14)	331	4,572	150,403	32.9
Secondary (age 15–21)[12]	85	1,936	46,769	24.2
Postsecondary	4	155[13]	1,082[13]	7.0[13]

Health: physicians (2000) 105 (1 per 12,977 persons); hospital beds (2000) 1,140 (1 per 1,199 persons); infant mortality rate per 1,000 live births (2001) 77.8.
Food (2000): daily per capita caloric intake 2,474 (vegetable products 95%, animal products 5%); 104% of FAO recommended minimum requirement.

Military

Total active duty personnel (2001): 800 (army 100%). *Military expenditure as percentage of GNP* (1999): 1.3% (world 2.4%); per capita expenditure U.S.$12.

[1]Includes 5 nonelective seats. [2]Kanifing includes the urban areas of Serekunda and Bakau. [3]Kanifing and Banjul city make up Greater Banjul. [4]Detail does not add to total given because of rounding. [5]Includes inland water area of 802 sq mi (2,077 sq km). [6]Based on land area only. [7]Low-income population in Banjul and Kanifing only; weights of consumer price index components. [8]Construction includes mining. [9]Indirect taxes. [10]Not adequately defined. [11]Imports c.i.f. in balance of trade and f.o.b. in commodities and trading partners. [12]Includes teacher training and vocational. [13]1994.

Internet resources for further information:
- **Official WWW Site of The Republic of The Gambia**
  http://www.Gambia.com
- **The Gambia Human Development Report**
  http://www.un.gm/nhdrtoc.htm

Georgia

Official name: Sak'art'velo (Georgia).
Form of government: unitary multiparty republic with a single legislative body (Parliament [235]).
Head of state and government: President, assisted by Minister of State.
Capital: T'bilisi (Tblisi).
Official language: Georgian[1].
Official religion: none[2].
Monetary unit: 1 Georgian lari = 100 tetri; valuation (Sept. 23, 2002) 1 U.S.$ = 2.18 lari; 1 £ = 3.39 lari.

Area and population

Autonomous republics	Capitals	area sq mi	area sq km	population 1993[3] estimate
Abkhazia[4]	Sokhumi (Sukhumi)	3,320	8,600	516,600
Ajaria (Adjara)	Bat'umi	1,158	3,000	386,700
Regions				
Guria	Ozurget'i			160,800
Imereti	K'ut'aisi			788,900
Kakheti	T'elavi			464,000
Kvemo Kartli	Rust'avi			601,500
Mts'khet'a-Mtianeti	Mts'khet'a	21,892	56,700	43,800
Ragha-Lechkhumi & Kvemo Svaneti	Ambrolauri			45,400
Samegrelo & Zemo Svaneti	Zugdidi			418,100
Samtskhe-Javakheti	Akhalts'ikhe			198,800
Shida Kartli[5]	Gori			485,900
City				
T'bilisi (Tblisi)	...	541	1,400	1,271,800
TOTAL		26,911	69,700	5,405,400[6]

Demography

Population (2002): 4,961,000.
Density (2002): persons per sq mi 184.3, persons per sq km 71.2.
Urban-rural (2000): urban 60.7%; rural 39.3%.
Sex distribution (2001): male 47.56%; female 52.44%.
Age breakdown (2001): under 15, 19.6%; 15–29, 24.0%; 30–44, 22.4%; 45–59, 15.6%; 60–74, 14.4%; 75 and over, 4.0%.
Population projection: (2010) 4,815,000; (2020) 4,785,000.
Ethnic composition (2000): Georgian 57.9%; Mingrelian 9.1%; Armenian 8.1%; Russian 6.3%; Azerbaijani 5.7%; Ossetian 3.0%; Greek 1.9%; Abkhazian 1.8%; other 6.2%.
Religious affiliation (1995): Christian 46.2%, of which Georgian Orthodox 36.7%, Armenian Apostolic 5.6%, Russian Orthodox 2.7%, other Christian 1.2%; Sunni Muslim 11.0%; other (mostly nonreligious) 42.8%.
Major cities (1997): T'bilisi (1998) 1,398,968; K'ut'aisi 240,000; Rust'avi 158,000; Bat'umi 137,100; Zugdidi 105,000[7].

Vital statistics

Birth rate per 1,000 population (2001): 11.2 (world avg. 21.2).
Death rate per 1,000 population (2001): 14.6 (world avg. 8.9).
Natural increase rate per 1,000 population (2001): –3.4 (world avg. 12.3).
Total fertility rate (avg. births per childbearing woman; 2001): 1.4.
Marriage rate per 1,000 population (1996): 3.7.
Life expectancy at birth (2001): male 61.0 years; female 68.3 years.
Major causes of death per 100,000 population (1995): diseases of the circulatory system 569.6; malignant neoplasms (cancers) 63.4; accidents, poisoning, and violence 44.7; diseases of the digestive system 30.3.

National economy

Budget (2000). Revenue: 913,300,000 lari (tax revenue 77.4%, of which value-added tax 31.7%, excise tax 13.5%, income tax 11.8%; extrabudgetary revenue 15.9%; nontax revenue 4.9%; grants 1.8%). Expenditures: 1,155,900,000 lari (current expenditure 94.7%; development expenditure and net lending 5.3%).
Public debt (external, outstanding; 2000): U.S.$1,609,700,000.
Population economically active (2000): total 1,748,800[8]; activity rate of total population 35.1% (participation rates [1993]: ages 16–65 [male], 16–60 [female] 55.6%; female 47.8%; unemployed [2000] 12.0%).

Price and earnings indexes (1995 = 100)

	1995	1996	1997	1998	1999	2000	2001[9]
Consumer price index	100.0	113.5	122.1	154.4	183.9	191.3	198.8
Annual earnings index	100.0	213.2	319.2	407.2	496.0	382.2	...

Production (metric tons except as noted). Agriculture, forestry, fishing (2001): corn (maize) 420,000, potatoes 380,000, tomatoes 310,000, wheat 306,000, grapes 180,000, apples 112,000, watermelons 70,000, sunflower seed 42,000, tea 30,000; livestock (number of live animals) 1,177,400 cattle, 545,000 sheep, 443,400 pigs; roundwood, n.a.; fish catch (1999) 1,600. Mining and quarrying (2000): manganese ore 59,100. Manufacturing (2000)[10]: steel 56,400[11]; cigarettes 300,000,000 units; wine 430,400 hectolitres; beer 181,640 hectolitres. Energy production (consumption): electricity (kW-hr; 2000) 7,400,000,000 (7,400,000,000); coal (metric tons; 2000) 7,300 (1997; 5,000); crude petroleum (barrels; 2000) 803,000 (803,000); petroleum products (metric tons; 2000) 10,600 (1997; 104,000); natural gas (cu m; 2000) 79,500,000 (1997; 914,935,000).

Gross national product (2000): U.S.$3,183,000,000 (U.S.$630 per capita).

Structure of net material product and labour force

	2000 in value '000,000 lari	2000 % of total value	1995 labour force[12]	1995 % of labour force
Agriculture	1,191.0	20.0	516,000	29.6
Mining				
Manufacturing	833.7	14.0	264,000	15.2
Public utilities				
Construction	226.3	3.8	90,000	5.2
Transp. and commun.	857.5	14.4	52,000	3.0
Trade, restaurants	899.2	15.1	257,000	14.8
Finance, real estate	101.2	1.7	10,000	0.6
Pub. admin., defense	190.6	3.2	35,000	2.0
Services	518.1	8.7	516,000	29.6
Other	1,137.5	19.1		
TOTAL	5,955.1	100.0	1,740,000	100.0

Household income and expenditure (1993). Average household size 4.0; income per household: n.a.; sources of income: wages and salaries 34.5%, benefits 21.9%, agricultural income 21.6%, other 22.0%; expenditure: taxes 42.5%, retail goods 32.3%, savings 16.4%, transportation 4.2%.
Tourism (U.S.$'000,000; 2000): receipts 413; expenditures 110.

Foreign trade[13]

Balance of trade (current prices)

	1995	1996	1997	1998	1999	2000
U.S.$'000,000	–337	–519	–657	–475	–382	–370
% of total	31.8%	56.5%	59.4%	64.1%	44.2%	36.0%

Imports (2000): U.S.$700,200,000 (mineral fuels 18.5%; wheat and flour 6.5%; medicines 5.2%; tobacco products 4.5%; sugar 3.8%; unspecified 52.9%). *Major import sources:* Turkey 16.0%; Russia 14.1%; United States 10.1%; Azerbaijan 8.5%; Germany 7.7%.
Exports (2000): U.S.$329,900,000 (scrap metals 11.5%; wine 8.6%; nuts 6.8%; fertilizers 4.9%; precious metallic ores 4.5%; ferroalloys 4.1%; crude oil 3.9%; aluminum waste 3.9%). *Major export destinations:* Turkey 22.7%; Russia 21.1%; Germany 10.4%; Azerbaijan 6.4%; Armenia 4.1%; Switzerland 4.1%.

Transport and communications

Transport. Railroads (1997): 1,546 km; (1995) passenger-km 371,000,000; (1993) metric ton-km cargo 1,750,000,000. Roads (1999): 20,215 km (paved 93%). Vehicles (1999): passenger cars 247,872; trucks and buses 43,421. Air transport (1997): passenger-km 206,000,000; metric ton-km cargo 840,000[14]; airports (2000) with scheduled flights 1.

Communications

Medium	date	unit	number	units per 1,000 persons
Daily newspapers	1996	circulation	0	—
Radio	1997	receivers	3,020,000	586
Television	1998	receivers	2,580,000	506
Telephones	2001	main lines	867,600	159
Cellular telephones	2001	subscribers	295,000	54
Internet	2001	users	25,000	4.6

Education and health

Education (1996–97)

	schools	teachers	students	student/ teacher ratio
Primary (age 6–9)	3,201	16,542	293,325	17.7
Secondary (age 10–16)	3,139[15]	55,817	424,465	7.6
Voc., teacher tr.	...	2,146	19,593	9.1
Higher	23	25,549	163,345	6.4

Food (2000): daily per capita caloric intake 2,412 (vegetable products 84%, animal products 16%); 92% of FAO recommended minimum requirement.
Health (1997): physicians 21,846 (1 per 236 persons); hospital beds 24,500 (1 per 210 persons); infant mortality rate per 1,000 live births (2001) 52.4.

Military

Total active duty personnel (2001): 28,490 (army 50.5%, air force 4.7%, navy 3.7%, paramilitary 41.1%). About 4,000 Russian troops remained in Georgia in mid-2001[16]. *Military expenditure as percentage of GNP* (1999): 1.2% (world 2.4%); per capita expenditure U.S.$33.

[1]Locally Abkhazian, in Abkhazia. [2]Special recognition is given to the Georgian Orthodox Church. [3]January 1. [4]Abkhazia has had de facto autonomy from Georgia since 1993. Its final status was unresolved in July 2002. [5]The northern 1,505 sq mi- (3,900 sq km-) area of Shida Kartli is the autonomous region of South Ossetia. In March 1997 the separatist region of South Ossetia was given this status by the Georgian government, but its final status was unresolved in July 2002. [6]Excludes population of 23,200 with unknown distribution by autonomous republic or district. [7]Includes internally displaced persons from Abkhazia. [8]Excludes informal sector, which was about 750,000 persons in 1998. [9]August. [10]Excludes Abkhazia and South Ossetia. [11]1998. [12]Employed persons in formal sector only. [13]Imports c.i.f.; exports f.o.b. [14]Orbi Georgian Airways. [15]1995–96. [16]Withdrawal of Russian troops from Georgia began in June 2001 with the closure of the first of four Russian military bases.

Internet resources for further information:
• **National Bank of Georgia**
  http://www.nbg.gov.ge
• **Social-Economic Situation in Georgia**
  http://www.parliament.ge/GENERAL/stat/emain.htm

Germany

Official name: Bundesrepublik
Deutschland (Federal Republic of
Germany).
Form of government: federal multiparty
republic with two legislative houses
(Federal Council [69]; Federal Diet [603]).
Chief of state: President.
Head of government: Chancellor.
Capital: Berlin, some
ministries remain in Bonn.
Official language: German.
Official religion: none.
Monetary unit: 1 euro (€) = 100 cents;
valuation (Sept. 23, 2002) 1 U.S.$ =
€1.02; 1 £ = €1.58[1].

Area and population

States[2] Administrative districts	Capitals	area sq mi	area sq km	population 2000[3] estimate
Baden-Württemberg	Stuttgart	13,804	35,752	10,475,900[4]
Freiburg	Freiburg im Breisgau	3,613	9,357	2,125,400
Karlsruhe	Karlsruhe	2,671	6,919	2,676,300
Stuttgart	Stuttgart	4,076	10,558	3,917,300
Tübingen	Tübingen	3,443	8,918	1,757,000
Bavaria	Munich	27,240	70,551[4]	12,155,000
Mittelfranken	Ansbach	2,798	7,246	1,683,300
Niederbayern	Landshut	3,988	10,330	1,170,200
Oberbayern	Munich	6,768	17,530	4,033,600
Oberfranken	Bayreuth	2,792	7,230	1,114,200
Oberpfalz	Regensburg	3,741	9,690	1,074,300
Schwaben	Augsburg	3,859	9,994	1,745,600
Unterfranken	Würzburg	3,294	8,532	1,333,800
Berlin	—	344	891	3,386,700
Brandenburg	Potsdam	11,381	29,476	2,601,200
Bremen	Bremen	156	404	663,100
Hamburg	Hamburg	292	755	1,704,700
Hesse	Wiesbaden	8,152	21,114[4]	6,052,000
Darmstadt	Darmstadt	2,874	7,445	3,719,400
Giessen	Giessen	2,078	5,381	1,063,500
Kassel	Kassel	3,200	8,289	1,269,100
Lower Saxony	Hannover	18,383	47,612[4]	7,898,800
Braunschweig	Braunschweig	3,126	8,097	1,669,600
Hannover	Hannover	3,493	9,046	2,152,800
Lüneburg	Lüneburg	5,986	15,505	1,660,700
Weser-Ems	Oldenburg	5,778	14,965	2,415,700
Mecklenburg-West Pomerania	Schwerin	8,946	23,170	1,789,300
North Rhine-Westphalia	Düsseldorf	13,158	34,078[4]	17,999,800[4]
Arnsberg	Arnsberg	3,090	8,002	3,814,300
Detmold	Detmold	2,517	6,518	2,048,600
Düsseldorf	Düsseldorf	2,042	5,289	5,264,500
Cologne (Köln)	Cologne (Köln)	2,844	7,365	4,263,700
Münster	Münster	2,665	6,903	2,608,800
Rhineland-Palatinate	Mainz	7,662[4]	19,846[4]	4,030,800[4]
Koblenz	Koblenz	3,117	8,072	1,516,200
Rheinhessen-Pfalz	Mainz	2,646	6,852	2,003,000
Trier	Trier	1,901	4,923	511,500
Saarland	Saarbrücken	992	2,570	1,071,500
Saxony	Dresden	7,109	18,413	4,459,700
Chemnitz	Chemnitz	2,354	6,097	1,638,900
Dresden	Dresden	3,062	7,930	1,724,700
Leipzig	Leipzig	1,693	4,836	1,096,100
Saxony-Anhalt	Magdeburg	7,895[4]	20,447[4]	2,648,700
Dessau	Dessau	1,652	4,280	552,400
Halle	Halle	1,710	4,430	876,100
Magdeburg	Magdeburg	4,532	11,738	1,220,200
Schleswig-Holstein	Kiel	6,089	15,770	2,777,300
Thuringia	Erfurt	6,244	16,171	2,449,100
TOTAL		137,846[4]	357,021[4]	82,163,500[4]

Demography

Population (2002): 82,506,000.
Major cities[5] (*urban agglomerations*[6]): Berlin 3,392,900[7]; Hamburg 1,701,800
(2,664,000); Munich 1,193,600 (2,291,000); Cologne 963,200 (3,050,000[8]);
Frankfurt am Main 644,700 (3,681,000); Essen 600,700 (6,531,000[8]);
Dortmund 590,300 (6,531,000[8]); Stuttgart 581,200 (2,672,000); Düsseldorf
568,500 (3,233,000[8]); Bremen 542,300 (880,000); Duisburg 521,300
(6,531,000[8]); Hannover 515,200 (1,283,000); Leipzig 490,000; Nuremberg
(Nürnberg) 486,400 (1,189,000).

Other principal cities (1999)

	population		population		population
Aachen	243,600	Hamm	181,500	Münster	264,700
Augsburg	254,500	Heidelberg	139,400	Neuss	149,100
Bielefeld	321,600	Herne	176,200	Oberhausen	222,300
Bochum	392,900	Karlsruhe	276,700	Oldenburg	154,100
Bonn	304,100	Kassel	196,700	Osnabrück	164,900
Braunschweig	246,800	Kiel	235,500	Paderborn	136,800
Chemnitz	266,000	Krefeld	242,800	Potsdam	129,500
Darmstadt	137,600	Leverkusen	161,100	Recklinghausen	125,200
Dresden	477,700	Lübeck	213,800	Regensburg	125,200
Erfurt	202,100	Ludwigshafen am Rhein	164,200	Rostock	205,900
Freiburg im Breisgau	201,000	Magdeburg	238,000	Saarbrücken	184,300
Gelsenkirchen	283,300	Mainz	185,600	Solingen	165,400
Göttingen	125,400	Mannheim	308,400	Wiesbaden	268,200
Hagen	206,400	Mönchengladbach	264,100	Wuppertal	370,700
Halle	258,400	Mülheim an der Ruhr	174,300	Würzburg	126,000

Density (2002): persons per sq mi 598.5, persons per sq km 231.1.
Urban-rural (1997[3]): urban 82.4%; rural 17.6%.

Population projection: (2010) 83,858,000; (2020) 84,741,000.
Sex distribution (2000[3]): male 48.79%; female 51.21%.
Age breakdown (2000[3]): under 15, 15.7%; 15–29, 17.6%; 30–44, 24.7%; 45–59,
19.1%; 60–74, 15.9%; 75 and over, 7.0%.
Ethnic composition (by nationality; 2000): German 88.2%; Turkish 3.4%, of
which Kurdish 0.7%; Italian 1.0%; Greek 0.7%; Serb 0.6%; Russian 0.6%;
Polish 0.4%; other 5.1%.
Religious affiliation (2000): Christian 75.8%, of which Protestant 35.6%
(including Lutheran 33.9%), Roman Catholic 33.5%, Orthodox 0.9%, independent Christian 0.9%, other Christian 4.9%; Muslim 4.4%; Jewish 0.1%;
nonreligious 17.2%; atheist 2.2%; other 0.3%.
Households (2000). Number of households 38,124,000; average household size
2.2; 1 person 36.0%, 2 persons 33.4%, 3 persons 14.7%, 4 persons 11.5%, 5
or more persons 4.4%.

Vital statistics

Birth rate per 1,000 population (2001): 9.0 (world avg. 21.2); legitimate 75.0%;
illegitimate 25.0%.
Death rate per 1,000 population (2001): 10.0 (world avg. 8.9).
Natural increase rate per 1,000 population (2001): –1.0 (world avg. 12.3).
Total fertility rate (avg. births per childbearing woman; 2000): 1.3.
Marriage rate per 1,000 population (2001): 4.7.
Divorce rate per 1,000 population (2001): 2.4.
Life expectancy at birth (1997–99): male 74.4 years; female 80.6 years.
Major causes of death per 100,000 population (1999): diseases of the circula-
tory system 494.7; malignant neoplasms (cancers) 256.8; diseases of the res-
piratory system 62.7; suicide 14.9.

Social indicators

Educational attainment (2000). Percentage of population age 25 and over having: primary and lower secondary 50.6%; intermediate secondary 17.9%;
vocational secondary 8.7%; post-secondary and higher (all levels) 22.8%.
Quality of working life. Average workweek (1998): 39.8 hours. Annual rate per
100,000 workers (1993) for: injuries or accidents at work 4,808; deaths, including commuting accidents, 6.7. Proportion of labour force insured for damages of income loss resulting from: injury, virtually 100%; permanent disability, virtually 100%; death, virtually 100%. Average days lost to labour
stoppages per 1,000 workers (2000): 0.3.
Access to services. Proportion of dwellings (1996) having: electricity, virtually
100%; piped water supply, virtually 100%; flush sewage disposal (1993)
98.4%; public fire protection, virtually 100%.
Social participation. Eligible voters participating in last (September 1998)
national election c. 81%. Trade union membership in total workforce (1994):
c. 27%. Practicing religious population (1994): 5% of Protestants and 25%
of Roman Catholics "regularly" attend religious services.
Social deviance (1996). Offense rate per 100,000 population for: murder and
manslaughter 3.3; sexual abuse 46.0, of which rape and forcible sexual assault
13.4, child molestation 7.3; assault and battery 116.9; theft 688.9.
Material well-being (2000[3]; median income). Households possessing: automobile 75.4%; telephone 96.7%; colour television receiver 95.5%; refrigerator
79.3%; washing machine 97.9%; home freezer 73.8%; personal computer
48.2%; video recorder 83.8%.

Recreational and leisure activities[9]

(Monthly household expenditures, 1997; median income)

Activity	DM	percentage
Vacations	203	24.0
Expenditures for motor vehicles	119	14.0
Sporting and camping equipment and sporting events	121	14.3
Televisions, radios, and their fees	91	10.7
Books, newspapers, and magazines	66	7.8
Gardening and pets	54	6.4
Games and toys	38	4.5
Visits to theatre and cinema	23	2.7
Photographic and moviemaking equipment and film	21	2.5
Tools	8	0.9
Other activities	103	12.2
TOTAL	847	100.0

National economy

Budget (2000). Revenue: DM 1,910,161,000,000 (taxes 84.7%, interest 7.7%).
Expenditures: DM 1,873,837,000,000 (pensions and other social security payments 34.4%, purchase of current goods and services 21.9%, personnel costs
18.4%).
Total national debt (May 2002): €715,800,000,000.
Production (value of production in DM except as noted; 1999–2000).
Agriculture, forestry, fishing: cereal grains 7,007,000,000, flowers and ornamental plants 3,010,000,000, sugar beets 2,541,000,000, grapes for wine
2,289,000,000, fruits 2,095,000,000, potatoes 2,024,000,000, vegetables
1,960,000,000, tree nurseries 1,870,000,000, oilseed crops 1,601,000,000; livestock (number of live animals; 2000) 27,049,000 pigs, 14,658,000 cattle,
2,100,000 sheep, 110,000,000 chickens; roundwood (2000) 37,634,000 cu m;
fish catch (metric tons; 1999) 312,492. Mining and quarrying (metric tons;
1998): potash 37,100,000. Manufacturing (value added at factor cost in DM
'000,000; 1996): capital equipment 252,226, of which machinery 90,213, transport equipment 80,418; electrical equipment 57,269; chemicals (including
pharmaceuticals) 60,842; food and beverages 39,184; plastics and other synthetic products 27,853; glass and ceramic products 22,730; furniture and other
wood products 16,651; paper products 12,948; textiles 8,636; clothing 5,467.
Construction (newly completed buildings, sq m; 1996): residential 43,937,000;
nonresidential 43,593,000.

Manufacturing, mining, and construction enterprises (1997)

	no. of enter-prises	no. of employees	wages as a % of avg. of all wages	annual gross production value (DM '000,000)[10]
Manufacturing	44,514	6,162,900	100.0	2,077,699
of which				
Road and motor vehicles	1,000	695,800	117.9	303,801
Machinery (nonelectric)	6,461	981,500	106.1	254,366
Chemical	1,709	500,500	121.2	220,367
Food and beverages	4,812	502,100	76.4	219,025
Machinery and appliances (electric)	2,248	446,000	105.2	210,357
Petroleum and natural gas	53	23,000	124.1	123,801
Rubber and plastic products	2,923	343,000	87.5	86,006
Glass and ceramics	3,747	257,400	89.5	70,439
Textiles	1,296	131,600	74.5	31,429
Wood and wood products	2,014	115,700	81.7	30,423
Mining and quarrying	787	169,000	105.3	29,094
Construction	24,848	1,403,000	100.0	249,327

Energy production (consumption): electricity (kW-hr; 2000) 557,004,000,000 ([1997] 544,063,000,000); hard coal (metric tons; 2001) 28,866,000 ([1997] 72,236,000); lignite (metric tons; 2001) 175,259,000 ([1997] 179,403,000); crude petroleum (barrels; 2001) 21,502,000 ([1997] 745,355,000); petroleum products (metric tons; 1997) 93,230,000 (113,289,000); natural gas (cu m; 2000) 23,387,000,000 ([1997] 108,390,000,000).

Gross national product (at current market prices; 2000): U.S.$2,063,734,000,000 (U.S.$25,120 per capita).

Structure of gross domestic product and labour force

	1999 in value DM '000,000	1999 % of total value	2000 labour force	2000 % of labour force
Agriculture	42,240	1.2	988,000	2.5
Public utilities }	82,600	2.4	290,000	0.7
Mining			152,000	0.4
Manufacturing	826,960	23.8	8,542,000	21.5
Construction	189,830	5.4	3,118,000	7.8
Transp. and commun.	204,630	5.9	2,008,000	5.1
Trade, restaurants	423,730	12.2	6,409,000	16.1
Finance, real estate }	1,077,270	30.9	4,256,000	10.7
Services			7,568,000	19.1
Pub. admin., defense	770,600	22.1	3,103,000	7.8
Other	−137,800[11]	−3.9[11]	3,297,000[12]	8.3[12]
TOTAL	3,480,060	100.0	39,731,000	100.0

Household income and expenditure. Average annual income per household (1998) DM 75,144 (U.S.$42,702); sources of take-home income[13]: wages 77.6%, self-employment 12.0%, transfer payments 10.4%; expenditure: rent 24.7%, food and beverages 13.9%, transportation 13.7%, entertainment, education, and leisure 11.8%, household operations, durables, and maintenance 7.0%, clothing and footwear 5.5%.

Financial aggregates[14]

	1995	1996	1997	1998	1999	2000	2001
Exchange rate, DM per[15]:							
U.S. dollar	1.4335	1.5548	1.7341	1.7597	0.9386	1.0854	1.1175
£	2.2219	2.6285	2.8399	2.9148	1.5188	1.6456	1.6092
SDR	2.1309	2.2357	2.4180	2.3556	1.3662	1.4002	1.4260
International reserves (U.S.$)							
Total (excl. gold; '000,000)	85,005	83,178	77,587	74,024	61,039	56,890	51,309
SDRs ('000,000)	2,001	1,907	1,788	1,868	1,959	1,763	1,793
Reserve pos. in IMF ('000,000)	5,210	5,468	5,946	8,023	6,419	5,460	5,901
Foreign exchange	77,794	75,083	69,853	64,133	52,661	49,667	43,615
Gold ('000,000 fine troy oz)	95.18	95.18	95.18	118.98	111.52	111.52	111.13
% world reserves	10.48	10.52	10.69	12.31	11.56	11.73	11.80
Interest and prices							
Central bank discount (%)	3.0	2.5	2.5	2.5	...	...	...
Govt. bond yield (%)	6.5	5.6	5.1	4.4	4.3	5.2	4.7
Industrial share prices (1995 = 100)[16]	100.0	114.1	156.3	200.0	207.3	258.7	197.3
Balance of payments (U.S.$'000,000,000)							
Balance of visible trade	+65.10	+69.38	+70.12	+76.91	+70.04	+57.51	+88.51
Imports, f.o.b.	458.48	453.20	439.90	465.71	472.69	492.33	481.44
Exports, f.o.b.	523.58	522.58	510.02	542.62	542.73	549.84	569.95
Balance of invisibles	−84.03	−77.35	−72.96	−83.02	−89.11	−77.90	−86.07
Balance of payments, current account	−18.93	−7.97	−2.84	−6.11	−19.07	−20.39	+2.44

Tourism (2000): receipts U.S.$17,879,000,000; expenditures U.S.$47,785,000,000.

Service enterprises (1991)

	no. of enter-prises	no. of employees	weekly wages as a % of all wages	annual turnover (DM '000,000)
Gas	151	37,000	...	42,228
Water	183	40,000	...	3,443
Electrical power	462	296,000	...	147,076
Transport				
air	133	57,390	...	20,270
buses	6,054	192,869	...	12,586
rail	1	416,199	...	14,697
shipping	1,449	9,076	...	...
Communications				
press	2,452	240,075	...	31,096
Postal services	17,616[17]	652,573	...	68,346
Hotels and restaurants	135,141	652,251	...	60,257
Wholesale trade	36,605[17]	1,214,000	...	1,015,984
Retail trade	152,629	2,241,000	...	605,755

Population economically active (2000): total 40,326,000; activity rate of total population 49.0% (participation rates[18]: ages 15–64, 70.7%; female 43.1%; unemployed 10.7%).

Price and earnings indexes (1995 = 100)

	1996	1997	1998	1999	2000	2001	2002[19]
Consumer price index	101.5	103.3	104.3	104.9	107.0	109.6	111.1
Hourly earnings index[20]	...	...	108.1	110.8	113.2	115.7	116.9

Land use (1994): forest 30.6%; pasture 15.1%; agriculture 19.9%; other 34.4%.

Foreign trade[21]

Balance of trade (current prices)

	1996	1997	1998	1999[22]	2000[22]	2001[22]
DM '000,000,000	+117.35	+137.35	+148.66	+77.33	+70.61	+108.99
% of total	8.0%	8.4%	8.4%	8.2%	6.3%	9.3%

Imports (2000): DM 1,064,308,800,000 (machinery and transport equipment 37.0%, of which road transport equipment 8.3%, electrical machinery other than office equipment 7.9%; chemicals and chemical products 8.9%, of which organic chemical products 2.5%, unfabricated plastics 1.4%; mineral fuels 8.7%, of which crude petroleum and petroleum products 6.5%, natural gas 1.8%; food and beverages 6.1%, of which fruits and vegetables 1.8%, meat and meat products 0.7%, coffee, tea, and cocoa 0.6%; iron and steel 2.2%; furniture 1.3%). *Major import sources:* France 9.6%; The Netherlands 8.8%; U.S. 8.5%; U.K. 7.0%; Italy 6.6%; Japan 4.9%; Belgium 4.8%; Austria 3.8%; Switzerland 3.4%.

Exports (2000): DM 1,167,343,300,000 (machinery and transport equipment 51.2%, of which road transport equipment 17.4%, electrical machinery other than office equipment 8.4%; chemicals and chemical products 12.7%, of which organic chemical products 2.4%, unfabricated plastics 2.2%). *Major export destinations:* France 11.4%; U.S. 10.2%; U.K. 8.3%; Italy 7.6%; The Netherlands 6.4%; Austria 5.3%; Belgium 5.1%; Spain 4.5%; Switzerland 4.3%; Poland 2.4%.

Transport and communications

Transport. Railroads (1999): length 51,209 mi[18], 82,413 km[18]; passengers carried 1,943,000,000; passenger-mi 45,725,000,000, passenger-km 73,587,000,000; short ton-mi cargo 48,874,000,000, metric ton-km cargo 71,356,000,000. Roads (1999): total length 143,372 mi, 230,735 km (paved 99%). Vehicles (2000[3]): passenger cars 42,423,300; trucks and buses 2,576,000. Air transport (1999): passengers carried 41,118,000; passenger-mi 55,219,396,000, passenger-km 88,867,173,000; short ton-mi cargo 4,519,788,000, metric ton-km cargo 6,598,776,000; airports (1997) 35.

Communications

Medium	date	unit	number	units per 1,000 persons
Daily newspapers	1996	circulation	25,500,000	311
Radio	1997	receivers	77,800,000	948
Television	1999	receivers	47,600,000	580
Telephones	2001	main lines	52,280,000	635
Cellular telephones	2001	subscribers	56,245,000	683
Personal computers	2000	units	27,640,000	336
Internet	2001	users	30,000,000	364

Education and health

Health (2000): physicians 294,676 (1 per 279 persons); dentists 63,156 (1 per 1,302 persons); hospital beds (1999) 565,268 (1 per 145 persons); infant mortality rate per 1,000 live births (2001) 4.3.

Education (1999–2000)

	schools	teachers	students	student/teacher ratio
Primary (age 6–10)	17,503	192,659	3,488,300	17.9
Secondary (age 10–19)	19,897	421,002	5,827,714	13.8
Voc., teacher tr.	9,580	112,577	2,656,450	23.5
Higher[23]	335	152,401	1,838,456	12.1

Food (1999): daily per capita caloric intake 3,411 (vegetable products 69%, animal products 31%); 128% of FAO recommended minimum requirement.

Military

Total active duty personnel (2001): 308,400 (army 68.7%, navy 8.4%, air force 22.9%); U.S. troops in Germany (2001): 71,000. *Military expenditure as percentage of GNP* (1999): 1.6% (world 2.4%); per capita expenditure U.S.$395.

[1]The Deutsche Mark (DM) was the former monetary unit; on Jan. 1, 2002, DM 1.96 = €1. [2]State names used in this table are English conventional. [3]January 1. [4]Detail does not add to total given because of rounding. [5]1999 estimate. [6]2000 estimate. [7]1999 city population estimate coextensive with urban agglomeration. [8]Population of 3 combined Rhine-Ruhr urban agglomerations equals 12,814,000. [9]Former West Germany only. [10]1996. [11]Less imputed bank service charges. [12]Including 3,127,000 unemployed. [13]1997. [14]End-of-period figures unless footnoted otherwise. [15]Beginning in 1999 exchange rates expressed in euros (€). [16]Period averages. [17]1990. [18]1998. [19]Average of first and second quarters. [20]In manufacturing, trade, transportation, and communications. [21]Imports are f.o.b. in balance of trade and c.i.f. in commodities and trading partners. [22]In billions of euros. [23]1995–96.

Internet resources for further information:
• **Federal Statistical Office of Germany (in English)**
 http://www.destatis.de/basis/e/bevoe/bev_tab4.htm

Ghana

Official name: Republic of Ghana.
Form of government: unitary multiparty
  republic with one legislative house
  (House of Parliament [200]).
Head of state and government:
  President.
Capital: Accra.
Official language: English.
Official religion: none.
Monetary unit: 1 cedi (₵) = 100
  pesewas; valuation (Sept. 23, 2002)
  1 U.S.$ = ₵8,192; 1 £ = ₵12,732.

Area and population

Regions[2]	Capitals	area sq mi	area sq km	population 1991[1] estimate
Ashanti	Kumasi	9,417	24,389	2,485,766
Brong-Ahafo	Sunyani	15,273	39,557	1,432,971
Central	Cape Coast	3,794	9,826	1,359,861
Eastern	Koforidua	7,461	19,323	2,003,235
Greater Accra	Accra	1,253	3,245	1,696,170
Northern	Tamale	27,175	70,384	1,389,105
Upper East	Bolgatanga	3,414	8,842	921,196
Upper West	Wa	7,134	18,476	526,398
Volta	Ho	7,942	20,570	1,432,971
Western	Sekondi-Takoradi	9,236	23,921	1,374,483
TOTAL		92,098[3]	238,533	14,622,156

Demography

Population (2002): 20,244,000.
Density (2002): persons per sq mi 219.8, persons per sq km 84.9.
Urban-rural (1999): urban 37.8%; rural 62.2%.
Sex distribution (1999): male 49.77%; female 50.23%.
Age breakdown (2000): under 15, 41.9%; 15–29, 27.7%; 30–44, 17.4%; 45–59, 7.8%; 60–74, 4.2%; 75 and over, 1.0%.
Population projection: (2010) 22,650,000; (2020) 25,223,000.
Doubling time: 37 years.
Ethnolinguistic composition (1983): Akan 52.4%; Mossi 15.8%; Ewe 11.9%; Ga-Adangme 7.8%; Gurma 3.3%; Yoruba 1.3%; other 7.5%.
Religious affiliation (2000): Christian 55.4%, of which Protestant 16.6%, African Christian 14.4%, Roman Catholic 9.5%; traditional beliefs 24.4%; Muslim 19.7%; other 0.5%.
Major cities (2001[1]): Accra 1,551,200; Kumasi 610,600; Tamale 259,200; Tema 225,900; Obuasi 118,000.

Vital statistics

Birth rate per 1,000 population (2001): 29.0 (world avg. 21.2); legitimate, n.a.; illegitimate, n.a.
Death rate per 1,000 population (2001): 10.3 (world avg. 8.9).
Natural increase rate per 1,000 population (2001): 18.7 (world avg. 12.3).
Total fertility rate (avg. births per childbearing woman; 2001): 3.8.
Life expectancy at birth (2001): male 55.9 years; females 58.7 years.
Major causes of death per 100,000 population: n.a.; however, principal infectious diseases as a percentage of outpatients (1989): malaria 43.8%, respiratory infections (including tuberculosis) 8.0%, diarrheal diseases 6.7%, intestinal worms 3.1%.

National economy

Budget (1996). Revenue: ₵1,997,600,000,000 (excise and value-added taxes 36.7%, of which petroleum tax 14.5%; import-export duties 27.3%; income taxes 21.7%; nontax revenue 14.4%). Expenditures (1995): ₵1,697,893,000,000 (1994: education 22.3%; debt service 20.1%; health 6.9%; transportation and communications 5.3%; social security and welfare 3.6%; defense 2.9%).
Public debt (external, outstanding; 2000): U.S.$5,529,000,000.
Production (metric tons except as noted). Agriculture, forestry, fishing (2000): roots and tubers 12,893,000 (of which cassava 7,845,000, yams 3,249,000, taro 1,707,000), cereals 1,686,000 (of which corn [maize] 1,014,000, sorghum 302,000, rice 210,000, millet 160,000), bananas and plantains 2,061,000, cacao 409,000, coconuts 310,000, oranges 270,000, tomatoes 216,000, peanuts (groundnuts) 212,000, sugarcane 147,000, palm kernels 34,000, lemons and limes 30,000, pulses 20,000; livestock (number of live animals) 2,739,000 goats, 2,516,000 sheep, 1,273,000 cattle, 352,000 pigs, 17,467,000 chickens; roundwood (2000) 21,765,000 cu m; fish catch (2000) 452,070. Mining and quarrying (2000): manganese (metal content) 287,000; bauxite 504,000; gold 2,317,000 troy oz; gem diamonds 736,000 carats. Manufacturing (value added in ₵; 1993): tobacco 71,474,700,000; footwear 60,350,600,000; chemical products 40,347,600,000; beverages 36,167,000,000; metal products 35,121,700,000; petroleum products 32,143,500,000; textiles 18,278,600,000; machinery and transport equipment 9,525,700,000. Construction (value added in ₵; 1994) 171,129,000,000. Energy production (consumption): electricity (kW-hr; 1997) 6,652,000,000 (6,426,000,000); coal (metric tons; 1998) none (3,000); crude petroleum (barrels; 1998) none (7,315,000); petroleum products (metric tons; 1998) 926,000 (1,077,000); natural gas, none (n.a.).
Tourism (2000): receipts U.S.$335,000,000; expenditures U.S.$100,000,000.
Household income and expenditure. Average household size (1984) 4.9; average annual income per household (1978) ₵9,600 (U.S.$[4]); sources of income: n.a.; expenditure: n.a.
Gross national product (1999): U.S.$7,451,000,000 (U.S.$400 per capita).

Structure of gross domestic product and labour force

	1996 in value ₵'000,000	1996 % of total value	1984 labour force	1984 % of labour force
Agriculture	4,895,000	46.0	3,310,967	59.4
Mining	190,000	1.8	26,828	0.5
Manufacturing	964,000	9.1	588,418	10.5
Construction	376,000	3.5	64,686	1.2
Public utilities	215,000	2.0	15,437	0.3
Transp. and commun.	431,000	4.0	122,806	2.2
Trade[5]	2,176,000	20.5	792,147	14.2
Finance	404,000	3.8	27,475	0.5
Pub. admin., defense	} 957,000	} 9.0	97,548	1.7
Services			376,168	6.7
Other	26,000[6]	0.26	157,624[7]	2.8[7]
TOTAL	10,633,000[3]	100.0[3]	5,580,104	100.0

Population economically active (1984): total 5,580,104; activity rate of total population 45.4% (participation rates: over age 15, 82.5%; female 51.2%; unemployed 2.8%).

Price and earnings indexes (1995 = 100)

	1995	1996	1997	1998	1999	2000	2001
Consumer price index	100.0	146.6	187.4	214.8	241.5	302.3	401.8
Monthly earnings index	...	...	...	...	...	...	...

Land use (1994): forest 42.2%; pasture 36.9%; agriculture 19.0%; other 1.9%.

Foreign trade

Balance of trade (current prices)

	1995	1996	1997	1998	1999	2000
U.S.$'000,000	−256.6	−366.0	−638.3	−805.5	−1,111.5	−842.9
% of total	4.6%	10.4%	17.6%	16.2%	20.8%	18.2%

Imports (1998): U.S.$2,896,900,000 (petroleum [all forms] 7.4%; unspecified 92.6%). *Major import sources* (1999): Nigeria 14.9%; U.K. 9.5%; Côte d'Ivoire 9.0%; U.S. 8.1%; France 7.7%.
Exports (1998): U.S.$2,091,400,000 (gold 32.9%; cacao 25.9%; wood products 8.2%; cocoa products 3.8%). *Major export destinations* (1999): Togo 12.6%; U.K. 11.6%; U.S. 9.4%; Italy 8.9%; The Netherlands 7.5%.

Transport and communications

Transport. Railroads (2000): route length 592 mi, 953 km; (1993) passenger-mi 731,400,000, passenger-km 1,177,000,000; (1994) short ton-mi cargo 86,097,000, metric ton-km cargo 125,700,000. Roads (1996): total length 24,000 mi, 38,700 km (paved 40%). Vehicles (1996): passenger cars 90,000; trucks and buses 45,000. Air transport (2001)[8]: passenger-mi 782,000,000, passenger-km 1,259,000,000; short ton-mi cargo 22,583,000, metric ton-km cargo 32,970,000; airports (1996) with scheduled flights 1.

Communications

Medium	date	unit	number	units per 1,000 persons
Daily newspapers	1996	circulation	250,000	14
Radio	1997	receivers	4,400,000	236
Television	1999	receivers	2,266,000	118
Telephones	2001	main lines	242,100	12
Cellular telephones	2001	subscribers	193,800	9.3
Personal computers	2001	units	70,000	3.3
Internet	2001	users	40,500	1.9

Education and health

Educational attainment (1984). Percentage of population age 25 and over having: no formal schooling 60.4%; primary education 7.1%; middle school 25.4%; secondary 3.5%; vocational and other postsecondary 2.9%; higher 0.6%. *Literacy* (2000): total population age 15 and over literate 8,070,000 (70.2%); males literate 4,520,000 (79.8%); females literate 3,550,000 (61.2%).

Education (1991–92)

	schools	teachers	students	student/ teacher ratio
Primary (6–12)	11,056	66,068	1,796,490	27.2
Secondary (13–20)	5,540	43,367	816,578	18.8
Voc., teacher tr.[9]	957	422	13,232	31.4
Higher[9]	16	700	9,274	13.2

Health: physicians (1994) 735 (1 per 22,970 persons); hospital beds (1994) 26,455 (1 per 638 persons); infant mortality rate per 1,000 live births (2001) 56.5.
Food (2000): daily per capita caloric intake 2,699 (vegetable products 96%, animal products 4%); 118% of FAO recommended minimum.

Military

Total active duty personnel (2001): 7,000 (army 71.4%, navy 14.3%, air force 14.3%). *Military expenditure as percentage of GNP* (1999): 0.8% (world 2.4%); per capita expenditure U.S.$3.

---

[1]January 1. [2]Government administration has been decentralized to the local level of 103 district assemblies, 4 municipal assemblies, and 3 metropolitan assemblies. [3]Detail does not add to total given because of rounding. [4]Unofficial 1978 exchange rate (7.5 to 9.9 times the official rate) does not permit meaningful conversion into other currencies. [5]Trade includes hotels. [6]Import duties and statistical adjustments less imputed bank service charges. [7]Unemployed only. [8]Ghana Airways only. [9]1989–90.

Internet resources for further information:
• Ghana Home Page http://www.ghanaweb.com/GhanaHomePage
• UNDP in Ghana http://www.undp-gha.org

Greece

Official name: Ellinikí Dhimokratía (Hellenic Republic).
Form of government: unitary multiparty republic with one legislative house (Greek Chamber of Deputies [300]).
Chief of state: President.
Head of government: Prime Minister.
Capital: Athens.
Official language: Greek.
Official religion: Eastern Orthodox.
Monetary unit: 1 euro (€) = 100 cents; valuation (Sept. 23, 2002) 1 U.S.$ = €1.02; 1 £ = €1.58[1].

Area and population

Regions[2]	Principal cities	area sq mi	area sq km	population 2001 census
Insular				
Aegean, Northern	Mitilíni	1,481	3,836	200,066
Aegean, Southern	Ermoúpolis	2,041	5,286	298,745
Crete	Iráklion	3,218	8,336	601,159
Ionian Islands	Kérkira	891	2,307	214,274
Mainland				
Attica	Athens	1,470	3,808	3,764,348
Epirus	Ioánnina	3,553	9,203	352,420
Greece, Central	Lamía	6,004	15,549	608,655
Greece, Western[3]	Pátrai	4,382	11,350	742,419
Macedonia, Central	Thessaloníki	7,393	19,147	1,862,833
Macedonia, Eastern and Thrace	Komotiní	5,466	14,157	604,254
Macedonia, Western	Kozáni	3,649	9,451	302,750
Peloponnese	Trípolis	5,981	15,490	632,955
Thessaly	Lárisa	5,420	14,037	754,893
TOTAL		50,949	131,957	10,939,771[4]

Demography

Population (2002): 10,994,000.
Density (2002): persons per sq mi 215.8, persons per sq km 83.3.
Urban-rural (2000): urban 60.1%; rural 39.9%.
Sex distribution (1998): male 49.29%; female 50.71%.
Age breakdown (1998): under 15, 15.6%; 15–29, 22.1%; 30–44, 21.5%; 45–59, 18.1%; 60–74, 16.3%; 75 and over, 6.5%.
Population projection: (2010) 11,064,000; (2020) 10,962,000.
Ethnic composition (2000)[5]: Greek 90.4%; Macedonian 1.8%; Albanian 1.5%; Turkish 1.4%; Pomak 0.9%; Roma (Gypsy) 0.8%; other 3.2%.
Religious affiliation (1995): Christian 95.2%, of which Eastern Orthodox 94.0%, Roman Catholic 0.5%; Muslim 1.3%; other 3.5%.
Major cities (1991): Athens 772,072 (urban agglomeration [2001] 3,120,000); Thessaloníki 383,967 (urban agglomeration [2000] 789,000); Piraeus (Piraiévs) 182,671[6]; Pátrai 152,570; Peristérion 137,288[6]; Iráklion 116,178.

Vital statistics

Birth rate per 1,000 population (2000): 11.7 (world avg. 22.5); (1998) legitimate 96.2%; illegitimate 3.8%.
Death rate per 1,000 population (2000): 10.5 (world avg. 9.0).
Natural increase rate per 1,000 population (2000): 1.2 (world avg. 13.5).
Total fertility rate (avg. births per childbearing woman; 2000): 1.3.
Marriage rate per 1,000 population (1998): 5.3.
Divorce rate per 1,000 population (1997): 0.8.
Life expectancy at birth (2000): male 75.9 years; female 81.2 years.
Major causes of death per 100,000 population (1998): diseases of the circulatory system 490.6; malignant neoplasms (cancers) 208.5; ill-defined conditions 81.6; diseases of the respiratory system 63.7.

National economy

Budget (1999). Revenue: Dr 12,409,000,000,000 (indirect taxes 47.2%, direct taxes 32.6%, nontax revenue 20.2%). Expenditures: Dr 17,737,000,000,000 (debt service 36.8%, health and social insurance 12.4%, education and culture 7.9%, agriculture 7.1%, defense 5.9%).
Public debt (1997): U.S.$18,331,000,000.
Tourism (2000): receipts U.S.$9,219,000,000; expenditures U.S.$4,558,000,000.
Production (metric tons except as noted). Agriculture, forestry, fishing (2000): sugar beets 2,906,000, olives 2,000,000, tomatoes 1,960,000, corn (maize) 1,850,000, wheat 1,770,000, seed cotton 1,250,000, grapes 1,200,000, oranges 950,000, peaches and nectarines 900,000, potatoes 890,000, apples 326,000, barley 255,000, tobacco 129,900; livestock (number of live animals) 9,041,000 sheep, 5,293,000 goats, 906,000 pigs; roundwood (1999) 2,215,260 cu m; fish catch (1999) 215,964. Mining and quarrying: bauxite (1999) 1,813,000; nickel (1998) 18,000[7]. Manufacturing (value added in Dr '000,000,000; 1999): food 573; paints, soaps, varnishes, drugs, and medicines 371; electrical machinery 287; textiles 259; cement, bricks, and tiles 227; beverages 214. Energy production (consumption): electricity (kW-hr; 1999) 44,724,000,000 ([1997] 36,528,000,000); hard coal (metric tons; 1997) none (1,153,000); lignite (metric tons; 1999) 61,464,000 ([1997] 58,678,000); crude petroleum (barrels; 1997) 3,145,000 (130,453,000); petroleum products (metric tons; 1997) 18,938,000 (15,669,000); natural gas (cu m; 1997) 52,177,000 (202,530,000).
Household income and expenditure. Average household size (1993–94) 2.9; income per household Dr 3,900,000 (U.S.$15,660); sources of income (1995): wages and salaries 36.6%, transfer payments 19.0%, other 44.4%; expenditure: food and beverages 32.7%, transportation and communications 13.5%, housing 11.5%, cafe/hotel expenditures 7.6%, household furnishings 7.4%.
Gross national product (2000): U.S.$126,269,000,000 (U.S.$11,960 per capita).

Structure of gross domestic product and labour force

	1999 in value Dr '000,000,000	1999 % of total value	1998 labour force	1998 % of labour force
Agriculture	2,645	6.9	704,200	15.8
Mining	187	0.5	18,300	0.4
Manufacturing	4,023	10.5	577,900	13.0
Construction	2,865	7.5	282,300	6.4
Public utilities	802	2.1	35,300	0.8
Transp. and commun.	2,206	5.8	244,800	5.5
Trade, restaurants	7,427	19.5	917,000	20.6
Finance, real estate	7,316	19.2	290,600	6.5
Pub. admin., defense	2,355	6.2	896,800	20.2
Services	4,659	12.2		
Other	3,662[8]	9.6[8]	478,500[9]	10.8[9]
TOTAL	38,147	100.0	4,445,700	100.0

Population economically active (1998): total 4,445,700; activity rate of total population 42.3% (participation rates: ages 15 and over, 50.1%; female 39.4%; unemployed [2000] 11.1%).

Price and earnings indexes (1995 = 100)

	1996	1997	1998	1999	2000	2001	2002
Consumer price index	108.2	114.7	119.6	122.8	126.6	130.9	132.7[10]
Hourly earnings index	108.6	118.3	123.9	...	...	...	...

Land use (1994): forest 20.3%; pasture 40.7%; agriculture 27.2%; other 11.8%.

Foreign trade[11]

Balance of trade (current prices)

	1996	1997	1998	1999	2000	2001
Dr '000,000,000	−4,312	−5,235	−5,730	−4,774	−6,751	−20,444[12]
% of total	48.6%	52.6%	47.2%	44.3%	46.2%	51.9%

Imports (1998): Dr 8,933,000,000,000 (machinery and transport equipment 34.7%, chemicals and chemical products 12.3%, food products 10.9%, mineral fuels 7.3%). *Major import sources:* Italy 15.9%; Germany 14.9%; France 8.6%; U.K. 6.4%; The Netherlands 6.2%; U.S. 4.6%.
Exports (1998): Dr 3,203,000,000,000 (food 18.4%, of which fruits and nuts 7.7%; clothing and apparel 16.8%; petroleum 6.4%; aluminum 4.2%; tobacco products 4.1%). *Major export destinations:* Germany 18.3%; Italy 11.9%; U.K. 7.0%; U.S. 4.7%; France 4.6%; Bulgaria 4.1%.

Transport and communications

Transport. Railroads (1999): route length 2,299 km; passenger-km 1,434,000,000; metric ton-km cargo 347,000,000. Roads (1999): total length 117,000 km (paved 92%). Vehicles (1998): passenger cars 2,675,676; trucks and buses 1,013,677. Air transport (1999)[13]: passenger-km 8,305,451,000; metric ton-km cargo 103,243,000; airports (1997) 36.

Communications

Medium	date	unit	number	units per 1,000 persons
Daily newspapers	1996	circulation	1,600,000	150
Radio	1997	receivers	5,020,000	470
Television	1999	receivers	5,100,000	471
Telephones	2001	main lines	5,607,700	529
Cellular telephones	2001	subscribers	7,962,000	751
Personal computers	2001	units	860,000	81
Internet	2001	users	1,400,000	132

Education and health

Educational attainment (1991). Percentage of population age 25 and over having: no formal schooling (illiterate) 6.8%; some primary education 10.6%; completed primary 39.7%; lower secondary 10.8%; higher secondary 20.6%; some postsecondary 4.9%; completed higher 6.6%. *Literacy* (2000): total population age 15 and over literate 9,080,000 (97.2%); males literate 4,570,000 (98.6%); females literate 4,510,000 (96.0%).

Education (1998–99)

	schools	teachers	students	student/ teacher ratio
Primary (age 6–12)	6,549	45,876	646,559	14.1
Secondary (age 12–18)	2,921	48,754	598,237	12.3
Voc., teacher tr.	637	11,270	139,422	12.4
Higher[14]	...	13,793	185,146	13.4

Health (1997): physicians 43,030 (1 per 248 persons); hospital beds 52,474 (1 per 204 persons); infant mortality rate per 1,000 live births (1999) 6.7.
Food (1999): daily per capita caloric intake 3,689 (vegetable products 78%, animal products 22%); 148% of FAO recommended minimum requirement.

Military

Total active duty personnel (2001): 159,170 (army 69.1%, navy 11.9%, air force 19.0%). *Military expenditure as percentage of GNP* (1999): 4.7% (world 2.4%); per capita expenditure U.S.$573.

[1]The drachma (Dr) was the former monetary unit; on Jan. 1, 2002, Dr 340.75 = €1. [2]Created for planning and economic development; local administration is based on 52 departments and one autonomous self-governing monastic region (Mount Athos). [3]Corresponds to the northwestern part of the Peloponnese. [4]Preliminary figure; final census total equals 10,964,595. [5]Government states there are no ethnic divisions in Greece. [6]Within Athens urban agglomeration. [7]Metal content of ores. [8]Taxes less imputed bank service charges and subsidies. [9]Unemployed. [10]July. [11]Imports c.i.f.; exports f.o.b. [12]In U.S.$'000,000. [13]Olympic Airways. [14]Includes higher technical education.

Internet resources for further information:
• **National Statistical Service of Greece http://www.statistics.gr**

Greenland

Official name: Kalaallit Nunaat (Greenlandic); Grønland (Danish) (Greenland).
Political status: integral part of the Danish realm with one legislative house (Parliament [31]).
Chief of state: Danish Monarch.
Heads of government: High Commissioner (for Denmark); Prime Minister (for Greenland).
Capital: Nuuk (Godthåb).
Official languages: Greenlandic; Danish.
Official religion: Evangelical Lutheran (Lutheran Church of Greenland).
Monetary unit: 1 Danish krone (Dkr) = 100 øre; valuation (Sept. 23, 2002) 1 U.S.$ = Dkr 7.56; 1 £ = Dkr 11.74.

Area and population	area		population
Counties			2002[1]
Communes	sq mi	sq km	estimate
Avanersuaq (Nordgrønland)	...	...	
Qaanaaq (Thule)	...	...	854
Kitaa (Vestgrønland)	...	...	
Aasiaat (Egedesminde)	...	...	3,404
Ilulissat (Jakobshavn)	...	...	4,781
Ivittuut (Ivigtut)	...	...	153
Kangaatsiaq (Kangåtsiaq)	...	...	1,505
Maniitsoq (Sukkertoppen)	...	...	3,703
Nanortalik	...	...	2,516
Narsaq (Narssaq)	...	...	2,051
Nuuk (Godthåb)	...	...	14,272
Paamiut (Frederikshåb)	...	...	2,014
Qaqortoq (Julianehåb)	...	...	3,365
Qasigiannguit (Christianshåb)	...	...	1,462
Qeqertarsuaq (Godhavn)	...	...	1,067
Sisimiut (Holsteinsborg)	...	...	5,960
Upernavik	...	...	2,903
Uummannaq (Umanaq)	...	...	2,738
Tunu (Østgrønland)	...	...	
Illoqqortoormiit (Scoresbysund)	...	...	549
Ammassalik	...	...	2,979
TOTAL (ICE-FREE)	158,475	410,449	
PERMANENT ICE	677,855	1,755,637	
TOTAL	836,330	2,166,086	56,542[2]

Demography

Population (2002): 56,600.
Density[3] (2002): persons per sq mi 0.36, persons per sq km 0.14.
Urban-rural (2001[1]): urban (town) 84.3%; rural (settlement) 15.7%.
Sex distribution (2002[1]): male 53.37%; female 46.63%.
Age breakdown (2002[1]): under 15, 26.4%; 15–29, 19.4%; 30–49, 35.4%; 50–64, 13.5%; 65 and over, 5.3%.
Population projection: (2010) 57,300; (2020) 58,200.
Doubling time: 76 years.
Ethnic composition (2000): Greenland Eskimo 79.1%; Danish 13.6%; other 7.3%.
Religious affiliation (2000): Protestant 69.2%, of which Evangelical Lutheran 64.2%, Pentecostal 2.8%; other Christian 27.4%; other/nonreligious 3.4%.
Major towns (2001[1]): Nuuk (Godthåb) 13,650; Sisimiut (Holsteinsborg) 5,165; Ilulissat (Jakobshavn) 4,165; Aasiaat (Egedesminde) 3,239; Qaqortoq (Julianehåb) 3,111.

Vital statistics

Birth rate per 1,000 population (2000): 16.8 (world avg. 22.5); (1993) legitimate 29.2%; illegitimate 70.8%.
Death rate per 1,000 population (2000): 7.6 (world avg. 9.0).
Natural increase rate per 1,000 population (2000): 9.2 (world avg. 13.5).
Total fertility rate (avg. births per childbearing woman; 2000): 2.3.
Marriage rate per 1,000 population (1995): 7.1.
Divorce rate per 1,000 population (1993): 2.7.
Life expectancy at birth (2000): male 64.5 years; female 71.7 years.
Major causes of death per 100,000 population (1995): diseases of the circulatory system 214.4, of which cerebrovascular disease 68.8, ischemic heart disease 64.9; malignant neoplasms (cancers) 198.7; suicides 90.5; accidents 80.6.

National economy

Budget (1998). Revenue: Dkr 4,304,000,000 (block grant from Danish government 59.8%; taxes and royalties for Greenland treasury 13.5%; import duties 11.3%; EEC fishery license fees 6.4%; other 6.6%). Expenditures (1997): Dkr 5,987,442,000 (current expenditure 93.3%, of which wages and salaries 35.9%, social welfare 22.3%, culture and education 15.3%, health 10.7%, defense 5.5%; capital [development] expenditure 6.7%).
Public debt (external, outstanding; 1995): U.S.$243,000,000.
Tourism (1997): number of overnight visitors 181,043.
Production (metric tons except as noted). Fishing, animal products: fish catch (1998) 372,974 (by local boats 128,630, of which shrimp 73,581, halibut 29,965, cod 11,776; by foreign boats 123,748); livestock (number of live animals; 1999) 22,000 sheep, 4,800 reindeer; animal products (value of external sales in Dkr '000; 1998) sealskins 31,044, polar bear skins 579. Mining[4]: none. Manufacturing: principally handicrafts and fish processing. Construction: residential (1992[1]) 18,624 sq m; nonresidential (1985) 12,300 sq m. Energy production (consumption): electricity (kW-hr; 1999) 250,000,000 (232,000,000); coal,

none (none); crude petroleum (barrels; 1999) none (1,307,000); petroleum products (metric tons; 1991) none (214,000); natural gas, none (none).
Gross national product (1998): U.S.$1,021,000,000 (U.S.$18,205 per capita).

Structure of gross domestic product and labour force				
	1998		2000	
	in value Dkr '000,000	% of total value	labour force	% of labour force
Fishing, hunting, and sheep farming	...	...	...	...
Mining	...	...	...	...
Manufacturing	...	...	...	...
Construction	...	...	...	...
Transp. and commun.	...	...	...	...
Trade, restaurants	...	...	...	...
Public utilities	...	...	...	...
Public administration	...	...	...	...
Private services	...	...	...	...
Other	...	...	...	...
TOTAL	7,719	100.0	31,518[1]	100.0

Population economically active (2000[1]): total 31,518; activity rate of total population 56.2% (participation rates: ages 15–60, 86.6%; female [1987] 43.4%; unemployed [1999] 10.0%).

Price and earnings indexes (January 1995 = 100)[5]						
	1996	1997	1998	1999	2000	2001
Consumer price index	100.7	101.6	102.1	103.0	104.7	107.9
Monthly earnings index	102.4	103.5	103.0	102.9	...	...

Household income and expenditure. Average household size (1998): 2.6; income per person (1997): Dkr 144,700 (U.S.$17,700); sources of income: n.a.; expenditure (1994): food, beverages, and tobacco 41.6%, housing and energy 22.4%, transportation and communications 10.2%, recreation 6.4%.
Land use (1994): forested 0.03%; meadows and pastures 0.69%; agricultural and under permanent cultivation, none; other (principally ice cap) 99.28%.

Foreign trade

Balance of trade (current prices)						
	1996	1997	1998	1999	2000	2001
Dkr '000,000	–578	–688	–1,038	–924	–742	–215
% of total	11.9%	15.1%	23.4%	19.3%	14.4%	4.6%

Imports (2001): Dkr 2,466,000,000 (food, beverages, and tobacco products 17.3%; mineral fuels 16.6%; goods for construction industry 9.2%; machinery 7.0%; transport equipment 3.6%; unspecified 10.7%). *Major import sources* (2000): Denmark 72.8%; Norway 8.9%; Japan 2.6%; Germany 2.4%; Sweden 1.8%.
Exports (2001): Dkr 2,251,000,000 (fish and fish products 87.2%, of which shrimp 54.8%, crab 11.4%). *Major export destinations* (2000): Denmark 86.0%; Japan 6.6%; U.S. 4.7%; Thailand 1.4%.

Transport and communications

Transport. Railroads: none. Roads (1998): total length 93 mi, 150 km (paved 60%). Vehicles (1998): passenger cars 2,242; trucks and buses 1,474. Merchant marine (1992): vessels (100 gross tons and over) 82; total deadweight tonnage, 54,169. Air transport (1998)[6]: passenger-mi 103,769,000, passenger-km 167,000,000; short ton-mi cargo 232,000[7], metric ton-km cargo 339,000; airports (1998) with scheduled flights 18.

Communications				units per 1,000
Medium	date	unit	number	persons
Daily newspapers	1996	circulation	1,000	18
Radio	1997	receivers	27,000	482
Television	1997	receivers	22,000	393
Telephones	1999	main lines	26,000	464
Cellular telephones	1999	subscribers	14,000	250

Education and health

Educational attainment: n.a. *Literacy* (1999): total population age 15 and over literate: virtually 100%.

Education (1998–99)				student/
	schools	teachers	students	teacher ratio
Primary (age 6–15)	88	975	9,341	9.6
Secondary (age 15–19)	3	...	1,746	5.9
Voc., teacher tr.[8]	8	110	650	
Higher[8]	2	35	200	5.7

Health (1998): physicians 84 (1 per 668 persons); hospital beds (1993) 465 (1 per 125 persons); infant mortality rate per 1,000 live births (2000) 18.3.

Military

Total active duty personnel. Denmark is responsible for Greenland's defense. Greenlanders are not liable for military service.

---

[1]January 1. [2]Includes 266 people not distributed by county. [3]Population density calculated with reference to ice-free area only. [4]Greenland's only mine closed in 1990. [5]All figures denote January. [6]Greenlandair only. [7]1985. [8]1986–87.

Internet resources for further information:
• **Greenland Home Rule http://www.gh.gl/english**
• **Statistics Greenland http://www.statgreen.gl**
• **Danmarks Statistik http://www.dst.dk/665**

Grenada

Official name: Grenada.
Form of government: constitutional monarchy with two legislative houses (Senate [13]; House of Representatives [15[1]]).
Chief of state: British Monarch represented by Governor-General.
Head of government: Prime Minister.
Capital: St. George's.
Official language: English.
Official religion: none.
Monetary unit: 1 East Caribbean dollar (EC$) = 100 cents; valuation (Sept. 23, 2002) 1 U.S.$ = EC$2.70; 1 £ = EC$4.20.

Area and population

Local Councils	Principal towns	area sq mi	area sq km	population 2001[2] census
Carriacou	Hillsborough	10	26 }	6,063
Petite Martinique	...	3	8 }	
St. Andrew	Grenville	38	99	24,661
St. David	...	17	44	11,476
St. George	...	25[3]	65[3]	31,651
St. John	Gouyave	14	35	8,557
St. Mark	Victoria	10	25	3,955
St. Patrick	Sauteurs	16	42	10,624
Town				
St. George's	—	3	3	3,908
TOTAL		133	344	100,895

Demography

Population (2002): 101,000.
Density (2002): persons per sq mi 759.4, persons per sq km 293.6.
Urban-rural (2000)[4]: urban 38.3%; rural 61.7%.
Sex distribution (2000): male 51.70%; female 48.30%.
Age breakdown (2000): under 15, 38.1%; 15–29, 33.3%; 30–44, 17.7%; 45–59, 4.9%; 60–74, 4.7%; 75 and over, 1.3%.
Population projection: (2010) 106,000; (2020) 112,000.
Doubling time: 60 years.
Ethnic composition (2000): black 51.7%; mixed 40.0%; Indo-Pakistani 4.0%; white 0.9%; other 3.4%.
Religious affiliation (1995): Roman Catholic 57.8%; Protestant 37.6%, of which Anglican 14.4%, Pentecostal 8.3%, Seventh-day Adventist 7.0%; other 4.6%, of which Rastafarian c. 3.0%.
Major localities (2001): St. George's 3,908 (urban agglomeration 35,559); Gouyave 3,100[5]; Grenville 2,300[5]; Victoria 2,100[5].

Vital statistics

Birth rate per 1,000 population (2001): 18.8 (world avg. 21.2); (1987) legitimate 18.1%; illegitimate 81.9%.
Death rate per 1,000 population (2001): 7.2 (world avg. 8.9).
Natural increase rate per 1,000 population (2001): 11.6 (world avg. 12.3).
Total fertility rate (avg. births per childbearing woman; 2000): 2.6.
Marriage rate per 1,000 population (1991): 4.3.
Divorce rate per 1,000 population (1991): 0.8.
Life expectancy at birth (2000): male 62.7 years; female 66.3 years.
Major causes of death per 100,000 population (1987): diseases of the circulatory system 264.3; malignant neoplasms (cancers) 82.8; endocrine and metabolic diseases 57.3; diseases of the respiratory system 45.6; diseases of the digestive system 38.2; ill-defined conditions 209.1.

National economy

Budget (1998). Revenue: EC$229,000,000 (current revenue 90.0%, of which tax on international trade 52.3%, general sales taxes 17.8%, income taxes 9.6%; grants from abroad 10.0%). Expenditures: EC$281,700,000 (current expenditure 73.7%, of which wages 37.2%, transfers 16.1%, debt 11.6%; capital expenditure 26.3%).
Public debt (external, outstanding; 2000): U.S.$180,900,000.
Tourism (2000): receipts from visitors U.S.$67,000,000; expenditures by nationals abroad U.S.$5,000,000.
Gross national product (at current market prices; 2000): U.S.$370,000,000 (U.S.$3,770 per capita).

Structure of gross domestic product and labour force

	1997 in value EC$'000,000[6]	1997 % of total value[6]	1991 labour force[7]	1991 % of labour force[7]
Agriculture	53.8	9.5	4,223	17.1
Quarrying	3.1	0.5	126	0.5
Manufacturing	39.9	7.0	1,881	7.6
Construction	41.7	7.3	3,168	12.9
Public utilities	28.7	5.1	350	1.4
Transportation and communications	139.1	24.5	1,614	6.5
Trade, restaurants	113.6	20.0	5,149	20.9
Finance, real estate	77.4	13.6	866	3.5
Pub. admin., defense	93.6	16.5	1,738	7.1
Services	15.7	2.8	3,372	13.7
Other	–38.7[8]	–6.8[8]	2,163	8.8
TOTAL	567.9	100.0	24,650	100.0

Production (metric tons except as noted). Agriculture, forestry, fishing (1999): coconuts 6,800, sugarcane 6,600, bananas 4,400, roots and tubers 3,000, nutmeg 2,500, grapefruit 2,000, mangoes 1,800, avocados 1,700, cacao 1,100, oranges 900, other crops include cotton, limes, cinnamon, cloves, and pimiento; livestock (number of live animals) 13,000 sheep, 7,000 goats, 5,300 pigs; roundwood, n.a.; fish catch (1998) 1,713. Mining and quarrying: excavation of gravel for local use. Manufacturing (value of production in EC$'000; 1997): wheat flour 13,390; soft drinks 9,798; beer 7,072; animal feed 5,852; rum 5,497; toilet paper 4,237; malt 4,192; stout 3,835; cigarettes 1,053. Construction: n.a. Energy production (consumption): electricity (kW-hr; 1996) 95,000,000 (95,000,000); coal, none (none); crude petroleum, none (none); petroleum products (metric tons; 1996) none (55,000); natural gas, none (none).
Household income and expenditure. Average household size (1991) 3.7; income per household (1988) EC$7,097 (U.S.$2,629); sources of income: n.a.; expenditure (1987): food, beverages, and tobacco 40.7%, household furnishings and operations 13.7%, housing 11.9%, transportation 9.1%, personal effects and medical care 8.6%.
Population economically active (1988): total 38,920; activity rate of total population 39.9% (participation rate: ages 15–65, 72.7%; female 48.6%; unemployed [1997] 17.0%).

Price and earnings indexes (1995 = 100)

	1995	1996	1997	1998	1999	2000
Consumer price index	100.0	102.0	103.0	104.7	105.0	108.1
Annual earnings index[9]	100.0	....	...	...	...	...

Land use (1994): forested 9.0%; meadows and pastures 3.0%; agricultural and under permanent cultivation 35.0%; other 53.0%.

Foreign trade

Balance of trade (current prices)

	1996	1997	1998	1999	2000
U.S.$'000,000	–122.5	–133.8	–137.1	–109.8	–133.1
% of total	71.1%	67.1%	59.9%	42.4%	44.1%

Imports (2000): U.S.$242,700,000 (machinery and transport equipment 30.9%; basic manufactures 17.2%; food 16.2%; chemicals and chemical products 6.8%). *Major import sources:* United States 37.9%; United Kingdom 8.4%; Japan 7.1%; Venezuela 5.0%; Canada 4.2%.
Exports (2000): U.S.$79,100,000 (domestic exports 95.0%, of which electronic components 54.7%, nutmeg 15.8%, fish 6.5%, cocoa beans 2.1%, paper products 2.1%; reexports 5.0%). *Major export destinations:* United States 35.9%; United Kingdom 3.1%; Canada 1.9%.

Transport and communications

Transport. Railroads: none. Roads (1996): total length 646 mi, 1,040 km (paved 61%). Vehicles (1991)[10]: passenger cars 4,739; trucks and buses 3,068. Merchant marine (1992): vessels (100 gross tons and over) 3; total deadweight tonnage 484. Air transport (1997)[11]: passengers 322,000; cargo 2,300 metric tons; airports (1998) with scheduled flights 2.

Communications

Medium	date	unit	number	units per 1,000 persons
Radio	1997	receivers	57,000	615
Television	1997	receivers	33,000	353
Telephones	2001	main lines	73,700	328
Cellular telephones	2001	subscribers	61,400	273
Personal computers	2001	units	13,000	130
Internet	2001	users	5,200	52

Education and health

Educational attainment (1991). Percentage of population age 25 and over having: no formal schooling 1.8%; primary education 74.9%; secondary 15.5%; higher 4.7%, of which university 2.8%; other/unknown 3.1%. *Literacy* (1995): total population age 15 and over literate 50,000 (85.0%).

Education (1996–97)

	schools	teachers	students	student/ teacher ratio
Primary (age 5–11)[12]	58	879	23,449	26.7
Secondary (age 12–16)[12]	19[13]	381[13]	7,367	19.3
Vocational	...	...	...	...
Higher[13, 14]	1	66	651	9.9

Health (1997): physicians 80 (1 per 1,236 persons); hospital beds 340 (1 per 290 persons); infant mortality rate per 1,000 live births (2001) 17.4.
Food (2000): daily per capita caloric intake 2,764 (vegetable products 76%, animal products 24%); 114% of FAO recommended minimum requirement.

Military

Total active duty personnel (1997)[15]: *Military expenditure as percentage of GNP:* n.a.; per capita expenditure, n.a.

[1]Excludes the speaker, who may be elected from outside its elected membership. [2]Preliminary noninstitutional figures. [3]St. George local council includes St. George's town. [4]Urban defined as St. George's town and St. George local council. [5]1991. [6]At factor cost. [7]Employed persons only. [8]Less imputed bank service charges. [9]Private sector only. [10]Registered vehicles only. [11]Point Salines airport. [12]Excludes private schools. [13]1994–95. [14]Excludes Grenada Teachers' College. [15]The 730-member police force includes an 80-member paramilitary unit and a 30-member coast guard unit.

Internet resources for further information:
• **Eastern Caribbean Central Bank** http://www.eccb-centralbank.org
• **Governments of the WWW: Grenada**
  http://www.gksoft.com/govt/en/gd.html

Guadeloupe

Official name: Département de la Guadeloupe (Department of Guadeloupe).
Political status: overseas department (France) with two legislative houses (General Council [42]; Regional Council [41]).
Chief of state: President of France.
Heads of government: Commissioner of the Republic (for France); President of the General Council (for Guadeloupe); President of the Regional Council (for Guadeloupe).
Capital: Basse-Terre.
Official language: French.
Official religion: none.
Monetary unit: 1 euro (€) = 100 centimes; valuation (Sept. 23, 2002) 1 U.S.$ = €1.02; 1 £ = €1.58[1].

Area and population

Arrondissements	Capitals	area sq mi	area sq km	population 1999 census
Basse-Terre[2]	Basse-Terre	330	855	175,691
Pointe-à-Pitre[3]	Pointe-à-Pitre	299	775	210,875
Saint-Martin-Saint-Barthélemy[4]	Marigot	29	74	35,930
TOTAL		658	1,705	422,496

Demography

Population (2002): 432,000.
Density (2002): persons per sq mi 656.5, persons per sq km 253.4.
Urban-rural (1999)[5]: urban 99.6%; rural 0.4%.
Sex distribution (1999): male 48.11%; female 51.89%.
Age breakdown (1999): under 15, 23.6%; 15–29, 22.4%; 30–44, 24.3%; 45–59, 15.7%; 60–74, 9.3%; 75 and over, 4.7%.
Population projection: (2010) 458,000; (2020) 479,000.
Doubling time: 62 years.
Ethnic composition (2000): Creole (mulatto) 76.7%; black 10.0%; Guadeloupe mestizo (French-East Asian) 10.0%; white 2.0%; other 1.3%.
Religious affiliation (1995): Roman Catholic 81.1%; Jehovah's Witness 4.8%; Protestant 4.7%; other 9.4%.
Major communes (1999): Les Abymes 63,054; Saint-Martin 29,078; Le Gosier 25,360; Baie-Mahault 23,389; Pointe-à-Pitre 20,948; Le Moule 20,827.

Vital statistics

Birth rate per 1,000 population (2000): 17.2 (world avg. 22.5); (1997) legitimate 37.0%; illegitimate 63.0%.
Death rate per 1,000 population (2000): 6.0 (world avg. 9.0).
Natural increase rate per 1,000 population (2000): 11.2 (world avg. 13.5).
Total fertility rate (avg. births per childbearing woman; 2000): 1.9.
Marriage rate per 1,000 population (1997): 4.7.
Divorce rate per 1,000 population (1997): 1.3.
Life expectancy at birth (2000): male 73.8 years; female 80.3 years.
Major causes of death per 100,000 population (1996): diseases of the circulatory system 183.7; malignant neoplasms (cancers) 134.8; accidents, violence, and poisoning 68.1; diseases of the respiratory system 32.1; diseases of the digestive system 31.4; endocrine and metabolic diseases 26.2; infectious and parasitic diseases 23.8.

National economy

Budget (1998). Revenue: F 4,227,000,000 (tax revenues 69.0%, of which direct taxes 42.5%, value-added taxes 25.1%; advances, loans, and transfers 26.8%). Expenditures: F 7,874,000,000 (current expenditures 70.6%, capital [development] expenditures 10.6%; advances and loans 18.8%).
Public debt: n.a.
Tourism (2000): receipts from visitors U.S.$418,000,000; expenditures, n.a.
Production (metric tons except as noted). Agriculture, forestry, fishing (1999): sugarcane 499,980, bananas 141,140, yams 9,030, pineapples 6,900, plantains 5,870, sweet potatoes 3,410, melons 3,240, tomatoes 3,080, lettuce 3,030, cucumbers and gherkins 2,620; livestock (number of live animals) 80,410 cattle, 63,000 goats, 15,000 pigs; roundwood (1998) 15,000 cu m; fish catch (1998) 9,084. Mining and quarrying (1993): pumice 210,000. Manufacturing (1996): cement 282,571; raw sugar 48,896; rum 66,483 hectolitres; other products include clothing, wooden furniture and posts, and metalware. Construction (buildings authorized; 1992): residential 358,474 sq m; nonresidential 160,084 sq m. Energy production (consumption): electricity (kW-hr; 1997) 1,211,-000,000 (1,211,000,000); coal, none (none); crude petroleum, none (none); petroleum products (metric tons; 1997) none (462,000); natural gas, none (none).
Population economically active (1998): total 182,200; activity rate of total population 41.8% (participation rates: ages [1995] 15–64, 73.2%; female 46.8%; unemployed 30.7%).

Price and earnings indexes (1995 = 100)

	1996	1997	1998	1999	2000	2001	2002[6]
Consumer price index	101.4	102.6	104.2	104.6	104.6	107.3	108.4
Monthly earnings index	...	...	...	...	...	...	...

Gross national product (1995): U.S.$3,877,000,000 (U.S.$9,145 per capita).

Structure of gross domestic product and labour force

	1995 in value F '000,000	1995 % of total value	1998 labour force	1998 % of labour force
Agriculture	1,080.7	4.1	8,200	4.5
Mining, manufacturing	1,744.9	6.6	7,900	4.3
Construction	1,880.1	7.2	13,000	7.1
Public utilities	...	...	...	...
Transp. and commun.	2,156.2	8.2	4,200	2.3
Trade, hotels	6,121.6	23.4	20,700	11.4
Finance, real estate	1,043.2	4.0	3,500	1.9
Pub. admin., defense	9,926.7	37.9	43,400	23.8
Services	3,210.2	12.2	24,400	13.4
Other	−957.4[7]	−3.6[7]	56,900[8]	31.2[8]
TOTAL	26,206.2	100.0	182,200	100.0[9]

Household income and expenditure. Average household size (1990) 3.4; income per household (1988) F 105,400 (U.S.$17,700); sources of income (1988): wages and salaries 78.9%, self-employment 12.7%, transfer payments 8.4%; expenditure (1994–95): housing 26.2%, food and beverages 21.4%, transportation and communications 14.1%, household durables 6.0%, culture and leisure 4.2%.
Land use (1994): forest 39.1%; pasture 14.2%; agriculture 16.0%; other 30.7%.

Foreign trade

Balance of trade (current prices)

	1993	1994	1995	1996	1997	1998
F '000,000	−7,309	−7,693	−8,655	−9,635	−9,274	−9,996
% of total	83.2%	82.0%	84.3%	83.6%	86.3%	88.2%

Imports (1998): F 10,663,000,000 (consumer goods 23.7%, food and agriculture products 21.1%, machinery and equipment 19.7%, transport vehicles and parts 12.3%). *Major import sources:* France 63.4%; Germany 4.4%; Italy 3.5%; Martinique 3.4%; U.S. 2.9%; Japan 1.9%.
Exports (1998): F 667,000,000 (1995: bananas 25.4%, sugar 11.4%, rum 4.4%, melons 2.9%). *Major export destinations:* France 68.5%; Martinique 9.4%; Italy 4.8%; Belgium-Luxembourg 3.3%; French Guiana 3.0%.

Transport and communications

Transport. Railroads: none. Roads (1998): total length 1,988 mi, 3,415 km (paved [1986] 80%). Vehicles (1993): passenger cars 101,600; trucks and buses 37,500. Merchant marine (1992): vessels (100 gross tons and over) 20; deadweight tonnage 4,430. Air transport (1998): passenger arrivals and departures 1,807,100; cargo handled 16,496 metric tons, cargo unloaded 5,493 metric tons; airports (1997) with scheduled flights 7.

Communications

Medium	date	unit	number	units per 1,000 persons
Daily newspapers	1995	circulation	35,000	81
Radio	1997	receivers	113,000	258
Television	1999	receivers	118,000	262
Telephones	2000	main lines	204,900	449
Cellular telephones	2001	subscribers	292,500	635
Personal computers	2001	units	100,000	217
Internet	2000	users	8,000	18

Education and health

Educational attainment (1990). Percentage of population age 25 and over having: incomplete primary, or no declaration 59.8%; primary education 14.5%; secondary 19.0%; higher 6.7%. *Literacy* (1982): total population age 15 and over literate 225,400 (90.1%); males literate 108,700 (89.7%); females literate 116,700 (90.5%).

Education (1998–99)

	schools	teachers	students	student/teacher ratio
Primary (age 6–10)	348	2,936	40,042	13.6
Secondary (age 11–17) Vocational	85	3,392	51,491	15.2
Higher[10]	1	...	10,919	

Health (1998): physicians 760 (1 per 550 persons); hospital beds 2,796 (1 per 149 persons); infant mortality rate per 1,000 live births (2000) 9.8.
Food (1995): daily per capita caloric intake 2,732 (vegetable products 75%, animal products 25%); 129% of FAO recommended minimum requirement.

Military

Total active duty personnel (2002): French troops in Antilles (Guadeloupe and Martinique) 4,000.

[1]French franc replaced by euro as of Jan. 1, 2002. [2]Comprises Basse-Terre 327 sq mi (848 sq km), pop. 172,693, and Îles des Saintes 5 sq mi (13 sq km), pop. 2,998. [3]Comprises Grande-Terre 230 sq mi (596 sq km), pop. 196,767; Marie-Galante 61 sq mi (158 sq km), pop. 12,488; La Désirade 8 sq mi (21 sq km), pop. 1,620; and the uninhabited Îles de la Petite-Terre. [4]Comprises the French part of Saint-Martin 21 sq mi (53 sq km), pop. 29,079; Saint-Barthélemy 8 sq mi (21 sq km), pop. 6,852; and the small, uninhabited island of Tintamarre. [5]Urban defined as locality with 2,000 or more inhabitants. [6]Includes external long-term private debt not guaranteed by the government. [7]Less imputed bank service charges. [8]Includes 55,900 unemployed. [9]Detail does not add to total given because of rounding. [10]University of Antilles-French Guiana, Guadeloupe campus.

Internet resources for further information:
• INSEE Guadeloupe
  http://www.insee.fr/fr/insee_regions/guadeloupe/home/home_page.asp

Guam

Official name: Teritorion Guam (Chamorro); Territory of Guam (English).
Political status: self-governing, organized, unincorporated territory of the United States with one legislative house (Guam Legislature [15]).
Chief of state: President of the United States.
Head of government: Governor.
Capital: Agana (Hagåtña).
Official languages: Chamorro; English.
Official religion: none.
Monetary unit: 1 United States dollar (U.S.$) = 100 cents; valuation (Sept. 23, 2002) 1 U.S.$ = £0.65.

Area and population	area		population[1]
Election Districts	sq mi	sq km	2000 census
Agana	1	3	1,100
Agana Heights	1	3	3,940
Agat	11	29	5,656
Asan	6	16	2,090
Barrigada	9	23	8,652
Chalan Pago-Ordot	6	16	5,923
Dededo	30	78	42,980
Inarajan	19	49	3,052
Mangilao	10	26	13,313
Merizo	6	16	2,163
Mongmong-Toto-Maite	2	5	5,845
Piti	7	18	1,666
Santa Rita	16	42	7,500
Sinajana	1	3	2,853
Talofofo	17	44	3,215
Tamuning	6	16	18,012
Umatac	6	16	887
Yigo	35	91	19,474
Yona	20	52	6,484
TOTAL	209[2]	541[2, 3]	154,805

Demography

Population (2002): 160,000.
Density (2002)[2]: persons per sq mi 737.3, persons per sq km 285.2.
Urban-rural (2002): urban 40.0%; rural 60.0%.
Sex distribution (2000): male 51.15%; female 48.85%.
Age breakdown (2000): under 15, 30.5%; 15–34, 32.4%; 35–59, 28.9%; 60–74, 6.7%; 75 and over, 1.5%.
Population projection: (2010) 184,000; (2020) 211,000.
Doubling time: 32 years.
Ethnic composition (2000): Pacific Islander 44.6%, of which Chamorro 37.0%; Asian 32.5%, of which Filipino 26.3%, Korean 2.5%; white 6.8%; mixed 13.9%; black 1.0%; other 1.2%.
Religious affiliation (1995): Roman Catholic 74.7%; Protestant 12.8%; other Christian 2.4%; other 10.1%.
Major populated places (2000): Tamuning 10,833; Mangilao 7,794; Yigo 6,391; Astumbo 5,207; Barrigada 4,417.

Vital statistics

Birth rate per 1,000 population (2002): 26.6 (world avg. 21.2); (1997) legitimate 50.1%; illegitimate 49.9%.
Death rate per 1,000 population (2002): 4.9 (world avg. 8.9).
Natural increase rate per 1,000 population (2002): 21.7 (world avg. 12.3).
Total fertility rate (avg. births per childbearing woman; 2002): 4.0.
Marriage rate per 1,000 population (1997): 9.5.
Divorce rate per 1,000 population (1995): 4.3.
Life expectancy at birth (2002): male 72.0 years; female 77.0 years.
Major causes of death per 100,000 population (1997): heart diseases 123.2; malignant neoplasms 55.9; accidents, poisonings, and violence 35.7; cerebrovascular disease 35.0; diabetes mellitus 20.9; suicide 20.2; pneumonia 10.8.

National economy

Budget (1997–98). Revenue: U.S.$738,100,000 (local taxes 68.7%, federal contributions 25.5%, interest 2.2%, licenses, fees, and permits 1.7%). Expenditures: U.S.$501,900,000 (current expenditures 80.2%, debt service 10.6%, capital expenditures 8.6%).
Production. Agriculture, forestry, fishing (value of production in U.S.$'000; 1996): eggplant 625, long beans 592, bananas 418, cucumbers 348, watermelons 232, papayas 101; livestock (number of live animals) 205,000 poultry, 4,000 pigs, 610 goats; fish catch (metric tons; 1998) 253, value of aquaculture production (1996) U.S.$1,442,000. Mining and quarrying: sand and gravel. Manufacturing (value of sales in U.S.$'000; 1997): printing and publishing 40,307; food processing 24,333; stone, clay, and glass products 16,914; fabricated metal products 4,367. Construction (gross value of building and construction permits in U.S.$; 1998): residential 125,207,000; nonresidential 196,681,000. Energy production (consumption): electricity (kW-hr; 1997) 825,000,000 (825,000,000); petroleum products (metric tons; 1997) none (1,329,000).
Household income and expenditure. Average household size (1998) 3.94; average annual income per household (1998) U.S.$47,374[4]; sources of income: n.a.; expenditure (1978): housing 28.6%, food 24.1%, transportation 18.0%, clothing 10.6%, entertainment 5.1%, medical care 4.7%.
Gross domestic product (1998): U.S.$3,302,700,000 (U.S.$20,660 per capita).

Structure of gross domestic product and labour force				
	1995		1999	
	in value U.S.$'000,000	% of total value	labour force[5]	% of labour force[5]
Agriculture	6	6	300	0.5
Manufacturing	6	6	1,880	3.0
Construction	379.0	12.5	6,490	10.2
Trade	622.9	20.6	13,690	21.6
Transp. and commun.	6	6	5,230	8.3
Finance	6	6	2,720	4.3
Pub. admin. (local)	513.3	16.9	19,760	31.2
Pub. admin., defense (federal)	452.7	14.9		
Services	486.9	16.1	13,280	21.0
Other	575.4[6]	19.0[6]	—	—
TOTAL	3,030.2	100.0	63,350	100.0[3]

Population economically active (1997): total 71,400; activity rate of total population 45.7% (participation rates: over age 16 [1994] 69.3%[7]; female [1994] 43.3%[7]; unemployed [June 1999] 15.2%).

Price and earnings indexes (1996 = 100)				
	1996	1997	1998	1999
Consumer price index	100.0	101.6	101.2	100.9
Hourly earnings index	...	...	...	...

Tourism (1999): receipts from visitors U.S.$1,908,000,000.
Land use (1998): forested 14.6%; meadows and pastures 14.5%; agricultural and under permanent cultivation 21.8%; other 49.1%.

Foreign trade

Balance of trade (current prices)						
	1991	1992	1993	1994	1995	1996
U.S.$'000,000	−358	−384	−355	−528	−584	−600
% of total	74.3%	74.4%	70.3%	86.3%	88.0%	88.2%

Imports (1998–99[8]): U.S.$205,800,000 (food products 34.2%; leather products including footwear 15.8%; motor vehicles and parts 14.3%; construction materials 6.4%; clothing 5.0%). *Major import sources:* n.a.
Exports (1999): U.S.$75,700,000 (food products 54.7%, of which fish 53.8%; petroleum and natural gas products 20.0%; tobacco products 6.7%). *Major export destinations:* Japan 53.9%; Federated States of Micronesia 18.6%; Palau 6.3%; Hong Kong 2.0%.

Transport and communications

Transport. Railroads: none. Roads (1999): total length 550 mi, 885 km (paved 76%). Vehicles (1995): passenger cars 79,800; trucks and buses 34,700. Merchant marine (1992): vessels (100 gross tons and over) 5, total deadweight tonnage 50; surface cargo loaded, unloaded, or transshipped (1998) 2,053,000 metric tons. Air transport (1998): passenger arrivals 1,375,000; passenger departures 1,378,000; cargo loaded and unloaded (1997) 35,295 metric tons; airports (1999) with scheduled flights 1.

Communications				units per 1,000
Medium	date	unit	number	persons
Daily newspapers	1996	circulation	28,000	178
Radio	1997	receivers	221,000	1,400
Television	1997	receivers	106,000	668
Telephones	2000	main lines	80,300	478
Cellular telephones	2000	subscribers	27,200	162
Internet	1999	users	5,000	30

Education and health

Educational attainment (1995). Percentage of population age 25 and over having: no formal schooling to some secondary education 26.9%; completed secondary 55.4%; completed higher 17.7%. *Literacy* (1990): total population age 15 and over literate 99.0%; males literate 99.0%; females literate 99.0%.

Education (1996)	schools	teachers	students	student/ teacher ratio
Primary (age 5–10)	24	1,091	18,896	17.3
Secondary (age 11–18) Vocational	6	943	18,068	19.2
Higher	5	...	3,383	...

Health (1999): physicians 130[9] (1 per 1,169 persons); hospital beds 192[10] (1 per 792 persons); infant mortality rate per 1,000 live births (2002) 10.0.

Military

Total active duty U.S. personnel (2001): 3,490 (army 1.2%; navy 53.0%; air force 45.8%).

[1]Includes active-duty military personnel, U.S. Department of Defense employees, their dependents, and Guamanian nationals. [2]Total area per most recent survey including area designated as inland water equals 217 sq mi (561 sq km). [3]Detail does not add to total given because of rounding. [4]Excludes U.S. military and dependents. [5]Employed persons only. [6]Other includes Agriculture, Manufacturing, Transportation and communications, and Finance. [7]Excludes nonimmigrant aliens and civilians living on military reservations. [8]Fiscal year November 1998–October 1999. [9]Members of Guam Medical Society only. [10]Guam Memorial Hospital only.

Internet resources for further information:
• **The Official Guam U.S.A. Website** http://ns.gov.gu
• **Government of Guam: Economic Overview** http://www.admin.gov.gu/commerce/economy.htm

Guatemala

Official name: República de Guatemala (Republic of Guatemala).
Form of government: republic with one legislative house (Congress of the Republic [113]).
Head of state and government: President.
Capital: Guatemala City.
Official language: Spanish.
Official religion: none
Monetary unit: 1 quetzal (Q) = 100 centavos; valuation (Sept. 23, 2002) 1 U.S.$ = Q 7.82; 1 £ = Q 12.16.

Area and population

Departments	Capitals	area sq mi	area sq km	population 2002 estimate[1]
Alta Verapaz	Cobán	3,695	9,569	883,463
Baja Verapaz	Salamá	1,198	3,104	212,202
Chimaltenango	Chimaltenango	757	1,960	449,137
Chiquimula	Chiquimula	912	2,361	328,987
El Progreso	Guastatoya (Progreso)	737	1,910	149,451
Escuintla	Escuintla	1,682	4,356	494,738
Guatemala	Guatemala City	856	2,218	2,732,085
Huehuetenango	Huehuetenango	2,813	7,285	932,836
Izabal	Puerto Barrios	3,468	8,981	347,211
Jalapa	Jalapa	792	2,050	285,121
Jutiapa	Jutiapa	1,235	3,199	369,697
Petén	Flores	12,987	33,635	360,691
Quetzaltenango	Quetzaltenango	810	2,098	711,252
Quiché	Santa Cruz del Quiché	3,927	10,172	616,287
Retalhuleu	Retalhuleu	712	1,844	249,894
Sacatepéquez	Antigua Guatemala	178	462	276,761
San Marcos	San Marcos	1,468	3,802	882,220
Santa Rosa	Cuilapa	1,134	2,936	331,260
Sololá	Sololá	405	1,050	325,738
Suchitepéquez	Mazatenango	930	2,409	419,785
Totonicapán	Totonicapán	403	1,043	377,554
Zacapa	Zacapa	1,032	2,673	223,185
TOTAL		42,130[2]	109,117	11,986,558[2]

Demography

Population (2002): 11,987,000.
Density (2002): persons per sq mi 284.5, persons per sq km 109.9.
Urban-rural (2000): urban 39.4%; rural 60.6%.
Sex distribution (2002): male 50.31%; female 49.69%.
Age breakdown (2002): under 15, 41.8%; 15–29, 28.1%; 30–44, 15.9%; 45–59, 8.8%; 60–74, 4.2%; 75 and over, 1.2%.
Population projection: (2010) 14,631,000; (2020) 18,123,000.
Doubling time: 25 years.
Ethnic composition (1994): Amerindian 42.8%; non-Amerindian 57.2%.
Religious affiliation (1995): Roman Catholic 75.9%, of which Catholic/traditional syncretist 25.0%; Protestant 21.8%; other Christian 1.3%; other 1.0%.
Major cities (1995)[3]: Guatemala City 1,167,495; Mixco 436,668; Villa Nueva 165,567; Chinautla 61,335; Amatitlan 40,229.

Vital statistics

Birth rate per 1,000 population (2000): 35.1 (world avg. 22.5).
Death rate per 1,000 population (2000): 6.9 (world avg. 9.0).
Natural increase rate per 1,000 population (2000): 28.2 (world avg. 13.5).
Total fertility rate (avg. births per childbearing woman; 2000): 4.7.
Marriage rate per 1,000 population (1995): 4.6.
Divorce rate per 1,000 population (1995): 0.05.
Life expectancy at birth (2000): male 63.5 years; female 69.0 years.
Major causes of death per 100,000 population (1988): infectious and parasitic diseases 121.6; diseases of the respiratory system 110.8; perinatal causes 58.7; malnutrition 50.2; dehydration 18.5.

National economy

Budget (1998). Revenue: Q 11,997,000,000 (tax revenue 90.3%, nontax revenue 8.9%). Expenditures: Q 14,828,000,000 (current expenditures 61.7%, of which disbursements for wages and salaries 25.3%, transfer payments 18.0%; capital expenditures 38.3%).
Public debt (external, outstanding; 2000): U.S.$3,146,000,000.
Tourism (2000): receipts U.S.$518,000,000; expenditures U.S.$182,000,000.
Production (metric tons except as noted). Agriculture, forestry, fishing (1999): sugarcane 15,459,000, corn (maize) 1,109,000, bananas 733,000, oil palm fruit 340,000, coffee 200,000, tomatoes 149,000; livestock (number of live animals) 2,300,000 cattle, 825,000 pigs, 24,000,000 chickens; roundwood (1998) 12,995,000 cu m; fish catch (1998) 10,847. Mining and quarrying (1997): gypsum 30,000; iron ore 3,300; antimony ore 880. Manufacturing (value added in Q '000,000; 1998[4]): food and beverage products 298; clothing and textiles 119; machinery and metal products 55. Construction (value of buildings authorized in Q '000,000; 1991)[5]: residential 170.2; nonresidential 127.5. Energy production (consumption): electricity (kW-hr; 1997) 4,132,000,000 (4,044,000,000); crude petroleum (barrels; 1997) 7,000,000 (6,100,000); petroleum products (metric tons; 1997) 713,000 (2,152,000).
Household income and expenditure. Average household size (1994) 5.2; income per household (1989) Q 4,306 (U.S.$1,529); sources of income: n.a.; expenditure (1981): food 64.4%, housing and energy 16.0%, transportation and communications 7.0%, household furnishings 5.0%, clothing 3.1%.
Gross national product (2000): U.S.$19,164,000,000 (U.S.$1,680 per capita).

Structure of gross domestic product and labour force

	1998 in value Q '000,000[4]	1998 % of total value	1995 labour force	1995 % of labour force
Agriculture	1,103	23.4	1,798,227	58.1
Mining	30	0.6	3,095	0.1
Manufacturing	640	13.6	420,928	13.6
Construction	113	2.4	126,898	4.1
Public utilities	162	3.4	9,285	0.3
Transp. and commun.	426	9.0	77,377	2.5
Trade	1,162	24.6	225,940	7.3
Finance, real estate	461	9.8	371,407	12.0
Pub. admin., defense	356	7.5		
Services	269	5.7		
Other	—	—	61,901[6]	2.0[6]
TOTAL	4,722	100.0	3,095,058	100.0

Population economically active (1996): total 3,183,173; activity rate of total population 29.1% (participation rates [1994] ages 15–64, 51.0%; female 19.5%; unemployed [1995] 1.4%[7]).

Price and earnings indexes (1995 = 100)

	1995	1996	1997	1998	1999	2000	2001
Consumer price index	100.0	111.1	121.3	129.8	136.1	144.2	155.2
Annual earnings index[8]	100.0	121.8	136.7	151.0	...	...	...

Land use (1998): forested and nonarable land 58.4%; meadows and pastures 24.0%; agricultural and under permanent cultivation 17.6%.

Foreign trade[9]

Balance of trade (current prices)

	1996	1997	1998	1999	2000	2001
U.S.$'000,000	−849.7	−1,198.7	−1,582.9	−1,613.0	−1,727.7	−2,768.2
% of total	17.3%	20.4%	23.5%	25.2%	24.3%	35.9%

Imports (1998): U.S.$4,650,900,000 (intermediate goods 34.9%, consumer goods 29.5%, capital goods 26.3%, lubricants and fuels 6.1%, construction materials 3.2%). *Major import sources:* United States 41.5%; Mexico 10.4%; Japan 4.5%; Venezuela 3.3%; Germany 2.8%.
Exports (1998): U.S.$2,846,700,000 (coffee 20.4%, sugar 11.0%, bananas 6.2%, petroleum 2.0%). *Major export destinations:* United States 32.2%; Germany 4.3%; Mexico 4.1%; Japan 2.2%.

Transport and communications

Transport. Railroads (1996): route length 884 km; passenger-km (1995) 16,580,000; metric ton-km cargo 85,615,000. Roads (1996): total length 13,100 km (paved 28%). Vehicles (1996): passenger cars 102,000; trucks and buses 97,000. Air transport (1995)[10]: passenger-km 500,000,000; metric ton-km cargo 70,000,000; airports (1996) 2.

Communications

Medium	date	unit	number	units per 1,000 persons
Daily newspapers	1996	circulation	338,000	33
Radio	1997	receivers	835,000	79
Television	1998	receivers	660,000	61
Telephones	2001	main lines	756,000	65
Cellular telephones	2001	subscribers	1,134,000	97
Personal computers	2001	units	150,000	13
Internet	2001	users	200,000	17

Education and health

Educational attainment (1994). Percentage of population age 25 and over having: no formal schooling 45.2%; incomplete primary education 20.8%; complete primary 18.0%; some secondary 4.8%; secondary 7.2%; higher 4.0%. *Literacy* (1995): total population age 15 and over literate 55.6%; males literate 62.5%; females literate 48.6%.

Education (1996)

	schools	teachers	students	student/teacher ratio
Primary (age 7–12)	12,409	43,403	1,510,811	34.8
Secondary (age 13–18)	1,274[11]	22,624	375,528	16.6
Voc., teacher tr.	626[11]			
Higher	5[12]	4,346[12]	80,228[13]	16.0[12]

Health (1988): physicians (1997) 9,812 (1 per 1,072 persons); hospital beds (1995) 10,974 (1 per 909 persons); infant mortality rate (2000) 47.0.
Food (2000): daily per capita caloric intake 2,171 (vegetable products 90%, animal products 10%); 99% of FAO recommended minimum.

Military

Total active duty personnel (2001): 31,400 (army 93.0%, navy 4.8%, air force 2.2%). *Military expenditure as percentage of GNP* (1999): 0.7% (world 2.4%); per capita expenditure U.S.$10.

[1]Adjusted for underenumeration in 1994 census. [2]Detail does not add to total given because of rounding. [3]Municipal population. [4]At prices of 1958. [5]Private construction in Guatemala City metropolitan area only. [6]Persons in activities not adequately defined. [7]Registered unemployed; majority of economically active population is estimated to be underemployed. [8]Based on employees entitled to social security. [9]Import figures are f.o.b. in balance of trade and c.i.f. for commodities and trading partners. [10]Aviateca Airlines only. [11]1991. [12]1989. [13]1995.

Internet resources for further information:
• **Banco de Guatemala (Spanish only)** http://www.banguat.gob.gt
• **Instituto Nacional de Estadistica** http://www.segeplan.gob.gt/ine/index.htm

Guernsey[1]

Official name: Bailiwick of Guernsey.
Political status: crown dependency
  (United Kingdom) with one legislative
  house (States of Deliberation [57[2, 3, 4]]).
Chief of state: British Monarch
  represented by Lieutenant Governor.
Head of government: [5].
Capital: St. Peter Port.
Official language: English.
Official religion: n.a.
Monetary unit: 1 Guernsey pound[6] = 100
  pence; valuation (Sept. 23, 2002)
  1 Guernsey pound = U.S.$1.55.

Area and population	area		population
	sq mi	sq km	2001 census[7]
Parishes of Guernsey	24.3	63.0	59,710
Castel	3.9	10.1	8,975
Forest	1.6	4.1	1,549
St. Andrew	1.7	4.5	2,409
St. Martin	2.8	7.3	6,267
St. Peter (St. Pierre du Bois)	2.4	6.2	2,188
St. Peter Port	2.6	6.6	16,488
St. Sampson	2.3	6.0	8,592
St. Saviour	2.4	6.3	2,696
Torteval	1.2	3.1	973
Vale	3.4	8.8	9,573
Dependencies of Guernsey	5.9	15.1	2,966
Alderney	3.1	7.9	2,294
Brechou	0.1	0.3	0
Herm	0.5	1.3	} 97
Jethou	0.1	0.2	
Lihou	0.1	0.2	0
Little Sark	0.4	1.0	} 575[8]
Sark (Great Sark)	1.6	4.2	
TOTAL	30.2	78.1	62,676

Demography

Population (2002)[9]: 63,000.
Density (2002)[9]: persons per sq mi 2,085.1, persons per sq km 806.3.
Sex distribution (2001): male 48.72%; female 51.28%.
Age breakdown (1996): under 15, 17.6%; 15–29, 20.6%; 30–44, 22.3%; 45–59,
  19.0%; 60–74, 13.2%; 75 and over, 7.3%.
Population projection[9]: (2010) 64,000; (2020) 65,000.
Doubling time: n.a.; doubling time exceeds 100 years.
Population by place of birth (1996): Guernsey 65.5%; United Kingdom 27.2%;
  Portugal 1.9%; Jersey 0.7%; Ireland 0.7%; Alderney 0.3%; Sark 0.1%; other
  3.6%.
Religious affiliation (c. 1990): Anglican 65.2%; other 34.8%.
Major cities (2001)[10]: St. Peter Port 16,488; Vale 9,573; Castel 8,975; St.
  Sampson 8,592; St. Martin 6,267.

Vital statistics

Birth rate per 1,000 population (2000): 10.5 (world avg. 22.5).
Death rate per 1,000 population (2000): 9.3 (world avg. 9.0).
Natural increase rate per 1,000 population (2000): 1.2 (world avg. 13.5).
Total fertility rate (avg. births per childbearing woman; 2000): 1.3.
Marriage rate per 1,000 population (1995): 6.0.
Divorce rate per 1,000 population (1993): 2.5.
Life expectancy at birth (2000): male 76.7 years; female 82.8 years.
Major causes of death per 100,000 population (1993): diseases of the circula-
  tory system 423.5; malignant neoplasms (cancers) 288.0; diseases of the res-
  piratory system 133.8; endocrine and metabolic disorders 25.4; accidents, poi-
  soning, and violence 22.0; diseases of the digestive system 11.8.

National economy

Budget (1999). Revenue: £306,991,000 (income tax 79.7%, customs duties and
  excise taxes 5.7%, document duties 2.7%, corporation taxes 2.1%, automobile taxes 1.9%). Expenditures: £244,418,000 (welfare 31.1%, health 26.2%,
  education 15.9%, administrative services 6.7%, law and order 4.9%, community services 4.1%).
Public debt: n.a.
Gross national product (at current market prices; 2000): U.S.$1,883,550,000
  (U.S.$30,840 per capita).

Structure of gross domestic product and labour force	1999		1996	
	in value £'000	% of total value	labour force	% of labour force
Horticulture, fishing	25,596	2.2	1,893	6.2
Mining	—	—	—	—
Manufacturing	38,812	3.4	2,084	6.8
Construction	59,623	5.2	2,676	8.7
Public utilities	[11]	[11]	447	1.5
Transp. and commun.	[12]	[12]	1,260	4.1
Finance, real estate[13]	706,483[11]	61.7[11]	5,928	19.3
Pub. admin., defense }	302,010[12]	26.4[12]	1,908	6.2
Services }			14,252	46.4
Other	12,998	1.1	245	0.8
TOTAL	1,145,522	100.0	30,693	100.0

Production (metric tons except as noted). Agriculture, forestry, fishing (1999):
  tomatoes 2,449[14], flowers 1,153,857 boxes, of which roses 287,915 boxes,
  freesia 184,467 boxes, carnations 161,273 boxes; livestock (number of live
  animals) 3,262 cattle; roundwood, n.a.; fish catch (1997)[15]: 4,368, of which
  crustaceans 2,934 (sea spiders and crabs 2,713), mollusks 743 (abalones, winkles, and conch 438), marine fish 691. Mining and quarrying: n.a.
  Manufacturing: milk 98,830 hectolitres. Construction: n.a. Energy production (consumption): electricity (kW-hr; 1999–2000), n.a. (273,013,000).
Household income and expenditure (1999). Average household size (2001) 2.5;
  expenditure (1996): housing 21.6%, food 12.7%, household goods and services 11.2%, recreation services 9.2%, transportation 8.5%, clothing and
  footwear 5.6%, personal goods 4.9%, energy 4.1%.
Population economically active (1999): total 31,153; activity rate of total population 48.8% (participation rates: ages 15–64, n.a.; female, n.a.; unemployed,
  n.a.).

Retail price and earnings indexes (1994 = 100)							
	1995	1996	1997	1998	1999	2000	2001
Consumer price index[16]	103.0	105.5	108.8	113.2	115.7	120.1	124.0
Earnings index	...	...	...	...	...	...	...

Tourism (1996): receipts U.S.$275,000,000.

Foreign trade

Imports (1997): principal imports, n.a. *Major import sources* (1997): mostly
  United Kingdom.
Exports (1999): £525,718,000 (mostly flowers and tomatoes). *Major export des-
  tinations* (1999): mostly United Kingdom.

Transport and communications

Transport. Railroads: n.a. Vehicles (2000): passenger cars 37,598; trucks and
  buses 7,338. Air transport: (2000) passenger arrivals 884,284; (1996) freight
  loaded and unloaded 7,616 metric tons; airports (1999) with scheduled flights
  2[17].

Communications				units per 1,000 persons
Medium	date	unit	number	
Daily newspapers	1998	circulation	15,784	260
Telephones	2001	main lines	55,000	877
Cellular telephones	2001	subscribers	31,500	502
Internet	2000	users	20,000	320

Education and health

Educational attainment: n.a. *Literacy* (1993): percentage of total population age
  15 and over literate 100.0%; males literate 100.0%; females literate 100.0%.

Education (1999)	schools	teachers	students	student/ teacher ratio
Primary (age 5–10)	22[18]	253	4,977	19.9
Secondary (age 11–16)	8[18]	295	3,900	13.2
Higher	1	...	211[19]	...

Health (1999): physicians 93 (1 per 654 persons); hospital beds, n.a.; infant mortality rate per 1,000 live births (2000) 5.1.
Food (2000)[20]: daily per capita caloric intake 3,334 (vegetable products 70%,
  animal products 30%); 132% of FAO recommended minimum requirement.

Military

Total active duty personnel[21]: n.a.

[1]Data excludes Alderney and Sark unless otherwise noted. [2]Elected only; excludes
those serving ex-officio. [3]Headed by the Bailiff. [4]Alderney and Sark have their own
parliaments. The States of Alderney has an elected president and 12 people's deputies.
The Chief Please of Sark consists of 40 *tenants* or landowners and 12 people's deputies.
[5]The government of Guernsey is conducted by committees appointed by the States of
Deliberation. [6]Equivalent in value to pound sterling (£). [7]Preliminary. [8]Estimated figure. [9]Includes Alderney, Sark, and other dependencies. [10]Parishes. [11]Public utilities and
trade included in Finance, real estate. [12]Transportation is included in Public administration, defense and Services. [13]Mostly from 79 banks (located offshore) and 581 insurance companies (352 offshore and 217 domestic). [14]1998. [15]Includes Jersey. [16]March.
[17]Includes one airport on Alderney. [18]1992. [19]Full-time students. [20]Data for the United
Kingdom. [21]The United Kingdom is responsible for defense.

Internet resources for further information:
• **The States of Guernsey**
  http://www.gov.gg

Guinea

Official name: République de Guinée (Republic of Guinea).
Form of government: unitary multiparty republic with one legislative house (National Assembly [114 seats]).
Head of state and government: President assisted by extraconstitutional Prime Minister.
Capital: Conakry.
Official language: French.
Official religion: none.
Monetary unit: 1 Guinean franc (GF) = 100 cauris; valuation (Sept. 23, 2002) 1 U.S.$ = GF 1,976; 1 £ = GF 3,072.

Area and population		area		population
Regions[1]	Capitals	sq mi	sq km	1983 census
Beyla	Beyla	6,738	17,452	161,347
Boffa	Boffa	1,932	5,003	141,719
Boké	Boké	3,881	10,053	225,207
Conakry	Conakry	119	308	705,280
Coyah (Dubréka)	Coyah	2,153	5,576	134,190
Dabola	Dabola	2,317	6,000	97,986
Dalaba	Dalaba	1,313	3,400	132,802
Dinguiraye	Dinguiraye	4,247	11,000	133,502
Faranah	Faranah	4,788	12,400	142,923
Forécariah	Forécariah	1,647	4,265	116,464
Fria	Fria	840	2,175	70,413
Gaoual	Gaoual	4,440	11,500	135,657
Guéckédou	Guéckédou	1,605	4,157	204,757
Kankan	Kankan	7,104	18,400	229,861
Kérouané	Kérouané	3,070	7,950	106,872
Kindia	Kindia	3,409	8,828	216,052
Kissidougou	Kissidougou	3,425	8,872	183,236
Koubia	Koubia	571	1,480	98,053
Koundara	Koundara	2,124	5,500	94,216
Kouroussa	Kouroussa	4,647	12,035	136,926
Labé	Labé	973	2,520	253,214
Lélouma	Lélouma	830	2,150	138,467
Lola	Lola	1,629	4,219	106,654
Macenta	Macenta	3,363	8,710	193,109
Mali	Mali	3,398	8,800	210,889
Mamou	Mamou	2,378	6,160	190,525
Mandiana	Mandiana	5,000	12,950	136,317
Nzérékoré	Nzérékoré	1,460	3,781	216,355
Pita	Pita	1,544	4,000	227,912
Siguiri	Siguiri	7,626	19,750	209,164
Télimélé	Télimélé	3,119	8,080	243,256
Tougué	Tougué	2,394	6,200	113,272
Yomou	Yomou	843	2,183	74,417
TOTAL		94,926[2]	245,857	5,781,014

Demography

Population (2002): 7,775,000.
Density (2002): persons per sq mi 81.9, persons per sq km 31.6.
Urban-rural (1998): urban 31.3%; rural 68.7%.
Sex distribution (1998): male 50.28%; female 49.72%.
Age breakdown (1999): under 15, 43.6%; 15–29, 26.9%; 30–44, 16.0%; 45–59, 9.0%; 60–74, 3.9%; 75 and over, 0.6%.
Population projection: (2010) 9,281,000; (2020) 11,440,000.
Doubling time: 31 years.
Ethnic composition (1996): Fulani 38.6%; Malinke 23.2%; Susu 11.0%; Kissi 6.0%; Kpelle 4.6%; other 16.6%.
Religious affiliation (1996): Muslim 85.0%; Christian 10.0%; other 5.0%.
Major cities (2001): Conakry 1,565,200; Kankan 88,800; Labé 64,500; Kindia 56,000; Nzérékoré 55,000; Kissidougou 40,400.

Vital statistics

Birth rate per 1,000 population (2001): 39.8 (world avg. 21.2).
Death rate per 1,000 population (2001): 17.5 (world avg. 8.9).
Natural increase rate per 1,000 population (2001): 22.3 (world avg. 12.3).
Total fertility rate (avg. births per childbearing woman; 2001): 5.4.
Life expectancy at birth (2001): male 43.5 years; female 48.4 years.

National economy

Budget (1998). Revenue: GF 624,500,000,000 (current revenues 79.5%, of which indirect taxes 34.8%, mining sector 20.2%, tax on trade 11.5%, direct taxes 7.7%, nontax revenue 5.3%; foreign aid 20.5%). Expenditures: GF 655,600,000,000 (wages and salaries 27.6%, goods and services 13.6%, interest 9.8%, transfers 8.1%; capital spending 38.2%).
Production (metric tons except as noted). Agriculture, forestry, fishing (1999): roots and tubers 1,064,888 (of which cassava 811,869, sweet potatoes 134,940, yams 88,635), fruits 996,078 (of which plantains 429,000, bananas 150,000, pineapples 71,858), paddy rice 750,000, vegetables and melons 420,000, sugarcane 220,000, peanuts (groundnuts) 173,682, corn (maize) 88,690; livestock (number of live animals) 2,368,000 cattle, 864,000 goats, 687,000 sheep, 54,000 pigs, 8,900,000 chickens; roundwood (1998) 8,650,000 cu m; fish catch (1997) 102,589. Mining and quarrying (2000): bauxite 15,000,000; alumina 550,000; gold 427,600 troy oz; diamonds 450,000 carats. Manufacturing (2000): cement 250,000. Energy production (consumption): electricity (kW-hr; 1997) 542,000,000 (542,000,000); petroleum products (metric tons; 1997) none (356,000).
Gross national product (2000): U.S.$3,303,000,000 (U.S.$450 per capita).

Structure of gross domestic product and labour force				
	1998		1983	
	in value GF '000,000,000[3]	% of total value[3]	labour force	% of labour force
Agriculture, forestry, fishing	824.8	20.6	1,423,615	78.2
Mining	630.3	15.7	12,241	0.7
Manufacturing	153.9	3.8	11,215	0.6
Construction	350.6	8.7	9,115	0.5
Public utilities	20.8	0.5	3,205	0.2
Transp. and commun.	243.6	6.1	29,496	1.6
Trade, finance	1,116.8	27.8	40,865	2.0
Pub. admin., defense Services	} 166.1	4.1	137,600	7.5
Other	505.8[4]	12.6[4]	155,679	8.5
TOTAL	4,012.7	100.0[2]	1,823,031	100.0

Public debt (external, outstanding; 2000): U.S.$2,940,000,000.
Population economically active (1997): total 3,321,000; activity rate of total population 44.8% (participation rates [1983]: ages 15–64, 63.5%; female 47.3%; unemployed, n.a.).

Price and earnings indexes (1995 = 100)					
	1994	1995	1996	1997	1998
Consumer price index	94.7	100.0	102.9	104.9	110.3
Annual salary index	...	...	...	...	...

Household income and expenditure. Average household size (1997): 4.1; average annual income per capita (1984) GS 7,660 (U.S.$305); expenditure (1985): food 61.5%, health 11.2%, clothing 7.9%, housing 7.3%.
Tourism (2000): receipts U.S.$7,000,000; expenditures U.S.$36,000,000.
Land use (1994): forest 27.3%; pasture 43.5%; agriculture 3.3%; other 25.9%.

Foreign trade

Balance of trade (current prices)						
	1994	1995	1996	1997	1998	1999
U.S.$'000,000	−169.7	−39.0	+111.2	+117.6	+137.4	+94.5
% of total	14.1%	3.2%	9.6%	10.3%	10.7%	7.5%

Imports (1997): U.S.$571,800,000 (capital goods 52.4%, consumer products 18.0%, food 17.1%, petroleum 12.5%). *Major import sources:* France 24.8%; U.S. 9.8%; Belgium 7.9%; Côte d'Ivoire 6.6%; China 5.6%.
Exports (1998): U.S.$709,200,000 (bauxite 45.7%, gold 17.7%, alumina 14.1%, diamonds 7.2%, fish 5.4%, coffee 3.3%). *Major export destinations:* U.S. 16.4%; Hong Kong 14.7%; Belgium 13.7%; Spain 12.4%; Ireland 12.2%.

Transport and communications

Transport. Railroads (2000): route length of operational lines for cargo (mostly bauxite) transport 170 mi, 274 km; (latest) passenger-km, n.a.[5]; metric ton-km cargo, n.a. Roads (1997): total length 30,500 km (paved 16.5%). Vehicles (1996): passenger cars 14,100; trucks and buses 21,000. Air transport (1998): passenger-km 50,000,000; metric ton-km cargo 5,000,000; airports (1998) 1.

Communications				units per 1,000
Medium	date	unit	number	persons
Daily newspapers	1988	circulation	13,000	2.0
Radio	1998	receivers	325,000	43
Television	1999	receivers	343,000	44
Telephones	2001	main lines	25,500	3.2
Cellular telephones	2001	subscribers	55,700	6.9
Personal computers	2001	units	32,000	4.0
Internet	2001	users	15,000	1.9

Education and health

Educational attainment of those age 6 and over having attended school (1983): primary 55.2%; secondary 32.7%; vocational 3.4%; higher 8.7%. *Literacy* (1995): percentage of total population age 15 and over literate 35.9%; males 49.9%; females 21.9%.

Education (1997–98)				student/
	schools	teachers	students	teacher ratio
Primary (age 7–12)	3,723	13,883	674,732	48.6
Secondary (age 13–18)	239	4,958	143,245	28.9
Voc., teacher tr.[6]	55	1,268	8,569	6.8
Higher[7, 8]	2	947	8,151	8.6

Health: physicians (1991) 920 (1 per 6,840 persons); hospital beds (1988) 3,382 (1 per 1,652 persons); infant mortality rate (2002) 127.1.
Food (2000): daily per capita caloric intake 2,353 (vegetable products 97%, animal products 3%); 102% of FAO recommended minimum requirement.

Military

Total active duty personnel (2001): 9,700 (army 87.6%, navy 4.1%, air force 8.2%). *Military expenditure as percentage of GNP* (1999): 1.6% (world 2.4%); per capita expenditure U.S.$7.

[1]Regions represent second-level administration; Guinea is divided into 7 provinces and 1 city (Conakry) at the first level of administration. [2]Detail does not add to total given because of rounding. [3]1994 prices. [4]Includes Services and indirect taxes. [5]Passenger service has been limited and irregular since the late 1980s. [6]1995–96. [7]1996–97. [8]Universities only.

Internet resources for further information:
• webGuinée http://www.guinee.net
• Official site of Guinea http://www.guinee.gov.gn

Guinea-Bissau

Official name: Républica da Guiné-Bissau (Republic of Guinea-Bissau).
Form of government: transitional regime with one legislative house (National People's Assembly [102]).
Chief of state: President.
Head of government: Prime Minister.
Capital: Bissau.
Official language: Portuguese.
Official religion: none.
Monetary unit: 1 CFA franc[1] (CFAF) = 100 centimes; valuation (Sept. 23, 2002) 1 U.S.$ = CFAF 667.00; 1 £ = CFAF 1,037.

Area and population		area		population
Regions	Chief towns	sq mi	sq km	1991 census
Bafatá	Bafatá	2,309	5,981	143,377
Biombo	Quinhámel	324	840	60,420
Bolama	Bolama	1,013	2,624	26,691
Cacheu	Cacheu	1,998	5,175	146,980
Gabú	Gabú	3,533	9,150	134,971
Oio	Bissorã	2,086	5,403	156,084
Quinara	Fulacunda	1,212	3,138	44,793
Tombali	Catió	1,443	3,736	72,441
Autonomous Sector				
Bissau	—	30	78	197,610
TOTAL		13,948[2]	36,125[2]	983,367

Demography

Population (2002): 1,345,000.
Density (2002)[3]: persons per sq mi 123.9, persons per sq km 47.8.
Urban-rural (2001): urban 32.4%; rural 67.6%.
Sex distribution (1997): male 48.52%; female 51.48%.
Age breakdown (1997): under 15, 42.7%; 15–29, 28.1%; 30–44, 15.4%; 45–59, 9.2%; 60–74, 3.8%; 75 and over, 0.8%.
Population projection: (2010) 1,614,000; (2020) 1,998,000.
Doubling time: 29 years.
Ethnic composition (1995): Balante 30%; Fulani 20%; Mandyako 14%; Malinke 13%; Pepel 7%; nonindigenous Cape Verdean mulatto 2%; other 14%.
Religious affiliation (2000): traditional beliefs 45.2%; Muslim 39.9%; Christian 13.2%, of which Roman Catholic 9.9%; other 1.7%.
Major cities (1997): Bissau 200,000 (urban agglomeration [2001] 292,000); Bafatá 15,000; Cacheu 14,000; Gabú 10,000.

Vital statistics

Birth rate per 1,000 population (2000): 39.6 (world avg. 22.5).
Death rate per 1,000 population (2000): 15.6 (world avg. 9.0).
Natural increase rate per 1,000 population (2000): 24.0 (world avg. 13.5).
Total fertility rate (avg. births per childbearing woman; 2000): 5.3.
Marriage rate per 1,000 population: n.a.
Divorce rate per 1,000 population: n.a.
Life expectancy at birth (2000): male 46.8 years; female 51.4 years.
Major causes of death per 100,000 population: n.a.; however, major diseases include tuberculosis of the respiratory system, whooping cough, typhoid fever, cholera, bacillary dysentery and amebiasis, malaria, pneumonia, and meningococcal infections; malnutrition is widespread.

National economy

Budget (1998). Revenue: CFAF 10,500,000,000 (foreign grants 37.1%; taxes on international trade 21.6%, of which import duties 12.9%; nontax revenues 19.8%, of which fishing licenses 7.3%; taxes on goods and services 10.7%; income taxes 8.2%). Expenditures: CFAF 30,200,000,000 (current expenditures 75.2%, of which scheduled external interest payments 27.0%; capital expenditures 24.8%).
Production (metric tons except as noted). Agriculture, forestry, fishing (1999): rice 130,000, oil palm fruit 80,000, roots and tubers 77,500, coconuts 44,000, cashew nuts 38,000, plantains 36,000, millet 30,000, peanuts (groundnuts) 18,000; livestock (number of live animals) 520,000 cattle, 340,000 pigs, 315,000 goats, 280,000 sheep; roundwood (1998) 589,000 cu m; fish catch (2000) 3,993, of which marine fish 3,508, shrimp 415. Mining and quarrying: extraction of construction materials only. Manufacturing (2000): processed wood 11,200; wood products 4,400; dried and smoked fish 3,500; soap 2,500; vegetable oils 34,000 hectolitres; distilled liquor 11,000 hectolitres. Energy production (consumption): electricity (kW-hr; 1999) 27,500,000 (10,200,000); coal, none (none); crude petroleum, none (none); petroleum products (metric tons; 1997) none (75,000); natural gas, none (none).
Population economically active (1992): total 471,000; activity rate of total population 46.9% (participation rates [1991]: over age 10, 67.1%; female 40.5%; unemployed, n.a.).

Price and earnings indexes (1995 = 100)							
	1996	1997	1998	1999	2000	2001	2002
Consumer price index	150.7	224.7	239.4	237.7	258.2	266.9	279.6[4]
Monthly earnings index	...	...	...	...	...	...	...

Public debt (external, outstanding; 2000): U.S.$818,300,000.
Gross national product (at current market prices; 2000): U.S.$217,000,000 (U.S.$180 per capita).

Structure of gross domestic product and labour force				
	1998		1994	
	in value CFAF '000,000	% of total value	labour force	% of labour force
Agriculture	74,831	61.7	365,000	77.2
Mining				
Manufacturing	11,134	9.2	21,000	4.5
Public utilities				
Construction	4,071	3.4		
Transportation and communications	2,333	1.9		
Trade	23,624	19.5	87,000	18.3
Finance, services	897	0.7		
Pub. admin., defense	3,067	2.5		
Other	1,357[5]	1.1[5]		
TOTAL	121,313[6]	100.0	473,000	100.0

Tourism: n.a.
Land use (1994): forested 38.1%; meadows and pastures 38.4%; agricultural and under permanent cultivation 12.1%; other 11.4%.
Household income and expenditure. Average household size (1996) 6.9; income per household: n.a; sources of income: n.a.; expenditure: n.a.

Foreign trade[7]

Balance of trade (current prices)					
	1997	1998	1999	2000	2001
U.S.$'000,000	−40.1	−38.9	−30.8	−41.7	−49.5
% of total	29.2%	42.9%	23.1%	25.1%	34.4%

Imports (2001): U.S.$96,700,000 (foodstuffs 18.7%, of which rice 6.6%; transport equipment 13.2%; equipment and machinery 7.7%; fuel and lubricants 6.2%; unspecified 39.3%). *Major import sources:* Portugal 30.9%; Senegal 28.3%; China 11.3%; The Netherlands 6.8%; Japan 5.8%.
Exports (2001): U.S.$47,200,000 (cashews 95.6%; cotton 2.3%; logs 1.5%). *Major export destinations:* India 85.6%; Portugal 3.8%; Senegal 2.5%; France 1.7%.

Transport and communications

Transport. Railroads: none. Roads (1999): total length 2,734 mi, 4,400 km (paved 10%). Vehicles (1996): passenger cars 7,120; trucks and buses 5,640. Merchant marine (1992): vessels (100 gross tons and over) 19; total deadweight tonnage 1,846. Air transport (1998): passenger-mi 6,200,000, passenger-km 10,000,000; short ton-mi cargo, n.a., metric ton-km cargo, n.a., airports (1997) with scheduled flights 2.

Communications				units per 1,000 persons
Medium	date	unit	number	
Daily newspapers	1996	circulation	6,000	5.1
Radio	1997	receivers	49,000	41
Television	1997	receivers	0	0
Telephones	2001	main lines	12,000	9.8
Internet	2001	users	4,000	3.3

Education and health

Educational attainment: n.a. *Literacy* (1995): total population age 15 and over literate 54.9%; males literate 68.0%; females literate 42.5%.

Education (1994–95)				student/ teacher ratio
	schools	teachers	students	
Primary (age 7–13)	...	...	100,369	...
Secondary (age 13–18)	...	...	7,000[8]	...

Health: physicians (1994) 184 (1 per 5,546 persons); hospital beds (1993) 1,300 (1 per 834 persons); infant mortality rate per 1,000 live births (2000) 112.3.
Food (1999): daily per capita caloric intake 2,245 (vegetable products 93%, animal products 7%); 97% of FAO recommended minimum requirement.

Military

Total active duty personnel (2001): 7,250[9] (army 93.8%, navy 4.8%, air force 1.4%). *Military expenditure as percentage of GNP* (1999): 2.7% (world 2.4%); per capita expenditure U.S.$4.

[1]Formerly pegged to the French franc and since Jan. 1, 2002, to the euro at the rate of €1 = CFAF 655.96. [2]Includes water area of about 3,089 sq mi (8,000 sq km). [3]Based on land area of 10,859 sq mi (28,125 sq km). [4]June. [5]Indirect taxes. [6]Detail does not add to total given because of rounding. [7]Imports c.i.f.; exports f.o.b. [8]1993–94. [9]Excludes 2,000 paramilitary (gendarmes).

Internet resources for further information:
- Afristat http://www.afristat.org
- Investir en Zone Franc http://www.izf.net/izf/Index.htm

Guyana

Official name: Co-operative Republic of Guyana.
Form of government: unitary multiparty republic with one legislative house (National Assembly [65[1]]).
Head of state and government: President.
Capital: Georgetown.
Official language: English.
Official religion: none.
Monetary unit: 1 Guyana dollar (G$) = 100 cents; valuation (Sept. 23, 2002) 1 U.S.$ = G$179.00; 1 £ = G$278.18.

Area and population

Administrative Regions		Capitals	area		population
			sq mi	sq km	1986 estimate
Region 1	(Barima–Waini)	Mabaruma	7,853	20,339	18,516
Region 2	(Pomeroon–Supenaam)	Anna Regina	2,392	6,195	41,966
Region 3	(Essequibo Islands–West Demerara)	Vreed en Hoop	1,450	3,755	102,760
Region 4	(Demerara–Mahaica)	Paradise	862	2,233	310,758
Region 5	(Mahaica–Berbice)	Fort Wellington	1,610	4,170	55,556
Region 6	(East Berbice–Corentyne)	New Amsterdam	13,998	36,255	148,967
Region 7	(Cuyuni–Mazaruni)	Bartica	18,229	47,213	17,941
Region 8	(Potaro–Siparuni)	Mahdia	7,742	20,052	5,672
Region 9	(Upper Takutu–Upper Essequibo)	Lethem	22,313	57,790	15,338
Region 10	(Upper Demerara–Berbice)	Linden	6,595	17,081	38,598
TOTAL			83,044[2]	215,083[2]	756,072

Demography

Population (2002): 775,000.
Density (2002)[3]: persons per sq mi 10.2, persons per sq km 3.9.
Urban-rural (2001): urban 36.7%; rural 63.3%.
Sex distribution (2000): male 48.49%; female 51.51%.
Age breakdown (2000): under 15, 30.6%; 15–29, 31.0%; 30–44, 21.0%; 45–59, 10.4%; 60–74, 5.1%; 75 and over, 1.9%.
Population projection: (2010) 774,000; (2020) 739,000.
Doubling time: 74 years.
Ethnic composition (1992–93): East Indian 49.4%; black (African Negro and Bush Negro) 35.6%; mixed 7.1%; Amerindian 6.8%; Portuguese 0.7%; Chinese 0.4%.
Religious affiliation (1995): Christian 40.9%, of which Protestant 27.5% (including Anglican 8.6%), Roman Catholic 11.5%, Ethiopian Orthodox 1.1%; Hindu 34.0%; Muslim 9.0%; other 16.1%.
Major cities (1997): Georgetown 230,000 (urban agglomeration [2001] 280,000); Linden 35,000; New Amsterdam 25,000; Corriverton 24,000.

Vital statistics

Birth rate per 1,000 population (2000): 17.9 (world avg. 22.5).
Death rate per 1,000 population (2000): 8.4 (world avg. 9.0).
Natural increase rate per 1,000 population (2000): 9.5 (world avg. 13.5).
Total fertility rate (avg. births per childbearing woman; 2000): 2.1.
Life expectancy at birth (2000): male 61.1 years; female 67.2 years.
Major causes of death per 100,000 population (1994)[4]: diseases of the circulatory system 274.3, of which cerebrovascular disease 99.2, ischemic heart diseases 75.2, diseases of pulmonary circulation and other forms of heart disease 57.9; accidents and violence 76.1; endocrine and metabolic disorders 58.9; diseases of the respiratory system 50.1.

National economy

Budget (1999): Revenue: G$36,544,000,000 (tax revenue 91.6%, of which consumption taxes 32.0%, income taxes on companies 22.2%, personal income taxes 15.5%, import duties 11.4%; nontax revenue 8.2%). Expenditures: G$41,983,000,000 (current expenditure 71.2%, of which debt charges 13.8%; development expenditure 28.8%).
Production (metric tons except as noted). Agriculture, forestry, fishing (1999): rice 365,469, raw sugar 321,438, coconuts 56,449, cassava (manioc) 25,957, plantains 14,000, bananas 11,177, pineapples 7,000; livestock (number of live animals) 220,000 cattle, 130,000 sheep, 11,600,000 chickens; roundwood 442,000 cu m; fish catch 54,450, of which shrimps and prawns 12,153. Mining and quarrying (2001): bauxite 2,011,901; gold 455,918 troy oz; diamonds 184,309 carats. Manufacturing (1999): flour 35,290; rum 137,800 hectolitres; beer and stout 129,200 hectolitres; soft drinks 3,975,000 cases; pharmaceuticals 7,600,000 tablets; garments 2,900,000 units. Construction: n.a. Energy production (consumption): electricity (kW-hr; 2001) 505,000,000 ([1997] 404,000,000); coal, none (none); crude petroleum, none (none); petroleum products (metric tons; 1997) none (333,000); natural gas, none (none).
Population economically active (1992–93): total 278,000; activity rate of total population 38.8% (participation rates: ages 15–64, 61.8%; female 34.1%; unemployed [1998] *c.* 12%).

Price and earnings indexes (1995 = 100)

	1995	1996	1997	1998	1999	2000	2001
Consumer price index[5]	100.0	107.1	110.9	116.0	124.7	131.9	134.0
Earnings index	...	...	...	...	...	...	...

Gross national product (at current market prices; 2000): U.S.$652,000,000 (U.S.$860 per capita).

Structure of gross domestic product and labour force

	1999		1980	
	in value G$'000,000	% of total value	labour force	% of labour force
Sugar	16,142[6]	13.4[6]	} 50,316	20.4
Other agriculture	17,543[7]	14.5[7]		
Fishing, forestry	8,851	7.3		
Mining	13,923	11.5	9,669	3.9
Manufacturing	3,681[8, 9]	3.1[8, 9]	28,980	11.8
Construction	4,771	4.0	7,024	2.8
Public utilities	[9]	[9]	2,850	1.2
Transp. and commun.	7,138	5.9	9,412	3.8
Trade	4,268	3.5	15,231	6.2
Finance, real estate	7,235	6.0	2,944	1.2
Pub. admin., defense	16,976	14.1	29,948	12.1
Services	1,570	1.3	29,295	11.9
Other	18,570[10]	15.4[10]	61,002[11]	24.7[11]
TOTAL	120,668	100.0	246,671	100.0

Public debt (external, outstanding; 2000): U.S.$1,209,000,000.
Household income and expenditure. Average household size (1997) 4.5.
Tourism: receipts from visitors (1999) U.S.$59,000,000; expenditures by nationals abroad (1997) U.S.$22,000,000.
Land use (1994): forested 83.8%; meadows and pastures 6.3%; agricultural and under permanent cultivation 2.5%; other 7.4%.

Foreign trade[12]

Balance of trade (current prices)

	1996	1997	1998	1999	2000	2001
U.S.$'000,000	−20.2	−34.2	−54.2	−25.2	−80.2	−93.6
% of total	1.7%	2.8%	4.7%	2.3%	7.4%	8.7%

Imports (2001): U.S.$583,900,000 (consumer goods 28.3%, fuels and lubricants 22.5%, capital goods 19.7%). *Major import sources* (1999)[13]: U.S. 29%; Trinidad and Tobago 18%; Netherlands Antilles 16%; U.K. 7%; Cuba 3%.
Exports (2001): U.S.$490,300,000 (gold 25.9%, sugar 22.3%, bauxite 12.4%, rice 10.2%, shrimp 10.1%, timber 6.7%). *Major export destinations* (1999)[13]: U.S. 22%; Canada 22%; U.K. 18%; Netherlands Antilles 11%; Jamaica 5%.

Transport and communications

Transport. Railroads: [14]. Roads (1999): total length 4,952 mi, 7,970 km (paved 7%). Vehicles (1995): passenger cars 24,000; trucks and buses 9,000. Air transport (1998)[15]: passenger-mi 144,000,000, passenger-km 231,000,000; (1996) short ton-mi cargo 2,300,000, metric ton-km cargo 3,300,000; airports (1996) with scheduled flights 1[16].

Communications

Medium	date	unit	number	units per 1,000 persons
Daily newspapers	1996	circulation	42,000	54
Radio	1997	receivers	420,000	539
Television	1999	receivers	60,000	77
Telephones	2001	main lines	79,900	92
Cellular telephones	2001	subscribers	39,500	45
Personal computers	2001	units	23,000	26
Internet	2001	users	95,000	109

Education and health

Educational attainment (1980). Percentage of population age 25 and over having: no formal schooling 8.1%; primary education 72.8%; secondary 17.3%; higher 1.8%. *Literacy* (1995): total population age 15 and over literate, *c.* 511,000 (98.1%); males literate, *c.* 254,000 (98.6%); females literate, *c.* 257,000 (97.5%).

Education (1996–97)

	schools	teachers	students	student/ teacher ratio
Primary (age 6–11)	420	3,461	102,000	29.5
Secondary (age 12–17)	...	2,150[17]	62,043	29.5[17]
Higher	...	612[17]	8,965	12.5[17]

Health: physicians (1998) 334 (1 per 2,326 persons); hospital beds 3,293 (1 per 236 persons); infant mortality rate per 1,000 live births (2000) 39.1.
Food (1999): daily per capita caloric intake 2,569 (vegetable products 84%, animal products 16%); 113% of FAO recommended minimum requirement.

Military

Total active duty personnel (2001): 1,600 (army 87.5%, navy 6.3%, air force 6.2%). *Military expenditure as percentage of GNP* (1998): 0.8% (world 2.4%); per capita expenditure U.S.$7.

---

[1]Includes 12 indirectly elected seats. [2]Includes inland water area equaling *c.* 7,000 sq mi (*c.* 18,000 sq km). [3]Based on land area only. [4]Projected rates based on about 78% of total deaths. [5]Weights of consumer price index components for Georgetown only. [6]Includes sugar manufacturing. [7]Includes rice manufacturing. [8]Excludes sugar and rice manufacturing. [9]Manufacturing includes Public utilities. [10]Indirect taxes less subsidies. [11]Represents "not stated." [12]Imports c.i.f.; exports f.o.b. [13]Estimated figures. [14]No public railways. [15]Scheduled traffic only. [16]International only; domestic air service is provided on a charter basis. [17]1995–96.

Internet resources for further information:
- **Bank of Guyana**
  http://www.bankofguyana.org.gy
- **UNDP Common Country Assessment**
  http://www.undp.org.gy/ccassess.pdf

Haiti

Official name: Repiblik Dayti (Haitian Creole); République d'Haïti (French) (Republic of Haiti).
Form of government: multiparty republic with two legislative houses (Senate [27[1]]; Chamber of Deputies [83]).
Chief of state: President.
Head of government: Prime Minister.
Capital: Port-au-Prince.
Official languages: Haitian Creole; French.
Official religion: none[2].
Monetary unit: 1 gourde (G) = 100 centimes; valuation (Sept. 23, 2002) 1 U.S.\$ = G 28.00; 1 £ = G 43.51.

Area and population		area		population
				1997
Departements	**Capitals**	sq mi	sq km	estimate
Artibonite	Gonaïves	1,924	4,984	1,052,834
Centre	Hinche	1,419	3,675	508,199
Grand'Anse	Jérémie	1,278	3,310	660,420
Nord	Cap-Haïtien	813	2,106	785,687
Nord-Est	Fort-Liberté	697	1,805	255,601
Nord-Ouest	Port-de-Paix	840	2,176	439,984
Ouest	Port-au-Prince	1,864	4,827	2,651,115
Sud	Les Cayes	1,079	2,794	671,112
Sud-Est	Jacmel	781	2,023	466,810
TOTAL		10,695	27,700	7,491,762[3]

Demography

Population (2002): 7,064,000[4].
Density (2002): persons per sq mi 660.5, persons per sq km 255.0.
Urban-rural (2001): urban 36.3%; rural 63.7%.
Sex distribution (2000): male 49.26%; female 50.74%.
Age breakdown (2000): under 15, 41.1%; 15–29, 28.7%; 30–44, 15.2%; 45–59, 8.6%; 60–74, 5.0%; 75 and over, 1.4%.
Population projection[4]: (2010) 7,950,000; (2020) 9,072,000.
Doubling time: 41 years.
Ethnic composition (2000): black 94.2%; mulatto 5.4%; other/unspecified 0.4%.
Religious affiliation (1995): Roman Catholic 68.5%[5]; Protestant 24.1%, of which Baptist 5.9%, Pentecostal 5.3%, Seventh-day Adventist 4.6%; other 7.4%.
Major cities (1997): Port-au-Prince 917,112 (metropolitan area 1,556,588); Carrefour 306,074[6]; Delmas 257,247[6]; Cap-Haïtien 107,026; Pétion-Ville 76,155[6].

Vital statistics

Birth rate per 1,000 population (2000): 32.0 (world avg. 22.5).
Death rate per 1,000 population (2000): 15.1 (world avg. 9.0).
Natural increase rate per 1,000 population (2000): 16.9 (world avg. 13.5).
Total fertility rate (avg. births per childbearing woman; 2000): 4.5.
Life expectancy at birth (2000): male 47.5 years; female 51.1 years.
Major causes of death per 100,000 population (1982)[7]: infectious and parasitic diseases 46.0; diseases of the circulatory system 11.9; diseases associated with malnutrition 8.5; ill-defined conditions 115.2.

National economy

Budget (2001)[8]. Revenue: G 6,509,000,000 (general sales tax 31.3%; customs duties 27.2%; individual taxes on income and profits 13.7%). Expenditures: G 8,728,000,000 (current expenditure 81.9%, of which interest on public debt 8.8%; capital expenditure 18.1%).
Production (metric tons except as noted). Agriculture, forestry, fishing (1999): sugarcane 1,000,100, cassava (manioc) 325,000, plantains 290,000, bananas 290,000, mangoes 225,000, corn (maize) 215,000, yams 195,000, sweet potatoes 172,000, rice 102,000, sorghum 96,000, avocados 45,000, coffee 28,000, sisal 5,700, cacao 4,500; livestock (number of live animals) 1,618,000 goats, 1,300,000 cattle, 800,000 pigs, 490,000 horses; roundwood (1998) 6,397,000 cu m; fish catch 5,000. Mining and quarrying: small amounts of limestone, calcareous clay, salt, and marble. Manufacturing (1999–2000): soap 30,070; rum 21,750 hectolitres; malt liquor and beer 18,800,000 bottles; articles assembled for reexport (gross export value in U.S.\$'000,000; 1999–2000) 270.3, of which garments 255.3, leather manufactures from domestic sources 3.6; sports equipment and toys 2.8; cement and essential oils (mostly amyris, neroli, and vetiver) are also manufactured. Energy production (consumption): electricity (kW-hr; 1997) 633,000,000 (633,000,000); coal (metric tons) none (none); crude petroleum, none (none); petroleum products (metric tons; 1997) none (453,000); natural gas, none (none).
Land use (1994): forested 5.1%; meadows and pastures 18.0%; agricultural and under permanent cultivation 33.0%; other 43.9%.
Population economically active (1996): total 3,209,000; activity rate of total population 49.3% (participation rates: ages 15–64 [1990] 64.8%; female 43.0%; unemployed unofficially about 60%).

Price and earnings indexes (1995 = 100)							
	1996	1997	1998	1999	2000	2001	2002
Consumer price index	120.6	145.4	160.8	174.8	198.7	226.9	244.5[9]
Daily earnings index[10]	100.0	100.0	100.0	100.0	100.0	100.0	...

Household income and expenditure. Average household size (1982) 4.4; average annual income of urban wage earners (1984): G 1,545 (U.S.\$309); expenditure (1996)[11]: food, beverages, and tobacco 49.4%, housing and energy 9.1%, transportation 8.7%, clothing and footwear 8.5%.
Public debt (external, outstanding; 2000): U.S.\$1,040,000,000.
Gross national product (2000): U.S.\$4,059,000,000 (U.S.\$510 per capita).

Structure of gross domestic product and labour force				
	1997–98[12]		1990	
	in value G '000,000[13]	% of total value	labour force	% of labour force
Agriculture, forestry	1,403	30.2	1,535,444	57.3
Mining	10	0.2	24,012	0.9
Manufacturing	330	7.1	151,387	5.6
Construction	562	12.1	28,001	1.0
Public utilities	42	0.9	2,577	0.1
Transp. and commun.	98	2.1	20,691	0.8
Trade, restaurants	622	13.4	352,970	13.2
Finance, real estate	366	7.9	5,057	0.2
Services	216	4.6 }	155,347	5.8
Pub. admin., defense	829	17.8 }		
Other	174[14]	3.7[14]	403,654[15]	15.1[15]
TOTAL	4,652	100.0	2,679,140	100.0

Tourism (2000): receipts from visitors U.S.\$54,000,000; expenditures by nationals abroad (1998) U.S.\$37,000,000.

Foreign trade[12, 16, 17]

Balance of trade (current prices)						
	1996	1997	1998	1999	2000	2001
U.S.\$'000,000	–469.8	–497.8	–522.7	–600.4	–698.0	–693.9
% of total	58.0%	54.8%	46.6%	46.9%	52.5%	54.2%

Imports (2001): U.S.\$1,061,500,000 (food and live animals 24.6%, basic manufactures 20.0%, machinery and transport equipment 16.5%, petroleum and derivatives 15.4%). *Major import sources* (1999)[18]: United States 60%; Dominican Republic 4%; Japan 3%; France 3%; Canada 3%.
Exports (2001): U.S.\$293,300,000 (reexports 85.7%, of which clothing 83.9%; handicrafts and related products [including wood carvings, paintings, woven sisal products, and ceramics] 2.7%; cacao 2.4%). *Major export destinations* (1999)[18]: United States 90%; Canada 3%; Belgium 2%, France 2%.

Transport and communications

Transport. Railroad (1998) none. Roads (1999): total length 2,585 mi, 4,160 km (paved 24%). Vehicles (1996): passenger cars 32,000; trucks and buses 21,000. Air transport (2000)[19]: passenger arrivals and departures 924,000; cargo unloaded and loaded 15,300 metric tons; airports (1997) with scheduled flights 2.

Communications				units per 1,000
Medium	**date**	**unit**	**number**	**persons**
Daily newspapers	1996	circulation	20,000	3.1
Radio	1997	receivers	415,000	63
Television	1997	receivers	38,000	5.8
Telephones	2001	main lines	80,000	10
Cellular telephones	2001	subscribers	91,500	11
Internet	2001	users	30,000	3.6

Education and health

Educational attainment (1986–87). Percentage of population age 25 and over having: no formal schooling 59.5%; primary education 30.5%; secondary 8.6%; vocational and teacher training 0.7%; higher 0.7%. *Literacy* (1995): total population age 15 and over literate 1,930,000 (45.0%); males literate 992,000 (48.0%); females literate 938,000 (42.2%).

Education (1994–95)	schools	teachers	students	student/ teacher ratio
Primary (age 6–12)	10,071	30,205	1,110,398	36.8
Secondary (age 13–18) } Voc., teacher tr. }	1,038	...	195,418	...
Higher[20, 21]	2	817	12,204	14.9

Health: physicians (1994–95) 641[22] (1 per 9,989 persons); hospital beds (1996) 5,241 (1 per 1,242 persons); infant mortality rate (2000) 97.1.
Food (1999): daily per capita caloric intake 1,977 (vegetable products 94%, animal products 6%); 87% of FAO recommended minimum requirement.

Military

Total active duty personnel: [23].

[1]Statutory membership. [2]Roman Catholicism has special recognition. [3]Official population projection based on 1982 census. [4]De facto estimate(s). [5]About 80% of all Roman Catholics also practice voodoo. [6]Within Port-au-Prince metropolitan area. [7]Public health facilities only. [8]Does not include projects financed with loans and grants. [9]April. [10]Standard minimum wage rate. [11]Weights of consumer price index components. [12]For fiscal year ending September 30. [13]At prices of 1975–76. [14]Indirect taxes including import duties. [15]Includes 63,975 not adequately defined and 339,679 officially unemployed. [16]Includes reexports. [17]Import figures are f.o.b. in balance of trade and c.i.f. in commodities and trading partners. [18]Estimated percentages. [19]Port-au-Prince Airport only. [20]Port-au-Prince universities only. [21]1997–98. [22]Public health services only. [23]The Haitian army was disbanded in 1995. The national police force had 5,300 personnel in 2001.

Internet resources for further information:
• **Embassy of Haiti (Washington, D.C.) (mostly French language)** http://www.haiti.org
• **Banque de la République d'Haïti** http://www.brh.net

Honduras

Official name: República de Honduras (Republic of Honduras).
Form of government: multiparty republic with one legislative house (National Assembly [128]).
Head of state and government: President.
Capital: Tegucigalpa[1].
Official language: Spanish.
Official religion: none.
Monetary unit: 1 Honduran lempira (L) = 100 centavos; valuation (Sept. 23, 2002) 1 U.S.$ = L 16.65; 1 £ = L 25.88.

Area and population

Departments	Administrative centres	area sq mi	area sq km	population 1996 estimate
Atlántida	La Ceiba	1,641	4,251	305,000
Choluteca	Choluteca	1,626	4,211	368,000
Colón	Trujillo	3,427	8,875	196,000
Comayagua	Comayagua	2,006	5,196	316,000
Copán	Santa Rosa de Copán	1,237	3,203	277,000
Cortés	San Pedro Sula	1,527	3,954	826,000
El Paraíso	Yuscarán	2,787	7,218	322,000
Francisco Morazán	Tegucigalpa	3,068	7,946	1,018,000
Gracias a Dios	Puerto Lempira	6,421	16,630	47,000
Intibucá	La Esperanza	1,186	3,072	158,000
Islas de la Bahía	Roatán	100	261	28,000
La Paz	La Paz	900	2,331	137,000
Lempira	Gracias	1,656	4,290	224,000
Ocotepeque	Nueva Ocotepeque	649	1,680	94,000
Olancho	Juticalpa	9,402	24,351	373,000
Santa Bárbara	Santa Bárbara	1,975	5,115	347,000
Valle	Nacaome	604	1,565	150,000
Yoro	Yoro	3,065	7,939	423,000
TOTAL		43,277[2]	112,088[2]	5,609,000

Demography

Population (2002): 6,561,000.
Density (2002)[3]: persons per sq mi 151.1, persons per sq km 58.3.
Urban-rural (2001): urban 53.7%; rural 46.3%.
Sex distribution (1999): male 48.94%; female 51.06%.
Age breakdown (1998): under 15, 42.6%; 15–29, 28.4%; 30–44, 16.2%; 45–59, 7.8%; 60–74, 3.9%; 75 and over, 1.1%.
Population projection: (2010) 7,683,000; (2020) 8,826,000.
Doubling time: 26 years.
Ethnic composition (2000): mestizo 86.6%; Amerindian 5.5%; black (including Black Carib) 4.3%; white 2.3%; other 1.3%.
Religious affiliation (1995): Roman Catholic 86.7%; Protestant 10.4%, of which Pentecostal 5.7%; other 2.9%.
Major cities (2000): Tegucigalpa 1,037,600[4]; San Pedro Sula 471,000; El Progreso 109,400; La Ceiba 107,200; Choluteca 96,900.

Vital statistics

Birth rate per 1,000 population (2000): 32.7 (world avg. 22.5).
Death rate per 1,000 population (2000): 5.3 (world avg. 9.0).
Natural increase rate per 1,000 population (2000): 27.4 (world avg. 13.5).
Total fertility rate (avg. births per childbearing woman; 2000): 4.3.
Life expectancy at birth (2000): male 67.9 years; female 72.1 years.
Major causes of death per 100,000 population (1983): diseases of the circulatory system 48.4; infectious and parasitic diseases 46.6; accidents and violence 42.2; diseases of the respiratory system 26.3.

National economy

Budget (1998). Revenue: L 13,197,000,000 (current revenue 99.8%, of which indirect taxes 65.1%, direct taxes 25.6%, nontax revenue 6.9%, transfers 2.2%). Expenditures: L 11,367,000,000 (current expenditure 72.6%; capital expenditure 27.4%).
Public debt (external, outstanding; 2000): U.S.$4,337,000,000.
Production (metric tons except as noted). Agriculture, forestry, fishing (1999): sugarcane 4,286,000, bananas 861,000, oil palm fruit 522,000, corn (maize) 478,000, plantains 250,000, coffee 164,000, oranges 79,000, cantaloupes 78,000, sorghum 71,000, pineapples 70,000; livestock (number of live animals) 2,061,000 cattle, 700,000 pigs, 18,000,0000 chickens; roundwood (1998) 7,176,000 cu m; fish catch (1998) 14,881. Mining and quarrying (1997): gypsum 28,000; zinc 25,500; salt 25,500; lead 3,400; gold 150 kilograms. Manufacturing (value added in L '000,000; 1996): food products 1,937.3; wearing apparel 1,266.4; beverages 699.6; nonmetallic mineral products 503.6; wood products 325.7; consumer chemicals 319.7. Construction (value of private construction in L '000,000; 1999)[5]: residential 813.8; nonresidential 890.7. Energy production (consumption): electricity (kW-hr; 1997) 3,097,000,000 (3,252,000,000); coal, none (none); crude petroleum (barrels; 1992) none (3,064,000); petroleum products (metric tons; 1996) none (1,157,000).
Household income and expenditure. Average household size (1988) 5.4; income per household: n.a.; sources of income (1985): wages and salaries 58.8%, transfer payments 1.8%, other 39.4%; expenditure (1986): food 44.4%, utilities and housing 22.4%, clothing and footwear 9.0%, household furnishings 8.3%, health care 7.0%, transportation 3.0%, other 5.9%.
Land use (1998): forested and other 67.9%; meadows and pastures 13.8%; agricultural and under permanent cultivation 18.3%.
Gross national product (at current market prices; 2000): U.S.$5,517,000,000 (U.S.$860 per capita).

Structure of gross domestic product and labour force

	1999 in value L '000,000[6]	% of total value	labour force	% of labour force
Agriculture	10,635	16.2	834,900	39.2
Mining	1,325	2.0	4,200	0.2
Manufacturing	12,916	19.6	249,000	11.7
Construction	3,516	5.4	158,300	7.4
Public utilities	3,208	4.9	20,100	0.9
Transp. and commun.	3,423	5.2	58,600	2.7
Trade	8,365	12.7	240,400	11.3
Finance, real estate	10,950	16.7	48,400	2.3
Public admin., defense	4,153	6.3 }	517,400	24.3
Services	7,261	11.0 }		
TOTAL	65,752	100.0	2,131,300	100.0

Population economically active (1999): total 2,131,300; activity rate of total population 33.4% (participation rates: over age 15 [1998] 61.2%; female [1998] 34.6%; unemployed [1998] 4.3%).

Price and earnings indexes (1995 = 100)

	1995	1996	1997	1998	1999	2000	2001
Consumer price index	100.0	123.8	148.8	169.2	188.9	209.8	230.1
Daily earnings index[7]	100.0	119.3	158.0	184.9	...	...	...

Tourism (2000): receipts U.S.$262,000,000; expenditures U.S.$99,000,000.

Foreign trade[8]

Balance of trade (current prices)

	1996	1997	1998	1999	2000	2001
U.S.$'000,000	−524	−703	−923	−1,424	−1,485	−1,600
% of total	16.6%	19.6%	22.6%	35.3%	35.1%	37.8%

Imports (1999): U.S.$2,727,800,000 (machinery and electrical equipment 20.8%, industrial chemicals 13.0%, transport equipment 12.1%, food products 10.3%, mineral fuels and lubricants 9.4%). *Major import sources:* United States 47.1%; Guatemala 7.4%; Mexico 4.8%; Japan 4.7%; Costa Rica 2.5%.
Exports (1999): U.S.$1,303,900,000 (coffee 20.5%, shrimp and lobsters 15.5%, melons 3.7%, lead and zinc 3.4%). *Major export destinations:* United States 35.4%; Germany 7.5%; El Salvador 6.4%; Guatemala 5.8%; Nicaragua 4.8%.

Transport and communications

Transport. Railroads (2000): serviceable lines c. 127 mi (c. 205 km); most track are out of use but not dismantled. Roads (1999): total length 9,073 mi, 14,602 km (paved 18%). Vehicles (1995): passenger cars 81,439; trucks and buses 170,006. Air transport (1995): passenger-mi 212,000,000, passenger-km 341,000,000; short ton-mi cargo 23,000,000, metric ton-km cargo 33,000,000; airports (1996) with scheduled flights 8.

Communications

Medium	date	unit	number	units per 1,000 persons
Daily newspapers	1996	circulation	320,000	55
Radio	1997	receivers	2,450,000	410
Television	1999	receivers	600,000	95
Telephones	2001	main lines	309,700	47
Cellular telephones	2001	subscribers	237,600	36
Personal computers	2001	units	80,000	12
Internet	2000	users	40,000	6.1

Education and health

Educational attainment (1988). Percentage of population age 10 and over having: no formal schooling 33.4%; primary education 50.1%; secondary education 13.4%; higher 3.1%. *Literacy* (1995): total population age 15 and over literate 72.7%; males literate 72.6%; females literate 72.7%.

Education (1999)

	schools	teachers	students	student/ teacher ratio
Primary (age 7–13)	8,768	33,431	1,099,714	32.9
Secondary (age 14–19) } Voc., teacher tr.	661[9]	14,539	187,561	12.9
Higher	8[9]	3,600	52,139	14.5

Health: physicians (1993) 3,803 (1 per 1,358 persons); hospital beds (1999) 5,720 (1 per 1,098 persons); infant mortality rate (2000) 31.3.
Food (2000): daily per capita caloric intake 2,395 (vegetable products 86%, animal products 14%); (1997) 106% of FAO recommended minimum.

Military

Total active duty personnel (2001): 8,300 (army 66.3%, navy 12.0%, air force 21.7%). *Military expenditure as percentage of GNP* (1999): 0.7% (world 2.4%); per capita expenditure U.S.$6.

---

[1]Tegucigalpa and the adjacent urban area of Comayagüela jointly form the capital according to the constitution. [2]Area as of 1992 judgment of the International Court of Justice is 43,433 sq mi (112,492 sq km); breakdown by department is not available. [3]Based on the revised area. [4]Population cited is for Central District (Tegucigalpa and Comayagüela). [5]Tegucigalpa, San Pedro Sula, and 10 other urban centres. [6]At factor cost. [7]Official minimum wages in all sectors. [8]Imports c.i.f.; exports f.o.b. [9]1995.

Internet resources for further information:
• **Banco Central de Honduras** http://www.bch.hn
• **Instituto Nacional de Estadística** http://www.ine.online.hn

Hong Kong

Official name: Xianggang Tebie Xingzhengqu (Chinese); Hong Kong Special Administrative Region (English).
Political status: special administrative region[1] (People's Republic of China) with one legislative house (Legislative Council [60[2]]).
Chief of state: President of China.
Head of government: Chief Executive.
Government offices: Central & Western District (formerly Victoria), Hong Kong Island.
Official languages: Chinese; English.
Official religion: none.
Monetary unit: 1 Hong Kong dollar (HK$) = 100 cents; valuation (Sept. 23, 2002) 1 U.S.$ = HK$7.80; 1 £ = HK$12.12.

Area and population		area	population
			2001
Area	sq mi	sq km	census
Hong Kong Island	31.0	80.4	1,335,469
Kowloon and New Kowloon	18.1	46.8	2,023,979
New Territories	375.0	971.3	3,343,046
Marine	—	—	5,895
TOTAL	424.1	1,098.5	6,708,389

Demography

Population (2002): 6,785,000.
Density (2002): persons per sq mi 15,999, persons per sq km 6,177.
Urban-rural (2001): urban 100.0%.
Sex distribution (2002): male 48.63%; female 51.37%.
Age breakdown (2002): under 15, 16.1%; 15–29, 20.6%; 30–44, 28.9%; 45–59, 19.4%; 60–74, 10.4%; 75 and over, 4.6%.
Population projection: (2010) 7,401,000; (2020) 8,083,000.
Place of birth (1996)[3]: Hong Kong 60.3%; China or Macau 33.7%; other 6.0%.
Religious affiliation (1994): Buddhist and Taoist 73.8%; Christian 8.4%, of which Protestant 4.3%, Roman Catholic 4.1%; New Religionist 3.2%; Muslim 0.8%; Hindu 0.2%; nonreligious/atheist 13.5%; other 0.1%.

Vital statistics

Birth rate per 1,000 population (2001): 7.2 (world avg. 21.2).
Death rate per 1,000 population (2001): 5.0 (world avg. 8.9).
Natural increase rate per 1,000 population (2001): 2.2 (world avg. 12.3).
Total fertility rate (avg. births per childbearing woman; 2000): 1.3.
Marriage rate per 1,000 population (2001): 4.8.
Life expectancy at birth (2001): male 78.4 years; female 84.6 years.
Major causes of death per 100,000 population (2000): malignant neoplasms (cancers) 167.7; diseases of the circulatory system 139.9; diseases of the respiratory system 86.2; accidents and poisoning 31.4; diseases of the genitourinary system 23.4; diseases of the digestive system 20.5.

National economy

Budget (2000–01). Revenue: HK$222,855,000,000 (earning and profit taxes 32.0%; capital revenue 23.9%; indirect taxes 23.2%, of which entertainment and stamp duties 11.3%, duties 3.3%). Expenditures: HK$278,388,000,000 (housing 18.7%; education 18.6%; health 11.6%; social welfare 10.2%; law and order 9.7%; transportation and public works 8.2%; environment and food 4.1%).
Gross domestic product (2000): U.S.$162,397,000,000 (U.S.$24,360 per capita).

Structure of gross domestic product and labour force				
	2000		1998	
	in value HK$'000,000	% of total value	labour force	% of labour force
Agriculture	920	0.1		
Mining	241	—	391,900	11.7
Manufacturing	71,655	5.6		
Construction	64,026	5.0	319,500	9.5
Public utilities	38,853	3.0	[4]	[4]
Transp. and commun.	125,724	9.8	363,300	10.8
Trade	324,622	25.2	973,900	29.0
Finance, insurance, and real estate	291,062	22.6	419,000	12.5
Pub. admin., defense, and services	252,435	19.6	705,300	21.0
Other	117,266[5]	9.1[5]	185,800[4, 6]	5.5[4, 6]
TOTAL	1,286,804	100.0	3,358,700	100.0

Production (metric tons except as noted). Agriculture, forestry, fishing (2000): vegetables 42,500, fruits and nuts 2,022, field crops 508, milk 259, eggs 3,710,000 units; livestock (number of live animals) 446,000 pigs[7], 120 cattle; roundwood (1996) 206,000 cu m; fish catch (2000) 157,012. Manufacturing (value added in HK$; 1999): publishing and printed materials 10,748,000,000; electrical and electronic products 8,279,000,000; textiles 7,276,000,000; wearing apparel 7,240,000,000; food 5,213,000,000; machinery and equipment 4,849,000,000; transport equipment 3,031,000,000; basic metals and fabricated metal products 2,667,000,000. Construction (1998)[8]: residential 1,564,000 sq m; nonresidential 1,652,000 sq m. Energy production (consumption): elec-

tricity (kW-hr; 1997) 28,943,000,000 (36,260,000,000); coal (metric tons; 1997) none (5,711,000); petroleum products (metric tons; 1997) none (3,358,000).
Population economically active (2000): total 3,382,700; activity rate of total population 49.3% (participation rates: over age 15, 60.7%; female 49.1%; unemployed 5.0%).

Price and earnings indexes (1995 = 100)						
	1995	1996	1997	1998	1999	2000	2001
Consumer price index	100.0	106.3	112.5	115.7	111.1	106.9	105.2
Daily earnings index	...	...	...	...	...	...	...

Household income and expenditure. Average household size (2001) 3.2; monthly income per household (1996) HK$17,500 (U.S.$2,300); sources of income: n.a.; expenditure (1994–95): food 29.5%, housing 28.8%, transportation and vehicles 7.8%, clothing and footwear 6.7%, durable goods 5.5%.
Tourism (2000): receipts from visitors U.S.$7,886,000,000.
Land use (1995): forested 20.1%; agricultural and under permanent cultivation 5.8%; fishponds 1.5%; built-on, scrublands, and other 72.6%.

Foreign trade[9]

Balance of trade (current prices)						
	1996	1997	1998	1999	2000	2001
HK$'000,000	−137,664	−159,141	−81,443	−43,718	−85,273	−87,208
% of total	4.7%	5.8%	2.9%	1.6%	2.6%	2.9%

Imports (2001): HK$1,568,194,000,000 (machinery and transport equipment 43.9%, manufactured goods 16.2%, chemicals and other related products 5.7%, food and beverages 4.1%, mineral fuels and lubricants 2.0%). *Major import sources:* China 43.5%; Japan 11.3%; Taiwan 6.9%; U.S. 6.7%; Singapore 4.6%; South Korea 4.5%.
Exports (2001): HK$153,520,000,000[10] (clothing accessories and apparel 47.1%, electrical machinery 13.2%, textile fabrics 5.3%, office and automatic data-processing machines 3.1%, jewelry 3.1%, printed materials 2.6%, telecommunications equipment 2.3%, watches and clocks 1.5%, articles of artificial resins and plastics 0.7%). *Major export destinations:* China 32.3%; U.S. 31.0%; U.K. 5.6%; Germany 3.8%; Taiwan 3.5%; The Netherlands 3.0%.

Transport and communications

Transport. Railroads (1995): route length 21 mi, 34 km; passenger-mi 2,231,-000,000, passenger-km 3,591,000,000; short ton-mi cargo 68,000,000[11], metric ton-km cargo 99,000,000[11]. Roads (2001): total length 1,187 mi, 1,911 km (paved 100%). Vehicles (2001): passenger cars 341,000; trucks and buses 132,000. Air transport (2001): passenger arrivals 11,533,000, passenger departures 11,488,000; airports (2000) with scheduled flights 1.

Communications				units per 1,000
Medium	date	unit	number	persons
Daily newspapers	1996	circulation	5,000,000	792
Radio	1998	receivers	3,700,000	553
Television	1998	receivers	1,749,000	262
Telephones	2001	main lines	3,926,000	584
Cellular telephones	2001	subscribers	5,701,700	848
Personal computers	2001	units	2,600,000	387
Internet	2001	users	3,100,000	461

Education and health

Educational attainment (1996). Percentage of population age 15 and over having: no formal schooling 9.5%; primary education 22.6%; secondary 46.6%; matriculation 6.1%; nondegree higher 4.8%; higher degree 10.4%.
Literacy (1995): total population age 15 and over literate 92.2%; males literate 96.0%; females literate 88.2%.

Education (2000–2001)				student/
	schools	teachers[12]	students	teacher ratio[12]
Primary (age 6–11)	816	22,344	493,979	22.0
Secondary (age 12–18)	525	24,453	456,693	18.5
Vocational	1[13]	1,058	22,279	21.0
Higher	28	5,892	59,479	10.1

Health (2000): physicians 10,130[14] (1 per 658 persons); hospital beds 35,100 (1 per 190 persons); infant mortality rate per 1,000 live births (2001) 2.6.
Food (1999): daily per capita caloric intake 3,231 (vegetable products 63%, animal products 37%); 141% of FAO recommended minimum requirement.

Military

Total active duty personnel (2001): 7,000 Chinese troops to intervene in local matters only at the request of the Hong Kong government.

[1]On July 1, 1997, Hong Kong reverted to China as a special administrative region in which the existing socioeconomic system would remain unchanged for a period of 50 years. [2]24 seats are directly elected by ordinary voters; the remaining 36 seats are elected/appointed by special interest groups and a committee. [3]Per special census. [4]Other includes Public utilities. [5]Indirect taxes less subsidies. [6]Includes 157,600 unemployed. [7]Excludes local pigs not slaughtered in abattoirs. [8]Usable floor area only. [9]Imports are c.i.f., exports f.o.b. [10]Excludes reexports valued at HK$1,327,467,000,000. [11]1994. [12]1999–2000. [13]The Hong Kong Institute of Vocational Education was formed in 1999. It is composed of the two former technical colleges and the seven former technical institutes. [14]Registered personnel; all may not be present and working in the country.

Internet resources for further information:
• **Census and Statistics Department http://www.info.gov.hk/censtatd**

Hungary

Official name: Magyar Köztársaság
(Republic of Hungary).
Form of government: unitary multi-party republic with one legislative
house (National Assembly [386]).
Chief of state: President.
Head of government: Prime Minister.
Capital: Budapest.
Official language: Hungarian.
Official religion: none.
Monetary unit: 1 forint (Ft) = 100
filler; valuation (Sept. 23, 2002)
1 U.S.$ = Ft 247.24;
1 £ = Ft 384.24.

Area and population

Counties	Capitals	area sq mi	area sq km	population 2001 census
Bács-Kiskun	Kecskemét	3,261	8,445	546,753
Baranya	Pécs	1,710	4,430	408,019
Békés	Békéscsaba	2,174	5,631	397,074
Borsod-Abaúj-Zemplén	Miskolc	2,798	7,247	745,154
Csongrád	Szeged	1,646	4,263	433,388
Fejér	Székesfehérvár	1,683	4,359	434,547
Györ-Moson-Sopron	Györ	1,579	4,089	434,956
Hajdú-Bihar	Debrecen	2,398	6,211	553,043
Heves	Eger	1,404	3,637	325,673
Jász-Nagykun-Szolnok	Szolnok	2,155	5,582	415,819
Komárom-Esztergom	Tatabánya	875	2,265	316,780
Nógrád	Salgótarján	982	2,544	220,576
Pest	Budapest[1]	2,468	6,393	1,080,759
Somogy	Kaposvár	2,331	6,036	335,463
Szabolcs-Szatmár-Bereg	Nyíregyháza	2,292	5,937	582,795
Tolna	Szekszárd	1,430	3,703	250,062
Vas	Szombathely	1,288	3,336	268,653
Veszprém	Veszprém	1,781	4,613	374,346
Zala	Zalaegerszeg	1,461	3,784	298,056
Capital City				
Budapest[1]		203	525	1,775,203
TOTAL		35,919	93,030	10,197,119

Demography

Population (2002): 10,162,000.
Density (2002): persons per sq mi 282.9, persons per sq km 109.2.
Urban-rural (2000): urban 63.6%; rural 36.4%.
Sex distribution (2001): male 47.70%; female 52.30%.
Age breakdown (2000): under 15, 17.1%; 15–29, 22.6%; 30–44, 20.2%; 45–59, 20.5%; 60–74, 14.0%; 75 and over, 5.6%.
Population projection: (2010) 9,916,000; (2020) 9,566,000.
Ethnic composition (2000): Hungarian 84.4%; Roma (Gypsy) 5.3%; Ruthenian 2.9%; German 2.4%; Romanian 1.0%; Slovak 0.9%; Jewish 0.6%; other 2.5%.
Religious affiliation (1998): Roman Catholic 57.8%; Reformed 17.7%; Lutheran 3.9%; Jewish 0.2%; nonreligious 18.5%; other/unknown 1.9%.
Major cities (2001): Budapest 1,775,203; Debrecen 211,038; Miskolc 184,129; Szeged 168,276; Pécs 162,502; Györ 129,415.

Vital statistics

Birth rate per 1,000 population (2001): 9.5 (world avg. 21.2); (2000) legitimate 71.0%; illegitimate 29.0%.
Death rate per 1,000 population (2001): 13.0 (world avg. 8.9).
Natural increase rate per 1,000 population (2001): –3.5 (world avg. 12.3).
Total fertility rate (avg. births per childbearing woman; 2000): 1.3.
Marriage rate per 1,000 population (2001): 4.3.
Life expectancy at birth (2000): male 67.1 years; female 75.6 years.
Major causes of death per 100,000 population (1999): diseases of the circulatory system 728.4; malignant neoplasms (cancers) 340.3.

National economy

Budget (1999). Revenue: Ft 4,955,000,000,000 (social security contributions 29.6%, value-added taxes 19.0%, personal income taxes 15.5%, excise taxes 9.4%). Expenditures: Ft 5,396,000,000,000 (current expenditures 93.9%, development expenditures 6.1%).
Production (metric tons except as noted). Agriculture, forestry, fishing (2000): corn (maize) 5,000,000, wheat 3,709,000, sugar beets 2,300,000, barley 905,000, apples 520,000, grapes 500,000, sunflower seeds 485,000; livestock (number of live animals) 5,335,000 pigs, 857,000 cattle; roundwood (1999) 4,287,500 cu m; fish catch (1997) 21,916. Mining and quarrying (1999): bauxite 935,000. Manufacturing (value added in Ft '000,000; 1998): refined petroleum products 296,000; food and beverages 278,800; electrical machinery and apparatus 218,000; transportation equipment 168,800; paints, soaps, and pharmaceuticals 100,800. Energy production (consumption): electricity (kW-hr; 2001) 33,986,000,000 ([1997] 33,348,000,000); hard coal (metric tons; 2001) 573,000 ([1999] 1,110,000); lignite (metric tons; 2001) 12,745,000 ([1999] 14,341,000); crude petroleum (barrels; 2001) 7,118,000 ([1999] 51,633,000); petroleum products (metric tons; 1997) 6,516,000 (6,393,000); natural gas (cu m; 2001) 3,417,000,000 ([1999] 12,365,000,000).
Land use (1994): forested 19.1%; meadows and pastures 12.4%; agricultural and under permanent cultivation 53.9%; other 14.6%.
Public debt (external, outstanding; 2000): U.S.$14,251,000,000.
Population economically active (1999): total 4,096,200; activity rate of total population 40.7% (participation rates: ages 15–64, 59.9%; female 44.5%; unemployed [2001] 5.7%).

Price and earnings indexes (1995 = 100)

	1995	1996	1997	1998	1999	2000	2001
Consumer price index	100.0	123.4	146.0	166.7	183.5	201.4	219.8
Annual earnings index	100.0	117.8	145.7	170.7	191.6	215.8	245.2

Tourism (U.S.$'000,000; 2000): receipts 3,429; expenditures 1,094.
Gross national product (2000): U.S.$47,249,000,000 (U.S.$4,710 per capita).

Structure of gross domestic product and labour force

	1999 in value Ft '000,000	% of total value	labour force	% of labour force
Agriculture, forestry	490,200	4.3	270,400	6.6
Mining	28,800	0.3	24,400	0.6
Manufacturing	2,374,300	20.8	928,900	22.7
Construction	457,800	4.0	253,000	6.2
Public utilities	392,700	3.4	89,800	2.2
Transp. and commun.	1,019,600	8.9	308,300	7.5
Trade, restaurants	1,338,100	11.7	650,700	15.9
Finance, real estate	1,928,800	16.9	264,800	6.5
Public administration, defense	723,400	6.3	301,900	7.4
Services	1,241,000	10.9	719,200	17.6
Other	1,441,900[2]	12.6[2]	284,700[3]	7.0[3]
TOTAL	11,436,500[4]	100.0[4]	4,096,200[4]	100.0[4]

Household income and expenditure. Average household size (1998) 2.5; income per household[5] (1998) Ft 1,828,441 (U.S.$8,528); sources of income (1998): wages 49.9%, transfers 17.9%, self-employment 17.2%, other 15.0%; expenditure (1999): food and beverages 33.6%; transportation and communications 14.9%; energy 14.6%; housing 8.0%.

Foreign trade

Balance of trade (current prices)

	1996	1997	1998	1999	2000	2001
Ft '000,000,000	–490.0	–378.4	–567.3	–707.1	–1,121.2	–916.9
% of total	10.3%	5.1%	5.4%	5.6%	6.6%	5.0%

Imports (2000): Ft 9,064,000,000,000 (electrical machinery 16.0%, nonelectrical machinery 14.4%, road vehicles 7.3%, computers and office machines 7.1%, telecommunications equipment 6.5%). *Major import sources:* Germany 25.5%; Russia 8.1%; Italy 7.5%; Austria 7.4%; Japan 5.3%.
Exports (2000): Ft 7,942,800,000,000 (office machines and computers 13.9%, electrical machinery 11.9%, telecommunications equipment 10.8%, power generating machinery 10.0%, road vehicles 8.8%). *Major export destinations:* Germany 37.2%; Austria 8.7%; Italy 5.9%; The Netherlands 5.4%; U.S. 5.3%.

Transport and communications

Transport. Railroads: (2000) route length 7,768 km; (1999) passenger-km 9,514,000,000; (1999) metric ton-km cargo 7,733,000,000. Roads (1999): total length 188,203 km (paved 43%). Vehicles (1999): passenger cars 2,255,526; trucks and buses 321,634. Air transport (1999): passenger-km 3,513,000,000; metric ton-km cargo 55,500,000; airports (1997) with scheduled flights 1.

Communications

Medium	date	unit	number	units per 1,000 persons
Daily newspapers	1996	circulation	1,895,000	186
Radio	1997	receivers	7,000,000	689
Television	1998	receivers	4,500,000	445
Telephones	2001	main lines	3,730,000	374
Cellular telephones	2001	subscribers	4,968,000	498
Personal computers	2001	units	1,000,000	100
Internet	2001	users	1,480,000	148

Education and health

Educational attainment (1990). Population age 25 and over having: no formal schooling 1.3%; primary education 57.9%; secondary 30.7%; higher 10.1%.

Education (1999–2000)

	schools	teachers	students	student/ teacher ratio
Primary (age 6–13)	3,696	82,829	960,601	11.6
Secondary (age 14–17)	1,054	32,317	386,579	12.0
Vocational	356	5,002	117,038	23.4
Higher	89	21,138	278,997	13.2

Health (1999): physicians 32,240[6] (1 per 312 persons); hospital beds 83,992 (1 per 120 persons); infant mortality rate per 1,000 live births (2001) 8.1.
Food (1998): daily per capita caloric intake 3,408 (vegetable products 69%, animal products 31%); 130% of FAO recommended minimum requirement.

Military

Total active duty personnel (2001): 33,810 (army 67.7%, air force 10.4%, headquarters staff 21.9%). *Military expenditure as percentage of GNP* (1999): 1.7% (world 2.4%); per capita expenditures U.S.$185.

[1]Budapest acts as the capital of Pest county even though it is administratively not part of Pest county. [2]Represents net taxes on commodities less imputed bank service charge. [3]Unemployed. [4]Detail does not add to total given because of rounding. [5]Adjusted disposable income including government transfers. [6]In active service.

Internet resources for further information:
• **Hungarian Central Statistical Office**
  http://www.ksh.hu/pls/ksh/docs/index_eng.html

Iceland

Official name: Lýdhveldidh Ísland (Republic of Iceland).
Form of government: unitary multiparty republic with one legislative house (Althing [63]).
Chief of state: President.
Head of government: Prime Minister.
Capital: Reykjavík.
Official language: Icelandic.
Official religion: Evangelical Lutheran.
Monetary unit: 1 króna (ISK) = 100 aurar; valuation (Sept. 23, 2002)
1 U.S.$ = ISK 87.91; 1 £ = ISK 136.61.

Area and population

Constituencies[1]	Principal centres	area sq mi	area sq km	population 2001[2] estimate
Austurland	Egilsstadhir	8,491	21,991	11,798
Nordhurland eystra	Akureyri	8,636	22,368	26,618
Nordhurland vestra	Saudhárkrókur	5,055	13,093	9,310
Reykjanes	...	765[3]	1,982[3]	82,459
Reykjavík	Reykjavík	3	3	112,268
Sudhurland	Selfoss	9,735	25,214	21,326
Vestfirdhir	Ísafjördhur	3,657	9,470	8,014
Vesturland	Borgarnes	3,360	8,701	14,457
TOTAL		39,699	102,819	286,250

Demography

Population (2002): 288,000.
Density (2002)[4]: persons per sq mi 31.3, persons per sq km 12.1.
Urban-rural (1999): urban 93.5%; rural 6.5%.
Sex distribution (2001): male 50.07%; female 49.93%.
Age breakdown (2000): under 15, 23.2%; 15–29, 22.7%; 30–44, 22.2%; 45–59, 16.9%; 60–74, 9.9%; 75 and over, 5.1%.
Population projection: (2010) 307,000; (2020) 331,000.
Doubling time: 79 years.
Ethnic composition (2000)[5]: Icelandic 96.9%; European 2.2%, of which Nordic 0.6%; Asian 0.5%; other 0.4%.
Religious affiliation (2000): Protestant 92.3%, of which Evangelical Lutheran 87.8%, other Lutheran 3.9%; Roman Catholic 1.5%; other and not specified 6.2%.
Major cities (2001): Reykjavík 112,268 (urban area 178,000); Kópavogur 24,229[6]; Hafnarfjördhur 20,223[6]; Akureyri 15,632; Gardhabær 8,445[6].

Vital statistics

Birth rate per 1,000 population (2000): 15.2 (world avg. 21.2); (1999) legitimate 37.4%; illegitimate 62.6%.
Death rate per 1,000 population (2000): 6.4 (world avg. 8.9).
Natural increase rate per 1,000 population (2000): 8.8 (world avg. 12.3).
Total fertility rate (avg. births per childbearing woman; 2000): 2.1.
Marriage rate per 1,000 population (2000): 6.3.
Divorce rate per 1,000 population (2000): 1.9.
Life expectancy at birth (1999–2000): male 77.6 years; female 81.4 years.
Major causes of death per 100,000 population (1997): diseases of the circulatory system 279.8, of which ischemic heart diseases 148.4, cerebrovascular disease 79.3; malignant neoplasms (cancers) 196.4; diseases of the respiratory system 68.3; injury and poisoning 38.4.

National economy

Budget (1998). Revenue: ISK 220,840,000,000 (indirect taxes 49.5%, of which value-added taxes 26.0%; direct taxes 44.6%; nontax revenue 5.9%). Expenditures: ISK 198,216,000,000 (1997; health and welfare 39.6%; education 14.3%; general administration 8.7%; communications 7.5%; cultural affairs 6.2%; agriculture 4.0%).
Public debt (2000): U.S.$2,242,600,000.
Production (metric tons except as noted). Agriculture, forestry, fishing (2000): potatoes 9,843, cereals 3,041, tomatoes 931, hay 2,363,342 cu m; livestock (number of live animals) 465,777 sheep, 73,995 horses, 72,135 cattle; fish catch (value in ISK '000,000; 2000) 57,858, of which cod 26,383, herring 5,728, redfish 4,570, shrimp 2,661, other 18,516. Mining and quarrying (2000): diatomite 28,300. Manufacturing (value added in ISK '000,000; 1996): preserved and processed fish 18,114; other food products 10,848; printing and publishing 6,914; fabricated metal products 6,640; nonferrous metals 2,932; wood furniture 2,379. Energy production (consumption): electricity (kW-hr; 2000) 7,676,000,000 (7,676,000,000); coal (metric tons; 1997) none (58,000); crude petroleum, none (none); petroleum products (metric tons; 1997) none (724,000).
Land use (1994): forested 1.2%; meadows and pastures 22.7%; agricultural and under permanent cultivation 0.1%; other 76.0%.
Population economically active (2000): total 160,100; activity rate of total population 55.6% (participation rates: ages 16–74, 83.5%; female 46.5%; unemployed 2.3%).

Price and earnings indexes (1995 = 100)

	1995	1996	1997	1998	1999	2000	2001
Consumer price index	100.0	102.3	104.1	105.9	109.3	114.9	122.1
Hourly earnings index	...	...	...	...	...	...	...

Tourism (2000): receipts U.S.$228,000,000; expenditures U.S.$467,000,000.
Gross national product (2000): U.S.$8,540,000,000 (U.S.$30,390 per capita).

Structure of gross domestic product and labour force

	2000 in value ISK '000,000[7]	2000 % of total value[7]	2000 labour force[8]	2000 % of labour force[8]
Agriculture	12,100	1.8	6,900	4.4
Fishing	39,700	5.9	6,100	3.9
Fish processing	27,000	4.0	6,700	4.3
Manufacturing	86,900	12.9	17,500	11.2
Construction	60,600	9.0	10,500	6.7
Public utilities	33,000	4.9	1,300	0.8
Transp. and commun.	60,600	9.0	10,600	6.8
Trade, restaurants	95,000	14.1	28,300	18.1
Finance, real estate	133,400	19.8	19,600	12.5
Public administration	97,000	14.4	7,000	4.5
Health, education, other services	61,300	9.1	41,900	26.8
Other	−33,000[9]	−4.9[9]	—	—
TOTAL	673,600	100.0	156,400[6]	100.0

Household income and expenditure. Average household size (1990)[10] 3.6; annual income per household (1995)[11] ISK 1,976,066 (U.S.$30,546); sources of income (1995): wages and salaries 74.1%, pension 10.5%, self-employment 2.7%, other 12.7%; expenditure (2000): transportation and communications 22.0%; food and beverages 20.1%, housing and energy 18.5%, recreation and education 12.4%.

Foreign trade[11]

Balance of trade (current prices)

	1995	1996	1997	1998	1999	2000	2001
ISK '000,000	+2,993	−10,304	−12,014	−39,516	−36,189	−55,331	−76,062
% of total	1.3%	3.9%	4.4%	12.6%	11.1%	15.7%	20.8%

Imports (2001): ISK 220,874,000,000 (machinery and apparatus 15.1%; road vehicles 12.4%; food products 8.4%; chemicals 8.3%; crude petroleum and petroleum products 8.3%). *Major import sources* (2000): Germany 11.9%; U.S. 11.0%; U.K. 9.0%; Norway 8.1%; Denmark 7.9%; The Netherlands 7.5%; Sweden 6.6%; Japan 4.9%.
Exports (2001): ISK 144,811,600,000 (marine products 62.5%, of which frozen fish 33.7%, salted fish 13.1%, lobster and shrimp 7.5%; manufactured products 31.3%). *Major export destinations* (2000): U.K. 19.3%; Germany 16.4%; U.S. 12.2%; The Netherlands 7.7%; Portugal 5.7%; France 4.6%; Spain 4.5%.

Transport and communications

Transport. Railroads: none. Roads (2000): total length 7,880 mi, 12,682 km (paved 28%). Vehicles (2001): passenger cars 158,936; trucks and buses 21,105. Air transport (2000)[12]: passenger-mi 2,308,000,000, passenger-km 3,714,000,000; short ton-mi cargo 68,102,000, metric ton-km cargo 109,600,000; airports (1996) with scheduled flights 24.

Communications

Medium	date	unit	number	units per 1,000 persons
Daily newspapers	1996	circulation	145,000	535
Radio	1997	receivers	260,000	950
Television	1999	receivers	145,000	523
Telephones	2001	main lines	190,600	664
Cellular telephones	2001	subscribers	235,400	820
Personal computers	2001	units	120,000	418
Internet	2001	users	195,000	679

Education and health

Educational attainment (2001): Percentage of population ages 25–64 having primary and some secondary education 36.6%; secondary 44.8%; higher 18.6%. *Literacy:* virtually 100%.

Education (1999–2000)

	schools[13]	teachers	students	student/ teacher ratio
Primary/lower secondary (age 7–15)	205	3,784	43,644	11.5
Upper Secondary (age 16–19)	35	1,297	20,256	15.6
Higher	14	799	10,543	13.2

Health: physicians (1999) 938 (1 per 296 persons); hospital beds (1993) 2,798[14] (1 per 95 persons); infant mortality rate (2000) 3.0.
Food (2000): daily per capita caloric intake 3,313 (vegetable products 58%, animal products 42%); 126% of FAO recommended minimum requirement.

Military

Total active duty personnel (2001): 125 coast guard personnel; NATO-sponsored U.S.-manned Iceland Defense Force: 1,640. *Military expenditure as percentage of GNP* (1999): none (world average 2.4%).

---

[1]Constituencies are electoral districts. Actual local administration is based on towns or rural districts. [2]December. [3]Reykjanes includes Reykjavík. [4]Population density calculated with reference to 9,191 sq mi (23,805 sq km) area free of glaciers (comprising 4,603 sq mi [11,922 sq km]), lava fields or wasteland (comprising 24,918 sq mi [64,538 sq km]), and lakes (comprising 1,064 sq mi [2,757 sq km]). [5]By country of birth. [6]Within Reykjavík urban area. [7]Breakdown by sector is estimated. [8]Employed only. [9]Indirect taxes, statistical discrepancy, and production of private nonprofit institution less imputed bank service charges and subsidies. [10]Based on sample survey. [11]Imports c.i.f.; exports f.o.b. [12]Icelandair only. [13]1996–97. [14]Excludes nursing wards in old-age homes.

Internet resources for further information:
• **Statistics Iceland http://www.statice.is**
• **Central Bank of Iceland http://www.sedlabanki.is**

India

Official name: Bharat (Hindi);
Republic of India (English).
Form of government: multiparty federal
republic with two legislative houses
(Council of States [245[1]], House of
the People [545[2]]).
Chief of state: President.
Head of government: Prime Minister.
Capital: New Delhi.
Official languages: Hindi; English.
Official religion: none.
Monetary unit: 1 Indian rupee
(Re, plural Rs) = 100 paise; valuation
(Sept. 23, 2002) 1 U.S.$ = Rs 48.81;
1 £ = Rs 75.23.

Oriya 3.32%; Punjabi 2.76%; Assamese 1.55%; Bhili/Bhilodi 0.66%; Santhali 0.62%; Kashmiri 0.47%[12]; Gondi 0.25%; Sindhi 0.25%; Nepali 0.25%; Konkani 0.21%; Tulu 0.18%; Kurukh 0.17%; Manipuri 0.15%; Bodo 0.14%; Khandeshi 0.12%; other 3.26%. Hindi (66.00%) and English (19.00%) are also spoken as lingua francas (second languages).
Religious affiliation (2000): Hindu 73.72%; Muslim 11.96%, of which Sunnī 8.97%, Shīʿī 2.99%; Christian 6.08%, of which Independent 2.99%, Protestant 1.47%, Roman Catholic 1.35%, Orthodox 0.27%; traditional beliefs 3.39%; Sikh 2.16%; Buddhist 0.71%; Jain 0.40%; Bahā'ī 0.12%; Zoroastrian (Parsi) 0.02%; other 1.44%.
Households (1991)[13]. Total households 151,032,898. Average household size 5.6; 1–2 persons 12.1%, 3–5 persons 44.4%, 6–8 persons 30.5%, 9 or more persons 13.0%. Average number of rooms per household 2.2; 1 room 40.5%, 2 rooms 30.6%, 3 rooms 13.8%, 4 rooms 7.1%, 5 rooms 3.2%, 6 or more rooms 3.9%, unspecified number of rooms 0.9%. Average number of persons per room 2.6.

Vital statistics

Birth rate per 1,000 population (2000): 24.8 (world avg. 22.5).
Death rate per 1,000 population (2000): 8.9 (world avg. 9.0).
Natural increase rate per 1,000 population (2000): 15.9 (world avg. 13.5).
Total fertility rate (avg. births per childbearing woman; 2000): 3.1.
Marital status of male (female) population age 6 and over (1992–93): single 48.3% (37.1%); married 47.5% (55.2%); widowed 3.6% (7.2%); divorced or separated 0.6% (0.5%).
Life expectancy at birth (2000): male 61.9 years; female 63.1 years.
Major causes of death per 100,000 population (1987)[14]: diseases of the circulatory system 227; infectious and parasitic diseases 215; diseases of the respiratory system 108; certain conditions originating in the perinatal period 108; accidents, homicide, and other violence 102; diseases of the digestive system 48; diseases of the nervous system 43; malignant neoplasms (cancers) 41; endocrine, metabolic, and nutritional disorders 30; diseases of the blood and blood-forming organs 25; ill-defined conditions 129.

Social indicators

Educational attainment (1991)[13, 15]. Percentage of population age 25 and over having: no formal schooling 57.5%; incomplete primary education 28.0%; complete primary or some secondary 7.2%; complete secondary or higher 7.3%.

Distribution of expenditure (1994)

percentage of household expenditure by decile/quintile

1	2	3	4	5	6	7	8	9	10 (highest)
4.1	5.1	—13.0—		—16.8—		—21.7—		14.3	25.0

Quality of working life. Average workweek (1989): 42 hours[16]. Rate of fatal (nonfatal) injuries per 100,000 industrial workers (1989) 17 (3,625)[16]. Agricultural workers in servitude to creditors (early 1990s) 10–20%.
Access to services (1991). Percentage of total (urban, rural) households having access to: electricity for lighting purposes 42.4% (75.8%, 30.5%); attached toilet or nearby latrine 23.7% (63.9%, 9.5%). Source of drinking water: piped water 32.3%, well 32.2%, hand pump or tube well 30.0%, river or canal 2.0%, public tank 1.3%, other 2.2%.
Social participation. Eligible voters participating in September/October 1999 national election: 59.6%. Trade union membership (1998): c. 16,000,000 (primarily in the public sector).
Social deviance (1990)[17]. Offense rate per 100,000 population for: murder 4.1; dacoity (gang robbery) 1.3; theft and housebreaking 56.6; riots 12.0. Rate of suicide per 100,000 population (1991): 9.0.
Material well-being (1994). Households possessing: black and white television receivers 18.8%, colour television receivers 6.3%, videocassette recorders 1.3%, refrigerators 6.9%, washing machines 2.3%.

National economy

Gross national product (2000): U.S.$454,800,000,000 (U.S.$450 per capita).

Area and population

States	Capitals	area sq mi	area sq km	population 2001 preliminary census
Andhra Pradesh	Hyderabad	106,204	275,068	75,727,541
Arunachal Pradesh	Itanagar	32,333	83,743	1,091,117
Assam	Dispur	30,285	78,438	26,638,407
Bihar	Patna	38,301	99,200	82,878,796
Chhattisgarh[3]	Raipur	52,199	135,194	20,795,956
Goa	Panaji	1,429	3,702	1,343,998
Gujarat	Gandhinagar	75,685	196,024	50,596,992
Haryana	Chandigarh	17,070	44,212	21,082,989
Himachal Pradesh	Shimla	21,495	55,673	6,077,248
Jammu and Kashmir	Srinagar	39,146	101,387	10,069,917
Jharkhand[3]	Ranchi	28,833	74,677	26,909,428
Karnataka	Bangalore	74,051	191,791	52,733,958
Kerala	Thiruvananthapuram (Trivandrum)	15,005	38,863	31,838,619
Madhya Pradesh	Bhopal	119,016	308,252	60,385,118
Maharashtra	Mumbai (Bombay)	118,800	307,690	96,752,247
Manipur	Imphal	8,621	22,327	2,388,634
Meghalaya	Shillong	8,660	22,429	2,306,069
Mizoram	Aizawl	8,139	21,081	891,058
Nagaland	Kohima	6,401	16,579	1,988,636
Orissa	Bhubaneshwar	60,119	155,707	36,706,920
Punjab	Chandigarh	19,445	50,362	24,289,296
Rajasthan	Jaipur	132,139	342,239	56,473,122
Sikkim	Gangtok	2,740	7,096	540,493
Tamil Nadu	Chennai (Madras)	50,216	130,058	62,110,839
Tripura	Agartala	4,049	10,486	3,191,168
Uttar Pradesh	Lucknow	93,933	243,286	166,052,859
Uttaranchal[3]	Dehra Dun	19,739	51,125	8,479,562
West Bengal	Kolkata (Calcutta)	34,267	88,752	80,221,171
Union Territories				
Andaman and Nicobar Islands	Port Blair	3,185	8,249	356,265
Chandigarh	Chandigarh	44	114	900,914
Dadra and Nagar Haveli	Silvassa	190	491	220,451
Daman and Diu	Daman	43	112	158,059
Lakshadweep	Kavaratti	12	32	60,595
Pondicherry	Pondicherry	190	492	973,829
National Capital Territory				
Delhi	Delhi	573	1,483	13,782,976
TOTAL		1,222,559[4, 5]	3,166,414[4]	1,027,015,247

Demography

Population (2002): 1,047,671,000.
Density (2002)[4]: persons per sq mi 856.9, persons per sq km 330.9.
Urban-rural (2001): urban 27.8%; rural 72.2%.
Sex distribution (2001): male 51.73%; female 48.27%.
Age breakdown (2000): under 15, 33.6%; 15–29, 27.7%; 30–44, 19.8%; 45–59, 11.9%; 60–74, 5.6%; 75 and over, 1.4%.
Population projection: (2010) 1,172,000,000; (2020) 1,316,000,000.
Doubling time: 44 years.
Major cities (2001; *urban agglomerations,* 2001): Greater Mumbai (Greater Bombay) 11,914,398 (16,368,084); Delhi 9,817,439 (12,791,458); Kolkata (Calcutta) 4,580,544 (13,216,546); Bangalore 4,292,223 (5,686,844); Chennai (Madras) 4,216,268 (6,424,624); Ahmadabad 3,515,361 (4,519,278); Hyderabad 3,449,878 (5,533,640); Pune (Poona) 2,540,069 (3,755,525); Kanpur 2,532,138 (2,690,486); Surat 2,433,787 (2,811,466); Jaipur 2,324,319 (2,324,-319); New Delhi[6] 294,783.

Other principal cities (2001)[7]

	population		population		population
Agra	1,259,979	Jodhpur	846,408	Shambajinagar	
Allahabad	1,193,266	Kalyan[9]	1,193,266	(Aurangabad)	873,037
(Prayag Raj)	990,298	Kota	537,371	Sholapur (Solapur)	873,037
Amritsar	975,695	Lucknow	2,207,340	Srinagar	894,940
Bhopal	1,433,875	Ludhiana	1,395,053	Thane (Thana)[9]	1,261,517
Chandigarh	808,796	Madurai	922,913	Thiruvanan-	
Coimbatore	923,085	Meerut	1,074,229	thapuram	
Faridabad	1,054,981	Mysore	742,261	(Trivandrum)	744,739
Ghaziabad	968,521	Nagpur	2,051,320	Tiruchirappalli	746,062
Guwahati	808,021	Nashik (Nasik)	1,076,967	Vadodara (Baroda)	1,306,035
Gwalior	826,919	Patna	1,376,950	Varanasi	
Howrah (Haora)[8]	1,008,704	Pimpri-		(Benares)	1,100,748
Hubli-Dharwad	786,018	Chinchwad[10]	1,006,417	Vijayawada	825,436
Indore	1,597,641	Rajkot	966,642	Vishakhapatnam	969,608
Jabalpur	951,469	Ranchi	846,454		

Linguistic composition (1991)[11]: Hindi 27.58% (including associated languages and dialects, 39.85%); Bengali 8.22%; Telugu 7.80%; Marathi 7.38%; Tamil 6.26%; Urdu 5.13%; Gujarati 4.81%; Kannada 3.87%; Malayalam 3.59%;

Budget (1999–2000). Revenue: Rs 3,288,000,000,000 (tax revenue 48.6%, of which excise taxes 19.4%, customs duties 15.3%, corporation taxes 9.4%; nontax revenue 36.5%, of which economic services 20.7%, interest receipts 10.0%; other sources of revenue 14.9%). Expenditures: Rs 3,288,000,000,000 (interest payments and debt servicing 26.8%; transportation 11.0%; defense 10.5%; grants in aid to state governments 9.4%; communications 7.2%; agriculture 5.0%; social services 4.7%).
Public debt (external, outstanding; 2000): U.S.$87,598,000,000.
Production (in '000 metric tons except as noted). Agriculture, forestry, fishing (2000): sugarcane 315,100, cereals 239,814 (of which rice 134,150, wheat 74,251, corn [maize] 11,500, sorghum 9,500, millet 9,000), fruits 49,199 (of

Structure of gross domestic product and labour force

	1999–2000[18] in value Rs '000,000,000[19]	1999–2000[18] % of total value	1993–94 labour force	1993–94 % of labour force
Agriculture, forestry	4,940	27.9	240,700,000	64.7
Mining	332	1.9	2,600,000	0.7
Manufacturing	2,793	15.8	39,100,000	10.5
Construction	1,039	5.9	11,900,000	3.2
Public utilities	440	2.5	1,500,000	0.4
Transp. and commun. }	3,600	20.3	10,400,000	2.8
Trade, restaurants }			27,500,000	7.4
Finance, real estate	2,075	11.7	}	
Pub. admin., defense }	2,504	14.1	} 38,300,000	10.3
Services }				
TOTAL	17,723	100.0[5]	372,000,000	100.0

which mangoes 15,642, bananas 13,900, oranges 3,000, apples 1,580, pineapples 1,440, lemons and limes 1,000), oilseeds 31,015[20] (of which rapeseed 6,120, peanuts [groundnuts] 6,100, soybeans 5,400, sunflower seeds 1,200, castor beans 810, sesame 620), pulses 14,237[20] (of which chickpeas 5,754[20], dry beans 3,600[20], pigeon peas 2,450[20]), coconuts 11,100, seed cotton 6,172, eggplants 6,100, jute 1,500, tea 749, tobacco 702, natural rubber 620, garlic 517, cashews 450, betel 315, coffee 282, ginger 235, pepper 58; livestock (number of live animals; 2000) 218,800,000 cattle, 123,000,000 goats, 93,772,000 water buffalo, 57,900,000 sheep, 16,500,000 pigs, 1,030,000 camels; roundwood (1999) 302,794,000 cu m, of which fuelwood 278,755,000 cu m, industrial roundwood 24,038,000; fish catch (metric tons; 1999) 5,352,000, of which freshwater fish 2,632,000, marine fish 2,248,000, crustaceans 377,000. Mining and quarrying (1999–2000): limestone 128,000; iron ore 48,100[21, 22]; bauxite 6,854; manganese 626[21]; chromium 509[21]; zinc 252[21]; copper 37[21]; gold 78,512 troy oz; gem diamonds 40,666 carats. Manufacturing (value added in Rs '000,000,000; 1999): iron and steel 188.1; industrial chemicals 167.7; paints, soaps, varnishes, drugs, and medicines 164.2; transport equipment 159.7; food products 139.0; textiles 136.8; electrical machinery 118.6; nonelectrical machinery 116.3; refined petroleum 79.2; cements, bricks, and tiles 67.2; fabricated metal products 39.5; nonferrous base metals 37.5.

Manufacturing enterprises (1995–96)[23]

	no. of factories	no. of persons engaged	avg. wages as a % of avg. of all wages	annual value added (Rs '000,000)[24]
Chemicals and chemical products,	9,206	758,500	140.3	237,093
of which synthetic fibres	395	97,100	183.8	68,420
fertilizers/pesticides	753	104,500	217.4	59,521
drugs and medicine	2,542	204,600	129.3	40,050
paints, soaps, and cosmetics	1,958	104,300	129.0	23,459
Transport equipment,	6,120	838,600	142.7	120,207
of which motor vehicles	3,758	392,400	162.4	77,240
motorcycles and bicycles	1,243	124,900	123.6	21,957
Textiles	16,228	1,579,400	80.2	99,855
Iron and steel	3,519	507,700	152.9	97,274
Nonelectrical machinery/apparatus	9,075	548,400	137.2	92,762
Food products,	22,878	1,285,900	60.4	92,163
of which refined sugar	1,285	341,000	92.0	28,125
Electrical machinery/apparatus,	5,472	443,700	149.4	84,320
of which industrial machinery	2,048	165,600	190.8	35,717
Refined petroleum	161	31,100	349.3	52,778
Bricks, cement, plaster products	10,067	394,500	70.3	49,413
Nonferrous basic metals	3,301	228,700	124.3	42,252
Fabricated metal products	7,984	277,700	98.6	32,565
Paper and paper products	2,742	175,200	99.5	26,380
Wearing apparel	3,463	263,700	55.0	23,485

Energy production (consumption): electricity (kW-hr; 2001) 509,209,000,000 ([1997] 465,867,000,000); hard coal (metric tons; 2001) 318,756,000 ([1997] 310,133,000); lignite (metric tons; 2001) 23,713,000 ([1997] 22,855,000); crude petroleum (barrels; 2001) 242,919,000 ([1997] 512,232,000); petroleum products (metric tons; 1997) 50,916,000 (69,390,000); natural gas (cu m; 2001) 29,016,000,000 ([1997] 19,430,000,000).

Financial aggregates[25]

	1996	1997	1998	1999	2000	2001	2002
Exchange rate, Rs per:							
U.S. dollar	35.93	39.28	42.48	43.49	46.75	48.18	49.03[26]
£	61.01	64.96	70.67	70.30	69.76	69.88	71.91[26]
SDR	51.67	53.00	59.81	59.69	60.91	60.55	63.28[26]
International reserves (U.S.$)							
Total (excl. gold; '000,000)	20,170	24,688	27,341	32,667	37,902	45,870	53,530[26]
SDRs ('000,000)	122	77	83	4	2	5	9[26]
Reserve pos. in IMF ('000,000)	306	287	300	671	637	614	631[26]
Foreign exchange ('000,000)	19,742	24,324	26,958	31,992	37,264	45,251	52,890[26]
Gold ('000,000 fine troy oz)	12.781	12.740	11.487	11.502	11.502	11.502	11.502[26]
% world reserves	1.4	1.4	1.2	1.2	1.2	1.2	1.2[26]
Interest and prices							
Central bank discount (%)	12.0	9.0	9.0	8.0	8.0	8.0	6.5[26]
Advance (prime) rate (%)	16.0	13.8	13.5	12.5	12.3	12.1	12.0[26]
Industrial share prices (1995 = 100)[27]	91.3	84.5	76.8	...	...	...	...
Balance of payments (U.S.$'000,000)							
Balance of visible trade	−10,052	−10,028	−10,752	−8,679	−12,193	...	...
Imports, f.o.b.	43,789	45,730	44,828	45,556	55,325	...	...
Exports, f.o.b.	33,737	35,702	34,076	36,877	43,132	...	...
Balance of invisibles	+4,096	+7,063	+3,849	+5,451	+7,995	...	...
Balance of payments, current account	−5,956	−2,965	−6,903	−3,228	−4,198	...	...

Land use (1994): forested 23.0%; meadows and pastures 3.8%; agricultural and under permanent cultivation 57.1%; other 16.1%.
Population economically active (1993–94): total 372,000,000; activity rate of total population c. 41% (participation rates: n.a.; female 32.5%; unemployed[28]).

Price and earnings indexes (1995 = 100)

	1995	1996	1997	1998	1999	2000	2001
Consumer price index	100.0	109.0	116.8	132.2	138.4	144.0	149.3
Monthly earnings index	100.0	98.2	93.9	...	...	...	...

Household income and expenditure. Average household size (1991)[13] 5.6; sources of income (1984–85): salaries and wages 42.2%, self-employed 39.7%, interest 8.6%, profits and dividends 6.0%, rent 3.5%; expenditure (1998–99): food, beverages, and tobacco 52.1%, transportation and communications 13.7%, housing and energy 10.2%, clothing and footwear 5.2%, health 4.4%.
Service enterprises (net value added in Rs '000,000,000; 1998–99): wholesale and retail trade 1,562; finance, real estate, and insurance 1,310; transport and storage 804; community, social, and personal services 763; construction 545; electricity, gas, and steam 287.
Tourism (2000): U.S.$3,168,000,000; expenditures U.S.$2,567,000,000.

Foreign trade[29, 30]

Balance of trade (current prices)

	1996–97	1997–98	1998–99	1999–2000	2000–01	2001–02
Rs '000,000	−200,030	−252,680	−385,080	−399,140	−273,020	−358,990
% of total	7.8%	9.5%	12.6%	11.0%	6.3%	8.0%

Imports (1999–2000): Rs 2,006,570,000,000 (crude petroleum and refined petroleum 22.3%; precious and semiprecious stones 11.6%; chemicals 6.0%; nonelectrical machinery 5.8%; electronic goods 5.6%). Major import sources: Belgium 7.7%; U.S. 7.5%; U.K. 5.8%; Switzerland 5.5%; Japan 5.1%; Saudi Arabia 4.8%; United Arab Emirates 4.5%; Malaysia 4.3%; Germany 3.9%.
Exports (1999–2000): Rs 1,607,430,000,000 (cut and polished diamonds and jewelry 20.0%; cotton ready-made garments 9.2%; cotton yarn, fabrics, and thread 7.9%; leather and leather manufactures 4.2%; drugs and pharmaceuticals 4.2%; fabricated metals 3.2%). Major export destinations: U.S. 22.2%; Hong Kong 6.7%; U.K. 5.6%; United Arab Emirates 5.6%; Germany 4.6%; Japan 4.5%; Belgium 3.6%; Italy 3.0%; Russia 2.5%.

Transport and communications

Transport. Railroads (1998–99): route length 39,028 mi, 62,809 km; (1999–2000) passenger-mi 261,254,000,000, passenger-km 420,449,000,000; (1999–2000) short ton-mi cargo 209,259,000,000, metric ton-km cargo 305,513,000,000. Roads (1999): total length 2,062,727 mi, 3,319,644 km (paved 46%). Vehicles (1997): passenger cars 4,662,000; trucks and buses 2,748,000. Air transport (2001)[31]: passenger-mi 11,969,000,000, passenger-km 19,263,000,000; short ton-mi cargo 308,451,000, metric ton-km cargo 450,331,000; airports (1996) with scheduled flights 66.

Communications

Medium	date	unit	number	units per 1,000 persons
Daily newspapers	1993	circulation	18,800,000	21
Radio	1997	receivers	116,000,000	120
Television	1999	receivers	75,000,000	75
Telephones	2001	main lines	34,732,100	34
Cellular telephones	2001	subscribers	5,725,200	5.6
Personal computers	2001	units	6,000,000	5.8
Internet	2001	users	7,000,000	6.8

Education and health

Literacy (2001): total population age 7 and over literate 566,715,000 (65.4%); males literate 339,969,000 (75.8%); females literate 226,746,000 (54.2%).

Education (1997–98)

	schools	teachers	students	student/teacher ratio
Primary (age 6–10)	610,763	1,871,542	108,781,792	58.1
Secondary (age 11–17)	261,736	2,081,223	57,433,776	27.6
Higher	26,491	651,766	6,944,069	10.7

Health: physicians (1992) 410,875 (1 per 2,173 persons); hospital beds (1993) 659,000 (1 per 1,364 persons); infant mortality rate (2000) 64.9.
Food (1999): daily per capita caloric intake 2,417 (vegetable products 92%, animal products 8%); 109% of FAO recommended minimum requirement.

Military

Total active duty personnel (2001): 1,263,000 (army 87.1%, navy 4.2%, air force 8.7%); personnel in paramilitary forces 1,089,700. Military expenditure as percentage of GNP (1999): 2.5% (world 2.4%); per capita expenditure U.S.$11.

[1]Council of States can have a maximum of 250 members; a maximum of 12 of these members may be nominated by the president. [2]Includes 2 nonelective seats. [3]Created November 2000. [4]Excludes 46,660 sq mi (120,849 sq km) of territory claimed by India as part of Jammu and Kashmir but occupied by Pakistan or China; inland water constitutes 9.6% of total area of India (including all of Indian-claimed Jammu and Kashmir). [5]Detail does not add to total given because of rounding. [6]Within Delhi urban agglomeration. [7]Preliminary figures. [8]Within Kolkata urban agglomeration. [9]Within Greater Mumbai urban agglomeration. [10]Within Pune urban agglomeration. [11]Mother tongue unless otherwise noted. [12]1981. [13]Excludes Jammu and Kashmir. [14]Projected rates based on about 3.5% of total deaths (317,392 registered deaths out of an estimated total of nearly 9,000,000 deaths). [15]No formal schooling (1991): males 43.3%, females 72.8%; complete secondary or higher education (1991): males 10.6%, females 3.7%. [16]Data apply to the workers employed in the "organized sector" only (28.2 million in 1997–98, of which 19.4 million are employed in the public sector and 8.8 million are employed in the private sector; few legal protections exist for the more than 350 million workers in the "unorganized sector." [17]Crimes reported to National Crime Records Bureau by police authorities of state governments. [18]April 1–March 31. [19]At factor cost. [20]1998. [21]Approximate metal content of ore. [22]2001. [23]Establishments using power with at least 10 workers on any workday and all establishments employing 20 or more workers. [24]In factor values. [25]End-of-period unless otherwise noted. [26]May. [27]Period average. [28]Average number of registered unemployed in February 2000 was 40,395,000. [29]Imports c.i.f.; exports f.o.b. [30]Fiscal year beginning April 1. [31]Air India and Indian Airlines.

Internet resources for further information:
- India Image: Directory of Government Web Sites http://www.nic.in
- Census of India http://www.censusindia.net
- Reserve Bank of India http://www.rbi.org.in
- India Infoline.com http://www.indiainfoline.com

Indonesia

Official name: Republik Indonesia (Republic of Indonesia).
Form of government: unitary multiparty republic with two legislative houses (People's Consultative Assembly [700[1]]; House of People's Representatives [500[2]]).
Head of state and government: President.
Capital: Jakarta.
Official language: Indonesian (Bahasa Indonesia).
Official religion: monotheism.
Monetary unit: 1 Indonesian rupiah (Rp) = 100 sen; valuation (Sept. 23, 2002) 1 U.S.$ = Rp 9,032; 1 £ = Rp 14,037.

Area and population

Island(s) Provinces	area sq km	population 2000 census[3]	Island(s) Provinces	area sq km	population 2000 census[3]
Bali and the Lesser			East Kalimantan	210,985	2,455,120
Sunda Islands[4]	73,135	11,112,702	South Kalimantan	36,535	2,985,240
Bali	5,633	3,151,162	West Kalimantan	146,807	4,034,198
East Nusa Tenggara	47,349	3,952,279	Maluku (Moluccas)	77,871	1,990,598
West Nusa Tenggara	20,153	4,009,261	Maluku	...	1,205,539
Celebes (Sulawesi)[5]	191,800	14,946,488	North Maluku	...	785,059
Central Sulawesi	63,689	2,218,435	Papua (Irian		
Gorontalo[6]	12,151	835,044	Jaya)[5, 11]	421,981	2,220,934
North Sulawesi	15,337	2,012,098	Sumatra[5]	482,393	43,309,707
Southeast Sulawesi	38,140	1,821,284	Aceh[9]	55,390	3,930,905
South Sulawesi	62,483	8,059,627	Bangka-Belitung[6]	[12]	900,197
Java[5]	127,499	121,352,608	Bengkulu	19,789	1,567,432
Banten[7]	8,232	8,098,780	Jambi	53,436	2,413,846
Central Java	32,549	31,228,940	Lampung	35,385	6,741,439
East Java	47,923	34,783,640	North Sumatra	71,680	11,649,655
Jakarta[8]	664	8,389,443	Riau	94,561	4,957,627
West Java	34,945	35,729,537	South Sumatra	109,254[12]	6,899,675
Yogyakarta[9]	3,186	3,122,268	West Sumatra	42,898	4,248,931
Kalimantan[5, 10]	547,891	11,331,558	**TOTAL**	**1,922,570**[4]	**206,264,595**[4]
Central Kalimantan	153,564	1,857,000			

Demography

Population (2002): 211,023,000.
Density (2002)[4]: persons per sq mi 284.3, persons per sq km 109.8.
Urban-rural (2002): urban 43.0%; rural 57.0%.
Sex distribution (2000): male 50.14%; female 49.86%.
Age breakdown (2000): under 15, 30.4%; 15–29, 29.3%; 30–44, 21.8%; 45–59, 11.3%; 60–74, 5.8%; 75 and over, 1.4%.
Population projection: (2010) 231,180,000; (2020) 254,702,000.
Ethnolinguistic composition (1990): Javanese 39.4%; Sundanese 15.8%; Indonesian (Malay) 12.1%; Madurese 4.3%; Minang 2.4%; other 26.0%.
Religious affiliation (2000): Muslim 76.5%, of which syncretistic religions 21.8%; Christian 13.1%, of which Protestant 5.7%, independent Christian 4.0%, Roman Catholic 2.7%; Hindu 3.4%; traditional beliefs 2.5%; nonreligious 1.9%; other 2.6%.
Major cities (1995): Jakarta (1996) 9,341,000; Surabaya (1996) 2,743,000; Bandung (1996) 2,429,000; Medan 1,909,700; Palembang 1,283,100; Tangerang 1,144,500; Semarang 1,097,800; Ujung Pandang 1,029,900.

Vital statistics

Birth rate per 1,000 population (2002): 20.3 (world avg. 21.2).
Death rate per 1,000 population (2002): 7.1 (world avg. 8.9).
Total fertility rate (avg. births per childbearing woman; 2002): 2.3.
Marriage rate per 1,000 population (1997–98): 8.1[13].
Life expectancy at birth (2002): male 65.0 years; female 69.0 years.
Major causes of death (percent distribution, 1986): infectious and parasitic diseases 43.5%; diseases of the respiratory system 21.9%; cardiovascular diseases 9.7%; diseases of the nervous system 6.0%.

National economy

Budget (1999–2000). Revenue: RP 188,428,500,000,000 (income tax 31.7%, oil and gas revenues 31.0%, value-added tax 17.6%, nontax revenue 9.1%, excise taxes 5.5%). Expenditures: RP 204,900,300,000,000 (development 23.9%, subsidies 22.9%, salaries 15.7%, debt repayment 10.1%, transfers 8.5%).
Production (metric tons except as noted). Agriculture, forestry, fishing (2000): rice 51,000,000, palm fruit oil 34,000,000, sugarcane 21,400,000, cassava 16,347,000, corn (maize) 9,169,000, natural rubber 1,488,000; livestock (number of live animals) 14,121,000 goats, 12,102,000 cattle, 7,502,000 sheep, 2,859,000 buffalo; roundwood (1999) 190,601,000 cu m; fish catch (1998) 3,699,000. Mining and quarrying (1998): copper concentrate 2,640,000; nickel ore 1,642,000; bauxite 513,000; gold 118,246 kg. Manufacturing (value added in RP '000,000,000; 1997)[14]: transport equipment 10,038.6; textiles 9,629.7; food products 9,028.1; electrical machinery 6,654.7; wood products, except furniture 6,092.8; industrial chemicals 5,019.3; paper and paper products 4,121.2. Energy production (consumption): electricity (kW-hr; 1997) 84,096,000,000 (84,096,000,000); coal (metric tons; 2001) 90,648,000 ([1997] 10,330,000); crude petroleum (barrels; 2001) 514,413,000 ([1997] 315,000,000); petroleum products (metric tons; 1997) 44,576,000 (42,492,000); natural gas (cu m; 2000) 82,326,000,000 ([1997] 39,818,000,000).
Gross national product (2000): U.S.$119,871,000,000 (U.S.$570 per capita).

Structure of gross domestic product and labour force

	1999 in value Rp '000,000,000	% of total value	labour force[15]	% of labour force[15]
Agriculture	218,044	19.5	38,378,000	43.2
Mining	112,638	10.1	726,000	0.8
Manufacturing	284,804	25.4	11,516,000	13.0
Construction	73,418	6.5	3,415,000	3.9
Public utilities	13,369	1.2	188,000	0.2
Transp. and commun.	66,077	5.9	4,206,000	4.7
Trade	183,627	16.4	17,529,000	19.7
Finance, real estate	55,098	4.9	634,000	0.7
Pub. admin., defense	56,745	5.1		
Services	55,622	5.0	12,225,000	13.8
Other	...	...	...	...
TOTAL	**1,119,442**	**100.0**	**88,817,000**	**100.0**

Public debt (external, outstanding; 2000): U.S.$69,161,000,000.
Population economically active (1999): total 94,800,000; activity rate 46.0% (participation rates: over age 15, 70.7%; unemployed 6.3%).

Price and earnings indexes (1995 = 100)

	1995	1996	1997	1998	1999	2000	2001
Consumer price index	100.0	108.0	115.2	181.7	218.9	227.0	253.1
Earnings index[16]	100.0	105.4	116.1	133.9	155.4	...	...

Household income and expenditure. Average household size (2000) 3.9.
Tourism (2000): receipts U.S.$5,749,000,000; expenditures U.S.$3,197,000,000.

Foreign trade[17]

Balance of trade (current prices)

	1995	1996	1997	1998	1999	2000
U.S.$'000,000	+6,533	+5,948	+10,075	+18,429	+20,644	+25,040
% of total	7.4%	6.3%	9.8%	22.4%	25.2%	23.7%

Imports (1998): U.S.$27,336,900,000 (machinery and transport equipment 36.3%, basic manufactures 16.6%, chemicals 15.1%, mineral fuels 9.8%, food and live animals 9.6%). *Major import sources:* Japan 15.7%; U.S. 12.9%; Singapore 9.3%; Germany 8.7%; Australia 6.4%; South Korea 5.6%.
Exports (1998): U.S.$48,847,600,000 (crude petroleum 8.3%, natural gas 7.8%, garments 5.4%, plywood 4.3%, processed rubber 2.3%). *Major export destinations:* Japan 18.7%; U.S. 14.4%; Singapore 10.6%; Australia 3.1%.

Transport and communications

Transport. Railroads (1999): route length 6,458 km; passenger-km 18,585,000,000; metric ton-km cargo 5,035,000,000. Roads (1997): length 341,467 km (paved 56%). Vehicles (1998): passenger cars 2,734,769; trucks and buses 2,189,876. Air transport (1999): passenger-km 12,389,000,000; metric ton-km cargo 340,932,000; airports (1996) 81.

Communications

Medium	date	unit	number	units per 1,000 persons
Daily newspapers	1996	circulation	4,665,000	23
Radio	1998	receivers	26,000,000	128
Television	1999	receivers	30,000,000	143
Telephones	2001	main lines	7,949,300	37
Cellular telephones	2001	subscribers	5,303,000	25
Personal computers	2001	units	2,300,000	11
Internet	2001	users	4,000,000	19

Education and health

Educational attainment (1990). Percentage of population age 25 and over having: no schooling 34.6%; less than complete primary 28.2%; primary 23.3%; secondary 12.5%; higher 1.4%. *Literacy* (1995 est.): total population age 15 and over literate 83.8%; males literate 89.6%; females literate 78.0%.

Education (1997–98)

	schools	teachers	students	student/ teacher ratio
Primary (age 7–12)	151,064	1,158,616	25,689,693	22.1
Secondary (age 13–18)	29,398	654,505	10,821,139	16.5
Voc., teacher tr.	4,006	127,270	1,862,060	14.6
Higher	1,391	181,545	2,051,001	11.3

Health: physicians (1996) 31,435 (1 per 6,259 persons); hospital beds (1997) 121,996 (1 per 1,638 persons); infant mortality rate (2002) 40.0.
Food (1999): daily per capita caloric intake 2,931 (vegetable products 95%, animal products 5%); (1997) 136% of FAO recommended minimum.

Military

Total active duty personnel (2001): 297,000 (army 77.4%, navy 13.5%, air force 9.1%). *Military expenditure as percentage of GNP* (1999): 1.1% (world 2.4%); per capita expenditure U.S.$7.

[1]Includes the 500 members of the House of People's Representatives plus 200 other appointees. [2]Includes 38 nonelective seats reserved for the military. [3]Adjusted figure. [4]Excludes area and population of East Timor. [5]Includes area and population of nearby islands. [6]Formally established February 2001. [7]Formally established November 2000. [8]Formally a metropolitan district. [9]Formally a special autonomous district. [10]Kalimantan is the name of the Indonesian part of the island of Borneo. [11]Locally West Papua; increased autonomy from October 2001. [12]South Sumatra includes Bangka-Belitung. [13]Muslim population only. [14]Medium and large establishments only. [15]Employed people only. [16]Based on minimum monthly wages. [17]Imports and exports are f.o.b. in balance of trade.

Internet resources for further information:
• Central Bureau of Statistics http://www.bps.go.id

Iran

Official name: Jomhūrī-ye Eslamī-ye Īrān (Islamic Republic of Iran).
Form of government: unitary Islamic republic with one legislative house (Islamic Consultative Assembly [290]).
Supreme political/religious authority: Leader[1].
Head of state and government: President.
Capital: Tehrān.
Official language: Farsī (Persian).
Official religion: Islam.
Monetary unit: 1 rial (Rls); valuation (Sept. 23, 2002) 1 U.S.$ = Rls 7,948; 1 £ = Rls 12,352.

Area and population

Provinces	area sq km	1996 census population	Provinces	area sq km	1996 census population
Ardabīl	17,881	1,168,000	Khūzestān	63,213	3,747,000
Āzārbāyjān-e Gharbī	37,463	2,496,000	Kohgīlūyeh va		
Āzārbāyjān-e Sharqī	45,481	3,326,000	Būyer Ahmad	15,563	544,000
Būshehr	23,168	744,000	Kordestān	28,817	1,346,000
Chahār Mahāll va			Lorestān	28,392	1,584,000
Bakhtīārī	16,201	761,000	Markazī	29,406	1,229,000
Eşfahān	107,027	3,923,000	Māzandarān	23,833	2,602,000
Fārs	121,825	3,817,000	Qazvīn	15,502	968,000
Gilan	13,952	2,242,000	Qom	11,237	853,000
Golestān	20,893	1,426,000	Semnān	96,816	501,000
Hamadān	19,547	1,678,000	Sīstān va		
Hormozgān	71,193	1,062,000	Balūchestān	178,431	1,723,000
Īlām	20,150	488,000	Tehrān	19,196	10,344,000
Kermān	181,814	2,004,000	Yazd	73,467	751,000
Kermānshāh	24,641	1,779,000	Zanjān	21,841	901,000
Khorāsān	302,966	6,048,000	TOTAL	1,629,918[2]	60,055,000

Demography

Population (2002): 65,457,000[3].
Density (2002): persons per sq mi 104.0, persons per sq km 40.2.
Urban-rural (2001): urban 64.7%; rural 35.3%.
Sex distribution (2000): male 50.73%; female 49.27%.
Age breakdown (2000): under 15, 34.4%; 15–29, 32.0%; 30–44, 17.9%; 45–59, 9.2%; 60–74, 5.1%; 75 and over, 1.4%.
Population projection: (2010) 73,150,000; (2020) 84,649,000.
Doubling time: 54 years.
Ethnic composition (1995): Persian 51%; Azerbaijani 24%; Gīlaki/Mazāndarānī 8%; Kurd 7%; Arab 3%; Lurī 2%; Balochi 2%; other 3%.
Religious affiliation (2000): Muslim 95.6% (Shī'ī 90.1%, Sunnī 5.5%); Zoroastrian 2.8%; Christian 0.5%; other 1.1%.
Major cities (1996): Tehrān 6,758,845; Mashhad 1,887,405; Eşfahān 1,266,072; Tabriz 1,191,043; Shīrāz 1,053,025; Karaj 940,968; Ahvāz 804,980.

Vital statistics

Birth rate per 1,000 population (2000): 18.3 (world avg. 22.5).
Death rate per 1,000 population (2000): 5.5 (world avg. 9.0).
Natural increase rate per 1,000 population (2000): 12.8 (world avg. 13.5).
Total fertility rate (avg. births per childbearing woman; 2000): 2.2.
Life expectancy at birth (2000): male 68.3 years; female 71.5 years.
Major causes of death per 100,000 population (1990)[4]: diseases of the circulatory system 304; accidents and violence 108; malignant neoplasms (cancers) 61; diseases of the respiratory system 48; infectious diseases 34.

National economy

Budget (2000–01). Revenue: Rls 150,212,000,000,000 (petroleum and natural gas revenue 55.2%; taxes 22.6%, of which corporate 8.9%; import duties 4.6%; other 17.6%). Expenditures: Rls 136,761,000,000,000 (current expenditure 65.1%; development expenditures 22.0%; other 12.9%).
Public debt (external, outstanding; 2000): U.S.$3,812,000,000.
Tourism (1999): receipts U.S.$662,000,000; expenditures U.S.$918,000,000.
Gross national product (2000): U.S.$106,707,000,000 (U.S.$1,680 per capita).

Structure of gross domestic product and labour force

	1999–2000		1996	
	in value Rls '000,000,000[5]	% of total value[5]	labour force	% of labour force
Agriculture, forestry	86,997	20.9	3,357,263	21.0
Petroleum, natural gas	35,044	8.4	119,884	0.7
Other mining	2,740	0.7		
Manufacturing	70,655	17.0	2,551,962	15.9
Construction	14,083	3.4	1,650,481	10.3
Public utilities	7,421	1.8	150,631	0.9
Transp. and commun.	34,387	8.3	972,792	6.1
Trade, restaurants	76,802	18.4	1,927,067	12.0
Finance, real estate	44,759	10.7	301,962	1.9
Pub. admin., defense	35,652	8.5	1,618,100	10.1
Services	8,628	2.1	1,664,402	10.4
Other	–9516	–0.26	1,712,028[7]	10.7[7]
TOTAL	416,698	100.0	16,026,572	100.0

Production (metric tons except as noted). Agriculture, forestry, fishing (1998): wheat 8,673,000, sugar beets 5,587,000, potatoes 3,433,000, tomatoes 3,400,000, grapes 2,350,000, rice 2,348,000, apples 2,200,000, barley 1,999,000, oranges 1,850,000, onions 1,667,000, corn (maize) 1,155,000, lemons 1,000,000,

dates 930,000, seed cotton 441,000, pistachios 291,000; livestock (number of live animals) 55,000,000 sheep, 8,100,000 cattle; roundwood (2000) 1,151,000 cu m; fish catch (1999) 419,000. Mining and quarrying (1998): copper ore 14,500,000; iron ore 12,300,000; gypsum 9,750,000; lead-zinc ore 1,520,000; chromite 860,000. Manufacturing (value added in U.S.$'000,000; 1995): iron and steel 1,393; food products 1,170; textiles 989; transport equipment 763; electrical machinery 716; bricks, tiles, and cement 703. Energy production (consumption): electricity (kW-hr; 2000–01) 120,611,000,000 (120,611,000,-000); coal (metric tons; 1997) 1,750,000 (1,320,000); crude petroleum (barrels; 1999–2000) 1,255,000,000 (496,000,000); petroleum products (metric tons; 1997) 50,135,000 (53,936,000); natural gas (cu m; 1999–2000) 80,000,000,000 (58,700,000,000).
Population economically active (2000–01): total 18,700,000; activity rate 29.3% (participation rates: over age 15 [1996] 44.0%; female [1996] 12.7%; unemployed 13.9%).

Price and earnings indexes (1997–98 = 100)

	1995–96	1996–97	1997–98	1998–99	1999–2000	2000–01
Consumer price index	68.4	88.4	100.0	118.1	141.8	159.7
Daily earnings index[8]	59.4	79.5	100.0	113.3	128.5	142.3

Household income and expenditure. Average household size (1999) 5.0; income per urban household (1988) Rls 1,339,970 (U.S.$19,536); sources of urban income (1988): wages 37.4%, self-employment 30.5%, other 32.1%; expenditure (1990–91): food, beverages, and tobacco 42.6%[9], housing and energy 24.9%, clothing 11.8%, household furnishings 6.4%.
Land use (1994): forest 7.0%; pasture 26.9%; agriculture 11.1%; other 55.0%.

Foreign trade

Balance of trade (current prices)

	1994–95	1995–96	1996–97	1997–98	1998–99	1999–2000
U.S.$'000,000	+7,633	+5,586	+7,910	+4,258	–1,168	+6,215
% of total	24.4%	17.9%	21.5%	13.1%	4.3%	18.7%

Imports (1998–99): U.S.$14,286,000,000 (nonelectrical machinery 24.4%, electrical machinery 10.6%, transportation equipment 9.3%, iron and steel 9.0%, grains and derivatives 6.1%). *Major import sources:* Germany 11.6%; Italy 8.3%; Japan 7.0%; Belgium 6.3%; U.A.E. 5.3%; Argentina 4.4%.
Exports (1998–99): U.S.$13,118,000,000 (petroleum and natural gas 75.7%, fruit 4.5%, carpets 4.3%, iron and steel 1.1%). *Major export destinations:* U.K. 16.8%; Japan 15.7%; Italy 8.6%; U.A.E. 6.7%; South Korea 5.0%; Greece 5.0%; Turkey 3.8%.

Transport and communications

Transport. Railroads (1999): route length 3,915 mi, 6,300 km; passenger-km 6,103,000,000[10]; metric ton-km cargo 14,400,000,000[10]. Roads (1997): length 102,976 mi, 165,724 km (paved 50%). Vehicles (1996): passenger cars 1,793,000; trucks and buses 692,000. Air transport (2000)[11]: passenger-km 6,228,670,000; metric ton-km cargo 72,150,000; airports (1996) 19.

Communications

Medium	date	unit	number	units per 1,000 persons
Daily newspapers	1996	circulation	1,651,000	28
Radio	1997	receivers	17,000,000	280
Television	1999	receivers	10,500,000	157
Telephones	2001	main lines	10,005,000	155
Cellular telephones	2001	subscribers	1,485,000	23
Personal computers	2001	units	4,500,000	70
Internet	2001	users	402,000	6.2

Education and health

Educational attainment (1986). Percentage of population age 25 and over having: no formal schooling 12.8%; secondary education 38.0%; higher 7.8%.
Literacy (1997): total population age 15 and over literate 73.4%; males literate 79.7%; females literate 65.9%.

Education (1997–98)

	schools	teachers	students	student/ teacher ratio
Primary (age 7–11)	63,101[12]	298,755[12]	8,938,000	30.9[12]
Secondary (age 12–18)[13]	...	280,309	8,776,792	31.3
Higher	...	40,477[12,14]	1,284,658	...

Health (1998–99): physicians 60,000 (1 per 1,033 persons); hospital beds 98,669 (1 per 628 persons); infant mortality rate (2000) 30.0.
Food (2000): daily per capita caloric intake 2,913 (vegetable products 91%, animal products 9%); 121% of FAO recommended minimum requirement.

Military

Total active duty personnel (2001): 513,000 (revolutionary guard corps 24.4%, army 63.4%, navy 3.5%, air force 8.7%). *Military expenditure as percentage of GNP* (1999): 2.9% (world 2.4%); per capita expenditure U.S.$106.

[1]Not required to be a supreme theological authority. [2]Detail does not add to total given because of rounding. [3]Excludes roughly 1.4 million Afghan refugees and about 220,000 Iraqi refugees in August 2002. [4]Projected rates based on about 20% of total deaths. [5]At factor cost. [6]Less imputed bank service charge. [7]Includes 1,455,000 unemployed. [8]Construction sector only. [9]Includes café and hotel expenditures. [10]1997. [11]Iran Air. [12]1996–97. [13]Includes vocational and teacher training. [14]Excludes private universities.

Internet resources for further information:
• Embassy of the Islamic Republic of Iran (London) http://www.iran-embassy.org.uk
• Statistical Centre of Iran http://www.sci.or.ir

Iraq

Official name: Al-Jumhūrīyah
al-'Irāqīyah (Republic of Iraq).
Form of government: unitary
multiparty[1] republic with one
legislative house (National Assembly
[220[2]]).
Head of state and government:
President.
Capital: Baghdad.
Official language: Arabic[3].
Official religion: Islam.
Monetary unit: 1 Iraqi dinar (ID) = 20
dirhams = 1,000 fils; valuation
(Sept. 23, 2002) 1 ID = U.S.$3.23 =
£2.08.

Area and population		area[4]		population
				1991
Governorates	**Capitals**	sq mi	sq km	estimate
Al-Anbār	Ar-Ramādī	53,208	137,808	865,500
Bābil	Al-Hillah	2,163	5,603	1,221,100
Baghdād	Baghdad	1,572	4,071	3,910,900
Al-Başrah[4]	Al-Başrah	7,363	19,070	1,168,800
Dhī Qār	An-Nāşirīyah	4,981	12,900	1,030,900
Diyālā	Ba'qūbah	6,828	17,685	1,037,600
Karbalā'	Karbalā'	1,944	5,034	567,600
Maysān	Al-'Amārah	6,205	16,072	524,200
Al-Muthannā	As-Samāwah	19,977	51,740	350,000
An-Najaf	An-Najaf	11,129	28,824	666,400
Nīnawā	Mosul	14,410	37,323	1,618,700
Al-Qādisiyah	Ad-Dīwānīyah	3,148	8,153	595,600
Şalāh ad-Dīn	Tikrīt	9,407	24,363	772,200
At-Ta'mīm	Karkūk (Kirkūk)	3,737	9,679	605,900
Wāsiţ	Al-kūt	6,623	17,153	605,700
Kurdish Autonomous				
Region[5]				
Dahūk	Dahūk	2,530	6,553	309,300
Irbīl	Irbīl	5,820	15,074	928,400
As-Sulaymānīyah	As-Sulaymānīyah	6,573	17,023	1,124,200
LAND AREA		167,618	434,128	
OTHER[6]		357	924	
TOTAL		167,975	435,052	17,903,000

Demography

Population (2002): 24,002,000.
Density (2002): persons per sq mi 142.9, persons per sq km 55.2.
Urban-rural (1999): urban 76.4%; rural 23.6%.
Sex distribution (2001): male 50.57%; female 49.43%.
Age breakdown (2000): under 15, 42.1%; 15–29, 30.4%; 30–44, 15.6%; 45–59, 7.4%; 60–74, 3.5%; 75 and over, 1.0%.
Population projection: (2010) 29,672,000; (2020) 36,908,000.
Doubling time: 25 years.
Ethnic composition (2000): Arab 64.7%; Kurd 23.0%; Azerbaijani 5.6%; Turkmen 1.2%; Persian 1.1%; other 4.4%.
Religious affiliation (2000): Shī'ī Muslim 62.0%; Sunnī Muslim 34.0%; Christian (primarily Chaldean rite and Syrian rite Catholic and Nestorian) 3.2%; other (primarily Yazīdī syncretist) 0.8%.
Major cities: Baghdad (2001) 4,958,000[7]; Irbīl (2000) 2,369,000[7]; Mosul (2000) 1,131,000[7]; Karkūk (1987) 418,624; Al-Başrah (1987) 406,296.

Vital statistics

Birth rate per 1,000 population (2001): 34.6 (world avg. 21.2).
Death rate per 1,000 population (2001): 6.2 (world avg. 8.9).
Natural increase rate per 1,000 population (2001): 28.4 (world avg. 12.3).
Total fertility rate (avg. births per childbearing woman; 2001): 4.8.
Marriage rate per 1,000 population (1997): 6.3.
Divorce rate per 1,000 population (1997): 1.3.
Life expectancy at birth (2001): male 65.9 years; female 68.0 years.
Major causes of death per 100,000 population (1995): infectious and parasitic diseases 311.6, diseases of the circulatory system 130.2, malignant neoplasms (cancers) 111.5, diseases of the respiratory system 99.5, accidents and violence 65.3.

National economy

Budget (1992). Revenue: ID 13,935,000,000. Expenditures: ID 13,935,000,000. Details of more recent budgets are not available.
Production (metric tons except as noted). Agriculture, forestry, fishing (2001): wheat 550,000, tomatoes 500,000, barley 465,000, dates 400,000, watermelons 380,000, oranges 270,000, grapes 265,000, cucumbers 215,000, cantaloupes 195,000, potatoes 150,000, rice 130,000; livestock (number of live animals) 6,780,000 sheep, 1,350,000 cattle; roundwood (2000) 110,309 cu m; fish catch (1999) 26,789. Mining and quarrying (2000): phosphate rock 300,000, sulfur 250,000. Manufacturing (value added in U.S.$'000,000; 1994): refined petroleum 127; bricks, tiles, and cement 100; industrial chemicals 79; food products 59; metal products 28. Energy production (consumption): electricity (kW-hr; 1999) 26,000,000,000 (31,563,000,000); coal, none (none); crude petroleum (barrels; 2001) 853,225,000 ([1997] 214,678,000); petroleum products (metric tons; 1997) 23,730,000 (21,531,000); natural gas (cu m; 1999) 4,000,000,000 (4,000,000,000).
Household income and expenditure (1988). Average household size 8.9; sources of income: self-employment 33.9%, wages and salaries 23.9%, transfers 23.0%, rent 18.6%; expenditure: food and beverages 50.2%, housing and energy 19.9%, clothing and footwear 10.6%.

Gross domestic product (2000): U.S.$20,000,000,000 (U.S.$900 per capita).

Structure of gross domestic product				
	2001		1996	
	in value ID '000,000[8]	% of total value	labour force	% of labour force
Agriculture	1,962,510	24.6	...	...
Mining			...	...
Manufacturing	786,249	9.8	...	...
Public utilities			...	...
Construction	253,375	3.2	...	...
Transp. and commun.	1,241,586	15.5	...	...
Trade	2,083,053	26.1	...	...
Finance, real estate	914,625	11.5	...	...
Pub. admin., defense	921,570	11.5	...	...
Services			...	...
Other	−177,923[9]	−2.2[9]	...	...
TOTAL	7,985,045	100.0	5,573,000	100.0

Public debt (external, outstanding; 1999): U.S.$23,000,000,000.
Population economically active (1996): total 5,573,000; activity rate of total population 27.6% (participation rates: ages 15–64, 45.7%; female 25.0%).

Price index (1995 = 100)							
	1990	1991	1992	1993	1994	1995	1996
Consumer price index	0.2	0.6	1.7[10]	5.2[10]	20[10]	100[10]	550[10]

Tourism (1997): receipts U.S.$13,000,000; expenditures, n.a.
Land use (1994): forest 0.4%; pasture 9.1%; agriculture 13.1%; other 77.4%.

Foreign trade[11, 12]

Balance of trade (current prices)[10]						
	1994	1995	1996	1997	1998	1999
U.S.$'000,000	−1,518	−1,968	−1,169	+471	+560	+560
% of total	66.5%	72.0%	44.4%	5.2%	6.0%	6.0%

Imports (1999): U.S.$4,400,000,000[10] (agricultural products 41.9%, of which cereals 17.5%; unspecified 58.1%). *Major import sources* (1996): Turkey 36.5%; Jordan 26.3%; Malaysia 3.7%; Australia 3.0%.
Exports (1999): U.S.$4,960,000,000[10] (mostly crude petroleum and petroleum products). *Major export destinations* (1996): Jordan 91.5%; Turkey 5.8%.

Transport and communications

Transport. Railroads (1999): route length 2,603 km; passenger-km 499,600,000; metric ton-km cargo 830,200,000. Roads (1999): total length 45,550 km (paved 84%). Vehicles (1998): passenger cars 735,521; trucks and buses 349,202. Air transport: [13].

Communications				units
Medium	date	unit	number	per 1,000 persons
Daily newspapers	1996	circulation	407,000	20
Radio	1997	receivers	4,850,000	229
Television	1997	receivers	1,750,000	78
Telephones	1999	main lines	675,000	30

Education and health

Educational attainment (1987). Percentage of population age 10 and over having: no formal schooling 52.8%; primary education 21.5%; secondary 11.6%; higher 4.1%; unknown 10.0%. *Literacy* (1995): total population age 15 and over literate 58.0%; males 70.7%; females 45.0%.

Education (1997–98)	schools	teachers	students	student/ teacher ratio
Primary (age 6–11)	8,333	141,935	3,029,386	21.3
Secondary (age 12–17)	2,822	54,846	1,020,823	18.6
Voc., teacher tr.	303	8,838	102,004	11.5
Higher	11	12,101	266,505	22.0

Health (1998): physicians 11,046 (1 per 1,937 persons); hospital beds 30,022 (1 per 713 persons); infant mortality rate per 1,000 live births (2001) 60.0.
Food (2000): daily per capita caloric intake 2,197 (vegetable products 96%, animal products 4%); 91% of FAO recommended minimum requirement.

Military

Total active duty personnel (2001): 429,000 (army 91.3%, navy 0.5%, air force 8.2%). *Military expenditure as percentage of GDP* (1999): 5.5% (world 2.4%); per capita expenditure U.S.$57.

[1]Multipartyism is officially authorized, but political power is in fact concentrated in a single-party apparatus. [2]Elective seats as of March 2000 elections; 30 additional seats allotted to the Kurdish Autonomous Region were filled by presidential appointment. [3]Kurdish is official in the Kurdish Autonomous Region only. [4]Includes territory ceded to Kuwait as of Jan. 15, 1993. [5]De facto self-government from 1992 through September 2002. [6]Territorial water at the mouth of the Shaţţ al-'Arab. [7]Urban agglomeration. [8]ESCWA estimate; in purchaser's value. [9]Imputed bank service charge. [10]Estimated figure(s). [11]Imports c.i.f.; exports f.o.b. [12]UN-imposed trade sanctions in place from August 1990 through September 2002. [13]Scheduled domestic and limited international air service resumed in 2000 and 2001, respectively.

Internet resources for further information:
• **Permanent Mission of Iraq to the United Nations (official site)**
  http://www.iraqi-mission.org
• **Iraq Foundation (unofficial)** http://www.iraqfoundation.org

Ireland

Official name: Éire (Irish); Ireland[1] (English).
Form of government: unitary multi-party republic with two legislative houses (Senate [60[2]]; House of Representatives [166]).
Chief of state: President.
Head of government: Prime Minister.
Capital: Dublin.
Official languages: Irish; English.
Official religion: none.
Monetary unit: 1 euro (€) = 100 cents; valuation (Sept. 23, 2002) 1 U.S.$ = €1.02; 1 £ = €1.58[3].

Area and population

Provinces Counties/County Boroughs (C.B.)	area sq km	population 2002[4] census	Provinces Counties/County Boroughs (C.B.)	area sq km	population 2002[4] census
Connacht	17,122	464,050	Wexford	2,351	116,543
Galway	5,940	143,052	Wicklow	2,025	114,719
Galway C.B. }		65,774	Munster	24,127	1,101,266
Leitrim	1,525	25,815	Clare	3,188	103,333
Mayo	5,398	117,428	Cork	7,460	324,843
Roscommon	2,463	53,803	Cork C.B. }		123,338
Sligo	1,796	58,178	Kerry	4,701	132,424
Leinster	19,633	2,105,449	Limerick	2,686	121,471
Carlow	896	45,845	Limerick C.B. }		54,058
Dublin C.B.	922[5]	495,101	Tipperary North Riding	1,996	61,068
Dun Laoghaire-Rathdown	5	191,389	Tipperary South Riding	2,258	79,213
Fingal	5	196,223	Waterford	1,838	56,954
Kildare	1,694	163,995	Waterford C.B. }		44,564
Kilkenny	2,062	80,421	Ulster (part of)	8,012	246,571
Laoighis	1,719	58,732	Cavan	1,891	56,416
Longford	1,044	31,127	Donegal	4,830	137,383
Louth	823	101,802	Monaghan	1,291	52,772
Meath	2,336	133,936	TOTAL LAND AREA	68,895[6]	
Offaly	1,998	63,702	INLAND WATER	1,390	
South Dublin	5	239,887	TOTAL	70,285[7]	3,917,336
Westmeath	1,763	72,027			

Demography

Population (2002): 3,926,000.
Density (2002)[8]: persons per sq mi 147.6, persons per sq km 57.0.
Urban-rural (1996): urban 58.0%; rural 42.0%.
Sex distribution (2002): male 49.66%; female 50.34%.
Age breakdown (2000): under 15, 21.9%; 15–29, 24.9%; 30–44, 21.1%; 45–59, 16.9%; 60–74, 10.3%; 75 and over, 4.9%.
Population projection: (2010) 4,253,000; (2020) 4,651,000.
Ethnic composition (2000): Irish 95.0%; British 1.7%, of which English 1.4%; Ulster Irish 1.0%; U.S. white 0.8%; other 1.5%.
Religious affiliation (1991): Roman Catholic 91.6%; Church of Ireland (Anglican) 2.5%; Presbyterian 0.4%; other 5.5%.
Major cities (2002)[9]: Dublin 495,101 (urban agglomeration 1,122,600); Cork 123,338; Galway 65,774; Limerick 54,058; Waterford 44,564.

Vital statistics

Birth rate per 1,000 population (2000): 14.3 (world avg. 22.5).
Death rate per 1,000 population (2000): 8.2 (world avg. 9.0).
Natural increase rate per 1,000 population (2000): 6.1 (world avg. 13.5).
Marriage rate per 1,000 population (2000): 5.1.
Total fertility rate (avg. births per childbearing woman; 2000): 1.9.
Life expectancy at birth (2000): male 74.1 years; female 79.7 years.
Major causes of death per 100,000 population (1998): heart and circulatory diseases 364.4, of which ischemic heart diseases 199.3; malignant neoplasms (cancers) 206.9; respiratory disease 131.8, of which pneumonia 62.0.

National economy

Budget (2000). Revenue: £Ir 21,741,000,000 (income taxes 33.0%, value-added tax 27.0%, excise taxes 15.4%). Expenditures: £Ir 19,297,000,000 (social welfare 27.9%, health 20.9%, education 14.9%, debt service 10.5%).
Public debt (1996): U.S.$47,876,000,000.
Gross national product (2000): U.S.$85,979,000,000 (U.S.$22,660 per capita).

Structure of gross domestic product and labour force

	2000			
	in value £Ir '000,000[10]	% of total value[10]	labour force	% of labour force
Agriculture	2,872	4.0	130,900	7.5
Mining } Manufacturing } Public utilities }	30,781	42.8	309,900	17.7
Construction			166,300	9.5
Transp. and commun. } Trade }	11,803	16.4	100,800	5.8
			362,800	20.8
Pub. admin., defense	2,460	3.4	77,800	4.5
Services } Finance }	24,612	34.2	310,100	17.8
			212,100	12.2
Other	–626[11]	–0.9[11]	74,900[12]	4.3[12]
TOTAL	71,912[6]	100.0[6]	1,745,600	100.0[6]

Tourism (2000): receipts U.S.$3,387,000,000; expenditures U.S.$2,957,000,000.
Production (metric tons except as noted). Agriculture, forestry, fishing (2000): sugar beets 1,564,000, barley 1,129,000, wheat 706,000, potatoes 381,000, oats 128,000, milk (1995) 51,900,000 hectolitres; livestock (number of live animals)

8,393,000 sheep, 6,607,500 cattle, 1,763,000 pigs; roundwood (2000) 2,673,000 cu m; fish catch (1999) 329,777. Mining and quarrying (1999): gypsum 480,000; zinc ore 199,300[13]; lead ore 44,100[13]. Manufacturing (value added in £Ir '000,000; 1995): office equipment and computers 2,163; basic chemicals 2,112; reproduction of recorded media 1,531; pharmaceuticals 884; alcoholic beverages 735. Construction (1998): residential 6,098,000 sq m; nonresidential 4,122,000 sq m. Energy production (consumption): electricity (kW-hr; 1997) 19,856,000,000 (19,856,000,000); coal (metric tons; 1997) none (3,070,000); crude petroleum (barrels; 1997) none (20,800,000); petroleum products (metric tons; 1997) 2,795,000 (5,616,000); natural gas (cu m; 1997) 1,012,000,000 (3,242,000,000).
Population economically active (2000): total 1,745,600; activity rate 46.1% (participation rates: ages 15–64, c. 68%; female 40.3%; unemployed 4.3%).

Price and earnings indexes (1995 = 100)

	1995	1996	1997	1998	1999	2000	2001
Consumer price index	100.0	101.7	103.2	105.7	107.4	110.7	118.9
Weekly earnings index	100.0	102.5	107.5	111.9	118.4	126.4	136.4

Household income and expenditure. Average household size (1997) 3.1; income per household (1994–95): £Ir 16,224 (U.S.$25,100); expenditure (1996)[14]: food and beverages 35.4%, transportation 13.9%, rent/household goods 11.6%.

Foreign trade[15]

Balance of trade (current prices)

	1995	1996	1997	1998	1999	2000[16]	2001[16]
£Ir '000,000	+7,206	+7,978	+9,454	+13,939	+17,855	+27,980	+35,500
% of total	14.9%	15.1%	15.4%	18.2%	20.5%	20.0%	23.7%

Imports (1999): £Ir 34,682,100,000 (machinery and transport equipment 51.5%, chemicals 11.2%, manufactured goods 11.0%, food 5.8%, petroleum and petroleum products 2.8%). *Major import sources:* U.K. 33.1%; U.S. 16.7%; Germany 6.2%; Japan 5.8%; France 4.1%.
Exports (1999): £Ir 52,537,200,000 (machinery and transport equipment 38.8%, chemical products 31.6%, manufactured goods 11.1%, food 8.2%). *Major export destinations:* U.K. 22.0%; U.S. 15.4%; Germany 11.9%; France 8.4%; The Netherlands 6.0%.

Transport and communications

Transport. Railroads (1999): route length 1,945 km; passenger-km 1,295,000,000; metric ton-km cargo 570,000,000. Roads (1999): length 92,500 km (paved 94%). Vehicles (2000): passenger cars 1,269,245; trucks and buses 188,814. Air transport (2000)[17]: passenger-km 9,385,039,000; metric ton-km cargo 1,005,296,000; airports (1996) 9.

Communications

Medium	date	unit	number	units per 1,000 persons
Daily newspapers	1996	circulation	543,000	150
Radio	1998	receivers	2,150,000	580
Television	1999	receivers	2,144,000	578
Telephones	2001	main lines	1,860,000	480
Cellular telephones	2001	subscribers	2,800,000	722
Personal computers	2001	units	1,500,000	387
Internet	2001	users	895,000	231

Education and health

Educational attainment (1991). Percentage of population age 15 and over having: primary education or no schooling 33.7%; secondary 42.7%; some postsecondary 12.6%; university or like institution 11.0%.

Education (1998–99)

	schools	teachers	students	student/teacher ratio
Primary (age 6–11)[18]	3,303	21,500	452,533	21.0
Secondary (age 12–18)	432	12,180	211,369	17.4
Voc., teacher tr.	330	8,640	151,136	17.5
Higher	24	5,644	107,213	19.0

Health: physicians (1998) 8,114 (1 per 457 persons); hospital beds (1995) 11,953[19] (1 per 301 persons); infant mortality rate (2000) 5.6.
Food (2000): daily per capita caloric intake 3,613 (vegetable products 68%, animal products 32%); 144% of FAO recommended minimum requirement.

Military

Total active duty personnel (2001): 10,460 (army 81.3%, navy 10.5%, air force 8.2%). *Military expenditure as percentage of GNP* (1999): 1.0% (world 2.4%); per capita expenditure U.S.$208.

---

[1]As provided by the constitution; the 1948 Republic of Ireland Act provides precedent for this longer formulation of the official name but, per official sources, "has not changed the usage *Ireland* as the name of the state in the English language." [2]Includes 11 nonelective seats. [3]The Irish pound was the former monetary unit; on Jan. 1, 2002, 1 £Ir = € 1.27. [4]Preliminary. [5]Dublin C.B. includes Dun Laoghaire-Rathdown, Fingal, and South Dublin. [6]Detail does not add to total given because of rounding. [7]Area per more recent survey is 70,273 sq km. [8]Land area only. [9]Populations for Ireland's five administrative county boroughs. [10]At factor cost. [11]Statistical discrepancy. [12]Unemployed. [13]Metal content of ores. [14]November. [15]Imports c.i.f.; exports f.o.b. [16]In millions of euros (€). [17]Aer Lingus only. [18]National schools only. [19]Acute-care public hospitals only.

Internet resources for further information:
• **Central Statistics Office (Ireland) http://www.cso.ie**
• **Central Bank of Ireland http://www.centralbank.ie**

Isle of Man

Official name: Isle of Man[1].
Political status: crown dependency (United Kingdom) with two legislative bodies[2] (Legislative Council [11[3]]; House of Keys [24]).
Chief of state: British Monarch represented by Lieutenant-Governor.
Head of government: Chief Minister assisted by the Council of Ministers.
Capital: Douglas.
Official language: English.
Official religion: none.
Monetary unit: 1 Manx pound (£M)[4] = 100 new pence; valuation (Sept. 23, 2002) 1 £M = U.S.$1.55.

Area and population

	area sq km	population 2001 census		area sq km	population 2001 census
Towns			**Parishes** (cont.)		
Castletown	0.4	3,100	Ballaugh	24.6	868
Douglas	6.7	25,347	Braddan	45.1	2,665
Peel	1.3	3,785	Bride	23.5	408
Ramsey	1.2	7,322	German	46.1	1,010
			Jurby	19.1	677
Villages			Lezayre	65.3	1,134
Laxey	5	1,725	Lonan	38.1[5]	1,393
Onchan	26.4	8,803	Malew	51.7	2,262
Port Erin	2.6	3,369	Marown	26.6	1,879
Port St. Mary	1.4	1,941	Maughold	36.2	941
			Michael	35.5	1,431
Parishes			Patrick	42.9	1,305
Andreas	31.9	1,152	Rushen	26.2	1,504
Arbory	18.1	1,714	Santon	17.2	580
			TOTAL	588.1	76,315

Demography

Population (2002): 76,900.
Density (2002): persons per sq mi 338.6, persons per sq km 130.8.
Urban-rural (1999): urban 76.3%; rural 23.7%.
Sex distribution (2001): male 48.97%; female 51.03%.
Age breakdown (2001): under 15, 17.9%; 15–29, 17.5%; 30–44, 22.6%; 45–59, 20.1%; 60–74, 13.6%; 75 and over, 8.3%.
Population projection: (2010) 80,000; (2020) 84,000.
Population by place of birth (2001): Isle of Man 48.0%; United Kingdom 45.2%, of which England 38.2%, Scotland 3.5%, Northern Ireland 2.3%, Wales 1.2%; Ireland 2.3%; other Europe 1.0%; South Africa 0.5%.
Religious affiliation (2000): Christian 63.7%, of which Anglican 40.5%, Methodist 9.9%, Roman Catholic 8.2%; other (mostly nonreligious) 36.3%.
Major towns (2001): Douglas 25,347; Onchan 8,803; Ramsey 7,322; Peel 3,785; Port Erin 3,369.

Vital statistics

Birth rate per 1,000 population (2000): 11.0 (world avg. 22.5); legitimate 66.2%; illegitimate 33.8%.
Death rate per 1,000 population (2000): 11.9 (world avg. 9.0).
Natural increase rate per 1,000 population (2000): –0.9 (world avg. 13.5).
Total fertility rate (avg. births per childbearing woman; 1999): 1.6.
Marriage rate per 1,000 population (2000): 5.5.
Divorce rate per 1,000 population (1996): 4.0.
Life expectancy at birth (1999): male 73.9 years; female 80.8 years.
Major causes of death per 100,000 population (1998): diseases of the circulatory system 504.3, of which ischemic heart diseases 247.3, cerebrovascular disease 96.7; neoplasms (cancers) 298.4; diseases of the respiratory system 225.2.

National economy

Budget (1999–2000). Revenue: £339,070,000 (customs duties and excise taxes 54.1%; income taxes 44.7%, of which resident 40.0%, nonresident 4.7%). Expenditures: £291,804,000 (health and social security 40.2%; education 18.8%; home affairs 6.8%; transportation 6.5%; tourism and recreation 5.5%).
Public debt: n.a.
Production. Agriculture, forestry, fishing (1998): main crops include hay, oats, barley, wheat, and orchard crops; livestock (number of live animals) 173,900 sheep, 34,000 cattle, 6,600 pigs; roundwood, n.a.; fish catch (value of catch in £; 1997): scallops 1,666,000, whitefish 244,000, herring 138,000. Mining and quarrying: sand and gravel. Manufacturing (value added in U.S.$; 1996–97): electrical and nonelectrical machinery/apparatus, textiles, other 103,700,000; food and beverages 18,600,000. Energy production (consumption): electricity (kW-hr; 1999–2000), n.a. (307,400,000); crude petroleum, none (n.a.); petroleum products, n.a. (n.a.); natural gas, none (n.a.).
Household income and expenditure. Average household size (2001) 2.4; income per household (1981–82)[6, 7] £7,479 (U.S.$13,721); sources of income (1981–82)[6, 7]: wages and salaries 64.1%, transfer payments 16.9%, interest and dividends 11.2%, self-employment 6.6%; expenditure (1981–82)[6, 7]: food and beverages 31.0%, transportation 14.9%, energy 11.0%, housing 7.9%, clothing and footwear 7.0%.
Gross national product (at current market prices; 1998–99): U.S.$1,485,000,000 (U.S.$20,030 per capita).

Structure of gross domestic product and labour force

	1997–98		2001	
	in value £'000[8]	% of total value[8]	labour force	% of labour force
Agriculture, fishing	10,726	1.5	543	1.4
Mining	} 80,981	11.2	3,185	8.0
Manufacturing				
Construction	44,587	6.2	2,512	6.3
Public utilities	15,062	2.1	515	1.3
Transp. and commun.	63,198	8.8	2,970	7.5
Trade, hotels	69,109	9.6	7,171	18.1
Finance, real estate, insurance	320,414[9]	44.5[9]	8,959	22.6
Pub. admin., defense	40,850	5.7	3,105	7.8
Services	167,826[9]	23.3[9]	10,090	25.4
Other	–93,071	–12.9	635[10]	1.6[10]
TOTAL	719,682	100.0	39,685	100.0

Population economically active (2001): total 39,685; activity rate of total population 52.0% (participation rates: ages 16 and over 64.2%; female 45.4%; unemployed 1.6%).

Price and earnings indexes (1995 = 100)

	1995	1996	1997	1998	1999	2000
Retail price index	100.0	102.9	105.2	108.3	110.4	113.4
Weekly earnings index[11]	100.0	102.9	110.0	115.0	120.3	123.3

Tourism: receipts from visitors (1999) U.S.$90,600,000; expenditures by nationals abroad, n.a.
Land use: n.a.

Foreign trade

Imports (1998): n.a. *Major import sources* (1998): mostly the United Kingdom. *Exports* (1998): traditional exports include scallops, herring, beef, lambs, and tweeds. *Major export destinations* (1998): mostly the United Kingdom.

Transport and communications

Transport. Railroads (1998): route length 32 mi, 52 km[12]. Roads (1998): total length, more than 500 mi, more than 805 km (paved, n.a.). Vehicles (1998): passenger cars 40,168; trucks and buses, n.a. Merchant marine (1999): vessels (100 gross tons and over) 219; total deadweight tonnage, n.a. Air transport (1998)[13]: passenger-mi 526,161,000, passenger-km 846,775,000; short ton-mi cargo 115,000, metric ton-km cargo 168,000; airports (1999) with scheduled flights 1.

Communications

Medium	date	unit	number	units per 1,000 persons
Daily newspapers	1997	circulation	—[14]	—
Television	1997	receivers	27,000	375
Telephones	1996	main lines	46,000	641

Education and health

Educational attainment: n.a. *Literacy:* n.a.

Education (1998–99)

	schools	teachers	students	student/teacher ratio
Primary (age 5–10)	33	...	6,210	...
Secondary (age 11–16)	5	...	4,732	...
Higher[15]	1	...	1,128[16]	...

Health: physicians (2000) 138 (1 per 547 persons); hospital beds (1998) 505 (1 per 143 persons); infant mortality rate per 1,000 live births (1998–2000 avg.) 4.5.
Food (1998)[17]: daily per capita caloric intake 3,257 (vegetable products 68%, animal products 32%); 129% of FAO recommended minimum requirement.

Military

Total active duty personnel: 18.

[1]Ellan Vannin in Manx Gaelic. [2]Collective name is Tynwald. [3]Includes 3 nonelected seats. [4]Equivalent in value to pound sterling (£). [5]Lonan includes Laxey. [6]Fiscal year ending March 31st. [7]Based on survey of 259 households; "high income" and "pensioner" households are excluded. [8]At factor cost. [9]Most GDP in 1999 was derived from 66 banks (most of which are "offshore"), 77 investment businesses, and 193 insurance companies. [10]Unemployed. [11]June only. [12]Length of three tourist (novel) railways operating in summer. [13]Manx Airlines. [14]Isle of Man has 2 weekly newspapers and 1 biweekly newspaper. [15]1997–98. [16]Includes enrollees at Isle of Man College and students abroad. [17]Data for United Kingdom. [18]The United Kingdom is responsible for defense.

Internet resources for further information:
• **Isle of Man Government**
  http://www.gov.im

Israel

Official name: Medinat Yisra'el (Hebrew); Isrā'īl (Arabic) (State of Israel).
Form of government: multiparty republic with one legislative house (Knesset [120]).
Chief of state: President.
Head of government: Prime Minister.
Capital: Jerusalem is the proclaimed capital of Israel and the actual seat of government, but recognition of its status as capital by the international community has largely been withheld pending final settlement of territorial and other issues through peace talks between Israel and the Arab parties concerned.
Official languages: Hebrew; Arabic.
Official religion: none.
Monetary unit: 1 New (Israeli) sheqel (NIS) = 100 agorot; valuation (Sept. 23, 2002) 1 U.S.$ = NIS 4.82; 1 £ = NIS 7.48.

Area and population

Districts	Capitals	area[1] sq mi	area[1] sq km	population 2001[2] estimate
Central (Ha Merkaz)	Ramla	493	1,276	1,457,500
Haifa (Hefa)	Haifa	333	863	818,500
Jerusalem (Yerushalayim)	Jerusalem	225	582	758,300
Northern (Ha Zafon)	Tiberias	1,275	3,302	1,083,300
Southern (Ha Darom)	Beersheba	5,494	14,231	899,400
Tel Aviv	Tel Aviv–Yafo	66	171	1,153,800
TOTAL		7,886	20,425	6,170,800[3]

Demography

Population (2002): 6,394,000.
Density (2002)[3]: persons per sq mi 810.8, persons per sq km 313.0.
Urban-rural (2000): urban 90.6%; rural 9.4%.
Sex distribution (2000): male 49.33%; female 50.67%.
Age breakdown (2000): under 15, 28.6%; 15–29, 25.1%; 30–44, 18.7%; 45–59, 14.5%; 60–74, 8.8%; 75 and over, 4.3%.
Population projection: (2010) 7,148,000; (2020) 7,894,000.
Ethnic composition (2000): Jewish 78.1%; Arab and other 21.9%.
Religious affiliation (2000): Jewish 78.1%; Muslim (mostly Sunnī) 15.1%; Christian 2.1%; Druze 1.6%; other 3.1%.
Major cities (2001[2]): Jerusalem 657,500; Tel Aviv–Yafo 354,400; Haifa 270,500; Rishon LeẔiyyon 202,200; Petaẖ Tiqwa 167,500; Ḥolon 165,700.

Vital statistics

Birth rate per 1,000 population (2000): 21.7 (world avg. 22.5); (1994)[4] legitimate 98.2%; illegitimate 1.8%.
Death rate per 1,000 population (2000): 6.0 (world avg. 9.0).
Natural increase rate per 1,000 population (2000): 15.7 (world avg. 13.5).
Total fertility rate (avg. births per childbearing woman; 2000): 3.0.
Marriage rate per 1,000 population (1999): 6.6.
Divorce rate per 1,000 population (1999): 1.7.
Life expectancy at birth (2000): male 76.6 years; female 80.4 years.
Major causes of death per 100,000 population (1997): diseases of the circulatory system 210; malignant neoplasms (cancers) 140; diabetes mellitus 42; accidents and violence 20; diseases of the respiratory system 19.

National economy

Budget (2000). Revenue: NIS 178,037,000,000 (tax revenue 74.6%, of which income tax and property tax 34.7%, value-added tax 26.0%, sales tax and fuel tax 4.7%; nontax revenue 18.5%; grants 6.9%). Expenditures: NIS 188,927,000,000 (defense 20.7%; education 14.8%; interest on loans 13.9%; labour and welfare 12.1%; health 8.5%).
Public debt (external, outstanding; 1999): U.S.$27,323,000,000.
Gross national product (2000): U.S.$104,128,000,000 (U.S.$16,710 per capita).

Structure of net domestic product and labour force

	1999 in value NIS '000,000[5]	1999 % of total value[5]	2000 labour force	2000 % of labour force
Agriculture	4,419	2.3	47,900	2.0
Manufacturing, mining	35,501	18.6	396,600	16.3
Construction	16,401	8.6	116,400	4.8
Public utilities	3,299	1.7	19,300	0.8
Transp. and commun.	13,122	6.9	144,900	6.0
Trade	21,526	11.2	295,600	12.1
Finance	51,754[6]	27.1[6]	433,700[6]	17.8[6]
Public and community services	48,297[7]	25.3[7]	712,100[7]	29.2[7]
Services	8,403[8]	4.4[8]	34,700[8]	1.4[8]
Other	−11,690[9]	−6.1[9]	233,800[10]	9.6[10]
TOTAL	191,032	100.0	2,435,000	100.0

Production (metric tons except as noted). Agriculture, forestry, fishing (2000): tomatoes 550,200, grapefruit 370,000, potatoes 348,600, oranges 300,000, seed cotton 112,000, corn (maize) 82,160, apples 81,500; livestock (number of live animals) 388,000 cattle, 350,000 sheep; roundwood (2000) 113,000 cu m; fish catch (1999) 24,661. Mining and quarrying (1999): phos-

phate rock 4,100,000, potash 1,750,000. Manufacturing (1996): cement 6,723,000; polyethylene 144,147[11]; sulfuric acid 130,000[11]; paper 114,403; cardboard 113,278; chlorine 34,630; wine 12,733,000 litres[11]. Construction (2000): residential 7,101,000 sq m; nonresidential 2,354,000 sq m. Energy production (consumption): electricity (kW-hr; 2000) 42,916,000 (39,317,-000); coal (metric tons; 1997) none (8,639,000); crude petroleum (barrels; 1997) 36,000 (80,340,000); petroleum products (metric tons; 1997) 9,637,000 (9,514,000); natural gas (cu m; 1997) 13,272,000 (13,272,000).
Population economically active (2000)[12]: total 2,435,000; activity rate 39.9% (participation rates: over ages 15, 54.3%; female 45.6%; unemployed 8.8%).

Price and earnings indexes (1995 = 100)

	1995	1996	1997	1998	1999	2000	2001
Consumer price index	100.0	111.3	121.3	127.9	134.5	136.0	137.6
Daily earnings index	100.0	113.9	130.8	143.9	155.4	160.1	...

Household income and expenditure (1999). Average household size 3.6; monthly income per household[12] (1995) NIS 6,125 (U.S.$2,034); sources of income (1993)[13]: salaries and wages 63.4%, allowances and assistance 18.9%, self-employment 14.6%; expenditure (1998): housing 23.7%, food, beverages, and tobacco 21.1%, household durable goods 8.2%.
Tourism (2000): receipts U.S.$3,819,000,000; expenditures U.S.$2,804,000,000.

Foreign trade

Balance of trade (current prices)

	1995	1996	1997	1998	1999	2000
U.S.$'000,000	−10,533	−11,010	−8,278	−6,349	−7,372	−4,346
% of total	21.7%	21.1%	15.5%	12.1%	12.5%	6.5%

Imports (2000): U.S.$35,749,500,000 (investment goods 21.3%; diamonds 17.0%; consumer goods 12.3%; fuel and lubricants 6.0%). *Major import sources:* U.S. 20.7%; Belgium 11.1%; Germany 8.1%; U.K. 7.6%; Italy 5.3%.
Exports (2000): U.S.$31,403,700,000 (machinery and transport equipment 39.7%; diamonds 23.7%; chemicals 13.4%; apparel 4.9%; food, beverages, and tobacco 3.1%). *Major export destinations:* U.S. 35.5%; U.K. 5.5%; Belgium 5.4%; Germany 4.5%; Hong Kong 3.4%; Japan 3.3%.

Transport and communications

Transport. Railroads (1999): route length 610 km; passenger-km 529,000,000; metric ton-km cargo 1,128,000,000. Roads (1999): total length 15,464 km (paved 100%). Vehicles (2000): passenger cars 1,316,765; trucks and buses 319,581. Air transport (2000)[14]: passenger-km 14,125,067,000; metric ton-km cargo 1,288,345,000; airports (1999) with scheduled flights 7.

Communications

Medium	date	unit	number	units per 1,000 persons
Daily newspapers	1997	circulation	1,650,000	288
Radio	1997	receivers	3,070,000	524
Television	1999	receivers	1,690,000	288
Telephones	2001	main lines	3,100,000	476
Cellular telephones	2001	subscribers	5,260,000	808
Personal computers	2001	units	1,600,000	246
Internet	2001	users	1,500,000	231

Education and health

Educational attainment (2000). Percentage of population age 15 and over having: no formal schooling 3.3%; primary 1.9%; secondary 57.4%; postsecondary, vocational, and higher 37.4%. *Literacy* (2000): total population age 15 and over literate 96.7%.

Education (2000–01)

	schools	teachers	students	student/ teacher ratio
Primary (age 6–13)	2,137	58,785	559,541	9.5
Secondary (age 14–17)[15]	707	76,915	473,092	6.2
Vocational, teacher tr.	113	...	118,605	...
Higher	7	10,171	219,763	21.6

Health (2000): physicians 21,500 (1 per 284 persons); hospital beds 38,577 (1 per 158 persons); infant mortality rate (2000) 5.1.
Food (2000): daily per capita caloric intake 3,562 (vegetable products 81%, animal products 19%); 139% of FAO recommended minimum.

Military

Total active duty personnel (2001): 163,500 (army 73.4%, navy 4.0%, air force 22.6%). *Military expenditure as percentage of GNP* (1999): 8.8% (world 2.4%); per capita expenditure U.S.$1,510.

---

[1]Excluding West Bank (2,278 sq mi [5,900 sq km]), Gaza Strip (140 sq mi [363 sq km]), Golan Heights (454 sq mi [1,176 sq km]), East Jerusalem (27 sq mi [70 sq km]), Sea of Galilee (63 sq mi [164 sq km]), and the Dead Sea (120 sq mi [310 sq km]). [2]January 1. [3]Includes 2002 population of Golan Heights (35,000) and East Jerusalem and excludes 2002 Jewish population of the West Bank and Gaza Strip (220,000). [4]Jewish population only. [5]At factor cost; 1999 GDP equals NIS 417,446,000,000. [6]Finance includes other business activities. [7]Public and community services includes education, health, and social services. [8]Services includes private households with domestic personnel. [9]Less imputed bank service charges. [10]Includes 213,800 unemployed. [11]1993. [12]Civilian labour force. [13]Urban population only. [14]El Al only. [15]Includes intermediate schools.

Internet resources for further information:
• **Central Bureau of Statistics (Israel) http://www.cbs.gov.il/engindex.htm**

Italy

Official name: Repubblica Italiana (Italian Republic).
Form of government: republic with two legislative houses (Senate [321[1]]; Chamber of Deputies [630]).
Chief of state: President.
Head of government: Prime Minister.
Capital: Rome.
Official language: Italian.
Official religion: none.
Monetary unit: 1 euro (€) = 100 cents; valuation (Sept. 23, 2002) 1 U.S.$ = €1.02; 1 £ = €1.58[2].

Area and population

Regions Provinces	Capitals	area sq mi	area sq km	population 2000 estimate[3]
Abruzzo	L'Aquila	4,168	10,794	1,279,016
Chieti	Chieti	999	2,587	390,133
L'Aquila	L'Aquila	1,944	5,034	303,839
Pescara	Pescara	473	1,225	294,168
Teramo	Teramo	752	1,948	290,876
Basilicata	Potenza	3,858	9,992	606,183
Matera	Matera	1,331	3,447	206,193
Potenza	Potenza	2,527	6,545	399,990
Calabria	Catanzaro	5,823	15,080	2,050,478
Catanzaro	Catanzaro	924	2,392	381,737
Cosenza	Cosenza	2,568	6,650	745,406
Crotone	Crotone	662	1,716	174,158
Reggio di Calabria	Reggio di Calabria	1,229	3,183	572,546
Vibo Valentia	Vibo Valentia	440	1,139	176,631
Campania	Naples	5,249	13,595	5,780,958
Avellino	Avellino	1,078	2,792	440,482
Benevento	Benevento	800	2,071	293,458
Caserta	Caserta	1,019	2,639	855,693
Napoli	Naples	452	1,171	3,099,366
Salerno	Salerno	1,900	4,922	1,091,959
Emilia-Romagna	Bologna	8,542	22,123	3,981,146
Bologna	Bologna	1,429	3,702	917,110
Ferrara	Ferrara	1,016	2,632	348,705
Forlì-Cesena	Forlì	969	2,510	354,426
Modena	Modena	1,039	2,690	625,766
Parma	Parma	1,332	3,449	397,092
Piacenza	Piacenza	1,000	2,589	266,085
Ravenna	Ravenna	718	1,859	350,646
Reggio nell'Emilia	Reggio nell'Emilia	885	2,292	449,285
Rimini	Rimini	154	400	272,031
Friuli-Venezia Giulia	Trieste	3,029	7,845	1,185,172
Gorizia	Gorizia	180	467	138,305
Pordenone	Pordenone	878	2,273	280,326
Trieste	Trieste	82	212	247,723
Udine	Udine	1,889	4,893	518,818
Lazio	Rome	6,642	17,203	5,264,077
Frosinone	Frosinone	1,251	3,239	494,019
Latina	Latina	869	2,251	510,109
Rieti	Rieti	1,061	2,749	150,587
Roma	Rome	2,066	5,352	3,817,133
Viterbo	Viterbo	1,395	3,612	292,229
Liguria	Genoa	2,092	5,418	1,625,870
Genova	Genoa	709	1,836	907,583
Imperia	Imperia	446	1,155	216,386
La Spezia	La Spezia	341	882	222,140
Savona	Savona	596	1,545	279,761
Lombardia	Milan	9,211	23,857	9,065,440
Bergamo	Bergamo	1,051	2,722	965,133
Brescia	Brescia	1,846	4,782	1,098,481
Como	Como	497	1,288	539,472
Cremona	Cremona	684	1,771	334,317
Lecco	Lecco	315	816	309,484
Lodi	Lodi	302	783	195,720
Mantova	Mantova	903	2,339	374,008
Milano	Milan	765	1,980	3,757,609
Pavia	Pavia	1,145	2,965	497,575
Sondrio	Sondrio	1,240	3,212	177,367
Varese	Varese	463	1,199	816,274
Marche	Ancona	3,743	9,693	1,460,989
Ancona	Ancona	749	1,940	444,056
Ascoli Piceno	Ascoli Piceno	806	2,087	369,791
Macerata	Macerata	1,071	2,774	302,648
Pesaro e Urbino	Pesaro	1,117	2,892	344,494
Molise	Campobasso	1,713	4,438	327,987
Campobasso	Campobasso	1,123	2,909	236,418
Isernia	Isernia	590	1,529	91,569
Piemonte	Turin	9,807[4]	25,399	4,287,465
Alessandria	Alessandria	1,375	3,560	430,983
Asti	Asti	583	1,511	210,347
Biella	Biella	352	913	189,506
Cuneo	Cuneo	2,665	6,903	557,430
Novara	Novara	530	1,373	343,556
Torino	Turin	2,637	6,830	2,214,282
Verbano-Cusio-Ossola	Verbania	858	2,221	160,751
Vercelli	Vercelli	806	2,088	180,610
Puglia	Bari	7,470	19,348	4,085,239
Bari	Bari	1,980	5,129	1,576,050
Brindisi	Brindisi	710	1,838	411,563
Foggia	Foggia	2,774	7,185	693,900
Lecce	Lecce	1,065	2,759	815,855
Taranto	Taranto	941	2,437	587,871
Sardegna	Cagliari	9,301	24,090	1,651,888
Cagliari	Cagliari	2,662	6,895	766,066
Nuoro	Nuoro	2,720	7,044	269,422
Oristano	Oristano	1,016	2,631	157,215
Sassari	Sassari	2,903	7,520	459,185
Sicilia (Sicily)	Palermo	9,926	25,709	5,087,794
Agrigento	Agrigento	1,175	3,042	469,288
Caltanissetta	Caltanissetta	822	2,128	282,256

Area and population (continued)

		sq mi	sq km	population
Catania	Catania	1,371	3,552	1,100,208
Enna	Enna	989	2,562	181,749
Messina	Messina	1,254	3,248	676,895
Palermo	Palermo	1,927	4,992	1,238,061
Ragusa	Ragusa	623	1,614	301,854
Siracusa	Siracusa	814	2,109	403,478
Trapani	Trapani	951	2,462	434,005
Toscana	Florence	8,877	22,992[5]	3,536,392
Arezzo	Arezzo	1,248	3,232	321,725
Firenze	Florence	1,365	3,536	953,973
Grosseto	Grosseto	1,739	4,504	215,445
Livorno	Livorno	468	1,213	334,223
Lucca	Lucca	684	1,773	375,103
Massa-Carrara	Massa-Carrara	447	1,157	199,534
Pisa	Pisa	945	2,448	386,298
Pistoia	Pistoia	373	965	269,265
Prato	Prato	133	344	228,027
Siena	Siena	1,475	3,821	252,799
Trentino-Alto Adige	Bolzano	5,258	13,618	936,256
Bolzano-Bozen	Bolzano	2,857	7,400	462,542
Trento	Trento	2,401	6,218	473,714
Umbria	Perugia	3,265	8,456	835,488
Perugia	Perugia	2,446	6,334	612,629
Terni	Terni	819	2,122	222,859
Valle d'Aosta	Aosta	1,259	3,262	120,343
Veneto	Venice	7,090	18,364	4,511,714
Belluno	Belluno	1,420	3,678	211,048
Padova	Padova	827	2,142	849,592
Rovigo	Rovigo	691	1,789	243,520
Treviso	Treviso	956	2,477	784,055
Venezia	Venice	950	2,460	814,581
Verona	Verona	1,195	3,096	821,563
Vicenza	Vicenza	1,051	2,722	787,355
TOTAL		116,324[5]	301,277[5]	57,679,895

Demography

Population (2002): 57,988,000.
Density (2002): persons per sq mi 498.4, persons per sq km 192.4.
Urban-rural (2000): urban 67.2%; rural 32.8%.
Sex distribution (2000): male 48.55%; female 51.45%.
Age breakdown (2000): under 15, 14.4%; 15–29, 19.5%; 30–44, 23.1%; 45–59, 19.1%; 60–74, 16.1%; 75 and over, 7.8%.
Population projection: (2010) 57,681,000; (2020) 55,802,000.
Doubling time: not applicable; population stable.
Ethnolinguistic composition (2000): Italian 96.0%; North African Arab 0.9%; Italo-Albanian 0.8%; Albanian 0.5%; German 0.4%; Austrian 0.4%; other 1.0%.
Religious affiliation (1996): Roman Catholic 81.7%; nonreligious 13.6%; Muslim 1.2%; other 3.5%.
Major cities (2000[3, 6]): Rome 2,643,581; Milan 1,300,977; Naples 1,002,619; Turin 903,703; Palermo 683,794; Genoa 636,104; Bologna 381,161; Florence 376,682; Catania 337,862; Bari 331,848; Venice 277,305.
National origin (1991): Italian 99.3%; foreign-born 0.7%, of which European 0.3%, African 0.2%, Asian 0.1%, other 0.1%.
Mobility (1991). Population living in the same commune as in 1986: 93.3%; another commune, same province 3.4%; different province 2.5%; abroad 0.8%.
Households. Average household size (1991) 2.7; composition of households: 1 person 19.5%, 2 persons 21.9%, 3 persons 25.2%, 4 persons 21.4%, 5 or more persons 12.0%. Family households (1991): 15,538,335 (73.8%); nonfamily 5,527,105 (26.2%), of which one-person 19.5%.
Immigration (1997): immigrants 162,857, from Europe 41.1%, of which EU countries 14.2%; Africa 25.5%; Asia 19.0%; Western Hemisphere 14.0%.

Vital statistics

Birth rate per 1,000 population (2000): 9.1 (world avg. 22.5); (1998) legitimate 91.0%; illegitimate 8.0%.
Death rate per 1,000 population (2000): 10.1 (world avg. 9.0).
Natural increase rate per 1,000 population (2000): –1.0 (world avg. 13.5).
Total fertility rate (avg. births per childbearing woman; 2000): 1.2.
Marriage rate per 1,000 population (1998): 4.8.
Divorce rate per 1,000 population (1994): 0.5.
Life expectancy at birth (2001): male 75.9 years; female 82.5 years.
Major causes of death per 100,000 population (1996): diseases of the circulatory system 418.3; malignant neoplasms 272.8; diseases of the respiratory system 56.2; accidents and violence 48.8; diseases of the digestive system 45.6.

Social indicators

Educational attainment (1995). Percentage of labour force age 15 and over having: basic literacy or primary education 40.4%; secondary 30.5%; postsecondary technical training 5.1%; some college 19.2%; college degree 4.3%.
Quality of working life. Average workweek (1995): 37.0 hours. Annual rate per 100,000 workers (1996) for: injury or accident 3,208; death 7.5. Percentage of labour force insured for damages or income loss (1992) resulting from: injury 100%; permanent disability 100%; death 100%. Number of working days lost to labour stoppages per 1,000 workers (1996): 97. Average duration of journey to work: n.a. Rate per 1,000 workers of discouraged (unemployed no longer seeking work; 1990): 1.1.
Material well-being. Rate per 1,000 of population possessing (1995): telephone 434; automobile 550; television 436.
Social participation. Eligible voters participating in last national election (May 13, 2001): 81.2%. Trade union membership in total workforce (1990): *c.* 28%.
Social deviance (1999). Offense rate per 100,000 population for: murder 1.4; rape 68.3; assault 210.4[7]; theft, including burglary and housebreaking 2,567; suicide 6.3[8].
Access to services (1999). Nearly 100% of dwellings have access to electricity, a safe water supply, and toilet facilities.

Leisure (1998). Favourite leisure activities (as percentage of household spending on culture): cinema 21.8%; sporting events 14.6%; theatre 13.8%.

National economy

Gross national product (2000): U.S.$1,163,211,000,000 (U.S.$20,160 per capita).

Structure of gross domestic product and labour force

| | 1999 | | | |
	in value (Lit '000,000,000)	% of total value	labour force	% of labour force
Agriculture	58,865	2.8	1,371,000	5.9
Mining	[9]	[9]		[9]
Manufacturing	558,617[9]	26.3[9]	5,252,000[9]	22.7[9]
Construction	94,722	4.4	1,508,000	6.5
Public utilities	[9]	[9]		[9]
Transp. and commun.	146,610	6.9	1,413,000	6.1
Trade	332,374	15.6	4,729,000	20.4
Finance	159,090	7.5	} 8,862,000	38.3
Pub. admin., defense	270,080	12.7		
Services	269,140	12.6		
Other	238,667[10]	11.2[10]	[11]	[11]
TOTAL	2,128,165	100.0	23,135,000	100.0[4]

Budget (1999). Revenue: Lit 620,534,000,000,000 (income taxes 46.9%, of which individual 37.5%, corporate 9.4%; value-added and excise taxes 30.6%). Expenditures: Lit 668,251,000,000,000 (1995; debt service 27.5%; social security 18.4%; education 9.1%; transportation 4.7%; defense 2.8%).
Public debt (1999): U.S.$766,000,000,000.
Tourism (2000): receipts U.S.$27,500,000,000; expenditures U.S.$15,693,000,000.

Manufacturing, mining, and construction enterprises (1995)

	no. of enter-prises	no. of employees[12]	hourly wages as a % of avg. of all wages	annual value added (Lit '000,000,000)
Manufacturing				
Metal products	5,780	360,979	...	36,249
Machinery (nonelectrical)	4,503	379,027	...	35,221
Industrial chemicals	1,206	180,836	...	27,505
Electrical machinery	2,962	303,439	...	26,306
Food products	2,549	224,025	...	22,878
Transport equipment	1,122	275,077	...	22,642
Printing, publishing[13]	2,086	148,757	...	16,150
Pottery, ceramics, and glass	2,128	149,586	...	14,361
Textiles[14]	3,514	215,387	...	14,335
Rubber and plastic products	1,836	123,119	...	12,711
Wearing apparel	2,436	114,059	...	7,279
Paper and paper products[13]	...	...	...	...
Petroleum and gas	108	22,566	...	4,221
Mining and quarrying	340	20,013	...	5,991
Construction	6,228	1,564,100	...	94,887

Production (metric tons except as noted). Agriculture, forestry, fishing (2001): sugar beets 12,000,000, corn (maize) 11,300,000, grapes 9,770,000, tomatoes 6,990,000, wheat 6,500,000, olives 2,780,000, oranges 2,270,000, apples 2,160,000, potatoes 2,100,000, peaches and nectarines 1,730,000, rice 1,300,000, barley 1,250,000, soybeans 1,100,000; livestock (number of live animals) 10,970,000 sheep, 8,400,000 pigs, 7,180,000 cattle, 100,000,000 chickens; roundwood (2000) 9,329,000 cu m; fish catch (1999) 540,523. Mining and quarrying (1998): rock salt 3,413,522; feldspar 2,503,541; barite 31,792; lead 10,102; zinc 5,242. Manufacturing (1998): cement 33,714,914[7]; crude steel 25,782,300; pig iron 10,792,700; glass 3,981,104[7]; textiles 2,340,600[15]; sulfuric acid 2,013,400; wine 56,896,000 hectolitres; beer 10,616,173 hectolitres[7]; olive oil (2000) 493,000 hectolitres; 6,995,818 washing machines[7]; 5,908,224 refrigerators[7]; 2,779,827 colour televisions[7]; 2,723,541 motorized road vehicles, of which 1,378,517 automobiles, 1,062,570 motorcycles, 282,454 trucks and buses. Construction (1998): residential 56,268,471 cu m; commercial 67,443,808 cu m.

Service enterprises (1997)

	no. of enter-prises[16]	no. of employees	hourly wage as a % of all wages	annual value added (Lit '000,000,000)
Public utilities	327	257,000[7]	...	102,495[7]
Transportation } Communications }	3,230	1,413,000	...	146,610
Finance	...	424,000[15]	...	159,090
Wholesale and retail trade	8,115	4,729,000	...	332,374
Pub. admin., services	...	4,251,900[15]	...	270,080

Energy production (consumption): electricity (kW-hr; 2001) 278,904,000,000 ([1997] 289,607,000,000); coal (metric tons; 1997) negligible (16,006,000); crude petroleum (barrels; 2001) 27,714,000 ([1997] 614,938,000); petroleum products (metric tons; 1997) 85,936,000 (90,037,000); natural gas (cu m; 2001) 15,298,000,000 ([1997] 58,001,000,000).
Population economically active (1999): total 23,135,000; activity rate of total population 40.1% (participation rates: ages 15–64, 57.7%[8]; female 38.2%; unemployed 11.4%).

Price and earnings indexes (1995 = 100)

	1996	1997	1998	1999	2000	2001
Consumer price index	104.0	106.1	108.2	110.0	112.8	115.9
Earnings index	103.2	106.9	109.9	112.4	114.7	116.6

Household income and expenditure (1995). Average household size 2.7; average annual income per household (1984) Lit 19,692,000 (U.S.$11,208); sources of income (1996): salaries and wages 38.8%, property income and self-employment 38.5%, transfer payments 22.0%; expenditure (1997): food and beverages 18.1%, housing 18.0%, transportation and communications 13.3%, recreation and education 8.4%.

Financial aggregates

	1995	1996	1997	1998	1999	2000
Exchange rate, Lit per:						
U.S. dollar	1,628.9	1,530.6	1,759.2	1,653.1	1,927.8	2,080.9
£	2,571.2	2,690.8	2,909.4	2,749.9	3,116.1	3,105.1
SDR	2,355.7	2,200.9	2,373.6	2,327.6	2,645.9	2,711.2
International reserves (U.S.$)						
Total (excl. gold; '000,000)	34,905	45,948	55,739	29,888	...	25,566
SDRs ('000,000)	53	29	67	111	168	238
Reserve pos. in IMF ('000,000)	1,963	1,855	2,241	4,330	3,546	2,906
Foreign exchange ('000,000)	32,942	44,064	54,431	25,447	18,623	22,423
Gold ('000,000 fine troy oz)	66.67	66.67	66.67	83.36	78.83	78.83
% world reserves	7.3	7.3	7.5	8.6	8.2	8.3
Interest and prices						
Central bank discount (%)	9.00	7.50	5.50	3.00	...	...
Govt. bond yield (%)	11.98	8.93	6.47	4.55	4.04	5.29
Industrial share prices						
(1990 = 100)	95.4	96.0	137.7	220.5	245.5	319.0
Balance of payments (U.S.$'000,000)						
Balance of visible trade	44,082	60,822	39,877	35,361	23,437	10,717
Imports, f.o.b.	−187,254	−190,021	−200,527	−206,941	−212,420	−228,019
Exports, f.o.b.	231,336	250,843	240,404	242,572	235,856	238,736
Balance of invisibles	−18,378	−20,823	−7,474	−15,363	−15,326	−16,477
Balance of payments, current account	25,704	−39,999	32,403	19,998	8,111	−5,760

Land use (1994): forest 23.0%; pasture 15.4%; agriculture 37.9%; other 23.7%.

Foreign trade[17]

Balance of trade (current prices)

	1995	1996	1997	1998	1999	2000
Lit '000,000,000	+45,514	+67,599	+51,541	+47,398	+24,853	+3,358
% of total	6.3%	9.5%	6.7%	5.2%	3.1%	0.3%

Imports (1999): Lit 394,271,000,000,000 (machinery and transport equipment 38.4%, of which transport equipment 15.1%; chemicals 13.6%; metal 9.8%; food 7.5%; textiles 5.2%; plastics 2.3%). *Major import sources:* Germany 19.0%; France 12.6%; The Netherlands 6.3%; U.K. 6.1%; U.S. 4.9%; Belgium-Luxembourg 4.6%; Spain 4.3%.
Exports (1999): Lit 419,124,000,000,000 (machinery and transport equipment 41.7%, of which transport equipment 11.5%, electrical machinery 9.8%; textiles and wearing apparel 10.7%; chemicals 8.9%; plastics 3.7%). *Major export destinations:* Germany 16.5%; France 13.0%; U.S. 9.5%; U.K. 7.1%; Spain 6.3%.

Transport and communications

Transport. Railroads: (1997) length 19,527 km; (1998) passenger-km 41,392,000,000; (1998) metric ton-km cargo 22,386,000,000. Roads (1997): total length 308,139 km (paved 100%). Vehicles (1998): passenger cars 31,370,000; trucks and buses 5,127,000. Air transport (2001)[18]: passenger-km 36,524,000,000; metric ton-km cargo 1,530,000,000; airports (1997) 34.

Communications

Medium	date	unit	number	units per 1,000 persons
Daily newspapers	1997	circulation	5,970,000	104
Radio	1997	receivers	50,500,000	880
Television	1998	receivers	28,000,000	488
Telephones	2001	main lines	27,303,000	471
Cellular telephones	2001	subscribers	48,698,000	839
Personal computers	2001	units	11,300,000	195
Internet	2001	users	16,000,000	278

Education and health

Literacy (1995): total population age 15 and over literate 48,100,000 (98.1%); males literate 23,800,000 (98.6%); females literate 24,300,000 (97.6%).

Education (1998–99)

	schools	teachers	students	student/teacher ratio
Primary (age 6–10)	19,073	281,909	2,859,379	10.1
Secondary (age 11–18)	8,695	208,620	1,775,009	8.5
Voc., teacher tr.	6,883	295,482	2,543,750	8.6
Higher[18, 19]	48	58,874	1,601,873	27.2

Health (1997): physicians (1993) 207,319 (1 per 193 persons); hospital beds 334,613 (1 per 172 persons); infant mortality rate (2001) 5.8.
Food (1999): daily per capita caloric intake 3,629 (vegetable products 74%, animal products 26%); 144% of FAO recommended minimum requirement.

Military

Total active duty personnel (2001): 230,350 (army 59.5%, navy 16.5%, air force 24.0%). *Military expenditure as percentage of GNP* (1999): 2.0% (world 2.4%); per capita expenditure U.S.$412.

[1]Includes 6 nonelective seats in May 2001 (4 presidential appointees and 2 former presidents serving ex officio). [2]The Italian lira (Lit) was the former monetary unit; on Jan. 1, 2002, Lit 1,936 = €1. [3]Resident population only. [4]Detail does not add to total given because of rounding. [5]The total area for Italy, per 1998 survey, is 301,337 sq km (116,347 sq mi). [6]January 1. [7]1995. [8]1996. [9]Manufacturing includes Mining and Public utilities. [10]Other includes indirect import charges and building rental less imputed bank service charges. [11]The 2,637,000 unemployed are not calculated separately. [12]Total number of persons engaged. [13]Printing, publishing includes Paper and paper products. [14]1993. [15]1997. [16]Enterprises with 20 or more persons engaged. [17]Imports c.i.f.; exports f.o.b. [18]Alitalia only. [19]Universities only. [20]1994–95.

Internet resources for further information:
• **National Statistical Institute http://www.istat.it/English**

Jamaica

Official name: Jamaica.
Form of government: constitutional monarchy with two legislative houses (Senate [21]; House of Representatives [60]).
Chief of state: British Monarch represented by Governor-General.
Head of government: Prime Minister.
Capital: Kingston.
Official language: English.
Official religion: none.
Monetary unit: 1 Jamaica dollar (J$) = 100 cents; valuation (Sept. 23, 2002) 1 U.S.$ = J$48.70; 1 £ = J$75.68.

Area and population		area		population
Parishes	**Capitals**	sq mi	sq km	2000[1] estimate
Clarendon	May Pen	462	1,196	228,300
Hanover	Lucea	174	450	67,500
Kingston	[2]	8	22	[3]
Manchester	Mandeville	321	830	188,800
Portland	Port Antonio	314	814	79,400
Saint Andrew	[2]	166	431	716,000[3]
Saint Ann	Saint Ann's Bay	468	1,213	164,900
Saint Catherine	Spanish Town	460	1,192	413,200
Saint Elizabeth	Black River	468	1,212	148,600
Saint James	Montego Bay	230	595	180,800
Saint Mary	Port Maria	236	611	112,800
Saint Thomas	Morant Bay	287	743	92,400
Trelawny	Falmouth	338	875	72,500
Westmoreland	Savanna-la-Mar	312	807	140,600
TOTAL		4,244	10,991	2,605,800

Demography

Population (2002): 2,630,000.
Density (2002): persons per sq mi 619.7, persons per sq km 239.3.
Urban-rural (2001): urban 55.6%; rural 44.4%.
Sex distribution (2001): male 48.96%; female 51.04%.
Age breakdown (2001): under 15, 29.7%; 15–29, 28.3%; 30–44, 22.4%; 45–59, 10.5%; 60–74, 6.3%; 75 and over, 2.8%.
Population projection: (2010) 2,798,000; (2020) 3,068,000.
Doubling time: 47 years.
Ethnic composition (2000): local black 77.0%; local mulatto 14.6%; Haitian 2.0%; East Indian 1.7%; black-East Indian 1.6%; other 3.1%.
Religious affiliation (1995): Protestant 39.0%, of which Pentecostal 10.5%, Seventh-day Adventist 6.1%, Baptist 5.3%; Roman Catholic 10.4%; Anglican 3.7%; other (including nonreligious) 46.9%[4].
Major cities (1991): Kingston 103,771[5] (metropolitan area 587,798); Spanish Town 92,383; Portmore 90,138; Montego Bay 83,446; May Pen 46,785.

Vital statistics

Birth rate per 1,000 population (2001): 21.2 (world avg. 21.2).
Death rate per 1,000 population (2001): 6.6 (world avg. 8.9).
Natural increase rate per 1,000 population (2001): 14.6 (world avg. 12.3).
Total fertility rate (avg. births per childbearing woman; 2001): 2.1.
Marriage rate per 1,000 population (1996): 7.4.
Life expectancy at birth (2001): male 73.5 years; female 77.5 years.
Major causes of death per 100,000 population (1991): diseases of the circulatory system 189.4; malignant neoplasms (cancers) 84.1; endocrine and metabolic disorders 51.3; diseases of the respiratory system 30.1.

National economy

Budget (2000–01). Revenue J$101,018,000,000 (tax revenue 86.2%, of which income taxes 35.1%, consumption taxes 26.4%, custom duties 8.4%; nontax revenue 7.7%; bauxite levy 2.7%; capital revenue 1.7%; grants 1.7%). Expenditures: J$104,171,000,000 (current expenditure 91.0%, of which debt interest 41.2%, wages 33.8%; capital expenditure 9.0%).
Production (metric tons except as noted). Agriculture, forestry, fishing (2001): sugarcane 2,400,000, yams 145,000, vegetables and melons 144,500, citrus fruits 140,000, bananas 130,000, coconuts 115,000, pumpkins, squash, and gourds 42,000, plantains 33,500, cabbages 23,000, carrots 22,000, tomatoes 21,500, sweet potatoes 19,000; livestock (number of live animals) 440,000 goats, 400,000 cattle, 180,000 pigs; roundwood (2001) 873,825 cu m; fish catch (1999) 12,658. Mining and quarrying (2001): bauxite 11,126,000; alumina 3,601,000; gypsum 331,000. Manufacturing (value added in constant 1991–95 prices, J$'000,000; 1995): machinery and equipment 593.6; food processing 580.3; petroleum products 351.3; rubber and plastic products 324.1; textiles and clothing 257.0; tobacco and tobacco products 255.2; metal and nonmetallic products 223.6. Energy production (consumption): electricity (kW-hr; 1997) 6,255,000,000 (6,255,000,000); coal, none (none); crude petroleum (barrels; 1997) none (7,828,000); petroleum products (metric tons; 1997) 1,104,000 (3,294,000); natural gas, none (none).
Population economically active (April 2001): total 1,105,800; activity rate of total population 42.4% (participation rates: ages 14 and over 63.0%; female 43.9%; unemployed 14.8%).

Price and earnings indexes (1995 = 100)							
	1995	1996	1997	1998	1999	2000	2001
Consumer price index	100.0	126.4	138.6	150.6	159.5	172.6	184.6
Earnings index	...	...	...	...	...	...	...

Gross national product (2000): U.S.$6,883,000,000 (U.S.$2,610 per capita).

Structure of gross domestic product and labour force				
	2000			
	in value J$'000,000	% of total value	labour force	% of labour force
Agriculture	20,765.5	6.9	195,700	17.7
Mining	13,826.6	4.6	4,600	0.4
Manufacturing	42,903.8	14.4	69,600	6.3
Construction	30,924.9	10.3	81,500	7.4
Public utilities	12,877.3	4.3	6,300	0.6
Transp. and commun.	31,704.3	10.6	59,400	5.4
Trade	78,184.6	26.2	206,300	18.7
Pub. admin., defense	36,326.7	12.2	254,800	23.0
Finance, real estate	42,756.9	14.3	53,100	4.8
Services	8,910.0	3.0	2,300	0.2
Other	−20,497.9[6]	−6.8[6]	171,800[7]	15.5[7]
TOTAL	298,682.7	100.0	1,105,400	100.0

Public debt (external, outstanding; 2000): U.S.$3,373,000,000.
Household income and expenditure. Average household size (1991) 4.2; average annual income per household (1988) J$8,356 (U.S.$1,525); sources of income (1989): wages and salaries 66.1%, self-employment 19.3%, transfers 14.6%; expenditure (1988)[8]: food and beverages 55.6%, housing 7.9%, fuel and other household supplies 7.4%, health care 7.0%, transportation 6.4%.
Tourism: receipts (2000) U.S.$1,332,600,000; expenditures U.S.$209,000,000.

Foreign trade

Balance of trade (current prices)							
	1994	1995	1996	1997	1998	1999	2000
U.S.$'000,000	−551.2	−829.3	−994.2	−1,120.8	−1,101.9	−1,654.8	−1,365.0
% of total	28.7%	18.7%	23.5%	24.8%	25.7%	40.1%	30.5%

Imports (2000): U.S.$2,921,000,000 (raw materials 53.4%, of which fuels 18.3%; consumer goods 30.6%, of which food 8.2%; capital goods 15.9%, of which machinery and apparatus 7.8%). *Major import sources* (2000): U.S. 44.8%; Trinidad and Tobago 10.0%; Japan 6.0%; France 5.0%; Venezuela 3.9%; U.K. 3.1%; Canada 3.1%; Mexico 2.6%.
Exports (2000): U.S.$1,556,000,000 (crude materials 62.0%, of which alumina 44.4%; food 18.7%; manufactured articles 7.9%; chemicals 5.5%; beverages and tobacco 4.0%; machinery and transport equipment 0.1%). *Major export destinations:* U.S. 39.1%; U.K. 11.5%; Canada 10.2%; Norway 9.1%; Japan 2.3%.

Transport and communications

Transport. Railroads (2000): route length 211 mi; 339 km; passenger-mi 12,127,000[7], passenger-km 19,516,000[7]; short ton-mi cargo 1,700,000, metric ton-km cargo 2,482,000. Roads (1999): total length 11,620 mi, 18,700 km (paved 70%). Vehicles (1999–2000): passenger cars 160,948; trucks and buses 55,596. Air transport (1999)[9]: passenger-mi 2,741,500,000, passenger-km 4,412,000,000; short ton-mi cargo 16,399,000, metric ton-km cargo 26,391,000; airports (2000) with scheduled flights 4.

Communications				units per 1,000
Medium	date	unit	number	persons
Daily newspapers	1996	circulation	158,000	63
Radio	1997	receivers	1,215,000	483
Television	1998	receivers	480,000	187
Telephones	2001	main lines	512,600	197
Cellular telephones	2001	subscribers	700,000	269
Personal computers	2001	units	130,000	50
Internet	2001	users	100,000	38

Education and health

Educational attainment (1982). Percentage of population age 25 and over having: no formal schooling 3.2%; some primary education 79.8%; some secondary 15.0%; complete secondary and higher 2.0%. *Literacy* (2000): total population age 15 and over literate 88%; males 83%; females 91%.

Education (1999–2000)				student/
	schools	teachers	students	teacher ratio
Primary (age 6–11)[10]	788[11]	9,908	325,298	32.8
Secondary (age 12–16)	134	8,903	167,098	18.8
Voc., teacher tr.	17	1,091	17,388	15.9
Higher[12]	1	418	8,191	19.6

Health (2000)[13]: physicians 435 (1 per 5,988 persons); hospital beds 3,511 (1 per 742 persons); infant mortality rate (2001) 14.2.
Food (2000): daily per capita caloric intake 2,693 (vegetable products 85%, animal products 15%); 120% of FAO recommended minimum requirement.

Military

Total active duty personnel (2001): 2,830 (army 88.3%; coast guard 6.7%; air force 5.0%). *Military expenditure as percentage of GNP* (1999): 0.8% (world 2.4%); per capita expenditure U.S.$19.

---

[1]Year end. [2]The parishes of Kingston and Saint Andrew are jointly administered from the Half Way Tree section of Saint Andrew. [3]Kingston included with Saint Andrew. [4]Includes *c.* 0.7% Rastafarian. [5]City of Kingston is coextensive with Kingston parish. [6]Less imputed service charges. [7]Unemployed. [8]Weights of consumer price index components. [9]Air Jamaica only. [10]Includes lower-secondary students at all-age schools. [11]1991–92. [12]1996–97. [13]Public health only.

Internet resources for further information:
• **Statistics Institute of Jamaica http://www.statinja.com**

Japan

Official name: Nihon (Japan).
Form of government: constitutional
monarchy with a national Diet
consisting of two legislative houses
(House of Councillors [247]; House of
Representatives [480]).
Symbol of state: Emperor.
Head of government: Prime Minister.
Capital: Tokyo.
Official language: Japanese.
Official religion: none.
Monetary unit: 1 yen (¥) = 100 sen;
valuation (Sept. 23, 2002) 1 U.S.$ =
¥123.26; 1 £ = ¥191.56.

Area and population

Regions Prefectures	Capitals	area sq mi	area sq km	population 2001[1] estimate
Chūbu				
Aichi	Nagoya	1,984	5,139	7,087,000
Fukui	Fukui	1,619	4,192	830,000
Gifu	Gifu	4,091	10,596	2,111,000
Ishikawa	Kanazawa	1,621	4,198	1,182,000
Nagano	Nagano	5,245	13,585	2,223,000
Niigata	Niigata	4,857	12,579	2,473,000
Shizuoka	Shizuoka	3,001	7,773	3,781,000
Toyama	Toyama	1,642	4,252	1,121,000
Yamanashi	Kōfu	1,723	4,463	890,000
Chūgoku				
Hiroshima	Hiroshima	3,269	8,467	2,879,000
Okayama	Okayama	2,738	7,092	1,953,000
Shimane	Matsue	2,559[2]	6,629[2]	761,000
Tottori	Tottori	1,349[2]	3,494[2]	613,000
Yamaguchi	Yamaguchi	2,358	6,107	1,524,000
Hokkaidō				
Hokkaidō (Territory)	Sapporo	32,247	83,520	5,679,000
Kantō				
Chiba	Chiba	1,989	5,151	5,968,000
Gumma	Maebashi	2,454	6,356	2,031,000
Ibaraki	Mito	2,353	6,094	2,992,000
Kanagawa	Yokohama	928	2,403	8,570,000
Saitama	Urawa	1,467	3,799	6,978,000
Tochigi	Utsunomiya	2,476	6,414	2,010,000
Kinki				
Hyōgo	Kōbe	3,236	8,381	5,571,000
Mie	Tsu	2,231	5,778	1,861,000
Nara	Nara	1,425	3,692	1,442,000
Shiga	Ōtsu	1,551	4,016	1,353,000
Wakayama	Wakayama	1,824	4,725	1,066,000
Kyūshū				
Fukuoka	Fukuoka	1,916	4,963	5,032,000
Kagoshima	Kagoshima	3,539	9,167	1,783,000
Kumamoto	Kumamoto	2,860	7,408	1,860,000
Miyazaki	Miyazaki	2,986	7,735	1,169,000
Nagasaki	Nagasaki	1,588	4,113	1,513,000
Ōita	Ōita	2,447	6,338	1,221,000
Saga	Saga	942	2,440	876,000
Ryukyu				
Okinawa	Naha	871	2,255	1,329,000
Shikoku				
Ehime	Matsuyama	2,190	5,672	1,491,000
Kagawa	Takamatsu	727	1,883	1,022,000
Kōchi	Kōchi	2,744	7,107	813,000
Tokushima	Tokushima	1,601	4,146	822,000
Tohoku				
Akita	Akita	4,484[3]	11,613[3]	1,184,000
Aomori	Aomori	3,714[3]	9,619[3]	1,474,000
Fukushima	Fukushima	5,322	13,784	2,125,000
Iwate	Morioka	5,898	15,277	1,413,000
Miyagi	Sendai	2,815	7,292	2,371,000
Yamagata	Yamagata	3,601	9,327	1,241,000
Metropolis				
Tōkyō[4]	Tokyo	836	2,166	12,138,000
Urban prefectures				
Kyōto[5]	Kyōto	1,781	4,613	2,646,000
Ōsaka[5]	Ōsaka	722	1,869	8,818,000
TOTAL		145,883[6, 7]	377,835[6, 7]	127,291,000[7]

Demography

Population (2002): 127,347,000.
Density (2002): persons per sq mi 872.8, persons per sq km 337.0.
Urban-rural (1999): urban 78.6%; rural 21.4%.
Sex distribution (2001[1]): male 48.9%; female 51.1%.
Age breakdown (2001[1]): under 15, 14.4%; 15–29, 19.8%; 30–44, 19.7%; 45–59, 21.9%; 60–74, 16.7%; 75 and over, 7.5%.
Population projection: (2010) 127,979,000; (2020) 125,722,000.
Doubling time: not applicable; doubling time exceeds 100 years.
Composition by nationality (1997[8]): Japanese 99.1%; Korean 0.5%; Chinese 0.2%; other 0.2%.
Place of birth (1995): 99.3% native-born; 0.7% foreign-born (mainly Korean).
Immigration (2001[8]): permanent immigrants/registered aliens admitted 1,686,444, from North and South Korea 37.7%, Taiwan, Hong Kong, and China 19.9%, Brazil 15.1%, Philippines 8.6%, Peru 2.7%, United States 2.6%, Thailand 1.7%, Indonesia 1.1%, United Kingdom 1.0%, Vietnam 0.6%, Canada 0.6%, India 0.6%, Pakistan 0.4%, other 7.4%.
Major cities (2000[1]): Tokyo 8,134,408; Yokohama 3,426,506; Ōsaka 2,598,589; Nagoya 2,171,378; Sapporo 1,822,300; Kōbe 1,493,595; Kyōto 1,467,705; Fukuoka 1,341,489; Kawasaki 1,249,851; Hiroshima 1,126,282; Kita-Kyūshū 1,011,491; Sendai 1,008,024.

Other principal cities (2000[1])

	population		population		population
Akashi	293,122	Kagoshima	552,099	Ōita	436,490
Akita	317,563	Kakogawa	266,175	Okayama	626,534
Amagasaki	466,161	Kanazawa	456,434	Okazaki	336,570
Aomori	297,763	Kashiwa	327,868	Omiya	456,164
Asahikawa	359,526	Kasugai	287,619	Ōtsu	288,232
Chiba	887,163	Kawagoe	330,737	Sagamihara	605,555
Fujisawa	379,191	Kawaguchi	459,952	Sakai	792,034
Fukui	252,274	Kōchi	330,613	Shimonoseki	252,390
Fukushima	291,117	Koriyama	334,845	Shizuoka	469,679
Fukuyama	378,793	Koshigaya	308,277	Suita	347,938
Funabashi	550,079	Kumamoto	662,123	Takamatsu	332,866
Gifu	402,748	Kurashiki	430,239	Takatsuki	357,440
Hachinohe	241,925	Machida	377,546	Tokorozawa	330,152
Hachiōji	536,000	Maebashi	284,156	Tokushima	268,116
Hakodate	287,648	Matsudo	464,836	Toyama	325,693
Hamamatsu	582,120	Matsuyama	473,397	Toyohashi	364,868
Higashi-Ōsaka	515,055	Miyazaki	305,777	Toyonaka	391,732
Himeji	478,312	Morioka	288,844	Toyota	351,068
Hirakata	402,586	Nagano	360,117	Urawa	484,834
Hiratsuka	254,630	Nagasaki	423,163	Utsunomiya	443,787
Ibaraki	260,644	Naha	301,107	Wakayama	386,501
Ichihara	278,277	Nara	366,196	Yamagata	255,333
Ichikawa	440,553	Neyagawa	250,837	Yao	274,779
Ichinomiya	273,709	Niigata	501,378	Yokkaichi	291,106
Iwaki	360,143	Nishinomiya	438,129	Yokosuka	428,836

Religious affiliation (1995): Shintō and related religions 93.1%[9]; Buddhism 69.6%; Christian 1.2%; other 8.1%.
Households (2000). Total households 46,376,000; average household size 2.7; composition of households 1 person 26.4%, 2 persons 25.5%, 3 persons 19.2%, 4 persons 17.3%, 5 persons 6.9%, 6 or more persons 4.7%. Family households 33,920,000 (73.2%); nonfamily 12,456,000 (26.8%), of which 1 person 12,268,000 (26.4%).

Type of household (1998)

Total number of occupied dwelling units: 43,922,000

	number of dwellings	percentage of total
by kind of dwelling		
exclusively for living	41,744,000	95.0
mixed use	124,000	0.3
combined with nondwelling	2,054,000	4.7
detached house	23,469,000	56.2
apartment building	16,420,000	39.3
tenement (substandard or overcrowded building)	1,735,000	4.2
other	120,000	0.3
by legal tenure of householder		
owned	26,468,000	60.3
rented	16,730,000	38.1
other	724,000	1.6
by kind of amenities		
flush toilet	36,461	83.0
bathroom	41,919	95.4
by year of construction		
prior to 1945	1,647,000	3.8
1945–70	8,077,000	18.9
1971–80	11,492,000	26.8
1981–90	11,973,000	28.0
1991–98 (Sept.)	9,650,000	22.5

Mobility (October 1990). Population living in same residence as in October 1985, 74.7%; different residence, same town 9.5%; same prefecture 7.9%; different prefecture 7.6%; different country 0.3%.

Vital statistics

Birth rate per 1,000 population (1999): 9.4 (world avg. 22.5); (1985) legitimate 99.0%; illegitimate 1.0%.
Death rate per 1,000 population (1999): 7.8 (world avg. 9.0).
Natural increase rate per 1,000 population (1999): 1.6 (world avg. 13.5).
Total fertility rate (avg. births per childbearing woman; 1999): 1.3.
Marriage rate per 1,000 population (1999): 6.1; average age at first marriage (1996) men 28.5 years, women 26.4 years.
Divorce rate per 1,000 population (1999): 2.0.
Life expectancy at birth (2000): male 77.5 years; female 84.0 years.
Major causes of death per 100,000 population (1999): malignant neoplasms (cancers) 229.3; circulatory diseases 229.0, of which cerebrovascular disease 109.7; pneumonia and bronchitis 74.2; accidents and adverse effects 56.4, of which suicide 24.8; nephritis, nephrotic syndrome, and nephrosis 14.0; cirrhosis of the liver 13.1; diabetes mellitus 10.1.

Social indicators

Educational attainment (1990). Percentage of population age 25 years and over having: primary education 34.3%; secondary 44.5%; postsecondary 21.2%.

Distribution of income (2000)

percentage of average household income by quintile

1	2	3	4	5 (highest)
11.2	15.3	18.7	23.0	31.7

Quality of working life. Average hours worked per month (2000): 154.9. Annual rate of industrial deaths per 100,000 workers (1998): 1.7. Proportion of labour force insured for damages or income loss resulting from injury, permanent disability, and death (1991): 50.1%. Average man-days lost to labour stoppages per 1,000,000 workdays (1998): 6.8. Average duration of journey to work (1996): 19.0 minutes (1983; 26.7% private automobile, 67.4% public transportation, 5.5% taxi, 0.4% other). Rate per 1,000 workers of discouraged (unemployed no longer seeking work: 1997): 89.4.

Access to services (1989). Proportion of households having access to: gas supply 64.6%; safe public water supply 94.0%; public sewage collection 89.4%.

Social participation. Eligible voters participating in last national election (June 2000): 62.5%. Population 15 years and over participating in social-service activities on a voluntary basis (1991): 26.3%. Trade union membership in total workforce (2002): 21.5%.

Social deviance (1999). Offense rate per 100,000 population for: homicide 1.0; rape 1.5; robbery 3.3; larceny and theft 1,505. Incidence in general population of: alcoholism, n.a.; drug and substance abuse, n.a. Rate of suicide per 100,000 population: 24.8.

Leisure/use of personal time

Discretionary daily activities (1996)
(Population age 10 years and over)

	weekly average hrs./min.
Total discretionary daily time	6:12
of which	
Hobbies and amusements	0:36
Sports	0:13
Learning (except schoolwork)	0:12
Social activities	0:04
Associations	0:27
Radio, television, newspapers, and magazines	2:59
Rest and relaxation	1:15
Other activities	0:20

Major leisure activities (1996)
(Population age 15 years and over)

	percentage of participation		
	male	female	total
Sports	81.7	70.5	76.1
Light gymnastics	25.9	30.6	28.3
Swimming	24.6	20.9	22.8
Bowling	33.7	24.6	29.2
Learning (except schoolwork)	30.7	30.6	30.6
Travel (1991)			
Domestic	72.7	68.3	70.4
Foreign	10.4	7.6	9.0

Material well-being (1994). Households possessing: automobile 79.7%; telephone, virtually 100%; colour television receiver 99.3%; refrigerator 98.9%; air conditioner 72.3%; washing machine 99.4%; vacuum cleaner 98.7%; videocassette recorder 82.8%; camera 86.8%; microwave oven 84.3%; compact disc player 53.8%.

National economy

Gross national product (at current market prices; 2000): U.S.$4,519,067,000,-000 (U.S.$35,620 per capita).

Structure of gross domestic product and labour force

	1999		2000	
	in value ¥'000,000,000	% of total value	labour force	% of labour force
Agriculture, fishing	7,625	1.5	3,260,000	4.8
Mining	671	0.1	50,000	0.1
Manufacturing	110,490	21.6	13,210,000	19.5
Construction	38,891	7.6	6,530,000	9.6
Public utilities	14,561	2.8	340,000	0.5
Transportation and communications	34,423	6.7	4,140,000	6.1
Trade	73,978	14.4	14,740,000	21.8
Finance	97,124	18.9	6,160,000	9.1
Pub. admin., defense	45,908	9.0	} 15,640,000	23.1
Services	110,281	21.5		
Other	−21,420[10]	−4.2[10]	3,590,000[11]	5.3[11]
TOTAL	512,530[7]	100.0[7]	67,660,000[7]	100.0[7]

Budget (2001–02). Revenue: ¥54,334,000,000,000 (income tax 34.2%; corporation tax 21.8%; value-added tax 18.6%; stamp and customs duties 2.8%). Expenditures: ¥66,731,000,000,000 (social security 26.3%; debt service 25.7%; public works 14.1%; national defense 7.4%).

Public debt (1998): U.S.$2,412,200,000,000 (¥278,847,900,000,000).

Population economically active (2000): total 67,660,000; activity rate of total population 52.7% (participation rates: age 15 and over, 63.7%[12]; female 40.7%; unemployed 4.7%).

Price and earnings indexes (1995 = 100)

	1995	1996	1997	1998	1999	2000	2001
Consumer price index	100.0	100.1	101.9	102.5	102.2	101.5	100.8
Monthly earnings index	100.0	101.9	103.4	103.1	103.6	104.6	104.7

Household income and expenditure (2000). Average household size 2.8; average annual income per household ¥6,601,000 (U.S.$61,120); sources of income (1994): wages and salaries 59.0%, transfer payments 20.5%, self-employment 12.8%, other 7.3%; expenditure (1999): food 23.7%, transportation and communications 10.6%, recreation 10.3%, fuel, light, and water charges 6.7%, housing 6.5%, clothing and footwear 5.4%, education 4.2%, furniture and household utensils 3.6%, medical care 3.5%.

Tourism (2000): receipts from visitors U.S.$3,373,000,000; expenditures by nationals abroad U.S.$31,886,000,000.

Land use (1994): forested 66.4%; meadows and pastures 1.8%; agricultural and under permanent cultivation 11.7%; other 20.1%.

Manufacturing and mining enterprises (1999)

	no. of establishments	avg. no. of persons engaged	annual wages as a % of all mfg. wages[13]	annual value added (¥'000,000,000)
Electrical machinery	27,522	1,604,000	104.3	17,800
Food, beverages, and tobacco	44,867	1,249,000	69.2	12,593
Transport equipment	13,327	857,000	126.3	12,494
Chemical products	5,280	371,000	134.4	11,476
Nonelectrical machinery	38,963	1,037,000	115.9	11,121
Fabricated metal products	42,385	728,000	97.5	6,775
Printing and publishing	25,275	517,000	118.2	6,700
Ceramic, stone, and clay	17,704	373,000	100.9	4,187
Plastic products	18,582	430,000	88.8	4,137
Iron and steel	5,223	243,000	136.5	3,824
Paper and paper products	9,717	250,000	99.4	2,910
Apparel products	25,820	440,000	50.3	1,847
Precision instruments	5,469	178,000	98.6	1,751
Nonferrous metal products	3,573	141,000	118.3	1,647
Rubber products	4,357	135,000	101.0	1,444
Textiles	12,304	201,000	80.0	1,371
Furniture and fixtures	13,003	172,000	85.5	1,226
Lumber and wood products	13,400	171,000	71.2	1,221
Petroleum and coal products	1,156	29,000	161.7	960
Leather products	3,932	48,000	66.2	285
Mining and quarrying	577	10,501	109.3	78

Energy production (consumption): electricity (kW-hr; 1998) 1,046,294,000,000 (1,046,294,000,000); coal (metric tons; 1998) 3,681,000 (132,849,000); crude petroleum (barrels; 1998) 3,298,000 (1,569,000); petroleum products (metric tons; 1998) 187,410,000, of which (by volume) diesel 32.8%, heavy fuel oil 21.7%, gasoline 21.7%, kerosene and jet fuel 12.0% (192,747,000); natural gas (cu m; 1998) 2,320,400,000 (68,211,000,000). Composition of energy supply by source (1998): crude oil and petroleum products 50.9%, coal 17.0%, nuclear power 14.2%, natural gas 12.8%, hydroelectric power 4.1%, other 1.0%. Domestic energy demand by end use (1998): mining and manufacturing 46.3%, residential and commercial 26.3%, transportation 25.2%, other 2.2%.

Financial aggregates

	1995	1996	1997	1998	1999	2000	2001
Exchange rate[14], ¥ per:							
U.S. dollar	102.30	116.00	129.95	115.60	102.20	114.90	131.80
£	158.56	196.97	214.11	192.30	165.20	171.45	191.16
SDR	152.86	166.80	175.34	162.77	140.27	149.70	165.64
International reserves (U.S.$)							
Total (excl. gold; '000,000)	183,250	216,648	219,648	215,471	286,916	354,902	395,155
SDRs ('000,000)	2,707	2,648	2,638	2,663	2,656	2,437	2,377
Reserve pos. in IMF ('000,000)	8,100	6,671	9,144	9,593	6,552	5,253	5,051
Foreign exchange ('000,000)	172,443	207,335	207,866	203,215	277,708	347,212	387,727
Gold ('000,000 fine troy oz)	24.23	24.23	24.23	24.23	24.23	24.55	24.60
% world reserves	2.7	2.7	2.7	2.5	2.6	2.6	2.6
Interest and prices							
Central bank discount (%)[14]	0.50	0.50	0.50	0.50	0.50	0.50	0.10
Govt. bond yield (%)	2.27	2.23	1.69	1.10	1.77	1.75	1.33
Industrial share prices (1995 = 100)	100.0	116.3	101.1	85.4	100.4	112.0	86.5
Balance of payments (U.S.$'000,000,000)							
Balance of visible trade	131.79	83.56	101.60	122.39	123.32	116.72	70.21
Imports, f.o.b.	296.93	316.72	307.64	251.66	280.37	342.80	313.38
Exports, f.o.b.	428.72	400.28	409.24	374.04	403.69	459.51	383.59
Balance of invisibles	−20.8	−17.68	−7.25	−1.69	−16.45	0.16	19.07
Balance of payments, current account	111.04	65.88	94.35	120.70	106.87	116.88	89.28

Retail and wholesale trade and services (1999)

	no. of establishments	avg. no. of employees	annual sales (¥'000,000,000)
Retail trade	1,406,884	8,029,000	143,833
Food and beverages	488,304	3,114,000	43,687
Grocery	50,125	804,000	17,024
Liquors	77,668	253,000	5,196
General merchandise	6,687	518,000	19,224
Department stores	2,064	489,000	18,555
Motor vehicles and bicycles	92,031	579,000	17,502
Furniture and home furnishings	133,890	584,000	13,045
Apparel and accessories	201,762	748,000	13,002
Gasoline service stations	68,858	459,000	11,020
Books and stationery	63,166	751,000	5,416
Wholesale trade	425,850	4,496,000	495,453
Machinery and equipment	100,260	1,197,000	133,507
Motor vehicles and parts	18,773	219,000	29,357
General machinery except electrical	38,140	364,000	29,214
General merchandise	1,641	54,000	63,977
Farm, livestock, and fishery products	43,653	457,000	50,284
Food and beverages	94,376	1,020,000	49,447
Minerals and metals	17,556	215,000	45,149
Building materials	49,432	385,000	29,200
Textiles, apparel, and accessories	36,593	400,000	25,526
Chemicals	16,438	168,000	24,072
Drugs and toilet goods	23,300	295,000	22,020

Production (metric tons except as noted). Agriculture, forestry, fishing (2001): rice 11,320,000, sugar beets 4,000,000, potatoes 2,900,000, cabbages 2,600,000, sugarcane 1,600,000, sweet potatoes 1,073,000, onions 1,000,000, apples 894,000, tomatoes 800,000, cucumbers 766,700, wheat 700,000, carrots 680,000, watermelons 580,600, lettuce 540,000, eggplant 476,900, pears 411,800, spinach 330,000, cantaloupes 315,000, persimmons 278,800, pumpkins 253,600, soybeans 240,000, grapes 234,200, taro 231,000, barley 220,000, yams 200,000, strawberries 200,000, peaches 174,600, peppers

170,900, plums 121,000, cauliflower 116,000; livestock (number of live animals) 9,785,000 pigs, 4,530,000 cattle, 297,000,000 chickens; roundwood (1999) 17,987,000 cu m; fish catch (2000) 5,752,178, of which squid 671,100, scallops 515,000, cod 398,900, crabs 42,000. Mining and quarrying (1999): limestone 180,193,000; silica stone 18,312,000; dolomite 3,648,000; pyrophyllite 694,000; zinc 64,263; lead 6,074; copper 1,038; silver 94,004 kg; gold 9,405 kg. Manufacturing (1999): crude steel 94,192,000; steel products 86,335,000[13]; cement 80,120,000; pig iron 74,520,000; sulfuric acid 6,493,000; plastic products 6,035,000[13]; fertilizers 4,156,000[13]; spun yarn 507,475[13]; newsprint 3,192,300; cotton fabrics 814,000,000 sq m[13]; synthetic fabrics 2,087,000 sq m[13]; finished products (in number of units) 552,269,000 watches and clocks, 30,350,000[15] air conditioners, 12,051,000[13] videocassette recorders, 10,326,000 cameras, 9,684,000[13] video cameras, 9,639,000[13] computers, 8,100,000 passenger cars, 6,056,000[13] facsimile machines, 5,975,000[12] bicycles, 4,851,000[13] electric refrigerators, 4,468,000[13] automatic washing machines, 3,444,000 colour television receivers, 2,959,000[13] microwave ovens, 2,252,000 motorcycles, 1,903,000[15] photocopy machines. Construction (value in ¥'000,000; 1996): residential 44,240,000; nonresidential 28,800,000.

Foreign trade

Balance of trade (current prices)

	1996	1997	1998	1999	2000	2001
¥'000,000,000	+6,737	+9,982	+13,991	+12,279	+10,734	+6,608
% of total	8.1%	10.9%	16.0%	14.8%	11.6%	7.2%

Imports (1999): ¥35,268,000,000,000 (machinery and transport equipment 31.3%, food products 14.3%, petroleum and petroleum products 10.5%, chemicals and chemical products 7.4%, textiles 5.4%). *Major import sources:* United States 21.7%; China 13.8%; South Korea 5.2%; Australia 4.1%; Taiwan 4.1%; Indonesia 4.0%; Germany 3.7%; Malaysia 3.5%; Thailand 2.9%; United Arab Emirates 2.8%.
Exports (1999): ¥47,548,000,000 (electrical machinery 24.3%, transport equipment 22.7%, chemicals 7.4%, scientific and optical equipment 5.0%, iron and steel products 3.2%, textiles and allied products 1.9%). *Major export destinations:* United States 30.7%; Taiwan 6.9%; China 5.6%; Hong Kong 5.3%; South Korea 5.2%; Germany 4.5%; Singapore 3.8%; United Kingdom 3.4%; The Netherlands 2.9%; Thailand 2.7%.

Trade by commodity group (1999)

		imports		exports	
SITC group		U.S.$'000,000	%	U.S.$'000,000	%
00	Food and live animals	39,312	12.7	...	...
01	Beverages and tobacco	4,765	1.5		
02	Crude materials, excluding fuels	23,653[16]	7.6[16]	2,909[16]	0.7[16]
03	Mineral fuels, lubricants, and related materials	49,949	16.1	...	...
04	Animal and vegetable oils, fats, and waxes	16	16	16	16
05	Chemicals and related products, n.e.s.	22,566	7.3	29,668	7.1
06	Basic manufactures	29,987	9.7	43,378	10.4
07	Machinery and transport equipment	85,117	27.5	285,923	68.5
08	Miscellaneous manufactured articles	48,200	15.5	38,128	9.1
09	Goods not classified by kind	5,776	1.9	2,505	0.6
	TOTAL	309,994[17]	100.0[17]	417,610[17]	100.0[17]

Direction of trade (1999)

	imports		exports	
	U.S.$'000,000	%	U.S.$'000,000	%
Africa	3,930	1.3	4,311	1.0
Asia	154,654	49.8	167,690	40.0
South America	6,907	2.2	4,830	1.2
North America and Central America	77,865	25.0	150,301	35.8
United States	67,529	21.7	130,195	31.0
other North and Central Am.	10,336	3.3	20,106	4.8
Europe	53,750	17.3	80,432	19.2
EU	42,820	13.8	74,542	17.8
Russia	3,767	1.2	483	0.1
other Europe	7,163	2.3	5,407	1.3
Oceania	15,416	5.0	10,233	2.4
TOTAL	310,733[17]	100.0[17]	419,207[17]	100.0[17]

Transport and communications

Transport. Railroads (1999): length 17,059 mi, 27,454 km; rolling stock—locomotives 1,787[18], passenger cars 25,973[18], freight cars 12,688[18]; passengers carried 21,750,000,000; passenger-mi 239,929,000,000, passenger-km 385,101,000,000; short ton-mi cargo 15,439,000,000, metric ton-km cargo 22,541,000,000. Roads (1999): total length 717,951 mi, 1,155,439 km (paved 73%). Vehicles (1999): passenger cars 51,164,000; trucks and buses 18,630,000. Merchant marine (1999): vessels (100 gross tons and over) 6,140; total deadweight tonnage 16,198,000. Air transport (1998): passengers carried 102,749,000; passenger-mi 97,744,600,000, passenger-km 157,305,000,000; short ton-mi cargo 4,920,000,000, metric ton-km cargo 7,183,000,000; airports (1996) with scheduled flights 73.

Distribution of traffic (1998)

	cargo carried[15] ('000,000 tons)	% of national[15] total	passengers carried ('000,000)	% of national total
Road	6,177	90.8	52,819	70.5
Rail (intercity)	74	1.1	22,014	29.4
Urban transport (1997)	—	—	13,149	...
road	—	—	10,385	...
rail (subways)	—	—	2,764	...
Inland water	547	8.0	148[15]	0.2[15]
Air	1	0.0	87	0.1
TOTAL	6,799	100.0[7]	74,918[7, 19]	100.0[19]

Communications

Medium	date	unit	number	units per 1,000 persons
Daily newspapers	1999	circulation	72,218,000	567
Radio	1997	receivers	120,500,000	955
Television	1997	receivers	86,500,000	686
Telephones	2001	main lines	76,000,000	597
Cellular telephones	2001	subscribers	72,796,000	572
Personal computers	2001	units	44,400,000	349
Internet	2001	users	57,900,000	455

Radio and television broadcasting (1994): total radio stations 1,340, of which commercial 481; total television stations 14,625, of which commercial 7,736. Commercial broadcasting hours (by percentage of programs; 1994): reports—radio 13.0%, television 21.0%; education—radio 3.4%, television 12.0%; culture—radio 14.9%, television 24.7%; entertainment—radio 67.6%, television 40.0%. Advertisements (daily average; 1994): radio 148, television 295.

Other communications media (2000)

Print	titles		Electronic	traffic ('000)
Books (new)	65,065		Telegram[15]	40,368
of which			Domestic	40,198
Social sciences	14,099		International	170
Fiction	11,484		Fax service[14]	1,212[20]
Arts	8,895			
Engineering	6,105			
Natural sciences	5,218			
History	4,634		Post	
Philosophy	2,997		Mail	25,708,000
Magazines/journals	4,396		Domestic	25,029,000
Weekly	142		International	679,000
Monthly	2,792		Parcels	319,000
			Domestic	299,000
Cinema			International	20,000
Feature films	644			
Domestic	282			
Foreign	362			

Education and health

Literacy: total population age 15 and over literate, virtually 100%.

Education (2000)

	schools	teachers	students	student/teacher ratio
Primary (age 6–11)	24,106	408,000	7,366,000	18.0
Secondary (age 12–17)	16,678	527,000	8,270,000	15.7
Higher	1,283	172,000	3,125,000	18.2

Health (1999): physicians 248,611 (1 per 508 persons); dentists 88,061 (1 per 1,436 persons); nurses 985,821 (1 per 128 persons); pharmacists 205,953 (1 per 614 persons); midwives 24,202 (1 per 5,223 persons); hospital beds 1,648,217 (1 per 77 persons), of which general 76.5%, mental 21.7%, other 1.8%; infant mortality rate per 1,000 live births (1999) 3.4.
Food (2000): daily per capita caloric intake 2,762 (vegetable products 79%, animal products 21%); 118% of FAO recommended minimum requirement.

Military

Total active duty personnel (2001): 239,800 (army 62.0%, navy 18.4%, air force 18.9%). *Military expenditure as percentage of GNP* (1999): 1.0% (world 2.4%); per capita expenditure U.S.$342.

[1]October 1. [2]Excludes Lake Naka (38 sq mi [98 sq km]), which is part of both Shimane and Tottori prefectures. [3]Excludes Lake Towada (23 sq mi [60 sq km]), which is part of both Akita and Aomori prefectures. [4]Part of Kantō geographic region. [5]Part of Kinki geographic region. [6]1987 survey (includes Lake Naka and Lake Towada); total area per 2000 survey equals 145,898 sq mi (377,873 sq km). [7]Detail does not add to total given because of rounding. [8]January 1. [9]Many Japanese practice both Shintōism and Buddhism. [10]Import duties and statistical discrepancy less imputed bank service charge. [11]Includes 3,200,000 unemployed. [12]1997. [13]1998. [14]End of period. [15]1996. [16]Crude materials includes Animal and vegetable oils, fats, and waxes. [17]Detail does not add to total given because of statistical discrepancies in the data. [18]1995. [19]Totals do not include Urban transport or Inland water. [20]Number of subscribers.

Internet resources for further information:
• **Bank of Japan** http://www.boj.or.jp/en/index.htm
• **Statistics Bureau and Statistics Center (Japan)** http://www.stat.go.jp/english/index.htm

Jersey

Official name: Bailiwick of Jersey.
Political status: crown dependency
(United Kingdom) with one legislative
house (States of Jersey [57])[1].
Chief of state: British Monarch
represented by Lieutenant Governor.
Head of government: [2].
Capital: Saint Helier.
Official language: English[3].
Official religion: none.
Monetary unit: 1 Jersey pound (£J) =
100 pence; valuation (Sept. 23, 2002)
1 Jersey pound = U.S.$1.55; at par
with the British pound.

Area and population	area		population
Parishes	sq mi	sq km	2001 census
Grouville	3.0	7.8	4,702
St. Brelade	4.9	12.8	10,134
St. Clement	1.6	4.2	8,196
St. Helier	3.3	8.6	28,310
St. John	3.4	8.7	2,618
St. Lawrence	3.7	9.5	4,702
St. Martin	3.8	9.9	3,628
St. Mary	2.5	6.5	1,591
St. Ouen	5.8	15.0	3,803
St. Peter	4.5	11.6	4,293
St. Saviour	3.6	9.3	12,491
Trinity	4.7	12.3	2,718
TOTAL	44.9	116.2	87,186

Demography

Population (2002): 87,400.
Density (2002): persons per sq mi 1,946.5, persons per sq km 752.2.
Sex distribution (2001): male 48.73%; female 51.27%.
Age breakdown (2001): under 15, 16.9%; 15–29, 18.4%; 30–44, 25.9%; 45–59, 19.7%; 60–74, 12.6%; 75 and over, 6.5%.
Population projection: (2010) 88,600; (2020) 89,100.
Population by place of birth (2001): Jersey 52.6%; United Kingdom, Guernsey, or Isle of Man 35.8%; Portugal 5.9%; France 1.2%; other 4.5%.
Religious affiliation (2000)[4]: Christian 86.0%, of which Anglican 44.1%, Roman Catholic 14.6%, other Protestant 6.9%, unaffiliated Christian 20.1%; nonreligious/atheist 13.4%; other 0.6%.
Major cities (2001)[5]: St. Helier 28,310; St. Saviour 12,491; St. Brelade 10,134.

Vital statistics

Birth rate per 1,000 population (2000): 11.6 (world avg. 22.5).
Death rate per 1,000 population (2000): 9.3 (world avg. 9.0).
Natural increase rate per 1,000 population (2000): 2.3 (world avg. 13.5).
Total fertility rate (avg. births per childbearing woman; 2000): 1.6.
Marriage rate per 1,000 population: n.a.
Divorce rate per 1,000 population: n.a.
Life expectancy at birth (2000): male 76.1 years; female 81.1 years.
Major causes of death per 100,000 population: n.a.

National economy

Budget (2000). Revenue: £388,389,000 (corporate income tax 43.0%, individual income tax 26.9%, self-employment tax 11.6%, spirits and tobacco tax 6.0%, international business 5.4%, tax on fuel 3.0%). Expenditures: £300,030,000 (current expenditure 79.2%, of which health 27.8%, education 21.3%, social security 20.5%; capital expenditure 20.8%).
Production. Agriculture, forestry, fishing: fruits and vegetables, mostly potatoes and greenhouse tomatoes; greenhouse flowers are important export crops; livestock (number of live animals; 1999) 7,315 cattle, of which about 4,500 dairy cattle; roundwood, none; fish catch (metric tons; 1997)[4]: 4,368, of which crustaceans 2,934 (including sea spiders and crabs 2,713), mollusks 743 (including abalones, winkles, and conch 438), marine fish 691. Mining and quarrying: n.a. Manufacturing: light industry, mainly electrical goods, textiles and clothing; dairy products (including 179 hectolitres of milk in 1999). Construction: n.a. Energy production (consumption): electricity (kW-hr; 1995) 266,000,000 (467,000,000); crude petroleum, none (n.a.); petroleum products, n.a. (n.a.); natural gas, none (n.a.).
Gross national product (at current market prices; 1995): U.S.$2,670,000,000 (U.S.$30,940 per capita).

Structure of gross domestic product and labour force	1996		2001	
	in value[6] £J '000,000	% of total value	labour force	% of labour force
Agriculture, fishing	74	5.0	1,750	3.8
Mining	...	...	4,320	9.3
Construction }				
Manufacturing	30	2.0	1,400	3.0
Public utilities	...	...	560	1.2
Transp. and commun.	...	...	2,590	5.6
Trade, hotels, restaurants	354[7]	24.0[7]	9,780	21.0
Finance, real estate[8]	811	55.0	11,340	24.3
Pub. admin., defense	...	... }	13,840	29.7
Services	...	...		
Other	206[9]	14.0[9]	1,022[10]	2.1[10]
TOTAL	1,475	100.0	46,602	100.0

Household income and expenditure. Average household size (1996) 2.4; income per household: n.a.; sources of income: n.a.; expenditure (1998–99)[11]: housing 20.1%, recreation 16.5%, transportation 12.8%, household furnishings 11.6%, food 11.5%, alcoholic beverages 6.0%, clothing and footwear 5.5%.
Population economically active (2001): total 46,602; activity rate of total population 53.4% (participation rates: ages 15–64, 81.7%; female 45.5%; unemployed 2.1%).

Price index (1995 = 100)[12]						
	1995	1996	1997	1998	1999	2000
Consumer price index	100.0	103.6	107.2	111.7	115.6	120.2

Public debt: none.
Tourism (1996): receipts U.S.$429,000,000; expenditures by nationals abroad, n.a.; number of visitors for at least one night 670,000.
Land use (1997): land under cultivation 56.8%; other 43.2%.

Foreign trade

Imports: [13]. *Major import sources* (1999): mostly the United Kingdom.
Exports: [13]; agricultural exports (1996): £45,400,000 (potatoes 61.2%, greenhouse tomatoes 17.2%, zucchini 6.4%, greenhouse carnations and narcissus 6.0%). *Major export destinations:* mostly the United Kingdom.

Transport and communications

Transport. Railroads: none. Roads (1995): total length 346 mi, 557 km (paved 100%). Vehicles (1995): passenger cars 58,491; trucks and buses 9,109. Air transport (1999)[14]: passenger-mi 553,291,000, passenger-km 890,438,000; short ton-mi cargo 632,000, metric ton-km cargo 923,000; airports (1999) with scheduled flights 1.

Communications				units per 1,000
Medium	date	unit	number	persons
Daily newspapers	1997	circulation	25,542	299
Telephones	2001	main lines	73,900	848
Cellular telephones	2001	subscribers	61,400	704
Internet	2000	users	8,000	92

Education and health

Educational attainment: n.a. *Literacy* (1996): total population age 15 and over literate 71,033 (100.0%).

Education (1996)	schools	teachers	students	student/ teacher ratio
Primary (age 5–10)	32	313[15]	6,906	...
Secondary (age 11–16)	14	373[15]	4,924	...
Voc., teacher tr.	...	...	...	...
Higher	1	...	1,298	...

Health (1995): physicians 95 (1 per 895 persons); hospital beds 651 (1 per 130 persons); infant mortality rate per 1,000 live births (2000) 5.7.
Food (1998): daily per capita caloric intake, n.a.

Military

Total active duty personnel (2000): none; defense is the responsibility of the United Kingdom.

[1]53 elected members include 12 senators popularly elected for six-year terms, 12 constables popularly elected triennially, and 29 deputies also popularly elected triennially; 4 nonelected members include the bailiff, the dean of Jersey, the attorney general, and the solicitor general. [2]Executive committees appointed by the States of Jersey (alternately called States Assembly). [3]Until the 1960s French was an official language of Jersey and is still used by the court and legal professions; Jerriais, a Norman-French dialect, is spoken by a small number of residents. [4]Includes Guernsey. [5]Population of parishes. [6]Calculation based on percentage distribution. [7]Represents tourism-related businesses. [8]Jersey is an international finance centre with 79 banks in 1998 and over 33,000 registered companies; of more than U.S.$160,000,000,000 deposited in the island, 62 percent is in foreign (not £J or £) currency. [9]Represents investment income from abroad received by residents. [10]Unemployed seeking work. [11]Weights of retail price index components. [12]June. [13]Customs ceased recording imports and exports as of 1980. [14]Jersey European Airways. [15]1990.

Internet resources for further information:
• **States of Jersey**
http://www.gov.je
• **An Introduction to Jersey**
http://www.adwebjersey.co.uk/states.html

Jordan

Official name: Al-Mamlakah
al-Urdunnīyah al-Hāshimīyah
(Al-Urdun) (Hashemite Kingdom of
Jordan).
Form of government: constitutional
monarchy with two legislative houses
(Senate [40[1]]; House of
Representatives [80]).
Head of state and government: King
assisted by Prime Minister.
Capital: Amman.
Official language: Arabic.
Official religion: Islam.
Monetary unit: 1 Jordan dinar
(JD) = 1,000 fils; valuation (Sept. 23,
2002) JD 1.00 = U.S.$1.41 = £0.91.

Area and population		area		population
				2000
Governorates	Capitals	sq mi	sq km	estimate[2]
'Ajlūn	'Ajlun	159	412	108,800
'Amman	Amman	3,178	8,231	1,864,500
Al-'Aqabah	Al-'Aqabah	2,542	6,583	98,500
Al-Balqā'	Aṣ-Ṣalt	415	1,076	321,400
Irbid	Irbid	626	1,621	874,200
Jarash	Jarash	155	402	144,100
Al-Karak	Al-Karak	1,242	3,217	197,000
Ma'ān	Ma'ān	12,804	33,163	95,600
Mādabā	Mādabā	775	2,008	125,000
Al-Mafraq	Al-Mafraq	10,207	26,435	225,900
Aṭ-Ṭafīlah	Aṭ-Ṭafīlah	816	2,114	74,500
Az-Zarqā'	Az-Zarqā'	1,575	4,080	770,800
TOTAL		34,495[3]	89,342	4,900,300

Demography

Population (2002): 5,260,000.
Density (2002): persons per sq mi 152.5, persons per sq km 58.9.
Urban-rural (2000): urban 74.2%; rural 25.8%.
Sex distribution (2001): male 52.35%; female 47.65%.
Age breakdown (2000): under 15, 37.9%; 15–29, 30.9%; 30–44, 18.3%; 45–59, 7.8%; 60–74, 4.2%; 75 and over, 0.9%.
Population projection: (2010) 6,427,000; (2020) 7,849,000.
Doubling time: 30 years.
Ethnic composition (2000): Arab 97.8%, of which Jordanian 32.4%, Palestinian 32.2%, Iraqi 14.0%, Bedouin 12.8%; Circassian 1.2%; other 1.0%.
Religious affiliation (2000): Sunnī Muslim 93.5%; Christian 4.1%; other 2.4%.
Major cities (1994): Amman 969,598; Az-Zarqā' 350,849; Irbid 208,329; Ar-Ruṣayfah 137,247; Wādī Essier 89,104; Al-'Aqabah 62,773.

Vital statistics

Birth rate per 1,000 population (2001): 25.4 (world avg. 21.2).
Death rate per 1,000 population (2001): 2.6 (world avg. 8.9).
Natural increase rate per 1,000 population (2001): 22.8 (world avg. 12.3).
Total fertility rate (avg. births per childbearing woman; 2001): 3.3.
Life expectancy at birth (2001): male 75.1 years; female 80.0 years.
Major causes of death per 100,000 population: n.a.

National economy

Budget (2000 est.). Revenue: JD 1,804,700,000 (taxes 53.3%, of which sales tax 28.8%, custom duties 14.7%, income and profits taxes 8.9%; nontax 33.5%, of which licenses and fees 13.2%; foreign grants 13.2%). Expenditures: JD 2,004,600,000 (current 85.7%, of which defense 26.5%, social security and other transfers 20.4%, wages 18.3%, interest expense 14.6%; capital expenditure 14.3%).
Public debt (external, outstanding; 2000): U.S.$7,055,000,000.
Production (metric tons except as noted). Agriculture, forestry, fishing (2000): tomatoes 354,300, cucumbers 135,600, olives 134,300, potatoes 97,100, watermelons 69,000, citrus fruit 124,700, zucchini 49,500, cabbages 38,300, apples 37,500, grapes 23,900, bananas 20,800; livestock (number of live animals) 1,850,000 sheep, 640,000 goats, 65,400 cattle, 18,000 camels; roundwood (2000) 226,143 cu m; fish catch (1999) 1,025. Mining and quarrying (2001): phosphate ore 5,878,100; potash 1,962,600. Manufacturing (value added in JD '000; 1997): chemicals 130,276; nonmetallic mineral products, pottery, and china 114,897; tobacco 96,380; food products 80,994; refined petroleum 60,028; plastic products 25,627. Construction (permits issued; 2000): residential 4,132,500 sq m; nonresidential 780,000. Energy production (consumption): electricity (kW-hr; 2001) 7,365,700,000 (7,365,700,000); crude petroleum (barrels; 1997) none (25,100,000); petroleum products (metric tons; 2001) 3,596,800 (3,596,800); natural gas (cu m; 2000) 283,000,000 (283,000,000).
Land use (1994): forest 0.8%; pasture 8.9%; agriculture 4.6%; other 85.7%.
Tourism (2000): receipts U.S.$722,000,000; expenditures U.S.$387,000,000.
Population economically active (1993): total 859,300; activity rate of total population 22.2% (participation rates: over age 15, 43.6%; female 14.0%; unemployed [1999] 14.4%).

Price and earnings indexes (1995 = 100)							
	1994	1995	1996	1997	1998	1999	2000
Consumer price index	97.7	100.0	106.5	109.7	113.1	113.8	114.6
Daily earnings index	...	...	...	...	...	...	...

Gross national product (2000): U.S.$8,360,000,000 (U.S.$1,710 per capita).

Structure of gross domestic product and labour force				
	2000		1993	
	in value JD '000,000	% of total value	labour force	% of labour force
Agriculture	116.7	1.9	54,995	6.4
Mining	157.4	2.6		
Manufacturing	792.0	13.2	91,086	10.6
Construction	203.9	3.4	60,151	7.0
Public utilities	134.6	2.2	6,015	0.7
Transp. and commun.	831.6	13.9	57,573	6.7
Trade[4]	602.5	10.1	129,754	15.1
Finance	1,071.3	17.9	24,920	2.9
Pub. admin., defense	1,079.1	18.0		
Services[5]	315.8	5.3	434,806	50.6
Other	687.3[6]	11.5[6]		
TOTAL	5,992.2	100.0	859,300	100.0

Household income and expenditure. Average household size (1997) 6.1; income per household (1997) JD 5,464 (U.S.$7,700); sources of income (1997): wages and salaries 52.4%, rent and property income 24.5%, transfer payments 12.8%, self-employment 10.3%; expenditure (1997): food and beverages 44.3%, housing and energy 23.5%, transportation 8.2%, clothing and footwear 6.2%, education 4.5%, health care 2.5%.

Foreign trade

Balance of trade (current prices)						
	1996	1997	1998	1999	2000	2001
JD '000,000	−1,851.0	−1,609.0	−1,436.5	−1,336.4	−1,872.8	−1,808.8
% of total	41.8%	38.2%	36.0%	34.0%	41.0%	35.7%

Imports (2000): JD 3,218,100,000 (machinery and transport equipment 28.6%; food and live animals 16.1%; mineral fuels 15.8%; chemicals and chemical products 10.6%; iron and steel 3.0%). *Major import sources:* Iraq 15.1%; Germany 11.5%; United States 10.0%; United Kingdom 4.6%; Japan 4.0%; Italy 3.6%.
Exports (2000): JD 1,345,300,000 (domestic goods 80.3%, of which chemicals and chemical products 25.8%, potash 10.3%, manufactured goods 8.4%, phosphate fertilizers 6.8%, fruits, vegetables, and nuts 5.3%, machinery and transport equipment 5.1%; reexports 19.7%). *Major export destinations[7]:* India 15.9%; Iraq 9.3%; Saudi Arabia 8.5%; United States 4.2%; China 3.0%; Kuwait 1.8%; Syria 1.5%.

Transport and communications

Transport. Railroads (1998): route length 677 km; passenger-km 2,000,000; metric ton-km cargo 596,000,000. Roads (1998): total length 7,133 km (paved 100%). Vehicles (1996): passenger cars 213,874; trucks and buses 79,153. Merchant marine (1995): vessels (1,000 gross tons and over) 1; total deadweight tonnage 15,794. Air transport (2001)[8]: passenger-km 3,848,000,000; metric ton-km cargo 181,408,000; airports (1999) 3.

Communications				units per 1,000
Medium	date	unit	number	persons
Daily newspapers	1996	circulation	250,000	57
Radio	1997	receivers	1,660,000	395
Television	1999	receivers	540,000	83
Telephones	2001	main lines	660,000	127
Cellular telephones	2001	subscribers	745,500	144
Personal computers	2001	units	170,000	33
Internet	2001	users	212,000	41

Education and health

Educational attainment (2000). Percentage of population age 25 and over having: no formal schooling 16.7%; primary education 49.2%; secondary 16.7%; postsecondary and vocational 9.5%; higher 8.2%. *Literacy* (2000): percentage of population age 15 and over literate 88.8%; males literate 94.9%; females literate 84.4%.

Education (1998–99)				student/
	schools	teachers	students	teacher ratio
Primary (age 6–14)	2,678	46,864	1,135,146	24.2
Secondary (age 15–17)	948	13,377	165,475	12.4
Voc., teacher tr.	53	2,213	31,961	14.4
Higher[9]	17	5,275	112,959	21.4

Health (1998): physicians 7,480 (1 per 625 persons); hospital beds 8,565 (1 per 546 persons); infant mortality rate per 1,000 live births (2001) 20.4.
Food (2000): daily per capita caloric intake 2,749 (vegetable products 88%, animal products 12%); 112% of FAO recommended minimum requirement.

Military

Total active duty personnel (2001): 100,240 (army 84.5%, navy 0.5%, air force 15.0%). *Military expenditure as percentage of GDP* (1999): 9.2% (world 2.4%); per capita expenditure U.S.$150.

---

[1]Appointed by king. [2]January 1. [3]Detail does not add to total given because of rounding. [4]Includes hotels. [5]Includes domestic help employed in households. [6]Net taxes on products less imputed bank service charges. [7]Domestic exports only. [8]Royal Jordanian airlines only. [9]1996–97.

Internet resources for further information:
• **Dept. of Statistics http://www.dos.gov.jo**
• **Jordan National Information System http://www.nic.gov.jo**

Kazakhstan

Official name: Qazaqstan Respūblīkasy (Republic of Kazakhstan).
Form of government: unitary republic with a Parliament consisting of two chambers (Senate [39[1]] and Assembly [77]).
Head of state and government: President assisted by Prime Minister.
Capital: Astana[2].
Official language: Kazakh[3].
Official religion: none.
Monetary unit: 1 tenge (T) = 100 tiyn; valuation (Sept. 23, 2002) free rate, 1 U.S.$ = 154.49 tenge; 1 £ = 240.09 tenge.

Area and population

Provinces	Capitals	area sq mi	area sq km	population 1999 census
Almaty (Alma-Ata)	Almaty (Alma-Ata)	86,500[4]	224,200[4]	1,559,522
Aqmola	Astana[2]	35,500[5, 6]	92,000[5, 6]	835,661
Aqtöbe	Aqtöbe	116,050	300,600	682,793
Atyraū	Atyraū	45,800	118,600	439,900
Batys Qazaqstan	Oral	58,400	151,300	617,624
Mangghystaū	Aqtaū	63,950	165,600	316,847
Ongtüstik Qazaqstan	Shymkent	45,300	117,300	1,976,689
Pavlodar	Pavlodar	48,200	124,800	806,034
Qaraghandy	Qaraghandy	165,250	428,000	1,411,401
Qostanay	Qostanay	44,000[5]	113,000[5]	1,019,560
Qyzylorda[7]	Qyzylorda	87,250[7]	226,000[7]	596,344[7]
Shyghys Qazaqstan	Shyghys Qazaqstan	109,400	283,300	1,530,792
Soltüstik Qazaqstan	Petropavl	47,500	123,200	725,932
Zhambyl	Zhambyl (Aullye-Ata)	55,700	144,300	983,935
Cities				
Almaty (Alma-Ata)	—	4	4	1,130,068
Astana[2]	—	6	6	319,318
TOTAL		1,052,100[8]	2,724,900	14,952,420

Demography

Population (2002): 14,884,000.
Density (2002): persons per sq mi 14.1, persons per sq km 5.5.
Urban-rural (2001): urban 56.3%; rural 43.7%.
Sex distribution (2001): male 48.07%; female 51.93%.
Age breakdown (2001): under 15, 26.7%; 15–29, 27.1%; 30–44, 21.5%; 45–59, 13.2%; 60–74, 9.2%; 75 and over, 2.3%.
Population projection: (2010) 15,314,000; (2020) 16,436,000.
Ethnic composition (1999): Kazakh 53.4%; Russian 30.0%; Ukrainian 3.7%; Uzbek 2.5%; German 2.4%; Tatar 1.7%; other 6.3%.
Religious affiliation (1995): Muslim (mostly Sunnī) 47.0%; Russian Orthodox 8.2%; Protestant 2.1%; other (mostly nonreligious) 42.7%.
Major cities (1999): Almaty (Alma-Ata) 1,130,068; Qaraghandy (Karaganda) 436,900; Shymkent (Chimkent) 360,100; Taraz 330,100; Astana 319,318.

Vital statistics

Birth rate per 1,000 population (2001): 14.9 (world avg. 21.2); (1996) legitimate 82.4%, illegitimate 17.6%.
Death rate per 1,000 population (2001): 10.0 (world avg. 8.9).
Natural increase rate per 1,000 population (2001): 4.9 (world avg. 12.3).
Total fertility rate (avg. births per childbearing woman; 2001): 2.0.
Life expectancy at birth (2002): male 58.3 years; female 71.1 years.
Major causes of death per 100,000 population (1996): diseases of the circulatory system 436.2; malignant neoplasms (cancers) 133.0; accidents, poisoning, and violence 101.1; diseases of the respiratory system 71.0.

National economy

Budget (2001). Revenue: 743,550,000,000 tenge (tax revenue 91.1%, of which income, profits, and taxes 34.8%, sales tax 29.3%, social security 17.5%, taxes on international trade 3.6%; nontax revenue 8.9%). Expenditures: 749,092,000,000 tenge (social security 24.9%, education 14.0%, public order 8.5%, health 8.3%, debt 6.7%, defense 4.3%).
Population economically active (2001): total 7,479,100; activity rate of total population 50.4% (participation rates: ages 16–59 [male], 16–54 [female] 73.6%; female 46%; unemployed 4.4%).

Price and earnings indexes (1995 = 100)

	1995	1996	1997	1998	1999	2000	2001
Consumer price index	100.0	139.3	163.4	175.0	189.6	214.6	228.3
Monthly earnings index	100.0	142.9	178.5	202.3	247.9	300.3	362.8

Production (metric tons except as noted). Agriculture, forestry, fishing (2001): wheat 12,910,000, barley 2,330,000, potatoes 1,600,000, tomatoes 428,000, corn (maize) 346,000, sugar beets 280,000, oats 253,500; livestock (number of live animals) 8,939,400 sheep and goats, 4,106,600 cattle, 976,000 horses, 1,076,000 pigs; roundwood (1998) 315,000 cu m; fish catch (1999) 26,951. Mining and quarrying (2000): copper 32,751,200; iron ore 16,157,000; nickel 7,000,000; bauxite 3,600,000; chromite 1,900,000. Manufacturing (value of production in '000,000 tenge; 2001): metallurgy 215,862; food 128,934; oil and nuclear energy 58,270; machinery 13,458; chemicals 13,258; electrical equipment 10,584; transport equipment 9,444; paper 6,880. Construction (2000): residential 1,650,000 sq m. Energy production (consumption): electricity (kW-hr; 1997) 52,000,000,000 (58,700,000,000); coal (metric tons; 2000) 74,872,400 ([1997] 46,274,000); crude petroleum (barrels; 2000) 258,872,000 ([1997]

66,828,000); petroleum products (metric tons; 1997) 8,249,000 (7,381,000); natural gas (cu m; 2000) 11,541,900,000 ([1997] 7,394,800,000).
Gross national product (2000): U.S.$18,773,000,000 (U.S.$1,260 per capita).

Structure of gross domestic product and labour force

	2000 in value '000,000 tenge	2000 % of total value	1998 labour force	1998 % of labour force
Agriculture	210,872	8.1	1,360,000	20.9
Manufacturing, mining, public utilities	864,727	33.3	877,000	13.5
Construction	134,575	5.2	223,000	3.4
Transp. and commun.	298,515	11.5	560,000	8.6
Trade	323,467	12.4	1,405,000	21.6
Finance			222,000	3.4
Pub. admin., defense	767,745	29.5	179,000	2.8
Services			1,035,000	15.9
Other	...	...	648,000[9]	10.0[9]
TOTAL	2,599,901	100.0	6,509,000	100.0[8]

Public debt (external, outstanding; 2000): U.S.$3,602,000,000.
Household income and expenditure. Average household size (1999) 3.6; income per household: n.a.; sources of income (2001): salaries and wages 72.1%, social benefits 9.2%, agricultural income 8.1%, other 10.6%; expenditure (2001): food and beverages 56.0%, housing 11.7%, clothing 7.9%, transportation 5.1%, health 2.6%, education 2.4%, other 14.3%.
Tourism (2000): receipts U.S.$356,000,000; expenditures U.S.$408,000,000.

Foreign trade[10]

Balance of trade (current prices)

	1996	1997	1998	1999	2000	2001
U.S.$'000,000	−335.0	−276.4	−750.1	+686.0	+2,154.2	+2,283.9
% of total	2.6%	2.0%	6.0%	5.7%	13.6%	15.2%

Imports (2001): U.S.$6,363,000,000 (2000; electrical equipment and mechanical tools 20.3%, vehicles 6.6%, nonfood consumer goods 6.4%, foodstuffs 3.4%, petroleum products 3.4%). *Major import sources:* Russia 50.1%; Germany 6.2%; U.S. 5.3%; U.K. 3.7%; Ukraine 1.9%; Uzbekistan 1.5%.
Exports (2001): U.S.$8,646,900,000 (2000; oil and gas condensate 46.9%, refined copper 6.7%, grain 5.3%, ferrous metals 3.1%). *Major export destinations:* Russia 21.8%; Italy 10.8%; Germany 7.3%; China 6.8%.

Transport and communications

Transport. Railroads: (2001) route length 13,500 km; passenger-km 10,384,000,000; metric ton-km cargo 135,653,000,000. Roads (1999): total length 109,445 km (paved 90%). Vehicles (1997): passenger cars 987,724; trucks and buses 291,114. Air transport (2001): passenger-km 1,901,100,000; metric ton-km cargo 44,000,000; airports (1999) with scheduled flights 20.

Communications

Medium	date	unit	number	units per 1,000 persons
Radio	1997	receivers	6,470,000	395
Television	1998	receivers	3,890,000	238
Telephones	2001	main lines	1,834,200	113
Cellular telephones	2001	subscribers	582,000	36
Personal computers	...	units	...	...
Internet	2001	users	100,000	6.2

Education and health

Educational attainment (1989). Population age 25 and over having: primary education or no formal schooling 16.2%; some secondary 19.8%; completed secondary and some postsecondary 54.1%; higher 9.9%. *Literacy* (1989): population age 15 and over literate 97.5%; males 99.1%; females 96.1%.

Education (2000–2001)

	schools	teachers	students	student/teacher ratio
Primary (age 7–13) Secondary (age 14–17)	8,408	...	3,085,000	...
Voc., teacher tr.	318	...	196,200	...
Higher	185	...	514,700	...

Health (2001): physicians 51,300 (1 per 289 persons); hospital beds 110,200 (1 per 134 persons); infant mortality rate per 1,000 live births (2001) 19.4.
Food (2000): daily per capita caloric intake 2,991 (vegetable products 78%, animal products 22%); 117% of FAO minimum requirement.

Military

Total active duty personnel (2001): 64,000 (army 70.3%, air force 29.7%). *Military expenditure as percentage of GNP* (1999): 0.9% (world avg. 2.4%); per capita expenditure U.S.$40.

[1]Includes 7 nonelective seats. [2]City of Akmola (Kazakh: Aqmola; new capital replacing Almaty) was renamed Astana on May 6, 1998. [3]Russian has equal status with Kazakh at state-owned organizations and bodies of local government per a law effective July 16, 1997. [4]Area of Almaty city included with Almaty province. [5]Excludes parts of the former Torghay province incorporated into Aqmola and Qostanay provinces in 1997. The total area of Torghay province was 43,150 sq mi (111,800 sq km). [6]Area of Astana city is included with Aqmola province. [7]Includes an area of 6,000 sq km enclosing the Bayqongyr (Baykonur) space launch facilities and the city of Bayqongyr (formerly Leninsk) leased to Russia in 1995 for a period of 20 years. [8]Detail does not add to total given because of rounding. [9]Includes 382,000 undistributed unemployed and 266,000 undistributed employed. [10]Imports and exports are f.o.b. in balance of trade.

Internet resources for further information:
• **National Bank of Kazakhstan** http://www.nationalbank.kz/eng
• **Agency on Statistics of Kazakhstan** http://www.kazstat.asdc.kz/indexe.htm

Kenya

Official name: Jamhuri ya Kenya
(Swahili); Republic of Kenya
(English).
Form of government: unitary multiparty
republic with one legislative house
(National Assembly [224[1]]).
Head of state and government:
President.
Capital: Nairobi.
Official languages: Swahili; English.
Official religion: none.
Monetary unit: 1 Kenya shilling[2]
(K Sh) = 100 cents; valuation (Sept. 23,
2002) 1 U.S.$ = K Sh 78.85;
1 £ = K Sh 122.54.

Indian
Ocean

Area and population

		area		population
Provinces	**Provincial headquarters**	sq mi	sq km	1999 census[3]
Central	Nyeri	5,087	13,176	3,724,159
Coast	Mombasa	32,279	83,603	2,487,264
Eastern	Embu	61,734	159,891	4,631,779
North Eastern	Garissa	48,997	126,902	962,143
Nyanza	Kisumu	6,240	16,162	4,392,196
Rift Valley	Nakuru	67,131	173,868	6,987,036
Western	Kakamega	3,228	8,360	3,358,776
Special area				
Nairobi	—	264	684	2,143,254
TOTAL		224,961[4]	582,646	28,686,607

Demography

Population (2002)[5]: 31,139,000.
Density (2002): persons per sq mi 138.4, persons per sq km 53.4.
Urban-rural (2002): urban 34.4%; rural 65.6%.
Sex distribution (2001): male 50.16%; female 49.84%.
Age breakdown (2001): under 15, 41.9%; 15–29, 32.1%; 30–44, 14.6%; 45–59, 7.0%; 60–74, 3.4%; 75 and over, 1.0%.
Population projection[5]: (2010) 33,068,000; (2020) 34,001,000.
Doubling time: 54 years.
Ethnic composition (1989): Kikuyu 17.7%; Luhya 12.4%; Luo 10.6%; Kalenjin 9.8%; Kamba 9.8%; other 39.7%.
Religious affiliation (2000): Christian 79.3%, of which Roman Catholic 22.0%, African Christian 20.8%, Protestant 20.1%; Muslim 7.3%; other 13.4%.
Major cities (1999): Nairobi 2,143,254; Mombasa 461,753[6]; Nakuru 231,262; Kisumu 192,733[6]; Meru 126,427; Eldoret 111,882[6].

Vital statistics

Birth rate per 1,000 population (2001): 28.5 (world avg. 21.2).
Death rate per 1,000 population (2001): 14.4 (world avg. 8.9).
Natural increase rate per 1,000 population (2001): 14.1 (world avg. 12.3).
Total fertility rate (avg. births per childbearing woman; 2000): 3.7.
Life expectancy at birth (2001): male 46.6 years; female 48.4 years.
Major causes of death per 100,000 population: n.a.; however, major infectious diseases include AIDS, malaria, gastroenteritis, venereal diseases, diarrhea and dysentery, trachoma, amebiasis, and schistosomiasis.

National economy

Budget (2001–02). Revenue: K Sh 206,665,600,000 (tax revenue 86.6%, of which income and profit taxes 29.0%, value-added tax 27.2%, import duties 15.3%, excise tax 15.1%; nontax revenue 13.4%). Expenditures: K Sh 235,-832,000,000 (recurrent expenditure 80.4%, of which administration 29.7%, education 22.2%, defense 6.1%, health 6.0%; development expenditure 19.6%).
Production (metric tons except as noted). Agriculture, forestry, fishing (2001): sugarcane 5,150,000, corn (maize) 2,700,000, cassava 950,000, sweet potatoes 535,000, potatoes 500,000, plantains 370,000, pineapples 280,000, pulses 240,000, tea 240,000, bananas 210,000, wheat 180,000, sorghum 133,000, coffee 75,000, coconuts 63,000, millet 50,000, barley 45,000, tomatoes 30,000, sisal 25,000, seed cotton 20,000, tobacco 18,000, cashew nuts 12,500, sunflower seeds 12,200; livestock (number of live animals) 12,500,000 cattle, 9,000,000 goats, 6,500,000 sheep; roundwood (2001) 21,803,900 cu m; fish catch (1999) 205,587, of which freshwater fish 95.0%. Mining and quarrying (2000): soda ash 238,200; fluorite 100,100; salt 16,400. Manufacturing (value added in K£'000[2]; 1995): food products 847,000; beverages and tobacco 249,000; machinery and transport equipment 226,000; chemical products 181,000; metal products 131,000; textiles 94,000; paper and paper products 86,000; plastic products 75,000; clothing and footwear 58,000. Construction (1990): residential 411,000 sq m; nonresidential 182,000 sq m. Energy production (consumption): electricity (kW-hr; 2001) 4,338,400,000 (3,654,800,000); coal (metric tons; 1997) none (114,000); crude petroleum (barrels; 1997) none (13,194,000); petroleum products (metric tons; 2001) 1,695,600 (2,385,200).
Household income and expenditure. Average household size (1998) 3.4; average annual income per household: n.a.; sources of income: n.a.; expenditure (1993–94): food 42.4%, housing and energy 24.1%, clothing and footwear 9.1%, transportation 6.4%, other 18.0%.
Tourism (2000): receipts from visitors U.S.$257,000,000; expenditures by nationals abroad U.S.$132,000,000.
Population economically active (1997): total 14,592,000; activity rate of total population 50.0% (participation rates [1985]: ages 15–64, 76.2%; female [1997] 46.1%; unemployed, n.a.).

Price and earnings indexes (1995 = 100)

	1995	1996	1997	1998	1999	2000	2001
Consumer price index	100.0	108.8	121.9	129.0	132.4	140.1	143.2
Earnings index	...	...	...	...	...	...	...

Public debt (external, outstanding; 2000): U.S.$5,180,000,000.
Gross national product (2000): U.S.$10,610,000,000 (U.S.$350 per capita).

Structure of gross domestic product and labour force

	2000		2001	
	in value K Sh '000,000	% of total value	labour force	% of labour force
Agriculture	134,010	19.9	312,500	5.0
Mining	1,143	0.2	5,200	0.1
Manufacturing	87,974	13.1	216,600	3.4
Construction	29,134	4.3	76,800	1.2
Public utilities	7,624	1.1	21,400	0.3
Transp. and commun.	49,890	7.4	84,300	1.3
Trade	150,253	22.4	156,900	2.5
Finance	106,798	15.9	83,800	1.3
Pub. admin., defense } Services	105,393	15.7	719,600	11.4
Other	—	—	4,624,400[7]	73.4[7]
TOTAL	672,219	100.0	6,301,500	100.0[4]

Land use (1994): forest 29.5%; pasture 37.4%; agriculture 8.0%; other 25.1%.

Foreign trade[8]

Balance of trade (current prices)

	1996	1997	1998	1999	2000	2001
K Sh '000,000	−50,260	−70,714	−71,780	−76,246	−113,277	−98,700
% of total	17.5%	22.8%	22.8%	23.8%	29.6%	24.3%

Imports (2000): K Sh 247,803,900,000 (machinery and transport equipment 29.1%, mineral fuels 26.1%, chemical products 13.2%, basic manufactures 11.1%, food and beverages 8.6%). *Major import sources:* U.A.E. 19.5%; U.K. 10.1%; South Africa 6.7%; Saudi Arabia 6.1%; Japan 5.1%; United States 4.1%; India 4.1%; Germany 3.5%.
Exports (2000): K Sh 134,527,100,000 (tea 29.3%, coffee 9.8%, petroleum products 7.9%, horticulture 7.8%, fruits and vegetables 6.5%, chemicals 5.6%, iron and steel 2.2%). *Major export destinations:* Uganda 17.9%; U.K. 13.9%; Tanzania 8.2%; Pakistan 7.4%; The Netherlands 5.4%; Egypt 5.3%; Germany 4.2%.

Transport and communications

Transport. Railroads (2000): route length 1,678 mi, 2,700 km; passenger-mi 187,600,000; passenger-km 302,000,000; short ton-mi cargo 967,000,000, metric ton-km cargo 1,557,000,000. Roads (1999): total length 39,600 mi, 63,800 km (paved 14%). Vehicles (2000): passenger cars 244,836; trucks and buses 96,726. Merchant marine (2000): vessels (100 gross tons and over) 38. Air transport (1998): passenger-mi 1,299,000,000, passenger-km 2,091,000,000; short ton-mi cargo 151,000,000, metric ton-km cargo 243,000,000; airports (1997) with scheduled flights 11.

Communications

Medium	date	unit	number	units per 1,000 persons
Daily newspapers	1996	circulation	263,000[9]	9.4[9]
Radio	1997	receivers	3,070,000	107
Television	1999	receivers	660,000	23
Telephones	2001	main lines	313,100	10
Cellular telephones	2001	subscribers	500,000	16
Personal computers	2001	units	175,000	5.6
Internet	2001	users	500,000	16

Education and health

Educational attainment: n.a. Literacy (1999): total population over age 15 literate 81.5%; males literate 88.3%; females literate 74.8%.

Education (2001)

	schools[10]	teachers	students	student/ teacher ratio
Primary (age 5–11)	15,906	185,720	6,314,500	34.0
Secondary (age 12–17)	2,878	48,129	818,200	17.0
Voc., teacher tr.	62		44,700	...
Higher[11]	14	4,392[10]	62,100	...

Health (2001): physicians 4,630 (1 per 6,645 persons); hospital beds 57,540 (1 per 535 persons); infant mortality rate per 1,000 live births (2001): 68.0.
Food (2000): daily per capita caloric intake 1,965 (vegetable products 88%, animal products 12%); 85% of FAO recommended minimum requirement.

Military

Total active duty personnel (2001): 24,400 (army 82.0%, navy 5.7%, air force 12.3%). *Military expenditure as percentage of GNP* (1999): 1.9% (world 2.4%); per capita expenditure U.S.$7.

---

[1]Includes 14 nonelective seats. [2]Kenya pound (K£) as a unit of account equals 20 K Sh. [3]Preliminary. [4]Detail does not add to total given because of rounding. [5]Not based on August 1999 census results. [6]1989 census. [7]Employed in informal sector, primarily in agriculture. [8]Import figures are c.i.f. [9]Circulation for four newspapers only. [10]1993. [11]Universities only.

Internet resources for further information:
• **Central Bank of Kenya** http://www.centralbank.go.ke/
• **Ministry of Finance and Planning** http://www.treasury.go.ke

Kiribati

Official name: Republic of Kiribati.
Form of government: unitary republic with a unicameral legislature (House of Assembly [42[1]]).
Head of state and government: President.
Capital: Bairiki, on Tarawa Atoll.
Official language: English.
Official religion: none.
Monetary unit: 1 Australian dollar ($A) = 100 cents; valuation (Sept. 23, 2002) 1 U.S.$ = $A 1.83; 1 £ = $A 2.84.

Area and population

Island Groups Islands	Capitals	area[2] sq mi	sq km	population 2000 census
Gilberts Group	Bairiki Islet	110	286[3]	78,158
Abaiang	Tuarabu	7	18	5,794
Abemama	Kariatebike	11	27	3,142
Aranuka	Takaeang	5	12	966
Arorae	Roreti	3	9	1,225
Banaba	Anteeren	2	6	276
Beru	Taubukinberu	7	18	2,732
Butaritari	Butaritari	5	13	3,464
Kuria	Tabontebike	6	16	961
Maiana	Tebangetua	6	17	2,048
Makin	Makin	3	8	1,691
Marakei	Rawannawi	5	14	2,544
Nikunau	Rungata	7	19	1,733
Nonouti	Teuabu	8	20	3,176
Onotoa	Buariki	6	16	1,668
Tabiteuea North	Utiroa	10	26	3,365
Tabiteuea South	Buariki	5	12	1,217
Tamana	Bakaka	2	5	962
Tarawa North	Abaokoro	6	15	4,477
Tarawa South	Bairiki	6	16	36,717
Line Group	Kiritimati	192	496	6,275
Northern		167	432	6,275
Kiritimati (Christmas)	London	150	388	3,431
Tabuaeran (Fanning)	Paelau	13	34	1,757
Teraina (Washington)	Washington	4	10	1,087
Southern (Caroline [Millennium], Flint, Malden, Starbuck, Vostok)		25	64	—
Phoenix Group (Birnie, Enderbury, Kanton [Canton], McKean, Manra [Sydney], Nikumaroro [Gardner], Orona [Hull], Rawaki [Phoenix])	Kanton	11	29	61
TOTAL		**313**	**811**	**84,494**

Demography

Population (2002): 90,600.
Density (2002)[4]: persons per sq mi 323.6, persons per sq km 124.8.
Urban-rural (2002): urban 40.0%; rural 60.0%.
Sex distribution (2000): male 49.40%; female 50.60%.
Age breakdown (1995): under 15, 41.2%; 15–29, 25.8%; 30–44, 18.3%; 45–59, 9.3%; 60–74, 4.4%; 75 and over, 1.0%.
Population projection: (2010) 104,000; (2020) 124,000.
Doubling time: 30 years.
Ethnic composition (1995): I-Kiribati 97.7%; mixed (part I-Kiribati and other) 1.5%; Tuvaluan 0.3%; European 0.2%; other 0.3%.
Religious affiliation (1995): Roman Catholic 54.3%; Kiribati Protestant (Congregational) 37.9%; Bahā'ī 2.6%; other Protestant 2.5%; other Christian (Mormon) 1.7%; other/nonreligious 1.0%.
Major cities (1999): Tarawa (urban area) 32,000.

Vital statistics

Birth rate per 1,000 population (2002): 31.6 (world avg. 21.2).
Death rate per 1,000 population (2002): 8.8 (world avg. 8.9).
Total fertility rate (avg. births per childbearing woman; 2002): 4.3.
Marriage rate per 1,000 population (1988): 5.2.
Life expectancy at birth (2002): male 57.6 years; female 63.6 years.
Major causes of death per 100,000 population (1993): senility without mention of psychosis 61.2; stroke 39.1; diarrhea 37.8; hepatitis 32.5; diabetes mellitus 28.6; malnutrition 23.4; meningitis 18.2.

National economy

Budget (1997). Revenue: $A 79,100,000 (nontax revenue 46.6%, tax revenue 20.4%, grants 33.0%). Expenditures: $A 79,100,000 (current expenditures 66.3%, of which wages 25.4%; capital expenditures 33.7%).
Public debt (external, outstanding; 1999): U.S.$9,500,000.
Tourism: receipts from visitors (2000) U.S.$2,100,000; expenditures by nationals abroad (1999) U.S.$2,000,000.
Land use (1994): forest 2.7%; agricultural and under permanent cultivation 50.7%; other 46.6%.
Production (metric tons except as noted). Agriculture, forestry, fishing (1999): coconuts 85,000, roots and tubers 6,500 (of which taro 1,600), vegetables and melons 5,000, bananas 4,700, tropical fruit 1,150; livestock (number of live animals) 9,500 pigs, 300,000 chickens; fish catch (1997) 23,000. Mining and quarrying: none. Manufacturing (1996): processed copra 9,321; other important products are processed fish, baked goods, clothing, and handi-

crafts. Energy production (consumption): electricity (kW-hr; 1997) 7,000,000 (7,000,000); petroleum products (metric tons; 1997) none (7,000).
Gross national product (2000): U.S.$86,000,000 (U.S.$950 per capita).

Structure of gross domestic product and labour force

	1996		1990	
	in value[5] $A '000	% of total[5] value	labour force	% of labour force
Agriculture, fishing	4,832	12.4	23,137[6]	71.0[6]
Mining	—	—	—	—
Manufacturing	344	0.9	622	1.9
Construction	1,024	2.6	339	1.0
Public utilities	947	2.4	301	0.9
Transp. and commun.	4,822	12.4	921	2.8
Trade	7,238	18.5	1,341	4.1
Finance	2,215	5.7	441	1.4
Pub. admin., defense	12,780	32.8	2,123	6.5
Services	1,346	3.4	2,286	7.0
Other	3,470[7]	8.9[7]	1,098[8]	3.4[8]
TOTAL	39,018	100.0	32,610	100.0

Population economically active (1995): total 38,407; activity rate of total population 49.5% (participation rates: over age 15, 84.0%; female 47.8%; unemployed 0.2%).

Price and earnings indexes (1990 = 100)

	1991	1992	1993	1994	1995	1996	1997
Consumer price index	103.7	109.2	115.6	123.0	127.4	126.7	126.6
Earnings index	...	...	...	...	...	...	...

Household income and expenditure. Average household size (1995) 6.5; income per household: n.a.; sources of income (1978): wages 69.7%, self-employment 21.4%, transfer payments 6.0%, other 2.9%; expenditure (1982): food 50.0%, tobacco and alcohol 14.0%, clothing 8.0%, transportation 8.0%, housing, energy, and household operation 7.5%.

Foreign trade

Balance of trade (current prices)[9]

	1993	1994	1995	1996	1997	1998
$A '000	−36,443	−29,303	−38,826	−40,382	−44,104	−43,790
% of total	80.7%	68.1%	69.0%	73.1%	72.3%	69.9%

Imports (1996): $A 47,829,000 (food and live animals 33.4%; machinery and transport equipment 18.1%; basic manufactures 14.6%; mineral fuels 10.3%; beverages and tobacco 6.7%; chemicals 6.6%; crude materials 2.1%). *Major import sources:* Australia 46.1%; Fiji 18.7%; Japan 8.6%; New Zealand 8.4%; China 5.9%; United States 3.3%.
Exports (1996): $A 7,447,000 (domestic exports 91.7%, of which copra 62.8%, pet fish 11.6%, fish and fish preparations 4.0%, seaweed 3.6%; reexports 8.3%). *Major export destinations* (1994): Japan 32.9%; United States 17.1%; Hong Kong 12.9%; Bangladesh 8.6%; Germany 8.6%; Malaysia 7.1%.

Transport and communications

Transport. Roads (1996): total length 416 mi, 670 km (paved 5%). Vehicles (1988): passenger cars 222; trucks and buses 115. Merchant marine (1992): vessels (100 gross tons and over) 7; total deadweight tonnage 2,685. Air transport (1996): passenger-mi 4,350,000, passenger-km 7,000,000; short ton-mi cargo 621,000, metric ton-km cargo 1,000,000; airports 9.

Communications

Medium	date	unit	number	units per 1,000 persons
Radio	1997	receivers	17,000	212
Television	1997	receivers	1,000	15
Telephones	2000	main lines	3,400	40
Cellular telephones	2000	subscribers	400	4.8
Personal computers	2001	units	2,000	25
Internet	2001	users	2,000	25

Education and health

Educational attainment (1995). Percentage of population age 25 and over having: no schooling 7.8%; primary education 68.5%; secondary or higher 23.7%.
Literacy (1995): population age 15 and over literate 90%.

Education (1997)

	schools	teachers	students	student/ teacher ratio
Primary (age 6–13)	86	727	17,594	24.2
Secondary (age 14–18)	9[10]	215	4,403	20.5
Voc., teacher tr.	10	23	333	14.5
Higher[11]	—	—	—	—

Health: physicians (1998) 26 (1 per 3,378 persons); hospital beds (1990) 283 (1 per 253 persons); infant mortality rate per 1,000 live births (2002) 52.6.
Food (1999): daily per capita caloric intake 2,982 (vegetable products 89%, animal products 11%); (1997) 131% of FAO recommended minimum.

---

[1]Includes two nonelective members. [2]Includes uninhabited islands. [3]Detail does not add to total given because of rounding. [4]Based on inhabited island areas (280 sq mi [726 sq km]) only. [5]1991 constant prices. [6]Includes 20,568 persons engaged in "village work" (subsistence agriculture or fishing). [7]Indirect taxes less subsidies and imputed bank service charge. [8]Includes 900 unemployed. [9]Exports do not include reexports. [10]Includes vocational. [11]54 students overseas in 1993.

Internet resources for further information:
• **United Nations Development Programme, Common Country Assessments**
  http://www.undp.org.fj/CCAs.htm

Korea, North

Official name: Chosŏn Minjujuŭi
In'min Konghwaguk (Democratic
People's Republic of Korea).
Form of government: unitary
single-party republic with one
legislative house (Supreme People's
Assembly [687]).
Chief of state: Chairman of the
National Defense Commission[1].
Head of government: Premier.
Capital: P'yŏngyang.
Official language: Korean.
Official religion: none.
Monetary unit: 1 won = 100
chŏn; valuation (Sept. 23, 2002)
1 U.S.$ = 2.20 won; 1 £ = 3.42 won.

Area and population		area		population[2]
				1987
Provinces	**Capitals**	sq mi	sq km	estimate
Chagang-do	Kanggye	6,551	16,968	1,156,000
Kangwŏn-do	Wŏnsan	4,306	11,152	1,227,000
North Hamgyŏng (Hamgyŏng-pukto)	Ch'ŏngjin	6,784[3]	17,570[3]	2,003,000[3]
North Hwanghae (Hwanghae-pukto)	Sariwŏn	3,091	8,007	1,409,000
North P'yŏngan (P'yŏngan-pukto)	Sinŭiju	4,707[4]	12,191[4]	2,380,000
South Hamgyŏng (Hamgyŏng-namdo)	Hamhŭng	7,324	18,970	2,547,000
South Hwanghae (Hwanghae-namdo)	Haeju	3,090	8,002	1,914,000
South P'yŏngan (P'yŏngan-namdo)	P'yŏngsan	4,470	11,577	2,653,000
Yanggang-do	Hyesan	5,528	14,317	628,000
Special cities				
Kaesŏng	—	485	1,255	331,000
Namp'o	—	291	753	715,000
Najin Sŏnbong[3]	—	...	...	...
P'yŏngyang	—	772	2,000	2,355,000
Special district				
Hyangsan-chigu	—	4	4	28,000
TOTAL		47,399	122,762	19,346,000

Demography

Population (2002): 22,224,000.
Density (2002): persons per sq mi 468.9, persons per sq km 181.0.
Urban-rural (1998): urban 62.2%; rural 37.8%.
Sex distribution (2000): male 48.48%; female 51.52%.
Age breakdown (2000): under 15, 25.6%; 15–29, 24.5%; 30–44, 24.7%; 45–59,
14.4%; 60–74, 9.0%; 75 and over, 1.8%.
Population projection: (2010) 23,753,000; (2020) 25,143,000.
Ethnic composition (1999): Korean 99.8%; Chinese 0.2%.
Religious affiliation (1980): atheist or nonreligious 68.3%; traditional beliefs
15.6%; Ch'ŏndogyo 13.9%; Buddhist 1.7%; Christian 0.5%.
Major cities (1993): P'yŏngyang 2,500,000[5, 6]; Namp'o 731,448; Hamhŭng 709,000;
Ch'ŏngjin 582,480; Kaesŏng 334,433; Sinŭiju 326,011.

Vital statistics

Birth rate per 1,000 population (2000): 20.4 (world avg. 22.5).
Death rate per 1,000 population (2000): 6.9 (world avg. 9.0).
Natural increase rate per 1,000 population (2000): 13.5 (world avg. 13.5).
Total fertility rate (avg. births per childbearing woman; 2000): 2.3.
Marriage rate per 1,000 population (1987): 9.3.
Divorce rate per 1,000 population (1987): 0.2.
Life expectancy at birth (2000): male 67.8 years; female 73.9 years.
Major causes of death per 100,000 population (1986); diseases of the cir-
culatory system 224.9; malignant neoplasms (cancers) 69.0; diseases of the
digestive system 51.6; diseases of the respiratory system 46.7; injuries and
poisoning 38.2; infectious and parasitic diseases 19.4.

National economy

Budget (1999). Revenue: 19,801,000,000 won (turnover tax and profits from
state enterprises). Expenditures: 20,018,200,000 won (1994; national economy 67.8%, social and cultural affairs 19.0%, defense 11.6%).
Population economically active (1997)[7]: total 11,898,000; activity rate of total
population 55.8% (participation rates [1988–93]: ages 15–64, 49.5%; female
46.0%; unemployed, n.a.).
Production (metric tons except as noted). Agriculture, forestry, fishing (2000):
rice 1,690,000, potatoes 1,402,000, corn (maize) 1,041,000, cabbages 630,000,
apples 650,000, sweet potatoes 468,000, soybeans 350,000, wheat 157,500,
pears 130,000, watermelons 104,000, peaches and nectarines 100,000, barley
88,500, cucumbers and gherkins 64,000, tomatoes 62,000, tobacco leaves
62,000, millet 45,000, oats 11,000; livestock (number of live animals) 2,970,000
pigs, 2,100,000 goats, 600,000 cattle, 190,000 sheep, 10,371,000 chickens;
roundwood (2000) 4,900,000 cu m; fish catch (1999): 278,500. Mining and
quarrying (2000): iron ore (metal content) 300,000; magnesite 1,000,000;
phosphate rock 350,000; sulfur 240,000; zinc 190,000; lead (metal content)
70,000; copper (metal content) 14,000; tungsten (metal content) 700,000; silver 50; gold 5,000 kg. Manufacturing (1999): cement 16,000,000; crude steel
8,100,000; pig iron 6,600,000; coke 3,400,000; steel semimanufactures
2,700,000[8]; chemical fertilizers 2,500,000[8]; meat 259,200[8]; gasoline 8,600,000[9]
barrels; textile fabrics 350,000,000 sq m[8]. Construction: n.a. Energy production (consumption): electricity (kW-hr; 1999) 28,600,000 (28,600,000); coal
(metric tons; 1999) 85,500,000 (87,600,000); crude petroleum (barrels; 1999)
none (26,000,000); petroleum products (metric tons; 1997) 2,785,000
(4,258,000).

Household income and expenditure. Average household size (1999) 4.6; average annual income per household: n.a.; sources of income: n.a.; expenditure:
n.a.
Public debt (external, outstanding; 1999): U.S.$12,000,000,000.
Gross national product (1999): U.S.$9,912,000,000 (U.S.$457 per capita).

Structure of gross domestic product and labour force				
	1999		1997	
	in value U.S.$'000,000	% of total value	labour force	% of labour force
Agriculture	...	25.0	3,853,000	32.4
Mining and manufacturing	}	} 60.0	}	}
Construction				
Public utilities				
Transp. and commun.			8,045,000	67.6
Trade				
Finance	...	...		
Pub. admin., defense	}	}		
Services	...	15.0		
Other				
TOTAL	22,600	100.0	11,898,000	100.0

Land use (1994): forested 61.2%; meadows and pastures 0.4%; agricultural
and under permanent cultivation 16.6%; other 21.8%.

Foreign trade[10]

Balance of trade (current prices)						
	1994	1995	1996	1997	1998	1999
U.S.$'000,000	−429.5	−880.0	−1,050	−390	−320	−450
% of total	20.4%	42.7%	36.3%	18.1%	22.2%	30.4%

Imports (1999): U.S.$965,000,000 (crude petroleum, coal and coke, industrial
machinery and transport equipment [including trucks], industrial chemicals,
textile yarn and fabrics, and grain are among the major imports). *Major
import sources* (1995): China 30.0%; Japan 15.8%; Austria 9.3%; Ukraine
5.9%.
Exports (1999): U.S.$515,000,000 (minerals [including lead, magnesite, zinc],
metallurgical products [iron and steel, nonferrous metals], cement, agricultural products [including fish, grain, fruit and vegetables, tobacco], and manufactured goods [textile fabrics, clothing] are among the major exports).
Major export destinations (1995): Japan 31.4%; Austria 17.3%; India 6.9%.

Transport and communications

Transport. Railroads (1999): length 8,533 km. Roads (1998): total length 14,544
mi, 23,407 km (paved 8%). Vehicles (1990): passenger cars 248,000. Merchant
marine (1992): vessels (100 gross tons and over) 100; total deadweight tonnage 951,222. Air transport (1997): passenger-mi 177,712,000, passenger-km
286,000,000; short ton-mi cargo 18,600,000; metric ton-km cargo 30,000,000;
airports (2001) with scheduled flights 1.

Communications				units
				per 1,000
Medium	**date**	**unit**	**number**	**persons**
Daily newspapers	1996	circulation	4,500,000	199
Radio	1997	receivers	3,360,000	146
Television	1997	receivers	1,200,000	52
Telephones	1999	main lines	1,100,000	46

Education and health

Educational attainment (1987–88). Percentage of population age 16 and over
having attended or graduated from postsecondary-level school: 13.7%.
Literacy (1997): 95%.

Education (1988)				student/
	schools	teachers	students	teacher ratio
Primary (age 6–9)	4,810	59,000	1,543,000	26.2
Secondary (age 10–15)	4,840	111,000	2,468,000	22.2
Voc., teacher tr.	...	...	...	...
Higher	46	23,000	325,000	14.1

Health (1993): physicians 61,200 (1 per 370 persons); hospital beds (1989)
290,590 (1 per 74 persons); infant mortality rate (2001) 22.5.
Food (2000): daily per capita caloric intake 2,185 (vegetable products 94%,
animal products 6%); 93% of FAO recommended minimum requirement.

Military

Total active duty personnel (2001): 1,082,000 (army 87.8%, navy 4.2%, air force
8.0%). *Military expenditure as percentage of GNP* (1997): 27.5% (world
2.4%); per capita expenditure U.S.$282.

---

[1]Position in effect from Sept. 5, 1998. It is defined as an enhanced military post with
revised constitutional powers. [2]Civilian population only; UN cites a 1993 census total
of 21,123,376, but details are not available. [3]North Hamgyŏng includes Najin Sŏnbong
special city created in 2001. [4]North P'yŏngan includes special district of Hyangsan-
chigu. [5]1996 estimate. [6]Urban agglomeration for 1999 equals 3,136,000. [7]The Democratic
People's Republic of Korea categorizes economically active as including students in
higher education, retirees, and heads of households, as well as those in the civilian
labour force. [8]1994. [9]1996. [10]Imports are f.o.b.

Internet resources for further information:
• **Korean News** http://www.kcna.co.jp
• **United States Department of Energy**
   http://www.eia.doe.gov/emeu/cabs/nkorea.html

Korea, South

Official name: Taehan Min'guk
  (Republic of Korea).
Form of government: unitary multiparty
  republic with one legislative house
  (National Assembly [273]).
Head of state and government:
  President, assisted by Prime Minister.
Capital: Seoul.
Official language: Korean.
Official religion: none.
Monetary unit: 1 won (W) = 100 chon;
  valuation (Sept. 23, 2002)
  1 U.S.$ = W 1,209; 1 £ = W 1,880.

Area and population		area		population
				2000
Provinces	**Capitals**	sq mi	sq km	census
Cheju	Cheju	713	1,846	512,541
Kangwŏn	Ch'unch'ŏn	6,399	16,572	1,484,536
Kyŏnggi	Suwŏn	3,913	10,135	8,937,752
North Chŏlla	Chŏnju	3,108	8,050	1,887,239
North Ch'ungch'ŏng	Ch'ŏngju	2,870	7,432	1,462,621
North Kyŏngsang	Taegu	7,345	19,024	2,716,218
South Chŏlla	Kwangju	4,628	11,987	1,994,287
South Ch'ungch'ŏng	Taejŏn	3,315	8,586	1,840,410
South Kyŏngsang	Masan	4,060	10,515	2,970,929
Metropolitan cities				
Inch'ŏn	Inch'ŏn	373	965	2,466,338
Kwangju	Kwangju	193	501	1,350,948
Pusan	Pusan	293	760	3,655,437
Sŏul (Seoul)	Seoul	234	606	9,853,972
Taegu	Taegu	342	886	2,473,990
Taejŏn	Taejŏn	208	540	1,365,961
Ulsan	Ulsan	408	1,056	1,012,110
TOTAL		38,402	99,461	45,985,289

Demography

Population (2002): 47,640,000.
Density (2002): persons per sq mi 1,240.6, persons per sq km 479.0.
Urban-rural (2002): urban 83.0%; rural 17.0%.
Sex distribution (2002): male 50.34%; female 49.66%.
Age breakdown (2002): under 15, 20.6%; 15–29, 24.1%; 30–44, 26.9%; 45–59, 16.5%; 60–74, 9.4%; 75 and over, 2.5%.
Population projection: (2010) 49,594,000; (2020) 50,650,000.
Doubling time: over 100 years.
Ethnic composition (2000): Korean 97.7%; Japanese 2.0%; U.S. white 0.1%; Han Chinese 0.1%; other 0.1%.
Religious affiliation (1995): religious 50.7%, of which Buddhist 23.2%, Protestant 19.7%, Roman Catholic 6.6%, Confucian 0.5%, Wonbulgyo 0.2%, Ch'ŏndogyo 0.1%, other 0.4%; nonreligious 49.3%.
Major cities (2000): Seoul 9,853,972; Pusan 3,655,437; Taegu 2,473,990; Inch'ŏn 2,466,338; Taejŏn 1,365,961.

Vital statistics

Birth rate per 1,000 population (2001): 11.6 (world avg. 21.2).
Death rate per 1,000 population (2001): 5.1 (world avg. 8.9).
Natural increase rate per 1,000 population (2001): 6.5 (world avg. 12.3).
Total fertility rate (avg. births per childbearing woman; 1999): 1.7.
Marriage rate per 1,000 population (2000): 7.0.
Divorce rate per 1,000 population (2000): 2.5.
Life expectancy at birth (2002): male 72.0 years; female 79.0 years.
Major causes of death per 100,000 population (2000): malignant neoplasms (cancers) 125.6; diseases of the circulatory system 124.6; accidents, poisoning, and violence 61.4; diseases of the respiratory system 34.3.

National economy

Budget (1998). Revenue: W 96,673,000,000,000 (taxes on income and profits 28.9%, taxes on goods and services 28.1%, nontax revenue 18.1%, social security contributions 10.9%, education tax 5.4%). Expenditures: W 115,689,000,000,000 (economic services 24.6%, education 15.4%, defense 11.8%, social security and welfare 10.6%, general public services 9.4%, housing and community amenities 6.3%).
Public debt (external, outstanding; 2000): U.S.$46,941,000,000.
Production (metric tons except as noted). Agriculture, forestry, fishing (2000): rice 7,067,000, cabbages 2,755,000, dry onions 936,000, tangerines 601,000, apples 491,000; livestock (number of live animals) 7,864,000 pigs, 2,486,000 cattle, 97,000,000 chickens; roundwood 1,722,000 cu m; fish catch (1998) 2,026,934. Mining and quarrying (1998): copper ore 226,000; iron ore 133,000; zinc concentrate 10,488. Manufacturing (2000): cement 51,424,000; finished steel 48,865,000; synthetic resin 8,657,000; computer peripherals U.S.$12,460,000,000; mobile phones U.S.$12,019,000,000; colour television receivers U.S.$1,773,000,000; motor vehicles 3,115,000 units. Construction (permits authorized; 2000): residential 41,283,000 sq m; nonresidential 39,775,000 sq m. Energy production (consumption): electricity (kW-hr; 1999) 239,328,000,000 ([1997] 248,653,000,000); coal (metric tons; 1999) 4,140,000 ([1997] 53,942,000); crude petroleum (barrels; 1997) none (873,000,000); petroleum products (metric tons; 1997) 97,118,000 (76,056,000); natural gas (cu m; 1997) none (15,620,000,000).
Household income and expenditure (2000)[1]. Average household size (1998) 3.6; income per household W 54,025,000 (U.S.$47,769); sources of income: wages 53.0%, other 47.0%; expenditure: food and beverages 27.5%, transportation and communications 16.4%, education and recreation 16.2%, clothing and

footwear 5.7%, utilities 5.1%, health care 4.1%, household durable goods 3.7%, housing 3.3%, other 18.0%.
Gross national product (2000): U.S.$421,069,000,000 (U.S.$8,910 per capita).

Structure of gross domestic product and labour force				
	2000			
	in value W '000,000,000[2]	% of total value[2]	labour force	% of labour force
Agriculture	24,859.8	6.0	2,288,000	10.4
Mining	1,439.4	0.3	18,000	0.1
Manufacturing	163,014.5	39.6	4,244,000	19.3
Construction	36,881.8	9.0	1,583,000	7.2
Public utilities	12,265.2	3.0		
Transp. and commun.	41,276.1	10.0		
Trade	58,469.5	14.2	12,928,000	58.9
Finance	83,860.0	20.4		
Pub. admin., defense	29,171.7	7.1		
Services	30,396.9	7.4		
Other	−69,946.4[3]	−17.0[3]	889,000[4]	4.1[4]
TOTAL	411,688.5	100.0	21,950,000	100.0

Population economically active (2000): total 21,950,000; activity rate 46.4% (participation rates: ages 15 and over, 60.7%; female [1998] 38.8%; unemployed 4.1%).

Price and earnings indexes (1995 = 100)							
	1995	1996	1997	1998	1999	2000	2001
Consumer price index	100.0	104.9	109.6	117.8	118.8	121.5	126.7
Monthly earnings index	100.0	112.2	118.0	114.3	131.3	142.5	151.5

Tourism (2000): receipts U.S.$6,811,000,000; expenditures U.S.$6,174,000,000.

Foreign trade[5]

Balance of trade (current prices)						
	1996	1997	1998	1999	2000	2001
U.S.$'000,000	−20,624	−8,452	+39,031	+23,934	+11,787	+9,341
% of total	7.4%	3.0%	17.3%	9.1%	3.5%	3.2%

Imports (2000): U.S.$160,481,000,000 (electric and electronic products 27.0%, crude petroleum 15.7%, machinery and transport equipment 13.2%, manufactured consumer goods 10.0%, chemicals 7.4%, iron and steel products 3.7%). *Major import sources:* Japan 19.8%; U.S. 18.2%; China 8.0%; Saudi Arabia 6.0%; Australia 3.7%; Malaysia 3.0%.
Exports (2000): U.S.$172,267,500,000 (electric and electronic products 36.0%, machinery and transport equipment 18.2%, chemicals 7.0%, crude materials and fuels 6.7%). *Major export destinations:* U.S. 21.8%; Japan 11.9%; China 10.7%; Hong Kong 6.2%; Taiwan 4.7%; Singapore 3.3%; U.K. 3.1%.

Transport and communications

Transport. Railroads (1998): length (2000) 6,706 km; passenger-km 30,072,-000,000; metric ton-km cargo 12,708,000,000. Roads (2000): total length 88,775 km (paved 76%). Vehicles (2000): passenger cars 8,084,000; trucks and buses 3,938,000. Air transport (1998): passenger-km 47,712,000,000; metric ton-km cargo 7,280,640,000; airports (1996) with scheduled flights 14.

Communications				units per 1,000
Medium	date	unit	number	persons
Daily newspapers	1995	circulation	17,700,000	394
Radio	1997	receivers	47,500,000	1,033
Television	1999	receivers	16,896,000	361
Telephones	2001	main lines	22,724,700	476
Cellular telephones	2001	subscribers	29,045,600	608
Personal computers	2001	units	12,000,000	251
Internet	2001	users	24,380,000	511

Education and health

Educational attainment (1995). Percentage of population age 25 and over having: no formal schooling 8.5%; primary education or less 17.7%; some secondary and secondary 53.1%; postsecondary 20.6%. *Literacy* (1995): total population age 15 and over literate 98.0%; males 99.3%; females 96.7%.

Education (1999)				student/
	schools	teachers	students	teacher ratio
Primary (age 6–13)	14,334	163,741	4,469,703	27.3
Secondary (age 14–19)	4,684	198,548	4,148,096	20.9
Vocational, teacher training	172	12,089	880,870	72.9
Higher[6]	158	41,226	1,587,667	38.5

Health (1999): physicians 69,724 (1 per 672 persons); hospital beds (1997) 220,427 (1 per 209 persons); infant mortality rate (2002): 7.0.
Food (2000): daily per capita caloric intake 3,073 (vegetable products 86%, animal products 14%); (1997) 131% of FAO recommended minimum.

Military

Total active duty personnel (2001): 683,000 (army 82.0%, navy 8.8%, air force 9.2%); U.S. military forces (2001): 36,000. *Military expenditure as percentage of GNP* (1999): 2.9% (world 2.4%); per capita expenditure U.S.$246.

---

[1]Excludes farm households. [2]At 1995 constant prices. [3]Import duties less imputed bank service charges. [4]Unemployed. [5]Imports c.i.f.; exports f.o.b. [6]Excludes graduate schools.

Internet resources for further information:
• **National Statistical Office http://www.nso.go.kr/eng**

Kuwait

Official name: Dawlat al-Kuwayt (State of Kuwait).
Form of government: constitutional monarchy with one legislative body (National Assembly [65[1]]).
Head of state and government: Emir[2].
Capital: Kuwait City[3].
Official language: Arabic.
Official religion: Islam.
Monetary unit: 1 Kuwaiti dinar (KD) = 1,000 fils; valuation (Sept. 23, 2002) 1 KD = U.S.$3.33 = £2.13.

Area and population		area		population
Governorates	Capitals	sq mi	sq km	2000 estimate
Al-Aḥmadī	Al-Aḥmadī	1,977	5,120	363,025
Al-Farwānīyah	Al-Farwānīyah	73	190	572,345
Al-Jahrā'	Al-Jahrā'	4,336	11,230	280,765
Al-'Aṣimah	Kuwait City	77	200	382,360
Ḥawallī	Ḥawallī	69	178	627,990
Islands[4]	—	347	900	...
TOTAL		6,880[5]	17,818	2,226,485[6]

Demography

Population (2002): 2,253,000.
Density (2002): persons per sq mi 327.5, persons per sq km 126.4.
Urban-rural (2001): urban 96.1%; rural 3.9%.
Sex distribution (2000): male 60.04%; female 39.96%.
Age breakdown (2000): under 15, 29.4%; 15–29, 28.2%; 30–44, 25.8%; 45–59, 12.6%; 60–74, 3.5%; 75 and over, 0.5%.
Population projection: (2010) 2,334,000; (2020) 2,439,000.
Doubling time: 36 years.
Ethnic composition (2000): Arab 74%, of which Kuwaiti 30%, Palestinian 17%, Jordanian 10%, Bedouin 9%; Kurd 10%; Indo-Pakistani 8%; Persian 4%; other 4%.
Religious affiliation (1995): Muslim 85%, of which Sunnī 45%, Shī'ī 30%; other Muslim 10%; other (mostly Christian and Hindu) 15.0%.
Major cities (1995): As-Sālimīyah 130,215; Qalīb ash-Shuyūkh 102,178; Ḥawallī 82,238; Kuwait City 28,859 (urban agglomeration [2001] 888,000).

Vital statistics

Birth rate per 1,000 population (2000): 22.0 (world avg. 22.5).
Death rate per 1,000 population (2000): 2.4 (world avg. 9.0).
Natural increase rate per 1,000 population (2000): 19.6 (world avg. 13.5).
Total fertility rate (avg. births per childbearing woman; 2000): 3.3.
Marriage rate per 1,000 population (1999): 7.0.
Divorce rate per 1,000 population (1999): 3.9.
Life expectancy at birth (2000): male 75.3 years; female 76.9 years.
Major causes of death per 100,000 population (1998): circulatory diseases 84.2; accidents and violence 31.7; cancers 22.9; congenital anomalies 12.4; endocrine and metabolic diseases 11.5; respiratory diseases 10.7.

National economy

Budget[7] (2001–02). Revenue: KD 2,224,000,000 (oil revenue 79.2%). Expenditures: KD 4,295,000,000 (transfers 21.2%, defense 20.9%, education 9.1%, economic development 8.0%, health 6.3%).
Tourism (2000): receipts from visitors U.S.$98,000,000; expenditures by nationals abroad U.S.$2,451,000,000.
Gross national product (2000): U.S.$35,771,000,000 (U.S.$18,030 per capita).

Structure of gross domestic product and labour force				
	1999			
	in value KD '000,000[8]	% of total value	labour force	% of labour force
Agriculture	35.7	0.4	22,619	1.8
Mining (oil sector)	3,354.4	37.1	7,581	0.6
Manufacturing	1,100.6	12.2	77,879	6.4
Construction	229.4	2.5	118,301	9.7
Public utilities	−42.8	−0.5	7,907	0.6
Transp. and commun.	505.9	5.6	41,584	3.4
Trade[9]	646.6	7.2	196,079	16.0
Finance and business services	1,278.6	14.2	45,821	3.7
Pub. admin., defense Services	2,277.8	25.2	614,876	50.1
Other	−353.4[10]	−3.9[10]	93,487[11]	7.6[11]
TOTAL	9,032.8	100.0	1,226,134	100.0[5]

Production (metric tons except as noted). Agriculture, forestry, fishing (2000): cucumber and gherkins 33,004, tomatoes 31,788, eggplants 12,002, onions 3,377, garlic 539; livestock (number of live animals) 450,000 sheep, 150,000 goats, 20,400 cattle, 8,900 camels; fish catch (1999) 6,535. Mining and quarrying (1997): sulfur 600,000; lime 40,000. Manufacturing (value added in KD '000,000; 1997): refined petroleum products 3,632; industrial chemicals 962; fabricated metal products 68; food products 55; clothing and apparel 37. Construction (floor area of new construction; 1998): residential 2,983,000 sq m; nonresidential 220,000 sq m. Energy production (consumption): electricity (kW-hr; 1998) 29,988,000,000 ([1997] 27,224,000,000); crude petroleum (barrels; 2000) 867,000,000 ([1998] 315,000,000); petroleum products (metric tons; 1997) 41,109,000 (7,722,000); natural gas (cu m; 1998) 11,081,000,000 (11,081,000,000).

Population economically active (1999): total 1,226,134; activity rate of total population 53.9% (participation rates [1995]: ages 15–59, 70.7%; female 26.1%; unemployed 0.7%).

Price and earnings indexes (1995 = 100)						
	1995	1996	1997	1998	1999	2000	2001
Consumer price index	100.0	103.6	104.2	104.4	100.9	101.3	103.3
Earnings index	...	...	...	...	...	...	...

Household income and expenditure. Average household size (1995) 3.9; sources of income (1986): wages and salaries 53.8%, self-employment 20.8%, other 25.4; expenditure (1992): food, beverages and tobacco 37.0%, housing and energy 18.7%, transportation 15.3%, household appliances and services 11.1%, clothing and footwear 10.0%, education and health 2.5%.
Land use (1994): forest 0.1%; pasture 7.7%; agriculture 0.3%; other 91.9%.

Foreign trade[12]

Balance of trade (current prices)					
	1996	1997	1998	1999	2000	2001
KD '000,000	+1,951	+1,813	+285	+1,378	+498	+2,842
% of total	28.0%	26.6%	5.2%	22.9%	10.2%	40.0%

Imports (1999): KD 2,318,305,000 (machinery and transport equipment 39.7%, manufactured goods 16.3%, food and live animals 14.9%, miscellaneous manufactured articles 14.5%, chemical products 8.7%). *Major import sources:* Japan 12.8%; U.S. 12.3%; Germany 7.7%; Saudi Arabia 6.2%; U.K. 5.8%; Italy 5.8%; France 3.7%; India 3.7%.
Exports (1999): KD 3,696,000,000 (crude petroleum and petroleum products 96.5%, chemicals 2.9%). *Major export destinations[13]:* Japan 27%; U.S. 14%; South Korea 13%; Singapore 10%; The Netherlands 8%; Pakistan 8%.

Transport and communications

Transport. Railroads: none. Roads (1997): total length 2,765 mi, 4,450 km (paved 81%). Vehicles (1998): passenger cars 747,042; trucks and buses 140,480. Merchant marine (1998): vessels (100 gross tons and over) 202; total deadweight tonnage (1992) 3,188,526. Air transport (2000): passenger-mi 3,813,469,000, passenger-km 6,137,195,000; short ton-mi cargo 151,120,000, metric ton-km cargo 243,204,000; airports (1999) with scheduled flights 1.

Communications				units per 1,000
Medium	date	unit	number	persons
Daily newspapers	1996	circulation	635,000	377
Radio	1997	receivers	1,175,000	678
Television	1999	receivers	910,000	520
Telephones	2001	main lines	472,000	240
Cellular telephones	2001	subscribers	489,000	248
Personal computers	2001	units	260,000	132
Internet	2001	users	200,000	101

Education and health

Educational attainment (1988). Percentage of population age 25 and over having: no formal schooling 44.8%; primary education 8.6%; some secondary 15.1%; complete secondary 15.1%; higher 16.4%. *Literacy* (1995): total population age 15 and over literate 79.3%; males literate 82.3%; females literate 76.0%.

Education (1998–99)				student/
	schools	teachers	students	teacher ratio
Primary (age 6–9)	179[14]	10,389	139,690	13.4
Secondary (age 10–17)	117[14]	19,702	228,810	11.6
Voc., teacher tr.	39	1,030	4,457	4.3
Higher[15]	1	942	15,726	16.7

Health (1998): physicians 3,447 (1 per 541 persons); hospital beds 4,389[16] (1 per 425 persons); infant mortality rate per 1,000 live births (2000) 11.5.
Food (2000): daily per capita caloric intake 3,132 (vegetable products 77%, animal products 23%); 129% of FAO recommended minimum requirement.

Military

Total active duty personnel (2001): 15,500 (army [including central staff] 71.0%, navy 12.9%, air force 16.1%); U.S. troops (2002) 10,000. *Military expenditure as percentage of GNP* (1999): 7.7% (world 2.4%); per capita expenditure U.S.$1,410.

[1]Fifty elected seats in National Assembly may include Cabinet ministers; Cabinet ministers not elected to National Assembly serve ex officio. [2]Assisted by prime minister. [3]Officially Al-Kuwayt; Kuwait is variant. [4]Bubian Island 333 sq mi (863 sq km) and Warba Island 14 sq mi (37 sq km). [5]Detail does not add to total given because of rounding. [6]Sum of governorate populations. Actual mid-year est. pop. is 2,228,363. [7]Approved budget. [8]In purchasers' prices. [9]Trade includes restaurants and hotels. [10]Includes import duties and imputed bank service charges. [11]Not stated. [12]Imports and exports are f.o.b. in the balance of trade table. [13]Estimated figures. [14]Government schools only. [15]University only. [16]Public hospitals only.

Internet resources for further information:
• Central Bank of Kuwait http://www.cbk.gov.kw
• Ministry of Planning
  http://www.mop.gov.kw/MopWebSite/english/default.asp

Kyrgyzstan

Official name: Respublika Kirgizstan (Kyrgyz); Kyrgyz Respublikasy (Russian) (Kyrgyz Republic).
Form of government: unitary multiparty republic with two legislative houses (Assembly of People's Representatives [45]; Legislative Assembly [60]).
Head of state and government: President assisted by Prime Minister.
Capital: Bishkek.
Official languages: Kyrgyz; Russian.
Official religion: none.
Monetary unit: 1 som (K.S.) = 100 tiyin; valuation (Sept. 23, 2002) 1 U.S.$ = K.S. 46.16; 1 £ = K.S. 71.74.

Area and population		area		population
Provinces	**Capitals**	sq mi	sq km	1999 census
Batken	Batken	6,600	17,000	382,426
Chüy (Chu)	Kara-Balta	7,800	20,200	770,811
Jalal-Abad	Jalal-Abad			
(Dzhalal-Abad)	(Dzhalal-Abad)	13,000	33,700	869,259
Naryn	Naryn	17,500	45,200	249,115
Osh	Osh	11,300	29,200	1,175,998
Talas	Talas	4,400	11,400	199,872
Ysyk-Köl	Ysyk-Köl			
(Issyk-Kul)	(Issyk-Kul)	16,600	43,100	413,149
City				
Bishkek (Frunze)	—	40	100	762,308
TOTAL		77,200[1,2]	199,900[1]	4,822,938

Demography

Population (2002): 5,002,000.
Density (2002): persons per sq mi 64.8, persons per sq km 25.0.
Urban-rural (1999): urban 34.3%; rural 65.7%.
Sex distribution (2001): male 48.84%; female 51.16%.
Age breakdown (2001): under 15, 35.0%; 15–29, 28.1%; 30–44, 18.6%; 45–59, 9.2%; 60–74, 7.0%; 75 and over, 2.1%.
Population projection: (2010) 5,473,000; (2020) 6,120,000.
Doubling time: 53 years.
Ethnic composition (1999): Kyrgyz 64.9%; Uzbek 13.8%; Russian 12.5%; Hui 1.1%; Ukrainian 1.0%; Uighur 1.0%; other 5.7%.
Religious affiliation (1997): Muslim (mostly Sunnī) 75.0%; Christian 6.7%, of which Russian Orthodox 5.6%; other (mostly nonreligious) 18.3%.
Major cities (1999): Bishkek (Frunze) 762,308; Osh 220,500; Jalal-Abad 74,200[3]; Tokmok 71,200[3]; Kara-Köl 64,300[3].

Vital statistics

Birth rate per 1,000 population (2001): 20.6 (world avg. 21.2); (1994) legitimate 83.2%; illegitimate 16.8%.
Death rate per 1,000 population (2001): 7.3 (world avg. 8.9).
Natural increase rate per 1,000 population (2001): 13.3 (world avg. 12.3).
Total fertility rate (avg. births per childbearing woman; 2001): 2.5.
Marriage rate per 1,000 population (1999): 5.6.
Divorce rate per 1,000 population (1999): 4.6.
Life expectancy at birth (2001): male 64.0 years; female 72.0 years.
Major causes of death per 100,000 population (1996): diseases of the circulatory system 278.5; diseases of the respiratory system 75.0; malignant neoplasms (cancers) 25.7; accidents, poisoning, and violence 21.4.

National economy

Budget (2000). Revenue: K.S. 9,896,000,000 (tax revenue 93.9%, of which taxes on goods and services 60.8%, taxes on income and profits 13.9%, taxes on international trade 2.8%; nontax revenue 6.1%). Expenditures: K.S. 11,850,000,000 (education 19.4%; health 11.0%; economic development 10.0%; defense 9.9%; social security 9.4%).
Public debt (external, outstanding; 2000): U.S.$1,223,600,000.
Land use (1994): forest 3.7%; pasture 45.4%; agriculture 7.2%; other 43.7%.
Population economically active (2000): total 1,905,400; activity rate of total population 39.0% (participation rates: ages 16–59 [male], 16–54 [female] 62.0%; female (1999) 44.9%; unemployed 7.6%).

Price and earnings indexes (1995 = 100)						
	1995	1996	1997	1998	1999	2000	2001
Consumer price index	100.0	131.9	162.9	179.9	244.5	290.2	327.7
Monthly earnings index	100.0	133.3	184.7	228.3	250.1	261.2	...

Production (metric tons except as noted). Agriculture, forestry, fishing (2000): grain 1,569,000, potatoes 1,046,000, vegetables and melons 747,000, sugarbeet 450,000, fruit 161,000, seed cotton 88,000; livestock (number of live animals) 3,570,000 sheep and goats, 825,000 cattle, 320,000 horses; roundwood (2000) 45,000 cu m; fish catch (1999) 198. Mining and quarrying (2000): antimony 1,500; mercury 700; gold 22,000 kg. Manufacturing (value of production in '000,000 som; 1994): textiles 1,112; processed foods 729; ferrous and nonferrous metals 678; machinery and metalwork 650; construction materials 258. Energy production (consumption): electricity (kW-hr; 2000) 14,886,-000,000 (12,054,000,000); coal (metric tons; 2000) 419,400 (1,141,600); crude petroleum (barrels; 2000) 564,000 (564,000); petroleum products (metric tons; 2000) 141,000 (420,000); natural gas (cu m; 2000) 31,900,000 (681,800,000).

Household income and expenditure. Average household size (1999) 4.3; income per household (1994) 4,359 som (U.S.$325); sources of income (1999): wages and salaries 55.2%, pensions and stipends 14.3%, income from agricultural products 4.1%, other 26.4%; expenditure (1990): food and clothing 48.0%, health care 13.1%, housing 5.9%, cultural affairs 5.2%, appliances 4.4%.
Gross national product (2000): U.S.$1,345,000,000 (U.S.$270 per capita).

Structure of gross domestic product and labour force				
	1999			
	in value K.S. '000,000	% of total value	labour force	% of labour force
Agriculture	17,002.7	34.9	924,300	48.6
Mining	} 10,964.6	} 22.5	9,500	0.5
Manufacturing			127,000	6.7
Public utilities			22,100	1.2
Construction	1,484.7	3.0	45,200	2.4
Transp. and commun.	2,355.9	4.8	65,800	3.5
Trade	6,317.7	13.0	195,200	10.3
Finance	126.4	0.3	35,800	1.9
Public admin., defense	2,111.7	4.3	65,700	3.5
Services	4,837.6	9.9	273,700	14.4
Other	3,542.7[4]	7.3[4]	136,800[5]	7.2[5]
TOTAL	48,744.0	100.0	1,901,100	100.0[2]

Tourism (2000): receipts from visitors, U.S.$14,000,000; expenditures by nationals abroad, U.S.$11,000,000.

Foreign trade[6]

Balance of trade (current prices)						
	1995	1996	1997	1998	1999	2000
U.S.$'000,000	−122.1	−251.7	−15.3	−220.8	−84.3	+8.8
% of total	13.0%	19.2%	1.2%	17.1%	8.4%	0.9%

Imports (2000): U.S.$502,100,000 (oil and gas 24.5%, machine-building equipment 22.1%, food products 11.4%, chemical products 9.0%, light industrial products 6.4%). *Major import sources:* Russia 26.4%; Uzbekistan 15.0%; Kazakhstan 11.4%; United States 10.7%; China 7.3%; Turkey 5.3%.
Exports (2000): U.S.$510,900,000 (nonferrous metals 45.8%, electricity 15.6%, machinery 9.9%, light industrial products 9.2%, agricultural products 9.2%, food 3.3%). *Major export destinations:* Germany 28.3%; Uzbekistan 17.5%; Russia 13.4%; China 8.6%; Kazakhstan 7.1%; Switzerland 6.7%.

Transport and communications

Transport. Railroads (1999): length 424 km; (1998) passenger-km 59,000,000; metric ton-km cargo 471,000,000. Roads (1999): total length 18,500 km (paved 91%). Vehicles (1999): passenger cars 187,734; trucks and buses, n.a. Air transport (1997): passenger-km 5,301,000,000; metric ton-km cargo 52,000,000; airports with scheduled flights 2.

Communications				units per 1,000
Medium	date	unit	number	persons
Daily newspapers	1996	circulation	67,000	15
Radio	1997	receivers	520,000	113
Television	1998	receivers	220,000	47
Telephones	2001	main lines	376,100	79
Cellular phones	2001	subscribers	27,000	5.4
Personal computers	...	units	...	...
Internet	2001	users	51,600	10.5

Education and health

Educational attainment (1999). Percentage of population age 15 and over having: primary education 6.3%; some secondary 18.3%; completed secondary 50.0%; some postsecondary 14.9%; higher 10.5%. *Literacy* (1999): total population age 15 and over literate 97.5%; males literate 98.5%; females literate 96.5%.

Education (1995–96)	schools	teachers	students[7]	student/ teacher ratio
Primary (age 6–13)	1,885	24,086	} 1,118,793	19.7
Secondary (age 14–17)	1,474[8]	38,915		12.8
Voc., teacher tr.	53[8]	3,371	38,793	9.5
Higher	23	3,691	124,553	13.5

Health (1997): physicians 15,100 (1 per 307 persons); hospital beds 40,700 (1 per 114 persons); infant mortality rate per 1,000 live births (2001) 39.0.
Food (2000): daily per capita caloric intake 2,871 (vegetable products 81%, animal products 19%); 111% of FAO recommended minimum.

Military

Total active duty personnel (2001): 9,000 (army 73.3%, air force 26.7%)[9].
Military expenditure as percentage of GNP (1999): 2.4% (world 2.4%); per capita expenditure U.S.$62.

[1]Includes c. 480 sq mi (c. 1,250 sq km) ceded to China in May 2002. [2]Detail does not add to total given because of rounding. [3]1991. [4]Taxes on products less imputed bank service charge. [5]Unemployed. [6]Imports and exports in balance of trade are f.o.b. [7]2000. [8]1993–94. [9]U.S. troops (June 2002) 1,000.

Internet resources for further information:
• **National Statistical Committee of the Kyrgyz Republic**
  http://nsc.bishkek.su/Eng/Home/Start.html
• **Embassy of the Kyrgyz Republic http://www.kyrgyzstan.org**

Laos

Official name: Sathalanalat Paxathipatai Paxaxôn Lao (Lao People's Democratic Republic).
Form of government: unitary single-party people's republic with one legislative house (National Assembly[1] [109]).
Chief of state: President.
Head of government: Prime Minister.
Capital: Vientiane (Viangchan).
Official language: Lao.
Official religion: none.
Monetary unit: 1 kip (KN) = 100 at; valuation (Sept. 23, 2002) managed floating rate, 1 U.S.$ = KN 7,600; 1 £ = KN 11,811.

Area and population

Provinces	Capitals	area sq mi	area sq km	population 1996 estimate
Attapu	Attapu	3,985	10,320	87,700
Bokèo	Houayxay	2,392	6,196	114,900
Bolikhamxai	Pakxan	5,739	14,863	164,900
Champasak	Pakxé	5,952	15,415	503,300
Houaphan	Xam Nua	6,371	16,500	247,300
Khammouan	Thakhek	6,299	16,315	275,400
Louangnamtha	Louangnamtha	3,600	9,325	115,200
Louangphrabang	Louangphrabang	6,515	16,875	367,200
Oudomxay	Xay	5,934	15,370	211,300
Phôngsali	Phôngsali	6,282	16,270	153,400
Salavan	Salavan	4,128	10,691	258,300
Savannakhét	Savannakhét	8,407	21,774	674,900
Special Region	...	2,743	7,105	54,200
Viangchan	Muang Phôn-Hông	6,149	15,927	286,800
Xaignabouli	Xaignabouli	6,328	16,389	293,300
Xékong	Thong	2,959	7,665	64,200
Xiangkhoang	Phônsavan	6,131	15,880	201,200
Municipalities				
Viangchan	Vientiane (Viangchan)	1,514	3,920	531,800
TOTAL		91,429[2]	236,800	4,605,300

Demography

Population (2002): 5,777,000.
Density (2002): persons per sq mi 63.2, persons per sq km 24.4.
Urban-rural (2002): urban 25.0%; rural 75.0%.
Sex distribution (1996): male 49.42%; female 50.58%.
Age breakdown (1996): under 15, 44.2%; 15–29, 25.4%; 30–44, 16.0%; 45–59, 8.7%; 60–74, 4.5%; 75 and over, 1.2%.
Population projection: (2010) 6,993,000; (2020) 8,637,000.
Doubling time: 30 years.
Ethnic composition (2000): Lao-Lum (Lao) 53.0%; Lao-Theung (Mon-Khmer) 23.0%; Lao-Tai (Tai) 13.0%; Lao-Soung (Miao [Hmong] and Man [Yao]) 10.0%; other (ethnic Chinese or Vietnamese) 1.0%.
Religious affiliation (2000): Buddhist 48.8%; traditional beliefs 41.7%; nonreligious 4.3%; Christian 2.1%; other 3.1%.
Major cities (1995): Vientiane 528,100; Louangphrabang 55,300; Savannakhét 47,500; Salavan 42,500; Pakxé 32,500.

Vital statistics

Birth rate per 1,000 population (2002): 36.0 (world avg. 21.2).
Death rate per 1,000 population (2002): 12.8 (world avg. 8.9).
Natural increase rate per 1,000 population (2002): 23.2 (world avg. 12.3).
Total fertility rate (avg. births per childbearing woman; 2001): 5.0.
Marriage rate per 1,000 population: n.a.
Divorce rate per 1,000 population: n.a.
Life expectancy at birth (2002): male 52.0 years; female 55.9 years.
Major causes of death per 100,000 population (incomplete, 1990): malaria 7.6; pneumonia 3.0; meningitis 1.5; diarrhea 1.2; tuberculosis 0.8.

National economy

Budget (2000–01). Revenue: KN 2,614,000,000,000 (taxes 66.6%, nontax revenue 17.3%, foreign grants 16.1%). Expenditures: KN 3,382,000,000,000 (capital expenditure 58.1%, current expenditure 41.9%).
Public debt (external, outstanding; 2000): U.S.$2,449,000,000.
Tourism (2000): receipts from visitors U.S.$114,000,000; expenditures by nationals abroad U.S.$17,000,000.
Population economically active (1989): total 1,888,000; activity rate of total population 49.0% (participation rates [1985]: ages 15–64, 84.2%; female 45.3%; unemployed [1994] 2.6%).

Price and earnings indexes (1995 = 100)

	1995	1996	1997	1998	1999	2000	2001
Consumer price index	100.0	113.0	144.1	275.2	628.7	786.4	847.8
Earnings index	...	...	...	...	...	...	...

Production (metric tons except as noted). Agriculture, forestry, fishing (1999): rice 2,103,000, sugarcane 174,000, corn (maize) 96,000, sweet potatoes 81,000, cassava 70,000, pineapples 34,000, melons 33,000, potatoes 33,000, oranges 28,000, seed cotton 26,000, bananas 22,000, coffee 18,000; livestock (number of live animals) 1,937,000 pigs, 1,497,000 cattle, 1,286,000 water buffalo, 200,-000 goats, 28,000 horses, 13,882,000 chickens; roundwood (1998) 4,591,000 cu m; fish catch (1997) 40,000. Mining and quarrying (1997): gypsum 145,000;

rock salt 18,000; tin (metal content) 618. Manufacturing (1998): plastic products 3,225; tobacco 1,000; detergent 912; nails 624; clothing 23,000,000 pieces; cigarettes 55,000,000 packs; beer 332,000 hectolitres; soft drinks 125,000 hectolitres. Construction: n.a. Energy production (consumption): electricity (kW-hr; 1997) 1,219,000,000 (495,000,000); coal (metric tons; 1997) 1,000 (1,000); crude petroleum, n.a. (n.a.); petroleum products (metric tons; 1997) none (112,000); natural gas, n.a. (n.a.).
Gross national product (2000): U.S.$1,519,000,000 (U.S.$290 per capita).

Structure of gross domestic product and labour force

	2000 in value KN '000,000[3]	2000 % of total value	1989 labour force	1989 % of labour force
Agriculture	584,000	51.8	1,359,000	72.0
Manufacturing	190,000	16.8		
Mining	6,000	0.5		
Construction	25,000	2.2		
Public utilities	31,000	2.8		
Transp. and commun.	63,000	5.6		
Trade	106,000	9.4	58,533	8.1
Finance	47,000	4.2		
Pub. admin., defense	31,000	2.8		
Services	35,000	3.1		
Other	9,000	0.8		
TOTAL	1,127,000	100.0	1,888,000	100.0

Household income and expenditure. Average household size (1995) 6.1%; average annual income per household KN 3,710 (U.S.$371); sources of income: n.a.; expenditure: n.a.
Land use (1994): forested 54.4%; meadows and pastures 3.5%; agricultural and under permanent cultivation 3.9%; other 38.2%.

Foreign trade[4]

Balance of trade (current prices)

	1996	1997	1998	1999	2000	2001
U.S.$'000,000	−366.8	−347.0	−183.3	−214.0	−205.0	−215.1
% of total	36.2%	32.6%	19.9%	25.6%	23.7%	24.3%

Imports (1998): U.S.$552,800,000 (consumption goods 42.3%; investment goods 41.0%, of which construction and electrical equipment 14.7%, motor vehicles 7.1%; materials for garment assembly 12.1%). *Major import sources* (1997): Thailand 52.0%; Vietnam 3.9%; Japan 1.6%; Hong Kong 1.5%; China 0.8%.
Exports (1998): U.S.$369,500,000 (wood products 34.3%; garments 20.8%; electricity 18.0%; coffee 14.3%). *Major export destinations* (1997): Vietnam 42.7%; Thailand 22.1%; France 6.3%; Belgium 5.6%; Germany 5.1%.

Transport and communications

Transport. Railroads: none. Roads (1996): total length 13,870 mi, 22,321 km (paved [1995] 14%). Vehicles (1996): passenger cars 16,320; trucks and buses 4,200. Merchant marine (1992): vessels (100 gross tons and over) 1; total deadweight tonnage 1,469. Air transport (1997): passenger-mi 29,000,000, passenger-km 48,000,000; short ton-mi cargo 3,000,000, metric ton-km cargo 5,000,000; airports (1996) with scheduled flights 11.

Communications

Medium	date	unit	number	units per 1,000 persons
Daily newspapers	1996	circulation	18,000	3.7
Radio	1997	receivers	730,000	145
Television	1999	receivers	51,000	9.6
Telephones	2001	main lines	52,600	9.3
Cellular telephones	2001	subscribers	29,500	5.2
Personal computers	2001	units	16,000	2.8
Internet	2001	users	10,000	1.8

Education and health

Educational attainment (1985). Percentage of population age 6 and over having: no schooling 49.3%; primary 41.2%; secondary 9.1%; higher 0.4%.
Literacy (1995): total population age 15 and over literate 56.6%; males literate 69.4%; females literate 44.4%.

Education (1996–97)

	schools	teachers	students	student/ teacher ratio
Primary (age 6–10)	7,896	25,831	786,335	30.4
Secondary (age 11–16)	750[5]	10,717	180,160	16.8
Voc., teacher tr.	139[6]	1,600[7]	9,400[7]	5.9[7]
Higher	9[5]	1,369	12,732	9.3

Health: physicians (1995) 3,100 (1 per 1,563 persons); hospital beds (1990) 10,364 (1 per 402 persons); infant mortality rate (2002) 91.0.
Food (1999): daily per capita caloric intake 2,152 (vegetable products 93%, animal products 7%); (1997) 97% of FAO recommended minimum requirement.

Military

Total active duty personnel (2001): 29,100 (army 85.9%, navy 2.1%, air force 12.0%). *Military expenditure as percentage of GNP* (1999): 2.0% (world 2.4%); per capita expenditure U.S.$5.

[1]Formerly known as the Supreme People's Assembly. [2]Detail does not add to total given because of rounding. [3]At constant 1990 prices. [4]Import figures are c.i.f. in balance of trade and commodities. [5]1989–90. [6]1988–89. [7]1995–96.

Internet resources for further information:
• Discovering Laos http://www.laoembassy.com/discover/index.htm

Latvia

Official name: Latvijas Republika
(Republic of Latvia).
Form of government: unitary multiparty
republic with a single legislative body
(Parliament, or Saeima [100]).
Chief of state: President.
Head of government: Prime Minister.
Capital: Riga.
Official language: Latvian.
Official religion: none.
Monetary unit: 1 lats (Ls; plural lati) =
100 santimi; valuation (Sept. 23, 2002)
1 U.S.$ = 0.60 lats; 1 £ = 0.94 lats.

Area and population

Cities	area sq km	population 2000 census	Districts	area sq km	population 2000 census
Daugavpils	72	115,265	Jelgava	1,604	37,371
Jelgava	60	63,652	Krāslava	2,285	36,836
Jūrmala	100	55,718	Kuldīga	2,502	38,169
Liepāja	60	89,448	Liepāja	3,594	46,817
Rēzekne	17	39,233	Limbaži	2,602	40,164
Riga	307	764,329	Ludza	2,569	35,125
Ventspils	46	43,928	Madona	3,346	46,459
			Ogre	1,840	63,064
Districts			Preiļi	2,041	41,735
Aizkraukle	2,565	41,968	Rēzekne	2,655	43,090
Alūksne	2,243	26,422	Rīga (Riga)	3,059	144,346
Balvi	2,386	30,624	Saldus	2,182	38,916
Bauska	1,882	53,197	Talsi	2,751	49,814
Cēsis	3,067	60,620	Tukums	2,447	54,200
Daugavpils	2,525	42,758	Valka	2,437	34,317
Dobele	1,633	40,246	Valmiera	2,365	60,390
Gulbene	1,877	28,194	Ventspils	2,472	14,620
Jēkabpils	2,998	56,348	TOTAL	64,589	2,377,383

Demography

Population (2002): 2,341,000.
Density (2002): persons per sq mi 93.9, persons per sq km 36.2.
Urban-rural (2000): urban 68.1%; rural 31.9%.
Sex distribution (2000): male 46.06%; female 53.94%.
Age breakdown (2000): under 15, 18.1%; 15–29, 21.2%; 30–44, 21.4%; 45–59, 18.3%; 60–74, 15.7%; 75 and over, 5.3%.
Population projection: (2010) 2,226,000; (2020) 2,125,000.
Ethnic composition (2000): Latvian 57.7%; Russian 29.6%; Belarusian 4.1%; Ukrainian 2.7%; Polish 2.5%; Lithuanian 1.4%; other 2.0%.
Religious affiliation (1995): Christian 39.6%, of which Protestant 16.7% (of which Lutheran 14.6%), Roman Catholic 14.9%, Orthodox 8.0%; Jewish 0.6%; other (mostly nonreligious) 59.8%.
Major cities (2000): Riga (2001) 755,600; Daugavpils 115,265; Liepāja 89,448; Jelgava 63,652; Jūrmala 55,718.

Vital statistics

Birth rate per 1,000 population (2001): 8.3 (world avg. 21.2); (1998) legitimate 62.9%; illegitimate 37.1%.
Death rate per 1,000 population (2001): 13.9 (world avg. 8.9).
Natural increase rate per 1,000 population (2001): –5.6 (world avg. 12.3).
Total fertility rate (avg. births per childbearing woman; 2000): 1.1.
Marriage rate per 1,000 population (2001): 3.9.
Divorce rate per 1,000 population (2001): 2.4.
Life expectancy at birth (1999): male 64.9 years; female 76.2 years.
Major causes of death per 100,000 population (1998): diseases of the circulatory system 775.6; malignant neoplasms (cancers) 231.8; accidents, poisoning, and violence 161.8; diseases of the digestive system 42.2.

National economy

Budget (1998). Revenue: Ls 1,577,400,000 (social security contributions 27.1%, value-added taxes 20.1%, personal income taxes 13.9%, excises 10.7%, nontax revenue 10.1%). Expenditures: Ls 1,572,300,000 (social security and welfare 34.4%, education 15.7%, health 9.4%, police 5.8%, defense 2.4%).
Production (metric tons except as noted). Agriculture, forestry, fishing (1999): grasses for forage and silage 13,800,000, hay 1,355,000, potatoes 795,500, sugar beets 451,500, wheat 351,900, barley 232,600, rye 88,700; livestock (number of live animals) 403,400 pigs, 375,700 cattle; roundwood (2001) 14,037,000 cu m; fish catch (1999) 125,827. Mining and quarrying (1998): peat 171,700; gypsum 119,100. Manufacturing (value added in Ls '000,000; 1998): alcoholic beverages 79.4; sawn wood 64.4; veneer/plywood 37.6; dairy products 30.5; wearing apparel 30.4; bakery products 29.8; fish processing 24.2. Energy production (consumption): electricity (kW-hr; 2001) 4,236,000,000 ([1998] 5,133,000,000); coal (1997) none (196,000); crude petroleum, none (none); petroleum products (1997) none (1,690,000); natural gas (cu m; 1997) none (1,143,000,000).
Household income and expenditure. Average household size (2000) 2.7; annual disposable income per household (1996) Ls 1,659 (U.S.$3,011); sources of income (1998): wages and salaries 55.8%, pensions and transfers 25.7%, self-employment 9.5%; expenditure (1998): food, beverages, and tobacco 46.4%, housing and energy 16.6%, transportation and communications 9.8%, clothing and footwear 6.9%.
Public debt (external, outstanding; 2000): U.S.$827,100,000.
Gross national product (2000): U.S.$6,925,000,000 (U.S.$2,920 per capita).

Structure of gross domestic product and labour force

	2000			
	in value Ls '000,000	% of total value	labour force	% of labour force
Agriculture, forestry	171.3	4.0	130,500[1,2]	11.5
Mining and quarrying	5.2	0.1	2,000	0.2
Manufacturing	553.4	12.8	171,300	15.1
Construction	258.0	6.0	57,900	5.1
Public utilities	149.6	3.4	23,300	2.1
Transp. and commun.	617.2	14.2	81,900	7.2
Trade, restaurants	736.1	17.0	177,500	15.7
Finance, real estate	587.6	13.6	59,700	5.3
Pub. admin., defense	249.2	5.7	71,300	6.3
Services	492.5	11.4	187,800	16.6
Other	512.9[3]	11.8[3]	168,400[4]	14.9
TOTAL	4,333.0	100.0	1,131,900[5]	100.0

Population economically active (2000)[1,2]: total 1,131,900; activity rate of total population 46.7% (participation rates: ages 15–64, 67.5%; female 48.5%; unemployed 14.6%).

Price and earnings indexes (1995 = 100)

	1996	1997	1998	1999	2000	2001	2002
Consumer price index	117.6	127.5	133.5	136.6	140.3	143.7	146.4[6]
Annual earnings index	114.9	139.7	148.8	154.7	159.7	167.5	…

Tourism (in U.S.$'000,000; 2000): receipts 131; expenditures 248.
Land use (1994): forested 44.4%; meadows and pastures 12.4; agricultural and under permanent cultivation 27.0%; other 16.2%.

Foreign trade[7]

Balance of trade (current prices)

	1996	1997	1998	1999	2000	2001
Ls '000,000	–483	–610	–812	–716	–803	–946
% of total	23.3%	23.9%	27.5%	26.2%	26.2%	27.4%

Imports (1999): Ls 1,724,000,000 (machinery and equipment 22.0%; chemicals and chemical products 12.0%; mineral fuels 11.4%; transport vehicles 8.3%; textiles and clothing 7.7%). *Major import sources:* Germany 15.2%; Russia 10.5%; Finland 9.1%; Lithuania 7.3%; Sweden 7.2%.
Exports (1999): Ls 1,008,000,000 (wood and paper products 37.3%, of which sawn wood 22.0%; textiles and clothing 15.4%; base and fabricated metals 11.5%). *Major export destinations:* Germany 16.9%; U.K. 16.4%; Sweden 10.7%; Lithuania 7.5%; Russia 6.6%.

Transport and communications

Transport. Railroads (2000): length 2,413 km; passenger-km (1999) 984,000,000; metric-km cargo (1999) 12,210,000,000. Roads (1999): total length 73,227 km (paved 39%). Vehicles (1999): passenger cars 525,572; trucks and buses 101,776. Air transport (1999): passenger-km 238,000,000; metric ton-km cargo 10,000,000; airports with scheduled flights (2001) 2.

Communications				units per 1,000 persons
Medium	date	unit	number	
Daily newspapers	1996	circulation	616,000	247
Radio	1997	receivers	1,760,000	713
Television	1999	receivers	1,808,000	755
Telephones	2001	main lines	724,800	308
Cellular telephones	2001	subscribers	656,800	279
Personal computers	2001	units	360,000	153
Internet	2001	users	170,000	72

Education and health

Educational attainment (2000). Percentage of population age 15 and over having: incomplete primary education 2.4%; complete primary 6.1%; lower secondary 26.5%; upper secondary 51.1%; higher 13.9%. *Literacy* (1995): percentage of total population age 15 and over literate 99.6%.

Education (1996–97)	schools	teachers	students	student/ teacher ratio
Primary	1,074	10,883[8]	146,653	13.5[8]
Secondary	…	24,112	196,148	8.1
Vocational	…	5,740	43,170	7.5
Higher	28	4,486	56,187	12.5

Health (1998): physicians 6,900 (1 per 355 persons); hospital beds 23,165 (1 per 106 persons); infant mortality rate per 1,000 live births (2001) 10.9.
Food (1999): daily per capita caloric intake 2,904 (vegetable products 75%, animal products 25%); 113% of FAO recommended minimum requirement.

Military

Total active duty personnel (2001): 6,500[9] (army 47.7%, navy 12.9%, air force 3.2%, national guard 36.2%). *Military expenditure as percentage of GNP* (1999): 0.9% (world 2.4%); per capita expenditure U.S.$59.

[1]Excludes military service. [2]As of November. [3]Indirect taxes less subsidies. [4]Includes 165,100 unemployed. [5]Detail does not add to total given because of rounding. [6]June. [7]Imports c.i.f.; exports f.o.b. [8]Full-time teachers only. [9]Excludes 3,500 border guards classified as paramilitary.

Internet resources for further information:
• Bank of Latvia http://www.bank.lv
• Central Statistical Bureau of Latvia http://www.csb.lv

Lebanon

Official name: Al-Jumhūrīyah
al-Lubnānīyah (Lebanese Republic).
Form of government: unitary multiparty
republic with one legislative house
(National Assembly [128])[1].
Chief of state: President.
Head of government: Prime Minister.
Capital: Beirut.
Official language: Arabic.
Official religion: none.
Monetary unit: 1 Lebanese pound
(£L) = 100 piastres; valuation
(Sept. 23, 2002) 1 U.S.$ = £L 1,514;
1 £ = £L 2,353.

Area and population

Governorates	Capitals	area sq mi	area sq km	population 1996 estimate
Bayrūt	Beirut (Bayrūt)	7	18	407,403
Al-Biqāʿ	Zahlah	1,653	4,280	399,890
Jabal Lubnān	Bʿabdā	753	1,950	1,145,458
Al-Janūb	Sidon (Saydā)	364	943	283,056
An-Nabaṭīyah	An-Nabaṭīyah	408	1,058	205,412
Ash-Shamāl	Tripoli (Ṭarābulus)	765	1,981	670,609
TOTAL		4,016[2]	10,400[2]	3,111,828

Demography

Population (2002): 3,678,000[3].
Density (2002): persons per sq mi 915.8, persons per sq km 353.7.
Urban-rural (2001): urban 90.1%; rural 10.9%.
Sex distribution (2000): male 48.44%; female 51.56%.
Age breakdown (2000): under 15, 27.9%; 15–29, 33.5%; 30–44, 19.0%; 45–59, 10.1%; 60–74, 7.2%; 75 and over, 2.3%.
Population projection: (2010) 4,056,000; (2020) 4,417,000.
Doubling time: 50 years.
Ethnic composition (2000): Arab 84.5%, of which Lebanese 71.2%, Palestinian 12.1%; Armenian 6.8%; Kurd 6.1%; other 2.6%.
Religious affiliation (1995): Muslim 55.3%, of which Shīʿī 34.0%, Sunnī 21.3%; Christian 37.6%, of which Catholic 25.1% (Maronite 19.0%, Greek Catholic or Melchite 4.6%), Orthodox 11.7% (Greek Orthodox 6.0%, Armenian Apostolic 5.2%), Protestant 0.5%; Druze 7.1%.
Major cities (1998): Beirut 1,100,000 (urban agglomeration; 2,115,000[4]); Tripoli 200,000; Sidon (Saydā) 140,000; Tyre (Ṣūr) 110,000; An-Nabaṭīyah 84,000; Jūniyah 75,000.

Vital statistics

Birth rate per 1,000 population (2000): 20.3 (world avg. 22.5).
Death rate per 1,000 population (2000): 6.4 (world avg. 9.0).
Natural increase rate per 1,000 population (2000): 13.9 (world avg. 13.5).
Total fertility rate (avg. births per childbearing woman; 2000): 2.1.
Life expectancy at birth (1999): male 68.9 years; female 73.7 years.
Major causes of death: n.a.

National economy

Budget (2000). Revenue: £L 4,091,435,000,000 (1998; tax revenue 74.6%, of which customs revenues 44.1%, income tax 9.0%, taxes on goods and services 8.4%, property tax 8.4%, miscellaneous taxes and fees 2.1%; nontax revenue 25.4%). Expenditures: £L 8,190,034,000,000 (current expenditures 81.1%, of which debt service 40.0%, public services 13.3%, defense 9.7%, education 8.3%, social security 6.4%, health 2.6%; capital expenditures 18.9%).
Production (metric tons except as noted). Agriculture, forestry, fishing (2000): tomatoes 335,000, sugar beets 330,000, potatoes 270,000, grapes 250,000, cucumbers and gherkins 190,000, oranges 160,000, apples 120,000, lemons and limes 109,000, olives 105,000, onions 85,000; livestock (number of live animals) 445,000 goats, 380,000 sheep, 77,000 cattle, 63,500 pigs, 32,000,000 chickens; roundwood (2000) 412,150 cu m; fish catch (1999) 3,860. Mining and quarrying (1996): lime 16,000; salt 4,000; gypsum 2,000. Manufacturing (1999): cement 2,715,000; flour 411,300; olive oil 6,000. Construction (1999): 6,700,000 sq m[5]. Energy production (consumption): electricity (kW-hr; 2000) 9,236,000,000 ([1998] 9,010,000,000); coal, n.a. (none); crude petroleum (barrels; 1998) none (1,358,000); petroleum products (metric tons; 1998) none (3,204,000).
Gross national product (2000): U.S.$17,355,000,000 (U.S.$4,010 per capita).

Structure of gross domestic product and labour force

	1995 in value U.S.$'000,000	1995 % of total value	labour force	% of labour force
Agriculture	380	4.0	143,900	14.0
Mining	—	—		
Manufacturing	1,235	13.0		
Construction	950	10.0	277,600	27.0
Public utilities	2,375[6]	25.0[6]		
Transp. and commun.				
Trade	2,660	28.0		
Finance				
Real estate and business services	1,900	20.0	606,500	59.0
Services				
Pub. admin., defense	6	6		
TOTAL	9,500	100.0	1,028,000	100.0

Population economically active (1995): total 1,028,000; activity rate of total population 25.4% (participation rates: over age 15 [1988] 44%; female c. 30%; unemployed n.a.).

Price and earnings indexes (1995 = 100)

	1995	1996	1997	1998	1999
Consumer price index[7]	100.0	108.0	110.8	113.4	116.1
Wages index	...	...	...	...	...

Public debt (external, outstanding; 2000): U.S.$7,034,000,000.
Household income and expenditure. Average household size (1998) 4.4; average annual income per household (1994) £L 2,400,000 (U.S.$1,430); sources of income (1974): wages 27.9%, transfers 3.0%, other 69.1%; expenditure (1966)[8]: food 42.8%, housing 16.8%, clothing 8.6%, health care 7.2%.
Tourism (2000): receipts from visitors U.S.$742,000,000.
Land use (1994): forested 7.8%; meadows and pastures 1.0%; agricultural and under permanent cultivation 29.9%; wasteland and other areas 61.3%.

Foreign trade[9]

Balance of trade (current prices)

	1996	1997	1998	1999	2000	2001
U.S.$'000,000	−6,643	−6,880	−6,408	−5,503	−5,514	−6,423
% of total	76.4%	84.1%	82.9%	80.3%	79.4%	78.7%

Imports (1999): U.S.$6,177,000,000 (food and live animals 15.2%; machinery and apparatus 14.6%; road vehicles 9.7%; refined petroleum 7.9%; nonmonetary gold 6.3%). *Major import sources:* Italy 10.9%; France 9.6%; Germany 8.9%; U.S. 8.1%; Switzerland 7.1%.
Exports (1999): U.S.$674,000,000 (food 13.7%, of which fruits and vegetables 8.8%; machinery and transport equipment 12.0%; precious metal jewelry 7.7%; apparel 5.7%; aluminum 4.9%). *Major export destinations:* Saudi Arabia 10.5%; U.A.E. 8.0%; France 7.7%; Switzerland 6.6%; U.S. 6.2%.

Transport and communications

Transport. Railroads: [10]. Roads (1996): total length 6,350 km (paved 95%). Vehicles (1997): passenger cars 1,299,398; trucks and buses 85,242. Merchant marine (1992): vessels (100 gross tons and over) 163; total deadweight tonnage 438,165. Air transport (2001)[11]: passenger-km 1,661,000,000; metric ton-km cargo 216,700,000; airports (1999) 1.

Communications

Medium	date	unit	number	units per 1,000 persons
Daily newspapers	1996	circulation	435,000	141
Radio	1997	receivers	2,850,000	907
Television	1998	receivers	1,120,000	351
Telephones	2000	main lines	681,000	195
Cellular telephones	2000	subscribers	743,000	213
Personal computers	2001	units	200,000	56
Internet	2000	users	300,000	86

Education and health

Educational attainment: n.a. *Literacy* (1995): total population age 15 and over literate 1,829,000 (92.4%); males literate 94.7%; females literate 90.3%.

Education (1996–97)

	schools	teachers	students	student/ teacher ratio
Primary (age 5–9)	2,160	...	382,309	...
Secondary (age 10–16)	...	...	292,002	...
Voc., teacher tr.	275[12]	7,745	55,848	7.2
Higher	20	10,444[13]	81,588[13]	7.8[13]

Health (1997): physicians 7,203 (1 per 476 persons); hospital beds (1995) 11,596 (1 per 319 persons); infant mortality rate per 1,000 live births (2000) 29.3.
Food (2000): daily per capita caloric intake 3,155 (vegetable products 87%, animal products 13%); 127% of FAO recommended minimum.

Military

Total active duty personnel (2001): Lebanese national armed forces 71,830 (army 97.5%, navy 1.1%, air force 1.4%). External regular military forces include: UN peacekeeping force in Lebanon (July 2002) 3,400; Syrian army 18,000. *Military expenditure as percentage of GNP* (1999): 4.0% (world 2.4%); per capita expenditure: U.S.$185.

---

[1]The current legislature was elected between August and September 2000; one-half of its membership is Christian and one-half Muslim/Druze. [2]Includes water area of 66 sq mi (170 sq km) not distributed by governorate. [3]Excludes about 375,000 Palestinian refugees. [4]2001. [5]Permits authorized. [6]Public utilities and Transportation and communications includes Public administration and defense. [7]ESCWA estimate for Beirut only. [8]Weights based on consumer price index components. For capital city only. [9]Imports are c.i.f. [10]Apart from a 14-mi (23-km) section delivering oil from the Zahrani refinery to a thermal power station serving Beirut, no passenger or general cargo track was in use in 2001. [11]For Middle East Airlines and Trans-Mediterranean Airways. [12]1994–95. [13]1995–96.

Internet resources for further information:
• **Central Administration for Statistics**
  http://www.cas.gov.lb
• **Central Bank of Lebanon**
  http://www.bdl.gov.lb

Lesotho

Official name: Lesotho (Sotho); Kingdom of Lesotho (English).
Form of government[1]: transitional regime with 2 legislative houses (Senate [33]; National Assembly [120]).
Chief of state: King.
Head of government: Prime Minister.
Capital: Maseru.
Official languages: Sotho; English.
Official religion: Christianity.
Monetary unit: 1 loti (plural maloti [M]) = 100 lisente; valuation (Sept. 23, 2002) 1 U.S.$ = M 10.63; 1 £ = M 16.52.

Area and population		area		population
				1995
Districts	Capitals	sq mi	sq km	estimate[2]
Berea	Teyateyaneng	858	2,222	206,200
Butha-Buthe	Butha-Buthe	682	1,767	135,400
Leribe	Hlotse	1,092	2,828	349,500
Mafeteng	Mafeteng	818	2,119	259,000
Maseru	Maseru	1,652	4,279	400,200
Mohale's Hoek	Mohale's Hoek	1,363	3,530	231,300
Mokhotlong	Mokhotlong	1,573	4,075	100,300
Qacha's Nek	Qacha's Nek	907	2,349	86,800
Quthing	Quthing	1,126	2,916	151,900
Thaba-Tseka	Thaba-Tseka	1,649	4,270	136,200
TOTAL		11,720	30,355	2,056,800

Demography

Population (2002): 2,208,000[3].
Density (2002)[3]: persons per sq mi 188.4, persons per sq km 72.7.
Urban-rural (1996): urban 16.9%; rural 83.1%.
Sex distribution (1996): male 49.20%; female 50.80%.
Age breakdown (1996): under 15, 43.1%; 15–29, 27.6%; 30–44, 15.0%; 45–59, 8.6%; 60–74, 4.8%; 75 and over, 0.9%.
Population projection[3]: (2010) 2,339,000; (2020) 2,382,000.
Doubling time: 50 years.
Ethnic composition (2000): Sotho 80.3%; Zulu 14.4%; other 5.3%.
Religious affiliation (2000): Christian 91.0%, of which Roman Catholic 37.5%, Protestant (mostly Presbyterian) 13.0%, African Christian 11.8%; other (mostly traditional beliefs) 9.0%.
Major urban centres (1996): Maseru 137,837; Teyateyaneng 48,869; Maputsoe 27,951; Hlotse 23,122; Mafeteng 20,804.

Vital statistics

Birth rate per 1,000 population (2002): 30.7 (world avg. 21.2).
Death rate per 1,000 population (2002): 16.8 (world avg. 8.9).
Natural increase rate per 1,000 population (2002): 13.9 (world avg. 12.3).
Total fertility rate (avg. births per childbearing woman; 2002): 4.0.
Life expectancy at birth (2002): male 46.3 years; female 47.8 years.
Major causes of death per 100,000 population: n.a.; however, major diseases include typhoid fever and infectious and parasitic diseases.

National economy

Budget (2000–01). Revenue: M 2,752,200,000 (customs receipts 40.9%, grants and nontax revenue 29.4%, income tax 11.4%, sales tax 10.2%). Expenditures: M 2,897,900,000 (personal emoluments 31.8%, capital expenditure 17.8%, subsidies and transfers 9.6%, interest payments 9.0%).
Production (metric tons except as noted). Agriculture, forestry, fishing (1999): corn (maize) 125,000, roots and tubers 85,000, sorghum 33,000, vegetables 19,000, wheat 15,000, fruit 14,000, dry beans 9,300, dry peas 3,000; livestock (number of live animals) 720,000 sheep, 560,000 goats, 510,000 cattle, 152,000 asses, 98,000 horses, 63,000 pigs, 1,700,000 chickens; roundwood (1998) 1,594,000 cu m; fish catch (1998) 30. Mining and quarrying (1998): diamonds 2,398 carats. Manufacturing (value added in U.S.$'000,000; 1995): food products 58; beverages 38; textiles 14; chemical products 9; metal products 4; wearing apparel 4. Construction (permits issued in M '000,000; 1999): residential 3.76; nonresidential 65.10. Energy production (consumption): electricity, data for Lesotho included with South Africa; coal, none (n.a); petroleum, none (n.a.); natural gas, none (n.a.).
Tourism (2000): receipts from visitors U.S.$24,000,000; expenditures by nationals abroad U.S.$9,000,000.
Population economically active (1993): total 617,871; activity rate of total population 45.1% (participation rates: ages 15–64 [1986] 79.8%; female 23.7%; unemployed [1992] 35.0%).

Price and earnings indexes (1995 = 100)						
	1995	1996	1997	1998	1999	2000	2001
Consumer price index	100.0	109.3	...	...	138.6	147.1	132.9
Annual earnings index[4]	100.0	114.2	126.1	146.9	164.6	179.3	...

Household income and expenditure. Average household size (1996) 5.0; average annual income per household (1986–87) M 2,832 (U.S.$1,297); sources of income (1986–87): transfer payments 44.7%, self-employment 27.8%, wages and salaries 22.4%, other 5.1%; expenditure (1989): food 48.0%, clothing 16.4%, household durable goods 11.9%, housing and energy 10.1%, transportation 4.7%.

Gross national product (2000): U.S.$1,181,000,000 (U.S.$580 per capita).

Structure of gross domestic product and labour force				
	2000–01		1986	
	in value M '000,000[5]	% of total value[5]	labour force	% of labour force
Agriculture	654.7	12.9	474,171	66.2
Mining	3.2	0.1	6,446	0.9
Manufacturing	565.3	11.1	19,339	2.7
Construction	785.5	15.5	31,516	4.4
Public utilities	223.2	4.4	1,433	0.2
Transp. and commun.	150.4	2.9	5,014	0.7
Trade	337.3	6.6	22,204	3.1
Finance	414.7	8.2	3,581	0.5
Pub. admin., defense	273.2	5.4	17,907	2.5
Services	277.5	5.5	126,780	17.7
Other	1,394.1[6]	27.4[6]	7,879	1.1
TOTAL	5,079.1	100.0	716,270[7]	100.0[7]

Public debt (external, outstanding; 2000): U.S.$697,800,000.
Land use (1998): meadows and pastures 65.9%; agricultural and under permanent cultivation 10.7%; other 23.4%.

Foreign trade[8]

Balance of trade (current prices)						
	1995	1996	1997	1998	1999	2000
U.S.$'000,000	−825.2	−811.8	−828.3	−672.5	−606.7	−516.5
% of total	72.1%	68.5%	67.9%	63.5%	63.7%	55.0%

Imports (1998): M 5,199,800,000 (1990; manufactured goods [excluding chemicals, machinery, and transport equipment] 42.5%; food and live animals 19.1%; machinery and transport equipment 15.3%; petroleum products 8.6%). *Major import sources:* Customs Union of Southern Africa 88.7%; Asia 7.2%; Europe 2.3%, of which European Economic Community 2.0%; the Americas 1.3%.
Exports (1998): M 1,109,600,000 (manufactured goods 71.6%; machinery and transport equipment 15.1%; food and live animals 4.0%; beverages and tobacco 3.5%; crude materials 1.8%). *Major export destinations:* Customs Union of Southern Africa 65.5%; the Americas 33.6%; Europe 0.5%.

Transport and communications

Transport. Railroads (1999): length 1.6 mi, 2.6 km. Roads (1996): total length 3,079 mi, 4,955 km (paved 18%). Vehicles (1996): passenger cars 12,610; trucks and buses 25,000. Merchant marine: vessels (100 gross tons and over) none. Air transport (1996): passenger-mi 3,900,000, passenger-km 6,200,000; short ton-mi cargo 395,000, metric ton-km cargo 577,000; airports (1997) with scheduled flights 1.

Communications				units per 1,000
Medium	date	unit	number	persons
Daily newspapers	1996	circulation	15,000	7.6
Radio	1997	receivers	104,000	52
Television	1999	receivers	33,000	16
Telephones	2000	main lines	22,200	10
Cellular telephones	2001	subscribers	33,000	15
Personal computers	...	units	...	...
Internet	2001	users	5,000	2.3

Education and health

Educational attainment (1986–87). Percentage of population age 10 and over having: no formal education 22.9%; primary 52.8%; secondary 23.2%; higher 0.6%. *Literacy* (1995): total population age 15 and over literate 849,700 (71.3%); males literate 468,000 (81.1%); females literate 381,700 (62.3%).

Education (1996–97)				student/
	schools	teachers	students	teacher ratio
Primary (age 6–12)	1,249	7,898	374,628	47.4
Secondary (age 13–17)	187[9]	2,817	67,454	23.9
Vocational	9[9]	61	678	11.1
Higher	1[9]	574	4,614	8.0

Health: physicians (1995) 105 (1 per 18,527 persons); hospital beds (1992) 2,400 (1 per 765 persons); infant mortality rate per 1,000 live births (2002) 82.6.
Food (1999): daily per capita caloric intake 2,300 (vegetable products 95%, animal products 5%); (1997) 101% of FAO recommended minimum requirement.

Military

Total active duty personnel (2001): 2,000[10]. *Military expenditure as percentage of GNP* (1999): 2.6% (world 2.4%); per capita expenditure U.S.$14.

[1]Traditionally a hereditary monarchy; the Interim Political Authority, which was mandated in December 1998 to make Lesotho more democratic, implemented a new electoral system that resulted in internationally judged free and fair elections in May 2002. [2]De jure population. [3]Excludes absentee miners working in South Africa. [4]Based on average annual wages, including overtime, of mine workers. [5]At 1995 prices. [6]Indirect taxes less imputed bank service charges. [7]Approximately 117,600 persons (c. 40% of Lesotho's adult male labour force) were employed as mine workers in South Africa in 1993; by May 2000 this figure had declined to 54,000. [8]Import figures are f.o.b. in balance of trade and c.i.f. in commodities and trading partners. [9]1993–94. [10]Royal Lesotho Defence Force.

Internet resources for further information:
• **Central Bank of Lesotho http://www.centralbank.org.ls**

Liberia

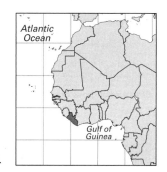

Official name: Republic of Liberia.
Form of government: multiparty republic with two legislative houses (Senate [26]; House of Representatives [64]).
Head of state and government: President.
Capital: Monrovia.
Official language: English.
Official religion: none.
Monetary unit: 1 Liberian dollar (L$) = 100 cents; valuation (Sept. 23, 2002) 1 U.S.$ = L$1.00[1]; 1 £ = L$1.55.

Area and population		area		population
				1999
Counties	Capitals	sq mi	sq km	estimate
Bomi	Tubmanburg	755	1,955	114,316
Bong	Gbarnga	3,127	8,099	299,825
Gbarpolu	Bopulu	2,982	7,723	2
Grand Bassa	Buchanan	3,382	8,759	215,338
Grand Cape Mount	Robertsport	2,250	5,827	120,141
Grand Gedeh	Zwedru	6,575[3]	17,029[3]	94,497[3]
Grand Kru	Barclayville	4	4	39,062
Lofa	Voinjama	4,493	11,367	351,492[2]
Margibi	Kakata	1,260	3,263	219,417
Maryland	Harper	2,066[4]	5,351[4]	71,977
Montserrado	Bensonville	1,058	2,740	843,783
Nimba	Sanniquellie	4,650	12,043	338,887
River Gee	Fish Town	3	3	3
Rivercess	Rivercess City	1,693	4,385	38,167
Sinoe	Greenville	3,959	10,254	79,241
TOTAL		38,250[5]	99,067[5, 6]	2,826,143

Demography

Population (2002): 3,288,000.
Density (2001)[5]: persons per sq mi 87.1, persons per sq km 33.6.
Urban-rural (2001): urban 45.5%; rural 54.5%.
Sex distribution (2001): male 49.42%; female 50.58%.
Age breakdown (2001): under 15, 43.2%; 15–29, 27.0%; 30–44, 15.1%; 45–59, 9.4%; 60–74, 4.2%; 75 and over, 1.1%.
Population projection: (2010) 4,073,000; (2020) 5,294,000.
Doubling time: 23 years.
Ethnic composition (1984): Kpelle 19.4%; Bassa 13.9%; Grebo 9.0%; Gio 7.8%; Kru 7.3%; Mano 7.1%; other 35.5%.
Religious affiliation (1995): traditional beliefs 63.0%; Christian 21.0%, of which Protestant 13.5%, African Christian 5.1%, Roman Catholic 2.4%; Muslim 16.0%.
Major cities (2002): Monrovia 543,000; Zwedru 33,800; Buchanan 27,000; Yekepa 22,500; Harper 19,600.

Vital statistics

Birth rate per 1,000 population (2001): 46.6 (world avg. 21.2).
Death rate per 1,000 population (2001): 16.4 (world avg. 8.9).
Natural increase rate per 1,000 population (2001): 30.2 (world avg. 12.3).
Total fertility rate (avg. births per childbearing woman; 2001): 6.4.
Marriage rate per 1,000 population: n.a.
Divorce rate per 1,000 population: n.a.
Life expectancy at birth (2001): male 50.0 years; female 52.9 years.
Major causes of death per 100,000 population: n.a.; however, major health problems include complications during pregnancy, malaria, pneumonia, anemia, malnutrition, measles, and AIDS. Violence and acts of war were major causes of both morbidity and mortality from 1990 onward.

National economy

Budget (2001). Revenue: U.S.$80,700,000 (tax revenue 85.1%, of which import duties 22.4%, maritime revenue 19.8%, stamps and land rental 15.9%, income and profit taxes 13.8%; grants 8.3%; nontax revenue 6.6%). Expenditures: U.S.$73,100,000 (current expenditures 76.2%, of which goods and services 42.1%, wages 27.9%, interest on debt 4.5%; development expenditures 23.8%).
Tourism: n.a.
Population economically active (1997): total 1,183,000; activity rate 51.4% (participation rates: ages 10–64 [1994] 64.0%; female 39.5%; unemployed [1996] 95%).

Price and earnings indexes (1998 = 100)				
	1998	1999	2000	2001
Consumer price index	100.0	104.3	114.0	118.2
Earnings index	...	...	...	...

Production (metric tons except as noted). Agriculture, forestry, fishing (2001): cassava 440,500, sugarcane 250,000, rice 183,400, oil palm fruit 174,000, natural rubber 135,000, bananas 110,000, plantains 39,500, yams 20,000, peanuts (groundnuts) 4,800, coffee 3,200, cacao beans 3,000; livestock (number of live animals) 220,000 goats, 210,000 sheep, 130,000 pigs, 36,000 cattle, 4,000,000 chickens; roundwood (2001) 5,261,930 cu m; fish catch (1999) 15,472. Mining and quarrying (1998): diamonds 150,000 carats; gold 500 kg. Manufacturing (1999): palm oil 42,000; cement 8,300[7]; cigarettes 22,000,000 units[8]; soft drinks 171,000 hectolitres[9]; beer 158,000 hectolitres[13]. Construction: n.a. Energy production (consumption): electricity (kW-hr; 1997) 493,000,000 (493,000,000);

coal, none (none); crude petroleum, none (none); petroleum products (metric tons; 1997) none (107,000); natural gas, none (none).
Public debt (external, outstanding; 2000): U.S.$1,040,000,000.
Household income and expenditure. Average household size (1983) 4.3; income per household: n.a.; sources of income: n.a.; expenditure: n.a.
Gross national product (1996): U.S.$1,174,000,000 (U.S.$490 per capita).

Structure of gross domestic product and labour force				
	2001		1994	
	in value U.S.$'000,000	% of total value	labour force	% of labour force
Agriculture	388.1	74.2	676,000	68.1
Mining	0.3	0.1		
Manufacturing	34.1	6.5		
Construction	7.8	1.5		
Public utilities	3.1	0.6	77,000	7.7
Transp. and commun.	23.2	4.4		
Trade	23.0	4.4		
Finance	14.7	2.8		
Pub. admin., defense	14.1	2.7		
Services	14.5	2.8	240,000	24.2
Other	...	...		
TOTAL	522.9	100.0	993,000	100.0

Land use (1994): forested 47.8%; meadows and pastures 20.8%; agricultural and under permanent cultivation 3.8%; other 27.6%.

Foreign trade

Balance of trade (current prices)						
	1996	1997	1998	1999	2000	2001
U.S.$'000,000	−2,718	−217.9	−118.5	−111.8	−69.0	−53.5
% of total	54.5%	81.1%	58.1%	50.1%	22.3%	17.4%

Imports (2001): U.S.$180,900,000 (food and live animals 31.1%, petroleum and petroleum products 19.5%, machinery and transport equipment 17.6%, basic manufactures 10.7%, chemicals 4.6%, beverages and tobacco 3.2%). *Major import sources* (1999): South Korea 27.4%; Japan 24.8%; Germany 14.1%; Singapore 7.1%; Croatia 5.2%.
Exports (2001): U.S.$127,400,000 (rubber 52.9%, logs and timber 46.2%, cocoa 0.4%, other 0.5%). *Major export destinations* (2001): Norway 23.8%; Germany 10.5%; France 7.5%; Singapore 6.5%; Belgium 4.8%; Italy 3.8%; Spain 3.4%; Turkey 3.1%; South Korea 2.0%.

Transport and communications

Transport. Railroads (1998): route length 304 mi, 490 km; short ton-mi cargo 534,000,000, metric ton-km cargo 860,000,000. Roads (1999): total length 6,600 mi, 10,600 km (paved 6%). Vehicles (1996): passenger cars 9,400; trucks and buses 25,000. Merchant marine (1992): vessels (100 gross tons and over) 1,672; total deadweight tonnage 97,373,965. Air transport (1992): passenger-mi 4,300,000, passenger-km 7,000,000; short ton-mi cargo 621,000, metric ton-km cargo 1,000,000; airports (2000) with scheduled flights 2.

Communications				units per 1,000
Medium	date	unit	number	persons
Daily newspapers	1996	circulation	35,000	16
Radio	1997	receivers	790,000	329
Television	1997	receivers	70,000	29
Telephones	1999	main lines	6,600	2.2

Education and health

Educational attainment, n.a. *Literacy* (1995): total population age 15 and over literate 705,000 (38.3%); males literate 523,000 (53.9%); females literate 182,000 (22.4%).

Education (1985)				student/
	schools	teachers	students	teacher ratio
Primary (age 6–12)	1,691	9,856	260,560	26.4
Secondary (age 13–18)	419			
Higher	3	472[7]	5,716[7]	...

Health: physicians (1992) 257 (1 per 8,333 persons); hospital beds, n.a.; infant mortality rate (2001) 132.4.
Food (2000): daily per capita caloric intake 2,076 (vegetable products 97%, animal products 3%); 90% of FAO recommended minimum requirement.

Military

Total active duty personnel: About 11,000–15,000 in all armed forces as of 2001. West African (ECOMOG) peacekeepers withdrew in January 1999 and the civil war resumed in April 1999. The fighting continued in late 2002. *Military expenditure as percentage of GNP* (1999): 1.2% (world 2.4%); per capita expenditure U.S.$2.

[1]Par value rate to U.S.$ ineffective from January 1998; the independent free market exchange rate was roughly L$74 = U.S.$1 in May 2002. [2]Population for Gbarpolu (created late 2000) included with Lofa. [3]Figures for River Gee (created mid-2000) included with Grand Gedeh. [4]Figures for Grand Kru included with Maryland. [5]Total area per more recent survey is 37,743 sq mi (97,754 sq km). [6]Detail does not add to total given because of rounding. [7]1993. [8]1992. [9]1988.

Internet resources for further information:
• Liberian Daily News Bulletin (link) http://www.africanews.org/west/liberia

Libya

Official name: Al-Jamāhīrīyah
al-'Arabīyah al-Lībīyah ash-Sha'bīyah
al-Ishtirākīyah al-Uẓmā (Socialist
People's Libyan Arab Jamahiriya).
Form of government: socialist state with
one policy-making body (General
People's Congress [760]).
Chief of state: Muammar al-Qaddafi
(de facto)[1]; Secretary of General
People's Congress (de jure).
Head of government: Secretary of the
General People's Committee (prime
minister).
Capital: Tripoli[2].
Official language: Arabic.
Official religion: Islam.
Monetary unit: 1 Libyan dinar
(LD) = 1,000 dirhams; valuation
(Sept. 23, 2002) 1 U.S.$ = LD 1.24;
1 £ = LD 1.92.

Area and population		area		population
Administrative regions[3]	Capitals	sq mi	sq km	1995 census[4]
Al-Bāṭin	...	...	...	151,240
Banghāzī	Banghāzī	...	...	665,615
Fazzān	...	...	...	314,029
Al-Jabal al-Akhḍar	Al-Bayḍā'	...	...	381,165
Al-Jabal al-Gharbī	Gharyān	...	...	316,970
Al-Jufrah	...	...	...	39,335
Miṣrātah (Misurata)	...	...	...	488,573
Najghaza	...	...	...	244,553
Sofuljin	...	...	...	76,401
Ṭarābulus	Tripoli (Ṭarābulus)	...	...	1,313,996
Al-Wāḥah	...	...	...	62,056
Al-Waṣṭa	...	...	...	240,574
Az-Zāwiyah	Az-Zāwiyah	...	...	517,395
TOTAL		679,362	1,759,540	4,811,902

Demography

Population (2002): 5,369,000.
Density (2002): persons per sq mi 7.9, persons per sq km 3.1.
Urban-rural (2000): urban 87.6%; rural 12.4%.
Sex distribution (2001): male 51.41%; female 48.59%.
Age breakdown (2001): under 15, 35.4%; 15–29, 31.7%; 30–44, 19.1%; 45–59, 8.0%; 60–74, 4.5%; 75 and over, 1.3%.
Population projection: (2010) 6,447,000; (2020) 7,740,000.
Doubling time: 29 years.
Ethnic composition (1995): Libyan Arab 78%; Berber 1%; other 21% (mostly Egyptians, Sudanese, and Chadians).
Religious affiliation (1995): Sunnī Muslim 97.0%; other 3.0%.
Major cities (1995): Tripoli 1,140,000; Banghāzī 650,000; Miṣrātah 280,000; Surt 150,000.

Vital statistics

Birth rate per 1,000 population (2001): 27.6 (world avg. 21.2).
Death rate per 1,000 population (2001): 3.5 (world avg. 8.9).
Natural increase rate per 1,000 population (2001): 24.1 (world avg. 12.3).
Total fertility rate (avg. births per childbearing woman; 2001): 3.6.
Marriage rate per 1,000 population: n.a.
Divorce rate per 1,000 population: n.a.
Life expectancy at birth (2001): male 73.5 years; female 77.9 years.
Major causes of death per 100,000 population: n.a.; however, the main causes of hospital mortality in 1987 were injuries and poisoning 15.5%, diseases of the circulatory system 11.6%, conditions originating in the perinatal period 11.4%, diseases of the respiratory system 7.0%, neoplasms (cancers) 4.4%.

National economy

Budget (2000). Revenue: LD 6,850,000,000 (oil revenues 69.1%, other 30.9%). Expenditures: LD 4,400,000,000 (1990–91; current expenditures 55.7%, of which municipalities 39.4%, education and scientific research 4.3%, health 2.7%; capital expenditures 44.3%, of which agriculture and land reclamation 13.6%, industry 5.3%).
Production (metric tons except as noted). Agriculture, forestry, fishing (2001): tomatoes 250,000, watermelons 215,000, potatoes 210,000, olives 190,000, dry onions 180,000, dates 132,500, wheat 130,000, barley 80,000; livestock (number of live animals; 2001) 5,100,000 sheep, 1,950,000 goats, 220,000 cattle, 72,000 camels, 25,000,000 chickens; roundwood 652,000 cu m; fish catch (1999) 32,550. Mining and quarrying (2000): lime 290,000; gypsum 175,000; salt 40,000. Manufacturing (value of production in '000,000 LD; 1996): base metals 212, electrical equipment 208, petrochemicals 175, food products 79, cement and other building materials 68. Energy production (consumption): electricity (kW-hr; 1999) 18,900,000,000 (17,577,000,000); coal (metric tons; 1997) none (5,000); crude petroleum (barrels; 2001) 490,294,000 ([1997] 114,348,000); petroleum products (metric tons; 1997) 14,266,000 (7,695,000); natural gas (cu m; 1997) 6,542,000,000 (5,442,000,000).
Land use (1994): forested 0.5%; meadows and pastures 7.6%; agricultural and under permanent cultivation 1.2%; desert and built-up areas 90.7%.
Population economically active (1996): total 1,224,000; activity rate of total population 26.1% (participation rates [1993]: ages 10 and over, 35.2%; female 9.8%; unemployed [2000] 30.0%).

Price index (1995 = 100)							
	1989	1990	1991	1992	1993	1994	1995
Consumer price index	33.9	38.4	42.9	49.3	59.2	76.9	100.0

Public debt (2000): n.a.[5]
Gross domestic product (2000): U.S.$38,000,000,000 (U.S.$6,200 per capita).

Structure of gross domestic product and labour force				
	1996			
	in value LD '000,000	% of total value	labour force	% of labour force
Agriculture	782.5	6.6	219,500	17.0
Mining and quarrying	3,036.5	25.8	31,000	2.5
Manufacturing	1,107.0	9.4	128,500	10.5
Construction	797.0	6.8	171,000	14.0
Public utilities	240.5	2.0	35,500	2.9
Transp. and commun.	1,025.5	8.7	104,000	8.5
Trade	1,345.5	11.4	73,000	6.0
Finance, insurance	739.5	6.3	22,000	1.8
Pub. admin., defense	2,247.5	19.1 }	439,500	35.9
Services	461.0	3.9		
TOTAL	11,782.5	100.0	1,224,000	100.0

Household income and expenditure. Average household size (1980) 5.1; income per household: n.a.; sources of income: n.a.; expenditure: n.a.
Tourism (2000): receipts U.S.$114,000,000; expenditures U.S.$17,000,000.

Foreign trade[6]

Balance of trade (current prices)						
	1994	1995	1996	1997	1998	1999
U.S.$'000,000	+1,026	+2,781	+2,519	+2,716	+471	+2,974
% of total	6.5%	18.2%	15.1%	15.9%	3.9%	25.7%

Imports (2000): U.S.$7,600,000,000 (1997; machinery 25.9%; food products 20.0%; road vehicles 10.1%; chemical products 7.5%). *Major import sources:* Italy 24.0%; Germany 12.0%; Tunisia 9.0%; U.K. 7.0%; France 6.0%.
Exports (2000): U.S.$13,900,000,000 (1997; crude petroleum 76.4%; refined petroleum 16.5%; iron and steel 1.5%). *Major export destinations:* Italy 33.0%; Germany 24.0%; Spain 10.0%; France 5.0%; Turkey 4.0%.

Transport and communications

Transport. Railroads: none. Roads (1999): total length 83,200 km (paved 57%). Vehicles (1996): passenger cars 809,514; trucks and buses 357,528. Merchant marine (1992): vessels (100 gross tons and over) 150; total deadweight tonnage 1,223,589. Air transport (2001): passenger-km 410,000,000; metric ton-km cargo 259,000; airports with scheduled flights: n.a.

Communications				units per 1,000
Medium	date	unit	number	persons
Daily newspapers	1996	circulation	71,000	14
Radio	1997	receivers	1,350,000	259
Television	1999	receivers	730,000	133
Telephones	2001	main lines	610,000	115
Cellular telephones	2001	subscribers	50,000	9.0
Internet	2001	users	20,000	3.6

Education and health

Educational attainment (1984). Percentage of population age 25 and over having: no formal schooling (illiterate) 59.7%; incomplete primary education 15.4%; complete primary 8.5%; some secondary 5.2%; secondary 8.5%; higher 2.7%. *Literacy* (1998): percentage of total population age 15 and over literate 78.1%; males literate 89.6%; females literate 65.4%.

Education (1995–96)				student/
	schools	teachers	students	teacher ratio
Primary (age 6–12)	2,737[7]	122,020	1,333,679	10.9
Secondary (age 13–18)	...	17,668	189,202[8]	...
Voc., teacher tr.	480	...	147,689[9]	...
Higher	13	...	126,348	...

Health: physicians (1997) 6,092 (1 per 781 persons); hospital beds (1998) 18,100[10] (1 per 312 persons); infant mortality rate (2001) 29.0.
Food (2000): daily per capita caloric intake 3,305 (vegetable products 89%, animal products 11%); 140% of FAO recommended minimum requirement.

Military

Total active duty personnel (2001): 76,000 (army 59.2%, navy 10.5%, air force 30.3%). *Military expenditure as percentage of GNP* (1995): 6.1% (world 2.4%); per capita expenditure U.S.$342.

---

[1]No formal titled office exists. [2]Policy-making body (General People's Congress) may meet in Surt or Tripoli. [3]Libya is divided into 25 administrative entities as of 1998. [4]Preliminary. [5]Libya had no foreign debt in 2000. [6]Imports f.o.b. in balance of trade and c.i.f. in commodities and trading partners. [7]1994–95. [8]1992–93. [9]1993–94. [10]Includes beds in clinics.

Internet resources for further information:
• CIA World Factbook—Libya
    http://www.odci.gov/cia/publications/factbook/geos/ly.html

Liechtenstein

Official name: Fürstentum Liechtenstein (Principality of Liechtenstein).
Form of government: constitutional monarchy with one legislative house (Diet [25]).
Chief of state: Prince.
Head of government: Prime Minister.
Capital: Vaduz.
Official language: German.
Official religion: none.
Monetary unit: 1 Swiss franc (Sw F) = 100 centimes; valuation (Sept. 23, 2002) 1 U.S.$ = Sw F 1.49; 1 £ = Sw F 2.31.

Area and population

	area		population
Regions			2001[1]
Communes	sq mi	sq km	estimate
Oberland (Upland)	48.3	125.2	21,906
Balzers	7.6	19.6	4,233
Planken	2.0	5.3	355
Schaan	10.3	26.8	5,454
Triesen	10.2	26.4	4,381
Triesenberg	11.5	29.8	2,556
Vaduz	6.7	17.3	4,927
Unterland (Lowland)	13.4[2]	34.8	10,957
Eschen	4.0	10.3	3,791
Gamprin	2.4	6.1	1,159
Mauren	2.9	7.5	3,288
Ruggell	2.9	7.4	1,744
Schellenberg	1.4	3.5	975
TOTAL	61.8[2]	160.0	32,863

Demography

Population (2002): 33,300.
Density (2002): persons per sq mi 538.8, persons per sq km 208.1.
Urban-rural (2001): urban 21.2%; rural 78.8%.
Sex distribution (2000): male 48.70%; female 51.30%.
Age breakdown (2000): under 15, 18.7%; 15–29, 22.3%; 30–44, 25.4%; 45–59, 19.4%; 60–74, 9.7%; 75 and over, 4.5%.
Population projection: (2010) 36,000; (2020) 38,000.
Doubling time: n.a.; doubling time exceeds 100 years.
Ethnic composition (2000): Liechtensteiner 65.5%; Swiss 11.9%; Austrian 6.2%; German 3.4%; Italian 2.8%; other 10.2%.
Religious affiliation (1998): Roman Catholic 80.0%; Protestant 7.5%; Muslim 3.3%; Eastern Orthodox 0.7%; atheist 0.6%; other 7.9%.
Major cities (1999): Schaan 5,262; Vaduz 5,106.

Vital statistics

Birth rate per 1,000 population (2000): 11.8 (world avg. 22.5); (1997) legitimate 86.0%; illegitimate 14.0%.
Death rate per 1,000 population (2000): 6.7 (world avg. 9.0).
Natural increase rate per 1,000 population (2000): 5.1 (world avg. 13.5).
Total fertility rate (avg. births per childbearing woman; 2000): 1.5.
Marriage rate per 1,000 population (1998): 13.2.
Divorce rate per 1,000 population (1994): 1.4.
Life expectancy at birth (2000): male 75.2 years; female 82.5 years.
Major causes of death per 100,000 population (1998): diseases of the circulatory system 284.2; malignant neoplasms (cancers) 128.0; old age 49.9; diseases of the respiratory system 31.2; accidents, poisonings, and acts of violence 28.1; diseases of the digestive tract 24.9.

National economy

Budget (1999). Revenue: Sw F 690,200,000 (taxes and duties 78.2%, investment income 11.3%, charges and fees 8.5%, real estate capital-gains taxes and death and estate taxes 2.0%). Expenditures: Sw F 537,200,000 (financial affairs 35.8%, social welfare 17.0%, education 15.1%, transportation 9.1%, general administration 9.4%, public safety 4.9%, health 4.7%).
Public debt: none.
Tourism (2001): 123,273 tourist overnight stays; receipts from visitors, n.a.; expenditures by nationals abroad, n.a.
Population economically active (2000): total 16,368; activity rate of total population 50.1% (participation rates: ages 15–64, 71.2%; female 40.3%; unemployed 1.8%).

Price and earnings indexes (1995 = 100)

	1993	1994	1995	1996	1997	1998	1999
Consumer price index	97.4	98.2	100.0	100.8	101.3	101.4	102.2
Earnings index	...	...	...	...	...	...	...

Household income and expenditure. Average household size (1990) 2.7; income per household: n.a.; sources of earned income (1987): wages and salaries 92.9%, self-employment 7.1%; expenditure (1990)[3]: rent 20.9%, food 17.7%, transportation 11.0%, education and self-improvement 9.7%, clothing 7.0%, health 4.7%.
Production (metric tons except as noted). Agriculture, forestry, fishing (2000): significantly market gardening, other crops include cereals and apples; livestock (number of live animals; 2000) 6,000 cattle, 3,000 pigs, 2,900 sheep; commercial timber (1998) 19,527 cu m; fish catch, n.a. Mining and quarrying: n.a. Manufacturing (1997): processed milk 13,304; milk for whipped cream 262; yogurt 82; cheese 3; wine (1993) 635.2 hectolitres; small-scale precision manufacturing includes optical lenses, electron microscopes, electronic equipment, and high-vacuum pumps; metal manufacturing, construction machinery, and ceramics are also important. Construction (1997): residential 344,515 cu m; nonresidential 282,145 cu m. Energy production (consumption): electricity (kW-hr; 1997) 75,842,000 (302,018,000[4]); coal (metric tons; 1996) none (24); petroleum products (metric tons; 1995) none (49,291); natural gas (cu m; 1994) none (19,350,000).
Gross national product (1998): U.S.$1,164,000,000 (U.S.$36,760 per capita).

Structure of gross domestic product and labour force

	1996		2000	
	in value U.S.$	% of total value	labour force	% of labour force
Agriculture	...	...	277	1.7
Manufacturing	...	...	4,393	26.8
Construction	...	...	1,448	8.8
Public utilities	...	...	163	1.0
Transportation and communications	...	...	561	3.4
Trade, public accommodation	...	...	2,287	14.0
Finance, insurance, real estate	...	...	1,282	7.8
Pub. admin., defense	...	...	1,253	7.7
Services	...	...	4,405	26.9
Other	...	...	299[5]	1.8[5]
TOTAL	714,000,000	100.0	16,368[6]	100.0[2]

Land use (latest): forested 34.8%; meadows and pastures 15.7%; agricultural and under permanent cultivation 24.3%; other 25.2%.

Foreign trade

Balance of trade (current prices)

	1992	1993	1994	1995	1996	1997	1998
Sw F '000,000	+947	+1,024	+1,043	+1,078	+1,165	+1,515	+2,394
% of total	30.6%	33.8%	33.1%	33.5%	34.0%	39.1%	49.1%

Imports (1997): Sw F 1,179,000,000 (machinery and transport equipment 35.2%; other finished goods 23.6%; metal products 12.5%; limestone, cement, and other building materials 12.4%; unrefined and semifabricated metal 5.7%; chemical products 5.2%). *Major import sources:* EU and Switzerland.
Exports (1997): Sw F 2,694,000,000 (machinery and transport equipment 49.2%; metal products 15.1%; other finished goods 12.7%; limestone, cement, and other building materials 9.8%; chemical products 7.7%; food and beverages 4.2%). *Major export destinations* (1998): EU 49.5%; Switzerland 12.7%; other 37.8%.

Transport and communications

Transport. Railroads (1998): length 11.5 mi, 18.5 km; passenger and cargo traffic, n.a. Roads (1999): total length 201 mi, 323 km. Vehicles (1999): passenger cars 21,150; trucks and buses (1998) 2,684. Merchant marine: none. Air transport: the nearest scheduled airport service is through Zürich, Switzerland.

Communications

Medium	date	unit	number	units per 1,000 persons
Daily newspapers	1998	circulation	17,900	565
Radio	1997	receivers	21,000	658
Television	1997	receivers	12,000	364
Telephones	1999	main lines	19,763	597

Education and health

Educational attainment (1990). Percentage of population not of preschool age or in compulsory education having: no formal schooling 0.3%; primary and lower secondary education 39.3%; higher secondary and vocational 47.6%; some postsecondary 7.4%; university 4.2%; other and unknown 1.1%.
Literacy: virtually 100%.

Education (1998–99)

	schools	teachers	students	student/ teacher ratio
Primary (age 7–12)	14	151	2,048	13.6
Secondary (age 13–19)	9	162	1,859	11.5
Vocational[7]	2	309	2,307	7.5

Health: physicians (1997) 41 (1 per 764 persons); hospital beds 108 (1 per 288 persons); infant mortality rate per 1,000 live births (2000) 5.7.
Food (1999)[8]: daily per capita caloric intake 3,600 (vegetable products 65%, animal products 35%); 134% of FAO recommended minimum requirement.

Military

Total active duty personnel: none; Liechtenstein has had no standing army since 1868. *Military expenditure as percentage of GNP:* none.

[1]January 1. [2]Detail does not add to total given because of rounding. [3]Household expenditures are taken from a 1986 Swiss sample survey; a similarity of consumption patterns is assumed. [4]2000. [5]Unemployed. [6]Excludes 10,643 foreign employees. [7]1997–98. [8]Figures are derived from statistics for Switzerland and Austria.

Internet resources for further information:
• Liechtenstein News
  http://www.news.li/index.htm

Lithuania

Official name: Lietuvos Respublika
  (Republic of Lithuania).
Form of government: unitary multi-
  party republic with a single legislative
  body, the Seimas (141).
Head of state: President.
Head of government: Prime Minister.
Capital: Vilnius.
Official language: Lithuanian.
Official religion: none.
Monetary unit: 1 litas (LTL) =
  100 centai; valuation (Sept. 23, 2002)
  1 U.S.$ = LTL 3.51; 1 £ = LTL 5.45[1].

Area and population		area		population
				2001
Provinces	Capitals	sq mi	sq km	census
Alytus	Alytus	2,095	5,425	187,769
Kaunas	Kaunas	3,112	8,060	701,529
Klaipėda	Klaipėda	2,011	5,209	385,768
Marijampolė	Marijampolė	1,723	4,463	188,634
Panevėžys	Panevėžys	3,043	7,881	299,990
Šiauliai	Šiauliai	3,297	8,540	370,096
Tauragė	Tauragė	1,703	4,411	134,275
Telšiai	Telšiai	1,680	4,350	179,885
Utena	Utena	2,780	7,201	185,962
Vilnius	Vilnius	3,768	9,760	850,064
TOTAL		25,212	65,300	3,483,972

Demography

Population (2002): 3,473,000.
Density (2002): persons per sq mi 137.8, persons per sq km 53.2.
Urban-rural (2001): urban 66.9%; rural 33.1%.
Sex distribution (2001): male 46.76%; female 53.24%.
Age breakdown (2001): under 15, 19.5%; 15–29, 21.2%; 30–44, 22.8%; 45–59, 17.2%; 60–74, 14.2%; 75 and over, 5.1%.
Population projection: (2010) 3,430,000; (2020) 3,427,000.
Ethnic composition (2001): Lithuanian 83.5%; Polish 6.7%; Russian 6.3%; Belarusian 1.2%; Ukrainian 0.7%; other 1.6%.
Religious affiliation (1995): Roman Catholic 72.2%; Orthodox 3.3%; Protestant 1.3%; other (mostly nonreligious) 23.2%.
Major cities (2001): Vilnius 542,287; Kaunas 378,943; Klaipėda 192,954; Šiauliai 133,883; Panevėžys 119,749; Alytus 71,491.

Vital statistics

Birth rate per 1,000 population (2001): 9.0 (world avg. 21.2); (2000) legitimate 77.4%; illegitimate 22.6%.
Death rate per 1,000 population (2001): 11.6 (world avg. 8.9).
Natural increase rate per 1,000 population (2001): –2.6 (world avg. 12.3).
Total fertility rate (avg. births per childbearing woman; 2000): 1.3.
Marriage rate per 1,000 population (2000): 4.6.
Divorce rate per 1,000 population (2000): 2.9.
Life expectancy at birth (2000): male 67.6 years; female 77.9 years.
Major causes of death per 100,000 population (1997): diseases of the circulatory system 613.9; malignant neoplasms (cancers) 199.7; accidents, injury, homicide 146.9.

National economy

Budget (1998). Revenue: LTL 9,378,000,000 (value-added tax 38.5%, individual income tax 25.8%, excise taxes 14.3%, nontax revenue 7.5%). Expenditures: LTL 9,916,000,000 (education 27.7%, police 12.3%, social security and welfare 10.0%, health 6.6%, defense 4.5%).
Gross national product (2000): U.S.$10,809,000,000 (U.S.$2,930 per capita).

Structure of gross national product and labour force					
	2000		1998		
	in value LTL '000,000	% of total value	labour force[2]	% of labour force[2]	
Agriculture, forestry	3,088	6.9	356,000	20.1	
Mining	} 8,983	} 20.0	3,100	0.2	
Manufacturing			286,900	16.2	
Construction	2,533	5.6	118,200	6.7	
Public utilities	1,689	3.7	40,600	2.3	
Transp. and commun.	4,974	11.1	96,900	5.5	
Trade, restaurants	6,699	14.9	265,400	15.0	
Finance, real estate	4,336	9.6	58,600	3.3	
Pub. admin., defense	2,770	6.2	69,100	3.9	
Services	5,602	12.5	361,300	20.4	
Other	4,256[3]	9.5[3]	113,700[4]	6.4[4]	
TOTAL	44,930	100.0	1,769,800	100.0	

Production (metric tons except as noted). Agriculture, forestry, fishing (1999): hay 2,621,000, potatoes 1,699,000, sugar beets 890,000, wheat 837,300, barley 835,000, cabbages 200,000, apples 100,000, oats 75,000, rapeseed 71,900; livestock (number of live animals) 1,168,000 pigs, 928,000 cattle; roundwood (2000) 5,500,000 cu m; fish catch (1999) 35,244. Mining and quarrying (1998): limestone 250,000; peat 195,300. Manufacturing (value of production in LTL '000,000; 1997): food and beverages 5,785; refined petroleum products 3,488; wearing apparel 1,378; textiles 1,312; chemicals and chemical products 1,222; wood and wood products (excluding furniture) 902. Energy production (consumption): electricity (kW-hr; 2000) 11,388,000,000 ([1997] 12,105,000,000); coal (metric tons; 1997) none (256,000); crude petroleum (barrels; 1997)

1,554,000 (36,782,000); petroleum products (metric tons; 1997) 5,151,000 (3,326,000); natural gas (cu m; 1997) none (2,148,000,000).
Public debt (external outstanding; 2000): U.S.$2,188,300,000.
Population economically active (1997)[5]: total 1,819,800; activity rate of total population 49.1% (participation rates: ages 14–64, 71.1%; female 47.3%; registered unemployed [2000] 11.5%).

Price and earnings indexes (1995 = 100)							
	1996	1997	1998	1999	2000	2001	2002
Consumer price index	124.6	135.7	142.5	143.6	145.1	146.9	148.1[6]
Annual earnings index	135.1	166.7	187.7	198.6	197.2	198.2	...

Household income and expenditure. Average household size (1997) 2.9; average annual household disposable income (1997): LTL 12,914 (U.S.$3,228); sources of income (1998): wages and salaries 52.7%, transfers 21.3%, self-employment 14.8%, other 11.2%; expenditure (1998): food, beverages, and expenditures in cafes/hotels 54.6%, housing and energy 12.4%, transportation and communications 8.6%, clothing and footwear 8.0%.
Land use (1994): forested 30.4%; meadows and pastures 7.6%; agricultural and under permanent cultivation 53.9%; other 8.1%.
Tourism (2000): receipts from visitors U.S.$391,000,000; expenditures by nationals abroad U.S.$253,000,000.

Foreign trade[7]

Balance of trade (current prices)						
	1996	1997	1998	1999	2000	2001
LTL '000,000	–4,815	–7,136	–8,332	–7,323	–6,588	–7,081
% of total	12.7%	18.8%	21.9%	23.4%	17.8%	16.2%

Imports (2000): LTL 21,826,000,000 (mineral fuels 23.3%, machinery/apparatus 15.7%, textiles and clothing 9.3%, chemicals and chemical products 9.1%, food products 8.3%). *Major import sources:* Russia 27.4%; Germany 15.1%; Poland 4.9%; United Kingdom 4.5%; France 4.2%.
Exports (2000): LTL 15,238,000,000 (mineral fuels 21.2%, textiles and clothing 18.6%, machinery/apparatus 10.6%, food products 9.4%, chemicals and chemical products 7.9%). *Major export destinations:* Latvia 15.0%; Germany 14.3%; United Kingdom 7.8%; Russia 7.1%; Poland 5.5%.

Transport and communications

Transport. Railroads (1998): route length 1,241 mi, 1,997 km; passenger-mi 444,000,000, passenger-km 715,000,000; short ton-mi cargo 5,661,000,000, metric ton-km cargo 8,265,000,000. Roads (1999): total length 45,764 mi, 73,650 km (paved 91%). Vehicles (1999): passenger cars 1,089,334; trucks and buses 102,414. Air transport (2001)[8]: passenger-mi 272,000,000; passenger-km 438,000,000; short ton-mi cargo 1,049,000, metric ton-km cargo 1,531,000; airports with scheduled flights (1996) 3.

Communications				units per 1,000
Medium	date	unit	number	persons
Daily newspapers	1996	circulation	344,000	93
Radio	1997	receivers	1,900,000	513
Television	1999	receivers	1,555,000	420
Telephones	2001	main lines	1,151,700	313
Cellular telephones	2001	subscribers	932,000	253
Personal computers	2001	units	260,000	71
Internet	2001	users	250,000	68

Education and health

Educational attainment (1989). Percentage of population age 25 and over having: no schooling 9.1%; incomplete and complete primary education 21.3%; incomplete and complete secondary 57.0%; postsecondary 12.6%. *Literacy* (1995): total population age 15 and over literate 99.2%.

Education (1996–97)				student/
	schools	teachers	students	teacher ratio
Primary (7–10)[9]	...	14,095	225,071	16.0
Secondary (11–18)[9]	...	32,172	325,480	10.1
Voc., teacher tr.[10]	104	5,078	56,400	11.1
Higher	...	13,136	83,645	6.4

Health (1998): physicians 14,622 (1 per 253 persons); hospital beds 35,612 (1 per 104 persons); infant mortality rate per 1,000 live births (2001) 7.9.
Food (1999): daily per capita caloric intake 2,959 (vegetable products 77%, animal products 23%); 116% of FAO recommended minimum requirement.

Military

Total active duty personnel (2001): 12,190[11] (army 61.5%, navy 4.8%, air force 6.6%, volunteer national defense force 27.1%). *Military expenditure as percentage of GNP* (1999): 1.3% (world 2.4%); per capita expenditure U.S.$87.

---

[1]Pegged to the euro from Feb. 2, 2002, at the rate of 1€ = LTL 3.45. [2]Annual average. [3]Taxes less imputed bank service charges and subsidies. [4]Unemployed. [5]As of September. [6]May. [7]Imports c.i.f.; exports f.o.b. [8]Lithuanian airlines. [9]Excludes special education. [10]1998–99. [11]Excludes 4,400 paramilitary in border police or coast guard.

Internet resources for further information:
• **Lithuanian Department of Statistics http://www.std.lt**
• **Bank of Lithuania http://www.lbank.lt/eng/default.htm**

Luxembourg

Official name: Groussherzogtum
Lëtzebuerg (Luxemburgian);
Grand-Duché de Luxembourg
(French); Grossherzogtum
Luxemburg (German) (Grand Duchy
of Luxembourg).
Form of government: constitutional
monarchy with two legislative houses
(Council of State [21][1]; Chamber of
Deputies [60]).
Chief of state: Grand Duke.
Head of government: Prime Minister.
Capital: Luxembourg.
Official language: none; Luxemburgian
(national); French (used for
most official purposes); German
(lingua franca).
Official religion: none.
Monetary unit: 1 € (euro) = 100 cents;
valuation (Sept. 23, 2002) 1 U.S.$ =
€1.02; 1 £ = €1.58[2].

Area and population

	area		population
Districts			2001
Cantons	sq mi	sq km	census
Diekirch	447	1,157	67,487
Clervaux	128	332	12,411
Diekirch	92	239	26,748
Redange	103	267	13,689
Vianden	21	54	2,920
Wiltz	102	265	11,719
Grevenmacher	203	525	51,960
Echternach	72	186	14,141
Grevenmacher	82	211	21,664
Remich	49	128	16,155
Luxembourg	349	904	320,317
Capellen	77	199	30,523
Esch	94	243	134,846
Luxembourg			
(Ville et Campagne)	92	238	131,652
Mersch	86	224	23,296
TOTAL	999	2,586	439,764

Demography

Population (2002): 447,000.
Density (2002): persons per sq mi 447.4, persons per sq km 172.9.
Urban-rural (2002): urban 91.9%; rural 8.1%.
Sex distribution (2001): male 49.26%; female 50.74%.
Age breakdown (2001): under 15, 18.9%; 15–29, 18.2%; 30–44, 25.4%; 45–59, 18.7%; 60–74, 13.1%; 75 and over, 5.7%.
Population projection: (2010) 491,000; (2020) 541,000.
Ethnic composition (nationality; 2001): Luxemburger 63.1%; Portuguese 13.4%; French 4.6%; Italian 4.3%; Belgian 3.4%; German 2.3%; English 1.0%; other 7.9%.
Religious affiliation (1996): Roman Catholic 95.1%; other 4.9%.
Major cities (2001)[3]: Luxembourg 76,687; Esch-sur-Alzette 27,186; Dudelange 17,348; Schifflange 7,854; Bettembourg 7,162.

Vital statistics

Birth rate per 1,000 population (2001): 12.4 (world avg. 21.2); (1998) legitimate 82.5%; illegitimate 17.5%.
Death rate per 1,000 population (2001): 8.8 (world avg. 8.9).
Natural increase rate per 1,000 population (2001): 3.6 (world avg. 12.3).
Total fertility rate (avg. births per childbearing woman; 2001): 1.7.
Marriage rate per 1,000 population (2001): 4.5.
Divorce rate per 1,000 population (2001): 2.3.
Life expectancy at birth (2001): male 74.2 years; female 81.0 years.
Major causes of death per 100,000 population (2001): circulatory diseases 328.1; malignant neoplasms (cancers) 214.2.

National economy

Budget (2002). Revenue: €5,977,200,000 (1998; income and excise taxes 58.2%, customs taxes 13.4%). Expenditures: €5,976,100,000 (1998; social security 21.3%, education 11.7%, transportation 8.2%, administration 6.5%, defense 2.7%, debt service 0.9%).
Public debt (1997): U.S.$668,420,000.
Production (metric tons except as noted). Agriculture, forestry, fishing (2000): barley 64,787, wheat 53,500, potatoes 23,430, oats 12,000, apples 11,950; livestock (number of live animals) 205,072 cattle, 80,141 pigs; roundwood (2000) 355,000 cu m. Mining and quarrying (1999): gypsum and anhydrite 400,000. Manufacturing (2000): rolled steel 4,519,000; crude steel 2,725,000; cement 748,600; wine 134,800 hectolitres. Construction (1999): residential 742,717 sq m; nonresidential 102,968 sq m. Energy production (consumption): electricity (kW-hr; 2000) 1,124,000,000 (6,445,000,000); coal (metric tons; 1997) none (194,000); crude petroleum, none (none); petroleum products (metric tons; 1997) none (1,615,000); natural gas (cu m; 1997) none (730,700,000).
Land use (1992): forested 34.2%; meadows and pastures 25.6%; agricultural and under permanent cultivation 23.2%; other 17.0%.
Tourism (1997): receipts from visitors U.S.$297,000,000.
Gross national product (2000): U.S.$18,439,000,000 (U.S.$42,060 per capita).

Structure of gross domestic product and labour force

	2000		2001	
	in value €'000,000	% of total value	labour force	% of labour force
Agriculture	133.1	0.6	3,600	1.3
Mining	27.4	0.1	} 35,800	12.9
Manufacturing	2,306.5	11.2		
Construction	1,236.6	6.0	27,100	9.8
Public utilities	217.9	1.1	1,600	0.6
Transp. and commun.	1,986.2	9.7	23,000	8.3
Trade	2,453.6	11.9	51,600	18.6
Finance	7,907.8	38.5	32,400	11.7
Pub. admin., defense	1,092.5	5.3	15,200	5.5
Services	2,179.9	10.6	86,700	31.3
Other	1,022.1[4]	5.0[4]	...	...
TOTAL	20,563.6	100.0	277,000	100.0

Population economically active (2001): total 277,000; activity rate of total population 63.0% (participation rates: ages 15–64 [1997] 51.4%; female [1997] 38.2%; unemployed [2001] 2.6%).

Price and earnings indexes (1995 = 100)

	1995	1996	1997	1998	1999	2000	2001
Consumer price index	100.0	101.4	102.8	103.8	104.8	108.1	111.0
Hourly earnings index	...	...	...	...	...	...	...

Household income and expenditure. Average household size (1991) 2.6; income per household (1992) Lux F 1,438,000 (U.S.$44,700); sources of income (1992): wages and salaries 67.1%, transfer payments 28.1%, self-employment 4.8%; expenditure (1994): food, beverages, and tobacco 19.7%, housing 17.3%, transportation and communications 16.2%, household goods and furniture 9.9%, clothing and footwear 8.2%, health 7.9%.

Foreign trade[5]

Balance of trade (current prices)

	1995	1996	1997	1998	1999	2000
Lux F '000,000	−62,400	−71,100	−82,800	−82,200	−109,400	−105,700
% of total	12.0%	13.9%	14.4%	8.0%	15.4%	13.4%

Imports (2000): €11,126,400,000 (machinery and other equipment 22.0%; fabricated metals 12.7%; transport equipment 12.1%; chemicals and chemical products 9.9%; food, beverages, and tobacco 5.2%). *Major import sources:* Belgium 37.1%; Germany 25.2%; France 12.9%; The Netherlands 4.8%; U.S. 3.5%; U.K. 2.9%.
Exports (2000): €8,483,400,000 (fabricated metals 30.0%; machinery and equipment 24.4%; basic manufactures 16.0%; chemicals and chemical products 6.7%; transport equipment 4.0%; food products 3.7%). *Major export destinations:* Germany 23.9%; France 21.0%; Belgium 12.6%; U.K. 7.6%; Italy 5.5%; The Netherlands 5.3%; U.S. 4.1%.

Transport and communications

Transport. Railroads (2001): route length 170 mi, 274 km; passenger-mi 215,000,000, passenger-km 346,000,000; short ton-mi cargo 394,000,000, metric ton-km cargo 634,000,000. Roads (1999): total length 3,209 mi, 5,166 km (paved 100%). Vehicles (2001): passenger cars 273,088; trucks and buses 21,490. Merchant marine (1992): vessels (100 gross tons and over) 54; total deadweight tonnage 2,603,611. Air transport (2001): passengers carried 1,625,000; cargo 510,965 metric tons; airports (2001) with scheduled flights 1.

Communications

Medium	date	unit	number	units per 1,000 persons
Daily newspapers	1996	circulation	135,000	325
Radio	1997	receivers	285,000	677
Television	1998	receivers	165,000	389
Telephones	2001	main lines	350,000	783
Cellular telephones	2001	subscribers	432,400	967
Personal computers	2001	units	230,000	515
Internet	2001	users	100,000	227

Education and health

Educational attainment: n.a. *Literacy* (2001): virtually 100% literate.

Education (2000–01)

	schools	teachers	students	student/teacher ratio
Primary (age 6–11)[6]	...	2,135	31,278	14.7
Secondary (age 12–18)	...	} 3,125	9,859	...
Voc., teacher tr.	...		21,359	...
Higher	5	...	2,533	...

Health (2001): physicians 1,123 (1 per 392 persons); hospital beds 3,035 (1 per 145 persons); infant mortality rate per 1,000 live births (2001) 4.7.
Food (1995): daily per capita caloric intake 3,530 (vegetable products 68%, animal products 32%); 134% of FAO recommended minimum.

Military

Total active duty personnel (2000): 899 (army 100.0%). *Military expenditure as percentage of GNP* (1999): 0.8% (world 2.4%); per capita expenditure U.S.$326.

[1]Has limited legislative authority. [2]The Luxembourg franc was the former monetary unit; on Jan. 1, 2002, Lux F 40.34 = €1. [3]Populations of localities (comparable to cities proper or towns proper). [4]Imputed bank service charges. [5]Imports c.i.f.; exports f.o.b. [6]Public schools only.

Internet resources for further information:
• STATEC: Luxembourg in Figures http://statec.gouvernement.lu

Macau[1]

Official name: Aomen Tebie Xingzhengqu (Chinese); Região Administrativa Especial de Macau (Portuguese) (Macau Special Administrative Region).
Political status: special administrative region (China) with one legislative house (Legislative Council [27[2]]).
Chief of state: President of China.
Head of government: Chief Executive.
Capital: Macau.
Official languages: Chinese; Portuguese.
Official religion: none.
Monetary unit: 1 pataca (MOP) = 100 avos; valuation (Sept. 23, 2002) 1 U.S.$ = MOP 8.03; 1 £ = MOP 12.48.

Area and population

Geographical areas	area		population
	sq mi	sq km	1991 census
Macau peninsula	3.3	8.5	326,460
Islands	5.3	13.8	10,148
Coloane	2.9	7.6	3,111
Taipa	2.4	6.2	7,037
Marine	—	—	2,856
Embankment[3]	1.4	3.5	—
TOTAL	10.0	25.8	339,464

Demography

Population (2002): 438,000.
Density (2002): persons per sq mi 43,800, persons per sq km 16,977.
Urban-rural (2002): urban, virtually 100%[4].
Sex distribution (2001): male 47.55%; female 52.45%.
Age breakdown (1999): under 15, 23.2%; 15–29, 22.9%; 30–44, 29.0%; 45–59, 15.0%; 60–74, 6.6%; 75 and over, 3.3%.
Population projection: (2010) 467,000; (2020) 501,000.
Doubling time: over 100 years.
Nationality (1991): Chinese 68.2%; Portuguese 27.9%; English 1.8%; other 2.1%.
Religious affiliation (1998): nonreligious 60.8%; Buddhist 16.7%; other 22.5%.
Major city (2000 est.): Macau 437,900.

Vital statistics

Birth rate per 1,000 population (2002): 9.0 (world avg. 21.2); legitimate, n.a.; illegitimate, n.a.
Death rate per 1,000 population (2002): 4.6 (world avg. 8.9).
Natural increase rate per 1,000 population (2002): 4.4 (world avg. 12.3).
Total fertility rate (avg. births per childbearing woman; 2002): 1.1.
Marriage rate per 1,000 population (2001): 2.8.
Divorce rate per 1,000 population (2001): 0.8.
Life expectancy at birth (2002): male 77.0 years; female 82.0 years.
Major causes of death per 100,000 population (1999): diseases of the circulatory system 107.9; malignant neoplasms (cancers) 83.7; diseases of the respiratory system 38.4; accidents, poisoning, and violence 26.3; diseases of the digestive system 12.1; diseases of the genitourinary system 9.4; infectious and parasitic diseases 7.5; endocrine and metabolic disorders 6.4; diseases of the nervous system 2.9.

National economy

Budget (1998). Revenue: MOP 14,831,099,000 (recurrent receipts 69.1%, autonomous agency receipts 21.4%, capital receipts 2.2%). Expenditures: 14,831,099,000 MOP (recurrent payments 61.1%, autonomous agency expenditures 21.4%, capital payments 17.5%).
Tourism: receipts from visitors (2000) U.S.$2,999,000,000; expenditures by nationals abroad (1999) U.S.$131,000,000.
Land use (1992): built-on area, wasteland, and other 100.0%.
Gross domestic product (at current market prices; 2000): U.S.$6,385,000,000 (U.S.$14,580 per capita).

Structure of labour force

	1998	
	labour force	% of labour force
Agriculture	300	0.1
Mining	100	—
Manufacturing	41,500	19.7
Construction	11,800	5.6
Public utilities	1,400	0.7
Transportation and communications	13,700	6.5
Trade	54,600	25.9
Finance	13,600	6.5
Public administration } Services	64,000	30.4
Other	9,700	4.6
TOTAL	210,700	100.0

Production (metric tons except as noted). Agriculture, forestry, fishing (1999): eggs 650; livestock (number of live animals) 500,000 chickens; fish catch (1997) 1,500. Quarrying (value added in '000,000 MOP; 1997): 13. Manufacturing (value added in MOP '000,000; 1997): wearing apparel 2,161; textiles 607; elec-

trical appliances 131; printing and publishing 97; nonmetallic mineral products 92; food products 83; footwear 53. Construction (1998): residential 742,955 sq m; nonresidential 226,237 sq m. Energy production (consumption): electricity (kW-hr; 1997) 1,409,000,000 (1,584,000,000); coal (metric tons) none (none); crude petroleum (barrels) none (none); petroleum products (metric tons; 1997) none (480,000); natural gas, none (none).
Public debt (long-term, external; 1999): U.S.$706,000,000.
Population economically active (1998): total 210,700; activity rate of total population 48.9% (participation rates: age 15–64, 70.2%; female 44.8%; unemployed [1999] 6.6%).

Price and earnings indexes (1995 = 100)

	1996	1997	1998	1999	2000	2001
Consumer price index[5]	99.4	102.8	103.0	99.7	98.1	96.2
Earnings index	...	...	...	...	...	...

Household income and expenditure. Average household size (1991) 3.5; income per household: n.a.; sources of income: n.a.; expenditure (1987–88): food 38.3%, housing 19.7%, education, health, and other services 12.1%, transportation 7.4%, clothing and footwear 6.8%, energy 4.0%, household durable goods 3.7%, other goods 8.0%.

Foreign trade[6]

Balance of trade (current prices)

	1996	1997	1998	1999	2000	2001
MOP '000,000	−32	+526	+1,487	+1,280	+2,283	−697
% of total	0.1%	1.6%	4.6%	3.8%	5.9%	1.9%

Imports (1998): MOP 15,596,446,000 (raw materials 54.1%, capital goods 14.2%, foodstuffs 9.3%, fuels and lubricants 6.3%). *Major import sources:* China 32.7%; Hong Kong 23.7%; European Economic Community 10.5%; Taiwan 9.9%; Japan 7.8%; United States 4.7%.
Exports (1998): MOP 17,083,616,000 (garments 76.4%, textiles 4.5%, machinery and mechanical appliances 3.5%, textile yarn and thread 3.1%, footwear 2.2%). *Major export destinations:* United States 47.7%; European Economic Community 30.5%; Hong Kong 7.6%; China 6.8%; Taiwan 1.5%; Japan 0.7%.

Transport and communications

Transport. Railroads: none. Roads (1996): total length 31 mi, 50 km (paved 100%). Vehicles (1998): passenger cars 45,184; trucks and buses 6,578. Merchant marine (1990): vessels 6; total gross tonnage 3,512. Air transport: none.

Communications

Medium	date	unit	number	units per 1,000 persons
Daily newspapers	1996	circulation	200,000	455
Radio	1997	receivers	160,000	356
Television	1999	receivers	125,492	287
Telephones	2001	main lines	176,400	394
Cellular telephones	2001	subscribers	194,500	434
Personal computers	2001	units	80,000	179
Internet	2001	users	101,000	225

Education and health

Educational attainment (1991). Population age 25 and over having: no formal schooling 13.1%; incomplete primary education 16.0%; completed primary 19.9%; some secondary 45.1%; post-secondary 5.9%. *Literacy* (1995): percentage of population age 15 and over literate 91.7%; males literate 95.6%; females literate 88.2%.

Education (1997–98)

	schools	teachers	students	student/ teacher ratio
Primary (age 6–11)	81	1,744	47,235	27.1
Secondary (age 12–18)	47	1,577	28,280	17.9
Teacher tr.	2	47	699	14.9
Higher	7	818	7,682	9.4

Health (1998): physicians 369 (1 per 1,167 persons); hospital beds 1,086 (1 per 396 persons); infant mortality rate per 1,000 live births (2002) 8.0.
Food (1998): daily per capita caloric intake 2,471 (vegetable products 76%, animal products 24%); 108% of FAO recommended minimum requirement.

Military

Total active duty personnel: Chinese troops (2001) 500.

---

[1]Macau reverted to Chinese sovereignty on Dec. 20, 1999. [2]Includes 10 directly elected seats, 7 seats appointed by the chief executive, and 10 seats appointed by special-interest groups. [3]Landfill called (Co Tai) links Coloane and Taipa. [4]About 1% of Macau's population live on sampans and other vessels. [5]Excluding rent; base year is July 1995–June 1996. [6]Import figures are c.i.f.

Internet resources for further information:
• **Government of Macau Special Administrative Region, P.R.C.**
　http://www.macau.gov.mo
• **Macau Census and Statistics Service**
　http://www.dsec.gov.mo

Macedonia

Official name[1]: Republika Makedonija
  (Republic of Macedonia).
Form of government: unitary multiparty
  republic with a unicameral legislative
  (Assembly [120]).
Head of state: President.
Head of government: Prime Minister.
Capital: Skopje.
Official languages[2]: Macedonian;
  Albanian.
Official religion: none.
Monetary unit: denar; valuation
  (Sept. 23, 2002) 1 U.S.$ = 62.30 denar;
  1 £ = 96.82 denar.

Area and population

Former administrative districts[3]	area sq km	population 1994 census	Former administrative districts[3]	area sq km	population 1994 census
Berovo	806	19,737	Negotino	734	23,094
Bitola	1,798	106,012	Ohrid	1,069	60,841
Brod	924	10,912	Prilep	1,675	93,248
Debar	274	26,449	Probištip	326	16,373
Delčevo	589	25,052	Radoviš	735	30,378
Demir Hisar	443	10,321	Resen	739	17,467
Gevgelija	757	34,767	Skopje	1,818	541,280
Gostivar	1,341	108,189	Štip	815	50,531
Kavadarci	1,132	41,801	Struga	507	62,305
Kičevo	854	53,044	Strumica	952	89,759
Kočani	570	48,105	Sveti Nikole	649	21,391
Kratovo	376	10,855	Tetovo	1,080	174,748
Kriva Palanka	720	25,112	Titov Veles	1,536	65,523
Kruševo	239	11,981	Valandovo	331	12,049
Kumanovo	1,212	126,543	Vinica	432	19,010
			TOTAL	25,713[4]	1,936,877

Demography

Population (2002): 2,031,000.
Density (2002): persons per sq mi 204.6, persons per sq km 79.0.
Urban-rural (2000): urban 62.0%; rural 38.0%.
Sex distribution (2001): male 50.06%; female 49.94%.
Age breakdown (2001): under 15, 22.9%; 15–29, 24.4%; 30–44, 21.5%; 45–59, 16.8%; 60–64, 11.2%; 65 and over, 3.2%.
Population projection: (2010) 2,057,000; (2020) 2,061,000.
Ethnic composition (2000): Macedonian 53.9%; Albanian 18.0%; Turkish 7.7%; Roma (Gypsy) 5.3%; Aromanian 5.0%; Serbian 2.1%; Croat 2.0%; other 6.0%.
Religious affiliation (1995): Serbian (Macedonian) Orthodox 54.2%; Sunnī Muslim 30.0%; other 15.8%.
Major cities (1994): Skopje 440,577; Bitola 75,386; Prilep 67,371; Kumanovo 66,237; Tetovo 50,376.

Vital statistics

Birth rate per 1,000 population (2001): 13.5 (world avg. 21.2); (1998) legitimate 90.5%; illegitimate 9.5%.
Death rate per 1,000 population (2001): 7.7 (world avg. 8.9).
Natural increase rate per 1,000 population (2001): 5.8 (world avg. 12.3).
Total fertility rate (avg. births per childbearing woman; 2001): 1.6.
Marriage rate per 1,000 population (1999): 7.0.
Life expectancy at birth (2001): male 71.8 years; female 76.4 years.
Major causes of death per 100,000 population (1997): diseases of the circulatory system 462.8; malignant neoplasms 138.3; diseases of the respiratory system 39.5; accidents, violence, and poisoning 32.4; diseases of the digestive system 15.9.

National economy

Budget (2002). Revenue: 53,089,000,000 denar (tax revenue 94.2%, of which value-added tax 33.7%, excise taxes 20.6%, income and profit tax 19.6%; import duties 10.0%; nontax revenue 5.8%). Expenditure: 59,979,000,000 denar (wages and salaries 29.5%, pensions 26.1%, goods and services 20.0%, interest 6.1%).
External debt (2000): U.S.$1,165,000,000.
Production (metric tons except as noted). Agriculture, forestry, fishing (2001): wheat 246,000, grapes 229,800, potatoes 176,000, tomatoes 126,300, corn (maize) 118,000; livestock (number of live animals) 1,251,000 sheep, 265,000 cattle, 204,000 pigs, 3,350,000 chickens; roundwood (2000) 1,052,000 cu m; fish catch (1999) 1,804 (all freshwater). Mining and quarrying (1999): copper 38,200; lead 12,300; zinc 10,200; refined silver 18,000 kg. Manufacturing (1998): cement 461,195; steel sheets 276,464; detergents 21,990; wool yarn 3,252; refrigerators 4,007 units; freezers 3,488 units; leather footwear 1,382,000 pairs; cotton fabric 13,700,000 sq m; cigarettes 7,009,000 units. Construction (value in '000,000 denars; 1998) residential 331; nonresidential 834. Energy production (consumption): electricity (kW-hr; 1997) 6,719,-000,000 (6,719,000,000); coal (metric tons; 1997) 6,700,000 (6,800,000); crude petroleum (barrels; 1997) none (2,932,000); petroleum products (metric tons; 1997) 385,000 (976,000); natural gas (cu m; 1997) none (n.a.).
Household income and expenditure (1994). Average household size 3.8; income per household Din 49,635 (U.S.$1,223); sources of income: wages and salaries 59.9%, transfer payments 17.0%, transfers from abroad 13.4%, other 9.7%; expenditure: food 42.2%, fuel and lighting 7.5%, clothing and footwear 7.4%, transportation and communications 7.2%, drink and tobacco 7.0%, health care 4.7%, education and entertainment 3.2%.

Gross national product (2000): U.S.$3,902,000,000 (U.S.$1,920 per capita).

Structure of gross domestic product and labour force

	2000			
	in value '000,000 denar	% of total value	labour force	% of labour force
Agriculture	23,368	9.9	123,038	15.2
Mining and manufacturing	43,660	18.5	148,633	18.3
Construction	11,675	4.9	35,712	4.4
Public utilities	10,085	4.3	10,627	1.3
Transp. and commun.	19,569	8.3	27,486	3.4
Trade	32,772	13.9	68,732	8.5
Finance	14,195	6.0	15,667	1.9
Pub. admin., defense	14,779	6.2	32,508	4.0
Services	66,108	28.0	118,419	14.6
Other			230,178[6]	28.4[6]
TOTAL	236,211	100.0	811,000	100.0

Population economically active (2000): total 811,000; activity rate 39.9% (participation rates: ages 15–64, 52.9%; female 38.5%; unemployed 28.4%).

Price and earnings indexes (1995 = 100)

	1996	1997	1998	1999	2000	2001
Consumer price index	102.7	103.8	104.4	103.6	109.7	115.7
Monthly earnings index[7]	102.2	102.6	107.2	113.2	...	...

Tourism (2000): receipts from visitors U.S.$37,000,000; expenditures by nationals abroad U.S.$34,000,000.

Foreign trade

Balance of trade (current prices)

	1995	1996	1997	1998	1999	2000
U.S.$'000,000	−514.9	−316.5	−387.6	−400	−392	−556
% of total	17.6%	11.0%	13.9%	13.2%	14.1%	17.4%

Imports (2000): U.S.$1,875,000,000 (machinery and transport equipment 19.6%, manufactured products 12.9%, mineral fuels 13.9%, food products and beverages 11.2%, chemical products 9.0%). *Major import sources:* Germany 12.1%; Ukraine 9.8%; Greece 9.6%; Russia 9.2%; Yugoslavia 9.2%; Slovenia 6.9%; Italy 5.3%; United States 4.0%.
Exports (2000): U.S.$1,319,000,000 (manufactured products 36.8%, machinery and transport equipment 6.3%, food products 5.0%, chemical products 4.5%, raw materials 3.7%). *Major export destinations:* Yugoslavia 25.2%; Germany 19.4%; United States 12.6%; Italy 6.6%; Greece 6.4%; Croatia 3.6%.

Transport and communications

Transport. Railroads (1999): length 575 mi, 925 km; passenger-mi 93,200,000, passenger-km 150,000,000; short ton-mi cargo 236,000,000, metric ton-km cargo 380,000,000. Roads (1998): length 7,154 mi, 11,513 km (paved 63%). Vehicles (1998): passenger cars 288,678; trucks and buses 24,745. Merchant marine: n.a. Air transport (2001)[8]: passenger-mi 104,000,000, passenger-km 168,000,000; short ton-mile cargo transported 80,778,000, metric tons cargo transported 130,000,000; airports (2001) with scheduled flights 2.

Communications

Medium	date	unit	number	units per 1,000 persons
Daily newspapers	1996	circulation	41,000	20
Radio	1997	receivers	410,000	204
Television	1999	receivers	500,000	248
Telephones	2001	main lines	538,000	264
Cellular telephones	2001	subscribers	223,300	109
Personal computers	2001	units	...	...
Internet	2001	users	70,000	34

Education and health

Educational attainment (1981). Percentage of population age 15 and over having: less than full primary education 45.3%; primary 28.1%; secondary 21.2%; postsecondary and higher 5.1%; unknown 0.3%. *Literacy* (1998): 94.6%.

Education (1998–99)

	schools	teachers	students	student/ teacher ratio
Primary (age 7–14)	1,041	13,604	255,150	18.8
Secondary (age 15–18)	95	5,372	87,420	16.3
Higher[9]	31	1,493	36,922	24.7

Health (1998): physicians 4,508 (1 per 445 persons); hospital beds 10,333 (1 per 194 persons); infant mortality rate per 1,000 live births (2001) 13.0.
Food (2000): daily per capita caloric intake 3,006 (vegetable products 83%, animal products 17%); 118% of FAO recommended minimum requirement.

Military

Total active duty personnel (2001): 16,000 (army 95.6%, air force 4.4%). *Military expenditure as percentage of GNP* (1999): 2.5% (world 2.4%); per capita expenditure U.S.$112.

[1]Member of the United Nations under the name The Former Yugoslav Republic of Macedonia. [2]Albanian was made an official language in June 2002. [3]Local government reorganized September 1996 from 34 administrative districts into 123 municipalities. [4]Total includes 280 sq km of inland water not distributed by district. [5]Contained metal. [6]Unemployed. [7]In service industries only. [8]Macedonian airline. [9]1999–2000.

Internet resources for further information:
• **National Bank of the Republic of Macedonia http://www.nbrm.gov.mk**

Madagascar

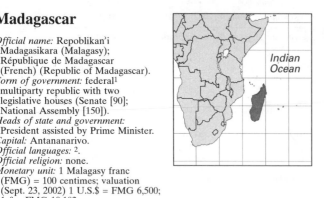

Official name: Repoblikan'i
 Madagasikara (Malagasy);
 République de Madagascar
 (French) (Republic of Madagascar).
Form of government: federal[1]
 multiparty republic with two
 legislative houses (Senate [90];
 National Assembly [150]).
Heads of state and government:
 President assisted by Prime Minister.
Capital: Antananarivo.
Official languages: [2].
Official religion: none.
Monetary unit: 1 Malagasy franc
 (FMG) = 100 centimes; valuation
 (Sept. 23, 2002) 1 U.S.$ = FMG 6,500;
 1 £ = FMG 10,102.

Area and population

Autonomous provinces[1]	Capitals	area sq mi	area sq km	population 1993 census
Antananarivo	Antananarivo	22,503	58,283	3,483,236
Antsirañana	Antsirañana	16,620	43,046	942,410
Fianarantsoa	Fianarantsoa	39,526	102,373	2,671,150
Mahajanga	Mahajanga	57,924	150,023	1,330,612
Toamasina	Toamasina	27,765	71,911	1,935,330
Toliary	Toliary	62,319	161,405	1,729,419
TOTAL		226,658	587,041	12,092,157

Demography

Population (2002): 16,473,000.
Density (2002): persons per sq mi 72.7, persons per sq km 28.1.
Urban-rural (2001): urban 30.1%; rural 69.9%.
Sex distribution (2000): male 49.70%; female 50.30%.
Age breakdown (2000): under 15, 45.0%; 15–29, 26.5%; 30–44, 15.8%; 45–59,
 7.9%; 60–74, 3.8%; 75 and over, 1.0%.
Population projection: (2010) 20,993,000; (2020) 28,405,000.
Doubling time: 23 years.
Ethnic composition (2000): Malagasy 95.9%, of which Merina 24.0%, Betsi-
 misaraka 13.4%, Betsileo 11.3%, Tsimihety 7.0%, Sakalava 5.9%; Makua
 1.1%; French 0.6%; Comorian 0.5%; Reunionese 0.4%; other 1.5%.
Religious affiliation (2000): Christian 49.5%, of which Protestant 22.7%,
 Roman Catholic 20.3%; traditional beliefs 48.0; Muslim 1.9%; other 0.6%.
Major cities (1993): Antananarivo 1,103,304; Toamasina 137,782; Antsirabe
 126,062; Fianarantsoa 109,248; Mahajanga 106,780.

Vital statistics

Birth rate per 1,000 population (2000): 42.9 (world avg. 22.5).
Death rate per 1,000 population (2000): 12.7 (world avg. 9.0).
Natural increase rate per 1,000 population (2000): 30.2 (world avg. 13.5).
Total fertility rate (avg. births per childbearing woman; 2000): 5.8.
Life expectancy at birth (2000): male 52.7 years; female 57.3 years.
Major causes of death per 100,000 population: n.a.; however, major causes of
 death in the 1990s included maternal and perinatal diseases, malaria, infec-
 tious and parasitic diseases, malnutrition, diarrhea, and respiratory diseases.

National economy

Budget (1999). Revenue: FMG 2,667,000,000,000 (taxes 96.7%, of which duties
 on trade 55.5%, value-added tax 15.0%, income tax 14.9%; nontax receipts
 3.3%). Expenditures: FMG 3,791,000,000,000 (current expenditure 57.4%, of
 which debt service 13.0%, general administration 10.8%, education 10.3%,
 defense 7.5%, health 4.0%, agriculture 1.5%; capital expenditure 42.6%).
Public debt (external, outstanding; 2000): U.S.$4,295,000,000.
Production (metric tons except as noted). Agriculture, forestry, fishing (2000):
 paddy rice 2,300,000, cassava 2,228,000, sugarcane 2,200,000, sweet potatoes
 476,000, potatoes 293,000, bananas 265,000, mangoes 206,000, corn (maize)
 155,000, taro 155,000, oranges 85,000, coconuts 85,000, dry beans 84,000, coffee 65,000, pineapples 52,000, peanuts (groundnuts) 35,000, seed cotton
 32,000; livestock (number of live animals) 10,364,000 cattle, 1,370,000 goats,
 900,000 pigs, 800,000 sheep, 20,000,000 chickens; roundwood (2000)
 10,359,000 cu m; fish catch (1999) 141,057. Mining and quarrying (2000):
 chromite ore 97,200; graphite 15,200; mica 800; gold 290 troy oz[3]; sapphires
 (value of exports in U.S.$'000,000; 1999) 12.5. Manufacturing (1998): refined
 sugar 79,775; cement 44,327; soap 14,513; cigarettes 3,303; beer 207,400 hectolitres; fuel oil 217,800 cu m; gas oil 110,800 cu m; kerosene 75,200 cu m;
 gasoline 92,700 cu m, shoes 511,000 pairs. Energy production (consumption):
 electricity (kW-hr; 1998) 642,000,000 (642,000,000); coal (metric tons; 1997)
 none (14,000); crude petroleum (barrels; 1997) none (1,539,000); petroleum
 products (metric tons; 1997) 193,000 (361,000); natural gas, none (n.a.).
Population economically active (1993): total 5,914,000; activity rate of total
 population 48.9% (participation rates [1995]: over age 10, 59.4%; female
 38.4%; unemployed, n.a.).

Price and earnings indexes (1995 = 100)

	1995	1996	1997	1998	1999	2000	2001
Consumer price index[4]	100.0	119.8	125.1	132.9	146.1	163.7	175.0
Annual earnings index	...	...	...	...	...	...	...

Gross national product (2000): U.S.$3,869,000,000 (U.S.$250 per capita).

Structure of gross domestic product and labour force

	1999 in value FMG '000,000[5]	1999 % of total value[5]	1993 labour force	1993 % of labour force
Agriculture	6,366.1	30.0	5,100,000	86.2
Manufacturing	2,916.7	13.8	86,000	1.5
Mining				
Public utilities	355.0	1.7	46,000	0.8
Construction				
Transp. and commun.	4,034.7	19.0	42,000	0.7
Trade	2,624.2	12.4	149,000	2.5
Finance	6	6		
Services	3,948.5[6]	18.6[6]	243,000	4.1
Pub. admin., defense	1,266.0	6.0	208,000	3.5
Other	−308[7]	−1.5[7]	40,000	0.7
TOTAL	21,202.6	100.0	5,914,000	100.0

Household income and expenditure. Average household size (1993) 4.6[8];
 average annual income per household: n.a.: expenditure (1983)[4, 9]: food
 60.4%, fuel and light 9.1%, clothing and footwear 8.6%, household goods
 and utensils 2.4%.
Land use (1994): forest 39.9%; pasture 41.3%; agriculture 5.3%; other 13.5%.
Tourism (2000): receipts from visitors U.S.$119,000,000; expenditures by
 nationals abroad U.S.$114,000,000.

Foreign trade

Balance of trade

	1994	1995	1996	1997	1998	1999
FMG '000,000,000	−161.9	−764.5	−840.4	−1,253.1	−1,480.3	−992.9
% of total	6.1%	19.6%	25.7%	35.5%	36.1%	26.4%

Imports (1998): FMG 2,748,989,000,000 (chemical products 14.9%; food 14.1%;
 minerals 11.2%, of which crude petroleum 7.1%; machinery and equipment
 9.3%). *Major import sources* (1999): France 24.1%; Iran 7.1%; Japan 6.2%;
 South Africa 6.0%; U.S. 4.0%.
Exports (1998): FMG 1,273,787,000,000 (coffee 17.2%, cotton fabrics 14.1%,
 minerals 11.3%, shrimp 6.0%, cloves and clove oil 3.9%, vanilla 3.0%).
Major export destinations (1998): France 39.4%; Mauritius 6.8%; U.S. 5.5%;
 Germany 4.5%; Italy 3.7%.

Transport and communications

Transport. Railroads: route length (1998) 680 mi, 1,095 km; passenger-mi
 21,748,000, passenger-km 35,000,000; short ton-mi cargo 44,117,000, metric
 ton-km cargo 71,000,000. Roads (1996): total length 30,967 mi, 49,837 km
 (paved 17%). Vehicles (1996): passenger cars 62,000; trucks and buses 16,460.
 Air transport (1998): passenger-mi 519,000,000, passenger-km 836,000,000;
 short ton-mi cargo 20,230,000, metric ton-km cargo 29,533,000; airports
 (1994) with scheduled flights 44.

Communications

Medium	date	unit	number	units per 1,000 persons
Daily newspapers	1996	circulation	66,000	4.6
Radio	1997	receivers	3,050,000	209
Television	1998	receivers	340,000	22
Telephones	2001	main lines	54,100	4.7
Cellular telephones	2001	subscribers	147,500	9.0
Personal computers	2001	users	40,000	2.4
Internet	2001	users	35,000	2.1

Education and health

Educational attainment: n.a. *Literacy* (1995): percentage of total population
 age 15 and over literate 45.7%; males literate 59.8%; females literate 32.0%.

Education (1995–96)

	schools	teachers	students	student/ teacher ratio
Primary (age 6–13)	13,325	44,145	1,638,187	37.1
Secondary (age 14–18)	1,142[10]	16,795	302,036	18.0
Voc., teacher tr.	61[11]	1,150	8,479	7.3
Higher	5[10]	921	18,458	20.0

Health: physicians (1996) 1,470 (1 per 9,351 persons); hospital beds (1989)
 10,900 (1 per 1,029 persons); infant mortality rate (2000) 87.0.
Food (2000): daily per capita caloric intake 2,007 (vegetable products 90%,
 animal products 10%); 88% of FAO recommended minimum requirement.

Military

Total active duty personnel (2001): 13,500 (army 92.6%, navy 3.7%, air force
 3.7%). *Military expenditure as percentage of GNP* (1999): 1.2% (world 2.4%);
 per capita expenditure U.S.$3.

---

[1]Each of the six autonomous provinces is adopting its own statutory laws per article 2
of the 1998 constitution. [2]The 1998 constitution identifies Malagasy as the "national"
language, although neither Malagasy nor French, the languages of the two official texts
of the constitution, is itself "official." [3]Official figure; figure for smuggled artisanal production in 2000 was estimated to be more than 60,000 troy oz. [4]Antananarivo only. [5]At
factor cost. [6]Services includes Finance. [7]Less imputed bank charges. [8]Malagasy households only. [9]Weights of consumer price index components; excludes housing. [10]1988–89.
[11]1987–88.

Internet resources for further information:
• **Madagascar Census Atlas**
  http://www.ons.dz/unfpa/pmappl/madagasc.htm

Malawi

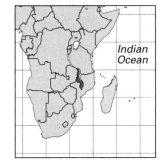

Indian
Ocean

Official name: Republic of Malawi.
Form of government: multiparty republic with one legislative house (National Assembly [192]).
Head of state and government: President.
Capital: Lilongwe[1].
Official language: none.
Official religion: none.
Monetary unit: 1 Malawi kwacha (MK) = 100 tambala; valuation (Sept. 23, 2002) 1 U.S.$ = MK 79.83; 1 £ = MK 124.06.

Area and population

Regions Districts	Capitals	area sq mi	area sq km	population 1998 census
Central	Lilongwe	13,742	35,592	4,066,340
Dedza	Dedza	1,399	3,624	486,682
Dowa	Dowa	1,174	3,041	411,387
Kasungu	Kasungu	3,042	7,878	480,659
Lilongwe	Lilongwe	2,378	6,159	1,346,360
Mchinji	Mchinji	1,296	3,356	324,941
Nkhotakota	Nkhotakota	1,644	4,259	229,460
Ntcheu	Ntcheu	1,322	3,424	370,757
Ntchisi	Ntchisi	639	1,655	167,880
Salima	Salima	848	2,196	248,214
Northern	Mzuzu	10,398	26,931	1,233,560
Chitipa	Chitipa	1,656	4,288	126,799
Karonga	Karonga	1,295	3,355	194,572
Likoma	Likoma	7	18	8,074
Mzimba	Mzimba	4,027	10,430	610,994
Nkhata Bay	Nkhata Bay	1,572	4,071	164,761
Rumphi	Rumphi	1,841	4,769	128,360
Southern	Blantyre	12,260	31,753	4,633,968
Balaka	Balaka	847	2,193	253,098
Blantyre	Blantyre	777	2,012	809,397
Chikwawa	Chikwawa	1,836	4,755	356,682
Chiradzulu	Chiradzulu	296	767	236,050
Machinga	Machinga	1,456	3,771	369,614
Mangochi	Mangochi	2,422	6,273	610,239
Mulanje	Mulanje	794	2,056	428,322
Mwanza	Mwanza	886	2,295	138,015
Nsanje	Nsanje	750	1,942	194,924
Phalombe	Phalombe	538	1,394	231,990
Thyolo	Thyolo	662	1,715	458,976
Zomba	Zomba	996	2,580	546,661
TOTAL LAND AREA		36,400	94,276	
INLAND WATER		9,347	24,208	
TOTAL		45,747	118,484	9,933,868

Demography

Population (2002): 10,520,000.
Density (2002)[2]: persons per sq mi 289.0, persons per sq km 111.6.
Urban-rural (2002): urban 15.1%; rural 84.9%.
Sex distribution (2001): male 49.39%; female 50.61%.
Age breakdown (2001): under 15, 44.4%; 15–29, 30.4%; 30–44, 13.5%; 45–59, 7.2%; 60–74, 3.7%; 75 and over, 0.8%.
Population projection: (2010) 11,480,000; (2020) 12,169,000.
Ethnic composition (2000): Chewa 34.7%; Maravi 12.2%; Ngoni 9.0%; Yao 7.9%; Tumbuka 7.9%; Lomwe 7.7%; Ngonde 3.5%; other 17.1%.
Religious affiliation (1995): Christian 50.3%, of which Protestant 20.5%, Roman Catholic 18.0%; Muslim 20.0%; traditional beliefs 10.0%; other 19.7%.
Major cities (1998): Blantyre 478,155; Lilongwe 435,964; Mzuzu 87,030.

Vital statistics

Birth rate per 1,000 population (2001): 37.8 (world avg. 21.2).
Death rate per 1,000 population (2001): 22.8 (world avg. 8.9).
Natural increase rate per 1,000 population (2001): 15.0 (world avg. 12.3).
Total fertility rate (avg. births per childbearing woman; 2001): 5.2.
Life expectancy at birth (2001): male 36.6 years; female 37.6 years.
Major causes of death per 100,000 population (1986)[3]: infectious and parasitic diseases 711, of which malaria 270, diarrheal diseases 148, measles 128; malnutrition 267; diseases of the respiratory system 265.

National economy

Budget (2000–01). Revenue: MK 31,233,000,000 (tax revenue 61.7%, of which income and profit tax 28.0%, sales tax 26.2%, import tax 7.6%; grants 33.1%; nontax revenue 5.2%). Expenditures: MK 37,303,000,000 (administration 33.4%; education 11.6%; social security 9.1%; health 6.1%).
Public debt (external, outstanding; 2000): U.S.$2,555,000,000.
Production (metric tons except as noted). Agriculture (2001): corn (maize) 2,500,000, potatoes 2,000,000, sugarcane 1,900,000, cassava 900,000, plantains 200,000, peanuts (groundnuts) 125,000, tobacco 100,000, bananas 93,000; livestock (number of live animals) 1,450,000 goats, 750,000 cattle, 250,000 pigs, 110,000 sheep; roundwood (2000) 9,964,000 cu m; fish catch (1999) 45,982. Mining and quarrying (1999): gemstones account for 95% of all mineral exports. Manufacturing (value added in MK '000,000; 1998): beverages 793; food products 571; chemicals 505, of which industrial 245; fabricated metal products 278. Construction (value in MK; 1994): 41,700,000[4]. Energy production (consumption): electricity (kW-hr; 1997) 878,000,000 (878,000,000); coal (metric tons; 1999) 43,800 (43,800); petroleum products (metric tons; 1997) none (199,000).
Land use (1994): forested 39.3%; meadows and pastures 19.6%; agricultural and under permanent cultivation 18.1%; other 23.0%.

Population economically active (1998): total 4,509,290; activity rate 45.4% (participation rates: age 10 and over 66.9%; female 50.2%; unemployed 1.1%).

Price and earnings indexes (1995 = 100)

	1994	1995	1996	1997	1998	1999	2000
Consumer price index	54.5	100.0	137.6	150.2	194.9	282.4	365.6
Earnings index	...	...	...	...	...	...	...

Gross national product (2000): U.S.$1,744,000,000 (U.S.$170 per capita).

Structure of gross domestic product and labour force

	2000 in value MK '000,000[5]	2000 % of total value[5]	1998 labour force	1998 % of labour force
Agriculture	5,210	39.2	3,765,827	83.6
Mining	188	1.4	2,499	0.1
Manufacturing	1,705	12.8	118,483	2.6
Construction	288	2.2	73,402	1.6
Public utilities	189	1.4	7,319	0.2
Transp. and commun.	552	4.2	32,623	0.7
Trade	2,760	20.8	257,389	5.7
Finance	1,242	9.3	13,957	0.3
Public administration	1,282	9.6	101,433	2.2
Services	271	2.0	85,996	1.9
Other	–387[6]	–2.9[6]	50,362[7]	1.1[7]
TOTAL	13,300	100.0	4,509,290	100.0

Household income and expenditure. Average household size (1998) 4.3; income per household: n.a.; sources of income: n.a.; expenditure (1990)[8]: food 55.5%, clothing and footwear 11.7%, housing 9.6%, household goods 8.4%.
Tourism: receipts (2000) U.S.$27,000,000; expenditures (1994) U.S.$15,000,000.

Foreign trade

Balance of trade (current prices)

	1996	1997	1998	1999	2000	2001
U.S.$'000,000	–140.5	–244.0	–40.7	–226.3	–157.7	–175.4
% of total	13.5%	18.4%	3.6%	20.2%	16.3%	17.7%

Imports (2001): U.S.$582,200,000 (1995: machinery 14.6%, transport equipment 13.0%, petroleum products 10.6%, food 10.6%, pharmaceutical products 7.9%, fertilizers 7.5%, textiles 5.1%). *Major import sources:* South Africa 39.7%; Zimbabwe 16.0%; Zambia 10.9%; U.S. 2.6%.
Exports (2001): U.S.$406,800,000 (tobacco 58.0%, sugar 11.3%, tea 11.2%, cotton 1.3%). *Major export destinations:* South Africa 19.1%; U.S. 15.4%; Germany 11.2%; Japan 7.6%; The Netherlands 5.4%; U.K. 3.9%; France 2.3%.

Transport and communications

Transport. Railroads (1995–96): route length 495 mi, 797 km; passenger-km 18,048,000; metric ton-km cargo 43,431,000. Roads (1998): total length 10,222 mi, 16,451 km (paved 19%). Vehicles (1996): passenger cars 27,000; trucks and buses 29,700. Air transport (2001)[9]: passenger-km 241,000,000; metric ton-km cargo 798,000; airports (1998) 5.

Communications

Medium	date	unit	number	units per 1,000 persons
Daily newspapers	1996	circulation	22,000[10]	2.3[10]
Radio	1997	receivers	2,600,000	258
Television	1999	receivers	27,000	2.5
Telephones	2001	main lines	54,100	4.7
Cellular telephones	2001	subscribers	55,700	4.8
Personal computers	2001	units	13,000	1.1
Internet	2001	users	20,000	1.7

Education and health

Educational attainment (1987). Percentage of population age 25 and over having: no formal education 55.0%; primary education 39.8%; secondary and higher 5.2%. *Literacy* (1998): total population age 15 and over literate 58.2%; males literate 73.2%; females literate 44.1%.

Education (1995–96)

	schools	teachers	students	student/teacher ratio
Primary (age 6–13)	3,706	49,138	2,887,107	58.8
Secondary (age 14–18)	94[11]	2,948	139,386	47.3
Teacher tr., voc.	13[11]	224	2,525	11.3
Higher	6[12]	329	3,872	11.8

Health: physicians (1989) 186 (1 per 47,634 persons); hospital beds (1987) 12,617 (1 per 627 persons); infant mortality rate (2001) 121.0.
Food (2000): daily per capita caloric intake 2,181 (vegetable products 98%, animal products 2%); 94% of FAO recommended minimum requirement.

Military

Total active duty personnel (2001): 5,000 (army 100%; navy, none; air force, none). *Military expenditure as percentage of GNP* (1999): 0.6% (world 2.4%); per capita expenditure U.S.$1.

[1]Judiciary meets in Blantyre. [2]Based on land area. [3]Estimates based on reported inpatient deaths in hospitals, constituting an estimated 8% of total deaths. [4]Cities of Blantyre, Lilongwe, and Mzuzu only. [5]At constant prices of 1994. [6]Less imputed bank service charges. [7]Unemployed. [8]Weights of consumer price index components, cities of Blantyre and Lilongwe only. [9]Air Malawi only. [10]Circulation for one newspaper only. [11]1989–90. [12]Universities only.

Internet resources for further information:
• National Statistical Office of Malawi http://www.nso.malawi.net

Malaysia

Official name: Malaysia.
Form of government: federal
  constitutional monarchy with two
  legislative houses (Senate [70[1]];
  House of Representatives [193]).
Chief of state: Yang di-Pertuan Agong
  (Paramount Ruler).
Head of government: Prime Minister.
Capital: Kuala Lumpur[2].
Official language: Malay.
Official religion: Islam.
Monetary unit: 1 ringgit, or Malaysian
  dollar (RM) = 100 cents; valuation[3]
  (Sept. 23, 2002) 1 U.S.\$ = RM 3.80;
  1 £ = RM 5.91.

Area and population		area		population
Regions				2000
States	Capitals	sq mi	sq km	census
East Malaysia				
Sabah	Kota Kinabalu	28,424	73,619	2,603,485
Sarawak	Kuching	48,050	124,450	2,071,506
West Malaysia				
(Peninsular Malaysia)				
Johor	Johor Baharu	7,331	18,987	2,740,625
Kedah	Alor Setar	3,639	9,425	1,649,756
Kelantan	Kota Baharu	5,801	15,024	1,313,014
Melaka	Melaka	638	1,652	635,791
Negeri Sembilan	Seremban	2,565	6,644	859,924
Pahang	Kuantan	13,886	35,965	1,288,376
Perak	Ipoh	8,110	21,005	2,051,236
Perlis	Kangar	307	795	204,450
Pulau Pinang	George Town	398	1,031	1,313,449
Selangor	Shah Alam	3,054	7,910	4,188,876[4]
Terengganu	Kuala Terengganu	5,002	12,955	898,825
Federal Territories				
Kuala Lumpur	—	94	243	1,379,310
Labuan	—	36	92	76,067
Putrajaya	—	19	50	4
TOTAL		127,355	329,847	23,274,690

Demography

Population (2002): 24,370,000.
Density (2002): persons per sq mi 191.4, persons per sq km 73.9.
Urban-rural (2002): urban 59.0%; rural 41.0%.
Sex distribution (2000[5]): male 50.45%; female 49.55%.
Age breakdown (1999): under 15, 33.5%; 15–29, 28.2%; 30–44, 21.0%; 45–59,
  11.3%; 60–74, 4.9%; 75 and over, 1.1%.
Population projection: (2010) 27,709,000; (2020) 31,378,000.
Doubling time: 37 years.
Ethnic composition (2000): Malay and other indigenous 61.3%; Chinese 24.5%;
  Indian 7.2%; other nonindigenous 1.1%; noncitizen 5.9%.
Religious affiliation (2000): Muslim 60.4%; Buddhist 19.2%; Christian 9.1%;
  Hindu 6.3%; Chinese folk religionist 2.6%; other 2.4%.
Major cities (2000[5]): Kuala Lumpur 1,297,526; Ipoh 566,211; Kelang 563,173;
  Petaling Jaya 438,084; Johor Baharu 384,613.

Vital statistics

Birth rate per 1,000 population (2002): 23.2 (world avg. 21.2).
Death rate per 1,000 population (2002): 4.4 (world avg. 8.9).
Natural increase rate per 1,000 population (2002): 18.8 (world avg. 12.3).
Total fertility rate (avg. births per childbearing woman; 2000): 3.1.
Life expectancy at birth (2002): male 70.4 years; female 75.3 years.
Major causes of death per 100,000 population (1997): diseases of the circula-
  tory system 59.7; accidents and violence 34.8; malignant neoplasms 22.3;
  infectious and parasitic diseases 18.6; respiratory diseases 10.2.

National economy

Budget (1999). Revenue: RM 59,157,000,000 (income tax 42.5%, taxes on
  goods and services 24.6%, nontax revenue 19.0%, taxes on international
  trade 9.1%). Expenditures: RM 71,429,000,000 (education 21.5%, defense
  and internal security 12.9%, interest payments 11.1%, health 6.2%, transport
  and communications 6.1%, social security 5.7%, agriculture 3.2%).
Tourism (2000): receipts from visitors U.S.\$4,936,000,000; expenditures by
  nationals abroad (1999) U.S.\$1,973,000,000.
Population economically active (1999): total 9,010,000; activity rate 39.7% (participation rates: ages 15–64, 60.6%; female [1997] 34.0%; unemployed 3.0%).

Price index (1995 = 100)							
	1995	1996	1997	1998	1999	2000	2001
Consumer price index	100.0	103.5	106.2	111.8	114.9	116.7	118.3

Production (metric tons except as noted). Agriculture, forestry, fishing (2000):
  palm fruit oil 56,600,000, rice 2,037,000, sugarcane 1,600,000, rubber 768,900,
  bananas 545,000, pineapples 134,000; livestock (number of live animals)
  1,829,000 pigs, 723,000 cattle, 120,000,000 chickens; roundwood 29,461,000 cu
  m; fish catch (1998) 1,153,719. Mining and quarrying (1998): iron ore 316,808;
  bauxite 134,077; copper concentrates 53,001; tin concentrates 5,756.
  Manufacturing (1999): cement 10,104,000; iron and steel bars and rods
  2,261,000; refined sugar 1,226,000; plywood 3,701,000 cu m; radio receivers
  32,957,000 units; automotive tires 24,984,000 units. Energy production (consumption): electricity (kW-hr; 1997) 58,675,000,000 (58,638,000,000); coal
  (metric tons; 2001) 540,000 ([1997] 2,636,000); crude petroleum (barrels;
  2001) 247,000,000[6] ([1997] 140,000,000); petroleum products (metric tons;

1997) 15,395,000 (19,655,000); natural gas (cu m; 2001) 46,378,000,000
  ([1997] 21,110,000,000).
Gross national product (2000): U.S.\$78,727,000,000 (U.S.\$3,380 per capita).

Structure of gross domestic product and labour force				
	1999			
	in value RM '000,000[7]	% of total value	labour force	% of labour force
Agriculture	17,998	9.3	1,389,000	15.4
Mining	13,973	7.3	42,000	0.5
Manufacturing	57,760	30.0	2,379,000	26.4
Construction	6,922	3.6	804,000	8.9
Public utilities	6,631	3.5	72,000	0.8
Transp. and commun.	15,592	8.1	442,000	4.9
Trade	29,154	15.1	1,449,000	16.1
Finance	23,753	12.3	420,000	4.7
Pub. admin., defense	14,195	7.4	875,000	9.7
Services	15,251	7.9	} 1,138,000	12.6
Other	−8,720[8]	−4.5[8]		
TOTAL	192,509	100.0	9,010,000	100.0

Public debt (external, outstanding; 2000): U.S.\$19,090,000,000.
Household income and expenditure. Average household size (2000) 4.5; annual income per household (1997) RM 31,280 (U.S.\$11,120); sources of income:
  n.a.; expenditure (1983): food 28.7%, transportation 20.9%, recreation and
  education 11.0%, housing 10.2%, household durable goods 7.7%.

Foreign trade[9]

Balance of trade (current prices)						
	1995	1996	1997	1998	1999	2000
U.S.\$'000,000	−103	+3,848	+3,510	+17,505	+22,644	+20,854
% of total	0.1%	2.6%	2.3%	13.9%	15.6%	11.8%

Imports (1998): RM 228,309,000,000 (machinery and transport equipment
  63.0%, basic manufactures 11.1%, chemicals 7.1%, food 4.6%, mineral fuels
  3.1%). *Major import sources:* Japan 20.8%; U.S. 17.4%; Singapore 14.0%;
  Taiwan 5.3%; South Korea 5.2%; Thailand 3.8%.
Exports (1998): RM 286,756,000,000 (machinery and transport equipment
  59.2%, basic manufactures 8.3%, animal and vegetable oils 7.5%, mineral
  fuels 6.2%, chemicals 3.5%, inedible crude materials 3.3%). *Major export destinations:* U.S. 21.9%; Singapore 16.5%; Japan 11.6%; The Netherlands 5.1%;
  Taiwan 4.5%; Hong Kong 4.2%; United Kingdom 3.8%.

Transport and communications

Transport. Railroads (1999): route length 2,227 km; passenger-km 1,332,000,-
  000[10]; metric ton-km cargo 912,000,000[10]. Roads (1998): total length 66,437
  km (paved 76%). Vehicles (1998): passenger cars 3,517,484; trucks and buses
  644,792. Air transport (1999): passenger-km 33,708,000,000; metric ton-km
  cargo 1,424,556,000; airports (1997) 39.

Communications				units per 1,000
Medium	date	unit	number	persons
Daily newspapers	1996	circulation	3,345,000	163
Radio	1997	receivers	9,100,000	434
Television	1999	receivers	3,800,000	174
Telephones	2001	main lines	4,738,000	199
Cellular telephones	2001	subscribers	7,128,000	300
Personal computers	2001	units	3,000,000	126
Internet	2001	users	5,700,000	239

Education and health

Educational attainment (1996). Percentage of population age 25 and over having: no formal schooling 16.7%; primary education 33.7%; secondary 42.8%;
  higher 6.8%. *Literacy* (1995): total population age 15 and over literate 83.5%;
  males literate 89.1%; females literate 78.1%.

Education (1998)				student/
	schools	teachers	students	teacher ratio
Primary (age 7–12)	7,124	154,829	2,872,000	18.5
Secondary (age 13–19)	1,486	97,083	1,866,000	19.2
Voc., teacher tr.	78	5,056	24,000	4.7
Higher	51	15,684[11]	230,000[11]	14.7[11]

Health (1998): physicians 15,016 (1 per 1,402 persons); hospital beds 42,398 (1
  per 497 persons); infant mortality rate per 1,000 live births (2002) 7.9.
Food (2000): daily per capita caloric intake 2,919 (vegetable products 81%,
  animal products 19%); 131% of FAO recommended minimum.

Military

Total active duty personnel (2001): 100,500 (army 79.6%, navy 12.4%, air force
  8.0%). *Military expenditure as percentage of GDP* (1999): 2.3% (world 2.4%);
  per capita expenditure U.S.\$78.

---

[1]Includes 40 appointees of the Paramount Ruler; the remaining 30 are indirectly elected at different times. [2]The transfer to the new federal administrative centre at Putrajaya
will occur between 1999 and 2012. [3]Pegged to the U.S. dollar at RM 3.80 = 1 U.S.\$
on Oct. 6, 2000. [4]Selangor includes population data for Putrajaya. [5]Preliminary.
[6]Production for Sabah and Sarawak only. [7]At constant prices of 1987. [8]Net bank service charges. [9]Import figures are f.o.b. in balance of trade. [10]Peninsular Malaysia and
Singapore. [11]1996.

Internet resources for further information:
• **Department of Statistics http://www.statistics.gov.my**
• **Malaysian Information Services (English) http://penerangan.gov.my**

Maldives

Official name: Divehi Jumhuriyya
  (Republic of Maldives).
Form of government: republic with one
  legislative house (Majlis[1] [42[2, 3]]).
Head of state and government:
  President.
Capital: Male.
Official language: Divehi.
Official religion: Islam.
Monetary unit: 1 Maldivian rufiyaa
  (Rf) = 100 laari; valuation (Sept. 23,
  2002) 1 U.S.$ = Rf 11.77;
  1 £ = Rf 18.29.

Area and population[4]		area		population
				2000
Administrative atolls	**Capitals**	**sq mi**	**sq km**	**census**
North Thiladhunmathi (Haa-Alifu)	Dhidhdhoo	...	...	14,161
South Thiladhunmathi (Haa-Dhaalu)	Nolhivaranfaru	...	...	16,956
North Miladhunmadulu (Shaviyani)	Farukolhu-funadhoo	...	...	11,406
South Miladhunmadulu (Noonu)	Manadhoo	...	...	10,429
North Maalhosmadulu (Raa)	Ugoofaaru	...	...	14,486
South Maalhosmadulu (Baa)	Eydhafushi	...	...	9,612
Faadhippolhu (Lhaviyani)	Naifaru	...	...	9,385
Male (Kaafu)	Thulusdhoo	...	...	13,474
Ari Atoll Uthuru Gofi (Alifu)	Rasdhoo	...	...	5,518
Ari Atoll Dhekunu Gofi (Alifu)	Mahibadhoo	...	...	7,803
Felidhu Atoll (Vaavu)	Felidhoo	...	...	1,753
Mulakatholhu (Meemu)	Muli	...	...	5,084
North Nilandhe Atoll (Faafu)	Magoodhoo	...	...	3,827
South Nilandhe Atoll (Dhaalu)	Kudahuvadhoo	...	...	5,067
Kolhumadulu (Thaa)	Veymandoo	...	...	9,305
Hadhdhunmathi (Laamu)	Hithadhoo	...	...	11,588
North Huvadhu Atoll (Gaafu-Alifu)	Viligili	...	...	8,249
South Huvadhu Atoll (Gaafu-Dhaalu)	Thinadhoo	...	...	11,886
Foammulah (Gnyaviyani)	Foahmulah	...	...	7,528
Addu Atoll (Seenu)	Hithadhoo	...	...	18,515
Capital island				
Male (Maale)		...	...	74,069
TOTAL		115	298	270,101

Demography

Population (2002): 281,000.
Density (2002): persons per sq mi 2,443, persons per sq km 943.0.
Urban-rural (2002): urban 27.0%; rural 73.0%.
Sex distribution (2002): male 50.74%; female 49.26%.
Age breakdown (2002): under 15, 37.7%; 15–29, 30.6%; 30–44, 17.8%; 45–59, 7.6%; 60–74, 5.2%; 75 and over, 1.1%.
Population projection: (2010) 318,000; (2020) 372,000.
Doubling time: 23 years.
Ethnic composition: the majority is principally of Sinhalese and Dravidian extraction; Arab, African, and Negrito influences are also present.
Religious affiliation: virtually 100% Sunnī Muslim.
Major city (2000): Male 74,069.

Vital statistics

Birth rate per 1,000 population (2002): 36.1 (world avg. 21.2).
Death rate per 1,000 population (2002): 6.1 (world avg. 8.9).
Natural increase rate per 1,000 population (2002): 30.0 (world avg. 12.3).
Total fertility rate (avg. births per childbearing woman; 2002): 5.4.
Marriage rate per 1,000 population (2001): 11.6.
Divorce rate per 1,000 population (2001): 5.5.
Life expectancy at birth (2002): male 68.0 years; female 67.0 years.
Major causes of death per 100,000 population (1988): rheumatic fever 106.0; ischemic heart diseases 65.0; bronchitis, emphysema, and asthma 61.0; tetanus 23.5; tuberculosis 13.0; accidents and suicide 10.0.

National economy

Budget (2000). Revenue: Rf 2,548,800,000 (nontax revenue 51.1%, taxation 40.8%, foreign aid 7.9%). Expenditures: Rf 2,819,900,000 (general public services 23.6%, education 17.8%, defense 16.8%, health 10.2%, housing 9.1%, transportation and communications 9.1%).
Public debt (external, outstanding; 2000): U.S.$185,300,000.
Production (metric tons except as noted). Agriculture, forestry, fishing (1999): vegetables and melons 25,300, coconuts 13,000, fruits (excluding melons) 8,850, roots and tubers (including cassava, sweet potatoes, and yams) 7,010; fish catch (2000) 132,427. Mining and quarrying: coral for construction materials. Manufacturing: details, n.a.; however, major industries include boat building and repairing, coir yarn and mat weaving, coconut and fish processing, lacquerwork, garment manufacturing, and handicrafts. Energy production (consumption): electricity (kW-hr; 1997) 66,000,000 (66,000,000); petroleum products (metric tons; 1997) none (99,000).
Tourism (2000): receipts from visitors U.S.$344,000,000; expenditures by nationals abroad U.S.$46,000,000.
Population economically active (1995): total 67,476; activity rate of total population 27.6% (participation rates: ages 15–64, 62.6%; female 27.1%; unemployed [1995] 0.9%).

Price index (1995 = 100)							
	1995	1996	1997	1998	1999	2000	2001
Consumer price index	100.0	106.3	114.3	112.7	116.0	114.7	115.4

Household income and expenditure (1990). Average household size 7.2; annual income per household Rf 2,616 (U.S.$274), sources of income: n.a.; expenditure (1981)[5]: food and beverages 61.8%, housing equipment 17.0%, clothing 8.0%, recreation and education 5.9%, transportation 2.6%, health 2.5%, rent 1.6%.
Gross national product (2000): U.S.$541,000,000 (U.S.$1,960 per capita).

Structure of gross domestic product and labour force				
	2000			
	in value Rf '000[6]	% of total value	labour force	% of labour force
Agriculture[7]	549,200	8.7	11,789	13.4
Mining	35,600	0.6	473	0.5
Manufacturing }	738,900	11.8	11,081	12.6
Public utilities }			1,132	1.3
Construction	166,800	2.6	3,691	4.2
Transp. and commun.	986,100	15.7	7,873	9.0
Trade	2,377,900	37.9	15,606	17.7
Finance	882,900	14.1	1,690	1.9
Pub. admin., defense	773,900	12.3 }	18,089	20.6
Services	136,400	2.2 }		
Other	−369,400	−5.9	16,563	18.8
TOTAL	6,278,300	100.0	87,987	100.0

Land use (1994): forested 3.3%; meadows and pastures 3.3%; agricultural and under permanent cultivation 10.0%; built-on, wasteland, and other 83.4%.

Foreign trade[8]

Balance of trade (current prices)						
	1996	1997	1998	1999	2000	2001
U.S.$'000,000	−206.3	−233.8	−235.3	−290.4	−266.1	−271.8
% of total	63.5%	61.5%	60.7%	69.5%	63.7%	64.1%

Imports (1996): Rf 3,551,289,000 (machinery and transport equipment 27.9%, basic manufactures 23.7%, food and live animals 21.4%, petroleum products 9.1%). *Major import sources:* Singapore 32.0%; India 12.0%; Malaysia 8.5%; Sri Lanka 7.6%; United Kingdom 3.6%; Japan 3.5%.
Exports (1996): Rf 699,190,000 (canned fish 28.0%, yellowfin tuna 20.5%, apparel and clothing 17.4%, dried skipjack tuna 11.0%). *Major export destinations:* United Kingdom 21.7%; Sri Lanka 18.3%; United States 10.2%; Germany 10.8%; Japan 10.6%; Thailand 9.5%.

Transport and communications

Transport. Railroads: none. Roads: total length, n.a. Vehicles (1999): passenger cars 3,037; trucks and buses 1,003. Merchant marine (1992): vessels (100 gross tons and over) 44; total deadweight tonnage 78,994. Air transport (1997): passengers carried 189,000; passenger-km 292,000,000; airports (1997) with scheduled flights 5.

Communications				units per 1,000 persons
Medium	date	unit	number	
Daily newspapers	1996	circulation	5,000	19
Radio	1997	receivers	34,000	129
Television	1999	receivers	10,650	38
Telephones	2001	main lines	27,200	101
Cellular telephones	2001	subscribers	18,400	68
Personal computers	2001	units	6,000	22
Internet	2001	users	10,000	37

Education and health

Educational attainment (1990). Percentage of population age 15 and over having: no standard passed 25.6%; primary standard 37.2%; middle standard 25.9%; secondary standard 6.3%; preuniversity 3.4%; higher 0.4%; not stated 1.2%. *Literacy* (1995): total population age 15 and over literate 93.2%; males literate 93.0%; females literate 93.3%.

Education (1998)				student/
	schools	teachers	students	teacher ratio
Primary (age 6–11)	228	1,992	48,895	24.5
Secondary (age 11–18)	99[9]	291[9]	15,933[10]	12.3[9]
Voc., teacher tr.	10[9]	52[9]	452[10]	8.9[9]
Higher	—	—	—	—

Health (1996): physicians 99 (1 per 1,995 persons); hospital beds 318 (1 per 806 persons); infant mortality rate per 1,000 live births (2002) 38.0.
Food (1999): daily per capita caloric intake 2,298 (vegetable products 81%, animal products 19%); (1997) 104% of FAO recommended minimum requirement.

Military

Total active duty personnel: Maldives maintains a single security force numbering about 700–1,000; it performs both army and police functions.

---

[1]Also known or translated as People's Majlis, Citizens' Council, or Citizens' Assembly. [2]Excludes eight nonelective seats. [3]The new constitution went into effect Jan. 1, 1998. [4]Maldives is divided into 20 administrative atolls corresponding to atoll groups; arrangement shown here is from north to south. Total area excludes 34,634 sq mi (89,702 sq km) of tidal waters. [5]Weights of consumer price index components. [6]At 1995 prices. [7]Primarily fishing. [8]Import figures are f.o.b. in balance of trade and c.i.f. for commodities and trading partners. [9]1986. [10]1992.

Internet resources for further information:
• **Ministry of Planning and National Development**
  http://www.planning.gov.mv

Mali

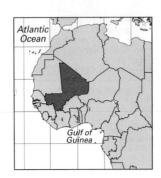

Official name: République du Mali (Republic of Mali).
Form of government: multiparty republic with one legislative house (National Assembly [147]).
Chief of state: President.
Head of government: Prime Minister.
Capital: Bamako.
Official language: French.
Official religion: none.
Monetary unit: 1 CFA franc (CFAF) = 100 centimes; valuation (Sept. 23, 2002) 1 U.S.$ = CFAF 667.00; 1 £ = CFAF 1,037[1].

Area and population

Regions	Capitals	area sq mi	area sq km	population 1998 census
Gao	Gao	65,858	170,572	495,178
Kayes	Kayes	46,233	119,743	1,424,657
Kidal	Kidal	58,467	151,430	65,524
Koulikoro	Koulikoro	37,007	95,848	1,620,811
Mopti	Mopti	30,509	79,017	1,405,370
Ségou	Ségou	25,028	64,821	1,652,594
Sikasso	Sikasso	27,135	70,280	1,839,747
Tombouctou	Timbuktu (Tombouctou)	191,743	496,611	496,312
District				
Bamako	Bamako	97	252	1,178,977
TOTAL		482,077	1,248,574	10,179,170[2]

Demography

Population (2002): 11,340,000.
Density (2002): persons per sq mi 23.5, persons per sq km 9.1.
Urban-rural (1998): urban 28.7%; rural 71.3%.
Sex distribution (2001): male 48.9%; female 51.1%.
Age breakdown (2001): under 15, 47.2%; 15–29, 26.8%; 30–44, 13.3%; 45–59, 7.9%; 60–74, 4.0%; 75 and over, 0.8%.
Population projection: (2010) 14,349,000; (2020) 18,984,000.
Doubling time: 23 years.
Ethnic composition (2000): Bambara 30.6%; Senufo 10.5%; Fula Macina (Niafunke) 9.6%; Soninke 7.4%; Tuareg 7.0%; Maninka 6.6%; Songhai 6.3%; Dogon 4.3%; Bobo 3.5%; other 14.2%.
Religious affiliation (2000): Muslim 82%; traditional beliefs 16%; Christian 2%.
Major cities (1998): Bamako 1,016,167; Sikasso 113,803; Ségou 90,898; Mopti (1996) 86,355; Gao (1996) 62,667.

Vital statistics

Birth rate per 1,000 population (2001): 48.8 (world avg. 21.2).
Death rate per 1,000 population (2001): 18.7 (world avg. 8.9).
Natural increase rate per 1,000 population (2001): 30.1 (world avg. 12.3).
Total fertility rate (avg. births per childbearing woman; 2001): 6.8.
Life expectancy at birth (2001): male 45.8 years; female 48.2 years.
Major causes of death per 100,000 population: n.a.; morbidity ([notified cases of illness] by cause as a percentage of all reported infectious disease; 1985): malaria 62.1%; measles 10.3%; amebiasis 10.3%; syphilis and gonococcal infections 6.0%; influenza 4.9%.

National economy

Budget (1999). Revenue: CFAF 356,000,000,000 (tax revenue 66.1%, grants 23.4%, nontax revenue 10.5%). Expenditures: CFAF 417,400,000,000 (current expenditure 46.3%, of which wages and salaries 15.6%, education 10.3%, defense 8.3%, interest on public debt 3.6%, health 2.8%; capital expenditure 53.7%).
Public debt (external, outstanding; 2000): U.S.$2,645,000,000.
Tourism (2000): receipts from visitors U.S.$71,000,000; expenditures by nationals abroad U.S.$41,000,000.
Population economically active (1997): total 5,042,000; activity rate of total population 51.5% (participation rates [1987] ages 15–64, 67.4%; female 46.3%; unemployed 0.8%).

Price and earnings indexes (1995 = 100)

	1995	1996	1997	1998	1999	2000	2001
Consumer price index	100.0	106.8	106.4	110.7	109.4	108.6	114.3
Hourly earnings index[3]	100.0	103.2	106.0	109.0[4]	...	...	...

Production (metric tons except as noted). Agriculture, forestry, fishing (2001): millet 802,500, rice 745,100, sorghum 591,700, seed cotton 480,000, corn (maize) 322,700, sugarcane 300,000, peanuts (groundnuts) 140,000, sweet potatoes 15,000; livestock (number of live animals) 14,550,000 goats and sheep, 6,200,000 cattle, 652,000 asses, 292,000 camels, 136,000 horses, 65,000 pigs; roundwood (2000) 6,596,900 cu m; fish catch (1999) 98,776. Mining and quarrying (1999): limestone 20,000[5]; phosphate 3,000[5]; iron oxide 708[5]; gypsum 500[5]; gold 23,689 kg; silver 250 kg. Manufacturing (1999): sugar 27,000; cement 20,000; soap 10,097[6]; soft drinks 68,609 hectolitres[6]; beer 41,690 hectolitres[6]; shoes 111,000 pairs[6]; cigarettes 114,928 cartons[6]. Construction: n.a. Energy production (consumption): electricity (kW-hr; 1997) 391,000,000 (391,000,000); coal, none (n.a.); crude petroleum, none (n.a.); petroleum products (metric tons; 1997) none (154,000); natural gas, none (n.a.).
Gross national product (2000): U.S.$2,548,000,000 (U.S.$240 per capita).

Structure of gross domestic product and labour force

	1999 in value CFAF '000,000	1999 % of total value	1987 labour force	1987 % of labour force
Agriculture	393,100	43.8	2,802,722	82.2
Mining	51,400	5.8	1,524	—
Manufacturing	71,500	8.0	186,243	5.5
Construction	} 42,400	4.7	13,065	0.4
Public utilities			3,157	0.1
Transp. and commun.	48,100	5.4	6,174	0.2
Trade	} 133,700	14.9	158,892	4.7
Finance			320	—
Pub. admin., defense	53,700	6.0	158,704	4.6
Services	51,400	5.7	...	...
Other	51,400[7]	5.7[7]	78,470	2.3
TOTAL	896,700	100.0	3,409,271	100.0

Household income and expenditure. Average household size (1997) 5.0; average annual income per household: n.a.; sources of income: n.a.; expenditure (1986–87)[8]: food 54.6%, clothing 14.2%, transportation and communications 11.9%, housing and energy 8.7%, household durable goods 4.2%.
Land use (1994): forested 5.7%; meadows and pastures 24.6%; forest 9.7%; agricultural and under permanent cultivation 2.1%; other 63.6%.

Foreign trade[9]

Balance of trade (current prices)

	1996	1997	1998	1999	2000	2001
CFAF '000,000,000	−173.3	−110.5	−117.5	−142.0	−33.4	+60.9
% of total	28.2%	14.4%	15.1%	16.9%	4.1%	5.9%

Imports (1999): CFAF 490,600,000,000 (machinery, appliances, and transport equipment 31.1%; petroleum products 14.3%; food products 13.9%; construction products 10.5%; chemicals 10.2%). *Major import sources:* African countries 49.9%, of which Côte d'Ivoire 18.9%; France 18.7%; China 4.4%; Germany 2.7%; Belgium-Luxembourg 2.4%.
Exports (1999): CFAF 348,600,000,000 (raw cotton and cotton products 43.9%; gold 40.8%; live animals 9.4%). *Major export destinations:* Western Europe, U.S., and other non-Asian industrial countries 52.7%; Asian countries 33.9%; African countries 8.4%.

Transport and communications

Transport. Railroads (1996): route length 453 mi, 729 km; passenger-mi 117,000,000, passenger-km 189,000,000; short ton-mi cargo 175,000,000, metric ton-km cargo 256,000,000. Roads (1996): total length 9,383 mi, 15,100 km (paved 12%). Vehicles (1996): passenger cars 26,190; trucks and buses 18,240. Merchant marine: vessels (100 gross tons and over) none. Air transport (1997)[10]: passenger-mi 150,400,000, passenger-km 242,000,000; short ton-mi cargo 23,600,000, metric ton-km cargo 38,000,000; airports (1999) 9.

Communications

Medium	date	unit	number	units per 1,000 persons
Daily newspapers	1997	circulation	45,000	4.6
Radio	1997	receivers	1,600,000	163
Television	1999	receivers	130,000	12
Telephones	2001	main lines	49,900	4.3
Cellular phones	2001	subscribers	45,300	3.9
Personal computers	2001	units	14,000	1.2
Internet	2001	users	30,000	2.6

Education and health

Educational attainment (1987). Percentage of population age 6 and over having: no formal schooling 86.0%; primary education 12.5%; secondary 1.2%; postsecondary and higher 0.3%. *Literacy* (1995): Percentage of total population age 15 and over literate 1,760,000 (31.0%); males literate 1,084,000 (39.4%); females literate 676,000 (23.1%).

Education (1997–98)

	schools	teachers	students	student/ teacher ratio
Primary (age 6–14)	2,511	10,853	862,875	79.5
Secondary (age 15–17)	307[11]	4,549[12]	166,372	...
Vocational	...	21,737	7,200	3.0
Higher	7	796[13]	13,847	17.4

Health: physicians (1993) 483 (1 per 18,376 persons); hospital beds (1987) 3,430 (1 per 2,253 persons); infant mortality rate per 1,000 live births (2001) 121.4.
Food (1999): daily per capita caloric intake 2,314 (vegetable products 91%, animal products 9%); 90% of FAO recommended minimum requirement.

Military

Total active duty personnel (2000): 7,350 (army 100.0%). *Military expenditure as percentage of GNP* (1999): 2.3% (world 2.4%); per capita expenditure U.S.$6.

---

[1]Formerly pegged to the French franc, and since Jan. 1, 2002, to the euro at the rate of €1 = CFAF 655.96. [2]Excludes 772,006 Malians living abroad. [3]Minimum wage for nonagricultural workers. [4]As of November 1. [5]1997. [6]1995. [7]Import taxes. [8]Weights of consumer price index components. [9]Imports are in c.i.f. [10]Represents 1/11 of the traffic of Air Afrique, which is operated by 11 West African states. [11]1991–92. [12]1995–96. [13]1996–97.

Internet resources for further information:
• **Embassy of Mali (Washington, D.C.)**
  http://www.maliembassy-usa.org
• **Investir en Zone Franc** http://www.izf.net/izf/Index.htm

Malta

Official name: Repubblikka ta' Malta (Maltese); Republic of Malta (English).
Form of government: unitary multiparty republic with one legislative house (House of Representatives [65]).
Chief of state: President.
Head of government: Prime Minister.
Capital: Valletta.
Official languages: Maltese; English.
Official religion: Roman Catholicism.
Monetary unit: 1 Maltese lira (Lm) = 100 cents = 1,000 mils; valuation (Sept. 23, 2002) 1 U.S.$ = Lm 0.42; 1 £ = Lm 0.65.

Area and population

Islands/statistical districts[2]	area sq mi	area sq km	population 2001[1] estimate
Comino }	27	70	2,335
Gozo			27,355
Malta	95	246	352,835
Northern District	30	78	46,034
Northern Harbour	12	32	118,059
South Eastern District	20	53	52,407
Southern Harbour	6	15	83,405
Western District	27	69	52,930
TOTAL	122	316[3]	382,525[4]

Demography

Population (2002): 386,000.
Density (2002): persons per sq mi 3,164, persons per sq km 1,222.
Urban-rural (2000): urban 90.5%; rural 9.5%.
Sex distribution (2000): male 49.49%; female 50.51%.
Age breakdown (2000): under 15, 20.3%; 15–29, 21.6%; 30–44, 20.8%; 45–59, 20.4%; 60–74, 12.0%; 75 and over, 4.9%.
Population projection: (2010) 394,000; (2020) 400,000.
Ethnic composition (by nationality; 2000): Maltese 93.8%; British 2.1%; Arab 2.0%; other 2.1%.
Religious affiliation (1996): Roman Catholic 93.4%; other 6.6%.
Major cities (1999[1]): Birkirkara 21,350; Qormi 17,881; Sliema 12,308; Hamrun 11,014; Valletta 7,100.

Vital statistics

Birth rate per 1,000 population (2001): 10.0 (world avg. 21.2); (2000) legitimate 89.4%; illegitimate 10.6%.
Death rate per 1,000 population (2001): 7.6 (world avg. 8.9).
Natural increase rate per 1,000 population (2001): 2.4 (world avg. 12.3).
Total fertility rate (avg. births per childbearing woman; 2000): 1.9.
Marriage rate per 1,000 population (1998): 6.3.
Divorce rate per 1,000 population: n.a.
Life expectancy at birth (2002): male 75.8 years; female 81.0 years.
Major causes of death per 100,000 population (1998): diseases of the circulatory system 353.1; malignant neoplasms 191.2; diseases of the respiratory system 79.7; endocrine and metabolic diseases of the blood 33.1; accidents, poisoning, and violence 26.5; diseases of the digestive system 23.6.

National economy

Budget (1999). Revenue: Lm 637,852,000 (direct taxes 42.7%; indirect taxes 32.6%; nontax revenue 23.1%; foreign grants 1.5%). Expenditures: Lm 690,965,000 (recurrent expenditures 84.6%, of which social security 27.2%[5], education 10.4%[5], health 10.0%[5], debt service 4.9%[5], defense 4.2%[5]; capital expenditure 15.4%).
Public debt (2001): U.S.$2,150,800,000.
Production (metric tons except where noted). Agriculture, forestry, fishing (1999): vegetables 58,850 (of which tomatoes 32,800, cabbage 3,500, melons 2,600, garlic 2,000, onions 1,200), potatoes 32,000, grapes 10,000, barley 2,000; livestock (number of live animals; 1999) 69,000 pigs, 21,000 cattle, 16,000 sheep, 9,050 goats; fish catch 979,432. Quarrying (value of production in Lm; 1996): 6,898,000. Manufacturing (value of sales in Lm; 1994–95): machinery and transport equipment 402,993,000; food 103,733,000; textiles and wearing apparel 80,813,000; paper and printing 40,610,000; chemicals 35,151,000. Construction (buildings completed; 1996): residential 3,360[6]; nonresidential 1,859. Energy production (consumption): electricity (kW-hr; 1997) 1,515,000,000 (1,515,-000,000); coal (metric tons; 1997) none (310,000); crude petroleum, none (n.a.); petroleum products (metric tons; 1997) none (344,000).
Population economically active (1998): total 144,824; activity rate of total population 38.4% (participation rates: ages 15–64 [1985] 45.9%; female 27.6%; unemployed 5.1%).

Price and earnings indexes (1995 = 100)

	1995	1996	1997	1998	1999	2000	2001
Consumer price index	100.0	102.5	105.7	108.2	110.5	113.1	116.4
Average weekly earnings	100.0	104.3	...	...	...	...	...

Household income and expenditure. Average household size (1985) 3.3; average annual income per household (1982) Lm 4,736 (U.S.$11,399); sources of income (1993): wages and salaries 63.8%, professional and unincorporated enterprises 19.3%, rents, dividends, and interest 16.9%; expenditure (1993): food and beverages 27.9%, transportation and communications 15.7%, household furnishings and operations 9.5%, recreation, entertainment, and education 7.2%, clothing and footwear 6.9%, housing 5.5%, health 3.3%, tobacco 2.6%.
Tourism (2000): receipts from visitors U.S.$614,000,000; expenditures by nationals abroad U.S.$201,000,000.
Gross domestic product (2000): U.S.$3,559,000,000 (U.S.$9,120 per capita).

Structure of gross domestic product and labour force

	1998 in value Lm '000	1998 % of total value	1998 labour force	1998 % of labour force
Agriculture	32,605	2.7	2,522	1.7
Manufacturing	271,334	22.7 }	33,924	23.4
Mining }			5,440	3.8
Construction }	36,073	3.0		
Public utilities	7	7	2,004	1.4
Transp. and commun.	75,819	6.3	10,199	7.0
Trade	136,096	11.4	24,256[8]	16.7[8]
Finance	96,941	8.1	5,370	3.7
Pub. admin., defense	279,887[7]	23.4[7]	32,151	22.2
Services	134,308	11.2	16,630	11.5
Other	134,869	11.3	12,328[9]	8.5[9]
TOTAL	1,197,932	100.0[3]	144,824	100.0[3]

Land use (1994): agricultural and under permanent cultivation 40.6%; other (infertile clay soil with underlying limestone) 59.4%.

Foreign trade[10]

Balance of trade (current prices)

	1995	1996	1997	1998	1999	2000	2001
Lm '000,000	−362.8	−383.7	−352.5	−335.1	−348.6	−472.1	−303.8
% of total	21.2%	23.5%	21.8%	19.2%	18.0%	18.7%	15.0%

Imports (1999): Lm 1,135,796,000 (machinery and transport equipment 52.3%, manufactured and semimanufactured goods 22.8%, food 8.8%, chemicals 7.3%, mineral fuels 5.2%). *Major import sources:* France 19.1%; Italy 16.7%; U.K. 10.9%; Germany 10.0%; Singapore 9.5%.
Exports (1999): Lm 712,481,000 (machinery and transport equipment 59.8%, other finished manufactured goods 30.5%, food and live animals 0.8%). *Major export destinations:* U.S. 22.0%; Singapore 17.5%; France 16.5%; Germany 13.1%; U.K. 8.9%; Italy 4.4%.

Transport and communications

Transport. Railroads: none. Roads (1997): total length 1,219 mi, 1,961 km (paved 94%). Vehicles (1998): passenger cars 185,247; trucks and buses 49,520. Merchant marine (1992): vessels (100 gross tons and over) 889; total deadweight tonnage 17,073,207. Air transport (1998): passenger-mi 1,172,-982,000, passenger-km 1,887,736,000; short ton-mi cargo 7,689,800; metric ton-km cargo 11,227,000; airports (1999) with scheduled flights 1.

Communications

Medium	date	unit	number	units per 1,000 persons
Daily newspapers	1996	circulation	54,000	145
Radio	1997	receivers	255,000	680
Television	1999	receivers	212,000	549
Telephones	2001	main lines	207,700	530
Cellular telephones	2001	subscribers	138,800	354
Personal computers	2001	units	90,000	230
Internet	2001	users	99,000	253

Education and health

Educational attainment (1967). Percentage of economically active population having: no formal schooling 60.4%; primary education 60.4%; lower secondary 3.4%; upper secondary 17.6%; technical secondary 3.9%; post-secondary and higher 3.9%. *Literacy* (2000): total population age 15 and over literate 279,000 (92.1%); males literate 138,000 (91.4%); females literate 141,000 (92.8%).

Education (1995–96)

	schools	teachers	students	student/teacher ratio
Primary (age 5–10)	111	1,990	35,479	17.8
Secondary (age 11–17)	59	2,679	29,907	20.9
Voc., teacher tr.	22	541	4,539	8.4
Higher[11]	1	470	5,805	12.3

Health (1996): physicians 925 (1 per 403 persons); hospital beds 2,140 (1 per 174 persons); infant mortality rate per 1,000 live births (2001) 4.3.
Food (1999): daily per capita caloric intake 3,482 (vegetable products 72%, animal products 28%); 139% of FAO recommended minimum requirement.

Military

Total active duty personnel (2001): 2,140 (army 100%). *Military expenditure as percentage of GNP* (1999): 0.8% (world 2.4%); per capita expenditure U.S.$73.

---

[1]January 1. [2]Actual local administration in 2001 was based on 68 local councils. [3]Detail does not add to total given because of rounding. [4]Excludes foreign workers and foreign residents (8,890 persons as of Jan. 1, 2001). [5]1997. [6]Dwellings completed. [7]Pub. admin., defense includes Public utilities. [8]Includes hotels and catering. [9]Includes 7,437 unemployed. [10]Import figures are c.i.f. in balance of trade and f.o.b. for commodities and trading partners. [11]1994–95.

Internet resources for further information:
• National Statistics Office http://www.nso.gov.mt

Marshall Islands

Official name: Majōl (Marshallese); Republic of the Marshall Islands (English).
Form of government: unitary republic with two legislative houses (Council of Iroij [12][1]; Nitijela [33]).
Head of state and government: President.
Capital: Majuro.
Official languages: Marshallese (Kajin-Majōl); English.
Official religion: none.
Monetary unit: 1 U.S. dollar (U.S.$) = 100 cents; valuation (Sept. 23, 2002) 1 U.S.$ = £0.64.

Area and population	area		population
Atolls/Islands	sq mi	sq km	1999 census
Ailinglaplap	5.67	14.68	1,959
Ailuk	2.07	5.36	514
Arno	5.00	12.95	2,069
Aur	2.17	5.62	537
Bikini	2.32	6.01	13
Ebon	2.22	5.75	902
Enewetak	2.26	5.85	853
Jabat	0.22	0.57	95
Jaluit	4.38	11.34	1,669
Kili	0.36	0.93	774
Kwajalein	6.33	16.39	10,903
Lae	0.56	1.45	332
Lib	0.36	0.93	147
Likiep	3.96	10.26	527
Majuro	3.75	9.71	23,682
Maloelap	3.75	9.71	856
Mejit	0.72	1.86	416
Mili	6.15	15.93	1,032
Namorik	1.07	2.77	772
Namu	2.42	6.27	903
Rongelap	3.07	7.95	19
Ujae	0.72	1.86	440
Ujelang	0.67	1.74	0
Utrik	0.94	2.43	433
Wotho	1.67	4.32	145
Wotje	3.16	8.18	866
Other atolls	4.10	10.62	0
TOTAL	70.07	181.48[2]	50,840[3]

Demography

Population (2002): 56,600.
Density (2002): persons per sq mi 807.8, persons per sq km 311.9.
Urban-rural (2001): urban 65.4%; rural 34.6%.
Sex distribution (1999): male 51.20%; female 48.80%.
Age breakdown (1999): under 15, 42.9%; 15–29, 28.7%; 30–44, 16.7%; 45–59, 8.2%; 60–74, 2.6%; 75 and over, 0.9%.
Population projection: (2010) 74,000; (2020) 94,000.
Doubling time: 19 years.
Ethnic composition (nationality; 2000): Marshallese 88.5%; U.S. white 6.5%; other Pacific islanders and East Asians 5.0%.
Religious affiliation (1995): Protestant 62.8%; Roman Catholic 7.1%; Mormon 3.1%; Jehovah's Witness 1.0%; other (mostly nonreligious) 26.0%.
Major cities: Majuro (1999) 23,676; Ebeye (1988) 8,324.

Vital statistics

Birth rate per 1,000 population (2000): 41.8 (world avg. 22.5).
Death rate per 1,000 population (2000): 4.9 (world avg. 9.0).
Natural increase rate per 1,000 population (2000): 36.9 (world avg. 13.5).
Total fertility rate (avg. births per childbearing woman; 2000): 6.6.
Life expectancy at birth (2000): male 63.7 years; female 67.4 years.
Major causes of death per 100,000 population (1990–93)[4]: infectious and parasitic diseases 169.9; circulatory diseases 155.1; respiratory diseases 105.1; malignant neoplasms (cancers) 68.4; digestive diseases 63.3; accidents, injuries, and violence 36.7.

National economy

Budget (1997–98). Revenue: U.S.$61,400,000 (U.S. government grants 59.7%, income tax 12.7%, import tax 10.7%, value-added and excise taxes 4.4%, fishing rights 2.9%, fees and charges 2.1%). Expenditures: U.S.$50,900,000 (wages and salaries 33.4%, goods and services 32.4%, capital expenditures 14.3%, interest payments 10.8%, subsidies 7.1%).
Production (metric tons except as noted). Agriculture, forestry, fishing (value of production for household consumption in U.S.$'000; 1999): fish 3,920; pork 1,496; breadfruit 646; chickens 591; coconuts 434; taro 166; bananas 108; foreign fish catch (1999) 12,993, of which Japanese 6,762. Mining and quarrying: for local construction only. Manufacturing (1999): copra 3,348; coconut oil and processed (chilled or frozen) fish are important products; the manufacture of handicrafts and personal items (clothing, mats, boats, etc.) by individuals is also significant. Construction (1994): value added U.S.$9,300,000. Energy production (consumption): electricity (kW-hr; 1994) 57,891,000 (57,891,000); coal, none (n.a.); gasoline, oil, and lubricants (barrels; 1988)[5] n.a. (84,588).
Public debt (external, outstanding; 1996–97): U.S.$124,900,000.
Gross national product (at current market prices; 1999): U.S.$99,000,000 (U.S.$1,950 per capita).

Structure of gross domestic product and labour force

	1996–97		1999	
	in value U.S.$'000	% of total value	labour force	% of labour force
Agriculture	14,400	14.8	2,355	16.0
Mining	300	0.3	—	—
Manufacturing	2,200	2.3	1,447	9.9
Public utilities	2,400	2.5	274	1.9
Construction	6,600	6.8	863	5.9
Transp. and commun.	6,400	6.6	867	5.9
Trade, restaurants, hotels	17,300	17.8	1,210	8.2
Finance, insurance, real estate	14,700	15.2	814	5.5
Public administration	12,100	12.5	} 5,119	34.9
Services	17,200	17.7		
Other	3,400[6]	3.5[6]	1,728[7]	11.8[7]
TOTAL	97,000	100.0	14,677	100.0

Land use (1989)[8]: forested 22.5%; meadows and pastures 13.5%; agricultural and under permanent cultivation 33.1%; other 30.9%.
Household income and expenditure. Average household size (1999) 7.8; annual median income per household (1999) U.S.$6,840; sources of income: n.a.; expenditure (1982): food 57.7%, housing 15.6%, clothing 12.0%, personal effects and other 14.7%.
Population economically active (1999): total 14,677; activity rate of total population 28.9% (participation rates: over age 15, 53.1%; female [1988] 30.1%; unemployed 9.5%).

Price and earnings indexes (1995 = 100)							
	1994	1995	1996	1997	1998	1999	2000
Consumer price index[9]	92.4	100.0	109.6	114.9	117.4	119.4	117.1
Earnings index	...	...	...	...	...	...	...

Tourism (2000): receipts U.S.$4,000,000; expenditures, n.a.

Foreign trade[10]

Balance of trade (current prices)						
	1994	1995	1996	1997	1998	1999
U.S.$'000,000	−48.2	−52.0	−53.6	−48.3	−61.5	−61.2
% of total	52.1%	53.0%	58.6%	65.6%	84.1%	79.9%

Imports (1997): U.S.$60,995,000 (mineral fuels and lubricants 23.4%, food, beverages, and tobacco 22.8%, machinery and transport equipment 9.5%, manufactured goods 7.4%, chemical products 6.6%). *Major import sources:* U.S. 47.2%; Guam 4.8%; Australia 4.0%; Singapore 3.4%; Japan 3.3%.
Exports (1997): U.S.$12,665,000 (chilled fish 78.2%, frozen fish 10.7%, crude coconut oil 9.6%). *Major export destinations:* U.S. *c.* 80.0%; other *c.* 20.0%.

Transport and communications

Transport. Roads: only Majuro and Kwajalein have paved roads. Vehicles (1995): passenger cars 1,374; trucks and buses 262. Air transport (2001)[11]: passenger-km 24,972,000; metric ton-km cargo 183,000; airports (1997) 25.

Communications				units per 1,000 persons
Medium	date	unit	number	
Telephones	2001	main lines	4,200	60
Cellular telephones	2001	subscribers	500	7.0
Internet	2001	users	900	13
Personal computers	2001	units	4,000	50

Education and health

Educational attainment (1999). Percentage of population age 25 and over having: no formal schooling 3.1%; elementary education 35.5%; secondary 46.5%; some higher 12.3%; undergraduate degree 1.7%; advanced degree 0.9%. *Literacy* (latest): total population age 15 and over literate 19,377 (91.2%); males literate 9,993 (92.4%); females literate 9,384 (90.0%).

Education (1994–95)	schools	teachers	students	student/teacher ratio
Primary (age 6–14)	103	669	13,355	20.0
Secondary (age 15–18)	12	144	2,400	16.7
Voc., teacher tr.	...	...	...	...
Higher	...	...	...	...

Health (1997): physicians 34 (1 per 1,785 persons); hospital beds 129 (1 per 470 persons); infant mortality rate per 1,000 live births (2000) 41.0.

Military

Under the 1984 Compact of Free Association, the United States provides for the defense of the Republic of the Marshall Islands.

[1]Council of Iroij is an advisory body only. [2]Detail does not add to total given because of rounding. [3]Detail does not add to total given because of statistical discrepancies. [4]Registered deaths only. [5]Import only. [6]Import duties less imputed bank service charges. [7]Represents sum of not stated and unemployed. [8]Data are for the former Trust Territory of the Pacific Islands. [9]Majuro only. [10]Imports c.i.f. in balance of trade table. [11]Air Marshall Islands only.

Internet resources for further information:
• RMI Online, Internet Guide to the Republic of the Marshall Islands http://www.rmiembassyus.org
• U.S. Office of Insular Affairs http://www.pacificweb.org

Martinique

Official name: Département de la Martinique (Department of Martinique).
Political status: overseas department (France) with two legislative houses (General Council [45]; Regional Council [41]).
Chief of state: President of France.
Heads of government: Prefect (for France); President of the General Council (for Martinique); President of the Regional Council (for Martinique).
Capital: Fort-de-France.
Official language: French.
Official religion: none.
Monetary unit: 1 euro (€) = 100 cents; valuation (Sept. 23, 2002) 1 U.S.$ = €1.02; 1 £ = €1.58[1].

Area and population

Arrondissements	Capitals	area sq mi	area sq km	population 1999 census
Fort-de-France	Fort-de-France	66	171	166,139
Le Marin	Le Marin	158	409	106,818
La Trinité	La Trinité	131	338	85,006
Saint-Pierre	Saint-Pierre	81	210	23,464
TOTAL		436	1,128	381,427

Demography

Population (2002): 386,000.
Density (2002): persons per sq mi 885.3, persons per sq km 342.2.
Urban-rural (2001): urban 95.2%; rural 4.8%.
Sex distribution (2001): male 49.47%; female 50.53%.
Age breakdown (2001): under 15, 23.1%; 15–29, 23.3%; 30–44, 26.3%; 45–59, 13.8%; 60–74, 9.1%; 75 and over, 4.4%.
Population projection: (2010) 397,000; (2020) 403,000.
Doubling time: 75 years.
Ethnic composition (2000): mixed race (black/white/Asian) 93.4%; French (metropolitan and Martinique white) 3.0%; East Indian 1.9%; other 1.7%.
Religious affiliation (1995): Roman Catholic 86.5%; Protestant 8.0% (mostly Seventh-day Adventist); Jehovah's Witness 1.6%; other 3.9%, including Hindu, syncretist, and nonreligious.
Major communes (1999): Fort-de-France 94,049; Le Lamentin 35,460; Le Robert 21,201; Schoelcher 20,845; Sainte-Marie 20,058.

Vital statistics

Birth rate per 1,000 population (2001): 15.8 (world avg. 21.2); (1997) legitimate 31.8%; illegitimate 68.2%.
Death rate per 1,000 population (2001): 6.4 (world avg. 8.9).
Natural increase rate per 1,000 population (2001): 9.4 (world avg. 12.3).
Total fertility rate (avg. births per childbearing woman; 2001): 1.4.
Marriage rate per 1,000 population (1997): 4.1.
Divorce rate per 1,000 population (1997): 1.1.
Life expectancy at birth (2001): male 79.1 years; female 77.7 years.
Major causes of death per 100,000 population (1996): diseases of the circulatory system 206.8; malignant neoplasms (cancers) 150.3; accidents, poisoning, and violence 47.2; diseases of the respiratory system 36.3; endocrine and metabolic disorders 27.8; diseases of the digestive system 27.2.

National economy

Budget (1999). Revenue: F 1,298,000,000 (general receipts from French central government and local administrative bodies 45.0%; tax receipts 34.0%, of which indirect taxes 19.5%, direct taxes 14.5%). Expenditures: F 1,298,000,000 (health and social assistance 42.0%; wages and salaries 16.7%; other administrative services 7.2%; debt amortization 5.0%).
Public debt (1994): U.S.$186,700,000.
Production (metric tons except as noted). Agriculture, forestry, fishing (2001): bananas 310,000, sugarcane 207,000, pineapples 20,800, plantains 16,000, roots and tubers 13,250, lettuce 7,800, yams 7,500, tomatoes 6,100, cucumbers and gherkins 4,000, melons 2,240, sweet potatoes 1,170, coconuts 1,150; livestock (number of live animals) 35,000 pigs, 34,000 sheep, 25,000 cattle, 17,000 goats; roundwood (2000) 12,000 cu m; fish catch (1999) 5,040. Mining and quarrying (1996): pumice 130,000; sand and gravel for local construction. Manufacturing (1998): cement 232,300; processed pineapples 20,210; sugar 6,543; rum 68,716 hectolitres; other products include clothing, fabricated metals, and yawls and sails. Construction (buildings authorized; 1998): residential permits 5,392; nonresidential 118,395 sq m. Energy production (consumption): electricity (kW-hr; 1998) 988,000,000 (988,000,000); coal, none (none); crude petroleum (barrels; 1997) none (5,900,000); petroleum products (metric tons; 1997) 740,000 (565,000); natural gas, none (none).
Household income and expenditure. Average household size (1999) 3.0; income per household (1996) F 194,387 (U.S.$38,900); sources of income (1989): wages and salaries 80%, other 20%; expenditure (1993): food and beverages 32.1%, transportation and communications 20.7%, housing and energy 10.6%, household durable goods 9.4%, clothing and footwear 8.0%, education and recreation 5.4%, health care 5.2%, other 8.6%.
Tourism (2000): receipts from visitors U.S.$302,000,000; expenditures by nationals abroad, n.a.; number of visitors 816,000.

Gross national product (1998): U.S.$4,888,000,000 (U.S.$12,875 per capita).

Structure of gross domestic product and labour force

	1995 in value F '000,000	1995 % of total value	1998 labour force	1998 % of labour force
Agriculture, fishing	1,151,952	4.1	7,650	4.6
Mining, manufacturing	1,502,161	5.3	7,103	4.3
Construction	2,249,756	7.9	10,405	6.3
Public utilities	973,068	3.4		
Transp. and commun.	1,797,425	6.3	4,383	2.6
Trade, restaurants, hotels	5,660,282	20.0	16,196	9.8
Finance, real estate, insurance	1,180,409	4.2	25,909	15.6
Pub. admin., defense	13,159,431	46.4	18,742	11.3
Services			25,667	15.5
Other	693,355[2]	2.4[2]	49,845[3]	30.0[3]
TOTAL	28,367,839	100.0	165,900	100.0

Population economically active (1998): total 165,900; activity rate of total population 43.7% (participation rates: ages 15–64, 70.7%; female 45.9%; unemployed [2000] 27.9%).

Price and earnings indexes (1995 = 100)

	1995	1996	1997	1998	1999	2000	2001
Consumer price index[4]	100.0	106.6	113.8	121.6	130.0	135.4	142.7
Monthly earnings index[5]	100.0	100.9	104.9	106.3	106.3	106.8	...

Land use (1998): forested 43.2%; meadows and pastures 12.5%; agricultural and under permanent cultivation 18.1%; other 26.2%.

Foreign trade[6]

Balance of trade (current prices)

	1995	1996	1997	1998	1999	2000
F '000,000	–8,604	–8,987	–8,676	–8,305	–8,891	–9,436
% of total	78.2%	80.5%	78.6%	71.0%	72.2%	71.0%

Imports (1999): F 10,605,600,000 (1996; consumer goods 23.9%, goods for intermediate consumption [inputs to the manufacturing process changed or destroyed in the final product] 15.9%, automobiles 15.0%, professional equipment 15.2%, energy products 8.3%). *Major import sources* (1998): France 64.2%; Germany 3.8%; Italy 3.6%; Venezuela 3.2%; United States 2.7%; U.K. 2.6%; Japan 1.8%.
Exports (1999): F 1,715,100,000 (1998; bananas 39.3%, refined petroleum 12.2%, rum 7.5%, yachts and boats 4.4%). *Major export destinations* (1998): France 51.8%; Guadeloupe 22.4%; U.K. 10.2%; Belgium 5.0%; French Guiana 3.2%.

Transport and communications

Transport. Railroads: none. Roads (1994): total length 1,291 mi, 2,077 km (paved [1988] 75%). Vehicles (1998): passenger cars 147,589; trucks and buses 35,615. Merchant marine (1992): vessels (100 gross tons and over) 6; total deadweight tonnage 1,121. Air transport (1998): passenger arrivals and departures 1,570,700; cargo handled 15,655 metric tons; airports (2000) 1.

Communications

Medium	date	unit	number	units per 1,000 persons
Daily newspapers	1996	circulation	32,000	83
Radio	1997	receivers	82,000	213
Television	1999	receivers	66,000	168
Telephones	2001	main lines	172,192	417
Cellular telephones	2001	subscribers	286,100	715
Personal computers	2001	units	52,000	130
Internet	1999	users	5,000	12.7

Education and health

Educational attainment (1990). Percentage of population age 25 and over having: incomplete primary, or no declaration 54.3%; primary education 18.0%; secondary 20.0%; higher 7.7%. *Literacy* (1982): total population age 15 and over literate 206,807 (92.5%); males literate 97,538 (91.8%); females literate 109,269 (93.2%).

Education (1998–99)

	schools	teachers	students	student/ teacher ratio
Primary (age 6–11)	272	2,631	55,163	21.0
Secondary (age 12–18)	77	3,341	38,405	11.5
Vocational	...	896[7]	9,380	...
Higher	1	998[8]	11,199	...

Health (1998): physicians 780 (1 per 487 persons); hospital beds 2,585 (1 per 128 persons); infant mortality rate per 1,000 live births (2001) 7.8.
Food (1998): daily per capita caloric intake 2,865 (vegetable products 75%, animal products 25%); 118% of FAO recommended minimum requirement.

Military

Total active duty personnel (2001): 3,800 French troops.

[1]The French franc was the former monetary unit; on Jan. 1, 2002, F 6.56 = €1. [2]Statistical discrepancy. [3]Unemployed. [4]Figures are end-of-year. [5]Based on minimum-level wage of public employees. [6]Imports c.i.f.; exports f.o.b. [7]1995–96. [8]1993–94.

Internet resources for further information:
• France Overseas http://www.outre-mer.gouv.fr
• INSEE: Martinique http://www.insee.fr/fr/insee_regions/Martinique

Mauritania

Official name: Al-Jumhūrīyah
al-Islāmīyah al-Mūrītānīyah (Arabic)
(Islamic Republic of Mauritania).
Form of government: unitary multiparty
republic with two legislative houses
(Senate [56]; National Assembly [81]).
Head of state and government:
President assisted by the Prime
Minister.
Capital: Nouakchott.
Official language: Arabic[1].
Official religion: Islam.
Monetary unit: 1 ouguiya (UM) =
5 khoums; valuation (Sept. 23, 2002)
1 U.S.$ = UM 272.51;
1 £ = UM 423.51.

Atlantic
Ocean
Gulf of
Guinea

Area and population

Regions	Capitals	area sq mi	area sq km	population 2000 census[2]
El-'Açâba	Kiffa	14,100	36,600	249,596
Adrar	Atar	83,100	215,300	60,847
Brakna	Aleg	13,000	33,800	240,167
Dakhlet Nouadhibou	Nouadhibou	8,600	22,300	75,976
Gorgol	Kaédi	5,300	13,600	248,980
Guidimaka	Sélibaby	4,000	10,300	186,697
Hodh ech-Chargui	Néma	70,600	182,700	275,288
Hodh el-Gharbi	'Ayoûn el-'Atroûs	20,600	53,400	219,167
Inchiri	Akjoujt	18,100	46,800	11,322
Tagant	Tidjikdja	36,800	95,200	61,984
Tiris Zemmour	Zouérate	97,600	252,900	53,586
Trarza	Rosso	26,200	67,800	252,664
Capital District				
Nouakchott	Nouakchott	400	1,000	611,883
TOTAL		398,000[3]	1,030,700	2,548,157

Demography

Population (2002): 2,656,000.
Density (2002): persons per sq mi 6.7, persons per sq km 2.6.
Urban-rural (1999): urban 56.5%; rural 43.5%.
Sex distribution (2000): male 48.68%; female 51.32%.
Age breakdown (2000): under 15, 46.2%; 15–29, 26.6%; 30–44, 15.6%; 45–59, 7.8%; 60–74, 3.3%; 75 and over, 0.5%.
Population projection: (2010) 3,243,000; (2020) 4,161,000.
Doubling time: 24 years.
Ethnic composition (1993)[4]: Moor 70% (of which about 40% "black" Moor [Harātīn, or African Sudanic] and about 30% "white" Moor [Bidan, or Arab-Berber]); other black African 30% (mostly Wolof, Tukulor, Soninke, and Fulani).
Religious affiliation (2000): Sunnī Muslim 99.1%; traditional beliefs 0.5%; Christian 0.3%; other 0.1%.
Major cities (1998): Nouakchott 611,883[5]; Nouadhibou 97,600; Kiffa 48,300; Kaédi 43,000; Rosso 35,000.

Vital statistics

Birth rate per 1,000 population (2001): 42.5 (world avg. 21.2).
Death rate per 1,000 population (2001): 13.3 (world avg. 8.9).
Natural increase rate per 1,000 population (2001): 29.2 (world avg. 12.3).
Total fertility rate (avg. births per childbearing woman; 2001): 6.1.
Life expectancy at birth (2001): male 49.2 years; female 53.7 years.

National economy

Budget (1997). Revenue: UM 44,800,000,000 (tax revenue 58.3%, of which taxes on goods and services 26.5%, import taxes 12.1%, income taxes 9.6%; nontax revenue 39.9%, of which fishing royalties and penalties 32.3%). Expenditures: UM 32,110,000,000 (wages and salaries 24.9%; interest on public debt 15.3%; defense 11.4%).
Land use (1994): forested 4.3%; meadows and pastures 38.3%; agricultural and under permanent cultivation 0.2%; desert 57.2%.
Production (metric tons except as noted). Agriculture, forestry, fishing (1999): rice 101,900, sorghum 74,800, dates 22,000, cow peas 22,000, pulses 12,000, millet 10,400; livestock (number of live animals) 6,200,000 sheep, 4,133,000 goats, 1,395,000 cattle, 1,185,000 camels; roundwood (1998) 15,000 cu m; fish catch (metric tons; 1997) 82,000, of which octopuses 23,500[6]. Mining and quarrying (gross weight; 1998): iron ore 11,411,000; gypsum 100,000. Manufacturing (1996): cow's milk 91,000[7]; goat's milk 77,000[7]; meat 58,200, of which fresh mutton and lamb 24,600, fresh beef and veal 10,200; hides and skins 4,600; cement, tiles, and bricks 5.9[8]; fabricated metal products 5.4[8]; paper and paper products 2.1[8]. Energy production (consumption): electricity (kW-hr; 1999) 226,700,000 ([1997] 153,000,000); coal (metric tons; 1997) none (6,000); crude petroleum (barrels; 1997) none (6,927,000); petroleum products (metric tons; 1997) 845,000 (932,000); natural gas, none (none).
Population economically active (1994): total 687,000; activity rate of total population 31.3% (participation rates: over age 10 [1991] 45.5%; female 22.9%).

Price and earnings indexes (1995 = 100)

	1995	1996	1997	1998	1999	2000	2001
Consumer price index[9]	100.0	104.7	109.5	118.3	123.1	127.1	133.1
Hourly earnings index[10]	100.0	100.0	100.0	100.0	100.0	...	...

Household income and expenditure. Average household size (1996): 5.3; expenditure (1990): food and beverages 73.1%, clothing and footwear 8.1%, energy and water 7.7%, transportation and communications 2.0%.
Gross national product (2000): U.S.$978,000,000 (U.S.$370 per capita).

Structure of gross domestic product and labour force

	1997 in value UM '000,000	1997 % of total value	1988 labour force	1988 % of labour force
Agriculture, livestock	37,117	22.2	225,238	38.5
Mining	16,075	9.6	6,322	1.1
Manufacturing	16,447	9.9	5,630	1.0
Public utilities	} 14,344	} 8.6	1,326	0.2
Construction			12,291	2.1
Transp. and commun.	12,627	7.6	8,378	1.4
Trade and finance	25,511	15.3	73,451	12.5
Services	11,270	6.8	} 86,807	} 14.8
Pub. admin., defense	16,852	10.1		
Other	16,688[11]	10.0[11]	166,366[12]	28.4[12]
TOTAL	166,930[3]	100.0[3]	585,809	100.0

Public debt (external, outstanding; 2000): U.S.$2,150,000,000.
Tourism (1999): receipts U.S.$28,000,000; expenditures U.S.$55,000,000.

Foreign trade

Balance of trade (current prices)

	1993	1994	1995	1996	1997	1998
U.S.$'000,000	+2.6	+47.4	+183.8	+133.9	+1.6	+40.0
% of total	0.3%	6.3%	23.9%	16.2%	0.2%	5.9%

Imports (1997): U.S.$403,400,000 (imports for National Industrial and Mining Company 20.2%; petroleum products 13.6%; investment including food aid 10.0%; equipment and machinery 6.5%). *Major import sources:* France 25.5%; Spain 7.5%; Germany 6.7%; Belgium-Luxembourg 6.4%; Thailand 5.1%.
Exports (1997): U.S.$405,000,000 (iron ore 52.4%; fish 47.6%, of which cephalopods 28.3%). *Major export destinations:* Japan 23.3%; Italy 16.7%; France 13.9%; Spain 8.3%; Belgium-Luxembourg 7.1%.

Transport and communications

Transport. Railroads (1998): route length 437 mi, 704 km; passenger-km, negligible; (1997) metric ton-km cargo 2,340,000,000. Roads (1996): total length 4,760 mi, 7,660 km (paved 11%). Vehicles (1996): passenger cars 18,810; trucks and buses 10,450. Air transport (1998)[13]: passenger-km 258,263,000; metric ton-km cargo 13,524,000; airports (1997) with scheduled flights 9.

Communications

Medium	date	unit	number	units per 1,000 persons
Daily newspapers	1996	circulation	1,000	0.4
Radio	1997	receivers	360,000	147
Television	1999	receivers	247,000	100
Telephones	2000	main lines	19,000	7.2
Cellular telephones	2000	subscribers	7,000	2.7
Personal computers	2001	units	27,000	9.8
Internet	2001	users	7,000	2.7

Education and health

Educational attainment (1988). Percentage of population age 25 and over having: no formal schooling 60.8%; primary and incomplete secondary 34.1%; secondary 3.8%; higher 1.3%. *Literacy* (1995): percentage of total population age 15 and over literate 37.7%; males literate 49.6%; females literate 26.3%.

Education (1995–96)

	schools	teachers	students	student/ teacher ratio
Primary (age 6–11)[14]	2,392	6,225	312,671	50.2
Secondary (age 12–17)	...	1,865	49,221	26.4
Voc., teacher tr.[15]	...	202	2,544	12.6
Higher	...	270	8,496	31.5

Health: physicians (1994) c. 200 (1 per 11,085 persons); hospital beds (1988) 1,556 (1 per 1,217 persons); infant mortality rate per 1,000 live births (2001) 75.2.
Food (1999): daily per capita caloric intake 2,702 (vegetable products 85%, animal products 15%); 117% of FAO recommended minimum requirement.

Military

Total active duty personnel (2001): 15,650 (army 95.8%, navy 3.2%, air force 1.0%). *Military expenditure as percentage of GNP* (1999): 4.0% (world 2.4%); per capita expenditure U.S.$14.

---

[1]The 1991 constitution names Arabic as the official language and the following as national languages: Arabic, Fulani, Soninke, and Wolof. [2]Preliminary figures. [3]Detail does not add to total given because of rounding. [4]Estimated figures. [5]2000 census. [6]Fish catch (1996) including foreign fishing vessels equals 564,200 metric tons. [7]1994. [8]1993 value added of production in U.S.$'000,000. [9]Nouakchott only. [10]Minimum wage. [11]Indirect taxes. [12]Mostly unemployed. [13]Data represent 1/11 of the total scheduled traffic of Air Afrique. [14]1996–97. [15]Excludes health-related programs.

Internet resources for further information:
• **Office National de la Statistique**
   http://www.ons.mr

Mauritius

Official name: Republic of Mauritius.
Form of government: republic with one legislative house (National Assembly [70[1]]).
Chief of state: President.
Head of government: Prime Minister.
Capital: Port Louis.
Official language: English.
Official religion: none.
Monetary unit: 1 Mauritian rupee (Mau Re; plural Mau Rs) = 100 cents; valuation (Sept. 23, 2002) 1 U.S.$ = Mau Rs 29.71; 1 £ = Mau Rs 46.17.

Area and population		area		population
Islands **Districts/Dependencies**	**Administrative Centres**	**sq mi**	**sq km**	**2000 census**
Mauritius		720	1,865	1,143,069
Black River	Tamarin	100	259	60,587
Flacq	Centre de Flacq	115	298	126,839
Grand Port	Mahébourg	100	260	106,665
Moka	Moka	89	231	75,479
Pamplemousses	Pamplemousses	69	179	122,252
Plaines Wilhems	Rose Hill	78	203	358,182
Port Louis	Port Louis	17	43	127,855
Rivière du Rempart	Poudre d'Or	57	148	98,854
Savanne	Souillac	95	245	66,356
Mauritian dependencies				
Agalega[2]	...	27	70	289
Cargados Carajos Shoals (Saint Brandon)[2]	—	0.4	1	0
Rodrigues[3]	Port Mathurin	40	104	35,779
TOTAL		788[4]	2,040[4]	1,179,137

Demography

Population (2002): 1,211,000.
Density (2002): persons per sq mi 1,536.8, persons per sq km 593.6.
Urban-rural (2000): urban 42.7%; rural 57.3%.
Sex distribution (2000): male 49.47%; female 50.53%.
Age breakdown (2000): under 15, 25.7%; 15–29, 25.6%; 30–44, 24.7%; 45–59, 15.1%; 60–74, 6.8%; 75 and over, 2.1%.
Population projection: (2010) 1,295,000; (2020) 1,387,000.
Doubling time: 72 years.
Ethnic composition (2000): Indo-Pakistani 67.0%; Creole (mixed Caucasian, Indo-Pakistani, and African) 27.4%; Chinese 3.0%; other 2.6%.
Religious affiliation (2000)[5]: Hindu 49.6%; Christian 32.2%, of which Roman Catholic 23.6%; Muslim 16.6%; Buddhist 0.4%; other 1.2%.
Major urban areas (2000)[5]: Port Louis 144,303; Beau Bassin-Rose Hill 103,872; Vacoas-Phoenix 100,066; Curepipe 78,920; Quatre Bornes 75,884.

Vital statistics

Birth rate per 1,000 population (2001): 16.3[6] (world avg. 21.2).
Death rate per 1,000 population (2001): 6.6[6] (world avg. 8.9).
Natural increase rate per 1,000 population (2001): 9.7[6] (world avg. 12.3).
Total fertility rate (avg. births per childbearing woman; 2001): 2.0[6].
Marriage rate per 1,000 population (1998): 9.4[6].
Divorce rate per 1,000 population (1997): 0.8[6].
Life expectancy at birth (2001): male 67.3 years; female 75.3 years.
Major causes of death per 100,000 population (1998): diseases of the circulatory system 331.0; malignant neoplasms (cancers) 65.0; diseases of the respiratory system 63.0; homicide, suicide, and accidents 44.0.

National economy

Budget (1997–98). Revenue: Mau Rs 18,501,000,000 (tax revenue 84.8%, of which import duties 33.3%, taxes on goods and services 32.5%, income tax 13.0%; nontax revenue 14.0%; grants 1.2%). Expenditures: Mau Rs 21,872,000,000 (social security 19.4%, government services 18.8%, education 16.0%, interest on debt 16.0%, economic services 11.4%, health 8.1%).
Tourism (2000): receipts from visitors U.S.$542,000,000; expenditures by nationals abroad U.S.$182,000,000.
Public debt (external, outstanding; 2000): U.S.$889,000,000.
Gross national product (2000): U.S.$4,449,000,000 (U.S.$3,750 per capita).

Structure of gross domestic product and labour force				
	1998			
	in value Mau Rs '000,000	% of total value	labour force[7]	% of labour force[7]
Agriculture	7,150	7.5	30,400	10.4
Mining	135	0.1	200	0.1
Manufacturing	20,650	21.6	111,200	38.0
Construction	4,940	5.2	8,900	3.0
Public utilities	1,900	2.0	3,200	1.1
Transp. and commun.	9,315	9.7	15,100	5.1
Trade	14,795	15.4	27,800	9.5
Finance	13,585	14.2	13,700	4.7
Pub. admin., defense	8,900	9.3	61,800	21.1
Services	4,860	5.1	17,900	6.1
Other	9,520[8]	9.9[8]	2,600	0.9
TOTAL	95,750	100.0	292,800[9]	100.0[9]

Production (metric tons except as noted). Agriculture, forestry, fishing (1999): sugarcane 3,500,000, vegetables 23,000, potatoes 15,000, roots and tubers 11,750, tomatoes 11,000, bananas 9,400, onions 6,750, cabbages 6,300, pineapples 1,500, peanuts (groundnuts) 600; livestock (number of live animals)

93,000 goats, 27,000 cattle, 20,000 pigs, 7,200 sheep; roundwood (1998) 14,760 cu m; fish catch (1998) 13,734. Manufacturing (value added in Mau Rs '000; 1994): apparel 5,065,000; beverages and tobacco 1,995,800; food products 1,580,400; metal and metal products 882,900; textile yarn and fabrics 676,400; chemical products 505,600. Construction (1998): residential 1,204,000 sq m; nonresidential 276,000 sq m. Energy production (consumption): electricity (kW-hr; 1998) 1,364,800 (1,364,800); coal (metric tons; 1998) none (86,300); petroleum products (metric tons; 1998) none (576,000).
Population economically active (1998): total 507,000; activity rate of total population 43.8% (participation rates: ages 12 and over, 55.6%; female 37.1%; unemployed 5.7%).

Price and earnings indexes (1995 = 100)							
	1995	1996	1997	1998	1999	2000	2001
Consumer price index	100.0	106.6	113.8	121.6	130.0	135.4	142.7
Earnings index	100.0	...	...	...	...	...	...

Household income and expenditure. Average household size (2000) 4.2; annual income per household (1996–97) Mau Rs 122,148 (U.S.$6,263); sources of income (1990): salaries and wages 48.4%, entrepreneurial income 41.2%, transfer payments 10.4%; expenditure (1996–97): food, beverages, and tobacco 45.2%, transportation and communications 14.2%, housing and household furnishings 13.2%, clothing and footwear 7.9%, recreation and education 6.0%, energy 4.4%, health 3.8%.
Land use (1994): forested 21.7%; meadows and pastures 3.4%; agricultural and under permanent cultivation 52.2%; other 22.7%.

Foreign trade

Balance of trade (current prices)						
	1994	1995	1996	1997	1998	1999
Mau Rs '000,000	−10,451	−7,607	−9,501	−6,381	−10,177	−17,019
% of total	17.8%	12.4%	13.1%	7.5%	11.4%	17.8%

Imports (1998): Mau Rs 49,811,000,000 (manufactured goods classified chiefly by material 34.6%, machinery and transport equipment 22.8%, food 13.8%, chemicals 7.8%, mineral fuels and lubricants 6.3%, inedible crude materials excluding fuels 3.9%, animal and vegetable oils and fats 1.3%). *Major import sources:* France 11.1%; South Africa 10.5%; India 9.3%; Taiwan 5.2%; United Kingdom 5.2%; Japan 5.1%; Hong Kong 5.0%; Germany 4.1%.
Exports (1998): Mau Rs 39,634,000,000 (clothing 55.9%, sugar 21.3%, yarn 3.7%, chemicals 0.5%, other 18.6%). *Major export destinations:* United Kingdom 32.3%; France 17.1%; United States 16.3%; Germany 5.3%; Italy 3.5%.

Transport and communications

Transport. Railroads: none. Roads (1998): total length 1,184 mi, 1,905 km (paved 93%). Vehicles (1998): passenger cars 46,300; trucks and buses 12,100. Air transport (1998)[10]: passenger-km 3,858,695; metric ton-km cargo 819,412,000; airports (1998) with scheduled flights 1.

Communications				units per 1,000
Medium	date	unit	number	**persons**
Daily newspapers	1996	circulation	85,000	76
Radio	1997	receivers	420,000	371
Television	1999	receivers	265,000	230
Telephones	2001	main lines	306,800	256
Cellular telephones	2001	subscribers	300,000	250
Personal computers	2001	units	130,000	108
Internet	2001	users	158,000	132

Education and health

Educational attainment (1990). Percentage of population age 25 and over having: no formal education 18.3%; incomplete primary 42.6%; primary 6.1%; incomplete secondary 18.0%; secondary 13.1%; higher 1.9%. *Literacy* (1995): percentage of total population age 15 and over literate 82.9%; males literate 87.1%; females literate 78.8%.

Education (1998)	schools	teachers	students	student/ teacher ratio
Primary (age 5–12)	285	5,065	130,505	25.7
Secondary (age 12–20)	133	4,820	94,364	19.6
Voc., teacher tr.	13	1,170[11]	5,496	...
Higher	3	461	6,429	13.9

Health (1998): physicians 1,033 (1 per 1,123 persons); hospital beds 3,826 (1 per 303 persons); infant mortality rate per 1,000 live births (2001) 13.8[6].
Food (1999): daily per capita caloric intake 2,972 (vegetable products 86%, animal products 14%); 131% of FAO recommended minimum requirement.

Military

Total active duty personnel: none; however, a special 1,500-person paramilitary force ensures internal security. *Military expenditure as percentage of GNP* (1999): 0.2% (world 2.4%); per capita expenditure U.S.$7.

[1]Includes 8 "bonus" seats allocated to minor parties. [2]Administered directly from Port Louis. [3]Local autonomy status granted by Mauritius in November 2001. [4]Detail does not add to total given because of rounding. [5]Based on census. [6]Excludes Agalega and Cargados Carajos Shoals. [7]Employed persons in large establishments only. [8]Indirect taxes less imputed bank service charges. [9]Total labour force equals 507,000 and includes 223,000 employees of small businesses or self-employed and 29,000 unemployed. [10]Air Mauritius only. [11]1997.

Internet resources for further information:
• Central Statistical Office http://statsmauritius.gov.mu

Mayotte

Official name: Collectivité Départementale de Mayotte (Departmental Collectivity of Mayotte)[1].
Political status: overseas dependency of France[2] with one legislative house (General Council [19]).
Chief of state: President of France.
Head of government: Prefect (for France); President of the General Council (for Mayotte).
Capitals: Dzaoudzi (French administrative); Mamoudzou (local administrative)[3].
Official language: French.
Official religion: none.
Monetary unit: 1 euro (€) = 100 cents; valuation (Sept. 23, 2002) 1 U.S.$ = €1.02; 1 £ = €1.58[4].

Area and population		area		population
Islands				1997
Communes	Capitals	sq mi	sq km	census
Grande Terre				
Acoua	Acoua	4.9	12.6	4,446
Bandraboua	Bandraboua	12.5	32.4	6,406
Bandrele	Bandrele	14.1	36.5	4,958
Boueni	Boueni	5.4	14.1	4,673
Chiconi	Chiconi	3.2	8.3	6,042
Chirongui	Chirongui	10.9	28.3	5,144
Dembeni	Dembeni	15.0	38.8	5,554
Kani-Keli	Kani-Keli	7.9	20.5	4,155
Koungou	Koungou	11.0	28.4	10,165
Mamoudzou	Mamoudzou	16.2	41.9	32,733
M'tsangamouji	M'tsangamouji	8.4	21.8	5,098
M'tzamboro	M'tzamboro	5.3	13.7	6,335
Ouangani	Ouangani	7.3	19.0	4,838
Sada	Sada	4.3	11.2	7,434
Tsingoni	Tsingoni	13.4	34.8	5,507
Petite Terre				
Dzaoudzi-Labattoir	Dzaoudzi	2.6	6.7	10,792
Pamandzi	Pamandzi	1.7	4.3	7,040
TOTAL		144.1	373.2[5]	131,320

Demography

Population (2002): 165,000.
Density (2002): persons per sq mi 1,145, persons per sq km 442.1.
Urban-rural (1985): urban 59.7%; rural 40.3%.
Sex distribution (2001): male 52.44%; female 47.56%.
Age breakdown (2001): under 15, 46.6%; 15–29, 24.9%; 30–44, 18.3%; 45–59, 7.4%; 60–74, 2.4%; 75 and over, 0.4%.
Population projection: (2010) 225,000; (2020) 304,000.
Doubling time: 20 years.
Place of birth (1997): Mayotte 73.6%[6]; nearby islands of the Comoros 19.9%[6]; metropolitan France 2.8%; other 3.7%.
Ethnic composition (2000): Comorian (Mauri, Mahorais) 92.3%; Swahili 3.2%; white (French) 1.8%; Makua 1.0%; other 1.7%.
Religious affiliation (2000): Sunnī Muslim 96.5%; Christian, principally Roman Catholic, 2.2%; other 1.3%.
Major towns (1997[7]): Mamoudzou 32,733; Dzaoudzi 10,792; Koungou 10,165.

Vital statistics

Birth rate per 1,000 population (2001): 44.4 (world avg. 21.2).
Death rate per 1,000 population (2001): 8.8 (world avg. 8.9).
Natural increase rate per 1,000 population (2001): 35.6 (world avg. 12.3).
Total fertility rate (avg. births per childbearing woman; 2001): 6.2.
Marriage rate per 1,000 population: n.a.; *marital status of adult population* (1997): monogamous marriage 48.5%, polygamous marriage 6.9%, other 44.6%.
Divorce rate per 1,000 population (1997): 16.2.
Life expectancy at birth (2000): male 57.8; female 62.0.
Major causes of death per 100,000 population: n.a.

National economy

Budget (1997). Revenue: F 1,022,400,000 (1993; current revenue 68.8%, of which subsidies 40.0%, indirect taxes 16.8%, direct taxes 4.9%; development revenue 31.2%, of which loans 11.6%, subsidies 7.9%). Expenditures: F 964,200,000 (current expenditure 75.2%, development expenditure 24.8%).
Public debt: n.a.
Production (metric tons except as noted). Agriculture, forestry, fishing (1997): bananas 30,200, cassava 10,000, cinnamon 27,533 kg, ylang-ylang 14,300 kg, vanilla 4,417 kg; livestock (number of live animals; 1997) 25,000 goats, 17,000 cattle, 2,000 sheep; roundwood, n.a.; fish catch (1999) 1,502. Mining and quarrying: negligible. Manufacturing: mostly processing of agricultural products and materials used in housing construction (including siding and roofing materials, joinery, and latticework). Construction (public works authorized in F '000; 1999): residential 128,991; nonresidential 119,294. Energy production (consumption): electricity (kW-hr; 1999) 68,387,000 (68,387,000); coal, none (none); crude petroleum, none (none); petroleum products, none (n.a.); natural gas, none (none).
Tourism (number of visitors; 1999): 21,000; receipts U.S.$10,000,000.
Gross national product (1998): U.S.$486,409,000 (U.S.$3,704 per capita).

Structure of gross domestic product and labour force

	1997			
	in value U.S.$'000	% of total value	labour force	% of labour force
Agriculture, forestry, and fishing	...	...	4,824	11.2
Mining	...	...	80	0.2
Manufacturing	...	...	1,083	2.5
Construction	...	...	3,840	9.0
Public utilities	...	...	399	0.9
Transp. and commun.	...	...	1,563	3.6
Trade	...	...	3,057	7.1
Finance, insurance, real estate	...	...	647	1.5
Pub. admin., defense	...	...	4,526	10.6
Services	...	...	5,074	11.8
Other	...	...	17,803[8]	41.5[8]
TOTAL	154,900	100.0	42,896	100.0[5]

Household income and expenditure. Average household size (1997) 4.6; expenditure (1991)[9]: food 42.2%, clothing and footwear 31.5%, household furnishings 8.8%, energy and water 6.8%, transportation 5.1%.
Population economically active (1997): total 42,896; activity rate of total population 32.7% (participation rates: ages 15–64, 58.6%; female 43.4%; unemployed 41.5%).

Price and earnings indexes (1995 = 100)					
	1995	1996	1997	1998	1999
Consumer price index	100.0	105.3	108.9	111.1	112.2
Monthly earnings index[10]	100.0	106.3	109.5	112.2	113.4

Land use (1987): meadows 35.0%; agricultural 29.0%; other 36.0%.

Foreign trade

Balance of trade (current prices)				
	1996	1997	1998	1999
F '000,000	−520.8	−620.4	−660.0	−615.7
% of total	92.9%	96.0%	95.7%	96.0%

Imports (1999): F 628,266,000 (1997; food products 23.8%; machinery 20.4%; transport equipment 10.4%; metals and metal products 10.3%; chemical products 7.7%). *Major import sources* (1997): France 66.0%; South Africa 14.0%; Asia 11.0%.
Exports (1999): F 12,540,000 (1997; domestic exports 37.2%, of which ylang-ylang 27.9%, vanilla 3.5%; reexports 62.8%). *Major export destinations* (1997): France 80.0%; Comoros 15.0%.

Transport and communications

Transport. Railroads: none. Roads (1998): total length 145 mi, 233 km (paved 77%). Vehicles (1998): 8,213. Merchant marine: n.a. Air transport (1998): passenger arrivals and departures 88,034; cargo unloaded and loaded 1,012 metric tons; airports (2000) with scheduled flights 1.

Communications				units per 1,000
Medium	date	unit	number	persons
Daily newspapers[11]	1998	circulation	...	...
Radio	1996	receivers	50,000	427
Television	1999	receivers	3,500	30
Telephones	2001	main lines	10,000	70

Education and health

Educational attainment (1991). Percentage of population age 25 and over having: no formal education 72.8%; primary 14.2%; lower secondary 7.5%; higher secondary 3.2%; higher 2.3%. *Literacy* (1997): total population age 15 and over literate 63,053 (86.1%).

Education (1997)	schools	teachers	students	student/ teacher ratio
Primary (age 6–11)	99	555[12]	24,681	38.9[12]
Secondary (age 12–18)	14	246[12]	10,616	16.2[12]
Voc., teacher tr.	2	17[13]	1,499	23.1[13]
Higher	—	—	—	

Health: physicians (1997) 57 (1 per 2,304 persons); hospital beds 186 (1 per 706 persons); infant mortality rate per 1,000 live births (2001) 69.5.

Military

Total active duty personnel (2001): 4,200 French troops are assigned to Mayotte and Réunion.

[1]The extraconstitutional status of departmental collectivity (between an overseas department and an overseas territory) was approved by the residents of Mayotte in mid-2000. [2]Final status of Mayotte has not yet been determined; it is claimed by Comoros as an integral part of that country. [3]Representatives of the French government in Mayotte continue to occupy offices in the original capital of Dzaoudzi. Local administrative (General Council) offices are in Mamoudzou. [4]The French franc was the former monetary unit; on Jan. 1, 2002, F 6.56 = €1. [5]Detail does not add to total given because of rounding. [6]Nearly all ethnic Comorian (a mixture of Bantu, Arab, and Malagasy peoples). [7]Population of communes. [8]Unemployed. [9]Weights of consumer price index components. [10]Based on minimum-level wage of public employees. [11]One weekly newspaper has a total circulation of 15,000. [12]1992–93. [13]1989–90.

Mexico

Official name: Estados Unidos Mexicanos (United Mexican States).
Form of government: federal republic with two legislative houses (Senate [128]; Chamber of Deputies [500]).
Head of state and government: President.
Capital: Mexico City.
Official language: Spanish.
Official religion: none.
Monetary unit: 1 Mexican peso[1] (Mex$) = 100 centavos; valuation (Sept. 23, 2002) 1 U.S.$ = Mex$10.27; 1 £ = Mex$15.96.

Area and population

States	Capitals	area sq mi	area sq km	population 2000 census
Aguascalientes	Aguascalientes	2,112	5,471	944,285
Baja California	Mexicali	26,997	69,921	2,487,367
Baja California Sur	La Paz	28,369	73,475	424,041
Campeche	Campeche	19,619	50,812	690,689
Chiapas	Tuxtla Gutiérrez	28,653	74,211	3,920,892
Chihuahua	Chihuahua	94,571	244,938	3,052,907
Coahuila de Zaragoza	Saltillo	57,908	149,982	2,298,070
Colima	Colima	2,004	5,191	542,627
Durango	Durango	47,560	123,181	1,448,661
Guanajuato	Guanajuato	11,773	30,491	4,663,032
Guerrero	Chilpancingo	24,819	64,281	3,079,649
Hidalgo	Pachuca	8,036	20,813	2,235,591
Jalisco	Guadalajara	31,211	80,836	6,322,002
México	Toluca	8,245	21,355	13,096,686
Michoacán de Ocampo	Morelia	23,138	59,928	3,985,667
Morelos	Cuernavaca	1,911	4,950	1,555,296
Nayarit	Tepic	10,417	26,979	920,185
Nuevo León	Monterrey	25,067	64,924	3,834,141
Oaxaca	Oaxaca	36,275	93,952	3,438,765
Puebla	Puebla	13,090	33,902	5,076,686
Querétaro de Arteaga	Querétaro	4,420	11,449	1,404,306
Quintana Roo	Chetumal	19,387	50,212	874,963
San Luis Potosí	San Luis Potosí	24,351	63,068	2,299,360
Sinaloa	Culiacán	22,521	58,328	2,536,844
Sonora	Hermosillo	70,291	182,052	2,216,969
Tabasco	Villahermosa	9,756	25,267	1,891,829
Tamaulipas	Ciudad Victoria	30,650	79,384	2,753,222
Tlaxcala	Tlaxcala	1,551	4,016	962,646
Veracruz–Llare	Xalapa (Jalapa)	27,683	71,699	6,908,975
Yucatán	Mérida	14,827	38,402	1,658,210
Zacatecas	Zacatecas	28,283	73,252	1,353,610
Federal District				
Distrito Federal	—	571	1,479	8,605,239
CONTINENTAL AREA		756,066[2]	1,958,201[2]	
LAND		736,949	1,908,690	
WATER		19,116	49,511	
INSULAR AREA[3]		1,979	5,127	
TOTAL		758,449[4]	1,964,375[4]	97,483,412

Demography

Population (2002): 100,977,000.
Density (2002): persons per sq mi 133.1, persons per sq km 51.4.
Urban-rural (1990): urban 71.3%; rural 28.7%.
Sex distribution (2000): male 49.28%; female 50.72%.
Age breakdown (2000): under 15, 33.8%; 15–29, 29.8%; 30–44, 19.1%; 45–59, 10.7%; 60–74, 5.2%; 75 and over, 1.4%.
Population projection: (2010) 112,062,000; (2020) 124,065,000.
Doubling time: 39 years.
Ethnic composition (2000): mestizo 64.3%; Amerindian 18.0%, of which detribalized 10.5%; Mexican white 15.0%; Arab 1.0%; Mexican black 0.5%; Spaniard 0.3%; U.S. white 0.2%; other 0.7%.
Religious affiliation (1995): Roman Catholic 90.4%; Protestant (including Evangelical) 3.8%; other 5.8%.
Major cities (2000): Mexico City 8,591,309; Guadalajara 1,647,000; Puebla 1,270,989; Ciudad Netzahualcóyotl 1,224,500; Juárez 1,190,000; Tijuana 1,150,000; Monterrey 1,108,400; León 1,019,510; Mérida 660,848; Chihuahua 650,000.
Place of birth (1990): 93.1% native-born; 6.9% foreign-born and unknown.
Mobility (1990). Population 5 years and older living in the same state as in 1985: 94.3%; different state 4.9%; unspecified 0.8%.
Households. Total households (2000) 21,948,000; distribution by size (1995): 1 person 5.7%, 2 persons 10.9%, 3 persons 15.8%, 4 persons 20.1%, 5 persons 17.7%, 6 persons 11.6%, 7 or more persons 18.2%. Family households (1990): 17,064,507 (98.4%); nonfamily 1,039,738 (1.3%); unspecified 256,554 (0.3%).
Emigration (1998): legal immigrants into the United States 131,600.

Vital statistics

Birth rate per 1,000 population (2000): 23.2 (world avg. 22.5); (1983) legitimate 72.5%; illegitimate 27.5%.
Death rate per 1,000 population (2000): 5.0 (world avg. 9.0).
Natural increase rate per 1,000 population (2000): 18.2 (world avg. 13.5).
Total fertility rate (avg. births per childbearing woman; 2000): 2.7.
Marriage rate per 1,000 population (1997): 7.5.
Divorce rate per 1,000 population (1995): 0.4.
Life expectancy at birth (2000): male 68.5 years; female 74.7 years.
Major causes of death per 100,000 population (1998): diseases of the circula-

tory system 104.1; malignant neoplasms (cancers) 57.6; diseases of the digestive system 43.5; diseases of the respiratory system 43.3; conditions originating in the perinatal period 20.7.

Social indicators

Access to services (1995). Proportion of dwellings having: electricity 93.2%; piped water supply 85.6%; drained sewage 74.7%.
Educational attainment (1995). Population age 15 and over having: no primary education 13.4%; some primary 22.8%; completed primary 19.3%; incomplete secondary 19.9%; complete secondary 16.3%; higher 8.3%.

Distribution of income (1994)

percentage of household income by quintile

1	2	3	4	5 (highest)
4.8	8.6	12.8	19.5	54.3

Quality of working life. Average workweek (1999): 44.4 hours[5]. Annual rate (1992) per 100,000 insured workers for: temporary disability 6,426; indemnification for permanent injury 239; death 18. Labour stoppages (1997): 39, involving 9,375 workers. Average duration of journey to work: n.a. Method of transport: n.a. Rate per 1,000 workers of discouraged (unemployed no longer seeking work): n.a.
Social participation. Eligible voters participating in last national election (2000): 64%. Population participating in voluntary work: n.a. Trade union membership in total workforce: n.a. Practicing religious population in total affiliated population: national average of weekly attendance (1993) 11%; (1970) weekly attendance 10% of urban dwellers, 25% of rural dwellers; yearly attendance 55% of urban dwellers, 73% of rural dwellers.
Social deviance (1991). Criminal cases tried by local authorities per 100,000 population for: murder 60.3; rape 22.4; other assault 301.0; theft 703.8. Incidence per 100,000 in general population of: alcoholism, n.a.; drug and substance abuse, n.a.[6]; suicide (1994) 2.47.
Material well-being. n.a.

National economy

Gross national product (2000): U.S.$497,025,000,000 (U.S.$5,070 per capita).

Structure of gross domestic product and labour force

	2000 in value Mex$'000,000[1, 7]	% of total value	labour force	% of labour force
Agriculture	203,797	4.1	7,060,700	17.8
Mining	70,178	1.4	155,600	0.4
Manufacturing	1,013,323	20.4	7,546,700	19.0
Construction	251,598	5.0	2,527,600	6.4
Public utilities	54,941	1.1	188,500	0.5
Transp. and commun.	556,409	11.2	1,730,500	4.4
Trade	1,066,845	21.4	10,368,900	26.2
Finance	605,319	12.2	1,470,900	3.7
Pub. admin., defense } Services	1,213,139	24.4	7,773,000	19.6
Other	−61,084[8]	−1.2[8]	811,500[9]	2.0[9]
TOTAL	4,974,465	100.0	39,633,900	100.0

Budget (2000). Revenue: Mex$866,231,000,000[1] (1997; income tax 30.9%, VAT 20.9%, social security contributions 12.3%, excise tax 9.9%, import duties 3.9%). Expenditures: Mex$936,738,000,000[1] (1997; education 22.1%, social security and welfare 18.0%, interest on public debt 13.7%).
Public debt (external, outstanding; 2000): U.S.$81,550,000,000.
Tourism (2000): receipts from visitors U.S.$8,295,000,000; expenditures by nationals abroad U.S.$5,499,000,000.

Manufacturing, mining, and construction enterprises (1993)

	no. of enterprises	no. of employees ('000)	yearly wages as a % of avg. of all wages[10]	value added (Mex$'000,000[1, 10])
Manufacturing	266,033	3,174.4	97.5	20,950,900
Metal products	46,667[11]	955.6[11]	114.2[11]	6,605,300[11]
Chemicals	7,321	371.2	152.3	4,228,000
Food, beverages, and tobacco	91,894	679.3	86.4	3,378,700
Textiles and apparel	44,071	530.6	80.0	2,414,800
Iron and steel	401	57.4	128.2	1,332,400
Nonmetallic mineral products	24,397	181.8	98.6	1,177,700
Paper and printing	15,022	193.2	100.0	1,127,900
Wood and wood products	31,549	162.6	62.8	497,000
Nonelectrical machinery and transport equipment	11	11	...11	11
Electrical machinery	11	11	...11	11
Other manufactures	4,711	42.7	...	189,200
Mining	2,845	95.6	161.0	1,643,800
Construction	5,308[10]	342.4[10]	62.1	1,414,800

Production (metric tons except as noted). Agriculture, forestry, fishing (2000): sugarcane 49,274,780, corn (maize) 17,988,060, sorghum 5,981,835, oranges 4,059,769, wheat 3,404,576, tomatoes 2,176,557, bananas 1,978,032, peppers 1,826,140, mangoes 1,499,382, lemons and limes 1,639,196, coconuts 1,213,000, watermelons 1,069,000, avocados 933,337, dry beans 914,379, pineapples 881,000, papayas 748,000, barley 732,706, grapes 446,470, rice 410,210, carrots 372,869, coffee (green) 353,999, cauliflower 205,000; livestock (number of live animals) 30,540,000 cattle, 14,900,000 pigs, 9,600,000 goats, 8,000,000 ducks, 6,250,000 horses, 5,950,000 sheep, 3,000,000 turkeys, 3,280,000 mules, 3,250,000 asses, 476,000,000 chickens; roundwood (2000) 24,122,000 cu m; fish catch (1999) 1,250,592. Mining and quarrying (1999): salt 8,900,000, iron 6,855,219, gypsum 4,100,000, silica 1,700,000, phosphate 950,649, sulfur 855,482, dolomite 415,284, fluorite 557,106, zinc 339,758, copper 340,148, barite 157,952, manganese 169,107, lead 131,402, silver 2,456,000 kg, gold 23,476 kg. Manufacturing (gross value of production in Mex$'000[1]; 1998): machinery and equipment 423,579,725; food, beverages, and tobacco products 279,104,375; chemical products 212,479,904; metal products 108,951,844; mineral products 55,612,499; paper and paper products 56,522,215; textiles 54,458,821. Construction (gross value of new construction, in Mex$'000,000[1]; 1985): residential 154,835; nonresidential 168,096.

Trade and service enterprises (1998)

	no. of establish- ments	no. of employees	yearly wage as a % of avg. of all wages[12]	annual income (Mex$'000,000[1])[13]
Trade	1,497,828	3,790,764	...	565,728,373
Wholesale	110,180	864,569	...	249,597,035
Retail	1,387,648	2,926,195	...	316,131,338
Boutiques (excluding food products)	536,900	1,192,597	...	108,507,889
Food and tobacco speciality stores	768,799	1,234,656	...	65,305,180
Automobile, tire, and auto parts dealers	41,236	164,493	...	47,888,576
Supermarkets and grocery stores	24,697	254,497	...	48,769,283
Gasoline stations	4,345	53,610	...	32,517,091
Other	11,671	26,342	...	13,143,319
Services[13]	711,843	2,766,750	85.2	200,001,682
Professional services	130,475	652,148	77.9	53,533,318
Food and beverage services	677	11,258	...	1,012,369
Transp. and travel agencies	9,967	62,767	133.4	11,858,406
Lodging	9,913	151,445	...	8,960,922
Automotive repair	112,293	252,950	...	7,263,560
Educational services (private)	20,622	247,086	134.3	10,815,238
Medical and social assistance	79,748	203,348	206.4	7,497,794
Amusement services (cinemas and theatres)	4,855	65,608	148.9	9,845,129
Recreation[13]	20,973	65,936	...	3,065,672
Other repair[13]	72,129	104,478	...	2,625,370
Commercial and professional[13] organizations	1,946	11,946	77.9	264,770
Other[13]	248,245	937,780	49.9	83,259,134

Energy production (consumption): electricity (kW-hr; 1997) 170,751,000,000 (172,212,000,000); coal (metric tons; 1997) 10,337,000 (11,538,000); crude petroleum (barrels; 1997) 1,099,400,000 (470,400,000); petroleum products (metric tons; 1997) 72,362,000 (83,281,000); natural gas (cu m; 1997) 29,708,000,000 (30,314,000,000).

Population economically active (1999): total 39,751,000; activity rate of total population 41.2% (participation rates: ages 15–64, 63.4%; female 33.5%; unemployed [2000] 4.0%).

Price and earnings indexes (1995 = 100)

	1995	1996	1997	1998	1999	2000	2001
Consumer price Index	100.0	134.4	162.1	187.9	219.1	239.9	255.1
Monthly earnings index	100.0	...	156.6	...	...	...	...

Household income and expenditure. Average household size (1999) 4.4; income per household (1989) Mex$3,461 (U.S.$1,384); sources of income (1992): wages and salaries 61.5%, property and entrepreneurship 29.1%, transfer payments 7.8%, other 1.6%; expenditure (1992): food, beverages, and tobacco 36.9%, housing (includes household furnishings) 25.2%, transportation and communications 10.1%, clothing and footwear 8.5%, recreation and entertainment 5.5%, health and medical services 3.5%.

Financial aggregates[1, 14]

	1994	1995	1996	1997	1998	1999	2000
Exchange rate, Mex$ per:							
U.S. dollar	3.375	6.419	7.599	7.919	9.136	9.560	9.456
£	5.164	10.132	11.867	12.969	15.133	15.470	14.336
SDR	7.774	11.361	11.289	10.906	13.890	13.059	12.472
International reserves (U.S.$)							
Total (excl. gold; '000,000)	6,278	16,847	19,433	28,797	31,799	31,782	35,509
SDRs ('000,000)	177	1,597	257	661	337	790	366
Reserve pos. in IMF ('000,000)	—	—	—	—	—	—	—
Foreign exchange	6,101	15,250	19,176	28,136	31,461	30,992	35,142
Gold ('000,000 fine troy oz)	0.43	0.51	0.26	0.19	0.22	0.16	0.25
% world reserves	0.05	0.06	0.03	0.02	0.03	0.02	0.02
Interest and prices							
Treasury bill rate	14.10	48.44	31.39	19.80	24.76	21.41	15.24
Balance of payments (U.S.$'000,000)							
Balance of visible trade,	−18,464	+7,089	+6,531	+623	−7,743	−5,581	−8,003
of which:							
Imports, f.o.b.	−79,347	−72,454	−89,469	−109,808	−125,243	−141,973	−174,458
Exports, f.o.b.	60,882	79,543	96,000	110,431	117,500	136,392	166,455
Balance of invisibles	−11,198	−8,665	−8,454	−8,077	−8,044	−8,473	−10,134
Balance of payments, current account	−29,662	−1,576	−2,328	−7,454	−15,724	−14,324	−18,137

Land use (1994): forest 25.5%; pasture 39.0%; agriculture 13.0%; other 22.5%.

Foreign trade

Balance of trade (current prices)

	1995	1996	1997	1998	1999	2000
U.S.$'000,000	−18,464	+6,531	+623	−7,742	−5,361	−8,003
% of total	13.2%	3.5%	0.3%	3.2%	1.9%	2.3%

Imports (2000): U.S.$174,458,000,000 (intermediate goods 76.6%; capital goods 13.8%; consumer goods 9.6%). *Major import sources:* U.S. 73.1%; Japan 3.7%; Germany 3.6%; Canada 2.3%; Italy 1.2%; China 1.1%.
Exports (2000): U.S.$166,455,000,000 (machinery and transport equipment 33.3%; electrical equipment 10.7%; crude petroleum 8.9%; agricultural goods 3.3%). *Major export destinations:* U.S. 88.7%; Europe 3.9%; Canada 2.0%; Japan 0.6%.

Trade by commodity group (1998)

	imports		exports	
SITC group	U.S.$'000,000	%	U.S.$'000,000	%
00 Food and live animals	5,285	4.2	6,135	5.2
01 Beverages and tobacco	...	...	1,035	0.9
02 Crude materials, excluding fuels	4,263	3.4	1,696	1.4
03 Mineral fuels, lubricants, and related materials	2,747	2.2	6,980	5.9
04 Animal and vegetable oils, fats, and waxes	590	0.5	—	—
05 Chemicals and related products, n.e.s.	10,718	8.6	4,231	3.6
06 Basic manufactures	21,537	17.2	11,976	10.2
07 Machinery and transport equipment	59,850	47.8	68,011	58.0
08 Miscellaneous manufactured articles	15,773	12.6	16,976	14.5
09 Goods not classified by kind	4,210	3.4	285	0.3
TOTAL[15]	125,193[16]	100.0[16]	117,325	100.0

Direction of trade (1999)

	imports		exports	
	U.S.$'000,000	%	U.S.$'000,000	%
Western Hemisphere	112,011	78.8	127,982	93.6
United States	105,267	74.1	120,393	88.1
Latin America and the Caribbean	3,795	2.7	5,198	3.8
Canada	2,949	2.0	2,391	1.7
Europe	15,208	10.7	5,889	4.3
EU	14,006	9.9	5,197	3.8
EFTA	776	0.5	455	0.3
Russia	—	—	—	—
Other Europe	426	0.3	237	0.2
Asia	13,354	9.4	2,353	1.7
Japan	5,083	3.6	776	0.6
Other Asia	8,271	5.8	1,577	1.1
Africa	398	0.3	159	0.1
Other	1,093	0.8	320	0.2
TOTAL	142,064	100.0	136,703	100.0[16]

Transport and communications

Transport. Railroads (1998): route length 16,543 mi, 26,623 km; passenger-mi 677,000,000, passenger-km 1,089,000,000; short ton-mi cargo 19,726,000,000, metric ton-km cargo 31,747,000,000. Roads (1999): total length 226,874 mi, 365,119 km (paved 29%). Vehicles (1999): passenger cars 9,842,006; trucks and buses 4,749,789. Air transport (2000): passenger-mi 19,887,000,000, passenger-km 32,005,000,000; short ton-mi cargo 2,089,000,000, metric ton-km cargo 3,050,000,000; airports (1997) 83.

Communications

Medium	date	unit	number	units per 1,000 persons
Daily newspapers	1996	circulation	9,030,000	97
Radio	1997	receivers	31,000,000	329
Television	1999	receivers	26,000,000	267
Telephones	2001	main lines	13,533,000	136
Cellular telephones	2001	subscribers	20,136,000	202
Personal computers	2001	units	6,900,000	69
Internet	2001	users	3,500,000	35

Education and health

Literacy (1995): total population age 15 and over literate 89.6%; males literate 91.8%; females literate 87.4%.

Education (2000–01)

	schools	teachers	students	student/ teacher ratio
Primary (age 6–12)	99,176	546,717	14,808,300	27.1
Secondary (age 12–18)	44,441	552,735	9,330,900	16.9
Voc., teacher tr.[17]	6,610	63,674	883,000	13.9
Higher	4,081	214,126	2,073,600	9.7

Health: physicians (1994) 146,021 (1 per 613 persons); hospital beds 107,288 (1 per 864 persons); infant mortality rate per 1,000 live births (2000) 26.2.
Food (2000): daily per capita caloric intake 3,165 (vegetable products 82%, animal products 18%); 136% of FAO recommended minimum requirement.

Military

Total active duty personnel (2001): 192,770 (army 74.7%, navy 19.2%, air force 6.1%). *Military expenditure as percentage of GNP* (1999): 0.6% (world 2.4%); per capita expenditure U.S.$27.

[1]The Mexican new peso, equivalent to 1,000 old Mexican pesos, was introduced on Jan. 1, 1993. On Jan. 1, 1996, the name of the currency was changed to Mexican peso. [2]Continental area per more recent survey equals 756,470 sq mi (1,959,248 sq km). [3]Uninhabited (nearly all Pacific) islands directly administered by federal government. [4]Total area based on most recent survey figure for continental area. [5]Manufacturing only. [6]Through 1982, cannabis remained the most abused drug. [7]At factor cost. [8]Imputed bank service charge. [9]Includes 650,000 unemployed persons. [10]1988. [11]Metal products include Nonelectrical machinery and transport equipment and Electrical machinery. [12]1984. [13]1993. [14]Exchange rates and treasury bill rates are expressed in period averages; international reserves are expressed in end-of-period rates. [15]Totals include adjustments of unspecified nature. [16]Detail does not add to total given because of rounding. [17]1996–97.

Internet resources for further information:
• **National Institute of Statistics, Geography, and Informatics**
  http://www.inegi.gob.mx/difusion/ingles/portadai.html

Micronesia

Pacific
Ocean

Official name: Federated States of
Micronesia.
Form of government: federal nonparty
republic in free association with the
United States with one legislative
house (Congress [14])[1].
Head of state and government:
President.
Capital: Palikir, on Pohnpei.
Official language: none.
Official religion: none.
Monetary unit: 1 U.S. dollar
(U.S.$) = 100 cents; valuation
(Sept. 23, 2002) 1 £ = U.S.$1.55.

Area and population

States Major Islands	area sq mi	area sq km	population 2000 census
Chuuk (Truk)	49.1	127.2	53,595
Weno (Moen) Islands	7.0	18.1	...
Kosrae	42.3	109.6	7,686
Kosrae Island	42.3	109.6	7,686
Pohnpei	133.3	345.2	34,486
Pohnpei Island	129.0	334.1	...
Yap	45.9	118.9	11,241
Yap Island	38.7	100.2	...
TOTAL	270.8[2]	701.4[2]	107,008

Demography

Population (2002): 109,000.
Density (2002): persons per sq mi 402.5, persons per sq km 155.4.
Urban-rural (2000): urban 28.5%; rural 71.5%.
Sex distribution (2000): male 50.64%; female 49.36%.
Age breakdown (2000): under 15, 40.3%; 15–29, 28.4%; 30–44, 16.9%; 45–59,
9.1%; 60–74, 3.9%; 75 and over, 1.4%.
Population projection: (2010) 125,000; (2020) 126,000.
Doubling time: 31 years.
Ethnic composition (2000): Chuukese/Mortlockese 48.8%; Pohnpeian 24.2%;
Yapese 9.2%; Kosraean 6.7%; Polynesian 1.4%; Asian 1.2%; other 8.5%.
Religious affiliation (2000): Christianity is the predominant religious tradition;
Roman Catholic 52.7%, Protestant 40.1%; the Kosraeans, Pohnpeians, and
Chuukese are mostly Protestant and the Yapese mostly Roman Catholic.
Major towns (2000): Weno, in Chuuk state 22,000; Tol, in Chuuk state 9,500;
Palikir, on Pohnpei 8,600; Kolonia, on Pohnpei 5,600; Colonia, on Yap 4,800.

Vital statistics

Birth rate per 1,000 population (2000): 26.7 (world avg. 22.5); legitimate, n.a.;
illegitimate, n.a.
Death rate per 1,000 population (2000): 3.9 (world avg. 9.0).
Natural increase rate per 1,000 population (2000): 22.8 (world avg. 13.5).
Total fertility rate (avg. births per childbearing woman; 2000): 3.8.
Marriage rate per 1,000 population: n.a.
Divorce rate per 1,000 population: n.a.
Life expectancy at birth (2000): male 66.5 years; female 67.6 years.
Major causes of death per 100,000 population (1997)[3]: diseases of the cere-
brovascular system 90.3; endocrine and metabolic diseases 64.4; homicide,
suicide, and accidents 55.4; diseases of the respiratory system 42.0; malignant
neoplasms (cancers) 34.0; infectious and parasitic diseases 26.8 (with especially high morbidity rates for tuberculosis and leprosy).

National economy

Budget (1997–98). Revenue: U.S.$152,300,000 (external grants 60.0%; tax rev-
enue 15.1%; fishing rights fees 13.4%). Expenditures: U.S.$154,700,000 (cur-
rent expenditures 79.6%, of which government services 71.4%, transfer payments 4.7%, debt services 3.4%; capital expenditure 20.4%).
Public debt (external, outstanding; 2000): U.S.$85,700,000.
Population economically active (2000): total 37,414; activity rate of total population 35.0% (participation rates: ages 15–64, 61.7%; female 42.9%; unemployed 22.0%).

Price and earnings indexes (1995 = 100)

	1994	1995	1996	1997	1998	1999
Price index	96.2	100.0	103.1	105.2	106.8	109.6
Annual wage index	103.2	100.0	97.5	94.2	...	...

Production (metric tons except as noted). Agriculture, forestry, fishing: n.a.;
however, Micronesia's major crops include coconuts (which provide annually more than 4,000 tons of copra), breadfruit, cassava, sweet potatoes, peppers, and a variety of tropical fruits (including bananas); livestock comprises mostly pigs and poultry; fish catch (1998) 15,393, of which skipjack tuna
15,000, yellowfin tuna 5,000. Mining and quarrying: quarrying of sand and
aggregate for local construction only. Manufacturing: n.a.; however, copra
and coconut oil, traditionally important products, are being displaced by
garment production; the manufacture of handicrafts and personal items
(clothing, mats, boats, etc.) by individuals is also important. Construction:
n.a. Energy production (consumption): electricity (kW-hr; 1997) 100,333,000
(100,333,000); coal, none (n.a.); crude petroleum, none (n.a.); petroleum
products (metric tons; 1992) none (77,000); natural gas, none (n.a.).

Household income and expenditure. Average household size (2000) 6.7; annual income per household U.S.$8,944 (median income; U.S.$4,618); sources of
income (1994): wages and salaries 51.8%, operating surplus 23.0%, social
security 2.1%; expenditure (1985): food and beverages 73.5%.
Land use (1984)[4]: forested 22.5%; meadows and pastures 13.5%; agricultural
and under permanent cultivation 33.5%; other 30.5%.
Gross national product (2000): U.S.$250,000,000 (U.S.$2,110 per capita).

Structure of gross domestic product and labour force

	1996 in value U.S.$'000,000	1996 % of total value	2000 labour force	2000 % of labour force
Agriculture and fishing[5]	34.7	19.1	15,216	40.7
Mining	0.7	0.4	1,164	3.1
Manufacturing	2.6	1.4		
Construction	1.9	1.0	781	2.1
Public utilities	2.0	1.1	360	1.0
Transp. and commun.	8.5	4.7	806	2.2
Finance	4.2	2.3	726	1.9
Services	3.1	1.7	1,445	3.9
Trade[6]	43.6	24.0	2,540	6.8
Public administration	80.4	44.3	6,137	16.4
Other	...	...	8,239[7]	22.0[7]
TOTAL	181.6[2]	100.0	37,414	100.0[2]

Tourism (1998): expenditures U.S.$4,383,000; number of visitors 16,283.

Foreign trade

Balance of trade (current prices)

	1992	1993	1994	1995	1996
U.S.$'000,000	−109.1	−93.7	−75.5	−59.1	−52.0
% of total	66.0%	41.4%	43.5%	48.0%	44.1%

Imports (1998): U.S.$82,486,915 (1997; food, beverages, and tobacco 41.9%;
manufactured goods 32.0%; machinery and transport equipment 28.4%;
petroleum products 11.2%; chemicals 4.4%). *Major import sources* (1997):
United States (including Guam) 72.5%; Japan 13.5%; Australia 6.6%.
Exports (1998): U.S.$8,037,207 (1997; marine products 89.2%; agricultural
products 4.4%, of which bananas 3.2%, copra 1.2%). *Major export destinations* (1992): Japan 80.0%; United States 9.3%; Guam 8.3%; South Pacific
Region 2.4%.

Transport and communications

Transport. Railroads: none. Roads (1990): total length 140 mi, 226 km (paved
17%). Vehicles (1998): passenger cars 2,044; trucks and buses 354. Merchant
marine (1997[8]): vessels (100 gross tons and over) 19; deadweight tonnage
9,200. Air transport: n.a.; airports (1997) with scheduled flights 4.

Communications

Medium	date	unit	number	units per 1,000 persons
Radio	1996	receivers	70,000	667
Television	1999	receivers	2,400	21
Telephones	2001	main lines	10,000	93
Cellular telephones	2001	subscribers	49,900	466
Internet	2000	users	4,000	37

Education and health

Educational attainment (2000). Percentage of population age 25 and over having: no formal schooling 12.3%; primary education 37.0%; some secondary
18.3%; secondary 12.9%; some college 18.4%. *Literacy* (2000): total population age 10 and over literate 72,140 (92.4%); males literate 36,528 (92.9%);
females literate 35,612 (91.9%).

Education (1997–98)

	schools	teachers	students	student/ teacher ratio
Elementary (age 6–12)	171	1,486	25,915	18.6
Secondary (age 13–18)	24	418	6,809	16.2
College	1	71	1,884	26.5

Health (1998): physicians 68 (1 per 1,677 persons); hospital beds (1997) 260 (1
per 447 persons); infant mortality rate per 1,000 live births (2000) 38.0.
Food: daily per capita caloric intake, n.a.

Military

External security is provided by the United States.

[1]On Nov. 3, 1986, the United States unilaterally terminated the UN trusteeship it held
over the Federated States of Micronesia (FSM), thus formally initiating their free-asso-
ciation political status. On Dec. 22, 1990, the United Nations Security Council joined
the Trusteeship Council, which had endorsed the termination of the trusteeship in May
1986. [2]Detail does not add to total given because of rounding. [3]Based on registered
deaths only. [4]Includes all areas formerly constituting the U.S. Trust Territory of the
Pacific Islands. [5]Includes subsistence farming and fishing. [6]Includes hotels. [7]Unem-
ployed. [8]January 1.

Internet resources for further information:
• **General Information on The FSM**
  http://www.boh.com/econ/pacific
• **U.S. Office on Insular Affairs**
  http://www.pacificweb.org

Moldova

Official name: Republica Moldova (Republic of Moldova).
Form of government: unitary parliamentary republic[1] with a single legislative body (Parliament [101]).
Head of state: President.
Head of government: Prime Minister.
Capital: Chişinău.
Official language: Romanian[2].
Official religion: none.
Monetary unit: 1 Moldovan leu (plural lei) = 100 bani; valuation (Sept. 23, 2002) free rate, 1 U.S.$ = 13.58 Moldovan lei; 1 £ = 21.10 Moldovan lei.

Area and population[3]

Counties	Capitals	area sq mi	area sq km	population 2002 estimate
Bălţi	Bălţi	1,576	4,081	501,900
Cahul	Cahul	941	2,438	189,900
Chişinău	Chişinău	1,073	2,780	381,500
Edineţ	Edineţ	1,231	3,187	282,800
Lăpuşna	Lăpuşna	1,327	3,436	276,300
Orhei	Orhei	1,100	2,850	300,500
Soroca	Soroca	1,221	3,162	276,700
Taraclia	Taraclia	395	1,022	45,800
Tighina	Tighina	1,119	2,899	169,300
Ungheni	Ungheni	971	2,516	260,200
City				
Chişinău	—	189	490	776,700
Autonomous Region				
Găgăuzia	Comrat	580	1,503	158,600
Disputed Territory[4]				
Stonga Nistruli (Transdniester)	...	1,343	3,479	627,100
TOTAL		13,066	33,843	4,247,300[5]

Demography

Population (2002): 3,621,000[6].
Density (2002): persons per sq mi 277.1, persons per sq km 107.0.
Urban-rural (2001): urban 41.4%; rural 58.6%.
Sex distribution (2001): male 47.66%; female 52.34%.
Age breakdown (2001): under 15, 22.4%; 15–29, 25.5%; 30–44, 21.1%; 45–59, 16.6%; 60–74, 11.0%; 75 and over, 3.4%.
Population projection: (2010) 3,550,000; (2020) 3,483,000.
Doubling time: not applicable; doubling time exceeds 100 years.
Ethnic composition (2000): Moldovan 48.2%; Ukrainian 13.8%; Russian 12.9%; Bulgarian 8.2%; Roma (Gypsy) 6.2%; Gagauz 4.2%; other 6.5%.
Religious affiliation (1995): Orthodox 46.0%, of which Romanian Orthodox 35.0%, Russian Orthodox 9.5%; Muslim 5.5%; Catholic 1.8%, of which Roman Catholic 0.6%; Protestant 1.7%; Jewish 0.9%; other (mostly nonreligious) 44.1%.
Major cities (1999): Chişinău 655,000; Tiraspol 200,700; Bălţi 156,600.

Vital statistics

Birth rate per 1,000 population (2001): 13.3 (world avg. 21.2); (1995) legitimate 87.7%; illegitimate 12.3%.
Death rate per 1,000 population (2001): 12.6 (world avg. 8.9).
Natural increase rate per 1,000 population (2001): 0.7 (world avg. 12.3).
Total fertility rate (avg. births per childbearing woman; 2001): 1.7.
Marriage rate per 1,000 population (1998): 6.0.
Life expectancy at birth (2001): male 60.2 years; female 69.3 years.
Major causes of death per 100,000 population (1994): circulatory diseases 500.7; cancers 136.1; accidents and violence 113.3; digestive system diseases 110.4.

National economy

Budget (1999). Revenue: 3,745,000,000 lei (value-added tax 25.1%, social fund contributions 20.9%, excise taxes 11.9%, profits tax 6.2%, duties and customs taxes 6.2%, personal income tax 5.9%). Expenditures: 4,535,000,000 lei (current expenditures 97.7%, of which interest payments 20.0%, social fund expenditures 19.6%, education 12.7%, health care 7.4%, national economy 6.3%; capital expenditure 2.3%).
Public debt (external, outstanding; 2000): U.S.$854,000,000.
Production (metric tons except as noted). Agriculture, forestry, fishing (2001): sugar beets 1,138,000, wheat 980,000, corn (maize) 825,400, grapes 430,150, potatoes 425,000, apples 132,000; livestock (number of live animals) 866,000 sheep, 543,000 pigs, 402,000 cattle; roundwood (2000) 58,300 cu m; fish catch (1999) 1,630. Mining and quarrying (1995): sand and gravel 376,000; gypsum 13,600. Manufacturing ('000,000 lei; 1995): food 1,446,824; machinery 383,153; construction materials 164,198; textiles 57,283. Construction (1994): 127,200,000 lei. Energy production (consumption): electricity (kW-hr; 1999) 3,819,000,000 (4,997,000,000); coal (metric tons; 1999) none (620,000); crude petroleum (barrels; 1999) none (none); petroleum products (metric tons; 1999) none (835,000); natural gas (cu m; 1999) none (2,100,000,000).
Population economically active (1994): total (1999) 1,682,000; activity rate of total population 44.8% (participation rates: ages 16–59 [male], 16–54 [female] 85.2%; female 53.0%; unemployed [1998] 2.0%).

Price and earnings indexes (1995 = 100)

	1995	1996	1997	1998	1999	2000	2001
Consumer price index	100.0	120.9	130.6	139.2	203.2	266.8	292.9
Earnings index	100.0	...	...	...	...	...	...

Gross national product (at current market prices; 2000): U.S.$1,428,000,000 (U.S.$400 per capita).

Structure of gross domestic product and labour force

	1999 in value '000,000 lei[7]	1999 % of total value	1999 labour force	1999 % of labour force
Agriculture	2,727.1	22.4	731,000	43.4
Manufacturing, mining	1,602.2	13.1	138,000	8.2
Public utilities	369.2	3.0	22,000	1.3
Construction	373.3	3.1	44,000	2.6
Transp. and commun.	1,054.7	8.6	70,000	4.2
Trade[8]	1,615.7	13.2	150,000	8.9
Finance	857.2	7.0	45,000	2.7
Pub. admin., defense	2,258.4 }	18.5	49,000	2.9
Services			246,000	14.6
Other	1,345.9[9]	11.0[9]	187,000[10]	11.1[10]
TOTAL	12,203.7	100.0[11]	1,682,000	100.0[11]

Tourism (2000): receipts from visitors U.S.$46,000,000; expenditures by nationals abroad U.S.$78,000,000.
Household income and expenditure. Average household size (1989) 3.4; income per household: n.a.; sources of income (1994): wages and salaries 41.2%, social benefits 15.3%, agricultural income 10.4%, other 33.1%; expenditure (1995): food and drink 49.1%, clothing 9.7%, health 4.1%.
Land use (1994): forest 10.6%; pasture 10.9%; agriculture 75.9%; other 2.6%.

Foreign trade

Balance of trade (current prices)

	1995	1996	1997	1998	1999	2000
U.S.$'000,000	−55	−252	−348	−388	−128	−136
% of total	3.6%	13.3%	16.4%	23.2%	12.0%	10.8%

Imports (1999): U.S.$597,000,000 (mineral products 38.2%, machinery 12.1%, textiles 11.6%, chemical products 8.0%, agricultural goods 6.6%). *Major import sources* (1997): Russia 28.4%; Ukraine 18.0%; Romania 8.6%; Germany 8.1%.
Exports (1999): U.S.$469,000,000 (food and agricultural goods 42.5%, textile products 13.9%, machinery 5.9%, metals and metal products 3.5%). *Major export destinations* (1997): Russia 58.2%; Romania 6.7%; U.S. 6.7%; Ukraine 5.6%.

Transport and communications

Transport. Railroads (1998): length 2,710 km; passenger-km 656,000,000; metric ton-km cargo 2,575,000,000. Roads (1999): total length 12,657 km (paved 87%). Vehicles (1999): passenger cars 232,278; trucks and buses 66,012. Air transport (1997): passenger-km 61,000,000; metric ton-km cargo 6,000,000; airports (2000) 1.

Communications

Medium	date	unit	number	units per 1,000 persons
Daily newspapers	1996	circulation	261,000	59
Radio	1997	receivers	3,220,000	736
Television	1998	receivers	1,300,000	297
Telephones	2001	main lines	676,100	154
Cellular telephones	2001	subscribers	210,000	48
Personal computers	2001	units	70,000	16
Internet	2001	users	60,000	14

Education and health

Educational attainment (1989). Percentage of population age 15 and over having: no formal schooling or some primary education 24.5%; some secondary 20.4%; secondary 46.4%; higher 8.7%. *Literacy* (2000): total population age 15 and over literate 98.9%; males 99.6%; females 98.3%.

Education (1996–97)

	schools[12]	teachers	students	student/ teacher ratio
Primary (age 7–13) }	1,700	14,097	320,725	22.8
Secondary (age 14–17) }		28,615[13]	419,256	...
Voc., teacher tr.	64	...	26,245	...
Higher	20	8,814	93,759	10.6

Health (1995): physicians 17,200 (1 per 250 persons); hospital beds 53,000 (1 per 82 persons); infant mortality rate per 1,000 live births (2001) 42.7.
Food (2000): daily per capita caloric intake 2,764 (vegetable products 86%, animal products 14%); 108% of FAO recommended minimum requirement.

Military

Total active duty personnel (2001): 8,220 (army 86.6%, air force 13.4%). *Military expenditure as percentage of GNP* (1999): 1.6% (world 2.4%); per capita expenditure U.S.$10.

---

[1]Moldova is officially a parliamentary republic from Oct. 27, 2000. [2]Officially designated Moldovan per constitution. [3]Local government structure reorganized in 1999. [4]Breakaway area from 1991. [5]Includes about 600,000 Moldovans working abroad (particularly in Western Europe). [6]Excludes about 600,000 Moldovans working abroad. [7]Excludes Stonga Nistruli (Transdniester). [8]Includes hotels. [9]Import and production taxes less subsidies. [10]Includes unemployed. [11]Detail does not add to total given because of rounding. [12]1995–96. [13]Secondary includes Voc., teacher tr.

Internet resources for further information:
• Moldova.Net http://www.moldova.net

Monaco

Official name: Principauté de Monaco
(Principality of Monaco).
Form of government: constitutional
monarchy with one legislative body
(National Council [18]).
Chief of state: Prince.
Head of government[1]: Minister of
State assisted by the Council of
Government.
Capital: [2].
Official language: French.
Official religion: Roman Catholicism.
Monetary unit: 1 euro
(€) = 100 centimes; valuation
(Sept. 23, 2002) 1 U.S.$ = €1.02;
1 £ = €1.58[3].

Area and population

Quarters[2]	Capitals	area sq mi	area sq km	population 1990 census
Fontvieille	—	0.13	0.33	1,961
La Condamine	—	0.23	0.61	12,158
Monaco-Ville	—	0.08	0.20	1,151
Monte-Carlo	—	0.32	0.82	14,702
TOTAL		0.76	1.96	29,972

Demography

Population (2002): 32,000.
Density (2002): persons per sq mi 42,105, persons per sq km 16,326.
Urban-rural (2000): urban 100%; rural 0%.
Sex distribution (2000): male 47.58%; female 52.42%.
Age breakdown (2000): under 15, 15.1%; 15–29, 14.0%; 30–44, 21.2%; 45–59,
21.3%; 60–74, 17.2%; 75 and over, 11.2%.
Population projection: (2000) 33,000; (2010) 34,200.
Doubling time: not applicable.
Ethnic composition (2000): French 45.8%; Ligurian (Genoan) 17.2%;
Moneguasque 16.9%; British 4.5%; Jewish 1.7%; other 13.9%.
Religious affiliation (2000): Christian 93.2%, of which Roman Catholic 89.3%;
Jewish 1.7%; nonreligious and other 5.1%.

Vital statistics

Birth rate per 1,000 population (2000): 22.8 (world avg. 22.5).
Death rate per 1,000 population (2000): 16.4 (world avg. 9.0).
Natural increase rate per 1,000 population (2000): 6.4 (world avg. 13.5).
Total fertility rate (avg. births per childbearing woman; 2000): 1.8.
Marriage rate per 1,000 population (1997): 6.0.
Divorce rate per 1,000 population (1997): 2.5.
Life expectancy at birth (2000): male 74.9 years; female 83.0 years.
Major causes of death per 100,000 population: n.a.; however, principal causes
are those of a developed country with an older population.

National economy

Budget (1997). Revenue: F 3,225,658,000 (value-added taxes 50.0%)[4].
Expenditures: F 3,139,854,000.
Public debt: n.a.
Production. Agriculture, forestry, fishing: some horticulture and greenhouse
cultivation; no agriculture as such. Mining and quarrying: none.
Manufacturing: in the 1990s, principal manufactures included chemicals, cos-
metics, perfumery, and pharmaceuticals; light electronics and precision instru-
ments; paper and card manufactures; fabricated plastics; and clothing.
Construction: n.a. Energy production (consumption): electricity (kW-hr;
1997), n.a. (403,000,000 [imported from France]); coal, none (n.a.); crude
petroleum, none (n.a.); natural gas, none (n.a.).
Gross domestic product (1994): U.S.$765,000,000[5] (U.S.$24,460 per capita).

Distribution of value of sales and labour force

	1992 in value F '000,000	1992 % of total value	1990 labour force[6]	1990 % of labour force[6]
Agriculture	...	...	41	0.3
Manufacturing	3,650	11.3	3,754	29.8
Construction	} 7	} 7	122	1.0
Public utilities				
Hotels, restaurants	1,140	3.5	1,445	11.5
Transportation and communications	...	...	} 3,491	} 27.8
Finance, real estate	3,780[7]	11.6[7]		
Services	23,870	73.6		
Pub. admin., defense	...	...	2,828	22.5
Other	—	—	893[8]	7.1[8]
TOTAL	32,440	100.0	12,574	100.0

Population economically active (1990): total 12,574 (42.0%); female participation in labour force 5,002 (39.8%); ages 17–64, 63.6%; unemployed (1996)
3.0%.

Price and earnings indexes (1995 = 100)

	1995	1996	1997	1998	1999	2000	2001
Consumer price index[9]	100.0	102.0	103.2	103.9	104.5	106.3	108.1
Earnings index	100.0	101.9	104.7	107.6	110.0	115.0	120.2

Household income and expenditure. Average household size (1998) 2.2; average annual income per household: n.a.; sources of income: n.a.; expenditure:
n.a.
Tourism (1999): 2,219 hotel rooms; 278,000 overnight stays.
Land use (2000): forested 0%; meadows and pastures 0%; agricultural and
under permanent cultivation 0%; built-up and other 100%.

Foreign trade

Monaco participates in a customs union (since 1963) with France; separate figures are not available.

Transport and communications

Transport. Railroads (1997): length 1.1 mi, 1.7 km; passengers 2,171,100; cargo
3,357 tons. Roads (1997): total length 31 mi, 50 km (paved 100%). Vehicles
(1997): passenger cars 21,120; trucks and buses 2,770. Merchant marine
(1997): vessels (100 gross tons and over) 9; total deadweight tonnage (1989)
4,959. Air transport (1999): traffic, not applicable; airports with scheduled
flights: none[10].

Communications

Medium	date	unit	number	units per 1,000 persons
Daily newspapers	1999	circulation	10,000	300
Radio	1997	receivers	34,000	1,030
Television	1997	receivers	25,000	758
Telephones	1999	main lines	33,000	990
Cellular telephones	1999	subscribers	12,000	360

Education and health

Education (1996–97)

	schools	teachers	students	student/ teacher ratio
Primary (age 6–10)	8	127	1,917	15.1
Secondary (age 11–17)	6	192	2,416	12.6
Vocational	4	89	532	6.0
Higher	1	...	112	...

Literacy: virtually 100%.
Health (1997): physicians 188 (1 per 170 persons); hospital beds 555 (1 per 58
persons); infant mortality rate per 1,000 live births (2000) 5.9.
Food: daily per capita caloric intake, n.a.; assuming consumption patterns similar to France (2000) 3,591 (vegetable products 62%, animal products 38%);
143% of FAO recommended minimum requirement.

Military

Defense responsibility lies with France according to the terms of the Versailles
Treaty of 1919.

[1]Under the authority of the prince. [2]The principality is a single administrative unit, and
no separate area within it is distinguished as capital. [3]French franc replaced by euro.
[4]The main sources of revenue in 1997 were financial activities (about 50%) and tourism
(about 25%); receipts from gambling had declined to about 4%. [5]UN estimate.
[6]Officially economically active per 1990 census; the employed labour force in 1998
(including many foreign workers) was 32,697. [7]Finance, real estate includes Construction
and Public utilities. [8]Includes not adequately defined. [9]The index is for France, which
is united with Monaco in a customs and monetary union. [10]Fixed-wing service is provided at Nice, France; helicopter service is available at Fontvieille; passengers carried
(1997) 131,038.

Internet resources for further information:
• **Welcome to Monaco (official guide)**
   http://www.monaco.mc/monaco/index.html
• **Monaco: Internet Resources**
   http://internet.ggu.edu/university_library/countries/Monaco.html

Mongolia

Official name: Mongol Uls (Mongolia).
Form of government: unitary multiparty republic with one legislative house (State Great Hural [76]).
Chief of state: President.
Head of government: Prime Minister.
Capital: Ulaanbaatar (Ulan Bator).
Official language: Khalkha Mongolian.
Official religion: none.
Monetary unit: 1 tugrik (Tug) = 100 möngö; valuation (Sept. 23, 2002) 1 U.S.$ = Tug 1,116; 1 £ = Tug 1,734.

Area and population

Provinces	Capitals	area[1] sq mi	area[1] sq km	population 2000 census
Arhangay	Tsetserleg	21,400	55,300	97,091
Bayan-Ölgiy	Ölgiy	17,600	45,700	91,068
Bayanhongor	Bayanhongor	44,800	116,000	84,779
Bulgan	Bulgan	18,800	48,700	61,776
Darhan-Uul	Darhan	1,270	3,280	83,271
Dornod	Choybalsan	47,700	123,600	75,373
Dornogoví	Saynshand	42,300	109,500	50,575
Dundgoví	Manalgovi	28,800	74,700	51,517
Dzavhan	Uliastay	31,900	82,500	89,999
Govĭ-Altay	Altay	54,600	141,400	63,673
Govĭ-Sümber	Choyr	2,140	5,540	12,230
Hentiy	Öndörhaan	31,000	80,300	70,946
Hovd	Hovd	29,400	76,100	86,831
Hövsgöl	Mörön	38,800	100,600	119,063
Ömnögoví	Dalandzadgad	63,900	165,400	46,858
Orhon	Erdenet	320	840	71,525
Övörhangay	Aryayheer	24,300	62,900	111,420
Selenge	Sühbaatar	15,900	41,200	99,950
Sühbaatar	Baruun-Urt	31,800	82,300	56,166
Töv	Dzüünmod	28,600	74,000	99,268
Uvs	Ulaangom	26,900	69,600	90,037
Autonomous municipality				
Ulaanbaatar	—	1,800	4,700	760,077
TOTAL	...	603,930[2]	1,564,160	2,373,493

Demography

Population (2002): 2,457,000.
Density (2002): persons per sq mi 4.1, persons per sq km 1.6.
Urban-rural (2000): urban 56.6%; rural 43.4%.
Sex distribution (2000): male 49.63%; female 50.37%.
Age breakdown (2000): under 15, 35.8%; 15–29, 30.2%; 30–44, 20.5%; 45–59, 8.3%; 60–69, 3.3%; 70 and over, 1.9%.
Population projection: (2010) 2,714,000; (2020) 3,113,000.
Doubling time: 47 years.
Ethnic composition (2000): Khalkha Mongol 81.5%; Kazakh 4.3%; Dörbed Mongol 2.8%; Bayad 2.1%; Buryat Mongol 1.7%; Dariganga Mongol 1.3%; Zakhchin 1.3%; Tuvan (Uriankhai) 1.1%; other 3.9%.
Religious affiliation (1995): Tantric Buddhist (Lamaism) 96.0%; Muslim 4.0%.
Major cities (2000): Ulaanbaatar (Ulan Bator) 760,077; Erdenet 68,310; Darhan 65,791; Choybalsan 41,714; Ulaangom 26,319.

Vital statistics

Birth rate per 1,000 population (2001): 21.8 (world avg. 21.2).
Death rate per 1,000 population (2001): 7.1 (world avg. 8.9).
Natural increase rate per 1,000 population (2001): 14.7 (world avg. 12.3).
Total fertility rate (avg. births per childbearing woman; 2001): 2.4.
Marriage rate per 1,000 population (2000): 5.0.
Divorce rate per 1,000 population (2000): 1.5.
Life expectancy at birth (2001): male 62.1 years; female 66.5 years.
Major causes of death per 100,000 population: n.a.; however, in the early 1990s, major causes of mortality included diseases of the cardiovascular system, the respiratory system, and the cerebrovascular system.

National economy

Budget (2001). Revenue: Tug 333,491,400,000 (taxes 75.0%, of which sales tax 26.8%, social security contributions 13.3%, special taxes 12.1%, income taxes 11.3%, custom duties 8.8%; nontax revenue 25.0%). Expenditures: Tug 423,985,500 (education, health, social services 58.4%; transfers to provincial governments 14.0%; capital investment 6.9%; wages 7.9%; defense 6.0%).
Public debt (external; 2000): U.S.$794,800,000.
Tourism (1999): receipts U.S.$36,000,000; expenditures U.S.$41,000,000.
Population economically active (2000): total 944,083; activity rate of total population 39.8% (participation rates: ages 15 and over 61.9%; female 50.8%; unemployed [2002] 11.5%).

Price and earnings indexes (1995 = 100)

	1995	1996	1997	1998	1999	2000	2001
Consumer price index	100.0	149.3	203.9	223.0	239.9	267.7	289.5
Monthly earnings index	100.0	146.4	185.4	234.4	...	...	...

Production (metric tons except as noted). Agriculture, forestry, fishing (2000): wheat 142,100, potatoes 58,900, vegetables and melons 44,000; livestock (number of live animals) 13,876,400 sheep, 10,077,500 goats, 3,097,600 cattle, 2,660,700 horses, 322,900 camels, 14,684 pigs; roundwood (2000) 631,000 cu m; fish catch (1999) 524. Mining and quarrying (2000): fluorspar 733,500; copper 357,800; molybdenum 2,843; gold 11,808 kg. Manufacturing (value added

by manufacturing in Tug '000,000; 1996): food products 10,261.3; textiles 6,522.8; beverages 3,316.6; clothing and apparel 2,782.6; nonmetallic mineral products 1,708.8; leather and footwear 1,374.1; wood products 847.0; printing 834.2; chemicals 724.9. Construction (1994): residential 120,400 sq m. Energy production (consumption): electricity (kW-hr; 2000) 2,946,000,000 (3,042,-000,000); coal (metric tons; 2000) 5,185,000 (4,986,000); petroleum products (metric tons; 1998) none (278,300).
Gross national product (2000): U.S.$947,000,000 (U.S.$390 per capita).

Structure of gross domestic product and labour force

	2000 in value Tug '000,000	% of total value	labour force[3]	% of labour force[3]
Agriculture	287,200	32.8	367,700	47.1
Mining	4	4	18,800	2.5
Manufacturing	211,500[4]	24.1[4]	56,600	7.3
Construction	30,200	3.4	13,700	1.8
Public utilities	4	4	15,900	2.1
Transp. and commun.	59,100	6.7	42,100	5.4
Trade	169,300	19.3	79,600	10.2
Finance, real estate	} 118,700	} 13.6	14,700	1.9
Public admin., defense			59,600	7.6
Services			100,000	12.8
Other	—	—	10,400	1.3
TOTAL	876,000	100.0[2]	779,100	100.0

Household income and expenditure (2000): Average household size 4.4; monthly income per household (1999) Tug 67,426 (U.S.$66); sources of income (1999): wages 36.4%, transfer payments 11.7%, self-employment 41.2%[5], other 10.7%; expenditure (1999): food 41.1%, housing 11.4%, clothing 9.7%, education 7.5%, transportation and communications 7.1%, healthcare 3.6%.
Land use (1998): forest and other 24.4%; pasture 74.8%; agriculture 0.8%.

Foreign trade[6]

Balance of trade (current prices)

	1994	1995	1996	1997	1998	1999
U.S.$'000,000	+97.7	+58.0	−26.6	−16.8	−158.1	−246.9
% of total	15.9%	6.5%	3.0%	1.8%	18.6%	13.9%

Imports (2000): U.S.$574,200,000 (1998; capital equipment 33.5%, energy 15.7%, food 13.9%, consumer goods 12.6%, raw materials and spare parts 10.8%). *Major import sources:* Russia 33.6%; China 20.5%; Japan 11.9%; South Korea 9.1%; United States 4.6%; Germany 4.6%.
Exports (2000): U.S.$432,300,000 (mineral products 59.3%, of which copper 33.1%; textiles 23.2%; cashmere 11.3%; wool, hides, and leather goods 6.2%). *Major export destinations:* China 58.9%; United States 19.9%; Russia 9.7%; Italy 3.1%; U.K. 2.4%.

Transport and communications

Transport. Railroads (2000): length 1,815 km; passenger-km (1999): 559,800,000; metric ton-km cargo 4,282,500. Roads (1999): total length 49,250 km (paved 4%). Vehicles (2000): passenger cars 44,100; trucks and buses 37,600. Air transport (1996): passenger-km 525,000,000; metric ton-km cargo 48,000,000; airports (2000) with scheduled flights 1.

Communications

Medium	date	unit	number	units per 1,000 persons
Daily newspapers	1996	circulation	68,000	27
Radio	1997	receivers	360,000	142
Television	2000	receivers	169,100	58
Telephones	2001	main lines	123,000	48
Cellular telephones	2001	subscribers	195,000	76
Personal computers	2001	units	35,000	14
Internet	2001	users	40,000	16

Education and health

Educational attainment (2000). Percentage of population age 10 and over having: no formal education 11.6%; primary education 23.5%; secondary 46.1%; vocational secondary 11.2%; higher 7.6%. *Literacy* (2000): percentage of total population age 15 and over literate 97.8%; males 98.0%; females 97.5%.

Education (2000–01)

	schools	teachers	students	student/ teacher ratio
Primary (age 6–12)	} 705	19,200	494,500	25.8
Secondary (age 13–16)				
Vocational (age 16–18)	36	865	12,177	14.1
Higher	172	4,920	84,970	17.2

Health (1999): physicians 6,162 (1 per 384 persons) hospital beds 17,877 (1 per 132 persons); infant mortality rate per 1,000 live births (2001) 53.5.
Food (2000): daily per capita caloric intake 1,981 (vegetable products 52%, animal products 48%); 82% of FAO recommended minimum.

Military

Total active duty personnel (2001): 9,100 (army 82.4%, air force 17.6%). *Military expenditure as percentage of GNP* (1999): 2.1% (world 2.4%); per capita expenditure U.S.$5.

[1]Rounded figures. [2]Detail does not add to total given because of rounding. [3]Employed only. [4]Manufacturing includes Mining and Public utilities. [5]Includes income from agricultural cooperatives. [6]Imports c.i.f. in balance of trade table.

Internet resources for further information:
• **National Statistical Office of Mongolia**
  http://nso.mn/eng/header.htm

Morocco

Official name: Al-Mamlakah al-Maghribīyah (Kingdom of Morocco).
Form of government: constitutional monarchy with two legislative houses (House of Councillors [270[1]]; House of Representatives [325]).
Chief of state and head of government: King assisted by Prime Minister.
Capital: Rabat.
Official language: Arabic.
Official religion: Islam.
Monetary unit: 1 Moroccan dirham (DH) = 100 Moroccan francs; valuation (Sept. 23, 2002) 1 U.S.$ = DH 10.67; 1 £ = DH 16.59.

Population (2000 estimate)[2]

Provinces	Administrative centres	Population
Chaouia-Ouardigha	Settat	1,637,000
Doukkala-Abda	Safi	1,934,000
Fès-Boulemane	Fès	1,517,000
Gharb-Chrarda-Béni Hsen	Kénitra	1,806,000
Grand Casablanca	Casablanca	3,422,000
Guelmim-Es Semara	Guelmim	424,000
Laâyoune-Bojador-Sakia El-Hamra	Laâyoune	207,000
Marrakech-Tensift-El Haouz	Marrakech	2,951,000
Meknès-Tafilalt	Meknès	2,065,000
Oriental	Oujda	1,877,000
Oued Eddahab-Lagouira[3]	Dakhla	48,000
Rabat-Salé-Zemmour-Zaër	Rabat	2,280,000
Sous-Massa-Draâ	Agadir	2,961,000
Tadla-Azilal	Béni Mellal	1,435,000
Tangier-Tetouan	Tangier	2,326,000
Taza-Al Hoceïma-Taounate	Al-Hoceïma	1,815,000
	TOTAL	28,705,000

Demography

Area[2]: 274,461 sq mi, 710,850 sq km.
Population (2002)[2]: 29,632,000.
Density (2002)[2]: persons per sq mi 108.0, persons per sq km 41.7.
Urban-rural (1999): urban 52.7%; rural 47.3%.
Sex distribution (1999): male 49.89%; female 50.11%.
Age breakdown (1999): under 15, 35.7%; 15–29, 28.9%; 30–44, 18.9%; 45–59, 9.2%; 60–74, 5.3%; 75 and over, 2.0%.
Population projection[2]: (2010) 33,601,000; (2020) 38,326,000.
Doubling time: 40 years.
Ethnolinguistic composition (1995): Arab 65%; Berber 33%; other 2%.
Religious affiliation (2000): Muslim (mostly Sunnī) 98.3%; Christian 0.6%; other 1.1%.
Major urban areas (1994): Casablanca 2,940,623; Rabat-Salé 1,385,872; Fès 774,574; Marrakech 745,541; Oujda 678,778; Agadir 550,200.

Vital statistics

Birth rate per 1,000 population (2002): 23.6 (world avg. 21.2).
Death rate per 1,000 population (2002): 5.9 (world avg. 8.9).
Natural increase rate per 1,000 population (2002): 17.7 (world avg. 12.3).
Total fertility rate (avg. birth per childbearing woman; 2002): 3.0.
Life expectancy at birth (2002): male 67.5 years; female 72.1 years.
Major causes of death (1989)[4]: childhood diseases 22.9%; circulatory diseases 15.4%; accidents 7.3%; infectious and parasitic diseases 6.3%; cancers 5.6%.

National economy

Budget. Revenue (1997): DH 79,747,000,000 (taxes on income and profits 25.2%; value-added tax 22.7%; excise taxes 17.9%; international trade 15.0%; stamp tax 4.4%). *Expenditures (1997):* DH 86,058,000,000 (current expenditure 78.7%, of which wages 39.7%, debt payment 20.1%; capital expenditure 21.3%).
Public debt (external, outstanding; 2000): U.S.$15,793,000,000.
Tourism (2000): receipts U.S.$2,040,000; expenditures U.S.$430,000,000.
Production (metric tons except as noted). Agriculture, forestry, fishing (1999): sugar beets 3,223,400, wheat 2,153,540, barley 1,473,980, sugarcane 1,372,900, potatoes 1,140,780, oranges 873,500, tomatoes 857,410; livestock (number of live animals) 16,576,400 sheep, 5,114,400 goats, 2,559,800 cattle, 979,800 asses, 150,000 horses, 100,000 chickens, 36,000 camels; roundwood (1998) 1,746,000 cu m; fish catch (1997) 625,000. Mining and quarrying (1996): phosphate rock 20,792,000; barite 283,000; zinc 152,000; lead 108,000; copper 38,000; silver 199. Manufacturing (value added in DH '000,000; 1996): food 39,280; chemical products 13,508; textiles 12,392. Construction (authorized, urban areas; 1994): residential 7,069,557 sq m; nonresidential 998,424 sq m. Energy production (consumption): electricity (kW-hr; 2001) 13,339,000,000 ([1997] 14,192,-000,000); coal (metric tons; 2001) 135,000 ([1997] 3,009,000); crude petroleum (barrels; 1997) 88,000 (43,460,000); petroleum products (metric tons; 1997) 5,056,000 (6,146,000); natural gas (cu m; 1997) 30,625,000 (30,625,000).
Population economically active (1998): total 5,137,539; activity rate 34.4% (participation rates: over age 15, 48.1%; female 23.8%; unemployed 19.0%).

Price and earnings indexes (1995 = 100)

	1995	1996	1997	1998	1999	2000	2001
Consumer price index	100.0	103.0	103.9	106.9	107.6	109.7	110.4
Earnings index[5]	100.0	101.1	...	...	...	...	...

Gross national product (2000): U.S.$33,940,000,000 (U.S.$1,180 per capita).

Structure of gross domestic product and labour force

	1996 in value DH '000,000	1996 % of total value	1993 labour force	1993 % of labour force
Agriculture	65,478	20.4	2,906,000	34.0
Mining	5,539	1.7		
Manufacturing	54,384	16.9		
Construction	13,515	4.2	2,650,000	31.0
Public utilities	24,568	7.7		
Transp. and commun.	18,152	5.7		
Trade	35,755	11.1		
Finance	...	...		
Pub. admin., defense	39,350	12.3	2,991,000	35.0
Services	39,724	12.4		
Other	24,454	7.6		
TOTAL	320,919	100.0	8,547,000	100.0

Household income and expenditure. Average household size (1998) 5.7; expenditure (1994)[6]: food 45.2%, housing 12.5%, transportation 7.6%.

Foreign trade[7]

Balance of trade (current prices)

	1996	1997	1998	1999	2000	2001
DH '000,000	−24,599	−23,655	−30,608	−25,171	−43,310	−43,423
% of total	17.0%	15.0%	18.0%	14.8%	21.6%	21.2%

Imports (2000): DH 121,983,000,000 (finished consumer products 23.5%, of which textiles and apparel 8.8%; finished industrial products 20.2%; mineral fuels 17.8%, of which crude petroleum 12.1%; food 11.7%, of which wheat 4.5%). *Major import sources:* France 24.3%; Spain 9.8%; U.K. 6.0%; U.S. 5.6%; Germany 4.9%.
Exports (2000): DH 78,673,000,000 (finished consumer products 37.5%, of which hosiery 11.2%; food 20.8%, of which crustaceans and mollusks 8.1%; phosphoric acid 6.8%; phosphates 5.8%; electronic components 5.3%). *Major export destinations:* France 33.6%; Spain 12.7%; U.K. 9.3%; Italy 7.6%; Germany 4.4%.

Transport and communications

Transport. Railroads (1996): route length 1,768 km; passenger-km 1,776,000,-000; metric ton-km cargo 4,757,000,000. Roads (1996): total length 57,810 km (paved 52%). Vehicles (1996): passenger cars 1,018,146; trucks and buses 278,075. Air transport (2001)[8]: passenger-km 7,362,000,000; metric ton-km cargo 76,005,000; airports (1998) 11.

Communications

Medium	date	unit	number	units per 1,000 persons
Daily newspapers	1996	circulation	704,000	27
Radio	1997	receivers	6,640,000	247
Television	1997	receivers	3,100,000	115
Telephones	2001	main lines	1,191,000	39
Cellular telephones	2001	subscribers	4,772,000	157
Personal computers	2001	units	400,000	13
Internet	2001	users	400,000	13

Education and health

Educational attainment (1982). Percentage of population age 25 and over having: no formal education 47.8%; some primary education 47.8%; some secondary 3.8%; higher 0.6%. *Literacy (1995):* total population over age 15 literate 43.7%; males literate 56.6%; females literate 31.0%.

Education (1996–97)

	schools	teachers	students	student/teacher ratio
Primary (age 7–12)	5,806	114,406	3,160,907	27.6
Secondary (age 13–17)	451[9]	84,202	1,345,589	16.0
Vocational[10]	...	...	96,460	...
Higher	13[11]	13,155	31,743	11.0

Health (1994): physicians 8,838 (1 per 2,923 persons); hospital beds 26,407 (1 per 978 persons); infant mortality rate (2001) 48.1.
Food (1999): daily per capita caloric intake 3,010 (vegetable products 94%, animal products 6%); 124% of FAO recommended minimum requirement.

Military

Total active duty personnel (2001): 198,500 (army 88.2%, navy 5.0%, air force 6.8%). *Military expenditure as percentage of GDP (1999):* 4.3% (world 2.4%); per capita expenditure U.S.$49.

[1]All seats indirectly elected; 162 by regional councils; 108 by industry, agriculture, and trade unions. [2]Includes Western Sahara, annexure of Morocco whose unresolved political status (from 1991) is to be eventually decided by a UN-sponsored referendum; Western Sahara area: 97,344 sq mi, 252,120 sq km; Western Sahara population (2002 est.) 256,000. [3]Includes Aousserd province created in late 1990s. [4]Registered deaths of urban population only. [5]Central government employees only. [6]Weights of consumer price index components. [7]Imports c.i.f.; exports f.o.b. [8]Royal Air Maroc only. [9]1994–95. [10]Excludes teacher training. [11]Universities only.

Internet resources for further information:
• Moroccan Central Statistical Office http://www.statistic.gov.ma

Mozambique

Official name: República de Moçambique (Republic of Mozambique).
Form of government: multiparty republic with a single legislative house (Assembly of the Republic [250]).
Head of state and government: President assisted by the Prime Minister.
Capital: Maputo.
Official language: Portuguese.
Official religion: none.
Monetary unit: 1 metical (Mt; plural meticais) = 100 centavos; valuation (Sept. 23, 2002) 1 U.S.$ = Mt 23,285; 1 £ = Mt 36,188.

Area and population		area		population
				2002
Provinces	**Capitals**	sq mi	sq km	estimate
Cabo Delgado	Pemba	31,902	82,625	1,525,634
Gaza	Xai-Xai	29,231	75,709	1,266,431
Inhambane	Inhambane	26,492	68,615	1,326,848
Manica	Chimoio	23,807	61,661	1,207,332
Maputo	Maputo	9,944	25,756	1,003,992
Nampula	Nampula	31,508	81,606	3,410,141
Niassa	Lichinga	49,828	129,055	916,672
Sofala	Beira	26,262	68,018	1,516,166
Tete	Tete	38,890	100,724	1,388,205
Zambézia	Quelimane	40,544	105,008	3,476,484
City				
Maputo	—	232	602	1,044,618
TOTAL LAND AREA		308,642[1]	799,379	
INLAND WATER		5,019	13,000	
TOTAL		313,661	812,379	18,082,523

Demography

Population (2002): 18,083,000.
Density (2002): persons per sq mi 57.7, persons per sq km 22.3.
Urban-rural (2000): urban 40.2%; rural 59.8%.
Sex distribution (2002): male 48.12%; female 51.88%.
Age breakdown (2001): under 15, 42.7%; 15–29, 29.2%; 30–44, 15.2%; 45–59, 8.4%; 60–74, 3.8%; 75 and over, 0.7%.
Population projection: (2010) 18,909,000; (2020) 19,022,000.
Doubling time: 54 years.
Ethnic composition (2000): Makuana 15.3%; Makua 14.5%; Tsonga 8.6%; Sena 8.0%; Lomwe 7.1%; Tswa 5.7%; Chwabo 5.5%; other 35.3%.
Linguistic composition (1997): Makua 26.3%; Tsonga 11.4%; Lomwe 7.6%; Sena 7.0%; Portuguese 6.5%; Chuaba 6.3%; other Bantu languages 33.0%; other 1.9%.
Religious affiliation (2000): traditional beliefs 50.4%; Christian 38.4%, of which Roman Catholic 15.8%, Protestant 8.9%; Muslim 10.5%.
Major cities (1997): Maputo 989,386; Matola 440,927; Beira 412,588; Nampula 314,965; Chimoio 177,608.

Vital statistics

Birth rate per 1,000 population (2001): 37.2 (world avg. 21.2).
Death rate per 1,000 population (2001): 24.2 (world avg. 8.9).
Natural increase rate per 1,000 population (2001): 13.0 (world avg. 12.3).
Total fertility rate (avg. births per childbearing woman; 2001): 4.8.
Life expectancy at birth (2001): male 37.3 years; female 35.6 years.

National economy

Budget (2001). Revenue: Mt 19,253,000,000 (grants 50.1%; tax revenue 44.6%, of which sales tax 27.9%, customs taxes 7.7%, individual income tax 7.7%; nontax revenue 5.3%). Expenditures: Mt 23,221,000,000 (current expenditures 45.2%, of which administrative salaries 21.1%, goods and services 10.3%, transfers 9.6%; capital expenditures 44.9%; net lending 9.9%).
Public debt (external, outstanding; 2000): U.S.$4,599,000,000.
Production (metric tons except as noted). Agriculture, forestry, fishing (2001): cassava 5,361,974, corn (maize) 1,143,263, sugarcane 397,276, sorghum 313,787, coconuts 300,000, rice 166,945, peanuts (groundnuts) 109,175, bananas 59,000, cashews 57,894; livestock (number of live animals) 1,320,000 cattle, 392,000 goats, 180,000 pigs, 125,000 sheep, 28,000,000 chickens; roundwood (2001) 18,043,000 cu m; fish catch (1999) 35,560. Mining and quarrying (2000): gold 23 kg[2]; semiprecious gemstones 3,400 carats. Manufacturing (gross production value in Mt '000,000; 1998): beverages and tobacco 1,753,706; food 1,238,569; chemicals 497,406; nonmetallic mineral products 485,289; machinery and transport equipment 226,169; textiles 209,169; iron and steel 76,042. Construction (value in Mt; 1994) 157,700,000. Energy production (consumption): electricity (kW-hr; 1997) 570,000,000 (1,174,000,000); coal (metric tons; 2000) 16,100 ([1997] 60,000); crude petroleum, none (none); petroleum products (metric tons; 1997) none (277,000); natural gas (cu m; 2000) 55,000,000 (n.a.).
Household income and expenditure. Average family size (1997) 4.1; income per household: n.a.; source of income (1992–93)[3]: wages and salaries 51.6%, self-employment 12.5%, barter 11.5%, private farming 7.7%; expenditure (1992–93)[3]: food, beverages, and tobacco 74.6%; housing and energy 11.7%; transportation and communications 4.7%; clothing and footwear 3.7%; education and recreation 1.4%; health 0.8%.

Population economically active (1999): total 9,985,000; activity rate 59.3% (participation rates [1980]: over age 15, 87.3%; female [1980] 52.4%; unemployed [1980] 1.7%).

Price and earnings indexes (1995 = 100)							
	1995	1996	1997	1998	1999	2000	2001
Consumer price index	100.0	146.9	156.3	157.1	160.3	174.9	195.3[4]
Monthly earnings index	...	...	...	...	...	...	...

Gross national product (2000): U.S.$3,746,000,000 (U.S.$270 per capita).

Structure of gross domestic product and labour force				
	2001		1991	
	in value Mt '000,000	% of total value	labour force	% of labour force
Agriculture	15,510,000	20.8	6,870,000	81.4
Mining	} 8,206,000	11.0		
Manufacturing				
Construction	8,761,000	11.7	} 766,000	9.1
Public utilities	1,573,000	2.1		
Transp. and commun.	11,982,000	16.0		
Finance	4,437,000	5.9		
Trade	13,643,000	18.3	} 798,000	9.5
Pub. admin., defense	5,320,000	7.1		
Services	5,243,000	7.0		
Other	...	...	...	...
TOTAL	74,675,000	100.0[1]	8,434,000	100.0

Land use (1994): forested 22.1%; meadows and pastures 56.1%; agricultural and under permanent cultivation 4.0%; other 17.8%.

Foreign trade[5]

Balance of trade (current prices)						
	1996	1997	1998	1999	2000	2001
U.S.$'000,000	−490	−530.0	−572.7	−916.1	−798.3	−413.9
% of total	55.4%	53.5%	53.9%	61.8%	52.3%	22.7%

Imports (2000): U.S.$1,162,300,000 (1996; machinery and transport equipment 32.3%, food and beverages 18.3%, basic manufactures 17.4%, petroleum products 9.6%). *Major import sources:* South Africa 49.8%; European Union 28.6%, of which Portugal 7.6%; Japan 4.6%; U.S. 3.5%.
Exports (2000): U.S.$364,000,000 (prawns 25.1%, electricity 18.4%, aluminum 16.5%, cotton 7.0%, cashews 5.6%). *Major export destinations:* Zimbabwe 17.7%; South Africa 14.6%; Portugal 11.6%; Spain 10.7%; U.S. 4.7%; Japan 4.2%.

Transport and communications

Transport. Railroads (1999): route length 1,940 mi, 3,123 km; passenger-mi 89,912,000, passenger-km 144,700,000; short ton-mi cargo 448,194,000, metric ton-km cargo 721,300,000. Roads (1996): total length 18,890 mi, 30,400 km (paved 19%). Vehicles (1995): passenger cars 84,000; trucks and buses 26,800. Air transport (1999): passenger-mi 193,681,000, passenger-km 311,700,000; short ton-mi cargo 3,790,000, metric ton-km cargo 6,100,000; airports (1997) with scheduled flights 7.

Communications				units per 1,000
Medium	date	unit	number	persons
Daily newspapers	1996	circulation	49,000	2.7
Radio	1997	receivers	730,000	40
Television	1999	receivers	95,000	5.0
Telephones	2001	main lines	89,400	4.4
Cellular telephones	2001	subscribers	169,900	8.4
Personal computers	2001	units	70,000	3.5
Internet	2001	users	15,000	0.7

Education and health

Literacy (2000): percentage of total population age 15 and over literate 43.8%; males literate 59.9%; females literate 28.4%.

Education (1997)	schools	teachers	students	student/ teacher ratio
Primary (7–12)	6,025	32,670	1,899,531	58.1
Secondary (13–18)	75	1,555	51,554	33.2
Voc., teacher tr.	25	565	12,001	21.2
Higher	3	954	7,156	7.5

Health: physicians (1996) 120[6] (1 per 124,697 persons); hospital beds (1997) 12,630 (1 per 1,210 persons); infant mortality rate (2001) 139.2.
Food (2000): daily per capita caloric intake 1,927 (vegetable products 97%, animal products 3%); 83% of FAO recommended minimum requirement.

Military

Total active duty personnel (2001): c. 11,100 (army 86%, navy 5%, air force 9%). *Military expenditure as percentage of GNP* (1999): 2.5% (world 2.4%); per capita expenditure U.S.$5.

---

[1]Detail does not add to total given because of rounding. [2]Official figures; unofficial artisanal production is 4,000–5,000 kg. [3]City of Maputo only. [4]Average of 2nd and 3rd quarters. [5]Import figures are c.i.f. [6]Government personnel only.

Internet resources for further information:
• Instituto Nacional de Estatística http://www.ine.gov.mz

Myanmar (Burma)

Official name: Pyidaungzu Myanma
Naingngandaw (Union of Myanmar).
Form of government: military regime.
Head of state and government:
Chairman of the State Peace and
Development Council.
Capital: Yangôn (Rangoon).
Official language: Burmese.
Official religion: none.
Monetary unit: 1 Myanmar kyat
(K) = 100 pyas; valuation[1] (Sept. 23,
2002) 1 U.S.$ = K 6.45; 1 £ = K 10.03.

Area and population

Divisions	Capitals	area sq mi	area sq km	population 1994 estimate
Irrawaddy (Ayeyarwady)	Bassein (Pathein)	13,567	35,138	6,107,000
Magwe (Magway)	Magwe (Magway)	17,305	44,820	4,067,000
Mandalay	Mandalay	14,295	37,024	5,823,000
Pegu (Bago)	Pegu (Bago)	15,214	39,404	4,607,000
Sagaing	Sagaing	36,535	94,625	4,889,000
Tenasserim (Tanintharyi)	Tavoy (Dawei)	16,735	43,343	1,187,000
Yangôn	Yangôn (Rangoon)	3,927	10,171	5,037,000
States				
Chin	Hakha	13,907	36,019	438,000
Kachin	Myitkyinä	34,379	89,041	1,135,000
Karen	Pa-an (Hpa-an)	11,731	30,383	1,323,000
Kayah	Loi-kaw	4,530	11,733	228,000
Mon	Moulmein (Mawlamyine)	4,748	12,297	2,183,000
Rakhine (Arakan)	Sittwe (Akyab)	14,200	36,778	2,482,000
Shan	Taunggyi	60,155	155,801	4,416,000
TOTAL		261,228	676,577	43,922,000

Demography

Population (2002): 42,238,000.
Density (2002): persons per sq mi 161.7, persons per sq km 62.4.
Urban-rural (2002): urban 29.0%; rural 71.0%.
Sex distribution (1997): male 49.65%; female 50.35%.
Age breakdown (1997): under 15, 33.3%; 15–29, 27.7%; 30–44, 19.8%; 45–59, 11.5%; 60 and over, 7.7%.
Population projection: (2010) 43,674,000; (2020) 44,775,000.
Doubling time: 58 years.
Ethnic composition (2000): Burman 55.9%; Karen 9.5%; Shan 6.5%; Han Chinese 2.5%; Mon 2.3%; Yangbye 2.2%; Kachin 1.5%; other 19.6%.
Religious affiliation (1983): Buddhist 89.4%; Christian 4.9%; Muslim 3.8%; traditional beliefs 1.2%; other 0.7%.
Major cities (1993 est.): Yangôn (Rangoon) 3,361,700; Mandalay 885,300; Moulmein (Mawlamyine) 307,600; Pegu (Bago) 190,900; Bassein (Pathein) 183,900.

Vital statistics

Birth rate per 1,000 population (2002): 23.5 (world avg. 21.2).
Death rate per 1,000 population (2002): 11.6 (world avg. 8.9).
Natural increase rate per 1,000 population (2002): 11.9 (world avg. 12.3).
Total fertility rate (avg. births per childbearing woman; 2002): 2.9.
Marriage rate per 1,000 population: n.a.
Divorce rate per 1,000 population: n.a.
Life expectancy at birth (2002): male 54.0 years; female 59.0 years.
Major causes of death per 100,000 population (1994): infectious and parasitic diseases 27.7; circulatory diseases 17.4; respiratory diseases 15.1; malignant neoplasms (cancers) 7.6; malnutrition 3.2.

National economy

Budget (1999–2000). Revenue: K 90,900,000,000 (nontax revenue 55.7%; revenue from taxes 43.8%, of which taxes on goods and services 19.0%, taxes on income 15.8%; foreign grants 0.5%). Expenditures: K 92,500,000,000 (defense 34.3%; interest payments 13.4%; agriculture and forestry 12.4%; education 10.7%; public works and housing 10.5%; general services 6.2%).
Public debt (external, outstanding; 2000): U.S.$5,360,000,000.
Tourism (2000): receipts from visitors U.S.$42,000,000; expenditures by nationals abroad U.S.$25,000,000.
Production (metric tons except as noted). Agriculture, forestry, fishing (1999): rice 17,075,000, sugarcane 5,429,000, pulses 1,895,000, peanuts (groundnuts) 562,000, plantains 423,000, corn (maize) 303,000, sesame seeds 210,000, seed cotton 158,000, opium poppy (2000) 1,085; livestock (number of live animals) 10,740,000 cattle, 6,100,000 ducks, 3,715,000 pigs, 2,391,000 buffalo; roundwood (1998) 22,430,000 cu m; fish catch (1997) 917,666. Mining and quarrying (1997–98): gypsum 40,642; copper concentrates 14,634; refined lead 1,585; tin concentrates 154; refined silver 9,381 kilograms. Manufacturing (1996): cement 513,000; fresh meat 116,000; fertilizers 66,000; refined sugar 43,000; cheese 29,000; butter 10,100; plywood 24,000 cu m; cigarettes 1,727,000,000 units; clay bricks 60,900,000 units. Construction (units; 1987–88)[2]: residential 1,193; nonresidential 1,483. Energy production (consumption): electricity (kW-hr; 1997) 4,211,000,000 (4,211,000,000); coal (metric tons; 1997) 59,000 (125,000); crude petroleum (barrels; 1997) 2,800,000 (7,300,000); petroleum products (metric tons; 1997) 890,000 (1,452,000); natural gas (cu m; 1997) 1,703,000,000 (1,703,000,000).
Household income and expenditure. Average household size (1994) 5.6; average annual income per household: n.a.; sources of income: n.a.; expenditure (1994)[3]: food and beverages 67.1%, fuel and lighting 6.6%, transportation 4.0%, charitable contributions 3.1%, medical care 3.1%.
Gross national product (1996): U.S.$119,334,000,000 (U.S.$2,610 per capita).

Structure of gross domestic product and labour force

	1999–2000 in value K '000,000	1999–2000 % of total value	1997–98 labour force[4]	1997–98 % of labour force[4]
Agriculture	1,312,285	59.9	12,093,000	65.9
Mining	10,842	0.5	121,000	0.7
Manufacturing	143,244	6.5	1,666,000	9.1
Construction	40,425	1.9	400,000	2.2
Public utilities	2,558	0.1	26,000	0.1
Transp. and commun.	105,669	4.8	495,000	2.7
Trade	524,403	23.9	1,781,000	9.7
Finance	2,215	0.1	1,485,000	8.1
Public administration	16,505	0.8		
Services	32,174	1.5	270,000	1.5
TOTAL	2,190,320	100.0	18,337,000	100.0

Population economically active (1997–98): total 19,743,000; activity rate of total population 42.5% (participation rates: ages 15–64 [1983] 64.2%; female [1987–88] 35.3%; unemployed 6.2%).

Price and earnings indexes (1995 = 100)

	1995	1996	1997	1998	1999	2000	2001
Consumer price index	100.0	116.3	150.8	228.5	270.5	270.2	327.2
Monthly earnings index	...	...	...	...	...	...	...

Land use (1994): forested 49.3%; meadows and pastures 0.5%; agricultural and under permanent cultivation 15.3%; other 34.9%.

Foreign trade[5]

Balance of trade (current prices)

	1996	1997	1998	1999	2000	2001
K '000,000	–3,612.5	–7,320.1	–10,183.5	–7,390.4	–6,252.2	–3,360.6
% of total	29.0%	40.3%	43.0%	34.3%	25.4%	9.9%

Imports (1997–98): K 12,735,900,000 (machinery and transport equipment 28.6%, intermediate raw materials 19.9%, basic manufactures 15.8%, capital construction materials 12.3%, consumer durable goods 4.3%). *Major import sources:* Singapore 31.1%; Japan 15.3%; Thailand 9.8%; China 9.4%; Malaysia 7.0%; South Korea 5.5%; Indonesia 4.8%.
Exports (1997–98): K 5,415,800,000 (pulses and beans 22.3%, teak 11.1%, fish and fish products 4.6%, hardwood 2.5%, rubber 2.1%). *Major export destinations:* India 22.6%; Singapore 13.2%; Thailand 11.9%; China 10.6%; Hong Kong 5.8%; Japan 3.8%; United States 3.5%.

Transport and communications

Transport. Railroads (1999): route length (1999–2000) 3,955 km; passenger-km 4,112,000,000; metric ton-km cargo 1,043,000,000. Roads (1996): total length 28,200 km (paved 12%). Vehicles (1996): passenger cars 27,000; trucks and buses 42,000. Air transport (1998): passenger-km 345,000,000; metric ton-km cargo 40,000,000; airports (1996) 19.

Communications

Medium	date	unit	number	units per 1,000 persons
Daily newspapers	1996	circulation	449,000	10
Radio	1997	receivers	4,200,000	96
Television	1999	receivers	323,000	7.2
Telephones	2001	main lines	281,200	5.8
Cellular telephones	2001	subscribers	13,800	0.3
Personal computers	2001	units	55,000	1.1
Internet	2001	users	10,000	0.2

Education and health

Educational attainment (1983). Percentage of population age 25 and over having: no formal schooling 55.8%; primary education 39.4%; secondary 4.6%; religious 0.1%; postsecondary 0.1%. *Literacy* (1995): total population age 15 and over literate 83.1%; males literate 88.7%; females literate 77.7%.

Education (1997–98)

	schools	teachers	students	student/ teacher ratio
Primary (age 5–9)	35,877	167,134	5,145,400	30.8
Secondary (age 10–15)	2,091	56,955	1,545,400	27.1
Voc., teacher tr.[6]	103	2,462	25,374	10.3
Higher	923	17,089	385,300	22.5

Health (1995–96): physicians 12,950 (1 per 3,114 persons); hospital beds 28,732 (1 per 1,404 persons); infant mortality rate per 1,000 live births (2002) 88.0.
Food (2000): daily per capita caloric intake 2,843 (vegetable products 96%, animal products 4%); 132% of FAO recommended minimum requirement.

Military

Total active duty personnel (2001): 444,000 (army 95.7%, navy 2.3%, air force 2.0%). *Military expenditure as percentage of GNP* (1999): 7.8% (world 2.4%); per capita expenditure U.S.$112.

[1]Pegged rate to the Special Drawing Right of the International Monetary Fund.
[2]Construction Corporation activity only. [3]Yangôn only. [4]Employed only. [5]Import figures are c.i.f. in balance of trade and in commodities and trading partners. [6]1994–95.

Internet resources for further information:
• Myanmar Home Page http://www.myanmar.com/e-index.html

Namibia

Official name: Republic of Namibia.
Form of government: republic with two
legislative houses (National Council[1]
[26]; National Assembly [72[2]]).
Head of state and government:
President.
Capital: Windhoek.
Official language: English.
Official religion: none.
Monetary unit: 1 Namibian dollar
(N$) = 100 cents; valuation (Sept. 23,
2002) 1 U.S.$ = N$10.63;
1 £ = N$16.52.

Area and population[3]		area		population
		sq mi	sq km	2001 census
Regions	**Chief towns**			
Erongo[3]	Omaruru	24,602	63,719	107,629
Hardap	Mariental	42,428	109,888	67,998
Karas	Keetmanshoop	62,288	161,324	69,677
Khomas	Windhoek	14,210	36,804	250,305
Kunene	Opuwo	55,697	144,254	68,224
Liambezi (Caprivi)	Katima Mulilo	7,541	19,532	79,852
Ohangwena	Oshikango	4,086	10,582	227,728
Okavango	Rundu	16,763	43,417	201,093
Omaheke	Gobabis	32,715	84,731	67,496
Omusati	Ongandjera	5,265	13,637	228,364
Oshana	Oshakati	2,042	5,290	161,977
Oshikoto	Tsumeb	10,273	26,607	160,788
Otjozondjupa	Grootfontein	40,667	105,327	135,723
TOTAL		318,580[4]	825,118[4]	1,826,854

Demography

Population (2002): 1,837,000.
Density (2002): persons per sq mi 5.8, persons per sq km 2.2.
Urban-rural (1999): urban 39.8%; rural 60.2%.
Sex distribution (2001): male 48.73%; female 51.27%.
Age breakdown (1999): under 15, 43.2%; 15–29, 28.6%; 30–44, 15.1%; 45–59, 7.7%; 60–74, 4.0%; 75 and over, 1.4%.
Population projection: (2010) 1,950,000; (2020) 1,999,000.
Doubling time: 59 years.
Ethnic composition (2000): Ovambo 34.4%; mixed race (black/white) 14.5%; Kavango 9.1%; Afrikaner 8.1%; San (Bushmen) and Bergdama 7.0%; Herero 5.5%; Nama 4.4%; Kwambi 3.7%; German 2.8%; other 10.5%.
Religious affiliation (2000): Protestant (mostly Lutheran) 47.5%; Roman Catholic 17.7%; African Christian 10.8%; traditional beliefs 6.0%; other 18.0%.
Major cities (2001): Windhoek 216,000[5]; Walvis Bay 40,849; Rehoboth 21,782; Oshakati (1991) 21,603; Rundu 19,597; Swakopmund (1991) 17,681.

Vital statistics

Birth rate per 1,000 population (2002): 34.2 (world avg. 21.2).
Death rate per 1,000 population (2002): 22.3 (world avg. 8.9).
Natural increase rate per 1,000 population (2002): 11.9 (world avg. 12.3).
Total fertility rate (avg. births per childbearing woman; 2002): 4.8.
Life expectancy at birth (2002): male 40.8 years; female 37.1 years.
Major causes of death per 100,000 population: n.a.; however, in the early 1990s, tuberculosis had become a serious problem (especially in the southern regions); AIDS cases, while few, were increasing exponentially.

National economy

Budget (1999–2000). Revenue: N$7,128,400,000 (customs taxes 31.4%, general sales tax 28.2%, individual income taxes 17.9%, nontax revenues 8.9%, mining taxes 3.1%). Expenditures: N$8,009,400,000 (1996–97; education 23.2%, health and welfare 10.3%, transportation 6.1%, defense 5.8%, social security 5.4%).
Public debt (external, outstanding 1998): U.S.$747,700,000.
Production (metric tons except as noted). Agriculture, forestry, fishing (1999): roots and tubers 260,000; cereals 71,100,000 (of which millet 46,300, corn [maize] 18,300, sorghum 3,300, wheat 3,000), fruits 10,000, vegetables and melons 10,000, pulses 8,000; livestock (number of live animals) 2,100,000 sheep, 2,000,000 cattle, 1,700,000 goats; fish catch (1998) 352,188. Mining and quarrying (2000): gem diamonds 1,542,000 carats; zinc (metal content) 40,266; copper (metal content) 5,070; uranium oxide 3,201; silver 536,000 troy oz; gold 79,000 troy oz. Manufacturing: n.a.; products include cut gems (primarily diamonds), fur products (karakul), processed foods (fish, meats, and dairy products), textiles, carved wood products, refined metals (copper and lead). Construction (value of buildings completed in N$'000,000; 1994): residential 347.7; nonresidential 160.4. Energy production (consumption): electricity (kW-hr; 1999) 1,948,000,000 (2,838,000,000); coal (metric tons; 1999) none (7,000); petroleum products (metric tons; 1999) none (7,000,000).
Population economically active: total (1991) 493,580; activity rate of total population, 34.9% (participation rates: ages 15–64, 61.3%; female 43.5%; unemployed 20.1%).

Price and earnings indexes (1995 = 100)						
	1996	1997	1998	1999	2000	2001
Consumer price index	108.0	117.5	124.8	135.5	147.7	161.8
Earnings index	...	...	...	...	...	...

Gross national product (2000): U.S.$3,569,000,000 (U.S.$2,030 per capita).

Structure of gross domestic product and labour force				
	1998		1991	
	in value N$'000,000	% of total value	labour force[6]	% of labour force[6]
Agriculture	1,804	10.7	189,929	38.5
Mining	1,876	11.2	14,686	3.0
Manufacturing	2,414	14.3	22,884	4.6
Construction	323	1.9	18,638	3.8
Public utilities	353	2.1	2,974	0.6
Transp. and commun.	613	3.6	9,322	1.9
Trade[7]	1,476	8.8	37,820	7.7
Finance	1,480	8.8	8,547	1.7
Services	507	3.0	}	
Public administration and defense	3,999	23.8	89,541	18.1
Other	1,981[8]	11.8[8]	99,239[9]	20.1[9]
TOTAL	16,826	100.0	493,580	100.0

Household income and expenditure. Average household size (2001) 5.1; average annual income per household (1980) R 3,223 (U.S.$4,143); sources of income (1992): wages and salaries 69.0%, income from property 25.6%, transfer payments 5.4%; expenditure: n.a.
Tourism (1998): receipts U.S.$288,000,000; expenditures U.S.$88,000,000.
Land use (1994): forested 15.2%; meadows and pastures 46.2%; agricultural and under permanent cultivation 0.8%; other 37.8%.

Foreign trade

Balance of trade (current prices)						
	1993	1994	1995	1996	1997	1998
N$'000,000	−136	−305	−470	−547	−1,252	−954
% of total	1.6%	3.0%	4.4%	4.3%	9.2%	6.3%

Imports (1998): N$8,021,000,000 (1994; machinery and transport equipment 27.1%, of which transport equipment 16.2%; food and live animals 22.3%; minerals and fuels 11.4%; chemical products 8.1%). *Major import sources* (1993): South Africa 87.0%[10]; Germany 3.0%; France 2.0%; Japan 2.0%.
Exports (1998): N$7,076,000,000 (manufactured products 46.7%, of which fish processing 28.4%; minerals 45.1%, of which diamonds 30.4%; food and live animals 8.0%, of which cattle 3.7%; karakul pelts 0.3%). *Major export destinations* (1993): U.K. 34.0%; South Africa 27.0%; Japan 10.0%; Spain 6.0%.

Transport and communications

Transport. Railroads: route length (1999) 1,480 mi, 2,382 km; (1995–96) passenger-km 48,300,000; (1995–96) metric ton-km 1,082,000,000. Roads (1996): total length 25,130 mi, 65,220 km (paved 7.7%). Vehicles (1996): passenger cars 74,875; trucks and buses 66,500[11]. Air transport (2001)[12]: passenger-km 624,000,000; metric ton-km cargo 72,575,000; airports (1997) 11.

Communications				units per 1,000 persons
Medium	**date**	**unit**	**number**	
Daily newspapers	1996	circulation	30,000	19
Radio	1997	receivers	232,000	143
Television	1999	receivers	65,000	38
Telephones	2001	main lines	117,400	66
Cellular telephones	2001	subscribers	100,000	56
Personal computers	2001	units	65,000	36
Internet	2001	users	45,000	25

Education and health

Educational attainment (1991). Percentage of population age 25 and over having: no formal schooling 35.1%; primary education 31.9%; secondary 28.5%; higher 4.5%. *Literacy* (2000): total population age 15 and over literate 830,200 (82.1%); males literate 416,000 (82.9%); females literate 414,200 (81.2%).

Education (1994)				student/ teacher ratio
	schools	teachers	students	
Primary (age 6–12)	933	10,912[13]	366,666	32.0[13]
Secondary (age 13–19)	114	2,534[14]	101,838	29.3[14]
Voc., teacher tr.	17	140[15]	1,503	11.9[15]
Higher	7	213[16]	6,523	11.8[16]

Health: physicians (1997) 458 (1 per 3,390 persons); hospital beds (1989) 6,997 (1 per 216 persons); infant mortality rate per 1,000 live births (2001) 71.7.
Food (1999): daily per capita caloric intake 2,096 (vegetable products 89%, animal products 11%); 92% of FAO recommended minimum requirement.

Military

Total active duty personnel (2001): 9,200 (army 97.8%, navy 2.2%[17]). *Military expenditure as percentage of GNP* (1999): 2.9% (world 2.4%); per capita expenditure U.S.$53.

---

[1]Mostly an advisory body. [2]72 elected and up to 6 appointed members. [3]Includes the 434 sq mi (1,124 sq km) former district of Walvis Bay (1992 population estimate, 23,000) that was jointly administered with South Africa from November 1992 to March 1994. [4]Detail does not add to total given because of rounding. [5]Urban agglomeration. [6]Includes more than 140,000 nonwage (informal) workers. [7]Includes hotels. [8]Includes import duties and excise taxes. [9]Unemployed. [10]Includes goods from other countries shipped via South Africa. [11]1995. [12]Air Namibia only. [13]1992. [14]1990. [15]1989. [16]1991. [17]Coast Guard for fishery protection.

Internet resources for further information:
• Namibia Fact Sheet http://www.emulateme.com/namibia.htm
• Bank of Namibia http://www.bon.com.na

Nauru

Official name: Naoero (Nauruan[1]); (Republic of Nauru).
Form of government: republic with one legislative house (Parliament [18]).
Head of state and government: President.
Capital: [2].
Official language: none[1].
Official religion: none.
Monetary unit: 1 Australian dollar ($A) = 100 cents; valuation (Sept. 23, 2002) 1 U.S.$ = $A 1.83; 1 £ = $A 2.84.

Area and population

Districts	area		population 1992 census[3]
	sq mi	sq km	
Aiwo	0.4	1.1	1,072
Anabar	0.6	1.5	320
Anetan	0.4	1.0	427
Anibare	1.2	3.1	165
Baitsi	0.5	1.2	450
Boe	0.2	0.5	750
Buada	1.0	2.6	661
Denigomodu	0.3	0.9	2,548
Ewa	0.5	1.2	355
Ijuw	0.4	1.1	206
Meneng	1.2	3.1	1,269
Nibok	0.6	1.6	577
Uaboe	0.3	0.8	447
Yaren	0.6	1.5	672
TOTAL	8.2	21.2	9,919

Demography

Population (2002): 12,300.
Density (2002): persons per sq mi 1,500, persons per sq km 580.2.
Urban-rural (2001): urban 100%.
Sex distribution (2001): male 50.50%; female 49.50%.
Age breakdown (2001): under 15, 40.3%; 15–29, 26.8%; 30–44, 19.0%; 45–59, 10.7%; 60–74, 3.0%; 75 and over, 0.2%.
Population projection: (2010) 14,300; (2020) 16,700.
Doubling time: 35 years.
Ethnic composition (1992): Nauruan 68.9%; other Pacific Islander 23.7%, of which Kiribati 12.8%, Tuvaluan 8.7%; Asian 5.9%, of which Filipino 2.5%, Chinese 2.3%; other 1.5%.
Religious affiliation (1995): Protestant 53.5%, of which Congregational 35.3%, Pentecostal 4.8%; Roman Catholic 27.5%; other 19.0%.
Major cities: none; population of Yaren district (1996) 700.

Vital statistics

Birth rate per 1,000 population (2001): 27.2 (world avg. 21.2); legitimate, n.a.; illegitimate, n.a.
Death rate per 1,000 population (2001): 7.2 (world avg. 8.9).
Natural increase rate per 1,000 population (2001): 20.0 (world avg. 12.3).
Total fertility rate (avg. births per childbearing woman; 2001): 3.6.
Marriage rate per 1,000 population (1995): 5.3.
Divorce rate per 1,000 population: n.a.
Life expectancy at birth (2001): male 57.7 years; female 64.9 years.
Major causes of death per 100,000 population: n.a.[4]

National economy

Budget (1999). Revenue: $A 38,700,000[5]. Expenditures: $A 37,200,000.
Public debt (external, outstanding; beginning of 1996): c. U.S.$150,000,000.
Tourism: receipts from visitors, virtually none; expenditures by nationals abroad, n.a.
Gross national product (at current market prices; 1997): U.S.$128,000,000 (U.S.$11,538 per capita).

Distribution of gross domestic product and labour force

	1997			
	in value U.S.$'000,000	% of total value	labour force[6, 7, 8]	% of labour force
Agriculture	...	...	...	...
Mining (phosphate)	...	...	528	24.7
Manufacturing	...	...	...	...
Construction	...	...	...	...
Public utilities	...	...	...	...
Transportation and communications	...	...	...	...
Hotels	...	...	137	6.4
Finance[9]	...	...	33	1.6
Services	...	...	...	...
Pub. admin.	...	...	1,238	58.0
Other	...	...	198	9.3
TOTAL	540	100.0	2,134	100.0

Production (metric tons except as noted). Agriculture, forestry, fishing (2001): coconuts 1,600, vegetables 450, tropical fruit (including mangoes) 275; almonds, figs, and pandanus are also cultivated, but most foodstuffs and beverages (including water) are imported; livestock (number of live animals) 2,800 pigs; roundwood, none; fish catch (1999) 250. Mining and quarrying (2001): phosphate rock (gross weight) 400,000. Manufacturing: none; virtually all consumer manufactures are imported. Construction: n.a. Energy pro-

duction (consumption): electricity (kW-hr; 1999) 30,000,000 (27,900,000); coal, none (n.a.); crude petroleum, none (n.a.); petroleum products (metric tons; 1997) none (45,000); natural gas, none (n.a.).
Population economically active (1992): 2,453[7, 10]; activity rate of total population 35.9% (participation rates: over age 15, n.a.; female, n.a.; unemployed, 18.2%).
Price and earnings indexes: [11].
Household income and expenditure. Average household size (1992) 10.0[6]; income per household: n.a.; sources of income: n.a.; expenditure: n.a.
Land use (1995): forested, nil; meadows and pastures, nil; agricultural and under permanent cultivation c. 10%[12]; other c. 90%[13].

Foreign trade

Balance of trade (current prices)

	1994	1995	1996	1997	1998	1999
U.S.$'000,000	+20.0	+0.2	+3.3	+10.1	+20.0	+20.0
% of total	33.3%	0.4%	4.6%	24.9%	33.3%	33.3%

Imports (1999): U.S.$20,000,000 (agricultural products 65.0%, of which food 45.0%; remainder 35.0%). *Major import sources* (1995): Australia more than 50%; United Kingdom c. 10%; New Zealand c. 10%.
Exports (1999): U.S.$40,000,000 (phosphate, virtually 100%). *Major export destinations* (1995): New Zealand c. 50%; Australia c. 25%.

Transport and communications

Transport. Railroads (2001): length 3 mi, 5 km; passenger traffic, n.a.; metric ton-km cargo, n.a. Roads (2001): total length 19 mi, 30 km (paved 79%). Vehicles (1989): passenger cars, trucks, and buses 1,448. Merchant marine (1992): vessels 2, total deadweight tonnage 5,791. Air transport (1996): passenger-mi 151,000,000, passenger-km 243,000,000; short ton-mi cargo 15,000,000, metric ton-km cargo 24,000,000; airports (2001) with scheduled flights 1.

Communications

Medium	date	unit	number	units per 1,000 persons
Daily newspapers	—	circulation	—	—
Radio	1997	receivers	7,000	609
Television	1997	receivers	500	48
Telephones	1998	main lines	1,700	149
Cellular telephones	1998	subscribers	850	75
Personal computers	1998	units	...	...
Internet	1998	users	...	...

Education and health

Educational attainment (1992)[7]. Percentage of population age 5 and over having primary education or less 77.4%; secondary education 12.9%; higher 4.1%; not stated 5.6%. *Literacy* (1999): total population age 15 and over literate 99%.

Education (1997)[7]

	schools	teachers	students	student/ teacher ratio
Primary (age 6–13) } Secondary (age 14–17) }	3	64	1,379	21.5
Vocational	3	53	1,113	21.0
Higher	—	—	—	—

Health: physicians (1995) 17 (1 per 637 persons); hospital beds (1990) 207 (1 per 46 persons); infant mortality rate per 1,000 live births (2001) 10.7.
Food (2000)[14]: daily per capita caloric intake 2,991 (vegetable products 70%, animal products 30%); 131% of FAO recommended minimum requirement.

Military

Total active duty personnel (2001): Nauru does not have any military establishment. The defense is assured by Australia, but no formal agreement exists.

---

[1]Nauruan is the national language; English is the language of business and government. [2]Government offices are located in Yaren district. [3]Preliminary. [4]Morbidity is often associated with dietary and social problems (particularly obesity and alcoholism). In 1989, 32% of adult Nauruans were diagnosed with diabetes mellitus. [5]Largely from phosphate exports. [6]Employed only. [7]Nauruan only. [8]Most non-Nauruans are phosphate industry contract workers. [9]400 offshore banks were registered in Nauru in mid-2001. [10]Excludes activity not stated. [11]Minimum wage remained constant between November 1992 and the end of 1997. [12]Cultivatable coastal strip. [13]Phosphate-extracted interior wasteland. [14]Data for Oceania.

Nepal

Official name: Nepal Adhirajya (Kingdom of Nepal).
Form of government: constitutional monarchy with a bicameral parliament consisting of two legislative houses (National Council [60[1]]; House of Representatives [205]).
Chief of state: King.
Head of government: Prime Minister.
Capital: Kathmandu.
Official language: Nepali.
Official religion: Hinduism.
Monetary unit: 1 Nepalese rupee (NRs) = 100 paisa (pice); valuation (Sept. 23, 2002) 1 U.S.$ = NRs 76.89; 1 £ = NRs 119.50.

Area and population		area		population
				2001
Development regions		sq mi	sq km	census
Zones	Capitals			
Eastern	Dhankuta	10,987	28,456	5,286,890
Central	Kathmandu	10,583	27,410	7,988,612
Western	Pokhara	11,351	29,398	4,571,013
Mid-western	Surkhet	16,362	42,378	2,707,244
Far-western	Dipayal	7,544	19,539	2,183,175
TOTAL		56,827	147,181	22,736,934[2]

Demography

Population (2002): 23,692,000.
Density (2002): persons per sq mi 416.9, persons per sq km 161.0.
Urban-rural (2002): urban 13.0%; rural 87.0%.
Sex distribution (2001): male 49.96%; female 50.04%.
Age breakdown (2001): under 15, 39.3%; 15–29, 27.0%; 30–44, 17.1%; 45–59, 10.1%; 60–74, 5.2%; 75 and over, 1.3%.
Population projection: (2010) 28,403,000; (2020) 34,813,000.
Doubling time: 29 years.
Ethnic composition (1991): Nepalese 53.2%; Bihari (including Maithili and Bhojpuri) 18.4%; Tharu 4.8%; Tamang 4.7%; Newar 3.4%; Magar 2.2%; Abadhi 1.7%; other 11.6%.
Religious affiliation (2001): Hindu 80.6%; Buddhist 10.7%; Muslim 4.2%; Kirat 3.6%; Christian 0.5%; other 0.4%.
Major cities (2001): Kathmandu 696,852; Biratnagar 166,902; Lalitpur 161,617; Pokhara 159,104; Birganj 112,031.

Vital statistics

Birth rate per 1,000 population (2002): 34.2 (world avg. 21.2).
Death rate per 1,000 population (2002): 10.0 (world avg. 8.9).
Natural increase rate per 1,000 population (2002): 24.2 (world avg. 12.3).
Total fertility rate (avg. births per childbearing woman; 2002): 4.5.
Life expectancy at birth (2002): male 60.0 years; female 59.0 years.
Major causes of death per 100,000 population: n.a.; however, the leading causes of mortality are infectious and parasitic diseases, diseases of the respiratory system, and diseases of the nervous system.

National economy

Budget (1999). Revenue: NRs 40,698,000,000 (taxes on goods and services 29.2%, taxes on international trade 23.9%, foreign grants 14.5%, income taxes 14.2%, state property revenues 8.4%, administrative fees 5.5%). Expenditures: NRs 58,391,000,000 (education 13.6%, transport and communications 11.4%, fuel and energy 9.0%, health 6.5%, agriculture 5.5%, housing 4.7%, defense 4.5%, public order 4.3%, general public services 3.7%).
Public debt (external, outstanding; 2000): U.S.$2,784,000,000.
Land use (1994): forested 42.0%; meadows and pastures 14.6%; agricultural and under permanent cultivation 17.2%; other 26.2%.
Tourism (2000): receipts from visitors U.S.$167,000,000; expenditures by nationals abroad U.S.$73,000,000.
Production (metric tons except as noted). Agriculture, forestry, fishing (1999): rice 3,710,000, sugarcane 1,972,000, corn (maize) 1,346,000, potatoes 1,091,000, wheat 1,086,000, millet 291,000, pulses 213,000; livestock (number of live animals) 7,030,698 cattle, 6,204,616 goats, 3,470,600 buffalo, 855,159 sheep, 825,132 pigs; roundwood (1998) 21,474,000 cu m; fish catch (1997) 23,206. Mining and quarrying (1997): limestone 369,000; salt 7,000; talc 6,800. Manufacturing (value added in U.S.$'000,000; 1995): textiles 78; food products 74; wearing apparel 54; tobacco products 41; nonmetal mineral products 35. Construction: n.a. Energy production (consumption): electricity (kW-hr; 1997) 1,232,000,000 (1,262,000,000); coal (metric tons; 1997) none (119,000); petroleum products (metric tons; 1997) none (509,000).
Population economically active (1991): total 7,339,586; activity rate of total population 39.7% (participation rates: ages 10 years and over, 57.0%; female 45.5%; unemployed [1996] 4.9%).

Price and earnings indexes (1995 = 100)							
	1995	1996	1997	1998	1999	2000	2001
Consumer price index	100.0	109.2	113.6	125.0	135.1	137.1	141.0
Monthly earnings index[3]	100.0	100.0	100.0	124.1	124.1	145.9	...

Gross national product (at current market prices; 2000): U.S.$5,584,000,000 (U.S.$240 per capita).

Structure of gross domestic product and labour force				
	1999–2000		1991	
	in value NRs '000,000[4]	% of total value[4]	labour force	% of labour force
Agriculture	145,597	38.7	5,961,788	81.2
Mining	1,719	0.5	2,367	—
Manufacturing	34,366	9.1	150,051	2.0
Construction	34,340	9.1	35,658	0.5
Public utilities	6,193	1.6	11,734	0.2
Transp. and commun.	27,692	7.4	50,808	0.7
Trade	42,977	11.4	256,012	3.5
Finance	36,441	9.7	20,847	0.3
Services	33,609	8.9	752,019	10.3
Other	13,499[5]	3.6[5]	98,302	1.3
TOTAL	376,433	100.0	7,339,586	100.0

Household income and expenditure (1984–85). Average household size (2001) 5.4; income per household NRs 14,796 (U.S.$853); sources of income: self-employment 63.4%, wages and salaries 25.1%, rent 7.5%, other 4.0%; expenditure: food and beverages 61.2%, housing 17.3%, clothing 11.7%, health care 3.7%, education and recreation 2.9%, transp. and commun. 1.2%, other 2.0%.

Foreign trade[6]

Balance of trade (current prices)						
	1995	1996	1997	1998	1999	2000
U.S.$'000,000	−960.9	−1,106.0	−1,278.1	−757.1	−881.9	−792.7
% of total	57.9%	58.7%	60.7%	44.0%	41.9%	33.5%

Imports (1996–97): NRs 96,006,000,000 (basic manufactured goods 47.6%; machinery and transport equipment 14.7%; chemicals 8.8%; mineral fuels and lubricants 7.5%; food and live animals, chiefly for food 6.6%; crude materials except fuels 5.5%). *Major import sources:* India 23.3%; Hong Kong 14.3%; Singapore 13.0%; Japan 11.2%; China 6.4%; New Zealand 5.1%.
Exports (1996–97): NRs 22,481,000,000 (basic manufactures 48.7%; miscellaneous manufactures 29.2%; food and live animals, chiefly for food 12.6%; chemicals and drugs 5.9%; crude materials except fuels 2.6%). *Major export destinations:* U.S. 34.4%; India 9.5%; Bangladesh 1.4%; China 0.9%.

Transport and communications

Transport. Railroads (1995–96): route length (1999) 59 km; passengers carried 1,379,000; freight handled 5,320 metric tons. Roads (1997): total length 7,700 km (paved 42%). Vehicles (1998–99): passenger cars 49,426; trucks and buses 30,620. Air transport (1997): passenger-km 908,000,000; metric ton-km cargo 99,000,000; airports (1996) with scheduled flights 24.

Communications				units per 1,000
Medium	date	unit	number	persons
Daily newspapers	1996	circulation	250,000	11
Radio	1997	receivers	840,000	38
Television	1999	receivers	150,000	6.7
Telephones	2001	main lines	298,100	13
Cellular telephones	2001	subscribers	17,300	0.7
Personal computers	2001	units	80,000	3.4
Internet	2001	users	60,000	2.5

Education and health

Educational attainment (1981). Percentage of population age 25 and over having: no formal schooling 41.2%; primary education 29.4%; secondary 22.7%; higher 6.8%. *Literacy* (1995): total population age 15 and over literate 27.5%; males literate 40.9%; females literate 14.0%.

Education (1999)	schools	teachers	students	student/ teacher ratio
Primary (age 6–10)	26,226	100,424	3,946,000	39.3
Secondary (age 11–15)	11,171	42,193	1,340,000	31.8
Vocational				
Higher	3[7]	4,925[8]	115,938	22.4[7]

Health (1996): physicians 872 (1 per 25,745 persons); hospital beds 3,604 (1 per 6,229 persons); infant mortality rate per 1,000 live births (2002) 72.0.
Food (2000): daily per capita caloric intake 2,435 (vegetable products 93%, animal products 7%); 111% of FAO recommended minimum.

Military

Total active duty personnel (2001): 46,000 (army 99.5%, air force 0.5%). *Military expenditure as percentage of GNP* (1999): 0.8% (world 2.4%); per capita expenditure U.S.$2.

---

[1]Includes 10 members nominated by the king. [2]Excludes an officially estimated 400,000 persons in wards where census enumerators were unable to conduct a head count; adjusted 2001 census total equals 23,150,000. [3]Minimum monthly wage rates for unskilled industrial workers; 1994–95 = 100. [4]Estimate. [5]Includes indirect taxes. [6]Import figures are f.o.b. in balance of trade and c.i.f. for commodities and trading partners. [7]1993. [8]1991.

Internet resources for further information:
• **Central Bureau of Statistics** http://www.census.gov.np
• **Central Bank of Nepal** http://www.nrb.org.np
• **National Planning Commission** http://npc.gov.np:8080

Netherlands, The

Official name: Koninkrijk der Nederlanden (Kingdom of The Netherlands).
Form of government: constitutional monarchy with a parliament (States General) comprising two legislative houses (First Chamber [75]; Second Chamber [150]).
Chief of state: Monarch.
Head of government: Prime Minister.
Seat of government: The Hague.
Capital: Amsterdam.
Official language: Dutch.
Official religion: none.
Monetary unit: 1 euro (€) = 100 cents; valuation (Sept. 23, 2002)
1 U.S.$ = €1.02; 1 £ = €1.58[1].

Area and population

Provinces	Capitals	area sq mi	area sq km	population 2001[2] estimate
Drenthe	Assen	1,035	2,680	474,506
Flevoland	Lelystad	931	2,412	328,936
Friesland	Leeuwarden	2,217	5,741	630,539
Gelderland	Arnhem	1,983	5,137	1,934,314
Groningen	Groningen	1,146	2,968	566,489
Limburg	Maastricht	853	2,209	1,142,679
Noord-Brabant	's-Hertogenbosch	1,962	5,082	2,375,116
Noord-Holland	Haarlem	1,567	4,059	2,534,599
Overijssel	Zwolle	1,321	3,421	1,086,280
Utrecht	Utrecht	556	1,439	1,117,997
Zeeland	Middelburg	1,133	2,934	374,920
Zuid-Holland	The Hague	1,331	3,446	3,420,700
TOTAL		16,034[3, 4]	41,528[4]	15,987,075

Demography

Population (2002): 16,142,000.
Density (2002)[5]: persons per sq mi 1,234.2, persons per sq km 476.5.
Urban-rural (2001): urban 89.6%; rural 10.4%.
Sex distribution (2002[2]): male 49.50%; female 50.50%.
Age breakdown (2000[2]): under 15, 18.6%; 15–29, 19.3%; 30–44, 24.2%; 45–59, 19.8%; 60–74, 12.1%; 75 and over, 6.0%.
Population projection: (2010) 16,913,000; (2020) 17,524,000.
Ethnic composition (by place of origin [including 2nd generation]; 2000[2]): Netherlander 82.5%; Indonesian 2.6%; Turkish 1.9%; Surinamese 1.9%; Moroccan 1.7%; Netherlands Antillean/Aruban 0.7%; other 8.7%[6].
Religious affiliation (1999[2]): Roman Catholic 31.0%; Reformed (NHK) 14.0%; other Reformed 7.0%; Muslim 4.5%; Hindu 0.5%; nonreligious 41.0%; other 2.0%.
Major urban agglomerations (2000[2]): Amsterdam 1,002,868; Rotterdam 989,956; The Hague 610,245; Utrecht 366,186; Eindhoven 302,274.

Vital statistics

Birth rate per 1,000 population (2001): 12.6 (world avg. 21.2); legitimate 72.8%; illegitimate 27.2%.
Death rate per 1,000 population (2001): 8.8 (world avg. 8.9).
Natural increase rate per 1,000 population (2001): 3.8 (world avg. 12.3).
Total fertility rate (avg. births per childbearing woman; 2001): 1.7.
Marriage rate per 1,000 population (2000): 5.3.
Life expectancy at birth (2001): male 75.8 years; female 80.7 years.
Major causes of death per 100,000 population (1999): diseases of the circulatory system 313.3; malignant neoplasms (cancers) 247.2; diseases of the respiratory system 90.8; accidents and violence 32.8.

National economy

Budget (1997). Revenue: f. 324,360,000,000 (social security taxes 41.1%; income and corporate taxes 24.8%; value-added and excise taxes 22.7%; property taxes 3.0%). Expenditures: f. 337,620,000,000 (social security and welfare 37.4%; health 14.8%; education 10.0%; interest payments 9.1%; defense 3.9%; transportation 3.5%).
Public debt (1999): U.S.$251,763,000,000.
Production (metric tons except as noted). Agriculture, forestry, fishing (2000): potatoes 8,200,000, sugar beets 5,504,000, wheat 1,183,000, onions 766,000, tomatoes 600,000, apples 575,000, barley 319,000, flowering bulbs and tubers 55,600 acres (22,500 hectares), of which tulips 24,000 acres (9,700 hectares), cut flowers/plants under glass 14,625 acres (5,917 hectares); livestock (number of live animals; 2000) 13,140,000 pigs, 4,200,000 cattle, 1,401,000 sheep; roundwood (1999) 1,044,000 cu m; fish catch (2000) 495,804. Manufacturing (value added in f. '000,000; 1998): food, beverages, and tobacco 24,323; chemicals and chemical products 15,009; printing and publishing 11,267; electric/electronic machinery 10,385. Energy production (consumption): electricity (kW-hr; 2000) 89,580,000,000 ([1999] 93,505,000,000); coal (metric tons; 1997) negligible (14,793,000); crude petroleum (barrels; 2000) 9,389,000 ([1997] 392,581,000); petroleum products (metric tons; 1997) 63,072,000 (31,863,000); natural gas (cu m; 2000) 67,864,000,000 ([1997] 51,783,000,000).
Household income and expenditure. Average household size (2000) 2.3; disposable income per household (1999) f. 51,600 (U.S.$26,444); sources of income (1996): wages 48.4%, transfers 28.5%, self-employment 11.3%; expenditure (1999): housing and energy 20.8%; transportation and communications 15.6%; food and beverages 14.8%; recreation and culture 11.1%.
Gross national product (2000): U.S.$397,544,000,000 (U.S.$24,970 per capita).

Structure of gross domestic product and labour force

	1999 in value f. '000,000	1999 % of total value	1998 labour force	1998 % of labour force
Agriculture	20,554	2.5	236,000	3.1
Mining	14,503	1.8	11,000	0.1
Manufacturing	125,570	15.2	1,104,000	14.3
Construction	43,091	5.2	451,000	5.8
Public utilities	13,046	1.6	47,000	0.6
Transp. and commun.	55,723	6.8	442,000	5.7
Trade	112,907	13.7	1,487,000	19.2
Finance, real estate	199,652	24.2	1,097,000	14.2
Pub. admin., defense	87,044	10.6	525,000	6.8
Services	84,717	10.3	1,811,000	23.4
Other	67,176[7]	8.1[7]	524,000[8]	6.8[8]
TOTAL	823,983	100.0	7,735,000	100.0

Population economically active (1998): total 7,735,000; activity rate of total population 49.3% (participation rates: ages 15–64, 72.9%; female 42.5%; unemployed [February 2001–January 2002] 2.0%).

Price and earnings indexes (1995 = 100)

	1996	1997	1998	1999	2000	2001	2002[9]
Consumer price index	102.0	104.2	106.3	108.6	111.4	116.4	120.6
Hourly earnings index	101.7	104.8	108.1	111.3	115.4	120.2	123.7

Tourism (2000): receipts U.S.$7,206,000,000; expenditures U.S.$12,198,000,000.
Land use (1994): forested 10.3%; meadows and pastures 31.0%; agricultural and under permanent cultivation 28.0%; other 30.7%.

Foreign trade[10]

Balance of trade (current prices)

	1996	1997	1998	1999	2000	2001
€'000,000	+28,361[11]	+32,732[11]	+26,926[11]	+9,325	+12,367	+23,682
% of total	5.2%	4.4%	4.5%	2.5%	2.8%	5.2%

Imports (2001): €217,151,000,000 (computers and related equipment 11.9%, chemicals and chemical products 11.4%, mineral fuels 10.1%, food 8.2%, road vehicles 7.0%). *Major import sources:* Germany 18.5%; U.S. 9.8%; Belgium-Luxembourg 9.3%; U.K. 8.9%; France 5.7%.
Exports (2001): €240,833,000,000 (chemicals and chemical products 15.4%, food 12.3%, computers and related equipment 11.7%, mineral fuels 9.2%). *Major export destinations:* Germany 25.6%; Belgium-Luxembourg 11.9%; U.K. 11.2%; France 10.3%; Italy 6.2%.

Transport and communications

Transport. Railroads (1999): length 2,808 km; passenger-km 14,330,000,000; metric ton-km cargo 3,521,000,000. Roads (1999): total length 116,500 km (paved 90%). Vehicles (2000): passenger cars 6,343,000; trucks and buses 826,000. Air transport (2001)[12]: passenger-km 57,848,000,000; metric ton-km cargo 4,464,000,000; airports (1996) 6.

Communications

Medium	date	unit	number	units per 1,000 persons
Daily newspapers	1996	circulation	4,753,000	306
Radio	1998	receivers	12,000,000	764
Television	1999	receivers	9,500,000	601
Telephones	2001	main lines	10,000,000	621
Cellular telephones	2001	subscribers	11,900,000	739
Personal computers	2001	units	6,900,000	429
Internet	2001	users	5,300,000	329

Education and health

Educational attainment (1999). Percentage of population ages 15–64 having: primary education 13.4%; lower secondary 10.4%; upper secondary/vocational 53.9%; tertiary vocational 15.5%; university 6.8%.

Education (1999–2000)[13]

	schools	teachers	students	student/teacher ratio
Primary (age 6–12)	7,224	...	1,543,000	...
Secondary (age 12–18)	635	...	861,000	...
Vocational[14]	65	...	250,000	...
Higher[15]	13	...	150,000	...

Health (1999): physicians 27,090 (1 per 582 persons); hospital beds 81,328 (1 per 194 persons); infant mortality rate per 1,000 live births (2001) 5.4.
Food (1999): daily per capita caloric intake 3,243 (vegetable products 64%, animal products 36%); 121% of FAO recommended minimum requirement.

Military

Total active duty personnel (2001): 50,430 (army 45.8%, navy 24.0%, air force 19.8%, paramilitary 10.4%). *Military expenditure as percentage of GNP* (1999): 1.8% (world 2.4%); per capita expenditure U.S.$445.

---

[1]The Netherlands guilder (f.) was the former monetary unit; on Jan. 1, 2002, f. 2.20 = €1. [2]January 1. [3]Detail does not add to total given because of rounding. [4]Includes inland water area totaling 1,343 sq mi (3,479 sq km) and coastal water totaling 1,612 sq mi (4,176 sq km). [5]Based on land area only (13,079 sq mi [33,873 sq km]). [6]Includes Netherlander-EU country 4.6%. [7]Imputed value added tax less subsidies and bank service charges. [8]Includes 337,000 registered unemployed. [9]April. [10]Imports c.i.f.; exports f.o.b. [11]In guilders. [12]KLM only. [13]Public schools only. [14]Colleges only. [15]Universities only.

Internet resources for further information:
• Statistics Netherlands http://www.cbs.nl/en

Netherlands Antilles

Official name: Nederlandse Antillen (Netherlands Antilles).
Political status: nonmetropolitan territory of The Netherlands with one legislative house (States of the Netherlands Antilles [22]).
Chief of state: Dutch Monarch represented by Governor.
Head of government: Prime Minister.
Capital: Willemstad.
Official language: Dutch.
Official religion: none.
Monetary unit: 1 Netherlands Antillean guilder (NA f.) = 100 cents;
valuation (Sept. 23, 2002)
1 U.S.$ = NA f. 1.78;
1 £ = NA f. 2.77.

Area and population

Island councils	Capitals	area sq mi	area sq km	population 2001 census
Leeward Islands				
Bonaire	Kralendijk	111	288	10,791
Curaçao	Willemstad	171	444	130,627
Windward Islands				
Saba	The Bottom	5	13	1,349
Sint Eustatius, or Statia	Oranjestad	8	21	2,292
Sint Maarten (Dutch part only)	Philipsburg	13	34	30,594
TOTAL		308	800	175,653

Demography

Population (2002): 175,000.
Density (2002): persons per sq mi 568.2, persons per sq km 218.8.
Urban-rural (2001): urban 69.6%; rural 30.4%.
Sex distribution (2001): male 46.98%; female 53.02%.
Age breakdown (2001): under 15, 24.2%; 15–29, 18.2%; 30–44, 25.5%; 45–59, 19.0%; 60–74, 9.4%; 75 and over, 3.7%.
Population projection: (2010) 175,000; (2020) 175,000.
Ethnic composition (2000): local black-other (Antillean Creole) 81.1%; Dutch 5.3%; Surinamese 2.9%; other (significantly West Indian black) 10.7%.
Religious affiliation (2001): Roman Catholic 72.0%; Protestant 16.0%; Spiritist 0.9%; Buddhist 0.5%; Jewish 0.4%; Bahā'ī 0.3%; Hindu 0.2%; Muslim 0.2%; other/unknown 4.3%.
Major cities: Willemstad (urban area; 1999) 123,000; Kralendijk (2001) 7,900; Philipsburg (2001) 6,300.

Vital statistics

Birth rate per 1,000 population (2001): 13.6 (world avg. 21.2); (1988)[1] legitimate 51.6%; illegitimate 48.4%.
Death rate per 1,000 population (2001): 6.4 (world avg. 8.9).
Natural increase rate per 1,000 population (2001): 7.2 (world avg. 12.3).
Total fertility rate (avg. births per childbearing woman; 2001): 2.1.
Marriage rate per 1,000 population (1999): 4.7.
Divorce rate per 1,000 population (1999): 2.6.
Life expectancy at birth (2001): male 72.8 years; female 77.2 years.
Major causes of death per 100,000 population (1993): infectious and parasitic diseases/diseases of the respiratory system 209.0; diseases of the circulatory system 180.2; malignant neoplasms (cancers) 117.7.

National economy

Budget (2000). Revenue: NA f. 621,300,000 (tax revenue 83.5%, of which sales tax 37.3%, import duties 20.6%, excise on gasoline 12.8%; nontax revenue 14.9%; grants 1.6%). Expenditures: NA f. 743,700,000 (current expenditures 92.6%, of which wages 35.3%, transfers 32.4%, goods and services 12.9%, interest payments 10.4%; development expenditures 7.4%).
Production (metric tons except as noted). Agriculture, forestry, fishing: [2]; livestock (number of live animals; 2001) 13,000 goats, 7,300 sheep, 2,600 asses, 135,000 chickens; roundwood, n.a.; fish catch (1999) 905. Mining and quarrying (1997): salt 432,225, sulfur by-product 27,600. Manufacturing (1996): residual fuel oil 5,013,000; gas-diesel oils 2,218,000; other manufactures include electronic parts, cigarettes, textiles, rum, and Curaçao liqueur. Energy production (consumption): electricity (kW-hr; 1999) 1,112,500,000 (1,112,-500,000); coal, none (none); crude petroleum (barrels; 1997) none (100,-289,000); petroleum products (metric tons; 1997) 9,966,000 (863,000); natural gas, none (none).
Land use (1998): forested, negligible; meadows and pastures, negligible; agricultural and under permanent cultivation 10.0%; other (dry savanna) 90.0%.
Tourism (2000): receipts from visitors U.S.$765,000,000; expenditures by nationals abroad U.S.$339,000,000.
Household income and expenditure. Average household size (2001) 2.9; income per household: n.a.; sources of income: n.a.; expenditure (1996)[3, 4]: housing 26.5%, transportation and communications 19.9%, food 14.7%, household furnishings 8.8%, recreation and education 8.2%, clothing and footwear 7.5%.
Gross national product (at current market prices; 1997): U.S.$2,609,000,000 (U.S.$12,490 per capita).

Structure of gross domestic product and labour force

	1997 in value NA f. '000,000	1997 % of total value	2001 labour force	2001 % of labour force
Agriculture, forestry }	28.7	0.6	441	0.5
Mining			131	0.2
Manufacturing	271.0	6.0	4,619	5.7
Construction	330.6	7.3	5,335	6.5
Public utilities	194.4	4.3	1,131	1.4
Transp. and commun.	500.1	11.0	5,410	6.6
Trade, hotels, restaurants	1,089.6	24.0	19,002	23.3
Finance, real estate, insurance	1,173.1	25.9	10,103	12.4
Pub. admin., defense	748.1	16.5	5,997	7.3
Services	423.2	9.3	15,961	19.6
Other	−221.7[5]	−4.9[5]	13,428[6]	16.5[6]
TOTAL	4,537.1	100.0	81,558	100.0

Population economically active (2001): total 81,558; activity rate of total population 46.4% (participation rates: ages 15–64, 68.7%; female 49.0%; unemployed 14.6%).

Price and earnings indexes (1996 = 100)

	1995	1996	1997	1998	1999	2000	2001
Consumer price index	96.5	100.0	103.3	104.4	104.8	110.9	117.0
Monthly earnings index[7]	...	100.0	100.0	100.0	...	...	...

Public debt (external, outstanding; 1999): U.S.$294,600,000.

Foreign trade

Balance of trade (current prices)

	1995	1996	1997	1998	1999	2000
NA f. '000,000	−1,939	−2,003	−1,998	−1,815	−1,905	−1,224
% of total	71.3%	70.8%	67.6%	62.6%	60.4%	68.9%

Imports (1999): NA f. 2,375,000,000 (nonpetroleum domestic imports 71.3%, crude petroleum and petroleum products 14.8%, imports of Curaçao free zone 13.9%). *Major import sources* (1998): Venezuela 35.3%; United States 21.0%; Mexico 9.8%; Italy 5.4%; The Netherlands 4.8%; Brazil 3.1%.
Exports (1999): NA f. 470,000,000 (reexports of Curaçao free zone 59.1%, nonpetroleum domestic exports 37.5%, petroleum products 3.4%). *Major export destinations* (1998): United States 17.5%; Guatemala 8.0%; Costa Rica 6.5%; The Bahamas 4.6%; Jamaica 4.1%; Chile 3.4%.

Transport and communications

Transport. Railroads: none. Roads (1992): total length 367 mi, 590 km (paved, 51%). Vehicles (1999): passenger cars 74,840; trucks and buses 17,415. Air transport (2000)[8]: passenger arrivals and departures 911,000; freight loaded and unloaded 14,500 metric tons; airports (2000) with scheduled flights 5.

Communications

Medium	date	unit	number	units per 1,000 persons
Daily newspapers	1996	circulation	70,000	341
Radio	1997	receivers	217,000	1,039
Television	1997	receivers	69,000	330
Telephones	1999	main lines	79,000	386
Cellular telephones	1998	subscribers	16,000	77

Education and health

Educational attainment (2001). Percentage of population 25 and over having: no formal schooling 0.8%; primary education 24.2%; lower secondary 42.8%; upper secondary 16.8%; higher 11.4%; unknown 4.0%. *Literacy* (1995): total population age 15 and over literate 194,900 (96.6%); males literate 93,300 (96.6%); females literate 101,600 (96.6%).

Education (1999–2000)

	schools	teachers	students	student/ teacher ratio
Primary (age 6–12)	90	1,139[9]	23,205	21.1[9]
Secondary (age 12–17)	22	46[9]	8,112	18.2[9]
Voc., teacher tr.	32	853[9]	7,576	9.7[9]
Higher	2	123	825	6.7

Health (1999): physicians 341 (1 per 616 persons); hospital beds 1,466 (1 per 142 persons); infant mortality rate per 1,000 live births (2001) 11.4.
Food (2000): daily per capita caloric intake 2,573 (vegetable products 68%, animal products 32%); 107% of FAO recommended minimum requirement.

Military

Total active duty personnel (2001): a 45-member Dutch naval/air force contingent is stationed in the Netherlands Antilles and Aruba.

[1]Excludes Sint Eustatius. [2]Mostly tomatoes, beans, cucumbers, gherkins, melons, and lettuce grown on hydroponic farms; aloes grown for export, divi-divi pods, and sour orange fruit are nonhydroponic crops. [3]Curaçao only. [4]Weights of consumer price index components. [5]Less imputed bank service charges. [6]Includes 11,876 unemployed. [7]Minimum wages only. [8]Curaçao airport only. [9]1996–97.

Internet resources for further information:
• Central Bank of the Netherlands Antilles http://www.centralbank.an

New Caledonia

Official name: Nouvelle-Calédonie (New Caledonia)[1].
Political status: overseas country[1] (France) with one legislative house (Congress[2] [54]).
Chief of state: President of France represented by High Commissioner.
Head of government: President.
Capital: Nouméa.
Official language: none[3].
Official religion: none.
Monetary unit: 1 franc of the Comptoirs français du Pacifique (CFPF) = 100 centimes; valuation (Sept. 23, 2002)[4] 1 U.S.$ = CFPF 121.25; 1 £ = CFPF 188.44.

Area and population		area		population
Provinces Island(s)	Capitals	sq mi	sq km	1996 census
Loyauté (Loyalty)	Wé	765	1,981	20,877
Maré		248	642	6,896
Lifou		466	1,207	10,007
Ouvéa		51	132	3,974
Nord (Northern)	Koné	3,305	8,561	41,413
Belep		27	70	923
New Caledonia (part)		3,278	8,491	40,490
Sud (Southern)	Nouméa	3,102	8,033	134,546
New Caledonia (part)		3,043	7,881	132,875
Pins		59	152	1,671
TOTAL		7,172	18,575	196,836

Demography

Population (2002): 218,000.
Density (2002): persons per sq mi 30.4, persons per sq km 11.7.
Urban-rural (2002): urban 79.0%; rural 21.0%.
Sex distribution (1996): male 51.23%; female 48.77%.
Age breakdown (1996): under 15, 30.7%; 15–29, 27.2%; 30–44, 21.3%; 45–59, 13.3%; 60–74, 5.9%; 75 and over, 1.6%.
Population projection: (2010) 240,000; (2020) 265,000.
Doubling time: 48 years.
Ethnic composition (1996): Melanesian 45.3%, of which local (Kanak) 44.1%, Vanuatuan 1.2%; European 34.1%; Wallisian or Futunan 9.0%; Indonesian 2.6%; Tahitian 2.6%; Vietnamese 1.4%; other 5.0%.
Religious affiliation (1995): Roman Catholic 61.3%; Protestant 14.5%, of which Presbyterian 12.3%; Muslim 2.7%; other Christian 2.3%; other 19.2%.
Major cities (1996): Nouméa 76,293 (urban agglomeration 118,823); Mont-Dore 20,780[5]; Dumbéa 13,888[5].

Vital statistics

Birth rate per 1,000 population (2002): 19.7 (world avg. 21.2); (1996) legitimate 36.4%; illegitimate 63.6%.
Death rate per 1,000 population (2002): 4.9 (world avg. 8.9).
Natural increase rate per 1,000 population (2002): 14.8 (world avg. 12.3).
Total fertility rate (avg. births per childbearing woman; 2002): 2.5.
Marriage rate per 1,000 population (2001): 4.3.
Divorce rate per 1,000 population (1999): 0.8.
Life expectancy at birth (2002): male 72.0 years; female 78.0 years.
Major causes of death per 100,000 population (1999): diseases of the circulatory system 143.5; malignant neoplasms (cancers) 119.9; accidents, poisonings, and violence 95.4; diseases of the respiratory system 52.0.

National economy

Budget (1999). Revenue: CFPF 77,477,000,000 (indirect taxes 49.7%, direct taxes 30.9%, French government subsidies 8.6%, tobacco excises 6.3%). Expenditures: CFPF 74,218,000,000 (current expenditure 93.4%, development expenditure 6.6%).
Production (metric tons except as noted). Agriculture, forestry, fishing (1999): roots and tubers 21,100, of which yams 11,000, sweet potatoes 3,000; coconuts 16,000; vegetables 3,785; fruit 3,021; cereals 1,870, of which maize (corn) 1,650; livestock (number of live animals) 120,000 cattle, 38,000 pigs, 390,000 chickens; roundwood (1998) 4,800 cu m; fish catch (1997) 3,421, of which shrimp 1,107, sea urchins and echinoderms 505. Mining and quarrying (metric tons; 1999): nickel ore 6,562,000, of which nickel content (1997) 110,000; cobalt (1997) 800. Manufacturing (metric tons; 1999): cement 92,714; ferronickel (metal content) 45,289; nickel matte (metal content) 11,353; other manufactures include beer, copra cake, and soap. Energy production (consumption): electricity (kW-hr; 1997) 1,567,000,000 (1,567,000,000); coal (metric tons; 1997) none (168,000); crude petroleum, none (none); petroleum products (metric tons; 1997) none (409,000); natural gas, none (none).
Tourism: receipts from visitors (2000) U.S.$110,000,000; expenditures by nationals abroad, n.a.
Population economically active (1996): total 80,589; activity rate of total population 40.9% (participation rates: over age 14, 57.3%; female 39.7%; unemployed 18.6%).

Price and earnings indexes (1995 = 100)[6]						
	1995	1996	1997	1998	1999	2000	2001
Consumer price index	100.0	101.7	103.7	104.0	104.1	106.5	108.9
Earnings index[7]	100.0	101.2	103.1	104.4	105.0	106.1	135.3

Public debt (external, outstanding; 1999): U.S.$746,000,000.
Gross national product (2000): U.S.$3,203,000,000 (U.S.$15,060 per capita).

Structure of gross domestic product and labour force				
	1997		1996	
	in value CFPF '000,000	% of total value	labour force	% of labour force
Agriculture	6,439	1.9	4,663	5.8
Mining	13,307	3.8	4,408[8]	5.5[8]
Manufacturing	38,766	11.1	3,072[9]	3.8[9]
Construction	17,447	5.0	6,890	8.5
Public utilities	5,370	1.5	697	0.8
Transp. and commun.	23,415	6.7	2,968	3.7
Trade	80,054	22.9	8,375	10.4
Finance	76,543	21.9	5,550	6.9
Services			17,218	21.4
Pub. admin., defense	87,919	25.2	10,536	13.1
Other	—	—	16,212[10]	20.1[10]
TOTAL	349,260	100.0	80,589	100.0

Household income and expenditure (1991). Average household size (1996) 3.8; average annual income per household CFPF 3,361,233 (U.S.$32,879)[11]; sources of income: wages and salaries 68.2%, transfer payments 13.7%, other 18.1%; expenditure: food and beverages 25.9%, housing 20.4%, transportation and communications 16.1%, recreation 4.8%.
Land use (1994): forested 38.7%; meadows and pastures 11.8%; agricultural and under permanent cultivation 0.7%; other 48.8%.

Foreign trade[12]

Balance of trade (current prices)						
	1996	1997	1998	1999	2000	2001
CFPF '000,000	–41,616	–40,949	–58,910	–68,125	–44,235	–63,830
% of total	28.8%	26.2%	42.0%	43.2%	22.7%	34.6%

Imports (1999): CFPF 112,888,000,000 (machinery and apparatus 20.0%, food 16.2%, transportation equipment 15.6%, mineral fuels 9.4%, chemicals and chemical products 7.8%). *Major import sources* (1998): France 52.2%; Australia 13.9%; New Zealand 5.3%; Singapore 4.2%; Japan 3.4%.
Exports (1999): CFPF 44,763,000,000 (ferronickel 54.8%, nickel ore 18.8%, nickel matte 13.9%, shrimp 4.2%). *Major export destinations:* Japan 32.2%; France 22.1%; Taiwan 8.4%; South Korea 7.6%; Australia 7.1%.

Transport and communications

Transport. Railroads: none. Roads (1996): total length 3,582 mi, 5,764 km (paved [1993] 52%). Vehicles: passenger cars (1996) 56,700; trucks and buses (1993) 21,200. Air transport (1999)[13]: passenger arrivals 171,887, passenger departures 170,815; freight unloaded 3,914 metric tons, freight loaded 1,163 metric tons; airports (1999) with scheduled flights 11.

Communications				units per 1,000 persons
Medium	date	unit	number	
Daily newspapers	1996	circulation	24,000	121
Radio	1997	receivers	107,000	533
Television	1999	receivers	101,000	480
Telephones	2000	main lines	51,000	237
Cellular telephones	2000	subscribers	49,900	232
Internet	2000	users	24,000	111

Education and health

Educational attainment (1996). Percentage of population age 14 and over having: no formal schooling 5.7%; primary education 28.9%; lower secondary 30.2%; upper secondary 24.6%; higher 10.5%. *Literacy:* n.a.

Education (2000)				student/ teacher ratio
	schools	teachers	students	
Primary (age 6–10)	204	1,809	23,748	13.1
Secondary (age 11–17) Vocational	72	2,283	28,198	12.4
Higher	4[14]	55	2,069	37.6

Health (1999): physicians 418 (1 per 497 persons); hospital beds 838 (1 per 248 persons); infant mortality rate per 1,000 live births (2002) 7.0.
Food (1999): daily per capita caloric intake 2,772 (vegetable products 73%, animal products 27%); (1997) 122% of FAO recommended minimum requirement.

Military

Total active duty personnel (2001): 3,100 French troops. *Military expenditure as percentage of GNP:* n.a.

[1]The Nouméa Accord granting New Caledonia limited autonomy (with likely independence by 2013) was formally signed on May 5, 1998, approved by referendum in New Caledonia in November 1998, and passed by both houses of the French Parliament by February 1999. [2]Operates in association with 3 provincial assemblies. [3]Kanak languages and French have special recognition per Nouméa Accord. [4]Pegged to the euro on January 1, 2002, at €1 = CFPF 119.25. [5]Within Nouméa urban agglomeration. [6]All figures are end-of-year. [7]Based on minimum hourly wage. [8]Includes metallurgy. [9]Excludes metallurgy. [10]Includes 1,194 military conscripts and 15,018 unemployed. [11]Includes both monetary (92%) and nonmonetary income (8%). [12]Imports c.i.f.; exports f.o.b. [13]La Tontouta international airport only. [14]1996.

Internet resources for further information:

- **Overseas Departments and Territories of France**
  http://www.outre-mer.gouv.fr/domtom/nouvcal/index.htm
- **New Caledonia Economic Development Agency** http://www.adecal.nc

New Zealand

Official name: New Zealand (English); Aotearoa (Māori).
Form of government: constitutional monarchy with one legislative house (House of Representatives [120[1]]).
Chief of state: British Monarch, represented by Governor-General.
Head of government: Prime Minister.
Capital: Wellington.
Official languages: English; Māori.
Official religion: none.
Monetary unit: 1 New Zealand dollar ($NZ) = 100 cents; valuation (Sept. 23, 2002) 1 U.S.$ = $NZ 2.12; 1 £ = $NZ 3.30.

Area and population

Islands Regional Councils	area		population 2001 census
	sq mi	sq km	
North Island	44,702	115,777	2,870,688
Auckland	...	...	1,173,639
Bay of Plenty	...	...	245,100
Gisborne[2]	...	...	44,142
Hawkes Bay	...	...	146,109
Manawatu-Wanganui	...	...	222,123
Northland	...	...	144,363
Taranaki	...	...	102,684
Waikato	...	...	364,986
Wellington	...	...	427,542
South Island	58,384	151,215	949,242
Canterbury	...	...	494,952
Marlborough[2]	...	...	42,528
Nelson[2]	...	...	43,560
Otago	...	...	194,487
Southland	...	...	94,371
Tasman[2]	...	...	44,880
West Coast	...	...	34,464
Offshore islands	1,368	3,542	819
TOTAL	104,454	270,534	3,820,749

Demography

Population (2002): 3,893,000[3].
Density (2002): persons per sq mi 37.3, persons per sq km 14.4.
Urban-rural (2002): urban 86.0%; rural 14.0%.
Sex distribution (2001): male 48.73%; female 51.27%.
Age breakdown (2001): under 15, 22.9%; 15–29, 20.1%; 30–44, 23.0%; 45–59, 17.9%; 60–74, 10.7%; 75 and over, 5.4%.
Population projection: (2010) 4,113,000; (2020) 4,352,000.
Ethnic composition (2001): European 73.8%; Māori (local Polynesian) 13.5%; Asian 6.1%; other Pacific Peoples (mostly other Polynesian) 6.0%; other 0.6%.
Religious affiliation (2001): Christian 55.2%, of which Anglican 15.3%, Roman Catholic 12.7%, Presbyterian 11.3%; nonreligious 26.9%; Buddhist 1.1%; Hindu 1.0%; other religions/not specified 15.8%.
Major cities (2001): Auckland 371,313 (urban agglomeration 1,087,152); Christchurch 342,285; Wellington 166,362; Hamilton 140,088; Dunedin 110,757.

Vital statistics

Birth rate per 1,000 population (2002): 14.2 (world avg. 21.2); (1996) legitimate 58.0%; illegitimate 42.0%.
Death rate per 1,000 population (2002): 7.6 (world avg. 8.9).
Natural increase rate per 1,000 population (2002): 6.6 (world avg. 12.3).
Total fertility rate (avg. births per childbearing woman; 2002): 1.8.
Life expectancy at birth (2002): male 75.0 years; female 81.0 years.
Major causes of death per 100,000 population (1996): diseases of the circulatory system 317.2; malignant neoplasms (cancers) 200.8; diseases of the respiratory system 86.5; accidents, suicide, homicide, and other violence 47.0.

National economy

Budget (2000–2001). Revenue: $NZ 37,156,000,000 (income taxes 59.4%, taxes on goods and services 34.4%, nontax revenue 6.2%). Expenditures: $NZ 37,019,000,000 (social welfare 37.0%, health 19.0%, education 17.6%).
Production (metric tons except as noted). Agriculture, forestry, fishing (2000): apples 482,000, wheat 360,000, barley 281,000, corn (maize) 174,000; livestock (number of live animals) 45,800,000 sheep, 9,457,000 cattle, 344,000 pigs; roundwood (1999) 17,953,000 cu m; fish catch (1998) 635,711. Mining and quarrying (1998): iron ore and sand concentrate 2,000,000; aluminum metal 315,600; silver 31,500 kg; gold 11,250 kg. Manufacturing (1996–97): wood pulp 1,405,300; chemical fertilizers 1,365,000; yarn 21,302; beer 343,457,000 litres; footwear 2,840,000 pairs[4]; carpets 9,980,000 sq m. Energy production (consumption): electricity (kW-hr; 1997) 36,219,000,000 (36,219,000,000); coal (metric tons; 1997) 3,370,000 (2,651,000); crude petroleum (barrels; 1997) 21,000,000 (38,000,000); petroleum products (metric tons; 1997) 4,911,000 (5,039,000); natural gas (cu m; 1997) 5,059,000,000 (5,060,000,000).
Household income and expenditure. Average household size (1996) 2.8; annual income per household[5] (1996–97) $NZ 59,444 (U.S.$40,143); sources of income (1998): wages and salaries 65.8%, transfer payments 15.2%, self-employment 9.8%, other 9.2%; expenditure (1996–97): housing 20.2%, transportation 18.2%, food 16.4%, household goods 13.7%, clothing 3.8%.
Tourism (2000): receipts U.S.$2,100,000,000; expenditures U.S.$1,786,000,000.
Gross national product (2000): U.S.$49,750,000,000 (U.S.$12,990 per capita).

Structure of gross domestic product and labour force

	2001–02		1999	
	in value $NZ '000,000[6]	% of total value	labour force	% of labour force
Agriculture	} 8,991	8.3	165,500	8.8
Mining			3,600	0.2
Manufacturing	16,886	15.6	278,400	14.8
Construction	3,872	3.6	109,500	5.8
Public utilities	2,041	1.9	8,900	0.5
Transp. and commun.	11,164	10.3	110,400	5.9
Trade	16,699	15.4	371,500	19.8
Finance	26,878	24.8	220,100	11.7
Pub. admin., defense	4,349	4.0	} 478,600	25.5
Services	13,328	12.3		
Other	4,152	3.8	131,700[7]	7.0[7]
TOTAL	108,360	100.0	1,878,200	100.0

Population economically active (2000): total 1,923,700; activity rate 50.1% (participation rates: over age 15, 66.2%; female 45.3%; unemployed 5.7%).

Price and earnings indexes (1995 = 100)

	1995	1996	1997	1998	1999	2000	2001
Consumer price index	100.0	102.3	103.5	104.8	104.7	107.4	110.3
Hourly earnings index[8]	100.0	103.7	107.2	...	...	...	...

Land use (1999): pasture 49.6%; agriculture 12.2%; forest and other 38.2%.

Foreign trade[9]

Balance of trade (current prices)

	1996	1997	1998	1999	2000	2001
$NZ '000,000	+1,162.0	+902.0	+812.0	–1,896	+338	+2,994
% of total	2.8%	2.2%	1.8%	3.9%	0.6%	4.8%

Imports (1999): $NZ 24,248,000,000 (machinery 24.6%; transport equipment 17.2%; mineral fuels 5.7%; textiles and textile products 4.7%; plastics 4.1%). *Major import sources:* Australia 22.1%; U.S. 17.7%; Japan 12.6%; China 5.1%; Germany 4.5%; U.K. 4.4%.
Exports (1998–99): $NZ 22,600,000,000 (food 47.2%; wood and wood products 10.6%; machinery 7.7%; metals and metal products 7.2%; wool 3.8%). *Major export destinations:* Australia 21.4%; U.S. 13.3%; Japan 12.7%; U.K. 6.2%; South Korea 3.9%; Germany 2.8%; China 2.7%.

Transport and communications

Transport. Railroads (1999): route length 3,912 km; passengers carried (1998) 11,751,000; metric ton-km cargo 3,960,000,000. Roads (1999): total length 92,075 km (paved 62%). Vehicles (1998–99): passenger cars 1,831,118; trucks and buses (1998) 368,723. Merchant marine (1992): vessels (100 gross tons and over) 139; total deadweight tonnage 279,805. Air transport[10] (1999): passenger-km 19,879,000,000; metric ton-km cargo 851,744,000; airports (1997) 36.

Communications

Medium	date	unit	number	units per 1,000 persons
Daily newspapers	1999	circulation	850,000	223
Radio	1997	receivers	3,750,000	997
Television	1999	receivers	1,975,000	518
Telephones	2001	main lines	1,833,600	471
Cellular telephones	2001	subscribers	2,417,000	621
Personal computers	2001	units	1,500,000	386
Internet	2001	users	1,091,900	281

Education and health

Educational attainment (1991). Percentage of population age 25 and over having: primary and some secondary education 54.9%; secondary 31.1%; higher 6.9%; not specified 7.1%. *Literacy:* virtually 100.0%.

Education (1999)

	schools	teachers	students	student/ teacher ratio
Primary (age 5–12)[11]	2,366	25,832	478,065	18.5
Secondary (age 13–17)	335	15,401	226,164	14.7
Voc., teacher tr.	29	5,428	111,855	20.6
Higher[12]	7	5,008	105,996	21.2

Health: physicians (1999) 13,360 (1 per 285 persons); hospital beds (2000) 31,425 (1 per 122 persons); infant mortality rate per 1,000 live births (2002) 6.0.
Food (1999): daily per capita caloric intake 3,152 (vegetable products 68%, animal products 32%); 119% of FAO recommended minimum requirement.

Military

Total active duty personnel (2001): 9,230 (army 48.2%, air force 30.3%, navy 21.5%). *Military expenditure as percentage of GNP* (1999): 1.2% (world 2.4%); per capita expenditure U.S.$156.

[1]Includes six elected seats allocated to Māoris. [2]Reorganized as a unitary authority that is administered by a district council with regional powers. [3]Excludes undercounts of the March 2001 preliminary census results. [4]1994–95. [5]Disposable income. [6]Constant 1995–96 prices. [7]Mostly unemployed. [8]In manufacturing. [9]Import figures are f.o.b. in balance of trade and c.i.f. in commodities and trading partners. [10]Air New Zealand only. [11]Includes composite schools that provide both primary and secondary education. [12]Universities only.

Internet resources for further information:
- Statistics New Zealand/Te Tari Tatau http://www.stats.govt.nz/statsweb.nsf
- The Press On-Line New Zealand News http://www.press.co.nz

Nicaragua

Official name: República de Nicaragua (Republic of Nicaragua).
Form of government: unitary multiparty republic with one legislative house (National Assembly [92[1]]).
Head of state and government: President.
Capital: Managua.
Official language: Spanish.
Official religion: none.
Monetary unit: 1 córdoba oro (C$) = 100 centavos; valuation (Sept. 23, 2002) 1 U.S.$ = C$14.43; 1 £ = C$22.43.

Area and population		area[2]		population
Departments	**Capitals**	sq mi	sq km	1998 estimate
Boaco	Boaco	1,613	4,177	150,744
Carazo	Jinotepe	417	1,081	160,705
Chinandega	Chinandega	1,862	4,822	383,658
Chontales	Juigalpa	2,502	6,481	159,603
Estelí	Estelí	861	2,230	188,462
Granada	Granada	402	1,040	170,129
Jinotega	Jinotega	3,714	9,620	294,333
León	León	2,107	5,457	359,588
Madriz	Somoto	659	1,708	115,935
Managua	Managua	1,338	3,465	1,196,422
Masaya	Masaya	236	611	270,954
Matagalpa	Matagalpa	2,627	6,804	417,465[3]
Nueva Segovia	Ocotal	1,194	3,093	163,400
Río San Juan	San Carlos	2,912	7,541	81,408
Rivas	Rivas	835	2,162	151,294
Autonomous regions				
North Atlantic	Puerto Cabezas	12,549	32,501	216,737[3]
South Atlantic	Bluefields	10,636	27,546	303,037
TOTAL LAND AREA		46,464	120,340[4]	
INLAND WATER		3,874	10,034	
TOTAL		50,337[4]	130,373[4]	4,803,102[5]

Demography

Population (2002): 5,024,000[6].
Density (2002)[7]: persons per sq mi 108.1, persons per sq km 41.7.
Urban-rural (2001): urban 56.5%; rural 43.5%.
Sex distribution (2000): male 49.96%; female 50.04%.
Age breakdown (2000): under 15, 39.7%; 15–29, 30.6%; 30–44, 17.0%; 45–59, 8.2%; 60–74, 3.7%; 75 and over, 0.8%.
Population projection: (2010) 5,839,000; (2020) 6,808,000.
Doubling time: 30 years.
Ethnic composition (1997): mestizo (Spanish/Indian) 69.0%; white 17.0%; black 9.0%; Amerindian 5.0%.
Religious affiliation (1995): Roman Catholic 72.9%; Protestant 16.7%, of which Evangelical 15.1%, Moravian 1.5%; nonreligious 8.5%; other 1.9%.
Major cities (1995): Managua (2001) 1,039,000[8]; León 123,865; Chinandega 97,387; Masaya 88,971; Granada 71,783; Estelí 71,550.

Vital statistics

Birth rate per 1,000 population (2000): 28.3 (world avg. 22.5).
Death rate per 1,000 population (2000): 4.9 (world avg. 9.0).
Natural increase rate per 1,000 population (2000): 23.4 (world avg. 13.5).
Total fertility rate (avg. births per childbearing woman; 2000): 3.3.
Life expectancy at birth (2000): male 66.8 years; female 70.8 years.
Major causes of death per 100,000 population (1994)[9]: diseases of the circulatory system 126; accidents, injuries, and violence 77; infectious and parasitic diseases 55; conditions originating in the perinatal period 53; diseases of the respiratory system 51.

National economy

Budget (1998). Revenue: C$6,581,000,000 (tax revenue 85.7%, of which import duties 23.0%, excise taxes on petroleum products 16.7%, general sales tax 14.2%, income taxes 12.3%; grants 10.3%). Expenditures: C$7,037,000,000 (current expenditure 67.2%; development expenditure 31.6%).
Public debt (external, outstanding; 2000): U.S.$5,602,000,000.
Production (metric tons except as noted). Agriculture, forestry, fishing (1999): sugarcane 3,748,000, corn (maize) 302,000, rice 137,000, dry beans 94,000, sorghum 83,000, oranges 71,000, bananas 69,000, coffee 65,000, manioc (cassava) 51,000, soybeans 31,500; livestock (number of live animals) 1,693,000 cattle, 400,000 pigs; roundwood (2000) 5,984,000 cu m; fish catch (2000) 28,008, of which crustaceans 11,379. Mining and quarrying (2000): gold 90,000 troy oz. Manufacturing (value added in C$'000,000; 2000[10]): food 1,936; beverages 1,261; cement, bricks, tiles 538; refined petroleum 212; chemical products 191. Energy production (consumption): electricity (kW-hr; 1998) 2,084,000,000 (1,392,000,000); coal, none (none); crude petroleum (barrels; 1997) none (5,468,000); petroleum products (metric tons; 1997) 735,000 (947,000); natural gas, none (none).
Tourism (2000): receipts from visitors U.S.$111,000,000; expenditures by nationals abroad U.S.$79,000,000.
Land use (1994): forested 26.3%; meadows and pastures 45.3%; agricultural and under permanent cultivation 10.5%; other 17.9%.
Population economically active (2000): total 1,815,300; activity rate of total population 35.8% (participation rates: 15–64, 64.1%; female 29.5%; unemployed 9.8%).

Price and earnings indexes (1995 = 100)							
	1995	1996	1997	1998	1999	2000	2001
Consumer price index	100	112	122	145	155	170	182
Monthly earnings index	100	106	119	138	167	...	...

Gross national product (2000): U.S.$2,053,000,000 (U.S.$410 per capita).

Structure of gross domestic product and labour force				
	2000		1999	
	in value C$'000,000	% of total value	labour force	% of labour force
Agriculture, forestry	9,818	32.3	655,300	37.9
Mining	221	0.7	11,700	0.7
Manufacturing	4,389	14.4	125,300	7.2
Construction	1,921	6.3	88,100	5.1
Public utilities	339	1.1	5,800	0.3
Transp. and commun.	1,023	3.4	49,700	2.9
Trade, restaurants	6,867	22.6	259,200	15.0
Finance, real estate	1,560	5.1	20,100	1.2
Pub. admin., defense	2,615	8.6	67,500	3.9
Services	1,642	5.4	261,500	15.1
Other	—	—	184,700[11]	10.7[11]
TOTAL	30,395	100.0[4]	1,728,900	100.0

Household income and expenditure. Average household size (1995) 5.8.

Foreign trade[12]

Balance of trade (current prices)						
	1996	1997	1998	1999	2000	2001
U.S.$'000,000	−577.1	−793.9	−823.7	−1,153.5	−962.2	−1,019.9
% of total	38.2%	40.8%	41.8%	51.4%	43.3%	46.0%

Imports (1999): U.S.$1,845,700,000 (capital goods 32.2%, nondurable consumer goods 23.9%, mineral fuels 8.7%). *Major import sources:* U.S. 34.5%; Costa Rica 11.4%; Guatemala 7.3%; Panama 6.9%.
Exports (1999): U.S.$543,800,000 (coffee 24.9%, manufactured products 19.9%, crustaceans 15.4%, beef 7.7%, raw sugar 5.6%, gold 5.6%). *Major export destinations:* U.S. 37.7%; El Salvador 12.5%; Germany 9.8%; Honduras 6.5%; Costa Rica 5.1%.

Transport and communications

Transport. Railroads:[13]. Roads (1999): total length 16,382 km (paved 11%). Vehicles (1998): passenger cars 52,220; trucks and buses 73,402. Air transport (1998): passenger-km 93,000,000; metric ton-km cargo 10,000,000; airports (1997) with scheduled flights 10.

Communications				units per 1,000
Medium	date	unit	number	persons
Daily newspapers	1996	circulation	135,000	30
Radio	1997	receivers	1,240,000	265
Television	1999	receivers	340,000	72
Telephones	2001	main lines	158,000	31
Cellular telephones	2001	subscribers	156,000	30
Personal computers	2000	units	50,000	9.9
Internet	2000	users	50,000	9.9

Education and health

Educational attainment (1995). Percentage of population age 25 and over having: no formal schooling 30.6%, no formal schooling (literate) 3.9%, primary education 39.2%, secondary 17.0%, technical 3.1%, incomplete undergraduate 2.2%; complete undergraduate 4.0%. *Literacy* (1995): total population age 15 and over literate 1,769,000 (74.0%); males literate 853,000 (74.4%); females literate 916,000 (73.6%).

Education (1997)				student/
	schools	teachers	students	teacher ratio
Primary (age 7–12)	7,224[14]	21,020[15]	783,002[14]	36.3[15]
Secondary (age 13–18)	451[16]	5,990[17]	220,670[17]	36.8[17]
Higher	10[16]	3,840	48,758	12.7

Health: physicians (1997) 3,725 (1 per 1,255 persons); hospital beds (1996) 6,666 (1 per 674 persons); infant mortality rate (2000) 34.8.
Food (1999): daily per capita caloric intake 2,314 (vegetable products 93%, animal products 7%); 103% of FAO recommended minimum requirement.

Military

Total active duty personnel (2001): 16,000 (army 87.5%, navy 5.0%, air force 7.5%). *Military expenditure as percentage of GNP* (1999): 1.2% (world 2.4%); per capita expenditure U.S.$5.

[1]Includes 2 unsuccessful 2001 presidential candidates meeting special conditions. [2]Lakes and lagoons are excluded from the areas of departments and autonomous regions. [3]1997 estimate. [4]Detail does not add to total given because of rounding. [5]De jure projection based on 1995 census. [6]De facto estimate. [7]Based on land area. [8]Population of urban agglomeration. [9]Projected rates based on about 55% of total deaths. [10]At prices of 1980. [11]Represents unemployed. [12]Imports f.o.b. in balance of trade and c.i.f. in commodities and trading partners. [13]Public railroad service ended in January 1994; private rail service (2000) 4 mi (6 km). [14]1998. [15]1996. [16]1994. [17]1995.

Internet resources for further information:
• **Central Bank of Nicaragua** http://www.bcn.gob.ni/english/default.htm

Niger

Official name: République du Niger
(Republic of Niger).
Form of government: multiparty republic
with one legislative house
(National Assembly [83]).
Head of state and government:
President, assisted by Prime Minister.
Capital: Niamey.
Official language: French.
Official religion: none.
Monetary unit: 1 CFA franc
(CFAF) = 100 centimes;
valuation (Sept. 23, 2002)
1 U.S.$ = CFAF 667.00;
1 £ = CFAF 1.037[1].

Area and population		area[2]		population
Departments	**Capitals**	sq mi	sq km	1990 estimate
Agadez	Agadez	244,869	634,209	189,000
Diffa	Diffa	54,138	140,216	227,000
Dosso	Dosso	11,970	31,002	982,000
Maradi	Maradi	14,896	38,581	1,415,000
Tahoua	Tahoua	41,188	106,677	1,373,000
Tillabéri	Tillabéri	34,604	89,623	1,818,000[3]
Zinder	Zinder	56,151	145,430	1,467,000
City				
Niamey	Niamey	259	670	[3]
TOTAL		458,075	1,186,408	7,471,000

Demography

Population (2002): 10,640,000.
Density (2002)[2]: persons per sq mi 21.8, persons per sq km 8.4.
Urban-rural (2000): urban 20.1%; rural 79.9%.
Sex distribution (2001): male 49.93%; female 50.07%.
Age breakdown (2001): under 15, 48.0%; 15–29, 26.3%; 30–44, 14.1%; 45–59, 7.8%; 60–74, 3.2%; 75 and over, 0.6%.
Population projection: (2010) 13,140,000; (2020) 16,800,000.
Doubling time: 26 years.
Ethnic composition (1988): Hausa 53.0%; Zerma- (Djerma-) Songhai 21.2%; Tuareg 10.4%; Fulani (Peul) 9.8%; Kanuri-Nanga 4.4%; Teda 0.4%; Arab 0.3%; Gurma 0.3%; other 0.2%.
Religious affiliation (2000): Sunnī Muslim 90.7%; traditional beliefs 8.7%; Christian 0.5%; other 0.1%.
Major cities (1988): Niamey 391,876 (urban agglomeration [2001] 821,000); Zinder 119,827; Maradi 110,005; Tahoua 49,948; Agadez 32,272.

Vital statistics

Birth rate per 1,000 population (2001): 50.7 (world avg. 21.2).
Death rate per 1,000 population (2001): 22.7 (world avg. 8.9).
Natural increase rate per 1,000 population (2001): 28.0 (world avg. 12.3).
Total fertility rate (avg. births per childbearing woman; 2001): 7.1.
Marriage rate per 1,000 population: n.a.
Divorce rate per 1,000 population: n.a.
Life expectancy at birth (2001): male 41.7 years; female 41.4 years.
Major causes of death: n.a.; however, among selected major causes of infectious disease registered at medical facilities were malaria, measles, diarrhea, meningitis, pneumonia, diphtheria, tetanus, viral hepatitis, and poliomyelitis; malnutrition and shortages of trained medical personnel are widespread.

National economy

Budget (2000). Revenue: CFAF 162,166,000,000 (taxes 63.4%, external aid and gifts 32.1%, nontax revenue 4.5%). Expenditures: CFAF 204,800,000,000 (current expenditures 67.6%, of which education 13.7%, defense 6.8%, economic services 4.5%, health 3.9%; development expenditures 32.4%).
Public debt (external, outstanding; 2000): U.S.$1,413,000,000.
Tourism (2000): receipts from visitors U.S.$24,000,000; expenditures by nationals abroad U.S.$28,000,000.
Gross national product (2000): U.S.$1,939,000,000 (U.S.$180 per capita).

Structure of gross domestic product and labour force				
	2000		1988	
	in value CFAF '000,000	% of total value	labour force[4]	% of labour force[4]
Agriculture	484,400	37.8	1,764,049	76.2
Mining	87,500	6.8	5,295	0.2
Manufacturing	87,000	6.8	65,793	2.8
Construction	24,100	1.9	13,742	0.6
Public utilities	28,800	2.2	1,778	0.1
Transp. and commun.	60,900	4.8	14,764	0.6
Trade and finance	237,100	18.5	210,354	9.1
Pub. admin., defense	109,600	8.6	59,271	2.6
Services	131,400	10.3	63,991	2.8
Other	29,600[5]	2.3[5]	116,657	5.0
TOTAL	1,280,400	100.0	2,315,694	100.0

Production (metric tons except as noted). Agriculture, forestry, fishing (2001): millet 2,414,394, sorghum 655,729, cowpeas 300,000, sugar cane 211,354, onions 271,218, cassava 105,494, peanuts (groundnuts) 129,336, tomatoes 99,226,000, rice 76,400, tobacco leaf 164; livestock (number of live animals) 6,900,000 goats, 4,500,000 sheep, 2,260,000 cattle, 580,000 asses, 415,000 camels, 105,000 horses; roundwood (2001) 8,406,463 cu m; fish catch (1999)

11,014. Mining and quarrying: salt (1997) 3,000; uranium (2000) 2,898. Manufacturing (value added in CFAF '000,000; 1998): paper and products 3,171; food 1,697; soaps and other chemical products 1,547; textiles 784. Construction (value added in CFAF; 1994): 16,100,000,000. Energy production (consumption): electricity (kW-hr; 2000) 199,200,000 (326,600,000); coal (metric tons; 1997) 174,000 (174,000); crude petroleum, none (none); petroleum products (metric tons; 2000) none (165,700); natural gas, none (none).
Population economically active (1988)[4]: total 2,315,694; activity rate of total population 31.9% (participation rates: ages 15–64, 55.2%; female 20.4%).

Price and earnings indexes (1995 = 100)							
	1995	1996	1997	1998	1999	2000	2001
Consumer price index	100.0	105.3	108.4	113.3	110.7	113.9	118.5
Annual earnings index	...	...	...	...	...	...	...

Household income and expenditure. Average household size (1998) 6.3; income per household: n.a.; expenditure (1987): food and beverages 43.1%, housing 22.8%, clothing 10.0%.
Land use (1994): forested 2.0%; meadows and pastures 8.2%; agricultural and under permanent cultivation 2.9%; other (largely desert) 86.9%.

Foreign trade

Balance of trade (current prices)						
	1995	1996	1997	1998	1999	2000
CFAF '000,000	−5,500	−2,300	−16,400	−21,100	−17,800	−29,200
% of total	1.9%	0.6%	4.9%	5.7%	4.8%	6.8%

Imports (2000): CFAF 230,400,000,000 (food products 27.5%, petroleum products 20.7%; capital goods 19.4%; intermediate goods 7.5%). *Major import sources:* France 20.1%; Côte d'Ivoire 13.2%; Nigeria 10.3%; Japan 6.2%; Germany 2.2%; Italy 1.5%.
Exports (2000): CFAF 201,200,000,000 (uranium 31.8%; livestock [mostly live cattle, sheep, and goats] 18.4%; cowpeas 6.7%). *Major export destinations:* France 48.1%; Nigeria 40.6%; Côte d'Ivoire 1.6%; Japan 0.5%.

Transport and communications

Transport. Railroads: none. Roads (1999): total length 6,276 mi, 10,100 km (paved 8%). Vehicles (1999): passenger cars 38,220, trucks and buses 15,200. Air transport (1998)[6]: passenger-mi 160,477,000, passenger-km 258,263,000; short ton-mi cargo 9,263,000, metric ton-km cargo 13,524,000; airports (1999) with scheduled flights 6.

Communications				units per 1,000
Medium	date	unit	number	persons
Daily newspapers	1996	circulation	2,000	0.2
Radio	1997	receivers	680,000	73
Television	1999	receivers	285,000	29
Telephones	2001	main lines	21,700	1.9
Cellular telephones	2001	subscribers	1,800	0.1
Personal computers	2001	units	6,000	0.5
Internet	2001	users	12,000	1.1

Education and health

Educational attainment (1988). Percentage of population age 25 and over having: no formal schooling 85.0%; Koranic education 11.2%; primary education 2.5%; secondary 1.1%; higher 0.2%. *Literacy* (1995): total population age 15 and over literate 641,000 (13.6%); males literate 482,000 (20.9%); females literate 159,000 (6.6%).

Education (1997–98)				student/
	schools	teachers	students	teacher ratio
Primary (age 7–12)	3,175	11,545	482,065	41.8
Secondary (age 13–19)[7]	...	3,579	97,675	27.3
Voc., teacher tr.[7]	...	215	2,145	10.0
Higher[8]	2	355	5,569	15.7

Health: physicians (1997) 324 (1 per 28,171 persons); hospital beds n.a.; infant mortality rate per 1,000 live births (2001) 123.6.
Food (2000): daily per capita caloric intake 2,089 (vegetable products 95%, animal products 5%); 88% of FAO recommended minimum requirement.

Military

Total active duty personnel (2001): 5,300 (army 98%, air force 2%). *Military expenditure as percentage of GNP* (1999): 1.2% (world 2.4%); per capita expenditure U.S.$2.

---

[1]Formerly pegged to the French franc and since Jan. 1, 2002, to the euro at the rate of 1€ = CFAF 655.96. [2]The departmental areas and total shown are based on old survey. The total area, according to a more recent survey, is 489,000 sq mi (1,267,000 sq km); but subtotals distributing this total among the departments remain unpublished. [3]Tillabéri includes Niamey. [4]Excluding nomadic population. [5]Import taxes and duties. [6]Represents 1/11 of the traffic of Air Afrique, which is operated by 11 West African states. [7]1996–97. [8]Université de Niamey and École Nationale d'Administration du Niger only.

Internet resources for further information:

- **The United Nations in Niger**
  http://www.un.ne
- **Investir en zone franc**
  http://www.izf.net/izf/Index.htm

Nigeria

Official name: Federal Republic of Nigeria.
Form of government: federal republic with two legislative bodies (Senate [109]; House of Representatives [360]).
Head of state and government: President.
Capital: Abuja.
Official language: English.
Official religion: none.
Monetary unit: 1 Nigerian naira (₦) = 100 kobo; valuation (Sept. 23, 2002) 1 U.S.$ = ₦129.00; 1 £ = ₦200.48.

Gulf of Guinea

Atlantic Ocean

Area and population

States[1]	area sq km	population 1995 estimate	States[1]	area sq km	population 1995 estimate
Abia	6,320	2,569,362[2]	Kebbi	36,800	2,305,768
Adamawa	36,917	2,374,892	Kogi	29,833	2,346,936
Akwa Ibom	7,081	2,638,413	Kwara	36,825	1,751,464
Anambra	4,844	3,094,783	Lagos	3,345	6,357,253
Bauchi	45,837	4,801,569[3]	Niger	76,363	2,775,526
Bayelsa	10,773	[4]	Nassarawa	27,117	[6]
Benue	34,059	3,108,754	Ogun	16,762	2,614,747
Borno	70,898	2,903,238	Ondo	14,606	4,343,230[5]
Cross River	20,156	2,085,926	Osun	9,251	2,463,185
Delta	17,698	2,873,711	Oyo	28,454	3,900,803
Ebonyi	5,670	[2]	Plateau	30,913	3,671,498[6]
Edo	17,802	2,414,919	Rivers	11,077	4,454,337[4]
Ekiti	6,353	[5]	Sokoto	25,973	4,911,118[7]
Enugu	7,161	3,534,633[2]	Taraba	54,473	1,655,443
Gombe	18,768	[3]	Yobe	45,502	1,578,172
Imo	5,530	2,779,028	Zamfara	39,762	[7]
Jigawa	23,154	3,164,134			
Kaduna	46,053	4,438,007	**Federal Capital Territory**		
Kano	20,131	6,297,165	Abuja	7,315	423,391
Katsina	24,192	4,336,363	TOTAL	923,768	98,967,768

Demography

Population (2002): 129,935,000.
Density (2002): persons per sq mi 364.4, persons per sq km 140.7.
Urban-rural (2002): urban 44.9%; rural 55.1%.
Sex distribution (2001): male 50.60%; female 49.40%.
Age breakdown (2001): under 15, 43.7%; 15–29, 27.8%; 30–44, 15.3%; 45–59, 8.6%; 60–74, 3.9%; 75 and over, 0.7%.
Population projection: (2010) 155,588,000; (2020) 187,437,000.
Ethnic composition (2000): Yoruba 17.5%; Hausa 17.2%; Igbo (Ibo) 13.3%; Fulani 10.7%; Ibibio 4.1%; Kanuri 3.6%; Egba 2.9%; Tiv 2.6%; Bura 1.1%; Nupe 1.0%; Edo 1.0%; other 25.0%.
Religious affiliation (2000): Christian 45.9%, of which independent Christian 15.0%, Anglican 13.0%, other Protestant 9.0%, Roman Catholic 8.0%; Muslim 43.9%; African indigenous 9.8%; other 0.4%.
Major cities (1991): Lagos 5,197,247 (urban agglomeration [2000] 13,427,000); Kano 2,166,554; Ibadan (2000) 1,731,000; Kaduna 993,642; Benin City 762,719; Port Harcourt 703,421; Maiduguri 618,278; Zaria 612,257; Ilorin 532,089.

Vital statistics

Birth rate per 1,000 population (2001): 39.7 (world avg. 21.2).
Death rate per 1,000 population (2001): 13.9 (world avg. 8.9).
Natural increase rate per 1,000 population (2001): 25.8 (world avg. 12.3).
Total fertility rate (avg. births per childbearing woman; 2001): 5.6.
Life expectancy at birth (2001): male 51.1 years; female 51.7 years.

National economy

Budget (2000). Revenue: ₦1,927,087,000,000 (tax revenue 33.1%, of which petroleum profit tax 17.3%; import duties, excise taxes, and fees 6.0%; non-tax revenue 66.9%, of which oil export proceeds 49.1%). Expenditures: ₦1,834,305,000,000 (1999; recurrent expenditure 75.6%, of which debt service 18.8%, education 5.2%, defense 4.6%; capital expenditure 24.4%).
Production (metric tons except as noted). Agriculture, forestry, fishing (2001): cassava 33,854,000, yams 26,201,000, sorghum 7,711,000, millet 6,105,000, corn (maize) 5,598,000, taro 3,866,000, rice 3,298,000, peanuts (groundnuts) 2,901,000, sweet potatoes 2,468,000, cow peas 2,150,000, plantains 1,902,000, tomatoes 879,000; livestock 24,300,000 goats, 20,500,000 sheep, 19,830,000 cattle, 4,855,000 pigs; roundwood (2001) 69,115,550 cu m; fish catch (1999) 477,365. Mining and quarrying (2000): limestone 2,000,000; marble 30,000. Manufacturing (value added in ₦'000,000; 1995): food and beverages 25,415; textiles 16,193; chemical products 11,181; machinery and transport equipment 5,639; paper products 2,828. Energy production (consumption): electricity (kW-hr; 1999) 18,700,000,000 ([1997] 14,830,000,000); coal (metric tons; 1999) 63,500 (72,500); crude petroleum (barrels; 2001) 757,498,000 (106,580,000); petroleum products (metric tons; 1997) 5,550,000 (6,175,000); natural gas (cu m; 2001) 757,498,000 (106,580,000).
Tourism (2000): receipts U.S.$200,000,000; expenditures U.S.$730,000,000.
Household income and expenditure. Avg. household size (1995) 4.7; annual income per household (1992–93) ₦15,000 (U.S.$760); sources of income (1979): self-employment 49.4%, wages 30.2%, interest 5.4%, rent 4.7%, transfer payments 4.3%; expenditures (1979): food 53.0%, fuel and light 11.4%, clothing 6.0%, transportation 4.7%, household goods 3.8%, other 21.1%.

Gross national product (2000): U.S.$32,705,000,000 (U.S.$260 per capita).

Structure of gross domestic product and labour force

	2000 in value ₦'000,000	2000 % of total value	1986 labour force	1986 % of labour force
Agriculture	1,191,989	28.5	13,259,000	43.1
Mining[8]	1,657,876	39.7	6,800	0.1
Manufacturing	166,247	4.0	1,263,700	4.1
Construction	31,017	0.7	545,600	1.8
Public utilities	2,212	0.1	130,400	0.4
Transp. and commun.	108,080	2.6	1,111,900	3.6
Trade, hotels	533,442	12.8	7,417,400	24.1
Finance	216,270	5.1	120,100	0.4
Pub. admin., defense	226,306	5.4 }	4,902,100	15.9
Services	53,688	1.3 }		
Other	−8,948[9]	−0.2[9]	2,008,500[10]	6.5[10]
TOTAL	4,178,179	100.0	30,765,500	100.0

Public debt (external, outstanding; 2000): U.S.$32,735,000,000.
Population economically active (1993–94): total 29,000,000; activity rate 31.0% (participation rates: ages 15–59, 64.4%; female 44.0%).

Price and earnings indexes (1995 = 100)

	1995	1996	1997	1998	1999	2000	2001
Consumer price index	100.0	129.3	139.9	154.3	164.6	176.0	215.7
Earnings index	...	...	...	...	...	...	...

Land use (1994): forest 15.7%; pasture 43.9%; agriculture 35.9%; other 4.5%.

Foreign trade

Balance of trade (current prices)

	1995	1996	1997	1998	1999	2000
₦'000,000	+108,681	+746,996	+395,946	+18,341	+128,904	+820,593
% of total	32.7%	39.9%	19.0%	4.3%	6.2%	24.6%

Imports (2000): U.S.$12,372,000,000 (1995; machinery and transport equipment 42.0%; manufactured goods [mostly iron and steel products, textiles, and paper products] 24.0%; chemicals 17.0%; food 8.4%). *Major import sources* (2000): U.K. 10.9%; U.S. 9.2%; France 8.9%; Germany 7.4%; China 6.3%; Italy 5.3%; The Netherlands 5.2%.
Exports (2000): U.S.$20,441,000,000 (crude petroleum 98.9%; ships and boats 0.3%; food products 0.3%). *Major export destinations* (2000): U.S. 46.1%; Spain 10.7%; India 6.1%; France 5.2%; Portugal 3.6%.

Transport and communications

Transport. Railroads (2000): length 3,505 km; passenger-km 179,000,000[11]; metric ton-km cargo 120,000,000[11]. Roads (1999): total length 62,598 km (paved 19%). Vehicles (1996): passenger cars 773,000; trucks and buses 68,300[12]. Merchant marine (2001): vessels (100 gross tons and over) 293. Air transport[13] (2000): passenger-km 111,566,000; metric ton-km cargo 2,068,000; airports (1998) 12.

Communications

Medium	date	unit	number	units per 1,000 persons
Daily newspapers	1996	circulation	2,500,000	24
Radio	1996	receivers	20,500,000	197
Television	1998	receivers	7,200,000	66
Telephones	2001	main lines	500,000	4.3
Cellular telephones	2001	subscribers	330,000	2.8
Personal computers	2001	units	800,000	6.8
Internet	2000	users	200,000	1.8

Education and health

Literacy (2000): total population age 15 and over literate 40,700,000 (64.1%); males literate 22,600,000 (62.3%); females literate 18,100,000 (56.2%).

Education (1994–95)

	schools	teachers	students	student/ teacher ratio
Primary (age 6–12)	38,649	435,210	16,191,000	37.2
Secondary (age 12–17)	6,074	152,596	4,451,000	29.2
Higher	31	12,103	228,000	18.8

Health (1995): physicians 27,230 (1 per 3,707 persons); hospital beds 68,350 (1 per 1,477 persons); infant mortality rate (2001) 73.3.
Food (2000): daily per capita caloric intake 2,850 (vegetable products 97%, animal products 3%); 121% of FAO recommended minimum requirement.

Military

Total active duty personnel (2001): 78,500 (army 79.0%, navy 8.9%, air force 12.1%). *Military expenditure as percentage of GNP* (1999): 1.7% (world 2.4%); per capita expenditure U.S.$13.

[1]In October 1996 six new states were created: Bayelsa, Ebonyi, Ekiti, Gombe, Nassarawa, and Zamfara. [2]Ebonyi is included partly in Abia and partly in Enugu. [3]Bauchi includes Gombe. [4]Rivers includes Bayelsa. [5]Ondo includes Ekiti. [6]Plateau includes Nassarawa. [7]Sokoto includes Zamfara. [8]Includes ₦1,653,212,000,000 (39.5%) from petroleum and natural gas. [9]Less subsidies. [10]Includes 1,263,000 unemployed. [11]1997. [12]1995 [13]Nigeria Airways only.

Internet resources for further information:
• **Nigeria High Commission (Canada)**
  http://www.nigeriahighcommottawa.com
• **Information on corporate Nigeria http://www.nigeriabusinessinfo.com**

Northern Mariana Islands

Pacific
Ocean

Official name: Commonwealth of the
Northern Mariana Islands.
Political status: self-governing
commonwealth in association
with the United States, having two
legislative houses (Senate [9];
House of Representatives [18])[1].
Chief of state: President of the
United States.
Head of government: Governor.
Capital: Capital Hill, Saipan.
Official languages: Chamorro,
Carolinian, and English.
Official religion: none.
Monetary unit: 1 dollar (U.S.$) = 100
cents; valuation (Sept. 23, 2002)
1 U.S.$ = £0.64.

Area and population		area		population
				2000
Municipal councils	Major villages	sq mi	sq km	census
Northern Islands[2]	...	55.3	143.2	6
Rota (island)	Songsong	32.8	85.0	3,283
Saipan (island)	San Antonio	46.5	120.4	62,392
Tinian[3]	San Jose	41.9	108.5	3,540
TOTAL		176.5[4]	457.1[4]	69,221[5]

Demography

Population (2002): 70,000.
Density (2002): persons per sq mi 396.6, persons per sq km 153.1.
Urban-rural (2002)[6]: urban 90.0%; rural 10.0%.
Sex distribution (2000): male 46.21%; female 53.79%.
Age breakdown (2000): under 15, 22.5%; 15–34, 45.8%; 35–59, 29.0%; 60–74, 2.3%; 75 and over, 0.4%.
Population projection: (2010) 70,000; (2020) 70,000.
Doubling time: 39 years.
Ethnic composition (2000)[7]: Filipino 26.2%; Chinese 22.1%; Chamorro 21.3%; Carolinian 3.8%; other Asian 7.5%; other Pacific Islander 6.6%; white 1.8%; multiethnic and other 10.7%.
Religious affiliation (1995)[8]: Roman Catholic 59.6%; Protestant 18.7%; other Christian 1.4%; other 20.3%.
Major villages (2000)[6, 9]: San Antonio 4,741; Garapan 3,588; Capital Hill 1,498; Songsong (on Rota) 1,411; San Jose (on Tinian) 1,361.

Vital statistics

Birth rate per 1,000 population (2002): 20.3 (world avg. 21.2); legitimate, 32.4%; illegitimate, 67.6%.
Death rate per 1,000 population (2002): 2.4 (world avg. 8.9).
Natural increase rate per 1,000 population (2002): 17.9 (world avg. 12.3).
Total fertility rate (avg. births per childbearing woman; 2002): 1.8.
Marriage rate per 1,000 population (1989): 28.5.
Divorce rate per 1,000 population (1986): 2.9.
Life expectancy at birth (2002): male 72.9 years; female 79.2 years.
Major causes of death per 100,000 population (1994–96 avg.): diseases of the circulatory system 53.3, of which cerebrovascular disease 25.8, ischemic heart diseases 21.8; malignant neoplasms (cancers) 33.3; accidents 29.8; diabetes mellitus 10.9.

National economy

Budget (1999–2000). Revenue: U.S.$297,200,000 (local revenue 83.3%, grants from U.S. Office of Insular Affairs for capital improvements 16.7%). Expenditures: U.S.$225,500,000 (education 22.0%, health and social welfare 19.3%, general government 16.0%, public safety 9.6%).
Tourism (1998): receipts from visitors, U.S.$394,000,000; expenditures by nationals abroad, n.a.
Land use (1990): forested, n.a.; meadows and pastures 3.7%; agricultural and under permanent cultivation 4.0%; other 92.3%.
Gross national product (1999): U.S.$664,600,000 (U.S.$9,600 per capita).

Structure of labour force		
	1995	
	labour force	% of labour force
Agriculture, forestry, and fishing	419	1.2
Mining and quarrying	...	...
Manufacturing	7,770	22.8
Public utilities	...	...
Construction	3,627	10.7
Transp. and commun.	2,540	7.5
Trade	5,980	17.6
Finance, insurance, and real estate	723	2.1
Pub. admin., defense	2,552	7.5
Services	10,429	30.6
Other	...	...
TOTAL	34,040	100.0

Production (metric tons except as noted). Agriculture, forestry, fishing (1989): melons 165, cucumbers 83, bananas 46, betelnuts 38, Chinese cabbage 33, coconuts 30, eggplant 23; livestock (number of live animals) 4,513 cattle, 1,260 pigs, 482 goats, 9,580 chickens; roundwood, n.a.; fish catch (1998) 235. Mining and quarrying: negligible amount of quarrying for building material.

Manufacturing (value of sales in U.S.$'000,000; 1997): garments 700; stone, glass, or ceramic products 21; food products 6. Construction (new permits in U.S.$'000,000; 1998): 63.3. Energy production (consumption): electricity (kW-hr) n.a.[10]; coal, none (none); crude petroleum, none (none); petroleum products, none (none); natural gas, none (none).
Population economically active (1995): total 37,393; activity rate of total population 63.5% (participation rates: ages 16 and over, 85.3%; female 48.1%; unemployed 7.1%).

Price index (1990 = 100)							
	1992	1993	1994	1995	1996	1997	1998
Consumer price index	116.9	122.0	125.4	127.7	131.5	132.9	132.5

Public debt (external, outstanding; 1999): U.S.$146,000,000.
Household income and expenditure. Average household size (1995) 4.0; average income per household (1995) U.S.$30,296; sources of income (1994): wages 83.9%, interest and rental 7.2%, self-employment 7.2%, transfer payments 1.7%.

Foreign trade

Balance of trade (current prices)			
	1989	1990	1991
U.S.$'000,000	−162	−138	−129
% of total	34.7%	25.3%	19.7%

Imports (1997): U.S.$836,200,000 (clothing and accessories 37.0%, foodstuffs 9.6%, petroleum and petroleum products 8.2%, transport equipment and parts 5.0%, construction materials 4.2%). *Major import sources:* Guam 35.6%, Hong Kong 24.0%, Japan 14.1%, South Korea 9.6%, United States 7.6%.
Exports (1999): U.S.$1,049,000,000 (clothing and accessories 99.9%). *Major export destinations:* nearly all to the United States.

Transport and communications

Transport. Railroads: none. Roads (1998): total length *c.* 225 mi, *c.* 360 km (paved, nearly 100%). Vehicles (1993): passenger cars 12,000; trucks and buses 6,300. Merchant marine (1992): vessels (100 gross tons and over) 2; total deadweight tonnage 856. Air transport (1999[11]): aircraft landings 23,853; boarding passengers 562,364; airports (1999) with scheduled flights 2[12].

Communications				units per 1,000
Medium	date	unit	number	persons
Radio	1999	receivers	10,500	152
Television	1999	receivers	4,100	59
Telephones	2000	main lines	26,800	506
Cellular telephones	2000	subscribers	3,000	57
Personal computers	...	units	...	...
Internet	...	users	...	...

Education and health

Educational attainment (1995). Percentage of population age 25 and over having: no formal schooling 0.7%; primary education, 5.5%; some secondary 13.5%; completed secondary 38.8%; some postsecondary 23.3%; completed undergraduate 18.2%. *Literacy* (1990): total population age 10 and over literate 35,490 (98.8%); males literate 18,790 (99.0%); females literate 16,700 (98.6%).

Education (1996–97)				student/
	schools	teachers	students	teacher ratio
Primary (age 6–11)	16[13]	597	6,952	18.4
Secondary (age 12–17)	9[13]		4,003	
Vocational	—	—	—	—
Higher[14]	1	...	845	...

Health: physicians (1986): 23 (1 per 1,326 persons); hospital beds (1998): 74 (1 per 899 persons); infant mortality rate per 1,000 live births (2002): 5.6.
Food: n.a.

Military

The United States is responsible for military defense; headquarters of the U.S. Pacific Command are in Hawaii.

[1]Residents elect a nonvoting representative to U.S. Congress. [2]Comprises the islands of Agrihan, Pagan, and Alamagan, as well as seven other uninhabited islands: Farallon de Pajaros (Uracas), Maug (East, West, and North islands), Asuncion, Guguan, Serigan, Anatahan, and Farallon de Medinilla. [3]Comprises Tinian island and Aguijan island. [4]Area measured at high tide; at low tide, total dry land area is 184.0 square miles (476.6 square km). [5]The 1995 census totaling 58,846 included 27,478 U.S. citizens and 31,368 aliens working primarily in the garment industry. [6]All of Saipan was designated an urban area in 2002. [7]Includes aliens. [8]Unofficial estimate. [9]All villages are unincorporated census designated places. [10]The installed electrical capacity in 1992 was 114,020 kilowatts. [11]Saipan International Airport only. [12]International flights are regularly scheduled at Saipan and at Rota; Tinian has nonscheduled domestic service. Additional domestic airports mainly handle charter flights. [13]1993–94. [14]Northern Marianas College; 1995–96.

Internet resources for further information:
- **Bank of Hawaii: Economics Research Center**
  http://www.boh.com/econ/pacific
- **CNMI: Central Statistics Division**
  http://www.commerce.gov.mp/csdhome.htm

Norway

Official name: Kongeriket Norge (Kingdom of Norway).
Form of government: constitutional monarchy with one legislative house (Parliament [165]).
Chief of state: King.
Head of government: Prime Minister.
Capital: Oslo.
Official language: Norwegian.
Official religion: Evangelical Lutheran.
Monetary unit: 1 Norwegian krone (NKr) = 100 øre; valuation (Sept. 23, 2002) 1 U.S.$ = NKr 7.50; 1 £ = NKr 11.66.

Area and population

Counties	Capitals	area[1] sq mi	sq km	population 2002[2] estimate
Akershus	—	1,898	4,917	477,325
Aust-Agder	Arendal	3,557	9,212	102,945
Buskerud	Drammen	5,763	14,927	239,793
Finnmark	Vadsø	18,779	48,637	73,732
Hedmark	Hamar	10,575	27,388	187,965
Hordaland	Bergen	6,036	15,634	438,253
Møre og Romsdal	Molde	5,832	15,104	243,855
Nordland	Bodø	14,798	38,327	237,503
Nord-Trøndelag	Steinkjer	8,647	22,396	127,457
Oppland	Lillehammer	9,726	25,191	183,235
Oslo	Oslo	175	454	512,589
Østfold	Moss	1,615	4,183	252,746
Rogaland	Stavanger	3,529	9,141	381,375
Sogn og Fjordane	Leikanger	7,189	18,620	107,280
Sør-Trøndelag	Trondheim	7,271	18,838	266,323
Telemark	Skien	5,913	15,315	165,710
Troms	Tromsø	10,032	25,984	151,673
Vest-Agder	Kristiansand	2,811	7,281	157,851
Vestfold	Tønsberg	856	2,216	216,456
TOTAL		125,004[3]	323,758[3]	4,524,066[4]

Demography

Population (2002): 4,537,000.
Density (2002): persons per sq mi 36.3, persons per sq km 14.0.
Urban-rural (1990): urban 75.0%; rural 25.0%.
Sex distribution (2002[2]): male 49.56%; female 50.44%.
Age breakdown (2002[2]): under 15, 20.0%; 15–29, 19.6%; 30–44, 22.3%; 45–59, 18.8%; 60–74, 11.5%; 75 and over, 7.8%.
Population projection: (2010) 4,702,000; (2020) 4,904,000.
Ethnic composition (by country of citizenship; 2002[2]): Norway 95.9%; Sweden 0.6%; Denmark 0.4%; United Kingdom 0.2%; Iraq 0.2%; Bosnia and Herzegovina 0.2%; United States 0.2%; Germany 0.2%; Pakistan 0.2%; Somalia 0.1%; Yugoslavia 0.1%; Finland 0.1%; Iran 0.1%; other 1.5%.
Major cities (2002)[5]: Oslo 512,589; Bergen 233,291; Trondheim 151,408.

Vital statistics

Birth rate per 1,000 population (2000): 13.2 (world avg. 22.5); (1999) legitimate 49.1%; illegitimate 50.9%.
Death rate per 1,000 population (2000): 9.8 (world avg. 9.0).
Natural increase rate per 1,000 population (2000): 3.4 (world avg. 13.5).
Total fertility rate (avg. births per childbearing woman; 1999): 1.9.
Marriage rate per 1,000 population (1998): 5.3.
Divorce rate per 1,000 population (2000): 2.2.
Life expectancy at birth (2000): male 76.0 years; female 81.4 years.
Major causes of death per 100,000 population (1996): malignant neoplasms (cancers) 250.2; ischemic heart disease 205.2; cerebrovascular disease 119.1.

National economy

Budget (2001). Revenue: NKr 829,345,000,000 (value-added taxes 30.7%, tax on income 28.6%, social security taxes 20.2%). Expenditures: NKr 617,372,000,000 (social security and welfare 37.8%, health 15.9%, education 13.6%, debt service 4.6%).
Land use (1994): forested 27.2%; meadows and pastures 0.4%; agricultural and under permanent cultivation 2.9%; built-up and other 69.5%.
Production (metric tons except as noted). Agriculture, forestry, fishing (2000): barley 649,400, potatoes 446,000, oats 372,400, wheat 293,000; livestock (number of live animals) 2,400,000 sheep, 1,042,000 cattle, 690,000 pigs; roundwood (1999) 8,424,000 cu m; fish catch (1999) 2,598,733, of which herring 807,635, cod 256,621[6], saithe 197,857, capelin 86,767. Mining and quarrying (1998)[7]: iron ore 621,000, ilmenite-titanium 589,500, copper 11,400, zinc 1,800. Manufacturing (value added in NKr '000,000; 1997): machinery and transport equipment 27,779; food products 25,646; paper and paper products 18,139; chemical products 10,421; wood products 4,616. Construction (1999): residential 2,919,000 sq m; nonresidential 3,768,000 sq m. Energy production (consumption): electricity (kW-hr; 1997) 111,551,000,000 (115,369,000,000); coal (metric tons; 1997) 386,000 (996,000); crude petroleum (barrels; 1997) 1,191,-000,000 (109,000,000); petroleum products (metric tons; 1997) 15,425,000 (8,648,000); natural gas (cu m; 1997) 47,485,000,000 (4,652,000,000).
Household income and expenditure. Average household size (2001) 2.3; consumption expenditure per household (1998) NKr 357,458 (U.S.$47,376); expenditure (1996–98): transportation 24.1%, housing 16.6%, food 12.9%, recreation and education 11.3%, household furniture and equipment 8.7%, clothing and footwear 6.1%.
Gross national product (2000): U.S.$155,064,000,000 (U.S.$34,530 per capita).

Structure of gross domestic product and labour force

	2001			
	in value NKr '000,000	% of total value	labour force	% of labour force
Agriculture	25,010	1.7	89,000	3.8
Mining	2,769	0.2	[8]	[8]
Crude petroleum and natural gas	311,274	20.6	32,000	1.4
Manufacturing	131,432	8.7	290,000[8]	12.3[8]
Construction	56,654	3.7	152,000	6.4
Public utilities	30,844	2.0	18,000	0.8
Transp. and commun.	119,351	7.9	169,000	7.1
Trade	141,378[9]	9.4[9]	398,000	16.9
Finance	247,619	16.4	273,000	11.6
Pub. admin., defense	233,950	15.5 }	855,000	36.2
Services	68,652	4.5 }		
Other	141,935	9.4	84,000[10]	3.5[10]
TOTAL	1,510,866[3]	100.0	2,362,000[3]	100.0

Population economically active (1999): total 2,333,000; activity rate of total population 52.4% (participation rates: ages 16–64 [1996] 79.1%; female 46.0%; unemployed 4.9%).

Price and earnings indexes (1995 = 100)

	1996	1997	1998	1999	2000	2001	2002
Consumer price index	101.3	103.9	106.2	108.7	112.0	115.4	116.9
Hourly earnings index	104.2	108.4[12]	...	...	...	...	...

Public debt (1998): U.S.$29,289,000,000.
Tourism (2000): receipts from visitors U.S.$1,937,000,000.

Foreign trade[13]

Balance of trade (current prices)

	1996	1997	1998	1999	2000	2001
NKr '000,000	+90,410	+90,189	+25,998	+84,886	+226,984	+233,805
% of total	16.4%	15.1%	4.5%	13.8%	32.1%	28.3%

Imports (2001): NKr 296,161,000,000 (machinery and transport equipment 42.1%, of which road vehicles 8.7%; ships 3.4%; metals and metal products 7.7%, of which iron and steel 2.6%; food products 6.7%, of which fruits and vegetables 1.4%; petroleum products 3.0%). *Major import sources:* Sweden 15.2%; Germany 12.6%; U.K. 7.9%; Denmark 7.1%.
Exports (2001): NKr 529,966,000,000 (petroleum products 48.5%; machinery and transport equipment 11.4%; metals and metal products 7.9%; food products 6.1%, of which fish 5.6%). *Major export destinations:* U.K. 19.6%; Germany 12.2%; The Netherlands 10.4%; Sweden 8.0%.

Transport and communications

Transport. Railroads (2001): route length 4,178 km; passenger-km 2,536,000,-000; metric ton-km cargo 2,451,000,000. Roads (2001): total length 91,545 km (paved 74%[14]). Vehicles (2001): passenger cars 1,872,862; trucks and buses 444,626. Merchant marine (1995): vessels (100 gross tons and over) 1,597; total deadweight tonnage 20,834,000. Air transport (2000): passenger-km 10,754,711,000; metric ton-km cargo 1,254,364,000; airports (1996) 50.

Communications

Medium	date	unit	number	units per 1,000 persons
Daily newspapers	1999	circulation	2,294,000	514
Radio	1996	receivers	4,000,000	913
Television	1999	receivers	2,900,000	650
Telephones	2001	main lines	3,262,000	723
Cellular telephones	2001	subscribers	3,737,000	828
Personal computers	2001	units	2,300,000	510
Internet	2001	users	2,700,000	598

Education and health

Educational attainment (1998). Percentage of population age 16 and over having: primary and lower secondary education 30.0%; higher secondary 45.9%; higher 20.8%; unknown 3.3%. *Literacy* (1998): virtually 100% literate.

Education (1998–99)

	schools	teachers	students	student/ teacher ratio
Primary (age 7–12)	3,277	44,972	569,044	12.7
Secondary (age 13–18) and vocational	703	21,068	197,765	9.4
Higher	82	11,590	184,063	15.9

Health: physicians (1996) 15,368 (1 per 285 persons); hospital beds (2000) 22,486 (1 per 199 persons); infant mortality rate (1999) 3.9.
Food (2000): daily per capita caloric intake 3,414 (vegetable products 66%, animal products 34%); 127% of FAO recommended minimum requirement.

Military

Total active duty personnel (2001): 25,800 (army 57.0%, navy 23.6%, air force 19.4%). *Military expenditure as percentage of GNP* (1999): 2.2% (world avg. 2.4%); per capita expenditure U.S.$742.

[1]Excludes Svalbard and Jan Mayen (24,360 sq mi [63,080 sq km]). [2]January 1. [3]Detail does not add to total given because of rounding. [4]Includes the Norwegian population of Svalbard and Jan Mayen, registered as residents in municipalities on the mainland. [5]Population of municipalities. [6]Norwegian catches on quotas bought from other countries are included. [7]Metal content of ore. [8]Manufacturing includes mining. [9]Includes hotels. [10]Unemployed. [11]June. [12]2nd quarter. [13]Imports c.i.f. in balance of trade. [14]1998.

Internet resources for further information:
• Statistics Norway http://www.ssb.no/www-open/english

Oman

Official name: Salṭanat 'Umān (Sultanate of Oman).
Form of government: monarchy with two advisory bodies (Council of State [52[1]]; Consultative Council [83]).
Head of state and government: Sultan.
Capital: Muscat[2].
Official language: Arabic.
Official religion: Islam.
Monetary unit: 1 rial Omani (RO) = 1,000 baizas; valuation (Sept. 23, 2002) 1 RO = U.S.$2.56 = £1.67.

Area and population

Regions	Capitals	area[3]		population
		sq mi	sq km	2000 estimate
Al-Bāṭinah	Ar-Rustāq; Ṣuḥār	4,850	12,500	667,053
Ad-Dākhilīyah	Nizwā; Samā'il	12,300	31,900	272,141
Ash-Sharqīyah	Ibrā; Ṣūr	14,200	36,800	307,000
Al-Wusṭā	Haymā'	30,750	79,700	20,000
Az-Zāhirah	Al-Buraymī; 'Ibrī	17,000	44,000	214,997
Governorates				
Masqaṭ	Muscat (Masqaṭ)	1,350	3,500	661,145
Musandam	Khaṣab	700	1,800	34,007
Ẓufār (Dhofar)	Salālah	38,350	99,300	224,993
TOTAL		119,500	309,500	2,401,336[4]

Demography

Population (2002): 2,522,000.
Density (2002): persons per sq mi 21.1, persons per sq km 8.1.
Urban-rural (2001): urban 76.5%; rural 23.5%.
Sex distribution (2000): male 56.8%; female 43.2%.
Age breakdown (1998): under 15, 36.8%; 15–29, 29.7%; 30–44, 22.1%; 45–59, 7.9%; 60 and over, 3.5%.
Population projection: (2010) 3,002,000; (2020) 3,733,000.
Doubling time: 21 years.
Ethnic composition (2000): Omani Arab 48.1%; Indo-Pakistani 31.7%, of which Balochi 15.0%, Bengali 4.4%, Tamil 2.5%; other Arab 7.2%; Persian 2.8%; Zanzibari (blacks originally from Zanzibar) 2.5%; other 7.7%.
Religious affiliation (1993): Muslim 87.7%, of which Ibāḍiyah Muslim *c.* 75% (principal minorities are Sunnī Muslim and Shī'ī Muslim); Hindu 7.4%; Christian 3.9%; Buddhist 0.5%; other 0.5%.
Major cities (1993): As-Sīb 155,000[5]; Salālah 116,000; Bawshar 107,500[5]; Ṣuḥār 84,300; 'Ibrī 76,000; Muscat 40,900 (urban agglomeration [2001] 540,000).

Vital statistics

Birth rate per 1,000 population (2000): 38.1 (world avg. 22.5).
Death rate per 1,000 population (2000): 4.2 (world avg. 9.0).
Natural increase rate per 1,000 population (2000): 33.9 (world avg. 13.5).
Total fertility rate (avg. births per childbearing woman; 2000): 6.1.
Life expectancy at birth (1999): male 69.7 years; female 74.0 years.
Major causes of death per 100,000 population: n.a.; however, the main causes of hospital deaths in 1995 were diseases of the circulatory system 34.1%, infectious diseases 11.1%, malignant neoplasms (cancers) 9.4%, perinatal problems 7.2%, diseases of the respiratory system 6.3%.

National economy

Budget (2000). Revenue: RO 2,284,300,000 (oil revenue 75.3%; other 24.7%). Expenditures: RO 2,608,200,000 (current expenditure 78.8%, of which civil ministries 41.0%, defense 30.6%, interest paid on loans 4.1%; capital development projects and subsidies 21.2%).
Public debt (external, outstanding; 2000): U.S.$2,673,000,000.
Gross national product (1998): U.S.$13,135,000,000 (U.S.$5,950 per capita).

Structure of gross national product and labour force

	2000			
	in value RO '000,000	% of total value	labour force	% of labour force
Agriculture, fishing	162.3	2.1	58,595	9.8
Mining	3,749.5	49.3	4,739	0.8
Manufacturing	397.8	5.2	68,304	11.4
Construction	116.3	1.5	116,711	19.5
Public utilities	78.0	1.0	1,188	0.2
Transp. and commun.	461.9	6.1	3,905	0.7
Trade, restaurants, hotels	865.5	11.4	158,509	26.6
Finance, real estate	591.1	7.8	6,097	1.0
Pub. admin., defense	699.8	9.2	102,942	17.2
Services	650.5	8.6	76,651	12.8
Other	−169.8[6]	−2.2[6]		
TOTAL	7,602.9	100.0	597,641[7]	100.0[4]

Tourism (2000): receipts U.S.$120,000,000; expenditures U.S.$341,000,000.
Household income and expenditure. Average household size (1999) 6.9; income per household: n.a.; sources of income: n.a.; expenditure (1990): housing and utilities 27.8%, food, beverage, and tobacco 26.4%, transportation 19.8%, clothing and shoes 7.8%, household goods and furniture 6.1%, education, health services, entertainment, and other 12.1%.
Production (metric tons except as noted). Agriculture, forestry, fishing (2000): vegetables and melons 165,000 (of which watermelons 32,000), dates 135,000, bananas 28,000, mangoes 12,000, onions 9,400, potatoes 5,700, papayas 2,900, tobacco leaf 2,450, wheat 1,400; livestock (number of live animals) 729,000 goats, 180,000 sheep, 149,000 cattle, 98,000 camels, 3,400,000 chickens; fish

catch (1999) 108,819. Mining and quarrying (2000): copper 26,000; chromite 15,000; silver 4,692 kg; gold 551 kg. Manufacturing (value of production in RO '000,000; 1993): textiles and apparel 78,200; food and beverages 72,930; chemical products 40,950; wood products 5,950; metal products 4,200; paper products 360; other major products include refined petroleum products. Construction (1998): number of residential permits 5,372; nonresidential permits 448; mixed 263. Energy production (consumption): electricity (kW-hr; 1999) 8,600,000,000 (8,600,000,000); crude petroleum (barrels; 2001) 350,300,000 (20,100,000); petroleum products (metric tons; 1997) 3,540,000 (1,889,000); natural gas (cu m; 2001) 9,100,000,000 (6,300,000,000).
Population economically active (1993)[8]: total 704,798; activity rate of total population 34.9% (participation rates: over age 15, 60.9%; female 9.7%; unemployed [1996] *c.* 20%).

Price and earnings indexes (1995 = 100)

	1995	1996	1997	1998	1999	2000	2001
Consumer price index	100.0	100.3	100.0	99.5	99.8	98.7	97.7
Earnings index	...	...	...	...	...	...	...

Land use (1994): meadows and pastures 4.7%; agricultural and under permanent cultivation 0.3%; other (mostly desert and developed area) 95.0%.

Foreign trade[9]

Balance of trade (current prices)

	1995	1996	1997	1998	1999	2000
RO '000,000	+700	+1,064	+1,001	−66.6	+977.9	+2,414.3
% of total	17.6%	23.2%	20.6%	1.5%	21.4%	38.4%

Imports (2000): RO 1,937,700,000 (machinery and transport equipment 43.1%; basic manufactured goods 16.0%; food and live animals 12.2%; beverages and tobacco 8.7%; miscellaneous manufactured articles 6.6%). *Major import sources:* United Arab Emirates 29.5%; Japan 18.1%; United Kingdom 5.8%; United States 5.4%; Germany 3.7%; South Korea 3.4%; India 3.3%; Saudi Arabia 2.7%.
Exports (2000): RO 4,352,000,000 (domestic exports 88.5%, of which petroleum 82.8%, manufactured goods 2.4% [of which copper and copper products 0.5%], food and live animals 1.9%, mineral fuels 0.7%; reexports 11.5%, of which machinery and transport equipment 7.8%). *Major export destinations*[10]: United Arab Emirates 40.1%; Saudi Arabia 8.4%; Iran 7.8%; Yemen 7.8%; United States 5.5%; United Kingdom 3.8%; Tanzania 2.9%.

Transport and communications

Transport. Railroads: none. Roads (1999): total length 20,518 mi, 33,020 km (paved 24%). Vehicles (1999): passenger cars 229,029; trucks and buses 110,717. Merchant marine (1998): vessels (100 gross tons and over) 20; total deadweight tonnage 15,000. Air transport (2000)[11]: passenger-mi 601,400,000, passenger-km 968,000,000; short ton-mi cargo 11,250,000, metric ton-km cargo 18,106,000; airports (1999) with scheduled flights 6.

Communications

Medium	date	unit	number	units per 1,000 persons
Daily newspapers	1996	circulation	63,000	28
Radio	1997	receivers	1,400,000	607
Television	1999	receivers	1,415,000	608
Telephones	2001	main lines	235,300	90
Cellular telephones	2001	subscribers	324,500	124
Personal computers	1999	units	85,000	32
Internet	2001	users	120,000	46

Education and health

Educational attainment (1993). Percentage of population age 15 and over having: no formal schooling (illiterate) 41.2%; no formal schooling (literate) 14.9%; primary 18.9%; secondary 21.1%; higher technical 2.0%; higher undergraduate 1.5%; higher graduate 0.1%; other 0.3%. *Literacy* (1995): percentage of total population age 15 and over literate 64.0%; males literate 74.6%; females literate 50.7%.

Education (1998–99)

	schools	teachers	students	student/ teacher ratio
Primary (age 6–14)	294	11,447	301,281	26.3
Secondary (age 15–17)[12]	674	12,646	227,026	18.0
Voc., teacher tr.	10	954	9,936	10.4
Higher[13]	1	695	6,605	9.5

Health (1998): physicians 3,061 (1 per 747 persons); hospital beds 5,075 (1 per 444 persons); infant mortality rate per 1,000 live births (2000) 23.3.

Military

Total active duty personnel (2001): 43,400 (army 57.6%, navy 9.7%, air force 9.4%, royal household 23.3%); U.S. troops in Oman (2002) 2,400. *Military expenditure as percentage of GNP* (1999): 15.3% (world 2.4%); per capita expenditure U.S.$726.

[1]All seats are nonelected. [2]Most ministries have moved to suburbs. [3]Approximate; no comprehensive survey of surface area has ever been carried out in Oman. [4]Detail does not add to total given because of rounding. [5]Within Muscat urban agglomeration. [6]Includes import taxes less bank service charges. [7]Employed only; includes 494,699 expatriate workers in private sector and 102,942 government employees, of which 74.0% are Omani. [8]Non-Omani workers constituted 61.3% of the labour force in 1993. [9]Imports c.i.f.; exports f.o.b. [10]Non-oil exports only; includes reexports. [11]Oman Air only. [12]Includes preparatory. [13]University only.

Internet resources for further information:
• **Ministry of Information http://www.omanet.com**
• **Central Bank of Oman http://www.cbo-oman.org/pub_annual.htm**

Pakistan

Official name: Islam-i Jamhuriya-e Pakistan (Islamic Republic of Pakistan).
Form of government: military regime with two legislative houses (Senate [92]; National Assembly [342]).
Chiefs of state and government: President[1] assisted by Prime Minister.
Capital: Islamabad.
Official language: Urdu.
Official religion: Islam.
Monetary unit: 1 Pakistan rupee (PRs) = 100 paisa; valuation (Sept. 23, 2002) 1 U.S.$ = PRs 59.18; 1 £ = PRs 91.97.

Arabian Sea

Area and population		area[2]		population
Provinces	**Capitals**	sq mi	sq km	1998 census[3]
Balochistan	Quetta	134,051	347,190	6,511,000
North-West Frontier	Peshawar	28,773	74,521	17,555,000
Punjab	Lahore	79,284	205,344	72,585,000
Sindh	Karachi	54,407	140,914	29,991,000
Federally Administered Tribal Areas	...	10,509	27,220	3,138,000
Federal Capital Area				
Islamabad	...	350	906	799,000
TOTAL		307,374	796,095	130,579,000

Demography

Population (2002)[3]: 145,960,000.
Density (2002): persons per sq mi 474.9, persons per sq km 183.3.
Urban-rural (2002)[3, 4]: urban 38.0%; rural 62.0%.
Sex distribution (2002)[3, 4]: male 51.92%; female 48.08%.
Age breakdown (1998)[3, 4]: under 15, 43.2%; 15–29, 26.9%; 30–44, 15.6%; 45–59, 8.8%; 60–74, 4.3%; 75 and over, 1.2%.
Population projection[3]: (2010) 169,396,000; (2020) 197,441,000.
Doubling time: 26 years.
Ethnic composition (2000): Punjabi 52.6%; Pashtun 13.2%; Sindhi 11.7%; Urdu-speaking muhajirs 7.5%; Balochi 4.3%; other 10.7%.
Religious affiliation (2000): Muslim 96.1%[5]; Christian 2.5%; Hindu 1.2%; others (including Ahmadiyah) 0.2%.
Major cities (1998): Karachi 9,269,000; Lahore 5,063,000; Faisalabad 1,977,000; Rawalpindi 1,406,000; Multan 1,182,000; Islamabad 525,000.

Vital statistics

Birth rate per 1,000 population (2002): 36.5 (world avg. 21.2).
Death rate per 1,000 population (2002): 9.8 (world avg. 8.9).
Natural increase rate per 1,000 population (2002): 26.7 (world avg. 12.3).
Total fertility rate (avg. births per childbearing woman; 2002): 4.1.
Life expectancy at birth (2002): male 61.0 years; female 61.0 years.
Major cause of death (percentage of total deaths; 1987): malaria 18.2%; childhood diseases 12.1%; diseases of digestive system 9.8%; diseases of respiratory system 9.2%; infection of intestinal tract 7.7%.

National economy

Budget (1999–2000). Revenue: PRs 505,921,000,000 (nontax receipts 23.5%, sales tax 23.1%, income taxes 21.3%, customs duties 12.2%, excise taxes 11.0%). Expenditures: PRs 573,788,000,000 (public-debt service 42.7%, defense 26.2%, development 11.8%, general administration 8.3%, grants and subsidies 5.9%).
Public debt (external, outstanding; 2000): U.S.$27,140,000,000.
Production (metric tons except as noted). Agriculture, forestry, fishing (2000): sugarcane 46,333,000, wheat 21,079,000, rice 7,000,000, seed cotton 5,735,000, potatoes 1,868,000, corn (maize) 1,351,000, chickpeas 565,000, rapeseed 260,000; livestock (number of live animals) 47,400,000 goats, 24,100,000 sheep, 22,700,000 buffalo, 22,000,000 cattle, 148,000,000 chickens; roundwood (1999) 33,075,000 cu m; fish catch (1998) 596,980. Mining and quarrying (1998–99): limestone 9,467,000; rock salt 1,190,000; gypsum 242,000; silica sand 158,000; chromite 18,000. Manufacturing (1998–99): cement 9,635,000; refined sugar 3,568,000; chemical fertilizers 3,543,000, of which urea 3,522,000; cotton yarn 1,540,000; vegetable ghee 842,000; industrial chemicals 387,000; jute textiles 85,500; cotton textiles 385,000,000 sq m; cigarettes 51,578,000,000 units; motor-vehicle tires 845,000 units; bicycles 504,000 units; sewing machines 29,700 units. Energy production (consumption): electricity (kW-hr; 1997–98) 59,088,000,000 ([1997] 59,119,000,000); coal (metric tons; 1997–98) 3,144,000 ([1997] 4,393,000); crude petroleum (barrels; 1997–98) 20,520,000 ([1997] 47,000,000); petroleum products (metric tons; 1997) 5,528,000 (15,712,000); natural gas (cu m; 1997–98) 19,809,000,000 ([1997] 18,466,000).
Population economically active (1999): total 38,590,000; activity rate of total population 28.7% (participation rates: ages 15–64, 43.1%; female [1996–97] 14.4%; unemployed 6.1%).

Price index (1995 = 100)							
	1995	1996	1997	1998	1999	2000	2001
Consumer price index	100.0	110.4	122.9	130.6	136.0	141.9	146.4

Gross national product (2000): U.S.$61,022,000,000 (U.S.$440 per capita).

Structure of gross domestic product and labour force				
	1999–2000		1999	
	in value PRs '000,000	% of total value	labour force	% of labour force
Agriculture	762,527	24.0	15,980,000	41.4
Mining	16,851	0.5	4,060,000	10.5
Manufacturing	448,531	14.1		
Construction	96,645	3.1	2,460,000	6.4
Public utilities	119,751	3.8	360,000	0.9
Transp. and commun.	305,919	9.6	2,070,000	5.4
Trade	442,475	14.0	5,290,000	13.7
Finance	230,404	7.3		
Pub. admin., defense	235,543	7.4	5,290,000	13.7
Services	264,279	8.3		
Other	250,760	7.9	3,080,000[6]	8.0[6]
TOTAL	3,173,685	100.0	38,590,000	100.0

Household income and expenditure (1988). Average household size 6.3; income per household PRs 25,572 (U.S.$1,420); sources of income: self-employment 56.0%, wages and salaries 22.0%, other 22.0%; expenditure: food 47.0%, housing 12.0%, clothing and footwear 8.0%, other 33.0%.
Tourism (2000): receipts U.S.$84,000,000; expenditures U.S.$252,000,000.
Land use (1999): pasture 6.5%; agriculture 28.4%; forest and other 65.1%.

Foreign trade[7]

Balance of trade (current prices)						
	1995–96	1996–97	1997–98	1998–99	1999–2000	2000–01
U.S.$'000,000	–3,704	–3,145	–1,868	–2,086	–1,412	–1,246
% of total	18.2%	16.3%	10.0%	12.2%	7.9%	6.5%

Imports (1999–2000): U.S.$10,361,000,000 (1998–99; petroleum products 14.7%, fixed vegetable oil and fats 8.9%, specialized machinery 6.9%, organic chemicals 5.6%, wheat 4.1%, general industrial machinery 3.7%, road vehicles and parts 3.4%, iron and steel manufactures 3.2%). *Major import sources* (1998–99): Japan 8.3%; U.S. 7.7%; Saudi Arabia 6.8%; United Arab Emirates 6.7%; Malaysia 6.7%; Kuwait 5.9%; U.K. 4.4%; China 4.2%; Germany 4.2%.
Exports (1999–2000): U.S.$8,569,000,000 (textile fabrics 18.1%, ready-made apparel and made-up articles 14.2%, cotton yarn 12.5%, rice 6.3%, leather goods 6.0%). *Major export destinations* (1998–99): U.S. 21.8%; Hong Kong 7.1%; Germany 6.6%; U.K. 6.6%; United Arab Emirates 5.4%; Japan 3.5%; France 3.2%; The Netherlands 3.1%; Italy 2.7%.

Transport and communications

Transport. Railroads (1998–99): route length 8,774 km; passenger-km 19,164,000,000; metric ton-km cargo 4,020,000,000. Roads (1997–98): total length 149,679 mi, 240,885 km (paved 55%). Vehicles (1998): passenger cars 1,167,635; trucks and buses 251,407. Air transport (1999): passenger-km 10,466,000,000; metric ton-km cargo 329,832,000; airports (1997) 35.

Communications				units per 1,000 persons
Medium	date	unit	number	
Daily newspapers	1995	circulation	2,800,000	21
Radio	1997	receivers	13,500,000	102
Television	1999	receivers	16,000,000	119
Telephones	2001	main lines	3,400,000	24
Cellular telephones	2001	subscribers	800,000	5.5
Personal computers	2001	units	600,000	4.1
Internet	2001	users	500,000	3.4

Education and health

Educational attainment (1990). Percentage of population age 25 and over having: no formal schooling 73.8%; some primary education 9.7%; secondary 14.0%; postsecondary 2.5%. *Literacy* (1995): total population age 15 and over literate 37.8%; males literate 50.0%; females literate 24.4%.

Education (1998–99)				student/ teacher ratio
	schools	teachers	students	
Primary (age 5–9)	163,746	374,500	17,298,000	46.2
Secondary (age 10–14)	27,526	262,800	5,664,000	21.6
Voc., teacher tr.	498	7,045	85,000	12.1
Higher	1,026	39,704	989,288	24.9

Health (1998): physicians 82,682 (1 per 1,638 persons); hospital beds 90,659 (1 per 1,494 persons); infant mortality rate per 1,000 live births (2002) 85.0.
Food (1999): daily per capita caloric intake 2,462 (vegetable products 83%, animal products 17%); 107% of FAO recommended minimum.

Military

Total active duty personnel (2001): 620,000 (army 88.7%, navy 4.0%, air force 7.3%). *Military expenditure as percentage of GNP* (1999): 5.9% (world 2.4%); per capita expenditure U.S.$25.

[1]Military leader (from October 1999) who was sworn in as president in June 2001 and was given three years to restore democracy by the Pakistani Supreme Court in May 2000. [2]Excludes 32,494 sq mi (84,159 sq km) area of Pakistani-administered Jammu and Kashmir (comprising both Azad Kashmir [AK] and the Northern Areas [NA]). [3]Excludes Afghan refugees (2002; c. 1,100,000) and the population of AK and NA (2002; c. 4,300,000). [4]Excludes Federally Administered Tribal Areas. [5]Mostly Sunnī, with Shīʿī comprising about 17% of total population. [6]Mostly unemployed. [7]Import figures are f.o.b.

Internet resources for further information:
• **Economic Survey, Ministry of Finance**
   http://www.finance.gov.pk/survey/main.html
• **Statistics Division: Government of Pakistan** http://www.statpak.gov.pk

Palau

Official name: Belu'u er a Belau
(Palauan); Republic of Palau
(English).
Form of government: unitary republic
with a national congress composed of
two legislative houses (Senate [14];
House of Delegates [16]).
Head of state and government:
President.
Capital: Koror (acting)[1].
Official languages[2]: Palauan; English.
Official religion: none.
Monetary unit: 1 U.S. dollar
(U.S.$) = 100 cents; valuation
(Sept. 23, 2002) 1 U.S.$ = £0.64.

Pacific
Ocean

Area and population

| | area | | population |
States	sq mi	sq km	2000 census
Aimeliik	20	52	272
Airai	17	44	2,104
Angaur	3	8	188
Hatohobei	1	3	23
Kayangel	1	3	138
Koror	7	18	13,303
Melekeok	11	28	239
Ngaraard	14	36	638
Ngarchelong	4	10	267
Ngardmau	18	47	286
Ngatpang	18	47	367
Ngchesar	16	41	280
Ngeremlengui	25	65	221
Ngiwal	10	26	193
Peleliu	5	13	571
Sonsorol	1	3	39
Other			
Rock Islands	18	47	—
TOTAL	188[3]	488[3]	19,129

Demography

Population (2002): 19,900.
Density (2002): persons per sq mi 105.9, persons per sq km 40.8.
Urban-rural (2002): urban 73.0%; rural 27.0%.
Sex distribution (2000): male 54.63%; female 45.37%.
Age breakdown (2000): under 15, 23.9%; 15–29, 24.2%; 30–44, 29.9%; 45–59,
14.2%; 60–74, 5.5%; 75 and over 2.3%.
Population projection: (2010) 22,200; (2020) 24,200.
Doubling time: 58 years.
Ethnic composition (1997): Palauan 74.5%; Filipino 16.0%; Chinese 3.2%;
other Micronesian and other 6.3%.
Religious affiliation (1995): Roman Catholic 38.4%; Protestant 24.7%;
Modekngei (marginal Christian sect) 26.5%; other 10.4%.
Major city (2000): Koror 13,303.

Vital statistics

Birth rate per 1,000 population (2002): 19.3 (world avg. 21.2).
Death rate per 1,000 population (2002): 7.1 (world avg. 8.9).
Natural increase rate per 1,000 population (2002): 12.2 (world avg. 12.3).
Total fertility rate (avg. births per childbearing woman; 2002): 2.5.
Marriage rate per 1,000 population: n.a.
Divorce rate per 1,000 population: n.a.
Life expectancy at birth (2002): male 66.1 years; female 72.5 years.
Major causes of death per 100,000 population (1993): diseases of the cir-
culatory system 192.9; malignant and benign neoplasms (cancers) 136.9;
accidents, poisoning, and violence 112.0; diseases of the respiratory system
43.6; infectious and parasitic diseases 43.6.

National economy

Budget (2002). Revenue: U.S.$70,058,000 (grants from the U.S. 49.4%, tax rev-
enue 36.0%, nontax revenue 14.6%). Expenditures: U.S.$79,691,000 (current
expenditure 74.6%, of which wages and salaries 38.1%; capital expenditure
25.4%).
Gross national product (at current market prices; 2000)[4]: U.S.$118,206,000
(U.S.$6,179 per capita).

Structure of gross domestic product and labour force

| | 2000 | | | |
	in value U.S.$'000	% of total value	labour force	% of labour force
Agriculture, fisheries	4,662	3.9	215	2.2
Mining	229	0.2		
Manufacturing	1,706	1.4	345	3.5
Public utilities	3,610	3.1	[5]	[5]
Construction	8,909	7.5	1,112	11.3
Transportation and communications	10,535	8.9	765[5]	7.8[5]
Trade	36,089	30.5	2,619	26.6
Finance	9,442	8.0	116	1.2
Public administration, defense	30,373	25.7	3,203	32.5
Services	10,059	8.5	1,246	12.6
Other	2,592[6]	2.2[6]	224[7]	2.3[7]
TOTAL	118,206	100.0[3]	9,845	100.0

Production (metric tons except as noted). Agriculture, forestry, fishing (value
of sales in U.S.$; 1993): eggs 262,701, fruit and vegetables 126,325, betel nuts
60,376, root crops (taro, cassava, sweet potatoes) 43,718; livestock (number
of live animals; 1984) 1,343 pigs, 82 cows, 52 goats, 9,500 poultry; roundwood,
n.a.; fish catch (1997) 1,500 (major species are parrot fish, snapper, unicorn
fish, and rabbitfish). Mining and quarrying: n.a. Manufacturing: includes
handicrafts and small items. Construction: n.a. Energy production (consumption): electricity (kW-hr; 1997) 208,000,000 (208,000,000); coal, none
(n.a.); crude petroleum, none (n.a.); petroleum products, none (78,000); natural gas, none (n.a.).
Public debt (external, outstanding; 2000): U.S.$20,000,000.
Tourism (2000): receipts from visitors U.S.$53,750,000.
Population economically active (2000): total 9,845; activity rate of total population 51.5% (participation rates: over age 15, 67.6%; female [1995] 39.6%;
unemployed 2.3%).
Land use: n.a.
Household income and expenditure. Average household size (2000) 5.7; income
per household (1989) U.S.$8,882; sources of income (1989): wages 63.7%,
social security 12.0%, self-employment 7.4%, retirement 5.5%, interest, dividend, or net rental 4.3%, remittance 4.1%, public assistance 1.0%, other
2.0%; expenditure (1997): food 42.2%, beverages and tobacco 14.8%, entertainment 13.1%, transportation 6.4%, clothing 5.7%, household goods 2.7%,
other 15.1%.

Foreign trade

Balance of trade (current prices)

	1994–95	1995–96	1996–97	1997–98	1998–99	1999–2000
U.S.$'000	–46,569	–58,517	–61,079	–52,127	–70,278	–115,619
% of total	62.7%	67.8%	72.1%	70.1%	72.1%	83.4%

Imports (1997–98): U.S.$63,222,000 (1997; machinery and transport equipment
27.8%; food, beverages, and tobacco 27.1%; manufactured articles 27.1%;
mineral fuels 13.2%; chemicals and related products 4.5%). *Major import
sources* (1997): United States 44.1%; Guam 19.3%; Japan 14.8%; Singapore
14.3%; Taiwan 5.4%; China 2.6%; Hong Kong 1.9%.
Exports (1997–98): U.S.$11,095,000 (mostly high-grade tuna; also garments
and handicrafts). *Major export destinations:* mostly Japan.

Transport and communications

Transport. Railroads: none. Roads (1993): total length 40 mi, 64 km (paved
59%). Vehicles (1994): passenger cars and trucks 4,271. Merchant marine
(1991): vessels (100 gross tons and over) 4; total deadweight tonnage, n.a. Air
transport (1993): passenger arrivals 50,366, passenger departures 49,376; airports (1997) with scheduled flights 1.

Communications

Medium	date	unit	number	units per 1,000 persons
Radio	1997	receivers	12,000	663.0
Television	1997	receivers	11,000	606.0
Telephones	1994	main lines	2,615	160.0

Education and health

Educational attainment (1997). Percentage of population age 25 and over having: no formal schooling 0.1%; some primary education 4.4%; completed primary 5.7%; some secondary 16.3%; completed secondary 41.0%; some postsecondary 13.0%; higher 19.5%. *Literacy* (1997): total population age 15 and
over literate 99.9%.

Education (1997)

	schools[8]	teachers[8]	students	student/ teacher ratio
Primary (age 6–13)	26	289	1,450	...
Secondary (age 14–18)	6	[9]	490	...
Higher[10]	1		130	...

Health (1990): physicians (1998) 20 (1 per 906 persons); hospital beds (1990)
70 (1 per 200 persons); infant mortality rate per 1,000 live births (1999) 17.7.
Food: daily per capita caloric intake, n.a.

Military

The United States is responsible for the external security of Palau, as specified in the Compact of Free Association of Oct. 1, 1994.

---

[1]New capital buildings at Melekeok on Babelthuap are to be completed in 2003.
[2]Sonsorolese-Tobian is also, according to official sources, considered an official language. [3]Detail does not add to total given because of rounding. [4]Gross domestic product. [5]Transportation and communications includes Public utilities. [6]Includes import
duties and imputed bank service charge. [7]Unemployed. [8]1987. [9]Included with primary.
[10]Palau Community College.

Internet resources for further information:
• **Republic of Palau Economic Report (Bank of Hawaii)**
  http://www.boh.com/econ/pacific/pal/2000/palau2000.pdf
• **Department of the Interior: Office of Insular Affairs**
  http://www.pacificweb.org/pwquickmenus.htm

Panama

Official name: República de Panamá (Republic of Panama).
Form of government: multiparty republic with one legislative house (Legislative Assembly [71]).
Head of state and government: President assisted by Vice Presidents.
Capital: Panama City.
Official language: Spanish.
Official religion: none.
Monetary unit: 1 balboa (B) = 100 cents; valuation (Sept. 23, 2002) 1 U.S.\$ = B 1.00; 1 £ = B 1.55.

Area and population

Provinces	Capitals	area sq mi	area sq km	population 2000 census
Bocas del Toro	Bocas del Toro	1,788	4,631	89,269
Chiriquí	David	2,498	6,471	368,790
Coclé	Penonomé	1,902	4,927	202,461
Colón	Colón	1,888	4,890	204,208
Darién[1]	La Palma	4,282	11,091	40,284[2]
Herrera	Chitré	904	2,341	102,465
Los Santos	Las Tablas	1,469	3,805	83,495
Panamá	Panama City	3,719	9,633	1,385,052
Veraguas	Santiago	4,119	10,668	209,076
Indigenous districts				
Emberá	Unión Chocó	1,698	4,398	8,246
Ngöbe Buglé	Quebrada Guabo	2,576	6,673	110,080
Kuna de Madungandí	...	895	2,319	3,305
Kuna de Wargandí[1]	...	299	775	[2]
Kuna Yala (San Blas)	El Porvenir	910	2,357	32,446
TOTAL		28,950[3]	74,979	2,839,177

Demography

Population (2002): 2,915,000.
Density (2002): persons per sq mi 100.7, persons per sq km 38.9.
Urban-rural (1999): urban 56.0%; rural 44.0%.
Sex distribution (2000): male 50.46%; female 49.54%.
Age breakdown (1999): under 15, 31.7%; 15–29, 27.4%; 30–44, 20.9%; 45–59, 12.0%; 60–74, 5.9%; 75 and over, 2.1%.
Population projection: (2010) 3,189,000; (2020) 3,486,000.
Doubling time: 51 years.
Ethnic composition (2000): mestizo 58.1%; black and mulatto 14.0%; white 8.6%; Amerindian 6.7%; Asian 5.5%; other 7.1%.
Religious affiliation (1995): Roman Catholic 80.2%; Protestant 15.0%, of which Pentecostal 8.4%; other Christian 1.6%; other 3.2%.
Major cities (2000): Panama City 415,964 (urban agglomeration [1999] 1,141,000); San Miguelito 293,745[4]; David 77,734[5]; Arraiján 63,753[5]; La Chorrera 55,871; Colón 42,133.

Vital statistics

Birth rate per 1,000 population (2000): 19.5 (world avg. 22.5).
Death rate per 1,000 population (2000): 5.0 (world avg. 9.0).
Natural increase rate per 1,000 population (2000): 14.5 (world avg. 13.5).
Total fertility rate (avg. births per childbearing woman; 2000): 2.3.
Marriage rate per 1,000 population (1997): 4.1[6].
Divorce rate per 1,000 population (1997): 0.7[6].
Life expectancy at birth (2002): male 73.1 years; female 78.7 years.
Major causes of death per 100,000 population (1997): diseases of the circulatory system 122.1; malignant neoplasms (cancers) 64.4; accidents 37.1; diseases of the respiratory system 25.4; infectious and parasitic diseases 21.2.

National economy

Budget (1997). Revenue: B 2,266,300,000 (tax revenue 70.3%, of which income taxes 20.2%, social security contributions 19.1%; nontax revenue 26.8%, of which entrepreneurial and property income 15.4%). Expenditures: B 2,341,300,000 (social security and welfare 20.5%; health 18.7%; education 18.3%; economic affairs 8.0%; defense 5.0%).
Production (metric tons except as noted). Agriculture, forestry, fishing (1999): sugarcane 2,050,000, bananas 650,000, rice 232,000, plantains 115,000, corn (maize) 89,800, yams 36,900, oranges 27,000, coffee 10,400, tobacco 2,200; livestock (number of live animals; 1999) 1,400,000 cattle, 252,000 pigs, 165,000 horses; roundwood (1998) 1,098,300 cu m; fish catch (value of production in B '000,000; 1998): fish 63, shrimps 40. Mining and quarrying (2001): limestone 270,000; gold 48,600 troy oz. Manufacturing (value of production in B '000,000; 1998): food products 1,203, of which meat 341, dairy products 144; refined petroleum 299; beverages 176; cement, bricks, and tiles 154. Energy production (consumption): electricity (kW-hr; 1997) 4,858,-000,000 ([1998] 3,416,000,000); coal (metric tons; 1997) none (57,000); crude petroleum (barrels; 1997) none (17,277,000); petroleum products (metric tons; 1997) 1,479,000 (1,440,000); natural gas (cu m; 1997) none (60,992,000).
Tourism (2000): receipts from visitors U.S.\$576,000,000; expenditures by nationals abroad U.S.\$187,000,000.
Household income and expenditure. Average household size (2000) 4.2; average annual income per household (1990) B 5,450 (U.S.\$5,450); expenditure (1983–84)[7]: food and beverages 34.9%, transportation and communications 15.1%, housing and energy 12.6%, education and recreation 11.7%.
Population economically active (1998)[6]: total 1,083,580; activity rate of total population 42.2%[8] (participation rates: ages 15–69 [1997] 64.3%, female [1997] 35.6%, unemployed 13.6%).

Price and earnings indexes (1995 = 100)

	1995	1996	1997	1998	1999	2000	2001
Consumer price index	100.0	101.3	102.5	103.2	104.5	106.0	106.3
Monthly earnings index	...	...	...	...	...	...	...

Public debt (external, outstanding; 2000): U.S.\$5,723,000,000.
Gross national product (2000): U.S.\$9,308,000,000 (U.S.\$3,260 per capita).

Structure of gross domestic product and labour force

	1998 in value B '000,000[9]	1998 % of total value[9]	labour force[6]	% of labour force[6]
Agriculture, fishing	545.1	7.9	171,560	15.8
Mining	17.0	0.2	934	0.1
Manufacturing	673.4	9.7	106,076	9.8
Construction	279.4	4.0	80,680	7.4
Public utilities	293.8	4.2	9,827	0.9
Transp. and commun.	901.1	13.0	69,176	6.4
Trade, restaurants	1,410.3	20.3	244,108	22.5
Finance, real estate	1,746.8	25.2	66,264	6.1
Pub. admin.	711.3	10.3	72,696	6.7
Services	397.0	5.7	224,118	20.7
Other	−42.3[10]	−0.6[10]	38,141	3.5
TOTAL	6,932.9	100.0[3]	1,083,580	100.0[3]

Land use (1994): forested 43.8%; meadows and pastures 19.8%; agricultural and under permanent cultivation 8.9%; other 27.5%.

Foreign trade[11, 12]

Balance of trade (current prices)

	1996	1997	1998	1999	2000	2001
B '000,000	−2,215	−2,358	−2,693	−2,695	−2,519	−2,053
% of total	66.2%	64.5%	65.6%	62.1%	49.1%	53.0%

Imports (1998): B 3,398,000,000 (machinery and apparatus 22.9%, transport equipment 15.1%, mineral fuels 10.3%, chemicals and chemical products 9.6%). *Major import sources:* U.S. 39.7%; Colón Free Zone 12.8%; Japan 9.0%; Mexico 4.8%; Ecuador 3.2%.
Exports (1998): B 705,000,000 (bananas 19.7%, shrimps 19.4%, fish 7.9%, sugar 3.6%, clothing 3.6%). *Major export destinations:* U.S. 40.0%; Sweden 7.2%; Costa Rica 6.6%; Spain 5.4%; Belgium 4.3%.

Transport and communications

Transport. Railroads (2000): route length 220 mi, 354 km. Roads (1997): total length 7,022 mi, 11,301 km (paved 33%). Vehicles: passenger cars (1996) 203,760; trucks and buses 74,637. Panama Canal traffic (2000–01): oceangoing transits 12,197; cargo 196,242,000 metric tons. Air transport (2001)[13]: passenger-km 3,004,000,000; metric ton-km cargo 25,235,000; airports (1996) 10.

Communications

Medium	date	unit	number	units per 1,000 persons
Daily newspapers	1996	circulation	166,000	63
Radio	1997	receivers	815,000	306
Television	1998	receivers	530,000	195
Telephones	2001	main lines	430,000	148
Cellular telephones	2001	subscribers	600,000	207
Personal computers	2001	units	110,000	38
Internet	2000	users	90,000	32

Education and health

Educational attainment (1990). Percentage of population age 25 and over having: no formal schooling 11.6%; primary 41.6%; secondary 28.7%; undergraduate 12.4%; graduate 0.7%; other/unknown 5.0%. *Literacy* (1995): total population age 15 and over literate 1,590,000 (90.8%).

Education (1997)

	schools	teachers	students	student/teacher ratio
Primary (age 6–11)	2,866	15,058	377,898	25.1
Secondary (age 12–17) Voc., teacher tr.	417	12,450	223,155	17.9
Higher	14	6,409	95,341	14.9

Health (1998): physicians 3,518 (1 per 772 persons); hospital beds 7,287 (1 per 373 persons); infant mortality rate per 1,000 live births (2002) 19.6.
Food (2000): daily per capita caloric intake 2,488 (vegetable products 77%, animal products 23%); 108% of FAO recommended minimum requirement.

Military

Total active duty personnel (2001): none; Panama has an 11,800-member national police force. *Military expenditure as percentage of GNP* (1999): 1.4% (world avg. 2.4%); per capita expenditure U.S.\$45.

---

[1]Kuna de Wargandí indigenous district (*comarca*) was created in 2000 from part of Darién province. [2]Darién includes Kuna de Wargandí. [3]Detail does not add to total given because of rounding. [4]District adjacent to Panama City within Panama City urban agglomeration. [5]Population of *cabecera*. [6]Excludes indigenous population. [7]Panama City only. [8]Estimated figure. [9]At prices of 1982. [10]Imputed finance service charges less import duties. [11]Imports c.i.f.; exports f.o.b. [12]Excludes Colón Free Zone (1998 imports f.o.b. B 5,319,000,000; 1998 reexports f.o.b. B 5,969,000,000, of which machinery and apparatus 28.4%, textiles and clothing 21.3%). [13]COPA only.

Internet resources for further information:
• **Contraloría General de la República Panamá**
  http://www.contraloria.gob.pa/index.htm

Papua New Guinea

Official name: Independent State of
Papua New Guinea.
Form of government: constitutional
monarchy with one legislative house
(National Parliament [109]).
Chief of state: British Monarch
represented by Governor-General.
Head of government: Prime Minister.
Capital: Port Moresby.
Official language: English[1].
Official religion: none.
Monetary unit: 1 Papua New Guinea
kina (K) = 100 toea; valuation
(Sept. 23, 2002) 1 U.S.$ = K 4.00;
1 £ = K 6.22.

Area and population

Provinces	Administrative centres	area sq mi	area sq km	population 2000 census
Central	Port Moresby (Central)	11,400	29,500	183,983
East New Britain	Rabaul	6,000	15,500	220,133
East Sepik	Wewak	16,550	42,800	343,181
Eastern Highlands	Goroka	4,300	11,200	432,972
Enga	Wabag	4,950	12,800	295,031
Gulf	Kerema	13,300	34,500	106,898
Madang	Madang	11,200	29,000	365,106
Manus	Lorengau	800	2,100	43,387
Milne Bay	Alotau (Samarai)	5,400	14,000	210,412
Morobe	Lae	13,300	34,500	539,404
National Capital District	Port Moresby	100	240	254,158
New Ireland	Kavieng	3,700	9,600	118,350
Oro (Northern)	Popondetta	8,800	22,800	133,065
Sandaun (West Sepik)	Vanimo	14,000	36,300	185,741
Simbu (Chimbu)	Kundiawa	2,350	6,100	259,703
Southern Highlands	Mendi	9,200	23,800	546,265
West New Britain	Kimbe	8,100	21,000	184,508
Western	Daru	38,350	99,300	153,304
Western Highlands	Mount Hagen	3,300	8,500	440,025
Autonomous region (pending)				
Bougainville[2]	Arawa (Buka)	3,600	9,300	175,160
TOTAL		178,704[3]	462,840	5,190,786

Demography

Population (2002): 5,426,000.
Density (2002): persons per sq mi 30.4, persons per sq km 11.7.
Urban-rural (2001): urban 17.6%; rural 82.4%.
Sex distribution (2000): male 51.30%; female 48.70%.
Age breakdown (2000): under 15, 38.8%; 15–29, 28.7%; 30–44, 17.1%; 45–59, 9.7%; 60–74, 4.7%; 75 and over, 1.0%.
Population projection: (2010) 6,496,000; (2020) 7,790,000.
Ethnic composition (1983)[4]: New Guinea Papuan 84.0%; New Guinea Melanesian 15.0%; other 1.0%.
Religious affiliation (1990): non-Anglican Protestant 64.3%, of which Evangelical Lutheran 23.2%, Uniting Church 12.7%, Seventh-day Adventist 8.1%, Pentecostal 7.1%; Roman Catholic 28.3%; Anglican 3.9%; other (mostly animists) 3.5%.
Major cities (1997): Port Moresby 271,813; Lae 113,118; Madang 32,117; Wewak 25,143; Goroka 17,269.

Vital statistics

Birth rate per 1,000 population (2000): 32.7 (world avg. 22.5).
Death rate per 1,000 population (2000): 8.0 (world avg. 9.0).
Natural increase rate per 1,000 population (2000): 24.7 (world avg. 13.5).
Total fertility rate (avg. births per childbearing woman; 2000): 4.4.
Life expectancy at birth (2000): male 61.1 years; female 65.3 years.
Major causes of death per 100,000 population (1993): acute respiratory infections 34.6; pneumonia 27.8; meningitis 7.6; conditions originating from perinatal period 6.2; malaria 3.8.

National economy

Budget (2000). Revenue: K 2,866,700,000 (tax revenue 72.5%, of which income tax 19.5%, corporate tax 18.3%, VAT 11.8%; foreign grants 18.9%, nontax revenue 8.6%). Expenditures: K 3,081,800,000 (current expenditure 70.8%, of which transfer to provincial governments 16.8%, interest payments 12.4%; development expenditure 29.2%).
Public debt (external, outstanding; 2000): U.S.$1,502,000,000.
Production (metric tons except as noted). Agriculture, forestry, fishing (2000): coconuts 826,000, bananas 700,000, sweet potatoes 480,000, sugarcane 430,000, palm oil 299,000, yams 220,000, taro 170,000, cassava 120,000, coffee 83,040, palm kernels 61,000, cacao 39,000, pineapples 11,500, tea 9,000, natural rubber 7,200; livestock (number of live animals) 1,500,000 pigs, 87,000 cattle, 3,600,000 chickens; roundwood (2000) 8,597,000 cu m; fish catch (1997) 53,763. Mining and quarrying (1999): copper (metal content) 187,900; silver 66,500 kg; gold 65,700 kg. Manufacturing (1998): palm oil 241,485; copra 124,349; coffee 80,700; cocoa 26,852; tea 7,923; rubber 5,645. Construction (value in K; 1998): total 193,500,000. Energy production (consumption): electricity (kW-hr; 1997) 1,161,900,000 (1,790,000,000[5]); coal (metric tons; 1997) none (1,000); crude petroleum (barrels; 1997) 29,000,000 (440,000); natural gas (cu m; 1997) 83,416,000 (83,416,000); petroleum products (metric tons; 1997) 52,000 (738,000).
Land use (1997): forested 92.3%; agricultural and under permanent cultivation 1.5%; meadows and pastures 0.2%; other 6.0%.

Gross national product (2000): U.S.$3,607,000,000 (U.S.$700 per capita).

Structure of gross domestic product and labour force

	2000 in value K '000,000	2000 % of total value	1980 labour force[6]	1980 % of labour force[6]
Agriculture	2,210	25.1	564,500	77.0
Mining	2,313	26.2	4,300	0.6
Manufacturing	806	9.1	14,000	1.9
Construction	628	7.2	21,600	2.9
Public utilities	119	1.3	2,800	0.4
Transp. and commun.	473	5.4	17,400	2.4
Trade	762	8.6	25,100	3.4
Finance	104	1.2	4,500	0.6
Pub. admin., defense } Services }	937	10.6	77,100	10.5
Other	468[7]	5.3[7]	1,500	0.2
TOTAL	8,820	100.0	732,800	100.0[3]

Population economically active (1990)[6]: total 1,715,330; activity rate 36.9% (participation rates: over age 10, 35.2%[8]; female 41.5%; unemployed 7.7%).

Price and earnings indexes (1995 = 100)

	1995	1996	1997	1998	1999	2000	2001
Consumer price index	100.0	111.6	116.0	131.8	151.5	175.1	191.4
Weekly earnings index	100.0	...	...	...	...	...	...

Tourism (1999): receipts U.S.$76,000,000; expenditures U.S.$53,000,000.

Foreign trade

Balance of trade (current prices)

	1996	1997	1998	1999	2000	2001
K '000,000	+1,318.0	+928.4	+1,356.1	+2,173.1	+1,937.0	+2,915.9
% of total	24.8%	17.9%	24.2%	28.5%	26.0%	31.6%

Imports (2000): K 2,758,100,000 (1998; nonelectrical machinery 18.3%; food and live animals 16.2%; transport equipment 14.8%; chemicals and chemical products 9.6%; fabricated metals 8.6%). *Major import sources* (1999): Australia 53.5%; Singapore 12.9%; Japan 5.6%; New Zealand 4.1%; U.S. 3.6%; China 2.6%.
Exports (2000): K 4,695,000,000 (gold 35.3%; crude petroleum 19.8%; copper 14.7%; coffee 7.0%; palm oil 5.2%; cocoa beans 2.8%). *Major export destinations* (1999): Australia 38.1%; Japan 16.9%; Germany 9.6%; U.S. 6.6%; South Korea 5.8%; China 4.0%; U.K. 2.7%.

Transport and communications

Transport. Railroads: none. Roads (1986): total length 19,736 km (paved 6%). Vehicles (1994): passenger cars 13,000; trucks and buses 32,000. Air transport (1997): passenger-km 735,000,000; metric ton-km cargo 86,000,000; airports (1999) with scheduled flights 42.

Communications

Medium	date	unit	number	units per 1,000 persons
Daily newspapers	1996	circulation	65,000	15
Radio	1997	receivers	410,000	91
Television	1999	receivers	60,000	13
Telephones	2000	main lines	64,800	14
Cellular telephones	2000	units	8,600	1.8
Internet	2001	users	300,000	61

Education and health

Educational attainment (1990). Percentage of population age 25 and over having: no formal schooling 82.6%; some primary education 8.2%; completed primary 5.0%; some secondary 4.2%. *Literacy* (1995 est.): total population age 15 and over literate 72.2%; males literate 81.0%; females literate 62.7%.

Education (1997)

	schools	teachers	students	student/ teacher ratio
Primary (age 7–12)	3,518	13,457[9]	587,788	...
Secondary (age 13–16)	159	2,415[10]	74,873	...
Voc., teacher tr.	128	878[10]	15,422	...
Higher	3	957[9]	9,220	...

Health: physicians (1998) 342 (1 per 13,708 persons); hospital beds (1989) 15,335 (1 per 234 persons); infant mortality rate (2000) 59.9.
Food (1999): daily per capita caloric intake 2,175 (vegetable products 90%, animal products 10%); 95% of FAO recommended minimum.

Military

Total active duty personnel (2001): 4,400 (army 86.4%, navy 9.1%, air force 4.5%). *Military expenditure as percentage of GNP* (1999): 1.1% (world 2.4%); per capita expenditure U.S.$7.

[1]The national languages are English, Tok Pisin (English Creole), and Motu. [2]Formal peace agreement signed on Aug. 30, 2001, ended nine years of civil war and promised Bougainville autonomy; funds for implementing autonomy were not available in October 2002. [3]Detail does not add to total given because of rounding. [4]Papua New Guinea has several thousand separate communities, most with only a few hundred people. [5]1996. [6]Citizens of Papua New Guinea over age 10 involved in "money-raising activities" only. [7]Import duties. [8]1980. [9]1995. [10]1992.

Internet resources for further information:
• **National Statistical Office of Papua New Guinea**
  http://www.nso.gov.pg
• **Bank of Hawaii Economic Report http://www.boh.com/econ/pacific**

Paraguay

Official name: República del Paraguay (Spanish); Tetä Paraguáype (Guaraní)(Republic of Paraguay).
Form of government: multiparty republic with two legislative houses (Senate [46[1]]; Chamber of Deputies [80]).
Head of state and government: President.
Capital: Asunción.
Official languages: Spanish; Guaraní.
Official religion: none[2].
Monetary unit: 1 Paraguayan Guaraní (Ø) = 100 céntimos; valuation (Sept. 23, 2002) 1 U.S.$ = Ø6,255; 1 £ = Ø9,721.

Area and population

Regions Departments	Capitals	area sq mi	area sq km	population 2000 estimate
Occidental		95,338	246,925	136,313
Alto Paraguay	Fuerte Olimpo	31,795	82,349	14,669
Boquerón	Filadelfia	35,393	91,669	38,451
Presidente Hayes	Pozo Colorado	28,150	72,907	83,193
Oriental		61,710	159,827	5,360,137
Alto Paraná	Ciudad del Este	5,751	14,895	705,137
Amambay	Pedro Juan Caballero	4,994	12,933	136,910
Asunción[3]	—	45	117	561,386
Caaguazú	Coronel Oviedo	4,430	11,474	461,937
Caazapá	Caazapá	3,666	9,496	143,889
Canindeyú	Salto del Guairá	5,663	14,667	145,841
Central	Asunción	952	2,465	1,333,889
Concepción	Concepción	6,970	18,051	191,911
Cordillera	Caacupé	1,910	4,948	215,516
Guairá	Villarrica	1,485	3,846	175,121
Itapúa	Encarnación	6,380	16,525	490,969
Misiones	San Juan Bautista	3,690	9,556	100,385
Ñeembucú	Pilar	4,690	12,147	88,285
Paraguarí	Paraguarí	3,361	8,705	247,175
San Pedro	San Pedro	7,723	20,002	361,786
TOTAL		157,048	406,752	5,496,450

Demography

Population (2002): 5,774,000.
Density (2002): persons per sq mi 36.8, persons per sq km 14.2.
Urban-rural (2000): urban 54.5%; rural 45.5%.
Sex distribution (2000): male 50.43%; female 49.57%.
Age breakdown (1999): under 15, 39.3%; 15–29, 26.2%; 30–44, 17.9%; 45–59, 9.9%; 60–74, 5.1%; 75 and over, 1.6%.
Population projection: (2010) 6,980,000; (2020) 8,570,000.
Ethnic composition (2000): mixed (white/Amerindian) 85.6%; white 9.3%, of which German 4.4%, Latin American 3.4%; Amerindian 1.8%; black 1.0%; other 2.3%.
Religious affiliation (1995): Roman Catholic 88.5%; Protestant 5.0%; other 6.5%.
Major cities (1992): Asunción 500,938 (urban agglomeration [2001] 1,302,000); Ciudad del Este 133,881; San Lorenzo 133,395[4]; Lambaré 99,572[4]; Fernando de la Mora 95,072[4].

Vital statistics

Birth rate per 1,000 population (2000): 31.3 (world avg. 22.5).
Death rate per 1,000 population (2000): 4.8 (world avg. 9.0).
Natural increase rate per 1,000 population (2000): 26.5 (world avg. 13.5).
Total fertility rate (avg. births per childbearing woman; 2000): 4.2.
Marriage rate per 1,000 population (1999): 3.6[5].
Life expectancy at birth (2000): male 71.2 years; female 76.3 years.
Major causes of death per 100,000 population (1998)[6]: diseases of the circulatory system 129; malignant neoplasms (cancers) 63; accidents 54; diseases of the respiratory system 40; infectious and parasitic diseases 29.

National economy

Budget (1999): Revenue: Ø4,011,200,000,000 (tax revenue 69.4%, of which taxes on goods and services 39.0%, income tax 13.4%, customs duties 10.3%, social security 6.7%; nontax revenue including grants 30.6%). Expenditures: Ø4,605,800,000,000 (current expenditure 75.6%; capital expenditure 24.4%).
Public debt (external, outstanding; 2000): U.S.$2,061,000,000.
Population economically active (1996): total 1,747,488; activity rate 35.3% (participation rates [1992]: ages 12 and over, 51.0%; female 23.8%; unemployed [1998] 7.2%).

Price index (1995 = 100)

	1995	1996	1997	1998	1999	2000	2001
Consumer price index	100.0	109.8	117.5	131.0	139.9	152.4	163.5

Production (metric tons except as noted). Agriculture, forestry, fishing (1999): cassava 3,500,000, soybeans 3,303,500, sugarcane 2,872,270, corn (maize) 817,000, oranges 230,632, seed cotton 202,283, lint cotton 120,000, sweet potatoes 79,365, bananas 69,968; livestock (number of live animals) 9,863,000 cattle, 2,500,000 pigs, 15,000,000 chickens; roundwood (1998) 8,097,000 cu m; fish catch (1998) 26,000. Mining and quarrying (1997): limestone 600,000; kaolin 66,700; gypsum 4,500. Manufacturing (value added in constant prices of 1982, Ø'000,000; 1998): food products 59,100; wood products and furniture 23,500; handicrafts 10,300; printing and publishing 9,200; leather and hides

7,000; textiles 6,600; nonmetal products 6,600; petroleum products 3,800.
Energy production (consumption): electricity (kW-hr; 2000) 51,500,000,000 (2,000,000,000); crude petroleum (barrels; 1997) none (1,158,000); petroleum products (metric tons; 1997) 149,000 (1,147,000).
Gross national product (2000): U.S.$7,933,000,000 (U.S.$1,440 per capita).

Structure of gross domestic product and labour force

	1998 in value Ø'000,000,000	1998 % of total value	1996 labour force	1996 % of labour force
Agriculture	7,037.2	28.3	559,042	32.0
Mining	119.6	0.5	2,568	0.1
Manufacturing	3,385.3	13.6	181,983	10.4
Construction	1,291.7	5.2	142,678	8.2
Public utilities	1,498.9	6.0	13,150	0.8
Transp. and commun.	1,216.0	4.9	55,972	3.2
Trade Finance	5,772.8	23.2	224,210	12.8
Pub. admin., defense	1,454.3	5.9	330,697	18.9
Services Other	3,077.9	12.4	237,188[7]	13.6[7]
TOTAL	24,853.7	100.0	1,747,488	100.0

Household income and expenditure. Average household size (2000) 4.4; sources of income (1989): wages and salaries 33.9%, transfer payments 2.5%.
Tourism (2000): receipts U.S.$101,000,000; expenditures U.S.$97,000,000.

Foreign trade[8]

Balance of trade (current prices)

	1994	1995	1996	1997	1998	1999
U.S.$'000,000	−1,323.6	−1,887.6	−1,807.0	−1,868.5	−1,866.4	−1,456.7
% of total	44.8%	50.5%	46.4%	46.2%	45.9%	41.8%

Imports (1998): U.S.$2,470,800,000 (machinery and transport equipment 30.6%, of which transport equipment 8.1%; food, beverages, and tobacco 23.7%; fuels and lubricants 7.6%; chemicals and pharmaceuticals 5.4%). *Major import sources:* Brazil 32.2%; U.S. 20.2%; Argentina 15.6%; Hong Kong 6.9%; Japan 2.7%.
Exports (1998): U.S.$1,014,100,000[9] (soybean flour 43.4%; cotton fibres 9.1%; vegetable oil 7.5%, of which soybean oil 6.0%; timber 6.9%; processed meats 6.7%; hides and skins 3.8%). *Major export destinations:* Brazil 28.1%; Argentina 25.7%; The Netherlands 15.3%; Japan 4.8%; Chile 4.7%.

Transport and communications

Transport. Railroads (1998): route length 441 km; passenger-km 3,000,000; metric ton-km cargo 5,500,000. Roads (1999): total length 29,500 km (paved 51%). Vehicles (2002): passenger cars 274,186; trucks 189,115. Air transport (2000): passenger-km 270,503,000; metric ton-km cargo 24,346,000; airports (1998) 5.

Communications

Medium	date	unit	number	units per 1,000 persons
Daily newspapers	1996	circulation	213,000	43
Radio	1997	receivers	925,000	182
Television	1999	receivers	1,100,000	205
Telephones	2001	main lines	288,800	51
Cellular telephones	2001	subscribers	1,150,000	204
Personal computers	2001	units	60,000	11
Internet	2001	users	80,000	14.2

Education and health

Educational attainment (1999). Percentage of population age 15 and over having: no formal schooling 5.5%; primary education 52.8%; secondary 34.0%; higher 7.6%; not stated 0.1%. *Literacy* (1999): percentage of total population age 15 and over literate 92.3%; males literate 94.1%; female literate 90.6%.

Education (1998)

	schools	teachers	students	student/ teacher ratio
Primary (age 7–12)	6,143	59,423	933,289	15.7
Secondary (age 13–18)[10]	1,846	17,668[11]	332,703	16.6[11]
Higher[11]	2	742[12]	42,302	...

Health (1995): physicians 3,730 (1 per 1,294 persons); hospital beds 6,759 (1 per 714 persons); infant mortality rate per 1,000 live births (2000) 30.8.
Food (2000): daily per capita caloric intake 2,533 (vegetable products 77%, animal products 23%); 110% of FAO recommended minimum requirement.

Military

Total active duty personnel (2001): 18,600 (army 80.1%, navy 10.8%, air force 9.1%). *Military expenditure as percentage of GNP* (1999): 1.1% (world 2.4%); per capita expenditure U.S.$15.

[1]Includes one nonelective seat. Former president Juan Carlos Wasmosy became senator-for-life in August 1998. [2]Roman Catholicism, although not official, enjoys special recognition in the 1992 constitution. [3]Asunción is the capital city, not a department. [4]Within Asunción urban agglomeration. [5]Civil Registry records only. [6]Reporting areas only (constituting about 67 percent of the total population). [7]Includes 171,312 unemployed. [8]Imports are f.o.b. [9]Excludes value of hydroelectricity exports to Brazil and Argentina. [10]Includes vocational and teacher training. [11]1996. [12]1993–94.

Internet resources for further information:
• **Banco Central del Paraguay**
  http://www.bcp.gov.py
• **Dirección General Estadística, Encuestas y Censos**
  http://www.dgeec.gov.py/index.htm

Peru

Official name: República del Perú
(Spanish) (Republic of Peru).
Form of government: unitary
multiparty republic with one
legislative house (Congress [120]).
Head of state and government:
President, assisted by Prime Minister.
Capital: Lima.
Official languages: Spanish; Quechua;
Aymara.
Official religion: Roman Catholicism.
Monetary unit: 1 nuevo sol (S/.) =
100 céntimos; valuation (Sept. 23, 2002)
1 U.S.$ = S/. 3.63; 1 £ = S/. 5.64.

Area and population

Departments[1]	area sq km	population 2002 estimate	Departments[1]	area sq km	population 2002 estimate
Amazonas	39,249	428,095	Loreto	368,852	907,341
Ancash	35,877	1,107,828	Madre de Dios	85,183	99,452
Apurímac	20,896	463,131	Moquegua	15,734	156,750
Arequipa	63,345	1,101,005	Pasco	25,320	264,702
Ayacucho	43,815	550,751	Piura	35,892	1,636,047
Cajamarca	33,318	1,498,567	Puno	71,999[2]	1,263,995
Cusco	72,104	1,208,689	San Martin	51,253	757,740
Huancavelica	22,131	443,213	Tacna	16,076	294,214
Huánuco	36,887	811,865	Tumbes	4,669	202,088
Ica	21,328	687,334	Ucayali	102,411	456,340
Junín	44,197	1,246,663	**Constitutional**		
La Libertad	25,500	1,506,122	**Province**		
Lambayeque	14,231	1,121,358	Callao	147	787,154
Lima	34,802	7,748,528	TOTAL	1,285,216[2]	26,748,972

Demography

Population (2002): 26,749,000.
Density (2002): persons per sq mi 53.9, persons per sq km 20.8.
Urban-rural (2000): urban 72.3%; rural 27.7%.
Sex distribution (2000): male 49.59%; female 50.41%.
Age breakdown (2000): under 15, 33.4%; 15–29, 29.1%; 30–44, 19.3%; 45–59, 10.9%; 60–74, 5.7%; 75 and over, 1.6%.
Population projection: (2010) 29,952,000; (2020) 33,923,000.
Doubling time: 40 years.
Ethnic composition (2000): Quechua 47.0%; mestizo 31.9%; white 12.0%; Aymara 5.4%; Japanese 0.5%; other 3.2%.
Religious affiliation (1995): Roman Catholic 88.8%; Protestant 6.7%; other Christian 1.5%; other 3.0%.
Major cities (1998 est.): metropolitan Lima 7,060,600; Arequipa 710,103; Trujillo 603,657; Chiclayo 469,200; Iquitos 334,013.

Vital statistics

Birth rate per 1,000 population (2002): 23.4 (world avg. 21.2).
Death rate per 1,000 population (2002): 5.7 (world avg. 8.9).
Natural increase rate per 1,000 population (2002): 17.7 (world avg. 12.3).
Total fertility rate (avg. births per childbearing woman; 2002): 2.9.
Life expectancy at birth (2002): male 68.2 years; female 73.1 years.
Major causes of death per 100,000 population (1989): diseases of the circulatory system 115.3; respiratory diseases 100.2; infectious diseases 84.5; malignant neoplasms 72.9; accidents, poisoning, and violence 53.6.

National economy

Budget (2000). Revenue: S/. 27,978,000,000 (taxes on goods and services 44.7%, income taxes 18.3%, nontax revenue 16.5%, import duties 10.3%, payroll tax 3.7%). Expenditures: S/. 32,900,000,000 (current expenditure 71.9%, capital expenditure 15.5%, interest payments 12.6%).
Public debt (external, outstanding; 2000): U.S.$19,205,000,000.
Tourism (2000): receipts U.S.$911,000,000; expenditures U.S.$531,000,000.
Production (metric tons except as noted). Agriculture, forestry, fishing (1999): sugarcane 6,900,000, potatoes 3,050,000, rice 1,947,000, plantains 1,344,000, corn (maize) 1,058,000, cassava 862,000; livestock (number of live animals) 13,700,000 sheep, 4,898,000 cattle, 2,784,000 pigs, 2,068,000 goats, 79,917,000 chickens; roundwood (1998) 9,157,000 cu m; fish catch (1998) 4,338,437. Mining and quarrying (2001): iron ore 3,892,000; zinc (metal) 201,498; copper (metal) 471,875; lead (metal) 121,181; silver (metal) 1,184; gold 4,438,000 troy oz. Manufacturing (value in S/. '000,000[3]; 1996): processed foods 275.1; base metal products 188.6; textiles and leather products 129.5; industrial chemicals 112.3; wood products 80.0. Construction (value in S/. '000,000[3]; 1996): residential 32.1; nonresidential 26.8. Energy production (consumption): electricity (kW-hr; 1997) 17,951,000,000 (17,953,000,000); coal (metric tons; 1997) 22,000 (310,000); crude petroleum (barrels; 1997) 44,000,000 (57,000,000); petroleum products (metric tons; 1997) 6,896,000 (7,866,000); natural gas (cu m; 1997) 142,000,000 (142,000,000).
Population economically active (1998): total 7,407,280; activity rate of total population 45.7% (participation rates: over age 15, 66.9%; female 43.8%; unemployed 7.7%).

Price and earnings indexes (1995 = 100)

	1995	1996	1997	1998	1999	2000	2001
Consumer price index	100.0	111.5	121.1	129.9	134.4	139.4	142.2
Monthly earnings index[4]	100.0	106.8	114.8	120.5	122.1	...	...

Gross national product (at current market prices; 2000): U.S.$53,392,000,000 (U.S.$2,080 per capita).

Structure of gross domestic product and labour force

	2000		1992	
	in value S/.'000[3]	% of total value	labour force	% of labour force
Agriculture	14,503,800	7.8	2,658,000	33.0
Mining	9,931,800	5.3	198,000	2.4
Manufacturing	27,882,300	14.9	840,000	10.4
Construction	10,294,400	5.5	300,000	3.7
Public utilities	3,943,000	2.1	25,000	0.3
Transp. and commun.	15,555,300	8.3	355,000	4.4
Trade	33,491,900	17.9	1,297,000	16.1
Finance	24,773,400	13.3	192,000	2.4
Services	46,380,200[5]	24.9[5]	2,199,000[6]	27.3[6]
TOTAL	186,756,200	100.0	8,064,000	100.0

Household income and expenditure. Average household size (1993) 5.1; income per household (1988) U.S.$2,173; sources of income (1991): business income 67.1%, wages 23.3%, transfers 7.6%, other 2.0%; expenditure (1990): food 29.4%, recreation and education 13.2%, household durables 10.1%, clothing and footwear 8.5%, transportation 7.5%, health 7.0%.
Land use (1998): forest and other 75.7%; pasture 21.1%; agricultural 3.2%.

Foreign trade[7]

Balance of trade (current prices)

	1996	1997	1998	1999	2000	2001
U.S.$'000,000	−1,996.5	−1,738.3	−2,477.2	−612.2	−303.0	−72.7
% of total	14.5%	11.3%	17.8%	4.8%	2.1%	0.5%

Imports (1998): U.S.$8,200,000,000 (raw and intermediate materials 41.3%, machinery 24.9%, consumer goods 23.0%, transport equipment 6.7%). *Major import sources:* U.S. 32.5%; Colombia 7.4%; Germany 5.6%; Venezuela 4.3%.
Exports (1998): U.S.$5,722,900,000 (gold 16.2%, copper and copper products 13.6%, zinc products 7.8%, fish meal fodder 6.8%, coffee 5.0%, petroleum and derivatives 3.9%, lead products 3.7%, silver 2.3%, tin 2.1%). *Major export destinations:* U.S. 32.3%; Japan 8.7%; United Kingdom 4.8%; Switzerland 4.2%; Spain 4.1%; Venezuela 3.9%; South Korea 3.4%.

Transport and communications

Transport. Railroads (2000): route length 1,608 km; (1996) passenger-km 171,091,000; (1996) metric ton-km cargo 850,329,000. Roads (1999): total length 78,128 km (paved 13%). Vehicles (1999): passenger cars 684,533; trucks and buses 403,652. Air transport (1998): passenger-km 3,014,000,000; metric ton-km cargo 286,000,000; airports (1996) 27.

Communications

Medium	date	unit	number	units per 1,000 persons
Daily newspapers	1996	circulation	2,000,000	84
Radio	1997	receivers	6,650,000	273
Television	1999	receivers	3,700,000	147
Telephones	2001	main lines	2,022,300	78
Cellular telephones	2001	subscribers	1,545,000	59
Personal computers	2001	units	1,250,000	48
Internet	2001	users	3,000,000	115

Education and health

Educational attainment (1993). Percentage of population age 15 and over having: no formal schooling 12.3%; less than primary education 0.3%; primary 31.5%; secondary 35.5%; higher 20.4%. *Literacy* (1995): total population age 15 and over literate 88.0%; males 93.5%; females 82.7%.

Education (1997)

	schools	teachers	students	student/ teacher ratio
Primary (age 6–11)	33,017	153,951	4,163,180	27.0
Secondary (age 12–16)	8,452[8]	106,614	1,969,501	18.5
Voc., teacher tr.[8]	2,531	12,392	256,763	20.7
Higher	994[8]	45,443	657,586	14.5

Health: physicians (1996) 24,708 (1 per 969 persons); hospital beds (1994) 42,979 (1 per 538 persons); infant mortality rate per 1,000 live births (2002) 38.2.
Food (2000): daily per capita caloric intake 2,624 (vegetable products 87%, animal products 13%); 112% of FAO recommended minimum requirement.

Military

Total active duty personnel (2001): 100,000 (army 60.0%, navy 25.0%, air force 15.0%). *Military expenditure as percentage of GNP* (1999): 2.4% (world 2.4%); per capita expenditure U.S.$45.

---

[1]The traditional local administrative structure of Peru is based on departments. The regional administrative structure introduced in the late 1980s has assumed limited authority because of a lack of funding from the central government. [2]Includes the 4,996 sq km area of the Peruvian part of Lake Titicaca. [3]At market prices. [4]Estimate for Lima metropolitan area only; private sector nominal wages. [5]Includes public administration, services, import duties, and other taxes on products. [6]Includes public administration and other. [7]Imports and exports in balance of trade is f.o.b. [8]1996.

Internet resources for further information:
• **Instituto Nacional de Estadística e Informática (Spanish)**
  http://www.inei.gob.pe
• **Banco Central de Reserva del Peru**
  http://www.bcrp.gob.pe/English/Index_eng.htm

Philippines

Pacific
Ocean

Official name: Republika ng Pilipinas
(Pilipino); Republic of the Philippines
(English).
Form of government: unitary republic
with two legislative houses (Senate
[24]; House of Representatives [260[1]]).
Chief of state and head of government:
President.
Capital: Quezon City/Manila[2].
Official languages: Pilipino; English.
Official religion: none.
Monetary unit: 1 Philippine peso
(₱) = 100 centavos; valuation (Sept. 23,
2002) 1 U.S.$ = ₱ 52.30;
1 £ = ₱ 81.27.

Area and population	area		population
Regions	sq mi	sq km	2000 census
Bicol	6,808	17,633	4,674,855
Cagayan Valley	10,362	26,838	2,813,159
Caraga	7,277	18,847	2,095,367
Central Luzon	7,039	18,231	8,030,945
Central Mindanao	5,549	14,373	2,598,210
Central Visayas	5,773	14,951	5,701,064
Eastern Visayas	8,275	21,432	3,610,355
Ilocos	4,958	12,840	4,200,478
National Capital (Metro Manila)	246	636	9,932,560
Northern Mindanao	5,418	14,033	2,747,585
Southern Mindanao	10,479	27,141	5,189,335
Southern Tagalog	18,117	46,924	11,793,655
Western Mindanao	6,194	16,042	3,091,208
Western Visayas	7,808	20,223	6,208,733
Autonomous Regions			
Cordillera	7,063	18,294	1,365,220
Muslim Mindanao	4,493	11,638	2,412,159
TOTAL	115,860[3]	300,076	76,498,735[4]

Demography

Population (2002): 79,882,000.
Density (2002): persons per sq mi 689.5, persons per sq km 266.2.
Urban-rural (2002): urban 60.0%; rural 40.0%.
Sex distribution (2000): male 50.37%; female 49.63%.
Age breakdown (2000): under 15, 36.2%; 15–29, 28.1%; 30–44, 19.0%; 45–59,
10.7%; 60–74, 4.8%; 75 and over, 1.2%.
Population projection: (2010) 92,426,000; (2020) 106,162,000.
Doubling time: 33 years.
Ethnolinguistic composition (by mother tongue of households; 1995): Pilipino
(Tagalog) 29.3%; Cebuano 23.3%; Ilocano 9.3%; Hiligaynon Ilonggo 9.1%;
Bicol 5.7%; Waray 3.8%; Pampango 3.0%; Pangasinan 1.8%; other 14.7%.
Religious affiliation (1996): Roman Catholic 82.9%; Protestant 5.4%; Muslim
4.6%; Aglipayan (Philippine Independent Church) 2.6%; other 4.5%.
Major cities (2000): Quezon City 2,173,831; Manila 1,581,082; Caloocan
1,177,604; Davao 1,147,116; Cebu 718,821; Zamboanga 601,794.

Vital statistics

Birth rate per 1,000 population (2002): 26.2 (world avg. 21.2); (1982) legitimate
93.9%; illegitimate 6.1%.
Death rate per 1,000 population (2002): 5.2 (world avg. 8.9).
Natural increase rate per 1,000 population (2002): 21.0 (world avg. 12.3).
Total fertility rate (avg. births per childbearing woman; 2002): 3.2.
Life expectancy at birth (2002): male 68.0 years; female 72.0 years.
Major causes of death per 100,000 population (1997): circulatory diseases 101.0;
respiratory diseases 70.1; accidents 39.9; malignant neoplasms (cancers) 37.5;
tuberculosis 32.2; diabetes mellitus 9.4.

National economy

Budget (2000). Revenue: ₱ 514,762,000,000 (income taxes 39.6%, taxes on
goods and services 27.1%, international duties 18.5%, nontax revenues
10.6%). Expenditures: ₱ 649,484,000,000 (debt service 20.0%, education
18.7%, transportation and communications 9.5%, public order and safety
7.0%, general administration 5.4%, defense 5.0%).
Production (metric tons except as noted). Agriculture, forestry, fishing (2000):
sugarcane 33,732,000, rice 12,415,000, coconuts 5,761,000, corn (maize)
4,486,000, bananas 4,156,000, pineapples 1,524,000; livestock (number of live
animals) 10,398,000 pigs, 6,780,000 goats, 3,018,000 buffalo, 142,000,000 chickens; roundwood (1999) 43,399,000 cu m; fish catch (1998) 1,827,971. Mining
and quarrying (1999): nickel ore 436,970; copper concentrate 98,857; chrome
concentrate 17,562; gold 29,109 kg; silver 16,387 kg. Manufacturing (gross
value added in ₱ '000,000; 1998)[5]: food products 246,300; electrical machinery 53,000; chemicals 49,100; petroleum and coal products 41,900. Energy
production (consumption): electricity (kW-hr; 2001) 46,340,000,000 ([1997]
39,816,000,000); hard coal (metric tons; 2001) 1,235,000 ([1997] 5,182,000);
crude petroleum (barrels; 1997) 300,000 (127,000,000); petroleum products
(metric tons; 1997) 16,281,000 (17,234,000); natural gas, none (none).
Household income and expenditure (2000). Average household size 5.0; income
per family ₱ 144,506 (U.S.$3,150); sources of income (1997): wages 45.6%,
entrepreneurial income 26.2%, rent 10.3%, transfers 6.8%, other 11.1%;
expenditure: food, beverage, and tobacco 45.0%, housing 15.1%, transportation 6.8%, fuel and power 6.2%, education 4.2%, personal care 3.6%.
Gross national product (at current market prices; 2000): U.S.$78,778,000,000
(U.S.$1,040 per capita).

Structure of gross domestic product and labour force				
	2000			
	in value P '000,000	% of total value	labour force	% of labour force
Agriculture	548,400	16.5	11,415,000	35.8
Mining	21,000	0.6	110,000	0.3
Manufacturing	745,700	22.4	2,700,000	8.5
Construction	161,400	4.9	1,485,000	4.7
Public utilities	96,900	2.9	121,000	0.4
Transp. and commun.	198,000	6.0	1,991,000	6.2
Trade	475,100	14.3	4,590,000	14.4
Finances	149,200	4.5	729,000	2.3
Services	926,900	27.9	5,751,000	18.1
Others	—	—	2,956,000[6]	9.3[6]
TOTAL	3,322,600	100.0	31,848,000	100.0

Public debt (external, outstanding; 2000): U.S.$33,429,000,000.
Population economically active (2000): total 31,848,000; activity rate 41.5%
(participation rates: ages 15–64, 65.0%; female [1995] 37.4%; unemployed
[July 2002] 11.2%).

Price and earnings indexes (1995 = 100)							
	1995	1996	1997	1998	1999	2000	2001
Consumer price index	100.0	109.0	115.4	126.6	135.1	141.0	149.6
Daily earnings index[7]	100.0	113.8	127.6	127.6	...	...	...

Tourism (2000): receipts U.S.$2,134,000,000; expenditures U.S.$1,005,000,000.

Foreign trade[8]

Balance of trade (current prices)						
	1996	1997	1998	1999	2000	2001
P '000,000	−299,998	−316,285	−69,991	+231,075	+385,576	+130,813
% of total	21.9%	17.5%	3.0%	8.8%	12.2%	4.2%

Imports (1999): U.S.$30,723,340,000 (chemicals 8.1%, mineral fuels and lubri-
cants 7.9%, power generating and specialized machinery 7.8%, telecommunications equipment and electrical machinery 7.6%, base metals 4.3%).
Major import sources: United States 20.7%; Japan 19.9%; South Korea 8.9%;
Singapore 5.7%; Taiwan 5.3%; Hong Kong 4.0%.
Exports (1999): U.S.$35,036,560,000 (electronics 56.2%, garments 6.5%, igni-
tion wiring sets 1.5%, woodcraft and furniture 1.4%, coconut oil 1.0%,
bananas 0.7%). *Major export destinations:* United States 29.6%; Japan 13.3%;
Taiwan 8.5%; The Netherlands 8.2%; Singapore 7.0%; Hong Kong 5.6%.

Transport and communications

Transport. Railroads (2000): route length 897 km; passenger-km 12,000,000;
metric ton-km cargo 660,000,000. Roads (1998): total length 199,950 km
(paved 39%). Vehicles (2000): passenger cars 763,834; trucks and buses
282,231. Air transport (1999)[9]: passenger-km 10,292,338,000; metric ton-km
cargo 240,918,000; airports (1996) with scheduled flights 21.

Communications				units
Medium	date	unit	number	per 1,000 persons
Daily newspapers	1996	circulation	5,700,000	82
Radio	1997	receivers	11,500,000	161
Television	1999	receivers	8,200,000	110
Telephones	2001	main lines	3,100,000	40
Cellular telephones	2001	subscribers	10,568,000	137
Personal computers	2001	units	1,700,000	22
Internet	2001	users	2,000,000	26

Education and health

Education attainment (1995). Percentage of population age 15 and over having: no schooling 3.7%; elementary education 35.8%; secondary 38.4%; postsecondary 21.9%; not stated 0.2%. *Literacy* (1995): total population age 15
and over literate 94.6%; males literate 95.0%; females literate 94.3%.

Education (1998–99)	schools	teachers	students	student/ teacher ratio
Primary (age 7–12)	39,011	328,517	12,474,886	38.0
Secondary (age 13–16) } Voc., teacher tr.	7,021	108,981	5,066,190	46.5
Higher	1,316	66,876[10]	2,017,972[10]	30.2[10]

Health: physicians (1993) 78,445 (1 per 849 persons); hospital beds (2000) 81,016
(1 per 948 persons); infant mortality rate per 1,000 live births (2002) 30.0.
Food (2000): daily per capita caloric intake 2,379 (vegetable products 85%,
animal products 15%); 105% of FAO recommended minimum.

Military

Total active duty personnel (2001): 107,000 (army 62.6%, navy 22.4%, air force
15.0%). *Military expenditure as percentage of GNP* (1999): 1.4% (world
2.4%); per capita expenditure U.S.$14.

---

[1]Includes 38 vacant seats. [2]And other Manila suburbs of the National Capital Region.
[3]Detail does not add to total given because of rounding. [4]Includes foreign-service
employees stationed abroad. [5]Manufacturing firms with 10 or more workers. [6]Mostly
unemployed. [7]Minimum wages in nonagricultural activities in the National Capital
Region. [8]Import figures are f.o.b. in balance of trade and c.i.f. for commodities and
trading partners. [9]Philippines Airlines only. [10]1995–96.

Internet resources for further information:
• **National Statistics Office http://www.census.gov.ph**
• **Government Website http://www.neda.gov.ph**

Poland

Official name: Rzeczpospolita Polska (Republic of Poland).
Form of government: unitary multiparty republic with two legislative houses (Senate [100]; Diet [460]).
Chief of state: President.
Head of government: Prime Minister.
Capital: Warsaw.
Official language: Polish.
Official religion: none[1].
Monetary unit: 1 zloty (Zł) = 100 groszy; valuation (Sept. 23, 2002) 1 U.S.$ = Zł 4.13; 1 £ = Zł 6.42.

Area and population

Provinces[2]	Capitals	area sq mi	area sq km	population 2001[3] estimate
Dolnośląskie	Wrocław	7,702	19,948	2,972,667
Kujawsko-pomorskie	Bydgoszcz/Toruń	6,938	17,970	2,099,724
Lubelskie	Lublin	9,697	25,114	2,232,054
Lubuskie	Gorzów Wielkopolski/ Zielona Góra	5,399	13,984	1,023,988
Łódzkie	Łódź	7,034	18,219	2,643,385
Małopolskie	Kraków	5,847	15,144	3,233,799
Mazowieckie	Warsaw (Warszawa)	13,744	35,598	5,072,335
Opolskie	Opole	3,634	9,412	1,084,665
Podkarpackie	Rzeszów	6,921	17,926	2,128,605
Podlaskie	Białystok	7,792	20,180	1,221,128
Pomorskie	Gdańsk	7,063	18,293	2,198,322
Śląskie	Katowice	4,747	12,294	4,847,600
Świętokrzyskie	Kielce	4,507	11,672	1,322,879
Warmińsko-Mazurskie	Olsztyn	9,345	24,203	1,468,313
Wielkopolskie	Poznań	11,516	29,826	3,360,899
Zachodniopomorskie	Szczecin	8,843	22,902	1,733,848
TOTAL		120,728[4]	312,685	38,644,211

Demography

Population (2002): 38,644,000.
Density (2002): persons per sq mi 319.9, persons per sq km 123.6.
Urban-rural (2000): urban 61.8%; rural 38.2%.
Sex distribution (2000): male 48.60%; female 51.40%.
Age breakdown (2000): under 15, 19.1%; 15–29, 24.3%; 30–44, 21.3%; 45–59, 18.7%; 60–74, 12.2%; 75 and over, 4.4%.
Population projection: (2010) 38,764,000; (2020) 39,003,000.
Ethnolinguistic composition (1997): Polish 94.2%; Ukrainian 3.9%; German 1.3%; Belarusian 0.6%.
Religious affiliation (1995): Roman Catholic 90.7%; Ukrainian Catholic 1.4%; Polish Orthodox 1.4%; Protestant 0.5%; Jehovah's Witness 0.5%; other (mostly nonreligious) 5.5%.
Major cities (2001[3]): Warsaw 1,610,471; Łódź 793,217; Kraków 741,510; Wrocław 633,857; Poznań 574,896; Gdańsk 456,754.

Vital statistics

Birth rate per 1,000 population (2001): 9.5 (world avg. 21.2); (2000) legitimate 87.9%; illegitimate 12.1%.
Death rate per 1,000 population (2001): 9.4 (world avg. 8.9).
Natural increase rate per 1,000 population (2001): 0.1 (world avg. 12.3).
Total fertility rate (avg. births per childbearing woman; 2000): 1.3.
Marriage rate per 1,000 population (2000): 5.5.
Divorce rate per 1,000 population (2000): 1.1.
Life expectancy at birth (2000): male 69.7 years; female 78.0 years.
Major causes of death per 100,000 population (1998): diseases of the circulatory system 450.9; malignant neoplasms (cancers) 168.6; accidents, poisoning, and violence 73.2; diseases of the respiratory system 36.5.

National economy

Budget (1998). Revenue: Zł 126,560,000,000 (income tax 39.1%, value-added tax 33.9%, excise tax 16.6%). Expenditures: Zł 139,752,000,000 (social security 18.0%, health 15.0%, education 8.1%, welfare 6.6%, defense 6.0%).
Gross national product (2000): U.S.$161,832,000,000 (U.S.$4,190 per capita).

Structure of gross domestic product and labour force

	1999 in value Zł '000,000	1999 % of total value	1998 labour force	1998 % of labour force
Agriculture	20,991	3.4	2,946,000	17.2
Mining	13,938	2.2	381,000	2.2
Manufacturing	112,645	18.1	3,205,000	18.7
Public utilities	18,580	3.0	265,000	1.5
Construction	47,143	7.6	1,071,000	6.2
Transp. and commun.	35,654	5.7	958,000	5.6
Trade, restaurants	118,578	19.0	2,336,000	13.6
Finance, real estate	74,651	12.0	818,000	4.8
Pub. admin., defense	26,892	4.3	779,000	4.5
Services	67,490	10.8	2,595,000	15.1
Other	86,752[5]	13.9[5]	1,808,000[6]	10.5[6]
TOTAL	623,317[4]	100.0	17,162,000	100.0[4]

Production (metric tons except as noted). Agriculture, forestry, fishing (1999): (gross value of production in Zł '000,000) potatoes 4,066, wheat 3,747, fruit 3,578, vegetables 3,484, rye 1,420, sugar beets 1,254; livestock (number of live animals) 18,538,000 pigs, 6,555,000 cattle; roundwood (1999) 24,300,000 cu m; fish catch (2000) 218,354. Mining and quarrying (1998): sulfur 1,672,000; copper ore (metal content) 432,243; silver (recoverable metal content) 1,108.

Manufacturing (value added in Zł '000,000; 1999): food products 13,764; beverages 13,582; transport equipment 10,596; nonelectrical machinery 7,542; electrical machinery 7,506. Energy production (consumption): electricity ('000,000 kW-hr; 2001) 142,584 ([1997] 140,576); hard coal ('000 metric tons; 2001) 103,896 ([1997] 104,337); lignite ('000 metric tons; 2001) 59,544 ([1997] 63,143); crude petroleum (barrels; 1997) 2,144,000 (110,424,000); petroleum products (metric tons; 1997) 14,153,000 (17,565,000); natural gas (cu m; 2001) 5,178,000,000 ([1997] 11,227,000,000).
Public debt (external, outstanding; 2000): U.S.$30,785,000,000.
Population economically active (1998): total 17,162,000; activity rate of total population 44.4% (participation rates: 15–64, 66.1%; female 45.7%; unemployed [May 2001–April 2002] 16.7%).

Price and earnings indexes (1995 = 100)

	1996	1997	1998	1999	2000	2001	2002[7]
Consumer price index	119.8	137.9	154.1	165.3	182.1	192.1	196.9
Annual earnings index	126.3	151.6	174.2	189.9	209.6	224.1	224.8

Household income and expenditure. Average household size (2000) 2.9; average annual income (1995) Zł 8,431 (U.S.$2,990); sources of income (1996): wages 43.9%, transfers 25.2%, self-employment 21.9%; expenditure (1999): food, beverages, and tobacco 32.3%, housing and energy 23.4%, transportation and communications 14.3%, recreation 6.6%.
Tourism (2000): receipts U.S.$6,100,000,000; expenditures U.S.$3,600,000,000.
Land use (1994): forest 28.8%; meadow 13.3%; agricultural and under permanent cultivation 47.0%; other 10.9%.

Foreign trade[8]

Balance of trade (current prices)

	1996	1997	1998	1999	2000	2001
Zł '000,000	−34,412	−54,418	−67,443	−73,656	−75,163	−58,138
% of total	20.7%	24.4%	26.2%	25.3%	21.4%	16.4%

Imports (1999): Zł 182,362,000,000 (machinery and transport equipment 38.2%, chemicals and chemical products 14.3%, mineral fuels and lubricants 7.2%, food 5.5%). *Major import sources:* Germany 25.2%; Italy 9.4%; France 6.8%; Russia 5.9%; U.K. 4.6%.
Exports (1999): Zł 108,706,000,000 (machinery and transport equipment 30.3%, food 8.5%, chemicals and chemical products 6.2%, mineral fuels and lubricants 5.0%). *Major export destinations:* Germany 36.1%; Italy 6.5%; The Netherlands 5.3%; France 4.8%; U.K. 4.0%.

Transport and communications

Transport. Railroads (2000[3]): length 22,981 km; (1999) passenger-km 26,198,000,000; (1999) metric ton-km cargo 55,471,000,000. Roads (1997): total length 381,046 km (paved 66%). Vehicles (2000[3]): passenger cars 9,283,000; trucks and buses 1,762,000. Air transport (2001[9]): passenger-km 6,052,000,000; metric ton-km cargo 69,039,000; airports (1997) 8.

Communications

Medium	date	unit	number	units per 1,000 persons
Daily newspapers	1996	circulation	4,351,000	113
Radio	1997	receivers	20,200,000	523
Television	1999	receivers	15,000,000	388
Telephones	2001	main lines	11,400,000	295
Cellular telephones	2001	subscribers	10,050,000	260
Personal computers	2001	units	3,300,000	85
Internet	2001	users	3,800,000	98

Education and health

Educational attainment (1995). Percentage of population age 15 and over having: no formal schooling/incomplete primary education 6.3%; primary 33.7%; secondary/vocational 53.2%; higher 6.8%. *Literacy* (2000): 99.8%.

Education (1999–2000)

	schools	teachers	students	student/ teacher ratio
Primary (age 7–12)	17,743	274,600	3,958,000	14.4
Secondary (age 13–18)	8,277	71,500	1,479,400	20.7
Voc., teacher tr.	8,066	89,900	1,552,300	17.3
Higher	287	78,100	1,431,900	18.3

Health (1999): physicians 90,086[3] (1 per 429 persons); hospital beds (2000[3]) 239,341 (1 per 161 persons); infant mortality rate per 1,000 live births (2001) 7.7.
Food (1999): daily per capita caloric intake 3,368 (vegetable products 73%, animal products 27%); 129% of FAO recommended minimum requirement.

Military

Total active duty personnel (2001): 206,045 (army 58.3%, navy 8.1%, air force 21.2%, paramilitary 12.4%). *Military expenditure as percentage of GNP* (1999): 2.1% (world 2.4%); per capita expenditure U.S.$173.

---

[1]Roman Catholicism has special recognition per 1997 concordat with Vatican City. [2]New administrative organization effective from Jan. 1, 1999. [3]January 1. [4]Detail does not add to total given because of rounding. [5]Taxes less subsidies. [6]Unemployed. [7]May. [8]Imports c.i.f.; exports f.o.b. [9]LOT only.

Internet resources for further information:
• **Polish Official Statistics**
  http://www.stat.gov.pl/english/index.htm

Portugal

Official name: República Portuguesa (Portuguese Republic).
Form of government: republic with one legislative house (Assembly of the Republic [230]).
Chief of state: President.
Head of government: Prime Minister.
Capital: Lisbon.
Official language: Portuguese.
Official religion: none.
Monetary unit: 1 euro (€) = 100 cents; valuation (Sept. 23, 2002) 1 U.S.$ = €1.02; 1 £ = €1.58[1].

Area and population

Continental Portugal		area		population
		sq mi	sq km	2001[2] census
Regions	**Principal cities**	34,284	88,796	9,869,100
Alentejo	Évora	10,398	26,931	535,500
Algarve	Faro	1,926	4,988	395,200
Centre (Centro)	Coimbra	9,138	23,668	1,782,300
Lisbon and Tagus Valley (Lisboa e Vale do Tejo)	Lisbon	4,607	11,931	3,468,900
North (Norte)	Porto	8,215	21,278	3,687,200
Insular Portugal				
Autonomous Regions		1,209	3,130	486,800
Azores (Açores)	Ponta Delgada	901[3]	2,333[3]	241,800
Madeira	Funchal	308[4]	797[4]	245,000
TOTAL		35,662[5]	92,365[5]	10,355,800[2]

Demography

Population (2002): 10,384,000.
Density (2002): persons per sq mi 291.1, persons per sq km 112.4.
Urban-rural (2001): urban 65.8%; rural 34.2%.
Sex distribution (2001): male 48.34%; female 51.66%.
Age breakdown (2000): under 15, 17.1%; 15–29, 23.0%; 30–44, 21.5%; 45–59, 17.8%; 60–74, 14.5%; 75 and over, 6.1%.
Population projection: (2010) 10,491,000; (2020) 10,407,000.
Ethnic composition (2000): Portuguese 91.9%; mixed race 1.6%[6]; Brazilian 1.4%; Marrano 1.2%; other European 1.2%; Han Chinese 0.9%; other 1.8%.
Religious affiliation (1995): Christian 94.8%, of which Roman Catholic 92.2%, Protestant 1.5%, other Christian (Jehovah's Witness 0.7%; Mormon 0.4%) 1.1%; Muslim 0.1%; other and nonreligious 5.1%.
Major cities (2001)[2]: Lisbon 564,657 (urban agglomeration 3,447,173); Porto 263,131; Amadora 175,872; Braga 164,193; Coimbra 148,474; Funchal 103,962.

Vital statistics

Birth rate per 1,000 population (2001): 11.5 (world avg. 21.2).
Death rate per 1,000 population (2001): 10.2 (world avg. 8.9).
Natural increase rate per 1,000 population (2001): 1.3 (world avg. 12.3).
Total fertility rate (avg. births per childbearing woman; 2001): 1.5.
Life expectancy at birth (2001): male 72.4 years; females 79.7 years.
Major causes of death per 100,000 population (1998): circulatory diseases 426.5; malignant neoplasms (cancers) 213.9; respiratory diseases 94.9.

National economy

Budget (1998). Revenue: Esc 7,633,800,000,000 (1997; social security contributions 22.5%, general sales tax 19.3%, individual income tax 14.9%, excise tax 11.6%, grants 9.2%, nontax revenue 9.1%). Expenditures: Esc 7,881,500,000,000 (1997; current expenditure 87.3%, development expenditure 12.7%).
Public debt (1996): U.S.$40,504,000,000.
Production (metric tons except as noted). Agriculture, forestry, fishing (2000): potatoes 1,250,000, tomatoes 1,075,000, corn (maize) 975,000, grapes 892,500, sugar beets 500,000, wheat 350,000, apples 316,000, olives 271,000, oranges 230,000, cork (1998) 163,000, rice 151,000, carrots 150,000, cabbages 140,000, pears 126,000; livestock (number of live animals) 5,900,000 sheep, 2,350,000 pigs, 1,250,000 cattle; roundwood (2000) 9,450,000 cu m; fish catch (1999) 215,230. Mining and quarrying (2000): marble 1,324,700; tin ore 1,200,000; copper (metal content) 76,200; silver 25; uranium 10. Manufacturing (value added in Esc '000,000; 1998): machinery and transport equipment 605,966, of which transport equipment 231,893; petroleum refining 517,170; wearing apparel and footwear 307,275; food and beverages 290,051; textiles 283,268; tobacco 187,220; printing and publishing 165,341. Energy production (consumption): electricity (kW-hr; 1998) 33,144,000,000 ([1997] 37,086,000,000); coal (metric tons; 1997) negligible (5,758,000); crude petroleum (barrels; 1997) none (90,452,000); petroleum products (metric tons; 1997) 11,333,000 (11,100,000); natural gas (cu m; 1997) none (103,328,000).
Tourism (2000): receipts U.S.$5,257,000,000; expenditures U.S.$2,230,000,000.
Land use (1994): forest 35.9%; pasture 10.9%; agriculture 31.5%; other 21.7%.
Population economically active (2001): total 5,200,600; activity rate of total population 50.1% (participation rates: ages 15–64 (1997), 68.5%; female 45.7%; unemployed 4.1%).

Price and earnings indexes (1995 = 100)

	1995	1996	1997	1998	1999	2000	2001
Consumer price index	100.0	103.1	105.3	108.3	110.8	114.0	118.9
Annual earnings index	...	...	...	...	...	...	...

Gross national product (at current market prices; 1999): U.S.$111,291,000,000 (U.S.$11,120 per capita).

Structure of gross domestic product and labour force

	1993		2000	
	in value Esc '000,000	% of total value	labour force	% of labour force
Agriculture	489,476	3.7	616,300	12.0
Mining	113,243	0.8	16,000	0.3
Manufacturing	3,417,963	25.8	1,081,200	21.1
Construction	699,267	5.3	593,500	11.6
Public utilities	551,164	4.2	28,900	0.6
Trade[7]	2,474,801	18.6	976,700	19.1
Finance	1,246,248	9.4	293,100	5.7
Transp. and commun.	825,319	6.2	180,400	3.5
Services	2,477,083	18.7	319,300	6.2
Pub. admin., defense	976,901	7.4	815,700	15.9
Other	...	...	204,600[8]	4.0[8]
TOTAL	13,271,465	100.0[9]	5,125,700	100.0

Household income and expenditure. Average household size (1999) 3.1; income per household: n.a.; sources of income (1994–95): wages and salaries 45.8%, property and entrepreneurial income 32.4%, transfer payments 21.5%; expenditure (1994–95): food 23.9%, housing 20.6%, transportation and communications 18.9%, clothing and footwear 6.3%, health 4.6%, other 25.7%.

Foreign trade[10]

Balance of trade (current prices)

	1995	1996	1997	1998	1999	2000
Esc '000,000,000	–1,527	–1,631	–1,945	–2,454	–2,903	–3,245
% of total	17.9%	17.7%	18.8%	21.6%	23.9%	24.3%

Imports (1999): Esc 7,519,000,000,000 (machinery and transport equipment 37.8%, of which road vehicles and parts 14.5%; basic manufactures 20.1%, of which textiles 5.8%; food products 10.4%; chemicals and chemical products 9.4%; mineral fuels 5.6%). *Major import sources* (1999): Spain 25.3%; Germany 14.7%; France 11.4%; Italy 7.7%; U.K. 7.7%; The Netherlands 4.8%.
Exports (1999): Esc 4,616,000,000,000 (machinery and transport equipment 34.1%, of which transport equipment 14.7%; textiles and wearing apparel 20.5%; footwear 6.5%; chemicals and chemical products 4.8%; food 3.8%; cork and wood products 3.8%). *Major export destinations* (1999): Germany 19.8%; Spain 18.1%; France 13.9%; U.K. 12.0%; U.S. 5.0%; Belgium 4.7%.

Transport and communications

Transport. Railroads (1998): route length 3,259 km; passenger-km 4,602,185; metric ton-km cargo 2,339,895,000. Roads (1996): total length 68,732 km (paved 88%). Vehicles (1998): passenger cars 3,200,000; trucks and buses 1,097,000. Merchant marine (1992): vessels (100 gross tons and over) 332; total deadweight tonnage 1,129,382. Air transport (2001): passenger-km 10,457,000,000; metric ton-km cargo 53,865,000; airports (2000) 16.

Communications

Medium	date	unit	number	units per 1,000 persons
Daily newspapers	1996	circulation	744,000	74
Radio	1997	receivers	3,020,000	298
Television	1999	receivers	5,600,000	547
Telephones	2001	main lines	4,369,700	424
Cellular telephones	2001	subscribers	7,977,500	774
Personal computers	2001	units	1,210,000	117
Internet	2001	users	3,600,000	349

Education and health

Educational attainment (1991). Percentage of population age 25 and over having: no formal schooling 16.1%; some primary education 61.5%; some secondary 10.6%; postsecondary 3.5%. *Literacy* (2000): total population age 15 and over literate 92.2%; males 94.8%; females 90.0%.

Education (1998–99)

	schools	teachers	students	student/ teacher ratio
Primary (age 5–11)	12,635	145,513	1,563,700	10.7
Secondary (age 12–19)				
Vocational	215	6,895	80,130[11]	...
Higher	282	16,192[11]	346,034	...

Health (1998): physicians 31,087 (1 per 321 persons); hospital beds 39,870 (1 per 250 persons); infant mortality rate per 1,000 live births (2000) 6.1.
Food (2000): daily per capita caloric intake 3,716 (vegetable products 72%, animal products 28%); 146% of FAO recommended minimum requirement.

Military

Total active duty personnel (2001): 43,600 (army 58.3%, navy 24.8%, air force 16.9%). *Military expenditure as percentage of GNP* (1999): 2.1% (world 2.4%); per capita expenditure U.S.$240.

---

[1]The escudo was the former monetary unit; on Jan. 1, 2002, 200.48 = €1. [2]Revised preliminary de jure figures; revised preliminary de facto census figure equals 10,148,000. [3]Includes the uninhabited Ilhéus in the Azores. [4]Includes the uninhabited Desertas and Selvagens islands associated with Madeira. [5]Includes the 169 sq mi (439 sq km) of water areas comprising the Tagus and Sado estuaries and the Aveiro lagoon. [6]Refugees and descendants of refugees from Angola, Cape Verde, or Mozambique. [7]Includes hotels. [8]Unemployed. [9]Detail does not add to total given because of rounding. [10]Imports c.i.f.; exports f.o.b. [11]1996–97.

Internet resources for further information:
• **Instituto Nacional de Estatística** http://www.ine.pt
• **Banco de Portugal** http://www.bportugal.pt

Puerto Rico

Official name: Estado Libre Asociado de Puerto Rico; Commonwealth of Puerto Rico.
Political status: self-governing commonwealth in association with the United States, having two legislative houses (Senate [27[1]]; House of Representatives [51[1]]).
Chief of state: President of the United States.
Head of government: Governor.
Capital: San Juan.
Official languages: Spanish; English.
Monetary unit: 1 U.S. dollar (U.S.$) = 100 cents; valuation (Sept. 23, 2002) 1 £ = U.S.$1.55.

Population (2000 census)

Municipio	population	Municipio	population	Municipio	population
Adjuntas	19,143	Fajardo	40,712	Naguabo	23,753
Aguada	42,042	Florida	12,367	Naranjito	29,709
Aguadilla	64,685	Guánica	21,888	Orocovis	23,844
Agunas Buenas	29,032	Guayama	44,301	Patillas	20,152
Aibonito	26,493	Guayanilla	23,072	Peñuelas	26,719
Añasco	28,348	Guaynabo	100,053	Ponce	186,475
Arecibo	100,131	Gurabo	36,743	Quebradillas	25,450
Arroyo	19,117	Hatillo	38,925	Rincón	14,767
Barceloneta	22,322	Hormigueros	16,614	Río Grande	52,362
Barranquitas	28,909	Humacao	59,035	Sabana Grande	25,935
Bayamón	224,044	Isabela	44,444	Salinas	31,113
Cabo Rojo	46,911	Jayuya	17,318	San Germán	37,105
Caguas	140,502	Juana Díaz	50,531	San Juan	434,374
Camuy	35,244	Juncos	36,452	San Lorenzo	40,997
Canóvanas	43,335	Lajas	26,261	San Sebastián	44,204
Carolina	186,076	Lares	34,415	Santa Isabel	21,665
Cataño	30,071	Las Marías	11,061	Toa Alta	63,929
Cayey	47,370	Las Piedras	34,485	Toa Baja	94,085
Ceiba	18,004	Loíza	32,537	Trujillo Alto	75,728
Ciales	19,811	Luquillo	19,817	Utuado	35,336
Cidra	42,753	Manatí	45,409	Vega Alta	37,910
Coamo	37,597	Maricao	6,449	Vega Baja	61,929
Comerío	20,002	Maunabo	12,741	Vieques	9,106
Corozal	36,867	Mayagüez	98,434	Villalba	27,913
Culebra	1,868	Moca	39,697	Yabucoa	39,246
Dorado	34,017	Morovis	29,965	Yauco	46,384
				TOTAL	3,808,610

Demography

Area: 3,515 sq mi, 9,104 sq km.
Population (2002): 3,856,000.
Density (2002): persons per sq mi 1,097.0, persons per sq km 423.5.
Urban-rural (2001): urban 75.6%; rural 24.4%.
Sex distribution (2000): male 48.14%; female 51.86%.
Age breakdown (2000): under 15, 23.8%; 15–34, 30.1%; 35–54, 25.7%; 55–64, 9.2%; 65 and over, 11.2%.
Population projection: (2010) 3,987,000; (2020) 4,092,000.
Doubling time: 90 years.
Ethnic composition (2000): local white 72.1%; black 15.0%; mulatto 10.0%; U.S. white 2.2%; other 0.7%.
Religious affiliation (1995): Roman Catholic 64.8%; Protestant 28.7%; other 6.5%.
Major urban agglomerations (1998): San Juan 2,004,054; Ponce 366,273; Caguas 315,921; Mayagüez 258,283; Arecibo 176,814.

Vital statistics

Birth rate per 1,000 population (2001): 15.4 (world avg. 21.2).
Death rate per 1,000 population (2001): 7.6 (world avg. 8.9).
Natural increase rate per 1,000 population (2001): 7.8 (world avg. 12.3).
Total fertility rate (avg. births per childbearing woman; 2000): 2.0.
Marriage rate per 1,000 population (1996): 8.7.
Life expectancy at birth (2001): male 72.9 years; female 81.1 years.
Major causes of death per 100,000 population (1993): heart disease 142.6; cancers 95.4; diabetes 55.1; cerebrovascular disease 38.0; pneumonia and influenza 29.2.

National economy

Budget. Revenue (1997–98): U.S.$8,784,000,000 (tax revenue 68.3%, of which income taxes 45.5%, excise taxes 15.5%, intergovernment transfers 31.7%). Expenditures (1997–98): U.S.$6,263,000,000 (welfare 25.6%; education 20.3%; debt service 9.0%; public safety and protection 8.7%; health 3.5%).
Public debt (outstanding; 1999): U.S.$22,678,200,000.
Tourism (2000): receipts U.S.$2,388,000,000; expenditures U.S.$931,000,000.
Production (in metric tons except as noted). Agriculture, forestry, fishing (1999): sugarcane 307,358, plantains 76,140, bananas 38,215, pineapples 19,204, mangoes 17,245, oranges 16,057, pumpkins, squash, and gourds 16,-329, coffee 11,567; livestock (number of live animals) 388,307 cattle, 174,748 pigs; roundwood, n.a.; fish catch (1997) 2,744 metric tons. Mining (value of production in U.S.$'000; 1999): crushed stone 57. Manufacturing (value added in U.S.$'000,000; 1997): chemicals, pharmaceuticals, and allied products 21,393; food 3,532; machinery and metal products 2,940; petroleum products 849; clothing 679. Energy production (consumption): electricity (kW-hr; 1996) 19,029,000,000 ([2001] 20,500,000,000); coal (metric tons; 2001) none (172,000); crude petroleum (barrels; 2001) none (58,400,000); petroleum products (metric tons; 1996) 5,877,000 (6,743,000); natural gas, none (none).

Gross national product (2001): U.S.$45,300,000,000 (U.S.$11,783 per capita).

Structure of gross domestic product and labour force

| | 1997–98 | | 1997 | |
	in value U.S.$'000,000	% of total value	labour force	% of labour force
Agriculture	402.2	0.7	31,000	2.4
Manufacturing	23,015.6	42.8	162,000	12.5
Mining }	1,323.3	2.5	1,000	0.1
Construction }			64,000	4.9
Public utilities }	4,068.9	7.6	15,000	1.1
Transp. and commun. }			44,000	3.4
Trade	6,989.7	13.0	228,000	17.6
Finance, real estate	6,898.4	12.8	37,000	2.9
Pub. admin., defense	5,246.0	9.7	261,000	20.1
Services	5,758.0	10.7	285,000	22.0
Other	123.3[2]	0.2[2]	170,000[3]	13.1[3]
TOTAL	53,825.4	100.0	1,298,000	100.0[4]

Population economically active (1997): total 1,298,000; activity rate 34.1% (participation rates: ages 16 and over, 48.0%; female 39.5%; unemployed 13.1%).

Price and earnings indexes (1995 = 100)

	1993	1994	1995	1996	1997	1998	1999
Consumer price index	93.5	96.2	100.0	105.1	110.8	117.0	123.2
Hourly earnings index[5]	...	...	...	...	...	...	...

Household income and expenditure (1999). Average family size (2000) 3.0; income per family U.S.$32,892; sources of income: wages and salaries 60.6%, transfers 31.3%, rent 6.5%, self-employment 6.1%; expenditure: food and beverages 18.8%, health care 17.8%, transportation 12.8%, housing 12.1%, household furnishings 11.6%, clothing 7.9%, recreation 7.7%.

Foreign trade

Balance of trade (current prices)

	1994	1995	1996	1997	1998	1999
U.S.$'000,000	+5,098	+4,995	+3,884	+2,559	+6,107	+9,602
% of total	13.3%	11.7%	9.2%	5.6%	10.1%	16.0%

Imports (1997–98): U.S.$27,308,700,000 (chemicals [all forms] 26.8%, electrical machinery 11.8%, food 10.2%, transport equipment 9.6%, petroleum and petroleum products 7.2%, nonelectrical machinery 6.8%, professional and scientific instruments 4.2%, clothing and textiles 4.2%). *Major import sources* (1995–96): U.S. 62.5%; Japan 6.4%; Dominican Republic 4.0%; U.K. 2.9%. *Exports* (1997–98): U.S.$33,416,400,000 (chemicals and chemical products 43.6%, nonelectrical machinery 13.2%, food 12.1%, electrical machinery 7.7%). *Major export destinations:* U.S. 88.5%; other 11.5%.

Transport and communications

Transport. Railroads (1988)[6]: length 59 mi, 96 km. Roads (1996): total length 8,948 mi, 14,400 km (paved 100%). Vehicles (1996): passenger cars 878,000; trucks and buses 190,000. Merchant marine: n.a. Air transport (1998): passenger arrivals and departures 9,285,000; cargo loaded and unloaded 275,500 metric tons[7]; airports (1998) with scheduled flights 7.

Communications

Medium	date	unit	number	units per 1,000 persons
Daily newspapers	1996	circulation	475,000	128
Radio	1997	receivers	2,700,000	724
Television	1998	receivers	1,250,000	333
Telephones	2001	main lines	1,330,000	336
Cellular telephones	2001	subscribers	1,211,000	307
Internet	2001	users	600,000	152

Education and health

Educational attainment (2000). Percentage of population age 25 and over having: no formal schooling to secondary education 25.4%; some upper secondary to some higher 60.0%; undergraduate or graduate degree 18.3%. *Literacy* (1995): total population age 15 and over literate 92.8%; males literate 92.7%; females literate 92.8%.

Education (1985–86)

	schools	teachers	students	student/ teacher ratio
Primary (age 5–12)	1,542	18,359	427,582	23.3
Secondary (age 13–18)	395	13,612	334,661	24.6
Voc., teacher tr.	52	...	149,191	...
Higher	45	9,045	156,818	17.3

Health: physicians (1992) 6,269 (1 per 575 persons); hospital beds (1993–94) 9,598 (1 per 381 persons); infant mortality rate (2001) 9.8.

Military

Total active duty personnel (2001): 2,840 U.S. personnel.

[1]Number of members per constitution. Excludes additional seats allotted to either the Senate or House of Representatives to meet 1/3 total representation requirements for minority parties per constitution. [2]Statistical discrepancy. [3]Unemployed. [4]Detail does not add to total given because of rounding. [5]Manufacturing sector only. [6]Privately owned railway for sugarcane transport only. [7]Handled by the Luis Muñoz Marín International Airport only.

Internet resources for further information:
• Estado Libre Asociado de Puerto Rico http://www.presupuesto.prstar.net
• Junta de Plantificacion http://www.jp.gobierno.pr

Qatar

Official name: Dawlat Qaṭar (State of Qatar).
Form of government: monarchy (emirate)[1]; Islamic law is the basis of legislation in the state.
Heads of state and government: Emir assisted by Prime Minister.
Capital: Doha.
Official language: Arabic.
Official religion: Islam.
Monetary unit: 1 riyal (QR) = 100 dirhams; valuation (Sept. 23, 2002) 1 U.S.$ = QR 3.64; 1 £ = QR 5.66.

Area and population

Municipalities	Capitals	area sq mi	area sq km	population 1997 census
Ad-Dawḥah (Doha)	—	51	132	264,009
Al-Ghuwayrīyah	Al-Ghuwayrīyah	240	622	1,716
Jarayān al-Bāṭinah	Jarayān al-Bāṭinah	1,434	3,715	4,742
Al-Jumaylīyah	Al-Jumaylīyah	991[2]	2,565[2]	9,836
Al-Khawr	Al-Khawr	385	996	17,793
Ar-Rayyān	Ar-Rayyān	343	889	169,774
Ash-Shamāl	Madinat ash-Shamāl	348	901	4,059
Umm Ṣalāl	Umm Ṣalāl Muḥammad	190	493	18,392
Al-Wakrah	Al-Wakrah	430	1,114	31,702
TOTAL		4,412[3]	11,427[3]	522,023

Demography

Population (2002): 606,000.
Density (2001): persons per sq mi 137.4, persons per sq km 53.0.
Urban-rural (2001): urban 92.9%; rural 7.1%.
Sex distribution (2000): male 65.9%; female 34.1%.
Age breakdown (2000): under 15, 26.3%; 15–29, 22.6%; 30–44, 27.1%; 45–59, 19.4%; 60–74, 4.1%; 75 and over, 0.5%.
Population projection: (2010) 679,000; (2020) 756,000.
Doubling time: 59 years.
Ethnic composition (2000): Arab 52.5%, of which Palestinian 13.4%, Qatari 13.3%, Lebanese 10.4%, Syrian 9.4%; Persian 16.5%; Indo-Pakistani 15.2%; black African 9.5%; other 6.3%.
Religious affiliation (2000): Muslim (mostly Sunnī) 82.7%; Christian 10.4%; Hindu 2.5%; other 4.4%.
Major cities (1997): Ad-Dawḥah (Doha) 264,009 (urban agglomeration [1999] 391,000); Ar-Rayyān 161,453; Al-Wakrah 20,205; Umm Ṣalāl 15,935.

Vital statistics

Birth rate per 1,000 population (2000): 16.1 (world avg. 22.5).
Death rate per 1,000 population (2000): 4.2 (world avg. 9.0).
Natural increase rate per 1,000 population (2000): 11.9 (world avg. 13.5).
Total fertility rate (avg. births per childbearing woman; 2000): 3.3.
Marriage rate per 1,000 population (1994): 2.8.
Divorce rate per 1,000 population (1994): 1.0.
Life expectancy at birth (2000): male 69.9 years; female 74.9 years.
Major causes of death per 100,000 population (1992): diseases of the circulatory system 56.9; injuries and poisoning 36.0; neoplasms (including benign neoplasms) 21.4; certain conditions originating in the perinatal period 11.1; diseases of the respiratory system 7.5; endocrine, metabolic, and nutritional diseases and immunity disorders 7.3; diseases of the digestive system 3.4; signs, symptoms, and ill-defined conditions 10.9.

National economy

Budget (1999–2000). Revenue: QR 14,098,000,000 (crude oil about 90%). Expenditures: QR 14,353,000,000 (current expenditure 91.7%, of which wages and salaries 37.5%; capital expenditure 8.3%).
Production (metric tons except as noted). Agriculture, forestry, fishing (2000): dates 16,500, tomatoes 11,000, pumpkin and squash 8,500, barley 4,650, dry onions 4,000, melons 3,450, watermelons 1,400; livestock (number of live animals; 2000) 215,000 sheep, 179,000 goats, 50,000 camels, 14,200 cattle; fish catch (1999) 4,207. Mining and quarrying (1996): limestone 900,000; sulfur 61,000; gypsum, sand and gravel, and clay are also produced. Manufacturing (value added in QR '000,000; 1998): industrial chemicals 516; fertilizers and pesticides 474; iron and steel 459; wearing apparel 235; pottery, china, and earthenware 194; cement and plaster 157; refined petroleum 112. Construction (1992): residential 12,420 units; nonresidential 1,416 units. Energy production (consumption): electricity (kW-hr; 1997) 6,868,-000,000 (6,868,000,000); coal, none (n.a.); crude petroleum (barrels; 2001) 243,788,000 ([1997] 22,500,000); petroleum products (metric tons; 1997) 5,367,000 (873,000); natural gas (cu m; 1997) 17,900,000,000 (17,900,000,000).
Tourism (1997): receipts and expenditures, n.a.; total number of tourists staying in hotels 435,000.
Population economically active (1997): total 280,122; activity rate of total population 53.7% (participation rates: ages 15–64, 59.7%; female 21.0%; unemployed, n.a.).

Price and earnings indexes (1995 = 100)

	1996	1997	1998	1999	2000	2001
Consumer price index	107.4	110.4	113.3	115.7	117.7	119.3
Earnings index	...	...	...	...	...	...

Gross national product (1998): U.S.$6,473,000,000 (U.S.$11,600 per capita).

Structure of gross domestic product and labour force

	2000 in value QR '000,000	2000 % of total value	1988 labour force	1988 % of labour force
Agriculture	290	0.7	4,544	1.6
Oil sector	27,200	51.6	7,657	2.6
Manufacturing	3,745	7.1	10,627	3.6
Construction	2,180	4.1	64,213	21.9
Public utilities	635	1.2	3,672	1.3
Transportation	2,080	3.9	11,877	4.1
Trade	3,350	6.4	34,246	11.7
Finance	4,710	8.9	6,172	2.1
Pub. admin., defense				
Services	8,490	16.1	149,560	51.1
Other				
TOTAL	52,680	100.0	292,568	100.0

Household income and expenditure. Average household size (1998) 7.0; income per household: n.a.; sources of income (1988): wages and salaries 80.8%, rents and royalties 10.6%, self-employment 5.6%, other 3.0%; expenditure (1993): food 28.7%, transportation 19.3%, housing 12.4%, clothing 10.6%, education 7.6%, health 1.2%.
Land use (1994): meadows and pastures 4.5%; agricultural and under permanent cultivation 0.7%; built-up, desert, and other 94.7%.

Foreign trade

Balance of trade (current prices)[4]

	1996	1997	1998	1999	2000	2001
QR '000,000	+4,546	+3,143	+7,134	+18,062	+31,538	+27,243
% of total	19.5%	12.6%	24.2%	52.4%	59.7%	52.5%

Imports (1999): QR 9,098,400,000 (machinery and transport equipment 34.6%, manufactured goods 19.0%, food and live animals 13.2%, chemicals and chemical products 8.2%, raw materials 3.1%). *Major import sources* (1999): United Kingdom 11.5%; United States 11.4%; Japan 10.3%; U.A.E. 8.0%; Saudi Arabia 7.1%; Germany 6.1%; France 4.9%; Italy 4.9%.
Exports (1999): QR 26,258,000,000 (1994; mineral fuels and lubricants 81.2%, chemicals and chemical products 10.4%, manufactured goods 5.9%). *Major export destinations* (1999): Japan 51.0%; South Korea 12.9%; Singapore 9.1%; U.S. 4.3%; Thailand 3.4%; U.A.E. 2.3%; India 1.1%.

Transport and communications

Transport. Railroads: none. Roads (1996): total length 764 mi, 1,230 km (paved 90%). Vehicles (1996): passenger cars 126,000; trucks and buses 64,000. Merchant marine (1998): vessels (100 gross tons and over) 64; total deadweight tonnage 744,181. Air transport (1999)[5]: passenger-mi 1,775,583,000, passenger-km 2,857,529,000; short ton-mi cargo 54,700,000, metric ton-km cargo 104,947,000; airports (1999) with scheduled flights 1.

Communications

Medium	date	unit	number	units per 1,000 persons
Daily newspapers	1995	circulation	90,000	161
Radio	1997	receivers	250,000	432
Television	1998	receivers	490,000	846
Telephones	2001	main lines	167,400	275
Cellular telephones	2001	subscribers	178,800	293
Personal computers	2001	units	100,000	163.9
Internet	2001	users	2,000,000	25.9

Education and health

Educational attainment (1986). Percentage of population age 25 and over having: no formal education 53.3%, of which illiterate 24.3%; primary 9.8%; preparatory (lower secondary) 10.1%; secondary 13.3%; postsecondary 13.3%; other 0.2%. *Literacy* (1995): total population age 15 and over literate 460,000 (79.4%); males literate 298,000 (79.2%); females literate 122,000 (79.9%).

Education (1995–96)[6]

	schools	teachers	students	student/ teacher ratio
Primary (age 6–11)	174	5,864	53,631	9.1
Secondary (age 12–17)	123	3,738	37,924	10.1
Vocational[7]	3	120	670	5.6
Higher[8]	1	643	8,475	13.2

Health: physicians (1996) 703 (1 per 793 persons); hospital beds (1995) 892 (1 per 555 persons); infant mortality rate per 1,000 live births (2000) 22.1.

Military

Total active duty personnel (2001): 12,330 (army 68.9%, navy 14.0%, air force 17.1%); U.S. troops (2002) 3,300. *Military expenditure as percentage of GNP* (1999): 10.0% (world 2.4%); per capita expenditure U.S.$1,470.

---

[1]Provisional constitution of 1970 provided limited constitutional forms but has not been fully implemented. [2]Includes the area of the unpopulated and formerly disputed (with Bahrain) Hawar Islands. The International Court of Justice awarded Hawar to Bahrain in early 2001. Qatar was awarded jurisdiction over some nearby islets. [3]Includes approximately 4 sq mi (10 sq km) of area not distributed by municipalities. [4]Imports f.o.b. in balance of trade and c.i.f. in commodities and trading partners. [5]Qatar Airways. [6]Public schools only; available detail for private schools (1991–92) included 17,728 primary students, 1,695 secondary students, and 1,465 teachers. [7]1994–95. [8]1996–97.

Internet resources for further information:
• **Qatar Ministry of Foreign Affairs** http://www.mofa.gov.qa
• **Qatar Central Bank** http://www.qcb.gov.qa

Réunion

Indian Ocean

Official name: Département de la Réunion (Department of Réunion).
Political status: overseas department (France) with two legislative houses (General Council [47]; Regional Council [45]).
Chief of state: President of France.
Heads of government: Prefect (for France); President of General Council (for Réunion); President of Regional Council (for Réunion).
Capital: Saint-Denis.
Official language: French.
Official religion: none.
Monetary unit: 1 euro (€) = 100 cents; valuation (Sept. 23, 2002) 1 U.S.$ = €1.02; 1 £ = €1.58[1].

Area and population

Arrondissements	Capitals	area sq mi	area sq km	population 1999 census
Saint-Benoît	Saint-Benoît	285	737	101,804
Saint-Denis	Saint-Denis	163	421	236,599
Saint-Paul	Saint-Paul	180	467	138,551
Saint-Pierre	Saint-Pierre	341	883	229,346
TOTAL		968[2, 3]	2,507[2, 3]	706,300

Demography

Population (2002): 743,000.
Density (2002): persons per sq mi 767.6, persons per sq km 296.4.
Urban-rural (1999): urban 71.6%; rural 28.4%[4].
Sex distribution (1999): male 49.15%; female 50.85%.
Age breakdown (1999): under 15, 27.0%; 15–29, 24.8%; 30–44, 24.4%; 45–59, 13.8%; 60–74, 7.2%; 75 and over, 2.8%.
Population projection: (2010) 812,000; (2020) 888,000.
Doubling time: 49 years.
Ethnic composition (2000): mixed race (black-white-South Asian) 42.6%; local white 25.6%; South Asian 23.0%, of which Tamil 20.0%; Chinese 3.4%; East African 3.4%; Malagasy 1.4%; other 0.6%.
Religious affiliation (1995): Roman Catholic 89.4%; Pentecostal 2.7%; other Christian 1.8%; other (mostly Muslim) 6.1%.
Major cities (1999): Saint-Denis 131,557[5] (agglomeration 158,139); Saint-Paul 87,712[5]; Saint-Pierre 68,915[5] (agglomeration 129,238); Le Tampon 60,323[5, 6]; Saint-Louis 43,519[5].

Vital statistics

Birth rate per 1,000 population (1999): 19.9 (world avg. 22.5); (1997) legitimate 41.5%; illegitimate 58.5%.
Death rate per 1,000 population (1999): 5.4 (world avg. 9.0).
Natural increase rate per 1,000 population (1999): 14.5 (world avg. 13.5).
Total fertility rate (avg. births per childbearing woman; 1997): 2.2.
Marriage rate per 1,000 population (1998): 4.8.
Divorce rate per 1,000 population (1997): 1.3.
Life expectancy at birth (2000): male 70.6 years; female 78.7 years.
Major causes of death per 100,000 population (1996): diseases of the circulatory system 170.7; malignant neoplasms (cancers) 98.0; accidents, suicide, and violence 53.0; diseases of the respiratory system 48.5.

National economy

Budget (1998). Revenue: F 4,624,000,000 (receipts from the French central government and local administrative bodies 52.7%, tax receipts 20.2%, loans 8.9%). Expenditures: F 4,300,000,000 (current expenditures 68.7%, development expenditures 31.3%).
Public debt (external, outstanding): n.a.
Tourism (2000): receipts U.S.$254,000,000; expenditures, n.a.
Gross national product (at current market prices; 1998): U.S.$5,070,000,000 (U.S.$7,270 per capita).

Structure of gross domestic product and labour force

	1995 in value F '000,000	1995 % of total value	1999 labour force	1999 % of labour force
Agriculture, fishing	1,392	3.6	9,562	3.2
Manufacturing, mining	3,101	8.0	13,424	4.5
Public utilities	1,761	4.5		
Construction			11,003	3.7
Transp. and commun.	1,753	4.5	5,494	1.8
Trade, restaurants	6,140	15.8	24,658	8.2
Finance, real estate, business services	9,823	25.4	16,076	5.4
Pub. admin., defense	16,524	42.7	40,019	13.4
Services			54,408	18.2
Other	−1,760[7]	−4.5[7]	124,203[8]	41.6[8]
TOTAL	38,734	100.0	298,847	100.0

Production (metric tons except as noted). Agriculture, forestry, fishing (1999): sugarcane 1,800,000, corn (maize) 17,000, cabbages 14,000, pineapples 13,000, tomatoes 11,500, bananas 10,000, pimento 430, ginger 95, vanilla 30, tobacco 20, geranium essence (1998) 6.3; livestock (number of live animals) 89,000 pigs, 38,000 goats, 27,000 cattle; roundwood (2000) 36,100 cu m; fish catch (2000) 5,091. Mining and quarrying: gravel and sand for local use.

Manufacturing (value added in F '000,000; 1997): food and beverages 1,019, of which meat and milk products 268; construction materials (mostly cement) 394; fabricated metals 258; printing and publishing 192. Energy production (consumption): electricity (kW-hr; 2000) 1,757,000,000 ([1997] 1,133,000,000); coal, none (none); crude petroleum, none (none); petroleum products (metric tons; 1997) none (511,000); natural gas, none (none).
Population economically active (1998): total 288,760; activity rate of total population 41.2% (participation rates: ages 15–64, 57.5%; female 44.3%; unemployed [2000] 36.5%).

Price and earnings indexes (December 1997 = 100)[9]

	1996	1997	1998	1999	2000	2001	2002
Consumer price index	98.6	100.0	100.9	101.9	104.1	106.2	108.8[10]
Monthly earnings index[11]	98.9	100.0	101.4	102.8	103.4	108.5	109.1[10]

Household income and expenditure. Average household size (1999) 3.3; average annual income per household (1997) F 136,800 (U.S.$23,438); sources of income (1997): wages and salaries and self-employment 41.8%, transfer payments 41.3%, other 16.9%; expenditure (1994–95): food and beverages 22.0%, transportation and communications 19.0%, housing and energy 10.0%, household furnishings 8.0%, recreation 6.0%.
Land use (1994): forested 35.2%; meadows and pastures 4.8%; agricultural and under permanent cultivation 19.6%; other 40.4%.

Foreign trade

Balance of trade (current prices)

	1996	1997	1998	1999	2000[12]	2001[12]
F '000,000	−13,180	−13,011	−14,095	−12,937	−2,494	−2,556
% of total	86.0%	83.9%	85.3%	85.3%	85.2%	84.8%

Imports (1998): F 15,310,000,000 (food and agricultural products 17.1%, transport equipment 14.7%, machinery and apparatus 13.4%, clothing and footwear 6.8%). *Major import sources:* France 66.0%; EC 14.0%.
Exports (1998): F 1,215,000,000 (sugar 58.9%, machinery, apparatus, and transport equipment 17.5%, rum 2.5%, lobster 1.7%). *Major export destinations:* France 70.0%; EC 9.0%; Madagascar 4.5%; Mauritius 2.3%.

Transport and communications

Transport. Railroads: [13]. Roads (1994): total length 1,711 mi, 2,754 km (paved [1991] 79%). Vehicles (1999): passenger cars 190,300; trucks and buses 44,300. Air transport (2000)[14]: passenger arrivals 736,499, passenger departures 730,980; cargo unloaded 17,206 metric tons, cargo loaded 8,934 metric tons; airports (1999) with scheduled flights 2.

Communications

Medium	date	unit	number	units per 1,000 persons
Daily newspapers	1996	circulation	83,000	123
Radio	1997	receivers	173,000	252
Television	1997	receivers	127,000	185
Telephones	1999	main lines	268,496	378
Cellular telephones	1998	subscribers	50,300	72

Education and health

Educational attainment (1986–87). Percentage of population age 25 and over having: no formal schooling 18.8%; primary education 44.3%; lower secondary 21.6%; upper secondary 11.0%; higher 4.3%. *Literacy* (1996): total population age 16–66 literate 373,487 (91.3%); males literate 179,154 (89.9%); females literate 194,333 (92.7%).

Education (1997–98)

	schools	teachers	students	student/teacher ratio
Primary (age 6–10)	351	...	76,364	...
Secondary (age 11–17)	111	...	96,811	...
Higher[15]	1	286	9,103	31.8

Health (2000): physicians 1,595 (1 per 449 persons); hospital beds (2000) 2,124 (1 per 337 persons); infant mortality rate per 1,000 live births (1999) 6.0.
Food (1999): daily per capita caloric intake, n.a.

Military

Total active duty personnel (2001): 4,200 French troops[16].

---

[1]The French franc was the former monetary unit; on Jan. 1, 2002, F 6.56 = €1. [2]Detail does not add to total given because of rounding. [3]Indian Ocean islets administered by France from Réunion are excluded from total. Islets between Africa and Réunion, which have no permanent population, are: Îles Glorieuses 1.9 sq mi (5.0 sq km), Île Juan de Nova 1.7 sq mi (4.4 sq km), Île Tromelin 0.4 sq mi (1.0 sq km), Bassas da India 0.1 sq mi (0.2 sq km), Île Europa 7.8 sq mi (20.2 sq km). The French overseas territory of French Southern and Antarctic Territories has been administered from Réunion since April 2000. It comprises 2 archipelagos and 2 islands in the South Indian Ocean as well as the French-claimed part of Antarctica. Non-Antarctic scientific pop. in summer (2000) 172; non-Antarctic area 4,844 sq mi (7,796 sq km). [4]Includes semi-urban. [5]Population of commune. [6]Within Saint-Pierre agglomeration. [7]Less imputed bank service charges. [8]Unemployed. [9]Indexes refer to December. [10]September. [11]Minimum salary in public administration. [12]In €'000,000. [13]No public railways; railways in use are for sugar industry. [14]Saint-Denis airport only. [15]University only. [16]Includes troops stationed on Mayotte.

Internet resources for further information:
• INSEE: Réunion
  http://www.insee.fr/fr/insee_regions/reunion/home/home_page.asp
• Ministère de l'Outre-mer (Paris)
  http://www.outre-mer.gouv.fr

Romania

Official name: România (Romania).
Form of government: unitary republic with two legislative houses (Senate [143]; Assembly of Deputies [345[1]]).
Chief of state: President.
Head of government: Prime Minister.
Capital: Bucharest.
Official language: Romanian.
Official religion: none.
Monetary unit: 1 Romanian leu (plural lei) = 100 bani; valuation (Sept. 23, 2002) 1 U.S.$ = 33,335 lei; 1 £ = 51,806 lei.

Area and population

	area	population		area	population
Countries	sq km	2002 census[2]	**Countries**	sq km	2002 census[2]
Alba	6,231	382,999	Iaşi	5,469	819,044
Arad	7,652	461,730	Ilfov	1,593	300,109
Argeş	6,801	653,903	Maramureş	6,215	510,688
Bacău	6,606	708,751	Mehedinţi	4,900	306,118
Bihor	7,535	600,223	Mureş	6,696	579,862
Bistriţa-Năsăud	5,305	312,325	Neamţ	5,890	557,084
Botoşani	4,965	454,023	Olt	5,507	490,276
Brăila	4,724	588,366	Prahova	4,694	829,224
Braşov	5,351	373,897	Sălaj	3,850	248,407
Buzău	6,072	494,982	Satu Mare	4,405	369,096
Călăraşi	5,074	324,629	Sibiu	5,422	422,224
Caraş-Severin	8,503	333,396	Suceava	8,555	690,941
Cluj	6,650	703,269	Teleorman	5,760	436,926
Constanţa	7,055	715,172	Timiş	8,692	677,744
Covasna	3,705	222,274	Tulcea	8,430	258,639
Dâmboviţa	4,036	541,326	Vâlcea	5,705	413,570
Dolj	7,413	734,823	Vaslui	5,297	455,550
Galaţi	4,425	619,522	Vrancea	4,863	390,268
Giurgiu	3,511	298,022	**Municipality**		
Gorj	5,641	387,407	Bucharest	227	1,921,751
Harghita	6,610	326,020	TOTAL	237,500	21,698,181
Hunedoara	7,016	487,115			
Ialomiţa	4,449	296,486			

Demography

Population (2002): 21,667,000.
Density (2002): persons per sq mi 236.3, persons per sq km 91.2.
Urban-rural (2002): urban 52.7%; rural 47.3%.
Sex distribution (2002): male 48.77%; female 51.23%.
Age breakdown (2000): under 15, 18.4%; 15–29, 24.1%; 30–44, 21.0%; 45–59, 17.7%; 60–74, 14.3%; 75 and over, 4.5%.
Population projection: (2010) 21,290,000; (2020) 20,647,000.
Ethnic composition (2002): Romanian 89.5%; Hungarian 6.6%; Roma (Gypsy) 2.5%; other 1.4%.
Religious affiliation (2002): Romanian Orthodox 86.7%; Protestant 6.4%; Roman Catholic 4.7%; Greek Orthodox 0.9%; Muslim 0.3%; other 1.0%.
Major cities (1997): Bucharest 2,027,512; Iaşi 348,399; Constanţa 344,876; Timişoara 334,098; Cluj-Napoca 332,792; Galaţi 331,360.

Vital statistics

Birth rate per 1,000 population (2000): 10.8 (world avg. 22.5).
Death rate per 1,000 population (2000): 12.3 (world avg. 9.0).
Natural increase rate per 1,000 population (2000): –1.7 (world avg. 13.5).
Total fertility rate (avg. births per childbearing woman; 2000): 1.4.
Marriage rate per 1,000 population (1995): 6.8.
Life expectancy at birth (2000): male 66.1 years; female 74.0 years.
Major causes of death per 100,000 population (1998): circulatory disease 738.6; cancers 173.4; diseases of the digestive system 71.6; respiratory disease 71.0.

National economy

Budget ('000,000,000,000 lei; 1996). Revenue: 76.7 (social security 23.0%, personal income tax 18.2%, value-added tax 15.2%). Expenditures: 85.6 (social security 28.2%, debt service 10.0%, education 9.6%, health 7.5%).
Public debt (external, outstanding; 2000): U.S.$6,430,000,000.
Population economically active (1998): total 11,577,300; activity rate 51.4% (participation rates: ages 15–64, 67.2%[3]; female 42.8%; unemployed 6.3%).

Price and earnings indexes (1995 = 100)

	1995	1996	1997	1998	1999	2000	2001
Consumer price index	100.0	138.8	353.7	562.7	820.4	1,195.1	1,607.0
Annual earnings index	100.0	149.0	295.0	502.9	719.6	1,006.0	1,413.3

Household income and expenditure. Average household size (1992) 3.1; income per household (1989) 73,500 lei (U.S.$4,940); sources of income (1982): wages 62.6%; expenditure (1989): food 51.1%, housing 16.4%.
Production (metric tons). Agriculture (2000): wheat 4,320,000, corn (maize) 4,200,000, potatoes 3,650,000, sugar beets 1,500,000, grapes 1,250,000; livestock (number of live animals) 7,972,000 sheep, 5,951,000 pigs, 3,154,000 cattle; roundwood (1998) 11,515,000 cu m; fish catch (1998) 9,020. Mining (2000): iron (metal content) 55,000; bauxite 135,000; zinc (metal content of concentrate) 27,455; lead (metal content of concentrate) 18,744; copper (metal content of concentrate) 16,079. Manufacturing (value-added in '000,000,000,000 lei; 1996): food products 5.8; beverages 3.0; iron and steel 1.6; glass products 1.5; textiles 1.4; motor vehicles 1.3; electrical machinery 0.9. Construction (1995): 9,300 dwelling units. Energy production (consumption): electricity (kW-hr; 2001)

53,640,000,000 ([1997] 57,369,000,000); hard coal (metric tons; 2000) 3,240,000 ([1997] 6,637,000); lignite (metric tons; 2001) 29,431,000 ([1997] 31,504,000); crude petroleum (barrels; 2001) 45,164,000 ([1997] 91,427,000); petroleum products (metric tons; 1997) 10,520,000 (10,941,000); natural gas (cu m; 2001) 12,172,000,000 ([1997] 16,744,000,000).
Gross national product (2000): U.S.$37,380,000,000 (U.S.$1,670 per capita).

Structure of gross domestic product and labour force

	1998			
	in value '000,000,000 lei	% of total value	labour force	% of labour force
Agriculture	20,662.0	19.1	4,342,200	37.5
Industry[4]	37,054.4	34.2	2,750,600	23.8
Construction	7,468.8	6.9	433,500	3.7
Transp. and commun.	9,374.3	8.6	529,400	4.6
Trade	10,907.5	10.1	1,068,000	9.2
Finance			81,800	0.7
Pub. admin. } Services }	18,011.1	16.6	} 1,639,500	14.2
Other	4,912.8	4.5	732,400[5]	6.3[5]
TOTAL	108,390.5[6]	100.0	11,577,300[6]	100.0

Tourism (2000): receipts U.S.$359,000,000; expenditures U.S.$420,000,000.

Foreign trade[7]

Balance of trade (current prices)

	1996	1997	1998	1999	2000	2001
U.S.$'000,000	–2,470.5	–1,980.3	–2,611.4	–1,087.4	–1,683.1	–2,972.9
% of total	13.2%	10.5%	13.6%	6.0%	7.5%	11.5%

Imports (1999): U.S.$10,395,300,000 (textile yarn, fabrics, and made-up articles 30.7%; chemicals and chemical products 10.6%; mineral fuels 10.1%; electrical machinery and apparatus 6.9%; food 5.8%). *Major import sources:* Italy 19.7%; Germany 17.1%; Russia 6.8%; France 6.7%; United Kingdom 4.2%.
Exports (1999): U.S.$8,503,000,000 (clothing and apparel 24.0%; iron and steel 8.6%; footwear 5.0%; chemicals and chemical products 4.9%; sawn wood 3.8%; refined petroleum 3.8%). *Major export destinations:* Italy 23.4%; Germany 17.8%; France 6.2%; Turkey 5.5%; U.K. 4.9%.

Transport and communications

Transport. Railroads (1997): length 11,365 km[8]; passenger-km 15,794,000,000; metric ton-km cargo 24,789,000,000. Roads (1996): length 153,358 km (paved 51%). Vehicles (1997): cars 2,605,565; trucks and buses 427,579. Air transport (1998): passenger-km 1,712,300,000; metric ton-km cargo 12,110,000; airports (1997) 8.

Communications

Medium	date	unit	number	units per 1,000 persons
Daily newspapers	1996	circulation	6,800,000	297
Radio	1997	receivers	7,200,000	319
Television	1999	receivers	7,000,000	312
Telephones	2001	main lines	4,094,000	183
Cellular telephones	2001	subscribers	3,860,000	172
Personal computers	2001	units	800,000	36
Internet	2001	users	1,000,000	45

Education and health

Educational attainment (1992). Percentage of population age 25 and over having: no schooling 5.4%; some primary education 24.4%; some secondary 63.2%; postsecondary 6.9%. *Literacy* (2000): total population age 15 and over literate 98.2%; males 99.1%; females 97.3%.

Education (1996–97)

	schools	teachers	students	student/ teacher ratio
Primary (age 6–9)	13,978	175,426	2,546,231	14.5
Secondary (age 10–17)	1,295	64,485	792,788	12.3
Voc., teacher tr.	1,692	10,942	351,900	32.2
Higher	102	23,447	354,488	15.1

Health: physicians (1998) 40,658 (1 per 543 persons); hospital beds (1992) 174,900 (1 per 130 persons); infant mortality rate (2002) 18.9.
Food (2000): daily per capita caloric intake 3,274 (vegetable products 79%, animal products 21%); 124% of FAO recommended minimum requirement.

Military

Total active duty personnel (2001): 103,000 (army 51.4%, navy 9.9%, air force 18.3%, other 20.4%). *Military expenditure as percentage of GNP* (2001): 1.6% (world 2.4%); per capita expenditure U.S.$97.

---

[1]Includes 18 nonelective seats. [2]Preliminary. [3]1992. [4]Mining, manufacturing, and public utilities. [5]Unemployed. [6]Detail does not add to total given because of rounding. [7]Imports f.o.b. in balance of trade and c.i.f. in commodities and trading partners. [8]1994.

Internet resources for further information:
• **Embassy of Romania (Washington, D.C.) http://www.roembus.org**
• **National Institute of Statistics http://www.insse.ro/NIS.htm**

Russia

Official name: Rossiyskaya Federatsiya (Russian Federation).
Form of government: federal multiparty republic with a bicameral legislative body (Federal Assembly comprising a Federation Council [178] and a State Duma [450]).
Head of state: President.
Head of government: Prime Minister.
Capital: Moscow.
Official language: Russian.
Official religion: none.
Monetary unit: 1 ruble (Rub) = 100 kopecks; valuation (Sept. 23, 2002) market rate, 1 U.S.$ = Rub 31.67; 1 £ = Rub 49.21.

Area and population

Federal districts[2]	Capitals	area sq mi	area sq km	population 2001[1] estimate
Central	Moscow (Moskva)	252,000	652,800	36,738,000
Belgorod (region)	Belgorod	10,500	27,100	1,499,000
Bryansk (region)	Bryansk	13,500	34,900	1,424,000
Ivanovo (region)	Ivanovo	9,200	23,900	1,205,000
Kaluga (region)	Kaluga	11,500	29,900	1,069,000
Kostroma (region)	Kostroma	23,200	60,100	774,000
Kursk (region)	Kursk	11,500	29,800	1,299,000
Lipetsk (region)	Lipetsk	9,300	24,100	1,235,000
Moscow (city)		[3]	[3]	8,546,000
Moskva (Moscow; region)	Moscow (Moskva)	18,200[3]	47,000[3]	6,436,000
Oryol (region)	Oryol	9,500	24,700	891,000
Ryazan (region)	Ryazan	15,300	39,600	1,271,000
Smolensk (region)	Smolensk	19,200	49,800	1,114,000
Tambov (region)	Tambov	13,200	34,300	1,257,000
Tula (region)	Tula	9,900	25,700	1,716,000
Tver (region)	Tver	32,500	84,100	1,575,000
Vladimir (region)	Vladimir	11,200	29,000	1,589,000
Voronezh (region)	Voronezh	20,200	52,400	2,437,000
Yaroslavl (region)	Yaroslavl	14,100	36,400	1,401,000
Far Eastern	Khabarovsk	2,400,000	6,215,900	7,107,000
Amur (region)	Blagoveshchensk	140,400	363,700	990,000
Chukot (autonomous district)	Anadyr	284,800	737,700	75,000
Kamchatka (region)	Petropavlovsk-Kamchatsky	66,000	170,800	355,000
Khabarovsk (territory)	Khabarovsk	304,500	788,600	1,496,000
Koryak (autonomous district)	Palana	116,400	301,500	29,000
Magadan (region)	Magadan	178,100	461,400	234,000
Primorye (territory)	Vladivostok	64,100	165,900	2,155,000
Sakha (republic)	Yakutsk	1,198,200	3,103,200	986,000
Sakhalin (region)	Yuzhno-Sakhalinsk	33,600	87,100	591,000
Yevreyskaya (autonomous region)	Birobidzhan	13,900	36,000	196,000
Northwest	St. Petersburg	648,000	1,677,900	14,371,000
Arkhangelsk (region)	Arkhangelsk	158,700	411,000	1,397,000
Kaliningrad (region)	Kaliningrad	5,800	15,100	947,000
Kareliya (republic)	Petrozavodsk	66,600	172,400	760,000
Komi (republic)	Kudymkar	160,600	415,900	1,126,000
Leningrad (region)	St. Petersburg	33,200[4]	85,900[4]	1,659,000
Murmansk (region)	Murmansk	55,900	144,900	988,000
Nenets (autonomous district)	Naryan-Mar	68,100	176,400	45,000
Novgorod (region)	Novgorod	21,400	55,300	720,000
Pskov (region)	Pskov	21,400	55,300	790,000
St. Petersburg (city)		[4]	[4]	4,628,000
Vologda (region)	Vologda	56,300	145,700	1,311,000
Siberia	Novosibirsk	1,974,800	5,114,800	20,675,000
Agin Buryat (autonomous district)	Aginskoye	7,300	19,000	79,000
Altay (republic)	Gorno-Altaysk	35,700	92,600	205,000
Altay (territory)	Barnaul	65,300	169,100	2,643,000
Buryatiya (republic)	Ulan-Ude	135,600	351,300	1,026,000
Chita (region)	Chita	159,300	412,500	1,168,000
Evenk (autonomous district)	Tyra	296,400	767,600	18,000
Irkutsk (region)	Irkutsk	287,900	745,500	2,586,000
Kemerovo (region)	Kemerovo	36,900	95,500	2,962,000
Khakassia (republic)	Abakan	23,900	61,900	578,000
Krasnoyarsk (territory)	Krasnoyarsk	274,100	710,000	2,970,000
Novosibirsk (region)	Novosibirsk	68,800	178,200	2,731,000
Omsk (region)	Omsk	53,900	139,700	2,147,000
Taymyr (Dolgano-Nenets) (autonomous district)	Dudinka	332,900	862,100	44,000
Tomsk (region)	Tomsk	122,400	316,900	1,065,000
Tuva (republic)	Kyzyl-Orda	65,800	170,500	310,000
Ust-Ordyn Buryat	Ust-Ordinsky	8,600	22,400	143,000
Southern	Rostov-na-Donu	227,300	589,200	21,523,000
Adygeya (republic)	Maykop	2,900	7,600	446,000
Astrakhan (region)	Astrakhan	17,000	44,100	1,013,000
Chechnia (republic)	Grozny	6,010	15,700	610,000
Dagestan (republic)	Makhachkala	19,400	50,300	2,160,000
Ingushetiya (republic)	Magas	1,390	3,600	460,000
Kabardino-Balkariya (republic)	Nalchik	4,800	12,500	784,000
Kalmykiya (republic)	Elista	29,400	76,100	314,000
Karachayevo-Cherkessia (republic)	Cherkessk	5,400	14,100	431,000
Krasnodar (territory)	Krasnodar	29,300	76,000	4,999,000
Rostov (region)	Rostov-na-Donu	38,900	100,800	4,317,000
Severnaya Osetiya–Alania (republic)	Vladikavkaz	3,100	8,000	677,000
Stavropol (territory)	Stavropol	25,700	66,500	2,654,000
Volgograd (region)	Volgograd	44,000	113,900	2,658,000
Urals	Yekaterinburg	690,600	1,788,900	12,565,000
Chelyabinsk (region)	Chelyabinsk	33,900	87,900	3,651,000
Khanty-Mansi (autonomous district)	Khanty-Mansiysk	202,000	523,100	1,402,000
Kurgan (region)	Kurgan	27,400	71,000	1,087,000
Sverdlovsk (region)	Sverdlovsk	75,200	194,800	4,573,000
Tyumen (region)	Tyumen	62,400	161,800	1,347,000
Yamalo-Nenets (autonomous district)	Salekhard	289,700	750,300	505,000

Area and population (continued)

		area sq mi	area sq km	population 2001[1] estimate
Volga	Nizhny Novgorod	400,100	1,035,900	31,840,000
Bashkortostan (republic)	Ufa	55,400	143,600	4,102,000
Chuvashiya (republic)	Cheboksary	7,100	18,300	1,353,000
Kirov (region)	Kirov	46,600	120,800	1,576,000
Komi-Permyak (autonomous district)	Syktyvkar	12,700	32,900	149,000
Mari-El (republic)	Toshkar-Ola	9,000	23,200	755,000
Mordoviya (republic)	Saransk	10,100	26,200	920,000
Nizhny Novgorod (region)	Nizhny Novgorod	28,900	74,800	3,633,000
Orenburg (region)	Orenburg	47,900	124,000	2,212,000
Penza (region)	Penza	16,700	43,200	1,518,000
Perm (region)	Perm	49,300	127,700	2,792,000
Samara (region)	Samara	20,700	53,600	3,279,000
Saratov (region)	Saratov	38,700	100,200	2,696,000
Tatarstan (republic)	Kazan	26,300	68,000	3,777,000
Udmurtia (republic)	Izhevsk	16,300	42,100	1,624,000
Ulyanovsk (Simbirsk; region)	Simbirsk	14,400	37,300	1,454,000
TOTAL		**6,592,800**	**17,075,400**	**144,819,000**

Demography

Population (2002): 143,673,000.
Density (2002): persons per sq mi 21.7, persons per sq km 8.4.
Urban-rural (2001): urban 73.1%; rural 26.9%.
Sex distribution (2001): male 46.68%; female 53.32%.
Age breakdown (2001): under 15, 13.3%; 15–29, 22.9%; 30–44, 23.0%; 45–59, 17.8%; 60 and over, 23.0%.
Population projection: (2010) 136,900,000; (2020) 129,700,000.
Ethnic composition (1997): Russian 86.6%; Tatar 3.2%; Ukrainian 1.3%; Chuvash 0.9%; Bashkir 0.7%; Chechen 0.6%; Mordovian 0.5%; Belorussian 0.3%; other 5.9%.
Religious affiliation (1997): Russian Orthodox 16.3%; Muslim 7.6%; other Orthodox 1.6%; Protestant 0.9%; Jewish 0.4%; Roman Catholic 0.3%; other Catholic 0.3%; other (mostly nonreligious) 72.6%.
Major cities (2001[1]): Moscow 8,546,000; St. Petersburg 4,628,000; Novosibirsk 1,393,000; Nizhny Novgorod 1,343,300; Yekaterinburg 1,256,900; Samara 1,146,400; Omsk 1,138,400; Kazan 1,090,200; Ufa 1,088,800; Chelyabinsk 1,081,100; Perm 1,004,800; Rostov-na-Donu 997,800.

Other principal cities (2001[1])

	population		population		population
Astrakhan	479,700	Lipetsk	519,200	Tolyatti	724,300
Barnaul	573,300	Naberezhnye Chelny	518,300	Tomsk	483,100
Irkutsk	587,200	Novokuznetsk	564,500	Tula	495,500
Izhevsk	650,300	Orenburg	516,600	Tyumen	500,200
Kemerovo	487,200	Penza	524,900	Vladivostok	598,600
Khabarovsk	603,500	Ryazan	523,400	Volgograd	982,900
Krasnodar	634,700	Saratov	864,400	Voronezh	901,800
Krasnoyarsk	875,700	Simbirsk (Ulyanovsk)	662,100	Yaroslavl	608,800

Migration (2000): immigrants 350,876; emigrants 161,046.
Refugees (2001): 808,280, of which from Kazakhstan 291,445, Uzbekistan 102,125, Tajikistan 85,101, Georgia 60,067.
Households (1999). Total family households 52,116,000; average household size 2.8; distribution by size (1995): 1 person 19.2%; 2 persons 26.2%; 3 persons 22.6%; 4 persons 20.5%; 5 persons or more 11.5%. Population in family households (1989): 87.0%, nonfamily population 13.0%.

Vital statistics

Birth rate per 1,000 population (2001): 8.7 (world avg. 21.2); legitimate 70.5%; illegitimate 29.5%.
Death rate per 1,000 population (2001): 15.4 (world avg. 8.9).
Natural increase rate per 1,000 population (2000): –6.7 (world avg. 12.3).
Total fertility rate (avg. births per childbearing woman; 2001): 1.3.
Life expectancy at birth (2001): male 59.0 years; female 72.2 years.
Major causes of death per 100,000 population (2000): circulatory diseases 849.4; accidents, poisoning, and violence 219.9, of which suicide 39.3, murder 28.3, alcohol poisoning 25.7; malignant neoplasms (cancers) 205.6; respiratory diseases 70.5; digestive diseases 44.6; infectious and parasitic diseases 25.0.

Social indicators

Educational attainment (1998). Percentage of population age 16 and over having: primary or no formal education 11.2%; some secondary 25.3%; secondary and some postsecondary 40.9%; higher and postgraduate 22.6%.
Quality of working life (2000). Average workweek: 40 hours. Annual rate per 100,000 workers of: injury or accident 510; industrial illness 18.1; death 14.9. Proportion of labour force insured for damages or income loss resulting from: injury 100%; permanent disability 100%; death 100%. Average days lost to labour strikes per 1,000 employees (1999): 35.7.
Access to services (1990). Proportion of dwellings having access to: electricity, virtually 100%; safe public water supply 94%; public sewage collection 92%; central heating 92%; bathroom 87%; gas 72%; hot water 79%.
Social participation. Eligible voters participating in last national election (2000): 64.2%. Trade union membership in total workforce (2000[5]): 100%. Practicing religious population in total affiliated population (1991): 32%.
Social deviance. Offense rate per 100,000 population (2000) for: murder 21.9; rape 5.4; serious injury 34.3; larceny-theft 1,023.2. Incidence per 100,000 population (2000) of: alcoholism (1992) 1,727.5; substance abuse 25.6; suicide 39.2.
Material well-being (1999). Durable goods possessed per 100 family households: automobile 37; radio receiver 100; television receiver 112; refrigerator or freezer 93; washing machine 80; camera 35; motorcycle 22; bicycle 51.

National economy

Public debt (external, outstanding: 2000): U.S.$111,419,000,000.
Budget (2000)[6]. Revenue: Rub 1,132,100,000,000 (tax revenue 85.2%, of which value-added tax 32.8%, profit tax 15.7%, individual income tax 11.6%, excise tax 6.0%; nontax revenue 14.8%). Expenditures: Rub

1,029,200,000 (interest on foreign debt 25.0%; defense 18.6%; social and cultural 13.0%; law enforcement 10.2%; administrative 2.4%).
Gross national product (2000): U.S.$241,027,000,000 (U.S.$1,660 per capita).

Structure of gross domestic product and labour force

	in value Rub '000,000	% of total value	labour force	% of labour force
		2000		
Agriculture	465,106.3	6.6	8,740,000	12.0
Mining } Manufacturing	2,040,866.8	28.9	14,297,000	19.6
Public utilities	187,168.6	2.6	3,361,000	4.6
Construction	421,115.7	6.0	5,080,000	7.0
Transp. and commun.	534,940.3	7.6	4,919,000	6.7
Trade	1,540,205.4	21.8	9,320,000	12.8
Finance	294,919.4	4.2	744,000	1.0
Services	426,268.6	6.0	14,643,000	20.1
Pub. admin., defense	337,199.3	4.8	2,858,000	3.9
Other	815,602.4[7]	11.5[7]	8,938,000[8]	12.3[8]
TOTAL	7,063,392.8	100.0	72,900,000	100.0

Production (metric tons except as noted). Agriculture, forestry, fishing (2001): wheat 46,871,000, potatoes 34,500,000, barley 19,500,000, sugar beets 14,539,000, vegetables (other than potatoes) 12,533,800, oats 8,010,000, rye 6,000,000, sunflower seeds 2,700,000, apples 1,800,000, millet 1,315,000, corn (maize) 831,000, peas 800,000, buckwheat 570,000, rice 497,000; livestock (number of live animals) 27,300,000 cattle, 15,700,000 pigs, 14,800,000 sheep; roundwood (2000) 158,100,000 cu m; fish catch (1999) 4,209,772. Mining and quarrying (2000): nickel 275,000; chrome ore 169,000,000; iron ore 86,800,000; tin 5,000,000; molybdenum 4,600,000; antimony 4,500,000; gold 4,113,000 troy oz; silver 270. Manufacturing (2000): crude steel 59,200,000; rolled steel 46,700,000; pig iron 44,600,000; cement 32,400,000; mineral fertilizers 12,213,000; sulfuric acid 8,300,000; cellulose 4,960,000; synthetic resins and plastics 2,576,000; cardboard 1,985,000; caustic soda 1,241,000; detergents 436,000; synthetic fibres 164,000; cotton fabrics 1,822,000,000 sq m; silk fabrics 178,000,000 sq m; linen fabrics 113,000,000 sq m; wool fabrics 54,600,000 sq m; cigarettes 290,000,000,000 units; watches 6,500,000 units; refrigerators 1,327,000 units; television receivers 1,116,000 units; passenger cars 959,000 units; washing machines 954,000 units; vacuum cleaners 745,000 units; bicycles 639,000 units; cameras 183,600 units; sewing machines 31,800 units; motorcycles 28,700 units; leather footwear 22,500,000 pairs; vodka and liquors 12,300,000 hectolitres; champagne 6,800,000 hectolitres; grape wine 2,401,000 hectolitres; beer 516,000 hectolitres; brandy 174,900 hectolitres. Construction (2000): residential 30,300,000 sq m; nonresidential (1995) 26,400,000 sq m.

Manufacturing, mining, and construction enterprises (1995)

	no. of enter- prises	no. of employees	monthly wages as a % of avg. of all wages	value added (Rub '000,000,000)
Manufacturing				
Machinery and metal products	48,905	4,842,000	80.1	27,234
Fuel and energy	1,758	1,554,000	228.9	44,211
Metallurgy	2,158	1,248,000	121.9	26,437
Chemicals	23,027	2,432,000	95.9	17,934
Light industry	23,007	1,368,000	60.1	2,931
Food	14,713	1,514,000	105.3	12,886
Other industries	19,073	2,085,000	...	4,685
Building materials	8,359	994,000	110.4	3,761

Energy production (consumption): electricity (kW-hr; 2000) 877,800,000,000 (863,700,000,000); hard coal (metric tons; 2000) 172,000,000 ([1997] 153,100,000); lignite (metric tons; 2000) 86,300,000 ([1997] 80,080,000); crude petroleum (barrels; 2000) 2,323,730,000 ([1997] 1,312,200,000); petroleum products (metric tons; 1997) 156,920,000 (102,980,000); natural gas (cu m; 2000) 584,000,000,000 ([1997] 308,646,800,000); peat (metric tons; 1997) 3,224,000 (3,224,000).
Population economically active (2000): total 72,900,000; activity rate of total population 49.9% (participation rates: ages over 15, 78.0%; female 47.6%; unemployed 12.3%).

Price and earnings indexes (1995 = 100)

	1995	1996	1997	1998	1999	2000
Consumer price index	100.0	121.8	111.0	184.4	136.5	164.8
Monthly earnings index	100.0	100.4	105.9	83.6	86.4	...

Household income and expenditure. Average household size (2000) 2.8; income per household: Rub 38,300 (U.S.$1,320); sources of income (2000): wages 61.4%, pensions and stipends 14.4%, income from entrepreneurial activities 15.9%, property income 7.1%, other 1.2%; expenditure (2000): food 47.6%, clothing 15.5%, furniture and household appliances 7.7%, housing 4.6%, transportation 2.6%.
Tourism (1999): receipts U.S.$7,510,000,000; expenditures U.S.$7,434,000,000.

Foreign trade[9]

Balance of trade (current prices)

	1995	1996	1997	1998	1999	2000
U.S.$'000,000	+20,152	+27,556	+19,749	+15,103	+34,234	+67,325
% of total	14.2%	18.4%	12.7%	11.3%	29.7%	52.8%

Imports (2000): U.S.$30,142,000,000 (machinery and transport equipment 30.6%, food 23.1%, chemicals 18.6%, ferrous and nonferrous metals 8.3%, textiles and clothing 4.8%, fuels and lubricants 4.6%, wood and wood products 3.8%). Major import sources (2000): Germany 11.5%; Belarus 11.1%; Ukraine 10.8%; U.S. 8.0%; Kazakhstan 6.5%; Italy 3.6%; France 3.3%; Finland 2.8%; Poland 2.1%.

Exports (2000): U.S.$97,467,000,000 (fuels and lubricants 53.5%, of which oil and oil products 24.3%, gas 16.0%; ferrous and nonferrous metals 17.1%; machinery and transport equipment 8.6%; chemicals 7.0%; precious metals 5.0%; forestry products 4.4%). Major export destinations: Germany 9.0%; U.S. 7.7%; Italy 7.0%; Belarus 5.4%; China 5.1%; Ukraine 4.9%; Poland 4.3%; The Netherlands 4.2%; Switzerland 3.9%; Finland 3.0%.

Trade by commodity group (2000)

SITC group	imports U.S.$'000,000	%	exports U.S.$'000,000	%
00 Food and live animals	6,977	23.1	1,299	1.3
02 Raw materials, excl. fuels	2,492	8.3	16,682	17.1
03 Mineral fuels, lubricants	1,383	4.6	52,142	53.5
05 Chemicals	5,621	18.7	6,801	7.0
65 Textile yarn, fabrics	1,451	4.8	655	0.7
07 Machinery and transport equipment	9,227	30.6	8,394	8.6
08 Misc. manufactured articles	2,991	9.9	11,494	11.8
TOTAL	30,142	100.0	97,467	100.0

Direction of trade (1999)

	imports U.S.$'000,000	%	exports U.S.$'000,000	%
Africa	404.3	1.0	1,115.9	1.5
Asia	4,447.2	11.0	12,776.6	17.1
Japan	455.7	1.1	2,124.7	2.8
South America	606.4	1.5	2,627.0	3.5
North and Central America	3,072.6	7.6	5,111.3	6.8
United States	2,389.5	5.9	4,714.0	6.3
Europe	31,898.5	78.9	53,022.1	71.0
EU	...	...	24,850.4	33.3
Eastern Europe	...	...	7,796.4	10.4
Other Europe	...	...	20,375.3	27.3
Oceania	246.0	0.6	10.1	0.1
TOTAL	40,429.0	100.0	74,663.0	100.0

Transport and communications

Transport. Railroads (2000): length 139,000 km; passenger-km 167,000,000,000; metric ton-km cargo 1,373,000,000. Roads (2000): total length 584,000 km (paved 91%). Vehicles (2000): passenger cars 20,247,800; trucks and buses (1999) 5,021,000. Air transport (2000): passenger-km 53,400,000,000; metric ton-km cargo 2,500,000,000; airports (1998) 75.

Distribution of traffic (2000)

	cargo carried ('000,000 tons)	% of national total	passengers carried ('000,000)	% of national total
Intercity transport			23,502	54.5
Road	550	21.5	22,033	51.1
Rail	1,046	40.9	1,419	3.3
Sea and river	134	5.2	27	0.1
Air	0.8	...	23	...
Pipeline	829	32.4	—	—
Urban transport			19,628	45.5
Road	—	—	} 19,628	45.5
Rail	—	—		
TOTAL	2,559.8	100.0	43,130	100.0

Communications

Medium	date	unit	number	units per 1,000 persons
Daily newspapers	1996	circulation	15,517,000	105
Radio	1997	receivers	61,500,000	417
Television	1999	receivers	62,000,000	425
Telephones	2001	main lines	35,700,000	243
Cellular telephones	2001	subscribers	5,560,000	38
Personal computers	2001	units	7,300,000	49.7
Internet	2001	users	4,300,000	29.3

Education and health

Health (2001): physicians 680,200 (1 per 213 persons); hospital beds 1,671,600 (1 per 87 persons); infant mortality rate per 1,000 live births (2000) 15.3.

Education (2000–01)

	schools	teachers	students	student/ teacher ratio
Primary (age 6–13) } Secondary (age 14–17)	67,000	1,696,000	20,073,800	11.8
Voc., teacher tr.	3,893	129,500	1,700,000	13.1
Higher	965	265,200	4,741,400	17.9

Food (2000): daily per capita caloric intake 2,917 (vegetable products 78%; animal products 22%); 114% of FAO recommended minimum.

Military

Total active duty personnel (2001): 1,026,100 (army 31.3%, navy 16.7%, air force 18.0%, strategic deterrent forces 14.5%, other 19.5%[10]). Military expenditure as percentage of GNP (1999): 5.6% (world 2.4%); per capita expenditure U.S.$239.

[1]January 1. [2]Federal districts were formally established in May 2000. [3]Moskva (Moscow; region) includes Moscow (city). [4]Leningrad region includes St. Petersburg city. [5]State enterprises only. [6]Federal budget only. [7]Taxes on products less subsidies and bank service charges. [8]Unemployed. [9]Imports c.i.f. [10]Represents 200,000 military personnel not included elsewhere (including Ministry of Defense staff and centrally controlled units for electronic warfare).

Internet resources for further information:
• **Russian Statistical Agency http://www.gks.ru/eng/default.asp**
• **Permanent Mission of the Russian Federation to the United Nations http://www.un.int/russia**

Rwanda

Official name: Repubulika y'u Rwanda
(Rwanda); République Rwandaise
(French); Republic of Rwanda
(English).
Form of government: transitional
regime[1] with one legislative body
(Transitional National Assembly
[74]).
Head of state and government:
President assisted by Prime Minister.
Capital: Kigali.
Official languages: Rwanda; French;
English.
Official religion: none.
Monetary unit: 1 Rwanda franc (RF);
valuation (Sept. 23, 2002)
1 U.S.$ = RF 475.35; 1 £ = RF 738.74.

Area and population

Prefectures	Capitals	area sq mi	area sq km	population 1991 census
Butare	Butare	709	1,837	766,839
Byumba[2]	Byumba	1,838	4,761	783,350
Cyangugu	Cyangugu	712	1,845	515,129
Gikongoro	Gikongoro	794	2,057	464,585
Gisenyi	Gisenyi	791	2,050	734,697
Gitarama	Gitarama	845	2,189	851,516
Kibungo[2]	Kibungo	1,562	4,046	655,368
Kibuye	Kibuye	658	1,705	470,747
Kigali	Kigali (city)	1,159	3,002	918,869
Kigali (city)	—	45	116	237,782
Ruhengeri	Ruhengeri	642	1,663	766,112
Umutara[2]	Nyagatare	...	...	...
TOTAL LAND AREA		9,757[3]	25,271	
TOTAL		10,169	26,338	7,164,994

Demography

Population (2002): 7,398,000.
Density (2002)[4]: persons per sq mi 758.2, persons per sq km 292.7.
Urban-rural (2001): urban 6.3%; rural 93.7%.
Sex distribution (2001): male 49.60%; female 50.40%.
Age breakdown (2001): under 15, 43.0%; 15–29, 30.4%; 30–44, 15.0%; 45–59, 7.3%; 60–74, 3.5%; 75 and over, 0.8%.
Population projection: (2010) 7,876,000; (2020) 8,027,000.
Doubling time: 47 years.
Ethnic composition (1996): Hutu 80.0%; Tutsi 19.0%; Twa 1.0%.
Religious affiliation (2000): Roman Catholic 51.0%; Protestant 28.8%; traditional beliefs 9.0%; Muslim 7.9%; independent Christian 2.1%; other 1.2%.
Major cities (1991): Kigali (1999) 369,000; Ruhengeri 29,578[5]; Butare 28,645[5]; Gisenyi 21,918[5].

Vital statistics

Birth rate per 1,000 population (2001): 34.0 (world avg. 21.2).
Death rate per 1,000 population (2001): 21.1 (world avg. 8.9).
Natural increase rate per 1,000 population (2001): 12.9 (world avg. 12.3).
Total fertility rate (avg. births per childbearing woman; 2001): 4.9.
Marriage rate per 1,000 population (1984)[6]: 2.5.
Life expectancy at birth (2001): male 38.4 years; female 39.7 years.
Major causes of death per 100,000 population: n.a.; however, principal causes in 1999 were malaria, bronchopneumonia, diarrhea, AIDS, pulmonary diseases, cerebrospinal meningitis, kwashiorkor, and road accidents.

National economy

Budget (2000). Revenue: RF 132,400,000,000 (grants 47.8%, taxes on goods and services 26.6%, income tax 13.5%, import and export duties 10.6%). Expenditures: RF 131,700,000,000 (current expenditures 67.7%, of which wages 27.8%, goods and services 18.1%, transfers 8.4%, defense 5.9%, debt payment 4.9%; capital expenditure 32.3%).
Production (metric tons except as noted). Agriculture, forestry, fishing (2001): plantains 2,103,100, sweet potatoes 1,136,600, potatoes 988,900, cassava 688,000, sorghum 174,900, corn [maize] 92,100, coffee 18,800; livestock (number of live animals) 756,522 goats, 732,123 cattle, 248,345 sheep, 177,220 pigs; roundwood (2001) 7,836,000 cu m; fish catch (1999) 6,773. Mining and quarrying (2001): cassiterite (tin ore) 555; wolframite (tungsten ore) 161; gold (1999) 10 kg. Manufacturing (value added in RF '000,000; 2000): food and nonalcoholic beverages 37,981; nonmetallic products 3,109; metal products 1,087; chemicals 965; textiles 791; paper 615. Energy production (consumption): electricity (kW-hr; 2000) 110,800,000 (210,770,000); petroleum products (metric tons; 1998) none (95,500); natural gas (cu m; 2000) 1,373,000,000 ([1996] 300,000).
Population economically active (1996): total 3,021,000; activity rate of total population 50.8% (participation rates: ages 14–74 [1989] 46.3%; female 49.0%; unemployed, n.a.).

Price and earnings indexes (1995 = 100)

	1995	1996	1997	1998	1999	2000
Consumer price index	100.0	107.4	120.3	127.8	124.7	129.6
Earnings index	100.0	120.0	...	...	...	...

Land use (1994): forested 10.1%; meadows and pastures 28.4%; agricultural and under permanent cultivation 47.4%; other 14.1%.

Gross national product (2000): U.S.$1,998,000,000 (U.S.$230 per capita).

Structure of gross domestic product and labour force

	2000 in value RF '000,000	2000 % of total value	1989 labour force	1989 % of labour force
Agriculture	292,300	41.4	2,832,557	90.1
Mining	11,500	1.6	4,691	0.2
Manufacturing	68,600	9.7	45,089	1.4
Construction	60,500	8.6	38,237	1.2
Public utilities	3,700	0.5	2,562	0.1
Transp. and commun.	49,700	7.0	7,333	0.2
Trade	71,000	10.1	80,026	2.6
Pub. admin., defense	52,800	7.5 }	123,147	3.9
Services	95,600	13.5 }		
Other	—	—	9,414	0.3
TOTAL	705,700	100.0[3]	3,143,056	100.0

Public debt (external, outstanding; 2000): U.S.$1,306,000,000.
Household income and expenditure. Average household size (1991) 4.7; average annual income per household (1983) RF 122,870 (U.S.$1,300); sources of income: n.a.; expenditure: n.a.
Tourism: receipts (1993) U.S.$2,000,000; expenditures (1992) U.S.$17,000,000.

Foreign trade

Balance of trade (current prices)

	1996	1997	1998	1999	2000	2001
U.S.$'000,000	−151.3	−184.5	−191.5	−186.7	−150.0	−161.9
% of total	55.0%	52.5%	59.9%	60.0%	45.5%	46.5%

Imports (2000): U.S.$239,800,000 (capital goods 22.1%, food 19.4%, energy products 18.7%, intermediate goods 18.1%). Major import sources (1999): Japan 13.1%; Belgium 12.8%; Kenya 12.5%; Saudi Arabia 8.0%; Germany 5.1%.
Exports (2000): U.S.$89,800,000 (tea 27.1%, coffee 25.1%, cassiterite and tin 1.1%). Major export destinations (1999): Kenya 62.4%; Tanzania 13.9%; Germany 7.9%; Belgium 6.5%.

Transport and communications

Transport. Railroads: none. Roads (1999): total length 7,460 mi, 12,000 km (paved 8%). Vehicles (1996): passenger cars 13,000; trucks 17,100. Air transport (2000)[7]: passengers embarked and disembarked 101,000; cargo loaded and unloaded 4,300 metric tons; airports (1998) with scheduled flights 2.

Communications

Medium	date	unit	number	units per 1,000 persons
Daily newspapers	1995	circulation	500	0.1
Radio	1997	receivers	601,000	101
Telephones	2001	main lines	21,500	2.7
Cellular telephones	2001	subscribers	65,000	8.2
Internet	2001	users	20,000	2.5

Education and health

Educational attainment: n.a. *Literacy* (1995): percentage of total population age 15 and over literate 67.0%; males literate 73.7%; females literate 60.6%.

Education (1991–92)

	schools	teachers	students	student/ teacher ratio
Primary (age 7–15)	1,710	18,937	1,104,902	58.3
Secondary (age 16–19)[8]	...	3,413	94,586	27.7
Higher[9]	3[10]	646	3,389	5.2

Health: physicians (1992) 150 (1 per 50,000 persons); hospital beds (1990) 12,152 (1 per 588 persons); infant mortality rate (2001) 107.0.
Food (2000): daily per capita caloric intake 2,077 (vegetable products 98%, animal products 2%); 90% of FAO recommended minimum requirement.

Military

Total active duty personnel (2001): 49,000–64,000 (army 100%). Military expenditure as percentage of GNP (1999): 4.5% (world 2.4%); per capita expenditure U.S.$12.

[1]Five-year transitional period from November 1994 was extended to July 2003 in June 1999. [2]Umutara prefecture created in 1996 from parts of Byumba and Kibungo prefectures. [3]Detail does not add to total given because of rounding. [4]Based on land area only. [5]De jure population only. [6]Excludes marriages not registered in court. [7]Kigali airport only. [8]Includes vocational and teacher training. [9]1989–90. [10]1985.

Internet resources for further information:
• Republic of Rwanda (official website)
  http://www.rwanda1.com/government/rwandalaunch.html
• Banque Nationale du Rwanda
  http://www.bnr.rw/bnrnet

Saint Kitts and Nevis

Official name: Federation of Saint Kitts and Nevis[1].
Form of government: constitutional monarchy with one legislative house (National Assembly [15[2]]).
Chief of state: British Monarch represented by Governor-General.
Head of government: Prime Minister.
Capital: Basseterre.
Official language: English.
Official religion: none.
Monetary unit: 1 Eastern Caribbean dollar (EC$) = 100 cents; valuation (Sept. 23, 2002) 1 U.S.$ = EC$2.70; 1 £ = EC$4.20.

Area and population		area		population
Islands	**Capitals**	sq mi	sq km	2001 census[3]
Nevis[4]	Charlestown	36.0	93.2	11,181
St. Kitts	Basseterre	68.0	176.2	34,703
TOTAL		104.0	269.4	45,884

Demography

Population (2002): 46,000.
Density (2002): persons per sq mi 444.2, persons per sq km 171.7.
Urban-rural (2000): urban 34.2%; rural 65.8%.
Sex distribution (2001): male 49.70%; female 50.30%.
Age breakdown (2000): under 15, 30.3%; 15–29, 24.9%; 30–44, 22.2%; 45–59, 11.2%; 60–74, 7.1%; 75 and over, 4.3%.
Population projection: (2010) 48,000; (2020) 53,000.
Doubling time: 72 years.
Ethnic composition (2000): black 90.4%; mulatto 5.0%; Indo-Pakistani 3.0%; white 1.0%; other/unspecified 0.6%.
Religious affiliation (1995): Protestant 84.6%, of which Anglican 25.2%, Methodist 25.2%, Pentecostal 8.4%, Moravian 7.6%; Roman Catholic 6.7%; Hindu 1.5%; other 7.2%.
Major towns (2001): Basseterre 13,033; Charlestown (1994) 1,411.

Vital statistics

Birth rate per 1,000 population (2000): 19.1 (world avg. 22.5); (1983) legitimate 19.2%; illegitimate 80.8%.
Death rate per 1,000 population (2000): 9.4 (world avg. 9.0).
Natural increase rate per 1,000 population (2000): 9.7 (world avg. 13.5).
Total fertility rate (avg. births per childbearing woman; 2000): 2.4.
Marriage rate per 1,000 population: n.a.
Divorce rate per 1,000 population: n.a.
Life expectancy at birth (2000): male 67.9 years; female 73.7 years.
Major causes of death per 100,000 population (1985): diseases of the circulatory system 443.2, of which cerebrovascular disease 220.5, diseases of pulmonary circulation and other heart disease 122.7; malignant neoplasms (cancers) 95.5.

National economy

Budget (1999). Revenue: EC$252,400,000 (tax revenue 72.8% of which taxes on income and profits 19.6%, consumption taxes 16.3%, import duties 15.4%, taxes on domestic goods and services 14.9%; nontax revenue 26.1%). Expenditures: EC$298,300,000 (current expenditure 88.4%; development expenditure 11.6%).
Production (metric tons except as noted). Agriculture, forestry, fishing (1999): sugarcane 196,784, tropical fruit 1,300, coconuts 1,000, roots and tubers 700, potatoes 211, pulses 210, cabbages 175, sweet potatoes 170, tomatoes 120, onions 75; sea island cotton is grown on Nevis; livestock (number of live animals) 14,500 goats, 8,000 sheep, 3,600 cattle, 3,000 pigs; roundwood, n.a.; fish catch (2000) 257. Mining and quarrying: excavation of sand for local use. Manufacturing (2001): raw sugar 20,193; carbonated beverages 45,000 hectolitres[5]; beer 20,000 hectolitres[5]; other manufactures include electronic components, garments, footwear, and batik. Construction (value added; 1994): EC$57,000,000. Energy production (consumption): electricity (kW-hr; 1997) 90,000,000 (90,000,000); coal, none (none); crude petroleum, none (none); petroleum products (metric tons; 1997) none (33,000); natural gas, none (none).
Gross national product (2000): U.S.$269,000,000 (U.S.$6,570 per capita).

Structure of gross domestic product and labour force				
	1999		1994	
	in value EC$'000,000	% of total value	labour force[6]	% of labour force[6]
Sugarcane	7.7	0.9	1,525[7]	9.2[7]
Other agriculture, forestry, fisheries	17.2	2.1	914	5.5
Mining	2.3	0.3	29	0.2
Manufacturing	70.5	8.7	1,290[8]	7.8[8]
Construction	89.4	11.0	1,745	10.5
Public utilities	12.9	1.6	416	2.5
Transp. and commun.	96.4	11.9	534	3.2
Trade, restaurants	162.8	20.1	3,367	20.3
Finance, real estate	112.8	13.9	3,708[9]	22.3[9]
Pub. admin., defense	129.5	16.0	2,738	16.5
Services	29.5	3.6	[9]	[9]
Other	80.7[10]	9.9[10]	342	2.1
TOTAL	811.8[11]	100.0[11]	16,608	100.0[11]

Household income and expenditure. Average household size (2001) 2.9; average annual income per wage earner (1994) EC$9,940 (U.S.$3,681); sources of income: n.a.; expenditure (1978)[12]: food, beverages, and tobacco 55.6%, household furnishings 9.4%, housing 7.6%, clothing and footwear 7.5%, fuel and light 6.6%, transportation 4.3%, other 9.0%.
Public debt (external, outstanding; 2000): U.S.$135,800,000.
Population economically active (1980): total 17,125; activity rate of total population 39.5% (participation rates: ages 15–64, 69.5%; female 41.0%; unemployed [1997] 4.5%).

Price and earnings indexes (1995 = 100)					
	1995	1996	1997	1998	1999	2000
Consumer price index	100.0	102.1	111.2	115.0	119.5	122.1
Earnings index	...	...	...	...	...	...

Land use (1994): forested 17%; meadows and pastures 3%; agricultural and under permanent cultivation 39%; other 41%.
Tourism: receipts from visitors (2000) U.S.$56,000,000; expenditures by nationals abroad (1998) U.S.$6,000,000.

Foreign trade

Balance of trade (current prices)					
	1995	1996	1997	1998	1999	2000
EC$'000,000	–217	–263	–291	–239	–245	–335
% of total	52.4%	43.3%	57.0%	47.5%	50.6%	56.2%

Imports (1997): EC$401,100,000 (machinery and transport equipment 30.3%, basic and miscellaneous manufactures 20.6%, food 16.1%, chemicals and chemical products 8.2%). *Major import sources:* United States 45.5%; Caricom countries 13.4%, of which Trinidad and Tobago 9.8%; United Kingdom 9.7%.
Exports (1997): EC$109,900,000 (food 56.0%, machinery and transport equipment [mostly electronic goods] 31.7%). *Major export destinations* (1997): United States 55.0%; United Kingdom 32.6%; Caricom countries 2.9%.

Transport and communications

Transport. Railroads (2000)[13]: length 36 mi, 58 km. Roads (1999): total length 155 mi, 250 km (paved 50%). Vehicles (1999): passenger cars 5,326; trucks and buses 3,742. Merchant marine (1992): vessels (100 gross tons and over) 1; total deadweight tonnage 550. Air transport: passenger arrivals (1992) 123,195[14]; passenger departures, n.a.; cargo handled, n.a.; airports (1998) with scheduled flights 2.

Communications				units per 1,000 persons
Medium	date	unit	number	
Radio	1997	receivers	28,000	701
Television	1997	receivers	10,000	264
Telephones	2000	main lines	21,900	568
Cellular telephones	2000	units	1,200	31
Personal computers	1999	units	8,000	190
Internet	1999	users	2,000	52

Education and health

Educational attainment (1980). Percentage of population age 25 and over having: no formal schooling 1.1%; primary education 29.6%; secondary 67.2%; higher 2.1%. *Literacy* (1990): total population age 15 and over literate 25,500 (90.0%); males literate 13,100 (90.0%); females literate 12,400 (90.0%).

Education (1997–98)				student/ teacher ratio
	schools	teachers	students	
Primary (age 5–12)	23	320	5,928	18.5
Secondary (age 13–17)	9	341	4,548	13.3
Higher[15]	1	51	394	7.7

Health (1998): physicians 50 (1 per 815 persons); hospital beds 244 (1 per 167 persons); infant mortality rate per 1,000 live births (2000): 16.7.
Food (2000): daily per capita caloric intake 2,685 (vegetable products 72%, animal products 28%); 111% of FAO recommended minimum requirement.

Military

Total active duty personnel: in July 1997 the National Assembly approved a bill creating a 50-member army. *Military expenditure as percentage of GNP* (1998): 3.5%[16] (world, n.a.); per capita expenditure U.S.$226[16].

[1]Both Saint Christopher and Nevis and the Federation of Saint Christopher and Nevis are officially acceptable, variant, short- and long-form names of the country. [2]Includes 4 nonelective seats. [3]Preliminary figures. [4]Nevis has full internal self-government. The Nevis legislature is subordinate to the National Assembly only with regard to external affairs and defense. [5]1995. [6]Employed persons only. [7]Includes sugar manufacturing. [8]Excludes sugar manufacturing. [9]Finance, real estate includes Services. [10]Net of indirect taxes less imputed service charge. [11]Detail does not add to total given because of rounding. [12]Weights of consumer price index components. [13]Light railway serving the sugar industry on Saint Kitts. [14]Saint Kitts airport only. [15]1992–93. [16]Includes expenditure for police.

Internet resources for further information:
• **Official Web site of the Government of St. Kitts & Nevis**
  http://www.stkittsnevis.net
• **Eastern Caribbean Central Bank**
  http://www.eccb-centralbank.org

Saint Lucia

Official name: Saint Lucia.
Form of government: constitutional
  monarchy with a Parliament consisting
  of two legislative chambers (Senate
  [11]; House of Assembly [17[1]]).
Chief of state: British Monarch
  represented by Governor-General.
Head of government: Prime Minister.
Capital: Castries.
Official language: English.
Official religion: none.
Monetary unit: 1 Eastern Caribbean
  dollar (EC$) = 100 cents; valuation
  (Sept. 23, 2002) 1 U.S.$ = EC$2.70;
  1 £ = EC$4.20.

Area and population

Districts	Capitals	area sq mi	area sq km	population 2001 census
Anse-la-Raye	Anse-la-Raye }	18	47	5,954
Canaries	Canaries			1,741
Castries	Castries	31	79	60,390
Choiseul	Choiseul	12	31	5,993
Dennery	Dennery	27	70	12,537
Gros Islet	Gros Islet	39	101	19,409
Laborie	Laborie	15	38	7,329
Micoud	Micoud	30	78	15,892
Soufrière	Soufrière	19	51	7,337
Vieux Fort	Vieux Fort	17	44	14,561
TOTAL		238[2]	617[2]	151,143[3]

Demography

Population (2002): 160,000.
Density (2002): persons per sq mi 672.3, persons per sq km 259.3.
Urban-rural (1998): urban 37.3%; rural 62.7%.
Sex distribution (2000): male 49.04%; female 50.96%.
Age breakdown (2000): under 15, 31.8%; 15–29, 29.6%; 30–44, 20.5%; 45–59,
  10.2%; 60–74, 5.3%; 75 and over, 2.6%.
Population projection: (2010) 177,000; (2020) 199,000.
Doubling time: 57 years.
Ethnic composition (2000): black 50%; mulatto 44%; East Indian 3%; white
  1%; other 2%.
Religious affiliation (2001): Roman Catholic 67.5%; Protestant 22.0%, of which
  Seventh-day Adventist 8.4%, Pentecostal 5.6%; Rastafarian 2.1%; nonreli-
  gious 4.5%; other/unknown 3.9%.
Major urban area (2001): Castries 35,070.

Vital statistics

Birth rate per 1,000 population (2000): 18.2 (world avg. 22.5); legitimate 14.3%;
  illegitimate 85.7%.
Death rate per 1,000 population (2000): 6.0 (world avg. 9.0).
Natural increase rate per 1,000 population (2000): 12.2 (world avg. 13.5).
Total fertility rate (avg. births per childbearing woman; 2000): 2.0.
Marriage rate per 1,000 population (2000): 4.1.
Divorce rate per 1,000 population (2000): 0.3.
Life expectancy at birth (2000): male 68.7 years; female 73.6 years.
Major causes of death per 100,000 population (1996): diseases of the circula-
  tory system 282.9; malignant neoplasms (cancers) 74.1; diseases of the respi-
  ratory system 41.5; infectious and parasitic diseases 37.4; endocrine and meta-
  bolic disorders 19.0; ill-defined conditions 63.2.

National economy

Budget (1998–99). Revenue: EC$469,900,000 (current revenue 86.9%, of
  which consumption duties on imported goods 24.4%; taxes on income and
  profits 21.9%; import duties 14.7%; nontax revenue 9.2%; grants 3.9%).
  Expenditures: EC$496,600,000 (current expenditures 69.4%; development
  expenditures and net lending 30.6%).
Production (metric tons except as noted). Agriculture, forestry, fishing (1999):
  bananas 80,000, mangoes 27,000, coconuts 12,000, yams 3,800, tropical fruit
  2,750, grapefruit 1,393, plantains 1,296, cassava 980, vegetables 950, oranges
  705; livestock (number of live animals; 1999) 14,750 pigs, 12,500 sheep, 12,450
  cattle, 9,800 goats; roundwood, n.a.; fish catch (2000) 1,759. Mining and quarrying: excavation of sand for local construction and pumice. Manufacturing
  (value of production in EC$'000; 1998): alcoholic beverages and tobacco
  31,120; paper products and cardboard boxes 28,747; electrical and electronic components 16,245; food 9,535; garments 6,563; textiles 3,999; refined
  coconut oil 2,330; copra 1,330. Construction (buildings approved; 1994): residential 61,400 sq m; nonresidential 41,350 sq. m. Energy production (consumption): electricity (kW-hr; 1998) 235,881,000 (213,000,000); coal, none
  (none); crude petroleum, none (none); petroleum products (metric tons;
  1997) none (65,000); natural gas, none (none).
Household income and expenditure. Average household size (2001) 3.3; income
  per household: n.a.; sources of income: n.a.; expenditure (1982)[4]: food 46.8%,
  housing 13.5%, clothing and footwear 6.5%, transportation and communications 6.3%, household furnishings 5.8%, other 21.1%.
Tourism: receipts from visitors (2000) U.S.$277,000,000; expenditures by
  nationals abroad (1997) U.S.$29,000,000.
Population economically active (1998): total 73,660; activity rate of total
  population 49.2% (participation rates: ages 15–64, 79.1%; female 44.4%;
  unemployed [2001] 18.9%).

Price and earnings indexes (1995 = 100)

	1995	1996	1997	1998	1999	2000	2001
Consumer price index	100.0	101.8	102.0	104.2	107.9	111.9	115.0[5]
Earnings index	...	...	...	...	...	...	...

Public debt (external, outstanding; 2000): U.S.$169,200,000.
Gross national product (at current market prices; 2000): U.S.$642,000,000
  (U.S.$4,120 per capita).

Structure of gross domestic product and labour force

	1998 in value EC$'000,000[6]	1998 % of total value[6]	1998 labour force[7]	1998 % of labour force
Agriculture	114	8.1	17,310	23.5
Mining	7	0.5	221	0.3
Manufacturing	83	5.9	6,850	9.3
Construction	103	7.3	5,893	8.0
Public utilities	73	5.2	1,105	1.5
Transportation and communications	253	18.0	4,788	6.5
Trade, restaurants	374	26.6	19,225	26.1
Finance, real estate	305	21.7	3,168	4.3
Pub. admin., defense	206	14.7	9,797	13.3
Services	51	3.6	1,252	1.7
Other	−165[8]	−11.7[8]	4,051	5.5
TOTAL	1,404	100.0[9]	73,660	100.0

Land use (1994): forested 13%; meadows and pastures 5%; agricultural and
  under permanent cultivation 30%; other 52%.

Foreign trade

Balance of trade (current prices)

	1995	1996	1997	1998	1999	2000
U.S.$'000,000	−197.4	−233.9	−271.1	−273.0	−298.9	−311.7
% of total	47.5%	59.5%	68.9%	68.7%	72.8%	78.2%

Imports (2000): U.S.$355,100,000 (machinery and transportation equipment
  24.6%; food products 20.0%; crude petroleum and petroleum products 9.3%;
  chemicals and chemical products 8.2%). *Major import sources:* United States
  37.5%; Caricom countries 21.7%, of which Trinidad and Tobago 14.4%;
  United Kingdom 8.5%; Japan 4.5%; Canada 3.8%.
Exports (2000): U.S.$43,400,000 (1999; bananas 58.4%; beer and ale 11.7%;
  clothing 6.0%; cardboard boxes 4.1%). *Major export destinations:* United
  Kingdom 55.9%; Caricom countries 26.6%, of which Barbados 10.3%,
  Antigua and Barbuda 4.8%; United States 14.8%.

Transport and communications

Transport. Railroads: none. Roads (1999): total length 750 mi, 1,210 km (paved
  5%). Vehicles (1997): passenger cars 14,783; trucks and buses 1,020. Air
  transport (2000)[10]: passenger arrivals and departures 726,000; cargo unloaded
  and loaded 4,200 metric tons; airports (2000) with scheduled flights 2.

Communications

Medium	date	unit	number	units per 1,000 persons
Radio	1997	receivers	100,000	668
Television	1997	receivers	40,000	267
Telephones	1999	main lines	44,465	289
Cellular telephones	1998	subscribers	1,900	12.5

Education and health

Educational attainment (2000). Percentage of population age 15 and over having: no formal schooling 6.5%; primary education 56.2%; secondary 27.5%;
  higher vocational 4.5%; university 2.7%; other/unknown 2.6%. *Literacy*
  (1995): about 82%.

Education (1997–98)

	schools	teachers	students	student/teacher ratio
Primary (age 5–11)	84	1,160	30,536	26.3
Secondary (age 12–16)	17	620	11,405	18.4
Vocational[11]	1	34	806	23.7
Higher[11]	1	389	870	2.4

Health (1998): physicians 60 (1 per 2,533 persons); hospital beds 521 (1 per 292
  persons); infant mortality rate per 1,000 live births (2000) 13.4.
Food (1999): daily per capita caloric intake 2,812 (vegetable products 77%,
  animal products 23%); 116% of FAO recommended minimum requirement.

Military

Total active duty personnel (2000): [12].

[1]Represents elected seats only. Attorney general and speaker serve ex officio. [2]Total
includes the uninhabited 30 sq mi (78 sq km) Central Forest Reserve. [3]Preliminary
enumerated household pop.; preliminary household pop. adjusted for underenumeration equals 157,775; total adjusted pop. (including institutionalized individuals but
excluding visitors) equals 158,361. [4]Castries area only. [5]July. [6]At factor cost in current
prices. [7]Based on the percentage given. [8]Less imputed bank service charges. [9]Detail
does not add to total given because of rounding. [10]Combined data for both Castries
and Vieux Fort airports. [11]1992–93. [12]The 300-member police force includes a specially trained paramilitary unit and a coast guard unit.

Internet resources for further information:
• **Saint Lucian Government Statistics Department**
  http://www.stats.gov.lc

Saint Vincent and the Grenadines

Official name: Saint Vincent and the Grenadines.
Form of government: constitutional monarchy with one legislative house (House of Assembly [21[1]]).
Chief of state: British Monarch represented by Governor-General.
Head of government: Prime Minister.
Capital: Kingstown.
Official language: English.
Official religion: none.
Monetary unit: 1 Eastern Caribbean dollar (EC$) = 100 cents; valuation (Sept. 23, 2002) 1 U.S.$ = EC$2.70; 1 £ = EC$4.20.

Area and population	area		population
Census Divisions[3]	sq mi	sq km	2000[2] estimate
Island of Saint Vincent			
Barrouallie	14.2	36.8	5,449
Bridgetown	7.2	18.6	7,894
Calliaqua	11.8	30.6	21,266
Chateaubelair	30.9	80.0	6,335
Colonarie	13.4	34.7	8,269
Georgetown	22.2	57.5	7,654
Kingstown (city)	1.9	4.9	16,209
Kingstown (suburbs)	6.4	16.6	11,274
Layou	11.1	28.7	6,281
Marriaqua	9.4	24.3	9,290
Sandy Bay	5.3	13.7	2,927
Saint Vincent Grenadines			
Nothern Grenadines	9.0	23.3	5,779
Southern Grenadines	7.5	19.4	2,990
TOTAL	150.3	389.3[4]	111,617

Demography

Population (2002): 113,000.
Density (2002): persons per sq mi 751.8, persons per sq km 290.3.
Urban-rural (2000): urban 54.4%; rural 45.6%.
Sex distribution (1999): male 50.50%; female 49.50%.
Age breakdown (1999): under 15, 31.3%; 15–29, 31.2%; 30–44, 19.6%; 45–59, 9.4%; 60–74, 5.9%; 75 and over, 2.6%.
Population projection: (2010) 116,000; (2020) 117,000.
Doubling time: 61 years.
Ethnic composition (1999): black 65.5%; mulatto 23.5%; Indo-Pakistani 5.5%; white 3.5%; black-Amerindian 2.0%.
Religious affiliation (1995): Protestant 57.6%; unaffiliated Christian 20.6%; Roman Catholic 10.7%; Hindu 3.3%; Muslim 1.5%; other/nonreligious 6.3%.
Major city (2000[2]): Kingstown 16,209.

Vital statistics

Birth rate per 1,000 population (2001): 18.0 (world avg. 21.2); (1999) legitimate 17.9%; illegitimate 82.1%.
Death rate per 1,000 population (2001): 6.6 (world avg. 8.9).
Natural increase rate per 1,000 population (2001): 11.4 (world avg. 12.3).
Total fertility rate (avg. births per childbearing woman; 2000): 2.1.
Marriage rate per 1,000 population (1999): 5.7.
Divorce rate per 1,000 population (1999): 0.6.
Life expectancy at birth (2000): male 70.6 years; female 74.1 years.
Major causes of death per 100,000 population (1997): diseases of the circulatory system 228.4; malignant neoplasms (cancers) 90.0; endocrine and metabolic disorders 56.6; diseases of the respiratory system 42.2; infectious and parasitic diseases 36.8.

National economy

Budget (1998). Revenue: EC$285,200,000 (current revenue 73.8%, of which income tax 25.1%, consumption duties on imports 23.3%, taxes on goods and services 9.3%, import duties 7.9%; grants 14.5%; nontax revenue 9.5%; capital revenue 2.2%). Expenditures: EC$303,100,000 (current expenditure 65.9%; development expenditure 34.1%).
Public debt (external, outstanding; 2000): U.S.$161,000,000.
Production (metric tons except as noted). Agriculture, forestry, fishing (1999): bananas 43,000, coconuts 23,600, eddoes and dasheens[5] 4,118, corn (maize) 2,000, sweet potatoes 1,500, oranges 960, ginger 499, arrowroot starch 165, nutmegs 98, soursops, guavas, mangoes, and papayas are also grown; livestock (number of live animals) 13,000 sheep, 9,400 pigs, 6,200 cattle; roundwood, n.a.; fish catch (2000) 7,294. Mining and quarrying: sand and gravel for local use. Manufacturing (export value of manufactures in U.S.$'000,000; 1995): packaged flour 8.7; packaged rice 6.4; other goods (mostly garments, sporting goods, and electronic goods) 8.1. Energy production (consumption): electricity (kW-hr; 1999) 95,900,000 (84,800,000); coal, none (none); crude petroleum, none (none); petroleum products (metric tons; 1997) none (43,000); natural gas, none (none).
Tourism: receipts from visitors (2000) U.S.$74,000,000; expenditures by nationals abroad (1998) U.S.$8,000,000.
Land use (1994): forested 36%; meadows and pastures 5%; agricultural and under permanent cultivation 28%; other 31%.
Gross national product (2000): U.S.$313,000,000 (U.S.$2,720 per capita).

Structure of gross domestic product and labour force

	1998		1991	
	in value EC$'000,000	% of total value	labour force	% of labour force
Agriculture, forestry, fishing	78.3	9.2	8,377	20.1
Mining	2.3	0.3	98	0.2
Manufacturing	49.5	5.8	2,822	6.8
Construction	101.9	11.9	3,535	8.5
Public utilities	40.6	4.7	586	1.4
Transp. and commun.	148.4	17.4	2,279	5.5
Trade, restaurants	128.6	15.1	6,544	15.7
Finance, real estate	71.6	8.4	1,418	3.4
Pub. admin., defense	129.6	15.2 }	7,696	18.5
Services	12.9	1.5 }		
Other	90.5[6]	10.6[6]	8,327[7]	20.0[7]
TOTAL	854.2	100.0[4]	41,682	100.0[3]

Population economically active (1991): total 41,682; activity rate of total population 39.1% (participation rates: ages 15–64, 67.5%; female 35.9%; unemployed [1996] more than 30%).

Price and earnings indexes (1995 = 100)

	1995	1996	1997	1998	1999	2000	2001
Consumer price index	100.0	104.4	104.9	107.1	108.2	108.4	109.3
Daily earnings index	...	...	...	...	...	...	...

Household income and expenditure. Average household size (1991) 3.9; income per household (1988) EC$4,579 (U.S.$1,696); sources of income: n.a.; expenditure: n.a.

Foreign trade[8]

Balance of trade (current prices)

	1996	1997	1998	1999	2000	2001
U.S.$'000,000	−85.5	−127.2	−142.5	−152.9	−115.6	−144.4
% of total	48.0%	58.2%	58.9%	60.7%	54.9%	63.5%

Imports (1999): U.S.$202,300,000 (basic manufactures 33.9%; machinery and transport equipment 24.1%; food products 21.2%; chemicals and chemical products 9.9%; fuels 5.5%). *Major import sources:* U.S. 37.5%; Caricom countries 23.2%, of which Trinidad and Tobago 15.7%; U.K. 12.0%; Japan 4.5%.
Exports (1998): U.S.$49,600,000 (domestic exports 90.7%, of which bananas 38.5%, packaged flour 13.6%, packaged rice 10.1%, eddoes and dasheens[5] 3.8%; reexports 9.3%). *Major export destinations:* Caricom countries 51.6%, of which Trinidad and Tobago 10.3%, St. Lucia 8.7%, Barbados 8.7%; U.K. 40.3%.

Transport and communications

Transport. Railroads: none. Roads (1999): total length 646 mi, 1,040 km (paved 31%). Vehicles (1999): passenger cars 7,989; trucks and buses 3,920. Merchant marine (1997): vessels (100 gross tons and over) 946; total deadweight tonnage 1,253,000. Air transport (1999): passenger arrivals 122,815; passenger departures 126,924; airports (1998) with scheduled flights 5.

Communications

Medium	date	unit	number	units per 1,000 persons
Radio	1995	receivers	65,000	591
Television	1995	receivers	17,700	161
Telephones	2001	main lines	24,900	220
Cellular telephones	2001	subscribers	2,400	21
Internet	2001	users	3,500	31
Personal computers	2001	units	13,000	116

Education and health

Educational attainment (1980). Percentage of population age 25 and over having: no formal schooling 2.4%; primary education 88.0%; secondary 8.2%; higher 1.4%. *Literacy* (1991): total population age 15 and over literate 64,000 (96.0%).

Education (1997–98)

	schools	teachers	students	student/ teacher ratio
Primary (age 5–11)	60	1,007	21,347	21.2
Secondary (age 12–18)	21	379	7,775	20.5
Voc., teacher tr.[9]	3	49[10]	415	...

Health (1998): physicians 59 (1 per 1,883 persons); hospital beds 209 (1 per 531 persons); infant mortality rate per 1,000 live births (1999) 17.7.
Food (1999): daily per capita caloric intake 2,540 (vegetable products 83%, animal products 17%); 105% of FAO recommended minimum requirement.

Military

Total active duty personnel (1992): 634-member police force includes a coast guard and paramilitary unit.

[1]Includes 6 nonelective seats; excludes speaker who may be elected from within or from outside of the House of Assembly membership. [2]January 1. [3]For statistical purposes and the election of legislative representatives only. [4]Detail does not add to total given because of rounding. [5]Varieties of taro roots. [6]Net of indirect taxes less imputed bank service charges. [7]Unemployed. [8]Imports c.i.f.; exports f.o.b. [9]1996–97. [10]1993–94.

Internet resources for further information:
• **Eastern Caribbean Central Bank http://www.eccb-centralbank.org**

Samoa[1]

Official name: Malo Sa'oloto Tuto'atasi o Samoa (Samoan); Independent State of Samoa (English).
Form of government: constitutional monarchy[2] with one legislative house (Legislative Assembly [49]).
Chief of state: Head of State.
Head of government: Prime Minister.
Capital: Apia.
Official languages: Samoan; English.
Official religion: none.
Monetary unit: 1 tala (SA$[3], plural tala) = 100 sene; valuation (Sept. 23, 2002) 1 U.S.$ = SA$3.31; 1 £ = SA$5.14.

Pacific Ocean

Area and population

Islands	area		population
Political Districts	sq mi	sq km	2001 census
Savai'i	659	1,707	42,400[4]
Fa'aseleleaga			...
Gaga'emauga			...
Gaga'ifomauga			...
Palauli			...
Satupa'itea			...
Vaisigano			...
Upolu	432	1,119	134,400[4]
A'ana			...
Aiga-i-le-Tai			...
Atua			...
Tuamasaga			...
Vaa-o-Fonoti			...
TOTAL	1,093[5]	2,831[5]	176,848[6]

Demography

Population (2002): 178,000.
Density (2002): persons per sq mi 162.9, persons per sq km 62.9.
Urban-rural (2002): urban 22.0%; rural 78.0%.
Sex distribution (2001): male 52.0%[4]; female 48.0%[4].
Age breakdown (1991): under 15, 40.6%; 15–29, 29.9%; 30–44, 14.6%; 45–59, 8.8%; 60–74, 5.0%; 75 and over, 1.1%.
Population projection: (2010) 186,000; (2020) 210,000.
Doubling time: 31 years.
Ethnic composition (1997): Samoan (Polynesian) 92.6%; Euronesian (European and Polynesian) 7.0%; European 0.4%.
Religious affiliation (1995): Mormon 25.8%; Congregational 24.6%; Roman Catholic 21.3%; Methodist 12.2%; Pentecostal 8.0%; Seventh-day Adventist 3.9%; other Christian 1.7%; other 2.5%.
Major city (2001): Apia 38,836.

Vital statistics

Birth rate per 1,000 population (2002): 28.0 (world avg. 21.2).
Death rate per 1,000 population (2002): 5.6 (world avg. 8.9).
Natural increase rate per 1,000 population (2002): 22.4 (world avg. 12.3).
Total fertility rate (avg. births per childbearing woman; 2002): 4.2.
Marriage rate per 1,000 population: n.a.
Divorce rate per 1,000 population: n.a.
Life expectancy at birth (2002): male 67.0 years; female 73.0 years.
Major causes of death (percent distribution; 1992): congestive heart failure 14.0%; malignant neoplasms (cancers) 11.0%; cerebrovascular diseases 8.0%; injury and poisoning 8.0%; pneumonia 6.0%; septicemia 6.0%; diabetes mellitus 4.0%; intestinal infectious diseases 2.0%.

National economy

Budget (2000–01). Revenue: SA$262,400,000 (tax revenue 66.6%; grants 24.8%; nontax revenue 8.6%). Expenditures: SA$281,700,000 (current expenditure 58.4%; development expenditure 36.6%; net lending 5.0%).
Production (metric tons except as noted). Agriculture, forestry, fishing (1999): coconuts 130,000, taro 36,900, bananas 10,000, papayas 10,000, pineapples 5,700, mangoes 4,900, avocados 1,700, cacao beans 400; livestock (number of live animals) 178,800 pigs, 26,000 cattle, 350,000 chickens; roundwood (1998) 131,000 cu m; fish catch (2000) 13,004. Mining and quarrying: n.a. Manufacturing (in WS$'000; 1990): beer 8,708; cigarettes 6,551; coconut cream 5,576; sawn wood 3,662; coconut oil 3,442; corned meat 2,905; soap 1,487; paints 1,457. Construction (permits issued in WS$; 1995): residential 7,749,000; commercial, industrial, and other 30,867,000. Energy production (consumption): electricity (kW-hr; 1997) 65,000,000 (65,000,000); coal, none (n.a.); crude petroleum, none (n.a.); petroleum products (metric tons; 1997) none (43,000).
Household income and expenditure. Average household size (1999) 5.4; income per household: n.a.; sources of income: n.a.; expenditure (1987)[7]: food 58.8%, transportation 9.0%, housing and furnishings 5.1%, fuel and lighting 5.0%, clothing 4.2%, other goods and services 1.9%, other 16.0%.
Tourism: receipts from visitors (2000) U.S.$40,000,000; expenditures by nationals abroad (1999) U.S.$4,000,000.
Land use (1994): forested 47.3%; meadows and pastures 0.4%; agricultural and under permanent cultivation 43.1%; other 9.2%.
Gross national product (at current market prices; 2000): U.S.$246,000,000 (U.S.$1,450 per capita).

Structure of gross domestic product and labour force

	2000		1986	
	in value WS$'000	% of total value	labour force	% of labour force
Agriculture	125,700	16.2	29,023	63.6
Mining	...	...		
Manufacturing	117,300	15.2 }	1,587	3.5
Construction	71,000	9.2	62	0.1
Public utilities	16,700	2.1	855	1.9
Transp. and commun.	87,300	11.3	1,491	3.3
Trade	155,600	20.1	1,710	3.7
Finance	52,500	6.8	842	1.8
Pub. admin., defense	67,100	8.7 }		
Services	85,500	11.0 }	9,436	20.7
Other	−5,000	−0.6	629	1.4
TOTAL	773,700	100.0	45,635	100.0

Population economically active (1994): total 47,207; activity rate of total population 28.7% (participation rates: ages 15–64 [1981] 48.6%; female [1991] 32.0%).

Price and earnings indexes (1995 = 100)

	1995	1996	1997	1998	1999	2000	2001
Consumer price index	100.0	105.4	112.6	115.1	115.4	116.5	121.2
Earnings index	...	...	...	...	...	...	...

Public debt (external, outstanding; 2000): U.S.$147,000.

Foreign trade[8]

Balance of trade (current prices)

	1996	1997	1998	1999	2000	2001
WS$'000	−222,258	−208,846	−242,409	−285,070	−301,774	−399,017
% of total	81.7%	73.0%	73.7%	69.8%	76.3%	78.7%

Imports (1997): WS$247,377,000 ([1996] food 33.9%, industrial supplies 26.4%, machinery 16.9%, petroleum products 11.8%, consumer goods 11.0%). *Major import sources:* New Zealand 37.9%; Australia 20.7%; United States 15.6%; Fiji 15.0%; Japan 4.5%; Hong Kong 0.9%; Singapore 0.5%.
Exports (1997): WS$38,531,000 (fresh fish 33.0%, copra 21.1%, coconut oil 18.1%, coconut cream 12.8%, beer 4.3%, kava 4.0%, copra meal 1.5%). *Major export destinations:* New Zealand 48.1%; American Samoa 15.3%; Australia 9.2%; United States 3.3%; Germany 2.9%.

Transport and communications

Transport. Railroads: none. Roads (1996): total length 491 mi, 790 km (paved 42%). Vehicles (1995): passenger cars 1,068; trucks and buses 1,169. Merchant marine (1997): vessels (100 gross tons and over) 7; total deadweight tonnage 6,501. Air transport (1998): passenger-km 250,000,000; metric ton-km cargo 24,000,000; airports (1997) with scheduled flights 3.

Communications

Medium	date	unit	number	units per 1,000 persons
Radio	1997	receivers	178,000	1,035
Television	1998	receivers	9,000	52
Telephones	2001	main lines	10,000	56
Cellular telephones	2001	subscribers	3,000	17
Personal computers	2001	units	1,000	6.7
Internet	2001	users	3,000	17

Education and health

Educational attainment (1981). Percentage of population age 25 and over having: some primary education 16.5%; complete primary 24.5%; some secondary 52.1%; complete secondary 3.1%; higher 2.0%; unknown 1.8%.
Literacy: virtually 100%.

Education (1998)

	schools	teachers	students	student/ teacher ratio
Primary (age 5–11)	155[9]	1,233[10]	35,749[10]	23.9[10]
Secondary (age 12–18)	...	665[9]	12,672[9]	19.1[9]
Higher[11]	1	28	328	11.7

Health: physicians (1996) 62 (1 per 2,919 persons); hospital beds (1991) 863 (1 per 255 persons); infant mortality rate per 1,000 live births (2002) 26.0.
Food (1992): daily per capita caloric intake 2,828 (vegetable products 74%, animal products 26%); 124% of FAO recommended minimum requirement.

Military

No military forces are maintained; New Zealand is responsible for defense.

---

[1]In July 1997 the short-form name of the country was officially changed from Western Samoa to Samoa. [2]According to the constitution, the current Head of State, paramount chief HH Malietoa Tanumafili II, will hold office for life. Upon his death, the monarchy will functionally cease, and future Heads of State will be elected by the Legislative Assembly. [3]Symbol of the monetary unit changed from WS$ to SA$ as of July 1997. [4]Rounded census figure. [5]Total includes 2 sq mi (5 sq km) of uninhabited islands. [6]Detail does not add to total given because of rounding. [7]Consumer price index components. [8]Imports c.i.f.; exports f.o.b. [9]1996. [10]1999. [11]National University of Samoa only.

Internet resources for further information:
• **Central Bank of Samoa** http://www.cbs.gov.ws

San Marino

Official name: Serenissima Repubblica di San Marino (Most Serene Republic of San Marino).
Form of government: unitary multiparty republic with one legislative house (Great and General Council [60]).
Head of state and government: Captains-Regent (2).
Capital: San Marino.
Official language: Italian.
Official religion: none.
Monetary unit: 1 euro (€) = 100 cents; valuation (Sept. 23, 2002) 1 U.S.$ = €1.02; 1 £ = €1.58[1].

Area and population

Castles	Capitals	area sq mi	area sq km	population 2000 estimate
Acquaviva	Acquaviva	1.88	4.86	1,454
Borgo Maggiore	Borgo	3.48	9.01	5,591
Chiesanuova	Chiesanuova	2.11	5.46	902
Città	San Marino	2.74	7.09	4,429
Domagnano	Domagnano	2.56	6.62	2,435
Faetano	Faetano	2.99	7.75	996
Fiorentino	Fiorentino	2.53	6.56	1,833
Montegiardino	Montegiardino	1.28	3.31	754
Serravalle/Dogano	Serravalle	4.07	10.53	8,547
TOTAL		23.63[2]	61.19	26,941

Demography

Population (2002): 27,700.
Density (2002): persons per sq mi 1,172.2, persons per sq km 452.7.
Urban-rural (1999): urban 96.2%; rural 3.8%.
Sex distribution (2000): male 48.34%; female 51.66%.
Age breakdown (2000): under 15, 15.7%; 15–29, 18.8%; 30–44, 25.5%; 45–59, 18.8%; 60–74, 14.0%; 75 and over, 7.2%.
Population projection: (2010) 30,700; (2020) 33,500.
Doubling time: not applicable; natural population growth is negligible.
Ethnic composition (1971[1]): Sammarinesi 83.1%; Italian 12.0%; other 4.8%.
Religious affiliation (2000): Roman Catholic 88.7%; Pentecostal 1.8%; other 9.5%.
Major cities (1997[3]): Serravalle/Dogano 4,802; Borgo Maggiore 2,394; San Marino 2,294; Murata 1,549; Domagnano 1,048.

Vital statistics

Birth rate per 1,000 population (2000): 10.8 (world avg. 22.5); (1985) legitimate 95.2%; illegitimate 4.8%.
Death rate per 1,000 population (2000): 7.0 (world avg. 9.0).
Natural increase rate per 1,000 population (2000): 3.8 (world avg. 13.5).
Total fertility rate (avg. births per childbearing woman; 2000): 1.3.
Marriage rate per 1,000 population (1992–96): 8.1.
Divorce rate per 1,000 population (1991–95): 1.0.
Life expectancy at birth (2000): male 77.6 years; female 85.0 years.
Major causes of death per 100,000 population (1994–98): disease of the circulatory system 338.3; malignant neoplasms (cancers) 224.5; accidents, violence, and suicide 60.9; diseases of the respiratory system 9.5.

National economy

Budget (1997). Revenue: Lit 411,000,000,000 (taxes on goods and services 37.2%; taxes on income and profits 31.6%; social security 19.7%). Expenditures: Lit 448,000,000,000 (current expenditures 90.4%, of which social security and subsidies 48.2%, wages and salaries 31.2%; capital expenditures 6.9%; other 2.7%).
Public debt (external outstanding; 2000): U.S.$3,873,000.
Tourism: number of tourist arrivals (1999) 3,148,000; receipts from visitors (1994) U.S.$252,500,000; expenditures by nationals abroad, n.a.
Population economically active (2000): total 19,072; activity rate of total population 73.1% (participation rates: ages 15–64, 88.4%[4]; female 40.8%; unemployed 2.2%).

Price and earnings indexes (1995 = 100)

	1993	1994	1995	1996	1997	1998	1999
Consumer price index	91.6	95.3	100.0	104.1	106.2	108.6	112.1
Annual earnings index	87.9	93.9	100.0	110.9	118.4	...	...

Household income and expenditure. Total number of households (1997[3]) 10,093; average household size 2.5; income per household: n.a.; sources of income: n.a.; expenditure (1991)[5]: food, beverages, and tobacco 22.1%, housing, fuel, and electrical energy 20.9%, transportation and communications 17.6%, clothing and footwear 8.0%, furniture, appliances, and goods and services for the home 7.2%, education 7.1%, health and sanitary services 2.6%, other goods and services 14.5%.
Production (metric tons except as noted). Agriculture, forestry, fishing[6]: wheat *c.* 4,400, grapes *c.* 700, barley *c.* 500; livestock (number of live animals; 1998) 831 cattle, 748 pigs. Manufacturing (1998): processed meats 324,073 kg, of which beef 226,570 kg, pork 87,764 kg, veal 7,803 kg; cheese 61,563 kg; butter 12,658 kg; milk 1,167,620 litres; yogurt 5,131 litres; other major products include electrical appliances, musical instruments, printing ink, paint, cosmetics, furniture, floor tiles, gold and silver jewelry, clothing, and postage stamps. Construction (new units completed; 1998): residential

69; nonresidential 165. Energy production (consumption): all electrical power is imported via electrical grid from Italy (consumption, n.a.); coal, none (n.a.); crude petroleum, none (n.a.); petroleum products, none (n.a.); natural gas, none (n.a.).
Gross national product (at current market prices; 1999): U.S.$715,300,000 (U.S.$26,600 per capita).

Structure of labour force (2000)

	labour force	% of labour force
Agriculture	244	1.3
Manufacturing	6,132	32.2
Construction and public utilities	1,603	8.4
Transportation and communications	435	2.3
Trade	3,278	17.2
Finance and insurance	574	3.0
Services	2,223	11.6
Public administration and defense	4,155	21.8
Other	428[7]	2.2[7]
TOTAL	19,072	100.0

Land use (1985): agricultural and under permanent cultivation 74%; meadows and pastures 22%; forested, built-on, wasteland, and other 4%.

Foreign trade

Balance of trade (current prices)

	1992	1993	1994	1995	1996
U.S.$'000,000	−50.3	−48.8	−41.2	−3.3	+22.6
% of total	1.4%	1.4%	1.3%	0.1%	0.7%

Imports (1996): U.S.$1,719,300,000 (manufactured goods of all kinds, oil, and gold). *Major import source:* Italy.
Exports (1996): U.S.$1,741,900,000 (manufactured goods, traditionally wine, wheat, woolen goods, furniture, wood, ceramics, building stone, dairy products, meat, and postage stamps). *Major export destination:* Italy.

Transport and communications

Transport. Railroads: none (nearest rail terminal is at Rimini, Italy, 17 mi [27 km] northeast). Roads (1999): total length 156 mi, 252 km. Vehicles (1999): passenger cars 26,320; trucks and buses 2,763. Merchant marine: vessels (100 gross tons and over) none. Air transport: airports with scheduled flights, none; there is, however, a heliport that provides passenger and cargo service between San Marino and Rimini, Italy, during the summer months.

Communications

Medium	date	unit	number	units per 1,000 persons
Daily newspapers	1996	circulation	2,000	72
Radio	1998	receivers	16,000	610
Television	1998	receivers	9,055	358
Telephones	1999	main lines	19,970	769
Cellular telephones	1999	subscribers	10,000	369

Education and health

Educational attainment (1997[3]). Percentage of population age 14 and over having: basic literacy[8] or primary education 35.6%; secondary 30.7%; some postsecondary 27.9%; higher degree 5.8%. *Literacy* (1997[3]): total population age 15 and over literate 21,885 (99.1%); males literate 10,546 (99.4%); females literate 11,339 (98.8%).

Education (2000–01)

	schools	teachers	students	student/ teacher ratio
Primary (age 6–10)	14	242	1,297	5.4
Secondary (age 11–18)[9]	8	227	1,978	8.7
Voc., teacher tr.[10]	...	49	380	7.8
Higher	1	27	961	35.6

Health (2000): physicians 117 (1 per 230 persons); hospital beds 141 (1 per 191 persons); infant mortality rate per 1,000 live births (2000) 6.3.
Food (2000)[11]: daily per capita caloric intake 3,661 (vegetable products 74%, animal products 26%); 146% of FAO recommended minimum requirement.

Military

Total active duty personnel (2000): none[12]. *Military expenditure as percentage of national budget* (1992): 1.0% (world 3.6%); per capita expenditure (1987) U.S.$155.

[1]Italian lira replaced by euro. [2]Detail does not add to total given because of rounding. [3]January 1. [4]1999. [5]Weighting coefficients for component expenditures are those of the 1991 official Italian consumer price index for the North-Central region of Italy. [6]Early 1980s. [7]Unemployed. [8]Includes 0.9 percent illiterate population. [9]Includes vocational schools. [10]1997–98. [11]Figures are for Italy. [12]Defense is provided by a public security force of about 50; all fit males ages 16–55 constitute a militia.

Internet resources for further information:
• San Marino http://www.esteri.sm/eindex.htm

São Tomé and Príncipe

Atlantic Ocean

Official name: República democrática de São Tomé e Príncipe (Democratic Republic of São Tomé and Príncipe).
Form of government: Multiparty republic with one legislative house (National Assembly [55]).
Chief of state: President.
Head of government: Prime Minister.
Capital: São Tomé.
Official language: Portuguese.
Official religion: none.
Monetary unit: 1 dobra (Db) = 100 cêntimos; valuation (Sept. 23, 2002) 1 U.S.\$ = Db 9,020; 1 £ = Db 14,017.

Area and population

Islands Districts	Capitals	area sq mi	area sq km	population 1997 estimate
São Tomé		332	859	126,973
Aqua Grande	São Tomé	6	16	49,541
Cantagalo	Santana	46	119	12,220
Caué	São João Angolares	104	268	5,838
Lemba	Neves	88	229	9,818
Lobata	Guadalupe	41	105	15,935
Mé-Zóchi	Trindade	47	122	33,621
Autonomous Island		55	142	5,705
Príncipe (Pagué)	Santo António	55	142	5,705
TOTAL		386	1,001	132,678

Demography

Population (2002): 147,000.
Density (2002): persons per sq mi 379.9, persons per sq km 146.5.
Urban-rural (1999): urban 46.0%; rural 54.0%.
Sex distribution (2001): male 49.28%, female 50.72%.
Age breakdown (2001): under 15, 47.7%; 15–29, 27.5%; 30–44, 12.6%; 45–59, 6.3%; 60–74, 4.5%; 75 and over, 1.4%.
Population projection: (2010) 171,000; (2020) 207,000.
Doubling time: 20 years.
Ethnic composition (2000): black-white admixture 79.5%; Fang 10.0%; angolares (descendants of former Angolan slaves) 7.6%; Portuguese 1.9%; other 1.0%.
Religious affiliation (1995): Roman Catholic, about 89.5%; remainder mostly Protestant, predominantly Seventh-day Adventist and an indigenous Evangelical Church.
Major cities (1997): São Tomé 49,541; Trindade 11,388[1]; Santana 6,190[1]; Neves 5,919[1]; Santo Amaro 5,878[1].

Vital statistics

Birth rate per 1,000 population (2001): 42.7 (world avg. 21.2).
Death rate per 1,000 population (2001): 7.5 (world avg. 8.9).
Natural increase rate per 1,000 population (2001): 35.2 (world avg. 12.3).
Total fertility rate (avg. births per childbearing woman; 2001): 6.0.
Marriage rate per 1,000 population: n.a.
Divorce rate per 1,000 population: n.a.
Life expectancy at birth (2001): male 64.2 years; female 67.1 years.
Major causes of death per 100,000 population (1987): malaria 160.6; direct obstetric causes 76.7; pneumonia 74.0; influenza 61.5; anemias 47.3; hypertensive disease 32.1.

National economy

Budget (2000). Revenue: Db 183,400,000,000 (grants 56.4%; taxes 32.4%, of which sales taxes 10.9%, import taxes 9.8%, income and profit taxes 9.1%; nontax revenue 11.2%). Expenditures: Db 244,400,000,000 (capital expenditure 63.3%; recurrent expenditure 36.7%, of which personnel costs 11.8%, debt service 10.0%, goods and services 6.2%, transfers 3.0%, defense 0.5%).
Public debt (external, outstanding; 2000): U.S.\$294,400,000.
Production (metric tons except as noted). Agriculture, forestry, fishing (2001): coconuts 25,500, taro 23,160, bananas 20,000, vegetables 7,000, cassava 5,324, cacao 3,418, fruits (other than melon) 2,400, corn (maize) 2,230, yams 1,300, coffee 18; livestock (number of live animals) 4,800 goats, 4,100 cattle, 2,600 sheep, 2,200 pigs; roundwood (2001) 9,000 cu m; fish catch (1999) 3,756, principally marine fish and shellfish. Mining and quarrying: some quarrying to support local construction industry. Manufacturing (value in Db; 1995): beer 880,000; clothing 679,000; lumber 369,000; bakery products 350,000; palm oil 228,000; soap 133,000; ceramics 87,000. Construction (1972): buildings authorized 44 (5,561 sq m, of which residential 3,698, mixed residential-commercial 1,361, commercial 502). Energy production (consumption): electricity (kW-hr; 2000) 26,050,000 (16,574,000); coal, none (n.a.); crude petroleum, none (n.a.); petroleum products (metric tons; 1997) none (25,000); natural gas, none (n.a.).
Household income and expenditure. Average household size (1981): 4.0; income per household: n.a.; sources of income: n.a.; expenditure (1995)[2]: food 71.9%, housing and energy 10.2%, transportation and communications 6.4%, clothing and other items 5.3%, household durable goods 2.8%, education and health 1.7%.
Population economically active (1994): total 51,789; activity rate of total population 40.8% (participation rates [1981] ages 15–64, 61.1%; female [1991] 32.4%; unemployed [1994] 29.0%).

Price and earnings indexes (1995 = 100)

	1995	1996	1997	1998	1999	2000
Consumer price index	100.0	137.6	175.8	209.7	233.6	233.9
Earnings index	...	...	...	...	...	...

Gross national product (2000): U.S.\$43,000,000 (U.S.\$290 per capita).

Structure of gross domestic product and labour force

	2000 in value Db '000,000	2000 % of total value	1998 labour force[3]	1998 % of labour force[3]
Agriculture	74,300	20.1	16,004	41.5
Mining	...	...	...	...
Manufacturing }	20,300	5.5	2,420	6.2
Public utilities }				
Construction	43,700	11.8	3,515	9.1
Transp. and commun. }	85,700	23.2	2,819	7.3
Trade }			5,350	13.9
Finance	32,100	8.7	215	0.6
Pub. admin., defense	84,800	22.9	3,338	8.7
Services	28,800	7.8	...	...
Other	...	...	4,921	12.8
TOTAL	369,700	100.0	38,582	100.0[4]

Tourism (1997): receipts from visitors U.S.\$2,000,000; expenditures by nationals abroad U.S.\$1,000,000.
Land use (1994): meadows and pastures 1.3%; agricultural and under permanent cultivation 54.0%; forest, built-on, wasteland, and other 44.7%.

Foreign trade

Balance of trade (current prices)

	1995	1996	1997	1998	1999	2000
U.S.\$'000,000	−18.3	−14.9	−13.9	−12.1	−18.0	−19.1
% of total	64.2%	60.3%	56.7%	56.3%	69.8%	74.9%

Imports (2000): U.S.\$22,300,000 (investment goods 52.9%, food and other agricultural products 20.2%, petroleum products 17.9%). *Major import sources:* Portugal 41.7%; Angola 13.0%; Japan 10.8%; Belgium 8.5%; France 7.6%; Gabon 3.1%; Germany 0.4%.
Exports (2000): U.S.\$3,200,000 (cocoa 90.6%). *Major export destinations:* The Netherlands 57.7%; Portugal 10.9%.

Transport and communications

Transport. Railroads: none. Roads (1999): total length 199 mi, 320 km (paved 68%). Vehicles (1996): passenger cars 4,040; trucks and buses 1,540. Merchant marine (2000): vessels (100 gross tons and over) 39; total deadweight tonnage 149,048. Air transport (1997): passenger-mi 6,000,000, passenger-km 9,000,000; short ton-mi cargo 700,000, short ton-km cargo 1,000,000; airports (2000) 2.

Communications

Medium	date	unit	number	units per 1,000 persons
Radio	1997	receivers	38,000	272
Television	1997	receivers	23,000	163
Telephones	2001	main lines	5,400	36
Internet	2001	users	9,000	60

Education and health

Educational attainment: n.a. *Literacy* (1991): total population age 15 and over literate 73.0%; males literate 85.0%; females literate 62.0%.

Education (1998)

	schools	teachers[5]	students	student/ teacher ratio
Primary (age 6–13)	71	638	20,287	34.1[5]
Secondary (age 14–18)[6]	11	415	11,814	29.6[5]
Voc., teacher tr.	...	...	...	...
Higher	...	...	...	...

Health: physicians (1996) 61 (1 per 2,147 persons); hospital beds (1983) 640 (1 per 158 persons); infant mortality rate per 1,000 live births (2001) 49.0.
Food (2000): daily per capita caloric intake 2,390 (vegetable products 96%, animal products 4%); 102% of FAO recommended minimum requirement.

Military

Total active duty personnel (2001): 18,043[7]. *Military expenditure as percentage of GNP* (1999): 1.0% (world 2.4%); per capita expenditure U.S.\$3.

[1]1981. [2]Weights based on CPI components. [3]Employed only. [4]Detail does not add to total given because of rounding. [5]1997. [6]Includes vocational. [7]Military manpower availability.

Saudi Arabia

Official name: Al-Mamlakah
al-'Arabīyah as-Sa'ūdīyah (Kingdom
of Saudi Arabia).
Form of government: monarchy[1].
Head of state and government: King.
Capital: Riyadh.
Official language: Arabic.
Official religion: Islam.
Monetary unit: 1 Saudi riyal
(SRls) = 100 halalah; valuation (Sept.
23, 2002) 1 U.S.$ = SRls 3.75;
1 £ = SRls 5.83.

Area and population

Geographic Regions Administrative Regions	Capitals	area sq mi	area sq km	population 2000 estimate
Al-Gharbīyah (Western)		121,637	315,039	7,304,025
Al-Bāḥah	Al-Bāḥah	3,830	9,921	476,382
Al-Madīnah al-Munawwarah	Medina (Al-Madīnah)	58,684	151,990	1,378,870
Makkah al-Mukarramah	Mecca (Makkah)	59,123	153,128	5,448,773
Al-Janūbīyah (Southern)		91,844	237,875	3,106,074
'Asīr	Abha	29,611	76,693	1,637,464
Jīzān	Jīzān	4,506	11,671	1,083,022
Najrān	Najrān	57,727	149,511	385,588
Ash-Shamālīyah (Northern)		138,256	358,081	1,197,700
Al-Ḥudūd ash-Shamālīyah (Northern Borders)	'Ar'ar	43,165	111,797	249,544
Al-Jawf	Sakākah	38,692	100,212	354,450
Tabūk	Tabūk	56,399	146,072	593,706
Ash-Sharqīyah (Eastern)		259,662	672,522	3,008,193
Ash-Sharqīyah (Eastern)	Ad-Dammām	259,662	672,522	3,008,913
Al-Wūsṭā (Central)		218,601	566,173	6,230,172
Ḥā'il	Ḥā'il	40,111	103,887	519,984
Al-Qaṣīm	Buraydah	22,412	58,046	979,858
Ar-Riyāḍ	Riyadh (Ar-Riyāḍ)	156,078	404,240	4,730,330
TOTAL		830,000	2,149,690	20,846,884[2]

Demography

Population (2002): 23,370,000[3].
Density (2002): persons per sq mi 28.2, persons per sq km 10.9.
Urban-rural (2001): urban 86.7%; rural 13.3%.
Sex distribution (2000): male 55.33%; female 44.67%.
Age breakdown (2000): under 15, 42.6%; 15–29, 22.8%; 30–44, 17.9%; 45–59,
12.1%; 60–74, 3.9%; 75 and over, 0.7%.
Population projection: (2010) 28,478,000; (2020) 36,460,000.
Doubling time: 22 years.
Ethnic composition (2000): Arab 88.1%, of which Saudi Arab 74.2%, Bedouin
3.9%, Gulf Arab 3.0%; Indo-Pakistani 5.5%; African black 1.5%; Filipino
1.0%; other 3.9%.
Religious affiliation (1992): Sunnī Muslim 93.3%; Shī'ī Muslim 3.3%; Christian
3.0%; other 0.4%.
Major urban agglomerations (2000): Riyadh 4,549,000; Jiddah 3,192,000; Mecca
1,335,000; Medina 891,000; Ad-Dammām 764,000.

Vital statistics

Birth rate per 1,000 population (2000): 37.5 (world avg. 22.5).
Death rate per 1,000 population (2000): 6.0 (world avg. 9.0).
Natural increase rate per 1,000 population (2000): 31.5 (world avg. 13.5).
Total fertility rate (avg. births per childbearing woman; 2000): 6.3.
Life expectancy at birth (2000): male 66.1 years; female 69.5 years.
Major causes of death per 100,000 population: n.a.

National economy

Budget (2000). Revenue: SRls 157,000,000,000 (oil revenues 75.1%). Expenditures: SRls 185,000,000,000 (defense and security 40.5%, human resource
development 26.6%, public administration, municipal transfers, and subsidies
16.5%, health and social development 8.9%).
Public debt: n.a.
Production (metric tons except as noted). Agriculture, forestry, fishing (2000):
wheat 2,046,000, alfalfa 1,400,000, dates 712,000, potatoes 394,000, watermelons 285,000, tomatoes 277,000, grapes 259,000, sorghum 204,000, barley
192,000, cantaloupes 140,500, dry onions 95,000; livestock (number of live
animals) 7,576,000 sheep, 4,305,000 goats, 400,000 camels, 297,000 cattle; fish
catch (1999) 51,949. Mining and quarrying (1999): gypsum 330,000; silver
20,000 kg; gold 9,000 kg. Manufacturing (value added in U.S.$'000,000; 1995):
industrial chemicals 3,014; cement, glass, and other nonmetal mineral products 943; refined petroleum 830; metal products 589; iron and steel 561; food,
beverages, and tobacco 493; plastic products 221. Energy production (consumption): electricity (kW-hr; 1996) 106,979,000,000 (106,979,000,000); coal,
none (none); crude petroleum (barrels; 2001) 2,862,000,000 ([1997]
603,789,000); petroleum products (metric tons; 1997) 94,298,000 (44,873,000);
natural gas (cu m; 1999) 46,200,000,000 ([1997] 43,400,000,000).
Population economically active (1994): total 5,614,000; activity rate of total
population 32.2% (participation rates [1988] ages 15–64, 59.1%, female 3.5%;
unemployed [1997] c. 25%).

Price and earnings indexes (1995 = 100)

	1995	1996	1997	1998	1999	2000	2001
Consumer price index	100.0	101.2	101.3	100.7	99.3	98.5	98.1
Earnings index	...	...	...	...	...	...	...

Gross national product (2000): U.S.$149,932,000,000 (U.S.$7,230 per capita).

Structure of gross domestic product and labour force

	2001 in value SRls '000,000	2001 % of total value	1990 labour force	1990 % of labour force
Agriculture	35,708	5.1	569,200	9.9
Petroleum and natural gas	238,492	34.1	46,800	0.8
Other mining	2,650	0.4	3,500	0.1
Manufacturing[4]	70,096	10.0	374,900	6.5
Construction	43,018	6.2	944,100	16.4
Public utilities	3,152	0.5	126,900	2.2
Transp. and commun.	30,500	4.4	262,300	4.5
Trade	49,506	7.1	898,300	15.6
Finance, real estate[5]	78,297	11.2	99,000	1.7
Pub. admin., defense	123,753	17.7	624,800	10.8
Services	23,130	3.3	} 1,822,000	31.6
Other	101[6]	—		
TOTAL	698,403	100.0	5,771,800	100.0[7]

Household income and expenditure. Average household size (1992) 6.1; income
per household: n.a.; sources of income: n.a.; expenditure (1994)[8]: food and
tobacco 38.5%, transportation and communications 16.4%, housing 15.2%,
clothing 8.8%, household furnishings 9.7%, education and entertainment
2.3%, other 9.1%.
Tourism (in U.S.$'000,000): receipts (1997) 1,420; expenditures, n.a.
Land use (1994): forested 0.8%; meadows and pastures 55.8%; agricultural and
under permanent cultivation 1.8%; built-on, waste, and other 41.6%.

Foreign trade[9]

Balance of trade (current prices)

	1995	1996	1997	1998	1999	2000
SRls '000,000,000	+82.2	+123.5	+119.8	+33.0	+85.1	+177.3
% of total	28.1%	37.3%	35.8%	12.8%	28.9%	43.9%

Imports (1999): SRls 104,980,000,000 (machinery and appliances 24.0%, transport equipment 14.5%, chemicals and chemical products 9.0%, base metals
and articles 8.4%, vegetables 7.3%, textiles and clothing 6.2%). *Major import
sources:* U.S. 18.9%; Japan 9.2%; U.K. 8.1%; Germany 7.3%; Italy 4.2%.
Exports (1999): SRls 190,100,000,000 (crude petroleum 72.8%; refined petroleum 15.8%; chemical products 4.8%; plastic products 1.9%). *Major export
destinations*[11]: U.S. 16.3%; Japan 14.9%; S. Korea 9.6%; Singapore 6.0%; The
Netherlands 4.2%.

Transport and communications

Transport. Railroads (1997–98): route length 1,390 km; passenger-km
222,000,000 metric ton-km cargo 856,000,000. Roads (1996): total length
162,000 km (paved 42.7%). Vehicles (1996): passenger cars 1,744,000; trucks
and buses 1,192,000. Merchant marine (1998): vessels (100 gross tons and
over) 279; total deadweight tonnage 1,278,000. Air transport (2001): passenger-km 20,216,000,000[12]; metric ton-km cargo 798,968,000[12]; airports (1998)
with scheduled flights 28.

Communications

Medium	date	unit	number	units per 1,000 persons
Daily newspapers	1996	circulation	1,105,000	59
Radio	1997	receivers	6,250,000	313
Television	1999	receivers	5,500,000	256
Telephones	2001	main lines	3,233,000	145
Cellular telephones	2001	subscribers	2,529,000	133
Personal computers	2001	units	1,400,000	63
Internet	2001	users	300,000	14

Education and health

Educational attainment (1986). Percentage of population age 25 and over having: no formal schooling 31.8%; primary, secondary, or higher education
68.2%. *Literacy* (1995): percentage of population age 15 and over literate
62.8%; males literate 71.5%; females literate 50.2%.

Education (1998–99)

	schools	teachers	students	student/ teacher ratio
Primary (age 6–12)	12,234	189,008	2,259,849	12.0
Secondary (age 13–18)	9,018	139,946	1,739,934	12.4
Voc., teacher tr.[13]	...	6,878	56,972	8.3
Higher[13]	72	9,427	165,545	17.6

Health (1995): physicians 30,306 (1 per 590 persons); hospital beds 41,916 (1
per 427 persons); infant mortality rate per 1,000 live births (2000) 52.9.
Food (2000): daily per capita caloric intake 2,875 (vegetable products 84%,
animal products 16%); 119% of FAO recommended minimum requirement.

Military

Total active duty personnel (2001): 126,500 (army 59.3%, navy 12.3%, air force
28.4%); U.S. military (2001) 5,200. *Military expenditure as percentage of GNP*
(1999): 14.9% (world 2.4%); per capita expenditure U.S.$996.

[1]Assisted by the Consultative Council consisting of 120 appointed members. [2]Detail
does not add to total given because of statistical discrepancy. [3]2002 pop. estimate
includes 6,030,000 expatriates (25.8% of the total population). [4]Includes refined petroleum. [5]Includes business services. [6]Other equals import duties less imputed bank services charge. [7]Detail does not add to total given because of rounding. [8]Urban middle-
income households only. [9]Imports c.i.f., exports f.o.b. [10]Includes reexports. [11]1998.
[12]Saudi Arabian Airlines only. [13]1997–98.

Internet resources for further information:
• Ministry of Information http://www.saudinf.com

Senegal

Official name: République du Sénégal (Republic of Senegal).
Form of government: multiparty republic with one legislative house (National Assembly [120])[1].
Head of state and government: President assisted by Prime Minister.
Capital: Dakar.
Official language: French.
Official religion: none.
Monetary unit: 1 CFA franc (CFAF) = 100 centimes; valuation (Sept. 23, 2002) 1 U.S.$ = CFAF 667.00; 1 £ = CFAF 1,037[2].

Area and population

Regions	Capitals	area sq mi	area sq km	population 1994 estimate
Dakar	Dakar	212	550	1,869,000
Diourbel	Diourbel	1,683	4,359	750,000
Fatick	Fatick	3,064	7,935	569,000
Kaolack	Kaolack	6,181	16,010	948,000
Kolda	Kolda	8,112	21,011	689,000
Louga	Louga	11,270	29,188	525,000
Saint-Louis	Saint-Louis	17,034	44,117	749,000
Tambacounda	Tambacounda	23,012	59,602	449,000
Thiès	Thiès	2,549	6,601	1,115,000
Ziguinchor	Ziguinchor	2,834	7,339	467,000
TOTAL		75,951	196,712	8,127,000[3]

Demography

Population (2002): 9,905,000.
Density (2002): persons per sq mi 130.4, persons per sq km 50.4.
Urban-rural (2000): urban 47.4%; rural 52.6%.
Sex distribution (2000): male 48.98%; female 50.02%.
Age breakdown (2000): under 15, 44.6%; 15–29, 27.5%; 30–44, 15.6%; 45–59, 7.7%; 60–74, 3.7%; 75 and over, 0.9%.
Population projection: (2010) 12,051,000; (2020) 15,023,000.
Doubling time: 24 years.
Ethnic composition (1988): Wolof 48.1%; Serer 12.6%; Peul (Fulani) and Tukulor 21.7%; Diola 5.0%; Malinke (Mandingo) 3.7%; other 8.9%.
Religious affiliation (1988): Sunnī Muslim 92.0%; traditional beliefs and other 6.0%; Christian (predominantly Roman Catholic) 2.0%.
Major cities (1994): Dakar 785,071 (urban agglomeration [1998] 1,905,000[4]); Thiès 216,381; Kaolack 193,115; Ziguinchor 161,680; Rufisque 138,837[5]; Saint-Louis 132,444.

Vital statistics

Birth rate per 1,000 population (2000): 37.9 (world avg. 22.5).
Death rate per 1,000 population (2000): 8.6 (world avg. 9.0).
Natural increase rate per 1,000 population (2000): 29.3 (world avg. 13.5).
Total fertility rate (avg. births per childbearing woman; 2000): 5.2.
Marriage rate per 1,000 population: n.a.[6]
Life expectancy at birth (2000): male 60.6 years; female 63.8 years.
Major causes of death (percentage of officially confirmed deaths from infectious diseases only; 1988): malaria 44.8%; tetanus 17.8%; meningitis 15.3%; tuberculosis of respiratory system 10.4%.

National economy

Budget (1997). Revenue: CFAF 432,200,000,000 (value-added taxes 30.3%, individual income tax 12.4%, taxes on petroleum products 9.1%, corporate income tax 6.7%). Expenditures: CFAF 432,200,000,000 (current expenditures 73.5%, of which education 19.0%, defense 9.3%, health 3.7%; development expenditure 26.5%).
Production (metric tons except as noted). Agriculture, forestry, fishing (2000): sugarcane 887,000, peanuts (groundnuts) 828,000, millet 506,000, watermelons 260,000, paddy rice 240,000, sorghum 147,000, mangoes 75,000, corn (maize) 66,000, oil palm fruit 64,000, onions 61,000, cassava 42,000; livestock (number of live animals) 4,300,000 sheep, 3,595,000 goats, 2,960,000 cattle, 510,000 horses; roundwood (1998) 4,934,000 cu m; fish catch (1998) 425,766. Mining and quarrying (1996): phosphate 1,376,000; salt 87,600[7]. Manufacturing (1996): tobacco 1,425,000; phosphates 1,384,000; cement 811,000; peanut oil 91,200; vegetable oil 84,200; sugar 68,400; soap 46,300. Construction (authorized; 1993)[5]: residential 357,000 sq m; nonresidential 235,000 sq m. Energy production (consumption): electricity (kW-hr; 1998) 1,160,000,000 (1,160,000,000); coal, none (none); crude petroleum (barrels; 1998) none (6,392,000); petroleum products (metric tons; 1998) 852,000 (895,000); natural gas, none (none).
Population economically active (1991): total 2,739,476; activity rate of total population 36.1% (participation rates [1988]: ages 15–60, 53.1%; female 25.6%; unemployed [1992] 24.4%).

Price and earnings indexes (1995 = 100)

	1995	1996	1997	1998	1999	2000	2001
Consumer price index[8]	100.0	102.8	104.4	105.6	106.5	107.2	110.5
Hourly earnings index	...	...	...	...	...	...	...

Household income and expenditure. Average household size (1991) 8.7; average annual income per household: n.a.; sources of income: n.a.; expenditure (early 1980s): food 49%, clothing and footwear 11%, housing 7%, education 6%.
Gross national product (2000): U.S.$4,714,000,000 (U.S.$490 per capita).

Structure of gross domestic product and labour force

	1997 in value CFAF '000,000,000	1997 % of total value	1991 labour force	1991 % of labour force
Agriculture	476.9	18.3	1,789,467	65.3
Mining	} 406.5	15.6	1,998	0.1
Manufacturing			161,124	5.9
Public utilities	51.3	2.0	...	...
Construction	126.5	4.8	60,935	2.2
Transp. and commun.	286.7	11.0	58,081	2.1
Trade[9]	649.5	24.9	378,241	13.8
Finance	...	...	4,623	0.2
Services	416.4	16.0	...	...
Pub. admin., defense	193.2	7.4	268,721	9.8
Other	—	—	16,286	0.6
TOTAL	2,607.0	100.0	2,739,476	100.0

Public debt (external, outstanding; 2000): U.S.$2,958,000,000.
Tourism (2000): receipts U.S.$140,000,000; expenditures (1999) U.S.$54,000,000.
Land use (1994): forested 39.5%; meadows and pastures 29.6%; agricultural and under permanent cultivation 12.2%; other 18.7%.

Foreign trade[10]

Balance of trade (current prices)

	1994	1995	1996	1997	1998	1999	2000
CFAF '000,000,000	−215.7	−219.8	−143.9	−154.7	−258.9	−273.2	−261.6
% of total	21.4%	20.3%	12.5%	12.5%	18.5%	17.8%	15.6%

Imports (1998): CFAF 793,000,000,000 (1995; agricultural products 34.5%, of which rice 7.1%, fixed vegetable oils 5.2%; capital goods 15.0%[11]; refined petroleum 11.0%[11]). *Major import sources:* France 35.8%; United States 5.9%; Germany 5.2%; Spain 4.6%; Nigeria 4.4%.
Exports (1998): CFAF 575,700,000,000 (1995[11]; fish and crustaceans 28.0%; chemical products 12.0%; peanut [groundnut] oil 11.0%; phosphates 3.0%). *Major export destinations:* France 9.8%; Mali 8.5%; Mauritania 3.9%; Cameroon 1.6%.

Transport and communications

Transport. Railroads: (1995) route length 761 mi, 1,225 km; (1993) passenger-mi 128,000,000, passenger-km 206,000,000; short ton-mi cargo 476,000,000, metric ton-km cargo 695,000,000. Roads (1996): total length 9,060 mi, 14,700 km (paved 29%). Vehicles (1996): passenger cars 85,488, trucks and buses 36,962. Air transport (1996)[12]: passenger-mi 139,644,000, passenger-km 224,736,000; short ton-mi cargo 11,247,000, metric ton-km cargo 16,420,000; airports (1996) with scheduled flights 7.

Communications

Medium	date	unit	number	units per 1,000 persons
Daily newspapers	1996	circulation	45,000	5.3
Radio	1997	receivers	1,240,000	141
Television	1998	receivers	370,000	41
Telephones	2001	main lines	237,200	24
Cellular telephones	2001	subscribers	390,800	40
Personal computers	2001	units	180,000	19
Internet	2001	users	100,000	10

Education and health

Educational attainment (1988). Percentage of population age 6–34 having: no formal schooling 62.6%; primary education 25.7%; secondary 8.4%; higher 0.8%; other 2.5%. *Literacy* (1995): percentage of total population age 15 and over literate 1,960,000 (37.3%); males literate 1,220,000 (47.2%); females literate 740,000 (27.6%).

Education (1996–97)

	schools	teachers	students	student/ teacher ratio
Primary (age 6–12)	3,530	16,567	954,758	57.6
Secondary (age 13–18)	359[13]	6,219	206,934	33.3
Vocational	19[13]	182[13]	4,624	40.1[13]
Higher[13, 14]	2	784	16,733	21.3

Health (1992): physicians 520 (1 per 14,825 persons); hospital beds 7,408 (1 per 1,041 persons); infant mortality rate per 1,000 live births (2000): 58.1.
Food (2000): daily per capita caloric intake 2,257 (vegetable products 91%, animal products 9%); 95% of FAO recommended minimum requirement.

Military

Total active duty personnel (2001): 9,400[15] (army 85.1%, navy 6.4%, air force 8.5%). *Military expenditure as percentage of GNP* (1999): 1.7% (world 2.4%); per capita expenditure U.S.$8.

[1]Replacement of former Senate (abolished January 2001) with new legislative advisory body was pending in late 2002. [2]Formerly pegged to the French franc and since Jan. 1, 2002, to the euro at the rate 1€ = CFAF 656.96. [3]Detail does not add to total given because of rounding. [4]Urbanized area of Pikine (1994 population estimate 855,287) is within Dakar urban agglomeration. [5]Within Dakar urban agglomeration. [6]In 1996 about half of all women lived in polygamous unions. [7]1994. [8]Capital region only. [9]Includes hotels. [10]Imports c.i.f.; exports f.o.b. [11]Estimated figure(s). [12]Represents 1/11 of total international scheduled traffic of Air Afrique (government-supported airline of 11 West African countries). [13]1992–93. [14]Universities only; 1994–95. [15]Excludes 1,170 French troops.

Internet resources for further information:
• **République du Sénégal (French language only)**
http://www.primature.sn

Seychelles

Indian
Ocean

Official name: Repiblik Sesel (Creole);
  Republic of Seychelles (English);
  République des Seychelles (French).
Form of government: multiparty
  republic with one legislative house
  (National Assembly [34]).
Head of state and government:
  President.
Capital: Victoria.
Official languages: none[1].
Official religion: none.
Monetary unit: 1 Seychelles rupee
  (SR) = 100 cents; valuation (Sept. 23,
  2002) 1 U.S.$ = SR 5.62;
  1 £ = SR 8.73.

Area and population		area		population
				1997
Island Groups	Capital	sq mi	sq km	census
Central (Granitic) group				
La Digue and satellites	—	6	15	1,998
Mahé and satellites	Victoria	59	153	67,338
Praslin and satellites	—	15	40	6,091
Silhouette	—	8	20	449
Other islands	—	2	4	0
Outer (Coralline) islands	—	86	223	0
TOTAL		176	455	75,876

Demography

Population (2002): 83,400.
Density (2002): persons per sq mi 473.9, persons per sq km 183.3.
Urban-rural (2002): urban 64.6%; rural 35.4%.
Sex distribution (2000): male 49.57%; female 50.43%.
Age breakdown (2000): under 15, 28.8%; 15–29, 29.6%; 30–44, 24.6%; 45–59,
  8.6%; 60–74, 5.8%; 75 and over, 2.6%.
Population projection: (2010) 93,000; (2020) 102,000.
Doubling time: 59 years.
Ethnic composition (2000): Seychellois Creole (mixture of Asian, African, and
  European) 93.2%; British 3.0%; French 1.8%; Chinese 0.5%; Indian 0.3%;
  other unspecified 1.2%.
Religious affiliation (1996): Roman Catholic 86.6%; other Christian (mostly
  Anglican) 9.3%; Hindu 1.3%; other 2.8%.
Major city (1999): Victoria 28,000.

Vital statistics

Birth rate per 1,000 population (2000): 18.6 (world avg. 22.5); (1998) legitimate
  24.7%; illegitimate 75.3%.
Death rate per 1,000 population (2000): 6.8 (world avg. 9.0).
Natural increase rate per 1,000 population (2000): 11.8 (world avg. 13.5).
Total fertility rate (avg. births per childbearing woman; 2000): 2.1.
Marriage rate per 1,000 population (2000): 6.0.
Divorce rate per 1,000 population (2000): 1.1.
Life expectancy at birth (2000): male 67.9 years; female 77.9 years.
Major causes of death per 100,000 population (2000): diseases of the cir-
  culatory system 190.0; malignant neoplasms (cancers) 89.0; accidents 61.0;
  diseases of the respiratory system 60.0; infectious and parasitic diseases
  35.9; diseases of the digestive system 23.0.

National economy

Budget (2000). Revenue: SR 1,332,700,000 (tax revenue 71.0%, of which customs taxes and duties 23.7%, sales tax 19.7%, tax on income and profit 18.3%;
  nontax revenue 25.3%; grants 3.7%). Expenditures: SR 1,674,800,000 (current expenditure 76.1%, of which debt service 15.7%, wages and salaries
  13.0%, education 8.1%, health 7.9%; capital expenditure 23.9%).
Tourism (2000): receipts from visitors U.S.$112,000,000; expenditures by
  nationals abroad U.S.$21,000,000.
Land use (1994): forested 11.1%; agricultural and under permanent cultivation 15.6%; built-on, wasteland, and other 73.3%.
Gross national product (1999): U.S.$573,000,000 (U.S.$7,050 per capita).

Structure of gross domestic product and labour force				
	2000			
	in value SR '000,000	% of total value	labour force[2]	% of labour force[2]
Agriculture	83.3	2.4	2,290	7.2
Manufacturing	498.8	14.5	3,835	12.0
Construction, mining	341.1	9.9	2,502	7.8
Public utilities	86.7	2.5	934	2.9
Trade	804.2	23.3	7,033	22.0
Transportation and communications	614.7	17.8	3,343	10.5
Finance	449.4[3]	13.0[3]	} 11,998	} 37.6
Pub. admin., defense	440.3	12.8		
Services	3	3		
Other	131.9[4]	3.8[4]	...	...
TOTAL	3,450.4	100.0	31,935	100.0

Production (metric tons except as noted). Agriculture, forestry, fishing (2001):
  coconuts 3,200, bananas 1,970, cinnamon 400, tea 236; livestock (number of
  live animals) 18,400 pigs, 5,250 goats, 1,500 cattle, 560,000 chickens; fish
  catch (2000) 4,768, of which (1998) jack 30.2%, snapper 18.3%, capitaine
  8.3%, mackerel 4.8%. Mining and quarrying (1998): guano 5,000. Manufac-

turing (2000): canned tuna 28,781; copra 377; tea 246; soft drinks 88,060;
  hectolitres; beer and stout 70,460 hectolitres; fruit juices 30,540 hectolitres;
  cigarettes 40,000,000 units. Energy production (consumption): electricity
  (kW-hr; 2000) 189,100,000,000 (166,500,000,000); coal, none (n.a.); crude
  petroleum, none (n.a.); petroleum products (metric tons; 2000) none
  (291,000); natural gas, none (n.a.).
Population economically active (2000): total 31,935; activity rate of total population 39.4% (participation rates: ages 15–64, 81.5%; female 43.0%; unemployed [1999] 11.5%).

Price and earnings indexes (1995 = 100)						
	1995	1996	1997	1998	1999	2000	2001
Consumer price index	100.0	98.9	99.5	102.1	108.6	115.4	122.4
Monthly earnings index	100.0	...	...	...	...	...	...

Public debt (external, outstanding; 2000): U.S.$134,400,000.
Household income and expenditure. Average household size (1997) 4.2; average annual income per household (1978) SR 18,480 (U.S.$2,658); sources of
  income: wages and salaries 77.2%, self-employment 3.8%, transfer payments
  3.2%; expenditure (1991–92): food and beverages 47.6%, housing 15.1%,
  clothing and footwear 8.6%, transportation 8.0%, energy and water 7.4%,
  recreation 6.7%, household and personal goods 6.6%.

Foreign trade

Balance of trade (current prices)					
	1995	1996	1997	1998	1999	2000
SR '000,000	–855.7	–1,188.7	–1,131.4	–1,140.1	–1,544.3	–476.5
% of total	62.8%	46.1%	49.4%	49.6%	50.0%	17.6%

Imports (2000): SR 1,591,400,000 (food, beverages, and tobacco 29.0%, manufactured goods 21.7%, machinery and transport equipment 20.3%, mineral
  fuels [including petroleum], lubricants, and related materials 17.0%, chemicals 7.2%). *Major import sources* (2000): South Africa 13.6%; France 11.5%;
  United Kingdom 10.6%; Italy 10.6%; Singapore 9.7%; United Arab Emirates
  2.1%; Thailand 1.4%.
Exports (2000): SR 1,114,900,000[5] (canned tuna 54.4%, petroleum products
  32.0%[6], other fish, including dried shark fins 4.5%, frozen prawns 1.6%, cinnamon bark 0.1%). *Major export destinations* (2000)[7]: United Kingdom
  44.4%; France 21.6%; Germany 12.1%; Italy 9.1%.

Transport and communications

Transport. Railroads: none. Roads (2000): total length 275 mi, 443 km (paved
  88%). Vehicles (2000): passenger cars 6,970; trucks and buses 2,483. Merchant
  marine (1992): vessels (100 gross tons and over) 9; total deadweight tonnage
  3,337. Air transport (2000): passenger arrivals 157,000, passenger departures
  158,000; metric ton cargo unloaded 4,592; metric ton cargo loaded 1,801; airports (2000) with scheduled flights 2.

Communications				units per 1,000 persons
Medium	date	unit	number	
Daily newspapers	1996	circulation	3,000	46
Radio	1997	receivers	42,000	560
Television	1998	receivers	12,000	149
Telephones	2001	main lines	21,400	267
Cellular telephones	2001	subscribers	44,100	552
Personal computers	2001	units	12,000	150
Internet	2001	users	9,000	112

Education and health

Educational attainment (1994). Percentage of population age 12 and over having: primary education 37.0%; some secondary 16.8%; complete secondary
  19.0%; vocational 15.2%; postsecondary 3.0%; not stated 9.0%. *Literacy*
  (2000): total population age 12 and over literate 91.0%; males literate 92.0%;
  females literate 91.0%.

Education (2001)				student/ teacher ratio
	schools	teachers	students	
Primary (age 6–15)	26	712	9,782	14.1
Secondary (age 16–18)	14	525	7,514	14.1
Voc., teacher tr.	11	216	1,740	8.1

Health (2000): physicians 105 (1 per 854 persons); hospital beds 420 (1 per 193
  persons); infant mortality rate per 1,000 live births (2000) 9.9.
Food (2000): daily per capita caloric intake 2,432 (vegetable products 80%,
  animal products 20%); 104% of FAO recommended minimum requirement.

Military

Total active duty personnel (2001): 450[8]. *Military expenditure as percentage of
  GNP* (1997): 3.8% (world 2.6%); per capita expenditure U.S.$194.

[1]Creole, English, and French are all national languages per 1993 constitution.
[2]Excludes unemployed, self-employed, and domestic workers. [3]Finance includes services. [4]Import duties less bank service charges. [5]Includes SR 402,800,000 of reexports. [6]Items reexported. [7]Domestic exports only. [8]All services form part of the army.

Internet resources for further information:
• Seychelles in Figures http://www.seychelles.net/hendrick

Sierra Leone

Official name: Republic of
Sierra Leone.
Form of government: republic with one
legislative body (Parliament [124[1]]).
Head of state and government:
President.
Capital: Freetown.
Official language: English.
Official religion: none.
Monetary unit: 1 leone (Le) = 100
cents; valuation (Sept. 23, 2002)
1 U.S.$ = Le 2,045; 1 £ = Le 3,178.

Area and population

Provinces		area		population
Districts	Capitals	sq mi	sq km	1985 census[2]
Eastern Province	Kenema	6,005	15,553	960,551
Kailahun	Kailahun	1,490	3,859	233,839
Kenema	Kenema	2,337	6,053	337,055
Kono	Sefadu	2,178	5,641	389,657
Northern Province	Makeni	13,875	35,936	1,259,641
Bombali	Makeni	3,083	7,985	317,729
Kambia	Kambia	1,200	3,108	186,231
Koinaduga	Kabala	4,680	12,121	183,286
Port Loko	Port Loko	2,208	5,719	329,344
Tonkolili	Magburaka	2,704	7,003	243,051
Southern Province	Bo	7,604	19,694	741,377
Bo	Bo	2,015	5,219	268,671
Bonthe (incl. Sherbro)	Bonthe	1,339	3,468	105,007
Moyamba	Moyamba	2,665	6,902	250,514
Pujehun	Pujehun	1,585	4,105	117,185
Western Area[3]	Freetown	215	557	554,243
TOTAL		27,699	71,740	3,515,812

Demography

Population (2002): 4,823,000.
Density (2002): persons per sq mi 174.1, persons per sq km 67.2.
Urban-rural (2000): urban 36.6%; rural 63.4%.
Sex distribution (2000): male 48.44%; female 51.56%.
Age breakdown (2000): under 15, 44.7%; 15–29, 26.1%; 30–44, 14.9%; 45–59, 9.2%; 60–74, 4.3%; 75 and over, 0.8%.
Population projection: (2010) 6,283,000; (2020) 8,036,000.
Doubling time: 27 years.
Ethnic composition (2000): Mende 26.0%; Temne 24.6%; Limba 7.1%; Kuranko 5.5%; Kono 4.2%; Fulani 3.8%; Bullom-Sherbro 3.5%; other 25.3%.
Religious affiliation (2000): Sunnī Muslim 45.9%; traditional beliefs 40.4%; Christian 11.4%; other 2.3%.
Major cities (1985): Freetown 469,776 (urban agglomeration [2001]; 837,000); Koidu–New Sembehun 80,000; Bo 26,000; Kenema 13,000; Makeni 12,000.

Vital statistics

Birth rate per 1,000 population (2000): 45.6 (world avg. 22.5).
Death rate per 1,000 population (2000): 19.6 (world avg. 9.0).
Natural increase rate per 1,000 population (2000): 26.0 (world avg. 13.5).
Total fertility rate (avg. births per childbearing woman; 2000): 6.1.
Life expectancy at birth (2000): male 42.4 years; female 48.2 years.
Major causes of death per 100,000 population: n.a.; however, the major diseases are malaria, tuberculosis, leprosy, measles, tetanus, and diarrhea.

National economy

Budget (1996–97). Revenue: Le 85,708,000,000 (customs duties 47.4%; excise taxes 25.4%; corporate income tax 9.5%; personal income tax 7.3%). Expenditures: Le 143,293,000,000 (recurrent expenditures 75.6%, of which transfers 24.4%, wages and salaries 19.8%, goods and services 18.9%, debt service 12.5%; capital expenditures 24.4%).
Gross national product (2000): U.S.$647,000,000 (U.S.$130 per capita).

Structure of gross domestic product and labour force

	1994–95		1997	
	in value Le '000,000	% of total value	labour force	% of labour force
Agriculture	275,327.5	38.8	1,052,000	63.8
Mining	119,229.2	16.8		
Manufacturing	61,475.3	8.6	297,000	18.0
Construction	15,788.2	2.2		
Public utilities	2,816.8	0.4		
Transp. and commun.	61,267.5	8.6		
Trade[4]	98,270.1	13.8		
Finance	14,732.2	2.1	300,000	18.2
Pub. admin., defense	19,844.9	2.8		
Services	12,308.9	1.7		
Other	29,329.7[5]	4.2[5]		
TOTAL	710,389.3[6]	100.0	1,649,000	100.0

Production (metric tons except as noted). Agriculture, forestry, fishing (1999): rice 247,235, cassava 239,597, oil palm fruit 163,000, pulses 40,000, peanuts (groundnuts) 29,010, plantains 26,000, tomatoes 25,000, sugarcane 21,000, sweet potatoes 20,000, coffee 17,350, sorghum 17,200, cacao beans 10,920, mangoes 6,500, millet 4,725; livestock (number of live animals) 400,000 cattle, 350,000 sheep, 190,000 goats, 52,000 pigs; roundwood (1998) 3,315,000 cu m; fish catch (1998) 52,700. Mining and quarrying (2000): rutile and ilmenite (titanium ores) (1994) 184,000[7]; diamonds 350,000 carats; gold 965 troy oz. Manufacturing (value added in Le '000,000; 1993): food 36,117; chemicals

10,560; earthenware 1,844; printing and publishing 1,171; metal products 1,073; furniture 647. Construction (value added in Le; 1994–95): 15,788,200,-000. Energy production (consumption): electricity (kW-hr; 1997) 242,000,000 (242,000,000); crude petroleum (barrels; 1997) none (1,700,000); petroleum products (metric tons; 1997) 177,000 (130,000).
Household income and expenditure. Average household size (1998) 6.3; average annual income per household (1984): U.S.$320; sources of income (1984): self-employment 61.6%, wages and salaries 27.9%, other 10.5%; expenditure (1989): food 66.2%, clothing 9.9%, housing 5.8%, transportation 4.4%, household goods 4.0%, recreation and education 3.8%, health 3.5%.
Public debt (external, outstanding; 2000): U.S.$969,000,000.
Population economically active (1996): total 1,610,000; activity rate of total population 34.8% (participation rates [1991]: ages 10–64, 53.3%; female 32.4%; unemployed [registered; 1992] 10.6%).

Price index (1995 = 100)

	1995	1996	1997	1998	1999	2000	2001
Consumer price index	100.0	123.1	141.5	191.8	257.2	255.1	260.4

Tourism (1999): receipts U.S.$8,000,000; expenditures U.S.$4,000,000.
Land use (1994): forest 28.5%; pasture 30.7%; agriculture 7.5%; other 33.3%.

Foreign trade[8]

Balance of trade (current prices)

	1996	1997	1998	1999	2000	2001
Le '000,000	−150,622	−64,598	−137,744	−142,509	−287,868	−312,580
% of total	63.6%	67.7%	86.8%	86.3%	84.3%	73.7%

Imports (1999): Le 153,856,000,000 (1995–96; food and live animals 51.6%; fuels 11.6%; chemicals 10.2%; machinery and transport equipment 8.9%; beverages and tobacco 2.7%; crude minerals 2.5%). *Major import sources* (1998): U.K. 20.0%; U.S. 13.0%; Belgium 7.5%; Italy 6.5%; Nigeria 5.5%.
Exports (1999): Le 11,347,000,000 (1995–96; mineral exports 56.4%, of which diamonds 50.6%, rutile [titanium ore] 5.7%; cocoa 5.0%; coffee 3.7%; reexports 4.8%). *Major export destinations* (1999): Belgium 40.8%; United States 7.5%; Spain 6.1%; U.K. 4.1%.

Transport and communications

Transport. Railroads (1995): length 52 mi, 84 km. Roads (1996): total length 7,270 mi, 11,700 km (paved 11%). Vehicles (1996): passenger cars 17,640; trucks and buses 10,890. Air transport (1996): passenger-mi 15,000,000, passenger-km 24,000,000; short ton-mi cargo 1,400,000, metric ton-km cargo 2,000,000; airports (1998) with scheduled flights 1.

Communications

Medium	date	unit	number	units per 1,000 persons
Daily newspapers	1996	circulation	20,000	4.7
Radio	1997	receivers	1,121,000	253
Television	1998	receivers	60,000	13
Telephones	2001	main lines	22,700	4.7
Cellular telephones	2001	subscribers	26,900	5.5
Personal computers	1999	units	100	—
Internet	2001	users	7,000	1.4

Education and health

Educational attainment (1985). Percentage of population age 5 and over having: no formal schooling 64.1%; primary education 18.7%; secondary 9.7%; higher 1.5%. *Literacy* (1995): total population age 15 and over literate 791,000 (31.4%); males literate 555,000 (45.4%); females 236,000 (18.2%).

Education (1992–93)

	schools	teachers	students	student/ teacher ratio
Primary (age 5–11)	1,643	10,595	267,425	25.2
Secondary (age 12–18)	167	4,313	70,900	16.4
Voc., teacher tr.	44	709	7,756	10.9
Higher[9]	2	257	2,571	10.0

Health: physicians (1996) 339 (1 per 13,696 persons); hospital beds (1988) 4,025 (1 per 980 persons); infant mortality rate per 1,000 live births (2000) 148.7.
Food (2000): daily per capita caloric intake 1,863 (vegetable products 97%, animal products 3%); 81% of FAO recommended minimum requirement.

Military

Total active duty personnel (2001): 6,000 (army 96.7%, navy 3.3%, air force, none)[10]. *Military expenditure as percentage of GNP* (1999): 3.0% (world 2.4%); per capita expenditure U.S.$4.

[1]Includes 12 paramount chiefs elected to represent each of the provincial districts. [2]Preliminary figures exclude adjustment for underenumeration; adjusted total is 3,760,000. [3]Not officially a province; the administration of the Western Area is split among Greater Freetown (the city and its suburbs) and other administrative bodies. [4]Includes hotels. [5]Import duties less imputed bank service charges. [6]Detail does not add to total given because of rounding. [7]Production was suspended after 1994 because of the civil war. [8]Import c.i.f.; exports f.o.b. [9]1990–91. [10]UN troops authorized from October 1999 numbered 17,100 in September 2002.

Internet resources for further information:
• **Sierra Leone Web** http://www.Sierra-Leone.org

Singapore

Official name: Hsin-chia-p'o
Kung-ho-kuo (Mandarin Chinese);
Republik Singapura (Malay);
Singapore Kudiyarasu (Tamil);
Republic of Singapore (English).
Form of government: unitary multiparty
republic with one legislative house
(Parliament [90[1]]).
Chief of state: President.
Head of state government: Prime
Minister.
Capital: Singapore.
Official languages: Chinese; Malay;
Tamil; English.
Official religion: none.
Monetary unit: 1 Singapore dollar
(S$) = 100 cents; valuation (Sept. 23,
2002) 1 U.S.$ = S$1.78; 1 £ = S$2.76.

Population (2000 census)	
De facto population	4,017,733[2]
De jure population	3,263,209[3]

Demography

Area: 263.6 sq mi, 682.7 sq km.
Population (2002): 4,204,000.
Density (2002): persons per sq mi 15,948, persons per sq km 6,158.
Urban-rural: urban 100.0%.
Sex distribution (2000)[4]: male 49.96%; female 50.04%.
Age breakdown (2000)[4]: under 15, 21.5%; 15–34, 30.1%; 35–54, 33.9%; 55–74,
12.1%; 75 and over, 2.4%.
Population projection: (2010) 4,670,000; (2020) 4,949,000.
Ethnic composition (2000)[4]: Chinese 76.8%; Malay 13.9%; Indian 7.9%.
Religious affiliation (2000)[5]: Buddhist 42.5%; Muslim 14.9%; Christian 14.6%;
Taoist 8.5%; Hindu 4.0%; traditional beliefs 0.6%; nonreligious 14.9%.

Vital statistics

Birth rate per 1,000 population (2001)[4]: 11.9 (world avg. 21.2).
Death rate per 1,000 population (2001)[4]: 4.4 (world avg. 8.9).
Natural increase rate per 1,000 population (2001)[4]: 7.5 (world avg. 12.3).
Total fertility rate (avg. births per childbearing woman; 2000)[4]: 1.4.
Marriage rate per 1,000 population (2000): 6.9.
Life expectancy at birth (2000): male 76.0 years; female 80.0 years.
Major causes of death per 100,000 population (2001)[4]: diseases of the circula-
tory system 164.4; malignant neoplasms (cancers) 130.5; diseases of the res-
piratory system 50.0; accidents and violence 31.0.

National economy

Budget (2000). Revenue: S$33,526,600,000 (income tax 40.0%, nontax revenue
24.6%, goods and services tax 6.7%, motor vehicle taxes 6.5%, customs and
excise duties 5.3%). Expenditures: S$18,896,900,000 (security 47.0%, education
20.6%, communications 12.8%, health 5.2%, trade and industry 2.1%).
Production (metric tons except as noted). Agriculture, forestry, fishing (2000):
vegetables and fruits 4,811; livestock (number of live animals) 2,000,000
chickens; fish catch (1999) 6,489. Mining and quarrying (value of output in
S$; 1994): granite 75,800,000. Manufacturing (value added in S$'000,000;
1996): electronic products 16,982.1; chemical products 3,326.5; machinery
and equipment 2,623.3; transport equipment 2,216.1; fabricated metal products 2,121.1; petroleum products 2,038.3. Construction (starts; 2000): residential 1,472,000 sq m; nonresidential 1,272,000 sq m. Energy production
(consumption): electricity (kW-hr; 1997) 26,188,000,000 (26,188,000,000);
crude petroleum (barrels; 1997) none (453,000,000); petroleum products
(metric tons; 1997) 53,592,000 (24,636,000).
Population economically active (2000): total 2,192,300[5]; activity rate of total
population 67.2% (participation rates: ages 15 and over, 85.6%; female
55.5%; unemployed 3.5%).

Price and earnings indexes (1995 = 100)							
	1995	1996	1997	1998	1999	2000	2001
Consumer price index	100.0	101.4	103.4	103.1	103.2	104.6	105.6
Monthly earnings index	100.0	105.8	111.8	114.9	118.0	128.4	131.4

Gross national product (at current market prices; 2000): U.S.$99,404,000,000
(U.S.$24,740 per capita).

Structure of gross domestic product and labour force				
	2000			
	in value S$'000,000[6]	% of total value[6]	labour force[7]	% of labour force[7]
Agriculture } Quarrying	190.8	0.1	12,600	0.6
Manufacturing	36,974.4	26.5	434,900	20.8
Construction	9,555.2	6.8	274,000	13.1
Public utilities	2,333.9	1.7	...	...
Transp. and commun.	19,557.0	14.0	196,500	9.4
Trade	27,272.2	19.5	401,300	19.2
Finance	35,666.1	25.5	322,500	15.4
Services	14,990.5	10.7	452,500	21.6
Other	−6,700.6[8]	−4.8[8]	500	—
TOTAL	139,839.5	100.0	2,094,800	100.0[9]

Household income and expenditure. Average household size (2000) 3.7; income
per household (2000) S$59,316 (U.S.$34,406); sources of income: n.a.; expenditure (1998): food 23.7%, transportation and communications 22.8%, housing costs and furnishings 21.6%, education 6.9%, clothing and footwear 4.1%,
health 3.3%, other 17.6%.
Tourism (2000): receipts from visitors U.S.$6,018,000,000; expenditures by
nationals abroad U.S.$4,970,000,000.

Foreign trade[10]

Balance of trade (current prices)						
	1996	1997	1998	1999	2000	2001
S$'000,000	−8,912	−10,993	+8,896	+6,147	+5,651	+10,335
% of total	2.5%	2.4%	2.5%	1.6%	1.2%	2.4%

Imports (2000): S$232,175,000,000 (office machines 12.4%, crude petroleum
6.5%, petroleum products 5.6%, telecommunications apparatus 4.7%, electric power machinery 4.7%, scientific instruments 3.7%, industrial machinery 2.1%). *Major import sources* (1999): U.S. 17.0%; Japan 16.6%; Malaysia
15.6%; China 5.1%; Thailand 4.7%; Taiwan 4.0%; South Korea 3.8%.
Exports (2000): S$237,826,000,000 (office machines 22.6%, petroleum products
7.2%, telecommunications apparatus 5.5%, electrical generators 3.4%, optical instruments 2.6%, industrial machinery 1.4%, clothing 1.3%). *Major
export destinations* (1999): U.S. 19.2%; Malaysia 16.6%; Hong Kong 7.7%;
Japan 7.4%; Taiwan 4.9%; Thailand 4.4%; United Kingdom 3.7%.

Transport and communications

Transport. Railroads (2000): length 117 km. Roads (1997): total length 3,017
km (paved 97%). Vehicles (2000): passenger cars 413,545; trucks and buses
147,325. Air transport (1999): passenger-km 64,528,800,000; metric ton-km
cargo 5,481,708,000; airports (2000) 1.

Communications				units per 1,000
Medium	date	unit	number	persons[4]
Daily newspapers	2000	circulation	1,197,301	367
Radio	1997	receivers	2,550,000	821
Television	1999	receivers	1,200,000	373
Telephones	2001	main lines	1,948,500	472
Cellular telephones	2001	subscribers	2,858,800	692
Personal computers	2001	units	2,100,000	508
Internet	2001	users	1,500,000	363

Education and health

Educational attainment (2000)[4]. Percentage of population age 15 and over having: no schooling 19.6%; primary education 23.1%; secondary 39.5%; postsecondary 17.8%. *Literacy* (1995)[4]: total population age 15 and over literate
90.8%; males literate 95.6%; females literate 86.1%.

Education (2000)				student/
	schools	teachers	students	teacher ratio
Primary (age 6–11)	201	12,287	305,992	24.5
Secondary (age 12–18)	180	11,340	201,107	17.7
Voc., teacher tr.	10	1,257	15,974	12.7
Higher	8	7,318	111,538	15.2

Health (2000): physicians 5,577 (1 per 585[4] persons); hospital beds 11,798 (1
per 277[4] persons); infant mortality rate per 1,000 live births (2001) 2.2.
Food (1988–90): daily per capita caloric intake 3,121 (vegetable products 76%,
animal products 24%); 136% of FAO recommended minimum requirement.

Military

Total active duty personnel (2001): 60,500 (army 82.7%, navy 7.4%, air force
9.9%). *Military expenditure as percentage of GNP* (1999): 4.8% (world 2.4%);
per capita expenditure U.S.$1,100.

---

[1]Includes 6 nonelective seats. [2]The de facto population figure includes citizens
(2,973,091), noncitizens with permanent residency status (290,118), and temporary residents (754,524). [3]The de jure population figure excludes temporary residents. [4]Based
on de jure population. [5]Based on de jure population aged 15 years and over. [6]At prices
of 1990. [7]Employed only. [8]Imputed bank service charges. [9]Detail does not add to total
given because of rounding. [10]Imports c.i.f., exports f.o.b.

Internet resources for further information:
• **Statistics Singapore http://www.singstat.gov.sg**

Slovakia

Official name: Slovenská Republika
(Slovak Republic).
Form of government: unitary multiparty
republic with one legislative house
(National Council [150]).
Chief of state: President.
Head of government: Prime Minister.
Capital: Bratislava.
Official language: Slovak.
Official religion: none.
Monetary unit: 1 Slovak koruna
(Sk) = 100 halura; valuation
(Sept. 23, 2002) 1 U.S.$ = Sk 43.85;
1 £ = Sk 68.15.

Area and population		area		population
Regions[1]	**Capitals**	sq mi	sq km	2001 census
Banská Bystrica	Banská Bystrica	3,651	9,455	662,121
Bratislava	Bratislava	793	2,053	599,015
Košice	Košice	2,607	6,753	766,012
Nitra	Nitra	2,449	6,343	713,422
Prešov	Prešov	3,472	8,993	789,968
Trenčín	Trenčín	1,738	4,501	605,582
Trnava	Trnava	1,602	4,148	551,003
Žilina	Žilina	2,621	6,788	692,332
TOTAL		18,933	49,035[2]	5,379,455[3]

Demography

Population (2002): 5,383,000.
Density (2002): persons per sq mi 284.3, persons per sq km 109.8.
Urban-rural (2002): urban 57.6%; rural 42.4%.
Sex distribution (2001): male 48.56%; female 51.44%.
Age breakdown (2001): under 15, 18.9%; 15–29, 25.1%; 30–44, 21.5%; 45–59, 18.9%; 60–74, 11.0%; 75 and over, 4.6%.
Population projection: (2010) 5,407,000; (2020) 5,361,000.
Doubling time: not applicable; population growth is negligible.
Ethnic composition (2001): Slovak 85.8%; Hungarian 9.7%; Rom (Gypsy) 1.7%; Czech 0.8%; Ruthenian and Ukrainian 0.7%; other 1.3%.
Religious affiliation (2001): Roman Catholic 68.9%; Protestant 9.2%, of which Slovak Evangelical 6.9%, Reformed Christian 2.0%; Greek Catholic 4.1%; Eastern Orthodox 0.9%; nonreligious and other 16.9%.
Major cities (2001): Bratislava 428,672; Košice 236,093; Prešov 92,786; Nitra 87,285; Žilina 85,400; Banská Bystrica 83,056.

Vital statistics

Birth rate per 1,000 population (2001): 10.5 (world avg. 21.2); (1999) legitimate 83.1%; illegitimate 16.9%.
Death rate per 1,000 population (2001): 9.3 (world avg. 8.9).
Natural increase rate per 1,000 population (2001): 1.2 (world avg. 12.3).
Total fertility rate (avg. births per childbearing woman; 2001): 1.3.
Marriage rate per 1,000 population (2001): 4.4.
Divorce rate per 1,000 population (2002): 1.8.
Life expectancy at birth (2001): male 70.0 years; female 78.2 years.
Major causes of death per 100,000 population (1999): diseases of the circulatory system 531; malignant neoplasms (cancers) 221; diseases of the digestive system 49; diseases of the respiratory system 48.

National economy

Budget (2000). Revenue: Sk 347,600,000,000 (tax revenue 87.4%, of which social security contribution 33.3%, value-added tax 20.3%, income tax 11.9%; nontax revenue 12.6%). Expenditures: Sk 378,800,000,000 (current expenditures 89.4%, of which social welfare 32.5%, wages 15.8%, health 12.8%, debt service 6.3%; investment 10.6%).
Production (metric tons except as noted). Agriculture, forestry, fishing (2001): wheat 1,894,000, sugar beets 1,293,140, corn [maize] 721,000, barley 685,200, potatoes 400,892, rapeseed 241,798, cabbages 157,500, sunflower seeds 136,214; livestock (number of live animals) 1,488,400 pigs, 646,100 cattle, 347,983 sheep; roundwood (2000) 5,213,000 cu m; fish catch (2000) 2,115. Mining and quarrying (2000): iron ore 750,000; gold (1998) 10,900 troy oz. Manufacturing (value added in Sk '000,000; 1998): food 10,203; nonelectrical machinery 10,116; transport equipment 9,422; crude steel and pig iron 8,204; electrical machinery 6,738; paper 6,346; refined petroleum 6,303; chemicals 6,286. Construction (1997): residential 281,298 dwellings. Energy production (consumption): electricity (kW-hr; 2000) 30,685,000,000 (22,957,000,000); coal (metric tons; 1997) 5,236,000 (4,875,000); crude petroleum (barrels; 1997) 462,800 (38,497,000); petroleum products (metric tons; 1997) 3,973,000 (1,998,000); natural gas (cu m; 2000) 358,800,000 ([1997] 5,743,400,000).
Population economically active (2001): total 2,665,837; activity rate of total population 49.6% (participation rates: ages 15–64, 79.6%; female 47.7%; unemployed 18.0%).

Price and earnings indexes (1995 = 100)							
	1995	1996	1997	1998	1999	2000	2001
Consumer price index	100.0	105.8	112.3	119.8	132.5	148.4	144.1
Annual earnings index	100.0	114.6	127.2	136.1	148.3	162.0	177.6

Household income and expenditure. Average household size (1999) 3.3; income per household (1999) Sk 74,010 (U.S.$2,100); sources of income: wages and salaries 68.0%, transfer payments 21.8%, other 10.2%; expenditure: food, beverages, and tobacco 26.3%, housing and energy 12.4%, transportation and communications 8.9%, clothing and footwear 7.3%.
Public debt (external, outstanding; 2000): U.S.$4,883,000,000.
Gross national product (2000): U.S.$19,969,000,000 (U.S.$3,700 per capita).

Structure of gross domestic product and labour force				
	2000		2001	
	in value Sk '000,000	% of total value	labour force[4]	% of labour force[4]
Agriculture	36,000	4.1	130,600	6.1
Mining and manufacturing	200,200	22.6	628,800[5]	29.6[5]
Construction	42,300	4.8	169,500	8.0
Public utilities	32,900	3.7	[5]	[5]
Transp. and commun.	90,100	10.1	162,100	7.6
Trade	134,200	15.1	327,300	15.4
Finance	[6]	[6]	142,600	6.7
Pub. admin., defense	106,100	12.0	157,800	7.4
Services	163,900[6]	18.5[6]	405,200	19.1
Other	81,500[7]	9.2[7]	...	...
TOTAL	887,200	100.0[2]	2,123,700[2, 8]	100.0[2, 8]

Tourism: receipts from visitors (2000) U.S.$432,000,000; expenditure by nationals abroad U.S.$295,000,000.
Land use (1994): forested 40.6%; meadows and pastures 17.0%; agricultural and under permanent cultivation 32.9%; other 9.5%.

Foreign trade

Balance of trade (current prices)						
	1995	1996	1997	1998	1999	2000
U.S.$'000,000	−228	−2,293	−2,081	−2,353	−1,093	−898
% of total	1.3%	11.5%	9.7%	9.9%	5.1%	3.6%

Imports (2000): U.S.$12,812,000,000 (machinery and transport equipment 35.6%; semimanufactured products 17.7%; mineral fuels 17.5%; chemicals and chemical products 10.9%). *Major import sources* (2000): Germany 25.0%; Czech Republic 18.7%; Russia 17.0%; Italy 6.2%; Austria 3.9%.
Exports (2000): U.S.$11,914,000,000 (machinery and transport equipment 39.4%; manufactured goods 26.6%; chemicals and chemical products 7.9%; mineral fuels 7.0%). *Major export destinations* (2000): Germany 26.7%; Czech Republic 20.0%; Italy 9.1%; Austria 8.3%; Poland 5.8%; Hungary 4.8%.

Transport and communications

Transport. Railroads (1998): length 3,673 km; passenger-km 3,092,000,000; metric ton-km cargo 11,754,000,000. Roads (1999): total length 17,710 km (paved, n.a.). Vehicles (2000): passenger cars 1,274,244; trucks and buses 121,634. Merchant marine: n.a. Air transport (2000): passenger-km 250,900,000; metric ton-km cargo 220,000; airports (2000) with scheduled flights 2.

Communications				units per 1,000
Medium	date	unit	number	persons
Daily newspapers	1996	circulation	989,000	184
Television	1999	receivers	2,250,000	417
Telephones	2001	main lines	1,556,300	288
Cellular telephones	2001	subscribers	2,147,300	397
Personal computers	2001	units	80,000	148
Internet	2000	users	650,000	120

Education and health

Educational attainment (1991). Percentage of adult population having: incomplete primary education 0.7%; primary and incomplete secondary 37.9%; complete secondary 50.9%; higher 9.5%; unknown 1.0%. *Literacy* (2001): total population age 15 and over literate 100%.

Education (2000–01)				student/
	schools	teachers	students	teacher ratio
Primary (age 6–14)	2,447	39,745	650,966	16.4
Secondary (age 15–18)	212	6,259	82,147	13.1
Voc., teacher tr.	368	11,255	111,128	9.9
Higher	20	9,047	125,896	13.9

Health (1999): physicians 19,171 (1 per 281 persons); hospital beds 60,169 (1 per 90 persons); infant mortality rate per 1,000 live births (2001) 9.0.
Food (2000): daily per capita caloric intake 3,133 (vegetable products 75%, animal products 25%); 127% of FAO recommended minimum requirement.

Military

Total active duty personnel (2001): 33,000 (army 60.0%, air force 30.9%, headquarters staff 9.1%). *Military expenditure as percentage of GNP* (1999): 1.8% (world 2.4%); per capita expenditure U.S.$187.

---

[1]Based on administrative reorganization effective from July 1996. [2]Detail does not add to total given because of rounding. [3]De jure figure; 2001 de facto census total equals 5,193,376. [4]Employed only. [5]Mining and manufacturing includes Public utilities. [6]Services includes Finance. [7]Bank service charges and indirect taxes. [8]Excluding 482,000 unemployed and women on regular and additional maternity leave and armed forces.

Internet resources for further information:
• **Statistical Office of the Slovak Republic** http://www.statistics.sk
• **National Bank of Slovakia**
  http://www.nbs.sk

Slovenia

Official name: Republika Slovenija (Republic of Slovenia).
Form of government: unitary multiparty republic with two legislative houses (National Council [40]; National Assembly [90]).
Head of state: President.
Head of government: Prime Minister.
Capital: Ljubljana.
Official language[1]: Slovene.
Official religion: none.
Monetary unit: 1 Slovene tolar (SIT; plural tolarjev) = 100 stotin; valuation (Sept. 23, 2002) 1 U.S.$ = 232.09 tolarjev; 1 £ = 360.69 tolarjev.

Area and population

Statistical regions[2]	Principal cities	area sq mi	area sq km	population 2002 preliminary census
Dolenjska	Novo mesto	653	1,690	135,484
Gorenjska	Kranj	825	2,137	194,476
Goriška	Nova Gorica	898	2,325	117,235
Koroška	Ravne na Koroškem	401	1,041	72,739
Notranjsko-kraška	Postojna	562	1,456	50,014
Obalno Kraško	Koper	403	1,044	100,238
Osrednjeslovenska	Ljubljana	1,367	3,540	485,843
Podravska	Maribor	838	2,170	307,273
Pomurska	Murska Sobota	516	1,337	120,397
Savinjska	Celje	920	2,384	251,493
Spodnjeposavska	Krško	342	885	67,873
Zasavska	Trbovlje	102	264	45,185
TOTAL		7,827	20,273	1,948,250

Demography

Population (2002): 1,948,000.
Density (2001): persons per sq mi 248.9, persons per sq km 96.1.
Urban-rural (2001): urban 49.1%; rural 50.9%.
Sex distribution (2000): male 48.84%; female 51.16%.
Age breakdown (2000): under 15, 16.1%; 15–29, 21.9%; 30–44, 23.4%; 45–59, 19.6%; 60–74, 14.0%; 75 and over, 5.0%.
Population projection: (2010) 1,962,000; (2020) 1,942,000.
Ethnic composition (2000): Slovene 89.8%; Croat 4.9%; Austrian 1.3%; German 1.0%; Serb 0.6%; other 2.4%.
Religious affiliation (1995): Christian 86.2%, of which Roman Catholic 82.7%, Orthodox 2.0%, Protestant 1.3%; Muslim 1.0%; other 12.8%.
Major cities (2000[3]): Ljubljana 270,986; Maribor 115,532; Kranj 51,923; Celje 49,572; Koper 47,905.

Vital statistics

Birth rate per 1,000 population (2001): 9.3 (world avg. 21.2); legitimate 64.4%; illegitimate 35.6%.
Death rate per 1,000 population (2001): 10.0 (world avg. 8.9).
Natural increase rate per 1,000 population (2001): –0.7 (world avg. 12.3).
Total fertility rate (avg. births per childbearing woman; 2001): 1.3.
Marriage rate per 1,000 population (2000): 3.6.
Divorce rate per 1,000 population (2000): 1.1.
Life expectancy at birth (2001): male 71.2 years; female 79.2 years.
Major causes of death per 100,000 population (2000): diseases of the circulatory system 377.5; malignant neoplasms (cancers) 242.7; accidents and violence 77.6; diseases of the respiratory system 74.4.

National economy

Budget (2000). Revenue: SIT 1,725,791,000,000 (taxes on goods and services 34.9%, social security contributions 32.0%, personal income tax 15.0%, nontax revenue 7.3%). Expenditures: SIT 1,781,311,000,000 (current expenditures 90.4%, development expenditures 9.6%).
Public debt (external, outstanding; 2000): U.S.$2,665,000,000.
Production (metric tons except as noted). Agriculture, forestry, fishing (2000): silage 1,900,000, sugar beets 467,000, corn (maize) 308,000, potatoes 194,000, wheat 150,000, grapes 98,000, apples 81,000; livestock (number of live animals) 552,000 pigs, 471,000 cattle; roundwood (1999) 2,133,000 cu m; fish catch (1997) 3,262. Mining and quarrying (1998): ferrosilicon 10,000; kaolin 10,000. Manufacturing (value added in SIT '000,000; 1997): base and fabricated metals 89,189; food, beverages, and tobacco products 81,998; chemicals and chemical products 81,408; electrical machinery 81,068; paper and paper products and printing and publishing 60,075. Energy production (consumption): electricity (kW-hr; 1999) 12,456,000,000 (10,432,000,000); coal (metric tons; 1998) 5,200,000 ([1997] 5,456,000); crude petroleum (barrels; 1999) 6,000 ([1997] 3,914,000); petroleum products (metric tons; 1997) 463,000 ([1998] 2,328,000); natural gas (cu m; 1999) 5,700,000 (996,000,000).
Land use (1994): forest 53.2%; pasture 24.8%; agricultural 11.6%; other 10.4%.
Household income and expenditure (1999). Average household size 2.84; income per household SIT 2,557,500 (U.S.$14,070); sources of income: wages 58.8%, transfers 29.7%, self-employment 7.0%, other 4.5%; expenditure: transportation and communications 18.9%, food and beverages 18.6%, housing 11.3%, recreation 8.2%, clothing and footwear 8.1%.
Gross national product (at current market prices; 2000): U.S.$19,979,000,000 (U.S.$10,050 per capita).

Structure of gross domestic product and labour force

	1999 in value SIT '000,000	% of total value	labour force[5]	% of labour force[5]
Agriculture, forestry	115,484	3.2	96,000	10.0
Mining	36,503	1.0	6,000	0.6
Manufacturing	866,778	23.8	278,000	28.9
Construction	193,157	5.3	45,000	4.7
Public utilities	96,060	2.6	8,000	0.8
Transp. and commun.	256,337	7.0	54,000	5.6
Trade, restaurants	457,620	12.6	143,000	14.9
Finance, real estate	517,280	14.2	70,000	7.3
Pub. admin., defense	180,101	5.0	49,000	5.1
Services	459,667	12.6	141,000	14.7
Other	458,450[6]	12.6[6]	71,000[7]	7.4[7]
TOTAL	3,637,437	100.0[8]	963,000[8]	100.0

Population economically active (1998): total 967,000; activity rate 49.6% (participation rates: ages 15–64, 69.1%; female 46.3%; unemployed[9] [2000] 12.2%).

Price and earnings indexes (1995 = 100)

	1995	1996	1997	1998	1999	2000	2001
Consumer price index	100.0	109.8	119.0	128.4	136.3	148.4	168.0
Annual earnings index	100.0	114.8	128.0	140.3	153.5	169.4	...

Tourism (2000): receipts U.S.$961,000,000; expenditures U.S.$461,000,000.

Foreign trade[10]

Balance of trade (current prices)

	1996	1997	1998	1999	2000	2001
U.S.$'000,000	–1,111	–985	–1,062	–1,537	–1,384	–893
% of total	6.3%	5.6%	5.5%	8.3%	7.3%	4.6%

Imports (2000): U.S.$10,115,000,000 (machinery and transport equipment 34.2%, other manufactured goods 21.9%, chemicals and chemical products 12.4%, mineral fuels 9.1%, food products 5.1%). *Major import sources:* Germany 19.0%; Italy 17.4%; France 10.3%; Austria 8.2%; Croatia 4.4%.
Exports (2000): U.S.$8,731,000,000 (machinery and transport equipment 36.0%, other manufactured goods 27.3%, chemicals and chemical products 11.2%, food products 2.3%). *Major export destinations:* Germany 27.2%; Italy 13.6%; Croatia 7.9%; Austria 7.5%; France 7.1%.

Transport and communications

Transport. Railroads (1999): length 746 mi, 1,201 km; passenger-km 625,000,000; metric ton-km cargo 2,784,000,000. Roads (1999): total length 12,507 mi, 20,128 km (paved 81%). Vehicles (1999): passenger cars 829,674; trucks and buses 67,111. Air transport (1999): passenger-mi 517,000,000, passenger-km 832,000,000; short ton-mi cargo 2,849,000, metric ton-km cargo 4,160,000; airports (1999) with scheduled flights 3.

Communications

Medium	date	unit	number	units per 1,000 persons
Daily newspapers	1996	circulation	397,000	199
Radio	1997	receivers	630,000	317
Television	1998	receivers	710,000	358
Telephones	2001	main lines	799,700	401
Cellular telephones	2001	subscribers	1,515,700	760
Internet	2001	users	600,000	301
Personal computers	2001	units	550,000	276

Education and health

Educational attainment (1991). Percentage of population age 25 and over having: no formal schooling 0.7%; incomplete and complete primary education 45.1%; incomplete and complete secondary 42.4%; higher 10.4%; unknown 1.4%. *Literacy* (2000): 99.7%.

Education (1998–99)

	schools	teachers	students	student/ teacher ratio
Primary (age 7–14)	444	15,140	189,564	12.5
Secondary (age 15–18)	201	8,816	116,672[11]	...
Higher	...	4,482	74,642	16.7

Health (1999): physicians 4,486 (1 per 440 persons); hospital beds 10,959 (1 per 180 persons); infant mortality rate per 1,000 live births 4.5.

Military

Total active duty personnel (2001): 7,600 (army 100%). *Military expenditure as percentage of GNP* (1999): 1.4% (world 2.4%); per capita expenditure U.S.$227.

---

[1]Hungarian and Italian are official in indigenous Hungarian and Italian communities. [2]Actual first-order administration is based on 192 municipalities. [3]Populations of municipalities, which may include nearby small towns and rural areas. [4]January. [5]Second quarter. [6]Corrections less imputed bank service charges. [7]Unemployed. [8]Detail does not add to total given because of rounding. [9]Registered. [10]Imports c.i.f.; exports f.o.b. [11]1997–98.

Internet resources for further information:
• **Statistical Office of the Republic of Slovenia**
  http://www.sigov.si/zrs/eng/index.html
• **Bank of Slovenia** http://www.bsi.si

Solomon Islands

Official name: Solomon Islands.
Form of government: constitutional monarchy with one legislative house (National Parliament [50]).
Chief of state: British Monarch represented by Governor-General.
Head of government: Prime Minister.
Capital: Honiara.
Official language: English.
Official religion: none.
Monetary unit: 1 Solomon Islands dollar (SI$) = 100 cents; valuation (Sept. 23, 2002) 1 U.S.$ = SI$7.51; 1 £ = SI$11.68.

Area and population

Provinces	Capitals	area sq mi	area sq km	population 1999 census
Central Islands	Tulagi	237	615	21,577
Choiseul	Taro	1,481	3,837	20,008
Guadalcanal	Honiara	2,060	5,336	60,275
Isabel	Buala	1,597	4,136	20,421
Makira-Ulawa	Kira Kira	1,231	3,188	31,006
Malaita	Auki	1,631	4,225	122,620
Rennell and Bellona	Tigoa	259	671	2,377
Temotu	Santa Cruz	334	865	18,912
Western	Gizo	2,114	5,475	62,739
Capital Territory				
Honiara	—	8	22	49,107
TOTAL		10,954[1]	28,370	409,042

Demography

Population (2002): 439,000.
Density (2002): persons per sq mi 40.1, persons per sq km 15.5.
Urban-rural (2002): urban 21.0%; rural 79.0%.
Sex distribution (1999): male 51.68%; female 48.32%.
Age breakdown (1996): under 15, 43.7%; 15–29, 28.7%; 30–44, 15.2%; 45–59, 8.1%; 60–74, 3.6%; 75 and over, 0.7%.
Population projection: (2010) 544,000; (2020) 667,000.
Doubling time: 21 years.
Ethnic composition (1986): Melanesian 94.2%; Polynesian 3.7%; other Pacific Islander 1.4%; European 0.4%; Asian 0.2%; other 0.1%.
Religious affiliation (1995): Christian 85.6%, of which Protestant 67.1% (including Church of Melanesia [Anglican] 31.0%), Roman Catholic 17.4%; traditional beliefs 3.1%; other 11.3%.
Major cities (1999): Honiara 49,107[2]; Noro 3,482; Gizo 2,960; Auki 1,606; Tulagi 1,333.

Vital statistics

Birth rate per 1,000 population (2002): 37.9 (world avg. 21.2).
Death rate per 1,000 population (2002): 4.7 (world avg. 8.9).
Natural increase rate per 1,000 population (2002): 33.2 (world avg. 12.3).
Total fertility rate (avg. births per childbearing woman; 2002): 5.3.
Marriage rate per 1,000 population: n.a.
Divorce rate per 1,000 population: n.a.
Life expectancy at birth (2002): male 68.0 years; female 71.0 years.
Major causes of death per 100,000 population (1990): respiratory diseases 22.4; diarrheal diseases 13.6; malaria 10.0.

National economy

Budget (1998). Revenue: SI$557,800,000 (foreign grants 33.0%, taxes on foreign trade 25.8%, income taxes 19.5%, taxes on goods and services 13.1%, nontax revenue 8.6%). Expenditures: SI$558,700,000 (capital expenditure 35.9%, administrative 28.6%, wages and salaries 27.2%, interest payments 8.3%).
Tourism: receipts from visitors (1999) U.S.$6,000,000; expenditures by nationals abroad U.S.$7,000,000.
Land use (1994): forested 87.5%; meadows and pastures 1.4%; agricultural and under permanent cultivation 2.0%; other 9.1%.
Gross national product (at current market prices; 2000): U.S.$278,000,000 (U.S.$620 per capita).

Structure of gross domestic product and labour force

	2000 in value SI$'000[3]	2000 % of total value	1993 labour force[4]	1993 % of labour force[4]
Agriculture	116,000	42.1	8,106	27.4
Mining	8,600	3.1		
Manufacturing	13,400	4.9 }	2,844	9.6
Construction	7,600	2.8	977	3.3
Public utilities	3,600	1.3	245	0.8
Transportation and communications	15,500	5.6	1,723	5.8
Trade	29,700	10.8	3,390	11.5
Finance	12,900	4.7	1,144	3.9
Pub. admin., defense }	68,000	24.7	4,303	14.6
Services }			6,845	23.1
Other	...	...	...	...
TOTAL	275,300	100.0	29,577	100.0

Household income and expenditure. Average household size (1999) 6.3; average annual income per household[5] (1991) U.S.$2,387; sources of income

(1983): wages and salaries 74.1%, self-employment, remittances, gifts, and other assistance 25.9%; expenditure (1992)[6]: food 46.8%, housing 11.0%, household operations 10.9%, transportation 9.9%, recreation and health 7.9%, clothing 5.7%, drinks and tobacco 5.0%.
Population economically active (1993): total 29,577[4]; activity rate of total population 8.3% (participation rates: ages 15–60 [1986] 98.6%; female 22.6%; unemployed [1999] 11%).

Price and earnings indexes (1995 = 100)

	1993	1994	1995	1996	1997	1998	1999
Consumer price index	80.5	91.2	100.0	111.8	120.8	135.7	146.9
Annual earnings index[4]	142.8	...	...	...	...	...	...

Production (metric tons except as noted). Agriculture, forestry, fishing (1999): coconuts 240,000, palm oil fruit 140,000, sweet potatoes 73,000, taro 32,000, yams 24,500, vegetables and melons 6,850, cacao beans 3,454; livestock (number of live animals) 58,000 pigs, 10,000 cattle, 185,000 chickens; roundwood (1998) 872,000 cu m; fish catch (2000) 23,443. Mining and quarrying (1998): gold 33,300 troy oz. Manufacturing (1997): palm oil 30,100, copra 23,500, coconut oil 3,900, cocoa 2,200, (1996) sawnwood 12,000 cu m. Construction (gross value in SI$ in Honiara; 1994): residential 9,508,000; nonresidential 11,151,000. Energy production (consumption): electricity (kW-hr; 1997) 32,000,000 (32,000,000); coal none (n.a.); petroleum products (metric tons; 1997) none (52,000); natural gas, none (n.a.).
Public debt (external, outstanding; 2000): U.S.$120,700,000.

Foreign trade[7]

Balance of trade (current prices)

	1994	1995	1996	1997	1998	1999
U.S.$'000,000	−0.06	+13.77	+10.96	−28.08	−18.07	+54.53
% of total	0.0%	4.3%	3.5%	8.2%	6.0%	19.9%

Imports (1996): SI$536,870,000 (machinery and transport equipment 30.3%, basic manufactured goods 22.2%, food and live animals 15.1%, mineral fuels and lubricants 11.3%). *Major import sources:* Australia 44.1%; Japan 12.5%; Singapore 7.0%; United States 2.1%; Thailand 1.8%; United Kingdom 1.6%.
Exports (1996): SI$656,300,000 (timber products 60.6%, fish products 18.3%, palm oil products 10.9%, copra 4.1%, cacao beans 2.2%). *Major export destinations:* Japan 40.1%; South Korea 19.4%; United Kingdom 18.4%; Thailand 3.8%; Australia 2.3%; Singapore 2.2%.

Transport and communications

Transport. Railroads: none. Roads (1996): total length 1,360 km (paved 2.5%). Vehicles (1993): passenger cars 2,052; trucks and buses 2,574. Merchant marine (1992): vessels (100 gross tons and over) 33; total deadweight tonnage 4,985. Air transport (1999): passenger-km 47,278,000; metric ton-km cargo 1,250,000; airports (1997) with scheduled flights 21.

Communications

Medium	date	unit	number	units per 1,000 persons
Radio	1997	receivers	57,000	141
Television	1998	receivers	6,000	14
Telephones	2001	main lines	7,400	16
Cellular telephones	2001	subscribers	1,000	2.1
Personal computers	2001	units	22,000	48
Internet	2001	users	2,000	4.3

Education and health

Educational attainment (1986)[8]. Percentage of population age 25 and over having: no schooling 44.4%; primary education 46.2%; secondary 6.8%; higher 2.6%. *Literacy* (1999): total population age 15 and over literate 181,000 (76%); males 102,500 (83%); females 78,500 (68%).

Education (1994)

	schools	teachers	students	student/ teacher ratio
Primary (age 7–12)	520	2,510	73,120	29.1
Secondary (age 13–18)	23	618	7,981	12.9
Voc., teacher tr.[9]	1	...	...	...
Higher[9]	1	...	...	...

Health: physicians (1999) 53 (1 per 7,692 persons); hospital beds (1997) 210 (1 per 1,957 persons); infant mortality rate per 1,000 live births (1999) 66.0.
Food (1999): daily per capita caloric intake 2,222 (vegetable products 92%, animal products 8%); (1997) 97% of FAO recommended minimum requirement.

Military

Total active duty personnel: no military forces are maintained, but the Solomon Islands Peace Plan of 2000 permits the establishment of a defense force.

[1]Detail does not add to total given because of rounding. [2]Urban agglomeration (2001) 78,000. [3]At 1985 factor cost. [4]Persons employed in the monetary sector only; 1990 = 100. [5]Public-service earnings. [6]Retail price index components. [7]Import figures are f.o.b. [8]Honiara only; a 1993 survey of rural households returned an average household income of U.S.$330. [9]Vocational and teacher training are carried out at the College of Higher Education.

Internet resources for further information:
• **Solomon Islands Government Ministries**
  http://www.commerce.gov.sb/Ministries/sigmin.htm
• **UN Common Country Assessment: Solomon Islands**
  http://www.undp.org.fj

Somalia[1]

Official name: Soomaaliya
(Somali)(Somalia).
Form of government: transitional
regime[2] with one legislative body
(Transitional National Assembly
[245[3]]).
Head of state and government:
President assisted by Prime Minister.
Capital: Mogadishu.
Official languages: Somali; Arabic.
Official religion: Islam.
Monetary unit: 1 Somali shilling
(So.Sh.) = 100 cents; valuation
(Sept. 23, 2002)
1 U.S.$ = So.Sh. 2,620[4];
1 £ = So.Sh. 4,072.

Area and population

Regions	Principal cities	area sq mi	area sq km	population 1980 estimate
Bakool[5]	Xuddur	10,000	27,000	148,700
Banaadir	Mogadishu (Muqdisho)	400	1,000	520,100
Bari[6]	Boosaaso	27,000	70,000	222,300
Bay[5]	Baydhabo	15,000	39,000	451,000
Galguduud	Dhuusamarreeb	17,000	43,000	255,900
Gedo[5]	Garbahaarrey	12,000	32,000	235,000
Hiiraan	Beledweyne	13,000	34,000	219,300
Jubbada Dhexe[5]	Bu'aale	9,000	23,000	147,800
Jubbada Hoose[5]	Kismaayo	24,000	61,000	272,400
Mudug[6]	Gaalkacyo	27,000	70,000	311,200
Nugaal[6]	Garoowe	19,000	50,000	112,200
Sanaag[7]	Ceerigaabo	21,000	54,000	216,500
Shabeellaha Dhexe	Jawhar	8,000	22,000	352,000
Shabeellaha Hoose[5]	Marka	10,000	25,000	570,700
Togdheer[7]	Burao	16,000	41,000	383,900
Woqooyi Galbeed[7]	Hargeysa	17,000	45,000	655,000
TOTAL		246,000[8]	637,000	5,074,000

Demography

Population (2002): 7,753,000.
Density (2002): persons per sq mi 31.5, persons per sq km 12.2.
Urban-rural (2001): urban 27.9%; rural 72.1%.
Sex distribution (2000): male 50.18%; female 49.82%.
Age breakdown (2000): under 15, 44.4%; 15–29, 26.8%; 30–44, 17.9%; 45–59,
6.6%; 60–74, 3.5%; 75 and over, 0.8%.
Population projection: (2010) 9,922,000; (2020) 13,023,000.
Doubling time: 24 years.
Ethnic composition (2000): Somali 92.4%[9]; Arab 2.2%; Afar 1.3%; other 4.1%.
Religious affiliation (1995): Sunnī Muslim 99.9%; other 0.1%.
Major cities (1990): Mogadishu 1,212,000[10]; Hargeysa 90,000; Kismaayo 90,000;
Berbera 70,000; Marka 62,000.

Vital statistics

Birth rate per 1,000 population (2001): 47.2 (world avg. 21.2).
Death rate per 1,000 population (2001): 18.4 (world avg. 8.9).
Natural increase rate per 1,000 population (2001): 28.8 (world avg. 12.3).
Total fertility rate (avg. births per childbearing woman; 2000): 7.1.
Life expectancy at birth (2001): male 45.0 years; female 48.3 years.

National economy

Budget (1991). Revenue: So.Sh. 151,453,000,000 (domestic revenue sources,
principally indirect taxes and import duties 60.4%; external grants and transfers 39.6%). Expenditures: So.Sh. 141,141,000,000 (general services 46.9%;
economic and social services 31.2%; debt service 7.0%).
Public debt (external, outstanding; 2000): U.S.$1,825,000,000.
Production (metric tons except as noted). Agriculture, forestry, fishing (1999):
fruits (excluding melons) 210,000, sugarcane 210,000, corn (maize) 150,000,
cassava 65,000, bananas 55,000, sorghum 55,000, sesame seed 22,000, beans
14,000, dates 10,000, seed cotton 4,550, other forest products include khat,
frankincense, and myrrh; livestock (number of live animals) 13,000,000
sheep, 12,000,000 goats, 6,000,000 camels, 5,000,000 cattle; roundwood
(2000) 9,338,000 cu m; fish catch (2000) 20,200. Mining and quarrying (2001):
gypsum 1,500; salt 1,000. Manufacturing (value added in So.Sh. '000,000;
1988): food 794; cigarettes and matches 562; hides and skins 420; paper and
printing 328; plastics 320; chemicals 202; beverages 144. Energy production
(consumption): electricity (kW-hr; 1998) 265,000,000 (246,000,000); coal,
none (none); crude petroleum (barrels; 1991) none (806,000); petroleum
products (metric tons; 1991) none (59,000); natural gas, none (none).
Household income and expenditure. Average household size (1980) 4.9; income
per household: n.a.; sources of income: n.a.; expenditure (1983)[11]: food and
tobacco 62.3%, housing 15.3%, clothing 5.6%, energy 4.3%, other 12.5%.
Population economically active (1991): total 3,215,000; activity rate of total
population 40.9% (participation rates [1987] over age 10, 63.1%; female
48.7%; unemployed n.a.).

Price and earnings indexes (1990 = 100)

	1989	1990	1991	1992	1993	1994	1995
Consumer price index[12]	100.0	240.0	372.2	507.4	630.7	749.8	872.1
Earnings index	...	...	...	...	...	...	...

Gross national product (1996): U.S.$706,000,000 (U.S.$110 per capita).

Structure of gross domestic product and labour force

	1991 in value So.Sh. '000,000	% of total value	labour force	% of labour force
Agriculture	867,500	64.5	2,275,000	70.8
Mining	2,700	0.2		
Manufacturing	59,200	4.4		
Construction	51,100	3.8	336,000	10.4
Public utilities	9,400	0.7		
Transp. and commun.	80,700	6.0		
Trade	125,000	9.3		
Finance	45,700	3.4		
Pub. admin., defense	80,700	6.0	604,000	18.8
Services	30,900	2.3		
Other	−8,100	−0.6		
TOTAL	1,344,900[8]	100.0	3,215,000	100.0

Tourism: n.a.
Land use (1994): forest 25.5%; pasture 68.6%; agriculture 1.6%; other 4.3%.

Foreign trade[13]

Balance of trade (current prices)

	1994	1995	1996	1997	1998	1999
U.S.$'000,000	−133	−48	−20	−30	−30	−30
% of total	32.8%	14.2%	6.2%	9.1%	9.1%	9.1%

Imports (1999): U.S.$180,000,000 (agricultural products 49.2%, of which
refined sugar 23.9%, wheat 14.3%, rice 9.4%; unspecified 50.8%). *Major
import sources:* Djibouti 27%; Kenya 12%; India 9%; Thailand 5%; United
Arab Emirates 4%.
Exports (1999): U.S.$150,000,000 (agricultural products 47.6%, of which live
sheep and goats 38.7%, bananas 5.3%; other [including bagged charcoal]
52.4%). *Major export destinations:* Yemen 29%; Saudi Arabia 28%; United
Arab Emirates 28%; Oman 6%.

Transport and communications

Transport. Railroads: none. Roads (1996): total length 13,700 mi, 22,100
km (paved 12%). Vehicles (1996): passenger cars 1,020; trucks and buses
6,440. Merchant marine (1992): vessels (100 gross tons and over) 28; total
deadweight tonnage 18,496. Air transport (1991): passenger-mi 81,000,000,
passenger-km 131,000,000; short ton-mi cargo 3,000,000, metric ton-km
cargo 5,000,000; airports (1998) with scheduled flights 1.

Communications

Medium	date	unit	number	units per 1,000 persons
Daily newspapers	1996	circulation	10,000	1.2
Radio	1997	receivers	470,000	53
Television	1997	receivers	135,000	15
Telephones	1999	main lines	15,000	2.1

Education and health

Educational attainment: n.a. *Literacy* (1995): percentage of total population age
15 and over literate 24%; males literate 36%; females literate 14%.

Education (1989–90)

	schools	teachers	students	student/ teacher ratio
Primary (age 6–14)	1,125	8,208	377,000	20.9
Secondary (age 15–18)	82	2,109	44,000	20.3
Voc., teacher tr.	21	498	10,400	9.7
Higher	1	549	4,640	

Health: physicians (1997) 265 (1 per 25,034 persons); hospital beds (1985) 5,536
(1 per 1,130 persons); infant mortality rate (2001) 124.0.
Food (2000): daily per capita caloric intake 1,628 (vegetable products 62%,
animal products 38%); 70% of FAO recommended minimum requirement.

Military

Total active duty personnel: clan warfare between 1991 and late 2002. *Military
expenditure as percentage of GNP* (1990): 0.9% (world 4.3%); per capita
expenditure U.S.$1.

---

[1]Proclamation of the "Republic of Somaliland" in May 1991 on territory corresponding to the former British Somaliland (which unified with the former Italian Trust
Territory of Somalia to form Somalia in 1960) had not received international recognition as of November 2002. This entity represented about a quarter of Somalia's territory. [2]From August 2000. [3]Includes 44 seats allotted to each of 4 major clans, 24 seats
allotted to minor clans and tribes, 25 seats allotted to women, and 20 nominees of
president. [4]In November 2002 about 19,000–20,200 So.Sh. equaled 1 U.S.$ on the black
market. [5]Part of "autonomous region" of South-western Somalia from April 2002. [6]Part
of "autonomous region" of Puntland from 1998. [7]Part of "Republic of Somaliland"
from 1991. [8]Detail does not add to total given because of rounding. [9]The Somali are
divided into six major clans, of which four are predominantly pastoral (representing *c.*
70% of the population) and two are predominantly agricultural (representing *c.* 20%
of the population); the remainder are urban dwellers with less clan identification. [10]2001.
[11]Mogadishu only. [12]Reported inflation rate. [13]Imports c.i.f.; exports f.o.b.

Internet resources for further information:
• **The ACG Somalia Page**
  http://www.abyssiniacybergateway.net/somalia
• **UN Development Programme in Somalia**
  http://www.so.undp.org

South Africa

Official name: Republic of South Africa (English).
Form of government: multiparty republic with two legislative houses (National Council of Provinces [90]; National Assembly [400]).
Head of state and government: President.
Capitals (de facto): Pretoria/Tshwane[1] (executive); Bloemfontein/Mangaung[1] (judicial); Cape Town (legislative).
Official languages: [2].
Official religion: none.
Monetary unit: 1 rand (R) = 100 cents; valuation (Sept. 23, 2002) 1 U.S.$ = R 10.63; 1 £ = R 16.52.

Area and population

Provinces	Capitals	area sq mi	area sq km	population 2002 estimate
Eastern Cape	Bisho	65,475	169,580	7,132,141
Free State	Bloemfontein	49,993	129,480	2,859,081
Gauteng	Johannesburg	6,568	17,010	8,106,190
KwaZulu–Natal	Pietermaritzburg	35,560	92,100	9,212,123
Limpopo	Polokwane	47,842	123,910	5,843,851
Mpumalanga	Nelspruit	30,691	79,490	3,156,272
Northern Cape	Kimberley	139,703	361,830	888,390
North West	Mafikeng/Mmabatho	44,911	116,320	3,659,902
Western Cape	Cape Town	49,950	129,370	4,313,959
TOTAL		470,693	1,219,090	45,171,909

Demography

Population (2002): 45,172,000.
Density (2002): persons per sq mi 96.0, persons per sq km 37.1.
Urban-rural (2002): urban 57.7%; rural 42.3%.
Sex distribution (2002): male 48.15%; female 51.85%.
Age breakdown (1996): under 15, 33.9%; 15–29, 28.6%; 30–44, 19.4%; 45–59, 9.9%; 60–74, 5.3%; 75 and over, 1.7%; unknown, 1.2%.
Population projection: (2010) 46,362,000; (2020) 45,167,000.
Ethnic composition (2000): black 77.6%, of which Zulu c. 22.0%, Xhosa c. 18.0%, Pedi c. 9.0%, Sotho c. 7.0%, Tswana c. 7.0%, Tsonga c. 3.5%, Swazi c. 3.0%; white 10.4%; Coloured 8.7%; Asian 2.5%; other 0.8%.
Religious affiliation (2000): Christian 83.1%, of which black independent churches 39.1%, Protestant 31.8%, Roman Catholic 7.1%; traditional beliefs 8.4%; Hindu 2.4%; Muslim 2.4%; nonreligious 2.4%; Bahā'ī 0.6%; Jewish 0.4%; other 0.3%.
Major urban agglomerations (2000)[3]: Cape Town 2,930,000; Durban 2,391,000[4]; Johannesburg 2,950,000[4]; Pretoria 1,590,000; Port Elizabeth 1,006,000[5].

Vital statistics

Birth rate per 1,000 population (2001): 19.8 (world avg. 21.2).
Death rate per 1,000 population (2001): 15.0 (world avg. 8.9).
Natural increase rate per 1,000 population (2001): 4.8 (world avg. 12.3).
Marriage rate per 1,000 population (1998): 3.4.
Total fertility rate (avg. births per childbearing woman; 2001): 2.4.
Life expectancy at birth (2001): male 50.7 years; female 51.4 years.
Major causes of death per 100,000 population (1993–94): accidents and violence 221.9; diseases of the circulatory system 102.3; infectious and parasitic diseases 51.8; ill-defined conditions 424.0.

National economy

Budget (2000–01). Revenue: R 213,385,700,000 (personal income taxes 42.8%, value-added taxes 24.3%, company income taxes 11.6%, other 21.3%). Expenditures: R 235,048,400,000 (transfer to provinces 46.3%, interest on public debt 19.6%, police and prisons 9.1%, defense 5.9%).
Public debt (external, outstanding; 2000): U.S.$9,088,000,000.
Production (in R '000,000 except as noted). Agriculture, forestry, fishing (in value of production; 2000): poultry 8,270, corn (maize) 5,654, beef 3,904, temperate fruits 2,975, sugarcane 2,530, vegetables 2,516, milk 2,229, wheat 2,100, citrus fruits 1,835, potatoes 1,599, sheep and goat meat 1,322; roundwood (2000) 30,616,000 cu m; fish catch (1999) 592,144 metric tons. Mining and quarrying (in value of sales; 2000): platinum-group metals 27,111; gold 25,272; rough diamonds 10,015,000 carats; coal 19,520; iron ore (1998) 2,492; copper (1998) 1,612; nickel (1997) 1,004. Manufacturing (in R '000,000 value added; 1996): food products 11,437; iron and steel 7,515; transport equipment 7,445; metal products 6,930; nonelectrical machinery 5,495; beverages 4,511; refined petroleum 3,926. Energy production (consumption): electricity (kW-hr; 1999) 203,532,000,000 ([1998] 187,517,000,000); coal (metric tons; 1999) 223,357,000 ([1997] 149,076,000[6]); crude petroleum (barrels; 1999) 5,493,000 ([1997] 159,061,000[6]); petroleum products (metric tons; 1997) 19,193,000[6] (17,252,000[6]); natural gas (cu m; 1999) 1,616,500,000[6] (1,616,500,000[6]).
Tourism (2000): receipts U.S.$2,707,000,000; expenditures U.S.$2,004,000,000.
Household income and expenditure. Average household size (1996) 4.5; average annual disposable income per household (1996)[7] R 47,600 (U.S.$11,070); expenditure (1998): food, beverages, and tobacco 31.3%; transportation 14.3%; housing 9.3%; household furnishings and operation 8.9%.
Population economically active (2000): total 13,527,000; activity rate of total population 31.2% (participation rates [1995]: over age 15, c. 53%; female 43.6%; unemployed [2000] 23.3%).

Price and earnings indexes (1995 = 100)

	1994	1995	1996	1997	1998	1999	2000
Consumer price index	92.0	100.0	107.4	116.5	124.6	130.5	138.1
Monthly earnings index	...	...	...	...	...	...	...

Gross national product (2000): U.S.$129,171,000,000 (U.S.$3,020 per capita).

Structure of gross domestic product and labour force

	2000 in value R '000,000	2000 % of total value	2000 labour force	2000 % of labour force
Agriculture	25,375	2.9	1,099,000	8.1
Mining	51,563	5.9	476,000	3.5
Manufacturing	148,875	17.0	1,498,000	11.1
Construction	22,152	2.5	567,000	4.2
Public utilities	22,995	2.6	78,000	0.6
Transp. and commun.	80,063	9.2	539,000	4.0
Trade	103,523	11.9	2,079,000	15.4
Finance, real estate	160,954	18.4	931,000	6.9
Pub. admin., defense	129,735	14.9	} 2,951,000	21.8
Services	48,358	5.5		
Other	79,644[8]	9.1[8]	3,309,000[9]	24.5[9]
TOTAL	873,637	100.0[10]	13,527,000	100.0[10]

Land use (1994): forest 6.7%; pasture 66.7%; agriculture 10.8%; other 15.8%.

Foreign trade

Balance of trade (current prices)

	1996	1997	1998	1999	2000	2001
U.S.$'000,000	+2,695	+2,324	+2,056	+4,073	+4,232	+4,966
% of total	4.7%	3.9%	3.6%	7.7%	7.2%	8.8%

Imports (2000): U.S.$27,202,000,000 (1997; machinery and apparatus 33.7%, petroleum and products 11.1%, basic manufactures 10.5%, chemicals and chemical products 10.5%, food 3.9%). *Major import sources* (1999): Germany 14.5%; U.S. 13.3%; U.K. 9.4%; Japan 7.5%; France 4.3%.
Exports (2000): U.S.$31,434,000,000 (1997; machinery and transport equipment 14.8%; pearls, precious and semiprecious stones 14.7%; gem diamonds 14.7%; chemicals 9.1%; food 8.9%; iron and steel 6.8%). *Major export destinations* (1999): U.K. 8.3%; U.S. 8.2%; Germany 7.0%; Japan 5.2%; Italy 4.2%; unspecified 21.8%.

Transport and communications

Transport. Railroads: route length (1998) 20,319 km[11]; passenger-km (1997–98) 1,775,000,000[11]; metric ton-km cargo (1997–98) 103,866,000,000. Roads (1999): length 331,265 km (paved 41%). Vehicles (1999): passenger cars 3,966,252; trucks and buses 1,904,871. Air transport (2000)[12]: passenger-km 19,320,000,000; metric ton-km cargo 677,048,000; airport (1996) 24.

Communications

Medium	date	unit	number	units per 1,000 persons
Daily newspapers	1996	circulation	1,288,000	31
Radio	1997	receivers	13,750,000	324
Television	1999	receivers	5,450,000	124
Telephones	2001	main lines	4,969,000	101
Cellular telephones	2001	subscribers	9,197,000	210
Personal computers	2001	units	3,000,000	69
Internet	2001	users	3,068,000	70

Education and health

Educational attainment (1994). Percentage of population age 25 and over having: no formal schooling 14.5%; primary/incomplete secondary 61.6%; secondary/incomplete higher 20.4%; complete higher 3.1%; other/unknown 0.4%. *Literacy* (1995): total population age 15 and over literate: 81.8%.

Education (1999)

	schools	teachers	students	student/ teacher ratio
Primary (age 6–12)	14,897	159,432	5,578,978	35.0
Secondary (age 13–17)[13]	8,493	152,305	5,008,932	32.9
Higher[14]	241	27,099[15]	669,115	...

Health: physicians (2000) 29,788 (1 per 1,453 persons); hospital beds (1998) 144,363 (1 per 290 persons); infant mortality rate (2001) 58.1.
Food (2000): daily per capita caloric intake 2,886 (vegetable products 87%, animal products 13%); 114% of FAO recommended minimum.

Military

Total active duty personnel (2001): 61,500 (army 67.9%, navy 8.1%, air force 15.0%, intraservice medical service 9.0%). *Military expenditure as percentage of GNP* (1999): 1.5% (world 2.4%); per capita expenditure U.S.$45.

---

[1]Renamed within larger municipality in December 2000. [2]Afrikaans; English; Ndebele; Pedi (North Sotho); Sotho (South Sotho); Swazi; Tsonga; Tswana (West Sotho); Venda; Xhosa; Zulu. [3]UN estimates. [4]Name change pending late 2002. [5]Known as Nelson Mandela Metropole in combination with the adjacent cities of Uitenhage and Despatch. [6]Includes Botswana, Lesotho, Namibia, and Swaziland. [7]Estimated figures. [8]Taxes on products less subsidies on products. [9]Includes 151,000 not adequately defined and 3,158,000 unemployed. [10]Detail does not add to total given because of rounding. [11]Excludes suburban lines. [12]SAA only. [13]Includes combined and intermediate. [14]Includes vocational. [15]1996.

Internet resources for further information:
• **South African Reserve Bank** http://www.resbank.co.za
• **Statistics South Africa** http://www.statssa.gov.za

Spain

Official name: Reino de España (Kingdom of Spain).
Form of government: constitutional monarchy with two legislative houses (Senate [259[1]]; Congress of Deputies [350]).
Chief of state: King.
Head of government: Prime Minister.
Capital: Madrid.
Official languages: Castilian Spanish[2].
Official religion: none.
Monetary unit: 1 euro (€) = 100 céntimos; valuation (Sept. 23, 2002) 1 U.S.$ = €1.02; 1 £ = €1.58[3].

Area and population		area		population
				2001
Autonomous communities	Capitals	sq mi	sq km	census
Andalucía	Seville	33,820	87,595	7,357,558
Aragón	Zaragoza	18,425	47,720	1,204,215
Asturias	Oviedo	4,094	10,604	1,062,998
Baleares (Balearic Islands)	Palma de Mallorca	1,927	4,992	841,669
Canarias (Canary Islands)	Santa Cruz de Tenerife	2,893	7,492	1,694,477
Cantabria	Santander	2,054	5,321	535,131
Castilla-La Mancha	Toledo	30,680	79,461	1,760,516
Castilla y León	Valladolid	36,380	94,224	2,456,474
Cataluña	Barcelona	12,399	32,113	6,343,110
Extremadura	Mérida	16,075	41,634	1,058,503
Galicia	Santiago de Compostela	11,419	29,575	2,695,880
La Rioja	Logroño	1,948	5,045	276,702
Madrid	Madrid	3,100	8,028	5,423,384
Murcia	Murcia	4,368	11,314	1,197,646
Navarra	Pamplona	4,012	10,391	555,829
País Vasco (Basque Country)	Vitoria (Gasteiz)	2,793	7,234	2,082,587
Valenciana	Valencia	8,979	23,255	4,162,776
Autonomous cities				
Ceuta	—	8	20	71,505
Melilla	—	5	12	66,411
TOTAL		195,379	506,030	40,847,371

Demography

Population (2002): 40,998,000.
Density (2002): persons per sq mi 209.8, persons per sq km 81.0.
Urban-rural (2002): urban 77.8%; rural 22.2%.
Sex distribution (2002): male 48.95%; female 51.05%.
Age breakdown (2002): under 15, 14.6%; 15–29, 21.7%; 30–44, 24.0%; 45–59, 18.0%; 60–74, 14.2%; 75 and over, 7.5%.
Population projection: (2010) 41,080,000; (2020) 40,135,000.
Ethnolinguistic composition (1991): Spanish 74.4%; Catalan 16.9%; other 8.7%.
Religious affiliation (2000): Roman Catholic 92.0%; Muslim 0.5%; Protestant 0.3%; other 7.2%.
Major cities (2001): Madrid 2,938,723; Barcelona 1,503,884; Valencia 738,441; Seville 684,633; Zaragoza 614,905.

Vital statistics

Birth rate per 1,000 population (2001): 10.0 (world avg. 21.2).
Death rate per 1,000 population (2001): 9.3 (world avg. 8.9).
Natural increase rate per 1,000 population (2001): 0.7 (world avg. 12.3).
Total fertility rate (avg. births per childbearing woman; 2001): 1.2.
Life expectancy at birth (2001): male 75.6 years; female 82.5 years.
Major causes of death per 100,000 population (1998): circulatory diseases 341.7; malignant neoplasms (cancers) 234.5; respiratory diseases 97.0; digestive diseases 48.1; accidents 42.8.

National economy

Budget (2002). Revenue: €108,824,300,000 (direct taxes 46.6%, of which income tax 27.2%; indirect taxes 41.8%, of which value-added tax on products 27.8%; other taxes 11.6%). Expenditures: €112,586,900,000 (public debt 15.7%; health 9.8%; pensions 5.7%; defense 5.6%; public works 4.4%).
Tourism (2000): receipts U.S.$31,454,000,000; expenditures U.S.$5,572,000,000.
Gross national product (2000): U.S.$595,255,000,000 (U.S.$15,080 per capita).

Structure of gross domestic product and labour force				
	2000			
	in value Ptas '000,000	% of total value	labour force	% of labour force
Agriculture	3,309,160	3.3	1,196,900	7.1
Mining	} 15,789,795	15.6	64,000	0.4
Manufacturing			2,927,900	17.4
Public utilities	3,955,530	3.9	97,600	0.6
Construction	8,056,403	8.0	1,776,800	10.5
Transp. and commun.	...	...	911,900	5.4
Trade and hotels			3,618,800	21.5
Finance	} 59,995,170	59.5	1,527,300	9.1
Services			3,802,800	22.6
Pub. admin., defense				
Other	9,766,668[4]	9.7[4]	920,200[5]	5.4[5]
TOTAL	100,872,726	100.0	16,844,200	100.0

Production (metric tons except as noted). Agriculture, forestry, fishing (2000): barley 11,283,100, sugar beets 8,343,800, wheat 7,333,100, grapes 5,646,400, olives 4,182,900, corn (maize) 3,866,700, tomatoes 3,597,000, potatoes 3,138,000, oranges 2,706,000; livestock (number of live animals) 23,700,000 sheep, 23,682,000 pigs, 6,203,000 cattle, 2,873,000 goats; roundwood (2000) 14,810,000 cu m; fish catch (1999) 1,485,000. Mining and quarrying (metal content in metric tons; 1999): zinc 109,400; lead 28,000; copper 3,500. Manufacturing (value added in Ptas '000,000,000; 1999): machinery 2,475; transport equipment 1,687; food products 1,585; chemical products 1,467; publishing products 431; wood products 387. Energy production (consumption): electricity (kW-hr; 2000) 212,244,000,000 ([1997] 187,128,000,000); hard coal (metric tons; 2000) 11,916,000 ([1997] 27,940,000); lignite (metric tons; 1997) 12,587,000 (12,805,000); crude petroleum (barrels; 2000) 1,711,000 ([1997] 331,765,000); petroleum products (metric tons; 1997) 48,528,000 (44,200,000); natural gas (cu m; 2000) 183,336,000 ([1997] 12,999,000,000).
Public debt (2001): €307,434,000,000.
Population economically active (2000): total 16,844,200; activity rate of total population 41.6% (participation rates: ages [1995] 16–64, 60.7%, female 38.3%; unemployed 22.9%).

Price and earnings indexes (1995 = 100)							
	1995	1996	1997	1998	1999	2000	2001
Consumer price index	100.0	103.6	105.6	107.5	110.0	113.8	116.8
Monthly earnings index	100.0	105.3	109.6	...	115.5	...	...

Household income and expenditure. Average household size (1999) 3.3; income per household (2000) Ptas 3,205,693 (U.S.$18,470); expenditure (1995): housing 26.0%, food 24.0%, transportation 12.8%, clothing and footwear 7.4%, household goods and services 6.1%.

Foreign trade[6]

Balance of trade (current prices)						
	1996	1997	1998	1999	2000	2001
U.S.$'000,000	−16,283	−13,407	−20,758	−30,339	−34,820	−31,500
% of total	7.3%	5.9%	8.5%	11.9%	13.0%	11.8%

Imports (2000): Ptas 27,643,097,000,000 (machinery 12.5%; energy products 12.0%; transportation equipment 10.9%; agricultural products 8.1%). *Major import sources:* France 17.1%; Germany 14.9%; Italy 14.3%; U.K. 7.0%.
Exports (2000): Ptas 20,482,039,900,000 (transport equipment 19.5%; agricultural products 12.9%; machinery 7.9%). *Major export destinations:* France 19.4%; Germany 12.4%; Portugal 9.4%; Italy 8.8%; U.K. 8.3%.

Transport and communications

Transport. Railroads (2000): route length 13,832 km; passenger-km 19,927,000,000; metric ton-km cargo 12,071,000,000. Roads (1999): length 346,548 km (paved 99%). Vehicles (2000): cars 17,449,000; trucks and buses 3,835,000. Air transport (1999): passenger-km 60,696,083,000; metric ton-km cargo 6,406,562,000; airports (1997) with scheduled flights 25.

Communications				units per 1,000
Medium	date	unit	number	persons
Daily newspapers	1996	circulation	3,931,000	99
Radio	1998	receivers	12,000,000	332
Television	1998	receivers	22,000,000	553
Telephones	2001	main lines	17,427,000	431
Cellular telephones	2001	subscribers	26,494,200	655
Personal computers	2001	units	6,800,000	168
Internet	2001	users	7,388,000	183

Education and health

Educational attainment (1997). Percentage of economically active population age 16 and over having: no formal schooling 6.4%[7]; primary 26.6%; secondary 58.9%; higher 8.1%. *Literacy* (1999): total population age 15 and over 97.6%; males 98.5%; females 96.7%.

Education (1999–2000)				student/
	schools	teachers	students	teacher ratio
Primary (age 6–11)	16,540[8]	174,638	2,539,925	14.5
Secondary (age 12–18)[9]	25,775[10]	285,179	3,399,645	11.9
Higher	1,415[10]	107,032	1,828,987	17.1

Health (1997): physicians 168,630 (1 per 236 persons); hospital beds (1999) 164,097 (1 per 244 persons); infant mortality rate (2001) 4.7.
Food (2000): daily per capita caloric intake 3,352 (vegetable products 73%, animal products 27%); 136% of FAO recommended minimum requirement.

Military

Total active duty personnel (2001): 143,450 (army 64.1%, navy 18.8%, air force 17.1%). *Military expenditure as percentage of GNP* (1999): 1.3% (world 2.4%); per capita expenditure U.S.$192.

---

[1]Includes 51 indirectly elected seats. [2]The constitution states that "Castilian is the Spanish official language of the State," but that "all other Spanish languages (including Euskera [Basque], Catalan, and Galician) will also be official in the corresponding Autonomous Communities." [3]The peseta (Pta) was the former monetary unit; on Jan. 1, 2002, Ptas 166.33 = €1. [4]Import taxes and value-added tax on products. [5]Includes 507,000 unemployed persons not previously employed. [6]Imports are f.o.b. in Balance of trade. [7]Includes illiterate. [8]1993–94. [9]Includes vocational. [10]1992–93.

Internet resources for further information:
• Banco de España http://www.bde.es
• National Institute of Statistics http://www.ine.es

Sri Lanka

Official name: Śri Lanka Prajatantrika Samajavadi Janarajaya (Sinhala); Ilangai Jananayaka Socialisa Kudiarasu (Tamil) (Democratic Socialist Republic of Sri Lanka).
Form of government: unitary multiparty republic with one legislative house (Parliament [225]).
Head of state and government: President assisted by Prime Minister.
Capitals: Colombo (executive); Sri Jayewardenepura Kotte (Colombo suburb; legislative and judicial).
Official languages: Sinhala; Tamil.
Official religion: none.
Monetary unit: 1 Sri Lanka rupee (SL Rs) = 100 cents; valuation (Sept. 23, 2002) 1 U.S.$ = SL Rs 96.20; 1 £ = SL Rs 149.50.

Area and population

Districts	Capitals	area sq mi	area sq km	population 2001 census[1]
Amparai	Amparai	1,705	4,415	589,344
Anuradhapura	Anuradhapura	2,772	7,179	746,466
Badulla	Badulla	1,104	2,861	774,555
Batticaloa	Batticaloa	1,102	2,854	486,447[2]
Colombo	Colombo	270	699	2,234,289
Galle	Galle	638	1,652	990,539
Gampaha	Gampaha	536	1,387	2,066,096
Hambantota	Hambantota	1,007	2,609	525,370
Jaffna	Jaffna	396	1,025	490,621[2]
Kalutara	Kalutara	617	1,598	1,060,800
Kandy	Kandy	749	1,940	1,272,463
Kegalle	Kegalle	654	1,693	779,774
Kilinochchi	Kilinochchi	494	1,279	127,263[2]
Kurunegala	Kurunegala	1,859	4,816	1,452,369
Mannar	Mannar	771	1,996	151,577[2]
Matale	Matale	770	1,993	442,427
Matara	Matara	495	1,283	761,236
Monaragala	Monaragala	2,177	5,639	396,173
Mullaitivu	Mullaitivu	1,010	2,617	121,667[2]
Nuwara Eliya	Nuwara Eliya	672	1,741	700,083
Polonnaruwa	Polonnaruwa	1,271	3,293	359,197
Puttalam	Puttalam	1,186	3,072	705,342
Ratnapura	Ratnapura	1,264	3,275	1,008,164
Trincomalee	Trincomalee	1,053	2,727	340,158[2]
Vavuniya	Vavuniya	759	1,967	149,835[2]
TOTAL		**25,332**	**65,610**	**18,732,255**

Demography

Population (2002): 18,870,000.
Density (2002): persons per sq mi 744.9, persons per sq km 287.6.
Urban-rural (2002): urban 25.0%; rural 75.0%.
Sex distribution (1999): male 50.97%; female 49.03%.
Age breakdown (1996): under 15, 28.0%; 15–29, 26.9%; 30–44, 22.5%; 45–59, 13.6%; 60–74, 7.0%; 75 and over, 2.0%.
Population projection: (2010) 20,096,000; (2020) 21,338,000.
Ethnic composition (2000): Sinhalese 72.4%; Tamil 17.8%; Sri Lankan Moor 7.4%; other 2.4%.
Religious affiliation (2000): Buddhist 68.4%; Hindu 11.3%; Christian 9.4%; Muslim 9.0%; other 1.9%.
Major cities (2001)[1]: Colombo 642,020; Dehiwala–Mount Lavinia 201,787; Moratuwa 177,190; Negombo 121,933; Kandy 110,049.

Vital statistics

Birth rate per 1,000 population (2002): 17.3 (world avg. 21.2); (1986) legitimate 96.3%; illegitimate 3.7%.
Death rate per 1,000 population (2002): 6.3 (world avg. 8.9).
Natural increase rate per 1,000 population (2002): 11.0 (world avg. 12.3).
Total fertility rate (avg. births per childbearing woman; 2002): 2.1.
Marriage rate per 1,000 population (1997): 8.9.
Life expectancy at birth (2002): male 70.0 years; female 76.0 years.
Major causes of death per 100,000 population (1989): diseases of the circulatory system 47.8; violence and poisoning 38.6; malignant neoplasms 26.7.

National economy

Budget (2000). Revenue: SL Rs 233,974,000,000 (sales and turnover tax 22.8%, excise taxes 19.9%, nontax revenue 13.8%, income taxes 12.5%, import duties 11.5%). Expenditures: SL Rs 329,012,000,000 (interest payments 21.1%, defense 11.7%, transport and communications 11.7%, social welfare 10.5%, education 9.5%, administration 8.5%).
Public debt (external, outstanding; 2000): U.S.$8,035,000,000.
Production (metric tons except as noted). Agriculture, forestry, fishing (2000): rice 2,767,000, coconuts 1,950,000, sugarcane 1,114,000, plantains 600,000; livestock (number of live animals) 1,616,700 cattle, 727,700 buffalo, 514,400 goats; roundwood (1999) 10,344,000 cu m; fish catch (1998) 266,100. Mining and quarrying (1998): limestone 950,000; titanium concentrate 23,000; graphite 5,000; gemstones U.S.$63,000,000. Manufacturing (value added, in U.S.$'000,000; 1995): food, beverages, and tobacco 601; textiles and apparel 391; petrochemicals 116. Energy production (consumption): electricity (kW-hr; 1997) 5,145,000,000 (5,145,000,000); coal (metric tons; 1997) none (negligible); crude petroleum (barrels; 1997) none (13,000,000); petroleum products (metric tons; 1997) 1,675,000 (2,399,000).

Gross national product (2000): U.S.$16,408,000,000 (U.S.$850 per capita).

Structure of gross domestic product and labour force

	2000 in value SL Rs '000,000[1]	% of total value[1]	labour force[3]	% of labour force[3]
Agriculture	222,100	19.8	2,290,000	33.4
Mining	21,700	1.9	77,800	1.1
Manufacturing	188,200	16.7	1,013,200	14.8
Construction	80,800	7.2	320,600	4.7
Public utilities			25,000	0.4
Transp. and commun.			278,100	4.1
Trade			767,700	11.2
Finance	612,300	54.4	122,600	1.8
Pub. admin., defense			1,153,700	16.8
Services				
Other			804,600[4]	11.7[4]
TOTAL	1,125,100	100.0	6,853,300	100.0

Population economically active: total (1997) 6,213,086; activity rate 40.2% (participation rates: ages 15 and over, 55.2%; female 32.4%; unemployed [2000] 8.0%[3]).

Price and earnings indexes (1995 = 100)

	1995	1996	1997	1998	1999	2000	2001
Consumer price index	100.0	115.9	127.0	138.9	145.4	154.4	176.3
Average wage index[5]	100.0	109.3	117.0	132.1	134.3	237.3	141.7

Household income and expenditure (1992). Average household size (1994) 4.6[3]; income per household SL Rs 116,100 (U.S.$2,600); sources of income: wages 48.5%, property income and self-employment 41.8%, transfers 9.7%; expenditure: food 58.6%, transportation 16.0%, clothing 8.4%.
Tourism (2000): receipts U.S.$253,000,000; expenditures U.S.$244,000,000.

Foreign trade

Balance of trade (current prices)

SL Rs '000,000	1996	1997	1998	1999	2000	2001
	−74,275	−41,449	−63,164	−91,443	−134,176	−98,075
% of total	14.1%	7.0%	9.4%	12.4%	13.8%	10.2%

Imports (1999): U.S.$5,981,000,000 (textile products 22.1%, machinery and equipment 11.3%, transport equipment 8.7%, petroleum 8.4%, processed foods 6.7%). *Major import sources:* Japan 10.4%; India 9.5%; Singapore 8.4%; U.K. 4.7%; U.S. 4.0%.
Exports (1999): U.S.$4,600,000,000 (clothing and accessories 52.7%, tea 13.5%, gems 4.7%, coconuts 1.8%). *Major export destinations:* U.S. 39.6%; U.K. 13.3%; Germany 4.8%; Japan 3.5%; The Netherlands 2.4%.

Transport and communications

Transport. Railroads (1998): route length 1,447 km; passenger-km 3,264,000,000; metric ton-km cargo 132,000,000. Roads (1996): total length 99,200 km (paved 40%). Vehicles (1996): passenger cars 107,000; trucks and buses 150,160. Air transport (1999): passenger-km 5,156,000,000; metric ton-km cargo 669,700,000; airports (1996) 1.

Communications

Medium	date	unit	number	units per 1,000 persons
Daily newspapers	1996	circulation	530,000	29
Radio	1997	receivers	3,850,000	211
Television	1999	receivers	1,900,000	102
Telephones	2001	main lines	828,000	43
Cellular telephones	2001	subscribers	720,000	38
Personal computers	2001	units	150,000	7.9
Internet	2001	users	150,000	7.9

Education and health

Educational attainment: n.a. *Literacy* (1995): percentage of population age 15 and over literate 90.2%; males literate 93.4%; females literate 87.2%.

Education (1995)

	schools	teachers	students	student/ teacher ratio
Primary (age 5–10)	9,657	70,537	1,962,498	27.8
Secondary (age 11–17)	5,771[6]	103,572	2,314,054	22.3
Voc., teacher tr.[7]	23	437	8,908	20.4
Higher	8[7]	2,636	63,660	24.2

Health (1999): physicians 6,938 (1 per 2,740 persons); hospital beds (1997) 52,298 (1 per 355 persons); infant mortality rate (2002) 20.0.
Food (2000): daily per capita caloric intake 2,405 (vegetable products 94%, animal products 6%); 108% of FAO recommended minimum.

Military

Total active duty personnel (2001): 120,500 (army 76.8%, navy 14.9%, air force 8.3%). *Military expenditure as percentage of GNP* (1999): 4.7% (world 2.4%); per capita expenditure U.S.$38.

[1]Provisional figures except for 7 districts experiencing civil war. [2]Registrar-general estimates. [3]Excludes the Northern and Eastern provinces where Tamils are in the majority. [4]Mainly unemployed. [5]Agricultural minimum rates. [6]1992. [7]1991.

Internet resources for further information:
• **Central Bank of Sri Lanka**
  http://www.centralbanklanka.org
• **Department of Census and Statistics**
  http://www.statistics.gov.lk

Sudan, The

Official name: Jumhūrīyat as-Sūdān
(Republic of the Sudan).
Form of government: military
regime[1] with one legislative body
(National Assembly [360[2]]).
Head of state and government:
President.
Capitals: Khartoum (executive);
Omdurman (legislative).
Official language: Arabic[3].
Official religion: [4].
Monetary unit: 1 Sudanese dinar (Sd)[5];
valuation (Sept. 23, 2002)
1 U.S.$ = Sd 258.70; 1 £ = Sd 402.05.

Area and population

States[6]	area sq km	population 2000 estimate	States[6]	area sq km	population 2000 estimate
Bahr el-Ghazal[7]	...	2,256,942	Red Sea	...	709,637
Blue Nile	...	633,129	River Nile	...	895,893
Equatoria	...	1,234,486	Sinnar	...	1,132,758
Gedaref	...	1,414,531	Southern Darfur	...	2,708,007
Gezira	...	3,310,928	Southern Kordofan	...	1,066,117
Kassalā	...	1,433,730	Upper Nile	...	1,342,943
Khartoum	...	4,740,290	Western Darfur	...	1,531,682
Northern	...	578,376	Western Kordofan	...	1,078,330
Northern Darfur	...	1,409,894	White Nile	...	1,431,701
Northern Kordofan	...	1,439,930	TOTAL	2,503,890[8]	30,349,304[9, 10]

Demography

Population (2002): 37,090,000.
Density (2002): persons per sq mi 38.3, persons per sq km 14.8.
Urban-rural (2002): urban 37.1%; rural 62.9%.
Sex distribution (2001): male 50.64%; female 49.36%.
Age breakdown (2001): under 15, 44.6%; 15–29, 27.6%; 30–44, 15.6%; 45–59,
8.4%; 60–74, 3.3%; 75 and over, 0.5%.
Population projection: (2000) 45,485,000; (2010) 56,162,000.
Doubling time: 25 years.
Ethnic composition (1983): Sudanese Arab 49.1%; Dinka 11.5%; Nuba 8.1%;
Beja 6.4%, Nuer 4.9%; Zande 2.7%; Bari 2.5%; Fur 2.1%; other 12.7%.
Religious affiliation (2000): Sunnī Muslim 70.3%; Christian 16.7%, of which
Roman Catholic c. 8%, Anglican c. 6%; traditional beliefs 11.9%; other 1.1%.
Major cities (1993): Omdurman 1,267,077; Khartoum 924,505; Khartoum North
879,105; Port Sudan 305,385; Kassalā 234,270; Nyala 228,778.

Vital statistics

Birth rate per 1,000 population (2001): 37.9 (world avg. 21.2).
Death rate per 1,000 population (2001): 10.0 (world avg. 8.9).
Natural increase rate per 1,000 population (2001): 27.9 (world avg. 12.3).
Total fertility rate (avg. births per childbearing woman; 2001): 5.3.
Life expectancy at birth (2001): male 55.9 years; female 58.1 years.
Major causes of death per 100,000 population: n.a.

National economy

Budget (1999–2000). Revenue: Sd 206,700,000,000[5] (import duties 26.0%, nontax revenue 25.8%, excise duties 11.9%, taxes on business profits 11.1%).
Expenditures: Sd 227,200,000,000[5] (current expenditure 85.8%, development
expenditure 14.2%).
Public debt (external, outstanding; 2000): U.S.$8,647,000,000.
Tourism (2000): receipts U.S.$5,000,000; expenditures U.S.$55,000,000.
Production (metric tons except as noted). Agriculture, forestry, fishing (2000):
sugarcane 4,982,000, sorghum 2,488,000, peanuts (groundnuts) 947,000, millet 481,000, wheat 303,000, sesame seeds 282,000, seed cotton 242,000, dates
176,000, tea 170,000, gum arabic (1998–99) 28,000; livestock (number of live
animals) 46,095,000 sheep, 38,548,000 goats, 37,093,000 cattle, 3,108,000
camels; roundwood (2000) 18,853,000 cu m; fish catch (1999) 50,500. Mining
and quarrying (2000): salt 50,000; gold 6,000 kg. Manufacturing (2000): raw
sugar 662,000; flour 600,000; cement 161,000; vegetable oils 120,000; cattle
hides and horsehides 8,500,000 units; shoes 50,000,000 pairs. Construction:
n.a. Energy production (consumption): electricity (kW-hr; 2000) 2,569,200,-
000 (1,337,000,000); coal, none (none); crude petroleum (barrels; 1999–
2000[11]) 60,700,000 ([1997] 6,441,000); petroleum products (metric tons; 2000)
1,913,600 (1,753,000); natural gas, none (none).
Gross national product (2000): U.S.$9,599,000,000 (U.S.$310 per capita).

Structure of gross domestic product and labour force

| | 2000 | | 1983 | |
	in value Sd '000,000,000[12]	% of total value[12]	labour force[13]	% of labour force[13]
Agriculture	1,040	42.6	4,028,705	63.5
Mining	21	0.9	6,534	0.1
Manufacturing	217	8.9	266,693	4.2
Construction	157	6.4	139,282	2.2
Public utilities	19	0.8	43,728	0.7
Transportation and communications	142	5.8	215,474	3.4
Trade, hotels	492	20.1	314,676	5.0
Finance	}			
Services	354	14.5	550,409	8.7
Pub. admin., defense	}			
Other	—	—	777,480[14]	12.2[14]
TOTAL	2,442	100.0	6,342,981	100.0

Population economically active (1993): total 8,866,000; activity rate of total
population 32.3% (participation rates: ages 15–64 [1983] 57.4%; female
22.3%; unemployed c. 30.0%).

Price and earnings indexes (1995 = 100)

	1995	1996	1997	1998	1999	2000	2001
Consumer price index	100.0	232.8	341.5	399.9	463.8	488.3	525.5
Earnings index	...	...	...	...	...	...	...

Household income and expenditure. Average household size: n.a.; income per
household: n.a.[15]; expenditure (1983): food and beverages 63.6%, housing
11.5%, household goods 5.5%, clothing and footwear 5.3%.
Land use (1994): forested 18.1%; meadows and pastures 46.3%; agricultural
and under permanent cultivation 5.5%; desert and other 30.1%.

Foreign trade[16]

Balance of trade (current prices)

	1995	1996	1997	1998	1999	2000
U.S.$'000,000	−629	−884	−985	−1,329	−635	+254
% of total	36.1%	41.6%	45.2%	52.7%	28.8%	7.6%

Imports (2000): U.S.$1,552,700,000 (1999; machinery and equipment 25.4%;
foodstuffs 19.5%, of which wheat and wheat flour 8.7%; petroleum products
13.0%; transport equipment 9.3%). *Major import sources:* Saudi Arabia
11.8%; France 8.6%; Italy 6.3%; U.A.E. 5.5%; Germany 5.4%; U.K. 5.1%.
Exports (2000): U.S.$1,806,700,000 (1999; crude petroleum 35.4%; sesame
seeds 16.3%; sheep and lambs 13.0%; gold 7.1%; cotton 5.8%). *Major export
destinations:* Saudi Arabia 18.1%; Japan 15.7%; U.K. 9.2%; South Korea
7.9%; Italy 7.1%.

Transport and communications

Transport. Railroads: route length (2000) 5,901 km; (1995–96) passenger-km
161,000,000; (1995–96) metric ton-km cargo 1,965,000,000. Roads (1999): total
length 11,900 km (paved 36%). Vehicles (1996): passenger cars 285,000;
trucks and buses 53,000. Air transport (2001): passenger-km 803,000,000; metric ton-km cargo 54,542,000; airports (1997) with scheduled flights 3.

Communications

Medium	date	unit	number	units per 1,000 persons
Daily newspapers	1996	circulation	737,000	24
Radio	1997	receivers	7,550,000	235
Television	1999	receivers	5,000,000	147
Telephones	2001	main lines	453,000	14
Cellular telephones	2001	subscribers	105,000	3.3
Personal computers	2001	units	115,000	3.6
Internet	2001	users	56,000	1.8

Education and health

Educational attainment (1983). Percentage of population age 25 and over having: no formal schooling 76.7%; complete secondary 2.0%; higher 0.8%.
Literacy (1998): total population age 15 and over literate 55.7%; males 68.0%;
females 43.4%.

Education (1999–2000)

	schools	teachers	students	student/ teacher ratio
Primary (age 7–12)	11,923	117,151	3,137,494	26.8
Secondary (age 13–18)	1,694	21,114	401,424	19.0
Vocational[17]	...	761	26,421	34.7
Higher[18]	19	1,417[17]	200,538	...

Health: physicians (1997) 3,423 (1 per 9,395 persons); hospital beds (1997)
22,656 (1 per 1,420 persons); infant mortality rate (2001) 68.7.
Food (2000): daily per capita caloric intake 2,444 (vegetable products 81%,
animal products 19%); 100% of FAO recommended minimum.

Military

Total active duty personnel (2001): 117,000 (army 96.2%, navy 1.2%, air force
2.6%). *Military expenditure as percentage of GNP* (1999): 4.8% (world 2.4%);
per capita expenditure U.S.$33.

[1]A state of emergency introduced Dec. 12, 1999, was extended through August 2002;
elections to National Assembly were held in December 2000. [2]Includes 90 indirectly
elected or appointed seats. [3]English has been designated the "principal" language in
southern Sudan. [4]Islamic law and custom are sources of national law per 1998 constitution. [5]The Sudanese dinar (Sd), introduced May 1992 at a value equal to 10
Sudanese pounds (LSd), officially replaced the Sudanese pound on March 1, 1999.
[6]Local administrative reorganization into 26 new states was announced in February
1994 and confirmed in June 1998. Names listed below are English-language variants;
six southern states are excluded. [7]Includes Western Bahr el-Ghazal and Northern Bahr
el-Ghazal. [8]Including c. 130,000 sq km of inland water area. [9]Summary total; actual
total per official source is 31,081,000. [10]Population estimates are unavailable for six
states in southern Sudan experiencing civil war since 1983. [11]Production from August
1999 through July 2000. [12]At factor cost. [13]Excludes nomads, the homeless, and institutionalized persons. [14]Includes 592,759 unemployed not previously employed.
[15]Average annual income of paid worker (1992) U.S.$216. [16]Imports c.i.f.; exports
f.o.b. [17]1996–97. [18]Universities only.

Internet resources for further information:
• **Ministry of Foreign Affairs**
   http://www.sudmer.com
• **Bank of Sudan**
   http://www.bankofsudan.org

Suriname

Official name: Republiek Suriname (Republic of Suriname).
Form of government: multiparty republic with one legislative house (National Assembly [51]).
Head of state and government: President.
Capital: Paramaribo.
Official language: Dutch.
Official religion: none.
Monetary unit: 1 Suriname guilder (Sf) = 100 cents; valuation (Sept. 23, 2002) 1 U.S.$ = Sf 2,178; 1 £ = Sf 3,386.

Area and population		area		population
				1996
Districts	Capitals	sq mi	sq km	estimate
Brokopondo	Brokopondo	2,843	7,364	7,200
Commewijne	Nieuw Amsterdam	908	2,353	20,900
Coronie	Totness	1,507	3,902	2,900
Marowijne	Albina	1,786	4,627	12,600
Nickerie	Nieuw Nickerie	2,067	5,353	33,600
Para	Onverwacht	2,082	5,393	14,400
Saramacca	Groningen	1,404	3,636	13,000
Sipaliwini	1	50,412	130,566	23,500
Wanica	Lelydorp	171	443	72,400
Town district				
Paramaribo	Paramaribo	71	183	222,800
TOTAL		63,251[2]	163,820[2]	423,400[3]

Demography

Population (2002): 436,000.
Density (2002): persons per sq mi 6.9, persons per sq km 2.7.
Urban-rural (1998): urban 51.0%; rural 49.0%.
Sex distribution (2000): male 50.77%; female 49.23%.
Age breakdown (2000): under 15, 32.1%; 15–29, 27.2%; 30–44, 22.7%; 45–59, 9.9%; 60–74, 6.4%; 75 and over, 1.7%.
Population projection: (2010) 450,000; (2020) 457,000.
Doubling time: 45 years.
Ethnic composition (1999): Indo-Pakistani 37.0%; Suriname Creole 31.0%; Javanese 15.0%; Bush Negro 10.0%; Amerindian 2.5%; Chinese 2.0%; white 1.0%; other 1.5%.
Religious affiliation (1995): Hindu 27.4%; Roman Catholic 21.0%; Muslim 19.6%; Protestant (mostly Moravian) 16.4%; other 15.6%.
Major cities (1996/1997): Paramaribo 222,800 (urban agglomeration 289,000); Lelydorp 15,600; Nieuw Nickerie 11,100; Mungo (Moengo) 6,800; Meerzorg 6,600.

Vital statistics

Birth rate per 1,000 population (2000): 21.1 (world avg. 22.5).
Death rate per 1,000 population (2000): 5.7 (world avg. 9.0).
Natural increase rate per 1,000 population (2000): 15.4 (world avg. 13.5).
Total fertility rate (avg. births per childbearing woman; 2000): 2.5.
Marriage rate per 1,000 population (1991): 4.9.
Divorce rate per 1,000 population (1991): 2.5.
Life expectancy at birth (2000): male 68.7 years; female 74.1 years.
Major causes of death per 100,000 population (1992): noncommunicable diseases 769.0; external and other causes 608.1; communicable and perinatal diseases 232.8; ill-defined diseases 279.0.

National economy

Budget (1996). Revenue: Sf 90,874,600,000 (direct taxes 42.2%; indirect taxes 32.2%; bauxite levy 25.0%; other 0.6%). Expenditures: Sf 96,957,700,000 (current expenditures 99.6%, of which wages and salaries 28.5%, transfers 13.7%, debt service 1.7%; capital expenditures 0.4%).
Production (metric tons except as noted). Agriculture, forestry, fishing (1999): rice 180,400, sugarcane 90,000, bananas 55,000, plantains 13,000, oranges 12,000, coconuts 9,400, cassava 4,000, cucumbers 3,220, watermelons 2,700, tomatoes 1,625, cabbage 990, grapefruit 940; livestock (number of live animals) 102,000 cattle, 25,000 pigs, 10,600 sheep, 10,000 goats, 2,200,000 chickens; roundwood (2000) 226,700 cu m; fish catch (2000) 16,200. Mining and quarrying (2000): bauxite 3,600,000; gold 9,600 troy oz[4]. Manufacturing (value of production at factor cost in Sf; 1993): food products 992,000,000; beverages 558,000,000; tobacco 369,000,000; chemical products 291,000,000; pottery and earthenware 258,000,000; wood products 180,000,000. Energy production (consumption): electricity (kW-hr; 1997) 1,626,000,000 (1,626,000,000); hard coal (metric tons) none (n.a.); crude petroleum (barrels; 2000) 4,400,000 ([1997] 1,451,000); petroleum products (metric tons; 1997) none (482,000); natural gas, none (none).
Household income and expenditure. Average household size (1998) 4.8; income per household: n.a.; sources of income: n.a.; expenditure: n.a.
Population economically active (1994): total 98,240; activity rate of total population 24.3% (participation rates[5, 6]: ages 15–64, 56.0%; female 37.5%; unemployed [1996] 10.7%).

Price and earnings indexes (1995 = 100)							
	1995	1996	1997	1998	1999	2000	2001
Consumer price index	100.0	99.3	106.4	126.6	251.8	...	556.3
Earnings index	...	...	...	...	...	...	...

Gross national product (at current market prices; 2000): U.S.$788,000,000 (U.S.$1,890 per capita).

Structure of gross domestic product and labour force				
	1996		1994	
	in value Sf '000,000[7]	% of total value[7]	labour force	% of labour force
Agriculture, forestry	104.4	7.0	19,940[8]	20.3[8]
Mining	190.8	12.9	3,181	3.2
Manufacturing	148.9	10.1	4,432	4.5
Construction	47.3	3.2	1,656	1.7
Public utilities	126.7	8.6	1,288	1.3
Transp. and commun.	139.3	9.4	2,112	2.1
Trade, hotels	123.9	8.4	4,383	4.5
Finance, real estate	551.3	37.2	1,954	2.0
Pub. admin., defense	289.0	19.5	38,552	39.2
Services	7.4	0.5	2,010	2.0
Other	−248.0[9]	−16.7[9]	18,732[10]	19.1[10]
TOTAL	1,481.0	100.0[3]	98,240	100.0[3]

Public debt (external, outstanding; 1996): U.S.$216,500,000.
Tourism (2000): receipts from visitors U.S.$16,000,000; expenditures by nationals abroad U.S.$23,000,000.
Land use (1994): forested 96.2%; meadows and pastures 0.1%; agricultural and under permanent cultivation 0.4%; other 3.3%.

Foreign trade[11]

Balance of trade (current prices)						
	1993	1994	1995	1996	1997	1998
Sf '000,000	+364	+3,486	−47,896	−27,145	+17,259	−24,180
% of total	9.4%	3.0%	10.2%	7.2%	3.2%	5.9%

Imports (1998): Sf 216,860,000,000 (machinery and transport equipment 31.9%, food and live animals 10.8%, road vehicles 10.2%, inorganic chemicals 8.5%, refined petroleum 8.1%). *Major import sources:* U.S. 41.2%; The Netherlands 25.0%; Trinidad and Tobago 9.6%; Netherlands Antilles 5.8%; Japan 5.5%.
Exports (1998): Sf 192,680,000,000 (metalliferous ores [mostly alumina and bauxite] 61.5%, rolled silver 11.6%, processed nickel 7.6%, fish 5.8%, rice 3.8%). *Major export destinations:* The Netherlands 21.3%; Norway 21.2%; U.S. 19.1%; Canada 11.0%; France 8.6%.

Transport and communications

Transport. Railroads (1997)[12]: length 187 mi, 301 km; passengers, not applicable; cargo, n.a. Roads (1996): total length 2,815 mi, 4,530 km (paved 26%). Vehicles (1996): passenger cars 46,408; trucks and buses 19,255. Air transport (1996): passenger-mi 548,885,000, passenger-km 883,347,000; short ton-mi cargo 65,865,000, metric ton-km cargo 106,000,000; airports (1998) with scheduled flights 1.

Communications				units per 1,000
Medium	date	unit	number	persons
Daily newspapers	1996	circulation	50,000	122
Radio	1997	receivers	300,000	728
Television	1999	receivers	98,000	236
Telephones	2001	main lines	77,400	176
Cellular telephones	2001	subscribers	84,100	191
Internet	2001	users	14,500	33

Education and health

Educational attainment: n.a. *Literacy* (1995): total population age 15 and over literate 271,000 (93.0%); males literate 137,000 (95.1%); females literate 134,000 (91.0%).

Education (1995–96)				student/
	schools	teachers	students	teacher ratio
Primary (age 6–11)	304	3,611	75,585	20.9
Secondary (age 12–18)	104	2,286	31,918	13.9
Teacher training	1	...	1,462	...
Higher	1	155	1,335	8.6

Health: physicians (1998) 166 (1 per 2,518 persons); hospital beds (1998) 1,449 (1 per 288 persons); infant mortality rate per 1,000 live births (2000) 25.1.
Food (2000): daily per capita caloric intake 2,652 (vegetable products 86%, animal products 14%); 118% of FAO recommended minimum requirement.

Military

Total active duty personnel (2001): 2,040[13] (army 78.4%, navy 11.8%, air force 9.8%). *Military expenditure as percentage of GNP* (1999): 1.8% (world 2.4%); per capita expenditure U.S.$33.

---

[1]No capital; administered from Paramaribo. [2]Area excludes 6,809 sq mi (17,635 sq km) of territory disputed with Guyana. [3]Detail does not add to total given because of rounding. [4]Recorded production; unrecorded production may be as high as 950,000 troy oz. [5]Districts of Wanica and Paramaribo only. [6]1992. [7]At factor cost; 1980 prices. [8]Derived value. [9]Indirect taxes less subsidies and imputed bank service charges. [10]Includes 11,300 unemployed. [11]Imports c.i.f.; exports f.o.b. [12]There are no public railways operating in Suriname. [13]All services are part of the army.

Internet resources for further information:
• Suriname http://www.sesrtcic.org/statistics/coustats.shtml

Swaziland

Official name: Umbuso weSwatini (Swazi); Kingdom of Swaziland (English).
Form of government[1]: monarchy with two legislative houses (Senate [30[2]]; House of Assembly [65[3]]).
Head of state and government: King, assisted by Prime Minister.
Capitals: Mbabane (administrative and judicial); Lozitha and Ludzidzini (royal); Lobamba (legislative).
Official languages: Swati (Swazi); English.
Official religion: none.
Monetary unit: 1 lilangeni[4] (plural emalangeni [E]) = 100 cents; valuation (Sept. 23, 2002) 1 U.S.$ = E 10.63; 1 £ = E 16.52.

Area and population		area		population
				1997
Districts	Capitals	sq mi	sq km	census
Hhohho	Mbabane	1,378	3,569	269,826
Lubombo	Siteki	2,296	5,947	201,696
Manzini	Manzini	1,571	4,068	292,100
Shiselweni	Nhlangano	1,459	3,780	217,100
TOTAL		6,704	17,364	980,722[5]

Demography

Population (2002): 1,124,000.
Density (2002): persons per sq mi 167.7; persons per sq km 64.7.
Urban-rural (2001): urban 26.7%; rural 73.3%.
Sex distribution (1997): male 48.28%; female 51.72%.
Age breakdown (1997): under 15, 42.5%; 15–29, 29.2%; 30–44, 15.5%; 45–59, 7.8%; 60–74, 3.3%; 75 and over, 1.2%; unknown 0.5%.
Population projection: (2010) 1,216,000; (2020) 1,296,000.
Doubling time: 55 years.
Ethnic composition (2000): Swazi 82.3%; Zulu 9.6%; Tsonga 2.3%; Afrikaner 1.4%; mixed (black-white) 1.0%; other 3.4%.
Religious affiliation (1995): Christian 66.7%, of which African indigenous 44.7%, Protestant 14.8%, Roman Catholic 5.3%; other (mostly traditional beliefs) 33.3%.
Major cities (1986): Manzini (2000) 80,000; Mbabane (2000) 60,000; Big Bend 9,676; Simunye/Ngomane 9,060; Mhlume 6,509.

Vital statistics

Birth rate per 1,000 population (2001): 31.0 (world avg. 21.2).
Death rate per 1,000 population (2001): 17.8 (world avg. 8.9).
Natural increase rate per 1,000 population (2001): 13.2 (world avg. 12.3).
Total fertility rate (avg. births per childbearing woman; 2001): 4.1.
Life expectancy at birth (2001): male 44.8 years; female 41.8 years.
Major causes of death (1992)[6]: accidents and injuries 15.8%; infectious intestinal diseases 13.3%; tuberculosis 10.3%; malnutrition 6.2%; respiratory diseases 5.3%; circulatory diseases 5.0%; digestive diseases 4.6%.

National economy

Budget (1999–2000). Revenue: E 2,436,400,000 (receipts from Customs Union of Southern Africa 50.1%; tax on income and profits 25.8%; sales tax 12.0%; foreign-aid grants 3.5%; property income 2.1%; fees, services, and fines 1.1%). Expenditures: E 2,630,700,000 (recurrent expenditure 78.2%, of which general administration 28.0%, education 17.3%, economic services 11.2%, justice and police 8.0%, health 6.5%, defense 4.8%).
Gross national product (2000): U.S.$1,451,000,000 (U.S.$1,390 per capita).

Structure of gross domestic product and labour force				
	1999		1986	
	in value E '000	% of total value	labour force	% of labour force
Agriculture	904,900	11.7	30,197	18.8
Mining	51,400	0.7	5,245	3.3
Manufacturing	2,148,700	27.7	14,742	9.2
Construction	278,800	3.6	7,661	4.8
Public utilities	117,700	1.5	1,315	0.8
Transp. and commun.	290,600	3.7	7,526	4.7
Trade	530,500	6.8	12,348	7.7
Finance	333,300	4.3	1,931	1.2
Pub. admin., defense	1,158,100	15.0	32,309	20.1
Services	82,100	1.1		
Other	1,849,700[7]	23.9[7]	47,081[8]	29.4[8]
TOTAL	7,746,000[9]	100.0	160,355	100.0

Population economically active (1986): total 160,355; activity rate of total population 23.5% (participation rates: ages 15 and over, 44.1%; female 34.2%; unemployed 27.0%).

Price and earnings indexes (1995 = 100)							
	1994	1995	1996	1997	1998	1999	2000
Consumer price index	89.1	100.0	106.4	114.0	123.3	130.8	146.7
Weekly earnings index[10]	...	100.0	100.0	95.7	95.7	98.3	...

Public debt (external, outstanding; 2000): U.S.$198,200,000.
Production (metric tons except as noted). Agriculture, forestry, fishing (1999): sugarcane 3,700,000, corn (maize) 113,000, oranges 31,200, grape-

fruit and pomelo 25,400, seed cotton 16,200, roots and tubers 8,300 (of which potatoes 6,000, sweet potatoes 2,300), pineapples 8,000, dry beans 5,000, peanuts (groundnuts) 4,600; livestock (number of live animals) 652,000 cattle, 438,000 goats, 31,000 pigs, 26,000 sheep, 980,000 chickens; roundwood (1998) 1,494,000 cu m; fish catch (1998) 60. Mining and quarrying (2000): asbestos 12,690; diamonds 64,000 carats[11]. Manufacturing (value added in U.S.$'000; 1994): food and beverages 244,000, of which beverage processing 153,000; paper and paper products 35,000; textiles 19,000; printing and publishing products 18,000; clothing 7,000; metal and metal products 7,000. Construction (value in E; 1996)[12]: residential 34,100,000; nonresidential 17,500,000. Energy production (consumption): electricity (kW-hr; 2000) 265,000,000 (702,000,000); coal (metric tons; 2000) 378,000 (n.a.); crude petroleum, n.a. (n.a.).
Household income and expenditure. Average household size (1986) 5.7; annual income per household (1985) E 332 (U.S.$151); sources of income (1985): wages and salaries 44.4%, self-employment 22.2%, transfers 12.2%, other 21.2%; expenditure (1985): food and beverages 33.5%, rent and fuel 13.4%, household durable goods 12.8%, transportation and communications 8.8%, clothing and footwear 6.0%, recreation 3.3%.
Tourism (2000): receipts U.S.$34,000,000; expenditures U.S.$36,000,000.

Foreign trade

Balance of trade (current prices)					
	1995	1996	1997	1998	1999
U.S.$'000,000	−197	−204	−127	−100	−130
% of total	10.2%	10.7%	6.2%	4.9%	6.6%

Imports (1998): U.S.$1,068,000,000 (machinery and transport equipment 26.2%; manufactured items 17.0%; foodstuffs 15.8%; chemicals 13.9%; minerals, fuels, and lubricants 11.8%). *Major import sources* (1997–98): South Africa 82.9%; U.K. 1.7%; U.S. 0.9%; Zimbabwe 0.2%; Spain 0.2%.
Exports (1998): U.S.$921,000,000 (sugar 11.0%; wood and wood products 8.1%; refrigerators 7.5%; cotton yarn 2.3%; paper and paper products 2.0%; canned fruits 1.4%; citrus fruits 1.3%; asbestos 1.0%). *Major export destinations* (1997): South Africa 74.0%; Italy 8.7%; Mozambique 5.2%; U.S. 2.4%; U.K. 2.1%; Zimbabwe 1.7%.

Transport and communications

Transport. Railroads (1995)[13]: length 187 mi, 301 km; passenger-mi 752,000,000[14], passenger-km 1,210,000,000[14]; short ton-mi cargo 1,993,000,000[15], metric ton-km cargo 2,910,000,000[15]. Roads (1996): total length 2,367 mi, 3,810 km (paved 29%). Vehicles (1997): passenger cars 31,882; trucks and buses 32,772. Air transport (1995)[16]: passenger-mi 30,710,000, passenger-km 49,423,000; short ton-mi cargo 87,000, metric ton-km cargo 127,000; airports (1997) with scheduled flights 1.

Communications				units per 1,000
Medium	date	unit	number	persons
Daily newspapers	1996	circulation	24,000	24.3
Radio	1997	receivers	155,000	153
Television	1999	receivers	110,000	104
Telephones	2001	main lines	32,000	32
Cellular telephones	2001	subscribers	66,000	65
Personal computers	1998	units	278	0.3
Internet	2001	users	14,000	14

Education and health

Educational attainment (1986). Percentage of population age 25 and over having: no formal schooling 42.1%; some primary education 23.9%; complete primary 10.5%; some secondary 19.2%; complete secondary and higher 4.3%.
Literacy (1995): total population age 15 and over literate 76.7%; males literate 78.0%; females literate 75.6%.

Education (1997)	schools	teachers	students	student/ teacher ratio
Primary (age 6–13)	529	6,094	205,829	33.8
Secondary (age 14–18)	175	3,067	58,197	19.0
Voc., teacher tr.[17]	5	228	2,958	13.0
Higher	1	190[17]	2,132	9.1[17]

Health: physicians (1996) 148 (1 per 6,663 persons); hospital beds (1984) 1,608 (1 per 396 persons); infant mortality rate per 1,000 live births (2001) 65.7.
Food (2000): daily per capita caloric intake 2,620 (vegetable products 85%, animal products 15%); 113% of FAO recommended minimum requirement.

Military

Total active duty personnel: n.a. *Military expenditure as percentage of GNP* (1999): 1.5% (world 2.4%); per capita expenditure U.S.$20.

[1]The Constitutional Review Committee appointed in August 1996 presented a draft constitution to the King in August 2001; promulgation of a new constitution expected by August 2003. [2]Includes 20 nonelective seats. [3]Includes 10 nonelective seats. [4]The lilangeni is at par with the South African rand. [5]Final results; includes 51,004 residents abroad. [6]Percentage of deaths of known cause at government, mission, and private hospitals. [7]Includes indirect taxes less imputed bank service charges and subsidies. [8]Includes 43,925 unemployed. [9]Detail does not add to total given because of rounding. [10]Manufacturing sector only. [11]1994. [12]Urban areas under the jurisdiction of the Manzini and Mbabane town councils only. [13]Swaziland's only passenger train service was terminated in May 2000. [14]1988. [15]1991. [16]Royal Swazi National Airways only; international flights only. [17]1993–94.

Internet resources for further information:
• **Central Bank of Swaziland http://www.centralbank.sz**
• **Swaziland on the Internet http://www.realnet.co.sz**

Sweden

Official name: Konungariket Sverige (Kingdom of Sweden).
Form of government: constitutional monarchy and parliamentary state with one legislative house (Parliament [349]).
Chief of state: King.
Head of government: Prime Minister.
Capital: Stockholm.
Official language: Swedish.
Official religion: none[1].
Monetary unit: 1 Swedish krona (SKr) = 100 ore; valuation (Sept. 23, 2002) 1 U.S.$ = SKr 9.21; 1 £ = SKr 14.31.

Area and population		area		population
				2002[2]
Counties	Capitals	sq mi	sq km	estimate
Blekinge	Karlskrona	1,136	2,941	150,036
Dalarna	Falun	10,885	28,193	276,765
Gävleborg	Gävle	7,024	18,192	277,171
Gotland	Visby	1,212	3,140	57,458
Halland	Halmstad	2,106	5,454	278,236
Jämtland	Östersund	19,090	49,443	127,953
Jönköping	Jönköping	4,044	10,475	327,917
Kalmar	Kalmar	4,313	11,171	234,776
Kronoberg	Växjö	3,266	8,458	176,955
Norrbotten	Luleå	38,190	98,911	253,945
Örebro	Örebro	3,288	8,517	273,419
Östergötland	Linköping	4,078	10,562	413,401
Skåne	Malmo	4,258	11,027	1,143,513
Södermanland	Nyköping	2,341	6,062	258,389
Stockholm	Stockholm	2,506	6,490	1,849,206
Uppsala	Uppsala	2,698	6,989	298,556
Värmland	Karlstad	6,790	17,586	273,716
Västerbotten	Umeå	21,390	55,401	254,936
Västernorrland	Härnösand	8,370	21,678	244,734
Västmanland	Västerås	2,433	6,302	258,855
Västra Götaland	Göteborg	9,244	23,942	1,507,182
TOTAL LAND AREA		158,662	410,934	
INLAND WATER		15,070	39,030	
TOTAL		173,732	449,964	8,937,119

Demography

Population (2002): 8,925,000.
Density (2002)[3]: persons per sq mi 56.2, persons per sq km 21.7.
Urban-rural (1999): urban 83.3%; rural 16.7%.
Sex distribution (2000): male 49.42%; female 50.58%.
Age breakdown (2000[4]): under 15, 18.5%; 15–29, 18.3%; 30–44, 20.8%; 45–59, 20.3%; 60–74, 13.3%; 75 and over, 8.8%.
Population projection: (2010) 9,114,000; (2020) 9,407,000.
Ethnic composition (1997[4]): Swedish 89.3%; Finnish 2.3%; Yugoslavian 0.8%; Iranian 0.6%; Bosnian 0.5%; other 6.5%.
Religious affiliation (1999): Church of Sweden 86.5% (nominally; about 30% nonpracticing); Muslim 2.3%; Roman Catholic 1.8%; Pentecostal 1.1%; other 8.3%.
Major cities (2001): Stockholm 754,948; Göteborg 471,267; Malmö 262,397; Uppsala 191,110; Linköping 134,039.

Vital statistics

Birth rate per 1,000 population (2001): 10.3 (world avg. 21.2); (1999) legitimate 48.2%; illegitimate 51.8%.
Death rate per 1,000 population (2001): 10.5 (world avg. 8.9).
Natural increase rate per 1,000 population (2001): –0.2 (world avg. 12.3).
Total fertility rate (avg. births per childbearing woman; 2001): 1.5.
Marriage rate per 1,000 population (2001): 4.0.
Divorce rate per 1,000 population (2001): 2.4.
Life expectancy at birth (2001): male 77.6 years; female 82.1 years.
Major causes of death per 100,000 population (1997): heart disease 508.8; malignant neoplasms (cancers) 240.0; cerebrovascular disease 116.2.

National economy

Budget (2000). Revenue: SKr 800,000,000,000 (value-added and excise taxes 33.2%, social security 28.2%, income and capital gains taxes 15.9%, property taxes 4.7%). Expenditures: SKr 698,068,000,000 (health and social affairs 29.3%, debt service 14.0%, defense 7.2%, education 4.9%).
Production (metric tons except as noted). Agriculture, forestry, fishing (2001): sugar beets 2,752,600, wheat 2,390,000, barley 1,600,000, potatoes 991,000, oats 990,000; livestock (number of live animals) 1,891,456 pigs; 1,713,000 cattle, 451,594 sheep; roundwood (2000) 55,250,000 cu m; fish catch (1999) 357,317. Mining and quarrying (1998): iron ore 20,930,000; zinc 297,000; copper 270,000. Manufacturing (value added, in SKr '000,000; 1999): transport equipment 76,274; machinery, except electrical 76,133; paper products 46,363; electrical machinery 40,603; food 21,474; wood products 15,825; iron and steel 14,671. Construction (dwellings completed; 2000): 12,984. Energy production (consumption): electricity (kW-hr; 2000) 144,966,000,000 (160,203,000,000); coal (metric tons; 1997) none (3,113,000); crude petroleum (barrels; 1997) none (146,382,000); petroleum products (metric tons; 1997) 18,840,000 (12,757,000); natural gas (cu m; 1997) none (856,941,000).
Household income and expenditure. Average household size (1999) 2.2; median income per household (1994) SKr 396,100 (U.S.$51,330); sources of income (1992): wages and salaries 58.9%, transfer payments 25.8%, self-employment 15.3%; expenditure (1995): housing and energy 29.6%, food 20.9%, transportation 16.1%, education and recreation 9.2%.

Gross national product (2000): U.S.$240,707,000,000 (U.S.$27,140 per capita).

Structure of gross domestic product and labour force				
	2000			
	in value SKr '000,000	% of total value	labour force	% of labour force
Agriculture	31,388	1.5	98,000	2.3
Mining	5,141	0.2	} 796,000	} 18.2
Manufacturing	394,526	18.9		
Public utilities	35,247	1.7		
Construction	80,752	3.9	225,000	5.2
Transp. and commun.	149,421	7.2	} 799,000	} 18.3
Trade	233,276	11.2		
Finance	467,906	22.5	553,000	12.7
Pub. admin., defense	397,001	19.1	223,000	5.1
Services	76,420	3.7	1,459,000	33.4
Other	211,670[5]	10.2[5]	209,000[6]	4.8[6]
TOTAL	2,082,148	100.0[7]	4,362,000	100.0

Public debt (2000): U.S.$61,046,000,000.
Population economically active (2000): total 4,362,000; activity rate of total population 49.1% (participation rates: ages 16–64, 77.9%; female 47.7%; unemployed 4.7%).

Price and earnings indexes (1995 = 100)							
	1995	1996	1997	1998	1999	2000	2001
Consumer price index	100.0	100.5	101.0	100.9	101.3	102.3	104.8
Hourly earnings index	100.0	107.2	111.4	115.4	118.2	122.1	125.4

Tourism (2000): receipts U.S.$4,034,000,000; expenditures U.S.$8,015,000,000.
Land use (1994): forest 68.0%; pasture 1.4%; agriculture 6.8%; other 23.8%.

Foreign trade

Balance of trade (current prices)						
	1995	1996	1997	1998	1999	2000
SKr '000,000	82,735	120,000	131,600	129,700	135,100	129,685
% of total	8.1%	11.8%	11.6%	10.7%	10.7%	16.3%

Imports (2000): SKr 666,864,000,000 (machinery and transport equipment 44.9%; manufactured goods 13.9%; chemicals 9.6%; food 5.3%). *Major import sources* (1999): Germany 17.6%; U.K. 9.5%; Norway 8.2%; Denmark 7.6%; U.S. 6.7%.
Exports (2000): SKr 796,549,000,000 (machinery and transport equipment 50.2%, of which electrical machinery 23.0%, road vehicles 11.4%; chemicals 9.4%; paper products 7.8%; iron and steel products 4.7%). *Major export destinations* (2000): Germany 11.0%; U.S. 9.5%; U.K. 9.4%; Norway 7.5%; Finland 6.2%; Denmark 5.9%.

Transport and communications

Transport. Railroads (2000[4]): length 6,811 mi, 10,961 km; (1999) passenger-km 7,638,000,000; metric ton-km cargo 19,088,000,000. Roads (2000[4]): total length 130,500 mi, 210,000 km (paved 74%). Vehicles (2000[4]): passenger cars 3,890,159; trucks and buses 352,897. Merchant marine (2000[4]): vessels (100 gross tons and over) 412; total deadweight tonnage 2,861,000. Air transport (2000[8]): passenger-km 11,261,000; metric ton-km cargo 286,404,000; airports (1996) 48.

Communications				units per 1,000 persons
Medium	date	unit	number	
Daily newspapers	1996	circulation	3,933,000	446
Radio	1997	receivers	8,250,000	932
Television	1999	receivers	4,900,000	553
Telephones	2001	main lines	6,585,000	740
Cellular telephones	2001	subscribers	6,867,000	771
Personal computers	2001	units	4,600,000	517
Internet	2001	users	5,000,000	562

Education and health

Educational attainment (2000[4]). Percentage of population age 16–64 having: primary education 32.0%; lower secondary education 28.0%; higher secondary 16.0%; some postsecondary 24.0%. *Literacy* (2000): virtually 100%.

Education (1999–2000)		schools	teachers	students	student/ teacher ratio
Primary (age 7–12)	}	5,048	100,827	1,034,881	10.3
Secondary (age 13–18)			30,295	312,936	10.3
Higher		64	29,487[9]	372,108	...

Health (2000): physicians 24,500 (1 per 362 persons); hospital beds 31,765 (1 per 279 persons); infant mortality rate per 1,000 live births (2000) 3.5.
Food (2000): daily per capita caloric intake 3,109 (vegetable 67%, animal 33%) 116% of FAO recommended minimum requirement.

Military

Total active duty personnel (2001): 33,900 (army 56.3%, navy 20.9%, air force 22.7%). *Military expenditure as percentage of GNP* (1999): 2.3% (world 2.4%); per capita expenditure U.S.$601.

[1]As of January 1, 2000, the Church of Sweden (Lutheran Church) ceased being the official religion. [2]September 30. [3]Density based on land area only. [4]January 1. [5]Includes statistical discrepancies less imputed bank service charges. [6]Includes 203,000 unemployed. [7]Detail does not add to total given because of rounding. [8]One-third of SAS. [9]1994–95.

Internet resources for further information:
• **Statistics Sweden http://www.scb.se/indexeng.asp**

Switzerland

Official name: Confédération Suisse (French); Schweizerische Eidgenossenschaft (German); Confederazione Svizzera (Italian) (Swiss Confederation)[1].
Form of government: federal state with two legislative houses (Council of States [46]; National Council [200]).
Head of state and government: President of the Federal Council.
Capitals: Bern (administrative); Lausanne (judicial).
Official languages: French; German; Italian; Romansh (locally).
Official religion: none.
Monetary unit: 1 Swiss Franc (Sw F) = 100 centimes; valuation (Sept. 23, 2002) 1 U.S.\$ = Sw F 1.49; 1 £ = Sw F 2.31.

Area and population		area		population
				2001[2]
Cantons	Capitals	sq mi	sq km	estimate
Aargau	Aarau	542	1,404	544,300
Appenzell Ausser-Rhoden[3]	Herisau	94	243	53,500
Appenzell Inner-Rhoden[3]	Appenzell	66	172	15,000
Basel-Landschaft[3]	Liestal	200	518	260,000
Basel-Stadt[3]	Basel	14	37	187,700
Bern	Bern	2,301	5,959	943,700
Fribourg	Fribourg	645	1,671	236,300
Genève	Geneva	109	282	408,800
Glarus	Glarus	264	685	38,500
Graubünden	Chur	2,743	7,105	186,700
Jura	Delémont	324	838	68,800
Luzern	Luzern	576	1,493	347,200
Neuchâtel	Neuchâtel	310	803	165,700
Nidwalden[3]	Stans	107	276	38,000
Obwalden[3]	Sarnen	190	491	32,400
Sankt Gallen	Sankt Gallen	782	2,026	449,400
Schaffhausen	Schaffhausen	115	298	73,300
Schwyz	Schwyz	351	908	130,200
Solothurn	Solothurn	305	791	244,000
Thurgau	Frauenfeld	383	991	227,300
Ticino	Bellinzona	1,086	2,812	310,200
Uri	Altdorf	416	1,077	35,200
Valais	Sion	2,017	5,224	276,200
Vaud	Lausanne	1,240	3,212	620,300
Zug	Zug	92	239	99,400
Zürich	Zürich	668	1,729	1,211,600
TOTAL		15,940	41,284	7,204,100[4, 5]

Demography

Population (2002): 7,282,000.
Density (2002): persons per sq mi 456.8, persons per sq km 176.4.
Urban-rural (2001): urban 67.3%; rural 32.7%.
Sex distribution (2001[2]): male 48.86%; female 51.14%.
Age breakdown (2001[2]): under 15, 17.4%; 15–29, 18.3%; 30–44, 24.4%; 45–59, 19.8%; 60–74, 13.0%; 75 and over, 7.1%.
Population projection: (2010) 7,448,000; (2020) 7,739,000.
National composition (2001[2])[5]: Swiss 80.2%; Yugoslav 4.8%; Italian 4.5%; Portuguese 1.9%; German 1.5%; Spanish 1.2%; other 5.9%.
Religious affiliation (1990): Roman Catholic 46.2%; Protestant 40.0%; Muslim 2.2%; Orthodox Christian 1.0%; Jewish 0.3%; other 10.3%.
Major urban agglomerations (2001[2]): Zürich 953,800; Geneva 464,000; Basel 401,500; Bern 319,600; Lausanne 289,600; Luzern 182,500.

Vital statistics

Birth rate per 1,000 population (2000): 11.0 (world avg. 22.5); legitimate 90.0%; illegitimate 10.0%.
Death rate per 1,000 population (2000): 8.7 (world avg. 9.0).
Natural increase rate per 1,000 population (2000): 2.3 (world avg. 13.5).
Total fertility rate (avg. births per childbearing woman; 2000): 1.5.
Marriage rate per 1,000 population (2001): 4.9.
Divorce rate per 1,000 population (2001): 2.1.
Life expectancy at birth (2000): male 76.9 years; female 82.6 years.
Major causes of death per 100,000 population (1998): diseases of the circulatory system 357.2; malignant neoplasms (cancers) 212.2; diseases of the respiratory system 63.8; accidents, suicide, violence 50.0.

National economy

Budget (2002)[6]: Revenue: Sw F 130,595,000,000 (1997; social security contributions 46.7%, taxes on goods and services 20.2%, income taxes 11.6%). Expenditures: Sw F 132,989,000,000 (1997; social security and welfare 50.5%, health 19.7%, economic affairs 10.4%, defense 5.2%, education 2.3%).
National debt (end of year; 2001): Sw F 106,810,000,000.
Tourism (2000): receipts from visitors U.S.\$7,500,000,000; expenditures by nationals abroad U.S.\$6,238,000,000.
Production (metric tons except as noted). Agriculture, forestry, fishing (2001): cow's milk (2000) 3,910,000, sugar beets 1,065,600, potatoes 526,000, wheat 519,600, barley 250,500, apples 170,000, grapes 170,000; livestock (number of live animals) 1,611,000 cattle, 1,556,000 pigs; roundwood (2001) 5,000,000 cu m; fish catch (1999) 2,975. Mining (1999): salt 300,000.[7] Manufacturing (value added in Sw F '000,000; 1998): nonelectrical machinery and transport equipment 20,757; chemicals and chemical products 13,026; fabricated metal products 8,143; food 5,667; electrical machinery 4,883. Energy production (consumption): electricity (kW-hr; 2000) 63,374,000,000 (56,304,000,000); coal (metric tons; 1997) none (133,000); crude petroleum (barrels; 1997) none (35,726,000); petroleum products (metric tons; 2000) 4,861,000 ([1997] 10,907,000); natural gas (cu m; 1997) negligible (2,801,700,000).
Gross national product (2000): U.S.\$273,829,000,000 (U.S.\$38,140 per capita).

Structure of gross domestic product and labour force				
	1994		2000	
	in value Sw F '000,000	% of total value	labour force	% of labour force
Agriculture	9,230	2.6	177,000	4.4
Manufacturing	80,997	23.0	705,000	17.7
Mining	...	...	5,000	0.1
Public utilities	7,741	2.2	24,000	0.6
Construction	24,749	7.0	299,000	7.5
Transp. and commun.	22,173	6.3	255,000	6.4
Trade, restaurants	61,092	17.3	875,000	22.0
Finance, insurance[8]	84,744	24.0	592,000	14.9
Pub. admin., defense	45,647	12.9	152,000	3.8
Services	27,769	7.9	824,000	20.7
Other	−11,218[9]	−3.2[9]	77,000[10]	1.9[10]
TOTAL	352,924[11]	100.0	3,985,000[12]	100.0

Population economically active (2000): total 3,985,000[12]; activity rate of total population 55.6% (participation rates: ages 15 and over, 67.4%; female 44.2%; unemployed [2001] 1.9%).

Price and earnings indexes (1995 = 100)							
	1995	1996	1997	1998	1999	2000	2001
Consumer price index	100.0	100.8	101.3	101.4	102.2	103.8	104.8
Annual earnings index	100.0	101.2	101.7	102.4	102.7	102.3	104.8

Household income and expenditure (2000). Average household size 2.4; average gross income per household Sw F 104,352 (U.S.\$64,400); sources of income (2000): work 72.4%, transfers 22.3%; expenditure (2000): housing 17.6%, taxes 13.6%, recreation, entertainment, restaurants 13.2%, social security contribution 9.5%, health 8.8%, food 8.3%, transportation 7.5%.

Foreign trade[13]

Balance of trade (current prices)						
	1996	1997	1998	1999	2000	2001
Sw F '000,000	+1,925	+330	+2,247	+1,030	−2,066	+1,665
% of total	1.0%	0.1%	1.0%	0.5%	0.8%	0.6%

Imports (2001): Sw F 130,052,000,000 (machinery 22.7%, chemical products 20.2%, vehicles 10.9%, food products 7.6%). *Major import sources:* Germany 32.2%; France 11.0%; Italy 10.2%; The Netherlands 5.9%; U.S. 5.3%.
Exports (2001): Sw F 131,717,100,000 (chemical products 31.8%; machinery 27.3%; precision instruments, watches, jewelry 16.4%; fabricated metals 7.9%). *Major export destinations:* Germany 22.2%; U.S. 10.6%; France 9.0%; Italy 8.0%; U.K. 5.3%; Japan 3.9%; Hong Kong 3.2%.

Transport and communications

Transport. Railroads: length (1999) 3,129 mi, 5,035 km; passenger-km 14,104,000,000; metric ton-km cargo 8,688,000,000. Roads (1998): total length 44,248 mi, 71,211 km. Vehicles (2001): passenger cars 3,629,713; trucks and buses 289,897. Air transport (2001)[14]: passenger-km 32,981,000,000; metric ton-km cargo 1,793,704,000; airports (1996) with scheduled flights 5.

Communications				units per 1,000
Medium	date	unit	number	persons
Daily newspapers	1996	circulation	2,383,000	337
Radio	1997	receivers	7,100,000	1,002
Television	1999	receivers	3,700,000	518
Telephones	2001	main lines	5,183,000	718
Cellular telephones	2001	subscribers	5,226,000	724
Personal computers	2001	units	3,600,000	500
Internet	2001	users	2,917,000	404

Education and health

Educational attainment (2000). Percentage of resident Swiss and resident alien population age 25–64 having: compulsory education 19.0%; secondary 56.8%; higher 24.2%.
Health (1999): physicians 27,863 (1 per 256 persons); hospital beds (1998) 45,959 (1 per 155 persons); infant mortality rate per 1,000 live births (2000) 3.3.
Food (2000): daily per capita caloric intake 3,293 (vegetable products 67%, animal products 33%); 122% of FAO recommended minimum.

Military

Total active duty personnel (2001): 3,600[15]. *Military expenditure as percentage of GNP* (1999): 1.2% (world 2.4%); per capita expenditure U.S.\$469.

[1]Long-form name in Romansh is Confederaziun Svizra. [2]January 1. [3]Demicanton; functions as a full canton. [4]Detail does not add to total given because of rounding. [5]Includes 1,424,370 resident aliens; excludes 71,957 refugees. [6]Consolidated central government. [7]Cut and polished diamond exports (1998): U.S.\$1,340,000,000. [8]Includes consulting services. [9]Import duties less imputed bank charges. [10]Unemployed. [11]GDP in 2000 was Sw F 404,392,000,000. [12]Labour force includes about 956,000 foreign workers. [13]Imports c.i.f.; exports f.o.b. [14]Swissair only. [15]Excludes 351,200 reservists.

Internet resources for further information:
• **Embassy of Switzerland (Washington, D.C.) http://www.swissemb.org**
• **Swiss Federal Statistical Office http://www.statistik.admin.ch/eindex.htm**

Syria

Official name: Al-Jumhūrīyah al-ʿArabīyah as-Sūrīyah (Syrian Arab Republic).
Form of government: unitary multiparty[1] republic with one legislative house (People's Council [250]).
Head of state and government: President.
Capital: Damascus.
Official language: Arabic.
Official religion: none[2].
Monetary unit: 1 Syrian pound (LS) = 100 piastres; valuation[3] (Sept. 23, 2002) 1 U.S.$ = LS 48.85; 1 £ = LS 75.92.

Area and population		area		population
Governorates	**Capitals**	**sq mi**	**sq km**	**1995 estimate**
Darʿā	Darʿā	1,440	3,730	623,000
Dayr az-Zawr	Dayr az-Zawr	12,765	33,060	722,000
Dimashq	Damascus	6,962	18,032	1,730,000
Ḥalab	Aleppo	7,143	18,500	3,035,000
Ḥamāh	Ḥamāh	3,430	8,883	1,120,000
Al-Ḥasakah	Al-Ḥasakah	9,009	23,334	1,050,000
Ḥimṣ	Homs	16,302	42,223	1,247,000
Idlib	Idlib	2,354	6,097	922,000
Al-Lādhiqīyah	Latakia	887	2,297	766,000
Al-Qunayṭirah	Al-Qunayṭirah (abandoned)	719[4]	1,861[4]	50,000
Ar-Raqqah	Ar-Raqqah	7,574	19,616	566,000
As-Suwaydāʾ	As-Suwaydāʾ	2,143	5,550	270,000
Ṭarṭūs	Ṭarṭūs	730	1,892	596,000
Municipality				
Damascus	—	41	105	1,489,000
TOTAL		71,498[4]	185,180[4]	14,186,000

Demography

Population (2002): 17,156,000.
Density (2002): persons per sq mi 240.0, persons per sq km 92.6.
Urban-rural (2001): urban 51.8%; rural 48.2%.
Sex distribution (2000): male 51.23%; female 48.77%.
Age breakdown (2000): under 15, 40.1%; 15–29, 30.6%; 30–44, 16.6%; 45–59, 7.4%; 60–74, 3.8%; 75 and over, 1.5%.
Population projection: (2010) 20,606,000; (2020) 24,676,000.
Doubling time: 27 years.
Ethnic composition (2000): Syrian Arab 74.9%; Bedouin Arab 7.4%; Kurd 7.3%; Palestinian Arab 3.9%; Armenian 2.7%; other 3.8%.
Religious affiliation (1992): Muslim 86.0%, of which Sunnī 74.0%, ʿAlawite (Shīʿī) 12.0%; Christian 5.5%; Druze 3.0%; other 5.5%.
Major cities (1994): Aleppo 1,591,400; Damascus 1,549,932; Homs 644,204; Latakia 306,535; Ḥamāh 229,000.

Vital statistics

Birth rate per 1,000 population (2001): 30.6 (world avg. 21.2).
Death rate per 1,000 population (2001): 5.2 (world avg. 8.9).
Natural increase rate per 1,000 population (2001): 25.4 (world avg. 12.3).
Total fertility rate (avg. births per childbearing woman; 2001): 3.9.
Marriage rate per 1,000 population (1995)[5]: 8.4.
Life expectancy at birth (2001): male 67.6 years; female 70.0 years.
Major causes of death per 100,000 population (1989): n.a.; however, the leading causes of mortality among the total population were diseases of the circulatory system 39.6%, injuries and poisoning 9.1%, diseases of the nervous system 7.4%, diseases of the respiratory system 7.4%.

National economy

Budget (1999). Revenue: LS 255,300,000,000 (current revenues 85.4%, capital [development] revenues 14.6%). Expenditures: LS 255,300,000,000 (current expenditures 56.4%, capital [development] expenditures 43.6%).
Public debt (external, outstanding; 2000): U.S.$15,930,000,000.
Gross national product (2000): U.S.$15,146,000,000 (U.S.$940 per capita).

Structure of gross domestic product and labour force				
	1999			
	in value LS '000,000[6]	**% of total value[6]**	**labour force**	**% of labour force**
Agriculture	196,743	24.0	1,163,672	25.7
Mining	} 221,416[7]	} 27.0[7]	10,868	0.2
Manufacturing			520,734	11.5
Construction	27,433	3.3	582,382	12.9
Public utilities	—[7]	[7]	3,386	0.1
Transp. and commun.	104,053	12.7	224,527	5.0
Trade	152,866	18.6	647,195	14.3
Finance	35,095	4.3	33,474	0.7
Pub. admin.	64,859	7.9 }	} 909,242	20.1
Services	18,862	2.3		
Other	...	...	431,778[8]	9.5[8]
TOTAL	821,327	100.0[9]	4,527,258	100.0

Production (metric tons except as noted). Agriculture, forestry, fishing (2000): wheat 3,104,969, sugar beets 1,300,000, seed cotton 930,000, grapes 451,000, olives 750,000, tomatoes 610,000, potatoes 450,000, oranges 400,000, apples 320,000, eggplants 128,000; livestock (number of live animals) 15,000,000 sheep, 1,200,000 goats, 905,000 cattle; roundwood (2000) 50,400 cu m; fish

catch (1999) 14,024. Mining and quarrying (1999): phosphate rock 2,127,000; gypsum 232,000; salt 104,000; marble blocks 16,000,000 cu m. Manufacturing (1998): cement 5,016,000; refined sugar 89,000; cottonseed cake 226,000; olive oil 145,000; soap 89,000; vegetable oil 65,000; glass and pottery products 57,000; television receivers 150,500 units; refrigerators 136,900 units. Construction (1993): residential 628,000 sq m; nonresidential 209,000 sq m. Energy production (consumption): electricity (kW-hr; 2000) 23,952,000,000 (21,568,000,000); crude petroleum (barrels; 1997) 192,433,000 (86,817,000); petroleum products (metric tons; 1997) 11,573,000 (10,473,000); natural gas (cu m; 1997) 3,588,000,000 (3,588,000,000).
Population economically active (1999): total 4,527,258; activity rate of total population 28.8% (participation rates: ages 10 and over, 32.9%; female 11.3%; unemployed 9.5%).

Price and earnings indexes (1995 = 100)							
	1994	**1995**	**1996**	**1997**	**1998**	**1999**	**2000**
Consumer price index	92.6	100.0	108.2	110.8	110.2	107.3	106.8
Earnings index	...	...	...	...	...	...	...

Average household size (1999): 5.0; income per household: n.a.; sources of income: n.a.; expenditure (1987)[10]: food 58.8%, rent, fuel, and light 16.0%, clothing 7.5%, household goods 5.8%, transportation 2.4%.
Tourism (2000): receipts U.S.$1,082,000,000; expenditures U.S.$640,000,000.
Land use (1994): steppe and pasture 45.2%; agricultural and under permanent cultivation 30.1%; forested 2.6%; other 22.1%.

Foreign trade[11]

Balance of trade (current prices)						
	1994	**1995**	**1996**	**1997**	**1998**	**1999**
LS '000,000	−21,550	−12,860	−15,500	−1,250	−11,280	−4,130
% of total	21.3%	13.8%	14.7%	1.4%	14.8%	5.0%

Imports (1999): LS 43,010,000,000 (basic metals and manufactures 16.9%, food and beverages 13.8%, machinery and transport equipment 13.0%, textiles 9.9%, chemicals and chemical products 8.9%, resins 5.8%). *Major import sources:* Germany 7.0%; France 5.7%; Italy 5.6%; Turkey 4.7%; United States 4.6%; Japan 4.1%; China 3.3%; Belgium 2.9%.
Exports (1999): LS 38,880,000,000 (crude petroleum and petroleum products 62.9%, fresh vegetables and fruits 12.4%, textiles and fabrics 7.2%, raw cotton 4.5%, live animals and meat 1.3%). *Major export destinations:* Italy 26.6%; France 20.6%; Turkey 9.2%; Saudi Arabia 8.3%; Spain 6.9%; Lebanon 4.0%.

Transport and communications

Transport. Railroads (2000)[12]: route length 2,676 km; (1998) passenger-km 181,575,000; (1998) metric ton-km cargo 1,440,000,000. Roads (1998): total length 41,451 km (paved 23%). Vehicles (1998): passenger cars 138,900; trucks and buses 282,664. Air transport (2000): passenger-km 1,421,537,000; metric ton-km cargo 20,813,000; airports (1999) with scheduled flights 5.

Communications				units per 1,000
Medium	**date**	**unit**	**number**	**persons**
Daily newspapers	1996	circulation	287,000	20
Radio	1997	receivers	4,150,000	278
Television	1999	receivers	1,070,000	66.4
Telephones	2001	main lines	1,807,600	109
Cellular telephones	2001	units	200,000	12
Personal computers	2001	units	270,000	16.3
Internet	2001	users	60,000	3.6

Education and health

Educational attainment (1984). Percentage of population age 10 and over having: no schooling 20.1%; knowledge of reading and writing 26.3%; primary education 29.3%; secondary 18.4%; certificate 3.3%; higher 2.7%. *Literacy* (1995): percentage of population age 15 and over literate 74.4%; males literate 88.3%; females literate 60.4%.

Education (1996–97)				student/
	schools	**teachers**	**students**	**teacher ratio**
Primary (age 6–11)	10,783	114,689	2,690,205	23.5
Secondary (age 12–18)	2,526[13]	52,182	865,042	16.6
Voc., teacher tr.	292[13]	12,479	92,622	7.4
Higher[14]	4[13]	4,773	215,734	45.2

Health (1998): physicians 22,293 (1 per 694 persons); hospital beds (1995) 17,623 (1 per 832 persons); infant mortality rate (2001) 33.8.
Food (1999): daily per capita caloric intake 3,038 (vegetable products 86.5%, animal products 13.5%); 123% of FAO recommended minimum.

Military

Total active duty personnel (2001): 321,000 (army 67.0%, navy 1.9%, air force 12.5%). *Military expenditure as percentage of GNP* (1999): 7.0% (world 2.4%); per capita expenditure U.S.$280.

[1]Parties ideologically compatible with the Baʿth Party. [2]Islam is required to be the religion of the head of state and is the basis of the legal system. [3]Exchange rate most commonly used for commerce; Syria had five different exchange rates in late 2001. [4]Includes territory in the Golan Heights recognized internationally as part of Syria. [5]Syrian Arabs only. [6]In purchasers' values. [7]Manufacturing and Mining includes Public utilities. [8]Unemployed. [9]Detail does not add to total given because of rounding. [10]Weights of consumer price index components for Damascus only. [11]Import figures are c.i.f. [12]Excludes length of Syrian part of railway opened in August 2000 linking Aleppo, Syria, and Mosul, Iraq. [13]1994–95. [14]University-level institutions only.

Taiwan

Official name: Chung-hua Min-kuo
(Republic of China).
Form of government: multiparty
republic with a Legislature
(Legislative Yuan [225])[1].
Chief of state: President.
Head of government: Premier.
Capital: Taipei.
Official language: Mandarin Chinese.
Official religion: none.
Monetary unit: 1 New Taiwan dollar
(NT$) = 100 cents; valuation (Sept. 23,
2002) 1 U.S.$ = NT$34.78;
1 £ = NT$54.04.

Area and population

Taiwan area Counties	area sq km	population 2002 estimate	Municipalities	area sq km	population 2002 estimate
Chang-hua	1,074	1,315,075	Chia-i	60	267,592
Chia-i	1,902	562,606	Chi-lung	133	390,764
Hsin-chu	1,428	449,416	Hsin-chu	104	375,862
Hua-lien	4,629	352,459	Kao-hsiung	154	1,504,061
I-lan	2,137	465,150	T'ai-chung	163	990,041
Kao-hsiung	2,793	1,232,847	T'ai-nan	176	742,574
Miao-li	1,820	560,722	Taipei	272	2,635,678
Nan-t'ou	4,106	541,385	**non-Taiwan area**		
P'eng-hu	127	92,424	**Counties**		
P'ing-tung	2,776	907,479	Kinmen		
T'ai-chung	2,051	1,506,242	(Quemoy)		
T'ai-nan	2,016	1,107,082	Lienchiang	179	67,214
T'ai-pei	2,052	3,625,669	(Matsu)		
T'ai-tung	3,515	244,631	TOTAL	36,179[2]	22,457,488
T'ao-yüan	1,221	1,777,100			
Yün-lin	1,291	743,415			

Demography

Population (2002)[3]: 22,457,000.
Density (2002)[2, 3]: persons per sq mi 1,607.7, persons per sq km 620.7.
Urban-rural (1991)[4]: urban 74.7%; rural 25.3%.
Sex distribution (2002)[3]: male 51.03%; female 48.97%.
Age breakdown (2002)[3]: under 15, 20.8%; 15–29, 24.9%; 30–44, 25.3%; 45–59, 16.7%; 60–74, 9.1%; 75 and over, 3.2%.
Population projection: (2010) 23,777,000; (2020) 24,876,000.
Ethnic composition (1997): Han Chinese, Chinese mainland minorities, and others 98.2%; indigenous tribal peoples 1.8%, of which Ami 0.6%.
Religious affiliation (1997)[5, 6]: Buddhism 22.4%; Taoism 20.7%; I-kuan Tao 4.3%; Protestant 1.6%; Roman Catholic 1.4%; other Christian 0.3%; Muslim 0.2%; Bahā'ī 0.1%; other (mostly Christian folk-religionists) 49.0%.
Major cities (2002): Taipei 2,635,678; Kao-hsiung 1,504,061; T'ai-chung 990,041; T'ai-nan 742,574; Chung-ho (1998) 388,174; Chi-lung 390,764.

Vital statistics

Birth rate per 1,000 population (2001): 11.7 (world avg. 21.2).
Death rate per 1,000 population (2001): 5.7 (world avg. 8.9).
Natural increase rate per 1,000 population (2001): 6.0 (world avg. 12.3).
Total fertility rate (avg. births per childbearing woman; 2000): 1.8.
Life expectancy at birth (2000): male 73.6 years; female 79.3 years.
Major causes of death per 100,000 population (2001)[4]: malignant neoplasms 147.6; cerebrovascular diseases 58.8; heart disease 49.2; accidents and suicide 42.6; diabetes 40.8; liver diseases 23.5; kidney diseases 18.2; pneumonia 16.8.

National economy

Budget (1999[7]). Revenue: NT$3,391,948,000,000 (income taxes 18.0%, business tax 9.1%, commodity tax 6.5%, land tax 6.4%, customs duties 4.6%). Expenditures: NT$3,371,702,000,000 (administration and defense 24.5%, education 19.4%).
Population economically active (1990): total 10,236,324; activity rate 50.5% (participation rates: ages 15–64, 72.5%; female 38.5%; unemployed [2000] 3.0%).

Price and earnings indexes (1995 = 100)

	1995	1996	1997	1998	1999	2000	2001
Consumer price index	100.0	103.1	104.0	105.7	105.9	107.2	107.2
Monthly earnings index[8]	100.0	104.2	108.9	112.0	115.8	119.2	...

Production (metric tons except as noted). Agriculture, forestry, fishing (2000): sugarcane 2,894,000, rice 1,559,000, citrus fruits 440,382, pineapples 357,535, bananas 198,454, sweet potatoes 198,000; livestock (number of live animals) 7,494,954 pigs, 202,491 goats, 161,700 cattle; timber 21,134 cu m; fish catch 1,356,275. Mining and quarrying (2000): marble 17,800,000. Manufacturing (2000): cement 17,572,303; steel ingots 17,302,396; paperboard 3,233,864; fertilizers 1,706,861; polyester filament 1,639,139; polyvinyl chloride plastics 1,386,933; telephones 4,722,353 units; televisions 1,153,217 units. Construction (2000): total residential and nonresidential 56,121,000 sq m. Energy production (consumption): electricity (kW-hr; 2001) 178,358,000,000 ([1996] 111,140,000,000); coal (metric tons; 2000) 83,400 ([1999] 40,700,000); crude petroleum (barrels; 2000) 234,000 (285,400,000); natural gas (cu m; 2000) 670,000,000 ([1999] 6,230,000,000).
Tourism (2000): receipts from visitors U.S.$3,738,000,000; expenditures by nationals abroad U.S.$6,376,000,000.

Gross national product (2001): U.S.$288,267,000,000 (U.S.$12,941 per capita).

Structure of gross domestic product and labour force[4]

	2000 in value NT$'000,000	% of total value	labour force[9]	% of labour force[9]
Agriculture	199,430	2.1	740,000	7.6
Mining	40,782	0.4	11,000	0.1
Manufacturing	2,549,927	26.3	2,655,000	27.1
Construction	336,703	3.5	832,000	8.5
Public utilities	207,271	2.1	36,000	0.4
Transp. and commun.	652,924	6.7	481,000	4.9
Trade	1,856,026	19.2	2,163,000	22.1
Finance	2,248,185	23.2	725,000	7.4
Pub. admin., defense	987,409	10.2	1,849,000	18.9
Services	912,265	9.4		
Other	−303,983[10]	−3.1[10]	293,000[11]	3.0[11]
TOTAL	9,686,939	100.0	9,785,000	100.0

Household income and expenditure (1999). Average household size (2002) 3.3; income per household NT$1,181,082 (U.S.$37,153); expenditure: food, beverage, and tobacco 25.1%, rent, fuel, and power 24.9%, education and recreation 13.0%, transportation 11.1%, health care 11.0%, clothing 4.1%, furniture 2.9%.

Foreign trade[12]

Balance of trade (current prices)

	1996	1997	1998	1999	2000	2001
U.S.$'000,000	+13,572	+7,656	+5,917	+10,901	+8,310	+15,629
% of total	6.2%	3.2%	2.7%	4.7%	2.8%	6.8%

Imports (2001): U.S.$107,237,400,000 (electronic machinery 25.4%, nonelectrical machinery 15.9%, minerals 13.1%, chemicals 12.2%, metals and metal products 10.3%, precision instruments, clocks, watches, and musical instruments 8.5%). *Major import sources:* Japan 36.0%; U.S. 17.0%; South Korea 6.3%; Germany 4.0%; Malaysia 3.9%; Singapore 3.1%.
Exports (2001): U.S.$122,866,300,000 (nonelectrical machinery, electrical machinery, and electronics 67.2%, textile products 12.4%, plastic articles 7.4%, transportation equipment 4.7%). *Major export destinations:* U.S. 22.5%; Hong Kong 21.9%; Japan 10.4%; Germany 3.6%; Singapore 3.3%.

Transport and communications

Transport. Railroads (2001): track length 3,733 km; passenger-km 12,269,000,000; metric ton-km cargo 1,010,000,000. Roads (2001): total length 36,624 km (paved 88%[13]). Vehicles (2001): passenger cars 4,825,581; trucks and buses 854,726. Air transport (1998): passenger-km 39,218,000,000; metric ton-km cargo 4,129,300,000; airports (1996) 13.

Communications

Medium	date	unit	number	units per 1,000 persons
Radio	1996	receivers	8,620,000	402
Television	1999	receivers	9,200,000	418
Telephones	2001	main lines	12,846,906	575
Cellular telephones	2001	subscribers	21,632,978	968
Personal computers	2001	units	5,000,000	223
Internet	2001	users	6,231,917	279

Education and health

Educational attainment (1999). Percentage of population age 25 and over having: no formal schooling 7.0%; less than complete primary education 6.3%; primary 21.3%; incomplete secondary 25.7%; secondary 21.8%; some college 10.4%; higher 7.5%. *Literacy* (1999): population age 15 and over literate 16,414,896 (94.6%); males 8,641,549 (97.6%); females 7,773,347 (91.4%).

Education (1999–2000)

	schools	teachers	students	student/ teacher ratio
Primary (age 6–12)	2,583	98,745	1,927,179	19.5
Secondary (age 13–18)	972	78,506	1,288,827	16.4
Vocational	199	20,203	467,207	23.1
Higher	141	41,949	994,283	23.7

Health (2001): physicians 30,562 (1 per 731 persons); hospital beds 127,676 (1 per 175 persons); infant mortality rate per 1,000 live births (2000) 7.1.

Military

Total active duty personnel (2001): 370,000 (army 64.9%, navy 16.8%, air force 18.4%). *Military expenditure as percentage of GNP* (1999): 5.2% (world 2.4%); per capita expenditure U.S.$690.

[1]The National Assembly became a nonstanding body with limited specialized authority per April 2000 amendment; the Legislature is the formal lawmaking body. [2]Total area per more recent survey is 36,188 sq km (13,972 sq mi). [3]Includes Quemoy and Matsu groups. [4]For Taiwan area only, excluding Quemoy and Matsu groups. [5]Formal subscribers to religious beliefs. [6]Almost all Taiwanese adults engage in religious practices stemming from one or a combination of traditional folk religions. [7]General government. [8]In manufacturing. [9]Civilian employed persons only. [10]Import duties less imputed bank service charge. [11]Unemployed. [12]Imports c.i.f. [13]1999.

Internet resources for further information:
• **The Republic of China Yearbook 2001**
  http://www.gio.gov.tw/taiwan-website/5-gp/yearbook/index.htm
• **Directorate-General of Budget, Accounting and Statistics (Taiwan)**
  http://www.dgbasey.gov.tw/english/dgbas_e0.htm
• **National Statistics of Taiwan, the Republic of China** http://www.stat.gov.tw

Tajikistan

Official name: Jumhurii Tojikistan (Republic of Tajikistan).
Form of government: parliamentary republic with two legislative houses (National Assembly [33[1]]; Assembly of Representatives [63]).
Chief of state: President.
Head of government: Prime Minister.
Capital: Dushanbe.
Official language: Tajik (Tojik).
Official religion: none.
Monetary unit: 1 somoni = 100 dinars[2]; valuation (Sept. 23, 2002)
1 U.S.$ = 2.75 somoni;
1 £ = 4.28 somoni.

Area and population		area		population
				2000
Oblasts	**Capitals**	sq mi	sq km	census
Khatlon (Qŭrghonteppa)	Qŭrghonteppa	9,500	24,600	2,151,000
Sughd	Khujand	10,100	26,100	1,870,000
Autonomous oblast				
Kŭhistoni Badakhshon (Gorno-Badakhshan)	Khorugh	24,600	63,700	206,000
City				
Dushanbe	—	100	300	562,000
Other[3]	—	11,000	28,400	1,338,000
TOTAL		55,300[4]	143,100[4]	6,127,000

Demography

Population (2002): 6,327,000.
Density (2002): persons per sq mi 114.4, persons per sq km 44.2.
Urban-rural (2000): urban 26.5%; rural 73.5%.
Sex distribution (2000): male 50.30%; female 49.70%.
Age breakdown (2000): under 15, 39.4%; 15–29, 27.7%; 30–44, 18.4%; 45–59, 7.6%; 60–74, 5.4%; 75 and over, 1.5%.
Population projection: (2010) 6,779,000; (2020) 7,787,000.
Doubling time: 39 years.
Ethnic composition (2000): Tajik 64.9%; Uzbek 25.9%; Russian 3.5%; Tatar 1.4%; Kyrgyz 1.3%; other 3.0%.
Religious affiliation (1995): Sunnī Muslim 80.0%; Shī'ī Muslim 5.0%; Russian Orthodox 1.5%; Jewish 0.1%; other (mostly nonreligious) 13.4%.
Major cities (2000): Dushanbe 562,000; Khujand 149,000; Kulyab 78,000; Kurgan-Tyube 60,000; Ura-Tyube 51,000.

Vital statistics

Birth rate per 1,000 population (2001): 24.7 (world avg. 21.2); (1994) legitimate 90.8%; illegitimate 9.2%.
Death rate per 1,000 population (2001): 6.4 (world avg. 8.9).
Natural increase rate per 1,000 population (2001): 18.3 (world avg. 12.3).
Total fertility rate (avg. births per childbearing woman; 2001): 4.4.
Marriage rate per 1,000 population (1994): 6.8.
Divorce rate per 1,000 population (1994): 0.8.
Life expectancy at birth (2001): male 65.0 years; female 71.0 years.
Major causes of death per 100,000 population (1993): diseases of the circulatory system 225.5; violence, poisoning, and accidents 184.0; diseases of the respiratory system 160.6; infectious and parasitic diseases 129.9; malignant neoplasms (cancers) 42.3; diseases of the digestive system 20.9.

National economy

Budget (2000). Revenue: 218,803,000 somoni (tax revenue 93.9%, of which taxes on aluminum and cotton 26.9%, value-added tax 20.3%, income and profit taxes 15.2%, customs duties 12.5%, excise taxes 4.1%; nontax revenue 5.4%; grants 0.7%). Expenditures: 225,410,000 somoni (current expenditures 78.2%, of which state authorities 19.7%, education 18.3%, state bodies and administration 12.0%, defense 9.7%, law enforcement 9.7%, health 7.4%; capital expenditures 21.8%).
Production (metric tons except as noted). Agriculture, forestry, fishing (2000): grain 550,000, vegetables and fruit 523,000, raw cotton 335,000, milk 310,000, potatoes 303,000, grapes 110,000; livestock (number of live animals) 2,222,000 sheep and goats, 1,062,000 cattle, 72,000 horses; roundwood, n.a.; fish catch (1999) 80. Mining and quarrying (2000): aluminum 520,000; lead (metal content of concentrate) 800; gold 2,700 kg. Manufacturing (value of production in '000,000 Tajik rubles[2]; 1996): ferrous and nonferrous metals 80,333; textiles 35,023; grain mill products 23,526; bakery products 16,908; basic chemicals 7,586; jewelry 3,552; processed fruits and vegetables 2,339. Energy production (consumption): electricity (kW-hr; 2000) 14,200,000,000 (12,500,000,000); coal (metric tons; 2001) 24,900 (122,000); crude petroleum (barrels; 1997) 183,000 (183,000); petroleum products (metric tons; 1997) none (1,116,000); natural gas (cu m; 1997) 41,000,000 (1,015,000,000).
Public debt (external, outstanding; 2000): U.S.$625,600,000.
Population economically active (2000): total 1,754,000; activity rate of total population 28.6% (participation rates: ages 15–59 [male], 15–54 [female] 55.0%; female [1996] 46.5%; unemployed 3.1%).

Price and earnings indexes (1995 = 100)							
	1994	1995	1996	1997	1998	1999	2000
Consumer price index	18.4	100.0	298.0	511.0	524.8	682.8	1,096.6
Monthly earnings index	47.7	100.0	383.7	680.6	1,175.1	1,487.7	2,048.6

Gross national product (2000): U.S.$1,109,000,000 (U.S.$180 per capita).

Structure of gross domestic product and labour force				
	2000			
	in value '000 somoni	% of total value	labour force	% of labour force
Agriculture	315,323	17.4	1,090,000	62.1
Mining	} 368,218	20.4	122,000	7.0
Manufacturing				
Public utilities	...	...	...	...
Construction	50,110	2.8	34,000	1.9
Transp. and commun.	58,585	3.2	37,000	2.1
Trade	185,455	10.3	29,000	1.7
Finance		...	...	...
Pub. admin., defense	} 459,290	25.4	25,000	1.4
Services			285,000	16.2
Other	369,786[5]	20.5[5]	132,000[6]	7.5[6]
TOTAL	1,806,767	100.0	1,754,000	100.0[7]

Tourism: receipts from visitors, n.a.; expenditures by nationals abroad, n.a.
Land use (1994): forest 3.8%; pasture 24.8%; agriculture 6.0%; other 65.4%.
Household income and expenditure. Average household size (1989) 6.1; (1995) income per household 18,744 Tajik rubles (U.S.$114); sources of income (1995): wages and salaries 34.5%, self-employment 34.0%, borrowing 2.4%, pension 2.0%, other 27.1%; expenditure: food 81.5%, clothing 10.2%, transport 2.5%, fuel 2.1%, other 3.7%.

Foreign trade[8]

Balance of trade (current prices)						
	1995	1996	1997	1998	1999	2000
U.S.$'000,000	−59	−16	−63	−145	−27	−47
% of total	3.6%	1.0%	4.1%	11.0%	2.0%	2.9%

Imports (2000): U.S.$864,000,000 (electricity 24.3%, alumina 21.3%, petroleum products and natural gas 14.2%, grain and flour 5.1%). *Major import sources* (1996): Uzbekistan 29.8%; Switzerland 14.9%; United Kingdom 11.7%; Russia 11.1%; Kazakhstan 7.8%; Turkmenistan 3.9%; Ukraine 2.9%.
Exports (2000): U.S.$792,000,000 (aluminum 49.6%, electricity 23.2%, cotton fibre 11.6%). *Major export destinations* (1996): The Netherlands 28.3%; Uzbekistan 24.8%; Switzerland 10.8%; Russia 10.2%; Kazakhstan 3.2%.

Transport and communications

Transport. Railroads (1999): length 299 mi, 482 km; passenger-mi 38,000,000, passenger-km 61,200,000; short ton-mi cargo 890,000,000, metric ton-km cargo 1,300,000,000. Roads (1996): total length 8,500 mi, 13,700 km (paved 83%). Vehicles (1996): passenger cars 680,000; trucks and buses 8,190. Air transport (2001)[9]: passenger-mi 376,000,000, passenger-km 605,000,000; short ton-mi cargo 3,316,000, metric ton-km cargo 4,841,000; airports (1997) 1.

Communications				units per 1,000
Medium	date	unit	number	persons
Daily newspapers	1996	circulation	120,000	21
Radio	1997	receivers	850,000	143
Television	1999	receivers	2,000,000	328
Telephones	2001	main lines	223,000	36
Cellular phones	2001	subscribers	1,600	0.3
Personal computers	...	units	...	...
Internet	2001	users	3,200	0.5

Education and health

Educational attainment (1989). Percentage of population age 25 and over having: primary education or no formal schooling 16.3%; some secondary 21.1%; completed secondary and some postsecondary 55.1%; higher 7.5%. *Literacy* (1998): percentage of total population age 15 and over literate 99.0%; males literate 99.5%; females literate 98.6%.

Education (1996–97)				student/
	schools	teachers	students	teacher ratio
Primary (age 6–13)	3,432	27,172	638,674	23.5
Secondary (age 14–17)[10]	...	112,532	688,150	6.1
Voc., teacher tr.	...	...	29,482[11]	...
Higher	8	...	76,613	...

Health (1998): physicians 14,292 (1 per 416 persons); hospital beds 36,920 (1 per 161 persons); infant mortality rate per 1,000 live births (2001) 54.0.
Food (2000): daily per capita caloric intake 1,720 (vegetable products 91%, animal products 9%); 67% of FAO recommended minimum requirement.

Military

Total active duty personnel (2001): 6,000 (army 100%); Russian troops (2002) 25,000. *Military expenditure as percentage of GNP* (1999): 1.3% (world 2.4%); per capita expenditure U.S.$13.

---

[1]Eight members are appointed by the President. [2]The somoni (equal to 1,000 Tajik rubles) was introduced on Oct. 30, 2000. [3]No oblast-level administration. [4]Includes c. 400 sq mi (c. 1,035 sq km) ceded to China in May 2002. [5]Includes 190,675,000 somoni in undistributed GDP and 179,111,000 somoni in indirect taxes. [6]Includes 78,000 undefined and 54,000 registered unemployed. [7]Detail does not add to total given because of rounding. [8]Import total in balance of trade is c.i.f. [9]Tajikistan Airlines only. [10]Excludes special education. [11]1994–95.

Internet resources for further information:
• **Interactive Central Asia Resource Project** http://www.icarp.org
• **Interstate Statistical Committee of the Commonwealth of Independent States** http://www.cisstat.com/eng/macro0.htm

Tanzania

Official name: Jamhuri ya Muungano wa Tanzania (Swahili); United Republic of Tanzania (English).
Form of government: unitary multiparty republic with one legislative house (National Assembly [275[1]]).
Head of state and government: President.
Seat of government: Dar es Salaam (pending capital, Dodoma)[2].
Official languages: Swahili; English.
Official religion: none.
Monetary unit: 1 Tanzania shilling (T Sh) = 100 cents; valuation (Sept. 23, 2002) 1 U.S.$ = T Sh 977.00; 1 £ = T Sh 1,518.

Area and population

Administrative regions	area sq km	population 2002 estimate	Administrative regions	area sq km	population 2002 estimate
Mainland Tanzania (Tanganyika)			Rukwa	68,635	1,158,956
			Ruvuma	63,498	1,204,656
Arusha[3]	82,306	2,154,899	Shinyanga	50,781	2,630,010
Dar es Salaam	1,393	2,373,840	Singida	49,341	1,133,115
Dodoma	41,311	1,751,383	Tabora	76,151	1,469,687
Iringa	56,864	1,761,424	Tanga	26,808	1,809,007
Kagera	28,388	1,984,547	**Autonomous territory**		
Kigoma	37,037	1,252,793	Zanzibar and Pemba[4]		
Kilimanjaro	13,309	2,097,165			
Lindi	66,046	884,524	Pemba	906	398,752
Mara	19,566	1,440,387	Zanzibar	1,554	604,910
Mbeya	60,350	2,229,706	TOTAL LAND AREA	883,749	
Morogoro	70,799	1,815,167	INLAND WATER	59,050	
Mtwara	16,707	1,152,920	TOTAL	942,799[5]	34,901,628
Mwanza	19,592	2,713,041			
Pwani (Coast)	32,407	880,739			

Demography

Population (2002): 34,902,000.
Density (2002)[6]: persons per sq mi 102.3, persons per sq km 39.5.
Urban-rural (2002): urban 33.3%; rural 66.7%.
Sex distribution (2001): male 49.72%; female 50.28%.
Age breakdown (2001): under 15, 44.8%; 15–29, 28.9%; 30–44, 14.2%; 45–59, 7.6%; 60–74, 3.6%; 75 and over, 0.9%.
Population projection: (2010) 41,805,000; (2020) 52,065,000.
Doubling time: 27 years.
Ethnolinguistic composition (1987): Nyamwezi and Sukuma 21.1%; Swahili 8.8%; Hehet and Bena 6.9%; Haya 5.9%; Makonde 5.9%; Nyakyusa 5.4%; Chagga 4.9%; other 41.1%.
Religious affiliation (1997): Christian *c.* 44%; Muslim *c.* 37%; animist *c.* 19%.

Vital statistics

Birth rate per 1,000 population (2001): 39.7 (world avg. 21.2).
Death rate per 1,000 population (2001): 13.0 (world avg. 8.9).
Natural increase rate per 1,000 population (2001): 26.7 (world avg. 12.3).
Total fertility rate (avg. births per childbearing woman; 2001): 5.4.
Life expectancy at birth (2001): male 51.0 years; female 53.0 years.
Major causes of death per 100,000 population: n.a.; however, the major diseases include HIV/AIDS, malaria, schistosomiasis, tuberculosis, and sleeping sickness.

National economy

Budget (1999–2000). Revenue: T Sh 777,644,700,000 (sales and excise tax 28.7%, income tax 26.9%, import duties 22.9%). Expenditures: T Sh 1,168,778,800,000 (current payments 58.2%, interest payments on debt 11.0%; capital expenditure 30.8%).
Public debt (external, outstanding; 2000): U.S.$6,325,000,000.
Tourism (2000): receipts from visitors U.S.$739,000,000; expenditures by nationals abroad U.S.$337,000,000.
Gross national product (2000)[7]: U.S.$9,013,000,000 (U.S.$270 per capita).

Structure of gross domestic product and labour force

	2000 in value T Sh '000,000[7]	% of total value	labour force	% of labour force
Agriculture	3,003,903	45.1	14,551,000	80.4
Mining	99,519	1.5		
Manufacturing	499,726	7.4		
Construction	343,354	5.2		
Public utilities	112,753	1.7		
Transp. and commun.	328,259	4.9		
Trade	823,025	12.4	3,537,000	19.6
Finance	377,996	5.7		
Pub. admin., defense	516,865	7.8		
Services	709,617	10.6		
Other	-151,359[8]	-2.3[8]		
TOTAL	6,663,658	100.0	18,088,000	100.0

Production (metric tons except as noted). Agriculture (2000): cassava 5,758,000, corn (maize) 2,009,000, sweet potatoes 798,000, bananas 703,000, sorghum 664,000, rice 508,000, seed cotton 123,000, cashew nuts 121,000, coffee 47,800, tobacco leaves 25,400, tea 23,600; livestock (number of live animals) 14,380,000 cattle, 9,950,000 goats, 4,200,000 sheep, 27,798,000 chick-

ens; roundwood (2000) 23,100,000 cu m; fish catch (1999) 310,300. Mining and quarrying (2000): gemstones (excluding diamonds) 150,800 kg; gold 15,060 kg; diamonds 354,400 carats. Manufacturing (2000): cement 833,000; sugar 135,300; petroleum products 117,000; iron sheets 25,000; rolled steel 11,200; beer 1,830,000 hectolitres; cigarettes 3,700,000,000 units; textiles 73,600,000 sq m. Energy production (consumption): electricity (kW-hr; 1997) 1,744,000,000 (1,744,000,000); coal (metric tons; 1997) 5,000 (5,000); crude petroleum (barrels; 1997) none (4,354,000); petroleum products (metric tons; 1997) 589,000 (665,000).
Population economically active (2000): total 18,088,000; activity rate 51.2% (participation rates [1991]: over age 10, 87.8%; female 40.0%).

Price index (1995 = 100)

	1995	1996	1997	1998	1999	2000	2001
Consumer price index	100.0	121.0	140.4	158.4	170.9	181.0	190.3

Household income and expenditure. Average household size (1998) 5.4; income per household: n.a.; sources of income: n.a.; expenditure (1994): food 64.2%, clothing 9.9%, housing 8.3%, energy 7.6%, transportation 4.1%.
Land use (1995): forested 37.0%; meadows and pastures 39.6%; agricultural and under permanent cultivation 4.2%; other 19.2%.

Foreign trade

Balance of trade (current prices)

	1994	1995	1996	1997	1998	1999
T Sh '000,000	-385,977	-433,525	-363,605	-379,905	-517,779	-809,445
% of total	42.1%	35.7%	29.2%	30.2%	36.6%	49.6%

Imports (1999): U.S.$1,630,600,000 (consumer goods 33.9%, machinery 20.9%, transport equipment 18.2%, food 10.8%). *Major import sources:* Japan 10.9%; U.K. 7.8%; U.S. 6.0%; Kenya 5.8%; India 5.6%.
Exports (1999): U.S.$541,000,000 (cashew nuts 18.3%, coffee 14.2%, minerals 13.2%, tobacco 8.0%, cotton 5.2%, tea 4.5%). *Major export destinations:* India 19.5%; U.K. 17.0%; Japan 8.0%; The Netherlands 5.7%; Singapore 4.5%; Germany 4.0%; Kenya 3.8%; U.S. 3.3%.

Transport and communications

Transport. Railroads (1997): length 3,569 km; passenger-journeys 694,000,000[9]; metric ton-km cargo 1,354,000,000[9]. Roads (1999): length 88,200 km (paved 4.2%). Vehicles (1996): passenger cars 23,760; trucks and buses 115,700. Air transport (2001)[10]: passenger-km 155,000,000; metric ton-km 2,772,000; airports (1999) with scheduled flights 11.

Communications

Medium	date	unit	number	units per 1,000 persons
Daily newspapers	1996	circulation	120,000	3.9
Radio	1997	receivers	8,800,000	280
Television	1999	receivers	690,000	20
Telephones	2001	main lines	148,500	4.1
Cellular telephones	2001	subscribers	427,000	12
Personal computers	2001	units	120,000	3.3
Internet	2001	users	300,000	8.3

Education and health

Educational attainment: n.a. *Literacy* (1999): percentage of population age 15 and over literate 74.7%; males 84.0%; females 65.7%.

Education (1997)[7]

	schools	teachers	students	student/ teacher ratio
Primary (age 7–13)	10,927	109,936	4,057,965	36.9
Secondary (age 14–19)	491[11]	11,434	225,607	19.7
Teacher training	40[11]	1,062	9,136	8.6
Higher[12]	...	1,650	12,776	7.7

Health (1993): physicians 1,365 (1 per 20,511 persons); hospital beds 26,820 (1 per 1,000 persons); infant mortality rate (2001) 79.4.
Food (2000): daily per capita caloric intake 1,906 (vegetable products 94%, animal products 6%); 82% of FAO recommended minimum requirement.

Military

Total active duty personnel (2001): 27,000 (army 85.2%, navy 3.7%, air force 11.1%). *Military expenditure as percentage of GNP* (1999): 1.4% (world 2.4%); per capita expenditure U.S.$4.

[1]Statutory number. [2]As of 2002 only the prime minister's office and legislature were located in Dodoma; the scheduled completion date for the move of all government offices to Dodoma is 2005. [3]Includes Manyara administrative region created in early 2002. [4]Has local internal government structure; Zanzibar has 3 administrative regions, Pemba has 2. [5]A recent survey indicates a total area of 945,090 sq km (364,901 sq mi). [6]Based on land area only. [7]Mainland Tanzania only. [8]Bank service charge. [9]Tanzanian Railways only; 1995. [10]Air Tanzania only. [11]1994. [12]1996.

Internet resources for further information:
• National Bureau of Statistics
  http://www.tanzania.go.tz/statistics.html#top
• Bank of Tanzania http://www.bot-tz.org

Thailand

Official name: Muang Thai, or Prathet Thai (Kingdom of Thailand).
Form of government: constitutional monarchy with two legislative houses (Senate [200]; House of Representatives [500]).
Chief of state: King.
Head of government: Prime Minister.
Capital: Bangkok.
Official language: Thai.
Official religion: Buddhism.
Monetary unit: 1 Thai baht (B) = 100 stangs; valuation (Sept. 23, 2002)
1 U.S.$ = B 43.33; 1 £ = B 67.34.

Area and population	area		population
Regions[1]	sq mi	sq km	2000 census
Bangkok Metropolis	604	1,565	6,355,144
Central	39,512	102,335	14,215,503
Northeastern	65,196	168,855	20,825,262
Northern	65,500	169,645	11,433,061
Southern	27,303	70,715	8,087,471
TOTAL	198,115	513,115	60,916,441

Demography

Population (2002): 63,430,000.
Density (2002): persons per sq mi 320.2, persons per sq km 123.6.
Urban-rural (2002): urban 31.0%; rural 69.0%.
Sex distribution (2000): male 49.24%; female 50.76%.
Age breakdown (1999): under 15, 26.0%; 15–29, 27.7%; 30–44, 23.3%; 45–59, 14.1%; 60–74, 7.2%; 75 and over, 1.7%.
Population projection: (2010) 67,435,000; (2020) 70,706,000.
Doubling time: 87 years.
Ethnic composition (2000): Tai peoples 81.4%, of which Thai (Siamese) 34.9%, Lao 26.5%; Han Chinese 10.6%; Malay 3.7%; Khmer 1.9%; other 2.4%.
Religious affiliation (2000): Buddhist 94.2%; Muslim 4.6%; Christian and other 1.2%.
Major cities (2000)[2]: Bangkok 5,680,380; Nonthaburi 522,669; Songkhla 273,113; Samut Prakan 268,583; Chon Buri 256,300.

Vital statistics

Birth rate per 1,000 population (2002): 14.0 (world avg. 21.2).
Death rate per 1,000 population (2002): 6.0 (world avg. 8.9).
Natural increase rate per 1,000 population (2002): 8.0 (world avg. 12.3).
Total fertility rate (avg. births per childbearing woman; 2002): 1.8.
Marriage rate per 1,000 population (1999)[2]: 5.7.
Divorce rate per 1,000 population (1999)[2]: 1.1.
Life expectancy at birth (2002): male 70.0 years; female 75.0 years.
Major causes of death per 100,000 population (1998): diseases of the heart 65.3; accidents, homicide, and poisonings 51.0; malignant neoplasms (cancers) 49.2; hypertension and cerebrovascular disease 10.6; pneumonia and other lung diseases 10.4; diseases of the liver and the pancreas 9.6.

National economy

Budget (2000). Revenue: B 794,700,000,000 (taxes on goods and services 40.5%; income taxes 29.6%; taxes on international trade 11.0%). Expenditures: B 949,500,000,000 (education 20.7%; transportation and communications 11.1%; defense 7.6%; agriculture 7.4%; health 7.3%; public order and safety 5.8%; social security 5.8%).
Production (metric tons except as noted). Agriculture, forestry, fishing (2000): sugarcane 51,210,472, rice 23,402,900, cassava 18,508,568, corn (maize) 4,571,450, pineapples 2,280,959, natural rubber 2,235,680, bananas 1,720,000, soybeans 346,127, tobacco 74,200; livestock (number of live animals) 7,682,000 pigs, 6,100,000 cattle, 2,100,000 buffalo, 172,000,000 chickens; roundwood (1999) 36,631,000 cu m; fish catch (1998) 2,900,320. Mining and quarrying (1998): limestone 37,251,000; gypsum 4,334,000; kaolin clay 266,000; zinc ore 195,122; lead ore 15,346; fluorite 3,743; tin concentrates 2,028. Manufacturing (1996): cement 38,739,000; refined sugar 6,323,000; crude steel 2,143,000; paper products 608,000; unwrought tin 10,981; beer 6,323,000 hectolitres. Energy production (consumption): electricity (kW-hr; 2000) 67,104,000,000 ([1997] 98,194,000,000); hard coal (metric tons; 1997) negligible (3,204); lignite (metric tons; 2001) 19,619,000 ([1997] 22,614,000]); 23,393,000 (25,818,000); crude petroleum (barrels; 2001) 21,900,000 ([1997] 278,000,000); petroleum products (metric tons; 1997) 36,727,000 (33,927,000); natural gas (cu m; 2001) 20,633,000,000 ([1997] 15,046,000,000).
Tourism (2000): receipts from visitors U.S.$7,112,000,000; expenditures by nationals abroad U.S.$2,068,000,000.
Land use (1998): meadows and pastures 1.6%; agricultural and under permanent cultivation 39.8%; forested and other 58.6%.
Population economically active (2000)[3]: total 33,973,000; activity rate of total population 54.4% (participation rates: over age 13, 69.7%; female 45.0%; unemployed 2.4%).

Price and earnings indexes (1995 = 100)							
	1995	1996	1997	1998	1999	2000	2001
Consumer price index	100.0	105.8	111.8	120.8	121.1	123.0	125.1
Monthly earnings index	100.0	108.5	117.0	...	...	...	...

Gross national product (2000): U.S.$121,602,000,000 (U.S.$2,000 per capita).

Structure of gross domestic product and labour force

	2000			
	in value B '000,000	% of total value	labour force[3]	% of labour force[3]
Agriculture	504,513	10.3	16,095,500	47.4
Mining	116,798	2.4	38,900	0.1
Manufacturing	1,570,842	32.0	4,784,800	14.1
Construction	150,333	3.1	1,280,000	3.8
Public utilities	146,155	3.0	172,500	0.5
Transp. and commun.	396,667	8.1	951,200	2.8
Trade	784,478	16.0	4,801,500	14.1
Finance	282,314	5.7	} 4,864,800	14.3
Pub. admin., defense	212,515	4.3		
Services	740,110	15.1		
Other	...	...	983,800[4]	2.9[4]
TOTAL	4,904,725	100.0	33,973,000	100.0

Public debt (external, outstanding; 2000): U.S.$29,418,000,000.
Household income and expenditure (1998). Average household size (2000) 3.9; average annual income per household B 149,904 (U.S.$3,624); sources of income: wages and salaries 40.1%, self-employment 29.8%, transfer payments 7.9%, other 22.2%; expenditure: food, tobacco, and beverages 37.7%, housing 21.4%, transportation and communications 13.3%, medical and personal care 5.1%, clothing 3.5%, education 2.3%.

Foreign trade[5]

Balance of trade (current prices)						
	1996	1997	1998	1999	2000	2001
U.S.$'000,000	−9,488	+1,572	+16,238	+14,013	+11,700	+8,582
% of total	8.0%	1.4%	18.2%	14.1%	9.4%	7.3%

Imports (1998): B 1,778,564,000,000 (electrical machinery 26.2%, power generating equipment 14.6%, mineral fuels and lubricants 8.0%, iron and steel products 8.0%, plastics 4.2%, organic chemicals 3.3%, aircraft and parts 2.7%). *Major import sources:* Japan 23.6%; U.S. 14.0%; Singapore 5.6%; Taiwan 5.2%; Malaysia 5.1%; Germany 4.3%; China 4.2%; South Korea 3.5%.
Exports (1998): B 2,242,579,000,000 (electrical machinery 18.9%, power generating equipment 18.6%, garments 6.1%, rubber products 4.1%, live fish 4.0%, meat and fish preparations 3.9%, cereals 3.9%). *Major export destinations:* U.S. 22.3%; Japan 13.7%; Singapore 8.6%; Hong Kong 5.1%; The Netherlands 4.0%; U.K. 3.9%; Malaysia 3.3%; China 3.2%.

Transport and communications

Transport. Railroads (1998[6]): route length 4,623 km; passenger-km 10,680,-000,000; metric ton-km cargo 2,832,000,000. Roads (1996): total length 64,600 km (paved 98%). Vehicles (1999): passenger cars 1,661,000; trucks and buses 2,855,000. Air transport (1999): passenger-km 38,345,195,000; metric ton-km cargo 1,670,717,000; airports (1996) 25.

Communications				units per 1,000
Medium	date	unit	number	persons
Daily newspapers	1996	circulation	3,800,000	64
Radio	1997	receivers	13,959,000	234
Television	1999	receivers	17,600,000	289
Telephones	2001	main lines	5,973,500	94
Cellular telephones	2001	subscribers	7,550,000	119
Personal computers	2001	units	1,700,000	27
Internet	2001	users	3,536,000	56

Education and health

Educational attainment (1990). Percentage of population age 25 and over having: no formal schooling 11.8%; primary education 71.3%; secondary 9.5%; postsecondary 6.6%; unknown 0.8%. *Literacy* (1995): total population age 15 and over literate 93.8%; males literate 96.0%; females literate 91.6%.

Education (1997–98)	schools	teachers	students	student/ teacher ratio
Primary (age 7–12)	34,001[7]	445,542[8]	5,927,902	19.3[8]
Secondary (age 13–18)	2,318[8]	107,025[8]	3,358,470	19.8[8]
Voc., teacher tr.	679[8]	40,116[8]	738,861	19.8[8]
Higher	102[8]	38,423[7]	1,522,142	31.8[7]

Health (1997): physicians 16,569 (1 per 3,553 persons); hospital beds 132,405 (1 per 445 persons); infant mortality rate (2002) 21.0.
Food (2000): daily per capita caloric intake 2,506 (vegetable products 89%, animal products 11%); 113% of FAO recommended minimum requirement.

Military

Total active duty personnel (2001): 306,000 (army 62.1%, navy 22.2%, air force 15.7%). *Military expenditure as percentage of GNP* (1999): 1.7% (world 2.4%); per capita expenditure U.S.$34.

---

[1]Actual local administration is based on 76 provinces. [2]Based on registration records. [3]August; economically active persons 13 years and over. [4]Mostly unemployed. [5]Import figures are f.o.b. in balance of trade and c.i.f. for commodities and trading partners. [6]Traffic data refer to fiscal year ending September 30. [7]1995–96. [8]1993.

Internet resources for further information:
• **National Statistical Office Thailand**
   http://www.nso.go.th
• **Bank of Thailand**
   http://www.bot.or.th/bothomepage/index/index_e.asp

Togo

Official name: République Togolaise (Togolese Republic).
Form of government: multiparty republic[1] with one legislative body (National Assembly [81]).
Chief of state: President[1].
Head of government: Prime Minister.
Capital: Lomé.
Official language: French.
Official religion: none.
Monetary unit: 1 CFA franc (CFAF) = 100 centimes; valuation (Sept. 23, 2002) 1 U.S.$ = CFAF 667.00; 1 £ = CFAF 1,037[2].

Area and population		area		population
Regions Prefectures	Capitals	sq mi	sq km	1989 estimate
Centrale	Sokodé			339,000
Sotouboua	Sotouboua	2,892	7,491	162,500
Tchamba	Tchamba	1,214	3,143	54,500
Tchaoudjo	Sokodé	984	2,549	122,000
De la Kara	Kara			531,500
Assoli	Bafilo	362	938	41,000
Bassar	Bassar	2,444	6,330	152,000
Binah	Pagouda	180	465	61,000
Doufelgou	Niamtougou	432	1,120	75,000
Kéran	Kandé	419	1,085	49,500
Kozah	Kara	653	1,692	153,000
Des Plateaux	Atakpamé			810,500
Amou	Amlamé	773	2,003	98,500
Haho	Notsé	1,406	3,641	139,000
Kloto	Kpalimé	1,072	2,777	233,500
Ogou	Atakpamé	2,349	6,083	204,000
Wawa	Badou	954	2,471	135,500
Des Savanes	Dapaong			410,500
Oti	Sansanné-Mango	1,453	3,762	98,500
Tône	Dapaong	1,869	4,840	312,000
Maritime	Lomé			1,299,500
Golfe	Lomé	133	345	560,000
Lacs	Aného	275	713	172,500
Vo	Vogan	290	750	125,000
Yoto	Tabligbo	483	1,250	187,000
Zio	Tsévié	1,288	3,337	255,000
TOTAL		21,925	56,785	3,391,000

Demography

Population (2002): 5,286,000.
Density (2002): persons per sq mi 241.1, persons per sq km 93.1.
Urban-rural (2002): urban 33.9%; rural 66.1%.
Sex distribution (2001): male 49.22%; female 50.78%.
Age breakdown (2001): under 15, 45.6%; 15–29, 28.1%; 30–44, 14.8%; 45–59, 7.5%; 60–74, 3.3%; 75 and over, 0.7%.
Population projection: (2010) 6,245,000; (2020) 7,197,000.
Ethnic composition (2000): Ewe 22.2%; Kabre 13.4%; Wachi 10.0%; Mina 5.6%; Kotokoli 5.6%; Bimoba 5.2%; Losso 4.0%; Gurma 3.4%; Lamba 3.2%; Adja 3.0%; other 24.4%.
Religious affiliation (1993): traditional beliefs 50%; Christian 35%, of which Roman Catholic 23%; Muslim 15%.
Major cities (1997): Lomé 375,000 (urban agglomeration [2001] 732,000); Sokodé 51,000; Kara 30,000; Kpalimé 30,000; Atakpamé 30,000.

Vital statistics

Birth rate per 1,000 population (2001): 37.0 (world avg. 21.2).
Death rate per 1,000 population (2001): 11.2 (world avg. 8.9).
Natural increase rate per 1,000 population (2001): 25.8 (world avg. 12.3).
Total fertility rate (avg. births per childbearing woman; 2001): 5.3.
Life expectancy at birth (2001): male 52.4 years; female 56.4 years.

National economy

Budget (1999). Revenue: CFAF 140,400,000,000 (tax revenue 80.1%; grants 10.5%; nontax revenue 9.4%). Expenditures: CFAF 173,700,000,000 (current expenditure 83.3%, of which wages 33.9%, materials and supplies 20.0%, transfers 13.8%, debt service 10.8%, other 4.8%; capital expenditure 16.7%).
Public debt (external, outstanding; 2000): U.S.$1,232,000,000.
Production (metric tons except as noted). Agriculture, forestry, fishing (2000): cassava 700,700, yams 563,300, corn (maize) 495,500, sorghum 154,800, vegetables 130,700, seed cotton 117,400, oil palm fruit 114,000, rice 81,400, coffee 15,200, cacao beans 6,600; livestock (number of live animals) 1,110,000 goats, 850,000 pigs, 740,000 sheep, 215,000 cattle, 7,500,000 chickens; roundwood (2000) 5,805,000 cu m; fish catch (1999) 23,100. Mining and quarrying (2000): phosphate rock 1,400,000; limestone is quarried for cement manufacture. Manufacturing (value added in CFAF '000,000; 1998): food products, beverages, and tobacco manufactures 41,400; metallic goods 12,000; nonmetallic manufactures 8,500; textiles, clothing, and leather 4,900; wood products 4,700; paper, printing, and publishing 4,300; chemicals 3,600. Construction (value added in CFAF; 1995): 19,958,000,000. Energy production (consumption): electricity (kW-hr; 1998) 48,320,000 ([1997] 282,200,000,); petroleum products (metric tons; 1998) none (231,000).
Household income and expenditure. Average household size (1999) 6.0; average annual income per household (1980) CFAF 102,000 (U.S.$452); sources of income: n.a.; expenditure (1987): food and beverages 45.9%, services 20.5%, household durable goods 13.9%, clothing 11.4%, housing 5.9%.
Gross national product (2000): U.S.$1,318,000,000 (U.S.$290 per capita).

Structure of gross domestic product and labour force				
	1999		2000	
	in value CFAF '000,000,000	% of total value	labour force	% of labour force
Agriculture	366.3	41.8	1,142,000	59.7
Mining	44.9	5.1		
Manufacturing	80.6	9.2		
Construction	32.3	3.7		
Public utilities	27.8	3.2		
Transp. and commun.	47.5	5.4	771,000	40.3
Trade and finance	150.7	17.2		
Pub. admin., defense	60.9	6.9		
Services	66.1	7.5		
TOTAL	877.1	100.0	1,913,000	100.0

Population economically active (2000): total 1,913,000; activity rate of total population 38.1% (participation rates over age 15, 70.7%; female 39.9%; unemployed ([1994]) 16–18%).

Price and earnings indexes (1995 = 100)						
	1995	1996	1997	1998	1999	2000	2001
Consumer price index	100.0	104.7	113.3	114.4	114.3	116.5	122.9
Hourly earnings index	...	...	...	...	...	...	...

Tourism (2000): receipts U.S.$5,000,000; expenditures U.S.$3,000,000.

Foreign trade[3]

Balance of trade (current prices)						
	1996	1997	1998	1999	2000	2001
CFAF '000,000,000	−114.5	−129.8	−224.2	−126.4	−144.7	−94.1
% of total	20.3%	20.8%	24.4%	20.8%	21.9%	22.1%

Imports (2001): CFAF 260,016,000,000 (1999; fuels 39.7%, manufactured goods 17.2%, machinery and transport equipment 11.1%, food 8.4%, chemicals 7.3%). *Major import sources* (1999): France 17.5%; Côte d'Ivoire 11.6%; Benin 6.0%; Italy 4.1%; The Netherlands 4.1%; Japan 3.7%.
Exports (2001): CFAF 165,922,000,000 (1999; cotton 24.2%, phosphates 18.0%, coffee 7.1%, cocoa 4.2%, tea 2.5%). *Major export destinations* (1999): Benin 16.6%; Ghana 10.9%; Canada 5.1%; Brazil 4.8%; Nigeria 4.1%; France 2.5%.

Transport and communications

Transport. Railroads (1999): route length 395 km; (1998) passenger-km 35,200,000; metric ton-km cargo 758,700,000. Roads (1999): total length 7,520 km (paved 32%). Vehicles (1996): passenger cars 79,200; trucks and buses 34,240. Merchant marine (2000): vessels (100 gross tons and over) 12; total deadweight tonnage (1992) 20,633. Air transport (1997)[4]: passenger-km 242,000,000; metric ton-km cargo 38,000,000; airports (1998) 2.

Communications				units per 1,000
Medium	date	unit	number	persons
Daily newspapers	1996	circulation	15,000	3.6
Radio	1998	receivers	720,000	167
Television	1999	receivers	100,000	21
Telephones	2001	main lines	48,100	11
Cellular telephones	2001	subscribers	95,000	20
Personal computers	2001	units	100,000	22
Internet	2001	users	50,000	11

Education and health

Educational attainment (1981). Percentage of population age 25 and over having: no formal schooling 76.5%; primary education 13.5%; secondary 8.7%; higher 1.3%. *Literacy* (1995): total population age 15 and over literate 51.7%; males 67.0%; females 37.0%.

Education (1996–97)				student/
	schools	teachers	students	teacher ratio
Primary (age 6–11)	3,283[5]	18,535	859,574	46.4
Secondary (age 12–18)	314[6]	4,736[6]	169,178	...
Vocational	...	653	9,076	13.9
Higher[7]	1	443	11,639	26.3

Health: physicians (1995) 320 (1 per 13,158 persons); hospital beds (1990) 5,307 (1 per 694 persons); infant mortality rate (2001) 70.4.
Food (1999): daily per capita caloric intake 2,527 (vegetable products 96%, animal products 4%); 110% of FAO recommended minimum requirement.

Military

Total active duty personnel (2001): 6,950 (army 93.5%, navy 2.9%, air force 3.6%). *Military expenditure as percentage of GNP* (1999): 1.8% (world 2.4%); per capita expenditure U.S.$5.

---

[1]Personal military-supported rule from 1967 continues under constitution approved by referendum in September 1992. [2]Formerly pegged to the French franc and since Jan. 1, 2002, to the euro at the rate of €1 = CFAF 655.96. [3]Import figures are c.i.f. [4]Includes 1/11 of the traffic of Air Afrique, which is operated by 11 West African states. [5]1995–96. [6]1990. [7]University only.

Internet resources for further information:
• **President of the Republic**
  http://www.republicoftogo.com/english/index.htm
• **Investir en Zone Franc** http://www.izf.net/izf/index.htm

Tonga

Official name: Pule'anga Fakatu'i 'o Tonga (Tongan); Kingdom of Tonga (English).
Form of government: constitutional monarchy with one legislative house (Legislative Assembly [30[1]]).
Head of state and government: King assisted by Privy Council.
Capital: Nuku'alofa.
Official languages: Tongan; English.
Official religion: none.
Monetary unit: 1 pa'anga[2] (T$) = 100 seniti; valuation (Sept. 23, 2002) 1 U.S.$ = T$2.21; 1 £ = T$3.43.

Area and population		area		population
				1996
Divisions	Capitals	sq mi	sq km	census
'Eua[3]	'Ohonua	33.7	87.4	4,934
Ha'apai[4]	Pangai	42.5	110.0	8,138
Niuas[5]	Hihifo	27.7	71.7	2,018
Tongatapu[3]	Nuku'alofa	100.6	260.5	66,979
Vava'u[4]	Neiafu	46.0	119.2	15,715
TOTAL LAND AREA		278.1[6]	720.3[6]	
INLAND WATER		11.4	29.6	
TOTAL		289.5	749.9	97,784

Demography

Population (2002): 101,000.
Density (2002)[7]: persons per sq mi 363.2, persons per sq km 140.2.
Urban-rural (2002): urban 39.0%; rural 61.0%.
Sex distribution (2000): male 50.87%; female 49.13%.
Age breakdown (1996): under 15, 39.1%; 15–29, 28.0%; 30–44, 15.1%; 45–59, 10.0%; 60–74, 6.0%; 75 and over, 1.8%.
Population projection: (2010) 104,000; (2020) 108,000.
Doubling time: 38 years.
Ethnic composition (1996): Tongan and part Tongan 98.2%; other 1.8%.
Religious affiliation (1998): Free Wesleyan 41.2%; Roman Catholic 15.8%; Mormon 13.6%; other (mostly other Protestant) 29.4%.
Major cities (1986): Nuku'alofa (1996) 22,400[8]; Neiafu 3,879; Haveluloto 3,070.

Vital statistics

Birth rate per 1,000 population (2002): 24.1 (world avg. 21.2).
Death rate per 1,000 population (2002): 5.6 (world avg. 8.9).
Natural increase rate per 1,000 population (2002): 18.5 (world avg. 12.3).
Total fertility rate (avg. births per childbearing woman; 2000): 4.2.
Marriage rate per 1,000 population (1992): 8.2.
Divorce rate per 1,000 population (1992): 1.1.
Life expectancy at birth (2000): male 71.0 years; female 73.0 years.
Major causes of death per 100,000 population (1993)[9]: circulatory diseases 58.1; nervous system diseases 51.0; senility 27.6; diabetes mellitus 17.3.

National economy

Budget (2000–01). Revenue: T$77,500,000 (foreign-trade taxes 45.7%, government services revenue 15.4%, direct taxes 13.2%, indirect taxes 10.2%, interest and rent 5.8%). Expenditures[10]: T$84,700,000 (general administration 20.9%, education 14.0%, health 10.2%, social security 6.7%, agriculture 6.5%, law and order 5.7%, defense 4.6%).
Public debt (external, outstanding; 2000): U.S.$58,000,000.
Production (metric tons except as noted). Agriculture, forestry, fishing (1999): yams 31,000, cassava 28,000, taro 27,200, coconuts 24,500, fruits 12,500, vegetables 7,308, sweet potatoes 5,137; livestock (number of live animals) 80,853 pigs, 13,939 goats, 11,400 horses, 9,318 cattle, 266,000 chickens; roundwood (1998) 4,600 cu m; fish catch (2000) 3,531. Mining and quarrying: coral and sand for local use. Manufacturing (output in T$'000,000; 1996): food products and beverages 8,203; paper products 1,055; chemical products 964; metal products 889; textile and wearing apparel 742; nonmetallic products 715. Energy production (consumption): electricity (kW-hr; 1997) 34,000,000 (34,000,000); crude petroleum (barrels) none (none); petroleum products (metric tons; 1997) n.a. (39,000).
Tourism: receipts (2000) U.S.$7,000,000; expenditures (1997) U.S.$3,000,000.
Gross national product (2000): U.S.$166,000,000 (U.S.$1,660 per capita).

Structure of gross domestic product and labour force				
	2000–2001		1996	
	in value T$'000,000	% of total value	labour force	% of labour force
Agriculture	70.4	25.4	9,953	29.3
Mining	0.9	0.3	43	0.1
Manufacturing	12.3	4.4	6,710	19.8
Construction	15.3	5.5	500	1.5
Public utilities	4.7	1.7	504	1.5
Transp. and commun.	19.3	7.0	1,209	3.6
Trade	32.0	11.6	2,506	7.4
Finance	33.9	12.2	657	1.9
Pub. admin., defense	43.4	15.7	3,701	10.9
Services	13.5	4.9	3,623	10.7
Other	31.4	11.3	4,502	13.3
TOTAL	277.1	100.0	33,908	100.0

Population economically active (1996): total 33,908; activity rate 34.7% (participation rates: ages 15 and over 57.0%; female 36.0%; unemployed 13.3%).

Price and earnings indexes (1995 = 100)							
	1995	1996	1997	1998	1999	2000	2001
Consumer price index	100.0	103.0	105.2	108.6	113.9	120.6	130.7
Quarterly earnings index	...	...	...	...	...	...	...

Household income and expenditure. Average household size (1996) 6.0; income per household: n.a.; sources of income: n.a.; expenditure (1991–92)[11]: food 43.2%, transportation 15.5%, household 14.2%, housing 6.4%, tobacco and beverages 5.4%, clothing and footwear 4.2%.
Land use (1994): forest 11.1%; pasture 5.6%; agriculture 66.7%; other 16.6%.

Foreign trade

Balance of trade (current prices)						
	1995–96	1996–97	1997–98	1998–99	1999–2000	2000–01
U.S.$'000,000	−53.8	−47.0	−66.2	−43.5	−43.0	−48.6
% of total	67.9%	64.0%	73.6%	64.3%	65.5%	68.3%

Imports (1999–2000): U.S.$54,300,000 (food and live animals 32.0%, basic manufactures 17.3%, machinery and transport equipment 15.7%, mineral fuels 14.7%, chemicals and chemical products 7.2%). *Major import sources:* U.S. 35.2%; Australia 23.0%; New Zealand 12.3%; Fiji 10.3%; Japan 6.1%.
Exports (1999–2000): U.S.$11,300,000 (squash 48.7%, fish 36.3%, manufactured goods 7.1%, vanilla beans 4.4%). *Major export destinations:* Japan 57.5%; U.S. 18.5%; New Zealand 7.6%; Australia 2.6%; Fiji 1.4%.

Transport and communications

Transport. Railroads: none. Roads (1996): total length 680 km (paved 27%). Vehicles (1998): passenger cars 6,419, commercial vehicles 9,189. Merchant marine (1992): vessels (100 gross tons and over) 15; total deadweight tonnage 13,740. Air transport (1998): passenger-km 10,000,000; metric ton-km cargo 1,000,000; airports (1996) with scheduled flights 6.

Communications				units per 1,000
Medium	date	unit	number	persons
Daily newspapers	1996	circulation	7,000	72
Radio	1997	receivers	61,000	619
Television	1997	receivers	2,000	21
Telephones	2000	main lines	9,700	99
Cellular telephones	1999	subscribers	140	1.4
Personal computers	...	units	...	...
Internet	1999	users	1,000	10

Education and health

Educational attainment (1996). Percentage of population age 25 and over having: primary education 26%; lower secondary 58%; upper secondary 8%; higher 6%; not stated 2%. *Literacy:* n.a.

Education (1994)				student/
	schools	teachers	students	teacher ratio
Primary (age 6–11)	115	701	16,540	23.6
Secondary (age 12–18)	38	809	15,702	19.4
Voc., teacher tr.	9	67	824	12.3
Higher[12]	1	19	226	11.9

Health: physicians (1997) 43 (1 per 2,279 persons); hospital beds (1992) 307 (1 per 320 persons); infant mortality rate per 1,000 live births (2002) 13.7.
Food (1992): daily per capita caloric intake 2,946 (vegetable products 82%, animal products 18%); 129% of FAO recommended minimum requirement.

Military

Total active duty personnel (1999): 125-member naval force; an air force was created in 1996. *Military expenditure as percentage of GNP* (1989): 4.9% (world 4.7%); per capita expenditure U.S.$21.

[1]Includes 12 nonelective seats and 9 nobles elected by the 33 hereditary nobles of Tonga. [2]The pa'anga was pegged at par to the Australian dollar through Feb. 8, 1991, but beginning Feb. 11, 1991, it was linked to a weighted basket of foreign currencies. [3]'Eua and Tongatapu together comprise Tongatapu island group. [4]Also the name of an island group. [5]Also known as Niuatoputapu island group. [6]Total includes 27.6 sq mi (71.5 sq km) of uninhabited islands. [7]Based on land area. [8]Population of urban agglomeration (2001) is 33,000. [9]Reported inpatient deaths at all hospitals. [10]Excludes amortization of public debt and sinking funds. [11]Current weight of consumer price index components. [12]1992.

Internet resources for further information:
• Tonga on the Net http://www.tongatapu.net.to

Trinidad and Tobago

Official name: Republic of Trinidad and Tobago.
Form of government: multiparty republic with two legislative houses (Senate [31]; House of Representatives [36[1]]).
Chief of state: President.
Head of government: Prime Minister.
Capital: Port of Spain.
Official language: English.
Official religion: none.
Monetary unit: 1 Trinidad and Tobago dollar (TT$) = 100 cents; valuation (Sept. 23, 2002) 1 U.S.$ = TT$6.07; 1 £ = TT$9.43.

Area and population

	area² sq km	population 1990 census		area² sq km	population 1990 census
Trinidad			**Cities**		
Counties			Port of Spain	10	50,878
Couva/Tabaquite/			San Fernando	8	30,092
Talparo	701		**Boroughs**		
Diego Martin	122		Arima	10	29,695
Mayaro/Rio Claro	907		Chaguanas	60	56,601
Penal/Debe	259	996,815	Point Fortin	23	20,025
Princes Town	551		**Tobago (Unitary State)**		
Sangre Grande	881		**Counties**		
San Juan/Laventille	200		Eastern Tobago	231	50,282
Siparia	570		Western Tobago	69	
Tunapuna/Piarco	526		TOTAL	5,128	1,234,388

Demography

Population (2002): 1,304,000.
Density (2002): persons per sq mi 658.4, persons per sq km 254.2.
Urban-rural (2002): urban 74.5%; rural 25.5%.
Sex distribution (2001): male 51.22%; female 48.78%.
Age breakdown (2001): under 15, 24.3%; 15–29, 27.1%; 30–44, 22.5%; 45–59, 15.5%; 60–74, 7.7%; 75 and over, 2.9%.
Population projection: (2010) 1,358,000; (2020) 1,420,000.
Ethnic composition (2000): black 39.2%; East Indian 38.6%; mixed 16.3%; Chinese 1.6%; white 1.0%; other/not stated 3.3%.
Religious affiliation (1990): six largest Protestant bodies 29.7%; Roman Catholic 29.4%; Hindu 23.7%; Muslim 5.9%; other 11.3%.
Major cities (1990): Chaguanas 56,601; Port of Spain 43,396[3]; San Fernando 30,115[4]; Arima 29,483[4]; Point Fortin 20,025; Scarborough 4,000.

Vital statistics

Birth rate per 1,000 population (2001): 12.8 (world avg. 21.2).
Death rate per 1,000 population (2001): 8.2 (world avg. 8.9).
Natural increase rate per 1,000 population (2001): 4.6 (world avg. 12.3).
Total fertility rate (avg. births per childbearing woman; 2001): 1.8.
Marriage rate per 1,000 population (1996): 5.6.
Divorce rate per 1,000 population (1996): 1.2.
Life expectancy at birth (2001): male 67.4 years; female 72.8 years.
Major causes of death per 100,000 population (1994): diseases of the circulatory system 286.4; malignant neoplasms (cancers) 94.3; endocrine and metabolic disorders 90.0; accidents, violence, and homicide 52.8.

National economy

Budget (2000). Revenue: TT$12,144,000,000 (income taxes 29.7%; petroleum sector 26.4%; sales tax 25.8%; taxes on international trade 6.4%; other taxes 1.6%; nontax revenues 10.1%). Expenditures: TT$12,068,000,000 (current expenditures 90.0%, of which transfers and subsidies 36.6%, wages 28.9%, interest payment 23.6%, other 0.9%; development expenditures 10.0%).
Production (metric tons except as noted). Agriculture, forestry, fishing (2000): sugarcane 1,500,000, coconuts 23,000, oranges 19,500, rice 7,200, pigeon peas 3,200, cocoa 1,536, coffee 553; livestock (number of live animals) 59,000 goats, 10,000,000 chickens; roundwood (2000) 116,500 cu m; fish catch (2000) 15,000. Mining and quarrying (2000): natural asphalt 9,900. Manufacturing (2000): anhydrous ammonia and urea (nitrogenous fertilizers) 3,718,700; methanol 2,480,200; steel billets 743,800; cement 742,700; steel wire rods 630,800; refined sugar 51,500; beer and stout 523,800 hectolitres; rum 146,000 hectolitres. Energy production (consumption): electricity (kW-hr; 1997) 4,848,000,000 ([1997] 4,848,000,000); coal, none (none); crude petroleum (barrels; 2000) 39,337,000 ([1997] 37,963,000); petroleum products (metric tons; 1997) 5,259,000 (1,310,000); natural gas (cu m; 2000) 15,483,000,000 ([1997] 8,136,000,000).
Household income and expenditure. Average household size (1998) 3.8; average income per household (1988) TT$21,760 (U.S.$5,661); expenditure (1993): food, beverages, and tobacco 25.5%, housing 21.6%, transportation 15.2%, household furnishings 14.3%, clothing and footwear 10.4%.
Tourism (1999): receipts from visitors U.S.$210,000,000; expenditures by nationals abroad (1998) U.S.$67,000,000.
Land use (1994): forested 45.8%; meadows and pastures 2.1%; agricultural and under permanent cultivation 23.8%; other 28.3%.
Gross national product (at current market prices; 2000): U.S.$6,415,000,000 (U.S.$4,930 per capita).

Structure of gross domestic product and labour force

	2000 in value TT$'000,000	% of total value	labour force	% of labour force
Agriculture	838.2	1.8	39,700	6.9
Petroleum, natural gas, quarrying	13,100.8[5]	26.1[5]	15,800[6]	2.8[6]
Manufacturing	3,887.9[6]	7.7[6]	54,300[5]	9.5[5]
Construction	4,672.4	9.3	68,200[7]	11.9[7]
Public utilities	865.6	1.7	[7]	[7]
Transp. and commun.	4,438.5	8.8	38,500	6.7
Trade	8,260.3	16.4	92,800	16.2
Finance, real estate	7,449.3	14.8		
Pub. admin., defense	3,738.1	7.4	192,400	33.6
Services	2,884.7	5.7		
Other	95.7[8]	0.2[8]	70,600[9]	12.3[9]
TOTAL	50,231.5	100.0[10]	572,300	100.0[10]

Population economically active (2000): total 572,300; activity rate of total population 44.2% (participation rates: ages 15 and over 61.4%; female 39.3%; unemployed 12.3%).

Price and earnings indexes (1995 = 100)

	1995	1996	1997	1998	1999	2000	2001
Consumer price index	100.0	103.4	107.2	113.2	117.1	121.2	126.0
Weekly earnings index[11]	100.0	102.5	109.5	114.9	...	...	...

Public debt (external, outstanding; 2000): U.S.$1,496,000,000.

Foreign trade[12]

Balance of trade (current prices)

	1995	1996	1997	1998	1999	2000
TT$'000,000	+3,938	+1,488	−2,818	−4,666	+398	+8,481
% of total	16.2%	5.5%	8.1%	14.1%	1.1%	16.9%

Imports (1999): TT$17,263,000,000 (machinery and apparatus 26.6%, fuels 20.1%, food 7.0%, transport equipment 5.6%). *Major import sources* (2000): United States 32.0%; Venezuela 18.4%; United Kingdom 4.3%; Japan 3.8%; Canada 3.3%.
Exports (1999): TT$17,661,200,000 (refined petroleum 32.7%, crude petroleum 13.0%, anhydrous ammonia 10.4%, iron and steel 5.8%, reexports 4.4%, methanol 1.7%). *Major export destinations* (2000): United States 42.6%; Caricom 23.8%, of which Jamaica 8.9%, Barbados 5.0%; EC (excluding United Kingdom) 5.7%.

Transport and communications

Transport. Railroads: none. Roads (1999): total length 7,900 km (paved 51%). Vehicles (1996): passenger cars 122,000; trucks and buses 24,000. Air transport (2001)[13]: passenger-km 2,496,000,000; metric ton-km cargo 56,236,000; airports (2000) with scheduled flights 2.

Communications

Medium	date	unit	number	units per 1,000 persons
Daily newspapers	1996	circulation	156,000	123
Radio	1997	receivers	680,000	535
Television	1999	receivers	435,000	338
Telephones	2001	main lines	311,800	239
Cellular telephones	2001	subscribers	225,400	173
Personal computers	2001	units	90,000	69
Internet	2001	users	120,000	92

Education and health

Educational attainment (1990). Percentage of population age 25 and over having: no formal schooling 4.5%; primary education 56.4%; secondary 32.1%; higher 3.4%; other/not stated 3.6%. *Literacy* (1999): total population age 15 and over literate 93.5%; males 95.4%, females 91.7%.

Education (1996–97)

	schools	teachers	students	student/teacher ratio
Primary (age 5–11)	476	7,311	181,030	24.8
Secondary (age 12–16)	...	5,070	104,349	20.6
Higher[14]	1	510	6,641	13.0

Health: physicians (1997) 1,074 (1 per 1,183 persons); hospital beds (1996) 6,622 (1 per 191 persons); infant mortality rate (2001) 25.6.
Food (2000): daily per capita caloric intake 2,760 (vegetable products 85%, animal products 15%); 114% of FAO recommended minimum requirement.

Military

Total active duty personnel (2001): 2,700 (army 74.1%, coast guard 25.9%). *Military expenditure as percentage of GNP* (1999): 1.4% (world 2.4%); per capita expenditure U.S.$78.

[1]Excludes speaker, who may be elected from outside the House of Representatives. [2]Area figures for counties are estimated. [3]1996. [4]1991. [5]Includes refined petroleum and petrochemicals. [6]Excludes refined petroleum and petrochemicals. [7]Construction includes public utilities. [8]Net of value-added taxes less imputed bank service charges. [9]Unemployed. [10]Detail does not add to total given because of rounding. [11]Manufacturing only. [12]Imports c.i.f.; exports f.o.b. [13]BWIA only. [14]1998–99; University of the West Indies, St. Augustine campus only.

Internet resources for further information:
• Central Bank of Trinidad and Tobago
  http://www.central-bank.org.tt

Tunisia

Official name: Al-Jumhūrīyah
at-Tūnisīyah (Republic of Tunisia).
Form of government: multiparty
republic[1] with one legislative house
(Chamber of Deputies [182]).
Chief of state: President.
Head of government: Prime Minister.
Capital: Tunis.
Official language: Arabic.
Official religion: Islam.
Monetary unit: 1 dinar (D) = 1,000
millimes; valuation (Sept. 23, 2002)
1 U.S.$ = D 1.39; 1 £ = D 2.16.

Area and population

Governorates	Capitals	area sq mi	area sq km	population 2001 estimate
Al-Ariānah	Al-Ariānah	192	498	373,400
Bājah	Bājah	1,374	3,558	318,800
Banzart	Bizerte (Banzart)	1,423	3,685	523,200
Bin ʿArūs	Bin ʿArūs	294	761	456,600
Jundūbah	Jundūbah	1,198	3,102	427,600
Al-Kāf	Al-Kāf	1,917	4,965	281,200
Madanīn	Madanīn	3,316	8,588	427,000
Al-Mahdīyah	Al-Mahdīyah	1,145	2,966	371,500
Manūbah	Manūbah	410	1,060	321,000
Al-Munastīr	Al-Munastīr	393	1,019	421,200
Nābul	Nābul	1,076	2,788	641,500
Qābis	Qābis	2,770	7,175	335,000
Qafşah	Qafşah	3,471	8,990	330,700
Al-Qaşrayn	Al-Qaşrayn	3,114	8,066	420,700
Al-Qayrawān	Al-Qayrawān	2,591	6,712	567,400
Qibilī	Qibilī	8,527	22,084	142,800
Safāqis	Safāqis	2,913	7,545	820,600
Sīdī Bū Zayd	Sīdī Bū Zayd	2,700	6,994	401,500
Siliānah	Siliānah	1,788	4,631	256,700
Sūsah	Sūsah	1,012	2,621	501,200
Tatāuīn	Tatāuīn	15,015	38,889	148,900
Tawzar	Tawzar	1,822	4,719	97,400
Tūnis	Tunis (Tūnis)	134	346	932,000
Zaghwān	Zaghwān	1,069	2,768	155,700
TOTAL		63,378[2]	164,150[2]	9,673,600

Demography

Population (2002): 9,764,000.
Density (2002): persons per sq mi 154.1, persons per sq km 59.5.
Urban-rural (2001): urban 66.2%; rural 33.8%.
Sex distribution (2000): male 50.40%; female 49.60%.
Age breakdown (2000): under 15, 29.7%; 15–29, 30.4%; 30–44, 21.2%; 45–59, 10.6%; 60–74, 6.8%; 75 and over, 1.3%.
Doubling time: 58 years.
Ethnic composition (2000): Tunisian Arab 67.2%; Bedouin Arab 26.6%; Algerian Arab 2.4%; Berber 1.4%; other 2.4%.
Religious affiliation (2000): Sunnī Muslim 98.9%; Christian 0.5%; other 0.6%.
Major cities (commune; 1994): Tunis 674,100 (urban agglomeration [2001] 1,927,000); Şafāqis 230,900; Al-Ariānah 152,700; Ettadhamen 149,200; Sūsah 125,000.

Vital statistics

Birth rate per 1,000 population (2001): 17.1 (world avg. 21.2).
Death rate per 1,000 population (2001): 5.0 (world avg. 8.9).
Total fertility rate (avg. births per childbearing woman; 2001): 2.1.
Marriage rate per 1,000 population (1995): 6.0.
Life expectancy at birth (2001): male 72.4 years; female 75.6 years.
Major causes of death (1992)[3]: complications of pregnancy and childbirth 31.6%, circulatory diseases 22.4%, accidents and poisoning 14.9%, respiratory diseases 7.2%.

National economy

Budget (2000). Revenue: D 7,625,000,000 (tax revenue 91.1%, of which goods and services 39.1%, income tax 20.0%, social security 17.8%, import duties 9.8%; nontax revenue 8.9%). Expenditures: D 8,454,000,000 (current expenditure 77.2%, of which interest on public debt 10.3%; development expenditure 22.8%).
Public debt (external, outstanding; 2000): U.S.$8,869,000,000.
Production (metric tons except as noted). Agriculture, forestry, fishing (2000): wheat 1,144,000, olives 1,000,000, tomatoes 905,000, barley 416,000, potatoes 295,000, oranges 116,000, apples 108,000, dates 104,000; livestock (live animals) 6,600,000 sheep, 1,400,000 goats, 790,000 cattle; roundwood (2000) 2,841,800 cu m; fish catch (2000) 90,100. Mining and quarrying (2000): phosphate rock 8,339,000; iron ore 182,000; zinc (metal content) 41,200. Manufacturing (2000): cement 5,398,900; phosphoric acid 845,000; flour 745,500; semolina 620,500; lime 432,000; crude steel 183,300. Energy production (consumption): electricity (kW-hr; 2001) 9,787,000,000 ([2000] 8,150,400,000); coal (metric tons; 1997) none (2,000); crude petroleum (barrels; 2001) 25,712,000 ([1996] 7,097,000); petroleum products (metric tons; 1997) 1,855,000 (3,230,000); natural gas (cu m; 2001) 2,143,100,000 ([1997] 2,107,300,000).
Household income and expenditure. Average household size (2000) 4.8; expenditure (1995): food and beverages 37.7%, housing and energy 22.2%, health and personal care 9.6%, transportation 8.9%, recreation 8.7%, other 12.9%.
Tourism (2000): receipts U.S.$1,496,000,000; expenditures U.S.$263,000,000.
Gross national product (2000): U.S.$20,057,000,000 (U.S.$2,100 per capita).

Structure of gross domestic product and labour force

	2000 in value D '000,000	2000 % of total value	1994 labour force	1994 % of labour force
Agriculture	3,248.3	12.2	501,000	21.6
Mining	234.5	0.9	36,800	1.6
Public utilities	1,287.6	4.8		
Manufacturing	4,889.0	18.3	455,700	19.6
Construction	1,252.4	4.7	305,800	13.2
Transp. and commun.	2,069.9	7.8	4	4
Trade	5,646.9	21.2	315,600	13.6
Finance				
Pub. admin., defense	3,590.9	13.5	667,100[4]	28.7[4]
Services				
Other	4,461.7[5]	16.7[5]	38,600	1.7
TOTAL	26,683.2[6]	100.0[6]	2,320,600	100.0

Population economically active (1997): total 3,502,000; activity rate of total population 37.9% (participation rates [1989]: ages 15–64, 42.2%; female [1997] 30.9%; unemployed [2000] 15.9%).

Price and earnings indexes (1995 = 100)

	1995	1996	1997	1998	1999	2000	2001
Consumer price index	100.0	103.7	107.5	110.9	113.9	117.2	119.4
Hourly earnings index	...	...	...	...	...	...	...

Land use (1994): forested 4.3%; meadows and pastures 20.0%; agricultural and under permanent cultivation 31.9%; other 43.8%.

Foreign trade[7]

Balance of trade (current prices)

	1996	1997	1998	1999	2000	2001
D '000,000	−2,126	−2,608	−2,944	−3,103	−3,723	−4,225
% of total	16.5%	17.5%	18.4%	18.2%	18.9%	18.2%

Imports (2000): D 11,728,000,000 (textiles, clothing, and leather 22.9%, non-electrical equipment 20.3%, electrical equipment 10.2%, transport equipment 10.2%). *Major import sources:* France 26.3%; Italy 19.1%; Germany 10.0%; U.S. 4.6%; Libya 3.7%.
Exports (2000): D 8,005,000,000 (textiles, clothing, and leather products 46.6%, mineral fuels and lubricants 12.1%, electrical equipment 10.1%, phosphates and phosphate derivatives 9.0%). *Major export destinations:* France 26.8%; Italy 23.0%; Germany 12.5%; Belgium 5.1%; Libya 3.6%.

Transport and communications

Transport. Railroads (2000): route length 2,169 km; passenger-km 1,196,000,-000; metric ton-km cargo 2,365,000,000. Roads (1997): total length 23,100 km (paved 79%). Vehicles (1996): passenger cars 269,000; trucks and buses 312,000. Air transport (2000)[8]: passenger-km 2,694,167,000; metric ton-km cargo 20,821,000; airports (1998) 5.

Communications

Medium	date	unit	number	units per 1,000 persons
Daily newspapers	1996	circulation	280,000	31
Radio	1997	receivers	2,060,000	224
Television	1999	receivers	1,800,000	190
Telephones	2001	main lines	1,056,000	109
Cellular telephones	2001	subscribers	389,200	40
Personal computers	2001	units	230,000	24
Internet	2001	users	400,000	41

Education and health

Educational attainment (1989). Percentage of population age 25 and over having: no formal schooling 54.9%; primary 26.9%; secondary 14.3%; higher 3.4%; unspecified 0.5%. *Literacy* (2000): total population age 10 and over literate 74.4%; males literate 83.5%; females literate 65.3%.

Education (1999–2000)

	schools	teachers	students	student/ teacher ratio
Primary (age 6–11)	4,497	60,912	1,413,795	23.2
Secondary (age 12–18)	1,301	52,432	965,607	18.4
Teacher tr.[9]	...	237	3,839	16.2
Higher	95	6,641[10]	180,044	18.3[10]

Health (2000): physicians 7,444 (1 per 1,284 persons); hospital beds (1999) 16,256 (1 per 581 persons); infant mortality rate (2001) 29.0.
Food (2000): daily per capita caloric intake 3,299 (vegetable products 89%, animal products 11%); 138% of FAO recommended minimum requirement.

Military

Total active duty personnel (2002): 35,000 (army 77.1%, navy 12.9%, air force 10.0%). *Military expenditure as percentage of GNP* (1999): 1.8% (world 2.4%); per capita expenditure U.S.$38.

---

[1]A single party dominates the political system in practice. [2]Total includes 3,714 sq mi- (9,620 sq km-) area of saline lakes that are not distributed by governorate. [3]12,000 reported deaths from urban areas only, including complete figures for Tunis. [4]Services includes Transportation and communications. [5]Indirect taxes less subsidies. [6]Detail does not add to total given because of rounding. [7]Imports c.i.f. [8]Tunis Air only. [9]1987–88. [10]1996–97.

Internet resources for further information:
• Tunisia Online http://www.tunisiaonline.com
• National Statistics Institute (French only) http://www.ins.nat.tn

Turkey

Official name: Türkiye Cumhuriyeti (Republic of Turkey).
Form of government: multiparty republic with one legislative house (Turkish Grand National Assembly [550]).
Chief of state: President.
Head of government: Prime Minister.
Capital: Ankara.
Official language: Turkish.
Official religion: none.
Monetary unit: 1 Turkish lira (LT) = 100 kurush; valuation (Sept. 23, 2002)
1 U.S.$ = LT 1,662,000;
1 £ = LT 2,582,914.

Area and population		area		population
Geographic regions[1]	Largest cities	sq mi	sq km	1997 estimate
Black Sea Coast	Samsun	31,388	81,295	6,816,009
Central Anatolia	Ankara	91,254	236,347	14,049,774
East Anatolia	Diyarbakır	68,074	180,180	7,351,461
Marmara and Aegean coasts	İzmir	33,035	85,560	13,677,750[2]
Mediterranean Coast	Adana	22,933	59,395	6,266,958
Southeast Anatolia	Gaziantep	15,347	35,880	3,205,251
Thrace	Istanbul (part)	9,175	23,764	7,168,094[2]
West Anatolia	Eskişehir	29,742	77,031	4,074,955
TOTAL		300,948	779,452	62,610,252

Demography

Population (2002): 69,359,000.
Density (2002): persons per sq mi 230.5, persons per sq km 89.0.
Urban-rural (2001): urban 66.2%; rural 33.8%.
Sex distribution (2000): male 50.57%; female 49.43%.
Age breakdown (2000): under 15, 29.1%; 15–29, 28.8%; 30–44, 21.5%; 45–59, 11.8%; 60–74, 6.8%; 75 and over, 2.0%.
Population projection: (2010) 75,656,000; (2020) 82,214,000.
Doubling time: 54 years.
Ethnic composition (2000)[3]: Turk 65.1%; Kurd 18.9%; Crimean Tatar 7.2%; Arab 1.8%; Azerbaijani 1.0%; Yoruk 1.0%; other 5.0%.
Religious affiliation (2000): Muslim 97.2%, of which Sunnī *c.* 67%, Shī'ī *c.* 30% (including nonorthodox Alevi *c.* 26%); Christian (mostly Eastern Orthodox) 0.6%; other 2.2%.
Major urban agglomerations (2001): Istanbul 10,243,000; Ankara 4,611,000; İzmir 3,437,000; Bursa (2000) 1,166,000; Adana (2000) 1,091,000.

Vital statistics

Birth rate per 1,000 population (2000): 18.7 (world avg. 22.5).
Death rate per 1,000 population (2000): 6.0 (world avg. 9.0).
Natural increase rate per 1,000 population (2000): 12.7 (world avg. 13.5).
Total fertility rate (avg. births per childbearing woman; 2000): 2.2.
Marriage rate per 1,000 population (1997): 7.8.
Divorce rate per 1,000 population (1997): 0.5.
Life expectancy at birth (2000): male 68.6 years; female 73.4 years.
Major causes of death per 100,000 population (1995)[4]: diseases of the circulatory system 322; malignant neoplasms (cancers) 71; accidents and violence 32; infectious and parasitic diseases 20; ill-defined conditions 129.

National economy

Budget (2000). Revenue: LT 33,756,347,000,000,000 (tax revenue 78.5%, nontax revenue 10.3%, special funds 9.7%, other 1.5%). Expenditures: LT 46,602,627,000,000,000 (interest payments 38.3%, personnel 24.7%, investments 5.5%).
Public debt (external, outstanding; 2000): U.S.$55,293,000,000.
Production (in '000 metric tons except as noted). Agriculture, forestry, fishing (2000): wheat 21,000, sugar beets 18,000, barley 8,000, tomatoes 6,800, potatoes 5,350, grapes 3,550, corn (maize) 2,800, apples 2,300, seed cotton 2,200, olives 1,700, cottonseed 1,500, oranges 1,035, sunflower seeds 825, lentils 590, hazelnuts 470, peaches 430, raisins 250[5], tobacco 189, tea 120[5], garlic 106[5], attar of roses 800 kg[6]; livestock (number of live animals) 29,435,000 sheep, 11,031,000 cattle, 615,000[7] angora goats; roundwood (2000) 17,767,000 cu m; fish catch (1999) 638,097. Construction (2000): residential 43,607,000 sq m; nonresidential 14,999,000 sq m. Mining (1999): boron minerals 2,600; chromite 770; copper ore (metal content) 45. Manufacturing (1995)[8]: refined petroleum 4,583; food products 3,944; textiles 3,907; transport equipment 3,048; iron and steel 2,453; paints, soaps, and pharmaceuticals 2,301. Energy production (consumption): electricity (kW-hr; 2001) 123,096,000,000 ([1997] 80,862,000,000); hard coal (metric tons; 2001) 3,719,000 ([1997] 12,537,000); lignite (metric tons; 2001) 57,157,000 ([1997] 59,503,000); crude petroleum (barrels; 2001) 18,218,000 ([1997] 192,771,000); petroleum products (metric tons; 1997) 22,914,000 (25,336,000); natural gas (cu m; 2000) 611,800,000 ([1997] 10,420,000,000).
Tourism (2000): receipts U.S.$7,636,000,000; expenditures U.S.$1,711,000,000.
Household income and expenditure (1994). Average household size (1999) 4.6; income per household LT 165,089,000 (U.S.$5,576); expenditure: food, tobacco, and café expenditures 38.5%, housing 22.8%, clothing 9.0%.
Population economically active (1997)[9]: total 22,359,000; activity rate of total population 35.8% (participation rates: ages 15–64, 53.1%; female 26.8%; unemployed [2000] 6.6%).

Price and earnings indexes (1995 = 100)							
	1995	1996	1997	1998	1999	2000	2001
Consumer price index	100.0	180.3	335.0	618.5	1,019.7	1,579.6	2,439.0
Annual earnings index[10]	100.0	190.4	376.8	650.3	...	...	...

Gross national product (2000): U.S.$202,131,000,000 (U.S.$3,100 per capita).

Structure of gross domestic product and labour force	2000		1998	
	in value LT '000,000,000,000	% of total value	labour force[9]	% of labour force[9]
Agriculture	12,749	14.5	8,918,000	39.6
Mining	} 20,347	} 23.2	154,000	0.7
Manufacturing			3,267,000	14.5
Construction	4,617	5.3	1,277,000	5.7
Public utilities	2,251	2.6	115,000	0.5
Transp. and commun.	12,419	14.1	957,000	4.3
Trade	17,567	20.0	2,860,000	12.7
Finance, real estate	8,090	9.2	511,000	2.3
Pub. admin., defense	9,000	10.3	} 3,026,000	} 13.4
Services	3,365	3.8		
Other	−2,645[11]	−3.0[11]	1,428,000[12]	6.3[12]
TOTAL	87,760	100.0	22,513,000	100.0

Land use (1994): forested 26.2%; meadows and pastures 16.1%; agricultural and under permanent cultivation 36.1%; other 21.6%.

Foreign trade[13]

Balance of trade (current prices)						
	1995	1996	1997	1998	1999	2000
U.S.$'000,000	−14,073	−20,403	−22,298	−18,947	−14,104	−26,659
% of total	24.5%	30.5%	29.8%	26.0%	21.0%	32.8%

Imports (2000): U.S.$53,983,000,000 (mineral fuels 17.6%; nonelectrical machinery 14.3%; electrical machinery 11.2%; transport equipment 10.1%; iron and steel 5.1%; chemicals 3.7%). *Major import sources:* Germany 13.2%; Italy 8.0%; U.S. 7.2%; France 6.5%; U.K. 5.0%.
Exports (2000): U.S.$27,324,000,000 (textiles and clothing 22.6%; electrical and electronic machinery 7.1%; vehicles 5.7%; iron and steel 5.7%). *Major export destinations:* Germany 18.8%; U.S. 11.2%; Russia and Eastern Europe 10.8%; U.K. 7.4%; Italy 6.3%; France 6.0%.

Transport and communications

Transport. Railroads (2000): length 5,388 mi, 8,671 km; passenger-km 6,122,000,000; metric ton-km cargo 10,032,000,000. Roads (2000): total length 238,379 mi, 383,636 km (paved [1997] 25%). Vehicles (2000): passenger cars 4,283,080; trucks and buses 1,488,016. Air transport (2000)[14]: passenger-km 16,492,416; metric ton-km cargo 379,630,000; airports (1996) 26.

Communications				units per 1,000 persons
Medium	date	unit	number	
Daily newspapers	1996	circulation	6,845,000	111
Radio	1997	receivers	11,300,000	181
Television	1999	receivers	21,500,000	331
Telephones	2001	main lines	18,900,000	285
Cellular telephones	2001	subscribers	20,000,000	302
Personal computers	2001	units	2,700,000	41
Internet	2001	users	2,500,000	38

Education and health

Educational attainment (1993). Percentage of population age 25 and over having: no formal schooling 30.5%; incomplete primary education 6.6%; complete primary 40.4%; incomplete secondary 3.1%; complete secondary or higher 19.1%; unknown 0.3%. *Literacy* (1995): total population age 15 and over literate 33,605,000 (82.3%); males literate 19,191,000 (91.7%); females literate 14,414,000 (72.4%).

Education (1996–97)	schools	teachers	students	student/ teacher ratio
Primary (age 6–10)	47,313	217,131	6,389,060	29.4
Secondary (age 11–16)	11,144	139,497	3,427,715	24.6
Voc., teacher tr.	4,046	72,537	1,333,177	18.4
Higher	817[15]	50,313	1,434,033	28.5

Health: physicians (1997) 73,659[16] (1 per 853 persons); hospital beds (1997) 144,984 (1 per 431 persons); infant mortality rate (2000) 48.9.
Food (2000): daily per capita caloric intake 3,416 (vegetable products 89%, animal products 11%); 136% of FAO recommended minimum requirement.

Military

Total active duty personnel (2002): 515,100 (army 78.0%, navy 10.3%, air force 11.7%). *Military expenditure as percentage of GNP* (1999): 5.3% (world 2.4%); per capita expenditure U.S.$154.

[1]Administratively divided into 81 provinces as of 2000. [2]Estimated figures. [3]Per unofficial source. [4]Projected rates based on about 42% of total deaths. [5]1998. [6]1993. [7]1997. [8]Value added in U.S.$'000,000. [9]Civilian population only. [10]Istanbul wage earners only. [11]Import duties less imputed bank charges. [12]Unemployed. [13]Imports c.i.f.; exports f.o.b. [14]Turkish Airlines only. [15]1995–96. [16]Includes assistant doctors.

Internet resources for further information:
• **Ministry of Foreign Affairs** http://www.mfa.gov.tr
• **Republic of Turkey** http://www.turkey.org
• **State Institute of Statistics** http://www.die.gov.tr

Turkmenistan

Official name: Türkmenistan (Turkmenistan).
Form of government: unitary republic with one legislative body (Majlis [Parliament; 50]).
Head of state and government: President assisted by the People's Council[1].
Capital: Ashgabat (formerly Ashkhabad).
Official language: Turkmen.
Official religion: none.
Monetary unit: manat; valuation (Sept. 23, 2002) 1 U.S.$ = 5,174 manat; 1 £ = 8,041 manat.

Area and population

Provinces	Capitals	area sq mi	area sq km	population 1999 estimate
Ahal	Ashgabat	37,500[2]	97,100[2]	722,800
Balkan	Nebitdag	53,500	138,600	424,700
Dashhowuz	Dashhowuz	28,100	72,700	1,059,800
Lebap	Turkmenabad (Chärjew)	36,000	93,200	1,034,700
Mary	Mary	33,400	86,400	1,146,800
City				
Ashgabat	—	2	2	604,700
TOTAL		188,500[3]	488,100[3]	4,993,500

Demography

Population (2002): 4,946,000.
Density (2002): persons, per sq mi 26.2, persons per sq km 10.1.
Urban-rural (2002): urban 44.9%; rural 55.1%.
Sex distribution (2001): male 49.44%; female 50.56%.
Age breakdown (2001): under 15, 37.9%; 15–29, 27.9%; 30–44, 23.7%; 45–59, 6.5%; 60–74, 3.5%; 75 and over, 0.5%.
Population projection: (2010) 5,651,000; (2020) 6,448,000.
Doubling time: 39 years.
Ethnic composition (1997): Turkmen 77.0%; Uzbek 9.2%; Russian 6.7%; Kazakh 2.0%; Tatar 0.8%; other 4.3%.
Religious affiliation (1995): Muslim (mostly Sunnī) 87.0%; Russian Orthodox 2.4%; other (mostly nonreligious) 10.6%.
Major cities (1999 est.): Ashgabat 605,000; Turkmenabad 203,000; Dashhowuz 165,000; Mary 123,000; Nebitdag 119,000.

Vital statistics

Birth rate per 1,000 population (2001): 28.6 (world avg. 21.2); (1998) legitimate 96.2%; illegitimate 3.8%.
Death rate per 1,000 population (2001): 8.0 (world avg. 8.9).
Natural increase rate per 1,000 population (2001): 20.6 (world avg. 12.3).
Total fertility rate (avg. births per childbearing woman; 2001): 3.5.
Marriage rate per 1,000 population (1998): 5.4.
Divorce rate per 1,000 population (1994): 1.5.
Life expectancy at birth (2001): male 57.5 years; female 64.8 years.
Major causes of death per 100,000 population (1994): diseases of the circulatory system 337.1; diseases of the respiratory system 150.3; infectious and parasitic diseases 75.7; accidents, poisoning, and violence 60.1; malignant neoplasms (cancers) 56.8; diseases of the digestive system 31.1.

National economy

Budget (1999). Revenue: 3,693,100,000,000 manat (value-added tax 25.6%, pension and social security fund 22.5%, repayments of scheduled gas 13.0%, excise tax 10.2%, personal income tax 6.1%). Expenditures: 3,894,300,000,000 manat (education 26.9%, pension and social security 15.6%, defense and security 14.9%, health 14.1%, agriculture 5.7%).
Public debt (external, outstanding; 2000): U.S.$1,731,000,000.
Production (metric tons except as noted). Agriculture, forestry, fishing (2001): seed cotton 1,800,000, wheat 1,200,000, vegetables and melons 347,000, watermelons 235,000, fruit excluding watermelons 185,000; livestock (number of live animals) 6,375,000 sheep and goats, 860,000 cattle, 5,000,000 poultry; roundwood (2000) 2,000,000 cu m; fish catch (1999) 9,292. Mining and quarrying (2000): gypsum 100,000, sodium sulfate 60,000, sulfur 9,000, iodine 150,000 kg[4]. Manufacturing (value of production in '000,000 manat; 1994): ferrous and nonferrous metals 278; machinery and metalworks 223; food products 129; chemical products 80; construction materials 52; wood products 31. Construction (1994): 1,700,000 sq m. Energy production (consumption): electricity (kW-hr; 1997) 9,400,000,000 (6,750,000,000); crude petroleum (barrels; 2001) 58,000,000 (19,000,000); petroleum products (metric tons; 1997) 3,886,000 (2,332,000); natural gas (cu m; 2001) 46,439,000,000 (7,362,000,000).
Household income and expenditure. Average household size (1998) 5.0; income per household: n.a.; sources of income (1996): wages and salaries 70.6%, pensions and grants 20.9%, self-employment (mainly agricultural income) 2.3%, nonwage income of workers 1.1%; expenditure (1996): goods 26.8%, services 13.5%, taxes and other payments 9.4%.
Land use (1994): forested 8.2%; meadows and pastures 61.6%; agricultural and under permanent cultivation 3.0%; other 27.2%.
Population economically active (1999): total 1,838,700; activity rate of total population 38.8% (participation rates [1995]: ages 16–59 [male], 16–54 [female] 81.0%; female 41.0%; unemployed 3.0%[5]).

Price and earnings indexes (1994 = 100)[6]

	1994	1995	1996	1997	1998
Consumer price index	100	1,362	7,431	27,502	32,122
Monthly earnings index	100	739	6,334	11,282	16,163

Gross national product (2000): U.S.$3,886,000,000 (U.S.$750 per capita).

Structure of gross domestic product and labour force

	1998 in value '000,000 manat	1998 % of total value	1999 labour force	1999 % of labour force
Agriculture	3,256,000	24.6	892,400	48.5
Mining			226,800	12.3
Manufacturing	3,862,000	29.2		
Public utilities			48,300	2.6
Construction	1,582,000	11.9	108,200	5.9
Transp. and commun.	1,372,000	10.4	90,700	4.9
Trade	687,000	5.2	115,800	6.4
Finance	...	...	12,600	0.7
Public administration, defense	...	...	28,800	1.6
Services	1,678,000	12.7	284,900	15.5
Other	804,000	6.1	30,200	1.6
TOTAL	13,241,000	100.0[3]	1,838,700	100.0

Tourism: receipts from visitors (1998) U.S.$192,000,000; expenditures (1997) U.S.$125,000,000.

Foreign trade[7]

Balance of trade (current prices)

U.S.$'000,000	1994	1995	1996	1997	1998
	+485	+536	+329	−231	−523
% of total	12.5%	15.4%	10.8%	13.0%	30.0%

Imports (1998): U.S.$1,137,100,000 (machinery and equipment 39.1%, food products 8.0%, chemicals 5.1%, medicines 1.8%). *Major import sources:* Ukraine 16.1%; Turkey 13.1%; Russia 11.6%; Germany 6.9%; U.S. 6.4%; Uzbekistan 5.2%; Armenia 3.0%.
Exports (1998): U.S.$614,100,000 (natural gas and oil products 54.6%, cotton 22.0%, electricity 5.2%). *Major export destinations:* Iran 24.1%; Turkey 18.3%; Azerbaijan 6.9%; U.K. 4.9%; Russia 4.7%; Tajikistan 4.5%.

Transport and communications

Transport. Railroads (1998): length 1,437 mi, 2,313 km; passenger-km (1996) 2,104,000,000, metric ton-km cargo (1996) 6,779,000,000. Roads (1999): total length 24,000 km (paved 81%). Vehicles (1995): passenger cars 220,000; trucks and buses 58,200. Air transport (2001)[8]: passenger-km 1,631,000,000; metric ton-km cargo 35,000,000; airports (2000) with scheduled flights 1.

Communications

Medium	date	unit	number	units per 1,000 persons
Radio	1997	receivers	1,225,000	289
Television	1998	receivers	865,000	201
Telephones	2001	main lines	387,600	80
Cellular phones	2001	subscribers	9,500	2.1
Internet	2001	users	8,000	1.6

Education and health

Educational attainment (1989). Percentage of population age 25 and over having: primary education or no formal schooling 13.6%; some secondary 21.3%; completed secondary and some postsecondary 56.8%; higher 8.3%. *Literacy* (1999): total population age 15 and over literate 98.0%.

Education (1994–95)

	schools	teachers	students	student/ teacher ratio
Primary (age 6–13)	1,900	72,900	940,600	12.9
Secondary (age 14–17)				
Voc., teacher tr.	78	...	26,000	...
Higher	15	...	29,435[9]	...

Health (1995): physicians 13,500 (1 per 330 persons); hospital beds 46,000 (1 per 97 persons); (2001) infant mortality rate per 1,000 live births 73.2.
Food (2000): daily per capita caloric intake 2,675 (vegetable products 83%, animal products 17%); 104% of FAO recommended minimum.

Military

Total active duty personnel (2001): 17,500 (army 82.9%; air force 17.1%). *Military expenditure as percentage of GNP* (1999): 3.4% (world 2.4%); per capita expenditure U.S.$122.

---

[1]The People's Council is the ultimate representative organ of governmental supervision and is composed of the president, membership of the Majlis, elected members, and a variety of ex officio members of national, provincial, and local government. [2]Ahal includes Ashgabat. [3]Detail does not add to total given because of rounding. [4]1999. [5]Every Turkmen citizen is guaranteed employment, so that unemployment does not officially exist. However, the 1995 Household Survey indicates an unemployment rate of about 3 percent of the labour force (defined as those actively seeking employment but not employed as a proportion of the labour force). [6]December. [7]Import data in balance of trade is c.i.f. [8]Turkmenavia only. [9]1995–96.

Internet resources for further information:
• **United Nations in Turkmenistan http://www.untuk.org**
• **Interstate Statistical Committee of the Commonwealth of Independent States http://www.cisstat.com/eng/macro0.htm**

Tuvalu

Official name: Tuvalu.
Form of government: constitutional monarchy with one legislative house (Parliament [12]).
Chief of state: British Monarch, represented by Governor-General.
Head of government: Prime Minister.
Capital: government offices are at Vaiaku, Fongafale islet, of Funafuti atoll.
Official language: none.
Official religion: none.
Monetary units[1]: 1 Tuvalu dollar = 1 Australian dollar ($T = $A) = 100 Tuvalu and Australian cents; valuation (Sept. 23, 2002) 1 U.S.$ = $A 1.83; 1 £ = $A 2.84.

Area and population

Islands[2]	area		population
	sq mi	sq km	2000 estimate
Funafuti	1.08	2.79	4,590
Nanumaga	1.07	2.78	770
Nanumea	1.49	3.87	1,010
Niulakita	0.16	0.42	3
Niutao	0.98	2.53	1,120[3]
Nui	1.09	2.83	690
Nukufetau	1.15	2.99	800
Nukulaelae	0.70	1.82	360
Vaitupu	2.16	5.60	1,410
TOTAL	9.90[4, 5]	25.63[4]	10,750

Demography

Population (2002): 10,900.
Density (2002): persons per sq mi 1,101, persons per sq km 425.
Urban-rural (2002): urban 54.0%; rural 46.0%.
Sex distribution (2000): male 48.65%; female 51.35%.
Age breakdown (2000): under 15, 33.7%; 15–29, 22.1%; 30–44, 21.9%; 45–59, 12.8%; 60–74, 7.3%; 75 and over, 2.2%.
Population projection: (2010) 13,000; (2020) 15,000.
Doubling time: 50 years.
Ethnic composition (2000): Tuvaluan (Polynesian) 96.3%; mixed (Pacific Islander/European/Asian) 1.0%; Micronesian 1.0%; European 0.5%; other 1.2%.
Religious affiliation (1995): Church of Tuvalu (Congregational) 85.4%; Seventh-day Adventist 3.6%; Roman Catholic 1.4%; Jehovah's Witness 1.1%; Bahā'i 1.0%; other 7.5%.
Major locality (1995): Fongafale, on Funafuti atoll, 4,000.

Vital statistics

Birth rate per 1,000 population (2002): 21.4 (world avg. 21.2); (1989) legitimate 82.2%; illegitimate 17.8%.
Death rate per 1,000 population (2002): 7.5 (world avg. 8.9).
Natural increase rate per 1,000 population (2002): 13.9 (world avg. 12.3).
Total fertility rate (avg. births per childbearing woman; 2002): 3.1.
Marriage rate per 1,000 population: n.a.
Divorce rate per 1,000 population: n.a.
Life expectancy at birth (2002): male 64.8 years; female 69.2 years.
Major causes of death per 100,000 population (1985): diseases of the digestive system 170.0; diseases of the circulatory system 150.0; diseases of the respiratory system 120.0; diseases of the nervous system 120.0; malignant neoplasms (cancers) 70.0; infectious and parasitic diseases 40.0; endocrine and metabolic disorders 20.0; ill-defined conditions 430.0.

National economy

Budget (1996). Revenue: $A 7,905,000 (nontax revenues 67.2%; taxes 32.8%). Expenditures: $A 8,203,000 (1987; capital [development] expenditures 68.9%, of which marine transport 20.7%, education 13.0%, fisheries 5.6%, health 3.1%; current expenditures 31.1%).
Public debt (external; 1993): U.S.$6,000,000.
Gross national product (1998): U.S.$14,700,000 (U.S.$1,400 per capita).

Structure of gross domestic product and labour force

	1998		1991	
	in value $A '000[6]	% of total value[6]	labour force	% of labour force
Agriculture, fishing, forestry	3,484	15.8	4,020	68.0
Mining	638	2.9	—	—
Manufacturing[7]	881	4.0	60	1.0
Construction	2,951	13.4	240	4.0
Public utilities	574	2.6	—	—
Transp. and commun.	1,380	6.2	60	1.0
Trade, hotels, and restaurants	2,972	13.5	240	4.0
Finance	2,376	10.8	—	—
Pub. admin., defense } Services	4,806	21.8	1,290	22.0
Other	1,983	9.0	...	...
TOTAL	22,045	100.0	5,910	100.0

Production (metric tons except as noted). Agriculture[8], forestry, fishing (1999): coconuts 1,800, bananas 180, hens' eggs 12, other agricultural prod-

ucts include breadfruit, pulaka (taro), pandanus fruit, sweet potatoes, and pawpaws; livestock (number of live animals) 27,000 chickens, 12,600 pigs, 7,000 ducks; forestry, n.a.; fish catch (1998) 400. Mining and quarrying[9]: n.a. Manufacturing: tiny amounts of copra, handicrafts, and garments. Overseas employment (2000) of Tuvaluan seafarers contributes about U.S.$5,000,000 annually to the Tuvalu economy. Energy production (consumption): electricity (kW-hr; 1992) 1,300,000 (1,300,000); coal, none (none); crude petroleum, none (n.a.); petroleum products, none (n.a.); natural gas, none (none).
Tourism (1998): receipts from visitors U.S.$200,000; expenditures by nationals abroad, n.a.
Population economically active (1991): total 5,910; activity rate of total population 65.3% (participation rates: ages 15–64, 85.5%; female [1979] 51.3%; unemployed [1979] 4.0%).

Price and earnings indexes (1990 = 100)

	1994	1995	1996	1997	1998	1999	2000
Consumer price index	103.7	109.0	109.8	111.5	112.4	113.5	119.5
Earnings index	...	...	...	...	...	...	...

Household income and expenditure. Average household size (1994): Funafuti 7.0, other islands 5.8; average annual gross income per household (1994): Funafuti $A 12,012 (U.S.$8,789), other islands $A 3,536 (U.S.$2,587); sources of income (1987): agriculture and other 45.0%, cash economy only 38.0%, overseas remittances 17.0%; expenditure (1992)[10]: food 45.5%, housing and household operations 11.5%, transportation 10.5%, alcohol and tobacco 10.5%, clothing 7.5%, other 14.5%.
Land use (1987): agricultural and under permanent cultivation 73.6%[11]; scrub 16.1%; other 10.3%.

Foreign trade

Balance of trade (current prices)

	1995	1996	1997	1998	1999	2000
$A '000	−6,373	−5,638	−7,771	−11,341	−14,353	−22,250
% of total	94.4%	88.6%	91.2%	98.8%	77.3%	89.1%

Imports (1999): $A 16,461,000 (food 26%, machinery and transport equipment 25%, refined petroleum 9%, chemicals and chemical products 5%, beverages and tobacco 5%). *Major import sources:* Australia 38%; Fiji 32%; New Zealand 11%; Japan 6%; China 2%.
Exports (1999): $A 2,108,000 (primarily copra, stamps, and handicrafts). *Major export destinations* (1995): South Africa 64%; Colombia 9%; Belgium-Luxembourg 9%.

Transport and communications

Transport. Railroads: none. Roads (2000): total length 28 km (paved, none). Vehicles[12]: n.a. Merchant marine (1992): vessels (100 gross tons and over) 6; total deadweight tonnage 16,005. Air transport: n.a.; airports (1997) 1.

Communications

Medium	date	unit	number	units per 1,000 persons
Radio	1997	receivers	4,000	384
Television	1996	receivers	100	13
Telephones	1999	main lines	630	55

Education and health

Educational attainment (mid-1990s). Percentage of population age 15 and over (on Funafuti) having: no formal schooling through completed primary education 31.9%; some secondary 46.6%; completed secondary to some higher 18.6%; completed higher 2.9%. *Literacy* (1990): total population literate in Tuvaluan 8,593 (95.0%); literacy in English estimated at 45.0%.

Education (1991)

	schools	teachers[13]	students	student/ teacher ratio
Primary (age 5–11)	11	72	1,906[14]	...
Secondary (age 12–18)	1	21	314	...
Vocational	1	10	58	...
Higher	—	—	—	—

Health (1999): physicians 8 (1 per 1,375 persons); hospital beds (1990) 30 (1 per 302 persons); infant mortality rate per 1,000 live births (2002): 22.0.

Military

Total active duty personnel: none; Tuvalu relies on Australian-trained volunteers from Fiji and Papua New Guinea.

---

[1]The value of the Tuvalu dollar is pegged to the value of the Australian dollar, which is also legal currency in Tuvalu. [2]Local government councils have been established on all islands except Niulakita. [3]Niutao includes Niulakita. [4]Another survey puts the area at 9.4 sq mi (24.4 sq km). [5]Detail does not add to total given because of rounding. [6]In purchasers' values. [7]Including cottage industry. [8]Because of poor soil quality, only limited subsistence agriculture is possible on the islands. [9]Research into the mineral potential of Tuvalu's maritime exclusive economic zone (289,500 sq mi [750,000 sq km] of the Pacific Ocean) is currently being conducted by the South Pacific Geo-Science Commission. [10]Weights of consumer price index components. [11]Capable of supporting coconut palms, pandanus, and breadfruit. [12]There are several cars, tractors, trailers, and light trucks on Funafuti; a few motorcycles are in use on most islands. [13]1990. [14]1994.

Internet resources for further information:
- **United Nations Development Programme, Common Country Assessments** http://www.undp.org.fj/CCAs.htm
- **Secretariat of Pacific Communities** http://www.spc.org

Uganda

Official name: Republic of Uganda.
Form of government: nonparty republic with one legislative house (Parliament [305[1]]).
Head of state and government: President.
Capital: Kampala.
Official language: English[2].
Official religion: none.
Monetary unit: 1 Uganda shilling (U Sh) = 100 cents; valuation (Sept. 23, 2002) 1 U.S.$ = U Sh 1,815; 1 £ = U Sh 2,821.

Indian Ocean

Area and population

Geographic regions[3]	Principal cities	area sq mi	area sq km	population 2002 preliminary census
Central	Kampala	23,749	61,510	6,625,239
Eastern	Jinja	15,426	39,953	6,208,351
Northern	Gulu	32,687	84,658	5,366,104
Western	Mbarara	21,204	54,917	6,351,327
TOTAL		93,065[4, 5]	241,038[4]	24,551,021

Demography

Population (2002): 24,378,000.
Density (2002)[6]: persons per sq mi 320.4, persons per sq km 123.7.
Urban-rural (1999–2000): urban 13.0%; rural 87.0%.
Sex distribution (2002): male 49.11%; female 50.89%.
Age breakdown (2000): under 15, 51.1%; 15–29, 26.2%; 30–44, 13.6%; 45–59, 5.7%; 60–74, 2.9%; 75 and over, 0.5%.
Population projection: (2010) 30,944,000; (2020) 41,258,000.
Doubling time: 27 years.
Ethnolinguistic composition (1991): Ganda 18.1%; Nkole 10.7%; Kiga 8.4%; Soga 8.2%; Lango 5.9%; Lugbara 4.7%; Gisu 4.5%; Acholi 4.4%.
Religious affiliation (1995): Christian 66%, of which Roman Catholic 33%, Protestant 33% (of which mostly Anglican); traditional beliefs 18%; Muslim 16%.
Major cities (1991): Kampala 1,274,000[7]; Jinja 61,000; Mbale 53,600; Masaka 49,100; Gulu 42,800; Entebbe 41,600.

Vital statistics

Birth rate per 1,000 population (2000): 48.0 (world avg. 22.5).
Death rate per 1,000 population (2000): 22.4 (world avg. 9.0).
Natural increase rate per 1,000 population (2000): 25.6 (world avg. 13.5).
Total fertility rate (avg. births per childbearing woman; 2000): 7.0.
Life expectancy at birth (2000): male 42.2 years; female 43.7 years.

National economy

Budget (1997–98). Revenue: U Sh 1,193,100,000,000 (taxes 62.7%, of which customs duties 25.5%, sales taxes 20.2%, income taxes 10.5%; grants 33.3%). Expenditures: U Sh 1,239,900,000,000 (current expenditures 58.7%, of which wages and salaries 20.6%, education 16.6%, security 11.0%, health 4.3%; capital expenditures 41.3%).
Public debt (external, outstanding; 2000): U.S.$2,997,000,000.
Production (metric tons except as noted). Agriculture, forestry, fishing (1999): plantains 9,400,000, cassava 3,400,000, sweet potatoes 2,520,000, sugarcane 1,600,000, corn (maize) 780,000, millet 638,000, sorghum 454,000, potatoes 449,000, coffee 198,000, peanuts (groundnuts) 183,000, rice 96,000; livestock (number of live animals) 5,700,000 cattle, 3,650,000 goats, 1,970,000 sheep, 960,000 pigs, 23,000,000 chickens; roundwood (1998) 15,649,000 cu m; fish catch (2000) 355,831. Mining and quarrying (2000): gold (officially reported export figure) 7,303 kg. Manufacturing (1998): cement 278,800; sugar 93,000; soap 36,100; metal products 22,400; meat 3,706; footwear 995,000 pairs; beer 552,000 hectolitres. Energy production (consumption): electricity (kW-hr; 1998) 1,282,800,000 (872,000,000); coal (metric tons) none (none); crude petroleum (barrels) none (none); petroleum products (metric tons; 1997) none (330,000); natural gas (cu m) none (none).
Tourism (1999): receipts from visitors U.S.$149,000,000; expenditures by nationals abroad U.S.$141,000,000.
Gross national product (2000): U.S.$6,699,000,000 (U.S.$300 per capita).

Structure of gross domestic product and labour force

	1998–99 in value U Sh '000,000	1998–99 % of total value	1991 labour force	1991 % of labour force
Agriculture	3,489,000	40.3	6,724,000	80.4
Mining	49,000	0.6		
Manufacturing	690,000	8.0	478,000	5.7
Construction	565,000	6.5		
Public utilities	108,000	1.2		
Transp. and commun.	335,000	3.9		
Trade	1,091,000	12.6		
Finance	1,279,000	14.8	1,163,000	13.9
Pub. admin., defense				
Services	281,000	3.2		
Other	778,000	9.0	...	...
TOTAL	8,665,000	100.0[5]	8,365,000	100.0

Population economically active (1991): total 8,365,000; activity rate of total population 49.6% (participation rates: ages 15–64, 78.9%[8]; female 35.2%).

Price and earnings indexes (1995 = 100)

	1995	1996	1997	1998	1999	2000	2001
Consumer price index	100.0	107.2	114.6	114.6	121.9	125.4	127.9
Earnings index	...	...	...	...	...	...	...

Household income and expenditure (1999–2000)[8]. Average household size 5.2; income per household U Sh 141,000 (U.S.$91[9]); sources of income: wages and self-employment 78.0%, transfers 13.0%, rent 9.0%; expenditure: food and beverages 51.0%, rent, energy, and services 17.0%, education 7.0%, household durable goods 6.0%, transportation 5.0%, health 4.0%.
Land use (1994): forest 31.5%; pasture 9.1%; agriculture 34.0%; other 25.4%.

Foreign trade[10]

Balance of trade (current prices)

	1996	1997	1998	1999	2000	2001
U Sh '000,000,000	−633.8	−831.1	−952.7	−1,207.0	−1,727.0	−1,995.9
% of total	34.1%	41.1%	50.1%	44.6%	53.2%	55.4%

Imports (1999): U.S.$1,015,200,000 (1998; machinery and apparatus 18.5%, food and live animals 11.4%, road vehicles 11.0%, refined petroleum 10.1%, pharmaceuticals 4.8%). *Major import sources:* Kenya 23.8%; U.K. 10.2%; Japan 8.1%; India 6.4%; U.S. 5.6%; United Arab Emirates 5.5%.
Exports (1999): U.S.$505,700,000 (unroasted coffee 52.8%, fish waste 8.0%, nonmonetary gold [excl. gold ores and concentrates] 6.6%, cotton 5.8%, fresh fish 4.7%). *Major export destinations:* U.K. 18.0%; Southern African Customs Union 6.5%; Kenya 6.3%; Singapore 4.9%; Switzerland 4.8%.

Transport and communications

Transport. Railroads (1998): route length 1,241 km; passenger-km (1996) 27,000,000; metric ton-km cargo (1996) 236,000,000. Roads (1996): total length 26,800 km (paved 7.7%). Vehicles (1996): passenger cars 35,361; trucks and buses 48,430. Merchant marine (1992): vessels (100 gross tons and over) 2; total deadweight tonnage 8,600[11]. Air transport (1997): passenger-km 52,117,000; metric ton-km cargo 5,000,000; airports (1998) 1.

Communications

Medium	date	unit	number	units per 1,000 persons
Daily newspapers	1997	circulation	40,000	2.1
Radio	1997	receivers	2,600,000	130
Television	1998	receivers	580,000	28.0
Telephones	2001	main lines	63,700	2.8
Cellular telephones	2001	subscribers	322,700	14
Personal computers	2001	units	70,000	3.1
Internet	2001	users	60,000	2.7

Education and health

Educational attainment (1991). Percentage of population age 25 and over having: no formal schooling or less than one full year 46.9%; primary education 42.1%; secondary 10.5%; higher 0.5%. *Literacy* (1999–2000): population age 10 and over literate 65.0%; males literate 74.0%; females literate 57.0%.

Education (1995)

	schools	teachers	students	student/ teacher ratio
Primary (age 5–11)[12]	8,531	76,134	2,636,409	34.6
Secondary (age 12–15)[12]	...	14,447	255,158	17.7
Voc., teacher tr.[12]	...	1,788	36,063	20.2
Higher	...	2,006	29,343	14.6

Health (1993): physicians 840 (1 per 22,399 persons); hospital beds (1989) 20,136 (1 per 817 persons); infant mortality rate (2000) 93.3.
Food (2000): daily per capita caloric intake 2,359 (vegetable products 94%, animal products 6%); 101% of FAO recommended minimum requirement.

Military

Total active duty personnel (2001): 50,000–60,000[13]. *Military expenditure as percentage of GNP* (1999): 2.3% (world 2.4%); per capita expenditure U.S.$6.

[1]Includes 10 ex officio members (ministers who are not elected to Parliament). [2]The constitution was translated into six local languages in 1999 including Ganda (Luganda), Acholi, Teso (Ateso), Lugbara, and two others. [3]The 39 administrative districts in Uganda as of 1994 were increased to 45 administrative districts in 1997. Eight additional administrative districts were announced in November 2000 and 3 more in July 2001, for a total of 56 administrative districts. [4]Includes water area of 16,984 sq mi (43,989 sq km); Uganda's portion of Lake Victoria comprises 11,954 sq mi (30,960 sq km). [5]Detail does not add to total given because of rounding. [6]Based on land area only. [7]Urban agglomeration; 2001. [8]Based on nationally representative household survey. [9]The household income for urban areas is U Sh 302,900 (U.S.$195). [10]Imports c.i.f.; exports f.o.b. [11]1988. [12]Public sector only. [13]Breakdown by branch of service is unavailable.

Internet resources for further information:
• Uganda Bureau of Statistics http://www.ubos.org
• Bank of Uganda http://www.bou.or.ug

Ukraine

Official name: Ukrayina (Ukraine).
Form of government: unitary multiparty republic with a single legislative body (Supreme Council [450]).
Head of state: President.
Head of government: Prime Minister.
Capital: Kiev (Kyyiv).
Official language: Ukrainian.
Official religion: none.
Monetary unit: hryvnya (pl. hryvnyas)[1]; (Sept. 23, 2002) free rate, 1 U.S.$ = 5.33 hryvnyas; 1 £ = 8.28 hryvnyas.

Area and population

	area	population		area	population
Autonomous republic	sq km	2001 census[2]	**Provinces**	sq km	2001 census[2]
Crimea (Krym)	26,100	2,031,000	Kyyiv (Kiev)	28,100	1,828,000
			Luhansk	26,700	2,546,000
Cities			Lviv	21,800	2,626,000
Kiev	800	2,602,000	Mykolayiv	24,600	1,264,000
Sevastopol	900	378,000	Odessa	33,300	2,468,000
			Poltava	28,800	1,630,000
Provinces			Rivne	20,100	1,173,000
Cherkasy	20,900	1,402,000	Sumy	23,800	1,300,000
Chernihiv	31,900	1,236,000	Ternopil	13,800	1,146,000
Chernivtsi	8,100	923,000	Vinnytsya	26,500	1,772,000
Dnipropetrovsk	31,900	3,560,000	Volyn	20,200	1,061,000
Donetsk	26,500	4,843,000	Zakarpatska	12,800	1,258,000
Ivano-Frankivsk	13,900	1,409,000	Zaporizhzhya	27,200	1,926,000
Kharkiv	31,400	2,910,000	Zhytomyr	29,900	1,389,000
Kherson	28,500	1,174,000	TOTAL	603,700	48,416,000[3]
Khmelnytsky	20,600	1,431,000			
Kirovohrad	24,600	1,129,000			

Demography

Population (2002): 48,120,000.
Density (2002): persons per sq mi 206.4, persons per sq km 79.7.
Urban-rural (2002): urban 68.0%; rural 32.0%.
Sex distribution (2001): male 46.25%; female 53.75%.
Age breakdown (2001): under 15, 17.3%; 15–29, 22.3%; 30–44, 21.7%; 45–59, 17.8%; 60–74, 15.7%; 75 and over, 5.2%.
Population projection: (2010) 45,930,000; (2020) 44,109,000.
Ethnic composition (2000): Ukrainian 70.4%; Russian 20.0%; Polish 2.3%; Rom (Gypsy) 1.3%; Ruthenian 1.1%; other/unspecified 4.9%.
Religious affiliation (1995): Ukrainian Orthodox (Russian patriarchy) 19.5%; Ukrainian Orthodox (Kiev patriarchy) 9.7%; Ukrainian Catholic (Uniate) 7.0%; Protestant 3.6%; other Orthodox 1.6%; Roman Catholic 1.2%; Jewish 0.9%; other (mostly nonreligious) 56.5%.
Major cities (2001): Kiev 2,602,000; Kharkiv 1,470,000; Dnipropetrovsk 1,064,000; Odessa 1,029,000; Donetsk 1,016,000; Zaporizhzhya 814,000.

Vital statistics

Birth rate per 1,000 population (2001): 9.3 (world avg. 21.2); (1993) legitimate 87.0%; illegitimate 13.0%.
Death rate per 1,000 population (2001): 16.4 (world avg. 8.9).
Natural increase rate per 1,000 population (2001): –7.1 (world avg. 12.3).
Total fertility rate (avg. births per childbearing woman; 2001): 1.3.
Life expectancy at birth (2001): male 60.6 years; female 72.0 years.
Major causes of death per 100,000 population (1995): circulatory diseases 874.0; neoplasms (cancers) 199.0; accidents 160.0; respiratory diseases 89.0.

National economy

Budget (2000). Revenue: 24,792,000,000 hryvnyas (tax revenue 87.0%, of which taxes on goods and services 29.1%, payroll tax 26.9%, income tax 24.8%, excise tax 2.6%, property tax 2.2%, other 1.4%; nontax revenue and grants 13.0%). Expenditures: 25,100,000,000 hryvnyas (social security 37.5%; education 11.6%; debt payment 8.7%; health 8.3%; defense 3.5%).
Production (metric tons except as noted). Agriculture, forestry, fishing (2001): wheat 21,333,000, sugar beets 15,489,000, potatoes 13,500,000, barley 10,156,000, corn (maize) 3,300,000, rye 1,500,000, oats 1,100,000; livestock (number of live animals) 9,914,000 cattle, 9,078,000 pigs, 1,770,000 sheep and goats; roundwood (2000) 5,920,000 cu m; fish catch (1999) 441,700. Mining and quarrying (1999): iron ore 47,709,000; manganese (metal content) 675,000; uranium 500,000. Manufacturing (value of production in '000,000 hryvnyas; 1998): iron and steel 14,525; food and beverages 12,974; nonelectrical machinery 3,838; fabricated metal products 2,919; industrial chemicals 2,741. Energy production (consumption): electricity (kW-hr; 2000) 171,000,000,000 ([1999] 168,600,-000,000); hard coal (2001) 82,896,000,000 ([1997] 81,509,000,000); lignite (2001) 1,035,000 ([1997] 1,915,000); crude petroleum (barrels; 2001) 27,150,000 ([2000] 126,290,000); petroleum products (barrels; 1997) 11,867,000 (15,468,000); natural gas (cu m; 2001) 15,954,000,000 ([1999] 78,013,000,000).
Population economically active (1999): total 21,824,000; activity rate of total population 43.6% (participation rates: ages 16–59 [male] 15–64 [female] 56.6%; female [1994] 51.0%; unemployed [2000] 6.4%).

Price and earnings indexes (1997 = 100)

	1997	1998	1999	2000	2001
Consumer price index	100.0	110.6	135.7	174.0	196.4[4]
Monthly earnings index	100.0	107.3	124.0	160.8	...

Gross national product (2000): U.S.$34,565,000,000 (U.S.$700 per capita).

Structure of gross domestic product and labour force

	1999			
	in value '000,000 hryvnyas	% of total value	labour force	% of labour force
Agriculture	14,300	11.2	4,927,000	26.2
Mining				
Manufacturing }	35,700	28.1	4,342,000	23.1
Public utilities				
Construction	5,600	4.4	974,000	5.2
Transp. and commun.	14,200	11.2	1,229,000	6.5
Trade	9,700	7.6	1,510,000	8.0
Finance				
Pub. admin., defense }	29,200	23.0	3,687,000	19.6
Services				
Other	18,400[5]	14.5[5]	2,121,000[6]	11.3[6]
TOTAL	127,100	100.0	18,790,000[7]	100.0[3]

Public debt (external; 2000): U.S.$8,139,000,000.
Tourism (1999): receipts U.S.$2,124,000,000; expenditures U.S.$1,774,000,000.
Household income and expenditure (1996). Average household size (1998) 3.0; income per household (1996) 4,968 hryvnyas[1] (U.S.$2,715); sources of income (1995): wages and salaries 66.4%, sales of agricultural products 9.3%, subsidies 6.9%, pensions 6.5%, remuneration from abroad 5.3%; expenditures (1995): food and beverages 43.1%, consumer goods 27.5%, services 7.2%, housing 6.7%, taxes 6.2%.

Foreign trade

Balance of trade (current prices)

	1995	1996	1997	1998	1999	2000
U.S.$'000,000	–2,702	–4,296	–4,205	–2,584	–482	–779
% of total	8.7%	12.1%	12.0%	8.6%	1.9%	2.5%

Imports (1999): U.S.$12,945,000,000 (fuel and energy products 39.9%; machinery 17.4%; chemicals and chemical products 11.3%; food and raw materials 7.0%). *Major import sources:* Russia 47.9%; Germany 7.3%; Turkmenistan 3.7%; U.S. 3.1%; Belarus 2.6%.
Exports (1999): U.S.$12,463,000,000 (ferrous and nonferrous metals 39.1%; food and raw materials 11.4%; machinery 11.1%; chemicals and chemical products 11.1%). *Major export destinations:* Russia 19.2%; China 5.9%; Turkey 5.4%; Germany 4.5%; Italy 3.7%; U.S. 3.5%.

Transport and communications

Transport. Railroads (1999): length 22,302 km; passenger-km 47,600,000,000; metric ton-km cargo 156,336,000,000. Roads (2000): total length 168,674 km (paved 97%). Vehicles (1997): passenger cars 5,210,774. Air transport (1998): passenger-km 1,720,000,000; metric ton-km cargo 188,000,000; airports (1998) with scheduled flights 12.

Communications

Medium	date	unit	number	units per 1,000 persons
Daily newspapers	1996	circulation	2,780,000	54
Radio	1997	receivers	45,050,000	889
Television	1998	receivers	21,000,000	418
Telephones	2001	main lines	10,669,600	212
Cellular telephones	2001	subscribers	2,224,600	44
Personal computers	2001	units	920,000	18
Internet	2001	users	600,000	12

Education and health

Educational attainment (1989). Percentage of population age 15 and over having: some primary education 6.8%; completed primary 13.8%; some secondary 18.4%; completed secondary 31.1%; some postsecondary 19.5%; higher 10.4%. *Literacy* (1999): percentage of total population age 15 and over literate 99.6%; males literate 99.7%; females literate 99.5%.

Education (2000–01)

	schools	teachers	students	student/ teacher ratio
Primary (age 6–13) }	22,200	577,000	6,764,000	11.7
Secondary (age 14–17)				
Voc., teacher tr.	1,008	...	545,900	...
Higher	979	...	1,930,900	...

Health (1998): physicians 150,382 (1 per 334 persons); hospital beds 508,030 (1 per 99 persons); infant mortality rate per 1,000 live births (2001) 21.4.
Food (2000): daily per capita caloric intake 2,871 (vegetable products 80%, animal products 20%); 112% of FAO recommended minimum requirement.

Military

Total active duty personnel (2001): 303,800 (army 49.8%, air force 31.6%, navy 4.3%, headquarters 14.3%). *Military expenditure as percentage of GNP* (1999): 3.0% (world 2.4%); per capita expenditure U.S.$103.

[1]On Sept. 2, 1996, the karbovanets, a transitional currency, was replaced by the hryvnya at a 100,000-to-1 ratio. [2]Preliminary. [3]Detail does not add to total given because of rounding. [4]May. [5]Less imputed bank service charges, net indirect taxes, and taxes on production. [6]Includes 1,174,500 unemployed. [7]Excludes about 3,000,000 self-employed.

Internet resources for further information:
• National Bank of Ukraine
  http://www.bank.gov.ua/ENGL/DEFAULT.htm

United Arab Emirates

Official name: Al-Imārāt al-ʿArabīyah al-Muttaḥidah (United Arab Emirates).
Form of government: federation of seven emirates with one appointive advisory body (Federal National Council [401]).
Chief of state: President.
Head of government: Prime Minister.
Capital: Abu Dhabi.
Official language: Arabic.
Official religion: Islam.
Monetary unit: 1 U.A.E. dirham (Dh) = 100 fils; valuation (Sept. 23, 2002) 1 U.S.\$ = Dh 3.67; 1 £ = Dh 5.71.

Area and population		area		population
Emirates	**Capitals**	**sq mi**	**sq km**	**2000 estimate**
Abū Zaby (Abu Dhabi)	Abu Dhabi	28,210[2]	73,060[2]	1,186,000
ʿAjmān (Ajman)	ʿAjmān	100	260	174,000
Dubayy (Dubai)	Dubai	1,510	3,900	913,000
Al-Fujayrah (Fujairah)	Al-Fujayrah	500	1,300	98,000
Raʾs al-Khaymah (Ras al-Khaimah)	Raʾs al-Khaymah	660	1,700	171,000
Ash-Shāriqah (Sharjah)	Sharjah	1,000	2,600	520,000
Umm al-Qaywayn (Umm al-Qaiwain)	Umm al-Qaywayn	300	780	46,000
TOTAL		32,280	83,600	3,108,000

Demography

Population (2002): 3,550,000.
Density (2002): persons per sq mi 110.0, persons per sq km 42.5.
Urban-rural (2001): urban 87.2%; rural 12.8%.
Sex distribution (2001): male 67.54%; female 32.46%.
Age breakdown (2001): under 15, 26.2%; 15–29, 29.2%; 30–44, 33.4%; 45–59, 9.6%; 60–74, 1.4%; 75 and over, 0.2%.
Population projection: (2010) 4,010,000; (2020) 4,552,000.
Doubling time: 50 years.
Ethnic composition (2000): Arab 48.1%, of which U.A.E. Arab 12.2%, U.A.E Bedouin 9.4%, Egyptian Arab 6.2%, Omani Arab 4.1%, Saudi Arab 4.0%; South Asian 35.7%, of which Pashtun 7.1%, Balochi 7.1%, Malayali 7.1%; Persian 5.0%; Filipino 3.4%; white 2.4%; other 5.4%.
Religious affiliation (1995): Muslim 96.0% (Sunnī 80.0%, Shīʿī 16.0%); other (mostly Christian and Hindu) 4.0%.
Major cities (1995): Dubai 669,181; Abu Dhabi 398,695; Sharjah 320,095; Al-ʿAyn 225,970; ʿAjmān 114,395; Raʾs al-Khaymah 77,550.

Vital statistics

Birth rate per 1,000 population (2001): 18.1 (world avg. 21.2).
Death rate per 1,000 population (2001): 3.8 (world avg. 8.9).
Natural increase rate per 1,000 population (2001): 14.3 (world avg. 12.3).
Total fertility rate (avg. births per childbearing woman; 2001): 1.6.
Marriage rate per 1,000 population (1999): 3.5.
Divorce rate per 1,000 population (1999): 0.9.
Life expectancy at birth (2001): male 71.8 years; female 76.9 years.
Major causes of death per 100,000 population (1998): cardiovascular diseases 44.1; accidents and poisoning 31.1; malignant neoplasms (cancers) 15.3; congenital anomalies 9.4.

National economy

Budget (1999). Revenue: Dh 52,003,000,000 (oil revenue 54.2%, non-oil revenue 45.8%). Expenditures: Dh 77,089,000,000 (current expenditures 66.2%, capital [development] expenditure 33.8%).
Gross national product (1999): U.S.\$52,098,000,000 (U.S.\$17,730 per capita).

Structure of gross domestic product and labour force				
	2000			
	in value Dh '000,000[3]	% of total value[3]	labour force	% of labour force
Agriculture	7,017	2.9	142,213	7.8
Crude petroleum production } Mining and quarrying	82,655	34.2	41,148	2.3
Manufacturing	28,846	11.9	194,765	10.7
Construction	17,247	7.1	344,179	18.9
Public utilities	4,627	1.9	17,759	1.0
Transp. and commun.	16,153	6.7	127,214	7.0
Trade	27,294	11.3	310,430	17.1
Finance, real estate	32,981	13.6	68,127	3.7
Pub. admin., defense	24,637	10.2	237,391	13.0
Services	5,441	2.2	295,774	16.2
Other	−5,010[4]	−2.0[4]	41,000[5]	2.3[5]
TOTAL	241,888	100.0	1,820,000	100.0

Public debt: n.a.
Tourism (2000): total number of tourist arrivals 3,907,000.
Production (metric tons except as noted). Agriculture, forestry, fishing (2000): tomatoes 780,000, dates 318,000, cantaloupes and watermelons 64,000, cabbages 58,132, pumpkins and squash 31,252, eggplants 28,068, lemons and limes 18,137, cucumbers and gherkins 14,836, mangoes 10,300; livestock (number of live animals) 1,200,000 goats, 467,281 sheep, 200,000 camels, 110,000 cattle, 14,650,000 chickens; fish catch (1999) 117,607. Mining and

quarrying (1998): sulfur 268,000; gypsum 110,000; chromite 54,000; lime 50,000. Manufacturing (value of production in Dh '000,000; 1998): chemical products (including refined petroleum) 10,096; textiles and wearing apparel 2,397; fabricated metal products 1,999; food, beverages, and tobacco 1,510; cement, bricks, and ceramics 1,409. Energy production (consumption): electricity (kW-hr; 1997) 20,571,000,000 (20,571,000,000); crude petroleum (barrels; 2001) 740,000,000 ([1997] 86,000,000); petroleum products (metric tons; 1997) 18,995,000 (7,190,000); natural gas (cu m; 2000) 39,000,000,000 ([1997] 28,839,000,000).
Population economically active (2001): total 1,947,000; activity rate of total population 59.2% (participation rates [1995]: over age 15, 55.4%; female 13.2%; unemployment [2000] 2.3%).

Price and earnings indexes (1995 = 100)							
	1993	1994	1995	1996	1997	1998	1999
Consumer price index	91.2	95.8	100.0	102.6	104.7	106.8	108.9
Annual earnings index	104.1	101.1	100.0	103.0	102.7	...	...

Household income and expenditure. Average household size (1999) 6.1; income per household: n.a.; sources of income: n.a.; expenditure (1991): rent, fuel, and light 23.9%, food 22.7%, transportation and communications 14.1%, durable household goods 11.6%, education, recreation, and entertainment 8.6%.
Land use (1994): forested, virtually none; meadows and pastures 2.4%; agricultural and under permanent cultivation 0.5%; built-on, wasteland, and other 97.1%.

Foreign trade

Balance of trade (current prices)						
	1996	1997	1998	1999	2000	2001
Dh '000,000,000	+27.2	+30.4	+6.2	+16.0	+41.7	+18.3
% of total	12.5%	12.2%	2.7%	6.6%	15.1%	6.9%

Imports (1997): Dh 109,100,000,000 (machinery and transport equipment 38.4%, basic manufactures 24.8%, food and live animals 9.7%, chemicals 6.1%, crude minerals 1.6%, mineral fuels 1.4%). *Major import sources:* Japan 10.2%; United States 9.4%; United Kingdom 8.7%; China 8.0%; Germany 6.9%; India 5.8%; Italy 5.2%; South Korea 5.1%.
Exports (1997): Dh 139,500,000,000 (domestic exports 76.0%, of which crude petroleum 37.6%, nonmonetary gold 11.8%, natural gas 7.1%, refined petroleum products 4.8%; reexports 24.0%). *Major export destinations:* Japan 36.2%; India 6.6%; Singapore 6.4%; South Korea 6.1%; Iran 3.7%; Oman 3.7%.

Transport and communications

Transport. Railroads: none. Roads (1999): total length 2,355 mi, 3,791 km (paved 100%). Vehicles (1996): passenger cars 201,000; trucks and buses 56,950. Air transport (2000)[6]: passenger-mi 12,149,300,000, passenger-km 19,552,500,000; short ton-mi cargo 887,000,000, metric ton-km cargo 1,427,500,000; airports (1999) with scheduled flights 6.

Communications				units per 1,000 persons
Medium	**date**	**unit**	**number**	
Daily newspapers	1996	circulation	384,000	170
Radio	1997	receivers	820,000	355
Television	1999	receivers	740,000	252
Telephones	2001	main lines	1,053,000	397
Cellular telephones	2001	subscribers	1,909,300	720
Personal computers	2001	units	420,000	158
Internet	2001	users	900,000	339

Education and health

Educational attainment (1995). Percentage of population age 10 and over having: no formal schooling 47.6%; primary education 27.8%; secondary 16.0%, higher 8.6%. *Literacy* (1995): total population age 15 and over literate 79.2%; males literate 78.9%; females literate 79.8%.

Education (1998–99)				student/ teacher ratio
	schools	teachers	students	
Primary (age 6–11)	...	16,148[7]	270,486	16.1[7]
Secondary (age 12–18)	...	12,388[8]	198,439	12.0[8]
Vocational	...	249[7]	3,113	7.7[7]
Higher	47	510[9]	17,950[7]	19.2[9]

Health (1999): physicians 6,059 (1 per 485 persons); hospital beds 7,448 (1 per 394 persons); infant mortality rate per 1,000 live births (2001) 16.7.
Food (2000): daily per capita caloric intake 3,192 (vegetable products 75%, animal products 25%); 132% of FAO recommended minimum requirement.

Military

Total active duty personnel (2001): 65,000 (army 90.8%, navy 3.1%, air force 6.2%). *Military expenditure as percentage of GDP* (1999): 4.1% (world 2.4%); per capita expenditure U.S.\$935.

[1]All appointed seats. [2]Approximate, based on reported total and on reported partial areas for smaller emirates. [3]At factor cost. [4]Imputed bank service charges. [5]Unemployed. [6]Emirates Air and one-fourth apportionment of Gulf Air. [7]1996–97. [8]1994–95. [9]1992–93.

Internet resources for further information:
• **Government of United Arab Emirates** http://www.uae.gov.ae
• **Central Bank of the United Arab Emirates** http://www.cbuae.gov.ae

United Kingdom

Official name: United Kingdom of Great Britain and Northern Ireland.
Form of government: constitutional monarchy with two legislative houses (House of Lords [709]; House of Commons [659]).
Chief of state: Sovereign.
Head of government: Prime Minister.
Capital: London.
Official language: English.
Official religion: Churches of England and Scotland "established" (protected by the state, but not "official") in their respective countries; no established church in Northern Ireland or Wales.
Monetary unit: 1 pound sterling (£) = 100 new pence; valuation (Sept. 23, 2002) 1 £ = U.S.$1.55; 1 U.S.$ = £0.64.

Sex distribution (2001): male 48.62%; female 51.38%.
Religious affiliation (2000): Christian 66.4%, of which Protestant 53.3% (Anglican 45.0%), Roman Catholic 9.6%, Orthodox 0.9%; Muslim 2.0%; Hindu 0.7%; Sikh 0.5%; Jewish 0.4%; other/nonreligious 30.0%.
Major cities (2000): Greater London 7,375,100; Birmingham 1,010,400; Leeds 726,100; Glasgow 609,400; Sheffield 530,100; Bradford 486,100; Liverpool 457,300; Edinburgh 453,400; Manchester 439,500; Bristol 406,200; Kirklees 395,100; Fife 350,400.
Mobility (1991)[6]. Population living in the same residence as 1990: 90.1%; different residence, same country (of Great Britain) 8.1%; different residence, different country of Great Britain 1.2%; from outside Great Britain 0.6%.
Households (1994)[6]. Average household size 2.4; 1 person 27%, 2 persons 34%, 3 persons 16%, 4 persons 15%, 5 persons 6%, 6 or more persons 2%. Family household: 16,900,000 (72.0%), nonfamily 6,600,000 (28.0%, of which 1-person 12.0%).
Immigration (1998): permanent residents 332,000, from Australia 7.5%, United States 5.7%, New Zealand 4.2%, South Africa 3.6%, Bangladesh, India, and Sri Lanka 3.0%, Canada 1.5%, Pakistan 1.2%, other 73.3%, of which EU 8.7%.

Vital statistics

Birth rate per 1,000 population (2000): 11.4 (world avg. 22.5); (1999) legitimate 61.2%; illegitimate 38.8%.
Death rate per 1,000 population (2000): 10.2 (world avg. 9.0).
Natural increase rate per 1,000 population (2000): 1.2 (world avg. 13.5).
Total fertility rate (avg. births per childbearing woman; 1999): 1.7.
Marriage rate per 1,000 population (1999): 5.1.
Divorce rate per 1,000 population (1999): 2.7.
Life expectancy at birth (1998–2000): male 75.4 years; female 80.2 years.
Major causes of death per 100,000 population (2000): diseases of the circulatory system 396.0, of which ischemic heart disease 207.6, cerebrovascular disease 100.2; malignant neoplasms (cancers) 257.2; diseases of the respiratory system 170.6, of which pneumonia 101.5; diseases of the digestive system 42.8; diseases of the genitourinary system 14.1; diseases of the endocrine system 13.7, of which diabetes mellitus 10.8; suicide 7.2.

Social indicators

Educational attainment (1999). Percentage of population age 25–64 having: up to lower secondary education only 38%; completed secondary 37%; higher 25%, of which at least some university 17%.

Distribution of disposable income (1998–99)

percentage of household income by quintile

1	2	3	4	5 (highest)
7.8	11.6	16.0	22.1	42.5

Quality of working life (2000). Average workweek (hours): male 41.2, female 37.4. Annual rate per 100,000 workers for (1996): injury or accident 553.6; death 1.0. Proportion of labour force (employed persons) insured for damages or income loss resulting from: injury 100%; permanent disability 100%; death 100%. Average days lost to labour stoppages per 1,000 employee workdays: 20. Principal means of transport to work (1991; London only): public transportation 81%, private automobile 15%, motor or pedal cycle 2%, other 2%.
Access to services (1991)[6]. Proportion of households having access to: bath or shower 98.7%; toilet 99.8%.
Social participation. Eligible voters participating in last national election (May 1997): 71.4%. Population age 16 and over participating in voluntary work (1987)[6]: 22%. Trade union membership in total workforce (1999) 27.0%.
Social deviance (1998–99). Offense rate per 100,000 population for: theft and handling stolen goods 3,574.2; burglary 1,599.8; violence against the person 387.9; fraud and forgery 291.9; robbery 111.3; sexual offense 58.6.
Leisure (1994). Favourite leisure activities (hours weekly): watching television 17.1; listening to radio 10.3; reading 8.8, of which books 3.8, newspapers 3.3; gardening 2.1.
Material well-being (2000). Households possessing: automobile 72.0%, telephone 93.0%, television receiver 98.3% (colour 95%)[7], refrigerator 98.5%, washing machine 92.0%, central heating 91.0%, video recorder 87.0%.

National economy

Budget (2000–01). Revenue: £372,561,000,000 (income tax 37.7%, customs and excise taxes 35.3%, social security contributions 15.8%). Expenditures: £354,867,000,000 (social protection 40.6%, health 15.5%, debt interest 7.6%, defense 7.5%).
Total national debt (March 31, 2000): £426,239,200,000 (U.S.$679,894,200,000).
Gross national product (at current market prices; 2000): U.S.$1,459,500,000,000 (U.S.$24,430 per capita).

Population (2001 census[1])

Countries[2]	population		population		population
England	49,138,831	Peterborough	156,060	Scotland	5,062,011
Counties		Plymouth	240,718	**Unitary Districts**	
Bedfordshire	381,571	Poole	138,299	Aberdeen City	212,125
Buckinghamshire	479,028	Portsmouth	186,704	Aberdeenshire	226,871
Cambridgeshire	552,655	Reading	143,124	Angus	108,400
Cheshire	673,777	Redcar and		Argyll and Bute	91,306
Cornwall	501,267	Cleveland	139,141	City of Edinburgh	448,624
Cumbria	487,607	Rutland	34,560	Clackmannanshire	48,077
Derbyshire	734,581	Slough	119,070	Dumfries and	
Devon	704,499	South		Galloway	147,765
Dorset	390,986	Gloucestershire	217,478	Dundee City	145,663
Durham	493,470	Southampton	245,644	East Ayrshire	120,235
East Sussex	492,324	Southend-on-Sea	160,256	East Dumbarton-	
Essex	1,310,922	Stockton-on-		shire	108,243
Gloucestershire	564,559	Tees	178,405	East Lothian	90,088
Hampshire	1,240,032	Stoke-on-Trent	240,643	East Renfrewshire	89,311
Hertfordshire	1,033,977	Swindon	180,061	Eilean Siar[5]	26,502
Isle of Wight[3]	132,719	Telford and		Falkirk	145,191
Kent	1,329,653	Wrenkin	158,285	Fife	349,429
Lancashire	1,134,976	Thurrock	143,042	Glasgow City	577,869
Leicestershire	609,579	Torbay	129,702	Highland	208,914
Lincolnshire	646,646	Warrington	191,084	Inverclyde	84,203
Norfolk	796,733	West Berkshire	144,445	Midlothian	80,941
North Yorkshire	569,660	Windsor and		Moray	86,940
Northamptonshire	629,676	Maidenhead	133,606	North Ayrshire	135,817
Northumberland	307,186	Wokingham	150,257	North Lanarkshire	321,067
Nottinghamshire	748,503	York	181,131	Orkney Islands	19,245
Oxfordshire	605,492	**Metropolitan**		Perth and Kinross	134,949
Shropshire	283,240	**Counties/Greater**		Renfrewshire	172,867
Somerset	498,093	**London**		Scottish Borders	106,764
Staffordshire	806,737	Greater London[4]	7,172,036	Shetland Islands	21,988
Suffolk	668,548	Greater		South Ayrshire	112,097
Surrey	1,059,015	Manchester	2,482,352	South Lanarkshire	302,216
Warwickshire	505,885	Merseyside	1,362,034	Stirling	86,212
West Sussex	753,612	South Yorkshire	1,266,337	West Dumbarton-	
Wiltshire	432,973	Tyne and Wear	1,075,979	shire	93,378
Worcestershire	542,107	West Midlands	2,555,596	West Lothian	158,714
Unitary Districts		West Yorkshire	2,079,217		
Bath and				Northern Ireland	1,685,267
NE Somerset	169,045	**Wales**	2,903,085	**Districts**	
Blackburn with		**Unitary Districts**		Antrim	48,366
Darwen	137,471	Blaenau Gwent	128,650	Ards	73,244
Blackpool	142,284	Bridgend	169,521	Armagh	54,263
Bournemouth	163,441	Caerphilly	305,340	Ballymena	58,610
Bracknell Forest	109,606	Cardiff	173,635	Ballymoney	26,894
Brighton and		Carmarthenshire	75,384	Banbridge	41,392
Hove	247,820	Ceredigion	109,597	Belfast	277,391
Bristol	380,615	Conway	93,092	Carrickfergus	37,659
Darlington	174,844	Denbighshire	148,565	Castlereagh	66,488
Derby	97,822	Flintshire	116,838	Coleraine	56,315
East Riding of		Gwynedd	66,828	Cookstown	32,581
Yorkshire	221,716	Isle of Anglesey	70,058	Craigavon	80,671
Halton	314,076	Merthyr Tydfil	55,983	Derry	105,066
Hartlepool	118,215	Monmouthshire	84,879	Down	63,828
Herefordshire	88,629	Neath and		Dungannon	47,735
Kingston upon		Port Talbot	134,471	Fermanagh	57,527
Hull	243,595	Newport	137,017	Larne	30,832
Leicester	279,923	Pembrokeshire	112,901	Limvady	32,422
Luton	184,390	Powys	126,344	Lisburn	108,694
Medway	249,502	Rhondda, Cynon,		Magherafelt	39,780
Middlesborough	134,847	Taff	231,952	Moyle	15,933
Milton Keynes	207,063	Swansea	223,293	Newry and Mourne	87,058
NE Lincolnshire	157,983	Torfaen	90,967	Newtownabbey	79,995
North Lincolnshire	152,839	The Vale of		North Down	76,323
North Somerset	188,556	Glamorgan	119,293	Omagh	47,952
Nottingham	266,995	Wrexham	128,477	Strabane	38,248
				TOTAL	58,789,194

Demography

Population (2002): 60,178,000.
Area: 94,248 sq mi, 244,101 sq km, of which England 50,351 sq mi, 130,410 sq km; Wales 8,015 sq mi, 20,758 sq km; Scotland 30,421 sq mi, 78,789 sq km; Northern Ireland (figures represent remainder) 5,461 sq mi, 14,144 sq km.
Density (2002): persons per sq mi 638.5, persons per sq km 246.5.
Urban-rural (1999): urban 88.2%; rural 10.8%.
Age breakdown (2001): under 15, 18.9%; 15–29, 18.8%; 30–44, 22.5%; 45–59, 18.9%; 60–74, 13.3%; 75 and over, 7.6%.
Population projection: (2010) 61,753,000; (2020) 63,887,000.
Ethnic composition (1998): white 93.2%; black 1.8%, of which Caribbean origin 0.9%, African origin 0.7%; Asian Indian 1.7%; Pakistani 1.2%; Bangladeshi 0.5%; Chinese 0.2%; other and not stated 1.4%.

Structure of gross domestic product and labour force

	2000			
	in value £'000,000	% of total value	labour force	% of labour force
Agriculture	8,912	0.9	342,000	1.2
Mining[8]	24,244	2.6	272,000	0.9
Manufacturing	155,531	16.5	3,958,000	13.5
Construction	43,287	4.6	1,188,000	4.0
Public utilities	15,677	1.7	135,000	0.5
Transp. and commun.	68,195	7.2	1,415,000	4.8
Trade[9]	130,782	13.9	4,095,000	13.9
Finance	234,379	24.8	988,000	3.4
Pub. admin., defense	144,580	15.3	5,979,000	20.3
Services	42,560	4.5	5,942,000	20.2
Other	75,268[10]	8.0[10]	5,098,000[11]	17.3[11]
TOTAL	943,412[12]	100.0	29,412,000	100.0

Land use (1994): forested 10.4%; meadows and pastures 45.9%; agricultural and under permanent cultivation 24.8%; other 18.9%.

Tourism (2000): receipts from visitors U.S.$19,544,000,000; expenditures by nationals abroad U.S.$36,267,000,000.

Production (metric tons except as noted). Agriculture, forestry, fishing (2001): wheat 12,060,000, sugar beets 10,000,000, barley 6,690,000, potatoes 6,647,000, rapeseed 1,129,000, oats 680,000, carrots 674,000, green peas 436,000; livestock (number of live animals) 42,000,000 sheep, 11,000,000 cattle, 6,500,000 pigs; roundwood (1999) 7,451,000 cu m; fish catch (1999) 992,552. Mining and quarrying (1999): china clay (kaolin) 2,304,000; ball clay and pottery clay 985,000. Manufacturing (value added in £'000,000; 1998): electrical and optical equipment 19,478; food and beverages 19,337; paper, printing, and publishing 17,717; iron and ferro-alloys 17,375; transport equipment 16,968; chemicals and chemical products 14,582; machinery and equipment 13,295; textiles and leather products 6,704. Construction (value in £; 1995)[6]: residential 7,135,000,000; nonresidential 13,877,000,000.

Financial aggregates

	1995	1996	1997	1998	1999	2000	2001
Exchange rate							
U.S. dollar per £	1.58	1.56	1.64	1.66	1.62	1.52	1.44
SDRs per £	1.04	1.18	1.22	1.18	1.18	1.14	1.15
International reserves (U.S.$)							
Total (excl. gold; '000,000,000)	42.02	39.90	32.32	32.21	35.87	43.89	37.32
SDRs ('000,000,000)	0.41	0.34	0.47	0.47	0.51	0.33	0.29
Reserve pos. in IMF							
('000,000,000)	2.42	2.43	2.97	4.38	5.28	4.28	5.05
Foreign exchange	39.18	37.12	28.88	27.36	30.08	39.28	31.94
Gold ('000,000 fine troy oz)	18.43	18.43	18.42	23.00	20.55	15.67	11.42
% world reserves	2.0	2.0	2.1	2.4	2.1	1.6	1.2
Interest and prices							
Central bank discount (%)	...	...	...	...	...	...	...
Govt. bond yield (%) long term	8.26	8.10	7.09	5.45	4.70	4.68	4.78
Industrial share prices							
(1995 = 100)	100.0	113.3	128.3	150.5	...	...	...
Balance of payments							
(U.S.$'000,000,000)							
Balance of visible trade,	−18,266	−18,870	−19,490	−35,020	−42,340	−43,580	−48,250
Imports, f.o.b.	259,154	278,400	−300,800	−305,800	−311,280	−326,760	−324,200
Exports, f.o.b.	240,888	259,530	281,310	271,780	268,940	283,180	275,950
Balance of invisibles	7,697	19,110	30,320	34,870	26,360	19,120	18,880
Balance of payments,							
current account	−10,569	240	10,830	−150	−15,980	−24,460	−29,370

Manufacturing, mining, and construction enterprises (1997)

	no. of establish-ments	no. of employees	annual wages as a % of avg. of all wages	annual value added (£'000,000)
Manufacturing				
Food, beverages, and tobacco	15,106	880,000	92.5	33,718
Paper and paper products;				
printing and publishing	62,641	879,000	113.8	31,386
Chemical products	8,242	532,000	127.0	28,814
Metal manufacturing	61,867	939,000	94.7	26,381
Machinery and equipment	28,199	759,000	107.9	25,727
Electrical and data-				
processing equipment	10,466	397,000	101.2	13,279
Transport equipment	2,723	249,000	116.4	9,698
Rubber and plastics	8,049	312,000	90.7	9,115
Textiles	11,615	335,000	76.2	7,465
Wood and wood products	15,851	157,000	74.2	3,696
Furniture	7,529	132,000	86.7	3,452
Clothing and footwear	8,640	185,000	56.7	3,333
Mining[13]				
Extraction of coal, mineral oil,				
and natural gas	358	80,000[14]	...	10,261
Extraction of minerals other				
than fuels	921	30,200	...	1,090
Construction[13]	199,363	1,016,000[14]	...	19,274

Retail trade enterprises (1992)

	no. of enter-prises	no. of employees	weekly wage as a % of all wages	annual turnover (£'000,000)[15]
Food and grocery,	60,119	854,000	...	51,462
of which				
large grocery	71	579,000	...	40,837
other grocery	18,557	95,000	...	4,086
meats	12,149	58,000	...	2,523
Household goods,	45,532	299,000	...	20,881
of which				
electrical and musical goods	10,887	87,000	...	7,270
furniture	11,927	60,000	...	4,575
Drink, confectionery, and tobacco,	46,671	254,000	...	13,810
of which				
tobacco and confectionery	41,502	215,000	...	10,880
Clothing and footwear,	24,923	264,000	...	12,428
of which				
women's, girls', and infants' wear	13,624	102,000	...	4,771
footwear	3,098	67,000	...	2,589
men's and boys' wear	3,751	37,000	...	2,063
Pharmaceuticals	7,560	87,000	...	5,231

Energy production (consumption): electricity (kW-hr; 2000) 341,808,000,000 ([1997] 361,529,000,000); hard coal (metric tons; 2000) 31,200,000 ([1999] 58,800,000); crude petroleum (barrels; 2000) 884,273,000 (620,500,000); petroleum products (metric tons; 1997) 89,779,000 (72,673,000); natural gas (cu m; 2000) 128,425,000,000 ([1997] 102,506,000,000).

Population economically active (2000): total 29,412,000, activity rate of total population 49.2% (participation rates: ages 16–64, 74.3%; female 44.5%; unemployed 5.5%).

Price and earnings indexes (1995 = 100)

	1995	1996	1997	1998	1999	2000	2001
Consumer price index	100.0	102.4	105.7	109.3	111.0	114.2	116.3
Monthly earnings index	100.0	103.5	108.0	113.5	119.0	124.4	129.8

Household income and expenditure (1999–2000). Average household size 2.3; average annual disposable income per household £17,170 (U.S.$27,750); sources of income: wages and salaries 67.0%, social security benefits 12.0%, income from self-employment 8.8%, dividends and interest 4.0%; expenditure: food and beverages 19.9%, transport and vehicles 16.7%, housing 16.6%, household goods 8.4%, clothing 5.7%, energy 3.1%.

Foreign trade

Balance of trade (current prices)

	1996	1997	1998	1999	2000	2001
£'000,000	−16,549	−15,540	−25,466	−29,765	−34,856	−37,271
% of total	4.7%	4.3%	7.2%	8.2%	8.6%	9.1%

Imports (2000): £218,036,000,000 (machinery and transport equipment 45.5%, of which electrical equipment 23.2%, road vehicles 10.6%; chemicals 9.4%, of which organic chemicals 2.4%, plastics 1.9%; clothing and footwear 4.8%; petroleum and petroleum products 4.1%; food 3.4%; textiles 2.0%; paper and paperboard 2.0%). *Major import sources:* U.S. 13.1%; Germany 12.7%; France 8.4%; The Netherlands 6.9%; Belgium-Luxembourg 5.3%; Japan 4.7%; Ireland 4.4%; Italy 4.3%; Spain 2.7%; Hong Kong 2.7%.

Exports (2002): £187,656,000,000 (machinery and transport equipment 46.7%, of which electrical equipment 22.6%, road vehicles 8.3%; chemicals 13.3%, of which medicinal products 3.8%, organic chemicals 3.0%; petroleum and petroleum products 8.3%; professional and scientific 3.9%; iron and steel products 1.5%; food 0.9%). *Major export destinations:* U.S. 15.7%; Germany 12.1%; France 9.9%; The Netherlands 8.0%; Ireland 6.6%; Belgium-Luxembourg 5.5%; Italy 4.5%; Spain 4.4%; Sweden 2.2%; Japan 2.0%; Switzerland 1.6%.

Transport and communications

Transport. Railroads (1999–2000)[6]: length 23,518 mi[16], 37,849 km[16]; passenger-mi 24,369,000,000[17], passenger-km 39,218,000,000[17]; ton-mi cargo 12,800,000,000, metric ton-km cargo 18,400,000,000. Roads (1999): total length 231,097 mi, 371,914 km (paved 100%). Vehicles (2000): passenger cars 22,758,000, trucks and buses 2,511,000. Merchant marine (1999): vessels (over 100 gross tons) 937; total deadweight tonnage 7,200,000. Air transport (2000): passenger-mi 105,924,300,000, passenger-km 170,469,000,000; short ton-mi cargo 3,534,200,000, metric ton-km cargo 5,159,900,000; airports (1997) 57.

Communications

Medium	date	unit	number	units per 1,000 persons
Daily newspapers	1996	circulation	19,332,000	332
Radio	1997	receivers	84,500,000	1,443
Television	1999	receivers	38,800,000	652
Telephones	2001	main lines	34,710,000	578
Cellular telephones	2001	subscribers	47,026,000	783
Personal computers	2001	units	22,000,000	366
Internet	1999	users	24,000,000	400

Education and health

Literacy (1990): total population literate, virtually 100%[18].

Education (1998–99)[19]

	schools	teachers	students	student/teacher ratio
Primary (age 5–10) }	31,956	226,696	5,028,684	22.2
Secondary (age 11–19) }		230,635	3,694,311	16.0
Voc., teacher tr.	...	...	586,000[20]	...
Higher[21, 22]	70	c. 48,000	c. 810,000	c. 17.0

Health: physicians (1993) 164,000 (1 per 355 persons); hospital beds (2000) 242,671 (1 per 246 persons); infant mortality rate (1999) 5.8.

Food (2000): daily per capita caloric intake 3,334 (vegetable products 70%, animal products 30%); 133% of FAO recommended minimum requirement.

Military

Total active duty personnel (2001): 211,430 (army 53.9%, navy 20.6%, air force 25.5%); U.S. troops (2001) 11,300. *Military expenditure as percentage of GNP* (1999): 2.5% (world 2.4%); per capita expenditure U.S.$615.

[1]Preliminary. [2]The reorganization of first-order administrative units was completed in 1999: England's former 46 counties (including 7 metropolitan counties) reorganized into 35 counties, 45 unitary districts, 6 metropolitan counties, and Greater London; Wales's former 8 counties reorganized into 22 unitary districts; Scotland's former 9 regions and 3 island councils organized into 32 unitary districts; Northern Ireland remained. [3]Only unitary district with county status. [4]Has administrative authority from July 2000. [5]Formerly Western Isles. [6]Great Britain only. [7]1992. [8]Includes petroleum extraction. [9]Includes hotels. [10]Plus rent and value-added taxes; less imputed bank service charges. [11]Includes 1,619,000 unemployed and 3,139,000 self-employed not distributed by sector and 207,000 military personnel. [12]Detail does not add to total given because of rounding. [13]1993. [14]1992. [15]Includes value-added taxes. [16]1990. [17]2000–01. [18]A survey in 1986–87, however, put the number of functional illiterates at 9–12% of the adult population. [19]Public sector only. [20]1992–93. [21]1994–95. [22]Universities only.

Internet resources for further information:
• Office for National Statistics http://www.statistics.gov.uk

United States

Official name: United States of America.
Form of government: federal republic with two legislative houses (Senate [100]; House of Representatives [435[1]]).
Head of state and government: President.
Capital: Washington, D.C.
Official language: none.
Official religion: none.
Monetary unit: 1 dollar (U.S.$) = 100 cents; valuation (Sept. 23, 2002) 1 U.S.$ = €0.98; 1 U.S.$ = £0.64.

Area and population

States	Capitals	area sq mi	area sq km	population 2000 census (unadjusted)
Alabama	Montgomery	51,718	133,950	4,447,100
Alaska	Juneau	587,875	1,522,595	626,932
Arizona	Phoenix	114,006	295,275	5,130,632
Arkansas	Little Rock	53,182	137,741	2,673,400
California	Sacramento	158,647	410,895	33,871,648
Colorado	Denver	104,100	269,619	4,301,261
Connecticut	Hartford	5,006	12,966	3,405,565
Delaware	Dover	2,026	5,247	783,600
Florida	Tallahassee	58,680	151,981	15,982,378
Georgia	Atlanta	58,930	152,629	8,186,453
Hawaii	Honolulu	6,459	16,729	1,211,537
Idaho	Boise	83,574	216,456	1,293,953
Illinois	Springfield	57,918	150,008	12,419,293
Indiana	Indianapolis	36,420	94,328	6,080,485
Iowa	Des Moines	56,276	145,755	2,926,324
Kansas	Topeka	82,282	213,110	2,688,418
Kentucky	Frankfort	40,411	104,664	4,041,769
Louisiana	Baton Rouge	47,719	123,592	4,468,976
Maine	Augusta	33,128	85,801	1,274,923
Maryland	Annapolis	10,455	27,078	5,296,486
Massachusetts	Boston	8,262	21,399	6,349,097
Michigan	Lansing	96,705	250,466	9,938,444
Minnesota	St. Paul	86,943	225,182	4,919,479
Mississippi	Jackson	47,695	123,530	2,844,658
Missouri	Jefferson City	69,709	180,546	5,595,211
Montana	Helena	147,046	380,849	902,195
Nebraska	Lincoln	77,359	200,360	1,711,263
Nevada	Carson City	110,567	286,368	1,998,257
New Hampshire	Concord	9,283	24,043	1,235,786
New Jersey	Trenton	7,790	20,176	8,414,350
New Mexico	Santa Fe	121,598	314,939	1,819,046
New York	Albany	53,013	137,304	18,976,457
North Carolina	Raleigh	52,672	136,420	8,049,313
North Dakota	Bismarck	70,704	183,123	642,200
Ohio	Columbus	44,828	116,104	11,353,140
Oklahoma	Oklahoma City	69,903	181,049	3,450,654
Oregon	Salem	97,052	251,364	3,421,399
Pennsylvania	Harrisburg	45,759	118,516	12,281,054
Rhode Island	Providence	1,213	3,142	1,048,319
South Carolina	Columbia	31,117	80,593	4,012,012
South Dakota	Pierre	77,121	199,743	754,844
Tennessee	Nashville	42,145	109,155	5,689,283
Texas	Austin	266,873	691,201	20,851,820
Utah	Salt Lake City	84,904	219,901	2,233,169
Vermont	Montpelier	9,615	24,903	608,827
Virginia	Richmond	40,598	105,149	7,078,515
Washington	Olympia	68,126	176,446	5,894,121
West Virginia	Charleston	24,232	62,761	1,808,344
Wisconsin	Madison	65,500	169,645	5,363,675
Wyoming	Cheyenne	97,819	253,351	493,782
District				
District of Columbia	—	68	176	572,059
TOTAL		3,675,031[2]	9,518,323[2]	281,421,906[3]

Demography

Population (2002): 287,602,000[4].
Density (2002)[4]: persons per sq mi 78.3, persons per sq km 30.2.
Urban-rural (2000): urban 77.2%; rural 22.8%.
Sex distribution (2000): male 49.06%; female 50.94%.
Age breakdown (2000): under 15, 21.4%; 15–29, 20.8%; 30–44, 23.3%; 45–59, 18.2%; 60–74, 10.4%; 75 and over, 5.9%.
Population projection: (2010) 307,668,000; (2020) 333,385,000.
Doubling time: not applicable; doubling time exceeds 100 years.
Population by race and Hispanic[5] origin (2000): non-Hispanic white 70.5%; Hispanic 12.5%; non-Hispanic black 12.3%; Asian and Pacific Islander 3.8%; American Indian and Eskimo 0.9%.
Religious affiliation (1995): Christian 85.3%, of which Protestant 57.9%, Roman Catholic 21.0%, other Christian 6.4%; Jewish 2.1%; Muslim 1.9%; nonreligious 8.7%; other 2.0%.
Mobility (2000). Population living in the same residence as in 1999: 84.0%; different residence, same county 9.0%; different county, same state 3.0%; different state 3.0%; moved from abroad 1.0%.
Households (2000). Total households 105,480,000 (married-couple families 54,493,000 [51.7%]). Average household size (2000) 2.7; 1 person 25.9%, 2 persons 32.1%, 3 persons 16.9%, 4 persons 14.9%, 5 or more persons 10.2%. Family households: 71,787,000 (68.1%); nonfamily 33,693,000 (31.9%), of which 1-person 80.8%.
Immigration (2000): permanent immigrants admitted 849,807, from Mexico 20.2%, former U.S.S.R. 5.2%, China 4.9%, the Philippines 4.8%, Africa 4.8%, India 4.6%, Vietnam 3.0%, Haiti 2.6%, El Salvador 2.6%, Canada 2.5%, Cuba 2.3%, Dominican Republic 2.1%, Jamaica 1.8%, South Korea 1.8%, other 36.8%. Refugees (end of 2000) 508,222[6]. Asylum seekers (end of 2000): 386,330[6].

Components of population change (1990–99)

States	Net change in population	Annual percentage change	Births	Deaths	Net migration
Alabama	329,473	0.8	568,961	387,158	147,670
Alaska	69,457	1.3	98,976	22,291	−7,228
Arizona	1,112,993	2.9	670,677	317,200	759,516
Arkansas	200,749	0.9	330,123	244,180	114,806
California	3,333,694	1.2	5,227,258	2,039,044	145,480
Colorado	761,660	2.3	513,908	225,699	473,451
Connecticut	−5,085	−0.1	423,922	268,782	−160,225
Delaware	87,370	1.3	97,768	58,165	47,767
Florida	2,173,173	1.7	1,781,648	1,370,234	1,761,759
Georgia	1,310,091	2.0	1,053,424	525,580	782,247
Hawaii	77,268	0.7	173,388	67,676	−28,444
Idaho	244,966	2.4	166,298	77,951	156,619
Illinois	697,768	0.6	1,735,493	971,944	−65,781
Indiana	398,745	0.8	779,368	482,740	102,117
Iowa	92,582	0.4	349,191	256,794	185
Kansas	176,464	0.7	348,226	215,686	43,924
Kentucky	273,933	0.8	494,758	340,897	120,072
Louisiana	150,209	0.4	629,286	362,228	−116,849
Maine	25,112	0.2	137,791	107,664	−5,015
Maryland	390,881	0.9	687,293	375,178	78,766
Massachusetts	158,744	0.3	778,803	506,880	−113,179
Michigan	568,488	0.6	1,287,572	763,166	44,082
Minnesota	399,843	0.9	603,264	338,093	134,672
Mississippi	193,144	0.8	389,349	246,225	50,020
Missouri	351,437	0.7	697,038	492,127	146,526
Montana	83,714	1.1	103,358	69,332	49,688
Nebraska	87,611	0.6	217,510	139,754	9,855
Nevada	607,578	4.5	227,622	110,437	490,393
New Hampshire	91,882	0.9	142,027	83,680	33,535
New Jersey	395,662	0.5	1,079,022	667,367	−15,993
New Mexico	224,775	1.5	254,934	111,862	81,703
New York	205,823	0.1	2,539,280	1,519,562	−813,895
North Carolina	1,018,341	1.6	967,386	586,354	637,309
North Dakota	−5,134	−0.1	78,833	54,150	−29,817
Ohio	409,539	0.4	1,454,713	957,171	−88,003
Oklahoma	212,468	0.7	437,373	298,499	73,594
Oregon	473,817	1.7	399,411	255,204	329,610
Pennsylvania	111,174	0.1	1,438,566	1,163,384	−164,008
Rhode Island	−12,645	−0.1	125,103	89,187	−48,561
South Carolina	399,426	1.2	498,067	301,259	202,618
South Dakota	37,129	0.6	98,048	62,765	1,846
Tennessee	606,332	1.3	687,916	463,719	382,135
Texas	3,057,806	1.8	3,025,567	1,254,005	1,286,244
Utah	406,986	2.3	369,419	98,393	135,960
Vermont	30,982	0.6	67,101	44,797	8,678
Virginia	683,715	1.1	872,681	477,233	288,267
Washington	889,692	1.8	729,025	372,964	533,631
West Virginia	13,451	0.1	198,388	184,750	−187
Wisconsin	358,492	0.8	637,733	412,353	133,112
Wyoming	26,013	0.6	60,099	32,704	−1,382
District					
District of Columbia	−87,900	−1.7	87,167	59,836	−115,231
TOTAL/RATE	23,899,888	1.0	36,820,132	20,934,303	8,014,059

Major cities (2000): New York 8,008,278; Los Angeles 3,694,820; Chicago 2,896,016; Houston 1,953,631; Philadelphia 1,517,550; Phoenix 1,321,045; San Diego 1,223,400; Dallas 1,188,580; San Antonio 1,144,646; Detroit 951,270.

Other principal cities (2000)

	population		population		population
Akron	217,074	Fresno	427,652	Omaha	390,007
Albuquerque	448,607	Honolulu	371,657	Pittsburgh	334,563
Anaheim	328,014	Indianapolis	791,926	Portland (Ore.)	529,121
Anchorage	260,283	Jacksonville	735,617	Raleigh	276,093
Arlington (Tex.)	332,969	Jersey City	240,055	Riverside	255,166
Atlanta	416,474	Kansas City (Mo.)	441,545	Rochester	219,773
Austin	656,562	Las Vegas	478,434	Sacramento	407,018
Bakersfield	247,057	Lexington (Ky.)	260,512	St. Louis	348,189
Baltimore	651,154	Lincoln	225,581	St. Paul	287,151
Baton Rouge	227,818	Long Beach	461,522	St. Petersburg	248,232
Birmingham	242,820	Louisville	256,231	San Francisco	766,733
Boston	589,141	Madison	208,054	San Jose	894,243
Buffalo	292,648	Memphis	650,100	Santa Ana	337,977
Charlotte	540,828	Mesa (Ariz.)	396,375	Seattle	563,374
Cincinnati	331,285	Miami	362,470	Shreveport	200,145
Cleveland	478,403	Milwaukee	596,974	Stockton	243,771
Colorado Springs	360,890	Minneapolis	382,618	Tampa	303,447
Columbus	711,470	Nashville	545,524	Toledo	313,619
Corpus Christi	277,454	New Orleans	484,674	Tucson	486,699
Denver	554,636	Newark	273,546	Tulsa	393,049
El Paso	563,662	Norfolk	234,403	Virginia Beach	425,257
Fort Wayne	205,727	Oakland	399,484	Washington, D.C.	572,059
Fort Worth	534,694	Oklahoma City	506,132	Wichita	344,284

Place of birth (2000): native-born 245,708,000 (89.6%); foreign-born 28,379,000 (10.4%), of which Mexico 7,841,000, the Philippines 1,222,000, China and Hong Kong 1,067,000, India 1,007,000, Cuba 952,000, Vietnam 863,000, El Salvador 765,000, South Korea 701,000.

Vital statistics

Birth rate per 1,000 population (2000): 14.7 (world avg. 22.5); (1999) legitimate 67.0%; illegitimate 33.0%.
Death rate per 1,000 population (2000): 8.7 (world avg. 9.0).
Natural increase rate per 1,000 population (2000): 6.0 (world avg. 13.5).
Total fertility rate (avg. births per childbearing woman; 2000): 2.0.
Marriage rate per 1,000 population (1999): 8.6; median age at first marriage (1991): men 26.3 years, women 24.1 years.
Divorce rate per 1,000 population (1998): 4.2.
Life expectancy at birth (2000): white male 74.8 years, black and other male (1996) 68.9 years; white female 80.4 years, black and other female 76.1 (1996) years.

Vital statistics (1999)

States	Live births	Birth rate per 1,000 population	Death rate per 1,000 population[7]	Infant mortality rate per 1,000 live births[7]	Abortion rate per 1,000 live births[8]	Life expectancy[9]
Alabama	62,122	14.2	10.1	10.2	248.8	73.6
Alaska	9,950	16.1	4.2	5.9	196.1	...
Arizona	81,145	17.0	8.2	7.5	248.3	76.1
Arkansas	36,729	14.4	10.8	8.9	170.5	74.3
California	518,508	15.6	6.9	5.8	434.8	75.9
Colorado	62,167	15.3	6.7	6.7	294.7	77.0
Connecticut	43,310	13.2	9.1	7.0	383.7	76.9
Delaware	10,676	14.2	8.9	9.6	582.5	74.8
Florida	197,023	13.0	10.6	7.2	466.3	75.8
Georgia	126,717	16.3	7.9	8.5	329.5	73.6
Hawaii	17,038	14.4	6.8	6.9	430.1	78.2
Idaho	19,872	15.9	7.5	7.2	111.1	76.9
Illinois	182,068	14.5	8.7	8.4	366.0	74.9
Indiana	86,031	13.1	8.9	7.6	169.1	75.4
Iowa	37,558	13.1	9.9	6.6	163.0	77.3
Kansas	38,782	14.6	9.3	7.0	268.8	76.8
Kentucky	54,403	13.7	9.6	7.5	152.7	74.4
Louisiana	67,136	15.4	9.2	9.1	228.7	73.0
Maine	13,616	10.9	9.8	6.3	215.8	73.1
Maryland	71,967	13.9	8.2	8.6	428.2	76.4
Massachusetts	80,939	13.1	9.0	5.1	502.5	74.8
Michigan	133,607	13.5	8.7	8.2	364.0	75.0
Minnesota	65,970	13.8	7.9	5.9	237.0	77.8
Mississippi	42,684	15.4	10.1	10.1	72.6	73.0
Missouri	75,432	13.8	10.1	7.7	150.7	75.3
Montana	10,785	12.2	9.0	7.4	270.3	76.2
Nebraska	23,907	14.3	9.1	7.3	172.4	76.9
Nevada	29,362	16.2	8.3	7.0	640.0	74.2
New Hampshire	14,041	11.7	8.1	4.4	204.1	76.7
New Jersey	114,105	14.0	8.8	6.4	531.4	75.4
New Mexico	27,191	15.6	7.7	7.2	185.9	75.7
New York	255,612	14.0	8.6	6.3	648.5	74.7
North Carolina	113,795	14.9	9.0	9.3	344.5	74.5
North Dakota	7,639	12.1	9.3	8.6	117.6	77.6
Ohio	152,584	13.6	9.5	8.0	266.1	75.3
Oklahoma	49,010	14.6	10.2	8.5	196.9	75.1
Oregon	45,204	13.6	9.0	5.4	373.8	76.4
Pennsylvania	145,347	12.1	10.6	7.1	270.1	75.4
Rhode Island	12,366	12.5	9.7	7.0	468.8	76.5
South Carolina	54,948	14.1	9.1	9.6	216.1	73.5
South Dakota	10,524	14.4	9.3	9.1	95.2	76.9
Tennessee	77,803	14.2	10.0	8.2	245.9	74.3
Texas	349,245	17.4	7.2	6.4	275.7	75.1
Utah	46,290	21.7	5.6	5.6	101.0	77.7
Vermont	6,567	11.1	8.4	7.0	294.1	76.5
Virginia	95,469	13.9	8.0	7.7	334.8	75.2
Washington	79,586	13.8	7.5	5.7	323.8	76.8
West Virginia	20,728	11.5	11.5	8.0	141.5	74.3
Wisconsin	68,208	13.0	8.8	7.2	192.6	76.9
Wyoming	6,129	12.8	8.0	7.2	...	76.2
District						
District of Columbia	7,522	14.5	11.4	12.5	2,333.3	68.0
TOTAL/RATE	3,959,417	14.5	8.7	7.2	349.8	75.8

Major causes of death per 100,000 population (1998): cardiovascular diseases 348.0, of which ischemic heart disease 170.1, cerebrovascular diseases 58.6, atherosclerosis 5.7; malignant neoplasms (cancers) 200.3; diseases of the respiratory system 74.9, of which pneumonia 34.0; accidents and adverse effects 36.2, of which motor-vehicle accidents 16.1; diabetes mellitus 24.0; AIDS 17.2; suicide 11.3; chronic liver disease and cirrhosis 9.3.

Death rates by major causes (1997)

States	Total death rate per 100,000 population	Circulatory diseases	Malignant neoplasms (cancers)	Pulmonary diseases	Suicide and homicide	Other
Alabama	1,001.5	381.0	221.7	66.8	23.9	308.1
Alaska	422.6	113.1	102.1	21.7	30.0	155.7
Arizona	813.7	277.9	185.5	54.5	26.1	269.7
Arkansas	1,103.7	433.0	240.3	97.5	25.9	307.0
California	696.0	264.6	161.1	51.8	19.4	199.1
Colorado	658.3	210.5	145.1	43.9	20.4	238.4
Connecticut	899.6	356.0	218.3	58.2	11.8	255.3
Delaware	889.9	319.7	228.1	47.4	16.3	278.4
Florida	1,054.3	408.2	260.0	68.4	22.0	295.7
Georgia	792.8	293.0	174.0	57.0	20.8	248.0
Hawaii	665.1	260.4	155.6	59.8	15.6	173.7
Idaho	741.7	266.8	160.9	58.7	20.9	234.4
Illinois	865.1	335.0	205.8	60.7	17.4	246.2
Indiana	906.0	349.4	210.3	65.3	19.8	261.2
Iowa	970.9	395.1	222.0	75.7	14.6	263.5
Kansas	915.3	346.6	201.1	66.2	18.4	283.0
Kentucky	972.3	382.8	229.5	64.0	19.1	276.9
Louisiana	919.3	330.8	214.9	58.1	28.2	287.3
Maine	965.6	356.3	239.9	63.5	12.8	293.1
Maryland	820.4	286.9	198.8	51.2	21.1	262.4
Massachusetts	893.9	325.5	223.7	55.7	10.3	278.7
Michigan	852.3	337.7	200.6	58.9	18.4	236.7
Minnesota	787.8	269.1	187.3	64.0	12.9	254.5
Mississippi	1,007.3	423.3	214.2	68.0	26.6	275.2
Missouri	1,005.6	410.3	221.4	68.6	21.1	284.2
Montana	884.0	301.8	203.5	61.9	25.0	291.8
Nebraska	922.3	364.5	195.4	66.5	14.5	281.4
Nevada	797.9	280.0	189.6	47.6	35.0	245.7
New Hampshire	806.5	297.7	205.8	58.8	13.8	230.4
New Jersey	895.8	341.8	225.5	51.3	11.8	265.4
New Mexico	731.5	233.7	159.9	44.4	26.8	266.7
New York	874.7	380.1	206.0	44.2	13.9	230.5
North Carolina	889.2	330.4	204.3	70.4	21.4	262.7
North Dakota	919.5	360.3	206.3	75.2	12.5	265.2
Ohio	941.7	368.3	220.7	61.5	14.5	276.7
Oklahoma	1,023.3	411.9	218.1	72.1	23.7	297.5
Oregon	887.0	311.0	208.7	79.2	20.6	267.5
Pennsylvania	1,064.3	420.1	251.1	69.6	18.2	305.3

Death rates by major causes (1997) (continued)

States	Total death rate per 100,000 population	Circulatory diseases	Malignant neoplasms (cancers)	Pulmonary diseases	Suicide and homicide	Other
Rhode Island	994.5	400.0	249.7	69.3	10.1	265.4
South Carolina	896.0	338.9	203.2	75.7	21.0	257.2
South Dakota	930.3	366.0	209.8	77.4	20.2	256.9
Tennessee	981.1	385.2	220.9	74.9	24.0	276.1
Texas	734.5	276.6	165.6	52.2	18.6	221.5
Utah	562.3	188.5	103.6	42.5	17.7	210.0
Vermont	857.9	314.6	208.8	58.9	12.4	263.2
Virginia	799.7	292.1	192.0	60.0	18.9	236.7
Washington	739.0	258.1	178.9	60.0	17.7	224.3
West Virginia	1,150.0	449.4	262.0	68.1	19.7	350.8
Wisconsin	868.4	336.1	204.6	71.2	15.2	241.3
Wyoming	780.6	265.4	175.9	48.6	24.2	266.5
District						
District of Columbia	1,158.7	369.0	254.8	63.5	54.8	416.6
U.S. RATE	864.7	331.3	201.6	59.7	18.8	253.3

Morbidity rates of infectious diseases per 100,000 population (1998): chlamydia 223.4; gonorrhea 131.7; chicken pox 30.5; AIDS 17.2; syphilis 14.0; salmonellosis 16.2; shigellosis 8.7; hepatitis A (infectious) 8.6; tuberculosis 6.8; lyme disease 6.2; hepatitis B (serum) 3.8; pertussis 2.7.

Leading cause of death by age group (1998)

	Number of deaths			Total death rate per 100,000 population	Percentage of all deaths
	Total	Male	Female		
All ages[10]	2,337,256	1,157,260	1,179,996	864.7	100.0
1 to 4 years	5,251	2,920	2,331	34.6	0.22
Accidents	1,935	1,155	780	12.7	0.08
Congenital anomalies	564	287	277	3.7	0.02
Malignant neoplasms	365	189	176	2.4	0.02
Homicide	399	223	175	2.6	0.02
Circulatory diseases	214	114	100	1.4	0.01
5 to 14 years	7,791	4,686	3,105	19.9	0.33
Accidents	3,254	2,086	1,158	8.3	0.14
Malignant neoplasms	1,013	582	431	2.6	0.04
Homicide	460	257	203	1.2	0.02
Circulatory diseases	326	191	135	0.9	0.01
Suicide	324	241	83	0.8	0.01
15 to 24 years	30,627	22,717	7,910	82.3	1.31
Accidents	13,349	9,887	3,462	35.9	0.57
Homicide	5,506	4,720	785	14.8	0.24
Suicide	4,135	3,532	603	11.1	0.18
Malignant neoplasms	1,699	1,029	670	4.6	0.07
Circulatory diseases	1,057	672	385	2.8	0.04
25 to 44 years	131,382	86,354	45,028	157.7	5.62
Accidents	27,172	20,232	6,940	32.6	1.16
Malignant neoplasms	21,407	9,684	11,723	25.7	0.92
Circulatory diseases	16,800	11,796	5,004	20.2	0.72
Suicide	12,202	9,700	2,502	14.6	0.52
HIV infection	8,658	6,509	2,149	10.4	0.37
45 to 64 years	380,203	231,861	146,342	664.0	16.27
Malignant neoplasms	132,771	70,736	62,035	231.9	5.68
Circulatory diseases	100,124	70,138	29,986	174.9	4.28
Accidents	18,286	12,971	5,315	31.9	0.78
Diabetes mellitus	13,091	7,139	5,952	22.9	0.56
Liver disease and cirrhosis	11,023	8,031	2,992	19.3	0.47
65 and over	1,753,220	792,612	960,608	5,096.4	75.01
Circulatory diseases	605,673	270,637	335,036	1,760.6	25.91
Malignant neoplasms	384,186	199,794	184,392	1,116.8	16.44
Pneumonia and influenza	82,989	35,790	47,199	241.2	3.55
Diabetes mellitus	48,974	20,862	28,112	142.4	2.10
Accidents	32,975	16,176	16,799	95.9	1.41

Incidence of chronic health conditions per 1,000 population (1996): chronic sinusitis 125.0; arthritis 126.8; deformities or orthopedic impairments 111.2; hypertension 106.8; hay fever 89.4; hearing impairment 83.1; heart conditions 77.9; asthma 55.0; chronic bronchitis 53.4; migraine 43.5.

Social indicators

Educational attainment (2000). Percentage of population age 25 and over having: primary and incomplete secondary 15.9%; secondary 33.1%; some postsecondary 25.4%; 4-year higher degree 17.0%; advanced degree 8.6%. Number of earned degrees (1998): bachelor's degree 1,183,033; master's degree 429,296; doctor's degree 45,925; first-professional degrees (in fields such as medicine, theology, and law) 78,353.

Distribution of income (1998)

percentage of disposable family income by quintile

1	2	3	4	5 (highest)
4.2	9.9	15.7	23.0	47.3

Quality of working life (1999). Average workweek: 39.5 hours. Annual death rate per 100,000 workers for (1999): 4.5; leading causes of occupational deaths: transportation incidents 43.4%, contact with objects/equipment 17.1%, assaults/violent acts 14.8%. Average days per 1,000 workdays lost to labour stoppages (2000): 1.8. Average duration of journey to work (1990): 22.4 minutes (private automobile 94.7%, of which drive alone 80.0%, carpool 14.7%; take public transportation 5.3%). Rate per 1,000 employed workers of discouraged workers (unemployed no longer seeking work; 2000): 1.8.

Access to services (1995). Proportion of occupied dwellings having access to: electricity, virtually 100.0%; safe public water supply 99.4% (12.6% from wells); public sewage collection 77.0%, septic tanks 22.8%.

Social participation. Eligible voters participating in last presidential election (2000): 51.2%. Population age 18 and over participating in voluntary work (1999): 66.0%. Trade-union membership in total workforce (2000): 14.9%.

Social deviance (1999). Offense rate per 100,000 population for: murder 5.7; rape 32.7; robbery 150.0; aggravated assault 336.0; motor-vehicle theft 421.0; burglary and housebreaking 770.0; larceny-theft 2,551.0; drug-abuse violation 583.7; drunkenness 200.2[8]. Estimated drug and substance users (population age 12 and over; 1999)[11]: cigarettes 57,296,000; binge alcohol[12] 44,486,000; marijuana 11,476,000; other illicit drugs 6,645,000. Rate per 100,000 population of suicide (1999): 10.7.

Crime rates per 100,000 population in metropolitan areas[13] (1999)

	violent crime				
	total	murder	rape	robbery	assault
Atlanta	2,794	35.6	79.9	1,014	1,665
Baltimore[14]	2,420	43.4	66.7	1,199	1,111
Boston	1,308	5.6	60.7	444	797
Chicago	...	22.9	....	731	1,172
Dallas	1,434	17.7	61.6	591	764
Detroit	2,277	43.0	81.8	811	1,342
Houston	1,166	13.1	40.5	452	660
Los Angeles	1,290	11.7	35.4	397	845
Miami	2,129	17.1	30.6	833	1,248
Minneapolis	1,399	13.3	128	593	665
New York	1,063	9.0	22.9	486	545
Pittsburgh	904	14.5	41.0	469	379
St. Louis	2,279	38.9	43.1	836	1,361
San Francisco	878	8.6	25.8	465	378
Washington, D.C.	1,628	46.4	47.8	644	889

	property crime			
	total	burglary	larceny	auto theft
Atlanta	11,015	2,134	7,058	1,824
Baltimore[14]	8,363	1,772	5,363	1,227
Boston	5,009	615	3,176	1,218
Chicago	6,198	1,083	3,988	1,126
Dallas	8,317	1,824	4,834	1,659
Detroit	8,246	1,894	3,579	2,774
Houston	5,973	1,340	3,579	1,053
Los Angeles	3,320	592	2,049	679
Miami	8,717	1,985	5,182	1,550
Minneapolis	7,299	1,574	4,631	1,094
New York	2,969	545	1,890	534
Pittsburgh	5,404	925	3,531	949
St. Louis	12,007	2,352	7,665	1,990
San Francisco	4,923	740	3,383	800
Washington, D.C.	6,434	976	4,176	1,282

Leisure (1997). Favourite leisure activities (percentage of total population age 18 and over that undertook activity at least once in the previous year): movie 66.0%, amusement park 57.0%, sports event 41.0%, exercise program 76.0%, home improvement 66.0%, charity 43.0%, playing sports 45.0%.

Material well-being (1995). Occupied dwellings with householder possessing: automobile 95.6%; telephone 93.9%; radio receiver 99.0%; television receiver 98.3%; videocassette recorder 81.0%; washing machine 78.3%; air conditioner 69.7%; cable television 63.4%.

Recreational expenditures (1999): U.S.$534,900,000,000 (television and radio receivers, computers, and video equipment 18.5%; sports supplies 11.8%; golfing, bowling, and other participatory activities 11.4%; nondurable toys and sports equipment 6.9%; magazines and newspapers 6.9%; books and maps 5.6%; spectator amusements 4.8%, of which theatre and opera 1.9%, movies 1.4%, spectator sports 1.5%; flowers, seeds, and potted plants 3.3%; other 29.3%).

National economy

Budget (2001). Revenue: U.S.$2,136,900,000,000 (individual income tax 48.8%, social-insurance taxes and contributions 36.4%, corporation income tax 10.4%, excise taxes 3.4%, customs duties 1.0%). Expenditures: U.S.$1,856,200,000,000 (social security and medicare 37.5%, defense 16.1%, interest on debt 11.1%, other 35.3%).

Total national debt (2000): U.S.$5,686,338,000,000.

Manufacturing, mining, and construction enterprises (1999)

	no. of enterprises	no. of employees	hourly wages as a % of all wages[15]	value added (U.S.$'000,000)
Manufacturing				
Electric and electronic machinery, and computers	24,383	2,201,000	100.9	186,600
Chemical and related products	13,534	886,000	131.0	176,300
Transportation equipment	13,042	1,906,000	137.2	174,100
Machinery, except electrical	30,177	1,398,000	113.2	158,200
Food and related products	26,734	1,464,000	90.1	131,400
Fabricated metal products	62,242	1,788,000	100.4	105,500
Printing and publishing	40,671	834,000	104.0	99,000
Paper and related products	5,883	559,000	118.0	57,000
Rubber and plastic products	16,646	1,047,000	92.2	55,800
Primary metals	5,900	598,000	119.9	54,900
Lumber and wood	17,473	595,000	85.4	44,100
Stone, clay, and glass products	16,541	510,000	102.9	41,000
Petroleum and coal products	2,226	109,000	162.1	28,600
Furniture and fixtures	20,206	623,000	84.6	25,900
Apparel and related products	16,721	575,000	66.3	25,500
Textile-mill products	7,152	584,000	79.8	25,300
Beverages and tobacco products	2,789	172,000	127.4	19,900
Leather and leather products	1,807	74,000	72.6	4,200
Miscellaneous manufacturing industries	31,470	734,000	85.1	27,600

Manufacturing, mining, and construction enterprises (1999) (continued)

	no. of enterprises	no. of employees	hourly wages as a % of all wages[15]	value added (U.S.$'000,000)
Mining[7]				
Oil and gas extraction	8,312	110,881	124.1	82,350
Coal mining	1,511	87,965	142.7	15,567
Nonmetallic, except fuels	5,344	95,887	112.0	12,253
Metal mining	493	45,467	126.2	7,387
Construction[7]				
Special trade contractors	414,602	3,441	130.4	307,743
General contractors and operative builders	199,289	1,342,953	124.3	198,827
Heavy construction contractors	42,557	880,400	121.5	105,639

Gross national product (2000): U.S.$9,860,800,000,000 (U.S.$35,040 per capita).

Structure of gross domestic product and labour force

	2001		2000	
	in value U.S.$'000,000,000	% of total value	labour force[16]	% of labour force[16]
Agriculture	140.6	1.4	3,457,000	2.5
Mining	139.0	1.4	521,000	0.4
Manufacturing	1,423.0	14.1	19,940,000	14.2
Construction	480.0	4.8	9,433,000	6.7
Public utilities	221.9	2.2	1,447,000	1.0
Transp. and commun.	597.6	5.9	9,433,000	6.7
Trade, hotels	1,700.9	16.9	27,832,000	19.8
Finance, real estate	2,076.9	20.6	8,294,000	5.9
Public administration, defense	1,281.3	12.7	7,082,000	5.0
Services	2,138.2	21.2	47,770,000	33.9
Other	−117.2[17]	−1.2[17]	5,654,000[18]	4.0[18]
TOTAL	10,082.2	100.0	140,863,000	100.0[19]

Gross domestic product and national income

(in U.S.$'000,000,000)

	1996	1997	1998	1999	2000
Gross domestic product	7,576.1	8,110.9	8,511.0	9,299.2	9,963.1
By type of expenditure					
Personal consumption expenditures	5,151.4	5,493.7	5,807.9	6,268.7	6,757.3
Durable goods	632.1	673.0	724.7	761.3	820.3
Nondurable goods	1,545.1	1,600.6	1,662.4	1,845.5	2,010.0
Services	2,974.3	3,220.1	3,420.8	3,661.9	3,927.0
Gross private domestic investment	1,117.0	1,256.0	1,367.1	1,650.1	1,832.7
Fixed investment	1,101.5	1,188.6	1,307.8	1,606.8	1,778.2
Changes in business inventories	15.4	67.4	59.3	43.3	54.5
Net exports of goods and services	−98.7	−93.4	−151.2	−254.0	−370.7
Exports	855.2	965.4	959.0	990.2	1,097.3
Imports	953.9	1,058.8	1,110.2	1,224.2	1,468.0
Government purchases of goods and services	1,406.4	1,454.6	1,487.1	1,634.4	1,743.7
Federal	523.1	520.2	520.6	568.6	595.2
State and local	886.8	934.4	966.5	1,003.8	1,148.6
By major type of product					
Goods output	2,799.8	2,978.5	3,104.0	3,510.2	3,793.4
Durable goods	1,232.3	1,343.8	1,416.2	1,687.3	1,843.9
Nondurable goods	1,567.5	1,634.8	1,687.8	1,831.9	1,949.5
Services	4,105.2	4,414.1	4,641.0	4,934.6	5,254.0
Structures	671.1	718.3	765.9	854.3	915.6
National income (incl. capital consumption adjustment)	6,164.2	6,646.5	6,994.7	7,469.7	8,002.0
By type of income					
Compensation of employees	4,448.5	4,687.2	4,981.0	5,299.8	5,638.2
Proprietors' income	527.7	551.2	577.2	663.5	710.4
Rental income of persons	150.2	158.2	162.6	143.4	140.0
Corporate profits	670.2	817.9	824.6	856.0	946.2
Net interest	403.3	432.0	449.3	507.1	567.2
By industry division (excl. capital consumption adjustment)					
Agriculture, forestry, fishing	114.1	106.0	104.2	109.2	...
Mining and construction	325.9	357.6	381.1	433.1	...
Manufacturing	1,069.1	1,150.0	1,168.7	1,193.3	...
Durable	628.6	659.4	684.2	704.6	...
Nondurable	440.5	491.6	484.4	488.7	...
Transportation	196.5	208.0	216.2	236.9	...
Communications	148.5	139.3	149.3	161.9	...
Public utilities	126.5	133.6	135.3	135.9	...
Wholesale and retail trade	857.8	927.4	989.2	1,077.0	...
Finance, insurance, real estate	1,037.0	1,192.0	1,273.5	1,366.9	...
Services	1,441.1	1,513.6	1,624.9	1,782.9	...
Government and government enterprise	843.1	877.5	906.3	953.2	...
Other	−8.9	−8.0	−20.4	−11.0	...

Business activity (1997): number of businesses 23,645,000 (sole proprietorships 72.6%, active corporations 19.9%, active partnerships 7.5%), of which services 10,114,000, wholesaling and retailing 4,455,000; business receipts U.S.$18,057,000,000,000 (active corporations 88.0%, sole proprietorships 4.8%, active partnerships 7.2%), of which wholesaling and retailing U.S.$5,136,000,000,000, services U.S.$2,130,000,000,000; net profit U.S.$1,270,000,000,000 (active corporations 72.0%, sole proprietorships 14.7%, partnerships 13.3%), of which services U.S.$203,000,000,000, wholesaling and retailing U.S.$10,000,000,000. New business starts and business failures (1995): total number of new business starts 168,158; total failures 71,194, of which commercial service 21,850, retail trade 12,952; failure rate per 10,000 concerns 90.0; current liabilities of failed concerns U.S.$37,507,000,000; average liability U.S.$526,830. Business expenditures for new plant and equipment (1995): total U.S.$594,465,000,000, of which trade, services, and communications U.S.$244,829,000,000, manufacturing businesses U.S.$172,308,000,000 (durable goods 53.0%, nondurable goods 47.0%), public utilities U.S.$42,816,000,000, transportation U.S.$37,021,000,000, mining and construction U.S.$35,985,000.

Components of gross domestic product (2001)

States	Gross state product (U.S.$'000,-000,000)	Personal income (U.S.$'000,-000,000)	Disposable personal income (U.S.$'000,-000,000)	Per capita disposable personal income (U.S.$)
Alabama	119.9	109.0	95.9	21,481
Alaska	27.7	19.7	17.2	27,131
Arizona	156.3	135.2	116.5	21,942
Arkansas	67.7	61.7	54.2	20,151
California	1,344.6	1,127.4	929.7	26,947
Colorado	167.9	145.6	122.3	27,683
Connecticut	159.3	143.6	115.6	33,765
Delaware	36.3	25.6	21.7	27,237
Florida	472.1	467.2	402.6	24,554
Georgia	296.1	238.4	203.7	24,296
Hawaii	42.4	35.0	30.4	24,810
Idaho	37.0	32.0	27.7	20,967
Illinois	457.3	408.9	345.9	27,711
Indiana	192.2	168.3	145.5	23,801
Iowa	89.6	79.7	69.4	23,754
Kansas	85.1	76.8	66.0	24,506
Kentucky	118.5	101.9	87.9	21,631
Louisiana	137.7	107.5	95.1	21,286
Maine	36.0	33.9	29.2	22,663
Maryland	186.1	187.9	156.9	29,197
Massachusetts	284.9	247.8	202.2	31,694
Michigan	325.4	295.1	251.3	25,158
Minnesota	184.8	163.0	137.3	27,622
Mississippi	67.3	61.9	55.4	19,401
Missouri	178.8	157.8	136.3	24,217
Montana	21.7	21.3	18.6	20,544
Nebraska	56.1	48.9	42.3	24,707
Nevada	42.4	62.9	54.0	25,637
New Hampshire	47.7	42.7	36.8	29,259
New Jersey	363.1	323.7	268.9	31,693
New Mexico	54.4	42.4	37.2	20,340
New York	799.2	682.2	559.0	29,402
North Carolina	281.7	224.4	192.9	23,567
North Dakota	18.3	16.2	14.4	22,691
Ohio	372.6	325.5	277.7	24,420
Oklahoma	91.8	85.8	74.8	21,613
Oregon	118.6	97.2	82.1	23,650
Pennsylvania	404.0	376.2	322.0	26,203
Rhode Island	36.5	31.8	27.3	25,769
South Carolina	113.4	99.9	87.0	21,423
South Dakota	23.2	19.9	17.7	23,454
Tennessee	178.4	153.6	136.7	23,819
Texas	742.3	607.5	533.4	25,015
Utah	68.5	54.9	47.2	20,803
Vermont	18.4	17.2	14.8	24,064
Virginia	261.4	232.1	193.9	26,972
Washington	219.9	189.1	160.3	26,773
West Virginia	42.3	40.9	36.2	20,068
Wisconsin	173.5	156.2	133.5	24,710
Wyoming	19.3	14.2	12.2	24,575
District				
District of Columbia	59.4	23.2	18.9	33,031
TOTAL/AVERAGE	9,941.5	8,621.0	7,316.0	25,688

Retail and wholesale trade and services (1999)

	no. of establish-ments	no. of employees	hourly wage as a % of all wages[15]	annual sales or receipts (U.S.$'000,000)[15]
Retail trade	1,111,300	14,777,000	68.7	3,105,585
Automotive dealers	123,900	1,804,000	93.5	927,141
Food stores	151,500	3,015,000	68.8	464,288
General merchandise group stores	38,100	2,445,000	74.7	417,852
Eating and drinking places	480,298	7,900,273	50.0[20]	303,905
Building materials, hardware, garden supply, and mobile home dealers	92,300	1,184,000	74.2	298,604
Gasoline service stations	121,100	930,000	93.5	199,420
Apparel and accessory stores	151,700	1,293,000	67.8	169,815
Drugstores and proprietary stores	82,400	938,000	79.8	152,780
Furniture, home furnishings, equipment stores	64,300	525,000	92.2	90,503
Electronics and appliances	45,200	384,000	75.1	88,678
Sporting goods, book and music stores	66,100	590,000	92.1	74,080
Liquor stores	28,100	131,000	...	23,400
Wholesale trade	450,030	5,972,022	110.1	2,755,500
Durable goods	290,053	3,527,913	114.9	1,435,100
Professional and commercial equipment	45,157	751,200	136.6	279,300
Machinery, equipment, and supplies	75,423	803,332	115.9	257,900
Electrical goods	38,512	507,297	117.5	239,500
Motor vehicles, automotive equipment	28,328	391,849	101.8	195,700
Computers and software	...	...	...	164,700
Metals and minerals, except petroleum	12,328	169,728	109.1	103,300
Lumber and other construction materials	14,901	169,013	101.8	71,500
Hardware, plumbing, heating equipment and supplies	21,472	237,954	106.4	65,500
Furniture and home furnishings	15,008	161,687	100.8	46,500
Miscellaneous durable goods	38,926	335,853	89.6	175,900
Nondurable goods	159,977	2,444,108	97.3	1,320,500
Groceries and related products	40,568	876,175	101.5	387,900
Petroleum and products	11,160	134,052	93.8	171,900
Drugs, drug proprietaries, and druggists' sundries	7,510	199,759	142.6	166,300
Farm-products raw materials	9,760	92,219	79.2	106,200
Apparel and accessories	20,284	208,649	97.6	94,200
Paper and paper products	15,368	228,588	104.9	79,000
Beer, wine, and distilled alcoholic beverages	4,720	152,969	115.0	71,700
Chemicals and allied products	15,410	159,824	119.7	60,000
Miscellaneous nondurable goods	35,197	391,874	84.0	184,300

Retail and wholesale trade and services (1999) (continued)

	no. of establish-ments	no. of employees	hourly wage as a % of all wages[15]	annual sales or receipts (U.S.$'000,000)[15]
Services	3,790,229	59,048,833	101.6	1,843,800[14]
Health	649,846	13,865,014	107.1	398,500[14]
Business, except computer services	610,981	5,418,473	100.9	304,400[14]
Computer and data-processing services	93,798	1,013,049	168.4	224,100[14]
Legal services	177,037	1,082,253	145.3	122,600[14]
Automotive repair, services, garages	164,898	842,606	86.7	99,600[14]
Management and public relations	46,528	2,788,278	139.6	101,300[14]
Hotels and motels	59,278	1,737,734	70.1	97,900[14]
Amusement and recreation	64,166	1,205,042	76.4	67,900[14]
Engineering services	103,430	1,212,838	139.5	108,600[14]
Personal services	195,107	1,261,383	72.2	53,100[14]
Motion pictures	23,102	293,369	111.4	67,900[14]

Daily consumption of water (1995)

(in gallons)

States	Total consumption ('000,000,000)	Per capita	Irrigation	Public consumption	Industrial processes	Thermo-electric
Alabama	6,967	1,670	139	875	753	5,200
Alaska	318	350	1	90	197	30
Arizona	6,775	1,620	5,670	846	197	62
Arkansas	8,326	3,540	5,940	419	187	1,780
California	45,072	1,130	28,900	5,740	802	9,630
Colorado	13,738	3,590	12,700	732	191	115
Connecticut	4,427	389	28	448	11	3,940
Delaware	1,483	1,050	48	101	64	1,270
Florida	18,079	509	3,470	2,360	649	11,600
Georgia	5,718	799	722	1,250	676	3,070
Hawaii	1,860	853	652	218	20	970
Idaho	13,330	13,000	13,000	254	76	...
Illinois	19,757	1,680	180	1,950	527	17,100
Indiana	9,000	1,570	116	784	2,410	5,690
Iowa	2,888	1,070	39	418	301	2,130
Kansas	5,101	2,040	3,380	384	77	1,260
Kentucky	4,358	1,150	12	521	375	3,450
Louisiana	9,506	2,270	769	677	2,580	5,480
Maine	314	178	27	135	16	136
Maryland	7,655	289	57	907	331	6,360
Massachusetts	5,499	189	82	759	88	4,570
Michigan	11,997	1,260	227	1,490	1,910	8,370
Minnesota	3,258	736	157	573	438	2,090
Mississippi	2,786	1,140	1,740	377	294	375
Missouri	6,937	1,320	567	757	63	5,550
Montana	8,813	10,200	8,550	161	80	22
Nebraska	10,403	6,440	7,550	328	175	2,350
Nevada	2,241	1,480	1,640	479	95	27
New Hampshire	1,296	388	6	130	50	1,110
New Jersey	6,091	269	125	1,120	486	4,360
New Mexico	3,451	2,080	2,990	337	69	55
New York	16,591	567	30	3,140	321	13,100
North Carolina	8,983	1,070	239	939	385	7,420
North Dakota	1,038	1,750	117	85	17	819
Ohio	10,427	944	27	1,560	650	8,190
Oklahoma	1,870	543	864	597	285	124
Oregon	7,130	2,520	6,170	572	379	9
Pennsylvania	9,606	802	16	1,730	1,930	5,930
Rhode Island	406	138	2	121	7	275
South Carolina	6,180	1,690	53	614	703	4,810
South Dakota	403	631	269	97	32	5
Tennessee	10,023	1,920	24	831	868	8,300
Texas	29,290	1,300	9,450	3,420	2,920	13,500
Utah	4,337	2,200	3,530	506	253	48
Vermont	534	967	4	66	12	452
Virginia	8,183	826	30	911	622	6,620
Washington	8,798	1,620	6,470	1,300	652	376
West Virginia	4,557	2,530	...	217	1,330	3,010
Wisconsin	7,134	1,420	169	692	453	5,820
Wyoming	7,028	14,700	6,590	100	118	220
District						
District of Columbia	10	18	...	...	1	10
TOTAL/AVERAGE	389,972	1,280	133,538	43,118	26,126	187,190

Production. Agriculture, forestry, fishing (value of production/catch in U.S.$'000,000 except as noted; 2000): corn (maize) 18,621, soybeans 13,073, wheat 5,970, cotton lint 4,781, grapes 3,063, potatoes 2,539, tobacco 2,056, oranges 1,752, apples 1,554, head lettuce 1,259, tomatoes 1,160, rice 1,073, strawberries 1,013, almonds 852, peanuts (groundnuts) 844, sorghum 822, onions 732, cottonseed 677, barley 632, bell peppers 614, broccoli 597, peaches 495, sweet corn 474, carrots 436, dry beans 423, grapefruit 423, cantaloupes 359, cabbage 332, lemons 318, avocados 318, sweet cherries 286, cauliflower 259, pears 255, sunflower seeds 241, watermelons 236, pecans 234; livestock (number of live animals; 2000) 98,048,000 cattle, 59,337,000 pigs, 7,215,000 sheep, 5,320,000 horses, 1,720,000,000 chickens; roundwood (2000) 500,434,000 cu m; fish and shellfish catch (1999) 3,095, of which fish 1,395 (including salmon 308, Alaska pollack 187), shellfish 1,700 (including shrimp 519, crabs 480). Mining (metal content in metric tons except as noted; 2001): iron 37,800,000; copper 1,340,000; zinc 830,000; lead 420,000; molybdenum 38,300; vanadium 2,700; mercury 57; silver 1,800,000 kg; gold 350,000 kg; helium 101,000,000 cu m. Quarrying (metric tons; 2000): crushed stone 1,300,000,000; sand and gravel 1,139,000,000; cement 75,000,000; clay 40,700,000; phosphate rock 34,200,000; common salt 45,000,000; gypsum 18,800,000; lime 20,000,000. Manufacturing (value added in U.S.$'000,000; 1999): transportation equipment 268,511, of which motor vehicle parts 86,310, motor vehicles 80,134, aerospace products and parts 73,897; computers and electronic products 265,442, of which semiconductors and related components 102,003; chemicals and chemical products 229,284, of which pharmaceuticals and medicine 74,108; food 177,659; fabricated metal products 142,451; nonelectrical machinery 138,798; paper and paper products

74,602; plastics 72,183; base metals 66,733; printing 62,428; electrical machinery 60,458. Construction (completed; 2000): private U.S.$640,654,000,000, of which residential U.S.$374,274,000,000, nonresidential U.S.$210,140,000,000; public U.S.$174,860,000,000.

Energy production (consumption): electricity (kW-hr; 2001) 3,778,500,000,000 ([1998] 3,399,600,000,000); coal (metric tons; 1998) 934,790,000 (846,813,000); lignite (metric tons; 1998) 78,593,000 (79,821,000); crude petroleum (barrels; 2001) 2,163,000,000 ([1998] 5,608,000,000); petroleum products (metric tons; 1998) 747,623,000 (757,728,000); natural gas (cu m; 2001) 549,557,000,000 ([1998] 601,880,000,000). Domestic production of energy by source (1998): coal 32.5%, natural gas 26.3%, crude petroleum 18.0%, nuclear power 9.8%, renewable energy 9.1%, other 0.9%.

Energy consumption by sector and state (1999)

('000,000,000,000 Btu)

States	Total	Residential	Commercial	Industrial	Transportation	Per capita ('000,000 Btu)
Alabama	2,005	341	226	977	461	459
Alaska	695	48	63	386	198	1,122
Arizona	1,220	279	267	222	453	255
Arkansas	1,204	193	124	589	297	472
California	8,375	1,416	1,237	2,824	2,899	253
Colorado	1,156	281	255	273	366	285
Connecticut	839	245	197	162	235	256
Delaware	279	56	45	107	71	370
Florida	3,853	1,018	810	680	1,346	255
Georgia	2,798	553	416	957	871	359
Hawaii	241	23	25	71	122	204
Idaho	518	96	87	210	126	414
Illinois	3,883	897	722	1,273	991	320
Indiana	2,736	484	301	1,306	645	460
Iowa	1,122	223	159	463	278	391
Kansas	1,050	201	169	392	288	396
Kentucky	1,830	316	219	851	444	462
Louisiana	3,615	325	237	2,249	805	827
Maine	529	98	58	260	113	422
Maryland	1,378	359	337	277	405	267
Massachusetts	1,569	412	325	391	441	254
Michigan	3,240	744	568	1,083	845	328
Minnesota	1,675	340	218	618	500	351
Mississippi	1,209	203	146	451	409	437
Missouri	1,209	432	334	380	623	323
Montana	412	62	48	196	107	467
Nebraska	602	130	111	166	194	361
Nevada	615	122	97	198	198	340
New Hampshire	335	82	56	97	101	279
New Jersey	2,589	540	541	645	863	318
New Mexico	635	93	106	202	234	365
New York	4,283	1,092	1,216	995	980	235
North Carolina	2,447	563	440	754	491	320
North Dakota	366	54	43	186	82	577
Ohio	4,323	867	632	1,855	969	384
Oklahoma	1,378	259	198	518	403	410
Oregon	1,109	238	191	352	328	335
Pennsylvania	3,716	859	583	1,290	984	310
Rhode Island	261	66	52	77	66	264
South Carolina	1,493	288	210	618	376	384
South Dakota	239	53	39	62	84	326
Tennessee	2,071	442	328	711	590	378
Texas	11,501	1,323	1,147	6,482	2,549	574
Utah	694	128	120	235	211	326
Vermont	165	43	29	40	53	278
Virginia	2,227	494	463	614	656	324
Washington	2,241	436	332	856	617	389
West Virginia	735	142	101	311	182	407
Wisconsin	1,811	376	285	717	432	345
Wyoming	422	36	42	224	120	879
District						
Dist. of Columbia	170	34	106	4	27	327
TOTAL/AVERAGE	95,682	18,382	15,059	35,917	26,325	351

Energy consumption by source (1999): petroleum and petroleum products 39.7%, natural gas 23.3%, coal 21.4%, nuclear electric power 8.1%, hydroelectric and thermal 7.5%; by end use: industrial 37.8%, residential and commercial 35.4%, transportation 26.8%.

Energy consumption by source and by state (1999)

('000,000,000,000 Btu)

States	Petroleum	Natural gas	Coal	Hydroelectric power	Nuclear electric power
Alabama	551	345	855	80	328
Alaska	253	420	11	9	0.0
Arizona	497	163	404	104	323
Arkansas	384	266	267	28	137
California	3,383	2,182	64	425	355
Colorado	426	318	355	17	0.0
Connecticut	440	135	0.0	14	135
Delaware	141	58	36	0.0	0.0
Florida	1,912	542	672	2	335
Georgia	1,044	341	790	28	334
Hawaii	214	3	3	1	0.0
Idaho	170	72	8	140	0.0
Illinois	1,340	1,058	837	2	868
Indiana	899	577	1,451	4	0.0
Iowa	419	236	416	10	39
Kansas	437	302	329	0.0	97
Kentucky	726	220	885	27	0.0
Louisiana	1,452	1,558	228	8	139
Maine	250	6	3	81	0.0
Maryland	584	201	304	15	141
Massachusetts	639	356	13	15	48
Michigan	1,098	930	823	11	155
Minnesota	661	346	336	59	142
Mississippi	483	346	138	0.0	90
Missouri	781	270	686	18	91
Montana	174	64	174	143	0.0
Nebraska	246	121	196	18	107
Nevada	221	157	180	29	0.0

Energy consumption by source and by state (1999) (continued)

('000,000,000,000 Btu)

States	Petroleum	Natural gas	Coal	Hydroelectric power	Nuclear electric power
New Hampshire	188	21	35	25	92
New Jersey	1,236	641	68	0.0	308
New Mexico	257	225	298	3	0.0
New York	1,653	1,251	188	265	393
North Carolina	937	229	708	40	399
North Dakota	123	59	412	28	0.0
Ohio	1,340	878	1,379	4	175
Oklahoma	500	543	334	32	0.0
Oregon	392	219	39	475	0.0
Pennsylvania	1,385	696	1,143	16	756
Rhode Island	99	86	0.1	10	0.0
South Carolina	467	163	403	7	540
South Dakota	115	36	46	71	0.0
Tennessee	713	286	626	74	289
Texas	5,565	3,982	1,535	13	391
Utah	262	169	382	13	0.0
Vermont	85	8	2	61	43
Virginia	864	275	402	6	301
Washington	878	277	96	988	65
West Virginia	220	147	977	10	0.0
Wisconsin	668	379	472	23	122
Wyoming	156	102	495	12	0.0
District					
District of Columbia	34	33	0.6	0.0	0.0
TOTAL	37,960	22,295	20,498	3,449	7,736

Household income[21] level by selected characteristics (1998)

Characteristics	Number of households ('000)	Number ('000) Under $15,000	Number ('000) $15,000–$34,999	Number ('000) $35,000–$74,999	Number ('000) $75,000 and over	Median income ($)
Total/Average	103,874	18,798	28,285	35,272	20,860	38,885
Age of householder						
15 to 24 years	5,770	1,743	2,269	1,483	274	23,564
25 to 34 years	18,819	2,699	5,453	7,694	2,973	40,069
35 to 44 years	23,968	2,626	5,376	9,916	6,051	48,451
45 to 54 years	20,158	2,078	3,950	7,744	6,387	54,148
55 to 64 years	13,571	2,370	3,271	4,580	3,350	43,167
65 years and over	21,589	7,311	7,964	4,247	1,824	21,729
Size of household						
One person	26,606	10,388	9,199	5,703	1,314	20,154
Two persons	34,262	4,233	10,106	12,807	7,115	41,512
Three persons	17,386	1,916	3,955	6,970	4,544	46,069
Four persons	15,030	1,180	2,808	6,259	4,784	55,886
Five persons	6,962	681	1,351	2,841	2,089	53,706
Six persons	2,367	267	555	856	690	49,080
Seven or more persons	1,261	132	309	495	324	46,646
Educational attainment of householder						
Total[22]	98,104	17,055	26,016	34,448	20,585	40,296
Less than 9th grade	7,047	3,314	2,455	1,070	208	16,154
Some high school	9,407	3,405	3,360	2,179	463	20,724
High school graduate	30,613	5,881	9,671	11,263	3,797	34,373
Some college, no degree	17,833	2,334	4,936	7,182	3,381	41,658
Associate degree	7,468	779	1,690	3,251	1,748	48,604
Bachelor's degree	16,781	936	2,867	6,535	6,442	62,188
Master's degree	5,961	265	769	2,911	2,784	71,086
Professional degree	1,623	93	145	414	971	95,309
Doctorate degree	1,373	48	122	413	789	84,100

Household income and expenditure. Average household size (2000) 2.7; median annual income per household (2001) U.S.$42,228, of which median Asian and Pacific Islander household U.S.$53,635, median non-Hispanic household U.S.$46,305, median Hispanic[5] household U.S.$33,565, median black (including Hispanic) household U.S.$29,470; sources of personal income (2000): wages and salaries 57.6%, self-employment 8.6%, transfer payments 8.5%, other 25.3%; expenditure (1999): transportation 18.9%, housing 18.9%, food at home 7.9%, household furnishings 7.2%, fuel and utilities 6.4%, food away from home 5.7%, recreation 5.5%, health 5.3%, wearing apparel 4.7%, education 1.7%, other 17.8%.

Financial aggregates

	1996	1997	1998	1999	2000	2001	2002[23]
Exchange rate, U.S.$ per:							
£[24]	1.56	1.65	1.66	1.62	1.49	1.44	1.49
SDR[24]	1.45	1.38	1.36	1.37	1.32	1.27	1.33
International reserves (U.S.$)[25]							
Total (excl. gold; '000,000,000)	64.04	58.91	70.71	60.50	56.60	57.63	67.31
SDRs ('000,000,000)	10.31	10.03	10.60	10.35	10.54	10.78	11.58
Reserve pos. in IMF ('000,000,000)	15.43	18.07	24.11	17.97	14.82	17.87	19.86
Foreign exchange ('000,000,000)	38.29	30.81	36.00	32.18	31.24	29.98	32.27
Gold ('000,000 fine troy oz)	261.66	261.61	261.78	261.67	261.61	262.00	262.00
% world reserves	28.86	29.52	27.09	27.13	27.52	27.83	28.14
Interest and prices							
Central bank discount (%)[25]	5.00	5.00	4.50	5.00	6.00	1.25	1.25
Govt. bond yield (%)[24]	6.44	6.35	5.26	5.49	6.22	4.08	3.01
Industrial share prices[24] (1995 = 100)	123.5	159.3	198.7	251.3	272.8	215.2	160.4
Balance of payments (U.S.$'000,000,000)							
Balance of visible trade	−189.25	−181.87	−231.10	−343.26	−449.57	−424.23	...
Imports, f.o.b.	−803.23	−870.57	−913.60	−1,029.92	−1,224.43	−1,145.98	...
Exports, f.o.b.	613.98	688.70	682.50	686.66	774.86	721.75	...
Balance of invisibles	40.52	52.58	87.25	5.86	4.88	30.85	...
Balance of payments, current account	−148.73	−129.29	−143.85	−337.4	−444.69	−393.40	...

Average employee earnings

	average hourly earnings in U.S.$		average weekly earnings in U.S.$	
	Feb. 1999	Feb. 2000	Feb. 1999	Feb. 2000
Manufacturing				
Durable goods	13.66	14.19	564.16	588.89
Lumber and wood products	11.26	11.61	453.78	469.04
Furniture and fixtures	11.06	11.50	440.17	457.70
Stone, clay, and glass products	13.64	13.99	576.96	593.18
Primary metal industries	15.41	16.29	673.42	723.28
Fabricated metal products	13.29	13.65	555.52	576.03
Machinery, except electrical	14.72	15.39	619.71	652.54
Electrical and electronic equipment	13.25	13.71	544.58	567.59
Transportation equipment	17.50	18.65	768.25	818.74
Instruments and related products	13.94	14.41	578.51	595.13
Miscellaneous manufacturing	11.17	11.56	442.33	455.46
Nondurable goods	12.97	13.38	525.29	543.23
Food and kindred products	11.91	12.25	489.50	501.03
Tobacco manufactures	17.80	17.32	662.16	680.68
Textile mill products	10.60	10.84	426.12	447.69
Apparel and other textile products	8.65	9.01	322.65	338.78
Paper and allied products	15.70	16.03	675.10	689.29
Printing and publishing	13.67	14.13	515.36	536.53
Chemicals and allied products	17.20	17.80	734.44	756.50
Petroleum and coal products	21.43	22.03	927.92	962.71
Rubber and miscellaneous plastics products	12.16	12.53	503.42	518.74
Leather and leather products	9.56	9.87	355.63	370.13
Nonmanufacturing				
Metal mining	18.16	18.63	793.59	815.99
Coal mining	19.11	19.40	865.68	873.00
Oil and gas extraction	16.98	16.68	696.18	738.47
Nonmetallic minerals, except fuels	14.81	15.22	662.00	672.02
Construction	16.66	17.37	633.08	672.09
Transportation and public utilities	15.56	16.06	606.84	613.49
Wholesale trade	14.38	14.96	550.75	571.47
Retail trade	8.98	9.34	256.83	266.19
Finance, insurance, and real estate	14.55	14.91	528.17	536.76
Hotels, motels, and tourist courts	9.20	9.53	280.60	289.71
Health services	14.06	14.55	462.57	480.15
Legal services	18.74	19.75	652.15	693.23
Miscellaneous services	18.38	18.67	637.79	681.46

Median household income[21]

(in constant 1999 U.S.$)

States	1995	1996	1997	1998	1999
Alabama	28,413	32,175	33,153	37,067	36,213
Alaska	52,422	56,042	49,818	51,812	51,509
Arizona	33,739	33,593	33,984	37,909	37,119
Arkansas	28,219	28,800	27,156	28,276	29,762
California	40,457	41,211	41,203	41,838	43,744
Colorado	44,499	43,482	44,876	47,628	48,346
Connecticut	43,993	44,723	45,657	47,535	50,798
Delaware	38,182	41,739	44,669	42,374	46,839
Florida	32,517	32,535	33,688	35,680	35,876
Georgia	37,276	34,505	38,056	39,519	39,433
Hawaii	46,844	44,354	42,490	41,729	44,373
Idaho	35,721	36,855	34,674	37,490	35,906
Illinois	41,618	41,999	42,852	44,132	46,392
Indiana	36,496	37,320	40,367	40,608	40,929
Iowa	38,829	35,262	35,067	37,837	41,238
Kansas	33,168	34,600	37,857	37,522	37,476
Kentucky	32,588	34,417	34,723	37,053	33,901
Louisiana	30,553	32,133	34,524	32,436	32,695
Maine	37,013	36,841	34,018	36,427	38,932
Maryland	44,865	46,713	48,459	51,121	52,310
Massachusetts	42,168	41,936	43,620	43,280	44,192
Michigan	39,820	41,650	40,214	42,745	46,238
Minnesota	41,467	43,525	44,182	48,984	47,240
Mississippi	29,011	28,326	29,582	29,763	32,540
Missouri	38,070	36,383	37,942	41,089	41,466
Montana	30,343	30,457	30,322	32,274	31,244
Nebraska	35,997	36,117	36,011	37,217	38,787
Nevada	39,446	40,923	40,331	40,634	41,680
New Hampshire	42,821	41,843	42,556	45,951	46,167
New Jersey	48,017	50,403	49,846	50,926	49,930
New Mexico	28,413	26,637	31,229	32,240	32,475
New York	36,105	37,599	37,159	38,220	40,058
North Carolina	34,959	37,802	37,202	36,630	37,340
North Dakota	31,799	33,416	32,864	30,973	32,877
Ohio	38,197	36,176	37,507	39,785	39,617
Oklahoma	28,763	29,133	32,543	34,472	32,919
Oregon	39,763	37,686	38,663	39,930	40,713
Pennsylvania	37,741	37,057	38,943	39,877	37,995
Rhode Island	38,654	39,273	36,119	41,585	42,936
South Carolina	31,780	36,808	35,564	34,002	36,563
South Dakota	32,334	31,351	30,823	33,510	35,982
Tennessee	31,719	32,694	31,800	34,844	36,536
Texas	35,024	35,117	36,408	36,573	38,978
Utah	39,879	39,328	44,401	45,277	46,094
Vermont	36,976	34,358	36,385	40,242	41,630
Virginia	39,597	41,635	44,590	44,312	45,750
Washington	38,882	38,943	46,256	48,468	45,639
West Virginia	27,198	26,808	28,533	27,294	29,433
Wisconsin	44,771	42,474	41,100	42,240	45,825
Wyoming	34,467	32,867	34,693	36,029	37,395
District					
District of Columbia	33,613	33,942	33,071	34,171	38,686
U.S. AVERAGE	37,251	37,686	38,411	39,744	40,816

Average annual expenditure of "consumer units" (households, plus individuals sharing households or budgets; 1999): total U.S.$37,027, of which housing U.S.$12,057, transportation U.S.$7,011, food U.S.$5,031, pensions and social security U.S.$3,436, health care U.S.$1,959, clothing U.S.$1,743, other U.S.$5,790.

Selected household characteristics (2000). Total number of households 104,705,000, of which (family households by race) white 84.8%, black 12.2%, other 3.0%; in central cities 31.4%[26], in suburbs 46.3%[26], outside metropolitan areas 22.3%[26]; (by tenure[26]) owned 64,045,000 (64.7%), rented 34,946,000 (35.3%); family households 72,025,000, of which married couple 76.8%, female head with own children[27] under age 18, 10.5%, female head without own children[27] under 18, 7.1%; nonfamily households 32,680,000, of which female living alone 47.6%, male living alone 34.2%, other 18.2%.

Population economically active (2000): total 140,863,000[16]; activity rate of total population 50.1% (participation rates: age 16 and over 67.2%; female 46.6%; unemployed [November 2002] 6.0%).

Price and earnings indexes (1995 = 100)

	1995	1996	1997	1998	1999	2000	2001
Consumer price index	100.0	102.9	105.3	107.0	109.3	113.0	116.2
Hourly earnings index[28]	100.0	103.3	106.4	109.1	112.4	116.2	120.0

Tourism (1999): receipts from visitors U.S.$94,657,000,000; expenditures by nationals abroad U.S.$80,756,000,000; number of foreign visitors 48,491,000,-000 (14,110,000 from Canada, 9,915,000 from Mexico, 11,243,000 from Europe); number of nationals traveling abroad 58,358,000 (17,743,000 to Mexico, 16,036,000 to Canada).

Land use (1997): forested 20.9%; meadows and pastures 27.1%; agricultural and under permanent cultivation 21.1%; other 30.9%.

Foreign trade

Balance of trade (current prices)

	1996	1997	1998	1999	2000	2001
U.S.$'000,000,000	−189.2	−181.9	−231.1	−343.3	−434.3	−410.2
% of total	13.4%	11.7%	14.5%	20.0%	21.7%	21.9%

Imports (2000): U.S.$1,216,743,000,000 (manufactured goods 84.8%, of which motor vehicles and parts 13.3%, electrical machinery 8.9%, computers and office equipment 7.5%, petroleum and petroleum products 7.4%, chemicals and chemical products 6.0%, wearing apparel 5.3%; food and live animals 3.1%). *Major import sources:* Canada 19.0%; Japan 12.0%; Mexico 11.2%; China 8.2%; Germany 4.8%; United Kingdom 3.6%; Taiwan 3.3%; South Korea 3.3%; France 2.4%; Italy 2.1%; Malaysia 2.1%; Singapore 1.6%; Thailand 1.3%; Philippines 1.1%; Brazil 1.1%.

Exports (2000): U.S.$782,429,000,000 (manufactured goods 79.7%, of which electrical machinery 11.4%, chemicals and related products 10.2%, motor vehicles 7.3%, scientific and precision equipment 3.9%; food and live animals 6.4%). *Major export destinations:* Canada 22.9%; Mexico 14.2%; Japan 8.3%; United Kingdom 5.3%; Germany 3.7%; South Korea 3.6%; Taiwan 3.1%; The Netherlands 2.8%; France 2.6%; Singapore 2.3%; Brazil 2.0%.

Trade by commodity group (2000)

	imports		exports	
SITC Group	U.S.$'000,000	%	U.S.$'000,000	%
00 Food and live animals	39,547[29]	3.1[29]	40,242[29]	5.4[29]
01 Beverages and tobacco	9,736	0.8	6,821	0.9
02 Crude materials, excluding fuels	24,086	1.9	29,014	3.9
03 Mineral fuels, lubricants, and related materials	139,706	11.1	13,813	1.9
04 Animal and vegetable oils, fat, and waxes	29	29	29	29
05 Chemicals and related products, n.e.s.	74,562	5.9	80,021	10.8
06 Basic manufactures	142,245	11.3	73,265	9.8
07 Machinery and transport equipment	563,304	44.8	382,362	51.4
08 Miscellaneous manufactured articles	210,503	16.7	86,191	11.6
09 Goods not classified by kind	52,899	4.2	30,295	4.1
TOTAL	1,258,080[30]	100.0[30]	743,404[30]	100.0[30]

Direction of trade (1999)

	imports		exports	
	U.S.$'000,000	%	U.S.$'000,000	%
Africa	17,969	1.7	9,911	1.4
South Africa	3,327	0.3	2,809	0.4
Other Africa	14,642	1.4	7,102	1.0
Americas	369,601	35.2	304,596	44.1
Canada	198,829	19.0	162,956	23.6
Caribbean countries and Central America	20,285	1.9	19,949	2.9
Mexico	109,499	10.4	86,383	12.5
South America	40,988	3.9	35,308	5.1
Asia	423,146	40.4	190,325	27.6
China	98,678	9.4	25,715	3.7
Japan	134,009	12.8	57,733	8.4
Other Asia	190,459	18.2	106,877	15.5
Europe	229,766	21.9	171,925	24.9
EU	199,581	19.0	151,865	22.0
Russia	6,094	0.6	2,186	0.3
Other Europe	24,091	2.3	17,874	2.6
Oceania	7,951	0.8	13,555	2.0
Australia	5,828	0.6	11,344	1.6
Other Oceania	2,123	0.2	2,211	0.3
TOTAL	1,048,435[30]	100.0	690,689[30]	100.0

Transport and communications

Transport. Railroads (1998): length 132,000 mi, 212,433 km; (1999) passenger-mi 13,402,000,000, passenger-km 21,568,000,000; short ton-mi cargo (1997) 1,421,000,000,000, metric ton-km cargo (1997) 2,075,000,000. Roads (1999): total length 3,944,598 mi, 6,348,227 km (paved 91%). Vehicles (2000): passenger cars 133,621,000; trucks and buses 87,107,000. Merchant marine (1999): vessels (1,000 gross tons and over) 579; total deadweight tonnage 16,747,000. Air transport (2000): passenger-mi 707,979,000,000, passenger-km 1,139,000,000,000; short ton-mi cargo 30,221,000,000, metric ton-km cargo 48,636,000,000; localities (1996) with scheduled flights 834[31]. Certified route passenger/cargo air carriers (1992) 77; operating revenue (U.S.$'000,000; 1991) 74,942, of which domestic 56,119, international 18,823; operating expenses 76,669, of which domestic 56,596, international 20,073.

Intercity passenger and freight traffic by mode of transportation (1999)

	cargo traffic ('000,000,000 ton-mi)	% of nat'l total	passenger traffic ('000,000,000 passenger-mi)	% of nat'l total
Rail	1,499	40.3	14	0.6
Road	1,093	29.4	1,885	78.5
Inland water	486	13.1	—	—
Air	14	0.4	501	20.9
Petroleum pipeline	623	16.8	—	—
TOTAL	3,715	100.0	2,400	100.0

Communications

Medium	date	unit	number	units per 1,000 persons
Daily newspapers	2000	circulation	55,773,000	198
Radio	1997	receivers	575,000,000	2,116
Television	1999	receivers	233,000,000	843
Telephones	2001	main lines	190,000,000	665
Cellular telephones	2001	subscribers	127,000,000	444
Personal computers	2001	units	178,000,000	623
Internet	2001	users	142,823,000	500

Other communications media (2000)

	titles		titles
Print			
Books (new)	122,108	Engineering	265
of which		Fine and applied arts	145
Agriculture	1,073	General interest	181
Art	5,980	History	151
Biography	3,899	Home economics	90
Business	4,068	Industrial arts	106
Education	3,378	Journalism and commun.	90
Fiction	14,617	Labour and industrial	
General works	1,318	relations	70
History	7,931	Law	273
Home economics	2,513	Library and information	
Juvenile	8,690	sciences	118
Language	2,536	Literature and language	158
Law	3,070	Mathematics and science	238
Literature	3,371	Medicine	182
Medicine	6,234	Philosophy and religion	130
Music	1,582	Physical education and	
Philosophy, psychology	5,556	recreation	151
Poetry, drama	2,479	Political science	136
Religion	6,206	Psychology	138
Science	8,464	Sociology and anthropology	149
Sociology, economics	14,908	Zoology	94
Sports, recreation	3,483		
Technology	8,582	**Cinema**	
Travel	3,170	Feature films	478
Periodicals[7]	3,731		
of which			(pieces of mail)
Agriculture	153		
Business and economics	262	**Post**[32]	
Chemistry and physics	170	Mail	201,576,000,000
Children's periodicals	78	Domestic	200,613,000,000
Education	203	International	963,000,000

Education and health

Literacy: n.a.

Education (2001–02)

	schools	teachers	students	student/teacher ratio
Primary (age 5–13)[33]	...	2,206,000	38,163,000	17.3
Secondary and vocational (age 14–17)	...	1,341,000	14,902,000	11.1
Higher, including teacher-training colleges	4,064[7]	1,012,000	15,300,000	15.1

Food (2000): daily per capita caloric intake 3,772 (vegetable products 72%, animal products 28%); 143% of FAO recommended minimum requirement. Per capita consumption of major food groups (kilograms annually; 2000): milk 259.5; fresh vegetables 125.8; fresh fruits 124.8; cereal products 113.6; red meat 74.2; potatoes 65.3; poultry products 47.6; sweeteners 37.2; fats and oils 31.2; fish and shellfish 21.4.
Health (1999): doctors of medicine 797,600[34] (1 per 341 persons), of which office-based practice 473,200 (including specialties in internal medicine 17.9%, general and family practice 14.0%, pediatrics 8.5%, obstetrics and gynecology 6.5%, general surgery 6.6%, psychiatry 5.2%, anesthesiology 5.6%, orthopedics 3.6%, ophthalmology 3.2%); doctors of osteopathy 43,500; nurses 2,271,000 (1 per 120 persons); dentists 196,000[35] (1 per 1,390 persons); hospital beds 994,000 (1 per 274 persons), of which nonfederal 94.5% (community hospitals 88.4%, psychiatric 9.3%, long-term general and special 2.1%), federal 5.5%; infant mortality rate per 1,000 live births (2000) 7.1.

Physicians and nurses (1999)[36]

	Physicians		Nurses	
States	Total	Rate per 100,000 population	Total	Rate per 100,000 population
Alabama	8,733	200	33,680	771
Alaska	1,054	170	7,350	1,186
Arizona	9,714	203	36,660	767
Arkansas	4,906	192	19,890	780
California	82,176	248	176,360	532
Colorado	9,914	244	31,230	770
Connecticut	11,859	361	32,660	995
Delaware	1,791	238	8,440	1,120
Florida	36,760	243	131,800	872
Georgia	16,470	211	56,880	728
Hawaii	3,184	269	9,540	805
Idaho	1,944	155	7,520	601
Illinois	31,928	263	110,270	909
Indiana	11,753	198	49,360	831
Iowa	5,009	175	31,220	1,088
Kansas	5,424	204	23,660	891
Kentucky	8,382	212	33,190	838
Louisiana	10,975	251	35,370	809
Maine	2,913	232	13,600	1,085
Maryland	19,592	379	44,210	855
Massachusetts	26,062	422	72,840	1,180
Michigan	22,246	226	83,370	845
Minnesota	12,125	254	51,970	1,088
Mississippi	4,533	164	21,700	784
Missouri	12,695	232	53,890	985
Montana	1,683	191	7,850	889
Nebraska	3,679	221	14,950	897
Nevada	3,209	177	11,420	631
New Hampshire	2,813	234	10,860	904
New Jersey	24,525	301	65,730	807
New Mexico	3,717	214	12,600	724
New York	71,840	395	170,930	939
North Carolina	18,166	237	71,550	935
North Dakota	1,420	224	7,460	1,177
Ohio	26,731	237	103,980	924
Oklahoma	5,614	167	20,500	610
Oregon	7,519	227	29,580	892
Pennsylvania	35,148	293	136,360	1,137
Rhode Island	3,362	339	11,680	1,179
South Carolina	8,294	213	32,410	834
South Dakota	1,379	188	7,400	1,009
Tennessee	13,626	248	49,210	897
Texas	41,084	205	132,110	659
Utah	4,312	202	13,870	651
Vermont	1,860	313	5,160	869
Virginia	16,717	243	57,560	837
Washington	13,616	237	44,740	777
West Virginia	3,962	219	16,130	893
Wisconsin	12,167	232	47,520	905
Wyoming	825	172	5,030	1,049
District				
District of Columbia	3,935	752	8,290	1,597
TOTAL/AVERAGE	693,345	245	2,271,340	833

Military

Total active duty personnel (2002): 1,414,000 (army 34.3%, navy 27.3%, air force 26.1%, marines 12.3%). *Military expenditure as percentage of GNP* (1999): 3.0% (world 2.4%); per capita expenditure U.S.$1,030. *Security assistance to the world* (2002): U.S.$7,209,000,000, for underwriting the purchase of U.S. weapons 50.6%, of which Israel 28.3%, Egypt 18.0%, Jordan 1.0%; for economic support 30.5%, of which Israel 10.0%, Egypt 9.1%, Jordan 2.1%; for the Andean Counterdrug Initiative 9.2%; for nonproliferation, antiterrorism, and de-mining 4.3%; for international narcotics and law enforcement 3.0%; for peacekeeping operations 1.9%.

[1]Excludes 4 nonvoting delegates from the District of Columbia, the U.S. Virgin Islands, American Samoa, and Guam; a nonvoting resident commissioner from Puerto Rico; and a nonvoting resident representative from the Northern Mariana Islands. [2]Total area per most recent official survey equals 3,675,267 sq mi (9,518,898 sq km), of which land area equals 3,536,278 sq mi (9,158,918 sq km), inland water area equals 78,937 sq mi (204,446 sq km), and Great Lakes water area equals 60,052 sq mi (155,534 sq km). [3]Excludes 230,000 military personnel overseas; adjusted census total announced December 2002 equaled 284,683,782. [4]Includes military personnel residing overseas. [5]Persons of Hispanic origin may be of any race. [6]Estimate of the UN High Commissioner of Refugees. [7]1998. [8]1995. [9]1989–91. [10]Includes deaths with age not known. [11]Individuals who used drugs at least once within month prior to survey. [12]Drinking 5 or more drinks on the same occasion on at least one day in the past 30 days per survey. [13]Estimated crimes include unreported crimes. [14]1997. [15]2000. [16]Excludes military personnel overseas. [17]Statistical discrepancy. [18]Unemployed. [19]Detail does not add to total given because of rounding. [20]1997; excludes tips. [21]Gross income from all sources, including transfer payments to individuals. [22]Householder 25 years old or older. [23]July. [24]Period average. [25]End-of-period. [26]1994. [27]"Own children" includes adopted children and stepchildren. [28]Manufacturing sector only. [29]Animal and vegetable oils included in Food and live animals. [30]Detail does not add to total given because of statistical discrepancies in the data. [31]Includes 292 localities in Alaska. [32]1999. [33]Primary includes kindergarten. [34]720,900 professionally active. [35]1996. [36]Nonfederal physicians and nurses only.

Internet resources for further information:
• **U.S. Census Bureau** http://www.census.gov
• **Statistical Abstract of the United States**
  http://www.census.gov/prod/www/statistical-abstract-us.html

Uruguay

Official name: República Oriental del Uruguay (Oriental Republic of Uruguay).
Form of government: republic with two legislative houses (Senate [31][1]; Chamber of Representatives [99]).
Head of state and government: President.
Capital: Montevideo.
Official language: Spanish.
Official religion: none.
Monetary unit: 1 peso uruguayo[2] ($U) = 100 centesimos; valuation (Sept. 23, 2002) 1 U.S.$ = $U 29.25; 1 £ = $U 45.46.

Atlantic Ocean

Area and population		area		population
				2001
Departments	**Capitals**	sq mi	sq km	estimate
Artigas	Artigas	4,065	11,928	78,075
Canelones	Canelones	1,751	4,536	503,359
Cerro Largo	Melo	5,270	13,648	85,881
Colonia	Colonia del Sacramento	2,358	6,106	125,946
Durazno	Durazno	4,495	11,643	57,561
Flores	Trinidad	1,986	5,144	25,471
Florida	Florida	4,022	10,417	68,562
Lavalleja	Minas	3,867	10,016	62,552
Maldonado	Maldonado	1,851	4,793	148,313
Montevideo	Montevideo	205	530	1,381,542
Paysandú	Paysandú	5,375	13,922	117,595
Río Negro	Fray Bentos	3,584	9,282	54,563
Rivera	Rivera	3,618	9,370	104,843
Rocha	Rocha	4,074	10,551	72,463
Salto	Salto	5,468	14,163	126,625
San José	San José de Mayo	1,927	4,992	104,635
Soriano	Mercedes	3,478	9,008	84,098
Tacuarembó	Tacuarembó	5,961	15,438	87,658
Treinta y Tres	Treinta y Tres	3,679	9,529	51,779
TOTAL LAND AREA		67,574	175,016	
INLAND WATER		463	1,199	
TOTAL		68,037	176,215	3,341,521

Demography

Population (2002): 3,383,000.
Density (2002): persons per sq mi 49.7, persons per sq km 19.2.
Urban-rural (1996): urban 88.7%; rural 11.3%.
Sex distribution (2001): male 48.43%; female 51.57%.
Age breakdown (2001): under 15, 24.6%; 15–29, 22.8%; 30–44, 19.7%; 45–59, 15.5%; 60–74, 11.8%; 75 and over, 5.6%.
Population projection: (2010) 3,566,000; (2020) 3,771,000.
Ethnic composition (2000): white (mostly Spanish, Italian, or mixed Spanish-Italian) 94.5%; mestizo 3.1%; mulatto 2.0%; other 0.4%.
Religious affiliation (1997): Roman Catholic 78.5%[3]; Protestant 4.5%; other Christian 3.5%; Jewish 0.9%; other 12.6%.
Major cities (1996): Montevideo 1,378,707; Salto 93,113; Paysandú 74,568; Las Piedras 66,584; Rivera 62,859.

Vital statistics

Birth rate per 1,000 population (2001): 16.1 (world avg. 21.2).
Death rate per 1,000 population (2001): 9.5 (world avg. 8.9).
Total fertility rate (avg. births per childbearing woman; 2001): 2.2.
Marriage rate per 1,000 population (2001): 4.2.
Divorce rate per 1,000 population (2001): 2.0.
Life expectancy at birth (2001): male 70.9 years; female 78.8 years.
Major causes of death per 100,000 population (1999): diseases of the circulatory system 330.4; malignant neoplasms 221.7; suicides, accidents, and injury 56.9.

National economy

Budget (1998). Revenue: $U 70,664,000,000 (taxes on goods and services 39.4%, social security contributions 28.6%, income taxes 12.6%, nontax revenue 7.1%, receipts from foreign trade 3.7%). Expenditures: $U 72,673,000,000 (social security and welfare 61.4%, general public services 7.4%, education 7.0%, health 5.8%, interest payments 4.7%).
Public debt (external, outstanding; 2000): U.S.$5,597,000,000.
Production (metric tons except as noted). Agriculture, forestry, fishing (1999): rice 1,328,000, wheat 377,000, corn (maize) 243,000, oranges 186,000, sugarcane 185,000, sunflower seed 161,000; livestock (number of live animals) 15,500,000 sheep, 10,700,000 cattle; roundwood (1998) 6,163,000 cu m. Mining and quarrying (2001): limestone 1,300,000; gold 67,000 troy oz; gypsum 183,000. Manufacturing (value added in $U '000,000; 1998): food products 6,955; refined petroleum 4,966; beverages 3,175; paints, soaps, and varnishes 2,337; textiles (excluding wearing apparel) 2,156. Energy production (consumption): electricity (kW-hr; 1997) 7,147,000,000 (7,003,000,000); crude petroleum (barrels; 1997) none (10,000,000); petroleum products (metric tons; 1997) 1,317,000 (1,665,000).
Land use (1998): forested and other 15.2%; meadows and pastures 77.3%; agricultural and under permanent cultivation 7.5%.
Household income and expenditure. Avg. household size (1999) 3.3; avg. annual income per household (1985) NUr$266,261[2] (U.S.$2,625); sources of income[4]: wages 53.5%, self-employment 17.0%, transfer payments and other 29.5%; expenditure (1982–83)[5]: food 39.9%, housing 17.6%, transportation and communications 10.4%, health care 9.3%, clothing 7.0%.

Gross national product (2000): U.S.$20,010,000,000 (U.S.$6,000 per capita).

Structure of gross domestic product and labour force				
	2000		1993	
	in value $U '000,000	% of total value	labour force	% of labour force
Agriculture	14,662	6.0	47,700	3.8
Mining	750	0.3	2,100	0.2
Manufacturing	40,966	16.9	254,300	20.2
Construction	14,312	5.9	86,400	6.9
Public utilities	10,212	4.2	16,900	1.3
Transp. and commun.	22,178	9.1	67,900	5.4
Trade	32,461	13.4	231,300	18.3
Finance	24,900	10.3	68,400	5.4
Pub. admin., defense	23,936	9.9 }		
Services	70,745	29.1 }	455,800	36.1
Other	−12,486[6]	−5.1[6]	30,200[7]	2.4[7]
TOTAL	242,636	100.0	1,261,000	100.0

Population economically active (1998): total 1,239,400[8]; activity rate 47.0% (participation rates: ages 14 and over, 60.4%; female 44.0%).

Price and earnings indexes (1995 = 100)							
	1995	1996	1997	1998	1999	2000	2001
Consumer price index	100.0	128.3	153.8	170.4	180.0	188.6	196.8
Monthly earnings index[9]	100.0	126.0	146.4	161.6	169.9	175.2	...

Tourism (2000): receipts U.S.$652,000,000; expenditures U.S.$281,000,000.

Foreign trade[10]

Balance of trade (current prices)					
	1995	1996	1997	1998	1999	2000
U.S.$'000,000	−563.0	−686.9	−704.4	−772.1	−896.6	−936.8
% of total	11.6%	12.3%	11.2%	12.0%	16.4%	16.4%

Imports (1999): U.S.$3,356,770,000 (machinery and appliances 22.2%; chemical products 14.6%; mineral products 11.6%; transport equipment 9.1%; processed foods 7.1%; synthetic plastics, resins, and rubber 7.0%; metal products 4.8%). *Major import sources* (1998): Argentina 22.0%; Brazil 20.8%; United States 12.1%; France 4.7%; Italy 4.6%; Spain 3.7%.
Exports (1999): U.S.$2,236,848,000 (live animals and live-animal products 30.1%; vegetable products 15.8%; textiles and textile products 11.8%; hides and skins 9.8%; processed foods 5.4%). *Major export destinations* (1998): Brazil 33.8%; Argentina 18.5%; United States 5.7%; Germany 4.0%.

Transport and communications

Transport. Railroads (1998): track length 3,002 km; passenger-km 14,000,000; metric ton-km cargo 244,000,000. Roads (1997): length 8,683 km[11] (paved 30%). Vehicles (1997): passenger cars 516,889; trucks and buses 50,264. Air transport (1998): passenger-km 642,000,000; metric ton-km cargo 70,000,000; airports (1997) 1.

Communications				units per 1,000
Medium	date	unit	number	persons
Daily newspapers	1996	circulation	950,000	293
Radio	1997	receivers	1,970,000	603
Television	1999	receivers	1,760,000	531
Telephones	2001	main lines	950,900	283
Cellular telephones	2001	subscribers	520,000	155
Personal computers	2001	units	370,000	110
Internet	2001	users	400,000	119

Education and health

Educational attainment (1996). Percentage of population age 25 and over having: no formal schooling 3.4%; primary education 53.6%; secondary 31.7%; higher 10.1%; unknown 1.2%. *Literacy* (2000 est.): population age 15 and over literate 97.7%; males 97.3%; females 98.1%.

Education (1997)				student/
	schools	teachers	students	teacher ratio
Primary (age 6–11)	2,410	16,721	348,195	20.8
Secondary (age 12–17)	413	19,104	192,399	10.1
Vocational	101	...	58,246	...
Higher	2	9,907[12]	79,691[12]	8.0[12]

Health (1999): physicians 12,357 (1 per 263 persons); hospital beds 6,651 (1 per 488 persons); infant mortality rate (2002) 14.3.
Food (2000): daily per capita caloric intake 2,879 (vegetable products 66%, animal products 34%); 108% of FAO recommended minimum.

Military

Total active duty personnel (2001): 23,900 (army 63.6%, navy 23.8%, air force 12.6%). *Military expenditure as percentage of GNP* (1999): 1.3% (world 2.4%); per capita expenditure U.S.$83.

---

[1]Includes the vice president, who serves as ex officio presiding officer. [2]The peso uruguayo (Uruguayan peso [$U]) replaced the new Uruguayan peso (NUr$) on March 1, 1993. [3]About 30–40% of Roman Catholics are estimated to be nonreligious. [4]Salaried employees only. [5]Weights of consumer price index components in Montevideo. [6]Includes indirect taxes less imputed bank service charges. [7]Includes unemployed not previously employed. [8]From urban areas only. [9]December 1995 = 100. [10]Import figures are f.o.b. in balance of trade. [11]Excludes streets under local control. [12]1996.

Internet resources for further information:
• **Instituto Nacional de Estadística—Uruguay** http://www.ine.gub.uy

Uzbekistan

Official name: Ŭzbekiston Respublikasi (Republic of Uzbekistan).
Form of government: multiparty republic with a single legislative body (Supreme Assembly [250]).
Heads of state and government: President assisted by Prime Minister.
Capital: Tashkent (Toshkent).
Official language: Uzbek.
Official religion: none.
Monetary unit: sum (plural sumy); valuation (Sept. 23, 2002) 1 U.S.$ = 788.69 sumy; 1 £ = 1,226 sumy.

Area and population

Autonomous republic	Administrative centres	area sq mi	area sq km	population 1993 estimate
Qoraqalpoghiston	Nuqus	63,700	164,900	1,343,000
Provinces				
Andijon	Andijon	1,600	4,200	1,899,000
Bukhoro	Bukhara (Bukhoro)	15,200	39,400	1,262,000
Farghona	Fergana (Farghona)	2,700	7,100	2,338,000
Jizzakh	Jizzakh	7,900	20,500	831,000
Khorazm	Urganch	2,400	6,300	1,135,000
Namangan	Namangan	3,100	7,900	1,652,000
Nawoiy	Nawoiy	42,800	110,800	715,000
Qashqadaryo	Qarshi	11,000	28,400	1,812,000
Samarqand	Samarkand (Samarqand)	6,300	16,400	2,322,000
Sirdaryo	Guliston	2,000	5,100	600,000
Surkhondaryo	Termiz	8,000	20,800	1,437,000
Tashkent (Toshkent)	Tashkent (Toshkent)	6,000[1]	15,600[1]	2,236,000
City				
Tashkent (Toshkent)	—	1	1	2,121,000
TOTAL		172,700	447,400	21,703,000

Demography

Population (2002): 25,484,000.
Density (2002): persons per sq mi 147.6, persons per sq km 57.0.
Urban-rural (2002): urban 36.6%; rural 63.4%.
Sex distribution (2001): male 49.55%; female 50.45%.
Age breakdown (2001): under 15, 36.4%; 15–29, 28.6%; 30–44, 19.6%; 45–59, 8.5%; 60–74, 5.4%; 75 and over, 1.5%.
Population projection: (2010) 28,538,000; (2020) 32,496,000.
Doubling time: 44 years.
Ethnic composition (1998): Uzbek 75.8%; Russian 6.0%; Tajik 4.8%; Kazakh 4.1%; Tatar 1.6%; other 7.7%.
Religious affiliation (2000): Muslim (mostly Sunnī) 76.2%; nonreligious 18.1%; Russian Orthodox 0.8%; Jewish 0.2%; other 4.7%.
Major cities (1999): Tashkent 2,142,700; Namangan 376,600; Samarkand 362,300; Andijon 323,900; Bukhara 237,900.

Vital statistics

Birth rate per 1,000 population (2001): 21.7 (world avg. 21.2); (1994) legitimate 96.5%; illegitimate 3.5%.
Death rate per 1,000 population (2001): 5.9 (world avg. 8.9).
Natural increase rate per 1,000 population (2001): 15.8 (world avg. 12.3).
Total fertility rate (avg. births per childbearing woman; 2001): 3.1.
Marriage rate per 1,000 population (1997): 7.7.
Divorce rate per 1,000 population (1994): 1.1.
Life expectancy at birth (2001): male 66.0 years; female 72.0 years.
Major causes of death per 100,000 population (1993): diseases of the circulatory system 303.6; diseases of the respiratory system 115.0; accidents, poisoning, and violence 50.0; cancers 48.7; infectious and parasitic diseases 38.4; diseases of the digestive system 31.8; diseases of the nervous system 10.3; endocrine and metabolic disorders 10.3.

National economy

Budget (1999). Revenue: 611,897,000,000 sumy (taxes on income and profits 30.5%, value-added tax 27.3%, excise taxes 22.8%, property and land taxes 12.1%, other 7.3%). Expenditures: 654,259,000,000 sumy (social and cultural affairs 36.7%, investments 18.7%, national economy 10.4%, transfers 10.4%, administration 2.2%, interest on debt 1.9%, other 19.2%).
Household income and expenditure (1995). Average household size (1998) 5.5; income per household 35,165 sumy (U.S.$1,040); sources of income: wages and salaries 63.0%, subsidies, grants, and nonwage income 34.9%, other 2.1%; expenditure: food and beverages 71%, clothing and footwear 14%, recreation 6%, household durables 4%, housing 3%.
Public debt (external, outstanding; 2000): U.S.$3,578,000,000.
Production (metric tons except as noted). Agriculture, forestry, fishing (2001): seed cotton 3,300,000, wheat 3,127,000, vegetables 2,700,000, fruit (except grapes) and berries 1,300,000, potatoes 800,000, grapes 650,000, rice 178,000, barley 58,000; livestock (number of live animals) 8,100,000 sheep, 5,344,000 cattle, 830,000 goats, 14,420,000 chickens; roundwood (2001) 24,980 cu m; fish catch (1999) 8,536. Mining and quarrying (2000): copper (metal content) 91,800; gold 62,276 kg. Manufacturing (metric tons except as noted; 1998): cement 3,358,000; cotton fibre 1,138,000; mineral fertilizer 897,000; steel 360,000; ferrous metal products 322,000; television sets 192,468 units; passenger cars 54,456 units; video recorders 50,096 units; refrigerators 16,000 units; tractors 3,000 units. Energy production (consumption): electricity (kW-hr; 1999) 45,108,000,000 ([1998] 46,100,000,000); hard coal (metric tons; 1997) 59,000 (75,000); lignite (metric tons; 1999) 2,904,000 ([1998] 2,792,000); crude petroleum (barrels; 1998) 59,400,000 (57,870,000); petroleum products (metric tons; 1998) 8,104,000 (6,934,000); natural gas (cu m; 2000) 56,350,000,000 (42,758,000,000).
Gross national product (2000): U.S.$8,843,000,000 (U.S.$360 per capita).

Structure of gross domestic product and labour force

	1999 in value '000,000 sumy	% of total value	labour force	% of labour force
Agriculture	521,627	26.9	3,091,000	35.0
Manufacturing and mining	283,425	14.6	1,126,000	12.8
Construction	149,803	7.7	578,000	6.5
Transp. and commun.	120,125	6.2	379,000	4.3
Trade	169,344	8.7	716,000	8.1
Finance				
Pub. admin., defense	399,882	20.6	2,003,000	22.7
Services				
Other	297,903[2]	15.3[2]	938,000[3]	10.6[3]
TOTAL	1,942,109	100.0	8,831,000[4]	100.0

Population economically active (1999): total 8,831,000; activity rate of total population 36.4% (participation rates: ages 16–59 [male], 16–54 [female] 70.4%; female [1994] 43.0%; unemployed 0.6%[5]).

Price and earnings indexes (1995 = 100)

	1994	1995	1996	1997	1998	1999
Consumer price index	44.4	100.0	...	...	...	...
Monthly earnings index	25.7	100.0	204.5	345.0	508.3	826.9

Tourism (1997): receipts U.S.$19,000,000.
Land use (1994): forested 2.9%; meadows and pastures 46.5%; agricultural and under permanent cultivation 10.1%; other 40.5%.

Foreign trade

Balance of trade (current prices)

	1993	1994	1995	1996	1997	1998
U.S.$'000,000	–378	+214	+237	–706	–72	+171
% of total	6.2%	3.8%	3.5%	9.1%	1.0%	3.0%

Imports (1998): U.S.$2,717,000,000 (machinery and metalworking products 49.6%, food products 20.9%, other 29.5%). *Major import sources:* Western Europe 30.6%; Russia 20.5%; Asia 14.2%; Kazakhstan 5.2%; Ukraine 3.2%.
Exports (1998): U.S.$2,888,000,000 (cotton fibre 41.5%, energy 22.7%, gold 6.0%, other 29.8%). *Major export destinations:* Western Europe 33.7%; Russia 22.6%; Asia 11.6%; Ukraine 5.4%; Kazakhstan 5.4%; Tajikistan 2.9%; Turkmenistan 2.5%.

Transport and communications

Transport. Railroads (2000): length 3,950 km; (1999) passenger-km 1,900,-000,000; (1999) metric ton-km cargo 13,900,000,000. Roads (1997): total length 84,400 km (paved 87%). Vehicles (1994): passenger cars 865,300; buses 14,500. Air transport (2000)[6]: passenger-km 3,732,000,000; metric ton-km cargo 76,600,000; airports (1998) with scheduled flights 9.

Communications

Medium	date	unit	number	units per 1,000 persons
Daily newspapers	1996	circulation	75,000	3.3
Television	1999	receivers	6,700,000	276
Telephones	2001	main lines	1,663,000	66
Cellular telephones	2001	subscribers	62,800	2.5
Internet	2001	users	150,000	5.9

Education and health

Educational attainment (1989). Percentage of population age 25 and over having: primary education or no formal schooling 13.3%; some secondary 19.8%; completed secondary and some postsecondary 57.7%; higher 9.2%. *Literacy* (1998): percentage of total population age 15 and over literate 88.0% (male 92.7%, female 83.4%).

Education (1995–96)

	schools	teachers	students	student/ teacher ratio
Primary (age 6–13)	9,300	413,000	5,090,000	12.3
Secondary (age 14–17)				
Voc., teacher tr.[7]	248	22,164[8]	240,100	...
Higher[8]	55	...	272,300	...

Health (1995): physicians 76,200 (1 per 302 persons); hospital beds 192,000 (1 per 120 persons); infant mortality rate per 1,000 live births (2001) 38.0.
Food (2000): daily per capita caloric intake 2,371 (vegetable products 82%, animal products 18%); 93% of FAO recommended minimum requirement.

Military

Total active duty personnel (2001): 78,100 (army 64.0%, air force 11.7%, other 24.3%)[9]. *Military expenditure as percentage of GNP* (1999): 1.7% (world 2.4%); per capita expenditure U.S.$38.

---

[1]Tashkent province includes Tashkent City. [2]Includes value-added taxes: excise taxes plus net import taxes minus subsidies. [3]Includes 882,600 persons on forced leave and 55,400 unemployed. [4]Detail does not add to total given because of rounding. [5]Official unemployment rate. [6]Uzbekistan Airways. [7]1998. [8]1992–93. [9]U.S. troops (June 2002) 1,000.

Internet resources for further information:
• Welcome to Uzbekistan http://www.gov.uz
• UNDP in Uzbekistan http://www.undp.uz

Vanuatu

Official name: Ripablik blong Vanuatu (Bislama); République de Vanuatu (French); Republic of Vanuatu (English).
Form of government: republic with a single legislative house (Parliament [52]).
Chief of state: President.
Head of government: Prime Minister.
Capital: Vila.
Official languages: Bislama; French; English.
Official religion: none.
Monetary unit: vatu (VT); valuation (Sept. 23, 2002) 1 U.S.$ = VT 136.78; 1 £ = VT 212.56.

Area and population

Provinces	Capitals	area sq mi	area sq km	population 1999 census
Malampa	Lakatoro	1,073	2,779	33,773
Penama	Longana	463	1,198	28,914
Sanma	Luganville	1,640	4,248	37,141
Shefa	Vila	562	1,455	55,900
Tafea	Isangel	628	1,627	29,412
Torba	Sola	341	882	8,079
TOTAL		4,707	12,190[1]	193,219[2]

Demography

Population (2002): 207,000.
Density (2002): persons per sq mi 44.0, persons per sq km 17.0.
Urban-rural (2002): urban 21.0%; rural 79.0%.
Sex distribution (1999): male 51.46%; female 48.54%.
Age breakdown (1999): under 15, 37.8%; 15–29, 29.4%; 30–44, 18.2%; 45–59, 9.7%; 60–74, 4.0%; 75 and over, 0.9%.
Population projection: (2010) 252,000; (2020) 313,000.
Doubling time: 27 years.
Ethnic composition (1999): Ni-Vanuatu 98.7%; European and other Pacific Islanders 1.3%.
Religious affiliation (1989): Christian 89.7%, of which Presbyterian 35.8%, Roman Catholic 14.5%, Anglican 14.0%, Seventh-day Adventist 8.2%; Custom (traditional beliefs) 4.6%; unknown 4.0%; nonreligious 1.7%.
Major towns (1999): Vila (Port-Vila) 30,139; Luganville 11,360.

Vital statistics

Birth rate per 1,000 population (2002): 31.6 (world avg. 21.2).
Death rate per 1,000 population (2002): 5.5 (world avg. 8.9).
Natural increase rate per 1,000 population (2002): 26.1 (world avg. 12.3).
Total fertility rate (avg. births per childbearing woman; 2002): 4.3.
Marriage rate per 1,000 population (1985): c. 7.4.
Divorce rate per 1,000 population (1985): less than 0.7.
Life expectancy at birth (2002): male 67.0 years; female 70.0 years.
Major causes of death per 100,000 population (1994)[3]: diseases of the circulatory system 39.0; diseases of the respiratory system 30.4; malignant neoplasms (cancers) 29.2; infectious and parasitic diseases 25.0; diseases of the digestive system 9.7.

National economy

Budget (1998). Revenue: VT 8,536,000,000 (taxes on international trade 33.0%; taxes on goods and services 32.0%; foreign grants 20.9%; nontax revenue 10.2%). Expenditures: VT 12,611,000,000 (current expenditure 58.0%, of which general public services 17.2%, education 13.2%, public order and safety 8.4%, health 6.6%, economic affairs and services 5.8%; capital expenditure 42.0%).
Public debt (external, outstanding; 2000): U.S.$67,200,000.
Household income and expenditure (1985)[4]. Average household size (1989) 5.1; income per household U.S.$11,299; sources of income: wages and salaries 59.0%, self-employment 33.7%; expenditure (1990)[4,5]: food and nonalcoholic beverages 30.5%, housing 20.7%, transportation 13.2%, health and recreation 12.3%, tobacco and alcohol 10.4%.
Production (metric tons except as noted). Agriculture, forestry, fishing (1999): coconuts 339,000, roots and tubers 65,000, bananas 12,500, vegetables and melons 9,800, peanuts (groundnuts) 1,750, cacao beans 1,500, corn (maize) 700; livestock (number of live animals) 151,000 cattle, 62,000 pigs, 12,000 goats, 320,000 chickens; roundwood (1998) 63,200 cu m; fish catch (2000) 73,490, of which tuna 71,120. Mining and quarrying: small quantities of coral-reef limestone, crushed stone, sand, and gravel. Manufacturing (value added in VT '000,000; 1995): food, beverages, and tobacco 645; wood products 423; fabricated metal products 377; paper products 125; chemical, rubber, plastic, and nonmetallic products 84; textiles, clothing, and leather 54. Energy production (consumption): electricity (kW-hr; 1997) 30,000,000 (30,000,000); coal, none (none); crude petroleum, none (none); petroleum products (metric tons; 1997) none (20,000); natural gas, none (none).
Land use (1994): forested 75.0%; meadows and pastures 2.0%; agricultural 11.8%; other 11.2%.
Population economically active (1999): total 76,370; activity rate of total population 40.9% (participation rates: ages 15–64, 78.2%; female 49.6%; unemployed, n.a.).

Price and earnings indexes (1995 = 100)

	1995	1996	1997	1998	1999	2000	2001
Consumer price index	100.0	100.9	103.8	107.2	109.3	112.0	116.1
Earnings index	...	...	...	...	...	...	...

Gross national product (2000): U.S.$226,000,000 (U.S.$1,150 per capita).

Structure of gross domestic product and labour force

	1999 in value VT '000,000	1999 % of total value	1989 labour force	1989 % of labour force
Agriculture	5,417	19.6	49,811	74.4
Mining	...	...	1	—
Manufacturing	989	3.6	891	1.3
Construction	877	3.2	1,302	1.9
Public utilities	594	2.2	109	0.2
Transportation and communications	1,697	6.1	1,031	1.5
Trade	10,927	39.6	2,713	4.1
Finance	2,127	7.7	646	1.0
Pub. admin., defense	3,635	13.2	} 7,892	11.8
Services	1,930	7.0		
Other	−606[6]	−2.2[6]	2,561	3.8
TOTAL	27,587	100.0	66,957	100.0

Tourism (2000): receipts from visitors U.S.$58,000,000; expenditures by nationals abroad U.S.$9,000,000.

Foreign trade[7]

Balance of trade (current prices)

	1995	1996	1997	1998	1999	2000
VT '000,000	−7,486	−7,520	−6,801	−6,943	−9,120	−8,673
% of total	54.1%	52.7%	45.4%	44.5%	57.8%	54.3%

Imports (1997): VT 10,888,000,000 (machinery and transport equipment 25.7%, food and live animals 19.7%, basic manufactures 15.2%, mineral fuels 10.6%, chemical products 6.2%, beverages and tobacco 3.6%). *Major import sources:* Australia 42.1%; France 13.5%; New Zealand 12.2%; Japan 7.3%; Fiji 6.0%.
Exports (1997): VT 4,087,000,000 (copra 49.0%, timber 12.3%, beef 10.2%, cacao beans 5.9%). *Major export destinations*[8]: European Union 45.9%; Bangladesh 12.6%; Japan 10.4%; New Caledonia 4.5%; Australia 2.3%.

Transport and communications

Transport. Railroads: none. Roads (1996): total length 665 mi, 1,070 km (paved 24%). Vehicles (1996): passenger cars 4,000; trucks and buses 2,600. Merchant marine (1992): vessels (100 gross tons and over) 280; total deadweight tonnage 3,259,594. Air transport (2001)[9]: passenger-mi 131,755,000, passenger-km 212,039,000; short ton-mi cargo 1,301,000, metric ton-km 1,899,000; airports (1996) with scheduled flights 29.

Communications

Medium	date	unit	number	units per 1,000 persons
Radio	1997	receivers	62,000	350
Television	1997	receivers	2,000	14
Telephones	2001	main lines	6,800	34
Cellular telephones	2001	subscribers	300	1.7
Personal computers	...	units	...	...
Internet	2001	users	5,500	27

Education and health

Educational attainment (1999). Percentage of population age 15 and over having: no formal schooling 18.0%; incomplete primary education 20.6%; completed primary 35.5%; some secondary 12.2%; completed secondary 8.5%; higher 5.2%, of which university 1.3%. *Literacy* (1998): total population age 15 and over literate 64%.

Education (1992)

	schools	teachers	students	student/ teacher ratio
Primary (age 6–11)[10]	272	852	26,267	30.8
Secondary (age 11–18)	27	220	4,269	19.4
Voc., teacher tr.	...	...	444	...
Higher	1[11]	13[12]	124[13]	...

Health (1997): physicians 21 (1 per 8,524 persons); hospital beds 573 (1 per 312 persons); infant mortality rate per 1,000 live births (2002) 29.0.
Food (1999): daily per capita caloric intake 2,766 (vegetable products 86%, animal products 14%); (1997) 121% of FAO recommended minimum.

Military

Total active duty personnel: Vanuatu has a paramilitary force of about 300.

---

[1]Detail does not add to total given because of rounding. [2]De facto figure; de jure figure equals 186,678. [3]Deaths reported to the Ministry of Health only. [4]Vila and Luganville only. [5]Weights of consumer price index components. [6]Imputed bank service charges. [7]Imports c.i.f.; exports f.o.b. [8]Destination of domestic exports only. [9]Air Vanuatu only. [10]Excludes independent private schools. [11]1989. [12]1983. [13]1991.

Internet resources for further information:
- **Vanuatu Statistics Office**
  http://www.statistics.gov.vu

Venezuela

Official name: República Bolivariana de Venezuela (Bolivarian Republic of Venezuela).
Form of government: federal multiparty republic with a unicameral legislature (National Assembly [165]).
Head of state and government: President.
Capital: Caracas.
Official languages: Spanish and Indian languages[1].
Official religion: none.
Monetary unit: 1 bolívar (B, plural Bs) = 100 céntimos; valuation (Sept. 23, 2002) 1 U.S.$ = Bs 1,467; 1 £ = Bs 2,279.

Area and population

States	Capitals	area sq mi	area sq km	population 2000 estimate
Amazonas	Puerto Ayacucho	69,554	180,145	100,325
Anzoátegui	Barcelona	16,700	43,300	1,140,369
Apure	San Fernando de Apure	29,500	76,500	466,931
Aragua	Maracay	2,708	7,014	1,481,453
Barinas	Barinas	13,600	35,200	583,521
Bolívar	Ciudad Bolívar	91,900	238,000	1,306,651
Carabobo	Valencia	1,795	4,650	2,106,264
Cojedes	San Carlos	5,700	14,800	262,154
Delta Amacuro	Tucupita	15,500	40,200	137,939
Falcón	Coro	9,600	24,800	747,672
Guárico	San Juan de Los Morros	25,091	64,986	638,638
Lara	Barquisimeto	7,600	19,800	1,581,121
Mérida	Mérida	4,400	11,300	744,986
Miranda	Los Teques	3,070	7,950	2,607,163
Monagas	Maturín	11,200	28,900	599,764
Nueva Esparta	La Asunción	440	1,150	377,701
Portuguesa	Guanare	5,900	15,200	830,441
Sucre	Cumaná	4,600	11,800	824,764
Táchira	San Cristóbal	4,300	11,100	1,031,158
Trujillo	Trujillo	2,900	7,400	587,280
Vargas	La Guaira	578	1,497	2
Yaracuy	San Felipe	2,700	7,100	518,902
Zulia	Maracaibo	24,400	63,100	3,209,626
Other federal entities				
Dependencias Federales[3]	—	50	120	...
Distrito Federal	Caracas	167	433	2,284,921[2]
TOTAL		353,841[4]	916,445	24,169,744

Demography

Population (2002): 25,093,000.
Density (2002): persons per sq mi 70.9, persons per sq km 27.4.
Urban-rural (2000): urban 87.1%; rural 12.9%.
Sex distribution (2000): male 50.31%; female 49.69%.
Age breakdown (2000): under 15, 34.0%; 15–29, 27.5%; 30–44, 20.2%; 45–59, 11.7%; 60–74, 5.2%; 75 and over, 1.4%.
Population projection: (2010) 28,716,000; (2020) 32,911,000.
Ethnic composition (1993): mestizo 67%; white 21%; black 10%; Indian 2%.
Religious affiliation (2000): Roman Catholic 89.5%; Protestant 2.0%; other Christian 1.4%; Spiritist 1.1%; nonreligious/atheist 2.2%; other 3.8%.
Major cities (2000): Caracas 1,975,787 (urban agglomeration [2001] 3,177,000); Maracaibo 1,764,038; Valencia 1,338,833; Barquisimeto 875,790; Ciudad Guayana 704,168.

Vital statistics

Birth rate per 1,000 population (2002): 20.2 (world avg. 21.2).
Death rate per 1,000 population (2002): 4.9 (world avg. 8.9).
Total fertility rate (avg. births per childbearing woman; 2002): 2.4.
Marriage rate per 1,000 population (2000): 3.8.
Divorce rate per 1,000 population (2000): 0.8.
Life expectancy at birth (2002): male 70.5 years; female 76.8 years.
Major causes of death per 100,000 population (1996): heart diseases 102.9; cancers 59.0; accidents 35.8; cardiovascular diseases 33.0.

National economy

Budget (1998). Revenue: Bs 9,017,475,000,000 (tax revenues 73.6%; nontax revenues 26.4%, of which oil revenues 24.9%). Expenditures: Bs 10,460,235,000,000 (subsidies 43.7%; goods and services 23.9%; capital expenditure 18.9%; debt service 11.8%).
Public debt (external, outstanding; 2000): U.S.$27,628,000,000.
Production (metric tons except as noted). Agriculture, forestry, fishing (1999): sugarcane 6,850,000, corn (maize) 1,024,000, bananas 1,000,394, rice 670,000, cassava 588,000, plantains 578,000, sorghum 402,000, potatoes 352,000; livestock (number of live animals) 15,992,400 cattle, 4,500,000 pigs, 4,000,000 goats, 110,000,000 chickens; roundwood (1998) 2,038,000 cu m; fish catch (1998) 506,177. Mining and quarrying (1998): iron ore 19,305,000; bauxite 4,633,000; gold 14,046 kg; diamonds (1997) 401,068 carats. Manufacturing (value added in 1984 Bs '000,000; 1997): ferrous and nonferrous metals 16,355; food products 13,277; chemicals 10,004; beverages 9,480; clothing, textiles, leather, and shoes 8,311; metal products 6,413. Energy production (consumption): electricity (kW-hr; 1997) 75,300,000,000 (75,145,000,000); coal (metric tons; 1999) 6,588,000 (419,000); crude petroleum (barrels; 2001) 972,000,000 ([1998] 374,000,000); petroleum products (metric tons; 1997) 59,974,000 (25,090,000); natural gas (cu m; 1997) 43,690,000,000 (43,690,000,000).
Gross national product (2000): U.S.$104,065,000,000 (U.S.$4,310 per capita).

Structure of gross domestic product and labour force

	2001 in value Bs '000,000[5]	2001 % of total value[5]	2000 labour force	2000 % of labour force
Agriculture	29,166	4.9	950,000	9.2
Petroleum and natural gas Mining	135,609	22.6	53,000	0.5
Manufacturing	113,618	18.9	1,191,000	11.5
Construction	33,467	5.6	741,000	7.2
Public utilities	11,276	1.9	58,000	0.6
Transp. and commun.	39,103	6.5	608,000	5.9
Trade	63,835	10.6	2,752,000	26.6
Finance	55,262	9.2		
Pub. admin., defense	46,208	7.7	2,598,000	25.2
Services	59,803	10.0		
Other	12,434	2.1	1,376,000[6]	13.3[6]
TOTAL	599,781	100.0	10,327,000	100.0

Population economically active (1997): total 9,507,125; activity rate 41.7% (participation rates: over age 15, 64.6%; female 35.9%; unemployed 10.6%).

Price index (1995 = 100)

	1995	1996	1997	1998	1999	2000	2001
Consumer price index	100.0	199.9	299.9	407.2	503.2	584.7	658.0

Household income and expenditure. Average household size (1990) 5.1; average annual income per household (1981) Bs 42,492 (U.S.$9,899); expenditure (1995): food 40.6%, housing 13.8%, transportation and communications 8.6%, clothing 5.3%, health 3.1%, education and recreation 2.9%.
Tourism (2000): receipts U.S.$563,000,000; expenditures U.S.$1,824,000,000.
Land use (1998): forest and other 75.3%; pasture 20.7%; agriculture 4.0%.

Foreign trade[7]

Balance of trade (current prices)

	1996	1997	1998	1999	2000	2001
Bs '000,000	+5,996.8	+3,858.3	+1,642.2	+5,201.4	+11,694.7	+5,658.0
% of total	44.3%	23.1%	9.6%	25.6%	37.1%	19.2%

Imports (2000): U.S.$9,907,500,000 (nonelectrical machinery 18.8%, chemicals and chemical products 13.8%, transport equipment 11.6%, electrical machinery 11.1%). *Major import sources:* U.S. 37.8%; Colombia 7.4%; Brazil 5.0%; Italy 4.4%; Mexico 4.3%.
Exports (2000): U.S.$21,602,200,000 (crude petroleum 58.9%, refined petroleum 26.6%, iron and steel 2.7%, aluminum 2.5%). *Major export destinations:* U.S. 59.6%; Netherlands Antilles 5.6%; Brazil 3.6%; Colombia 2.8%.

Transport and communications

Transport. Railroads (1996): length (1994) 627 km; passenger-km 149,905; metric ton-km cargo 54,474,000. Roads (1999): total length 96,155 km (paved 34%). Vehicles (1997): passenger cars 1,505,000; trucks and buses 542,000. Merchant marine (1992): vessels (over 100 gross tons) 271; total deadweight tonnage 1,355,419. Air transport (1998): passenger-km 3,133,000,000; metric ton-km cargo 332,000,000; airports (1997) with scheduled flights 20.

Communications

Medium	date	unit	number	units per 1,000 persons
Daily newspapers	1996	circulation	4,600,000	206
Radio	1997	receivers	10,750,000	472
Television	1998	receivers	4,300,000	185
Telephones	2001	main lines	2,758,300	112
Cellular telephones	2001	subscribers	6,489,900	264
Personal computers	2001	units	1,300,000	53
Internet	2001	users	1,300,000	53

Education and health

Educational attainment (1993). Percentage of population age 25 and over having: no formal schooling 8.0%; primary education or less 43.7%; some secondary and secondary 38.3%; postsecondary 10.0%. *Literacy* (1995 est.): total population age 15 and over literate 91.1%; males 91.8%; females 90.3%.

Education (1996–97)

	schools	teachers	students	student/ teacher ratio
Primary (age 7–12)	14,601	202,195	4,262,221	21.1
Secondary (age 13–17)[8]	2,177	39,601	377,984	9.5
Higher	99[9]	43,833[9]	717,192	12.6[10]

Health (1997): physicians 28,341 (1 per 804 persons); hospital beds 38,924 (1 per 585 persons); infant mortality rate (2002) 24.6.
Food (1999): daily per capita caloric intake 2,229 (vegetable products 84%, animal products 16%); (1997) 90% of FAO recommended minimum.

Military

Total active duty personnel (2001): 82,300 (army 69.3%, navy 22.2%, air force 8.5%). *Military expenditure as percentage of GNP* (1999): 1.4% (world 2.4%); per capita expenditure U.S.$61.

[1]31 indigenous Indian languages were made official in May 2002. [2]Distrito Federal includes Vargas. [3]A new federal entity (the Caribbean Federal Territory) was under consideration in late 2001. [4]Detail does not add to total given because of rounding. [5]At constant 1984 prices. [6]Mostly unemployed. [7]Imports and exports are f.o.b. in balance of trade. [8]Includes vocational and teacher training. [9]1990–91. [10]1991–92.

Internet resources for further information:
• Banco Central de Venezuela http://www.bcv.org.ve

Vietnam

Official name: Cong Hoa Xa Hoi Chu
Nghia Viet Nam (Socialist Republic
of Vietnam).
Form of government: socialist republic
with one legislative house (National
Assembly [498]).
Head of state: President.
Head of government: Prime Minister.
Capital: Hanoi.
Official language: Vietnamese.
Official religion: none.
Monetary unit: 1 dong (D) = 10
hao = 100 xu; valuation (Sept. 23, 2002)
1 U.S.$ = D 15,340; 1 £ = D 23,841.

Area and population

Economic regions[1]	Principal cities	area		population 1999 census
		sq mi	sq km	
Central Highlands	Buon Ma Thuot	17,740	45,946	3,062,293
Mekong River Delta	Long Xuyen	15,274	39,559	16,131,984
North Central Coast	Hue	19,758	51,174	10,007,215
North East	Thai Nguyen	25,871	67,005	10,860,417
North West	Hoa Binh	15,426	39,955	2,227,686
Northeastern South Region	Ho Chi Minh City	16,437	42,572	12,708,882
Red River Delta	Hanoi	4,833	12,517	14,800,066
South Central Coast	Da Nang	13,040	33,773	6,525,841
TOTAL		128,379[2]	332,501[2]	76,324,384[2]

Demography

Population (2002): 80,200,000.
Density (2002): persons per sq mi 624.7, persons per sq km 241.2.
Urban-rural (1999): urban 23.5%; rural 76.5%.
Sex distribution (1999): male 49.15%; female 50.85%.
Age breakdown (2001): under 15, 32.1%; 15–29, 29.4%; 30–44, 21.1%; 45–59, 9.7%; 60–74, 5.8%; 75 and over, 1.9%.
Population projection: (2010) 88,684,000; (2020) 100,205,000.
Doubling time: 46 years.
Ethnic composition (2000): Vietnamese 85.0%; Han Chinese 3.5%; Montagnards 1.9%; Tho (Tay) 1.6%; Tai 1.5%; Muong 1.4%; Khmer 1.2%; Nung 1.0%; other 2.9%.
Religious affiliation (1995): Buddhist 66.7%; Christian 8.7%, of which Roman Catholic 7.7%, Protestant 1.0%; Cao Dai (a New-Religionist group) 3.5%; Hoa Hao (a New-Religionist group) 2.1%; other 19.0%.
Major cities (1992): Ho Chi Minh City 4,549,000[3]; Hanoi 2,154,900[4]; Haiphong 783,133; Da Nang 382,674; Buon Ma Thuot 282,095; Nha Trang 221,331; Hue 219,149; Can Tho 215,587.

Vital statistics

Birth rate per 1,000 population (2000): 21.6 (world avg. 22.5).
Death rate per 1,000 population (2000): 6.3 (world avg. 9.0).
Natural increase rate per 1,000 population (2000): 15.3 (world avg. 13.5).
Total fertility rate (avg. births per childbearing woman; 2000): 2.5.
Life expectancy at birth (2000): male 66.8 years; female 71.9 years.

National economy

Budget (1998). Revenue: D 73,000,000,000,000 (tax revenue 80.8%, of which taxes on trade 20.4%, corporate income taxes 17.9%, turnover taxes 16.2%; nontax revenues 16.3%; grants 2.9%). Expenditures: D 80,200,000,000,000 (current expenditures 67.6%, of which social services 30.4%; capital expenditures 25.6%; other 6.8%).
Public debt (external, outstanding; 2000): U.S.$11,546,000,000.

Structure of gross domestic product and labour force

	1998		1997	
	in value D '000,000,000[5]	% of total value	labour force	% of labour force
Agriculture, forestry, fishing	57,422	23.5	25,400,000	68.5
Public utilities	5,099	2.1	200,000	0.5
Mining	15,063	6.2	200,000	0.5
Manufacturing	42,613	17.4	3,300,000	8.9
Construction	20,434	8.3	1,000,000	2.7
Transp. and commun.	9,548	3.9	900,000	2.4
Trade and restaurants	49,210	20.1	3,200,000	8.6
Finance, insurance	16,287	6.7	700,000	1.9
Pub. admin., defense, services, other	29,065	11.9	2,200,000	5.9
TOTAL	244,741	100.0[6]	37,000,000[6]	100.0[6]

Gross national product (2000): U.S.$30,439,000,000 (U.S.$390 per capita).
Tourism (1997): receipts from visitors U.S.$88,000,000; expenditures by nationals abroad, n.a.
Production (metric tons except as noted). Agriculture, forestry, fishing (2000): rice 32,554,000, sugarcane 15,145,000, cassava 2,036,000, corn (maize) 1,929,000, sweet potatoes 1,658,000, bananas 1,269,000, coconuts 940,000, coffee 802,000, oranges 427,000, groundnuts (peanuts) 353,000, natural rubber 291,000, pineapples 291,000, pimento 75,000, tea 69,700; livestock (number of live animals) 54,500,000 ducks, 20,194,000 pigs, 4,137,000 cattle, 2,897,000 buffalo; roundwood (1999) 36,730,000 cu m, of which fuelwood 32,174,000 cu m, industrial roundwood 4,556,000 cu m; fish catch (2000) 1,442,000, of which marine fish 1,008,000. Mining and quarrying (1998): phosphate rock (gross weight) 860,000; tin (metal content) 5,000. Manufacturing (gross value of pro-

duction in D '000,000,000; 1998[5]): food and beverages 36.5; cement, bricks, pottery, and glass 13.7; textiles 8.4; chemicals and chemical products 8.1; footwear and leather tanning 7.1; electric and electronic products 6.2. Energy production (consumption): electricity (kW-hr; 1998) 21,847,000,000 ([1997] 19,253,000,000); coal (metric tons; 1998) 10,800,000 ([1997] 6,984,000); crude petroleum (barrels; 1998) 83,000,000 ([1997] 293,200); petroleum products (metric tons; 1997) 38,000 (5,691,000); natural gas (cu m; 1997) 11,550,000 (11,550,000).
Population economically active (1989): total 30,521,019; activity rate 47.4% (participation rates: ages 15–64, 79.9%; female 51.7%; unemployed [1997] 10.3%).

Price and earnings indexes (1995 = 100)

	1995	1996	1997	1998	1999	2000	2001
Consumer price index	100.0	105.7	109.1	117.0	121.8	119.7	119.2
Earnings index	...	...	...	...	...	...	...

Household income and expenditure. Average household size (1989) 4.8; income per household (1990)[7] D 577,008 (U.S.$93); sources of income: n.a.; expenditure (1990): food 62.4%, clothing 5.0%, household goods 4.6%, education 2.9%, housing 2.5%.
Land use (1994): forested 29.6%; meadows and pastures 1.0%; agricultural and under permanent cultivation 21.5%; other 47.9%.

Foreign trade[8]

Balance of trade (current prices)

	1996	1997	1998	1999	2000
U.S.$'000,000	−2,775	−1,247	−989	+972	+375
% of total	32.1%	6.4%	5.0%	4.4%	1.3%

Imports (1998): U.S.$11,527,000,000 (machinery equipment [including aircraft] 17.8%; petroleum products 7.2%; textiles, clothing, and leather 7.1%; iron and steel 4.5%; unspecified 50.1%). *Major import sources:* Singapore 13.4%; South Korea 12.1%; Japan 11.8%; Taiwan 10.8%; China 9.1%.
Exports (1998): U.S.$9,365,000,000 (garments 14.4%; crude petroleum 13.2%; rice 10.9%; footwear 10.7%; fish, crustaceans, and mollusks 8.7%; coffee 6.3%). *Major export destinations:* Japan 18.0%; Germany 9.2%; U.S. 6.2%; France 5.8%; Australia 5.4%.

Transport and communications

Transport. Railroads (1999): route length 1,952 mi, 3,142 km; passenger-mi 1,694,000,000, passenger-km 2,727,000,000; short ton-mile cargo 958,000,000, metric ton-km cargo 1,398,000,000. Roads (1996): total length 58,000 mi, 93,300 km (paved 25%). Vehicles (1994): passenger cars, trucks, and buses 200,000. Air transport (1999)[9]: passenger-mi 2,380,000,000, passenger-km 3,831,000,000; short ton-mile cargo 67,436,000, metric ton-km cargo 98,455,000; airports (1997) with scheduled flights 12.

Communications

Medium	date	unit	number	units per 1,000 persons
Daily newspapers	1996	circulation	300,000	4.1
Radio	1997	receivers	8,200,000	109
Television	1999	receivers	14,500,000	187
Telephones	2001	main lines	3,049,900	38
Cellular telephones	2001	subscribers	1,251,200	15
Personal computers	2001	units	800,000	10
Internet	2001	users	400,000	4.9

Education and health

Educational attainment (1989). Percentage of population age 25 and over having: no formal education (illiterate) 16.6%; incomplete and complete primary 69.8%; incomplete and complete secondary 10.6%; higher 2.6%; unknown 0.4%. *Literacy* (2000): percentage of population age 15 and over literate 93.3%; males 95.7%; females 91.0%.

Education (1997–98)

	schools	teachers	students	student/ teacher ratio
Primary (age 7–12)	...	324,431	10,431,337	32.2
Secondary (age 13–18)	...	226,491	6,642,350	29.3
Vocational[10]	...	9,336	172,400	18.5
Higher	109[11]	23,522[10]	509,300[10]	21.7[10]

Health (1999): physicians 37,100 (1 per 2,092 persons); hospital beds (1997) 197,900 (1 per 380 persons); infant mortality rate per 1,000 live births (2000) 31.1.
Food (2000): daily per capita caloric intake 2,583 (vegetable products 89%, animal products 11%); 120% of FAO recommended minimum requirement.

Military

Total active duty personnel (2002): 484,000 (army 85.1%, navy 8.7%, air force 6.2%). *Military expenditure as percentage of GNP* (1997): 2.4% (world 2.5%); per capita expenditure U.S.$44.

---

[1]Eight economic regions are divided into 57 provinces and 4 municipalities as of the administrative reorganization of 1997. [2]Total represents sum of parts; actual reported total figure may differ. [3]1999. [4]1993. [5]Estimated figures at prices of 1994. [6]Detail does not add to total given because of rounding. [7]Wage workers and government officials only. [8]Imports are f.o.b. in balance of trade and c.i.f. in commodities and trading partners. [9]Vietnam Airlines only. [10]1996–97. [11]1995–96.

Internet resources for further information:
• **Ministry of Foreign Affairs http://www.mofa.gov.vn**

Virgin Islands (U.S.)

Official name: Virgin Islands of the United States.
Political status: organized unincorporated territory of the United States with one legislative house (Senate [15]).
Chief of state: President of the United States.
Head of government: Governor.
Capital: Charlotte Amalie.
Official language: English.
Official religion: none.
Monetary unit: 1 U.S. dollar (U.S.$) = 100 cents; valuation (Sept. 23, 2002) 1 £ = U.S.$1.55.

Area and population

Islands[1]	Principal Towns	area sq mi	area sq km	population 2000 census
St. Croix	Christiansted	84	218	53,234
St. John	Cruz Bay[2]	20	52	4,197
St. Thomas	Charlotte Amalie	32	83	51,181
TOTAL		136	353	108,612[3]

Demography

Population (2002): 110,000.
Density (2002): persons per sq mi 808.8, persons per sq km 311.6.
Urban-rural (1998): urban 45.7%; rural 54.3%.
Sex distribution (2000): male 46.91%; female 53.09%.
Age breakdown (2000): under 15, 27.8%; 15–29, 22.4%; 30–44, 17.9%; 45–59, 19.1%; 60–74, 9.7%; 75 and over, 3.1%.
Population projection: (2010) 116,000; (2020) 124,000.
Doubling time: 70 years.
Ethnic composition (1995): black 76.7%, of which Hispanic 6.7%; white 10.4%, of which Hispanic 1.5%; other 12.9%, of which Hispanic 9.1%.
Religious affiliation (2000): Christian 96.3%, of which Protestant 51.0% (including Anglican 13.0%), Roman Catholic 27.5%, independent Christian 12.2%; nonreligious 2.2%; other 1.5%.
Major towns (2000): Charlotte Amalie 11,004 (urban agglomeration 18,914); Christiansted 2,637; Frederiksted 732.

Vital statistics

Birth rate per 1,000 population (2001): 15.9 (world avg. 21.2); (1998) legitimate 30.2%[4]; illegitimate 69.8%.
Death rate per 1,000 population (2001): 5.5 (world avg. 8.9).
Natural increase rate per 1,000 population (2001): 10.4 (world avg. 12.3).
Total fertility rate (avg. births per childbearing woman; 2001): 2.3.
Marriage rate per 1,000 population (1993): 35.1.
Divorce rate per 1,000 population (1993): 4.5.
Life expectancy at birth (2001): male 74.4 years; female 82.4 years.
Major causes of death per 100,000 population (1997): diseases of the heart 111.3; malignant neoplasms (cancers) 103.9; cerebrovascular diseases 44.5; diabetes mellitus 32.3; accidents 31.4; homicide 27.1.

National economy

Budget. Revenue (1998): U.S.$459,485,000 (personal income tax 45.7%, gross receipts tax 18.5%, property tax 9.9%, corporate income tax 5.4%, excise tax 3.7%). Expenditures (1998): U.S.$398,394,000 (education 30.4%, health 17.8%, executive branch 7.8%, public safety 7.6%, public works 6.3%, College of the Virgin Islands 5.7%).
Production. Agriculture, forestry, fishing (value of sales in U.S.$'000; 1998): milk 1,263, livestock and livestock products 655 (of which cattle and calves 439, hogs and pigs 46), ornamental plants and other nursery products 364, vegetables 329 (notably tomatoes and cucumbers), fruits and nuts 185 (notably mangoes, bananas, and avocados), poultry 21; livestock (number of live animals) 3,636 cattle, 3,074 sheep, 2,944 goats, 1,436 hogs and pigs, 3,538 chickens; roundwood, n.a.; fish catch (1998) 910 metric tons. Mining and quarrying: sand and crushed stone for local use. Manufacturing (U.S.$'000[5]; 1997): food and food products 31,949; stone, clay, and glass products 21,897; print and publishing 21,127; transportation equipment 4,920; fabricated metal products 3,352. Construction: n.a. Energy production (consumption): electricity (kW-hr; 1997) 1,079,000,000 (1,079,000,000); coal (metric tons; 1997) none (252,000); crude petroleum (barrels; 1997) none (120,212,000); petroleum products (metric tons; 1997) 15,142,000 (2,290,000); natural gas, none (none).
Tourism (2001): receipts from visitors U.S.$1,196,000,000; number of hotel rooms 5,049; occupancy percentage 56.6%; expenditures by nationals abroad, n.a.
Household income and expenditure. Average household size (2000) 2.6; average annual income per household (2000) U.S.$34,991; sources of income (1984): wages and salaries 65.7%, transfer payments 13.0%, interest, dividends, and rent 12.7%, self-employment 2.6%; expenditure, n.a.
Population economically active (2000)[6]: total 50,933; activity rate of total population 46.9% (participation rates: ages 16–64, 72.5%[7]; female 47.8%[7]; unemployed 8.6%).

Price and earnings indexes (1995 = 100)

	1994	1995	1996	1997
Consumer price index	...	...	...	...
Hourly earnings index[8]	93.0	100.0	115.6	109.9

Gross national product (at current market prices; 1997): U.S.$2,666,000,000 (U.S.$18,287 per capita).

Structure of gross domestic product and labour force

	1989 in value U.S.$'000,000	1989 % of total value	1995 labour force[9]	1995 % of labour force[9]
Agriculture, fishing	...	...	3,110	6.5
Mining	...	...	[10]	[10]
Manufacturing	...	...	2,370[11]	5.0[11]
Construction	...	...	1,140[10]	2.4[10]
Public utilities	...	...	[11]	[11]
Transp. and commun.	...	...	2,560	5.4
Trade, hotels, restaurants	...	...	9,740	20.4
Finance, insurance, real estate	...	...	1,830	3.8
Pub. admin., defense	...	...	13,770	28.8
Services	...	...	10,490	21.9
Other	...	...	2,800[12]	5.8[12]
TOTAL	1,344[13]	100.0	47,810	100.0

Public debt (1999): U.S.$1,200,000,000.
Land use (1994): forested 5.9%; meadows and pastures 26.5%; agricultural and under permanent cultivation 20.6%; other 47.0%.

Foreign trade[14]

Balance of trade (current prices)

	1996	1997	1998	1999	2000	2001
U.S.$'000,000	+56.6	−372.3	−120.3	−99.4	−149.5	−374.5
% of total	0.8%	5.1%	2.2%	1.5%	1.4%	4.2%

Imports (2001): U.S.$4,608,700,000[15]. *Major import sources:* United States 15.8%; other countries 84.2%.
Exports (2001): U.S.$4,234,200,000[16]. *Major export destinations* (1995): United States 92.7%; other countries 7.3%.

Transport and communications

Transport. Railroads: none. Roads (1996): total length 532 mi, 856 km (paved, n.a.). Vehicles (1993): passenger cars 51,000; trucks and buses 13,300. Merchant marine (1992): vessels (100 gross tons and over) 1. Shipping (1988): cruise ship arrivals 1,228; passenger arrivals 1,062,010. Air transport (1989)[17]: passenger arrivals and departures 1,897,000; cargo loaded and unloaded 4,600 metric tons; airports (1999) with scheduled flights 2.

Communications

Medium	date	unit	number	units per 1,000 persons
Daily newspapers	1996	circulation	42,000	364
Radio	1996	receivers	107,000	927
Television	1996	receivers	67,000	580
Telephones	2000	main lines	69,000	570
Cellular telephones	2000	subscribers	35,000	289
Internet	1999	users	12,000	100

Education and health

Educational attainment (1997). Percentage of population age 25 and over having: incomplete primary education 4.4%; completed lower secondary 18.5%; incomplete upper secondary 27.3%; completed upper secondary 24.0%; incomplete undergraduate 14.0%; completed undergraduate 11.8%. *Literacy:* n.a.

Education (1997–98)[18]

	schools	teachers	students	student/ teacher ratio
Primary (age 5–12)	62[19]	777	11,926	15.3
Secondary (age 12–18)	...	782	9,982	12.8
Higher	1	266[19]	3,103	11.0[19]

Health (1989): physicians 130 (1 per 780 persons); hospital beds 252 (1 per 402 persons); infant mortality rate per 1,000 live births (2001) 9.4.
Food: daily per capita caloric intake, n.a.

Military

Total active duty personnel: no domestic military force is maintained; the United States is responsible for defense and external security.

---

[1]May be administered by officials assigned by the governor. [2]Census designated place. [3]De jure figure. [4]Percentage of legitimate births may be an underestimation due to the common practice of consensual marriage. [5]Figures are for value of sales. [6]Excludes armed forces. [7]1990. [8]Service workers only. [9]Employed labour force as of September 30; excludes armed forces. [10]Construction includes Mining. [11]Manufacturing includes Public utilities. [12]Includes 2,740 unemployed. [13]Tourism accounts for more than 70% of gross domestic product. [14]Imports c.i.f. [15]Breakdown of 1992 imports from U.S. only, totaling U.S.$1,768,000,000: crude petroleum 60.7%, food and beverages 4.5%, iron and steel (all forms) 4.5%, fuel oils 3.2%. [16]Breakdown of 1999 exports to U.S. only, totaling U.S.$2,971,899,000: petroleum products 90.4%, chemicals and chemical products 2.4%, antibiotics 0.4%, alcoholic beverages 0.3%. [17]St. Croix and St. Thomas airports. [18]Public schools only. [19]1992–93.

Internet resources for further information:
• **U.S. Department of the Interior: Pacific Web**
  http://www.pacificweb.org
• **U.S. Census Bureau: Economic Census of Outlying Areas**
  http://www.census.gov/csd/oat

Yemen

Official name: Al-Jumhūrīyah al-Yamanīyah (Republic of Yemen).
Form of government: multiparty republic with two legislative houses (Consultative Council [111 nonelected seats]; House of Representatives [301]).
Head of state: President.
Head of government: Prime Minister.
Capital: Sanaa.
Official language: Arabic.
Official religion: Islam.
Monetary unit: 1 Yemeni Rial (YRls) = 100 fils; valuation (Sept. 23, 2002) 1 U.S.$ = YRls 176.39; 1 £ = YRls 274.13.

Area and population

Governorates	Capitals	area[1] sq mi	area[1] sq km	population 2000 estimate
Abyān	Zinjibār	8,297	21,489	420,243
'Adan[2]	Aden	2,695	6,980	503,794
'Amrān[2]	'Amrān	…	…	955,978
Al-Baydā'	Al-Baydā'	4,310	11,170	562,851
Al-Dāli'[2]	Al-Dāli'	…	…	403,488
Dhamār	Dhamār	3,430	8,870	1,199,998
Hadramawt	Al-Mukallā	59,991	155,376	873,119
Hajjah	Hajjah	3,700	9,590	1,361,084
Al-Hudaydah	Al-Hudaydah	5,240	13,580	1,942,251
Ibb	Ibb	2,480	6,430	2,018,878
Al-Jawf	Al-Jawf	…	…	433,235
Lahij	Lahij	4,928	12,766	650,044
Al-Mahrah	Al-Ghaydah	25,618	66,350	70,318
Al-Mahwīt	Al-Mahwīt	830	2,160	451,624
Ma'rib	Ma'rib	15,400	39,890	226,488
Sa'dah	Sa'dah	4,950	12,810	596,334
San'ā'	Sanaa	7,745	20,063	1,352,389
Shabwah	'Atāq	28,536	73,908	454,786
Ta'izz	Ta'izz	4,020	10,420	2,295,990
City				
Sanaa	—	95	247	1,488,108
TOTAL		3	3	18,261,000

Demography

Population (2002): 19,495,000.
Density (2002)[4]: persons per sq mi 91.0, persons per sq km 35.1.
Urban-rural (2001): urban 25.0%; rural 75.0%.
Sex distribution (2000): male 50.98%; female 49.02%.
Age breakdown (2000): under 15, 47.5%; 15–29, 27.8%; 30–44, 13.2%; 45–59, 7.1%; 60–74, 3.3%; 75 and over, 1.1%.
Population projection: (2010) 24,887,000; (2020) 32,401,000.
Doubling time: 21 years.
Ethnic composition (2000): Arab 92.8%; Somali 3.7%; black 1.1%; Indo-Pakistani 1.0%; other 1.4%.
Religious affiliation (1995): Muslim 99.9%, of which Sunnī *c.* 60%, Shī'ī *c.* 40%; other 0.1%.
Major cities (1994): Sanaa 954,400 (urban agglomeration [2001] 1,410,000); Aden 398,300; Ta'izz 317,600; Al-Hudaydah 298,500; Al-Mukallā 122,400.

Vital statistics

Birth rate per 1,000 population (2001): 43.4 (world avg. 21.2).
Death rate per 1,000 population (2001): 9.6 (world avg. 8.9).
Natural increase rate per 1,000 population (2001): 33.8 (world avg. 12.3).
Total fertility rate (avg. births per childbearing woman; 2001): 3.4.
Life expectancy at birth (2001): male 58.5 years; female 62.1 years.
Major causes of death per 100,000 population: n.a.; however, infant, child, and maternal mortality were very high in the late 1990s.

National economy

Budget (2000). Revenue: YRls 388,950,000,000 (1999; tax revenue 90.1%, of which oil revenue 64.1%, taxes on income and profits 9.4%, customs duties 7.8%; nontax revenue 9.9%). Expenditures: YRls 422,250,000,000 (1999; wages and salaries 23.0%; defense 18.1%; economic development 17.5%; interest on debt 13.8%; subsidies 7.7%).
Population economically active (1999): total 4,118,000; activity rate of total population 24.3% (participation rates [1994]: age 15 and over, 45.8%; female 18.2%; unemployed [1995] 30%).

Price index (1995 = 100)

	1993	1994	1995	1996	1997	1998	1999
Consumer price index	44.0	64.0	100.0	130.0	137.0	148.0	167.9

Production (metric tons except as noted). Agriculture, forestry, fishing (2000): sorghum 401,212, tomatoes 244,720, potatoes 213,445, oranges 175,095, grapes 162,315, wheat 137,166, bananas 94,114, onions 70,838, millet 67,234, papayas 64,195; livestock (number of live animals) 4,760,389 sheep, 4,214,170 goats, 1,282,975 cattle, 500,000 asses, 185,000 camels, 28,000,000 chickens; roundwood (1998) 324,000 cu m; fish catch (1999) 123,252. Mining and quarrying (1999): salt 149,000; gypsum 103,000. Manufacturing (value of production in YRls '000,000; 1996): food, beverages, and tobacco 43,927; chemicals and chemical products 42,369; nonmetallic mineral products 8,571; paper products 8,562; basic metal industries 3,040; clothing, textiles, and leather 1,693; wood products 392. Construction: n.a. Energy production (consumption): electricity (kW-hr; 1999) 2,633,000,000 ([1997]

2,482,000,000); coal, none (none); crude petroleum (barrels; 2001) 165,200,000 ([1997] 42,700,000); petroleum products (metric tons; 1997) 5,692,000 (4,937,000); natural gas (cu m; 2000) none (none).
Gross national product (2000): U.S.$6,554,000,000 (U.S.$370 per capita).

Structure of gross domestic product and labour force

	1999 in value YRls '000,000[5]	1999 % of total value[5]	1999 labour force	1999 % of labour force
Agriculture	186,054	17.5	1,996,000	48.5
Mining	296,447	27.9	13,000	0.3
Manufacturing	83,829	7.9	206,000	5.0
Public utilities	8,401	0.8	382,000	9.3
Construction	41,867	3.9	21,000	0.5
Transp. and commun.	127,814	12.0	210,000	5.1
Trade	106,790	10.0	440,000	10.7
Finance, real estate	62,429	5.9	49,000	1.2
Pub. admin., defense	121,982	11.5	389,000	9.4
Services	19,009	1.8	412,000	10.0
Other	8,935[6]	0.8[6]	…	…
TOTAL	1,063,557	100.0	4,118,000	100.0

Household income and expenditure. Average household size (1998) 7.1; income per household YRls 29,035 (U.S.$217).
Tourism (2000): receipts U.S.$64,000,000; expenditures U.S.$83,000,000.
Public debt (external, outstanding; 2000): U.S.$4,525,000,000.
Land use (1994): forest 3.8%; pasture 30.4%; agriculture 2.9%; other 62.9%.

Foreign trade[7]

Balance of trade

	1996	1997	1998	1999	2000	2001
U.S.$'000,000	+636.9	+490.2	−669.9	+431.9	+1,755.1	+905.5
% of total	13.5%	10.9%	18.3%	9.7%	27.4%	16.4%

Imports (1999): U.S.$1,535,900,000 (food and live animals 36.2%, of which cereals and related products 17.1%; machinery 15.3%; chemicals and chemical products 8.5%; mineral fuels 7.4%). *Major import sources:* U.A.E. 11.7%; Saudi Arabia 10.2%; U.S. 5.5%; Australia 4.8%; U.K. 4.7%; Kuwait 4.6%.
Exports (1999): U.S.$2,435,800,000 (crude petroleum 87.5%; petroleum products 8.0%; coffee 0.5%; fish 0.5%). *Major export destinations:* China 28.8%; Thailand 25.5%; South Korea 14.5%; Singapore 8.6%.

Transport and communications

Transport. Railroads: none. Roads (1996): total length 64,725 km (paved 8.1%). Vehicles (1996): passenger cars 240,567; trucks and buses 291,149. Air transport (2000): passenger-km 1,574,000,000; metric ton-km cargo 32,000,000; airports (1998) with scheduled flights 12.

Communications

Medium	date	unit	number	units per 1,000 persons
Daily newspapers	1996	circulation	230,000	15
Radio	1997	receivers	1,050,000	64
Television	1999	receivers	5,000,000	286
Telephones	2001	main lines	423,200	22
Cellular telephones	2001	subscribers	152,000	8.0
Internet	2001	users	17,000	0.9
Personal computers	2001	units	37,000	1.9

Education and health

Educational attainment (1998). Percentage of population age 10 and over having: no formal schooling 49.5%; reading and writing ability 32.2%; primary education 11.0%; secondary education 4.6%; higher 2.7%. *Literacy* (1998): percentage of total population age 10 and over literate 50.5%; males literate 71.8%; females literate 29.1%.

Education (1996–97)

	schools	teachers	students	student/ teacher ratio
Primary (age 7–12)	11,013[8]	90,478	2,699,788	29.8
Secondary (age 13–18)[9]	1,224[10]	11,130[10]	354,288	…
Voc., teacher tr.[9, 10]	125	369	15,074	40.9
Higher	2	1,991	65,675	…

Health (1998): physicians 3,883 (1 per 4,211 persons); hospital beds 9,143 (1 per 1,788 persons); infant mortality rate per 1,000 live births (2001) 68.5.
Food (2000): daily per capita caloric intake 2,002 (vegetable products 93%, animal products 7%); 84% of FAO recommended minimum requirement.

Military

Total active duty personnel (2001): 54,000 (army 90.7%, navy 2.8%, air force 6.5%). *Military expenditure as percentage of GNP* (1999): 6.1% (world 2.4%); per capita expenditure U.S.$22.

---

[1]Governorate area figures are based on a pre-1998 survey and are sometimes rounded. [2]Created in 1998 from parts of three other governorates. [3]An agreement to resolve the long-undemarcated northeastern boundary with Saudi Arabia (which increased Yemen's total area to roughly 214,300 sq mi [555,000 sq km]) was signed in June 2000. [4]Based on the total area estimate of 214,300 sq mi (555,000 sq km). [5]In purchasers' value at current prices. [6]Includes import duties of 31.0 million Yemeni Rials less imputed bank service charges. [7]Imports c.i.f. in balance of trade and f.o.b. in commodities and trading partners. [8]1993–94. [9]Public schools only, which comprise the vast majority of schools in Yemen. [10]1994–95.

Internet resources for further information:
• **The Yemen Times** http://www.yementimes.com
• **Central Bank of Yemen** http://www.centralbank.gov.ye

Yugoslavia[1]

Official name: Savezna Republika Jugoslavija (Federal Republic of Yugoslavia).
Form of government: federal multiparty republic with two legislative houses (Chamber of Republics [40]; Chamber of Citizens [138]).
Chief of state: Federal President.
Head of government: Prime Minister.
Capital: Belgrade.
Official language: Serbian (Serbo-Croatian).
Official religion[2]: none.
Monetary unit: 1 Yugoslav new dinar (second) = 100 paras; valuation (Sept. 23, 2002) 1 U.S.$ = 62.21 Yugoslav new dinars; 1 £ = 96.68 Yugoslav new dinars[3].

Area and population

Republics	Capitals	area		population
		sq mi	sq km	2001 estimate
Montenegro (Crna Gora)	Podgorica	5,333	13,812	658,000
Serbia (Srbija)	Belgrade	21,609	55,968	5,731,000
Autonomous province[4]				
Vojvodina	Novi Sad	8,304	21,506	1,937,000
Geographical region				
Kosovo (Kosova)[5]	Priština	4,203	10,887	2,325,000
TOTAL		39,449	102,173	10,651,000

Demography

Population (2002): 10,664,000.
Density (2002): persons per sq mi 270.3, persons per sq km 104.4.
Urban-rural (2002): urban 51.7%; rural 48.3%.
Sex distribution (1999): male 49.53%; female 50.47%.
Age breakdown (1991): under 15, 22.8%; 15–29, 21.6%; 30–44, 21.7%; 45–59, 17.1%; 60–74, 12.2%; 75 and over, 3.5%; unknown, 1.1%.
Population projection: (2010) 10,545,000; (2020) 10,330,000.
Ethnic composition (2000): Serb 62.1%; Albanian 17.1%; Montenegrin 4.3%; Hungarian 4.3%; Croat 3.1%; Bosniak Muslim 1.8%; Romany (Gypsy) 1.4%; Slovak 0.9%; Romanian 0.8%; other 4.2%.
Religious affiliation (1995): Serbian Orthodox 62.6%; Muslim 19.0%; Roman Catholic 5.8%; other, mostly nonreligious 12.6%.
Major cities (2000): Belgrade 1,168,454; Novi Sad 179,626; Niš 175,391; Kragujevac 147,305; Podgorica 117,875; Subotica 100,386.

Vital statistics

Birth rate per 1,000 population (2000): 11.8 (world avg. 22.5).
Death rate per 1,000 population (2000): 11.1 (world avg. 9.0).
Natural increase rate per 1,000 population (2000): 0.7 (world avg. 13.5).
Total fertility rate (avg. births per childbearing woman; 2000): 2.0.
Life expectancy at birth (2000): male 69.8 years; female 74.9 years.
Major causes of death per 100,000 population (1997): diseases of the circulatory system 585.0; malignant neoplasms (cancers) 169.0; accidents, violence, and poisoning 45.0; diseases of the respiratory system 39.0.

National economy

Budget (2001)[6]. Revenue: 421,000,000,000 Yugoslav new dinars (tax revenue 91.5%, of which social security tax 26.8%, VAT 26.2%, income tax 12.5%, excise tax 11.9%; nontax revenue 8.5%). Expenditure: 477,000,000,000 Yugoslav new dinars (transfers 50.1%, wages 20.7%, other 29.2%).
Public debt (external, outstanding; 2000): U.S.$6,074,000,000.
Production (metric tons except as noted). Agriculture, forestry, fishing (2001): corn (maize) 3,828,000, wheat 2,949,000, sugar beets 2,500,000, potatoes 690,446, plums 370,000, grapes 362,628, cabbages 285,317, watermelons 244,407; livestock (number of live animals) 4,372,000 pigs, 1,917,000 sheep, 1,831,000 cattle, 21,118,000 poultry; roundwood (2000) 1,140,000 cu m; fish catch (2000) 9,940. Mining and quarrying (1998): copper ore 19,939,000; lead-zinc ore 1,249,000; aluminum and ingots 100,000; magnesite 81,000; salt 19,305; asbestos ore 19,000; refined silver 34,000 kg. Manufacturing (1998): cement 2,418,000; crude steel 949,000; wheat flour 830,000; pig iron 826,000; sulfuric acid 211,000; nitric acid 185,000; electrolytic copper 94,000; welded pipes 43,000; rolled copper 27,055; refined lead 24,000; medicines 22,871. Construction (residential units constructed; 2000): 12,732. Energy production (consumption): electricity (kW-hr; 2001) 34,594,000,000 (34,594,000,000); coal (metric tons; 2001) 32,225,000 (32,225,000); crude petroleum (barrels; 2001) 5,534,000,000 (5,534,000,000); petroleum products (metric tons; 1998) 763,000 ([1997] 1,285,000); natural gas (cu m; 1998) 731,000,000 ([1997] 2,944,000,000).
Tourism (2000): receipts from visitors U.S.$26,000,000; expenditures, n.a.
Population economically active (2001)[7]: total 3,092,000; activity rate 37.1% (1998; participation rates: over age 15, 58.3%; female [1995] 43.7%; [2001] unemployed 27.5%[7]).

Price and earnings indexes (1997 = 100)

	1997	1998	1999	2000	2001
Consumer price index	100.0	129.9	188.2	348.0	613.4
Annual earnings index	100.0	132.4	163.0	318.6	690.5

Gross domestic product (2000): U.S.$10,028,000,000 (U.S.$940 per capita).

Structure of gross material product and labour force

	1999[7]		2001[7]	
	in value '000,000 Yugoslav new dinars	% of total value	labour force	% of labour force
Agriculture	37,227	18.9	90,000	2.9
Mining	50,102	25.5	684,000	22.1
Manufacturing				
Construction	8,220	4.2	104,000	3.4
Public utilities	7,879	4.0	55,000	1.8
Transp. and commun.	16,439	8.4	140,000	4.5
Trade	17,669	9.0	271,000	8.8
Finance	16,912	8.6	101,000	3.3
Pub. admin., defense	10,274	5.2	73,000	2.4
Services	17,133	8.7	362,000	11.7
Other	14,661[8]	7.5[8]	1,212,000[9]	39.2[9]
TOTAL	196,516	100.0	3,092,000	100.0[10]

Household income and expenditure[7]. Average household size (2000) 4.2; income per household (2000) 93,185 Yugoslav new dinars (U.S.$7,280); sources of income (2000): wages and salaries 50.6%, pensions 21.2%, self-employment 9.5%, other 18.7%; expenditure (2000): food 47.0%, fuel and light 9.9%, beverages and tobacco 7.3%, clothing and footwear 6.6%, transportation and communications 6.2%, health 5.6%, education 2.1%, housing 1.3%, other 14.0%.

Foreign trade

Balance of trade (current prices)

	1997	1998	1999	2000	2001
U.S.$'000,000	−2,431	−1,991	−1,798	−1,988	−2,934
% of total	33.9%	25.8%	37.5%	36.6%	43.5%

Imports (2001): U.S.$4,837,000,000 (machinery and transport equipment 21.3%, mineral fuels 20.7%, chemicals 14.4%, food and live animals 9.1%). *Major import sources:* Russia 14.2%; Germany 12.2%; Italy 10.3%; Greece 4.5%; Hungary 4.0%.
Exports (2001): U.S.$1,903,000,000 (manufactured goods 19.1%, food 14.5%, machinery and transport equipment 12.8%, chemicals 7.0%). *Major export destinations:* Italy 16.4%; Bosnia 13.1%; Germany 12.1%; Macedonia 9.2%; Switzerland 8.4%; Russia 4.2%; Greece 3.3%; Hungary 3.3%; U.K. 2.9%.

Transport and communications

Transport. Railroads (2000): length 4,058 km; passenger-km 1,436,000,000; metric ton-km cargo 1,969,000,000. Roads (2000): total length 44,777 km (paved 63%). Vehicles (1998): passenger cars 1,863,315; trucks and buses 158,667. Merchant marine (2000): cargo vessels 15. Air transport (2000): passenger-mi 608,300,000, passenger-km 979,000,000; short ton-mi cargo 4,740,000,000, metric ton-km cargo 7,629,000,000; airports (2000) 5.

Communications

Medium	date	unit	number	units per 1,000 persons
Daily newspapers	1995	circulation	1,363,000	256
Radio	1997	receivers	1,384,000	131
Television	1999	receivers	2,900,000	272
Telephones	2001	main lines	2,443,900	229
Cellular telephones	2001	subscribers	1,997,800	187
Personal computers	2001	units	250,000	23
Internet	2001	users	600,000	56

Education and health

Educational attainment (1991). Percentage of population age 15 and over having: less than full primary education 33.5%; primary 25.0%; secondary 32.2%; postsecondary and higher 9.3%. *Literacy* (1991): total population age 10 and over literate 93.0%; males literate 97.2%; females literate 88.9%.

Education (2000–01)

	schools	teachers	students	student/ teacher ratio
Primary (age 7–14)	4,087	48,868	787,423	16.1
Secondary (age 15–18)	518	26,740	355,424	13.3
Higher	51	1,612	50,901	31.6

Health (2000): physicians 27,010 (1 per 394 persons); hospital beds 56,928 (1 per 187 persons); infant mortality rate per 1,000 live births (2000) 13.0.
Food (2000): daily per capita caloric intake 2,570 (vegetable products 61%, animal products 39%); 101% of FAO recommended minimum.

Military

Total active duty personnel (2001)[11]: 105,500 (army 74.9%, air force 18.5%, navy 6.6%). *Military expenditure as percentage of government expenditure* (1991): 3.9% (world 4.0%); per capita expenditure U.S.$176.

[1]Official name change per constitution to Serbia and Montenegro was pending in November 2002. [2]Government gives "preferential treatment" to the Serbian Orthodox Church according to the U.S. Department of State, *Country Reports on Human Rights Practices for 2001.* [3]Montenegro and Kosovo (Kosova) adopted the euro on Jan. 1, 2002. [4]Vojvodina is administratively part of the Republic of Serbia. [5]Region under interim UN administration from mid-1999. [6]Consolidated general government. [7]Excludes Kosovo. [8]Taxes on products less subsidies. [9]Includes 850,000 unemployed and 574,000 undistributed workers in small enterprises. [10]Detail does not add to total given because of rounding. [11]38,600 troops from over 30 NATO and non-NATO countries were deployed in Kosovo in 2002.

Internet resources for further information:
• Federal Statistical Office of Yugoslavia http://www.szs.sv.gov.yu/homee.htm
• Federal Republic of Yugoslavia Official Web Site http://www.gov.yu

Zambia

Official name: Republic of Zambia.
Form of government: multiparty
republic with one legislative house
(National Assembly [158[1]]).
Head of state and government:
President.
Capital: Lusaka.
Official language: English.
Official religion: none[2].
Monetary unit: 1 Zambian kwacha
(K) = 100 ngwee; valuation (Sept. 23,
2002) 1 U.S.$ = K 4,500;
1 £ = K 6,993.

Area and population

Provinces	Capitals	area sq mi	area sq km	population 2000 census[3]
Central	Kabwe	36,446	94,394	1,006,766
Copperbelt	Ndola	12,096	31,328	1,657,646
Eastern	Chipata	26,682	69,106	1,300,973
Luapula	Mansa	19,524	50,567	784,613
Lusaka	Lusaka	8,454	21,896	1,432,401
North-Western	Solwezi	48,582	125,827	610,975
Northern	Kasama	57,076	147,826	1,407,088
Southern	Livingstone	32,928	85,283	1,302,660
Western	Mongu	48,798	126,386	782,509
TOTAL		290,585[4]	752,612[4]	10,285,631

Demography

Population (2002): 9,959,000.
Density (2002): persons per sq mi 34.3, persons per sq km 13.2.
Urban-rural (2001): urban 43.9%; rural 56.1%.
Sex distribution (2000): male 49.30%; female 50.70%.
Age breakdown (2000): under 15, 47.6%; 15–29, 30.6%; 30–44, 12.4%; 45–59,
5.5%; 60–74, 3.1%; 75 and over, 0.8%.
Population projection: (2010) 11,482,000; (2020) 13,365,000.
Doubling time: 35 years.
Ethnolinguistic composition (1990): Bemba peoples 39.7%; Maravi (Nyanja)
peoples 20.1%; Tonga peoples 14.8%; North-Western peoples 8.8%; Barotze
peoples 7.5%; Tumbuka peoples 3.7%; Mambwe peoples 3.4%; other 2.0%.
Religious affiliation (1995): Christian 47.8%, of which Protestant 22.9%,
Roman Catholic 16.9%, African Christian 5.6%; traditional beliefs 27.0%;
Muslim 1.0%; other 24.2%.
Major cities (1990): Lusaka 982,362 (urban agglomeration [1999] 1,577,000);
Ndola 370,000; Kitwe 290,000; Chingola 167,954; Kabwe 159,000; Mufulira
152,944.

Vital statistics

Birth rate per 1,000 population (2000): 41.9 (world avg. 22.5); legitimate, n.a.;
however, marriage is both early and universal, suggesting that legitimate
births are a relatively high proportion of all births.
Death rate per 1,000 population (2000): 22.1 (world avg. 9.0).
Natural increase rate per 1,000 population (2000): 19.8 (world avg. 13.5).
Total fertility rate (avg. births per childbearing woman; 2000): 5.6.
Life expectancy at birth (2000): male 37.1 years; female 37.4 years.
Major causes of death per 100,000 population: n.a.

National economy

Budget (1999). Revenue: K 1,430,400,000 (1998; tax revenue 71.5%, of which
income tax 24.9%, excise taxes 13.8%, value-added tax 13.1%, company
income tax 5.9%; grants 26.0%; nontax revenue 2.5%). Expenditures: K
1,874,300,000 (1998; current expenditures 65.0%, of which debt service
21.7%, education 7.7%, transfers 7.7%, health 5.7%, defense 1.4%; capital
expenditures 35.0%).
Public debt (external, outstanding; 2000): U.S.$4,448,000,000.
Production (metric tons except as noted). Agriculture, forestry, fishing (2001):
sugarcane 1,800,000, corn (maize) 980,000, cassava 950,000, fruits and vegetables 380,000 (of which onions 27,000, tomatoes 25,000, oranges 3,500),
wheat 75,000, seed cotton 62,000, millet 55,000, peanuts (groundnuts) 55,000,
sweet potatoes 53,000, soybeans 30,000, sorghum 27,000, potatoes 11,000,
sunflower seeds 7,500, tobacco 3,200; livestock (number of live animals)
2,400,000 cattle, 1,270,000 goats, 340,000 pigs, 150,000 sheep, 30,000,000
chickens; roundwood (2000) 8,053,000 cu m; fish catch (1999) 71,507. Mining
and quarrying (1999): copper (metal content) 260,000; cobalt (metal content)
4,700; silver 8,000 kg; gold 740 kg[5]. Manufacturing (value added in K '000,000;
1994): food products 39,765.1; beverages 36,596.5; chemicals and pharmaceuticals 32,141.5; textiles 15,358.5; tobacco 14,060.2; iron and steel, nonferrous metals, and fabricated metal products 13,874.6. Construction (value
added in K; 1995): 45,663,000,000. Energy production (consumption): electricity (kW-hr; 1997) 7,795,000,000 (6,315,000,000); coal (metric tons; 1997)
360,000 (355,000); crude petroleum (barrels; 1997) none (4,215,000); petroleum products (metric tons; 1997) 517,000 (455,000); natural gas, none (n.a.).
Household income and expenditure. Average household size (1997) 5.0; average annual income per household: n.a.; sources of income: n.a.; expenditure:
n.a.
Tourism (1999): receipts U.S.$85,000,000; expenditures, n.a.
Population economically active (1996): total 3,454,000; activity rate of total
population 38.2% (participation rates [1991]: over age 10, 52.6%; female
29.6%; unemployed, n.a.).

Price and earnings indexes (1996 = 100)

	1996	1997	1998	1999	2000	2001
Consumer price index	100.0	123.3	153.5	214.1	266.1	308.6[6]
Earnings index	...	...	...	...	...	...

Gross national product (2000): U.S.$3,026,000,000 (U.S.$300 per capita).

Structure of gross domestic product and labour force

	1998 in value K '000,000	1998 % of total value	1990 labour force	1990 % of labour force
Agriculture	1,080,000	17.3	1,872,000	68.9
Mining	378,000	6.1	56,800	2.1
Manufacturing	713,000	11.4	50,900	1.9
Construction	316,000	5.1	29,100	1.1
Public utilities	241,000	3.9	8,900	0.3
Transp. and commun.	362,000	5.8	25,600	0.9
Trade	1,201,000	19.2	30,700	1.1
Finance	1,014,000	16.2	24,200	0.9
Pub. admin., defense Services	560,000	9.0	111,600	4.1
Other	376,000[7]	6.0[7]	506,100	18.6
TOTAL	6,241,000	100.0	2,716,000[4]	100.0[4]

Land use (1994): forest 43.0%; pasture 40.4%; agriculture 7.1%; other 9.5%.

Foreign trade

Balance of trade (current prices)

	1994	1995	1996	1997	1998
U.S.$'000,000	+63	−8	−62	−27	−148
% of total	3.0%	0.3%	3.0%	1.1%	7.8%

Imports (1998): U.S.$1,022,000,000 (1995; machinery 24.5%, transport equip-
ment 13.4%, chemicals and chemical products 13.3%, crude petroleum
11.3%, cereals and related products 6.5%). Major import sources (1999):
South Africa 50.3%; Zimbabwe 9.3%; U.K. 5.9%; Saudi Arabia 5.7%.
Exports (1998): U.S.$873,600,000 (copper 49.3%, cobalt 17.7%, nonmetal
exports 33.0%). Major export destinations (1999): Japan 11.3%; U.K. 8.5%;
India 6.6%; Thailand 5.7%; Saudi Arabia 4.8%; U.S. 4.5%; Germany 4.1%.

Transport and communications

Transport. Railroads (1997)[8]: length 787 mi, 1,266 km; passenger-mi 166,-
000,000, passenger-km 267,000,000; short ton-mi cargo 316,000,000, metric
ton-km cargo 462,000,000. Roads (1999): total length 24,170 mi, 38,898 km
(paved 18%). Vehicles (1996): passenger cars 157,000; trucks and buses
81,000. Merchant marine: vessels (100 gross tons and over) none. Air transport (1994): passenger-mi 266,000,000, passenger-km 428,000,000; short ton-
mi cargo 34,000,000, metric ton-km cargo 54,000,000; airports (1998) 4.

Communications

Medium	date	unit	number	units per 1,000 persons
Daily newspapers	1996	circulation	114,000	14
Radio	1997	receivers	1,030,000	120
Television	1999	receivers	1,300,000	156
Telephones	2001	main lines	85,400	8.0
Cellular telephones	2001	subscribers	98,300	9.0
Internet	2001	users	25,000	2.4
Personal computers	2001	units	75,000	7.0

Education and health

Educational attainment (1993)[9]. Percentage of population age 14 and over having: no formal schooling 18.6%; some primary education 54.8%; some secondary 25.1%; higher 1.5%. Literacy (1995): population age 15 and over literate 3,890,000 (78.2%); males literate 2,060,000 (85.6%); females literate
1,830,000 (71.3%).

Education (1996)

	schools	teachers	students	student/ teacher ratio
Primary (age 7–13)	3,907	38,528[10]	1,670,000	...
Secondary (age 14–18)	246	...	255,000	...
Voc., teacher tr.	4	...	...	...
Higher	2	640	4,797[11]	7.0

Health: physicians (1993) 786 (1 per 10,917 persons); hospital beds (1989) 22,461
(1 per 349 persons); infant mortality rate per 1,000 live births (2000) 92.4.
Food (2000): daily per capita caloric intake 1,912 (vegetable products 95%,
animal products 5%); 83% of FAO recommended minimum requirement.

Military

Total active duty personnel (2001): 21,600 (army 92.6%; navy, none; air force
7.4%). Military expenditure as percentage of GNP (1999): 1.0% (world 2.4%);
per capita expenditure U.S.$3.

[1]Includes 8 nonelective seats. [2]In 1996 Zambia was declared a Christian nation per the
preamble of a constitutional amendment. [3]Preliminary and unadjusted for under-
count/overcount. [4]Detail does not add to total given because of rounding. [5]In 1999
legal and illegal exports of emeralds were estimated to equal U.S.$20,000,000 (about
20% of world total). [6]Average of June–July. [7]Less imputed bank service charge.
[8]Excludes Tanzania-Zambia Railway Authority (TAZARA) data. [9]Based on a sample
survey of 35,502 persons. [10]1995. [11]1998.

Internet resources for further information:
• Zambian National WWW Server (Zamnet) http://www.zamnet.zm

Zimbabwe

Official name: Republic of Zimbabwe.
Form of government: multiparty republic with one legislative house (House of Assembly [150[1]]).
Head of state and government: President.
Capital: Harare.
Official language: English.
Official religion: none.
Monetary unit: 1 Zimbabwe dollar (Z$) = 100 cents; valuation (Sept. 23, 2002) 1 U.S.$ = Z$55.45; 1 £ = Z$86.17.

Area and population		area		population
				1992
Provinces	**Capitals**	sq mi	sq km	census
Bulawayo[2]	—	185	479	620,936
Harare[2]	—	337	872	1,478,810
Manicaland	Mutare	14,077	36,459	1,537,676
Mashonaland Central	Bindura	10,945	28,347	857,318
Mashonaland East	Marondera	12,444	32,230	1,033,336
Mashonaland West	Chinhoyi	22,178	57,441	1,116,928
Masvingo	Masvingo	21,840	56,566	1,221,845
Matabeleland North	Lupane	28,967	75,025	640,957
Matabeleland South	Gwanda	20,916	54,172	591,747
Midlands	Gweru	18,983	49,166	1,302,214
TOTAL		150,872	390,757	10,401,767

Demography

Population (2002): 11,377,000.
Density (2002): persons per sq mi 75.4, persons per sq km 29.1.
Urban-rural (2001): urban 36.0%; rural 64.0%.
Sex distribution (2001): male 50.52%; female 49.48%.
Age breakdown (2000): under 15, 39.6%; 15–29, 33.1%; 30–44, 14.8%; 45–59, 7.2%; 60–74, 4.1%; 75 and over, 1.2%.
Population projection: (2010) 11,057,000; (2020) 9,997,000.
Doubling time: 62 years.
Ethnic composition (2000): Shona 67.1%; Ndebele 13.0%; Chewa 4.9%; British 3.5%; other 11.5%.
Religious affiliation (1995): Christian 45.4%, of which Protestant (including Anglican) 23.5%, African indigenous 13.5%, Roman Catholic 7.0%; animist 40.5%; other 14.1%.
Major cities (1992): Harare 1,184,169; Bulawayo 620,936; Chitungwiza 274,035; Mutare 131,808; Gweru 124,735.

Vital statistics

Birth rate per 1,000 population (2001): 31.0 (world avg. 21.2).
Death rate per 1,000 population (2001): 19.7 (world avg. 8.9).
Natural increase rate per 1,000 population (2001): 11.3 (world avg. 12.2).
Total fertility rate (avg. births per childbearing woman; 2001): 1.9.
Life expectancy at birth (2001): male 43.1 years; female 39.7 years.
Major causes of death per 100,000 population (1990): infectious and parasitic diseases 64.7; accidents and poisoning 44.4; diseases of the circulatory system 40.9; diseases of the respiratory system 39.5; malignant neoplasms (cancers) 28.4; diseases of the digestive system 12.1; diseases of the nervous system 9.4; endocrine and metabolic disorders 4.9.

National economy

Budget (1997–98). Revenue: Z$57,596,000,000 (tax revenue 93.0%, of which income tax 48.0%, sales tax 20.4%, customs duties 17.3%, excise tax 4.2%; nontax revenue 7.0%). Expenditures: Z$70,332,000,000 (recurrent expenditures 92.1%, of which goods and services 48.5%, interest payments 25.0%, transfer payments 18.4%).
Population economically active (1992): total 3,600,000; activity rate of total population 34.6% (participation rates: over age 15, 63.4%; female 39.8%; unemployed 7.2%[3]).

Price and earnings indexes (1995 = 100)							
	1995	1996	1997	1998	1999	2000	2001
Consumer price index	100.0	121.4	144.2	190.1	301.3	469.6	830.0
Earnings index	...	...	...	...	...	...	...

Production (metric tons except as noted). Agriculture, forestry, fishing (1999): sugarcane 4,657,000, corn (maize) 1,520,000, wheat 320,000, seed cotton 268,000, tobacco 193,000, cassava 170,000, vegetables (including melons) 122,000, peanuts (groundnuts) 113,000, soybeans 107,000, sorghum 85,000, bananas 82,000, oranges 72,000, millet 53,000; livestock (number of live animals) 5,500,000 cattle, 2,770,000 goats, 525,000 sheep, 272,000 pigs, 15,000,000 chickens; roundwood (1998) 8,378,000 cu m; fish catch (1998) 16,386. Mining and quarrying (value of production in Z$'000,000; 2000): gold 8,521; asbestos 2,776; coal 2,690; nickel 2,178; chrome 778; granite 552. Manufacturing (value in Z$; 1994): foodstuffs 6,746,300,000; metals and metal products 5,662,700,000; chemicals and petroleum products 3,314,800,000; beverages and tobacco 3,208,400,000; textiles 2,607,700,000; clothing and footwear 1,732,200,000; paper, printing, and publishing 1,553,700,000; transport equipment 1,454,400,000; wood and furniture 1,136,500,000; nonmetallic mineral products 1,076,600,000; other manufactured goods 323,300,000. Energy production (consumption): electricity (kW-hr; 2000) 7,016,000,000 ([1999] 10,926,000,000); coal (metric tons; 2000) 3,986,000 ([1997] 5,095,000); crude

petroleum, none (none); petroleum products (metric tons; 1997) none (1,395,000).
Public debt (external, outstanding; 2000): U.S.$2,948,000,000.
Household income and expenditure. Average household size (1992) 4.8; income per household Z$1,689 (U.S.$2,628); sources of income: n.a.; expenditure (1990[4]): food, beverages, and tobacco 39.1%, housing 18.7%, clothing and footwear 9.8%, transportation 8.4%, education 7.6%, household durable goods 7.2%, health 2.8%, recreation 2.0%, other 4.4%.
Gross national product (2000): U.S.$5,851,000,000 (U.S.$460 per capita).

Structure of gross domestic product and labour force				
	1996		1995	
	in value Z$'000,000[5]	% of total value[5]	labour force[6]	% of labour force[6]
Agriculture	15,283	20.0	334,000	26.9
Mining	3,846	5.0	59,000	4.7
Manufacturing	14,668	19.2	185,900	15.0
Construction	1,943	2.5	71,800	5.8
Public utilities	2,409	3.2	9,500	0.8
Transp. and commun.	4,200	5.5	50,900	4.1
Trade	15,630	20.5	100,600	8.2
Finance	7,896	10.4	21,100	1.7
Pub. admin., defense	3,324	4.4	406,800	32.8
Services	5,472	7.2		
Other	1,572[7]	2.1[7]	...	...
TOTAL	76,243	100.0	1,239,600	100.0

Tourism: receipts (2000) U.S.$125,000,000; expenditures (1998) U.S.$131,000,000.

Foreign trade[8]

Balance of trade (current prices)						
	1995	1996	1997	1998	1999	2000
U.S.$'000,000	+89	+249	−230	−95	+248	+272
% of total	2.0%	5.2%	4.5%	2.4%	6.9%	8.2%

Imports (1999): U.S.$2,208,000,000 (machinery and transport equipment 34.1%, chemicals and chemical products 16.4%, petroleum products 9.7%, food 4.7%, electricity 3.9%). *Major import sources* (2000): South Africa 38.4%; U.S. 6.0%; U.K. 4.8%; Botswana 4.3%; Japan 4.1%.
Exports (1999): U.S.$1,924,000,000 (tobacco 31.8%, gold sales 11.9%, ferroalloys 8.7%, cotton lint 5.8%, horticultural products [including cut flowers] 4.3%). *Major export destinations* (2000): South Africa 15.0%; U.K. 8.7%; Germany 7.8%; Japan 7.3%; U.S. 5.7%; China 5.2%.

Transport and communications

Transport. Railroads (1998): route length 2,759 km; passenger-km 408,223,000; metric ton-km cargo 4,603,000. Roads (1996): total length 18,338 km (paved 47%). Vehicles (1996): passenger cars 323,000; trucks and buses 32,000. Air transport (2001)[9]: passenger-km 723,000,000; metric ton-km cargo 28,829,000; airports (1997) with scheduled flights 7.

Communications				units per 1,000 persons
Medium	date	unit	number	
Daily newspapers	1996	circulation	209,000	19
Radio	1997	receivers	1,140,000	102
Television	1999	receivers	2,074,000	183
Telephones	2001	main lines	253,700	19
Cellular telephones	2001	subscribers	329,000	24
Personal computers	2001	units	165,000	12
Internet	2001	users	100,000	7.3

Education and health

Educational attainment (1992). Percentage of population age 25 and over having: no formal schooling 22.3%; primary 54.3%; secondary 13.1%; higher 3.4%. *Literacy* (1995): percentage of total population age 15 and over literate 85.1%; males literate 90.4%; females literate 79.9%.

Education (1998)				student/ teacher ratio
	schools	teachers	students	
Primary (age 7–13)	4,706	64,538	2,507,098	38.8
Secondary (age 14–19)	1,530	30,482	847,296	27.8
Voc., teacher tr.[10]	25	1,479	27,431	18.5
Higher[11]	28[10]	3,581	46,492	13.0

Health: physicians (1996) 1,603 (1 per 6,904 persons); hospital beds (1996) 22,975 (1 per 501 persons); infant mortality rate (2001) 65.3.
Food (2000): daily per capita caloric intake 2,117 (vegetable products 93%, animal products 7%); 89% of FAO recommended minimum requirement.

Military

Total active duty personnel (2001): 39,000 (army 89.7%, air force 10.3%). *Military expenditure as percentage of GNP* (1999): 5.0% (world 2.4%); per capita expenditure U.S.$23.

---

[1]Includes 30 nonelective seats. [2]City with provincial status. [3]Does not take into consideration seasonal unemployment of communal workers; 1986–87. [4]Based on consumer price index. [5]At factor cost. [6]Wage-earning workers only. [7]Less imputed bank service charges. [8]Imports are f.o.b. in balance of trade and c.i.f. in commodities and trading partners. [9]Air Zimbabwe only. [10]1992. [11]Includes postsecondary vocational and teacher training at the higher level.

Internet resources for further information:
• Reserve Bank of Zimbabwe http://www.rbz.co.zw

Comparative National Statistics

World and regional summaries

region/bloc	area and population, 2002						gross national product, 2000						labour force, 1990		
	area		population			population projection, 2020	total ('000,000 U.S.$)	% agriculture	% industry	% services	growth rate, 1990–99	GNP per capita (U.S.$)	total ('000)	% male	% female
	square miles	square kilometres	total	per sq mi	per sq km										
World	52,405,501	135,729,680	6,188,991,000	118.1	45.6	7,277,448,300	31,252,121	4	28	68	2.5	5,330	2,353,806	63.8	36.2
Africa	11,717,218	30,347,469	826,835,000	70.6	27.2	1,155,595,000	550,247	16	30	53	2.5	730	242,784	65.6	34.4
Central Africa	2,552,966	6,612,155	96,752,000	37.9	14.6	153,453,000	25,549	17	36	21	1.3	540	26,428	64.7	35.3
East Africa	2,473,626	6,406,665	253,267,000	102.4	39.5	352,790,000	66,770	28	17	54	2.9	270	85,082	58.8	41.2
North Africa	3,288,763	8,517,861	179,457,000	54.6	21.1	238,802,000	244,873	16	33	51	3.3	1,450	40,016	84.6	15.4
Southern Africa	1,032,546	2,674,283	52,020,000	50.4	19.5	52,235,000	140,652	3	28	68	1.3	2,850	14,532	64.3	35.7
West Africa	2,369,317	6,136,505	245,338,000	103.5	40.0	358,315,000	72,403	31	30	38	3.0	310	76,726	63.8	36.2
Americas	16,239,588	42,060,357	845,400,000	52.1	20.1	1,020,635,000	12,126,348	2	23	75	3.0	14,870	293,723	66.5	33.5
Anglo-America[3]	8,306,759	21,514,416	318,973,000	38.4	14.8	368,699,000	10,252,979	1	22	76	3.0	32,830	135,438	58.7	41.3
Canada	3,855,101	9,984,670	31,244,000	8.1	3.1	35,187,000	647,829	3	27	70	2.8	21,130	13,360	60.2	39.8
United States	3,615,214	9,363,364	287,602,000	79.6	30.7	333,385,000	9,601,505	1	22	77	3.0	34,100	122,005	58.6	41.4
Latin America	7,932,829	20,545,941	526,427,000	66.4	25.6	651,936,000	1,873,369	7	29	64	3.4	3,720	158,285	73.1	26.9
Caribbean	90,681	234,862	37,393,000	412.4	159.2	43,396,000	124,590	5	33	56	2.8	3,330	13,813	66.9	33.1
Central America	201,571	522,067	37,052,000	183.8	71.0	51,369,000	63,867	17	21	63	4.4	1,770	9,520	78.5	21.5
Mexico	758,449	1,964,375	100,976,000	133.1	51.4	124,065,000	497,025	4	27	69	2.8	5,070	30,487	72.9	27.1
South America	6,882,128	17,824,637	351,006,000	51.0	19.7	433,106,000	1,187,887	8	30	63	3.6	3,580	104,465	73.6	26.4
Andean Group	2,111,959	5,469,951	129,428,000	61.3	23.7	164,832,000	270,788	9	32	59	3.8	2,380	34,715	75.6	24.4
Brazil	3,287,291	8,514,047	174,619,000	53.1	20.5	210,817,000	610,058	8	31	60	3.0	3,580	55,026	72.6	27.4
Other South America	1,482,878	3,840,639	46,959,000	31.7	12.2	57,457,000	307,041	5	24	70	4.8	6,500	14,724	72.4	27.6
Asia	12,268,332	31,774,846	3,758,725,000	306.4	118.3	4,358,451,000	8,491,380	8	35	57	3.7	2,400	1,464,452	64.5	35.5
Eastern Asia	4,539,179	11,756,425	1,513,559,000	333.4	128.7	1,671,199,000	6,470,963	4	36	59	3.1	4,340	775,590	57.4	42.6
China	3,696,116	9,572,900	1,284,211,000	347.4	134.2	1,433,111,000	1,062,919	18	49	33	10.8	840	669,693	56.7	43.3
Japan	145,898	377,873	127,347,000	872.9	337.0	125,722,000	4,519,067	2	33	66	1.4	35,620	62,202	62.1	37.9
South Korea	38,402	99,461	47,640,000	1,240.6	479.0	50,650,000	421,069	6	49	45	5.7	8,910	18,664	66.2	33.8
Other Eastern Asia	658,764	1,706,191	54,361,000	82.5	31.9	61,716,000	467,908	1	22	73	5.5	8,940	25,031	58.8	41.2
South Asia	1,939,156	5,022,393	1,398,328,000	721.1	278.4	1,628,488,000	563,681	28	23	48	5.5	460	411,136	77.4	22.6
India	1,222,559	3,166,414	1,047,671,000	856.9	330.9	1,316,000,000	454,800	28	24	48	5.9	450	322,944	74.8	25.2
Pakistan	307,374	796,095	145,960,000	474.9	183.3	197,441,000	61,022	24	18	58	3.5	440	33,698	87.5	12.5
Other South Asia	409,223	1,059,884	204,697,000	500.2	193.1	115,047,000	47,859	35	28	36	4.9	590	54,494	86.2	13.8
Southeast Asia	1,742,700	4,513,573	525,686,000	301.7	116.5	641,859,000	661,194	21	30	49	5.3	1,290	189,297	63.0	37.0
Southwest Asia	4,047,297	10,482,455	321,152,000	79.3	30.6	416,905,000	795,542	10	36	52	2.8	2,620	88,429	69.4	30.6
Central Asia	1,545,721	4,003,400	56,643,000	36.6	14.1	69,328,000	33,915	16	25	58	-4.3	610	20,728	54.8	45.2
Gulf Cooperation Council	993,336	2,572,729	32,973,000	33.2	12.8	48,799,000	261,751	4	51	45	2.2	8,880	6,511	91.7	8.3
Iran	629,315	1,629,918	65,457,000	104.0	40.2	84,649,000	106,707	21	30	50	3.4	1,680	15,253	82.0	18.0
Other Southwest Asia	878,926	2,276,408	166,079,000	189.0	73.0	214,129,000	393,169	11	28	57	4.0	2,530	45,936	68.7	31.3
Europe	8,892,753	23,032,135	726,169,000	81.7	31.5	704,486,300	9,627,957	3	27	70	1.3	13,260	340,666	57.1	42.9
Eastern Europe	7,437,203	19,262,274	332,594,000	44.7	17.3	301,661,000	719,022	7	32	61	-3.2	2,140	171,080	50.6	49.4
Russia	6,592,846	17,075,400	143,673,000	21.8	8.4	129,661,000	241,027	7	35	59	-6.0	1,660	72,286	47.6	52.4
Ukraine	233,090	603,700	48,120,000	206.4	79.7	44,109,000	34,595	11	30	59	-10.8	700	25,401	48.0	52.0
Other Eastern Europe	611,267	1,583,174	140,801,000	230.3	88.9	127,891,000	443,400	7	30	62	1.3	3,140	73,393	54.4	45.6
Western Europe	1,455,551	3,769,861	393,575,000	270.4	104.4	402,825,300	8,908,935	2	27	71	1.8	22,850	169,586	63.6	36.4
European Union (EU)	1,249,718	3,236,756	380,616,000	304.6	117.6	388,981,000	8,457,121	2	27	71	1.8	19,950	163,771	63.6	36.4
France	210,026	543,965	59,440,000	283.0	109.3	61,371,000	1,438,293	3	22	75	1.5	24,090	25,404	60.1	39.9
Germany	137,847	357,021	82,259,000	596.7	230.4	84,741,000	2,063,734	1	31	68	1.4	25,120	38,981	60.7	39.3
Italy	116,347	301,337	57,988,000	498.4	192.4	55,802,000	1,163,211	3	31	67	1.4	20,160	23,339	68.1	31.9
Spain	195,379	506,030	40,998,000	209.8	81.0	40,135,000	595,255	3	24	73	2.3	15,080	14,456	75.5	24.5
United Kingdom	94,248	244,101	60,178,000	638.5	246.5	63,887,000	1,459,500	1	26	73	2.5	24,430	27,766	61.4	38.6
Other EU	495,872	1,284,302	79,753,000	160.8	62.1	83,045,000	1,737,128	3	25	72	2.4	22,140	33,825	63.4	36.6
Non-EU	205,833	533,105	12,959,000	63.0	24.3	13,844,300	451,814	2	29	67	1.7	35,640	5,815	61.9	38.1
Oceania	3,287,609	8,514,873	31,862,000	9.7	3.7	38,281,000	456,189	4	21	74	3.9	14,780	12,181	63.0	37.0
Australia	2,969,908	7,692,030	19,702,000	6.6	2.6	22,587,000	388,252	3	22	76	4.1	20,240	20,240	61.9	38.1
Pacific Ocean Islands	317,701	822,843	12,160,000	38.3	14.8	15,694,000	67,937	9	21	64	2.9	5,810	4,218	65.0	35.0

[1]Refers only to the outstanding long-term external public and publicly guaranteed debt of the 137 countries that report under the World Bank's Debtor Reporting System (DRS). [2]World total includes

Africa

Americas

Asia

economic indicators							social indicators									region/bloc
pop. per 1,000 ha of arable land, 2002	electricity consump-tion (kW-hr per capita), 1998	trade ('000,000 U.S.$), 1999			debt ('000,000 U.S.$), 1999[1]		life expec-tancy (years), 2000		health			food (% FAO recom-mended minimum), 1998	literacy (%) (latest)		
		imports (c.i.f.)	exports (f.o.b.)	balance	total	% of GNP	male	female	pop. per doctor (latest)	infant mor-tality per 1,000 births, 2001	pop. having safe water (%); (1989–98)		male	female	
4,570	2,428	5,785,724	5,667,433	−118,291	1,464,107	24.0	64.3	68.3	730	55.2	76	118	83.7	71.0	World
4,600	521	124,113	119,194	−4,919	236,331	48.0	51.1	53.1	2,560	86.7	57	104	65.9	45.5	Africa
4,450	114	6,281	11,402	+5,122	34,588	134.3	47.3	50.4	12,890	107.3	44	83	77.7	56.4	Central Africa
5,760	139	18,145	9,269	−8,876	45,902	77.9	44.9	46.3	13,620	94.8	44	84	65.4	44.1	East Africa
4,460	749	48,990	36,052	−12,938	87,534	44.0	63.2	66.7	890	59.0	82	125	64.8	40.1	North Africa
3,160	4,221	32,634	32,131	−503	10,458	7.7	50.2	52.4	1,610	63.1	70	116	81.6	80.0	Southern Africa
4,280	140	18,064	30,341	+12,277	57,849	79.6	50.3	51.5	6,260	85.6	52	113	58.4	37.5	West Africa
2,370	6,511	1,640,288	1,264,753	−375,535	398,042	20.6	68.6	74.8	520	25.1	83	128	91.3	89.9	Americas
1,430	14,427	1,275,874	931,894	−343,979	—	—	74.3	80.0	370	6.8	91	140	96.1	95.7	Anglo-America[3]
690	17,486	215,555	238,778	+23,223	—	—	76.0	83.0	540	5.1	100	119	96.6	96.6	Canada
1,630	14,089	1,059,220	692,784	−366,436	—	—	74.1	79.7	360	6.9	90	142	95.7	95.3	United States
3,940	1,805	364,414	332,859	−31,555	398,042	20.6	65.2	71.6	690	32.4	78	119	87.8	85.6	Latin America
6,600	1,702	54,781	47,226	−7,555	10,091	26.6	67.3	72.0	380	43.8	77	102	83.8	83.0	Caribbean
5,940	712	21,925	12,058	−9,868	24,967	41.2	67.1	72.5	950	34.3	76	105	73.6	68.1	Central America
4,070	1,933	145,556	136,263	−9,293	87,531	18.6	68.5	74.7	810	26.2	85	135	91.8	87.4	Mexico
3,630	1,890	142,151	137,312	−4,839	275,453	20.2	63.8	70.6	710	32.9	76	117	88.4	87.0	South America
8,950	1,580	48,780	59,046	+10,266	87,634	26.6	68.0	71.7	830	31.0	79	106	92.6	88.7	Andean Group
3,280	2,177	60,793	51,120	−9,673	95,233	13.0	58.5	67.6	770	38.0	76	122	83.3	83.2	Brazil
1,610	1,726	32,578	27,146	−5,432	92,586	30.4	71.8	78.4	410	20.9	71	129	96.0	95.7	Other South America
7,890	1,183	1,475,600	1,676,841	+201,241	595,398	20.9	65.9	68.9	970	53.5	75	117	81.2	63.7	Asia
11,360	1,788	919,675	1,082,099	+162,425	166,210	12.1	69.9	74.3	610	34.2	71	125	91.4	77.0	Eastern Asia
10,350	926	165,699	194,931	+29,232	108,163	11.1	69.0	73.0	620	37.0	67	126	89.9	72.7	China
28,460	8,285	309,995	417,610	+107,616	—	—	77.5	84.0	530	3.4	97	123	100.0	100.0	Japan
27,710	5,218	119,751	143,685	+23,934	57,231	14.2	72.0	79.0	740	7.0	93	131	99.3	96.7	South Korea
18,910	3,686	324,230	325,873	+1,643	816	94.7	71.3	77.2	500	31.0	96	107	95.9	91.4	Other Eastern Asia
6,890	439	67,099	51,878	−15,221	139,322	24.4	61.4	62.3	2,100	70.4	80	108	62.4	35.5	South Asia
6,480	505	42,425	33,207	−9,218	82,380	18.5	61.9	63.1	1,920	64.9	81	112	65.5	37.7	India
6,850	419	10,159	8,383	−1,776	28,514	48.5	61.0	60.0	1,840	85.0	79	106	50.0	24.4	Pakistan
10,250	116	14,515	10,287	−4,228	28,428	41.3	59.2	60.0	5,080	80.6	78	89	53.5	30.9	Other South Asia
9,940	686	301,916	349,480	+47,564	186,531	37.6	65.9	69.8	3,120	40.0	70	120	91.8	83.3	Southeast Asia
3,690	2,301	186,911	193,385	+6,473	103,335	25.5	66.4	71.0	610	45.2	79	116	86.7	72.4	Southwest Asia
1,900	2,399	9,215	10,877	+1,662	9,819	25.1	63.1	71.0	330	45.4	85	98	98.8	96.1	Central Asia
8,910	7,140	65,737	91,749	+26,013	1,768	12.8	67.8	71.3	620	45.7	95	122	73.8	55.8	Gulf Cooperation Council
4,570	1,573	12,622	19,726	+7,104	6,184	5.6	68.3	71.5	1,200	30.0	95	117	78.4	65.8	Iran
4,220	1,688	99,338	71,032	−28,306	85,563	35.5	66.4	70.6	690	49.3	65	122	87.8	68.1	Other Southwest Asia
2,510	5,738	2,459,253	2,531,996	+72,742	232,295	28.0	66.2	74.2	300	9.4	99	125	99.0	97.5	Europe
1,550	4,355	227,417	220,533	−6,884	232,295	28.0	63.5	73.9	290	15.4	95	116	99.1	96.6	Eastern Europe
1,150	5,488	40,429	74,663	+34,234	120,375	32.1	59.9	72.4	240	15.3	…	111	99.5	96.8	Russia
1,480	3,385	11,846	11,582	−265	10,027	26.7	60.6	72.0	330	21.7	97	112	99.5	97.4	Ukraine
2,450	3,534	175,142	134,288	−40,854	101,893	24.4	68.2	76.1	370	13.7	94	122	98.7	96.1	Other Eastern Europe
5,260	6,960	2,231,837	2,311,463	+79,627	—	—	68.6	74.3	300	5.0	100	134	98.9	98.2	Western Europe
5,180	6,696	2,109,241	2,152,830	+43,589	—	—	68.3	74.1	290	5.1	100	134	98.8	98.1	European Union (EU)
3,220	7,613	286,593	296,025	+9,432	—	—	74.8	82.9	330	4.5	100	141	98.9	98.7	France
6,970	6,785	464,318	535,530	+71,212	—	—	74.4	80.6	290	4.3	100	128	100.0	100.0	Germany
7,260	5,244	216,451	230,094	+13,643	—	—	75.9	82.5	180	5.8	100	143	97.8	96.4	Italy
3,080	5,014	147,866	111,493	−36,373	—	—	75.6	82.5	240	5.0	99	136	98.1	95.1	Spain
10,240	6,329	327,576	273,492	−54,084	—	—	75.4	80.2	720	5.8	100	129	100.0	100.0	United Kingdom
4,960	8,113	666,438	706,196	+39,758	—	—	42.5	45.8	320	5.2	100	132	97.9	97.2	Other EU
9,170	14,899	122,595	158,633	+36,038	—	—	76.4	81.9	480	3.7	100	123	99.9	99.9	Non-EU
96,340	8,140	86,469	74,649	−11,821	2,042	33.7	0.5	0.5	480	26.2	86	117	96.3	94.0	Oceania
390	10,520	65,515	58,016	−7,499	—	—	76.6	82.0	400	6.0	95	120	99.5	99.5	Australia
5,620	4,029	20,955	16,633	−4,322	2,042	33.7	67.1	71.6	770	42.8	68	111	89.8	82.7	Pacific Ocean Islands

U.S.$64,255,000,000 undistributable by region.   [3]Anglo-America includes Canada, the United States, Greenland, Bermuda, and St. Pierre and Miquelon.

Europe

Eastern Europe

Oceania

Government and international organizations

This table summarizes principal facts about the governments of the countries of the world, their branches and organs, the topmost layers of local government constituting each country's chief administrative subdivisions, and the participation of their central governments in the principal intergovernmental organizations of the world.

In this table "date of independence" may refer to a variety of circumstances. In the case of the newest countries, those that attained full independence after World War II, the date given is usually just what is implied by the heading—the date when the country, within its present borders, attained full sovereignty over both its internal and external affairs. In the case of longer established countries, the choice of a single date may be somewhat more complicated, and grounds for the use of several different dates often exist. The reader should refer to appropriate Britannica articles on national histories and relevant historical acts. In cases of territorial annexation or dissolution, the date given here refers either to the final act of union of a state composed of smaller entities or to the final act of separation from a larger whole (*e.g.,* the separation of Bangladesh from Pakistan in 1971).

The date of the current, or last, constitution is in some ways a less complicated question, but governments sometimes do not, upon taking power, either adhere to existing constitutional forms or trouble to terminate the previous document and legitimize themselves by the installation of new constitutional forms. Often, however, the desire to legitimize extraconstitutional political activity by associating it with existing forms of long precedent leads to partial or incomplete modification, suspension, or abrogation of a constitution, so that the actual day-to-day conduct of government may be largely unrelat-

ed to the provisions of a constitution still theoretically in force. When a date in this column is given in italics, it refers to a document that has been suspended, abolished by extraconstitutional action, or modified extensively.

The characterizations adopted under "type of government" represent a compromise between the forms provided for by the national constitution and the more pragmatic language that a political scientist might adopt to describe these same systems. For an explanation of the application of these terms in the Britannica World Data, *see* the Glossary at page 533.

The positions denoted by the terms "chief of state" and "head of government" are usually those identified with those functions by the constitution. The duties of the chief of state may range from largely ceremonial responsibilities, with little or no authority over the day-to-day conduct of government, to complete executive authority as the effective head of government. In certain countries, an official of a political party or a revolutionary figure outside the constitutional structure may exercise the powers of both positions.

Membership in the legislative house(s) of each country as given here includes all elected or appointed members, as well as ex officio members (those who by virtue of some other office or title are members of the body), whether voting or nonvoting. The legislature of a country with a unicameral system is shown as the upper house in this table.

The number of administrative subdivisions for each country is listed down to the second level. A single country may, depending on its size, complexity, and historical antecedents, have as many as five levels of administrative subordination or it may have none at all. Each level of subordination may have several kinds of subdivisions.

Government and international organizations

country	date of independence[a]	date of current or last constitution[b]	type of government	executive branch[c] chief of state	head of government	legislative branch[d] upper house (members)	lower house (members)	admin. subdivisions first-order (number)	second-order (number)	seaward claims territorial (nautical miles)	fishing/ economic (nautical miles)
Afghanistan	Aug. 19, 1919	—	[1]	————president————		—	—	...	...	—	2
Albania	Nov. 28, 1912	Nov. 28, 1998	republic	president	prime minister	140	—	12	36	12	2
Algeria	July 5, 1962	Dec. 7, 1996[3]	republic	president	prime minister	144	389	48	553	12	4
American Samoa	—	July 1, 1967	territory (U.S.)	U.S. president	governor	18	20	4	14	12	200
Andorra	Dec. 6, 1288	May 4, 1993	parl. coprincipality	[6]	head of govt.	28		7	...	—	—
Angola	Nov. 11, 1975	Aug. 27, 1992	republic	————president[7]————		220[8]	—	18	163	20	200
Antigua and Barbuda	Nov. 1, 1981	Nov. 1, 1981	constitutional monarchy	British monarch	prime minister	17	17[9]	30	—	12[10]	200[10]
Argentina	July 9, 1816	Aug. 24, 1994[11]	federal republic	————president[12]————		72	257	24	503	12	200
Armenia	Sept. 23, 1991	July 5, 1995	republic	president	prime minister	131	—	11	...	—	—
Aruba	—	Jan. 1, 1986	overseas territory (Neth.)	Dutch monarch	[13]	21	—	...	...	12	200
Australia	Jan. 1, 1901	July 9, 1900	federal parl. state[15]	British monarch	prime minister	76	150	8	c. 900	12	200
Austria	Oct. 30, 1918	Oct. 1, 1920[16]	federal state	president	chancellor	64	183	9	99	—	—
Azerbaijan	Aug. 30, 1991	Aug. 24, 2002[17]	republic	————president[18]————		125[8]	—	...	...	...	...
Bahamas, The	July 10, 1973	July 10, 1973	constitutional monarchy	British monarch	prime minister	16	40	—	—	12	200
Bahrain	Aug. 15, 1971	Feb. 14, 2002	constitutional monarchy	monarch	prime minister	40	40	...	—	12	19
Bangladesh	March 26, 1971	Dec. 16, 1972	republic	president	prime minister	330	—	7	64	12	200
Barbados	Nov. 30, 1966	Nov. 30, 1966	constitutional monarchy	British monarch	prime minister	21	28	—	—	12	200
Belarus	Aug. 25, 1991	Nov. 27, 1996[20]	republic	————president[18]————		62[8]	110[8]	7	118	—	—
Belgium	Oct. 4, 1830	Feb. 17, 1994	fed. const. monarchy	monarch	prime minister	71[21]	150	22	589	12	19
Belize	Sept. 21, 1981	Sept. 21, 1981	constitutional monarchy	British monarch	prime minister	8	29	23	...	12[24]	200
Benin	Aug. 1, 1960	Dec. 2, 1990	republic	————president————		83	—	12	77	200	200
Bermuda	June 8, 1968	dependent territory (U.K.)		British monarch	[25]	11	40	11	—	12	200
Bhutan	March 24, 1910	—	[26]	monarch	chairman CM	150	—	20	196	—	—
Bolivia	Aug. 6, 1825	Feb. 2, 1967	republic	————president————		27	130	9	112	—	—
Bosnia and Herzegovina	March 3, 1992	Dec. 14, 1995[27]	federal republic	[28]	chairman CM	15	42	2	10[29]	...	...
Botswana	Sept. 30, 1966	Sept. 30, 1966	republic	————president————		15[30]	47	18	...	—	—
Brazil	Sept. 7, 1822	Oct. 5, 1988[16]	federal republic	————president————		81	513	27	5,561	12	200
Brunei	Jan. 1, 1984	*Sept. 29, 1959*[31]	monarchy (sultanate)	————sultan————		21[30]	—	4	...	12	200
Bulgaria	Oct. 5, 1908	July 12, 1991	republic	president	prime minister	240	—	28	259	12	200
Burkina Faso	Aug. 5, 1960	June 11, 1991	republic	president	prime minister	178[30]	111	45	382	—	—
Burundi	July 1, 1962	July 23, 2001[32]	republic[1]	————president[33]————		178	—	17	...	—	—
Cambodia	Nov. 9, 1953	March 4, 1999[34]	constitutional monarchy	king	prime minister	61	122	24	183	12	200
Cameroon	Jan. 1, 1960	Jan. 18, 1996	republic	president	prime minister	180	—	10	56	50	2
Canada	July 1, 1867	April 17, 1982	federal parl. state[15]	Canadian GG[35]	prime minister	105	301	13	...	12	200
Cape Verde	July 5, 1975	Sept. 25, 1992	republic	president	prime minister	72	—	17	...	12[10]	200[10]
Central African Republic	Aug. 13, 1960	Jan. 14, 1995	republic	president	prime minister	109	—	17	69	—	—
Chad	Aug. 11, 1960	April 14, 1996	republic	president	prime minister	155	—	28	107	—	—
Chile	Sept. 18, 1810	March 11, 1981	republic	————president————		48	120	13	51	12	200
China	1523 BC	Dec. 4, 1982	people's republic	president	premier SC	2,989	—	31	332	12	2
Colombia	July 20, 1810	July 5, 1991	republic	————president————		102	166	33	1,097	12	200
Comoros	July 6, 1975	June 5, 2002[36]	federal republic	————president[37]————		...	...	3	...	12[10]	200[10]
Congo, Dem. Rep. of the	June 30, 1960	*April 9, 1994*	republic[1]	————president————		300	—	11	...	12	200
Congo, Rep. of the	Aug. 15, 1960	Aug. 10, 2002	republic	————president————		66[8]	137[8]	16	47	200	2
Costa Rica	Sept. 15, 1821	Nov. 9, 1949	republic	————president————		57	—	7	81	12	200
Côte d'Ivoire	Aug. 7, 1960	July 23, 2000[38]	republic	————president[18]————		225	—	19	...	12	200
Croatia	June 25, 1991	Dec. 22, 1990	republic	president	prime minister	151	—	21	123	12	...
Cuba	May 20, 1902	Feb. 24, 1976	socialist republic	————president————		601	—	15	169	12	200
Cyprus[40]	Aug. 16, 1960	Aug. 16, 1960	republic	————president————		56[41]	—	...	647	12	2
Czech Republic	Jan. 1, 1993	Jan. 1, 1993	republic	president	prime minister	81	200	14	76	—	—
Denmark	c. 800	June 5, 1953	constitutional monarchy	monarch	prime minister	179	—	16	275	3	200
Djibouti	June 27, 1977	Sept. 15, 1992	republic	————president————		65	—	5	...	12	200
Dominica	Nov. 3, 1978	Nov. 3, 1978	republic	president	prime minister	32	—	37	...	12	200
Dominican Republic	Feb. 27, 1844	Nov. 28, 1966	republic	————president————		32	150	32	160	6	200
East Timor	May 20, 2002	March 22, 2002[42]	republic	president	prime minister	88	—	4	13	...	...
Ecuador	May 24, 1822	Aug. 10, 1998	republic	————president————		123	—	22	214	200	200

Finally, in the second half of the table are listed the memberships each country maintains in the principal international intergovernmental organizations of the world. This part of the table may also be utilized to provide a complete membership list for each of these organizations as of Dec. 1, 2002.

Notes for the column headings

a. The date may also be either that of the organization of the present form of government or the inception of the present administrative structure (federation, confederation, union, etc.).
b. Constitutions whose dates are in italic type had been wholly or substantially suspended or abolished as of late 2002.
c. For abbreviations used in this column see the list on the facing page.
d. When a legislative body has been adjourned or otherwise suspended, figures in parentheses indicate the number of members in the legislative body as provided for in constitution or law.
e. States contributing funds to or receiving aid from UNICEF in 1997.
f. 15 nations with judicial representation in ICJ in 2002.
g. Palestine (Liberation Organization) also a member.

International organizations, conventions

ACP	African, Caribbean, and Pacific (Cotonou Agreement) states
ADB	Asian Development Bank
APEC	Asia-Pacific Economic Co-operation
AU	African Union
CARICOM	Caribbean Community and Common Market
ECOWAS	Economic Community of West African States
EU	The European Union
FAO	Food and Agriculture Org.
FZ	The Franc Zone
GCC	Gulf Cooperation Council
I-ADB	Inter-American Development Bank
IAEA	International Atomic Energy Agency
IBRD	International Bank for Reconstruction and Development
ICAO	International Civil Aviation Org.
ICJ	International Court of Justice
IDA	International Development Association
IDB	Islamic Development Bank
IFC	International Finance Corporation
ILO	International Labour Org.
IMF	International Monetary Fund
IMO	International Maritime Org.
ITU	International Telecommunication Union
LAS	League of Arab States (Arab League)
OAS	Organization of American States
OPEC	Organization of the Petroleum Exporting Countries
PC	Pacific Community
UNCTAD	United Nations Conference on Trade and Development
UNESCO	United Nations Educational Scientific and Cultural Org.
UNICEF	United Nations Children's Fund
UNIDO	United Nations Industrial Development Org.
UPU	Universal Postal Union
WHO	World Health Org.
WIPO	World Intellectual Property Org.
WMO	World Meteorological Org.
WTO	World Trade Org.

Abbreviations used in the executive-branch column

CM	Council of Ministers
FC	Federal Council
GG	Governor-General
GPC	General People's Committee
NDC	National Defense Commission
PC	People's Council
PNA	Palestine National Authority
SC	State Council
SPDC	State Peace and Development Council

membership in international organizations

United Nations (date of admission)	UNCTAD*	UNICEF*e	ICJ*f	FAO	IAEA	IBRD	ICAO	IDA	IFC	ILO	IMF	IMO	ITU	UNESCO	UNIDO	UPU	WHO	WIPO	WMO	WTO	The Commonwealth	AU	EU	GCC	LASg	OAS	PC	ACP	ADB	APEC	CARICOM	ECOWAS	FZ	I-ADB	IDBg	OPEC	country
1946	•	•		•	•	•	•	•	•	•	•	•	•	•	•	•	•	•	•										•						•		Afghanistan
1955	•	•		•	•	•	•	•	•	•	•	•	•	•	•	•	•	•	•																•		Albania
1962	•	•		•	•	•	•	•	•	•	•	•	•	•	•	•	•	•	•	5		•			•										•	•	Algeria
—					•							•	•			•		•	•	5							•										American Samoa
1993	•						•						•	•		•	•	•	•	5																	Andorra
1976	•	•		•		•	•	•	•	•	•	•	•	•	•	•	•	•	•	•		•						•							•		Angola
1981	•	•		•		•	•	•	•	•	•	•	•	•	•	•	•	•	•	•	•					•		•			•				•		Antigua and Barbuda
1945	•	•		•	•	•	•	•	•	•	•	•	•	•	•	•	•	•	•	•						•		•						•			Argentina
1992	•	•		•	•	•	•	•	•	•	•	•	•	•	•	•	•	•	•	5									•						•		Armenia
—									•		14		•		•		•		•																		Aruba
1945	•	•		•	•	•	•	•	•	•	•	•	•	•		•	•	•	•	•	•					•		•	•	•				•			Australia
1955	•	•		•	•	•	•	•	•	•	•	•	•	•	•	•	•	•	•	•			•						•					•			Austria
1992	•	•		•	•	•	•	•	•	•	•	•	•	•	•	•	•	•	•	5									•						•		Azerbaijan
1973	•	•		•		•	•	•	•	•	•	•	•	•	•	•	•	•	•	5	•					•		•			•			•			Bahamas, The
1971	•	•		•		•	•	•	•	•	•	•	•	•	•	•	•	•	•	•				•	•										•		Bahrain
1974	•	•		•	•	•	•	•	•	•	•	•	•	•	•	•	•	•	•	•	•							•	•						•		Bangladesh
1966	•	•		•		•	•	•	•	•	•	•	•	•	•	•	•	•	•	•	•					•		•			•			•			Barbados
1945	•	•		•	•	•	•	•	•	•	•	•	•	•	•	•	•	•	•	5									•						•		Belarus
1945	•	•		•	•	•	•	•	•	•	•	•	•	•	•	•	•	•	•	•			•						•					•			Belgium
1981	•	•		•		•	•	•	•	•	•	•	•	•	•	•	•	•	•	•	•					•		•			•			•			Belize
1960	•	•		•		•	•	•	•	•	•		•	•	•	•	•	•	•	•		•						•				•	•		•		Benin
—																																					Bermuda
1971	•	•		•		•	•	•	•	•	•		•	•	•	•	•	•	•	5									•					•			Bhutan
1945	•	•		•	•	•	•	•	•	•	•	•	•	•	•	•	•	•	•	•						•								•			Bolivia
1992	•	•		•	•	•	•	•	•	•	•	•	•	•	•	•	•	•	•	5									•						•		Bosnia and Herzegovina
1966	•	•		•		•	•	•	•	•	•		•	•	•	•	•	•	•	•	•	•						•						•		Botswana
1945	•	•	•	•	•	•	•	•	•	•	•	•	•	•	•	•	•	•	•	•						•		•						•			Brazil
1984	•	•		•		•	•	•	•	•	•	•	•	•	•	•	•	•	•	•	•								•						•		Brunei
1955	•	•		•	•	•	•	•	•	•	•	•	•	•	•	•	•	•	•	•									•						•		Bulgaria
1960	•	•		•		•	•	•	•	•	•		•	•	•	•	•	•	•	•		•						•	•			•	•		•		Burkina Faso
1962	•	•		•		•	•	•	•	•	•		•	•	•	•	•	•	•	•		•						•						•		Burundi
1955	•	•		•	•	•	•	•	•	•	•	•	•	•	•	•	•	•	•	5		•							•					•			Cambodia
1960	•	•		•	•	•	•	•	•	•	•	•	•	•	•	•	•	•	•	•	•	•						•				•	•		•	•	Cameroon
1945	•	•	•	•	•	•	•	•	•	•	•	•	•	•	•	•	•	•	•	•	•					•	•	•	•	•				•			Canada
1975	•	•		•		•	•	•	•	•	•	•	•	•	•	•	•	•	•	5		•						•				•			•		Cape Verde
1960	•	•		•		•	•	•	•	•	•		•	•	•	•	•	•	•	•		•						•					•		•		Central African Republic
1960	•	•		•		•	•	•	•	•	•		•	•	•	•	•	•	•	•		•						•					•		•		Chad
1945	•	•		•	•	•	•	•	•	•	•	•	•	•	•	•	•	•	•	•						•		•	•	•				•			Chile
1945	•	•	•	•	•	•	•	•	•	•	•	•	•	•	•	•	•	•	•	•							•		•	•				•			China
1945	•	•		•	•	•	•	•	•	•	•	•	•	•	•	•	•	•	•	•						•								•			Colombia
1975	•	•		•		•	•	•	•	•	•		•	•	•	•	•	•	•			•			•			•						•	•		Comoros
1960	•	•		•		•	•	•	•	•	•		•	•	•	•	•	•	•	•		•						•						•	•		Congo, Dem. Rep. of the
1960	•	•		•		•	•	•	•	•	•		•	•	•	•	•	•	•	•		•						•				•	•		•		Congo, Rep. of the
1945	•	•		•	•	•	•	•	•	•	•	•	•	•	•	•	•	•	•	•						•		•						•			Costa Rica
1960	•	•		•		•	•	•	•	•	•		•	•	•	•	•	•	•	•		•						•				•	•		•		Côte d'Ivoire
1992	•	•		•	•	•	•	•	•	•	•	•	•	•	•	•	•	•	•	•									39						•		Croatia
1945	•	•		•	•	•	•	•	•	•	•	•	•	•	•	•	•	•	•	•															•		Cuba
1960	•	•		•	•	•	•	•	•	•	•	•	•	•	•	•	•	•	•	•	•		5												•		Cyprus40
1993	•	•		•	•	•	•	•	•	•	•	•	•	•	•	•	•	•	•	•			5												•		Czech Republic
1945	•	•		•	•	•	•	•	•	•	•	•	•	•	•	•	•	•	•	•			•						•					•			Denmark
1977	•	•		•		•	•	•	•	•	•	•	•	•	•	•	•	•	•	•		•			•			•							•		Djibouti
1978	•	•		•		•	•	•	•	•	•	•	•	•	•	•	•	•	•	•	•					•		•			•			•			Dominica
1945	•	•	•	•	•	•	•	•	•	•	•	•	•	•	•	•	•	•	•	•						•		•						•			Dominican Republic
2002	•	•		•		•	•	•	•	•	•	•	•	•	•	•	•	•	•															•			East Timor
1945	•	•		•	•	•	•	•	•	•	•	•	•	•	•	•	•	•	•	•						•								•			Ecuador

Government and international organizations (continued)

country	date of independence[a]	date of current or last constitution[b]	type of government	executive branch[c] chief of state	head of government	legislative branch[d] upper house (members)	lower house (members)	admin. subdivisions first-order (number)	second-order (number)	seaward claims territorial (nautical miles)	fishing/ economic (nautical miles)
Egypt	Feb. 28, 1922	Sept. 11, 1971	republic	president	prime minister	454	—	27	186	12[43]	200[43]
El Salvador	Jan. 30, 1841	Dec. 20, 1983	republic	president		84	—	14	262	200	200
Equatorial Guinea	Oct. 12, 1968	Nov. 16, 1991[38]	republic	president	prime minister	80	—	7	18	12	200
Eritrea	May 24, 1993	[44]	republic[1]	president		150	—	6	...	12	...
Estonia	Feb. 24, 1918	July 3, 1992	republic	president	prime minister	101	—	15	46	12	...
Ethiopia	c. 1000 BC	Aug. 22, 1995[45]	federal republic	president	prime minister	108	546	11	57	—	—
Faroe Islands	—	April 1, 1948	part of Danish realm	Danish monarch	[46]	32	—	9	48	3	200[47]
Fiji	Oct. 10, 1970	July 27, 1998	republic	president	prime minister	32	72	4	15	12[10]	200[10]
Finland	Dec. 6, 1917	March 1, 2000	republic	president	prime minister	200	—	6	20	12[48]	12
France	August 843	Oct. 4, 1958[16]	republic	president	prime minister	321	577	22	96	12	200
French Guiana	—	Feb. 28, 1983	overseas dept. (Fr.)	French president	[49]	19	31	2	22	12	200
French Polynesia	—	Sept. 6, 1984	overseas territory (Fr.)	French president	[50]	49	—	5	48	12	200
Gabon	Aug. 17, 1960	March 26, 1991	republic	president	prime minister	91	120	9	37	12	200
Gambia, The	Feb. 18, 1965	Jan. 16, 1997	republic	president		53	—	8	45	12	200
Gaza Strip	—	May 4, 1994[51]	interim authority	chairman PNA		89	—	5	...	...	...
Georgia	April 9, 1991	Oct. 17, 1995[52]	republic	president[53]		235	—	12	74	...	...
Germany	May 5, 1955	May 23, 1949	federal republic	president	chancellor	69	603	16	32	12[47]	200
Ghana	March 6, 1957	Jan. 7, 1993	republic	president		200	—	10	110	12	200
Greece	Feb. 3, 1830	April 6, 2001[54]	republic	president	prime minister	300	—	53	448	6/10	2
Greenland	—	May 1, 1979	part of Danish realm	Danish monarch	[46]	31	—	18	...	3	200
Grenada	Feb. 7, 1974	Feb. 7, 1974	constitutional monarchy	British monarch	prime minister	13	15	9	...	12	200
Guadeloupe	—	Feb. 28, 1983	overseas dept. (Fr.)	French president	[49]	42	41	3	34	12	200
Guam	—	Aug. 1, 1950	territory (U.S.)	U.S. president	governor	15	—	...	—	12	200
Guatemala	Sept. 15, 1821	Jan. 14, 1986	republic	president		113	—	22	313	12	200
Guernsey	—	Jan. 1, 1949[16]	crown dependency (U.K.)	British monarch[55]	[56]	59	—	2	10	3	12
Guinea	Oct. 2, 1958	Dec. 23, 1990[57]	republic	president[58]		114	—	8	34	12	200
Guinea-Bissau	Sept. 10, 1974	May 11, 1991	republic[1]	president	prime minister	102	—	9	37	12	200
Guyana	May 26, 1966	Oct. 6, 1980	cooperative republic	president		65	—	10	71	12	200
Haiti	Jan. 1, 1804	March 29, 1987	republic	president	prime minister	27	83	9	41	12	200
Honduras	Nov. 5, 1838	Jan. 20, 1982	republic	president		128	—	18	297	12	200
Hong Kong	—	July 1, 1997	[59]	Chinese president	chief executive	60	—	18	...	12	2
Hungary	Nov. 16, 1918	Oct. 18, 1989[57]	republic	president	prime minister	386	—	20	195	—	—
Iceland	June 17, 1944	June 17, 1944	republic	president	prime minister	63	—	124	—	12	200
India	Aug. 15, 1947	Jan. 26, 1950	federal republic	president	prime minister	245	545	35	593	12	200
Indonesia	Aug. 17, 1945	Aug. 17, 1945	republic	president		700	500	30	...	12[10]	200[10]
Iran	Oct. 7, 1906	Dec. 2–3, 1979	Islamic republic	president[60]		290	—	28	282	12	50[61]
Iraq	Oct. 3, 1932	Sept. 22, 1968[62]	republic	president		250	—	18	96	12	2
Ireland	Dec. 6, 1921	Dec. 29, 1937	republic	president	prime minister	60	166	34	86	12	200
Isle of Man	—	1961[16]	crown dependency (U.K.)	British monarch[55]	chief minister	11	24	24	—	12[63]	...
Israel	May 14, 1948	June 1950[16]	republic	president	prime minister	120	—	6	15	12	...
Italy	March 17, 1861	Jan. 1, 1948	republic	president	prime minister	321	630	20	103	12	2
Jamaica	Aug. 6, 1962	Aug. 6, 1962	constitutional monarchy	British monarch	prime minister	21	60	13	—	12	200
Japan	c. 660 BC	May 3, 1947	constitutional monarchy	[64]	prime minister[66]	247	480	47	3,233	12[65]	200
Jersey	—	Jan. 1, 1949[16]	crown dependency (U.K.)	British monarch[55]	[66]	57	—	12	—	3	...
Jordan	May 25, 1946	Jan. 8, 1952	constitutional monarchy	king[18]		40	80	12	18	3	2
Kazakhstan	Dec. 16, 1991	Sept. 6, 1995	republic	president[18]		39	77	16	...	—	—
Kenya	Dec. 12, 1963	Dec. 12, 1963	republic	president		224	—	8	...	12	200
Kiribati	July 12, 1979	July 12, 1979	republic	president		42	—	3	6	12[10]	200[10]
Korea, North	Sept. 9, 1948	Sept. 5, 1998[67]	socialist republic	chairman NDC	premier	687	—	14	172	12	200
Korea, South	Aug. 15, 1948	Feb. 25, 1988	republic	president[18]		273	—	16	195	12[68]	12
Kuwait	June 19, 1961	Nov. 16, 1962	const. mon. (emirate)	emir[18]		50[69]	—	5	—	12	2
Kyrgyzstan	Aug. 31, 1991	May 5, 1993	republic	president[18]		45	60	7	39	—	—
Laos	Oct. 23, 1953	Aug. 15, 1991	republic	president	prime minister	109	—	18	133	—	—
Latvia	Nov. 18, 1918	Nov. 7, 1922	republic	president	prime minister	100	—	33	70	12	...
Lebanon	Nov. 26, 1941	Sept. 21, 1990	republic	president	prime minister	128	—	6	c. 700	12	2
Lesotho	Oct. 4, 1966	April 2, 1993	[1], [70]	king	prime minister	33[30]	120	10	...	—	—
Liberia	July 26, 1847	Aug. 20, 1995[71]	republic	president		26	64	15	...	200	2
Libya	Dec. 24, 1951	March 2, 1977	socialist state[72]	leader[73]	sec. GPC	760	—	25	...	12[74]	2
Liechtenstein	July 12, 1806	Oct. 5, 1921	constitutional monarchy	prince	head of govt.	25	—	11	—	—	—
Lithuania	Feb. 16, 1918	Nov. 6, 1992	republic	president	prime minister	141	—	10	61	12	...
Luxembourg	May 10, 1867	Oct. 17, 1868	constitutional monarchy	grand duke	prime minister	21[30]	60	3	12	—	—
Macau	—	Dec. 20, 1999	[59]	Chinese president	chief executive	27	—	...	—	...	...
Macedonia	Nov. 17, 1991	Nov. 16, 2001[75]	republic	president	prime minister	120	—	123	...	—	—
Madagascar	June 26, 1960	April 8, 1998	federal republic	president[18]		90	150	6	113	12	200
Malawi	July 6, 1964	May 18, 1994	republic	president		192	—	3	27	—	—
Malaysia	Aug. 31, 1957	Aug. 31, 1957	fed. const. monarchy	paramount ruler	prime minister	70	193	16	134	12	200
Maldives	July 26, 1965	Jan. 1, 1998	republic	president		42[69]	—	21	201	12[10]	43
Mali	Sept. 22, 1960	Feb. 25, 1992	republic	president	prime minister	147	—	9	49	—	—
Malta	Sept. 21, 1964	Dec. 13, 1974	republic	president	prime minister	65	—	1	68	12	25
Marshall Islands	Dec. 22, 1990	May 1, 1979	republic	president		12[30]	33	...	—	12[10]	200
Martinique	—	Feb. 28, 1983	overseas dept. (Fr.)	French president	[49]	45	41	4	34	12	200
Mauritania	Nov. 28, 1960	July 21, 1991	republic	president[18]		56	81	13	53	12	200
Mauritius	March 12, 1968	March 12, 1992	republic	president	prime minister	70	—	11	130	12	200
Mayotte	—	July 11, 2001	dept. collectivity (Fr.)	French president	[76]	19	—	17	...	12	200
Mexico	Sept. 16, 1810	Feb. 5, 1917	federal republic	president		128	500	32	2,443	12	200
Micronesia	Dec. 22, 1990	Jan. 1, 1981	federal republic	president		14	—	4	74	12	200
Moldova	Aug. 27, 1991	Aug. 27, 1994	parliamentary republic	president	prime minister	101	—	13	...	—	—
Monaco	Feb. 2, 1861	Dec. 17, 1962	constitutional monarchy	prince	min. of state[77]	18	—	—	—	12	2
Mongolia	March 13, 1921	Feb. 12, 1992	republic	president	prime minister	76	—	22	342	—	—
Morocco	March 2, 1956	Oct. 7, 1996	constitutional monarchy	king[18]		270	325	17[78]	71[78]	12	200
Mozambique	June 25, 1975	Nov. 30, 1990	republic	president		250	—	11	112	12	200
Myanmar (Burma)	Jan. 4, 1948	Jan. 4, 1974	republic	chairman SPDC		(492)	—	14	58	12	200
Namibia	March 21, 1990	March 21, 1990	republic	president		26	72[69]	13	—	12	200
Nauru	Jan. 31, 1968	Jan. 31, 1968	republic	president		18	—	1	—	12	200
Nepal	Nov. 13, 1769	Nov. 9, 1990	constitutional monarchy	king	prime minister	60	205	5[79]	75	—	—

membership in international organizations																																					country
United Nations (date of admission)	UN organs* and affiliated intergovernmental organizations																				The Commonwealth	regional multipurpose						economic									
	UNCTAD*	UNICEF*e	ICJ*f	FAO	IAEA	IBRD	ICAO	IDA	IFC	ILO	IMF	IMO	ITU	UNESCO	UNIDO	UPU	WHO	WIPO	WMO	WTO		AU	EU	GCC	LAS^g	OAS	PC	ACP	ADB	APEC	CARICOM	ECOWAS	FZ	I-ADB	IDB^g	OPEC	
1945	•	•	•	•	•	•	•	•	•	•	•	•	•	•	•	•	•	•	•	•		•			•										•		Egypt
1945	•	•		•		•	•	•	•	•	•	•	•	•	•	•	•	•	•	•		•				•		•									El Salvador
1968	•	•		•		•	•	•	•	•	•	•	•	•	•	•	•	•	•	5		•						•							•		Equatorial Guinea
1993	•	•		•	•	•	•	•	•	•	•	•	•	•	•	•	•	•	•	•		•						•									Eritrea
1991	•	•		•	•	•	•	•	•	•	•	•	•	•	•	•	•	•	•	•			5														Estonia
1945	•	•		•	•	•	•	•	•	•	•	•	•	•	•	•	•	•	•	5		•						•									Ethiopia
—													•			•	•	•	•																		Faroe Islands
1970	•	•		•		•	•	•	•	•	•	•	•	•	•	•	•	•	•	•	•						•	•	•								Fiji
1955	•	•		•	•	•	•	•	•	•	•	•	•	•	•	•	•	•	•	•			•						•						•	•	Finland
1945	•	•	•	•	•	•	•	•	•	•	•	•	•	•	•	•	•	•	•	•			•				•						•	•			France
—											•					•	•	•	•								•								•		French Guiana
—											•					•	•	•	•								•								•		French Polynesia
1960	•	•		•		•	•	•	•	•	•	•	•	•	•	•	•	•	•	•		•	•					•					•	•	•		Gabon
1965	•	•	•	•		•	•	•	•	•	•	•	•	•	•	•	•	•	•	•	•							•						•			Gambia, The
—		•															•																				Gaza Strip
1992	•	•		•	•	•	•	•	•	•	•	•	•	•	•	•	•	•	•	•									•						•		Georgia
1973	•	•	•	•	•	•	•	•	•	•	•	•	•	•	•	•	•	•	•	•		•	•					•						•			Germany
1957	•	•		•	•	•	•	•	•	•	•	•	•	•	•	•	•	•	•	•	•	•						•				•		•			Ghana
1945	•	•		•	•	•	•	•	•	•	•	•	•	•	•	•	•	•	•	•			•				•						•	•			Greece
—																•																					Greenland
1974	•	•		•		•	•	•	•	•	•	•	•	•	•	•	•	•		•	•					•		•			•			•			Grenada
—																•	•	•	•								•					•					Guadeloupe
—																•									•												Guam
1945	•	•		•	•	•	•	•	•	•	•	•	•	•	•	•	•	•	•	•						•								•			Guatemala
—																•																					Guernsey
1958	•	•		•		•	•	•	•	•	•	•	•	•	•	•	•	•	•	•		•						•				•	•	•	•		Guinea
1974	•	•		•		•	•	•	•	•	•	•	•	•	•	•	•	•	•	•		•						•				•	•	•	•		Guinea-Bissau
1966	•	•		•		•	•	•	•	•	•	•	•	•	•	•	•	•	•	•	•					•		•			•			•	•		Guyana
1945	•	•		•	•	•	•	•	•	•	•	•	•	•	•	•	•	•	•	•						•		•			5			•			Haiti
1945	•	•		•		•	•	•	•	•	•	•	•	•	•	•	•	•	•	•						•								•			Honduras
—		•									14		•			•		•	•	•									•	•							Hong Kong
1955	•	•	•	•	•	•	•	•	•	•	•	•	•	•	•	•	•	•	•	•			5												•		Hungary
1946	•	•		•	•	•	•	•	•	•	•	•	•	•	•	•	•	•	•	•															•		Iceland
1945	•	•		•	•	•	•	•	•	•	•	•	•	•	•	•	•	•	•	•	•								•					•			India
1950	•	•		•	•	•	•	•	•	•	•	•	•	•	•	•	•	•	•	•									•	•					•	•	Indonesia
1945	•	•		•	•	•	•	•	•	•	•	•	•	•	•	•	•	•	•						•				•						•	•	Iran
1945	•	•		•	•	•	•	•	•	•	•	•	•	•	•	•	•	•	•						•										•	•	Iraq
1955	•	•		•	•	•	•	•	•	•	•	•	•	•	•	•	•	•	•	•			•														Ireland
—																	•																	•			Isle of Man
1949	•	•		•	•	•	•	•	•	•	•	•	•		•	•	•	•	•	•															•		Israel
1955	•	•		•	•	•	•	•	•	•	•	•	•	•	•	•	•	•	•	•			•						•						•		Italy
1962	•	•		•	•	•	•	•	•	•	•	•	•	•	•	•	•	•	•	•	•					•		•			•			•			Jamaica
1956	•	•	•	•	•	•	•	•	•	•	•	•	•	•	•	•	•	•	•	•								•	•	•				•			Japan
—																•	•																				Jersey
1955	•	•	•	•	•	•	•	•	•	•	•	•	•	•	•	•	•	•	•	•					•									•			Jordan
1992	•	•		•	•	•	•	•	•	•	•	•	•	•	•	•	•	•	•	5									•						•		Kazakhstan
1963	•	•		•	•	•	•	•	•	•	•	•	•	•	•	•	•	•	•	•	•	•						•						•			Kenya
1999	•	•		•		•	•	•		•	•	•	•	•		•	•		•	•	•	•					•	•									Kiribati
1991	•	•		•			•			•		•	•	•	•	•	•		•	•								•						•			Korea, North
1991	•	•		•	•	•	•	•	•	•	•	•	•	•	•	•	•	•	•	•									•	•							Korea, South
1963	•	•		•	•	•	•	•	•	•	•	•	•	•	•	•	•	•	•	•				•	•				•					•	•	•	Kuwait
1992	•	•		•	•	•	•	•	•	•	•	•	•	•	•	•	•	•	•	•									•					•	•		Kyrgyzstan
1955	•	•		•		•	•	•	•	•	•	•	•	•	•	•	•	•	•	5									•								Laos
1991	•	•		•	•	•	•	•	•	•	•	•	•	•	•	•	•	•	•	•			5												•		Latvia
1945	•	•		•	•	•	•	•	•	•	•	•	•	•	•	•	•	•	•	5					•									•			Lebanon
1966	•	•		•		•	•	•	•	•	•	•	•	•	•	•	•	•	•	•	•	•						•						•			Lesotho
1945	•	•		•	•	•	•	•	•	•	•	•	•	•	•	•	•	•	•	•		•						•						•			Liberia
1955	•	•		•		•	•	•	•	•	•	•	•	•	•	•	•	•	•	•		•			•									•	•	•	Libya
1990	•	•			•		•			•		•	•	•	•	•	•	•	•	•			5														Liechtenstein
1991	•	•		•	•	•	•	•	•	•	•	•	•	•	•	•	•	•	•	•			5														Lithuania
1945	•	•		•	•	•	•	•	•	•	•	•	•	•	•	•	•	•	•	•			•											•			Luxembourg
—											14		14			•	•	•	•	5																	Macau
1993	•	•		•	•	•	•	•	•	•	•	•	•	•	•	•	•	•	•	5																	Macedonia
1960	•	•	•	•		•	•	•	•	•	•	•	•	•	•	•	•	•	•	•		•						•					•		•		Madagascar
1964	•	•		•	•	•	•	•	•	•	•	•	•	•	•	•	•	•	•	•	•	•						•						•			Malawi
1957	•	•		•	•	•	•	•	•	•	•	•	•	•	•	•	•	•	•	•	•								•	•				•			Malaysia
1965	•	•		•		•	•	•	•	•	•	•	•	•	•	•	•	•	•	•	•								•					•			Maldives
1960	•	•		•	•	•	•	•	•	•	•	•	•	•	•	•	•	•	•	•		•						•				•	•	•	•		Mali
1964	•	•		•	•	•	•	•	•	•	•	•	•	•	•	•	•	•	•	•	•		5					•						•			Malta
1991	•	•		•		•	•	•	•		•	•	•	•		•	•		•								•	•	•								Marshall Islands
—																•	•											•					•				Martinique
1961	•	•		•		•	•	•	•	•	•	•	•	•	•	•	•	•	•	•		•			•			•				•	•	•	•		Mauritania
1968	•	•		•		•	•	•	•	•	•	•	•	•	•	•	•	•	•	•	•	•						•					•	•			Mauritius
—																	•																	•			Mayotte
1945	•	•		•	•	•	•	•	•	•	•	•	•	•	•	•	•	•	•	•						•				•				•			Mexico
1991	•	•		•		•	•	•	•		•	•	•	•		•	•		•	•							•	•	•								Micronesia
1992	•	•		•	•	•	•	•	•	•	•	•	•	•	•	•	•	•	•	•									•						•		Moldova
1993	•	•		•		•	•			•	•	•	•	•		•	•	•	•	•																	Monaco
1961	•	•		•	•	•	•	•	•	•	•	•	•	•	•	•	•	•	•	•									•						•		Mongolia
1956	•	•		•	•	•	•	•	•	•	•	•	•	•	•	•	•	•	•	•		•			•									•			Morocco
1975	•	•		•		•	•	•	•	•	•	•	•	•	•	•	•	•	•	•	•	•						•						•			Mozambique
1948	•	•		•	•	•	•	•	•	•	•	•	•	•	•	•	•	•	•	•									•	•							Myanmar (Burma)
1990	•	•		•	•	•	•	5	•	•	•	•	•	•	•	•	•	•	•	•	•	•						•	•					•			Namibia
1999	•	•		•			•				•		•	•		•	•		•	•							•	•	•							Nauru
1955	•	•		•		•	•	•	•	•	•	•	•	•	•	•	•	•	•	5								•	•								Nepal

Government and international organizations (continued)

country	date of independence[a]	date of current or last constitution[b]	type of government	executive branch[c] chief of state	executive branch[c] head of government	legislative branch[d] upper house (members)	legislative branch[d] lower house (members)	admin. subdivisions first-order (number)	admin. subdivisions second-order (number)	seaward claims territorial (nautical miles)	seaward claims fishing/economic (nautical miles)
Netherlands, The	March 30, 1814	Feb. 17, 1983	constitutional monarchy	monarch	prime minister	75	150	12	536	12	200
Netherlands Antilles	—	Dec. 29, 1954	overseas territory (Neth.)	Dutch monarch	[13]	22	—	5	—	12	200
New Caledonia	—	February 1999	overseas country (Fr.)	French president[80]	president	54	—	3	33	12	200
New Zealand	Sept. 26, 1907	June 30, 1852[16]	constitutional monarchy	British monarch	prime minister	120	—	16	74	12	200
Nicaragua	April 30, 1838	Jan. 9, 1987	republic	——president——		92	—	17	151	200	200
Niger	Aug. 3, 1960	Aug. 9, 1999	republic	——president[18]——		83	—	8	35	—	—
Nigeria	Oct. 1, 1960	May 5, 1999	federal republic	——president——		109	360	37	768	30	200
Northern Mariana Is.	—	Jan. 9, 1978	commonwealth (U.S.)	U.S. president	governor	9	18	4	—	12	200
Norway	June 7, 1905	May 17, 1814	constitutional monarchy	king	prime minister	165	—	19	435	4	200
Oman	Dec. 20, 1951	Nov. 6, 1996[81]	monarchy (sultanate)	——sultan——		—[82]—		8	60	12	200
Pakistan	Aug. 14, 1947	Aug. 14, 1973	republic	——president[18]——		92	342	16[83]	106	12	200
Palau	Oct. 1, 1994	Jan. 1, 1981	republic	——president——		14	16	16	—	3	200
Panama	Nov. 3, 1903	May 20, 1983[34]	republic	——president[37]——		71	—	14	74	200	2
Papua New Guinea	Sept. 16, 1975	Sept. 16, 1975	constitutional monarchy	British monarch	prime minister	109	—	20	267	12[10]	200[10]
Paraguay	May 14, 1811	June 22, 1992	republic	——president——		46	80	18	217	—	—
Peru	July 28, 1821	Dec. 29, 1993	republic	——president[18]——		120	—	25	194	200	200
Philippines	July 4, 1946	Feb. 11, 1987	republic	——president——		24	220[8]	16	80	...	200[10]
Poland	Nov. 10, 1918	Oct. 17, 1997	republic	president	prime minister	100	460	16	373	12	84
Portugal	c. 1140	April 25, 1976	republic	president	prime minister	230	—	7	308	12	200
Puerto Rico	—	July 25, 1952	commonwealth (U.S.)	U.S. president	governor	27[85]	51[85]	78	...	12	200
Qatar	Sept. 3, 1971	July 1970[62]	monarchy	——emir[18]——		35[30]	—	9	—	12	86
Réunion	—	Feb. 28, 1983	overseas dept. (Fr.)	French president	[49]	47	45	4	24	12	200
Romania	May 21, 1877	Dec. 13, 1991	republic	president	prime minister	143	345	42	2,687	12[43]	200[43]
Russia	Dec. 8, 1991	Dec. 24, 1993	federal republic	president	prime minister	178	450	7	89	12	200
Rwanda	July 1, 1962	May 5, 1995[87]	republic[1]	——president[18]——		74	—	12	154	—	—
St. Kitts and Nevis	Sept. 19, 1983	Sept. 19, 1983	constitutional monarchy	British monarch	prime minister	15	—	1	—	12	200
St. Lucia	Feb. 22, 1979	Feb. 22, 1979	constitutional monarchy	British monarch	prime minister	11	17[9]	10	—	12	200
St. Vincent	Oct. 27, 1979	Oct. 27, 1979	constitutional monarchy	British monarch	prime minister	21	—	...	—	12	200
Samoa	Jan. 1, 1962	Oct. 28, 1960	[88]	head of state	prime minister	49	—	11	—	12	200
San Marino	855	Oct. 8, 1600	republic	——captains-regent (2)——		60	—	9	—	—	—
São Tomé and Príncipe	July 12, 1975	Sept. 10, 1990	republic	president	prime minister	55	—	1	6	12[10]	200[10]
Saudi Arabia	Sept. 23, 1932	[89]	monarchy	——king——		120[30]	—	13	103	12	2
Senegal	Aug. 20, 1960	Jan. 7, 2001[138]	republic	——president[18]——		120	—	10	30	12[43]	200[43]
Seychelles	June 29, 1976	June 21, 1993	republic	——president——		34	—	...	...	12	200
Sierra Leone	April 27, 1961	Oct. 1, 1991	republic	——president——		124	—	4	12	200	2
Singapore	Aug. 9, 1965	June 3, 1959[16]	republic	president	prime minister	90	—	—	—	3	12
Slovakia	Jan. 1, 1993	2001[90]	republic	president	prime minister	150	—	8	79	—	—
Slovenia	June 25, 1991	Dec. 23, 1991	republic	president	prime minister	40	90	192	—	...	...
Solomon Islands	July 7, 1978	July 7, 1978	constitutional monarchy	British monarch	prime minister	50	—	10	183	12[10]	200[10]
Somalia	July 1, 1960	July–August 2000[91]	republic[1]	——president[18]——		245	—	3	...	200	200
South Africa	May 31, 1910	June 30, 1997	republic	——president——		90	400	9	360	12	200
Spain	1492	Dec. 29, 1978	constitutional monarchy	king	prime minister	259	350	19	50	12	200[92]
Sri Lanka	Feb. 4, 1948	Sept. 7, 1978	republic	——president——		225	—	25	...	12	200
Sudan, The	Jan. 1, 1956	June 30, 1998	military regime	——president——		360	—	26	66	12	2
Suriname	Nov. 25, 1975	Nov. 25, 1987	republic	——president——		51	—	10	...	12	200
Swaziland	Sept. 6, 1968	Sept. 6, 1968	monarchy	——king[18]——		30[30]	65[30]	4	55	—	—
Sweden	before 836	Jan. 1, 1975	constitutional monarchy	king	prime minister	349	—	21	289	12	19
Switzerland	Sept. 22, 1499	Jan. 1, 2000	federal state	——president FC——		46	200	26	187	—	—
Syria	April 17, 1946	March 14, 1973	republic	——president——		250	—	14	47	35	2
Taiwan	Oct. 25, 1945	Dec. 25, 1947[16]	republic	president	premier	225	—	2	25	24	200
Tajikistan	Sept. 9, 1991	Nov. 6, 1994	republic	president	prime minister	33	63	4	...	—	—
Tanzania	Dec. 9, 1961	April 25, 1977	republic	——president——		275	—	1	26	12	200
Thailand	1350	Oct. 11, 1997	constitutional monarchy	king	prime minister	200	500	76	795	12	200
Togo	April 27, 1960	Sept. 27, 1992[38]	republic	president	prime minister	81	—	5	21	30	200
Tonga	June 4, 1970	Nov. 4, 1875	constitutional monarchy[93]	——monarch——		30	—	...	...	12	200
Trinidad and Tobago	Aug. 31, 1962	July 27, 1976	republic	president	prime minister	31	36	16	...	12[10]	200[10]
Tunisia	March 20, 1956	June 1, 1200[234]	republic	president	prime minister	182	—	24	257	12	2
Turkey	Oct. 29, 1923	Oct. 3, 2001[94]	republic	president	prime minister	550	—	81	849	12[95]	19
Turkmenistan	Oct. 27, 1991	May 18, 1992	republic	——president PC——		50	—	6	...	—	—
Tuvalu	Oct. 1, 1978	Oct. 1, 1986	constitutional monarchy	British monarch	prime minister	12	—	8	—	12[10]	200[10]
Uganda	Oct. 9, 1962	Oct. 8, 1995	republic	——president[18]——		305	—	56	...	—	—
Ukraine	Aug. 24, 1991	June 28, 1996	republic	president	prime minister	450	—	27	485	12	200
United Arab Emirates	Dec. 2, 1971	Dec. 2, 1971	federation of emirates	president	prime minister	40[30]	—	7	—	12	200
United Kingdom	Dec. 6, 1921	[96]	constitutional monarchy	monarch	prime minister	709	659	3	...	12[63]	200
United States	July 4, 1776	March 4, 1789	federal republic	——president——		100	435	51	3,043	12	200
Uruguay	Aug. 25, 1828	Feb. 15, 1967	republic	——president——		31	99	19	...	200	200
Uzbekistan	Aug. 31, 1991	Dec. 8, 1992	republic	——president[18]——		250	—	14	162	—	—
Vanuatu	July 30, 1980	July 30, 1980	republic	president	prime minister	52	—	6	...	12[10]	200[10]
Venezuela	July 5, 1811	Dec. 20, 1999	federal republic	——president——		165	—	25	332	12	200
Vietnam	Sept. 2, 1945	April 15, 1992	socialist republic	president	prime minister	498	—	8	61	12	200
Virgin Islands (U.S.)	—	July 22, 1954	territory (U.S.)	U.S. president	governor	15	—	...	...	12	200
West Bank	—	May 4, 1994[51]	interim authority	——chairman PNA——		89	—	11	...	—	—
Western Sahara	—	—	annexure of Morocco			—	—	...	...	12	200
Yemen	December 1918	Sept. 29, 1994[98]	republic	president	prime minister	111	301	20	...	12	200
Yugoslavia	Dec. 1, 1918	April 27, 1992	federal republic	federal president	prime minister	40	138	3	24[99]	...	...
Zambia	Oct. 24, 1964	May 28, 1996[3]	republic	——president——		158	—	9	57	—	—
Zimbabwe	April 18, 1980	April 18, 1980	republic	——president——		150	—	...	...	—	—

[1]Transitional government. [2]Territorial sea claim. [3]Date president signed new constitution. [4]Varies between 32 and 52 nautical miles. [5]Observer. [6]President of France and Bishop of Urgell, Spain. [7]President annulled post of prime minister in January 1999. [8]Statutory number of seats. [9]Excludes possible ex officio members. [10]Measured from claimed archipelagic baselines. [11]Promulgation date of significant amendments to July 9, 1853, constitution. [12]Assisted by the ministerial coordinator. [13]Executive responsibilities divided between (for The Netherlands) the governor and (locally) the prime minister. [14]Associate member. [15]Formally a constitutional monarchy. [16]Evolving body of constitutional law. [17]Date of referendum approving significant constitutional amendments. [18]Assisted by the prime minister. [19]Defined by equidistant line. [20]Legal status is controversial. [21]Excludes children of the monarch serving ex officio from age 18. [22]10 provincial councils; 5 region/community councils. [23]6 districts; 8 town boards. [24]3 nautical miles from the mouth of the Sarstoon River (southern boundary with Guatemala) to Ranguana Caye. [25]Executive responsibilities divided between (for the U.K.) the governor and (locally) the premier. [26]Resembles a constitutional monarchy without a formal constitution. [27]Date of international treaty confirming the existence of a single state under the final international authority of the high representative. [28]Tripartite presidency. [29]Cantons only; Republika Srpska has no cantons. [30]Body with limited or no legislative authority. [31]Sections of the constitution have been suspended since 1962. [32]Implementation date of Arusha Accords. [33]Assisted by the vice president. [34]Date significant amendments adopted. [35]Governor-general can exercise all the powers of the reigning monarch of the Commonwealth. [36]Effective date of new government. [37]Assisted by vice presidents. [38]Date of referendum approving new constitution. [39]Suspended membership. [40]Republic of Cyprus only. [41]24 seats reserved for Turkish Cypriots are not occupied. [42]Date constituent assembly approved and decreed new constitution. [43]Zone defined by geographic coordinates. [44]Constitution approved by the constituent assembly on May 23, 1997, had not been promulgated as of November 2002. [45]Date new republic was formally established. [46]Executive responsibilities divided between (for Denmark) the high commissioner and (locally) the prime minister. [47]Or agreed boundaries or median line. [48]3 nautical miles in the Gulf of Finland. [49]Executive responsibilities divided among (for France) the prefect and (locally) the president of the General Council and the president of the Regional Council. [50]Executive responsibilities divided

United Nations (date of admission)	UN organs★ and affiliated intergovernmental organizations																				The Common-wealth	regional multipurpose						economic									country
	UNCTAD★	UNICEF★e	ICJ★f	FAO	IAEA	IBRD	ICAO	IDA	IFC	ILO	IMF	IMO	ITU	UNESCO	UNIDO	UPU	WHO	WIPO	WMO	WTO		AU	EU	GCC	LAS9	OAS	PC	ACP	ADB	APEC	CARICOM	ECOWAS	FZ	I-ADB	IDB9	OPEC	
1945	•	•	•	•	•	•	•	•	•	•	•	•	•	•	•	•	•	•	•	•			•					•						•			Netherlands, The
—											•			14		•	•		•	•																	Netherlands Antilles
—	•	•														•	•		•	•							•		•	•				•			New Caledonia
1945	•	•	•	•	•	•	•	•	•	•	•	•	•	•	•	•	•	•	•	•	•					•	•							•			New Zealand
1945	•	•		•	•	•	•	•	•	•	•	•	•	•	•	•	•	•	•	•						•								•			Nicaragua
1960	•	•		•	•	•	•	•	•	•	•	•	•	•	•	•	•	•	•	•		•						•				•	•	•			Niger
1960	•	•		•	•	•	•	•	•	•	•	•	•	•	•	•	•	•	•	•	•	•						•				•	•	•		•	Nigeria
—																•	•											•									Northern Mariana Is.
1945	•	•	•	•	•	•	•	•	•	•	•	•	•	•	•	•	•	•	•	•														•			Norway
1971	•	•		•	•	•	•	•	•	•	•	•	•	•	•	•	•	•	•	•				•	•			•						•		•	Oman
1947	•	•	•	•	•	•	•	•	•	•	•	•	•	•	•	•	•	•	•	•	39							•	•					•			Pakistan
1994	•	•		•		•	•	•		•	•			•		•	•		•	•						•	•		•					•			Palau
1945	•	•		•	•	•	•	•	•	•	•	•	•	•	•	•	•	•	•	•						•								•			Panama
1975	•	•		•	•	•	•	•	•	•	•	•	•	•	•	•	•	•	•	•	•						•	•	•	•				•			Papua New Guinea
1945	•	•		•	•	•	•	•	•	•	•	•	•	•	•	•	•	•	•	•						•								•			Paraguay
1945	•	•		•	•	•	•	•	•	•	•	•	•	•	•	•	•	•	•	•						•				•				•			Peru
1945	•	•		•	•	•	•	•	•	•	•	•	•	•	•	•	•	•	•	•									•	•				•			Philippines
1945	•	•		•	•	•	•		•	•	•	•	•	•	•	•	•	•	•	•			•											•			Poland
1955	•	•		•	•	•	•	•	•	•	•	•	•	•	•	•	•	•	•	•			•											•			Portugal
—			14																	14																	Puerto Rico
1971	•	•		•	•	•	•	•	•	•	•	•	•	•	•	•	•	•	•	•				•	•			•						•		•	Qatar
—																	•																•				Réunion
1955	•	•		•	•	•	•	•	•	•	•	•	•	•	•	•	•	•	•	•								•						•			Romania
1991	•	•	•	•	•	•	•	•	•	•	•	•	•	•	•	•	•	•	•	5		•												•			Russia
1962	•	•		•		•	•	•	•	•	•	•	•	•	•	•	•	•	•	•		•						•					•	•			Rwanda
1983	•	•		•		•	•	•	•	•	•	•	•	•	•	•	•	•	•	•	•					•		•			•			•			St. Kitts and Nevis
1979	•	•		•		•	•	•	•	•	•	•	•	•	•	•	•	•	•	•	•					•		•			•			•			St. Lucia
1980	•	•		•		•	•	•	•	•	•	•	•	•	•	•	•	•	•	•	•					•		•			•			•			St. Vincent
1976	•	•		•		•	•	•	•	•	•	•	•	•	•	•	•	•	•	5	•						•	•						•			Samoa
1992	•	•		•	•	•	•	•		•	•	•	•	•	•	•	•	•	•	•														•			San Marino
1975	•	•		•	•	•	•	•	•	•	•	•	•	•	•	•	•	•	•	5		•						•					•	•			São Tomé and Príncipe
1945	•	•		•	•	•	•	•	•	•	•	•	•	•	•	•	•	•	•	5				•	•			•						•		•	Saudi Arabia
1960	•	•		•	•	•	•	•	•	•	•	•	•	•	•	•	•	•	•	•		•						•		•	•		•	•			Senegal
1976	•	•		•	•	•	•	•	•	•	•	•	•	•	•	•	•	•	•	5	•	•						•						•			Seychelles
1961	•	•	•	•		•	•	•	•	•	•	•	•	•	•	•	•	•	•	•	•	•						•				•		•			Sierra Leone
1965	•	•		•	•	•	•	•	•	•	•	•	•	•	•	•	•	•	•	•	•								•	•				•			Singapore
1993	•	•		•	•	•	•	•	•	•	•	•	•	•	•	•	•	•	•	•				5					•	•				•			Slovakia
1992	•	•		•	•	•	•	•	•	•	•	•	•	•	•	•	•	•	•	•				5									•	•			Slovenia
1978	•	•		•		•	•	•	•	•	•	•	•	•	•	•	•	•	•	•	•						•	•	•	•				•			Solomon Islands
1960	•	•		•		•	•	•	•	•	•	•	•	•	•	•	•	•	•	•		•			•			•					•	•			Somalia
1945	•	•		•	•	•	•	•	•	•	•	•	•	•	•	•	•	•	•	•	•	•						•						•			South Africa
1955	•	•		•	•	•	•	•	•	•	•	•	•	•	•	•	•	•	•	•			•			•								•			Spain
1955	•	•		•	•	•	•	•	•	•	•	•	•	•	•	•	•	•	•	•	•						•		•					•	•		Sri Lanka
1956	•	•		•	•	•	•	•	•	•	•	•	•	•	•	•	•	•	•	5		•			•			•						•	•		Sudan, The
1975	•	•		•		•	•	•	•	•	•	•	•	•	•	•	•	•	•	•						•		•			•			•	•		Suriname
1968	•	•		•	•	•	•	•	•	•	•	•	•	•	•	•	•	•	•	•	•	•						•						•			Swaziland
1946	•	•		•	•	•	•	•	•	•	•	•	•	•	•	•	•	•	•	•			•			•								•			Sweden
2002	•	•	•	•	•	•	•	•	•	•	•	•	•	•	•	•	•	•	•	•														•			Switzerland
1945	•	•		•	•	•	•	•	•	•	•	•	•	•	•	•	•	•	•	•		•			•			•						•			Syria
—													•							•																	Taiwan
1992	•	•		•	•	•	•	•	•	•	•	•	•	•	•	•	•	•	•	5		•	•						•	•				•			Tajikistan
1961	•	•		•	•	•	•	•	•	•	•	•	•	•	•	•	•	•	•	•	•	•						•	•					•			Tanzania
1946	•	•		•	•	•	•	•	•	•	•	•	•	•	•	•	•	•	•	•							•		•	•				•			Thailand
1960	•	•		•	•	•	•	•	•	•	•	•	•	•	•	•	•	•	•	•		•						•				•	•	•			Togo
1999	•	•		•		•	•	•	•	•	•	•	•	•	•	•	•	•	•	5	•						•	•						•			Tonga
1962	•	•		•	•	•	•	•	•	•	•	•	•	•	•	•	•	•	•	•	•					•		•			•			•			Trinidad and Tobago
1956	•	•		•	•	•	•	•	•	•	•	•	•	•	•	•	•	•	•	•		•			•			•						•	•		Tunisia
1945	•	•	•	•	5	•	•	•	•	•	•	•	•	•	•	•	•	•	•	•			•						•					•	•		Turkey
1992	•	•		•	•	•	•	5	•	•	•	•	•	•	•	•	•	•	•	•		•							•					•	•		Turkmenistan
2000	•	•		•		•	•	•	•	•	•	•	•	•	•	•	•	•	•	•	•						•	•						•			Tuvalu
1962	•	•		•	•	•	•	•	•	•	•	•	•	•	•	•	•	•	•	•	•	•						•						•			Uganda
1945	•	•		•	5	•	•	•	•	•	•	•	•	•	•	•	•	•	•	5														•			Ukraine
1971	•	•		•	•	•	•	•	•	•	•	•	•	•	•	•	•	•	•	•				•	•			•						•	•	•	United Arab Emirates
1945	•	•	•	•	•	•	•	•	•	•	•	•	•	•	•	•	•	•	•	•	•		•					•	•					•			United Kingdom
1945	•	•	•	•	•	•	•	•	•	•	•	•	•	•	•	•	•	•	•	•						•	•		•	•				•			United States
1945	•	•		•	•	•	•	•	•	•	•	•	•	•	•	•	•	•	•	•						•								•			Uruguay
1992	•	•		•	•	•	•	•	•	•	•	•	•	•	•	•	•	•	•	5		•							•	•				•			Uzbekistan
1981	•	•		•		•	•	•	•	•	•	•	•	•	•	•	•	•	•	•	•						•	•		•	•				•			Vanuatu
1945	•	•		•	•	•	•	•	•	•	•	•	•	•	•	•	•	•	•	•						•		•						•		•	Venezuela
1977	•	•		•	•	•	•	•	•	•	•	•	•	•	•	•	•	•	•	5								•	•	•				•			Vietnam
—																	•																				Virgin Islands (U.S.)
—																							97														West Bank
—																																					Western Sahara
1947	•	•		•		•	•	5	5	•	•	•	•	•	•	•	•	•	•	5					•			•						•			Yemen
1945	•	•		•	•	•	•	•	•	•	•	•	•	•	•	•	•	•	•	•			•											•			Yugoslavia
1964	•	•		•		•	•	•	•	•	•	•	•	•	•	•	•	•	•	•	•	•						•						•			Zambia
1980	•	•		•	•	•	•	•	•	•	•	•	•	•	•	•	•	•	•	•	39	•	•					•						•			Zimbabwe

between (for France) the high commissioner and (locally) the president of the territorial government. [51]Date of agreement providing for Palestinian self-rule. [52]Significantly amended in 1999, 2000, and 2001. [53]Assisted by the minister of state. [54]Date parliament approved constitutional amendments for 78 articles. [55]Represented by the lieutenant governor. [56]Executive committees appointed by the States of Deliberation. [57]Transitional constitution. [58]Assisted by extraconstitutional prime minister. [59]Special administrative region (China). [60]Shares coexecutive authority with spiritual leader. [61]Sea of Oman only; median line boundaries in Persian Gulf. [62]Provisional constitution. [63]Median line boundary between the Isle of Man and the United Kingdom. [64]The emperor is the symbol of state. [65]3 nautical miles in 5 straits. [66]Executive committees appointed by the States Assembly. [67]Essentially 1992 constitution with new preamble. [68]3 nautical miles in Korea Strait. [69]Elected seats only. [70]Traditionally a hereditary monarchy. [71]Date of peace accord. [72]Formally a *jamahiriya,* translated as "the masses of people"; in fact, a military dictatorship. [73]De facto chief of state. [74]Based on Gulf of Sidra (32° 30′ N), in part. [75]Date parliament adopted significant constitutional amendments. [76]Executive responsibilities divided between (for France) the prefect and (locally) the president of the General Council. [77]Under prince's authority. [78]Includes Western Sahara annexure. [79]Development regions. [80]Represented by high commissioner. [81]Basic law promulgated by sultan. [82]Has 2 consultative bodies with advisory authority only. [83]Includes federally administered tribal areas; excludes Jammu and Kashmir. [84]Defined by international treaties. [85]Excludes additional seats for both houses of the legislature to meet 1/3 total representation requirements for minority parties per constitution. [86]Limits of continental shelf or median boundaries. [87]Date constitution adopted by transitional legislature. [88]Mixed political system approximating a constitutional monarchy. [89]Royal decrees from March 1, 1992, created first written rules of governance. [90]Many significant constitutional amendments became effective in 2001. [91]Transitional national charter. [92]Atlantic Ocean only. [93]In practice resembles a system of monarchical absolutism. [94]Date parliament approved 34 amendments. [95]Black Sea and Mediterranean Sea; 6 nautical miles in Aegean Sea. [96]Based on evolving body of statutes and common law. [97]Membership held by the Sahrawi Arab Democratic Republic. [98]Effective date of significant amendments. [99]Serbia only excluding Kosovo.

Area and population

This table provides the area and population for each of the countries of the world and for all but the smallest political dependencies having a permanent civilian population. The data represent the latest published and unpublished data for both the surveyed area of the countries and their populations, the latter both as of a single year (2002) to provide the best comparability and as of a recent census to provide the fullest comparison of certain demographic measures that are not always available between successive national censuses. The 2002 midyear estimates represent a combination of national, United Nations (UN) or other international organizations, and *Encyclopædia Britannica* estimates so as to give the best fit to available published series, to take account of unpublished information received via Internet, facsimile, or correspondence, and to incorporate the results of very recent censuses for which published analyses are not yet available.

One principal point to bear in mind when studying these statistics is that all of them, whatever degree of precision may be implied by the exactness of the numbers, are estimates—all of varying, and some of suspect, accuracy—even when they *contain* a very full enumeration. The United States—which has a long tradition both of census taking and of the use of the most sophisticated analytical tools in processing the data—is unable to determine within 1.2% (the estimated 2000 undercount) its total population nationally. And that is an *average* underenumeration. In states and larger cities, where enumeration of particular populations, including illegal, is more difficult, the accuracy of the enumerated count may be off as much as 3.1% at a state level (in New Mexico, for instance) and by a greater percent for a single city. The high accuracy attained by census operations in China may approach 0.25% of rigorously maintained civil population registers. Other national census operations not so based, however, are inherently less accurate. For example, Ethiopia's first-ever census in 1984 resulted in figures that were 30% or more above prevailing estimates; Nigeria's 1991 census corrected decades of miscounts and was well below prevailing estimates. An undercount of 2–8% is more typical, but even census operations offering results of 30% or more above or below prevailing estimates can still represent well-founded benchmarks from which future planning may proceed. The editors have tried to take account of the range of variation and accuracy in published data, but it is difficult to establish a value for many sources of inaccuracy unless some country or agency has made a conscientious effort to establish both the relative accuracy (precision) of its estimate and the absolute magnitude of the quantity it is trying to measure—for example, the number of people in Cambodia who died at the hands of the Khmer Rouge. If a figure of 2,000,000 is adopted, what is its accuracy: ± 1%, 10%, 50%? Are the original data documentary or evidentiary, complete or incomplete, analytically biased or unbiased, in good agreement with other published data?

Many similar problems exist and in endless variations: What is the extent of eastern European immigration to western Europe in search of jobs? How many registered and unregistered refugees from Afghanistan, Sierra Leone, or Burundi are there in surrounding countries? How many undocumented aliens are there in the United Kingdom, Japan, or the United States? How many Tamils have left Sri Lanka as a result of civil unrest in their homeland? How many Amerindians exist (remain, preserving their original language and a mode of life unassimilated by the larger national culture) in the countries of South America?

Still, much information is accurate, well founded, and updated regularly.

Area and population

country	area			population (latest estimate)					population (recent census)				
	square miles	square kilometres	rank	total midyear 2002	rank	density per sq mi	per sq km	% annual growth rate 1997–2002	census year	total	male (%)	female (%)	urban (%)
Afghanistan	251,825	652,225	41	27,756,000	38	110.2	42.6	3.6	1979	13,051,358[1]	51.4	48.6	15.1
Albania	11,082	28,703	142	3,108,000	131	280.5	108.3	-0.3	1989	3,182,417	51.5	48.5	35.7
Algeria	919,595	2,381,741	11	31,261,000	34	34.0	13.0	1.5	1998	29,272,343	50.6	49.4	80.8
American Samoa	77	200	206	60,000	207	779.2	300.0	2.0	2000	57,291	51.4[2]	48.6[2]	33.4[2]
Andorra	181	468	194	66,400	204	367.4	142.1	0.5	2000[3]	65,971	52.2	47.8	93.0[4]
Angola	481,354	1,246,700	24	10,593,000	72	22.0	8.5	2.1	1970	5,673,046	52.1	47.9	14.2
Antigua and Barbuda	171	442	196	76,400	201	446.7	172.9	2.1	1991	63,896	48.2	51.8	36.2
Argentina	1,073,400	2,780,092	8	36,446,000	33	34.0	13.1	1.0	1991	32,615,528	48.9	51.1	88.4
Armenia	11,484	29,743	141	3,008,000	132	261.9	101.1	0.7	1989	3,287,677	49.3	50.7	67.8
Aruba	75	193	207	91,600	196	1,221.3	474.6	1.2	1991	66,687	49.2	50.8	...
Australia	2,969,910	7,692,030	6	19,702,000	51	6.6	2.6	1.2	1996	17,892,423	49.5	50.5	89.3
Austria	32,378	83,858	115	8,077,000	87	249.5	96.3	0.0	1991	7,795,786	48.2	51.8	64.5
Azerbaijan	33,400	86,600	113	8,176,000	86	244.8	94.4	0.8	1999	7,953,000	48.8	51.2	56.9[4]
Bahamas, The	5,382	13,939	159	309,000	175	57.4	22.2	1.4	1990	255,095	49.0	51.0	64.3
Bahrain	268	694	187	672,000	161	2,507.5	968.0	2.7	1991	508,037	57.9	42.1	88.4
Bangladesh	56,977	147,570	93	133,377,000	8	2,340.9	903.8	1.6	1991	111,455,185	51.4	48.6	20.2
Barbados	166	430	197	270,000	178	1,626.5	627.9	0.4	1990[6]	257,083	47.7	52.3	37.9[7]
Belarus	80,153	207,595	85	9,933,000	79	123.9	47.8	-0.4	1999	10,045,237[6]	47.0[6]	53.0[6]	69.3[6]
Belgium	11,787	30,528	139	10,280,000	75	872.1	336.7	0.2	1991	9,978,681	48.9	51.1	96.6[8]
Belize	8,867	22,965	150	251,000	180	28.3	10.9	2.3	2000	240,204	50.5	49.5	47.7
Benin	43,484	112,622	101	6,788,000	94	156.1	60.3	3.1	1992	4,915,555	48.6	51.4	35.7
Bermuda	21	54	213	63,600	205	3,029.0	1,178.0	0.6	1991[6]	58,460	48.5	51.5	100.0
Bhutan	18,150	47,000	131	721,000	160	39.7	15.3	3.1	...	...	51.6[10]	48.4[10]	7.0[10]
Bolivia	424,164	1,098,581	28	8,401,000	85	19.8	7.6	1.9	1992	6,420,792	49.4	50.6	57.5
Bosnia and Herzegovina	19,741	51,129	127	3,964,000	119	200.8	77.5	3.5	1991	4,377,033	49.9	50.1	39.6
Botswana	224,848	582,356	47	1,679,000	146	7.5	2.9	2.0	1991	1,326,796	47.8	52.2	23.9
Brazil	3,287,292	8,514,047	5	174,619,000	5	53.1	20.5	1.6	1991	146,825,475	49.4	50.6	75.6
Brunei	2,226	5,765	168	351,000	174	157.7	60.9	2.2	1991	260,482	52.8	47.2	66.6
Bulgaria	42,846	110,971	103	7,890,000	88	184.1	71.1	-0.8	2001	7,977,646	48.7	51.3	67.2[11]
Burkina Faso	105,946	274,400	73	12,603,000	64	119.0	45.9	2.8	1996	10,312,609	48.2	51.8	15.0[10]
Burundi	10,740	27,816	145	6,373,000	98	593.4	229.1	3.0	1990[6]	5,292,793	48.6	51.4	6.3
Cambodia	69,898	181,035	89	13,414,000	62	191.9	74.1	2.4	1998	11,437,656	48.2	51.8	20.9
Cameroon	183,569	475,442	53	16,185,000	58	88.2	34.0	2.5	1987	10,516,232	49.0	51.0	38.3
Canada	3,855,103	9,984,670	2	31,244,000	35	8.1	3.1	0.8	1996	28,846,761	49.1	50.9	77.9
Cape Verde	1,557	4,033	170	453,000	166	290.9	112.3	2.3	2000	434,812	48.4	51.6	53.3
Central African Republic	240,324	622,436	43	3,643,000	125	15.2	5.9	1.8	1988	2,688,426	49.1	50.9	36.5
Chad	495,755	1,284,000	21	8,997,000	82	18.1	7.0	3.4	1993	6,279,931	47.9	52.1	21.4
Chile	291,930	756,096	38	15,082,000	60	51.7	19.9	1.2	1992	13,348,401	49.1	50.9	83.5
China	3,696,100	9,572,900	3	1,284,211,000	1	347.5	134.2	1.0	2000	1,265,830,000	51.6	48.4	36.1
Colombia	440,762	1,141,568	26	41,008,000	28	93.0	35.9	1.7	1993	33,109,840	49.2	50.8	70.3[7]
Comoros	719	1,862	176	583,000	163	810.8	313.1	2.4	1991	446,817	49.5	50.5	28.5
Congo, Dem. Rep. of the	905,354	2,344,858	12	52,557,000	23	58.1	22.4	2.0	1984	29,671,407	49.2	50.8	29.1[12]
Congo, Rep. of the	132,047	342,000	63	2,899,000	134	22.0	8.5	2.0	1984[6]	1,909,248	48.7	51.3	52.0
Costa Rica	19,730	51,100	128	3,960,000	120	200.7	77.5	2.5	2000	3,824,593	50.0	50.0	51.9[10]
Côte d'Ivoire	123,863	320,803	68	16,805,000	56	135.7	52.4	2.3	1988	10,815,694	51.1	48.9	39.0
Croatia	21,831	56,542	126	4,405,000	116	201.8	77.9	0.4	1991	4,784,265	48.5	51.5	54.3
Cuba	42,804	110,861	104	11,267,000	68	263.2	101.6	0.4	1993	10,904,466	50.3	49.7	74.4
Cyprus[13]	3,572	9,251	165	907,000	155	253.9	98.0	1.2	1992[6, 14]	615,013	49.8	50.2	67.7
Czech Republic	30,450	78,866	117	10,210,000	76	335.3	129.5	-0.2	1991	10,302,215	48.5	51.5	75.2
Denmark	16,640	43,098	133	5,377,000	105	323.1	124.8	0.4	1999[3]	5,313,577	49.4	50.6	85.0
Djibouti	8,950	23,200	149	473,000	165	52.8	20.4	1.8	1983	273,974	51.9	48.1	82.8[12]
Dominica	290	750	184	71,700	202	247.2	95.6	-0.6	1991	71,183	49.8	50.2	...
Dominican Republic	18,792	48,671	130	8,833,000	84	470.0	181.5	1.7	1993	7,293,390	48.7	51.3	56.1
East Timor	5,639	14,604	158	797,000	157	141.3	54.6	-0.1	1990	747,750	51.7	48.3	7.8
Ecuador	105,037	272,045	74	13,095,000	63	124.7	48.1	1.9	1990	9,648,189	49.7	50.3	55.4

The sources of these data are censuses; national population registers (cumulated periodically); registration of migration, births, deaths, and so on; sample surveys to establish demographic conditions; and the like.

The statistics provided for area and population by country are ranked, and the population densities based on those values are also provided. The population densities, for purposes of comparison within this table, are calculated on the bases of the 2002 midyear population estimate as shown and of total area of the country. Elsewhere in individual country presentations the reader may find densities calculated on more specific population figures and more specialized area bases: land area for Finland (because of its many lakes) or ice-free area for Greenland (most of which is ice cap). The data in this section conclude with the estimated average annual growth rate for the country (including both natural growth and net migration) during the five-year period 1997–2002.

In the section containing census data, information supplied includes the census total (usually de facto, the population actually present, rather than de jure, the population legally resident, who might be anywhere); the male-female breakdown; the proportion that is urban (usually according to the country's own definition); and finally an analysis of the age structure of the population by 15-year age groups. This last analysis may be particularly useful in distinguishing the type of population being recorded—young, fast-growing nations show a high proportion of people under 30 (many countries in sub-Saharan Africa and the Middle East have about 40% of their population under 15 years), while other nations (for example, Sweden, which suffered no age-group losses in World War II) exhibit quite uniform proportions.

Finally, a section is provided giving the population of each country at 10-year intervals from 1950 to 2020. The data for years past represent the best available analysis of the published data by the country itself, by the demographers of the UN, demographers of the U.S. Bureau of the Census, International Data Base, or by the editors of Britannica. The projections for 2010 and 2020 similarly represent the best fit of available data through the autumn of 2002. The evidence of the last 30 years with respect to similar estimates published about 1970, however, shows how cloudy is the glass through which these numbers are read. In 1970 no respectable Western analyst would have imagined proposing that mainland China could achieve the degree of birth control that it apparently has since then (as evidenced by the results of 1982 and 1990 censuses); on the other hand, even the Chinese admit that their methods have been somewhat Draconian and that they have already seen some backlash in terms of higher birth rates among those who have so far postponed larger families. How much is "some" by 2010? Compound that problem with all the social, economic, political, and biological factors (including the impact of AIDS) that can affect 217 countries' populations, and the difficulty facing the prospective compiler of such projections may be appreciated.

Specific data about the vital rates affecting the data in this table may be found in great detail in both the country statistical boxes in "The Nations of the World" section and in the *Vital statistics, marriage, family* table, beginning at page 802.

Percentages in this table for male and female population will always total 100.0, but percentages by age group may not, for reasons such as non-response on census forms, "don't know" responses (which are common in countries with poor birth registration systems), and the like.

age distribution (%)						population (by decade, '000s)								country
0–14	15–29	30–44	45–59	60–74	75 and over	1950	1960	1970	1980	1990	2000	2010 projection	2020 projection	
44.5	26.9	15.8	8.6	3.6	0.6	8,150	9,829	12,431	14,985	14,750	25,889	33,864	41,735	Afghanistan
33.0	28.9	18.5	11.7	5.9	1.9	1,227	1,623	2,157	2,671	3,258	3,100	3,248	3,497	Albania
36.2	30.6	17.7	8.9	5.1	1.5	8,956	10,800	14,330	18,666	24,698	30,386	35,022	40,365	Algeria
38.1[2]	29.0[2]	18.1[2]	9.4[2]	4.3[2]	1.1[2]	19	20	27	32	47	58	71	86	American Samoa
15.4	20.9	29.3	18.6	10.5	5.3	6	8	19	33	53	66	70	74	Andorra
41.7	23.2	17.0	7.4	3.8	1.0	4,118	4,797	5,606	6,741	8,056	10,145	12,646	15,750	Angola
30.4	27.8	20.5	10.2	7.7	3.4	45	55	66	69	64	74	80	84	Antigua and Barbuda
30.6	23.3	19.3	13.9	9.6	3.3	17,150	20,616	23,962	28,094	32,527	36,446	39,904	43,630	Argentina
30.3	25.7	20.8	13.6	6.4	3.2	1,354	1,867	2,520	3,067	3,271	3,050	3,021	3,007	Armenia
24.4	22.0	27.0	16.1	7.2	3.0	51	57	61	60	64	91	95	98	Aruba
21.5[5]	22.3[5]	23.1[5]	17.1[5]	11.0[5]	5.0[5]	8,219	10,315	12,552	14,741	17,065	19,222	21,091	22,587	Australia
17.4	23.7	21.6	17.2	13.4	6.7	6,935	7,048	7,447	7,549	7,729	8,110	8,170	8,265	Austria
31.8	25.6	24.1	9.5	7.6	1.4	2,896	3,895	5,172	6,165	7,166	8,048	8,545	8,985	Azerbaijan
32.2	30.8	19.7	10.6	5.0	1.8	79	110	170	210	256	304	325	334	Bahamas, The
31.7	28.4	28.2	8.0	3.1	0.6	110	149	210	334	503	638	758	859	Bahrain
41.5	25.2	16.2	8.1	4.3	1.1	45,646	54,622	67,403	88,077	109,897	129,194	150,392	169,613	Bangladesh
24.1	27.1	22.1	11.4	9.9	5.4	209	232	235	249	261	268	278	284	Barbados
19.5	21.8	23.4	16.4	—18.9—		7,745	8,190	9,040	9,650	10,186	10,005	9,645	9,339	Belarus
18.2	21.8	22.5	16.9	14.1	6.6	8,639	9,153	9,690	9,859	9,967	10,251	10,318	10,265	Belgium
43.9[9]	27.9[9]	14.9[9]	7.2[9]	4.4[9]	1.6[9]	68	90	120	146	189	241	288	329	Belize
48.6	24.2	14.5	6.6	4.1	1.9	1,673	2,055	2,620	3,444	4,656	6,396	8,411	10,588	Benin
19.5	24.0	26.8	16.4	—13.3—		37	43	53	55	59	63	67	69	Bermuda
40.2[10]	26.0[10]	17.4[10]	10.1[10]	5.2[10]	1.1[10]	...	...	...	...	519	678	853	1,038	Bhutan
41.2	26.2	16.8	8.9	—6.5—		2,766	3,434	4,346	5,441	6,574	8,094	9,449	10,691	Bolivia
23.5[8]	26.3[8]	22.6[8]	16.9[8]	8.9[8]	2.7[8]	2,662	3,240	3,703	4,092	4,424	3,836	4,103	4,182	Bosnia and Herzegovina
42.8	27.3	14.3	7.3	4.1	2.2	430	497	584	903	1,304	1,634	1,585	1,391	Botswana
34.7	28.1	19.3	10.6	5.7	1.6	53,444	72,594	95,847	118,617	143,581	169,358	191,662	210,817	Brazil
34.5	29.3	24.2	7.9	—4.1—		45	83	128	185	258	336	408	475	Brunei
20.5[11]	19.2[11]	—39.8[11]—		—20.5[11]—		7,251	7,867	8,490	8,862	8,718	8,012	7,229	6,528	Bulgaria
47.9[5]	26.8[5]	12.9[5]	7.6[5]	3.9[5]	0.9[5]	4,376	4,866	5,626	6,939	9,037	11,946	15,424	19,402	Burkina Faso
46.4	25.3	15.4	7.0	4.0	1.7	2,363	2,812	3,513	4,138	5,285	6,055	7,669	9,553	Burundi
42.8	26.1	17.2	8.5	4.3	1.1	4,346	5,433	6,938	6,613	9,630	12,798	16,218	19,870	Cambodia
46.4	24.5	14.6	8.7	4.1	1.6	4,888	5,609	6,727	8,747	11,761	15,422	19,202	22,869	Cameroon
19.9	20.9	25.7	17.2	11.1	5.2	13,737	17,909	21,324	24,561	27,634	30,750	33,132	35,187	Canada
43.6[10]	24.8[10]	17.1[10]	5.8[10]	6.3[10]	2.4[10]	146	197	269	296	342	435	532	619	Cape Verde
43.2	27.5	15.0	9.2	4.1	0.8	1,260	1,467	1,827	2,244	2,803	3,513	4,135	4,672	Central African Republic
48.1	24.6	14.7	7.2	4.2	1.3	2,608	3,042	3,728	4,535	6,018	8,425	11,616	15,772	Chad
29.4	27.3	21.2	12.2	7.2	2.5	6,082	7,608	9,496	11,147	13,100	14,724	16,492	18,203	Chile
27.7[2]	31.0[2]	20.7[2]	12.1[2]	6.9[2]	1.7[2]	556,613	667,070	818,316	981,242	1,133,683	1,261,379	1,357,864	1,433,111	China
34.5	28.5	20.1	10.0	5.3	1.6	11,592	15,953	21,430	26,583	32,859	39,686	46,109	52,199	Colombia
47.6[8]	27.0[8]	13.1[8]	7.7[8]	3.5[8]	1.0[8]	148	183	236	334	429	549	734	950	Comoros
47.3[12]	25.9[12]	14.1[12]	8.1[12]	3.8[12]	0.8[12]	13,569	16,462	21,395	28,129	37,991	49,815	66,471	87,913	Congo, Dem. Rep. of the
44.7	27.2	13.3	9.1	4.6	0.7	768	931	1,183	1,620	2,218	2,785	3,425	4,129	Congo, Rep. of the
32.1[10]	27.1[10]	21.6[10]	11.7[10]	5.6[10]	1.9[10]	862	1,236	1,731	2,246	2,869	3,810	4,620	5,303	Costa Rica
46.8	27.3	15.0	7.5	2.8	0.6	2,860	3,565	5,427	8,261	11,919	15,981	20,003	23,748	Côte d'Ivoire
19.4	20.7	22.7	18.3	12.9	4.5	3,837	4,036	4,205	4,383	4,508	4,282	4,559	4,615	Croatia
22.3	29.4	21.3	14.8	8.4	3.9	5,850	7,028	8,572	9,780	10,603	11,199	11,514	11,721	Cuba
25.4	22.0	22.3	15.4	10.2	4.7	494	573	615	658	751	890	944	993	Cyprus[13]
21.0	21.8	22.6	16.8	12.7	5.1	8,925	9,539	9,805	10,326	10,363	10,243	10,101	9,859	Czech Republic
18.2	19.2	22.4	20.5	12.6	7.1	4,271	4,581	4,929	5,123	5,140	5,337	5,525	5,706	Denmark
39.4	32.9	16.9	7.4	2.8	0.6	60	78	158	279	370	451	579	729	Djibouti
33.3	28.3	16.3	9.7	—11.8—		51	60	70	75	72	72	72	72	Dominica
36.5[15]	29.5[15]	18.4[15]	9.6[15]	4.8[15]	1.2[15]	2,353	3,231	4,423	5,697	7,098	8,554	9,995	11,489	Dominican Republic
...	...	...	...	...	...	433	501	605	581	740	737	1,019	1,161	East Timor
38.8	28.5	17.3	9.0	4.7	1.7	3,387	4,439	5,970	7,961	10,264	12,646	14,899	16,904	Ecuador

Area and population (continued)

country	area			population (latest estimate)					population (recent census)				
	square miles	square kilo-metres	rank	total midyear 2002	rank	density		% annual growth rate 1997–2002	census year	total	male (%)	female (%)	urban (%)
						per sq mi	per sq km						
Egypt	385,210	997,690	30	66,341,000	17	172.2	66.5	2.0	1996	59,312,914	51.2	48.8	42.6
El Salvador	8,124	21,041	151	6,354,000	99	782.1	302.0	1.9	1992	5,118,599	48.6	51.4	50.4
Equatorial Guinea	10,831	28,051	144	498,000	164	46.0	17.8	2.5	1983	300,060	48.8	51.2	28.2
Eritrea	46,774	121,144	99	3,981,000	118	85.1	32.9	3.4	1984	2,703,998	49.9	50.1	15.1
Estonia	17,462	45,227	132	1,359,000	148	77.8	30.0	–0.7	2000	1,376,700[6]	46.1	53.9	74.3[10]
Ethiopia	437,794	1,133,882	27	67,673,000	16	154.6	59.7	2.8	1994	53,477,265	50.3	49.7	14.4[12]
Faroe Islands	540	1,399	178	47,400	210	87.8	33.9	1.5	1999[3]	45,409	51.8	48.2	...
Fiji	7,055	18,272	155	824,000	156	116.8	45.1	1.0	1996	775,077	50.8	49.2	46.4
Finland	130,559	338,145	64	5,201,000	109	39.8	15.4	0.2	1990	4,998,478	48.5	51.5	79.7
France	210,026	543,965	49	59,440,000	21	283.0	109.3	0.4	1999	58,518,748	48.6	51.4	75.5
French Guiana	33,399	86,504	114	172,000	186	5.1	2.0	3.0	1999	157,274	50.4	49.6	77.8[4]
French Polynesia	1,544	4,000	171	242,000	181	156.7	60.5	1.7	1996	219,521	51.9	48.1	40.1[4]
Gabon	103,347	267,667	76	1,233,000	152	11.9	4.6	1.1	1993	1,011,710	49.3	50.7	73.2
Gambia, The	4,127	10,689	163	1,418,000	147	343.6	132.7	2.8	1993	1,038,145	50.1	49.9	36.7
Gaza Strip	140	363	200	1,269,000	151	9,064.3	3,495.9	4.8	1995[3, 17]	1,054,000	50.9	49.1	...
Georgia	26,911	69,700	121	4,961,000	112	184.3	71.2	–0.8	1989	5,443,359	47.2	52.8	55.7
Germany	137,847	357,021	62	82,506,000	12	598.5	231.1	0.0	1998[3]	82,037,000	48.8	51.2	87.5[10]
Ghana	92,098	238,533	81	20,244,000	50	219.8	84.9	1.9	1984	12,296,081	49.3	50.7	32.0
Greece	50,949	131,957	96	10,994,000	69	215.8	83.3	0.6	1991	10,264,156	49.3	50.7	58.9
Greenland	836,330	2,166,086	13	56,600	208	0.07	0.03	0.2	2000[3]	56,124	53.4	46.6	81.5
Grenada	133	344	202	101,000	194	759.4	293.6	0.4	1991	95,597	48.8	51.2	33.5
Guadeloupe	658	1,705	177	432,000	171	656.5	253.4	0.8	1999	422,496	48.1	51.9	99.7[4]
Guam	217	561	191	160,000	188	737.3	285.2	1.6	1990	133,152	53.3	46.7	38.2
Guatemala	42,130	109,117	105	11,987,000	65	284.5	109.9	2.6	1994	8,331,874	49.3	50.7	35.0
Guernsey	30	78	211	63,000	206	2,100.0	807.7	0.4	1996[18]	58,681	48.1	51.9	...
Guinea	94,926	245,857	78	7,775,000	89	81.9	31.6	1.0	1996	7,165,750	48.8	51.2	26.0
Guinea-Bissau	13,948	36,125	137	1,345,000	149	96.4	37.2	2.4	1991	983,367	48.4	51.6	20.3[8]
Guyana	83,044	215,083	84	775,000	158	9.3	3.6	–0.1	1991	701,704	49.2	50.8	35.4[12]
Haiti	10,695	27,700	146	7,064,000	93	660.5	255.0	1.4	1982	5,053,792	48.5	51.5	20.6
Honduras	43,433	112,492	102	6,561,000	96	151.1	58.3	2.5	1988	4,376,839	49.6	50.4	39.4
Hong Kong	424	1,099	180	6,785,000	95	16,002.4	6,173.8	0.9	2001	6,715,000	49.0	51.0	100.0
Hungary	35,919	93,030	110	10,162,000	77	282.9	109.2	–0.2	1990	10,375,323	48.1	51.9	61.8
Iceland	39,699	102,819	106	288,000	176	7.3	2.8	1.2	1999[3]	278,717	50.1	49.9	93.5
India	1,222,559	3,166,414	7	1,047,671,000	2	856.9	330.9	1.7	2001	1,027,015,247	51.7	48.3	27.8
Indonesia	742,308	1,922,570	16	211,023,000	4	284.3	109.8	1.3	1990	178,631,196	49.9	50.1	30.9
Iran	629,315	1,629,918	18	65,457,000	18	104.0	40.2	1.4	1996	60,055,488	50.8	49.2	61.3
Iraq	167,975	435,052	58	24,002,000	44	142.9	55.2	2.9	1997	22,017,983	49.7	50.3	74.5[12]
Ireland	27,133	70,273	120	3,926,000	121	144.7	55.9	1.3	1996	3,626,087	49.6	50.4	57.0
Isle of Man	227	588	190	76,900	200	338.8	130.8	1.0	1996[6]	71,714	48.5	51.5	74.7
Israel[21, 22]	7,886	20,425	152	6,394,000	97	810.8	313.0	2.4	1995[6, 23]	5,548,523	49.3	50.7	92.9[12]
Italy	116,347	301,337	71	57,988,000	22	498.4	192.4	0.2	1991	57,103,833	48.6	51.4	67.1[24]
Jamaica	4,244	10,991	162	2,630,000	136	619.7	239.3	0.7	1991	2,374,193	49.0	51.0	50.4
Japan	145,898	377,873	61	127,347,000	10	872.8	337.0	0.2	1995	125,570,246	49.0	51.0	78.1
Jersey	45	116	210	87,400	198	1,942.2	753.4	0.4	1996	85,150	48.6	51.4	...
Jordan[25]	34,495	89,342	112	5,260,000	108	152.5	58.9	3.1	1994	4,139,458	52.2	47.8	78.3
Kazakhstan	1,052,090	2,724,900	9	14,884,000	61	14.1	5.5	–0.6	1999	15,049,100	48.5[26]	51.5[26]	57.2[26]
Kenya	224,961	582,646	46	31,139,000	36	138.4	53.4	1.7	1999	28,686,607	49.5	50.5	32.2[4]
Kiribati	313	811	182	90,600	197	289.5	111.7	1.8	1995	77,658	49.5	50.5	36.5
Korea, North	47,399	122,762	98	22,224,000	48	468.9	181.0	0.8	1993	21,213,378	48.7	51.3	58.9
Korea, South	38,402	99,461	108	47,640,000	25	1,240.6	479.0	0.7	1995[6]	44,608,726	50.2	49.8	81.0[12]
Kuwait	6,880	17,818	156	2,253,000	141	327.5	126.4	0.9	1995	1,575,983	58.0	42.0	97.0[12]
Kyrgyzstan	77,200	199,900	86	5,002,000	111	64.8	25.0	1.5	1999	4,822,938	49.4	50.6	34.8
Laos	91,429	236,800	83	5,777,000	101	63.2	24.4	2.5	1995	4,581,258	49.5	50.5	20.7[12]
Latvia	24,938	64,589	124	2,341,000	140	93.9	36.2	–0.9	2000	2,375,339	46.0	54.0	69.2
Lebanon	4,016	10,400	164	3,678,000	124	915.8	353.7	1.4	1970	2,126,325	50.8	49.2	60.1
Lesotho	11,720	30,355	140	2,208,000	142	188.4	72.7	1.7	1996[6]	1,960,069	49.2	50.8	16.9
Liberia	37,743	97,754	109	3,288,000	130	87.1	33.6	7.4	1984	2,101,628	50.6	49.4	38.8
Libya	679,362	1,759,540	17	5,369,000	106	7.7	3.0	2.4	1995[6]	4,404,986	50.8	49.2	85.3[12]
Liechtenstein	62	160	209	33,300	212	537.1	208.1	1.3	1999[3]	32,426	48.7	51.3	22.2[4]
Lithuania	25,212	65,300	123	3,473,000	128	137.8	53.2	–0.5	1989	3,689,779	47.4	52.6	68.0
Luxembourg	999	2,586	173	447,000	167	447.4	172.9	1.3	1991	384,634	49.0	51.0	85.9[8]
Macau	10.0	25.8	214	438,000	169	43,800.0	16,976.7	0.9	1991	339,464	48.5	51.5	97.0
Macedonia	9,928	25,713	148	2,031,000	143	204.6	79.0	0.3	1994	1,945,932	50.4	49.6	58.7
Madagascar	226,658	587,041	45	16,473,000	57	72.7	28.1	3.1	1993[6]	12,092,157	49.5	50.5	26.4[12]
Malawi	45,747	118,484	100	10,520,000	73	230.0	88.8	1.6	1998	9,933,868	49.0	51.0	14.0
Malaysia	127,355	329,847	66	24,370,000	43	191.4	73.9	2.9	2000	22,202,614	50.4	49.6	50.6[9]
Maldives	115	298	204	281,000	177	2,443.5	943.0	1.8	2000	269,010	51.2	48.8	25.5[29]
Mali	482,077	1,248,574	23	11,340,000	67	23.5	9.1	3.1	1987	7,696,348	48.9	51.1	22.0
Malta	122	316	203	386,000	172	3,163.9	1,221.5	0.6	1995	378,132	49.4	50.6	90.3[4]
Marshall Islands	70	181	208	56,600	208	808.6	312.7	2.8	1999	50,865	51.2	48.8	64.5[30]
Martinique	436	1,128	179	386,000	172	885.3	342.2	0.5	1999	381,427	47.4	52.6	94.6[4]
Mauritania	398,000	1,030,700	29	2,656,000	135	6.7	2.6	2.5	2000	2,548,157	48.7	51.3	57.7[10]
Mauritius	788	2,040	175	1,211,000	153	1,536.8	593.6	1.1	1990	1,056,827	49.9	50.1	39.3
Mayotte	144	374	199	165,000	187	1,145.8	441.2	4.7	1997	131,320	50.7	49.3	...
Mexico	758,449	1,964,375	15	100,977,000	11	133.1	51.4	1.7	2000	97,361,711	48.6	51.4	71.3
Micronesia	271	701	186	109,000	193	402.2	155.5	–0.5	1994	105,506	51.1	48.9	28.0[12]
Moldova	13,066	33,843	138	3,620,000	126	277.1	107.0	–1.1	1989	4,337,592	47.5	52.5	46.9
Monaco	0.76	1.96	217	32,000	213	42,105.3	16,326.5	0.5	1990	29,972	47.5	52.5	100.0
Mongolia	603,909	1,564,116	19	2,457,000	138	4.1	1.6	1.3	2000	2,382,500	49.6	50.4	58.6
Morocco[32]	177,117	458,730	55	29,376,000	37	165.9	64.0	1.6	1994	25,821,571[33]	49.7[33]	50.3[33]	51.7[33]
Mozambique	313,661	812,379	35	18,083,000	54	57.7	22.3	2.4	1997	16,099,246	47.9	52.1	28.6
Myanmar (Burma)	261,228	676,577	40	42,238,000	27	161.7	62.4	0.7	1983	35,307,913	49.6	50.4	24.0
Namibia	318,580	825,118	34	1,837,000	145	5.8	2.2	2.3	1991	1,401,711	48.6	51.4	32.8
Nauru	8.2	21.2	216	12,300	216	1,500.0	580.2	2.1	1992	9,919	51.2	48.8	100.0
Nepal	56,827	147,181	94	23,692,000	45	416.9	161.0	2.3	1991	18,491,097	49.9	50.1	9.6

age distribution (%)						population (by decade, '000s)								country
0–14	15–29	30–44	45–59	60–74	75 and over	1950	1960	1970	1980	1990	2000	2010 projection	2020 projection	
37.7	27.6	18.6	10.4	5.0	0.7	20,461	26,085	33,329	40,546	51,959	63,978	74,986	84,896	Egypt
38.7	28.7	16.0	9.2	5.4	1.9	1,940	2,582	3,604	4,566	5,100	6,123	7,293	8,494	El Salvador
41.7	25.1	15.7	11.2	5.3	1.0	211	244	270	256	368	474	604	755	Equatorial Guinea
46.1	23.0	15.9	8.9	4.4	1.6	1,140	1,420	1,831	2,382	3,103	3,659	5,097	6,382	Eritrea
17.7[10]	22.1[10]	21.4[10]	18.4[10]	15.0[10]	5.4[10]	1,101	1,216	1,365	1,473	1,571	1,369	1,316	1,279	Estonia
46.1[16]	26.0[16]	15.1[16]	8.3[16]	3.8[16]	0.7[16]	20,175	24,252	29,673	36,413	48,335	64,117	82,312	103,163	Ethiopia
23.8	19.4	21.0	18.2	11.3	1.8	31	35	39	43	48	46	50	52	Faroe Islands
35.4	27.4	20.7	11.4	4.2	0.9	289	394	520	634	737	808	872	918	Fiji
19.3	20.5	24.6	17.1	12.9	5.7	4,009	4,430	4,606	4,800	4,986	5,176	5,267	5,317	Finland
17.9	20.2	21.9	18.7	13.6	7.7	41,736	45,684	50,770	53,880	56,710	58,893	60,975	62,179	France
34.0	24.2	23.3	12.5	4.3	1.7	27	33	49	68	116	162	220	297	French Guiana
33.7	27.3	21.6	11.4	5.0	1.0	62	84	117	151	197	233	272	304	French Polynesia
33.8[15]	23.7[15]	17.0[15]	17.4[15]	6.9[15]	1.2[15]	416	446	514	806	1,069	1,208	1,309	1,386	Gabon
43.8	27.7	15.1	6.8	3.5	1.4	305	391	502	676	962	1,367	1,833	2,365	Gambia, The
50.3	25.8	13.1	6.2	3.7	0.9	...	...	370	456	630	1,147	1,872	2,623	Gaza Strip
24.8	24.1	19.2	17.5	10.8	3.6	3,516	4,147	4,694	5,048	5,457	5,020	4,815	4,785	Georgia
15.8	17.9	24.6	19.3	15.5	6.9	68,377	72,674	77,709	78,275	79,635	82,207	83,858	84,741	Germany
45.0	26.4	14.6	8.1	4.1	1.8	5,297	6,958	8,789	10,998	15,360	19,534	22,650	25,223	Ghana
19.3	22.2	20.3	18.3	14.1	5.9	7,566	8,327	8,793	9,643	10,161	10,913	11,064	10,962	Greece
27.1	19.2	29.3	16.4	——8.0——		23	32	46	50	56	56	57	58	Greenland
42.5[8]	30.4[8]	12.9[8]	6.6[8]	5.5[8]	2.1[8]	76	90	95	89	95	100	106	112	Grenada
23.6	22.4	24.3	15.7	9.3	4.7	206	265	320	327	388	426	458	479	Guadeloupe
30.0	30.0	22.6	10.8	5.5	1.1	60	67	86	107	134	155	184	211	Guam
44.0	26.1	15.8	8.3	——5.8——		2,969	3,963	5,243	6,820	8,749	11,385	14,631	18,123	Guatemala
17.6	20.6	22.3	19.0	13.2	7.3	44	45	51	53	61	62	64	65	Guernsey
44.1[5]	26.5[5]	15.9[5]	9.0[5]	3.9[5]	0.6[5]	2,586	3,019	3,587	4,320	5,936	7,466	9,281	11,440	Guinea
43.9[8]	26.5[8]	16.1[8]	8.8[8]	3.7[8]	1.0[8]	573	617	620	789	996	1,286	1,614	1,998	Guinea-Bissau
35.4[8]	31.5[8]	17.8[8]	9.0[8]	4.8[8]	1.5[8]	428	560	714	759	759	772	774	739	Guyana
39.2	26.9	15.6	10.0	5.4	2.9	3,097	3,723	4,605	5,056	6,028	6,868	7,950	9,072	Haiti
46.8	25.8	14.4	7.9	3.8	1.4	1,431	1,952	2,683	3,635	4,772	6,250	7,683	8,826	Honduras
16.5	21.6	29.0	18.0	10.6	4.3	1,974	3,074	3,942	5,063	5,705	6,665	7,401	8,083	Hong Kong
21.3	19.4	22.5	17.9	13.4	5.6	9,338	9,984	10,337	10,693	10,367	10,203	9,916	9,566	Hungary
23.3	22.7	22.4	16.5	10.0	5.1	143	176	204	228	255	281	307	331	Iceland
33.1[19]	27.8[19]	19.9[19]	12.1[19]	5.6[19]	1.5[19]	369,880	445,857	555,042	690,462	850,558	1,014,807	1,171,746	1,315,729	India
36.6	28.3	18.1	10.6	5.2	1.1	75,449	92,701	119,467	145,868	177,562	206,265	231,180	254,702	Indonesia
44.3	26.6	15.1	8.2	4.8	0.8	16,913	21,554	28,359	38,783	54,134	63,664	73,150	84,649	Iran
43.8[20]	30.2[20]	14.5[20]	6.9[20]	3.6[20]	1.0[20]	5,163	6,822	9,413	13,233	18,135	22,676	29,672	36,908	Iraq
26.7	24.1	20.2	13.8	10.6	4.6	2,969	2,834	2,954	3,421	3,506	3,826	4,253	4,651	Ireland
17.6	19.0	20.6	19.5	14.4	8.9	55	49	52	64	69	76	80	84	Isle of Man
29.2	25.0	19.6	13.1	9.1	4.0	...	2,114	2,958	3,862	4,613	6,098	7,148	7,895	Israel[21, 22]
15.9	23.7	20.9	18.4	14.4	6.7	47,104	50,200	53,822	56,434	56,749	57,762	57,681	55,802	Italy
34.4	30.6	16.6	9.0	——9.4——		1,403	1,629	1,891	2,133	2,369	2,597	2,798	3,068	Jamaica
15.9	21.5	19.7	22.0	15.0	5.9	83,200	93,419	103,720	116,807	123,478	126,867	127,979	125,722	Japan
15.5[9]	24.9[9]	23.5[9]	17.0[9]	11.9[9]	6.8[9]	57	63	71	76	84	87	89	89	Jersey
41.3	31.8	14.6	8.1	3.4	0.8	1,095	1,384	1,795	2,183	3,306	4,970	6,427	7,849	Jordan[25]
31.9[26]	26.3[26]	19.4[26]	13.2[26]	6.9[26]	2.3[26]	6,693	9,982	13,106	14,994	16,708	14,869	15,314	16,436	Kazakhstan
47.8[26]	27.6[26]	13.1[26]	6.6[26]	3.4[26]	1.5[26]	6,121	8,157	11,272	16,685	23,767	30,340	33,068	34,001	Kenya
41.2	25.8	18.3	9.3	4.4	1.0	33	41	49	58	71	88	104	124	Kiribati
29.5[15]	31.9[15]	21.3[15]	11.0[15]	5.0[15]	1.2[15]	9,471	10,392	13,912	17,114	20,019	21,688	23,753	25,143	Korea, North
23.0	27.6	25.7	14.5	7.4	1.9	21,147	25,012	32,241	38,124	42,869	47,008	49,594	50,650	Korea, South
25.4[27]	26.4[27]	34.4[27]	11.1[27]	——2.7[27]——		145	292	748	1,358	2,141	2,253	2,334	2,439	Kuwait
37.5[26]	27.0[26]	16.3[26]	10.9[26]	6.2[26]	2.1[26]	1,740	2,173	2,965	3,631	4,395	4,884	5,473	6,120	Kyrgyzstan
45.4[12]	26.5[12]	14.9[12]	8.1[12]	4.2[12]	1.0[12]	1,886	2,309	2,845	3,293	4,210	5,497	6,993	8,637	Laos
21.4[26]	21.7[26]	20.3[26]	19.2[26]	12.0[26]	5.3[26]	1,936	2,115	2,361	2,525	2,672	2,373	2,226	2,125	Latvia
42.6	23.8	16.7	9.1	——7.7——		1,364	1,786	2,383	3,086	3,147	3,578	4,056	4,417	Lebanon
43.1	27.6	15.0	8.6	4.8	0.9	726	859	1,067	1,344	1,732	2,143	2,339	2,382	Lesotho
43.2	28.2	14.7	7.7	4.4	1.8	824	1,055	1,397	1,892	2,190	3,164	4,073	5,294	Liberia
45.4[12]	26.4[12]	14.7[12]	9.1[12]	3.7[12]	0.6[12]	961	1,338	1,999	3,065	4,140	5,115	6,447	7,740	Libya
18.7	20.6	25.8	20.5	9.7	4.7	14	16	21	26	29	33	36	38	Liechtenstein
22.6	23.8	20.0	17.9	10.9	4.8	2,553	2,765	3,138	3,436	3,702	3,501	3,430	3,427	Lithuania
17.3	21.5	23.8	17.5	12.8	7.1	296	314	339	364	382	436	491	541	Luxembourg
24.1	27.2	29.4	9.6	7.3	2.3	188	169	221	243	332	431	467	501	Macau
24.8	24.1	22.3	15.8	10.6	2.4	1,225	1,366	1,574	1,792	1,893	2,031	2,057	2,061	Macedonia
45.1[15]	26.8[15]	15.1[15]	7.7[15]	4.3[15]	1.0[15]	4,620	5,482	6,766	8,677	11,522	15,506	20,993	28,405	Madagascar
45.7[28]	29.2[28]	13.2[28]	7.5[28]	3.7[28]	0.7[28]	2,817	3,450	4,489	6,129	8,442	10,233	11,480	12,169	Malawi
36.7[9]	27.6[9]	20.0[9]	9.9[9]	4.6[9]	1.2[9]	6,187	7,908	10,466	13,764	17,857	23,242	27,709	31,378	Malaysia
46.4[29]	26.2[29]	14.3[29]	7.7[29]	4.3[29]	0.9[29]	79	92	115	155	215	271	318	372	Maldives
46.1	23.9	15.0	8.9	4.9	1.2	3,688	4,486	5,525	6,731	8,228	10,686	14,349	18,984	Mali
21.9	20.9	22.5	18.8	11.6	4.3	308	329	326	324	354	381	394	400	Malta
51.0[30]	24.5[30]	14.6[30]	5.5[30]	3.6[30]	0.8[30]	11	15	22	31	45	57	74	94	Marshall Islands
22.0	21.0	24.4	16.0	11.1	5.5	222	252	287	326	360	383	398	403	Martinique
46.2[10]	26.6[10]	15.6[10]	7.8[10]	3.3[10]	0.5[10]	960	1,057	1,227	1,550	1,969	2,527	3,243	4,161	Mauritania
29.7	28.9	22.3	10.9	6.6	1.6	479	662	829	966	1,059	1,187	1,295	1,387	Mauritius
43.5	29.9	15.6	6.6	2.7	1.7	17	25	35	52	89	151	225	304	Mayotte
38.3	29.4	16.6	8.9	4.5	1.7	27,737	36,945	50,596	67,570	81,700	98,152	112,062	124,065	Mexico
46.4[31]	26.8[31]	12.6[31]	8.5[31]	4.5[31]	1.1[31]	30	40	57	73	98	108	115	116	Micronesia
27.9	22.9	21.0	15.6	9.7	2.9	2,341	3,004	3,595	4,002	4,245	3,664	3,550	3,483	Moldova
12.3	16.7	21.2	20.4	17.9	10.8	18	21	24	27	30	32	33	34	Monaco
41.9[26]	29.2[26]	14.6[26]	8.5[26]	——5.8[26]——		747	931	1,248	1,663	2,097	2,396	2,714	3,113	Mongolia
37.0[16]	29.6[16]	17.3[16]	9.2[16]	5.4[16]	1.5[16]	8,953	11,640	15,126	19,206	23,986	28,460	33,300	37,970	Morocco[32]
43.5[20]	28.6[20]	15.1[20]	8.5[20]	3.6[20]	0.7[20]	6,250	7,472	9,304	12,103	14,276	17,244	18,909	19,022	Mozambique
38.6	28.7	15.5	9.0	5.2	1.1	19,488	22,836	27,386	33,281	38,519	41,735	43,674	44,775	Myanmar (Burma)
41.7	28.8	14.7	7.8	——6.9——		464	591	765	975	1,409	1,772	1,950	1,999	Namibia
41.8	25.0	20.7	8.2	——2.8——		3	4	7	8	10	12	14	17	Nauru
42.3	25.7	16.7	9.7	4.7	0.9	8,502	9,839	11,880	14,559	18,142	22,647	28,403	34,813	Nepal

Area and population (continued)

country	area square miles	area square kilometres	rank	population (latest estimate) total midyear 2002	rank	density per sq mi	density per sq km	% annual growth rate 1997–2002	census year	total	male (%)	female (%)	urban (%)
Netherlands, The	16,034	41,528	134	16,142,000	59	1,006.7	388.7	0.7	2000	15,864,000	49.5	50.5	89.4[10]
Netherlands Antilles	308	800	183	175,000	185	568.2	218.8	–1.1	1992	189,474	47.9	52.1	...
New Caledonia	7,172	18,575	154	218,000	182	30.4	11.7	1.6	1996	196,836	51.2	48.8	60.4
New Zealand	104,454	270,534	75	3,893,000	122	37.3	14.4	0.7	1996	3,681,546	49.1	50.9	85.0
Nicaragua	50,337	130,373	97	5,024,000	110	99.8	38.5	2.3	1995	4,357,099	49.3	50.7	54.4
Niger	489,000	1,267,000	22	10,640,000	71	21.8	8.4	2.8	1988	7,228,552	49.5	50.5	15.3
Nigeria	356,669	923,768	32	129,935,000	9	364.4	140.7	2.7	1991	88,514,501	50.3	49.7	35.0[7]
Northern Mariana Islands	184	477	193	70,000	203	380.4	146.8	2.3	1995	58,846	49.8	50.2	28.0[2]
Norway	125,004	323,758	67	4,537,000	115	36.3	14.0	0.6	1990	4,247,546	49.4	50.6	72.0
Oman	119,500	309,500	70	2,522,000	137	20.9	8.1	2.3	1993	2,018,074	58.4	41.6	71.7
Pakistan[34]	307,374	796,095	36	145,960,000	6	474.9	183.3	2.3	1998	130,579,571	52.0	48.0	33.3
Palau	188	488	192	19,900	215	105.9	40.8	2.0	2000	19,129	54.6	45.4	71.4[29]
Panama	28,950	74,979	118	2,915,000	133	100.7	38.9	1.7	2000	2,839,177	50.5	49.5	56.3
Papua New Guinea	178,704	462,840	54	5,426,000	103	30.4	11.7	2.9	2000	5,130,000	51.9	48.1	15.2[2]
Paraguay	157,048	406,752	59	5,774,000	102	36.8	14.2	2.5	1992	4,123,550	50.2	49.8	50.5
Peru	496,225	1,285,216	20	26,749,000	39	53.9	20.8	1.6	1993	22,639,443	49.7	50.3	70.1
Philippines	115,860	300,076	72	79,882,000	14	689.5	266.2	2.2	1995	68,613,706	50.4	49.6	54.0[12]
Poland	120,728	312,685	69	38,644,000	30	319.9	123.6	0.0	1988	37,878,641	48.7	51.3	61.2
Portugal	35,662	92,365	111	10,384,000	74	291.2	112.4	0.4	2001	10,318,084[6]	48.3[6]	51.7[6]	48.2[9]
Puerto Rico	3,515	9,104	166	3,856,000	123	1,097.0	423.6	0.7	2000	3,808,610	48.1	51.9	71.2[2]
Qatar	4,412	11,427	161	606,000	162	137.4	53.0	2.8	1997	522,023	65.6	34.4	91.4[12]
Réunion	968	2,507	174	743,000	159	767.6	295.4	1.7	1999	706,180	49.1	50.9	70.3[4]
Romania	91,699	237,500	82	21,667,000	49	236.3	91.2	–0.5	1992	22,760,449	49.1	50.9	54.4
Russia	6,592,800	17,075,400	1	143,673,000	7	21.7	8.4	–0.5	1989	147,400,537	46.9	53.1	73.6
Rwanda	10,169	26,338	147	7,398,000	91	727.5	280.9	0.8	1991	7,164,994	48.7	51.3	5.4
St. Kitts and Nevis	104	269	205	46,200	211	444.2	171.7	1.1	1991	40,618	49.1	50.9	48.9[7]
St. Lucia	238	617	189	160,000	188	672.3	259.3	1.3	1991	133,308	48.5	51.5	44.1[7]
St. Vincent and the Grenadines	150	389	198	113,000	191	751.8	290.3	0.4	1991	106,499	49.9	50.1	24.6
Samoa	1,093	2,831	172	178,000	184	162.9	62.9	0.9	1991	161,298	52.5	47.5	21.2
San Marino	24	61	212	27,700	214	1,154.2	454.1	1.5	1997	25,872[3]	49.3	50.7	96.0[12]
São Tomé and Príncipe	386	1,001	181	147,000	190	379.9	146.5	1.7	1991	117,504	49.4	50.6	44.1[24]
Saudi Arabia	830,000	2,149,690	14	23,370,000	46	28.2	10.9	3.2	1992	16,948,388	55.9	44.1	77.3[7]
Senegal	75,951	196,712	87	9,905,000	80	130.4	50.4	2.6	1988	6,928,405	48.7	51.3	38.6
Seychelles	176	455	195	83,400	199	473.9	183.3	1.5	1997	75,876	49.5	50.5	54.8[12]
Sierra Leone	27,699	71,740	119	4,823,000	114	174.1	67.2	3.2	1985	3,517,530	49.6	50.4	31.8
Singapore	264	683	188	4,204,000	117	15,924.2	6,155.2	2.1	2000[6]	3,263,209	50.0	50.0	100.0
Slovakia	18,933	49,035	129	5,383,000	104	284.3	109.8	0.0	1991	5,268,935	48.9	51.1	56.8
Slovenia	7,827	20,273	153	1,948,000	144	248.9	96.1	–0.4	1991	1,974,839	48.5	51.5	48.9
Solomon Islands	10,954	28,370	143	439,000	168	40.1	15.5	2.8	1986	285,176	51.9	48.1	15.7
Somalia	246,000	637,000	42	7,753,000	90	31.5	12.2	3.2	1975	4,089,203	50.1	49.9	25.4
South Africa	470,693	1,219,090	25	45,172,000	26	96.0	37.1	1.9	1996	40,583,573	48.1	51.9	53.7
Spain	195,379	506,030	51	40,998,000	29	209.8	81.0	0.6	1991	38,999,181	49.1	50.9	75.3
Sri Lanka	25,332	65,610	122	18,870,000	53	744.9	287.6	1.1	1981	14,848,364	50.8	49.2	21.5
Sudan, The	966,757	2,503,890	10	37,090,000	32	38.4	14.8	2.9	1993	24,940,683	50.2	49.8	31.3[12]
Suriname	63,251	163,820	92	436,000	170	6.9	2.7	0.6	1980	354,860	49.5	50.5	49.1[12]
Swaziland	6,704	17,364	157	1,124,000	154	167.7	64.7	2.1	1997	929,718	47.3	52.7	23.1
Sweden	173,732	449,964	56	8,925,000	83	51.4	19.8	0.2	1999[3]	8,861,426	49.4	50.6	83.3[4]
Switzerland	15,940	41,284	135	7,282,000	92	456.8	176.4	0.5	1990[36]	6,873,687	49.3	50.7	68.9
Syria	71,498	185,180	88	17,156,000	55	240.0	92.6	2.6	1994	13,812,284	50.7	49.3	52.2[12]
Taiwan	13,972	36,188	136	22,457,000	47	1,607.3	620.6	0.8	1990[6]	20,393,628	52.1	47.9	74.5
Tajikistan	55,300	143,100	95	6,327,000	100	114.4	44.2	1.6	1989	5,108,576	49.7	50.3	32.6
Tanzania	364,901	945,090	31	34,902,000	33	95.6	36.9	3.1	1988	23,174,336	48.9	51.1	18.5
Thailand	198,115	513,115	50	63,430,000	19	320.2	123.6	1.0	2000	60,606,947	49.2	50.8	31.1
Togo	21,925	56,785	125	5,286,000	107	241.1	93.1	2.8	1981	2,719,567	48.7	51.3	15.2
Tonga	290	750	185	101,000	194	347.3	134.1	0.6	1996[6]	97,784	50.7	49.3	32.1
Trinidad and Tobago	1,980	5,128	169	1,304,000	150	658.6	254.3	0.5	1990	1,234,388	50.1	49.9	64.8
Tunisia	63,378	164,150	91	9,764,000	81	154.1	59.5	1.2	1994	8,785,711	50.6	49.4	61.0
Turkey	300,948	779,452	37	69,359,000	15	230.5	89.0	2.1	1997	62,865,574	50.7[2]	49.3[2]	65.0
Turkmenistan	188,500	488,100	52	4,946,000	113	26.2	10.1	1.5	1995	4,483,251	49.6	50.4	46.0
Tuvalu	9.9	25.6	215	10,900	217	1,101.0	425.8	2.2	1991	9,043	48.4	51.6	42.5
Uganda	93,065	241,038	80	24,378,000	42	261.9	101.1	3.4	1991	16,671,705	49.1	50.9	11.3
Ukraine	233,100	603,700	44	48,120,000	24	206.4	79.7	–1.0	1989	51,706,746	46.3	53.7	66.9
United Arab Emirates	32,280	83,600	116	3,550,000	127	110.0	42.5	6.2	1995	2,411,041	66.6	33.4	77.3
United Kingdom	94,248	244,101	79	60,178,000	20	638.5	246.5	0.4	1991[6]	56,467,000	48.4	51.6	89.1[7]
United States	3,615,215[37]	9,363,364[37]	4	287,602,000	3	79.6	30.7	1.1	2000	281,421,906	49.1	50.9	75.2[2]
Uruguay	68,037	176,215	90	3,383,000	129	49.7	19.2	1.1	1996	3,151,662	48.4	51.6	89.3
Uzbekistan	172,700	447,400	57	25,484,000	40	147.6	57.0	1.5	1989	19,905,158	49.3	50.7	40.7
Vanuatu	4,707	12,190	160	207,000	183	44.0	17.0	2.8	1999	193,219	51.5	48.5	21.5
Venezuela	353,841	916,445	33	25,093,000	41	70.9	27.4	2.0	1990	19,405,429	49.7	50.3	84.0
Vietnam	128,379	332,501	65	80,200,000	13	624.7	241.2	1.6	1999	76,324,753	49.2	50.8	23.5
Virgin Islands (U.S.)	136	352	201	110,000	192	808.8	312.5	0.6	1990	101,809	48.3	51.7	37.2
West Bank[38]	2,270	5,900	167	2,414,000	139	1,063.4	409.2	4.4	1995[3, 17]	1,707,000	51.2	48.8	...
Western Sahara	97,344	252,120	77	256,000	179	2.6	1.0	2.3	1994	252,146	...	...	90.7
Yemen	214,300	555,000	48	19,495,000	52	91.0	35.1	3.4	1994	14,587,807	51.2	48.8	23.5
Yugoslavia	39,449	102,173	107	10,664,000	70	270.3	104.4	0.1	1991	10,394,026	49.6	50.4	53.2[7]
Zambia	290,585	752,612	39	9,959,000	78	34.3	13.2	2.0	1990	7,818,447	49.2	50.8	42.0
Zimbabwe	150,872	390,757	60	11,377,000	66	75.4	29.1	0.4	1992	10,412,548	48.8	51.2	30.6

[1]Settled population only. [2]1990 census. [3]Civil register; not a census. [4]1999 estimate. [5]1996 estimate. [6]Data are for de jure population. [7]1990 estimate. [8]1991 estimate. [9]1991 census. [10]2000 estimate. [11]1992 census. [12]1995 estimate. [13]Data are for the island of Cyprus (excepting census information). [14]Republic of Cyprus only. [15]1993 estimate. [16]1994 estimate. [17]Projections from 1995 demographic survey. [18]Data exclude Alderney (population 2,297) and Sark (population 604). [19]2001 estimate. [20]1997 estimate. [21]Area figures exclude the West Bank, East Jerusalem, Gaza Strip, and Golan Heights. [22]Population figures include Golan Heights and East Jerusalem and exclude Israelis in the West Bank and Gaza Strip. [23]Includes East

0–14	15–29	30–44	45–59	60–74	75 and over	1950	1960	1970	1980	1990	2000	2010 projection	2020 projection	country
		age distribution (%)							population (by decade, '000s)					
18.6	19.3	24.2	19.8	12.1	6.0	10,027	11,417	12,958	14,150	14,952	15,926	16,913	17,524	Netherlands, The
26.0	23.9	25.5	14.3	7.3	3.0	112	136	163	174	188	177	175	175	Netherlands Antilles
30.7	27.2	21.3	13.3	5.9	1.6	59	79	110	140	171	211	240	265	New Caledonia
23.0	22.3	23.0	16.2	10.6	4.9	1,909	2,377	2,820	3,144	3,417	3,831	4,113	4,352	New Zealand
45.1	27.5	15.0	7.2	3.7	1.4	1,098	1,493	2,053	2,804	3,643	4,813	5,839	6,808	Nicaragua
48.7	24.8	14.6	6.8	3.6	1.5	2,482	3,168	4,182	5,629	7,627	10,076	13,140	16,800	Niger
45.5[8]	26.0[8]	15.3[8]	8.8[8]	3.8[8]	0.6[8]	31,797	39,914	51,099	69,593	92,483	123,338	155,588	187,437	Nigeria
24.6	31.9	31.6	9.6	1.8	0.5	6	9	10	17	44	70	70	70	Northern Mariana Islands
18.8	22.9	22.1	15.1	13.9	7.2	3,265	3,581	3,877	4,086	4,241	4,487	4,702	4,904	Norway
41.0	25.5	21.9	7.8	2.9	0.9	489	499	779	1,060	1,625	2,416	3,002	3,733	Oman
43.2	26.9	15.6	8.8	4.3	1.2	39,448	50,387	65,706	85,219	109,710	139,760	169,396	197,441	Pakistan[34]
23.9	24.2	29.9	14.2	5.5	2.3	7	9	12	13	15	19	22	24	Palau
32.0	26.8	20.6	12.0	6.1	2.5	893	1,148	1,531	1,950	2,335	2,846	3,189	3,486	Panama
41.9[2]	28.5[2]	16.6[2]	8.7[2]	— 3.2[2] —		1,412	1,747	2,288	2,991	3,758	5,187	6,496	7,790	Papua New Guinea
40.1	27.6	18.7	8.3	4.2	1.1	1,351	1,774	2,351	3,136	4,219	5,496	6,980	8,570	Paraguay
37.0	28.6	17.7	9.8	— 7.0 —		7,632	9,931	13,193	17,324	21,753	25,939	29,958	33,923	Peru
38.3	28.4	18.3	9.5	4.3	1.2	20,988	27,561	36,850	48,286	60,937	76,797	92,426	106,162	Philippines
25.4	21.2	23.3	15.5	10.4	4.2	24,824	29,561	32,526	35,578	38,057	38,651	38,764	39,003	Poland
20.0[9]	23.7[9]	20.2[9]	17.1[9]	13.7[9]	5.3[9]	8,405	8,826	9,040	9,766	9,896	10,320	10,491	10,407	Portugal
23.8	23.2	20.6	17.1	10.5	4.8	2,218	2,360	2,721	3,210	3,529	3,816	3,987	4,092	Puerto Rico
29.7[20]	30.7[20]	31.0[20]	7.0[20]	1.4[20]	0.2[20]	47	59	151	229	423	579	679	756	Qatar
27.0	24.8	24.4	13.8	7.2	2.8	244	338	447	507	601	722	812	888	Réunion
22.4	22.9	20.8	17.1	— 16.8 —		16,311	18,403	20,253	22,201	23,207	21,881	21,290	20,647	Romania
23.1	22.0	21.9	17.6	11.2	4.2	101,937	119,906	130,392	138,660	148,292	145,555	136,948	129,661	Russia
45.6	28.6	12.4	8.4	3.9	0.9	2,439	3,032	3,769	5,139	6,962	7,229	7,876	8,027	Rwanda
36.9[8]	31.8[8]	14.5[8]	6.0[8]	6.9[8]	3.8[8]	49	51	46	44	41	45	48	53	St. Kitts and Nevis
36.8	29.4	16.3	8.7	6.3	2.5	79	86	101	115	134	156	177	199	St. Lucia
37.2	29.5	16.1	8.3	6.4	2.5	67	80	86	99	105	112	116	117	St. Vincent and the Grenadines
40.5	30.0	14.6	8.7	— 6.0 —		82	111	143	155	160	175	186	210	Samoa
14.6	20.5	25.9	18.5	13.8	6.7	13	15	19	21	23	27	31	34	San Marino
46.9	26.2	12.2	8.0	— 6.7 —		60	64	74	94	117	142	171	207	São Tomé and Príncipe
41.8	26.8	20.4	7.0	3.0	1.0	3,860	4,718	6,109	9,949	15,847	22,010	28,478	36,460	Saudi Arabia
47.5	26.1	13.6	7.8	— 5.0 —		2,500	3,187	4,158	5,538	7,327	9,421	12,051	15,023	Senegal
28.8	27.4	22.6	10.6	7.5	3.1	34	42	54	63	70	81	93	102	Seychelles
43.9[35]	25.6[35]	15.7[35]	9.6[35]	4.5[35]	0.7[35]	1,944	2,241	2,656	3,236	4,061	4,405	6,283	8,036	Sierra Leone
21.5	21.2	28.4	18.2	8.2	2.5	1,022	1,639	2,075	2,414	3,047	4,018	4,670	4,949	Singapore
25.0	22.7	22.8	14.6	10.7	4.2	3,463	3,994	4,528	4,984	5,298	5,401	5,407	5,361	Slovakia
20.0	22.4	23.7	17.4	11.9	4.6	1,467	1,580	1,727	1,901	1,998	1,990	1,962	1,942	Slovenia
47.3	25.7	13.9	8.1	— 4.9 —		107	126	163	232	335	416	544	667	Solomon Islands
45.6	24.9	15.5	7.4	— 5.4 —		2,438	2,956	3,667	5,791	6,675	7,253	9,922	13,023	Somalia
33.9	28.6	19.4	9.8	5.3	1.8	13,683	17,396	22,656	29,064	36,376	43,291	46,362	45,167	South Africa
19.4	24.9	20.0	16.5	13.6	5.6	27,868	30,303	33,779	37,636	38,798	40,599	41,080	40,135	Spain
35.3	29.6	17.9	10.6	5.2	1.4	7,678	9,889	12,514	14,747	16,511	18,510	20,096	21,338	Sri Lanka
43.0	27.0	16.4	9.3	3.7	0.6	8,051	10,589	13,788	19,064	26,627	35,080	45,485	56,162	Sudan, The
39.3	29.5	13.8	10.0	4.5	2.8	208	285	373	355	395	431	450	457	Suriname
44.3	28.6	14.4	7.7	3.4	1.6	277	352	455	606	852	1,083	1,216	1,296	Swaziland
18.5	18.3	20.7	20.3	13.3	8.9	7,041	7,498	8,081	8,310	8,559	8,872	9,114	9,407	Sweden
16.8	22.8	23.2	18.0	12.5	6.7	4,715	5,429	6,270	6,362	6,712	7,184	7,448	7,739	Switzerland
44.7	28.2	14.8	7.3	— 5.0 —		3,495	4,533	6,258	8,774	12,436	16,306	20,606	24,676	Syria
27.1	27.8	23.1	12.3	7.9	1.8	7,619	10,668	14,583	17,642	20,279	22,185	23,777	24,876	Taiwan
42.9	28.1	13.8	9.0	4.6	1.6	1,532	2,083	2,942	3,968	5,213	6,151	6,779	7,787	Tajikistan
45.8	26.7	13.5	7.8	4.5	1.7	7,935	10,260	13,842	18,939	24,460	32,894	41,805	52,065	Tanzania
28.8[2]	30.4[2]	21.2[2]	12.3[2]	5.7[2]	1.6[2]	20,010	26,392	35,037	46,538	56,096	62,317	67,435	70,706	Thailand
49.8	24.8	13.1	6.8	3.3	2.0	1,172	1,456	1,964	2,596	3,691	5,019	6,245	7,197	Togo
39.1	28.0	15.1	10.0	6.0	1.8	50	65	80	92	96	100	104	108	Tonga
33.5	27.2	19.9	10.7	6.4	2.3	668	828	941	1,082	1,227	1,291	1,358	1,420	Trinidad and Tobago
34.8	28.5	18.8	9.6	6.4	1.9	3,517	4,149	5,099	6,443	8,154	9,563	10,472	11,223	Tunisia
35.0[2]	28.6[2]	18.4[2]	10.9[2]	5.6[2]	1.6[2]	21,122	28,217	35,758	44,439	56,098	67,456	75,656	82,214	Turkey
40.5[26]	28.8[26]	15.5[26]	9.1[26]	4.7[26]	1.4[26]	1,211	1,594	2,189	2,861	3,668	4,809	5,651	6,448	Turkmenistan
34.6	24.0	20.7	11.3	— 9.2 —		5	5	6	8	9	10	13	15	Tuvalu
47.3	27.7	13.1	6.9	3.7	1.3	5,522	7,262	9,728	12,298	16,447	22,813	30,944	41,258	Uganda
21.5	21.0	20.6	18.5	10.7	7.7	36,906	42,783	47,317	50,034	51,892	49,235	45,930	44,109	Ukraine
26.3	29.2	33.2	9.6	1.4	0.3	70	90	223	1,042	1,844	3,247	4,010	4,552	United Arab Emirates
19.1	21.9	21.2	16.7	14.1	7.0	50,290	52,372	55,632	56,330	57,567	59,756	61,753	63,887	United Kingdom
21.4	20.8	23.3	18.2	10.4	5.9	152,271	180,671	204,879	227,726	249,806	282,339	307,668	333,384	United States
25.1	22.9	19.6	15.1	12.2	5.1	2,194	2,531	2,824	2,914	3,041	3,321	3,566	3,771	Uruguay
40.8	28.4	15.0	9.3	4.7	1.8	6,314	8,559	11,973	15,977	20,515	24,741	28,538	32,496	Uzbekistan
45.5[26]	26.6[26]	15.2[26]	8.4[26]	3.7[26]	0.6[26]	52	66	85	117	147	197	252	313	Vanuatu
38.3	28.1	18.6	9.3	4.5	1.2	5,094	7,579	10,721	15,091	19,502	24,170	28,716	32,911	Venezuela
39.0[26]	28.7[26]	16.0[26]	9.1[26]	5.6[26]	1.6[26]	27,367	33,648	42,898	53,005	65,792	78,137	88,684	100,205	Vietnam
28.9	23.7	22.0	16.0	7.3	2.2	27	32	63	100	102	109	116	124	Virgin Islands (U.S.)
44.6	28.4	14.0	7.4	4.4	1.2	...	...	608	733	1,011	2,209	3,271	4,172	West Bank[38]
...	...	...	...	...	...	14	32	76	126	191	245	301	357	Western Sahara
47.6[16]	28.7[16]	11.9[16]	7.4[16]	3.6[16]	0.7[16]	4,316	5,247	6,332	8,219	11,590	18,261	24,887	32,401	Yemen
22.8	21.6	21.7	17.1	12.2	3.5	7,131	8,050	8,691	9,522	10,156	10,633	10,545	10,330	Yugoslavia
47.3	28.2	12.9	7.3	3.5	0.7	2,553	3,254	4,252	5,700	7,851	9,582	11,482	13,365	Zambia
45.1	28.3	14.0	7.2	3.9	1.2	2,853	4,011	5,515	7,170	10,103	11,343	11,057	9,997	Zimbabwe

Jerusalem and Israelis in the West Bank, Gaza Strip, and Golan Heights. [24]1992 estimate. [25]Excludes the West Bank. [26]1989 census. [27]1998 official country estimate including nonresidents. [28]1998 estimate. [29]1995 census. [30]1988 census. [31]1980 census. [32]Excludes Western Sahara, an annexure of Morocco. [33]Includes Western Sahara. [34]Excludes Afghan refugees (2002; c. 1.1 million) and the area (32,494 sq mi [84,159 sq km]) and population (2002; c. 4.3 million) of Pakistani-occupied Jammu and Kashmir. [35]1985 estimate. [36]Includes resident aliens; excludes seasonal workers. [37]Includes inland water area of 78,937 sq mi (204,446 sq km); excludes Great Lakes water area of 60,052 sq mi (155,534 sq km). [38]Excludes East Jerusalem.

Major cities and national capitals

The following table lists the principal cities or municipalities (those exceeding 100,000 in population [75,000 for Anglo-America, Australia, and the United Kingdom]) of the countries of the world, together with figures for each national capital (indicated by a ★), regardless of size.

Most of the populations given refer to a so-called city proper, that is, a legally defined, incorporated, or chartered area defined by administrative boundaries and by national or state law. Some data, however, refer to the municipality, or commune, similar to the medieval city-state in that the city is governed together with its immediately adjoining, economically dependent areas, whether urban or rural in nature. Some countries define no other demographic or legal entities within such communes or municipalities, but many identify a centre, seat, head (*cabecera*), or locality that corresponds to the most densely populated, compact, contiguous core of the municipality. Because the amount of work involved in carefully defining these "centres" may be considerable, the necessary resources usually exist only at the time of a national census (generally 5 or 10 years apart). Between censuses, therefore, it may be possible only to track the growth of the municipality as a whole. Thus, in order to provide the most up-to-date data for cities in this table, figures referring to municipalities or communes may be given (identified by the abbreviation "MU"), even though the country itself may define a smaller, more closely knit city proper. Specific identification of municipalities is provided in this table *only* when

the country also publishes data for a more narrowly defined city proper; it is *not* provided when the sole published figure is the municipality, whether or not this is the proper local administrative term for the entity.

Populations for urban agglomerations as defined by the United Nations are occasionally inset beneath the populations of cities proper. Specifically that is when the urban agglomeration populations are at least three times the size of cities proper.

For certain countries, more than one form of the name of the city is given, usually to permit recognition of recent place-name changes or of *forms* of the place-name likely to be encountered in press stories if the title of the city's entry in the *Encyclopædia Britannica* is spelled according to a different romanization or spelling policy.

Chinese names for China are usually given in their Pinyin spelling, the official Chinese system encountered in official documents and maps. For Taiwan, the Wade-Giles spelling of place-names is used.

Sources for this data were often national censuses and statistical abstracts of the countries concerned, supplemented by Internet sources.

Internet sources for further information
• City Population: http://www.citypopulation.de/cities.html
• The World Gazetteer: http://www.gazetteer.de/st/stata.htm

Major cities and national capitals

country / city	population
Afghanistan	
(early 1990s est.)	
Herāt	186,800
★ Kābul	700,000[1]
agglomeration	2,454,000[2]
Kandahār	
(Qandahār)	237,500
Mazār-e Sharīf	127,800
Albania (1999 est.)	
★ Tiranë	279,000
Algeria (1998)	
★ Algiers	1,519,570
Annaba	348,554
Batna	242,514
Béchar	131,010
Bejaïa	147,076
Biskra (Beskra)	170,956
Blida (el-Boulaida)	226,512
Bordj Bou Arreridj	128,535
Constantine	
(Qacentina)	462,187
Djelfa	154,265
Ech-Cheliff	
(el-Asnam)	179,768
El-Eulma	105,130
El-Wad	104,801
Ghardaïa	110,724
Ghilizane	104,285
Guelma	108,734
Jijel	106,003
Khenchela	106,082
Médéa	123,535
Mostaganem	124,399
Oran (Wahran)	692,516
Saïda	110,865
Sétif (Stif)	211,859
Sidi bel Abbès	180,260
Skikda	152,335
Souq Ahras	115,882
Tébessa (Tbessa)	153,246
Tihert	145,332
Tlemcen (Tilimsen)	155,162
Touggourt	113,625
Wargla (Ouargla)	129,402
American Samoa (1990)	
★ Fagatogo (legislative and judicial)	2,323[3]
★ Utulei (executive)	930[3]
Andorra (1999 est.)	
★ Andorra la Vella	21,513
Angola (1999 est.)	
Huambo	400,000[4]
★ Luanda	2,555,000
Antigua and Barbuda (1991)	
★ Saint John's	22,342
Argentina (1999 est.)	
Almirante Brown	550,000
Avellaneda	342,193
Bahía Blanca	281,161
Belén de Escobar	192,992

country / city	population
Berazategui	296,759
★ Buenos Aires	2,904,192
agglomeration	12,423,000
Caseros	341,398
Catamarca	140,000
Comodoro Rivadavia	144,074
Concordia	131,716
Córdoba	1,275,585
Corrientes	325,628
Esteban Echeverría	234,188
Florencio Valera	331,358
Formosa	197,057
General San Martín	409,879
General Sarmiento	209,450
Godoy Cruz	205,955
Hurlingham	165,986
Ituzaingo	154,437
José Carlos Paz	219,624
La Matanza (San Justo)	1,241,264
La Plata	556,308
La Rioja	138,074
Lanús	470,000
Las Heras	183,511
Lomas de Zamora	609,621
Mar del Plata	579,483
Mendoza	119,681
Mercedes	100,876
Merlo	430,213
Moreno	398,023
Morón	340,645
Neuquén	327,374
Paraná	256,602
Pilar	166,587
Posadas	250,000
Quilmes	550,069
Resistencia	280,000
Río Cuarto	150,000
Rosario	1,000,000
Salta	457,223
San Carlos de Bariloche	105,093
San Fernando	146,896
San Isidro	296,935
San Juan	120,000
San Luis	146,855
San Miguel	246,503
San Miguel de Tucumán	519,252
San Nicolás de los Arroyos	132,909
San Rafael	111,066
San Salvador de Jujuy	226,961
Santa Fe	400,000
Santiago del Estero	202,876
Tigre	299,376
Trelew	101,425
Vicente López	279,464
Villa Krause	100,000
Villa Nueva	224,116
Armenia (1995 est.)	
Gyumri (Kumayri; Leninakan)	120,000[5]
★ Yerevan	1,248,700

country / city	population
Aruba (1998 est.)	
★ Oranjestad	28,000
Australia (1998 est.)	
Adelaide UC[6]	978,100[7]
Adelaide	12,922
Charles Sturt	103,012
Marion	77,547
Onkaparinga	146,367
Port Adelaide Enfield	101,225
Salisbury	112,344
Tea Tree Gully	96,972
Brisbane UC[6]	1,291,117[7]
Brisbane	848,741
Ipswich	132,232
Logan	165,924
Canberra-Queanbeyan UC[6]	322,723[7]
★ Canberra	306,000
Melbourne UC[6]	2,865,329[7]
Banyule	119,486
Bayside	88,449
Boroondara	157,208
Brimbank	158,032
Casey	160,845
Dandenong	132,091
Darebin	129,005
Frankston	111,081
Glen Eira	122,535
Hobsons Bay	80,825
Hume	126,350
Kingston	132,895
Knox	141,016
Manningham	112,563
Maroondah	97,321
Melbourne	44,619
Monash	161,996
Moonee Valley	111,898
Moreland	137,258
Port Philip	78,680
Stonnington	90,546
Whitehorse	145,611
Whittlesea	111,040
Wyndham	80,931
Perth UC[6]	1,096,829[7]
Gosnells	79,372
Melville	95,854
Perth	5,957
Stirling	175,569
Wanneroo	154,641
Sydney UC[6]	3,276,207[7]
Bankstown	167,839
Blacktown	248,525
Blue Mountains	75,855
Campbelltown	149,489
Canterbury	140,435
Fairfield	190,920
Gosford	155,144
Holroyd	86,280
Liverpool	137,066
Parramatta	144,366
Penrith	171,420
Randwick	125,359

country / city	population
Rockdale	90,372
Ryde	97,598
South Sydney	83,752
Sydney	24,883
Other cities	
Ballarat	80,330
Bendigo	86,451
Cairns	118,834
Geelong	186,307
Gold Coast	380,270
Lake Macquarie	180,826
Newcastle	139,171
Shoalhaven	81,253
Toowoomba	86,968
Townsville	87,235
Wollongong	185,397
Austria (2001)	
Graz	226,424
Innsbruck	113,826
Linz	186,298
Salzburg	144,816
★ Vienna	1,562,676
Azerbaijan (1997 est.)	
★ Baku (Baky)	1,727,200
Gäncä (Gyandzha)	291,900
Sumqayit (Sumgait)	248,500
Bahamas, The (1999 est.)	
★ Nassau	214,000[8]
Bahrain (1999 est.)	
★ Al-Manāmah	162,000
Bangladesh (1991)	
Barisal	170,232
Bogra	120,170
Brahmanbaria	109,032
Chittagong	1,392,860
Comilla	135,313
★ Dhaka (Dacca)	3,612,850
agglomeration	11,726,000[2]
Dinajpur	127,815
Jamalpur	103,556
Jessore	139,710
Khulna	663,340
Mymensingh	188,713
Naogaon	101,266
Narayanganj	276,549
Nawabganj (Nowabganj)	130,577
Pabna	103,277
Rajshahi	294,056
Rangpur	191,398
Sylhet	117,396
Tangail	106,004
Tongi	168,702
Barbados (1990)	
★ Bridgetown	6,070
agglomeration	133,000[2]
Belarus (1998 est.)	
Baranovichi (Baranavichy)	173,000
Bobruysk (Babrujsk)	227,000

country / city	population
Borisov (Barysau)	153,000
Brest (Bierascie)	297,000
Gomel (Homiel)	513,000
Grodno (Horadnia)	306,000
Lida	100,000
★ Minsk	1,717,000
Mogilyov (Mahilou)	369,000
Mozyr (Mazyr)	109,000
Orsha (Vorsha)	138,000
Pinsk	132,000
Soligorsk	102,000
Vitebsk (Viciebsk)	364,000
Belgium (2000 est.)	
Antwerp	446,525
Brugge (Bruges)	116,246
★ Brussels	133,859
agglomeration	1,121,000[2]
Charleroi	200,827
Ghent	224,180
Liège (Luik)	185,639
Namur	105,419
Schaerbeek	105,692
Belize (2000)	
★ Belmopan	8,130
Benin (1992)	
★ Cotonou (official)	533,212
Djougou	132,192
Parakou	106,708
★ Porto-Novo (de facto)	177,660
Bermuda (1995 est.)	
★ Hamilton	1,100
Bhutan (1999 est.)	
★ Thimphu	28,000
Bolivia (2000 est.)	
Cochabamba	607,129
El Alto	568,919
★ La Paz (administrative)	1,000,899
Oruro	232,311
Potosí	147,351
Quillacollo	132,579
Santa Cruz	1,016,137
★ Sucre (judicial)	192,238
Tarija	135,679
Bosnia and Herzegovina (1997 est.)	
Banja Luka	160,000
★ Sarajevo	360,000
Botswana (1997 est.)	
★ Gaborone	183,487
Brazil (2000)[9]	
Águas Lindas de Goiás	105,216
Alagoinhas	112,339
Alvorada	182,864
Americana	181,650
Ananindeua	391,994
Anápolis	279,752
Angra dos Reis	114,237

country city	population
Aparecida de Golânia	334,994
Apucarana	100,241
Aracaju	460,898
Araçatuba	164,440
Araguaina	105,701
Arapiraca	152,281
Araraquara	173,086
Barbacena	103,522
Barra Mansa	164,963
Barreiras	115,331
Barueri	208,028
Bauru	310,208
Belém	1,271,615
Belford Roxo	433,120
Belo Horizonte	2,229,697
Betim	295,480
Blumenau	241,987
Boa Vista	196,942
Botucatu	103,793
Bragança Paulista	110,982
★ Brasília	1,954,442
Cabo (de Santo Agostinho)	134,356
Cabo Frio	106,326
Cachoeirinha	107,472
Cachoeiro de Itapemirim	154,771
Camaçari	153,829
Camaragibe	128,627
Campina Grande	336,218
Campinas	951,824
Campo Grande	654,832
Campos	363,489
Canoas	305,711
Carapicuíba	343,668
Cariacica	312,542
Caruaru	217,084
Cascavel	228,340
Castanhal	121,174
Catanduva	104,195
Caucaia	225,854
Caxias	103,276
Caxias do Sul	333,201
Chapecó	134,210
Colombo	174,971
Contagem	531,715
Cotia	148,082
Criciúma	152,903
Cubatão	107,260
Cuiabá	475,632
Curitiba	1,586,898
Diadema	356,389
Divinópolis	177,729
Dourados	149,679
Duque de Caxias	767,724
Embu	206,781
Feira de Santana	431,458
Ferraz	140,777
Florianópolis	321,778
Fortaleza	2,138,234
Foz do Iguaçu	256,349
Franca	281,869
Francisco Morato	133,085
Franco de Rocha	100,241
Garanhuns	103,283
Goiânia	1,083,396
Governador Valadares	235,881
Gravataí	211,969
Guarapuava	141,575
Guarujá	265,076
Guarulhos	1,048,280
Hortolândia	151,669
Ibirité	132,131
Ilhéus	161,898
Imperatriz	218,555
Indaiatuba	144,528
Ipatinga	210,777
Itaboraí	176,767
Itabuna	190,888
Itajaí	141,932
Itapecerica da Serra	127,783
Itapetininga	111,774
Itapevi	162,421
Itaquaquecetuba	272,416
Itu	123,881
Jaboatão	567,319
Jacareí	183,444
Jaú	106,954
Jequié	130,207
João Pessoa	594,922
Joinville	414,350
Juàzeiro	132,796
Juàzeiro do Norte	201,950
Juiz de Fora	443,359
Jundiaí	299,669
Lages	152,320
Lauro de Freitas	108,111
Limeira	237,959
Londrina	433,264
Luziânia	129,905

country city	population
Macaé	125,118
Macapá	270,077
Maceió	794,894
Magé	193,784
Manaus	1,394,724
Marabá	134,258
Maracanaú	174,037
Marília	189,533
Maringá	283,792
Mauá	363,112
Mogi Guaçu	116,117
Moji das Cruzes	301,551
Montes Claros	288,534
Mossoró	197,067
Natal	709,422
Nilópolis	153,572
Niterói	458,465
Nossa Senhora de Socorro	130,255
Nova Friburgo	151,820
Nova Iguaçu	915,364
Novo Hamburgo	231,833
Olinda	361,300
Osasco	650,993
Palmas	133,471
Paranaguá	122,179
Parnaíba	124,942
Parnamirim	107,927
Passo Fundo	163,748
Patos de Minas	111,159
Paulista	262,072
Pelotas	300,952
Petrolina	166,113
Petrópolis	270,489
Pindamonhangaba	118,793
Pinhais	100,601
Piracicaba	316,518
Poços de Caldas	130,594
Ponta Grossa	266,552
Porto Alegre	1,320,069
Porto Velho	273,496
Praia Grande	191,811
Presidente Prudente	185,150
Queimados	121,681
Recife	1,421,947
Ribeirão das Neves	245,143
Ribeirão Pires	104,336
Ribeirão Preto	502,333
Rio Branco	226,054
Rio Claro	163,341
Rio de Janeiro	5,850,544
Rio Grande	179,422
Rio Verde	106,109
Rondonópolis	141,660
Sabará	111,897
Salvador	2,439,881
Santa Bárbara d'Oeste	167,574
Santa Luzia	184,026
Santa Maria	230,464
Santa Rita	100,259
Santarém	186,518
Santo André	648,443
Santos	415,543
São Bernardo do Campo	688,161
São Caetano do Sul	140,144
São Carlos	183,369
São Gonçalo	889,828
São João de Meriti	449,562
São José	167,268
São José do Rio Prêto	336,998
São José dos Campos	532,403
São José dos Pinhais	183,259
São Leopoldo	192,756
São Luís	834,968
São Paulo	9,785,640
São Vicente	302,541
Sapucaia do Sul	121,739
Serra	320,965
Sete Lagoas	180,211
Sobral	134,371
Sorocaba	487,907
Sumaré	193,266
Susano (Suzano)	221,192
Taboão da Serra	197,460
Taubaté	229,810
Teófilo Otoni	102,500
Teresina	676,596
Teresopolis	114,688
Timon	111,967
Uberaba	243,406
Uberlândia	487,887
Uruguaiana	118,181
Varginha	103,499
Várzea Grande	210,849
Viamão	210,873
Vila Velha	343,567
Vitória	291,889

country city	population
Vitória da Conquista	225,430
Volta Redonda	242,773
Brunei (1991)	
★ Bandar Seri Begawan	21,484
agglomeration	85,000[2]
Bulgaria (1999 est.)	
Burgas	195,255
Dobrich	100,399
Pleven	121,952
Plovdiv	342,584
Ruse	166,467
Sliven	105,530
★ Sofia	1,122,302
Stara Zagora	147,939
Varna	299,801
Burkina Faso (1993 est.)	
Bobo Dioulasso	300,000
Koudougou	105,000
★ Ouagadougou	690,000
Burundi (1994 est.)	
★ Bujumbura	300,000
Gitega	101,827[10]
Cambodia (1999 est.)	
★ Phnom Penh	938,000
Cameroon (1992 est.)	
Bafoussam	120,000
Bamenda	110,000[5]
Douala	1,200,000
Garoua	160,000
Maroua	140,000
Nkongsamba	112,000[5]
★ Yaoundé	800,000
Canada (1996)	
Abbotsford	105,403
Barrie	79,191
Brampton	268,251
Brantford	84,764
Burlington	136,976
Burnaby	179,209
Calgary	768,082
Cambridge	101,429
Cape Breton	114,733
Coquitlam	101,820
Delta	95,411
East York	107,822
Edmonton	616,306
Etobicoke	328,718
Gatineau	100,702
Gloucester	104,022
Guelph	95,821
Halifax	113,910
Hamilton	322,352
Kamloops	76,394
Kelowna	89,442
Kitchener	178,420
Laval	330,343
London	325,646
Longueuil	127,977
Markham	173,383
Mississauga	544,382
Montreal	1,016,376
Montréal-Nord	81,581
Nepean	115,100
Niagara Falls	76,917
North York	589,653
Oakville	128,405
Oshawa	134,364
★ Ottawa	323,340
Pickering	78,989
Prince George	75,150
Quebec	167,264
Regina	180,400
Richmond	148,867
Richmond Hill	101,725
Saanich	101,388
Saint Catharines	130,926
Saint-Hubert	77,042
Saint John's	101,936
Saskatoon	193,647
Sault Sainte Marie	80,054
Scarborough	558,960
Sherbrooke	76,786
Sudbury	92,059
Surrey	304,477
Thunder Bay	113,662
Toronto	653,734
Vancouver	514,008
Vaughan	132,549
Waterloo	77,949
Windsor	197,694
Winnipeg	618,477
York	146,534

country city	population
Cape Verde (2000)	
★ Praia	94,757
Central African Republic (1995 est.)	
★ Bangui	553,000
Chad (1993; MU)	
Abéché	187,936
Bongor	196,713
Doba	185,461
Moundou	282,103
★ N'Djamena	530,965
Sarh	193,753
Chile (1999 est.)	
Antofagasta	243,038
Arica	178,547
Calama	121,326
Chillán	162,969
Concepción	362,589
Copiapó	114,615
Coquimbo	126,886
Iquique	159,815
La Serena	123,166
Los Angeles	109,606
Osorno	126,645
Puente Alto	363,012
Puerto Montt	128,945
Punta Arenas	120,148
Quilpué	114,617
Rancagua	202,067
San Bernardo	223,055
★ Santiago (administrative)	202,010[11]
agglomeration	4,640,635
Talca	174,858
Talcahuano	269,265
Temuco	253,451
Valdívia	122,166
★ Valparaíso (legislative)	283,489
Viña del Mar	330,736
China (1999 est.)[12]	
Acheng	234,057
Aksu	220,415
Altay	106,665
Anda	180,795
Ankang	173,450
Anlu	112,529
Anning	128,275
Anqing	356,920
Anqiu	193,258
Anshan	1,285,849
Anshun	217,215
Anyang	527,982
Baicheng	269,732
Baise	119,150
Baishan	253,631
Baiyin	258,885
Baoding	570,167
Baoji	447,105
Baoshan	100,797
Baotou	1,092,819
Bazhong	137,627
Bei'an	217,980
Beihai	196,256
★ Beijing (Peking)	6,633,929
Beiliu	140,015
Beining	101,273
Beipiao	202,807
Bengbu	506,239
Benxi	827,203
Bijie	101,171
Binzhou	230,174
Botou	103,337
Bozhou	253,544
Cangzhou	304,010
Cenxi	113,589
Changchun	2,072,324
Changde	384,433
Changge	117,166
Changji	192,000
Changning	134,592
Changsha	1,334,036
Changshu	264,472
Changyi	133,754
Changzhi	387,002
Changzhou	772,700
Chaohu	280,409
Chaoyang (Fujian)	389,558
Chaoyang (Liaoning)	295,302
Chaozhou	257,521
Chengde	298,895
Chengdu	2,146,126
Chenghai	166,621
Chenzhou	274,338
Chibi	158,125
Chifeng	453,946

country city	population
Chongqing (Chungking)	3,193,889
Chuxiong	115,887
Chuzhou	187,985
Cixi	132,588
Conghua	128,328
Da'an	153,718
Dachuan	200,785
Dafeng	153,147
Dali	175,847
Dalian	2,000,944
Dandong	578,723
Dangyang	114,885
Danjiangkou	152,396
Danyang	211,875
Danzhou	212,572
Daqing	811,154
Dashiqiao	186,201
Datong	928,293
Daye	128,561
Dehui	149,275
Dengzhou	119,036
Dexing	104,945
Deyang	246,221
Dezhou	310,538
Dingzhou	131,992
Donggang	104,971
Dongguan	378,354
Dongsheng	113,436
Dongtai	231,444
Dongying	479,941
Dujiangyan	154,867
Dunhua	257,190
Duyun	150,950
Emeishan	124,471
Enping	164,929
Enshi	125,937
Ezhou	301,248
Fangchenggang	119,444
Fanyu	345,275
Feicheng	301,981
Fengcheng (Guangdong)	173,112
Fengcheng (Jiangxi)	221,652
Fengnan	121,767
Foshan	411,107
Fu'an	100,793
Fujin	123,280
Fuqing	139,426
Fushun	1,271,113
Fuxin	682,966
Fuyang (Anhui)	319,816
Fuzhou	1,057,372
Gaizhou	175,467
Ganzhou	271,952
Gao'an	130,520
Gaomi	224,162
Gaoming	121,732
Gaoyao	142,335
Gaoyou	135,728
Gaozhou	204,028
Gejiu	218,921
Genhe	173,188
Gongyi	118,985
Gongzhuling	352,978
Guanghan	121,228
Guangshui	137,189
Guangyuan	257,411
Guangzhou (Canton)	3,306,277
Guichi	103,860
Guigang	290,829
Guilin	458,333
Guiping	151,341
Guixi	102,536
Guiyang	1,320,566
Gujiao	104,560
Haicheng	259,725
Haikou	438,262
Hailar	209,294
Hailin	242,389
Hailun	154,148
Haimen	355,232
Haining	122,973
Hami	205,310
Hancheng	108,702
Hanchuan	171,827
Handan	1,005,834
Hangzhou	1,346,148
Hanzhong	215,284
Harbin	2,586,978
Hebi	276,808
Hechi	108,942
Hechuan	202,218
Hefei	1,000,655
Hegang	591,254
Heihe	112,961
Helong	135,328
Hengshui	212,516
Hengyang	584,346
Heshan	117,049

Major cities and national capitals (continued)

country / city	population	country / city	population	country / city	population	country / city	population	country / city	population
Heyuan	164,986	Linhai	127,378	Shihezi	330,535	Xuchang	275,743	Itagüí	228,985
Heze	307,445	Linhe	186,234	Shijiazhuang	1,338,796	Xuzhou	1,044,729	Maicao	108,053
Hezhou	113,031	Linjiang	114,072	Shishou	140,634	Ya'an	119,320	Manizales	337,580
Hohhot	754,749	Linqing	143,203	Shiyan	377,232	Yakeshi	391,627	Medellín	1,861,265
Honghu	201,421	Linyi	569,419	Shizuishan	313,842	Yan'an	133,226	Montería	248,245
Hongjiang	130,713	Linzhou	110,526	Shouguang	202,067	Yancheng	332,125	Neiva	300,052
Hongta	110,048	Liu'an	282,880	Shuangcheng	172,936	Yangchun	206,440	Palmira	226,509
Houma	103,578	Liupanshui	502,327	Shuangliao	135,663	Yangjiang	295,672	Pasto	332,396
Huadian	197,759	Liuyang	133,723	Shuangyashan	431,170	Yangquan	447,229	Pereira	381,725
Huadu	195,921	Liuzhou	775,823	Shulan	208,723	Yangzhou	395,048	Popayán	200,719
Huai'an	155,657	Liyang	292,482	Shunde	339,392	Yanji	329,112	Santa Marta	359,147
Huaibei	574,904	Longhai	101,884	Shuozhou	134,645	Yantai	818,646	★ Santafé de Bogotá, D.C.	6,260,862
Huaihua	225,414	Longjing	144,940	Sihui	125,065	Yanzhou	199,491	Sincelejo	220,704
Huainan	823,395	Longkou	221,823	Siping	382,652	Yibin	288,039	Soacha	272,058
Huaiyin	320,841	Longyan	237,385	Songyuan	303,821	Yichang	481,277	Sogamoso	107,728
Huanggang	241,268	Loudi	222,375	Songzi	148,183	Yicheng	116,586	Soledad	295,058
Huangshan	130,623	Lufeng	260,804	Suihua	262,117	Yichun (Heilongjiang)	802,931	Tuluá	152,488
Huangshi	569,384	Luoding	338,722	Suining	229,229	Yichun (Jiangxi)	198,799	Tunja	109,740
Huazhou	183,394	Luohe	306,565	Suizhou	333,766	Yima	116,760	Valledupar	263,247
Huichun	134,379	Luoyang	1,002,178	Suqian	115,368	Yinchuan	469,180	Villavicencio	273,140
Huiyang	192,713	Luzhou	371,843	Suzhou (Anhui)	325,724	Yingcheng	120,499		
Huizhou	287,178	Ma'anshan	393,174	Suzhou (Jiangsu)	845,687	Yingde	205,782	**Comoros** (1995 est.)	
Hulin	152,353	Macheng	175,322	Tai'an	518,117	Yingkou	498,300	★ Moroni	34,168
Huludao	447,986	Manzhouli	143,711	Taicang	119,862	Yingtan	110,671		
Huzhou	296,962	Maoming	302,022	Taishan	355,017	Yining	230,429	**Congo, Dem. Rep. of the**	
Jiamusi	579,093	Meihekou	255,514	Taixing	185,270	Yixing	258,808	(1994 est.)	
Ji'an (Jiangxi)	178,957	Meizhou	230,419	Taiyuan	1,768,530	Yiyang	297,000	Boma	135,284
Jiangdu	182,208	Mianyang	396,055	Taizhou (Jiangsu)	219,968	Yizheng	166,358	Bukavu	201,569
Jiangjin	222,571	Mingguang	112,715	Taizhou (Zhejiang)	239,271	Yong'an	130,688	Butembo	109,406
Jiangmen	333,154	Mishan	153,717	Tangshan	1,210,842	Yongcheng	118,659	Goma	109,094
Jiangyan	149,706	Mudanjiang	641,347	Taonan	156,464	Yongchuan	186,482	Kalemi	101,309
Jiangyin	339,420	Muling	134,632	Tengzhou	452,009	Yongzhou	276,669	Kananga	393,030
Jiangyou	221,960	Nan'an	108,684	Tianchang	167,508	Yuanjiang	140,406	Kikwit	182,142
Jianyang (Sichuan)	161,496	Nanchang	1,264,739	Tianjin (Tientsin)	4,835,327	Yuanping	101,689	★ Kinshasa	4,655,313
Jiaohe	170,881	Nanchong	390,603	Tianmen	367,036	Yuci	243,948	Kisangani	417,517
Jiaonan	186,424	Nanhai	381,322	Tianshui	301,570	Yueyang	448,249	Kolwezi	417,810
Jiaozhou	188,192	Nanjing (Nanking)	2,388,915	Tiefa	165,956	Yuhang	152,429	Likasi	299,118
Jiaozuo	536,021	Nankang	102,222	Tieli	272,841	Yulin (Guangxi)	190,418	Lubumbashi	851,381
Jiaxing	261,465	Nanning	984,061	Tieling	313,991	Yulin (Shaanxi)	106,391	Matadi	172,730
Jiayuguan	114,510	Nanping	230,931	Tongchuan	304,809	Yumen	116,194	Mbandaka	169,841
Jieyang	204,134	Nantong	468,215	Tonghua	362,577	Yuncheng	172,620	Mbuji-Mayi	806,475
Jilin	1,165,418	Nanyang	477,128	Tongliao	305,885	Yunfu	168,371	Mwene-Ditu	137,459
Jimo	149,083	Nehe	128,191	Tongling	292,721	Yushu	171,692	Tshikapa	180,860
Jinan	1,713,036	Neijiang	320,777	Tongxiang	109,976	Yuyao	136,464	Uvira	115,590
Jinchang	141,578	Ning'an	143,722	Tongzhou	365,003	Yuzhou	133,619		
Jincheng	200,659	Ningbo	704,819	Tumen	102,191	Zalantun	143,273	**Congo, Rep. of the**	
Jingdezhen	315,036	Ningguo	108,767	Ulanhot	182,128	Zaoyang	211,295	(1992 est.)	
Jingjiang	136,204	Panjin	471,729	Ürümqi	1,258,457	Zaozhuang	741,421	★ Brazzaville	937,579
Jingmen	388,780	Panshi	165,101	Wafangdian	305,249	Zengcheng	197,023	Pointe-Noire	576,206
Jingzhou	596,860	Panzhihua	488,911	Weifang	621,125	Zhangjiagang	168,546		
Jinhua	199,649	Penglai	114,440	Weihai	287,872	Zhangjiajie	115,896	**Costa Rica** (2000 est.)	
Jining (Inner Mongolia)	206,514	Pengzhou	122,074	Weinan	210,079	Zhangjiakou	660,504	★ San José	344,349[13]
Jining (Shandong)	427,256	Pingdingshan	619,694	Wendeng	183,952	Zhangqiu	207,212		
Jinjiang	126,102	Pingdu	198,558	Wenling	134,074	Zhangshu	112,600	**Côte d'Ivoire**	
Jinzhou	658,589	Pingliang	124,447	Wenzhou	512,523	Zhangye	114,592	(1995 est.)	
Jishou	114,650	Pingxiang	392,286	Wuchang	227,856	Zhangzhou	231,333	★ Abidjan (de facto; legislative)	3,199,000[2]
Jiujiang	361,645	Pizhou	159,194	Wuchuan	184,812	Zhanjiang	588,583	Bouaké	330,000
Jiutai	198,316	Pulandian	166,331	Wudalianchi	157,547	Zhaodong	227,218	Daloa	123,000
Jixi	752,840	Puning	312,498	Wuhai	316,718	Zhaoqing	311,571	Korhogo	109,445[14]
Jiyuan	241,406	Putian	145,051	Wuhan	3,911,824	Zhaotong	104,382	★ Yamoussoukro (de jure; administrative)	110,000
Jurong	108,555	Puyang	289,232	Wuhu	495,765	Zhaoyuan	172,646		
Kaifeng	569,300	Qianjiang	313,500	Wujiang	176,514	Zhengzhou	1,465,069	**Croatia** (2001)	
Kaili	149,939	Qidong	231,611	Wujin	141,495	Zhenjiang	469,977	Rijeka	147,709
Kaiping	188,795	Qilin	210,230	Wuwei	181,328	Zhijiang	126,808	Split	173,692
Kaiyuan (Liaoning)	132,481	Qingdao	1,702,108	Wuxi	940,858	Zhongshan	390,060	★ Zagreb	682,598[15]
Kaiyuan (Yunnan)	104,329	Qingyuan	193,284	Wuxian	176,694	Zhongxiang	224,442		
Karamay	225,251	Qingzhou	193,996	Wuxue	142,136	Zhoukou	189,377	**Cuba** (1994 est.)	
Kashgar (Kashi)	205,056	Qinhuangdao	485,143	Wuzhou	253,159	Zhoushan	196,368	Bayamo	137,663
Korla	200,374	Qinzhou	172,379	Xiamen (Amoy)	593,401	Zhuanghe	161,223	Camagüey	293,961
Kuitun	144,048	Qiongshan	144,979	Xi'an (Sian)	2,294,790	Zhucheng	145,952	Ciego de Ávila	104,060[5]
Kunming	1,350,640	Qiqihar (Tsitsihar)	1,115,766	Xiangcheng	103,692	Zhuhai	371,116	Cienfuegos	132,038
Kunshan	177,003	Qitaihe	289,111	Xiangfan	597,604	Zhuji	116,116	Guantánamo	207,796
Laiwu	382,785	Qixia	115,089	Xiangtan	518,783	Zhumadian	204,020	★ Havana	2,198,392[16]
Laixi	118,709	Quanzhou	281,906	Xiangxiang	103,871	Zhuozhou	109,390	Holguín	242,085
Laiyang	166,824	Qufu	157,201	Xianning	249,234	Zhuzhou	528,958	Las Tunas	126,930
Laizhou	206,786	Quzhou	151,122	Xiantao	412,434	Zibo	1,458,060	Manzanillo	109,471[5]
Langfang	241,984	Renqiu	158,242	Xianyang	460,976	Zigong	464,497	Matanzas	123,843
Langzhong	112,118	Rizhao	322,190	Xiaogan	224,026	Zixing	123,747	Pinar del Río	128,570
Lanxi	103,792	Rongcheng	203,263	Xiaoshan	220,815	Ziyang	145,665	Santa Clara	205,400
Lanzhou	1,429,673	Rugao	276,028	Xiaoyi	117,133	Zoucheng	302,856	Santiago de Cuba	440,084
Laohekou	162,343	Rui'an	164,563	Xichang	174,781	Zunyi	464,945		
Lechang	177,572	Rushan	116,166	Xingcheng	120,431			**Cyprus** (1998 est.)	
Leiyang	163,278	Ruzhou	102,691	Xinghua	199,023	**Colombia** (1999 est.)		Limassol	152,900
Leizhou	226,310	Sanhe	108,252	Xingning	206,712	Armenia	281,422	★ Lefkosia (Nicosia)	194,100[17]
Lengshuijiang	176,182	Sanmenxia	189,084	Xingping	108,491	Barrancabermeja	178,020		
Leping	129,376	Sanming	199,201	Xingtai	387,081	Barranquilla	1,223,260	**Czech Republic**	
Leqing	103,118	Sanshui	145,279	Xinhui	269,528	Bello	333,470	(2000 est.)	
Leshan	410,423	Sanya	161,869	Xining	604,812	Bucaramanga	515,555	Brno	383,569
Lhasa	121,568	Shanghai	8,937,171	Xinmin	123,655	Buenaventura	224,336	Olomouc	103,015
Lianjiang	246,638	Shangqiu	317,948	Xintai	381,637	Buga	110,699	Ostrava	321,263
Lianyuan	133,059	Shangrao	168,263	Xinxiang	583,408	Cali	2,077,386	Plzeň	167,534
Lianyungang	447,918	Shangyu	116,279	Xinyang	366,304	Cartagena	805,757	★ Prague	1,186,855
Liaocheng	275,271	Shangzhi	228,273	Xinyi (Guangdong)	170,368	Cartago	125,884		
Liaoyang	570,483	Shantou	831,949	Xinyi (Jiangsu)	127,496	Cúcuta	606,932	**Denmark** (2000 est.; MU)	
Liaoyuan	391,841	Shanwei	171,380	Xinyu	250,666	Dos Quebradas	159,363	Ålborg	161,161
Liling	135,453	Shaoguan	431,053	Xinzheng	136,980	Envigado	135,848	Århus	284,846
Linchuan	232,592	Shaoxing	233,954	Xinzhou	143,840	Florencia	108,574	★ Copenhagen	495,699
Linfen	257,684	Shaoyang	311,261	Xishan	171,316	Floridablanca	221,913	Odense	183,912
Lingbao	114,053	Shenyang	3,876,289	Xuanwei	120,046	Girardot	110,963		
Lingyuan	141,481	Shenzhen	899,111	Xuanzhou	136,914	Ibagué	393,664		

country / city	population
Djibouti (1995 est.)	
★ Djibouti	383,000
Dominica (1991)	
★ Roseau	15,853
Dominican Republic (1993)	
La Romana	140,204
San Francisco de Macorís	108,485
San Pedro de Macorís	124,735
Santiago	365,463
★ Santo Domingo	1,609,966[18]
East Timor (1999 est.)	
★ Dili	65,000
Ecuador (1997 est.)	
Ambato	160,302
Cuenca	255,028
Duran	135,675
Eloy Alfaro	120,364[4]
Esmeraldas	117,722
Guayaquil	1,973,880
Ibarra	119,243
Loja	117,365
Machala	197,350
Manta	156,981
Milagro	119,371
Portoviejo	167,956
Quevedo	120,640
★ Quito	1,487,513
Riobamba	117,270
Santo Domingo	183,219
Egypt (1996)	
Alexandria	3,328,196
Al-ʿArīsh	100,447
Aswān	219,017
Asyūṭ	343,498
Banhā	145,792
Banī Suwayf	172,032
Bilbays	113,608
Būr Saʿīd (Port Said)	469,533
★ Cairo	6,789,479
Damanhūr	212,203
Al-Fayyūm	260,964
Al-Ismāʿīlīyah	254,477
Al-Jīzah (Giza)	2,221,868
Kafr ad-Dawwar	231,978
Kafr ash-Shaykh	124,819
Al-Maḥallah al-Kubrā	395,402
Mallawī	119,283
Al-Manṣūrah	369,621
Al-Minyā	201,360
Mīt Ghamr	101,801
Qinā	171,275
Sawhāj	170,125
Shibīn al-Kawm	159,909
Shubrā al-Khaymah	870,716
As-Suways (Suez)	417,610
Ṭanṭā	371,010
Al-Uqṣur (Luxor)	360,503
Az-Zaqāzīq	267,351
El Salvador (1992)	
Mejicanos	131,972[19]
San Miguel	127,696
★ San Salvador	415,346
Santa Ana	139,389
Soyapango	261,122[19]
Equatorial Guinea (1995 est.)	
★ Malabo	47,500
Eritrea (1995 est.)	
★ Asmara	431,000
Estonia (2000 est.)	
★ Tallinn	404,000
Tartu	101,000
Ethiopia (1994)	
★ Addis Ababa	2,112,737
Dire Dawa	164,851
Gonder	112,249
Harer (Harar)	131,139
Jima	106,842
Nazret	127,842
Faroe Islands (2000 est.)	
★ Tórshavn	16,474
Fiji (1996)	
★ Suva	77,366

country / city	population
Finland (2000 est.)	
Espoo	209,667
★ Helsinki	551,123
Oulu	117,670
Tampere	193,174
Turku	172,107
Vantaa	176,386
France (1999)	
Aix-en-Provence	134,222
Amiens	135,501
Angers	151,279
Besançon	117,304
Bordeaux	215,118
Boulogne-Billancourt	106,367
Brest	149,634
Caen	113,987
Clermont-Ferrand	137,140
Dijon	149,867
Grenoble	153,317
Le Havre	190,651
Le Mans	146,105
Lille	182,228
Limoges	133,960
Lyon	445,257
Marseille	797,486
Metz	123,776
Montpellier	225,392
Mulhouse	110,359
Nancy	103,605
Nantes	268,695
Nice	342,738
Nîmes	133,424
Orléans	112,833
★ Paris	2,123,261
agglomeration	9,608,000[2]
Perpignan	105,115
Reims	187,206
Rennes	206,229
Rouen	106,035
Saint-Étienne	179,755
Strasbourg	263,940
Toulon	159,389
Toulouse	390,413
Tours	132,820
Villeurbanne	124,215
French Guiana (1999)	
★ Cayenne	50,594
French Polynesia (1996)	
★ Papeete	25,353
agglomeration	121,000[2]
Gabon (1993)	
★ Libreville	362,386
Gambia, The (1993)	
★ Banjul	42,407
agglomeration	270,540
Gaza Strip (1999 est.)	
★ Gaza (Ghazzah; acting administrative centre)	388,031
Jabālyah	113,901[20]
Khān Yūnus	123,175[20]
Georgia (1997 est.)	
Batʿumi (Batumi)	137,100
Kʿutʿaisi (Kutaisi)	240,000
Rustʿavi (Rustavi)	158,000
★ Tʿbilisi (Tbilisi)	1,398,968[16]
Zugdidi	105,000[21]
Germany (1999 est.)	
Aachen	243,600
Augsburg	254,500
Bergisch Gladbach	105,963[16]
★ Berlin	3,392,900
Bielefeld	321,600
Bochum	392,900
Bonn	304,100
Bottrop	121,500
Braunschweig	246,800
Bremen	542,300
Bremerhaven	123,800
Chemnitz	266,000
Cologne (Köln)	963,200
Cottbus	112,200
Darmstadt	137,600
Dortmund	590,300
Dresden	477,700
Duisburg	521,300
Düsseldorf	568,500
Erfurt	202,100
Erlangen	100,600
Essen	600,700
Frankfurt am Main	644,700

country / city	population
Freiburg im Breisgau	201,000
Fürth	109,700
Gelsenkirchen	283,300
Gera	115,800
Göttingen	127,366[16]
Hagen	206,400
Halle	258,500
Hamburg	1,701,800
Hamm	181,500
Hannover	515,200
Heidelberg	139,400
Heilbronn	119,900
Herne	176,200
Hildesheim	105,405[16]
Ingolstadt	114,500
Kaiserslautern	100,300
Karlsruhe	276,700
Kassel	196,700
Kiel	235,500
Koblenz	108,700
Krefeld	242,800
Leipzig	490,000
Leverkusen	161,100
Lübeck	213,800
Ludwigshafen	164,200
Magdeburg	238,000
Mainz	185,600
Mannheim	308,400
Moers	106,704[16]
Mönchengladbach	264,100
Mülheim an der Ruhr	174,300
Munich (München)	1,193,600
Münster	264,700
Neuss	149,206[16]
Nürnberg	486,400
Oberhausen	222,300
Offenbach am Main	116,400
Oldenburg	154,100
Osnabrück	164,900
Paderborn	131,851[16]
Pforzheim	117,500
Potsdam	129,500
Recklinghausen	126,241[16]
Regensburg	125,200
Remscheid	119,500
Reutlingen	109,882[16]
Rostock	205,900
Saarbrücken	186,402[16]
Salzgitter	113,700
Schwerin	104,200
Siegen	110,847[16]
Solingen	165,400
Stuttgart	581,200
Ulm	116,000
Wiesbaden	268,200
Witten	103,872[16]
Wolfsburg	122,200
Wuppertal	370,700
Würzburg	126,000
Zwickau	104,900
Ghana (1998 est.)	
★ Accra	1,446,000
Kumasi	578,000
Tamale	229,000
Tema	300,000
Greece (1991)	
★ Athens	772,072
Iráklion	116,178
Kallithéa	114,233
Larissa	112,777
Pátrai (Patras)	153,344
Peristérion	137,288
Piraiévs (Piraeus)	182,671
Thessaloníki	383,967
Greenland (2000 est.)	
★ Nuuk (Godthåb)	13,838
Grenada (1991)	
★ Saint George's	4,621
agglomeration	35,000[2]
Guadeloupe (1999)	
★ Basse-Terre	12,549
Guam (1995 est.)	
★ Hagåtña (Agana)	2,000
Guatemala (1994)	
★ Guatemala City	823,301
agglomeration	3,119,000[2]
Mixco	209,791[22]
Villa Nueva	101,295[22]
Guernsey (1996)	
★ St. Peter Port	16,194

country / city	population
Guinea (1999 est.)	
★ Conakry	1,764,000
Guinea-Bissau (1999 est.)	
★ Bissau	274,000
Guyana (1999 est.)	
★ Georgetown	275,000
Haiti (1997 est.)	
Cap-Haïtien	107,026
Carrefour	306,074
Delmas	257,247
★ Port-au-Prince	917,112
Honduras (1999 est.)	
El Progreso	104,100
La Ceiba	103,400
San Pedro Sula	452,100
★ Tegucigalpa	988,400[23]
Hong Kong (2001 est.)	
★ Hong Kong	6,732,100[24]
Hungary (2000 est.)	
★ Budapest	1,811,552
Debrecen	203,648
Györ	127,119
Kecskemét	105,606
Miskolc	172,357
Nyíregyháza	112,419
Pécs	157,332
Szeged	158,158
Székesfehérvár	105,119
Iceland (1999 est.)	
★ Reykjavík	109,184
India (1991)	
Abohar	107,163
Adoni	136,182
Agartala	157,358
Agra	891,790
Ahmadabad	2,876,710
Ahmadnagar	181,339
Aizawl	155,240
Ajmer	402,700
Akola	328,034
Alandur	125,244
Alappuzha (Alleppey)	174,666
Alibag	328,640
Aligarh	480,520
Allahabad (Prayag Raj)	792,858
Alwar	205,086
Ambala	119,338
Ambattur	215,424
Amravati	421,576
Amritsar	708,835
Amroha	137,061
Anand	110,266
Anantapur	174,924
Ara (Arrah)	157,082
Asansol	262,188
Avadi	183,215
Baharampur	115,144
Bahraich	135,400
Bally	184,474
Balurghat	119,796
Bangalore	2,660,088
Bankura	114,876
Baranagar (Barahanagar)	224,821
Barasat	102,660
Barddhaman (Burdwan)	245,079
Bareilly	587,211
Barrackpore	133,265
Basirhat	101,409
Bathinda (Bhatinda)	159,042
Beawar	105,363
Belgaum	326,399
Bellary	245,391
Bhagalpur	253,225
Bharatpur	148,519
Bharuch (Broach)	133,102
Bhatpara	304,952
Bhavnagar	402,338
Bhilainagar	395,360
Bhilwara	183,965
Bhimavaram	121,314
Bhind	109,755
Bhiwandi	379,070
Bhiwani	121,629
Bhopal	1,062,771
Bhubaneshwar	411,542
Bhuj	102,176
Bhusawal	145,143
Bid (Bhir)	112,434

country / city	population
Bidar	108,016
Bidhan Nagar	100,048
Bihar Sharif	201,323
Bijapur	186,939
Bikaner	416,289
Bilaspur	179,833
Bokaro (Bokaro Steel City)	333,683
Brahmapur	210,418
Budaun	116,695
Bulandshahr	127,201
Burhanpur	172,710
Burnpur	174,933
Champdani	101,067
Chandannagar	120,378
Chandigarh	504,094
Chandrapur	226,105
Chennai (Madras)	3,841,396
Chhapra	136,877
Chittoor	133,462
Coimbatore	816,321
Cuddalore	144,561
Cuddapah	121,463
Cuttack	403,418
Dabgram	147,217
Darbhanga	218,391
Davanagere	266,082
Dehra Dun	270,159
Delhi	7,206,704
Dewas	164,364
Dhanbad	151,789
Dhule (Dhulia)	278,317
Dibrugarh	120,127
Dindigul	182,447
Durg	150,645
Durgapur	425,836
Eluru	212,866
Erode	159,232
Etawah	124,072
Faizabad	124,437
Faridabad	617,717
Farrukhabad-cum-Fatehgarh	194,567
Fatehpur	117,675
Fīrozabad	215,128
Gadag-Betigeri	134,051
Gandhidham	104,585
Gandhinagar	123,359
Ganganagar	161,482
Gaya	219,675
Ghaziabad	454,156
Gondia	109,470
Gorakhpur	505,566
Gudivada	101,656
Gulbarga	304,099
Guna	100,490
Guntakal	107,592
Guntur	471,051
Gurgaon	121,486
Guwahati (Gauhati)	584,342
Gwalior	690,765
Habra	100,223
Haldia	100,347
Haldwani-cum-Kathgodam	104,195
Halisahar	114,028
Haora (Howrah)	950,435
Hapur	146,262
Haridwar (Hardwar)	147,305
Hathras	113,285
Hindupur	104,651
Hisar (Hissar)	172,677
Hoshiarpur	122,705
Hubli-Dharwad	648,298
Hugli-Chunchura	151,806
Hyderabad	3,145,939
Ichalkaranji	214,950
Imphal	198,535
Indore	1,091,674
Ingraj Bazar (English Bazar)	139,204
Jabalpur	741,927
Jaipur	1,458,183
Jalandhar (Jullundur)	509,510
Jalgaon	242,193
Jalna	174,985
Jammu	225,000[5, 25]
Jamnagar	341,637
Jamshedpur	478,950
Jaunpur	136,062
Jhansi	300,850
Jodhpur	666,279
Junagadh	130,484
Kakinada	279,980
Kalyan	1,014,557
Kamarhati	266,889
Kanchipuram	144,955
Kanchrapara	100,194
Kanpur	1,874,409

Major cities and national capitals (continued)

country / city	population
Karimnagar	148,583
Karnal	173,751
Katihar	135,436
Khammam	127,992
Khandwa	143,133
Kharagpur	177,989
Kochi (Cochin)	564,589
Kolhapur	406,370
Kolkata (Calcutta)	4,399,819
Kollam (Quilon)	139,852
Korba	124,501
Kota	537,371
Kozhikode (Calicut)	419,831
Krishnanagar	121,110
Kukatpalle	186,963
Kulti-Barakar	108,518
Kumbakonam	139,483
Kurnool	236,800
Lalbahadur Nagar	155,514
Latur	197,408
Lucknow	1,619,115
Ludhiana	1,042,740
Machilipatnam (Masulipatam)	159,110
Madurai	940,989
Mahbubnagar	116,833
Malegaon	342,595
Malkajgiri	127,178
Mandya	120,265
Mangalore	273,304
Mango	108,100
Mathura	226,691
Maunath Bhanjan	136,697
Medinipur (Midnapore)	125,498
Meerut	753,778
Mira-Bhayandar	175,605
Miraj	121,593
Mizapur-cum-Vindhyachal	169,336
Modinagar	101,660
Moga	108,304
Moradabad	429,214
Morena	147,124
Mumbai (Bombay)	9,925,891
Munger (Monghyr)	150,112
Murwara (Katni)	163,431
Muzaffarnagar	240,609
Muzaffarpur	241,107
Mysore	480,692
Nadiad	167,051
Nagercoil	190,084
Nagpur	1,624,752
Naihati	132,701
Nanded (Nander)	275,083
Nandyal	119,813
Nashik (Nasik)	656,925
Navadwip	125,037
Navsari	126,089
Nellore	316,606
New Bombay	307,724
★ New Delhi	301,297
Neyveli	118,080
Nizamabad	241,034
Noida	146,514
North Barrackpore	100,606
North Dum Dum	149,965
Ongole	100,836
Palghat (Palakkad)	123,289
Pali	136,842
Pallavaram	111,866
Panihati	275,990
Panipat	191,212
Parbhani	190,255
Pathankot	123,930
Patiala	238,368
Patna	917,243
Pilibhit	106,605
Pimpri-Chinchwad	517,083
Pondicherry	203,065
Porbandar	116,671
Proddatur	133,914
Pune	1,566,651
Puri	125,199
Purnia (Purnea)	114,912
Qutubullapur	106,591
Rae Bareli	129,904
Raichur	157,551
Raiganj	151,045
Raipur	438,639
Raj Nandgaon	125,371
Rajahmundry	324,851
Rajapalaiyam	114,202
Rajkot	559,407
Ramagundam	214,384
Rampur	243,742
Ranchi	599,306
Ratlam	183,375
Raurkela Civil Township	140,408
Raurkela Steel Township	215,509
Rewa	128,981
Rishra	102,815
Rohtak	216,096
Sagar	195,346
Saharanpur	374,945
Salem	366,712
Sambalpur	131,138
Sambhal	150,869
Sangli	193,197
Satna	156,630
Shahjahanpur	237,713
Shambajinagar (Aurangābād)	573,272
Shantipur	109,956
Shiliguri (Siliguri)	216,950
Shillong	131,719
Shimoga	179,258
Shivpuri	108,277
Sholapur (Solapur)	604,215
Shrirampur	137,028
Sikandarabad (Secunderabad) Cantonment	171,148
Sikar	148,272
Silchar	115,483
Sirsa	112,841
Sitapur	121,842
Sonipat (Sonepat)	143,922
South Dum Dum	232,811
Srinagar	700,000[5, 25]
Surat	1,498,817
Surendranagar	106,110
Tambaram	107,187
Tenali	143,726
Thalassery (Tellicherry)	103,579
Thane (Thana)	803,389
Thanjavur	202,013
Thiruvananthapuram (Trivandrum)	524,006
Tiruchchirappalli	387,223
Tirunelueli	135,825
Tirupati	174,369
Tirupper (Tiruppur)	235,661
Tiruvannamalai	109,196
Tiruvottiyur	168,642
Titagarh	114,085
Tonk	100,079
Tumkur	138,903
Tuticorin	199,854
Udaipur	308,571
Ujjain	362,266
Ulhasnagar	369,077
Uluberia	155,172
Unnao	107,425
Uttarpara-Kotrung	101,268
Vadodara (Baroda)	1,031,346
Valparai	106,523
Varanasi (Benares)	929,270
Vellore	175,061
Vijayawada	701,827
Vishakhapatnam	752,037
Vizianagaram	160,359
Warangal	447,657
Wardha	102,985
Yamunanagar	144,346
Yavatmal (Yeotmal)	108,578

Indonesia (1995 est.)[26]

city	population
Ambon	249,312
Balikpapan	338,752
Banda Aceh	143,360[10]
Bandar Lampung	457,927[10]
Bandung	2,356,120
Banjarmasin	482,931
Bekasi	644,284[10]
Bengkulu	146,395[10]
Binjai	127,184[10]
Blitar	112,986[10]
Bogor	285,114
Cianjur	114,335[10]
Cibinong	101,317[10]
Cilacap	206,928[10]
Cilegon-Merak	116,981[10]
Cimahi	344,607[10]
Ciomas	187,379[10]
Ciparay	111,467[10]
Ciputat	270,815[10]
Cirebon	254,406
Citeurup	105,079[10]
Denpasar	345,150[10]
Depok (West Java)	106,825[10]
Depok (Yogyakarta)	661,495[10]
★ Jakarta	9,112,652
Jambi	385,201
Jember	218,529[10]
Karawang (Krawang)	145,041[10]
Kediri	253,760
Klaten	103,327[10]
Kupang	129,259[10]
Lhokseumawe	109,569[10]
Madiun	171,532
Magelang	123,800
Malang	716,862
Manado	332,288
Mataram	275,089[10]
Medan	1,843,919
Padang	534,474
Palembang	1,222,764
Palu	142,767[10]
Pangkalpinang	108,377[10]
Pasuruan	133,685[9]
Pekalongan	301,504
Pekanbaru	438,638
Pemalang	103,540[10]
Pematang Siantar	203,056
Percut	129,036[10]
Pondokgede	263,152[10]
Pontianak	409,632
Probolinggo	120,770
Purwokerto	202,452[10]
Salatiga	103,000
Samarinda	399,175
Semarang	1,104,405
Serang	122,429[10]
Sukabumi	125,766
Surabaya	2,663,820
Surakarta	516,594
Taman	106,975[10]
Tangerang	887,952[10]
Tanjung Balai	101,644[10]
Tanjung Karang	680,332
Tasikmalaya	179,766[10]
Tebingtinggi	129,300
Tegal	289,744
Ujung Pandang	1,060,257
Waru	124,282[10]
Yogyakarta	418,944

Iran (1996)

city	population
Ābādān	206,073
Ahvāz	804,980
Āmol	159,092
Andīmeshk	106,923
Arāk	380,755
Ardabīl	340,386
Bābol	158,346
Bandar 'Abbās	273,578
Bandar-e Būshehr (Būshehr)	143,641
Bīrjand	127,608
Bojnūrd	134,835
Borūjerd	217,804
Būkān	120,020
Dezfūl	202,639
Emāmshahr (Shāhrūd)	104,765
Eṣfahān (Isfahan)	1,266,072
Gonbad-e Kavus	111,253
Gorgān	188,710
Hamadān	401,281
Īlām	126,346
Islāmshahr (Eslāmshahr)	265,450
Karaj	940,968[27]
Kāshān	201,372
Kermān	384,991
Kermānshāh (Bākhtarān)	692,986
Khomeynīshahr	165,888
Khorramābād	272,815
Khorramshahr	105,636
Khvoy (Khoy)	148,944
Mahābād	107,799
Malāyer	144,373
Marāgheh	132,318
Marv Dasht	103,579
Mashhad (Meshed)	1,887,405
Masjed-e Soleymān	116,882
Najafābād	178,498
Neyshābūr	158,847
Orūmīyeh	435,200
Qā'emshahr	143,286
Qarchak	142,690
Qazvīn	291,117
Qods	138,278
Qom	777,677
Rasht	417,748
Sabzevār	170,738
Sanandaj	277,808
Saqqez	115,394
Sārī	195,882
Sāveh	111,245
Shahr-e Kord	100,477
Shīrāz	1,053,025
Sīrjān	135,024
Tabrīz	1,191,043
★ Tehrān	6,758,845
Vāramīn	107,233
Yazd	326,776
Zābol	100,888
Zāhedān	419,518
Zanjān	286,295

Iraq (1987)

city	population
Al-'Amārah	208,797
★ Baghdad	4,689,000[2, 28]
Ba'qūbah	114,516[29]
Al-Baṣrah	406,296
Al-Ḥillah	268,834
Dīwanīyah	196,519
Irbīl	485,968
Karbalā'	296,705
Karkūk	418,624
Al-Kūt	183,183
Mosul	664,221
An-Najaf	309,010
An-Nāṣirīyah	265,937
Ar-Ramādī	192,556
As-Sulaymānīyah	364,096

Ireland (1996)

city	population
Cork	127,092[30]
★ Dublin	480,996[30]

Isle of Man (1996)

city	population
★ Douglas	23,487

Israel (1999 est.)

city	population
Ashdod	155,800
Bat Yam	137,000
Beersheba (Be'er Sheva')	163,700
Bene Beraq	133,900
Haifa (Ḥefa)	265,700
Ḥolon	163,100
★ Jerusalem (Yerushalayim, Al-Quds)	633,700
Netanya	154,900
Petaḥ Tiqwa	159,400
Ramat Gan	126,900
Rishon LeZiyyon	188,200
Tel Aviv–Yafo	348,100

Italy (2000 est.)[31]

city	population
Bari	331,848
Bergamo	117,837
Bologna	381,161
Brescia	191,317
Cagliari	165,926
Catania	337,862
Ferrara	132,127
Florence (Firenze)	376,682
Foggia	154,891
Forlì	107,475
Genoa (Genova)	636,104
Latina	114,099
Livorno	161,673
Messina	259,156
Milan (Milano)	1,300,977
Modena	176,022
Monza	119,516
Naples (Napoli)	1,002,619
Novara	102,037
Padua (Padova)	211,391
Palermo	683,794
Parma	168,717
Perugia	156,673
Pescara	115,698
Prato	172,473
Ravenna	138,418
Reggio di Calabria	179,617
Reggio nell'Emilia	143,664
Rimini	131,062
★ Rome (Roma)	2,643,581
Salerno	142,055
Sassari	120,803
Siracusa (Syracuse)	126,282
Taranto	208,214
Terni	107,770
Trento	104,906
Trieste	216,459
Turin (Torino)	903,703
Venice (Venezia)	277,305
Verona	255,268
Vicenza	109,738

Jamaica (1991)

city	population
★ Kingston	103,771
agglomeration	655,000[2]

Japan (1995)

city	population
Abiko	124,257
Ageo	206,090
Aizuwakamatsu	119,640
Akashi	287,606
Akishima	107,292
Akita	311,948
Amagasaki	488,586
Anjō	149,464
Aomori	294,167
Asahikawa	360,568
Asaka	110,789
Ashikaga	165,828
Atsugi	208,627
Beppu	128,255
Chiba	856,878
Chigasaki	212,874
Chōfu	198,574
Daitō	128,838
Ebetsu	115,495
Ebina	113,430
Fuchu	216,211
Fuji	229,187
Fujieda	124,822
Fujinomiya	119,536
Fujisawa	368,651
Fukaya	100,285
Fukui	255,604
Fukuoka	1,284,795
Fukushima	285,754
Fukuyama	374,517
Funabashi	540,817
Gifu	407,134
Habikino	117,735
Hachinohe	242,654
Hachiōji	503,363
Hadano	164,722
Hakodate	298,881
Hamamatsu	561,606
Handa	106,452
Higashi-Hiroshima	113,939
Higashi-Kurume	111,097
Higashi-Murayama	135,112
Higashi-Ōsaka	517,232
Hikone	103,508
Himeji	470,986
Hino	166,537
Hirakata	400,144
Hiratsuka	253,822
Hirosaki	177,972
Hiroshima	1,108,888
Hitachi	199,244
Hitachinaka	146,750
Hōfu	118,803
Hoya	100,260
Ibaraki	258,233
Ichihara	277,061
Ichikawa	440,555
Ichinomiya	267,362
Iida	106,772
Ikeda	104,293
Ikoma	106,726
Imabari	120,214
Iruma	144,402
Ise	102,632
Isesaki	120,236
Ishinomaki	121,208
Itami	188,431
Iwaki	360,598
Iwakuni	107,386
Iwatsuki	109,546
Izumi	157,300
Joetsu	132,205
Kadoma	140,506
Kagamigahara	131,955
Kagoshima	546,282
Kakogawa	260,567
Kamakura	170,329
Kanazawa	453,975
Kariya	125,305
Kashihara	121,988
Kashiwa	317,750
Kasugai	277,589
Kasukabe	200,121
Kawachi-Nagano	117,082
Kawagoe	323,353
Kawaguchi	448,854
Kawanishi	144,539
Kawasaki	1,202,820
Kiryū	120,377
Kisarazu	123,499
Kishiwada	194,818
Kita-Kyūshū	1,019,598
Kitami	110,452
Kobe	1,423,792
Kochi	321,999
Kodaira	172,946
Kofu	201,124
Koganei	109,279
Kokubunji	105,786
Komaki	137,165
Komatsu	107,965
Koriyama	326,833
Koshigaya	298,253

country city	population	country city	population	country city	population	country city	population	country city	population
Kumagaya	156,429	Ueda	123,284	Chŏng-ŭp	139,011	**Macau** (2000 est.)		Cuautla Morelos	137,000
Kumamoto	650,341	Uji	184,830	Chŏnju	563,153	★ Macau	440,000	Cuernavaca	330,000
Kurashiki	422,836	Urawa	453,300	Ch'unch'ŏn	234,528			Culiacán	536,942[34]
Kure	209,485	Urayasu	123,654	Ch'ungju	205,206	**Macedonia** (1994)		Durango	430,000
Kurume	234,433	Utsunomiya	435,357	Hanam	115,812	★ Skopje (Skopije)	444,299	Ecatepec	
Kusatsu	101,828	Wakayama	393,885	Iksan (Iri)	322,685			(de Morelos)	1,619,000
Kushiro	199,323	Yachiyo	154,509	Inch'ŏn (Incheon)	2,308,188	**Madagascar** (1993)		Ensenada	222,687[34]
Kuwana	103,044	Yaizu	115,931	Kangnŭng	220,403	★ Antananarivo	1,103,304	General Escobedo	230,000
Kyōto	1,463,822	Yamagata	254,488	Kimch'ŏn	147,027	Antsirabe	126,062	Gómez Palacio	210,000
Machida	360,525	Yamaguchi	135,579	Kimhae	256,370	Fianarantsoa	109,248	Guadalajara	1,647,000
Maebashi	284,788	Yamato	203,933	Kimje	115,427	Mahajanga	106,780	Guadalupe	668,500
Matsubara	134,457	Yao	276,664	Kŏje	147,562	Toamasina	137,782	Hermosillo	544,889[34]
Matsudo	461,503	Yatsushiro	107,709	Kongju	131,229			Heroica Nogales	
Matsue	147,416	Yokkaichi	285,779	Koyang	518,282	**Malawi** (1998 est.)		(Nogales)	157,000
Matsumoto	205,523	Yokohama	3,307,136	Kumi	311,431	★ Blantyre (executive;		Huixquilucan	110,000
Matsuyama	460,968	Yokosuka	432,193	Kunp'o	235,233	judicial)	478,155	Iguala	105,000
Matsuzaka	122,449	Yonago	134,762	Kunsan	266,569	★ Lilongwe (ministerial;		Irapuato	320,000
Minō	127,542	Zama	118,159	Kuri	142,173	financial; legislative)	435,964	Ixtapaluca	240,000
Misato	133,600			Kwangju	1,257,636			Jiutepec	140,000
Mishima	107,890	**Jersey** (1996)		Kwangmyŏng	350,914	**Malaysia** (1991)		Juárez	
Mitaka	165,721	★ St. Helier	27,523	Kwangyang	122,052	Alor Setar	125,026	(Ciudad Juárez)	1,190,000
Mito	246,347			Kyŏngju	273,968	George Town (Pinang)	219,376	La Paz	162,795[34]
Miyakonojō	132,714	**Jordan** (1994)		Kyŏngsan	173,746	Ipoh	382,633	León	1,019,510[34]
Miyazaki	300,068	★ Amman	969,598	Masan	441,242	Johor Baharu	328,646	Los Mochis	200,000
Moriguchi	157,306	Irbid	208,329	Miryang	121,501	Kelang (Port Kelang)	243,698	Los Reyes la Paz	213,040[34]
Morioka	286,478	Ar-Ruṣayfah	137,247	Mokp'o	247,452	Kota Baharu	219,713	Matamoros	370,000
Muroran	109,766	Az-Zarqā'	350,849	Naju	107,831	★ Kuala Lumpur	1,145,075	Mazatlán	325,000
Musashino	135,051			Namwon	103,544	Kuala Terengganu	228,659	Mérida	660,848[34]
Nagano	358,516	**Kazakhstan** (1999)		Namyangju	229,060	Kuantan	198,356	Metepec	160,000
Nagaoka	190,470	Almaty (Alma-Ata)	1,129,400	P'ohang	508,899	Kuching	147,729	Mexicali	550,000
Nagareyama	146,245	Aqtaū (Aktau;		Poryŏng	122,604	Petaling Jaya	254,849	★ Mexico City	8,591,309[34]
Nagasaki	438,635	Shevchenko)	143,400	Puch'ŏn	779,412	Sandakan	126,092	Minatitlán	150,000
Nagoya	2,152,184	Aqtöbe (Aktyubinsk)	253,100	Pusan (Busan)	3,814,325	Selayang Baru	124,606	Monclova	192,000
Naha	301,890	★ Astana (Aqmola;		P'yŏngt'aek	312,927	Seremban	182,584	Monterrey	1,108,400
Nara	359,218	Tselinograd)	313,000	Sach'ŏn	113,494	Shah Alam	101,773	Morelia	549,404[34]
Narashino	152,887	Atyraū (Guryev)	142,500	Sangju	124,116	Sibu	126,384	Naucalpan	840,000
Neyagawa	258,443	Ekibastuz	127,200	★ Seoul (Sŏul)	10,231,217	Sungai Petani	115,719	Nezahualcóyotl	1,224,500
Niigata	494,769	Kökshetaū (Kokchetav)	123,400	Shihŭng	133,443	Taiping	183,165	Nicolás Romero	218,000
Niihama	127,917	Oral (Uralsk)	195,500	Sŏngnam	869,094			Nuevo Laredo	309,000
Niiza	144,726	Öskemen		Sŏsan	134,746	**Maldives** (1995)		Oaxaca	252,586[34]
Nishinomiya	390,389	(Ust-Kamenogorsk)	311,000	Sunch'ŏn	249,263	★ Male	62,973	Orizaba	118,400
Nobeoka	126,629	Pavlodar	300,500	Suwŏn	755,550			Pachuca	231,089[34]
Noda	119,790	Petropavl		Taegu	2,449,420	**Mali** (1996 est.)		Piedras Negras	125,000
Numazu	212,241	(Petropavlovsk)	203,500	Taejŏn	1,272,121	★ Bamako	809,552	Poza Rica de Hidalgo	151,500
Obihiro	171,715	Qaraghandy		Tongyŏng	131,717	Ségou	106,799	Puebla	1,270,989[34]
Odawara	200,103	(Karaganda)	436,900	Ŭijŏngbu	276,111			Puerta Vallarta	150,000
Ōgaki	149,759	Qostanay (Kustanay)	221,400	Ŭiwang	108,788	**Malta** (1999 est.)		Querétaro	535,468[34]
Ōita	426,979	Qyzylord (Kzyl-Orda)	157,400	Ulsan	967,429	★ Valletta	7,100	Reynosa	398,000
Okayama	615,757	Rūdny	109,500	Wŏnju	237,460	agglomeration	102,000	Salamanca	140,000
Okazaki	322,621	Semey (Semipalatinsk)	269,600	Yŏngch'ŏn	113,511			Saltillo	560,000
Okinawa	115,336	Shymkent (Shimkent;		Yŏngju	131,097	**Marshall Is.** (1999)		San Cristóbal	
Ōme	137,234	Chimkent)	360,100	Yŏsu	183,596	★ Majuro	23,676	de las Casas	112,000
Ōmiya	433,755	Taraz (Auliye-Ata;						San Luis Potosí	628,134[34]
Ōmuta	145,085	(Dzhambul)	330,100	**Kuwait** (1995)		**Martinique** (1999)		San Luis Río Colorado	125,000
Ōsaka	2,602,421	Temirtaū	170,500	As-Sālimīyah	130,215	★ Fort-de-France	94,049	San Nicolás de los	
Ōta	143,057			★ Kuwait (Al-Kuwayt)	28,859			Garzas	495,540[34]
Ōtaru	157,022	**Kenya** (1999)		agglomeration	1,165,000[2]	**Mauritania** (1999 est.)		San Pablo	
Ōtsu	276,332	Eldoret	111,882[32]	Qalīb ash-Shuyūkh	102,178	★ Nouakchott	881,000	de las Salinas	150,000
Oyama	150,115	Kisumu	192,733[32]					San Pedro Garza	
Saga	171,231	Machakos	143,274	**Kyrgyzstan** (1999 est.)		**Mauritius** (1999 est.)		García	126,000
Sagamihara	570,597	Meru	126,427	★ Bishkek (Frunze)	619,000[28]	★ Port Louis	147,648	Soledad de Graciano	
Sakai	802,993	Mombasa	461,753[32]	Osh	220,500[33]	Beau Bassin/Rose Hill	101,273	Sanchez	170,000
Sakata	101,230	★ Nairobi	2,143,254					Tampico	294,789[34]
Sakura	162,624	Nakuru	231,262	**Laos** (1999 est.)		**Mayotte** (1997; MU)		Tapachula	180,000
Sapporo	1,757,025	Nyeri	101,238	★ Vientiane (Viangchan)	534,000	★ Dzaoudzi (French		Tehuacán	204,358[34]
Sasebo	244,909					administrative)	10,796	Tepic	265,681[34]
Sayama	162,240	**Kiribati** (1990)		**Latvia** (2000 est.)		★ Mamoudzou (local		Texcoco (de Mora)	105,000
Sendai	971,297	★ Bairiki	2,226	Daugavpils	114,510	administrative)	32,774	Tijuana	1,150,000
Seto	129,393	agglomeration	32,000[2]	★ Rīga	788,283			Tlalnepantla	715,000
Shimizu	240,174					**Mexico** (2000 est.)		Tlaquepaque	460,000
Shimonoseki	259,795	**Korea, North** (1987 est.)		**Lebanon** (1998 est.)		Acapulco	619,253[34]	Toluca	435,000
Shizuoka	474,092	Anju	186,000	Baalbek (Ba'labakk)	150,000	Aguascalientes	594,056[34]	Tonala	310,000
Sōka	217,930	Ch'ŏngjin	582,480[1]	★ Beirut (Bayrūt)	1,500,000	Atizapán de Zaragoza		Torreón	505,000
Suita	342,760	Haeju	195,000	Jūniyah	100,000	(Ciudad López		Tultitlan (Buenavista)	192,000
Suzuka	179,800	Hamhŭng-Hŭngnam	709,000[1]	Tripoli (Ṭarābulus)	160,000	Mateos)	467,000	Tuxtla Gutiérrez	425,000
Tachikawa	157,884	Hŭich'ŏn	163,000			Boca del Río	124,000	Uruapan	227,000
Tajimi	101,270	Kaesŏng	334,433[1]	**Lesotho** (1996 est.)		Campeche	195,000	Valle de Chalco (Xico)	323,000
Takamatsu	331,004	Kanggye	211,000	★ Maseru	160,100	Cancún	400,000	Veracruz	410,000
Takaoka	173,607	Kimch'aek (Songjin)	179,000	agglomeration	373,000[2]	Celaya	270,000	Villahermosa	330,605[34]
Takarazuka	202,544	Kusŏng	177,000			Chalco	123,000	Xalapa (Jalapa	
Takasaki	238,133	Namp'o	731,448[1]	**Liberia** (1999 est.)		Chetumal	118,000	Enríquez)	375,000
Takatsuki	362,270	★ P'yŏngyang	3,136,000[2, 28]	★ Monrovia	479,000[28]	Chihuahua	650,000	Zacatecas	113,780[34]
Tama	148,113	Sinp'o	158,000			Chilpancingo	140,000	Zamora de Hidalgo	121,000
Tokorozawa	320,406	Sinŭiju	326,011[1]	**Libya** (1995 est.)		Chimalhuacán	488,000	Zapopan	912,000
Tokushima	268,706	Sunch'ŏn	356,000	Banghāzī	650,000	Ciudad Acuña			
Tokuyama	108,671	Tanch'ŏn	284,000	Miṣrātah	280,000	(Acuña)	108,000	**Micronesia** (1995)	
★ Tokyo	7,967,614	Tōkch'ŏn	217,000	Surt (Sirte)	150,000	Ciudad Apodaca		★ Palikir	—
Tomakomai	169,328	Wŏnsan	274,000	★ Tripoli (Ṭarābulus)	1,140,000	(Apodaca)	273,000		
Tondabayashi	121,690					Ciudad del Carmen	115,000	**Moldova** (1999 est.)	
Tottori	146,330	**Korea, South** (1995)		**Liechtenstein** (2000 est.)		Ciudad Madero	182,012[34]	Bălți (Beltsy)	156,600
Toyama	325,375	Andong	188,443	★ Vaduz	5,043	Ciudad Obregón	250,000	★ Chişinău (Kishinyov)	655,000
Toyohashi	352,982	Ansan	510,314			Ciudad Santa Catarina		Tighina (Bendery)	128,000[33]
Toyokawa	114,380	Anyang	591,106	**Lithuania** (2000 est.)		(Santa Catarina)	226,500	Tiraspol	200,700
Toyonaka	398,908	Asan	154,663	Kaunas	412,614	Ciudad Valles	105,000		
Toyota	341,079	Ch'angwŏn	481,694	Klaipėda	202,484	Ciudad Victoria		**Monaco** (2000 est.)	
Tsu	163,156	Chech'ŏn	137,070	Panevėžys	133,696	(Victoria)	248,000	★ Monaco	31,700
Tsuchiura	132,243	Cheju (Jeju)	258,511	Šiauliai	146,570	Coacalco	250,000		
Tsukuba	156,012	Chinhae	125,997	★ Vilnius	577,969	Coatzacoalcos	229,000	**Mongolia** (2000 est.)	
Tsuruoka	100,538	Chinju	329,886			Colima	119,186[34]	★ Ulaanbaatar (Ulan	
Ube	175,116	Ch'ŏnan	330,259	**Luxembourg** (1999 est.)		Córdoba	138,000	Bator)	691,000
		Ch'ŏngju	531,376	★ Luxembourg	79,800	Cuautitlán Izcalli	435,000		

Major cities and national capitals (continued)

country city	population
Morocco (1994)	
Agadir	155,240
Beni-Mellal	140,212
Casablanca	2,940,623
El-Jadida	119,083
Fès	541,162
Kenitra	292,627
Khouribga	152,090
Ksar el-Kebir	107,065
Marrakech	621,914
Meknès	459,958
Mohammedia	170,083
Nador	112,450
Oujda	365,582
★ Rabat	623,457
Safi	262,276
Salé	504,420
Tanger	521,735
Temera	126,303
Tétouan	277,516
Mozambique (1997)	
Beira	412,588
Chimoio	177,608
★ Maputo (Lourenço	
Marques)	989,386
Matola	440,927
Mocuba	124,650
Nacala	164,309
Nampula	314,965
Quelimane	153,187
Tete	104,832
Xai-Xai	103,251
Myanmar (Burma)	
(1993 est.)	
Bassein (Pathein)	183,900
Henzada	104,700
Lashio	107,600
Mandalay	885,300
Meiktila	129,700
Mergui	122,700
Monywa	138,600
Moulmein	
(Mawlamyine)	307,600
Myingyan	103,600
Pegu (Bago)	190,900
Pyay (Prome, Pye)	105,700
Sittwe (Akyab)	137,600
Taunggyi	131,500
★ Yangôn (Rangoon)	3,361,700
Namibia (1997 est.)	
★ Windhoek	169,000
Nauru (1992)	
★ Yaren	672
Nepal (2000 est.; MU)	
Biratnagar	168,544
Birganj	103,880
★ Kathmandu	701,499
Lalitpur (Patan)	157,475
Pokhara	168,806
Netherlands, The	
(1999 est.)	
Almere	136,157
Amersfoort	123,367
★ Amsterdam (capital)	727,053
Apeldoorn	152,860
Arnhem	137,222
Breda	159,042
Dordrecht	119,462
Ede	101,542
Eindhoven	199,877
Emmen	105,497
Enschede	148,814
Groningen	171,193
Haarlem	148,262
Haarlemmermeer	109,377
Leiden	117,389
Maastricht	121,479
Nijmegen	151,864
Rotterdam	592,665
's-Hertogenbosch	128,009
★ The Hague (seat of	
government)	440,743
Tilburg	190,559
Utrecht	232,718
Zaanstad	135,126
Zoetermeer	108,899
Zwolle	104,431
Netherlands Antilles	
(1999 est.)	
★ Willemstad	123,000
New Caledonia (1996)	
★ Nouméa	76,293

country city	population
New Zealand	
(1999 est.)	
Auckland	381,800
Christchurch	324,200
Dunedin	119,600
Hamilton	117,100
Manukau	281,800
North Shore	187,700
Waitakere	170,600
★ Wellington	166,700
Nicaragua (1995)	
León	123,865
★ Managua	864,201
Niger (1994 est.)	
★ Niamey	420,000
Zinder	100,000
Nigeria (1991)	
Aba	500,183
Abeokuta	352,735
★ Abuja	107,069
Ado-Ekiti	156,122
Akure	239,124
Awka	104,682
Bauchi	206,537
Benin City	762,719
Bida	111,245
Calabar	310,839
Damaturu	141,897
Ede	142,363
Effon-Alaiye	158,977
Enugu	407,756
Gboko	101,281
Gombe	163,604
Gusau	132,393
Ibadan	1,835,300
Ife	186,856
Ijebu-Ode	124,313
Ikare	103,843
Ikire	111,435
Ikorodu	184,674
Ikot Ekpene	119,402
Ilawe-Ekiti	104,049
Ilesha	139,445
Ilorin	532,089
Ise	108,136
Iseyin	170,936
Iwo	125,645
Jimeta	141,724
Jos	510,300
Kaduna	993,642
Kano	2,166,554
Katsina	259,315
★ Lagos	5,195,247
agglomeration	12,763,000[2]
Maiduguri	618,278
Makurdi	151,515
Minna	189,191
Mubi	128,900
Nnewi	121,065
Ogbomosho	433,030
Okene	312,775
Okpogho	105,127
Ondo	146,051
Onitsha	350,280
Oshogbo	250,951
Owerri	119,711
Owo	157,181
Oyo	369,894
Port Harcourt	703,421
Sagamu	127,513
Sango Otta	103,332
Sapele	109,576
Sokoto	329,639
Suleja	105,075
Ugep	134,773
Umuahia	147,167
Warri	363,382
Zaria	612,257
Northern Mariana Is.	
(1995 est.)	
★ Capital Hill[35]	2,698
Norway (2000 est.; MU)	
Bærum	101,494
Bergen	229,496
★ Oslo	507,467
Stavanger	108,818
Trondheim	148,859
Oman (1993)	
As-Sīb	155,000
Bawshar	107,500
★ Muscat	40,900
agglomeration	887,000[2]
Salālah	116,000

country city	population
Pakistan (1998)	
Abbottabad	105,999[36]
Bahawalnagar	109,642
Bahawalpur	403,408[36]
Burewala	149,857
Chiniot	169,282
Chishtian Mandi	101,659
Daska	101,500
Dera Ghazi Khan	188,149
Faisalabad	
(Lyallpur)	1,977,246
Gojra	114,967
Gujranwala	1,124,799
Gujrat	250,121
Hafizabad	130,216
Hyderabad	1,151,274[36]
★ Islamabad	524,500
Jacobabad	137,773
Jaranwala	103,308
Jhang Sadar	292,214
Jhelum	145,847
Kamoke	150,984
Karachi	9,269,265[36]
Kasur	241,649
Khairpur	102,188
Khanewal	132,962
Khanpur	117,764
Kohat	125,271[36]
Lahore	5,063,499[36]
Larkana	270,366
Mardan	244,511[36]
Mingaora	174,469
Mirpur Khas	184,465
Multan	1,182,441[36]
Muridike	108,578
Muzaffargarh	121,641
Nawabshah	183,110
Okara	200,901
Pakpattan	107,791
Peshawar	988,055[36]
Quetta	560,307
Rahimyar Khan	228,479
Rawalpindi	1,406,214[36]
Sadiqabad	141,509
Sahiwal	207,388
Sargodha	455,360[36]
Shekhupura	271,875
Shikarpur	133,259
Sialkot	417,597[36]
Sukkur	329,176
Tando Adam	103,363
Wah	198,431[36]
Palau (2000)	
★ Koror	13,303
Panama (2000)	
★ Panama City	415,964
San Miguelito	293,745[37]
Papua New Guinea	
(1999 est.)	
Lae	113,118[38]
★ Port Moresby (National	
Capital District)	298,145
Paraguay (1992)	
★ Asunción	500,938
Ciudad del Este	133,881
San Lorenzo	133,395
Peru (1998 est.)	
Arequipa	710,103
Ayacucho	118,960
Cajamarca	108,009
Chiclayo	469,200
Chimbote	298,800
Chincha Alta	130,000
Cusco	278,590
Huancayo	305,039
Huánuco	129,688
Ica	194,820
Iquitos	334,013
Juliaca	180,000
Lima agglomeration	7,060,600
Ate	324,799[33]
Callao	407,904[33]
Carabayllo	115,000[33]
Chorrillos	238,739[33]
Comas	434,690[33]
El Agustino	159,707[33]
Independencia	191,151[33]
La Victoría	213,239[33]
★ Lima	316,322[33]
Los Olivos	281,115[33]
Lurigancho	110,347[33]
Puente Piedra	131,000[33]
Rímac	190,836[33]
San Borja	109,233[33]

country city	population
San Juan de	
Lurigancho	652,681[33]
San Juan de	
Miraflores	329,023[33]
San Martin de Porras	411,000[33]
San Miguel	126,825[33]
Santa Anita	131,519[33]
Santiago de Surco	224,866[33]
Ventanilla	105,824[33]
Villa el Salvador	296,000[33]
Villa Maria del Triunfo	301,505[33]
Piura	308,155
Pucallpa	220,866
Puno	101,578
Sullana	170,000
Tacna	215,683
Trujillo	603,657
Philippines (2000)	
Angeles	263,971
Antipolo	200,000[39]
Bacolod	429,076
Bacoor	305,699
Baguio	252,386
Baliuag	119,675
Biñan	201,186
Binangonan	187,691
Butuan	120,000[39]
Cagayan de Oro	345,000[39]
Cainta	242,511
Calamba	160,000[39]
Cebu	718,821
Cotabato	163,849
Dagupan	130,328
Dasmariñas	250,000[39]
Davao	700,000[39]
Dumaguete	102,265
General Mariano	
Alvarez	112,446
General Santos	250,000[39]
Iloilo	365,820
Kalookan (Caloocan)	1,177,604
Lapu-Lapu	217,019
Las Piñas	472,780
Lucena	196,075
Makati	444,867
Malabon	338,855
Malolos	175,291
Mandaluyong	278,474
Mandaue	259,728
★ Manila	1,581,082
Metro Manila	9,932,560
Marawi	131,090
Marikina	391,170
Meycauayan	163,037
Muntinlupa	379,310
Naga	137,810
Navotas	230,403
Olongapo	194,260
Parañaque	449,811
Pasay	354,908
Pasig	505,058
★ Quezon City	2,173,831
San Fernando	221,857
San Jose del Monte	117,680
San Pablo	105,000[39]
San Pedro	231,403
Santa Rosa	185,633
Tacloban	178,639
Tagig	467,375
Taytay	198,183
Valenzuela	485,433
Zamboanga	135,000[39]
Poland (1999 est.)	
Białystok	283,937
Bielsko-Biała	180,307
Bydgoszcz	386,855
Bytom	205,560
Chorzów	121,708
Częstochowa	257,812
Dąbrowa Górnicza	131,037
Elbląg	129,782
Gdańsk	458,988
Gdynia	253,521
Gliwice	212,164
Gorzów Wielkopolski	126,019
Grudziadz	102,434
Jastrzębie-Zdrój	102,294
Kalisz	106,641
Katowice	345,934
Kielce	212,383
Koszalin	112,375
Kraków	740,666
Legnica	109,335
Łódź	806,728
Lublin	356,251
Olsztyn	170,904
Opole	129,553

country city	population
Płock	131,011
Poznań	578,235
Radom	232,262
Ruda Śląska	159,665
Rybnik	144,582
Rzeszów	162,049
Słupsk	102,370
Sosnowiec	244,102
Szczecin	416,988
Tarnów	121,494
Toruń	206,158
Tychy	133,178
Wałbrzych	136,923
★ Warsaw (Warszawa)	1,618,468
Włocławek	123,373
Wrocław	637,877
Zabrze	200,177
Zielona Góra	118,182
Portugal (2001)	
Amadora	174,788
Braga	105,000
Coimbra	103,000
Funchal	102,521
★ Lisbon	556,797
agglomeration	3,754,000[2]
Porto	262,928
Puerto Rico (2000)	
Bayamón	203,499[40]
Carolina	168,164[40]
Ponce	155,038[40]
★ San Juan	421,958[40]
agglomeration	1,366,000[2]
Qatar (1997)	
★ Doha	264,009
Ar-Rayyān	161,453
Réunion (1999)	
★ Saint-Denis	131,557
Romania (1997 est.)	
Arad	184,619
Bacău	209,689
Baia Mare	149,496
Botoşani	129,285
Brăila	234,648
Braşov	317,772
★ Bucharest	2,027,512
Buzău	149,080
Cluj-Napoca	332,792
Constanţa	344,876
Craiova	312,891
Drobeta-Turnu Severin	117,882
Galaţi	331,360
Iaşi	348,399
Oradea	223,288
Piatra Neamţ	125,121
Piteşti	187,181
Ploieşti	253,414
Râmnicu Vâlcea	119,340
Satu Mare	129,886
Sibiu	168,949
Suceava	118,162
Timişoara	334,098
Târgu Mureş	165,534
Russia (1999 est.)	
Abakan	169,000
Achinsk	122,400
Almetyevsk	141,000
Angarsk	266,600
Arkhangelsk	366,200
Armavir	166,600
Arzamas	111,300
Astrakhan	488,000
Balakovo	206,300
Balashikha	134,200
Barnaul	586,200
Belgorod	339,100
Berezniki	182,200
Biysk	225,700
Blagoveshchensk	220,900
Bratsk	252,500
Bryansk	461,100
Cheboksary	458,000
Chelyabinsk	1,086,300
Cherepovets	324,500
Cherkessk	122,200
Chita	314,300
Dimitrovgrad	137,200
Dzerzhinsk	278,900
Elektrostal	147,600
Elista	101,700
Engels	189,100
Glazov	106,000
Grozny (Dzhokhar)	186,000
Irkutsk	596,400
Ivanovo	463,400

country / city	population
Izhevsk	655,300
Kaliningrad	427,200
Kaliningrad (*Moscow oblast*)	134,000[38]
Kaluga	342,400
Kamensk-Uralsky	192,000
Kamyshin	126,000
Kansk	107,500
Kazan	1,100,800
Kemerovo	496,300
Khabarovsk	614,000
Khimki	133,500
Kineshma	100,000
Kirov	466,100
Kiselyovsk	111,100
Kislovodsk	120,800
Kolomna	151,500
Kolpino	141,200
Komsomolsk-na-Amure	295,100
Kostroma	289,300
Kovrov	161,200
Krasnodar	643,400
Krasnoyarsk	877,800
Kurgan	367,200
Kursk	445,400
Leninsk-Kuznetsky	115,600
Lipetsk	521,600
Lyubertsy	165,100
Magadan	121,800
Magnitogorsk	428,100
Makhachkala	334,900
Maykop	167,000
Mezhdurechensk	104,500
Miass	166,900
Michurinsk	121,800
★ Moscow	8,389,700
Murmansk	382,700
Murom	143,200
Mytishchi	155,700
Naberezhnye Chelny (Brezhnev)	518,300
Nakhodka	159,800
Nalchik	234,700
Nevinnomyssk	132,700
Nikolo-Beryozovka (Neftekamsk)	116,500
Nizhnekamsk	222,000
Nizhnevartovsk	235,600
Nizhny Novgorod (Gorky)	1,364,900
Nizhny Tagil	395,800
Noginsk	117,800
Norilsk	146,500
Novgorod	231,700
Novocheboksarsk	123,600
Novocherkassk	186,500
Novokuybyshevsk	116,400
Novokuznetsk	562,800
Novomoskovsk	139,600
Novorossiysk	204,300
Novoshakhtinsk	103,100
Novosibirsk	1,402,400
Novotroitsk	109,700
Obninsk	108,500
Odintsovo	127,600
Oktyabrsky	111,700
Omsk	1,157,600
Orekhovo-Zuyevo	125,500
Orenburg	526,800
Orsk	274,400
Oryol	346,500
Penza	533,300
Perm	1,017,100
Pervouralsk	136,400
Petropavlovsk-Kamchatsky	196,700
Petrozavodsk	282,500
Podolsk	195,900
Prokopyevsk	240,500
Pskov	202,900
Pyatigorsk	133,100
Rostov-na-Donu	1,017,300
Rubtsovsk	163,900
Ryazan	531,300
Rybinsk (Andropov)	241,800
Saint Petersburg (Leningrad)	4,169,400
Salavat	156,400
Samara (Kuybyshev)	1,168,000
Saransk	316,600
Sarapul	106,800
Saratov	881,000
Sergiev Posad (Zagorsk)	111,800
Serov	100,400
Serpukhov	134,600
Severodvinsk	231,800
Seversk	118,600[39]

country / city	population
Shakhty	224,400
Shchyolkovo	104,900[39]
Simbirsk (Ulyanovsk)	671,700
Smolensk	355,700
Sochi	359,300
Solikamsk	106,400
Stary Oskol	211,800
Stavropol	345,100
Sterlitamak	263,600
Surgut	276,100
Syktyvkar	230,900
Syzran	188,100
Taganrog	287,600
Tambov	315,100
Tobolsk	100,000[39]
Tolyatti	720,300
Tomsk	481,400
Tula	513,100
Tver (Kalinin)	457,100
Tyumen	503,800
Ufa	1,088,900
Ulan-Ude	371,400
Usolye-Sibirskoye	104,100
Ussuriysk	158,400
Ust-Ilimsk	105,500
Velikiye Luki	117,100
Vladikavkaz (Ordzhonikidze)	310,600
Vladimir	339,200
Vladivostok	613,100
Volgodonsk	179,200
Volgograd	1,000,000
Vologda	304,300
Volzhsky	289,500
Voronezh	908,000
Votkinsk	102,000
Yakutsk	195,500
Yaroslavl	620,600
Yekaterinburg (Sverdlovsk)	1,272,900
Yelets	120,300
Yoshkar-Ola	249,800
Yuzhno-Sakhalinsk	179,900
Zelenodolsk	100,600
Zelenograd	206,800
Zheleznodorozhny	100,400
Zlatoust	198,400

Rwanda (1996 est.)
★ Kigali	356,000

St. Kitts and Nevis (1994 est.)
★ Basseterre	12,605

St. Lucia (1997 est.)
★ Castries	16,187
agglomeration	57,000[2]

St. Vincent and the Grenadines (1999 est.)
★ Kingstown	16,175

Samoa (1999 est.)
★ Apia	38,000

San Marino (1997 est.)
★ San Marino	2,294

São Tomé and Príncipe (1991)
★ São Tomé	43,420

Saudi Arabia (1992)
Abhā	112,316
'Ar'ar	108,055
Buraydah	248,636
Ad-Dammām	482,321
Hafar al-Bāṭin	137,793
Ḥā'il	176,757
Al-Hufūf	225,847
Jiddah	2,046,251
Al-Jubayl	140,828
Khamīs Mushayt	217,870
Al-Kharj	152,071
Al-Khubar	141,683
Mecca (Makkah)	965,697
Medina (Al-Madīnah)	608,295
Al-Mubarraz	219,123
★ Riyadh (Ar-Riyāḍ)	2,776,096
Tabūk	292,555
Aṭ-Ṭā'if	416,121
Ath-Thuqbah	125,650
Yanbu' al-Baḥr	119,819

Senegal (1998 est.)
★ Dakar	1,999,000[2, 28]
Kaolack	200,000
Mbour	109,317[33]
Rufisque	185,142[33]
Saint-Louis	180,000[33]

country / city	population
Thiès	320,000
Ziguinchor	180,555[33]

Seychelles (1997)
★ Victoria	24,701[28]

Sierra Leone (1999 est.)
★ Freetown	822,000[28]

Singapore (2000 est.)[41]
★ Singapore	3,278,000

Slovakia (2000 est.)
★ Bratislava	448,292
Košice	241,874

Slovenia (2000 est.)
★ Ljubljana	270,986

Solomon Islands (2000 est.)
★ Honiara	50,100

Somalia (1999 est.)
★ Mogadishu	1,162,000[28]

South Africa (1996)[28]
Alberton	147,948
Benoni	365,467
★ Bloemfontein[42] (de facto judicial)	333,769
Boksburg	260,905
Botshabelo	177,971
Brakpan	171,359
★ Cape Town (de facto legislative)	2,415,408
Carletonville	164,367
Durban	2,117,650
East London	212,323
Johannesburg	1,480,530
Kimberley	170,432
Klerksdorp	137,318
Krugersdorp	203,168
Mdantsane	182,998
Midrand	126,400
Newcastle	219,682
Paarl	140,376
Pietermaritzburg	378,126
Port Elizabeth	749,921
Potchefstroom	101,682
★ Pretoria[43] (de facto executive)	1,104,479
Rustenburg	104,537
Somerset West	112,489
Soweto	1,098,094
Springs	160,795
Tembisa	282,272
Uitenhage	192,120
Vanderbijlpark	253,335
Vereeniging	346,780
Verwoerdburg	114,575
Welkom	203,296
Westonaria	113,932
Witbank	167,183

Spain (1998 est.)
Albacete	145,454
Alcalá de Henares	163,831
Alcorcón	143,970
Algeciras	101,972
Alicante (Alacant)	272,432
Almería	168,025
Badajoz	134,710
Badalona	209,606
Barakaldo	98,649
Barcelona	1,505,581
Bilbao	358,467
Burgos	161,984
Cádiz	143,129
Cartagena	175,628
Castellón de la Plana (Castelló de la Plana)	137,741
Córdoba	309,961
Coruña, A (Coruña, La)	243,134
Donostia–San Sebastián	178,229
Elche (Elx)	191,713
Fuenlabrada	167,458
Getafe	143,629
Gijón	265,491
Granada	241,471
Hospitalet de Llobregat	248,521
Huelva	139,991
Jaén	107,184
Jerez de la Frontera	181,602
Laguna, La	127,945
Leganés	173,163
León	139,809

country / city	population
Lleida (Lérida)	112,207
Logroño	125,617
★ Madrid	2,881,506
Málaga	528,079
Mataró	103,265
Móstoles	195,311
Murcia	349,040
Ourense (Orense)	107,965
Oviedo	199,549
Palma (de Mallorca)	319,181
Palmas de Gran Canaria, Las	352,641
Pamplona (Iruña)	171,150
Sabadell	184,859
Salamanca	158,457
Santa Coloma de Gramanet	120,958
Santa Cruz de Tenerife	211,930
Santander	184,165
Sevilla (Seville)	701,927
Tarragona	112,795
Terrassa (Tarrasa)	165,654
Valencia (València)	739,412
Valladolid	319,946
Vigo	283,110
Vitoria–Gasteiz	216,527
Zaragoza (Saragossa)	603,367

Sri Lanka (1997 est.; MU)
★ Colombo (administrative)	800,982
Dehiwala-Mount Lavinia	220,780
Galle	123,616
Jaffna	145,600
Kandy	150,532
Moratuwa	213,000
Negombo	136,850
★ Sri Jayawardenepura Kotte (legislative and judicial)	118,000[44, 45]

Sudan, The (1993)
Al-Fāshir	141,884
Juba	114,980
Kassalā	234,270
★ Khartoum (executive)	924,505
Khartoum North	879,105
Kūstī	173,599
Nyala	228,778
★ Omdurman (legislative)	1,267,077
Port Sudan	305,385
Al-Qaḍārif	189,384
Al-Ubayyiḍ	228,096
Wad Madanī	218,714

Suriname (1999 est.)
★ Paramaribo	233,000[28]

Swaziland (1998 est.)
★ Lobamba (legislative)	…
★ Lozitha (royal)	…
★ Ludzidzini (royal)	…
★ Mbabane (administrative)	60,000

Sweden (2000 est.; MU)
Göteborg	462,470
Helsingborg	116,870
Jönköping	116,344
Linköping	132,500
Malmö	257,574
Norrköping	122,212
Örebro	123,503
★ Stockholm	743,703
Umeå	103,970
Uppsala	188,478
Västerås	125,433

Switzerland (1999 est.)
Basel (Bâle)	168,735
★ Bern (Berne)	123,254
Geneva (Genève)	172,809
Lausanne	114,161
Zürich	336,821

Syria (1994)
Aleppo (Ḥalab)	1,582,930
★ Damascus (Dimashq)	1,394,322
Dar'ā	180,093[44]
Dayr az-Zawr	140,459
Dūmā	131,158[44]
Ḥamāh	264,348
Ál-Ḥasakah	106,000[46]
Homs (Ḥimṣ)	540,133

country / city	population
Jaramānah	138,469[44]
Latakia (al-Ladhiqiyah)	311,784
Al-Qāmishlī	144,286
Ar-Raqqah	165,195
Ṭarṭūs	136,812[44]

Taiwan (2000 est.)
Chang-hua	227,715
Chi-lung (Keelung)	385,201
Chia-i	265,109
Chung-ho	392,176
Chung-li	318,649
Feng-shan	318,562
Féng-yüan	161,032
Hsi-chih	154,976
Hsin-chu	361,958
Hsin-chuang	365,048
Hsin-tien	263,603
Hua-lien	108,407
Kao-hsiung	1,475,505
Lu-chou	160,516
Nan-t'ou	104,723
Pa-te	161,700
Pan-ch-'iao (T'ai-pei-hsien)	523,850
P'ing-chen	188,344
P'ing-tung	214,727
San-ch'ung	380,084
Shu-lin	151,260
T'ai-chung	940,589
T'ai-nan	728,060
T'ai-p'ing	165,524
T'ai-tung	111,039
★ Taipei (T'ai-pei)	2,641,312
Ta-li	171,940
T'ao-yuan	316,438
T'u-ch'eng	224,897
Yung-ho	227,700
Yung-k'ang	193,005

Tajikistan (1998 est.)
★ Dushanbe	513,000
Khujand (Khudzhand; Leninabad)	163,000[1]

Tanzania (1988)
Arusha	102,544
★ Dar es Salaam	1,747,000[4]
★ Dodoma (legislative)	189,000[4]
Mbeya	130,798
Morogoro	117,760
Mwanza	172,287
Tanga	137,364
Zanzibar	157,634

Thailand (1999 est.)
★ Bangkok (Krung Thep)	6,320,174[34]
Chiang Mai	171,594
Hat Yai	156,812
Khon Kaen	126,500[39]
Nakhon Ratchasima	181,400[39]
Nakhon Si Thammarat	105,176
Nonthaburi	292,100[39]
Pak Kret	140,725[38]
Surat Thani	112,504
Ubon Ratchathani	116,300[39]
Udon Thani	156,038

Togo (1999 est.)
★ Lomé	790,000[28]

Tonga (1999 est.)
★ Nuku'alofa	37,000

Trinidad and Tobago (1996 est.)
★ Port-of-Spain	43,396

Tunisia (1994)
Aryānah	152,700
Ettadhamen	149,200
Kairouan	102,600
Ṣafāqis (Sfax)	230,900
Sūsah	125,000
★ Tunis	674,100

Turkey (1997)
Adana	1,041,509
Adıyaman	212,475
Afyon	113,510
Aksaray	101,187
Alanya	117,311
★ Ankara	2,984,099
Antakya (Hatay)	139,046
Antalya	512,086
Aydın	133,757
Balıkesir	189,987
Batman	212,726
Bismil	101,409

Major cities and national capitals (continued)

county / city	population
Bursa	1,066,559
Çorlu	123,266
Çorum	147,112
Denizli	233,651
Diyarbakır	511,640
Edirne	115,083
Elazığ	250,534
Erzincan	102,304
Erzurum	298,735
Eskişehir	454,536
Gaziantep	712,800
Gebze	235,211
Hatay	139,046
İçel (Mersin)	501,398
İskenderun	161,728
Isparta	134,271
Istanbul	8,260,438
İzmir	2,081,556
Kahramanmaraş (Maras)	303,594
Karabük	103,806
Karaman	104,154
Kayseri	498,233
Kınkkale	203,496
Kiziltepe	112,015
Kocaeli (İzmit)	198,200
Konya	623,333
Kütahya	162,319
Malatya	400,248
Manisa	201,340
Ordu	117,699
Osmaniye	160,854
Sakarya (Adapazarı)	183,265
Samsun	338,387
Siirt	107,067
Sivas	232,352
Sultanbeyli	144,932
Tarsus	190,184
Tekirdağ	100,557
Trabzon	182,552
Urfa (Şanlıurfa)	410,762
Uşak	124,356
Van	226,965
Viranşehir	106,363
Zonguldak	106,176
Turkmenistan (1999 est.)	
★ Ashkhabad (Ashgabat)	605,000
Chärjew (Chardzhev; Chardzhou)	203,000
Dashhowuz (Dashkhovuz; Tashauz)	165,000
Mary	123,000
Nebitdag	119,000
Tuvalu (1999 est.)	
★ Funafuti	6,000
Uganda (1999 est.)	
★ Kampala	1,154,000[28]
Ukraine (1998 est.)	
Alchevsk	120,900
Berdyansk	132,300
Bila Tserkva (Belaya Tserkov)	215,200
Cherkasy (Cherkassy)	310,600
Chernihiv (Chernigov)	310,800
Chernivtsi (Chernovtsy)	259,000
Dniprodzerzhynsk (Dneprodzerzhinsk)	275,000
Dnipropetrovsk (Dnepropetrovsk)	1,122,400
Donetsk	1,065,400
Horlivka (Gorlovka)	309,300
Ivano-Frankivsk (Ivano-Frankovsk)	237,400
Kam'yanets-Podilskyy (Kamenets-Podolsky)	108,000
Kerch	167,400
Kharkiv (Kharkov)	1,521,400
Kherson	358,700
Khmelnytskyy (Khmelnitsky)	260,100
★ Kiev (Kyyiv)	2,620,900
Kirovohrad	270,200
Kostyantynivka (Konstantinovka)	100,100
Kramatorsk	190,800
Krasnyy Luch	104,500
Kremenchuk (Kremenchug)	240,700
Kryvyy Rih (Krivoy Rog)	715,400
Luhansk (Voroshilovgrad)	475,300
Lutsk	217,900
Lviv (Lvov)	793,700
Lysychansk (Lisichansk)	119,000
Makiyivka (Makeyevka)	394,800
Mariupol (Zhdanov)	504,400
Melitopol	171,000
Mykolayiv (Nikolayev)	517,900
Nikopol	152,000
Odesa (Odessa)	1,027,400
Oleksandriya (Aleksandriya)	101,000
Pavlohrad	130,000
Poltava	317,300
Rivne (Rovno)	244,900
Sevastopol	356,000
Simferopol	341,000
Slov'yansk (Slavyansk)	129,600
Stakhanov	104,500
Sumy	299,800
Syeverodonetsk	129,200
Ternopil (Ternopol)	235,100
Uzhhorod	125,500
Vinnytsya (Vinnitsa)	389,100
Yenakiyeve (Yenakiyevo)	108,700
Yevpatoriya	113,500
Zaporizhzhya (Zaporozhye)	863,100
Zhytomyr (Zhitomir)	297,700
United Arab Emirates (1995)	
★ Abu Dhabi (Abū Zaby)	398,695
'Ajmān	114,395
Al-'Ayn	225,970
Dubai (Dubayy)	669,181
Sharjah (Ash-Shāriqah)	320,095
United Kingdom	
England[47] (1999 est.)	
Barnsley	220,937
Birmingham	961,041
Blackburn with Darwen	136,612
Blackpool	151,200
Bolton	258,584
Bournemouth	160,700
Bracknell Forest	110,000
Bradford	457,344
Brighton and Hove	245,000
Bristol	399,600
Bury	176,760
Calderdale	191,585
Cambridge	91,933
Canterbury	123,947
Carlisle	100,562
Chester	115,971
Coventry	294,387
Darlington	101,000
Derby	235,238
Doncaster	288,854
Dudley	304,615
Durham	80,669
Exeter	98,125
Gateshead	199,588
Gloucester	101,608
Halton	123,038
Kingston upon Hull	266,900
Kirklees	373,127
Knowsley	152,091
Lancaster	123,856
Leeds	680,722
Leicester	270,493
Lincoln	81,987
Liverpool	452,450
★ London (Greater London)	7,187,300[16, 48]
Luton	181,500
Manchester	404,861
Milton Keynes	204,415
Newcastle upon Tyne	259,541
North Tyneside	192,286
Norwich	120,895
Nottingham	284,000
Oldham	216,531
Oxford	134,800
Peterborough	159,900
Plymouth	255,800
Poole	139,200
Portsmouth	190,400
Reading	142,851
Rochdale	202,164
Rotherham	251,637
St. Albans	128,700
St. Helens	178,764
Salford	220,463
Sandwell	290,091
Sefton	289,542
Sheffield	501,202
Slough	108,000
Solihull	199,859
South Tyneside	154,697
Southampton	214,859
Southend	172,300
Stockport	284,395
Stockton-on-Tees	179,000
Stoke-on-Trent	254,300
Sunderland	289,040
Swindon	177,118
Tameside	216,431
Thurrock	132,283
Torbay	119,674
Trafford	212,731
Wakefield	310,915
Walsall	259,488
Warrington	187,000
Wigan	306,521
Winchester	96,386
Windsor and Maidenhead	132,465
Wirral	330,795
Wolverhampton	242,190
Worcester	89,481
York	175,925
Northern Ireland[49]	
Belfast	297,200
Craigavon	79,100
Derry (Londonderry)	104,700
Lisburn	106,600
Newtonabbey	79,600
Scotland[50]	
Aberdeen	213,070
Dundee	146,690
Edinburgh	450,180
Glasgow	619,680
Wales[51]	
Cardiff	315,040
Conwy	110,600
Neath Port Talbot	139,459
Newport	136,800
Rhondda, Cynon, Taff	240,117
Swansea	230,200
Torfaen	90,527
Wrexham	125,200
United States (2000)	
Abilene (Texas)	115,930
Akron (Ohio)	217,074
Albany (Ga.)	76,939
Albany (N.Y.)	95,658
Albuquerque (N.M.)	448,607
Alexandria (Va.)	128,283
Alhambra (Calif.)	85,804
Allentown (Pa.)	106,632
Amarillo (Texas)	173,627
Anaheim (Calif.)	328,014
Anchorage (Alaska)	260,283
Ann Arbor (Mich.)	114,024
Antioch (Calif.)	90,532
Arden-Arcade (Calif.)[52]	96,025
Arlington (Texas)	332,969
Arlington (Va.)[52]	189,453
Arlington Heights (Ill.)	76,031
Arvada (Colo.)	102,153
Athens (Ga.)	100,266
Atlanta (Ga.)	416,474
Augusta (Ga.)	195,182
Aurora (Colo.)	276,393
Aurora (Ill.)	142,990
Austin (Texas)	656,562
Bakersfield (Calif.)	247,057
Baldwin Park (Calif.)	75,837
Baltimore (Md.)	651,154
Baton Rouge (La.)	227,818
Beaumont (Texas)	113,866
Beaverton (Ore.)	76,129
Bellevue (Wash.)	109,569
Berkeley (Calif.)	102,743
Billings (Mont.)	89,847
Birmingham (Ala.)	242,820
Bloomington (Minn.)	85,172
Boise (Idaho)	185,787
Boston (Mass.)	589,141
Boulder (Colo.)	94,673
Brandon (Fla.)[52]	77,895
Brick Township (N.J.)[52]	76,119
Bridgeport (Conn.)	139,529
Brockton (Mass.)	94,304
Brownsville (Texas)	139,722
Buena Park (Calif.)	78,282
Buffalo (N.Y.)	292,648
Burbank (Calif.)	100,316
Cambridge (Mass.)	101,355
Camden (N.J.)	79,904
Canton (Mich.)[52]	76,366
Canton (Ohio)	80,806
Cape Coral (Fla.)	102,286
Carlsbad (Calif.)	78,247
Carrollton (Texas)	109,576
Carson (Calif.)	89,730
Cary (N.C.)	94,536
Cedar Rapids (Iowa)	120,758
Chandler (Ariz.)	176,581
Charleston (S.C.)	96,650
Charlotte (N.C.)	540,828
Chattanooga (Tenn.)	155,554
Cheektowaga (N.Y.)[52]	79,988
Chesapeake (Va.)	199,184
Chicago (Ill.)	2,896,016
Chula Vista (Calif.)	173,556
Cicero (Ill.)	85,616
Cincinnati (Ohio)	331,285
Citrus Heights (Calif.)	85,071
Clarksville (Tenn.)	103,455
Clearwater (Fla.)	108,787
Cleveland (Ohio)	478,403
Clifton (N.J.)	78,672
Clinton Township (Mich.)[52]	95,648
Colorado Springs (Colo.)	360,890
Columbia (Md.)[52]	88,254
Columbia (Mo.)	84,531
Columbia (S.C.)	116,278
Columbus (Ga.)	185,781
Columbus (Ohio)	711,470
Compton (Calif.)	93,493
Concord (Calif.)	121,780
Coral Springs (Fla.)	117,549
Corona (Calif.)	124,966
Corpus Christi (Texas)	277,454
Costa Mesa (Calif.)	108,724
Cranston (R.I.)	79,269
Dallas (Texas)	1,188,580
Daly City (Calif.)	103,621
Davenport (Iowa)	98,359
Davie (Fla.)	75,720
Dayton (Ohio)	166,179
Dearborn (Mich.)	97,775
Decatur (Ill.)	81,860
Denton (Texas)	80,537
Denver (Colo.)	554,636
Des Moines (Iowa)	198,682
Detroit (Mich.)	951,270
Dover Township (N.J.)[52]	86,327
Downey (Calif.)	107,323
Duluth (Minn.)	86,918
Durham (N.C.)	187,035
East Los Angeles (Calif.)[52]	124,283
Edison (N.J.)[52]	97,687
El Cajon (Calif.)	94,869
El Monte (Calif.)	115,965
El Paso (Texas)	563,662
Elgin (Ill.)	94,487
Elizabeth (N.J.)	120,568
Erie (Pa.)	103,717
Escondido (Calif.)	133,559
Eugene (Ore.)	137,893
Evansville (Ind.)	121,582
Everett (Wash.)	91,488
Fairfield (Calif.)	96,178
Fall River (Mass.)	91,938
Fargo (N.D.)	90,599
Farmington Hills (Mich.)	82,111
Fayetteville (N.C.)	121,015
Federal Way (Wash.)	83,259
Flint (Mich.)	124,943
Fontana (Calif.)	128,929
Fort Collins (Colo.)	118,652
Fort Lauderdale (Fla.)	152,397
Fort Smith (Ark.)	80,268
Fort Wayne (Ind.)	205,727
Fort Worth (Texas)	534,694
Fremont (Calif.)	203,413
Fresno (Calif.)	427,652
Fullerton (Calif.)	126,003
Gainesville (Fla.)	95,447
Garden Grove (Calif.)	165,196
Garland (Texas)	215,768
Gary (Ind.)	102,746
Gilbert (Ariz.)	109,697
Glendale (Ariz.)	218,812
Glendale (Calif.)	194,973
Grand Prairie (Texas)	127,427
Grand Rapids (Mich.)	197,800
Greeley (Colo.)	76,930
Green Bay (Wis.)	102,313
Greensboro (N.C.)	223,891
Gresham (Ore.)	90,205
Hammond (Ind.)	83,048
Hampton (Va.)	146,437
Hartford (Conn.)	121,578
Hawthorne (Calif.)	84,112
Hayward (Calif.)	140,030
Henderson (Nev.)	175,381
Hialeah (Fla.)	226,419
High Point (N.C.)	85,839
Hollywood (Fla.)	139,357
Honolulu (Hawaii)[52]	371,657
Houston (Texas)	1,953,631
Huntington Beach (Calif.)	189,594
Huntsville (Ala.)	158,216
Independence (Mo.)	113,288
Indianapolis (Ind.)	791,926
Inglewood (Calif.)	112,580
Irvine (Calif.)	143,072
Irving (Texas)	191,615
Jackson (Miss.)	184,256
Jacksonville (Fla.)	735,617
Jersey City (N.J.)	240,055
Joliet (Ill.)	106,221
Kalamazoo (Mich.)	77,145
Kansas City (Kan.)	146,866
Kansas City (Mo.)	441,545
Kendall (Fla.)[52]	75,226
Kenosha (Wis.)	90,352
Killeen (Texas)	86,911
Knoxville (Tenn.)	173,890
Lafayette (La.)	110,257
Lakeland (Fla.)	78,452
Lakewood (Calif.)	79,345
Lakewood (Colo.)	144,126
Lancaster (Calif.)	118,718
Lansing (Mich.)	119,128
Laredo (Texas)	176,576
Las Vegas (Nev.)	478,434
Lawrence (Kan.)	80,098
Lawton (Okla.)	92,757
Lewisville (Texas)	77,737
Lexington (Ky.)	260,512
Lincoln (Neb.)	225,581
Little Rock (Ark.)	183,133
Livonia (Mich.)	100,545
Long Beach (Calif.)	461,522
Los Angeles (Calif.)	3,694,820
Louisville (Ky.)	256,231
Lowell (Mass.)	105,167
Lubbock (Texas)	199,564
Lynn (Mass.)	89,050
McAllen (Texas)	106,414
Macon (Ga.)	97,255
Madison (Wis.)	208,054
Manchester (N.H.)	107,006
Memphis (Tenn.)	650,100
Mesa (Ariz.)	396,375
Mesquite (Texas)	124,523
Metairie (La.)[52]	146,136
Miami (Fla.)	362,470
Miami Beach (Fla.)	87,933
Midland (Texas)	94,996
Milwaukee (Wis.)	596,974
Minneapolis (Minn.)	382,618
Mission Viejo (Calif.)	93,102
Mobile (Ala.)	198,915
Modesto (Calif.)	188,856
Montgomery (Ala.)	201,568
Moreno Valley (Calif.)	142,381
Naperville (Ill.)	128,358
Nashua (N.H.)	86,605
Nashville (Tenn.)	545,524
New Bedford (Mass.)	93,768
New Haven (Conn.)	123,626
New Orleans (La.)	484,674
New York City (N.Y.)	8,008,278
Newark (N.J.)	273,546
Newport News (Va.)	180,150
Newton (Mass.)	83,829
Norfolk (Va.)	234,403

[1]1993 estimate. [2]1999 estimate. [3]Eight villages, including Fagatogo, Utulei, and Pago Pago, are collectively known as Pago Pago (1999 agglomeration pop. 14,000). [4]1995 estimate. [5]1991 estimate. [6]Urban Centre ("urban agglomeration") as defined by 1996 census. [7]1996 census. [8]Estimated population of New Providence and adjacent islands. [9]Preliminary census populations for urban areas of municípios. [10]1990 census. [11]1992 census. [12]Excludes agricultural population within city limits. [13]San Jose canton. [14]1988 census. [15]As of 1998 administrative reorganization. [16]1998 estimate. [17]Excludes Lefkoşa (Turkish Nicosia), whose population per 1996 census was 36,834. [18]Population of the urban area of the National District. [19]Within San Salvador metropolitan area. [20]1997 census. [21]Includes internally displaced persons from Abkhazia. [22]Within Guatemala City metropolitan area. [23]Population includes Comayagüela. [24]Urban population; Hong Kong is 100% urban. [25]Census not taken because of civil unrest. [26]Urban population (may or may not be city proper; not urban agglomeration). [27]Population of Greater Karaj. [28]Urban agglomeration(s). [29]1985 estimate. [30]County borough population. [31]Commune population. [32]1989 census. [33]1996 estimate. [34]2000 census. [35]Census designated place on the island of Saipan. [36]Includes

county / city	population	county / city	population	county / city	population	county / city	population	county / city	population
Norman (Okla.)	95,694	Rockford (Ill.)	150,115	Thornton (Colo.)	82,384	★ Tashkent		Hue	219,149
North Charleston (S.C.)	79,641	Roseville (Calif.)	79,921	Thousand Oaks		(Toshkent)	2,124,000	Long Xuyen	132,681
North Las Vegas		Roswell (Ga.)	79,334	(Calif.)	117,005	Urganch (Urgench)	135,000[1]	My Tho	108,404
(Nev.)	115,488	Sacramento (Calif.)	407,018	Toledo (Ohio)	313,619			Nam Dinh	171,699
Norwalk (Calif.)	103,298	St. Louis (Mo.)	348,189	Topeka (Kan.)	122,377	Vanuatu (1999 est.)		Nha Trang	221,331
Norwalk (Conn.)	82,951	St. Paul (Minn.)	287,151	Torrance (Calif.)	137,946	★ Vila	30,139	Phan Thiet	114,236[32]
Oakland (Calif.)	399,484	St. Petersburg (Fla.)	248,232	Trenton (N.J.)	85,403			Qui Nhon	163,385
Oceanside (Calif.)	161,029	Salem (Ore.)	136,924	Troy (Mich.)	80,959	Venezuela (2000 est.)[53]		Rach Gia	141,132
Odessa (Texas)	90,943	Salinas (Calif.)	151,060	Tucson (Ariz.)	486,699	Acarigua	166,720	Thai Nguyen	127,643
Ogden (Utah)	77,226	Salt Lake City (Utah)	181,743	Tulsa (Okla.)	393,049	Barcelona	311,475	Vinh	112,455
Oklahoma City		San Angelo (Texas)	88,439	Tuscaloosa (Ala.)	77,906	Barinas	228,598	Vung Tau	145,145
(Okla.)	506,132	San Antonio (Texas)	1,144,646	Tyler (Texas)	83,650	Barquisimeto	875,790		
Olathe (Kan.)	92,962	San Bernardino		Vacaville (Calif.)	88,625	Baruta	213,373	Virgin Islands (U.S.)	
Omaha (Neb.)	390,007	(Calif.)	185,401	Vallejo (Calif.)	116,760	Cabimas	214,000	(1990)	
Ontario (Calif.)	158,007	San Buenaventura		Virginia Beach (Va.)	425,257	Calabozo	102,000	★ Charlotte Amalie	12,331
Orange (Calif.)	128,821	(Ventura) (Calif.)	100,916	Visalia (Calif.)	91,565	★ Caracas	1,975,787		
Orem (Utah)	84,324	San Diego (Calif.)	1,223,400	Vista (Calif.)	89,857	Carúpano	121,892	West Bank (1997)	
Orlando (Fla.)	185,951	San Francisco (Calif.)	776,733	Waco (Texas)	113,726	Catia la Mar	118,466	Hebron (Al-Khalīl)	119,401
Overland Park (Kan.)	149,080	San Jose (Calif.)	894,943	Warren (Mich.)	138,247	Ciudad Bolívar	312,691	Nābulus	100,231
Oxnard (Calif.)	170,358	San Leandro (Calif.)	79,452	Warwick (R.I.)	85,808	Ciudad Guayana		★ Rām Allāh (Ramallah)	
Palm Bay (Fla.)	79,413	San Mateo (Calif.)	92,482	★ Washington, D.C.	572,059	(San Felix		(acting administrative	
Palmdale (Calif.)	116,670	Sandy (Utah)	88,418	Waukegan (Ill.)	87,901	de Guayana)	704,168	centre)	18,017
Paradise (Nev.)[52]	186,070	Sandy Springs (Ga.)[52]	85,781	Waterbury (Conn.)	107,271	Ciudad Ojeda	103,835		
Parma (Ohio)	85,655	Santa Ana (Calif.)	337,977	West Covina (Calif.)	105,080	Coro	158,763	Western Sahara	
Pasadena (Calif.)	133,936	Santa Barbara (Calif.)	92,325	West Palm Beach		Cúa	101,868	(1998 est.)	
Pasadena (Texas)	141,674	Santa Clara (Calif.)	102,361	(Fla.)	82,103	Cumaná	269,428	Laayoune (El Aaiún)	164,000[54]
Paterson (N.J.)	149,222	Santa Clarita (Calif.)	151,088	West Valley City		El Límon	119,602		
Pembroke Pines		Santa Maria (Calif.)	77,423	(Utah)	108,896	El Tigre	119,609	Yemen (1994)	
(Fla.)	137,427	Santa Monica (Calif.)	84,084	Westland (Mich.)	86,602	Guacara	137,816	Aden	398,300
Peoria (Ariz.)	108,364	Santa Rosa (Calif.)	147,595	Westminster (Calif.)	88,207	Guanare	112,000	Al-Hudaydah	298,500
Peoria (Ill.)	112,936	Savannah (Ga.)	131,510	Westminster (Colo.)	100,940	Guarenas	170,204	Ibb	103,300
Philadelphia (Pa.)	1,517,550	Schaumburg (Ill.)	75,386	Whittier (Calif.)	83,680	Guatire	115,264	Al-Mukallā	122,400
Phoenix (Ariz.)	1,321,045	Scottsdale (Ariz.)	202,705	Wichita (Kan.)	344,284	Los Teques	183,142	★ San'ā'	954,400
Pittsburgh (Pa.)	334,563	Scranton (Pa.)	76,415	Wichita Falls (Texas)	104,197	Maracaibo	1,764,038	Ta'izz	317,600
Plano (Texas)	222,030	Seattle (Wash.)	563,374	Wilmington (N.C.)	75,838	Maracay	459,007		
Plantation (Fla.)	82,934	Shreveport (La.)	200,145	Winston-Salem (N.C.)	185,776	Mariara	101,115	Yugoslavia (2000 est.)[55]	
Pomona (Calif.)	149,473	Silver Spring (Md.)[52]	76,540	Worcester (Mass.)	172,648	Maturín	283,318	★ Belgrade	
Pompano Beach (Fla.)	78,191	Simi Valley (Calif.)	111,351	Yonkers (N.Y.)	196,086	Mérida	230,101	(Beograd)	1,194,878
Port St. Lucie (Fla.)	88,769	Sioux City (Iowa)	85,013	Youngstown (Ohio)	82,026	Ocumare del Tuy	101,707	Kragujevac	154,489
Portland (Ore.)	529,121	Sioux Falls (S.D.)	123,975	Yuma (Ariz.)	77,515	Petare	520,982	Níš	182,583
Portsmouth (Va.)	100,565	Somerville (Mass.)	77,478			Puerto Cabello	169,959	Novi Sad	182,778
Providence (R.I.)	173,618	South Bend (Ind.)	107,789	Uruguay (1996)		Puerto La Cruz	205,635	Podgorica	
Provo (Utah)	105,166	South Gate (Calif.)	96,375	★ Montevideo	1,378,707	Punto Fijo	109,362	(Titograd)	130,875
Pueblo (Colo.)	102,121	Southfield (Mich.)	78,296			San Cristóbal	307,184	Priština	186,611
Quincy (Mass.)	88,025	Spokane (Wash.)	195,629	Uzbekistan (1998 est.)		Santa Teresa	126,930	Prizren	115,711
Racine (Wis.)	81,855	Spring Valley (Nev.)[52]	117,390	Andijon (Andizhan)	288,000	Turmero	226,084		
Raleigh (N.C.)	276,093	Springfield (Ill.)	111,454	Angren	132,000[1]	Valencia	1,338,833	Zambia (1990)	
Rancho Cucamonga		Springfield (Mass.)	152,082	Bukhoro (Bukhara)	220,000	Valera	116,036	Chingola	167,954
(Calif.)	127,743	Springfield (Mo.)	151,580	Chirchiq (Chirchik)	156,000[1]			Kabwe	166,519
Reading (Pa.)	81,207	Stamford (Conn.)	117,083	Farghona (Fergana)	203,000	Vietnam (1992 est.)		Kitwe	338,207
Redding (Calif.)	80,865	Sterling Heights		Jizzakh (Dzhizak)	116,000[1]	Bien Hoa	273,879[32]	Luanshya	146,275
Redwood City (Calif.)	75,402	(Mich.)	124,471	Marghilon (Margilan)	129,000[1]	Cam Pha	109,086	★ Lusaka	1,577,000[2, 28]
Reno (Nev.)	180,480	Stockton (Calif.)	243,771	Namangan	291,000	Cam Ranh	114,041[32]	Mufulira	152,944
Rialto (Calif.)	91,873	Sunnyvale (Calif.)	131,760	Nawoiy (Navoi)	115,000[1]	Can Tho	215,587	Ndola	376,311
Richardson (Texas)	91,802	Sunrise (Fla.)	85,779	Nukus	185,000[1]	Da Lat	106,409		
Richmond (Calif.)	99,216	Sunrise Manor (Nev.)[52]	156,120	Olmaliq (Almalyk)	116,000[1]	Da Nang	382,674	Zimbabwe (1998 est.)	
Richmond (Va.)	197,790	Syracuse (N.Y.)	147,306	Qarshi (Karshi)	177,000[1]	Haiphong	783,133	Bulawayo	790,000
Riverside (Calif.)	255,166	Tacoma (Wash.)	193,556	Qüqon (Kokand)	184,000[1]	★ Hanoi	1,073,760	Chitungwiza	600,000
Roanoke (Va.)	94,911	Tallahassee (Fla.)	150,624	Samarqand		Ho Chi Minh City		Gweru	170,000
Rochester (Minn.)	85,806	Tampa (Fla.)	303,447	(Samarkand)	388,000	(Saigon)	3,015,743	★ Harare	1,686,000[2, 28]
Rochester (N.Y.)	219,773	Tempe (Ariz.)	158,625			Hong Gai	127,484	Kwekwe	100,000
								Mutare	165,000

cantonment(s). [37]Urban district adjacent to Panama City. [38]1997 estimate. [39]2000 estimate. [40]Urban population. [41]Urban population; Singapore is 100% urban. [42]Bloemfontein was absorbed into the larger municipality of Manguang in December 2000. [43]Pretoria was absorbed into the larger municipality of Tshwane in December 2000. [44]1994 estimate. [45]Population refers to Kotte only. [46]1992 estimate. [47]All cities and borough councils of England after the local government reorganization of 1995–98. [48]32 borough councils, not listed separately, constitute London (Greater London). [49]Cities and borough councils of Northern Ireland with more than 75,000 population. [50]Cities of Scotland after the local government reorganization of 1994–96. Borough councils do not exist in Scotland. [51]Cities and boroughs in Wales with more than 75,000 population after the local government reorganization of 1994–96. [52]Unincorporated place. [53]Projections based on 1990 census. [54]Urban population of Laayoune and northern Western Sahara. [55]Unofficial estimate.

Language

This table presents estimated data on the principal language communities of the countries of the world. The countries, and the principal languages (occasionally, language families) represented in each, are listed alphabetically. A bullet (●) indicates those languages that are official in each country. The sum of the estimates equals the 2000 population of the country given in the "Area and population" table.

The estimates represent, so far as national data collection systems permit, the distribution of mother tongues (a mother tongue being the language spoken first and, usually, most fluently by an individual). Many countries do not collect any official data whatever on language use, and published estimates not based on census or survey data usually span a substantial range of uncertainty. The editors have adopted the best-founded distribution in the published literature (indicating uncertainty by the degree of rounding shown) but have also adjusted or interpolated using data not part of the base estimate(s). Such adjustments have not been made to account for large-scale refugee movements, as these are of a temporary nature.

A variety of approaches have been used to approximate mother-tongue distribution when census data were unavailabe. Some countries collect data on ethnic or "national" groups only; for such countries ethnic distribution often had to be assumed to conform roughly to the distribution of language communities. This approach, however, should be viewed with caution, because a minority population is not always free to educate its children in its own language and because better economic opportunities often draw minority group members into the majority-language community. For some countries, a given individual may be visible in national statistics only as a passport-holder of a foreign country, however long he may remain resident. Such persons, often guest workers, have sometimes had to be assumed to be speakers of the principal language of their home country. For other countries, the language mosaic may be so complex, the language communities so minute in size, scholarly study so inadequate, or the census base so obsolete that it was possible only to assign percentages to entire groups, or families, of related languages, despite their mutual unintelligibility (Papuan and Melanesian languages in Papua New Guinea, for instance). For some countries in the Americas, so few speakers of any single indigenous language remain that it was necessary to combine these groups as *Amerindian* so as to give a fair impression of their aggregate size within their respective countries.

No systematic attempt has been made to account for populations that may legitimately be described as bilingual, unless the country itself collects data on that basis, as does Bolivia or the Comoros, for example. Where a nonindigenous official or excolonial language constitutes a lingua franca of the country, however, speakers of the language as a second tongue are shown in italics, even though very few may speak it as a mother tongue. No comprehensive effort has been made to distinguish between dialect communities *usually* classified as belonging to the same language, though such distinctions were possible for some countries—*e.g.*, between French and Occitan (the dialect of southern France) or among the various dialects of Chinese.

In giving the names of Bantu languages, grammatical particles specific to a language's autonym (name for itself) have been omitted (the form *Rwanda* is used here, for example, rather than *kinyaRwanda* and *Tswana* instead of *seTswana*). Parenthetical alternatives are given for a number of languages that differ markedly from the name of the people speaking them (such as Kurukh, spoken by the Oraon tribes of India) or that may be combined with other groups sometimes distinguishable in national data but appearing here under the name of the largest member—*e.g.*, "Tamil (and other Indian languages)" combining data on South Asian Indian populations in Singapore. The term *creole* as used here refers to distinguishable dialectal communities related to a national, official, or former colonial language (such as the French creole that survives in Mauritius from the end of French rule in 1810).

Internet resources for further information:
- *Ethnologue* (13th ed.; Summer Institute of Linguistics)
  http://www.sil.org/ethnologue
- Joshua Project 2000—People's List (Christian interfaith missionary database identifying some 2,000 ethnolinguistic groups)
  http://www.ad2000.org/peoples/index.htm
- U.S. Census Bureau: http://www.census.gov/ftp/pub/ipc/www/idbconf.html (especially tables 57 and 59)
- Living Languages of the Americas (Summer Institute of Linguistics)
  http://www.sil.org/lla

Language

Major languages by country	Number of speakers
Afghanistan[1]	
Indo-Aryan languages	
Pashai	160,000
Iranian languages	
Balochi	240,000
● Dari (Persian)	
Chahar Aimak	730,000
Hazara	2,280,000
Tajik	5,280,000
Nuristani group	200,000
Pamir group	160,000
● Pashto	13,560,000
Turkic languages	
Turkmen	500,000
Uzbek	2,280,000
Other	490,000
Albania[1]	
● Albanian	3,419,000
Greek	65,000
Macedonian	5,000
Other	1,000
Algeria	
● Arabic	26,280,000
Berber	4,280,000
English	...
French	*6,000,000*
American Samoa	
● English	2,000
English (lingua franca)	*64,000*
● Samoan	59,000
Tongan	2,000
Other	2,000
Andorra[2]	
● Catalan (Andorran)	22,000
French	5,000
Portuguese	7,000
Spanish	29,000
Other	4,000
Angola[1]	
Ambo (Ovambo)	240,000
Chokwe	430,000
Herero	70,000
Kongo	1,340,000
Luchazi	240,000
Luimbe-Nkangala	550,000
Lunda	120,000
Luvale (Luena)	360,000
Mbunda	120,000
Mbundu	2,190,000
Nyaneka-Nkhumbi	550,000
Ovimbundu (Umbundu)	3,770,000
● Portuguese	*3,600,000*
Other	160,000

Major languages by country	Number of speakers
Antigua and Barbuda	
● English	71,000
English/English Creole	67,000
Other	4,000
Argentina	
Amerindian languages	110,000
Italian	650,000
● Spanish	35,860,000
Other	410,000
Armenia	
● Armenian	3,560,000
Azerbaijani (Azeri)	100,000
Other	160,000
Aruba	
● Dutch	5,000
English	9,000
Papiamento	74,000
Spanish	7,000
Other	1,000
Australia	
Aboriginal languages	51,000
Arabic	187,000
Cantonese	219,000
Dutch	46,000
● English	15,561,000
English (lingua franca)	*18,500,000*
French	44,000
German	111,000
Greek	299,000
Hungarian	30,000
Indonesian Malay	30,000
Italian	423,000
Macedonian	79,000
Maltese	51,000
Mandarin	101,000
Pilipino (Filipino)	78,000
Polish	70,000
Portuguese	27,000
Russian	35,000
Serbo-Croatian	118,000
Spanish	100,000
Turkish	49,000
Vietnamese	154,000
Other/not stated	1,303,000
Austria	
Czech	19,000
● German	7,444,000
Hungarian	34,000
Polish	19,000
Romanian	17,000
Serbo-Croatian	176,000
Slovene	30,000
Turkish	123,000
Other	230,000

Major languages by country	Number of speakers
Azerbaijan	
Armenian	160,000
● Azerbaijani (Azeri)	7,170,000
Lezgi (Lezgian)	180,000
Russian	240,000
Other	310,000
Bahamas, The	
● English	...
English/English Creole	260,000
French (Haitian)	
Creole	30,000
Bahrain[2]	
● Arabic	470,000
English	...
Other	220,000
Bangladesh[1]	
● Bengali	126,260,000
Chakma	480,000
English	*3,400,000*
Garo	120,000
Khasi	100,000
Marma (Magh)	250,000
Mro	40,000
Santhali	90,000
Tripuri	90,000
Other	1,770,000
Barbados	
Bajan (English	
Creole)	254,000
● English	...
Other	13,000
Belarus	
● Belarusian	6,560,000
Polish	50,000
● Russian	3,190,000
Ukrainian	130,000
Other	60,000
Belgium[2, 3]	
Arabic	160,000
● Dutch (Flemish;	
Netherlandic)	6,080,000
● French (Walloon)	3,350,000
● German	100,000
Italian	250,000
Spanish	50,000
Turkish	90,000
Other	180,000
Belize	
● English	128,000
English Creole (lingua	
franca)	*190,000*
Garifuna (Black Carib)	17,000
German	4,000
Mayan languages	24,000

Major languages by country	Number of speakers
Spanish	80,000
Spanish (lingua franca)	*140,000*
Benin[1]	
Adja	710,000
Aizo (Ouidah)	550,000
Bariba	550,000
Dendi	140,000
Djougou	190,000
Fon	2,540,000
● French	*600,000*
Fula (Fulani)	360,000
Somba (Ditamari)	420,000
Yoruba (Nago)	780,000
Other	150,000
Bermuda	
● English	63,000
Portuguese	*6,000*
Bhutan[1]	
Assamese	100,000
● Dzongkha (Bhutia)	330,000
Nepali (Hindi)	230,000
Bolivia	
● Aymara	270,000
Guaraní	10,000
● Quechua	680,000
● Spanish	3,480,000
Spanish-Amerindian	
(multilingual),	3,830,000
of which	
Spanish-Aymara	*1,650,000*
Spanish-Guaraní	*30,000*
Spanish-Quechua	*2,160,000*
Other	70,000
Bosnia and Herzegovina[1]	
● Bosnian	1,690,000
● Croatian	650,000
● Serbian	1,190,000
Other	310,000
Botswana[1]	
● English (lingua franca)	*630,000*
Khoekhoe (Hottentot)	39,000
Ndebele	20,000
San (Bushman)	55,000
Shona	196,000
Tswana	1,189,000
Tswana (lingua franca)	*1,260,000*
Other	77,000
Brazil[1]	
Amerindian languages	170,000
German	910,000
Italian	700,000
Japanese	630,000
● Portuguese	162,160,000
Other	1,540,000

Major languages by country	Number of speakers
Brunei	
Chinese	31,000
English	10,000
● Malay	153,000
Malay-Chinese	3,000
Malay-English	97,000
English-Chinese	7,000
Malay-Chinese-	
English	13,000
Other	18,000
Bulgaria[1]	
● Bulgarian	6,800,000
Macedonian	200,000
Romany	300,000
Turkish	770,000
Other	100,000
Burkina Faso[4]	
Dogon	40,000
French	40,000
● French (lingua franca)	*4,900,000*
Fula (Fulani)	1,150,000
Gur (Voltaic) languages	
Bwamu	260,000
Gouin (Cerma)	70,000
Grusi (Gurunsi) group	
Ko	20,000
Lyele	290,000
Nuni	140,000
Sissala	10,000
Lobi	230,000
Mossi (Moore) group	
Dagara	370,000
Gurma	680,000
Kusaal	20,000
Mossi (Moore)	6,000,000
Senufo group	
Minianka	—
Senufo	170,000
Kru languages	
Seme (Siamou)	20,000
Mande languages	
Bobo	270,000
Busansi (Bisa)	430,000
Dyula (Jula)	310,000
Marka	200,000
Samo	280,000
Tamashek (Tuareg)	110,000
Other	850,000
Burundi[1]	
● French	*560,000*
● Rundi	5,930,000
Hutu	5,000,000
Tutsi	880,000
Twa	60,000
Other[5]	120,000

Major languages by country	Number of speakers
Cambodia[1]	
Cham	290,000
Chinese	380,000
● Khmer	10,960,000
Vietnamese	680,000
Other[6]	60,000
Cameroon[1]	
Chadic languages	
Buwal	300,000
Hausa	190,000
Kotoko	170,000
Mandara (Wandala)	870,000
Masana (Masa)	610,000
● English	7,700,000
● French	4,600,000
Niger-Congo languages	
Adamawa-Ubangi languages	
Chamba	370,000
Gbaya (Baya)	190,000
Mbum	200,000
Atlantic languages	
Fula (Fulani)	1,480,000
Benue-Congo languages	
Bamileke (Medumba)-Widikum (Mogha-mo)-Bamum (Mum)	2,860,000
Basa (Bassa)	170,000
Duala	1,680,000
Fang (Pangwe)-Beti-Bulu	3,030,000
Ibibio (Efik)	20,000
Igbo	80,000
Jukun	100,000
Lundu	420,000
Maka	760,000
Tikar	1,140,000
Tiv	400,000
Wute	50,000
Saharan languages	
Kanuri	50,000
Semitic languages	
Arabic	150,000
Other	120,000
Canada	
● English	18,218,000
● French	7,158,000
English-French	116,000
English-other	269,000
French-other	39,000
English-French-other	10,000
Arabic	160,000
Chinese	772,000
Cree	83,000
Dutch	144,000
Eskimo (Inuktitut) languages	29,000
German	486,000
Greek	131,000
Italian	523,000
Pilipino (Filipino)	144,000
Polish	230,000
Portuguese	228,000
Punjābī	218,000
Spanish	230,000
Ukrainian	175,000
Vietnamese	115,000
Other	1,293,000
Cape Verde	
Crioulo (Portuguese Creole)	401,000
● Portuguese	...
Central African Republic	
Banda	820,000
● French	*900,000*
Gbaya (Baya)	830,000
Mandjia	520,000
Mbum	220,000
Ngbaka	270,000
Nzakara	60,000
● Sango (lingua franca)	*3,100,000*
Sara	230,000
Zande (Azande)	70,000
Other	500,000
Chad[1]	
● Arabic	1,040,000
Bagirmi	130,000
Fitri-Batha	390,000
● French	*2,530,000*
Fula (Fulani)	210,000
Gorane	530,000
Hadjarai	560,000
Kanem-Bornu	760,000
Lac-Iro	50,000
Mayo-Kebbi	970,000
Ouaddai	740,000
Sara	2,330,000
Tandjile	550,000
Other	180,000
Chile[1]	
Araucanian (Mapuche)	1,460,000
Aymara	80,000
Rapa Nui	35,000
● Spanish	13,640,000
China[1]	
Achang	30,000
Bulang (Blang)	90,000
Ch'iang (Qiang)	220,000
Chinese (Han)	1,159,850,000
Cantonese (Yüeh [Yue])	*50,000,000*
Hakka	*28,000,000*
Hsiang (Xiang)	*39,000,000*
Kan (Gan)	*22,000,000*
● Mandarin	*899,000,000*
Min	*39,000,000*
Wu	*83,000,000*
Ching-p'o (Jingpo)	130,000
Chuang (Zhuang)	17,230,000
Daghur (Daur)	130,000
Evenk (Ewenki)	30,000
Gelo	490,000
Hani (Woni)	1,400,000
Hui	9,570,000
Kazak	1,240,000
Korean	2,140,000
Kyrgyz	160,000
Lahu	460,000
Li	1,240,000
Lisu	640,000
Manchu	10,930,000
Maonan	80,000
Miao	8,230,000
Mongol	5,350,000
Mulam	180,000
Na-hsi (Naxi)	310,000
Nu	30,000
Pai (Bai)	1,770,000
Pumi	30,000
Puyi (Chung-chia)	2,830,000
Salar	100,000
She	700,000
Shui	380,000
Sibo (Xibe)	190,000
Tai (Dai)	1,140,000
Tajik	40,000
Tibetan	5,110,000
Tu (Monguor)	210,000
T'u-chia (Tujia)	6,350,000
Tung (Dong)	2,800,000
Tung-hsiang (Dongxiang)	420,000
Uighur	8,030,000
Wa (Va)	390,000
Yao	2,370,000
Yi	7,310,000
Other	990,000
Colombia[1]	
Amerindian languages	360,000
Arawakan	40,000
Cariban	30,000
Chibchan	180,000
Other	110,000
English Creole	50,000
● Spanish	41,880,000
Comoros	
● Arabic	...
● Comorian	434,000
Comorian-French	75,000
Comorian-Malagasy	32,000
Comorian-Arabic	10,000
Comorian-Swahili	3,000
Comorian-French-other	23,000
● French	*120,000*
Other	3,000
Congo, Dem. Rep. of the[1]	
Boa	1,220,000
Chokwe	950,000
● English	...
● French	*4,000,000*
Kongo	8,340,000
Kongo (lingua franca)	*16,000,000*
Lingala (lingua franca)	*36,000,000*
Luba	9,340,000
Lugbara	840,000
Mongo	7,000,000
Ngala and Bangi	3,000,000
Rundi	2,000,000
Rwanda	5,340,000
Swahili (lingua franca)	*25,000,000*
Teke	1,420,000
Zande (Azande)	3,170,000
Other	9,340,000
Congo, Rep. of the[1]	
Bobangi	30,000
● French	*1,500,000*
Kongo	1,460,000
Kota	30,000
Lingala (lingua franca)	...
Maka	50,000
Mbete	140,000
Mboshi	330,000
Monokutuba (lingua franca)	*1,700,000*
Punu	90,000
Sango	80,000
Teke	490,000
Other	150,000
Costa Rica	
Chibchan languages	11,000
Bribrí	7,000
Cabécar	4,000
Chinese	7,000
English Creole	73,000
● Spanish	3,553,000
Côte d'Ivoire[1]	
Akan (including Baule and Anyi)	4,800,000
● French	*8,000,000*
Gur ([Voltaic] including Senufo and Lobi)	1,870,000
Kru (including Bete)	1,680,000
Malinke (including Dyula and Bambara)	1,830,000
Southern Mande (including Dan and Guro)	1,230,000
Other (non-Ivoirian population)	4,570,000
Croatia	
● Serbo-Croatian (Croatian)	4,110,000
Other	170,000
Cuba	
● Spanish	11,148,000
Cyprus (island)[1]	
● Greek	640,000
● Turkish	190,000
Other	30,000
Czech Republic[1]	
Bulgarian	3,000
● Czech	8,338,000
German	48,000
Greek	3,000
Hungarian	20,000
Moravian	1,322,000
Polish	60,000
Romanian	1,000
Romany	33,000
Russian	5,000
Ruthenian	2,000
Silesian	44,000
Slovak	314,000
Ukrainian	8,000
Other	70,000
Denmark[2]	
Arabic	39,000
● Danish	5,050,000
English	20,000
German	26,000
South Slavic languages	39,000
Turkish	47,000
Other	119,000
Djibouti[1]	
Afar	160,000
● Arabic	50,000
● French	*70,000*
Somali	200,000
Gadaboursi	...
Issa	...
Issaq	...
Other	40,000
Dominica	
● English	...
English Creole	76,000
French Creole	*69,000*
Dominican Republic	
French (Haitian) Creole	170,000
● Spanish	8,270,000
East Timor	
● Portuguese	70,000
Tetum (Tetun)	530,000
Other	270,000
Ecuador	
Quechuan (and other Amerindian languages)	890,000
● Spanish	11,760,000
Egypt[1]	
● Arabic	65,080,000
Other	790,000
El Salvador	
● Spanish	6,123,000
Equatorial Guinea[1]	
Bubi	50,000
Fang	390,000
● French	...
Krio (English Creole)	...
● Spanish	...
Other	40,000
Eritrea	
Cushitic languages	
Afar	180,000
Bilin	130,000
Hadareb (Beja)	160,000
Saho	120,000
Nilotic languages	
Kunama	110,000
Nara	90,000
Semitic languages	
Arabic (Rashaida)	10,000
Tigré	1,310,000
Tigrinya	2,030,000
Estonia[1]	
Belarusian	21,000
● Estonian	936,000
Finnish	13,000
Russian	403,000
Ukrainian	36,000
Other	26,000
Ethiopia[1]	
Afar	1,210,000
Agew (Awngi)	610,000
Amharic	18,750,000
Berta	150,000
Gedeo	550,000
Gumuz	130,000
Gurage	2,720,000
Hadya–Libida	1,090,000
Kaffa	720,000
Kambata	800,000
Kimant	200,000
Oromo (Oromifa)	20,380,000
Sidamo	2,170,000
Somali	3,990,000
Tigrinya	3,780,000
Walaita	3,900,000
Other	5,730,000
Faroe Islands	
● Danish	...
● Faroese	46,000
Fiji[1]	
● English	*170,000*
Fijian	416,000
Hindi	358,000
Other	45,000
Finland	
Finnish	4,789,000
Russian	26,000
Sami (Lapp)	2,000
Swedish	293,000
Other	68,000
France	
Arabic[7]	1,490,000
English[7]	80,000
● French[7, 8, 9]	55,100,000
Basque	100,000
Breton	*800,000*
Catalan (Rousillonais)	*260,000*
Corsican	*80,000*
Dutch (Flemish)	*90,000*
German (Alsatian)	*1,000,000*
Occitan	*700,000*
Italian[7]	260,000
Polish[7]	50,000
Portuguese[7]	680,000
Spanish[7]	220,000
Turkish[7]	210,000
Other[7]	750,000
French Guiana	
Amerindian languages	3,000
● French	...
French/French Creoles	155,000
Other	7,000
French Polynesia[10]	
Chinese	13,000
● French	188,000
Polynesian languages	213,000
● Tahitian	...
Other	46,000
Gabon[1]	
Fang	430,000
● French	*1,000,000*
Kota	40,000
Mbete	170,000
Mpongwe (Myene)	180,000
Punu, Sira, Nzebi	200,000
Teke	20,000
Other	160,000
Gambia, The[1]	
● English	...
Gambians	
Aku (Krio)	8,000
Atlantic languages	
Diola (Jola)	126,000
Fula (Fulani)	221,000
Manjak	22,000
Serer	33,000
Wolof	172,000
Mande languages	
Bambara	10,000
Malinke	466,000
Soninke	105,000
Other	17,000
non-Gambians	188,000
Gaza Strip	
Arabic	1,141,000
Hebrew	6,000
Georgia	
Abkhaz	90,000
Armenian	350,000
Azerbaijani (Azeri)	280,000
● Georgian (Kartuli)	3,590,000
Ossetian	120,000
Russian	450,000
Other	160,000
Germany[2]	
● German	75,060,000
Greek	360,000
Italian	610,000
Polish	280,000
South Slavic languages	1,190,000
Turkish	2,110,000
Kurdish	*400,000*
Other	2.590,000
Ghana[1]	
Akan	10,240,000
● English	*1,370,000*
Ewe	2,320,000
Ga-Adangme	1,520,000
Gurma	650,000
Hausa (lingua franca)	11,700,000
Mole-Dagbani (Moore)	3,090,000
Yoruba	260,000
Other	1,450,000
Greece	
● Greek	10,400,000
Turkish	100,000
Other	60,000
Greenland[2]	
● Danish	7,000
● Greenlandic	49,000
Grenada	
● English	...
English/English Creole	102,000
Guadeloupe	
● French	...
French/French Creole	407,000
Other	21,000
Guam	
● Chamorro	45,000
Chinese	2,000
Chuukese (Trukese)	2,000
● English	58,000
English (lingua franca)	*153,000*
Japanese	4,000
Korean	5,000
Palauan	2,000
Philippine languages	31,000
Other	6,000
Guatemala	
Garífuna (Black Carib)	30,000
Mayan languages	3,990,000
Cakchiquel	1,020,000
Kekchí	550,000
Mam	310,000
Quiché	1,150,000
● Spanish	7,370,000
Guernsey	
● English	64,000
Norman French	...
Guinea[1]	
Atlantic languages	
Basari-Konyagi	90,000
Fula (Fulani)	2,880,000
Kissi	450,000
Other	230,000
● French	*700,000*
Mande languages	
Kpelle	350,000
Loma	170,000
Malinke	1,730,000
Susu	820,000
Yalunka	220,000
Other	520,000
Other	10,000
Guinea-Bissau[1]	
Balante	390,000
Crioulo (Portuguese Creole)	*570,000*
Ejamat	30,000
French	*130,000*
Fula (Fulani)	280,000
Malinke	170,000
Mandyako	140,000
Mankanya	50,000
Pepel	130,000
● Portuguese	*140,000*
Other	100,000
Guyana	
Amerindian languages	
Arawakan	11,000
Cariban	17,000
● English	...
English/English Creoles	764,000

Language (continued)

Major languages by country	Number of speakers
Haiti	
● French	1,400,000
● Haitian (French) Creole	6,868,000
Honduras	
English Creole	12,000
Garifuna (Black Carib)	82,000
Miskito	11,000
● Spanish	6,307,000
Other	78,000
Hong Kong	
Chinese	
● Cantonese	6,014,000
Cantonese (lingua franca)	6,500,000
Chiu Chau	95,000
Fukien (Min)	129,000
Hakka	113,000
Putonghua (Mandarin)	75,000
Putonghua (lingua franca)	1,230,000
Sze Yap	27,000
● English	150,000
English (lingua franca)	2,140,000
Japanese	14,000
Pilipino (Filipino)	7,000
Other	163,000
Hungary	
German	40,000
● Hungarian	9,870,000
Romanian	10,000
Romany	50,000
Serbo-Croatian	20,000
Slovak	10,000
Other	20,000
Iceland[2]	
● Icelandic	268,000
Other	12,000
India	
Afro-Asiatic languages	
Arabic	30,000
Austroasiatic languages	
Ho	1,140,000
Kharia	270,000
Khasi	1,090,000
Korku	560,000
Munda	500,000
Mundari	1,030,000
Santhali	6,250,000
Savara (Sora)	330,000
Other Austroasiatic	190,000
Dravidian languages	
Gondi	2,550,000
Kannada	39,240,000
Khond	260,000
Koya	320,000
Kui	770,000
Kurukh (Oraon)	1,710,000
Malayalam	36,400,000
Tamil	63,510,000
Telugu	79,100,000
Tulu	1,860,000
Other Dravidian	660,000
English	210,000
● English (lingua franca)	193,000,000
Indo-Iranian (Indo-Aryan) languages	
Assamese	15,670,000
Bengali	83,390,000
Bhili (Bhilodi)	6,680,000
Barel	560,000
Bhilali	560,000
Gujarati	48,730,000
Halabi	640,000
● Hindi	404,100,000
Awadhi	580,000
Baghelkhandi	1,660,000
Bagri	710,000
Banjari	1,060,000
Bhojpuri	27,680,000
Bundelkhandi	1,990,000
Chhattisgarhi	12,690,000
Dhundhari	1,160,000
Garhwali	2,240,000
Harauti	1,480,000
Haryanvi	430,000
Hindi	279,690,000
Kangri	590,000
Khortha (Khotta)	1,260,000
Kumauni	2,060,000
Lamani (Banjari)	2,460,000
Magahi (Magadhi)	12,660,000
Maithili	9,310,000
Malvi	3,560,000
Mandeali	530,000
Marwari	5,600,000
Mewari	2,530,000
Nagpuri	930,000
Nimadi	1,700,000
Pahari	2,610,000
Rajasthani	15,970,000
Sadani (Sadri)	1,880,000
Surgujia	1,250,000
Surjapuri	440,000
Other Hindi dialects	7,390,000
Hindi (lingua franca)	669,000,000
Kashmiri	4,720,000
Khandeshi	1,170,000
Konkani	2,110,000
Lahnda	30,000
Marathi	74,860,000
Nepali (Gorkhali)	2,490,000
Oriya	33,620,000
Punjabi	28,010,000
Sanskrit	60,000
Sindhi	2,540,000
Kachchhi	680,000
Urdu	52,010,000
Sino-Tibetan languages	
Adi	190,000
Angami	120,000
Ao	210,000
Bodo/Boro	1,460,000
Dimasa	110,000
Garo	810,000
Karbi/Makir	440,000
Konyak	170,000
Lotha	100,000
Lushai (Mizo)	650,000
Manipuri (Meithei)	1,520,000
Miri/Mishing	470,000
Nissi/Dafla	210,000
Rabha	170,000
Sema	200,000
Tangkhul	120,000
Thado	130,000
Tripuri	830,000
Kokbarak	620,000
Other Sino-Tibetan languages	1,810,000
Other	5,290,000
Indonesia	
Balinese	3,480,000
Banjarese	3,660,000
Batak	4,650,000
Buginese	4,610,000
● Indonesian (Malay)	25,350,000
Javanese	82,540,000
Madurese	9,060,000
Minangkabau	4,940,000
Sundanese	33,010,000
Other	38,040,000
Iran[1]	
Armenian	300,000
Iranian languages	
Bakhtyari (Luri)	1,050,000
Balochi	1,430,000
● Farsi (Persian)	28,610,000
Farsi (lingua franca)	51,900,000
Gilaki	3,310,000
Kurdish	5,720,000
Luri	2,710,000
Mazandarani	2,260,000
Other	1,360,000
Semitic languages	
Arabic	1,350,000
Other	150,000
Turkic languages	
Afshari	710,000
Azerbaijani (Azeri)	10,540,000
Qashqa'i	800,000
Shahsavani	380,000
Turkish (mostly Pishagchi, Bayat, and Qajar)	450,000
Turkmen	980,000
Other	130,000
Iraq[1]	
● Arabic	17,490,000
Assyrian	190,000
Azerbaijani (Azeri)	390,000
Kurdish	4,300,000
Persian	190,000
Other	130,000
Ireland	
● English	3,720,000
● Irish[11]	60,000
Irish	1,230,000
Isle of Man	
● English	73,000
Israel[12]	
● Arabic	1,100,000
● Hebrew	3,850,000
Russian	550,000
Other	610,000
Italy[1]	
Albanian	120,000
Catalan	30,000
French	310,000
German	310,000
Greek	40,000
● Italian	54,290,000
Rhaetian	740,000
Friulian	720,000
Ladin	20,000
Romany	110,000
Sardinian	1,530,000
Slovene	120,000
Other	130,000
Jamaica	
● English	...
English/English Creoles	2,460,000
Hindi and other Indian languages	50,000
Other	100,000
Japan[2]	
Ainu	15,000
Chinese	240,000
English	80,000
● Japanese	125,800,000
Korean	660,000
Philippine languages	90,000
Other	50,000
Jersey	
● English	89,000
French	...
Norman French	6,000
Jordan[1]	
● Arabic	4,880,000
Armenian	50,000
Kabardian (Circassian)	50,000
Kazakhstan[1]	
Azerbaijani (Azeri)	90,000
Belarusian	150,000
German	460,000
● Kazakh	6,860,000
Korean	90,000
Russian	5,180,000
Tatar	290,000
Uighur	170,000
Ukrainian	740,000
Uzbek	340,000
Other	550,000
Kenya[1]	
Bantu languages	
Bajun (Rajun)	70,000
Basuba	120,000
Embu	360,000
Gusii (Kisii)	1,870,000
Kamba	3,420,000
Kikuyu	6,340,000
Kuria	180,000
Luhya	4,200,000
Mbere	120,000
Meru	1,660,000
Nyika (Mijikenda)	1,450,000
Pokomo	80,000
Swahili	10,000
● Swahili (lingua franca)	20,000,000
Taita	300,000
Cushitic languages	
Oromo languages	
Boran	140,000
Gabbra	60,000
Gurreh	160,000
Orma	60,000
Somali languages	
Degodia	190,000
Ogaden	50,000
Somali	310,000
● English (lingua franca)	2,700,000
Nilotic languages	
Kalenjin	3,270,000
Luo	3,870,000
Masai	480,000
Sambur	150,000
Teso	260,000
Turkana	410,000
Semitic languages	
Arabic	80,000
Other	680,000
Kiribati[1]	
● English	23,000
Kiribati (Gilbertese)	91,000
Tuvaluan (Ellice)	500
Other	600
Korea, North[1]	
Chinese	30,000
● Korean	21,650,000
Korea, South[1]	
Chinese	50,000
● Korean	47,220,000
Kuwait	
● Arabic	1,550,000
Other	440,000
Kyrgyzstan[1]	
Azerbaijani (Azeri)	20,000
German	30,000
Kazakh	50,000
● Kyrgyz	2,920,000
● Russian	790,000
Tajik	40,000
Tatar	60,000
Ukrainian	80,000
Uzbek	690,000
Other	210,000
Laos[1]	
● Lao-Lum (Lao)	2,910,000
Lao-Soung (Miao [Hmong] and Man [Yao])	550,000
Lao-Tai (Tai)	710,000
Lao-Theung (Mon-Khmer)	1,260,000
Other[13]	50,000
Latvia[1]	
Belarusian	90,000
● Latvian	1,340,000
Lithuanian	30,000
Polish	50,000
Russian	780,000
Ukrainian	70,000
Other	40,000
Lebanon[1]	
● Arabic	3,330,000
Armenian	210,000
French	860,000
Other	40,000
Lesotho[1]	
● English	510,000
● Sotho	1,820,000
Zulu	320,000
Liberia[1]	
Atlantic (Mel) languages	
Gola	130,000
Kissi	130,000
● English	630,000
Krio (English Creole)	2,800,000
Kru languages	
Bassa	440,000
Belle	20,000
De (Dewoin, Dey)	10,000
Grebo	280,000
Krahn	120,000
Kru (Krumen)	230,000
Mande (Northern) languages	
Gbandi	90,000
Kpelle	610,000
Loma	180,000
Malinke (Mandingo)	160,000
Mende	20,000
Vai	110,000
Mande (Southern) languages	
Gio (Dan)	250,000
Mano	220,000
Other	160,000
Libya	
● Arabic	4,910,000
Berber	50,000
Other[14]	150,000
Liechtenstein[2]	
● German	28,000
Italian	1,000
Other	3,000
Lithuania[1]	
Belarusian	50,000
● Lithuanian	3,020,000
Polish	260,000
Russian	300,000
Ukrainian	40,000
Other	30,000
Luxembourg[2]	
Belgian	15,000
Dutch	4,000
English	5,000
French	19,000
German	11,000
Italian	20,000
Luxemburgian	278,000
Portuguese	257,000
Other	30,000
Macau	
Chinese	
● Cantonese (Yüeh [Yue])	380,000
Mandarin	5,000
Other Chinese languages	40,000
English	2,000
● Portuguese	10,000
Other	5,000
Macedonia[1]	
Albanian	467,000
● Macedonian	1,358,000
Romany	46,000
Serbo-Croatian	41,000
Turkish	81,000
Vlach	9,000
Other	39,000
Madagascar[1]	
French	2,300,000
Malagasy	15,340,000
Other	160,000
Malawi[1]	
Chewa (Maravi)	6,060,000
● English	540,000
Lomwe	1,910,000
Ngoni	690,000
Yao	1,370,000
Other	350,000
Malaysia	
Bajau	150,000
Chinese	1,350,000
Chinese-others	760,000
Dusun	240,000
English	120,000
English-others	260,000
English (lingua franca)	7,100,000
Iban	550,000
Iban-others	90,000
● Malay	10,030,000
Malay-others	3,560,000
Tamil	900,000
Tamil-others	10,000
Other	5,240,000
Maldives	
● Divehi (Maldivian)	285,000
Mali[1]	
Afro-Asiatic languages	
Berber languages	
Tamashek (Tuareg)	780,000
Semitic languages	
Arabic (Mauri)	170,000
● French	1,100,000
Niger-Congo languages	
Atlantic languages	
Fula (Fulani) and Tukulor	1,490,000
Dogon	430,000
Gur (Voltaic) languages	
Bwa (Bobo)	260,000
Mossi (Moore)	40,000
Senufo and Minianka	1,280,000
Mande languages	
Bambara	3,410,000
Bambara (lingua franca)	8,500,000
Bobo Fing	10,000
Dyula (Jula)	310,000
Malinke, Khasonke, and Wasulunka	710,000
Samo (Duun)	70,000
Soninke	940,000
Nilo-Saharan languages	
Songhai	770,000
Other	30,000
Malta[1]	
● English	13,000
English (lingua franca)	95,000
● Maltese	364,000
Other	5,000
Marshall Islands[2]	
● English	51,600
● Marshallese	50,000
Other	1,600
Martinique	
● French	...
French/French Creole	372,000
Other	13,000
Mauritania[1]	
● Arabic	...
French	270,000
Fula (Fulani)	30,000
Hassānīyah Arabic	2,170,000
Soninke	70,000
Tukulor	140,000
Wolof	180,000
Zenaga	30,000
Other	40,000
Mauritius	
Bhojpuri	226,000
Bhojpuri-other	25,000
Chinese	4,000
● English	2,000
French	41,000
French Creole	732,000
French Creole-other	105,000
Hindi	15,000
Marathi	8,000
Tamil	9,000
Telugu	7,000
Urdu	8,000
Other	3,000
Mayotte[15]	
● Arabic	...
Mahorais (local dialect of Comorian Swahili)	137,000
Other Comorian Swahili dialects	60,000
Malagasy	53,000
● French	66,000
Other	10,000
Mexico	
Amerindian languages	7,800,000
Amuzgo	40,000
Aztec (Nahuatl)	1,770,000
Chatino	40,000
Chinantec	160,000
Chocho	20,000

Major languages by country	Number of speakers
Chol	190,000
Chontal	50,000
Cora	20,000
Cuicatec	20,000
Huastec	180,000
Huave	20,000
Huichol	30,000
Kanjobal	20,000
Mame	20,000
Mayo	60,000
Mazahua	200,000
Mazatec	240,000
Mixe	140,000
Mixtec	570,000
Otomí	420,000
Popoluca	50,000
Purépecha (Tarasco)	140,000
Tarahumara	80,000
Tepehua	10,000
Tepehuan	30,000
Tlapanec	100,000
Tojolabal	50,000
Totonac	310,000
Trique	20,000
Tzeltal	390,000
Tzotzil	350,000
Yaqui	20,000
Yucatec (Mayan)	1,050,000
Zapotec	580,000
Zoque	70,000
Other	350,000
● Spanish	91,080,000
Spanish-Amerindian languages	*6,350,000*
Micronesia	
Chuukese (Trukese)	49,000
English	1,000
Kosraean	9,000
Mortlockese	9,000
Palauan	500
Pohnpeian	28,000
Woleaian	4,000
Yapese	7,000
Other	11,000
Moldova	
Bulgarian	70,000
Gagauz	140,000
● Romanian (Moldovan)	2,660,000
Russian	990,000
Ukrainian	370,000
Other	60,000
Monaco[2]	
English	2,000
● French	13,000
Italian	5,000
Monegasque	5,000
Other	6,000
Mongolia[1]	
Bayad	46,000
Buryat	41,000
Darhat	17,000
Dariganga	34,000
Dörbet	65,000
Dzakhchin	26,000
Kazakh	142,000
● Khalkha (Mongolian)	1,890,000
Khalkha (lingua franca)	*2,150,000*
Ould	10,000
Torgut	12,000
Tuvan (Uryankhai)	24,000
Other	94,000
Morocco	
● Arabic	18,730,000
Berber	9,510,000
French	*11,500,000*
Other	580,000
Mozambique	
Bantu languages	
Chuabo	1,200,000
Lomwe	1,450,000
Makua	5,020,000
Sena	1,340,000
Tsonga (Changana)	2,180,000
Other Bantu languages	6,300,000
● Portuguese	1,240,000
Portuguese (lingua franca)	*7,570,000*
Other	360,000
Myanmar (Burma)[1]	
● Burmese	28,780,000
Burmese (lingua franca)	*33,400,000*
Chin	910,000
Kachin (Ching-p'o)	570,000
Karen	2,600,000
Kayah	170,000
Mon	1,010,000
Rakhine (Arakanese)	1,880,000
Shan	3,530,000
Other	2,290,000
Namibia	
Afrikaans	168,000
Caprivi	83,000
● English	14,000
English (lingua franca)	*340,000*
German	16,000
Herero	142,000
Kavango (Okavango)	172,000
Nama	221,000
Ovambo (Ambo [Kwanyama])	897,000
San (Bushman)	34,000
Tswana	8,000
Other	17,000
Nauru	
Chinese	1,000
English	900
English (lingua franca)	*10,700*
Kiribati (Gilbertese)	2,100
Nauruan	6,800
Tuvaluan (Ellice)	1,000
Nepal	
Austroasiatic (Munda) languages	
Santhali	40,000
English	*7,300,000*
Indo-Aryan languages	
Bengali	40,000
Bhojpuri	1,840,000
Dhanwar	30,000
Hindi	230,000
Hindi (Awadhi dialect)	500,000
Maithili	2,930,000
● Nepali (Eastern Pahari)	12,430,000
Rajbansi	110,000
Tharu	1,330,000
Urdu	270,000
Tibeto-Burman languages	
Bhutia (Sherpa)	160,000
Chepang	30,000
Gurung	300,000
Limbu	340,000
Magar	570,000
Newari	920,000
Rai and Kiranti	590,000
Tamang	1,210,000
Thakali	10,000
Thami	20,000
Other	790,000
Netherlands, The[2]	
Arabic	130,000
● Dutch	15,228,000
Dutch and Frisian	600,000
Turkish	103,000
Other	435,000
Netherlands Antilles	
● Dutch	...
English	18,000
Papiamento	190,000
Other	13,000
New Caledonia[1]	
● French	72,000
Indonesian	5,000
Melanesian languages	95,000
Polynesian languages	25,000
Vietnamese	3,000
Other	11,000
New Zealand	
● English	3,338,000
English-Māori	149,000
● Māori	14,000
Other	334,000
Nicaragua	
English Creole	27,000
Misumalpan languages	
Miskito	79,000
Sumo	8,000
● Spanish	4,697,000
Other	2,000
Niger[1]	
Atlantic languages	
Fula (Fulani)	980,000
Berber languages	
Tamashek (Tuareg)	1,050,000
Chadic languages	
Hausa	5,340,000
Hausa (lingua franca)	*7,100,000*
● French	*1,500,000*
Gur (Voltaic) languages	
Gurma	30,000
Saharan languages	
Kanuri	450,000
Teda (Tubu)	40,000
Semitic languages	
Arabic	30,000
Songhai and Zerma	2,140,000
Other	20,000
Nigeria[1]	
Arabic	300,000
Bura	1,900,000
Edo	4,200,000
● English/English Creole (lingua franca)	*56,000,000*
Fula (Fulani)	13,900,000
Hausa	26,300,000
Hausa (lingua franca)	*62,000,000*
Ibibio	6,900,000
Igbo (Ibo)	22,200,000
Ijo (Ijaw)	2,200,000
Kanuri	5,100,000
Nupe	1,500,000
Tiv	2,800,000
Yoruba	26,300,000
Other	9,600,000
Northern Mariana Islands	
● Carolinian	3,400
● Chamorro	21,500
Chinese	5,100
Chuukese (Trukese)	1,700
● English	3,400
English (lingua franca)	*65,100*
Japanese	1,400
Korean	4,700
Palauan	2,500
Philippine languages	24,500
Other	3,600
Norway[2]	
Danish	18,000
English	24,000
● Norwegian	4,332,000
Swedish	13,000
Other	100,000
Oman	
● Arabic (Omani)	1,850,000
Other	560,000
Pakistan	
Balochi	4,260,000
Brahui	1,730,000
English (lingua franca)	*16,000,000*
Pashto	18,600,000
Punjabi	
Punjabi	68,190,000
Hindko	3,440,000
Sindhi	
Saraiki	13,910,000
Sindhi	16,660,000
● Urdu	10,760,000
Other	4,030,000
Palau	
Chinese	300
● English	600
English (lingua franca)	*18,700*
● Palauan	15,500
Philippine languages	1,800
Other	700
Panama	
Amerindian languages	
Bokotá	5,000
Chibchan	
Guaymí (Ngöbe Buglé)	150,000
Kuna	57,000
Teribe	3,000
Chocó	
Emberá	18,000
Wounaan	3,000
Arabic	16,000
Chinese	8,000
English	...
English Creoles	395,000
● Spanish	2,168,000
Papua New Guinea[1]	
● English	*140,000*
Melanesian languages	990,000
Motu	*160,000*
Papuan languages	3,840,000
Tok Pisin (English Creole)	*3,200,000*
Other	100,000
Paraguay	
German	50,000
● Guaraní	2,210,000
Guaraní-Spanish	2,670,000
Portuguese	170,000
● Spanish	360,000
Other	40,000
Peru	
Amerindian languages	
● Aymara	590,000
● Quechua	4,220,000
Other	180,000
● Spanish	20,470,000
Other	200,000
Philippines	
Aklanon	560,000
Bantoanon	70,000
Bicol	4,340,000
Bilaan	40,000
Bontoc	60,000
Butuanon	80,000
Cebuano	17,760,000
Chavacano	470,000
Chinese	70,000
Davaweno (Mansaka)	520,000
● English (lingua franca)	*39,700,000*
Hiligaynon	6,950,000
Ibaloi (Nabaloi)	130,000
Ibanag	280,000
Ifugao	210,000
Ilocano	7,110,000
Ilongot	110,000
Kalinga	130,000
Kankanai	290,000
Kinaray-a (Hamtikanon)	480,000
Maguindanao	1,110,000
Manobo	510,000
Maranao	970,000
Masbateño	530,000
Palawano	80,000
Pampango	2,280,000
Pangasinan	1,380,000
● Pilipino (Filipino; Tagalog)	22,350,000
Romblon	240,000
Samal	480,000
Sambal	200,000
Subanon	310,000
Surigaonon	560,000
Tau Sug	880,000
Tboli	100,000
Tinggian	70,000
Tiruray	70,000
Waray-Waray	2,910,000
Yakan	150,000
Other	1,500,000
Poland	
Belarusian	190,000
German	500,000
● Polish	37,730,000
Ukrainian	230,000
Portugal[2]	
● Portuguese	9,910,000
Other	100,000
Puerto Rico	
● English	20,000
● Spanish	2,010,000
Spanish-English	1,840,000
Other	50,000
Qatar[2]	
● Arabic	240,000
Other[16]	360,000
Réunion	
Chinese	20,000
Comorian	20,000
● French	*220,000*
French Creole	660,000
Malagasy	10,000
Tamil	*140,000*
Other	10,000
Romania	
Bulgarian	9,000
Czech	5,000
German	97,000
Hungarian	1,612,000
Polish	3,000
● Romanian	20,343,000
Romany (Tigani)	164,000
Russian	31,000
Serbo-Croatian	33,000
Slovak	18,000
Tatar	22,000
Turkish	27,000
Ukrainian	63,000
Other	5,000
Russia	
Adyghian	120,000
Armenian	360,000
Avar	530,000
Azerbaijani (Azeri)	280,000
Bashkir	970,000
Belarusian	430,000
Buryat	360,000
Chechen	880,000
Chuvash	1,370,000
Dargin	340,000
Georgian (Kartuli)	90,000
German	350,000
Ingush	210,000
Kabardian	370,000
Kalmyk	150,000
Karachay	150,000
Kazakh	560,000
Komi-Permyak	100,000
Komi-Zyryan	240,000
Kumyk	270,000
Lak	100,000
Lezgi (Lezgian)	240,000
Mari	520,000
Mordvin	730,000
Ossetian	370,000
Romanian	110,000
Romany	130,000
● Russian	126,420,000
Tabasaran	90,000
Tatar	4,690,000
Tuvan	200,000
Udmurt	500,000
Ukrainian	1,860,000
Uzbek	100,000
Yakut	360,000
Other	1,440,000
Rwanda	
● English	...
● French	*500,000*
● Rwanda	7,299,000
St. Kitts and Nevis	
● English	...
English/English Creole	39,000
St. Lucia	
● English	31,000
English/French Creole	126,000
St. Vincent and the Grenadines	
● English	...
English/English Creole	112,000
Other	1,000
Samoa	
● English	1,000
● Samoan	85,000
Samoan-English	93,000
San Marino[1]	
● Italian (Romagnolo)	26,800
São Tomé and Príncipe	
Crioulo (Portuguese Creole)	124,000
English	...
French	1,000
● Portuguese	...
Other	18,000
Saudi Arabia[1]	
● Arabic	20,920,000
Other	1,100,000
Senegal	
● French	*3,500,000*
Senegalese	
Bambara	90,000
Diola	490,000
Fula (Fulani)-Tukulor	2,170,000
Malinke (Mandingo)	370,000
Serer	1,250,000
Soninke	130,000
Wolof	4,800,000
Wolof (lingua franca)	*8,000,000*
Other	440,000
non-Senegalese	220,000
Seychelles	
English	3,000
English (lingua franca)	*29,000*
French	1,000
French (lingua franca)	*78,000*
Seselwa (French Creole)	75,000
Other	3,000
Sierra Leone[1]	
Atlantic languages	
Bullom-Sherbro	200,000
Fula (Fulani)	200,000
Kissi	120,000
Limba	440,000
Temne	1,660,000
● English	*500,000*
Krio (English Creole [lingua franca])	*4,400,000*
Mande languages	
Kono-Vai	270,000
Kuranko	180,000
Mende	1,810,000
Susu	80,000
Yalunka	180,000
Other	90,000
Singapore[1]	
Chinese	2,517,000
● English	*1,226,000*
● Malay	456,000
● Mandarin Chinese	*1,421,000*
● Tamil (and other Indian languages)	259,000
Other	43,000
Slovakia[1]	
Czech, Moravian, and Silesian	59,000
German	5,000
Hungarian	569,000
Polish	3,000
Romany	90,000
Ruthenian, Ukrainian, and Russian	35,000
● Slovak	4,626,000
Other	15,000
Slovenia	
Hungarian	9,000
Serbo-Croatian	155,000
● Slovene	1,725,000
Other	74,000

Language   (continued)

Major languages by country	Number of speakers
Solomon Islands[1]	
● English	*9,000*
Melanesian languages	399,000
Papuan languages	40,000
Polynesian languages	17,000
Solomon Island Pidgin (English Creole)	*163,000*
Other	10,000
Somalia[1]	
● Arabic	...
English	...
● Somali	7,130,000
Other	120,000
South Africa	
● Afrikaans	6,220,000
● English	3,700,000
Nguni	
● Ndebele	630,000
● Swazi	1,080,000
● Xhosa	7,700,000
● Zulu	9,840,000
Sotho	
● North Sotho (Pedi)	3,950,000
● South Sotho	3,320,000
● Tswana (Western Sotho)	3,530,000
● Tsonga	1,880,000
● Venda	940,000
Other	620,000
Spain	
Basque (Euskera)	630,000
● Castilian Spanish	29,860,000
Catalan (Català)	6,770,000
Galician (Gallego)	2,560,000
Other	300,000
Sri Lanka	
English	10,000
English-Sinhala	1,060,000
English-Sinhala-Tamil	690,000
English-Tamil	220,000
● Sinhala	11,610,000
Sinhala-Tamil	1,800,000
● Tamil	3,780,000
Other	60,000
Sudan, The[1]	
● Arabic	17,320,000
Arabic (lingua franca)	*21,000,000*
Bari	860,000
Beja	2,240,000
Dinka	4,050,000
Fur	720,000
Lotuko	520,000
Nubian languages	2,840,000
Nuer	1,720,000
Shilluk	600,000
Zande (Azande)	950,000
Other	3,260,000
Suriname	
● Dutch	*110,000*
English/English Creole	410,000
Sranantonga	170,000
Sranantonga-other	170,000
Other (mostly Hindī, Javanese, and Saramacca)	90,000
Swaziland[1]	
● English	*50,000*
● Swazi	970,000
Zulu	20,000
Other	80,000
Sweden[2]	
Arabic	68,000
Danish	41,000
English	32,000
Finnish	209,000
German	45,000
Iranian languages	49,000
Norwegian	46,000
Polish	39,000
South Slavic languages	116,000
Spanish	56,000
● Swedish	7,937,000
Turkish	29,000
Other	197,000
Switzerland	
● French	1,380,000
● German	4,570,000
● Italian	550,000
Romansch	40,000
Other	640,000

Major languages by country	Number of speakers
Syria[1]	
● Arabic	14,680,000
Kurdish	1,470,000
Other	160,000
Taiwan	
Austronesian languages	
Ami	138,000
Atayal	89,000
Bunun	42,000
Paiwan	68,000
Puyuma	10,000
Rukai	11,000
Saisiyat	6,000
Tsou	7,000
Yami	4,000
Chinese languages	
Hakka	2,440,000
● Mandarin	4,460,000
Min (South Fukien)	14,800,000
Other	120,000
Tajikistan	
Russian	610,000
● Tajik (Tojik)	3,920,000
Uzbek	1,460,000
Other	310,000
Tanzania[1]	
Chaga (Chagga), Pare	1,730,000
● English	*3,800,000*
Gogo	1,390,000
Ha	1,210,000
Haya	2,080,000
Hehet	2,430,000
Iramba	1,010,000
Luguru	1,730,000
Luo	290,000
Makonde	2,080,000
Masai	350,000
Ngoni	470,000
Nyakusa	1,910,000
Nyamwesi (Sukuma)	7,450,000
Shambala	1,510,000
● Swahili	3,120,000
Swahili (lingua franca)	*32,000,000*
Tatoga	260,000
Yao	860,000
Other	5,430,000
Thailand[1]	
Chinese	7,570,000
Karen	220,000
Malay	2,270,000
Mon-Khmer languages	
Khmer	790,000
Kuy	670,000
Other	220,000
Tai languages	
Lao	16,790,000
● Thai (Siamese)	32,820,000
Other	430,000
Other	640,000
Togo[1]	
Atlantic (Mel) languages	
Fula (Fulani)	68,000
Benue-Congo languages	
Ana (Ana-Ife)	126,000
Nago	13,000
Yoruba	10,000
Chadic languages	
Hausa	14,000
● French	*2,500,000*
Gur (Voltaic) languages	
Basari	88,000
Chakossi (Akan)	59,000
Chamba	49,000
Dye (Gangam)	47,000
Gurma	170,000
Kabre	692,000
Konkomba	71,000
Kotokoli (Tem)	289,000
Moba	270,000
Mossi (Moore)	13,000
Namba (Lamba)	153,000
Naudemba (Losso)	206,000
Tamberma	28,000
Yanga	15,000
Kwa languages	
Adja (Aja)	157,000
Adele	10,000
Ahlo	9,000
Akposo	134,000
Ane (Basila)	284,000

Major languages by country	Number of speakers
Anlo	4,000
Anyaga	10,000
Ewe	1,164,000
Fon	50,000
Hwe	6,000
Kebu	58,000
Kpessi	4,000
Peda-Hula (Pla)	20,000
Watyi (Ouatchi)	517,000
Other	212,000
Tonga	
● English	*30,000*
● Tongan	98,000
Other	2,000
Trinidad and Tobago	
● English	...
English Creole[17]	37,000
Hindi	45,000
Trinidad English	1,208,000
● Other	3,000
Tunisia	
● Arabic	6,710,000
Arabic-French	2,520,000
Arabic-French-English	300,000
Arabic-other	10,000
Other-no Arabic	30,000
Other	30,000
Turkey[1]	
Arabic	900,000
Kurdish[18]	6,960,000
● Turkish	57,510,000
Other	300,000
Turkmenistan[1]	
Armenian	37,000
Azerbaijani (Azeri)	40,000
Balochi	40,000
Kazakh	96,000
Russian	329,000
Tatar	40,000
● Turkmen	3,745,000
Ukrainian	25,000
Uzbek	448,000
Other	85,000
Tuvalu	
English	...
Kiribati (Gilbertese)	800
Tuvaluan (Ellice)	10,000
Uganda[1]	
Bantu languages	
Amba	90,000
Ganda (Luganda)	4,220,000
Gisu (Masaba)	1,050,000
Gwere	380,000
Kiga (Chiga)	1,950,000
Konjo	510,000
Nkole (Nyankole and Hororo)	2,500,000
Nyole	320,000
Nyoro	690,000
Ruli	100,000
Rundi	140,000
Rwanda	750,000
Samia	310,000
Soga	1,920,000
Swahili (lingua franca)	*8,200,000*
Toro	680,000
Central Sudanic languages	
Lugbara	1,100,000
Madi	180,000
Ndo	230,000
● English	*2,500,000*
Nilotic languages	
Acholi	1,030,000
Alur	550,000
Kakwa	120,000
Karamojong	490,000
Kumam	160,000
Lango	1,370,000
Padhola	350,000
Sebei (Kupsabiny)	150,000
Teso	1,400,000
Other (mostly Gujarati and Hindi)	580,000
Ukraine	
Belarusian	150,000
Bulgarian	160,000
Hungarian	150,000
Polish	30,000
Romanian	330,000
Russian	16,310,000
● Ukrainian	32,110,000
Other	430,000

Major languages by country	Number of speakers
United Arab Emirates[2]	
● Arabic	1,270,000
Other[16]	1,750,000
United Kingdom	
● English	58,090,000
Scots-Gaelic	80,000
Welsh	570,000
Other	970,000
United States	
Amharic	40,000
Arabic	420,000
Armenian	180,000
Bengali	50,000
Cajun	40,000
Chinese (including Formosan)	1,550,000
Czech	110,000
Danish	40,000
Dutch	170,000
English	237,320,000
English (lingua franca)	*267,000,000*
Finnish	60,000
French	2,030,000
French Creole (mostly Haitian)	220,000
German	1,850,000
Greek	460,000
Gujarati	120,000
Hebrew	170,000
Hindi (including Urdu)	400,000
Hungarian	180,000
Ilocano	50,000
Italian	1,560,000
Japanese	510,000
Korean	750,000
Kru (Gullah)	80,000
Lithuanian	70,000
Malayalam	40,000
Miao (Hmong)	100,000
Mon-Khmer (mostly Cambodian)	150,000
Navajo	180,000
Norwegian	100,000
Pennsylvania Dutch	100,000
Persian	240,000
Polish	860,000
Portuguese	510,000
Punjābī	60,000
Romanian	80,000
Russian	290,000
Samoan	40,000
Serbo-Croatian	140,000
Slovak	100,000
Spanish	20,720,000
Swedish	90,000
Syriac	40,000
Tagalog	1,010,000
Tai (including Laotian)	250,000
Turkish	50,000
Ukrainian	120,000
Vietnamese	610,000
Yiddish	250,000
Other	810,000
Uruguay	
● Spanish	3,140,000
Other	140,000
Uzbekistan[1]	
Kazakh	1,010,000
Russian	1,490,000
Tajik	1,190,000
Tatar	400,000
● Uzbek	18,770,000
Other	1,910,000
Vanuatu[19]	
● Bislama (English Creole)	120,000
● English	60,000
● French	30,000
Other	2,000
Venezuela	
Amerindian languages	
Goajiro	160,000
Warrau (Warao)	20,000
Other	150,000
● Spanish	23,310,000
Other	520,000
Vietnam[1]	
Bahnar	170,000
Cham	120,000
Chinese (Hoa)	1,100,000
French	*380,000*
Hre	120,000

Major languages by country	Number of speakers
Jarai	300,000
Khmer	1,090,000
Koho	110,000
Man (Mien, or Yao)	580,000
Miao (Meo, or Hmong)	690,000
Mnong	80,000
Muong	1,120,000
Nung	870,000
Rade (Rhadé)	240,000
Roglai	90,000
San Chay (Cao Lan)	140,000
San Diu	120,000
Sedang	120,000
Stieng	60,000
Tai	1,280,000
Tho (Tay)	1,460,000
● Vietnamese	68,400,000
Other	160,000
Virgin Islands (U.S.)	
● English	98,000
French	3,000
Spanish	16,000
Other	3,000
West Bank[20]	
Arabic	2,010,000
Hebrew	170,000
Western Sahara	
Arabic	245,000
Yemen[1]	
● Arabic	17,400,000
Other	70,000
Yugoslavia[1]	
Albanian	1,760,000
Hungarian	350,000
Macedonian	50,000
Romanian	40,000
Romany	150,000
● Serbo-Croatian (Serbian)	8,020,000
Serbo-Croatian (lingua franca)	*10,100,000*
Slovak	70,000
Vlach	20,000
Other	200,000
Zambia[21]	
Bemba group	
Bemba	2,850,000
Bemba (lingua franca)	*5,000,000*
Bisa	110,000
Lala	230,000
Lamba	210,000
Other	400,000
● English	110,000
English (lingua franca)	*1,800,000*
Lozi (Barotse) group	
Lozi (Barotse)	610,000
Other	110,000
Mambwe group	
Lungu	70,000
Mambwe	110,000
Mwanga (Winawanga)	130,000
Other	10,000
North-Western group	
Kaonde	220,000
Lunda	190,000
Luvale (Luena)	170,000
Other	260,000
Nyanja (Maravi) group	
Chewa	550,000
Ngoni	160,000
Nsenga	410,000
Nyanja (Maravi)	750,000
Nyanja (lingua franca)	*2,500,000*
Other	60,000
Tonga (Ila-Tonga) group	
Ila	90,000
Lenje	150,000
Tonga	1,050,000
Other	120,000
Tumbuka group	
Senga	70,000
Tumbuka	280,000
Other	10,000
Other	90,000
Zimbabwe	
● English	250,000
English (lingua franca)	*5,300,000*
Ndebele (Nguni)	1,840,000
Nyanja	260,000
Shona	8,180,000
Other	810,000

[1]Figures given represent ethnolinguistic groups.   [2]Data refer to nationality (usually resident aliens holding foreign passports).   [3]Data are partly based on place of residence.   [4]Majority of population speak Moore (language of the Mossi); Dyula is language of commerce.   [5]Swahili also spoken.   [6]English and French also spoken.   [7]Based on "nationality" at 1982 census.   [8]Includes naturalized citizens.   [9]French is the universal language throughout France; traditional dialects and minority languages are retained regionally in the approximate numbers shown, however.   [10]Data reflect multilingualism; 2000 population estimate is 233,000.   [11]Refers to Irish speakers in Gaeltacht areas.   [12]Includes the population of the Golan Heights and East Jerusalem; excludes the Israeli population in the West Bank and Gaza Strip.   [13]English and French also spoken.   [14]English and Italian also spoken.   [15]Data reflect ability to speak the language, not mother tongue; 2000 population estimate is 156,000.   [16]Mostly Pakistanis, Indians, and Iranians.   [17]Spoken on Tobago only.   [18]Other estimates of the Kurdish population range from 6 percent to 20–25 percent.   [19]Data reflect multilingualism; 2000 population is 190,000.   [20]Excludes East Jerusalem.   [21]Groups are officially defined geographic divisions; elements comprising them are named by language.

Religion

The following table presents statistics on religious affiliation for each of the countries of the world. An assessment was made for each country of the available data on distribution of religious communities within the total population; the best available figures, whether originating as census data, membership figures of the churches concerned, or estimates by external analysts in the absence of reliable local data, were applied as percentages to the estimated 2001 midyear population of the country to obtain the data shown below.

Several concepts govern the nature of the available data, each useful separately but none the basis of any standard of international practice in the collection of such data. The word "affiliation" was used above to describe the nature of the relationship joining the religious bodies named and the populations shown. This term implies some sort of formal, usually documentary, connection between the religion and the individual (a baptismal certificate, a child being assigned the religion of its parents on a census form, maintenance of one's name on the tax rolls of a state religion, etc.) but says nothing about the nature of the individual's personal religious practice, in that the individual may have lapsed, never been confirmed as an adult, joined another religion, or may have joined an organization that is formally atheist.

The user of these statistics should be careful to note that not only does the nature of the affiliation (with an organized religion) differ greatly from country to country, but the social context of religious practice does also. A country in which a single religion has long been predominant will often show more than 90% of its population to be *affiliated*, while in actual fact, no more than 10% may actually *practice* that religion on a regular basis. Such a situation often leads to undercounting of minority religions (where someone [head of household, communicant, child] is counted at all), blurring of distinctions seen to be significant elsewhere (a Hindu country may not distinguish Protestant [or even Christian] denominations; a Christian country may not distinguish among its Muslim or Buddhist citizens), or double-counting in countries where an individual may conscientiously practice more than one "religion" at a time.

Until 1989 communist countries had for long consciously attempted to ignore, suppress, or render invisible religious practice within their borders. Countries with large numbers of adherents of traditional, often animist, religions and belief systems usually will have little or no formal methodology for defining the nature of local religious practice. On the other hand, countries with strong missionary traditions, or good census organizations, or few religious sensitivities may have very good, detailed, and meaningful data.

The most comprehensive works available are DAVID B. BARRETT (ed.), *World Christian Encyclopedia* (2001); and PETER BRIERLEY, *World Churches Handbook* (1997).

Religion

Religious affiliation	2001 population	Religious affiliation	2001 population	Religious affiliation	2001 population	Religious affiliation	2001 population	Religious affiliation	2001 population
Afghanistan		**Azerbaijan**		Roman Catholic	710,000	**Central African Republic**		**Cuba**	
Sunnī Muslim	23,090,000	Shīʿī Muslim	5,299,000	other	350,000	Roman Catholic	660,000	Roman Catholic	4,420,000
Shīʿī Muslim	2,310,000	Sunnī Muslim	2,271,000	**Botswana**		Muslim	560,000	Protestant	270,000
other	490,000	other	535,000	African Christian	490,000	traditional beliefs	550,000	other (mostly Santeria)	6,500,000
				Protestant	170,000	Protestant	520,000		
Albania		**Bahamas, The**		Roman Catholic	60,000	other	1,290,000	**Cyprus**	
Muslim	1,200,000	Protestant	135,000	other (mostly				Greek Orthodox	630,000
Roman Catholic	520,000	Roman Catholic	50,000	traditional beliefs)	870,000	**Chad**		Muslim (mostly Sunnī)	200,000
Albanian Orthodox	320,000	Anglican	32,000			Muslim	4,690,000	other (mostly	
other	1,050,000	other	77,000	**Brazil**		Roman Catholic	1,770,000	Christian)	40,000
				Roman Catholic		Protestant	1,250,000		
Algeria		**Bahrain**		(including syncretic		traditional beliefs	640,000	**Czech Republic**	
Sunnī Muslim	30,550,000	Shīʿī Muslim	420,000	Afro-Catholic cults		other	350,000	Roman Catholic	4,010,000
Ibādīyah Muslim	180,000	Sunnī Muslim	140,000	having Spiritist				Evangelical Church of	
other	90,000	other	140,000	beliefs and rituals)	124,470,000	**Chile**		Czech Brethren	200,000
				Evangelical Protestant	39,850,000	Roman Catholic	11,810,000	Czechoslovak Hussite	180,000
American Samoa		**Bangladesh**		other	7,800,000	Evangelical		Silesian Evangelical	30,000
Congregational	23,800	Muslim	112,660,000			Protestant	1,910,000	Eastern Orthodox	20,000
Roman Catholic	11,300	Hindu	16,260,000	**Brunei**		other	1,690,000	atheist and	
other	23,400	other	2,360,000	Muslim	222,000			nonreligious	4,100,000
				other	121,000	**China**		other	1,730,000
Andorra		**Barbados**				nonreligious	661,390,000		
Roman Catholic	60,000	Anglican	89,000	**Bulgaria**		Chinese folk-		**Denmark**	
other	7,000	Protestant	80,000	Bulgarian Orthodox	5,690,000	religionist	256,260,000	Evangelical Lutheran	4,600,000
		Roman Catholic	12,000	Muslim (mostly		atheist	152,990,000	Muslim	120,000
Angola		other	88,000	Sunnī)	940,000	Buddhist	108,110,000	other	640,000
Roman Catholic	6,440,000			other	1,320,000	Christian	76,540,000		
Protestant	1,550,000	**Belarus**				Muslim	18,360,000	**Djibouti**	
African Christian	710,000	Belarusian		**Burkina Faso**		traditional beliefs	1,280,000	Sunnī Muslim	434,000
other	1,660,000	Orthodox	3,151,000	Muslim	5,960,000			other	27,000
		Roman Catholic	1,772,000	traditional beliefs	4,180,000	**Colombia**			
Antigua and Barbuda		other	5,062,000	Christian	2,040,000	Roman Catholic	39,590,000	**Dominica**	
Protestant	30,000			other	80,000	other	3,480,000	Roman Catholic	50,000
Anglican	23,000	**Belgium**						Protestant	12,000
Roman Catholic	8,000	Roman Catholic	8,310,000	**Burundi**		**Comoros**		other	10,000
other	10,000	nonreligious	600,000	Roman Catholic	4,050,000	Sunnī Muslim	555,000		
		other	1,360,000	nonreligious	1,160,000	other	11,000	**Dominican Republic**	
Argentina				other (mostly				Roman Catholic	7,110,000
Roman Catholic	29,920,000	**Belize**		Protestant)	1,020,000	**Congo, Dem. Rep. of the**		Protestant	560,000
Protestant	2,040,000	Roman Catholic	143,000			Roman Catholic	21,990,000	other	1,020,000
Muslim	730,000	Protestant	67,000	**Cambodia**		Protestant	16,950,000		
Jewish	500,000	Anglican	17,000	Buddhist	10,780,000	African Christian	7,170,000	**East Timor**	
nonreligious	880,000	other	20,000	Chinese folk-religionist	600,000	traditional beliefs	5,740,000	Roman Catholic	780,000
other	3,430,000			traditional beliefs	550,000	Muslim	750,000	Protestant	50,000
		Benin		Muslim	290,000	other	1,040,000	Muslim	30,000
Armenia		Voodoo		other	500,000			other	40,000
Armenian Apostolic		(traditional beliefs)	3,390,000			**Congo, Rep. of the**			
(Orthodox)	2,454,000	Roman Catholic	1,370,000	**Cameroon**		Roman Catholic	1,430,000	**Ecuador**	
other	1,353,000	Muslim	1,320,000	Roman Catholic	4,180,000	Protestant	490,000	Roman Catholic	11,910,000
		other	500,000	traditional beliefs	3,750,000	African Christian	360,000	Protestant	440,000
Aruba				Muslim	3,350,000	other	610,000	other	530,000
Roman Catholic	80,000	**Bermuda**		Protestant	3,270,000				
other	18,000	Anglican	23,700	other	1,250,000	**Costa Rica**		**Egypt**	
		Methodist	10,400			Roman Catholic	3,380,000	Sunnī Muslim	58,060,000
Australia		Roman Catholic	8,800	**Canada**		Protestant	360,000	Coptic Orthodox[1]	6,520,000
Roman Catholic	5,230,000	other	20,900	Roman Catholic	14,010,000	other	190,000	other	660,000
Anglican	4,260,000			Protestant	8,620,000				
Uniting Church	1,460,000	**Bhutan**		Anglican	2,490,000	**Côte d'Ivoire**		**El Salvador**	
Presbyterian	740,000	Lamaistic Buddhist	510,000	Eastern Orthodox	440,000	Muslim	6,340,000	Roman Catholic	4,880,000
other Protestant	1,400,000	Hindu	140,000	Jewish	360,000	Roman Catholic	3,400,000	Protestant	1,070,000
Orthodox	540,000	other	40,000	Muslim	290,000	traditional beliefs	2,790,000	other	290,000
nonreligious	3,220,000			Buddhist	190,000	nonreligious	2,220,000		
other	2,510,000	**Bolivia**		Hindu	180,000	Protestant	870,000	**Equatorial Guinea**	
		Roman Catholic	7,540,000	Sikh	170,000	other	770,000	Roman Catholic	390,000
Austria		Protestant	770,000	nonreligious	3,880,000			other	110,000
Roman Catholic	6,060,000	other	210,000	other	380,000	**Croatia**			
Protestant (mostly						Roman Catholic	3,890,000	**Eritrea**	
Lutheran)	430,000	**Bosnia and Herzegovina**		**Cape Verde**		Serbian Orthodox	250,000	Eritrean Orthodox	1,980,000
atheist and		Sunnī Muslim	1,690,000	Roman Catholic	370,000	Sunnī Muslim	100,000	Muslim	1,920,000
nonreligious	690,000	Serbian Orthodox	1,180,000	other	35,000	Protestant	30,000	other	400,000
other	890,000					other	130,000		

Religion (continued)

Religious affiliation	2001 population
Estonia	
Estonian Orthodox	277,000
Evangelical Lutheran	187,000
other	899,000
Ethiopia	
Ethiopian Orthodox	33,110,000
other Christian	7,090,000
Muslim (mostly Sunnī)	21,710,000
traditional beliefs	3,180,000
other	820,000
Faroe Islands	
Evangelical Lutheran	38,000
other	9,000
Fiji	
Christian (mostly Methodist and Roman Catholic)	437,000
Hindu	316,000
Muslim	65,000
other	9,000
Finland	
Evangelical Lutheran	4,420,000
other	770,000
France	
Roman Catholic	38,690,000
nonreligious	9,230,000
Muslim	4,180,000
atheist	2,380,000
Protestant	720,000
Jewish	590,000
other	3,290,000
French Guiana	
Roman Catholic	91,000
other	77,000
French Polynesia	
Protestant	119,000
Roman Catholic	94,000
other	25,000
Gabon	
Roman Catholic	690,000
Protestant	220,000
African Christian	170,000
other	160,000
Gambia, The	
Muslim (mostly Sunnī)	1,340,000
other	70,000
Gaza Strip	
Muslim (mostly Sunnī)	1,190,000
other	20,000
Georgia	
Georgian Orthodox	1,828,000
Sunnī Muslim	549,000
Armenian Apostolic (Orthodox)	279,000
Russian Orthodox	133,000
other (mostly nonreligious)	2,200,000
Germany	
Protestant (mostly Evangelical Lutheran)	29,330,000
Roman Catholic	27,590,000
Muslim	3,660,000
atheist	1,800,000
other (mostly nonreligious)	20,020,000
Ghana	
traditional beliefs	4,860,000
Muslim	3,910,000
Protestant	3,310,000
African Christian	2,870,000
Roman Catholic	1,890,000
other	3,050,000
Greece	
Greek Orthodox	10,010,000
Muslim	360,000
other	500,000
Greenland	
Evangelical Lutheran	36,500
other	19,800
Grenada	
Roman Catholic	54,000
Anglican	14,000
other	34,000

Religious affiliation	2001 population
Guadeloupe	
Roman Catholic	350,000
other	82,000
Guam	
Roman Catholic	118,000
Protestant	19,000
other	21,000
Guatemala	
Roman Catholic	8,880,000
Evangelical Protestant	2,540,000
other	270,000
Guernsey	
Anglican	42,000
other	22,000
Guinea	
Muslim	6,470,000
Christian	760,000
other	380,000
Guinea-Bissau	
traditional beliefs	590,000
Muslim	530,000
Christian	170,000
other	20,000
Guyana	
Hindu	264,000
Protestant	145,000
Roman Catholic	89,000
Muslim	70,000
Anglican	67,000
other	142,000
Haiti	
Roman Catholic	4,770,000
Protestant	1,590,000
other	610,000
Honduras	
Roman Catholic	5,740,000
Evangelical Protestant	690,000
other	200,000
Hong Kong	
Buddhist and Taoist	4,970,000
Protestant	290,000
Roman Catholic	280,000
other	1,200,000
Hungary	
Roman Catholic	6,120,000
Protestant	2,470,000
nonreligious	750,000
other	850,000
Iceland	
Evangelical Lutheran	260,000
other	20,000
India	
Hindu	759,350,000
Sunnī Muslim	92,380,000
traditional beliefs	34,930,000
Shī'ī Muslim	30,790,000
independent	30,750,000
Sikh	22,290,000
Protestant	15,130,000
Roman Catholic	13,940,000
Buddhist	7,290,000
Jain	4,160,000
atheist	1,670,000
Bahā'ī	1,190,000
Zoroastrian (Parsi)	210,000
nonreligious	12,910,000
other	3,000,000
Indonesia	
Muslim	185,060,000
Protestant	12,820,000
Roman Catholic	7,600,000
Hindu	3,880,000
Buddhist	2,190,000
other	660,000
Iran	
Shī'ī Muslim	57,180,000
Sunnī Muslim	3,460,000
Zoroastrian	1,780,000
Bahā'ī	430,000
Christian	340,000
other	250,000
Iraq	
Shī'ī Muslim	13,890,000
Sunnī Muslim	8,510,000
Christian	750,000
other	180,000

Religious affiliation	2001 population
Ireland	
Roman Catholic	3,500,000
other	320,000
Isle of Man	
Anglican	30,000
Methodist	7,000
Roman Catholic	6,000
other	31,000
Israel	
Jewish[2]	4,960,000
Muslim (mostly Sunnī)	930,000
other	360,000
Italy	
Roman Catholic	46,260,000
nonreligious and atheist	9,600,000
Muslim	680,000
other	1,350,000
Jamaica	
Protestant	1,020,000
Roman Catholic	270,000
Anglican	100,000
other	1,230,000
Japan	
Shintoist[3]	118,270,000
Buddhist[3]	88,490,000
Christian	1,470,000
other	10,250,000
Jersey	
Anglican	55,000
Roman Catholic	21,000
other	14,000
Jordan	
Sunnī Muslim	4,800,000
Christian	210,000
other	120,000
Kazakhstan	
Muslim (mostly Sunnī)	6,988,000
Russian Orthodox	1,216,000
Protestant	318,000
other (mostly nonreligious)	6,345,000
Kenya	
Roman Catholic	6,780,000
African Christian	6,400,000
Protestant	6,170,000
traditional beliefs	3,540,000
Anglican	2,900,000
Muslim	2,240,000
Orthodox	720,000
other	2,030,000
Kiribati	
Roman Catholic	50,000
Congregational	36,000
other	9,000
Korea, North	
atheist and nonreligious	15,000,000
traditional beliefs	3,430,000
Ch'ŏndogyo	3,050,000
other	480,000
Korea, South	
nonreligious	23,490,000
Buddhist	11,040,000
Protestant	9,370,000
Roman Catholic	3,160,000
Confucian	230,000
Wonbulgyo	90,000
other	290,000
Kuwait	
Sunnī Muslim	1,020,000
Shī'ī Muslim	680,000
other Muslim	230,000
other (mostly Christian and Hindu)	340,000
Kyrgyzstan	
Muslim (mostly Sunnī)	3,701,000
Russian Orthodox	276,000
other (mostly nonreligious)	958,000
Laos	
Buddhist	2,750,000
traditional beliefs	2,350,000
other	540,000

Religious affiliation	2001 population
Latvia	
Roman Catholic	350,000
Evangelical Lutheran	345,000
Russian Orthodox	181,000
other (mostly nonreligious)	1,482,000
Lebanon	
Shī'ī Muslim	1,230,000
Sunnī Muslim	770,000
Maronite Catholic	690,000
Druze	260,000
Greek Orthodox	220,000
Armenian Apostolic (Orthodox)	190,000
Greek Catholic (Melchite)	170,000
other	110,000
Lesotho	
Roman Catholic	820,000
Protestant	280,000
African Christian	260,000
traditional beliefs	170,000
Anglican	100,000
other	550,000
Liberia	
traditional beliefs	1,390,000
Christian	1,270,000
Muslim	520,000
other	60,000
Libya	
Sunnī Muslim	5,040,000
other	200,000
Liechtenstein	
Roman Catholic	26,000
other	7,000
Lithuania	
Roman Catholic	2,660,000
Russian Orthodox	90,000
other (mostly nonreligious)	940,000
Luxembourg	
Roman Catholic	400,000
other	40,000
Macau	
nonreligious	271,000
Buddhist	75,000
other	100,000
Macedonia	
Serbian (Macedonian) Orthodox	1,210,000
Sunnī Muslim	580,000
other	260,000
Madagascar	
traditional beliefs	7,670,000
Roman Catholic	3,250,000
Protestant	3,630,000
other	1,420,000
Malawi	
Roman Catholic	2,600,000
Protestant	2,070,000
African Christian	1,770,000
Muslim	1,560,000
traditional beliefs	820,000
other	1,730,000
Malaysia	
Muslim	10,770,000
Chinese folk-religionist	5,450,000
Christian	1,880,000
Hindu	1,660,000
Buddhist	1,500,000
other	1,350,000
Maldives	
Sunnī Muslim	273,000
other	2,000
Mali	
Muslim	9,010,000
traditional beliefs	1,760,000
Christian	220,000
other	10,000
Malta	
Roman Catholic	363,000
other	21,000
Marshall Islands	
Protestant	32,800
Roman Catholic	3,700
other	15,700

Religious affiliation	2001 population
Martinique	
Roman Catholic	336,000
other	52,000
Mauritania	
Sunnī Muslim	2,720,000
other	20,000
Mauritius	
Hindu	610,000
Roman Catholic	330,000
Muslim	190,000
other	70,000
Mayotte	
Sunnī Muslim	153,000
Christian	5,000
Mexico	
Roman Catholic	90,370,000
Protestant	3,820,000
other Christian	1,820,000
other (mostly nonreligious)	3,970,000
Micronesia	
Roman Catholic	63,600
Protestant	40,100
other	14,200
Moldova	
Romanian Orthodox	1,263,000
Russian (Moldovan) Orthodox	342,000
other (mostly nonreligious)	2,007,000
Monaco	
Roman Catholic	28,000
other	4,000
Mongolia	
Tantric Buddhist (Lamaist)	2,340,000
Muslim	100,000
Morocco	
Muslim (mostly Sunnī)	28,730,000
other	500,000
Mozambique	
traditional beliefs	9,750,000
Roman Catholic	3,060,000
Muslim	2,040,000
Protestant	1,720,000
African Christian	1,400,000
other	1,400,000
Myanmar (Burma)	
Buddhist	37,560,000
Christian	2,060,000
Muslim	1,610,000
traditional beliefs	480,000
Hindu	210,000
other	70,000
Namibia	
Protestant (mostly Lutheran)	850,000
Roman Catholic	320,000
African Christian	200,000
other	430,000
Nauru	
Protestant	6,100
Roman Catholic	3,300
other	2,700
Nepal	
Hindu	19,180,000
traditional beliefs	2,350,000
Buddhist	2,050,000
Muslim	970,000
Christian	600,000
other	140,000
Netherlands, The	
Roman Catholic	4,950,000
Dutch Reformed Church (NHK)	2,240,000
Reformed Churches	1,120,000
Muslim	720,000
nonreligious	6,550,000
other	400,000
Netherlands Antilles	
Roman Catholic	152,000
other	54,000
New Caledonia	
Roman Catholic	132,000
Protestant	31,300
other	52,200

Religious affiliation	2001 population
New Zealand	
Anglican	674,000
Roman Catholic	505,000
Presbyterian	489,000
Methodist	130,000
Baptist	57,000
Mormon	44,000
Ratana	39,000
nonreligious	954,000
other	969,000
Nicaragua	
Roman Catholic	3,590,000
Protestant	810,000
other (mostly nonreligious)	520,000
Niger	
Sunnī Muslim	9,390,000
traditional beliefs	900,000
other	70,000
Nigeria	
Muslim	55,600,000
traditional beliefs	12,500,000
Christian	58,100,000
other	500,000
Northern Mariana Islands	
Roman Catholic	53,600
other	19,700
Norway	
Evangelical Lutheran (Church of Norway)	3,990,000
other	530,000
Oman	
Ibāḍīyah Muslim	1,840,000
Sunnī Muslim	350,000
Hindu	190,000
Christian	100,000
other	20,000
Pakistan	
Sunnī Muslim	113,950,000
Shīʿī Muslim	25,010,000
Christian	3,560,000
Hindu	1,730,000
other	370,000
Palau	
Roman Catholic	7,600
Modekne	5,200
Protestant	4,900
other	2,100
Panama	
Roman Catholic	2,330,000
Protestant	420,000
other	150,000
Papua New Guinea	
Protestant	3,180,000
Roman Catholic	1,500,000
Anglican	210,000
other	420,000
Paraguay	
Roman Catholic	4,990,000
Protestant	280,000
other	370,000
Peru	
Roman Catholic	23,170,000
Protestant	1,730,000
other (mostly nonreligious)	1,190,000
Philippines	
Roman Catholic	63,530,000
Protestant	4,160,000
Muslim	3,500,000
Aglipayan	2,010,000
Church of Christ (Iglesia ni Cristo)	1,790,000
other	1,620,000
Poland	
Roman Catholic	35,050,000
Polish Orthodox	550,000
other (mostly nonreligious)	3,050,000
Portugal	
Roman Catholic	9,520,000
other	810,000

Religious affiliation	2001 population
Puerto Rico	
Roman Catholic	2,480,000
Protestant	1,080,000
other	270,000
Qatar	
Muslim (mostly Sunnī)	490,000
Christian	60,000
other	40,000
Réunion	
Roman Catholic	599,000
Hindu	33,000
other	102,000
Romania	
Romanian Orthodox	19,460,000
Roman Catholic	1,140,000
other	1,810,000
Russia	
Russian Orthodox	23,580,000
Muslim	10,980,000
Protestant	1,320,000
Jewish	590,000
other (mostly nonreligious)	107,960,000
Rwanda	
Roman Catholic	3,730,000
Protestant	1,530,000
traditional beliefs	660,000
Muslim	580,000
Anglican	570,000
other	260,000
St. Kitts and Nevis	
Anglican	10,000
Methodist	10,000
other	15,000
Pentecostal	7,000
other	12,000
St. Lucia	
Roman Catholic	125,000
Protestant	20,000
other	13,000
St. Vincent and the Grenadines	
Anglican	20,000
Pentecostal	17,000
Methodist	12,000
Roman Catholic	12,000
other	52,000
Samoa	
Mormon	46,200
Congregational	44,000
Roman Catholic	38,100
Methodist	21,800
other	29,100
San Marino	
Roman Catholic	24,000
other	3,000
São Tomé and Príncipe	
Roman Catholic	111,000
African Christian	16,000
other	20,000
Saudi Arabia	
Sunnī Muslim	20,490,000
Shīʿī Muslim	840,000
Christian	840,000
Hindu	250,000
other	330,000
Senegal	
Sunnī Muslim	9,010,000
traditional beliefs	640,000
Roman Catholic	480,000
other	160,000
Seychelles	
Roman Catholic	69,800
other	10,800
Sierra Leone	
Sunnī Muslim	2,490,000
traditional beliefs	2,190,000
Christian	620,000
other	130,000
Singapore	
Buddhist and Taoist	1,695,000
Muslim	495,000

Religious affiliation	2001 population
Christian	485,000
Hindu	133,000
nonreligious	493,000
other	21,000
Slovakia	
Roman Catholic	3,270,000
Slovak Evangelical	340,000
other (mostly nonreligious)	1,800,000
Slovenia	
Roman Catholic	1,650,000
other	340,000
Solomon Islands	
Protestant	173,000
Anglican	149,000
Roman Catholic	83,000
other	75,000
Somalia	
Sunnī Muslim	7,364,000
other	125,000
South Africa	
Christian	36,220,000
independents	17,040,000
Protestant	13,860,000
Roman Catholic	3,090,000
traditional beliefs	3,660,000
Hindu	1,050,000
Muslim	1,050,000
Bahā'ī	260,000
Jewish	170,000
nonreligious	1,050,000
other	130,000
Spain	
Roman Catholic	36,920,000
Muslim	200,000
other (mostly nonreligious)	3,010,000
Sri Lanka	
Buddhist	13,270,000
Hindu	2,190,000
Muslim	1,750,000
Roman Catholic	1,300,000
other	900,000
Sudan, The	
Sunnī Muslim	25,360,000
Christian	6,020,000
traditional beliefs	4,300,000
other	390,000
Suriname	
Hindu	119,000
Roman Catholic	91,000
Muslim	85,000
Protestant	71,000
other	68,000
Swaziland	
African Christian	480,000
Protestant	160,000
traditional beliefs	120,000
other	340,000
Sweden	
Church of Sweden (Lutheran)	7,690,000
other	1,200,000
Switzerland	
Roman Catholic	3,330,000
Protestant	2,890,000
other	1,000,000
Syria	
Sunnī Muslim	12,380,000
Shīʿī Muslim	2,010,000
Christian	920,000
Druze	500,000
other	920,000
Taiwan	
nonreligious	10,670,000
Buddhist	5,100,000
Taoist	4,040,000
I Kuan Tao	990,000
Protestant	440,000
Roman Catholic	320,000
Tien Te Chiao	210,000
Tien Ti Chiao	190,000
Confucianism (Li)	150,000
Hsuan Yuan Chiao	140,000
Muslim	50,000

Religious affiliation	2001 population
Shinto (Tenrikyo)	20,000
Bahā'ī	20,000
Tajikistan	
Sunnī Muslim	4,920,000
Shīʿī Muslim	310,000
Russian Orthodox	90,000
atheist	120,000
other (mostly nonreligious)	820,000
Tanzania	
Christian	18,260,000
Muslim	11,520,000
traditional beliefs	5,830,000
other	620,000
Thailand	
Buddhist	57,920,000
Muslim	2,850,000
Christian	440,000
other	40,000
Togo	
traditional beliefs	1,940,000
Roman Catholic	1,250,000
Sunnī Muslim	970,000
Protestant	530,000
other	450,000
Tonga	
Free Wesleyan	44,000
Roman Catholic	16,000
other	41,000
Trinidad and Tobago	
Roman Catholic	380,000
Hindu	308,000
Protestant	244,000
Anglican	142,000
Muslim	76,000
other	149,000
Tunisia	
Sunnī Muslim	9,720,000
other	104,000
Turkey	
Muslim (mostly Sunnī)	64,360,000
nonreligious	1,340,000
other	530,000
Turkmenistan	
Muslim (mostly Sunnī)	4,752,000
Russian Orthodox	129,000
other (mostly nonreligious)	581,000
Tuvalu	
Congregational	9,400
other	1,600
Uganda	
Roman Catholic	10,050,000
Anglican	9,450,000
Muslim (mostly Sunnī)	1,250,000
traditional beliefs	1,050,000
other	2,190,000
Ukraine	
Ukrainian Orthodox (Russian patriarchy)	9,491,000
Ukrainian Orthodox (Kiev patriarchy)	4,746,000
Ukrainian Autocephalous Orthodox	332,000
Ukrainian Catholic (Uniate)	3,417,000
Protestant	1,736,000
Roman Catholic	576,000
Jewish	423,000
other (mostly nonreligious)	28,044,000
United Arab Emirates	
Sunnī Muslim	2,490,000
Shīʿī Muslim	500,000
other	120,000
United Kingdom	
Christian	49,510,000
Anglican	26,140,000
Roman Catholic	5,590,000
Protestant	5,020,000
Eastern Orthodox	370,000
other Christian	12,390,000
Muslim	1,220,000
Hindu	440,000
Jewish	310,000

Religious affiliation	2001 population
Sikh	240,000
other (mostly nonreligious and atheist)	8,240,000
United States	
Christian (professing)	242,011,000
Christian (affiliated)	196,929,000
independent	80,639,000
Protestant	66,287,000
Roman Catholic	59,542,000
Eastern Orthodox	5,915,000
Anglican	2,464,000
other Christian	10,348,000
multi-affiliated Christians	-28,266,000
Christian (unaffiliated)	45,082,000
non-Christian	44,056,000
nonreligious	25,745,000
Jewish	5,771,000
Muslim	4,242,000
Buddhist	2,515,000
atheist	1,181,000
Hindu	1,059,000
New-Religionist	832,000
Bahā'ī	773,000
Ethnic religionist	447,000
Sikh	240,000
Chinese folk-religionist	80,000
other	1,171,000
Uruguay	
Roman Catholic	2,590,000
Protestant	150,000
Mormon	50,000
Jewish	30,000
other	480,000
Uzbekistan	
Muslim (mostly Sunnī)	19,156,000
Russian Orthodox	195,000
other (mostly nonreligious)	5,804,000
Vanuatu	
Presbyterian	70,000
Roman Catholic	28,000
Anglican	27,000
other	69,000
Venezuela	
Roman Catholic	22,050,000
other	2,590,000
Vietnam	
Buddhist	53,290,000
Roman Catholic	6,180,000
New-Religionist	
Cao Dai	2,810,000
Hoa Hao	1,690,000
other	16,500,000
Virgin Islands (U.S.)	
Protestant	56,000
Roman Catholic	41,000
other	24,000
West Bank	
Muslim (mostly Sunnī)	1,860,000
Jewish[4]	230,000
Christian and other	180,000
Western Sahara	
Sunnī Muslim	250,000
other	1,000
Yemen	
Muslim (mostly Sunnī)	18,050,000
other	20,000
Yugoslavia	
Serbian Orthodox	6,680,000
Sunnī Muslim	2,030,000
Roman Catholic	620,000
other (mostly nonreligious)	1,350,000
Zambia	
traditional beliefs	2,640,000
Protestant	2,240,000
Roman Catholic	1,650,000
other	3,240,000
Zimbabwe	
African Christian	4,580,000
traditional beliefs	3,430,000
Protestant	1,400,000
Roman Catholic	1,090,000
other	870,000

[1] Official 1986 census figure is 5.9 percent. [2] Includes the Golan Heights and East Jerusalem; excludes the West Bank and Gaza Strip. [3] Many Japanese practice both Shintoism and Buddhism. [4] Excludes East Jerusalem.

statistics, marriage, family

table provides some of the basic measures of the factors that influence size, direction, and rates of population change within a country. The accuracy of these data depends on the effectiveness of each respective national system for registering vital and civil events (birth, death, marriage, etc.) and on the sophistication of the analysis that can be brought to bear upon the data so compiled.

Data on birth rates, for example, depend not only on the completeness of registration of births in a particular country but also on the conditions under which those data are collected: Do all births take place in a hospital? Are the births reported comparably in all parts of the country? Are the records of the births tabulated at a central location in a timely way with an effort to eliminate inconsistent reporting of birth events, perinatal mortality, etc.? Similar difficulties attach to death rates but with the added need to identify "cause of death." Even in a developed country such identifications are often left to nonmedical personnel, and in a developing country with, say, only one physician for every 10,000 population, there will be too few physicians to perform autopsies to assess accurately the cause of death after the fact and also too few to provide ongoing care at a level where records would permit inference about cause of death based on prior condition or diagnosis.

Calculating natural increase, which at its most basic is simply the difference between the birth and death rates, may be affected by the differing degrees of completeness of birth and death registration for a given country. The total fertility rate may be understood as the average number of children that would be borne per woman if all childbearing women lived to the end of their childbearing years and bore children at each age at the average rate for that age. Calculating a meaningful fertility rate requires analysis of changing age structure of the female population over time,

changing mortality rates among mothers and their infants, and changing medical practice at births, each improvement of natural survivorship or medical support leading to greater numbers of live-born children and greater numbers of children who survive their first year (the basis for measurement of infant mortality, another basic indicator of demographic conditions and trends within a population).

As indicated above, data for causes of death are not only particularly difficult to obtain, since many countries are not well equipped to collect the data, but also difficult to assess, as their accuracy may be suspect and their meaning may be subject to varying interpretation. Take the case of a citizen of a less developed country who dies of what is clearly a lung infection: Was the death complicated by chronic malnutrition, itself complicated by a parasitic infestation, these last two together so weakening the subject that he died of an infection that he might have survived had his general health been better? Similarly, in a developed country: Someone may die from what is identified in an autopsy as a cerebrovascular accident, but if that accident occurred in a vascular system that was weakened by diabetes, what was the actual cause of death? Statistics on causes of death seek to identify the "underlying" cause (that which sets the final train of events leading to death in motion) but often must settle for the most proximate cause or symptom. Even this kind of analysis may be misleading for those charged with interpreting the data with a view to ordering health-care priorities for a particular country. The eight groups of causes of death utilized here include most, but not all, of the detailed causes classified by the World Health Organization and would not, thus, aggregate to the country's crude death rate for the same year. Among the lesser causes excluded by the present classification are: benign neoplasms; nutritional disorders; anemias; mental disorders; kidney and genito-urinary

Vital statistics, marriage, family

country	vital rates						causes of death (rate per 100,000 population)							
	year	birth rate per 1,000 population	death rate per 1,000 population	infant mortality rate per 1,000 live births	rate of natural increase per 1,000 population	total fertility rate	year	infectious and parasitic diseases	malignant neoplasms (cancers)	endocrine and metabolic disorders	diseases of the nervous system	diseases of the circulatory system	diseases of the respiratory system	diseases of the digestive system	accidents, poisoning, and violence
Afghanistan	2000	41.8	18.0	149.3	23.8	5.9	...	...	...	...	...	...	...	...	...
Albania	2000	19.5	6.0	41.3	13.5	2.4	1993	10.8	53.8	5.1	24.1	187.0	84.5	16.5	41.7
Algeria	2000	19.8	5.5	51.1	14.3	2.8	...	...	...	...	...	...	...	...	...
American Samoa	2000	25.8	4.3	10.6	21.5	3.6	1990	16.4[4]	46.8	16.4[5]	...	131.1[6]	65.6[7]	...	58.5
Andorra	1999	12.6[8]	3.1[8]	4.1[9]	9.5[8]	1.2[10]	...	...	...	...	...	...	...	...	...
Angola	2000	46.9	25.0	195.8	21.9	6.5	...	...	...	...	...	...	...	...	...
Antigua and Barbuda	2000	20.2	6.0	23.0	14.2	2.3	1995	10.4	96.2	57.7	13.3	242.6	42.9	19.2	37.0
Argentina	2000	18.6	7.6	18.3	11.0	2.5	1996	28.1	145.7	19.1[5]	9.7	297.3	64.8	32.5	52.2
Armenia	2000	11.0	9.5	41.5	1.5	1.5	1997	9.2	96.5	32.6	4.4	336.6	38.9	23.9	37.9
Aruba	2000	13.1	6.1	6.5	7.0	1.8	1998	26.1	118.0	29.3[5]	4.3	184.0	35.9	14.1	52.2
Australia	2000	13.0	7.6	6.0	5.4	1.8	1995	6.0	190.0	23.0	17.0	296.0	52.0	21.0	41.0
Austria	1999	9.5	9.4	4.4	0.1	1.3	1997	2.5	233.5	19.9	0.5[14]	532.6	29.9	28.4	54.9
Azerbaijan	2001	13.7	6.2	83.4[10]	7.5	1.6	1995	29.7	61.9	11.8	11.3	335.3	84.9	34.3	45.9
Bahamas, The	2000	19.5	6.8	17.0	12.7	2.3	1995	13.3	85.6	36.3	0.7	160.1	26.6	14.4	40.0
Bahrain	2000	20.6	3.9	20.5	16.7	2.8	1998	5.4	37.8	22.7	4.6	85.9	22.7	13.3	14.5
Bangladesh	2000	27.0	9.1	73.0	17.9	3.0	...	...	...	...	...	...	...	...	...
Barbados	2000	13.6	8.7	12.4	4.9	1.6	1995	27.3	162.5	149.2	22.7	365.5	55.7	34.1	36.0
Belarus	1999	9.3	14.2	11.5	-4.9	1.3[19]	1997	8.8	191.9	8.7[20]	11.5	673.9	68.7	27.5	154.5
Belgium	2000	10.9	10.1	4.8	0.8	1.5	1994	13.4	275.0	21.7	29.2	383.4	92.5	42.6	68.5
Belize	2000	32.3	4.8	26.0	27.5	4.1	1995	23.5	37.7	22.1	6.9	118.9	47.5	16.1	67.3
Benin	2000	44.8	14.5	90.8	30.3	6.3	...	...	...	...	...	...	...	...	...
Bermuda	1999	13.2	7.1	3.2[21]	6.1	1.8	1990	...	181.5	...	...	344.4	25.2	...	38.6
Bhutan	2001	35.2	9.0	56.0	26.2	5.2	...	...	...	...	...	...	...	...	...
Bolivia	2000	31.9	23.3	62.0[23]	23.3	3.7	...	...	...	...	...	...	...	...	...
Bosnia and Herzegovina	2000	12.9	7.9	25.2	5.0	1.7	1989	9.9	122.6[24]	12.6	11.9	344.1	29.0	29.2	47.1
Botswana	2001	28.8	24.8	63.2	4.0	3.7	...	...	...	...	...	...	...	...	...
Brazil	2000	18.8	9.4	38.0	9.4	2.1	1996	33.5	65.9	23.3[20]	9[13]	159.1	56.4	25.9	75.9
Brunei	1999	22.3	2.8	6.0	19.5	2.7	...	...	...	...	...	...	...	...	...
Bulgaria	1999	8.8	13.6	14.6	-4.8	1.2	1998	9.4	192.9	25.4	9.7	954.4	67.6	38.8	60.7
Burkina Faso	2000	45.3	17.0	108.5	28.3	6.4	...	...	...	...	...	...	...	...	...
Burundi	2000	40.5	16.4	71.5	24.1	6.3	...	...	...	...	...	...	...	...	...
Cambodia	2001	35.9	10.7	76.0	25.2	5.0	...	...	...	...	...	...	...	...	...
Cameroon	2000	36.6	11.9	70.9	24.7	4.9	...	...	...	...	...	...	...	...	...
Canada	2000	11.3	7.4	5.4	3.9	1.6	1997	8.3	195.6	23.7	21.9	264.8	66.8	25.4	43.5
Cape Verde	2000	29.7	7.4	54.6	22.3	4.2	...	...	...	...	...	...	...	...	...
Central African Republic	2000	37.5	18.4	106.7	19.1	5.0	...	...	...	...	...	...	...	...	...
Chad	2000	48.8	15.7	96.7	33.1	5.7	...	...	...	...	...	...	...	...	...
Chile	2000	17.2	5.5	9.6	11.7	2.2	1994	14.2	111.9	16.5	8.6	149.5	61.2	37.2	63.6
China	2001	14.9	7.0	38.0	7.9	1.8	1994[26]	15.2	117.7	17.2[20]	4.4	206.4	125.3	25.3	56.6
Colombia	2000	22.9	5.7	24.7	17.2	2.7	1994	13.7	58.3	15.2	4.6	125.3	34.3	15.7	119.5
Comoros	2000	40.0	9.6	86.3	30.4	5.4	...	...	...	...	...	...	...	...	...
Congo, Dem. Rep. of the	2000	46.4	15.4	101.6	31.0	6.9	...	...	...	...	...	...	...	...	...
Congo, Rep. of the	2000	38.6	16.4	101.6	22.2	5.1	...	...	...	...	...	...	...	...	...
Costa Rica	1999	21.7	4.2	11.8	17.5	2.6	1994	9.7	80.0	12.6	8.5	126.6	40.6	24.6	49.7
Côte d'Ivoire	2000	40.8	16.6	95.1	24.2	5.8	...	...	...	...	...	...	...	...	...
Croatia	1999	9.9	11.4	7.4	-1.5	1.9[10]	1996	8.8	227.2	25.4[20]	8.0	547.4	41.4	52.1	70.7
Cuba	2000	12.7	7.3	7.5	5.4	1.6	1995	12.8	133	25.9	11.1	305.5	64.1	24.9	84.6
Cyprus	1999	12.8	7.6	8.1[10]	5.2	2.0	...	...	...	...	...	...	...	...	...
Czech Republic	1999	8.7	10.7	4.6	-2.0	1.1	1998	2.6	272.1	15.0	11.6	586.7	39.9	40.4	68.1
Denmark	2000	12.6	10.9	5.0	1.7	1.7	1996	10.1	289.2	16.5	15.3	428.4	108.1	46.1	64.1

diseases not classifiable under the main groups; maternal deaths (for which data *are* provided, however, in the "Health services" table); diseases of the skin and musculoskeletal systems; congenital and perinatal conditions; and general senility and other ill-defined (ill-diagnosed) conditions, a kind of "other" category.

Expectation of life is probably the most accurate single measure of the quality of life in a given society. It summarizes in a single number all of the natural and social stresses that operate upon individuals in that society. The number may range from as few as 40 years of life in the least developed countries to as much as 80 years for women in the most developed nations. The lost potential in the years separating those two numbers is prodigious, regardless of how the loss arises—wars and civil violence, poor public health services, or poor individual health practice in matters of nutrition, exercise, stress management, and so on.

Data on marriages and marriage rates probably are less meaningful in terms of international comparisons than some of the measures mentioned above because the number, timing, and kinds of social relationships that substitute for marriage depend on many kinds of social variables—income, degree of social control, heterogeneity of the society (race, class, language communities), or level of development of civil administration (if one must travel for a day or more to obtain a legal civil ceremony, one may forgo it). Nevertheless, the data for a single country say specific things about local practice in terms of the age at which a man or woman typically marries, and the overall rate will at least define the number of legal civil marriages, though it cannot say anything about other, less formal arrangements (here the figure for the legitimacy rate for children in the next section may identify some of the societies in which economics or social constraints may operate to limit the number of marriages that are actually confirmed on

civil registers). The available data usually include both first marriages and remarriages after annulment, divorce, widowhood, or the like.

The data for families provide information about the average size of a family unit (individuals related by blood or civil register) and the average number of children under a specified age (set here at 15 to provide a consistent measure of social minority internationally, though legal minority depends on the laws of each country). When well-defined family data are not collected as part of a country's national census or vital statistics surveys, data for households have been substituted on the assumption that most households worldwide represent families in some conventional sense. But increasing numbers of households worldwide are composed of unrelated individuals (unmarried heterosexual couples, aged [or younger] groups sharing limited [often fixed] incomes for reasons of economy, or homosexual couples). Such arrangements do not yet represent great numbers overall. Increasing numbers of census programs, however, even in developing countries, are making more adequate provision for distinguishing these nontraditional, often nonfamily households.

Internet resources for further information:
- World Health Organization (World)
  http://www.who.ch
- Pan American Health Organization (the Americas)
  http://www.paho.org
- National Center for Health Statistics (U.S.)
  http://www.cdc.gov/nchs
- U.S. Census Bureau: International Data Base (World)
  http://www.census.gov/ipc/www/idbprint.html

expectation of life at birth (latest year)		nuptiality, family, and family planning																country
		marriages			age at marriage (latest)						families (F), households (H) (latest)							
		year	total number	rate per 1,000 population	groom (percent)			bride (percent)			families (households)		children		induced abortions			
male	female				19 and under	20–29	30 and over	19 and under	20–29	30 and over	total ('000)	size	number under age 15	percent legitimate	number	ratio per 100 live births		
46.6	45.1	...	...	...	...	...	...	...	...	...	H 2,110	H 6.2	H 2.8[1]	...	...	...	Afghanistan
68.8	74.9	1997	25,260	6.8	1.5[2]	80.4[2]	18.1[2]	24.0[2]	71.4[2]	4.6[2]	F 675	F 3.9	F 1.6	...	...	...	Albania
68.3	71.0	1996	156,870	5.6	0.7[3]	67.1[3]	32.2[3]	29.8[3]	61.4[3]	8.8[3]	H 4,102	H 7.1	H 3.0	...	...	...	Algeria
70.7	79.8	1993	325	6.1	...	...	...	...	...	...	H 7	H 7.0	H 2.7	72.0	...	...	American Samoa
80.6	86.6	1998	208	3.2	...	...	...	...	...	...	...	...	...	...	...	...	Andorra
37.1	39.6	...	...	...	...	...	...	...	...	...		H 5.0			...	...	Angola
68.2	72.8	1998	1,418	22.1	1.0[11]	37.4[12]	61.6	3.7[11]	52.4[12]	43.9	H 18	H 3.2	H 1.2	23.4	...	...	Antigua and Barbuda
71.7	78.6	1996	148,721	4.2	5.6	71.5	22.9	26.0	58.6	15.4	H 10,097	H 3.2	H 1.0	67.5	...	...	Argentina
62.0	71.0	1995	14,200	4.2	5.0[13]	73.8[13]	21.2[13]	39.3[13]	49.9[13]	10.8[13]	H 559	H 4.5	H 1.8	86.0	30,571	59.8	Armenia
75.0	81.9	1998	564	6.1	...	...	...	...	...	...	H 19	H 3.6		57.5	...	...	Aruba
76.0	81.0	1996	109,386	6.0	0.7	54.5	44.8	3.6	63.6	32.8	H 6,636	H 2.6	H 0.6	75.0	...	...	Australia
75.1	80.9	1998	39,143	4.8	1.1[15]	49.9[15]	49.0[15]	4.2[15]	62.0[15]	33.8[15]	H 3,058	H 2.6	H 0.5	69.5	...	...	Austria
68.0	75.0	1994	47,147	6.3	1.2[16]	80.4[16]	18.4[16]	24.8[16]	63.9[16]	11.3[16]	H 1,381	H 5.2	H 1.7	94.8	42,134	23.2	Azerbaijan
68.3	73.9	1996	2,628	9.3	...	14.0	86.0	—	26.1	73.9	H 74	H 3.9		45.7	...	...	Bahamas, The
70.6	75.5	1998	3,677	5.7	2.6[17]	65.4[17]	32.0[17]	28.0[17]	54.6[17]	17.4[17]	H 67	H 6.5	H 2.2	100.0	...	...	Bahrain
59.0	60.0	1997	1,181,000	9.7	...	...	...	...	...	...	H 19,980	H 5.6			...	...	Bangladesh
70.4	75.6	1995	3,564	13.5	0.1[18]	40.2[18]	59.7[18]	1.4[18]	53.6[18]	44.9[18]	H 67	H 3.5	H 1.5	26.9	723	19.6	Barbados
62.2	73.9	1997	69,735	6.8	5.4[15]	69.8[15]	24.8[15]	27.1[15]	53.1[15]	19.8[15]	H 2,796	H 3.6	H 0.8	82.2	174,098	181.7	Belarus
74.5	81.3	1996	50,601	5.0	0.6[17]	59.5[17]	39.9[17]	4.0[17]	66.3[17]	29.7[17]	F 3,613	F 2.7	F 0.5	88.7	...	...	Belgium
68.7	73.3	1997	1,543	6.6	6.3[17]	58.4[17]	35.3[17]	23.4[17]	51.0[17]	25.6[17]	H 42	H 5.3	H 2.2	40.3	990	15.1	Belize
49.2	51.2	...	...	...	...	...	...	...	...	...		H 5.9			...	...	Benin
74.9	78.9	1994	944	15.4	0.2[22]	37.4[22]	62.4[22]	1.5[22]	49.4[22]	49.1[22]	H 24	H 2.5	H 0.5	61.7	92	11.0	Bermuda
61.0	64.0	...	...	...	...	...	...	...	...	...		H 5.4			...	...	Bhutan
66.3	61.2	...	...	...	...	...	...	...	...	...	H 1,655	H 3.8	H 1.6	80.9	...	...	Bolivia
68.8	74.4	1991	27,923	6.0	2.3	74.2	23.5	28.6	58.9	12.5	H 1,203	H 3.4	H 1.1	92.6	...	...	Bosnia and Herzegovina
36.8	37.5	1986	1,638	1.5	—	33.0	67.0	5.0	69.2	25.8	H 125	H 5.7	H 2.0	28.8	17	0.1	Botswana
58.5	67.6	1995	...	4.7	7.0[13]	68.7[13]	24.3[13]	31.2[13]	54.3[13]	14.5[13]	F 39,768	F 3.9		1.2	...	...	Brazil
74.0	76.0	1995	1,793	6.1	10.6[25]	50.1[25]	39.3[25]	11.4[25]	54.7[25]	33.9[25]	H 45	H 5.8	H 2.0	99.6	...	...	Brunei
67.5	74.6	1996	...	4.3	3.4[17]	73.1[17]	23.5[17]	26.9[17]	60.4[17]	12.7[17]	H 2,795	H 3.0		74.3	97,023	134.8	Bulgaria
46.3	47.2	...	...	...	...	...	...	...	...	...		H 6.2			...	...	Burkina Faso
45.2	47.2	...	...	...	...	...	...	...	...	...		H 5.0			...	...	Burundi
54.0	59.0	...	...	...	...	...	...	...	...	...		H 5.6			...	...	Cambodia
54.0	55.6	...	...	...	...	...	...	...	...	...		H 5.7			...	...	Cameroon
76.0	83.0	1995	160,256	5.4	0.9	49.3	49.8	3.6	57.9	38.5	H 11,580	H 2.5	H 0.6	83.8	70,549	18.7	Canada
65.6	72.3	1994	1,200	3.2	...	...	...	...	...	...	F 59	F 5.1		28.9	...	...	Cape Verde
42.3	45.8	...	...	...	...	...	...	...	...	...		H 5.9			...	...	Central African Republic
48.5	52.6	...	...	...	...	...	...	...	...	...		H 5.0			...	...	Chad
72.4	79.2	1996	83,547	5.8	4.7	67.5	27.8	18.6	62.2	19.2	H 3,537	H 3.8		61.9	67	—	Chile
69.0	73.0	1994	9,290,027	7.8	...	...	...	...	...	...	H 278.6[27]	H 4.1	H 1.1	...	10,500,000	47.7	China
66.4	74.3	...	...	...	...	...	...	...	...	...	F 4,772	F 5.3	F 2.5	75.2	...	...	Colombia
57.8	62.2	...	...	...	...	...	...	...	...	...		H 5.6			...	...	Comoros
47.6	50.8	...	...	...	...	...	...	...	...	...		H 2.3			...	...	Congo, Dem. Rep. of the
44.5	50.5	...	...	...	...	...	...	...	...	...	H 326	H 4.7	H 2.0		...	...	Congo, Rep. of the
74.2	79.9	1997	22,422	6.5	7.1[17]	60.9[17]	32.0[17]	26.3[17]	52.0[17]	94.7[17]	H 772	H 4.1		50.3	...	...	Costa Rica
43.7	46.6	...	...	...	...	...	...	...	...	...		H 8.0			...	...	Côte d'Ivoire
70.0	77.5	1997	24,517	5.3	1.2[15]	65.2[15]	33.6[15]	13.9[15]	66.8[15]	19.3[15]	H 1,544	H 3.1	H 0.6	92.7	12,339	22.9	Croatia
73.8	78.5	1997	60,220	5.4	5.2[17]	51.8[17]	43.0[17]	18.0[17]	49.4[17]	32.6[17]	F 2,860	F 3.7	H 1.6	...	83,963	57.1	Cuba
75.3	80.1	1996	5,761	7.8	0.8	54.6	44.6	8.1	64.2	27.7	H 160	H 3.5	H 1.1	99.6	...	...	Cyprus
71.1	78.2	1997	57,086	5.6	3.7[15]	66.5[15]	29.8[15]	15.0[15]	65.8[15]	19.2[15]	H 3,557	H 2.9		79.4	48,086	53.2	Czech Republic
74.3	79.1	1997	34,108	6.5	0.4[17]	36.2[17]	63.4[17]	1.4[17]	47.9[17]	50.7[17]	H 2,027	H 2.2		53.5	17,720	53.2	Denmark

Vital statistics, marriage, family   (continued)

country	vital rates						causes of death (rate per 100,000 population)								
	year	birth rate per 1,000 population	death rate per 1,000 population	infant mortality rate per 1,000 live births	rate of natural increase per 1,000 population	total fertility rate	year	infectious and parasitic diseases	malignant neoplasms (cancers)	endocrine and metabolic disorders	diseases of the nervous system	diseases of the circulatory system	diseases of the respiratory system	diseases of the digestive system	accidents, poisoning, and violence
Djibouti	2000	41.0	14.9	103.3	26.1	5.8	...	...	...	...	...	...	...	...	...
Dominica	2000	18.3	7.3	17.1	11.0	2.0	1994	23.1	125.0	59.8	9.5	237.8	38.0	21.7	28.5
Dominican Republic	2000	25.2	4.7	35.9	20.5	3.0	1985[28]	85	45	155[5]	7[14]	165	41	25	*56*
East Timor[29]	...	...	...	...	...	...									
Ecuador	2000[1]	26.5	5.5	35.1	21.0	3.2	1995	29.7	50.8	17.5	7.2	80.8	46.0	23.1	65.1
Egypt	2000	25.4	7.8	62.3	17.6	3.2	1992	49.0	22.4	17.3	9.5	313.5	83.4	33.5	28.8
El Salvador	2000	29.0	6.3	29.2	22.7	3.4	1994[30]	42	52	9[5]	2[14]	124	36	14	135
Equatorial Guinea	2000	38.1	13.4	94.8	24.7	4.9	...	...	...	...	...	...	...	...	...
Eritrea	2000	42.7	12.3	76.7	30.4	5.9	...	...	...	...	...	...	...	...	...
Estonia	2000	9.6	13.5	8.4	–3.9	1.2	1995	13.7	221.1	8.2	13.0	771.9	42.5	36.0	198.8
Ethiopia	2000	45.1	17.6	101.3	27.5	7.1	...	...	...	...	...	...	...	...	...
Faroe Islands	2000	13.6	8.7	6.9	22.3	2.3	1992	4.3	191.3	14.9[5]	—	352.8	59.5	14.9	57.4
Fiji	2000	23.5	5.8	14.5	17.7	2.9	...	...	...	...	...	...	...	...	...
Finland	1999	11.2	9.5	4.2	1.7	1.7	1995	7.7	196.6	12.5	20.1	459.7	73.6	38.0	85.8
France	2000	12.3	9.1	4.8	3.2	1.7	1994	12.8	207.7	27.8	20.7	288.2	63.9	43.9	76.1
French Guiana	2000	22.4	4.8	14.0	17.6	3.2	1989	61.7	58.1	16.3	10.9	114.3	20.9	13.6	98.0
French Polynesia	2001	20.7	4.8	9.0	15.9	2.5	1994–95	14.0	104.0	14.0	10.0	123.0	47.0	17.0	52.0
Gabon	2001	27.4	17.2	94.9	10.2	3.7	...	...	...	...	...	...	...	...	...
Gambia, The	2000	42.3	13.2	79.3	29.1	5.8	...	...	...	...	...	...	...	...	...
Gaza Strip	2000	43.1	4.3	26.0	38.8	6.6	...	...	...	...	...	...	...	...	...
Georgia	2000	10.9	14.5	52.9	–3.6	1.4	1990	12.7	100.8	14.6	4.3	548.4	43.3	8.5	56.1
Germany	2000	9.4	10.5	4.8	–1.1	1.4	1995	7.4	260.7	34.5	18.0	525.7	66.0	51.2	48.2
Ghana	2001	29.0	10.3	56.5	18.7	3.8	...	...	...	...	...	...	...	...	...
Greece	2000	11.7	10.5	6.7[23]	1.2	1.3	1998	6.7	213.4	8.3	9.4	492.4	54.9	22.1	42.8
Greenland	2000	16.9	7.6	18.3	9.3	2.4	1995	29.5	198.7	3.9	1.8	214.4	9.6	5.7	206.5
Grenada	2000	23.2	8.0	14.6	15.2	3.2	1987	9.6	82.8	57.3	7.4	264.3	45.6	38.2	...
Guadeloupe	2000	17.3	6.0	9.8	11.3	1.9	1996	23.8	134.8	26.2	...	183.7	32.1	31.4	68.1
Guam	2001	27.0	4.8	10.0	22.2	4.0	1994	1.4	60.0	26.5[5]	6.8	141.8	27.9	1.4	64.1
Guatemala	2000	35.1	6.9	47.0	28.2	4.7	...	...	...	...	...	...	...	...	...
Guernsey	2000	10.5	9.3	5.1	1.2	1.3	1996	5.3	282.3	15.9	15.9	441.1	150.0	49.4	24.7
Guinea	2001	39.8	17.5	120.0	22.3	5.4	...	...	...	...	...	...	...	...	...
Guinea-Bissau	2000	39.6	15.6	112.3	24.0	5.3	...	...	...	...	...	...	...	...	...
Guyana	2000	17.9	8.4	39.1	9.5	2.1	1994	38.9	33.5	45.7	10.6	212.8	44.5	27.6	59.0
Haiti	2000	32.0	15.1	97.1	16.9	4.5	...	...	...	...	...	...	...	...	...
Honduras	2000	32.7	5.3	31.3	27.4	4.3	...	...	...	...	...	...	...	...	...
Hong Kong	2000	8.1	5.1	2.9	3.0	1.3	1998	14.4	160.5	7.4	3.9	126.7	99.6	21.0	21.2
Hungary	1999	9.4	14.2	8.4	–4.8	1.3	1995	7.9	322.0	20.1	11.5	721.4	63.0	115.6	111.5
Iceland	1999	14.8	6.9	2.4	7.9	2.0	1995	6.7	176.4	3.7	19.5	308.6	82.0	3.0	56.6
India	2000	24.8	8.9	64.9	15.9	3.1	...	...	...	...	...	...	...	...	...
Indonesia[29]	2001	20.8	7.2	42.0	13.6	2.4	...	...	...	...	...	...	...	...	...
Iran	2000	18.3	5.5	30.0	12.8	2.2	1990[34]	*34*	*61*	*12*[20]	*26*	*304*	*48*	*24*	*108*
Iraq	2000	35.0	6.4	62.5	28.6	4.9	...	...	...	...	...	...	...	...	...
Ireland	2000	14.5	8.1	5.6	6.4	1.9	1997	4.8	205.6	10.8[5]	0.2[14]	369.9	153.4	9.4	38.4
Isle of Man	1999	12.3	13.5	3.7[35]	–1.2	1.6	1998	2.8	298.4	11.1	31.8	504.3	225.2	38.7	52.5
Israel	2000	21.7	6.0	5.1	15.7	3.0	1995	10.4	148.9	23.4	11.5	278.4	26.5	23.1	35.8
Italy	2000	9.1	10.0	5.9	–0.9	1.2	1995	13.3	258.2	34.7	20.3	424.3	59.1	47.0	49.0
Jamaica	2000	20.0	5.1	14.6	14.9	2.8[36]	1991	8.1	84.1	51.3	7.5	189.5	30.2	14.1	8.4
Japan	1999	9.3	7.8	3.4	1.5	1.4	1997	14.6	220.0	12.4	7.0	237.7	98.0	30.0	52.4
Jersey	2000	11.7	9.3	5.7	2.4	1.6	...	...	...	...	...	...	...	...	...
Jordan	2000	26.2	2.6	21.1	23.6	3.4	...	...	...	...	...	...	...	...	...
Kazakhstan	2001	16.5	10.1	43.0	6.4	2.0	1996	45.7	133.0	10.9	1.4	436.2	71.0	32.9	101.1
Kenya	2000	29.4	14.1	68.7	15.3	3.7	...	...	...	...	...	...	...	...	...
Kiribati	2000	33.1	8.4	56.8[23]	24.7	4.4[23]	...	...	...	...	...	...	...	...	...
Korea, North	2000	20.4	6.9	24.3	13.5	2.3	...	...	...	...	...	...	...	...	...
Korea, South	1999	15.3	5.8	10.0	9.5	1.7	1997	10.8	115.4	20.2	5.1	121.5	24.4	34.4	70.6
Kuwait	2000	22.0	2.4	11.5	19.6	3.3	1997	5.4	22.7	10.6	3.1	84.6	11.0	4.7	34.8
Kyrgyzstan	2001	20.6	7.3	39.0	13.3	2.5	1996	12.6	25.7	8.3	1.5	278.5	75.0	9.8	21.4
Laos	2001	36.5	13.1	91.0	23.4	5.0	...	...	...	...	...	...	...	...	...
Latvia	1999	8.0	13.5	11.4	–5.5	1.2	1998	19.5	231.8	12.2[20]	12.7	775.6	34.6	42.2	161.8
Lebanon	2000	20.3	6.4	29.3	13.9	2.1	...	...	...	...	...	...	...	...	...
Lesotho	2000	31.7	14.6	83.0	17.1	4.2	...	...	...	...	...	...	...	...	...
Liberia	2000	47.2	16.6	134.6	30.6	6.4	...	...	...	...	...	...	...	...	...
Libya	2000	27.7	3.5	30.1	24.2	3.7	...	...	...	...	...	...	...	...	...
Liechtenstein	2000	11.8	6.7	5.7	5.1	1.5	1997	23.0[13]	199.7	...	6.6[13]	613.9	29.0	22.6	146.9
Lithuania	2000	9.2	10.5	8.5	–1.3	1.4	1995	16.4	203.2	8.0	10.3	654.2	40.5	32.1	176.0
Luxembourg	2000	12.5	8.9	4.8	3.6	1.7	1995	4.6	248.5	21.7	14.9	375.1	61.5	40.2	59.0
Macau	2001	9.4	4.5	8.0	4.9	1.1	1998	10.0	77.8	3.9	1.7	117.1	39.3	11.1	23.9
Macedonia	2000	13.7	7.7	13.4	6.0	1.8	1997	17.6	138.3	24.1[5]	28.0	462.8	39.5	15.9	32.4
Madagascar	2000	42.9	12.7	87.0	30.2	5.8	...	...	...	...	...	...	...	...	...
Malawi	2000	38.5	22.4	122.3	16.1	6.3	...	...	...	...	...	...	...	...	...
Malaysia	2001	23.5	4.4	7.9	19.1	3.1[23]	1997	15.2	19.8	3.8	1.1	37.2	8.7	2.1	13.2
Maldives	2001	36.3	6.3	43.0	30.0	5.5	...	...	...	...	...	...	...	—	...
Mali	2000	49.2	19.1	123.3	30.1	6.9	...	...	...	...	...	...	...	...	...
Malta	2000	12.8	7.7	5.9	5.1	1.9	1997	5.1	281.9	25.1	12.8	354.1	70.9	26.1	28.5
Marshall Islands	2000	41.8	4.9	41.0	36.9	6.6	1993[37]	169.9	68.4	...	—	155.1	105.1	63.3	36.7
Martinique	2000	16.1	6.4	8.0	9.7	1.8	1996	21.9	150.1	27.7	...	206.6	36.3	27.2	47.2
Mauritania	2000	43.4	14.0	78.1	29.4	6.3	...	...	...	...	...	...	...	...	...
Mauritius	2000	16.7	6.8	17.7	9.9	2.0	1996	12.1	56.8	24.9	0.8	291.2	34.9	21.7	46.2
Mayotte	2000	45.3	9.1	71.3	36.2	6.3	...	...	...	...	...	...	...	...	...
Mexico	2000	23.2	5.1	26.2	18.1	2.7	1995	22.0	52.9	46.9	6.7	106.8	47.1	42.1	62.4
Micronesia	2000	27.1	6.0	33.5	21.1	3.8	...	...	...	...	...	...	...	...	...
Moldova	2000	12.9	12.6	43.3	0.3	1.8	1995	14.6	133.3	10.7	11.8	559.4	76.3	114.7	113.7
Monaco	2000	9.9	13.1	5.9	–3.2	1.8	...	...	...	...	...	...	...	...	...
Mongolia	2001	22.4	7.5	61.0	14.9	2.4	1994[38]	33	118	3	14	200	110	55	64
Morocco	2001	24.2	5.9	48.1	18.3	3.0	1992	10.2	14.0	12.2	4.9	35.5	9.5	7.9	19.2

expectation of life at birth (latest year) male	female	nuptiality, family, and family planning — marriages: year	total number	rate per 1,000 popu-lation	groom (percent) 19 and under	20–29	30 and over	bride (percent) 19 and under	20–29	30 and over	families (households) total ('000)	size	children number under age 15	percent legiti-mate	induced abortions number	ratio per 100 live births	country
49.0	52.7	...	...	...	...	...	...	...	...	...	...	H 5.6	...	96.8	...	...	Djibouti
70.5	76.3	1996	230	3.1	—	37.0	63.0	2.7	56.2	41.1	H 19	H 3.6	H 2.2	24.1	...	...	Dominica
71.1	75.4	1994	14,883	2.0	...	...	...	...	...	...	H 1,804	H 3.9	...	32.8	562	0.5	Dominican Republic
...	...	...	...	...	...	...	...	...	...	...	...	...	...	...	...	...	East Timor[29]
68.3	74.0	1996	72,094	6.2	12.6	61.7	25.7	32.6	51.4	16.0	...	H 4.1	...	67.9	...	...	Ecuador
61.3	65.5	1994	451,817	3.2	3.4	58.7	37.9	11.2	77.1	11.7	H 9,733	H 4.9	H 2.1	100.0	...	...	Egypt
66.1	73.5	1994	27,761	5.1	6.6[25]	54.8[25]	38.6[25]	21.5[25]	51.4[25]	27.1[25]	H 1,092	H 4.8	...	29.4	...	...	El Salvador
51.5	55.7	...	...	...	...	...	...	...	...	...	...	H 4.5	...	...	...	...	Equatorial Guinea
53.4	58.3	1992	68	...	...	...	...	...	...	...		[31,32]	...	...	...	...	Eritrea
65.4	76.1	1998	5,430	3.7	3.2[15]	56.4[15]	40.4[15]	13.9[15]	53.9[15]	32.2[15]	H 427	H 3.1	H 0.8	47.8	16,887	127.1	Estonia
44.4	45.9	...	...	...	...	...	...	...	...	...	...	H 4.5[31,32]	...	...	...	...	Ethiopia
75.0	81.9	1990	203	4.3	...	...	...	...	...	...	F 14	F 3.0	F 0.9	57.5	26	3.3	Faroe Islands
65.5	70.5	1995	7,903	9.9	...	...	...	...	...	...	F 97	F 6.0	F 2.5	82.7	...	...	Fiji
73.7	81.0	1998	24,023	4.7	1.0[15]	47.1[15]	51.9[15]	3.5[15]	55.9[15]	40.6[15]	H 2,270	H 2.2	...	61.3	10,437	17.2	Finland
74.9	82.9	1997	283,984	4.8	0.2[17]	51.9[17]	47.9[17]	1.4[17]	63.2[17]	35.4[17]	H 20,899	H 2.6	H 1.0	63.9	157,886	22.2	France
72.8	79.6	1992	716	5.3	...	...	...	...	...	...	H 33	H 3.4	H 1.2	20.3	388	16.8	French Guiana
70.0	75.0	1996	1,200	5.7	...	...	...	...	...	...	H 40	H 4.3	H 1.7	40.5	...	...	French Polynesia
48.5	50.8	...	...	...	...	...	...	...	...	...	H 136	H 4.0	...	...	...	...	Gabon
50.9	54.7	...	...	...	...	...	...	...	...	...	...	H 8.3	...	...	...	...	Gambia, The
69.6	72.1	...	...	...	...	...	...	...	...	...	...	...	...	...	...	...	Gaza Strip
60.9	68.2	1996	19,253	3.7	9.1	59.4	31.5	32.7	51.2	16.1	H 1,244	H 4.1	H 1.1	82.3	43,549	77.3	Georgia
74.3	80.8	1997	422,319	5.1	0.7[15]	44.6[15]	54.7[15]	3.7[15]	56.3[15]	40.0[15]	H 37,457	H 2.2	H 0.3	82.0	97,937	12.8	Germany
55.9	58.7	...	...	...	...	...	...	...	...	...	H 2,355	H 4.9	H 2.2	...	...	...	Ghana
75.9	81.2	1998	55,489	5.3	0.9[17]	53.6[17]	45.5[17]	9.6[17]	68.9[17]	21.5[17]	H 2,990	H 3.3	H 0.7	96.7	12,289	12.1	Greece
64.5	71.7	1996	208	3.7	1.1[2]	44.6[2]	54.3[2]	2.7[2]	59.6[2]	37.7[2]	F 31	F 1.8	F 0.5	29.2	962	80.7	Greenland
62.7	66.3	1991	...	4.3	...	...	...	...	...	...	H 24	H 3.7	H 2.2	18.1	...	...	Grenada
73.8	80.3	1997	1,936	4.7	0.5[2]	51.4[2]	48.0[2]	7.2[2]	61.4[2]	31.4[2]	H 112	H 3.4	H 0.9	37.0	561	8.7	Guadeloupe
72.0	77.0	1995	1,507	10.1	3.0[25]	55.5[25]	41.5[25]	9.2[25]	59.3[25]	31.5[25]	H 31	H 4.0	H 1.3	50.1	...	...	Guam
63.5	69.0	1997	51,526	4.9	18.3	56.1	25.6	41.1	40.8	18.1	H 1,806	H 5.2	...	34.8	...	...	Guatemala
76.7	82.8	1996	340	5.8	...	...	...	...	...	...	H 21	H 2.6	H 0.5	73.2	...	...	Guernsey
43.5	48.4	...	...	...	...	...	...	...	...	...	H 1,064	H 4.1	...	...	...	...	Guinea
46.8	51.4	...	...	...	...	...	...	...	...	...	H 124	H 6.9	H 2.8	11.3	...	...	Guinea-Bissau
61.1	67.2	...	...	...	...	...	...	...	...	...	H 150	H 5.1	H 2.1	...	...	...	Guyana
47.5	51.1	...	...	...	...	...	...	...	...	...	H 1,147	H 4.4	H 1.8	...	...	...	Haiti
67.9	72.1	...	...	...	...	...	...	...	...	...	H 463	H 5.7	H 2.8	...	...	...	Honduras
77.0	82.2	1999	31,300	4.6	0.9[15]	42.7[15]	56.4[15]	3.0[15]	63.5[15]	33.5[15]	H 1,840	H 3.3	...	94.5	17,600	25.2	Hong Kong
66.3	75.1	1998	45,500	4.5	3.7[15]	69.1[15]	27.2[15]	17.5[15]	64.8[15]	17.7[15]	F 3,058	F 2.9	F 0.8	72.0	76,600	72.8	Hungary
77.5	81.4	1998	1,238	5.6	0.1[15]	40.7[15]	59.2[15]	1.2[15]	55.6[15]	43.2[15]	H 85	H 2.9	H 1.3	37.4	858	19.8	Iceland
61.9	63.1	...	...	...	...	...	...	...	...	...	H 151,033	H 5.6	H 2.4	...	581,215	...	India
65.0	69.0	1992–93[33]	1,423,774	7.6	...	...	...	...	...	...	H 39,695	H 4.5	H 1.8	...	...	...	Indonesia[29]
68.3	71.5	1996	479,263	7.8	...	...	...	...	...	...	H 9,759	H 4.8	H 2.2	...	...	...	Iran
65.5	67.6	1992	144,055	7.8	...	...	...	...	...	...	H 1,873	H 8.9	H 4.1	...	...	...	Iraq
74.1	79.7	1999	18,526	4.9	0.7[13]	62.2[13]	37.1[13]	1.6[13]	74.7[13]	23.7[13]	H 541	H 3.3	H 1.3	65.5	...	...	Ireland
73.9	80.8	1998	435	6.0	0.2	39.5	60.3	1.6	45.1	53.3	H 29,377	H 2.4	...	68.1	...	...	Isle of Man
76.6	80.5	1997	32,510	5.6	3.5[13]	74.0[13]	22.5[13]	21.2[13]	68.3[13]	10.5[13]	H 1,355	H 3.7	H 1.1	98.5	16,903	14.7	Israel
75.9	82.4	1997	275,381	4.8	0.6[17]	56.2[17]	43.2[17]	4.8[17]	71.5[17]	23.7[17]	F 19,766	F 2.6	F 0.5	90.2	134,137	25.5	Italy
73.3	77.3	1996	18,708	7.4	...	...	...	...	...	...	H 554	H 4.2	H 1.4	14.9	...	...	Jamaica
77.5	84.0	1996	795,000	6.3	1.2	61.6	37.2	2.6	77.0	20.4	H 43,447	H 2.8	...	99.0	338,867	28.1	Japan
76.1	81.1	1994	542	6.4	...	...	...	...	...	...	H 29	H 2.6	H 0.4	88.1	296	28.0	Jersey
74.9	79.9	1996	102,558	6.4	4.4[17]	70.0[17]	25.6[17]	37.3[17]	54.7[17]	8.0[17]	H 11,891	H 6.1	H 3.4	...	...	...	Jordan
59.0	71.0	1996	102,558	6.4	6.0	71.5	22.5	27.9	56.5	15.6	H 3,824	H 4.0	H 1.4	86.6	193,462	76.4	Kazakhstan
47.0	49.0	...	...	...	...	...	...	...	...	...	H 1,938	H 3.4	H 2.7	...	...	...	Kenya
56.5	62.4	...	...	...	...	...	...	...	...	...	H 11	H 6.6	H 2.5	...	...	...	Kiribati
67.8	73.9	...	...	...	...	...	...	...	...	...	H 4,054	H 4.8	H 1.7	...	...	...	Korea, North
70.5	78.4	1995	320,395	7.1	0.3	67.7	32.0	1.7	86.1	12.2	H 12,961	H 3.7	H 1.0	99.5	...	...	Korea, South
75.3	76.9	1997	9,612	5.3	6.1[25]	72.2[25]	21.7[25]	35.9[25]	53.3[25]	10.8[25]	H 246	H 3.9	H 1.6	100.0	...	...	Kuwait
64.0	72.0	1995	26,866	6.0	5.4	79.0	15.6	38.1	52.0	9.9	H 856	H 4.2	H 1.9	83.2	27,111	23.1	Kyrgyzstan
53.0	55.0	...	...	...	...	...	...	...	...	...	...	H 6.0	...	...	...	...	Laos
64.9	76.2	1998	9,641	3.9	—	61.7	38.3	—	69.0	31.0	H 732	H 2.7	H 0.8	62.9	24,227	122.5	Latvia
68.9	73.7	...	...	...	...	...	...	...	...	...	H 405	H 5.3	H 2.2	...	...	...	Lebanon
49.8	51.8	...	...	...	...	...	...	...	...	...	H 330	H 4.8	H 2.0	...	...	...	Lesotho
49.6	52.5	...	...	...	...	...	...	...	...	...	H 474	H 5.0	...	...	...	...	Liberia
73.3	77.7	...	...	...	...	...	...	...	...	...	F 383	F 5.4	F 2.9	...	...	...	Libya
75.2	82.5	1998	423	13.2	—	54.5	44.5	0.0	66.3	29.2	H 8	H 3.0	H 0.7	86.0	...	...	Liechtenstein
67.6	77.9	1997	18,769	5.0	7.1[15]	68.5[15]	24.4[15]	23.0[15]	57.8[15]	19.2[15]	H 1,000	H 2.9	H 0.8	82.0	27,829	71.0	Lithuania
73.8	80.6	1997	2,007	4.8	0.9[15]	49.1[15]	50.0[15]	4.0[15]	61.6[15]	34.4[15]	H 145	H 2.6	H 0.5	82.5	...	...	Luxembourg
77.0	81.0	1998	1,451	3.4	0.6[15]	38.6[15]	60.8[15]	2.8[15]	58.0[15]	39.2[15]	H 99	H 3.5	H 0.9	99.3	...	...	Macau
71.6	76.2	1998	13,993	7.0	5.0	75.1	19.9	26.5	63.8	9.7	H 468	H 3.8	H 1.3	90.5	18,754	57.9	Macedonia
52.7	57.3	...	...	...	...	...	...	...	...	...	H 1,709	H 4.7	H 2.0	...	...	...	Madagascar
37.2	38.0	...	...	...	...	...	...	...	...	...	...	H 4.3	...	...	...	...	Malawi
70.3	75.2	...	...	...	...	...	...	...	...	...	H 3,580	H 4.9	...	...	...	...	Malaysia
68.0	66.0	1995	4,998	19.7	13.7[18]	58.2[18]	29.1[18]	...	...	...	...	H 7.2	...	...	...	...	Maldives
45.5	47.8	...	...	...	...	...	...	...	...	...	H 1,364	H 5.0	...	...	...	...	Mali
75.5	80.6	1998	2,376	6.3	2.0[15]	74.0[15]	24.0[15]	9.5[15]	76.0[15]	14.5[15]	H 76	H 3.3	H 1.2	91.8	...	...	Malta
63.7	67.4	...	...	...	...	...	...	...	...	...	H 5	H 8.7	...	...	...	...	Marshall Islands
75.5	80.6	1993	1,555	4.2	0.1[25]	46.8[25]	53.1[25]	3.3[25]	61.5[25]	35.2[25]	H 107	H 3.3	H 0.8	34.1	1,753	30.6	Martinique
48.7	52.9	...	...	...	...	...	...	...	...	...	H 246	H 5.0	...	...	...	...	Mauritania
67.0	75.0	1997	10,887	9.5	1.8[15]	56.2[15]	42.0[15]	25.8[15]	54.0[15]	20.2[15]	F 155	F 5.3	F 2.0	72.8	...	...	Mauritius
57.4	61.6	...	...	...	...	...	...	...	...	...	H 19	H 4.9	H 2.3	89.2	...	...	Mayotte
68.5	74.7	1996	670,523	6.9	14.0	65.1	20.9	32.5	54.7	12.8	H 17,152	H 5.1	H 2.0	72.5	28,734	1.0	Mexico
66.7	70.6	...	...	...	...	...	...	...	...	...	H 11	H 6.8	...	...	...	...	Micronesia
59.9	69.2	1996	26,089	6.0	8.2[17]	70.0[17]	21.8[17]	38.2[17]	45.0[17]	16.8[17]	H 1,144	H 3.4	H 1.1	89.6	44,252	78.4	Moldova
74.9	83.0	...	...	...	...	...	...	...	...	...	H 14	H 2.2	H 0.3	96.8	...	...	Monaco
61.0	65.0	1996	14,200	6.0	...	...	...	...	...	...	F 428	F 4.8	...	...	...	...	Mongolia
67.2	71.7	...	...	...	...	...	...	...	...	...	H 2,819	H 5.8	H 2.5	...	...	...	Morocco

Vital statistics, marriage, family (continued)

country	year	birth rate per 1,000 population	death rate per 1,000 population	infant mortality rate per 1,000 live births	rate of natural increase per 1,000 population	total fertility rate	year	infectious and parasitic diseases	malignant neo-plasms (cancers)	endocrine and metabolic disorders	diseases of the nervous system	diseases of the circulatory system	diseases of the respiratory system	diseases of the digestive system	accidents, poisoning, and violence
Mozambique	2000	38.0	23.3	139.9	14.5	4.9	...	...	...	...	...	...	...	...	...
Myanmar (Burma)	2000	24.2	11.7	89.0	12.5	3.0	...	...	...	...	...	...	...	...	...
Namibia	2001	34.7	20.9	71.7	13.8	4.8	...	...	...	...	...	...	...	...	...
Nauru	2000	22.9	5.1	11.1[23]	17.8	3.8[23]	...	...	...	...	...	...	...	...	...
Nepal	2001	34.7	10.3	74.0	24.4	4.6	...	...	...	...	...	...	...	...	...
Netherlands, The	1999	12.7	8.9	5.2	3.8	1.6[10]	1995	7.6	236.1	28.1	13.3	335.1	81.8	32.6	33.5
Netherlands Antilles	1999	13.7	6.5	11.7[10]	7.2	2.1[10]	1995[39]	16.7	149.0	61.7	9.9	71.6	40.8	21.4	47.6
New Caledonia	2001	20.1	4.9	7.0	15.2	2.5	1996	17.6	110.6	8.1[16]	14.6	124.2	60.3	19.6	63.7
New Zealand	2001	14.7	6.9	5.9	7.8	2.0	1996	5.6	200.7	22.1	12.3	317.2	86.4	20.9	46.7
Nicaragua	2000	28.3	4.9	34.8	23.4	3.3	1994[38]	68	62	25	12	156	64	29	120
Niger	2000	51.5	23.2	124.9	28.3	7.2	...	...	...	...	...	...	...	...	...
Nigeria	2000	40.2	13.7	74.2	26.5	5.7	...	...	...	...	...	...	...	...	...
Northern Mariana Islands	2000	20.7	2.2	5.9[23]	18.5	1.8[23]	1994–96	40	33.3	10.9[5]	—	53.3	12.6[40]	—	47.0
Norway	2000	13.2	9.8	3.9	3.4	1.9[23]	1994	8.3	238.3	16.4	16.4	450.1	102.2	29.8	51.8
Oman	2000	38.1	4.2	23.3	33.9	6.1	...	...	...	...	...	...	...	...	...
Pakistan	2001	36.8	10.0	89.0	26.8	5.2	...	...	...	...	...	...	...	...	...
Palau	2000	21.1	7.2	17.7[23]	13.9	2.5[23]	1993	43.6	136.9	...	...	192.9	43.6	...	112.0
Panama	2000	19.5	5.0	20.8	14.5	2.3	1997	21.2	64.4	18.2[5]	1.3[14]	122.1	25.4	9.6	37.1
Papua New Guinea	2000	32.7	8.0	59.9	24.7	4.4	...	...	...	...	...	...	...	...	...
Paraguay	2000	31.3	4.8	30.8	26.5	4.2	1994[41]	29	53	18	6	162	31	18	48
Peru	2000	24.5	5.8	40.6	18.7	3.0	...	...	...	...	...	...	...	...	...
Philippines	2001	26.7	5.3	31.0	21.4	3.3	1996	66.7	42.9	11.0[5]	7.1	136.3	76.9	22.4	43.4
Poland	1999	9.9	9.9	8.9	0.0	1.4[10]	1995	6.4	202.3	14.0	8.1	504.5	34.3	33.0	74.5
Portugal	2000	11.5	10.2	6.1	1.3	1.5	1995	10.2	201.7	43.9	10.0	438.9	80.2	45.7	59.8
Puerto Rico	2000	15.5	7.7	9.7	7.8	1.9	1993	59.4	122.2	66.7	19.2	242.3	80.5	43.9	34.1
Qatar	2000	16.1	4.2	22.1	11.9	3.3	1992	3.4	21.4[24]	7.3[22]	2.6	59.9	7.5	3.4	36.0
Réunion	2000	21.8	5.6	8.7	16.2	1.3	1993	14.9	99.7	22.5	16.0	170.1	41.5	59.5[42]	65.3
Romania	2000	10.8	12.3	19.8	-1.5	1.4	1995	14.1	164.1	10.4	8.8	736.1	75.8	68.2	78.7
Russia	2000	8.3	14.7	16.9	-6.4	1.3	1998	19.0	203.0	11.0[13]	10.9[13]	749.0	57.0	38.0	185.0
Rwanda	2000	35.8	21.0	120.1	14.8	5.1	...	...	...	...	...	...	...	...	...
St. Kitts and Nevis	2000	19.1	9.4	16.7	9.7	2.4	1995	57.8	108.0	55.3	20.1	482.4	65.3	50.3	45.2
St. Lucia	2000	22.2	5.4	16.8	16.8	2.4	1995	20.7	98.6	79.3	13.8	226.9	29.7	21.4	50.3
St. Vincent and the Grenadines	2000	18.3	6.2	17.7[23]	12.1	2.1	1997	36.8	90.0	56.6	14.4	228.4	42.2	28.8	—
Samoa	2001	28.2	5.7	27.0	22.5	4.3	1992[37]	3.1	11.2	9.9	3.1	24.2	9.9	6.8	2.5
San Marino	2000	10.9	7.7	6.3	3.2	1.3	1991–95	...	229.4	2.4[5]	...	324.8	10.7	...	45.2
São Tomé and Príncipe	2000	43.0	7.8	50.4	35.2	6.1	...	...	...	...	...	...	...	...	...
Saudi Arabia	2000	37.5	6.0	52.9	31.5	6.3	...	...	...	...	...	...	...	...	...
Senegal	2000	37.9	8.6	58.1	29.3	5.2	...	...	...	...	...	...	...	...	...
Seychelles	2000	18.0	6.7	17.7	11.3	1.9	1994	43.3	128.6	16.2	16.2	288.4	98.8	39.3	43.3
Sierra Leone	2000	45.6	19.6	148.7	26.0	6.1	...	...	...	...	...	...	...	...	...
Singapore	2000	13.6	4.5	2.5	9.1	1.6	1995	12.4	130.5	10.9	3.0	186.1	97.5	13.7	37.3
Slovakia	2000	10.2	9.8	8.3	0.4	1.3	1997	4.0	209.0	12.0	5.0	529.0	70.0	41.0	69.0
Slovenia	1999	8.8	9.5	4.5	-0.7	1.2	1997	4.4	243.9	36.4	9.0	381.1	81.0	55.2	88.6
Solomon Islands	2001	38.3	4.8	22.0	33.5	5.4	...	...	...	...	...	...	...	...	...
Somalia	2000	47.7	18.7	125.8	29.0	7.2	...	...	...	...	...	...	...	...	...
South Africa	2000	21.6	14.7	58.9	6.9	2.5	1995	71.3	55.8	20.5	10.2	98.5	51.9	15.1	112.0
Spain	2000	9.8	9.1	5.0	0.7	1.2[23]	1995	5.9	219.8	23.1	0.4	333.6	28.0	20.4	41.3
Sri Lanka	2000	17.5	5.8	17.0	11.7	2.1	...	...	...	...	...	...	...	...	...
Sudan, The	2000	38.6	10.3	70.2	28.3	5.5	...	...	...	...	...	...	...	...	...
Suriname	2000	21.1	5.7	25.1	15.4	2.5	1992[43]	40	68	40	11	193	37	32	71
Swaziland	2000	40.6	20.4	109.0	20.2	5.9	...	...	...	...	...	...	...	...	...
Sweden	2000	10.0	10.6	3.5	-0.6	1.5	1995	8.6	234.6	23.2	14.3	525.5	85.8	33.8	48.9
Switzerland	1999	11.0	8.7	3.4	2.3	1.5	1994	16.3	238.7	23.3[20]	18.1	381.5	64.2	27.1	69.3
Syria	2000	31.1	5.3	34.8	25.8	4.1	...	...	...	...	...	...	...	...	...
Taiwan	2000	13.8	5.7	7.1	8.1	1.8	1992	...	101.5	23.7[5]	...	140.1[18]	24.3[44]	18.2[44]	63.7[44]
Tajikistan	2001	24.7	6.4	54.0	18.3	4.4	1993	128.3	40.7	8.8[2,20]	7.9[2]	222.8	158.7	20.7	181.3
Tanzania	2000	40.2	12.9	81.0	27.3	5.5	...	...	...	...	...	...	...	...	...
Thailand	2001	16.1	6.0	18.0	10.1	1.8	1994	27.6	49.0	7.5	11.0	89.8	91.4	18.4	73.8
Togo	2000	38.0	11.2	71.6	26.8	5.5	...	...	...	...	...	...	...	...	...
Tonga	2000	27.2	6.1	37.9[23]	21.1	3.6[23]	1992	16.3	54.9	15.2	6.1	158.5	31.5	18.3	4.1
Trinidad and Tobago	1997	14.5	7.2	17.1	7.3	1.8[10]	1994	11.6	94.4	119.3	14.7	286.5	49.0	28.6	52.8
Tunisia	2000	17.1	5.6	25.8	11.5	2.1	...	...	...	...	...	...	...	...	...
Turkey	2000	18.7	6.0	48.9	12.7	2.2	1993[44]	24	80	9[5]	2[13]	369	19	10	33
Turkmenistan	2000	28.9	9.0	73.3	19.9	1.8	1994	75.7	55.4	11.2	7.6	337.2	150.3	7.6	60.1
Tuvalu	2000	21.4	7.8	26.2[19]	13.6	3.1[19]	...	...	...	...	...	...	...	...	...
Uganda	2000	48.0	18.4	93.3	29.6	7.0	...	...	...	...	...	...	...	...	...
Ukraine	2000	7.9[45]	13.9[45]	21.7	-6.0[45]	1.3	1996	17.7	192.5	8.3[20]	1.2	784.5	75.3	4.9	157.2
United Arab Emirates	2000	18.0	3.7	8.8[23]	14.3	3.3	...	...	...	...	...	...	...	...	...
United Kingdom	2000	11.7	10.4	5.6	1.3	1.7	1997	6.8	261.2	13.8	18.5	442.1	165.8	39.5	32.7
United States	1999	14.3	8.7	6.9	5.6	2.0	1997	19.6[46]	201.6	30.3	21.0	354.4	85.2	29.5	55.9
Uruguay	2000	17.4	9.1	15.1	8.3	2.4	1990	16.0	222.8	25.5	16.2	378.4	76.3	39.1	61.7
Uzbekistan	2001	21.7	5.9	38.0	15.8	3.1	1993	38.0	48.2	9.4[25]	8.9[25]	300.3	113.8	31.4	49.5
Vanuatu	2001	32.1	5.6	30.0	26.5	4.4	1994[37]	25.0	29.2	9.1	5.5	39.0	30.4	9.7	9.1
Venezuela	2000	21.1	4.9	26.2	16.2	2.5	1994	33.0	60.5	24.1	7.4	144.7	31.9	19.3	74.1
Vietnam	2000	21.6	6.3	31.1	15.3	2.5	...	...	...	...	...	...	...	...	...
Virgin Islands (U.S.)	2000	16.0	5.4	9.6	10.6	2.3	...	...	...	...	...	...	...	...	...
West Bank	2000	36.7	4.5	22.3	32.2	5.0	...	...	...	...	...	...	...	...	...
Western Sahara	2000	45.1	16.1	133.6	29.0	6.6	...	...	...	...	...	...	...	...	...
Yemen	2000	43.4	9.9	70.3	33.5	7.1	...	...	...	...	...	...	...	...	...
Yugoslavia	1997	12.4	10.6	14.3	1.8	1.7	1995	9.0	167.7[24]	23.8	10.1	573.7	40.9	28.3	42.2
Zambia	2000	41.9	22.1	92.4	19.8	5.6	...	...	...	...	...	...	...	...	...
Zimbabwe	2000	25.0	22.4	62.3	2.6	3.3	1990	64.7	28.4	4.9	9.4	40.8	39.5	12.1	44.9

[1]Excludes nomadic tribes. [2]1991. [3]1986. [4]Septicemia only. [5]Diabetes mellitus only. [6]Cerebrovascular disease and heart disease only. [7]Chronic obstructive pulmonary diseases, pneumonia, and influenza only. [8]Official government figures. [9]1998–2000 average. [10]2000. [11]Under 21 years of age. [12]21–29 years of age. [13]1994. [14]Meningitis only. [15]1996. [16]1989. [17]1995. [18]1993. [19]1998. [20]Includes nutritional disorders. [21]1996–98 average. [22]1990. [23]1999. [24]Includes benign neoplasms (cancers). [25]1992. [26]Results based on a sample population of about 100,000. [27]Millions of households. [28]Projected rates based on about 60 percent of the total deaths. [29]Indonesia includes East Timor. [30]Projected rates based on about 75 percent of the total deaths.

expectation of life at birth (latest year) male	female	marriages year	total number	rate per 1,000 population	groom (percent) 19 and under	20–29	30 and over	bride (percent) 19 and under	20–29	30 and over	families (households) total ('000)	size	children number under age 15	percent legitimate	induced abortions number	ratio per 100 live births	country
38.3	36.7	...	...	...	...	...	...	...	...	...	F 1,860	F 4.4	F 2.0	73.1	...	...	Mozambique
59.0	63.0	...	...	...	...	...	...	...	...	...	...	H 5.6	...	...	...	...	Myanmar (Burma)
42.5	38.7	...	...	...	...	...	...	...	...	...	...	H 5.2	...	...	...	...	Namibia
57.0	64.1	1995	57	5.3	...	...	...	...	...	...	H 1	H 8.0	H 2.6	...	...	...	Nauru
59.0	59.0	...	...	...	...	...	...	...	...	...	H 3,345	H 5.6	H 2.3	...	...	...	Nepal
75.2	80.7	1998	87,000	5.5	0.5[15]	47.4[15]	52.1[15]	3.2[15]	60.9[15]	35.9[15]	H 6,185	H 2.3	H 0.4	77.3	22,441	11.8	Netherlands, The
72.6	77.0	1998	1,276	6.1	...	...	...	...	...	...	H 41	H 3.7	H 2.1	51.6	...	...	Netherlands Antilles
72.0	77.0	1999	934	4.5	0.1[12]	46.5[12]	53.4[12]	5.0[12]	61.2[12]	33.8[12]	H 51	H 3.8	...	36.4	...	...	New Caledonia
75.7	80.8	1996	21,506	6.0	0.8[12]	50.6[12]	48.6[12]	3.2[12]	60.8[12]	36.0[12]	H 1,178	H 2.8	H 0.7	58.0	11,460	19.3	New Zealand
66.8	70.8	1991	13,122	3.3	...	...	...	...	...	...	H 752	H 5.8	...	...	...	...	Nicaragua
41.4	41.1	...	...	...	...	...	...	...	...	...	H 1,130	H 6.3	...	...	...	...	Niger
51.6	51.6	...	...	...	...	...	...	...	...	...	H 21,283	H 4.7	...	...	...	...	Nigeria
72.0	78.4	...	...	...	...	...	...	...	...	...	H 7	H 4.6	H 1.5	51.2	...	...	Northern Mariana Islands
75.6	81.1	1996	23,172	5.3	0.4	43.5	56.1	2.1	59.1	38.8	H 1,864	H 2.3	...	51.0	13,672	22.6	Norway
69.7	74.0	...	...	...	...	...	...	...	...	...	...	H 8.0	...	...	...	...	Oman
61.0	60.0	...	...	...	...	...	...	...	...	...	...	H 6.3	...	...	...	...	Pakistan
65.2	71.5	...	...	...	...	...	...	...	...	...	...	H 4.9	...	...	...	...	Palau
72.7	78.3	1995	8,841	3.4	2.4	52.3	45.3	10.4	57.2	32.4	H 524	H 4.4	H 1.5	25.5	...	...	Panama
61.1	65.3	...	...	...	...	...	...	...	...	...	H 674	H 4.6	...	...	...	...	Papua New Guinea
71.2	76.3	1994	23,649	5.0	4.2[25]	64.8[25]	31.0[25]	30.4[25]	50.2[25]	19.4[25]	H 868	H 4.7	1.9	68.7	...	...	Paraguay
67.6	72.5	1993	90,000	4.1	...	...	...	...	...	...	H 3,099	H 5.1	...	57.8	...	...	Peru
68.0	72.0	1993	474,407	7.1	4.9	66.3	28.8	18.0	63.8	18.2	F 9,566	F 5.7	F 2.4	93.9	2,315	...	Philippines
69.0	77.6	1996	203,641	5.3	2.8	77.2	20.0	16.6	70.5	12.9	F 9,435	F 3.6	F 0.9	95.0	491	0.1	Poland
72.2	79.5	1997	63,542	6.5	3.1[15]	70.0[15]	26.9[15]	13.9[15]	68.1[15]	18.0[15]	H 3,150	H 3.1	H 0.8	85.5	...	...	Portugal
71.1	80.3	1996	32,572	8.7	8.5	53.8	37.7	19.4	49.3	31.4	H 1,005	H 3.6	H 1.0	59.6	...	...	Puerto Rico
69.9	74.9	1996	1,641	2.9	4.9	67.5	27.6	29.6	59.7	10.7	H 61	H 6.4	...	...	...	...	Qatar
69.3	76.2	1996	3,313	4.9	1.2[22]	65.2[22]	33.6[22]	12.5[22]	66.8[22]	20.7[22]	H 185	H 3.5	...	44.1	4,302	31.7	Réunion
66.1	74.0	1997	147,105	6.5	2.6[15]	76.0[15]	21.4[15]	25.4[15]	62.1[15]	12.5[15]	H 7,115	H 3.1	...	...	456,221	197.2	Romania
59.9	72.4	1995	1,074,900	7.3	6.5	64.5	29.0	28.5	47.7	23.8	H 40,426	H 3.2	H 0.8	70.5	2,766,362	202.8	Russia
38.6	40.1	...	...	...	...	...	...	...	...	...	H 1,509	H 4.7	2.3	94.9	...	...	Rwanda
67.9	73.7	...	...	...	...	...	...	...	...	...	H 12	H 3.7	H 1.4	19.2	...	...	St. Kitts and Nevis
68.7	76.1	1997	467	3.1	0.8[16]	34.4[16]	64.8[16]	3.5[16]	45.1[16]	51.4[16]	H 33	H 4.0	H 2.0	14.2	...	...	St. Lucia
70.6	74.1	1997	508	4.6	1.0[25]	37.0[25]	62.0[25]	4.8[25]	46.3[25]	48.9[25]	H 27	H 3.9	H 2.0	...	...	...	St. Vincent and the Grenadines
67.0	73.0	1997	...	4.6	0.5[18]	51.0[18]	48.5[18]	8.0[18]	65.0[18]	27.0[18]	F 20	F 7.8	F 3.8	43.5	...	...	Samoa
77.6	85.0	1996	191	7.5	0.6[16]	75.1[16]	24.3[16]	5.3[16]	85.3[16]	9.5[16]	H 9	H 2.6	H 0.4	95.2	...	...	San Marino
63.8	66.7	...	...	...	...	...	...	...	...	...	...	H 4.0	...	...	...	...	São Tomé and Príncipe
66.1	69.5	...	...	...	...	...	...	...	...	...	H 1,513	H 6.1	...	...	...	...	Saudi Arabia
60.6	63.8	...	...	...	...	...	...	...	...	...	...	H 8.7	...	...	...	...	Senegal
64.9	76.1	1996	875	11.4	2.0[13]	45.8[13]	42.2[13]	11.2[13]	51.5[13]	29.6[13]	H 13	H 4.8	H 1.9	27.2	387	22.8	Seychelles
42.4	48.2	...	...	...	...	...	...	...	...	...	...	H 6.6	...	...	...	...	Sierra Leone
76.0	80.0	1997	25,667	6.9	0.5	57.3	42.2	3.1	74.5	22.4	H 662	H 4.2	H 1.3	...	14,362	29.6	Singapore
69.7	78.0	1996	27,484	5.1	6.0[17]	76.2[17]	17.8[17]	27.4[17]	62.4[17]	10.2[17]	...	H 3.2	...	83.1	35,879	58.4	Slovakia
71.0	79.0	1996	7,555	3.8	0.5	63.2	36.3	5.8	72.7	21.5	H 637	H 3.1	...	64.4	10,218	54.4	Slovenia
68.0	70.0	...	...	...	...	...	...	...	...	...	...	H 5.8	...	...	...	...	Solomon Islands
44.7	47.9	...	...	...	...	...	...	...	...	...	...	H 4.9	...	...	...	...	Somalia
50.4	51.8	1995	148,148	3.6	0.3	39.7	60.0	2.8	54.9	42.3	H 8,688	H 4.6	...	75.9	...	...	South Africa
74.4	81.6	1996	194,635	5.0	1.2[17]	62.5[17]	36.3[17]	5.0[17]	72.8[17]	22.2[17]	F 10,665	F 3.5	...	89.5	47,832	13.1	Spain
71.0	76.0	1996	170,444	9.3	1.3	64.3	34.4	16.7	67.1	16.2	H 3,282	H 4.6	...	96.3	...	...	Sri Lanka
55.5	57.7	...	...	...	...	...	...	...	...	...	H 3,471	H 5.3	...	...	...	...	Sudan, The
68.7	74.1	1995	2,249	5.5	...	...	...	...	...	...	...	H 4.8	...	...	...	...	Suriname
39.5	41.4	...	...	...	...	...	...	...	...	...	H 122	H 5.7	...	...	1,145	...	Swaziland
77.0	82.4	1996	33,484	3.4	0.3	40.5	59.2	1.5	54.0	44.5	H 3,670	H 2.1	H 0.5	46.1	32,117	33.7	Sweden
76.7	82.6	1997	37,575	5.3	0.4[15]	43.6[15]	56.0[15]	2.8[15]	58.8[15]	38.4[15]	H 3,250	H 2.1	0.4	91.2	...	...	Switzerland
67.4	69.6	1994	115,994	8.4	...	...	...	...	...	...	F 1,151	H 6.2	F 2.4	...	...	...	Syria
73.6	79.3	1998	145,678	6.7	1.5[22]	62.3[22]	36.2[22]	6.0[22]	77.7[22]	16.3[22]	H 5,964	H 3.6	H 1.0	97.2	...	...	Taiwan
65.0	71.0	1994	38,820	6.8	10.7	80.6	8.7	49.6	45.7	4.7	H 799	H 6.1	H 2.7	93.0	35,709	22.0	Tajikistan
51.3	53.2	...	...	...	...	...	...	...	...	...	H 3,435	H 5.2	H 2.3	...	...	...	Tanzania
71.0	76.0	1995	470,751	7.9	...	...	...	...	...	...	H 15,551	H 3.8	...	...	...	...	Thailand
52.8	56.7	...	...	...	...	...	...	...	...	...	H 479	H 6.0	...	...	...	...	Togo
67.7	72.2	1994	748	7.7	16.3	63.0	20.7	5.1	65.0	29.9	F 15	F 6.3	F 2.7	80.6	...	...	Tonga
65.4	70.6	1996	7,118	5.6	4.3	54.9	40.8	20.0	52.8	27.2	H 301	H 3.8	H 1.3	...	9	—	Trinidad and Tobago
72.1	75.4	1997	57,100	6.2	...	60.5[25]	39.5[25]	24.7[25]	62.7[25]	20.2[25]	H 1,703	H 5.1	H 1.9	99.8	23,300	10.9	Tunisia
68.6	73.4	1996	486,734	7.8	5.9[17]	74.5[17]	19.6[17]	31.4[17]	58.5[17]	10.1[17]	...	H 4.5	...	...	...	...	Turkey
57.3	64.7	1993	42,106	10.7	3.0[16]	87.4[16]	9.6[16]	16.1[16]	77.1[16]	6.8[16]	H 598	H 5.6	H 2.4	96.5	39,068	31.3	Turkmenistan
62.7	65.1	...	...	...	...	...	...	...	...	...	H 1	H 6.4	H 2.2	82.2	...	...	Tuvalu
42.2	43.7	...	...	...	...	...	...	...	...	...	H 2,766	H 4.8	...	...	...	...	Uganda
60.6	72.0	1997	345,000	6.5	7.5	68.4	24.1	35.2	45.9	18.9	H 14,507	H 3.2	H 0.8	89.2	957,022	159.5	Ukraine
71.6	76.6	1995	...	2.7	...	...	...	...	...	...	H 247	H 5.3	...	...	...	...	United Arab Emirates
75.0	80.5	1995	282,900	5.5	0.8	49.1	50.1	3.6	57.4	39.0	H 29,533	H 2.4	H 1.7	63.2	167,297	22.8	United Kingdom
74.1	79.7	1996	2,324,000	8.8	4.3[22]	51.8[22]	43.9[22]	10.9[22]	55.8[22]	35.3[22]	H 96,391	H 2.6	F 1.0	67.2	1,359,145	32.0	United States
71.9	78.8	1996	17,596	5.5	6.9[25]	57.2[25]	35.9[25]	23.5[25]	51.4[25]	25.1[25]	H 863	H 3.3	H 0.9	73.8	...	...	Uruguay
66.0	72.0	1994	176,300	7.8	11.2	80.7	8.1	49.3	45.3	5.4	H 3,415	H 5.5	H 2.4	95.8	120,434	18.3	Uzbekistan
67.0	70.0	...	...	...	...	...	...	...	...	...	H 28	H 5.1	H 2.2	...	113	2.4	Vanuatu
70.1	76.3	1996	81,951	3.7	9.5	58.7	31.8	27.9	51.7	20.4	H 2,707	H 5.3	H 2.2	47.0	...	...	Venezuela
66.8	71.9	...	...	...	...	...	...	...	...	...	H 12,958[47]	H 4.8[47]	H 1.9[47]	...	...	...	Vietnam
74.2	82.5	1993	3,646	35.1	0.4	33.6	66.0	1.9	45.9	52.2	H 32	H 3.1	H 1.0	30.2	...	...	Virgin Islands (U.S.)
70.4	73.9	...	...	...	...	...	...	...	...	...	...	...	...	...	...	...	West Bank
48.7	51.3	...	...	...	...	...	...	...	...	...	...	...	...	...	...	...	Western Sahara
58.1	61.6	...	...	...	...	...	...	...	...	...	H 1,848	H 5.6	...	...	...	...	Yemen
69.9	74.7	1997	56,004	5.3	2.3[17]	64.5[17]	33.2[17]	18.7[17]	63.5[17]	17.8[17]	H 2,870	H 3.6	H 0.9	...	91,474	65.1	Yugoslavia
37.1	37.4	...	...	...	...	...	...	...	...	...	H 1,370	H 4.4	H 2.1	...	...	...	Zambia
39.2	36.4	...	...	...	...	...	...	...	...	...	H 2,166	H 4.8	1.1	95.8	...	...	Zimbabwe

[31]Ethiopia includes Eritrea. [32]Based on a sample registration scheme. [33]Muslims only. [34]Projected rates based on about 20 percent of the total deaths. [35]1997–99 average. [36]1997. [37]Registered deaths only. [38]Projected rates based on about 45 percent of the total deaths. [39]Includes Aruba. [40]Diseases of the respiratory system included in infectious and parasitic diseases. [41]Reporting areas only (constituting about 75 percent of the total population). [42]Includes all deaths associated with alcoholism. [43]Projected rates based on about 70 percent of the total deaths. [44]Projected rates based on about 35 percent of the total deaths. [45]Average of April to September only. [46]Of which AIDS, 6.2. [47]Private households only.

National product and accounts

This table furnishes, for most of the countries of the world, breakdowns of (1) gross national product (GNP)—its global and per capita values, and purchasing power parity (PPP), (2) growth rates (1990–99) and principal industrial and accounting components of gross domestic product (GDP), and (3) principal elements of each country's balance of payments, including international goods trade, invisibles, external public debt outstanding, and tourism payments.

Measures of national output. The two most commonly used measures of national output are GDP and GNP. Each of these measures represents an aggregate value of goods and services produced by a specific country. The GDP, the more basic of these, is a measure of the total value of goods and services produced entirely within a given country. The GNP, the more comprehensive value, is composed of both domestic production (GDP) and the net income from current (short-term) transactions with other countries. When the income received from other countries is greater than payments to them, a country's GNP is greater than its GDP. In theory, if all national accounts could be equilibrated, the global summation of GDP would equal GNP.

In the first section of the table, data are provided for the nominal and real GNP. ("Nominal" refers to value in current prices for the year indicated and is distinguished from a "real" valuation, which is one adjusted to eliminate the effect of recent inflation [most often] or, occasionally, of deflation between two given dates.) Both the total and per capita values of this product are denominated in U.S. dollars for ease of comparison, as is a new value for GNP per capita adjusted for purchasing power parity.

The latter is a concept that provides a better approximation of the ability of equivalent values of two (or more) national currencies to purchase comparable quantities of goods and services in their respective domestic markets and may differ substantially from two otherwise equal GNP per capita values based solely on currency exchange rates. Beside these are given figures for average annual growth of total and per capita real GNP. GNP per capita provides a rough measure of annual national income per person, but values should be compared cautiously, as they are subject to a number of distortions, notably of exchange rate, but also of purchasing power parity and in the existence of elements of national production that do not enter the monetary economy in such a way as to be visible to fiscal authorities (e.g., food, clothing, or housing produced and consumed within families or communal groups or services exchanged). For reasons of comparability, the majority of the data in this section are taken from the World Bank's *The World Bank Atlas* (annual).

The internal structure of the national product. GDP/GNP values allow comparison of the relative size of national economies, but further information is provided when these aggregates are analyzed according to their industrial sectors of origin, component kinds of expenditure, and cost components.

The distribution of GDP for ten industrial sectors, usually compiled from national sources, is aggregated into three major industrial groups:

1. The primary sector, composed of agriculture (including forestry and fishing) and mineral production (including fossil fuels).

National product and accounts

country	gross national product (GNP), 1999 nominal ('000,000 U.S.$)	per capita nominal (U.S.$)	per capita purchasing power parity (PPP; U.S.$)	GDP avg growth 1990–99 real GDP (%)	population (%)	real GDP per capita (%)	primary agriculture	mining	secondary manufacturing	construction	public utilities	tertiary transp., communications	trade	financial svcs.	other svcs.	government	other
Afghanistan	5,666[1]	250[1]	...	...	...	...	...	...	...	...	...	...	...	...	...	...	...
Albania	3,146	930	3,240	3.4	0.6	2.8	54	2	12[2]	13	2	3	—18—			13	—
Algeria	46,548	1,550	4,840	1.7	2.2	–0.5	11	23	10	11	—	—24—				13	8
American Samoa	253[1]	4,300[1]	...	...	...	...	...	...	...	...	...	...	...	...	...	...	...
Andorra	850[3]	13,100[3]	...	...	...	...	...	...	...	...	...	...	...	...	...	...	...
Angola	3,276	270	1,100	–0.5	2.3	–2.8	13	45	6	6	—	—18—			—11—		1
Antigua and Barbuda	606	8,990	9,870	3.8	1.1	2.7	3	1	2	10	3	17	19	14	6	15	10
Argentina	296,097	7,550	11,940	4.9	1.3	3.6	5[3]	2[3]	20[3]	6[3]	2[3]	6[3]	14[3]	18[3]	—24[3]—		3[3]
Armenia	1,878	490	2,360	–3.1	0.8	–3.9	31	2	22[2]	9	2	5	9	—25—			–1
Aruba	1,728[4,5]	18,700[4,5]	...	...	...	...	...	...	...	...	...	...	...	...	...	...	...
Australia	397,345	20,950	23,850	4.1	1.2	2.9	3	4	13	6	2	8	10	16	33	4	1
Austria	205,741	25,430	24,600	1.9	0.5	1.4	3	1	24	7	3	8	19	18	6	10	1
Azerbaijan	3,705	460	2,450	–9.5	1.2	–10.7	20[3]	2	25[2,3]	14[3]	2	10[3]	—31[3]—				—
Bahamas, The	3,288[3]	11,830[3]	...	...	...	...	1[6]	15[6]	17[6]	6[6]	2[6]	11[6]	11[6]	19[6]	5[6]	19[6]	–6[6]
Bahrain	4,909[4]	7,640[4]	...	...	...	...	1[7]	17[7]	22[7]	6[7]	2[7]	9[7]	11[7]	18[7]	5[7]	19[7]	–10[7]
Bangladesh	41,071	370	1,530	4.7	1.6	3.1	23	1	18	7	1	10	15	11	11	2	1
Barbados	2,294	8,600	14,010	1.8	0.3	1.5	6	1	10	8	4	8	35	—17—		12	–1
Belarus	26,299	2,620	6,880	–3.1	–0.2	–2.9	13	8	36[8]	7	4	12	12	—16—			11
Belgium	252,051	24,650	25,710	1.7	0.3	1.4	1[3]	—	21[3]	5[3]	2[3]	8[3]	12[3]	14[3]	7[3]	24[3]	6[3]
Belize	673	2,730	4,750	3.2	2.5	0.7	18	1	13	5	2	12	15	8	6	6	14
Benin	2,320	380	920	5.0	3.2	1.8	38[3]	8	9[3,8]	4[3]	1[3]	7[3]	18[3]	9[3]	—7[3]—		7[3]
Bermuda	2,128[3]	34,950[3]	...	...	...	...	...	...	...	...	...	...	...	...	...	...	...
Bhutan	399	510	1,260	6.1	2.7	3.4	38	2	12	11	11	8	7	5	—9—		–3
Bolivia	8,092	990	2,300	4.2	2.4	1.8	15	11	18	5	1	12	9	13	6	10	—
Bosnia and Herzegovina	4,706	1,210	...	...	...	...	12	...	24	6	3	9	19	4	14	8	—
Botswana	5,139	3,240	6,540	3.8	2.0	1.8	3	36	5	6	2	4	18	8	4	14	—
Brazil	730,424	4,350	6,840	3.0	1.5	1.5	7[3]	13	19[3]	9[3]	3[3]	5[3]	7[3]	20[3]	11[3]	13[3]	5[3]
Brunei	7,209[4]	22,280[4]	...	...	...	...	3	8	37[8]	7	1	4	10	9	—33—		–4
Bulgaria	11,572	1,410	5,070	–2.8	–0.7	–2.1	19	1	17	3	4	7	7	2	—29—		11
Burkina Faso	2,602	240	960	4.2	2.8	1.4	30	8	20[8]	5	1	4	12	—22—			6
Burundi	823	120	570	–3.9	1.1	–5.0	46	1[9]	9	5	9	4	4	—2—		18	11
Cambodia	3,023	260	1,350	5.2	3.3	1.9	51	—	6	7	1	4	15	5	7	3	1
Cameroon	8,798	600	1,490	1.3	2.8	–1.5	41	5	10	4	1	—35—					4
Canada	614,003	20,140	25,440	2.8	1.1	1.7	2	4	18	6	3	8	12	16	24	6	1
Cape Verde	569	1,330	4,450	4.6	1.4	3.2	12	—	10	9	—	18	19	12	7	14	–1
Central African Republic	1,035	290	1,150	2.0	2.3	–0.3	49	4	8	4	1	2	12	—6—		6	8
Chad	1,555	210	840	2.5	3.4	–0.9	37	1	12	2	1	—24—		—9—		11	3
Chile	69,602	4,630	8,410	7.1	1.5	5.6	7	9	15	5	2	9	18	17	6	2	10
China	979,894	780	3,550	10.8	1.3	9.5	18	2	42[2]	7	2	6	8	—18—			1
Colombia	90,007	2,170	5,580	3.3	1.9	1.4	14	4	14	5	...	8	12	—34—		9	—
Comoros	189	350	1,430	–0.1	3.0	–3.1	40	...	4	6	1	5	25	3	1	13	2
Congo, Dem. Rep. of the	5,433[4]	110[4]	...	...	...	...	58[7]	47	67	27	27	37	17[7]	—67—		17	17
Congo, Rep. of the	1,571	550	540	–0.8	2.5	–3.3	11[7]	33[7]	8[7]	2[7]	1[7]	12[7]	9[7]	—87—		13[7]	37
Costa Rica	12,828	3,570	7,880	5.0	2.0	3.0	15	8	19[8]	2	3	6	21	12	8	14	—
Côte d'Ivoire	10,387	670	1,540	3.6	3.0	0.6	28	2	20[2]	5	2	8	15	—12—		8	4
Croatia	20,222	4,530	7,260	0.4	–0.6	1.0	7	8	24[8]	6	3	8	12	13	—14—		13
Cuba	18,600[5]	1,700[5]	...	...	...	...	7[3]	23	37[3]	5[3]	23	4[3]	21[3]	23	—19[3]—		23
Cyprus[10]	9,086	11,950	19,080	4.2	1.4	2.8	4	—	11	8	2	9	20	19	10	14	3
Czech Republic	51,623	5,020	12,840	0.9	–0.0	0.9	4	2	32[2]	7	2	9	12	17	—13—		6
Denmark	170,685	32,050	25,600	2.4	0.4	2.0	4[3]	13	20[3]	6	2[3]	10[3]	13[3]	19[3]	6[3]	22[3]	–3[3]
Djibouti	511	790	...	–3.0	2.1	–5.1	3	—	5	8	5	17	16	10	5	20	11
Dominica	238	3,260	5,040	2.4	0.6	1.8	20	1	9	8	5	17	14	14	1	19	–8
Dominican Republic	16,130	1,920	5,210	5.7	1.8	3.9	12	2	17	12	2	12	20	9	8	8	–2
East Timor	113[4,5]	130[4,5]	...	...	...	...	...	...	...	...	...	...	...	...	...	...	...
Ecuador	16,841	1,360	2,820	2.1	2.1	0.0	17[3]	15[3]	15[3]	2[3]	1[3]	9[3]	15[3]	12[3]	6[3]	7[3]	1[3]

2. The secondary sector, composed of manufacturing, construction, and public utilities.

3. The tertiary sector, which includes transportation and communications, trade (wholesale and retail), restaurants and hotels, financial services (including banking, real estate, insurance, and business services), other services (community, social, and personal), and government services.

The category "other" contains adjustments such as import duties and bank service charges that are not distributed by sector.

There are three major domestic components of GDP expenditure: private consumption (analyzed in greater detail in the "Household budgets and consumption" table), government spending, and gross domestic investment. The fourth, nondomestic, component of GDP expenditure is net foreign trade; values are given for both exports (a positive value) and imports (a negative value, representing obligations to other countries). The sum of these five percentages, excluding statistical discrepancies and rounding, should be 100% of the GDP.

Balance of payments (external account transactions). The external account records the sum (net) of all economic transactions of a current nature between one country and the rest of the world. The account shows a country's net of overseas receipts and obligations, including not only the trade of goods and merchandise but also such invisible items as services, interest and dividends, short- and long-term investments, tourism, transfers to or from overseas residents, etc. Each transaction gives rise either to a foreign claim for payment, recorded as a deficit (*e.g.*, from imports, capital outflows), or a foreign obligation to pay, recorded as a surplus (*e.g.*, from exports, capital inflows) or a domestic claim on another country. Any international transaction automatically creates a deficit in the balance of payments of one country and a surplus in that of another. Values are given in U.S. dollars for comparability.

External public debt. Because the majority of the world's countries are in the less developed bloc, and because their principal financial concern is often external debt and its service, data are given for outstanding external public and publicly guaranteed long-term debt rather than for total public debt, which is the major concern in the developed countries. For comparability, the data are given in U.S. dollars. The data presented in the table come from the World Bank's *Global Development Finance* (formerly *World Debt Tables*).

Tourist trade. Net income or expenditure from tourism (in U.S. dollars for comparability) is often a significant element in a country's balance of payments. Receipts from foreign nationals reflect payments for goods and services from foreign currency resources by tourists in the given country. Expenditures by nationals abroad are also payments for goods and services, but in this case made by the residents of the given country as tourists abroad. The majority of the data in this section are compiled by the World Tourism Organization.

gross domestic product (GDP) by type of expenditure, 1998 (%)						external public debt outstanding (long-term, disbursed only), 1999							balance of payments, 1999 (current external transactions; '000,000 U.S.$)				tourist trade, 1997 ('000,000 U.S.$)		country
consumption		gross domestic invest-ment	foreign trade		total ('000,000 U.S.$)	creditors (%)		debt service				net transfers		current balance of payments	receipts from foreign nationals	expendi-tures by nationals abroad	
private	govern-ment		exports	imports		offi-cial	private	total ('000,000 U.S.$)	repayment (%)		goods, merchan-dise	invisibles					
									princi-pal	inter-est							
...	...	...	...	...	...	...	...	...	...	...	...	...	...	1	1	Afghanistan
...	...	...	...	...	849.1	70.7	29.3	27.1	28.4	71.6	−663.0	507.6	−155.4	27	5	Albania
51	17	27	28	−23	25,913	71.3	28.7	4,885	64.7	35.3	3,360	−3,340	20	20	64	Algeria
...	...	...	...	...	...	...	...	...	...	...	...	...	...	10	...	American Samoa
...	...	...	...	...	...	...	...	...	...	...	...	...	...	...	...	Andorra
...	...	...	...	...	9,248	39.6	60.4	1,099	89.6	10.4	1,463.5[4]	−3,323.1[4]	−1,857.6[4]	9	73	Angola
58	22	32	73	−84	...	...	...	...	...	...	−321.3[4]	232.7[4]	−88.6[4]	260	26	Antigua and Barbuda
71		20	10	−13	84,568	24.8	75.2	12,170	48.1	51.9	−770	−11,676	−12,446	5,069	2,680	Argentina
103	11	19	19	−53	681.9	100.0	—	39.8	64.6	35.4	−474.0	167.0	−307.1	7	41	Armenia
73	13	11	2		...	...	...	...	...	...	−591.7	258.5	−333.2	666	130	Aruba
59	18	24	20	−22	...	...	...	...	...	...	−9,730	−13,340	−23,070	9,026	6,129	Australia
55	20	26	44	−45	...	...	...	...	...	...	−3,649	−2,098	−5,747	12,393	10,992	Austria
78[3]	12[3]	38[3]	28[3]	−55[3]	493.3	91.1	8.9	49.8	81.5	18.5	−408.2	−191.5	−599.7	159	72	Azerbaijan
66[7]	15[7]	23[7]	54[7]	−58[7]	...	...	...	...	...	...	−1,428.2	756.3	−671.9	1,416	250	Bahamas, The
51	21	18	78	−68	...	...	...	...	...	...	672.1	−1,012.5	−340.4	260	129	Bahrain
78	14	13	19	−23	16,962	99.4	0.6	675	72.3	27.7	−1,962.1	1,670.6	−291.5	59	170	Bangladesh
59	21	20	58	−57	359.1	75.4	24.6	84.2	64.4	35.6	−691.7	565.9	−125.8	717	74	Barbados
58	20	27	60	−65	851	52.8	47.2	141	64.5	35.5	−570.0	376.3	−193.7	25	114	Belarus
54	21	21	76	−72	...	...	...	...	...	...	6,642	6,732	13,374	5,275	8,275	Belgium
65	17	27	52	−61	294.6	73.6	26.4	40.2	59.6	40.4	−128.8	51.4	−77.4	87	30	Belize
81	9	18	27	−35	1,472	99.8	0.2	56	64.3	35.7	−158.3[4]	6.8[4]	−151.5[4]	31	7	Benin
...	...	...	...	...	...	...	...	...	...	...	...	...	...	474	148	Bermuda
36[1]	29[1]	44[1]	34[1]	−44[1]	181.8	100.0	—	6.9	71.0	29.0	−24.8[4]	−21.7[4]	−46.5[4]	6	...	Bhutan
75	14	23	20	−32	3,864	99.4	0.6	257	57.0	43.0	−488.0	−67.8	−555.8	170	172	Bolivia
100		38	35	−73	1,826	92.6	7.4	388	64.3	35.7	−2,072.0	1,284.6	−787.4	15	...	Bosnia and Herzegovina
28	29	28	56	−41	442.3	95.2	4.8	82.5	74.7	25.3	674.5	−157.7	516.8	184	140	Botswana
64	18	21	7	−10	95,233	33.8	66.2	24,374	72.1	27.9	−1,261	−24,139	−25,400	2,595	6,583	Brazil
...	...	...	...	...	...	...	...	...	...	...	175[4]	1,910[4]	2,085[4]	39	...	Brunei
72	15	14	44	−45	7,602	32.8	67.2	632	49.5	50.5	−1,081.0	396.3	−684.7	368	222	Bulgaria
81	10	24	15	−30	1,295	99.7	0.3	53	69.8	30.2	−184.5	−38.6	−223.1	39	32	Burkina Faso
96	12	3	8	−19	1,050	99.9	0.1	20	70.0	30.0	−42.3	15.3	−27.0	1	10	Burundi
96[1]	7[1]	16[1]	28[1]	−46[1]	2,136	100.0	—	28	51.8	48.2	−209.5	143.5	−66.0	143	12	Cambodia
71	9	18	26	−27	7,614	95.2	4.8	346	47.8	52.2	112.4	−343.7	−231.3	39	107	Cameroon
59	20	20	41	−40	...	...	...	...	...	...	22,756	−25,029	−2,273	8,770	11,304	Canada
68	23	40	25	−57	265.1	95.7	4.3	21.6	84.7	15.3	−185.6[4]	127.6[4]	−58.0[4]	15	17	Cape Verde
84	12	14	16	−25	830.1	96.1	3.9	11.9	60.9	39.1	−8.3[4]	−79.1[4]	−87.4[4]	5	39	Central African Republic
90	10	15	18	−33	1,045	98.5	1.5	27	61.1	38.9	−50.3[4]	−155.8[4]	−206.1[4]	9	24	Chad
67	11	26	25	−29	5,655	37.1	62.9	780	60.1	39.9	1,664	−1,744	−80	1,021	946	Chile
46	12	38	4		108,163	46.6	53.4	15,668	68.2	31.8	36,207	−20,540	15,667	12,074	10,166	China
68	19	20	15	−22	19,434	39.6	60.4	4,775	65.5	34.5	1,776	−1,837	−61	955	958	Colombia
91[1]	15[1]	19[1]	20[1]	−45[1]	179.9	100.0	—	7.1	87.3	12.7	−35.6[4]	40.8[4]	5.2[4]	26	8	Comoros
81[7]	5[7]	9[7]	28[7]	−23[7]	8,188	93.8	6.2	—	—	—	830[1]	−1,375[1]	−515[1]	2	7	Congo, Dem. Rep. of the
46	16	26	67	−55	3,932	80.1	19.9	—	—	—	644.1	−885.7	−241.6	3	36	Congo, Rep. of the
56	16	28	50	−50	3,186	64.0	36.0	475	70.3	29.7	659.6	−1,309.1	−649.5	719	358	Costa Rica
64	11	19	44	−37	9,699	74.8	28.2	992	53.8	46.2	1,832.3[4]	−2,144.9[4]	−312.6[4]	88	282	Côte d'Ivoire
59[1]	29[1]	22[1]	42[1]	−52[1]	5,433	26.3	73.7	667	47.1	52.9	−3,298.7	1,776.5	−1,522.2	2,529	521	Croatia
71[1]	24[1]	7[1]	16[1]	−18[1]	...	...	...	...	...	...	...	...	...	1,338	...	Cuba
64	19	25	44	−52	...	...	...	...	...	...	−2,309.2	2,075.5	−233.7	1,639	278	Cyprus[10]
52	19	30	60	−61	13,440	8.6	91.4	2,470	62.5	37.5	−1,902	870	−1,032	3,647	2,380	Czech Republic
51	26	21	35	−33	...	...	...	...	...	...	6,689	−3,725	2,964	3,156	4,128	Denmark
79	24	15	45	−64	252.7	100.0	—	3.0	68.3	31.7	−179.7[4]	165.3[4]	−14.4[4]	4	5	Djibouti
58[3]	21[3]	34[3]	51[3]	−63[3]	89.0	100.0	—	9.3	75.3	23.7	−58.4	29.0	−29.4	37	7	Dominica
75	8	26	47	−56	3,665	80.5	19.5	331	52.3	47.7	−2,904.4	2,475.2	−429.2	2,107	242	Dominican Republic
...	...	...	...	...	...	...	...	...	...	...	...	...	...	...	...	East Timor
70	12	25	25	−32	12,756	42.7	57.3	1,382	45.2	54.8	1,655	−700	955	290	227	Ecuador

National product and accounts (continued)

country	gross national product (GNP), 1999 nominal ('000,000 U.S.$)	per capita nominal (U.S.$)	per capita purchasing power parity (PPP; U.S.$)	real GDP (%)	popu-lation (%)	real GDP per capita (%)	agri-culture	mining	manu-factur-ing	con-struc-tion	public util-ities	transp., commu-nications	trade	finan-cial svcs.	other svcs.	govern-ment	other
Egypt	86,544	1,380	3,460	4.6	2.2	2.4	16[3]	8	27[3,8]	5[3]	2[3]	11[3]	19[3]	6[3]	—7[3]—		7[3]
El Salvador	11,806	1,920	4,260	4.6	1.8	2.8	12	—	22	4	2	8	19	12	7	14	—
Equatorial Guinea	516	1,170	3,910	18.9	2.6	16.3	22	61	—	3	1	1	4	1	2	5	—
Eritrea	779	200	1,040	5.6	3.4	2.2	15	—	13	11	1	9	20	4	1	17	9
Estonia	4,906	3,400	8,190	−1.2	−0.9	−0.3	6	1	14	5	3	12	18	13	14	4	10
Ethiopia	6,524	100	620	5.3	2.9	2.4	46	8	7[8]	3	2	6	9	7	8	13	−1
Faroe Islands	976[4]	24,620[4]	...	...	...	...	...	...	...	...	...	...	...	...	...	...	...
Fiji	1,848	2,310	4,780	2.2	1.0	1.2	16	3	15	5	5	14	16	14	—20—		−8
Finland	127,764	27,730	22,600	2.4	0.4	2.0	4	—	22	4	2	8	11	11	9	16	13
France	1,453,211	24,170	23,020	1.5	0.4	1.1	3[3]	13	22[3]	5[3]	3[3]	6[3]	14[3,11]	5[3]	18[3,11]	19[3]	6[3]
French Guiana	1,543[7]	10,580[7]	...	..	...	...	...	...	...	...	...	...	...	...	...	...	...
French Polynesia	3,908	16,930	22,200	1.6	1.7	−0.1	...	...	...	...	...	...	...	...	...	...	...
Gabon	3,987	3,300	5,280	1.8	1.2	0.6	7[3]	43[3]	6[3]	4[3]	1[3]	5[3]	8[3]	—11[3]—		9[3]	6[3]
Gambia, The	415	330	1,550	3.0	3.6	−0.6	24	—	5	5	2	14	17	7	5	9	12
Gaza Strip	1,368[4,5]	1,320[4,5]	...	...	...	...	13	—	10	8	2	5	15	23	8	16	—
Georgia	3,362	620	2,540	...	...	...	32	2	13[2]	4	2	11	11	11	—13—		5
Germany	2,103,804	26,620	23,510	1.4	0.4	1.0	1	2	25[2]	5	2	—17—		30	—21—		1
Ghana	7,451	400	1,850	4.1	2.5	1.6	36	5	9	9	3	4	7	4	3	10	10
Greece	127,648	12,110	15,800	2.5	0.7	1.8	14[3]	13	14[3]	6[3]	2[3]	7[3]	14[3]	3[3]	11[3]	19[3]	9[3]
Greenland	1,142[3]	20,380[3]	...	...	...	...	...	...	...	...	...	...	...	...	...	...	...
Grenada	334	3,440	6,300	2.9	0.7	2.2	9[3]	13	7[3]	7[3]	5[3]	24[3]	20[3]	14[3]	3[3]	16[3]	−6[3]
Guadeloupe	3,706[5,7]	9,200[5,7]	...	...	...	...	...	...	...	...	...	...	...	...	...	...	...
Guam	3,301[4,5]	20,660[4,5]	...	...	...	...	...	...	...	...	...	...	...	...	...	...	...
Guatemala	18,625	1,680	3,630	4.2	2.7	1.5	23	1	14	2	3	9	25	10	6	8	−1
Guernsey[12]	1,902	29,810	...	...	...	...	...	...	...	...	...	...	...	...	...	...	...
Guinea	3,556	490	1,870	3.9	2.4	1.5	21	16	4	9	1	6	—28—		9	4	2
Guinea-Bissau	194	160	630	0.7	2.6	−1.9	62	2	9[2]	3	2	2	19	—1—		3	1
Guyana	651	760	3,330	5.6	0.4	5.2	29	14	9[13]	5	13	6	4	6	1	11	15
Haiti	3,584	460	1,470	−2.1	1.3	−3.4	30	—	7	12	1	2	13	8	5	18	4
Honduras	4,829	760	2,270	3.6	3.3	0.3	19	2	19	5	5	5	12	17	11	6	−1
Hong Kong	165,122	24,570	22,570	3.7	1.8	1.9	—	—	6	6	3	9	23	24	—19—		10
Hungary	46,751	4,640	11,050	1.1	−0.3	1.4	6[3]	8	20[3,8]	4[3]	3[3]	9[3]	10[3]	16[3]	13[3]	6[3]	13[3]
Iceland	8,197	29,540	27,210	2.7	0.9	1.8	9[3]	—	13[3]	6[3]	3[3]	6[3]	10[3]	15[3]	5[3]	14[3]	18[3]
India	441,834	440	2,230	5.9	1.8	4.1	25	2	15	4	2	7	14	10	6	5	10
Indonesia	125,043	600	2,660	4.6	1.6	3.0	19	13	26	5	1	5	15	8	3	4	1
Iran	113,729	1,810	5,520	3.4	1.5	1.9	20	12	16	4	2	8	17	10	2	10	−1
Iraq	11,500[1,5]	600[1,5]	...	...	...	...	...	...	...	...	...	...	...	...	...	...	...
Ireland	80,559	21,470	22,460	6.8	0.7	6.1	81	14	38[1,14]	14	14	—18[1]—		—31[1]—		51	...
Isle of Man	1,319[4,5]	18,270[4,5]	...	...	...	...	2[3]	—	12[3]	7[3]	3[3]	10[3]	12[3]	59[3]	4[3]	6[3]	−15[3]
Israel	99,574	16,310	18,070	5.2	2.9	2.3	2[3]	2	19[2,3]	9	2	6[3]	12[3]	30[3]	—28[3]—		−6[3]
Italy	1,162,910	20,170	22,000	1.4	0.2	1.2	3[1]	41	16[1]	5[1]	6[1]	6[1]	19[1]	5[1]	13[1]	22[1]	11
Jamaica	6,311	2,430	3,390	0.4	1.0	−0.6	7	5	14	10	2	11	23	12	3	12	1
Japan	4,054,545	32,030	25,170	1.4	0.3	1.1	2[3]	—	24[3]	10[3]	3[3]	7[3]	12[3]	19[3]	20[3]	8[3]	−5[3]
Jersey	2,670[1,5]	30,940[1,5]	...	...	...	...	...	...	...	...	...	...	...	...	...	...	...
Jordan	7,717	1,630	3,880	5.4	4.3	1.1	3	3	12	4	2	14	11	16	5	18	12
Kazakhstan	18,732	1,250	4,790	−6.1	−1.2	−4.9	8	2	22[2]	4	2	11	17	—37—		1
Kenya	10,696	360	1,010	2.3	2.6	−0.3	30[1]	—	10[1]	5[1]	1[1]	8[1]	19[1]	18[1]	—8[1]—		—
Kiribati	81	910	...	3.6	2.6	1.0	12[1]	—	1[1]	3[1]	2[1]	12[1]	19[1]	6[1]	3[1]	33[1]	9[1]
Korea, North	17,700[3]	740[3]	...	...	...	...	...	...	...	...	...	...	...	...	...	...	...
Korea, South	397,910	8,490	15,530	5.7	1.0	4.7	5	—	31	10	2	7	11	20	8	8	−2
Kuwait	35,152[3]	22,110[3]	...	...	...	...	—	31	12	3	—	6	10	14	—26—		−2
Kyrgyzstan	1,465	300	2,420	−5.4	1.0	−6.4	41	2	17[2]	3	2	2	12	—14—		3	8
Laos	1,476	290	1,430	6.5	2.7	3.8	52	—	17	3	2	6	12	3	1	3	1
Latvia	5,913	2,430	6,220	−4.7	−1.0	−3.7	8[1]	8	19[1,8]	4[1]	5[1]	—51[1]—		13[1]
Lebanon	15,796	3,700	...	7.0	1.3	5.7	...	...	...	...	...	...	...	...	...	...	...
Lesotho	1,158	550	2,350	4.3	2.2	2.1	12[1]	—	14[1]	18[1]	3[1]	3[1]	10[1]	8[1]	11	18[1]	13[1]
Liberia	1,174[1]	490[1]	...	...	...	...	78	2	5	2	—	5	3	3	2	2	−2
Libya	32,663[4,5]	6,700[4,5]	...	...	...	...	...	...	...	...	...	...	...	...	...	...	...
Liechtenstein	714[1,5]	23,000[1,5]	...	...	...	...	...	...	...	...	...	...	...	...	...	...	...
Lithuania	9,751	2,640	6,490	−4.0	−0.1	−3.9	9	8	17[8]	8	4	9	16	9	11	6	11
Luxembourg	18,545	42,930	41,230	5.2	1.4	3.8	1	—	17	7	1	—24—		45	—19—		−14
Macau	6,161	14,200	16,940	3.7	3.0	0.7	...	...	...	...	...	...	...	...	...	...	...
Macedonia	3,348	1,660	4,590	−0.7	0.8	−1.5	10	8	22[8]	6	3	6	13	6	—19—		15
Madagascar	3,712	250	790	1.8	3.0	−1.2	33	8	—12[8]—		—42—		5	8
Malawi	1,961	180	570	2.0	1.1	0.9	36	1	13	2	1	4	25	9	2	10	−3
Malaysia	76,944	3,390	7,640	7.4	2.7	4.7	9	8	28	4	3	8	16	13	—16—		−5
Maldives	322	1,200	...	6.3	2.4	3.9	16	2	7[13]	11	13	7	20	—29—		8
Mali	2,577	240	740	3.7	2.6	1.1	44	6	9	5	—	5	—16—		7	4	4
Malta	3,492	9,210	...	5.0	0.8	4.2	2	15	19	3[15]	7	6	10	17	9	14	13
Marshall Islands	99	1,950	...	...	...	...	15[3]	—	2[3]	7[3]	2[3]	7[3]	18[3]	15[3]	—30[3]—		43[3]
Martinique	4,271[3,5]	11,320[3,5]	...	...	...	...	...	...	...	...	...	...	...	...	...	...	...
Mauritania	1,001	390	1,550	4.3	3.0	1.3	22[3]	10[3]	10[3]	—9[3]—		8[3]	15[3]	—7[3]—		10[3]	9[3]
Mauritius	4,157	3,540	8,950	5.1	1.2	3.9	7	—	21	5	2	10	15	14	5	9	12
Mayotte	486[4]	3,700[4]	...	...	...	...	...	...	...	...	...	...	...	...	...	...	...
Mexico	428,877	4,440	8,070	2.8	1.8	1.0	5	1	21	5	1	11	20	14	—23—		−1
Micronesia	212	1,830	...	−0.2	1.6	−1.8	19[1]	—	1[1]	1[1]	1[1]	5[1]	24[1]	3[1]	3[1]	42[1]	1[1]
Moldova	1,481	410	2,100	−11.0	−0.2	−10.8	21	8	17[8]	4	2	4	7	6	—12—		27
Monaco	793[1,5]	25,000[1,5]	...	...	...	...	...	...	...	...	...	...	...	...	...	...	...
Mongolia	927	390	1,610	0.8	1.4	−0.6	33	8	24[8]	3	—	7	19	—14—		2
Morocco	33,715	1,190	3,320	2.1	1.7	0.4	15[3]	2[3]	18[3]	5[3]	9[3]	6[3]	19[3]	—13[3]—		13[3]
Mozambique	3,804	220	810	6.9	3.1	3.8	32	—	8	8	1	11	23	—	12	3	2
Myanmar (Burma)	55,700[3,5]	1,190[3,5]	...	...	...	...	53	—	6	2	—	5	30	2	—2—		2
Namibia	3,211	4,890	5,580	3.2	2.4	0.8	9[3]	12[3]	12[3]	3[3]	3[3]	4[3]	9[3]	8[3]	3[3]	23[3]	14[3]
Nauru	128[4]	11,540[4]	...	...	...	...	...	...	...	...	...	...	...	...	...	...	...
Nepal	5,173	220	1,280	4.8	2.5	2.3	38	1	9	10	2	8	11	10	—9—		2

consumption: private	consumption: government	gross domestic investment	foreign trade: exports	foreign trade: imports	external debt total ('000,000 U.S.$)	creditors official (%)	creditors private (%)	debt service total ('000,000 U.S.$)	repayment principal (%)	repayment interest (%)	net transfers goods, merchandise	net transfers invisibles	current balance of payments	receipts from foreign nationals	expenditures by nationals abroad	country
74	10	22	17	-23	25,998	97.9	2.1	1,478	56.8	43.2	-9,928	8,293	-1,635	3,727	1,347	Egypt
86	10	17	23	-36	2,649	91.8	8.2	254	54.3	45.7	-1,358.9	1,117.0	-241	75	75	El Salvador
...	...	...	102	-173	207.9	93.7	6.3	1.7	58.8	41.2	26.5[4]	-400.1[4]	-373.6[4]	2	8	Equatorial Guinea
...	...	...	...	...	253.8	100.0	—	3.9	16.7	83.3	-498.9[4]	323.5[4]	-175.4[4]	75	...	Eritrea
59	22	29	78	-88	205.5	81.8	18.2	61.2	80.5	19.5	-877.5	582.9	-294.6	465	118	Estonia
79	14	18	16	-26	5,360	97.6	2.4	147	62.6	37.4	-797.1	480.9	-316.2	36	40	Ethiopia
...	...	...	...	...	...	...	...	...	...	...	51.6[4]	102.4[4]	154.0[4]	...	...	Faroe Islands
72	18	12	67	-69	120.7	100.0	—	29.2	75.3	24.7	-115.6	128.3	12.7	297	53	Fiji
39	21	19	50	-30	...	...	...	...	...	...	11,655	-4,067	7,588	1,963	2,270	Finland
54	24	19	26	-23	...	...	...	...	...	...	19,390	17,190	36,580	28,009	16,576	France
...	...	...	...	...	...	...	...	...	...	...	...	...	...	...	...	French Guiana
...	...	...	...	...	...	...	...	...	...	...	...	...	...	359	...	French Polynesia
40[3]	11[3]	26[3]	64[3]	-42[3]	3,290	96.1	3.9	487	52.6	47.4	202.5[3]	34.6[3]	237.1[3]	7	178	Gabon
76	17	18	51	-62	425.4	100.0	—	16.6	67.2	32.8	-69.0[4]	52.7[4]	-16.3[4]	32	16	Gambia, The
...	...	...	...	...	...	...	...	...	...	...	...	...	...	...	...	Gaza Strip
...	...	...	...	...	1,308	99.8	0.2	80	48.1	51.9	-533.9	335.5	-198.4	416	228	Georgia
57	19	22	29	-27	...	...	...	...	...	...	72,000	-91,310	-19,310	16,509	46,200	Germany
77	10	25	34	-47	5,647	91.2	8.8	391	68.3	31.7	-1,111.5	345.5	-766.0	266	22	Ghana
71	15	21	18	-25	...	...	...	...	...	...	-17,947	12,845	-5,102	3,771	1,325	Greece
...	...	...	...	...	...	...	...	...	...	...	...	...	...	...	...	Greenland
61	18	44	53	-76	122.2	93.9	6.1	6.4	73.4	26.6	-133.4[4]	43.9[4]	-89.5[4]	61	5	Grenada
...	...	...	...	...	...	...	...	...	...	...	...	...	...	499	...	Guadeloupe
...	...	...	...	...	...	...	...	...	...	...	...	...	...	...	...	Guam
87	6	16	19	-27	3,129	80.0	20.0	313	58.5	41.5	1,445.1	-2,471.0	-1,025.9	325	119	Guatemala
...	...	...	...	...	...	...	...	...	...	...	...	...	...	...	...	Guernsey[12]
77	7	17	22	-23	3,057	99.1	0.9	114	61.4	38.6	94.5	-246.1	-151.6	5	23	Guinea
100	9	11	15	-35	837.1	99.9	0.1	8.6	44.2	55.8	-14.4	-12.6	-27.0	...	...	Guinea-Bissau
43[3]	20[3]	43[3]	78[3]	-84[3]	1,238	96.6	3.4	74	52.7	47.3	-25	-50	-75	39	22	Guyana
— 103 —			13	-29	1,049	100.0	—	43	65.1	34.9	-469.7	410.1	-59.6	97	37	Haiti
67	10	30	44	-51	4,231	96.7	3.3	296	59.3	40.7	-709.1	172.3	-536.8	146	62	Honduras
61	9	30	127	-127	...	...	...	...	...	...	-3,159	14,635	11,476	9,242	...	Hong Kong
62	11	29	51	-53	16,064	14.0	86.0	3,282	69.5	30.5	-2,189	83	-2,106	2,582	1,153	Hungary
62	21	22	35	-39	...	...	...	...	...	...	-308	-292	-600	173	324	Iceland
66	13	23	12	-13	82,380	71.1	28.9	8,221	62.7	37.3	-8,029	5,245	-2,784	3,152	1,342	India
53	4	35	40	-33	72,554	75.5	24.5	9,192	59.5	40.5	20,644	-14,859	5,785	5,437	2,436	Indonesia
65	13	22	8	-8	6,184	59.4	40.6	2,971	86.6	13.4	6,215	-1,488	4,727	327	253	Iran
...	...	...	...	...	...	...	...	...	...	...	...	...	...	13	...	Iraq
51	13	24	84	-72	...	...	...	...	...	...	24,178	-23,583	595	3,189	2,223	Ireland
...	...	...	...	...	...	...	...	...	...	...	...	...	...	...	...	Isle of Man
61	30	20	32	-43	...	...	...	...	...	...	-4,408	2,527	-1,881	2,741	3,570	Israel
60	18	20	24	-22	...	...	...	...	...	...	20,383	-14,079	6,304	29,714	16,631	Italy
67	18	29	43	-56	2,905	77.5	22.5	648	52.3	47.7	-1,137.7	882.0	-255.7	1,131	181	Jamaica
61	10	26	11	-9	...	...	...	...	...	...	123,320	-16,450	106,870	4,326	33,041	Japan
...	...	...	...	...	...	...	...	...	...	...	...	...	...	...	...	Jersey
70	27	25	49	-70	7,546	83.2	16.8	559	52.6	47.4	-1,460.1	1,865.0	404.9	774	398	Jordan
75	11	18	32	-37	2,995	77.0	23.0	629	71.7	28.3	343.7	-514.7	-171.0	289	445	Kazakhstan
74	16	17	25	-32	5,385	90.2	9.8	533	78.9	21.1	-829.2	840.2	11.0	377	194	Kenya
...	...	...	...	...	...	...	...	...	...	...	-31.6[1]	29.3[1]	-2.3[1]	2	4	Kiribati
...	...	...	...	...	...	...	...	...	...	...	...	...	...	...	...	Korea, North
55	11	21	48	-35	57,231	27.1	72.9	23,000	81.4	18.6	28,371	-3,894	24,477	5,116	6,262	Korea, South
56	31	14	45	-47	...	...	...	...	...	...	5,571	-509	5,062	188	2,558	Kuwait
88	18	16	36	-58	1,130.4	97.2	2.8	16.5	8.2	91.8	-84.4	-168.9	-253.3	7	4	Kyrgyzstan
...	...	...	...	...	2,471	100.0	—	29	69.0	31.0	-189.5	68.4	-121.1	73	21	Laos
64	26	23	48	-61	864.8	70.2	29.8	41.4	50.7	49.3	-1,027	380	-647	192	326	Latvia
...	...	...	...	...	5,568	16.4	83.6	653	45.6	54.4	...	...	...	1,000	...	Lebanon
116	20	46	27	-109	661.8	91.6	8.4	44.6	55.8	44.2	-606.7	385.9	-220.8	20	8	Lesotho
...	...	...	...	...	1,062	80.7	19.3	—	—	—	-118.5[4]	76.6[4]	-41.9[4]	...	...	Liberia
55[3]	27[3]	12[3]	29[3]	-23[3]	...	...	...	...	...	...	2,974	-838	2,136	6	215	Libya
...	...	...	...	...	...	...	...	...	...	...	...	...	...	...	...	Liechtenstein
63	25	24	47	-59	1,891.5	34.2	65.8	166.7	54.3	45.7	-1,404.6	210.6	-1,194.0	399	290	Lithuania
46	17	21	116	-99	...	...	...	...	...	...	-2,449	3,761	1,312	297	...	Luxembourg
40	11	18	76	-46	...	...	...	...	...	...	...	...	...	2,947	153	Macau
74	18	23	43	-58	1,135	75.4	24.6	377	85.0	15.0	-420.3	108.6	-311.7	14	27	Macedonia
89	7	12	21	-30	4,023	99.1	0.9	147	46.9	53.1	-154[4]	-147[4]	-301[4]	73	48	Madagascar
85	14	14	30	-42	2,596	99.3	0.7	44	62.5	37.5	-93.0[1]	-0.3[1]	-92.7[1]	7	17	Malawi
42	10	27	114	-93	18,929	24.2	75.8	2,278	52.3	47.7	22,648	-10,042	12,606	2,703	2,478	Malaysia
...	...	...	...	...	192.5	84.9	15.1	16.7	73.7	26.3	-262.6	192.6	-70.0	286	38	Maldives
70	14	24	24	-33	2,798	100.0	—	85	75.3	24.7	9.7[3]	-187.7[3]	-178.0[3]	26	42	Mali
62	20	23	88	-94	...	...	...	...	...	...	-571.4	449.0	-112.4	664	191	Malta
...	...	...	...	...	...	...	...	...	...	...	-35.8[3]	52.2[3]	16.4[3]	3	...	Marshall Islands
...	...	...	...	...	...	...	...	...	...	...	...	...	...	400	...	Martinique
69[3]	20[3]	17[3]	42[3]	-49[3]	2,138	99.1	0.9	88	68.2	31.8	40.0[4]	37.2[4]	77.2[4]	11	24	Mauritania
63	12	25	67	-67	1,155	45.8	54.2	161	62.4	37.6	-547.2	494.9	52.4	475	177	Mauritius
...	...	...	...	...	...	...	...	...	...	...	...	...	...	...	...	Mayotte
68	9	24	31	-33	87,531	24.9	75.1	16,015	61.4	38.6	-5,581	-8,585	-14,166	7,594	3,892	Mexico
...	...	...	...	...	...	...	...	...	...	...	-52.0[3]	115.8[3]	63.8[3]	...	...	Micronesia
71	24	30	— -25 —		722	82.5	17.5	98	55.1	44.9	-128.0	83.3	-44.7	4	...	Moldova
...	...	...	...	...	...	...	...	...	...	...	...	...	...	...	...	Monaco
65[3]	16[3]	23[3]	13	-53	816.3	97.4	2.6	20.9	57.2	42.8	-56.4	-55.8	-112.2	22	21	Mongolia
65	18	22	22	-26	17,284	75.9	24.1	2,985	64.6	35.4	-2,448	2,277	-171	1,443	315	Morocco
88	9	23	12	-32	4,625	99.7	0.3	68	47.8	52.2	-491.0[4]	61.7[4]	-429.3[4]	...	...	Mozambique
— 89 —		12	0	-1	5,333	90.1	9.9	88	72.7	27.3	-1,035.2	669.5	-365.7	34	25	Myanmar (Burma)
55[3]	31[3]	20[3]	53[3]	-58[3]	...	...	...	...	...	...	-172.6[4]	334.4[4]	161.8[4]	336	99	Namibia
...	...	...	...	...	...	...	...	...	...	...	...	...	...	...	...	Nauru
81	9	21	24	-35	2,910	99.3	0.7	99	69.7	30.3	-880.7	891.3	10.6	119	103	Nepal

National product and accounts (continued)

country	GNP 1999 nominal ('000,000 U.S.$)	GNP per capita nominal (U.S.$)	GNP per capita PPP (U.S.$)	GDP 1990–99 real GDP (%)	population (%)	real GDP per capita (%)	agriculture	mining	manufacturing	construction	public utilities	transp., communications	trade	financial svcs.	other svcs.	government	other
Netherlands, The	397,384	25,140	24,410	2.7	0.6	2.1	3	2	17	5	2	7	15	26	11	12	—
Netherlands Antilles	2,400[3,5]	11,500[3,5]	...	...	...	...	17	—	7[7]	7[7]	4[7]	13[7]	25[7]	17[7]	9[7]	18[7]	-17
New Caledonia	3,169	15,160	21,130	1.4	2.2	-0.8	2[3]	4[3]	11[3]	5[3]	2[3]	7[3]	23[3]	—20[3]—		25[3]	-1[3]
New Zealand	53,299	13,990	17,630	3.0	1.2	1.8	7	1	17	3	3	11	15	22	—22—		1
Nicaragua	2,012	410	2,060	3.3	2.9	0.4	28	2	21	5	3	5	18	7	4	8	-1
Niger	1,974	190	740	1.8	2.8	-1.0	37[3]	4[3]	7[3]	2[3]	2[3]	6[3]	17[3]	—21[3]—			4[3]
Nigeria	31,600	260	770	2.4	2.9	-0.5	37	26	5	1	—	3	16	5	1	1	5
Northern Mariana Is.	665	9,600	...	...	...	...	...	...	...	...	...	...	...	...	...	...	...
Norway	149,280	33,470	28,140	3.8	0.6	3.2	2	11	12	4	2	9	10	17	5	16	12
Oman	13,135[4]	5,950[4]	...	...	...	...	2[1]	43[1]	4[1]	2[1]	1[1]	6[1]	13[1]	8[1]	8[1]	12[1]	1[1]
Pakistan	62,915	470	1,860	3.5	2.5	1.0	24	—	15	3	4	9	15	8	7	7	8
Palau	129[4,5]	7,140[4,5]	...	...	...	...	5	—	1	8	—	16	27	12	7	22	2
Panama	8,657	3,080	5,450	4.3	1.9	2.4	8	—	10	4	4	13	21	25	6	10	-1
Papua New Guinea	3,834	810	2,260	4.9	2.6	2.3	24	26	9	6	1	5	9	1	—13—		6
Paraguay	8,374	1,560	4,380	2.5	2.7	-0.2	28	—	14	5	6	5	23	3	10	6	
Peru	53,705	2,130	4,480	5.0	1.8	3.2	6[3]	2[3]	19[3]	11[3]	1[3]	4[3]	16[3]	14[3]	13[3]	7[3]	7[3]
Philippines	77,967	1,050	3,990	3.2	2.3	0.9	17	1	22	6	3	5	14	12	11	10	-1
Poland	157,429	4,070	8,390	4.6	0.2	4.4	5	3	22	8	3	6	21	15	3	13	1
Portugal	110,175	11,030	15,860	2.4	0.1	2.3	...	...	...	...	...	...	...	...	...	...	
Puerto Rico	25,380[3]	7,010[3]	...	...	...	...	1[1]	15	41[1]	2[1,15]	16	8[1,16]	14[1]	13[1]	11[1]	11[1]	-1[1]
Qatar	6,473[4]	11,600[4]	...	...	...	...	1[3]	38[3]	7[3]	7[3]	1[3]	4[3]	8[3]	10[3]	—24[3]—		...
Réunion	5,680[3]	8,260[3]	...	...	...	...	...	...	...	...	...	...	...	...	...	...	...
Romania	33,034	1,470	5,970	-0.9	-0.4	-0.5	19[1]	2	34[1,2]	7[1]	2	9[1]	10[1]	—17[1]—			4[1]
Russia	328,995	2,250	6,990	-6.0	-0.1	-5.9	7	2	33[2]	8	2	—23—		14	9	6	-1
Rwanda	2,041	250	880	-2.7	0.3	-3.0	44	—	13	7	—	4	11	—15—		7	-1
St. Kitts	259	6,330	10,400	4.2	-0.7	4.9	6[1]	—	11[1]	12[1]	2[1]	16[1]	23[1]	16[1]	4[1]	18[1]	-8[1]
St. Lucia	590	3,820	5,200	2.4	1.5	0.9	7	—	5	6	4	15	23	15	3	13	9
St. Vincent	301	2,640	4,990	3.3	0.7	2.6	9	—	6	12	5	17	15	8	2	15	11
Samoa	181	1,070	4,070	2.0	0.6	1.4	17[3]	...	19[3]	5[3]	2[3]	11[3]	17[3]	11[3]	7[3]	9[3]	2[3]
San Marino	883[3,5]	34,330[3,5]	...	...	...	...	...	...	...	...	...	...	...	...	...	...	...
São Tomé and Príncipe	40	270	...	1.1	2.0	-0.9	23[3]	—	4[3]	15[3]	—	—19[3]—		8[3]	9[3]	22[3]	—
Saudi Arabia	139,365	6,900	11,050	2.2	3.3	-1.1	6[1]	36[1]	9[1]	9[1]	1	6[1]	7[1]	5[1]	3[1]	17[1]	2[1]
Senegal	4,685	500	1,400	3.7	3.1	0.6	18	5	13[5]	5	2	12	—21—		20	9	
Seychelles	520	6,500	...	2.9	1.6	1.3	3	—	14	9	3	15	24	10	2	13	7
Sierra Leone	653	130	440	-4.9	2.1	-7.0	39[7]	17[7]	9[7]	2[7]	—	9[7]	14[7]	2[7]	2[7]	3[7]	4[7]
Singapore	95,429	24,150	22,310	6.6	1.9	4.7	—	—	24	9	2	14	19	28	—11—		-7
Slovakia	20,318	3,770	10,430	1.8	0.2	1.6	4	1	23	5	3	8	—22—		—29—		5
Slovenia	19,862	10,000	16,050	2.4	-0.1	2.5	4[3]	13	25[3]	5[3]	3[3]	7[3]	13[3]	14[3]	12[3]	5[3]	11[3]
Solomon Islands	320	750	2,050	3.7	3.4	0.3	48[1]	—	3[1]	7[1]	2[1]	6[1]	9[1]	4[1]	—21[1]—		—
Somalia	706[1]	110[1]	...	...	...	...	...	...	...	...	...	...	...	...	...	...	...
South Africa	133,569	3,170	8,710	1.2	1.4	-0.2	4	7	19	3	3	10	13	18	—23—		
Spain	583,082	14,800	17,850	2.3	0.3	2.0	4[1]	2	24[1,2]	8[1]	2	—59[1]—					5[1]
Sri Lanka	15,578	820	3,230	5.3	1.3	4.0	19	2	15	7	1	10	19	9	—13—		5
Sudan, The	9,435	330	...	...	...	...	41	—	9	6	1	6	20	—14—			3
Suriname	684[4]	1,660[4]	...	...	...	...	12[1]	11[1]	13[1]	3[1]	9[1]	15[1]	12[1]	14[1]	—13[1]—		-2[1]
Swaziland	1,379	1,350	4,380	2.3	2.5	-0.2	12	1	27	4	2	4	7	4	1	15	23
Sweden	236,940	26,750	22,510	1.6	0.4	1.2	2[1]	—	20[1]	5[1]	3[1]	6[1]	11[1]	23[1]	4[1]	19[1]	7[1]
Switzerland	273,856	38,380	28,760	0.6	0.7	-0.1	...	...	...	...	...	...	...	...	...	...	...
Syria	15,172	970	3,450	5.5	2.8	2.7	28[1]	7[1]	4[1]	4[1]	1[1]	11[1]	26[1]	5[1]	2[1]	10[1]	...
Taiwan	297,953[4]	13,900[4]	...	...	...	...	3	—	27	4	2	7	17	23	10	10	-3
Tajikistan	1,749	280	...	...	...	...	20	2	28[2]	2	2	—18—		—22—			10
Tanzania	8,515	260	500	3.0	3.1	-0.1	43[3]	13	6[3]	4[3]	2[3]	5[3]	12[3]	12[3]	2[3]	7[3]	6[3]
Thailand	121,051	2,010	5,950	4.9	1.1	3.8	14	2	28	5	3	8	14	—26—			—
Togo	1,398	310	1,380	2.7	3.2	-0.5	42	6	9	3	2	5	17	—8—		7	—
Tonga	172	1,732	...	1.1	0.4	0.7	32	—	3	5	2	7	11	10	—18—		12
Trinidad and Tobago	6,142	4,750	7,690	2.5	0.5	2.0	2	21	8	10	—	—18—		12	17	9	3
Tunisia	19,757	2,090	5,700	4.5	1.6	2.9	12	1	18	5	5	8	—24—		14		13
Turkey	186,490	2,900	6,440	3.7	1.5	2.2	17	1	19	6	2	14	20	—13—		9	-1
Turkmenistan	3,205	670	3,340	-6.6	3.0	-9.6	25	2	30[2]	12	2	10	5	—13—			5
Tuvalu	7[1]	650[1]	...	...	...	...	22[7]	2[7]	3[7]	14[7]	2[7]	4[7]	14[7]	10[7]	—28[7]—		...
Uganda	6,794	320	1,160	7.1	3.1	4.0	41[1]	—	7[1]	7[1]	1[1]	4[1]	12[1]	7[1]	5[1]	4[1]	12[1]
Ukraine	41,991	840	3,360	-10.8	-0.5	-10.3	11	2	25[2]	5	2	13	8	—25—			13
United Arab Emirates	48,673[4]	17,870[4]	...	...	...	...	2[1]	35[1]	9[1]	9[1]	1[1]	6[1]	13[1]	13[1]	2[1]	11[1]	-1[1]
United Kingdom	1,403,843	23,500	22,220	2.5	0.4	2.1	1	2	18	5	2	7	13	23	4	15	10
United States	8,879,500	31,910	31,910	3.0	1.0	2.0	2[3]	13	17[3]	4[3]	3[3]	6[3]	17[3]	19[3]	20[3]	13[3]	—
Uruguay	20,604	6,220	8,750	3.7	0.7	3.0	11	—	20	4	4	10	14	21	—15—		1
Uzbekistan	17,613	720	2,230	-1.2	1.9	-3.1	26	2	15[2]	8	2	6	8	—21—			16
Vanuatu	227	1,180	2,880	2.3	3.1	-0.8	23	—	5	5	2	7	34	7	—17—		-1
Venezuela	87,313	3,680	5,420	1.7	2.2	-0.5	5	12	16	7	2	10	18	16	9	6	-1
Vietnam	28,733	370	1,860	8.0	1.8	6.2	26	8	—33[8]—			4	19	7	—12—		-1
Virgin Islands (U.S.)	2,666[3]	18,290[3]	...	...	...	...	...	...	...	...	...	...	...	...	...	...	...
West Bank	2,758[4,5]	1,680[4,5]	...	...	...	...	7	2	17[2]	11	2	17	14	11	19[17]	10	13
Western Sahara	605[5,18]	300[5,18]	...	...	...	...	...	...	...	...	...	...	...	...	...	...	...
Yemen	6,080	360	730	3.5	3.9	-0.4	24	17	10	4	2	7	14	6	2	14	...
Yugoslavia	13,742[4]	1,290[4]	...	...	...	...	20	8	36[8]	6	3	12	19	—5—			-1
Zambia	3,222	330	720	-0.4	2.0	-2.4	17	6	11	5	4	6	19	16	—9—		7
Zimbabwe	6,302	530	2,690	1.9	1.3	0.6	14[7]	5[7]	18[7]	2[7]	3[7]	5[7]	18[7]	9[7]	11[7]	4[7]	11[7]

consumption private	consumption government	gross domestic investment	exports	imports	external public debt total ('000,000 U.S.$)	creditors official (%)	creditors private (%)	debt service total ('000,000 U.S.$)	repayment principal (%)	repayment interest (%)	net transfers goods, merchandise	net transfers invisibles	current balance of payments	receipts from foreign nationals	expenditures by nationals abroad	country
59	14	20	55	−49	...	...	...	...	...	...	17,940	−704	17,236	6,219	10,232	Netherlands, The
67[7]	28[7]	19[7]	72[7]	−85[7]	...	...	...	...	...	...	−1,064[4]	1,008[4]	−56[4]	576	243	Netherlands Antilles
...	...	...	...	...	...	...	...	...	...	...	...	...	...	110	...	New Caledonia
65	15	19	31	−30	...	...	...	...	...	...	−435	−3,161	3,596	2,093	1,451	New Zealand
94	14	34	36	−78	5,799	93.3	6.7	137	43.1	56.9	−1,133.2	481.0	−652.2	74	65	Nicaragua
82[3]	16[3]	12[3]	19[3]	−29[3]	1,424	100.0	—	19	52.6	47.7	−17.6[5]	−134.1[5]	−151.7[5]	18	24	Niger
64	14	29	32	−38	22,423	74.3	25.7	835	67.2	32.8	4,288	−3,782	506	118	1,816	Nigeria
...	...	...	...	...	...	...	...	...	...	...	...	...	...	672	...	Northern Mariana Is.
50	22	28	37	−37	...	...	...	...	...	...	10,119	−4,105	6,014	2,226	4,496	Norway
55	24	23	37	−39	1,768	37.4	62.6	711	82.3	17.7	2,918	−3,110	−192	108	47	Oman
72	12	17	16	−17	28,514	92.5	7.5	1,597	63.1	36.9	−1,874[4]	−4	−1,874[4]	117	364	Pakistan
...	...	...	...	...	...	...	...	...	...	...	...	...	...	227	...	Palau
58	16	33	90	−97	5,678	23.6	76.4	619	45.7	54.3	−1,415.0	39.0	−1,376.0	374	164	Panama
55[7]	16[7]	18[7]	49[7]	−37[7]	1,517	95.6	4.4	160	66.9	33.1	856.0	−761.3	94.7	72	81	Papua New Guinea
86	8	23	28	−45	1,672	96.7	3.3	183	62.3	37.7	−334.4	270.8	−63.6	753	195	Paraguay
72	9	24	12	−17	20,709	79.7	20.3	1,957	41.3	58.7	−616	−1,206	−1,822	805	485	Peru
73	13	20	51	−58	33,568	63.8	36.2	5,097	68.1	31.9	4,958	2,952	7,910	2,831	1,936	Philippines
63	16	27	25	−32	33,151	75.6	24.4	2,162	39.1	60.9	−15,072	2,585	−12,487	8,679	6,900	Poland
66	20	26	28	−40	...	...	...	...	...	...	−13,766	4,137	−9,629	4,277	2,164	Portugal
...	...	...	...	...	...	...	...	...	...	...	...	...	...	2,046	869	Puerto Rico
...	...	...	...	...	...	...	...	...	...	...	...	...	...	...	...	Qatar
...	...	...	...	...	...	...	...	...	...	...	...	...	...	249	...	Réunion
76	15	18	26	−34	5,985	64.4	35.6	2,754	85.7	14.3	−1,092	−205	−1,297	526	783	Romania
58	19	15	31	−23	120,375	59.1	40.9	4,470	42.9	57.1	36,130	−11,482	24,648	6,900	10,113	Russia
94	9	16	6	−24	1,162	99.9	0.1	20	60.0	40.0	−140.6	138.1	−2.5	...	...	Rwanda
76[1]	18[1]	24[1]	44[1]	−63[1]	131.7	73.4	26.6	16.9	54.4	45.6	...	...	...	72	6	St. Kitts
69	15	19	65	−68	125.6	88.5	11.5	16.4	63.4	36.8	−201.2[4]	160.2[4]	−41.0[4]	282	29	St. Lucia
74	19	32	47	−72	159.8	63.2	36.8	12.6	49.2	50.8	−119.4[4]	75.1[4]	−44.3[4]	70	7	St. Vincent
...	...	...	...	...	156.5	100.0	—	4.8	70.8	29.2	−97.5	78.7	18.8	41	5	Samoa
66[1]	12[1]	17[1]	234[1]	−229[1]	...	...	...	...	...	...	22.6[1]	−11.9[1]	10.7[1]	...	...	San Marino
...	...	...	...	...	232.2	100.0	—	3.9	64.1	35.9	−12.1[4]	3.6[4]	−8.5[4]	2	1	São Tomé and Príncipe
41	32	21	36	−31	...	...	...	...	...	...	25,039	−24,627	412	1,420	...	Saudi Arabia
76	10	20	32	−38	3,111	99.7	0.3	179	68.2	31.8	−284.3[4]	174.6[4]	−109.7[4]	160	77	Senegal
51	27	37	65	−81	132.2	81.6	18.4	23.4	76.3	23.7	−232.4	118.4	−114.0	122	30	Seychelles
81	11	4	14	−10	938	99.4	0.6	7	57.1	42.9	−126.7[7]	0.2[7]	−126.5[7]	57	2	Sierra Leone
39	10	33	——18——		...	...	...	...	...	...	11,303	9,951	21,254	6,843	3,224	Singapore
50	22	39	64	−75	4,457	29.6	70.4	639	67.9	32.1	−1,109	−46	−1,155	546	439	Slovakia
56	21	25	57	−58	...	...	...	...	...	...	−1,245.2	462.8	−782.4	1,188	544	Slovenia
...	...	...	...	...	120.4	97.2	2.8	5.5	72.7	27.3	54.5	−33.1	21.5	7	9	Solomon Islands
...	...	...	...	...	1,859	98.2	1.8	—	...	...	...	...	...	...	...	Somalia
63	20	16	26	−25	9,148	—	100.0	3,162	78.5	21.5	4,150	−4,683	−533	2,297	1,947	South Africa
62	16	22	29	−28	...	...	...	...	...	...	−30,339	16,623	−13,716	26,651	4,467	Spain
71	10	25	36	−42	8,182	92.6	7.4	401	64.1	35.9	−707.4	214.4	−493.0	212	180	Sri Lanka
91	4	18	6	−19	8,852	84.8	15.2	12	45.8	54.2	−475.9	11.1	−464.8	4	34	Sudan, The
...	...	...	...	...	...	...	...	...	...	...	−27.2[4]	−127.7[4]	−154.9[4]	17	4	Suriname
63	25	34	76	−99	205.5	100.0	—	29.0	64.3	35.7	−110.8	128.0	17.2	40	37	Swaziland
50	27	17	44	−38	...	...	...	...	...	...	15,714	−9,732	5,982	3,572	6,579	Sweden
60	15	21	40	−36	...	...	...	...	...	...	723	28,476	29,199	7,902	6,904	Switzerland
69	11	20	30	−31	16,142	93.3	6.7	206	61.7	38.3	216	−15	201	1,035	545	Syria
61	14	22	49	−47	...	...	...	...	...	...	10,531[4]	−6,803[4]	3,728[4]	3,402	6,500	Taiwan
...	...	...	...	...	594.9	90.7	9.3	22.6	88.7	11.3	−38[3]	−36[3]	−74[3]	...	...	Tajikistan
85	8	15	19	−28	6,595	96.7	3.3	150	59.3	40.7	−876.0	69.1	−806.9	392	407	Tanzania
50	10	24	56	−40	31,011	71.3	28.7	4,255	60.0	40.0	14,013	1,585	12,428	7,048	1,888	Thailand
81	11	14	34	−40	1,263	100.0	—	26	81.4	18.6	−98.0	−29.1	−127.1	13	19	Togo
...	...	...	...	...	63.5	98.0	2.0	4.3	81.4	18.6	−67.1[4]	47.8[4]	−19.3[4]	14	3	Tonga
62	16	26	48	−54	1,485	46.3	53.7	401	74.1	25.9	−740.8[4]	97.3[4]	−643.5[4]	108	75	Trinidad and Tobago
60	16	28	42	−46	9,487	67.5	32.5	1,359	63.8	36.2	−2,141	1,698	−443	1,423	160	Tunisia
67	12	24	24	−27	50,095	25.8	74.2	8,559	64.0	36.0	−10,443	9,083	−1,360	8,088	1,716	Turkey
...	...	...	...	...	1,678	23.7	76.3	449	86.2	13.8	−523.0[4]	−411.5[4]	−934.5[4]	74	125	Turkmenistan
...	...	...	...	...	...	...	...	...	...	...	...	...	...	0.3	...	Tuvalu
83[3]	10[3]	15[3]	12[3]	−21[3]	3,564	98.0	2.0	126	65.1	34.9	−596.4	45.6	−550.8	135	137	Uganda
59	23	21	40	−43	10,027	61.5	38.5	1,277	62.4	37.6	244	1,414	1,658	270	305	Ukraine
45[1]	16[1]	26[1]	77[1]	−65[1]	...	...	...	...	...	...	8,254[3]	−1,553[3]	6,701[3]	535	...	United Arab Emirates
65	18	18	27	−28	...	...	...	...	...	...	−42,350	26,370	−15,980	20,039	27,710	United Kingdom
67	15	20	11	−13	...	...	...	...	...	...	−343,260	11,780	−331,480	73,268	51,220	United States
71	14	16	22	−22	5,108	42.1	57.9	917	61.6	38.4	−868.4	263.4	−605.0	759	264	Uruguay
...	...	...	...	...	3,421	54.8	45.2	461	65.7	34.3	171[4]	−210[4]	−39[4]	19	...	Uzbekistan
49[5]	27[5]	34[5]	47[5]	−57[5]	63.4	100.0	—	1.6	53.1	46.9	−51.5	48.4	−3.1	51	5	Vanuatu
73	8	20	20	−20	25,216	18.9	81.1	4,148	54.6	45.4	7,606	−3,917	3,689	1,086	2,381	Venezuela
71	7	29	42	−49	20,529	82.2	17.8	1,347	75.8	24.2	−981[4]	−86[4]	−1,067[4]	88	...	Vietnam
...	...	...	...	...	...	...	...	...	...	...	...	...	...	601	...	Virgin Islands (U.S.)
...	...	...	...	...	...	...	...	...	...	...	...	...	...	...	...	West Bank
...	...	...	...	...	...	...	...	...	...	...	...	...	...	...	...	Western Sahara
61[3]	16[3]	28[3]	43[3]	−48[3]	3,729	95.3	4.7	100	46.0	54.0	357.9	219.2	577.1	69	81	Yemen
...	...	...	...	...	7,416	44.4	55.6	—	—	—	...	...	...	41	...	Yugoslavia
79	16	14	29	−38	4,498	99.3	0.7	416	69.5	30.5	−148[4]	−121[4]	−269[4]	75	59	Zambia
70[3]	17[3]	20[3]	38[3]	−46[3]	3,211	88.7	11.3	480	71.6	28.4	79[4]	−423[4]	−344[4]	230	118	Zimbabwe

[1]1996. [2]Manufacturing includes mining and public utilities. [3]1997. [4]1998. [5]Gross domestic product (GDP). [6]1994. [7]1995. [8]Manufacturing includes mining. [9]Mining includes public utilities. [10]Republic of Cyprus only. [11]Services includes hotels. [12]Excludes Alderney and Sark. [13]Manufacturing includes public utilities. [14]Manufacturing includes mining, construction, and public utilities. [15]Construction includes mining. [16]Transportation, communications includes public utilities. [17]Services includes transportation, communications. [18]1991.

Employment and labour

This table provides international comparisons of the world's national labour forces—giving their size; composition by demographic component and employment status; and structure by industry.

The table focuses on the concept of "economically active population," which the International Labour Organisation (ILO) defines as persons of all ages who are either employed or looking for work. In general, the economically active population does not include students, persons occupied solely in domestic duties, retired persons, persons living entirely on their own means, and persons wholly dependent on others. Persons engaged in illegal economic activities—smugglers, prostitutes, drug dealers, bootleggers, black marketeers, and others—also fall outside the purview of the ILO definition. Countries differ markedly in their treatment, as part of the labour force, of such groups as members of the armed forces, inmates of institutions, the unemployed (both persons seeking their first job and those previously employed), seasonal and international migrant workers, and persons engaged in informal, subsistence, or part-time economic activities. Some countries include all or most of these groups among the economically active, while others may treat the same groups as inactive.

Three principal structural comparisons of the economically active total are given in the first part of the table: (1) participation rate, or the proportion of the economically active who possess some particular character-istic, is given for women and for those of working age (usually ages 15 to 64), (2) activity rate, the proportion of the total population who *are* economically active, is given for both sexes and as a total, and (3) employment status, usually (and here) grouped as employers, self-employed, employees, family workers (usually unpaid), and others.

Each of these measures indicates certain characteristics in a given national labour market; none should be interpreted in isolation, however, as the meaning of each is influenced by a variety of factors—demographic structure and change, social or religious customs, educational opportunity, sexual differentiation in employment patterns, degree of technological development, and the like. Participation and activity rates, for example, may be high in a particular country because it possesses an older population with few children, hence a higher proportion of working age, or because, despite a young population with many below working age, the economy attracts eligible immigrant workers, themselves almost exclusively of working age. At the same time, low activity and participation rates might be characteristic of a country having a young population with poor employment possibilities or of a country with a good job market distorted by the presence of large numbers of "guest" or contract workers who are not part of the domestic labour force. An illiterate woman in a strongly sex-differentiated labour force is likely to begin and end as a family or

Employment and labour

country	year	economically active population										distribution by economic sector			
		total ('000)	participation rate (%)		activity rate (%)			employment status (%)				agriculture, forestry, fishing		manufacturing; mining, quarrying; public utilities	
			female	ages 15–64	total	male	female	employers, self-employed	employees	unpaid family workers	other	number ('000)	% of econ. active	number ('000)	% of econ. active
Afghanistan	1979	3,941	7.9	49.1	30.3	54.2	4.9	52.2	33.8	14.0	—	2,369	60.1	494	12.5
Albania	1994	1,340	47.0[3]	92.0[3, 4]	57.4[3]	60.8[3]	54.0[3]	...	...	...	...	534	39.9	845[5]	6.3[5]
Algeria	1987	5,341	9.2	44.3	23.6	42.4	4.4	16.8	61.7	2.6	18.9	725	13.6	622	11.6
American Samoa	1990	14.2	41.1	52.6[8]	30.4	34.8	25.7	2.1	92.6	0.2	5.1	0.3	2.3	4.8	33.7
Andorra	1989	25	45.6	74.3	55.1	...	...	...	...	...	...	0.3	1.2	2.7	11.0
Angola	1996	4,581	37.3	65.1[10]	40.0	50.8	29.5	...	...	...	...	3,170	69.2	528	11.5[11]
Antigua and Barbuda	1991	26.8	45.6	69.7	45.1	50.9	39.6	12.1	82.8	0.7	4.4	1.0	3.9	1.9	7.3
Argentina	1995	14,345	36.7	64.5	41.5	53.5	29.9	28.0[13]	60.4[13]	5.0[13]	6.6[13]	1,201[14]	12.0[14]	2,136[14]	21.3[14]
Armenia	1996	1,584	...	75.1[16]	42.1	...	...	...	...	...	...	587	37.1	255	16.1
Aruba	1991	31.1	42.5	67.1	46.7	54.5	39.0	7.0	86.4	0.3	6.3	0.2	0.5	2.3	7.3
Australia	1998[18]	9,343	43.3	73.3[19]	49.8	56.6	43.0	12.7	78.2	0.7	8.4	442	4.7	1,311	14.0
Austria	1998[18]	3,888	43.1	70.7	48.1	56.5	40.3	9.7[20]	87.4[20]	3.0[20]	—	246	6.3	842	21.6
Azerbaijan	1998	3,744	47.8	64.4[16, 20]	47.1	50.1	44.2	...	...	...	...	1,085	29.0	367	9.8
Bahamas, The	1994	139	47.5	77.8	50.7	54.8	46.8	11.6[22]	85.1[22]	0.3[22]	3.0[22]	6.9	5.0	7.3	5.3
Bahrain	1991	226	17.5	66.8	44.6	63.5	18.5	5.1	88.5	0.1	6.3	5	2.3	33	14.6
Bangladesh	1995–96[18]	56,014	38.1	73.7	46.0	55.8	35.7	28.8	12.1	39.1	20.0	34,530	61.6	4,211	7.5
Barbados	1995[18]	137	49.5	79.9	51.8	54.6	49.1	8.8[24]	76.4[24]	0.2[24]	14.6[24]	6.3	4.6	15.6	11.4
Belarus	1999	4,542	52.4	78.2[16]	45.3	46.0	44.7	...	...	...	...	672	14.8	1,258	27.7
Belgium	1992	4,237	42.3	51.5[25]	42.2	49.8	34.9	12.7	72.4	3.4	11.5	95	2.2	788	18.6
Belize	1996	75.5	30.8	58.5[26]	34.1	47.2	21.0	26.2[20]	59.2[20]	4.9[20]	9.8[20]	18.3[13]	31.4[13]	7.0[13]	12.0[13]
Benin	1992	2,085	42.6	73.4	43.0	50.6	35.7	58.4	5.3	30.5	5.8	1,148	55.0	162	7.8
Bermuda	1995	34.1	50.0	63.5[13]	55.8	57.4	54.4	9.7[13]	84.0[13]	0.1[13]	6.2[13]	0.5	1.5	1.4	4.2
Bhutan		...	...	...	...	...	...	...	...	...	...	...	...	...	...
Bolivia	1992	2,530	38.2	64.0	39.4	48.7	30.4	41.2	31.5	7.1	20.2	984	38.9	281	11.1
Bosnia and Herzegovina	1990[5]	1,026	36.9	...	22.7	...	...	...	...	...	...	39	3.8	519	50.5
Botswana	1995	440	46.6	65.4	29.9	33.1	27.0	7.9	62.7	7.9	21.5	54	12.2	47	10.8
Brazil	1997	75,213	40.4	66.9	48.2	58.7	38.1	26.3[22]	62.3[22]	7.7[22]	3.7[22]	16,771	22.3	9,281	12.3
Brunei	1991	112	32.9	67.6	43.0	54.6	30.0	3.5	91.4	0.4	4.7	2.2	1.9	11.6	10.4
Bulgaria	1995	3,738	48.4[28]	68.8[28]	46.3[28]	48.7[28]	44.1[28]	8.4	75.9	0.9	14.8	783	20.9	1,003	26.8
Burkina Faso	1995	5,250	45.5	75.8[10]	50.9	56.0	45.9	...	...	...	...	4,397	83.8	298	5.7[11]
Burundi	1990	2,780	52.6	91.4	52.5	51.2	53.8	62.8	5.1	30.3	1.8	2,574	92.6	37	1.3
Cambodia	1993	4,010	55.8	86.2	43.1	39.5	46.4	...	...	...	...	2,454[14]	74.4[14]	220[11, 14]	6.7[11, 14]
Cameroon	1991	4,740	33.2	58.9[10]	40.0	53.9	26.3	60.2[22]	14.6[22]	18.0[22]	7.1[22]	2,856	60.3	628[11]	13.2[11]
Canada	1998[18]	15,631	45.3	75.4	51.0	56.3	45.9	15.8	75.5	0.4	8.3	586	3.7	2,601	16.6
Cape Verde	1990	121	37.1	64.3	35.3	46.9	24.9	24.7	53.7	2.0	19.6	29.9	24.8	6.8	5.7
Central African Republic	1988	1,187	46.8	78.3	48.2	52.2	44.3	75.3	8.0	8.1	8.6	881	74.2	31	2.6
Chad	1991	2,016	18.2	51.6[10]	35.3	56.5	14.7	...	...	...	...	1,489	73.9	149[11]	7.4[11]
Chile	1998[18]	5,852	33.4	59.9	39.3	52.8	26.0	26.4[19]	64.6[19]	3.2[19]	5.8[19]	809	13.8	1,015	17.3
China	1990	657,290	44.9	85.0	57.9	61.8	53.7	...	...	...	...	467,926	71.2	87,275	13.3
Colombia	1985	9,558	32.8	49.4[29]	34.3	46.6	22.3	...	...	...	...	2,412[14]	28.5[14]	1,231[14]	14.5[14]
Comoros	1996	252	38.9	59.2	37.2	44.8	29.3	47.6[14]	25.6[14]	— 26.8[14] —		189	74.7	18[11]	7.1[11]
Congo, Dem. Rep. of the	1996	14,082	35.0	47.9[10]	31.1	40.9	21.6	...	...	...	...	9,124	64.8	2,267[11]	16.1[11]
Congo, Rep. of the	1984	563	45.6	54.0	29.5	33.0	26.2	64.3	31.4	1.2	3.1	294	52.2	50	8.8
Costa Rica	1998	1,377	32.6	59.7[25]	41.2	55.8	26.7	24.0[19]	72.2[19]	3.3[19]	0.6[19]	271	19.7	231	16.8
Côte d'Ivoire	1988	4,263	32.3	66.6	39.4	52.2	26.0	...	...	...	...	2,628	61.6	100	2.3
Croatia	1991	2,040	42.9	65.2	45.3	53.9	37.4	12.7	73.7	2.0	11.6	341	16.7	571	28.0
Cuba	1988	4,570	36.1	56.9[25]	44.2	56.2	32.1	5.7[30]	94.1[30]	0.2[30]	—	79[30]	22.3[30]	668[30]	18.9[30]
Cyprus[31, 32]	1995	303	38.6	71.5	47.0	57.8	36.2	18.7[28]	73.1[28]	6.1[28]	2.1[28]	31	10.1	48	15.9
Czech Republic	1997	5,215	44.1	72.5	50.6	58.2	43.5	12.8	81.6	0.4	5.2	296	5.7	1,617	31.0
Denmark	1998	2,848	46.3	80.3	53.7	58.3	49.2	8.7	85.8	—	5.5	103	3.6	572	20.1
Djibouti	1996	396	41.4	96.3[10]	67.2	79.7	55.0	...	...	...	...	288	72.7	56[11]	14.1[11]
Dominica	1991	26.4	34.5	62.4	38.0	50.0	26.1	29.2[33]	50.6[33]	1.9[33]	18.3[33]	7.3	27.9	2.3	8.8
Dominican Republic	1981	1,915	28.9	53.6	33.9	48.1	19.7	36.5	51.3	3.3	8.9	420	22.0	243	12.7
East Timor		...	...	...	...	...	...	...	...	...	...	...	...	...	...
Ecuador	1990	3,360	26.4	55.7	34.8	51.5	18.3	45.7	42.5	4.4	7.4	1,036	30.8	404	12.0
Egypt	1995[18]	17,725	22.0	49.8	29.9	45.9	13.4	24.7[28]	50.0[28]	16.4[28]	9.0[28]	5,221	30.2	2,405	13.9
El Salvador	1997	2,256	36.7	61.4	38.2	50.2	27.0	31.7	48.5	7.4	12.4	607	26.9	373	16.5
Equatorial Guinea	1983	103	35.7	66.7	39.2	52.5	26.9	29.0	16.0	29.9	25.1	59.4	57.9	1.8	1.8
Eritrea		...	...	...	...	...	...	...	...	...	...	...	...	...	...
Estonia	1998	711	47.7	71.8[34]	48.9	54.9	43.6	4.8[19]	85.2[19]	0.8[19]	9.2[19]	61	8.6	165	23.2

traditional agricultural worker. Loss of working-age men to war, civil violence, or emigration for job opportunities may also affect the structure of a particular labour market.

The distribution of the economically active population by employment status reveals that a large percentage of economically active persons in some less developed countries falls under the heading "employers, self-employed." This occurs because the countries involved have poor, largely agrarian economies in which the average worker is a farmer who tills his own small plot of land. In countries with well-developed economies, "employees" will usually constitute the largest portion of the economically active.

Caution should be exercised when using the economically active data to make intercountry comparisons, as countries often differ in their choices of classification schemes, definitions, and coverage of groups and in their methods of collection and tabulation of data. The population base containing the economically active population, for example, may range, in developing countries, from age 9 or 10 with no upper limit to, in developed countries, age 18 or 19 upward to a usual retirement age of from 55 to 65, with sometimes a different range for each sex. Data on female labour-force participation, in particular, often lack comparability. In many less developed countries, particularly those dominated by the Islamic faith,

a cultural bias favouring traditional roles for women results in the under-counting of economically active women. In other less developed countries, particularly those in which subsistence workers are deemed economically active, the role of women may be overstated.

The second major section of the table provides data on the distribution by economic (also conventionally called industrial) sector of the economically active population. The data usually include such groups as unpaid family workers, members of the armed forces, and the unemployed, the last distributed by industry as far as possible.

The categorization of industrial sectors is based on the divisions listed in the *International Standard Industrial Classification of All Economic Activities*. The "other" category includes persons whose activities were not adequately defined and the unemployed who were not distributable by industrial sector.

A substantial part of the data presented in this table is summarized from various issues of the ILO's *Year Book of Labour Statistics*, which compiles its statistics both from official publications and from information submitted directly by national census and labour authorities. The editors have supplemented and updated ILO statistical data with information from Britannica's holdings of relevant official publications and from direct correspondence with national authorities.

construction number ('000)	construction % of econ. active	transportation, communications number ('000)	% of econ. active	trade, hotels, restaurants number ('000)	% of econ. active	finance, real estate number ('000)	% of econ. active	public administration, defense number ('000)	% of econ. active	services number ('000)	% of econ. active	other number ('000)	% of econ. active	country
51	1.3	66	1.6	138	3.5	[1]	[1]	[1]	[1]	749[1]	19.0[1]	78[2]	2.0[2]	Afghanistan
33[5]	2.5[5]	195	1.4[5]	3[5]	0.2[5]	3[5]	0.2[5]	16[5]	1.2[5]	145[5]	10.8[5]	505[6]	37.7[6]	Albania
690	12.9	216	4.1	391	7.3	143	2.7	[7]	[7]	1,180[7]	22.1[7]	1,374	25.7	Algeria
1.2	8.3	0.8	5.5	1.8	13.0	0.3	2.1	1.4	10.0	2.8	19.8	0.7[9]	5.1[9]	American Samoa
2.9	11.8	...	...	6.0	24.2	1.3	5.4	2.6	10.3	4.1	16.7	0.1	0.5	Andorra
[11]	[11]	[12]	[12]	[12]	[12]	[12]	[12]	[12]	[12]	883[12]	19.3[12]	—	—	Angola
3.1	11.6	2.4	9.0	8.5	31.9	1.5	5.4	[7]	[7]	6.4[7]	23.9[7]	1.9	7.0	Antigua and Barbuda
1,003[14]	10.0[14]	460[14]	4.6[14]	1,702[14]	17.0[14]	396[14]	3.9[14]	[7]	[7]	2,399[7,14]	23.9[7,14]	736[14,15]	7.3[14,15]	Argentina
68	4.3	24	1.5	110	6.9	[1]	[1]	[1]	[1]	350[1]	22.1[1]	190[17]	12.0[17]	Armenia
3.2	10.4	2.3	7.5	11.0	35.4	2.4	7.8	[7]	[7]	8.6[7]	27.7[7]	1.1[17]	3.5[17]	Aruba
654	7.0	567	6.1	2,279	24.4	1,310	14.0	444	4.7	1,884	20.2	454[17]	4.9[17]	Australia
341	8.8	250	6.4	844	21.7	387	9.9	256	6.6	712	18.3	12[2]	0.3[2]	Austria
150	4.0	167	4.5	772	20.6	10	0.3	[7]	[7]	618[7]	16.5[7]	574[21]	15.3[21]	Azerbaijan
11.6	8.3	11.2	8.1	44.2	31.8	12.9	9.3	10.7	7.7	29.7	21.4	4.5[23]	3.2[23]	Bahamas, The
27	11.8	14	6.1	30	13.2	17	7.6	41	18.1	43	19.0	16[17]	7.3[17]	Bahrain
1,015	1.8	2,308	4.1	6,068	10.8	213	0.4	[7]	[7]	5,092[7]	9.1[7]	2,585[17]	4.6[17]	Bangladesh
12.2	8.9	5.9	4.3	35.3	25.8	8.4	6.1	[7]	[7]	48.8[7]	35.7[7]	4.3[2]	3.1[2]	Barbados
336	7.4	332	7.3	504	11.1	[1]	[1]	[1]	[1]	1,345[1]	29.6[1]	95[9]	2.1[9]	Belarus
245	5.8	257	6.1	634	15.0	342	8.1	[7]	[7]	1,393[7]	32.9[7]	484[17]	11.4[17]	Belgium
4.1[13]	7.0[13]	2.9[13]	5.0[13]	10.0[13]	17.2[13]	1.8[13]	3.1[13]	5.4[13]	9.2[13]	6.0[13]	10.3[13]	2.8[13]	4.8[13]	Belize
52	2.5	53	2.5	433	20.7	3	0.1	[7]	[7]	165[7]	7.9[7]	71[21]	3.4[21]	Benin
1.7	5.0	2.2	6.4	10.8	31.6	5.2	15.3	[7]	[7]	12.3[7]	35.9[7]	—	—	Bermuda
...	...	...	...	...	...	...	...	...	...	...	...	...	...	Bhutan
129	5.1	117	4.6	232	9.2	54	2.1	59	2.3	350	13.8	323[15]	12.7[15]	Bolivia
75	7.3	69	6.7	131	12.8	39	3.8	[7]	[7]	155[7]	15.1[7]	—	—	Bosnia and Herzegovina
41	9.3	8	1.8	54	12.3	12	2.7	60	13.6	69	15.7	95[17]	21.6[17]	Botswana
4,583	6.1	2,759	3.7	9,223[27]	12.3[27]	1,287	1.7	[7]	[7]	25,436[7,27]	33.8[7,27]	5,882[9]	7.8[9]	Brazil
14.1	12.6	5.4	4.8	15.4	13.8	5.8	5.2	[7]	[7]	52.1[7]	46.6[7]	5.3[17]	4.7[17]	Brunei
188	5.0	251	6.7	357	9.5	51	1.4	76	2.0	532	14.2	497[17]	13.3[17]	Bulgaria
[11]	[11]	[12]	[12]	[12]	[12]	[12]	[12]	[12]	[12]	558[12]	10.6[12]	—	—	Burkina Faso
20	0.7	9	0.3	26	0.9	2.0	0.1	[7]	[7]	85[7]	3.1[7]	27[17]	1.0[17]	Burundi
[11]	[11]	[12]	[12]	[12]	[12]	[12]	[12]	[12]	[12]	625[12,14]	18.9[12,14]	—	—	Cambodia
[11]	[11]	[12]	[12]	[12]	[12]	[12]	[12]	[12]	[12]	1,256[12]	26.5[12]	—	—	Cameroon
857	5.5	1,128	7.2	3,585	22.9	2,336	14.9	820	5.2	3,252	20.8	468[2]	3.0[2]	Canada
22.7	18.8	6.1	5.1	12.7	10.6	0.8	0.7	[7]	[7]	17.4[7]	14.4[7]	24.1	20.0	Cape Verde
6	0.5	7	0.6	92	7.8	0.7	0.1	[7]	[7]	70[7]	5.9[7]	100[17]	8.5[17]	Central African Republic
[11]	[11]	[12]	[12]	[12]	[12]	[12]	[12]	[12]	[12]	377[12]	18.7[12]	—	—	Chad
533	9.1	456	7.8	1,075	18.4	437	7.5	[7]	[7]	1,478[7]	25.3[7]	47[15]	0.8[15]	Chile
11,890	1.8	11,814	1.8	25,631	3.9	8,268	1.3	[7]	[7]	34,053[7]	5.2[7]	10,434	1.6	China
242[14]	2.9[14]	353[14]	4.2[14]	1,262[14]	14.9[14]	278[14]	3.3[14]	[7]	[7]	1,998[7,14]	23.6[7,14]	691[14,15]	8.2[14,15]	Colombia
[11]	[11]	[12]	[12]	[12]	[12]	[12]	[12]	[12]	[12]	461[12]	18.2[12]	—	—	Comoros
[11]	[11]	[12]	[12]	[12]	[12]	[12]	[12]	[12]	[12]	2,691[12]	19.1[12]	—	—	Congo, Dem. Rep. of the
25	4.5	29	5.1	67	11.8	3	0.5	[7]	[7]	85[7]	15.1[7]	10	2.0	Congo, Rep. of the
89	6.5	75	5.5	267	19.4	35	2.6	[7]	[7]	385[7]	27.9[7]	23[23]	1.7[23]	Costa Rica
85	2.0	118	2.8	530	12.4	[1]	[1]	[1]	[1]	591[1]	13.9[1]	210[2]	4.9[2]	Côte d'Ivoire
93	4.5	112	5.5	223	10.9	58	2.8	104	5.1	204	10.0	329[17]	16.1[17]	Croatia
313[30]	8.8[30]	249[30]	7.0[30]	306[30]	8.6[30]	[1]	[1]	[1]	[1]	1,086[1,30]	30.7[1,30]	128[30]	3.6[30]	Cuba
26	8.7	19	6.2	77	25.4	23	7.6	[7]	[7]	65[7]	21.6[7]	13	4.4	Cyprus[31,32]
501	9.6	392	7.5	871	16.7	358	6.9	328	6.3	762	14.6	90[17]	1.7[17]	Czech Republic
185	6.5	191	6.7	467	16.4	321	11.3	175	6.1	821	28.8	18[23]	0.6[23]	Denmark
[11]	[11]	[12]	[12]	[12]	[12]	[12]	[12]	[12]	[12]	52[12]	13.2[12]	—	—	Djibouti
2.8	10.7	1.2	4.6	3.7	13.9	0.8	3.1	1.5	5.8	3.4	13.1	3.2[17]	12.3[17]	Dominica
81	4.3	40	2.1	192	10.0	22	1.2	[7]	[7]	363[7]	18.9[7]	553[15]	28.9[15]	Dominican Republic
...	...	...	...	...	...	...	...	...	...	...	...	...	...	East Timor
197	5.9	131	3.9	477	14.2	81	2.4	[7]	[7]	838[7]	24.9[7]	196[15]	5.8[15]	Ecuador
984	5.7	912	5.3	1,609	9.3	286	1.7	[7]	[7]	4,000[7]	23.2[7]	1,858[23]	10.8[23]	Egypt
159	7.1	103	4.6	462	20.5	32	1.4	[7]	[7]	485[7]	21.5[7]	36[2]	1.6[2]	El Salvador
1.9	1.9	1.8	1.7	3.1	3.0	0.4	0.4	[7]	[7]	8.4[7]	8.2[7]	25.8[17]	25.2[17]	Equatorial Guinea
...	...	...	...	...	...	...	...	...	...	...	...	...	...	Eritrea
48	6.8	60	8.4	105	14.8	44	6.2	37	5.2	122	17.2	68[9]	9.6[9]	Estonia

Employment and labour (continued)

country	year	economically active population total ('000)	participation rate (%) female	ages 15–64	activity rate (%) total	male	female	employment status (%) employers, self-employed	employees	unpaid family workers	other	distribution by economic sector agriculture, forestry, fishing number ('000)	% of econ. active	manufacturing; mining, quarrying; public utilities number ('000)	% of econ. active
Ethiopia	1995	24,606	41.1	72.2	43.3	50.3	36.5	58.5[35]	6.5[35]	34.0[35]	1.0[35]	21,605	87.8	419	1.7
Faroe Islands	1977	17.6	27.2	64.0	41.9	58.2	23.9	11.9	86.1	...	2.0	3.3	18.8	3.9	21.9
Fiji	1986	241	21.2	56.0	33.7	52.4	14.5	33.6	42.2	16.3	7.9	106	44.1	22	9.0
Finland	1998	2,532	47.0	73.1	49.1	53.4	45.1	11.9	75.2	0.6	12.3	154	6.1	508	20.1
France	1994[18]	25,871	44.9	67.7	44.8	50.6	39.2	10.2	77.4	—	12.4	1,048	4.1	4,432	17.4
French Guiana	1990	48.8	38.2	67.3	42.5	50.5	33.9	10.6	62.7	2.5	24.2	4.2	8.6	3.1	6.4
French Polynesia	1988	75	37.1	64.8	39.9	48.2	30.9	13.0	55.0	4.0	28.0	7.6	10.0	5.4	7.2
Gabon	1991	504	36.9	56.0[10]	43.9	53.9	30.7	...	...	...	...	338	67.1	71[11]	14.1[11]
Gambia, The	1983	326	46.3	78.2	47.3	51.1	43.6	0.5	78.0	14.3	7.1	240	73.7	9	2.9
Gaza Strip	1996	173	9.0	36.3[25]	18.0	32.0	3.2	15.7	46.8	6.7	30.8	9.0	5.2	17.0[36]	9.8[36]
Georgia	1993	1,920	...	58.1[16, 28]	35.7	...	...	...	...	...	...	562	29.3	303	15.8
Germany	1998	39,709	43.1	70.7	48.4	56.5	40.7	9.1	80.3	1.0	9.6	1,200	3.0	10,019	25.2
Ghana	1984	5,580	51.2	82.5[25]	45.4	44.9	45.8	67.7	15.7	12.2	4.4	3,311	59.3	631	11.3
Greece	1997[18]	4,294	39.2	61.3	40.9	53.0	31.5	29.9	49.2	10.7	10.2	773	18.0	680	15.8
Greenland	1976	21.4	33.4	63.5[25]	43.1	53.0	31.4	12.6	82.5	0.4	4.5	3.2	15.1	3.3	15.3
Grenada	1988	38.9	48.6	72.7[35]	39.9	42.9	37.2	16.0[30]	64.2[30]	0.8[30]	19.0[30]	5.6	14.3	3.3	8.6
Guadeloupe	1990	172	45.5	66.4	44.5	49.6	39.7	13.2	53.7	2.0	31.1	8.4	4.9	9.6	5.6
Guam	1990	66.1	37.4	75.7[8]	49.7	58.4	39.7	2.4	94.4	0.1	3.1	0.5	0.8	3.5	5.3
Guatemala	1999	3,489	22.0	55.0	31.5	48.6	14.0	32.7[33]	47.6[33]	16.2[33]	3.5[33]	1,416[33]	48.9[33]	405[33]	14.0[33]
Guernsey[38]	1996	30.7	44.7	76.4	52.3	60.1	45.1	13.0	87.0	—	—	1.9	6.2	2.5	8.2
Guinea	1983	1,823	39.4	63.5	39.1	48.7	30.1	36.2	15.6	37.6	10.6	1,424	78.1	27	1.5
Guinea-Bissau	1995	491	39.9	65.5[10]	45.8	55.9	36.0	...	...	...	...	373	76.0	20[11]	4.1[11]
Guyana	1992–93	278	34.1	61.8	38.8	51.9	26.0	14.3[14]	63.8[14]	1.9[14]	20.0[14]	50[14]	20.4[14]	41[14]	16.8[14]
Haiti	1990	2,679	40.0	64.8	41.1	50.3	32.3	59.1	16.5	10.4	14.0	1,535	57.3	178	6.6
Honduras	1998[18]	2,135	36.9	61.2[25]	36.9	49.2	25.0	40.6	48.0	11.4	—	738	34.6	380	17.8
Hong Kong	1998[18]	3,359	39.3	70.0	51.1	61.9	40.3	9.9[19]	87.4[19]	0.7[19]	1.9[19]	10	0.3	434	12.9
Hungary	1998[18]	4,011	44.4	58.4	39.3	45.8	33.4	10.6	80.3	0.7	8.4	301	7.5	1,115	27.8
Iceland	1998	152.1	47.1	86.6[8]	55.4	59.2	52.2	17.3	80.3	0.3	2.1	12.8	8.4	27.1	17.8
India	1991	314,131	28.6	60.7[25, 30]	37.5	51.6	22.3	8.8[30]	16.3[30]	3.6[30]	71.3[30]	191,341	60.9	30,423	9.7
Indonesia	1998	92,735	38.8	65.3[25]	45.4	55.8	35.0	42.7[34]	33.0[34]	17.1[34]	7.2[34]	39,415	42.5	10,756	11.6
Iran	1996–97	16,027	12.7	46.8[13]	26.7	45.8	6.9	39.7[13]	45.4[13]	2.3[13]	12.6[13]	3,205[13]	21.8[13]	2,243[13]	15.2[13]
Iraq	1988	4,127	12.0	45.3	24.7	42.3	6.1	25.4[39]	59.5[39]	11.4[39]	3.7[39]	477	11.6	439	10.6
Ireland	1997	1,539	39.1	62.7	42.0	51.6	32.6	17.4	71.1	1.1	10.4	145	9.4	314	20.4
Isle of Man	1991	33.2	42.3	73.2	47.6	56.9	38.9	15.8	80.1	—	4.1	1.2	3.7	3.9	11.6
Israel	1998[18]	2,272	44.3	53.5[25]	40.3	45.2	35.5	13.2	77.7	0.5	8.6	50	2.3	434	19.1
Italy	1994[18]	22,680	36.9	57.4	40.1	52.1	28.8	21.4	62.8	4.0	11.8	1,573	6.9	4,837	21.3
Jamaica	1998	1,129	45.6	69.3[40]	43.9	48.7	39.2	32.3	49.9	1.9	15.9	218[19]	20.0[19]	107[19]	9.8[19]
Japan	1998	67,930	40.7	72.6	53.7	65.1	42.9	11.2	79.0	5.4	4.4	3,440	5.1	14,620	21.5
Jersey	1991	47.5	43.2	66.9[25]	56.5	66.1	47.5	12.6	84.0	...	3.4	2.2	4.7	3.8	8.0
Jordan	1993	859	11.4[42]	43.2[42]	22.2	...	...	22.8[43]	67.2[43]	0.8[43]	9.2[43]	55	6.4	97	11.3
Kazakhstan	1995	6,976	...	71.8[16, 20]	40.8	...	...	...	...	...	...	1,442	20.7	1,372	19.7
Kenya	1996	12,269	38.5	63.6[10]	43.9	53.9	33.8	...	...	...	...	9,100	74.2	1,062[11]	8.7[11]
Kiribati	1990	32.6	46.4	75.6[25]	45.1	48.9	41.4	71.9	25.3	...	2.8	23.1	71.0	0.9	2.8
Korea, North	1985	9,084	46.0	75.3	44.6	48.6	40.6	...	...	...	...	3,726[24]	44.1[24]	2,790[11, 24]	33.0[11, 24]
Korea, South	1998[18]	21,390	39.8	60.7[25]	45.9	54.9	36.8	26.8	57.0	9.3	6.8	2,450	11.5	4,246	19.9
Kuwait	1997	1,217	23.5	61.5[42]	55.1	69.0	33.2	3.9[42]	94.1[42]	0.1[42]	1.9[42]	9[42]	1.3[42]	69[42]	9.4[42]
Kyrgyzstan	1998	1,705	46.1	...	37.2	41.1	33.5	...	...	...	...	831	48.7	104	6.1
Laos	1995	2,166	56.4	83.3	47.3	46.2	52.8	...	...	...	...	1,393[14]	75.7[14]	130[11, 14]	7.1[11, 14]
Latvia	1997	1,186	48.1	70.2	48.0	54.0	42.9	11.1	69.3	5.0	14.6	203	17.1	233	19.6
Lebanon	1997	1,362	21.6	49.3	34.0	55.2	14.2	...	...	...	...	132[44]	19.1[44]	131[44]	18.9[44]
Lesotho	1986	504	27.0	44.0	31.6	47.3	16.7	16.8	55.7	20.5	7.0	131	25.9	142	28.2
Liberia	1984	704	41.0	56.3	33.5	39.1	27.8	59.1	21.6	14.4	5.0	481	68.3	31	4.4
Libya	1991	1,169	9.3	37.1[10]	24.8	42.9	4.9	...	...	...	...	129	11.0	372[11]	31.8[11]
Liechtenstein	1996	16.2	40.3	71.3	52.0	63.7	40.8	6.4	90.8	0.1	2.7	0.3	2.0	4.9	30.2
Lithuania	1998	1,835	47.9	71.7[26]	49.5	54.8	44.9	14.1	69.1	0.2	16.6	317	17.2	411	22.4
Luxembourg	1991[45]	168	36.5	62.5	43.5	56.4	31.2	9.2	85.3	1.1	4.4	5	3.2	26	15.8
Macau	1998[18]	210.7	35.3	70.7[40]	50.2	58.2	43.0	8.0	85.9	1.6	4.5	0.4	0.2	44.5	21.1
Macedonia	1996	789	39.1	60.6	39.6	48.1	31.1	...	...	...	...	103	13.0	165	20.9
Madagascar	1996	5,984	38.2	58.7	39.2	48.9	29.8	...	...	...	...	4,381	73.2	926[11]	15.5[11]
Malawi	1987	3,458	51.0	89.4	43.3	43.9	42.8	4.9	16.2	77.6	1.3	2,968	85.8	114	3.3
Malaysia	1998[18]	8,884	33.5	64.4	40.1	52.0	27.5	21.1[20]	71.4[20]	7.5[20]	—	1,617	18.2	1,986	22.4
Maldives	1990	56.4	19.9	50.2	26.5	41.3	10.8	39.7	49.3	4.5	6.5	14.1	25.0	9.4	16.6
Mali	1987	3,438	37.4	67.4	44.7	57.2	32.7	35.4	5.2	57.6	1.8	2,803	81.5	191	5.6
Malta	1990	132	25.4	47.4[13]	37.2	56.1	18.7	14.1[48]	77.4[48]	...	8.5[48]	3	2.5	38	28.8
Marshall Islands	1988	11.5	30.1	54.1[28]	26.5	37.7	14.8	21.6	58.9	7.1	12.5	2.2	18.7	1.0	9.0
Martinique	1990	165	47.5	68.1	45.9	49.8	42.2	9.5	56.9	1.5	32.1	8.4	5.1	9.7	5.9
Mauritania	1995	704	23.0	44.3[10]	31.0	48.1	14.1	...	...	...	...	437	62.1	84[11]	11.9[11]
Mauritius[49]	1995	484	32.9	63.5	42.9	58.1	28.0	15.1	72.9	2.1	9.9	65	13.5	142	29.4
Mayotte	1991	27.3	29.4	56.4	28.9	39.2	17.7	12.0	42.9	7.3	37.8	3.1	11.4	1.3	4.7
Mexico	1998	39,507	33.7	65.4	41.3	56.1	27.2	30.1[20]	53.8[20]	13.6[20]	2.6[20]	7,842	19.8	7,473	18.9
Micronesia	1990	30.5	29.8[14]	60.6	30.3	...	...	2.7[14]	74.4[14]	0.1[14]	22.7[14]	12.7	41.5	1.6	5.2
Moldova	1996	1,686	...	68.7[16, 19]	39.1	...	...	...	...	...	...	711	42.2	195	11.6
Monaco	1990	12.6	39.7	...	42.0	53.2	31.8	17.4	75.1	0.3	7.2	—	0.3	2.7	21.8
Mongolia	1998	841	48.0	64.3[51]	36.7	38.8	34.6	...	...	...	...	300[20]	35.5[20]	124[20]	14.7[20]
Morocco	1982	5,999	19.7	48.9	29.3	47.1	11.6	27.1	40.5	17.6	14.8	2,352	39.2	1,016	16.9
Mozambique	1996	9,318	46.3	83.2[10]	56.3	61.1	51.5	...	...	...	...	7,360	79.0	987[11]	10.6[11]
Myanmar (Burma)	1997–98[18]	18,337	35.3[48]	64.2[48]	40.2[48]	52.4[48]	28.2[48]	41.4[48]	27.4[48]	30.2[48]	1.0[48]	12,093	65.9	1,831	9.9
Namibia	1991	494	43.6	61.3	35.2	39.9	30.5	17.8	49.1	17.9	15.2	190	38.5	41	8.2
Nauru	1977	2.2	...	...	30.5	...	...	...	...	...	...	...	...	...	...
Nepal	1991	7,340	40.4	57.0[10]	40.0	47.8	32.2	75.8	21.4	2.3	0.4	5,962	81.2	164	2.2
Netherlands, The	1998	7,735	42.5	72.9	49.3	57.2	41.5	10.0	84.8	0.8	4.4	236	3.1	1,162	15.0
Netherlands Antilles	1992	87.8	45.1	68.6	46.3	53.1	40.1	...	...	...	...	0.5	0.6	8.4	9.6
New Caledonia	1989	66	37.5	70.7[53]	40.2	49.1	30.8	16.3	64.3	1.6	17.8	7.8	11.8	6.2	9.3
New Zealand	1998[18]	1,864	45.0	74.0	49.2	54.9	43.6	18.1[20]	73.6[20]	0.8[20]	7.5[20]	161	8.6	326	17.5
Nicaragua	1998	1,630	29.5	61.2	34.1	48.9	19.8	...	...	...	...	457[28]	31.4[28]	183[28]	12.5[28]

construction number ('000)	construction % of econ. active	transportation, communications number ('000)	transportation, communications % of econ. active	trade, hotels, restaurants number ('000)	trade, hotels, restaurants % of econ. active	finance, real estate number ('000)	finance, real estate % of econ. active	public administration, defense number ('000)	public administration, defense % of econ. active	services number ('000)	services % of econ. active	other number ('000)	other % of econ. active	country
61	0.2	103	0.4	936	3.8	19	0.1	[7]	[7]	1,252[7]	5.1[7]	210[2]	0.9[2]	Ethiopia
2.0	11.1	1.9	11.1	2.1	11.9	0.3	1.9	[7]	[7]	3.5[7]	20.1[7]	0.6	3.2	Faroe Islands
12	4.9	13	5.5	26	10.8	6	2.5	[7]	[7]	377	15.2[7]	20[17]	8.2[17]	Fiji
163	6.4	178	7.0	366	14.5	269	10.6	148	5.8	653	25.8	95[23]	3.8[23]	Finland
1,443	5.7	1,397	5.5	3,716	14.6	2,340	9.2	[7]	[7]	7,733[7]	30.3[7]	3,376[17]	13.2[17]	France
4.4	9.1	1.9	3.8	4.2	8.5	1.7	3.5	[7]	[7]	17.5[7]	35.9[7]	11.8[9]	24.2[9]	French Guiana
5.5	7.4	2.8	3.7	10.3	13.7	1.2	1.5	[7]	[7]	21.5[7]	28.6[7]	21.1[17]	28.0[17]	French Polynesia
[11]	[11]	[12]	[12]	[12]	[12]	[12]	[12]	[12]	[12]	95[12]	18.8[12]	—	—	Gabon
4	1.3	8	2.5	17	5.1	5	1.4	8	2.5	9	2.9	25	7.7	Gambia, The
17.8	10.3	5.7	3.3	20.8	12.0	[1]	[1]	[1]	[1]	49.3[1, 36]	28.5[1, 36]	53.3[9]	30.8[9]	Gaza Strip
125	6.5	107	5.6	117	6.1	20	1.0	49	2.6	479	24.9	158[17]	8.2[17]	Georgia
3,760	9.5	2,090	5.3	6,924	17.4	4,098	10.3	3,174	8.0	8,182	20.6	262[2]	0.7[2]	Germany
65	1.2	123	2.2	792	14.2	27	0.5	98	1.7	376	6.7	158[9]	2.8[9]	Ghana
262	6.1	264	6.1	933	21.7	268	6.2	285	6.6	593	13.8	235[23]	5.5[23]	Greece
3.1	14.6	1.8	8.6	2.7	12.6	0.3	1.6	[7]	[7]	6.3[7]	29.5[7]	0.6	2.8	Greenland
3.5	9.1	1.7	4.4	5.4	13.9	0.8	2.0	[7]	[7]	5.9[7]	15.3[7]	12.7[17]	32.5[17]	Grenada
14.0	8.1	7.0	4.0	15.0	8.7	2.8	1.6	[7]	[7]	60.8[7]	35.2[7]	54.9[17]	31.8[17]	Guadeloupe
8.0	12.1	4.5	6.8	11.5	17.5	3.9	6.0	17.7	26.7	14.5	21.9	2.0[9]	3.1[9]	Guam
114[33]	3.9[33]	72[33]	2.5[33]	375[33]	12.9[33]	38[33]	1.3[33]	[7]	[7]	417[7]	14.4[7]	60[17]	2.1[17]	Guatemala
2.7	8.7	1.3	4.1	7.0	22.9	8.2	26.6	1.9	6.2	5.0	16.2	0.2	0.8	Guernsey[38]
9	0.5	29	1.6	37	2.0	4	0.2	[7]	[7]	138[7]	7.5[7]	156	8.5	Guinea
[11]	[11]	[12]	[12]	[12]	[12]	[12]	[12]	[12]	[12]	98[12]	20.0[12]	—	—	Guinea-Bissau
7[14]	2.8[14]	9[14]	3.8[14]	15[14]	6.2[14]	3[14]	1.2[14]	30[14]	12.1[14]	29[14]	11.9[14]	61[14, 17]	24.7[14, 17]	Guyana
28	1.0	21	0.8	353	13.2	5	0.2	[7]	[7]	155[7]	5.8[7]	404[17]	15.1[17]	Haiti
111	5.2	55	2.6	440	20.6	52	2.5	[7]	[7]	359[7]	16.8[7]	—	—	Honduras
349	10.4	377	11.2	1,024	30.5	431	12.8	[7]	[7]	718[7]	21.4[7]	16[2]	0.5[2]	Hong Kong
257	6.4	315	7.9	640	16.0	258	6.4	313	7.8	747	18.6	67[23]	1.7[23]	Hungary
11.0	7.2	11.0	7.2	25.7	16.9	14.4	9.5	7.1	4.7	41.4	27.2	1.3[2]	1.1[2]	Iceland
5,543	1.8	8,108	2.6	21,296	6.8	[1]	[1]	[1]	[1]	29,312[1]	9.3[1]	28,199	9.0	India
3,522	3.8	4,154	4.5	16,814	18.1	618	0.7	[7]	[7]	12,394[7]	13.4[7]	5,063[9]	5.5[9]	Indonesia
1,372[13]	9.3[13]	762[13]	5.2[13]	1,238[13]	8.4[13]	195[13]	1.3[13]	[7]	[7]	3,518[7, 13]	23.9[7, 13]	2,203[13, 17]	14.9[13, 17]	Iran
461	11.2	266	6.4	282	6.8	42	1.0	[7]	[7]	2,160[7]	52.3[7]	—	—	Iraq
128	8.3	69	4.5	295	19.2	140	9.1	75	4.8	312	20.3	61[17]	4.0[17]	Ireland
3.4	10.3	2.4	7.3	6.1	18.4	4.4	13.1	[7]	[7]	10.4[7]	31.4[7]	1.4[9]	4.1[9]	Isle of Man
144	6.3	130	5.7	377	16.6	304	13.4	115	5.1	606	26.7	111[17]	4.9[17]	Israel
1,641	7.2	1,080	4.8	4,221	18.6	1,514	6.7	[7]	[7]	5,134[7]	22.6[7]	2,676[9]	11.8[9]	Italy
66[19]	6.1[19]	40[19]	3.7[19]	196[19]	17.9[19]	47[19]	4.3[19]	[7]	[7]	237[7, 19]	21.7[7, 19]	180[17, 19]	16.5[17, 19]	Jamaica
6,670	10.0	4,170	6.1	15,150[41]	22.3[41]	5,930	8.7	[7]	[7]	16,010[7, 41]	23.6[7, 41]	1,810[17]	2.7[17]	Japan
4.4	9.3	2.4	5.0	6.8	14.4	7.4	15.6	3.1	6.5	15.7	33.1	1.6[17]	3.4[17]	Jersey
60	7.0	58	6.7	130	15.1	25	2.9	[7]	[7]	435[7]	50.6[7]	—	—	Jordan
364	5.2	507	7.3	1,035	14.8	334	4.8	[7]	[7]	1,664[7]	23.9[7]	258[17]	3.7[17]	Kazakhstan
[11]	[11]	[12]	[12]	[12]	[12]	[12]	[12]	[12]	[12]	2,107[12]	17.2[12]	—	—	Kenya
0.3	1.0	0.9	2.8	1.3	4.1	0.4	1.4	2.1	6.5	2.3	7.0	1.1[17]	3.4[17]	Kiribati
[11]	[11]	[12]	[12]	[12]	[12]	[12]	[12]	[12]	[12]	1,939[12, 24]	22.9[12, 24]	—	—	Korea, North
1,876	8.8	1,218	5.7	5,911	27.6	1,962	9.2	752	3.5	2,713	12.7	270[15]	1.3[15]	Korea, South
115[42]	15.7[42]	38[42]	5.2[42]	83[42]	11.4[42]	22[42]	3.0[42]	[7]	[7]	384[7, 42]	52.6[7, 42]	11[2, 42]	1.5[2, 42]	Kuwait
51	3.0	75	4.4	178	10.4	15	0.9	61	3.6	258	15.2	132	7.7	Kyrgyzstan
[11]	[11]	[12]	[12]	[12]	[12]	[12]	[12]	[12]	[12]	3,161[12, 14]	17.2[12, 14]	—	—	Laos
69	5.8	96	8.1	198	16.7	57	4.8	67	5.6	209	17.6	55	4.6	Latvia
43[44]	6.2[44]	48[44]	7.0[44]	115[44]	16.5[44]	24[44]	3.5[44]	[7]	[7]	200[7, 44]	28.8[7, 44]	—	—	Lebanon
28	5.5	8	1.6	24	4.7	2	0.5	[7]	[7]	157[7]	31.1[7]	13	2.6	Lesotho
4	0.6	14	2.0	47	6.7	[1]	[1]	[1]	[1]	63[1]	9.0[1]	64[17]	9.1[17]	Liberia
[11]	[11]	[12]	[12]	[12]	[12]	[12]	[12]	[12]	[12]	668[12]	57.1[12]	—	—	Libya
1.1	7.0	0.5	3.2	2.4	14.8	1.3	7.8	1.0	6.4	4.1	25.4	0.6[17]	3.4[17]	Liechtenstein
128	7.0	119	6.5	302	16.4	70	3.8	82	4.4	347	18.9	61[2]	3.3[2]	Lithuania
14	8.4	11	6.3	29	17.5	15	9.2	21	12.8	31	18.7	14[21]	8.1[21]	Luxembourg
23.0	10.9	14.3	6.8	60.0	28.5	14.4	6.8	16.5	7.8	36.6	17.4	1.0	0.5	Macau
36	4.5	27	3.4	77	9.8	15	1.9	28	3.5	88	11.1	251[46]	31.9[46]	Macedonia
[11]	[11]	[12]	[12]	[12]	[12]	[12]	[12]	[12]	[12]	677[12]	11.3[12]	—	—	Madagascar
46	1.4	25	0.7	94	2.7	6	0.2	[7]	[7]	147[7]	4.3[7]	57	1.7	Malawi
746	8.4	422	4.7	1,616	18.2	426	4.8	[7]	[7]	1,788[7]	20.1[7]	284	3.2	Malaysia
3.2	5.6	5.3	9.4	8.9	15.7	1.1	1.9	[7]	[7]	11.8[7]	21.0[7]	2.7[47]	4.7[47]	Maldives
13	0.4	6	0.2	159	4.6	0.3	—	75	2.2	84	2.4	107	3.1	Mali
6	4.4	9	6.9	13	9.8	5	3.7	[7]	[7]	53[7]	40.0[7]	5[9]	3.8[9]	Malta
1.1	9.4	0.5	4.7	1.4	12.1	0.8	7.3	[7]	[7]	3.1[7]	26.4[7]	1.4[17]	12.5[17]	Marshall Islands
9.3	5.6	6.7	4.0	14.0	8.5	3.0	1.8	[7]	[7]	59.1[7]	35.8[7]	54.8[17]	33.2[17]	Martinique
[11]	[11]	[12]	[12]	[12]	[12]	[12]	[12]	[12]	[12]	183[12]	26.0[12]	—	—	Mauritania
46	9.6	29	5.9	76	15.6	14	2.8	27	5.5	62	12.8	23[2]	4.8[2]	Mauritius[49]
3.1	11.4	1.5	5.4	2.0	7.2	0.1	0.4	[7]	[7]	5.7[7]	21.0[7]	10.5[17]	38.4[17]	Mayotte
2,189	5.5	1,730	4.4	8,777	22.2	1,518	3.8	1,630	4.1	8,051	20.4	298[17]	0.8[17]	Mexico
1.8	6.1	[50]	[50]	[50]	[50]	[50]	[50]	6.3	20.8	3.7[50]	12.1[50]	4.1[9]	13.5[9]	Micronesia
55	3.3	66	3.9	271	16.1	47	2.8	30	1.8	285	16.9	26	1.5	Moldova
0.7	5.3	...	...	2.5	20.2	1.0	8.0	2.8	22.4	1.9	14.9	0.9[21]	7.1[21]	Monaco
33	3.9	38	4.4	62	7.3	[1]	[1]	[1]	[1]	123[1, 20]	14.5[1, 20]	166[20, 21]	19.7[20, 21]	Mongolia
437	7.3	141	2.3	498	8.3	[52]	[52]	533	8.9	474[52]	7.9[52]	548[2]	9.1[2]	Morocco
[11]	[11]	[12]	[12]	[12]	[12]	[12]	[12]	[12]	[12]	971[12]	10.4[12]	—	—	Mozambique
400	2.2	495	2.7	1,781	9.7	...	...	[7]	[7]	1,485[7]	8.1[7]	270	1.5	Myanmar (Burma)
19	3.8	9	1.9	38	7.7	9	1.7	[7]	[7]	67[7]	1.2[7]	183[17]	37.1[17]	Namibia
...	...	...	...	...	...	...	...	...	...	...	...	...	...	Nauru
36	0.5	51	0.7	256	3.5	20	0.3	[7]	[7]	752[7]	10.3[7]	98	1.3	Nepal
451	5.8	442	5.7	1,487	19.2	1,097	14.2	525	6.8	1,833	23.7	498[17]	6.4[17]	Netherlands, The
6.5	7.4	5.0	5.7	20.9	23.8	8.2	9.3	[7]	[7]	24.8[7]	28.2[7]	13.4[9]	15.3[9]	Netherlands Antilles
4.5	6.8	3.1	4.7	9.5	14.3	2.5	3.8	[7]	[7]	22.0[7]	33.4[7]	13.5[9]	16.0[9]	New Caledonia
120	6.5	109	5.8	398	21.3	224	12.0	[7]	[7]	493[7]	26.4[7]	33[17]	1.8[17]	New Zealand
32[28]	2.2[28]	32[28]	2.2[28]	201[28]	13.8[28]	16[28]	1.1[28]	79[28]	5.4[28]	195[28]	13.4[28]	265[9, 28]	18.2[9, 28]	Nicaragua

Employment and labour (continued)

country	year	economically active population										distribution by economic sector			
		total ('000)	participation rate (%)		activity rate (%)			employment status (%)				agriculture, forestry, fishing		manufacturing; mining, quarrying; public utilities	
			female	ages 15–64	total	male	female	employers, self-employed	employees	unpaid family workers	other	number ('000)	% of econ. active	number ('000)	% of econ. active
Niger	1988[54]	2,316	20.4	55.2	31.9	51.1	13.0	51.4	5.0	40.3	3.3	1,764	76.2	73	3.1
Nigeria	1986[18]	30,766	33.3	58.8	31.1	41.1	20.9	64.6	18.8	10.7	5.9	13,259	43.1	1,401	4.6
Northern Mariana Islands	1990	26.6	43.2	83.6[8]	61.3	66.2	55.9	1.4	96.1	0.2	2.3	0.6	2.3	6.0	22.5
Norway	1998	2,317	46.2	80.8	52.3	56.9	47.8	7.4	88.7	0.6	3.2	104	4.5	375	16.2
Oman	1993	705	9.7	60.9	34.9	54.0	8.1	5.2	91.0	0.1	3.7	64	9.1	79	11.3
Pakistan	1996–97[18]	36,407	15.2	51.0	28.7	47.0	9.0	40.6[55]	34.2[55]	19.1[55]	6.1[55]	15,148	41.6	4,222	11.6
Palau	1990	6.1	36.9	64.1[8]	40.2	47.1	32.1	2.5	89.5	0.2	7.8	0.4	7.1	0.2	3.0
Panama	1998	1,049	35.5	66.4	38.4	49.0	27.6	23.9	59.5	2.7	13.9	180	17.2	118	11.3
Papua New Guinea	1980[56]	733	39.8	35.2[10]	24.6	28.3	20.5	72.7	26.4	—	0.9	564	77.0	21	2.9
Paraguay	1982	1,039	19.7	57.5	34.3	54.8	13.6	43.1	37.7	9.2	9.9	446	42.9	129	12.4
Peru	1995	8,906	34.7	60.9	37.8	49.8	26.1	39.8[30]	41.8[30]	8.4[30]	10.0[30]	2,693[20]	32.5[20]	1,091[20]	13.2[20]
Philippines	1998[18]	31,278	37.6	67.9	41.1	51.4	30.8	36.2[19]	41.7[19]	13.7[19]	8.4[19]	11,272	36.0	2,931	9.4
Poland	1998[18]	16,197	45.7	66.1	44.4	49.5	39.5	21.3	69.0	4.5	5.2	3,045	17.7	4,272	24.9
Portugal	1998[18]	5,000	45.0	70.3	50.2	57.3	43.6	24.2	68.0	0.8	7.0	651	13.0	1,243	24.9
Puerto Rico	1998[18]	1,320	42.2	54.5	34.2	41.0	27.9	13.6[34]	85.2[34]	0.7[34]	0.6[34]	35	2.7	203	15.4
Qatar	1988	293	11.2	80.8	53.7	77.3	22.2	1.8[44]	97.7[44]	—	0.5[44]	4.5	1.6	22.0	7.5
Réunion	1990[18]	234	41.1	60.3	39.1	46.8	31.6	8.4	53.1	1.1	37.4	11	4.8	11	4.8
Romania	1998	11,577	45.6	69.0	51.4	57.1	45.9	21.1	55.9	16.7	6.3	4,411	38.1	2,950	25.5
Russia	1996	68,264	46.6	71.9[51]	46.2	52.7	40.5	...	...	...	...	10,079	14.8	15,950	23.4
Rwanda	1996	3,719	47.5	67.5[10]	45.6	48.4	42.8	...	...	...	...	3,375	90.7	133[11]	3.6[11]
St. Kitts and Nevis	1980	17.1	41.0	69.5	39.5	48.4	31.2	9.7	78.5	0.4	11.4	4.5	26.1	3.8	22.3
St. Lucia	1991	53.1	40.3	67.6	39.9	49.1	31.2	21.0[14]	55.8[14]	1.6[14]	21.6[14]	11.6	21.8	7.5	14.0
St. Vincent	1991	41.7	35.9	67.5	39.1	50.3	28.0	18.2	59.6	2.1	20.1	8.4	20.1	3.5	8.4
Samoa	1986	45.6	18.8	48.6[30]	29.0	44.5	11.6	21.1[30]	43.5[30]	35.0[30]	0.4[30]	29.0	63.6	2.4	5.4
San Marino	1998	18.5	39.6	77.9	58.4	66.6	49.2	13.9	79.3	0.2	6.6	0.2	1.4	5.8	31.2
São Tomé and Príncipe	1991	35	33.6	59.1	30.1	40.5	20.0	25.8	68.6	0.7	4.9	13.6	38.4	1.8	5.0
Saudi Arabia	1988	5,369	3.6	59.1	36.3	54.9	3.6	...	...	...	...	192	3.6	595	11.1
Senegal	1995	3,508	38.3	62.1[10]	42.2	52.0	32	...	...	...	...	2,719	77.5	259[11]	7.4[11]
Seychelles	1993[57]	28.1	...	...	38.9	...	...	...	...	...	...	2.2	7.7	4.6[11]	16.4[11]
Sierra Leone	1995	1,648	31.7	54.1[10]	36.5	50.9	22.7	...	...	...	...	964	58.5	319[11]	19.4[11]
Singapore	1998[18]	1,932	41.8	69.0	51.6	60.8	42.6	12.2	83.6	1.0	3.2	4	0.2	429	22.2
Slovakia	1998[18]	2,464	45.6	67.0	45.7	51.1	40.6	6.0	81.9	—	12.1	185	7.5	710	28.8
Slovenia	1998	982	46.3	69.1	49.6	54.5	44.7	11.5	74.7	6.1	7.6	110	11.2	332	33.8
Solomon Islands	1993[58]	29.6	25.6[44]	24.9[44,59]	13.7[44]	19.7[44]	7.3[44]	29.6[44]	68.6[44]	—	1.8[44]	8.1	27.4	3.1	10.4
Somalia	1996	3,667	39.3	59.9[10]	38.8	47.1	29.9	...	...	...	...	2,446	66.7	417[11]	11.4[11]
South Africa[60]	1991	11,624	39.4	69.3[53]	37.5	45.5	29.5	7.0	74.8	...	18.2	1,224	10.5	2,361	20.3
Spain	1998[18]	16,265	39.2	62.6	41.6	51.9	31.8	11.9	62.4	0.9	24.7	1,286	7.9	2,965	18.2
Sri Lanka	1998	6,693	35.8	58.8[25]	43.4	55.9	30.9	24.9[34]	54.2[34]	7.8[34]	13.1[34]	2,472	36.9	1,028	15.4
Sudan, The	1983[54]	6,343	29.1	57.4	35.1	50.0	20.4	...	...	...	...	4,029	63.5	317	5.0
Suriname	1994[61]	89.8	35.1	52.3	45.2	59.4	31.4	...	...	...	...	4.8	5.3	10.7	11.9
Swaziland	1996	371	37.7	60.5[10]	42.3	55.0	30.6	...	...	...	...	231	62.3	44[11]	11.9[11]
Sweden	1998	4,255	47.5	76.5[8]	48.0	50.9	45.1	9.5	83.6	0.4	6.5	109	2.6	849	20.0
Switzerland	1998[18, 45]	3,975	44.2	67.9[25]	55.9	63.9	48.4	12.8[19]	84.3[19]	2.9[19]	—	179	4.5	715	18.0
Syria	1998[18]	4,411	17.5	51.2	28.3	46.9	9.8	31.0[13]	49.3[13]	13.0[13]	6.7[13]	917[13]	26.3[13]	471[13]	13.5[13]
Taiwan	1996[18]	9,310	39.2	58.4[25]	43.4	51.3	35.0	21.7	67.5	8.1	2.6	918	9.9	2,471	26.5
Tajikistan	1996	1,778	46.5	63.5[16, 20]	30.3	32.5	28.2	...	...	...	...	1,026	57.7	202	11.4
Tanzania	1996	15,170	46.6	74.1[10]	49.7	53.6	45.9	...	...	...	...	11,738	77.4	725[11]	4.8[11]
Thailand	1998[18, 62]	33,352	45.1	73.6[25]	54.5	60.0	49.0	31.2[63]	40.3[63]	19.5[63]	9.1[63]	16,472	49.4	4,449	13.3
Togo	1995	1,575	35.4	57.1[10]	38.1	49.7	26.7	70.3[30]	10.4[30]	11.3[30]	8.0[30]	1,059	67.2	183[11]	11.6[11]
Tonga	1990	32.0	33.0	57.0	33.6	45.2	22.0	33.7	45.4	16.8	4.1	11.7	36.5	5.1	15.8
Trinidad and Tobago	1998	559	38.3	65.4[34]	47.1	57.2	36.6	17.2	69.1	1.6	12.1	41	7.4	88	15.8
Tunisia	1989	2,361	20.9	50.6	29.8	46.5	12.7	20.9	54.9	7.4	16.8	510	21.6	418	17.7
Turkey	1998[18]	23,415	29.0	54.8	36.6	51.4	21.5	27.6[20]	41.5[20]	27.7[20]	3.2[20]	9,601	41.0	3,852	16.5
Turkmenistan	1996	1,680	40.0	71.9[16]	36.1	43.9	28.5	...	...	...	...	746	44.4	165	9.8
Tuvalu	1991	5.9	51.3[43]	85.5	65.3	...	...	0.3[43]	22.2[43]	— 77.5[43] —		4.2	68.0	0.1	2.0
Uganda	1996	9,636	39.9	68.9[10]	44.0	53.2	34.8	...	...	...	...	7,440	77.2	637[11]	6.6[11]
Ukraine	1998	25,936	50.9	74.9	51.6	54.6	49.0	...	...	...	...	5,074	19.6	4,227	16.3
United Arab Emirates	1990	690	10.4[42]	69.0[42]	47.0[42]	67.6[42]	12.9[42]	6.8[14]	92.7[14]	0.1[14]	0.5[14]	43	6.3	94	13.6
United Kingdom	1998	28,713	44.3	76.2[20]	49.2	55.7	43.0	11.2[20]	76.7[20]	0.5[20]	11.6[20]	479	1.7	5,592	19.5
United States	1998[18]	137,674	46.3	79.4[53]	50.9	55.9	46.1	7.5	87.9	0.1	4.5	3,724	2.7	23,723	17.2
Uruguay	1998[64]	1,239	44.0	71.3	47.0	55.8	39.1	22.9[28]	72.3[28]	2.3[28]	2.5[28]	47	3.8	215	17.3
Uzbekistan	1998	8,800	...	72.3	36.7	...	...	...	...	...	...	3,467	39.4	1,114	12.7
Vanuatu	1989	67.0	46.3	85.0	47.0	49.0	44.9	...	...	...	...	49.8	74.4	1.0	1.5
Venezuela	1997[18]	9,507	35.9	67.2	41.7	53.2	30.1	30.2[20]	61.8[20]	1.7[20]	6.3[20]	940	9.9	1,430	15.0
Vietnam	1989	30,521	51.7	79.9	47.4	47.0	47.7	...	...	...	...	20,471	67.1	3,390	11.1
Virgin Islands (U.S.)	1990[18]	47.4	47.8	70.3	46.6	50.3	43.1	7.6	85.5	0.2	6.7	0.6	1.2	3.7	7.8
West Bank	1996	356.9	16.1	42.2[25]	22.7	37.7	7.4	24.5	49.0	8.1	18.5	41.3	11.6	51.8[36]	14.5[36]
Western Sahara	...	...	...	...	...	...	...	...	...	...	...	...	...	...	...
Yemen	1988	3,029	31.6	52.6	26.4	36.8	16.4	...	...	...	...	2,152	71.1	129	4.3
Yugoslavia	1996	3,182	43.4[19]	58.7[25, 34]	30.1	...	...	...	...	...	...	104	3.3	903	28.4
Zambia	1996	3,507	30.3	54.5	36.1	50.9	21.7	22.9[14]	42.5[14]	3.6[14]	31.0[14]	2,322	66.2	428[11]	12.2[11]
Zimbabwe	1992	3,601	39.6	62.4	34.6	42.8	26.7	24.1	43.9	9.2	22.8	2,110[66]	64.7[66]	179[66]	5.5[66]

[1]Services includes finance, real estate and public administration, defense. [2]Unemployed, not previously employed only. [3]Includes emigrant workers (352,000). [4]Ages 15–59 (male) and 15–54 (female). [5]State sector only. [6]Includes nonagricultural private sector (241,000) and unemployed (261,000). [7]Services includes public administration, defense. [8]Ages 16–64. [9]Unemployed only. [10]Over age 10. [11]Manufacturing; mining, quarrying; public utilities includes construction. [12]Services includes transportation, communications; trade, hotels, restaurants; finance, real estate and public administration, defense. [13]1991. [14]1980. [15]Includes unemployed, not previously employed. [16]Ages 16–59 (male) and 16–54 (female). [17]Mostly unemployed. [18]Excludes all or some classes or elements of the military. [19]1994. [20]1993. [21]Includes unemployed. [22]1990. [23]Mostly unemployed, not previously employed. [24]1982. [25]Over age 15. [26]Ages 14–64. [27]Services includes restaurants and hotels. [28]1992. [29]Over age 12. [30]1981. [31]Republic of Cyprus only. [32]1993 population economically active for Turkish Republic of Northern Cyprus is 75,947. [33]1989. [34]1995.

construction		transportation, communications		trade, hotels, restaurants		finance, real estate		public administration, defense		services		other		country
number ('000)	% of econ. active	number ('000)	% of econ. active	number ('000)	% of econ. active	number ('000)	% of econ. active	number ('000)	% of econ. active	number ('000)	% of econ. active	number ('000)	% of econ. active	
14	0.6	15	0.6	209	9.0	2	0.1	[7]	[7]	123[7]	5.3[7]	117[21]	5.0[21]	Niger
546	1.8	1,112	3.6	7,417	24.1	120	0.4	[7]	[7]	4,902[7]	15.9[7]	2,009[17]	6.5[17]	Nigeria
5.8	21.7	1.4	5.3	5.3	19.8	1.0	3.8	1.4	5.3	4.5	16.9	0.6[9]	2.3[9]	Northern Mariana Islands
145	6.3	170	7.3	411	17.7	229	9.9	152	6.6	655	28.3	75	3.2	Norway
108	15.3	25	3.5	104	14.8	17	2.5	166	23.5	111	15.8	30[23]	4.3[23]	Oman
2,330	6.4	1,971	5.4	5,021	13.8	338	0.9	[7]	[7]	5,395[7]	14.8[7]	1,982[23]	5.4[23]	Pakistan
0.9	14.2	0.4	6.6	1.1	18.7	0.2	2.9	0.8	13.7	1.6	26.1	0.5[9]	7.8[9]	Palau
72	6.9	66	6.3	232	22.1	59	5.6	74	7.0	205	19.5	43[23]	4.1[23]	Panama
22	2.9	1.7	2.4	25	3.4	4	0.6	[7]	[7]	777[7]	10.5[7]	2	0.2	Papua New Guinea
70	6.7	31	2.9	86	8.3	18	1.7	[7]	[7]	174[7]	16.8[7]	86[15]	8.3[15]	Paraguay
308[20]	3.7[20]	364[20]	4.4[20]	1,352[20]	16.3[20]	197[20]	2.4[20]	[7]	[7]	2,887[7, 20]	27.6[7, 20]	—	—	Peru
1,511	4.8	1,885	6.0	4,328[27]	13.8[27]	695	2.2	[7]	[7]	5,631[7, 27]	18.0[7, 27]	3,024[17]	9.7[17]	Philippines
1,248	7.3	1,015	5.9	2,641	15.4	866	5.0	844	4.9	2,754	16.0	511[23]	3.0[23]	Poland
539	10.8	184	3.7	953	19.1	277	5.5	309	6.2	798	16.0	45[2]	0.9[2]	Portugal
103	7.8	50	3.8	266[41]	20.2[41]	44	3.3	[7]	[7]	602[7, 41]	45.6[7, 41]	17[23]	1.3[23]	Puerto Rico
64.2	22.0	11.9	4.1	34.2	11.7	6.2	2.1	[7]	[7]	149.6[7]	51.1[7]	—	—	Qatar
17	7.1	7	3.1	18	7.7	3	1.3	[7]	[7]	79[7]	33.9[7]	87[17]	37.4[17]	Réunion
471	4.1	545	4.7	1,134	9.8	245	2.1	522	4.5	1,006	8.7	291[23]	2.5[23]	Romania
5,516	8.1	5,219	7.6	7,165	10.5	5,077	7.4	2,726	4.0	14,229	20.8	2,314	3.4	Russia
[11]	[11]	[12]	[12]	[12]	[12]	[12]	[12]	[12]	[12]	212[12]	5.7[12]			Rwanda
0.4	2.5	0.3	1.6	1.3	7.3	0.8	4.7	1.0	5.7	2.9	17.0	2.2[17]	12.8[17]	St. Kitts and Nevis
5.0	9.3	2.7	5.0	11.1	20.8	1.9	3.6	[7]	[7]	9.2[7]	17.2[7]	4.3	8.2	St. Lucia
3.5	8.5	2.3	5.5	6.5	15.7	1.4	3.4	[7]	[7]	7.7[7]	18.5[7]	8.3[9]	20.0[9]	St. Vincent
0.1	0.1	1.5	3.3	1.7	3.7	0.8	1.8	[7]	[7]	9.4[7]	20.7[7]	0.6	1.4	Samoa
1.5	8.2	0.4	1.9	2.8	15.2	1.4	7.8	2.3	12.4	2.8	15.2	1.3[21]	6.8[21]	San Marino
2.9	8.1	2.2	6.2	4.5	12.6	0.2	0.5	[7]	[7]	8.0[7]	22.5[7]	2.4	6.7	São Tomé and Príncipe
1,181	22.0	321	6.0	964	18.0	151	2.8	[7]	[7]	1,965[7]	36.6[7]	—	—	Saudi Arabia
[11]	[11]	[12]	[12]	[12]	[12]	[12]	[12]	[12]	[12]	530[12]	15.1[12]			Senegal
[11]	[11]	3.4	12.2	5.2	18.6	1.0	3.4	2.6	9.1	5.6	20.0	3.6[17]	12.6[17]	Seychelles
[11]	[11]	[12]	[12]	[12]	[12]	[12]	[12]	[12]	[12]	365[12]	22.1[12]			Sierra Leone
136	7.0	212	11.0	415	21.5	300	15.5	119	6.2	307	15.9	9[2]	0.5[2]	Singapore
222	9.0	176	7.2	368	14.9	127	5.2	162	6.6	400	16.2	113[23]	4.6[23]	Slovakia
56	5.7	53	5.4	163	16.6	68	6.9	42	4.3	134	13.6	2.3[23]	2.4[23]	Slovenia
1.0	3.3	1.7	5.8	3.4	11.5	1.1	3.9	4.3	14.6	6.8	23.1	—	—	Solomon Islands
[11]	[11]	[12]	[12]	[12]	[12]	[12]	[12]	[12]	[12]	804[12]	21.9[12]			Somalia
526	4.5	497	4.3	1,358	11.7	504	4.3	[7]	[7]	2,641[7]	22.7[7]	2,513[17]	21.6[17]	South Africa[60]
1,546	9.5	828	5.1	3,387	20.8	1,331	8.2	905	5.6	2,634	16.2	1,382[23]	8.5[23]	Spain
309	4.6	268	4.0	594	8.9	117	1.8	[7]	[7]	1,007[7]	15.0[7]	897[17]	13.4[17]	Sri Lanka
139	2.2	215	3.4	294	4.6	21	0.3	[7]	[7]	550[7]	8.7[7]	777[23]	12.3[23]	Sudan, The
4.2	4.6	5.1	5.6	11.4	12.7	3.5	3.9	[7]	[7]	35.7[7]	39.7[7]	14.6[17]	16.3[17]	Suriname
[11]	[11]	[12]	[12]	[12]	[12]	[12]	[12]	[12]	[12]	96[12]	25.9[12]	—	—	Swaziland
244	5.7	285	6.7	663	15.6	519	12.2	218	5.1	1,328	31.2	39[23]	0.9[23]	Sweden
297	7.5	244	6.1	899	22.6	572	14.4	153	3.8	791	19.9	125	3.1	Switzerland
341[13]	9.8[13]	167[13]	4.8[13]	378[13]	10.9[13]	25[13]	0.7[13]	[7]	[7]	951[7, 13]	27.3[7, 13]	235[9, 13]	6.8[9, 13]	Syria
928	10.0	472	5.1	1,976	21.2	567	6.1	324	3.5	1,412	15.2	242[9]	2.6[9]	Taiwan
68	3.8	58	3.3	69	3.9	1	1	1	1	309[1]	17.3[1]	46[9]	2.6[9]	Tajikistan
[11]	[11]	[12]	[12]	[12]	[12]	[12]	[12]	[12]	[12]	2,708[12]	17.8[12]	—	—	Tanzania
1,280	3.8	923	2.8	4,464	13.4	1	1	1	1	4,584[1]	13.7[1]	1,222[17]	3.7[17]	Thailand
[11]	[11]	[12]	[12]	[12]	[12]	[12]	[12]	[12]	[12]	331[12]	21.0[12]	—	—	Togo
1.3	3.9	1.8	5.7	2.6	8.1	1.2	3.7	[7]	[7]	7.1[7]	22.0[7]	1.3[9]	4.2[9]	Tonga
84	14.9	38	6.8	99	17.6	43	7.7	[7]	[7]	165[7]	29.6[7]	1	0.1	Trinidad and Tobago
248	10.5	96	4.1	217	9.2	15	0.7	[7]	[7]	444[7]	18.8[7]	412[17]	17.5[17]	Tunisia
1,464	6.3	996	4.3	3,075	13.1	536	2.3	[7]	[7]	3,260[7]	13.9[7]	631[2]	2.7[2]	Turkey
155	9.2	83	4.9	107	6.4	55	3.3	25	1.5	300	17.9	44	2.6	Turkmenistan
0.2	4.0	0.1	1.0	0.2	4.0	—	—	[7]	[7]	1.3[7]	22.0[7]	—	—	Tuvalu
[11]	[11]	[12]	[12]	[12]	[12]	[12]	[12]	[12]	[12]	1,559[12]	16.2[12]	—	—	Uganda
1,092	4.2	1,400	5.4	1,514	5.8	213	0.8	[7]	[7]	5,886	22.7	6,509	25.1	Ukraine
119	17.3	72	10.4	101	14.7	19	2.7	[7]	[7]	241[7]	35.0[7]	—	—	United Arab Emirates
2,037	7.1	1,846	6.4	5,695	19.8	4,085	14.2	1,612	5.6	6,857	23.9	509[23]	1.8[23]	United Kingdom
9,094	6.6	8,075	5.9	28,740[41]	20.9[41]	16,151	11.7	[7]	[7]	47,623[7, 41]	34.6[7, 41]	543[23]	0.4[23]	United States
93	7.5	71	5.7	249	20.1	77	6.2	[7]	[7]	465[7]	37.5[7]	23[2]	1.9[2]	Uruguay
841	9.6	362	4.1	715	8.1	284	3.2	[7]	[7]	1,691[7]	19.2[7]	326	3.7	Uzbekistan
1.3	1.9	1.0	1.5	2.7	4.1	0.6	1.0	[7]	[7]	7.9[7]	11.8[7]	2.6	3.8	Vanuatu
841	8.8	578	6.1	2,169	22.8	523	5.5	[7]	[7]	2,616[7]	27.5[7]	410[23]	4.3[23]	Venezuela
581	1.9	576	1.9	1,880	6.2	90	0.3	305	1.0	1,374	4.5	1,854[17]	6.1[17]	Vietnam
5.7	12.0	3.7	7.8	10.3	21.8	3.6	7.7	5.1	10.8	7.8	16.4	6.9	14.6	Virgin Islands (U.S.)
60.8	17.0	15.7	4.4	52.6	14.8	1	1	1	1	68.6[1, 36]	19.2[1, 36]	66.0[9]	18.5[9]	West Bank
...	...	...	...	...	...	...	...	...	...	...	...	...	...	Western Sahara
178	5.9	90	3.0	84	2.8	4	0.1	[7]	[7]	391[7]	12.9[7]	—	—	Yemen
130	4.1	142	4.5	557[65]	17.5[65]	77	2.4	92	2.9	356	11.2	819[9]	25.7[9]	Yugoslavia
[11]	[11]	[12]	[12]	[12]	[12]	[12]	[12]	[12]	[12]	757[12]	21.6[12]	—	—	Zambia
51[66]	1.6[66]	76[66]	2.3[66]	128[66]	3.9[66]	24[66]	0.7[66]	[7]	[7]	397[7, 66]	12.2[7, 66]	277[17, 66]	8.5[17, 66]	Zimbabwe

[35]1984. [36]Services includes public utilities. [37]Ages 15–65. [38]Excludes Alderney and Sark. [39]1977. [40]Ages 14–64. [41]Services includes hotels. [42]1988. [43]1979. [44]1986. [45]Excludes foreign border workers. [46]Includes unemployed, emigrant workers, and employees in private nonagricultural sector. [47]Includes unemployed, previously employed. [48]1983. [49]Island of Mauritius only. [50]Services includes transportation, communications; trade, hotels, restaurants; and finance, real estate. [51]Ages 15–59. [52]Services includes finance, real estate. [53]Ages 20–64. [54]Excludes nomadic population. [55]1996–97. [56]Citizens over age 10 involved in money-raising activities only. [57]Excludes domestic workers (private households), self-employed, and family workers. [58]Wage earners only. [59]Over age 14. [60]Excludes the former black independent states of Bophuthatswana, Ciskei, Transkei, and Venda. [61]Districts of Wanica and Paramaribo only. [62]August survey. [63]1994; February survey. [64]Urban areas only. [65]Includes arts and crafts and owners and employees of private shops. [66]1986–87.

Crops and livestock

This table provides comparative data for selected categories of agricultural production for the countries of the world. The data are taken mainly from the United Nations Food and Agriculture Organization's (FAO's) annual *Production Yearbook* and the online FAOSTAT statistics database (http://apps.fao.org/default.htm).

The FAO depends largely on questionnaires supplied to each country for its statistics, but, where no official or semiofficial responses are returned, the FAO makes estimates, using incomplete, unofficial, or other similarly limited data. And, although the FAO provides standardized guidelines upon which many nations have organized their data collection systems and methods, persistent, often traditional, variations in standards of coverage, methodology, and reporting periods reduce the comparability of statistics that *can* be supplied on such forms. FAO data are based on calendar-year periods; that is, data for any particular crop refer to the calendar year in which the harvest (or the bulk of the harvest) occurred.

In spite of the often tragic food shortages in a number of countries in recent years, worldwide agricultural production is probably more often underreported than overreported. Many countries do not report complete domestic production. Some countries, for example, report only crops that are sold commercially and ignore subsistence crops produced for family or communal consumption, or barter; others may limit reporting to production for export only, to holdings above a certain size, or represent a sampling only.

Methodological problems attach to much smaller elements of the agricultural whole, however. The FAO's cereals statistics relate, ideally, to weight or volume of crops harvested for dry grain (excluding cereal crops used for grazing, harvested for hay, or harvested green for food, feed, or silage). Some countries, however, collect the basic data they report to the FAO on sown or cultivated areas instead and calculate production statistics from estimates of yield. Millet and sorghum, which in many European and North American countries are used primarily as livestock or poultry feed, may be reportable by such countries as animal fodder only, while elsewhere many nations use the same grains for human consumption and report them as cereals. Statistics for tropical fruits are frequently not compiled by producing countries, and coverage is not uniform, with some countries reporting only commercial fruits and others including those consumed for

Crops and livestock

country	crops grains production ('000 metric tons) 1989–91 average	2000	grains yield (kg/hectare) 1989–91 average	2000	roots and tubers[a] production ('000 metric tons) 1989–91 average	2000	roots and tubers[a] yield (kg/hectare) 1989–91 average	2000	pulses[b] production ('000 metric tons) 1989–91 average	2000	pulses[b] yield (kg/hectare) 1989–91 average	2000	fruits[c] production ('000 metric tons) 1989–91 average	2000	vegetables[d] production ('000 metric tons) 1989–91 average	2000
Afghanistan	2,754	1,913	1,200	795	217	235	16,291	16,786	32	50	913	1,351	615	615	466	652
Albania	792	580	2,609	2,610	88	180	8,409	14,400	20	32	729	926	153	133	377	652
Algeria	2,481	1,226	823	622	962	950	8,862	14,615	49	38	477	435	1,026	1,491	1,087	2,588
American Samoa	...	...	...	...	2	2	3,721	3,361	...	...	...	...	1	1	—	...
Andorra	...	...	...	...	...	...	...	...	...	...	...	...	...	...	...	...
Angola	298	550	350	619	1,815	3,331	4,220	6,071	35	68	273	356	414	423	250	240
Antigua and Barbuda	—	—	—	—	—	—	5,171	4,811	...	...	...	...	9	8	2	2
Argentina	19,916	38,110	2,342	3,522	2,279	3,990	18,183	25,659	249	358	1,105	1,155	5,915	6,531	2,802	3,480
Armenia	282[1]	216	1,500[1]	1,155	365[1]	320	12,080[1]	9,143	3[1]	1	1,714[1]	509	237[1]	227	444[1]	395
Aruba	...	...	...	...	...	...	...	...	...	...	...	...	...	...	...	...
Australia	21,390	30,589	1,665	1,710	1,127	1,333	28,301	32,001	1,530	1,764	1,025	864	2,345	3,016	1,504	1,799
Austria	5,115	4,457	5,443	5,383	810	496	24,907	20,908	119	70	3,555	2,397	946	1,036	455	613
Azerbaijan	1,130[1]	1,530	1,733[1]	2,372	153[1]	450	8,179[1]	11,250	...	21	...	3,443	803[1]	481	771[1]	917
Bahamas, The	1	—	1,522	2,168	1	1	6,900	5,330	1	—	1,199	718	12	22	27	21
Bahrain	...	...	...	...	—	—	14,112	16,000	—	—	836	1,091	14	22	10	12
Bangladesh	28,032	37,785	2,530	3,246	1,643	2,085	9,744	10,959	512	500	699	757	1,329	1,340	1,332	1,785
Barbados	2	2	2,656	2,500	7	7	9,271	9,024	1	1	1,261	1,254	3	3	7	12
Belarus	6,749[1]	4,820	2,610[1]	1,970	9,623[1]	8,500	12,975[1]	12,143	235[1]	380	1,335[1]	1,689	561[1]	262	917[1]	1,247
Belgium[2]	2,236	2,511	6,094	7,168	1,838	3,000	37,421	46,154	18	16	4,062	4,600	372	735	1,438	1,784
Belize	28	49	1,640	2,112	4	4	21,838	21,765	3	5	763	962	134	311	5	5
Benin	566	872	860	1,043	2,102	3,853	9,354	10,825	60	92	552	673	180	221	211	234
Bermuda	...	...	...	...	1	1	20,985	20,735	...	...	...	...	—	—	3	3
Bhutan	102	159	1,089	1,456	52	56	9,910	10,750	2	2	800	800	64	64	9	10
Bolivia	881	1,257	1,426	1,619	1,160	1,562	6,058	7,471	30	32	1,079	1,010	853	1,358	384	587
Bosnia and Herzegovina	1,176[1]	1,311	3,230[1]	2,771	230[1]	365	4,672[1]	8,795	19[1]	19	1,086[1]	1,270	130[1]	146	533[1]	689
Botswana	60	22	308	217	7	13	5,385	7,059	18	17	562	515	11	2	17	17
Brazil	37,702	46,597	1,868	2,690	27,229	26,272	12,567	13,598	2,471	3,063	473	690	30,895	39,910	5,605	7,138
Brunei	1	—	1,793	...	2	2	3,344	4,286	...	...	...	...	5	6	8	9
Bulgaria	8,872	4,545	4,121	2,574	495	566	11,987	10,885	89	41	1,021	819	1,576	743	1,792	1,766
Burkina Faso	1,975	2,453	717	827	70	61	6,032	6,080	56	72	746	935	71	73	229	229
Burundi	296	245	1,299	1,249	1,420	1,462	6,800	6,856	262	219	1,020	842	1,638	1,598	210	200
Cambodia	2,591	3,857	1,431	1,965	105	111	5,366	7,351	9	11	500	438	239	320	472	470
Cameroon	907	1,489	1,182	1,731	2,371	3,356	7,704	8,048	72	176	534	725	1,876	2,456	499	1,676
Canada	52,915	51,315	2,470	2,801	2,903	4,569	24,683	28,887	633	4,439	1,564	1,675	752	785	2,036	2,156
Cape Verde	10	11	287	333	18	9	9,099	7,965	9	3	184	94	15	15	7	17
Central African Republic	103	176	845	1,163	816	961	3,551	3,356	16	31	941	1,069	202	255	60	83
Chad	677	1,248	565	524	628	593	4,692	4,415	35	56	682	691	74	95	109	113
Chile	2,997	2,593	3,862	4,507	858	999	14,315	17,435	131	58	1,156	1,046	1,943	3,781	1,943	2,596
China	390,173	408,431	4,192	4,736	141,074	188,320	14,980	18,224	4,575	4,279	1,354	1,477	21,900	70,432	128,265	278,592
Colombia	4,090	3,362	2,471	3,048	4,342	4,931	11,973	12,206	167	141	691	1,007	5,024	6,732	1,433	1,325
Comoros	19	21	1,289	1,338	58	69	4,884	5,274	7	12	833	1,034	54	62	5	6
Congo, Dem. Rep. of the	1,471	1,621	803	778	19,477	16,748	7,913	13,280	204	168	602	534	3,321	3,013	513	426
Congo, Rep. of the	11	2	885	687	725	864	6,712	7,159	7	8	704	772	156	195	42	42
Costa Rica	262	287	2,775	3,556	152	111	20,865	16,908	34	16	524	544	2,119	3,267	116	334
Côte d'Ivoire	1,241	1,827	884	1,241	4,291	4,996	5,618	5,665	8	8	667	667	1,627	1,956	450	534
Croatia	2,562[1]	2,070	4,128[1]	4,046	517[1]	500	8,085[1]	9,091	221[1]	26	1,914[1]	2,209	539[1]	565	259[1]	504
Cuba	547	555	2,346	2,694	666	775	4,398	5,808	13	17	260	377	1,424	1,343	509	378
Cyprus	107	47	1,901	1,038	187	123	22,328	24,127	2	1	967	1,229	369	381	125	143
Czech Republic	6,622[3]	6,455	4,101[3]	3,910	1,652[3]	1,476	19,261[3]	21,330	175[3]	86	2,371[3]	2,107	496[3]	557	541[3]	492
Denmark	9,211	9,598	5,887	6,224	1,394	1,502	36,010	39,528	481	195	4,303	2,912	88	84	304	309
Djibouti	—	—	...	...	...	...	...	...	...	...	...	...	...	...	22	24
Dominica	—	—	...	...	29	27	9,292	9,251	—	—	450	400	97	72	6	6
Dominican Republic	531	556	3,951	3,690	243	246	7,085	6,890	98	46	937	866	1,560	1,299	245	458
East Timor[4]	...	...	...	...	...	...	...	...	...	...	...	...	...	...	...	...
Ecuador	1,422	2,341	1,718	2,588	500	979	6,596	11,661	40	59	489	723	4,446	8,368	389	418
Egypt	12,672	20,046	5,526	7,494	1,904	2,074	21,762	21,998	542	418	2,951	2,311	4,456	6,576	8,923	13,563
El Salvador	785	793	1,840	2,181	38	89	15,090	14,674	55	72	802	855	290	227	146	145
Equatorial Guinea	...	...	...	...	77	81	2,484	2,531	...	...	...	...	16	20	...	...
Eritrea	175[3]	270	740[3]	531	109[3]	120	2,804[3]	3,093	36[3]	41	545[3]	573	4[3]	4	303[3]	25
Estonia	638[1]	647	1,665[1]	1,781	590[1]	457	13,743[1]	12,026	1[1]	4	1,452[1]	948	33[1]	20	75[1]	55

subsistence as well. Figures on wild fruits and berries are seldom included in national reports at all. FAO vegetable statistics include vegetables and melons grown for human consumption only. Some countries do not make this distinction in their reports, and some exclude the production of kitchen gardens and small family plots, although in certain countries, such small-scale production may account for 20 to 40 percent of total output.

Livestock statistics may be distorted by the timing of country reports. Ireland, for example, takes a livestock enumeration in December that is reported the following year and that appears low against data for otherwise comparable countries because of the slaughter and export of animals at the close of the grazing season. It balances this, however, with a June enumeration, when numbers tend to be high. Milk production as defined by the FAO includes whole fresh milk, excluding milk sucked by young animals but including amounts fed by farmers or ranchers to livestock, but national practices vary. Certain countries do not distinguish between milk cows and other cattle, so that yield per dairy cow must be estimated. Some countries do not report egg production statistics (here given of metric tons), and external estimates must be based on the numbers of chickens

and reported or assumed egg-laying rates. Other countries report egg production by number, and this must be converted to weight, using conversion factors specific to the makeup by species of national poultry flocks.

Metric system units used in the table may be converted to English system units as follow:

metric tons × 1.1023 = short tons
kilograms × 2.2046 = pounds
kilograms per hectare × 0.8922 = pounds per acre.

The notes that follow, keyed by references in the table headings, provide further definitional information.

a. Includes such crops as potatoes and cassava.
b. Includes beans and peas harvested for dry grain only. Does not include green beans and green peas.
c. Excludes melons.
d. Includes melons, green beans, and green peas.
e. From cows only.
f. From chickens only.

livestock													country
cattle		sheep		hogs		chickens		milke				eggsf		
stock ('000 head)		stock ('000 head)		stock ('000 head)		stock ('000 head)		production ('000 metric tons)		yield (kg/animal)		production (metric tons)		
1989–91 average	2000	1989–91 average	2000	1989–91 average	2000	1989–91 average	2000	1989–91 average	2000	1989–91 average	2000	1989–91 average	2000	
1,600	3,478	14,173	18,000	...	...	7,073	7,000	507	2,100	633	1,207	14,300	18,000	Afghanistan
657	720	1,645	1,941	183	81	4,864	4,000	403	815	1,384	1,701	15,033	21,000	Albania
1,366	1,650	17,302	18,200	5	6	73,000	110,000	595	1,000	940	1,250	122,000	120,000	Algeria
—	—	—	—	11	11	34	37	—	—	...	...	30	30	American Samoa
...	...	...	...	...	...	...	...	...	...	...	...	...	...	Andorra
3,117	4,042	240	350	802	800	6,117	6,000	151	191	483	473	4,000	4,000	Angola
16	16	13	12	2	2	87	90	6	6	936	968	173	150	Antigua and Barbuda
52,633	55,000	28,139	14,500	2,633	4,200	42,333	65,000	6,375	9,800	2,621	4,000	298,453	286,000	Argentina
522[1]	479	858[1]	510	130[1]	71	3,209[1]	2,850	394[1]	470	...	1,793	11,242[1]	18,000	Armenia
...	...	1	—	1	—	50		...	...	...	...	...	...	Aruba
23,086	26,716	165,046	115,693	2,617	2,433	56,000	96,000	6,514	11,183	3,945	5,153	179,000	200,000	Australia
2,546	2,150	284	361	3,762	3,790	14,000	14,000	3,344	3,350	3,805	4,716	94,284	92,000	Austria
1,726[1]	1,945	4,714[1]	5,390	841	20	21,267[1]	14,000	798[1]	1,011	...	1,108	37,333[1]	29,000	Azerbaijan
4	1	39	6	12	6	1,733	5,000	1	1	1,000	1,000	1,000	1,000	Bahamas, The
14	11	20	18	...	...	1,000	...	19	14	2,602	1,970	2,800	3,000	Bahrain
23,173	23,652	871	1,121	...	...	90,253	139,000	741	755	206	206	57,000	132,000	Bangladesh
28	23	40	41	29	33	3,437	4,000	14	8	1,784	1,688	2,000	1,000	Barbados
6,216[1]	4,326	332[1]	92	4,397[1]	3,566	47,573[1]	30,000	5,660[1]	4,320	...	2,335	193,200[1]	187,000	Belarus
3,264	3,085	174	152	6,439	7,322	33,000	45,000	3,875	3,600	4,313	5,538	168,171	220,000	Belgium[2]
51	59	4	3	26	24	987	1,000	7	7	1,159	1,059	1,000	2,000	Belize
1,037	1,438	869	645	479	470	23,333	23,000	16	21	130	130	17,000	17,000	Benin
1	1	...	...	1	...	75	...	1	...	2,901	...	472	...	Bermuda
402	...	49	...	69	...	250	...	29	...	257	257	317	...	Bhutan
5,542	6,725	7,573	8,752	2,160	2,793	23,697	74,000	113	213	1,399	1,689	47,333	37,000	Bolivia
438[1]	462	518[1]	662	404[1]	150	5,167[1]	3,000	303[1]	270	...	892	17,833[1]	3,000	Bosnia and Herzegovina
2,694	2,350	317	350	16	6	2,080	4,000	113	102	350	350	2,000	3,000	Botswana
147,797	167,471	20,061	15,000	33,643	27,425	557,282	1,006,000	15,004	22,134	780	1,380	1,244,227	1,400,000	Brazil
2	2	...	...	17	6	2,254	6,000	...	...	...	...	3,083	4,000	Brunei
1,548	682	8,226	2,549	4,219	1,512	34,167	14,000	1,999	1,200	3,370	2,799	129,127	90,000	Bulgaria
3,937	4,704	5,049	6,585	510	610	17,028	22,000	101	163	156	172	15,000	18,000	Burkina Faso
431	320	352	120	92	50	4,000	4,000	33	19	350	285	3,040	3,000	Burundi
2,178	3,000	...	...	1,601	2,600	9,000	13,000	17	20	170	170	9,000	12,000	Cambodia
4,660	5,900	3,407	3,880	1,344	1,430	17,333	30,000	116	125	500	500	11,867	14,000	Cameroon
11,165	12,786	595	695	10,505	12,242	110,000	158,000	7,915	8,090	5,800	7,324	319,000	357,000	Canada
18	22	6	8	115	640	1,000	...	2	5	447	638	1,000	2,000	Cape Verde
2,589	2,950	134	210	430	650	3,000	4,000	46	62	224	264	1,000	1,000	Central African Republic
4,298	5,595	1,926	2,500	14	21	3,950	5,000	116	151	270	270	4,000	4,000	Chad
3,402	4,134	4,803	4,144	1,144	2,465	32,000	...	1,353	2,060	1,862	1,350	96,000	95,000	Chile
79,282	104,582	112,299	131,095	360,247	437,551	2,127,000	3,625,000	4,410	7,838	1,562	1,639	6,701,000	19,235,000	China
24,383	26,000	2,547	2,200	2,627	2,800	58,000	100,000	3,897	5,740	963	990	237,000	350,000	Colombia
47	52	13	20	...	...	392	440	4	4	500	500	1,000	1,000	Comoros
1,535	822	934	925	1,050	1,049	25,000	22,000	8	5	851	825	8,143	7,000	Congo, Dem. Rep. of the
65	77	104	116	49	46	2,000	2,000	1	1	500	500	1,170	1,000	Congo, Rep. of the
2,181	1,715	3	3	270	390	14,000	17,000	431	707	1,308	1,537	19,000	27,150	Costa Rica
1,101	1,350	1,137	1,393	361	280	24,333	30,000	18	24	150	168	13,000	18,000	Côte d'Ivoire
566[1]	427	502[1]	528	1,264[1]	1,233	11,665[1]	11,000	643[1]	641	...	2,424	51,167[1]	49,000	Croatia
4,922	4,700	385	310	2,184	2,800	27,876	15,000	1,100	618	1,866	1,200	120,000	74,000	Cuba
50	56	300	240	281	455	3,000	4,000	98	133	4,746	5,583	8,000	11,000	Cyprus
2,234[3]	1,574	205[3]	84	4,179[3]	3,688	25,574[3]	30,000	3,207[3]	2,708	...	4,946	154,226[3]	176,000	Czech Republic
2,227	1,850	164	143	9,390	11,551	16,000	20,000	4,710	4,465	6,227	7,271	83,000	78,000	Denmark
188	269	433	465	...	...	...	...	7	8	350	350	...	...	Djibouti
9	13	7	8	4	5	129	...	5	6	902	910	155	225	Dominica
2,283	1,904	115	105	543	539	31,227	46,000	345	398	1,701	1,657	35,000	61,000	Dominican Republic
...	...	...	...	...	...	...	...	...	...	...	...	...	...	East Timor[4]
4,351	5,110	1,417	2,870	2,213	2,130	52,000	130,000	1,529	1,996	2,092	2,009	51,000	57,000	Ecuador
2,771	3,180	3,310	4,450	24	30	38,000	88,000	974	1,645	689	1,089	144,000	170,000	Egypt
1,213	1,121	5	5	305	300	5,200	8,000	268	401	999	1,148	46,000	53,000	El Salvador
5	5	35	36	5	5	228	245	...	...	...	...	175	190	Equatorial Guinea
1,290[3]	1,800	1,520[3]	1,540	...	...	4,300[3]	4,600	30[3]	41	...	190	5,934[3]	1,000	Eritrea
595[1]	286	116[1]	29	588[1]	281	3,965[1]	2,000	834[1]	600	...	3,750	22,487[1]	17,000	Estonia

Crops and livestock (continued)

country	grains production ('000 metric tons) 1989–91 average	2000	grains yield (kg/hectare) 1989–91 average	2000	roots and tubers[a] production ('000 metric tons) 1989–91 average	2000	roots and tubers yield (kg/hectare) 1989–91 average	2000	pulses[b] production ('000 metric tons) 1989–91 average	2000	pulses yield (kg/hectare) 1989–91 average	2000	fruits[c] production ('000 metric tons) 1989–91 average	2000	vegetables[d] production ('000 metric tons) 1989–91 average	2000
Ethiopia	7,197	7,845	1,409[3]	1,151	2,000[3]	4,140	3,659[3]	7,289	978[3]	747	890[3]	777	228[3]	221	568[3]	575
Faroe Islands	...	...	...	...	1	2	13,663	13,636	—	—	...	...	...	...	...	...
Fiji	30	19	2,289	2,143	36	72	3,739	9,508	—	—	773	1,000	13	13	9	18
Finland	3,845	4,006	3,360	3,380	845	816	20,656	20,400	14	14	2,549	2,222	22	23	205	239
France	57,683	66,542	6,240	7,261	5,213	6,652	29,853	3,985	3,310	2,078	4,735	4,444	10,561	11,137	7,628	7,938
French Guiana	22	20	4,199	2,536	32	14	10,178	5,906	...	...	...	...	7	13	9	20
French Polynesia	...	...	...	...	11	12	12,752	12,778	...	...	...	...	8	7	7	1
Gabon	23	32	1,599	1,728	376	436	5,424	5,888	—	—	639	667	268	304	30	35
Gambia, The	99	144	1,076	1,112	6	6	3,000	3,000	4	4	267	267	4	4	8	8
Gaza Strip	1	1	510	529	23	35	22,624	21,875	...	...	...	...	168	137	140	158
Georgia	457[1]	327	1,823[1]	1,003	223[1]	480	10,300[1]	13,333	...	9	...	928	745[1]	564	1,205[1]	634
Germany	37,910	45,304	5,534	6,369	14,057	12,639	27,747	41,831	337	561	2,770	2,826	4,752	4,793	2,867	2,499
Ghana	1,155	1,686	1,076	1,292	6,608	12,892	8,143	10,725	18	15	102	100	1,147	2,449	414	698
Greece	5,491	4,171	3,727	3,289	1,052	892	19,880	18,938	41	41	1,512	1,598	4,005	4,010	4,070	4,124
Greenland	...	...	...	...	...	...	...	...	...	...	...	...	...	...	...	...
Grenada	—	—	1,000	1,000	4	4	5,214	5,336	1	1	1,080	1,132	26	18	2	3
Guadeloupe	...	...	...	...	20	17	9,649	10,826	—	—	577	3,833	129	159	24	23
Guam	—	—	2,000	2,000	2	2	14,904	14,904	...	...	...	...	2	2	4	5
Guatemala	1,413	1,199	1,950	1,750	61	92	4,861	7,077	135	130	916	816	811	1,263	511	523
Guernsey	...	...	...	...	...	...	...	...	...	...	...	...	...	...	...	...
Guinea	632	973	1,052	1,307	578	1,122	7,320	5,972	60	60	857	857	840	994	432	840
Guinea-Bissau	200	212	1,556	1,398	69	82	6,911	7,087	2	2	960	622	62	74	21	25
Guyana	218	603	3,197	4,086	35	42	10,027	10,000	1	2	612	593	49	40	10	9
Haiti	405	431	996	932	770	769	3,785	3,891	100	75	655	658	1,005	1,037	277	226
Honduras	664	607	1,403	1,370	30	34	8,836	7,223	71	85	746	704	1,399	945	197	269
Hong Kong	—	—	—	—	—	—	—	—	...	...	...	...	4	4	116	59
Hungary	14,592	9,956	5,160	3,623	1,230	768	16,713	17,067	347	118	2,249	1,990	2,184	1,309	1,937	1,279
Iceland	...	...	...	...	11	10	9,159	14,286	...	...	...	...	2	—	2	4
India	195,478	239,914	1,911	2,372	21,280	30,550	15,906	18,024	13,604	13,480	568	564	27,138	49,199	48,971	61,698
Indonesia[4]	51,258	60,169	3,814	4,031	19,270	19,248	11,522	11,555	666	901	1,393	1,603	5,497	7,478	4,336	6,397
Iran	12,973	12,513	1,363	1,627	2,387	3,450	17,394	20,783	398	475	584	571	7,088	11,550	7,743	12,863
Iraq	2,541	795	927	284	196	150	15,980	6,250	19	29	995	1,061	1,457	1,215	2,855	1,908
Ireland	1,950	1,963	6,374	7,134	577	500	25,060	29,412	8	19	4,798	4,524	24	19	235	216
Isle of Man	...	...	...	...	...	...	...	...	...	...	...	...	...	...	...	...
Israel	234	134	2,968	2,354	209	357	32,359	38,551	9	12	1,334	1,906	1,715	1,343	1,143	1,705
Italy	17,921	20,744	4,005	4,989	2,340	2,089	19,637	24,762	221	123	1,430	1,777	17,569	19,413	14,436	15,338
Jamaica	3	2	1,232	1,221	225	291	12,534	16,907	6	5	898	1,114	383	416	108	190
Japan	13,946	12,769	5,645	6,260	5,539	4,554	25,459	26,009	145	105	1,670	1,831	4,838	4,306	14,471	12,851
Jersey	...	...	...	...	...	...	...	...	...	...	...	...	...	...	...	...
Jordan	105	52	1,040	901	59	93	25,459	26,009	6	5	690	837	247	225	709	781
Kazakhstan	22,521[1]	11,583	1,040[1]	945	2,303[1]	1,694	9,742[1]	10,615	96[1]	20	782[1]	764	160[1]	106	1,096[1]	2,192
Kenya	2,893	2,197	1,567	1,329	1,536	1,855	8,200	7,275	219	230	312	329	888	981	629	649
Kiribati	...	...	...	...	7	9	7,449	8,148	...	...	...	...	5	6	4	5
Korea, North	8,244	3,118	3,152	2,443	1,051	1,870	13,414	8,348	325	280	922	848	1,304	1,350	4,344	3,810
Korea, South	8,412	7,498	5,891	6,362	939	1,106	21,133	23,163	45	30	1,134	1,102	2,019	2,468	9,729	10,980
Kuwait	1	3	4,143	2,815	1	29	19,530	25,961	...	...	...	...	2	10	92	130
Kyrgyzstan	1,339[1]	1,550	2,271[1]	2,670	321[1]	1,033	12,190[1]	15,892	...	...	...	...	97[1]	130	291[1]	732
Laos	1,443	2,232	2,688	3,189	246	158	8,150	8,535	12	15	780	954	130	173	89	288
Latvia	1,072[1]	928	1,739[1]	2,194	1,161[1]	747	13,147[1]	14,600	6[1]	3	1,480[1]	1,497	73[1]	52	256[1]	121
Lebanon	80	96	1,955	2,424	249	271	18,708	20,008	28	43	1,631	2,095	1,223	1,313	798	1,324
Lesotho	170	149	805	934	47	90	15,553	16,667	9	11	481	764	18	13	24	18
Liberia	191	200	1,035	1,290	422	440	7,253	6,801	3	3	517	500	111	149	73	76
Libya	284	238	680	728	141	210	7,891	7,000	12	19	1,126	1,379	307	381	708	905
Liechtenstein	...	...	...	...	...	...	...	...	...	...	...	...	...	...	...	...
Lithuania	2,319[1]	2,658	1,974[1]	2,713	1,316[1]	1,792	11,213[1]	16,392	30[1]	145	1,239[1]	2,185	145[1]	79	306[1]	321
Luxembourg[2]	...	...	...	...	...	...	...	...	...	...	...	...	...	...	...	...
Macau	...	...	...	...	7	...	13,394	...	1	...	...	...	—	...	1	...
Macedonia	583[1]	621	2,453[1]	2,867	127[1]	165	9,534[1]	12,445	29[1]	28	1,348[1]	2,555	342[1]	357	462[1]	523
Madagascar	2,541	2,460	1,943	1,761	3,160	3,152	6,359	6,489	67	99	883	909	790	854	328	344
Malawi	1,560	2,463	1,104	1,620	506	2,600	4,294	8,229	253	234	560	562	485	511	252	256
Malaysia	1,886	2,094	2,710	2,910	497	469	9,683	9,306	...	...	633	750	1,126	1,066	334	488
Maldives	...	...	1,125	4,400	7	7	4,537	4,355	...	...	...	...	9	10	20	28
Mali	2,114	2,952	907	1,171	23	34	4,721	4,250	40	98	172	349	15	41	307	320
Malta	8	12	3,422	4,008	17	35	13,181	19,612	1	1	2,336	2,556	14	8	52	64
Marshall Islands	...	...	...	...	...	...	...	...	...	...	...	...	...	...	...	...
Martinique	...	...	...	...	23	18	10,917	10,456	...	1	...	...	273	356	24	28
Mauritania	131	263	831	1,011	6	6	1,933	2,115	28	34	385	330	16	25	11	12
Mauritius	2	—	3,885	5,200	19	18	18,659	19,604	1	2	708	...	8	9	43	85
Mayotte	...	...	...	...	...	...	...	...	...	...	...	...	...	...	...	...
Mexico	23,553	29,550	2,350	2,451	1,302	1,722	11,790	21,553	1,412	1,460	704	595	9,430	12,363	6,604	9,621
Micronesia	...	...	...	...	...	...	...	...	...	...	...	...	...	...	...	...
Moldova	2,274[1]	2,021	3,019[1]	2,348	504[1]	342	7,989[1]	4,866	107[1]	49	1,537[1]	1,092	1,562[1]	749	689[1]	583
Monaco	...	...	...	...	...	...	...	...	...	...	...	...	...	...	...	...
Mongolia	719	190	1,104	956	128	70	10,613	10,747	3	1	708	833	...	...	42	47
Morocco	7,457	2,006	1,346	368	975	1,103	16,319	18,003	386	186	790	743	2,310	2,578	2,941	2,231
Mozambique	629	1,476	404	949	4,122	4,741	4,322	5,826	87	130	301	342	368	260	197	126
Myanmar (Burma)	14,111	20,643	2,738	3,138	212	356	8,579	9,836	434	1,655	674	648	957	1,284	2,027	3,369
Namibia	103	140	482	437	212	255	8,610	8,500	8	9	1,097	1,096	10	11	9	11
Nauru	...	...	...	...	...	...	...	...	...	...	...	...	—	—	...	...
Nepal	5,680	6,986	1,885	2,087	826	1,238	7,398	8,850	168	218	597	729	415	457	962	1,252
Netherlands, The	1,327	1,649	6,909	7,472	6,947	8,200	40,168	44,809	85	19	4,109	4,203	507	756	3,470	3,711
Netherlands Antilles	...	...	...	...	...	...	...	...	...	...	...	...	...	...	...	...
New Caledonia	1	2	1,837	3,736	21	21	6,023	5,778	—	—	393	600	4	3	5	4
New Zealand	783	870	4,886	6,648	277	518	30,899	39,808	62	52	2,941	2,984	806	925	576	995
Nicaragua	453	751	1,483	1,842	77	85	11,790	10,366	69	114	621	652	303	260	35	31

livestock														country
cattle		sheep		hogs		chickens		milk[e]		yield		eggs[f]		
stock ('000 head)		stock ('000 head)		stock ('000 head)		stock ('000 head)		production ('000 metric tons)		(kg/animal)		production (metric tons)		
1989–91 average	2000	1989–91 average	2000	1989–91 average	2000	1989–91 average	2000	1989–91 average	2000	1989–91 average	2000	1989–91 average	2000	
29,575[3]	35,000	21,700[3]	21,000	20[3]	24	54,200[3]	56,000	738[3]	930	...	204	73,370[3]	75,000	Ethiopia
2	2	67	68	...	...	...	...	...	...	...	...	...	...	Faroe Islands
274	350	—	7	88	115	3,000	4,000	58	58	1,705	1,800	2,000	4,000	Fiji
1,352	1,087	59	107	1,322	1,351	6,000	6,000	2,712	2,500	5,666	6,452	73,000	59,000	Finland
21,407	20,527	11,196	10,004	11,999	14,635	198,306	233,000	26,334	24,890	4,797	5,630	903,413	1,050,000	France
15	9	4	3	9	11	202	190	—	—	...	581	250	450	French Guiana
8	10	—	—	33	37	100	150	2	1	2,207	2,000	1,000	2,000	French Polynesia
30	36	161	198	160	213	2,217	3,000	1	2	250	250	1,500	1,980	Gabon
333	370	127	195	11	14	1,000	1,000	7	7	175	175	1,000	1,000	Gambia, The
3	3	24	24	...	...	3,000	4,000	7	8	4,000	4,000	5,000	8,000	Gaza Strip
1,051[1]	1,122	1,160[1]	560	525[1]	411	15,113[1]	8,000	450[1]	721	...	1,243	12,717[1]	24,000	Georgia
20,048	14,658	3,824	2,100	33,350	27,049	116,263	108,000	30,976	28,420	4,931	5,880	989,000	880,000	Germany
1,159	1,285	2,199	2,565	495	350	9,682	18,000	23	33	130	130	10,000	19,000	Ghana
651	590	8,684	9,041	1,002	906	27,213	28,000	646	770	2,523	4,400	123,000	110,000	Greece
...	...	21	22	...	...	...	...	...	...	...	...	...	...	Greenland
4	4	11	13	3	5	260	...	1	1	...	800	1,000	1,000	Grenada
70	80	4	4	28	15	311	200	1	...	506	...	1,000	2,000	Guadeloupe
—	—	...	...	4	4	170	...	...	...	...	...	367	1,000	Guam
2,052	2,300	432	551	602	825	14,633	24,000	312	320	680	711	68,000	109,000	Guatemala
...	...	...	...	...	...	...	...	...	...	...	...	...	...	Guernsey
1,491	2,368	429	687	24	54	5,800	9,000	42	62	185	185	6,000	9,000	Guinea
412	530	239	285	290	345	1,000	1,000	12	13	170	170	1,000	1,000	Guinea-Bissau
138	220	129	130	42	20	2,000	13,000	19	13	840	828	1,000	7,000	Guyana
1,067	1,430	120	152	330	1,000	5,167	6,000	25	41	250	250	4,000	4,000	Haiti
2,412	1,950	10	14	589	800	9,436	18,000	346	729	911	1,157	28,000	41,000	Honduras
2	—	—	—	296	110	5,678	3,000	2	—	...	2,236	1,497	10	Hong Kong
1,619	873	2,050	934	7,996	5,335	50,950	26,000	2,733	2,091	4,977	5,532	254,000	177,000	Hungary
75	72	540	465	18	43	450	180	112	107	3,509	3,972	3,000	2,000	Iceland
191,897	218,800	43,706	57,900	11,193	16,500	294,000	402,000	22,259	30,900	880	917	1,161,000	1,782,000	India
10,390	12,102	6,008	9,353	6,008	7,502	577,000	800,000	335	384	1,094	1,151	366,000	406,000	Indonesia[4]
7,382	8,100	44,754	55,000	—	—	162,000	250,000	2,480	4,403	1,014	1,243	310,000	538,000	Iran
1,416	1,350	7,804	6,780	...	...	63,000	23,000	297	319	730	750	64,450	14,000	Iraq
5,923	6,708	5,523	5,393	1,125	1,763	9,000	12,000	5,376	5,448	3,849	4,320	33,000	32,000	Ireland
...	...	...	...	...	...	...	...	...	...	...	...	...	...	Isle of Man
340	388	383	350	122	163	23,000	28,000	964	1,194	8,783	9,787	105,000	92,000	Israel
8,541	7,184	11,088	10,970	9,150	8,403	138,000	100,000	10,893	11,741	3,724	5,499	687,000	768,000	Italy
382	400	2	1	192	180	7,167	11,000	51	53	1,000	1,000	26,000	28,000	Jamaica
4,772	4,658	30	11	11,673	9,980	338,000	298,000	8,169	8,500	5,825	6,641	2,446,228	2,508,000	Japan
...	...	...	...	...	...	...	...	...	...	...	...	...	...	Jersey
35	57	1,660	1,600	...	...	14,000	25,000	60	145	2,485	3,085	32,420	50,000	Jordan
9,336[1]	3,998	33,688[1]	9,776	2,610[1]	1,034	50,400[1]	18,000	5,327[1]	3,600	...	1,829	176,667[1]	86,000	Kazakhstan
13,583	13,794	9,241	7,000	125	170	24,667	27,000	2,297	2,250	499	480	41,440	50,000	Kenya
...	...	...	...	9	12	259	300	...	...	...	124	...	140	Kiribati
1,293	600	385	190	3,215	2,970	21,000	10,000	88	90	2,379	2,308	146,000	95,000	Korea, North
2,149	2,486	3	1	4,792	7,864	70,336	97,000	1,752	2,244	5,944	7,357	399,000	465,000	Korea, South
14	20	197	450	...	...	17,000	33,000	21	42	3,226	606	6,390	20,000	Kuwait
1,124[1]	932	8,261[1]	3,264	257[1]	105	9,867[1]	2,200	918[1]	1,090	...	2,225	22,000[1]	12,000	Kyrgyzstan
853	987	...	...	1,397	1,101	8,165	12,000	9	6	200	200	4,000	8,000	Laos
1,068[1]	378	154[1]	27	865[1]	405	5,397[1]	3,000	1,212[1]	823	...	4,003	25,033[1]	26,000	Latvia
65	77	222	380	46	64	23,000	32,000	94	205	2,826	3,254	35,000	42,000	Lebanon
550	520	1,450	750	62	65	967	2,000	24	24	290	250	826	2,000	Lesotho
38	36	222	210	123	120	3,800	4,000	1	1	130	130	3,904	4,000	Liberia
238	143	5,100	5,100	...	...	15,867	25,000	99	135	1,202	1,205	33,917	59,000	Libya
6	6	3	3	3	3	...	...	13	12	4,645	4,444	...	...	Liechtenstein
1,761[1]	898	52[1]	14	1,579[1]	936	10,860[1]	6,000	2,128[1]	1,560	...	3,156	41,167[1]	37,000	Lithuania
...	...	...	...	...	...	...	...	...	...	...	...	...	...	Luxembourg[2]
...	...	...	...	...	...	450	500	...	...	...	...	638	...	Macau
282[1]	290	2,425[1]	1,600	176[1]	197	4,458[1]	3,000	127[1]	180	...	1,837	25,653[1]	22,000	Macedonia
10,254	10,364	737	800	1,431	900	13,062	20,000	476	535	273	282	15,050	15,000	Madagascar
862	760	151	115	236	240	11,500	15,000	37	35	460	461	11,203	20,000	Malawi
677	723	212	175	2,577	1,829	62,377	120,000	29	42	486	477	287,000	413,000	Malaysia
...	...	...	...	...	...	...	...	...	...	...	...	...	...	Maldives
5,007	6,200	6,072	6,000	59	65	22,000	25,000	123	152	245	245	11,880	12,000	Mali
21	19	6	16	101	80	1,000	1,000	24	48	3,851	5,535	7,000	8,000	Malta
...	...	...	...	...	...	...	...	...	...	...	...	...	...	Marshall Islands
37	30	46	42	39	33	347	250	2	2	756	763	1,000	2,000	Martinique
1,350	1,435	5,067	6,200	...	...	3,800	4,000	97	102	350	350	4,250	5,000	Mauritania
34	29	7	7	12	20	2,200	4,000	25	60	2,500	1,714	4,200	5,000	Mauritius
...	...	...	...	...	...	...	...	...	...	...	...	...	...	Mayotte
32,194	30,293	5,862	5,900	15,715	13,690	240,218	476,000	6,336	9,474	992	1,393	1,066,065	1,666,000	Mexico
...	14	...	...	...	...	...	32	...	185	...	...	...	175	Micronesia
962[1]	416	1,300[1]	974	1,468[1]	705	17,767[1]	14,000	998[1]	550	...	2,321	35,833[1]	32,000	Moldova
...	...	...	...	...	...	...	...	...	...	...	...	...	...	Monaco
2,694	3,500	14,266	14,000	166	19	351	72	320	285	348	320	2,000	340	Mongolia
3,284	2,675	13,528	17,300	9	8	71,200	100,000	929	1,150	521	879	171,000	180,000	Morocco
1,373	1,320	120	125	167	180	21,833	28,000	63	60	170	170	11,333	14,000	Mozambique
9,269	10,964	275	390	2,355	3,914	23,989	44,000	422	612	392	415	35,208	83,000	Myanmar (Burma)
2,104	2,063	3,289	2,100	18	17	1,717	2,200	76	75	401	403	1,000	2,000	Namibia
...	...	...	...	3	3	5	5	...	...	...	...	16	16	Nauru
6,274	7,031	903	900	571	870	12,000	18,000	252	337	366	407	16,133	22,000	Nepal
4,918	4,200	1,663	1,401	13,747	13,140	92,050	106,000	11,198	10,800	6,040	7,200	644,480	660,000	Netherlands, The
1	1	6	7	3	2	125	135	—	—	1,278	1,250	432	1,000	Netherlands Antilles
122	123	3	1	37	40	317	1,000	4	4	600	600	1,367	2,000	New Caledonia
7,987	9,457	57,861	45,800	404	344	9,067	13,000	7,572	12,014	2,835	3,600	46,000	51,000	New Zealand
1,693	1,660	4	4	565	400	4,000	10,000	162	231	797	981	25,500	30,000	Nicaragua

Crops and livestock (continued)

country	grains production ('000 metric tons) 1989–91 average	grains production 2000	grains yield (kg/hectare) 1989–91 average	grains yield 2000	roots and tubers[a] production ('000 metric tons) 1989–91 average	roots and tubers production 2000	roots and tubers yield (kg/hectare) 1989–91 average	roots and tubers yield 2000	pulses[b] production ('000 metric tons) 1989–91 average	pulses production 2000	pulses yield (kg/hectare) 1989–91 average	pulses yield 2000	fruits[c] production ('000 metric tons) 1989–91 average	fruits production 2000	vegetables[d] production ('000 metric tons) 1989–91 average	vegetables production 2000
Niger	2,120	2,738	341	368	180	158	5,570	5,167	312	658	127	172	44	48	274	286
Nigeria	18,100	22,405	1,165	1,212	35,155	64,236	10,370	9,507	1,383	2,158	719	417	6,644	8,900	4,272	7,783
Northern Mariana Islands	...	...	...	...	...	...	...	...	...	...	...	...	...	...	...	...
Norway	1,410	1,322	3,943	3,894	452	446	24,246	24,800	—	—	...	...	100	28	182	144
Oman	5	6	2,124	2,173	5	6	25,208	21,923	...	...	...	...	184	210	155	173
Pakistan	21,038	29,923	1,784	2,401	1,052	2,298	11,467	16,859	1,044	924	553	597	3,871	5,409	3,193	5,042
Palau	...	...	...	...	...	...	...	...	...	...	...	...	...	...	...	...
Panama	336	401	1,884	2,704	66	79	5,901	11,888	9	10	526	442	1,225	1,062	65	162
Papua New Guinea	4	11	2,330	3,981	1,253	1,251	7,270	7,219	2	3	500	526	1,076	1,213	357	387
Paraguay	818	1,266	1,838	2,257	3,479	3,582	15,109	14,312	55	55	959	786	523	533	268	302
Peru	1,983	3,313	2,473	3,116	2,293	4,750	8,066	10,640	107	208	896	1,125	1,922	3,431	918	1,947
Philippines	14,350	16,901	2,018	2,583	2,761	2,704	6,851	6,700	60	58	908	773	8,341	9,804	4,211	4,726
Poland	27,594	22,341	3,231	2,535	33,247	24,232	18,350	19,376	635	305	1,857	2,064	1,792	2,131	5,797	5,700
Portugal	1,673	1,686	2,019	2,737	1,403	1,274	11,596	14,457	51	30	590	574	2,176	1,713	2,063	2,369
Puerto Rico	—	—	7,462	4,000	28	9	6,499	11,246	2	—	569	609	255	179	43	31
Qatar	3	6	2,910	3,418	—	—	9,611	10,375	...	...	...	741	8	18	30	55
Réunion	12	17	5,559	6,724	15	9	11,006	13,043	1	1	1,429	...	44	49	45	68
Romania	18,286	9,594	3,084	1,844	3,159	3,650	10,517	13,129	149	64	889	1,159	2,295	1,947	3,215	4,105
Russia	92,890[1]	64,088	1,612[1]	1,610	36,603[1]	32,597	10,673[1]	10,030	2,880[1]	913	1,383[1]	962	2,989[1]	2,608	10,411[1]	14,809
Rwanda	289	240	1,161	993	1,641	2,124	4,553	4,339	216	231	726	795	3,020	2,272	131	261
St. Kitts and Nevis	...	...	...	...	1	1	3,611	2,861	—	—	1,000	1,000	1	1	—	1
St. Lucia	—	—	699	...	11	11	4,350	3,928	—	—	2,133	2,000	176	128	1	1
St. Vincent and the Grenadines	2	2	3,348	3,333	19	12	4,539	4,525	—	—	1,000	1,000	78	49	3	4
Samoa	...	...	...	...	41	41	5,002	6,164	...	...	...	...	51	43	1	1
San Marino	...	...	...	...	...	...	...	...	...	...	...	...	...	...	...	...
São Tomé and Príncipe	3	2	2,015	2,230	6	33	7,346	9,054	...	...	...	...	10	21	3	6
Saudi Arabia	4,214	2,452	4,177	4,214	59	394	19,121	25,088	7	8	1,832	1,841	832	1,192	1,987	1,821
Senegal	996	963	823	746	67	48	3,990	2,897	19	35	337	314	105	131	197	396
Seychelles	...	...	...	...	...	...	5,000	5,000	...	...	...	...	2	2	2	2
Sierra Leone	566	222	1,224	1,078	139	271	5,220	4,671	38	52	652	673	163	163	189	182
Singapore	...	...	...	...	—	—	13,933	10,000	...	...	...	...	1	—	8	5
Slovakia	3,494[3]	2,201	4,068[3]	2,705	566[3]	419	13,232[3]	15,474	161[3]	58	2,313[3]	2,055	285[3]	254	528[3]	411
Slovenia	486[1]	502	4,131[1]	5,230	379[1]	194	13,756[1]	19,736	71[1]	5	777[1]	1,594	255[1]	206	771[1]	104
Solomon Islands	1	5	...	...	107	134	17,595	16,947	2	4	1,175	1,296	15	16	6	7
Somalia	497	313	715	565	50	76	10,421	10,000	13	15	263	250	271	216	65	73
South Africa	12,734	13,245	2,053	2,630	1,336	1,737	16,611	22,269	146	96	1,178	955	3,744	4,760	2,021	2,270
Spain	19,306	24,602	2,489	3,600	5,334	3,156	19,439	25,370	238	389	755	840	13,503	14,971	11,026	11,822
Sri Lanka	2,370	2,804	2,924	2,370	547	329	8,845	8,213	50	26	780	618	743	834	578	650
Sudan, The	2,771	3,292	497	501	137	169	2,670	2,595	103	253	1,064	1,593	773	973	922	1,134
Suriname	229	175	3,770	3,499	3	5	11,900	12,000	—	—	690	727	75	81	26	21
Swaziland	127	73	1,401	1,299	9	7	1,665	1,872	5	7	569	957	141	99	13	11
Sweden	5,677	6,200	4,594	5,055	1,132	1,310	32,977	37,222	91	140	2,494	2,669	171	94	261	310
Switzerland	1,331	1,138	6,352	6,387	731	584	37,867	42,628	8	11	4,264	3,516	634	727	308	292
Syria	2,601	3,503	668	1,249	407	450	17,543	20,000	131	198	577	684	1,370	1,880	1,690	1,686
Taiwan	...	...	...	...	...	...	...	...	...	...	...	...	...	...	...	...
Tajikistan	256[1]	455	944[1]	1,198	151[1]	250	12,215[1]	12,500	7[1]	9	742[1]	1,948	248[1]	299	623[1]	490
Tanzania	4,138	3,556	1,389	822	8,167	6,498	8,824	5,637	437	433	501	565	2,093	1,874	1,185	1,166
Thailand	23,624	28,262	2,149	2,463	21,775	18,773	14,245	16,268	377	285	751	806	6,371	7,610	2,514	2,782
Togo	505	759	809	955	913	1,376	7,992	7,247	22	52	202	293	49	49	152	131
Tonga	...	...	...	...	99	92	6,551	10,008	...	...	...	...	15	13	20	7
Trinidad and Tobago	17	12	2,816	2,927	10	12	9,757	10,315	3	4	1,460	2,566	62	80	17	25
Tunisia	1,611	1,095	1,115	923	205	290	12,592	10,741	73	93	663	819	670	933	1,477	2,154
Turkey	28,283	26,657	2,065	2,018	4,321	5,476	22,388	25,935	1,946	1,349	885	974	9,117	10,610	17,963	22,099
Turkmenistan	1,038[1]	1,768	2,870[1]	2,619	32[1]	28	4,750[1]	5,620	...	8	...	2,000	158[1]	206	539[1]	363
Tuvalu	...	...	...	...	...	...	...	...	...	...	...	...	1	1	—	—
Uganda	1,597	2,111	1,483	1,539	5,360	7,842	6,335	7,803	493	585	774	568	8,384	10,195	421	549
Ukraine	37,208[1]	23,760	2,957[1]	1,949	19,129[1]	13,037	12,040[1]	8,357	2,840[1]	680	2,300[1]	1,789	2,597[1]	2,561	5,750[1]	6,040
United Arab Emirates	2	1	1,912	...	4	5	19,300	19,464	...	...	...	...	205	378	270	1,129
United Kingdom	22,644	23,983	6,168	7,165	6,333	6,640	35,916	40,151	745	686	3,401	3,757	515	307	3,580	2,996
United States	292,217	343,866	4,580	5,865	18,530	24,025	32,089	41,047	1,623	1,535	1,839	1,879	25,256	32,570	31,092	37,698
Uruguay	1,230	1,817	2,411	3,326	215	172	7,514	11,701	6	6	979	982	394	541	117	147
Uzbekistan	2,281[1]	3,048	1,714[1]	2,281	468[1]	656	10,083[1]	12,148	...	4	...	667	985[1]	1,422	3,760[1]	3,095
Vanuatu	1	...	515	538	49	65	10,139	13,000	...	...	...	...	18	20	8	10
Venezuela	2,037	1,958	2,484	2,938	682	951	8,676	11,314	57	35	585	730	2,579	2,508	514	1,223
Vietnam	20,008	34,484	3,081	4,120	4,758	4,010	7,432	7,700	187	244	639	736	3,096	4,098	3,625	4,849
Virgin Islands (U.S.)	...	...	...	...	...	...	...	...	...	...	...	...	...	...	...	...
West Bank	...	30	...	...	...	17	...	...	...	2	...	...	...	153	...	228
Western Sahara	...	3	...	794	...	...	...	...	...	...	...	...	...	...	...	...
Yemen	693	695	871	693	153	214	12,223	12,661	64	70	1,424	1,207	314	613	536	553
Yugoslavia	7,613[1]	5,238	3,102[1]	2,566	766[1]	690	6,928[1]	6,610	100[1]	107	1,438[1]	1,259	1,391[1]	1,116	1,045[1]	1,106
Zambia	1,467	1,435	1,569	1,570	704	1,084	6,517	6,384	15	15	629	516	105	101	274	270
Zimbabwe	2,391	2,513	1,488	1,406	127	208	4,792	4,856	50	50	694	760	170	200	153	147

livestock														country
cattle		sheep		hogs		chickens		milk[e]		yield		eggs[f]		
stock ('000 head)		stock ('000 head)		stock ('000 head)		stock ('000 head)		production ('000 metric tons)		(kg/animal)		production (metric tons)		
1989–91 average	2000	1989–91 average	2000	1989–91 average	2000	1989–91 average	2000	1989–91 average	2000	1989–91 average	2000	1989–91 average	2000	
1,712	2,217	3,100	4,300	37	39	17,833	20,000	140	168	393	400	9,000	9,000	Niger
14,650	19,830	12,477	20,500	3,319	4,855	122,120	126,000	350	386	239	243	313,000	435,000	Nigeria
...	...	...	...	...	...	...	...	...	...	...	...	...	...	Northern Mariana Islands
959	1,042	2,202	2,400	696	690	4,000	23,000	1,944	1,759	5,854	5,429	51,046	49,000	Norway
137	149	141	180	...	...	3,000	3,000	18	19	420	420	6,000	6,000	Oman
17,677	22,000	25,703	24,100	...	...	78,000	148,000	3,525	8,039	842	1,179	211,000	331,000	Pakistan
...	...	...	...	...	...	...	...	...	...	...	...	...	...	Palau
1,401	1,360	...	...	228	280	8,000	12,000	129	157	1,162	1,309	11,117	14,000	Panama
103	87	4	6	997	1,550	3,000	4,000	—	—	...	100	3,000	4,000	Papua New Guinea
7,985	9,910	422	413	2,443	2,700	15,065	25,000	224	330	1,904	2,399	35,000	68,000	Paraguay
4,126	4,903	12,484	14,400	2,417	2,788	62,406	81,000	788	1,048	1,323	2,015	104,000	163,000	Peru
1,644	2,553	30	30	7,968	10,398	77,000	142,000	15	10	1,036	1,037	297,000	539,000	Philippines
9,875	6,083	3,934	362	20,056	17,122	58,196	50,000	15,560	11,731	3,260	3,890	410,255	425,000	Poland
1,355	1,245	5,531	5,850	2,531	2,330	19,667	28,000	1,500	1,850	3,734	5,256	85,400	110,000	Portugal
595	388	7	8	204	175	11,241	12,000	396	357	4,233	3,933	16,690	15,143	Puerto Rico
10	14	126	215	...	...	2,932	4,000	10	11	1,592	1,600	3,000	4,000	Qatar
20	27	2	2	88	89	6,916	11,000	7	14	627	964	4,117	5,000	Réunion
6,029	3,155	12,675	5,951	12,675	7,972	121,000	72,000	3,450	4,500	1,867	2,727	354,367	300,000	Romania
51,939[1]	27,500	46,998[1]	14,000	31,820[1]	18,300	582,667[1]	340,000	45,088[1]	31,560	...	2,447	2,233,333[1]	1,867,000	Russia
592	725	387	320	117	160	1,292	1,000	85	85	579	739	2,000	2,000	Rwanda
4	4	14	7	2	3	56	70	...	...	...	...	347	300	St. Kitts and Nevis
12	12	16	13	12	15	223	260	1	1	1,396	1,389	528	1,000	St. Lucia
6	6	13	13	10	10	205	200	1	1	1,351	1,370	1,000	1,000	St. Vincent and the Grenadines
24	26	...	...	186	179	356	350	1	1	1,000	1,000	192	200	Samoa
...	...	...	...	...	...	...	...	...	...	...	...	...	...	San Marino
4	4	2	3	3	2	124	290	—	—	...	170	175	315	São Tomé and Príncipe
195	297	6,370	7,576	...	...	76,000	130,000	274	601	6,254	8,035	113,005	136,000	Saudi Arabia
2,616	2,960	3,500	4,300	295	330	19,667	45,000	98	105	360	360	15,000	33,000	Senegal
2	1	...	...	18	18	293	1,000	—	—	...	6	1,000	2,000	Seychelles
333	420	271	365	50	52	5,900	6,000	17	21	250	250	7,000	8,000	Sierra Leone
—	—	—	—	300	190	3,000	2,000	...	...	...	...	17,000	16,000	Singapore
1,030[3]	665	412[3]	340	2,162[3]	1,593	13,321[3]	12,000	1,206[3]	1,099	...	4,467	79,549[3]	65,000	Slovakia
488[1]	471	23[1]	73	574[1]	558	10,420[1]	7,000	569[1]	634	...	3,132	19,712[1]	23,000	Slovenia
11	12	...	...	53	59	144	185	1	1	650	650	288	372	Solomon Islands
3,967	5,100	12,117	13,100	9	4	2,833	3,000	425	530	398	400	2,000	3,000	Somalia
12,920	13,700	32,060	28,700	1,480	1,535	46,000	61,000	2,426	2,667	2,637	2,667	213,000	339,000	South Africa
5,125	6,203	23,800	23,700	16,720	23,682	75,000	128,000	6,100	5,900	3,728	4,820	649,413	522,000	Spain
1,690	1,617	25	12	88	74	9,000	10,000	172	220	271	319	46,033	51,000	Sri Lanka
20,593	37,093	20,179	42,800	...	...	32,371	42,000	2,252	3,072	480	480	33,212	45,000	Sudan, The
91	106	9	12	29	32	8,000	2,000	17	13	1,832	1,857	3,033	5,000	Suriname
712	610	24	30	23	33	1,133	3,000	42	35	274	302	...	1,000	Swaziland
1,704	1,713	408	437	2,243	1,918	11,433	8,000	3,401	3,300	6,097	7,717	116,333	107,000	Sweden
1,845	1,600	392	450	1,793	1,450	5,912	7,000	3,892	3,910	4,954	5,356	38,000	38,000	Switzerland
786	905	14,571	14,500	1	1	14,405	22,000	782	1,150	2,314	2,556	75,133	120,000	Syria
157	...	...	...	8,813	10,509[5]	80,119	101,838[5]	204	318[5]	4,349	4,802[5]	...	...	Taiwan
1,238[1]	1,042	2,110[1]	1,593	491[1]	1	4,029[1]	1,000	472[1]	306	...	593	14,667[1]	1,000	Tajikistan
13,047	14,380	3,551	4,200	320	350	20,567	28,000	516	685	169	207	41,000	58,000	Tanzania
5,513	6,100	161	41	4,766	7,200	109,000	172,000	137	469	1,886	2,231	430,033	515,000	Thailand
247	215	1,164	740	617	850	6,070	8,000	8	7	225	225	6,000	6,000	Togo
11	9	...	...	94	81	221	266	—	—	...	2	287	28	Tonga
55	35	14	12	53	41	10,000	10,000	11	10	1,593	1,552	9,000	9,000	Trinidad and Tobago
626	790	5,935	6,600	6	6	39,367	37,000	393	890	1,420	1,618	52,250	80,000	Tunisia
12,037	11,031	43,195	29,435	10	5	73,181	237,000	8,183	8,800	1,352	1,600	369,080	660,000	Turkey
962[1]	850	5,793[1]	5,600	203[1]	46	6,900[1]	4,000	565[1]	900	...	1,765	14,933[1]	16,000	Turkmenistan
...	...	...	...	12	13	29	27	...	...	...	...	12	12	Tuvalu
4,777	5,966	1,350	1,980	797	970	18,667	25,000	418	511	350	350	15,000	20,000	Uganda
22,597[1]	10,627	6,658[1]	1,060	16,437[1]	10,073	180,352[1]	105,000	18,363[1]	12,400	...	2,283	664,865[1]	477,000	Ukraine
49	110	255	467	...	...	7,000	15,000	5	9	210	157	10,000	13,000	United Arab Emirates
11,980	11,133	29,241	42,261	7,519	6,482	124,076	157,000	14,976	14,461	5,206	6,190	616,000	588,000	United Kingdom
96,316	98,048	11,384	7,215	54,557	59,337	1,333,000	1,720,000	66,423	76,294	6,673	8,388	4,048,000	5,011,000	United States
9,019	10,800	25,359	13,032	217	380	8,000	13,000	980	1,422	1,562	1,755	26,000	37,000	Uruguay
5,273[1]	5,268	8,681[1]	8,917	524[1]	80	26,867[1]	14,000	3,622[1]	3,692	...	1,605	96,833[1]	69,000	Uzbekistan
124	152	...	...	59	62	306	320	2	3	202	203	312	280	Vanuatu
13,311	15,800	551	781	2,801	4,900	60,000	110,000	1,564	1,311	1,285	1,278	119,000	168,000	Venezuela
3,153	4,137	...	...	12,224	20,194	77,228	196,000	36	42	800	800	97,000	165,000	Vietnam
8	8	3	3	3	3	30	35	2	2	2,725	2,703	120	160	Virgin Islands (U.S.)
...	12	...	352	...	...	...	...	...	27	...	35	...	15,000	West Bank
...	...	...	29	...	...	...	...	...	...	...	...	...	...	Western Sahara
1,154	1,283	3,682	4,760	...	...	16,385	28,000	152	172	600	600	18,000	31,000	Yemen
1,925[1]	1,452	2,701[1]	1,917	3,876[1]	4,087	21,920[1]	21,000	1,841[1]	1,825	...	2,100	96,833[1]	76,000	Yugoslavia
2,845	2,373	59	140	296	330	16,033	29,000	77	64	300	300	26,000	46,000	Zambia
6,147	5,550	584	530	300	275	12,000	16,000	440	310	417	310	16,000	21,000	Zimbabwe

[1]1992–94 average. [2]Belgium includes Luxembourg. [3]1993–95 average. [4]Indonesia includes East Timor. [5]1995.

Extractive industries

Extractive industries are generally defined as those exploiting in situ natural resources and include such activities as mining, forestry, fisheries, and agriculture; the definition is often confined, however, to nonrenewable resources only. For the purposes of this table, agriculture is excluded; it is covered in the preceding table.

Extractive industries are divided here into three parts: mining, forestry, and fisheries. These major headings are each divided into two main subheadings, one that treats production and one that treats foreign trade. The production sections are presented in terms of volume except for mining, and the trade sections are presented in terms of U.S. dollars. Volume of production data usually imply output of primary (unprocessed) raw materials only, but, because of the way national statistical information is reported, the data may occasionally include some processed and manufactured materials as well, since these are often indistinguishably associated with the extractive process (sulfur from petroleum extraction, cured or treated lumber, or "processed" fish). This is also the case in the trade sections, where individual national trade nomenclatures may not distinguish some processed and manufactured goods from unprocessed raw materials.

Mining. In the absence of a single international source publication or standard of practice for reporting volume or value of mineral production, single-country sources predominantly have been used to compile mining production figures, supplemented by U.S. Bureau of Mines data, by the United Nations' *National Accounts Statistics* (annual; 2 parts), and by industry sources, especially *Mining Journal's Mining Annual Review*. Each country has its own methods of classifying mining data, which do not always accord with the principal mineral production categories adopted in this table—namely, "metals," "nonmetals," and "energy." The available data have therefore been adjusted to accord better with the definition of each group. Included in the "metal" category are all ferrous and nonferrous metallic ores, concentrates, and scrap; the "nonmetal" group includes all nonmetallic minerals (stone, clay, precious gems, etc.) except the mineral fuels; the last group, "energy," is composed predominantly of the natural hydrocarbon fuels, though it may also include manufactured gas.

The contribution (value) of each national mineral sector to its country's gross domestic product is given, as is the distribution by group of that contribution (to gross domestic product and to foreign trade), although statistics regarding the value of mineral production are less readily available in country sources than those regarding trade or volume of minerals produced. Figures for value added by mineral output, though not always available, were sought first, as they provide the most consistent standard to compare the importance of minerals both within a particular national economy and among national mineral sectors worldwide. Where value added to the gross domestic product was not available, gross value of production or sales was substituted and the exception footnoted. Figures for value of production are reported here in millions of U.S. dollars to permit comparisons to be made from country to country. Comparisons can also be made as to the relative importance of each mineral group within a given country.

Extractive industries

country	mining % of GDP, 1998	year	total ('000,000 U.S.$)	by kind (%) metals[a]	non-metals[b]	energy[c]	trade year	exports total ('000,000 U.S.$)	exports metals[a]	non-metals[b]	energy[c]	imports total ('000,000 U.S.$)	imports metals[a]	non-metals[b]	energy[c]
Afghanistan	...	...	...	...	...	...	1997	0.1	—	100.0	—	...	...	...	...
Albania	...	1994[1]	81.4	46.1	0.8	53.1	1997	16.5	93.9	6.1	—	12.9	—	34.9	65.1
Algeria	23.0	1998	10,895.7	—	—	100.0	1996	8,931.6	—	0.2	99.8	22.4	—	—	100.0
American Samoa	...	1998	...	—	100.0	—	...	...	...	...	...	...	...	...	...
Andorra	...	...	...	...	...	...	...	...	...	...	...	...	...	...	...
Angola	60.9[2]	1997	3,935.1	—	7.7	92.3	1997	212.6	—	90.4	9.6	...	...	...	...
Antigua and Barbuda	1.5	1998	9.0[12]	—	100.0	—	1997	...	...	...	...	...	...	...	...
Argentina	2.4[2]	1997	7,821.8[3]		100.0		1997	2,429.7[4]	—	—	100.0[4]	419.5	65.2	1.6	33.2
Armenia	...	1998	...		100.0		1997	106.9	—	100.0	—	187.2	50.5	49.5	—
Aruba	...	1998	...	—	100.0	—	1997	1.4	—	100.0	—	...	...	...	...
Australia	4.4	1998	15,105.6	...	...	...	1997	17,083.6	40.1	3.6	56.3	3,181.5	3.4	9.0	87.6
Austria	0.5	1995	819.3	2.5	53.5	44.0	1997	484.0[4]	38.5[4]	61.2[4]	0.3[4]	3,055.2	16.7	10.2	73.1
Azerbaijan	...	...	...	...	...	...	1994	...	...	...	...	224.1	—	—	100.0
Bahamas, The	...	1998	...	—	100.0	—	1997	1.2	100.0	—	—	...	...	...	...
Bahrain	13.6	1998	841.2	—	1.5	98.5	1996	2,471.1[6]	0.6[6]	—	99.3[6]	2,002.2	15.8	0.6	83.7
Bangladesh	1.0	1997–98	417.6	—	47.4	52.6	1996	...	...	...	...	80.0	—	77.5	22.5
Barbados	1.0	1998	4.6[3]	—	100.0[3]		1997	0.1	100.0	—	—	8.3	—	43.4	56.6
Belarus	...	1998	...		100.0		1997	175.2	—	92.5	7.5	39.6	—	100.0	—
Belgium	0.3[2]	1997	617.8		100.0		1997	13,490.0	8.2	88.6	3.3	21,328.3	12.4	54.9	32.7
Belize	0.5	1998	2.5	—	100.0	—	1997	...	...	...	...	3.4	—	14.7	85.3
Benin	0.7[5]	1995	14.4[8]	—	100.0[8]		...	...	...	...	...	14.0	—	100.0	—
Bermuda	...	...	...	...	...	...	1997	...	...	...	...	1.7	—	29.4	70.6
Bhutan	2.3[2]	1997	8.5		100.0		1994	2.9	—	82.8	17.2	...	...	...	...
Bolivia	11.1	1998	686.1		49.5	50.5	1997	377.7	72.9	1.1	26.0	17.7	85.9	14.1	—
Bosnia and Herzegovina	...	...	...	...	...	...	1997	2.9	—	—	100.0	...	...	...	...
Botswana	37.6	1997–98	1,950.6	11.4[9]	88.0[9]	0.7[9]	...	10	...	...	...	...	...	...	...
Brazil	0.8[2]	1997	6,760.5	...	...	...	1997	3,454.5	92.4	7.6	—	5,433.9	8.2	4.4	87.4
Brunei	36.7	1998	1,777.6		8.5	91.5	1997	1,970.2[6]	—	—	100.0[6]	9.3	—	100.0	—
Bulgaria	1.4	1998	167.4	...	...	...	1997	120.4	37.7	62.3	—	1,166.2	13.4	3.4	83.2
Burkina Faso	...	1998	...		100.0		...	...	...	...	...	...	...	...	...
Burundi	0.6[2]	1995	6.2	...	...	...	...	...	...	...	...	...	...	...	...
Cambodia	0.3	1998	8.8	—	100.0	...	...	...	...	...	...	...	...	...	...
Cameroon	5.5	1997–98	491.5	—	—	100.0	1996	628.8	—	—	100.0	187.6	16.4	4.0	79.6
Canada	3.7	1998	21,998.8	19.4	12.0	68.6	1997	22,630.2	16.3	3.7	79.9	10,037.9	24.5	6.4	69.1
Cape Verde	0.3[9]	1994	0.9	—	100.0	—	...	...	...	...	...	...	...	...	...
Central African Republic	3.8	1998	39.8[11]		100.0[11]	—	1997	104.1	—	100.0	—	0.8[4]	—	100.0[4]	—
Chad	...	...	...	...	...	...	...	...	...	...	...	...	...	...	...
Chile	8.5	1998	3,555.7		100.0		1997	2,553.3	96.9	3.1	—	1,505.5	4.1	—	95.9
China	...	...	...	...	...	...	1997	5,786.1	2.5	24.5	73.0	10,446.5	32.9	5.6	61.5
Colombia	5.5[4]	1996	4,735.4	...	...	...	1997	3,363.5	0.1	4.2	95.7	86.1	20.0	80.0	—
Comoros	—	1998	...	—	100.0	—	...	...	...	...	...	...	...	...	...
Congo, Dem. Rep. of the	22.8[6]	1995	288.6		100.0		1995	302.7	—	84.5	15.5	3.4	—	100.0	—
Congo, Rep. of the	40.6[13]	1996[13]	978.8[13]	...	...	...	1995	939.5	—	0.3	99.7	5.2	—	48.1	51.9
Costa Rica	...	...	...	...	...	...	1997	5.1	100.0	—	—	123.1[4]	—	7.0[4]	93.0[4]
Côte d'Ivoire	0.2[13]	1998[13]	28.1[13]	...	...	...	1997	132.0	—	100.0	—	489.9[4]	—	3.2[4]	96.8[4]
Croatia	0.4	1998	96.9	...	...	...	1997	135.0	23.1	14.1	62.8	772.7	—	7.3	92.7
Cuba	...	...	...	...	...	...	1997	...	...	...	...	13.3	—	100.0	—
Cyprus	0.3[14]	1998[14]	25.1	—	100.0	—	1997[14]	20.6	46.6	53.4	—	167.9	—	12.9	87.1
Czech Republic	...	...	...	...	...	...	1997	651.0	23.9	11.0	65.1	2,175.5	13.0	4.1	82.9
Denmark	1.4[2]	1997	2,023.8	—	100.0		1997	1,193.7	15.2	6.9	77.8	1,004.3	7.7	18.6	73.7
Djibouti	—	1998	...	—	100.0	—	...	...	...	...	...	...	...	...	...
Dominica	0.9	1998	2.0	—	100.0	—	1996	0.9	—	100.0	—	1.1	—	—	100.0
Dominican Republic	2.0	1998	309.3		100.0		1994	2.7	—	100.0	—	...	...	...	...
East Timor	...	...	...	...	...	...	...	...	...	...	...	...	...	...	...
Ecuador	7.8	1997	1,560.0		6.8[15]	93.2[15]	1997	1,404.8	—	—	100.0	95.0	—	9.4	90.6

Since the data for value of mineral production are obtained mostly from country sources, there is some variation (from a standard calendar year) in the time periods to which the data refer. In addition, the time period for which production data are available does not always correspond with the year for which mineral trade data are available.

The Standard International Trade Classification (SITC), Revision 3, was used to determine the commodity groupings for foreign trade statistics. The actual trade data for these groups is taken largely from the United Nations' *International Trade Statistics Yearbook* (2 vol.) and national sources.

Forestry. Data for the production and trade sections of forestry are based on the Food and Agriculture Organization (FAO) of the United Nations' *Yearbook of Forest Products*. Production of roundwood (all wood obtained in removals from forests) is the principal indicator of the volume of each country's forestry sector; this total is broken down further (as percentages of the roundwood total) into its principal components: fuelwood and charcoal, and industrial roundwood. The latter group was further divided to show its principal component, sawlogs and veneer; lesser categories of industrial roundwood could not be shown for reasons of space. These included pitprops (used in mining, a principal consumer of wood) and pulpwood (used in papermaking and plastics). Value of trade in forest products is given for both imports and exports, although exports alone tend to be the significant indicator for producing countries, while imports of wood are rarely a significant fraction of the trade of most importing countries.

Fisheries. Data for nominal (live weight) catches of fish, crustaceans, mollusks, etc., in all fishing areas (marine areas and inland waters) are taken from the FAO *Yearbook of Fishery Statistics* (*Catches and Landings*). Total catch figures are given in metric tons; the catches in inland waters and marine areas are given as percentages of the total catch, as are the main kinds of catch—fish, crustaceans, and mollusks. The total catch figures exclude marine mammals, such as whales and seals; and such aquatic animal products as corals, sponges, and pearls; but include frogs, turtles, and jellyfish. The subtotals by kind of catch, however, exclude the last group, which do not belong taxonomically to the fish, crustaceans, or mollusks.

Figures for trade in fishery products (including processed products and preparations like oils, meals, and animal feeding stuffs) are taken from the FAO's *Yearbook of Fishery Statistics* (*Commodities*). Value figures for trade in fish products are given for both imports and exports.

The following notes further define the column headings:
a. Includes ferrous and nonferrous metallic ores, concentrates, and scraps, such as iron ore, bauxite and alumina, copper, zinc, gold (except unwrought or semimanufactured), lead, or uranium.
b. Includes natural fertilizers; stone, sand, and aggregate; and pearls, precious and semiprecious stones, worked and unworked.
c. Includes hydrocarbon solids, liquids, and gases.
1 cubic metre = 35.3147 cubic feet
1 metric ton = 1.1023 short tons

forestry						fisheries, 1999								country
production of roundwood, 2000				trade (value, '000 U.S.$), 1999		catch (nominal)						trade (value, '000 U.S.$)		
total ('000 cubic metres)	fuelwood, charcoal (%)	industrial roundwood (%)		exports	imports	total ('000 metric tons)	by source (%)		by kind of catch (%)			exports	imports	
		total	sawlogs, veneer				marine	inland	fish	crustaceans	mollusks			
8,283	78.8	21.2	10.3	...	1,090	1.2	—	100.0	100.0	—	—	...	...	Afghanistan
409	84.5	15.5	15.5	7,063	17,158	2.7	70.3	29.7	90.8	0.7	8.5	4,804	3,965	Albania
2,795	83.9	16.1	2.4	...	375,546	105.7	100.0	—	96.3	3.6	0.1	2,374	13,268	Algeria
...	...	...	...	...	302[2]	0.5	100.0	—	99.6	0.2	0.2	...	...	American Samoa
...	...	...	...	...	6,383	—	—	100.0	100.0	—	—	...	...	Andorra
6,676	83.3	16.7	1.0	1,635	5,124	177.5	96.6	3.4	98.3	1.4	0.3	10,043	14,523	Angola
...	...	...	...	...	4,604	3.2	100.0	—	69.3	29.2	1.4	644	2,373	Antigua and Barbuda
5,741	19.2	80.8	—	224,651	755,695	1,024.8	98.8	1.2	63.1	2.9	34.1	807,042	88,368	Argentina
365[5]	100.0[5]	—	—	...	386	0.4	—	100.0	100.0	—	—	494	3,136	Armenia
...	...	...	...	6	7,321	0.2	100.0	—	100.0	—	—	...	17,753	Aruba
22,938	11.8	88.2	43.5	709,553	1,523,192	216.3	98.6	1.4	61.5	25.8	12.7	899,040	485,072	Australia
13,276	21.5	78.5	60.5	4,085,669	2,318,823	0.4	—	100.0	100.0	—	—	10,689	204,997	Austria
...	...	...	...	206	28,116	4.7	—	100.0	100.0	—	—	3,850	846	Azerbaijan
17	—	100.0	100.0	...	30,414	10.5	100.0	—	16.9	78.5	4.5	69,591	4,400	Bahamas, The
—	—	—	—	...	25,821	10.3	100.0	—	65.5	34.1	0.4	6,925	3,203	Bahrain
33,629	98.1	1.9	0.5	14,405	92,529	924.1	37.0	63.0	96.6	3.4	—	297,585	2,050	Bangladesh
5	—	100.0	100.0	...	35,503	0.3	100.0	—	100.0	—	—	951	11,044	Barbados
6,136	15.1	84.9	51.6	73,918	63,254	0.5	—	100.0	88.9	—	11.1	14,028	54,905	Belarus
4,400	12.5	87.5	58.0	3,734,032[7]	4,136,516[7]	29.9	98.2	1.8	92.9	5.0	2.1	447,598[7]	1,063,195[7]	Belgium
188	67.2	32.8	32.8	3,763	4,003	39.9	100.0	—	64.3	5.4	30.3	21,163	1,724	Belize
6,140	94.6	5.4	0.6	931	12,324	38.5	22.2	77.8	80.1	19.9	—	1,928	3,457	Benin
...	...	...	...	...	...	0.5	100.0	—	91.1	8.9	—	...	7,569	Bermuda
1,751	97.4	2.6	1.0	156	2,159	0.3	—	100.0	100.0	—	—	...	...	Bhutan
1,906	72.7	27.3	26.3	25,409	40,384	6.1	—	100.0	100.0	—	—	4	2,938	Bolivia
40	100.0	100.0	100.0	72,219	23,986	2.5	—	100.0	100.0	—	—	...	9,781	Bosnia and Herzegovina
1,702	93.8	6.2	—	...	15,410	2.0	—	100.0	100.0	—	—	54	5,218	Botswana
197,897	57.6	42.4	23.6	2,579,776	811,923	655.0	73.3	26.7	90.6	8.7	0.6	138,232	289,808	Brazil
296	26.7	73.3	69.6	...	8,426	3.2	99.2	0.8	96.7	2.2	1.1	184	8,881	Brunei
4,766	44.2	55.8	34.1	75,289	77,741	10.6	76.6	23.4	64.0	—	36.0	5,774	13,307	Bulgaria
11,095	95.4	4.6	—	...	14,780	7.6	—	100.0	100.0	—	—	5	1,674	Burkina Faso
1,799	83.9	16.1	12.3	...	1,700	9.2	—	100.0	100.0	—	—	334	8	Burundi
8,157	87.3	12.7	5.0	35,010	8,910	269.1	14.2	85.8	98.0	1.3	0.7	30,525	2,796	Cambodia
15,279	82.0	18.0	11.6	386,415	18,650	95.0	63.2	36.8	99.6	0.4	—	6,152	19,783	Cameroon
185,659	2.6	97.4	78.9	25,469,746	3,777,382	1,021.9	96.0	4.0	62.5	26.2	11.4	2,617,759	1,338,973	Canada
...	...	...	...	...	2,519	10.4	100.0	—	99.6	0.4	—	1,852	1,013	Cape Verde
3,548	75.7	24.3	15.6	46,659	...	15.0	—	100.0	100.0	—	—	61	448	Central African Republic
1,969	61.4	38.6	0.7	116	1,650	84.0	—	100.0	100.0	—	—	...	28	Chad
27,972	38.6	61.4	42.1	1,530,190	185,022	5,050.5	100.0	—	97.1	0.8	2.1	1,696,819	54,569	Chile
291,330[12]	65.6[12]	34.4[12]	19.1[12]	6,778,898[12]	25,536,650[12]	17,240.0	98.3	1.7	69.9	17.6	12.5	2,959,530	1,127,412	China
17,845	95.4	4.6	4.5	78,486	316,615	117.9	75.6	24.4	94.8	5.0	0.2	183,668	71,028	Colombia
9	—	100.0	100.0	...	185	12.2	—	100.0	100.0	—	—	1	774	Comoros
50,754	92.7	7.3	0.5	20,754	3,968	208.4	1.9	98.1	99.8	0.2	—	431	41,905	Congo, Dem. Rep. of the
3,243	80.1	19.9	8.5	75,946	1,769	43.7	41.7	58.3	86.0	5.3	8.7	1,720	18,631	Congo, Rep. of the
5,397	69.0	31.0	25.9	20,837	240,616	25.7	90.4	9.6	96.1	3.6	0.3	148,321	25,359	Costa Rica
13,396	76.9	23.1	16.3	225,923	45,038	76.0	82.9	17.1	98.7	1.2	0.1	132,249	162,354	Côte d'Ivoire
3,486	31.4	68.6	54.9	229,147	290,892	19.3	97.9	2.1	93.0	1.5	5.5	34,845	34,825	Croatia
1,593	74.5	25.5	8.0	60	24,509	67.3	93.1	6.9	61.4	22.7	15.9	93,296	22,484	Cuba
25	26.4	73.6	579.7	2,127	37,192	5.3	98.7	1.3	93.8	2.8	3.4	4,343	31,891	Cyprus
14,441	6.5	93.5	55.5	868,057	667,290	4.2	—	100.0	100.0	—	—	25,922	73,795	Czech Republic
3,086	32.4	67.6	42.8	398,653	1,329,135	1,405.0	100.0	—	92.4	0.8	6.9	2,884,334	1,771,500	Denmark
—	—	—	—	...	4,475	0.4	100.0	—	100.0	—	—	130	1,253	Djibouti
...	...	...	...	...	8,358	1.2	100.0	—	100.0	—	—	...	1,595	Dominica
562	98.9	1.1	0.6	578	211,782	8.5	91.6	8.4	74.2	10.4	15.4	700	53,102	Dominican Republic
...	...	...	...	...	...	0.5	100.0	—	98.4	1.4	0.2	...	...	East Timor
11,340	47.8	0.1	45.6	72,103	224,328	497.9	99.9	0.1	99.6	0.4	—	954,471	5,060	Ecuador

Extractive industries (continued)

country	% of GDP, 1998	mineral production (value added) year	total ('000,000 U.S.$)	metals[a]	non-metals[b]	energy[c]	trade year	exports total ('000,000 U.S.$)	metals[a]	non-metals[b]	energy[c]	imports total ('000,000 U.S.$)	metals[a]	non-metals[b]	energy[c]
Egypt	9.8[9]	1994	5,151.3	—	1.0	99.0	1997	704.6	—	5.2	94.8	381.9	40.7	19.2	40.1
El Salvador	0.4	1998	47.6	100.0	—	—	1997	...	...	...	...	151.9	—	5.4	94.6
Equatorial Guinea	61.3	1998	279.6	—	—	100.0	...	...	...	...	...	...	...	...	...
Eritrea	0.1	1998	0.5	—	100.0	—	...	...	...	...	...	...	...	...	...
Estonia	1.0	1998	54.2	—	—	100.0	1997	76.5	79.0	—	21.0	113.1	27.9	20.2	52.0
Ethiopia	0.5	1997–98	33.3	—	100.0	—	1995	...	...	...	...	68.4	—	—	100.0
Faroe Islands	0.2[4]	1996	1.7	...	...	...	...	...	...	...	...	...	...	...	...
Fiji	3.4[4]	1996	42.5	—	100.0	—	1994	0.8	100.0	—	—	5.8	—	41.4	58.6
Finland	0.2	1998	307.4	—	100.0	—	1997	295.9	64.2	33.1	2.8	3,383.4	28.5	8.5	63.1
France	0.8[6]	1995	11,521.0	4.8	14.3	81.0	1997	2,335.7	46.6	32.5	20.9	20,162.7	9.2	5.2	85.5
French Guiana	...	1998	...	—	100.0	—	...	...	...	...	...	...	...	...	...
French Polynesia	...	...	...	...	...	...	1997	191.4	—	100.0	—	...	...	...	...
Gabon	41.8[4]	1996	2,382.8	4.0	—	96.0	1996	2,621.1	2.4	—	97.6	6.7	—	50.7	49.3
Gambia, The	—	1998	...	—	100.0	—	1995	...	...	...	...	1.4	—	—	100.0
Gaza Strip	...	...	...	...	...	...	...	...	...	...	...	...	...	...	...
Georgia	...	...	...	...	...	...	...	...	...	...	...	...	...	...	...
Germany	...	...	...	...	...	...	1997	5,631.4	43.6	21.0	35.3	30,568.8	16.3	5.6	78.1
Ghana	5.2	1998	388.6	—	100.0	—	1997	225.2	—	100.0	—	56.5	100.0	—	—
Greece	0.6[2]	1997	707.9	...	...	...	1997	310.3	40.9	35.9	23.2	1,393.2	6.9	7.2	85.9
Greenland	...	...	...	...	...	...	1997	...	...	...	...	1.6	—	100.0	—
Grenada	1.4	1998	1.3	—	100.0	—	1996	...	...	...	...	2.4	—	25.0	75.0
Guadeloupe	...	1998	...	—	100.0	—	...	...	...	...	...	...	...	...	...
Guam	...	1998	...	—	100.0	—	...	...	...	...	...	...	...	...	...
Guatemala	0.6	1998	30.0	...	...	...	1997	102.9	—	6.2	93.8	172.1	—	—	100.0
Guernsey	...	...	...	...	...	...	...	...	...	...	...	...	...	...	...
Guinea	15.7	1998	645.4[17]	—	100.0[17]	—	1997	396.7	80.3	19.7	—	...	...	...	...
Guinea-Bissau	...	1998	...	—	100.0	—	...	...	...	...	...	...	...	...	...
Guyana	13.6	1998	98.0	—	100.0	—	1997	94.3	100.0	—	—	...	...	...	...
Haiti	0.2	1998	1.8	—	100.0	—	...	...	...	...	...	...	...	...	...
Honduras	1.8	1998	82.3	—	100.0	—	1997	30.6	100.0	—	—	10.1	—	—	100.0
Hong Kong	0.02	1998	39.1	—	100.0	—	1997	2,264.8	27.2	72.8	—	4,639.9	12.9	75.8	11.2
Hungary	0.4[2]	1997	181.5	15.6	26.5	57.9	1997	136.5	99.6	—	0.4	1,747.1	1.9	3.5	94.6
Iceland	...	1998	...	—	100.0	—	1997	19.7	34.0	66.0	—	50.7	68.6	21.5	9.9
India	1.0	1996–97	3,268.9	...	...	...	1997	5,168.2	13.3	86.2	0.5	10,499.3[4]	7.8[4]	31.2[4]	61.0[4]
Indonesia	12.9	1998	12,704.4	—	34.7	65.3	1997	13,660.2	12.7	0.9	86.4	2,138.5	16.9	14.5	68.6
Iran	7.2	1998–99	13,441.8	—	9.1	90.9	1995	18,525.9	1.0	0.4	98.6	1,271.4	17.5	7.5	75.0
Iraq	...	...	...	...	...	...	...	...	...	...	...	...	...	...	...
Ireland	...	...	...	...	...	...	1997	538.5	75.1	16.5	8.4	825.7	14.4	12.9	72.7
Isle of Man	...	1998	...	—	100.0	—	...	...	...	...	...	...	...	...	...
Israel	...	...	...	...	...	...	1997	6,948.8	0.5	99.5	—	7,117.3	0.2	73.3	26.5
Italy	...	...	...	...	...	...	1997	851.4	34.6	57.2	8.2	16,573.7	15.0	9.3	75.7
Jamaica	4.5	1998	310.3	97.2	2.8	—	1997	682.4	100.0	—	—	105.8	—	—	100.0
Japan	0.2[4]	1996	9,863.9	...	...	...	1997	1,315.4	44.0	56.0	—	67,595.7	12.8	5.8	81.4
Jersey	...	...	...	...	...	...	...	...	...	...	...	...	...	...	...
Jordan	3.3	1998	239.3	—	100.0	—	1997	353.6	5.0	95.0	—	416.7[6]	0.6[6]	8.8[6]	90.6[6]
Kazakhstan	...	...	...	...	...	...	1996	837.9	18.9	12.8	68.4	170.9	29.9	25.8	44.3
Kenya	0.2[6]	1995	14.1	—	100.0	—	1997	40.4	—	100.0	—	227.3[4]	—	2.6[4]	97.4[4]
Kiribati	...	...	...	...	...	...	1995	...	...	...	...	0.1	—	100.0	—
Korea, North	...	...	...	...	...	...	1997	90.6	30.8	36.9	32.3	52.7[6]	—	36.1[6]	63.9[6]
Korea, South	0.4	1998	1,141.7	...	...	...	1997	238.6	13.9	53.9	32.2	23,311.9[4]	12.8[4]	3.0[4]	84.2[4]
Kuwait	39.5[6]	1995	10,513.4	—	—	100.0	1997	14,130.4	0.2[4]	—	99.8[4]	60.7	—	100.0	—
Kyrgyzstan	...	...	...	...	...	...	1996	15.8	75.9	—	24.1	118.2	2.5	4.8	92.7
Laos	0.4	1998	5.8	—	100.0	—	...	...	...	...	...	...	...	...	...
Latvia	0.5	1998	116.4	—	100.0	—	1997	32.3	85.1	—	14.9	148.9	13.7	8.1	78.2
Lebanon	...	...	...	...	...	...	1997	130.5	31.0	69.0	—	132.8	—	100.0	—
Lesotho	0.01[4]	1996	0.1	—	100.0	—	[10]	...	...	...	...	14.8	—	100.0	—
Liberia	2.4	1998	8.6	—	100.0	—	1997	15.7	100.0	—	—	...	...	...	...
Libya	25.8[4]	1996	8,441.7	—	7.1	92.9	1997	9,451.2[6]	—	—	100.0[6]	51.2	100.0	—	—
Liechtenstein	...	...	...	...	...	...	...	...	...	...	...	...	...	...	...
Lithuania	0.5	1998	49.3	—	33.9[2]	66.1[2]	1997	130.7	48.7	—	51.3	850.6	2.4	7.0	90.6
Luxembourg	0.2	1998	24.8	—	100.0	—	[7]	...	...	...	...	...	...	...	...
Macau	...	...	...	...	...	...	1997	...	...	...	...	17.3	—	20.8	79.2
Macedonia	...	...	...	...	...	...	1995	29.5	68.1	31.9	—	41.8	6.7	39.5	53.8
Madagascar	0.3[9]	1994	5.2	—	100.0	—	1997	26.6	40.6	59.4	—	79.5	—	—	100.0
Malawi	1.0[9]	1994	12.8	...	...	...	1995	...	...	...	...	5.1	—	62.7	37.3
Malaysia	7.9	1998	3,675.2[3]	...	...	...	1996	5,509.7	2.4	2.3	95.3	1,175.0	43.1	32.2	24.7
Maldives	1.6	1998	2.2	—	100.0	—	...	...	...	...	...	...	...	...	...
Mali	5.5	1998	81.7	—	100.0	—	1997	7.0	—	100.0	—	...	...	...	...
Malta	...	1998	...	—	100.0	—	1996	3.5[6]	97.9[6]	2.1[6]	—	10.2	—	100.0	—
Marshall Islands	0.3[6]	1995	0.3	—	100.0	—	...	...	...	...	...	...	...	...	...
Martinique	...	1998	...	—	100.0	—	1995	4.1	19.4	38.3	42.3	102.5	—	—	100.0
Mauritania	9.6[2]	1997	105.9	—	100.0	—	1997	301.6	100.0	—	—	...	...	...	...
Mauritius	0.1	1998	5.6	—	100.0	—	1996	56.2	—	73.8	26.2	56.2	—	73.8	26.2
Mayotte	...	...	...	...	...	...	...	...	...	...	...	...	...	...	...
Mexico	1.2	1998	5,128.4	...	...	...	1997	11,181.6	4.8	2.3	93.0	1,715.3	39.7	25.2	35.1
Micronesia	...	...	...	...	...	...	...	...	...	...	...	...	...	...	...
Moldova	...	1998	...	—	100.0	—	1997	18.7[6]	100.0[6]	—	—	147.5	—	—	100.0
Monaco	...	...	...	...	...	...	...	...	...	...	...	...	...	...	...
Mongolia	...	...	...	...	...	...	1996	254.1	90.9	9.1	—	...	...	...	...
Morocco	2.2[2]	1997	746.5	...	...	...	1997	751.1	23.6	76.4	—	1,449.6	—	11.3	88.7
Mozambique	...	...	...	...	...	...	1996	8.4	72.6	27.4	—	3.3	—	100.0	—
Myanmar (Burma)	0.4	1998–99	1,107.3	...	...	...	1997	39.0	—	100.0	—	...	...	...	...
Namibia	11.7[2]	1997	382.8	—	100.0	—	[10]	...	...	...	...	...	...	...	...
Nauru	...	1998	...	—	100.0	—	1997	151.6	—	100.0	—	...	...	...	...
Nepal	0.5	1998–99	26.8	—	100.0	—	1995	...	...	...	...	9.1	51.6	—	48.4

forestry						fisheries, 1999								country
production of roundwood, 2000				trade (value, '000 U.S.$), 1999		catch (nominal)						trade (value, '000 U.S.$)		
total ('000 cubic metres)	fuelwood, charcoal (%)	industrial roundwood (%)		exports	imports	total ('000 metric tons)	by source (%)		by kind of catch (%)			exports	imports	
		total	sawlogs, veneer				marine	inland	fish	crustaceans	mollusks			
2,883	95.4	4.6	—	11,855	794,951	380.5	40.8	59.2	94.5	4.1	1.4	1,442	153,061	Egypt
5,170	87.4	12.6	12.6	14,360	124,786	15.2	83.9	16.1	24.8	71.1	4.1	33,596	6,640	El Salvador
811	55.1	44.9	44.9	89,885	...	7.0	84.3	15.7	90.8	7.2	2.0	2,565	2,508	Equatorial Guinea
2,285	99.9	0.1	0.1	...	6,833	7.0	100.0	—	98.7	1.1	0.2	973	54	Eritrea
8,910	18.4	81.6	32.0	391,529	112,763	111.8	97.2	2.8	88.9	11.1	—	77,582	30,951	Estonia
89,925	97.3	2.7	—	...	8,894	15.9	—	100.0	100.0	—	—	...	42	Ethiopia
...	...	...	...	221	4,162	358.0	100.0	—	94.1	4.2	1.7	436,000	15,372	Faroe Islands
483	7.7	92.3	40.6	18,189	8,189	36.7	84.7	15.3	56.2	3.4	40.3	22,266	17,294	Fiji
54,263	7.6	92.4	47.9	10,925,450	887,491	160.6	77.1	22.9	99.9	0.1	—	21,493	118,244	Finland
50,170	22.0	78.0	52.8	5,683,978	7,492,308	578.1	99.2	0.8	86.4	3.5	10.1	1,107,169	3,280,940	France
120	49.8	50.2	42.6	2,481	2,424	7.7	100.0		45.5	54.5		40,495[2]	5,136[2]	French Guiana
...	...	...	...	...	22,201	12.4	99.6	0.4	99.5	0.4	0.1	2,263	6,891	French Polynesia
5,397	48.6	51.4	51.4	380,793	4,799	52.9	84.9	15.1	94.2	5.4	0.4	13,148	6,876	Gabon
618	81.8	18.2	17.2	...	1,416	30.0	91.7	8.3	97.9	1.8	0.3	4,643	848	Gambia, The
...	...	...	...	...	...	3.6	100.0	—	88.1	6.3	5.7	...	...	Gaza Strip
...	...	...	...	11,952	5,749	1.5	93.3	6.7	100.0	—	—	208	2,471	Georgia
37,634	6.8	93.2	62.2	9,923,976	10,776,915	238.9	90.4	9.6	92.0	8.0	—	966,300	2,288,523	Germany
21,907	94.4	5.6	5.2	187,175	24,016	492.8	84.9	15.1	99.1	0.9	—	95,813	20,321	Ghana
2,171	63.3	36.7	31.5	77,993	737,282	136.7	84.5	15.5	78.8	2.5	18.7	278,208	308,553	Greece
—	—	—	—	77	7,179	160.3	100.0	—	48.8	51.2	—	261,255	1,412	Greenland
...	...	...	...	—	5,167	1.6	100.0	—	95.2	4.4	0.4	3,530	2,534	Grenada
15	98.0	2.0	2.0	...	30,639	9.2	100.0	—	92.9	1.6	5.5	266[2]	30,393[2]	Guadeloupe
...	...	...	...	...	...	0.2	100.0	—	98.7	0.4	0.9	...	...	Guam
13,300	96.2	3.8	3.8	17,449	137,727	11.0	36.7	63.3	71.8	28.0	0.2	28,148	6,794	Guatemala
...	...	...	...	...	...	[16]	[16]	[16]	[16]	[16]	[16]	...	...	Guernsey
8,651	92.5	7.5	1.6	6,024	4,542	87.1	95.4	4.6	98.1	0.5	1.5	22,131	14,490	Guinea
592	71.3	28.7	6.8	610	71,424	5.0	96.0	4.0	81.3	2.4	16.3	6,318	487	Guinea-Bissau
467	2.4	97.6	93.1	36,047	3,239	53.8	98.9	1.1	77.7	22.3	—	34,461	475	Guyana
6,501	96.3	3.7	3.4	...	13,221	5.0	90.0	10.0	86.0	5.0	9.0	9,264	7,990	Haiti
7,413	88.5	11.5	11.5	43,309	59,836	7.2	98.6	1.4	53.7	21.8	24.4	97,207	14,805	Honduras
21[5]	100.0[5]	—	—	2,508,240[5]	3,101,116[5]	127.8	100.0	—	90.4	3.8	5.9	383,398	1,593,661	Hong Kong
5,902	44.0	56.0	23.4	353,145	618,345	7.5	—	100.0	97.6	—	2.4	6,948	39,552	Hungary
—	—	—	—	648	65,695	1,736.3	100.0	—	96.7	2.6	0.7	1,379,379	80,693	Iceland
302,794	92.1	7.9	6.1	54,971	789,321	3,316.8	79.2	20.8	89.3	7.9	2.8	1,019,579	20,188	India
190,601	83.5	16.5	13.0	4,757,769	947,593	4,149.4	92.9	7.1	90.9	6.6	2.6	1,527,092	86,555	Indonesia
1,151	16.5	83.5	26.9	...	201,165	387.2	63.0	37.0	97.3	1.2	1.5	23,945	58,002	Iran
177	66.7	33.3	14.1	...	4,341	24.6	53.2	46.8	100.0	—	—	...	1,277	Iraq
2,673	2.7	97.3	59.4	237,008	730,167	285.9	98.9	1.1	90.0	7.4	2.6	343,826	115,853	Ireland
...	...	...	...	...	...	2.6	100.0	—	3.6	9.0	87.3	...	...	Isle of Man
113	11.5	88.5	31.9	34,467	695,578	5.9	63.5	36.5	94.8	3.2	2.0	8,496	129,891	Israel
9,329	60.9	39.1	22.1	2,581,755	7,096,128	294.2	98.2	1.8	59.0	6.0	35.1	356,976	2,728,568	Italy
706	60.0	40.0	18.7	...	71,424	8.5	94.7	5.3	79.1	4.8	16.1	13,905	32,487	Jamaica
19,031	1.4	98.6	70.4	1,729,858	12,348,306	5,176.5	98.6	1.4	77.0	3.7	19.3	719,839	14,748,712	Japan
...	...	...	...	...	...	3.6[16]	100.0[16]	—[16]	25.7[16]	67.3[16]	7.0[16]	...	...	Jersey
11	63.6	36.4	—	5,420	104,204	0.5	31.4	68.6	100.0	—	—	1,231	21,020	Jordan
315[5]	100.0	—	—	598	48,398	25.8	—	100.0	100.0	—	—	12,257	11,903	Kazakhstan
29,908	93.4	6.6	1.5	2,064	38,124	205.3	3.2	96.8	99.5	0.4	0.2	32,415	5,339	Kenya
...	...	...	...	...	769[5]	48.2	100.0	—	97.0	—	3.0	5,611	299	Kiribati
7,000	78.6	21.4	14.3	15,192	8,781	210.0	90.5	9.5	95.2	—	4.8	71,535	2,579	Korea, North
1,722	1.6	98.4	36.1	1,515,287	2,967,578	2,119.7	99.7	0.3	64.0	4.4	31.5	1,393,428	1,140,022	Korea, South
...	...	...	...	13	97,708	6.3	100.0	—	88.5	11.5	—	4,721	22,111	Kuwait
42[5]	74.5[5]	25.5[5]	21.9[5]	225	9,892	—	100.0	—	100.0	—	—	...	2,287	Kyrgyzstan
4,869	82.2	17.8	15.1	26,657	1,704	30.0	—	100.0	100.0	—	—	99	1,157	Laos
14,488	11.6	88.4	58.7	600,131	47,946	125.4	99.5	0.5	97.5	2.5	—	51,849	36,097	Latvia
412	98.3	1.7	1.7	4,885	166,234	3.6	99.4	0.6	94.4	3.5	2.1	...	19,863	Lebanon
1,594	100.0	—	—	...	...	0.03	—	100.0	100.0	—	—	18	18	Lesotho
3,037	88.9	11.1	5.2	24,492	1,635	15.5	74.1	25.9	97.6	0.2	2.2	64	1,412	Liberia
652	82.2	17.8	9.7	...	33,260	32.5	100.0	—	100.0	—	—	32,654	12,561	Libya
13[5]	30.8[5]	69.2[5]	69.2[5]	...	...	—	...	...	...	...	...	...	...	Liechtenstein
5,346	22.4	77.6	52.4	171,231	113,279	33.6	94.9	5.1	87.6	12.4	—	33,560	52,499	Lithuania
259	6.9	93.1	43.6	[7]	[7]	—	100.0	...	...	...	...	[7]	[7]	Luxembourg
...	...	...	...	1,841	14,022	1.5	100.0	...	68.0	29.3	2.7	2,852	13,236	Macau
1,047	83.6	16.4	15.7	9,093	150,166	0.1	—	100.0	100.0	—	—	129	9,994	Macedonia
10,359	98.9	1.1	0.8	23,784	5,061	131.6	77.2	22.8	89.5	0.9	9.5	101,061	5,661	Madagascar
9,964	94.8	5.2	1.3	688	5,265	45.4	—	100.0	100.0	—	—	302	236	Malawi
29,461	26.2	73.8	68.6	3,114,963	1,000,476	1,251.8	99.7	0.3	78.3	8.5	13.2	299,437	258,747	Malaysia
...	...	...	...	14	4,220	133.5	100.0	—	99.6	—	0.4	38,907	...	Maldives
6,597	93.7	6.3	0.1	1,648	8,731	98.5	—	100.0	100.0	—	—	378	1,211	Mali
...	...	...	...	—	62,831	1.0	100.0	—	95.7	2.3	1.9	6,751	19,442	Malta
...	...	...	...	...	1,923	0.4	100.0	—	100.0	—	—	1,482	120	Marshall Islands
12	83.3	16.7	16.7	110	22,864	5.0	100.0	—	98.0	2.0	—	168[2]	38,658[2]	Martinique
16	62.5	37.5	6.3	...	6,000	47.8	89.5	10.5	64.7	—	35.2	99,348	524	Mauritania
25	48.0	52.0	28.0	3,741	67,773	12.0	100.0	—	97.2	0.3	2.5	38,558	32,642	Mauritius
...	...	...	...	...	...	1.5	100.0	—	100.0	—	—	3[2]	161[2]	Mayotte
24,122	67.1	32.9	27.0	281,218	2,106,097	1,202.2	92.4	7.6	80.6	7.7	11.7	649,787	125,723	Mexico
...	...	...	...	...	2,110	11.9	100.0	—	99.6	0.2	0.2	459	3,280	Micronesia
58	50.6	49.4	7.7	3,303	23,350	0.5	—	100.0	100.0	—	—	1,381	2,763	Moldova
...	...	...	...	...	...	0.004	100.0	—	100.0	—	—	...	...	Monaco
631	29.5	70.5	70.5	6,289	2,944	0.5	—	100.0	100.0	—	—	232	33	Mongolia
1,123	49.2	50.8	15.7	74,985	336,920	745.4	99.7	0.3	83.2	0.1	16.7	750,764	10,509	Morocco
18,043	92.7	7.3	0.7	14,072	10,075	35.6	69.8	30.2	100.0	—	—	76,861	10,341	Mozambique
22,574	85.2	14.8	10.4	239,712	18,874	851.6	84.8	15.2	98.7	1.3	0.1	158,560	559	Myanmar (Burma)
[19]	[19]	[19]	[19]	...	36,449	299.2	99.5	0.5	91.3	8.4	0.3	344,017	...	Namibia
...	...	...	...	235	205[5]	0.3	—	100.0	100.0	—	—	...	...	Nauru
21,962	97.2	2.8	2.8	1,199	2,572	12.8	—	100.0	100.0	—	—	269	261	Nepal

Extractive industries (continued)

country	mining % of GDP, 1998	mineral production (value added) year	total ('000,000 U.S.$)	by kind (%) metals[a]	non-metals[b]	energy[c]	trade (value) year	exports total ('000,000 U.S.$)	by kind (%) metals[a]	non-metals[b]	energy[c]	imports total ('000,000 U.S.$)	by kind (%) metals[a]	non-metals[b]	energy[c]
Netherlands, The	2.7[6]	1995[3]	9,620.1[3]	...	...	...	1997	6,275.9	19.2	8.5	72.3	12,803.2	12.5	5.9	81.6
Netherlands Antilles	...	1998	...	—	100.0	—	1995	901.5	...	0.1	99.9	900.5	—	—	100.0
New Caledonia	10.7[2]	1997	352.1	100.0	—	—	1997	208.9	100.0	—	—	12.9	—	—	100.0
New Zealand	...	1996	...	...	...	...	1996	110.9	31.3	0.4	68.3	854.0	21.1	13.5	65.5
Nicaragua	1.6	1998	34.0	—	100.0	—	1997	4.0	100.0	—	—	130.0	—	4.6	95.4
Niger	3.5[9]	1994	62.5	—	100.0	—	...	...	...	...	...	...	...	...	...
Nigeria	26.0	1998	33,716.8	—	0.5	99.5	1995	11,131.5	—	—	100.0	19.9	1.5	98.5	...
Northern Mariana Islands															
Norway	10.9	1998	16,068.2	—	1.8	98.2	1997	24,255.2	0.4	1.0	98.6	1,820.3	73.2	11.3	15.5
Oman	40.6[2]	1997	6,361.2	—	0.7	99.3	1996	5,768.3	—	0.1	99.9	70.7	78.8	21.2	—
Pakistan	0.5	1997–98	301.4	...	...	...	1997	57.3	—	1.4	98.6	338.9	50.5	7.5	42.0
Palau	0.1	1998	0.1	—	100.0	—	...	...	...	...	...	...	...	...	...
Panama	0.2	1998	10.5	—	100.0	—	1996	6.7	100.0	...	...	324.5	—	—	100.0
Papua New Guinea	26.0	1998	975.2	—	64.0	36.0	1995	1,123.1	48.0	—	52.0	...	...	...	...
Paraguay	0.3	1998	29.2	—	100.0	—	1996	...	...	...	...	124.9	—	66.9	33.1
Peru	10.9	1998	2,378.8	—	67.9[6, 20]	32.1[6]	1997	1,150.6	79.1	0.1	20.8	564.2	0.4	—	99.6
Philippines	0.7	1998	489.1	57.7[6]	41.3[6]	1.0[6]	1997	567.7	55.4	25.5	19.1	4,078.1	14.2	4.1	81.7
Poland	2.9	1998	4,613.0	—	...	...	1997	1,400.6[4]	-7.0[4]	11.6[4]	81.4[4]	3,751.2	11.7	6.5	81.8
Portugal	0.5[6]	1995	529.3	40.2	59.6	0.2	1997	391.8	57.0	35.6	7.5	2,369.2	0.7	7.7	91.6
Puerto Rico	...	...	...				...	...							
Qatar	38.1[2]	1997	3,502.7[3]	...	...	...	1995	3,000.3	—	0.1	99.9	51.3[9]	75.3[9]	24.7[9]	—
Réunion	...	1998	...	—	100.0	—	1995	0.9	100.0	...	...	15.0	—	—	100.0
Romania	3.3[9]	1994	990.9	—	16.1	83.9	1997	75.6	62.6	37.4	—	1,723.1[9]	9.7[9]	3.7[9]	86.6[9]
Russia	...	1997	...	...	...	...	1997	32,522.7	5.6	1.0	93.4	560.0[6]	60.2[6]	16.9[6]	23.0[6]
Rwanda	0.06	1998	1.2	...	...	...	...	...	...	...	...	...	...	...	...
St. Kitts and Nevis	0.3[6]	1995	0.6	—	100.0	—	1997	...	...	...	...	2.1	—	33.3	66.7
St. Lucia	0.5	1998	2.6	—	100.0	—	1996	...	...	...	...	5.1	—	49.0	51.0
St. Vincent	0.3	1998	0.9	—	100.0	—	1997	1.6	—	18.8	81.3	1.6[6]	—	18.8[6]	81.3[6]
Samoa	...	...					...								
San Marino	...	...					...								
São Tomé and Príncipe	...	1998	—	—	100.0	—	...	...	...	...	...	...	...	...	...
Saudi Arabia	37.2[2]	1997	54,352.5	—	1.1	98.9	1997	50,116.9[2]	0.1[2]	—	99.9[2]	136.7	88.6	11.4	—
Senegal	0.2	1998	6.3	—	100.0	—	1995	55.8	7.3	92.7	—	102.6	—	13.5	86.5
Seychelles	...	1998	—	—	100.0	—	1996	...	...	...	...	0.5	—	100.0	—
Sierra Leone	16.8[22]	1994–95	117.7	—	100.0	—	1995	16.7	25.4	74.6	—	0.6	—	100.0	—
Singapore	0.02	1998	14.3	—	100.0	—	1997	787.1	31.0	41.7	27.3	8,895.9	0.7	9.0	90.3
Slovakia	0.9	1998	178.8	...	...	...	1997	68.5	28.0	72.0	—	1,106.3	8.9	4.1	87.0
Slovenia	1.0[2]	1997	182.6	...	...	...	1997	28.6	100.0	—	—	386.4	23.4	17.1	59.4
Solomon Islands	...	1998	...	—	100.0[23]	—	1996	...	...	...	...	2.0	—	—	100.0
Somalia	...	...													
South Africa	6.5	1998	8,003.2	...	...	...	1997[10]	7,936.4	23.4	51.1	25.4	3,452.8	9.7	14.3	76.0
Spain	...	...	...	...	...	...	1997	771.2	39.7	55.0	5.3	12,200.5[4]	16.5[4]	4.2[4]	79.3[4]
Sri Lanka	1.9	1998	269.4[24]	—	100.0[24]	—	1995	216.5	—	100.0	—	271.1	—	40.0	60.0
Sudan, The	0.3	1998	27.4	...	...	...	1995	...	...	...	...	34.1	—	—	100.0
Suriname	10.9[4]	1996	58.9[25]	...	...	...	1997	594.7	100.0	—	—	15.9[6]	—	31.4[6]	68.6[6]
Swaziland	0.7	1998	8.9	...	...	...	[10]	...	...	...	...	...	...	...	...
Sweden	0.3[6]	1995	634.3	59.2[9]	40.8[9]	—	1997	1,127.6	83.8	11.2	5.0	4,369.9	13.4	6.2	80.4
Switzerland	...	1998	...	—	100.0	—	1997	1,931.1	15.0	85.0	—	4,056.5	3.0	69.0	28.0
Syria	6.6[9]	1994	2,594.1[8]	—	100.0[8]	—	1995	2,675.5	—	1.4	98.6	21.6	—	—	100.0
Taiwan	0.3[6]	1995	791.6	—	79.6	20.4	1995	843.7	...	— 35.8 —		8,035.8	— 35.8 —		64.2
Tajikistan	...	...	...	...	...	...	1997	1.0	—	100.0	—	228.0[4]	—	100.0[4]	—
Tanzania	1.3	1998	111.9	...	...	...	...	...	...	...	...	...	...	...	...
Thailand	1.8[2]	1997	2,756.6	—	100.0	—	1997	1,334.0	9.3	74.9	15.7	5,929.7	4.7	14.2	81.1
Togo	5.8	1998	88.3	—	100.0	—	1997	145.3	—	100.0	—	...	...	...	...
Tonga	0.3[6]	1995	0.4	—	100.0	—	1995	0.1	—	100.0	—	1.3	—	46.2	53.6
Trinidad and Tobago	12.2	1998	708.6	—	—	100.0	1996	492.4	—	—	100.0	476.9	12.7	2.1	85.1
Tunisia	5.6	1998	1,456.4	—	17.1	82.9	1997	438.9	2.7	11.6	85.7	367.1	—	32.4	67.6
Turkey	1.1	1998	2,160.5	...	...	...	1997	325.8	61.7	38.3	—	5,709.8	21.0	3.3	75.7
Turkmenistan	9.7[2]	1997	204.0	—	—	100.0	1997	489.9	—	0.2	99.8	...	...	...	...
Tuvalu	0.9[6]	1995	0.1	—	100.0	—	...	...	...	...	...	...	...	...	...
Uganda	0.3[26]	1995–96	15.8	—	100.0	—	1996	...	...	...	...	11.2	—	100.0	—
Ukraine	...	1997	...	...	...	...	1997	1,421.6	60.4	19.7	19.8	6,790.7	3.4	3.1	93.5
United Arab Emirates	33.4[9]	1994[3]	12,269.1[3]	...	...	...	1996	23,700.1	0.5	0.5	99.0	233.3	17.1	82.9	—
United Kingdom	1.7	1998	21,115.8	—	8.5	91.5	1997	18,681.6	5.5	32.6	61.8	16,302.2	16.2	38.7	45.1
United States	1.5[2]	1997	120,500.0	4.8	9.5	85.7	1997	13,394.6	35.4	33.2	31.4	80,065.7	5.6	12.8	81.6
Uruguay	0.2	1997	47.6	—	100.0	—	1997	...	...	...	...	229.7	—	6.4	93.6
Uzbekistan	...	...	...	...	...	...	1997	114.5	—	—	100.0	13.9	100.0	—	—
Vanuatu	...	1998	...	—	100.0	—	1994	...	...	...	...	0.5	—	—	100.0
Venezuela	12.1	1998	10,676.5	—	6.4	93.6	1997	12,510.3	1.8	—	98.2	132.3	41.5	58.5	—
Vietnam	6.2	1998	1,091.3	—	9.4	90.6	1997	103.2	1.8	—	98.8	32.1	—	100.0	—
Virgin Islands (U.S.)	...	1998	...	—	100.0	—	...	...	...	...	...	...	...	...	...
West Bank	...	...					...								
Western Sahara	...	...					...								
Yemen	9.8[9]	1994	1,788.2[8]	—	100.0[8]	—	1995	1,424.0	—	—	100.0	208.4	—	—	100.0
Yugoslavia	9.5[9]	1994	981.7	12.0	3.1	84.9	1997	16.8	32.1	—	67.9	708.7	23.6	5.9	70.6
Zambia	6.1	1998	203.0	...	...	...	1995	12.9	—	100.0	—	1.7	100.0	—	—
Zimbabwe	6.9[9]	1994	336.1	...	...	...	1997	95.9	4.9	94.3	0.8	35.3[4]	17.8[4]	37.1[4]	45.0[4]

[1]Gross value of production (output). [2]1997. [3]Mostly crude petroleum and natural gas. [4]1996. [5]1998. [6]1995. [7]Belgium includes Luxembourg. [8]Mostly crude petroleum. [9]1994. [10]South Africa includes Botswana, Lesotho, Namibia, and Swaziland. [11]Mostly diamonds, some gold. [12]China includes Taiwan. [13]Petroleum sector only. [14]Republic of Cyprus only. [15]1993. [16]Jersey includes

total ('000 cubic metres)	fuelwood, charcoal (%)	industrial roundwood (%) total	industrial roundwood (%) sawlogs, veneer	exports	imports	total ('000 metric tons)	marine	inland	fish	crusta-ceans	mollusks	exports	imports	country
1,039	15.4	84.6	55.1	2,706,468	5,705,731	514.6	99.6	0.4	87.2	2.8	9.9	1,744,665	1,304,585	Netherlands, The
...	...	...	...	1,535	19,459	0.9	100.0	—	99.4	—	0.6	1,198	6,380	Netherlands Antilles
5	—	100.0	58.3	...	11,595	3.2	100.0	—	96.1	2.8	1.1	18,766	5,677	New Caledonia
17,953	—	100.0	40.4	1,303,550	310,844	594.1	99.8	0.2	93.4	0.7	5.9	712,256	52,445	New Zealand
4,306	94.7	5.3	5.3	11,725	16,267	20.6	94.6	5.4	46.7	52.3	1.0	78,596	7,843	Nicaragua
6,666	93.8	6.2	—	...	6,334	11.0	—	100.0	100.0	—	—	154	458	Niger
100,637	90.6	9.4	7.1	33,457	172,331	455.6	69.4	30.6	92.0	7.2	0.8	19,662	209,959	Nigeria
...	...	...	...	...	51[5]	0.2	100.0	—	99.5	0.5	—	...	...	Northern Mariana Islands
8,173	8.1	91.9	50.1	1,831,746	1,009,845	2,620.1	100.0	—	97.5	2.5	—	3,764,790	612,469	Norway
...	...	...	...	...	17,179	108.8	100.0	—	92.6	0.5	6.9	38,243	5,077	Oman
33,075	92.7	7.3	5.4	...	137,040	654.5	72.5	27.5	93.6	4.9	1.6	141,476	816	Pakistan
...	...	...	...	...	1,123	1.8	100.0	—	98.0	2.0	—	290	87	Palau
1,052	96.7	3.3	3.3	5,440	67,462	120.5	100.0	—	90.8	7.7	1.5	194,898	15,125	Panama
8,597	64.4	35.6	35.6	168,807	12,439	53.7	74.9	25.1	96.9	3.1	—	25,173	7,819	Papua New Guinea
8,097	52.1	47.9	42.2	88,064	31,132	25.0	—	100.0	100.0	—	—	36	1,592	Paraguay
9,157	80.0	20.0	17.7	71,644	166,328	8,429.3	99.5	0.5	98.4	0.2	1.3	788,411	16,833	Peru
43,399	91.8	8.2	1.1	52,996	606,710	1,870.5	92.3	7.7	88.1	4.2	7.7	372,274	121,492	Philippines
25,652	6.0	94.0	44.1	862,220	1,251,300	235.1	94.1	5.9	89.6	8.3	2.1	282,354	260,653	Poland
9,878	6.1	84.8	32.7	1,185,978	913,640	207.7	100.0	—	90.3	2.3	7.4	278,586	1,017,066	Portugal
...	...	...	...	...	...	2.1	100.0	—	59.2	7.7	33.1	21	21	Puerto Rico
...	...	...	...	...	15,654	4.2	100.0	—	98.8	1.2	—	28	2,053	Qatar
36	85.9	14.1	11.6	342	69,029	5.8	100.0	—	95.5	4.5	—	19,662	33,053	Réunion
13,148	23.1	76.9	46.7	355,924	172,019	7.8	32.0	68.0	100.0	—	—	7,109	31,911	Romania
158,100	33.1	66.9	30.3	3,190,431	358,552	4,141.2	92.6	7.4	95.9	2.1	2.0	1,247,518	199,065	Russia
7,836	95.7	4.3	1.1	...	2,407	6.4	—	100.0	100.0	—	—	...	61	Rwanda
...	...	...	...	33	1,797	0.4	100.0	—	81.5	5.7	12.8	...	729	St. Kitts and Nevis
...	...	...	...	—	11,692	1.7	100.0	—	96.8	1.7	1.5	6,172	5,186	St. Lucia
...	...	...	...	8	18,545	15.6	100.0	—	100.0	—	—	927	1,537	St. Vincent
131	53.4	46.6	44.3	1,357	2,542	9.8	100.0	—	99.5	0.3	0.2	11,700	5,984	Samoa
...	...	...	...	...	...	—	100.0	—	100.0	—	—	...	...	San Marino
9	—	100.0	100.0	504[5]	196[5]	3.8	100.0	—	99.0	—	1.0	3,836	137	São Tomé and Príncipe
...	...	...	...	19,256	778,185	46.9	100.0	—	87.9	10.4	1.7	10,134	99,412	Saudi Arabia
5,037	84.2	15.8	0.8	...	45,293	418.1	90.4	9.6	87.8	1.5	10.7	301,498	3,784	Senegal
...	...	...	...	99	1,416	37.8	100.0	—	99.7	—	0.2	12,318	12,904	Seychelles
3,419	96.4	3.6	0.1	1,264	2,053	59.4	75.6	24.4	94.9	3.9	1.2	15,654	3,267	Sierra Leone
120[5]	—	100.0	100.0	502,202	889,039	5.1	100.0	—	75.4	14.3	10.3	390,062	475,224	Singapore
5,783	5.9	94.1	42.2	431,828	237,213	1.4	—	100.0	100.0	—	—	1,895	32,269	Slovakia
2,253	23.6	76.4	49.7	399,531	296,900	2.0	88.8	11.2	98.6	—	1.4	6,597	29,280	Slovenia
872	15.8	84.2	84.2	51,070	...	82.3	100.0	—	99.9	—	0.1	64,170	75	Solomon Islands
8,329	98.7	1.3	0.3	132[5]	257[5]	20.3	98.8	1.2	95.6	2.0	2.5	4,058	170	Somalia
30,616[19]	39.2[19]	60.8[19]	19.6[19]	827,673	487,114	588.0	99.8	0.2	98.2	0.5	1.3	260,056[18]	55,691[18]	South Africa
14,810	11.1	88.9	38.4	1,626,053	3,813,488	1,167.2	99.3	0.7	86.8	3.1	10.1	1,604,237	3,286,831	Spain
10,344	93.9	6.1	0.6	2,862	81,534	271.6	90.1	9.9	98.7	1.1	0.2	74,120	59,775	Sri Lanka
9,682	77.6	22.4	1.3	1,040	16,928	49.5	11.1	88.9	99.7	—	0.3	88	280	Sudan, The
93	1.1	98.9	96.8	3,249	1,353	13.0	98.5	1.5	98.0	2.0	—	11,640	3,600	Suriname
890	62.9	37.1	29.2	62,000	...	0.1	—	100.0	100.0	—	—	2,242	9,738	Swaziland
61,800	9.5	90.5	49.7	9,720,885	1,615,641	351.3	99.6	0.4	98.9	1.1	—	477,992	715,463	Sweden
10,428	20.1	79.9	73.9	1,937,022	2,393,070	1.8	—	100.0	100.0	—	—	3,031	375,700	Switzerland
50	31.5	68.5	31.7	1,040	141,790	7.9	32.7	67.3	99.1	0.9	—	183	49,546	Syria
...	...	...	...	...	...	1,099.7	99.9	0.1	70.2	2.6	27.2	1,763,572	556,873	Taiwan
...	...	...	...	80	4,131	...	—	100.0	100.0	—	—	54	143	Tajikistan
39,846	94.2	5.8	0.8	5,939	22,531	310.0	16.1	83.9	99.1	—	0.9	60,202	1,975	Tanzania
36,631	92.2	7.9	0.1	758,925	1,006,210	3,004.9	92.5	7.5	86.7	4.3	9.0	4,109,860	840,679	Thailand
1,232	74.5	25.5	5.4	974	4,355	22.9	78.2	21.8	100.0	—	—	1,498	12,222	Togo
2	—	100.0	100.0	...	2,065	3.7	100.0	—	94.3	5.5	0.2	2,625	872	Tonga
44	22.7	77.3	77.3	2,032	65,952	15.0	100.0	—	95.0	5.0	—	12,315	8,009	Trinidad and Tobago
2,842	92.5	7.5	0.7	14,709	151,980	92.1	99.1	0.9	81.6	7.8	10.6	82,118	13,276	Tunisia
17,767	41.3	58.7	29.1	82,545	969,948	575.1	91.3	8.7	97.1	0.4	2.5	98,196	59,207	Turkey
...	...	...	...	501	3,880	8.8	—	100.0	100.0	—	—	316	99	Turkmenistan
...	...	...	...	—	323[5]	0.4	100.0	—	100.0	—	—	326	...	Tuvalu
16,998	81.3	18.7	6.2	...	17,781	226.1	—	100.0	100.0	—	—	24,221	78	Uganda
10,008	17.6	82.4	62.0	132,755	235,646	407.9	98.9	1.1	98.1	1.4	0.6	75,079	96,776	Ukraine
...	...	...	...	7,290	297,934	117.6	100.0	—	99.9	0.1	—	29,436	28,872	United Arab Emirates
7,451	3.1	96.9	57.1	2,192,065	8,983,645	837.8	99.8	0.2	85.3	7.5	7.2	1,427,853	2,276,998	United Kingdom
500,434	14.4	85.6	49.6	14,783,367	23,721,067	4,749.6	99.2	0.8	79.0	8.3	12.7	2,945,014[21]	9,407,307[21]	United States
6,163	70.3	29.7	22.3	77,918	97,102	103.0	97.6	2.4	79.7	3.3	17.0	98,981	13,418	Uruguay
...	...	...	...	240	37,231	2.9	—	100.0	100.0	—	—	44	2,688	Uzbekistan
63	38.0	62.0	62.0	3,074	...	94.6	100.0	—	99.1	0.3	0.6	738	681	Vanuatu
2,713	33.6	66.4	59.7	65,999	297,987	411.9	91.4	8.6	86.2	2.2	11.6	134,120	40,409	Venezuela
36,730	87.6	12.4	6.6	47,277	132,913	1,200.0	93.8	6.3	70.8	22.3	6.9	940,473	13,801	Vietnam
...	...	...	...	...	...	0.8	100.0	—	100.0	—	—	...	...	Virgin Islands (U.S.)
...	...	...	...	...	...	...	—	—	...	...	...	...	...	West Bank
...	...	...	...	...	...	...	...	...	...	...	...	...	...	Western Sahara
—	—	—	—	...	44,915	123.3	100.0	—	96.2	0.4	3.4	19,789	4,636	Yemen
1,140	4.4	95.6	95.6	44,990	166,400	1.3	33.9	66.1	96.6	0.8	2.6	225	43,088	Yugoslavia
8,053	89.6	10.4	4.0	...	8,809	67.3	—	100.0	100.0	—	—	205	1,404	Zambia
9,253	87.7	12.3	10.1	31,415	33,293	12.4	—	100.0	100.0	—	—	1,462	9,925	Zimbabwe

Guernsey. [17]Mostly bauxite and diamonds. [18]South Africa includes Lesotho. [19]South Africa includes Namibia. [20]Includes coal mining. [21]United States includes Puerto Rico. [22]1994–95. [23]Mostly gold. [24]Mostly precious and semiprecious stones. [25]Mostly bauxite. [26]1995–96.

Manufacturing industries

This table provides a summary of manufacturing activity by industrial sector for the countries of the world, providing figures for total manufacturing value added, as well as the percentage contribution of 29 major branches of manufacturing activity to the gross domestic product. U.S. dollar figures for total value added by manufacturing are given but should be used with caution because of uncertainties with respect to national accounting methods; purchasing power parities; preferential price structures and exchange rates; labour costs; and costs for material inputs influenced by " most favored" international trade agreements, barter, and the like.

Manufacturing activity is classified here according to a modification of the International Standard Industrial Classification (ISIC), revision 2, published by the United Nations. A summary of the 2-, 3-, and 4-digit ISIC codes (groups) defining these 29 sectors follows, providing definitional detail beyond that possible in the column headings.

The collection and publication of national manufacturing data is usually carried out by one of three methods: a full census of manufacturing (usually done every 5 to 10 years for a given country), a periodic survey of manufacturing (usually taken at annual or other regular intervals between censuses), and the onetime sample survey (often limited in geographic, sectoral, or size-of-enterprise coverage). The full census is, naturally, the most complete, but,

since up to 10 years may elapse between such censuses, it has sometimes been necessary to substitute a survey of more recent date but less complete coverage. In addition to national sources, data published by the United Nations Industrial Development Organization (UNIDO), especially its *International Yearbook of Industrial Statistics* and *Industrial Development Global Report;* occasional publications of the International Monetary Fund (IMF); and other sources have been used.

ISIC code(s)	Products manufactured
31	Food, beverages, and tobacco
311 + 312	food including prepared animal feeds
313	alcoholic and nonalcoholic beverages
314	tobacco manufactures
32	Textiles, wearing apparel, and leather goods
321	spinning of textile fibres, weaving and finishing of textiles, knitted articles, carpets, rope, etc.
322	wearing apparel (including leather clothing; excluding knitted articles and footwear)
323 + 324	leather products (including footwear; excluding wearing apparel), leather substitutes, and fur products

Manufacturing industries

country	year	total manufacturing value added ('000,000 U.S.$)	(31) food (311 + 312)	bever-ages (313)	tobacco manufac-tures (314)	(32) textiles (exc. wearing apparel) (321)	wearing apparel (322)	leather and fur products (323 + 324)	(33) wood products (exc. furniture) (331)	wood furniture (332)	(34) paper, paper products (341)	printing and pub-lishing (342)	(35) industrial chemi-cals (351)	paints, soaps, etc. (352 exc. 3522)	drugs and medicines (3522)
Afghanistan	1988–89[1]	435	18.3	1.9	—	8.0	0.4	16.7	—0.5—		0.9	4.9	4.8	0.2	2.7
Albania	1996[2, 3, 4]	283	34.8	7.5	10.7	—	0.9	1.4	0.5	—	—	0.2	0.1	0.4	
Algeria	1995	4,147	15.0	3.2	4.1	2.8	2.6	1.2	1.9	0.9	2.2	0.3	0.4	—2.4—	
American Samoa	1993[5, 6]	326	99.5[7]	...	...	...	...	...	...	...	...	...	...	...	...
Andorra	1997[8]	48	1.1	6.1	2.2	—————15.7————			0.9	4.4[9]	0.7	10.6	—3.4—		
Angola	1989	319	20.0	——12.2——		————11.6————			——3.7——		——0.3——		9.1[10]	10	10
Antigua and Barbuda	1995	8.4	...	...	...	...	...	...	...	...	...	...	...	...	...
Argentina	1993[12]	29,622	16.0	6.0	6.2	4.4	2.4	2.4	1.2	1.2[9]	2.0	5.1	2.2	3.6	3.8
Armenia	1995[2, 12]	322	36.8	3.7	1.3	1.9	6.1	1.1	0.4	0.3	0.1	0.8	3.9	—1.3—	
Aruba	1994	89[13]	...	...	...	...	...	...	...	...	...	...	...	...	...
Australia	1995	65,859	15.2	3.4	0.6	2.7	1.9	0.6	2.9	1.8	2.4	8.0	3.2	—4.7—	
Austria	1995[3, 5]	41,735	8.7	2.3	...	3.8	1.3	0.7	4.6	3.8[9]	4.7	4.6	...	...	2.1
Azerbaijan	1996[2, 5]	1,483	1.1	0.2	0.4	13.0	...	...	1.0	...	...	0.2	—3.2—		
Bahamas, The	1992[5]	95	7.4	38.9	—	0.3	3.6	—	—	3.5	...	10.0	...	22.0	...
Bahrain	1992	761	5.0	1.1	—	—	6.5	0.1	0.1	8.4	0.4	4.4	5.6	—	...
Bangladesh	1991–92[12, 14]	1,899	12.7	0.6	12.2	23.5	10.2	3.9	0.7	0.1	2.9	1.2	5.6	4.5	5.8
Barbados	1995	289	18.0	16.9	2.4	0.7	2.1	—	—	1.4	1.0	8.3	5.9	—4.1—	
Belarus	1994[2, 5, 15]	3,006	16.2	...	...	7.0	2.1	2.6	—5.4[16]—		—16—		16.3[10]	10	10
Belgium	1995	53,712	15.4	2.0	0.7	4.3	2.3	0.1	0.6	3.6	2.2	4.6	11.5	—3.8—	
Belize	1992[12]	59	45.9	7.5	3.9	——3.8——			5.5	2.7	1.1	1.5	—14.1—		
Benin	1990	59	20.6	13.1	—	3.2	5.5	6.9	3.6	5.2	—	2.5	—	—9.5—	
Bermuda	1995	170	...	...	...	...	...	...	...	...	...	...	...	...	...
Bhutan	1989[12]	21	6.0	10.1	—	——5.6——			18.1	2.7	0.4	1.0	21.5	—1.7—	
Bolivia	1995[12, 19]	910	20.9	13.5	0.6	2.6	0.6	1.5	2.6	0.5	1.6	1.9	0.5	1.1	1.8
Bosnia and Herzegovina	1991	4,021	9.1	2.6	1.7	5.9	4.5	3.3	6.3	4.2	3.9	1.4	5.5	—4.1—	
Botswana	1995	212	32.5	12.7	—	8.0	5.2	2.8	2.4	1.4	2.8	2.8	1.4	—1.4—	
Brazil	1995	277,242	13.7	1.4	1.2	4.6	2.2	2.6	0.7	0.8	3.6	2.2	8.9	—4.7—	
Brunei	1995	314	...	...	...	...	...	...	...	...	...	...	...	...	...
Bulgaria	1995[20]	5,498	9.3	3.3	3.1	5.9	3.5	3.6	1.6	1.4	1.2	2.0	2.0	—1.9—	
Burkina Faso	1995	162	47.2	15.5	1.2	13.7	1.2	4.4	—	1.2	—	1.2	0.6	—	
Burundi	1995	117	54.7	21.4	5.1	9.4	—	—	0.9	—	—	0.9	—	—1.7—	
Cambodia	1995[12, 14]	71	——14.2——		5.9	0.7	——21.7——		—10.4[21]—		21	0.5	—	—0.3—	
Cameroon	1995–96[12]	543	19.4	21.0	2.3	10.3	0.3	—	13.0	0.1	1.9	0.5	—	—4.2—	
Canada	1995[12]	126,465	9.6	2.5	1.0	1.6	1.8	0.3	4.9	2.3[9]	10.5	5.6	5.2	3.2	1.9
Cape Verde	1990	14	33.1	0.6	26.8	...	8.0	2.0	...	...	...	9.2	...	...	...
Central African Republic	1995	36	27.0	13.5	21.6	...	—	—	13.5	2.7	...	5.4	2.7	—5.4—	
Chad	1998	200	...	...	...	...	—	—	—	—	—	—	...	...	...
Chile	1995[12, 22]	16,538	20.4	5.0	3.4	2.6	2.2	1.8	3.3	0.8	9.6	3.5	2.9	4.6	2.5
China	1996	174,971	6.9	3.1	5.2	7.1	3.1	1.9	1.6	0.5	2.3	1.2	—9.5—		2.5
Colombia	1995[12, 14]	14,781	19.9	9.6	0.5	6.4	3.3	1.4	0.6	0.5	4.6	3.8	5.9	6.0	4.6
Comoros	1996	11	...	...	...	...	...	...	...	...	...	...	...	...	...
Congo, Dem. Rep. of the	1990	808	86.7	5.4	1.9	0.6	0.2	0.6	0.1	0.2	—	0.1	0.9	—0.1—	
Congo, Rep. of the	1995	86	26.7	24.4	7.0	2.3	1.2	2.3	3.5	2.3	1.2	1.2	3.5	—4.7—	
Costa Rica	1996[5, 12]	1,381	31.6	15.0	2.6	1.8	3.3	0.8	1.3	1.2	3.7	3.4	6.6	3.9	1.6
Côte d'Ivoire	1995	1,395	17.6	4.3	6.0	10.9	2.2	0.9	5.9	0.8	0.2	0.6	5.5	—1.2—	
Croatia	1995	6,539	17.3	3.9	3.6	5.2	5.1	2.1	3.7	2.7	2.0	3.0	3.3	—8.0—	
Cuba	1995	4,077[20]	15.7	5.4	39.9	3.6	1.9	1.2	1.0	0.8	0.2	1.2	1.9	—7.8—	
Cyprus[23]	1996	1,018[12]	17.8	7.9	7.2	3.6	8.0	2.3	6.0	4.3	2.4	5.3	0.5	3.1	1.3
Czech Republic	1998[24]	12,054	——13.5——			——5.8——		0.9	—2.3—		—4.5—		—6.7—		
Denmark	1995	33,560	19.3	3.5	0.9	2.3	1.0	0.4	2.0	2.7	2.7	6.7	5.1	—7.0—	
Djibouti	1992[26]	13	——5.0——			——3.0——			—	—	—0.3—		—	—1.0—	
Dominica	1997[3, 5]	13	0.1	...	—	—	...	...	...	...	—	—	—	98.1	...
Dominican Republic	1990	1,298	31.9	13.8	5.2	3.5	1.2	3.0	0.2	1.5	2.9	1.7	1.6	—3.4—	
East Timor	...	...	...	...	...	...	...	...	...	...	...	...	...	...	...
Ecuador	1996[12, 14]	2,134	20.1	6.1	0.3	4.5	0.8	1.2	1.3	0.9	3.8	2.3	2.0	2.8	1.7
Egypt	1994–95[3, 27]	6,050	13.6	1.7	2.0	10.0	2.3	0.1	0.8	0.3	1.8	1.4	5.1	3.4	3.8
El Salvador	1996[12, 19, 28]	1,012	16.1	8.5	3.0	6.7	11.4	0.8	0.1	0.7	2.9	4.4	2.6	11.6	4.5
Equatorial Guinea	1990[2]	1.9	27.6	4.1	...	...	2.6	...	...	49.3	...	1.2	—13.8—		
Eritrea	1996[12, 14]	53	——65.7——			—2.6—		5.5	...	...	—2.2—		—12.6—		
Estonia	1996[2, 5]	2,134	26.8	6.1	...	8.4	4.3	1.4	8.0	5.8	1.6	4.5	2.5	5.5	0.8

ISIC code(s)		Products manufactured
33		Wood and wood products
	331	sawlogs, wood products (excluding furniture), cane products, and cork products
	332	wood furniture
34		Paper and paper products, printing and publishing
	341	wood pulp, paper, and paper products
	342	printing, publishing, and bookbinding
35		Chemicals and chemical, petroleum, coal, rubber, and plastic products
	351	basic industrial chemicals (including fertilizers, pesticides, and synthetic fibres)
	352 minus 3522	chemical products not elsewhere specified (including paints, varnishes, and soaps and other toiletries)
	3522	drugs and medicines
	353 + 354	refined petroleum and derivatives of petroleum and coal
	355	rubber products
	356	plastic products (excluding synthetic fibres)
36		Glass, ceramic, and nonmetallic mineral products
	361 + 362	pottery, china, glass, and glass products
	369	bricks, tiles, cement, cement products, plaster products, etc.

ISIC code(s)		Products manufactured
37		Basic metals
	371	iron and steel
	372	nonferrous basic metals and processed nickel and cobalt
38		Fabricated metal products, machinery and equipment
	381	fabricated metal products (including cutlery, hand tools, fixtures, and structural metal products)
	382 minus 3825	nonelectrical machinery and apparatus not elsewhere specified
	3825	office, computing, and accounting machinery
	383 minus 3832	electrical machinery and apparatus not elsewhere specified
	3832	radio, television, and communications equipment (including electronic parts)
	384 minus 3843	transport equipment not elsewhere specified
	3843	motor vehicles (excluding motorcycles)
	385	professional and scientific equipment; photographic and optical goods; watches and clocks
39		Other manufactured goods
	390	jewelry, musical instruments, sporting goods, artists' equipment, toys, etc.

		(36)			(37)		(38)								(39)	country
refined petroleum and products	rubber products	plastic products	pottery, china, and glass	bricks, tiles, cement, etc.	iron and steel	non-ferrous metals	fabricated metal products	nonelec-trical mach-inery	office equip., com-puters	electrical equip.	radio, tele-vision	transport equip. exc. motor vehicles	motor vehicles	profes-sional equip.	jewelry, musical instru-ments	
(353 + 354)	(355)	(356)	(361 + 362)	(369)	(371)	(372)	(381)	(382 exc. 3825)	(3825)	(383 exc. 3832)	(3832)	(384 exc. 3843)	(3843)	(385)	(390)	
—	—	2.1	—1.1—		0.4	—	0.6	—	—	—	—	—	0.1	—	37.1	Afghanistan
18.6	0.1	0.3	—	6.8	2.6	13.1	0.6	1.0	—	0.3	—	—	—	—	0.3	Albania
3.8	0.4	0.9	1.3	9.5	15.3	0.9	12.5	—1.5—		—5.8—		—8.5—		1.4	1.3	Algeria
...	...	...	...	...	—0.8—		...	...	...	...	...	...	...	...	...	American Samoa
...	0.1	2.4	0.2	1.0			0.7	—5.3—		—19.8—		0.1	13.4	3.0	8.0	Andorra
20.0	10	10	—11.3—		—1.9—			—5.0—				—4.7—		11	0.3[11]	Angola
...	...	...	...	...	...	...	...	...	...	...	...	...	...	...		Antigua and Barbuda
9.1	0.9	3.0	1.2	2.4	2.4	0.8	4.6	5.6	0.2	2.2	1.4	0.6	7.6	0.7	0.8	Argentina
0.3	0.8	0.1	0.5	5.0	0.2	2.1	2.2	—4.2—		—6.6—		—0.6—		3.6	16.1	Armenia
...	...	...	...	...	...	...	...	...	...	...	...	...	...	...	...	Aruba
3.5	0.9	3.6	1.1	3.9	3.8	7.2	7.3	—6.2—		—4.6—		—8.7—		0.9	0.8	Australia
...	0.8	3.3	2.4	4.4	5.0	1.6	9.2	10.5	0.1	4.9	6.2	0.9	4.6	1.8	1.6	Austria
47.6	0.6		...	...	0.1	—	...	1.1	—	0.8	0.1	0.5	—	0.3	...	Azerbaijan
...	...	...	...	7.0	2.6	—	—	—	—	—	—	—	—	—	...	Bahamas, The
13.7	0.8	—		4.5	4.4	33.4	0.3	—0.4—		3.4	—	3.4	—	—	4.1	Bahrain
0.4	0.5	0.4	1.0	1.7	3.6	0.1	1.2	0.4	—	1.2	0.5	0.8	3.7	—	0.6	Bangladesh
—	6.6	14.9	0.7	2.8	—	—	6.9	—3.8—		—2.4—		—1.0—		—	0.3	Barbados
7.6	10	10	—5.5—		—3.0—				—26.8—					...	Belarus
1.0	0.6	5.4	2.5	2.1	4.7	1.8	7.1	—7.1—		—7.8—		—7.0—		0.5	1.3	Belgium
—	—0.3[17]—		17	6.2	—	—	2.0	—		—0.1—		—4.2—		—	1.1	Belize
—	—	—	0.5	24.6	—	—	4.8	—	—	—	—	—	—	—	—	Benin
...	...	...	...	...	...	...	...	...	...	...	...	...	...	...	...	Bermuda
...	0.7	2.2	—29.0—		...	...	—1.0[18]—								18	Bhutan
36.4	—	1.5	0.7	6.0	—	2.4	1.1	0.3	...	0.4	...	0.1	0.3	0.1	0.8	Bolivia
2.3	0.3	1.3	0.5	3.2	5.5	3.4	10.8	—5.0—		—3.3—		—8.6—		2.6	0.7	Bosnia and Herzegovina
—	0.5	0.5	—	—	—	—	2.4	—0.9—		—0.9—		—1.4—		—	19.8	Botswana
5.0	1.1	2.4	0.8	3.6	5.7	1.5	4.0	—7.8—		—8.4—		—10.6—		0.9	1.5	Brazil
...	...	...	...	...	...	...	...	...	...	...	...	...	...	...		Brunei
1.6[20]	0.7	0.6	3.2	2.1	18.6	3.9	5.9	—6.6—		—5.4—		—5.5—		...	7.2	Bulgaria
—	1.2	0.6	—	—	1.2	—	0.6	—		—0.6—		—1.2—		—	8.1	Burkina Faso
—	—	0.9		1.7			2.6	—	—	—	—	—	—	—	0.9	Burundi
...	—17.4—		—24.6—		—3.8—		0.5	—	—	—	—	—	—	—	0.1	Cambodia
2.4	10.7	0.6	—	2.9	—	7.5	0.6	—	—	—1.1—		—	—	—	1.0	Cameroon
1.6	1.4	2.2	0.8	1.7	3.5	3.3	5.5	5.3	0.7	2.1	3.9	3.6	12.2	0.5	1.5	Canada
...	...	...	...	...	...	...	...					—20.1—		...	0.2	Cape Verde
—	—	—	—	—	—	—	2.7	...	...	—	—	—2.7—		—	2.7	Central African Republic
...	...	...	...	...	...	...	...	...	...	...	...	...	...	...	...	Chad
6.0	1.0	2.8	1.0	3.5	2.4	11.5	3.7	2.2	—	1.1	0.2	0.8	0.8	0.2	0.2	Chile
3.8	1.3	2.2	—7.3—		6.9	2.1	3.4	—8.6—		5.1	4.6	—6.4—		1.0	2.5	China
5.2	1.2	3.2	2.3	5.3	2.4	0.4	3.4	1.9	—	2.0	0.6	0.8	2.6	0.5	1.0	Colombia
			—	—	—	—									—	Comoros
0.1	—	—	—	0.2	...	...	0.4	—0.3—		—0.2—		—0.5—		—	1.5	Congo, Dem. Rep. of the
—	2.3		—	1.2	—	—	7.0	—2.3—		—3.5—		—3.5—		—	—	Congo, Rep. of the
3.0	1.7	4.3	1.2	2.7	...	0.1	2.2	—1.4—		1.0	3.8	1.0	0.2	...	0.2	Costa Rica
22.0	1.3	—	0.1	1.9	0.1	0.1	4.9	—0.1—		—0.4—		—7.6—		2.2	3.2	Côte d'Ivoire
3.2	0.3	1.6	1.5	4.0	2.6	0.9	4.5	—5.7—		—6.9—		—8.2—		0.4	0.3	Croatia
...	2.4	2.1	0.5	0.9	0.7	0.9	1.7	—1.7—		—0.9—		—3.5—		0.3	3.0	Cuba
1.2	0.4	3.5	0.4	10.2	—	—	7.3	—2.7—		1.2	—	0.3	0.8	0.1	2.1	Cyprus[23]
1.4	—4.7—		—8.2—		—16.7[25]—		25	—11.8—		—9.2[26]—		—10.4—		26	3.9	Czech Republic
1.5	0.4	2.9	0.7	3.6	1.0	0.3	8.1	—12.9—		—4.9—		—4.7—		2.9	2.6	Denmark
			—0.1—		—0.1—					—13.0—					77.5	Djibouti
				...			...								...	Dominica
16.2	0.8	1.6	0.7	3.5	1.8	0.2	3.7	—0.5—		—0.8—		—0.1—		0.2	0.2	Dominican Republic
...	...	...	...	...	...	...	...	...	...	...	...	...	...	...	...	East Timor
32.7	1.1	3.5	1.2	5.4	1.3	0.4	2.1	1.4	—	1.4	—	0.1	1.3	—	0.4	Ecuador
17.4	0.4	1.1	0.9	10.6	1.8	2.5	3.6	7.3	0.2	3.1	0.6	1.1	2.4	0.4	0.1	Egypt
10.2	0.4	3.1	0.1	5.1	0.8	—	2.2	1.3	—	1.6	0.8	—	...	0.1	0.9	El Salvador
...	...	...	...	0.8	...	...	0.6	...	...	...	...	...	...	...	...	Equatorial Guinea
...	—2.0—		—7.1—		—0.2[25]—		25			—0.5—				0.2	1.4	Eritrea
0.3	0.1	1.5	1.4	3.3	—	—	5.4	2.7	0.5	2.4	1.2	2.1	2.0	0.8	0.8	Estonia

Manufacturing industries (continued)

country	year	total manufacturing value added ('000,000 U.S.$)	(31) food (311 + 312)	beverages (313)	tobacco manufactures (314)	(32) textiles (exc. wearing apparel) (321)	wearing apparel (322)	leather and fur products (323 + 324)	(33) wood products (exc. furniture) (331)	wood furniture (332)	(34) paper, paper products (341)	printing and publishing (342)	(35) industrial chemicals (351)	paints, soaps, etc. (352 exc. 3522)	drugs and medicines (3522)
Ethiopia	1995–96[12,29]	435	25.3	22.7	4.4	9.8	1.2	7.5	1.7	1.2	1.7	3.6	−0.2	3.2	0.8
Faroe Islands	1997[6]	389	95.8	—	—	—	0.1	0.1	—	—	—	—	—	3.1	—
Fiji	1994	160	42.6	6.1	—	—13.8—		1.3	9.7	1.9	3.8	5.1	—	3.1	—
Finland	1995	27,928	8.3	1.4	0.2	1.1	1.1	0.4	4.9	1.5[9]	22.5	6.1	3.9	1.4	1.2
France	1995	297,536	10.5	2.3	1.2	2.4	1.8	0.9	1.7	1.6	2.6	5.6	3.4	—5.6—	
French Guiana	1991[14]	45	...	...	...	—31—			—38.2[31]—		...	...	...	...	...
French Polynesia	1993[5]	214	—27.2—		...	...	...	...	...	...	...	...	...	...	...
Gabon	1995	243	9.1	7.0	6.2	0.8	1.7	—	18.1	2.5	0.8	1.2	4.1	—1.7—	
Gambia, The	1995[12,19]	9.2	—65.0—		—	—8.3—			—6.2[33]—		—	4.2	8.8[10]	10	10
Gaza Strip[34]	...	...													
Georgia	1997	503	...	...	...	...	...	...	...	...	...	...	...	...	...
Germany	1994[24]	598,758	—8.7—		2.3	1.4	0.8	0.3	1.3	35	2.4	4.6		—11.7—	
Ghana	1993[12,24]	610	8.4	9.1	18.1	4.6	—0.5—		15.2	0.8	1.8	1.3	0.9	—8.9—	
Greece	1995[3,14]	10,741	18.3	6.3	2.0	7.0	5.8	1.4	1.6	1.5[9]	3.2	3.7	2.5	—8.5—	
Greenland	1991	27	...	...	...	...	...	...	...	...	...	...	...	...	...
Grenada	1995[2,37]	19	29.1	55.2	2.4	—	...	—	...	...	7.0	—	—	6.3	...
Guadeloupe	1995	152	...	...	...	...	...	...	...	...	...	...	...	...	...
Guam	1997[1,5]	165	—14.8—			47			47			24.4		47	
Guatemala	1995	1,468	28.7	6.2	3.1	5.7	2.5	1.2	0.8	0.5	1.5	4.5	3.5	—16.4—	
Guernsey	1997[5,6]	85	...	38		38				7.8[38]		18.5			
Guinea	1996	143	...	...	...	...	...	...	...	...	...	...	...	...	...
Guinea-Bissau	1995	19	...	...	...	...	...	...	...	...	...	...	...	...	...
Guyana	1998[5,39]	58	43.2[40]	...	...	...	...	...	...	...	...	...	—	...	...
Haiti	1996[5]	64	35.0	2.9	8.5	—19.1—			...	...	...	...		—11.4—	
Honduras	1996[3,19]	575	28.8	10.4	2.9	2.5	18.8	1.0	4.8	1.5	2.9	2.2	0.4	3.7	1.0
Hong Kong	1996	10,666	7.0	2.2	1.5	11.5	13.3	0.3	0.2	0.1	2.1	13.9	—2.7—		
Hungary	1998[2,14]	30,856	16.2	2.1	0.7	1.9	1.8	0.8	1.4	0.9	1.9	2.1	3.2	1.8	3.0
Iceland	1995	933	47.3	2.1	—	2.1	1.5	1.1	0.2	3.6	1.2	9.7	1.0	2.2	—
India	1994–95[3,41]	29,199	9.8	1.0	1.9	11.3	2.6	0.8	0.3	—	2.0	1.7	10.2	3.6	3.8
Indonesia	1996[3,24]	39,847	8.4	1.0	9.5	10.3	3.5	3.2	6.3	1.1	3.4	1.8	5.6	2.0	1.5
Iran	1995	9,147	12.8	2.2	0.8	10.8	0.3	0.9	0.7	0.3	1.7	0.9	4.7	—5.4—	
Iraq	1995	567	9.9	3.4	1.2	3.5	1.2	3.5	—	0.2	3.5	1.4	9.2	—1.1—	
Ireland	1995[3,42]	26,040	18.1	4.5	0.8	1.0	1.0	0.2	0.4	0.5[9]	1.4	12.1	13.6	4.8	5.5
Isle of Man	1996–97[3,5]	120	—15.2—		...	...		...	...		...	...		...	...
Israel	1995[12,19]	13,521	10.3	1.7	0.2	3.3	4.5	0.7	1.1	1.6	2.2	5.5	5.6	—3.3—	
Italy	1995	156,300	7.2	1.5	0.5	6.7	3.9	3.0	1.3	2.4	2.7	3.4	3.5	—6.4—	
Jamaica	1996[12,14]	916	25.4	11.5	10.6	—6.2—		0.6	0.2	2.4	—3.9—		9.5[10]	10	10
Japan	1995	1,363,980	8.1	2.0	0.3	2.5	1.1	0.4	1.5	1.0[9]	2.8	5.7	4.1	2.9	3.3
Jersey	1991	45	...	...	...	...	...	...	...	...	...	...	...	...	...
Jordan	1995[12]	1,000	11.3	5.2	13.5	2.9	2.5	1.1	1.0	3.0[9]	2.9	3.1	7.6	2.7	4.8
Kazakhstan	1996[2,5]	7,167	13.5	1.1	2.0	2.6	0.5	0.1	0.1	0.4	—	0.5	3.4	4.1	0.1
Kenya	1995	814	31.7	9.6	1.5	5.8	1.6	1.4	1.7	0.7	4.4	2.4	1.8	—6.6—	
Kiribati	1992	0.68	...	...	...	...	...	...	...	...	...	...	...	...	...
Korea, North		...	...	...	...	...	...	...	...	...	...	...	...	...	...
Korea, South	1996[19]	216,564	—7.1—		1.8	5.2	3.0	1.3	0.8	35	2.3	2.8	—9.2—		
Kuwait	1995[12]	3,148	4.3	1.4	—	0.7	3.7	0.1	0.7	1.5	1.0	0.7	4.7	0.7	—
Kyrgyzstan	1996[2]	408	33.9	4.7	2.7	17.3	1.7	1.5	0.3	0.5	—	0.9	—	0.1	0.1
Laos	1990[2]	66	4.5	7.4	16.3	—	5.1	0.3	40.1	5.0	—	1.2	—4.0—		
Latvia	1996[3,5]	947	27.6	11.5	...	6.3	4.0	1.2	9.1	2.3[9]	1.0	5.4	0.1	1.5	2.2
Lebanon	1994	1,679	—25.2—		1.9	3.3	9.6	3.0	—3.4—		2.4	2.4	2.4	—	
Lesotho	1995	134	43.3	28.4	...	10.4	3.0	2.2	...	0.7	...	1.5	—6.7—		
Liberia	1995	78	...	...	...	...	...	...	...	...	...	...	...	...	...
Libya	1995	857	4.3	2.2	9.4	3.7	3.3	8.5	0.3	0.2	0.3	1.0	7.0	—5.2—	
Liechtenstein	1997[5,6,45]	1,830	—4.2—											—7.8—	
Lithuania	1996[2,5]	3,590	26.9	4.2	...	7.3	6.2	1.4	2.8	2.2[9]	1.5	2.0	...	0.4	0.8
Luxembourg	1995	2,459	4.8	3.1	0.8	7.0	0.6	...	0.3	0.5	3.7	2.1	3.7	—4.8—	
Macau	1996[5,12]	425	2.6	0.9	47	16.9	59.8	1.1	0.1	0.7	0.3	2.2	—	0.4	0.8
Macedonia	1996	603	19.7	4.8	7.5	5.9	8.0	3.9	0.2	2.1	0.9	4.6	5.5	—5.1—	
Madagascar	1995	127	15.0	11.8	0.8	35.4	3.1	2.4	0.8	0.8	3.9	1.6	—	—6.3—	
Malawi	1995	153	35.3	5.9	1.3	7.8	—	...	1.3	—	2.0	5.2	7.8	—9.8—	
Malaysia	1995[3]	23,810	8.4	0.8	1.2	3.0	2.0	0.2	5.7	1.5	1.8	2.8	5.7	1.9	0.3
Maldives	1997	13[48]	...	...	—	...	...	—	—	—	...	...	—	...	...
Mali	1990	96	18.4	1.2	13.1	36.5	10.3	0.1	0.1	—	0.4	0.8	0.8	—0.7—	
Malta	1996	700	7.7	7.9	1.4	1.9	9.0	2.7	0.2	4.6	1.2	6.9	0.3	2.5	1.0
Marshall Islands	1997	2.2	...	...	...	...	...	...	...	...	...	...	...	...	...
Martinique	1995	207	...	...	...	...	...	...	...	...	...	...	...	...	...
Mauritania	1993	35	—42.9—		...	...	...	...	...	...	6.0	—	...	—18.8—	
Mauritius	1995[3,49]	826	17.1	—7.7—		7.2	43.5	1.2	—1.6—		—1.5—		—5.2—		
Mayotte	1992	...	...	...	...	...	...	...	...	...	...	...	...	...	...
Mexico	1995	54,750	15.4	6.4	1.9	4.9	1.9	1.4	1.2	0.8	2.7	2.6	6.3	—7.3—	
Micronesia	1992	2.2[6]	[51]	...	...	...	91.0	...	...	...	...	...		1.6[51]	...
Moldova	1996[2,12,52]	862	46.2	17.9	6.2	2.9	1.9	2.0	0.8	1.9	2.1	0.6	—	0.6	0.5
Monaco		...	...	...	...	...	...	...	...	...	...	...	...	...	...
Mongolia	1996[12]	54	34.9	11.3	—	22.2	9.5	4.7	2.5	0.3[9]	—	2.9		0.8	1.7
Morocco	1996[5]	5,295	17.1	4.3	13.1	8.9	7.7	1.3	1.1	0.4	2.5	1.2	10.9	2.9	1.9
Mozambique	1996[2]	246	26.9	30.9	1.8	3.8	0.4	0.1	0.4	0.6	1.1	2.5	1.6	—5.9—	
Myanmar (Burma)	1993	858[53]	14.8	20.4	4.6	26.4	...	...	1.9	0.7	5.7	...	0.2	2.0	1.6
Namibia	1996[5]	327	21.1[54]	...	...	...	...	...	...	...	...	...	...	...	...
Nauru	1989	—	—	...	...	—	...	...	—	...	...				
Nepal	1996–97[5,12,14]	381	13.6	9.1	12.0	25.9	6.3	1.3	1.4	0.9[9]	1.7	1.3	...	3.4	2.4
Netherlands, The	1995	56,417	14.8	4.0	5.2	2.0	0.4	0.2	1.0	0.9	3.5	8.3	8.6	—5.5—	
Netherlands Antilles	1995	157	...	...	...	...	...	...	...	...	...	...	...	...	...
New Caledonia	1992[5]	341	—15.4—												
New Zealand	1995	9,878	25.1	3.0	0.6	2.9	2.3	1.1	4.6	1.8	7.7	7.8	3.6	—3.1—	
Nicaragua	1997[5]	313	39.9	25.6	7.6	1.6	0.1	1.1	2.4	0.5	0.5	1.8	—3.1—		

refined petroleum and products (353 + 354)	rubber products (355)	plastic products (356)	pottery, china, and glass (361 + 362)	bricks, tiles, cement, etc. (369)	iron and steel (371)	nonferrous metals (372)	fabricated metal products (381)	nonelectrical machinery (382 exc. 3825)	office equip., computers (3825)	electrical equip. (383 exc. 3832)	radio, television (3832)	transport equip. exc. motor vehicles (384 exc. 3843)	motor vehicles (3843)	professional equip. (385)	jewelry, musical instruments (390)	country
—	1.2	1.4	0.5	7.1	3.0	—	1.9	0.2	—	—	—	—	1.8	—	—	Ethiopia
—	—	—	—	—	—	—	—	—	—	—	3.4	—	—	—	0.7	Faroe Islands
—	0.5	2.0	—	3.0[30]	30	—	3.2	1.2	—	—	—	0.4	1.0	—	1.2	Fiji
0.8	0.7	2.3	0.7	1.9	6.5		4.0	11.2	0.5	3.8	6.9	3.0	1.2	1.7	0.6	Finland
6.4	1.2	2.7	1.6	2.9	2.8	1.9	8.0	7.8		10.6		11.1		1.6	1.7	France
...	...	...	61.8[32]		32					32					...	French Guiana
...	...	...					35.4								...	French Polynesia
10.3	—	—	0.8	5.8	2.1	2.1	8.7	0.8		5.4		7.0		0.4	3.3	Gabon
—	10	10	—	—	1.8		4.8	0.8						—	33	Gambia, The
...	...	...	...	...	...	...	...	...	...	...	...	...	...	...	...	Gaza Strip[34]
...	...	...	...	...	...	...	...	...	...	...	...	...	...	...	...	Georgia
4.4	4.5		...	3.8	4.0		6.7	13.2	1.3	7.4	2.1	1.8	12.0	2.7	2.7[35]	Germany
8.1	0.6	2.6	4.4		0.7	8.2	3.4	0.3		1.5		0.6[36]		—	36	Ghana
5.2	0.3	3.2	6.3		2.8	3.9	3.6	3.2	0.1	2.2	1.7	4.0	0.6	0.3	0.6	Greece
...	...	...	...	...	...	...	...	...	...	...	...	...	...	...	...	Greenland
...	...	...	...	...	...	...	...	...	...	...	...	...	...	...	...	Grenada
...	...	...	...	...	...	...	...	...	...	...	...	...	...	...	...	Guadeloupe
...	...	...	10.3		...	...	2.6				47				0.6	Guam
1.1	2.5	4.0	2.5	4.8	2.7	0.1	2.5	0.8		3.4		0.3		0.2	0.4	Guatemala
...	...	...	...	...	...	...	...	8.8		...	34.3	4.0	...	...	...	Guernsey
...	...	...	...	...	...	...	...	...	...	...	...	...	...	...	...	Guinea
...	...	...	...	...	...	...	...	...	...	...	...	...	...	...	...	Guinea-Bissau
—	—	—	...	3.5	...	...	...	...	...	...	...	...	...	...	...	Guyana
...	...	...	...	...	...	...	12.1	...	...	...	...	...	...	...	...	Haiti
0.2	1.1	3.3	0.1	7.5	0.5	0.2	3.6	0.7	—	0.9	0.1	—	0.2	0.1	0.7	Honduras
0.1	0.1	2.8	3.0		1.0		4.5	7.0	5.5	0.9	9.7	3.7		3.2	3.7	Hong Kong
5.8	0.8	2.7	1.1	2.1	3.0	2.2	4.1	4.8	7.3	5.1	5.9	0.7	15.0	1.1	0.4	Hungary
—	—	2.9	0.5	3.8	2.2	4.6	7.9	—	—	—	—	2.0	—	—	3.9	Iceland
5.2	1.6	1.0	0.6	3.5	9.0	2.7	2.4	6.1	0.9	5.5	3.1	3.0	4.7	0.7	0.8	India
0.2	1.9	2.0	1.7	2.3	9.3	1.2	4.2	1.4	—	3.9	3.3	5.7	4.3	0.3	0.7	Indonesia
0.7	2.1	1.6	1.7	7.7	15.2	3.6	4.5	4.0		7.8		8.3		0.7	0.4	Iran
25.2	0.5	1.4	0.7	18.2	4.1	—	4.8	2.3		4.4		0.4		—	—	Iraq
43	0.7	1.5	2.5		0.1	0.4	1.9	3.2	13.3	3.2	2.1	0.8	0.7	3.8	1.7[43]	Ireland
...	...	...	...	...	...	...	...	...	...	...	...	...	...	...	...	Isle of Man
2.1	0.6	5.4	0.6	3.6	1.2	0.8	12.0	3.3		22.6		5.2		1.4	1.2	Israel
2.5	1.7	2.9	1.5	4.2	3.7	1.3	7.1	13.8		8.1		7.5		2.2	1.0	Italy
9.3	10	10	5.9		44		14.2[44]								0.2	Jamaica
1.3	1.2	3.6	1.4	2.9	4.3	1.2	7.5	10.9	2.4	5.0	8.5	1.2	9.4	1.9	1.7	Japan
...	...	...	...	...	...	...	...	...	...	...	...	...	...	...	...	Jersey
5.4	0.2	3.1	0.1	15.7	3.0	0.9	4.5	1.9	—	1.0	1.0	—	1.2	0.2	0.4	Jordan
8.1	0.2	0.1	0.4	1.2	8.3	17.6	1.5	2.6	...	0.6	...	...	—	0.1	0.1	Kazakhstan
0.7	3.1	3.3	0.5	3.6	1.7	—	6.3	0.6		5.7		3.4		0.1	1.7	Kenya
—	—	—	—	—	—	—	...	...	...	...	...	...	...	...	...	Kiribati
...	...	...	...	...	...	...	...	...	...	...	...	...	...	...	...	Korea, North
2.9	3.8		4.6		6.3		5.5	8.5	1.2	3.7	15.1	3.1	8.6	1.1	2.2[35]	Korea, South
65.4	0.1	1.5	0.5	4.8	0.7	—	3.5	1.5	—	1.3	—	0.6	0.1	—	0.6	Kuwait
—	0.1	0.2	3.6	8.4	—	9.2	0.6	5.8	0.2	5.6	—	0.1	0.9	0.8	0.9	Kyrgyzstan
—	0.5		0.1	3.8	—	—	10.8	0.5		0.2		—	—	—	0.1	Laos
0.1	—	0.8	0.7	1.9	—	0.1	3.1	5.2	0.2	2.3	1.5	5.0	0.4	0.4	1.4	Latvia
1.6	—	3.2	12.0		4.9		8.9	2.2		2.1		1.0		—	10.5	Lebanon
...	...	...	...	0.7	...	...	3.0	...	...	...	...	...	...	...	...	Lesotho
...	...	...	...	...	...	...	...	...	...	...	...	...	...	...	...	Liberia
27.2	0.1	0.8	0.2	21.7	...	...	0.5	—	—	—	—	—	—	—	4.0	Libya
...	...	...	...	...	1.0		15.3	50.0						...	...	Liechtenstein
18.0	0.1	0.9	1.0	2.5	0.2	—	1.4	3.3	0.1	1.8	3.3	2.0	0.2	0.6	0.6[46]	Lithuania
0.2	10.6	2.3	3.9	7.5	15.9	3.5	12.2	7.2		3.1		0.7		1.5	0.1	Luxembourg
—	47	0.3	...	3.0	—	—	2.0	0.3	—	3.3	...	1.2	—	—	3.7	Macau
0.4	0.1	1.2	0.8	0.6	6.2	—	5.4	1.1		9.5		4.7		0.3	1.7	Macedonia
7.9	0.8	0.8	—	2.4	—	—	3.1	—		2.4		0.8		—	—	Madagascar
—	0.7	3.3	—	1.3	—	—	5.9	4.6		1.3		0.7		—	5.9	Malawi
3.2	4.6	3.8	1.2	4.3	1.4	1.0	4.2	4.3	0.7	4.1	24.9	1.7	3.4	1.2	0.8	Malaysia
—	—	—	—	...	—	—	...	...	...	...	...	...	...	...	...	Maldives
0.7	0.3	0.4	—	1.3	—	—	6.2	0.5		1.7		6.5		—	—	Mali
—	3.2	2.4	0.4	3.3	—	—	3.8	1.0	0.3	4.4	23.6	1.1	0.1	3.8	5.3	Malta
...	...	...	...	...	...	...	...	...	...	...	...	...	...	...	...	Marshall Islands
...	...	...	16.8		...	...	15.5	—	...	...	—	...	...	—	...	Martinique
—	0.3	1.6	3.9		1.0		1.6	1.6[50]		0.9		50		1.7	2.6	Mauritania
...	...	...	...	...	...	...	...	...	...	...	...	...	...	...	...	Mayotte
11.6	1.4	1.8	2.2	1.7	4.1	1.1	3.9	3.1		3.1		9.3		2.0	1.9	Mexico
...	...	...	...	...	...	...	...	...	...	...	...	...	...	...	7.4	Micronesia
—	—	0.3	2.6	3.7	0.1	0.1	0.8	5.0	0.1	0.5	1.3	0.2	—	0.7	0.8	Moldova
...	...	...	...	...	...	...	...	...	...	...	...	...	...	...	...	Monaco
—	—	—	0.1	5.7	-1.5	—	-0.1	0.1	—	0.3	2.0	0.3	0.4	0.7	1.0	Mongolia
...	1.0	1.5	1.4	9.3	1.1	0.3	3.9	0.8	0.5	2.1	0.8	0.3	3.0	0.2	0.1	Morocco
0.2	2.6	1.7	0.3	13.3	0.8	0.5	2.2	0.2		0.7		1.4		—	0.1	Mozambique
...	0.5	0.2	...	0.5	6.1	7.0	0.2	...	...	0.7	—	...	1.5	...	5.0	Myanmar (Burma)
...	...	...	...	...	...	...	...	...	...	...	...	...	...	...	...	Namibia
—	—	—	—	—	—	—	...	...	...	...	...	...	...	...	—	Nauru
0.2	1.3	1.7	0.1	7.2	1.6	0.1	4.8	0.1	—	2.2	0.3	—	—	—	0.5	Nepal
2.4	0.5	3.3	1.7	2.3	2.8	0.1	6.8	8.2		11.4		4.5		0.9	0.3	Netherlands, The
...	...	...	...	...	...	...	...	...	...	...	...	...	...	...	...	Netherlands Antilles
...	...	...	...	...	...	43.2	...	...	...	...	...	...	...	...	...	New Caledonia
1.5	0.7	3.6	1.3	2.1	1.8	2.3	7.7	4.8		4.4		4.4		0.4	1.3	New Zealand
4.5	0.1	...	7.4		...	...	0.7	0.3		...		0.2		...	...	Nicaragua

Manufacturing industries (continued)

country	year	total manufacturing value added ('000,000 U.S.$)	(31) food (311 + 312)	beverages (313)	tobacco manufactures (314)	(32) textiles (exc. wearing apparel) (321)	wearing apparel (322)	leather and fur products (323 + 324)	(33) wood products (exc. furniture) (331)	wood furniture (332)	(34) paper, paper products (341)	printing and publishing (342)	(35) industrial chemicals (351)	paints, soaps, etc. (352 exc. 3522)	drugs and medicines (3522)
Niger	1996[12]	9.8	—23.2—			—1.2—			—0.5—		—35.5—		—21.8—		
Nigeria	1995	7,884	17.6	15.3	1.9	10.4	0.1	3.1	0.5	0.9	3.8	3.4	0.3	—11.7—	
Northern Mariana Islands	1997[1,5]	762	—0.7—			[47]	91.8	[47]	[47]	[47]	[47]	0.7	—0.3—		
Norway	1995[14]	16,835	—20.7—			1.0	0.4	0.1	3.4	2.1[9]	6.7	9.3	6.7	1.2	2.0
Oman	1995	660	12.1	3.0	—	2.0	6.2	0.1	2.3	2.1[9]	1.3	2.4	0.9	3.5	1.3
Pakistan	1995	7,550	15.2	1.3	7.1	18.7	2.1	1.7	0.3	0.2	1.7	1.8	9.8	—7.9—	
Palau	1998	1.2[56]	...	...	...	...	...	...	...	...	...	...	...	...	...
Panama	1995	694	43.5	10.0	3.6	0.8	2.6	1.1	1.4	1.3	4.0	2.8	1.4	—5.5—	
Papua New Guinea	1989	451	48.4	13.1	4.9	—	0.4	—	11.6	2.0	1.1	2.4	1.1	—1.1—	
Paraguay	1995	904	30.6	10.0	0.7	7.4	0.3	5.3	18.8	1.8	0.1	4.6	0.8	—0.8—	
Peru	1995	7,485	14.8	13.2	0.9	8.7	0.9	0.6	0.6	0.5	1.1	3.2	3.0	—7.7—	
Philippines	1995[12,14]	15,323	18.9	8.4	4.7	3.1	4.7	0.5	0.7	0.5[9]	2.0	1.4	2.5	5.2	4.0
Poland	1996	27,032	—16.1—		0.8	3.7	4.6	1.7	3.7	4.4[57]	2.0	4.8	—8.4—		
Portugal	1995[12]	20,472	7.5	2.6	4.2	8.5	6.5	3.9	3.5	1.7	4.9	4.3	2.0	1.7	1.6
Puerto Rico	1997[5]	36,427	4.0	5.7	...	0.2	1.9	0.6	...	0.1[9]	0.4	1.2	2.5	2.3	54.0
Qatar	1994	694	3.6	0.2		0.3	7.1	0.1	1.0	2.0	0.1	3.4	28.0	0.4	—
Réunion	1994	371	34.5	12.3	—	—0.5—		—	—3.8—		5.0[58]	6.3	...	—3.7—	
Romania	1995[5,59]	9,387	18.8	8.9	0.7	4.4	6.6	1.7	3.3	3.4[9]	1.3	1.1	3.5	2.4	1.8
Russia	1995	58,394[53]	15.0	1.5	0.3	2.1	1.2	0.7	1.6	0.9	3.1	0.7	6.2	1.5	0.8
Rwanda	1990	178	29.1	18.1	11.2	...	...	...	4.4	0.9	1.0	1.3	9.0	—	
St. Kitts and Nevis	1995[5]	21	16.0[61]	...	...	...	...	...	...	...	...	...	...	...	...
St. Lucia	1995[2,37]	46	10.0	—27.6—		2.4	7.2	...	...	...	40.8	...	...	...	...
St. Vincent	1997[3]	19	...	...	...	...	...	...	...	...	...	...	...	...	...
Samoa	1995[5]	25	...	...	...	—	—	—	...	...	...	...	...	...	...
San Marino	...	...	...	...	...	...	...	...	...	...	...	...	...	...	...
São Tomé and Príncipe	1993[2]	4.6	26.3	20.7	—	—	26.3	—	—15.1—		—	1.2	—	6.6	
Saudi Arabia	1995	7,461	5.8	0.5	0.3	0.4	0.1	0.1	0.1	0.5	2.2	1.0	40.4	—2.3—	
Senegal	1996[12]	309[62]	36.1[62]	3.9	3.9	3.2		0.2	0.3	0.1	1.3	1.9	21.1	6.0	3.4
Seychelles	1989	26	—79.6—			—0.6—			—2.1—		—6.0—		—4.1—		
Sierra Leone	1993[12]	92	37.0	21.6	10.5	—	1.0	0.1	0.3	1.2	0.2	2.2	—20.2—		
Singapore	1996[3,14]	26,157	2.8	0.8	—	0.2	0.7	0.1	0.2	0.6[9]	1.3	4.5	1.6	3.6	4.1
Slovakia	1996	3,277	10.5[53]	2.9	...	2.4[53]	3.3	1.6	1.9	1.6[9]	4.9[53]	2.7	6.7	0.9	2.9
Slovenia	1995[12]	5,857	8.4	2.3	0.6	3.4	4.1	3.3	2.8	3.0	6.1	4.3	7.8	—6.4—	
Solomon Islands	1995	8.2	—	...	...	—	...	...	...	...	...	...	...	...	...
Somalia	1990	36	21.6	6.3	37.5	10.5	0.8	2.0	—	7.3	-0.6	0.3	0.4	—5.1—	
South Africa	1995	29,071	10.4	5.7	0.4	3.2	2.8	1.3	1.3	1.1	5.0	3.4	5.0	—4.9—	
Spain	1996	95,026	11.6	3.9	0.7	3.0	2.3	1.6	2.2	2.5	3.2	5.2	4.3	—6.2—	
Sri Lanka	1993[12,19]	1,267	14.8	12.4	11.8	8.3	20.1	1.9	0.6	0.2	2.5	1.1	0.9	4.5	0.3
Sudan, The	1990	1,179	40.0	3.0	16.7	11.9	0.4	5.4	0.2	0.2	2.1	6.4	0.7	—2.2—	
Suriname	1992[2,3,37]	700	33.4	22.3	12.3	...	1.5	1.6	8.7	1.4	0.7	1.6	...	—8.3—	
Swaziland	1995[3,5,14]	335	27.5	42.0	...	0.4	3.0	...	1.2	0.8	17.9	1.1	—	0.2	...
Sweden	1994[3,14]	35,125	7.2	1.2	0.5	1.0	0.2	0.1	4.9	1.1	9.8	5.8	3.9	1.8	5.4
Switzerland	1994	60,111	8.1	1.4	0.8	1.8	1.0	0.5	4.6	3.0	1.9	7.4	7.4	—5.9—	
Syria	1995	3,805	12.0	5.8	3.8	20.2	1.2	2.1	2.2	0.2	0.4	0.8	0.2	—0.9—	
Taiwan	1997	78,385	—6.6—		1.4	6.3	2.2	0.7	0.5	0.8	1.9	1.1	7.6	—2.1—	
Tajikistan	1996[2,5]	864	26.1[53]	0.2	0.6	18.9[53]	0.5	0.1[53]	—	0.1	—	0.1[53]	4.7[53]	0.1[53]	...
Tanzania	1995	119	10.7	5.8	10.7	17.4	0.8	1.7	1.7	0.8	3.3	3.3	14.9	—2.5—	
Thailand	1994[12,14]	38,122	9.3	3.9	2.9	8.0	9.4	0.6	1.3	0.4	1.7	4.6	0.9	0.7	0.7
Togo	1995[5]	59	15.3	40.7	...	16.9	—	6.8	—	—	—	1.7	10.2	—24.9—	
Tonga	1994[2,12]	13	—45.1—			1.1	1.5	2.0	1.3	[63]	[63]	5.0			
Trinidad and Tobago	1995	862	12.0	9.1	3.3	0.2	0.9	0.2	0.4	1.0	2.8	2.5	36.5	1.4	0.1
Tunisia	1996[12]	5,216	9.4	2.9	6.5	7.0	14.9	4.0	—4.8—		—2.2—		4.8	2.8	0.6
Turkey	1997	42,524	8.2	2.5	2.0	11.7	4.3	0.4	0.6	0.4	1.6	1.4	4.5	—7.7—	
Turkmenistan	1992[2,5,15]	801	13.3	...	...	18.9	1.2	0.4	—0.3[16]—		—[16]—		3.2[10]	[10]	[10]
Tuvalu	1995[3]	0.35	...	—	...	—	...	—	—	—	—	...	...	...	...
Uganda	1989	155	42.8	11.9	8.9	8.0	1.3	1.5	0.1	4.0	0.9	1.4	0.3	0.7	5.1
Ukraine	1996[3,5]	27,508	24.1	3.4	0.6	1.4[53]	0.6	0.6	0.7	0.7	0.9	0.4	6.2	1.0[53]	0.8
United Arab Emirates	1993[2]	6,621	—8.7—			—4.7—			—2.8—		—2.8—		—53.8—		
United Kingdom	1996	283,255	10.6	2.7	1.2	2.9	1.7	0.6	1.3	2.2[9]	3.1	9.2	4.6	3.8	3.1
United States	1996	1,749,662	8.2	2.0	1.5	1.9	2.2	0.3	2.4	1.6[9]	4.1	7.5	4.7	3.0	3.4
Uruguay	1996[19]	3,755	24.9	10.9	4.6	5.6	3.0	3.2	0.3	0.4	2.4	4.2	1.6	—8.3—	
Uzbekistan	1992[2,5,15]	2,147	12.6	...	...	21.4	3.1	1.9	—1.3[16]—		—[16]—		5.4[10]	[10]	[10]
Vanuatu	1994[5]	11	—37.5—			—6.8—			—24.8—		—7.5—		—6.3[67]—		
Venezuela	1996[12,19]	15,621	11.3	4.0	12.7	1.8	1.9	0.9	0.4	0.5	1.7	1.5	7.8	3.4	1.3
Vietnam	1997[2,5]	12,096	—32.7—		4.1	—10.3—		4.9	5.6[68]	...	[68]	1.5	—7.0—		
Virgin Islands (U.S.)	1997[1,5]	146	—22.0—			[47]	0.8	[47]	1.1	[47]	—	14.5	[47]		
West Bank[34]	1994	314	12.9	0.1	0.5	2.8	19.2	4.7	2.5	1.3	2.2	0.5	0.4	2.0	1.0
Western Sahara	...	...	...	...	...	...	...	...	...	...	...	...	...	...	...
Yemen	1996[2,14]	1,153	—40.4—			—1.5—			—0.4—		—7.9—		—39.0—		
Yugoslavia	1996	4,439	20.0	6.9	1.9	4.2	2.7	2.0	1.8	1.8	1.9	5.2	2.1	—9.4—	
Zambia	1995	450	19.2	17.1	6.7	9.8	1.1	0.7	3.3	1.1	0.9	2.2	4.9	—10.5—	
Zimbabwe	1995–96[3]	1,627	14.9	13.9	4.3	9.0	3.0	2.5	2.6	1.8	2.3	3.0	3.9[77]	2.1	2.9

[1]Gross output in value of sales. [2]Gross output of production. [3]In factor values. [4]State sector only except food and beverages. [5]Complete ISIC detail is not available. [6]Value of manufactured exports. [7]Canned tuna and salmon. [8]Value of manufactured exports (excluding duty-free reexports). [9]Includes metal furniture. [10]351 includes 352, 355, and 356. [11]390 includes 385. [12]In producer's prices. [13]Estimated figure includes agriculture. [14]Establishments employing 10 or more persons. [15]Includes extraction of petroleum, natural gas, metals, and nonmetals. [16]33 includes 34. [17]355 and 356 includes 361 + 362. [18]38 includes 39. [19]Establishments employing five or more persons. [20]Excludes petroleum refining. [21]33 includes 341. [22]Establishments employing 50 or more persons. [23]Republic of Cyprus only. [24]Establishments employing 20 or more persons. [25]37 includes 381. [26]383 includes 385. [27]Private establishments employing 10 or more persons and all public establishments. [28]Excludes establishments processing coffee or cotton. [29]Establishments employing 10 or more persons and using power-driven machines. [30]369 includes 371. [31]33 includes 32. [32]36 includes 37 and 38. [33]34 includes 39. [34]West Bank includes Gaza Strip. [35]390 includes 332. [36]384 includes 390. [37]Selected industries only. [38]332 includes 313 and 321. [39]Includes public

refined petroleum and products	rubber products	plastic products	pottery, china, and glass	bricks, tiles, cement, etc.	iron and steel	non-ferrous metals	fabricated metal products	nonelectrical machinery	office equip., computers	electrical equip.	radio, television	transport equip. exc. motor vehicles	motor vehicles	professional equip.	jewelry, musical instruments	country
(353 + 354)	(355)	(356)	(361+ 362)	(369)	(371)	(372)	(381)	(382 exc. 3825)	(3825)	(383 exc. 3832)	(3832)	(384 exc. 3843)	(3843)	(385)	(390)	
			10.3		...	...				7.6					...	Niger
	1.9	2.8	0.4	5.8	1.0	1.9	3.7	1.1		2.0		9.8		—	0.5	Nigeria
[47]	[47]	[47]	2.8				—					0.2			[47]	Northern Mariana Islands
0.8	0.2	1.7	0.8	2.4	2.7	6.5	4.3	6.6	0.3	3.4	1.8	11.0[55]	1.3	1.8	0.9	Norway
27.9	—	1.5	1.5	16.5	—	6.0	5.8	1.3		1.6	—	0.1	0.1	—	0.4	Oman
3.1	0.9	0.6	1.1	8.3	6.5	—	0.8	3.0		4.6		2.8		0.2	0.3	Pakistan
...	...	...	...	...	...	...	...	...	...	...	...	...	...	...	...	Palau
5.8	0.2	4.1	0.6	4.8	1.2	0.4	2.2	...	...	0.9	...	1.2	0.2	0.1	0.3	Panama
—	—	0.4	0.7	1.6	...	—	6.7	1.3		0.7		2.4		...	...	Papua New Guinea
4.3	—	1.9	0.6	3.0	—	1.3	1.2	0.2		0.1		0.7		0.1	5.5	Paraguay
18.2	0.8	2.4	1.1	4.0	2.0	6.0	3.1	1.5		1.6		2.0		0.3	1.8	Peru
10.5	1.3	1.8	1.3	3.3	3.6	1.6	1.6	0.7	1.3	3.1	7.9	0.8	3.2	0.3	0.9	Philippines
1.9	4.5		6.3		5.5		6.8	9.2	0.3	4.0	1.8	3.1	4.3	1.9	[57]	Poland
13.8	0.6	1.7	3.5	5.1	1.0	0.5	6.1	3.2	0.1	3.3	2.0	1.6	3.1	0.5	1.0	Portugal
2.3	—	1.0	1.6		0.2		1.1	7.3		2.6	5.4	—	0.3	4.2	0.4	Puerto Rico
31.5	—	0.8	—	6.7	11.4	—	2.8	—		0.1		0.3		—	0.2	Qatar
—	—	[58]	...	16.8	—	—	12.2	5.0							—	Réunion
2.2	1.4	1.0	5.3		5.6	1.3	4.2	8.5	0.2	2.9	2.2	0.9	3.4	1.4	0.9	Romania
7.3	1.4	0.5	1.1	6.0	8.8	9.3	1.8	12.5	0.5	3.2	[47]	2.1[60]	1.5	1.0	1.6	Russia
—	—	—	—	11.7	—	—	10.3	0.9		0.8		1.4			...	Rwanda
...	...	...	...	...	...	...	...	...	...	12.0		...	...	...	...	St. Kitts and Nevis
...	...	...	...	...	...	...	...	...	...	...	...	...	...	...	1.2	St. Lucia
...	...	...	...	...	...	...	...	...	...	...	...	...	...	...	...	St. Vincent
—	—	—	—	...	—	—	—	...	...	...	...	...	21.0	—	...	Samoa
...	...	...	...	...	...	...	...	...	...	...	...	...	...	...	...	San Marino
			3.8		—	—	—	...	...	...	...	—		...	—	São Tomé and Príncipe
13.1	0.1	3.0	0.5	12.2	7.5	0.4	5.3	1.0		2.0		0.6			0.6	Saudi Arabia
3.7	—	1.6	—	7.4	—	—	4.1	0.5		-0.1	—	1.1	0.4		—	Senegal
			5.2		—	—	2.4								—	Seychelles
			3.5		...		2.1								0.1	Sierra Leone
5.5	0.3	2.5	0.5	1.5	0.4	0.1	5.9	6.7	25.6	2.9	18.9	5.7	0.3	2.1	0.5	Singapore
5.4	2.4	2.3	3.1	3.2[53]	9.0	3.6[53]	2.3	9.3[53]	0.3	3.0[53]	1.4	2.6[53]	3.6	1.7[53]	0.8[53]	Slovakia
0.4	1.6	2.4	3.7		10.2	1.6	7.3	5.9		7.9		3.9		2.0	0.7	Slovenia
—	—	—	—	—	—	—	—					0.9		—	—	Solomon Islands
1.6	—	0.5	—	3.0	—	—	1.1	—		—		0.9			1.7	Somalia
5.9	1.3	2.6	1.5	3.4	9.3	3.2	6.3	6.3		4.7		8.0		0.9	2.0	South Africa
1.4	1.6	3.1	1.9	5.7	5.3	1.9	8.3	7.3		5.5		11.1		1.0	1.0	Spain
1.4	4.2	1.4	1.8	2.9	1.1	0.2	1.3	0.9	0.2	1.1	0.1	1.6	0.3	—	2.1	Sri Lanka
1.3	0.8	1.2	0.1	0.5	0.1	0.7	2.6	0.1		1.2		2.1		—	0.1	Sudan, The
...	0.7	0.6	5.3		...		...					0.9		0.2	0.5	Suriname
		0.2	0.1	0.5			2.2	2.8					0.2		—	Swaziland
1.2	0.7	1.4	0.7	1.6	4.8	1.3	7.7	11.9	0.8	3.1	5.6	2.7	10.5	2.8	0.3	Sweden
2.0	0.8	2.3	1.7	2.7	1.2	1.9	6.4	12.8		16.9		1.7		5.4	0.4	Switzerland
17.1	0.3	0.6	4.7	7.1	—	0.6	14.0	2.4		2.4		0.5		—	0.3	Syria
7.7	1.1	5.3	3.2		7.8		7.0	4.7		21.7		7.5		0.9	2.0	Taiwan
...	—	—	0.3	1.4[53]	...	41.6	...	0.7[53]		1.7		3.3		0.4[53]	1.8[53]	Tajikistan
4.1	0.8	1.7	—	5.8	1.7	2.5	4.1	0.8		1.7		3.3			1.3	Tanzania
11.5	1.7	1.2	1.0	3.7	3.0	0.4	3.2	17.4	—	2.4	3.1	1.7	3.7	0.3	1.3	Thailand
...	...	...	—	3.4	3.4	...	3.8					4.1			—	Togo
			4.7									4.1			6.4[63]	Tonga
10.5	0.2	0.5	1.2	3.6	8.2	—	1.4	0.3	—	1.4	0.3	0.1	0.1	[11]	1.9[11]	Trinidad and Tobago
16.8	0.8	1.4[64]	2.5	6.9	1.5	3.0[65]	[65]	0.4		3.0	[66]	0.2	1.8	[66]	1.8[66]	Tunisia
10.0	1.9	2.9	3.0	4.0	7.2	1.1	2.9	5.8		7.5		7.8		0.4	0.2	Turkey
55.7	[10]	[10]	4.0		0.1			0.8							...	Turkmenistan
—	—	—	—	—	—	—	—	—	—	—	—	—	—	—	...	Tuvalu
—	0.2	—	—	2.5	3.0	—	4.7	0.7		1.3	0.5	0.1	—	—	—	Uganda
4.8	2.2	0.1	1.0	4.6	23.6	1.6	5.2	5.6	0.1	2.1[53]		2.9[53]	0.8	0.6[53]	0.1[53]	Ukraine
			8.3		8.2		3.7			9.2					1.4	United Arab Emirates
1.9	1.1	3.9	1.6	1.9	3.7		6.9	8.5	2.1	3.4	3.5	3.6	6.6	3.0	1.2	United Kingdom
1.8	1.1	3.2	0.9	1.7	2.2	1.8	6.2	8.3	2.3	3.5	7.0	4.0	6.1	5.6	1.5	United States
14.9	0.7	2.5	1.0	2.3	1.6	0.2	2.8	0.8		1.7		0.9		0.6	0.4	Uruguay
12.4	[10]	[10]	5.4		12.2					13.2					...	Uzbekistan
			[67]		11.4[25]		[25]								...	Vanuatu
15.8	2.2	1.6	2.3	2.9	7.0	6.1	2.7	1.7	—	1.7	0.1	0.3	5.9	0.3	0.3	Venezuela
	2.9		10.7		7.6[25]		[25]	1.8		5.1		3.5			...	Vietnam
			15.0				2.3	[47]				3.4		19.8	1.9	Virgin Islands (U.S.)
—	—	2.1	0.6	26.6	0.1	—	10.6	1.3		0.4		—	0.5	0.1	7.6	West Bank[34]
...	...	...	...	...	...	...	...	...	...	...	...	...	...	...	—	Western Sahara
			7.9		2.8										—	Yemen
0.9	2.0	1.8	1.4	4.9	1.6	2.6	7.8	4.5		6.3		5.6		0.5	0.4	Yugoslavia
4.2	1.8	1.3	-0.2	3.3	1.3	—	5.3	1.1		3.3		0.7		—	0.2	Zambia
[69]	2.7	1.3	0.4	5.3	8.4	0.8	6.3	1.2		3.3	0.2	0.7	2.6	0.2	0.7	Zimbabwe

utilities. [40]Sugar and rice manufacturing only. [41]Establishments with electric power and employing 10 or more workers and all establishments employing 20 or more workers. [42]Establishments employing three or more persons. [43]390 includes 353 + 354. [44]38 includes 37. [45]Excludes exports destined for Switzerland. [46]Includes recycled waste and scrap. [47]Data withheld for reasons of confidentiality. [48]Includes public utilities. [49]Statistical breakdown is based on 89.3% of total manufacturing value added (U.S.$737,000,000); detail for some establishments employing nine or fewer employees is unavailable. [50]382 includes 384. [51]Coconut soap includes coconut oil. [52]Excludes Transdniester area and city of Tighina (Bendery). [53]Sum of available data. [54]Fish and meat processing. [55]Includes petroleum platforms (6.2% of total). [56]Includes mining. [57]332 includes 390. [58]341 includes 356. [59]State enterprises only; state enterprises account for about 80% of all industrial output. [60]Excludes shipbuilding and aircraft. [61]Refined sugar only. [62]Excludes fish processing. [63]39 includes 332 and 341. [64]Includes synthetic fibres. [65]372 includes 381. [66]390 includes 3832 and 385. [67]35 includes 36. [68]331 includes 341. [69]351 includes 353 + 354.

Energy

This table provides data about the commercial energy supplies (reserves, production, consumption, and trade) of the various countries of the world, together with data about oil pipeline networks and traffic. Many of the data and concepts used in this table are adapted from the United Nations' *Energy Statistics Yearbook.*

Electricity. Total installed electrical power capacity comprises the sum of the rated power capacities of all main and auxiliary generators in a country. "Total installed capacity" (kW) is multiplied by 8,760 hours per year to yield "Total production capacity" (kW-hr).

Production of electricity comprises the total gross production of electricity by publicly or privately owned enterprises and also that generated by industrial establishments for their own use, but it usually excludes consumption by the utility itself. Measured in millions of kilowatt-hours (kW-hr), annual production of electricity ranges generally between 50% and 60% of total production capacity. The data are further analyzed by type of generation: fossil fuels, hydroelectric power, and nuclear fuel.

The great majority of the world's electrical and other energy needs are met by the burning of fossil hydrocarbon solids, liquids, and gases, either for thermal generation of electricity or in internal combustion engines. Many renewable and nontraditional sources of energy are being developed worldwide (wood, biogenic gases and liquids, tidal, wave, and wind power, geothermal and photothermal [solar] energy, and so on), but collectively these sources are still negligible in the world's total energy consumption. For this reason only hydroelectric and nuclear generation are considered here separately with fossil fuels.

Trade in electrical energy refers to the transfer of generated electrical output via an international grid. Total electricity consumption (residential and nonresidential) is equal to total electricity requirements less transformation and distribution losses.

Coal. The term coal, as used in the table, comprises all grades of anthracite, bituminous, subbituminous, and lignite that have acquired or may in the future, by reason of new technology or changed market prices, acquire an economic value. These types of coal may be differentiated according to heat content (density) and content of impurities. Most coal reserve data are based on proven recoverable reserves only, of all grades of coal. Exceptions are footnoted, with proven in-place reserves reported only when recoverable reserves are unknown. Production figures include deposits removed from both surface and underground workings as well as quantities used by the producers themselves or issued to the miners. Wastes recovered from mines or nearby preparation plants are excluded from production figures.

Natural gas. This term refers to any combustible gas (usually chiefly methane) of natural origin from underground sources. The data for production cover, to the extent possible, gas obtained from gas fields,

Energy

country	electricity												coal		
	installed capacity, 1998 ('000 kW)	production, 1998		power source, 1998			trade, 1998		consumption				reserves, latest ('000,000 metric tons)	pro-duction, 1998 ('000 metric tons)	con-sump-tion, 1998 ('000 metric tons)
		capacity ('000,000 kW-hr)	amount ('000,000 kW-hr)	fossil fuel (%)	hydro-power (%)	nuclear fuel (%)	exports ('000,000 kW-hr)	imports ('000,000 kW-hr)	amount, 1998 ('000,000 kW-hr)	per capita, 1998 (kW-hr)	resi-dential, 1998 (%)	non-resi-dential, 1998 (%)			
Afghanistan	494	4,327	485	35.1	64.9	—	—	95	580	27	...	...	66	2	2
Albania	1,892	16,574	5,068	1.6	98.4	—	692	1,068	5,444	1,738	42.9[1]	57.1[1]	15[2]	59	39
Algeria	6,042	52,928	23,615	99.6	0.4	—	262	255	23,608	785	28.4	71.6	40	23	651
American Samoa	35	307	130	100.0	—	—	—	—	130	2,063	...	...	—	—	—
Andorra	...								...		...	...			...
Angola	462	4,047	1,063	10.0	90.0	—	...	...	1,063	88	29.4[1]	70.6[1]	...	—	—
Antigua and Barbuda	26	228	99	100.0	—	—	—	—	99	1,478	...	...	...	...	...
Argentina	23,032	201,760	74,135	54.1	35.9	10.0	1,080	6,434	79,489	2,201	47.3	52.7	430	289	1,415
Armenia	3,005	26,324	6,190	49.5	24.8	25.7	—	—	6,190	1,751	...	...	...	...	5
Aruba	90	788	470	100.0	—	—	—	—	470	5,000	...	...	...	...	...
Australia	39,694	347,719	194,834	91.6	8.4	—	—	—	194,834	10,520	...	...	82,090	284,559	126,327
Austria	18,258	159,940	57,437	32.6	67.4	—	10,467	10,304	57,274	7,036	...	...	25	1,140	4,632
Azerbaijan	5,239	45,894	17,985	89.2	10.8	—	648	903	18,240	2,378	19.5[1]	80.5[1]	...	—	1
Bahamas, The	401	3,513	1,532	100.0	—	—	—	—	1,532	5,176	...	...	...	—	—
Bahrain	1,120	9,811	5,773	100.0	—	—	—	—	5,773	9,703	53.1[1]	46.9[1]	...	—	—
Bangladesh	3,490	30,572	13,857	93.8	6.2	—	—	—	13,857	111	37.7	62.3	1,756[2]	...	173
Barbados	156	1,367	747	100.0	—	—	—	—	747	2,787	78.4	21.6	...	—	—
Belarus	7,498	65,682	23,492	99.9	0.1	—	2,073	12,747	34,166	3,312	17.1[1]	82.9[1]	...	—	730
Belgium	14,969	131,128	85,833	44.5	1.7	53.8	6,435	7,828	87,226	8,601	...	...	—	312	11,596
Belize	43	377	183	63.9	36.1	—	—	25	208	904	71.0	29.0	...	...	...
Benin	15	131	6	100.0	—	—	—	305	311	54	64.1	35.9	...	...	...
Bermuda	146	1,279	530	100.0	—	—	—	—	530	8,281	...	...	...	...	...
Bhutan	356	3,119	1,801	—	100.0	—	1,357	8	452	226	...	...	...	50	68
Bolivia	1,043	9,137	3,710	56.1	43.9	—	3	13	3,720	468	48.9	51.1	0.9	—	—
Bosnia and Herzegovina	2,719	23,818	2,538	38.8	61.2	—	199	423	2,762	752	...	...	...	1,794	1,794
Botswana	3	3	3	3	3	3	3	3	3	3	26.3	73.7	4,300	3	3
Brazil	65,209	571,231	321,588	8.4	90.6	1.0	8	39,412	360,992	2,177	26.7	73.3	11,929	5,516	17,636
Brunei	479	4,196	1,725	100.0	—	—	—	—	1,725	5,476	53.7	46.3	—	—	—
Bulgaria	12,088	105,891	41,711	51.5	8.0	40.5	4,211	564	38,064	4,566	53.1	46.9	2,711	30,111	33,220
Burkina Faso	78	683	298	60.4	39.6	—	—	—	298	26	...	...	...	...	...
Burundi	43	377	123	1.6	98.4	—	—	30	153	24	73.8	26.2	...	...	...
Cambodia	35	307	215	62.8	37.2	—	—	—	215	20	...	...	...	...	...
Cameroon	627	5,493	2,765	3.3	96.7	—	—	—	2,765	193	...	...	...	1	1
Canada	115,037	1,007,724	561,805	28.2	59.1	12.7	44,665	17,299	534,439	17,486	...	...	6,578	75,368	59,492
Cape Verde	7	61	41	100.0	—	—	—	—	41	100	...	...	...	—	—
Central African Republic	43	377	104	21.2	78.8	—	—	—	104	30	69.3	30.7	2.7	...	...
Chad	29	254	91	100.0	—	—	—	—	91	13	...	...	...	...	...
Chile	8,423	73,785	35,503	55.1	44.9	—	—	—	35,503	2,395	30.0	70.0	1,181	975	5,790
China	231,167	2,025,023	1,166,200	81.0	17.8	1.2	2,976	17	1,163,241	926	25.3	74.7	114,500	1,250,000	1,228,106
Colombia	11,736	102,807	45,960	33.0	67.0	—	64	85	45,981	1,127	70.9	29.1	6,748	33,671	4,195
Comoros	5	44	17	88.2	11.8	—	—	—	17	26	...	...	...	...	...
Congo, Dem. Rep. of the	3,197	28,006	5,429	0.4	99.6	—	1,045	52	4,436	90	33.2[1]	66.8[1]	88	96	142
Congo, Rep. of the	118	1,034	443	0.7	99.3	—	—	119	562	202	52.7[1]	47.3[1]	...	...	...
Costa Rica	1,474	12,912	5,788	7.7	81.0	11.3	148	77	5,717	1,488	71.1	28.9	...	...	...
Côte d'Ivoire	1,173	10,275	2,765	38.7	61.3	—	—	—	2,765	193	26.1	73.9	...	...	...
Croatia	3,825	33,507	10,899	49.8	50.2	—	428	3,782	14,253	3,181	68.0	32.0	39	51	394
Cuba	3,988	34,935	14,768	99.1	0.9	—	—	—	14,768	1,340	52.8	47.2	...	—	15
Cyprus	699	6,123	2,954	100.0	—	—	—	—	2,954	3,831	82.4	17.6	...	—	26
Czech Republic	13,852	121,344	65,112	76.9	2.9	20.2	10,844	8,383	62,651	6,093	...	...	5,678	67,529	59,274
Denmark	12,140	106,346	46,104	93.2	0.1	6.7[4]	7,610	3,280	41,774	7,927	...	...	—	—	9,311
Djibouti	85	745	187	100.0	—	—	—	—	187	300	...	...	...	...	...
Dominica	8	70	39	48.7	51.3	—	—	—	39	549	...	...	...	...	...
Dominican Republic	2,198	19,254	7,555	68.7	31.3	—	—	—	7,555	918	72.3	27.7	...	...	81
East Timor	...	...	...	...	...	...	...	...	...	...	...	...	...	...	...
Ecuador	3,935	34,471	10,896	33.6	66.4	—	—	—	10,896	895	56.8	43.2	24	...	...

petroleum fields, or coal mines that is actually collected and marketed. (Much natural gas in Middle Eastern and North African oil fields is flared [burned] because it is often not economical to capture and market it.) Manufactured gas is generally a by-product of industrial operations such as gasworks, coke ovens, and blast furnaces. It is usually burned at the point of production and rarely enters the marketplace. Production of manufactured gas is, therefore, only reported as a percentage of domestic gas consumption.

Crude petroleum. Crude petroleum is the liquid product obtained from oil wells; the term also includes shale oil, tar sand extract, and field or lease condensate. Production and consumption data in the table refer, so far as possible, to the same year so that the relationship between national production and consumption patterns can be clearly seen; both are given in barrels.

Proven reserves are that oil remaining underground in known fields whose existence has been "proved" by the evaluation of nearby producing wells or by seismic tests in sedimentary strata known to contain crude petroleum, and that is judged recoverable within the limits of present technology and economic conditions (prices). The published proven reserve figures do not necessarily reflect the true reserves of a country, because government authorities or corporations often have political or economic motives for withholding or altering such data.

The estimated exhaustion rate of petroleum reserves is an extrapolated ratio of published proven reserves to the current rate of withdrawal/production. Present world published proven reserves will last about 40 to 45 years at the present rate of withdrawal, but there are large country-to-country variations above or below the average.

Data on petroleum and refined product pipelines are provided because of the great importance to both domestic and international energy markets of this means of bringing these energy sources from their production or transportation points to refineries, intermediate consumption and distribution points, and final consumers. Their traffic may represent a very significant fraction of the total movement of goods within a country. Available data for petroleum pipelines are often incomplete and their basis varies internationally, some countries reporting only international shipments, others reporting domestic shipments of 50 kilometres or more, and so on.

For data in the hydrocarbons portions of the table (coal, natural gas, and petroleum), extensive use has been made of a variety of international sources, such as those of the United Nations, the International Energy Agency (of the Organization for Economic Cooperation and Development), the World Energy Council (in its *World Energy Resources* [triennial]); the U.S. Department of Energy (especially its *International Energy Annual*); and of various industry surveys, such as those published by the *International Petroleum Encyclopedia* and *World Oil*.

natural gas						crude petroleum							country
published proven reserves, 2002 ('000,000,000 cu m)	production		consumption			reserves, 2002		production, 1998 ('000,000 barrels)	consumption, 1998 ('000,000 barrels)	refining capacity, 2002 ('000 barrels per day)	pipelines (latest)		
	natural gas, 1998 ('000,000 cu m)	manufactured gas, 1998 (% of total gas consumption)	amount, 1998 ('000,000 cu m)	residential, 1998 (%)	nonresidential, 1998 (%)	published proven ('000,000 barrels)	years to exhaust proven reserves				length (km)	traffic ('000,000 metric ton-km)	
99	137	...	137	...	...	...	...	—	—	—	251	...	Afghanistan
3.8	17	65.5	17	13.0[1]	87.0[1]	206	86	2.4	2.4	26	251	8	Albania
4,955	79,762	29.1	28,074	11.9[1]	88.1[1]	9,200	30	310	159	450	6,910	...	Algeria
...	...	...	...	...	...	...	...	—	—	—	—	—	American Samoa
...	...	...	...	...	...	...	...	—	—	—	—	—	Andorra
113	565	5.4	565	. ...	...	5,970	22	270	14	39	179	—	Angola
...	...	...	...	...	...	...	...	—	—	—	—	—	Antigua and Barbuda
758	35,923	10.2	35,479	22.9[1]	77.1[1]	2,881	9.5	302	191	639	6,990	...	Argentina
...	...	...	1,454	...	...	...	...	—	...	...	—	—	Armenia
...	...	...	...	...	...	...	...	—	2.4	280	—	—	Aruba
2,265	33,224	19.2	22,168	...	...	2,828	17	165	218	848	3,000	...	Australia
24	1,615	12.7	8,352	...	...	86	13	6.8	65	209	777	8,165	Austria
850	5,400	3.1	5,400	...	...	1,178	14	83	83	442	1,760	1,705	Azerbaijan
...	—	—	...	...	...	...	...	—	—	—	—	—	Bahamas, The
91	7,957	3.2	7,957	...	...	125	8.9	14	91	249	72	...	Bahrain
292	8,344	0.2	8,344	40.3	59.7	57	...	...	5.4	33	—	—	Bangladesh
0.1	37	13.3	37	34.8	65.2	2.5	4.2	0.6	1.0	4	—	—	Barbados
2.8	271	4.0	16,513	8.1[1]	91.9[1]	198	15	13	84	493	2,570	—	Belarus
—	0.1	16.9	18,237	...	...	...	...	—	235	791	1,328	1,168	Belgium
...	...	...	...	...	...	...	...	—	—	—	—	—	Belize
1.2	...	...	...	...	...	8.2	21	0.4	...	—	—	—	Benin
...	...	...	...	...	...	...	...	—	—	—	—	—	Bermuda
...	...	...	...	...	...	...	...	—	—	—	—	—	Bhutan
775	3,444	20.0	1,578	0.1[1]	99.9[1]	441	32	14	14	63	2,380	...	Bolivia
...	—	...	284	...	...	...	...	—	...	...	174	—	Bosnia and Herzegovina
...	...	3	...	...	...	—	...	—	3	—	—	—	Botswana
222	6,100	49.8	6,100	2.6	97.4	8,465	24	360	562	1,786	7,742	...	Brazil
239	8,924	1.2	1,371	3.5[1]	96.5[1]	1,160	20	59	1.5	9	553	—	Brunei
1.5	31	15.2	4,142	...	...	15	75	0.2	41	115	525	244	Bulgaria
...	...	...	...	...	...	...	...	—	—	—	—	—	Burkina Faso
...	...	...	...	...	...	...	...	—	—	—	—	—	Burundi
...	...	...	...	...	...	...	...	—	—	—	—	—	Cambodia
110	—	95.6	...	...	...	400	9.3	43	3.7	42	—	—	Cameroon
1,691	177,211	29.9	86,315	...	...	4,858	7.6	641	510	1,944	23,564	99,908	Canada
...	...	...	...	...	...	...	...	—	—	—	—	—	Cape Verde
...	...	...	...	...	...	...	...	—	—	—	—	—	Central African Republic
...	...	...	...	...	...	...	...	—	—	—	—	—	Chad
38	1,819	24.7	3,636	8.7	91.3	150	79	1.9	68	205	1,540	...	Chile
1,212	25,902	49.3	22,540	31.8	68.2	24,000	20	1,179	1,268	4,528	12,397	60,132	China
142	6,524	22.5	6,524	29.9	70.1	1,850	7.0	264	111	286	4,935	...	Colombia
...	...	...	...	...	...	...	...	—	—	—	—	—	Comoros
1.0	—	...	—	—	—	187	22	8.5	0.6	15	390	...	Congo, Dem. Rep. of the
119	3.4	58.0	3.4	...	...	1,506	16	95	4.3	21	25	...	Congo, Rep. of the
—	—	—	—	—	—	...	...	—	0.4	15	176	...	Costa Rica
30	—	59.4	—	—	—	100	11	9.3	31	65	—	—	Côte d'Ivoire
34	1,529	20.3	2,575	16.3[1]	83.7[1]	92	7.7	12	39	293	690	951	Croatia
14	24	71.3	24	3.4[1]	96.6[1]	314	26	12	18	301	—	—	Cuba
—	—	71.8	—	—	—	...	...	—	7.9	27	—	—	Cyprus
2.1	239	20.1	10,825	...	...	15	13	1.2	46	198	736	2,078	Czech Republic
87	7,091	11.1	4,063	...	...	1,113	13	88	61	176	688	1,385	Denmark
...	...	...	...	...	...	...	...	—	—	—	—	—	Djibouti
...	...	...	...	...	...	...	...	—	—	—	—	—	Dominica
...	—	7.9	...	...	...	—	...	—	19	49	104	...	Dominican Republic
...	...	...	...	...	...	...	...	—	...	...	—	—	East Timor
109	318	30.4	318	—	—	2,115	14	147	57	176	2,158	...	Ecuador

Energy (continued)

country	electricity												coal		
	installed capacity, 1998 ('000 kW)	production, 1998 capacity ('000,000 kW-hr)	amount ('000,000 kW-hr)	power source, 1998 fossil fuel (%)	hydro-power (%)	nuclear fuel (%)	trade, 1998 exports ('000,000 kW-hr)	imports ('000,000 kW-hr)	consumption amount, 1998 ('000,000 kW-hr)	per capita, 1998 (kW-hr)	residential, 1998 (%)	non-residential, 1998 (%)	reserves, latest ('000,000 metric tons)	production, 1998 ('000 metric tons)	consumption, 1998 ('000 metric tons)
Egypt	17,499	153,291	57,100	79.0	21.0	—	—	—	57,100	865	74.4	25.6	22	—	1,487
El Salvador	996	8,725	3,821	47.8	39.5	12.7[4]	23	61	3,859	640	67.4	32.6	...	...	...
Equatorial Guinea	5	44	21	90.5	9.5	—	—	—	21	49	...	...	...	...	...
Eritrea	5	5	5	5	5	...	—	—	5	5	5	5	...	...	...
Estonia	2,624	22,986	8,521	99.9	0.1	—	528	138	8,131	5,690	55.4	44.6	...	12,464	13,963
Ethiopia	456[5]	3,995[5]	1,676[5]	5.8[5]	94.2[5]	—	—	—	1,676[5]	27[5]	35.6[5]	64.4[5]	61	—	—
Faroe Islands	92	806	183	55.7	43.7	0.6[4]	—	—	183	4,256	...	...	—	—	—
Fiji	200	1,752	535	20.6	79.4	—	—	—	535	672	22.0	78.0	...	—	20
Finland	14,905	130,568	70,168	47.4	21.4	31.2	276	9,582	79,474	15,420	...	...	...	...	4,017
France	112,435[6]	984,931[6]	504,582[6]	9.8[6]	13.1[6]	77.1[6]	62,152[6]	4,590[6]	447,020[6]	7,613[6]	...	...	36	6,112[6]	25,001[6]
French Guiana	139	1,218	453	100.0	—	—	—	—	453	2,713	55.4	44.6	...	...	...
French Polynesia	89	780	361	62.6	37.4	—	—	—	361	1,648	...	...	...	...	...
Gabon	379	3,320	1,277	35.4	64.6	—	—	—	1,277	1,094	41.9	58.1	...	...	...
Gambia, The	29	254	77	100.0	—	—	—	—	77	63	...	...	...	...	...
Gaza Strip	...	...	...	...	...	...	...	...	...	...	...	...	...	...	...
Georgia	4,558	39,928	8,069	21.0	79.0	—	796	698	7,971	1,576	...	...	...	14	29
Germany	115,443	1,011,281	556,400	67.2	3.8	29.0	38,953	38,315	555,762	6,785	...	...	66,000	211,374	239,748
Ghana	1,187	10,398	6,662	0.1	99.9	—	232	4	6,434	336	7.2	92.8	...	—	3
Greece	10,146	88,879	46,363	91.1	8.7	0.2[4]	890	2,500	47,973	4,526	...	...	2,874	60,884	61,940
Greenland	106	929	260	100.0	—	—	—	—	260	4,643	...	...	183	...	...
Grenada	15	131	110	100.0	—	—	—	—	110	1,183	72.9	27.1	...	...	...
Guadeloupe	417	3,653	1,211	100.0	—	—	—	—	1,211	2,734	...	...	...	...	...
Guam	302	2,646	830	100.0	—	—	—	—	830	5,155	...	...	...	...	...
Guatemala	1,454	12,737	4,456	53.4	46.6	—	61	23	4,418	409	67.3	32.7	...	...	...
Guernsey	...	...	...	...	...	...	...	...	...	...	...	...	...	...	...
Guinea	186	1,629	545	65.1	34.9	—	—	—	545	74	...	...	...	...	...
Guinea-Bissau	11	96	53	100.0	—	—	—	—	53	46	...	...	...	...	...
Guyana	202	1,770	830	99.4	0.6	—	—	—	830	976	...	...	...	...	...
Haiti	264	2,313	691	59.8	40.2	—	—	—	691	87	44.1	55.9	13[2]	...	...
Honduras	518	4,538	3,690	47.5	52.5	—	1	42	3,731	607	69.5	30.5	21[2]	...	...
Hong Kong	11,312	99,093	31,414	100.0	—	—	610	7,760	38,564	5,790	25.2[1]	74.8[1]	...	—	7,102
Hungary	7,012	61,425	37,188	62.1	0.4	37.5	3,302	4,042	37,928	3,749	65.5	34.5	1,097	14,650	16,607
Iceland	1,245	10,906	6,281	0.1	89.5	10.4[4]	—	—	6,281	22,757	...	...	—	—	70
India	107,453	941,288	494,380	80.6	16.7	2.7	86	1,585	495,879	505	53.5	46.5	84,396	321,166	335,260
Indonesia	22,867	200,315	90,027	81.3	15.8	2.9[4]	—	—	90,027	436	46.9	53.1	5,370	60,321	14,034
Iran	30,627	268,293	103,412	93.2	6.8	—	—	—	103,412	1,573	31.6[1]	68.4[1]	1,710	1,169	1,466
Iraq	9,500	83,220	30,346	98.1	1.9	—	—	—	30,346	1,392	...	...	—	—	—
Ireland	4,412	38,649	21,387	94.3	5.6	0.1	73	152	21,612	5,871	...	...	14	—	2,918
Isle of Man	...	...	...	100.0	—	—	—	—	...	...	...	...	...	...	...
Israel	7,860	68,854	37,964	99.9	0.1	—	1,055	—	36,909	6,168	61.6	38.4	...	—	9,284
Italy	68,422[7]	599,377[7]	260,241[7]	80.2[7]	18.2[7]	1.6[4,7]	901[7]	41,633[7]	300,973[7]	5,244[7]	...	...	34	189[7]	16,413[7]
Jamaica	1,182	10,354	6,480	97.8	2.2	—	—	—	6,480	2,553	36.2	63.8	...	—	71
Japan	245,258	2,148,460	1,046,294	58.1	9.8	32.1	—	—	1,046,294	8,285	...	...	773	3,681	132,849
Jersey	...	...	...	...	...	...	...	...	...	...	...	...	...	...	...
Jordan	1,295	11,344	6,745	99.8	0.2	—	—	4	6,741	1,069	66.1	33.9	...	—	...
Kazakhstan	18,960	166,090	49,144	87.5	12.5	—	3,441	7,252	52,955	3,245	10.6[1]	89.4[1]	34,000	69,773	47,310
Kenya	889	7,788	4,439	13.8	73.8	12.4[4]	—	146	4,585	158	38.8	61.2	...	—	65
Kiribati	2	18	7	100.0	—	—	—	—	7	86	...	...	...	...	...
Korea, North	9,500	83,220	30,989	35.7	64.3	—	—	—	30,989	1,327	...	...	600	84,910	86,583
Korea, South	47,983	420,331	240,587	60.2	2.5	37.3	—	—	240,587	5,218	41.8	58.2	78	4,361	55,892
Kuwait	6,997	61,294	30,514	100.0	—	—	—	—	30,514	16,849	93.3	6.7	...	...	...
Kyrgyzstan	3,690	32,324	11,615	14.4	85.6	—	7,125	6,399	10,889	2,345	25.4[1]	...	812	680	1,466
Laos	256	2,243	1,225	3.5	96.5	—	774	46	497	96	...	...	...	1	—
Latvia	2,103	18,422	5,796	25.5	74.5	—	385	914	6,325	2,609	59.5	40.5	...	—	146
Lebanon	1,400	12,264	9,011	91.3	8.7	—	—	300	9,311	2,918	54.5[1]	45.5[1]	...	—	121
Lesotho	3	3	3	3	3	3	3	3	3	3	...	...	...	3	3
Liberia	334	2,926	498	62.5	37.5	—	—	—	498	187	...	...	...	—	5
Libya	4,600	40,296	19,496	100.0	—	—	—	—	19,496	3,652	...	...	—	—	5
Liechtenstein	8	8	8	8	8	8	8	8	8	8	...	...	...	...	8
Lithuania	5,791	50,729	17,631	18.0	5.1	76.9	6,466	384	11,549	3,126	16.2[1]	83.8[1]	...	...	219
Luxembourg	1,268	11,108	1,159	9.9	90.1	—	924	6,338	6,573	15,576	...	...	...	—	152
Macau	352	3,084	1,539	100.0	—	—	1	173	1,711	3,728	87.2	12.8	...	—	—
Macedonia	1,494	13,087	7,048	84.6	15.4	—	2	—	7,046	3,525	44.5[1]	55.5[1]	...	8,176	8,501
Madagascar	220	1,927	785	34.9	65.1	—	—	—	785	52	31.7	68.3	1,075[2]	—	15
Malawi	185	1,621	877	2.2	97.8	—	2	—	875	85	67.4	32.6	1.8	—	17
Malaysia	13,604	119,171	60,471	92.1	7.9	—	5	—	60,466	2,824	48.4	51.6	3.6	351	2,633
Maldives	25	219	82	100.0	—	—	—	—	82	303	...	...	...	...	...
Mali	114	999	398	42.0	58.0	—	—	—	398	37	99.0	1.0	...	...	...
Malta	250	2,190	1,518	100.0	—	—	—	—	1,518	3,953	29.2[1]	70.8[1]	...	—	320
Marshall Islands	9[9]	867[9]	...	...	...	...	...	...	...	...	...	...	...	...	...
Martinique	396	3,469	1,080	100.0	—	—	—	—	1,080	2,776	...	...	...	...	...
Mauritania	105	920	155	81.3	18.7	—	—	—	155	61	...	...	...	—	6
Mauritius	364	3,189	1,283	91.7	8.3	—	—	—	1,283	1,122	64.7	35.3	...	—	68
Mayotte	...	...	...	...	...	...	...	...	...	...	...	...	...	...	...
Mexico	45,615	399,587	183,841	78.3	13.5	8.2[4]	272	1,705	185,274	1,933	36.9	63.1	1,211	11,232	12,034
Micronesia	...	...	...	...	...	...	...	...	...	...	...	...	...	...	...
Moldova	1,022	8,953	4,584	98.2	1.8	—	—	1,916	6,500	1,485	...	...	...	—	546
Monaco	6	6	6	6	6	6	6	6	6	6	...	...	...	6	6
Mongolia	901	7,893	2,745	100.0	—	—	60	367	3,052	1,183	...	...	24,000[2]	5,057	5,092
Morocco	4,037	35,364	13,440	86.9	13.1	—	—	705	14,145	517	54.5	45.5	5.4	269	3,497
Mozambique	2,383	20,875	7,345	7.1	92.9	—	5,677	350	2,018	107	33.2[1]	66.8[1]	212	18	34
Myanmar (Burma)	1,402	12,282	4,139	77.1	22.9	—	—	—	4,139	94	75.5	24.5	1.8	59	65
Namibia	3	3	3	3	3	3	3	3	3	3	...	...	...	3	3
Nauru	10	88	32	100.0	—	—	—	—	32	2,909	...	...	...	...	...
Nepal	327	2,865	1,202	13.2	86.8	—	63	210	1,349	59	59.5	40.5	1.8	16	339

natural gas — published proven reserves, 2002 ('000,000,-000 cu m)	natural gas — production — natural gas, 1998 ('000,000 cu m)	natural gas — production — manufactured gas, 1998 (% of total gas consumption)	natural gas — consumption — amount, 1998 ('000,000 cu m)	natural gas — consumption — residential, 1998 (%)	natural gas — consumption — non-residential, 1998 (%)	crude petroleum — reserves, 2002 — published proven ('000,000 barrels)	crude petroleum — reserves, 2002 — years to exhaust proven reserves	crude petroleum — production, 1998 ('000,000 barrels)	crude petroleum — consumption, 1998 ('000,000 barrels)	crude petroleum — refining capacity, 2002 ('000 barrels per day)	pipelines (latest) — length (km)	pipelines (latest) — traffic ('000,000 metric ton-km)	country
1,533	12,356	11.9	12,356	5.1[1]	94.9[1]	2,948	10	292	213	726	1,767	...	Egypt
—	—	13.9	—	—	—	...	...	—	6.7	22	—	—	El Salvador
100	—	...	...	...	...	12	0.4	30	0.3	—	—	—	Equatorial Guinea
...	...	5	...	...	...	...	...	...	5	15	—	—	Eritrea
...	...	11.9	636	8.2[1]	91.8[1]	—	—	—	8.4	...	—	—	Estonia
25	—	100.0[5]	—	—	—	0.4	...	—	1.2[5]	—	—	—	Ethiopia
...	...	...	...	...	...	...	...	—	—	—	—	—	Faroe Islands
...	...	...	...	...	...	...	...	—	—	—	—	—	Fiji
—	—	28.8	4,027	...	...	...	...	—	84	239	—	—	Finland
14	2,279	17.8[6]	44,650[6]	32.4[1,6]	67.6[1,6]	149	12	12	661[6]	1,896	7,546	24,429	France
...	...	...	...	...	...	...	...	—	—	—	—	—	French Guiana
...	...	...	...	...	...	...	...	—	—	—	—	—	French Polynesia
99	654	1.7	654	19.7[1]	80.3[1]	2,499	19	133	5.3	17	284	...	Gabon
...	...	...	...	...	...	...	...	—	—	—	—	—	Gambia, The
...	...	...	...	...	...	...	...				—	—	Gaza Strip
8.5	—	...	820	...	...	35	39	0.9	0.4	106	670	...	Georgia
254	23,229	14.1	110,619	...	...	364	17	21	787	2,259	2,240	37,250	Germany
23	—	94.8	—	—	—	17	...	...	7.3	45	—	—	Ghana
1.0	47	65.5	864	...	...	9	4.3	2.1	133	407	573	...	Greece
...	...	...	...	...	...	...	...	—	—	—	—	—	Greenland
...	...	...	...	...	...	...	...	—	—	—	—	—	Grenada
...	...	...	...	...	...	...	...	—	—	—	—	—	Guadeloupe
...	—	—	—	...	...	...	...	—	—	—	—	—	Guam
2.8	11	2.8	11	...	...	526	57	9.2	6.7	16	275	...	Guatemala
...	...	...	...	...	...	...	...	—	—	—	—	—	Guernsey
...	...	...	...	...	...	...	...	—	—	—	—	—	Guinea
...	...	...	...	...	...	...	...	—	—	—	—	—	Guinea-Bissau
...	...	...	...	...	...	...	...	—	—	—	—	—	Guyana
...	...	...	...	...	...	...	...	—	—	—	—	—	Haiti
...	...	...	...	...	...	...	...	—	12	...	—	—	Honduras
...	—	18.2	2,590	—	—	—	—	—	—	—	—	—	Hong Kong
65	3,803	6.6	12,538	...	...	111	13	8.4	53	161	1,204	2,470	Hungary
...	...	...	...	...	...	...	...	—	7.3	—	—	—	Iceland
437	26,455	14.2	26,455	1.3[1]	98.7[1]	4,840	19	251	544	2,135	5,692	...	India
2,478	75,271	13.3	25,749	2.7[1]	97.3[1]	5,000	10	495	342	993	2,961	...	Indonesia
26,600	49,573	8.4	51,436	26.8[1]	73.2[1]	89,700	68	1,317	454	1,484	9,800	...	Iran
3,188	2,950	48.2	2,950	...	...	112,500	146	773	188	418	5,075	...	Iraq
20	1,645	3.5	3,278	...	...	—	...	—	22	71	—	—	Ireland
...	...	...	...	...	...	...	...	—	...	—	—	—	Isle of Man
42	12	118.7	12	—	100.0[1]	3.8	—	—	86	220	998	—	Israel
191	19,013	11.2[7]	62,438[7]	...	...	622	16	38	622[7]	2,283	3,851	13,981	Italy
—	—	26.0	—	—	—	...	...	—	8.8	34	10	—	Jamaica
40	2,301	30.1	71,037	...	...	59	18	3.3	1,560	4,786	406	...	Japan
...	...	...	...	...	...	...	...	—	—	—	—	—	Jersey
5.7	270	36.3	270	—	—	0.9	...	...	25	90	209	...	Jordan
1,841	7,679	2.0	8,400	...	...	5,417	31	176	56	427	6,965	26,581	Kazakhstan
—	—	100.0	—	...	...	...	...	—	16	90	483	...	Kenya
...	...	...	...	...	...	...	...	—	—	—	—	—	Kiribati
...	...	...	...	...	...	...	...	—	14	71	217	...	Korea, North
—	—	38.8	14,622	...	...	...	...	—	827	2,560	455	...	Korea, South
1,489	9,491	40.2	9,491	25.0[1]	75.0[1]	96,500	128	753	316	773	917	...	Kuwait
5.7	18	...	1,017	...	...	40	67	0.6	1.0	10	—	—	Kyrgyzstan
...	...	...	...	...	...	...	...	—	—	—	136	...	Laos
...	...	...	1,244	10.5[1]	89.5[1]	...	...	—	...	...	1,530	6,569	Latvia
—	...	...	...	...	...	...	...	—	...	38	72	...	Lebanon
—	—	3	—	...	...	...	...	—	3	—	—	—	Lesotho
—	—	—	—	...	...	...	...	—	...	15	—	—	Liberia
1,328	6,360	17.6	5,474	...	...	29,500	58	507	98	343	4,826	...	Libya
—	—	8	—	...	...	...	...	—	8	—	—	—	Liechtenstein
—	...	22.4	1,882	9.3[1]	90.7[1]	12	6.0	2.0	47	263	105	3,457	Lithuania
...	—	5.0	754	...	...	...	...	—	...	—	48	—	Luxembourg
...	...	...	...	...	...	...	...	—	—	—	—	—	Macau
...	...	34.6	...	...	...	...	...	—	5.6	51	—	—	Macedonia
2.8	—	75.0	—	...	...	...	...	—	1.6	15	—	—	Madagascar
...	...	...	...	...	...	...	...	—	—	—	—	—	Malawi
2,337	38,375	11.1	19,126	0.3	99.7	3,000	12	260	134	515	1,307	...	Malaysia
...	...	...	...	...	...	...	...	—	—	—	—	—	Maldives
...	...	...	...	...	...	...	...	—	—	—	—	—	Mali
...	...	...	...	...	...	...	...	—	—	—	—	—	Malta
...	...	...	...	...	...	...	...	—	—	...	—	—	Marshall Islands
—	—	161.5	...	...	...	...	...	—	5.8	17	—	—	Martinique
...	...	88.4	...	...	...	...	...	—	6.9	—	—	—	Mauritania
...	...	...	...	...	...	...	...	—	—	—	—	—	Mauritius
...	...	...	...	...	...	...	...	—	—	—	—	—	Mayotte
1,103	31,480	21.3	32,613	...	...	26,941	24	1,116	485	1,525	38,350	...	Mexico
...	...	...	...	...	...	...	...	—	—	—	—	—	Micronesia
...	—	...	3,373	11.6[1]	88.4[1]	...	...	—	...	...	—	—	Moldova
...	...	6	6	6	6	...	...	—	6	—	—	—	Monaco
...	...	...	...	...	...	...	...	—	3.3	—	—	—	Mongolia
1.3	37	23.4	37	—	100.0[1]	1.8	...	...	47	155	362	...	Morocco
57	—	...	...	...	...	...	...	—	...	—	595	...	Mozambique
346	1,641	1.2	1,641	0.3[1]	99.7[1]	50	19	2.7	7.3	32	1,343	...	Myanmar (Burma)
85	—	3	—	—	—	...	...	—	3	—	—	—	Namibia
...	—	—	—	...	...	...	...	—	—	—	—	—	Nauru
...	...	...	...	...	...	...	...	—	—	—	—	—	Nepal

Energy (continued)

country	electricity installed capacity, 1998 ('000 kW)	production, 1998 capacity ('000,000 kW-hr)	production, 1998 amount ('000,000 kW-hr)	power source, 1998 fossil fuel (%)	hydro-power (%)	nuclear fuel (%)	trade, 1998 exports ('000,000 kW-hr)	imports ('000,000 kW-hr)	consumption amount, 1998 ('000,000 kW-hr)	per capita, 1998 (kW-hr)	residential, 1998 (%)	nonresidential, 1998 (%)	coal reserves, latest ('000,000 metric tons)	coal production, 1998 ('000 metric tons)	coal consumption, 1998 ('000 metric tons)
Netherlands, The	20,164	176,637	90,903	95.0	0.1	4.9	420	12,234	102,717	6,552	...	...	497	—	15,006
Netherlands Antilles	220	1,927	1,490	100.0	—	—	—	—	1,490	6,995	...	...		...	
New Caledonia	253	2,216	1,568	69.5	30.5	—	—	—	1,568	7,612	...	...	1.8	—	165
New Zealand	7,960	69,730	37,566	28.4	64.9	6.7[4]	—	—	37,566	9,896	...	...	572	3,317	2,330
Nicaragua	614	5,379	2,153	50.3	19.1	30.6[4]	—	43	2,196	457	70.7	29.3			
Niger	105	920	234	100.0	—	—	—	198	432	43	56.0	44.0	70	174	174
Nigeria	5,881	51,518	15,716	65.1	34.9	—	...	—	15,716	148	50.1[1]	49.9[1]	190	59	59
Northern Mariana Islands	...	...	...	...	...	...	...	...	...	...	...	...	...	...	...
Norway	29,277	256,467	117,043	0.6	99.4	—	4,415	8,046	120,674	27,277	...	...	0.9	328	985
Oman	2,135	18,703	10,672	100.0	—	—	—	—	10,672	4,480	...	...			
Pakistan	15,658	137,164	62,104	63.9	35.5	0.6	—	—	62,104	419	72.3	27.7	2,265	3,159	4,119
Palau	62	543	208	85.6	14.4	—	—	—	208	10,947	...	...	—	—	—
Panama	1,094	9,583	4,498	29.0	71.0	—	23	57	4,532	1,638	79.5	20.5	—	—	59
Papua New Guinea	490	4,292	1,795	72.1	27.9	—	—	—	1,795	390	27.9	72.1	...	...	1
Paraguay	7,054	61,793	50,930	0.1	99.9	—	45,208	—	5,722	1,096	79.0	21.0	—	—	—
Peru	5,191	45,473	18,583	25.7	74.3	—	—	1	18,584	749	67.7	32.3	1,060	21	451
Philippines	11,601	101,625	41,192	65.5	17.8	16.7[4]	—	—	41,192	565	65.3	34.7	332	1,002	5,287
Poland	29,469	258,148	142,789	97.0	3.0	—	8,082	4,608	139,315	3,598	41.8	58.2	22,160	177,965	155,685
Portugal	9,787	85,734	38,985	66.1	33.5	0.4[4]	3,700	3,974	39,259	3,978	...	...	36	—	5,099
Puerto Rico	4,430	38,807	20,360	99.4	0.6	—	—	—	20,360	5,344	...	...			175
Qatar	1,899	16,635	8,170	100.0	—	—	—	—	8,170	14,111	74.9	25.1	...	...	...
Réunion	434	3,802	1,566	64.4	35.6	—	—	—	1,566	2,296	...	...	...	...	...
Romania	22,558	197,608	53,496	54.8	35.3	9.9	715	1,181	53,962	2,401	27.1	72.9	1,457	26,231	31,304
Russia	210,957	1,847,983	827,133	68.2	19.3	12.5	26,275	8,261	809,119	5,488	36.1	63.9	157,010	235,319	228,699
Rwanda	34	298	166	2.4	97.6	—	—	15	178	27	...	...	...	...	...
St. Kitts and Nevis	16	140	92	100.0	—	—	—	—	92	2,359	...	...			
St. Lucia	22	193	116	100.0	—	—	—	—	116	773	...	...			
St. Vincent and the Grenadines	16	140	85	74.1	25.9	—	—	—	85	759	...	...			
Samoa	19	166	65	61.5	38.5	—	—	—	65	374	...	...			
San Marino	7	7	7	7	7	7	7	7	7	7	...	...		7	7
São Tomé and Príncipe	6	53	15	46.7	53.3	—	—	—	15	106	...	...	...	...	...
Saudi Arabia	22,575	197,757	112,691	100.0	—	—	—	—	112,691	5,584	47.2[1]	52.8[1]	...	...	...
Senegal	235	2,059	1,252	100.0	—	—	—	—	1,252	139	16.7	83.3	...	...	...
Seychelles	28	245	159	100.0	—	—	—	—	159	2,092	24.3	75.7	...	...	...
Sierra Leone	126	1,104	242	100.0	—	—	—	—	242	53	...	...	...	...	—
Singapore	5,665	49,625	28,283	100.0	—	—	—	—	28,283	8,137	16.0[1]	84.0[1]	...	—	—
Slovakia	7,778	68,135	25,465	37.3	17.9	44.8	157	1,447	26,755	4,976	20.6[1]	79.4[1]	172	3,951	10,323
Slovenia	2,571	22,522	13,718	38.1	25.1	36.8	2,630	706	11,794	5,918	24.8[1]	75.2[1]	275	4,891	5,489
Solomon Islands	12	105	32	100.0	—	—	—	—	32	77	...	...	...	...	...
Somalia	79	692	278	100.0	—	—	—	—	278	27	...	...	...	...	...
South Africa	35,897[3]	314,458[3]	193,946[3]	92.2[3]	0.8[3]	7.0[3]	4,532[3]	3,078[3]	192,492[3]	4,221[3]	28.5	71.5	49,520	225,901[3]	159,436[3]
Spain	50,081	438,710	195,280	50.8	18.3	30.9	5,562	8,964	198,682	5,014	...	...	660	25,962	38,995
Sri Lanka	1,747	15,304	5,683	31.1	68.9	—	—	—	5,683	308	62.7	37.3	...	—	10
Sudan, The	606	5,309	1,346	29.4	70.6	—	—	—	1,346	48	18.6[1]	81.4[1]	...	—	—
Suriname	425	3,723	1,621	20.2	79.8	—	—	—	1,621	3,915	...	...	...	—	—
Swaziland	3	3	3	3	3	3	3	3	3	3	...	...	208	3	3
Sweden	33,949	297,393	158,277	6.3	47.0	46.7	16,799	6,102	147,580	16,629	...	...	0.9	...	2,917
Switzerland	16,692[8]	146,222[8]	62,909[8]	3.9[8]	55.1[8]	41.0[8]	29,561[8]	23,607[8]	56,955[8]	7,769[8]	...	...	—	—	108[8]
Syria	4,510	39,508	19,841	86.4	13.6	—	—	—	19,841	1,294	34.6[1]	65.4[1]	...	—	—
Taiwan	26,680	233,717	142,964	67.8	7.4	24.8	—	—	128,130	5,858	35.2	64.8	0.9	79	...
Tajikistan	4,443	38,921	14,422	1.9	98.1	—	3,724	3,969	14,667	2,438	14.6[1]	85.4[1]	...	20	126
Tanzania	543	4,757	1,747	13.8	86.2	—	—	—	1,747	54	36.6[1]	63.4[1]	200	5	5
Thailand	21,500	188,340	94,769	94.5	5.5	—	153	1,623	96,239	1,596	58.3	41.7	1,268	20,163	22,132
Togo	34	298	34	93.6	6.4	—	—	321	415	94	...	...	...	...	...
Tonga	7	61	34	100.0	—	—	—	—	34	347	...	...	...	...	...
Trinidad and Tobago	1,150	10,074	5,191	100.0	—	—	—	—	5,191	4,046	35.3	64.7	...	...	1
Tunisia	2,290	20,060	8,958	99.2	0.8	—	130	126	8,954	959	54.1	45.9	...	—	—
Turkey	23,351	204,555	111,022	61.9	38.0	0.1[4]	298	3,298	114,022	1,768	...	...	3,689	67,383	77,673
Turkmenistan	3,930	34,427	9,416	99.9	0.1	—	4,059	950	6,307	1,464	...	...	...	...	—
Tuvalu	...	...	...	...	...	...	...	...	...	...	...	...	...	...	...
Uganda	189	1,656	1,273	0.4	99.6	—	159	—	1,114	54	...	...	...	...	...
Ukraine	53,868	471,884	172,822	47.3	9.2	43.5	10,728	10,056	172,150	3,385	...	...	34,153	77,176	83,706
United Arab Emirates	5,710	50,020	31,392	100.0	—	—	—	—	31,392	13,341	...	...	...	...	...
United Kingdom	73,405	643,028	358,714	70.0	1.9	28.1	162	12,630	371,182	6,329	...	...	1,500	41,420	60,483
United States	792,839	6,945,270	3,833,979	72.4	8.4	19.2	12,730	39,513	3,860,762	14,089	...	...	248,257	1,013,383	926,634
Uruguay	2,179	19,088	9,570	9.5	90.5	—	2,234	78	7,414	2,254	76.0	34.0	...	...	1
Uzbekistan	11,709	102,571	45,900	87.5	12.5	—	5,100	6,000	46,800	1,985	...	...	4,000	2,923	2,920
Vanuatu	11	96	30	100.0	—	—	—	—	30	165	...	...	...	...	...
Venezuela	21,275	186,369	80,904	28.4	71.6	—	—	—	80,904	3,481	23.8	76.2	479	7,456	1,327
Vietnam	4,981	43,634	21,694	45.9	51.1	3.0[4]	—	—	21,694	280	32.6[1]	67.4[1]	150	11,672	6,162
Virgin Islands (U.S.)	323	2,829	1,082	100.0	—	—	—	—	1,082	11,511	...	...	...	—	254
West Bank	...	...	...	...	...	...	...	...	...	...	...	...			
Western Sahara	56	491	87	100.0	—	—	—	—	87	316	...	...	...	...	...
Yemen	810	7,096	2,507	100.0	—	—	—	—	2,507	148	...	...	1[2]	...	...
Yugoslavia	11,779	103,184	40,651	69.9	30.1	—	268	—	40,383	3,797	41.4[1]		16,255	44,072	44,124
Zambia	2,275	19,903	7,603	0.5	99.5	—	1,500	20	6,123	697	33.0	67.0	10	205	203
Zimbabwe	2,011	17,616	6,677	71.2	28.8	—	—	3,100	9,777	859	42.6	57.4	502	5,047	4,758

| natural gas | | | | | | crude petroleum | | | | | | | country |
| published proven reserves, 2002 ('000,000,-000 cu m) | production | | consumption | | | reserves, 2002 | | production, 1998 ('000,000 barrels) | consumption, 1998 ('000,000 barrels) | refining capacity, 2002 ('000 barrels per day) | pipelines (latest) | | |
	natural gas, 1998 ('000,000 cu m)	manufactured gas, 1998 (% of total gas consumption)	amount, 1998 ('000,000 cu m)	residential, 1998 (%)	non-residential, 1998 (%)	published proven ('000,000 barrels)	years to exhaust proven reserves				length (km)	traffic ('000,000 metric ton-km)	
1,615	84,541	18.6	51,225	...	...	107	8.9	12	400	1,206	1,383	5,503	Netherlands, The
—	...	117.2	...	...	...	...	...	—	103	320	—	—	Netherlands Antilles
...	...	...	...	...	...	...	...	—	...	...	—	—	New Caledonia
59	4,457	9.0	4,456	...	...	90	5.3	17	40	106	160	...	New Zealand
—	—	51.3	—	—	—	...	...	—	6.2	20	56	...	Nicaragua
...	—	—	—	—	—	...	...	—	—	—	—	—	Niger
4,502	5,900	1.4	5,900	—	100.0[1]	24,000	34	709	58	439	5,042	...	Nigeria
...	...	...	...	...	...	...	...	—	...	...	—	—	Northern Mariana Islands
2,186	49,569	23.6	6,792	...	...	9,447	8.3	1,142	106	310	5,747	3,485	Norway
864	6,029	1.4	6,029	...	...	5,506	17	327	27	85	1,300	...	Oman
681	18,738	1.2	18,738	41.2	58.8	298	14	21	49	239	1,135	...	Pakistan
—	—	—	—	—	—	—	—	—	...	...	—	—	Palau
—	—	35.6	61	—	—	...	...	—	17	60	130	...	Panama
425	83	...	83	—	—	238	8.2	29	0.4	—	—	...	Papua New Guinea
—	...	...	...	...	...	...	...	—	1.1	8	—	—	Paraguay
245	724	36.1	724	61.4[1]	38.6[1]	323	7.7	42	60	182	800	...	Peru
105	—	44.8	—	—	—	178	593	0.3	121	420	357	...	Philippines
164	4,818	23.7	14,109	45.0[1]	55.0[1]	115	43	2.7	119	382	2,280	18,448	Poland
—	—	29.6	831	...	...	...	...	—	99	304	80	—	Portugal
—	—	127.8	...	...	...	...	...	—	48	49	—	—	Puerto Rico
21,456	19,580	7.6	19,580	—	100.0[1]	15,207	70	218	28	58	235	—	Qatar
—	...	...	...	...	...	...	...	—	...	...	—	—	Réunion
121	14,881	13.1	19,918	9.6[1]	90.4[1]	1,154	25	47	92	504	4,229	2,257	Romania
48,139	635,485	5.1	412,137	11.2[1]	88.8[1]	48,573	22	2,162	1,216	5,435	63,000	1,899,000	Russia
57	0.2	—	0.2	...	...	...	...	—	...	...	—	—	Rwanda
...	...	...	...	...	...	...	...	—	—	—	—	—	St. Kitts and Nevis
...	...	...	...	...	...	...	...	—	—	—	—	—	St. Lucia
...	...	...	...	...	...	...	...	—	—	—	—	—	St. Vincent and the Grenadines
...	...	...	...	...	...	...	...	...	...	...	—	—	Samoa
...	...	...[7]	...[7]	...	...	...	...	...	...[7]	—	—	—	San Marino
...	...	...	...	...	...	...	...	—	—	—	—	—	São Tomé and Príncipe
6,349	46,819	42.5	46,819	...	...	261,750	83	3,135	670	1,745	6,550	...	Saudi Arabia
—	—	13.1	...	...	...	...	...	—	6.4	27	—	—	Senegal
...	...	...	...	...	...	...	...	—	—	—	—	—	Seychelles
—	...	...	...	...	...	...	...	—	1.7	10	—	—	Sierra Leone
—	—	338.7	—	—	—	...	...	—	453	1,259	—	—	Singapore
14	284	10.1	8,066	20.9[1]	79.1[1]	9	23	0.4	40	115	...	...	Slovakia
3.4	7	...	877	7.7[1]	92.3[1]	7	...	—	1.8	14	290	128	Slovenia
...	—	...	—	—	—	...	...	—	...	...	15	...	Solomon Islands
5.7	—	...	—	...	...	...	...	—	...	10	—	—	Somalia
23	1,383	58.5[3]	1,383	...	...	16	0.3	54	167[3]	469	2,679	...	South Africa
0.5	118	24.6	13,348	...	...	21	5.3	4.0	449	1,294	2,059	6,872	Spain
—	—	39.8	—	...	...	...	...	—	15	50	62	...	Sri Lanka
113	—	58.3	...	...	...	563	—	—	7.6	122	815	...	Sudan, The
—	...	—	...	...	...	74	49	1.5	1.2	7	—	—	Suriname
...	...	3	...	...	...	...	...	...	3	...	—	—	Swaziland
...	...	39.7	849	...	...	...	...	...	145	424	—	—	Sweden
—	—	15.5[8]	2,884[8]	...	...	...	...	...	37[8]	132	318	234	Switzerland
241	5,125	5.2	5,125	...	...	2,500	13	189	87	242	1,819	...	Syria
76	929	...	6,400	37.5	62.5	4	4.4	0.9	308	920	3,400	...	Taiwan
5.7	29	...	767	...	...	12	120	0.1	0.1	...	—	—	Tajikistan
28	—	100.0	...	...	...	...	...	...	4.3	15	982	...	Tanzania
377	15,605	15.8	15,627	—	100.0[1]	516	52	10	249	682	67	...	Thailand
—	...	...	...	...	...	...	...	...	...	...	—	—	Togo
...	...	...	...	...	...	...	...	...	...	...	—	—	Tonga
557	8,492	6.3	8,492	1.8[1]	98.2[1]	716	16	45	52	160	1,051	...	Trinidad and Tobago
76	1,661	4.7	2,311	3.7[1]	96.3[1]	308	9.9	31	24	34	883	...	Tunisia
8.6	581	18.7	11,176	...	...	296	13	23	198	719	4,059	2,994	Turkey
2,860	12,808	...	9,891	...	...	546	12	47	40	237	250	694	Turkmenistan
...	...	...	...	...	...	...	...	...	...	...	—	—	Tuvalu
...	...	...	...	...	...	...	...	...	...	...	—	—	Uganda
1,121	17,967	4.5	70,925	...	...	395	14	29	100	1,026	8,500	38,402	Ukraine
6,006	37,069	29.6	30,349	...	...	97,800	121	808	89	515	830	...	United Arab Emirates
695	110,575	10.0	108,216	...	...	4,930	5.3	927	623	1,784	3,926	11,666	United Kingdom
4,889	581,153	16.4	655,388	21.3	78.7	22,045	9.8	2,261	5,608	16,564	276,000	843,586	United States
—	—	84.5	...	...	...	...	...	—	13	37	—	—	Uruguay
1,875	48,107	0.6	45,070	...	...	594	15	39	36	222	290	200	Uzbekistan
...	...	...	...	...	...	...	...	...	...	...	—	—	Vanuatu
4,225	36,032	18.0	36,032	13.1	86.9	77,685	66	1,186	388	1,282	6,850	...	Venezuela
193	13	...	13	...	...	600	6.7	89	0.3	—	150	...	Vietnam
—	—	101.4	...	...	...	...	...	...	121	525	—	—	Virgin Islands (U.S.)
...	...	...	...	...	...	...	...	...	...	...	—	—	West Bank
...	...	...	...	...	...	...	...	...	...	...	—	—	Western Sahara
481	...	100.0	...	...	...	4,000	28	142	40	130	676	...	Yemen
48	665	2.0	2,370	...	...	78	11	6.8	21	158	545	...	Yugoslavia
—	—	396.0	...	...	...	...	...	...	2.9	24	1,724	...	Zambia
...	—	78.5	—	—	—	...	...	...	...	—	212	...	Zimbabwe

[1]1995. [2]Estimated reserves in place. [3]South Africa includes Botswana, Lesotho, Namibia, and Swaziland. [4]Geothermally generated electricity. [5]Ethiopia includes Eritrea. [6]France includes Monaco.
[7]Italy includes San Marino. [8]Switzerland includes Liechtenstein. [9]1993.

Transportation

This table presents data on the transportation infrastructure of the various countries and dependencies of the world and on their commercial passenger and cargo traffic. Most states have roads and airports, with services corresponding to the prevailing level of economic development. A number of states, however, lack railroads or inland waterways because of either geographic constraints or lack of development capital and technical expertise. Pipelines, one of the oldest means of bulk transport if aqueducts are considered, are today among the most narrowly developed transportation modes worldwide for shipment of bulk materials. Because the principal contemporary application of pipeline technology is to facilitate the shipment of hydrocarbon liquids and gases, coverage of pipelines will be found in the "Energy" table. It is, however, also true that pipelines now find increasing application for slurries of coal or other raw materials.

While the United Nations' *Statistical Yearbook, Monthly Bulletin of Statistics,* and *Annual Bulletin of Transport Statistics* provide much data on infrastructure and traffic and have established basic definitions and classifications for transportation statistics, the number of countries covered is limited. Several commercial publications maintain substantial databases and publishing programs for their particular areas of interest: highway and vehicle statistics are provided by the International Road Federation's annual *World Road Statistics;* the International Union of Railway's *International Railway Statistics* and Jane's *World Railways* provide similar data for railways; Lloyd's *Register of Shipping Statistical Tables* summarizes the world's

merchant marine; the *Official Airline Guide,* the International Civil Aviation Organization's *Digest of Statistics: Commercial Air Carriers,* and the International Air Transport Association's *World Air Transport Statistics* have also been used to supplement and update data collected by the UN. Because several of these agencies are commercially or insurance-oriented, their data tend to be more complete, accurate, and timely than those of intergovernmental organizations, which depend on periodic responses to questionnaires or publication of results in official sources. All of these international sources have been extensively supplemented by national statistical sources to provide additional data. Such diversity of sources, however, imposes limitations on the comparability of the statistics from country to country because the basis and completeness of data collection and the frequency and timeliness of analysis and publication may vary greatly. Data shown in italic are from 1994 or earlier.

The categories adopted in the table also have special problems of comparability. Total road length is subject to wide international variation of interpretation, as "roads" can mean anything from mere tracks to highly developed highways. Each country also has individual classifications that differ according to climate, availability of road-building materials, traffic patterns, administrative responsibility, and so on. "Paved roads," by contrast, is a much more tightly definable category, but the proportion of paved to total roads may be distorted by the less comparable total road statistics. Automobile and truck and bus fleet statistics, which are usually

Transportation

country	roads and motor vehicles (latest)								railroads (latest)					
	roads			motor vehicles			cargo		track length		traffic			
	length		paved (per-cent)	auto-mobiles	trucks and buses	persons per vehicle	short ton-mi ('000)	metric ton-km ('000)	mi	km	passengers		cargo	
	mi	km									passen-ger-mi ('000,000)	passen-ger-km ('000,000)	short ton-mi ('000,000)	metric ton-km ('000,000)
Afghanistan	13,000	21,000	13	31,000	25,000	401	*1,993*	*2,910*	16	25	...	...	...	...
Albania	11,000	18,000	30	90,766	34,378	25	550	803	416	670	72	116	0.01	0.02
Algeria	63,643	102,424	69	725,000	780,000	19	9,589	14,000	2,451[2]	3,945[2]	1,135	1,826	1,465	2,139
American Samoa	*217*	*350*	*43*	*4,672*	*199*	*11*	...	...	—	—	—	—	—	—
Andorra	167	269	74	35,358	4,238	1.6	...	...	—	—	—	—	—	—
Angola	45,128	72,626	25	207,000	25,000	41	...	...	1,834[2]	2,952[2]	*203*	*326*	*1,178*	*1,720*
Antigua and Barbuda	155	250	...	13,588	1,342	4.3	...	...	—	—	—	—	—	—
Argentina	135,630	218,276	29	4,901,608	1,379,044	5.7	...	...	21,100[2]	33,958[2]	5,656	9,102	6,234	9,102
Armenia	5,238	8,431	100	1,300	4,460	655	146	213	516	830	29	46	201	324
Aruba	*236*	*380*	*100*	38,834	990	2.4	...	...	—	—	—	—	—	—
Australia	502,356	808,465	40	9,719,900	2,214,900	1.6	*786,643*	*1,148,480*	22,233[2,7]	35,780[2,7]	7,152	11,510	87,262	127,400
Austria	124,000	200,000	100	4,009,604	328,591	1.9	10,773	15,670	3,506	5,643	4,953[7]	7,971[7]	10,617[7]	15,500[7]
Azerbaijan	28,502	45,870	94	281,100	104,300	21	484	706	1,317	2,120	342	550	3,160	4,613
Bahamas, The	1,522	2,450	57	89,263	17,228	2.6	...	...	—	—	—	—	—	—
Bahrain	1,966	3,164	77	149,636	32,213	3.4	...	...	—	—	—	—	—	—
Bangladesh	126,773	204,022	12	54,784	69,394	991	...	...	1,699[2]	2,734[2]	3,094	4,980	567	828
Barbados	1,025	1,650	96	43,711	10,583	4.9	...	...	—	—	—	—	—	—
Belarus	33,186	53,407	99	1,132,843	8,867	8.9	6,323	9,232	3,410	5,488	10,485	16,874	20,911	30,529
Belgium	89,353	143,800	97	4,491,734	453,122	2.1	25,586	37,355	2,100[2]	3,380[2]	4,570	7,354	5,063	7,392
Belize	1,398	2,250	18	9,695	11,698	11	...	...	—	—	—	—	—	—
Benin	4,217	6,787	20	37,772	8,058	123	...	...	359	578	75.7	121.8	193.5	311.4
Bermuda	140	225	100	21,220	4,007	2.4	...	...	—	—	—	—	—	—
Bhutan	2,041	3,285	61	2,590	1,367	348	...	...	—	—	—	—	—	—
Bolivia	30,696	49,400	6	223,829	138,536	21	*1,133*	*1,654*	2,187[2]	3,519[2]	84.9	136.7	359.0	524.2
Bosnia and Herzegovina	13,574	21,846	52	96,182	10,919	30	*2,708*	*3,954*	641	1,031	19.3	31.1	63.6	92.8
Botswana	11,388	18,327	25	30,517	59,710	17	...	...	603	971	60	96	545	795
Brazil	1,030,652	1,658,677	9	21,313,351	3,743,836	6.5	*178,359*	*260,400*	18,458[2]	29,706[2]	8,676	12,667	96,741	141,239
Brunei	1,064	1,712	75	91,047	15,918	2.9	...	...	12[13]	19[13]	—	—	—	—
Bulgaria	23,190	37,320	92	1,730,506	251,382	4.2	4,300	6,278	4,020	6,470	2,341	3,767	3,071	4,484
Burkina Faso	7,519	12,100	16	38,220	17,980	190	...	...	386[2]	622[2]	126	202	31	45
Burundi	8,997	14,480	7	19,200	18,240	145	...	...	—	—	—	—	—	—
Cambodia	22,226	35,769	8	52,919	13,574	171	822	1,200	409	649	37	60	25	36
Cameroon	30,074	48,400	8	98,000	64,350	88	*175*	*255*	625[2]	1,006[2]	197	317	556	812
Canada	560,415	901,903	35	13,887,270	3,694,125	1.7	94,584	138,090	40,639	65,403	906	1,458	205,146	299,508
Cape Verde	680	1,095	78	3,280	820	94	...	...	—	—	—	—	—	—
Central African Republic	14,900	24,000	2	9,500	7,000	195	41	60	—	—	—	—	—	—
Chad	20,800	33,400	1	10,560	14,550	293	580	850	—	—	—	—	—	—
Chile	49,590	79,800	14	1,323,800	687,500	7.5	...	...	5,410[2]	8,707[2]	377	606	1,984	2,896
China	794,405	1,278,474	93	6,548,300	6,278,900	96	375,580	548,338	35,781	57,584	229,657	369,598	843,302	1,236,200
Colombia	71,808	115,564	12	762,000	672,000	27	21	31	2,007[2]	3,230[2]	9.6	15.5	504.3	736.2
Comoros	559	900	76	9,100	4,950	36	...	...	—	—	—	—	—	—
Congo, Dem. Rep. of the	95,708	154,027	2	787,000	60,000	55	...	...	3,193	5,138	18[14]	29[14]	121[14]	176[14]
Congo, Rep. of the	7,950	12,800	10	37,240	15,520	49	*46*	*67*	556	894	150	242	92	135
Costa Rica	22,119	35,597	17	294,083	163,428	7.6	2,103	3,070	590[2]	950[2]	3.7	5.9	45.8	66.8
Côte d'Ivoire	31,300	50,400	10	293,000	163,000	32	...	...	397[2]	639[2]	80[17]	129[17]	40[17]	58[17]
Croatia	17,475	28,123	82	1,124,825	117,794	3.4	1,774	2,590	1,694	2,726	619	996	1,321	1,928
Cuba	37,815	60,858	49	172,574	185,495	31	*2,482*	*3,623*	2,987	4,807	1,219	1,962	763	1,075
Cyprus	6,620	10,654	58	234,976	108,452	2.4	...	...	—	—	—	—	—	—
Czech Republic	78,234	125,905	44	3,695,792	426,684	2.5	23,227	33,911	6,469	9,444	4,323	6,957	11,447	16,713
Denmark	44,389	71,663	100	1,854,060	335,690	2.4	14,639	21,372	1,704[2]	2,743[2]	3,304	5,318	1,387	2,025
Djibouti	1,796	2,890	13	9,200	2,040	38	...	...	*66*	*106*	361	762	144	232
Dominica	485	780	50	6,581	2,825	7.8	...	...	—	—	—	—	—	—
Dominican Republic	7,829	12,600	49	224,000	151,550	21	...	...	1,083[2]	1,743[2]	...	...	...	...
East Timor	...	...	...	...	...	...	...	...	...	...	...	...	...	...
Ecuador	26,841	43,197	19	464,902	52,630	23	2,712	3,959	600[2]	966[2]	28	45	686	1,002

based upon registration, are relatively accurate, though some countries round off figures, and unregistered vehicles may cause substantial undercount. There is also inconsistent classification of vehicle types; in some countries a vehicle may serve variously as an automobile, a truck, or a bus, or even as all three on certain occasions. Relatively few countries collect and maintain commercial road traffic statistics.

Data on national railway systems are generally given for railway track length rather than the length of routes, which may be multitracked. Siding tracks usually are not included, but some countries fail to distinguish them. The United States data include only class 1 railways, which account for about 94 percent of total track length. Passenger traffic is usually calculated from tickets sold to fare-paying passengers. Such statistics are subject to distortion if there are large numbers of nonpaying passengers, such as military personnel, or if season tickets are sold and not all the allowed journeys are utilized. Railway cargo traffic is calculated by weight hauled multiplied by the length of the journey. Changes in freight load during the journey should be accounted for but sometimes are not, leading to discrepancies.

Merchant fleet and tonnage statistics collected by Lloyd's registry service for vessels over 100 gross tons are quite accurate. Cargo statistics, however, reflect the port and customs requirements of each country and the reporting rules of each country's merchant marine authority (although these, increasingly, reflect the recommendations of the International

Maritime Organization); often, however, they are only estimates based on customs declarations and the count of vessels entered and cleared. Even when these elements are reported consistently, further uncertainties may be introduced because of ballast, bunkers, ships' stores, or transshipped goods included in the data.

Airport data are based on scheduled flights reported in the commercial *Official Airline Guide* and are both reliable and current. The comparability of civil air traffic statistics suffers from differing characteristics of the air transportation systems of different countries; data for an entire country may be two to three years behind those for a single airport.

Outside of Europe, where standardization of data on inland waterways is necessitated by the volume of international traffic, comparability of national data declines markedly. Calculations as to both the length of a country's waterway system (or route length of river, lake, and coastal traffic) and the makeup of its stock of commercially significant vessels (those for which data will be collected) are largely determined by the nature and use of the country's hydrographic net—its seasonality, relief profile, depth, access to potential markets—and inevitably differ widely from country to country. Data for coastal or island states may refer to scheduled coastwise or interisland traffic.

merchant marine (latest)				air					canals and inland waterways (latest)				country
fleet (vessels over 100 gross tons)	total dead-weight tonnage ('000)	international cargo (latest)		airports with sched-uled flights (latest)	traffic (latest)				length		cargo		
		loaded metric tons ('000)	off-loaded metric tons ('000)		passengers		cargo		mi	km	short ton-mi ('000,000)	metric ton-km ('000,000)	
					passenger-mi ('000,000)	passenger-km ('000,000)	short ton-mi ('000,000)	metric ton-km ('000,000)					
—	—	—	—	3	171.5[1]	276.0[1]	26[1]	38[1]	750	1,200	...	...	Afghanistan
24	81.0	120	2,040	1	2.2	3.5	0.22	0.32	46	74	24	35	Albania
149	1,093.4	63,110	15,700	28	1,803[3]	2,901[3]	12.5[3]	18.3[3]	...	...	...	...	Algeria
				3	...	...	...	...	...	...	...	...	American Samoa
3	0.1	380	581	3	—	—	—	—	—	—	—	—	Andorra
123	73.9	23,288	1,261	17	385[4]	620[4]	60[4]	97[4]	805	1,295	...	...	Angola
292	997.4	28	113	2	157	252	0.1	0.2	...	...	...	...	Antigua and Barbuda
423	1,173.1	69,372	19,536	39	7,292[5]	11,735[5]	895[5]	1,307[5]	6,804	10,950	19,326	28,215	Argentina
...	...	...	...	1	356	572	5.9	9.5	...	...	...	...	Armenia
6	6	...	...	1	318	511	...	...	...	...	...	...	Aruba
695	3,857.3	35,664	43,360	400	46,647	75,071	1,156	1,688	5,200	8,368	31,891	46,560	Australia
26	208.5	1,479	5,766	6	7,742	12,460	247	361	218	351	7,938	11,590	Austria
69	...	...	...	3	1,025	1,650	125	183	...	...	3,112	5,008	Azerbaijan
1,061	33,081.7	5,920	5,705	22	87	140	0.32	0.455	...	...	...	...	Bahamas, The
87	192.5	13,285	3,512	1	1,762[8]	2,836[8]	81.3[8]	118.7[8]	...	...	...	...	Bahrain
301	566.8	948	10,404	8	2,154	3,466	95	139	5,000	8,046	...	...	Bangladesh
37	84.0	206	538	1	93[9]	149[9]	0.8[10]	1.1[10]	...	...	...	...	Barbados
...	18,373.0	...	...	1	864	1,390	7	10	1,092	1,757	71	103	Belarus
232	218.5	360,984	367,680	2	12,042	19,379	389	568	957	1,540	3,993	5,830	Belgium
32	45.7	255	277	9	...	...	...	...	513	825	...	...	Belize
12	0.2	339	1,738	1	160.5[11]	258.3[11]	8.4[11]	13.5[11]	...	...	...	...	Benin
94	5,206.5	130	470	1	...	...	...	...	...	...	...	...	Bermuda
—	—	—	—	1	29	46	—	—	—	—	—	—	Bhutan
1	15.8	...	...	14	1,223	1,968	28.7	41.9	6,214	10,000	90	132	Bolivia
...	...	...	...	1	25.1	40.4	0.29	0.43	...	...	...	...	Bosnia and Herzegovina
—	—	—	—	7	35.3[12]	56.8[12]	0.1[12]	0.2[12]	...	...	...	...	Botswana
635	9,348.3	239,932	146,452	139	21,765	35,028	891	1,031	31,069	50,000	56,030	81,803	Brazil
51	349.7	42	1,308	1	1,742	2,803	75.0	109.5	130	209	...	...	Brunei
107	391	5,290	20,080	3	1,259	2,026	18.9	30.4	292	470	487	711	Bulgaria
—	—	—	—	2	134.9	217.2	23.4	34.2	...	...	...	...	Burkina Faso
1	0.4	35	188	1	1.2	2.0	...	...	...	...	...	...	Burundi
3	3.8	11	95	8	26.1	42.0	0.3	0.4	2,300	3,700	51	75	Cambodia
47	39.8	2,385	2,497	5	348	560	57	91	1,299	2,090	...	...	Cameroon
1,185	2,896.8	187,716	94,536	269	42,379	68,202	1,224	1,787	1,860	3,000	...	...	Canada
42	30.9	144	299	9	106	171	13.2	19.2	...	...	...	...	Cape Verde
—	—	53	126	1	139.6[12]	224.7[12]	11.2[12]	16.4[12]	500	800	185	270	Central African Republic
—	—	—	—	1	145	233	25	37	1,240	2,000	...	...	Chad
392	854.9	29,532	18,144	23	6,618	10,651	1,443	2,107	450	725	5,629	8,218	Chile
2,390	20,658.0	1,146,084	101,688	113	49,725	80,024	2,291	3,345	68,537	110,300	1,329,187	1,940,580	China
101	403.0	49,332	15,288	43	3,723	5,991	573	836	11,272	18,140	1.7	2.5	Colombia
6	3.6	12	107	2	1.9	3.0	...	...	...	...	...	...	Comoros
27	30.7	2,395	1,453	22	173[15]	279[15]	29[15]	42[15]	9,300	15,000	678	990	Congo, Dem. Rep. of the
22	10.8	708	533	10	160[11]	258[11]	9.6	14	696	1,120	...	...	Congo, Rep. of the
24	8.4	3,017	3,972	14	2,167[16]	3,487[16]	61.9[16]	90.4[16]	454	730	...	...	Costa Rica
51	98.6	4,173	7,228	5	191[18]	307[18]	30[18]	44[18]	609	980	...	...	Côte d'Ivoire
203	140.9	4,416	7,680	4	474	763	2.0	3.0	580	933	43	63	Croatia
393	924.6	8,092	15,440	14	2,202	3,543	38.5	56.2	149	240	108	158	Cuba
1,416	36,198.1	1,344	4,308	2	1,685	2,711	26	38	...	...	...	...	Cyprus
18[19]	514.1[19]	759	409	2	2,705	4,354	21	30	413	664	627	915	Czech Republic
456	7,589.1	21,060	38,292	13	3,340[20]	5,376[20]	117[20]	171[20]	259	417	1,100	1,600	Denmark
10	4.1	414	958	1	42	67	4	6	...	...	...	...	Djibouti
7	3.2	103	181	2	...	...	...	...	...	...	...	...	Dominica
28	10.4	1,668	4,182	7	9.8	15.8	7.9	11.6	...	...	...	...	Dominican Republic
...	...	...	...	...	...	...	...	...	...	...	...	...	East Timor
154	504.1	11,783	1,958	14	574	924	79	116	932	1,500	...	...	Ecuador

Transportation   (continued)

country	roads and motor vehicles (latest)								railroads (latest)					
	roads		paved (per-cent)	motor vehicles			cargo		track length		traffic			
	length			auto-mobiles	trucks and buses	persons per vehicle	short ton-mi ('000,000)	metric ton-km ('000,000)	mi	km	passengers		cargo	
	mi	km									passen-ger-mi ('000,000)	passen-ger-km ('000,000)	short ton-mi ('000,000)	metric ton-km ('000,000)
Egypt	39,800[21]	64,000[21]	78[21]	1,154,753	510,766	37	21,600	31,500	2,989	4,810	35,211	56,667	2,820	4,117
El Salvador	6,232	10,029	20	177,488	184,859	16	...	...	349[2]	562[2]	4.4	7.1	12	17
Equatorial Guinea	1,740	2,800	13	6,500	4,000	37	...	...	—	—	—	—	—	—
Eritrea	2,491	4,010	22	5,940	...	...	...	...	43	70	...	...	...	...
Estonia	10,209	16,430	51	451,000	86,900	2.7	2,691	3,929	636	1,024	149	238	4,808	7,020
Ethiopia	12,117	19,500	15	52,012	39,936	642	...	...	486[22]	782[22]	98	157	73	106
Faroe Islands	285	458	...	14,608	3,455	2.5			—	—	—	—	—	—
Fiji	3,200	5,100	20	49,712	33,928	9.4			370[13]	595[13]	...	...	...	...
Finland	48,340	77,900	65	2,069,055	300,048	2.2	19,884	29,030	3,626[2]	5,836[2]	2,122	3,415	6,680	9,753
France	547,200	893,500	100	27,480,000	5,610,000	1.8	114,382	166,995	19,486[2]	31,821[2]	40,100	64,500	37,000	54,000
French Guiana	706	1,137	40	29,100	10,600	3.2	...	...	—	—	—	—	—	—
French Polynesia	549	884	44	37,000	15,300	4.0	...	...	—	—	—	—	—	—
Gabon	4,760	7,670	8	24,750	16,490	28	...	...	506	814	53	85	345	503
Gambia, The	1,678	2,700	35	8,640	9,000	68			—	—	—	—	—	—
Gaza Strip	...	...	...	37,061	8,105	23			—	—	—	—	—	—
Georgia	12,862	20,700	93	427,000	41,510	11	288	420	961	1,546	219	349	2,150	3,139
Germany	143,372	230,735	99	42,323,672	2,550,222	1.8	176,337	257,447	54,188	87,207	41,321	66,500	48,875	71,356
Ghana	24,000	38,700	40	90,000	45,000	133	873	1,275	592[2]	953[2]	731.4	1,177	93.9	137.1
Greece	72,700	117,000	92	2,675,676	1,013,677	2.9	12,000	17,000	1,555[2]	2,503[2]	1,108	1,783	226	330
Greenland	93	150	60	2,242	1,474	15			—	—	—	—	—	—
Grenada	646	1,040	61	4,739	3,068	12			—	—	—	—	—	—
Guadeloupe	2,122	3,415	80	101,600	37,500	2.9			—	—	—	—	—	—
Guam	550	885	76	79,800	34,700	1.3			—	—	—	—	—	—
Guatemala	8,140	13,100	28	102,000	97,000	51			549[2]	884[2]	10.3	16.6	58.6	85.6
Guernsey	...	...	...	37,598	7,338	1.4			—	—	—	—	—	—
Guinea	18,952	30,500	16	14,100	21,000	219			411[2]	662[2]	25.8	41.5	5.0	7.3
Guinea-Bissau	2,734	4,400	10	7,120	5,640	91			—	—	—	—	—	—
Guyana	4,952	7,970	7	24,000	9,000	22			116[13]	187[13]	...	...	...	...
Haiti	2,585	4,160	24	32,000	21,000	121			—	—	—	—	—	—
Honduras	9,073	14,602	18	81,439	170,006	22			614	988	4.8	7.7	20.7	30.2
Hong Kong	1,183	1,904	100	332,000	133,000	14	...	...	21[2]	34[2]	2,231	3,591	68	99
Hungary	116,944	188,203	43	2,255,526	321,634	4.0	10,950	15,987	4,827[2]	7,768[2]	5,912	9,514	5,297	7,733
Iceland	7,691	12,378	25	151,409	19,428	1.6	318	464	—	—	—	—	—	—
India	2,062,727	3,319,644	46	4,189,000	2,234,000	148	656	958	39,028[2]	62,809[2]	261,254	420,449	209,259	305,513
Indonesia	212,177	341,467	56	2,734,769	2,189,876	41	17,000	25,000	4,013[2]	6,458[2]	11,548	18,585	3,449	5,035
Iran	102,976	165,724	50	1,793,000	692,000	24	46,750	68,250	3,915[2]	6,300[2]	3,792	6,103	9,863	14,400
Iraq	29,453	47,400	86	772,986	323,906	18			1,263[2]	2,032[2]	973	1,566	1,129	1,649
Ireland	57,477	92,500	94	1,269,245	188,814	2.6	4,041	5,900	1,209[2]	1,945[2]	870	1,400	342	500
Isle of Man	500	805	58	40,168	4,925	1.6			32[2]	52[2]	...	...	...	...
Israel	9,609	15,464	100	1,316,765	319,581	3.7	2,993	4,370	379[2]	610[2]	329	529	773	1,128
Italy	191,468	308,139	100	31,370,000	5,127,000	1.6	131,154	191,482	12,133	19,527	25,720	41,392	15,333	22,386
Jamaica	11,800	19,000	71	160,948	55,596	12			129[2]	208[2]	12.1	19.5	1.7	2.5
Japan	718,300	1,156,000	73	51,222,000	18,425,000	1.8	205,942	300,670	16,937	27,258	241,674	388,938	15,699	22,920
Jersey	346	557	100	58,491	9,922	1.3			—	—	—	—	—	—
Jordan	4,432	7,133	100	213,874	79,153	15	19,133	27,934	421[2]	677[2]	3.7	6.0	915	1,336
Kazakhstan	78,166	125,796	83	973,323	361,920	11	3,176	4,637	8,388[2]	13,500[2]	5,505	8,859	64,987	94,879
Kenya	39,600	63,800	14	278,000	81,200	78	134	196	1,885[2]	3,034[2]	239	385	813	1,309
Kiribati	416	670	5	222	115	260			—	—	—	—	—	—
Korea, North	14,526	23,377	8	248,000	...	...			5,302	8,533	2,100	3,400	6,200	9,100
Korea, South	55,162	88,775	76	8,084,000	3,938,000	3.9	51,031	74,504	4,165	6,703	18,686	30,072	8,704	12,708
Kuwait	2,765	4,450	81	747,042	140,480	2.3			—	—	—	—	—	—
Kyrgyzstan	11,495	18,500	91	146,000	...	...	695	1,015	264	424	58	93	323	472
Laos	13,870	22,321	14	16,320	4,200	242	16	23	—	—	—	—	—	—
Latvia	34,761	55,942	38	431,816	95,329	4.7	2,814	4,108	1,499	2,413	611	984	8,363	12,210
Lebanon	3,946	6,350	95	1,299,398	85,242	2.5			138	222	5.3	8.6	29	42
Lesotho	3,079	4,955	18	12,610	25,000	53			1.6	2.6	...	...	...	...
Liberia	6,600	10,600	6	9,400	25,000	59	...	...	304[2]	490[2]	...	...	534	860
Libya	50,704	81,600	57	809,514	357,528	4.0			12	19	...	...	...	...
Liechtenstein	201	323	...	21,150	2,684	1.4			12	19	...	...	...	...
Lithuania	44,350	71,375	91	980,910	105,022	3.4	3,843	5,611	1,241[2]	1,997[2]	463	745	5,376	7,849
Luxembourg	3,209	5,166	100	263,683	20,228	1.5	2,437	3,558	170[2]	274[2]	193	310	410	660
Macau	31	50	100	45,184	6,578	8.2			—	—	—	—	—	—
Macedonia	7,154	11,513	63	288,678	24,745	6.4	612	894	575	925	93	150	279	408
Madagascar	30,967	49,837	17	62,000	16,460	140	220	321	680[2]	1,095[2]	22	35	44	71
Malawi	10,222	16,451	19	27,000	29,700	171	—	—	495[2]	797[2]	16	26	34	49
Malaysia	41,282	66,437	76	3,517,484	644,792	5.1	...	...	1,384[2]	2,227[2]	828[31]	1,332[31]	625[31]	912[31]
Maldives	...	...	...	1,716	586	114			—	—	—	—	—	—
Mali	9,383	15,100	12	26,190	18,240	213			398[2]	641[2]	577.6	929.6	371	542.8
Malta	1,219	1,961	94	185,247	49,520	1.6			—	—	—	—	—	—
Marshall Islands	...	...	...	1,374	262	29			—	—	—	—	—	—
Martinique	1,299	2,091	75	108,300	32,200	2.6			—	—	—	—	—	—
Mauritania	4,760	7,660	11	18,810	10,450	82			437[2]	704[2]	...	...	1,603	2,340
Mauritius	1,184	1,905	93	46,300	12,100	20			—	—	—	—	—	—
Mayotte	145	233	77	6,553		20			—	—	—	—	—	—
Mexico	199,824	321,586	37	8,607,000	4,426,000	7.1	122,663	179,085	16,543[2]	26,623[2]	286	460	32,106	46,874
Micronesia	140	226	17	...	...	...			—	—	—	—	—	—
Moldova	7,643	12,300	87	166,757	67,638	18	697	1,018	819	1,318	213	343	816	1,191
Monaco	31	50	100	21,120	2,770	1.3			1	2	...	...	...	...
Mongolia	31,000	50,000	3	39,921	31,061	33	84.4	123.2	1,128	1,815	634	1,020	2,392	3,492
Morocco	35,921	57,810	52	1,018,146	278,075	21	1,429	2,086	1,099[2]	1,768[2]	1,104	1,776	3,258	4,757
Mozambique	18,890	30,400	19	4,900	7,520	1,431	75	110	1,940	3,123	317	510	781	1,140
Myanmar (Burma)	17,523	28,200	12	27,000	42,000	587	71	103.7	2,458[2]	3,955[2]	2,453	3,948	674	984
Namibia	40,526	65,220	8	74,875	66,500	12			1,480	2,382	21.6	34.7	738	1,077
Nauru	19	30	79	1,448		6.3			3[13]	5[13]	...	...	4.7	6.8
Nepal	4,785	7,700	42	47,541	29,371	306	984	1,437	37[2]	59[2]	...	...	...	...

merchant marine (latest)				air						canals and inland waterways (latest)				country
fleet (vessels over 100 gross tons)	total dead-weight tonnage ('000)	international cargo (latest)		airports with sched-uled flights (latest)	traffic (latest)					length		cargo		
		loaded metric tons ('000)	off-loaded metric tons ('000)		passengers		cargo		mi	km	short ton-mi ('000,000)	metric ton-km ('000,000)	
					passenger-mi ('000,000)	passenger-km ('000,000)	short ton-mi ('000,000)	metric ton-km ('000,000)					
444	1,685.2	15,012	22,044	11	5,638	9,074	185	270	2,175	3,500	452	660	Egypt
15	...	221	1,023	1	1,355	2,181	10.9	16.0	...	...	...	...	El Salvador
3	6.7	110	64	1	4	7	0.7	1.0	...	...	...	...	Equatorial Guinea
...	...	...	...	2	...	...	...	...	...	...	...	...	Eritrea
234	680.4	30,024	5,784	1	103.6	166.7	0.6	0.9	199	320	1.4	2.1	Estonia
27	84.3	234	1,242	31	1,190	1,915	225	328	...	...	...	...	Ethiopia
191	59.8	223	443	1	...	...	...	...	...	...	...	...	Faroe Islands
64	60.4	568	625	13	742	1,195	51.6	75.4	126	203	...	...	Fiji
263	989.3	39,312	38,052	27	8,026	12,916	216	316	3,880	6,245	127,945	186,797	Finland
729	4,981.0	64,704	189,504	61	55,344[23]	89,067[23]	3,271[23]	4,775[23]	3,562	5,732	5,436	7,936	France
7	0.7	73	447	8	...	...	...	...	286	460	...	...	French Guiana
41	16.5	15	666	17	...	...	...	...	...	...	...	...	French Polynesia
29	30.2	12,828	212	17	452	728	68	100	994	1,600	...	...	Gabon
11	2.0	185	240	1	31	50	3	5	250	400	...	...	Gambia, The
—	...	...	...	1	...	...	...	...	—	—	...	...	Gaza Strip
54	1,108	...	...	1	78.9	127.1	0.5	0.8	...	...	3,740	5,460	Georgia
1,375	6,832.3	74,568	138,864	35	55,219	88,867	4,520	6,599	4,188	6,740	44,019	64,267	Germany
155	131.0	2,424	2,904	1	407	655	20	30	803	1,293	75	110	Ghana
1,872	45,276.6	16,464	45,024	36	5,160	8,305	71	103	50	80	585	854	Greece
82	17.2	298	288	18	104	167	0.23	0.34	...	...	...	...	Greenland
3	0.5	21	193	2	...	...	...	...	...	...	...	...	Grenada
20	4.4	349	2,285	7	...	...	...	...	...	...	...	...	Guadeloupe
5	0.1	195	1,524	1	...	...	...	...	...	...	...	...	Guam
8	0.4	2,096	3,822	2	311	500	48	70	162	260	...	...	Guatemala
—	—	...	...	2	...	...	...	...	...	...	...	...	Guernsey
23	1.7	16,760	734	1	32	52	3	5	805	1,295	...	...	Guinea
19	1.8	46	283	2	6.2	10.0	0.7	1.0	...	...	...	...	Guinea-Bissau
82	13.5	1,730	673	1	154	248	2.3	3.3	3,660	5,900	...	...	Guyana
4	0.4	170	704	2	...	...	...	...	60	100	...	...	Haiti
966	1,437.3	1,316	1,002	8	212[24]	341[24]	23[24]	33[24]	289	465	...	...	Honduras
387	11,688.6	36,132[25]	80,820[25]	1	...	...	...	...	...	...	...	...	Hong Kong
15	93.2	...	...	1	2,183	3,513	38	56	853	1,373	1,069	1,561	Hungary
394	114.9	1,162	1,733	24	2,273	3,658	50.9	74.4	...	...	58	84	Iceland
888	10,365.9	61,880	102,630	66	11,456	18,436	329	481	10,054	16,180	202,000	295,000	India
2,014	3,130.2	310,246	208,871	81	7,698	12,389	234	341	13,409	21,579	17,000	25,000	Indonesia
403	8,345.3	32,148	37,404	19	3,871	6,229	49	72	562	904	...	...	Iran
131	1,578.8	97,830	8,638	...	976	1,570	37.4	54.6	631	1,015	...	...	Iraq
189	208.6	6,367	17,637	9	4,018	6,466	88.8	129.6	435	700	...	...	Ireland
101	2,836.5	6	203	1	526.1	846.8	0.1	0.2	...	...	...	...	Isle of Man
58	723.4	12,876	20,916	7	8,777[26]	14,125[26]	882[26]	1,288[26]	...	...	...	...	Israel
1,966	7,149.5	48,252	234,120	34	18,312[27]	29,471[27]	835[27]	1,219[27]	918	1,477	85,681	125,092	Italy
12	16.2	8,802	5,285	4	1,038[28]	1,670[28]	20.2[28]	29.5[28]	...	...	...	...	Jamaica
6,140	16,198	124,548	754,464	73	97,745	157,305	4,920	7,183	1,100	1,770	155,468	226,980	Japan
—	—	...	...	1	...	...	...	...	...	...	...	...	Jersey
5	113.6	7,308	5,328	2	2,526	4,065	150.1	219.2	...	...	19,202	28,035	Jordan
...	...	...	...	20	1,509	2,429	162	237	2,425	3,903	97	141	Kazakhstan
29	11.6	1,596	3,228	11	1,062[29]	1,709[29]	126[29]	203[29]	...	...	...	...	Kenya
7	2.7	15	26	9	4.4	7.0	0.6	1.0	3	5	...	...	Kiribati
100	951.2	635	5,520	1	178	286	19	30	1,400	2,253	...	...	Korea, North
2,138	11,724.9	255,888	448,416	14	29,647	47,712	4,987	7,281	1,000	1,609	22,920	33,462	Korea, South
209	3,188.5	51,400	4,522	1	3,813	6,137	151	243	...	...	...	...	Kuwait
...	...	...	...	2	2,739	4,408	44.7	65.2	290	466	41	6.0	Kyrgyzstan
1	1.5	...	—	11	30	48	3	5	2,850	4,587	68	100	Laos
261	1,436.9	45,144	3,888	1	185	298	6	9	66	106	19,241	28,091	Latvia
163	438.2	152	1,150	1	1,315	2,116	218	319	...	...	...	...	Lebanon
—	—	—	—	1	3.9	6.2	0.4	0.6	—	—	—	—	Lesotho
1,672	97,374.0	21,653	1,608	1	4.3	7.0	0.7	1.0	...	...	...	...	Liberia
150	1,223.6	62,491	7,808	12	264[30]	425[30]	23[30]	34[30]	—	—	...	...	Libya
—	—	...	...	—	...	...	...	...	...	...	...	...	Liechtenstein
52	373.9	12,864	2,796	3	190.5	306.6	1.8	2.6	229	369	8.9	13	Lithuania
54	2,603.6	—	—	1	79.5	232	606.9	886.1	23	37	205	300	Luxembourg
6	0.1	755	3,935	—	—	—	—	—	...	...	...	...	Macau
...	...	...	...	2	553.5	890.7	239.2	349.2	...	...	...	...	Macedonia
85	82.1	540	984	44	519	836	20.2	29.5	...	...	1.2	1.8	Madagascar
1	0.3	...	...	5	68	110	10	14	89	144	1,683	2,457	Malawi
552	2,916.3	39,756	54,852	39	20,945	33,708	976	1,425	4,534	7,296	...	...	Malaysia
44	79.0	27	78	5	44	71	...	...	...	...	...	...	Maldives
—	—	—	—	9	150	242	26	38	1,128	1,815	18	27	Mali
889	17,073.2	309	1,781	1	1,173	1,888	7.7	11.2	...	...	...	...	Malta
35	4,182.4	29	123	25	17	28	0.003	0.005	...	...	...	...	Marshall Islands
6	1.1	960	1,584	1	...	...	...	...	...	...	...	...	Martinique
126	23.9	10,400	724	9	160.5	258.3	9.2	13.5	...	...	...	...	Mauritania
35	152.2	966	2,753	1	2,398	3,859	561.2	819.4	...	...	...	...	Mauritius
1	1.1	158	31	1	...	...	...	...	...	...	...	...	Mayotte
635	1,495.3	134,400	67,500	83	14,864	23,922	1,779	2,597	1,800	2,900	14,806	21,616	Mexico
19	9.2	...	...	4	...	...	...	...	...	...	...	...	Micronesia
...	...	...	...	1	0.1	0.2	0.7	1.0	263	424	172	251	Moldova
1	...	...	...	—	...	...	...	...	...	...	...	...	Monaco
...	...	...	...	1	326	525	33	48	247	397	0.1	0.2	Mongolia
492	586.2	24,228	27,972	11	2,789	4,489	260	380	...	...	...	...	Morocco
107	31.6	2,800	3,400	7	239	384	6	9	2,330	3,750	57	83	Mozambique
144	1,354.0	1,788	3,456	19	272	438	2.2	3.2	7,954	12,800	240	351	Myanmar (Burma)
30	5.9	1,132	644	11	470	756	16	23	...	...	...	...	Namibia
2	5.8	1,650	59	1	151[32]	243[32]	15[32]	24[32]	...	...	...	...	Nauru
—	—	—	—	24	532	856	64	93	...	...	...	...	Nepal

Transportation   (continued)

country	roads length mi	roads length km	roads paved (percent)	motor vehicles automobiles	motor vehicles trucks and buses	persons per vehicle	cargo short ton-mi ('000,000)	cargo metric ton-km ('000,000)	track length mi	track length km	passengers passenger-mi ('000,000)	passengers passenger-km ('000,000)	cargo short ton-mi ('000,000)	cargo metric ton-km ('000,000)
Netherlands, The	77,379	124,530	91	6,343,000	826,000	2.2	98,445	143,727	1,745	2,808	8,904	14,330	2,412	3,521
Netherlands Antilles	367	590	51	75,105	17,753	2.2	...	...	—	—	—	—	—	—
New Caledonia	3,582	5,764	52	56,700	21,200	2.6	...	...	—	—	—	—	—	—
New Zealand	57,213	92,075	62	1,831,118	351,494	1.7	...	...	2,431[2]	3,912[2]	285	458	2,712	3,960
Nicaragua	11,200	18,000	10	73,000	61,650	33	...	...	—	—	—	—	—	—
Niger	6,276	10,100	8	38,220	15,200	169	1,044	1,524	—	—	—	—	—	—
Nigeria	38,897	62,598	19	773,000	68,300	131	...	...	2,178	3,505	100	161	74	108
Northern Mariana Islands	225	360	100	12,113	6,479	3.0	—	—	—	—	—	—	—	—
Norway	56,470	90,880	74	1,813,642	447,583	2.0	10,086	14,726	2,489[2]	4,006[2]	1,609	2,589	1,467	2,142
Oman	20,518	33,020	24	229,029	110,717	6.9	...	...	—	—	—	—	—	—
Pakistan	149,679	240,885	55	1,167,635	251,407	95	66,304	96,802	5,452[2]	8,774[2]	11,908	19,164	2,753	4,020
Palau	40	64	59	4,271		3.8	...	...	...	...	...	...	...	...
Panama	7,022	11,301	33	203,760	74,637	9.4	...	...	220[2]	354[2]	242	389	1,096	1,600
Papua New Guinea	12,263	19,736	6	13,000	32,000	93	...	...	—	—	—	—	—	—
Paraguay	18,330	29,500	10	71,000	50,000	41	...	...	274[2]	441[2]	1.9	3.0	3.8	5.5
Peru	45,836	73,766	12	557,042	359,374	26	...	...	1,238[2]	1,992[2]	132	212	0.8	1.1
Philippines	124,243	199,950	39	745,144	263,037	73	...	...	557[2]	897[2]	7.5	12	452	660
Poland	234,286	377,048	66	9,283,000	1,762,000	3.5	47,632	69,542	14,280	22,981	16,279	26,198	37,994	55,471
Portugal	42,708	68,732	88	3,200,000	1,097,000	2.4	16,984	24,796	2,025[2]	3,259[2]	2,860	4,602	1,603	2,340
Puerto Rico	8,948	14,400	100	878,000	190,000	3.5	...	...	—	—	—	—	—	—
Qatar	764	1,230	90	126,000	64,000	2.9	...	...	—	—	—	—	—	—
Réunion	1,711	2,754	79	190,300	44,300	3.0	...	...	—	—	—	—	—	—
Romania	95,175	153,170	51	2,408,000	409,550	8.0	14,898	21,750	7,062	11,365	7,658	12,324	10,909	15,927
Russia	354,628	570,719	79	19,717,800	5,021,000	5.9	14,384	21,000	93,800	151,000	88,048	144,700	825	1,205
Rwanda	9,528	14,900	9	13,000	17,100	188	140	200	—	—	—	—	—	—
St. Kitts and Nevis	199	320	43	5,200	2,300	5.3	...	...	22	36	—	—	—	—
St. Lucia	750	1,210	5	14,783	1,020	9.5	...	...	—	—	—	—	—	—
St. Vincent and the Grenadines	646	1,040	31	6,089	3,670	11	...	...	—	—	—	—	—	—
Samoa	491	790	42	1,068	1,169	74	...	...	—	—	—	—	—	—
San Marino	157	252	...	25,571	2,636	0.9	...	...	—	—	—	—	—	—
São Tomé and Príncipe	199	320	68	4,040	1,540	24	...	...	—	—	—	—	—	—
Saudi Arabia	101,000	162,000	43	1,744,000	1,192,000	6.6	57,859	84,473	864[2]	1,390[2]	138	222	586	856
Senegal	9,134	14,700	29	85,488	36,962	72	375	547	761	1,225	128	206	476	695
Seychelles	263	424	87	7,120	1,980	8.5	...	...	—	—	—	—	—	—
Sierra Leone	7,270	11,700	11	17,640	10,890	163	36	53	52	84	...	...	...	...
Singapore	1,875	3,017	97	413,545	147,325	5.8	...	...	73	117	31[31]	31[31]	31[31]	31[31]
Slovakia	10,953	17,627	...	1,135,914	100,254	4.4	5,804	8,474	2,282	3,673	1,844	2,968	6,753	9,859
Slovenia	7,771	12,507	81	829,674	67,111	2.2	1,986	2,900	746	1,201	388	625	1,907	2,784
Solomon Islands	845	1,360	3	2,052	2,574	75	...	...	—	—	—	—	—	—
Somalia	13,732	22,100	12	1,020	6,440	866	...	...	—	—	—	—	—	—
South Africa	205,838	331,265	41	3,966,252	2,069,536	7.2	1,053	1,538	12,626[2]	20,319[2]	1,103	1,775	71,142	103,866
Spain	215,335	346,548	99	16,847,000	3,659,000	2.0	85,801	125,268	8,595[2]	13,832[2]	11,525	18,547	7,959	11,620
Sri Lanka	61,640	99,200	40	107,000	150,160	71	21	30	899[2]	1,447[2]	2,028	3,264	90	132
Sudan, The	7,394	11,900	36	285,000	53,000	93	...	...	2,855[2]	4,595[2]	100	161	1,346	1,965
Suriname	2,815	4,530	26	46,408	19,255	6.4	...	...	187	301	...	...	...	...
Swaziland	2,367	3,810	29	31,882	32,772	17	...	...	187	301	752	1,210	1,993	2,910
Sweden	130,500	210,000	74	3,890,159	352,897	2.1	22,798	33,285	6,811	10,961	4,746	7,638	13,074	19,088
Switzerland	44,248	71,211	96	3,467,275	313,646	1.9	9,932	14,500	3,129	5,035	8,764	14,104	5,951	8,688
Syria	25,756	41,451	23	138,900	282,664	37	1,075	1,570	1,507[2]	2,425[2]	113	182	934	1,364
Taiwan	12,660	20,375	89	4,716,000	833,000	4.0	12,651	18,470	2,410	3,879	7,833	12,606	808	1,179
Tajikistan	8,500	13,700	83	680	8,190	667	34	50	295	474	77	124	1,449	2,115
Tanzania	54,805	88,200	4	23,760	115,700	229	...	...	2,218	3,569	2,324	3,740	927	1,354
Thailand	40,141	64,600	98	1,661,000	2,855,000	14	...	...	2,873[2]	4,623[2]	6,636	10,680	1,940	2,832
Togo	4,673	7,520	32	79,200	34,240	39	...	...	245[2]	395[2]	10.3	16.5	34	49
Tonga	423	680	27	1,140	780	51	...	...	—	—	—	—	—	—
Trinidad and Tobago	5,170	8,320	51	122,000	24,000	8.7	...	...	—	—	—	—	—	—
Tunisia	14,354	23,100	79	269,000	312,000	16	678	990	1,348[2]	2,169[2]	743	1,196	1,620	2,365
Turkey	238,380	383,636	25	4,283,080	1,488,016	11	104,255	152,210	5,388	8,671	3,804	6,122	6,871	10,032
Turkmenistan	8,500	13,700	83	220,000	58,200	16	335	489	1,317	2,120	1,307	2,104	4,643	6,779
Tuvalu	5	8	—	...	...	...	...	...	...	...	...	...	...	...
Uganda	16,653	26,800	8	35,361	48,430	249	...	...	771[2]	1,241[2]	17	27	162	236
Ukraine	107,111	172,378	95	4,885,691	...	...	12,534	18,300	14,021	22,564	29,577	47,600	107,081	156,336
United Arab Emirates	2,356	3,791	100	201,000	56,950	9.6	...	...	—	—	—	—	—	—
United Kingdom	231,096	371,914	100	23,393,000	2,368,000	2.3	117,504	171,553	23,518[44]	37,849[44]	23,800	38,300	12,603	18,400
United States	3,906,292	6,286,396	91	131,839,000	79,778,000	1.3	1,051,045	1,534,500	137,900	222,000	14,000	22,500	1,421,000	2,075,000
Uruguay	5,395	8,683	30	516,889	50,264	5.6	500	730	1,288[2]	2,073[2]	87.4	140.6	123	180
Uzbekistan	52,444	84,400	87	865,300	14,500	25	1,248	1,822	2,271	3,655	1,553	2,500	11,580	16,907
Vanuatu	665	1,070	24	4,000	2,600	27	...	...	—	—	—	—	—	—
Venezuela	59,443	95,664	36	1,505,000	542,000	10	...	...	390[2]	627[2]	93.1	149.9	37.3	54.5
Vietnam	58,000	93,300	25	200,000		358	1,462	2,134	1,952[2]	3,142[2]	1,694	2,727	958	1,398
Virgin Islands (U.S.)	532	856	100	51,000	13,300	1.7	...	...	—	—	—	—	—	—
West Bank	...	...	...	88,056	24,324	18	...	...	...	...	...	...	...	...
Western Sahara	3,900	6,200	23	6,284	424	20	...	...	—	—	—	—	—	—
Yemen	40,218	64,725	8	240,567	291,149	29	...	...	—	—	—	—	—	—
Yugoslavia	31,377	50,497	60	1,400,000	132,000	6.9	852	1,244	2,528	4,069	1,003	1,614	1,760	2,570
Zambia	24,170	38,898	18	157,000	81,000	37	...	...	787	1,266	166	267	316	462
Zimbabwe	11,395	18,338	18	323,000	32,000	31	...	...	1,714[2]	2,759[2]	253.6	408.2	3.2	4.6

[1]Ariana Afghan Airlines only. [2]Route length. [3]Air Algérie International flights only. [4]TAAG airline only. [5]Aerolineas Argentinas only. [6]Included in Netherlands Antilles. [7]Government railways only. [8]Portion of Gulf Air traffic. [9]Caribbean Airways only. [10]Caribbean Air Cargo only. [11]Air Afrique only. [12]Air Botswana only. [13]For industrial purposes only. [14]Zaire National Railways only. [15]Air Zaire only. [16]LASCA only. [17]Traffic between Ouagadougou, Burkina Faso, and Abidjan, Côte d'Ivoire. [18]Air Ivoire only. [19]Data refer to former Czechoslovakia. [20]Including SAS international and domestic traffic. [21]National roads only. [22]Includes 62 mi (100 km) of the Chemin de Fer Djibouti-Ethiopien (CDE) in Djibouti. [23]Air France and UTA only. [24]TAN and SAHSA airlines only. [25]Includes

merchant marine (latest)		international cargo (latest)		air	traffic (latest)				canals and inland waterways (latest)				country
fleet (vessels over 100 gross tons)	total dead-weight tonnage ('000)	loaded metric tons ('000)	off-loaded metric tons ('000)	airports with scheduled flights (latest)	passengers passenger-mi ('000,000)	passenger-km ('000,000)	cargo short ton-mi ('000,000)	metric ton-km ('000,000)	length mi	km	cargo short ton-mi ('000,000)	metric ton-km ('000,000)	
399	2,874	91,920	305,232	6	36,109	58,112	2,679	3,911	3,135	5,046	27,887	40,714	Netherlands, The
154[33]	1,053.6[33]	215	517	6	234[34]	377[34]	1.2[34]	1.8[34]	...	...	...	...	Netherlands Antilles
17	18.1	1,040	930	11	145[35]	233[35]	3.4[35]	4.9[35]	...	...	...	...	New Caledonia
139	279.8	20,640	13,308	36	12,352	19,879	584	852	1,000	1,609	1,503	2,195	New Zealand
25	1.3	320	1,629	10	49	79	6	9	1,379	2,220	...	...	Nicaragua
—	—	—	—	6	160.5	258.3	9.3	13.5	186	300	14	20	Niger
271	733.3	86,993	11,346	12	70	112	1.3	2.1	5,328	8,575	...	...	Nigeria
2	0.9	33	205	2	...	...	...	...	...	...	...	...	Northern Mariana Islands
1,597	20,834	151,116	25,788	50	6,444[20]	10,371[20]	821[20]	1,199[20]	980	1,577	7,640	11,154	Norway
26	11.7	43,525	5,303	6	601[8]	968[8]	11[8]	18[8]	...	...	...	...	Oman
73	513.8	6,408	31,008	35	6,503	10,466	226	330	...	...	...	...	Pakistan
4	...	...	64	1	...	...	...	...	...	...	...	...	Palau
5,217	79,255.6	117,924	76,800	10	853	1,373	14.9	21.8	497	800	...	...	Panama
87	40.9	2,463	1,784	42	457	735	59	86	6,798	10,940	...	...	Papua New Guinea
38	38.5	...	...	5	134	215	13	19	1,900	3,100	...	...	Paraguay
623	615.6	10,197	5,077	27	1,637	2,634	172	251	5,300	8,600	...	...	Peru
1,499	13,807.1	16,980	52,596	21	6,395[36]	10,292[36]	165[36]	241[36]	2,000	3,219	...	...	Philippines
644	4,314.3	33,360	15,864	8	2,878	4,632	55	80	2,369	3,812	753	1,100	Poland
332	1,129.3	7,572	37,740	16	6,278	10,104	159	232	510	820	...	...	Portugal
13	...	...	...	7	...	...	...	...	...	...	...	...	Puerto Rico
64	744	18,145	2,588	1	1,776[8]	2,858[8]	72[8]	105[8]	...	...	...	...	Qatar
7	33.5	454	2,302	2	...	...	...	...	...	...	...	...	Réunion
439	4,845.5	11,676	18,972	12	1,446	2,327	33.8	49.4	1,002	1,613	2,947	4,302	Romania
4,543	16,592.3	7,092	744	75	33,181	53,400	1,575	2,300	55,357	89,089	44,962	65,643	Russia
—	—	—	—	2	1.2	2.0	...	...	...	...	...	...	Rwanda
1	0.6	24	36	2	...	...	...	...	...	...	...	...	St. Kitts and Nevis
7	2.1	138	547	2	...	...	...	...	...	...	...	...	St. Lucia
946	1,253	72	128	5	...	...	...	...	...	...	...	...	St. Vincent and the Grenadines
7	6.5	48	144	3	165	265	18	26	—	—	—	—	Samoa
—	—	—	—	—	...	...	...	...	—	—	—	—	San Marino
4	2.3	16	45	2	6	9	0.7	1.0	...	...	...	...	São Tomé and Príncipe
279	1,278	214,070	46,437	28	11,774	18,949	1,815	2,650	...	...	...	...	Saudi Arabia
183	27.5	1,396	2,894	7	139.6[30]	224.7[30]	11.2[30]	16.4[30]	557	897	...	...	Senegal
9	3.3	47	543	2	389	626	48	70	...	...	...	...	Seychelles
62	18.4	2,310	589	1	68[37]	110[37]	1.4[37]	2.0[37]	500	800	447	652	Sierra Leone
946	14,929.2	326,040	188,234	1	40,096	64,529	3,755	5,482	...	...	...	...	Singapore
...	...	...	...	2	143.8	231.4	0.5	0.7	107	172	1,046	1,527	Slovakia
13	346.5	2,460	5,952	3	517	832	2.8	4.2	...	...	21,900	31,973	Slovenia
33	5.0	278	349	21	29[38]	47[38]	0.9	1.3	...	...	...	...	Solomon Islands
28	18.5	324	1,007	1	81	131	3.0	5.0	...	...	...	...	Somalia
219	282.5	114,331	22,203	24	12,005[39]	19,320[39]	464[39]	677[39]	...	...	...	...	South Africa
2,190	5,077.3	55,752	169,848	25	37,715	60,696	4,388	6,407	649	1,045	21,836[40]	31,880[40]	Spain
66	472.6	9,288	16,632	1	3,204	5,156	459	670	267	430	0.7	1	Sri Lanka
16	62.2	1,543	4,300	3	330[41]	531[41]	14[41]	20[41]	3,300	5,310	...	...	Sudan, The
24	15.7	1,595	1,265	1	549[42]	883[42]	66[42]	106[42]	746	1,200	...	...	Suriname
—	—	—	—	1	30.7	49.4	0.09	0.1	—	—	—	—	Swaziland
430	2,881	61,320	75,528	48	6,997[20]	11,261[20]	196[20]	286[20]	1,275	2,052	5,708	8,334	Sweden
24	602.8	...	...	5	19,739	31,767	1,216	1,776	13	21	34	49	Switzerland
94	210.4	2,136	5,112	5	884	1,422	14	21	541	870	...	...	Syria
649	9,241.3	182,127	301,275	13	24,369	39,218	2,828	4,129	...	...	274	400	Taiwan
...	...	...	...	1	1,386	2,231	140	205	...	...	...	...	Tajikistan
43	48.5	1,249	2,721	11	114	184	2.0	2.9	...	...	...	...	Tanzania
351	1,194.5	42,495	74,579	25	23,826	38,345	1,145	1,671	2,300	3,701	...	...	Thailand
8	20.6	391	1,274	2	139.6	224.7	11.2	16.4	31	50	...	...	Togo
15	13.7	15	104	6	7	11	0.7	1.0	...	...	...	...	Tonga
53	17.5	9,622	10,961	2	1,783	2,869	38	55	...	...	...	...	Trinidad and Tobago
77	443.3	6,792	13,152	5	1,674	2,694	13	21	...	...	...	...	Tunisia
880	7,114.3	24,756	78,168	26	10,248[43]	16,492[43]	260[43]	380[43]	750	1,200	189	276	Turkey
...	...	...	...	1	970	1,562	98	143	240	387	5.5	8.0	Turkmenistan
6	16.0	...	...	1	...	...	...	...	...	...	...	...	Tuvalu
2	8.6	...	...	1	32.4	52.1	3	5	...	...	...	...	Uganda
...	...	77,004	7,116	12	1,225	1,972	18	27	2,734	4,400	3,973	5,800	Ukraine
276	1,491.7	88,153	9,595	6	12,150[8]	19,553[8]	978[8]	1,428[8]	...	...	...	...	United Arab Emirates
1,631	4,355	177,228	178,572	57	99,628	160,336	3,373	4,925	716	1,153	36,302	53,000	United Kingdom
509	18,585	392,076[45]	713,880[45]	834	619,500	997,000	18,116	26,449	25,778	41,485	356,188	520,026	United States
93	172.5	710[46]	1,450[46]	1	398	640	42	62	1,000	1,600	...	...	Uruguay
...	...	...	...	9	2,150	3,460	220	321	684	1,100	...	...	Uzbekistan
280	3,259.6	80	55	29	110.8	178.3	1.3	1.9	...	...	...	...	Vanuatu
271	1,355.4	101,435	17,932	20	3,600	5,800	438	639	4,400	7,100	8.9	13	Venezuela
230	872.8	303	1,510	12	2,380	3,831	67	98	11,000	17,702	1,339	1,955	Vietnam
1	...	105.5	648.3	2	...	...	...	...	...	...	...	...	Virgin Islands (U.S.)
—	—	—	—	—	—	—	—	—	...	...	...	...	West Bank
—	—	40	15	1	...	...	...	...	...	...	...	...	Western Sahara
40	13.7	1,936	7,829	12	978	1,574	22	32	365	587	...	...	Yemen
462[47]	5,173.1[47]	360	972	5	551	887	4,112	6,003	...	...	905	1,322	Yugoslavia
—	—	—	—	4	192	308	6.8	9.9	1,398	2,250	...	...	Zambia
—	—	—	—	7	544	875	24	35	...	...	...	...	Zimbabwe

transshipments. [26]El Al only. [27]Alitalia only. [28]Air Jamaica only. [29]Kenya Airways only. [30]International traffic only. [31]Peninsular Malaysia and Singapore. [32]Air Nauru only. [33]Includes Aruba. [34]Antillean Airlines only. [35]Air Caledonie only. [36]Philippine Air Lines only. [37]Sierra Leone Airlines international traffic only. [38]Solair only. [39]SAA only. [40]Coastal shipping only. [41]Sudan Airways only. [42]Suriname Airways only. [43]Turkish Airlines only. [44]British Railways only; excludes Northern Ireland. [45]Includes Puerto Rico. [46]Port of Montevideo only. [47]Data refer to Yugoslavia as constituted prior to 1991.

Communications

Virtually all the states of the world have a variety of communications media and services available to their citizens: book, periodical, and newspaper publishing (although only daily papers are included in this table); postal services; and telecommunications systems: radio and television broadcasting, telephones (fixed and mobile), facsimile (fax) machines, personal computers (PCs), and access to the Internet. Unfortunately, the availability of information about these services often runs behind the capabilities of the services themselves. Certain countries publish no official information; others publish data analyzed according to a variety of fiscal, calendar, religious, or other years; still others, while they possess such data almost simultaneously with the end of the business or calendar year, may not see them published except in company or parastatal reports of limited distribution. Even when such data are published in national statistical summaries, it may be only after a delay of up to several years.

The data also differ in their completeness and reliability. Figures for book production, for example, generally include all works published in separate bindings except advertising works, timetables, telephone directories, price

lists, catalogs of businesses or exhibitions, musical scores, maps, atlases, and the like. The figures include government publications, school texts, theses, offprints, series works, and illustrated works, even those consisting principally of illustrations. Figures refer to works actually published during the year of survey, usually by a registered publisher, and deposited for copyright. A book is defined as a work of 49 or more pages; a work published simultaneously in more than one country is counted as having been published in each. A periodical is a publication issued at regular or stated intervals and, in Unesco's usage, directed to the general public. Newspaper statistics are especially difficult to collect and compare. Newspapers continually are founded, cease publication, merge, or change frequency of publication. Data on circulation are often incomplete, slow to be aggregated at the national level, or regarded as proprietary. In some countries no daily newspaper exists.

Post office statistics are compiled mainly from the Universal Postal Union's annual summary *Statistique des services postaux*. Postal services, unlike the other media discussed earlier, tend most often to be operated by

Communications

country	publishing (latest)							postal services				telecommunications	
	books		periodicals		daily newspapers			post offices, 1998				radio, 1997	
	number of titles	number of copies ('000)	number of titles	number of copies ('000)	number	total circulation ('000)	circulation per 1,000 persons	number	persons per office	pieces of mail handled ('000,000)	pieces handled per person	receivers (all types; '000)	receivers per 1,000 persons
Afghanistan	2,795	3,741	...	...	12	113	6	373	50,400	0.5	—	2,750	132
Albania	381	5,710	143	3,477	5	116	34	698[2]	4,840[2]	3.2	0.6	810	259
Algeria	670	...	48	803	5	1,080	38	3,223[1]	9,140[1]	736[1]	21[1]	7,100	242
American Samoa	...	...	...	...	2	5.0	93	...	...	...	...	57	929
Andorra	57	...	...	...	3	4.0	58	...	...	...	...	16	227
Angola	22	419	...	...	5	128	11	80[1]	145,000[1]	1.2	0.1	630	54
Antigua and Barbuda	...	...	...	...	1	6.0	91	16[5]	4,375[5]	...	...	36	542
Argentina	9,850	39,663	...	...	181	4,320	123	6,678[1]	5,340[1]	472[1]	11[1]	24,300	681
Armenia	396[6]	20,212[6]	44	541	11	85	23	...	17,500	0.7[7]	0.2[7]	850	239
Aruba	...	...	...	...	13	73	852	4	17,500	10	90	50	557
Australia	10,835	...	...	...	65	5,730	297	3,922	4,780	4,732	225	25,500	1,391
Austria	8,056[8]	...	2,481	...	17	2,382	294	2,436	3,320	3,133[1]	372[1]	6,080	751
Azerbaijan	542	2,643	49	801	6	210	28	1,673[1]	4,560[1]	12[1]	1.3[1]	175	23
Bahamas, The	...	...	...	...	3	28	100	138	2,170	61[10]	51[10]	215	739
Bahrain	40[6]	...	26	73	4	67	117	13	49,200	55	50	338	580
Bangladesh	...	...	...	...	37	1,117	9.0	9,093[1]	13,400[1]	589[1]	4.3[1]	6,150	50
Barbados	...	...	...	...	2	53	199	16	16,900	39	114	237	888
Belarus	3,809	59,073	155	3,765	10	1,899	187	3,852	2,640	709	67	3,020	292
Belgium	13,913	...	13,706	...	30	1,625	160	1,637[5]	6,205[5]	3,713	346	8,075	797
Belize	70	—	...	...	4	23.5	0.5	134[1]	1,720[1]	4.0[1]	12[1]	133	591
Benin	84[6]	42[6]	...	...	1	12	2.2	178	32,500	9.6	1.2	620	110
Bermuda	...	...	...	...	1	17	270	14[2]	4,500[2]	15[2]	240[2]	82	1,296
Bhutan	...	...	...	...	...	...	...	106[1]	17,540[1]	1.8[1]	0.7[1]	37	19
Bolivia	...	...	...	...	18	420	55	171	46,500	9.9	0.7	5,250	675
Bosnia and Herzegovina	...	...	...	...	3	518	146	210	20,050	9.8	1.6	940	267
Botswana	158[6]	...	14	177	1	40	27	180	8,720	54	26	237	154
Brazil	21,574[11]	104,397	...	...	380	6,472	55	11,713	13,800	5,223	32	71,000	434
Brunei	45[6]	56[6]	15	132	1	21	69	18	17,200	20	52	93	302
Bulgaria	4,840	20,317	772	1,740	17	2,145	253	3,303	2,500	156[2]	18[2]	4,510	537
Burkina Faso	12[6]	14[6]	37	24	4	14	1.3	85	130,000	7.3[12]	...	370	34
Burundi	...	...	...	...	1	20	3.2	28	225,000	16	1.3	440	69
Cambodia	...	...	...	...	...	...	...	56	204,000	3.2	0.2	1,340	128
Cameroon	...	...	...	...	2	91	6.7	377[1]	37,000[1]	6.1[1, 13]	0.41[1, 13]	2,270	163
Canada	19,900	...	1,400	37,108	107	4,718	158	18,607[10]	1,570[10]	10,715[12, 14]	370[12, 14]	32,300	1,067
Cape Verde	...	...	...	...	...	...	...	54	7,780	1.6	2.1	73	183
Central African Republic	...	...	...	...	3	6.0	1.8	35	99,710	...	...	283	83
Chad	...	...	...	...	1	2.0	0.2	36	201,900	13	1.0	1,670	236
Chile	2,469	4,095	417	3,450	52	1,411	99	710	20,870	343[13]	23[13]	5,180	354
China	100,951	5,945[15]	6,486	205,060	44	48,000	42	112,204	11,200	6,967[1]	5.5[1]	417,000	335
Colombia	1,481	11,314	...	...	37	1,800	49	1,354	30,200	116[3]	2.2[1]	21,000	524
Comoros	...	...	...	...	...	...	...	37	17,800	0.4	0.3	90	141
Congo, Dem. Rep. of the	64[6]	535[6]	...	...	9	124	2.7	497	98,870	...	...	18,030	376
Congo, Rep. of the	...	...	3	34	6	20	7.8	114[2]	22,720[2]	1.8[2]	0.5[2]	341	126
Costa Rica	963	...	...	...	6	320	88	134	24,900	32[1]	6.9[1]	980	261
Côte d'Ivoire	...	...	...	...	12	231	17	373	38,300	31	1.9	2,260	161
Croatia	1,718	...	352	6,357	10	515	114	1,168	3,910	299	60	1,510	337
Cuba	932	4,610	14	285	17	1,300	118	1,855	5,990	12[13]	1.1[13]	3,900	352
Cyprus	930	1,776	39	338	9	84	111	777	990	64	67	310	406
Czech Republic	10,244	...	1,168	81,387	21	2,620	256	3,369	3,050	803	72	8,270	803
Denmark	12,352	...	157	6,930	37	1,628	311	1,169	4,530	1,828[2]	335[2]	6,020	1,145
Djibouti	...	...	7	6.0	...	...	...	12	51,700	16[2]	12[2]	52	84
Dominica	...	...	...	...	...	...	...	64[10]	1,090[10]	2.9[2]	30	46	647
Dominican Republic	...	...	...	...	12	416	52	239	33,900	9.8[16]	1.3[16]	1,440	178
East Timor	...	...	...	...	...	...	...	...	...	...	...	18	21
Ecuador	12[6]	19[6]	199	...	24	820	70	315	38,600	13	0.4	4,150	348
Egypt	2,215	92,353	258	2,373	17	2,400	38	7,488	8,810	317	3.3	20,500	317
El Salvador	...	...	45	774	5	278	48	289	20,900	18	1.9	2,750	465
Equatorial Guinea	...	...	...	...	1	2.0	4.9	23[10]	17,000[10]	...	...	180	428
Eritrea	106	420	...	...	...	...	...	37[5]	91,900[5]	2.3	0.5	345	100
Estonia	2,628	6,662	517	2,323	15	255	173	560	2,550	75	43	1,010	698

a single national service, to cover a country completely, and to record traffic data according to broadly similar schemes (although the details of *classes* of mail handled may differ). Some countries do not enumerate domestic traffic or may record only international traffic requiring handling charges. Data for some kinds of telecommunications apparatus are relatively easy to collect; telephones, for example, must be installed, and service recorded so that it may be charged. But in most countries the other types of apparatus mentioned above may be purchased by anyone and used whenever desired. As a result, data on distribution and use of these types of apparatus may be collected in a variety of ways—on the basis of numbers of subscribers, licenses issued, periodic sample surveys, trade data, census or housing surveys, or private consumer surveys. Data on broadcast media refer to receivers; data on telephones to "main lines," or the lines connecting a subscriber's apparatus (fixed or mobile) to the public, switched net. Information on fax machines and PCs is estimated only, as noted above. "Users" refers to the number of people with access to computers connected to the Internet.

The *Statistical Yearbook* of Unesco contains extensive data on book, periodical, and newspaper publishing, and on radio and television broadcasting that have been collected from standardized questionnaires. The quality and recency of its data, however, depend on the completion and timely return of each questionnaire by national authorities. The commercially published annual *World Radio TV Handbook* (Andrew G. Sennitt, editor) is a valuable source of information on broadcast media and has complete and timely coverage. It depends on data received from broadcasters, but, because some do not respond, local correspondents and monitors are used in many countries, and some unconfirmed or unofficial data are included as estimates. The statistics on telecommunications apparatus and computers are derived mainly from the UN-affiliated International Telecommunication Union's *World Telecommunication Development Report* (annual).
... Not available.
— None, nil, or not applicable.

television, 1999		telephones, 2001		cellular phones, 2001		fax, 1999		personal computers, 2001		Internet users, 2001	country
receivers (all types; '000)	receivers per 1,000 persons	main lines ('000)	per 1,000 persons	cellular subscriptions ('000)	subscriptions per 1,000 persons	receivers ('000)	receivers per 1,000 persons	units ('000)	units per 1,000 persons	number ('000)	
270[1]	12[1]	29	1.3	...	...	...	...	...	...	...	Afghanistan
430[3]	112[3]	198	64	350	113	18.3	4.8	30	10	10	Albania
3,300	107	1,880	61	100	3.2	7.0[1]	0.2[1]	220	7.1	60	Algeria
14[1]	212[1]	14	237	2.4	41	...	...	...	...	...	American Samoa
30[3]	400[3]	35	530	24[4]	356[4]	5.0[3]	67[3]	...	...	7.0[4]	Andorra
190	15	80	7.7	87	8.3	...	...	17	1.6	60	Angola
31[3]	413[3]	37	487	25	329	...	...	...	...	5[4]	Antigua and Barbuda
10,600	290	8,108	225	6,975	193	873[3]	2.4[3]	2,000	55.4	3,000	Argentina
840[3]	238[3]	529	175	25	8.3	0.45	0.15	30	9.9	50[4]	Armenia
20[1]	204[1]	37	408	53	582	0.5[2]	6.9[2]	...	...	...	Aruba
13,400	706	10,060	517	11,169	574	900[1]	48[1]	10,000	514	7,200	Australia
4,200[3]	514[3]	3,810	472	6,566	814	285[2]	35[2]	2,270[4]	282[4]	2,600	Austria
1,950[3]	253[3]	866	107	620	76	2.5[2]	0.1[2]	0.4[9]	—	25	Azerbaijan
67[1]	223[1]	123	403	61	198	0.5[2]	6.9[2]	...	...	17	Bahamas, The
270	406	174	266	300	457	6.9	10	100	153	140	Bahrain
940	7.4	514	3.9	520	4.0	40[2]	0.3[2]	250	1.9	150	Bangladesh
78	290	124[4]	460[4]	29[4]	106[4]	1.8[2]	6.7[2]	25	93	10[4]	Barbados
3,300	321	2,858	287	138	14	24	2.3	...	...	422	Belarus
5,300	522	5,074	494	7,960	775	190[5]	19[5]	3,500[4]	341[4]	2,881	Belgium
42	179	35	143	28	114	0.5[2]	2.6[2]	33	134	18	Belize
65[3]	11[3]	59	9.0	125	19	1.1[5]	0.2[5]	11	1.7	25	Benin
66[3]	1,031[3]	56	893	13	211	...	...	32	508	25[9]	Bermuda
13	20	14	20	...	...	1.5[3]	2.3[3]	4.0	5.7	2.5	Bhutan
960	118	514	62	744	90	...	...	170	21	120[4]	Bolivia
385[2]	100[2]	450	115	233	60	...	...	...	...	45	Bosnia and Herzegovina
33	20	150[4]	90[4]	278	166	3.5[1]	2.2[1]	65	39	25	Botswana
56,000	333	37,431	218	28,746	167	500[1]	3.0[1]	10,800	63	8,000	Brazil
205	637	81	234	95	276	2.0[2]	18[2]	25	73	35	Brunei
3,400[3]	411[3]	2,914	366	1,550	195	1.5[1]	1.8[1]	361[4]	45[4]	605	Bulgaria
120[3]	10[3]	58	4.7	75	6.1	0.1	—	17	1.4	21	Burkina Faso
100	15	20	3.2	20	3.2	4.0[5]	0.6[5]	...	...	6.0	Burundi
98	9.0	34	2.6	224	17	3.0[1]	0.3[1]	20	1.5	10	Cambodia
480[3]	33[3]	101	6.4	310	20	...	...	60	3.8	45	Cameroon
21,450[1]	703[1]	20,319	613	9,924	300	1,075[1]	36[1]	12,000	362	13,500[4]	Canada
2.0	4.8	62	140	32	71	1.0[5]	2.5[5]	...	...	12.0	Cape Verde
20	5.6	9.9	2.8	11.0	3.1	0.3[1]	0.1[1]	7.0	2.0	2.0	Central African Republic
10[3]	1.4[3]	11	1.3	22	2.5	0.2	0.03[1]	12	1.4	4.0	Chad
3,600	240	3,703	249	5,272	354	40[1]	2.7[1]	1,300	87	3,102	Chile
370,000	292	179,034	140	144,812	114	2,000[1]	1.6[1]	25,000	20	33,700	China
8,273	199	7,300	181	3,160	78	242	5.8	1,800	45	1,154	Colombia
1.0[1]	1.5[1]	8.9	15.7	...	...	0.2[2]	0.2[2]	4.0	7.1	2.5	Comoros
150[5]	3.0[5]	20	0.4	150	2.9	5.0[2]	0.1[2]	...	...	6.0	Congo, Dem. Rep. of the
33[1]	12[1]	22	7.7	150	53	0.1[2]	0.4[2]	12	4.2	0.5[9]	Congo, Rep. of the
900	229	945	243	311	78	8.5[1]	2.2[1]	700	180	384	Costa Rica
1,000[3]	69[3]	294	18	729	44	...	...	100	6.1	70	Côte d'Ivoire
1,250	285	1,700	388	1,755	400	50[1]	11[1]	400	91	250[4]	Croatia
2,750	246	573	51	8.1	0.7	...	...	220	20	120	Cuba
120	178	435	482	314	349	7.0[14]	11[14]	170	188.5	150	Cyprus
5,000	487	3,846	376	6,769	662	102	9.9	1,250[4]	122[4]	1,400	Czech Republic
3,300	621	3,882	724	3,954	738	250[2]	48[2]	2,300[4]	429[4]	2,400	Denmark
30	48	9.9	22	0.3	0.6	0.1	0.2	7.0	15.2	3.3	Djibouti
6.0[1]	79[1]	23[4]	303[4]	1.2	15.6	0.3[2]	4.0[2]	6.0	78	6.0[4]	Dominica
770[1]	92[1]	940	108	1,073	124	2.5[2]	0.3[2]	...	...	186	Dominican Republic
...	...	...	...	...	...	...	...	...	...	...	East Timor
2,500[3]	201[3]	1,336	104	859	67	...	...	300	23	328	Ecuador
11,400	183	6,650	102	2,794	43	34	0.5	1,000	15	600	Egypt
1,177	191	598	96	800	128	...	...	140	22	50[4]	El Salvador
4.0[1]	9.0[1]	6.9	14	15	31	0.1[2]	0.3[2]	3.0	6.2	0.9	Equatorial Guinea
60	16	32	8.4	92	24	0.8[2]	0.2[2]	7.0	1.8	10	Eritrea
800	555	504	369	651	477	13	8.7	250	183	430	Estonia

Communications (continued)

country	publishing (latest) books number of titles	number of copies ('000)	periodicals number of titles	number of copies ('000)	daily newspapers number	total circulation ('000)	circulation per 1,000 persons	postal services post offices, 1998 number	persons per office	pieces of mail handled ('000,000)	pieces handled per person	telecommunications radio, 1997 receivers (all types; '000)	receivers per 1,000 persons
Ethiopia	240	674	...	...	4	86	1.5	534	112,000	27	0.3	11,750	202
Faroe Islands	...	...	...	...	1	6.0	136	42[1]	1,190[1]	10[1]	161[1]	26	582
Fiji	401	2,256	...	...	1	40	50	318	2,520	40	35	500	636
Finland	13,104	...	5,711	...	56	2,332	455	1,601	3,220	1,614	305	7,770	1,498
France	34,766	1,041	2,672	120,018	117	12,700	218	17,038	3,450	26,115	436	55,300	946
French Guiana	...	...	...	...	1	2.0	7.0	...	...	...	...	104	650
French Polynesia	...	...	...	...	4	24	108	97	2,370	28	102	128	574
Gabon	...	...	...	...	2	33	30	108	11,000	5.9	2.2	208	183
Gambia, The	14[17]	10[17]	10	885	1	2.0	1.7	...	...	...	...	196	165
Gaza Strip	...	...	...	...	...	...	...	...	...	...	...	...	...
Georgia	581[6]	834[6]	...	...	9	84	111	1,190[1]	4,560[1]	1,025[10, 13]	188[10, 13]	3,020	590
Germany	71,515	...	9,010	395,036	375	25,500	311	14,500	5,650	21,105[1]	249[1]	77,800	948
Ghana	28	648	121	774	4	250	14	1,010	18,800	225	3.4	4,400	236
Greece	4,225	...	...	...	156	1,622	153	1,225	8,590	392[5, 12]	375[5, 12]	5,020	475
Greenland	...	...	...	...	2	1.0	18	75[1]	800[1]	7.8[1]	72[1]	27	483
Grenada	...	...	4	89	1[18]	4.0[18]	45[18]	58[10]	1,550[10]	...	...	57	615
Guadeloupe	...	...	...	...	1	35	81	...	...	...	...	113	258
Guam	...	...	...	...	1	26	180	...	...	...	...	221	1,400
Guatemala	...	...	...	...	7	338	33	540[10]	19,700[10]	79[10]	7.7[10]	835	79
Guernsey	...	...	...	...	...	...	...	18	3,440	10[12]	169[12]	...	...
Guinea	...	...	3	5.0	...	...	...	96	47,400	7.9	0.4	357	49
Guinea-Bissau	...	...	...	...	1	6.0	5.4	18[5]	60,600[5]	311[2, 19]	0.32[2, 19]	49	43
Guyana	42[6]	508[6]	...	...	2	42	50	85[1]	10,000[1]	4.0[1, 13]	4.7[1, 13]	420	498
Haiti	...	...	...	...	4	20	2.5	85	90,000	1.2[19]	0.2[19]	415	53
Honduras	22	80	...	...	7	320	55	435[2]	13,700[2]	35[2]	3.0[2]	2,450	410
Hong Kong	...	...	598	...	52	5,000	800	125	53,500	1,254	175	3,700[5]	586[5]
Hungary	9,193	53,194	1,203	14,927	40	1,895	189	3,236	3,120	1,046	103	7,010	690
Iceland	1,527	...	938	384	5	145	535	94[5]	2,870[5]	73[5]	254[5]	260	950
India	11,903	...	...	...	3,037	22,969	27	153,021	6,240	16,394	16	116,000	120
Indonesia	4,018[17]	8,103[17]	115	4,173	69	4,665	23	20,139	10,200	758	3.4	31,500	155
Iran	15,073	87,861	318	6,166	32	1,651	24	13,715	4,490	274	4.2	17,000	263
Iraq	...	...	...	...	4	407	20	...	...	69	2.1	4,850	229
Ireland	...	...	...	...	6	543	153	1,912	1,940	748	170	2,550	697
Isle of Man	...	...	...	...	...	...	...	36	1,940	215[,7]	300[5, 7]	...	...
Israel	2,310[20]	9,368[20]	...	...	34	1,650	291	664	8,990	601	95	3,070	524
Italy	35,236	278,821	9,951	80,469	74	5,985	105	13,967[1]	4,120[1]	5,850[1]	99[1]	50,500	880
Jamaica	...	...	...	...	3	158	63	688	3,690	67	19	1,215	483
Japan	56,221[6]	400,013[6]	2,926	...	122	72,705	580	24,678	5,120	25,731[1]	202[1]	120,500	956
Jersey	...	...	...	...	...	...	...	23[1]	3,650[1]	62[1]	468[1]	...	...
Jordan	511	2,673[6]	31	43	4	250	45	687	9,170	118[1]	17[1]	1,660	271
Kazakhstan	1,226	21,014	...	...	3	500	30	3,580	4,700	201[2, 12]	0.01[2, 12]	6,470	395
Kenya	300[6]	452	...	...	4	263	9.4	1,033	28,100	413	14	3,070	108
Kiribati	...	...	...	...	...	...	...	25[1]	3,200[1]	1.9[1]	1.2[1]	17	212
Korea, North	...	...	...	...	3	4,500	200	...	...	...	...	3,360	146
Korea, South	30,487[6]	142,804[6]	...	...	60	18,000	394	3,610	12,900	3,631	77	47,500	1,039
Kuwait	196[21]	6,107	...	...	8	635	376	51[1]	35,500[1]	99[14]	68[14]	1,175	678
Kyrgyzstan	351	1,980	...	...	3	67	15	914[1]	5,080[1]	39[1, 12]	8.5[1, 12]	520	119
Laos	88[6]	995[6]	...	...	3	18	4.0	106	48,700	5.2	0.9	730	145
Latvia	1,965	7,734	213	1,660	24	616	246	978	2,500	37	12	1,760	715
Lebanon	...	...	...	...	15	435	141	268[1]	11,700[1]	3.9[1]	1.2[1]	2,850	907
Lesotho	...	...	...	...	2	15	7.6	157	13,100	64	16	104	52
Liberia	...	...	...	...	6	35	16	34[5]	8,260[5]	...	...	790	329
Libya	26	2,645	...	...	4	71	14	342	15,600	39	3.5	1,350	259
Liechtenstein	...	...	...	...	2	19	606	12[5]	2,500[5]	17[10]	0.6[10]	21	658
Lithuania	3,645	14,915	269	...	19	344	92	978[1]	3,790[1]	51	11	1,900	513
Luxembourg	681	...	508	...	5	135	327	106	3,960	169	340	285	683
Macau	67	99	16	...	10	197	448	17	25,300	19	30	160	356
Macedonia	892	2,496	74	347	3	41	19	294	6,800	27	11	410	206
Madagascar	119	296	55	108	5	66	4.6	764	19,700	26	1.5	3,050	209
Malawi	117[6, 22]	9,174[6, 22]	...	...	1	25	2.6	314	34,100	44	3.4	2,600	258
Malaysia	5,843	29,040	25	996	42	3,345	163	1,382	7,490	993[7]	96[7]	9,100	434
Maldives	...	...	...	...	2	5.0	18	249[1]	1,080[1]	2.5	5.9	34	129
Mali	14[6]	28[6]	...	...	3	12	1.2	124	86,200	3.4	0.2	570	55
Malta	404	...	359	...	2	48	130	51[13]	7,450[13]	14[13]	34[13]	255	669
Marshall Islands	...	...	...	...	...	...	...	...	...	...	...	...	...
Martinique	...	...	...	...	1	30	78	...	...	...	...	82	213
Mauritania	...	...	...	...	2	1.0	0.5	61	41,500	4.2	0.5	360	146
Mauritius	80	163	62	...	6	85	76	101	11,500	63	47	420	371
Mayotte	...	...	...	...	...	...	...	...	...	...	...	50[5]	427[5]
Mexico	...	...	158	13,097	295	9,030	97	9,432	10,600	1,133	9.4	31,000	329
Micronesia	...	...	...	...	...	...	...	...	...	...	...	70[5]	667[5]
Moldova	921	2,779	76	196	4	261	59	1,276	3,430	41	8.1	3,220	736
Monaco	41	722	3	38	1	8.0	263	...	...	...	...	34	1,039
Mongolia	285[6]	959[6]	45	6,361	4	68	27	339[1]	7,050[1]	1.1[1]	0.3[1]	360	142
Morocco	918	1,836	...	...	22	704	27	1,469	18,900	240	7.7	6,640	247
Mozambique	...	3,490	...	...	2	49	2.7	353	47,900	6.8	0.1	730	40
Myanmar (Burma)	3,660	4,038	...	...	5	449	10	1,238	37,500	88[2]	1.9[2]	4,200	96
Namibia	106	...	...	...	4	30	19	115	14,400	66[12]	4.0[12]	232	143
Nauru	...	...	...	...	...	...	...	1[1]	10,000[1]	...	...	7.0	609
Nepal	...	...	...	...	29	250	11	4,156	5,260	29[5, 7]	1.4[5, 7]	840	38
Netherlands, The	34,067	...	367	19,283	38	4,753	305	2,387	6,580	7,009[23]	447[23]	15,300	980
Netherlands Antilles	...	...	...	...	6	70	334	16	12,625	...	...	217	1,031
New Caledonia	...	...	...	...	3	24	127	54	3,700	21	75	107	527
New Zealand	...	...	126	3,991	23	804	223	...	...	...	...	3,750	997
Nicaragua	...	...	...	...	4	135	30	183	26,300	8.3	1.2	1,240	265

television, 1999		telephones, 2001		cellular phones, 2001		fax, 1999		personal computers, 2001		Internet users, 2001	country
receivers (all types; '000)	receivers per 1,000 persons	main lines ('000)	per 1,000 persons	cellular subscriptions ('000)	subscriptions per 1,000 persons	receivers ('000)	receivers per 1,000 persons	units ('000)	units per 1,000 persons	number ('000)	
350	5.7	310	4.7	28	0.4	3.1	0.1	75	1.1	25	Ethiopia
15[1]	333[1]	25[9]	556[9]	11[9]	244[9]	...	...	...	...	...	Faroe Islands
89	110	90	111	76	93	2.8	3.5	50	61	15	Fiji
3,320	643	2,845	548	4,044	780	198[1]	381	2,200	424	4,303	Finland
36,500	623	34,033	575	35,922	607	2,800[1]	471[1]	20,000	338	15,653	France
30[1]	172[1]	49	293	18	108	...	...	...	...	...	French Guiana
43	186	53	221	67	282	3.0[3]	13[3]	...	...	16	French Polynesia
300	251	39	32	120[4]	98[4]	0.5[1]	0.4[1]	15	12	15[4]	Gabon
4.0	3.2	35	25	43	31	1.1[1]	0.9[1]	18	13	17	Gambia, The
...	...	...	...	...	...	...	...	...	...	...	Gaza Strip
2,580[3]	473[3]	868	174	295	59	0.5[10]	0.1[10]	0.7[9]	0.1[9]	25	Georgia
47,660	580	52,280	634	56,245	683	6,500	79	27,640[4]	336[4]	30,000	Germany
2,266	115	242	12	194	9.7	5.0	0.3	70	3.5	41	Ghana
5,100	480	5,608	511	7,962	725	40	3.8	860	78	1,400	Greece
22[1]	393[1]	26	468	17	298	...	...	...	...	20	Greenland
33	355	33	325	6.4	63	0.3	3.1	13	129	5.2	Grenada
118	262	205[4]	478[4]	293	682	3.4[2]	8.1[2]	100	233	8.0[4]	Guadeloupe
106	646	80[4]	508[4]	27[4]	172[4]	3.4	8.1	...	...	5.0[4]	Guam
660[3]	60[3]	756	65	1,134	97	10	1.0	150	13	200	Guatemala
...	...	55	873	32	500	0.7	11	...	...	20[4]	Guernsey
343	44	26	3.3	56	7.3	3.2	0.4	32	4.2	15	Guinea
...	...	12	9.1	...	...	0.5[3]	0.4[3]	...	...	4.0	Guinea-Bissau
60	70	80	103	40	51	...	...	23	30	95	Guyana
38	5.5	80	12	92	13	...	...	...	...	30	Haiti
600	95	310	48	238	37	...	...	80	13	40[4]	Honduras
2,884[3]	429[3]	3,926	584	5,702	848	390	58	2,600	387	3,100	Hong Kong
4,500	448	3,730	366	4,968	488	180	18	1,000	98	1,480	Hungary
145	520	191	669	235	826	4.1[14]	15[14]	120	421	195	Iceland
75,000	75	34,732	34	5,725	5.5	150[1]	0.2[1]	6,000	5.8	7,000	India
30,000	143	7,949	38	5,303	25	185	0.9	2,300	11	4,000	Indonesia
10,500	157	10,006	155	1,485	23	30	0.5	4,500	70	402	Iran
1,750[1]	78[1]	675[9]	29[9]	...	...	...	...	...	...	...	Iraq
1,505	406	1,860	480	2,800	722	100[1]	27[1]	1,500	387	895	Ireland
...	...	...	...	...	...	...	...	...	...	...	Isle of Man
2,000	328	3,100	497	5,260	842	140	25	1,600	256	1,500	Israel
28,000[3]	488[3]	27,303	472	48,698	841	1,800	31	11,300	195	16,000	Italy
480[3]	188[3]	513	197	700	268	1.6[14]	0.6[14]	130	50	100	Jamaica
91,000	719	76,000	598	72,796	573	16,000[1]	126[1]	44,400	349	57,900	Japan
...	...	74	849	61	706	0.7	8.0	...	...	8.0[4]	Jersey
540	83	660	129	746	146	52[3]	8.0[3]	170	33	212	Jordan
3,890[3]	239[3]	1,834[4]	124[4]	582	39	2.0	0.1	...	...	100[4]	Kazakhstan
660	22	313	10	500	16	3.8	0.1	175	5.7	500	Kenya
10[1]	122[1]	3.4[4]	38[4]	0.4[4]	4.5[4]	0.2	2.5	2.0	23	2.0	Kiribati
1,200	51	1,100[9]	50[9]	...	...	3.0	0.1	...	...	...	Korea, North
16,896	361	22,725	480	29,046	614	400	8.6	12,000	254	24,380	Korea, South
910	480	472	211	489	218	60	32	260	116	200	Kuwait
220[3]	47[3]	376[4]	76[4]	27	5.5	...	...	...	...	52[4]	Kyrgyzstan
51	10	53	9.3	30	5.3	0.5[10]	0.1[10]	16	2.8	10	Laos
1,808	741	725	307	657	279	0.9[2]	0.3[2]	360	153	170	Latvia
1,120[3]	346[3]	682[4]	188[4]	743[4]	205[4]	3.0[12]	1.1[12]	200	55	300[4]	Lebanon
33	16	22	10	33	15	0.6[2]	0.3[2]	...	...	5.0	Lesotho
70[1]	24[1]	6.6	2.0	...	...	...	...	...	...	...	Liberia
730[1]	133[1]	610	116	50	9.5	...	...	...	...	20	Libya
12[1]	375[1]	18	546	9.5	288	...	...	...	...	...	Liechtenstein
1,555	420	1,152	331	932	268	6.2[1]	1.7[1]	260	75	250	Lithuania
165[3]	385[3]	350	792	432	978	30	70	230	520	100[4]	Luxembourg
125	286	176	407	195	448	6.3	14	80	184	101	Macau
500[3]	249[3]	538	265	223	110	3.0	1.5	2.2[9]	1.1[9]	70	Macedonia
340[3]	22[3]	58	3.7	148	9.2	...	...	40	2.5	35	Madagascar
27	2.5	54	5.2	56	5.4	1.3	0.1	13	1.3	20	Malawi
3,800	174	4,738	199	7,128	300	175[3]	8.0[3]	3,000	126	5,700	Malaysia
11	40	27	99	18	67	3.5[2]	14[2]	6.0	21.7	10.0	Maldives
130[3]	12[3]	50	4.5	45	4.1	...	...	14	1.3	30	Mali
212	549	208	541	139	362	6.0[5]	16[5]	90	234	99	Malta
...	...	4.2	78	0.5	9.3	...	...	4.0	74	0.9	Marshall Islands
66[1]	168[1]	172[4]	447[4]	286	743	20[2]	52[2]	52	135	99[9]	Martinique
247	96	19	7.3	...	...	3.3	1.3	27	10	7.0	Mauritania
265	230	307	256	300	250	32	28	130	108	158	Mauritius
3.5[5]	305[5]	10	63	...	...	...	...	...	...	...	Mayotte
26,000	267	13,533	136	20,136	202	285[1]	2.9[1]	6,900	69	3,500	Mexico
2.4	21	10	93	...	...	0.5[3]	4.3[3]	...	...	4.0[4]	Micronesia
1,300	297	676	186	210	58	0.7	0.2	70	19.3	60	Moldova
25[1]	758[1]	33[3]	1,000[3]	12[3]	364[3]	...	...	...	...	...	Monaco
152[3]	58[3]	123	51	195	80	7.9	3.0	35	14	40	Mongolia
4,600	165	1,191	41	374	13	18[1]	0.6[1]	400	14	400	Morocco
95	5	89	5.1	170	9.6	7.2[10]	0.4[10]	70	4.0	15	Mozambique
323	7.2	281	6.7	14	0.3	2.5	0.1	55	1.3	10	Myanmar (Burma)
65	38	117	65	100	55	...	...	65	36	45	Namibia
0.5[1]	0.1[1]	1.7[3]	0.2[3]	0.8[3]	0.1[3]	...	...	...	...	...	Nauru
150	6.7	298	13	17	0.7	8.0	0.4	80	3.5	60	Nepal
9,500	600	10,000	623	11,900	742	600[1]	38[1]	6,900	430	5,300	Netherlands, The
69[1]	321[1]	79[9]	367[9]	16[3]	74[3]	...	...	...	...	...	Netherlands Antilles
101	481	51[4]	238[4]	50[4]	233[4]	2.2[10]	12[10]	...	...	24[4]	New Caledonia
1,975	518	1,834	475	2,417	626	65[2]	18[2]	1,500	389	1,092	New Zealand
340	69	159[4]	32[4]	156	32	...	...	50	10	50	Nicaragua

Communications (continued)

country	books number of titles	books number of copies ('000)	periodicals number of titles	periodicals number of copies ('000)	daily newspapers number	daily newspapers total circulation ('000)	daily newspapers circulation per 1,000 persons	post offices 1998 number	post offices 1998 persons per office	post offices 1998 pieces of mail handled ('000,000)	post offices 1998 pieces handled per person	radio 1997 receivers (all types; '000)	radio 1997 receivers per 1,000 persons
Niger	5[6]	11[6]	...	...	1	2	0.2	53	190,000	3.4	0.3	680	70
Nigeria	1,314	18,800	...	...	25	2,740	27	3,971	26,800	391	2.0	23,500	226
Northern Mariana Islands	...	...	...	...	...	...	...	...	...	...	...	115[5]	190[5]
Norway	6,900[8,20]	...	8,017	...	83	2,578	593	1,534[1]	210[1]	2,524[1]	555[1]	4,030	917
Oman	7[6]	21[6]	15	...	4	63	27	90[2]	23,700[2]	43	7.1	1,400	607
Pakistan	124	714	...	...	264	2,840	22	13,294	9,820	413	2.9	13,500	94
Palau	...	...	...	...	...	...	...	...	...	...	...	12	663
Panama	...	...	...	...	7	166	62	176	15,700	18	4.4	815	299
Papua New Guinea	122	...	...	...	2	65	15	108[24]	39,800[24]	39[24]	10[24]	410	91
Paraguay	152	...	...	...	5	213	43	326	16,000	4.6	0.5	925	182
Peru	612	1,836	...	...	74	2,000	85	963	25,800	43	1.3	6,650	273
Philippines	1,507	14,718[6]	1,570	9,468	47	5,700	82	3,023[10]	22,600[10]	3,205[5]	125	11,500	161
Poland	14,104	80,306	5,260	75,358	55	4,351	113	7,836	4,930	2,503	63	20,200	522
Portugal	7,868[11]	26,942	984	10,208	27	740	75	3,712	2,660	1,201	117	3,020	306
Puerto Rico	...	...	...	...	3	475	127	...	...	...	...	2,700	714
Qatar	209[17]	2,205	11	47	5	90	161	26	20,800	20[13]	38[13]	256	450
Réunion	69	...	...	...	3	55	83	...	...	...	...	173	257
Romania	7,199	38,374	987	...	69	6,800	297	6,324	3,560	327	14	7,200	319
Russia	36,237	421,387	2,751	387,832	285	15,517	105	43,900[1]	3,350[1]	5,614[1,7]	381[1,7]	61,500	417
Rwanda	...	...	15	101	1	0.5	0.1	39	169,000	3.8	0.4	601	101
St. Kitts and Nevis	...	...	10	44	...	...	...	7	5,710	2.6	46	28	701
St. Lucia	...	...	...	...	...	...	...	63	2,380	2.3[12]	15[12]	111	746
St. Vincent and the Grenadines	...	...	...	...	1	1.0	9.0	41[1]	2,680[1]	...	...	77	690
Samoa	...	...	...	...	...	...	...	38	4,470	0.9	3.0	178	1,035
San Marino	...	...	15	9	3	2.0	72	10[5]	3,000[5]	...	...	16	610
São Tomé and Príncipe	...	...	...	...	...	...	...	18	7,780	0.3	0.6	38	272
Saudi Arabia	3,900[6]	14,493[6,22]	471	...	13	1,105	59	1,421	14,200	1,246	45	6,250	321
Senegal	...	...	...	...	1	45	5.3	134	69,200	12	0.7	1,240	141
Seychelles	...	...	...	...	1	3.0	46	5	16,000	5.2	49	42	560
Sierra Leone	...	...	...	...	1	20	4.7	54[2]	83,500[2]	1.1[2]	0.1[2]	1,121	253
Singapore	...	...	...	...	8	1,095	324	939	4,120	772[1]	184[1]	2,550	744
Slovakia	3,800	6,139	424	8,725	19	989	185	1,728	3,120	518	90	3,120	581
Slovenia	3,441	6,267	784	...	7	397	206	545	3,630	387	189	805	403
Solomon Islands	...	...	...	...	...	...	...	127	3,150	4.3[2]	11[2]	57	141
Somalia	...	...	...	...	2	10	1.2	...	...	...	...	470	53
South Africa	5,418	31,349	11	2,149	17	1,288	34	2,449	17,200	2,170[7]	52[7]	13,750	355
Spain	46,330	192,019	...	...	94	3,931	99	4,093	9,620	4,565	112	13,100	331
Sri Lanka	4,115	19,650	...	...	9	530	29	4,282	4,380	463	23	3,850	211
Sudan, The	...	...	...	...	5	737	27	491	57,600	4.4[5]	0.1[5]	7,550	272
Suriname	47[6]	21[6]	...	...	4	50	116	33	12,400	...	...	300	728
Swaziland	...	...	...	...	3	24	27	60[1]	15,200[1]	21[1]	18[1]	155	168
Sweden	13,496	...	373	19,242	94	3,933	446	1,720[5]	5,140[5]	4,570[5]	503[5]	8,250	932
Switzerland	15,371	...	60	4,561	88	2,383	330	3,630[5]	1,950[5]	4,230[10]	601[10]	7,100	979
Syria	598	310[5]	30	192	8	287	20	619	25,200	19	1.0	4,150	278
Taiwan	...	...	...	...	...	4,000	188	...	...	...	...	8,620[5]	402[5]
Tajikistan	132[6]	997[6]	11	130	2	120	20	706[1]	8,570[1]	3.0[1]	0.4[1]	850	143
Tanzania	172[6]	364[6]	...	...	3	120	3.9	612	52,400	55	1.3	8,800	280
Thailand	8,142	...	1,522	...	30	3,800	65	4,265	14,300	1,315	21	13,959	234
Togo	...	...	...	...	1	15	3.6	50[1]	86,400[1]	8.3[1]	0.7[1]	940	219
Tonga	...	...	...	...	1	7.0	71	1.8[14]	55,600[14]	4.0[14]	40[14]	61	400
Trinidad and Tobago	26	30	...	...	4	156	121	245	5,220	30[2]	16[2]	680	533
Tunisia	720	6,000[22]	170	1,748	8	280	31	947[2]	9,740[2]	117[2]	12[2]	2,060	224
Turkey	6,546	...	3,554	...	57	6,845	111	16,984	3,740	1,088	16	11,300	178
Turkmenistan	450[6]	5,493[6]	...	...	...	...	...	1,673[5]	2,730[5]	275[5]	6.0[5]	1,225	289
Tuvalu	...	...	...	...	...	...	...	...	...	...	...	4.0	384
Uganda	288	2,229[20]	26	158	2	40	2.1	313	67,200	18[1]	0.5[1]	2,600	130
Ukraine	6,225	68,876	717	2,521	44	2,780	54	15,227	3,320	374	6.3	45,050	882
United Arab Emirates	293[22]	5,117[22]	80	922	7	384	170	243	11,190	182	39	820	355
United Kingdom	107,263	...	...	...	99	19,332	332	18,760	3,130	19,556	325	84,500	1,443
United States	68,175	...	11,593	...	1,520	59,990	212	38,159	7,090	197,688	729	575,000	2,116
Uruguay	934	1,970	...	...	36	950	296	942	3,490	16	6.0	1,970	603
Uzbekistan	1,003	30,914	81	684	3	75	3.0	3,044[1]	7,700[1]	12[1]	0.4[1]	10,800	465
Vanuatu	...	...	...	...	...	...	...	...	...	...	...	62	350
Venezuela	3,468[6]	7,420[6]	...	...	86	4,600	206	407	57,600	141	5.1	10,750	472
Vietnam	5,581	83,000	338	2,710	10	300	4.0	3,075	25,200	...	...	8,200	107
Virgin Islands (U.S.)	...	...	...	...	3	42	326	9[1]	2,000[1]	3.6[10,13]	0.2[10,13]	107	1,119
West Bank	...	...	...	...	...	...	...	...	...	...	...	...	...
Western Sahara	...	...	...	...	...	...	...	...	...	...	...	56	211
Yemen	...	...	...	...	3	230	15	265	64,400	5.5	0.1	1,050	64
Yugoslavia	5,367	16,669	395	...	18	1,128	110	1,783	5,940	242	19	3,150	296
Zambia	...	...	...	...	3	114	14	195	45,000	16	0.8	1,030	120
Zimbabwe	232	...	28	680	2	209	19	296	42,800	137	9.4	1,140	102

television, 1999		telephones, 2001		cellular phones, 2001		fax, 1999		personal computers, 2001		Internet users, 2001	country
receivers (all types; '000)	receivers per 1,000 persons	main lines ('000)	per 1,000 persons	cellular subscriptions ('000)	subscriptions per 1,000 persons	receivers ('000)	receivers per 1,000 persons	units ('000)	units per 1,000 persons	number ('000)	
285	27	22	2.1	1.8	0.2	0.3[2]	0.0[2]	6.0	0.6	12	Niger
7,200[3]	66[3]	500	3.9	330	2.6	6.8[2]	0.1[2]	800	6.3	200[4]	Nigeria
...	...	27[4]	383[4]	3.0[4]	43[4]	...	...	...	...	...	Northern Mariana Islands
2,900	648	3,262	723	3,737	828	220[1]	49[1]	2,300	510	2,700	Norway
1,415	575	235	95	325	132	6.4[1]	2.6[1]	85	34	120	Oman
16,000	119	3,400	24	800	5.6	268	2.0	600	4.2	500	Pakistan
...	...	...	...	...	...	...	...	...	...	20[9]	Palau
530[3]	188[3]	430	149	600	208	0.8	0.2	110	38	90[4]	Panama
60	13	65[4]	12[4]	8.6[4]	1.6[4]	0.8[10]	0.2[10]	300	57	135[4]	Papua New Guinea
1,100	205	289	51	1,150	204	1.7[14]	0.4[14]	80	14	60	Paraguay
3,700	147	2,022	77	1,545	59	15[2]	0.6[2]	1,250	48	3,000	Peru
8,200	110	3,100	40	10,568	135	50[3]	0.7[3]	1,700	22	2,000	Philippines
15,000	387	11,400	295	10,050	260	55[2]	1.4[2]	3,300	85	3,800	Poland
5,600	560	4,370	421	7,978	769	70	7.0	1,210	117	3,600	Portugal
1,250[3]	321[3]	1,330	346	1,211	315	543[14]	149[14]	...	...	600	Puerto Rico
490[3]	832[3]	167	280	179	300	10[3]	18[3]	100	168	40	Qatar
127[1]	184[1]	268	366	50	68.2	1.9[2]	2.9[2]	...	...	...	Réunion
7,000	312	4,094	188	3,860	177	21[2]	0.9[2]	800	37	1,000	Romania
62,000[3]	421[3]	35,700	247	5,560	39	53[3]	0.4[3]	7,300	51	4,300	Russia
10[1]	1.7[1]	22	2.9	65	8.9	0.5[2]	0.1[2]	...	...	20	Rwanda
10[1]	256[1]	22[4]	476[4]	1.2[4]	26[4]	...	...	8.0	174	2.0[9]	St. Kitts and Nevis
32[1]	208[1]	44[9]	286[9]	1.9[3]	12[3]	...	...	...	...	...	St. Lucia
18[1]	159[1]	25[4]	222[4]	2.4[4]	21[4]	...	...	13	116	3.5[4]	St. Vincent and the Grenadines
9.0[3]	51[3]	10	57	3.0	17	0.5[3]	2.8[3]	1	5.7	3.0	Samoa
9.0[1]	346[1]	20[9]	769[9]	9.6	356	...	...	...	...	...	San Marino
23[1]	160[1]	5.4	38	...	...	0.2[2]	15[2]	...	...	9.0	São Tomé and Príncipe
5,500	263	3,233	143	2,529	111	150[2]	8.2[2]	1,400	62	300	Saudi Arabia
370[3]	40[3]	237	25	391	41	...	...	180	19	100	Senegal
16	200	21	261	44	538	0.6	7.5	12	146	9.0	Seychelles
60[3]	13[3]	23	4.9	27	5.8	2.5	0.5	...	...	7.0	Sierra Leone
1,200	308	1,949	472	2,859	692	100[3]	32[3]	2,100	508	1,500	Singapore
2,250	417	1,556	289	2,147	399	54[3]	10[3]	800	149	650[4]	Slovakia
710[3]	357[3]	800	406	1,516	770	21[3]	11[3]	550	279	600	Slovenia
6.0[3]	14[3]	7.4	17	1.0	2.3	0.8	1.9	22	52	2.0	Solomon Islands
135[1]	14[1]	15[9]	2.0[9]	...	...	...	...	...	...	...	Somalia
5,450[3]	124[3]	4,969	112	9,197	208	150[1]	3.4[1]	3,000	68	3,068	South Africa
22,000	547	17,427	427	26,494	649	700[5]	17[5]	6,800	168	7,388	Spain
1,900	102	828	44	720	39	11[10]	0.6[10]	150	8.0	150	Sri Lanka
5,000	173	453	13	105	2.9	25	0.9	115	3.2	56	Sudan, The
98[3]	236[3]	77	178	84	194	...	...	...	...	15	Suriname
110	112	32	29	66	60	1.2[5]	1.2[5]	...	...	14	Swaziland
4,700[3]	530[3]	6,585	740	6,867	772	450[5]	51[5]	5,000	562	4,600	Sweden
3,700	518	5,183	717	5,226	723	207[5]	29[5]	3,600[4]	498[4]	2,917	Switzerland
1,070	66	1,808	108	200	12	22	1.4	270	16	60	Syria
9,220	417	12,847	575	21,633	968	430[10]	20[10]	5,000	224	7,550	Taiwan
2,000	328	223	36	1.6	0.3	2.1	0.3	...	...	3.2	Tajikistan
690	21	148	4.1	427	13	2.0[14]	0.1[14]	120	3.5	300	Tanzania
17,600	289	5,974	95	7,550	120	150[1]	2.5[1]	1,700	27	3,536	Thailand
100	22	48	9.3	95	18	18	4.0	100	19	50	Togo
2.0[1]	20[1]	9.7[4]	97[4]	0.1[9]	1.0[9]	0.2[2]	2.0[2]	...	...	1.0[9]	Tonga
1,430	1,107	312	240	225	174	5.0[3]	3.9[3]	90	69	120	Trinidad and Tobago
1,800	190	1,056	109	389	40	31[1]	3.3[1]	230	24	400	Tunisia
21,500	332	18,901	276	20,000	292	108[1]	1.7[1]	2,700	39	2,500	Turkey
865[3]	197[3]	388	80	9.5[4]	1.9[4]	...	...	...	...	8.0	Turkmenistan
0.1[5]	9.1[5]	0.6[9]	55[9]	...	...	...	...	...	...	...	Tuvalu
580[3]	27[3]	64	2.7	323	14	3.0[5]	0.1[5]	70	3.0	60	Uganda
21,000[3]	415[3]	10,670	219	2,225	46	48	0.9	920	19	600	Ukraine
740	252	1,053	311	1,909	564	18	6.1	420	124	900	United Arab Emirates
38,800	652	34,710	579	47,026	784	1,992[5]	33[5]	22,000	367	24,000	United Kingdom
233,000	844	190,000	667	127,000	446	21,000[1]	78.0[1]	178,000	625	142,823	United States
1,760	531	951	283	520	155	0.6	0.2	370	110	400	Uruguay
6,700	276	1,663	66	63	2.5	2.2	0.1	...	...	150	Uzbekistan
2.0[1]	11[1]	6.8	34	0.3	1.5	0.6[2]	3.6[2]	...	...	5.5	Vanuatu
4,300[3]	181[3]	2,758	112	6,489	264	70[1]	3.0[1]	1,300	53	1,300	Venezuela
14,500	184	3,050	39	1,251	16	31	0.4	800	10	400	Vietnam
6.8[1]	57[1]	69[4]	562[4]	35[4]	321[4]	...	...	...	...	12[9]	Virgin Islands (U.S.)
...	...	257	72	40[1]	14[1]	...	...	...	...	60	West Bank
6.0[5]	24[5]	...	...	...	...	...	...	...	...	...	Western Sahara
5,000	286	423	22	152	8.1	2.8[2]	0.2[2]	37	2.0	17	Yemen
2,900[3]	273[3]	2,444	230	1,998	188	20	1.9	250	24	600	Yugoslavia
1,300	145	85	8.7	98	10	1.0	0.1	75	7.7	25	Zambia
2,074	180	254	22	329	29	4.1[3]	0.4[3]	165	15	100	Zimbabwe

[1]1997. [2]1995. [3]1998. [4]2000. [5]1996. [6]First editions only. [7]Domestic and foreign-dispatched only. [8]Not including school textbooks. [9]1999. [10]1994. [11]Including reprints. [12]Domestic only. [13]Foreign-dispatched and foreign-received only. [14]1993. [15]Millions of copies. [16]1985. [17]School textbooks and government publications only. [18]1980. [19]Foreign-received only. [20]Not including government publications. [21]Government publications only. [22]School textbooks only. [23]Domestic and foreign-received only. [24]1991.

Trade: external

The following table presents comparative data on the international, or foreign, trade of the countries of the world. The table analyzes data for both imports and exports in two ways: (1) into several major commodity groups defined in accordance with the United Nations system called the Standard International Trade Classification (SITC) and (2) by direction of trade for each country with major world trading blocs and partners. These commodity groupings are defined by the SITC code numbers beneath the column headings. The single-digit numbers represent broad SITC categories (in the SITC, called "sections"); the double-digit numbers represent subcategories ("divisions") of the single-digit categories (27 is a subcategory of 2); the three-digit number is a subcategory ("group") of the double-digit (667 is a subcategory of 66). Where a plus or minus sign is used before one of these SITC numbers, the SITC category or subcategory is being added to or subtracted from the aggregate implied by the total of the preceding sections. The SITC commodity aggregations used here are listed in the table at the end of this headnote. The full SITC commodity breakdown for the system used here is presented in the 1975 United Nations publication *Standard International Trade Classification, Revision 2.*

The SITC was developed by the United Nations through its Statistical Commission as an outgrowth of the need for a standard system of aggregating commodities of external trade to provide international comparability of foreign trade statistics. The United Nations Statistical Commission has defined external merchandise trade as "all goods whose movement into or out of the customs area of a country compiling the statistics adds to or subtracts from the material resources of the country." Goods passing through a country for transport only are excluded, but goods entering for reexport, or deposited (as in a bonded warehouse, or free trade area) for reimport, are included. Statistics in this table refer only to goods and exclude purely financial transactions that are covered in the "Finance" and "National product and accounts" tables. Gold for fabrication (*e.g.,* as jewelry) is included; monetary and reserve gold are excluded.

For purposes of comparability of data, total value of imports and exports is given in this table in U.S. dollars. Conversions from currencies other than U.S. dollars are determined according to the average market rates for the year for which data are supplied; these are mainly as calculated by the International Monetary Fund (IMF) or other official sources. The commodity categories are given in terms of percentages of the total value of the country's import or export trade (with the exclusions noted above). Value is based on transaction value: for imports, the value at which the goods were purchased by the importer plus the cost of transportation and insurance to the frontier of the importing country (c.i.f. [cost, insurance,

Trade: external

country	year	imports total value ('000,000 U.S.$)	food and agricultural raw materials (0+1+2-27-28+4)	mineral ores and concentrates (27+28+667)	fuels and other energy (3)	manufactured goods totala (5+6-667+7+8+9)	of which chemicals and related products (5)	of which machinery and transport equipment (7)	of which othera (6-667+8+9)	from European Union (EU)b	from United States	from Eastern Europec	from Japan	from all otherd
Afghanistan	1996[1]	359.0	—19.9[2]—		2.7	77.4[3]	—	15.2	62.2[3]	16.5[4]	1.1[4]	8.3[4]	25.3[4]	48.8[4]
Albania	1998	840.8	28.4	0.3	3.9	67.4	8.9	16.3	42.2	81.6	1.0	6.3	0.1	11.0
Algeria	1999	9,161.9	30.1	0.2	1.7	68.1	11.7	33.1	23.2	56.2	8.4	4.8	3.9	26.7
American Samoa	1996[6]	499.0	—40.5[2,7]—		16.9[7]	42.6[3,7]	2.3[7]	7.4[7]	32.9[3,7]	0.1[7]	78.2[7]	—[7]	2.0[7]	19.6[7]
Andorra	1998	1,080.5	24.2	3.9	3.5	68.4	10.7	25.8	31.9	88.2	2.3	0.2	3.2	6.1
Angola	1999	2,143.0	—33.6[2,5]—		0.3[5]	66.1[3,5]	9.1[5]	30.1[5]	26.9[3,5]	46.0	13.2	4.3	0.7	35.8
Antigua and Barbuda	1998	357.5	—15.7[2]—		8.4	75.9[3]	5.9	27.2	42.8[3]	10.1	26.6	—		63.3
Argentina	1999	25,508.0	6.4	1.0	2.8	89.7	17.5	46.4	25.8	29.1	19.6	1.4	4.2	45.8
Armenia	1999	810.9	26.7	10.5	21.6	41.3	10.1	13.9	17.3	31.1	10.9	22.2	0.2	35.5
Aruba	1998	832.5[10]	21.7	4.1	—	74.2	10.4	36.9	26.9	12.0	72.0	—	1.9	14.1
Australia	1999	65,514.5	5.9	0.7	5.9	87.5	11.1	47.0	29.3	22.4	20.5	0.2	13.2	43.6
Austria	1999	66,003.5	9.0	0.7	4.0	86.4	10.0	41.2	35.2	70.3	5.4	8.5	2.6	13.2
Azerbaijan	1999	1,035.7	21.2	1.0	6.3	71.5	6.1	41.5	23.9	18.4	8.0	29.4	5.4	38.9
Bahamas, The	1998	1,816.4	—19.0[2]—		6.2	74.8[3]	8.8	30.6	35.4[3]	1.6[11]	91.5[11]	0.3[4,11]	0.3[4,11]	6.3[11]
Bahrain	1996	4,092.6	12.3	5.3	40.9	41.5	5.2	15.7	20.7	18.9	6.7	0.2	3.7	70.6
Bangladesh	1998[13]	7,018.0	20.7	0.6	7.5	71.2	8.7	19.6	42.9	12.3	4.3	1.7	6.8	74.9
Barbados	1999	1,067.3	19.1	0.9	6.2	73.8	10.3	32.0	31.6	16.4	42.5	0.1	7.9	33.2
Belarus	1999	6,673.7	15.0	1.7	23.0	60.2	12.8	20.4	27.0	19.8	1.9	70.4	0.5	7.3
Belgium	1999	160,708.4	11.8	8.7	6.0	73.6	16.0	31.1	26.5	70.6	7.5	2.5	2.6	16.8
Belize	1999	366.3	17.2	0.2	15.3	67.3	9.2	27.3	30.8	7.8	51.7	—	2.3	38.2
Benin	1998	807.0	29.8	0.8	20.8	48.6	7.9	17.2	23.5	45.7	5.9	2.9	4.4	41.2
Bermuda	1995	680.2	21.5	2.1	6.0	70.4	7.8	25.3	37.3	6.4	49.8	—		43.9
Bhutan	1997	137.4	22.8[8]	0.5[8]	11.4[8]	65.2[8]	8.5[8]	30.3[8]	26.5[8]	3.5	0.6	0.1	16.9	79.0[17]
Bolivia	1999	1,835.4	10.6	0.2	3.6	85.6	12.9	44.7	28.0	12.5	23.9	0.2	8.6	54.9
Bosnia and Herzegovina	1998	1,193.2	—24.3[2]—		5.7	70.0[3]	10.5	28.2	31.3[3]	40.5	2.3	13.7[4]	1.0[4]	42.6[4]
Botswana	1997	2,261.9	16.6	2.7	5.6	75.0	7.3	37.6	30.2	8.2	...	—		91.8[20]
Brazil	1998	60,793.2	11.8	0.8	9.3	78.1	16.2	43.8	18.1	28.8	23.6	1.1	5.6	40.9
Brunei	1998	1,566.0	16.9	1.8	0.6	80.7	5.5	32.3	42.8	15.2	15.0	—	6.4	63.4
Bulgaria	1997	4,932.0	11.3	4.3	30.5	54.0	10.3	16.2	27.4	37.7	3.8	37.0	0.8	20.7
Burkina Faso	1997	529.9	—25.6[2,5]—		11.6[5]	62.8[3,5]	18.5[5]	20.8[5]	23.5[3,5]	46.1	4.2	1.8	5.5	42.3
Burundi	1999	132.0	13.0[22]	0.6[22]	12.4[22]	74.0[22]	14.1[22]	21.3[22]	38.6[22]	42.9	2.0	0.3	2.9	52.0
Cambodia	1998	1,080.3	17.2[22,23]	...	11.7[22]	...	6.5[22,23]	17.0[22,23]	...	8.2	3.6	0.3	6.6	81.3
Cameroon	1999	1,315.8	16.2[25]	3.2[25]	15.7[25]	64.9[25]	14.6[25]	27.6[25]	22.7[25]	52.9	4.9	1.5	5.4	35.3
Canada	1999	215,554.9	6.6	1.3	3.4	88.7	8.2	53.2	27.3	10.2	67.0	0.4	4.7	17.6
Cape Verde	1997	261.0	37.1	0.1	5.9	56.9	5.2	27.0	24.8	69.7	10.0	2.2	3.2	14.9
Central African Republic	1996	179.9	25.9	0.4	8.1	65.6	7.9	37.4	20.3	48.6	1.7	—	8.7	41.1
Chad	1995	215.2	24.7	0.5	17.9	57.0	7.2	23.8	25.9	51.3	6.5	0.4	2.4	39.5
Chile	1999	13,891.5	9.4	0.7	13.5	76.4	13.4	36.6	26.4	20.4	21.5	0.6	4.5	53.0
China	1999	165,699.1	8.3	2.6	5.4	83.6	14.3	41.9	27.4	15.4	11.8	3.0	20.4	49.5
Colombia	1999	10,659.1	15.0	0.6	2.5	81.9	21.9	34.3	25.7	18.1	37.4	0.6	4.9	38.9
Comoros	1998	47.8	37.8[9,23]	...	12.4[9]	49.8[9]	1.1[9,23]	7.2[9,23]	41.5[9]	47.3	0.2	0.2	3.8	48.5
Congo, Dem. Rep. of the	1995	889.2	—20.0[27]—		13.8[27]	66.2[27]	4.4[27]	45.5[27]	16.3[27]	37.1	0.8[4]	0.3	1.3	60.5[4]
Congo, Rep. of the	1995	555.9	21.7	0.4	19.6	58.3	13.9	20.2	24.2	45.4	8.0	0.1	2.2	44.3
Costa Rica	1999	5,986.5	8.2	0.2	5.4	86.1	13.2	30.8	42.1	9.4	54.8	0.5	5.0	30.4
Côte d'Ivoire	1996	2,615.7	19.3	1.0	25.2	54.5	11.9	23.3	19.3	47.5	5.2	1.8	4.4	41.1
Croatia	1999	7,777.4	9.9	0.6	11.1	78.4	11.7	34.7	32.0	56.5	3.2	15.1	1.8	23.4
Cuba	1996	3,480.6	—23.7[2]—		27.9	48.3[3]	8.7	16.1	23.5[3]	31.1	0.2	5.8	1.3	61.6
Cyprus	1999	3,618.0	20.7	0.5	8.7	70.0	9.2	27.4	33.5	52.6	10.8	5.3	6.7	24.5
Czech Republic	1999	28,837.4	7.7	1.0	6.6	84.7	11.2	40.3	33.2	64.0	4.1	17.1	2.0	12.8
Denmark	1999	44,316.6	15.0	0.5	3.1	81.4	9.7	35.8	35.9	71.3	4.5	3.9	1.9	18.4
Djibouti	1991	214.4	38.3	0.2	9.1	52.3	6.0	15.5	30.8	46.6	3.7	0.7[4]	7.2	41.8
Dominica	1999	132.8	25.3	0.2	6.4	68.1	12.6	25.9	29.6	14.5	41.5	0.1	7.2	36.7
Dominican Republic	1994	3,440.0	13.7[28]	0.3[28]	35.2[28]	50.7[28]	11.7[28]	23.2[28]	15.9[28]	2.0[4]	37.4[4]	—[4]	1.5[4]	59.1[4]
East Timor	...	...	...	...	...	...	...	...	...	...	...	...	...	...
Ecuador	1999	3,017.2	14.0	0.5	8.2	77.3	22.0	28.8	26.5	14.2	30.4	2.1	4.7	48.6

and freight] valuation); for exports, the value at which the goods were sold by the exporter, including the cost of transportation and insurance to bring the goods onto the transporting vehicle at the frontier of the exporting country (f.o.b. [free-on-board] valuation).

The largest part of the information presented here comes from the United Nations' *International Trade Statistics Yearbook*. This source is supplemented by the United Nations' *Commodity Trade Statistics* and by national and regional information. In some cases where the original data were only available for an alternative trade classification, an approximation has been made of the SITC commodity groupings. For some countries, where the amounts involved are very small, estimates have been made for selected categories.

The notes that follow further define the column headings.
a. Also includes any unallocated commodities.
b. EU of 15 countries (Austria, Belgium, Denmark, Finland, France, Germany, Greece, Ireland, Italy, Luxembourg, The Netherlands, Portugal, Spain, Sweden, and the United Kingdom).
c. Includes Albania, Bulgaria, Czech Republic, Hungary, Poland, Romania, Slovakia, and European republics of the former U.S.S.R. (Belarus, Estonia, Latvia, Lithuania, Moldova, Russia, and Ukraine).
d. May include value of trade shown as not available (…) in any of the four preceding columns. May include any unspecified areas or countries.

... Not available.
— None, less than 0.05%, or not applicable.
Detail may not add to 100.0 or indicated subtotals because of rounding.

SITC category codes	
0	food and live animals chiefly for food
1	beverages and tobacco
2	crude materials, inedible, except fuels
27	crude fertilizers and crude minerals (excluding coal, petroleum, and precious stones)
28	metalliferous ores and metal scrap
3	mineral fuels, lubricants, and related materials (including coal, petroleum, natural gas, and electric current)
4	animal and vegetable oils, fats and waxes
5	chemicals and related products not elsewhere specified
6	manufactured goods classified chiefly by material
667	pearls, precious and semiprecious stones, unworked or worked
7	machinery and transport equipment
8	miscellaneous manufactured articles
9	commodities and transactions not classified elsewhere

exports									direction of trade (%)					country
total value ('000,000 U.S.$)	Standard International Trade Classification (SITC) categories (%)													
	food and agricultural raw materials (0 + 1 + 2 − 27 − 28 + 4)	mineral ores and concentrates (27 + 28 + 667)	fuels and other energy (3)	manufactured goods				to European Union (EU)[b]	to United States	to Eastern Europe[c]	to Japan	to all other[d]	
				total[a] (5 + 6 − 667 + 7 + 8 + 9)	of which chemicals and related products (5)	of which machinery and transport equipment (7)	of which other[a] (6 − 667 + 8 + 9)						
166.0	—— 63.0[2, 5] ——		...	37.0[3, 5]	...	...	...	19.3[4]	3.0[4]	8.4[4]	0.6[4]	68.7[4]	Afghanistan
207.7	18.6	10.5	1.2	69.9	0.4	2.8	66.6	92.5	1.7	0.7	—	5.1	Albania
12,525.3	0.4	0.2	97.1	2.3	1.0	0.5	0.8	63.9	14.0	0.3	0.5	21.2	Algeria
399.0	100.0[4]	—	—	—	—	—	—	—[5]	100.0[5]	—[5]	—[5]	—[5]	American Samoa
57.8	11.9	1.5	—	86.7	6.5	30.7	49.5	87.4	0.2	0.3	8.5	3.6	Andorra
4,404.0	0.3[8]	3.2[8]	96.5[8]	—[8]	—[8]	—[8]	—[8]	16.9	53.1	—	0.2	29.8	Angola
36.2	—— 5.1[2] ——		17.5	77.3[3]	7.9	28.9	40.5[3]	19.4[9]	24.7[9]	2.7[9]	—[9]	53.2[9]	Antigua and Barbuda
23,125.9	51.3	2.4	12.0	34.3	7.3	11.9	15.1	20.4	11.3	0.9	2.3	65.0	Argentina
231.7	11.4	48.0	8.3	32.3	0.9	8.7	22.7	46.0	6.9	16.8	0.2	30.1	Armenia
42.8[10]	23.4	2.8	—	73.7	1.9	44.9	26.9	10.2	55.1	0.1	0.1	34.5	Aruba
56,015.9	26.8	11.9	16.7	44.6	4.3	12.6	27.6	10.6	8.1	0.2	16.2	65.0	Australia
59,271.6	7.9	0.7	1.2	90.1	7.1	40.5	42.5	64.4	4.5	11.5	1.3	18.3	Austria
929.2	8.9	2.3	78.6	10.2	2.5	3.8	3.9	45.6	3.2	13.4	—	37.8	Azerbaijan
300.3	—— 38.8[2] ——		—	61.2[3]	22.3	26.1	12.9[3]	31.4	56.5	1.0[4]	0.3[4]	10.7	Bahamas, The
4,602.0	2.1	0.4	66.5	31.0	3.2	1.0	26.7	1.6	2.3	—	4.3	91.8[12]	Bahrain
5,057.0	8.9	—	0.2	90.8	0.9	1.1	88.9	43.0	39.4	0.9	2.4	14.2	Bangladesh
250.7	30.8	0.2	13.3	55.7	14.8	16.0	24.9	17.6	17.6	—	0.1	64.7	Barbados
5,908.9	—— 11.5[2] ——		9.1	79.4[3]	15.3	27.3	36.8[3]	8.9	1.4	73.7	0.1	15.9	Belarus
176,026.2	11.2	7.7	2.9	78.1	18.3	28.9	30.9	75.8	5.3	2.8	1.2	14.8	Belgium
175.7	81.7	—	0.9	17.4	1.9	1.5	13.9	38.1	48.4	—	0.1	13.4	Belize
332.9	63.6	30.0	1.4	5.1	0.3[4]	1.0	3.8[4]	37.1	0.8	0.1	0.2	61.9	Benin
62.9	5.6[14]	3.1[14, 15]	45.6[14]	45.8[14, 16]	9.5[14]	18.5[14]	17.8[14, 16]	6.4	49.8	—	—	43.9	Bermuda
117.9	30.9[8]	3.5[8]	25.6[8, 18]	40.1[8]	20.3[8]	—[8]	19.7[8]	0.2	0.1	—	0.3	99.5[19]	Bhutan
1,401.9	28.1	16.4	5.3	50.2	0.9	25.0	24.3	20.6	33.2	0.1	0.5	45.6	Bolivia
185.3	—— 37.3[2] ——		4.3	58.4[3]	3.9	11.0	43.5[3]	35.8	2.9	1.0[4]	0.1[4]	60.2[4]	Bosnia and Herzegovina
2,923.6	3.3	75.1	—	21.7	1.5	11.9	8.3	56.9	...	—	...	43.1[21]	Botswana
51,120.0	33.4	7.7	0.7	58.2	6.2	24.6	27.4	28.9	19.3	2.2	4.3	45.2	Brazil
2,306.8	—	—	88.6	11.4	0.2[4]	4.8	6.4[4]	2.0	9.1	—	53.1	35.7	Brunei
4,939.7	16.6	2.0	7.6	73.9	16.9	11.1	45.8	43.3	2.6	17.3	0.8	36.0	Bulgaria
194.1	83.5[5]	0.5[5]	—[5]	16.0[5]	0.1[5]	1.0[5]	14.9[5]	32.5	1.8	—	1.1	64.6	Burkina Faso
64.6	85.1[22]	—[22]	—[22]	14.9[22]	1.4[22]	—[22]	13.4[22]	59.9	2.8	0.2	0.3	36.8	Burundi
796.1	88.9[22, 24]	...	...	...	...	...	...	16.5	36.8	0.4	1.0	45.4	Cambodia
1,587.7	49.5[25]	0.1[25]	36.2[25]	14.3[25]	1.1[25]	1.1[25]	12.1[25]	70.6	2.5	0.2	0.3	26.3	Cameroon
238,778.0	13.6	1.5	8.5	76.4	5.2	42.6	28.6	5.6	85.9	0.2	2.4	6.0	Canada
81.5	5.3	0.5	28.8	65.4	0.2	51.2	14.0	55.2	1.1	—	—	43.7[26]	Cape Verde
115.1	25.4	60.1	0.2	14.3	—	7.5	6.8	95.1	—	—	—	4.8	Central African Republic
251.6	88.2[14]	—[14]	—[14]	11.9[14]	6.5[14]	3.1[14]	2.3[14]	76.6[4]	2.4[4]	0.8[4]	2.4[4]	17.7[4]	Chad
15,619.2	37.7	14.4	0.5	47.3	4.8	3.2	39.4	26.2	18.0	0.2	14.6	41.0	Chile
194,930.9	7.3	0.7	2.4	89.6	5.2	30.1	54.2	15.5	21.5	1.7	16.6	44.6	China
11,565.4	28.9	1.1	40.6	29.4	3.0	2.6	16.7	16.7	50.3	0.7	2.1	30.2	Colombia
4.0	57.9[9]	—[9]	—[9]	42.1[9]	21.0[9, 23]	—[9]	21.2[9]	80.0	2.5	—	—	17.5	Comoros
742.8	13.1[14]	58.5[2, 14, 15]	11.1[14]	17.3[3, 14, 16]	0.2[14]	1.2[14]	15.9[3, 14, 16]	23.3	14.5	—	—	62.1	Congo, Dem. Rep. of the
1,089.8	9.3	0.3	87.6	2.7	—	0.4	2.3	41.3	28.5	—	0.3	29.9	Congo, Rep. of the
6,283.1	30.8	0.2	0.4	68.6	3.7	46.5	18.4	22.4	51.9	0.9	2.0	22.7	Costa Rica
4,274.7	—— 69.3[2] ——		15.4	15.4[3]	3.7	2.0	9.6[3]	56.4	8.2	3.6	0.2	31.7	Côte d'Ivoire
4,279.7	14.4	0.8	7.8	77.1	11.7	29.1	36.3	48.8	2.4	5.2	0.1	43.4	Croatia
1,848.9	69.8	23.6[2]	0.2[4]	6.4[3, 4]	3.1	0.1[4]	3.2[3, 4]	25.8	—	32.0	3.9	38.2	Cuba
997.0	47.9	1.5	6.0	44.6	7.5	16.9	20.2	40.0	4.0	12.4	0.2	43.4	Cyprus
26,842.6	6.7	0.7	2.9	89.8	6.6	43.1	40.0	69.2	2.4	19.2	0.3	8.9	Czech Republic
49,027.8	23.4	0.4	3.8	72.4	10.7	27.9	33.9	61.6	4.5	4.3	2.9	26.7	Denmark
17.3	32.5	—	—	67.5	0.4	8.3	58.7	62.6	0.8	—	0.9	35.7	Djibouti
54.3	42.5	2.8	—	54.7	50.3	2.2	2.2	34.6	6.4	—	—	58.9	Dominica
2,007.8	20.7	0.1	—	79.2[29]	2.6	11.6	65.1[29]	8.7	84.6	—	0.8	5.9	Dominican Republic
...	...	...	...	...	...	...	...	...	...	...	...	...	East Timor
4,451.1	58.0	—	33.2	8.8	1.8	1.4	5.6	18.4	38.4	2.4	2.5	38.3	Ecuador

Trade: external   (continued)

country	year	imports total value ('000,000 U.S.$)	food and agricultural raw materials (0 + 1 + 2 − 27 − 28 + 4)	mineral ores and concentrates (27 + 28 + 667)	fuels and other energy (3)	manufactured goods total[a] (5 + 6 − 667 + 7 + 8 + 9)	of which chemicals and related products (5)	of which machinery and transport equipment (7)	of which other[a] (6 − 667 + 8 + 9)	from European Union (EU)[b]	from United States	from Eastern Europe[c]	from Japan	from all other[d]
Egypt	1999	15,962.1	27.2	1.9	6.1	64.8	11.5	26.2	27.1	35.5	14.4	6.6	3.3	40.3
El Salvador	1999	3,128.1	20.8	0.3	11.5	67.3	14.2	27.6	25.5	7.9	37.5	1.0	4.1	49.5
Equatorial Guinea	1990	61.6	13.5	3.4	7.7	75.4	3.9	58.2	13.3	31.5	39.9	—	0.3[4]	28.3
Eritrea	1998	526.8	—21.8[2]		1.5	76.7[3]	5.7	38.3	32.7[3]	32.3[31]	4.2	—	4.0	59.5
Estonia	1999	4,107.4	16.2	1.4	6.9	75.5	10.6	34.3	30.6	57.8	4.4	22.5	4.7	10.6
Ethiopia	1995	1,141.0	15.7	0.2	11.1	73.0	14.0	35.5	23.5	39.6	12.9	0.6	8.4	38.4
Faroe Islands	1999	477.5	22.7	0.4	8.1	68.7	6.5	36.5	25.7	54.7	1.3	3.0	2.4	38.5
Fiji	1997	965.2	—16.6[2]		14.1	69.3[3]	7.8	20.6	40.9[3]	4.6	5.2	0.1	6.9	83.2
Finland	1999	31,614.1	8.9	3.7	8.5	78.8	10.7	43.2	24.9	55.7	7.9	11.3	6.2	18.9
France[32]	1999	286,592.9	11.0	0.9	6.6	81.4	12.2	39.8	29.4	61.6	8.8	3.1	3.6	23.0
French Guiana	1995	783.3	18.8	0.1	5.3	75.8	8.0	42.2	25.6	76.9	3.3	0.5	1.4	17.9
French Polynesia	1994	880.7	20.4[33]	0.2[33]	5.4[33]	74.1[33]	6.4[33]	35.9[33]	31.8[33]	44.8	13.9	—	4.0	37.3
Gabon	1996	898.1	19.8	0.4	3.4	76.4	10.7	39.3	26.4	68.1	10.4	0.3	6.0	15.2
Gambia, The	1998	257.2	—45.5[2]		6.3	48.2[33]	4.4	20.6	23.2[3]	48.4	5.5	0.9	2.8	42.3
Gaza Strip[34]	1994	339.3	...	...	...	...	...	...	...	...	...	...	...	100.0[35]
Georgia	1998	884.3	19.2	0.7	24.9	55.3	7.9	30.0	17.4	31.0	15.4[4]	26.2	0.5[4]	27.0
Germany	1999	464,318.0	9.5	1.3	5.7	83.5	8.7	36.5	38.3	52.4	8.1	9.5	4.9	25.1
Ghana	1999	3,003.8	14.7	0.2	17.7	67.3	10.3	37.7	19.4	43.6	8.7	0.9	2.8	43.9
Greece	1999	26,570.2	15.0	0.5	5.8	78.8	12.2	37.5	29.1	64.1	5.5	5.6	4.3	20.5
Greenland	1999	418.3	18.8	0.4	9.0	71.8	4.1	26.2	41.5	81.2	2.1	0.5	3.2	12.9
Grenada	1999	202.2	22.7	0.3	9.1	68.0	6.4	29.0	32.6	12.1	41.8	0.2	5.4	40.4
Guadeloupe	1995	1,901.3	22.6	0.3	5.8	71.3	9.5	32.0	29.8	77.8	3.3	0.3	2.2	16.5
Guam	1992	450.0	16.9[37]	0.1[37]	46.9[37]	36.2[37]	2.3[37]	19.1[37]	14.8[37]	...	23.4[37]	...	19.9[37]	56.6[37]
Guatemala	1999	4,554.3	14.1	0.2	9.9	75.9	16.3	35.4	24.2	9.0	41.6	0.9	4.0	44.5
Guernsey[38]	...	...	...	...	...	...	...	...	...	...	...	...	...	...
Guinea	1997	619.7	—25.1[2]		10.3	64.5[3]	7.0	35.4	22.1[3]	54.5	7.6	1.5	5.7	30.6
Guinea-Bissau	1995	56.8	43.8	0.2	16.2	39.8	4.9	22.9	12.0	42.8[1]	0.7	0.9	9.3	46.3
Guyana	1993	483.8	9.0	...	16.7	74.3	5.1	44.5	24.7	21.9[4]	27.9[4]	0.4[4]	18.2[4]	31.6[4]
Haiti	1997[6]	706.5	—40.2[2]		10.6	49.3[3]	7.3	15.8	26.1[3]	12.7[4]	57.5[4]	0.4[4]	4.5[4]	24.9[4]
Honduras	1999	2,651.9	17.3	0.2	9.3	73.2	14.6	31.4	27.2	7.1	48.8	0.6	4.0	39.4
Hong Kong	1999	180,710.6	6.2	2.2	2.1	89.6	6.3	38.5	44.7	9.3	7.0	0.3	11.6	71.8
Hungary	1999	28,008.2	4.6	0.4	5.9	89.1	9.0	49.8	30.3	64.4	3.5	13.5	4.1	14.5
Iceland	1999	2,315.5	11.5	3.8	5.5	79.3	7.7	41.8	29.8	55.9	10.9	4.8	5.6	22.7
India	1999[1]	42,425.0	10.9	11.5	19.0	58.5	12.3	15.8	30.5	25.3	8.6	2.0	5.8	58.3
Indonesia	1998	27,336.9	17.1	1.5	10.1	71.3	14.7	36.2	20.3	21.5	12.9	0.8	15.7	49.2
Iran	1999	12,621.8	23.2	1.5	1.7	73.6	14.8	38.3	20.4	40.9	0.5	5.7	4.7	48.3
Iraq	1990	4,833.9	—31.5[2]—		0.4	68.1[3]	8.8	30.3	28.9[3]	45.7[4]	10.8[4]	3.0[4]	4.6[4]	35.9[4]
Ireland	2001	51,165.5	7.6	0.5	3.9	88.0	11.1	52.8	24.1	58.1	15.2	1.5	3.5	21.6
Isle of Man[38]	...	...	...	...	...	...	...	...	...	...	...	...	...	...
Israel	1999	31,085.6	7.3	19.1	5.8	67.8	9.3	35.3	23.2	46.3	20.3	0.8	3.5	29.0
Italy[39]	1999	216,450.7	13.7	1.6	6.6	78.1	12.7	35.3	30.1	60.5	4.9	5.5	2.5	26.6
Jamaica	1997	3,112.9	18.4	0.1	13.1	68.3	9.0	28.2	31.1	12.8	49.3	0.3	6.4	31.2
Japan	1999	309,994.5	19.2	3.5	16.1	61.2	7.3	27.5	26.5	13.8	21.8	1.5	—	63.0
Jersey	1980	537.1	23.9	0.4	9.3	66.5	6.5	24.8	35.2	84.9[40]	...	...	...	15.1
Jordan	1998	3,828.5	25.1	0.8	9.3	64.8	12.6	28.6	23.7	32.7	9.5	4.8	5.9	47.1
Kazakhstan	1999	3,682.7	11.0	2.1	9.4	77.6	9.4	43.8	24.3	25.3	9.5	43.9	3.2	18.1
Kenya	1999	2,785.6	14.9	0.3	15.8	69.0	16.2	30.5	22.3	32.3	6.8	1.7	7.8	51.4
Kiribati	1995	34.1	40.5	0.3	10.3	49.0	7.0	14.7	27.3	1.1	3.1	—	7.6	88.2
Korea, North	1999	1,255.0[4]	...	...	...	...	...	...	...	14.7[4]	1.0[4]	5.7[4]	12.8[4]	65.7[4]
Korea, South	1999	119,751.3	9.2	3.1	19.2	68.6	9.1	36.4	23.0	10.5	20.8	1.7	20.2	46.7
Kuwait	1999	7,616.7	17.7	0.9	0.6	80.7	8.4	39.7	32.5	30.5	12.3	1.0	12.8	43.4
Kyrgyzstan	1999	599.7	14.0	1.3	20.3	64.4	10.8	30.4	23.1	18.3	9.0	22.0	2.0	48.7
Laos	1995	587.2	—36.8[2]—		6.1	57.1[3]	...	29.3	27.8[3]	2.0[4]	0.9	0.7[4]	11.8	84.6
Latvia	1999	2,946.8	14.4	1.0	10.8	73.8	12.8	29.8	31.2	54.5	2.0	35.6	0.2	7.6
Lebanon	1999	6,177.3	—21.9[2]—		9.0	69.1[3]	10.8	24.6	33.7[3]	46.4	8.1	5.8	4.2	35.5
Lesotho	1999	865.5	—39.2[2, 8]—		1.1[8]	59.7[3, 8]	10.0[8]	6.6[8]	43.1[3, 8]	1.6	0.1[4]	—[4]	0.1[4]	98.2[42]
Liberia	1999	209.6[44]	—36.5[2]—		24.2	39.2[3]	7.1	18.6	13.6[3]	23.6[4, 45]	1.5[4, 45]	3.2[4, 45]	24.8[4, 45]	47.0[4, 45]
Libya	1997	5,592.9	—23.9[2]—		0.2	75.9[3]	7.5	36.0	32.4[3]	55.4	1.4	0.9	8.1	34.2
Liechtenstein	1999	831.4	4.4[4]	0.3[2, 4]	1.0[4]	94.3[3, 4]	3.9[4]	45.2[4]	45.1[3, 4]	...	...	...	...	...
Lithuania	1999	4,834.5	13.8	1.8	14.8	69.6	12.3	25.9	31.4	49.7	2.9	41.0	1.6	4.8
Luxembourg	1999	9,888.7	12.3	3.4	4.0	80.2	8.8	39.5	31.9	82.9	9.8	0.9	1.4	5.0
Macau	1998	1,947.7	12.9	0.1	6.5	80.5	4.1	15.0	61.4	10.5	4.7	—	7.8	77.0
Macedonia	1998	1,914.7	18.6	0.7	8.5	72.1	10.5	19.1	42.5	36.3	5.3	20.0	0.9	37.5
Madagascar	1999	505.3	14.2	0.1	24.2	61.4	11.2	26.8	23.4	32.2	3.0	0.3	5.1	59.4
Malawi	1995	500.5	14.5	0.6	11.1	73.6	22.5	27.6	23.6	31.9	2.6	0.5	5.0	60.0
Malaysia	1999	64,939.2	6.8	0.9	3.1	89.2	7.3	61.7	20.2	11.7	17.6	0.7	21.0	49.0
Maldives	1997	348.8	25.3	1.7	11.1	61.9	4.6	28.1	29.2	12.7	1.5	0.1	3.2	82.7
Mali	1997	680.8	—20.2[2]—		20.9	59.0[3]	17.2	21.4	20.3[3]	35.7	3.5	2.6	3.0	55.1
Malta	1999	2,840.2	11.3	0.3	5.2	83.3	7.0	52.5	23.8	65.4	8.5	0.8	2.7	22.6
Marshall Islands	1996	72.7	—32.4[2]—		39.0	28.6[3]	0.1	10.7	17.8[3]	...	55.6	...	4.1	40.4
Martinique	1995	1,969.8	20.4	0.2	7.5	71.9	10.3	32.4	29.2	76.8	2.9	0.2	2.2	17.9
Mauritania	1996	426.7	—27.0[2]—		29.2	43.8[3]	3.0	24.8	15.9[3]	63.5	0.3	1.4	0.8	34.0
Mauritius	1999	2,275.9	15.8	2.1	7.1	74.9	6.5	31.1	37.3	32.5	4.2	0.3	5.9	57.1
Mayotte	1997	141.1	—23.8[2, 4]—		5.0	71.2[3, 4]	7.7	30.8	32.7[3, 4]	66.0[46]	...	...	...	34.0
Mexico	1999	145,556.2	6.8	0.5	2.1	90.6	8.2	50.3	32.0	9.0	74.4	0.3	3.5	12.8
Micronesia	1998	49.4	—37.3[2]—		8.9	53.8[3]	3.6	20.0	30.2[3]	...	45.7	...	14.0	40.4
Moldova	1999	573.1	7.9	0.6	37.5	54.0	9.1	15.4	29.6	27.3	3.9	61.6	1.0	6.3
Monaco[32]	...	...	...	...	...	...	...	...	...	...	...	...	...	...
Mongolia	1996	450.9	14.9	0.3	19.3	65.5	5.0	39.7	20.7	14.7	2.3	39.0	11.7	32.2
Morocco	1997	7,877.5	22.0	2.3	16.5	59.1	12.2	24.2	22.7	52.1	6.5	5.6	2.6	33.2
Mozambique	1998	817.3	26.7	1.1	8.1	64.1	7.7	35.0	21.4	18.2	5.3	0.2	4.0	72.3
Myanmar (Burma)	1996	1,914.0	—8.7[2]—		4.4	86.9[3]	8.6	27.0	51.3[3]	2.6	4.9	—	22.5	69.9
Namibia	1997	1,675.0	—23.3[2, 4]—		5.9	69.4[3, 4]	11.2	29.7	28.4[3, 4]	3.9[31]	4.1	1.0[31]	0.2	90.7[47]
Nauru	1994	31.8	87.8	...	...	12.2	...	2.8	9.3	...	...	...	...	...
Nepal	1998	1,313.2	12.2	1.1	12.5	74.3	6.9	16.0	51.4	7.7	1.6	0.6	3.2	86.9

total value ('000,000 U.S.$)	food and agricultural raw materials (0+1+2−27−28+4)	mineral ores and concentrates (27+28+667)	fuels and other energy (3)	manufactured goods total[a] (5+6−667+7+8+9)	of which chemicals and related products (5)	of which machinery and transport equipment (7)	of which other[a] (6−667+8+9)	to European Union (EU)[b]	to United States	to Eastern Europe[c]	to Japan	to all other[d]	country
3,500.9	16.8	1.0	36.9	45.3	7.5	0.9	36.8	35.3	12.4	1.3	1.3	49.7	Egypt
1,164.2	42.8	0.1	4.7	52.4	14.4	3.5	34.5	14.2	21.3	1.2	0.7	62.5	El Salvador
61.7	48.6	—	—	51.4	0.1	39.8[30]	11.5	47.2	—	—	—	52.8	Equatorial Guinea
27.9	—75.1[2]—		...	24.9[3]	2.1	2.4	20.4[3]	10.0[31]	2.0	...	13.2	74.8	Eritrea
2,937.7	22.4	2.7	4.5	70.3	6.8	24.6	38.9	62.7	2.5	26.5	0.3	7.9	Estonia
421.9	86.0	—	2.9	11.2	0.3	—	10.8	51.7	6.4	0.5	13.0	28.5	Ethiopia
477.9	94.7	—	—	5.3	0.1	3.8	1.4	82.3	4.6	2.3	1.2	9.6	Faroe Islands
591.5	—41.3[2]—		—	58.7[3]	0.7	0.6	57.4[3]	22.5	10.7	—	5.0	61.8	Fiji
41,765.5	8.4	0.4	2.5	88.7	6.0	42.7	40.0	55.5	7.8	11.7	1.7	23.3	Finland
296,025.3	13.3	0.5	2.2	84.0	13.4	44.0	26.6	64.2	7.8	3.0	1.5	23.5	France[32]
158.2	33.6	0.1	0.2	66.1	1.4	33.0	31.7	77.6	1.0	—	—	21.3	French Guiana
226.2	5.9[33]	31.3[33]	—[33]	62.8[33]	1.6[33]	38.6[33]	22.6[33]	32.7	8.4	—	45.8	13.1	French Polynesia
3,145.6	13.3	2.0	82.7	1.9	0.4	0.4	1.1	11.5	64.1	0.1	2.1	22.3	Gabon
25.6	—80.5[2]—			19.5[3]	0.8	10.2	8.6[3]	72.3	0.4	2.3	0.8	24.2	Gambia, The
49.4	...	...	...	...	...	...	...	...	...	...	...	100.0[36]	Gaza Strip[34]
192.4	36.5	5.3	11.2	47.0	12.2	7.6	27.2	19.1	5.8	36.2	0.3[4]	38.7	Georgia
535,530.4	5.2	0.6	1.1	93.2	12.6	49.2	31.4	55.6	10.1	8.7	2.0	23.6	Germany
1,269.7	61.1	2.8	4.4	31.7	1.1	3.0	27.7	59.8	5.5	1.0	4.0	29.8	Ghana
10,149.8	31.5	1.8	10.1	56.6	6.8	10.1	39.7	49.7	5.9	13.8	0.6	30.1	Greece
289.5	95.2	—	1.4	3.4	—	0.5	2.9	85.4	1.7	—	8.3	4.5	Greenland
36.3	76.9	—	—	23.1	3.6	3.3	16.3	42.1	18.7	—	—	39.1	Grenada
162.0	52.3	0.6	—	47.0	1.1	36.5	9.4	77.0	3.4	—	—	19.6	Guadeloupe
86.1	—69.5[2]—		0.7	29.7[3]	0.7	3.8	25.2	2.3[4]	—	—	57.5	40.2	Guam
2,458.2	61.7	0.3	3.5	34.4	13.1	2.3	19.0	11.8	34.3	1.2	2.4	50.3	Guatemala
...	...	...	...	...	...	...	...	...	...	...	...	...	Guernsey[38]
684.5	6.8	67.1	1.3	24.8	9.7	2.1	13.1	63.5	20.7	1.9	—	13.8	Guinea
23.6	88.1	—	4.7	7.2	—	6.4	0.8	40.3	—	—	—	59.7	Guinea-Bissau
404.0	43.5[23]	47.3[23]	—	9.2	...	...	...	35.9[4]	22.8[4]	—[4]	2.1[4]	39.2[4]	Guyana
110.1	—15.8[2]—		—	84.2[3]	5.6	3.1	75.5[3]	11.5	86.3	—	0.2	2.0	Haiti
761.0	66.2	1.1	0.5	32.2	5.8	3.0	23.4	14.2	57.3	0.1	3.5	24.9	Honduras
174,402.8	3.1	1.4	0.4	95.1	5.3	34.8	55.0	16.1	23.8	0.4	5.4	54.3	Hong Kong
25,012.2	9.7	0.4	1.6	88.2	5.6	57.1	25.6	76.2	5.2	9.3	0.3	8.9	Hungary
2,009.7	70.4	0.7	0.1	28.8	0.5	7.0	21.3	64.1	15.1	0.8	5.0	15.0	Iceland
33,207.4	18.8	17.1	0.4	63.7	9.3	7.1	47.3	27.0	21.7	2.9	5.0	43.5	India
48,847.6	15.8	3.1	19.3	61.8	4.3	9.5	48.0	15.9	14.4	0.7	18.7	50.3	Indonesia
19,726.0	4.6	0.5	85.4	9.5	1.2	0.5	7.8	40.3[25]	—[25]	0.7[25]	17.1[25]	41.8[25]	Iran
6,659.0	0.8	0.3[15]	96.8	2.1[16]	1.2	0.2	0.7[16]	26.6[4]	33.6[4]	6.8[4]	9.5[4]	23.5[4]	Iraq
82,794.9	7.7	0.6	0.3	91.4	34.9	41.0	15.6	61.8	17.0	1.3	3.5	16.4	Ireland
...	...	...	...	...	...	...	...	...	...	...	...	...	Isle of Man[38]
25,839.9	5.0	31.8	0.5	62.6	14.1	30.4	18.1	29.7	35.5	2.2	3.2	29.4	Israel
230,093.8	7.4	0.3	1.2	91.1	8.6	38.8	43.7	57.0	12.9	5.8	1.6	22.8	Italy[39]
1,386.1	23.6	53.1	0.2	23.0	3.4	1.7	18.0	26.4	37.8	6.6	1.2	28.0	Jamaica
417,610.2	1.1	0.3	0.3	98.3	7.1	68.5	22.7	17.9	31.1	0.4	—	50.6	Japan
209.2	27.6	4.3[41]		68.0	1.2	31.1	35.7	67.3[40]	...	...	...	32.7	Jersey
1,382.3	16.9	27.0	0.1	56.0	32.4	4.6	19.0	7.0	0.6	0.9	1.0	90.5	Jordan
5,592.2	9.3	4.5	40.9	45.3	6.1	4.9	34.3	23.0	1.4	27.7	0.4	47.5	Kazakhstan
1,662.5	65.9	2.7	8.4	23.0	6.3	0.9	15.8	33.5	2.3	0.4	0.9	62.9	Kenya
7.2	85.3	—	—	14.7	—	—	14.7	2.2	10.4	—	—	87.4	Kiribati
782.0[4]	...	...	...	...	...	...	...	14.8[4]	—[4]	3.7[4]	23.3[4]	58.2[4]	Korea, North
143,685.4	2.9	0.1	4.1	92.9	7.4	54.2	31.3	14.1	20.6	1.6	11.0	52.6	Korea, South
12,140.1	0.6[4]	0.3[4]	90.6	8.5[4]	5.8	1.3	1.4[4]	11.8[4]	11.6[4]	—[4]	22.9[4]	53.7[4]	Kuwait
453.8	22.0	4.7	11.8	61.5	3.3	9.7	48.5	38.2	2.5	21.0	0.2	38.1	Kyrgyzstan
347.9	—35.4[2]—		7.0	57.5[3]	...	5.1	52.4[3]	9.7[4]	3.2	3.2[4]	0.6	83.3	Laos
1,723.8	36.5	2.3	2.9	58.3	6.0	6.1	46.2	62.6	5.7	26.1	0.2	5.4	Latvia
673.6	—24.9[2]—		0.1	75.1[3]	13.6	12.0	49.5[3]	26.0	6.2	1.2	0.6	66.0	Lebanon
172.5	—15.3[2]—		—	84.7[3]	0.5	10.6	73.6[3]	0.2	44.6[4]	—[4]	—[4]	55.2[43]	Lesotho
58.9[44]	—99.3[2]—			0.7[3]	—	—	0.7[3]	66.0[4,45]	5.3[4,45]	2.7[4,45]	—[4,45]	26.0[4,45]	Liberia
9,028.7	0.4[4]	—[4]	94.8	4.9[4]	3.3	—[4]	1.6[4]	77.7	—	0.6	0.1[4]	21.6[4]	Libya
1,917.7	5.4[4]	0.2[2,4]	0.1[4]	94.2[3,4]	8.0[4]	61.0[4]	25.2[3,4]	38.0[4]	...	...	...	62.0[4]	Liechtenstein
3,003.8	18.5	1.4	14.4	65.7	10.8	16.6	38.2	50.1	4.4	37.9	0.3	7.3	Lithuania
7,343.5	7.9	0.4	0.1	91.6	5.5	24.6	61.4	84.7	4.0	2.6	0.6	8.1	Luxembourg
2,134.7	2.3	—	0.4	97.3	0.8	5.0	91.6	30.5	47.7	0.1	0.7	21.1	Macau
1,310.7	18.3	2.2	0.8	78.8	4.8	7.5	66.5	44.1	13.3	8.3	0.2	34.2	Macedonia
232.8	42.0	10.4	2.4	45.2	2.9	0.9	41.5	56.7	5.4	0.9	1.4	35.5	Madagascar
433.4	90.2	—	—	9.8	0.4	2.0	7.4	47.7	13.2	3.5	5.0	30.6	Malawi
84,511.9	10.9	0.2	6.8	82.1	3.2	62.3	16.6	15.7	21.9	0.3	11.6	50.4	Malaysia
70.2	79.1	0.1[4]	—	20.9	0.1[4]	—	20.8	25.9	21.9	0.1	15.2	36.8	Maldives
302.4	—92.5[2]—		0.7	6.8[3]	—	0.7	6.1[3]	2.4	—	—	—	97.5	Mali
1,979.6	3.3	0.1	2.9	93.6	2.3	63.5	27.9	48.7	21.3	0.3	2.6	27.1	Malta
19.5	—83.5[2]—			16.5[3]	...	...	16.5[3]	...	80.0[4]	...	...	20.0[4]	Marshall Islands
241.9	62.3	1.0	17.8	18.9	2.1	13.0	3.8	78.0	2.6	—	—	19.3	Martinique
517.4	51.7	41.5	4.6	2.2	—	0.9	1.2	51.5	1.1	4.5	20.6	22.2	Mauritania
1,562.5	24.3	2.6	—	73.1	0.7	1.0	71.3	70.9	17.8	0.1	0.5	10.8	Mauritius
3.5	21.3[24,25]	—[24,25]	—[24,25]	78.7[24,25]	78.7[24,25]	—[24,25]	—[24,25]	80.0[46]	...	...	...	20.0	Mayotte
136,262.8	6.1	0.5	7.1	86.3	3.2	59.6	23.4	3.8	88.4	0.1	0.6	7.1	Mexico
3.3	—93.2[2]—		—	6.8[3]	...	...	6.8[3]	...	...	...	94.6	5.4	Micronesia
462.3	65.3	3.5	0.2	31.0	2.9	7.4	20.7	20.5	3.1	70.5	—	5.8	Moldova
...	...	...	...	...	...	...	...	...	...	...	...	...	Monaco[32]
424.3	29.9	59.9	—	10.2	0.6	1.7	7.8	13.6	0.2	63.1	0.5	22.5	Mongolia
4,674.2	33.5	13.2	1.9	51.3	20.8	3.0	27.5	60.7	3.5	2.3	5.5	27.9	Morocco
244.6	63.5	0.5	15.4	20.6	0.4[4]	9.2	11.1	26.3	5.7	0.8	4.8	62.4	Mozambique
883.1	—77.3[2]—		0.6	22.2[3]	—	1.1	21.1[3]	4.3	4.9	—	7.3	83.5	Myanmar (Burma)
1,359.2	36.5	43.8	...	19.7	...	...	...	...	3.0[4,5]	—	—[4,5]	97.0[4,5]	Namibia
31.2	—	100.0	—	—	—	—	—	...	...	...	...	...	Nauru
408.7	8.7	0.1	—	91.2	3.4	0.2	87.6	33.7	26.3	0.2	0.7	39.1	Nepal

Trade: external (continued)

country	year	imports total value ('000,000 U.S.$)	food and agricultural raw materials (0+1+2-27-28+4)	mineral ores and concentrates (27+28+667)	fuels and other energy (3)	manufactured goods total[a] (5+6-667+7+8+9)	of which chemicals and related products (5)	of which machinery and transport equipment (7)	of which other[a] (6-667+8+9)	from European Union (EU)[b]	from United States	from Eastern Europe[c]	from Japan	from all other[d]
Netherlands, The	1999	167,875.5	13.2	1.1	7.6	78.1	10.3	41.9	25.9	53.5	9.9	3.5	4.5	28.6
Netherlands Antilles	1995	1,832.5	—12.9[2]—		55.2	31.9[3]	4.5	12.7	14.7[3]	13.1	19.9	—	1.7	65.4
New Caledonia	1997	924.2	—20.3[2]—		11.7	68.0[3]	7.7	33.3	27.0[3]	41.9	5.3	—	4.3	48.5
New Zealand	1999	14,318.4	8.8	1.7	6.2	83.3	11.9	43.2	28.2	18.6	16.7	0.4	12.4	51.9
Nicaragua	1999	1,723.1	19.4	0.5	8.2	71.9	15.2	29.8	26.9	4.9	33.2	0.8	5.3	55.8
Niger	1998	420.0	42.2	2.2	14.9	40.7	9.8	13.2	17.7	43.0	7.3	1.3	3.2	45.3
Nigeria	1999	5,766.9	28.5	1.1	1.8	68.6	15.7	27.7	25.3	48.6	15.6	1.6	3.1	31.1
Northern Mariana Islands	1997	836.2	—11.8[2]—		8.2	80.0[3]	2.5[4]	6.0[4]	71.6[3,4]	—[4]	7.6	—[4]	14.1	78.3
Norway	2001	32,936.6	9.2	4.7	4.2	81.9	9.5	42.1	30.2	65.7	7.1	5.5	3.7	17.9
Oman	1999	4,673.7	23.2	1.2	1.4	74.3	7.1	41.4	25.8	24.3	6.4	0.6	15.2	53.5
Pakistan	1999	10,159.1	22.3	1.2	20.8	55.7	18.7	22.2	14.8	17.3	6.4	1.4	7.6	67.3
Palau	1997	72.9	—25.4[2]—		12.0	62.5[3]	4.1	25.4	33.1[3]	...	44.1	...	14.8	41.1
Panama	1999	3,515.2	12.0	0.2	11.6	76.2	10.9	36.0	29.3	8.9	35.7	0.3	7.2	47.9
Papua New Guinea	1998	1,360.1	19.7	0.3	2.5	77.5	9.6	38.9	29.0	2.7	9.5	0.1	12.3	75.5
Paraguay	1999	1,905.9	17.3	0.2	11.6	70.9	11.9	36.0	23.0	14.0	13.7	0.2	6.1	66.0
Peru	1999	6,822.9	16.7	0.2	9.7	73.4	14.7	34.9	23.8	15.7	27.5	0.9	7.0	48.9
Philippines	1998	31,529.9	10.1	1.5	7.1	81.3	7.7	57.5	16.1	9.5	21.8	0.7	20.2	47.8
Poland	1999	45,876.1	8.4	1.1	7.2	83.2	13.5	37.7	31.9	65.0	3.6	13.7	2.0	15.6
Portugal	1999	39,828.6	14.8	0.5	6.8	77.8	9.3	39.1	29.5	78.1	2.8	1.3	2.7	15.0
Puerto Rico	1999[13]	27,308.7	17.3[14]	0.3[14]	10.6[14]	71.8[14]	25.4[14]	21.8[14]	24.7[14]	11.3	48.4	0.4[4]	4.3	35.6
Qatar	1994	1,927.4	15.8	2.7	0.6	80.8	7.0	39.7	34.2	33.9	10.6	1.4[4]	13.4	40.8
Réunion	1995	2,711.1	21.5	0.2	4.7	73.6	10.7	29.8	33.1	80.1	0.6	0.1	2.1	17.2
Romania	1999	10,395.3	8.8	2.2	10.1	78.9	10.6	26.3	42.0	60.4	3.5	16.9	1.1	18.1
Russia	1999	40,429.0	20.1	3.1[2]	2.0	74.8[3]	7.2	18.7	48.9[3]	36.6	7.9	25.9	1.5	28.0
Rwanda	1999	240.2	21.1[4]	2.5	16.8	59.5[4]	6.5	25.9	27.1[4]	27.6[4]	3.3	2.1[4]	13.1	54.0
St. Kitts and Nevis	1997	147.2	21.3	0.5	7.5	70.9	7.1	28.9	34.9	12.2	56.0	0.1	4.2	27.6
St. Lucia	1998	328.2	28.7	0.6	7.3	63.4	8.0	22.1	33.4	19.0	40.2	0.1	5.3	35.5
St. Vincent and the Grenadines	1999	200.7	25.5	0.4[4]	5.6	68.6	8.6	24.2	35.7	22.9	38.4	0.1	4.6	34.0
Samoa	1996	99.0	—35.0[2]—		11.8	53.2[3]	—[4]	16.9[4]	36.3[3]	2.1	14.0	—	3.8	80.0
San Marino[39]	1996	1,719.3	...	...	...	...	...	...	...	...	...	...	...	...
São Tomé and Príncipe	1999	21.9	—21.9[2,23]—		17.4	60.7[3]	...	49.3	11.4[3]	63.0[31]	—	—	10.0	26.9
Saudi Arabia	1998	30,012.3	16.5	0.8	0.2	82.5	9.1	37.6	35.8	31.3	17.7	1.0	8.6	41.4
Senegal	1999	1,604.4	30.9	0.9	10.2	58.0	11.8	25.9	20.4	54.8	4.1	2.5	3.4	35.3
Seychelles	1998	383.1	24.9	0.1[4]	9.4	65.6	5.4	29.4[4]	30.9	42.9	3.3	—	3.5	50.4
Sierra Leone	1995	136.3	—47.9[2]—		17.4	34.8[3]	7.6	14.7	12.5[3]	48.4[4]	8.1[4]	2.8[4]	0.8[4]	39.8[4]
Singapore	1999	111,060.9	4.5	0.6	9.1	85.8	5.8	60.1	19.9	12.7	17.1	0.5	16.6	53.0
Slovakia	1999	11,300.4	7.9	1.9	9.1	81.0	10.3	36.8	34.0	51.7	2.6	35.5	1.6	8.6
Slovenia	1999	10,081.4	9.4	1.6	6.5	82.6	11.3	36.9	34.4	68.8	2.9	10.2	1.9	16.1
Solomon Islands	1997	184.5	—17.9[2]—		8.6	73.5[3]	4.9	37.7	30.9[3]	3.4	2.1	—	14.9	79.6
Somalia	1999	285.0[4]	30.3[51]	0.2[51]	4.6[51]	64.9[51]	5.1[51]	37.1[51]	22.7[51]	8.4[4]	1.1[4]	—[4]	—[4]	90.5[4]
South Africa	1999	26,694.9	6.9	3.1	10.2	79.8	12.2	38.2	29.4	42.7	13.7	0.5	7.8	35.3
Spain	1999	147,865.9	12.4	1.7	7.2	78.7	10.7	43.0	25.0	67.3	5.5	2.3	3.2	21.7
Sri Lanka	1999	5,338.2	16.4	3.2	5.7	74.7	8.4	23.2	43.2	15.9	4.0	0.3	10.5	69.3
Sudan, The	1998	2,058.6	16.2	0.5	10.4	72.9	11.0	30.2	31.7	29.4	—	1.7	7.1	61.8
Suriname	1998	540.8	14.9	0.6	11.3	73.2	14.4	31.9	26.8	28.6	41.2	—	5.5	24.8
Swaziland	1998	1,136.6[1]	22.5[1]	0.4[1]	11.4[1]	65.8[1]	11.3[1]	26.4[1]	28.0[1]	5.4[1]	0.9[1]	—[1]	1.9[1]	91.8[1,52]
Sweden	1999	68,468.6	8.7	1.1	6.0	84.2	10.0	42.4	31.9	68.9	5.9	4.6	2.9	17.8
Switzerland[53]	1999	79,857.1	7.6	3.0	3.0	86.4	16.5	34.5	35.4	77.8	7.1	2.7	2.9	9.5
Syria	1999	3,611.3	24.1	0.8	2.5	72.5	9.9	19.7	42.9	32.1	4.8	14.5	4.3	44.2
Taiwan	2000	139,865.4	5.7	1.2	9.3	83.7	11.1	50.2	22.4	11.1	17.9	1.5	27.5	41.9
Tajikistan	1999	663.0	12.1	—58.6—		29.4	12.5	10.6	6.2	12.5	0.3	22.0	0.1	65.1
Tanzania	1999	1,588.0	18.4	0.3	8.0	73.2	10.4	39.4	23.4	30.6	5.1	0.4	8.2	55.7
Thailand	1999	50,309.1	7.9	2.2	9.7	80.2	10.8	43.1	26.3	11.7	12.8	1.2	24.4	50.0
Togo	1999	668.2	18.5	0.9	39.7	40.8	7.3	11.1	22.5	39.4	1.4	2.2	3.7	53.3
Tonga	1999	72.8	35.7	0.9	12.7	50.6	7.7	17.5	25.4	0.8	12.9	—	5.4	80.9
Trinidad and Tobago	1999	2,743.8	12.5	0.6[4]	21.0	65.9	9.0	34.0	22.9	12.7	40.3	0.4	5.1	41.5
Tunisia	1999	8,336.9	11.1	1.3	6.7	80.9	8.1	34.2	38.6	71.4	4.3	2.9	2.5	18.9
Turkey	1999	40,686.7	8.3	2.3	11.0	78.4	15.2	37.6	25.6	52.6	7.6	10.4	3.4	25.9
Turkmenistan	1998	980.7	9.1	0.8	7.2	82.9	10.1	45.7	27.1	16.1	7.4	36.5	0.8	39.2
Tuvalu	1999	8.1	35.0	—2	9.0	56.0[3]	5.0	25.0	26.0[3]	1.5	0.3	0.3	6.2	91.6
Uganda	1999	1,015.2	16.5	1.2	12.3	70.0	14.4	27.3	28.2	23.8	5.6	0.1	8.1	62.4
Ukraine	1999	11,846.1	8.9	3.4[2]	44.0	43.7[3]	9.2	17.5	16.9[3]	20.3	3.4	58.4	0.8	17.1
United Arab Emirates	1992	17,414.0	11.6	0.7	1.7	86.1	5.5	35.1	45.4	33.5	8.9	0.5	16.6	40.5
United Kingdom[38]	2001	327,576.1	9.9	3.3	4.4	82.3	10.4	44.0	28.0	50.5	13.3	3.1	4.1	29.0
United States[55]	1999	1,059,220.1	6.2	1.6	7.5	84.7	5.9	46.2	32.6	19.0	—	1.1	12.7	67.2
Uruguay	1999	3,356.3	13.6	0.5	11.3	74.7	17.2	31.2	26.3	18.7	11.3	2.2	2.1	65.8
Uzbekistan	1998	3,288.7	19.3[9]	1.3[9]	1.4[9]	78.0[9]	9.0[9]	43.1[9]	25.9[9]	17.9	7.5	23.6	0.3	50.8
Vanuatu	1999	95.6	—24.2[2]—		7.0	68.8[3]	5.8	30.2	32.8[3]	4.9	5.3	—	5.1	84.6
Venezuela	1999	13,554.0	14.2	0.7	2.6	82.5	11.8	43.1	27.6	25.8	38.5	0.3	3.4	32.0
Vietnam	1997	11,592.1	—8.1[2]—		10.3	81.6[3]	16.8	29.6	35.1[3]	11.0	2.2	2.0	13.0	71.8
Virgin Islands (U.S.)	1995	3,200.3	...	...	68.6[22]	...	...	...	...	...	32.7	...	...	...
West Bank[34]	1994	102.5[57]	...	...	...	...	...	...	...	...	...	...	...	...
Western Sahara	...	...	...	...	...	...	...	...	...	...	...	...	...	...
Yemen	2000	2,324.0	37.2	0.2[2]	12.0	50.7[3]	9.7	20.8	20.2[3]	17.5	4.4	0.9	3.2	74.0
Yugoslavia	1998	4,849.3	15.0	2.8	15.9	66.4	13.7	20.5	32.2	42.6	2.7	23.0	1.3	30.5
Zambia	1995	708.3	12.2	1.8[2]	13.2	72.9[3]	13.3	37.9	21.7[3]	22.3	2.8	0.1	6.4	68.5
Zimbabwe	1999	2,126.2	10.5	1.5	11.6	76.4	16.8	35.2	24.4	22.2	4.8	0.4	4.1	68.5

[1]Year ending March. [2]Excluding precious stones, etc. (667). [3]Including precious stones, etc. (667). [4]Estimate. [5]1991. [6]Year ending September 30. [7]Percentage of the total excluding fish imports or the cannery (52.1% of the overall total), and government purchases (0.1%) in 1993. [8]1994. [9]1995. [10]Excluding mineral fuels; overall totals on a balance of payments basis, f.o.b.: imports U.S.$1,518,200,000, exports U.S.$1,164,800,000. [11]Percentage of non-oil imports. [12]Includes 66.5% for special categories. [13]Year ending June 30. [14]1992. [15]Including metals. [16]Excluding metals. [17]Includes 69.4% from India. [18]Mainly electricity. [19]Includes 94.6% to India. [20]Includes 72.2% from South Africa. [21]Includes 19.4% to Switzerland. [22]1993. [23]Main items only. [24]Domestic exports only. [25]1996. [26]Includes 24.9% for bunkers and ship stores. [27]1987. [28]1985. [29]Includes 9.1% for ferronickel. [30]Includes 38.7% for ships and boats. [31]Main countries only. [32]Figures for France include Monaco. [33]1988. [34]Total external trade for West Bank and Gaza Strip in 1999: imports U.S.$2,629,000,000, exports U.S.$372,100,000. [35]Includes 82.4% from

exports total value ('000,000 U.S.$)	Standard International Trade Classification (SITC) categories (%) food and agricultural raw materials (0 + 1 + 2 − 27 − 28 + 4)	mineral ores and concentrates (27 + 28 + 667)	fuels and other energy (3)	manufactured goods total[a] (5 + 6 − 667 + 7 + 8 + 9)	of which chemicals and related products (5)	of which machinery and transport equipment (7)	of which other[a] (6 − 667 + 8 + 9)	direction of trade (%) to European Union (EU)[b]	to United States	to Eastern Europe[c]	to Japan	to all other[d]	country
170,538.3	20.7	0.8	6.8	71.8	13.5	36.2	22.0	72.5	4.3	3.2	1.1	19.0	Netherlands, The
1,355.8	6.9	2.0	85.1	6.0	1.0	1.7	3.3	14.3	13.9	—	0.2	71.5	Netherlands Antilles
529.4	—	39.5	—	60.5	—	—	60.5[48]	36.1[4]	11.3[4]	—[4]	29.8[49]	22.7	New Caledonia
12,474.0	58.8	0.4	2.2	38.6	7.1	10.2	21.3	17.7	13.6	0.6	12.6	55.5	New Zealand
508.5	84.5	0.3	0.9	14.2	1.7	1.1	11.4	22.9	36.3	2.7	0.7	37.4	Nicaragua
336.8	32.7	39.5	0.7	27.1	1.0	13.3	12.8	4.3	0.1	—	—	95.5	Niger
21,330.8	0.4	—	98.9	0.6	0.1	0.4	0.2	22.0	33.9	—	1.0	43.1	Nigeria
263.0[5]	—[5]	—[5]	—[5]	100.0[5]	—[5]	—[5]	100.0[5]	—[5]	100.0[5]	—[5]	—[5]	—[5]	Northern Mariana Islands
58,939.4	7.3	0.6	61.7	30.4	5.2	11.4	13.8	75.7	7.7	2.3	1.7	12.6	Norway
7,230.9	4.5	0.3	76.9	18.3	1.0	11.6	5.7	1.7	1.2	0.1	23.2	73.8	Oman
8,383.2	14.4	0.2	0.9	84.4	0.8	1.2	82.4	29.3	23.0	0.5	3.5	43.7	Pakistan
11.8	69.1[49]	—[49]	—[49]	30.9[49]	—[49]	—[49]	30.9[49]	—[49]	8.0[49]	—[49]	58.8[49]	33.2[49]	Palau
707.1	72.5	1.0	9.1	17.5	5.5	0.1	11.9	22.3	44.7	0.2	1.0	31.7	Panama
1,819.8	30.4	42.5	21.4	5.7	—	3.2	2.5	19.2[4]	3.6	0.9[4]	5.1	71.2[50]	Papua New Guinea
740.8	84.3	0.4	0.1	15.2	2.5	0.7	12.0	37.9	7.8	—	0.3	53.9	Paraguay
5,932.1	26.6	11.8	4.2	57.4	2.7	1.0	53.7	25.4	29.1	0.9	4.3	40.2	Peru
29,496.4	7.5	0.9	0.5	91.1	1.1	72.1	17.9	20.3	34.4	0.3	14.4	30.7	Philippines
27,375.0	11.0	0.7	5.0	83.3	5.8	29.6	47.9	70.6	2.8	16.6	0.2	9.8	Poland
24,493.6	10.1	1.1	1.8	87.0	4.8	34.1	48.1	83.2	5.0	1.0	0.4	10.4	Portugal
33,416.4	15.8[14]	0.1[14]	2.6[14]	81.5[14]	43.7[14]	21.7[14]	16.2[14]	2.7	82.0	—	0.7	14.6	Puerto Rico
3,212.9	0.5	0.2	73.8	25.4	15.9	1.4	8.1	1.9[4]	2.5[4]	—[4]	55.6[4]	40.0[4]	Qatar
208.7	78.6	0.5	0.2	20.7	1.7	12.7	6.2	79.9	0.6	—	6.1	13.4	Réunion
8,503.0	10.4	2.4	4.9	82.3	4.9	16.8	60.6	65.6	3.7	9.1	0.2	21.3	Romania
74,663.0	4.6	2.3[32]	41.8	51.4[3]	5.2	6.8	39.3[3]	33.3	6.3	26.0	2.8	31.5	Russia
54.5	83.3	—	—	16.7	—	—	16.7	14.7	—	—	—	85.3	Rwanda
41.1	58.2	—	—	41.8	0.2	37.2	4.4	33.7	57.4	—	4.6	4.4	St. Kitts and Nevis
53.9	72.5	0.1	—	27.5	1.5	6.9	19.1	63.2	15.6	—	0.4	20.8	St. Lucia
49.4	81.4	—[4]	—	18.6	0.8	8.7	9.1	42.3	3.2	—	—	54.5	St. Vincent and the Grenadines
10.1	89.2[2] (food + mineral + fuels)			10.8[3]	...	...	10.8[3]	16.8	18.8	—	2.0	62.4	Samoa
1,741.9	...	...	...	...	...	...	...	...	...	...	...	...	San Marino[39]
3.9	74.4[23]	...		25.6	...	...	25.6	100.0	—	—	—	—	São Tomé and Príncipe
39,807.0	1.5	0.2	84.3	14.0	9.2	1.4	3.4	18.3	15.9	—	14.5	51.3	Saudi Arabia
471.3	16.2	9.4	17.2	57.2	35.9	10.9	10.4	21.0	0.3	—	0.2[4]	78.5	Senegal
121.4	75.0	0.1[4]	21.9	3.0	...	2.2	0.7	71.3	0.1	—	3.6	25.0	Seychelles
76.1	13.3	77.0	—	9.7	—	—	9.7	65.3[4]	13.3[4]	1.0[4]	1.5[4]	18.9[4]	Sierra Leone
114,681.8	3.4	0.3	8.0	88.3	7.8	66.2	14.3	15.2	19.2	0.3	7.4	57.8	Singapore
10,190.7	5.9	1.1	4.7	88.4	6.5	38.7	43.2	59.5	1.4	31.7	0.1	7.2	Slovakia
8,545.9	5.4	0.3	0.6	93.7	10.7	35.5	47.4	66.1	3.0	9.7	0.2	21.0	Slovenia
156.5	96.5[2] (food + mineral + fuels)			3.5[3]	...	...	3.5[3]	24.9	0.1	—	39.7	35.2	Solomon Islands
119.0[4]	95.4[14]	2.3[14]	—[14]	2.3[14]	—[14]	2.3[14]	—[14]	0.8[4]	0.1[4]	—[4]	—[4]	99.1[4]	Somalia
26,709.6	11.8	11.4	8.4	68.4	6.8	14.9	46.7	32.1	10.3	0.5	6.8	50.3	South Africa
111,493.0	15.9	0.8	2.2	81.1	8.7	43.3	29.1	72.2	4.4	2.4	1.0	20.0	Spain
4,467.3	22.9	3.4	0.3	73.4	0.6	4.2	68.6	29.4	39.9	2.9	3.5	24.3	Sri Lanka
534.7	80.5	0.3	—	19.2	—	4.5	14.7	33.6	—	0.7	2.7	63.0	Sudan, The
480.5	13.0	61.5	4.5	21.1	—	0.9	20.2	32.8	19.1	3.7	3.8	40.5	Suriname
965.6	54.5	1.3	1.0	43.2	16.4	9.4	17.3	10.5	5.2	—	—	84.2	Swaziland
84,784.5	7.0	0.9	2.3	89.7	8.9	47.3	33.4	58.4	9.2	4.7	2.4	25.3	Sweden
80,299.8	3.2	2.0	0.2	94.5	28.6	30.5	35.4	61.2	12.4	2.8	4.0	19.6	Switzerland[53]
3,389.0	19.4	1.0	68.4	11.3	0.4[4]	0.2[4]	10.6[4]	62.2	1.3	1.9	0.3[4]	34.3	Syria
148,129.3	2.4	0.1	1.1	96.4	6.2	58.4	31.7	14.9	23.5	0.6	11.2	49.8	Taiwan
689.0	4.0	25.6 (mineral + fuels)		70.3	1.3	1.0	68.0	35.4	0.2	20.5	0.1	43.7	Tajikistan
642.1	82.9	3.1	0.3	13.6	0.8	5.9	7.0	39.1	2.4	1.2	7.1	50.2	Tanzania
58,423.1	20.0	1.4	1.8	76.7	5.0	41.9	29.7	16.8	21.7	0.5	14.1	46.8	Thailand
360.3	46.2	18.3	3.7	31.8	0.6	4.9	26.3	13.6	0.6	2.1	—	83.8	Togo
11.3	91.9	—	—	8.1	1.5	2.2	4.4	0.9	25.5	—	55.0	18.6	Tonga
2,805.7	8.4	0.1[4]	54.1	37.4	18.9	3.7	14.8	10.9	41.4	0.1	0.2	47.4	Trinidad and Tobago
5,788.0	11.8	1.3	7.2	79.7	11.6	12.5	55.6	80.5	0.7	0.7	0.2	17.9	Tunisia
26,587.2	16.7	1.1	1.3	80.9	3.4	18.9	58.6	54.0	9.2	7.1	0.5	29.3	Turkey
614.1	32.6	0.8	58.5	8.1	0.7	0.2	7.2	7.8	0.5	6.1	—	85.5	Turkmenistan
1.4	92.2[54]	—[54]	—[54]	7.8[54]	—[54]	—[54]	7.8[54]	78.7	—	6.6	—	14.7	Tuvalu
505.7	89.3	0.7	0.2	9.7	0.6	1.5	7.7	35.2	1.8	4.2	3.8	55.0	Uganda
11,581.6	15.0	10.1[2] (mineral + fuels)		74.9[3]	11.0	11.5	52.4[3]	18.4	3.8	37.3	0.5	40.0	Ukraine
24,756.3	0.3	0.1	96.6	3.0	0.2	0.2	2.6	7.0[4]	3.7[4]	0.1[4]	35.7[4]	53.9[4]	United Arab Emirates
273,491.9	5.8	3.1	8.2	83.0	14.6	46.4	21.9	57.5	15.5	2.7	2.0	22.3	United Kingdom[38]
692,783.9	9.5	1.3	1.5	87.7	10.1	53.2	24.4	21.9	—	0.7	8.3	69.1	United States[55]
2,237.0	55.2	0.3	0.6	43.9	5.7	7.5	30.7	19.6	6.9	0.8	1.1	71.6	Uruguay
3,528.0	63.3[4,9]	4.1[4,9]	10.7[9]	21.9[9]	2.8[9]	2.4[9]	16.6[9]	23.8	1.8	20.7	1.1[4]	52.6	Uzbekistan
22.5	87.0[8]	—[8]	—[8]	13.0[8]	—[8]	1.0[8]	12.0[8]	43.6	4.4	—	19.6	32.4	Vanuatu
20,076.3	2.8	1.0	81.4	14.8	3.5	1.5	9.7	5.7	51.6	0.1	1.2	41.5	Venezuela
9,185.0	34.1[2] (food + mineral)		18.0	48.0[3]	1.2	8.2	38.6[3]	16.1	3.2	2.7	18.2	59.7	Vietnam
3,026.3	...	...	83.3[22, 56]	...	...	...	...	...	92.7	...	...	...	Virgin Islands (U.S.)
22.6[58]	...	...	...	...	...	...	...	...	...	...	...	...	West Bank[34]
...	...	...	...	...	...	...	...	...	...	...	...	...	Western Sahara
4,079.0	2.5	0.1[2]	96.5	0.9[3]	0.3	0.3	0.3[3]	1.2	6.1	—	2.1	90.6	Yemen
2,858.2	18.1	0.3	2.8	78.9	9.9	10.1	58.9	38.6	0.8	12.9	0.1	47.6	Yugoslavia
1,055.1	3.3	1.5	3.3	92.0	0.2	1.5	90.3	13.2	6.1	0.8	15.5	64.4	Zambia
1,887.2	60.4	5.7	1.8	32.0	2.6	2.3	27.1	34.6	5.8	3.0	7.1	49.4	Zimbabwe

Israel.   [36]Includes 69.2% to Israel and 25.1% to Jordan.   [37]1983.   [38]Figures for United Kingdom include Guernsey, Isle of Man, and Jersey (data for Jersey is also shown separately).   [39]Figures for Italy include San Marino and Vatican City State.   [40]United Kingdom only.   [41]Including coins.   [42]Includes 89.5% from rest of Customs Union of Southern Africa.   [43]Includes 53.9% to rest of Customs Union of Southern Africa.   [44]Excluding external trade in ships.   [45]Including external trade in ships.   [46]France only.   [47]Includes 84.3% from South Africa.   [48]Includes 52.5% for ferro-alloys.   [49]1984.   [50]Includes 58.1% for areas not specified.   [51]1986.   [52]Includes 82.9% from South Africa.   [53]Figures for Switzerland include Liechtenstein, also shown separately.   [54]1989.   [55]Figures for United States include American Samoa, Guam, Puerto Rico, and Virgin Islands (U.S.), also shown separately.   [56]Exports of refined petroleum to United States only.   [57]Excluding imports from Israel (90.9% in 1987).   [58]Excluding exports to Israel (70.3% in 1987).

Household budgets and consumption

This table provides international data on household income, on the consumption expenditure of households for goods and services, and on the principal object of such expenditure (in most countries), food consumption (by kind). For purposes of this compilation, income comprises pretax monetary payments and payment in kind. The first part of the table provides data on distribution of income by households and by sources of income; the second part analyzes the largest portion of income use—consumption expenditure. Such expenditure is defined as the purchase of goods and services to satisfy current wants and needs. This definition excludes income expended on taxes, debts, savings and investments, and insurance policies. The third and last part of the table focuses on food, which usually, and often by a wide margin, represents the largest share of consumer spending worldwide. The data provided include daily available calories per capita and consumption of major food groups.

For both sources of income and consumption expenditure, the primary basis of analysis for most countries is the household, an economic unit that can be as small as a single person or as large as an extended family. For some of the countries that do not compile information by household, the table provides data on personal income and personal expenditure—*i.e.*, the income and expenditure of all the individuals constituting a society's households. When no expenditure data at all is available, the table reports the weights of each major class of goods and services making up a given country's consumer (or retail) price index (CPI). The weighting of the components of the CPI usually reflects household spending patterns within the country or its principal urban or rural areas.

The data on distribution of income show, collectively for an entire country, the proportion of total income earned (occasionally, expended) by households constituting the lowest quintile and highest decile (poorest 20% and wealthiest 10%) within the country. These figures show the degree to which either group represents a disproportionate share of poverty or wealth.

The data on sources of income illuminate patterns of economic structure in the gaining of an income. They indicate, for example, that in poor, agrarian countries income often derives largely from self-employment (usually farming) or that in industrial countries, with well-developed systems of salaried employment and social welfare, income derives mainly from wages and salaries and secondarily from transfer payments (*see* note a). Because household sizes and numbers of income earners vary so greatly internationally, and because the frequency and methodology of household and CPI surveys do not permit single-year comparisons for more than a few countries at once, no summary of total *household* income or expenditure was possible. Instead, U.S. dollar figures are supplied for *per capita* private final consumption expenditure (for a single, recent year) that are more comparable internationally and refer to the same date. The figures on distribution of consumption expenditure by end use reveal patterns of personal and family use of disposable income and indicate, inter alia, that in developing countries, food may absorb 50% or more of disposable income, while in the larger household budgets of the developed countries, by contrast, food purchases may account for only 20–30% of spending. Each category of expenditure betrays similar complexities of local habit, necessity, and aspiration.

The reader should exercise caution when using these data to make intercountry comparisons. Most of the information comes from single-country surveys, which often differ markedly in their coverage of economically or demographically stratified groups, in sample design, or in the methods

Household budgets and consumption

country	income (latest) percent received by — lowest 20% of households	highest 10% of households	by source (percent) — wages, salaries	self-employment	transfer payments[a]	other[b]	consumption expenditure — per capita private final, U.S.$ (1995)	by kind or end use (percent of household or personal budget; latest) — food[c]	housing[d]	clothing[e]	health care	energy, water	education
Afghanistan	...	...	20.7	28.0	8.2	43.1	...	33.9	3.0	...	1.1	0.7	...
Albania	...	...	53.0	4.0	11.5	31.5	680	...	...	...	...	...	...
Algeria	7.0[1]	26.8[1]	43.1	38.3	18.6	1.8	810	52.3	6.7[2]	8.6	2.8	[2]	[3]
American Samoa	...	...	...	...	...	...	1,880[4]	32.9	20.4[5]	5.2	...	...	...
Andorra	...	...	...	...	...	...	...	...	...	...	...	...	...
Angola	...	...	...	...	...	...	370	74.1[6]	10.2[2,6]	5.5[6]	1.8[6]	[2,6]	2.7[6]
Antigua and Barbuda	...	...	...	...	...	...	4,050	42.9	23.3	7.5	...	5.5	...
Argentina	4.4	35.2	53.9	31.5	1.5	12.7	6,620	40.1	9.3	8.0	7.9	9.0	2.6
Armenia	...	...	24.5	13.6[7]	5.5	56.4	360	69.6	...	17.4	...	...	...
Aruba	...	...	...	...	...	...	11,190	26.9	9.9	8.4	2.9	8.5	1.9
Australia	5.9	25.4	72.7	7.5	13.0	6.8	12,040	18.7	18.5	5.6	7.1	2.2	1.6
Austria	10.4	19.3	55.7	[8]	24.4	19.9[8]	16,020	28.1	14.5	8.5	5.8	4.0	0.4
Azerbaijan	...	...	70.2	10.8[7]	19.0	—	460	42.2	...	13.6	4.8	—	...
Bahamas, The	3.6	32.1	...	...	...	...	3,950[9]	13.8	32.8	5.9	4.4	...	5.3
Bahrain	...	...	...	...	...	...	2,240	32.4	21.2	5.9	2.3	2.2	2.3
Bangladesh	8.7[1]	28.6[1]	18.7	48.3	7.5	25.5	170[10]	63.3	8.8	5.9	1.1	8.4	1.2
Barbados	7.0	44.0[11]	...	...	...	...	4,860	45.8	16.8	5.1	3.8	5.2	[3]
Belarus	11.4[1]	20.0[1]	47.1	7.3[9]	45.6	—	610	29.0	2.7	...	...	...	...
Belgium	9.5[12]	20.2[12]	49.6	10.9	20.7	18.8	16,550	18.3	11.4	7.0	10.5	6.2	[3]
Belize	...	...	84.1		— 15.9 —		1,780	34.0	9.0	8.8	1.6	9.1	2.3
Benin	8.0	39.0	26.3		— 73.7 —		240	37.0	10.0	14.0	5.0	2.0	4.0
Bermuda	7.2	24.7	65.3	9.0	3.3	22.4	12,690[13]	14.6	27.7	4.9	7.6	3.3	3.8
Bhutan	...	...	...	...	...	...	170	72.3	...	21.2	...	3.7	...
Bolivia	5.6[12]	31.7[12]	...	...	...	...	690	46.6	7.8	5.1	2.1	4.7	0.3
Bosnia and Herzegovina	...	...	53.2	12.0	18.2	16.6	1,890[14]	44.7	1.6	8.3	3.4	7.8	[3]
Botswana	3.7	42.9	73.3	15.4	10.8	0.4	1,030	39.5[15]	11.8	5.6	2.3	2.5	4.9
Brazil	2.5[12]	47.6[12]	62.4	14.7	10.9	12.0	4,420	25.3	21.3[2]	12.9	9.1	[2]	[3]
Brunei	...	...	...	...	...	...	...	45.1	2.6	6.1	...	2.4	[3]
Bulgaria	8.5[1]	22.5[1]	34.7	23.6[7]	14.8	—	1,470	47.0	4.1	7.4	3.2	4.3	[3]
Burkina Faso	5.5[1]	39.5[1]	...	...	...	...	220	38.7[6]	5.1[6]	4.4[6]	5.2[6]	13.7[6]	[3]
Burundi	7.9[1]	26.6[1]	...	...	...	...	190	59.6[6]	4.4[6]	11.1[6]	...	5.8[6]	...
Cambodia	6.9[1]	33.8[1]	...	...	...	...	280	...	...	...	...	...	...
Cameroon	...	...	41.4	52.6	3.0	3.0	570	49.1	18.0[2]	7.6	8.6	[2]	...
Canada	7.5[12]	23.8[12]	57.0	13.7	20.7	8.6	11,460	13.4	24.5[2]	5.3	4.7	[2]	3.1
Cape Verde	...	...	...	...	...	...	920	60.0	8.5	2.5	0.5	4.9	[17]
Central African Republic	2.0[1]	47.7[1]	...	...	...	...	350	70.5[6]	0.6[6]	9.5[6]	1.0[6]	6.5[6]	...
Chad	8.0	30.0	...	...	...	...	170	45.3[6]	...	3.5[6]	11.9[6]	5.8[6]	...
Chile	3.5[12]	46.1[12]	— 75.1 —		12.0	12.9	2,940	27.9	15.2	22.5	...	...	...
China	5.9[12]	30.4[12]	21.6	72.2	— 6.2 —		260	49.9[15,18]	6.8[18]	13.7[18]	2.9[18]	...	2.3[18]
Colombia	3.0[12]	46.1[12]	45.1	35.4	14.2	5.3	1,540	45.0	7.8	4.5	6.4	2.2	1.7
Comoros	...	...	25.6	64.5	8.7	1.2	350	67.3	2.3	11.6	3.2	3.8	[3]
Congo, Dem. Rep. of the	...	...	...	...	...	...	190	61.7	11.5[2]	9.7	2.6	[2]	[3]
Congo, Rep. of the	7.0	43.5	...	...	...	...	870	37.0	6.0	6.0	6.0	3.0	8.0
Costa Rica	4.0[12]	34.7[12]	61.0	22.6	9.6	6.8	1,600	39.1	12.1[2]	9.4	3.7	[2]	[3]
Côte d'Ivoire	7.1[1]	28.8[1]	44.9	49.9	— 5.2 —		480	48.0	7.8	10.0	0.7	8.5	...
Croatia	9.3[1]	21.6[1]	40.2	40.8	12.1	6.9	3,790	37.8	2.9	8.6	4.3	7.6	[3]
Cuba	...	...	57.3	— 42.7 —			1,510[9]	26.7	...	...	...	2.5	...
Cyprus	...	...	76.3	5.9	14.4	3.4	8,300	22.7	5.5	10.0	3.1	1.3	1.4
Czech Republic	10.3[12]	22.4[12]	— 66.7 —		27.6	5.7	2,620	26.7	5.5[2]	7.3	[19]	[2]	...
Denmark	9.6[12]	20.5[12]	63.3	14.6	25.9	-3.8	17,730	17.9	22.9	5.2	2.2	6.1	1.9
Djibouti	...	...	51.6	36.0	10.5	1.9	590	50.3	6.4	1.7	2.4	13.1	...
Dominica	...	...	...	...	...	...	2,110	43.1	16.1	6.5	...	5.4	...
Dominican Republic	4.3[12]	37.8[12]	41.7	31.8	1.5	25.0	1,150	46.0	10.0	3.0	8.0	5.0	3.0
East Timor	...	...	...	...	...	...	...	...	...	...	...	...	...
Ecuador	5.4[1]	33.8[1]	17.4	76.9	3.6	2.1	1,040	36.1	9.0	10.1	4.2	3.3	[17]

employed for collection, classification, and tabulation of data. Further, the reference period of the data varies greatly; while a significant portion of the data is from 1980 or later, information for some countries dates from the 1970s. This older information is typeset in italic. Finally, intercountry comparisons of annual personal consumption expenditure may be misleading because of the distortions of price and purchasing power present when converting a national currency unit into U.S. dollars.

The table's food consumption data include total daily available calories per capita (food supply), which amounts to domestic production and imports minus exports, animal feed, and nonfood uses, and a percentage breakdown of the major food groups that make up food supply.

The data for daily available calories per capita provide a measure of the nutritional adequacy of each nation's food supply. The following list, based on estimates from the United Nations Food and Agriculture Organization (FAO), indicates the regional variation in recommended daily minimum nutritional requirements, which are defined by factors such as climatic ambience, physical activity, and average body weight: Africa (2,320 calories), formerly Centrally Planned Asia (2,300 calories), Far East (2,240 calories), Latin America (2,360 calories), Near East (2,440 calories).

The breakdown of diet by food groups describes the character of a nation's food supply. A typical breakdown for a low-income country might show a diet with heavy intake of vegetable foods, such as cereals, potatoes, or cassava. In the high-income countries, a relatively larger portion of total calories derives from animal products (meat, eggs, and milk). The reader should note that these data refer to total national *supply* and often do not reflect the differences that may exist within a single country.

In compiling this table, Britannica editors rely on both numerous national reports and principal secondary sources such as the World Bank's *World Development Report* (annual), the International Labour Organisation's *Sources and Methods: Labour Statistics vol. 1 Consumer Price Indices* (3rd ed.), the UN's *Yearbook of National Accounts Statistics* (annual) and *National Accounts Statistics: Compendium of Income Distribution Statistics,* and the FAO's *Food Balance Sheets.*

The following terms further define the column headings:

a. Includes pensions, family allowances, unemployment payments, remittances from abroad, and social security and related benefits.
b. Includes interest and dividends, rents and royalties, and all other income not reported under the three preceding categories.
c. Includes alcoholic and nonalcoholic beverages and meals away from home when identifiable. Excludes tobacco except as noted.
d. Rent, maintenance of dwellings, and taxes only; excludes energy and water (heat, light, power, and water) and household durables (furniture, appliances, utensils, and household operations), shown separately.
e. Includes footwear.
f. Furniture, appliances, and utensils; usually includes expenditure on household operation.
g. Includes expenditure on cultural activities other than education.
h. May include data not shown separately in preceding categories, including meals away from home (*see* note c).
i. Represents pure fats and oils only.
j. Consists mainly of peas, beans, and lentils; spices; stimulants; alcoholic beverages (when combined with "other"); sugars and honey; and nuts and oilseeds.

transportation, communications	household durable goods[f]	recreation[g]	personal effects, other[h]	daily available calories per capita	cereals	potatoes, cassava	meat, poultry	fish	eggs, milk	fruits, vegetables	fats, oils[i]	other[j]	country
...	...	...	61.3	1,716	83.4	1.1	4.1	—	2.4	2.6	3.8	2.6	Afghanistan
12.0	...	...	...	2,976	51.1	1.8	5.1	0.1	16.9	6.0	9.0	10.0	Albania
17.8	4.5	4.6[3]	8.5	3,020	60.3	2.2	2.7	0.3	6.1	5.1	13.8	9.5	Algeria
	5	1.1	22.6	...	...	...	...	...	...	...	...	...	American Samoa
...	...	...	...	3,348	22.6	4.7	13.4	2.4	9.3	6.7	21.6	19.4	Andorra
3.9[6]	...	...	1.8[6]	...	...	...	...	...	...	...	...	...	Angola
10.0	...	...	*10.8*	2,450	25.8	1.0	15.8	1.7	11.3	7.9	16.4	20.2	Antigua and Barbuda
11.6	...	7.5	5.9	3,144	29.5	5.2	16.5	0.5	10.3	4.5	15.4	18.0	Argentina
...	6.6	...	28.7	2,356	52.3	6.7	5.3	0.1	7.0	6.5	11.7	10.4	Armenia
15.5	9.1	3.1	11.9	2,659	28.2	2.3	18.9	1.4	10.8	5.0	13.6	19.7	Aruba
15.1	7.0	7.5	16.7	3,190	22.7	3.2	15.5	0.8	11.8	5.3	17.0	23.5	Australia
16.3	7.8	7.1	7.5	3,531	20.7	3.1	13.8	0.6	11.4	5.5	21.5	23.4	Austria
5.1	6.5	0.7	27.1	2,191	66.6	2.7	4.6	0.1	9.7	5.1	2.8	8.4	Azerbaijan
14.8	8.9	4.9	9.2	2,546	30.1	1.4	18.8	1.1	5.9	8.6	9.3	24.9	Bahamas, The
8.5	9.8	6.4	9.0	...	...	...	...	...	...	...	...	...	Bahrain
0.9	...	...	10.4	2,050	81.6	1.3	0.8	0.9	1.5	1.1	5.6	7.2	Bangladesh
10.5	8.1	4.8[3]	—	2,978	31.6	3.9	12.6	2.3	6.6	3.4	12.8	26.8	Barbados
...	...	...	68.3	3,136	36.2	9.9	10.5	0.1	10.2	2.6	12.0	18.7	Belarus
13.4	10.6	6.8[3]	15.8	3,606	20.4	5.2	8.6	1.1	10.8	6.5	25.7	21.7	Belgium
13.7	8.0	...	9.4	2,922	34.0	1.4	6.3	0.4	7.5	9.6	10.2	30.7	Belize
14.0	5.0	...	9.0	2,571	37.5	36.9	2.2	0.7	0.8	2.6	5.3	14.0	Benin
7.3	16.6	10.8	3.4	2,921	22.8	2.6	15.7	2.7	7.8	12.4	15.2	20.8	Bermuda
...	0.7	...	2.1	...	...	...	...	...	...	...	...	...	Bhutan
17.7	9.7	2.7	3.3	2,214	40.7	6.6	11.2	0.1	3.7	8.6	11.4	17.7	Bolivia
6.0	4.1	3.5[3]	2.3	2,801	64.6	5.6	4.3	0.1	3.7	4.5	3.7	13.4	Bosnia and Herzegovina
13.1	13.8	3.1	3.4	2,159	46.9	1.8	6.3	0.5	8.9	2.5	11.6	21.6	Botswana
15.0	...	...	16.4	2,926	30.9	4.3	10.8	0.4	8.3	4.5	12.6	28.2	Brazil
17.2	*8.3*	*8.9[3]*	*9.4*	2,851	48.0	1.2	13.0	1.3	6.4	5.0	6.3	18.9	Brunei
6.6	4.0	3.0[3]	21.5	2,740	37.6	2.1	10.7	0.3	12.1	5.4	15.6	16.3	Bulgaria
18.6[6]	3.0[6]	2.3[3, 6]	9.0[6]	2,149	73.2	0.7	2.6	0.1	1.9	0.9	5.2	15.5	Burkina Faso
...	6.0[6]	...	13.1[6, 16]	1,578	16.7	30.0	1.3	0.4	0.8	10.3	1.5	39.0	Burundi
...	...	...	...	2,078	77.9	1.3	6.2	0.8	0.5	2.9	4.7	5.7	Cambodia
13.0	...	2.4	1.3	2,209	41.7	16.3	3.4	0.8	1.4	13.7	9.1	13.6	Cameroon
14.3	8.8	8.0	17.9	3,167	24.9	2.9	11.4	1.1	8.8	6.6	20.5	23.8	Canada
8.8	6.9	17	7.9[17]	3,099	40.3	2.5	5.8	1.5	4.9	3.1	17.6	24.2	Cape Verde
4.1[6]	0.8[6]	1.3[6]	5.7[6]	2,056	18.9	35.9	6.4	0.3	1.5	6.2	13.7	17.1	Central African Republic
...	...	...	33.5[6]	2,171	53.8	9.4	2.3	0.5	2.2	1.5	7.1	23.2	Chad
6.4	...	...	28.0	2,844	38.7	3.4	12.5	1.2	6.7	4.8	12.4	20.3	Chile
4.7[18]	5.3[18]	2.4[18]	12.0[18]	2,972	54.7	5.6	13.2	13.2	2.6	5.3	7.3	10.1	China
18.5	5.7	...	8.2	2,559	32.5	7.2	7.2	0.4	8.7	7.9	11.9	24.2	Colombia
2.2	3.0	2.5[3]	4.1	1,858	42.7	15.6	1.8	2.4	1.1	8.0	10.3	18.1	Comoros
5.9	4.8	3.8[3]	—	1,701	19.2	56.3	1.9	0.6	0.1	6.5	6.3	9.1	Congo, Dem. Rep. of the
15.0	4.0	...	15.0	2,241	25.4	37.9	3.1	2.2	1.5	6.2	11.7	11.9	Congo, Rep. of the
11.6	10.9	4.4[3]	8.8	2,781	32.9	1.9	5.3	0.5	9.5	5.0	14.1	30.9	Costa Rica
12.2	3.4	...	9.4	2,695	42.5	24.7	1.9	0.7	0.9	8.7	11.2	9.4	Côte d'Ivoire
9.3	4.5	4.1[3]	1.5	2,479	31.2	8.4	4.2	0.3	10.6	7.5	11.9	25.8	Croatia
5.4	...	...	65.4	2,473	37.3	5.3	5.3	0.8	4.9	5.1	9.6	31.7	Cuba
15.6	10.5	6.3	23.6	3,474	25.6	2.4	14.7	1.0	12.7	8.0	12.7	22.9	Cyprus
3.1	4.5	0.8[19]	52.7	3,292	27.6	4.4	10.1	0.7	9.6	4.3	17.9	25.4	Czech Republic
15.5	6.1	8.3	13.9	3,443	25.4	3.8	11.7	1.4	9.9	4.9	17.6	25.3	Denmark
...	1.5	...	24.6	2,074	51.3	0.2	4.5	0.2	4.8	1.6	17.9	19.4	Djibouti
11.6	6.0	...	11.3	2,996	23.9	9.1	10.6	1.6	8.7	12.5	6.9	26.7	Dominica
4.0	8.0	...	13.0	2,277	28.3	2.8	7.6	0.7	5.2	10.1	19.1	26.4	Dominican Republic
...	...	...	...	...	...	...	...	...	...	...	...	...	East Timor
12.8	5.5	17	19.0[17]	2,724	34.5	2.7	5.8	0.6	6.6	4.4	20.6	24.8	Ecuador

Household budgets and consumption   (continued)

country	income (latest) percent received by — lowest 20% of households	highest 10% of households	by source (percent) wages, salaries	self-employment	transfer payments[a]	other[b]	consumption expenditure per capita private final, U.S.$ (1995)	by kind or end use (percent of household or personal budget; latest) food[c]	housing[d]	clothing[e]	health care	energy, water	education
Egypt	9.8[1]	25.0[1]	...	...	...	...	740	50.2	10.5[2]	10.9	2.7	[2]	[3]
El Salvador	3.4[12]	40.5[12]	...	...	...	...	1,520	37.0[18]	12.1[18]	6.7[18]	4.2[18]	3.6[18]	3.7[18]
Equatorial Guinea	...	...	57.0[6]	42.0[6]	—	1.0[6]	310	62.0[6]	...	10.0[6]	6.0[6]	...	...
Eritrea	...	...	...	...	...	...	170	...	...	...	...	...	...
Estonia	6.2[12]	26.2[12]	53.0	5.7	12.8	28.5	1,390	41.0	9.6	8.4	[19]	6.5	3.1
Ethiopia	7.1[1]	33.7[1]	0.2	79.5	—	20.3	87	49.0	7.0	6.0	3.0	7.0	4.0
Faroe Islands	...	...	88.3	11.7	...	...	...	40.9	11.0	8.0	...	18.9	...
Fiji	3.7	37.8	81.5	9.1	—	9.4	1,430[10]	34.7	15.6[2]	9.3	2.4	[2]	[3]
Finland	10.0[12]	21.6[12]	70.3	7.4	9.7	12.6	13,260	22.5	16.9	5.0	4.8	4.6	[3]
France	7.2[12]	25.1[12]	51.1	14.1	27.5	7.3	15,810	17.4	16.2	6.1	9.8	3.8	0.7
French Guiana	...	...	74.6		25.4		...	30.0[15]	16.1[2]	6.7	4.4	[2]	[3]
French Polynesia	...	...	61.9	18.5	16.6	3.0	4,310[20]	39.6	9.7	6.3	1.0	8.1	1.0
Gabon	3.3	54.4	...	...	...	...	4,060	...	...	...	...	...	...
Gambia, The	...	...	...	...	...	...	330	58.0[21]	5.1[21]	17.5[21]	...	5.4[21]	...
Gaza Strip	...	...	...	...	...	...	910[22]	...	...	...	...	...	...
Georgia	...	...	34.5	21.6[7]	21.7	22.0	430	38.3	...	14.8	...	0.3	...
Germany	8.2[12]	23.7[12]	57.9	[8]	21.3	20.8[8]	16,850	19.0	16.9	7.9	3.5	4.1	[3]
Ghana	8.4[1]	26.1[1]	41.6[23]	47.1[23]	—	11.3[23]	290	57.4	11.5[2]	14.3	1.3	[2]	[3]
Greece	7.5[12]	25.3[12]	34.0	22.8	17.0	26.2	8,140	29.9	14.1	6.5	3.1	3.3	0.5
Greenland	...	...	...	...	...	...	11,110	30.1	10.0	7.7	0.3	5.4	...
Grenada	...	...	...	...	...	...	1,650	40.7[15]	11.9	5.2	[24]	3.9	[3]
Guadeloupe	...	...	78.9	13.7	7.4	—	4,080[27]	31.6[15]	11.3[2]	9.3	4.6	[2]	[3]
Guam	...	...	...	...	...	...	...	24.1	28.6	10.6	4.8	...	...
Guatemala	2.1[12]	46.6[12]	...	...	...	...	1,180	64.4	16.0[2]	3.1	0.6	[2]	0.3
Guernsey	...	...	...	...	...	...	...	23.7	12.1	7.5	...	8.2	...
Guinea	6.4[1]	32.0[1]	...	...	...	...	510	61.5	7.3[2]	7.9	11.1	[2]	...
Guinea-Bissau	2.1[1]	42.4[1]	...	...	...	...	230	...	...	...	...	...	...
Guyana	4.0	40.0[11]	73.0	...	6.3	20.7	...	42.5[15]	21.4	8.6	...	5.2	[3]
Haiti	...	...	...	...	...	...	320	51.1[15]	4.3	8.7	2.2	...	[3]
Honduras	3.4[12]	42.1[12]	58.3	[8]	1.8	39.9[8]	450	44.4	22.4[2]	9.1	7.0	[2]	[3]
Hong Kong	...	...	55.0		19.2	5.8	13,880	15.1	15.7[2]	21.3	5.0	[2]	0.5
Hungary	8.8[12]	24.8[12]	73.1	2.7	10.2	14.0	4,270	38.1	5.7	7.4	1.5	6.1	0.7
Iceland	4.7	27.3	...	...	...	...	15,850	31.3	16.0	7.5	2.3	2.9	1.3
India	8.1[1]	33.5[1]	42.2	39.7	18.1		210	52.2	6.1[25]	10.0	2.4	4.7[25]	1.8
Indonesia	8.0[12]	30.3[12]	42.1	41.5	2.5	13.9	640	47.5[18]	20.1[2,18]	5.5[18]	...	[2]	...
Iran	3.8	41.7	37.4[18]	30.5[18]	32.1[18]		1,040	42.6[15]	24.9[2]	11.8	3.9	[2]	[3]
Iraq	...	...	23.9	33.9	23.0	18.6	1,710[13]	50.2	19.9[2]	10.6	1.6	[2]	[3]
Ireland	6.7[12]	27.4[12]	58.6	13.3	19.9	8.2	9,650	30.5	7.1	7.4	3.2	6.1	2.4
Isle of Man	6.4	26.6	64.1	6.6	16.9	12.4	...	31.0	7.9	7.0	...	11.0	...
Israel	6.9[12]	26.9[12]	63.4[18,26]	14.6[18,26]	18.9[18,26]	3.1[18,26]	9,930	23.8	19.8	5.3	6.2	2.4	2.9
Italy	8.7[12]	21.8[12]	41.7	25.9	20.3	12.1	11,860	19.5	10.0	9.8	6.7	3.8	0.7
Jamaica	7.0[1]	28.9[1]	63.6	13.9	14.0	8.5	1,770	35.7	5.7	4.6	2.8	4.9	0.2
Japan	10.6[12]	21.7[12]	59.3	11.1	19.5	10.1	24,670	22.6	6.7	6.0	2.7	5.6	5.3
Jersey	...	...	...	...	...	...	...	28.3	14.9	8.3	...	6.5	...
Jordan	7.6[1]	29.8[1]	51.4	11.1	13.7	23.8	1,020	40.6	15.8	6.7	2.2	5.0	3.5
Kazakhstan	6.7[1]	26.3[1]	67.7	5.8[7]	16.9	9.6	1,290	29.6	2.6	...	...	...	...
Kenya	5.0	34.9	...	...	...	...	220	46.5	10.0	7.7	2.2	2.6	1.0
Kiribati	...	...	69.7	21.4	6.0	2.9	370[4]	50.0[15]	7.5[2,5]	8.0	...	[2]	...
Korea, North	...	...	...	...	...	...	...	46.5[27]	0.6[27]	29.9[27]	...	3.3[27]	...
Korea, South	7.5[1]	24.3[1]	53.8	25.1	13.1	8.0	5,390	29.7	4.1	7.7	5.0	4.0	14.2
Kuwait	...	...	53.8	20.8	25.4		...	28.1[15]	15.5	8.1	0.7	9.6	[3]
Kyrgyzstan	6.3[12]	31.7[12]	67.3		32.7		670	33.5	2.2	...	...	...	...
Laos	9.6[1]	26.4[1]	...	...	...	...	140[9]	...	...	...	...	...	...
Latvia	7.6[12]	25.9[12]	67.0	5.4[7]	17.4	10.2	2,400	51.6	...	...	...	...	...
Lebanon	5.0	45.0	27.9	...	3.0	69.1	3,010	42.8[6]	16.8[6]	8.6[6]	7.2[6]	4.5[6]	3.9[6]
Lesotho	2.8[1]	43.4[1]	22.4	27.8	44.7	5.1	530	48.0[15]	10.1	16.4	...	...	...
Liberia	5.0	73.0[11]	...	...	...	...	330[9]	34.4[6]	14.9[6]	13.8[6]	...	5.0[6]	...
Libya	...	...	...	...	...	...	2,330[9]	37.2[15]	32.2[2]	6.9	3.3	[2]	[3]
Liechtenstein	...	...	...	...	...	...	...	21.3[15]	18.0	6.6	7.7	4.4	[3]
Lithuania	7.8[1]	25.6[1]	66.4	9.7	18.7	5.2	1,910	50.3	...	...	...	...	...
Luxembourg	10.0	34.0[11]	67.1	4.8	28.1	—	15,140[28]	12.8	13.7	5.9	7.3	6.1	[3]
Macau	...	...	65.0	18.1	7.0	9.9	5,480	39.2[15]	17.5	6.8	4.0	5.2	[3]
Macedonia	...	...	57.7	17.2	16.2	9.0	1,010	40.6	1.9	7.8	3.0	7.8	[3]
Madagascar	5.1[1]	36.7[1]	58.8[6,29]	14.1[6,29]	—	27.1[6,29]	220	59.0	6.0	6.0	2.0	6.0	4.0
Malawi	10.4	40.1	83.3	6.0	—	11.7	109	30.0	4.0	9.0	4.0	5.0	10.0
Malaysia	4.5[12]	37.9[12]	...	...	...	...	2,090	28.7	10.2[2]	4.3	2.5	[2]	0.6
Maldives	...	...	...	...	...	...	270[9]	57.4	1.6	8.0	2.5	...	[3]
Mali	4.6[1]	40.4[1]	...	...	...	...	200	57.0	2.0	6.0	2.0	6.0	4.0
Malta	...	...	63.8	19.3	—	16.9	5,380	31.2	3.5	7.6	3.5	2.0	0.4
Marshall Islands	...	...	...	...	...	...	...	57.7	15.6[2,5]	12.0	...	[2]	...
Martinique	...	...	80.0	...	...	20.0	4,840[6]	32.1[15]	10.6[2]	8.0	5.2	[2]	[3]
Mauritania	6.2[1]	29.9[1]	...	...	...	...	470	73.1	2.5	8.1	0.9	7.7	0.4
Mauritius	4.0	46.7	51.7	29.0	11.2	8.1	2,290	41.9	8.8	8.4	3.0	6.4	2.9
Mayotte	...	...	...	...	...	...	...	42.2	...	31.5	...	6.8	...
Mexico	3.6[12]	42.8[12]	61.5	29.1	7.8	1.6	2,110	36.6[15]	13.3[2]	8.4	3.4	[2]	[3]
Micronesia	...	...	51.8	23.0	2.1	23.1	...	73.5	...	...	...	...	...
Moldova	6.9[12]	25.8[12]	41.2	10.4	15.3	33.1	220	...	...	...	...	...	...
Monaco	...	...	...	...	...	...	...	...	...	...	...	...	...
Mongolia	7.3[1]	24.5[1]	72.1	9.5[7]	9.7	8.7	230	39.1	5.9[2]	23.4	0.5	[2]	2.9
Morocco	6.5[1]	30.9[1]	...	...	...	...	900	38.0	7.0	11.0	5.0	2.0	8.0
Mozambique	6.5[1]	31.7[1]	51.6		48.4		57	74.6	11.7	3.7	0.8	...	[3]
Myanmar (Burma)	8.0	40.0[11]	...	...	...	...	750[28]	49.1[6]	10.4[6]	15.3[6]	2.4[6]	4.0[6]	5.9[6]
Namibia	...	...	67.1	27.5	5.4	...	1,050	...	...	...	...	...	...
Nauru	...	...	...	...	...	...	...	...	...	...	...	...	...
Nepal	7.6[1]	29.8[1]	25.1	63.4	11.5		170	61.2	17.3	11.7	3.7	...	[3]

				food consumption, 1998									country
				daily available calories per capita	percent of total calories derived from:								
transportation, communications	household durable goods[f]	recreation[g]	personal effects, other[h]		cereals	potatoes, cassava	meat, poultry	fish	eggs, milk	fruits, vegetables	fats, oils[i]	other[j]	
4.7	5.0	3.3[3]	12.7	3,282	65.4	1.6	2.9	0.6	2.1	6.9	6.1	14.3	Egypt
10.2[18]	5.7[18]	4.3[18]	12.5[18]	2,522	53.4	1.5	2.6	0.2	6.3	3.5	7.7	24.9	El Salvador
...	...	...	22.0[6]	...	...	...	...	...	...	...	...	...	Equatorial Guinea
...	...	...	...	1,744	73.4	4.4	0.6	0.0	1.9	0.1	0.7	18.8	Eritrea
9.2	2.3	5.0[19]	15.0	3,058	38.5	5.3	8.9	1.6	12.7	4.3	13.3	15.4	Estonia
8.0	2.0	...	14.0	1,805	66.3	13.1	3.2	0.0	1.9	0.6	2.8	12.1	Ethiopia
...	6.6	...	14.6	...	...	...	...	...	...	...	...	...	Faroe Islands
13.8	9.3	4.3[3]	10.6	2,852	42.3	6.9	8.5	1.4	3.0	1.8	18.7	17.3	Fiji
14.8	6.3	9.5[3]	15.6	3,180	33.6	4.2	16.3	2.0	15.7	3.9	12.9	18.6	Finland
16.1	7.7	6.9	15.3	3,541	24.3	3.4	16.5	1.2	12.0	4.7	19.7	18.3	France
17.5	7.9	6.2[3]	11.2	2,818	32.4	7.9	13.2	2.1	7.5	7.0	10.5	19.3	French Guiana
16.4	4.4	4.0	9.5	2,924	33.6	4.0	13.3	4.4	6.1	3.0	13.6	22.1	French Polynesia
...	...	...	...	2,560	29.5	17.9	7.3	3.1	2.4	16.4	7.9	15.5	Gabon
...	...	...	14.0[21]	2,559	54.0	0.7	1.3	1.9	1.4	0.9	17.7	22.1	Gambia, The
...	...	...	...	...	...	...	...	...	...	...	...	...	Gaza Strip
...	5.9	...	40.7	2,252	60.5	4.8	4.9	0.2	7.6	4.8	3.0	14.2	Georgia
17.8	9.4	10.6[3]	10.8	3,402	22.5	4.1	11.7	0.8	10.3	5.7	21.6	23.3	Germany
3.3	3.8	3.9[3]	4.5	2,684	26.2	48.2	1.2	1.8	0.2	9.6	4.6	8.3	Ghana
17.5	6.9	5.2	13.0	3,630	29.1	3.5	8.9	1.2	11.8	8.6	20.0	16.8	Greece
8.0	9.2	15.5	13.8	...	...	...	...	...	...	...	...	...	Greenland
9.1	13.7	4.6[3]	10.9[24]	2,681	25.3	2.5	9.1	1.5	9.5	9.2	13.1	29.8	Grenada
20.5	9.3	4.7[3]	8.7	2,732	37.8	2.6	10.8	2.6	8.5	8.4	13.1	16.1	Guadeloupe
18.0	...	5.1	8.8	...	...	...	...	...	...	...	...	...	Guam
7.0	5.0	0.9	2.7	2,159	55.3	0.4	3.6	0.1	5.1	3.1	7.0	25.4	Guatemala
15.7	8.3	...	24.7	3,257	22.8	6.1	14.4	1.0	11.6	5.0	19.1	20.0	Guernsey
5.1	2.9	4.1	0.1	2,315	42.9	15.6	0.9	1.2	1.0	13.0	14.7	10.8	Guinea
...	...	...	...	2,411	61.2	7.4	4.6	0.2	1.4	4.2	13.0	8.1	Guinea-Bissau
4.8	2.9	6.4[3]	8.2	2,476	47.3	3.8	4.8	4.2	5.4	2.8	4.1	27.6	Guyana
7.6	9.2	5.3[3]	11.6	1,876	46.7	8.8	3.3	0.3	2.0	7.4	8.8	22.8	Haiti
3.0	8.3	2.4[3]	3.1	2,343	46.7	0.3	3.6	0.3	8.6	6.7	11.9	21.9	Honduras
8.4	17.5	8.1	8.4	3,200	27.1	1.6	20.0	3.3	5.2	4.0	19.7	19.2	Hong Kong
15.2	8.8	5.9	10.6	3,408	25.4	3.6	10.1	0.2	8.4	5.4	22.7	24.1	Hungary
14.5	7.6	9.6	7.0	3,222	20.7	3.2	14.3	3.6	14.6	4.0	13.4	26.2	Iceland
10.6	3.1	1.8	5.7	2,466	62.7	1.6	0.9	0.4	4.5	3.2	8.5	18.3	India
...	2.9[18]	...	24.0	2,850	64.6	5.8	2.2	1.3	0.6	2.3	7.8	15.4	Indonesia
5.0	6.4	1.7[3]	3.7	2,822	51.2	3.2	4.3	0.3	3.8	11.2	10.8	15.1	Iran
6.5	6.7	0.8[3]	3.7	2,419	59.4	1.2	1.4	0.1	1.9	8.0	19.5	8.6	Iraq
14.0	7.2	8.9	13.1	3,622	26.8	6.0	13.1	0.8	11.3	4.0	16.5	21.4	Ireland
14.9	5.7	...	22.5	3,257	22.8	6.1	14.4	1.0	11.6	5.0	19.1	20.0	Isle of Man
12.9	10.8	4.3	11.6	3,466	33.5	2.5	8.2	0.9	7.6	8.6	18.3	20.3	Israel
13.2	9.5	8.4	18.4	3,608	31.8	1.9	11.1	1.1	8.9	7.2	22.0	15.9	Italy
12.4	5.5	2.1	26.1	2,711	30.5	9.3	8.5	0.8	5.3	7.2	13.1	25.3	Jamaica
11.0	3.7	9.5	26.9	2,874	40.7	2.5	5.8	6.3	6.5	4.3	12.0	21.8	Japan
13.9	7.1	...	21.0	3,257	22.8	6.1	14.4	1.0	11.6	5.0	19.1	20.0	Jersey
11.2	6.1	4.0	4.9	2,791	52.7	1.1	5.1	0.2	5.4	3.9	15.3	16.3	Jordan
...	...	...	67.8	2,517	54.4	4.1	9.1	0.2	12.0	2.1	7.4	10.8	Kazakhstan
8.4	9.4	3.1	9.1	1,968	52.4	8.6	3.7	0.5	7.2	3.2	9.3	15.3	Kenya
8.0	5	...	26.5	2,977	34.7	8.3	4.6	4.6	1.6	4.6	7.2	34.4	Kiribati
...	3.8[27]	...	15.9	1,899	64.5	1.1	3.1	1.3	1.0	7.6	5.8	15.5	Korea, North
11.3	5.0	—— 19.0 ——		3,069	49.7	1.1	9.6	3.0	2.2	7.1	9.7	17.7	Korea, South
13.7	11.2	5.2[3]	7.9	3,059	36.8	1.9	11.2	0.5	9.8	8.4	10.2	21.2	Kuwait
...	...	...	64.3	2,535	58.3	6.7	8.7	—	13.0	2.1	3.6	7.6	Kyrgyzstan
...	...	...	...	2,175	77.7	3.8	4.4	0.7	0.5	2.2	2.3	8.5	Laos
...	...	...	54.8	2,994	32.7	8.4	6.0	0.9	12.9	3.8	15.3	20.0	Latvia
5.4[6]	2.6[6]	1.9[6]	6.3[6]	3,285	34.6	3.9	4.9	0.4	5.2	15.9	13.9	21.2	Lebanon
4.7	11.9	...	8.8	2,210	75.5	4.3	3.4	—	1.1	1.4	3.1	11.2	Lesotho
...	6.1[6]	...	25.8[6]	1,979	41.5	20.4	2.0	0.4	0.5	5.5	19.8	10.0	Liberia
9.4	4.6	8.5[3]	2.5	3,267	46.3	2.0	4.8	0.3	5.7	7.3	17.0	16.7	Libya
13.3	5.8	16.3[3]	6.6	3,222	22.1	2.3	14.8	0.8	12.5	6.1	18.7	22.7	Liechtenstein
...	...	...	49.7	3,104	45.5	7.8	8.9	0.9	6.9	5.3	10.1	14.6	Lithuania
19.1	10.8	4.2[3]	20.1	3,606	20.4	5.2	8.6	1.1	10.8	6.5	25.7	21.7	Luxembourg
8.2	3.0	8.8[3]	7.3	2,471	36.3	0.7	15.7	2.3	4.7	3.7	20.7	15.8	Macau
6.5	4.2	3.3[3]	1.8	2,938	39.7	3.3	7.0	0.3	5.2	6.9	15.7	21.8	Macedonia
4.0	1.0	...	12.0	2,001	53.0	21.1	5.5	0.7	3.1	3.8	4.4	8.3	Madagascar
10.0	3.0	...	25.0	2,226	59.0	15.8	1.3	0.4	0.5	4.2	4.0	14.7	Malawi
20.9	7.7	11.0	14.1	2,901	41.6	2.1	9.2	3.1	5.2	3.4	12.5	22.8	Malaysia
2.6	17.0	5.9[3]	5.0	2,451	43.5	3.2	1.4	13.1	4.3	5.6	5.2	23.7	Maldives
10.0	1.0	...	12.0	2,118	69.9	0.5	4.2	0.8	4.6	1.2	7.4	11.3	Mali
16.4	9.9	7.1	18.4	3,382	30.8	4.0	8.8	1.6	11.3	7.9	11.5	24.0	Malta
...	5	...	14.7	...	...	...	...	...	...	...	...	...	Marshall Islands
20.7	9.4	5.4[3]	8.6	2,865	30.0	4.2	12.1	2.9	8.5	11.0	8.7	22.5	Martinique
2.0	1.2	4.0	0.1	2,640	54.8	0.4	4.0	0.9	10.8	1.2	9.9	18.1	Mauritania
10.0	6.4	—	12.2	2,944	44.7	1.3	4.8	1.2	6.3	3.0	16.6	22.2	Mauritius
5.1	8.8	...	5.6	...	...	...	...	...	...	...	...	...	Mayotte
10.0	11.8	5.5[3]	11.0	3,144	46.2	0.8	8.2	0.7	6.0	4.0	11.3	22.8	Mexico
...	...	...	26.5	...	...	...	...	...	...	...	...	...	Micronesia
...	...	...	...	2,763	48.4	4.2	4.0	0.1	8.9	6.6	8.2	19.7	Moldova
...	...	...	...	3,541	24.3	3.4	16.5	1.2	6.3	3.0	16.6	22.2	Monaco
3.5	8.0	0.4	16.2	2,010	47.0	2.2	27.2	—	10.4	1.2	4.7	7.2	Mongolia
8.0	5.0	...	16.0	3,165	59.7	2.0	2.8	0.5	2.0	5.4	10.4	17.3	Morocco
...	...	1.4[3]	7.9	1,911	41.2	37.3	1.4	0.2	0.6	1.4	8.9	9.1	Mozambique
3.8[6]	0.5[6]	1.1[6]	7.5[6]	2,832	76.3	0.5	2.0	1.0	0.9	2.6	7.0	9.6	Myanmar (Burma)
...	...	...	...	2,107	48.6	13.9	5.6	0.6	3.4	1.9	5.1	20.9	Namibia
...	...	...	...	...	...	...	...	...	...	...	...	...	Nauru
1.2	...	2.9[3]	2.0	2,170	76.8	3.4	2.0	0.1	3.8	2.5	4.4	7.0	Nepal

Household budgets and consumption   (continued)

country	income (latest)						consumption expenditure						
	percent received by		by source (percent)				per capita private final, U.S.$ (1995)	by kind or end use (percent of household or personal budget; latest)					
	lowest 20% of households	highest 10% of households	wages, salaries	self-employment	transfer payments[a]	other[b]		food[c]	housing[d]	clothing[e]	health care	energy, water	education
Netherlands, The	7.3[1]	25.1[1]	48.2	10.7	29.1	12.0	15,290	13.6	14.9	7.1	12.9	3.1	0.7
Netherlands Antilles	...	...	...	...	...	...	6,050[10]	24.4[30]	10.4[30]	8.7[30]	2.2[30]	8.3[30]	1.2[30]
New Caledonia			68.2	18.1	13.7		5,410[31]	25.9	23.3[2,5]	3.5	3.2	[2]	...
New Zealand	2.7[12]	29.8[12]	65.8	9.8	15.2	9.1	10,300	20.0	19.4	4.4	2.9	3.2	1.5
Nicaragua	4.2[1]	39.8[1]	...	...	...	...	360						
Niger	2.6	35.4					210	50.5	19.1[5]	7.3	...	...	...
Nigeria	4.4[1]	40.8[1]	30.2[18]	46.3[18]	0.9[18]	22.6[18]	350[32]	48.0	3.0	5.0	3.0	1.0	4.0
Northern Mariana Islands	...	...	...	...	...	...		49.2[15]	19.5[2,5]	9.1	[19]	[2]	...
Norway	9.7[12]	21.8[12]	58.8	9.9	24.2	7.1	16,570	23.5	13.7	7.0	5.4	6.2	0.6
Oman	...	...	...	...	...	...	3,000	40.6	24.6	5.1	2.4	3.2	[3]
Pakistan	9.5[1]	27.6[1]	22.0	56.0	——22.0——		300	37.0	11.0	6.0	1.0	5.0	1.0
Palau	...	...	63.7	7.4	18.5	10.4	...	...	...	...	...	...	...
Panama	3.6[1]	35.7[1]	60.8[6]	12.8[6]	13.2[6]	13.2[6]	1,570	34.9	12.6[2]	5.1	3.5	[2]	[3]
Papua New Guinea	4.5[1]	40.5[1]	57.3	[8]	1.1	41.6[8]	1,140	40.9	12.5[5]	6.2	...	4.9	...
Paraguay	2.3	46.6	33.9	[8]	2.5	63.6[8]	1,590	48.7	16.4	9.7	3.4	—	1.5
Peru	4.4[12]	35.4[12]	31.2	65.1	3.7	...	1,820	44.1[15]	6.8[2]	10.1	2.7	[2]	[3]
Philippines	5.4[1]	36.6[1]	45.7	42.5	3.4	8.4	800	56.8	4.1[2]	3.9	...	[2]	...
Poland	7.7[12]	26.3[12]	34.0	4.3	20.7	41.0	1,940	41.2	2.8	10.9	8.1	1.0	[3]
Portugal	7.3[12]	28.4[12]	46.4	[8]	21.8	31.8[8]	6,860	34.8	2.0	10.3	4.5	3.0	1.4
Puerto Rico	3.2	34.7	56.3	6.4	29.5	7.8	5,640[10]	20.6	11.8[2]	7.4	11.6	[2]	3.1
Qatar	...	...	80.8	5.6	...	13.6	3,600[4]	24.5	35.1[5]	9.1	1.0	1.9	4.3
Réunion	...	...	68.9	[8]	16.0	15.1[8]	4,820[31]	22.4	11.8	7.9	2.2	2.2	[3]
Romania	8.9[12]	22.7[12]	62.6	——37.4——			1,570	51.1	16.4[2,6]	15.7	1.2	[2]	[3]
Russia	4.4[1]	38.7[1]	68.5	6.4	15.7	12.1	1,180	34.8	4.2	22.3	...	...	...
Rwanda	9.7[1]	24.2[1]	10.4[33]	47.7[33]	13.9[33]	28.0[33]	130	32.1[33]	13.1[33]	9.4[33]	1.3[33]	1.2[33]	[33]
St. Kitts and Nevis	...	...	...	...	...	...	2,480[28]	55.6[15]	7.6	7.5	...	6.6	...
St. Lucia	...	...	...	...	...	...	...	49.6[15]	13.5	6.5	2.3	4.5	[3]
St. Vincent and the Grenadines	...	...	...	...	...	...	1,700	59.8	6.3	7.7	...	6.2	...
Samoa	...	...	49.4	22.8	...	27.8	710[1]	58.8	5.1[5]	4.2	...	5.0	...
San Marino	...	...	...	...	...	...	...	22.1	20.9[2]	8.0	2.6	[2]	[3]
São Tomé and Príncipe	...	...	...	...	...	...	270						
Saudi Arabia	...	...	...	...	...	...	2,980	52.2[18,34]	17.2[18,34]	6.6[18,34]	2.1[18,34]	1.8[18,34]	1.1[18,34]
Senegal	6.4[1]	33.5[1]	51.6[6]	——48.4[6]——			380	49.0	7.0	11.0	2.0	4.0	6.0
Seychelles	4.1	35.6	77.2	3.8	3.2	15.8	3,410[32]	53.9	13.6	4.2	0.4	9.1	...
Sierra Leone	1.1[1]	43.6[1]	27.9	61.6	——10.5——		190	63.8	5.8[2]	7.3	4.5	[2]	[3]
Singapore	5.1	33.5	81.2	16.8	——2.0——		11,710	18.7	10.2[2]	7.1	4.6	[2]	1.4
Slovakia	11.9[12]	18.2[12]	76.7	8.7	14.4[8]		1,580	26.8	7.6[2]	8.9	...	[2]	...
Slovenia	8.4[12]	20.7[12]	52.4	13.0	23.4	11.2	5,460	30.8	18.3	8.5	5.0	7.3	[3]
Solomon Islands	...	...	74.1	——25.9——			820[4]	46.8	21.9[2,5]	5.7	[19]	[2]	...
Somalia	...	...	...	...	...	...	...	62.3[6,15]	15.3[6]	5.6[6]	...	4.3[6]	...
South Africa	2.9[1]	45.9[1]	73.6	[8]	4.9	21.5[8]	1,970	29.3	12.6[2]	7.5	4.5	[2]	1.4
Spain	7.5[12]	25.2[12]	48.5	27.5	19.5	4.5	8,840	21.6[15]	12.6[2]	8.6	4.7	[2]	[3]
Sri Lanka	8.0[1]	28.0[1]	48.5	[8]	9.7	41.8[8]	520	48.0	1.9	10.1	1.8	3.3	0.8
Sudan, The	4.0	34.6	...	...	...	...	1,050[35]	63.6	11.5	5.3	4.1	3.8	[3]
Suriname	...	...	74.6	...	3.2	22.2	5,960[10]	39.9[6]	4.4[6]	11.0[6]	3.6[6]	6.9[6]	2.6[6]
Swaziland	2.8	54.5	44.4	22.2	12.2	21.2	500	33.5[15]	13.4[2]	6.0	1.8	[2]	[3]
Sweden	9.6[12]	20.1[12]	58.9	9.7	25.8	5.6	13,680	21.3	19.9	8.6	3.2	4.9	0.1
Switzerland	6.9[12]	25.2[12]	63.6	[8]	16.5	19.9[8]	26,060	27.0[15]	13.1	4.4	9.9	7.7	[3]
Syria	...	...	40.7	...	25.1	34.2	2,210	58.8[15]	16.0[2]	7.5	...	[2]	[3]
Taiwan	7.1	25.5	64.5	19.7	4.5	11.3	12,230	26.8	22.5	5.6	7.8	3.0	5.6
Tajikistan	...	...	64.3	5.6[7]	30.1	—	340	65.3	...	...	...	...	...
Tanzania	6.8[1]	30.1[1]	28.1	34.2	3.5	34.2	150	66.7	8.3	9.9	1.3	7.6	...
Thailand	6.4[1]	32.4[1]	36.4	45.0	0.9	17.7	1,540	29.0	11.6	8.0	1.7		0.5
Togo	8.0	30.5	...	...	...	...	210	42.5[6]	13.4[2,6]	11.5[6]	5.0[6]	[2,6]	[3,6]
Tonga	...	...	...	...	...	...		49.3	10.5	5.6	0.3	2.7	...
Trinidad and Tobago	2.6	33.6	...	...	...	...	2,050	25.5[15]	21.6	10.4	[19]	...	1.5
Tunisia	5.9[1]	30.7[1]	...	...	...	...	1,260	39.0	10.7	6.0	3.0	5.1	1.8
Turkey	5.8[1]	32.3[1]	24.1	51.4	10.8	13.7	1,940	38.5	22.8[2]	9.0	2.6	[2]	1.4
Turkmenistan	6.1[1]	31.7[1]	56.6	26.0[7]	14.4	3.0	570[10]	...	...	...	...	...	...
Tuvalu	...	...	17.9	76.1		6.0	...	45.5	11.5[5]	7.5	...	...	...
Uganda	6.6[1]	31.2[1]	...	...	...	...	260	57.1[6,15]	...	5.5[6]	...	7.3[6]	...
Ukraine	8.6[1]	26.4[1]	66.4	9.3	13.4	10.9	490	41.3	1.7	...	...	1.2	[3]
United Arab Emirates	...	...	...	...	...	...	7,940	24.1	23.7	9.1	1.1	1.2	3.9
United Kingdom	6.6[12]	27.3[12]	66.2	9.8	13.9	11.0	12,020	17.1	21.7	6.0	...	4.6	2.2
United States	5.2[12]	30.5[12]	64.4	9.0	19.3	7.3	18,840	15.4	14.9	6.9	17.0	3.5	2.2
Uruguay	5.4[12]	32.7[12]	53.5	17.0	——29.5——		4,140	39.9	17.6[2]	7.0	9.3	[2]	1.3
Uzbekistan	7.4[12]	25.2[12]	59.8	18.5	21.7	—	950						
Vanuatu	...	...	59.0	33.7	——7.3——		680	30.5[15]	29.0[2,5]	4.7	[19]	[2]	...
Venezuela	3.7[12]	37.0[12]	...	...	...	...	2,490	30.4	11.5	10.6	2.9	3.0	0.8
Vietnam	8.0[1]	29.9[1]	17.2	64.6	17.6	0.5	280	62.4	2.5	5.0	...	...	2.9
Virgin Islands (U.S.)	...	...	65.7	2.6	13.0	12.7	...	25.3[36]	24.9[36]	5.4[36]	...	6.5[36]	...
West Bank	...	...	...	...	...	...	1,380[22]	...	...	...	...	...	...
Western Sahara	...	...											
Yemen	6.1[1]	30.8[1]	...	...	...	...	310	61.0[37]	13.2[37]	...	1.1[37]	6.1[37]	...
Yugoslavia	...	...	41.7	15.8	12.7	29.8	2,480[15]	51.6	1.4	7.4	5.2	8.4	[3]
Zambia	4.2[1]	39.2[1]	79.9	17.8	1.3	1.0	220	36.0	7.0	10.0	8.0	4.0	14.0
Zimbabwe	4.0[1]	46.9[1]	92.0	1.0	...	7.0	580	30.1[15]	6.5	10.3	7.1	8.9	6.0

[1]Data refer to consumption shares by fractiles of persons.   [2]Housing includes energy, water.   [3]Recreation includes education.   [4]1988.   [5]Housing includes household durable goods.   [6]Capital city only.   [7]Agricultural self-employment only.   [8]Other includes self-employment.   [9]1989.   [10]1993.   [11]Highest 20%.   [12]Data refer to income shares by fractiles of persons.   [13]1985.   [14]1990.   [15]Includes tobacco.   [16]Includes wage taxes.   [17]Personal effects, other includes education and recreation.   [18]Urban areas only.   [19]Recreation includes health care.   [20]1984.   [21]Low-income population in Banjul

transportation, communications	household durable goods[f]	recreation[g]	personal effects, other[h]	daily available calories per capita	cereals	potatoes, cassava	meat, poultry	fish	eggs, milk	fruits, vegetables	fats, oils[i]	other[j]	country
13.3	7.1	9.7	17.6	3,282	17.1	4.5	15.0	1.0	15.0	6.1	16.1	25.1	Netherlands, The
19.5[30]	10.0[30]	4.2[30]	10.1[30]	2,659	28.2	2.3	18.9	1.4	10.8	5.0	13.6	19.7	Netherlands Antilles
16.1	[5]	6.7	21.3	2,812	30.9	6.1	13.1	1.5	8.6	3.9	16.0	19.9	New Caledonia
17.1	10.9	——— 20.6 ———		3,315	22.1	4.1	15.1	1.3	11.1	7.4	16.8	22.3	New Zealand
...	...	...	...	2,208	50.4	1.3	2.4	0.1	4.3	2.7	10.9	27.9	Nicaragua
	[5]	...	23.1	1,966	70.5	3.2	2.6	0.1	2.2	1.7	4.4	15.2	Niger
3.0	6.0	...	27.0	2,882	45.8	18.6	2.4	0.4	1.0	4.4	14.1	13.3	Nigeria
8.3	[5]	13.9[19]	—	...	...	...	...	...	...	...	...	...	Northern Mariana Islands
12.8	6.9	8.8	15.1	3,425	27.4	4.3	10.7	3.5	12.2	4.9	17.7	19.2	Norway
8.9	7.1	4.1[3]	4.0	...	...	...	...	...	...	...	...	...	Oman
13.0	5.0	...	21.0	2,447	57.0	0.9	3.1	0.2	8.5	2.9	13.2	14.3	Pakistan
...	...	...	...	...	...	...	...	...	...	...	...	...	Palau
15.1	8.4	11.7[3]	8.7	2,476	37.0	2.7	7.5	1.1	7.4	5.7	16.1	22.5	Panama
13.0	[5]	...	22.5	2,168	31.2	25.4	7.7	1.3	0.6	17.6	6.2	9.9	Papua New Guinea
4.5	6.2	2.3	7.3	2,577	27.8	13.9	11.5	0.4	7.3	4.3	16.2	18.7	Paraguay
7.3	7.5	7.6[3]	13.9	2,420	35.7	13.4	4.3	1.8	4.5	6.4	11.6	22.4	Peru
5.0	12.8	...	17.3	2,280	51.7	4.2	8.8	3.0	2.2	8.3	5.9	15.9	Philippines
8.9	8.3	15.0[3]	3.8	3,351	34.4	7.4	10.4	1.0	8.6	4.5	15.6	18.0	Poland
15.4	8.6	4.4	15.6	3,691	28.6	6.3	10.8	2.4	8.3	7.1	17.0	19.6	Portugal
11.8	11.2	7.9	14.7	...	...	...	...	...	...	...	...	...	Puerto Rico
13.0	[5]	——— 11.1 ———		...	...	...	...	...	...	...	...	...	Qatar
24.9	6.0	10.1[3]	12.5	3,308	41.4	1.7	11.9	1.5	5.2	5.0	9.8	23.5	Réunion
6.6	[5]	4.5[3]	4.5	3,263	49.5	4.5	7.4	0.1	11.3	4.5	10.5	12.2	Romania
...	9.4	...	30.8	2,835	41.3	8.0	9.0	1.6	10.3	3.4	9.6	20.6	Russia
1.7[33]	5.3[33]	0.4[33]	35.5[33]	2,035	22.4	23.1	1.1	—	1.4	25.9	5.5	—	Rwanda
4.3	9.4	...	9.0	2,766	24.9	2.6	13.6	1.9	8.6	4.6	11.6	32.1	St. Kitts and Nevis
6.3	5.8	3.2[3]	8.3	2,842	34.3	4.8	14.0	1.3	6.8	9.3	6.9	22.7	St. Lucia
3.7	6.6	...	9.7	2,554	35.2	4.3	10.4	1.1	6.1	5.2	9.6	28	St. Vincent and the Grenadines
9.0	[5]	...	17.9	...	...	...	...	...	...	...	...	...	Samoa
17.6	7.2	7.1[3]	14.5	3,608	31.8	1.9	11.1	1.1	8.9	7.2	22.0	15.9	San Marino
...	...	...	...	2,201	28.3	15.4	1.4	2.1	0.8	17.0	10.6	24.3	São Tomé and Príncipe
4.5[18,34]	5.9[18,34]	...	8.6[18,34]	2,888	46.6	1.1	7.3	0.4	4.9	10.1	11.4	18.2	Saudi Arabia
5.0	2.0	...	12.0	2,277	57.5	1.0	3.7	2.8	2.4	2.0	18.7	11.9	Senegal
6.4	6.6	1.4	4.4	2,462	37.3	1.2	5.6	5.1	6.5	5.8	11.5	27.1	Seychelles
4.4	3.9	3.8[3]	4.8	2,045	53.4	10.4	1.0	1.4	0.6	2.9	17.6	12.8	Sierra Leone
13.8	8.9	13.1	23.3	...	...	...	...	...	...	...	...	...	Singapore
...	3.9	...	26.2	2,953	27.3	4.3	10.5	0.3	8.9	4.7	20.8	23.2	Slovakia
12.7	3.3	6.1[3]	8.0	2,950	35.4	3.5	11.1	0.4	12.0	5.3	15.2	17.2	Slovenia
9.9	[5]	[19]	15.7	2,130	33.3	36.3	3.1	3.7	0.6	2.7	2.9	17.4	Solomon Islands
...	...	...	12.1[6]	1,531	33.4	1.5	8.7	0.2	28.4	2.8	7.4	17.5	Somalia
16.7	10.0	6.3	11.7	2,909	53.0	2.0	7.0	0.5	4.8	2.8	11.7	18.1	South Africa
15.3	7.1	7.0[3]	23.1	3,348	22.6	4.7	13.4	2.4	9.3	6.7	21.6	19.4	Spain
17.0	3.9	2.4	10.8	2,314	51.3	2.9	0.9	1.9	3.4	4.5	2.9	32.3	Sri Lanka
1.5	5.5	0.7[3]	4.0	2,444	56.5	0.6	5.1	0.1	13.3	2.9	9.5	11.9	Sudan, The
9.5[6]	12.3[6]	5.8[6]	4.0[6]	2,633	41.2	2.3	7.0	1.6	4.8	6.2	12.5	24.5	Suriname
8.8	12.8	3.3[3]	20.4	2,503	48.1	1.3	6.4	—	5.2	1.8	6.2	31.0	Swaziland
15.7	6.6	10.9	8.8	3,114	25.6	3.6	10.2	1.8	14.1	5.2	18.9	20.7	Sweden
12.9	5.1	9.8[3]	10.1	3,222	22.1	2.3	14.8	0.8	12.5	6.1	18.7	22.7	Switzerland
2.4	5.8	2.1[3]	7.4	3,378	53.9	1.2	3.8	0.1	6.6	5.6	12.9	15.9	Syria
10.7	2.2	1.1	4.7	...	...	...	...	...	...	...	...	...	Taiwan
...	...	...	34.7	2,176	67.9	0.1	2.8	—	3.4	4.3	12.2	9.2	Tajikistan
4.1	1.4	0.7	—	1,999	49.0	19.5	2.6	1.1	2.2	5.4	6.8	13.6	Tanzania
12.9	10.9	4.2	14.9	2,462	47.1	1.9	6.6	2.6	2.8	5.7	6.1	27.3	Thailand
9.5[6]	4.4[6]	5.1[3,6]	8.6[6]	2,513	50.7	29.2	2.3	1.3	0.6	1.3	7.2	7.5	Togo
5.8	10.6	0.5	14.7	...	...	...	...	...	...	...	...	...	Tonga
15.2	14.3	[17]	6.2[17]	2,711	36.8	2.8	4.5	0.9	6.8	3.8	14.6	29.9	Trinidad and Tobago
9.0	11.2	7.1	7.1	3,297	52.9	1.8	3.0	0.5	4.6	6.2	15.8	15.3	Tunisia
8.8	9.0	5.6	2.3	3,554	48.4	3.7	2.5	0.4	6.9	7.9	15.1	15.1	Turkey
...	...	...	...	2,684	57.7	0.5	7.6	0.1	8.2	3.4	16.4	6.1	Turkmenistan
10.5	[5]	...	25.0	...	...	...	...	...	...	...	...	...	Tuvalu
5.9[6]	...	...	24.2[6]	2,216	20.4	23.4	3.2	0.8	1.9	25.8	2.2	22.3	Uganda
...	6.8	6.3[3]	43.9	2,878	44.5	8.8	5.8	0.7	10.3	3.4	10.8	15.7	Ukraine
14.1	11.6	4.7	6.5	3,372	33.8	1.6	11.5	1.4	9.5	14.3	10.3	17.7	United Arab Emirates
15.1	8.0	15.9	11.6	3,257	22.8	6.1	14.4	1.0	11.6	5.0	19.1	20.0	United Kingdom
13.9	1.5	5.8	18.9	3,757	23.6	2.9	11.9	0.8	11.7	5.2	17.9	26.1	United States
10.4	6.3	3.1	5.1	2,866	28.9	3.7	19.1	0.6	12.3	4.0	11.0	20.3	Uruguay
...	...	...	...	2,564	55.8	2.1	6.9	—	9.4	4.1	15.3	6.2	Uzbekistan
13.2	[5]	12.3[19]	10.3	2,737	21.4	30.7	9.2	1.6	1.5	6.4	8.9	20.3	Vanuatu
7.1	4.5	2.7	26.4	2,358	34.9	3.1	6.6	1.7	6.5	7.3	15.2	24.7	Venezuela
...	4.6	...	22.6	2,422	70.9	4.0	7.6	1.3	0.5	3.9	3.2	8.6	Vietnam
11.7[36]	4.3[36]	...	21.9[36]	...	...	...	...	...	...	...	...	...	Virgin Islands (U.S.)
...	...	...	...	...	...	...	...	...	...	...	...	...	West Bank
...	...	...	...	...	...	...	...	...	...	...	...	...	Western Sahara
1.9[37]	3.0[37]	...	13.7[37]	2,087	68.7	1.0	2.7	0.7	1.8	3.0	8.2	13.9	Yemen
5.7	1.6	2.4[3]	16.3	2,963	29.4	2.3	16.3	0.2	11.4	6.8	17.8	15.8	Yugoslavia
5.0	1.0	...	15.0	1,950	64.9	14.5	2.7	0.8	1.3	1.5	3.4	10.9	Zambia
1.1	12.9	0.6	16.5	2,153	60.5	2.1	2.3	0.3	3.1	1.0	11.9	18.8	Zimbabwe

food consumption, 1998 — percent of total calories derived from:

and Kombo St. Mary only. [22]1986. [23]Urban areas of Eastern region only. [24]Personal effects, other includes health care. [25]Housing includes water. [26]Wage earners only. [27]Workers and clerical workers only. [28]1992. [29]Malagasy households only. [30]Curaçao only. [31]1987. [32]1994. [33]Rural areas only. [34]Middle-income population only. [35]1991. [36]St. Thomas only. [37]Data refer to former Yemen Arab Republic.

Health services

The provision of health services in most countries is both a principal determinant of the quality of life and a large and growing sector of the national economy. This table summarizes the basic indicators of health personnel; hospitals, by kind and utilization; mortality rates that are most indicative of general health services; external controls on health (adequacy of food supply and availability of safe drinking water); and sources and amounts of expenditure on health care. Each datum refers more or less directly to the availability or use of a particular health service in a country, and, while each may be a representative measure at a national level, each may also conceal considerable differences in availability of the particular service to different segments of a population or regions of a country. In the United States, for example, the availability of physicians ranges from about one per 730 persons in the least well-served states to one per 260 in the best-served, with a rate of one per 150 in the national capital. In addition, even when trained personnel exist and facilities have been created, limited financial resources at the national or local level may leave facilities underserved; or lack of good transportation may prevent those most in need from reaching a clinic or hospital that could help them.

Definitions and limits of data have been made as consistent as possible in the compilation of this table. For example, despite wide variation worldwide in the nature of the qualifying or certifying process that permits an individual to represent himself as a physician, organizations such as the World Health Organization (WHO) try to maintain more specific international standards for training and qualification. International statistics presented here for "physicians" refer to persons qualified according to WHO standards and exclude traditional health practitioners, whatever the local custom with regard to the designation "doctor." Statistics for health personnel in this table uniformly include all those actually working in the health service field, whether in the actual provision of services or in teaching, administration, research, or other tasks. One group of practitioners for

whom this type of guideline works less well is that of midwives, whose training and qualifications vary enormously from country to country but who must be included, as they represent, after nurses, perhaps the largest and most important category of health auxiliary worldwide. The statistics here refer to those midwives working in some kind of institutional setting (a hospital, clinic, community health-care centre, or the like) and exclude rural noninstitutional midwives and traditional birth attendants.

Hospitals also differ considerably worldwide in terms of staffing and services. In this tabulation, the term hospital refers generally to a permanent facility offering inpatient services and/or nursing care and staffed by at least one physician. Establishments offering only outpatient or custodial care are excluded. These statistics are broken down into data for general hospitals (those providing care in more than one specialty), specialized facilities (with care in only one specialty), local medical centres, and rural health-care centres; the last two generally refer to institutions that provide a more limited range of medical or nursing care, often less than full-time. Hospital data are further analyzed into three categories of administrative classification: public, private nonprofit, and private for profit. Statistics on number of beds refer to beds that are maintained and staffed on a full-time basis for a succession of inpatients to whom care is provided.

Data on hospital utilization refer to institutions defined as above. Admission and discharge, the two principal points at which statistics are normally collected, are the basis for the data on the amount and distribution of care by kind of facility. The data on numbers of patients exclude babies born during a maternal confinement but include persons who die before being discharged. The bed-occupancy and average length-of-stay statistics depend on the concept of a "patient-day," which is the annual total of daily censuses of inpatients. The bed-occupancy rate is the ratio of total patient-days to potential days based on the number of beds; the average length-of-stay rate is the ratio of total patient-days to total admissions. Bed-occu-

Health services

country	health personnel							hospitals										
										kinds (%)				ownership (%)			hos-pital
	year	physicians	dentists	nurses	pharma-cists	midwives	popu-lation per physi-cian	year	number	gen-eral	spe-cial-ized	medical centres	rural	govern-ment	private non-profit	private for profit	beds per 10,000 pop.
Afghanistan	1997	2,556	232	4,182	464	...	9,090	1988–93	...	...	...	...	...	...	...	...	3
Albania	1995	4,848	1,332	14,559	772[2]	9,936[2]	668	1993	40	...	...	...	...	100.0	—	—	31
Algeria	1996	27,650	7,837	...	3,866	...	1,015	1996[3]	186	...	...	...	...	...	...	...	12
American Samoa	1991	26	7[6]	140[6]	2[6]	1[6]	1,885	1990	1	100.0	—	—	—	100.0	—	—	27
Andorra	1998	166	35	188	59	6	434	1996	1	100.0	—	—	—	100.0	—	—	28
Angola	1997	736	...	10,942	...	411	13,228	1990	58	...	...	...	...	...	...	...	12
Antigua and Barbuda	1996	75	12	187	13	31	915	1998	3	50.0	50.0	—	—	100.0	—	—	42
Argentina	1992	88,800	21,900[8]	18,000[8]	...	...	376	1997	1,235	...	...	...	...	56.8	— 43.2 —		22
Armenia	1998	18,000[9]	9	18,258	144	1,750	292[9]	1998	183[10]	...	...	...	...	100.0	—	—	28
Aruba	1997	103	21	515	15	3	874	1999	2	50.0	—	50.0	—	100.0	...	...	32
Australia	1997–98	47,400	8,800	148,300	15,600	...	395	1996–97	1,222	...	...	...	...	61.0	— 39.0 —		95
Austria	1998	33,698	1,534	35,834	2,137[12]	1,056	240	1998	329	37.7	62.3	...	...	...	...	...	92
Azerbaijan	1998	28,850	2,426	62,213	2,560	10,843	274	1997	762	...	...	...	...	100.0	...	...	92
Bahamas, The	1996	419	72	648	52[4]	...	673	1997	5	60.0	20.0	20.0	—	60.0	— 40.0 —		38
Bahrain	1997	620	56	1,755	124	...	1,000	1994	12	58.3	42.7	...	—	75.0	16.7	8.3	30[13]
Bangladesh	1997	27,546	938	15,408	7,485[4]	13,211	4,627	1997	976	...	...	...	...	69.3	— 30.7 —		4
Barbados	1993	330	42	869	138[11]	377[11]	797	1995	9	66.7	33.3	—	—	80.0	—	20.0	74
Belarus	1999	39,007	4,522	47,343	3,152[12]	5,826	261	1999	276	55.4	—	— 44.6 —		100.0	—	—	68
Belgium	1998	39,420	7,360	109,187	14,597	6,602	259	1993	363	80.4	19.6	—	—	38.6	61.4	—	76
Belize	1998	155	26	404	30	230	1,542	1998	7	...	...	...	...	100.0	—	—	23
Benin	1995	312	16	1,116	85	432	17,538	1993	...	...	...	...	...	...	...	...	2
Bermuda	1996	96	22	522	29	...	639	1996	2	50.0	50.0	—	—	...	...	...	40
Bhutan	1997	101	9[4]	355[13]	5[4]	326[13]	6,128	1997	28	...	...	...	...	...	...	...	16
Bolivia	1996	4,346	444	2,062	...	...	1,747	1996	336	10.7[13]	8.9[13]	23.5[13]	56.8[13]	...	...	...	11
Bosnia and Herzegovina	1998	4,813	640	15,241	370	1,565[8]	699	1996	...	...	...	...	...	...	...	...	48
Botswana	1994	339	...	3,329	...	...	4,395	1994	30	53.3	3.3	43.3	—	...	...	...	23
Brazil	1997	205,828	137,600	67,760	51,847	...	774	1997	6,410	— 100.0 —		—	—	35.5	— 64.5 —		31
Brunei	1996	259	26	1,229	15[13]	278[13]	1,181	1995	10	90.0	—	—	10.0	90.0	— 10.0 —		33
Bulgaria	1998	28,823	5,324	47,434	1,230	5,923	286	1998	288	— 71.2 —		28.8	—	...	...	...	104
Burkina Faso	1991[14]	341	19	2,627	113	339	27,158	1993	78	— 14.1 —		85.9	—	100.0	—	—	5
Burundi	1996	329	9[4]	1,131	55[4]	...	16,507	1996	...	...	...	...	...	...	...	...	0.7
Cambodia	1998	3,464	210	8,608	262[11]	3,359	3,367	1988[3]	188	...	...	...	...	100.0	—	—	16
Cameroon	1996	1,031	56	5,112	206[6]	70	13,510	1988	629	— 27.0 —		— 73.0 —		72.3	— 27.7 —		27
Canada	1996	55,006	15,636	232,869	22,197	...	539	1989	1,079	81.8	16.6	1.6	—	95.8	—	4.2	54[10]
Cape Verde	1996	66	...	213	6	...	5,818	1996	65	8.0	—	92.0	—	100.0	—	—	15[15]
Central African Republic	1995	112	16	282	22[4]	157	28,600	1990	255	— 21.1[16] —		— 78.9[16] —		79.7[16]	— 20.3[16] —		14[8]
Chad	1994	228	14	1,014	10	159	30,260	1994	...	...	...	...	...	...	...	...	13
Chile	1996	13,857	5,817	6,738	1,830[14]	5,369[14]	1,040	1994	198	...	...	...	...	89.4	— 10.6 —		31
China	1998	1,999,500[9, 17]	9	1,218,000	440,000	51,000	621[17]	1998	69,105	11.2	13.4	— 75.4 —		100.0	—	—	23
Colombia	1997	40,355	22,121	46,187	...	...	1,102	1997	1,657	...	...	...	...	...	...	...	1
Comoros	1997	64	6[4]	180	6[4]	74	7,765	1995	...	...	...	...	...	...	...	...	29
Congo, Dem. Rep. of the	1996	3,224	514	20,652	59[4]	...	14,492	1986	400	...	...	...	...	52.5	— 47.5 —		21
Congo, Rep. of the	1995	632	35[4]	4,663	175[4]	160	4,083	1990	...	...	...	...	...	...	...	...	33
Costa Rica	1997	5,500	1,420	3,720	1,362	...	641	1997	29	...	...	...	...	87.9	—	12.1	14
Côte d'Ivoire	1996	1,318	219[4]	4,568	135[4]	2,196	11,108	1993	...	...	...	...	...	...	...	...	5
Croatia	1998	9,766	2,802	20,216	1,940	1,407	436	1997	70	52.8	47.2	—	—	...	...	...	63
Cuba	1996	60,129	9,600	76,013	...	...	183	1993	244	...	...	—	—	100.0	—	—	65
Cyprus[18]	1997	1,725	594	2,942	668[13]	120[19]	486	1997[20]	103	71.8	22.1	—	6.1	10.0[19]	0.9[19]	89.1[19]	48
Czech Republic	1999	38,828	6,383	91,213	4,785	4,602	265	1999	365	59.2	40.8	—	—	70.7	— 29.3 —		67
Denmark	1995	15,175	4,605	36,944	747	1,046	345	1992	163	42.9	57.1	—	—	42.9	57.1	—	35

pancy rates may exceed 100% because stays of partial days are counted as full days.

Two measures that give health planners and policy makers an excellent indication of the level of ordinary health care are those for mortality of children under age five and for maternal mortality. The former reflects the probability of a newborn infant dying before age five. The latter refers to deaths attributable to delivery or complications of pregnancy, childbirth, the puerperium (the period immediately following birth), or abortion. A principal source for the former data was WHO's *The World Health Report* (annual) and for the latter, the UN Development Programme's *Human Development Report* (annual).

Levels of nutrition and access to safe drinking water are two of the most basic limitations imposed by the physical environment in which health-care activities take place. The nutritional data are based on reported levels of food supply (whether or not actually consumed), referred to the recommendations of the United Nations' Food and Agriculture Organization for the necessary daily intake (in calories) for a moderately active person of average size in a climate of a particular kind (fewer calories are needed in a hot climate) to remain in average *good* health. Excess intake in the many developed countries ranges to more than 40% above the minimum required to maintain health (the excess usually being construed to diminish, rather than raise, health). The range of deficiency is less dramatic numerically but far more critical to the countries in which deficiencies are chronic, because the deficiencies lead to overall poor health (raising health service needs and costs), to decreased productivity in nearly every area of national economic life, and to the loss of social and economic potential through early mortality. By "safe" water is meant only water that has no substantial quantities of chemical or biological pollutants—*i.e.*, quantities sufficient to cause "immediate" health problems. Data refer to the proportion of persons having "reasonable access" to an "adequate" supply

of water within a "convenient" distance of the person's dwelling, as these concepts are interpreted locally.

The data on health care expenditure were excerpted from a joint effort by the WHO and the World Bank to create better analytical tools by which the interrelations among health policy, health care delivery systems, and human health might be examined against the more general frameworks of government operations, resource allocation, and development process. First published in the World Bank's *World Development Report 1993: Investing in Health* and, the following year, in the World Health Organization's *Global Comparative Assessments in the Health Sector* (edited by C.J.L. Murray and A.D. Lopez), the database and underlying methodology are expected to provide a continuing basis for international comparisons and policy analysis. The first two of ten volumes of the final results appeared in 1996 as *The Global Burden of Disease* and *Global Health Statistics* by the same editors.

Expenditures were tabulated for direct preventative and curative activities and for public health and public education programs having direct impact on health status—family planning, nutrition, and health education—but not more indirect programs like environmental, waste removal, or relief activities. Public, parastatal (semipublic, *e.g.*, social security institutions), international aid, and household expenditure reports and surveys were utilized to build up a comprehensive picture of national, regional, and world patterns of health care expenditures and investment that could not have been assembled from any single type of source. For reasons of space, public and parastatal are combined as the former.

Internet resources for further information:
- Most Recent Values of W.H.O. Global Health-For-All Indicators (for personnel and general indicators)
  http://www.who.int/htl/countrysup/countrye.htm

No comparable source exists for hospitals.

admissions or discharges					bed occu-pancy rate (%)	aver-age length of stay (days)	mortality		popu-lation with access to safe water 1994–98 (%)	food supply (% of FAO require-ment) 1998	total health expenditures, 1990					country
rate per 10,000 pop.	by kinds of hospital (%)						under age 5 per 1,000 live newborn 1997	maternal mortality per 100,000 live births 1990–97			as percent of GDP	per capita (U.S.$)	by source (percent)			
	general	special-ized	medical centres	rural									public	private	inter-national aid	
...	...	...	...	...	...	...	257	...	10	73[1]	...	...	...	...	...	Afghanistan
...	...	...	...	...	...	...	40	65	...	124	4.00	26	84.0	16.0	...	Albania
371	...	...	...	...	49.3[4]	5[4]	39	220	90[5]	126	6.95	149	76.9	23.0	0.1	Algeria
965	100.0	—	—	—	38.4	4	...	...	...	...	...	...	...	...	...	American Samoa
...	...	...	...	...	...	...	6	...	...	...	...	...	...	...	...	Andorra
238	...	...	...	...	44.5[7]	16[7]	292	1,500	32	82	...	...	...	...	...	Angola
647	...	...	...	...	50.0[7]	8[7]	21	150	88	99	4.55	241	59.1	37.3	3.6	Antigua and Barbuda
560[3]	...	...	...	...	52.0[3]	7[3]	24	44	81	134	4.21	137	60.1	39.7	0.2	Argentina
...	...	...	...	...	...	...	30	35	...	92	4.17	152	59.8	40.2	—	Armenia
...	...	...	...	...	92.2[11]	...	...	...	...	...	...	...	...	...	...	Aruba
...	...	...	...	...	...	4.5	6	9	95	120	7.67	1,294	69.6	30.4	—	Australia
2,650	...	...	...	...	80.1	10	5	10	100[5]	134	8.38	1,711	66.4	33.6	—	Austria
...	...	...	...	...	...	...	46	37	...	86	4.27	99	61.2	38.8	—	Azerbaijan
837[3]	...	...	...	...	85.4[3]	12[3]	21	...	94	105	...	...	...	...	...	Bahamas, The
...	...	...	...	...	...	...	22	46	100[5]	...	4.62	324	63.0	36.9	0.1	Bahrain
...	...	...	...	...	...	...	109	440	95	89	3.19	6	24.8	56.7	18.5	Bangladesh
810[11]	93.5[11]	6.5[11]	—	—	88.3[11]	32[11]	12	0	100[5]	123	5.04	323	64.3	33.8	1.9	Barbados
...	...	...	...	...	...	...	27	22	100	123	3.19	157	68.7	31.3	—	Belarus
1,963	96.0	4.0	—	—	84.4	12	7	10	100[5]	137	7.50	1,449	82.5	17.5	—	Belgium
...	...	...	...	...	...	...	43	140	83	129	5.88	23	48.4	41.0	10.7	Belize
...	...	...	...	...	...	...	167	500	56	112	4.32	19	26.3	36.4	37.3	Benin
1,313	97.0	3.0	—	—	75.0	8	...	...	...	116	...	...	...	...	...	Bermuda
...	...	...	...	...	...	...	121	380	58	...	5.05	10	41.1	30.4	28.5	Bhutan
250	...	...	...	...	48.0	6	96	390	80	93	4.01	25	39.9	39.6	20.5	Bolivia
529[6, 7]	...	...	...	...	82.4[6, 7]	11[6, 7]	19	10	...	110	...	...	...	...	...	Bosnia and Herzegovina
...	...	...	...	...	93.1[6]	...	49	330	90	93	6.19	139	61.8	21.6	16.5	Botswana
740	...	...	...	...	...	6	44	220	76	122	4.20	146	65.7	33.9	0.4	Brazil
...	...	...	...	...	...	...	10	0	90[5]	127	...	...	...	...	...	Brunei
...	...	...	...	...	...	...	19	15	99[5]	110	5.36	121	81.4	18.6	—	Bulgaria
...	...	...	...	...	...	...	169	930	78[5]	91	8.46	7	9.8	17.9	72.3	Burkina Faso
...	...	...	...	...	...	...	176	1,300	52	68	3.28	30	42.4	48.3	9.3	Burundi
...	...	...	...	...	...	...	167	470	30	94	...	...	...	...	...	Cambodia
...	...	...	...	...	...	...	145	550	54	98	2.62	27	26.4	61.7	11.9	Cameroon
...	...	...	...	...	...	14	7	6	100	119	9.05	1,945	74.1	25.9	—	Canada
...	...	...	...	...	...	...	73	55	65[5]	132	6.32	64	20.7	25.5	53.7	Cape Verde
...	...	...	...	...	...	...	173	1,100	38	91	4.19	18	26.5	37.5	36.0	Central African Republic
...	...	...	...	...	...	...	198	830	54	91	6.22	7	27.6	24.7	47.7	Chad
749[3]	...	...	...	...	69.9[3]	7[3]	13	23	96	117	4.73	100	70.1	29.1	0.7	Chile
418[13]	— 60.4[13] —		— 39.6[13] —		66.9[13]	15[13]	47	60	67	126	3.51	11	58.5	40.9	0.6	China
614[6]	41.4[6]	16.7[6]	— 41.9[6] —		57.2[6]	6[6]	30	80	96	119	3.98	51	44.0	54.4	1.6	Colombia
...	...	...	...	...	...	...	93	500	53[5]	79	5.40	28	46.3	29.2	24.5	Comoros
...	...	...	...	...	...	...	207	870	42	77	2.38	5	8.5	64.8	26.7	Congo, Dem. Rep. of the
...	...	...	...	...	...	...	108	890	34	101	3.99	50	47.1	40.7	12.1	Congo, Rep. of the
958[8]	...	...	...	...	78.2[8]	6[8]	14	29	100	124	6.51	132	73.6	25.2	1.2	Costa Rica
...	...	...	...	...	...	...	150	600	42	117	3.35	28	48.7	47.9	3.4	Côte d'Ivoire
1,578	70.0	30.0	—	—	83.0	13	9	12	96	98	...	...	...	...	...	Croatia
1,376[8]	...	...	...	...	...	...	8	24	93	107	...	...	...	...	...	Cuba
522	...	...	...	...	78.9	6	9	0	100[5]	140	3.96	...	62.9	26.8	10.3	Cyprus[18]
1,982	97.6	2.4	—	—	79.0[13]	9	7	9	100[5]	133	5.94[21]	169[21]	84.9[21]	15.1[21]	—	Czech Republic
1,253	92.9	7.1	—	—	80.4	8	6	10	100	128	6.30	1,588	84.2	15.8	—	Denmark

Health services (continued)

country	year	physicians	dentists	nurses	pharma-cists	midwives	popu-lation per physi-cian	year	number	general	spe-cial-ized	medical centres	rural	govern-ment	private non-profit	private for profit	hos-pital beds per 10,000 pop.
Djibouti	1996	60	7	315	8	...	7,100	1993	8	—25.0—		—75.0—		100.0	...	...	27[6]
Dominica	1998	38	10	361	27[10]	...	2,000	1994	53	1.9	—		98.1	100.0	—	—	25
Dominican Republic	1997	17,315	1,879	8,600	372	...	464	1992[3]	723	—7.9—		—92.1—		...	...	...	12[10]
East Timor	...	...	...	...	...	...	...	...	...					...	...	...	...
Ecuador	1995	15,212	1,788	5,212	906[19]	802	753	1995	474	17.0	8.0	—75.0—		26.0	11.3	62.7	16
Egypt	1998	129,000	15,211	141,770	20,254[12]	...	490	1998	7,411	4.5	—95.5—			87.9	—12.1—		19
El Salvador	1997	6,177	5,604	12,851	...	1,940[8]	936	1993	78	...	...	...	...	61.5	1.3	37.2	17
Equatorial Guinea	1996	105	4	169	...	9	4,086	1988	...					...	...	...	29
Eritrea	1996	108	4	574	...	79	33,240	1993	10					...	...	...	9
Estonia	1998	4,471	987	9,088[22]	775	22	336	1998	78					87.2	—12.8—		73
Ethiopia	1988	1,466	...	3,496	364	...	30,195	1986–87	86	...	...	...	...				3
Faroe Islands	1995	85	40	412	10	19	529	1994	3	33.3	—		66.7	100.0	—	—	64
Fiji	1997	409	36	1,742	...	...	1,919	1997	25								23
Finland	1998	15,407	4,828	111,408	7,472	4,019	334	1994[7]	380								98
France	1997	177,585	39,736	291,287	58,609	12,718	330	1997	4,186	—91.6—			8.4	25.4	—74.6—		113
French Guiana	1994	213	38	495	47	40	669	1996	25	...	...	...	...	10		15	143
French Polynesia	1999	384	94	599	51	54[19]	599	1999	7								37
Gabon	1989	448	32	759	71	240	2,504	1988	27								51
Gambia, The	1997	43	...	155	6	102	28,791	1994	13	15.4	—	—84.6—		...	...	...	7
Gaza Strip	1999[23]	...	...	...	...	...	...	1995	6					83.3	—16.7—		9
Georgia	1998	22,236	1,800	24,174	469	1,586	229	1997	422[4]	...	...	...	...	100.0	—	—	48
Germany	1998	287,164	62,274	785,190	47,341	9,271	286	1996	2,269					49.21[9]	36.01[9]	14.81[9]	72
Ghana	1996[14]	1,117	36	12,970	676	9,583	16,127	1991	121	90.9	9.1	—	—	60.3	—39.7—		16[10]
Greece	1995	40,995	10,667	30,967[10]	8,147[12]	1,837[10]	255	1996	356	49.7	50.3	—	—				50
Greenland	1997	83	28	528	10[8]	11	674	1990	16	6.3	—	—	93.7	100.0	—	—	75
Grenada	1996	96	14	232	47	...	582	1996[7]	3	100.0	—	—	—	100.0	—	—	35
Guadeloupe	1996	690	129	1,640	220	140	597	1995	29	...	...	...	...	44.8	—55.2—		76
Guam	1986	147	...	594[22]	...	22	823	1998	1	...	...	...	...	...	...	...	...
Guatemala	1997	9,812	1,367	13,247[19]	...	18,924[19]	1,072	1985	35[13]	...	...	...	...	...	...	...	11[13]
Guernsey	1993	79	...	...	...	...	804	1993	1	100.0	—	—	—	100.0	—	—	
Guinea	1995	930	22[16]	3,983	197[8]	372	7,688	1991	38	—100.0—		...	...	100.0	—	—	5
Guinea-Bissau	1996	194	11	1,277	12[16]	148	6,015	1993	16					62.5	—37.5—		13
Guyana	1996	214	35	504	40	165	3,612	1994	30					83.3	—16.7—		30
Haiti	1996	773	95[10]	2,630	...	...	8,418	1994	49								10
Honduras	1997	4,896	989	6,152	975[19]	...	1,202	1994	61					47.5	—52.5—		9
Hong Kong	1999	9,580	2,052	38,320	1,368	...	714	1995	88	...	...	...	...	78.4	—21.6—		49
Hungary	1998	36,143	5,671	51,965	4,789	2,227	279	1998	167	...	...	...	...	...	...	...	83
Iceland	1998	893	288	2,370	228	235	307	1995	57	89.0	11.0	—	—	...	...	...	147
India	1998[24]	512,352	19,523[19]	449,351[19]	...	...	1,916	1998	15,067[8]	...	...	...	...	55.0[8]	—45.0[8]—		27
Indonesia	1997	31,887[9]	9	155,911[22]	5,440[12]	22	6,267[9]	1997	1,090	...	...	...	...	...	...	...	6
Iran	1997	50,770	9,427	136,030	6,816	7,387	1,195	1997	685	...	...	...	...	83.5	—16.5—		16
Iraq	1998	11,769	1,220	50,499	2,525	...	1,818	1993	185	...	...	...	...	...	...	...	14
Ireland	1998	8,114	1,712	59,021	2,882	15,228	457	1996	62[3,7]	100.0	—	—	—	100.0	—	—	33
Isle of Man	1998	117	26	...	25[12]	...	615	1986	3	33.3	33.3	—	33.3	100.0	—	—	...
Israel	1998	22,345	6,733	35,579	3,511	1,080	260	1995	259	18.5	81.5	—	—	12.0	51.7	36.3	61
Italy	1997	318,616	37,039	280,263	58,662	...	180	1997	1,589	91.5	8.5	—	—	59.2	—40.8—		65
Jamaica	1996	421	57	1,241	52	273	5,974	1996	24	75.0	25.0	—	—	75.0	—25.0—		24
Japan	1997	240,908	85,518	960,477	194,300	23,615	525	1997	9,413	88.7	11.3	—	—	73.5	—26.5—		131
Jersey	1995	95	...	...	...	...	895	1990	6	16.7	83.3	—	—	100.0	—	—	88
Jordan	1997	7,250	2,140	12,929	3,363	86[113]	602	1994	63	...	...	...	...	42.9	—57.1—		18[25]
Kazakhstan	1998	53,207	3,783	97,824	9,903	8,456	283	1996	1,518	...	...	...	...	100.0	—	—	123
Kenya	1995	3,606	600	24,610	605[19]	...	7,575	1994	846	—35.1—		—64.9—		...	...	...	14
Kiribati	1998	26	4	208	...	...	3,385	1990	1	...	...	...	...	...	...	...	40
Korea, North	1995	64,006	...	38,792	...	12,931	337	1989	...	...	...	...	...	...	...	...	135
Korea, South	1997	62,609	15,383	133,920	45,820	8,516	735	1997	6,446	70.0	30.0	—	—	...	...	...	47
Kuwait	1997	3,419	470	8,593	633[25]	19[13]	529	1995	24	...	...	...	...	66.7	—	33.3	31
Kyrgyzstan	1998	14,355	1,307	35,768	320	3,472	332	1994	348[13]	89.1	—	10.9	—	100.0	—	—	101[13]
Laos	1996	1,208	214	5,354	...	...	1,603	1995	25	0.7[4]	—99.3[4]—			100.0	—	—	254[4]
Latvia	1998	6,900	1,064	13,445	292[10]	81	355	1998	150	51.2[10]	4.1[10]	28.8[10]	15.9[10]	97.5	2.5	—	94
Lebanon	1997	7,203	2,744	3,430	1,715	...	476	1995	153	...	...	...	...	10.5	—89.5—		22
Lesotho	1995	105	10	1,169	60[14]	914	18,524	1987	22	90.9	9.1	—	—	54.5	45.5	—	15
Liberia	1997	53	2	136	...	99	43,434	1988	92	—37.0—		—63.0—		...	...	...	
Libya	1997	6,092	619[25]	17,136[25]	1,095[25]	...	781	1991	...	...	...	...	...	...	...	...	41
Liechtenstein	1997	41	18		2	...	764	1998	1	...	...	...	...	...	...	...	34
Lithuania	1999	14,578	2,316	37,448	2,143	1,611	254	1999	186	...	...	...	...	100.0	—	—	94
Luxembourg	1998	1,164	282	3,347	297	94	368	1994	34	50.0	50.0	—	—	...	...	...	109
Macau	1998	532	31	706	48	...	800	1994	30	6.7	—	93.3	—	46.7	—53.3—		22
Macedonia	1998	4,110	1,046	9,833	300	1,342	490	1994	58[25]	27.4	24.2	—48.4—		100.0	—	—	52[25]
Madagascar	1996	1,470	137	2,969	19[4]	1,471	9,351	1990	...	...	...	...	...	...	...	...	9
Malawi	1989	186	...	284	5	...	49,118	1987	395	12.2	0.8	—87.0—		59.2	—40.8—		16
Malaysia	1997	14,258	1,865	24,550	...	5,872	1,519	1997	337	...	...	...	...	35.1	—64.9—		20
Maldives	1995	100	...	281	134	461	2,533	1996	5	20.0	—	80.0	—	100.0	—	—	12
Mali	1994	419	9	1,167	57[27]	267	21,269	1987	...	...	...	...	...	...	...	...	4
Malta	1998	987	135	4,158	186	291	383	1996	7	...	...	...	...	71.4	—28.6—		57
Marshall Islands	1997	34	4	141	...	6	1,794	1997	2	100.0	—	—	—	100.0	—	—	21
Martinique	1996	680	130	1,700	230	150	547	1993	8[13]	...	...	...	...	...	...	...	56[13]
Mauritania	1995	323	47	1,461	6[8]	237	7,251	1990	16	...	...	...	...	100.0	—	—	7
Mauritius	1998	1,033	144	2,826[22]	250	22	1,117	1998	13	73.9[10]	17.4[10]	8.7[10]	—	60.9[10]	4.3[10]	34.8[10]	33
Mayotte	1985	9	1	51	1	2	7,427	1994	2	100.0	—	—	—	100.0	—	—	9
Mexico	1997	116,047	8,926	161,303	...	...	812	1993	1,888[25]	...	...	...	...	53.9	—46.1—		9[25]
Micronesia	1999	76	16	368	7[19]	...	1,737	1993	4	100.0	—	—	—	100.0	—	—	31
Moldova	1998	14,959	1,761	37,355	2,885	3,723	286	1996	312	...	...	...	...	100.0	—	—	125
Monaco	1997	188	22	500[13]	67[13]	11[13]	170	1997	1	100.0	—	—	—	100.0	—	—	173
Mongolia	1998	5,676	315	7,169	1,113[19]	...	411	1997	407	...	...	...	...	...	...	...	78
Morocco	1997	12,534	1,090	28,610	2,997	87[4]	2,173	1993[28]	201	48.8	—	51.2	—	100.0	—	—	10

admissions or discharges					bed occu-pancy rate (%)	aver-age length of stay (days)	mortality		popu-lation with access to safe water 1994–98 (%)	food supply (% of FAO require-ment) 1998	total health expenditures, 1990					country
rate per 10,000 pop.	by kinds of hospital (%)						under age 5 per 1,000 live newborn 1997	maternal mortality per 100,000 live births 1990–97			as percent of GDP	per capita (U.S.$)	by source (percent)			
	general	special-ized	medical centres	rural									public	private	inter-national aid	
	...	...	...	...			156	...	90[5]	89	...	...	...	...	...	Djibouti
1,026	...	...	...	...	94.6	8	20	65	96[5]	124	8.06	192	65.1	20.4	14.5	Dominica
470	...	...	...	...	...	...	53	230	79	101	3.72	38	52.7	43.3	4.0	Dominican Republic
	...	...	...	...			...	...	...	...			...	...	...	East Timor
508	...	...	...	...	53.1	6	39	160	68	119	4.14	44	55.9	37.3	6.8	Ecuador
317	...	...	...	...			73	170	87	131	2.61	28	30.3	62.0	7.7	Egypt
...	...	...	...	...	54.9[3,11]	6[3,11]	36	160	66	110	5.86	58	29.7	55.6	14.7	El Salvador
...	...	...	...	...	...	...	172	...	95[5]	68	7.60	28	36.6	20.7	42.7	Equatorial Guinea
	...	...	...	...			116	1,000	22	75			...	...	...	Eritrea
1,952	76.7[10]	21.5[10]	—	1.8[10]	75.1	10	23	50	100	120	3.62	228	53.0	47.0	—	Estonia
...	...	...	...	...			175	1,400	25	78	3.80	4	41.3	39.9	18.8	Ethiopia
...	...	...	...	...	86.4	12	...	...	...	...			...	...	...	Faroe Islands
...	...	...	...	...	...	...	24	38	77[5]	125	3.76	70	54.9	38.3	6.9	Fiji
2,322	...	...	...	...	70.9	11	4	6	100	117	7.82	2,046	83.3	16.7	—	Finland
2,128	...	...	...	...	...	...	5	10	100	141	9.40	1,869	74.2	25.8	—	France
1,714[19]	...	...	...	...	70.3[19]	8[19]	...	...	84	125	...	...	...	...	...	French Guiana
...	...	...	...	...	...	...	...	...	...	129			...	...	...	French Polynesia
...	...	...	...	...	...	...	145	500	67	109	4.10	164	52.7	40.9	6.4	Gabon
...	...	...	...	...	...	...	87	1,100	69	108	7.53	22	28.3	20.7	51.0	Gambia, The
752	...	...	...	...	74.9	3	...	...	...	...			...	...	...	Gaza Strip
...	...	...	...	...			23	60	...	88	4.45	152	62.5	37.5	—	Georgia
1,812[19]	...	...	...	...	82.8[19]	13[19]	5	8	100[5]	128	8.73	1,511	72.7	27.3	—	Germany
...	...	...	...	...	...	...	107	210	65	117	3.50	15	35.0	51.8	13.2	Ghana
1,370	81.0	19.0	—	—	66.0	9	8	10	99[5]	145	5.39	359	76.0	24.0	—	Greece
2,450	29.2	—	—	70.8	69.4	8	...	...	...	...	...	...	...	...	...	Greenland
774[8]	100.0	—	—	—	59.1[8]	7[8]	29	0	85[5]	111	5.96	133	68.8	27.8	3.5	Grenada
2,154	...	...	...	...	84.0	10	...	...	90	113	...	...	...	...	...	Guadeloupe
...	...	...	...	...			...	...	...	...			...	...	...	Guam
284	...	...	...	...	57.7	9	55	190	68	99	3.70	27	44.2	43.2	12.6	Guatemala
1,100	100.0	—	...	...			...	...	...	...			...	...	...	Guernsey
...	...	...	...	...			201	670	46	100	3.90	17	39.7	40.3	20.0	Guinea
...	...	...	...	...	...	...	220	910	43	104	8.15	16	31.3	18.9	49.8	Guinea-Bissau
...	...	...	...	...	...	...	82	180	91[5]	109	10.37	42	40.7	15.1	44.2	Guyana
...	...	...	...	...	...	...	132	1,000	37	83	6.99	27	26.3	54.8	19.0	Haiti
459[19]	...	...	...	...	...	...	45	220	78	104	4.54	52	56.7	35.7	7.7	Honduras
1,811	...	...	...	...	...	...	6	7	100[5]	143	5.69	687	19.5	80.5	0.0	Hong Kong
2,502	...	...	...	...	77.0	10	11	15	100[5]	130	5.95	185	84.4	15.6	—	Hungary
2,828[11]	94.0[11]	6.0[11]	—	—	86.5[11]	12[11]	5	6	100[5]	121	8.34	1,884	87.5	12.5	—	Iceland
...	...	...	...	...	...	...	108	440	81	112	6.00	21	20.0	78.4	1.6	India
...	...	...	...	...	...	...	60	450	74	132	2.01	12	25.6	66.7	7.7	Indonesia
...	...	...	...	...			35	37	95	117	2.54	244	56.9	43.1	0.0	Iran
645[4]	...	...	...	...	42.4[4]	4[4]	122	310	81	100	...	...	...	...	...	Iraq
1,470	100.0	—	—	—	82.2	7	7	10	100[5]	144	7.22	876	81.1	18.9	—	Ireland
...	...	...	...	...	...	...	...	...	...	...			...	...	...	Isle of Man
1,979	...	...	...	...	91.2	10	6	5	99	135	4.20	480	49.3	50.6	0.1	Israel
1,743	90.4	9.6	—	—	72.0	9	6	7	100[5]	143	7.54	1,449	77.7	22.3	—	Italy
242[3]	81.7[3]	18.3[3]	...	...	53.7	5	11	120	86	121	5.04	83	57.4	33.2	9.5	Jamaica
...	...	...	...	...	...	...	6	8	97	123	6.45	1.538	74.5	25.5	—	Japan
1,718	84.0	16.0	—	—	...	...	...	...	...	...			...	...	...	Jersey
478[3]	...	...	...	...	68.1[3]	4[3]	24	41	97	114	3.77	55	36.9	52.3	10.8	Jordan
...	...	...	...	...	...	...	44	70	93	98	4.44	154	62.3	37.7	—	Kazakhstan
...	...	...	...	...	...	...	87	370	44	85	4.33	16	40.0	37.9	22.1	Kenya
...	...	...	...	...	...	...	78[10]	...	99[5]	131	...	...	...	...	...	Kiribati
...	...	...	...	...	...	...	30	110	100	81			...	...	...	Korea, North
629[13]	97.5[13]	2.5[13]	...	...	65.5[13]	13[13]	6	20	93	131	6.61	365	40.9	58.9	0.2	Korea, South
950[3,10]	72.2[3,10]	27.8[3,10]	—	—	64.9[3,10]	7[3,10]	13	5	100[5]	126	4.86	541	64.2	35.6	0.1	Kuwait
1,775	95.5	—	4.5	—	75.6	15	68	65	79	99	4.97	118	66.7	33.3	—	Kyrgyzstan
...	...	...	...	...	...	...	122	650	44	98	2.53	5	17.4	60.7	21.9	Laos
2,210	78.4[10]	4.6[10]	13.8[10]	3.2[10]	76.5	13	22	45	100	117	3.87	220	56.1	43.9	—	Latvia
...	...	...	...	...	...	...	37	100	94	132	...	...	...	...	...	Lebanon
221[7]	...	...	...	...	...	...	137	610	62	97	8.32	26	38.3	26.5	35.2	Lesotho
...	...	...	...	...	...	...	235	...	46	86	8.24	4	19.9	11.8	68.3	Liberia
...	...	...	...	...	...	...	25	75	97	138	...	...	...	...	...	Libya
...	...	...	...	...	...	...	7	...	100[5]	...			...	...	...	Liechtenstein
2,001[13]	...	...	...	...	74.4[13]	15[13]	24	18	100	121	3.58	159	72.0	28.0	—	Lithuania
1,941	94.6	5.4	—	—	75.0	16	7	0	100[5]	137	6.56	1,662	91.4	8.6	—	Luxembourg
329	...	...	...	...	64.4	16	...	...	...	108	...	...	...	...	...	Macau
995	67.2	6.1	—26.7—		68.5	14	23	11	...	116	...	...	...	...	...	Macedonia
...	...	...	...	...	...	...	158	490	40	88	2.56	7	29.0	49.6	21.4	Madagascar
...	...	...	...	...	...	...	215	620	47	96	4.98	11	35.0	41.7	23.3	Malawi
717[3,6]	...	...	...	...			11	39	78	130	2.96	71	44.0	55.8	0.2	Malaysia
256[19,26]	...	...	...	...	71.4[19,26]	4[19,26]	74	350	60	111	...	...	...	...	...	Maldives
...	...	...	...	...	...	...	239	580	66	90	5.19	15	24.9	46.7	28.4	Mali
...	...	...	...	...	...	...	10	...	100[5]	136	5.38	349	68.3	31.7	0.0	Malta
...	...	...	...	...	...	...	92[10]	...	82	...	...	...	...	...	...	Marshall Islands
2,092	...	...	...	...	73.7	10	...	...	94	118	...	...	...	...	...	Martinique
...	...	...	...	...	...	...	183	550	37	114	3.80	18	28.5	41.5	30.0	Mauritania
1,446[3,10]	...	...	...	...	74.6[3,10]	5[3,10]	23	30	98	130	4.40	100	47.8	39.0	13.3	Mauritius
...	...	...	...	...	...	...	...	...	...	...			...	...	...	Mayotte
403[3,8]	...	...	...	...	64.7[3,8]	5[3,8]	35	48	85	135	3.17	89	49.3	49.8	0.9	Mexico
...	...	...	...	...			24	...	100[5]				...	...	...	Micronesia
...	...	...	...	...	...	...	35	42	98	108	3.91	143	74.4	25.6	—	Moldova
...	...	...	...	...	...	...	5	...	100	140	...	...	...	...	...	Monaco
205	...	...	...	...	...	...	150	150	45	83	6.63	58	83.0	15.1	1.9	Mongolia
255	...	...	...	...	63.8	8	72	230	65	131	2.55	26	33.6	63.3	3.1	Morocco

Health services (continued)

country	health personnel							hospitals		kinds (%)				ownership (%)			hospital beds per 10,000 pop.
	year	physicians	dentists	nurses	pharma-cists	midwives	popu-lation per physi-cian	year	number	gen-eral	spe-cial-ized	medical centres	rural	govern-ment	private non-profit	private for profit	
Mozambique	1990	387	108	3,533	353	1,139	36,320	1990	238	4.2	0.8	— 95.0 —		100.0	—	—	8[19]
Myanmar (Burma)	1999	12,313	871	10,820	...	9,162	3,367	1996	737	...	...	...	...	...	...	...	7
Namibia	1997	495	67	2,817	91[8]	1,954	3,388	1992	47	...	...	...	...	91.5	— 8.5 —		45[8]
Nauru	1995	17	...	62	...	...	624	...	...	...	...	...	...	...	...	...	...
Nepal	1997	874	45[13]	3,845	18[13]	1,621[13]	26,316	1997	74	...	...	...	...	...	...	...	2
Netherlands, The	1997	33,618	7,319	124,000[19]	2,622	1,357	462	1998	222	64.4	35.6	—	—	...	...	...	53
Netherlands Antilles	1998	339	62	1,198	42	11	617	1998	11	38.3	36.3	25.4	—	...	...	...	70
New Caledonia	1996	362	107	852	74	61	549	1996	9	12.5[4]	12.5[4]	75.0[4]	—	62.5[4]	— 37.5[4] —		45
New Zealand	1997	12,399	1,467	29,000	3,634	2,114	303	1996	368	...	...	...	...	32.3	— 67.7 —		59
Nicaragua	1995	4,551	1,099	2,577	...	...	957	1994	56	46.4	7.1	46.4					11
Niger	1997	325	19	2,126	29[4]	511	28,560	1987	...	...	...	...	...	...	...	...	5
Nigeria	1993	21,739	1,335	80,186	6,474[11]	62,386	3,707	1985	11,588	6.6	0.5	— 92.9 —		81.4	— 18.6 —		7[13]
Northern Mariana Islands	1986	23	4	103	2	2	1,324	1988	1	100.0	—	—	—	100.0	—	—	19
Norway	1998	18,304	5,230	81,548	2,531	2,619	242	1994	...	...	...	...	...	...	...	...	51
Oman	1998	3,061	201	7,453	435	65	773	1998	62	— 8.1 —		— 91.9 —		25.8	— 74.2 —		36
Pakistan	1997	78,470	3,159	28,661	47,618[25]	20,869[13]	1,836	1997	5,118	— 7.6[10] —		— 92.4[10] —		...	...	...	6
Palau	1998	20	2	26	...	1	900	1998	1	...	...	...	...	...	...	...	374
Panama	1998	3,518	784	3,203	756	...	773	1998	60	...	...	...	...	...	...	...	27
Papua New Guinea	1998	342	127	3,141	...	...	13,708	1993	...	...	...	...	...	...	...	...	34
Paraguay	1995	3,730	1,279	1,875	433	1,547	1,294	1995	...	...	...	...	...	...	...	...	14
Peru	1996	23,249	1,197	16,043	4,789	3,832	1,030	1996	472	...	...	...	...	50.2	— 49.8 —		13
Philippines	1996	36,375	1,668	5,663	...	13,750	1,923	1996	1,738	96.5	3.1	0.5	—	34.5	— 65.5 —		12
Poland	1998	91,121	17,869	215,295	20,139	25,014	424	1998	765	93.8	6.2	—	—	100	—	—	54
Portugal	1998	31,097	3,319	37,775	7,505	827	320	1993	335	43.0	18.8	38.2	—	74.3	14.7	11.0	41[13]
Puerto Rico	1989–92	6,269	902	19,666	2,111	120	558	1994	72	83.3	8.3	8.3	—	36.1	30.6	33.3	26
Qatar	1999[14]	703	117	1,612	285	...	793	1995	4	25.0	75.0	—	—	100.0	—	—	18
Réunion	1999	1,346	337	2,906	284	176	520	1998	19	85.5	— 14.5 —			71.0	— 29.0 —		39
Romania	1998	41,415	5,379	92,057	1,643	8,913	543	1995	414	...	...	...	...	99.5	— 0.5 —		77
Russia	1998	618,718	47,322	1,615,000	9,112	91,853	238	1998	11,200	37.4[10]	17.2[10]	—	45.4[10]	99.8	— 0.2 —		119
Rwanda	1989	272	7	835	25	...	24,697	1985[3]	220	— 13.6 —		— 86.4 —		100.0	—	—	9[6]
St. Kitts and Nevis	1998	50	8	274	21	...	846	1998	4	50.0	— 50.0 —			...	...	...	62
St. Lucia	1997	81	13	312	13	...	1,876	1998	6	25.0[11]	25.0[11]	—	50.0[11]	...	...	...	14
St. Vincent	1998	59	6	267	27[8]	...	2,075	1997	11	...	...	...	...	77.8[11]	— 22.2[11] —		19
Samoa	1996	62	7	281	6[11]	65	2,919	1992	36	2.8	—	—	97.2	100.0	—	—	34
San Marino	1998	84	...	...	...	...	309	1998	...	...	...	...	...	...	...	...	58
São Tomé and Príncipe	1996	61	7	167	1[6]	39	2,147	...	...	...	...	...	...	...	...	...	...
Saudi Arabia	1997	33,110	3,191	65,821	4,189	...	602	1996	290	...	...	...	...	74.1	— 25.9 —		22
Senegal	1996	649	93	1,876	322	588	13,656	1996	17	...	...	...	...	...	...	...	9
Seychelles	1998	93	15	342	7	...	849	1997	7	14.3	14.3	71.4	—	100.0	—	—	54
Sierra Leone	1996	339	19	1,532	...	218	13,696	1998	219	— 25.6[16] —		— 74.4[16] —		...	...	...	8
Singapore	1998	5,147	914	15,570	858[25]	487[25]	615	1997	23	...	...	...	...	43.5	— 56.5 —		35
Slovakia	1998	19,030	2,598	38,168	1,822	2,119[13]	283	1991	111	72.1	27.9	—	—	100.0	—	—	92[13]
Slovenia	1998	4,501	1,201	3,125	887	...	440	1998	28	57.7	42.3	—	—	...	...	...	56
Solomon Islands	1997	31	...	464	...	283	13,258	1997	11	100.0	—	—	—	75.0	25.0	—	51
Somalia	1997	265	13	1,327	70	540[15]	25,034	1988	...	...	...	...	...	...	...	...	7
South Africa	1998	29,369	4,387	174,754	9,948	...	1,459	1998	704	...	...	...	...	51.1	— 48.9 —		34
Spain	1996	165,560	14,877	177,034	43,221	6,314	240	1994	783	57.5	18.5	— 24.0 —		42.5	— 57.5 —		40
Sri Lanka	1999	6,881	471	19,362	848	7,899	2,740	1995[3]	407	...	...	...	...	100.0	—	—	26
Sudan, The	1996	2,818	219	18,158	344	...	11,110	1986	...	...	...	...	...	...	...	...	8
Suriname	1996	305	31	631	14	40	1,373	1998	...	...	...	...	...	...	...	...	34
Swaziland	1996	149	7[4]	1,264[4]	13[4]	...	6,617	1986	24	— 41.7 —		— 58.3 —		...	...	...	...
Sweden	1997	27,511	13,446	72,625	5,953	6,351	322	1996	...	...	...	...	...	...	...	...	43
Switzerland	1998	22,965	3,470	55,387	4,373	1,884	310	1997	...	...	...	...	...	...	...	...	66
Syria	1998	22,293	11,456	29,259	8,205	6,063[13]	694	1995	294	...	...	...	...	20.5	— 79.5 —		12
Taiwan	1998	27,168	7,900	71,215	22,761	704	804	1998	700	...	...	...	...	13.7	— 86.3 —		57
Tajikistan	1998	12,291	1,125	29,597	734	3,999	498	1994	449	...	...	...	...	98.2	— 1.8 —		88
Tanzania	1995	1,277	218	26,536	...	13,953	24,389	1993	173[8]	...	...	...	...	...	...	...	10
Thailand	1995	14,181	2,920	54,262	5,867	9,713	4,192	1996	1,397	93.6	6.4	—	—	65.8	— 34.2 —		21
Togo	1995	320	29	1,252	65[8]	438	13,168	1990	...	...	...	...	...	...	...	...	16
Tonga	1997	43	9	309	...	30	2,279	1993	4	...	...	...	...	...	...	...	28
Trinidad and Tobago	1997	949	141	1,378[22]	518	[22]	1,339	1997	77	...	...	...	...	...	...	...	37
Tunisia	1997	6,464	1,200	26,409	1,570	...	1,429	1994[3]	163	— 13.5 —		— 86.5 —		100.0	—	—	18
Turkey	1998	77,375	13,428	69,701	21,486	41,181	826	1997	1,078	75.3[10]	8.8[10]	— 15.9[10] —		84.3[10]	— 15.7[10] —		23
Turkmenistan	1997	14,022	1,010	21,436	1,566	3,664	333	1994	368	...	...	...	...	100.0	—	—	115
Tuvalu	1999	8	1	33	...	10	1,375	1985	8	11.1	—	—	88.9	100.0	—	—	36
Uganda	1996	840[19]	42	3,897	...	2,835	22,399[19]	1989	81	...	...	...	...	...	...	...	12
Ukraine	1998	150,382	19,615	370,171	23,488	29,523	334	1997	3,400	...	...	...	...	100.0	...	...	99
United Arab Emirates	1997	4,749	644[25]	8,450[25]	2,007[25]	...	553	1996	50	...	...	...	...	72.0	— 28.0 —		29
United Kingdom	1998	82,803	20,216	299,010	33,759[11]	24,801[6]	716	1997	...	...	...	...	...	...	...	...	42
United States	1998	756,700	196,000	2,162,000	184,000[13]	3,000[13]	357	1998	6,097	88.0	12.0	—	—	25.3	49.2	25.5	38
Uruguay	1998	11,964	3,921	2,369	1,009	586	269	1997	118	...	...	...	...	75.4	— 24.6 —		35
Uzbekistan	1998	74,230	5,869	243,166	746	16,235	324	1995	192	...	...	...	...	...	...	...	84
Vanuatu	1997	21	3[13]	259[13]	6[13]	33[13]	8,524	1995	90	5.6	—	21.1	73.3	100.0	—	—	32
Venezuela	1997	53,818	13,000	46,305	8,571	...	423	1997	556	...	...	...	...	37.0	— 63.0 —		17
Vietnam	1998	36,683	...	42,797	6,500[19]	13,450	2,083	1994	12,500	...	...	...	...	...	...	...	27
Virgin Islands (U.S.)	1985	167	...	...	...	...	622	1985	...	...	...	...	...	...	...	...	49
West Bank	1993[23]	1,344	445	2,279	149	56	1,536	1995	17	...	...	...	...	52.9	— 47.1 —		9
Western Sahara	1994	100	...	...	24	...	2,504	...	...	...	...	...	...	...	...	...	...
Yemen	1998	3,883	245[25]	7,578[13]	613	385[10]	4,211	1998	81	...	...	...	...	...	...	...	55
Yugoslavia	1997	22,498	4,209	...	2,032	...	471	1997	...	...	...	...	...	...	...	...	55
Zambia	1995	601	26[4]	9,853	24[4]	311[4]	14,496	1987	965	8.2	0.3	19.0	72.5	80.9	19.1	—	29[19]
Zimbabwe	1995	1,522	142	14,095	411[19]	3,078	7,196	1993[3]	1,378	0.9	2.6	83.7	12.7	100.0	—	—	19[13]

[1]1997. [2]1987. [3]Government hospitals only. [4]1990. [5]Data refer to a period other than 1994–95, differ from the standard definition, or refer to only part of the country. [6]1989. [7]General hospitals only. [8]1991. [9]Physicians include dentists. [10]1994. [11]1992. [12]Number of pharmacies. [13]1995. [14]Government-employed personnel only. [15]1987. [16]1988. [17]Includes doctors of traditional Chinese medicine. [18]Republic of Cyprus only. [19]1993. [20]Excludes psychiatric hospitals. [21]Data refer to former Czechoslovakia. [22]Nurses include midwives. [23]West Bank includes Gaza Strip. [24]Registered personnel; all may

admissions or discharges — rate per 10,000 pop.	general	specialized	medical centres	rural	bed occupancy rate (%)	average length of stay (days)	mortality — under age 5 per 1,000 live newborn 1997	maternal mortality per 100,000 live births 1990–97	population with access to safe water 1994–98 (%)	food supply (% of FAO requirement) 1998	total health expenditures 1990 — as percent of GDP	per capita (U.S.$)	public	private	international aid	country
...	...	...	...	...	...	...	209	1,100	46	82	5.86	5	21.0	25.7	53.3	Mozambique
...	...	...	...	...	...	...	114	230	60	131	...	...	...	...	..	Myanmar (Burma)
...	...	...	...	...	...	...	75	230	83	92	3.92	45	47.8	41.3	10.9	Namibia
...	...	...	...	...	...	...	30	...	...	...	...	...	...	...	...	Nauru
...	...	...	...	...	...	...	104	540	71	99	4.54	7	23.0	51.7	25.4	Nepal
1,028	96.7	3.3	—	—	70.1	10	6	7	100	122	8.03	1,501	72.6	27.4	—	Netherlands, The
...	...	...	...	...	...	...	...	...	...	110	...	...	...	...	...	Netherlands Antilles
1,165[4,7]	...	...	...	...	84.8[4,7]	8[4,7]	...	...	...	123	...	...	...	...	...	New Caledonia
1,332[3]	...	...	...	...	64.0[3]	6[3]	7	15	100[5]	126	7.37	925	81.7	18.3	—	New Zealand
769	—76.2—		23.8	—	...	...	57	160	78	98	8.61	34	56.9	22.5	20.6	Nicaragua
...	...	...	...	...	...	...	285	590	61	84	4.98	16	24.5	31.3	34.1	Niger
...	...	...	...	...	...	...	187	1,000	49	122	2.72	10	36.5	57.4	6.1	Nigeria
1,550	100.0	—	—	—	54.7	4	...	...	...	...	...	...	...	...	...	Northern Mariana Islands
1,515	96.4	3.6	—	—	83.0	10	4	6	100	128	7.35	1,835	95.7	4.3	—	Norway
911	...	...	...	...	...	...	18	21	85	...	4.22	209	59.5	40.1	0.5	Oman
...	...	...	...	...	...	...	136	340	79	106	3.48	12	47.4	47.1	5.5	Pakistan
1,582	...	...	...	...	48.5	6	34	...	88	...	...	...	...	...	...	Palau
1,239	...	...	...	...	52.5	8	20	85	93	107	7.13	142	72.6	23.1	4.3	Panama
...	...	...	...	...	...	...	112	370	41	95	4.44	37	59.1	36.1	4.8	Papua New Guinea
...	...	...	...	...	...	...	33	190	60	112	2.97	35	35.1	58.2	6.7	Paraguay
...	...	...	...	...	...	...	56	270	67	103	3.21	61	56.1	41.7	2.2	Peru
538	...	...	...	...	62.1	5	46	210	85	101	2.15	16	46.7	46.4	6.9	Philippines
1,288[11]	96.0[11]	4.0[11]	—	...	72.5[11]	14[11]	11	8	100[5]	128	5.07	84	80.3	19.7	—	Poland
1,146	86.3	10.5	3.2	—	74.5	10	8	8	100[5]	151	6.99	383	61.7	38.3	—	Portugal
1,101	94.0	4.3	1.7	—	63.1	5	...	...	...	...	...	...	...	...	...	Puerto Rico
...	...	...	...	...	71.7[11,29]	7[11,29]	20	10	100[5]	...	4.73	630	63.0	36.9	0.0	Qatar
1,951[10]	...	...	...	...	79.8[10]	7[10]	...	...	100[5]	146	...	...	...	...	...	Réunion
...	...	...	...	...	...	...	26	41	100[5]	123	3.87	58	61.4	38.6	—	Romania
2,320	...	...	...	...	85.0	14	22	49	...	111	3.02	159	66.8	33.2	—	Russia
85	...	...	...	...	42.8[27]	7[27]	170	1,300	66[5]	88	3.44	10	15.0	45.2	39.8	Rwanda
1,068[7,11]	...	...	...	...	49.3[7,11]	9[7,11]	37	130	100[5]	114	5.99	212	58.1	27.8	14.1	St. Kitts and Nevis
890[11,27]	...	...	...	...	...	...	29	30	85	117	7.18	169	75.6	23.0	1.4	St. Lucia
728	...	...	...	...	68.2	7	21	43	89	106	5.69	102	68.5	28.8	2.7	St. Vincent
894	70.8	—	—	29.2	32.9	5	27	...	68	...	2.94	20	6.1	54.2	39.7	Samoa
...	...	...	...	...	...	...	6	...	100[5]	...	...	...	...	...	...	San Marino
...	...	...	...	...	...	...	78	...	82	94	9.22	38	28.8	17.0	54.2	São Tomé and Príncipe
...	...	...	...	...	...	...	28	130	95	119	4.76	260	64.3	35.7	0.0	Saudi Arabia
...	...	...	...	...	...	...	124	560	81	96	3.66	29	45.1	38.0	16.9	Senegal
1,744[30]	...	...	...	...	76.4[30]	5[30]	18	...	97[5]	105	6.03	289	50.2	28.0	21.9	Seychelles
...	...	...	...	...	...	...	316	1,800	34[5]	89	2.43	4	19.6	30.9	49.5	Sierra Leone
1,127[25]	...	...	...	...	73.1[10]	8[10]	4	6	100	...	1.87	215	58.3	41.6	0.1	Singapore
1,679[13]	94.9[13]	5.1[13]	—	—	73.2[13]	14[13]	11	9	...	120	...	...	...	...	...	Slovakia
1,643	...	...	...	...	78.4	10	6	11	...	116	...	...	...	...	...	Slovenia
...	...	...	...	...	...	...	28	550	...	93	2.18	117	43.2	50.5	6.3	Solomon Islands
...	...	...	...	...	...	...	211	...	31	66	1.51	8	7.3	41.1	51.6	Somalia
...	...	...	...	...	...	...	82	230	87	119	5.56	77	57.5	42.5	0.0	South Africa
1,053	...	...	...	...	76.7[8]	12[8]	5	6	99	136	6.59	831	78.4	21.6	—	Spain
1,464[4]	...	...	...	...	...	...	19	60	57	104	3.74	18	40.4	51.1	8.6	Sri Lanka
...	...	...	...	...	...	...	115	550	73	104	3.33	34	11.0	84.5	4.5	Sudan, The
766[31]	...	...	...	...	68.8[31]	10[31]	36	110	72[5]	116	2.88	93	37.9	58.0	4.1	Suriname
...	...	...	...	...	...	...	94	230	50	108	7.22	64	43.6	22.2	34.2	Swaziland
1,906[10]	...	...	...	...	82.2[10]	8[10]	4	5	100[5]	116	8.79	2,343	89.3	10.7	—	Sweden
...	...	...	...	...	...	...	5	5	100	120	7.52	2,520	68.5	31.5	—	Switzerland
352[3,19]	...	...	...	...	75.5[3,19]	3[3,19]	33	110	86	136	2.07	41	16.6	79.4	4.0	Syria
...	...	...	...	...	...	...	8	8	90	...	4.30	323	53.0	47.0	0.0	Taiwan
1,492	...	...	...	...	70.2	15	76	85	60	85	5.98	100	72.6	27.4	—	Tajikistan
...	...	...	...	...	...	...	143	530	66	86	4.73	4	14.4	31.6	54.0	Tanzania
...	...	...	...	...	...	...	38	44	81	110	4.98	72	20.4	78.7	0.9	Thailand
...	...	...	...	...	...	...	125	640	55	109	4.10	18	40.4	38.5	21.2	Togo
622[11]	...	...	...	...	56.2[11]	10[11]	23	...	95	...	6.46	63	60.3	25.0	14.8	Tonga
1,114[3,7]	...	...	...	...	70.7[3,7]	6[3,7]	17	90	97	112	4.54	180	62.4	36.9	0.6	Trinidad and Tobago
...	...	...	...	...	...	...	33	70	98	126	4.91	76	63.8	33.3	3.0	Tunisia
709	...	...	...	...	...	...	45	130	92	141	3.94	76	36.2	63.3	0.5	Turkey
...	...	...	...	...	...	...	78	110	74	105	4.99	125	66.4	33.2	0.4	Turkmenistan
1,368	40.9	—	—	59.1	51.5[7]	12.2[7]	56	...	100[5]	...	2.66	472	34.0	66.0	0.1	Tuvalu
...	...	...	...	...	...	...	137	510	46	95	3.40	8	13.3	53.0	33.7	Uganda
...	...	...	...	...	...	...	23	30	97	112	3.30	131	69.7	30.3	—	Ukraine
...	...	...	...	...	...	...	10	3	97	132	2.66	472	34.0	66.0	0.1	United Arab Emirates
...	...	...	...	...	...	...	7	7	100	129	6.11	1,039	84.9	15.1	—	United Kingdom
1,180[32]	...	...	...	...	61.8[32]	6[32]	8	8	90	142	12.71	2,765	44.1	55.9	—	United States
477[3]	...	...	...	...	78.8[3]	9[3]	21	21	93	107	4.62	123	53.8	44.8	1.4	Uruguay
...	...	...	...	...	...	...	58	21	90	100	5.90	116	72.1	27.9	—	Uzbekistan
567	...	...	...	...	41.9	6	50	...	77	120	5.68	67	51.5	25.7	22.8	Vanuatu
601[3]	...	...	...	...	69.7[3]	6[3]	25	65	79	96	3.60	88	54.2	45.6	0.1	Venezuela
...	...	...	...	...	...	...	43	160	45	112	2.11	3	39.3	47.4	13.3	Vietnam
...	...	...	...	...	...	...	...	...	...	...	...	...	...	...	...	Virgin Islands (U.S.)
711	...	...	...	...	80.9	4	...	...	...	...	...	...	...	...	...	West Bank
...	...	...	...	...	...	...	...	...	...	...	...	...	...	...	...	Western Sahara
...	...	...	...	...	...	...	100	1,400	61	86	3.19	20	34.7	54.1	11.3	Yemen
1,154	...	...	...	...	72.0	12	21	10	76	117	5.11[33]	264[33]	80.4[33]	19.6[33]	—	Yugoslavia
1,249	—75.7—		—24.3—		68.5	7	202	650	38	84	3.16	17	65.4	30.6	4.1	Zambia
546	...	...	...	...	69.8	7	80	400	79	90	6.23	39	40.3	48.7	11.0	Zimbabwe

not be present and working in the country. [25]1996. [26]Central hospital only. [27]General and specialized hospitals only. [28]Public sector only. [29]Hamad General Hospital only. [30]Victoria Hospital only. [31]Paramaibo hospitals (1,213 beds) only. [32]5,037 community hospitals only. [33]Data refer to the former Socialist Federal Republic of Yugoslavia.

Social protection

This table summarizes three principal areas of social protective activity for the countries of the world: social security, crime and law enforcement, and military affairs. Because the administrative structure, financing, manning, and scope of institutions and programmed tasks in these fields vary so greatly from country to country, no well-accepted or well-documented body of statistical comparisons exists in international convention to permit objective assessment of any of these subjects, either from the perspective of a single country or internationally. The data provided within any single subject area do, however, represent the most consistent approach to problems of international comparison found in the published literature for that field.

The provision of social security programs to answer specific social needs, for example, is summarized simply in terms of the existence or nonexistence of a specific type of benefit program because of the great complexity of national programs in terms of eligibility, coverage, term, age limits, financing, payments, and so on. Activities connected with a particular type of benefit often take place at more than one governmental level, through more than one agency at the same level, or through a mixture of public and private institutions. The data shown here are summarized from the U.S. Social Security Administration's *Social Security Programs Throughout the World* (biennial). A bullet symbol (●) indicates that a country has at least one program within the defined area; in some cases it may have several. A blank space indicates that no program existed providing the benefit shown; ellipses [...] indicate that no information was available as to whether a program existed.

Data given for social security expenditure as a percentage of total central governmental expenditure are taken from the International Monetary Fund's *Government Finance Statistics Yearbook,* which provides the most comparable analytic series on the consolidated accounts of central governments, governmentally administered social security funds, and independent national agencies, all usually separate accounting entities, through which these services may be provided in a given country.

Data on the finances of social security programs are taken in large part from the International Labour Office's *The Cost of Social Security* (triennial), supplemented by national data sources.

Figures for criminal offenses known to police, usually excluding civil offenses and minor traffic violations, are taken in part from Interpol's *International Crime Statistics* (annual) and a variety of national sources. Statistics are usually based on the number of offenses reported to police, not the number of offenders apprehended or tried in courts. Attempted offenses are counted as the offense that was attempted. A person identified as having committed multiple offenses is counted only under the most serious offense. Murder refers to all acts involving the voluntary taking of life, including infanticide, but excluding abortion, or involuntary acts such as those normally classified as manslaughter. Assault includes "serious," or aggravated, assault—that involving injury, endangering life, or perpetrated with the use of a dangerous instrument. Burglary involves theft from the premises of another; although Interpol statistics are reported as "breaking and entering," national data may not always distinguish cases of forcible

Social protection

country	social security							finances									
	programs available, 1999					expenditures, 1999 (% of total central govt.)[f]	year	receipts					expenditures			
	old-age, invalidity, death[a]	sickness and maternity[b]	work injury[c]	unemployment[d]	family allowances[e]			total ('000,000 natl. cur.)	insured persons (%)	employers (%)	government (%)	other (%)	total ('000,000 natl. cur.)	benefits (%)	administration (%)	other (%)
Afghanistan	●	●	●		●	...	...	...	...	...	...	...	...	...	...	...
Albania	●	●	●	●	●	20.1	1990	967.0	—	—	88.8	11.2	1,440.0	99.5	——0.5——	
Algeria	●	●	●	●	●	...	1990	27,700.0	...	...	...	...	28,748.0	61.8	30.6	7.6
American Samoa	●	...	...	...	...	...	1990						13.0	100.0	...	...
Andorra	●	●	●		●	...	1993	11,832.2	...	...	...	...	7,937.2	90.2	4.6	5.2
Angola	...	...	...	...	...	...										
Antigua and Barbuda	●	●				...	1983	13.0	29.2	48.7	—	22.1	4.2	66.1	33.9	...
Argentina	●	●	●	●	●	48.4	1989	1,015,837.0	28.8	45.0	16.6	9.6	989,009.0	95.0	5.0	—
Armenia	●	●	●	●	●	...	...	...	...	...	...	...	...	...	...	...
Aruba	●		●	...	...	6	1998	197.1					179.0	...	...	...
Australia	●	●	●	●	●	35.5	1998–99	...	...	...	...	1.9	41,825	99.6	0.3	—
Austria	●	●	●	●	●	42.0	1989	425,417.0	30.1	45.9	21.1	2.9	412,134.0	96.5	2.3	1.2
Azerbaijan	●	●	●	●	●	33.1	...	...	...	...	...	...	...	...	...	...
Bahamas, The	●	●	●		●	6.9	1989	95.9	22.9	38.5	2.1	36.5	43.5	71.1	27.2	1.7
Bahrain	●		●			4.8	1989	39.6	12.3	40.2	—	47.5	9.7	69.8	20.9	9.3
Bangladesh	●	●	●			...	1989	73.6	12.4	37.5	2.4	47.7	34.1	94.0	6.0	—
Barbados	●	●	●	●		...	1989	191.7	38.0	40.8	1.5	19.7	149.1	93.5	5.8	0.7
Belarus	●	●	●	●	●	33.3	1986	3,199.0	—	—	93.2	6.8	3,199.0	100.0	—	—
Belgium	●	●	●	●	●	...	1986	1,347,070.0	24.4	39.7	31.6	4.3	1,322,636.0	94.5	4.3	1.2
Belize	●		●			5.9[7]	1989	15.3	8.9	53.2	—	38.0	3.9	56.7	43.3	—
Benin	●	●	●		●	...	1989	3,551.9	16.8	81.4	—	1.8	4,500.9	69.3	28.1	2.6
Bermuda	●					...	...	...	...	...	...	...	...	...	...	...
Bhutan	...	...	●	...	...	...	1990						26.0[8]	...	...	...
Bolivia	●	●	●		●	25.0	1989	346.6	29.3	47.7	11.2	11.8	340.2	84.9	14.3	0.8
Bosnia and Herzegovina	●	●	●	●	●	...	...	...	...	...	...	...	...	...	...	...
Botswana	●		●			1.1[10]	1996	—	—	—	—	—	65.0[8]	...	...	...
Brazil	●	●	●	●	●	47.2[11]	1989	71,847.0	24.4	51.0	20.0	4.6	68,957.0	61.9	18.6	19.5
Brunei	●	...	●	...	●	...	1984						39.5	...	...	...
Bulgaria	●	●	●	●	●	32.8	1989	6,016.8	—	71.4	28.1	0.5	6,000.1	96.6	3.3	0.1
Burkina Faso	●	●	●		●	0.1[12]	1989	8,816.5	15.6	62.9	—	21.5	4,975.3	69.5	30.4	0.1
Burundi	●		●		●	5.1	1989	1,991.5	31.6	47.6	—	20.8	1,563.9	74.8	16.8	8.4
Cambodia	...	...	●	...	●	...	...	...	...	...	...	...	...	...	...	...
Cameroon	●	●	●		●	0.5	1989	41,331.8	13.1	64.8	—	22.1	41,332.0	70.6	28.8	0.6
Canada	●	●	●	●	●	53.2	1989	130,306.6	9.9	15.6	64.4	10.1	115,764.2	96.9	2.5	0.6
Cape Verde	●	●	●		●	...	1989	697.7	26.5	58.5	—	15.0	316.7	82.4	16.1	1.5
Central African Republic	●	●	●		●	...	1989	3,604.0	8.4	76.0	—	15.6	3,247.0	64.6	32.9	2.5
Chad	●		●		●	...	1989	1,172.8	12.6	77.6	—	9.8	634.5	43.0	51.4	5.6
Chile	●	●	●	●	●	35.7	1989	1,186,056.0	32.8	2.7	37.9	26.6	798,770.0	83.9	14.7	1.4
China	●	●	●	●		22.4	1989	57,446.2	—	99.4	—	0.6	54,654	98.4	0.6	1.0
Colombia	●	●	●		●	12.4	1989	294,438.0	24.8	56.0	0.2	19.0	257,455.0	85.5	11.5	3.0
Comoros	...	...	...	...	...	...	1983	40.7	100.0	—	—	—	54.3	17.4	62.3	20.3
Congo, Dem. Rep. of the	●	●	●		●	—	1986	1,238.3	28.6	60.2	—	11.2	1,044.2	27.9	72.1	—
Congo, Rep. of the	●	●	●		●	...	1983	15,272.8	12.1	80.2	—	7.7	7,256.7	66.6	21.3	12.1
Costa Rica	●	●	●		●	23.1	1989	36,407.3	33.2	44.4	1.2	21.2	31,049.8	89.0	4.1	6.9
Côte d'Ivoire	●	●	●		●	...	1989	27,288.4	19.3	75.4	—	5.3	20,593.5	100.0	—	—
Croatia	●	●	●	●	●	38.6	...	...	...	...	...	...	...	...	...	...
Cuba	●	●	●			...	1989	2,284.8	—	37.4	62.6	—	2,284.8	96.7	—	3.3
Cyprus[15]	●	●	●	●	●	24.5	1989	217.5	24.7	40.3	17.3	17.7	117.7	98.4	1.6	—
Czech Republic	●	●	●	●	●	37.7	1989[17]	132,748.0	—	3.9	96.1	—	132,748.0	99.7	0.3	—
Denmark	●	●	●	●	●	40.1	1989	225,965.6	4.3	5.0	88.2	2.5	218,258.2	97.0	3.0	—
Djibouti	●	●	●		●	...	1979	1,352.2					1,115.7	...	...	...
Dominica	●	●	●			...	1986	12.3	22.6	50.9	—	26.5	4.4	68.0	32.0	—
Dominican Republic	●	●	●			6.7	1986	77.9	20.1	72.9	—	6.8	74.3	75.9	24.1	—
East Timor[19]	...	...	...	...	...	...										
Ecuador	●	●	●	●		1.9[3]	1988	71,286.0	37.0	50.0	—	13.0	52,032.4	86.0	14.0	—

entry. Automobile theft excludes brief use of a car without the owner's permission, "joyriding," and implies intent to deprive the owner of the vehicle permanently. Criminal offense data for certain countries refer to cases disposed of in court, rather than to complaints. Police manpower figures refer, for the most part, to full-time, paid professional staff, excluding clerical support and volunteer staff. Personnel in military service who perform police functions are presumed to be employed in their principal activity, military service.

The figures for military manpower refer to full-time, active-duty military service and exclude reserve, militia, paramilitary, and similar organizations. Because of the difficulties attached to the analysis of data on military manpower and budgets (including problems such as data withheld on national security grounds, or the publication of budgetary data specifically intended to hide actual expenditure, or the complexity of long-term financing of purchases of military matériel [how much was actually spent as opposed to what was committed, offset by nonmilitary transfers, etc.]), extensive use is made of the principal international analytic tools: publications such as those of the International Institute for Strategic Studies (*The Military Balance*) and the U.S. Arms Control and Disarmament Agency (*World Military Expenditures and Arms Transfers*), both annuals.

The data on military expenditures are from the sources identified above, as well as from the IMF's *Government Finance Statistics Yearbook* and country statistical publications.

The following notes further define the column headings:

a. Programs providing cash payments for *each* of the three types of long-term benefit indicated to persons (1) exceeding a specified working age (usually 50–65, often 5 years earlier for women) who are qualified by a term of covered employment, (2) partially or fully incapacitated for their usual employment by injury or illness, and (3) qualified by their status as spouse, cohabitant, or dependent minor of a qualified person who dies.

b. Programs providing cash payments (jointly, or alternatively, medical services as well) to occupationally qualified persons for *both* of the short-term benefits indicated: (1) illness and (2) maternity.

c. Programs providing cash or medical services to employment-qualified persons who become temporarily or permanently incapacitated (fully or partially) by work-related injury or illness.

d. Programs providing term-limited cash compensation (usually 40–75% of average earnings) to persons qualified by previous employment (of six months minimum, typically) for periods of involuntary unemployment.

e. Programs providing cash payments to families or mothers to mitigate the cost of raising children and to encourage the formation of larger families.

f. Includes welfare.

g. A police officer is a full-time, paid professional, performing domestic security functions. Data include administrative staff but exclude clerical employees, volunteers, and members of paramilitary groups.

h. Includes all active-duty personnel, regular and conscript, performing national security functions. Excludes reserves, paramilitary forces, border patrols, and gendarmeries.

crime and law enforcement (latest)					population per police officer[g]	military protection							arms trade, 1999 ('000,000 U.S.$)		country
offenses reported to the police per 100,000 population						manpower, 2002[h]		expenditure, 1999							
total	personal		property			total ('000)	per 1,000 population	total '000,000	per capita	% of central government expenditure	% of GDP or GNP	imports	exports	
	murder	assault	burglary	automobile theft										
...	...	...	...	...	540[1]	2	2	408[3]	...	...	...	0	0	Afghanistan
168.8	26.2	5.8	10.7	14.1	550	27.0	8.7	72	21	4.5	1.3	30	0	Albania
178.0	0.7	67.6	13.7	1.7	840	136.7	4.3	1,830	60	12.6	4.0	550	0	Algeria
3,006	8.0	494.0	588.0	6.0	460	4	4	...	...	...	...	...	...	American Samoa
2,616	0	16.7	515.2	110.6	220	—		...	...	...	...	...	...	Andorra
143.5	8.7	15.3	30.5	3.7	14[5]	100.0	9.4	2,460	248	41.1	21.2	350	0	Angola
4,977	4.7	475.0	1,984.4	35.9	120	0.2	2.6	...	...	...	...	...	...	Antigua and Barbuda
631.0	6.0	68.2	43.0	117.1	1,270	69.9	1.9	4,300	118	9.1	1.6	90	0	Argentina
264.4	4.1	4.7	16.6	0.7	...	44.6	14.8	570	170	20.2	5.8	10	0	Armenia
5,461	1.2	180.0	451.3	202.5	...	4	4	—				...	...	Aruba
7,003	3.7	708.5	2,926.2	684.8	438	50.9	2.6	7,060	372	7.6	1.8	1,100	550	Australia
6,095	1.4	3.0	944.0	34.7	470	34.6	4.2	1,690	208	1.5	0.8	30	30	Austria
176	4.2	2.4	10.3	0.4	...	72.1	8.8	927	120	24.4	6.6	10	0	Azerbaijan
4,870	27.1	61.5	1,560.2	415.7	125	0.9	2.9	...	...	...	...	...	...	Bahamas, The
1,390	1.6	0.5	380.1	207.6	180	10.7	15.9	415	666	18.9	8.1	70	0	Bahrain
90	2.8	4.3	4.3	1.1	2,560	137.0	1.0	624	5.0	10.1	1.3	80	0	Bangladesh
3,813	8.6	161.9	1,080.8	105.5	280	0.6	2.2	12	44	1.4	0.5	0	0	Barbados
1,282.4	11.6	20.6	197.9	59.9	...	79.8	8.0	925	89	4.1	1.3	0	310	Belarus
8,478	5.3	535.8	2,031.3	376.5	640	39.3	3.8	3,600	352	3.1	1.4	350	30	Belgium
...	12.8	20.0	600.0	4.0	290	1.1	4.3	11	47	5.4	1.6	0	0	Belize
297	5.1	102.0	4.6	0.6	3,250	4.6	0.7	34	5.0	8.3	1.4	5	0	Benin
8,871	5.1	221.7	1,949.2	...	370	4	4	—	—	—	—	...	...	Bermuda
...	...	...	...	...	...	...	...	...	...	...	...	0	0	Bhutan
660	28.6	59.4	0.9	...	...	31.5	3.7	148	18	8.0	1.8	10	0	Bolivia
402	2.5	2.6	...	...	...	19.8[9]	5.0[9]	276	75	24.3	4.5	40	0	Bosnia and Herzegovina
8,281	12.7	431.9	1.9	73.1	750	9.0	5.4	222	142	9.8	4.7	40	0	Botswana
779.1	11.2	255.7	5.2	61.2	...	287.6	1.6	9,920	58	5.5[7]	1.9	180	20	Brazil
932.9	1.5	1.2	79.8	57.5	100	7.0	19.9	295	897	11.5	4.0	20	0	Brunei
1,170.7	7.3	1.9	402.9	94.5	...	68.5	8.7	1,240	158	8.7	3.0	10	200	Bulgaria
9	0.4	1.7	—	—	...	6.0	0.5	42	4	5.9	1.6	0	0	Burkina Faso
156	9.7	10.8	2.0	0.2	...	40.0	6.2	49	8	26.7	7.0	60	0	Burundi
...	...	...	...	...	1,980	106	7.9	332	28	26.0	4.0	5	0	Cambodia
78	0.4	1.2	1.2	5.1	1,170	14.1	0.9	148	10	10.6	1.8	5	0	Cameroon
8,121	4.0	140.3	1,044.4	529.4	8,640	52.3	1.7	8,320	269	5.9	1.4	1,000	550	Canada
...	...	...	...	...	110	1.2	2.6	5	13	2.2	0.9	5	0	Cape Verde
135	1.6	22.8	2.7	...	2,740[1]	2.6	0.7	29	8	15.4	2.8	0	0	Central African Republic
...	...	...	...	...	990	25.4	2.8	37	5	12.7	2.4	10	0	Chad
1,366	4.5	84.8	488.0	12.9	470	80.5	5.3	1,990	133	12.3	3.0	100	10	Chile
128	0.2	5.2	45.2	6.9	1,360[13]	2,270.0	1.8	88,900	71	22.2	2.3	675	320	China
790	56.3	61.8	57.9	75.3	420	158.0	3.9	2,670	68	15.9	3.2	60	0	Colombia
...	...	...	...	...	960	14	14	...	...	...	...	...	...	Comoros
...	...	...	...	...	910	81.4	1.5	5,150	102	41.4[7]	14.4	110	0	Congo, Dem. Rep. of the
32	1.5	4.7	0.2	0.2	870	10.0	3.4	58	21	8.4	3.5	0	0	Congo, Rep. of the
868	5.3	11.1	232.4	23.1	480	—		69	19	2.0	0.5	0	0	Costa Rica
67	2.5	73.1	19.5	11.9	4,640	8.1	0.5	82	5	3.4	0.8	0	0	Côte d'Ivoire
1,216	6.1	24.1	290.9	38.6	...	51.0	11.6	2,090	491	14.2	6.4	10	10	Croatia
...	...	...	...	...	650	46.0	4.1	630	57	...	1.9	0	0	Cuba
689	1.9	17.7	203.3	3.0	180	10.0[16]	11.0[16]	309	411	9.3	3.4	340	0	Cyprus[15]
4,142	2.6	71.7	831.4	263.0	640[17]	49.5	4.8	3,000	292	6.3	2.3	220	80	Czech Republic
9,300	4.1	20.8	1,899	638.1	600	22.7	4.3	2,780	524	4.2	1.6	290	10	Denmark
252	4.2	124.2	45.0	0.5	...	6.0	12.7	23	51	12.7	4.3	0	0	Djibouti
9,567	7.9	682.4	1,736	77.6	300	18	18	...	...	...	...	...	...	Dominica
...	15.8	28.4	154.0	14.0	580	24.5	2.8	123	15	4.4	0.7	20	0	Dominican Republic
...	...	...	...	...	...	20	20	...	...	...	...	...	...	East Timor[19]
587	25.9	35.6	164.5	52.9	260	59.5	4.5	479	38	16.2	3.7	20	0	Ecuador

Social protection (continued)

country	social security — programs available, 1999					expenditures, 1999 (% of total central govt.)[f]	finances — year	receipts total ('000,000 natl. cur.)	insured persons (%)	employers (%)	government (%)	other (%)	expenditures total ('000,000 natl. cur.)	benefits (%)	administration (%)	other (%)
	old-age, invalidity, death[a]	sickness and maternity[b]	work injury[c]	unemployment[d]	family allowances[e]											
Egypt	●	●	●	●		0.5[7]	1989	2,443.5	22.8	41.0	2.0	34.2	1,685.6	93.4	6.6	—
El Salvador	●	●	●			2.7	1989	465.3	27.1	51.7	—	21.2	368.3	78.1	21.9	—
Equatorial Guinea	●	●	●		●	...	1989	141.0	7.1	92.9	—	—	134.0	49.3	50.7	—
Eritrea	...	...	●	...	...	...	...									
Estonia	●	●	●	●	●	32.5	...	90.1	...	...	...	...	...	...	...	...
Ethiopia	●		●			5.0[10]	1989[21]	190.9	32.8	65.3	—	1.9	153.7	98.3	1.7	—
Faroe Islands	●	...	...		●	...	...									
Fiji	●		●			4.1[10]	1989	153.5	20.9	33.8	0.8	44.5	75.47	95.3	4.7	...
Finland	●	●	●	●	●	36.4	1989	118,589.0	7.7	41.1	44.0	7.2	106,235	96.3	3.7	—
France	●	●	●	●	●	39.3[22]	1989	1,700,202.0	77.7	—	20.4	1.9	1,669,096.0	95.5	3.7	0.8
French Guiana	●	...	●	...	●	...	1991	1,071.5	...				997.1	...		
French Polynesia	●	●	●		●	...	1990	19,268.0	...				17,832.0	...		
Gabon	●		●		●	...	1989	3,415.0	—	44.3	29.3	26.4	2,737.0	55.2	44.8	—
Gambia, The	●		●			3.0[3]	1982	—	...				5.6	...		
Gaza Strip	...	...	...	...	...	—	...									
Georgia	●	●	●	●	●	33.9	...									
Germany	●	●	●	●	●	50.0[10]	1989[23]	522,172.0	36.9	34.3	26.1	2.7	507,604.0	97.1	2.8	0.1
Ghana	●		●			4.3	1989	17,920.8	21.1	52.9	—	26.0	4,147.7	13.3	64.0	22.7
Greece	●	●	●	●	●	17.9[11]	1989	1,314,421.0	24.9	38.4	30.8	5.9	1,349,693.0	92.5	7.5	—
Greenland	●	...	...		●	...	...									
Grenada	●	●				8.6[24]	1989	24.1	20.1	60.3	3.2	16.3	13.5	93.1	6.9	—
Guadeloupe	●	...	●	...	●	...	1994	2,607.3	...				5,883.4	...		
Guam	●				●	...	1989	...					7.3	...		
Guatemala	●	●	●			...	1989	348.5	29.1	54.8	—	16.1	279.7	82.7	14.6	2.7
Guernsey	●	●	●	●	●	...	1999	103,560	—45.0—		40.7	14.3	85,468	94.8	5.2	...
Guinea	●				●	...	1989	3,387.0	0.4	90.3	—	9.3	1,108.1	54.9	45.1	—
Guinea-Bissau	...	...	●	...	...	8.8[22]	1986	138.0	22.8	63.4	10.3	3.8	61.9	59.6	40.4	—
Guyana	●	●	●			...	1994	1,070.8	...				1,373.7	...		
Haiti	●		●			5.1[25]	1977	60.5	—26.6—		69.9	3.5	52.4	92.7	7.3	—
Honduras	●	●	●			...	1986	166.2	23.9	40.8	3.3	32.0	76.8	84.6	15.4	—
Hong Kong	●		●		●	...	1998–99	...					26,939	...		
Hungary	●	●	●	●	●	21.9	1994	798,000.0	...				737,000.0	...		
Iceland	●	●	●	●	●[27]	21.8	1997	14,799	—	—	—	—	96,094	98.2	1.8	—
India	●	●	●			...	1989	43,913.8	23.8	27.7	5.3	43.2	13,775.8	90.0	8.2	1.8
Indonesia	●		●			5.3	1989	239,477.0	50.7	49.3	—	—	181,499.0	12.3	15.8	71.9
Iran	●	●	●		●	15.9	1986	346,460.0	83.2	0.1	8.2	8.5	167,879.0	43.4	6.3	50.0
Iraq	●	●	●			...	1977	107.8	9.9	55.6	21.9	12.6	71.0	94.0	2.4	3.6
Ireland	●	●	●	●	●	27.1	1989	4,627.5	16.3	24.8	57.7	1.2	4,612.9	95.2	4.7	0.1
Isle of Man	●	●	●	●	●	...	1985	...					14.4	...		
Israel	●	●	●	●	●	25.9	1989	13,851.1	31.1	27.7	35.0	6.2	13,593.3	81.7	15.4	2.9
Italy	●	●	●	●	●	...	1989	278,383.0	16.5	51.4	30.0	2.1	100,251.0	89.3	2.0	8.7
Jamaica	●		●			1.0	1989	374.3	11.5	13.6	43.8	31.1	273.6	92.6	7.4	—
Japan	●	●	●	●	●	36.8[24]	1989	59,571,299.0	27.4	31.6	24.4	16.6	46,684,159.0	94.3	1.7	4.0
Jersey	●	●	●	●	●	9.5[22,25]	1991	60.9	—63.8—		23.4	12.8	52.8	...		
Jordan	●		●			15.5	1986	53.6	28.7	55.3	—	16.0	9.5	77.4	14.0	8.6
Kazakhstan	●	●	●	●	●	46.3	...									
Kenya	●		●			2.7	1989	4,262.0	18.2	13.7	10.0	58.1	1,857.8	53.8	46.1	0.1
Kiribati	●					...	...									
Korea, North	...	...	...	...	...	...	...									
Korea, South	●	●	●			10.8[7]	1996	7,425,400.0	—	62.2	—	—	9,656,600.0	...		
Kuwait	●				●	20.4	1989	445.8	7.1	13.2	54.3	25.4	206.5	97.0	3.0	—
Kyrgyzstan	●	●	●	●	●	10.2	...									
Laos	●	...	●	...	●	...	...									
Latvia	●	●	●	●	●	43.1	...									
Lebanon	●	●			●	5.2	...									
Lesotho	...	...	●	...	...	1.1[29]	1992	—	...				12.0[8]	...		
Liberia	●	●	●			...	1983	2.9	—	69.0	13.8	17.2	2.6	54.4	45.6	...
Libya	●	●	●			...	1989	314.3	21.6	25.4	50.2	2.8	260.0	77.5	19.5	3.0
Liechtenstein	●	●	●	●	●	...	...									
Lithuania	●	●	●	●		36.3	...						24,981.7	...		
Luxembourg	●	●	●	●	●	52.3[24]	1989	72,471.8	24.2	34.6	34.4	6.8	65,214.4	97.2	2.4	0.4
Macau	●	...	●	...	●	...	1998	223.2	...				207.4	...		
Macedonia	●	●	●	●	●	...	1996	24,482	...							
Madagascar	●		●		●	1.5	1989	15,229.0	22.2	77.8	—	—	14,542.0	81.2	18.8	...
Malawi	●					...	1986	—	...				5.4	...		
Malaysia	●		●			7.0	1989	7,958.7	20.7	40.2	—	39.1	2,826.5	97.0	3.0	—
Maldives	...	...	...	...	...	2.8	1990	...					7.1	...		
Mali	●	●	●		●	...	1986	8,128.8	16.6	74.3	—	9.1	7,924.6	63.7	34.7	1.6
Malta	●	●	●	●	●	34.4	1989	82.2	26.1	31.6	42.3	—	110.7	92.5	7.5	—
Marshall Islands	●		●			...	...									
Martinique	●	...	●	...	●	...	1998	3,913.1	...				8,429.6	...		
Mauritania	●	●	●		●	...	1989	808.4	1.5	90.4	—	8.1	735.2	63.5	31.2	5.3
Mauritius	●		●		●	12.3	1989	1,733.5	2.9	47.9	31.7	17.5	1,072.7	95.2	3.0	1.8
Mayotte	...	...	...	...	...	...	...									
Mexico	●	●	●			20.6	1989	16,011,795.0	20.9	54.8	12.9	11.4	14,562,293.0	79.9	15.5	4.6
Micronesia	●					...	...									
Moldova	●	●	●	●	●	40.2	...									
Monaco	●	●	●	●	●	...	...									
Mongolia	●	●			●	25.3	1989	2,431.6	—	—	20.8	79.2	2,304.6	100.0	—	—
Morocco	●		●		●	9.3	1989	4,660.5	20.6	47.5	12.9	19.0	3,040.7	94.8	5.0	0.2
Mozambique	●	...	...			...	1986	228.2	—	86.2	13.7	0.1	145.0	100.0	—	...
Myanmar (Burma)	●	●	●			1.6	1986	44.3	19.9	59.6	18.5	2.0	35.9	51.5	15.6	32.9
Namibia	●		●		●	6.8[12,25]	...									
Nauru	●	●	●		●	...	...									
Nepal	●		●			2.3	1985	—	...				59.3	...		

crime and law enforcement (latest)					population per police officer[g]	military protection								country
offenses reported to the police per 100,000 population						manpower, 2002[h]		expenditure, 1999				arms trade, 1999 ('000,000 U.S.$)		
total	personal		property			total ('000)	per 1,000 population	total '000,000	per capita	% of central government expenditure	% of GDP or GNP	imports	exports	
	murder	assault	burglary	automobile theft										
3,693	1.6	0.7	...	3.1	580	443.0	6.4	2,390	36	9.3[7]	2.7	700	0	Egypt
879	36.9	71.1	...	82.0	1,000	16.8	2.6	110	18	8.8	0.9	10	0	El Salvador
...	...	...	...	...	190	1.3	2.6	19	40	16.5	3.2	0	0	Equatorial Guinea
161.9	2.7	10.3	5.8	...	...	172.2	43.3	208	52	51.1	7.4	170	20	Eritrea
3,565	13.8	28.3	1,659.2	169.8	...	5.5	4.0	173	120	4.5	1.5	10	0	Estonia
258.3	6.5	77.8	1.4	1.4	1,100[21]	252.5	3.7	533	9	29.1	8.8	270	0	Ethiopia
						4	4	—	—	—	—	...	...	Faroe Islands
2,370	2.9	44.1	427.9	44.4	407	3.5	4.2	35	42	5.4	2.0	0	0	Fiji
14,350	0.7	34.9	1,739.7	33.2	640	31.9	6.1	1,770	344	4.5	1.4	400	50	Finland
6,097	3.4	162.7	632.4	511.0	630	260.4	4.4	38,900	658	5.9	2.7	800	2,900	France
8,936	27.2	178.7	1,367.3	150.6	...	4	4	—	—	—	—	...	...	French Guiana
1,799	0.9	98.9	232.7	...	...	4	4	—	—	—	—	...	...	French Polynesia
114	1.4	17.9	2.3	7.5	1,290	4.7	3.8	93	78	7.3	2.4	0	0	Gabon
89	0.4	10.6	5.6	...	3,310	0.8	0.6	5	4	5.4	1.3	0	0	Gambia, The
4,355	...	...	...	...	...	—	—	...	...	...	...	...	...	Gaza Strip
286	4.7	99.5	21.1	0.8	...	17.5	3.5	165	33	7.0	1.2	10	30	Georgia
7,682	3.5	139.6	1,377.4	114.3	...	296.0	3.6	32,600	395	4.7	1.6	1,300	1,900	Germany
...	2.2	418.9	1.5	...	620	7.0	0.3	62	3	3.1	0.8	0	0	Ghana
3,641	3.0	68.2	356.8	166.5	380	177.6	16.2	6,060	573	16.4	4.7	1,900	90	Greece
9,360	18.1	845.0	1,883.5	...	340	4	4	—	—	—	—	...	...	Greenland
8,543	7.8	98.9	582.2	...	230	18	18	...	...	—	...	...	...	Grenada
5,793	13.2	215.2	821.5	453.9	...	4	4	—	—	—	—	...	...	Guadeloupe
10,080	7.9	169.3	634.2	333.6	...	4	4	—	—	—	—	...	...	Guam
510	27.4	77.1	27.9	58.1	670	31.4	2.6	121	10	5.0	0.7	0	0	Guatemala
...	...	...	...	...	...	4	4	—	—	—	—	...	...	Guernsey
18.4	0.5	0.7	0.7	0.1	1,140	9.7	1.2	54	7	7.4	1.6	0	0	Guinea
129	0.5	8.7	4.0	0.2	...	7.3	5.4	6	4	6.1	2.7	0	0	Guinea-Bissau
1,277	19.1	246.0	365.8	32.2	190	1.4	1.8	5	7	2.0	0.8	0	0	Guyana
701	...	...	...	...	400	26	26	...	...	...	...	0	0	Haiti
392	154.0	44.4	4.3	25.8	1,040	8.3	1.3	34	6	2.6	0.7	10	0	Honduras
1,122	1.0	117.1	133.4	15.3	221	4	4	—	—	—	—	...	...	Hong Kong
5,011	4.1	76.6	804.4	41.3	237	33.4	3.3	1,880	185	3.9	1.7	80	10	Hungary
31,332	0.7	15.8	920.3	...	940	4	4	—	—	—	—	10	0	Iceland
594	4.6	...	15.6	...	820	1,100.0	1.0	11,300	11	14.6	2.5	700	10	India
120.9	1.0	4.4	1.8	1.7	1,119	230	1.1	1,450	7	5.3	1.1	450	100	Indonesia
77	0.5	47.7	...	...	...	520.0	7.9	6,880	106	11.2	2.9	150	10	Iran
197	7.1	34.7	...	...	140	389.0	18.2	1,250	57	...	5.5	5	0	Iraq
1,696	1.4	12.4	479.8	16.3	310	10.5	2.7	779	208	2.6	1.0	40	0	Ireland
2,867	0.7	12.3	921.4	60.6	...	4	4	—	—	—	—	...	...	Isle of Man
6,254	2.2	491.8	990.1	501.7	210	161.5	25.3	8,700	1,510	18.5	8.8	2,400	600	Israel
4,214	4.4	46.4	...	537.0	680	216.8	3.7	23,700	412	4.7	2.0	700	380	Italy
1,871	37.2	511.4	135.7	7.2	430	2.8	1.1	51	19	2.1	0.8	10	0	Jamaica
1,773	1.0	16.0	206.0	34.0	480	239.9	1.9	43,200	342	6.1	1.0	3,000	20	Japan
...	...	...	...	...	...	4	4	—	—	—	—	...	...	Jersey
1,256	6.3	14.0	31.0	52.2	630	100.2	19.0	725	150	27.5	9.2	70	0	Jordan
932	15.9	...	...	3.4	...	60	4.0	671	40	5.3	0.9	160	10	Kazakhstan
484	6.4	54.1	76.9	9.7	1,500	24.4	0.8	200	7	7.1	1.9	5	0	Kenya
261	5.1	11.6	38.6	...	330	—	—	...	...	...	...	...	...	Kiribati
...	...	...	...	...	460	1,082.0	48.7	4,260	199	...	18.8	30	140	Korea, North
3,494	2.1	64.6	7.0	...	506	686.0	14.3	11,600	246	11.0	2.9	2,200	20	Korea, South
1,346	1.5	36.4	75.9	56.7	80	15.5	6.9	2,690	1,410	20.8	7.7	725	0	Kuwait
987	10.4[28]	12.6	482.4	...	...	8.5	1.7	285	62	14.0	2.4	0	0	Kyrgyzstan
...	...	...	...	...	280	29.1	5.0	28	5	11.1	2.0	0	0	Laos
2,097	9.3	18.6	56.1	129.0	...	5.5	2.4	144	59	2.5	0.9	5	0	Latvia
3,063	5.5	209.7	78.0	30.0	530	71.8	19.5	653	185	11.0	4.0	10	0	Lebanon
2,357	50.4	156.9	250.4	30.8	1,130	2.0	0.9	29	14	6.5	2.6	0	0	Lesotho
...	...	...	...	...	1,570	30	30	6	2	8.3	1.2	0	0	Liberia
1,065	2.1	5.4	...	...	...	76.0	14.2	1,490[7]	342[7]	19.7[7]	6.1[7]	20	30	Libya
...	...	114.3	614.3	153.6	660	31	31	...	...	...	...	...	...	Liechtenstein
2,029	9.0	10.4	585.6	96.7	...	13.5	3.9	314	87	3.9	1.3	20	0	Lithuania
6,280	17.2	89.0	1,152.8	182.0	829	0.9	2.0	141	326	2.0	0.8	50	0	Luxembourg
1,698	5.4	34.0	250.5	26.6	...	4	4	...	...	...	...	...	...	Macau
1,102	5.4	26.9	...	44.7	...	12.3	6.1	228	112	10.4	2.5	20	0	Macedonia
112	0.6	12.0	0.7	0.1	2,900	13.5	0.8	45	3	7.4	1.2	0	0	Madagascar
850	3.1	82.2	13.1	...	1,670	5.3	0.5	10	1	2.2	0.6	0	0	Malawi
604	3.1	25.9	155.6	20.8	760	100.0	4.1	1,660	78	9.3	2.3	925	0	Malaysia
2,353	1.9	3.3	36.1	...	35,710	—	—	...	...	...	...	...	...	Maldives
10.0	0.7	1.5	0.8	0.3	160	7.4	0.7	58	6	8.7	2.3	0	0	Mali
1,841	3.0	35.2	1,079.2	243.9	230	2.1	5.4	28	73	1.8	0.8	0	0	Malta
2,273	...	...	...	...	400	32	32	—	—	—	—	...	...	Marshall Islands
						4	4	—	—	—	—	...	...	Martinique
6,305	5.8	184.9	641.2	192.8	710	15.7	5.9	37	14	18.9	4.0	0	0	Mauritania
95.4	0.8	27.0	7.3	2.5	240	—	—	9	7	0.9	0.2	0	0	Mauritius
2,712	2.9	7.8	116.0	...	...	4	4	—	—	—	—	...	...	Mayotte
...	...	...	...	...	...	192.8	1.9	2,700	27	3.8	0.6	160	30	Mexico
108	7.3	30.2	...	...	...									
						32	32	—	—	—	—	...	...	Micronesia
957	9.9	11.1	50.4	15.6	...	7.2	2.0	43	10	1.6	0.5	0	20	Moldova
3,430	—	46.7	106.7	70.0	...	—	—	...	...	...	...	...	...	Monaco
1,010	30.0	74.7	486.0	2.1	120	9.1	3.7	18	5	5.9	2.1	0	0	Mongolia
366	1.4	6.7	...	...	840	196.3	6.7	1,450	49	13.5	4.3	130	0	Morocco
166	4.2	9.2	45.9	...	...	33	33	94	5	9.1	2.5	5	0	Mozambique
64.5	1.9	26.9	0.1	0.1	650	325.0	7.7	4,650	112	189.3	7.8	60	0	Myanmar (Burma)
2,006	26.3	533.6	602.0	65.8	...	9.0	4.9	91	53	7.2	2.9	130	0	Namibia
...	25.0	400.0	100.0	...	110	—	—	...	...	...	...	...	...	Nauru
9	2.8	1.1	0.8	...	1,000	51.0	2.2	44	2	5.7	0.8	0	0	Nepal

Social protection (continued)

country	old-age, invalidity, death[a]	sickness and maternity[b]	work injury[c]	unemployment[d]	family allowances[e]	expenditures, 1999 (% of total central govt.)[f]	year	receipts total ('000,000 natl. cur.)	insured persons (%)	employers (%)	government (%)	other (%)	expenditures total ('000,000 natl. cur.)	benefits (%)	administration (%)	other (%)
Netherlands, The	●	●	●	●	●	37.4[7]	1989	154,427.0	37.3	30.3	19.0	13.4	135,609.0	96.9	3.1	—
Netherlands Antilles	●	...	●	●	...	12.9[6,24]	1998	317.0	100.0	—	—	—	275.0	...	...	...
New Caledonia	...	...	...	...	...		1987	15,834.0	...	...	...	...	14,598.0	...	...	...
New Zealand	●	●	●	●	●	39.8	1989	14,266.0	1.0	4.7	92.5	1.8	14,372.3	95.6	2.8	1.6
Nicaragua	●	●	●		...	14.7[24]	1989	647,454.8	13.5	49.1	7.6	29.8	452,038.6	82.4	17.6	—
Niger	●		●		●	...	1989	5,634.9	9.4	90.6	—	—	3,804.2	62.5	—	37.5
Nigeria	●		●			...	1989	54.0	50.0	50.0	—	—	22.6	42.5	57.5	—
Northern Mariana Islands	●	...	●	...	...											
Norway	●	●	●	●	●	39.0[11]	1989	158,105.0	18.3	31.4	46.6	3.7	131,578.2	98.7	1.3	—
Oman	●	...	●	...	...	6.0	1995	—					...	...	...	...
Pakistan	●	●	●			...	1989	9,321.4	1.3	8.0	84.3	6.4	8,092.0	97.4	1.2	1.4
Palau	●															
Panama	●	●	●[12]			18.7	1989	496.7	31.0	39.5	7.1	22.4	452.8	94.0	4.8	1.2
Papua New Guinea	●		●			2.3	1983	45.0	40.5	32.1	8.0	19.4	9.4	82.3	9.7	8.0
Paraguay	●	●	●			16.2[22]	1993						253,341	...	...	...
Peru	●	●	●			...	1989	1,363,280.6	30.2	65.1	4.7	—	1,435,134.1	78.5	21.5	—
Philippines	●	●	●			4.1	1989	19,213.6	22.2	32.3	—	45.5	7,878.3	87.3	12.3	—
Poland	●	●	●	●	●	51.2	1989	11,572,248.0	2.1	70.2	25.1	2.6	11,452,165.0	98.8	1.2	—
Portugal	●	●	●	●	●	27.3[3]	1989	833,442.5	31.3	50.1	13.4	5.2	756,410.8	94.6	4.2	1.2
Puerto Rico	●	●	●	●	●	...	1980						1,041.3	100.0		
Qatar	...	...	...	...	...	...	1986	80.0	—	—	100.0	—	80.0	100.0	—	—
Réunion							1998						13,200.0	...	...	...
Romania	●	●	●	●	●	29.8	1989	90,561.2	—	48.9	51.1	—	90,561.2	100.0	...	...
Russia	●	●	●	●	●	37.4										
Rwanda	●		●				1989	2,350.0	23.9	39.8	—	36.3	965.8	60.8	39.2	—
St. Kitts and Nevis	●	●	●			...	1989	14.3	...	...	...	...	7.9	...	...	...
St. Lucia	●	●	●			...	1986	14.6	28.6	28.6	—	42.8	3.4	61.4	38.6	—
St. Vincent and the Grenadines	●	●	●			10.7	1989	—	...	...	...	...	—	...	...	...
Samoa						—										
San Marino	●	●	●			...	1983	51,673.0	12.0	48.7	36.1	3.2	46,179.0	95.7	3.7	0.6
São Tomé and Príncipe	●	●				...	1986	46.4	37.7	56.3	—	6.0	23.7	100.0	—	—
Saudi Arabia	●		●			...	1989	1,761.4	26.8	73.2	—	—	4,292.9	100.0	—	—
Senegal	●		●		●	2.6[12,25]	1989	17,202.0	—	47.6	51.4	1.0	15,371.0	84.6	11.1	4.3
Seychelles	●	●	●			15.1	1983	69.1	30.1	60.2	—	9.7	42.7	69.6	4.9	25.5
Sierra Leone	●					2.3[3]	1990						153.00	100.00	...	...
Singapore	●	●	●			1.6	1989	7,531.9	49.1	35.3	0.1	15.6	5,045.8	78.0	0.6	21.4
Slovakia	●	●	●	●	●	29.2	1998	74,205	...	...	...	...	87,916	...	...	...
Slovenia	●	●	●	●	●	43.6										
Solomon Islands	●		●			...	1989	20.9	27.8	41.1	—	31.1	17.4	89.7	10.3	—
Somalia	●		●			...										
South Africa	●	●	●	●		3.5[7]	1994	2,034	—	100.0	—	—	2,260.0	...	...	...
Spain	●	●	●	●	●	38.5	1989	8,320,972.0	15.9	53.9	27.9	2.3	8,038,090.0	94.3	2.6	3.1
Sri Lanka	●		●		●	11.8	1989	15,399.9	22.0	24.4	29.1	24.5	5,819.0	98.5	1.3	0.2
Sudan, The	●		●			...	1989	62.0	24.9	0.5	—	74.6	14.7	37.5	62.5	—
Suriname	●	...			●	...	1989	73.0	24.7	75.3	—	—	70.6	100.0	—	—
Swaziland	●		●			0.4	1986	10.7	31.4	31.4	—	37.2	3.9	45.8	54.2	—
Sweden	●	●	●	●	●	46.3	1989	446,909.7	2.8	37.9	50.8	8.5	439,997.3	93.7	3.3	3.0
Switzerland	●	●	●	●	●	49.1	1989	45,800.1	45.6	22.6	25.9	5.9	41,745.7	91.5	3.0	5.5
Syria	●		●			5.4[11]	1989	3,147.9	30.4	60.9	...	5.6	1,455.9	95.7	4.2	0.1
Taiwan	●	●	●		●	13.8[3]	...	...	...	...	...	...	...	...	...	...
Tajikistan	●	●	●	●	●	18.7										
Tanzania	●		●			...	1989	3,275.8	25.9	25.9	—	48.2	2,780.7	5.8	14.1	80.1
Thailand	●	●	●			5.8	1989	654.0	—	60.2	—	39.8	260.0	88.2	11.8	—
Togo	●		●		●	...	1989	10,162.0	8.1	61.5	—	30.4	5,844.0	77.5	22.5	—
Tonga	...	...	...			0.8[12]										
Trinidad and Tobago	●	●	●			14.3[24]	1989	584.9	12.0	24.1	39.7	24.2	438.4	85.6	11.1	3.3
Tunisia	●	●	●		●	17.8	1989	325.3	36.9	63.1	—	—	358.3	...	...	...
Turkey	●	●	●			9.5	1989	12,075,809.0	28.5	32.9	22.8	15.8	10,241,427.0	97.2	2.2	0.6
Turkmenistan	●	●	●			...										
Tuvalu	●	...	...			...	1981						0.1	67.6	32.4	—
Uganda	●		●			...	1989	265.9	32.1	64.3	1.1	2.5	145.0	0.3	76.8	22.9
Ukraine	●	●	●	●	●	50.1	1989	20,350.0	...	...	...	...	20,350.0	100.0	—	—
United Arab Emirates	●	...	...			3.4	1989	182.2	17.3	6.2	0.5	76.0	182.2	100.0	—	—
United Kingdom	●	●	●	●	●	36.5	1989	92,157.0	18.1	24.9	52.9	4.1	88,294.0	93.8	3.3	2.9
United States	●	●	●	●	●	28.7	1989	804,909.0	25.5	33.9	28.8	11.8	627,653.0	95.5	3.3	1.2
Uruguay	●	●	●	●	●	59.3	1989	535,507.0	31.4	37.3	26.0	5.3	548,591.0	93.6	5.4	1.0
Uzbekistan	●	●	●		●	...										
Vanuatu	●					...										
Venezuela	●	●	●		●	...	1986	7,457.6	21.3	40.7	12.7	25.3	6,355.7	86.1	14.9	—
Vietnam	●					10.6	...	...	...	...	...	...	...	...	...	...
Virgin Islands (U.S.)	●	...	...	●	●	...		...	...	...	...	...	...	...	...	...
West Bank						...		...	...	...	...	...	...	...	...	...
Western Sahara	...	...	...	...	...	...		...	...	...	...	...	...	...	...	...
Yemen	●	...	...			...		...	...	...	...	...	...	...	...	...
Yugoslavia	●	●	●	●	●	6.0[45]	1998[45]	2,777,651.0	63.3	32.2	3.4	1.1	2,732,679.0	90.3	1.9	7.8
Zambia	●		●			1.2	1986	179.2	28.4	28.4	—	43.2	67.7	40.6	59.4	—
Zimbabwe	●		●			18.2[7]	1983	167.0	25.9	7.6	64.2	2.3	112.2	93.7	6.2	0.1

[1]Rural areas. [2]National army is being formed in early 2002. [3]1990. [4]Political dependency; defense is the responsibility of the administering country. [5]Includes civilian militia. [6]Netherlands Antilles includes Aruba. [7]1997. [8]Includes welfare. [9]In 2002 about 12,000 troops of the NATO Commanded Stabilization Forces were stationed in Bosnia and Herzegovina to assure implementation of the Dayton Accords. [10]1996. [11]1998. [12]1991. [13]Local officers only. [14]Military defense is the responsibility of France. [15]Republic of Cyprus only. [16]National Guard only. [17]Data refer to former Czechoslovakia. [18]Paramilitary unit of country participating in the U.S.-sponsored Regional Security System, a defense pact among eastern Caribbean countries. [19]Indonesia includes East Timor, except where noted. [20]UN forces of 5,199 troops including 117 observers are stationed in East Timor. [21]Ethiopia includes Eritrea. [22]1993. [23]Former West Germany. [24]1995. [25]Social Security only. [26]Haitian army was disbanded in 1995, and a National Police Force of 5,300 was formed in 2002. [27]Coverage is through the tax system. [28]Includes attempted murders. [29]1992. [30]As of 2002 there were between 11,000

crime and law enforcement (latest)					population per police officer[g]	military protection								country
offenses reported to the police per 100,000 population						manpower, 2002[h]		expenditure, 1999				arms trade, 1999 ('000,000 U.S.$)		
total	personal		property			total ('000)	per 1,000 population	total '000,000	per capita	% of central government expenditure	% of GDP or GNP	imports	exports	
	murder	assault	burglary	automobile theft										
7,808	10.9	242.8	3,100.4	239.0	510	49.6	3.1	7,030	445	5.9	1.8	775	140	Netherlands, The
5,574[34]	...	396	3,455	...	330	4	4	—	—	—	—	...	...	Netherlands Antilles
...	...	...	...	...	...	4	4	—	—	—	—	...	...	New Caledonia
13,854	3.9	546.3	2,352.9	788.6	630	8.7	2.2	587	156	3.5	1.2	575	0	New Zealand
1,069	25.6	203.8	110.7	...	905[5]	14	2.8	24	5	2.9	1.2	0	0	Nicaragua
99	0.9	16.6	1.0	0.7	2,350[35]	5.3	0.5	24	2	6.4	1.2	0	0	Niger
312	...	...	...	...	1,140	78.5	0.6	1,560	13	8.1	1.6	0	0	Nigeria
245	3.8	92.6	73.7	20.8	...	4	4	—	—	—	—	...	...	Northern Mariana Islands
9,769	2.3	66.1	95.0	465.8	660	26.6	5.9	3,310	742	5.0	2.2	480	20	Norway
331	1.5	1.8	...	14.9	430	41.7	16.5	1,780	726	36.3	15.3	30	0	Oman
318	7.1	2.2	10.4	9.0	720	620.0	4.2	3,520	25	27.9	5.9	1,000	10	Pakistan
...	...	...	323.0	...	...	32	32	...	...	...	...	...	...	Palau
419	2.0	11.8	25.1	77.7	180	—	—	124	45	5.1	1.4	5	0	Panama
766	8.6	66.7	63	22.0	720	3.1	0.6	36	7	3.7	1.1	0	0	Papua New Guinea
418	11.5	54.2	21.4	30.5	310	18.6	3.2	84	15	3.9	1.1	10	0	Paraguay
218	3.2	24.1	7.8	3.6	730	110.0	4.1	1,200	45	12.3	2.4	30	0	Peru
...	13.1	14.9	...	3.3	1,160	106.0	1.3	1,110	14	7.3	1.4	110	0	Philippines
2,901	2.8	79.2	936.8	185.0	370	163.0	4.2	6,690	173	6.1	2.1	40	30	Poland
661	3.1	1.5	115.3	40.4	660	43.6	4.2	2,410	240	5.4	2.1	60	0	Portugal
2,339	16.2	101.8	412.4	1,521	380	4	4	—	—	—	—	...	...	Puerto Rico
1,079	2.1	7.1	34.1	11.5	...	12.4	20.5	1,060	1,470	22.9	10.0	120	0	Qatar
2,097	7.8	123.1	181.3	137.9	220	4	4	—	—	—	—	...	...	Réunion
2,206	7.1	5.8	367.8	30.4	...	99.2	4.6	2,190	97	4.7	1.6	200	40	Romania
20,514	21.3	32.6	669.1	25.6	...	988.1	6.9	35,000	239	22.4	5.6	470	3,100	Russia
...	45.1	114.3	...	0.3	4,650	36	36	87	12	22.7	4.5	30	0	Rwanda
3,808	12.0	434.0	1,790	...	300	18	18	...	...	...	...	...	...	St. Kitts and Nevis
4,386	17.0	1,193.0	778.0	...	430	18	18	...	...	...	...	...	...	St. Lucia
3,977	10.3	986.9	...	...	250	18	18	...	...	...	...	...	...	St. Vincent and the Grenadines
...	...	...	...	...	...	37	37	—	—	—	—	...	...	Samoa
...	4.1	...	...	...	...									San Marino
558	4.0	...	...	...	400	—	—	1	3	1.3	1.2	0	0	São Tomé and Príncipe
149	0.5	0.2	...	45.4	280	124.5	5.3	21,200	996	43.2	14.9	7,700	0	Saudi Arabia
123	0.5	8.8	2.1	8.2	730	9.4	0.9	81	8	8.2	1.7	0	0	Senegal
5,361	3.7	43.4	378.0	40.9	120	0.2	2.4	...	...	...	...	...	...	Seychelles
...	...	...	...	...	600	38	38	20	4	13.5	3.0	10	0	Sierra Leone
783	1.0	2.4	40.1	55.2	230	60.5	14.4	4,400	1,100	20.5	4.8	950	20	Singapore
1,740	2.4	204.6	504.3	142.4	...	26.2	4.9	1,010	187	4.4	1.8	20	10	Slovakia
3,138	3.6	20.7	427.3	25.6	...	9.0	4.6	436	227	3.4	1.4	10	0	Slovenia
...	...	...	...	...	620	—	—	...	...	...	...	0	0	Solomon Islands
144	1.5	8.0	31.2	...	540	39	39	18[3]	3[3]	...	0.9[3]	20	0	Somalia
7,140.8	121.9	595.6	896.6	262.7	870	60.0	1.3	1,960	45	5.0	1.5	50	30	South Africa
4,449	2.7	23.4	562.8	343.3	580	178.0	4.3	7,560	192	6.1	1.3	750	70	Spain
280	8.2	10.8	54.7	...	860	157.9[40]	8.4[40]	729	38	18.4	4.7	40	0	Sri Lanka
...	10.2	46.3	66.6	4.7	740	117.0	3.4	424	12	46.8	4.8	10	0	Sudan, The
17,819	7.6	1,824.4	...	...	...	1.8	4.1	14	33	5.4	1.8	10	0	Suriname
3,962	18.1	471.7	706.8	54.1	610	—	—	21	20	4.6	1.5	0	0	Swaziland
12,982	4.5	42.5	1,615.1	658.9	330	33.9	3.8	5,330	601	5.5	2.3	230	675	Sweden
7,030	2.7	73.3	1,065.9	1,065.5	640	3.5	0.5	3,400	469	5.1	1.2	1,100	50	Switzerland
42	1.0	—	15.6	2.7	1,970	319.0	18.6	4,450	280	25.1	7.0	210	0	Syria
799	8.2	...	...	124.9	720	370.0	15.2	15,200	690	23.8[7]	5.2	2,600	20	Taiwan
317	2.5	4.6	...	...	...	6.0	0.9	80	13	9.4	1.3	0	0	Tajikistan
1,714	7.7	1.7	96.6	0.9	1,330	27.0	0.8	122	4	10.1	1.4	5	0	Tanzania
351	7.7	25.4	9.9	3.3	530	306.0	4.8	2,040	34	6.1	1.7	330	0	Thailand
11	...	...	...	...	1,970	9.5	1.8	25	5	9.4	1.8	0	0	Togo
2,727	1.0	108.5	541.7	14.8	330	37	37	—	—	—	—	...	...	Tonga
1,170	9.7	31.0	452.7	80.6	280	2.7	2.0	92	78	5.5	1.4	0	0	Trinidad and Tobago
1,419	1.2	165.1	60.1	10.2	340	35.0	3.6	357	38	5.4	1.8	10	0	Tunisia
547	3.9	120.0	...	28.9	1,570	514.9	7.4	9,950	154	13.9	5.3	3,200	70	Turkey
...	...	...	...	...	...	17.5	3.5	542	122	16.0	3.4	10	0	Turkmenistan
...	...	...	...	—	290	...	...	...	...	...	...	...	...	Tuvalu
316	9.9	54.8	19.3	8.3	1,090	41	41	140	6	13.9	2.3	30	0	Uganda
1,115	10.0	14.7	224.3	7.6	...	302.3	6.3	5,110	103	8.2	3.0	10	550	Ukraine
2,604.7	3.0	10.1	5.1	23.0	...140	41.5	11.7	2,180	935	39.6	4.1	950	0	United Arab Emirates
9,823[42]	2.8[42]	405.2[42]	1,832.7[42]	752.9[42]	350	210.5	3.5	36,500	615	6.9	2.5	2,600	5,200	United Kingdom
5,374	9.0	430.2	1,041.8	591.2	318	1,414.0	4.9	281,000	1,030	15.7	3.0	1,600	33,000	United States
3,002	7.7	162.5	52.3	130.1	170	23.9	7.0	275	83	4.1	1.3	10	0	Uruguay
328	3.2	3.0	33.2	2.3	...	43	43	933	38	5.3	1.7	0	10	Uzbekistan
...	...	...	...	...	450	—	—	...	...	...	...	...	...	Vanuatu
1,106	22.1	152.2	358.2	239.4	320	82.3	3.3	1,420	61	7.1	1.4	310	0	Venezuela
74	1.5	8.5	...	...	...	484.0	6.0	3,230[7]	44[7]	11.6[7]	2.5[7]	70	0	Vietnam
10,441	22.3	1,943.2	3,183.7	954	240	4	4	—	—	—	—	...	...	Virgin Islands (U.S.)
2,226	...	...,	...	...	...	—	—	...	...	...	...	...	...	West Bank
...	...	...	...	...	...	4	4	—	—	—	—	...	...	Western Sahara
634[44]	5.3	3.2	1.2	3.6	1,940	66.5	3.4	374	22	18.0	6.1	30	0	Yemen
1,268	...	...	...	...	140[45]	74.5	7.0	1,200[7]	114[7]	55.0[3, 45]	4.9[3, 45]	10	0	Yugoslavia
666	9.8	9.5	153.5	9.6	540	21.6	2.2	31	3	3.5	1.0	0	0	Zambia
5,619	9.0	198.4	435.9	13.4	750	36.0	3.2	263	23	12.1	5.0	10	0	Zimbabwe

and 15,000 in all armed forces. West African peacekeepers withdrew in January 1999 and the civil war resumed in some areas. [31]Military defense is the responsibility of Switzerland. [32]Military defense is the responsibility of the United States. [33]Forces are estimated between 10,000 and 11,150. [34]Curaçao only. [35]Includes paramilitary forces. [36]Forces are estimated between 60,000 and 75,000. [37]Military defense is the responsibility of New Zealand. [38]A new U.K.-trained national army was formed in 2002 and has an initial strength between 13,000 and 14,000. [39]Following the 1991 revolution, no national armed forces have yet been formed. [40]Includes 42,300 recalled reservists. [41]Forces estimated between 50,000 and 60,000. [42]England and Wales. [43]Forces estimated between 50,000 and 55,000. [44]Former Yemen Arab Republic. [45]Data refer to Yugoslavia as constituted prior to 1991.

Education

This table presents international data on education analyzed to provide maximum comparability among the different educational systems in use among the nations of the world. The principal data are, naturally, numbers of schools, teachers, and students, arranged by four principal levels of education—the first (primary); general second level (secondary); vocational second level; and third level (higher). Whenever possible, data referring to preprimary education programs have been excluded from this compilation. The ratio of students to teachers is calculated for each level. These data are supplemented at each level by a figure for enrollment ratio, an indicator of each country's achieved capability to educate the total number of children potentially educable in the age group usually represented by that level. At the first and second levels this is given as a net enrollment ratio and at the third level as a gross enrollment ratio. Two additional comparative measures are given at the third level: students per 100,000 population and proportion (percentage) of adults age 25 and over who have achieved some level of higher or postsecondary education. Data in this last group are confined as far as possible to those who have completed their educations and are no longer in school. No enrollment ratio is provided for vocational training at the second level because of the great variation worldwide in the academic level at which vocational training takes place, in the need of countries to encourage or direct students into vocational programs (to support national development), and, most particularly, in the age range of students who normally constitute a national vocational system (some will be as young as 14, having just completed a primary cycle; others will be much older).

At each level of education, differences in national statistical practice, in national educational structure, public-private institutional mix, training and deployment of teachers, and timing of cycles of enrollment or completion of particular grades or standards all contribute to the problems of comparability among national educational systems.

Reporting the number of schools in a country is not simply a matter of counting permanent red-brick buildings with classrooms in them. Often the resources of a less developed country are such that temporary or outdoor facilities are all that can be afforded, while in a developed but sparsely settled country students might have to travel 80 km (50 mi) a day to find a classroom with 20 students of the same age, leading to the institution of measures such as traveling teachers, radio or televisual instruction at home under the supervision of parents, or similar systems. According to UNESCO definitions, therefore, a "school" is defined only as "a body of students . . . organized to receive instruction."

Such difficulties also limit the comparability of statistics on numbers of teachers, with the further complications that many at any level must work part-time, or that the institutions in which they work may perform a mixture of functions that do not break down into the tidy categories required by a table of this sort. In certain countries teacher training is confined to higher education, in others as a vocational form of secondary training, and so on. For purposes of this table, teacher training at the secondary level has been treated as vocational education. At the higher level, teacher training is classified as one more specialization in higher education itself.

The number of students may conceal great variation in what each country defines as a particular educational "level." Many countries do, indeed, have a primary system composed of grades 1 through 6 (or 1 through 8) that passes students on to some kind of postprimary education. But the age of intake, the ability of parents to send their children or to permit them to finish that level, or the need to withdraw the children seasonally for agricul-

Education

country	year	first level (primary)					general second level (secondary)					vocational second level[a]	
		schools	teachers[c]	students[d]	student/ teacher ratio	net enroll-ment ratio[b]	schools	teachers[c]	students[d]	student/ teacher ratio	net enroll-ment ratio[b]	schools	teachers[c]
Afghanistan	1995	2,146	21,869	1,312,197	60.0	29	...	19,085	512,815	26.9	14	...	...
Albania	1996	1,782	31,369	558,101	17.8	102	162[1]	4,147	71,391	17.2	...	259[1]	2,174
Algeria	1997	15,426	170,956	4,674,947	27.3	94	3,954	151,948	2,618,242	17.2	56	...	...
American Samoa	1996	32	524[2]	9,971	...	...	9	245[2]	3,624	...	...	1	21[2]
Andorra	1997	12	...	5,424	...	...	6	...	2,655	...	...	...	...
Angola	1992	...	31,062[1]	989,443	...	...	...	5,138[1]	199,099	...	...	...	566[1]
Antigua and Barbuda	1997	58	559	12,229	21.9	...	13	389	4,260	11.0	...	1[3]	16[3]
Argentina	1997	22,437	309,081	5,153,256	16.7	96	7,623[4]	238,791[4]	2,463,608[4]	10.3[4]	42	4	4
Armenia	1998	1,407	61,965	602,600	9.7	...	...	57,325	365,025	6.4	...	69[5]	4
Aruba	1998	33	397	8,456	21.3	...	15[4]	470[4]	7,157[4]	15.2[4]	4	4	4
Australia	1998	7,709	104,603	1,869,852	17.9	95	2,468	104,477	1,329,000	12.7	89	...	28,900[3]
Austria	1998	3,680	38,491	385,207	10.0	87	1,837[6]	55,337	480,200	8.7	88	981	26,248
Azerbaijan	1998	4,515	36,800	700,900	19.0	...	...	85,300	905,500	10.6	...	78	...
Bahamas, The	1997	113	1,540	34,199	22.2	98	...	1,352	27,970	20.7	86	...	...
Bahrain	1997	124[3, 8]	3,536[3, 8]	72,876	...	98	...	2,305[3, 8]	49,897	...	83	...	820[3, 8]
Bangladesh	1996	75,595	242,252[5]	17,580,000	...	64	12,858	135,217[5]	5,788,000	...	18	156	8,800
Barbados	1996	79	994	18,519	18.6	78	21	1,263	21,455	17.0	74	...	...
Belarus	1998	4,835[9]	115,300[9]	1,580,000[9]	10.9[9]	85	9	9	9	9	...	150	...
Belgium	1996	4,401	82,168[10]	742,796	...	98	1,727	115,262	737,823	6.4	88	304[11]	...
Belize	1998	247	2,015	53,118	26.4	99	30	726	11,260	15.5	29	...	...
Benin	1997	3,072	13,957	779,329	55.8	63	145[5]	5,352	146,135	27.3	...	14[5]	283[5]
Bermuda	1997	26	478	5,883	18.3	...	...	355	3,726	10.5	...	...	...
Bhutan	1994	243	1,611	60,089	37.3	...	34	544	7,299	13.4	...	8	95
Bolivia	1995	...	51,763[12]	1,538,454	24.7[12]	91	...	12,434[4, 12]	293,158[4]	17.6[4, 12]	29	...	4
Bosnia and Herzegovina	1991	2,205	23,369	539,875	23.1	98	238	9,030	172,063	19.1	...	...	...
Botswana	1997	714	11,454	322,268	28.1	81	274	6,772	116,076	17.1	44	50	2,618
Brazil	1998	187,497	1,460,469	35,845,742	24.5	90	17,602	380,222	6,968,531	18.3	19	...	...
Brunei	1998	184[10]	3,858[10]	58,548[10]	15.2[10]	91	38	2,636	30,956	11.7	68	9	516
Bulgaria	1999	3,011[9]	65,885[9]	887,213[9]	13.5[9]	92	9	9	9	9	74	545	20,386
Burkina Faso	1996	3,568	14,037	702,204	50.0	31	252	4,152	137,257	33.0	7	41	731
Burundi	1993	1,418	10,400	651,086	62.6	52	113[12]	2,562	55,713	21.7	5	...	...
Cambodia	1998	5,026	43,282	2,011,772	46.5	100	440[11]	16,820	302,751	18.0	...	65[11]	2,315
Cameroon	1995	6,801	40,970	1,896,722	46.3	67	...	14,917	459,068	30.8	11	...	5,885
Canada	1996	12,685	148,565	2,448,144	16.5	95	3,780	133,275	2,505,389	18.8	91	...	...
Cape Verde	1994	370[12]	2,657	78,173	29.4	100	...	438	11,808	27.0	48	...	94[14]
Central African Republic	1991	930	4,004	308,409	77.0	53	46[4]	845[4]	46,989[4]	55.6[4]	...	4	4
Chad	1996	2,660	9,395	591,493	63.0	46	153	2,468	90,100	36.5	...	18	216
Chile	1995	8,702	80,155	2,149,501	26.8	89	...	51,042	679,165	13.3	58	...	...
China	1997	628,840	5,794,000	139,954,000	24.2	101	78,642	3,587,000	60,179,000	16.8	...	14,190	598,000
Colombia	1996	48,933	193,911	4,916,934	25.4	85	7,895[4]	165,976[4]	2,323,653	...	46	4	4
Comoros	1996	327	1,508	78,527	52.1	52	...	591	21,192	35.9	...	...	...
Congo, Dem. Rep. of the	1995	14,885	121,054	5,417,506	44.8	54	4,276[4, 11]	59,325[4, 11]	1,514,323[4]	...	17	4	...
Congo, Rep. of the	1997	1,612	6,926	489,546	70.7	96	...	5,466	190,409	34.8	...	...	1,746
Costa Rica	1998	3,711	19,235	529,637	27.5	89	353	10,943	202,415	18.5	40	...	...
Côte d'Ivoire	1996	7,401	40,529	1,662,285	41.0	55	147	15,959	489,740	30.7	...	...	1,424[3]
Croatia	1998	2,127	10,365	206,121	19.9	82	1,110	19,776	266,115	13.5	66	442	13,000
Cuba	1997	9,864[16]	78,625	1,028,880	13.0	101	...	71,025	778,028	11.0	59[16]	...	27,267[16]
Cyprus[17]	1997	376	4,159	64,761	15.6	96	125[4]	5,757[4]	61,266[4]	10.6[4]	93	4	4
Czech Republic	1998	8,067[18]	83,972[18]	1,186,246[18]	14.1[18]	91	367	11,658	83,010	7.1	89	1,776	54,204
Denmark	1996	2,536[3]	33,100	336,690	10.2	99	153[3]	37,000	321,448	8.7	88	237[3]	13,100

tural work all make even even a simple enrollment figure difficult to assess in isolation. All of these difficulties are compounded when a country has instruction in more than one language or when its educational establishment is so small that higher, sometimes even secondary, education cannot take place within the country. Enrollment figures in this table may, therefore, include students enrolled outside the country.

Student-teacher ratio, however, usually provides a good measure of the ratio of trained educators to the enrolled educable. In general, at each level of education both students and teachers have been counted on the basis of full-time enrollment or employment, or full-time equivalent when country statistics permit. At the primary and secondary levels, net enrollment ratio is the ratio of the number of children within the usual age group for a particular level who are actually enrolled to the total number of children in that age group ($\times$ 100). This ratio is usually less than (occasionally, equal to) 100 and is the most accurate measure of the completeness of enrollment at that particular level. It is not always, however, the best indication of utilization of teaching staff and facilities. Utilization, provided here for higher education only, is best seen in a gross enrollment ratio, which compares total enrollment (of all ages) to the population within the normal age limits for that level. For a country with substantial adult literacy or general educational programs, the difference may be striking: typically, for a less developed country, even one with a good net enrollment ratio of 90 to 95, the gross enrollment ratio may by 20%, 25%, even 30% higher, indicating the heavy use made by the country of facilities and teachers at that level.

Literacy data provided here have been compiled as far as possible from data for the population age 15 and over for the best comparability inter-nationally. Standards as to what constitutes literacy may also differ markedly; sometimes completion of a certain number of years of school is taken to constitute literacy; elsewhere it may mean only the ability to read or write at a minimal level testable by a census taker; in other countries studies have been undertaken to distinguish among degrees of functional literacy. When a country reports an official 100% (or near) literacy rate, it should usually be viewed with caution, as separate studies of "functional" literacy for such a country may indicate 10%, 20%, or even higher rates of inability to read, or write, effectively. Substantial use has been made of UNESCO literacy estimates, both for some of the least developed countries (where the statistical base is poorest) and for some of the most fully developed, where literacy is no longer perceived as a problem, thus no longer in need of monitoring.

Finally, the data provided for public expenditure on education are complete in that they include all levels of public expenditure (national, state, local) but are incomplete for certain countries in that they do not include data for private expenditure; in some countries this fraction of the educational establishment may be of significant size. Occasionally data for external aid to education may be included in addition to domestic expenditure.

The following notes further define the column headings:
a. Usually includes teacher training at the second level.
b. Latest.
c. Full-time.
d. Full-time; may include students registered in foreign schools.

students[d]	student/ teacher ratio	third level (higher)			student/ teacher ratio	gross enroll-ment ratio[b]	students per 100,000 popula-tion[b]	percent of population age 25 and over with post-secondary education[b]	literacy[b]				public expenditure on education (percent of GNP)[b]	country
		institutions	teachers[c]	students[d]					over age	total (%)	male (%)	female (%)		
...	...	...	...	12,800	...	2.0	165	3.0	15	36.3	51.0	20.8	2.0	Afghanistan
18,504	8.5	10[1]	2,348	34,257	14.6	12.0	1,007	...	10	91.8	95.5	88.0	3.1	Albania
...	...	...	19,910	347,410	17.4	10.9	1,236	...	15	63.3	75.1	51.3	5.1	Algeria
160[2]	7.6[2]	1	...	...	...	...	...	22.6	15	95.9	95.6	96.3	8.2	American Samoa
...	...	—	—	932	—	...	...	...	15	100.0	100.0	100.0	...	Andorra
22,401	...	1	787	6,.331	8.0	0.7	71	...	15	41.7	55.6	28.5	4.9	Angola
46[3]	2.9[3]	1	16	46	2.9	...	...	...	15	90.0	...	...	2.7	Antigua and Barbuda
4	4	1,831	117,104	936,832	8.0	38.0	3,117	12.0	15	96.9	96.9	96.9	3.5	Argentina
25,200[5]	...	15	4,420	38,500	8.7	12.0	976	...	15	98.8	99.4	98.1	2.0	Armenia
4	4	2	53	394	7.4	...	...	7.0	15	95.0	...	...	4.9	Aruba
985,000[3]	34.1[3]	92	32,663	671,853	20.6	80.0	5,552	...	15	99.5	...	...	5.5	Australia
307,548	11.7	77	20,356	232,377	11.4	48.0	2,970	6.1	15	100.0	100.0	100.0	5.4	Austria
23,500	...	23	17,900	120,870	6.6	17.0	1,516	...	15	97.3	98.9	95.9	3.0	Azerbaijan
...	...	17	160[7]	3,463[7]	21.6[7]	18.0	1,445	13.5	15	96.1	95.4	96.8	4.0	Bahamas, The
7,287	...		558	7,011	12.6	20.0	1,445	10.3	15	87.6	91.0	82.7	4.4	Bahrain
29,923[5]	16.1[5]	1,268[5]	36,000[5]	1,032,635[5]	28.7[5]	4.0	399	1.3	15	40.8	51.7	29.5	2.2	Bangladesh
...	...	4		6,622	...	29.0	2,602	3.3	15	97.4	98.0	96.8	7.2	Barbados
125,600	14.3	59	16,300	224,500	13.8	44.0	3,177	12.5	15	99.4	99.7	99.2	5.9	Belarus
569,041	...	151	38,014	358,214	9.4	56.0	3,494	...	15	100.0	100.0	100.0	3.1	Belgium
...	...	12		228	2,753	12.1	...	...	6.6	14	70.3	...	...	5.0	Belize
4,873[5]	17.2[5]	165[5]	962	14,085	14.6	3.0	253	1.3	15	37.5	47.8	23.6	3.2	Benin
...	...	1		543	...	...	...	18.4	15	96.9	96.7	97.0	3.7	Bermuda
1,822[1]	12.2[1]	2[1]	571	2,055	9.1[1]	...	...	...	15	47.3	61.1	33.6	4.1	Bhutan
4	4	...	4,261[2]	109,503[2]	25.7[2]	21.0	2,154	9.9	15	85.6	92.1	79.4	4.9	Bolivia
...	...	44		2,802	37,541	13.4	...	...	...	10	85.5	96.5	76.6	...	Bosnia and Herzegovina
9,829	3.8	1	1,001	9,660	9.6	6.0	596	1.4	15	77.2	74.4	79.8	8.6	Botswana
...	...	900	173,705[13]	1,948,200[13]	11.2[13]	15.0	1,094	...	15	85.3	85.5	85.4	5.1	Brazil
2,553	4.9	4	370	2,080	5.6	7.0	518	9.4	15	91.6	94.7	88.2	2.5	Brunei
201,736	10.0	86	42,829	258,240	6.0	41.0	3,103	15.0	15	98.5	99.1	98.0	3.2	Bulgaria
9,539	13.0	9	632	9,531	15.1	0.9	83	...	15	23.0	31.2	13.1	3.6	Burkina Faso
...	...	8	556	4,256	7.6	0.8	74	0.6	15	48.1	56.3	40.5	4.0	Burundi
16,350[11]	...	9[11]	784[11]	11,652[11]	14.9[11]	1.0	98	1.0	15	65.3	79.7	53.4	2.9	Cambodia
91,779	15.6	...	1,086[12]	33,177[12]	30.5[12]	3.0	289	...	15	75.4	81.8	69.2	2.9	Cameroon
...	...	265	64,100[5]	980,251[5]	14.4[5]	88.0	5,997	21.4	15	96.6	...	...	6.9	Canada
2,289	...	...	...	...	...	...	...	...	15	73.5	84.3	65.3	4.0	Cape Verde
4	4	1	136	2,823	20.8	1.0	131	2.0	15	46.5	59.6	34.5	2.3	Central African Republic
2,926	13.5	8	288	3,446	12.0	0.6	54	...	15	53.6	66.9	40.8	1.7	Chad
...	...	...	18,084[11, 15]	367,094	...	31.0	2,546	12.3	15	95.7	95.9	95.5	3.6	Chile
9,773,000	16.3	1,020	405,000	3,174,000	7.8	6.0	473	2.0	15	85.0	92.3	77.4	2.3	China
928,474	...	266	75,568	673,353	8.9	17.0	1,768	10.4	15	91.8	91.8	91.8	4.4	Colombia
...	...	...	...	348	...	0.6	57	...	15	56.2	63.5	49.1	3.9	Comoros
4	4	...	...	52,501	...	2.0	212	1.3	15	77.3	86.6	67.7	1.0	Congo, Dem. Rep. of the
23,606	13.5	...	1,341[3]	16,602[3]	12.4[3]	7.0	582	3.0	15	80.7	87.5	74.4	6.1	Congo, Rep. of the
...	...	40[13]		83,106[13]	...	30.0	2,919	...	15	95.6	95.5	95.7	5.4	Costa Rica
11,037[3]	7.8[3]	...	1,657[3]	43,147[3]	26.0[3]	6.0	396	8.7	15	46.8	54.6	38.5	5.0	Côte d'Ivoire
150,792	11.6	79	6,532	90,021	13.8	28.0	1,905	6.4	15	98.3	99.4	97.3	5.3	Croatia
244,253[16]	9.0[16]	351	22,967[16]	104,595	5.3[16]	12.0	1,013	5.9	15	96.4	96.5	96.4	6.7	Cuba
4	4	35	812	9,982	12.3	23.0	1,383	17.0	15	96.9	98.7	95.0	4.5	Cyprus[17]
419,843	7.7	272	18,061	203,598	11.3	24.0	1,867	8.5	15	100.0	100.0	100.0	5.1	Czech Republic
123,234	9.4	158[3]	9,600	169,783	17.7	48.0	3,189	19.6	...	100.0	100.0	100.0	8.1	Denmark

Education   (continued)

country	year	first level (primary)					general second level (secondary)					vocational second level[a]	
		schools	teachers[c]	students[d]	student/ teacher ratio	net enroll- ment ratio[b]	schools	teachers[c]	students[d]	student/ teacher ratio	net enroll- ment ratio[b]	schools	teachers[c]
Djibouti	1997	81[3]	1,005[3]	33,960	...	32	26[4,12]	628[3,4]	11,628[4]	...	12	4	4
Dominica	1998	63	587	13,636	23.2	...	15	293	5,455	18.6	...	...	...
Dominican Republic	1995	4,001	42,135	1,462,722	34.7	81	...	10,757	240,441	22.4	22	...	1,297
East Timor	...	...	...	...	...	...	...	...	...	...	...	...	...
Ecuador	1997	17,367	74,601	1,888,172	25.3	92	...	62,630[4,11]	765,073[4]	...	...	...	4
Egypt[19]	1997	18,522[16]	310,116	7,499,303	24.2	93	7,307[5,16]	259,618	4,835,938	18.6	64	1,351[5]	138,277
El Salvador	1996	5,025	34,496	1,130,900	32.8	78	...	9,255	143,588	15.5	22	...	...
Equatorial Guinea	1994	781	1,381	75,751	54.9	...	...	466	14,511	31.1	...	...	122
Eritrea	1996	537	5,828	241,725	41.5	30	86[11]	2,031	78,902	38.8	16	4[11]	174
Estonia	1996	727	...	125,718	...	87	...	9,299	95,342	10.3	83	84	1,793
Ethiopia	1995	9,276	83,113	2,722,192	32.8	32	...	22,779	747,142	32.8	...	...	826
Faroe Islands	1995	62	554[9]	4,898	...	...	6	9	3,041	...	...	...	...
Fiji	1997	697[5]	5,011	142,781	28.5	99	147[5]	3,519	70,098	19.9	...	...	625[2]
Finland	1997	4,392	39,966	592,500	14.8	98	454	5,766	131,900	22.9	93	35[5]	15,063
France	1995	41,244	216,962	4,071,599	18.8	100	11,212[4]	473,673[4]	6,003,797[4]	12.7[4]	95	4	4
French Guiana	1996	78[5]	802	17,006	21.2	...	22[12]	875	13,585	15.5	...	...	210
French Polynesia	1995	278	2,949	48,160	16.3	103	38	1,745	25,541	14.6	61	...	...
Gabon	1996	1,147	4,944	250,606	50.7	...	48	2,683	72,888	27.2	...	11	412
Gambia, The	1995	250[5]	3,158[5]	113,419	33.4[5]	65	32[4,5]	1,126[4,5]	31,567	24.1[4,5]	20	4	4
Gaza Strip	1997	1,118	15,903	656,353	41.3	...	...	7,634	54,692	7.2	...	...	316
Georgia	1997	3,201	16,542	293,325	17.7	77	3,139	55,817	424,465	7.6	74	...	2,146
Germany	1998	17,829	198,116	3,697,806	18.7	86	19,668	413,993	5,720,092	13.8	88	9,754	110,185
Ghana	1992	11,056	66,068	1,796,490	27.2	...	5,540	43,367	816,578	18.8	...	571	4221
Greece	1997	8,651	46,785	652,040	13.9	90	3,044	56,899	682,201	12.0	87	682	13,783
Greenland	1999	88	975	9,341	9.6	...	3	...	1,746	...	...	...	...
Grenada	1997	58	879	23,449	26.7	...	19[3]	381[3]	7,367	19.3	...	...	...
Guadeloupe	1999	348	2,936	38,092[5]	...	...	88[4]	3,392[4]	51,366[4,5]	13.4[4,5]	...	4	4
Guam	1998	24	469	20,248	43.2	...	11	622	17,091	27.5	...	2	370[1]
Guatemala	1995	11,495	43,731	1,470,754	33.6	72	2,308[4]	23,807[4]	372,006[4]	15.6[4]	10	626[12]	4
Guernsey	1993	22[2]	236	4,697	19.9	...	8[2]	276	3,642	13.2	...	...	...
Guinea	1998	3,723	13,883	674,732	48.6	42	239	4,958	143,245	28.9	9	55[16]	1,268[16]
Guinea-Bissau	1995	...	...	100,369	...	47	...	...	7,000	...	3	...	...
Guyana	1997	420	3,461	102,000	29.5	87	...	2,150	62,043	29.5	66	...	...
Haiti	1995	10,071	30,205	1,110,398	36.8	26	1,038	...	195,418	...	22	...	...
Honduras	1999	8,768	33,431	1,111,264	33.2	90	661[3,4]	14,539[4]	189,000[4]	13.0[4]	21	4	4
Hong Kong	1998	832	20,038	476,682	23.8	90	507	23,077	455,392	19.7	69	9	...
Hungary	1999	3,732	83,404	964,248	11.6	97	1,545	40,130	504,829	12.6	86	1,245	26,344
Iceland	1997	198	3,877	31,100	8.0	98	37	1,454	17,970	12.4	87	...	...
India	1997	598,354	1,789,733	110,393,406	61.7	...	274,944	2,738,205	65,359,339	23.9	...	...	...
Indonesia	1997	173,883	1,327,218	28,236,283	21.3	95	41,847	863,389	12,442,813	14.4	45	3,894	123,505
Iran	1997	63,101	298,755	9,238,393	31.2	90	18,445[1]	280,309	8,776,792	31.3	71	...	20,418[3]
Iraq	1996	8,145	145,455	2,903,923	20.0	76	2,635[3]	49,884	1,075,490	21.6	37	310[3]	9,903
Ireland	1997	3,254	18,968	476,632	25.1	92	440	12,694	375,518	29.6	86	324	8,305
Isle of Man	1999	33	...	6,210	...	...	5	...	4,732	...	...	...	...
Israel	1998	1,651	57,738	532,070	9.2	...	653	62,054	414,405	...	...	338	17,141[11]
Italy	1997	19,890	289,504	2,809,699	9.7	100	16,973	315,920	2,648,535	8.4	67	7,732	305,582
Jamaica	1997	788[2]	9,512	293,863	30.9	95	126[3]	8,377[3]	228,533	...	64[3]	18[3]	950[3]
Japan	1997	24,376	420,901	7,855,387	18.7	103	16,753	546,337	8,852,840	16.2	99	62	4,384
Jersey	1990	32	...	5,794	...	...	14	...	4,405	...	...	1	...
Jordan	1996	2,531	51,721	1,074,877	20.8	89	741[5]	6,309	109,906	17.4	42	54[5]	2,306
Kazakhstan	1997	8,611[16]	262,000[16]	1,342,035	...	...	...	178,900[5]	1,743,623	...	...	239	...
Kenya	1995	15,906	181,975	5,544,998	30.5	91	2,878	41,484	632,388	15.2	11	62	1,147[14]
Kiribati	1997	86	727	17,594	24.2	...	9	215	4,403	20.5	...	...	23
Korea, North	1988	4,810[13]	59,000	1,543,000	26.2	...	4,840[13]	111,000	2,468,000	22.2	...	...	...
Korea, South	1997	5,721	138,670	3,783,986	27.3	93	4,612	202,335	4,517,008	22.3	97	166	13,282
Kuwait	1997	258	9,863	142,265	14.4	62	416	19,402	213,266	11.0	61	38	793
Kyrgyzstan	1996	1,885	24,086	473,077	19.7	95	1,474[5]	38,915	498,849	12.8	...	535[5]	3,371
Laos	1997	7,896	25,831	786,335	30.4	72	750[1]	10,717	180,160	16.8	22	...	1,600[16]
Latvia	1998	638	10,883	146,653	13.5	89	380	24,112	196,148	8.1	79	123	5,470
Lebanon	1997	2,160	...	382,309	...	76	...	...	292,002	...	...	275	7,745
Lesotho	1997	1,249	7,898	374,628	47.4	70	187[3]	2,817	67,454	23.9	18	9[5]	61
Liberia	1987	...	...	...	...	...	...	...	...	...	...	...	...
Libya	1996	2,733[5]	122,020	1,333,679	10.9	96	...	17,668	170,573	9.7	62	480	...
Liechtenstein	1998	14	134	2,021	15.1	...	10[4]	198[4]	4,121[4]	20.8[4]	...	4	4
Lithuania	1997	2,292	14,093	225,071	16.0	...	...	32,172	325,480	10.1	80	104	5,078
Luxembourg	1997	...	1,844	28,232	15.3	...	...	2,673	9,463	3.5	...	...	2,904[3,14]
Macau	1998	81	1,744	47,235	27.1	...	47	1,577	28,280	17.9	53	2	47
Macedonia	1998	1,043	13,376	256,275	19.2	94	93[4]	5,226[4]	84,059[4]	16.1[4]	51	4	4
Madagascar	1996	13,325	44,145	1,638,187	37.1	61	...	16,795	302,036	18.0	...	...	1,150
Malawi	1996	3,706	49,138	2,887,107	58.7	103	...	2,948	139,386	47.2	2	...	475
Malaysia	1997	7,084	150,681	2,870,667	19.1	102	1,460	91,659	1,767,946	19.3	...	101	5,472
Maldives	1998	228	1,992	48,895	24.5	...	...	...	15,933[2]	...	...	...	...
Mali	1998	2,511	10,853	862,875	79.5	31	307[2]	4,549[16]	166,372	...	5	...	21,731
Malta	1998	99	1,457	35,261	24.2	100	75	2,458	27,178	11.1	79	22	626
Marshall Islands	1995	103	669	13,355	20.0	...	12	144	2,400	16.7	...	...	...
Martinique	1997	273	2,603	55,569	21.3	...	76[16]	2,888	36,605	12.7	...	...	896[16]
Mauritania	1997	2,392	6,225	312,671	50.2	57	...	1,865[16]	49,221[16]	26.4[16]	...	...	202
Mauritius	1998	285	5,065	130,505	25.7	98	133	4,820	94,364	19.6	33	13	1,170[13]
Mayotte	1997	88[1]	555[11]	25,805[10]	...	...	8	246[11]	6,190	...	...	2[1]	171
Mexico	1996	94,844	516,051	14,623,400	28.3	101	25,000	467,686	7,589,400	16.2	51	6,571[11]	77,347[11]
Micronesia	1995	174	...	27,281	...	...	24	...	6,898	...	...	...	...
Moldova	1997	1,700[9]	14,097	320,725	22.8	...	9	28,615[4]	419,256	...	...	64	4
Monaco	1997	8	127	1,917	15.1	...	6	192	2,416	12.6	...	4	89
Mongolia	1997	308	7,587	234,193	30.9	81	337	12,503	184,100	14.7	53	36	668
Morocco	1998	5,730	116,638	3,317,153	28.4	74	1,406	82,589	1,328,789	16.1	20	71[14]	2,951[3,14]

students[d]	student/ teacher ratio	third level (higher) institutions	teachers[c]	students[d]	student/ teacher ratio	gross enroll- ment ratio[b]	students per 100,000 popula- tion[b]	percent of population age 25 and over with post- secondary education[b]	literacy[b] over age	total (%)	male (%)	female (%)	public expenditure on education (percent of GNP)[b]	country
4	4	1[12]	13[12]	130[18]	...	0.2	26	...	15	51.4	65.0	38.4	3.6	Djibouti
...	...	2[11]	34[11]	48[11]	14.2[11]	...	...	1.7	15	90.0	...	...	5.5	Dominica
22,795	17.6	...	9,041[15]	176,995[15]	19.6[15]	23.0	...	...	15	83.8	84.0	83.7	2.3	Dominican Republic
...	...	...	...	...	...	...	...	...	...	...	...	...	...	East Timor
4	...	21	12,856[1]	206,541[1]	16.1[1]	20.0	2,012	12.7	15	91.9	93.6	90.2	3.5	Ecuador
1,912,040	13.8	16[15]	38,828[5,15]	850,051	...	20.0	1,900	4.6	15	55.3	66.6	43.7	4.8	Egypt[19]
...	...	...	5,919	112,266	19.0	18.0	1,933	6.4	15	78.7	81.6	76.1	2.5	El Salvador
2,105	17.3	...	58	578	10.0	...	164	...	15	83.2	92.5	74.5	1.7	Equatorial Guinea
4,268	24.5	1	136	3,081	22.7	1.0	95	...	15	20.0	...	...	1.8	Eritrea
16,870	9.4	37	...	40,621	...	42.0	2,956	13.7	15	99.7	99.9	99.6	7.2	Estonia
9,103	11.0	...	1,937	32,671	16.9	0.6	62	1.0	15	38.7	43.9	33.4	4.0	Ethiopia
2,090[5]	...	1[12]	20[12]	91[12]	4.6[12]	...	...	...	15	99.0	99.0	99.0	...	Faroe Islands
7,283[2]	11.6[2]	...	277[12]	7,908[12]	28.5[12]	12.0	757	4.5	15	92.9	95.0	90.9	5.4	Fiji
251,600	16.7	29	8,134	168,996	20.8	74.0	4,190	15.4	15	100.0	100.0	100.0	7.5	Finland
4	4	1,062	52,613	2,083,129	39.6	51.0	3,600	11.4	...	98.8	98.9	98.7	6.0	France
2,404	11.4	1	...	324[11]	16.9	...	...	6.4	15	83.0	83.6	82.3	...	French Guiana
...	...	...	...	301[12]	...	1.0	...	...	15	95.0	94.9	95.0	9.8	French Polynesia
7,664	18.6	2[2,15]	299[2,15]	3,000[2,15]	10.0[2,15]	...	650	...	15	70.8	79.8	62.2	2.9	Gabon
4	4	...	155[5]	1,591[5]	10.3[5]	2.0	148	...	15	36.5	43.8	29.6	4.9	Gambia, The
1,775	5.7	5	2,473	49,599	20.0	...	...	...	...	...	...	...	...	Gaza Strip
19,593	9.1	23	25,549	163,345	6.4	30.0	3,002	...	15	99.5	99.7	99.4	5.2	Georgia
2,838,416	25.8	296	161,383	1,813,348	11.2	47.0	2,628	...	15	100.0	100.0	100.0	4.8	Germany
13,232[1]	31.4[1]	16[1]	700[1]	9,274[1]	13.2[1]	0.6	127	...	15	70.2	79.5	61.2	4.2	Ghana
135,365	9.8	18	16,057	363,180	22.6	47.0	3,149	8.7	15	97.2	98.6	96.0	3.1	Greece
...	...	...	...	...	...	...	...	...	15	100.0	100.0	100.0	...	Greenland
...	...	1[3]	66[3]	651[3]	9.9[3]	...	...	1.5	15	85.0	...	...	4.7	Grenada
4	4	1[5]	121[5]	4,673[5]	38.6[5]	...	...	5.2	15	90.1	89.7	90.5	...	Guadeloupe
4,369	...	1	192[1]	3,533	...	...	...	39.9	15	99.0	99.0	99.0	8.5	Guam
4	4	...	...	80,228	...	8.0	755	2.2	15	68.7	76.2	61.1	1.7	Guatemala
...	...	—	...	...	...	...	...	...	15	100.0	100.0	100.0	...	Guernsey
8,151[16]	6.8[16]	2[16]	947[16]	8,151[16]	8.6[16]	1.0	108	...	15	41.1	55.1	27.0	1.9	Guinea
...	...	...	...	...	...	...	...	0.1	15	36.8	53.0	21.4	...	Guinea-Bissau
...	...	...	612	8,965	12.5	11.0	954	1.8	15	98.5	99.0	98.1	5.0	Guyana
...	...	2[20]	817[20]	12,204[20]	14.9[20]	1.0	...	0.7	15	48.6	51.0	46.5	1.5	Haiti
4	4	8	3,676[3]	56,077	...	10.0	985	3.3	15	72.2	72.5	72.0	3.6	Honduras
42,003	...	18	...	91,748	...	22.0	1,635	14.5	15	93.4	96.5	90.0	2.9	Hong Kong
362,633	13.8	89	21,351	163,164	7.6	24.0	1,926	10.1	15	99.4	99.5	99.3	4.6	Hungary
...	...	10	508	7,972	15.7	37.0	2,787	...	15	100.0	100.0	100.0	5.4	Iceland
...	...	8,407[5]	286,000[5]	5,007,000[5]	17.5[5]	7.0	642	7.3	15	55.8	68.6	42.1	3.2	India
1,767,181	14.3	1,667	180,471	2,703,886	15.0	11.0	1,167	2.3	15	87.0	91.9	82.1	1.4	Indonesia
368,218[3]	18.0[3]	...	40,477	579,070	14.3	18.0	1,599	...	15	76.9	83.7	70.0	4.0	Iran
122,939	12.4	12	11,685	232,896	19.9	12.0	...	4.1	15	58.0	70.7	45.0	4.0	Iraq
96,821	11.7	30	4,872	107,501	22.1	41.0	3,618	13.1	15	100.0	100.0	100.0	6.0	Ireland
...	...	...	...	1,128	...	...	...	...	...	...	...	...	...	Isle of Man
106,393	...	7	9,546	181,038	19.0	41.0	3,598	11.2	15	96.1	97.9	94.3	7.6	Israel
2,597,449	8.5	56[15]	48,891[15]	1,595,642[15]	32.6	47.0	3,103	3.8	15	98.5	98.9	98.1	4.9	Italy
15,898[3]	16.7[3]	15[3]	...	24,200[3]	...	8.0	803	2.7	15	86.7	82.5	90.7	7.5	Jamaica
56,294	12.8	1,243	166,051	3,136,834	18.9	41.0	3,139	20.7	15	100.0	100.0	100.0	3.6	Japan
...	...	...	...	...	...	...	...	...	15	100.0	100.0	100.0	...	Jersey
35,579	15.4	55	4,821	99,020	20.5	27.0	2,542	...	15	89.8	94.9	84.4	7.9	Jordan
177,679	...	69[3]	27,189[3]	260,043[16]	...	33.0	2,806	12.4	15	97.5	99.1	96.1	4.4	Kazakhstan
11,700[14]	10.2[4]	14[11,15]	4,392[1,15]	88,180[11]	...	2.0	143	...	15	82.5	89.0	76.0	6.5	Kenya
333	14.5	—	...	...	...	...	...	...	15	90.0	...	...	6.3	Kiribati
220,000	...	519[13]	27,000	390,000	14.4	...	...	...	15	95.0	...	...	...	Korea, North
745,689	56.1	742	53,300	1,469,819	27.6	68.0	5,609	21.1	15	97.8	99.2	96.4	3.7	Korea, South
3,779	4.8	1	1,691	29,509	17.5	19.0	2,247	16.4	15	82.3	84.3	79.9	5.0	Kuwait
32,005	9.5	23	3,691	49,744	13.5	12.0	1,115	...	15	97.0	98.6	95.5	5.3	Kyrgyzstan
9,400[16]	5.9[16]	9[1]	1,369	12,732	9.3	3.0	253	...	15	61.8	73.6	50.5	2.1	Laos
45,672	8.3	28	4,486	56,187	12.5	33.0	2,244	13.4	15	99.8	99.8	99.6	6.3	Latvia
55,848	7.2	20	10,444	81,588	7.8	27.0	2,712	...	15	86.1	92.3	80.4	2.5	Lebanon
678	11.1	1	574	4,614	8.0	2.0	222	...	15	83.9	73.6	93.6	8.4	Lesotho
...	...	...	472	5,095	10.8	2.0	...	...	15	53.4	69.9	36.8	5.7	Liberia
155,483	...	13	...	126,348	...	17.0	1,358	2.7	15	79.8	90.9	67.6	7.1	Libya
4	4	...	...	...	...	...	...	...	15	100.0	100.0	100.0	...	Liechtenstein
56,400	11.1	15	13,136	83,645	6.4	31.0	2,244	12.6	15	99.5	99.7	99.4	5.5	Lithuania
19,346	...	1	200[3]	957	...	10.0	...	10.8	15	100.0	100.0	100.0	4.0	Luxembourg
699	14.9	7	818	7,682	9.4	28.0	1,700	5.9	15	93.2	96.4	90.1	...	Macau
4	4	30	1,385	36,167	26.1	20.0	1,415	6.7	10	89.1	94.2	83.8	5.1	Macedonia
8,479	7.3	...	921	18,458	20.0	3.0	174	...	15	80.2	87.7	72.9	1.9	Madagascar
2,228	4.7	6	531[3]	5,561	...	0.6	58	0.4	15	60.3	74.5	46.7	5.4	Malawi
36,573	6.9	48	14,960	210,724	14.1	12.0	971	6.9	15	87.5	91.5	83.6	4.9	Malaysia
45[2]	...	—	—	—	—	...	...	1.7	15	96.3	96.3	96.4	6.4	Maldives
7,200	3.0	7	796	13,847	17.4	1.0	73	...	15	40.3	47.9	33.2	2.2	Mali
4,159	6.6	1	770	7,146	9.3	29.0	1,595	...	15	92.1	91.4	92.8	5.1	Malta
...	...	...	...	...	...	...	...	...	15	91.2	92.4	90.0	...	Marshall Islands
11,101[16]	12.4[16]	1	99[5]	3,079	45.3[5]	...	...	5.6	15	97.4	96.0	97.1	...	Martinique
2,544	12.6	4	270	8,496	31.5	4.0	374	1.3	15	39.9	50.6	29.5	5.1	Mauritania
5,496	...	3	461	6,429	13.9	6.3	594	1.9	15	84.3	87.7	81.0	4.6	Mauritius
839[11]	...	...	—	—	...	...	...	...	15	91.9	...	...	...	Mayotte
1,076,700[11]	13.9[11]	10,341	163,843	1,532,800	9.4	16.0	1,586	9.2	15	91.0	93.1	89.1	4.9	Mexico
...	...	...	...	1,461[5]	...	...	...	...	15	76.7	67.0	87.2	...	Micronesia
26,245	...	20	8,814	93,759	10.6	27.0	2,110	11.3	15	98.9	99.6	98.3	10.6	Moldova
532	6.0	1	...	112	...	...	...	...	...	...	...	...	...	Monaco
11,308	16.9	86	4,471	44,088	9.8	17.0	1,753	23.4	15	99.3	99.2	99.3	5.7	Mongolia
22,415[14]	...	68	9,667	266,507	27.5	11.0	1,132	...	15	48.9	61.9	36.0	5.3	Morocco

Education   (continued)

country	year	first level (primary)					general second level (secondary)					vocational second level[a]	
		schools	teachers[c]	students[d]	student/ teacher ratio	net enroll- ment ratio[b]	schools	teachers[c]	students[d]	student/ teacher ratio	net enroll- ment ratio[b]	schools	teachers[c]
Mozambique	1997	6,025	32,670	1,899,531	57.8	40	75	1,555	51,554	33.1	8	25	565
Myanmar (Burma)	1998	35,877	167,134	5,145,400	30.8	...	2,091	56,955	1,545,600	27.1	...	103[3]	2,462[3]
Namibia	1995	933[5]	10,912[2]	368,222	32.0[2]	91	114[5]	3,943[2]	101,838[5]	...	36	175[5]	56[2]
Nauru	1995	10	138	2,207	16.0	...	4	46	...	...	...	1	...
Nepal	1996	22,218	89,378	3,447,607	38.6	...	7,582[4]	36,127[4]	1,121,335[4]	31.0[4]	...	4	4
Netherlands, The	1999	7,238	99,031[12]	1,534,000	...	100	666	89,370[12]	856,000	...	84	143	18,613[12]
Netherlands Antilles	1998	85[16]	1,111	24,061	21.7	...	21	461[16]	8,372	...	...	33	623[16]
New Caledonia	1996	279	1,622	22,942	14.1	98	46	2,021[4]	20,360	...	72	14	4
New Zealand	1998	2,282	23,119	445,868	19.3	100	339	15,228	224,290	14.7	90	29	5,309
Nicaragua	1997	7,224	21,020[16]	783,002	...	77	451[5]	5,990[3]	220,670[3]	36.8[3]	18	...	...
Niger	1998	3,175	11,545	482,065	41.8	24	...	3,579	97,675	27.3	6	...	215
Nigeria	1995	38,649	435,210	16,191,000	37.2	...	6,074	152,596	4,451,000	29.2	...	...	...
Northern Mariana Islands	1993	18	183	4,666	25.5	...	9[4]	152[4]	3,044[4]	20.0[4]	...	4	4
Norway	1997	3,287	39,385	487,398	12.4	100	714[4]	21,105[4]	208,280[4]	9.9[4]	97	4	4
Oman	1997	429	11,925[16]	311,955	...	69	128[1]	11,896	205,046	17.2	49	25[1]	342[5]
Pakistan	1998	158,511[10]	346,000[10]	16,642,000[10]	48.0[10]	...	25,913	259,200	5,545,000	21.4	...	673	7,546
Palau	1997	...	172	1,450	8.4	...	...	60	490	8.2	...	...	...
Panama	1997	2,866	15,058	377,898	25.1	91	417	12,450	223,155	17.9	51	...	...
Papua New Guinea	1995	2,790	13,652	525,995	38.5	...	135[1]	2,415[2]	68,818	24.1[2]	...	117[1]	878[2]
Paraguay	1996	5,928	41,713	895,777	21.5	91	804[4]	17,668	293,651[4]	...	38	4	...
Peru	1997	33,017	153,951	4,163,180	27.0	91	8,085[3]	106,614	1,969,501	18.5	55	2,425[3]	12,293[3]
Philippines	1997	37,645	341,183	11,902,501	34.9	101	5,880[5]	154,705[4]	4,888,246[4]	31.6[4]	59	1,261[1]	4
Poland	1998	19,299	322,600	4,896,400	15.2	95	1,847	39,200	757,500	19.3	85	9,320	89,900
Portugal	1996	12,884	145,462[9]	1,339,744	...	104	664	[9]	477,221	...	78	262	6,895
Puerto Rico	1986	1,542	18,359	427,582	23.3	...	395	13,612	334,661	24.6	...	52	...
Qatar	1996[8]	174	5,864	53,631	9.1	80	123[3]	3,738[3]	36,964[3]	9.9[3]	69	3	120
Réunion	1998	351	...	76,364	...	...	111[4]	6,343	96,811	15.3	...	4	1,120[16]
Romania	1997	13,978[18]	175,426[18]	2,546,231[18]	14.5[18]	95	1,295[21]	64,485[21]	792,788[21]	12.3[21]	73	1,692	10,942
Russia	1999	69,613[9]	1,811,000[9]	21,966,900[9]	12.1[9]	93	[9]	[9]	[9]	[9]	[9]	3,590	[9]
Rwanda	1992	1,710	18,937	1,104,902	58.3	75	...	3,413[4]	94,586[4]	27.7[4]	8	...	4
St. Kitts and Nevis	1998	28	320	5,928	18.5	...	9	341	4,548	13.3	...	...	...
St. Lucia	1998	84	1,160	30,536	26.3	...	17	620	11,405	18.4	...	1[11]	341[11]
St. Vincent and the Grenadines	1998	60	1,007	21,347	21.2	...	21	379	7,775	20.5	...	3	32[16]
Samoa	1995	155	1,475	35,811	24.3	96	...	...	...	...	45	...	...
San Marino	1998	14	225	1,211	5.4	...	3	148	700	4.7	...	...	445
São Tomé and Príncipe	1997	69	638	21,760	34.1	...	10	415	12,280	29.6	...	...	...
Saudi Arabia	1997	11,509	175,458	2,256,185	12.9	61	7,667	115,907	1,505,072	13.0	42	...	6,133
Senegal	1997	3,530	16,567	954,758	57.6	60	359[11]	6,219	206,934	33.3	16	19[11]	182[11]
Seychelles	1999	25	656	9,868	15.0	...	13	545	7,774	14.3	...	12	218
Sierra Leone	1993	1,643	10,595	267,425	25.2	...	167	4,313	70,900	16.4	...	44	709
Singapore	1997	196	11,189	280,108	25.0	93	165	10,673	209,835	19.7	44	10	1,315
Slovakia	1998	2,482	39,535	645,941	16.3	...	198	5,849	80,116	13.7	...	365	10,104
Slovenia	1997	824	7,283	98,866	13.5	95	153	8,665	131,573	15.2	...	...	5,908
Solomon Islands	1994	520	2,514	60,493	24.1	...	23	618	7,981	12.9	...	1	...
Somalia	1990	...	...	377,000	...	10	...	...	44,000	...	3	...	...
South Africa	1996	20,863[9]	224,896	8,159,430	36.3	103	9	128,611[5]	3,749,449[5]	29.2[5]	58	187[5]	10,807[5]
Spain	1997	16,540[5]	163,105	2,682,894	16.4	105	25,775[4, 11]	245,118[4]	2,946,191	...	74	4	4
Sri Lanka	1998	10,947[9]	194,823[9]	4,278,124[9]	22.0[9]	...	[9]	[9]	[9]	[9]	[9]	36	623
Sudan, The	1997	11,158	102,987	3,000,048	24.1	54	2,578[2]	15,504	405,583	26.2	...	...	761
Suriname	1996	304	3,611	75,585	20.9	...	104	2,286	31,918	13.9	...	1	...
Swaziland	1997	529	6,094	205,829	33.8	91	165[5]	2,954[16]	57,330[16]	19.4[16]	38	5[5]	228[5]
Sweden	1997	4,936	81,800	958,972	11.7	102	641	28,305	310,000	10.9	99	...	...
Switzerland	1998	...	...	462,262	...	100	...	...	421,025	...	79	...	...
Syria	1997	10,783	114,689	2,690,205	23.5	91	2,526[3]	52,182	865,042	16.6	38	292[3]	12,479
Taiwan	1998	2,540	92,104	1,905,690	20.7	...	1,151[4]	99,411[4]	1,874,747[4]	18.9[4]	...	4	4
Tajikistan	1997	3,432	27,172	638,674	23.5	...	...	112,532	688,150	6.1	...	75[3]	...
Tanzania	1996[22]	10,892[5]	108,874	3,942,888	36.2	48	491[5]	11,689	199,093	17.0	...	40[5]	1,062
Thailand	1997	34,412[11]	445,542[11]	5,909,618	...	...	2,318[11]	107,025[11]	3,267,449	...	...	679[11]	40,116[11]
Togo	1997	3,283[16]	18,535	859,574	46.4	81	314[11]	4,736[16]	169,178	...	18	...	653
Tonga	1994	115	701	16,540	23.6	...	47	809	15,702	19.4	...	9	67[1]
Trinidad and Tobago	1997	478	7,311	181,030	24.8	88	...	5,070[4]	104,349[4]	20.6[4]	65	...	4
Tunisia	1997	4,428	60,101	1,450,916	24.1	98	712[3]	45,411	882,730	19.4	...	...	237[16]
Turkey	1997	47,313	217,131	6,389,060	29.4	99	11,144	143,322	3,427,715	23.9	51	4,046	75,507
Turkmenistan	1995	1,900[9]	72,900[9]	940,600[9]	12.9[9]	...	[9]	[9]	[9]	[9]	...	78	...
Tuvalu	1994	12	72[1]	1,906	...	...	2	31	345	...	...	1	10[1]
Uganda	1995[8]	8,531	76,134	2,636,409	34.6	...	...	14,447	255,158	17.7	...	...	1,788
Ukraine	1996	21,900[9]	576,000[3, 9]	7,007,000[9]	12.4[3, 9]	...	9	9	9	9	9	782	9
United Arab Emirates	1997	...	16,148	259,509	16.1	78	...	12,388[3]	178,839	12.0	71	9	249[14]
United Kingdom	1997	23,312	283,492	5,328,219	18.5	99	...	312,038	4,435,000	13.2	91	...	152,098
United States	1998	88,223[8, 9]	1,874,000	34,681,000	18.5	95	9	1,217,000	17,494,000	14.4	90	...	...
Uruguay	1997	2,410	16,721	348,195	20.8	93	413	19,104	192,399	10.1	...	101	...
Uzbekistan	1996	9,300[9]	413,000[9]	5,090,000[9]	12.3[9]	...	9	9	9	9	...	248	22,164[11]
Vanuatu	1992	272	852	26,267	30.8	...	...	220	4,269	19.4	17	...	...
Venezuela	1997	15,894[11]	182,192	4,262,221	23.4	84	1,621[2, 4]	43,369[4]	377,984[4]	8.7[4]	22	4	4
Vietnam	1998	13,092[5]	324,431	10,431,337	32.2	...	6,298[5]	209,500	6,642,350	31.7	...	451[5]	9,336
Virgin Islands (U.S.)	1993[8]	62	790	14,544	18.4	...	...	541[12]	12,502	17.2[12]	...	—	—
West Bank	1997	1,193[9]	15,912[9]	431,565[9]	27.1[9]	...	9	9	9	9	...	...	...
Western Sahara	1995[8]	40	925	32,257	34.9	...	13	1,267	10,541	8.3	...	...	...
Yemen	1997[14]	11,013[5]	90,478	2,699,788	29.8	...	1,224[3]	13,787	286,405	20.8	...	125[3]	369[3]
Yugoslavia	1999	4,431	52,294	864,199	16.5	69	561	27,766	367,587	13.2	62	...	...
Zambia	1996	3,907	38,528[3]	1,670,000	...	75	...	...	255,000	...	16	...	...
Zimbabwe	1996	4,659	63,718	2,493,791	39.1	...	1,536	28,354	751,349	26.5	...	25[2]	1,479[2]

students[d]	student/ teacher ratio	third level (higher) institutions	teachers[c]	students[d]	student/ teacher ratio	gross enroll- ment ratio[b]	students per 100,000 popula- tion[b]	percent of population age 25 and over with post- secondary education[b]	literacy[b] over age	total (%)	male (%)	female (%)	public expenditure on education (percent of GNP)[b]	country
12,001	21.2	3	954	7,158	7.5	0.5	40	0.1	15	43.8	59.9	28.4	4.1	Mozambique
25,374[3]	10.3[3]	51	17,089	385,300	22.5	5.0	564	2.0	15	84.7	89.0	80.6	1.2	Myanmar (Burma)
1,503[5]	...	75	331[12]	11,344	...	8.0	738	4.0	15	82.1	82.9	81.2	9.1	Namibia
									15	99.0	...	...	...	Nauru
[4]	[4]	3[2]	4,925[12]	105,694	...	5.0	501	0.6	15	41.4	59.1	21.8	3.2	Nepal
517,000	...	13	...	147,000	...	47.0	3,176	...	15	100.0	100.0	100.0	5.1	Netherlands, The
8,524	...	1	97	686	7.1	...	...	8.8	15	96.6	96.6	96.6	...	Netherlands Antilles
5,916	...	4	79	1,749	22.1	5.0	...	7.5	15	57.9	57.4	58.3	13.5	New Caledonia
105,186	19.8	7	4,973	107,837	21.7	63.0	4,508	39.1	15	100.0	100.0	100.0	7.3	New Zealand
...	...	10[5]	3,840	48,758	12.7	12.0	1,231	...	15	64.3	64.2	64.4	3.9	Nicaragua
2,145	10.0	2	355	5,569	15.7	0.7	55	...	15	15.7	23.5	8.3	2.3	Niger
...	...	31	12,103	228,000	18.8	4.0	367	...	15	64.1	72.3	56.2	0.7	Nigeria
[4]	[4]	...							15	96.3	96.9	95.6	...	Northern Mariana Islands
[4]	[4]	89	11,515	181,741	15.8	54.5	4,164	18.7	15	100.0	100.0	100.0	7.4	Norway
2,350[5]	6.9[5]	5[1]	1,162	13,251	11.4	8.0	532	...	15	71.3	80.4	61.7	4.5	Oman
95,000	12.6	984	34,078	1,052,782	30.9	3.0	291	2.5	15	43.3	57.6	27.8	2.7	Pakistan
...	...	...	...	130	...	...	...	...	15	97.6	98.3	96.6	...	Palau
...	...	14	6,409	95,341	14.9	30.0	3,024	13.2	15	91.9	92.6	91.3	5.1	Panama
9,941	12.9[2]	21	...	13,663	...	3.0	318	...	15	76.0	81.7	67.7	4.7	Papua New Guinea
[4]	[4]	2	742[11]	42,302	...	10.0	1,049	6.6	15	93.3	94.4	92.2	4.0	Paraguay
270,576[3]	22.0[3]	886	45,443	657,586	14.2	26.0	3,268	20.6	15	89.9	94.7	85.4	2.9	Peru
...	[4]	975[5]	56,880[12]	2,022,106[16]	...	29.0	2,981	22.0	15	95.4	95.5	95.2	3.4	Philippines
1,599,900	17.8	246	73,300	1,091,500	14.9	25.0	1,884	7.9	15	99.8	99.8	99.8	7.5	Poland
25,234	3.7	278	16,087	319,525	19.9	39.0	3,060	7.7	15	92.2	94.8	90.0	5.8	Portugal
149,191	...	45	9,045	171,625[16]	...	...	...	28.7	15	93.8	93.7	94.0	8.2	Puerto Rico
670	5.6	1	643	8,475	13.2	27.0	1,518	13.3	15	81.3	80.5	83.2	3.4	Qatar
13,547[16]	12.1[16]	1	286	8,663	30.3	...	...	...	15	87.1	84.8	89.2	...	Réunion
351,900	32.2	102	23,477	354,488	15.1	23.0	1,817	5.6	15	98.2	99.1	97.3	3.6	Romania
1,676,000	...	913	282,400	3,597,900	12.7	43.0	2,998	14.1	15	99.4	99.8	99.2	3.5	Russia
[4]	[4]	...	646[1]	3,389[1]	5.2[1]	0.4	...	...	15	67.0	73.7	60.6	3.8	Rwanda
...	...	1[11]	51[11]	394[11]	7.7[11]	...	...	2.3	15	90.9	90.0	90.0	3.8	St. Kitts and Nevis
808[11]	23.7[11]	1	157[16]	2,760[16]	17.6[16]	...	...	3.4	15	82.0	...	...	9.8	St. Lucia
415	...	...	...	...	...	...	...	1.4	15	96.0	...	...	6.3	St. Vincent and the Grenadines
...	...	...	...	...	...	...	...	5.6	15	100.0	100.0	100.0	4.2	Samoa
455[5]	10.3[5]	...	...	...	...	...	...	...	15	99.1	99.4	98.8	...	San Marino
...	...	...	...	...	...	...	...	0.3	15	54.2	70.2	39.1	3.8	São Tomé and Príncipe
51,916	8.5	68[15]	8,998[15]	165,262[15]	18.4[15]	16.0	1,455	...	15	77.0	84.1	67.2	7.5	Saudi Arabia
7,301[11]	40.1[11]	2	965[15]	24,081[15]	25.0[15]	3.0	297	...	15	37.3	47.2	27.6	3.7	Senegal
2,002	9.2	...	...	...	...	...	...	4.6	15	84.2	82.9	85.7	7.9	Seychelles
7,756	10.9	1	257[12]	2,571[12]	10.0[12]	2.0	119	1.5	15	36.3	50.7	22.6	0.9	Sierra Leone
9,906	7.5	7	7,764	97,392	12.5	39.0	2,722	7.6	15	92.4	96.4	88.5	3.0	Singapore
116,681	11.5	18	8,544	83,942	9.8	22.0	1,903	9.5	15	100.0	100.0	100.0	5.0	Slovakia
80,885	13.7	37	3,907	51,009	13.1	38.0	2,775	10.4	15	100.0	100.0	100.0	5.7	Slovenia
...	...	...	...	...	...	...	...	...	15	54.1	62.4	44.9	3.8	Solomon Islands
10,400	...	1	549[12]	4,640[12]	...	0.5	...	...	15	24.0	36.0	14.0	0.4	Somalia
140,531[5]	13.0[5]	...	27,099[5]	617,897[5]	22.8[5]	19.0	1,664	1.5	15	85.1	85.8	84.5	8.0	South Africa
1,029,606	...	...	88,922	1,741,528	19.6	51.0	4,017	8.4	15	97.7	98.6	96.8	5.0	Spain
11,652	18.7	12	3,050	38,192	12.5	5.0	474	1.1	15	91.6	94.5	88.9	3.4	Sri Lanka
26,421	34.7	6	1,417	52,260	36.9	3.0	272	0.8	15	57.1	68.3	46.0	1.4	Sudan, The
1,462	...	1	155	1,335	8.6	...	1,124	...	15	94.2	95.9	92.6	3.5	Suriname
2,958[5]	13.0[5]	1	467	5,658	12.1	6.0	642	3.3	15	79.8	80.9	78.7	5.7	Swaziland
...	...	64	33,498[13]	275,217[13]	8.2[13]	50.0	2,972	21.0	15	100.0	100.0	100.0	8.3	Sweden
198,452	...	...	7,709[3]	151,021	...	33.0	2,066	11.5	15	100.0	100.0	100.0	5.4	Switzerland
92,622	7.4	...	4,733[3, 15]	215,734[3]	...	16.0	1,559	...	15	74.4	88.3	60.4	3.1	Syria
[4]	[4]	139	38,806	856,186	22.1	...	...	...	15	94.0	97.6	90.2	5.2	Taiwan
29,482[3]	...	10[3]	5,200[3]	76,613	...	20.0	1,864	11.7	15	99.2	99.6	98.9	2.2	Tajikistan
12,571	11.8	...	1,650	12,776	7.7	0.6	43	2.0	15	75.2	84.1	66.6	3.4	Tanzania
658,474	...	102	25,171[16]	481,936[16]	19.1[16]	22.0	2,096	5.1	15	95.6	97.2	94.0	4.6	Thailand
9,076	13.8	1	443	11,639	26.3	4.0	317	1.3	15	57.1	72.2	42.6	4.5	Togo
824	...	1	53	226[2]	...	...	...	2.8	15	92.8	92.9	92.8	4.7	Tonga
[4]	[4]	3	...	6,007	...	7.7	771	3.4	15	98.2	99.0	97.5	4.4	Trinidad and Tobago
3,839[16]	16.2[16]	...	6,641	121,787	18.3	14.0	1,330	2.8	15	70.8	81.4	60.1	7.7	Tunisia
1,333,177	17.6	863	53,805	1,222,362	22.7	21.0	1,960	10.8	15	85.2	93.6	76.7	2.2	Turkey
26,000	...	15	...	29,435[16]	...	22.0	2,072	...	15	97.7	98.8	96.6	3.9	Turkmenistan
58[12]	...	—	—	—	—	...	...	7.0	15	95.0	...	...	...	Tuvalu
36,063	20.2	...	2,006	29,343	14.6	2.0	154	0.5	15	67.3	77.7	57.1	2.6	Uganda
618,000	...	255[15]	...	922,800[15]	...	41.0	2,977	...	15	98.4	99.5	97.4	7.3	Ukraine
1,925[14]	7.7[14]	4	510[11]	17,950	...	12.0	801	...	15	76.5	75.5	79.5	1.8	United Arab Emirates
2,435,321	16.0	...	89,241	1,820,849	20.4	52.0	3,135	...	15	100.0	100.0	100.0	5.3	United Kingdom
...	...	5,758[11]	940,000	14,350,000	15.3	81.0	5,339	46.5	15	95.5	95.7	95.3	5.4	United States
58,246	...	2	7,165	62,026	8.7	30.0	2,487	10.1	15	97.8	97.4	98.2	3.3	Uruguay
240,100[13]	...	55[13]	...	272,300[13]	...	32.0	2,938	...	15	97.2	98.5	96.0	7.7	Uzbekistan
444	...	1	...	124[12]	...	...	...	...	15	52.9	57.3	47.8	4.8	Vanuatu
[4]	[4]	99[12]	36,232	717,192	19.8	28.0	2,820	11.8	15	93.0	93.3	92.7	5.2	Venezuela
179,907	19.3	104[5]	23,522	509,300	21.7	7.0	404	2.6	15	93.3	95.7	91.0	3.0	Vietnam
—	—	1	266	2,924	11.0	...	...	24.4	...	...	...	...	7.5	Virgin Islands (U.S.)
...	...	22	1,598	30,622	19.2	...	...	...	...	...	...	...	...	West Bank
...	...	—	...	...	...	...	...	...	...	...	...	...	...	Western Sahara
1,222	...	2	1,991[3]	65,675	...	4.0	419	...	15	46.4	67.4	25.0	7.0	Yemen
67,883	...	83	10,998	147,981	13.5	22.0	1,674	...	15	93.3	97.6	89.2	...	Yugoslavia
7,982[12]	...	2	640	4,470	7.0	2.0	241	1.5	15	78.0	85.2	71.2	2.2	Zambia
27,431[2]	18.5[2]	28[2]	3,581[3]	43,200[3]	12.1[3]	7.0[3]	638	4.9	15	90.0	90.1	89.9	7.1	Zimbabwe

[1]1990. [2]1992. [3]1995. [4]General second level includes vocational second level. [5]1994. [6]Includes upper primary. [7]College of the Bahamas only. [8]Public schools only. [9]First level includes general second level. [10]Includes preschool. [11]1993. [12]1991. [13]1997. [14]Excludes teacher training. [15]Universities only. [16]1996. [17]Republic of Cyprus only. [18]Includes lower secondary. [19]Data exclude 1,770 primary and 1,449 secondary schools in the Al-Azhar education system. [20]Port-au-Prince universities only. [21]Upper second level only. [22]Mainland Tanzania only.

BIBLIOGRAPHY AND SOURCES

The following list indicates the principal documentary sources used in the compilation of *Britannica World Data*. It is by no means a complete list, either for international or for national sources, but is indicative more of the range of materials to which reference has been made in preparing this compilation.

While *Britannica World Data* has long been based primarily on print sources, many rare in North American library collections, the burgeoning resources of the Internet can be accessed from any appropriately equipped personal computer (PC). At this writing, more than 100 national statistical offices had Internet sites and there were also sites for central banks, national information offices, individual ministries, and the like.

Because of the relative ease of access to these sites for PC users, uniform resource locators (URLs) for mainly official sites have been added to both country statements (at the end, in boldface) and individual Comparative National Statistics tables (at the end of the headnote) when a source providing comparable international data existed. Many sites exist that are narrower in coverage or less official and that may also serve the reader (on-line newspapers; full texts of national constitutions; business and bank sites) but space permitted the listing of only the top national and intergovernmental sites. Sites that are wholly or predominantly in a language other than English are so identified.

International Statistical Sources

Asian Development Bank. *Asian Development Outlook* (annual); *Key Indicators of Developing Member Countries of ADB* (annual).
Billboard Books. *World Radio TV Handbook* (annual).
Caribbean Development Bank. *Annual Report.*
Christian Research. *World Churches Handbook* (1997).
Comité Monétaire de la Zone Franc. *La Zone Franc: Rapport* (annual).
Eastern Caribbean Central Bank. *Report and Statement of Accounts* (annual).
Europa Publications Ltd. *Africa South of the Sahara* (annual); *The Europa Year Book* (2 vol.); *The Far East and Australasia* (annual); *The Middle East and North Africa* (annual).
Food and Agriculture Organization. *Food Balance Sheets; Production Yearbook; Trade Yearbook; Yearbook of Fishery Statistics* (2 vol.); *Yearbook of Forest Products.*
Her Majesty's Stationery Office. *The Commonwealth Yearbook.*
Instituts d'Émission d'Outre-Mer et des Départements d'Outre-Mer (France). *Bulletin trimestriel* (quarterly); *Rapport annuel.*
Inter-American Development Bank. *Economic and Social Progress in Latin America* (annual).
Inter-Parliamentary Union. *Chronicle of Parliamentary Elections and Developments* (annual); *World Directory of Parliaments* (annual).
International Air Transport Association. *World Air Transport Statistics* (annual).
International Bank for Reconstruction and Development/The World Bank. *Statistical Handbook 19**: States of the Former USSR* (annual); *World Bank Atlas* (annual); *Global Development Finance* (2 vol.; annual); *World Development Report* (annual).
International Civil Aviation Organization. *Civil Aviation Statistics of the World* (annual); *Digest of Statistics.*
International Institute for Strategic Studies. *The Military Balance* (annual).
International Labour Organisation. *Year Book of Labour Statistics; The Cost of Social Security: Basic Tables* (triennial).

International Monetary Fund. *Annual Report on Exchange Arrangements and Exchange Restrictions; Direction of Trade Statistics Yearbook; Government Finance Statistics Yearbook; International Financial Statistics* (monthly, with yearbook).
International Road Federation. *World Road Statistics* (annual).
International Telecommunication Union. *Yearbook of Statistics: Telecommunication Services* (annual).
Jane's Publishing Co., Ltd. *Jane's World Railways* (annual).
Keesing's Worldwide LLC. *Keesing's Record of World Events* (monthly except August).
Macmillan Press Ltd. *The Statesman's Year-Book.*
Middle East Economic Digest Ltd. *Middle East Economic Digest* (semimonthly).
Mining Journal, Ltd. *Mining Annual Review* (2 vol.).
Organization for Economic Cooperation and Development. *Economic Surveys* (annual); *Financing and External Debt of Developing Countries* (annual).
Organization of Eastern Caribbean States. *Statistical Booklet* (irreg.).
Oxford University Press. *World Christian Encyclopedia* (David B. Barrett, ed. [2001, 2 vol.]).
Pan American Health Organization. *Health Conditions in the Americas* (2 vol.; quadrennial).
PennWell Publishing Co. *International Petroleum Encyclopedia* (annual).
René Moreux et Cie. *Marchés tropicaux & Méditerranéens* (weekly).
Secretariat of the Pacific Community. *Population Profile* (assorted countries).
United Nations (UN). *Demographic Yearbook; Energy Balances and Electricity Profiles* (biennial); *Industrial Commodities Statistics Yearbook; Energy Statistics Yearbook; International Trade Statistics Yearbook* (2 vol.); *Monthly Bulletin of Statistics; Population Studies* (irreg.); *National Accounts Statistics* (2 parts; annual); *Population and Vital Statistics Report* (quarterly); *Statistical Yearbook; World Population Prospects 19*** (biennial).
UN: Economic Commission for Africa. *African Socio-Economic Indicators* (annual); *African Statistical Yearbook* (2 vol. in 4 parts); *Economic and Social Survey of Africa* (annual).
UN: Economic Commission for Europe. *Annual Bulletin of Housing and Building Statistics for Europe; Annual Bulletin of Transport Statistics for Europe.*
UN: Economic Commission for Latin America. *Economic Survey of Latin America and the Caribbean* (2 vol.; annual); *Statistical Yearbook for Latin America and the Caribbean.*
UN: Economic and Social Commission for Asia and the Pacific. *Statistical Indicators for Asia and the Pacific* (quarterly); *Statistical Yearbook for Asia and the Pacific.*
UN: Economic and Social Commission for Western Asia. *Demographic and Related Socio-Economic Data Sheets* (irreg.); *National Accounts Studies of the ESCWA Region* (irreg.); *The Population Situation in the ESCWA Region* (irreg.); *Prices and Financial Statistics in the ESCWA Region* (irreg.); *Statistical Abstract of the Region of the Economic and Social Commission for Western Asia* (annual).
UN: Educational, Scientific, and Cultural Organization. *Statistical Yearbook.*
United Nations Industrial Development Organization. *Industrial Development Review Series* (irreg.); *Industrial Development: Global Report* (annual); *International Yearbook of Industrial Statistics.*
United States: Central Intelligence Agency, *The World Factbook* (annual); Dept. of Commerce, *World Population Profile* (biennial); Dept. of Health and Human Services, *Social Security Programs Throughout the World* (semiannual, 4 vol.); Dept. of Interior, *Minerals Yearbook* (3 vol. in 6 parts); Dept. of State, *Background Notes* (irreg.).
World Health Organization. *World Health Statistics Annual; World Health Statistics Quarterly.*
World Tourism Organization. *Compendium of Tourism Statistics* (annual).

National Statistical Sources

Afghanistan. *Preliminary Results of the First Afghan Population Census (1979).*
Albania. *Population and Housing Census 1989; Statistical Yearbook of Albania.*
Algeria. *Annuaire statistique; Recensement général de la population et de l'habitat, 1998; Algeria: Recent Economic Developments* (IMF Country Staff Report [2001]).

American Samoa. *American Samoa Statistical Digest* (annual); *Report on the State of the Island* (U.S. Department of the Interior [annual]); *2000 Census of Population and Housing* (U.S.).
Andorra. *Anuari Estadístic* (annual); *L'Andorre en Chiffres* (annual); *Recull Estadístic General de la Població Andorra 90.*
Angola. *Angola—Recent Economic Developments* (IMF Staff Country Report [2000]); *Perfil estatístico de Angola* (annual).
Antigua. *Antigua and Barbuda—Statistical Annex* (IMF Staff Country Report [1999]); *Statistical Yearbook; 1991 Population and Housing Census.*
Argentina. *Anuario estadístico de la República Argentina; Censo nacional de población, hogares y vivienda 2001.*
Armenia. *Recent Economic Development and Selected Issues* (IMF Staff Country Report [1999]); *Statisticheskii Yezhegodnik Armenii* (Statistical Yearbook of Armenia).
Aruba. *Statistical Yearbook; Central Bank of Aruba Bulletin* (quarterly); *Fourth Population and Housing Census October 14, 2000.*
Australia. *Monthly Summary of Statistics, Australia; Social Indicators* (annual); *Year Book Australia; 2001 Census of Population and Housing.*
Austria. *Grosszählung 2001* (General Census 2001). *Sozialstatistische Daten* (irreg.); *Statistisches Jahrbuch für die Republik Österreich.*
Azerbaijan. *Azerbaijan Republic: Selected Issues and Statistical Appendix* (IMF Staff Country Report [2002]); *Statistical Yearbook of Azerbaijan.*
Bahamas, The. *Census of Population and Housing 2000; Statistical Abstract* (annual); *Central Bank of The Bahamas Annual Report and Statement of Accounts.*
Bahrain. *Statistical Abstract* (annual); *The Population, Housing, Buildings and Establishments Census 2001.*
Bangladesh. *Bangladesh Population Census, 1991; Statistical Yearbook of Bangladesh; Bangladesh: Recent Economic Developments* (IMF Staff Country Report [2000]).
Barbados. *Barbados Economic Report* (annual); *Monthly Digest of Statistics; Barbados: Statistical Appendix* (IMF Staff Country Report [2000]).
Belarus. *Narodnoye Khozyaystvo Respubliki Belarus: Statisticheskiy Yezhegodnik* (National Economy of the Republic of Belarus: Statistical Yearbook).
Belgium. *Annuaire statistique de la Belgique; Recensement de la population et des logements au 1er mars 1991.*
Belize. *Abstract of Statistics* (annual); *Belize Economic Survey* (annual); *Central Bank of Belize Annual Report and Accounts; 2000 Population Census: Major Findings.*
Benin. *Annuaire statistique; Recensement général de la population et de l'habitation* (1992).
Bermuda. *Bermuda Digest of Statistics* (annual); *Report of the Manpower Survey* (annual); *The 1991 Census of Population and Housing.*
Bhutan. *Statistical Yearbook of Bhutan.*
Bolivia. *Anuario estadístico; Censo de población y vivienda 2001; Compendio estadístico* (annual); *Estadísticas socio-económicas* (annual); *Resumen estadístico* (annual).
Bosnia and Herzegovina. *Bosnia and Herzegovina: Statistical Appendix* (IMF Staff Country Report [2002]).
Botswana. *Statistical Bulletin* (quarterly); *2001 Population and Housing Census; Botswana—Selected Issues and Statistical Appendix* (IMF Staff Country Report [1999]).
Brazil. *Anuário Estatístico do Brasil; Censo Demográfico 2000.*
Brunei. *Brunei Statistical Yearbook; Summary Tables of the Population Census 1991.*
Bulgaria. *Prebroyavaneto na naselenieto kŭm 01.03.2001 godina* (Census of Population of March 1, 2001); *Statisticheskii godishnik na Republika Bŭlgariya* (Statistical Yearbook of the Republic of Bulgaria).
Burkina Faso. *Burkina Faso: Selected Issues and Statistical Annex* (IMF Staff Country Report [2002]); *Recensement général de la population du 10 au 20 decembre 1985.*
Burundi. *Annuaire statistique; Recensement général de la population, 1990; Burundi: Statistical Annex* (IMF Staff Country Report [2000]).
Cambodia. *1998 Population Census of Cambodia; Cambodia: Statistical Appendix* (IMF Staff Country Report [2002]).

Cameroon. *Cameroon—Statistical Appendix* (IMF Staff Country Report [2000]); *Recensement général de la population et de l'habitat 1987.*

Canada. *Canada Year Book* (biennial); *Census Canada 2001: Population.*

Cape Verde. *Boletím Anual de Estatística; Cape Verde—Recent Economic Developments* (IMF Staff Country Report [2001]); *O Recenseamento Geral da População e Habitação 2000.*

Central African Republic. *Annuaire statistique; Central African Republic—Statistical Annex* (IMF Staff Country Report [2000]); *Recensement général de la population 1988.*

Chad. *Annuaire statistique; Recensement general de la population et de l'habitat 1993; Chad: Statistical Appendix* (IMF Staff Country Report [2002]).

Chile. *Chile XVII censo nacional de población y VI de vivienda, 24 de abril 2002; Compendio estadístico* (annual).

China, People's Republic of. *People's Republic of China Year-Book; Statistical Yearbook of China; 10 Percent Sampling Tabulation on the 1990 Population Census of the People's Republic of China.*

Colombia. *Colombia estadística* (annual); *Censo 93 informacion de vivienda; Colombia: Statistical Appendix* (IMF Staff Country Report [2001]).

Comoros. *Banque Centrale des Comoroes Rapport Annuel* (Central Bank of Comoros Annual Report); *Recensement général de la population et de l'habitat 15 septembre 1980.*

Congo, Dem. Rep. of the (Zaire). *Annuaire statistique* (irreg.); *Recensement Scientifique de la Population du 1er juillet 1984.*

Congo, Rep. of the. *Annuaire statistique; Recensement général de la population et de l'habitat de 1984.*

Costa Rica. *Anuario estadístico; Costa Rica at a Glance* (annual); *IX censo nacional de población y V de vivienda, 2001.*

Côte d'Ivoire. *Côte d'Ivoire—Selected Issues and Statistical Appendix* (IMF Staff Country Report [2000]); *Recensement général de la population et de l'habitat 1988.*

Croatia. *Census of Population, Households and Dwellings 31st March 2001; Statistical Yearbook.*

Cuba. *Anuario estadístico; Censo de población y viviendas, 1981.*

Cyprus. *Census of Industrial Production* (annual); *Census of Population 1992; Economic Report* (annual); *Statistical Abstract* (annual).

Czech Republic. *Statistická ročenka České Republiky* (Statistical Yearbook of the Czech Republic).

Denmark. *Folke-og boligtaellingen, 1981* (Population and Housing Census); *Statistisk årbog* (Statistical Yearbook).

Djibouti. *Annuaire statistique de Djibouti; Djibouti: Statistical Annex* (IMF Staff Country Report [1999]).

Dominica. *Dominica—Statistical Annex* (IMF Staff Country Report [2000]); *Population and Housing Census 1991; Statistical Digest* (irreg.).

Dominican Republic. *Cifras Dominicanas* (irreg.); *Censo nacional de población y vivienda, 1993.*

Ecuador. *Serie estadística* (quinquennial); *VI censo de población y V de vivienda 2001.*

Egypt. *Census Population, Housing, and Establishment, 1996; Statistical Yearbook.*

El Salvador. *Anuario estadístico* (irreg.); *Censos nacionales: V censo de población y IV de vivienda (1992); El Salvador en cifras* (annual); *Indicadores económicos y sociales* (annual).

Equatorial Guinea. *Censos nacionales, I de población y I de vivienda—4 al 17 de julio de 1983; Equatorial Guinea—Recent Economic Developments* (IMF Staff Country Report [1999]).

Eritrea. *Eritrea—Selected Issues* (IMF Staff Country Report [2000]).

Estonia. *2000 Population and Housing Census; Eesti Statistika Aastaraamat* (Estonia Statistical Yearbook).

Ethiopia. *1994 Population and Housing Census of Ethiopia; Ethiopia Statistical Abstract* (annual); *Ethiopia—Recent Economic Developments* (IMF Staff Country Report [1999]).

Faroe Islands. *Rigsombudsmanden på Færøerne: Beretning* (annual); *Statistical Bulletin* (annual).

Fiji. *Key Statistics* (annual); *Current Economic Statistics* (quarterly); *1996 Census of the Population and Housing.*

Finland. *Economic Survey* (annual); *Population Census 1990; Statistical Yearbook of Finland.*

France. *Annuaire statistique de la France; Données sociales* (triennial); *Recensement général de la population de 1999; Tableaux de l'Economie Française* (annual).

French Guiana. *Recensement général de la population de 1999; Tableaux economiques regionaux: Guyane* (biennial).

French Polynesia. *Résultats du recensement général de la population de la Polynésie Française, du 6 Septembre 1996; Tableaux de l'economie polynesienne* (irreg.); *Te avei'a: Bulletin d'information statistique* (monthly).

Gabon. *Recensement général de la population et de l'habitat 1993; Situation économique, financière et sociale de la République Gabonaise* (annual).

Gambia, The. *The Gambia—Selected Issues* (IMF Staff Country Report [2000]).

Gaza Strip. *Judaea, Samaria, and Gaza Area Statistics Quarterly; Palestinian Statistical Abstract* (annual).

Georgia. *Georgia—Recent Economic Developments and Selected Issues* (IMF Staff Country Report [2001]); *Narodnoye Khozyaystvo Gruzinskoy SSR* (National Economy of the Georgian S.S.R. [annual]).

Germany. *Statistisches Jahrbuch für die Bundesrepublik Deutschland; Volkszählung vom 25. Mai 1987* (Census of Population).

Ghana. *Ghana—Statistical Appendix* (IMF Staff Country Report [2000]); *Population Census of Ghana, 1984; Quarterly Digest of Statistics.*

Greece. *Recensement de la population et des habitations, 2001; Statistical Yearbook of Greece.*

Greenland. *Grønland* (annual); *Grønlands befolkning* (Greenland Population [annual]).

Grenada. *Abstract of Statistics* (annual); *Grenada—Statistical Appendix* (IMF Staff Country Report [2001]). *2001 Population and Housing Census.*

Guadeloupe. *Recensement général de la population de 1999: Guadeloupe; Tableaux economiques regionaux: Guadeloupe* (biennial).

Guam. *Guam Annual Economic Review; 2000 Census of Population and Housing* (U.S.).

Guatemala. *Anuario estadística; Censo nacional instituto nacional de estadística 1994: X nacional de población y V de habitación.*

Guernsey. *Guernsey Census 2001; Statistical Digest* (annual); *Economic and Statistics Review* (annual).

Guinea. *Guinea—Statistical Appendix* (IMF Staff Country Report [2000]).

Guinea-Bissau. *Guinea-Bissau—Statistical Appendix* (IMF Staff Country Report [2002]); *Recenseamento Geral da População e da Habitação, 1991.*

Guyana. *Bank of Guyana: Annual Report and Statement of Accounts; Guyana: Statistical Appendix* (IMF Staff Country Report [2001]).

Haiti. *Banque de la République d'Haiti: Rapport Annuel; Haiti: Selected Issues* (IMF Staff Country Report [2002]). *Résultats préliminaires du recensement général (Septembre 1982).*

Honduras. *Anuario estadístico; Censo nacional de población y vivienda, 1988; Honduras—Statistical Appendix* (IMF Staff Country Report [2000]); *Honduras en cifras* (annual).

Hong Kong. *Annual Digest of Statistics; Hong Kong* (annual); *Hong Kong 2001 Population Census; Hong Kong Social and Economic Trends* (biennial).

Hungary. *Statisztikai évkönyv* (Statistical Yearbook); *2001, Evi népszámlálás* (Census of Population 2001).

Iceland. *Hagtidhindi* (monthly); *Landshagir* (Statistical Yearbook of Iceland [annual]); *Iceland in Figures* (annual).

India. *Census of India, 2001; Economic Survey* (annual); *Statistical Abstract* (annual).

Indonesia. *Indonesia: An Official Handbook* (irreg.); *Hasil Sensus penduduk Indonesia, 2000* (Census of Population); *Statistical Yearbook of Indonesia.*

Iran. *National Census of Population and Housing, October 1996; Iran Statistical Yearbook; Islamic Republic of Iran: Selected Issues and Statistical Appendix* (IMF Staff Country Report [2002]).

Iraq. *Annual Abstract of Statistics.*

Ireland. *Census of Population of Ireland, 2002; National Income and Expenditure* (annual); *Statistical Yearbook of Ireland* (annual).

Isle of Man. *Census Report 2001; Isle of Man Digest of Economic and Social Statistics* (annual).

Israel. *1995 Census of Population and Housing; Statistical Abstract* (annual).

Italy. *Statistica agraria; Statistiche demografiche* (4 parts); *Statistiche dell'istruzione; Annuario statistico Italiano; 13º Censimento generale della popolazione e delle Abitazioni 20 Ottobre 1991.*

Jamaica. *Economic and Social Survey* (annual); *Statistical Abstract* (annual); *Statistical Yearbook of Jamaica; Population Census 2001.*

Japan. *Japan Statistical Yearbook; Statistical Indicators on Social Life* (annual); *1995 Population Census of Japan.*

Jersey. *Report of the Census for 2001; Statistical Digest* (annual); *An Introduction to Jersey* (irreg.).

Jordan. *Population and Housing Census 1994; Central Bank of Jordan Report* (annual); *National Accounts* (irreg.); *Statistical Yearbook.*

Kazakhstan. *Statistichesky Yezhegodnik* (Statistical Yearbook); *1999 Population Census.*

Kenya. *Economic Survey* (annual); *Population Census 1999; Statistical Abstract* (annual); *Kenya—Selected Issues and Statistical Appendix* (IMF Staff Country Report [2002]).

Kiribati. *Annual Abstract of Statistics; Kiribati Population Census 2000; Kiribati—Statistical Appendix* (IMF Staff Country Report [1997]).

Korea, North. *North Korea: A Country Study* (1994); *The Population of North Korea* (1990).

Korea, South. *Korea Statistical Yearbook; Social Indicators in Korea* (annual); *2000 Population and Housing Census.*

Kuwait. *Annual Statistical Abstract; General Census of Population and Housing and Buildings 1995.*

Kyrgyzstan. *Statistichesky Yezhegodnik Kyrgyzstana* (Statistical Yearbook of Kyrgyzstan).

Laos. *Lao People's Democratic Republic: Selected Issues and Statistical Appendix* (IMF Staff Country Report [2002]).

Latvia. *Statistical Yearbook of Latvia; Latvijas Republikas 2000 Iedzivotāju Skaits* (2000 Census of Population of the Republic of Latvia).

Lebanon. *Lebanon: A Country Study* (1989).

Lesotho. *Lesotho—Statistical Annex* (IMF Staff Country Report [2002]); *Statistical Yearbook; 1996 Population Census.*

Liberia. *Economic Survey* (annual); *Liberia: Statistical Appendix* (IMF Staff Country Report [2002]).

Libya. *Libya Population Census, 1995.*

Liechtenstein. *Statistisches Jahrbuch; Volkszählung, 1990* (Census of Population); *Liechtenstein in Figures* (annual).

Lithuania. *Gyventojų ir Bustų Surašymu Skypius 2001* (Population and Housing Census 2001); *Lietuvos Statistikos Metraštis* (Lithuanian Statistical Yearbook).

Luxembourg. *Annuaire statistique; Bulletin du STATEC* (monthly); *Recensement général de la population du 15 février 2001.*

Macau. *Anuário Estatístico; XIII Recenseamento Geral da População, 1991.*

Macedonia. *Former Yugoslav Republic of Macedonia: Selected Issues and Statistical Appendix* (IMF Staff Country Report [2002]); *Statistical Yearbook of the Republic of Macedonia.*

Madagascar. *Madagascar: Selected Issues and Statistical Appendix* (IMF Staff Country Report [2001]); *Recensement général de la population et de l'habitat, aout 1993; Situation économique* (annual).

Malawi. *1998 Population and Housing Census; Malawi Statistical Yearbook; Malawi Yearbook; Malawi: Selected Issues and Statistical Appendix* (IMF Staff Country Report [2002]).

Malaysia. *Population and Housing Census of Malaysia 2000; Yearbook of Statistics; Malaysia: Statistical Appendix* (IMF Staff Country Report [2001]).

Maldives. *Population and Housing Census of Maldives 2000; Statistical Year Book of Maldives.*

Mali. *Annuaire statistique du Mali; Recensement general de la population et de l'habitat (du 1er au 9 mars 1998); Mali: Selected Issues and Statistical Annex* (IMF Staff Country Report [2002]).

Malta. *Annual Abstract of Statistics; Quarterly Digest of Statistics.*

Marshall Islands. *Marshall Islands Statistical Abstract* (annual); *Report on the State of the Islands* (U.S. Department of the Interior [annual]); *Population and Housing Census 1999.*

Martinique. *Recensement de la population de 1999. Martinique; Tableaux economiques regionaux: Martinique* (biennial).

Mauritania. *Recensement général de la population et de l'habitat 2000. Annuaire Statistique; Mauritania—Statistical Appendix* (IMF Staff Country Report [2000]).

Mauritius. *Annual Digest of Statistics; 2000 Housing and Population Census of Mauritius; Mauritius in Figures* (annual); *Mauritius: Selected Issues and Statistical Appendix* (IMF Staff Country Report [2002]).

Mayotte. *Bulletin Trimestriel* (quarterly) and *Rapport Annuel* (Institut d'Emission, France); *Recensement de la population de Mayotte: août 1997.*

Mexico. *Anuario estadístico; XII Censo general de población y vivienda, 2000; Anuario estadístico de los Estados Unidos Mexicanos.*

Micronesia. *Micronesia—Recent Economic Developments* (IMF Staff Country Report [1998]); *FSM Statistical Yearbook* (annual).

Moldova. *Republic of Moldova: Recent Economic Developments* (IMF Country Report [2001]); *Republica Moldova in Cifre* (annual).

Monaco. *Recensement general de la population 1990.*

Mongolia. *Mongolian Statistical Yearbook* (annual); *Mongolia: Selected Issues and Statistical Appendix* (IMF Staff Country Report [2002]); *2000 Population and Housing Census of Mongolia.*

Morocco. *Annuaire statistique du Maroc; Recensement général de la population et de l'habitat de 1994.*

Mozambique. *Anuário Estatístico; Republic of Mozambique—Statistical Appendix* (IMF Staff Country Report [2002]); *II Recenseamento Geral da População e habitação, 1997.*

Myanmar (Burma). *Myanmar—Statistical Appendix* (IMF Staff Country Report [2001]); *Report to the Pyithu Hluttaw on the Financial, Social, and Economic Conditions for 19*** (annual); *Statistical Abstract* (irreg.); *1983 Population Census.*

Namibia. *2001 Population and Housing Census; Statistical/Economic Review* (annual).

Nauru. *Population Profile* (irreg.).

Nepal. *Economic Survey* (annual); *Statistical Pocket Book* (irreg.); *Statistical Yearbook of Nepal; National Population Census* 2001.

Netherlands, The. *Statistical Yearbook of the Netherlands.*

Netherlands Antilles. *Fourth Population and Housing Census Netherlands Antilles 2001; Statistical Yearbook of the Netherlands Antilles.*

New Caledonia. *Images de la population de la Nouvelle-Calédonie principaux resultats du recensement 1996; Tableaux bilan economique* (annual); *New Caledonia Facts and Figures* (annual).

New Zealand. *2001 New Zealand Census of Population and Dwellings; New Zealand Official Yearbook.*

Nicaragua. *Censos Nacionales 1995; Compendio Estadístico* (annual); *Nicaragua—Statistical Appendix* (IMF Staff Country Report [2001]).

Niger. *Annuaire statistique; Niger—Statistical Annex* (IMF Staff Country Report [2002]); *2ème Recensement général de la population 1988.*

Nigeria. *Annual Abstract of Statistics; Nigeria: A Country Study* (1992); *Nigeria—Statistical Appendix* (IMF Staff Country Report [2001]).

Northern Mariana Islands. *CNMI Population Profile; Report on the State of the Islands* (U.S. Department of the Interior [annual]); *2000 Census of Population and Housing (U.S.).*

Norway. *Folke-og boligtelling 2001* (Population and Housing Census); *Industristatistikk* (annual); *Statistisk årbok* (Statistical Yearbook).

Oman. *General Census of Population, Housing, and Establishments* (1993); *Statistical Yearbook; Bank of Oman Annual Report.*

Pakistan. *Economic Survey* (annual); *Pakistan Statistical Yearbook; Population Census of Pakistan, 1998.*

Palau. *Statistical Yearbook; Census 2000; Republic of Palau: Recent Economic Developments* (IMF Staff Country Report [2002]).

Panama. *Indicadores económicos y sociales* (annual); *X censo nacional de poblacion y vivienda realizados el 14 de mayo del 2000; Panama en cifras* (annual).

Papua New Guinea. *Papua New Guinea: Recent Economic Developments* (IMF Staff Country Report [2000]); *Summary of Statistics* (annual); *2000 National Population Census.*

Paraguay. *Anuario estadístico del Paraguay; Censo nacional de población y viviendas, 1992; Paraguay: Recent Economic Developments* (IMF Staff Country Report [2001]).

Peru. *Censos nacionales; IX de población: IV de vivienda, 11 de julio de 1993; Compendio estadístico* (3 vol.; annual); *Informe estadístico* (annual); *Peru: Selected Issues* (IMF Staff Country Report [2001]).

Philippines. *Philippine Statistical Yearbook; 2000 Census of Population and Housing.*

Poland. *Narodowy spis powszechny 2002* (National Population and Housing Census); *Rocznik statystyczny* (Statistical Yearbook).

Portugal. *Anuário Estatístico; XIV Recenseamento Geral da População: IV Recenseamento Geral da Habitação, 2001.*

Puerto Rico. *Estadísticas socioeconomicas* (annual); *Informe económico al gobernador* (Economic Report to the Governor [annual]); *2000 Census of Population and Housing (U.S.).*

Qatar. *Annual Statistical Abstract; Economic Survey of Qatar* (annual); *Qatar Year Book; Qatar Central Bank Annual Report; Population and Housing Census 1993.*

Réunion. *Recensement général de la population de 1999; Tableau Economique de la Réunion* (biennial).

Romania. *Anuarul statistic al României* (Statistical Yearbook); *Census of Population and Housing March 27, 2002.*

Russia. *Demograficheskiy Yezhegodnik Rossii* (Demographic Yearbook of Russia); *Rossiysky Statistichesky Yezhegodnik* (Russian Statistical Yearbook).

Rwanda. *Bulletin de Statistique: Supplement Annuel; Recensement general de la population et de l'habitat 1991; Rwanda: Statistical Annex* (IMF Staff Country Report [2002]).

St. Kitts and Nevis. *Annual Digest of Statistics; St. Christopher and Nevis: Recent Economic Developments* (IMF Staff Country Report [2000]).

St. Lucia. *Annual Statistical Digest; St. Lucia: Selected Issues and Statistical Appendix* (IMF Staff Country Report [2002]); *2001 Population and Housing Census.*

St. Vincent and the Grenadines. *Digest of Statistics* (annual); *Population and Housing Census 2001; St. Vincent and the Grenadines: Statistical Appendix* (IMF Staff Country Report [2002]).

Samoa (Western Samoa). *Annual Statistical Abstract; Census of Population and Housing, 2001; Samoa: Statistical Appendix* (IMF Staff Country Report [1999]).

San Marino. *Bollettino di Statistica* (quarterly); *Annuario Statistico Demografico* (irreg.); *Republic of San Marino: Selected Issues and Statistical Appendix* (IMF Staff Country Report [2001]).

São Tomé and Príncipe. *1º Recenseamento Geral da População e da Habitação 1991; Sao Tome: Statistical Appendix* (IMF Staff Country Report [2002]).

Saudi Arabia. *Saudi Arabian Monetary Agency: Annual Report; Saudi Arabia Population and Housing Census 1992.*

Senegal. *Recensement de la population et de l'habitat 2001; Situation économique du Senegal* (annual); *Senegal: Selected Issues* (IMF Staff Country Report [2001]).

Seychelles. *Statistical Abstract* (annual); *Seychelles in Figures* (annual); *National Population and Housing Census 1997.*

Sierra Leone. *Sierra Leone—Recent Economic Developments* (IMF Staff Country Report [1997]).

Singapore. *Census of Population, 2000; Singapore Yearbook; Yearbook of Statistics Singapore; Singapore: Selected Issues* (IMF Staff Country Report [2001]).

Slovakia. *Sčítanie Obyvatel'ov, Domov a Btov 2001* (Population and Housing Census 2001); *Statistical Yearbook of the Slovak Republic; Slovak Republic: Selected Issues and Statistical Appendix* (IMF Staff Country Report [2002]).

Slovenia. *Slovenija Popis 2002* (Slovenia Population Census 2002); *Statistični Letopis Republike Slovenija* (Statistical Yearbook of the Republic of Slovenia); *Republic of Slovenia: Statistical Appendix* (IMF Staff Country Report [2002]).

Solomon Islands. *Solomon Islands 1999 Population Census; Solomon Islands—Statistical Appendix* (IMF Staff Country Report [1998]).

Somalia. *The CIA World Factbook* (annual).

South Africa. *The People of South Africa Population Census, 1996; South Africa: Official Yearbook of the Republic of South Africa; Stats in Brief* (annual).

Spain. *Anuario estadístico; Censo de población de 2001.*

Sri Lanka. *Census of Population and Housing, 2001; Sri Lanka Statistical Abstract* (irreg.); *Statistical Pocketbook of the Democratic Socialist Republic of Sri Lanka* (annual); *Sri Lanka: Selected Issues and Statistical Appendix* (IMF Staff Country Report [2002]).

Sudan, The. *Sudan—Statistical Appendix* (IMF Staff Country Report [2000]); *Fourth Population Census, 1993; Sudan in Figures* (annual); *Sudan: Statistical Appendix* (IMF Staff Country Report [2000]).

Suriname. *General Population Census 1980; Statistisch Jaarboek van Suriname; Suriname—Recent Economic Developments* (IMF Staff Country Report [1997]).

Swaziland. *Annual Statistical Bulletin; Report on the 1997 Swaziland Population Census; Swaziland—Selected Issues and Statistical Appendix* (IMF Staff Country Report [2000]).

Sweden. *Folk-och bostadsräkningen, 1990* (Population and Housing Census); *Statistisk årsbok för Sverige* (Statistical Abstract of Sweden [annual]).

Switzerland. *Recensement fédéral de la population, 2000; Statistisches Jahrbuch* (Statistical Yearbook).

Syria. *General Census of Housing and Inhabitants, 1994; Statistical Abstract* (annual).

Taiwan. *The Republic of China Yearbook; Social Indicators of the Republic of China* (annual); *Statistical Abstract* (annual); *Statistical Yearbook of the Republic of China; Taiwan Statistical Data Book* (annual); *1990 Census of Population and Housing.*

Tajikistan. *General Population Census of the Republic of Tajikistan 2000; Republic of Tajikistan: Statistical Appendix* (IMF Staff Country Report [2001]); *Narodnoye Khozyaystvo Tadzhikskoy SSR* (National Economy of the Tadzhik S.S.R. [annual]).

Tanzania. *Tanzania—Statistical Annex* (IMF Staff Country Report [2000]); *Tanzania in Figures* (annual); *Tanzania Statistical Abstract* (irreg.); *1988 Population Census.*

Thailand. *Statistical Handbook of Thailand* (annual); *Statistical Yearbook; Population and Housing Census 2000; Thailand: Statistical Appendix* (IMF Staff Country Report [2001]).

Togo. *Annuaire statistique du Togo; Recensement général de la population et de l'habitat 1993; Togo—Selected Issues* (IMF Staff Country Report [1999]).

Tonga. *Population Census, 1996; Tonga—Statistical Appendix* (IMF Staff Country Report [2001]).

Trinidad and Tobago. *Central Bank of Trinidad and Tobago: Annual Economic Survey; 1990 Population and Housing Census; Trinidad and Tobago: Statistical Appendix* (IMF Staff Country Report [2001]).

Tunisia. *Annuaire statistique de la Tunisie; Recensement général de la population et des logements, 1994; Tunisia: Selected Issues* (IMF Staff Country Report [2002]).

Turkey. *2000 Genel Nüfus Sayımı* (2000 Census of Population); *Türkiye İstatistik Yilliği* (Statistical Yearbook of Turkey).

Turkmenistan. *1995 Population and Housing Census of the Republic of Turkmenistan; Turkmenistan v tsifrakh* (Turkmenistan in figures [annual]).

Tuvalu. *Tuvalu Country Profile 2000.*

Uganda. *2002 National Population and Housing Census; Uganda: Selected Issues and Statistical Appendix* (IMF Staff Country Report [1999]).

Ukraine. *Perepis Naselennya 2002* (Population Census 2002); *Statistichniy Shchorichnik Ukraini* (Statistical Yearbook of Ukraine).

United Arab Emirates. *Statistical Yearbook* (Abu Dhabi); *United Arab Emirates—Recent Economic Developments* (IMF Staff Country Report [1999]); *Central Bank of UAE Report* (annual).

United Kingdom. *Annual Abstract of Statistics; Britain: An Official Handbook* (annual); *Census 2001; General Household Survey* series (annual).

United States. *Agricultural Statistics* (annual); *Current Population Reports; Digest of Education Statistics* (annual); *Minerals Yearbook* (3 vol. in 6 parts); *National Transportation Statistics* (annual); *Statistical Abstract* (annual); *U.S. Exports: SIC-Based Products* (annual); *U.S. Imports: SIC-Based Products* (annual); *Vital and Health Statistics* (series 1–20); *2000 Census of Population and Housing.*

Uruguay. *Anuario estadístico; VII Censo general de poblacion III de hogares y V de viviendas, 22 de mayo de 1996; Uruguay—Recent Economic Developments* (IMF Country Report [2001]).

Uzbekistan. *Narodnoye Khozyaystvo Respubliki Uzbekistan* (National Economy of Uzbekistan [annual]); *Republic of Uzbekistan; Uzbekistan—Recent Economic Developments* (IMF Staff Country Report [2000]).

Vanuatu. *National Population Census 1999; Vanuatu Statistical Yearbook; Vanuatu—Recent Economic Developments* (IMF Staff Country Report [2000]).

Venezuela. *Anuario estadístico; Censo general de la población y vivienda 2001; Encuesta de hogares por muestreo* (annual); *Encuesta industrial* (annual).

Vietnam. *Nien Giam Thong Ke* (Statistical Yearbook); *Tong Dieu Tra Dan So Viet Nam—1999* (Vietnam Population Census—1999); *Vietnam—Selected Issues and Statistical Appendix* (IMF Staff Country Report [2002]).

Virgin Islands of the United States. *2000 Census of Population and Housing* (U.S.).

West Bank. *Population, Housing and Establishment Census—1997; Palestinian Statistical Abstract.*

Western Sahara. *Recensement general de la population et de l'habitat* (1994 [Morocco]).

Yemen. *Population of Yemen: 1994 Census; Republic of Yemen: Selected Issues* (IMF Country Staff Report [2001]).

Yugoslavia. *Popis stanovištva, domaćinstava, stanova i poljoprivrednih gazdinstava 1991 godine* (Census of Population, Households, Housing, and Agricultural Holdings 1991); *Statistical Pocket Book* (annual); *Statistički godišnjak Jugoslavije* (Statistical Yearbook of Yugoslavia).

Zambia. *Zambia—Statistical Appendix* (IMF Staff Country Report [1999]); *2000 Census of Population, Housing, Agriculture.*

Zimbabwe. *Population Census 1992; Statistical Yearbook* (irreg.); *Zimbabwe—Statistical Appendix* (IMF Staff Country Report [2002]).

Index

This index covers both *Britannica Book of the Year* (cumulative for 10 years) and *Britannica World Data*.

Entries in dark type are titles of major articles in the *Book of the Year*; an accompanying year in dark type gives the year the reference appears, and the accompanying page number in light type **shows where the article appears. References for previous years are preceded by the year in dark type. For example, "Education 03:204; 02:206; 01:204; 00:191; 99:209; 98:201; 97:203; 96:191; 95:174; 94:154" indicates that the article "Education" appeared every year from 1994 through 2003. Other references that appear with a page number but without a year refer to references from the current yearbook.**

Indented entries in light type that follow dark-type article titles refer by page number to some other places in the text where the subject of the article is discussed. Light-type entries that are not indented refer by page number to subjects that are not themselves article titles. Names of people covered in biographies and obituaries from previous years are followed by the abbreviation "(biog.)" or "(obit.)" with the year in **dark type** and a page number in light type, e.g., Elizabeth, the Queen Mother, Queen (obit.) **03:108**. Biographies and obituaries for the current year appear under the main entry. In cases where a person has both a biography and an obituary, the words appear as subentries under the main entry and are alphabetized accordingly, e.g.:

Lebed, Aleksandr Ivanovich
  biography **97:**80
  obituary **03:**120

References to illustrations are by page number and are preceded by the abbreviation *il.*

The index uses word-by-word alphabetization (treating a word as one or more characters separated by a space from the next word). Please note that "St." is treated as "Saint." As of this year, "Mc" is alphabetized as "Mc" rather than "Mac."

A

Aaliyah, *or* Aaliyah Dana Haughton (obit.) **02:**104
Aamodt, Kjetil Andre 349
AAS (gardening award): *see* All-America Selections
Abacha, Sani
  biography **98:**65
  chronology 22
  obituary **99:**90
Abadi, Agha Hasan (obit.) **96:**73
ABB (Swiss-Swed. co.) 198
Abbott, George Francis (obit.) **96:**73
ABC (Am. co.): *see* American Broadcasting Company
'Abd al-'Aziz, 'Abdullah ibn: *see* Abdullah, Crown Prince
'Abd al-Aziz, Ahmed ibn Salman ibn: *see* Bin Salman, Prince Ahmed
Abdul Kalam, A.P.J., *or* Avul Pakir Jainulabdeen Abdul Kalam (biog.) **03:**67
Abdul Rauf Hasan Khalil Museum (Jeddah, Saud.Arab.) 234
Abdullah, Crown Prince, *or* 'Abdullah ibn 'Abd al-'Aziz
  biography **03:**67
  chronology 15
  Egypt 426
  Jordan 454
  Saudi Arabia 490, *il.*
Abdullah II
  biography **00:**35
  Egypt 426
  Jordan 454
Abe Kobo (obit.) **94:**54
Abeles, Sir (Emil Herbert) Peter (obit.) **00:**76
Abidine Ben Ali, Zine al- 505
Abidjan (C.I.) 419
Abiola, Moshood Kashimawo Olawale (obit.) **99:**90
Abkhazia (aut.area, Georgia) 433
ABL (U.S. mil. tech.): *see* Airborne Laser
ABM Treaty: *see* Anti-Ballistic Missile Treaty
Abouela, Leila 259
Abraham, Sir Edward Penley (obit.) **00:**76
Abrahams, William Miller (obit.) **99:**90
Abram, Morris Berthold (obit.) **01:**98
Abrams, Harriet Elizabeth: *see* Worth, Irene

Abravanel, Maurice (obit.) **94:**54
Abs, Hermann Josef (obit.) **95:**60
ABT: *see* American Ballet Theatre
Abu Ali Mustafa, *or* Mustafa az-Zibri (obit.) **02:**104
Abu Dhabi (U.A.E.) 509
Abu Nidal, *or* Sabri al-Banna (obit.) **03:**98
  chronology 38
Abu Sayyaf 9, 38, 481, *il.* 482
Abu Seif, Salah (obit.) **97:**91
Abu Sitta, Sobhi: *see* Atef, Muhammad
Abu Zayd, Nasr Hamid (biog.) **01:**67
Abubakar, Abdulsalam (biog.) **99:**65
Abuja (Nig.) 476
Abzug, Bella (obit.) **99:**90
AC (pol. party, Mauritania): *see* Action for Change
Academy Awards, *or* Oscars (motion pictures)
  chronology 19
  Film Awards *table* 297
Acaenoplax hayae (polychaete) 242
"Accelerating Changes in Mexico" (spotlight) **96:**443
accounting industry 194
Accra (Ghana) 436
Aceh (Sum., Indon.) 53, 443
Achebe, Chinua 45
Ackermann, Ronny 350
Ackroyd, Peter 244
acquired immune deficiency syndrome: *see* HIV/AIDS
acquisition, corporate: *see* merger and acquisition, corporate
Action for Change, *or* AC (pol. party, Mauritania) 466
Acton, Sir Harold Mario Mitchell (obit.) **95:**60
AD (pol. party, Austl.): *see* Australian Democrats
"Adagio for Strings" (Barber) 283
Adami, Eddie Fenech 466
Adamjee Jute Mills (factory, Bangla.) 401
Adamkus, Valdas V. (biog.) **99:**65
  Lithuania 54, 462
Adams, Alice 247
Adams, Diana (obit.) **94:**54
Adams, Douglas Noël (obit.) **02:**104
Adams, Gerry (biog.) **95:**39
  Northern Ireland 512
Adams, John Coolidge (biog.) **98:**65
  classical music 283
Adams, Scott (biog.) **96:**52
Adams, Victoria: *see* Beckham, Victoria

"Adaptation" (motion picture) 295
Adcock, Joseph Wilbur ("Joe") (obit.) **00:**76
Adderley, Nathaniel ("Nat") (obit.) **01:**98
Addis Ababa (Eth.) 429
Addison, John Mervyn (obit.) **99:**90
Adelphia Communications Corp. 194
ADEMA (pol. party, Mali): *see* Alliance for Democracy in Mali
Ademola, Sir Adetokunbo Adegboyaga (obit.) **94:**54
Adhikari, Man Mohan (obit.) **00:**76
"Adieux à la reine, Les" (Thomas) 252
Adler, Lawrence Cecil ("Larry") (obit.) **02:**104
Adler, Mortimer Jerome (obit.) **02:**105
adoption
  Cambodian infants 409
"Adults 'Toon In" (photo essay) **99:**270
Advanced Composites 99:171; **98:**167; **97:**168; **96:**147; **95:**132
Advertising Industry 99:157; **98:**152; **97:**154; **96:**133; **95:**121; **94:**181
  AOL Time Warner 172
  e-mail spam 171
  newspapers 272
  radio 272
  television 269
Aerial Sports **94:**278
Aerosmith (Am. rock group) (biog.) **02:**73
Aerospace Industry 99:158; **98:**153; **97:**155; **96:**134; **95:**121; **94:**181
Afanasyev, Viktor Grigoryevich (obit.) **95:**60
afghani (currency) 390
Afghanistan 03:390; **02:**384; **01:**387; **00:**378; **99:**399; **98:**389; **97:**388; **96:**366; **95:**367; **94:**402
  chronology 10–54
  education 205
  food aid 146
  immigration controversy 396
  international law 225
  international relations
    Canada 411
    Japan 452
    Nauru 473
    Tajikistan 503
    United Nations 381
    United States 513
  Kabul Zoo 215
  libraries 233
  military affairs 277
  modern warfare techniques 280
  opium 228
  refugees 316
  television 271
  "U.S. Military Bases In and Around Afghanistan" (map) **02:**384
  wildlife conservation 213
  see also Qaeda, al-; Taliban; WORLD DATA
Africa, Horn of (reg., E.Af.) 11
African Affairs **94:**352
  airline industry 201
  economic affairs 189
  literature 248
  multinational and regional organizations 385
  refugees 316
  United Kingdom 512
  United Nations AIDS program 381
  see also Middle Eastern and North African affairs; and individual countries by name
African Americans, *or* Black Americans
  chronology 21, 54
  death penalty study 231
  Olympic Games 345
African Cup of Nations (assoc. football) 337
African National Congress, *or* ANC (pol. party, S.Af.) 495
African Political Systems (map) **97:**417

African Union 33, 385, *il.* 384
African Union–Civil Society, Organization for 385
African Unity, Organization of, *or* OAU
  African Union 385
  Central African Republic 412
  Madagascar 464
"Africa's Second Liberation" (spotlight) **95:**453
"Africa's Struggle Against AIDS" (special report) **00:**450
"After Nature" (Sebald) 244
"After the Quake: Stories," *or* "Kami no kodomotachi wa mina odoru" (Murakami) 260
"Afterplay" (play) 293
Afwerki, Isaias 428
AG (pol. party, Austl.): *see* Australian Green Party
Ağaoğlu, Adalet 258
Agar, John (obit.) **03:**98
Agassi, Andre (biog.) **00:**35
Agbéyomé Kodjo, Gabriel 504
Agenda 21 (internat. treaty) 209
Agnew, Spiro Theodore (obit.) **97:**91
Agrawal, Manindra 261
Agriculture, U.S. Department of, *or* USDA 34, 46, 147
Agriculture and Food Supplies 03:146; **02:**152; **01:**146; **00:**128; **99:**124; **98:**123; **97:**123; **96:**103; **95:**90; **94:**83
  botany 238
  crop yields in Africa 46
  special reports **02:**154; **01:**150; **99:**132
  U.S. Food and Agribusiness Exhibition 421
  see also bovine spongiform encephalopathy; foot-and-mouth disease; genetically modified food; WORLD DATA; and individual countries by name
"agua grande, El" (Hiriart) 255
Aguilar Manzo, Luis (obit.) **98:**90
Ahern, Bertie 26, 447, *il.* 467
Ahmadabad (India) 16
Ahmed, Iajuddin 400
Ahrens, Geert-Hinrich 391
Ahtisaari, Martti (biog.) **00:**37
  chronology 22
Ai Qing (obit.) **97:**91
AIA (Am. org.): *see* American Institute of Architects
aid
  humanitarian: *see* humanitarian aid
  welfare: *see* Social Protection
AIDS: *see* HIV/AIDS
Aigner, Ladislas ("Lucien") (obit.) **00:**76
Aikman, Troy Kenneth (biog.) **97:**65
air pollution 212
Airborne Laser, *or* ABL (U.S. mil. tech.) 282
Airbus Industrie (Eur. consortium) 201
airport
  Civil Engineering Projects *table* 158
  see also Aviation
Ajax (assoc. football) 336
Ajit (obit.) **99:**90
Ajodhia, Jules Rattankoemar 499
Akayev, Askar 458
Ake, Claude (obit.) **97:**91
Akebono (biog.) **94:**33
Akerlof, George A. (biog.) **02:**68
Akesson, Birgit (obit.) **02:**105
Aki Basho 356
Akihito 451
Akii-Bua, John (obit.) **98:**90
Akilia (is., Atl.O.) 180
Akilov, Akil 502
Akin, Azra 53
AKO Literatuur Prijs 250
AKP (pol. party, Tur.): *see* Justice and Development Party
Aksu, Ali 180
Akutagawa Prize 260
  Literary Prizes *table* 245
AL (Am. sports org.): *see* American League
Al Hilal (assoc. football) 337
